W9-BUH-392

WITHDRAWN

AMERICAN NATIONAL BIOGRAPHY

EDITORIAL ADVISORY BOARD

Joyce Appleby

Dan T. Carter

William H. Chafe

Eric Foner

George M. Frederickson

Douglas Greenberg

Neil Harris

Nathan Irvin Huggins (*deceased*)

Stanley N. Katz

Linda K. Kerber

Edmund S. Morgan

Thomas G. Paterson

Barbara Gutmann Rosenkrantz

Maris A. Vinovskis

AMERICAN
NATIONAL BIOGRAPHY

Published under the auspices of the
AMERICAN COUNCIL OF LEARNED SOCIETIES

General Editors

John A. Garraty
Mark C. Carnes

VOLUME 16

OXFORD UNIVERSITY PRESS
New York   1999   Oxford

OXFORD UNIVERSITY PRESS

Oxford New York
Athens Auckland Bangkok Bogotá
Buenos Aires Calcutta Cape Town Chennai
Dar es Salaam Delhi Florence Hong Kong Istanbul
Karachi Kuala Lumpur Madrid Melbourne Mexico City
Mumbai Nairobi Paris São Paulo Singapore
Taipei Tokyo Toronto Warsaw
and associated companies in
Berlin Ibadan

Copyright © 1999 by the American Council of Learned Societies

Published by Oxford University Press, Inc.,
198 Madison Avenue, New York, New York 10016
http://www.oup-usa.org

Oxford is a registered trademark of Oxford University Press

All rights reserved. No part of this publication may be reproduced,
stored in a retrieval system, or transmitted, in any form or by any means,
electronic, mechanical, photocopying, recording, or otherwise,
without the prior permission of Oxford University Press.

Funding for this publication was provided in part by
the Andrew W. Mellon Foundation, the Rockefeller Foundation,
and the National Endowment for the Humanities,
a federal agency.

Library of Congress Cataloging-in-Publication Data

American national biography / general editors, John A. Garraty, Mark C. Carnes
p.   cm.
"Published under the auspices of the American Council of Learned Societies."
Includes bibliographical references and index.
1. United States—Biography—Dictionaries.   I. Garraty, John Arthur,
1920–   .   II. Carnes, Mark C. (Mark Christopher), 1950–   .
III. American Council of Learned Societies.
CT213.A68   1998   98-20826   920.073—dc21   CIP
ISBN 0-19-520635-5 (set)
ISBN 0-19-512795-1 (vol. 16)

Printing (last digit): 9 8 7 6 5 4 3 2 1

Printed in the United States of America
on acid-free paper

NEWARK PUBLIC LIBRARY
NEWARK, OHIO 43055-5087

485 3280

M

CONTINUED

MOSLER, Henry (6 June 1841–21 Apr. 1920), painter, was born Heinrich Mosler in Troplowitz, Silesia, the son of Gustav Mosler and Sophie Weiner. The family came to the United States in 1849 at the height of German-Jewish immigration; they lived at various times in New York City; Cincinnati, Ohio; Nashville, Tennessee; and Richmond, Indiana. Henry Mosler received his first training as an illustrator in Nashville, Tennessee, where he was apprenticed to a wood engraver. The family settled permanently in Cincinnati in 1859. There the young artist simultaneously worked as a wood engraver and studied painting with James Henry Beard, a local portrait and genre painter.

In 1861 Mosler was hired as an artist-reporter for *Harper's Weekly* to document the Union Army of the Ohio. For the next year and a half he traveled with the troops through Kentucky, Tennessee, and Alabama, recording troop movement, camp life, and military skirmishes. Using money he had earned working for *Harper's*, he left the United States in 1863 for Europe. He spent two and a half years at the Düsseldorf Academy with the painters Heinrich Mücke and Albert Kindler, perfecting his skills in portraiture and period history painting. He worked in Paris for the last six months of this trip in the atelier of Ernest Hébert, a painter of history, genre, and portraiture.

Mosler returned in 1866 to Cincinnati, where he stayed for most of the next eight years. He had numerous commissions for portraits, which are documented in his carefully detailed account book. During this period of his career Mosler's work related to the Jewish community, for Cincinnati was the center of Reform Judaism (the liberal branch of Judaism) in America. Mosler executed a painting of the exterior of Plum Street Temple, which was built in 1866 for the congregation of Rabbi Isaac Mayer Wise, the leader of Reform Judaism. He also painted portraits of several key personalities within the community including Wise's first wife Therese Bloch Wise and the Orthodox Rabbi Bernard Illowy and his wife Catherine Schiff Illowy. Other subjects that Mosler pursued during these years were landscapes and American genre themes. Among the most significant is his interpretation of the former Confederacy in a painting titled *Lost Cause*, commissioned by Colonel Albert Berry, a former officer of the Army of the Kentucky. In 1870 Mosler spent a little less than a year in New York City, where he established a studio in the Dodsworth Building and developed working relationships with the dealers Goupil and Knoedler.

Mosler had married Sarah Cahn of Cincinnati in 1869; they had five children. Mosler returned to Europe in 1874, spending the next three years in Munich. He studied on an informal basis with Karl von Piloty, the director of the Munich Academy, and Alexander von Wagner, who taught classes in painting techniques. He participated in the rediscovery of baroque art and the use of bravura painting techniques of Franz Hals. He also was influenced by the contemporary German artist Wilhelm Liebl, who advocated spontaneous painting of commonplace rustic scenes.

Mosler moved in 1877 to France, where he lived until his final return to the United States in 1894. He established an atelier for male and female students and exhibited annually at the Paris Salon. *Le Retour*, his entry to the 1879 salon, received an honorable mention and was the first painting by an American artist to be purchased for the French collection of contemporary art, which was housed in the Luxembourg Gallery. The painting was set in a humble Breton home replete with all the trappings of domestic life of the picturesque region of France. Its success was cause for Mosler to specialize in Breton genre, a region of interest to a large group of American painters: "I became a peasant among the peasants of Brittany and if I have been able to depict with some sincerity the homely pathos and charm of their lives, it is because I have lived in their homes as one of them" (Mosler, 1907). He spent many of his summers in Brittany or nearby Normandy making drawings for paintings. His Breton paintings include beautiful young women in distinctive Breton dress, customs of courtship and marriage, artisans in their workshops, and everyday family life. During these years he also took sketching tours through Switzerland, Germany, and Italy and trips back to the United States for family visits and professional purposes. In 1885 he was commissioned by H. H. Warner to paint three enormous paintings (seven by eleven feet) on American subjects: one on the husking bee and two on Native American themes that necessitated his going on a study trip to Arizona and New Mexico.

Mosler returned permanently to the United States and settled in New York. Like many of his American colleagues, he tried to emulate his experience abroad, establishing a studio in Carnegie Hall Studios, where he also conducted classes. He was elected an associate member of the National Academy of Design. He purchased a home in Margaretville in the Catskills, where he painted out-of-doors with his advanced students. He focused on subjects of American colonial history and contemporary domestic genre. His more freely painted landscapes during these late years reveal some awareness of impressionism and realism. A very prolific artist, Mosler continued to be active until the end of his life. He died in New York.

In 1895 W. A. Cooper wrote, "The stories his pictures tell need no title. They touch all the emotion of the soul" (*Godey's Magazine*, 1895). And in 1907 Florence Finch Kelly stated: "For it is life, the human appeal, the interest that the human being always feels in other human beings, that have inspired his brush. At his summer home in the Catskills, in Spain, Brittany, Egypt, Germany, wherever he has lived, he has worked always to put upon canvas the daily life of the people around him." These quotes from Mosler's own time confirm the strong appeal of his narrative genre paintings to nineteenth-century American audiences.

• Mosler's papers are in the Archives of American Art and the American Jewish Archives at Hebrew Union College–Jewish Institute of Religion in Cincinnati, Ohio. See Barbara Gilbert, *Henry Mosler Rediscovered: A Nineteenth-Century American-Jewish Artist* (1996). See also Florence Finch Kelly, "The Art of Henry Mosler," *Broadway Magazine*, Sept. 1907, p. 727. An obituary is in the *New York Times*, 22 Apr. 1920.

BARBARA C. GILBERT

MOSS, Howard (22 Jan. 1922–16 Sept. 1987), poet and editor, was born in New York City, the son of David Leonard Moss, a prosperous importer and manufacturer, and Sonya Schrag. Because Moss was a sickly infant, his parents relocated to nearby Rockaway Beach, where he spent his childhood and adolescence. When he was still very young, his father, a Lithuanian immigrant, brought Moss's grandparents to the United States; they eventually became Moss's primary caregivers. Moss once wrote, "I sometimes had the feeling I was growing up in two places at once: Rockaway Beach and Lithuania."

Moss was educated in the public school system of Belle Harbor, New York. In 1939 he enrolled at the University of Michigan but was expelled after only one year for participating in a dormitory workers' labor protest. He then transferred to the University of Wisconsin, from which he graduated in 1943. Other study included one summer at Harvard University in 1942 and graduate work at Columbia University in 1946.

Moss's first employment after college was as a copyboy and later a book reviewer at *Time*. He quit *Time* in 1945 to work at a series of jobs—at the Office of War Information; at Vassar College, where he taught English for two years; and at *Junior Bazaar*, where he was fiction editor for one year. In 1948 he joined the *New Yorker* as fiction editor; by 1950 he had become poetry editor, a position he occupied until his death.

Moss's career as a poet, playwright, and critic was eclipsed by his fame and influence as poetry editor of the *New Yorker*. During his long tenure, Moss turned the magazine into America's most important venue for new poetry and established the reputations of numerous now-celebrated poets, including Elizabeth Bishop, Sylvia Plath, Anne Sexton, Mark Strand, W. S. Merwin, and Galway Kinnell.

Moss began publishing poetry of his own while he was still in college. In 1944 he won *Poetry* magazine's Janet Sewall David award. At age twenty-four he published his first collection, *The Wound and the Weather* (1946). Influenced by W. H. Auden, Wallace Stevens,

and sometimes William Butler Yeats, this early poetry is accomplished but often stiff and mannered. In Moss's next two volumes, *The Toy Fair* (1954) and *Summer in the Air* (1957), the poet continues his elegant style and iambic line but begins to deepen his themes, reflecting often on mortality and the memories of love. Moss's mastery of the lyric was perhaps most clear in *Finding Them Lost and Other Poems* (1965), which received more unqualified praise than any of his previous books. In *Second Nature* (1968) Moss began to loosen his verse structures. His next volume of poetry, *Selected Poems* (1971), gathering the strongest of his earlier verse and seven previously unpublished poems, won the National Book Award.

Notes from the Castle (1979), considered by some critics to be Moss's finest book of poetry, reveals the delight in pun and irony that is characteristic of Moss, but also his reverence for the natural world and the sense of the poet as translator of the text of nature.

Moss's other poetic works are *A Winter Come, a Summer Gone: Poems, 1946–1960* (1960), which samples his first three books and adds fourteen new poems; *Travel: A Window* (1973); *Buried City* (1975), which won critical praise for its evocations of New York City; *A Swim off the Rocks: Light Verse* (1976), with its parodies of Shakespearean sonnets among other humorous poems; a book of juvenile poetry, *Tigers and Other Lilies* (1977); *Rules of Sleep* (1984); and his last published volume of poetry, *New Selected Poems* (1985), for which he won the Lenore Marshall/*Nation* poetry prize.

Throughout his career Moss has been recognized as a poet of verbal play, metaphorical ingenuity, and adherence to traditional structures and values. He has also been criticized as a poet of the *New Yorker*–style poem—reticent, muted, and blandly urbane. Most of his critics would agree that he was both a musical and a visual poet, a poet of charm and precision, and one whose poems depend more on intellect than on emotion. His themes are those of mortality, the bleakness and promise of the city, and the ordinary losses and gains of life. He moved from his earlier, more abstract poetry gradually toward the concrete; he also moved toward greater flexibility and freedom within the confines of traditional rhythms.

Moss wrote four plays, *The Folding Green* (1954), *Garden Music* (1966), *The Oedipus Mah-Jong Scandal* (1968), and *The Palace at 4 A.M.* (1972), and three collections of critical essays, *Writing against Time: Critical Essays and Reviews* (1969), *Whatever Is Moving* (1981), and *Minor Monuments: Selected Essays* (1986). Two other critical books are on single authors: *Chekhov* (1972) and his most famous critical work, *The Magic Lantern of Marcel Proust* (1962). He also edited collections of Edward Lear and John Keats and translated *The Cemetery by the Sea* (*Le Cimitière Marin*) (1985) by Paul Valéry.

"Moss has been . . . too quiet and almost quietistic to attract really wide attention," wrote Harold Bloom in the *New Republic* (29 Nov. 1975). Yet, as editor, Moss's impact on twentieth-century poetry was immeasurable. David Ray has commented, "Without people like Howard Moss we could, indeed, have no literary culture" (*Contemporary Poets*, 4th ed., ed. James Vinson and D. L. Kirkpatrick [1985], p. 598).

Howard Moss, who never married, died in New York City.

• Howard Moss's manuscript collections are in the Syracuse University Library, New York, and the Lilly Library, Indiana University, Bloomington. Criticism of Moss's work has been limited to reviews, of which there are dozens, and a few longer essays. An important critical study is Richard Howard's essay on Moss, "Beginnings Spin a Web Where Endings Spawn," in *Alone with America: Essays on the Art of Poetry in the United States* (1969). Other essays and interviews include Laurence Lieberman, *Unassigned Frequencies: American Poetry in Review, 1964–1977* (1977); Karl Malkoff, *Crowell's Handbook of Contemporary American Poetry* (1973); and William Packard, ed., *The Craft of Poetry: Interviews from "New York Quarterly"* (1974). Obituaries are in the *Washington Post*, 19 Sept. 1987, and the *New Yorker*, 5 Oct. 1987.

MELISSA FABROS

MOSSELL, Nathan Francis (27 July 1856–27 Oct. 1946), physician and hospital founder and administrator, was born in Hamilton, Ontario, Canada, the son of Aaron Mossell, a brick manufacturer, and Eliza Bowers; both parents were freeborn African Americans from Baltimore, Maryland, who had moved to Canada to escape racial discrimination. When the Civil War ended and slavery was abolished, Aaron Mossell moved his family back to the United States. In 1865 they settled in Lockport, New York, a small town near Rochester.

In Lockport the Mossell children were assigned to a separate all-black school. Mossell's father successfully petitioned the Lockport Board of Education to close the all-black school, and Nathan and the other black children were allowed to attend integrated schools. The Mossell family's home life was highly religious: his father donated the bricks for the first African Methodist Episcopal Zion church in Lockport.

After graduation from high school in Lockport in 1873, Nathan Mossell moved to Philadelphia, where he worked to acquire funds for college. He enrolled at Lincoln University in Lincoln, Pennsylvania, in 1875 and graduated in 1879 with a B.A. degree. During his four years at Lincoln University he taught Sunday school at the Bethel A.M.E. Zion Church in Wilmington, Delaware.

In 1879 Mossell gained admission to the Medical School of the University of Pennsylvania, from which he graduated with high honors in 1882. He was the first African American to apply to the University's medical program and the first to graduate. In the year before his medical school graduation he married Gertrude Bustill; they had two daughters.

After medical school Mossell worked in the outpatient clinic of the University Hospital. Because of racial attitudes, he was reluctantly given this position only through the influence of his former professors. Concurrently he completed a postgraduate course at the Philadelphia Polyclinic. He was refused membership, again because of his race, in the Philadelphia County Medical Society. After a bitter struggle and with letters of support from his former professors, he was accepted into the society in 1888, the first African American member.

In 1885 Mossell went to Europe for advanced medical training. He studied surgery at Guy's Hospital and St. Thomas Hospital in London, England. Back in Philadelphia, however, he was unable to gain a hospital staff appointment. Furthermore, he was disturbed that none of the more than twenty-four hospitals in the Philadelphia area would admit African-American medical graduates to internships, or African-American women into their nurse training programs. Mossell was convinced of the necessity of better hospital care for African Americans and of training opportunities for black doctors and nurses. Several medical colleges in Philadelphia offered to assist him in establishing a hospital if he would agree that it would be segregated. Mossell and other black leaders refused this offensive condition.

Mossell was against hospitals exclusively for black people, which he thought were a wasteful duplication of effort and perpetuation of a caste system. However, the great needs of Philadelphia's African-American community and discrimination at other hospitals forced him to act against his philosophy. In June 1895 Mossell convened other doctors to lay plans for establishing a hospital for patients of all races; it would provide a place for black physicians to treat their patients and to gain professional development, and for African-American interns and nurses to acquire training. With public fund-raising, church donations, and the work of African-American women volunteers led by Gertrude Mossell, a three-story building was leased at 1512 Lombard Street and outfitted as a fifteen-bed facility. Frederick Douglass Memorial Hospital and Training School opened on 31 October 1895. Eighty-six percent of the funds needed to open the hospital and to operate it during the first year were raised in the African-American community. Some blacks, however, criticized Mossell for conceding to race prejudice; some whites argued that there were already enough charitable hospitals.

Each year during its first decade Douglass Hospital's outpatient and inpatient censuses increased. Some of the first patients were veterans of the Spanish-American War. Beginning in 1905 annual state funding of $6,000 was gained in recognition of the number of poor patients being served. From the founding of Douglass Hospital until early 1931, Mossell served as both superintendent and medical director. The administrative and professional duties were separated in 1931 and he retained the post of medical director.

In early 1905 Mossell faced opposition from a segment of Douglass's professional staff. The board of directors requested his resignation. Some physicians had accused Mossell of retarding the professional growth of younger physicians by limiting their assignments to perform operations. Others faulted him for what they judged to be a turning of the hospital from a quasi-public institution to a more private one. Mossell overcame the attacks on him during 1905, with strong community support. In late 1905 a dissident group of doctors failed to get the board of managers to reorganize the hospital to free it from all appearances of being a private institution. They ended their affiliation with Douglass and established Mercy Hospital, which opened in 1907. The split between the supporters of Douglass and Mercy hospitals continued until the mid-1940s, when a merger was proposed. Mossell felt that a single hospital would better serve the growing African-American population of Philadelphia and provided strong leadership toward the eventual merger forming Mercy-Douglass Hospital, which was not realized until two years after his death.

Mossell was a leading organizer of African-American medical affairs and politics. In 1895 he was a founder of the National Medical Association (NMA), established by African-American physicians because they were barred from the American Medical Association and its local chapters. In 1900 he helped to establish the Philadelphia Academy of Medical and Allied Sciences, an NMA chapter. In 1907 he served as the eighth president of the NMA.

Medicine was not the only field in which Mossell combated racial discrimination and championed civil rights. In 1905 he joined the Niagara Movement, organized by William E. B. DuBois, which called for immediate and full civil rights for African Americans. The Niagara Movement led to the founding of the National Association for the Advancement of Colored People (NAACP) in 1910. Mossell spearheaded protests in Philadelphia against the anti-black novel, *The Clansmen*, and a Hollywood film, *Birth of a Nation*, based on the novel. He led a fight in Philadelphia in 1944 to have African-American youth admitted to Girard College, a privately funded but publicly administered institution.

Mossell died at his home in Philadelphia. For more than forty years he was a pioneering hospital developer and a forceful advocate for black-controlled hospitals, essential during a time when medical training and hospital practice for African-American physicians and nurses were severely limited in the United States.

• A memorial biography of Mossell is William Montague Cobb, "Nathan Francis Mossell, 1856–1946," *Journal of the National Medical Association* 46 (Mar. 1954): 118–30. His involvement with Douglass Hospital is discussed by Vanessa S. Gamble, *Making a Place for Ourselves: The Black Hospital Movement 1920–1945* (1995), pp. 19–21, 26–28, 32. Obituaries are in the *Philadelphia Inquirer* and the *Philadelphia Evening Bulletin*, both 28 Oct. 1946, and the *Pittsburgh Courier*, 2 Nov. 1946.

ROBERT C. HAYDEN

MOST, Johann Joseph (5 Feb. 1846–17 Mar. 1906), anarchist leader, was born in Augsburg, Germany, the son of Josef Most, a legal copyist, and Viktoria Hinterhuber, a governess. Most's youth was bitter and gave him a fierce hatred of authority. The city authorities gave a marriage license to his impoverished parents only two years after his birth, a social stain in his devout Catholic hometown. A jaw infection left him with a twisted face, crushed his hopes to join the stage, for which he was gifted, and made him the target of lifelong ridicule. Then his mother died in 1856, and his stepmother was cruel and abusive.

Thrown out of school for indiscipline, Most became a bookbinder. He wandered through Central Europe and experienced the misery created by unfettered capitalism. In 1867 he joined the International Workingmen's Association, or First International. In 1868 he went to Vienna to help workers protest a ban on labor unions, was jailed, and in 1871 was banned from Austria for life. A gifted writer and speaker, Most then became a militant in the Social-Democratic party (SPD) in Germany. He edited labor papers such as the *Berlin Freie Presse*, wrote labor songs such as the popular "Arbeitsmaenner," was elected to the Reichstag in 1874 and 1877 by the city of Chemnitz, and was repeatedly jailed for his fiery speeches.

In summer 1878 two attempts to kill Emperor William I were wrongly blamed on the SPD, and the government banned the party till 1890. Most and the SPD leadership left for London. There, Most offended Karl Marx, the icon of the movement, by attacking his tenet that a centralized dictatorship of the proletariat must precede a classless communist society. Most objected that this would lead to oppression and that workers were well able create a classless society at once after they took power. In January 1879, without clearance from the party, Most issued the weekly *Freiheit* and urged German workers to revolt. But the SPD leaders feared provoking a futile bloodbath, and in May 1880 they expelled him and his followers from the party. In 1881 the British jailed Most for sixteen months for lauding the killing of Czar Alexander II and shut down *Freiheit* in 1882 for praising the killing of Lord Frederick Cavendish by Irish patriots. Most left for the United States, arriving in New York on 12 December 1882.

Most was now an anarchist. Rejecting the individualist anarchism advocated by the American Benjamin Tucker because it provided no solution to mass poverty, he became the leading American advocate of the Communist anarchism of the Russian Peter Kropotkin who visited Most in 1897 and 1901. Kropotkin advocated a society of autonomous small groups of workers sharing from a common pool according to their needs. But Most's significance came from his call for revolution. He believed that the liberal bourgeoisie would never agree to social reforms nor allow workers to gain power by democratic means. Once they understood this and were emboldened by witnessing acts of terrorism against figures of authority, workers would rise.

Most organized the scattered local anarchists, then mainly German immigrants, wrote the platform adopted by the 1883 anarchist convention in Pittsburgh, and revived the disbanded First International as a framework for agitation. Besides *Freiheit*, he wrote pamphlets, such as *The God-Plague and Epidem-*

ic Religion (1883), The Science of Revolutionary Warfare (1885), a bomb-making guide, and The Property Beast (1887). He gained followers in Germany and the United States. Wretched living conditions, the repression of labor unions, and the execution of four anarchists framed for the 1886 Chicago Haymarket bombing shocked the urban workers Alex Berkman and Emma Goldman, Russian-Jewish immigrants who met Most in 1888–1889.

In Germany the police broke the revolutionary cells created by Most's followers. In 1892, after Berkman's failed attempt to stir strikers against Carnegie Steel in Homestead, Pennsylvania, by trying to kill its chairman Henry Clay Frick, Most realized U.S. workers would not rise. But when he repudiated terrorism, many followers were outraged. Goldman, his former lover and now Berkman's, even horsewhipped him. By the time he died in Cincinnati on a lecture tour, Most had become a somewhat quixotic figure of the radical left.

From 1873 to 1880 Most was married to Klara Haensch. They divorced, after an unknown number of children died young, because his activism made family life impossible. He may have married again, though evidence is inconclusive. Helene Minkin, a Russian-Jewish immigrant who shared his ideals, became his common-law wife in 1893; they had two children.

At his memorial in New York, radical leaders such as Goldman, Max Baginski, and Lucy Parsons eulogized Most before 20,000 mourners as a man who had devoted his life to free the poor. To mainstream America, however, he was the terrorist mastermind. Though never involved in a terrorist act, he was constantly harassed by the police and was jailed at Blackwell's Island in New York in 1886–1887, 1891–1892, and 1902–1903. At his memorial Goldman cried, "Most is dead, his ideas live!" The New York Times hailed the death of a "mad dog."

Most left no permanent mark. His words comforted desperate workers during the Gilded Age but mainly helped conservatives demonize the labor movement. His ideals became obsolete amid the social reforms of the Progressive Era. Freiheit closed in 1909. The Italian and Jewish immigrants who then were the bulk of the small American anarchist movement largely forgot the Germans who had preceded them and in the 1930s adopted the individualist pacifism Most had loathed.

• Most left no papers. He expressed his thought in Freiheit, in his pamphlets, and in his Memorien—Erlebtes, Erforschtes und Erdachtes (1903–1907). Works by people who knew him are Rudolf Rocker, Johann Most: Das Leben eines Rebellen (1924); Emma Goldman, "Johann Most," American Mercury 8 (June 1926): 158–66; and Max Nomad, "Johann Most, Terrorist of the Word," in Apostles of Revolution (1939). A more recent study is Frederic Trautmann, The Voice of Terror: A Biography of Johann Most (1980). His political activities are discussed notably in Andrew R. Carlson, Anarchism in Germany (1972); James Joll, The Anarchists (1964); William Reichert, Partisans of Freedom (1976); and Paul Avrich, The

Haymarket Tragedy (1984). Little is known about his private life, though Avrich, Anarchist Voices (1995), includes a 1979 interview with Most's son John Most about their family life.

THOMAS REIMER

MOSTEL, Zero (28 Feb. 1915–8 Sept. 1977), actor and painter, was born Samuel Joel Mostel in Brooklyn, New York, the son of Israel Mostel and Celia (originally Zina) Druchs, Orthodox Jewish immigrants who ran a kosher vineyard and slaughterhouse. Although Mostel was raised in a religious household and later displayed a special affinity for Jewish characters, his father was not a rabbi as has often been reported; Mostel's penchant for improvisation extended to his autobiography, and he creatively refashioned his past in interviews throughout his life. Most notably, he sometimes attributed his numeric nickname to his "financial standing in the community" (as he testified to the House Committee on Un-American Activities in 1955), but he more regularly credited the label to his supposedly undistinguished schoolwork. Despite these suggested derivations, his stage name may simply have been the innovation of an early publicist. In 1939 he married Clara Sverd; they were divorced in 1941.

Mostel graduated from the City College of New York in 1935 and briefly worked toward a master's degree in art at New York University, where he planned a thesis on Honoré Daumier. During this abortive year of graduate study, he taught a few art classes and began doing stand-up comedy in venues ranging from private parties to public museums, eventually making his formal professional debut at Café Society Downtown in 1942. Success here led rapidly to regular appearances in radio variety programs and then Broadway revues and musicals, beginning with Keep 'em Laughing at the Forty-fourth Street Theatre that same year. In 1943 he made his first film appearance, in Metro-Goldwyn-Mayer's Du Barry Was a Lady. He also toured nightclubs nationally with a varied act that included the satiric political character, Senator Polltax T. Pellagra. At this point in his career, Mostel already exhibited the boyish charm, intensity, and larger-than-life presence that would later lead critics to proclaim him a theatrical "heavyweight"—a description that his generous girth gave a notably literal twist. Life magazine proclaimed Mostel virtually the funniest man in America.

Perhaps his only unsuccessful engagement in this blossoming career came in 1943, when Mostel was inducted into the army and then honorably discharged within the year for disputed and possibly political reasons. A more successful engagement followed in 1944, when he married Katherine "Kate" Harkin; they had two children. The longevity of this marriage helps contextualize Mostel's reputation as a womanizer, a perception fueled by his spirited depiction of such lecherous characters as Pseudolus and Max Bialystock.

Mostel began a promising television career by appearing in a series of sketches called "Off the Record"

(1948). But such ventures were soon ended by the one credit no actor could afford: Mostel's name appeared on the various unofficial blacklists of the Red Scare of the 1950s. He was eventually compelled to appear before the HUAC in 1955. During that appearance, he wedded histrionic skill with political conviction by pleading the Fifth Amendment in pantomime, refusing to answer questions by wiggling his five fingers at the unamused committee. In an interview following the televised hearing, Mostel ironically thanked the committee for facilitating his first television appearance in several years. Years later he more directly testified to the devastating effects the blacklist had on his and others' careers by playing a largely autobiographical character in a film about the period, *The Front* (1976); the humiliating Catskill resort incident depicted there recreated his own experience in 1952.

When Mostel finally returned to television in 1959, he appeared in "The World of Sholom Aleichem." This association with Yiddish stories continued in his most acclaimed theatrical role, Tevye, the beleaguered milkman, in *Fiddler on the Roof*. The Antoinette Perry (Tony) award Mostel won for this performance in 1964 followed closely on the Tony award he earned for the dual roles of Pseudolus and Prologus in *A Funny Thing Happened on the Way to the Forum* (1962–1964). Though he would later successfully reprise Tevye onstage (1977), these years unquestionably mark the zenith of his theatrical career. From 1966, when he recreated Pseudolus for the film version of *Forum*, until his death, Mostel primarily acted in motion pictures, giving performances that brought mixed reviews but great financial reward in movies such as *The Producers* (1967), *The Great Bank Robbery* (1969), and *Rhinoceros* (1974).

Although Mostel will always be identified with the musical theater, he considered himself a serious dramatic actor, and a number of performances throughout his career attest to his potential as a tragicomedian. He had striking critical success as Leopold Bloom in *Ulysses in Nighttown*, for which he was given the 1958 "Obie" (Off-Broadway) award for best actor; he also earned the International Critics Circle award in 1959 for the show's European tour. He played Estragon in a televised version of *Waiting for Godot* (1960) and was John (Jean) in the English-language production of Ionesco's *Rhinoceros*, for which he received his first Tony in 1961. The latter role demonstrated Mostel's pantomimic skills and vocal range as he transformed himself onstage from sniveling gentleman to snorting beast without the aid of makeup. (Other "Johns" have depended on repeated offstage costume changes to approximate the same effect.) Mostel died in Philadelphia while rehearsing the part of Shylock in Arnold Wesker's modernization of *The Merchant of Venice*.

Although Mostel was almost universally praised as a physical comedian and often ranked beside Bert Lahr and even Charlie Chaplin, his acting evoked a wider range of responses. Several critics praised his histrionic range and ability to blend the serious and the silly; other observers, especially later in his career, criticized Mostel for always "playing Zero" regardless of the role. However valid the charge may have been (or eventually became), it surely underestimates the extent to which the offstage "Zero" was himself a complex and consciously created character. Close observers report that Mostel was almost always performing, whether on the stage or the street corner. According to one story, an unsuspecting passerby once marveled that the rotund, balding actor was "the spitting image" of Zero Mostel; Mostel promptly proved the point by spitting on him. Whether one considers this response outrageous or irrepressible, it vividly displays the improvisational instincts that produced Mostel's best and worst performances—his most sensitive portrayals as well as his self-indulgent shtick.

No portrait of this actor's life would be complete without some mention of his work in the visual arts. Throughout his life Mostel painted prolifically, and he often claimed that he acted only to support his art. In his own view, he was most himself, and perhaps his best self, in his paintings, whose varied styles and technical achievement are notable. Given his dual artistic ambitions, it seems only fitting that one of his two children, Joshua, has made acting his career while the other, Tobias, chose painting.

• The New York Public Library for the Performing Arts, Lincoln Center, has an extensive file of clippings on and interviews with Mostel, as well as some archival footage. Of particular interest is a typescript of "The Art of Comedy," a lecture he presented at the Harvard Loeb Drama Center in 1962. A full-length biography, Jared Brown, *Zero Mostel: A Biography* (1989), offers a particularly revealing treatment of his blacklist period and the stylistic origins of his talent in the Yiddish theater. Also of interest are the reminiscences in Kate Mostel, in *170 Years of Show Business: Kate Mostel and Madeline Gilford, with Jack Gilford and Zero Mostel* (1978); the memorial anecdotes in "Mostel Remembered," *New York Times*, 18 Sept. 1977; and the concise overview of his early career in the *New Yorker*, 28 Oct. 1961, pp. 72–78. Max Waldman's monograph (1965) reproduces a collection of Mostel's drawings, and several brief accounts such as "Infinite Zero," *Newsweek*, 13 Jan. 1964, describe his ambitions. Short photographic essays such as *Zero Reads a Book*, *Zero's Book of Villains*, and *The Sesame Street Book of Opposites* vividly illustrate his pantomimic versatility. An obituary is in the *New York Times*, 10 Sept. 1977.

RICHARD L. BARR

MOTEN, Bennie (13 Nov. 1894–2 Apr. 1935), musician, composer, and bandleader, was born Benjamin Moten in Kansas City, Missouri. Little is known about Moten's father; his mother was a pianist. At age twelve he began performing as a baritone horn player in Lacy Blackburn's Juvenile Brass Band. As a teenager Moten switched to ragtime piano, studying with Charlie Watts and Scrap Harris, two of Scott Joplin's former pupils. By age twenty-four Moten was leading his own trio, B. B. and D., with Bailey Handcock on vocals and Duke Lankford on drums, which worked for over a year. In 1921 Moten formed a six-piece band consisting of Lamar Wright on cornet, Thamon Hayes on trombone, Woodie Walder on clarinet, Willie Hall on drums, George Tall on banjo, and himself on piano. The group worked at Kansas City clubs.

In 1923 Ralph Peer, talent scout and chief of artists and repertoire for the Okeh Record Company, an independent label that maintained a significant "race catalog," auditioned Moten's band and signed the group for its first recording session in September 1923 in St. Louis with blues singers Ada Brown and Mary Bradford. The Bennie Moten Orchestra recording was only part of a very active year during which Freddie Keppard and Doc Cook's Ginger Snaps, Sidney Bechet with Clarence Williams's Blue Five, and Louis Armstrong with King Oliver's Creole Jazz Band also made recordings. Yet Moten's group managed to set itself apart from other bands.

In November 1924 Moten's orchestra, with the addition of Harry Cooper on trumpet, Harlan Leonard on alto saxophone, and Al "Abe" Bolar on tuba, recorded a second time for Okeh. Cooper's addition created a three-piece brass section, while Leonard's addition made for a complete reed section, the first in a Kansas City band. Bolar on tuba strengthened the 2/4 metric concept. Along with Thamon Hayes's composition of the parade-style chart *South*, the November 1924 session began to lead the Moten orchestra away from New Orleans style toward a new type of swing based primarily on section riffs and fluid solo lines. The trend of doubling and tripling instrumentation fostered by Moten led toward simple improvised "head" arrangements. The remaining significant aspect of Kansas City swing, a strong 4/4 rhythm, was not realized until the acquisition of Walter Page, string bassist and tubist, from the Blue Devils in the winter of 1931. Moten recorded a final session for Okeh in May 1925 in Kansas City. The old mechanical recording techniques used in the previous sessions were replaced by electrical methods. Stronger performances of blues with significant interplay among brass and reeds were featured on the session. In 1926 Peer moved to Victor, taking Moten and most of Okeh's strongest talent with him. Moten was associated with Victor from 1926 to 1932. The Moten orchestra was the only Southwest band that held a record contract.

The status of Moten's band was quite high in Kansas City. The band had no serious hometown rival other than the George E. Lee orchestra. The band also received acclaim along the Atlantic seaboard, where its 2/4 rhythms proved to be a novelty to audiences. Moten divided the earnings equally during this period, creating an appealing and stable atmosphere for the band. A recording session in Chicago on 13–14 December 1926 listed the following personnel: Lamar Wright (cornet); Thamon Hayes (trombone); Harlan Leonard, Woodie Walder, and LaForest Dent (reeds); Bennie Moten (piano); Sam Tall (banjo); Vernon Page (tuba); and Willie McWashington (drums).

Moten's success continued into 1928 with a renewed contract at Victor. Thamon Hayes's *South* became a runaway bestseller in September, ranked just below Duke Ellington on the lists. Ballrooms and theaters along the East Coast booked Moten's orchestra during its several Camden, New Jersey, recording sessions. However, because of its conspicuous absence in Kansas City, Moten's group was losing ground to other bands such as the Blue Devils and Lee's band, which were viewed by local audiences as the unadulterated Kansas City style.

The band returned to Kansas City at the height of its national popularity. Moten increased efforts to recruit Blue Devils members Bill Basie, Oran "Hot Lips" Page, and Eddie Durham. In the summer of 1929 Basie and Durham signed on. Durham's versatility on guitar and trombone, as well as his talent as a composer and arranger, along with Basie's energy and rhythmic vitality boosted the quality of the ensemble. Although he still played piano on a second piano alongside Basie, Moten turned his efforts toward management and direction of the band. His nephew Ira "Buster" Moten joined the group, playing both accordion and piano. Trumpeter Hot Lips Page and vocalist Jimmy Rushing next left the Blue Devils to join Moten. With the brass section increased to five, and Rushing ideal for the band, the next Victor session demonstrated advances in technical and musical cohesion.

In the winter of 1931 one of Moten's rivals finally capitulated. Walter Page, bassist and leader of the Blue Devils, joined the Moten orchestra, replacing Vernon Page. Walter's addition brought the final element central to the Kansas City style. Since he performed on both tuba and string bass, Walter Page was able on the bass to present a new rhythmic vitality in a 4/4 beat, while preserving the earlier two-beat style on tuba. With Walter on board, Moten's orchestra was in position to dominate jazz in the Southwest.

Musicians who subsequently joined Moten's ranks included trombonist Dan Minor (formerly with Alphonso Trent), alto saxophonist Eddie Barefield (Eli Rice Cotton Pickers), Joe Keyes on trumpet (Johnson's Joymakers), and young tenor saxophonist Ben Webster (Coy's Black Aces). The windfall of talent afforded Moten one of the most spectacular bands in jazz history, yet a serious rift occurred among its members. The newcomers demonstrated contempt for what they perceived to be limited performing abilities of the older members. The earlier members resented the fact that the band had grown away from its original Kansas City style; they also believed that Moten's change to a payroll system enabled him to siphon extra money for himself. Many of the older members left Moten and formed their own band to attempt to preserve the earlier style.

Nevertheless, Moten's group recorded in October 1931 and continued to gain momentum. By 13 December 1932, the band's last session for Victor, the ensemble was highly polished and turned out its best recordings ever. The twelve members of the 1932 band included Joe Keyes, Lips Page, and Dee Stewart on trumpet; Dan Minor and Eddie Durham on trombone; Eddie Barefield, Ben Webster, and Jack Washington on reeds; and a rhythm section that featured

Bill Basie, Leroy Berry, Walter Page, and Willie McWashington. Some of the works that resulted from this session were *Toby*, *Moten's Swing*, *Blue Room*, *New Orleans*, *Milenburg Joys*, and *Prince of Wails*.

Because of the flexibility of the rhythm section and the cohesiveness of the horn sections, many of the pieces in the Moten book were by this time either riff-based blues or head arrangements. With head arrangements, the basic tune of the piece was worked out in advance. Never written down, they would be played from memory, which allowed each performance to retain uniqueness and variety. In Moten's riff-based blues, a distinctly Kansas City specialty, usually short rhythmic and harmonic patterns were established and played over blues set up by the rhythm section. These works generated a sense of flow and allowed highly interactive exchanges among the reed, brass, and rhythm sections, balanced with rhythmically charged solos.

Moten's orchestra, even with no shortage of work, ran into other obstacles during the depression. Venues sometimes closed down unexpectedly, leaving players stranded with no way home but riding the railcars. The band soon restricted its activity to Kansas City, where work was still available. Moten slowly reduced the band's numbers from an all-time high of fifteen in 1932 to six players by 1933. Nonetheless, players such as tenor saxophonist Lester Young continued to play with the band.

In 1935 Moten sent the band ahead for a lengthy stint at the Rainbow Ballroom in Denver, remaining behind for a tonsillectomy. The surgeon was a personal friend of Moten's, and the evening before the surgery, both men spent the night on the town. The next morning, for whatever reason, the surgery went wrong, and Moten died on the operating table. Leadership of the band temporarily went to Buster Moten and Bill "Count" Basie. The band eventually became the Count Basie Orchestra.

Moten was the pivotal figure in the development of jazz in Kansas City and the Southwest. He was responsible for developing the swing-era jazz orchestra or big band, with its reed, brass, and rhythm sections. The orchestra evolved the genres of riff-based blues and memorized head arrangements, and many members of the orchestra were outstanding musicians in their own right.

• Significant sources for biographical information include Ross Russell, *Jazz Style in Kansas City and the Southwest* (1983), and Nathan W. Pearson, Jr., *Goin' to Kansas City* (1987), which details Moten's career via interviews with members of his band. Gunther Schuller, *Early Jazz: Its Roots and Musical Development* (1968), provides a contextual framework for Moten's career. See also liner notes to *Bennie Moten's Kansas City Orchestra: South (1926–1929)* (Bluebird 3139-2-RB) and *Basie Beginnings: Bennie Moten's Kansas City Orchestra (1929–1932)* (Bluebird 9768-2-RB) for additional information about specific time spans in Moten's career.

DAVID E. SPIES

MOTEN, Lucy Ellen (1851–24 Aug. 1933), teacher educator, was born in Fauquier County, Virginia, near White Sulphur Springs, the daughter of Benjamin Moten, a U.S. Patent Office clerk, and Julia Withers. Taking advantage of their status as free blacks, the Motens moved to the District of Columbia when Lucy was only a child to secure the best possible education for their precocious daughter. Lucy attended Washington's pay schools until 1862, when she was admitted to the district's first public schools for African Americans. After attending the preparatory and normal departments of Howard University, Lucy Moten began teaching in the primary grades of the local public schools and taught there continuously, except for a two-year interruption, from 1870 until 1883. In 1873 Moten moved to Salem, Massachusetts, to attend the State Normal School, from which she graduated in 1875.

In 1883 Frederick Douglass recommended that Moten be appointed to fill the vacant principalship of the Miner Normal School, a public teacher training institution for black primary teachers in the District of Columbia. Although impressed with her experience and academic credentials, the members of the Board of Trustees of the Miner School were concerned that Moten's youth and physical attractiveness made her unsuited for such a responsible position. Only after she assured the trustees that she would refrain from theatergoing, cardplaying, and dancing were they convinced that she was the right person for the job.

From 1883 to 1920 Moten ran the Miner Normal School with an iron hand. She was a strict taskmaster who demanded that her students maintain the highest personal and professional standards. She never challenged them, however, to do anything that she was unwilling to do herself and over time won their universal respect. Moten strongly urged the students with whom she worked to continue to educate themselves. She maintained a high standard in this regard by spending much of her spare time away from Miner furthering her own professional development. The same year she assumed the principalship at Miner, she graduated from the Spencerian Business College with honors. She worked closely with Alfred Townsend, a well-known elocution teacher, to sharpen her public speaking abilities.

Moten participated in countless professional conferences to increase her stock of pedagogical knowledge. She believed that all teachers should know something about health, physiology, and anatomy and attended medical school at Howard University to master these subjects, earning her M.D. in 1897. She employed the medical knowledge she had accumulated by initiating a series of lectures at Miner on health and hygiene. She spent many of her summers in the South teaching in vacation schools for veteran teachers and also found time to continue graduate work in education at New York University.

Moten's energy and enthusiasm for teaching were legendary and inspired at least two generations of African-American educators in the District of Columbia.

During the thirty-seven years that she was the principal of Miner Normal School, Moten took an active part in preparing most of the black primary teachers subsequently employed in the Washington Public Schools. She became so successful, in fact, in furnishing African-American teachers for the District of Columbia that by 1890 the local school board was recommending that prospective teachers from around the country enroll at Miner to benefit from her outstanding leadership. To maintain the highest educational standards, Moten worked unceasingly for more rigorous admissions standards, smaller class sizes, and a larger, better trained, and better compensated faculty. Most of all she sought to make the Miner curriculum more demanding and relevant. In 1896 she successfully expanded the school's program from one to two years, and by the end of her tenure she had laid the foundation for extending the program to a full four years.

Moten probably worked hardest to ensure that the teachers with whom she worked were as committed to character development as they were to fostering academic success. This meant that she expected them to maintain habits of strict integrity and intellectual honesty, to be models of self-control and patience, to remain sympathetic and cheerful at all times, and to cultivate a refined aesthetic taste. To Moten, manners, morals, and intellect were all equally important, especially for teachers preparing to instruct the very young. Her dignity, grace, and decency remained the moral standard by which her students proudly gauged their own contributions to the profession of teaching.

In 1914 Miner Normal School opened a new building modeled on a design suggested by Moten. An avid traveler and Anglophile, she had long admired the architecture of Christ's College at Cambridge University and urged the architects who planned the new Miner facility to base their design on this well-known English college. She also insisted, often over the objections of the board of education, which worried about the added expense, that the classrooms and hallways be well ventilated and well lighted and that in general the new building reflect the latest technology regarding the conditions most conducive to good education.

After Moten retired from Miner she lived most of the rest of her life in New York City and never married. She died tragically in 1933 when a taxicab struck her in New York's Times Square. Even in death her contributions to education continued. She left $51,000 to Howard University, requesting that the money be made available to students wishing to visit and study abroad. Finally, in recognition of Moten's important impact on primary education in the District of Columbia, a Washington elementary school was named for her in 1954.

• Apparently, Moten's personal papers were not preserved, leaving few primary sources from which to reconstruct her life. The annual reports that she wrote for Miner Normal School remain one of the few surviving primary sources. They can be found in the annual reports of the District of Columbia Public Schools. Brief references to the character and accomplishments of Moten are in the oral histories of Norma Boyd and Julia Hamilton Smith in the *Black Women Oral History Project* (10 vols., 1992). Of the secondary sources available about Moten, the most useful are Henrietta Hatter, "History of Miner Teachers College" (master's thesis, Howard Univ., 1939), and Thomasine Carothers, "Lucy Ellen Moten, 1851–1933," *Journal of Negro History* 19 (19 Jan. 1934): 102–6. An obituary is in the *Washington Post*, 8 March 1934.

STEPHEN PRESKILL

MOTEN, Pierce Sherman (28 July 1878–1 Feb. 1965), physician, was born in Winchester, Texas, the son of Pierce Moten, a farmer and businessman, and Amanda (maiden name unknown). His mother, who died when he was young, had planned for her sons to attend college. Moten studied in segregated public schools and pursued many interests, hoping to escape the sharecropper's life.

New York Age editor T. Thomas Fortune convinced Moten's father to send Moten to Tuskegee Institute because of the school's academic reputation in the African-American community and the employment opportunities available to Moten while he attended school there. Moten enrolled in Tuskegee in September 1896. Expressing an interest in medicine, he was employed in the doctor's office and drug room. After two years Moten was recommended for a position in a Tuskegee drugstore owned by a white physician, Dr. Smith. He learned to fill prescriptions and earned a prescription clerk certificate.

Moten continued to work in Tuskegee's drug room "with my heart and hopes set on the day I would become a doctor." In 1900 he graduated from Tuskegee. He directed Dr. C. L. Swain's Columbus, Georgia, drug store for one month, returning to Tuskegee when Booker T. Washington asked him to manage the school hospital's drug room. Moten also studied premedical courses with George Washington Carver and Roscoe C. Bruce, the Harvard-educated head teacher of Tuskegee's academic department.

By June 1902 Moten had moved to Montgomery, Alabama, where he was employed by Dr. Alfred C. Dungee in his office and drugstore. Dungee had worked with Dr. Cornelius N. Dorsette and kept Montgomery's primary black health center, the Hale Infirmary, operating after Dorsette's death. While working for Dungee, Moten received an emergency call to attend to a young boy who had been stabbed in his chest. The knife had penetrated the heart's chamber. Dungee ordered Moten to call Dr. Luther Leonidas Hill, a white physician. Moten held a kerosene lamp as Hill successfully sutured the wound in a pioneering procedure that was reported in international medical journals.

Moten resolved to become a physician. He enrolled in premedical courses at Walden University in Nashville and completed a medical degree at its affiliate, Meharry Medical College, in 1906. During vacations Moten worked at the Chicago Armour Packing Company and Pullman Company to finance his studies. He was permitted to listen to lectures at the College of Physicians and Surgeons at the University of Chicago. In his training to become a physician, Moten benefited from his pharmaceutical expertise.

While waiting for the results of the Alabama state medical board examination, Moten visited friends in Quincy, Florida, and passed that state's medical boards. He established a practice there and married Eula Lee Moore Young, whose adoptive father, the president of Florida A&M College, had taught at Tuskegee. The couple had four children. In 1912 Moten relocated to Birmingham, Alabama, where he established a medical practice the next year. After World War I, the Courts of Calanthe of Alabama asked Moten to be medical director of that fraternal organization. Moten planned and managed a 32-bed hospital for the group.

During the depression, Moten became acutely aware of the inferior medical facilities for the Birmingham black community. Most black women delivered infants at home because the county hospital was overcrowded, and white patients were given priority. Some women in labor who were turned away gave birth on the hospital's grounds. Moten observed one woman deliver her baby on the sidewalk outside the hospital. He was shocked that no one, including himself, offered her or the baby assistance. Moten immediately contacted city leaders and determined to provide adequate delivery services for black women. He admitted that the "mental picture that I saw of myself and others made me determined to do my part to help correct this horrible situation." Because "the weakest link in our race 'chain' is the lack of concern and interest on the part of our men, for the welfare of Negro women and children" ("Dr. Pierce S. Moten," *Journal of the National Medical Association*) he gathered a group of doctors and citizens to create an "emergency station" for expectant mothers located at Thirty-second Street and Sixth Avenue, South.

The public embraced the Southside Clinic, and Moten planned for expansion as demand increased. He was encouraged by support from white politicians and Rosenwald Foundation representatives who secured funds for modernization. By 1937 the new building, called the Slossfield Center, provided services in obstetrics, gynecology, and pediatrics. Moten directed obstetrics, developed postgraduate positions for black physicians, and secured accreditation for the hospital. He achieved reforms while battling political, social, and legal obstacles.

The Slossfield Center became a social center for the black community, hosting annual homecoming celebrations. Because no black schools were located nearby, Moten and his staff directed the construction of a playground and a schoolbuilding for children. He petitioned the Birmingham Board of Education for supplies, and the school gradually grew to more than 1,000 students and thirty-five teachers. Moten lauded, "A dream has become a reality, the community spirit is still moving."

In addition to serving the Slossfield Clinic, Moten was general superintendent of the Tuggle Hospital in Birmingham and on staff at Holy Family Hospital in Ensley, where he had helped draft the constitution and bylaws to gain accreditation. He also was vice president of the Alabama State Medical, Dental, and Pharmaceutical Association and participated in the National Medical Association. He was especially concerned with preserving the history of black medicine. Moten prepared an autobiographical account and was featured on the cover of the July 1961 *Journal of the National Medical Association*. The journal's editor advised readers, "May his story serve as an inspiration for those who still work with him and for those who must carry on."

Moten received honors from his community and peers. Dr. Frederick D. Patterson, a former president of Tuskegee Institute, declared in a letter to Moten of 15 December 1960, "You have written a chapter in the history of medical aid to Negroes in Birmingham, Alabama, and the South, which is an outstanding contribution by any standards and worthy of preservation in the historical annals of medical education."

A civic and club leader, Moten belonged to the Elks and the American Woodmen and was president of the Birmingham chapter of the Knights of Pythias. He devotedly attended the Sixth Avenue Baptist Church, South, and was an ordained minister of the gospel. After suffering for three weeks, Moten died at the Holy Family Hospital in Birmingham.

The *Birmingham World*, an African-American newspaper, eulogized Moten as "the family doctor, a collector of research in his profession, an investigator of facts surrounding maternity cases, organizer of clinics and builder of a hospital." The editor remarked that "To the end, Dr. Moten remained youthful in spirit, hopeful in outlook, and steadfast in his faith in the achieving potential of our group." Remembering him as "distinguished in looks, dignified in manners, and inquisitive in spirit," the newspaper summarized Moten's medical achievements: "Misunderstood at times, taunted by skeptics, shunned by the satisfied, challenged by the timid, and opposed by the selfish, he refused to take down nor give up on those projects and ideas he considered for the good of the community" (6 Feb. 1965).

• There is no known collection of Moten's papers. A biographical account is "Dr. Pierce S. Moten," *Journal of the National Medical Association* 53 (July 1961): 432–35. Secondary sources include Herbert M. Morais, *The History of the Afro-American in Medicine* (1976), and E. H. Beardsley, "Making Separate, Equal: Black Physicians and the Problems of Medical Segregation in the Pre–World War II South," *Bulletin of the History of Medicine* 57 (Fall 1983): 382–96.

ELIZABETH D. SCHAFER

MOTHER ANGELA. *See* Angela.

MOTHER CABRINI. *See* Cabrini, Frances Xavier.

MOTHER JONES. *See* Jones, Mother.

MOTHERWELL, Robert (24 Jan. 1915–16 July 1991), artist, was born in Aberdeen, Washington, the son of Robert Motherwell II, a banker, and Margaret Hogan. His family moved to California when he was three. He demonstrated talent as a painter at an early age, winning a fellowship to the Otis Art Institute in Los Angeles at the age of eleven; he studied there from 1926 to 1929. He then studied painting briefly in 1932 at the California School of Fine Arts in San Francisco. Despite this early training in the fine arts, Motherwell pursued a degree in philosophy at Stanford University, receiving his B.A. in 1937. He wrote an undergraduate thesis on psychoanalytic theory, a subject that remained a lifelong interest and ultimately had a great effect on his art. In 1935 he had visited Europe, where he became deeply interested in French literature, specifically the writings of André Gide. In 1937 he enrolled in a graduate program in philosophy at Harvard University, where he took courses in aesthetics and started a thesis on aesthetic ideas in Eugène Delacroix's *Journals*. Motherwell returned to Europe again in 1938, and in 1940 he moved to New York City.

In 1942 Motherwell married Maria Emilia Ferreira y Moyers; they had no children. Motherwell began summering in the Hamptons on Long Island in 1943; for most of the decade he lived there year-round, and his house served as a nexus for his fellow artists. Painters Mark Rothko and Clyfford Still spent the summer with him in 1948, and also among his friends were Herbert Ferber, Adolph Gottlieb, Barnett Newman, David Smith, and Bradley Walker Tomlin.

In 1950, a year after divorcing his first wife, he married Betty Little, with whom he had two daughters before their divorce in 1957. The couple moved from Long Island to New York City in 1951. In 1956 Motherwell spent his first summer in Provincetown on Cape Cod; the next year he bought a house there and returned every summer for the rest of his life.

When he first arrived in New York in 1940, Motherwell began to study with art historian Meyer Schapiro at Columbia University. Schapiro, however, encouraged him to give up art history in order to study painting, although Motherwell maintained his dual interest in art and academia throughout his career. Evidence of his scholarly side dates from 1943, when he began to edit two series of books, the Documents of Modern Art and the Documents of Twentieth-century Art, of which his own influential book, *The Dada Painters and Poets: An Anthology* (1951), was later a part. Throughout his career he retained his links to the academic world as a committed teacher, conducting courses at the University of Oregon, Oberlin College, Brown University, and Columbia University. He was on the faculty of the influential Black Mountain College in North Carolina from 1945 to 1951, and he was an associate professor of art at Hunter College from 1951 to 1958.

Thanks to Schapiro, Motherwell became acquainted with the European surrealists, many of whom had relocated to New York during World War II. From this time he became increasingly drawn to surrealism, a natural development given his longstanding interest in psychoanalytic theory. But Motherwell was more interested in surrealist theory than he was in surrealist imagery, which he found too literary and representational for his taste. Surrealist theory provided Motherwell a catalyst for his emerging style. The essence of surrealist art lay in the principle of automatism, a visual correlate to free association. The artist begins with no preconceived notion, allowing the brush to guide him, rather than consciously guiding it himself. This "artful scribbling" proved a rich vein for Motherwell to mine; it lent itself to the development of an abstract vocabulary that he would employ throughout his career.

Motherwell's stock characters, a set of biomorphic forms, were developed from these automatist experiments. They were already in evidence in *Pancho Villa Dead or Alive* (1943, Museum of Modern Art, N.Y.), in which Motherwell alternated the geometric passages and ovoid forms that were more fully developed in his series Elegy for the Spanish Republic, begun in 1949. *Pancho Villa*, however, is more figurative and more densely patterned than the Elegies would be. The Elegy paintings are characterized by simplicity and sobriety: a progression of loosely brushed black ovoid and oblong forms nestle against one another, tongue-in-groove, on a white ground, forming a processional rhythm across a monumental horizontal canvas. The somber mood is occasionally broken by equally loose patches of color accenting the totemic forms. This combination of gestural areas with more evenly painted passages earned for Motherwell the reputation of a key bridging figure among the abstract expressionists—his work combined various aspects of both action and color field painting.

Motherwell, who produced more than 150 Elegies in all, could not have sustained the series on the basis of formal considerations alone. A compelling subject matter gave the paintings their substance. Begun in homage to the Spanish Republic, which was crushed by the Spanish Civil War in the 1930s, the Elegies over time acquired more universal resonances. In 1962 Motherwell explained, "The Spanish Elegies are not 'political' but my private insistence that a terrible death happened that should not be forgot[ten] . . . The pictures are also general metaphors of the contrast between life and death, and their interrelation." The latter concept is most evident in the paintings' alternating womblike and phallic forms, which reduce life to its most primal, and perhaps most dangerous, elements. The Elegies demonstrate that although he worked abstractly, Motherwell's most powerful works are not contentless. His conviction that abstractions could carry significant human themes led him in 1948 to found a short-lived informal art school, Subject of the Artist, along with painters William Baziotes and Barnett Newman and the sculptor David Hare. The curriculum comprised a series of Friday night lectures, whose purpose was to emphasize that abstract art was not about nothing, held on Eighth Street in Greenwich Village.

Motherwell in 1955 began his Je t'aime series, a suitable title coming from a Francophile. The series is characterized by loose expressionist brushwork. Bright bands of color surround the vigorously scribbled, centrally inscribed title phrase, acting as a check to the unbounded passion the words express. The Je t'aimes are a joyous counterpoint to the more sober Elegies.

Another successful series was the Opens, begun in 1967. The Opens are diametrically opposed to the Elegies, both in style and content. The latter are more muscularly brushed and are strongly motivated by Motherwell's political convictions. The Opens, which were born serendipitously, perhaps come as close as Motherwell ever got to work based on purely formal considerations. The Opens are Motherwell's response to minimalism, filtered through his abstract expressionist sensibility. Struck by the proportion between a small painting lying backward against a larger finished canvas in his studio, he immediately traced its shape on the larger one. An Open consists of a large monochrome color field brushed with subtle gestural variations. On this field Motherwell drew three sides of a rectangle, with the edge of the canvas completing the shape. By providing a window into the void, the rectangle incorporates illusionary space into an otherwise nonobjective world. As monochrome color flows through the window, two-dimensional space is disrupted with a reminder of pictorial illusionism.

Motherwell moved freely between painting, printmaking, and collage. As with painting, the printmaking that he did was largely self-taught, although he studied engraving in 1941 with Kurt Seligmann and in 1945 with Stanley William Hayter at Atelier 17. His devotion to printmaking is unique among the abstract expressionists; over the course of his career he produced more than 430 prints. While his prints deal to a certain extent with the same material as his paintings, his collages stand in stark contrast. Motherwell's first collages date to 1943, and he continued to explore this medium throughout his career. While Motherwell's paintings convey his concern for the universal, he considered collage a more intimate medium. As a result of this autobiographical focus, his collages are more delicate and lyrical than his paintings, but they tend to be painterly. They are composed of bits of ephemera, which he collected, and interspersed with gentle gestural strokes. Motherwell frequently employs bits of sheet music in his collages as in *Collage with German Music and Canvas* (1974, private collection). Although he could not read music, Motherwell found sheet music visually pleasing, likening the demarcation of notes to abstract calligraphy.

An interest in calligraphy is a thread running though much of Motherwell's oeuvre. It is apparent in his collages, as well as in the large darkly brushed areas of the Elegies floating on white ground. Motherwell found the lack of distinction between abstraction and representation evinced by Asian calligraphy compelling. Moreover, he saw an affinity between calligraphy and the technique of free association, which he learned from the surrealists. He observed, "You learn from Japanese calligraphy to let the hand take over: then you begin to watch the hand as though it is not yours, but as though it is someone else's hand, and begin to look at it critically." Some of Motherwell's later paintings isolate the calligraphic gestures that he had been incorporating into earlier work. *Ancestral Presence* (1976, Chrysler Museum, Norfolk, Va.), explores the craggy edges and delicate bleedings of the hand-painted gesture writ large. Motherwell was married to painter Helen Frankenthaler from 1958 until 1971. In 1970 he gave up his Manhattan studio in favor of a house in Greenwich, Connecticut. He married Renate Pensold, a photographer, in 1972, and they remained together until his death at his summer home in Provincetown.

Motherwell was as much a scholar as he was an artist. As the most educated of the abstract expressionists, he became an eloquent propagandist for the movement and for modernism in general. He understood that abstract expressionism was a natural progression in modernism's evolution. As he wrote, "Every intelligent painter carries the whole culture of modern painting in his head. It is his real subject, of which everything he paints is both an homage and a critique, and everything he says a gloss."

• The majority of Motherwell's papers are at the Dedalus Foundation in Bedford Hills, Conn. The most comprehensive study of his work is H. H. Arnason, *Robert Motherwell* (1977, rev. ed. 1982), for which Motherwell himself wrote the notes on the plates. On his early work, see Robert Saltonstall Mattison, *Robert Motherwell: The Formative Years* (1987). The Albright Knox Art Gallery organized a retrospective, *Robert Motherwell* (1983). See also Jack Flam, *Motherwell* (1991); Frank O'Hara, *Robert Motherwell* (1965); and Stephanie Terenzio's catalogue raisonné, *The Prints of Robert Motherwell* (1984, rev. ed. 1990). Motherwell's writings are gathered in *The Collected Writings of Robert Motherwell* (1992), ed. Stephanie Terenzio. An obituary is in the *New York Times*, 18 July 1991.

PAMELA A. COHEN

MOTLEY, John Lothrop (15 Apr. 1814–29 May 1877), historian and diplomat, was born in Dorchester, Massachusetts, the son of Thomas Motley, a well-to-do merchant, and Anna Lothrop. Both parents were members of the Brahmin caste of New England, and their son would enjoy the advantages of that elite class. After attending the Round Hill School in Northampton, Massachusetts—where he was taught German by George Bancroft, the author of the twelve-volume *History of the United States* (1834–1882)—Motley entered Harvard in 1827. He was bright and had a facility for languages, especially German, but he was negligent in his studies and had to be suspended. Upon returning to Harvard he applied himself and was elected to Phi Beta Kappa before graduating with an A.B. in 1831. Following graduation Motley studied abroad for three years, first in Göttingen, where he formed a friendship with Prince Otto von Bismarck, and then at the University of Berlin, where he studied law and perfected his German. He returned to America in 1835 and was later admitted to the bar, but he never practiced. In 1837 the Unitarian Motley met and married Mary Benjamin, an Episcopalian; they had four children, one of whom died in early childhood.

Motley began his literary career in 1838 with "Goethe," an article on the German poet and dramatist Johann Wolfgang von Goethe in the *New York Review*, followed the next year by a critical survey, "Goethe's Works," in the same magazine. Motley's first novel, *Morton's Hope*, a historical romance, also appeared in 1839. The little critical attention it received was negative: it was condemned for its flawed plot, diction, and characterization. Motley's second historical novel, *Merry Mount* (1849), was better received and showed the author's skill in creating vivid scenes and depicting historical characters. These forays into the field of historical fiction were ultimately beneficial to Motley because they revealed to him that his strengths lay not in writing fiction, for which he had to create plots, but in writing history, for which he could dramatically render actual events and people.

Before he began his career as a historian, Motley served briefly as the secretary of the U.S. legation at St. Petersburg, Russia, in 1841–1842—the first of several diplomatic posts he would hold. The severe climate, low pay, and separation from his family influenced Motley to resign his post and return home. The experience provided him, however, with subjects for his first historical publication, a long article in the *North American Review* in 1845 on Peter the Great that displayed Motley's skill as a biographer and a painter of scenes. Two other *North American Review* articles followed: "The Novels of Balzac" (1847) and "Polity of the Puritans" (1849). In 1849, the year *Merry Mount* was published, Motley served one term in the Massachusetts House of Representatives, an experience that did not engender further political ambitions.

The favorable response to his historical essays in the *North American Review* no doubt contributed to Motley's becoming a historian, and in 1850 he chose for his subject the early Dutch Republic. Similarities between the struggles of the Dutch provinces against Catholic Spain and those of the American colonies against Britain influenced his theme. A memorable visit to another Brahmin historian, William Hickling Prescott, who was writing a history of the reign of Philip II of Spain, encouraged Motley to undertake his project and to make use of Prescott's library. Motley spent the years from 1851 to 1856 in research in libraries in Europe. The three-volume *The Rise of the Dutch Republic* (1856) received immediate popular and critical acclaim (by 1857 15,000 copies had been sold in London). Praised by scholars on the Continent and soon translated into Dutch, German, and Russian, the history was commended by important historical writers in America, including Washington Irving, Bancroft, and Prescott. Shared theories of historical composition accounted for Motley's reception by his fellow American writers. Like Francis Parkman, Prescott, and Bancroft, Motley was a romantic historian who

combined the literary qualities of the epic novel—drama, spectacle, heroic characterization, and unified themes—with careful research from original sources.

After returning to America following the publication of his history, Motley enjoyed the social life of Boston and his membership in the Saturday Club with Oliver Wendell Holmes (later his biographer), Nathaniel Hawthorne, Louis Agassiz, James Russell Lowell, Henry Wadsworth Longfellow, and Prescott. His newly won fame, according to Holmes, made Motley a citizen of the world. Although he would return to America for brief visits, Motley spent his mature years abroad. His return to England and the Continent in 1858 to research his second history provided him with the opportunity to associate with the British aristocracy, among whom he formed friendships.

While residing in England in 1860 Motley completed the first two volumes of *The History of the United Netherlands*, which continued the account of the Dutch revolt against Spain. He was commended for his archival research and use of unpublished manuscripts, and for the labor and art that he invested in his descriptions that put the reader in the scenes described. Before returning to work on the history, Motley, a Republican, published two letters in *The Times* (London) in 1861 explaining the causes of the Civil War and soliciting support for the Union. The letters were influential in gaining for him the post of minister to Austria, in which he served with distinction from 1861 to 1867. According to friends, Motley was eminently qualified for diplomatic service, possessing linguistic skills, charm of conversation, sparkling wit, and according to William Amory, fellow member of the Massachusetts Historical Society, "a manly elegance of person." Insulted by queries put to him by William Henry Seward, the secretary of state, concerning a report alleging that he had made offensive remarks against President Andrew Johnson, Motley resigned his post in 1867.

In 1868 Motley published volumes three and four of *The History of the Netherlands*, which were memorable for their vivid portraits of Elizabeth I of England and Philip II. Returning with his family to Boston that same year, he made a speech in support of General Grant's candidacy for the presidency, which resulted in his appointment as ambassador to the Court of St. James. A conflict between President Ulysses S. Grant and Charles Sumner, the historian's friend and supporter for the post, caused Motley to be recalled in 1870. Bitter over the event, he returned to writing history and established residence at The Hague in 1871 to research his final work. In 1874 he completed *The Life and Death of John Barneveld, Advocate of Holland*, regarded by a contemporary Dutch historian of the same subject as the most classical of Motley's works. At the end of that year Motley's wife died, and the historian, experiencing failing health, made his final visit to America in 1875. His remaining years were spent in England, where he died, near Dorchester.

Motley was a member of the French Academy of Moral and Political Sciences, the Royal Academy of

Arts and Sciences of Amsterdam, the Royal Society of Antiquaries in England, the American Philosophical Society in Philadelphia, and the Historical Society of Utrecht. His reputation as a historian rests on his literary talent rather than objective scholarship. Although he assiduously investigated archival holdings and sought out original manuscripts, he consistently read and interpreted his sources from the point of view of a nineteenth-century American Protestant committed to a belief in religious and political progress. He was dogmatic in assigning virtue and vice, respectively, to the Dutch and Spanish figures in his histories. Consequently, his portraits of Philip II, the duke of Alva, and Margaret of Palma, although striking, are exceptionally biased. Philip II, he recorded, "was prolix with his pen, not from affluence, but from paucity of ideas. He took refuge in a cloud of words, sometimes to conceal his meaning, oftener to conceal the absence of any meaning, thus mystifying not only others but himself " (*The Rise of the Dutch Republic*, vol. 1, p. 125). Motley did not or could not view the age he described in light of its own time, and he invariably judged it by the more humane practices of his own. Although not satisfying modern expectations of an objective account of the past, Motley remains an excellent narrator who brought a colorful age to life.

• Motley's papers are at the Massachusetts Historical Society, the Houghton Library at Harvard University, and the library of the University of Rochester. For Motley's letters, see George William Curtis, ed., *The Correspondence of John Lothrop Motley* (2 vols., 1889), and Susan St. John Mildmay (his daughter) and Herbert St. John Mildmay, eds., *John Lothrop Motley and His Family: Further Letters and Records* (1910). Biographies include Oliver Wendell Holmes, *John Lothrop Motley: A Memoir* (1879), and J. Guberman, *The Life of John Lothrop Motley* (1973). See also David Levin, *History as Romantic Art: Bancroft, Prescott, Motley, and Parkman* (1959), Chester Penn Higby and B. T. Schantz, *John Lothrop Motley: Representative Selections, with Introduction, Bibliography and Notes* (1939), Harry Elmer Barnes, *A History of Historical Writing* (1937), Van Wyck Brooks, *The Flowering of New England: 1815–1865* (1936), and Eric F. Goldman, "The Historians," in *Literary History of the United States*, ed. Robert Spiller et al. (1975).

DONALD DARNELL

MOTLEY, Willard Francis (14 July 1909–4 Mar. 1965), novelist, was born in Chicago, Illinois, the son of Florence Motley. He was reared by his maternal grandparents, Archibald Motley, Sr., a Pullman porter, and Mary Huff. An African American, Motley grew up in a South Side Chicago neighborhood with few black families. He began his literary career precociously, writing a column for the *Chicago Defender*, a black weekly, under the pen name "Bud Billiken." After his graduation from Englewood High School in 1929, however, he found it difficult to break into print and embarked on several cross-country trips—to the East Coast by bicycle and to the West Coast by automobile—in search of adventures to turn into fiction. For the same reason, he left his grandparents' middle-class home for an apartment in a slum. By the end of the

1930s he began to publish in travel and outdoor magazines and in *Commonweal*, and in 1940, while working for the Federal Writers' Project of the WPA, he began work on a naturalistic novel.

Knock on Any Door (1947) was based on Motley's experiences during the 1930s, including a thirty-day jail term in the Laramie County Jail in Wyoming for siphoning gas; a visit to a Colorado reform school after he encountered one of the inmates staring wistfully through the fence and impulsively befriended him; his reporting for the writers project; and informal research visits to Chicago area courtrooms, prisons, and the execution chamber of the Cook County Jail. The protagonist, Nick Romano, is introduced as an innocent altar boy, but after his father loses his business in the depression, Nick begins an escalating conflict with the law. He graduates from petty theft to armed robbery to the murder of a policeman, from reform school to county jail to the electric chair, a victim of the twin environmental influences of poverty and harsh penal institutions.

The novel was Motley's greatest popular and critical success. It sold 350,000 copies during its first two years in print, was condensed by *Omnibook* and a King Features comic strip, was excerpted in an eleven-page picture story in *Look*, and was filmed by Columbia Pictures in 1949, with Humphrey Bogart in a major role. Favorable reviews appeared in large-circulation journals such as *Saturday Review* and *Atlantic Monthly*. In *The Radical Novel in the United States*, Walter Rideout called the book one of the top ten radical novels of the 1940s.

In 1951 Motley moved to Mexico, partly to escape the racism of his own country and partly to escape the notoriety that accompanied his early success as a writer, eventually buying a house near Mexico City. Although he never married, Motley had a family life there with his adopted son, Sergio López. His second novel, *We Fished All Night* (1951), was less successful than his first book, partly because of its loose structure and partly because Motley attempted to treat too many themes, including Chicago politics, labor unions, the conflicts faced by racial and ethnic minorities, and the plight of veterans returning from World War II. More experimental in form than *Knock on Any Door*, the book was nevertheless seen by most critics as a step backward for Motley.

With *Let No Man Write My Epitaph* (1958), Motley returned to the Romano family for a sequel about the lives of Nick Romano's former mistress Nellie Watkins, their illegitimate son, Nick, Jr., and Nick's younger brother Louie. Like Nick in the earlier novel, all three characters face problems with the law, but these problems are compounded by the growing menace of narcotics, as both Nellie and Nick, Jr., become addicted to heroin.

In his earlier work Motley had been studiously color blind, seeking to be identified as a novelist rather than a black novelist. In *Epitaph*, however, he offered a limited view of the African-American experience by treating the sensitive topic of interracial romance.

Louie Romano falls in love with Judy, a black waitress, and each tries to introduce the other to his or her world, only to realize the enormity of the gap between the two cultures. Besides Judy, who comes from a middle-class family much like his own, Motley also creates an array of sympathetically depicted lower-class black characters within the drug culture in which Nellie lives. His views had changed considerably over the years: in 1947 he had refused to allow his publishers to identify him as a Negro in publicity releases, but a decade later he was moving toward his final position, that it was necessary to "stand up and be counted."

Motley's third novel received mixed reviews. Perhaps the most thoughtful, by Granville Hicks, perceptively contrasted the "powerful directness" of *Knock on Any Door* with the distracting multiple plots of *Epitaph* and disapproved of Motley's graceless use of sociological statistics. Although the novel sold only modestly in its hardcover edition, it was reprinted in paperback in 1959 and was the basis for a film with an impressive cast, including James Darren, Shelley Winters, Burl Ives, Ella Fitzgerald, and Ricardo Montalban.

In his final years Motley attempted to employ the insights he had gained in Mexico. He wrote a nonfiction book, "My House Is Your House," documenting both his love for his adopted country and his feeling of wonder at its cultural peculiarities, but was unable to find a publisher. Instead of this good-humored book, Motley's literary exploitation of his Mexican experience became a posthumously published novel, *Let Noon Be Fair* (1966). As Motley's new publisher prodded him to produce a bestseller, he turned *Noon* into a sordid exposé of the deterioration of a charming Mexican village into a tourist trap where Mexican opportunists prey on amoral North American tourists who, in turn, come south to prey on a people they viewed as naive potential victims.

Motley's last years were unhappy, filled with rejections and poverty. After his American royalties were attached by the Internal Revenue Service in 1963 for nonpayment of income taxes, he had to subsist on occasional sales of chapters from "My House Is Your House" to *Rogue*, a Chicago-based men's magazine, and on the European royalties from his first three books. Besides "My House Is Your House," Motley completed "Remember Me to Mama," a novel for which he could not find a publisher; he also experimented with other short stories to screen plays. He died in a Mexico City hospital of intestinal gangrene brought on by poor nutrition and perhaps by alcohol abuse.

• Motley's papers are in three collections. Most of his manuscripts and a number of notes, letters, journals, and clippings are in the library of Northern Illinois University. See Craig Abbott and Kay Van Mol, "The Willard Motley Papers at NIU," *Resources for American Literary Study* 7 (Spring 1977): 3–26. A smaller number of manuscripts and a large number of notes, letters, and clippings are in the library of the University of Wisconsin. See Jerome Klinkowitz, James Giles, and John T. O'Brien, "The Willard Motley Papers at UW," *Resources for American Literary Study* 2 (Autumn 1972): 218–73. The manuscript of *Knock on Any Door*, less the first eighty-seven pages, is in the James Weldon Johnson Collection, Beinecke Rare Book Room and Manuscript Library, Yale University.

Motley's "The Almost White Boy" appears in *Soon, One Morning: New Writing by American Negroes*, ed. Herbert Hill (1963). Diaries covering the years 1926 through 1943 appear in *The Diaries of Willard Motley*, ed. Jerome Klinkowitz (1979). The most thorough biographical-critical study is Robert E. Fleming, *Willard Motley* (1976). An obituary is in the *New York Times*, 5 Mar. 1965.

ROBERT E. FLEMING

MOTT, Charles Stewart (2 June 1875–18 Feb. 1973), industrialist and philanthropist, was born in Newark, New Jersey, the son of John Coon Mott, a cider and vinegar maker, and Isabella Turnbull Stewart. Charles grew up in the New York City metropolitan area. His father urged him to stay in the family business, but Charles wanted to study mechanical engineering. As a compromise, he enrolled in night classes at the Stevens Institute of Technology in 1892 while working days with his father. During the summer of 1893 Mott did a tour of sea duty after enlisting in the New York State Naval Militia. A year later his father sent him first to Copenhagen to study yeast cultures and then to Munich to study fermentation. In September 1895 Mott reenrolled at the Stevens Institute, and in June 1897 he received a degree in mechanical engineering.

In 1898 Mott saw action as a gunner's mate first class on the USS *Yankee* during the war against Spain. After the war, he helped manage several family-owned businesses including the Weston-Mott Company, a wheel and axle manufacturer in Utica, New York. After his father died suddenly in June 1899, Mott began to work full time as secretary and superintendent at the Weston-Mott factory. A local businessman, William G. Doolittle, joined Mott as a partner during the firm's transition to automotive parts production.

In 1900 he married Ethel Culbert Harding of New York City. The couple moved to Utica and eventually to Flint, Michigan, where they raised three children. Ethel died in 1924. Mott's personal life remained unsettled for the next decade. He married Mitties Rathbun Butterfield of Detroit in 1927. This marriage ended with his wife's death just a year later. Mott was briefly married to, and then divorced from, Dee Van Balkom Furey in 1929. In 1934 Mott married the daughter of a cousin, Ruth Rawlings of El Paso, Texas. Charles and Ruth Mott also had three children. They lived in Flint together the rest of his life.

In September 1901 Mott had purchased his first automobile, a Utica-built Remington Model C. Mott was soon an automotive aficionado. He was elected first president of the Automobile Club of Utica and was a founder of the American Automobile Association. Mott's business life also became tied to the automobile industry. In 1902 Weston-Mott plunged into crisis when the market for wire wheels collapsed. Mott saved the company by personally directing the design and production of a new kind of front and rear axle technology for the burgeoning automobile industry. Orders for the new axles poured in, forcing Weston-Mott to quadruple its production capacity by 1905.

That same year, William C. Durant convinced Mott to move the company from Utica to Flint, where it was housed in a new factory across the street from Durant's fast-growing Buick Motor Company. In 1907 Mott became Weston-Mott's sole owner when William Doolittle died. During the next five years, Weston-Mott constantly expanded to keep up with the growth of orders from Buick and other automobile companies. By 1913 Weston-Mott was the world's largest manufacturer of automobile axles. Durant's new General Motors Corporation bought 49 percent of Weston-Mott in 1908. In 1913 General Motors completely absorbed Weston-Mott in a deal that made Mott GM's largest individual stockholder and a member of the board of directors.

In 1912 Mott, a lifelong Republican, was persuaded to run for public office at the head of an "Independent Citizens" coalition put together to defeat the Socialist mayor of Flint. Mott was elected mayor that year and was reelected in 1913. He proved to be a very effective reformer. Mott created a professional staff to administer local government, improved Flint's water and sewer systems, began paving the city's streets, and successfully pushed ordinances regulating health, factory conditions, and child welfare through the city council. Although he was defeated in bids for a third term in 1914 and 1915, Mott remained politically ambitious. Mott was again elected mayor of Flint in April 1918 but spent most of that year supervising the motors branch of the Army Quartermaster Corps. In November 1918, just three days before the armistice, Mott resigned as mayor of Flint to accept a commission as a major in the U.S. Army. He was decommissioned in January 1919. After touring Europe with a group of General Motors executives later that year, Mott decided to run for governor of Michigan. His third place finish in the 1920 Republican primary ended his political career.

Mott had been made a General Motors vice president in 1916. In 1922 he was appointed to the corporation's governing body, the executive committee. Like his close friend, GM president Alfred P. Sloan, Jr., Mott had a rigorous analytical mind, an austere demeanor, and an enormous capacity for work. During the mid-1920s Mott helped Sloan reorganize General Motors automotive and parts production. In 1929 he moved from the executive committee to the finance committee. Mott retired as a senior vice president in 1937 but remained on GM's board of directors and its audit committee until his death.

Throughout his life, Mott cultivated other business interests that added to his considerable wealth. He was at various times the major stockholder and an executive officer of the U.S. Sugar Company, Northern Sugar Company, Coleman Stove Company, Sterling Motors, and Northern Illinois Water Company, as well as several Michigan banks and department stores.

In 1929 Mott made national headlines when he put up $3.5 million of his own money to protect depositors of the faltering Union Industrial Bank in Flint. By 1940 Mott's investments had made him one of the fifteen richest people on earth.

Mott soon became a renowned philanthropist. He made large gifts to the University of Michigan's Children's Hospital, Wayne State University Medical School, the University of Chicago's Industrial Relations Center, and the Stevens Institute of Technology. He was especially generous within his adopted hometown of Flint, Michigan. Mott provided land and capital for Flint's downtown cultural center, its community college, the local branch of the University of Michigan, the city's largest park, and a local summer camp for children. Most importantly, in 1926 he established the Charles Stewart Mott Foundation with an initial grant of 2,000 shares of General Motors stock. Before his death, Mott added more than two million shares of GM stock to the foundation's endowment. The Mott Foundation pioneered the development of "community schools" in Flint neighborhoods during the 1930s. The community schools provided adult education, youth recreation, and health programs in public school buildings during afternoons and evenings. By the 1950s the Mott Community Schools had become a model for similar programs in cities across the United States. Mott was honored for this work by President Dwight D. Eisenhower in a White House ceremony on 11 January 1955.

As an engineer and corporate executive, Mott made a significant contribution to the automotive revolution in American history. Ultimately, however, his philanthropic activities were more important. Through his personal generosity and the work of the Mott Foundation, he was able to turn a significant part of the wealth he generated through the automobile industry into enduring educational and social institutions that improved the quality of life in Flint and other cities across the United States.

• Collections of Mott's papers may be found in Flint, Mich., at the Charles Stewart Mott Foundation, the GMI Engineering and Management Institute Historical Collections, and at the Applewood Museum. A biography is Clarence H. Young and William A. Quinn, *Foundation for Living: The Story of Charles Stewart Mott and Flint* (1963), which stresses Mott's philanthropic activities.

RONALD EDSFORTH

MOTT, Frank Luther (4 Apr. 1886–23 Oct. 1964), journalism historian and educator, was born in What Cheer, Iowa, the son of David Charles Mott, a newspaper editor and publisher, and Mary E. Tipton. Mott learned the newspaper business from his father's newspapers, the *What Cheer Patriot* and the *Tipton Advertiser*, and at the *El Reno Daily American* in Oklahoma, where he worked during school breaks while a student to help pay for his expenses. He studied literature and philosophy at Simpson College at Indianola, Iowa, and then transferred in his senior year to the

University of Chicago, where he received a bachelor of philosophy degree in 1907. Mott spent ten years as a publisher and editor at small-town newspapers in Iowa, the *Marengo Republican* (1907–1913) and the *Grand Junction Globe* (1913–1917), after which he finished his M.A. (1919) and then received a Ph.D. (1928) in English from Columbia University. He married Vera H. Ingram, a Simpson College classmate, in 1910; they had one daughter.

Mott began his academic career as a professor of English first at Simpson College (1919–1921) and then at the University of Iowa (1921–1925), where he was coeditor of *Midland Magazine*. In 1927 he was made professor of journalism and director of the Iowa School of Journalism. In 1942 he became the third dean of the Missouri School of Journalism, where he built the graduate program (1942–1951) and the school's academic scholarship. After stepping down as dean in 1951, Mott taught as professor emeritus and dean emeritus until his retirement in 1956. Known by Missouri students for his histrionics as a lecturer in the required undergraduate course, the famed "History and Principles of Journalism," he began by explaining, "History throws light on the growth and meaning of principles, and the principles give meaning to history." Mott's lectures demonstrated journalism examples through historical accounts. One session nearly always included his dramatic recitation of "The Face on the Barroom Floor," a lesson in colorful reporting. Beloved by graduate students, he held a "Literature of Journalism" seminar weekly in his book-lined home study, where he passed out tea and coffee and cookies to his visitors. After World War II, he assisted in the special training of journalists for the U.S. military as chief of the journalism section of the army's American University of Biarritz, France (1945–1946), and adviser to General Douglas MacArthur's staff in Japan and to Japanese leaders about journalism education (1947).

Over the course of his lifetime Mott wrote more than a dozen books and 100 articles. He began with fiction, *Six Prophets Out of the Middle West* (1917), and short stories. "The Man with the Good Face" (1921), which was reprinted the next year in *O'Brien's Best Short Stories*, and *The Literature of Pioneer Life in Iowa* (1923). His fiction efforts pale beside his more successful nonfiction writings. He wrote *Rewards of Reading* (1926) and later collaborated with artist Grant Wood on the monograph *Revolt against the City* (1935). For decades, American journalism students used as a history text his *American Journalism: A History of Newspapers in the United States through 250 Years, 1690 to 1940* (1941). One reviewer described it as a history of "American folkways, as reflected in its press."

Mott's best-known work was the monumental five-volume series, *A History of American Magazines* (vol. 1, 1930; vols. 2 and 3, 1938; vol. 4, 1957), a major American history reference. The series was Mott's life's work, beginning with his Ph.D. dissertation and continuing until his last illness. It gave scholars for the first time a detailed chronology of the great editors, their national influence, and their salaries to authors.

In 1939 he received a Pulitzer Prize for history for the second and third volumes. After publishing the fourth volume in 1957, covering 1885–1905, he received Columbia University's Bancroft Prize for history and the 1958 National Research Award of Kappa Tau Alpha, the journalism scholastic fraternity. His unfinished fifth volume was published posthumously (1968). Mott's achievement remained for decades after his death the definitive history of American magazines.

Mott also wrote *Jefferson and the Press* (1943), *Golden Multitudes* (1947), a history of bestsellers in America, and *The News in America* (1952). He reminisced in *Time Enough, Essays in Autobiography* (1962) with personal sketches of the small towns of the Midwest. Just before his death in Columbia, Missouri, he completed *The Missouri Reader* (1964), a collection of stories, essays, poems, sketches, and folktales about the state, including "The Pronunciation of 'Missouri.'"

Mott's faith in the power of journalism was built on the concept that "the whole history of American journalism is a history of the leadership of great editors and publishers. And it is a mistake to assert, as some do, that the day of the great paper, the great editor, the great newspaper writer and the great publisher is past." In the monograph *A Free Press* (1958), he stressed the importance of the free press in a democracy, "if those decisions are to be made intelligently, they must be based upon adequate knowledge possessed by people concerning events and conditions." He recorded in his diary, "It is a public service that the journalist performs and should be looked upon as such by the laws and by legislature." Mott's critics contend that he became an academic rather a practicing journalist. Iowa colleague George Gallup insisted that "he did not qualify as a real newspaperman."

His peers recognized his vast scholarship and leadership. He served as editor in chief of *Journalism Quarterly* (1930–1934), the first scholarly journal in the field, and as chair of the National Council for Research in Journalism (1934–1938). He was the first elected president of the American Association of Schools and Departments of Journalism (1929). With George Gallup, he founded the high school journalism society *Quill and Scroll*.

Mott was one of the founding giants of journalism education. With his texts and well-known teaching skills, he helped shape the pedagogy of the new discipline of academic journalism and became one of the most prominent educators in the field. He gave the field of journalism academic credence and, according to his *New York Times* obituary, is credited with "having developed the University of Missouri School of Journalism into one of the foremost institutions of its kind."

• Mott's papers, correspondence, and diaries on tape are in the Western Manuscripts Collection, State Historical Society of Missouri. Additional material is held in the University of Iowa archives. The journalism faculty files are in the Missouri School of Journalism. The most complete assessment of his career is in Max Lawrence Marshall, "Frank Luther Mott:

Journalism Educator" (Ph.D. diss., Univ. of Missouri, 1968). Obituaries are in the *Columbia Missourian* and the *Kansas City Star*, both 23 Oct. 1964, and the *New York Times*, 24 Oct. 1964.

BETTY HOUCHIN WINFIELD

MOTT, Gershom (7 Apr. 1822–29 Nov. 1884), army officer and businessman, was born in Lamberton (now part of Trenton), New Jersey, the son of Gershom Mott and Phoebe Rose Scudder. Educated at Trenton Academy, he became a clerk in a New York City dry goods store at the age of fourteen. In 1847, when the Mexican War was in its second year, Mott obtained a commission as second lieutenant in the Tenth U.S. Infantry. This regiment, however, never left the United States, so Mott was denied combat. Mustered out at the end of the war, he married Elizabeth Smith in 1849. The marriage produced one child. Mott worked first as customs collector for the port of Lamberton and later, beginning in 1850, for the Bordentown, Delaware & Raritan Canal Company. In 1855 he moved on to a position as teller for the Bordentown Banking Company.

With the Civil War already four months old and the battle of Bull Run (Manassas) having demonstrated the need for large forces, the Fifth New Jersey Volunteer Infantry was organized at Trenton on 17 August 1861. Mott was selected to be its lieutenant colonel. The regiment became part of Major General George B. McClellan's Army of the Potomac and was transferred to the Virginia Peninsula for McClellan's campaign there in the spring of 1862. On 5 May it was among the troops that clashed with a Confederate rear guard at Williamsburg, and Mott distinguished himself sufficiently to win promotion to colonel of the Sixth New Jersey two days later. That regiment he led through the battle of Seven Pines (31 May-1 June 1862), where it saw action on the second day. In the Seven Days' battles (25 June-1 July 1862), it remained in reserve. Transferred back to northern Virginia that summer along with the rest of the Army of the Potomac, Mott and his regiment were in the thick of the fighting at the second battle of Bull Run (Second Manassas) on 30 August 1862, and Mott was seriously wounded. During his convalescence he was promoted to brigadier general of volunteers (7 Sept. 1862), and when he returned to the army the following February, he was given command of the Third Brigade of Major General Hiram G. Berry's Second Division of the III Corps. At the battle of Chancellorsville (1–4 May 1863), Mott was again seriously wounded. He returned to duty and to command of his brigade that fall in time to take part in Major General George G. Meade's Mine Run campaign, an abortive attempt to gain a tactical advantage against Confederate Robert E. Lee.

The following spring the badly depleted III Corps was broken up and consolidated into other units. Mott's brigade became part of the Fourth Division of the II Corps on 25 March 1864. Less than six weeks later, on 2 May, he was given command of the division. This would have been a difficult task in any case, since the division had seen much hard service, was badly depleted, resented the disbanding of the III Corps, and was largely demoralized. Mott's task was made even harder by the fact that the Army of the Potomac advanced across the Rapidan on the third day of his command and was locked in pitched battle with Lee the following day in a dense forest that was every commander's nightmare. On the second day of this battle of the Wilderness (6 May), Mott's division broke and ran for the rear. The result of the battle as a whole was indecisive, and the Union commander, Lieutenant General Ulysses S. Grant, advanced to encounter Lee again at nearby Spotsylvania Court House (8–21 May). There, on 10 May, Mott's division was given the duty of advancing to support an assaulting column commanded by Colonel Emory Upton. Though Upton's column achieved a local tactical breakthrough, Mott's division was hit by enfilading artillery fire as it moved in support. Once again the demoralized troops fled to the rear. Three days later the division was consolidated into a single brigade in Major General David B. Birney's Third Division of the II Corps. Mott was disgruntled at this effective demotion to brigade command, but presented with the alternative of being mustered out of the army, he had no choice. He led his new brigade ably through the battles of the North Anna and Cold Harbor.

When, on 18 June 1864, Birney was transferred to other duties, Mott succeeded to command of the division. He gained recognition for his performance at the battle of the Crater (30 July 1864) outside Petersburg and was brevetted major general. He continued in command of the division throughout the Petersburg siege (15 June 1864-2 Apr. 1865), and for a couple of days in February 1865, he actually exercised command of the corps. He took part in the Appomattox campaign but was not present at Lee's surrender (9 Apr. 1865). On 1 December 1865 he was promoted to the full rank of major general, to date from 26 May of that year. On 20 February 1866 he resigned from the army.

Thereafter Mott followed various civilian pursuits, turning down an offer of a commission as colonel of the Thirty-third U.S. Infantry in 1868. In 1866 he became paymaster for the Camden & Amboy Railroad and in 1875 took the post of treasurer of the state of New Jersey. The following year he became keeper of the state prison, a position he held for five years. In 1882 he became a member of the Riparian Commission of New Jersey. Simultaneously he held the office of commander of the New Jersey National Guard and was also a member of the iron-foundry firm of Thompson & Mott. He died in New York City.

• For further information on Mott see Ezra J. Warner, *Generals in Blue: Lives of the Union Commanders* (1964); U.S. War Department, *The War of the Rebellion: A Compilation of the Official Records of the Union and Confederate Armies* (128 vols., 1880–1901); Ulysses S. Grant, *Personal Memoirs of U.S. Grant* (2 vols., 1886); and Bruce Catton, *A Stillness at Appomattox* (1953).

STEVEN E. WOODWORTH

MOTT, James (29 June 1788–26 Jan. 1868), merchant and reformer, was born at Cowneck (later North Hempstead), New York, the son of Adam Mott, a farmer and miller, and Anne Mott (Mott was both her maiden and her married name). Both parents were descended from a seventeenth-century Quaker emigrant from England, and Mott was brought up in a close-knit community of Long Island Friends. He received his education at a Friends' boarding school at Nine Partners in New York's Dutchess County. He excelled at Nine Partners and, after ten years, was appointed an assistant teacher and then a teacher. At the school he met Lucretia Coffin, another student who became a teacher (at lower salary because of her sex), to whom he became engaged. When her family moved from Massachusetts to Philadelphia in 1809, he moved there too and began work as an assistant in her father's cut-nail business. In April 1811 they were married in Pine Street Meetinghouse and began what was to be celebrated as an exemplary marriage of reformers.

Mott left the nail business in the economic uncertainties after the War of 1812 and in the early 1820s began to achieve some prosperity as a merchant in the cotton trade. After the death of their first son (the second of six children), the Motts in their grief became intensely religious. Lucretia gained her first public-speaking success as a minister in Friends' meetinghouses. The Motts played a leading part in the "Great Separation" of 1827 in the Society of Friends. Like other followers of Elias Hicks, they were disowned by the orthodox for stressing the guidance of the inner light and the importance of human reason instead of more evangelical views of Jesus's divinity and spiritual authority. The Motts also followed Hicks's denunciation of slavery and teachings against the use of the products of slavery. Not only did this mean avoidance of cotton, sugar, and rag paper in their home, but it also required Mott to reexamine his profitable business dealing in cotton goods. In 1829 he had a "free produce" store in Philadelphia, and the next year he went into the wool commission business, in which he eventually prospered.

Mott was an active member of Philadelphia's Free Produce Society. This organization, like the Pennsylvania Anti-Slavery Society of which Mott was a charter member, was all male, while Lucretia Mott was a key figure in female antislavery organizations. By the end of the 1830s, however, abolitionists were bitterly divided over this kind of segregation by sex, and Lucretia Mott had joined Angelina and Sarah Grimké, Abigail Kelly, and others, as abolitionist women who could not be relegated to subordinate roles. The Motts were delegates to the World's Anti-Slavery Convention held in London in 1840, but the convention refused to recognize women except as observers. In *Three Months in Great Britain* (1841), Mott gives his account of these events, which reflected international schisms among both Quakers and abolitionists and gave impetus to the creation of an American women's rights movement. Mott himself presided at the Seneca Falls women's rights convention of 1848. Thus that famous convention, which issued bold expressions of women's rights, could not be criticized for having let a woman preside (though women did preside at similar conventions thereafter).

This instance of quietly lending respectability to the women's movement was typical of Mott's role in his marriage as his wife rose to fame as an abolitionist and feminist. The Swedish novelist Fredrika Bremer described him in 1850 as "a strong old gentleman, . . . obscured somewhat by the publicity of his wife's glory. It is said that he is pleased by it, and it does him honor" (*Homes of the New World* [1853], vol. 1, p. 432). By traveling with his wife and giving affectionate support to her throughout all her activities, he shielded her from attacks that other women reformers experienced. He was better at correspondence than she was. Within the various movements in which they participated their marriage was widely admired as a true partnership; within the women's movement he was revered.

In 1852 Mott retired from business. In 1857 the Motts moved from the city to a farm outside Philadelphia, but they remained active in reform activities, and their home remained a haven for fugitive slaves. In his retirement Mott took increasing interest in educational opportunities for young Quakers. He was one of the incorporators of Swarthmore College in 1864 and served on its board of managers. He died of pneumonia while visiting a daughter in Brooklyn. When his granddaughter Anna Davis Hallowell took responsibility for writing the life of Lucretia Mott, she found it so intertwined with James Mott's that it was impossible to recount one without the other.

• The Motts' papers are in the Friends Historical Library at Swarthmore College. For published information on James Mott's life, see Anna Davis Hallowell, *James and Lucretia Mott* (1984), which extracts extensively from the family papers. See also the biographies of his wife, including Otelia Cromwell, *Lucretia Mott* (1958), and Margaret Hope Bacon, *Valiant Friend: The Life of Lucretia Mott* (1980). For an appreciative treatment of James Mott's role as a model abolitionist husband, see Blanche Glassman Hersh, *The Slavery of Sex: Feminist Abolitionists in America* (1978). An obituary is in the *New York Tribune*, 27 Jan. 1868.

LEWIS PERRY

MOTT, John R. (25 May 1865–31 Jan. 1955), ecumenical and missionary activist, was born in Livingston Manor, New York, the son of John Stitt Mott and Elmira Dodge, farmers. The family soon moved to Pottsville, Iowa, where his father became a successful lumber and hardware merchant as well as mayor. The younger Mott added the middle initial to his name during childhood to distinguish himself from his father. After attending local schools he entered the preparatory department of Upper Iowa University in

1881 and remained there until 1885. He then transferred to Cornell University, where he studied history and graduated with a Ph.D. in 1888. He married Leila Ada White, a teacher and the sister of religious leaders John Campbell and Wilbert Webster White, in 1891; the Motts had four children. Leila Mott died in 1952, and Mott married Agnes Peter the following year.

Mott held salaried positions with the Young Men's Christian Association of the United States from 1888 until his retirement in 1928. He was at the same time an unpaid officer of numerous student, missionary, and ecumenical organizations—work supported by wealthy donors such as Cleveland H. Dodge, Cyrus McCormick, Jr., Nettie Fowler McCormick, John D. Rockefeller, Jr., and James Stokes. Their contributions made possible the travel, conferences, and personal staff with which Mott carried out his multiple responsibilities and also supported him during the twenty years of continued activity in global Christian affairs that followed 1928.

The evangelical Methodist piety, with an emphasis on personal "holiness," that Mott learned from his parents led him to a conversion experience at the age of thirteen. He became a charter member of the Upper Iowa college YMCA and an officer of the Cornell Christian Association. An encounter with English college athlete and evangelist J. E. K. Studd in January 1886 led him to consecrate himself to Christian service, and in July of that year he was among the one hundred students at evangelist Dwight L. Moody's Mount Hermon, Massachusetts, student conference who pledged to become foreign missionaries. Although he was also one of four who agreed at the time to tour colleges for a year to recruit other students, Mott decided instead to return to Cornell, where he became president of the Christian Association, and after graduation he accepted a one-year position as traveling secretary of the national YMCA College Committee.

The appointment was renewed, and in 1890 Mott was made senior student secretary. He became associate general secretary of the foreign department as well in 1901, with responsibility for YMCAs around the world. In 1915 he gave up both positions to become general secretary of the national association. He was elected life chairman of the World's Alliance of YMCAs in 1926 and served actively, after retiring from his paid position in the American association in 1928, until 1947.

Mott's involvement in the YMCA led to leadership positions in the Student Volunteer Movement for Foreign Missions (SVM) and in the World's Student Christian Federation (WSCF). When the spontaneous student movement begun at Mount Hermon was organized into the SVM in 1888, Mott became secretary of its executive committee, a position he held until 1921. By the 1920s the SVM, which functioned cooperatively as the missionary department of the YMCA and other student Christian organizations, had enlisted more than 8,000 missionaries for American Protestant foreign mission boards. Mott was determined also to bring Christian students of different countries together into one organization. He helped create the World's Student Christian Federation in 1895 and served as its general secretary until 1920 and chairman from 1920 to 1928.

Mott's involvement with foreign missions expanded when the Foreign Missions Conference of North America, a consortium of denominational mission boards he helped form in 1893, delegated him to the planning committee for the 1910 world missionary conference in Edinburgh, Scotland. His skill at chairing the conference sessions and at arguing for and chairing the ongoing Continuation Committee created to coordinate missionary efforts earned him a global reputation as a missionary leader. A 1912–1913 tour of Great Britain, Europe, India, China, Korea, and Japan combined student evangelism and YMCA visits with promotion of the Continuation Committee. Mott encouraged the Asian Christians to form national councils capable of representing them in international meetings on the same level as the European and American organizations. While in China, Mott declined President Woodrow Wilson's appointment as U.S. ambassador to that nation.

Wilson did secure Mott's participation in the 1916 Joint High Commission with Mexico, intended to defuse the tensions caused by General John H. Pershing's pursuit into Mexico of Pancho Villa, and in the 1917 Root Mission to Russia, sent to reinforce democratic tendencies in that country's new provisional government. The Foreign Missions Conference sent Mott and others to the Versailles Peace Conference to defend the rights of missionaries and the cause of religious freedom. During and after the war—the Continuation Committee did not meet after the fall of 1913—Mott traveled to Europe and used his many personal connections to advance various relief programs. At home, he made the YMCA a major social service organization for military personnel: he proposed and became general secretary of the YMCA War Work Council in 1917, was a member of the Federal Council of Churches' General War-Time Commission of the Churches, and in 1918 directed a large and successful united fundraising campaign for the service organizations working with soldiers. After the war he was chairman of the executive committee of the overly ambitious Interchurch World Movement of 1919 and of its successor, the Rockefeller-supported Institute of Social and Religious Research, from 1923 to 1934. He endorsed the institute's Laymen's Foreign Missions Inquiry and its theologically liberal report, written by William E. Hocking, *Re-Thinking Missions* (1932). Conservative "mainline" mission leaders such as Robert E. Speer were critical of the report's view of Christianity as one among many equally legitimate religions that were evolving together into a single world faith. Others, including the SVM's Robert P. Wilder, were troubled by the "social gospel" influence that made social welfare and political reform missionary concerns. While maintaining close ties with his conservative colleagues, Mott was more accepting of both theological and social liberalism.

By the 1920s the global coordination of Christian missions and organizations was Mott's central interest. In 1921 he resigned as SVM and WSCF secretary, and in 1928 as YMCA general secretary, in order to devote more time to the new International Missionary Council (IMC), inspired by the Edinburgh Continuation Committee. As IMC chairman until 1941, Mott traveled almost continuously. He encouraged the gradually but steadily increasing involvement in ecumenical organizations of Greek, Russian, and other Orthodox Christians and of the indigenous "younger" churches growing out of former missions. Mott chaired the influential IMC meetings held in Jerusalem in 1928 and Tambaram (Madras) in 1938. The first conference identified secularism, rather than other religions, as the major challenge Christianity faced. The second conference began to grapple with communism and fascism as well.

Now the world's best-known ecumenist, Mott participated in the 1937 conferences of American Episcopalian Charles Brent's Faith and Order movement (Oxford) and Swedish Lutheran Nathan Soderblom's Life and Work movement (Edinburgh). He strongly supported the proposal for a world council of churches advanced at Oxford, and at a 1938 meeting in Utrecht he was chosen vice chairman of the administrative committee charged with bringing the council into being. He chaired the meetings of the North American members of that committee from 1937 to 1946, was made one of five provisional presidents in 1946, helped plan the inaugural meeting of the council in Amsterdam in 1948, chaired that meeting's business committee, and was proclaimed honorary president of the World Council of Churches. Numerous honorary degrees and other awards preceded and followed that one, including the sharing of the 1946 Nobel Peace Prize with American economist and peace activist Emily Greene Balch. Mott was active until just before his death, at the age of eighty-nine, in Orlando, Florida. Always a Methodist, he had been made an honorary canon of the Washington Cathedral (Episcopal), of which his second wife was an active member, and was buried there.

John Mott was essentially a professional ecumenical Christian organizer, speaker, fundraiser, and administrator. His often simultaneous commitments to cooperative religious organizations reflected changes in both U.S. and world Protestantism from the late nineteenth to the mid-twentieth century, as those commitments gradually shifted from American foreign missions and American students to emerging national churches and international ecumenical organizations. Seen by Europeans—especially after the 1910 Edinburgh missionary conference—as the personification of a typically American, activist, and theologically weak Protestantism, Mott's personal piety and charm, and his openness to various forms of Christianity, nevertheless endeared him to diverse Christians worldwide. A widely known and respected ecumenical statesman for more than sixty years, Mott provided a personal link between various organizations, groups of Christians, and individual leaders and in so doing contributed significantly to their growing sense of membership in a global ecumenical Christian community.

• Mott's personal papers are in the Yale Divinity School Library and the YMCA Historical Library in New York City. The SVM archives are at Yale. Mott published many of his speeches and short written pieces in six volumes of *Addresses and Papers* (1946–1947). Mott's organizing and speaking were more important than his books, but among his books were *Strategic Points in the World's Conquest* (1897), *The Evangelization of the World in this Generation* (1900), *The Future Leadership of the Church* (1908), *The Decisive Hour of Christian Missions* (1910), *The Present World Situation* (1914), *The World's Student Christian Federation: Origin, Achievements, Forecast* (1920), and *Five Decades and a Forward View* (1939).

Biographies include Basil Mathews, *John R. Mott: World Citizen* (1934); a chapter in G. Sherwood Eddy, *Pathfinders of the World Missionary Crusade* (1945); Galen Fisher, *John R. Mott, Architect of Co-operation and Unity* (1952); and Robert C. Mackie et al., *Layman Extraordinary: John R. Mott, 1865–1955* (1965). The most recent and exhaustive study is C. Howard Hopkins, *John R. Mott, 1865–1955: A Biography* (1979), which includes a bibliography of Mott's major publications.

Standard studies of the organizations and movements in which Mott participated include Hopkins, *History of the YMCA in North America* (1951), Kenneth Scott Latourette, *World Service, A History of the Foreign Work and World Service of the Young Men's Christian Association of the U.S. and Canada* (1957), and Clarence P. Shedd, *History of the World's Alliance of YMCAs* (1955), on the YMCA; Robert P. Wilder, *The Student Volunteer Movement* (1935), and Clifton J. Phillips, "Changing Attitudes in the Student Volunteer Movement of Great Britain and North America," in *Missionary Ideologies in the Imperialist Era: 1880–1920*, ed. Torben Christensen and William R. Hutchison (1982), on the SVM; Ruth Rouse, *The World's Student Christian Federation: A History of the First Thirty Years* (1948), on the WSCF; William R. Hogg, *Ecumenical Foundations: A History of the International Missionary Council* (1952); and Rouse and C. S. Neill, eds., *A History of the Ecumenical Movement, 1517–1948* (1954), and Samuel McCrea Cavert, *Church Cooperation and Unity in America: A Historical Review: 1900–1970* (1970), on the ecumenical movement. An obituary appears in the *New York Times*, 1 Feb. 1955, and Mott's longtime Scottish colleague John H. Oldham published a tribute in the *Ecumenical Review*, Apr. 1955, pp. 256–59.

ROBERT A. SCHNEIDER

MOTT, Lucretia Coffin (3 Jan. 1793–11 Nov. 1880), abolitionist and feminist, was born on Nantucket Island, Massachusetts, the daughter of Thomas Coffin, Jr., a ship captain, and Anna Folger, a shopkeeper. The second of five children, Lucretia was raised in a family strongly shaped by their membership in the Society of Friends (Quakers), which includes among its tenets the equality of women and men. This abstract notion of equal abilities and worth was made concrete by her mother's success as a small shopkeeper during her father's frequent and prolonged absences.

As a child Lucretia was shocked by the horrors of slavery recounted in English Quaker and prolific author Priscilla Wakefield's *Mental Improvement* (1819).

Other shaping forces included her regular attendance at Quaker Meetings, where worship consisted of sitting in silence until any member, male or female, felt moved by the Holy Spirit to speak. After the capture of his ship in 1802 by a Spanish man-of-war, her father retired from the sea in 1803 and the next year moved the family to Boston, where he became a merchant. Lucretia and a sister boarded at the Quaker school, Nine Partners, in Dutchess County, in New York. While a student there she became a "Hicksite," an avid follower of Elias Hicks, a fiery Quaker abolitionist. After completing the course work at Nine Partners, Lucretia stayed on as a teacher's assistant and was struck by the unfairness in salary differences between male and female instructors. It was also at Nine Partners that she met teacher James Mott, the grandson of Nine Partners' superintendent.

The Coffin family moved in 1809 to Philadelphia, where Thomas Coffin entered into business, investing all his capital in a factory for the manufacture of cut nails, a new product of the Industrial Revolution. Lucretia soon followed, bringing with her James Mott, who boarded with the family and became her father's partner. Lucretia and James were married in 1811; they had six children, five of whom survived to adulthood. In 1815 Lucretia's father died, leaving her mother with heavy debts. The Motts, too, suffered financial hardship. Undaunted, Anna Coffin set about shopkeeping again, and Lucretia taught school while her husband reestablished a business career. James Mott worked in his uncle's cotton mill, sold plows, and was a bank clerk before entering the wholesale business. His boycott of slave products led him to trade primarily in wool rather than cotton. In 1817 tragedy struck again with the death of the Motts' three-year-old son. About a year later, Lucretia suddenly began speaking in Meeting, simply but powerfully, and in 1821 she was formally recognized as a minister with a genuine gift.

Lucretia Mott never shied from controversy and quickly became embroiled in the various squabbles among the Society of Friends, siding with the Hicksites against the Orthodox when a schism over authority and creed rocked the Quakers in 1827. Increasingly, however, her attention focused on the evils of slavery. She and her husband refused to sell or use any products created with slave labor. When she preached in Meeting for others to join their boycott, she gained prominence as an abolitionist. She was in great demand as a speaker and traveled extensively throughout the Northeast.

The Motts struck up a close friendship with renowned abolitionist publisher William Lloyd Garrison in 1830. Faced with the exclusion of women from the formally organized abolitionist groups, in December 1833 Lucretia Mott was one of the founders of the Philadelphia Female Anti-Slavery Society. Her dedication to equality at all levels included her social as well as her political life; the Motts were enormously popular hosts who seemed perpetually to have a houseful of guests of both races.

James and Lucretia Mott were equally devoted to the abolition of slavery, yet James frequently deferred to his wife's more powerful oratory and firm leadership within the movement. The endless criticism her outspokenness inspired did not deter her from speaking, but as her fame spread she suffered increasingly from dyspepsia. Not all of her time was absorbed by the fight against slavery, however, as she dedicated enormous energies to her relationships with various members of her extended family and to housekeeping tasks, which she seemed genuinely to enjoy.

In 1837 Mott attended the First Anti-Slavery Convention of American Women, an event she helped to organize, held in New York City. She devoted her speeches increasingly to the intertwined causes of feminism and antislavery, attracting large audiences. Like her colleagues Angelina and Sarah Grimké, Mott received harsh criticism, even from fellow antislavery advocates, for speaking to "promiscuous" audiences, that is, groups comprised of both women and men. Among proslavery forces Mott was denounced as a racial "amalgamator" and more than once was threatened by unruly, violent mobs. A pacifist, she believed that only moral weapons should be used to win the battle against slavery.

The "woman question" ultimately divided the American Anti-Slavery Society into two factions in 1840. That spring James and Lucretia Mott were named delegates from Pennsylvania to the World's Anti-Slavery Convention, which was held in London in June. The first order of business of the all-male convention was to discuss the admission of women delegates. Ninety percent of the delegates were opposed, and Lucretia Mott thus officially attended only as a visitor, but her presence nevertheless established her as a leading figure in both the women's rights and antislavery movements. Moreover, at the convention's end, she and abolitionist turned leading women's rights activist Elizabeth Cady Stanton resolved to call a meeting in the United States to advocate the rights of women.

After she returned to Philadelphia, Mott launched an extensive speaking trip that included several appearances in slave-owning regions. She personally carried the antislavery cause to President John Tyler. Struck by her assertiveness and speaking skills, Tyler remarked at their parting, "I would like to hand Mr. [John] Calhoun [famous debater and leader of the slave-owning southerners in the House] over to you" (*Valiant Friend*, p. 105).

In her dedication to women's issues, Mott advocated both short-term relief and long-term reform, including equal pay for equal work. Eight years after the idea was conceived at the World's Anti-Slavery Convention, Mott and Stanton held, in Seneca Falls, New York, their first annual women's rights convention. The cornerstone of the gathering was a revised U.S. Declaration of Independence, titled the Declaration of Sentiments, which borrowed heavily from the stirring language and demands for rightful equality of the original: "We hold these truths to be self-evident: That all men and women are created equal." The Seneca Falls convention and its declaration provoked a storm of controversy.

In 1851 James Mott retired from the wool business. The passage of the Fugitive Slave Act in the previous year intensified the Motts' commitment to pacifism as well as to alleviating the plight of slaves, joint commitments that they insisted were not mutually exclusive. In 1855 they were involved in a slave rescue, and Lucretia was unrelenting in her devotion to feminism as well; she developed a friendship with women's rights leader Susan B. Anthony.

The Civil War horrified Mott, whose pacifism left her increasingly isolated during the war years. She rejoiced, however, when war ultimately brought slavery to an end but almost immediately found herself immersed in the conflict over the inclusion of the word "male" in the Fourteenth Amendment (to qualify voters). While some pled for women to be patient, arguing that it was "the Negroes' hour," others took the position that the votes of virtuous, wealthy, and educated white women were needed to offset those of the former slaves. Mott rejected both positions, insisting on the right of both sexes and all races to vote.

James Mott died in 1868. Despite her sorrow, the next year Lucretia chaired the annual meeting of the American Equal Rights Association. Dismayed over the irreconcilable conflict concerning the Fourteenth Amendment, Mott joined with Anthony and Stanton to form the National Woman Suffrage Association, devoted to creating a federal amendment granting women the vote. Also in 1869 Mott was active in the plans for the opening of a Quaker institute of higher learning, Swarthmore College. When the college had been chartered in 1864, she and James had insisted it be co-educational.

Despite increasing frailty, Mott continued to travel, speak, and contribute her energies to a variety of causes. For years she was vice president of the Universal Peace Union. In 1870 she was elected president of the Pennsylvania Peace Society, an office she held until her death. In 1876, the centennial of the Declaration of Independence, she presided on the Fourth of July at the National Woman Suffrage Association convention in Philadelphia, where she, Stanton, and Anthony continued to demand women's rights. Two years later, at the age of eighty-five, she attended the thirtieth anniversary of the first Seneca Falls convention. She died in Chelton Hills, outside Philadelphia, surrounded by her remaining children and grandchildren.

Lucretia Mott spoke frequently on the underlying unity of the various reforms she advocated. She urged the development of women's mental powers and their admission into the professions and promoted reform of all laws that were detriments to women's access to equal property rights, education, and the like. Women's inability to vote, she maintained, was only one of many roadblocks. Unlike some of her contemporaries, however, Mott refused to claim the moral superiority of women but was instead dedicated to achieving equality for all of America's disadvantaged and disenfranchised, including Indians, women, slaves, and free blacks. Increasingly libertarian in her religious interpretations, Mott grew to believe that a new spirit was at work in the world that demanded active involvement in reform. An enormously inspirational speaker and a tireless organizer, Lucretia Mott was one of her country's earliest, and most radical, feminists and reformers.

• Lucretia Mott's papers, including two diaries and the bulk of her letters, are in the Friends Historical Library of Swarthmore College. A large collection of her letters is among the William Lloyd Garrison Papers, Sophia Smith Collection, Smith College. Mott nearly always spoke extemporaneously, so an unknown number of her speeches are unrecorded. Many, however, were recorded stenographically, to varying degrees of accuracy. *Lucretia Mott: Her Complete Speeches and Sermons*, ed. Dana Greene (1980), is well organized and includes an annotated index of the proper names that appear most frequently. More recent assessments of Mott's contributions are in Cheree Carlson, "Defining Womanhood: Lucretia Coffin Mott and the Transformation of Femininity," *Western Journal of Communication* 58 (Spring 1994), and Margaret Hope Bacon, "Lucretia Mott: Pioneer of Peace," *Quaker History* 82 (Fall 1993). Also see Bacon's scholarly full-length biography, *Valiant Friend: The Life of Lucretia Mott* (1980), which includes a bibliography as well as a listing of the members of the Mott extended family and a list of Mott's most significant sermons and speeches. For a brief account of Mott's life, see Constance Buel Burnett, *Five for Freedom* (1953). The Mott marriage is discussed in *James and Lucretia Mott: Life and Letters*, edited by their granddaughter, Anna Davis Hallowell (1884).

NANCY C. UNGER

MOTT, Valentine (20 Aug. 1785–26 Apr. 1865), surgeon and medical educator, was born at Glen Cove, Long Island, New York, the son of Henry Mott, a medical practitioner, and Jane Way. Mott entered the study of medicine in 1804 as the apprentice of a relative, Valentine Seaman of New York. He attended lectures in the medical department of Columbia College for two terms, receiving his medical degree in 1806. Mott then traveled to London for postgraduate study as a house pupil at Guy's Hospital, where the leading surgical teacher was Astley Cooper. After a year in London, Mott attended medical lectures at Edinburgh. He returned to New York City in the fall of 1809 and by 1810 had established a significant reputation as a skilled surgeon.

Mott was selected as an anatomical demonstrator at his alma mater by Wright Post, the professor of surgery, and he also began teaching a private course in surgical anatomy in 1810. He was elected professor of surgery the next year. In 1813 Columbia College combined with the newer College of Physicians and Surgeons of New York, and Mott served as professor of surgery in the new institution until 1826, when a dispute between the faculty and the trustees resulted in the resignation of the faculty en masse.

Mott was known more for his practice than for his teaching, even though many of his most famous operations took place in a teaching context. In May 1818 he was called to see Michael Bateman, a 57-year-old sailor suffering from an aneurysm of the right subclavian artery. Mott determined during the operation that tying the innominate artery was the only available therapy. Although there were no interoperative complications, the patient experienced a massive postoperative hemorrhage on the twenty-fourth day and died two days later. Mott published an account of the operation that convinced surgeons around the world of the possibility of tying the innominate artery. However, few successes resulted for years.

Mott married Louisa Dunmore Mums in 1819; they had nine children. His surgical reputation attracted large numbers of private pupils, and at the same time his practice grew substantially. Mott's fees, when patients could afford them, were among the highest in the country.

Mott performed all the duties of a general family physician for his private patients while increasing his referral practice as a surgeon. The ligation of arteries as a treatment of an aneurysm was the most innovative and radical surgical therapy of Mott's generation, and relatively few surgeons had the training and courage to attempt the major vessels in the preanesthetic era. Mott successfully ligated the common iliac artery in 1927 for the first time and had a record of artery ligation probably without equal in the era.

Mott also had extraordinary success in operations for cancers (although it must be remembered that operative success was a short-term survival measurement and not the long-term survival of twentieth-century cancer therapy). He excised portions of the jaw at least four times. He considered his excision of the clavicle, in 1828, his most difficult operation. In 1841 Mott removed a fibroid tumor from the nose by division of the nasal and maxillary bones to secure adequate surgical exposure, and the patient recovered. He also amputated the hip in a youth with a broken femur that would not heal. He was well known for his reconstructive operations, particularly in cases of hare-lip. He twice undertook the surgical treatment of spina bifida, managing the congenital affliction as a form of cleft-spine. In company with other leading surgeons of the period Mott was an accomplished lithotomist, operating for bladder stones 165 times with only seven deaths during his career.

After the resignation of the Columbia faculty in 1826, the professors attempted to form a rival school associated with Rutgers University in New Jersey. The questionable status of the degrees, awarded in New York on a New Jersey charter, undermined the school, and the Rutgers experiment ended in 1830. Mott then rejoined Columbia, where he taught until 1834 when deteriorating health forced his resignation, and he took an extensive vacation in Europe. He returned to New York in 1841 to assume the chair of surgery in the new New York University. His health again deteriorated in 1850, and he took another European trip to rest, returning to New York University in 1851 and retiring in 1853. During the Civil War, Mott served as a surgical consultant to the surgeon general

of the army and as a member of various committees and boards of the U.S. Sanitary Commission. In retirement he suffered increasingly from angina and poor circulation in his legs. He died in New York City, having succumbed to gangrene; he left a limited bibliography but a profound example.

• Collections of Mott's papers are in the National Library of Medicine and in the Library of the New York Academy of Medicine as well as occasional papers in other medical history collections. The best biographical study is Samuel D. Gross, *Memoir of Valentine Mott* (1868). A modern paper by Ira Rutkow, "Valentine Mott (1785–1865), the Father of American Vascular Surgery: A Historical Perspective," *Surgery* 85 (1979): 441–50, offers a helpful overview.

THE EDITORS

MOUET DE LANGLADE, Charles-Michel (May 1729–c. 1801), trader, military officer, and Indian agent, was baptized on 9 May 1729 at Michilimackinac (now Mackinaw City, Michigan), the son of Augustin Mouet de Langlade, a French trader, and Domitilde, the sister of Nissowaquet, a prominent Ottawa chief. Though the only son of this marriage, Charles had numerous and important relations among the Ottawa by virtue of his mother's previous marriage to a trader named Villenueve. He was educated in part by Jesuit priests at Michilimackinac. At the age of ten he accompanied his uncle Nissowaquet on a successful war party down the Mississippi against the Chickasaw. Here he gained great prestige among the Ottawa, who had been defeated twice previously by the Chickasaw. By 1750 he enrolled in the French colonial regulars as a cadet.

Langlade's first expedition in the colonial regulars helped shape the course of the French and Indian War. On 21 June 1752 Langlade led a force drawn from the powerful and influential "Three Fires" confederacy of Ottawa, Potawatomi, and Ojibwa (Chippewa) Indians of the *pays d'en haut* (upper Great Lakes area) in a raid against the Miami village of Pickawillany, near present day Piqua, Ohio. The village was the headquarters of a rebellious group of pro-British Miami in the Iroquois Confederacy under the leadership of Memeskia (known variously as La Demoiselle or "Old Briton"), a Piankashaw chief who used the strategic site of the village, which marked the convergence of several trading trails, to entertain British traders from Pennsylvania and influence other western Indians. Memeskia's recent break with the French alliance in the Ohio Valley represented a precipitous decline in French influence in that region, jeopardizing their trading network down through to Louisiana, and initiated a series of further defections among other tribes seeking British trade goods and alliances. Memeskia's defiance was finally curbed by Langlade and his Indian allies in a successful surprise attack, after which the captured Memeshia was killed, boiled, and eaten. In the aftermath of this incident, the Miami appealed to their British and Indian allies, but no help was forthcoming and the Miami, along with the rest of the rebellious tribes from the *pays d'en haut*, were forced to return to the French alliance in the face of this terrifying blow. With few exceptions, the Indians of the *pays d'en haut* remained loyal to the French until the end of the French and Indian War.

In 1754 Langlade married Charlotte-Ambroisine Bourassa; they had two daughters. Then, promoted to ensign on 15 March 1755, Langlade and his Three Fires tribesmen claimed to have been present at and, indeed, to have planned the ambush that led to the defeat of Edward Braddock near Fort Duquesne (Pittsburgh, Pennsylvania) in 1755. This victory and the rich booty from the attack helped lure many of Langlade's Indian allies to Montcalm's campaign down the Champlain Valley in 1756–1757. Langlade, already renowned among his mother's Ottawa and his father's Canadians, led one of the largest contingents of the thousand volatile warriors from the *pays d'en haut* who turned out for this campaign, and he was directly responsible for 337 Ottawa drawn from seven separate bands in what was later to become Michigan, including his uncle, the war chief Nissowaquet.

Langlade and his Indian allies were most instrumental in curbing English scouting. After ambushing a scouting party of Robert Rogers's Rangers, Langlade and Ottawa and Potawatomi warriors went on the offensive and, among other feats, thoroughly defeated a large force of New York and New Jersey militia under Colonel John Parker. The skirmishing and Indian patrols on this campaign helped keep the British in the dark about French plans and strength and sealed the fate of Fort William Henry. After the fall of the fort, Langlade was posted among his Indian allies by a worried Montcalm, specifically to try to curb potential Indian hostilities toward the British soldiers who were allowed to march away by the terms of the surrender. The anger of the Indians over the loss of promised booty and scalps, however, overcame any influence Langlade may have had, and the result was the "massacre" at Fort William Henry romanticized by James Fenimore Cooper in his *Last of the Mohicans*.

Later that year, and perhaps because of his services in the summer campaign, Governor Vaudreuil made Langlade second in command at Michilimackinac. However, he was soon back in service in the eastern theater, where he led a contingent of Indian auxiliaries at the siege of Quebec in 1759. It has been asserted that it was Langlade and his allies who first encountered the detachment sent by Wolfe to reconnoiter up the Montmorency River on 26 July, and had the reinforcements he had requested of Lévis arrived in time, they would have repelled the foothold gained by the British. The following year, in Montreal, he was promoted to lieutenant and then ordered out of the town before its surrender to Amherst. Upon receiving the news, the Michilimackinac commander deserted his post and left Langlade to deliver the town to the British, who arrived to take command in September 1761.

Langlade, like many other Canadians, quickly adjusted to life under his new colonial masters. His distinguished record of service in the pay of the British began almost immediately when Pontiac's uprising became general in 1763. Langlade gave warning of an attack to the British commander of Michilimackinac, George Etherington, whom he then saved, along with William Leslye and Alexander Henry, when the warning went unheeded and the post fell.

After the uprising, Langlade moved to La Baye (Green Bay, Wisconsin), where he and his father had already established a flourishing trading post. Here he was able to live peacefully for a number of years with his growing family. Langlade also had a number of business interests to manage besides the trade at La Baye. In October 1755 he established a trading post at the mouth of Grand River (Grand Haven, Michigan). Ultimately, it was in Wisconsin that Langlade had perhaps his most lasting influence, where his prominence among the early settlers earned him the appellation "Father of Wisconsin."

Langlade also saw considerable service in the American Revolution. Promoted to captain in the Indian department, Langlade helped raise Indian auxiliaries to defend Montreal in 1776, and with Luc de la Corne, joined Burgoyne in the summer of 1777 in his ill-fated campaign down the Champlain Valley with at least 100 Ottawas and other western Indians. Though most of Burgoyne's Indian allies left early in the campaign, Langlade was able to convince his followers to stay until after the battle of Bennington. Returning to the west in 1778, Langlade was asked to gather an Indian force to aid Henry Hamilton against rebels at Vincennes (now in Indiana) led by George Rogers Clark. In 1780 Langlade also led an unsuccessful expedition with his Indian allies into Illinois country to assist in the attack on Spanish St. Louis (now in Missouri).

After the Revolution, Langlade retained his position in the Indian department and returned to his life of trading. He lived an active life right up until his death in Green Bay, Wisconsin. He apparently enjoyed recounting tales of the ninety-nine battles in which he had supposedly participated. Though his life was hardly typical, certainly the ease in which he moved between the various Indian, French, and English cultures he encountered was representative of the fluid nature of cultural boundaries in eighteenth-century colonial North America. Moreover, Langlade's mediating role between European and Indian societies highlights the influence and impact of the cultural middle ground that he occupied as a synethnic, but also in general the nature and importance of the Amerindian contribution in shaping the contours of European life in America.

• Langlade's ubiquitous presence on the North American landscape in the eighteenth century is reflected in the varied collections of sources that contribute to his story. Though no single repository of his papers exists, helpful sources can be found in the Wisconsin State Historical Society, the Ontario Historical Society, the Public Archives of Canada, the Newberry Library, and the Archives Nationales. Some of his papers, and papers relating to him, have been printed in the "Langlade Papers, 1737–1800," Wisconsin Historical Society

Collections 8 (1879): 209–23, and throughout volumes 1–19, as well as in the *Michigan Pioneer Collection* vols. 8–27.

Accounts of Langlade's life are few, and most are dated. A good starting place is the biographical sketch by his grandson, printed in the Wisconsin State Historical Society *Collections* 3 (1857): 195–295, together with an account by Joseph Tassé in the same publication, vol. 7 (1876): 123–88, and another in vol. 18 (1908): 130–32. There is also a manuscript at the Wisconsin Historical Society by Benjamin Sulte, "Origines de Langlade." By far, the best single source on Langlade's full and varied life is the account given by Paul Trap in the *Dictionary of Canadian Biography*, vol. 4 (1979), pp. 563–64. More often, Langlade makes cameo appearances in various histories. Some of the more important of these are Ian K. Steele, *Warpaths: Invasions of North America* (1994), which describes Langlade's role in the Pickawillany affair in detail, as does Richard White, *The Middle Ground: Indians, Empires, and Republics in the Great Lakes Region, 1650–1815* (1991), and David Edmunds, "Pickawillany: French Military Power versus British Economics," *Western Pennsylvania Historical Magazine* 58 (1975): 169–84. Langlade's subsequent role in the French and Indian War is best dealt with in Ian K. Steele, *Betrayals: Fort William Henry and the "Massacre"* (1990), while John Burgoyne's *State of the Expedition from Canada . . .* (1780; repr. 1969), is the best source for Langlade's role in that affair.

MICHAEL A. MCDONNELL

MOULTON, Ebenezer (25 Dec. 1709–Mar. 1783), Baptist minister and political activist, was born in Windham, Connecticut, the son of Robert Moulton and Hannah Grove, farmers. He had no formal education. Early in his life he developed an interest in religious work. In 1736 he joined his parents in starting a new Baptist congregation in South Brimfield, Massachusetts, for which he was later ordained a regular Baptist minister (1741). He was ordained to the ministry by John Callendar of Newport, an old-order Baptist, which for the time defined Moulton's theological position as Five Principle Calvinistic, emphasizing redemption for the elect of God. One of Moulton's first official actions in South Brimfield was to organize a congregational petition to the Massachusetts General Assembly for exemption from the religious tax.

In 1748 Moulton experienced the new birth preached by the itinerant revivalists, particularly George Whitefield, and identified with New Light beliefs, including evangelical conversion experience, transformed lifestyle, devotion to prayer, study of scripture, evangelism, and witness of one's faith. A popular exponent of the revival, he preached widely in Massachusetts, Connecticut, and Rhode Island to Baptists and Separate Congregationalists. His preaching style and emphases eventually divided the congregation at South Brimfield; in 1749 a schism took place in which he became the pastor of the New Light faction. He traveled widely, proclaiming the need for revival among the Congregational churches; often this drew the wrath of local authorities, and he was treated severely. In 1749 after preaching at Sturbridge, Massachusetts, and baptizing over sixty adherents, he was imprisoned as a fanatic who promoted sedition and disturbed public tranquility. Later that year on a visit

to Titicut, Massachusetts, he baptized several members of Isaac Backus's Separate congregation (in Backus's absence), and he helped to constitute a new closed-communion Separate Baptist church. His church at South Brimfield became a center of Baptist influence; he assisted in forming churches and ordaining ministers. His objective seems to have been to draw together the themes of New Light religious experience with regular Baptist polity, and he became the prime architect of the growth of Massachusetts Baptists following the Great Awakening.

Beginning in 1749 Moulton was a major catalyst in uniting the Baptist community in New England in support of a favorable tax exemption. While the older Baptists (in contrast with the New Lights) had enjoyed an exemption from the payment of religious taxes, the Massachusetts legislature abrogated the exemption act of 1747, fearing the growth of revivalistic Baptists who would apply for the exemption. Moulton and several representatives from Baptist churches in Massachusetts, Rhode Island, and Connecticut lobbied to have the Massachusetts General Assembly modify the exemption laws to allow all the Baptists (and other nonconformists) the privilege of the exemption. On 7 March 1750 twelve leaders met at Providence, Rhode Island, at the instigation of Moulton and John Proctor of Boston, Massachusetts, to draft a petition to the legislature. The resulting document was an important step in the origins of Baptist denominational organization in America. Moulton favored petitioning the king, if the petition was denied in Boston. In 1753 the General Assembly passed an unfavorable exemption law, and Baptists again resorted to conventions and petitions to redress the situation. Moulton, joined by Thomas Green of Leicester, Massachusetts, helped write a new petition in 1754 that rehearsed the history of Baptists in the colony and the desire for freedom of conscience. The authorities, however, dismissed the petition, as well as other attempts over the next four years, as indecent assaults on the laws of the province. Moulton and other signers of the petitions narrowly escaped arrest.

Moulton's personal fortunes fared as poorly as his political activism. His congregation at South Brimfield could not support him, so he opened a mercantile business, which thrived for a time. When the French and Indian War ended and competition increased in northern New England, Moulton became insolvent and fled his creditors and pastoral assignment for Nova Scotia.

Moulton arrived in Yarmouth, Nova Scotia, in 1763 and became a surveyor of lands and a justice of the peace. He took up preaching, traveling in the Annapolis Valley between Windsor and Yarmouth. He became involved in a dispute at Yarmouth over closed communion and revivalism that divided the congregation. At Horton, in 1765, Moulton started what became the first Baptist congregation in Canada but was again forced to withdraw from that village under pressure from the Congregationalist community. He tended a small farm and preached infrequently at Cape

Forchu, Nova Scotia, until about 1771. Hearing that his Massachusetts creditors no longer pressed their claims, he returned to South Brimfield, where he died.

• Moulton published no materials and is known primarily through the diary of Isaac Backus and the records of South Brimfield (now Wales) Baptist Church, Mass. Moulton's contribution to the Separate movement and the petition campaign are covered in William G. McLoughlin, *New England Dissent, 1630–1833: Baptists and the Separation of Church and State* (2 vols., 1971), and McLoughlin, *Diary of Isaac Backus* (3 vols., 1979). McLoughlin's work is based on the older Isaac Backus, *A History of New England, with Particular Reference to the Denomination of Christians Called Baptists* (2 vols., 1871). Clarence Charles Goen, *Revivalism and Separatism in New England* (1962), reveals some unique data on Moulton's career. On the Nova Scotia phase of Moulton's career, consult M. W. Armstrong, *The Great Awakening in Nova Scotia, 1776–1809* (1948).

WILLIAM H. BRACKNEY

MOULTON, Forest Ray (29 Apr. 1872–7 Dec. 1952), theoretical astronomer and mathematician, was born in a log cabin near LeRoy, Michigan, the son of Belah G. Moulton and Mary C. Smith, farmers. His father, a Civil War veteran, had claimed 160 acres in the then still-forested region between Grand Rapids and Traverse City and had cleared and plowed it himself. His mother named Forest, the first of their eight children, for "a perfect ray of light and happiness in that dense forest." There was no school at first, and Moulton learned mostly at home from his parents and grandparents, then taught in a rural school himself before entering Albion College. He graduated with an A.B. in 1894 and a year later entered the University of Chicago as a graduate student. There he received a Ph.D. in astronomy and mathematics, the first awarded at Chicago, in 1899, summa cum laude. Moulton, who had been a part-time instructor in his last two years as a student at Albion, became an assistant in 1896, his second year at Chicago (also the year he married Estella L. Gillette, with whom he would have five children). He became an associate in 1898 and continued to rise through the ranks from instructor to full professor, which he reached in 1912. The main part of the University of Chicago astronomy department was at Yerkes Observatory in Williams Bay, Wisconsin, specializing in observational astrophysics, while Moulton was the department's chief representative on the campus, working in theoretical astronomy and teaching it and mathematics.

Moulton, like many scientists of his generation, particularly those who had grown up on farms or in tiny, isolated hamlets, was a great believer in science and technology. In fifty years they had transformed his life—and America itself—from rural LeRoy to the healthy, prosperous, thriving Chicago. He saw mathematics as "the basis of all science" and did his best to promote links between it and technology at the University of Chicago. The other senior professors in mathematics, however, were world experts in their own specialized, abstract subjects and had little interest in the institute of pure and applied mathematics that Moulton wished to set up on the campus. The university administration was equally uninterested in it, and in 1926, during the post–World War I era of prosperity and a booming stock market, Moulton resigned his faculty position to become a director of the Utilities Power and Light Company in Chicago and an adviser to its president. Although this holding company came perilously close to collapsing in 1933, during the Great Depression, it survived, and Moulton remained a member of its board of directors until 1937. In 1930 he was named a trustee and the director of concessions of the Century of Progress International Exposition (more commonly known as the Chicago World's Fair of 1933), then still in the planning stage. He operated the concessions successfully in spite of the depression and brought in considerable revenue to the fair. This project closed its books in 1936, and the next year Moulton began serving as permanent secretary of the American Association for the Advancement of Science, the largest scientific society in the country, its members ranging from top-flight researchers to college and even high-school teachers. He remained in this post, renamed administrative secretary in 1946, until 1948. Moulton and his wife had divorced in 1936, and in 1939 he married Alicia Pratt; they were divorced in 1951. Two years after his retirement from the AAAS, he moved to Evanston, Illinois, where one of his brothers was a professor of mathematics at Northwestern University, and he died at nearby Wilmette.

As a student at the University of Chicago, Moulton had studied astronomy under Thomas Jefferson Jackson See (with whom he later had several scientific controversies) and Kurt Laves. Moulton had also begun working with the older Thomas C. Chamberlin, professor of geology, on what they called the planetesimal hypothesis of the origin of the solar system. Chamberlin, convinced by geological evidence that the earth was much older than the tens of millions of years then widely believed on the authority of British physicist Lord Kelvin, conceived and developed a picture of the formation of the planets from rocky "planetesimals" rather than from gaseous nebulae, the earlier model. Moulton provided the mathematical calculations and the theoretical reasoning, based on orbital dynamics, that made quantitative many of Chamberlin's intuitive ideas outside of geology (see Moulton, 1900). Their picture, generally called the Chamberlin–Moulton hypothesis, traced the formation of the planetesimals to a chance close passage of another star past the sun. Their gravitational interaction was supposed to have pulled out tidal filaments from both stars, which cooled and solidified in small lumps. Although the Chamberlin-Moulton hypothesis was later overturned by the rebirth of the nebular theory in a more physically accurate form, many parts of it, particularly those having to do with the internal heat of the earth and with the angular momenta of the planets, have remained valid.

Moulton was a master of celestial mechanics and published many other papers, particularly on special cases in the three-body problem and applications to the motion of the moon (under the gravitational forces of the earth and sun) and of the satellites of other planets. He wrote *An Introduction to Celestial Mechanics* (1902), which became a widely used text and was translated into German and Russian; he revised it for a second edition in 1914. Moulton also wrote two, more elementary textbooks, *An Introduction to Astronomy* (1906) and *Descriptive Astronomy* (1912). He was generally considered an excellent teacher, and among the students he inspired to go on to research careers in astronomy, the most famous was Edwin Hubble. In 1921 Moulton, representing astronomy, helped plan and teach, along with fifteen other senior Chicago faculty members, a new survey course on the natural sciences that became the basis for *The Nature of the World and Man* (1926). Widely used in similar survey courses throughout the country, the book was reissued as *The World and Man as Science Sees Them* (1937), and two years later Moulton edited the second, revised edition of it. At the University of Chicago he was one of the first professors to give series of radio talks on science, aimed at general popular education. Later, in Washington, Moulton had a regular radio science program and published his popular astronomy book, *Consider the Heavens* (1935).

After U.S. entry into World War I, Moulton was commissioned a major and put in charge of the Ballistics Branch of the Army Ordnance Department at Aberdeen, Maryland. He brought in many other mathematicians and with them revolutionized the methods of calculating the trajectories of artillery projectiles, essentially a problem in applied celestial mechanics with the added complication of air resistance. In place of the older analytic methods, Moulton introduced advanced numerical calculations, based on mathematical formulae designed to produce the maximum accuracy with the minimum number of computational steps, carried out by armies of human computers. He wrote up this work in his book *New Methods in Exterior Ballistics* (1926). He also did other, more theoretical research in mathematics, nearly all of it in the general area of differential equations and the convergence of series. His textbook on this subject was *Differential Equations* (1930).

When Moulton became permanent secretary of the AAAS in 1937, the association was a relatively small organization with quarters in the Smithsonian Institution in Washington, D.C. Moulton perfectly expressed the desire of the majority of its members to make science more relevant to society. He supervised the expansion of the association (its membership more than doubled in his years at the helm), fundraising for its new home on Dupont Circle, and the initiation and publication of many symposia, particularly on the application of science to human health and welfare. Moulton played a major role in the association's taking over of the magazines *Science* and *Scientific Monthly* from the family of J. McKeen Cattell, who had founded them, and in making them over into the organs of the AAAS.

Moulton was an important figure in theoretical cosmogony and later became a leader in popularizing science. His textbooks, talks, and popular books had a major influence on astronomers, college graduates in general, and even popular readers and radio listeners.

• The most important collection of Moulton's scientific letters is in the University of Chicago Archives, Special Collections Department, Regenstein Library, especially in the papers of Thomas C. Chamberlin. There are smaller collections of his letters in the Presidents' Papers and the William Rainey Harper Papers there and in the Director's Papers in the Yerkes Observatory Archives, Williams Bay, Wisc. The best published memorial biography of him is by Charles E. Gasteyer, "Forest Ray Moulton," National Academy of Sciences, *Biographical Memoirs* 41 (1970): 341–55; it contains a complete bibliography. An anonymous article, "The Washington Moultons, Forest Ray '94 and Harold Glenn, 1907," in *Io Triumphe*, Mar. 1947, 19–22 (the Albion College alumni magazine), contains important information on his childhood and his remarkable family but is inaccurate in much of its description of his scientific career. Two books, Peter J. Kuznick, *Beyond the Laboratory: Scientists as Political Activists in 1930s America* (1987), and Dael Wolfle, *Renewing a Scientific Society: The American Association for the Advancement of Science from World War II to 1970* (1989), contain useful information on Moulton's career with the AAAS. The best historical account of his cosmogonical research activities is in Stephen G. Brush, "A Geologist among Astronomers: The Rise and Fall of the Chamberlin-Moulton Cosmology," *Journal for the History of Astronomy* 9 (1978): 1–41, 77–104. Probably Moulton's most important research paper on this work is "An Attempt to Test the Nebular Hypothesis by an Appeal to the Laws of Dynamics," *Astrophysical Journal* 11 (1900): 103–30. An obituary by his friend and contemporary Anton J. Carlson, "Forest Ray Moulton: 1872–1952," *Science* 117 (1953): 545–46, gives a good picture of his educational and AAAS activities but is incorrect in some of its dates.

DONALD E. OSTERBROCK

MOULTON, Louise Chandler (10 Apr. 1835–10 Aug. 1908), poet, was born Ellen Louise Chandler in Pomfret, Connecticut, the daughter of Lucius Lemuel Chandler and Louisa Rebecca Clark, farmers. She was educated locally at Christ Church Hall in Connecticut. An imaginative child, Ellen Louise wrote poems and stories from an early age and at fourteen had a poem published in a Norwich, Connecticut, newspaper. Her biographers note that her Calvinist upbringing influenced the strongly religious and often melancholy tone of her poetry. Her first book was published when she was eighteen. "I called it 'This, That, and the Other,' because it was made up of short stories, sketches (too brief and immature to call essays), and the rhymes into which, from the first, I put more of myself than into any other form of expression. Strangely enough, the book sold largely" (quoted in Whiting, p. 19); *This, That, and the Other* (1854) sold 20,0000 copies. She contributed sentimental stories to the "gift-books" popular in the mid-nineteenth century, producing one of these volumes herself, *The Book of the Boudoir: A Gift for All Seasons, Edited by Ellen Louise.* Shortly after her first book was published, Ellen Louise entered Mrs. Willard's Female Seminary in Troy, New York, and at commencement in 1855 was selected class poet. Her first novel, *June Clifford: A Tale*, was published that year. Over the next two decades she published children's stories, narrative sketches, and reviews in a number of journals, including the *Atlantic Monthly*, *Godey's*, *Youth's Companion*, the *New York Tribune*, and the *Boston Sunday Herald*.

In August 1855 Ellen Louise married William Upham Moulton of Boston, editor and publisher of the *True Flag*, one of the journals in which she had been published. Moving to Boston, she found herself in the midst of the literary life, meeting Ralph Waldo Emerson, Oliver Wendell Holmes, John Greenleaf Whittier, and Henry Wadsworth Longfellow. These writers and many others attended the Friday afternoon salon she hosted at the Moulton home at 28 Rutland Square. According to her biographer Lilian Whiting, Moulton's home "came to be well known to every Bostonian and to whomever among visitors was interested in things literary. It was the cosmopolitan centre of social life in the city" (p. 107). Her weekly literary receptions continued for three decades, and she extended this tradition by holding a Friday salon in London as well during her residence there.

In 1876 Moulton made the first of many voyages to England; until the last two years of her life she spent every summer there. Her literary friendships in the United States opened doors for her in Great Britain and Europe as well. To some, Moulton appeared as a literary ambassador. American author Thomas Wentworth Higginson wrote to her in 1887, "Few American women, perhaps none, have succeeded in establishing such a pleasant intermedian position before English and American literature as have you" (quoted in Whiting, p. 134). Her circle included William Dean Howells, Robert Browning, George Eliot, Thomas Hardy, Frances Hodgson Burnett, and Elizabeth Stoddard. In both Boston and London her life was filled with a demanding round of social engagements and literary activities, and her correspondence with friends and colleagues on both sides of the Atlantic was voluminous; she also corresponded with those seeking her assistance or advice.

Moulton devoted considerable energy to publicizing the work of others. One of her English friends, poet Philip Bourke Marston, requested that she be his literary executor, and after his death in 1887 she had several volumes of his works published. In 1894 she published an edition of the work of an English poet, Arthur O'Shaughnessy: *Arthur O'Shaughnessy: His Life and Works, with Selections from His Poems*. Anna Eichberg Lane, who was married to the English publisher John Lane, had attended Moulton's salon in Boston as well as in London. She recalled that Moulton introduced her to Henry Harland, editor of the *Yellow Book*, and its publisher, Lane; she credited Moulton for bringing the pre-Raphaelite authors and "the most distinguished of the younger English writ-

ers" published in the *Yellow Book* to the attention of American readers (Whiting, pp. 276–81).

Moulton's first volume of poems, *Swallow Flights* (its name inspired by a lyric of Tennyson) was published in England in 1877; the American version was titled simply *Poems*. Additional volumes of collected verse are *In the Garden of Dreams* (1889) and *At the Wind's Will* (1899). Her poetry was traditional in form. Reviewers praised the lyricism of her verse and her particular expertise in the sonnet. Her subjects were generally love and religion. Moulton also published collections of stories and sketches, *Some Women's Hearts* (1874), *Ourselves and Our Neighbors* (1887), and *Miss Eyre from Boston and Others* (1889); tales for children, including *Stories Told at Twilight* (1890) and *In Childhood's Country* (1896); and informal accounts of her travel experiences in Europe, *Random Rambles* (1881) and *Lazy Times in Spain and Elsewhere* (1896).

Her health declining, Moulton traveled to England for the last time in the summer of 1906. Her final sonnet was composed in 1907 to honor Julia Ward Howe's eighty-seventh birthday. Moulton died at her home in Boston, leaving her collection of hundreds of books, many of them autographed copies of works by the leading writers of the day, to the Boston Public Library.

• Moulton's papers are in the American Antiquarian Society, Worcester, Mass.; and the Library of Congress. There are two biographical accounts written by her contemporaries: Lilian Whiting, *Louise Chandler Moulton: Poet and Friend* (1910); and a fifteen-page essay by Harriet Prescott Spofford introducing the 1909 edition of *The Poets and Sonnets of Louise Chandler Moulton*. Spofford, also a New England writer and a close friend of the poet, published an essay about Moulton in *A Little Book of Friends* (1916).

JANE S. GABIN

MOULTRIE, James, Jr. (27 Mar. 1793–Apr. 1869), physician and educator, was born in Charleston, South Carolina, the son of James Moultrie, a physician; his mother's name is unknown. He was in the fourth successive generation of Moultries to practice medicine in South Carolina. His early education at Hammersmith, England, was cut short by the growing tensions between Great Britain and the United States, which would culminate in the War of 1812. After receiving a Bachelor of Arts degree from South Carolina College, he studied medicine at the University of Pennsylvania, from which he graduated in 1812.

Throughout Moultrie's career, his medical practice was often associated with the sort of public institutions that could provide him with material for his studies in physiology and pathology. He began work in Charleston in 1812 at the Marine Hospital, and shortly thereafter also at the Negro Hospital. During this time there was a smallpox outbreak in Charleston. The resulting cadavers afforded him a great deal of experience with smallpox as well as the opportunity to pursue his interests in pathology and physiology. With the onset of the War of 1812, Moultrie worked in a civil capacity as surgeon for the hospital at Hamstead, South Carolina.

Eventually he succeeded his father as physician to the port of Charleston and physician to the city jail. In 1818 he married Sara Louisa Shrewsbury; they had no children.

Moultrie was elected president of the state medical society in 1820 and 1821. Over the course of the next decade, he was an active participant in the disputes over the regulation of the profession and the institution of a medical college in the state. Once the state legislature was convinced to provide appropriation, a medical college was chartered; it opened its doors in 1833 with Moultrie as chair of physiology, a position he held until 1867. In 1834 Moultrie was elected the first president of the new Medical Society of the State of South Carolina.

At this time, medical training was chiefly a matter of apprenticeship and acquired skills, and formal lectures at the medical school lasted only four months. Although by 1828 state law required that an applicant hold a diploma from "some medical college," this could be waived if the applicant passed examination by the faculty of the Medical College of South Carolina. Moultrie proposed an overhaul of medical education, along the lines of the great schools of Europe. Writing in 1836, Moultrie called for more extensive premedical education, higher standards for medical faculty, and more clinical training in the college. He also insisted that lectures should run for six to eight months and that a mandatory minimum of three or four years study should be established. Although he pursued these goals throughout his life, it would be many decades before such standards were adopted in U.S. medical schools.

In 1847 Moultrie was in the six-man South Carolina delegation to the Philadelphia convention that established the American Medical Association. He also served as the AMA's first vice president and was elected president at its Charleston meeting in 1851.

Although the state medical society continued to meet until the outbreak of the Civil War, a new South Carolina Medical Association, with strong ties to the national association, was founded in 1848. Moultrie was its first president. It was chiefly through this organization that he was able to establish standards for medical practice and licensure within the state and, with limited success, work to improve the standards of medical education in South Carolina. He died in Charleston.

• Shortly before his death, Moultrie prepared a genealogy that was published as "The Moultries of South Carolina, from a Sketch by the Late Dr. James Moultrie, with Annotations by A. S. Salley, Jr." *South Carolina Historical and Genealogical Magazine* 5 (1904): 247–60. His most important work is *Memorial on the State of Medical Education in South Carolina Delivered to the South Carolina Society for the Advancement of Learning* (1836). A significant secondary source on Moultrie is Joseph I. Waring, *History of Medicine in South Carolina, 1825–1900* (1967), which includes a portrait and a list of Moultrie's publications.

CHARLES D. KAY

MOULTRIE, John, Jr. (18 Jan. 1729–19 Mar. 1798), politician and planter, was born in Charleston, South Carolina, the son of John Moultrie, a prominent physician, and Lucretia Cooper, the daughter of Dr. Barnard Christian Cooper. In a family with two physicians, Moultrie was predisposed toward medicine as a career. He received his early medical training under his father until 1746, when he went to University of Edinburgh in Scotland. Three years later Moultrie became the first native-born American to graduate with a degree in medicine from Edinburgh. His thesis, *Dissertatio Medica Inauguralis de Febre Maligna Biliosa Americae*, was the first monograph to provide exhaustive clinical observations on the nature of yellow fever in North America. Translated into French and German, Moultrie's thesis went through several editions, enduring as an authority on the subject for more than one hundred years.

Moultrie returned to Charleston in 1749; he possibly practiced medicine, although there is no evidence of such activity. In fact, his marriage in 1753 to Dorothy Morton, a "very agreeable young widow with a large fortune," removed the necessity for pursuing a medical career (*South Carolina Gazette*, 30 Apr. 1753). Moultrie's wife died four years later, leaving him with one daughter. In January 1762 Moultrie eloped with Eleanor Austin, the daughter of George Austin, a wealthy merchant and captain in the Royal Navy, who strongly disapproved of his daughter marrying below her station. Only Moultrie's appointment as lieutenant governor of East Florida in 1771 produced a reconciliation between Austin and the couple. Six children resulted from this union.

An ambitious young man, Moultrie engaged in a wide range of activities. He entered Charleston's social scene by joining the city's Library Society in 1750 and the Freemasons three years later. Moultrie began his public career in 1756 when the governor appointed him justice of the peace for Berkeley County. Five years later he won a special election to the assembly, representing Prince Frederick Parish. Moultrie served as tax collector for St. James Goose Creek Parish in 1766. He devoted most of his attention, though, to managing his plantations in Goose Creek Parish, where he grew mainly rice and indigo.

As hostilities increased between the colonists and Cherokees in the South Carolina backcountry during the 1750s, Moultrie received a commission in 1757 as an ensign in the Charleston Regiment and was later promoted in 1760 to major in the Provincial Regiment. During the following year Lieutenant Colonel James Grant, who commanded British regulars sent to aid the colony, relied on Moultrie as one of the leaders in his expedition against the Cherokees. Moultrie took 220 men to the settlement of Ninety-Six to guard a growing magazine of supplies. Moultrie and his men did little fighting; instead, in the words of Henry Laurens, they "died like dogs" due to the "inclemency of the weather & the want of proper hospitals & other conveniences" (Laurens papers, vol. 3, p. 319).

The hardship suffered in this expedition, as well as Moultrie's support for Grant in his feud with Colonel Thomas Middleton of the Provincials over who outranked the other in the campaign, did not go unrewarded. For when Grant, recently appointed governor of the new British province of East Florida (acquired from Spain in 1763), began forming a government, he asked his compatriot Moultrie to sit as a member of the council. In his initial inspection of the colony, Moultrie was encouraged by the mild temperature and fertility of the land. With high expectations of economic and political success, Moultrie accepted Grant's offer. Less than two years later, the council named him president of that body, a position he held until 1771. With thoughts of permanent settlement, Moultrie quickly acquired land, eventually amassing 14,300 acres. Here he built two plantations ("Bella Vista" and "Rozetta") maintained by 180 slaves. During these periods when Moultrie fulfilled his official duties in East Florida he and his family resided at the 1,000 acre Bella Vista plantation overlooking the Matanzas River about four miles from St. Augustine. The centerpiece of the plantation was a two-story stone mansion surrounded by a park, gardens, a bowling green, stocked fish ponds, and walks—all set within an abundant variety of aesthetically planted trees, shrubs, and flowers.

A progressive and prosperous planter, Moultrie cultivated a variety of goods, including citrus crops, fruits, rice, indigo, and sugar. He also produced naval stores from the thousands of acres of pine forests on his estates and even experimented with the production of alcoholic beverages such as wine and rum. Moultrie's varied activities enabled him, in his own words, to live "clear of debt in plenty, ease and some elegance" (Seibert, p. 237).

Exhausted by poor health and the difficulties of governing an undeveloped colony, Grant returned to Britain in May 1771, leaving Moultrie as acting governor until a full-time replacement could be located. The Crown confirmed his appointment because Mrs. Moultrie, Grant noted, "would not have agreed to leave her favorite Carolina upon any other terms." Grant also emphasized that "such a man leaving the Province would be a great misfortune to the Country" (*East Florida Papers*, no. 551, p. 183). Thirty inhabitants of St. Augustine addressed a memorial to Moultrie congratulating him on his appointment and urging him to establish a legislature to alleviate the "*wretched condition* [emphasis in text] of the Country" left by Grant (*South Carolina Gazette*, 23 May 1771).

Moultrie's tenure as acting governor of East Florida was steeped in personal and political conflict. Much of the contention revolved around the establishment of a legislative assembly. Moultrie, who favored government by the executive, opposed a legislature, while Chief Justice William Drayton and Dr. Andrew Turnbull, both influential members of the council, strongly favored an elected assembly. Turnbull was especially antagonistic toward Moultrie because he had expected to succeed Grant as governor. Both Drayton and Turnbull resigned their seats on the council over their differences with Moultrie. Although royal authorities restored Drayton to the council, Moultrie suspended him in August 1773 because his actions "tended so much to subvert good order, and good Government" (*East Florida Papers*, no. 553, p. 197). Despite such hindrances, Moultrie successfully promoted road construction, drainage, and the cultivation of profitable commodities such as indigo, rice, sugar, and naval stores. He also encouraged significant construction and strengthened the colonies' defense against Indians. On 1 May 1774 Patrick Tonyn replaced Moultrie as chief executive of East Florida.

When war erupted between the colonies and Britain one year later, Moultrie, who still held his appointment as lieutenant governor, remained zealously loyal to the Crown and was rewarded with a commission as colonel in the local militia. Although there is no evidence that Moultrie led troops in battle, he did encourage his neighbors to grow additional provisions to keep civilians and soldiers well supplied during the war. On Britain's cession of Florida to Spain in July 1784, Moultrie sent his slaves to the Bahamas, sold his livestock and possessions, and accompanied his family to England, where his wife and sons had inherited property from Moultrie's father-in-law. He became dependent on his wife's income until 1787 when he received £4,479 of his £9,432 claim for property lost as a result of the cession of East Florida. Moultrie passed the remainder of his years quietly in Shropshire, where he died.

Moultrie abandoned a promising career in medicine to pursue the life of a gentleman planter and politician. For nearly twenty years he was one of East Florida's pillars of government, rendering crucial guidance to the successful development of the young colony. His progressive and profitable agricultural methods, moreover, provided a model for others seeking to establish plantations in Florida.

• Nearly all of John Moultrie's extant letters are located at the South Carolina Historical Society in Charleston. This collection of sixty-five documents pertains to his correspondence while at Edinburgh University and courtship letters to his second wife, Eleanor Austin. A few additional letters are located in the Ballindalloch Castle Muniments in Scotland. Copies of his medical thesis are located at the University of Maryland, Baltimore; College of Physicians, Philadelphia; and the University of Wisconsin, Madison, Medical School. For correspondence relating to Moultrie's political career in East Florida, see the *East Florida Papers*, British Public Records, Colonial Office, class 5 files, nos. 540, 545, 551–54, and 563. Moultrie's "Memorial," published in William Seibert, *Loyalists in East Florida, 1774–1795*, vol. 2 (1929), provides detailed information on his plantations and other lands owned in East Florida.

There is no full-length biography. Joseph I. Waring, *History of Medicine in South Carolina, 1670–1825* (1964), provides information on Moultrie's medical training; Charles Mowat, *East Florida as a British Province, 1763–1784* (1964), provides a penetrating analysis of Moultrie's feud with Turnbull and Drayton; Eleanor Townshend, "John Moultrie, Junior, M.D. 1729–1798," *Annales of Medical History*, 3d ser., 2 (1940): 98–109, is a general account of his life; while Philip

M. Hamer et al., eds., *The Papers of Henry Laurens* (1968–), contains interesting material about Moultrie's years in South Carolina.

KEITH KRAWCZYNSKI

MOULTRIE, William (23 Nov. 1730–27 Sept. 1805), revolutionary war general and governor, was born in Charleston, South Carolina, the son of John Moultrie, a physician, and Lucretia Cooper. The elder Moultrie had emigrated from Scotland and settled in Charleston in about 1729. Nothing is known of William Moultrie's youth, but he certainly had a basic education. In 1749 he married Elizabeth Damaris de St. Julien; they had two children before Elizabeth died. In 1779 Moultrie married Hannah Motte Lynch, widow of Thomas Lynch. From the property his first wife brought him and from his own acquisitions, Moultrie established a large plantation, "Northampton," with two hundred slaves, located in St. John's Parish, Berkeley County.

For most of the period from the early 1750s to the outbreak of the Revolution, Moultrie sat in the South Carolina Commons House of Assembly. He was appointed a captain of a South Carolina militia company on 16 September 1760 and in 1761 accompanied Colonel Thomas Middleton's regiment on an expedition into the Cherokee country led by the British lieutenant colonel James Grant. In 1772 Moultrie was one of the commissioners who settled the boundary line between North Carolina and South Carolina west of the Catawba River. By 1774 he was a militia colonel. Elected to the First Continental Congress in 1774, he declined to serve.

With the coming of the Revolution, Moultrie was a deputy to both the First and Second South Carolina Provincial Congresses, 1775–1776, and he was a member of the First South Carolina General Assembly after the adoption of the state constitution in March 1776. On 17 June 1775 Moultrie was commissioned colonel of the Second South Carolina Regiment, created by the Provincial Congress. In December 1775 he led a raid on an encampment of escaped slaves on Sullivan's Island, killing fifty blacks who would not surrender and making prisoners of the rest.

In June 1776 Moultrie commanded a nearly completed fort on Sullivan's Island at the mouth of Charleston Harbor. General Charles Lee, whom George Washington had sent to help arrange the defenses of Charleston, advised Moultrie to abandon the fort, suggesting it would become a "slaughter pen" if attacked by the British. Moultrie, with the backing of John Rutledge, president of the South Carolina General Assembly, declined to evacuate the post. On 28 June 1776 a large British expeditionary force under General Henry Clinton and Admiral Sir Peter Parker launched an assault on Fort Sullivan. With only 435 troops and less than 5,000 pounds of powder, Moultrie, assisted by about 750 troops under Colonel William Thompson at the east end of the island, conducted a telling artillery fire that tore into the rigging and hulls of the British ships. British cannonading of the fort did little damage because the walls, consisting of sand encased in spongy palmetto logs, absorbed the shock. Troubled also by navigational problems, the British force withdrew after a full day of battle. In a few days the enemy flotilla headed back to New York City. On 20 July 1776 Congress passed a resolution expressing "the thanks of the United States" to Moultrie and his soldiers for repelling, "with so much valor," the attack "by the fleet and army of His Britannic Majesty." Congress named Moultrie a brigadier general on 16 September 1776. On 20 September 1776 his unit was taken into the service of the Continental army.

Moultrie was inactive in the field during 1777 and 1778. He helped raise troops for an invasion of Florida, which was thwarted because the South Carolina government did not provide the necessary funds. In 1778 Moultrie was elected to the state senate. For 1779 and early 1780 his Continentals operated largely as a separate wing of General Benjamin Lincoln's southern army. Moultrie's engagement with a British force at Port Royal (Beaufort) on 3 February 1779 forced the British to evacuate to Savannah. On 20 June 1779 Moultrie and Lincoln's troops launched an unsuccessful assault on British entrenchments on James and Johns islands at Stono Ferry. Owing to the fact that Lincoln had left Moultrie in command of American troops at Charleston, Moultrie did not join Lincoln's troops and the naval force under French admiral Charles Hector Theodat comte d'Estaing for the unsuccessful siege of Savannah in October 1779. Linking up with Lincoln's army in Charleston in spring 1780, Moultrie was made a prisoner of war when the whole of Lincoln's army surrendered on 12 May 1780. Moultrie was interned, along with other Continental army officers, at Haddrell's Point (now Mount Pleasant), opposite Charleston. Knowing that Moultrie had two brothers who were Loyalists, Lord Charles Montagu, a former colonial governor of South Carolina who was attempting to recruit a British regiment from American prisoners, in March 1781 offered Moultrie a British colonelcy and command of a regiment in Jamaica. Moultrie bore the insult to his patriotism gently but informed Montagu that not even "the fee simple of that valuable island of Jamaica should induce me to part with my integrity" (William Moultrie, vol. 2, p. 170). Moultrie was exchanged on 9 February 1782 in "composition" (that is, along with other American prisoners) for Lieutenant General John Burgoyne. Moultrie became the last major general appointed by Congress during the Revolution on 15 October 1782.

After the war Moultrie had a busy civic life. He was elected to the state house of representatives in 1783, and the next year he served as lieutenant governor. As governor from 1785 to 1787 he sought to establish a sound money system and to encourage the revival of trade. He supported the legislature's prohibition of immediate recovery of debts contracted before 26 February 1782, which was aimed at British creditors. Elected to the state senate in 1787, the next year he was a member of the South Carolina convention to ratify the Constitution, for which he voted. Moultrie was president of the state Society of the Cincinnati from

1783 until his death, the Company for the Inland Navigation from Santee to Cooper (rivers), and the Board of Trustees of the College of Charleston.

A Federalist in politics, Moultrie again served a two-year term as governor from 1792 to 1794. During his second governorship he ordered out of the state any free blacks who had emigrated from St. Domingue, the site of an uprising, and persuaded the legislature to establish two divisions of militia. In about December 1793 he issued a proclamation forbidding South Carolinians to enlist in an expedition against Spanish possessions in America being planned by the erstwhile French emissary to the United States, Edmond Charles Genêt.

Moultrie retired when his term ended. In addition to rice, he began cultivating cotton on his plantation and probably some tobacco, which he predicted would eventually become a major crop in South Carolina. He died at Northampton.

Moultrie was criticized for not always making the best use of opportunities and available manpower while a commander in the field, particularly at Port Royal and Stono Ferry. However, he had an unassailable reputation as South Carolina's "much beloved and revered patriot" (*Charleston Courier*, 28 Sept. 1805). The site of his plantation was inundated by Lake Moultrie, formed in 1942 by the Santee-Cooper (rivers) hydroelectric and navigation project.

• The South Carolina Department of Archives and History, Columbia, has correspondence and messages of the governors and legislative records. Moultrie's interpretive narrative of the war in the South and his war correspondence and other related documents are in William Moultrie, *Memoirs of the American Revolution So Far As It Related to the States of North and South Carolina, and Georgia* (2 vols., 1802; repr. 1968). A brief biography is in Cecil B. Hartley, *Heroes and Patriots of the South* (1860). Early vital statistics are in A. S. Salley, Jr., ed., *Register of St. Philip's Parish, Charles Town, South Carolina, 1720–1758* (1904). For Moultrie's role as boundary commissioner, see Charles S. Davis, ed., "The Journal of William Moultrie while a Commissioner on the North and South Carolina Boundary Survey, 1772," *Journal of Southern History* 8 (1942): 549–55. For genealogy and some information on Moultrie, see Gerrard Moultrie, "The Moultries," *South Carolina Historical and Genealogical Magazine* 5 (1904): 229–60. Particularly useful works relating to Moultrie and the southern campaigns are Edward McCrady, *The History of South Carolina in the Revolution, 1775–1780*, vol. 3 (1901; repr. 1969), and David B. Mattern, *Benjamin Lincoln and the American Revolution* (1995). Jerome J. Nadelhaft, *The Disorders of War: The Revolution in South Carolina* (1981), discusses political issues and legislation to 1788. Harriott H. Ravenel, *Charleston: The Place and the People* (1931), has items of interest pertaining to Moultrie. Biographies of contemporary S.C. leaders provide political context, chiefly Marvin R. Zahnizer, *Charles Cotesworth Pinckney: Founding Father* (1967). An obituary is in the *Charleston Courier*, 28 Sept. 1805.

HARRY M. WARD

MOUNT, William Sidney (26 Nov. 1807–19 Nov. 1868), painter, was born in Setauket, Long Island, New York, the son of Thomas Shepard Mount, a farmer and innkeeper, and Julia Ann Hawkins. Thomas Mount died when William was seven, and Julia Mount and her children subsequently moved to her father's farm in nearby Stony Brook. William's younger sister Ruth took lessons in watercolor painting in 1819, and he observed her at work: "A picture was then and always has been to me an object of great attraction," he later wrote in his autobiographical notes. "I had no idea at that time of ever becoming a painter, but, my mind from my earliest recollection was always awakened to the sublime and beautiful in nature." His eldest brother, Henry Smith Mount, was the first member of the family to make a living as an artist, setting up as an ornamental sign painter in New York City. In 1824 William was apprenticed to Henry and worked for his brother for three years. He desired to improve his skills and entered the National Academy of Design as one of its first students in 1826. There he drew from casts of antique sculpture and from engravings. Upon completion of his apprenticeship he returned to Stony Brook, which he always preferred to New York City.

Mount painted his first portrait—a self-portrait in which he holds a flute—and his first nonportrait picture, *Christ Raising the Daughter of Jairus* (both Museums at Stony Brook), in 1828. The naive style of both betrays his background as a sign painter. *Christ Raising the Daughter of Jairus* was exhibited later that year at the National Academy of Design, where it attracted the attention of the academy's president, Samuel F. B. Morse. Mount painted several other compositions with religious or literary themes, including *Saul and the Witch of Endor* (1828, National Museum of American Art) and *Celadon and Amelia* (1829, Museums at Stony Brook). However, soon discovering that history painting was not remunerative, he took up portrait painting, a shift he later described as "not wholly a sacrifice . . . for I found that portraits improved my colouring."

In the spring of 1829 William and another brother, Shepard Alonzo Mount, opened a studio in New York City. However, because it was easier to secure commissions by going to the sitter, Shepard duly took up a career as an itinerant portrait painter, traveling up and down the East Coast. William, who preferred to remain in New York, came to the conclusion that "we had materials enough at home to make original painters" (quoted in Frankenstein, p. 20) and in 1830 commenced painting the genre subjects for which he is best known. *Rustic Dance after a Sleigh Ride* (1830, Museum of Fine Arts, Boston) depicts a roomful of young people watching two couples dance to music provided by a black fiddler. Although still rather naive in style, it is much better executed than his paintings of only a year before. Mount exhibited his painting at the National Academy of Design in 1830; it received much favorable attention from the press, which encouraged him to portray other scenes of rural life. His technique in *Dancing on the Barn Floor* (1831, Museums at Stony Brook) shows a marked improvement over the course of a year; the painting convincingly depicts both the movement of the human body and the dancing couple's pleasure as a seated fiddler plays merrily outside the barn.

Mount's genre paintings attracted much attention from critics as well as collectors, and he established a successful practice in portraiture (nearly all of his sitters lived either on Long Island or in New York City). Although his work in this area is very competent, he seldom reached the level of such leading portraitists as Thomas Sully, Chester Harding, Henry Inman, or John Neagle. His best portraits are of family and friends, and he painted a particularly sensitive likeness of his sister's field hand, Reuben Merrill (1832, Museums at Stony Brook), which well captures Reuben's quiet and unassuming manner. Other notable portraits include those of his older brothers Henry (1832) and Shepard (1847) (both Museums at Stony Brook), the New York architect Martin Euclid Thompson (1830, Metropolitan Museum of Art), and the Reverend Zachariah Greene (1829, Museums at Stony Brook). A later depiction of Greene, *Great-Grandfather's Tale of the Revolution—A Portrait of the Reverend Zachariah Greene* (1852, Metropolitan Museum of Art), shows the old minister—a revolutionary war veteran—telling his great-grandchildren about the war while sitting before a copy of Jean Antoine Houdon's life mask of George Washington. Apart from family members and friends, most of Mount's sitters were prosperous New York businessmen and their wives. Occasionally he painted public figures; the most notable of these was Commodore Matthew Calbraith Perry (U.S. Naval Academy Museum, Annapolis).

It is Mount's genre paintings, however, that attracted the admiration of his contemporaries and that have ensured his lasting fame in the history of American art. He may be considered America's equivalent of Sir David Wilkie, the Scottish painter whose scenes of everyday life in Great Britain were popular on both sides of the Atlantic. (Contemporary American critics favorably compared the two.) Mount knew Wilkie's work through engravings, and such prints occasionally served as a source of inspiration. The composition of his *Bargaining for a Horse* (1835, New-York Historical Society) owes much to Wilkie's *The Errand Boy*, painted ten years earlier, especially in the treatment of the horse. Nevertheless, Mount's painting is an original, lively, and clever portrayal of two men negotiating the purchase of a horse, their discussion symbolized by each man whittling a stick. That same year he painted *The Truant Gamblers* (also known as *Undutiful Boys*; New-York Historical Society), which depicts four boys in a barn playing heads-and-tails, their game about to be interrupted by the angry farmer who owns the barn. Both paintings were commissions by the noted collector and patron of the arts Luman Reed, also the patron of such notable artists as Thomas Cole and Asher B. Durand. Reed died in 1836, but by then Mount's career as a genre painter had taken off. He had also received a favorable mention from William Dunlap when the latter published his *History of the Rise and Progress of the Arts of Design in the United States* in 1834. Among Mount's other notable paintings of the 1830s are *After Dinner* (1834, Yale University Art Gallery), which shows a young man playing the violin for two companions; *Raffling for the Goose* (1837, Metropolitan Museum of Art); and *Catching Rabbits* (1839, Museums at Stony Brook), which depicts a boy triumphantly displaying a caught rabbit while another boy resets the trap; it was exhibited in Paris in 1850.

Mount painted most of his pictures in and around his hometown of Setauket, using his family and neighbors and the local buildings as models and painting outdoors as much as possible. His adherence to plein air painting (as it came to be called) contributed greatly to the quality of his work. A notable example is *Farmers Nooning* (1836, Museums at Stony Brook), which shows a group of farmhands lazing in a field. His indoor genre subjects were also popular, however, and often are as striking as his outdoor scenes. Mount considered *The Long Story* (1837, Corcoran Gallery of Art), which depicts a gentleman telling a story to a tavernkeeper while a traveler standing nearby listens in, to be his best painting up to that time, and he sold it to Robert Gilmor, a prominent patron of the arts from Baltimore. *The Painter's Triumph* (1838, Pennsylvania Academy of the Fine Arts), in which an educated artist displays his latest work to a plain, middle-class farmer, illustrates Mount's belief that America's cultural tastes are elevated by the fine arts.

Mount's skill reached its peak in the 1840s. *Cider Making* (1840, Metropolitan Museum of Art) is a wonderfully detailed representation of the processing of apples into cider. Some critics have viewed the painting as a veiled commentary on the 1840 presidential campaign in which Whig candidate William Henry Harrison was touted as a man who preferred a log cabin and hard cider to a fancy mansion and imported French wines; if any such meaning was intended, it certainly was secondary to Mount's primary purpose of depicting a working cider mill. *Eel Spearing at Setauket* (New York State Historical Association), probably his masterpiece, was painted in 1845. It depicts a black woman and a young white boy in a boat on a small stream; as the woman searches for eels, the boy paddles. Most of Mount's paintings have humorous overtones, but *Eel Spearing* is a matter-of-fact portrayal of an activity that was common on Long Island until well into the twentieth century. The critics of his day liked it less than his other paintings, probably because it lacked the humor they had come to expect. Whatever it may lack in joviality is more than compensated for by its timelessness and excellent workmanship, including its astonishingly natural representation of light. Other noteworthy works painted in the 1840s include *Ringing the Pig* (1843, New York State Historical Association) and *Loss and Gain* (1847, Museums at Stony Brook), the latter showing an old codger trying to rescue his overturned jug of liquor.

Mount's other passion, besides art, was music, and music played an important role in his art as well as in his life. Many of his paintings focused on music and dance, for example, *Dance of the Haymakers* (1845,

Museums at Stony Brook). In his earliest portrait, a self-portrait, he holds a flute; his earliest genre painting depicts a dance; he also made a drawing of the Setauket Military Band (c. 1840, Museums at Stony Brook). The artistic culmination of his interest in music may be said to be *The Power of Music* (1847, Cleveland Museum of Art) and the series of paintings of musicians he did between 1849 and 1856. In *The Power of Music* a fiddler is depicted inside a barn (the same barn seen in *Dance of the Haymakers*) playing for two other men while just outside the barn a black farmhand pauses to listen. Beginning in 1849 Mount painted several of what he called "fancy pictures," lifesize representations of a single musician with an instrument. These were not portraits of specific individuals but rather depictions of a type of American character in the act of making music. The first of these, *Just in Tune* (Museums at Stony Brook), shows a young man tuning his violin. It was followed by *Right and Left* (1850, Museums at Stony Brook), its title reflected in the subject, a left-handed fiddler; *The Banjo Player* (1856, Museums at Stony Brook), and *The Bone Player* (1856, Museum of Fine Arts, Boston). All were subsequently reproduced as lithographs published by Goupil and Co. With the exception of the fiddler in *Just in Tune*, the subjects of these paintings are black men. Mount was, in fact, virtually alone among American artists of the period in painting sympathetic portraya's of blacks. With the exception of *Rustic Dance after a Sleigh Ride*, in which both the black fiddler and the white dancers are rendered as semicaricatures, the paintings that feature black people present them realistically and with sensitivity.

Mount's interest in music went beyond painting musicians. An accomplished fiddler, in 1852 he invented and patented a new type of violin he called the Cradle of Harmony. It differed from conventional violins in having a shape similar to that of a guitar, a concave rather than a convex back, and f-shaped sound holes in reverse. The bigger sound produced by Mount's instrument was a boon to the rural fiddler, who often was the only musician at a country dance and therefore needed to produce a large sound. Mount collected folk tunes and owned a large collection of musical manuscripts; he also composed the occasional tune. The Cradle of Harmony was not his only invention; he subsequently designed and created a portable studio that enabled him to paint outdoors in all types of weather.

Other noteworthy works from the 1850s are *California News* (1850, Museums at Stony Brook), which portrays a group of Stony Brook residents (among them Mount's brother Shepard) discussing the gold rush; and *The "Herald" in the Country* (1853, Museums at Stony Brook), which depicts two men in the woods discussing a news item in the *New York Herald*. Sometime between 1852 and 1856 Mount painted the enigmatic *The Banjo Player* (Detroit Institute of Arts), a puzzling work that neither he nor contemporary critics ever mentioned. It depicts a lone banjo player, seated in the by now familiar barn, playing a tune. Mount

evidently intended to add two dancing figures but never did so.

As the 1850s progressed, Mount's work became more uneven, probably due to his increasingly chronic poor health. Such paintings as *Coming to the Point* (1854, New-York Historical Society), a reworking of *Bargaining for a Horse*; and *Catching Crabs* (1865) and *Catching a Tune* (1866) (both Museums at Stony Brook) are sadly inferior to his best work. Perhaps the finest of his late paintings is *Long Island Farmhouses* (1862, Metropolitan Museum of Art), which depicts the home of his brother Robert and the neighboring Brewster homestead in Setauket. It was in Robert's home that Mount, a lifelong bachelor, died, one week before his sixty-first birthday. He was buried in the cemetery of the Presbyterian church in Setauket.

Mount may be regarded as the most important American genre painter of the nineteenth century. He reached artistic maturity when he was only twenty-three and maintained a consistently high level of proficiency until his fifties, when declining health interfered with his abilities. His paintings, better than those of any of his contemporaries, portray rural life in nineteenth-century America, and the skill with which he painted them makes his pictures equally valuable as historical documents and as works of art.

• Mount's papers, including his diaries, notebooks, and correspondence, belong to the Museums at Stony Brook in Stony Brook, N.Y., which also owns the largest collection of his work. Other institutions that own paintings by him include the New York State Historical Association, Cooperstown; the Metropolitan Museum of Art, New York; the Pennsylvania Academy of the Fine Arts, Philadelphia; the Corcoran Gallery of Art, Washington D.C.; the National Museum of American Art, Washington, D.C.; the New-York Historical Society, New York; and the Museum of Fine Arts, Boston. Mount wrote a series of autobiographical notes, the manuscripts of which are owned by the Museums at Stony Brook. A series of fifty-six articles by Edward P. Buffet published in the *Port Jefferson* (New York) *Times* from 1 Dec. 1923 to 12 June 1924 constitutes the first modern biography; complete sets of this series belong to the Museums at Stony Brook, the New York Public Library, and the Metropolitan Museum of Art. Alfred Frankenstein, *William Sidney Mount* (1975), is a rambling but comprehensive account of the artist's life and career. (Mary) Bartlett Cowdrey and Hermann Warner Williams, Jr., *William Sidney Mount* (1944), discusses the genre paintings in detail but not his work in portraiture. David Cassedy and Gail Shrott's catalog *William Sidney Mount: Works in the Collection of the Museums at Stony Brook* (1983) contains a short biographical sketch. Self-portraits are owned by the Museums at Stony Brook and by the Pennsylvania Academy of the Fine Arts; Mount was also twice painted by his good friend Charles Loring Elliott, in 1848 (Museums at Stony Brook) and around 1850 (National Gallery of Art, Washington, D.C.). The Pennsylvania Academy also owns a copy by David Johnson of the 1848 portrait.

DAVID MESCHUTT

MOUNTAIN CHIEF (1848?–2 Feb. 1942), Piegan warrior and tribal leader, was born at Old Man River in Alberta, Canada, the son of Mountain Chief, a chief of the Piegans, and Charging across Quartering. Married at least five times, he had at least six children. Mountain Chief (Nena-es-toko), who was also called Big Brave and later adopted the name Frank Mountain Chief, was born into the southern Piegan (Pikuni) tribe, one of three tribal groups that made up the Blackfoot confederacy. These groups occupied roughly the area stretching from present-day southern Alberta and Saskatchewan to Montana. The southern Piegans eventually settled in Montana, where they were commonly called the Blackfeet. Mountain Chief's life spanned the crucial period of the transformation of these native people from nomadic, feared warriors into reservation Indians.

Several Blackfeet bore the name Mountain Chief, and Frank Mountain Chief is sometimes confused with his father, also called Mountain Chief, who died in 1872. Frank Mountain Chief's early life was closely tied to the events that were shaped in part by his father, a noted warrior and tribal leader. Frank Mountain Chief came from a large family that included his father's five wives, all sisters, and some twenty children. Frank Mountain Chief's father gained recognition among his tribe and notoriety among the whites as a fearless warrior and eventually became head chief of the Piegans. He was one of the signatories of the Blackfeet treaty of 1855, the first treaty between the American government and the Blackfeet, a treaty gathering that Frank Mountain Chief witnessed. This treaty ceded to the United States all of the Blackfeet territory south of the Missouri River and presaged several later land cessions in which Frank Mountain Chief took part.

As a young man Frank Mountain Chief followed in the steps of his father and became recognized as a fearless warrior in fights against tribal enemies and white people alike. In 1866 he was one of the leaders of a Blackfeet expedition against the Gros Ventres and the Crows in Cypress Hills, Alberta, that resulted in the killing of more than 300 of the Blackfeet's enemies. In 1867 Mountain Chief led a fight against the Kootenais during which he nearly lost his life in a hand-to-hand combat.

In 1869, during the so-called Blackfeet War (1865–1870), Frank Mountain Chief's father suffered abuse and humiliation at the hands of white men in Fort Benton, and his uncle and a young companion were murdered on the street of Fort Benton. The simmering enmity between whites and Indians as well as the personal abuse caused Mountain Chief, Sr., his sons, and his followers to escalate their attacks on white ranches, freighters, and travelers. The culmination of these raids was the murder of a prominent Montana resident, Malcolm Clark, a white man married to a Piegan woman.

Mountain Chief, Sr., gave the murderers, all Piegans, a safe haven and was singled out by the Americans as one of the principal Blackfeet hostiles. The punishment of Mountain Chief's band became one of the objectives of a military expedition launched in the winter of 1870, headed by Colonel E. M. Baker. Unfortunately, Baker either mistakenly or deliberately attacked instead the band of chief Heavy Runner, who was friendly toward the whites, while encamped on the Marias River. The resulting encounter, denounced as the Baker Massacre or Marias Massacre, caused an outcry among Indian reformers in the East as an example of the government's heavy-handed dealings with the Indians and ended the debate over the transfer of Indian affairs to the military. In Montana the Baker Massacre effectively ended Blackfeet resistance to the presence of whites in Montana.

At peace with the whites, Frank Mountain Chief continued to fight tribal enemies. In 1871 he led a band of Blackfeet in a successful encounter with the Crees near Fort Whoop Up, a whiskey traders' fort near Lethbridge, Alberta. In this fight he killed two enemies with his spear. In 1873 he received a serious leg wound in a fight with the Crows, which left him lame for the rest of his life. By 1882 he had participated in one of the last intertribal fights on Milk River.

In the 1880s the traditional nomadic and hunting lifestyle of Frank Mountain Chief and his fellow tribesmen ended with their confinement to the reservation. Frank Mountain Chief became concerned with the survival and the security of his tribe, and in 1887 he participated in a land cession agreement that broke up the large northern reservation into three separate agencies. The Blackfeet's share of the cession secured tribal income for the following ten years. In 1895 Mountain Chief took part in a second land cession, involving the opening to miners of the so-called St. Mary's Strip, the area eventually designated Glacier National Park.

In the early 1900s Mountain Chief was widely acknowledged as an elder statesman of the Blackfeet. He served as a member of the tribal council and made several trips to various parts of the country and to Washington, D.C., as head of tribal delegations. He met presidents William McKinley, Theodore Roosevelt, William Taft, and Woodrow Wilson. A scheduled ten-minute interview with Wilson turned into an hour meeting during which Mountain Chief, through an interpreter, gave his opinion on woman suffrage.

Mountain Chief remained deeply concerned with the security of his tribe, especially regarding the allotment of land under the Blackfeet Allotment Act passed in 1907. The issue of land allotment and sale of surplus lands split the tribe between the growing population of "progressive" mixed-bloods and the more traditional full-bloods. In 1909 Mountain Chief and other prominent tribal leaders signed a letter protesting the historical erosion of tribal lands due to government policy and advocating the retention of tribal lands for future generations. Mountain Chief remained concerned with questions of land throughout the next several years as a heated intratribal debate and congressional hearings over the future of the Blackfeet reservation continued. During this time Mountain Chief remained torn between a desire to preserve the tribal lands and a realization that government policy favored the dispersal of Indian real estate.

In his later years Mountain Chief remained a respected public figure in Montana, taking part in various public functions. In 1922 he participated in a ceremony adopting Queen Marie of Rumania into the Blackfeet tribe. He enjoyed a long-standing friendship with General Hugh L. Scott, member of the Board of Indian Commissioners, Indian reformer, and student of the sign language of the Plains Indians. In 1931 Scott filmed Mountain Chief at Browning, Montana, recounting in sign language the many war exploits of his youth. Although he became blind in old age, Mountain Chief, the last hereditary chief of the northern Piegans, remained in good health until his sudden death at Browning.

• Information on Frank Mountain Chief is sketchy and scattered in several sources. Primary sources that mention Mountain Chief include the Blackfeet agency records, part of the Museum of the Plains Indians Archives, now housed in the archival collections at the Denver Federal Archives and Records Center in Denver, Colo. Other archival sources are in the biographical files of the Montana Historical Society, Helena. These include *Great Falls Tribune*, 5 Feb. 1942; *Montana Newspaper Association Inserts*, 19 July 1926; *Rocky Mountain Husbandman*, 19 Feb. 1942; and *Browning Chief*, 6 Feb. 1942. References to Blackfeet history in general and to Mountain Chief's father and the struggle over the northern plains are included in the standard work on the Blackfeet by John C. Ewers, *The Blackfeet: Raiders on the Northwestern Plains* (1958). Also useful is an account of Blackfeet life in Keith C. Seele, ed., *Blackfeet and Buffalo: Memories of Life among the Indians by James Willard Schultz* (1962). The story of the Baker Massacre is treated by Paul A. Hutton, "Phil Sheridan's Pyrric Victory: The Piegan Massacre, Army Politics, and the Transfer Debate," *Montana*, Spring 1982, pp. 32–43. For an account of the politics of Blackfeet land cessions, see Hana Samek, *The Blackfoot Confederacy, 1880–1920: A Comparative Study of Canadian and U.S. Indian Policy* (1987). Genealogical information is in *Blackfeet Heritage, 1907–1908: Blackfeet Indian Reservation, Browning, Montana* (n.d.). Photographs of Mountain Chief are included in William E. Farr, *The Reservation Blackfeet, 1882–1945: A Photographic History of Cultural Survival* (1984).

HANA SAMEK

MOURNING DOVE (1884?–1936), the first traditional Native American woman novelist, was born Christine Quintasket in a canoe crossing the Kootenay River near Bonner's Ferry, Idaho, the daughter of Joseph Quintasket and Lucy Stuikin, tribal leaders and farmers. Although her parents were prominent members of the Okanogan and Colville tribes of the Interior Salish, they were poor. Christine realized that education might be her only means of advancement. During the 1890s she studied at Goodwin Catholic Mission near Kettle Falls, Washington, and in 1900 at a government school at Fort Spokane. Several years later, she joined the staff at Fort Shaw School near Great Falls, Montana. There she married Hector McLeod in 1909, a member of the Flathead band, but they soon separated.

She decided to write a novel conveying the emotional depth and range of native peoples to counter the stereotype of the stoic Native American that she found so offensive. She moved to Portland, Oregon, around 1912 and produced the first draft, under the pen name "Morning Dove" (Humishuma). The next year she enrolled at a business school in Calgary to hone her grammar and writing skills. About 1914 she met Lucullus Virgil McWhorter, a Yakima businessman, who edited the novel and arranged for its publication as *Cogewea: The Half-Blood* in 1927.

Around 1917 Mourning Dove taught on the Inkameep Okanagan Reserve in British Columbia, where she was active in local politics. She used her salary to buy a typewriter and began, with the encouragement of McWhorter and others, to record stories from Salishan elders, including her parents.

In 1919 she married Fred Galler, a Wenatchi also enrolled among the Colville Confederated Tribes, and moved to East Omak, Washington, on her home reservation. There she prepared a collection of stories, designed, with the help of McWhorter and Hester Dean Guie, a Yakima newspaperman, to appeal to a white audience. The stories were published under the title *Coyote Stories* in 1933. In 1921 she adopted the spelling "Mourning Dove," adding tragic overtones to her lifelong efforts.

Mourning Dove led a double life, a private one as Christine Quintasket, a woman migrant laborer struggling to make ends meet, and a public one as a writer, lecturer, and politician among the Confederated Tribes of the Colville Reservation of north-central Washington State. During the early 1930s, as her works began to be published and she became politically active, some whites denied that she had the education or ability to write. In reply, she drafted several versions of an autobiography, providing a superb overview of female life among Interior Salishan tribes, which was not published until 1990.

Living at Omak, she formed organizations of women to promote crafts and to intervene in legal disputes between Native Americans and whites. In 1935 she was the first woman elected to the Colville tribal council.

The demands of a lifetime of physical labor in addition to writing and involvement in tribal affairs led to Mourning Dove's increasing complaints of a "nervous [sic]" disposition. She died at Medical Lake, Washington, of "exhaustion from manic depressive psychosis."

Her legacy includes opening the way for a succession of powerful women leaders on the tribal council, growing fame as a woman who wrote despite considerable personal and financial obstacles, and a published record that continues to help Native Americans and whites understand each other.

• Various of Mourning Dove's letters and papers are in the Lucullus Virgil McWhorter Collection at the Holland Library of Washington State University and the Erna Gunther Collection at the Archives of the University of Washington. Mourning Dove is best understood through her own writings. Besides the works mentioned in the text, see *Mourning Dove: A Salishan Autobiography*, ed. Jay Miller (1990). Different versions of her stories were published as *Tales of the Okanogans*, ed. Donald Hines (1976), and *Mourning Dove's*

Stories, ed. Clifford E. Trafzer and Richard D. Scheuerman (1991). See also Jay Miller, "Mourning Dove: The Author as Cultural Mediator," in *Being and Becoming Indian: Biographical Studies of North American Frontiers*, ed. James Clifton (1989).

JAY MILLER

MOURSUND, Walter Henrik (13 Aug. 1884–2 Apr. 1959), physician and medical educator, was born in Fredericksburg, in the Texas Hill Country, the son of Norwegian-born Albert Wadel Moursund, a locally prominent lawyer, district judge, and member of the Texas legislature, and Henrikke Marion Mowinckle, a native Texan also of Norwegian lineage. Following graduation from high school in 1902, Moursund studied medicine at the University of Texas Medical Branch in Galveston and received his M.D. in 1906. After an internship in clinical pathology at Galveston's John Sealy Hospital, he devoted four years to practicing medicine in a series of small Texas towns but was dissatisfied with the life and prospects of a general practitioner. In 1907 he married Freda Adelaide Plate of Seguin, Texas; they had four children.

A chance meeting with a former professor of pathology led Moursund in 1911 to join Dr. Alfred E. Mayer by becoming an assistant in pathology and bacteriology at Baylor University College of Medicine, which had been founded in Dallas in 1900 and affiliated since 1903 with Baylor University, a Baptist institution in Waco, Texas. Moursund became full professor in 1912 and functioned as a secretary and registrar of the medical school in 1914–1915. During World War I he served as a medical officer at several army posts within Texas, becoming a commanding medical officer of the Eighth Corps Area Laboratory. Returning to Baylor after the war as professor of clinical pathology, he also became pathologist for the Texas Baptist Memorial Sanitarium. In 1923 he was appointed dean of the college of medicine.

Although he had intended to retire as dean in 1941, Moursund forsook his personal plans in order to defend Baylor's college of medicine against a powerful group of Dallas philanthropists and civic leaders who in 1939 had organized the Southwestern Medical Foundation. These men, who were supported by many of the city's practitioners, envisioned Dallas as the locus of a huge medical center serving the greater Southwest and argued that the medical school at the center's hub would improve its fundraising opportunities if it was independent of denominational control. Baylor's trustees resisted this effort to divest the medical school of its Baptist connection, thereby jeopardizing the school's prospects of survival. As Moursund later wrote, "It would have been extremely difficult, if not impossible, for Baylor's medical college to have continued in Dallas." An invitation from the M. D. Anderson Foundation of Houston proposed that Baylor relocate its medical college to become the cornerstone of the new Texas Medical Center in Houston. Throughout this controversy Moursund stayed at the Baylor helm, assuring the school's vitality and direct-ing its removal to Houston in 1943. Until his retirement in 1953, he guided Baylor through the initial stages of its growth into the large biomedical research and teaching institution that it has since become. His three decades as dean may constitute the longest tenure of any comparable medical educator/administrator in American history.

Moursund was enormously respected by medical students, many of whom were helped through difficult times by his counsel and support. A man of high professional standards, he was also a compassionate mentor who linked medical education with clinical applications because most of his Baylor students became practitioners. "The study of medicine is a terrific grind," he observed. "If one can follow students through the full four years of their schooling, their development of knowledge and ability is wonderful to see." But concurrently he attracted to Baylor several research-oriented bioscientists, the most prominent being Michael E. DeBakey, who advanced Baylor's transformation from a regional school of modest ambitions to a national center of major stature. In 1956 Moursund wrote the only published history of his institution. He died in Houston.

• Moursund's papers are located at the Harris County Medical Archive of the Houston Academy of Medicine–Texas Medical Center Library in Houston. Archives and Oral History Office at Baylor College of Medicine contains administrative records that document Moursund's deanship. Accessible at the Texas Collection of Baylor University at Waco are his occasional communications with senior officials of that institution. His book, *A History of Baylor University College of Medicine, 1900–1953* (1956), offers more description and chronology than self-scrutiny. In 1958 he compiled "Medicine in Greater Houston, 1836–1956," an unpublished manuscript of 583 pages, and in 1957 he wrote a personal memoir, "For My Children: A Full Life," also unpublished. An obituary appears in the *Houston Post*, 3 Apr. 1959.

CHARLES T. MORRISSEY

MOWATT, Anna Cora (5 Mar. 1819–21 July 1870), actress and author, was born Anna Cora Ogden in Bordeaux, France, the daughter of Samuel Gouverneur Ogden, an American shipping merchant, and Eliza Lewis. At age seven Anna returned with her family to New York City, where she attended various private schools, including Mrs. Okill's on Eighth Street. A highly imaginative child, Anna wrote, staged, and acted in amateur theatricals put on by her large family. She also read widely and claimed to have read all of Shakespeare's plays before she was ten. In 1834, at age fifteen, she married James Mowatt, a wealthy attorney thirteen years her senior. Since her parents would not consent to the marriage because of her youth, the couple eloped. The newlyweds moved to "Melrose," an estate in the Flatbush section of Brooklyn. At Melrose Mowatt was tutored in languages and literature. She began writing poetry, and some of her work was published under the pseudonym Isabel, including an epic poem called *Pelayo; or, The Cavern of Cavadonga* (1836).

Mowatt took a lengthy trip to Europe with relatives in 1837 to recuperate from a bout of tuberculosis. Her husband joined her in Europe in 1838. Mowatt continued writing while abroad, and her verse drama *Gulzara; or, The Persian Slave* was presented as a family theatrical on her return from Europe in August 1840. The play was published the following year in the *New World*. Though traveling temporarily restored Mowatt's health, tuberculosis would continue to recur throughout her life. To help cope with her poor health Mowatt turned to various nonmedical treatments, such as mesmerism, and practiced the Swedenborgian religion. Her husband's health also began to fail, and by 1841 he was unable to practice law because of poor eyesight. To make matters worse, he lost his fortune through speculation. This dire financial situation impelled Mowatt to earn income through her dramatic and literary talents. In the winter of 1841–1842 she gave a series of poetry readings in Boston, Massachusetts, Providence, Rhode Island, and New York City, using the works of Sir Walter Scott and other popular contemporary poets as material. The novelty of a "female elocutionist" and of a society woman giving a public performance drew sellout crowds, but Mowatt found the tour exhausting and did not repeat it.

In 1842 Mowatt and her husband, who had no children of their own, became guardians of three children from a poverty-stricken New York City family. Turning to writing as a way of making money, Mowatt was a regular contributor to *Graham's Magazine*, the *Ladies Companion*, the *Democratic Review*, *Godey's Lady's Book*, and other periodicals from 1842 to 1844. Using various pseudonyms, she wrote sketches of famous people she had met and essays contrasting American and European manners. She also worked as a ghostwriter on articles by English author Sarah Stickney Ellis ("Mrs. Ellis") about cooking, needlework, care for the sick, and other domestic subjects. Using the pen name Henry C. Browning, she wrote a biography, *The Life of Goethe* (1844), and as Helen Berkley she wrote a novel, *The Fortune Hunter* (1844). Her first literary effort to appear under her own name was *Evelyn* (1845), a two-volume novel that was published after she had achieved notoriety in the theater.

At the suggestion of her close friend journalist Epes Sargent, Mowatt turned to writing for the professional theater. Her first and best known play, *Fashion*, a five-act comedy lampooning the pretensions of American high society, premiered at New York City's Park Theatre in March 1845. Although similar in style to other comedies of the time, the play was praised for its sparkling wit and for the accuracy of its satire. *Fashion* enjoyed great critical and commercial success in New York and was soon produced in Philadelphia and other cities. Its popularity has endured, and it is one of the few American plays from the first half of the nineteenth century to be regularly revived. (One notable revival was staged by the Provincetown Players in New York City in 1924.)

Finding the profits from playwrighting too meager to put her on a sound financial footing—especially af-

ter the repeated failure of her husband's business enterprises—Mowatt decided to become an actress. Her decision to go on the stage shocked and alienated many of her upper-class friends, who held the acting profession in ill repute. Strengthened by the full support of her husband and her father, Mowatt made her professional acting debut as Pauline in *The Lady of Lyons* at the Park Theatre in June 1845. Her good looks, mellifluous voice, and intellectual understanding of drama helped to compensate for her lack of professional experience. Mowatt quickly became an acting sensation, and during her first year on the stage she performed in all the major cities of the United States in a variety of plays, including *The Lady of Lyons*, *School for Scandal*, and her own *Fashion*. She also tackled Shakespearean roles, including Juliet, Rosalind, and Beatrice. Despite a grueling schedule of traveling and performing, she wrote another play, *Armand, the Child of the People*, and added it to her acting repertoire in September 1847.

Mowatt's most important asset as an actress was her highly emotional personality. Abandoning herself to the sentiments of her characters, she exhibited a naturalness and sincerity that audiences found a refreshing change from the polished style of trained performers. "Mrs. Mowatt is the first American actress of stature to use feminine emotionalism as her principal method and appeal. Undoubtedly the force of her example and the effect of her success influenced many other actresses to adopt her style," wrote Garff B. Wilson in *A History of American Acting* (p. 117). Though Mowatt was popular with audiences, she was never fully accepted by her fellow performers, who dismissed her as a dilettante. Mowatt's ability to function successfully in the theatrical world without losing her aura of upper-class breeding helped to make the acting profession more socially acceptable.

Late 1847 Mowatt sailed for England to play a brief series of provincial and London performances. Her reception by British theatergoers was so overwhelming that she stayed in England for more than three years, playing long engagements at London's Princess and Marylebone theaters. Mowatt's husband, who had accompanied her to England, died in London in 1851. Distraught by his death and by the knowledge that he had invested most of her earnings in a fraudulent theater management scheme, she returned to the United States in the summer of 1851. Mowatt toured American cities with a repertory of plays before being diagnosed with malaria in early 1853. While recuperating at her father's home in New York City she wrote *Autobiography of an Actress*. Published in 1854, the book was well received by critics and enjoyed brisk sales. It is still considered a valuable source of knowledge on the theatrical world of the 1840s and 1850s.

Having regained her health, Mowatt toured during the 1853–1854 season. Three days after the tour ended in June 1854, she married William Foushee Ritchie, editor of the *Richmond Enquirer*, and abandoned her acting career. While living in Virginia with Ritchie, with whom she had no children, Mowatt was active in the Mount Vernon Ladies' Association, which oversaw the restoration of George Washington's home. During this period she also wrote two works of fiction, *Mimic Life* (1856), a collection of tales based on her theatrical experiences, and *Twin Roses* (1857), a novel.

Mowatt's marriage to the aristocratic and profligate Ritchie proved unhappy. Their relationship was further strained by political differences: Mowatt was a staunch Unionist while the slaveholding Ritchie supported states' rights. In late 1860 Mowatt moved to New York City to nurse her ailing father and never lived with Ritchie again. Claiming that the Civil War made it impossible for her to return to Virginia, she spent the next few years with relatives and friends in New York, France, and Italy. In 1865 she settled in England. Although she grew increasingly ill from tuberculosis, she continued to write and published several fictional works, including *Fairy Fingers* (1865), *The Mute Singer* (1866), and *The Clergyman's Wife and Other Sketches* (1867). Poor health forced her to decline numerous acting offers. She died at Twickenham, near London.

• There is a small collection of material on Mowatt at the Schlesinger Library at Radcliffe College, Cambridge, Mass. Eric Wollencott Barnes, *The Lady of Fashion* (1954), is a biography. Discussions of Mowatt's career are in Garff B. Wilson, *A History of American Acting* (1966), Jack A. Vaughn, *Early American Dramatists* (1981), and Claudia D. Johnson, *American Actress: Perspective on the Nineteenth Century* (1984). See also *Cosmopolitan Art Journal*, Dec. 1858, pp. 28–31; Marius Blesi, "The Life and Letters of Anna Cora Mowatt" (Ph.D. diss., Univ. of Virginia, 1938); and Kelly Shaver Taylor, "The Rhetoric of Self-Fashioning in Works of Anna Cora Mowatt" (Ph.D. diss., Louisiana State Univ., 1994). An obituary is in the *New York Times*, 30 July 1870.

MARY C. KALFATOVIC

MOWBRAY, George Mordey (5 May 1814–21 June 1891), chemist and explosives manufacturer, was born in Brighton, England; the names of his parents are unknown. Mowbray recounted of his early life only that he studied organic chemistry in England, France, and Germany before becoming a pharmaceutical manufacturer, then a drug wholesaler in England. A voyage prescribed for poor health took him to South America, where he became interested in the nitrate industry. Continuing his journey around the Horn, he fetched up in the gold fields of California; working as an assayer, chemist, and amateur surgeon to the miners restored his energy. He married Annie Fade, a native of Kent, England, apparently around 1857, though whether he returned to England for that purpose is not clear. They had no children of their own, but they adopted Annie Mowbray's orphaned nephew, Henry Siddons, who took their surname. They took up residence in New York in 1858, and Mowbray became a research chemist for the wholesale drug firm of Schieffelin Brothers and Company.

In 1859 Mowbray met Edwin L. Drake, who had just drilled the first producing oil well in America. The two cigar aficionados smoked a full box of Ha-

vanas, and by morning Mowbray had secured for Schieffelin Brothers the New York distribution rights to the output of Drake's Seneca Oil Company. Mowbray built and operated for Drake the first petroleum refinery on Oil Creek in Titusville, Pennyslvania, and patented early methods for cracking petroleum. There he learned to "shoot" dormant wells with nitroglycerine, a technique introduced in 1863 in Titusville by the Roberts Torpedo Company, which licensed Alfred Nobel's formulas in 1866.

When the petroleum industry collapsed at the close of the Civil War, despite Mowbray's successful lobbying to repeal the federal tax on oil, the chemist turned to circumventing Nobel's patents for nitroglycerine. Mowbray's own patents involved low-temperature processing and compressed air. He dripped a mixture of nitric and sulfuric acids into exceptionally pure glycerol agitated by air bubbled through earthenware pots cooled in an ice bath; he then carefully washed and neutralized the compound. When accidents and delays occasioned by importing Nobel nitroglycerine stalled construction of the Hoosac Tunnel in western Massachusetts, the Troy and Greenfield Railroad hired Mowbray to do the blasting. Building a factory in North Adams, Massachusetts, in 1867, he distilled his own nitric acid, constructed an electrical detonation system, manufactured his own fuses and cable insulation, and supervised every aspect of the blasting. He recorded the experience in the first treatise on high explosives published in the United States, *Tri-Nitro-Glycerine, as Used in the Construction of the Hoosac Tunnel* (privately printed 1871, commercial editions 1872 and 1874).

The Nobel-licensed United Blasting Company unsuccessfully sued Mowbray for patent infringement in 1870. That year his daily production of 250 pounds of explosives, coupled with the discovery that freezing nitroglycerin reduced its sensitivity, enabled Mowbray to accelerate progress. By the day in 1873 when he personally blew the last sixteen feet of rock in the tunnel, Mowbray had demonstrated that high explosives could transform a continent. He licensed factories in Ontario, Ohio, and Kentucky; the last, in Maysville, supplied explosives for construction on the Chesapeake and Ohio Railroad in 1878. The North Adams factory also shipped thousands of pounds of nitroglycerin to the builders of the Canadian Pacific Railroad in Ontario and Manitoba (1877). Mowbray's laboratories trained a generation of American explosives specialists, although he would entrust long-distance delivery only to his adopted son, who rode on the freight trains to reassure nervous conductors.

The Mowbray enterprises never suffered a lethal accident, but patent battles finally destroyed them. The substance in dispute was "Mica Blasting Powder," nitroglycerine granulated with minute particles of mica to control its force, originally compounded in 1873. Because the powder closely resembled dynamite (nitroglycerine mixed with a silica called kieselguhr), the Nobel-licensed Atlantic Giant Powder Company in 1875 charged Mowbray with infringement. The Supreme Court ruled against Mowbray in 1879; in 1880 he closed his factory.

The following year the newly-incorporated American Zylonite Company hired Mowbray as chief chemist and technical manager to oversee the development of commercial celluloid products ranging from candy boxes to film. (Years later Henry Siddons Mowbray, who became a celebrated artist, noted with regret that he never introduced his friend Eadweard Muybridge to Mowbray; had he done so, he thought, the course of photography and motion pictures would have been altered.)

Mowbray's experiments with pyroxylin and camphor led him instead to the use of plastic nitrocellulose in gunpowders. He devised an ingenious mechanism for rapid, continuous nitration of paper or cotton. In 1886 news of Mowbray's experiments with smokeless powder fabricated by soaking nitrated fabrics (or "fluffy" guncotton) in nitroglycerin attracted the attention of Hiram and Hudson Maxim of the Maxim and Nordenfeldt Company in England, which was trying to compound a high-velocity smokeless powder for adoption by the British War Office. Because the Maxims were competing against Nobel, Mowbray agreed to help; he suggested binding nitroglycerin and guncotton with castor oil (an ingredient of zylonite). Both Nobel and the Maxims, however, lost the contract to Abel and Dewar, who invented cordite, but Maxim and Nordenfeldt purchased in advance any gunpowder patents Mowbray might secure. Hudson Maxim, who started the Maxim Powder and Torpedo Company in New Jersey in 1890, formed an alliance with Mowbray's assistant, Robert C. Schüpphaus. Mowbray was by that time too ill to take an active role, but his formulas were embodied in "Maxim-Schüpphaus Powder," a product perforated to control the rate of combustion; DuPont bought the rights in 1898, when it was adopted by the U.S. Navy.

Long before the success of that product, patent wars again overtook Mowbray: the Celluloid Company proved that American Zylonite had infringed its patents and took over the latter enterprise in 1890. Mowbray died in North Adams, Massachusetts.

• Many references to Mowbray, his enterprises, and his patents can be found in the manuscripts and letter files of the Hagley Museum and Library on the old DuPont estate in Wilmington, Delaware. The most important source on Mowbray is Arthur Pine Van Gelder and Hugo Schlatter, *History of the Explosives Industry in America* (1927). Henry Siddons Mowbray *H. Siddons Mowbray, Mural Painter, 1858–1928* (1928), a short autobiography by Mowbray's adopted son, provides personal glimpses, as does Hudson Maxim's anecdotal *Dynamite Stories* (1916). The Schieffelin Company's centennial pamphlet, *Respice, Adspice, Prospice: One Hundred Years of Business Life, 1794–1894* (1894), contains only a paragraph on the Titusville plant. Paul H. Giddens, *The Birth of the Oil Industry* (1938), recounts Mowbray's encounter with Edwin Drake and their association, as well as Mowbray's efforts to repeal the federal oil tax. "One Hundred Years of Oil," a centennial edition of the *Titusville Herald* (24 Aug. 1959) contains material on Mowbray's early experiments with nitroglycerine. *Scientific American*, 8 Dec. 1866, carries

Mowbray's first advertisement for nitroglycerine. For Mowbray's engineering feat see Carl R. Byron, *A Pinprick of Light: The Troy and Greenfield Railroad and Its Hoosac Tunnel* (1978). The two major patent infringement suits against Mowbray are *United Blasting Oil Company of New York v. George Mowbray et al.* (1870), in U.S. Circuit Court for the Western District of Pennsylvania, and *Atlantic Giant Powder Company v. George M. Mowbray et al.* (1875), in U.S. Circuit Court for the District of Massachusetts. An obituary is in the *Boston Transcript*, 23 June 1891.

JOSEPH W. SLADE

MOWER, Joseph Anthony (22 Aug. 1827–6 Jan. 1870), soldier, was born in Woodstock, Vermont, the son of Nathaniel Mower and Sophia Holmes, farmers. When he was six his family moved to Lowell, Massachusetts, where he received a public school education. In 1843 he returned to his native state and for two years studied at Norwich University. He left the carpenter's trade in 1846 to enlist in the Mexican War, serving for two years as a private soldier. In 1851 he married Betsey A. Bailey; the number of their children, if any, is unknown. Four years later, pursuing his enthusiasm for military life, he secured a direct commission into the army as second lieutenant, First U.S. Infantry. A few months after the Civil War began, Mower attained the rank of captain.

Stationed in Missouri when fighting broke out, Mower soon came to the attention of local authorities. When another transplanted New Englander, Colonel Joseph B. Plummer of the Eleventh Missouri Volunteers, was named a brigadier general late in 1861, he recommended Mower to replace him. Following Mower's conspicuous service in command of a siege train in the battle of New Madrid, 12–13 March 1862, the Eleventh Missouri decided that he was "a fit man to command," and on 3 May Mower was elected to the vacant colonelcy. From the first he proved a popular choice. The regiment came to regard him as strict but fair-minded, a plain-spoken leader worthy of admiration for his good judgment, his grace under fire, and his "eagle eye" for defensible terrain.

Less than a week after assuming command of his regiment, Mower received a regular army brevet for gallantry at Farmington, Mississippi. He moved up to brigade command in Major General William S. Rosecrans's Army of the Mississippi three months later. After the battle of Iuka, 19 September 1862, in which Mower, with a part of his brigade, came to the timely support of embattled comrades, Rosecrans noted that the colonel's "gallantry is equaled only by his energy." On the second day of the fighting at Corinth, 4 October, Mower had his horse shot from under him and received a wound in the neck while leading a reconnaissance-in-force; he fell into Confederate hands, only to be rescued when the enemy retreated late in the day. By year's end, Mower had risen to brigadier general of volunteers while receiving yet another brevet in the regular service.

At the outset of the Vicksburg campaign, Mower took command of a brigade in Major General William

T. Sherman's Fifteenth Corps. In a brief time he became a valued subordinate in the eyes of both Sherman and Major General Ulysses S. Grant, commander of the Army of the Tennessee. In mid-May Sherman successfully entrusted him with destroying the military potential of Jackson, Mississippi, stronghold of Confederate general Joseph E. Johnston, by burning large portions of it to the ground. Early in June Grant dispatched Mower on reconnaissance missions to Mechanicsburg, Mississippi, and Richmond, Louisiana. After Vicksburg's fall in July, Mower was given a series of semi-independent commands in southern Mississippi, northern Louisiana, and Middle Tennessee. In March 1864 he led a detachment of Grant's army to the Department of the Gulf and distinguished himself throughout the Red River campaign, particularly at Fort de Russy (14 Mar.), Pleasant Hill (9 Apr.), and Yellow Bayou (18 May). Despite his efforts, the campaign closed in Union defeat, whereupon Mower returned to district command in Tennessee and Mississippi. In that capacity he guarded territory that had long been the objective of Major General Nathan Bedford Forrest, the Confederacy's most successful cavalry commander.

Following Forrest's defeat of a large Union force at Brice's Crossroads, 10 June 1864, Sherman vowed to track him down with forces under "two officers at Memphis who will fight all the time, [Major General] A. J. Smith and Mower." Later Sherman vowed that "if Mower will whip Forrest I will pledge him my influence for a Major General and will ask the President as a personal favor to hold a vacancy for him." Sherman was as good as his word: Mower received his second star 12 August, one month after his four brigades overtook Forrest near Tupelo, Mississippi, repulsed a series of attacks, and inflicted hundreds of casualties, including the slight wounding of Forrest himself. A day after his promotion, Mower again defeated Forrest's command at Hurricane Creek, Mississippi, forcing a portion of the rebel force to quit the field in confusion. In September and October, still detached from Sherman's Military Division of the Mississippi, Mower drove his First Division, Sixteenth Corps, relentlessly in pursuing Major General Sterling Price's raiders through Missouri. Following Price's rout at Westport on 23 October, Mower rejoined Sherman, now in Atlanta, and prepared to accompany him on his March to the Sea.

For a time after reaching Atlanta, Mower led the Seventeenth Corps, although he reverted to divisional command when Sherman moved toward the coast. Although his command fought few pitched battles on the road to Savannah, it saw heavy fighting outside the city on 9–11 December. After the fall of the citadel, Mower ranged northward through the Carolinas. His command forced its way through miles of swamps to defeat rebel forces along the Salkehatchie River (3 Feb. 1865). The division was also successful in action on the South Edisto River (9 Feb.) and near Cheraw, South Carolina (3 Mar.). In these and other actions

Mower so distinguished himself that on 2 April he was given command of the Twentieth Corps.

Unlike many of his prewar colleagues, Mower elected to remain in the regular army, at reduced rank, when the volunteer service was disbanded. In July 1866 he was commissioned colonel of the newly organized Thirty-ninth U.S. Infantry, composed of black troops. Three years later he was transferred to the command of another black regiment, the Twenty-fifth Infantry. In the postwar years he commanded a series of occupation areas in the South, notably the Eastern District of Texas, the Fifth Military District at New Orleans (1867–1868), and later the Department of Louisiana. For a part of this period he also served as assistant commissioner of the Freedmen's Bureau in Louisiana. While on duty in New Orleans, he died suddenly of pneumonia.

Mower was one of the few Civil War commanders to achieve distinction in, successively, regimental, brigade, division, and corps command; never was he elevated beyond his ability. Even fewer Union officers attained as many citations and brevets for gallantry as he did. A major reason for his consistent success was his willingness to fight on any terrain, against any opposition, if he believed that skill and daring could carry the day. Late in the war Sherman, who placed his utmost trust in Mower, called him "the boldest young soldier we have."

• No body of Mower papers is known to exist, although a letter book he kept while commanding the Fifth Military District is in the Duke University Library. A family chronicle is W. L. Mower, *Mower Family History: A Genealogical Record of the Maine Branch* (1923). Mower's Civil War battle and campaign reports can be found in *The War of the Rebellion: A Compilation of the Official Records of the Union and Confederate Armies* (128 vols., 1880–1901), ser. 1, vols. 8, 17 (pt. 1), 24 (pt. 2), 34 (pt. 1), 39 (pt. 1), 44, and 47 (pt. 1). Glimpses of Mower in regimental command can be gleaned from D. McCall, *Three Years in the Service: A Record of the Doings of the 11th Reg. Missouri Vols.* (1864). Sherman mentions him prominently in his *Personal Memoirs* (1875), and an artillery commander observes him in Richard Harwell and Philip N. Racine, eds., *The Fiery Trail: A Union Officer's Account of Sherman's Last Campaigns* (1986). Mower's record as brigade, division, and corps leader receives prominent attention in several biographies and campaign studies, notably B. H. Liddell Hart, *Sherman: Soldier, Realist, American* (1929); Lloyd Lewis, *Sherman: Fighting Prophet* (1932); Albert Castel, *Decision in the West: The Atlanta Campaign of 1864* (1992); and Burke Davis, *Sherman's March* (1980). A series of obituaries can be found in the *Army and Navy Journal*, 15 and 22 Jan. and 26 Mar. 1870.

EDWARD G. LONGACRE

MOWRER, Edgar Ansel (8 Mar. 1892–2 Mar. 1977), and **Paul Scott Mowrer** (14 July 1887–7 Apr. 1971), foreign correspondents, were born in Bloomington, Illinois, the sons of Rufus Mowrer, a traveling salesman, and Nell Scott. Their mother was "rich in untutored talents," and Paul recalled that she read them poetry and fiction and sang them songs. His stories of their childhood in *House of Europe* (1945) suggest that

Nell's imagination rubbed off on her sons. Their father, frequently on the road, spent time with the boys when he was at home, teaching them about the outdoors. The family moved to Chicago in 1898 after Rufus's company failed.

Paul graduated from Hyde Park High School in 1905 and started working as a reporter for the *Chicago Daily News*. Though he had always intended to pursue a literary career and continued to write poetry, he enjoyed the newspaper life. For two and a half years he took classes at the University of Michigan but did not pursue a degree. In the summers he worked for the *Daily News*, and during the school year he edited the *Michigan Daily*. By the time he left Ann Arbor in 1908, he had done such a successful job with the student paper that the university paid him $300, which he used for a "graduation" trip to Europe. He returned to Chicago and the *Daily News* and in 1909 married his college sweetheart, Winifred Adams of Kansas City. The couple had two children. In 1910, against the advice of his supervisor at the paper and over the protests of his co-workers, he applied for a job in the paper's Paris bureau, and he and Winifred moved to France. Paul was one of a group of journalists, many raised in the American Midwest, who went to Europe at the start of the new century to work and take part in the exciting world of European literature and ideas they had been exposed to in college.

Edgar graduated from Hyde Park High School in 1909 and enrolled at the University of Michigan. After a year he transferred to the University of Chicago, but he spent only a semester there before he sailed for France to visit Paul in Paris and study at the Sorbonne. After a year in Paris Edgar returned to the United States and finished college at the University of Michigan, where he edited the literary magazine. When he graduated in 1913, Edgar returned to France to pursue his literary education, but when war came, his brother drafted him to work for the *Daily News*.

In Europe Paul served first as the *Daily News* Paris correspondent, next as the Paris bureau chief, and eventually as head of the European service for the *Daily News*. Covering the First World War from his Paris base, Paul realized that the news was on the front line, so he roped his brother into covering the Paris office while he roamed the front. When French officials kept Paul from the front, he returned to Paris and sent his brother to Belgium. He also called on friends from French literary circles to cover those places that were off-limits to Americans.

The war coverage Edgar did for his brother proved his worth to the *Daily News* editors, and in 1915 they assigned him to a regular posting in Rome. In 1916 he married Lilian Thomson, a British woman he had met during his first trip abroad. They had one child.

When the United States entered the war in 1917, Paul was assigned by the French government to the elite corps of reporters allowed to cover Allied efforts. While he covered the war, his wife and two young sons moved to the countryside to avoid the bombs in Paris.

At the war's end, Paul headed the *Chicago Daily News* coverage of the peace conference at Versailles.

After the peace treaty was signed, Paul settled down to cover the numerous diplomatic and economic conferences the world powers held as they attempted to adjust the balance of power. In addition he made periodic reporting trips around Europe and to Morocco. One journey led to his first book, *Balkanized Europe: A Study of Political Analysis and Reconstruction* (1921). Still posted in Rome, Edgar had also begun writing books with *Immortal Italy* (1922), praised as a contribution to the understanding of Italian political development. Over the years the two wrote a number of books on politics and current affairs in Europe. In 1924 Paul got permission from the home office to transfer his brother from Rome to Berlin. Edgar's coverage and analysis of Benito Mussolini suggested that he was just the person the paper needed to get beneath the surface of what was happening in Germany.

Paul and Edgar were among a group of American journalists in Europe who were developing a serious, interpretive approach to foreign coverage. While not the first American correspondents abroad, these men and women played a formative role in professionalizing the job, defining—through their own experiences—what a foreign correspondent's job should be and pressing editors and publishers at home to give them the resources to do what needed to be done. It is not a coincidence that their efforts coincided with the emergence of the United States as a world power, for it was as the witnesses and investigators of this new American role that they redefined their profession. At home their efforts were recognized. Paul received the first Pulitzer Prize for international reporting for his 1928 coverage of efforts to develop a league of nations and the rival peace plans of the jockeying European powers. The judges' criteria were "fair, judicious, well balanced and well informed interpretive writing, which shall make clear the significance of the subject covering in the correspondence or which shall promote international understanding and appreciation."

In 1933 Edgar ran into trouble with the Nazis. Familiar with Italian fascism, he understood the ramifications of Hitler's rise to power. In *Germany Turns the Clock Back* (1932) he predicted that under Hitler Germany would lead the world into another war. Many Berlin correspondents were harassed and expelled by the Nazis, but as president of the Foreign Press Association Edgar came in for particular attention. He finally left in 1933 when German officials said they could no longer guarantee his safety. His 1932 German coverage won Edgar his own Pulitzer Prize.

After a short visit to the United States, Edgar returned to Paris to take over as Paris bureau chief from Paul, who after twenty-four years abroad was heading back to the home office of the *Chicago Daily News*. He and Winifred had divorced, and Paul married Hadley Richardson, Ernest Hemingway's first wife, in 1933. They had no children. Spending a year as an editorial writer, he stepped in as the paper's editor in 1935.

Taking side trips to China, Spain, and the Soviet Union, Edgar remained at the Paris bureau until 1940, when the city fell to the Germans. Lilian meanwhile had written *Journalist's Wife* (1937), which told the story of their marriage and their years in Europe. In 1940 Edgar was assigned to cover Washington, D.C., for the *Daily News* and continued to write books about political affairs abroad. From 1941 to 1943 he served as deputy director of the Office of Facts and Figures and later the Office of War Information and broadcast news analyses from Washington. He quit the post when the State Department refused to allow him to travel to North Africa for the office because of his outspoken disagreements with U.S. policies toward the Vichy government and his criticism of the State Department's handling of nisei residents of the United States. His resignation became a cause célèbre, and under political pressure from Washington, his old employers in Chicago would not touch him. After six weeks the *New York Post* hired him as a commentator on world affairs, and he headed to the war fronts of Europe and North Africa.

Paul retired as editor for the *Chicago Daily News* in 1944 but in 1945 took a job as European editor for the *New York Post*, a job he held for four years. When he left the *Post*, he and Hadley retired to Tamworth, New Hampshire, where he devoted himself to his poetry until his death there.

After the war Edgar continued to write books on world affairs and worked as a syndicated columnist and broadcast commentator. He gained a reputation for his fiercely anti-Soviet views. From 1957 to 1960 he served as the editor in chief for North America for the magazine *Western World*, a monthly dedicated to preserving the Atlantic community. He retired to Wonalancet, New Hampshire, in 1969. He and Lilian were on the Portuguese island of Madeira when he died.

Paul and Edgar Mowrer were among a group of American correspondents who were pioneers in the professionalization of foreign reporting from Europe. Witness to some of the most dramatic events of the twentieth century, Edgar said he had "a ringside seat" to history, a claim that his brother could certainly also have made. Both gained attention and respect not only for their reporting but also for their books of commentary about world affairs and the emergence of the United States as a world power.

• Two telling accounts of the Mowrers' lives are Paul Scott Mowrer, *House of Europe* (1945), and Edgar Ansel Mowrer, *Triumph and Turmoil* (1968). Both men are among the correspondents whose work is the focus of Morrell Heald, *Transatlantic Vistas: American Journalists in Europe, 1900–1940* (1988). Both have entries in Joseph P. McKerns, ed., *Biographical Dictionary of American Journalism* (1989). Paul Mowrer wrote three books and ten books of poetry and a play. Edgar wrote ten books and numerous articles. Their Pulitzer Prize–winning stories can be found in vol. 1 of *Outstanding International Press Reporting: Pulitzer Prize Winning Articles*

in Foreign Correspondence, ed. Heinz-Dietrich Fischer (1984). The *New York Times*, 4 Mar. 1977, ran a fairly thorough obituary of Edgar Mowrer.

CATHERINE CASSARA

MOWRER, Orval Hobart (23 Jan. 1907–20 June 1982), psychologist, was born near Unionville, Missouri, the son of John A. Mowrer and Sallie Todd, farmers. Mowrer's father died unexpectedly when Mowrer was thirteen, and the family was subsequently forced to sell the family home and make separate living arrangements. A serious bout of depression at age fourteen prompted Mowrer to become interested in psychology, and he pursued this subject when he later attended the University of Missouri in Columbia. After completing his studies in 1929, he began study at Johns Hopkins University, where under Knight Dunlap he obtained a Ph.D. in experimental psychology in 1932. He married Willie Mae Cook in 1931; they had three children. Postdoctoral fellowships carried Mowrer from 1932 to 1936, when he was appointed instructor in psychology at Yale University.

At Yale, Mowrer involved himself in the interdisciplinary program that the Laura Spelman Rockefeller Memorial Fund supported at Yale's Institute of Human Relations. He made fundamental contributions to the incorporation of psychoanalytic ideas in learning theory during the 1930s, particularly in regard to mechanisms of avoidant behavior. In 1939 he collaborated on the influential *Frustration and Aggression*. During Mowrer's primary appointment from 1940 to 1948 in the College of Education at Harvard University, he spent 1944–1945 at the Office of Strategic Services in Washington, D.C. In 1948 he became a research professor of psychology at the University of Illinois in Urbana. There he continued the research on avoidance learning in laboratory rats that he had begun at Yale, contributed to the psychology of language and psychotherapy (particularly group therapy), and made daring efforts to incorporate into psychotherapy the concerns that religions had traditionally addressed. He was president of the American Psychological Association in 1953–1954. He retired from the University of Illinois in 1975.

Mowrer's work belongs to "neobehaviorism," that phase of behaviorism that followed early versions promoted by John B. Watson and others in the 1920s. Mowrer's reputation in psychology grew out of his development, in the late 1930s, of the fruitful "two-factor theory of avoidance reactions" (Mowrer, 1947). Freudian ideas—for example, that culturally mandated repression of impulses generates anxiety and that neurotic symptoms are, in part, efforts to deal with anxiety—provided the conceptual inspiration for this theory, but Mowrer's theory was tested primarily in research on animal learning in the somewhat artificial tasks (typically, avoiding signaled shock) of the behavioral psychology laboratory. Such cross-boundary fertilization was characteristic of work done under Clark Hull's leadership at Yale during the 1930s and 1940s. Mowrer's theory went beyond the Hullian theoretical framework of stimulus-response elements affected by reinforcement mechanisms, in suggesting two distinct mechanisms (that is, "two factors") for the learning of anxiety and the learning of symptoms.

At Harvard from 1940 to 1948 Mowrer continued to enlarge this framework of applying learning theory to normal and abnormal personality development, the role of language (for example, Mowrer, 1954), and "the neurotic paradox" that self-defeating (neurotic) behavior continues although it should (according to reinforcement theories) disappear through extinction or punishment. At a residential facility for children in New Haven, the Children's Community Center, he and his wife developed one of the earliest examples of a behavior therapy based on Pavlovian ideas, a highly effective procedure for treating enuresis.

Mowrer's year at the Office of Strategic Services exposed him to the ideas of the influential American psychiatrist Harry Stack Sullivan, who taught at the Washington School of Psychiatry; this encounter radically altered Mowrer's ideas about the origin of neurosis, moving him away from the *intra*personal, Freudian viewpoint to a recognition of the importance of *inter*personal factors in the neurotic individual's current life. In the late 1940s Mowrer began to provide informal counseling for troubled individuals and to reformulate the Freudian picture of the neurotic as an excessively socialized (that is, repressed) individual. Mowrer, thus, maintained two lines of inquiry in the 1950s, one in learning theory and the other in psychotherapy.

In 1960 Mowrer published two volumes that completed his work in the learning-theory area, *Learning Theory and Behavior* and *Learning Theory and the Symbolic Processes*. The first book reflected a major departure from Hullian ideas; in it Mowrer rejected the stimulus-response formula and the idea of reinforcement of instrumental behavior, instead emphasizing the role of Pavlov-type conditioning of (hypothetical) emotional states. Pavlovian-conditioned signals of reward evoke an emotional state that intensifies ongoing instrumental action; signals of pain or punishment produce emotions that inhibit the action. That is, rewards and punishments do not change the strength of habits; instead pleasurable (and painful) consequences exert modulating influences on performance by means of the emotional results of anticipating pleasure (or pain). Mowrer's innovative work cast him in the role of a transition figure between behavioristic and cognitivist theory.

After these two books, Mowrer turned his efforts almost entirely to psychotherapy and addressed such topics as sin, guilt, and confession; morality, ethics, and religion; and therapy in a societal context. Mowrer's stance troubled psychologists whose attitudes were positivistic and agnostic and whose professional ideals required scientific objectivity and value-neutral inquiry. (Perhaps as a result Mowrer's contributions to psychotherapy were less influential than his work in learning theory.) Mowrer's work led him to conclude that neurotic discomfort does not result from excessively scrupulous conformity to cultural moral guidelines—as Freud had taught—but from transgression of moral codes, consequent guilt, efforts to hide these "sins" from important persons, and a generalized pattern of dishonesty and inauthenticity in interpersonal dealings. The therapeutic innovation ("integrity groups") that he and his wife developed was carried out formally through coursework for mental-health professionals at the University of Illinois and informally through self-help groups in the community. Though integrity-group practices may have reflected Mowrer's personal struggles in their emphasis on honesty and responsible social conduct, the practices were influenced by two large cultural movements, the self-help movement and the group-process movement. These movements blossomed during a period, from the mid-1960s into the 1970s, of widespread distrust of the "establishment." It was widely assumed, or feared, that the primary institutions of Western society (community, family, church, corporate and military structures, etc.) would be swept away by social change and replaced by democratic, grass-roots institutions. Unlike writers who espoused individual self-actualization as the ultimate good, the Mowrers belonged to the camp of those seeking to reinvigorate existing systems of community and morality.

Mowrer will be remembered as an influential experimental psychologist and a courageous, innovative psychotherapist. His lifelong struggle with depression was a major motivating force for his contributions to therapy. He died in Urbana.

• The University of Illinois Archives has four boxes of Mowrer correspondence, papers, and manuscripts that cover the years 1928–1982. His autobiography (to the early 1970s) appeared in *A History of Psychology in Autobiography*, Vol. 6, ed. Gardner Lindzey (1974); his account of the succeeding years is contained in a posthumously published collection of his articles, *Leaves from Many Seasons* (1983), which contains a comprehensive bibliography through 1981.

Contributions to learning theory appeared in *Psychological Review* 45 (1938): 61–91, and 46 (1939): 553–65; and *Harvard Educational Review* 17 (1947): 102–48. For his theory of language, see "The Psychologist Looks at Language," *American Psychologist* 9 (1954): 660–94. His work on enuresis is retrospectively described in Mowrer, "Enuresis: The Beginning Work—What Really Happened," *Journal of the History of the Behavioral Sciences* 16 (1980): 25–30.

Mowrer's psychotherapeutic concern with sin provoked popular notice in 14 Sept. 1959 issues of *Time* (p. 69) and *Newsweek* (p. 108). *The Crisis in Psychiatry and Religion* (1961) identified, in these two major institutions, inadequate conceptualizations of difficulties that people have in living, and *The New Group Therapy* (1964) presented innovative solutions. A mature description of the Mowrers' group therapy is included in "Integrity Groups: Principles and Procedures," *Counseling Psychologist* 3 (1972): 7–32. Obituaries are in J. McV. Hunt, *American Psychologist* 39 (Aug. 1984): 912–14, and in the *Champaign-Urbana* (Ill.) *News-Gazette*, 23 June 1982.

STEPHEN R. COLEMAN

MOXHAM, Arthur James (19 Sept. 1854–16 May 1931), engineer, was born in Neath, South Wales, the son of Egbert Moxham, a landscape painter and itinerant engineer, and Catherine Morgan. He graduated from Clapton Orphan Asylum, a day school, in 1869 and emigrated to the United States to live with his aunt Dora Morgan Coleman in Louisville, Kentucky. At the age of fifteen, he became an office boy and apprentice ironmaster in the Louisville Rolling Mill Company, owned and operated by Dora's husband, Thomas Cooper Coleman.

Within nine years, Moxham was supervising business and floor operations at Coleman's Clay Street rolling mill and had become an accomplished ironmaster, holding several patents for iron-strengthening techniques. He married Helen Jilson Coleman in 1876; they had five children. When Coleman and his partner Bidermann du Pont invested in the construction of the Birmingham (Ala.) Rolling Mill in 1878, they asked Moxham to help design and supervise its start-up operations. There he began rolling experiments for a new offset street (girder) rail design invented by his boyhood friend from Louisville, Tom L. Johnson. In 1882 they contracted with the Cambria Iron Company of Johnstown, Pennsylvania, to roll the rail design from steel blooms rather than iron, and incorporated the Johnson Steel Street Rail Company. Production of the Johnson rail began in January 1883, and castings were commissioned to local foundries and machine shops. Moxham relocated his family to Johnstown and established a small finishing yard near the Cambria Iron plant to design and lay out trackwork for horsecar systems.

In its first years, the Johnson Company did a steady business providing custom rolled and cast steel trackwork for both horsecar and rapidly developing cable systems, and Moxham was able to capitalize and build a large trackwork mill and layout yard on the Cambria Iron right-of-way in Woodvale, Pennsylvania. In 1888 he designed and built his own rolling mill, including both steel and iron foundries, four miles south of Johnstown along the Stonycreek River. When Frank Sprague demonstrated that electrification of street rail systems was practical, also in 1888, the Johnson Company's business began to expand dramatically, by some accounts reaching 90 percent of market share in steel street rail and trackwork production during the period between 1888 and 1892 when most cities built electrified trolley systems. Protected by over 200 patents on rolling processes, roll design, trackwork design, and finishing machinery, the Johnson Company defined the market in street rail trackwork design and finishing for the next decade.

When the trackwork mill in Woodvale was destroyed in the Great Johnstown Flood of 1889, Moxham integrated the company's engineering and finishing operations into the mill on the Stonycreek site, in a municipality named after him by his business partner Tom Johnson. Within two years he expanded mill operations to include design and installation of entire railway systems, experimented with various steel alloys and continuous welding techniques, established regional engineering and sales offices in ten major cities across the country (and one in England), and was

actively exploring the prospect of building his own primary mill. In 1894 Moxham began construction of a major blast furnace and rolling mill complex at Lorain, Ohio, which would, on completion, become known as the Lorain Steel Company. The rolling operations were moved to the Lorain site in 1895, leaving the iron foundries and the trackwork finishing mill in Johnstown. However, the Lorain project ran short of capital in the hard years after the panic of 1893, and its blast furnaces were not completed until 1899.

A sophisticated steel engineering and finishing operation with an established national and international market, the Johnson Company was an attractive industrial commodity during the steel merger movement of the late 1890s. It was purchased in 1898 by Federal Steel (which as a conglomerate became part of the U.S. Steel merger four years later). Moxham retired for a year but was enticed to take over mill construction and start-up operations for Dominion Iron & Steel Company in Cape Breton, Nova Scotia, in 1899. Dominion was to be one of the first integrated steel mills in Canada, but difficulties with ore quality and undercapitalization forced Moxham over a period of three years to convert entirely to open hearth furnaces and delay construction of the rolling mill. Though steel was successfully made in 1902, Moxham resigned later that year when the company changed ownership. Why he left is the subject of debate. The standard family reason given was the death of his son, a plant foreman, in a plant accident; shortly thereafter, the son's wife died in childbirth, and the child did not survive. But business concerns may also have prompted Moxham's departure: for years he had been at odds with his board over his desire to use increased capital investment to overcome technological start-up problems, and his efforts to secure additional capital for investment were frustrated. He returned to Great Neck, Long Island, where he had established a second residence during his years in Lorain.

Within the year, Moxham was drawn onto the board of directors of the new Du Pont Company by its president, Coleman du Pont, who had apprenticed for four years under Moxham as manager of the Johnson Company's finishing mill in Johnstown while Moxham was building the Lorain works. Moxham remained with the Du Pont Company as director of product development until the company was sold to Pierre S. du Pont in 1915. That same year Moxham formed the Aetna Explosives Company, but its inability to get significant domestic munitions contracts, perhaps because of Moxham's noncitizen status, forced the company into receivership in 1917. He spent his later years experimenting with ore purification methods in Goshen, West Virginia, and Odessa, Delaware.

As a roll engineer and iron and steel foundryman, Moxham was primarily responsible for converting street rail production from iron to steel, and organized and managed the company that custom-designed and milled trackwork for most of the original electrified trolley systems in the United States. He died in Great

Neck and is buried in Cave Hill Cemetery in Louisville.

• For additional information see the papers of Moxham, Johnson, and Pierre S. du Pont in the manuscript collection of the Hagley Library, Wilmington, Del. The most complete discussion of Moxham's life is James R. Alexander, *Jaybird: A. J. Moxham and the Manufacture of the Johnson Rail* (1991). Other important sources include Alfred Chandler and Stephen Salisbury, *Pierre S. du Pont and the Making of the Modern Corporation* (1970). Also useful are Michael Massouh, "Technological and Managerial Innovation: The Johnson Company, 1883–1889," *Business History Review* 50 (1976): 46–68, and Alexander, "Technological Innovation in Early Street Railways: The Johnson Rail in Retrospective," *Railroad History* 164 (1991): 64–85. A substantive obituary is in the *Johnstown Tribune Democrat*, 19 May 1931.

JAMES R. ALEXANDER

MOXOM, Philip Stafford (10 Aug. 1848–13 Aug. 1923), clergyman, was born in Markham, Ontario, Canada, the son of Job Hibbard Moxom, a clergyman, and Anne Turner. While Philip was still a boy, the family moved to Illinois, and during the Civil War both father and son served in diverse ways in the Union army, the former as a second lieutenant, the latter initially as a "captain's boy" and, later, as a cavalryman.

Following the war, Moxom attended Kalamazoo College from 1866 to 1868 and Shurtleff College from 1868 to 1870. In 1871, after a brief time in a Kalamazoo law office, Philip had an unusual experience that led him into Christian ministry. He was invited to speak in the church from which his father had just resigned, the Baptist church of Bellevue, Michigan. The congregation was so taken with his eloquence that he was invited to be the pastor. He took this to be a special "call" and accepted. That same year he married Isabel Elliott; they had four children.

After a brief tenure at Bellevue, he spent three years as pastor of a small Baptist church in Albion, Michigan. Sensing the need for further theological studies, he entered the Rochester Theological Seminary (Baptist) in 1875 and earned a B.D. degree three years later.

From 1879 to 1885 he served as senior minister in the First Baptist Church of Cleveland, and from 1885 to 1893 he was pastor of the First Baptist Church of Boston. During these years he became well known for his eloquence from the pulpit and his liberal attitudes toward social and theological issues. He was selected to deliver an address on the Christian understanding of immortality at the World's Parliament of Religions held in Chicago in September 1893. The invitation to participate in the conference was a compliment to his scholarship and ecumenical Christian commitment. He attained greater visibility from this presentation than from anything else he ever did.

By this point Moxom had grown beyond the rather narrow Baptist outlook. He was especially chagrined with the Baptist policy of immersion and what was termed "closed communion," which allowed only those baptized in the "Baptist way" to receive communion. Two months after his address in Chicago, he resigned his Baptist pulpit with no other immediate position in sight. Offers from numerous churches and denominations came quickly, however, and in 1894 Moxom became pastor of the South Congregational Church in Springfield, Massachusetts, and served there until his retirement due to ill health in December 1917.

During his years in Springfield, he expanded his influence by participating in varied organizations (the Appalachian Mountain Club, the American Oriental Society, and the Society of Biblical Literature and Exegesis, among others), by preaching at universities, and through scholarly and homiletical publications. Moxom was especially active at peace conferences in the United States and Europe. He was also active in missionary societies, and in June of 1900 he preached a sermon before the Congregational Home Missionary Society entitled "Belief in God the Essential Condition of National Permanence and Prosperity," which was later published. It is an excellent example of American civil religion in the early twentieth century. His more expansive and scholarly publications included *The Aim of Life* (1894); *From Jerusalem to Nicaea* (1895; repr. 1896, 1898); *The Religion of Hope* (1896); and *Two Masters: Browning and Turgenief* (1912). His published sermons ranged widely in topics from "Our Problem with the Negro in America" to "The Industrial Revolution."

Moxom was equally at home in international gatherings and in student groups. Honest in his scholarship and Christian commitment, he was a man of genuine character and peace. His wide-ranging experiences were a perfect background for his openness, his sensitivity to numerous social issues, and his liberal religious views in his mature years. He died at his home in Springfield, Massachusetts.

• Clippings from the *Springfield Republican* reflecting Moxom's years in Springfield are in the public library there. In addition to his scholarly books, also see his sermons and pamphlets, such as "Christian Socialism" (1894); "The Insufficiency of Religious Toleration" (1905); "A New Theology: A Contribution to Progressive Christian Orthodoxy" (1883?); "The Pastor as Teacher" (1911); "The Place of the Christian Minister in Modern Life" (1899); and "The Strength of Youth" (1901). A tribute is in the *Congregationalist*, 23 Aug. 1923, p. 245.

GEORGE H. SHRIVER

MOZIER, Joseph (22 Aug. 1812–3 Oct. 1870), sculptor, was born in Burlington, Vermont. His parents' names are not known. As a young man he lived in Mount Vernon, Ohio, before settling in New York, where he became a very successful dry-goods merchant. Until 1845 his artistic interests were but an avocation, but in that year he retired from business and sailed for Italy to study sculpture. After a brief period in Florence he moved to Rome, where he would make his home for the remainder of his life.

While most midcentury sculptors had to make their living by modeling portraits, either busts or commemorative statues, and created imaginative works in between portrait commissions, Mozier throughout his career devoted himself almost totally to making ideal pieces based on literary, scriptural, or historical themes. The popularity of these pieces made it unnecessary for him to engage in portraiture. Translated into marble, these statues were richly anecdotal and possessed a profusion of details that captured the admiration of Victorian patrons from the United States and Europe. A list of titles of his works reflects the literary taste of the upper middle class among his contemporaries. His *Wept of the Wish-ton-Wish* was inspired by James Fenimore Cooper's popular novel, while the *White Lady of Avenel* was taken from the writings of Sir Walter Scott. His *Il Penseroso* was derived from Milton, as was his *Peri*, an image of the angel who waits patiently at the gates of heaven. A poem by William Cullen Bryant was the source for *Indian Girl*, while Friedrich Heinrich Karl de la Motte-Fouqué's melodramatic romance *Undine* was the inspiration for a statue by Mozier that won a grand prize in Rome in 1867. Mozier frequently turned to the Old Testament for subjects, as in works such as *Queen Esther*, *Jephthah's Daughter*, and *Rebecca at the Well* (New-York Historical Society). His *Pocahontas* was especially popular, and several marble replicas of it were produced in his busy Roman studio. His style was an extension of the neoclassicism of the earlier part of the century; much of the interest in his work derived from the beauty of the white marble and the rich narrative provided by the carefully wrought details, rather than from the aesthetics of sculptural form itself.

Although Mozier's work seems to have suited the taste of many well-to-do patrons of his day, critics—contemporary and later—did not always praise them. Nathaniel Hawthorne, a regular visitor to the numerous studios of Rome in the late 1850s and early 1860s and a friend of several sculptors, recorded his impressions of a visit to Mozier's rooms on 3 April 1858: "[Mozier] seems to have a good deal of vogue as a sculptor. . . . his cleverness and ingenuity appear in homely subjects, but are quite lost in attempts at a higher ideality. . . . he has a groupe of the 'Prodigal Son' [which] is now taking shape out of an immense block of marble, and will be as indestructible as the [ancient statue of] Laocoon; an idea at once awful and ludicrous, when we consider that it is at best but a respectable production." Twenty years later, another critic gave higher praise to the *Prodigal Son*, which had by then been given to the Pennsylvania Academy of the Fine Arts: "There is much pure pathos in this composition, which appeals with directness and force to the hearts of those who pause in their rambles through the galleries of the Academy to gaze on it" (Clark, *Great American Sculptures* [1874], p. 121). In 1903 Lorado Taft commented derisively on the excessive attention lavished on the anecdotal details of the *Wept of the Wish-ton-Wish*, details that had found such favor with Mozier's patrons: "Though evidently beyond his depth in anatomical subtleties, the sculptor demonstrates his conscience and his joy in the work by

a triumphant display of the seamstress's art; there is a 'masterly' hem which is carried without faltering around the entire border of the mantle, and in which the stone stitches are as accurate as though done by a sewing machine" (*History of American Sculpture* [1924], p. 110). Taft also observed that Mozier's *Rizpah* "is so bad that the curators apparently do not know what to do with it." By the time Adeline Adams wrote her biography of Mozier for the *Dictionary of American Biography* (1934) the *Rizpah* had been consigned to "seclusion," that is, to a storage room, for the taste for marmorean storytelling sculptures of this sort had long since passed.

While Hawthorne can hardly be said to be unbiased in his assessment of Mozier, several lines from his Italian notebooks do tell us something of the sculptor's personality: "after all this time [in Italy] he is still intensely American in everything but the most external surface of his manners . . . and might—for any polish or refinement that I can discern in him—still be a country shopkeeper in the interior of New York or New England. . . . Mr. [Mozier] is sensible, shrewd, keen, clever; an ingenious workman, no doubt, with tact enough, and not destitute of taste; very agreeable and lively in his conversation." In the twenty-five years after he left his native land, Mozier made only one return visit to it, in connection with an exhibition of his works at the Tenth Street Studio in New York. He died in Faido, Switzerland.

• For more information on Mozier, see William J. Clark, *Great American Sculptures* (1874); Rodman J. Sheirr, "Joseph Mozier and His Handiwork," *Potter's American Monthly* 6 (Jan. 1876): 24–28. Samuel Osgood, "American Artists in Italy," *Harper's New Monthly Magazine* 41 (Aug. 1870): 420–25; Lorado Taft, *History of American Sculpture* (1924; rev. ed., 1930); and William H. Gerdts, "American Sculpture: The Collection of James H. Ricau," *Antiques* 86 (Sept. 1964): 291–98. An obituary is in the *New York Times*, 30 Oct. 1870.

WAYNE CRAVEN

MUDGE, Isadore Gilbert (14 Mar. 1875–May 1957), reference librarian, was born in Brooklyn, New York, the oldest child of Alfred Mudge, a lawyer, and Mary Gilbert Ten Brook, daughter of Andrew Ten Brook, the one-time librarian of the University of Michigan. Mudge graduated from Brooklyn's Adelphi Academy in 1893 and enrolled that fall in Cornell University, where her paternal step-grandfather, Charles K. Adams, was president. Earning her bachelor of philosophy degree in 1897, she was inspired by George Lincoln Burr, an archivist, medieval historian, and librarian, to pursue librarianship as a career. An excellent undergraduate student, she was elected to Phi Beta Kappa as a junior.

The New York State Library School in Albany accepted Mudge in the fall of 1897, and she earned a bachelor of library science degree with distinction in 1900, having studied with Dunkin Van Rensselaer Johnston, who systemized the teaching of reference work. Despite being an avowed easterner, she accepted the dual post of head reference librarian at the University of Illinois Library and instructor in the University of Illinois Library School, under the able direction of Katherine Lucinda Sharp. After working for three years there to develop the reference collection with the view of helping Illinois students become independent learners, she resigned to accept the position of head librarian at Bryn Mawr in 1903. She worked there until 1908, when she left to pursue several projects, including two articles for *Library Journal* in 1910 and 1911, each titled "Some Reference Books," with the respective year appended; a Thackeray dictionary (1910); and a bibliography of philosopher Henri Bergson's writings (1913). She also taught part-time as an instructor of reference and documents at Simmons College (1910–1912).

Mudge joined the library staff at Columbia University in 1911. Nicholas Murray Butler, president of the university, became an early supporter of her efforts to build on the university's meager reference collection; in fact, he found her "incredibly resourceful in meeting his varied reference and bibliographic needs." Her work at Columbia became a platform for professional advocacy. Indeed, Mudge influenced other reference collections by arguing that any library needed several specific types of sources. Essential would be "the possession of certain basic works, a dictionary, an encyclopedia, an atlas, a biographical dictionary," but she also believed that a "book of quotations, handbook of statistics, a state or government manual, are needed everywhere."

By 1927 Mudge began teaching "Bibliography and Bibliographic Methods" in Columbia's newly merged School of Library Service, where she was an associate professor. To encapsulate her thinking succinctly, she coined the phrase "material, mind, and method"—by which she meant reference librarians needed to know books, possess the mental characteristics of success (e.g., good memory, high intelligence, and strong perseverance), and methodically answer reference questions by clarification and classification by type of source. The Mudge method was undoubtedly articulated to her students in numerous reference classes but never widely disseminated; so it remained private knowledge until her disciple and student, Margaret Hutchins, published this idea in the January 1937 issue of the *Library Quarterly*.

Mudge's landmark achievement is the *Guide to Reference Books*, a comprehensive bibliography of reference tools that she compiled for the American Library Association through four major revisions between 1917 (the third edition contained 1,790 titles in 235 pages) and 1936 (her sixth edition contained 3,873 titles in 504 pages). For many novices in this field, it served as an introductory textbook as well because of its valuable prefatory pages. According to John Waddell, her biographer, Mudge had early on "conceived the idea of a textbook for beginning library students; before she had advanced sufficiently in her planning to approach A. L. A. . . . Miss [Alice B.] Kroeger at the next A. L. A. conference told Mudge of *her* plan and showed her a draft of the text for comment." Shortly

after Kroeger's untimely death in 1909, ALA in 1910 asked Mudge to take over the work, which she did by compiling a needed two-year supplement to the second edition.

Reviewing Mudge's career at Columbia, Constance M. Winchell, Mudge's protégé, said: "Probably no other one person has contributed so much to raising the standards of reference collections and reference service in the libraries of this and other countries." In recognition of her outstanding effort and of her serving as a role model for succeeding generations, the American Library Association established the Isadore Gilbert Mudge Citation in 1958 to be given to those librarians who make a "distinguished contribution to reference librarianship." Perhaps it is only slightly hyperbolic to say, as does Waddell, that Mudge was "the best known and most influential reference librarian in the history of American librarianship" when she retired in 1941. A semi-invalid toward the end of her life, she died in the College Manor Nursing Home, Lutherville, Maryland.

• Some of Mudge's papers are extant in the Special Collections department of the Columbia University library. For further information, see John N. Waddell, "Career of Isadore Gilbert Mudge: A Chapter in the History of Reference Librarianship," (Ph.D. diss., Columbia Univ., 1973), and John V. Richardson Jr., "Learning Reference Work: The Paradigm," in Richardson, *Knowledge-based Systems for General Reference Work: Applications, Problems, and Progress* (1995).

JOHN V. RICHARDSON JR.

MUDGE, James (5 Apr. 1844–7 May 1918), Methodist minister and religion scholar, was born in West Springfield, Massachusetts, the son of James Mudge, a Methodist minister, and Harriet Wilde Goodridge. He grew up in Methodist parsonages in South Harwich and Lynn, Massachusetts. In 1861 Mudge entered Wesleyan University in Middletown, Connecticut, where he received an A.B. in literature in 1865, an A.M. in 1868, and an S.T.D. in 1891.

Between 1865 and 1867 Mudge taught Greek and Latin at a school in Pennington, New Jersey. He then studied at Boston University School of Theology, where he received an S.T.B. in 1870. In 1868 he became a probationary member of the New England Annual Conference of the Methodist Episcopal church, and he was ordained an elder in 1870. Between 1870 and 1873 he served as the pastor of a church in Wilbraham, Massachusetts. He married Martha Maria Wiswell, a school teacher, in April 1873; they had four children.

Soon after his marriage Mudge received an appointment as a missionary to India. Upon his arrival in Lucknow, he became editor of the *Lucknow Witness*, a Methodist missionary periodical. Between 1873 and 1883 he published a wide range of catechisms and devotional literature, in both English and Hindustani, that appeared in the *Lucknow Witness* and other church periodicals in India and the United States. He also served as the pastor of an English-speaking congregation in Lucknow from 1878 until 1882.

In 1882 Mudge took up missionary work in Shahjahanpore, India. However, he decided soon after this move to return to America and resume his pastoral ministry in the New England Conference. From 1883 until his retirement in 1913, he served a number of small membership churches in Massachusetts. An active leader of the New England Conference, he served as secretary from 1889 until his death. Between 1888 and 1904 he was an instructor of missions at the Boston University School of Theology and a frequent lecturer at numerous colleges and universities throughout the United States. From 1908 to 1912 he was the book review editor for *Zion's Herald*, a prominent journal of northern Methodism.

Mudge writings include works on church history, missions, and theology, as well as poetry and devotional literature. His writings established him as one of American Methodism's most respected writers and scholars. His most notable publication was his 1895 book, *Growth in Holiness*. This book emerged in the context of the late nineteenth-century holiness debate that was raging within many Protestant denominations, especially within Methodism. Holiness theology centered primarily on the teachings of the American evangelist, Phoebe Palmer, who believed that authentic conversion did not end when an individual accepted divine grace (i.e., justification by faith alone). Rather, Christians needed to undergo a second conversion after justification that enabled them to mirror in their lives the perfect will and intent of God. This "second blessing," or Christian perfection, reflected what Methodist founder John Wesley called sanctification. Critics argued that holiness theology perverted Wesley's definition of sanctification, criticizing the movement's tendency to view sanctification as a necessary component of salvation. In *Growth in Holiness*, Mudge affirmed a moderating position on holiness, maintaining the traditional doctrine that believers were to be sanctified after they were justified but arguing that sanctification was not an instantaneous event. Rather, sanctification was a lifelong process of spiritual growth. Mudge castigated holiness groups for their "tendency to schism," criticizing "the sectarian and divisive tendencies" within the movement. His middle-of-the-road stance on the holiness question was well received by prominent spokespersons within Methodism. One reviewer remarked that *Growth in Holiness* compared favorably with Thomas à Kempis's *Imitation of Christ* for its impact upon the contemporary church.

Mudge's contemporaries described him as "progressive and independent in his thinking" with persuasive gifts as a preacher, teacher, and writer. At a time when religious publications enjoyed an extensive circulation in America, his writings were widely read. An editor of *Zion's Herald* commented that "few writers in the whole church had a more distinctive gift or were read with equal pleasure." In all, Mudge published close to 24,000 articles and reviews, and wrote, edited, or contributed to over 100 books.

Mudge died in Malden, Massachusetts, not long after attending the annual meeting of the New England Conference.

• Selected holdings related to Mudge and New England Methodism may be found in the New England Methodist Historical Society, Boston, Mass. Mudge's other books include *History of Methodism* (1878), *Life of Love* (1902), *History of the New England Conference* (1910), and *The Perfect Life* (1911). His edited works include *Honey from Many Hives* (1899) and *Heart Religion as Described by John Wesley* (1913). For a discussion of his connection to the late nineteenth-century holiness debate see Emory Bucke, ed., *The History of American Methodism*, vol. 2 (1964), and Frederick Norwood, *The Story of American Methodism* (1974). An obituary is in the *Boston Transcript*, 7 May 1918.

CHRISTOPHER H. EVANS

MUELLER, John Howard (13 June 1891–16 Feb. 1954), bacteriologist, was born in Sheffield, Massachusetts, the son of John Henry Mueller, a Unitarian minister, and Sarah Eva Pease. As a young boy he moved with his family to Illinois, where he grew up. He studied biology at Illinois Wesleyan University and received his B.S. in 1912; he then taught biology and chemistry as a graduate assistant at the University of Louisville, where he received his M.S. in 1914. Having developed an interest in pathology, he took a course in it in the summer of 1914 at Columbia University's College of Physicians and Surgeons. His instructors were so impressed with his ability that they helped him obtain an Alonzo Clark Fellowship in Pathology to continue his studies at Columbia. He received his Ph.D. in pathology in 1916. That same year he married Mary R. Gilbert, with whom he had no children.

After obtaining his doctorate Mueller took a position as an assistant pathologist at New York's Presbyterian Hospital. In 1917 he enlisted in the U.S. Army Sanitary Corps as a private and went to France as a member of the Presbyterian Hospital Unit. In this capacity he took part in the study of trench fever, a highly infectious disease, first diagnosed in 1915, that became a major medical problem during World War I. He played a significant role in demonstrating that trench fever is transmitted by body lice.

After being discharged as a first lieutenant in 1919 Mueller returned to the College of Physicians and Surgeons as an instructor in bacteriology. He was promoted to assistant professor in 1920 and associate professor in 1922. His research focused on determining which chemical substances contribute to the growth of pathogenic bacteria in an effort to verify his hypothesis that the metabolism of these bacteria is closely related to animal metabolism in that both require substances found in animal tissue. Moreover, he suspected that, although most of these substances would be common chemical compounds, some of them would be new compounds produced and used only in bacterial metabolism. By experimenting with the effect of hydrolyzed animal protein on the growth of *Streptococcus hemolyticus*, in 1922 he discovered methionine, a sulfur-containing amino acid that can be synthesized from other amino acids by microorganisms but not by mammals.

In 1923 Mueller left Columbia to accept a position as an assistant professor in Harvard Medical School's Department of Bacteriology and Immunology. For the next seven years he postponed his work on bacterial nutrition to devote his efforts to other bacteriological studies of potentially great importance to the treatment of human diseases. After working for four years with residue antigens extracted from yeast, tuberculin, and a strain of pneumobacillus, he spent the better part of three frustrating years attempting to verify the work of the English researcher W. E. Gye, which had suggested that cancer in humans is caused by viral infection.

In 1930, when Mueller was promoted to associate professor, he returned to the study of the culture requirements of bacteria, focusing on *Corynebacterium diphtheriae*, the bacillus that causes diphtheria. In order to quantify the degree to which a particular chemical compound contributed to the growth of a colony of diphtheria bacteria, he measured the amount of nitrogen produced by the colony, using the micro-Kjeldahl method, a tedious procedure whereby the nitrogen is combined with sulfuric acid to form ammonium sulfate that must then be alkalized, distilled, and titrated before it can be measured. By 1934 Mueller and his associates had determined which amino acids play an essential role in the growth of *C. diphtheriae* and that certain strains of diphtheria bacteria differed in their capability to synthesize some or all of these amino acids. By 1937 he had isolated niacin and beta-alanine, for which he was able to substitute pantothenic acid from liver; he demonstrated that both substances were required for growth by all strains of diphtheria bacteria.

These findings led almost immediately to significant improvements in both the quality and quantity of diphtheria toxin produced for use in human immunization. However, the full implication of Mueller's work was not known until the early 1950s, when biochemical researchers, spurred on by his findings, discovered that niacin and pantothenic acid, both of which are part of the vitamin B complex, also play essential roles in animal metabolism—the first as a coenzyme in the citric acid cycle, and the second in the interconnection of carbohydrate, fat, and protein metabolism. As a result of these findings biochemists could proclaim with confidence the value of their discipline as a tool for understanding the growth and development of virtually all living organisms.

In 1942 Mueller was made full professor and head of the Department of Bacteriology and Immunology, a position he held until his death. Having completed his work with *C. diphtheriae*, he devoted the bulk of his research to arriving at a similar understanding of the growth requirements of *Clostridium tetani*, the tetanus bacillus, and *Neisseria gonorrhoeae*, which causes gonorrhea. He also investigated the various factors influencing the production of tetanus toxin.

Mueller contributed to the American effort during World War II by serving as a consultant to the secretary of war (1941–1945), to the Federal Security Agency (1942–1944), and to the U.S. Army's Chemical Warfare Service (1944–1946). He was elected to the National Academy of Sciences and the American Academy of Arts and Sciences. He died in West Roxbury, Massachusetts.

Mueller's work contributed significantly to a better understanding of bacteriology by shedding light on the nutritional needs of pathogenic bacteria. Just as importantly, it also showed that the principles of biochemistry are universally applicable to understanding the metabolisms of living organisms from the smallest bacterium to the largest mammal.

• Mueller's papers are in the Harvard University Library. A biography, including a bibliography, is A. M. Pappenheimer, Jr., "John Howard Mueller," National Academy of Sciences, *Biographical Memoirs* 57 (1987): 307–21. An obituary is in the *New York Times*, 18 Feb. 1954.

CHARLES W. CAREY, JR.

MUGAR, Stephen Pabken (5 Mar. 1901–16 Oct. 1982), businessman and philanthropist, was born in Harpoot, Armenia (Turkey), the son of Sarkis Mugar and Vosgitel (maiden name unknown). The Mugar family immigrated to the United States in 1906 and joined other family members in Boston. Mugar's father, using $200 borrowed from relatives, purchased the Star Market in nearby Watertown Square. Stephen, his father, mother, and three sisters worked in the market. Stephen graduated from the Boston High School of Commerce in 1919 and took night courses at the Bentley School of Accounting and Finance in Boston (now Bentley College in Waltham, Mass.). When his father died in an automobile accident in 1923, Stephen took over the management of the market.

As the depression was deepening, Mugar added a second store in 1932 in Newton, then a third store in 1937 in Wellesley. In 1948 he built another store across from his Newton operation. According to the *Boston Globe*, it was "built without posts, following an airline hanger design, . . . [and] was probably the most modern market in New England" (17 Oct. 1982). In 1964, when William Callahan, chairman of the Massachusetts Turnpike Authority, announced that it was extending the state's major highway into Boston and that the highway would go through his Newton market, Mugar decided to acquire the air rights over the turnpike at his Newton site. Mugar believed that he could continue to use a valuable shopping site by rebuilding the supermarket directly above the turnpike. No one had ever written a lease for supermarket air rights, but "the Massachusetts Judicial Supreme Court ruled in his favor and the Star Market became the only supermarket in the country built on air rights. It was typical of his ingenuity" (*Boston Globe*, 17 Oct. 1982). In 1960 Mugar purchased the popular regional Brigham's ice cream store chain, which included five Turnstyles. Four years later, he merged his sixty-two

New England Star Markets, eighty Brigham's ice cream stores, and five Turnstyles into a billion-dollar, Chicago-based firm, the Jewel Tea Company, of which he was a major stockholder. He remained chairman of the board until his retirement in 1969. After retirement, Mugar became active nationally as a real estate developer.

In 1960 Mugar was a member of a U.S. State Department delegation to the U.S.S.R. to study marketing techniques and food distribution. President Lyndon Johnson granted him the Democracy in Action Award in 1966. Other awards included the Medal for Distinguished Service to Higher Education and the Distinguished Service Award from Brandeis University, the Americanism Medal from the National Society of the Daughters of the American Revolution, the Golden Door Award from the International Institute of Boston, the Americanism Award from the Massachusetts American Legion, the Human Relations Award from the National Conference of Christians and Jews, the 1975 Citizen of the Year Award from the Armenian-American Citizens League, the Susan Colgate Cleveland Medal for Distinguished Service from Colby-Sawyer College, and the First Distinguished Service Award from the Armenian Assembly. Massachusetts governor John Volpe appointed him in 1968 to serve on a committee to examine a proposal to modernize the commonwealth's government that was submitted to the general court and enacted into law in 1969. In 1969–1970 Mugar served on the board of directors of the United States Bicentennial Corporation.

Mugar was a longtime overseer of the Boys Clubs of Boston; a founding member of the Hundred Club of Massachusetts (to benefit families of police and fire personnel killed in the line of duty); a trustee of Boston University, Colby-Sawyer College, Northeastern University, and Suffolk University; and a fellow of Brandeis University.

Mugar was also a founder of the Armenian Assembly of America in 1972 and contributed to and supported the National Association for Armenian Studies and Research, the Armenian Missionary Association of America, the Armenian General Benevolent Union, the Diocese of the Armenian Church of North America, and a number of local, national, and international Armenian churches.

Mugar was a major philanthropist in the greater Boston area. "I chose Greater Boston because this is where my customers are," he said. "The gifts are to show my appreciation to my customers for all the help they gave us. It's really paying something you feel that you owe. Giving while you're living is a wonderful thing. You see the great benefit. It is a source of happiness to me" (*Boston Globe*, 17 Oct. 1982). Colleges and universities that benefited from his giving include Colby-Sawyer College, Boston University, Brandeis University, Haigazian College (Beirut), the Massachusetts Institute of Technology, Northeastern University, Suffolk University, and the Fletcher School of Law and Diplomacy at Tufts University.

In 1937 Mugar married Marian Graves. The couple had two children, David and Carolyn. David Mugar took over the family enterprises.

Mugar was a prominent New England example of what the work ethic in action can do in a capitalistic democracy, and it was said of him, "He practices the true meaning of brotherhood with his kindness and love in giving so much. He touches you with love and from that moment on you remember him with your heart" (*Boston Globe*, 17 Oct. 1982). Mugar died in Boston.

• The Mugar Family Papers are in the Boston University Mugar Memorial Library. An obituary is in the *Boston Globe*, 17 Oct. 1982.

PAUL H. TEDESCO

MUHAMMAD, Elijah (10 Oct. 1897–25 Feb. 1975), leader of the Nation of Islam, was born Robert Poole in Sandersville, Georgia, the son of William Poole, an itinerant Baptist preacher and sharecropper, and Mariah Hall, a domestic for local white families. In 1900 the family moved to Cordele, Georgia, where Muhammad went to public school until the fourth grade when he dropped out to supplement his family's income as a laborer in sawmills and with the Cherokee Brick Company. In 1919 he married Clara Evans of Cordele, and they had two daughters and six sons.

With thousands of other African Americans from the rural South, Muhammad migrated to Detroit, Michigan, in the early 1920s. A depressed southern agricultural economy, hampered by boll weevil infestation of cotton crops and increasing mechanization of farm labor, forced many small farmers to join the great migration to the booming industrial cities of the North. Muhammad and some of his brothers found work in the automobile plants of Detroit. In 1931 he met Master Wallace Fard (or Wali Farad), a peddler of sundry goods in Detroit's ghettos, who claimed that he had a message of redemption for the "Asiatic black man." Using the Bible and the Qur'ān, the Muslim scripture, Fard began proselytizing among poor people in July 1930, starting with meetings in houses until he had enough members to rent a storefront, which he called Temple of Islam No. 1. Through his hard work, disciplined devotion, and intelligence, Robert Poole was chosen by Fard to be his chief aide. Fard made him a "minister of Islam" and changed his name to Elijah Muhammad.

Fard mysteriously disappeared in 1934, claiming that he was going back to Mecca. With no traces of their leader, the Nation of Islam split into several contending factions, and violent squabbles erupted. Fearing for their lives, Muhammad led his followers to several midwestern cities before finally settling in Chicago in 1936. Temple of Islam No. 2 was established in Chicago as the main headquarters for the fledgling Nation of Islam. With only thirteen members at the beginning, the Nation of Islam experienced its growth spurt only after Muhammad's incarceration from 1943 to 1946 for refusing the draft during World War II.

His imprisonment demonstrated his faith and contributed to his emergence as a confident leader. In 1950 at a Savior's Day rally, several hundred members attended. Muhammad also instituted the worship of Master Fard as Allah, a black man as god, and stated that he himself was Allah's messenger or prophet. As the main leader of the Nation of Islam, he was always addressed with the honorific "the Honorable." Muhammad built on the teachings of Fard and combined aspects of Islam and Christianity with the black nationalism of Marcus Garvey into a "proto-Islam," where aspects of Islamic teachings and practices were used to coat a message of black nationalism that had a strong racial slant. Muhammad also installed the ritual of celebrating Master Fard's birthdate, 26 February, as Savior's Day, a special time for gathering the members of the Nation in Chicago.

In the racial mythology of the Nation of Islam, the black man was the "original man." Whites were created as a hybrid race by a black mad scientist named Yacub, and they were to rule for a period of 6,000 years through deceit and "tricknology." At the end of that period, a battle of Armageddon will occur, and black people will emerge victorious and resume their rightful place as rulers of the earth. In this mythology the usual color valences of the English language are reversed: white is associated with evil and death, and black with goodness and life. Whites are also viewed as "devils." In the lives of many poor black people, this mythology functioned as a theodicy, an explanation of the injustices, pain, and suffering that they were experiencing in a deeply segregated American society.

Muhammad's message of racial separation focused on the recognition of the true black identity and stressed economic independence. "Knowledge of Self" and "Do for Self" became the rallying cries in Muhammad's sermons and writings, *The Supreme Wisdom: The Solutions to the So-Called Negroes' Problems* (1957) and *Message to the Black Man* (1965). Muhammad stressed that black people had lost the knowledge of their true selves, so that they were viewed by the wider society as "Negroes" or as "coloreds" and not as the "original black man." Moreover, he understood the vulnerability of the black psyche, and he hammered away at the slave mentality that had encumbered the demeanor and lifestyle of African Americans. As a means of getting black people to find a new identity, he had them drop their surnames, which most of them had inherited from their slave masters, and replaced them with an "X." X meant an unknown quantity; it also meant ex-slave, ex-Christian, ex-smoker, and ex-alcoholic. By reforming the mental attitudes and the behavior of his followers, he set about creating a new nation of black people.

In a similar manner, Muhammad placed priority on economic independence for members of the Nation of Islam. They could not be on welfare and had to work. It was best if they owned their own businesses. So members of the Nation set up hundreds of small businesses, such as bakeries, grocery stores, restaurants, and outlets for fish and bean pies. The men of the movement were required to sell a weekly quota of the Nation's newspaper, *Muhammad Speaks*, which became the main financial support for the movement. The Nation had also established its own educational system in 1932; although it was called the University of Islam, the focus was on the years from elementary to high school. Members of the Nation also followed Muhammad's strict dietary rules outlined in his book *How to Eat to Live* (1972), which enjoined one meal per day and complete abstention from pork, drugs, tobacco, and alcohol. He also instituted a Ramadan fast of one week during the month of December, mainly to counter the pervasive influence of the Christmas celebration of Christians in African-American communities.

In *Message to the Black Man* Muhammad taught that black people were not Americans, that they owed no allegiance to the American flag, and that they should not join the military. Muhammad spent four years in a federal prison for encouraging draft refusal during World War II and for refusing the draft himself. Several of his sons also spent time in prison for refusing the draft during the Korean War. The eventual goal of the movement was to create a separate black nation, a homeland for black people. The actual place or territory of this black nation—whether it would be in the United States, Africa, or elsewhere—was never specified.

Two internal organizations within the Nation of Islam were created for men and women. The Muslim Girls Training (MGT) provided classes for training young women in the domestic arts, housekeeping, cooking, and raising children. The private sphere of the home was the realm for women. Women could not go out alone at night; they had to be escorted by a Muslim male. The Fruit of Islam was set up as the security arm of the Nation. Trained in the martial arts, security techniques, and military drill, they guarded the ministers and leaders of the Nation. Everyone entering a Muslim temple or attending a national meeting was subject to body searches by the Fruit or the MGT. At national meetings, drill competitions were held for Fruit of Islam groups from different cities. Muhammad's brother-in-law, Raymond Sharieff, was the chief commander of the national Fruit of Islam.

The Nation of Islam reached its peak years through the efforts of Minister Malcolm X, with whom Elijah Muhammad had corresponded when Malcolm was in prison. After his release in 1952, Malcolm became an indefatigable organizer and proselytizer for the Nation. He founded many temples of Islam on the East Coast, throughout the South, and on the West Coast. Malcolm was a favorite visitor in Muhammad's home, and he was regarded as his seventh son. As a charismatic speaker, Malcolm encouraged the rapid spread of the Nation of Islam in the 1950s and early 1960s. He also started *Muhammad Speaks* in May 1960 in the basement of his home. Muhammad appointed Malcolm as the minister of Temple No. 7 in Harlem, the most important temple outside Chicago, and in 1962 he named Malcolm his national representative. However, in December 1963, after President John F. Kennedy was assassinated in Dallas, Muhammad ordered a three-month period of public silence for Malcolm as a result of Malcolm's comment that the assassination was an expression of the violence inherent in the culture of white America. His ill-spoken words inflamed the American public. As the period of silence was extended beyond three months, Malcolm eventually resigned from the Nation of Islam and began his own organizations. He also publicly accused Muhammad of fathering a number of illegitimate children with several of his secretaries. Malcolm was assassinated on 22 February 1965 at the Audubon Ballroom in Harlem. Muhammad and the leadership of the Nation denied any involvement in Malcolm's death.

Muhammad appointed one of Malcolm's protégés, Minister Louis Farrakhan from Boston, to become the national representative and minister of Temple No. 7 in Harlem. During its peak years in the 1960s, the Nation of Islam had close to 500,000 devoted followers, influencing millions more particularly during the period of increased cultural awareness among blacks from 1967 to 1975. It also accumulated an economic empire worth more than $80 million, which included farms in Georgia and Alabama, a modern printing press operation for its newspaper, a bank, and plans for establishing a Muslim hospital and university. As a person suffering from respiratory illnesses, Muhammad also had a large house in Phoenix, Arizona, where he often spent the winters.

Although he had only a third-grade education, Muhammad became the leader of the most enduring black militant movement in the United States. He was a shrewd judge of character and was able to control and contain a number of fiery, charismatic personalities in his movement. He died in Chicago and was succeeded by the fifth of his six sons, Wallace Deen Muhammad. After Wallace disbanded the Nation of Islam and led many of its members into the fold of Sunni Islam, or orthodox Islam, Farrakhan resurrected the Nation of Islam in 1978, using the teachings of Elijah Muhammad as its primary vehicle. Farrakhan also instituted a second Savior's Day celebration in his Nation, honoring the birthdate of Elijah Muhammad.

• Elijah Muhammad also wrote *Birth of a Savior* (1964). A biography is Claude Andrew Clegg III, *An Original Man: The Life and Times of Elijah Muhammad* (1997). Sources on the Nation of Islam and Black Muslims include E. U. Essien-Udom, *Black Nationalism* (1962), and C. Eric Lincoln, *The Black Muslims in America* (1961).

LAWRENCE H. MAMIYA

MUHLENBERG, Frederick Augustus (25 Aug. 1818–21 Mar. 1901), college president, was born in Lancaster, Pennsylvania, the son of Frederick Augustus Hall Muhlenberg, M.D., and Elizabeth Schaum. A member of a prominent Lutheran family, his grandfather Henry Muhlenberg, was a noted botanist and president of Franklin College. Muhlenberg entered the sophomore class of Pennsylvania College (now Gettysburg College) in 1833. After one year he trans-

ferred to Jefferson College (now Washington and Jefferson College), where he first demonstrated his facility in languages. He graduated in 1836, then studied at the Princeton Theological Seminary in 1837–1838. Returning to Lancaster, he taught in a private, classical school, and in 1840 was appointed a professor at Franklin College. Muhlenberg married Catharine Anna Muhlenberg in 1848; they had six sons.

Muhlenberg was involved in the uniting of Franklin and Marshall Colleges in 1849 and in the subsequent transfer of the Lutheran interest in Franklin College to Pennsylvania College in Gettysburg. He taught Greek at Pennsylvania College from 1850 until 1867 and was apparently a respected scholar and a demanding but well-liked instructor. He was also a college librarian. After being ordained a Lutheran minister in 1854, he frequently led services in local parishes.

In 1867 Muhlenberg was persuaded to accept appointment as the first president of Muhlenberg College in Allentown, Pennsylvania. The college, named for his great-grandfather, was established to encourage young men to enter the Lutheran ministry. He devoted the next ten years to securing faculty, students, an endowment, and adequate buildings. He also taught Greek, moral philosophy, and religion. When he resigned in 1876 to take a position as professor of Greek at the University of Pennsylvania, the college was securely established.

While teaching at the University of Pennsylvania, Muhlenberg continued to be active in Lutheran affairs, including preaching Sunday services. He retired his professorship in 1888 and moved to Reading, Pennsylvania, in 1889 to live with a son. In 1891, however, Thiel College, a Lutheran institution in Greenville, Pennsylvania, named him president at a time when the college was in a period of turmoil because of financial difficulty, high faculty turnover, and general student unrest. He successfully reorganized the college, but, following a stroke, he resigned the presidency in 1893 and returned to Reading, where he died.

Muhlenberg's students remembered him as a fine scholar and dedicated teacher. Beyond his students, many of whom entered the ministry, Muhlenberg shaped three Lutheran colleges in Pennsylvania.

• There is no significant collection of the papers of Frederick Augustus Muhlenberg. The major biographical sources are I. M. Stevenson, "Rev. F. A. Muhlenberg, D.D., LL.D." in *American Lutheran Biographies*, ed. J. C. Roseland (1890); Henry E. Jacobs, "Frederick Augustus Muhlenberg, D.D., LL.D.," in *Muhlenberg College*, ed. S. E. Ochsenford (1892); and S. E. Ochsenford, "Frederick Augustus Muhlenberg, D.D., LL.D.," *The Muhlenberg* 8 (Apr. 1901): 251–54.

DANIEL J. WILSON

MUHLENBERG, Frederick Augustus Conrad (1 Jan. 1750–4 June 1801), politician, was born at the German settlement of Trappe (formerly Providence), Pennsylvania, the son of Henry Melchior Muhlenberg, a prominent Lutheran minister, and Anna Maria Weiser. At the age of thirteen he was sent with his brothers, John Peter Gabriel and Gotthilf Henry

Ernest (known as Henry), to Germany to receive a college education. In Halle he attended the Orphan House (boarding school) of the Franckesche Stiftungen and then the University, where he studied the classical languages, history, and theology. In September 1770 he returned with Gotthilf via London to America, and on 25 October 1770 was ordained a minister of the United Evangelical Lutheran Congregations in Reading, Pennsylvania. In 1771 he married Catharine Schaefer, the daughter of a Philadelphia sugar refiner. They had seven children. From 1770 to 1773 he served as pastor on a rural circuit including Tulpehocken, Schaeferstown, Manheim, Warwick, White Oaks, and Lebanon. In September 1773 he accepted a call from the German-speaking Swamp Church (Christ Church) congregation in New York City. In the following years he grew sympathetic to the patriotic cause, although he still refused to mix politics with religion. When the British occupation of New York became imminent in the summer of 1776 he removed to Philadelphia, and in May 1777 he again fled with his family before the approaching British army to New Hanover. There he preached at several locations and continued as a member of the ministerium until 1780. Financial necessity compelled him to enter the business world. He became a partner in two Philadelphia firms and opened a small store at Trappe, which, however, was mainly run by his wife.

During the revolutionary turmoil of the late 1770s, pastoral duties no longer satisfied him. He became increasingly unsure of his call to the ministry and turned instead to politics. His unsolicited nomination by the Pennsylvania Assembly in February 1779 as one of the state's three delegates to the Continental Congress turned out to be the starting point of a long and distinguished career in local and national politics. On 3 March 1779 he took—much to his father's chagrin—the seat vacated by Edward Biddle. In October 1779, having been elected to the Pennsylvania Assembly on the radical (constitutionalist) ticket, the legislature unanimously renewed his congressional mandate. He acted as chairman of the medical committee of Congress, which directed the army hospital service. In October 1780 his term expired and according to the stipulations of the Articles of Confederation he became ineligible for reelection for three years. Having won the confidence of the German community in and around Philadelphia, he was, however, regularly reelected to the state legislature, serving as Speaker of the Assembly from 1780 to 1783. In 1784 he was appointed justice of the peace and register of wills and deeds of newly organized Montgomery County.

Although he had entered politics as a radical, he soon took a moderate position more in line with the mentality and interests of his constituency. During the 1780s he became increasingly convinced that both the unicameral state constitution of 1776 and the Articles of Confederation needed revising in order to complete, as he wrote, "the Triumph of Reason, Justice & Good Order amongst us." As Philadelphia County delegate he presided over the council of censors (1783–1784),

which discussed changes to the Pennsylvania constitution. This body, however, lacked the two-thirds majority required for calling a state constitutional convention. On the national level, as president of the Pennsylvania ratifying convention, he contributed to the success of the reform efforts in November–December 1787, when he urged the speedy adoption of the new U.S. Constitution. As a contributor to German-language newspapers he kept federalist propaganda alive until the summer of 1788, when ratification from the required number of nine states was finally assured.

In November 1788 he was elected on the Federalists' Lancaster ticket as a congressman-at-large to the first House of Representatives under the new Constitution, receiving the highest number of votes (8,726) given to any candidate from Pennsylvania. On 4 March 1789 he arrived with his brother John at the temporary seat of government in New York City. Widely appreciated as an experienced, urbane politician able to reconcile clashing party interests, the members of the House chose him as their first Speaker on 1 April 1789. His main responsibility was "to preserve decorum and order" and to convey a sense of pomp and circumstance through civic ritual. He was also charged with assigning members to all committees unless otherwise directed by the House. His corpulence contributed to his commanding presence, although it was also the subject of satire. The Speaker's position prevented Muhlenberg from playing an active role in the House's deliberations. His regular correspondence with Benjamin Rush and Tench Coxe in Philadelphia shows, however, that he supported both the strengthening of executive powers and the adoption of the amendments later known as the Bill of Rights. He welcomed assumption of the states' war debts, but was disappointed in his bid for a permanent residence of Congress at Lancaster, Pennsylvania.

Muhlenberg was reelected three times to Congress as representative for the district comprising Philadelphia and Bucks counties or as a Pennsylvania congressman-at-large, serving again as Speaker of the House in the Third Congress (1793–1795). When the federal capital was moved to Philadelphia, he made his home a center of social life for members of Congress. Until 1796 he managed to preserve his Federalist electoral base in Pennsylvania while keeping up good working relations with the Democratic-Republicans in Congress. Less successful was his bid for the governorship of his home state: he ran twice on the Federalist ticket but was defeated in 1793 by Thomas Mifflin and in 1796 by Thomas McKean.

The passionate public debate over the Jay Treaty marked the peak as well as the end of his political career. After ratification of the treaty by the Senate, a resolution was introduced in the House on 29 April 1796, "That it is expedient to make the necessary appropriations for carrying the Treaty with Great Britain into effect." When the House, resolving itself into a committee of the whole, was evenly divided over the resolution, Muhlenberg as chairman cast the tie-breaking vote appropriating money for the Jay Treaty.

He knew that this decision could cost him his popularity in Pennsylvania, where opposition against the Jay Treaty ran high, but he felt that he had acted in the best interests of the country. Held responsible by Pennsylvania voters for the passage of the treaty, he fell from political grace. On 4 May 1796 he was even attacked and stabbed by his psychologically unstable brother-in-law, Bernard Schaefer. Badly defeated at the polls in the fall of 1796, he was never again nominated for an electoral office. He remained active in politics, however, and grew more sympathetic to the Democratic-Republican cause. This ideological shift was accelerated when President John Adams (1735–1826) denied him the post of treasurer of the mint. On 8 January 1800 Governor McKean appointed him collector general of the Pennsylvania land office, and he settled down in the state capital, Lancaster. The following year he was again mentioned as a serious contender for the governorship. When he suffered a stroke and died in Lancaster, William Duane wrote to Thomas Jefferson, "There is no other character among the Germans of talents and standing equal to the deceased; his capacity as a German writer was admired, and there does not appear to be any one equal to him left" (Wallace, p. 291).

Muhlenberg's name figures prominently in a story that circulated widely in nineteenth-century Germany, was later revived by Nazi propagandists, and persisted even after World War II. It relates that German would have become the official language of the United States had it not been for Frederick Muhlenberg, who voted the proposal down in Congress. The kernel of truth in this legend is that Muhlenberg considered it essential for his fellow German Americans to master the English language, and that he disapproved of the idea of publishing federal laws and resolutions in German as well as in English.

Historians have criticized Muhlenberg for not following a clear party line and for acting inconsistently. In reality he deserves credit for his efforts at mediating and building bridges between Federalists and Democratic-Republicans and thereby helping to stabilize the young republic. His greatest achievement, however, seems to have been to provide "ethnic leadership" and to further the involvement and integration of German Americans into the political process of the United States.

• Much of the biographical material on the early years of Muhlenberg is in the papers and the published volumes of the journal and the correspondence of his father Henry Melchior Muhlenberg. Frederick Muhlenberg's diary, which he kept from 1770 to 1774, is in the possession of Trinity Lutheran Church, Reading, Penn. It was translated by J. W. Early and published in the *Lutheran Church Review* 24 (1905): 127–37, 388–90, 562–71, 682–94; and vol. 25 (1906): 134–47, 345–56. Additional papers are in the Lutheran Archives, Mount Airy, Penn., the Frederick Nicolls Collection, Reading, Penn., and the Gratz collection, Historical Society of Pennsylvania. The best biographical source is Paul A. W. Wallace, *The Muhlenbergs of Pennsylvania* (1950; repr. 1970). Muhlenberg's congressional career is outlined in Charlene B.

Bickford et al., eds., *Documentary History of the First Federal Congress. Debates in the House of Representatives: Third Session*, vol. 14 (1995), pp. 792–97. See also Oswald Seidensticker, "Frederick Augustus Conrad Muhlenberg, Speaker of the House of Representatives, in the First Congress, 1789," *Pennsylvania Magazine of History and Biography* 12 (1889): 184–206; Henry M. M. Richards, "Frederick Augustus Conrad Muhlenberg," *Pennsylvania-German* 3 (1902): 51–60; and Fredrick S. Weiser, ed., *The Weiser Family* (1960).

JÜRGEN HEIDEKING

MUHLENBERG, Henry (17 Nov. 1753–23 May 1815), Lutheran clergyman and botanist, was born Gotthilf Heinrich Ernst Muhlenberg in Trappe, Pennsylvania, the son of Heinrich (Henry) Melchior Muhlenberg, a patriarch of the Lutheran church in America, and Anna Maria Weiser, the daughter of the Indian interpreter Conrad Weiser. Henry Muhlenberg, as he signed his letters in English and as he was known to his friends, attended school at his birthplace, later in Philadelphia when the family moved there in 1761, and when only nine was sent with his two older brothers to Halle, in Saxony, at whose orphanage his father had been a teacher. There Muhlenberg learned Latin, Greek, and Hebrew but had only a year at the university. Although the University of Halle had a famous botanical garden, his studies focused on theology and ecclesiastical history.

Shortly after his return to Philadelphia in 1770, despite his tender age, Muhlenberg was ordained in Reading and then served for several years as his father's assistant. A decade later he accepted a call to Holy Trinity Church in Lancaster, where he was pastor until his death there. Late in life he agreed to serve as first principal of Franklin College, which later became Franklin and Marshall College after an 1853 merger. A fellow clergyman characterized his preaching as "perspicuous and direct," remarking that his message "came fairly within the range of the common mind" and observed that his pulpit presence "was no less impressive and paternal than his matter was instructive—he seemed like a father tenderly and earnestly addressing his children." Muhlenberg also ministered to the physical ills of his flock, prescribing medicines shipped to him from Halle as well as botanical remedies he collected himself.

While still in Philadelphia he had married Mary Catherine Hall in 1774; they had eight children. Like his brothers, one of whom became a major general in the Revolution, Muhlenberg was devoted to the patriot cause and on the approach of the British army had to flee from Philadelphia disguised as an Indian. It was during his forced rustication in Trappe that he took up botany as an avocation and began combing the surrounding countryside for specimens for his herbarium. Self-taught in botany, Muhlenberg turned to European botanists as soon as the revolutionary war was over, sending them plants for identification and exchanging his duplicates for European plant specimens. He also began corresponding with virtually all the Americans having any knowledge of botany, often obtaining from them seeds that he then planted in his own garden to observe the living plants. He tried on himself the reported medicinal effects of plants, and he made many contributions to Johann David Schöpf's *Materia Medica Americana* (1787) without receiving any credit from its author. He missed no chance to enlarge his knowledge of plants; late in life he remarked in a letter that "in winter, I collect, near the fire-side, our Lichens on the fire-wood."

His herbarium (now at the Academy of Natural Sciences of Philadelphia) was the earliest professional one collected by a native-born American, but Muhlenberg was not credited for many of his discoveries when his new plants were first published in Europe by correspondents such as Johann Hedwig. He seldom complained; having waited as long as ten to fifteen years for one of his European colleagues to verify the identification of a plant, he was mostly interested to see that it was correctly described and often did not devise a name for it himself. "In giving information," wrote the botanist W. P. C. Barton, "he was conscientious as truth itself, and his patience and industry in correcting the errors and confusions in botany, have scarce a parallel." Having little desire for fame as the first to name a plant, he urged as early as 1785 that all American botanists should thoroughly study the plants of their own regions; then, by their joint efforts, they could produce a complete Flora Americana. Many to whom he wrote about this scheme agreed with him, but few tried to carry out their end of the bargain.

Muhlenberg worked so slowly and carefully that his first published paper, an "Index florae Lancastriensis," did not appear until 1793 in the *Transactions* of the American Philosophical Society, followed by a supplement six years later. The "Index" contained no descriptions, but in 1801 Carl Willdenow published in Berlin Muhlenberg's notes on the genera *Juglans*, *Fraxinus*, and *Quercus*, which did describe several new species. In 1803 Willdenow also published for him ten new species of willows, and as the six volumes of Willdenow's edition of Linnaeus's *Species plantarum* came out, other new species were attributed to Muhlenberg in them. The only other botanical publication by Muhlenberg to appear during his lifetime was his *Catalogus plantarum Americae Septentrionalis* (1813). The *Catalogus* also did not give descriptions, but it did list 853 genera and about 3,700 species of native and naturalized plants, and in it Muhlenberg carefully acknowledged the thirty-one individuals from whom he had obtained either specimens or seeds from regions not familiar to him personally. Since it took four years to print this book of 122 pages, it is easy to see why his published output was modest. An enlarged edition appeared after the author's death, as did also his *Descriptio uberior plantarum graminum et plantarum Calamarium Americae Septentrionalis* (1817), prepared for the press by his son F. A. Muhlenberg and his Philadelphia friend Zaccheus Collins. He was also the joint author (with Benedict J. Schipper) of a two-volume German-English dictionary that included a German grammar (1812).

Few botanists have written so much but published so little. Muhlenberg left a two-volume bound manuscript titled "Descriptio uberior plantarum Lancastriensium" that the Philadelphia publisher S. W. Conrad announced for publication, though it never appeared. Muhlenberg's meticulously prepared manuscript daybooks contain botanical observations and other notes on natural history made from 1785 to the year of his death. In all, it has been estimated that he left more than 6,000 pages of unpublished descriptive botany, made all the harder to use by being written in a minuscule hand, in English, Latin, and an obsolete form of German.

Although physically so robust that he could walk the sixty miles between Lancaster and Philadelphia without undue fatigue, during the last year of his life Muhlenberg suffered a paralytic stroke that left him with limited speech and unable to write. Nevertheless, with his daughter acting as amanuensis he kept up his large correspondence, and he began learning to read for a second time, starting with the alphabet. Suddenly one day all his faculties returned at once. Finally, after several more small attacks, apoplexy carried him away in the course of a day.

• Muhlenberg left a rich legacy of manuscripts concerning the early history of botany in the United States. Twenty-four volumes of his unpublished writings on botany and natural history are at the American Philosophical Society; about 400 letters addressed to him by fellow naturalists are at the Historical Society of Pennsylvania. Harvard has his letters to Stephen Elliott, the Academy of Natural Sciences of Philadelphia his letters to Zaccheus Collins, Ohio University his letters to Manasseh Cutler, the Hunt Institute his letters to Franz Carl Mertens, and the Linnean Society of London his letters to J. E. Smith. His pastorate is documented by twelve volumes of manuscript sermon notes at the Lutheran Archives Center at Philadelphia (which also has a collection of letters on both religious and scientific subjects) and by approximately 700 pages of church records at Holy Trinity in Lancaster kept during his tenure there. Muhlenberg College has some of his letters to his son. Muhlenberg's scientific career is best summed up in two articles: E. D. Merrill and Shiu-ying Hu, "Work and Publications of Henry Muhlenberg," *Bartonia* 25 (1949): 1–66, and C. Earle Smith, Jr., "Henry Muhlenberg—Botanical Pioneer," *Proceedings of the American Philosophical Society* 106 (1962): 443–60. William Darlington printed some of Muhlenberg's letters in *Reliquiae Baldwinianae* (1843) and in *Memorials of John Bartram and Humphry Marshall* (1849). See also Paul A. W. Wallace, *The Muhlenbergs of Pennsylvania* (1950). His pastoral career is treated in William B. Sprague, *Annals of the American Pulpit*, vol. 9 (1869), where the Reverend Benjamin Keller comments on his pulpit manner and a grandson relates family memories of him. An obituary is in *Poulson's American Daily Advertiser*, 26 May 1815.

CHARLES BOEWE

MUHLENBERG, Henry Augustus Philip (13 May 1782–11 Aug. 1844), clergyman and member of the U.S. Congress, was born in Lancaster, Pennsylvania, the son of Henry Muhlenberg, a Lutheran minister and botanist, and Mary Catherine Hall. He received his education under the personal direction of his father, who in 1787 became the founding president of Franklin College in Lancaster. Henry A. Muhlenberg received his theological training from his uncle, John C. Kunze, who was a Lutheran pastor in New York City and also professor of Oriental languages at Columbia College. In April 1803, while still a candidate for ordination, Muhlenberg accepted the pastorate of the Trinity Lutheran Church of Reading, Pennsylvania; he was ordained in 1804. In 1805 he married Mary Elizabeth Hiester, who died in 1806 while giving birth to their first child (who survived). In 1808 he married Rebecca Hiester, the sister of his first wife. They had six children. During his quarter-century as minister in the church at Reading, Muhlenberg became renowned as a preacher and was an influential member of the Evangelical Lutheran Synod of Pennsylvania, serving as its secretary (1821–1824) and as its president (1825–1828).

Muhlenberg, a longtime supporter of the Jeffersonian Democratic-Republican party, began an active role in politics when his father-in-law, Joseph Hiester, was elected governor of Pennsylvania in 1820. Muhlenberg acted as informal adviser during Hiester's three-year term and handled requests from those seeking the governor's influence and patronage. In the fluid political party situation of the 1820s, Muhlenberg was among those Pennsylvanians forming a coalition of former Jeffersonian Democratic-Republicans and former Federalists behind the presidential candidacy of Andrew Jackson. This element of the nascent Jacksonian party, led by James Buchanan, became known as the "Amalgamators." Muhlenberg's relationship to Governor Hiester and his reputation as a clergyman among the German Lutherans helped to draw many Pennsylvania Germans into the Jacksonian camp.

In 1828 Muhlenberg resigned his pastorate, accepted the nomination of local Jacksonians for a seat in the U.S. House of Representatives, and was elected. He served five terms in Congress, supporting Jackson loyally. He publicly supported Jackson's war upon the Second Bank of the United States, while privately expressing reservations about the total destruction of the bank. He excused himself from voting on the recharter of the bank in 1832, since he had just inherited stock in the bank from his late father-in-law. He supported the Tariff of 1832 but voted also for the reductions in the Compromise Tariff of 1833 after the South Carolina nullification crisis. From 1831 to 1838 he served as chair of the Committee on Revolutionary War Claims.

In the early 1830s the Jacksonian party in Pennsylvania was torn by increasing factionalism. The Amalgamators were at odds with the "Eleventh Hour Men," former supporters of John C. Calhoun for the presidency before 1828 and now Jacksonians under the leadership of Samuel D. Ingham, who was Jackson's secretary of the treasury from 1829 to 1831. Governor George Wolf, elected in 1829, was of the Ingham faction. Most of the Amalgamators, opposing a third term for Wolf in 1835, supported Muhlenberg for the governor's post. The divided party produced rival state conventions that year, one nominating Wolf, the other nominating Muhlenberg. The resulting bitter struggle between the "Wolves" and the "Muhls" in the election brought disaster to the Jacksonian party and gave the governorship to Joseph Ritner, who was supported by the Anti-Masonic party and the Whigs. Muhlenberg was reelected to Congress in 1836.

As the gubernatorial campaign of 1838 approached, a renewed rivalry between Muhlenberg and Wolf for the Democratic nomination seemed once again in prospect. Seeking to repair the division in the party, Senator Buchanan sought federal appointments for both contenders, which would effectively remove them from active state politics. Muhlenberg rejected suggestions that he accept the posts of secretary of the navy and of minister to Russia. Later, President Martin Van Buren granted Wolf the post of collector of the Port of Philadelphia, while Muhlenberg agreed to become the first U.S. minister to Austria. He resigned his seat in the House of Representatives in February 1838 and arrived in Vienna later that spring. His two-year diplomatic mission was concerned mostly with matters of commerce and trade. His efforts to have American tobacco admitted to the Austrian market failed, since the Austrian state tobacco monopoly protected tobacco raised within the empire. After two years Muhlenberg tired of the diplomatic service and became concerned for the health of his wife and daughter in Austria. His request to return to the United States was granted in 1840.

Upon his return to Reading, Muhlenberg remained in temporary retirement from politics, his wife having died in January 1841. In 1843 he came out as a candidate for the Democratic nomination for governor in 1844. The Democratic State Convention of 1844 nominated him over Francis Shunk. The party avoided a factional split, and prospects seemed good for Muhlenberg's election. In late July Buchanan wrote to him, "There is a glorious career before you, should Providence spare your life and health." Fate, however, decreed otherwise: two weeks later, and two months before the election, Muhlenberg suffered a stroke at his home in Reading and died. The Democrats hastily nominated Shunk, who won the election in October.

Muhlenberg carried on a family tradition of leadership both in the church and in politics. He played a central role in shaping the new Jacksonian Democratic party in Pennsylvania and in leading Pennsylvanians of German stock into the Democratic organization. While he proved to be a strong supporter of Jacksonianism in Congress, the intractable factionalism of the party in Pennsylvania prevented his rise to higher office.

• Muhlenberg papers are in the Historical Society of Berks County, Reading, and in the American Philosophical Society, Philadelphia. His tenure as Lutheran pastor is described in Jacob Fry, *History of Trinity Lutheran Church, Reading, Pa.* (1894). The most complete summary of his political career is Gayle K. Steele, "Henry Augustus Philip Muhlenberg: An Historical Biography" (M.A. thesis, Pennsylvania State Univ., 1966). See also Philip S. Klein, *Pennsylvania Politics, 1817–1832: A Game without Rules* (1940); Philip S.

Klein, *President James Buchanan: A Biography* (1962); and Charles M. Snyder, *The Jacksonian Heritage: Pennsylvania Politics, 1833–1848* (1958). A laudatory memorial is in the *United States Magazine and Democratic Review*, Jan. 1845, pp. 67–78.

JAMES M. BERGQUIST

MUHLENBERG, Henry Melchior (6 Sept. 1711–7 Oct. 1787), clergyman, was born Heinrich Melchior Mühlenberg in Einbeck in the electorate of Hannover (now in Germany), the son of Nicolaus Mühlenberg, a shoemaker, and Anna Maria Kleinschmidt. His father died when Muhlenberg was twelve, and the boy had to discontinue his studies in the German and Latin school in Einbeck to support himself by doing manual labor. Nine years later he was able to resume his secondary education; with the support of patrons, he matriculated in the faculty of theology at the University of Göttingen. On graduating in 1737, he served as preceptor at the orphan school of Halle, thus coming under the influence of the Pietism for which the city was known.

Originally selected by the authorities in Halle to be a missionary in East India, Muhlenberg was instead called in 1739 to serve as pastor and teacher in a parish in Grosshennersdorf in Upper Lusatia in Germany. While Muhlenberg was there, the head of the institutions at Halle, Gotthilf August Francke, invited him to come to see him. On Muhlenberg's thirtieth birthday Francke offered him a call to serve for three years as pastor of three congregations in Pennsylvania: Philadelphia, New Hanover, and Providence (later called Trappe). Thrown into deep turmoil by this turn of events, Muhlenberg ultimately accepted the call and, after traveling to England, sailed from Gravesend on 13 June 1742 on the *Georgia Packet* for North America.

On arrival in Philadelphia on 25 November 1742, Muhlenberg encountered difficulties in maintaining his claim to be the duly ordained pastor of the three congregations that had called him. Among his main rivals and opponents were not only self-appointed pastors but also the founder and leader of Moravian Pietism, Nikolaus Ludwig von Zinzendorf. The church body, initially referred to by names such as general conference, association of pastors, synod, or united congregations, was organized in 1748. As the first person to gather it in congregations, Muhlenberg provided the leadership in the organization of this body and did so in a collegial manner. He exercised oversight of the calling, ordaining, and placing of pastors, which led to the exclusion of the self-appointed pastors, who were often defrocked individuals who had left Europe. Muhlenberg was also successful upon his arrival in wresting control of the congregations from Zinzendorf.

In 1745, a little less than three years after his arrival in the New World, Muhlenberg married Anna Maria Weiser, the daughter of Johann Conrad Weiser, Jr. Seven of their eleven children reached adulthood. Three sons are generally better known than their father. John Peter Gabriel Muhlenberg served as a brigadier general in the Continental army during the revolutionary war, Frederick Augustus Conrad Muhlenberg was the first Speaker of the House of Representatives in the Continental Congress, and Henry (Gotthilf Heinrich Ernst) Muhlenberg gained a notable reputation as a botanist.

Like other immigrants from continental Europe, Muhlenberg elected to become naturalized and became a citizen of Pennsylvania on 24 September 1754. At this time and in the succeeding years, the waves of German immigrants arriving in North America also led to an increase in membership in Muhlenberg's Philadelphia congregation and to tensions within it. Addressing a conflict in 1762 between the congregation and the elders concerning whether he should remain as its senior pastor, Muhlenberg devised a plan enabling members of the congregation to vote to resolve the conflict. In announcing the plan, he asked the elders and congregation members to send or bring their votes in writing to his home. Every member, even the poorest, had a vote, "whether man or woman, widower or widow, married or unmarried, whether in possession of a pew or not." Although initially in his ministry he had been disdainful of deciding matters by majority vote, that very method resolved a severe conflict in his congregation.

Muhlenberg was careful to discreetly hide his inner political commitments under the cover of his religious ones. Nevertheless, upon repeal of the Stamp Act in 1766, he preached a sermon of prayer and thanksgiving. The repeal brought him a sense of relief, in no small part because of his double allegiance to England's king, George III, who was ruler in Muhlenberg's adopted country and also elector of the state of Hannover, the country of Muhlenberg's birth. Emphasizing the importance he attached to the repeal of the Stamp Act, Muhlenberg published the sermon, titled (abridged and translated) *Testimony to the Goodness and Solemnity of God toward His Covenant People for the Repeal of the Stamp Act, Delivered 1 August 1766* (1766), the only publication of his voluminous writing in the New World apart from a preface he wrote for a hymnal published in 1786.

Muhlenberg was the leading spirit in organizing the first permanent Lutheran church body in North America. He labored primarily in Pennsylvania and New Jersey and exercised influence in New York, New England, Nova Scotia, and Georgia. At the time of his death, the number of German Lutheran congregations in this field had increased from perhaps nine or ten in 1742 to probably more than two hundred. While he was likely the only regularly ordained German Lutheran pastor in Pennsylvania in the year of his arrival, by 1787 at least twenty-five pastors were members of the church organized under his leadership, which after 1790 was called the Evangelical Lutheran Ministerium of Pennsylvania and Adjacent States. He died in Trappe, Pennsylvania. The epitaph engraved in Latin on his grave reflects his role in church and society, reading in translation, "Who and what he was future times will know without a monument of stone."

• The two main depositories of documents in the form of diaries, correspondence, opinions, and papers of Muhlenberg are the Archives of the Francke Institutions in Halle, Germany, and the Lutheran Archives Center in Philadelphia, Pa. Four volumes of Muhlenberg's correspondence have been published in Berlin, Kurt Aland, ed., *Die Korrespondenz Heinrich Melchior Mühlenbergs aus der Anfangszeit des deutschen Luthertums in Nordamerika* (1986–1993). *The Journals of Henry Melchior Muhlenberg*, ed. and trans. Theodore G. Tappert and John W. Doberstein (3 vols., 1942, 1948, 1958), is a translation of his diaries in the Lutheran Archives Center. *The Correspondence of Heinrich Melchior Mühlenberg*, ed. and trans. John W. Kleiner and Helmut T. Lehmann (1993), is an English translation of his correspondence in 1740–1747. The most comprehensive though undocumented biography of Muhlenberg is William Julius Mann, *Life and Times of Henry Melchior Muhlenberg* (1887). Muhlenberg and his family are the subjects of Paul A. W. Wallace, *The Muhlenbergs of Pennsylvania* (1950). Leonard Richard Riforgiato, *Missionary of Moderation: Henry Melchior Muhlenberg and the Lutheran Church in English America* (1971), includes a discussion of Muhlenberg's theological commitments. Critical analyses of Muhlenberg, all in *Lutheran Quarterly*, include Karl-Otto Strohmidel, "Henry Melchior Muhlenberg's European Heritage" (Spring 1992): 5–34; Paul A. Baglyos, "Muhlenberg in the American Lutheran Imagination" (Spring 1992): 35–50; Helmut T. Lehmann and J. Woodrow Savacool, "Muhlenberg's Ministry of Healing" (Spring 1992): 51–68; and Faith E. Rohrbough, "The Political Maturation of Henry Melchior Muhlenberg" (Winter 1996): 385–405.

HELMUT T. LEHMANN

MUHLENBERG, John Peter Gabriel (1 Oct. 1746–1 Oct. 1807), revolutionary soldier and politician, also known as Peter Muhlenberg, was born in the German settlement of Trappe, Pennsylvania, the son of Henry Melchior Muhlenberg, a Lutheran minister, and Anna Maria Weiser. Tall and strong as a boy, impulsive but shy, he was drawn to the military. From 1760 to 1763 he attended the Academy of Philadelphia but preferred fishing and hunting to his studies. In April 1763 his father sent him, together with two brothers, to Halle, Germany, to give them the advantages of a better education than was available at the time in Pennsylvania. John Peter's mentors at the Franckesche Stiftungen, however, found him unsuited to study for the ministry and thought him better qualified for a career in commerce.

On the advice of Gotthilf August Francke, Muhlenberg contracted himself in September 1763 to serve for a term of six years as an apprentice to a merchant in the city of Lübeck. Unfortunately his master turned out to be a petty grocer who exploited Muhlenberg's labor and kept him a virtual prisoner. After enduring this hardship for almost three years, he ran away and enlisted in the Royal American Regiment of Foot of the British army. As the secretary to one of the officers he returned to Philadelphia and in January 1767 was given an honorable discharge. He then went to a private English school for several months until Charles Magnus von Wrangel, provost of the Swedish Luther-

ans, offered to train him as a catechist and teacher in the American church. He soon began to preach in Swedish and German Lutheran churches, winning much praise from his congregations. In February 1769 he was licensed as a Lutheran minister and, assisting his father, took charge of the churches at Bedminster and New Germantown, New Jersey. In 1770 he married Anna Barbara "Hannah" Meyer, daughter of a successful potter. Together they had six children.

In May 1770 Muhlenberg accepted a call from the German Lutheran congregation at Woodstock, Dunmore County, in Virginia's Shenandoah Valley. Since the Anglican church was the state's established church, he had to travel to London to seek ordination. In King's Chapel on 25 April 1772 he was ordained a priest by the bishop of London. Back in Virginia he got involved in the patriotic cause and became a follower of Patrick Henry. When the freeholders of Woodstock discussed possible reactions to the Boston Port Act on 16 June 1774, he was chosen moderator and headed a committee that drew up "Resolves" protesting the British policy. He acted as chairman of a committee of correspondence and represented Dunmore County in the House of Burgesses, which met 1–6 August 1774 in Williamsburg. On his father's advice he resigned all his political offices, but in 1775 he was reelected chairman of the Committee of Correspondence and Safety of Dunmore County. In March he served as a delegate to the Virginia Convention, held in St. John's Church, where Henry delivered his famous "liberty or death" speech. When his brother Frederick Muhlenberg criticized him for mixing politics with religion, he wrote back, "Whether I choose or not, I am to be a politician" (Wallace, p. 113). On 12 January 1776 he accepted the appointment of the convention at Williamsburg as a colonel and went home to recruit his regiment. His farewell sermon to the Woodstock congregation, given on 21 January 1776 reportedly climaxed in the phrase: "There is a time to pray and a time to fight, and that time has now come!" Whether he really made the dramatic gesture of throwing off his gown in the pulpit, revealing his uniform beneath it, remains controversial.

Lacking any professional military experience, the "fighting parson" commanded the Eighth Virginia (German) Regiment of the Continental army. The regiment took part in the successful defense of Charleston in June 1776 but was weakened, mainly by illnesses, during the following campaign in Georgia. At this time Muhlenberg contracted a disease of the liver which troubled him for the remainder of the war and eventually caused his death. On 21 February 1777 he was commissioned brigadier general and summoned to George Washington's camp at Morristown. His brigade was put under the command of General Nathanael Greene and fought with distinction at the battles of Brandywine (Sept. 1777) and Germantown (Oct. 1777). He was stationed at Valley Forge that winter and the next year commanded two Virginia brigades in the second line, or Corps de Reserve, at Monmouth Court House. After spending the winter of 1778–1779 at army headquarters in Middlebrook, New Jersey, he went into action in New York, where his brigade contributed to General Anthony Wayne's success at Stony Point in July 1779. During the first years of the war he established his reputation as a good disciplinarian and a bold but safe commander who understood general strategic problems. He was held in high esteem by Washington and Baron von Steuben, who sought his advice and valued his reliability and efficiency.

When the British again threatened the South, Washington and the Board of War sent him back to Virginia and assigned him the task of raising fresh troops for the defense of Charleston. Against great odds he began in April 1780 to recruit and train troops in Fredericksburg, doubling his efforts after the fall of Charleston in the following month. Later that year and in the spring of 1781, as von Steuben's second in command, he distinguished himself in defensive actions against the invading forces of Banastre Tarleton, Benedict Arnold, and Charles Cornwallis. Fighting under the marquis de Lafayette, he played a major role in the siege of Yorktown. When his brigade attacked and captured one of the two remaining British redoubts on 14 October 1781, Cornwallis's surrender became inevitable. However, Alexander Hamilton, who had led the advance force, received most of the attention for this action. On 30 September 1783 Muhlenberg was promoted to the rank of brevet major general, and on 3 November 1783 he retired from the service. He was one of the founders of the Virginia chapter of the Society of the Cincinnati.

He declined an invitation from his congregation to return to Woodstock, arguing that "it would never do to mount the parson after the soldier" (H. A. Muhlenberg, p. 290). Appointed by the Virginia assembly to survey the military bounty lands assigned to the veterans of the Virginia line of the Continental army, he made a journey to Louisville at the Falls of the Ohio. After returning in June 1784, he reported to Congress about Indian opposition to the settlement project. He moved to Pennsylvania, where his former German neighbors elected him Montgomery County representative on the supreme executive council in 1784. At the end of his three-year term he served as vice president of the state (1787–1788). In 1787 he became a trustee of Franklin College in Lancaster, which was established for the German-speaking inhabitants of Pennsylvania.

At the elections for the First Federal Congress, Pennsylvania anti-Federalists nominated Muhlenberg to their Harrisburg ticket because of his popularity among German Americans. He was elected a representative at large in the First Congress and on 4 March 1789, together with his brother Frederick, took his seat at Federal Hall in New York City. His correspondence with Benjamin Rush in Philadelphia shows him especially interested in amending the Constitution by a Bill of Rights and in the question of the location of the federal capital, but his actual contributions to the First Congress were minimal. Most of his committee service reflected his expertise in military affairs, and

only once did he address his colleagues on the floor of the House. In the funding controversy he opposed Hamilton and joined the anti-administration forces. He was defeated for reelection but returned as representative to the Third and Sixth Congresses in 1793–1795 and 1799–1801. Ideologically a Democratic-Republican, he remained in the political background and acted as a "political balance wheel" (Wallace, p. 274), exerting a stabilizing influence on both the state and national level.

In 1797 Muhlenberg went west for a second time to survey his bounty lands on the Scioto but returned to his parents' house at Trappe. Two years later he managed Thomas McKean's successful campaign for the governorship of Pennsylvania and in February 1801, as a member of the House of Representatives, he helped to elect Thomas Jefferson president. He was considered a stalwart of the Democratic-Republican party in Pennsylvania, and a newspaper correspondent called him "the Moses of the German Israelites" (Wallace, p. 290). On 18 February 1801 he was elected to the U.S. Senate, but after attending the special session in March he resigned in order to accept a lucrative appointment as supervisor of U.S. customs in the district of Pennsylvania. From 1803 until his death he served as collector of customs for the port of Philadelphia. An active Lutheran layman, he supported bilingual pastoral services in Philadelphia and in 1806 helped to organize the English-speaking St. John's Church. He died at his suburban home at Gray's Ferry on the Schuylkill and was buried at Augustus Church at Trappe.

• Much of the biographical material for the early years of J. P. G. Muhlenberg is to be found in the papers and the published volumes of the journal and the correspondence of his father, Henry Melchior Muhlenberg. John Peter Muhlenberg's journal of his visit to London in 1772 is published in the *Lutheran Church Review* 4 (1885): 294–300. Additional papers are in the Lutheran Archives at Mount Airy, Penn., the Frederick Nicolls Collection, Reading, Penn., and the Gratz Collection at the Historical Society of Pennsylvania. The first detailed (but not always reliable) account was given by his great-nephew, Henry A. Muhlenberg, *The Life of Major-General Peter Muhlenberg, of the Revolutionary Army* (1849). Almost a century later a second biography was published by Edward W. Hocker, *The Fighting Parson of the American Revolution: A Biography of General Peter Muhlenberg, Lutheran Clergyman, Military Chieftain, and Political Leader* (1936). The most complete modern assessment is Paul A. W. Wallace, *The Muhlenbergs of Pennsylvania* (1950; repr. 1970). A biographical article concentrating on J. P. G. Muhlenberg's service in Congress is included in Charlene B. Bickford et al., eds., *Debates in the House of Representatives: Third Session, Documentary History of the First Federal Congress* (1995). See also "General John Peter G. Muhlenberg," *Pennsylvania-German* 3 (1902): 3–21; Wilhelm Germann, "The Crisis in the Early Life of General Peter Mühlenberg," *Pennsylvania Magazine of History and Biography* 37 (1913): 298–329, 450–70 (trans. from H. A. Rattermann's *Deutsch-Amerikanisches Magazin* [1886–1887]); Thomas N. Rightmyer, "The Holy Orders of Peter Muhlenberg," *Historical Magazine of the Protestant Episcopal Church* 30 (1961): 183–97; and George M. Smith, "The Reverend Peter Muhlenberg: A Symbiotic Adventure in Virginia, 1772–1783," *Society for the History of the Germans in Maryland* 36 (1975): 51–65.

JÜRGEN HEIDEKING

MUHLENBERG, William Augustus (16 Sept. 1796–8 Apr. 1877), Episcopal clergyman, was born in Philadelphia, Pennsylvania, the son of Henry William Muhlenberg, a wine merchant, and Mary Catherine Sheaff. He belonged to the first generation of his family for whom English was the native tongue. As a result, at the age of five he began attending the English language services of Christ Episcopal Church and thus grew up in that church instead of the German Lutheran church of his ancestors. Muhlenberg graduated from the University of Pennsylvania in 1815 and then studied for the Episcopal priesthood under the supervision of Jackson Kemper, who later became a noted missionary bishop. Upon his ordination to the diaconate in 1817, he became an assistant of Bishop William White (1748–1836), the rector of Christ Church, Philadelphia. Ordained to the priesthood in 1820, he became rector of St. James Church in Lancaster, Pennsylvania, a town near Philadelphia. He never married.

From the beginning of his career he worked to adapt the church's activity to an urban community. In Philadelphia, then the largest city in the United States, he reformed the services of Christ Church by bringing in more congregational participation to make the church more attractive to the rank and file of city dwellers. In Lancaster he took the lead in establishing a public school system, founding a Sunday school in his parish, and in establishing a public library.

Muhlenberg made a significant change in his career in 1826, when he moved to Long Island near the burgeoning metropolis of New York, which in 1820 had replaced Philadelphia as the nation's largest city. There he founded a school, the Flushing Institute, which in 1838 was expanded into St. Paul's College at College Point, Long Island. The institute and the college attracted students from the eastern United States and made Muhlenberg a nationally known figure. Methods put into practice at these two schools anticipated by the better part of a century the Progressive movement in education. He also introduced ritualistic practices in his chapels such as candles, incense, and flowers to relieve the drab services that made chapel going the terror of students at that time. His school served as a model for others founded in these years, among them St. Paul's in Hanover, New Hampshire; Episcopal High School in Alexandria, Virginia; and St. James near Hagerstown, Maryland.

Muhlenberg made another dramatic change in his career in 1845 when, at the age of fifty, he established the Church of the Holy Communion in New York City. This church was a model for the "institutional church" that emphasized services to the community, such as employment agencies, English language classes, medical services, parish schools, and social work. The church caught national attention because all of its pews were free, which went against the current practice of selling or renting pews to support the church. To assist in its numerous works Muhlenberg founded the Sisterhood of the Holy Communion, an order of women devoted to teaching, nursing, and social work. He continued his interest in reforming church services by introducing, among other things, a celebration of the Holy Communion every Sunday, weekday services, and a boys' choir. He also continued the ritualistic practices that he had started at his schools.

His interest in medical care led him to establish an infirmary at the church, which was staffed by the sisters. This work expanded into a hospital, St. Luke's, in New York City, modeled on St. Bartholomew's Hospital in London. St. Luke's in turn became a model for urban hospitals throughout the United States and abroad. The first nurses were the sisters from the Church of the Holy Communion. Muhlenberg became the director of the hospital when it opened in 1858 but continued a close relationship with the church.

Meanwhile, Muhlenberg had emerged as a major force for church unity. While still an educator he published a pamphlet entitled *Hints on Catholic Union* (1835). The climax of his career came in 1853, when he presented to the House of Bishops a memorial for a broader approach to church unity than that held by the Episcopal church at that time. He did not advocate unifying all denominations into one church. Rather, he envisioned a group of "concentric" churches in communion with each other that would be united through a federal council and have a unified ministry. Each church would be self-governing, however, and maintain its separate identity.

His interest in improving church services was lifelong. He published an expanded hymnal while at Lancaster. At his school and at the Church of the Holy Communion he introduced ritualistic practices that he had learned as a boy attending a Roman Catholic church in Philadelphia. He also advocated a revision of the historic Book of Common Prayer. In this area he anticipated many of the reforms of the modern liturgical movement.

In theology Muhlenberg called himself an Evangelical Catholic, a term he may have learned from his friend Dr. Philip Schaff, a prominent church historian. By this term, he meant that Catholicism and Protestantism were different aspects of Christianity and that evangelical Christians could use ritual from the Catholic tradition to make their services more attractive.

In 1870 he founded a housing project for industrial workers on Long Island called St. Johnland. Its purpose was to form an ecumenical housing project that would embody the ideas Muhlenberg had advocated throughout his life. He called it a Christian Socialist experiment. Because of his death (at St. Johnland), the multifaceted project was never completed.

Muhlenberg was one of the first major religious leaders in the United States to see that the Christian church must adopt new methods, new kinds of organization, and new institutions to meet the needs of an urban-industrial society. Most of his ideas had precedents or were already advocated by contemporary movements. He was, however, able to discern those movements that had a significant impact on the church and society in the late nineteenth century and become an effective advocate. He is ranked by historians of the Episcopal church as one of the most influential figures produced by that church. His vision was of a church that permeated society with the social ideals of Christianity, ameliorating the problems spawned by the urban-industrial revolution.

• The best manuscript source on Muhlenberg is the Kemper papers in the library of the Wisconsin State Historical Society, which include the lifelong correspondence between Muhlenberg and his close friend Bishop Kemper. The best single source is the biography written after his death by his longtime associate Anne Ayres, *Life and Work of William Augustus Muhlenberg*, 5th ed. (1894). Acting on instructions that Muhlenberg gave before his death, Ayres destroyed all of his papers after writing the biography. She also edited two volumes of Muhlenberg's published works entitled *Evangelical Catholic Papers* (1875, 1877). Muhlenberg edited for two years (1851–1853) a weekly paper, the *Evangelical Catholic*, to publicize his views. There is a file of this paper in the Library of the General Theological Seminary in New York City. The only full-scale biography is Alvin W. Skardon, *Church Leader in the Cities: William Augustus Muhlenberg* (1971), which has a voluminous bibliography and a bibliographical essay.

ALVIN W. SKARDON

MUIR, John (21 Apr. 1838–24 Dec. 1914), naturalist, conservationist, and writer, was born in Dunbar, Scotland, the son of Daniel Muir and Anne Gilrye, farmers. He was educated in Dunbar's common school and by his father's insistence that he memorize a Bible chapter every day. With his father and two siblings, John migrated to Wisconsin in 1849; the rest of the family soon followed. On the family's homestead near Portage, Daniel worked John, just entering his teens, as if he were an adult field hand, inflicting corporal punishment; John Muir later believed that this hard farm labor stunted his growth. The boy's escape was to devour every book that he came across, and when his father forbade his reading at night, he devised a sort of wooden alarm clock attached to his bed. This "early-rising machine" awakened him very early in the morning, and he would read until it was time for his exhausting chores.

An exhibit of Muir's inventions at the state fair (1860) led the University of Wisconsin to admit him as a student, but he did not bother to take his degree in 1863, preferring to study his own interests, practical geology and botany, rather than university-approved subjects. By making field trips in Wisconsin, neighboring states, and Canada, Muir increased his knowledge of nature, especially of plants. Already a phenomenal "pedestrian," as long-distance hikers were then called, he next walked from Indianapolis to Cedar Key, Florida, keeping a detailed nature diary,

published after his death as *A Thousand-Mile Walk to the Gulf* (1916).

In 1868 Muir went to California, heading directly from San Francisco to the Sierra Nevada, on foot. Seeing the Sierra in the distance, from the summit of Pacheco Pass in the Coast Range, he mused that the early Spaniards should have called the mountains not the Snowy Range, but the Range of Light. He fell in love with the Sierra and was entranced by its Yosemite Valley. He assumed the task of protecting the valley from degradation and made it his home for six years. All the while, he undertook expeditions into the surrounding forests and peaks to make notes and sketches in his journals, the source of future books. During his High Sierra explorations, Muir found sixty-five glaciers and developed the then radical theory that the great granite valley of Yosemite was not a down-dropped *graben*, or block of the earth's surface, but a gash carved by the abrasion of eons of glaciation. He engaged for years in a running battle with Josiah D. Whitney, the state geologist, and Clarence King of the U.S. Geological Survey. Both denigrated his ideas as the ravings of an ignorant sheepherder (Muir had briefly herded a flock in the Sierra, before he realized how destructive these "hooved locusts" were to the land). In the end, Muir proved to be right and the scientists wrong.

In 1880 Muir married Louie Wanda Strentzel, daughter of a Polish horticulturalist, John Strentzel. They had two children. In 1881 he joined the arctic expedition searching for G. W. DeLong's vanished *Jeannette* party. In Alaska he explored Glacier Bay and discovered the Muir Glacier. For a decade Muir made his home on a rented, then purchased, portion of a fruit ranch in the Alhambra Valley, just outside Martinez, California; his home there is now a National Historic Site. With his love and knowledge of botany, it was easy for Muir to master horticulture, and by 1891 he had made enough money for his family to live comfortably while he retired to natural history research in the field. He continued his Sierra wanderings and also investigated Nevada, Utah, and the Pacific Northwest. Later in 1903 and 1904, he extended his travels to Europe, Asia, Australia, and New Zealand.

Although he came to be a fine prose stylist, Muir never found writing easy. Nonetheless, he contributed articles to *Scribner's* and *Century* and won a special ally in the editor of the latter magazine, Robert Underwood Johnson, whom he took camping in Yosemite to show him the damage done to the Sierra Nevada by grazing sheep. Johnson helped Muir campaign for the establishment of Yosemite National Park, which became reality in 1890. In 1892 Muir organized the Sierra Club to foster conservation of wild lands, particularly the Sierra and Yosemite. He served as the club's president until his death. In 1896–1897 he influenced a federal forestry commission and President Grover Cleveland to establish thirteen forest reserves (today national forests) all over the country. Private interests initially negated most of this protection, but articles by Muir finally won public, press, and congressional support and the reestablishment of the reservations.

Muir's incessant writing of articles and books, his lobbying, and his personal example made him more instrumental than other naturalists in creating a strong conservation or preservation (now known as environmentalism and ecology) movement in the United States. He won the all-important friendship and support of President Theodore Roosevelt when he took him on a Yosemite camping trip in 1903. The result of their combined efforts was the designation of more national forests, national monuments such as Muir Woods, and national parks such as Sequoia.

John Muir is of such transcendent importance as an activist-conservationist that his worth as a naturalist is sometimes underestimated and his considerable skill as a writer obscured. His prose is as timeless as his message. His first book, *The Mountains of California* (1894), is probably his best, but *My First Summer in the Sierra* (1911) is a strong rival. Other worthy volumes are *Our National Parks* (1901), *Stickeen* (1909), and *The Yosemite* (1912). *Travels in Alaska* (1915) , *The Cruise of the Corwin* (1917), and *Steep Trails* (1918) appeared posthumously.

Muir was profoundly depressed when he lost his last battle against development, his effort to save the Yosemite-like Hetch Hetchy Valley from San Francisco, which seized the great gorge as a reservoir site to supply water to the city. His grief may have contributed to his death in Los Angeles; he was buried at his Martinez orchard-ranch.

• Muir's papers are scattered among the Bancroft Library, University of California, Berkeley; the University of the Pacific Library, Stockton, Calif.; the Humanities Research Center, University of Texas, Austin; and other archives. At least eight of his books were reprinted in the Sierra Club's John Muir Library Series. Literature by and about John Muir is abundant, starting with his *The Story of My Boyhood and Youth* (1913). A valuable source is William F. Kimes and Maymie Kimes, *John Muir: A Reading Bibliography* (1977). An early major study was W. F. Badé's *The Life and Letters of John Muir* (1924). It was followed by *John of the Mountains* (1938), an edition of Muir's unpublished journals, and *Son of the Wilderness: The Life of John Muir* (1945), both by Linnie Marsh Wolfe. James Mitchell Clarke, *The Life and Adventures of John Muir* (1979), is illustrated by many of the naturalist's field sketches. Among newer titles are S. Fox, *John Muir and His Legacy: The American Conservation Movement* (1981); Sally M. Miller, *John Muir: Life and Work* (1993); and Thurman Wilkins, *John Muir: Apostle of Nature* (1995). An obituary is in the *Los Angeles Times*, 25 Dec. 1914.

RICHARD H. DILLON

MULDOON, William (25 May 1852–3 June 1933), wrestler, physical culturist, and New York State athletic commissioner, was born in Caneadea, New York, the son of Patrick Muldoon, a farmer, and Maria Donohue. Muldoon's parents met and married in Dublin, Ireland, where Patrick had traveled from his native Portumna, near Galway, with the intention of studying for the priesthood. Patrick took employment with a surveying company and set sail for Canada. Eventually, the Muldoons settled in Caneadea, a tiny farming community in Allegany County, New York.

William was the seventh of ten children. As a youth Muldoon exhibited unusual levels of physical strength and a rather quick temper.

Muldoon's eldest brother, John Muldoon, served during the Civil War in the New York Sixth Cavalry (Ira Harris Guard), Company I, from 1861 until being discharged on 30 November 1864. His highest rank attained was first lieutenant. William idolized John, who returned to Caneadea in poor health and became increasingly debilitated before his death at age thirty-two. In later years Muldoon began to claim his brother's service record as his own, altering his own birth year to 1845 to make Civil War service plausible and claiming to have been promoted to the rank of colonel. Eventually the erroneous 1845 birthdate and the mendacious war service stories became such widely accepted facets of Muldoon's biography that the majority of secondary accounts of his life (as well as his own as-told-to biography written by Edward Van Every) contain the incorrect information.

Muldoon moved to New York City around 1870, a few years before his family relocated to Belfast, New York. He held various heavy labor jobs in the city for several years, including driving a cart and employment as a stevedore. During this time he began to cultivate his interest in wrestling matches. He built his reputation as a wrestler in local "dives" that featured wrestling contests, eventually attracting the attention of Harry Hill, the proprietor of the largest sporting saloon and dance hall in New York City. Hill, who was well connected with the Tammany Hall Democratic political machine in New York, employed Muldoon and introduced him to prominent local politicians and men such as Richard K. Fox, the publisher of the *National Police Gazette*. These connections enabled Muldoon to secure a position in the New York City's Twenty-ninth Precinct police force in 1876. Promoted from patrolman to roundsman in 1877, he joined the detective squad the following year.

In 1877 Muldoon helped to establish the first Police Athletic Association in New York City. He also gained recognition as the police force wrestling champion. In his burgeoning professional wrestling career, he defeated an increasingly illustrious list of opposition. On 14 May 1879, and again on 18 January 1880, Muldoon defeated France's Thiebault Bauer at Gilmore's Garden in New York City to gain recognition as the world's Greco-Roman wrestling champion. The following year he quit the police force to tour the country with his wrestling championship.

Muldoon gained national notoriety during his decade of wrestling tours, eventually creating his own traveling entourage of wrestlers, strongmen, and boxers called "Muldoon's Combinations," and helped the sport of wrestling reach its first wave of national popularity. He also appeared in several theatrical productions, most notably in 1882 as Charles the Wrestler in the Maurice Barrymore–Helena Modjeska production of Shakespeare's *As You Like It*, and in engagements posing in replication of classical Greek and Roman statuary.

In 1889 Muldoon, who had served as a wrestling and boxing trainer on a periodic basis since his days with the Police Athletic Association, agreed to serve as the trainer and second for his longtime acquaintance John L. Sullivan, who had a big prizefight upcoming with Jake Kilrain. Muldoon took the overweight and alcoholic Sullivan to his family's farm in Belfast in order to commence training. Muldoon gained wide acclaim for getting Sullivan into shape and then coaching him to victory against Kilrain in their famous bare-knuckle match.

During the 1890s Muldoon began to curtail his own wrestling career and spent much of his time training other wrestlers and boxers on his farm. His counsel on health, diet, and fitness became increasingly sought by well-to-do businessmen, setting the foundation for what was to become a profitable business for him. In 1900 Muldoon bought a large plot of land in Purchase, New York, near White Plains. He soon established a health resort, dubbed the Olympia, on the grounds. Three years later Muldoon donated his property in Belfast to the Roman Catholic church and devoted his full attention to the Olympia. Guests at the Olympia included railroad magnate and Republican senator Chauncey Depew, actor John Barrymore, and most notably, writer Theodore Dreiser and Secretary of State Elihu Root. At once fascinated and repulsed by Muldoon, Dreiser wrote a largely unflattering character sketch of him in the book *Twelve Men* (1919) substituting the name "Culhane" for Muldoon. Root checked into the Olympia in 1907 and again the following year to overcome bouts of severe physical and mental exhaustion. Muldoon's rehabilitation methods, which included extensive calisthenics, horseback riding, and use of a medicine ball, combined techniques utilized to train pugilists with then-popular beliefs of the healthful benefits of bucolic living. Muldoon's charges were put through the paces from the crack of dawn until the early evening. Although sometimes questioned for his harshness, Muldoon's purported high success ratio kept the clients coming. As a result Muldoon gained the reputation of being able to repair the ravages of alcoholism, mental anguish, or sedentary living within a few weeks.

Muldoon's acquaintances with Depew, Root, Theodore Roosevelt, and General Leonard Wood served to make him a visible figure in New York state and national politics. During the 1910s Muldoon was a vocal advocate for the preparedness movement, supporting mandatory peacetime military training for all males and advocating physical culture instruction in schools. He was also an active member of the Grand Army of the Republic, by now having assumed credit for his brother's Civil War military career. In 1920 Muldoon, a Democrat by party affiliation, aided Leonard Wood's New York State campaign staff during Wood's unsuccessful run for the Republican presidential nomination.

In 1921 Muldoon was elected as the first chairman of the New York State Athletic Commission, which had been reestablished after the first commission was disbanded in 1917. He held the chairmanship for three years and then served on the commission panel until his death. Muldoon's regulation code for boxing and wrestling events was copied almost verbatim by many other state commissions during the 1920s as prize-fighting became more widely legalized in the United States. Muldoon's reign as boxing czar largely paralleled Judge Kenesaw Mountain Landis's stewardship over baseball, and Muldoon earned the nickname "The Iron Duke" for his austere edicts and perceived inflexibility. As commission chairman, Muldoon supported the color barrier that prevented African-American fighters from fighting white opponents. His most impassioned stance as chairman, however, came on the issue of banning smoking from Madison Square Garden. Muldoon's experiences as an athlete and a physical culturist led him to become fiercely opposed to the use of tobacco products, and he stood firmly behind his unpopular decision. In 1928 he and Gene Tunney created the Tunney-Muldoon Trophy, to be awarded to the heavyweight boxing champion.

Muldoon, who is generally reported to have been a lifelong bachelor (although some later sources claim that he had two short-lived marriages), died at his home in Purchase. He was entombed after a military funeral several days later.

• Muldoon's papers are located primarily at the Charles Dawson History Center, West Harrison, N.Y. Assorted papers, the Muldoon family Bible, and other information related to Muldoon and his family are at the Belfast Public Library, Belfast, N.Y. See also John Muldoon's military records and the papers of the New York State Athletic Commission at the New York State Archives, Albany, and the John Muldoon Papers, Manuscripts and Special Collections, New York State Public Library, Albany. Alvin Fay Harlow corrected erroneous "standard" bibliographical information in "Muldoon, William," *Dictionary of American Biography*, supp. 1 (1944). A good modern scholarly assessment of Muldoon's relationship with John L. Sullivan is Michael T. Isenberg, *John L. Sullivan and His America* (1988), although some of his basic biographical information on Muldoon was culled from inaccurate sources. Most of the widely available sources of biographical information on Muldoon contain inaccuracies, generally related to his birthdate and military record. These sources include Edward Van Every, *Muldoon: The Solid Man of Sport* (1929), Associated Press Biographical Sketch Number 847 (the primary source for most newspaper obituaries on Muldoon); and many of the newspaper articles about Muldoon that appeared during his later life.

WILLIAM MELTZER

MULFORD, Clarence Edward (3 Feb. 1883–10 May 1956), writer, was born in Streator, Illinois, the son of Clarence Cohansey Mulford, a boiler designer, and Minnie Grace Kline. The only child of the transient manufacturing engineer, Mulford preferred reading dime novels to schoolwork. After graduating from Utica (N.Y.) Academy in 1900, he decided against college and moved to New York City, where he joined the *Municipal Journal and Engineer* as a reporter. In 1907 he became a marriage license clerk in Brooklyn, a job he held until 1925, by which time he was earning far more money from his fiction writing.

Mulford's best-known fictional creation was the rugged cowboy Hopalong Cassidy. Popular in books, Hoppy achieved even greater fame as portrayed in a series of sixty-six low-budget motion pictures starring actor William Boyd. To Mulford's dismay, the celluloid Cassidy as depicted by studio-hired screenwriters was a clean-shaven, sanitized hero, not his gruff, tobacco-chewing, salt-of-the-earth cowpuncher of prose. Hopalong generated the first television merchandising bonanza when Boyd took the hero to the then-new medium in 1949 and promoted the character on everything from lunch boxes to hair tonic. *Time* reported in 1950, with only slight exaggeration, that U.S. supplies of black dyes were severely strained in keeping up with demand for products featuring the black-garbed hero.

Writing didn't come easily to Mulford. His early short stories, particularly, went through many revisions. He made his first sale to *Metropolitan Magazine* in 1904. Editor Caspar Whitney accepted eight Cassidy tales for *Outing Magazine* beginning in 1905. Mulford's first book, *Bar-20* (1907), collected these early short stories. His second, *The Orphan* (1908), was his first attempt at a novel and contains romantic elements reminiscent of Owen Wister's *The Virginian*. Mulford returned to his original characters for *Hopalong Cassidy* (1910). Bill Cassidy, Red Connor, Johnny Nelson, Buck Peters, Tex Ewalt, and others would thread in and out of an interconnected series of eighteen books over a 34-year period, in a western tapestry that touched on all facets of range history, from trail drives to ranch life to cowtowns.

The writer took inspiration from the gritty realism of Andy Adams's *The Log of a Cowboy* and the heroic gunfighters of Wister. He never developed great skill in characterization (most of his cowboys are indistinguishable), or in plotting (several storylines were repeated over the years). He explained that he never outlined his work ahead of time. "My characters are placed in a given setting and then I watch their reactions to what happens." Mulford introduced Cassidy in *Bar-20* as "a combination of irresponsibility, humor and good nature, love of fighting, and nonchalance when face to face with danger. His most prominent attribute was that of always getting into trouble without any intention of doing so; in fact, he was much aggrieved and surprised when it came."

Mulford refused to romanticize outlaws. Shanghai McHenry, who shows up in three novels, has almost become likable by *Hopalong Cassidy Takes Cards* (1937). Betraying his old gang, he claims he's reformed. When he is mortally shot, Hopalong observes that Shanghai would never have fit in with the Bar-20, where loyalty is paramount. Mulford asserted that his reliance on research was an advantage to accurate writing. He amassed primary reference materials and painstakingly wrote out 17,000 note cards on every topic of western American history, he said, except

mining. "I saw the West through the eyes of over two hundred different people," he told an interviewer. "This has proved an invaluable help in adding authenticity of location, style and everything dealing with the locale of my stories." When he did finally visit the West, in 1924, he was enormously disappointed (for one thing, the dry air spoiled his cigars).

Mulford's later books, in a style less stilted than the early ones, hold up the best. In *Trail Dust* (1934), for example, one can almost taste the grit as the Bar-20 crew tangles with phony trail cutters and survives a fierce thunderstorm and stampede. Mulford is confident in characterization and interplay. *Hopalong Cassidy and the Eagle's Brood* (1931) is an ambitious saga bringing together the Bar-20 crew and the heroes of three other Mulford novels in a humorous and well-paced adventure. *Hopalong Cassidy Takes Cards* finds the hero serving as a sheriff in Montana.

Ranking behind only Zane Grey and Max Brand as a popular western writer, Mulford in 1920 was still living with his widowed mother. That year he married longtime friend Eva E. Wilkinson, a divorcée with a daughter. They had no children of their own. After Mulford quit his Civil Service job, the family moved to a village home in Fryeburg, Maine, in 1926. The writer was now semiretired, earning $10,000 or more a year from his writing career. His hobbies included model shipbuilding, stamp collecting, amateur astronomy, and ham radio. He built a shooting range and collected weapons, including a Sharps rifle reputed to have been used to kill Sitting Bull. He had the Colt firearms firm make him a large-caliber revolver capable of hitting a target at 500 yards—just as Hopalong's did in one book.

With the exception of a 1920 version of *The Orphan* featuring William Farnum, Hollywood shrugged off Mulford's early attempts at selling his books for the movies. Then in 1935 producer Harry "Pop" Sherman obtained rights to the Cassidy series; Mulford didn't write screenplays or in any way participate in the movie-making. The first picture came out that year, featuring white-haired Boyd. Contrary to his expectations, Mulford hated the pictures. "Imagine, Hoppy wearing clothes like those Bill Boyd wears," he griped. "Why, it's absolute nonsense. If Hoppy ever showed up in a saloon in duds like that they'd shoot him down on sight."

The series remained in production for fourteen years. Mulford gave up writing after *Hopalong Cassidy Serves a Writ* (1941), in part out of creative frustration (the movie Hoppy was more popular now than the print version), and in part out of income tax considerations (he had a comfortable royalty from the pictures, and book sales were reenergized). He held no personal grudge against Boyd, and the two—a short, wizened writer and a tall, glowing movie actor—made quite a contrast when they posed for photos in 1949 on Boyd's visit to Fryeburg to negotiate television rights. Mulford's farsighted agent Daniel Nye had withheld those rights in the 1935 movie contracts, and the writer now enjoyed an even greater financial windfall. With six movies being made each year in the late 1930s, Mulford was earning $15,000 annually from movie rights, in addition to his book royalties. Records are not available, but indications are his earnings soared even higher in the 1950s; he received a percentage of the merchandising when the Cassidy name or image appeared on everything from chewing gum to wastebaskets.

Mulford died following lung surgery in Portland, Maine. His books have never gone out of print. Ironically, videocassette sales of the motion pictures and the hardcover reprinting forty years later of 1950s pastiche Hoppy novels written by Louis L'Amour under the pseudonym Tex Burns reenergized in the 1990s Mulford's name with the public.

• Mulford's papers, including his writing log and books from his western Americana reference collection, are in the Fryeburg (Maine) Library. His extensive hand-annotated card reference collection is held by the Library of Congress. Joseph A. Perham's master's thesis for the University of Maine, Orono, "Reflections on Hopalong Cassidy: A Study of Clarence E. Mulford" (1966), is an early assessment of the writer's career, but Bernard A. Drew, *Hopalong Cassidy: The Clarence E. Mulford Story* (1991), is the most complete biography and bibliography. Francis M. Nevins, *The Films of Hopalong Cassidy* (1988), contains brief biographical background but concentrates on cinematic history and is the most thorough of several books celebrating the Boyd depiction of Mulford's character. Nevins, *Bar-20: The Life of Clarence E. Mulford, Creator of Hopalong Cassidy, with Seven Original Stories Reprinted* (1993), covers similar biographical territory as Drew.

BERNARD A. DREW

MULHOLLAND, William (11 Sept. 1855–22 July 1935), engineer, was born in Belfast, County Antrim, Ireland, the son of Hugh Mulholland, a British Postal Service employee, and Ellen Deakers. Educated in the Dublin public schools, Mulholland spent some time at the Christian Brothers College (equivalent to an American high school) but did not complete his studies. Differences with his father led him at age fifteen to leave Ireland. He spent the next four years as a sailor on the merchant ship *Gleniffer* and in 1874 arrived in New York City. He then worked as a sailor on the Great Lakes and as a lumberjack in Michigan for a year. In 1875 he became a clerk in his uncle's drygoods store in Pittsburgh, Pennsylvania. While there he read Charles Nordhoff's *California: For Health, Pleasure and Residence* and decided to try his luck on the West Coast. In December 1876, accompanied by his brother Hugh, William took the Panama route to California, walking across the isthmus to save the $25 railroad fare. Arriving in San Francisco in February 1877, the brothers bought horses and rode south to Los Angeles.

In the 1870s Los Angeles was a small town of fewer than 10,000 people. Mulholland first found employment digging artesian wells in nearby Compton. In the spring of 1878 he found a job as a ditch tender with the privately owned Los Angeles City Water Company. His duties included keeping the *zanjas* (open water ditches) and the Los Angeles River free of bushes, trees, and other objects. He studied engineering in his spare time and rose in the company ranks until 1886, when he was appointed its superintendent. In July 1890 Mulholland married Lillie Ferguson; they had five children.

Benefiting from the real estate boom of the 1880s, transcontinental railroad connections, and a national advertising campaign that extolled southern California's climate and economic opportunities, Los Angeles had grown by 1900 into a major metropolitan area. With the city's population reaching 100,000, the Los Angeles City Water Company became unable to provide adequate service to city water users. After four years of litigation, the city bought out the company's control of the water distribution system. Mulholland had remained objective and neutral during the dispute. Recognizing his expertise, the city appointed him superintendent and chief engineer of the now municipally operated waterworks. Mulholland was faced with the growing demand for water service by an ever-increasing population and the limited capacity of the Los Angeles River. To sustain the city's growth, a new source of water needed to be found.

In 1904 Mulholland was approached by Fred Eaton, his predecessor as superintendent of the Los Angeles City Water Company. Eaton was interested in purchasing a ranch in the Eastern Sierra region, an area from which the Owens River flowed south through Inyo County and provided water for a small number of Eastern Sierra farms and ranches. Eaton saw an opportunity to make money by obtaining water rights to the Owens River and selling surplus water to Los Angeles, 250 miles to the south. Connection between valley and city would be made through construction of an aqueduct. Mulholland was intrigued by Eaton's ambitious scheme and accompanied him on a trip to the Eastern Sierra. He decided that a gravity-flow aqueduct was a feasible plan that would provide both water and electricity at minimum expense.

The Los Angeles Board of Water Commissioners, concerned over the increasing demands for water by the growing city, expressed considerable interest in Eaton's idea. Meanwhile, the U.S. Reclamation Service was conducting preliminary surveys in the Owens Valley area, which was under consideration for a federal reclamation project. Mulholland persuaded Eaton that the federal government would never permit a privately operated aqueduct to remove water from a region where a public reclamation project was planned. Eaton agreed to support the aqueduct as a wholly municipal enterprise, though he retained control of certain properties he had optioned, particularly Long Valley, the most feasible location for a storage reservoir.

Meanwhile, a group of Los Angeles businessmen, led by *Los Angeles Times* publisher Harrison Gray Otis and transit line owner Moses Sherman, also a member of the board of water commissioners, had formed a syndicate to purchase property in the San Fernando Valley. This syndicate would greatly benefit from an aqueduct that terminated in the northeast corner of the San Fernando Valley, the best place for the terminus from an engineering standpoint. Eaton went around Owens Valley, purchasing water rights from farmers who mistakenly believed he was acting as an agent for the Reclamation Service. By late spring of 1905 Eaton had turned the options over to the board of water commissioners. Los Angeles newspapers had agreed to keep the maneuver a secret, but the *Los Angeles Times* leaked the story on 5 July 1905, with the headline "Titanic Project to Give City a River."

Owens Valley residents were outraged at what they perceived as a betrayal of their interests by the federal government. They accused Joseph B. Lippincott, the Reclamation Service engineer in charge of the surveys, of collusion with the city to steal the valley's water. A federal investigation cleared Lippincott of wrongdoing but blamed him for poor judgment.

Mulholland was not personally involved in the purchase of the water rights options and had no connection with the real estate syndicate. His main concern was providing water to the people of Los Angeles. Rainfall in southern California averaged about fifteen inches a year, but there had been prolonged periods of drought, and the Los Angeles River could supply at most a city population of 250,000. By 1905 the population of Los Angeles had reached 200,000 with thousands more continuing to be attracted by the city boosterism and advertising. The city scheduled an election for 7 September 1905 on the purchase of the water rights and the necessary engineering surveys for $1.5 million. Although there was some opposition, the voters overwhelmingly approved the proposal. On 12 June 1907 the voters approved $23 million in bonds for the construction of the aqueduct. Los Angeles also gained the approval of President Theodore Roosevelt, who declared that the needs of urban Los Angeles took precedence over the rural Owens Valley.

In addition to his duties as chief engineer of the Bureau of Water Works and Supply, Mulholland assumed command of the aqueduct construction project. Surveys of the route were carefully taken. Contemporaries considered the project second only to the building of the Panama Canal. Mulholland hired talented young engineers to supervise the field work, and the project provided employment for more than 5,000 workers. Construction began in 1908. Mulholland's estimates of time and cost proved astonishingly prescient. By the end of 1913 the aqueduct was completed at under the estimated cost.

To celebrate the completion of the aqueduct, Los Angeles planned a gala event for 5 November 1913. Some 40,000 people gathered at the Aqueduct Cascades at Sylmar in the San Fernando Valley. Mulholland's wife, stricken with cancer, was unable to attend the celebration. One after another, civic dignitaries orated in praise of the city's accomplishment. Mulholland had insisted on keeping in close communication regarding his ailing wife before he would attend the event. When it was his turn to speak, Mulholland proclaimed, "There it is. Take it!" as the headgates were opened, and Owens River water flowed down the cascade.

During the next ten years Mulholland gained an international reputation as an expert on water resource development. He served as a consultant to cities such as Sacramento, Seattle, and San Francisco. Among the social organizations to which he belonged were the California, Sunset, and Celtic clubs, and professionally he was a member of the American Society of Civil Engineers, the Engineers and Architects of Southern California, and the Seismological Society of America. Honorary memberships were bestowed on him by the American Water Works Association, the National Association of Power Engineers, and the Tau Beta Pi fraternity.

Even as honors and awards came his way, Mulholland continued to supervise the growth of the city's water system, which in 1925 was merged with the power bureau to become the Los Angeles Department of Water and Power. Mulholland had believed that Owens River water would take care of the city's long-range water needs, but by the early 1920s the city's growth had outstripped the most liberal population projections. In 1920 the population of Los Angeles was 576,000; ten years later it topped a million. A prolonged drought prompted Mulholland to begin preliminary surveys of a second aqueduct that would connect Los Angeles to the Colorado River. Meanwhile, new problems were developing in the Owens Valley.

When the Owens River Aqueduct was completed in 1913, Eastern Sierra residents resigned themselves to the realities of the situation. The city's intake lay south of the more developed area of Owens Valley, where irrigation canals had been dug and where Bishop had become a small but important town serving the surrounding region. Finding its water needs in a dry period were falling short of availability, Los Angeles began in the 1920s buying Owens Valley farms and letting the land return to its natural state. Bishop merchants protested a policy that adversely affected their businesses as the valley began to dry up. Los Angeles also purchased control of the major ditch companies that utilized Owens River water. In retaliation against the city's policies, some people resorted to violence, dynamiting the aqueduct numerous times between 1924 and 1927. Mulholland angrily issued orders that submachine guns be given to guards and that the aqueduct be patrolled.

The "water war," as it came to be called, ended dramatically in August 1927 when the leading Owens Valley bank closed its doors, and the bank's owners, the Watterson brothers, who had been leaders in the dispute against Los Angeles, were indicted. Shocked residents learned that the bankers had embezzled funds from depositors. Many Owens Valley residents lost their life savings as the result of the bank failure. Ironically, Eaton lost control of his Long Valley property because the bank had a note on the ranch. Mulholland and Eaton had ended their friendship over Eaton's refusal to allow the city to construct a storage reservoir at Long Valley in Mono County, north of Inyo County.

Mulholland constructed more than two dozen reservoirs along the aqueduct route, but the lack of a major storage reservoir in the Eastern Sierra caused him to decide to have such a facility built in southern California. In 1924 construction began on the St. Francis Dam in San Francisquito Canyon, north of the San Fernando Valley. This dam was completed in 1926 and, when filled to capacity, contained more than 38,000 acre-feet of water.

Shortly before midnight on 12 March 1928, the St. Francis Dam collapsed. More than 450 people were killed by the terrible flood. Several investigating committees attempted to determine why the dam had failed. Theories ranged from use of substandard materials to defective foundation rock. For many years it was generally believed that inadequate exploration of the foundations had caused the dam to be imperfectly built. Not until the 1990s did a geological examination reveal a subterranean fault that no investigation of the 1920s could have found.

Mulholland himself suspected sabotage—the last round of water war dynamiting—but did not advance this view at the coroner's inquest. He said, "I alone am the man," when asked who was responsible for the disaster. Before the year ended he resigned as chief engineer of the Department of Water and Power and went into retirement, though he continued to serve as an adviser on city water problems. In December 1934 Mulholland had a cerebral hemorrhage, which left him incapacitated, and he died in Los Angeles the following July.

Mulholland's contributions to his adopted city were remembered both during and after his lifetime. In 1924 the Mulholland Highway was dedicated in his honor. Mulholland Dam in Hollywood, completed in 1927, was named for him. After his death, funds were collected for a memorial fountain to be erected at Los Feliz Boulevard and Riverside Drive, where he had begun his career as a ditch tender. Mulholland Junior High School in Van Nuys is also named for him.

Although during his lifetime Mulholland had made enemies, he was respected by all for his dedication and integrity. Lippincott, who left the Reclamation Service in 1906 to become Mulholland's assistant chief engineer on the aqueduct construction project, said in his 1941 profile of Mulholland, "The true success of a man's life may be gauged by the benefit he has rendered the community in which he has lived. By that standard Mulholland should be judged as one of our very best citizens." Mulholland witnessed the growth of Los Angeles from a small town to the dominant city in southern California, and he was in large part responsible for that growth through his commitment to long-range planning for the water resources necessary for a thirsty city.

• Mulholland's long record of service to the Los Angeles Department of Water and Power is open to qualified researchers in the DWP Archives. The most recent examination of his life and work is Margaret Leslie Davis, *Rivers in the Desert: William Mulholland and the Inventing of Los Angeles* (1993). Important recent studies on the Los Angeles–Owens Valley water controversy include Abraham Hoffman, *Vision or Villainy: Origins of the Owens Valley–Los Angeles Water Controversy* (1981); William Kahrl, *Water and Power: The Conflict over Los Angeles' Water Supply in the Owens Valley* (1982); and Remi Nadeau, *The Water Seekers*, 3d ed. (1993). Biographical studies include Robert W. Matson, *William Mulholland: A Forgotten Forefather* (1976); Joseph B. Lippincott, "William Mulholland—Engineer, Pioneer, Raconteur," *Civil Engineering* 11 (Feb. and Mar. 1941): 105–7, 161–64; and H. A. Van Norman, "William Mulholland," American Society of Civil Engineers, *Transactions* 101 (1936): 1604–8. An obituary is in the *Los Angeles Times*, 23 July 1935.

ABRAHAM HOFFMAN

MULLAN, John (31 July 1830–28 Dec. 1909), army explorer, road builder, and lawyer, was born in Norfolk, Virginia, the son of John Mullan, a civil servant, and Mary Bright. The eldest of ten children, Mullan grew up in Annapolis, Maryland, where his father was postmaster at the U.S. Naval Academy. He received his education, beginning at the age of nine, at St. John's College in Annapolis, from which he received a B.A. in 1847 and an M.A. in 1855. Family tradition holds that Mullan sought a personal interview with President James Polk, who subsequently tendered him an appointment to the U.S. Military Academy. Whether or not this is true, it is likely that Mullan's father's connections with the military establishment played a role.

Mullan enrolled at West Point in 1848, graduating fifteenth in his class in 1852, whereupon he received a commission as a lieutenant in the artillery. The next year he volunteered for assignment to the northern railway survey headed by Governor Isaac I. Stevens of Washington Territory. This began a ten-year period of exploration and road building in the Pacific Northwest that is the basis for Mullan's reputation. The army transferred Mullan to the topographical engineers, and Stevens assigned him to a party bringing supplies up the Missouri River to Fort Benton. When he arrived in late summer, Mullan received his first independent assignment to explore the area of present Montana south and west of Fort Benton with particular attention to the Rocky Mountain passes. He located the pass that now bears his name near present Helena and located a route from the Missouri River to Clark's Fork, which he correctly suggested would be practical for either a wagon road or a railroad.

Impressed by Mullan's first effort, Stevens left him behind in the Bitterroot Valley to act as an unofficial emissary to the Flatheads and to continue explorations. During the winter of 1853–1854, Mullan explored the rugged territory south of the Bitterroot Valley as far as Fort Hall. Typical of the hardship was the crossing of Medicine Lodge Pass on the present Montana-Idaho boundary through three-foot-high snow drifts, strong winds, and below-freezing temperatures. Mullan with characteristic understatement described the day's travel as "uncomfortable." He also explored routes across the Bitterroots in present northern Idaho before rendezvousing with Stevens in Olympia late in 1854. In his official report, Stevens praised

Mullan for his contributions to geographic knowledge garnered under circumstances when most men, Stevens believed, would have refused to venture out. Mullan had detailed the terrain of the northern Rockies and Bitterroots while maintaining a harmonious relationship with the Flatheads and other tribes.

Early in 1855 Stevens sent Mullan to Washington, D.C., to lobby for funds to continue the survey's work and for a railroad along the northern route. Both objectives failed primarily because of the sectional dispute. Mullan returned to military duty during 1855–1857, serving in Florida, in Baton Rouge, and at Baltimore's Fort McHenry. In 1857 Stevens became the delegate to Congress from Washington Territory. Realizing that a railroad was unlikely at any time in the near future, he pushed for construction of a military road from the head of navigation at Fort Benton to the Walla Walla Valley. Congress made an appropriation of $100,000, and Stevens successfully lobbied for Mullan's appointment to head the project.

On arriving in the territory Mullan found himself in the middle of a war occasioned by the defeat of Colonel Edward Steptoe's command. Mullan was attached to the punitive expedition of Colonel George Wright as an aide and topographical engineer and participated in that capacity at the battles of Four Lakes and Spokane Plain near present Spokane in 1858. With the Indians subdued, but in some cases still hostile, Mullan began his road building the next year, proceeding north from Walla Walla to Lake Coeur d'Alene, then turning east toward Fort Benton, retracing the route he had explored during the railroad survey. Additional appropriations allowed Mullan to complete the more than 600-mile route by 1863, although wagons had begun to move over the road well before completion. The road represented a major engineering effort for which Mullan deservedly received high praise (and a promotion to captain in 1862); however, even when the road was finished, sections of it remained barely passable for wagons. Although the route, which came to be called the Mullan Road, proved useful for the movement of goods into the expanding Inland Empire of the Pacific Northwest, particularly after the discovery of gold in 1863, it never met the high expectations of its adherents. The major supply routes were from the south and west, and most immigrants continued to follow the Oregon Trail rather than the more northerly alternative. Mullan produced two major reports and an immigrant guide during this period, "Topographical Memoir of Colonel Wright's Campaign" (1859), "Report on the Construction of a Military Road from Fort Walla Walla to Fort Benton" (1863), and *Miners' and Travelers' Guide . . . via the Missouri and Columbia Rivers* (1865).

Upon completion of the road, Mullan returned east, where he married Rebecca Williamson of Baltimore on 28 April 1863; the union produced five children, of whom three survived infancy. Despite the fact that the nation was in the middle of the Civil War, Mullan resigned from the army and returned to Washington Territory, where, in partnership with three of his brothers, he began ranching in the Walla Walla Valley. His reasons for leaving the military are not entirely clear. Rebecca Mullan later said that he wanted to provide financially not only for her but also for other members of his family. It is also possible that Mullan, a lifelong Democrat, did not ardently support the Lincoln administration's war policies. The ranch failed, apparently at least in part due to family squabbling, and equally unsuccessful was a mail contract Mullan secured to connect Chico, California, with the Idaho gold mines. The mail contract failed, according to the Mullans, because of a more favorable contract granted to a competitor by the Radical Republicans.

In 1867 Mullan moved to San Francisco, where he continued law studies he had begun sometime earlier, and after a few months was admitted to the bar. Combining his engineering knowledge with the new profession, he become successful in the practice of land law. In the mid-1870s Mullan became the agent for California, Oregon, Nevada, and Washington to collect a variety of claims believed owed to citizens by the federal government. Apparently to better prosecute these claims, Mullan in 1878 moved to Washington, D.C., where he practiced law until ill health forced his retirement around 1904. He died in Washington, D.C. Among his clients was the Catholic Board of Missions, whose interests in western Indian reservations he pursued. This had led in the 1890s to Mullan being retained by the Spokane and Coeur d'Alene tribes, against whom he had fought in 1858, as their attorney in the capital.

John Mullan worked diligently to fill in the details of the geography of the upper Rocky Mountain region that was known only in broad outline before the 1850s. The culmination of his work was one of the first roads in the far West built, to the extent possible given the funds available, according to the engineering standards of the industrial age.

• There are no collections of Mullan papers in public repositories. His official correspondence is scattered throughout various record groups in the National Archives, in particular those of the Bureau of Indian Affairs and the Department of the Army. His most important reports, "Topographical Memoir of Colonel Wright's Campaign" and "Report on the Construction of a Military Road from Fort Walla Walla to Fort Benton" are published as Senate Exec. Doc. no. 32, 35th Cong., 2d Sess. and Senate Exec. Doc. no. 43, 37th Cong., 3d Sess., respectively. Scholarly books or articles on Mullan have not yet been published. Two accounts rely heavily on a memoir written by Rebecca Mullan in the 1890s, Louis C. Coleman and Leo Reiman, comps., *Captain John Mullan; His Life; Building the Mullan Road; As It Is Today and Interesting Tales of Occurrences along the Road* (1968), and Addison Howard, "Captain John Mullan," *Washington Historical Quarterly* 25 (1934): 185–202. The best assessment of Mullan is the brief note by Samuel Flagg Bemis, "Captain John Mullan and the Engineers' Frontier," *Washington Historical Quarterly* 14 (1923): 201–5.

KENT D. RICHARDS

MULLANE, Anthony John (20 Feb. 1859–26 Apr. 1944), major league baseball player, was born in Cork, Ireland, the son of Irish immigrants who came to the

United States when he was five years old. (The names of his parents and other details of his early and personal life are unknown.) A gifted athlete, Mullane grew proficient in boxing, roller skating, ice skating, and baseball and was an accomplished musician. He decided to concentrate on baseball since the sport was becoming recognized as the national pastime.

Mullane first played professional baseball in 1880 when he signed a contract with an independent team in Akron, Ohio. He joined the Detroit Wolverines of the National League the following season, but he hurt his right arm during a field meet in which he was credited with throwing a ball 416 feet, 7¾ inches. While recovering, he learned to effectively throw left-handed. Although he became an ambidextrous pitcher, he told a sportswriter many years later that he "never called on my left hand unless we were playing an exhibition game, or in practice for the amusement of my friends." Still, he was able to use his ambidexterity to great advantage. Since ballplayers then wore no gloves, he was able to field and throw with either hand, and his pickoff move was said to be remarkable.

In 1882 Mullane, who stood 5'10½" and weighed 165 pounds, joined the Louisville Eclipse in a new major league, the American Association. He pitched in 55 games, won 30, and threw the league's first no-hitter against Cincinnati on 11 September. The next year he switched teams again, to the St. Louis Browns, and won 35 games against only 15 losses.

Before the 1884 season Mullane signed a contract to play for the St. Louis Maroons of the Union Association, still another new major league. Before a pitch was thrown, however, he switched back to the American Association's Toledo Blue Stockings when they agreed to meet his salary demand. There he won a career-high 36 games and sometimes pitched to catcher Moses Fleetwood Walker, the last African-American to play major league baseball before the imposition of a color line.

The Toledo franchise lasted only one season, after which Mullane's contract was sold back to the Browns. He refused to accept this deal and signed instead with the Cincinnati Red Stockings. A protest from the St. Louis owner, Chris Von der Ahe, led to Mullane's suspension for all of 1885. In 1886 he rejoined Cincinnati and remained with the Red Stockings until the middle of the 1893 season.

Mullane won 33 games in 1886 and 31 in 1887, giving him five consecutive 30-win seasons, and he had 26 wins in 1888. On 30 June 1892 he hooked up with Addison Gumbert of the Chicago Colts to fashion the longest major league game played to that date, a 7–7 tie ended by darkness after twenty innings. Both pitchers pitched the entire game, and neither gave up a run after the fifth inning.

Mullane also played every other position except catcher. Hitting both left- and right-handed, he compiled a .243 batting average in 2,720 at-bats.

Mullane was a free spirit and a dandy who did not smoke, drink, or gamble. His handlebar mustache and elegant attire earned him the nickname "Count" and

made him a great favorite with fans. Cincinnati's owner, Aaron Stern, who noticed that female attendance increased sharply whenever Mullane pitched, established an early version of Ladies' Day by announcing that Mullane would start every home game the Red Stockings played on a Tuesday.

Despite his sober demeanor, Mullane regularly battled club owners to get the salary he thought he deserved. In 1892 he left the Red Stockings, then in the National League, after refusing to take a pay cut, and he played a while for Butte, Montana, in the Mountain League. In June 1893 the Reds traded him to the Baltimore Orioles, from where he was dealt during the next season to the Cleveland Spiders. He dropped to the minor leagues in 1895, playing for St. Paul in the Western League for three seasons and for Toronto in the Eastern League in 1899.

In all, Mullane won 284 major league games against 220 losses. He led the American Association twice in shutouts and once in games started, strikeouts, and winning percentage. He never played on a championship team, and today he is largely forgotten except by students of nineteenth-century baseball.

After his baseball career was over, Mullane became a police detective in Chicago. He was married several times and had at least one child. He died in Chicago.

• There is no scholarly biography of Mullane. Clipping files on him are held by the National Baseball Library, Cooperstown, N.Y., and by the *Sporting News*, St. Louis, Mo. Obituaries are in the *Chicago Tribune*, 27 Apr. 1944, and the *Sporting News*, 4 May 1944.

STEVEN P. GIETSCHIER

MULLANY, James Robert Madison (26 Oct. 1818–17 Sept. 1887), naval officer, was born in New York City, the son of Colonel James Robert Mullany, a quartermaster general of the U.S. Army, and Maria Burger. His private life is obscure, but he was twice married and had at least one son.

Mullany entered the U.S. Navy as a midshipman in January 1832, when he was only thirteen. He served in the Mediterranean on the frigates *Constellation* and *United States* until 1838, when he was promoted to passed midshipman, signifying that he was qualified for promotion to lieutenant. During the 1840s he served in both the Brazil Squadron (on the *Dolphin*) and the Home Squadron (on the *Missouri*) and as acting master of the *Somers*. From 1844 to 1848 he served as one of many officers on the Coast Survey, taking and recording soundings and preparing charts. During the war with Mexico (1846–1848), Mullany participated in the naval expedition to Tabasco, and after the war he served on the sloop *St. Louis* and the frigate *Brandywine* in the Brazil Squadron (1848–1850).

Mullany's most important service was during the Civil War. He was the commanding officer of the *Wyandotte* at Pensacola in the spring of 1861 and participated in the relief expedition to Fort Pickens on 12 April. Promoted to commander in October, Mullany was assigned in April 1862 to the side-wheel steamer

Bienville, a command he retained for the rest of the war. In that capacity he served first under Rear Admiral Samuel F. Du Pont, who commanded the South Atlantic Blockading Squadron, and later under Rear Admiral David G. Farragut, who commanded the West Gulf Blockading Squadron.

While serving in the South Atlantic Blockading Squadron (Apr. 1862–Mar. 1863), Mullany compiled a reputation as a reliable and conscientious skipper. His vessel captured a total of eleven blockade runners during the war, including the iron steamer *Patras* (27 May 1862), which was carrying a cargo valued at $400,000. When the Navy Department transferred Mullany and the *Bienville* to the West Gulf Blockading Squadron, Du Pont wrote to Farragut, "They have sent you one of my best ships, indeed my best blockader, with a tiptop captain."

In August 1864 Mullany participated in the naval attack on Mobile Bay. Because the *Bienville* was undergoing repairs, Farragut temporarily assigned Mullany to command the steam sloop *Oneida*. The U.S. squadron entered Mobile Bay in pairs on 5 August 1864, with the *Oneida* at the very end of the line lashed to the *Galena*'s starboard side, closest to the Confederate forts guarding the entrance. As a result, the *Oneida* took a heavy pounding from the guns of Fort Morgan. At one point a shell exploded the *Oneida*'s starboard boiler, scalding sixteen crewmen. Inside Mobile Bay, Mullany's vessel was one of several to take on the Confederate ironclad *Tennessee*. Mullany was wounded several times in the fight, including a severe wound in his left arm incurred when the *Tennessee* raked the *Oneida* from astern. Eventually his left arm had to be amputated. Afterward Farragut specifically commended Mullany for his gallant conduct during the engagement.

After the war Mullany was promoted to captain (July 1866), and in 1870 he became commodore of the Mediterranean Squadron. He subsequently served as commanding officer of the Philadelphia Navy Yard (1872–1874) and the North Atlantic Squadron (1874–1876). He was promoted to rear admiral in June 1874. Admiral Mullany retired in 1879 and died at his home in Bryn Mawr, Pennsylvania.

• Mullany's papers are in the Floyd T. Starr Collection at the Historical Society of Pennsylvania in Philadelphia. The raw data on Mullany's Civil War service is in *The Official Records of the Union and Confederate Navies in the War of the Rebellion* (30 vols., 1894–1922). Mullany is also prominently mentioned in Samuel F. Du Pont, *Samuel Francis Du Pont: A Selection from His Civil War Letters*, ed. John D. Hayes (3 vols., 1969), and in John B. Marchand, *Charleston Blockade: The Journals of John B. Marchand, U.S. Navy, 1861–1862*, ed. Craig L. Symonds (1976).

CRAIG L. SYMONDS

MULLEN, Arthur Francis (31 May 1873–14 July 1938), attorney and Democratic politician, was born in Kingston, Ontario, the son of James Mullen and Emily Clancy, farmers. Mullen moved with his parents to Nebraska when he was nine years old. After graduating from normal schools in Fremont and Wayne, Mullen taught school for three years before reading law in Nebraska and serving as deputy treasurer of Holt County. He completed his legal education at the University of Michigan, from which he was graduated in 1900. Returning to Nebraska, he served three terms as Holt's county attorney from 1901 to 1907. In 1903 Mullen married Mary Theresa Dolan, with whom he had two children.

During 1908 Mullen became active in statewide politics as the Nebraska campaign manager for William Jennings Bryan, the Democratic presidential candidate. Although Bryan lost the election, he carried his home state by a narrow margin, thanks to Mullen's efforts. Mullen later became an outspoken political opponent of Bryan, whom he accused of deserting progressivism and betraying political allies.

From 1910 to 1911 Mullen filled an unexpired term as the state's attorney general. As attorney general Mullen argued *Shallenberger v. First State Bank of Holstein* (1911), in which the U.S. Supreme Court sustained the constitutionality of a Nebraska statute that provided public guaranty of bank deposits. The Court's decision in that case helped to signal its growing receptivity toward progressive legislation. In 1911 Mullen moved to Omaha, where he maintained a law office for most of the remainder of his life. He had a wide-ranging commercial practice and also served as counsel in many cases involving public issues.

Mullen's most significant case was *Meyer v. Nebraska* (1923), in which he successfully appealed the conviction of a Lutheran parochial schoolteacher who had been fined for violating a Nebraska law that prohibited the teaching of foreign languages in elementary schools. In striking down the law, the U.S. Supreme Court endorsed many of Mullen's arguments about the sanctity of personal rights. It declared that the Fourteenth Amendment of the Constitution prohibits the states from infringing various individual liberties, including the right to engage in one's chosen vocation, to acquire useful knowledge, to worship freely, and to marry, establish a home, and raise children.

In addition to nullifying prohibitions on foreign language instruction that had been enacted by many states in the wake of World War I, the Court's decision in *Meyer* helped to retard a resurgence of nativism that threatened the rights of ethnic and religious minorities. Mullen, a devout Roman Catholic, perceived that the language laws were part of a broader assault on parochial education. *Meyer* provided the doctrinal basis for the Supreme Court's 1925 decision in *Pierce v. Society of Sisters*, which invalidated an Oregon law that required elementary school age children to attend public schools. The *Meyer* and *Pierce* decisions eventually provided the basic precedents for the Court's recognition of a right to privacy.

Active in Democratic politics during most of his life, Mullen served as Democratic national committeeman in Nebraska from 1916 to 1920 and again from 1924 to 1934. In this capacity he worked for abolition of the rule requiring a two-thirds vote for presidential nominations at national conventions. The abolition of the rule in 1936 helped prevent the type of fractious conventions that sometimes had produced weak compromise candidates. Mullen served as floor leader for Franklin D. Roosevelt at the Democratic National Convention in 1932. His role in helping to arrange for Roosevelt's selection of John Nance Garner as vice president enabled Roosevelt to win the critical votes of the Texas delegation. After the convention Mullen served as vice chairman of Roosevelt's campaign committee and was instrumental in winning support for Roosevelt among midwestern progressives.

After trying unsuccessfully to be named attorney general and turning down an appointment to the U.S. Court of Appeals for the Eighth Circuit, Mullen opened an office in Washington in 1933, where he practiced law for several years. Although Mullen remained an admirer of Roosevelt, he became increasingly critical of many Roosevelt programs that enhanced the power of the president at the expense of Congress and the states. Like many other progressives who retained a suspicion of concentrated economic and political power, Mullen warned that the expansion of the federal government threatened individual freedom. Ill health caused Mullen to close his Washington office late in 1937 and return to his home in Omaha, where he died.

Mullen was one of the most influential progressive midwestern Democrats of his era and a significant example of a progressive whose advocacy of social and economic reform was tempered by a devotion to states' rights. Mullen's most lasting legacy and the accomplishment of which he was most proud was his victory in *Meyer v. Nebraska*, which expanded the U.S. Supreme Court's role as a guardian of personal liberty against infringements by the states.

• Mullen's papers, including court briefs and correspondence with significant political figures, are located at Creighton University in Omaha. His autobiography, *Western Democrat*, was published posthumously in 1940. His role in the language cases is discussed in Thomas O'Brien Hanley, "A Western Democrat's Quarrel with the Language Laws," *Nebraska History* 50 (Summer 1969): 151–71. An obituary is in the *New York Times*, 15 July 1938.

WILLIAM G. ROSS

MULLER, Hermann Joseph (21 Dec. 1890–5 Apr. 1967), geneticist, was born in New York City, the son of Hermann Joseph Muller, a manufacturer of objects of art in metal, and Frances M. Lyons. Muller attended Morris High School in the Bronx; he was interested in science and helped organize a science club in high school and a biology club in college. He went on to Columbia University, obtaining his bachelor's degree in zoology in 1910 and his master's degree in physiology a year later. While at Columbia, Muller studied with the Nobel Prize–winning geneticist Thomas Hunt Morgan and honed his research skills experimenting with the fruit fly, which would feature in many of his major discoveries. Muller left for a year to attend Cornell Medical School but returned to Colum-

bia for his doctorate, which he received in 1915 or 1916. While completing his Ph.D., Muller was recruited by Julian Huxley to teach genetics at the Rice Institute and soon became head of the department. In 1918 he left to become a zoology instructor at Columbia, where he stayed for two years.

In 1920 Muller moved to the University of Texas as associate professor of zoology; he was promoted to professor in 1925. He married Jessie Marie Jacobs in 1923; they had one child. His work on the genetics of fruit flies led to his discovery, in 1927, that when the flies were irradiated by X rays, obvious mutations soon occurred. There were flies with no wings, one wing, two or more wings, and even flies with no legs and two heads. His landmark article "Artificial Transmutation of the Gene," published in *Science* (66: 84–87) the same year, summarized the findings.

As early as 1932 Muller's views on genetics in reference to humans were making their way into the newspapers. In an article in the *New York Times* (24 Aug. 1932), Muller was quoted as saying, "Individual economic considerations rather than considerations of the genetic worth of the future generations must in the main govern human reproduction, in so far as the latter is voluntary at all, and eugenics must remain an idle dream." At the Third International Congress of Eugenics, Muller criticized those who believed that the "lower classes" were genetically inferior; he noted, according to the same *New York Times* article, "Certain slum districts of our cities constitute veritable factories for the production of criminality among those who happen to be born in them, whether their parents were of the criminal class or not."

That same year Muller's research, done with N. Timofeev-Ressovsky of the Kaiser Wilhelm Institute for Animal Research in Berlin, was also noted in the popular press. They presented their work at the Sixth International Congress of Genetics in Ithaca, New York, showing how X rays or gamma rays could qualitatively alter genes. They noted that mutations resulted not only from subtracting or adding part of the gene but also from rearranging the parts of the gene itself; they went on to speculate that desirable genetic changes might be possible.

During his tenure at Texas, Muller had the opportunity to take leaves to work first in Germany and then in the Soviet Union. In the USSR he first worked as senior geneticist at the Institute of Genetics in Leningrad (1933–1934) and then moved to Moscow, where he stayed until 1937. While in Moscow Muller reportedly was able to create diverse mutations of fruit flies generated by X-ray radiation. Having been divorced from his first wife in 1934, Muller married Dorothea J. Kantorowicz in 1939; they had one child.

After leaving the politically hostile Soviet Union for his own safety, Muller took the position of research associate and lecturer at the Institute for Animal Genetics at the University of Edinburgh. In Muller's obituary in the *New York Times* he is quoted as saying, "I went to Russia hopefully but became disillusioned when I saw how genetics was being perverted by dictator Stalin to fit the Communist party line." Part of that perversion manifested itself in purges of the Soviet scientific community in the 1930s and 1940s; many were taken away from their homes and universities to be executed or exiled. Muller also came to disagree and publicly denounce the ideas of the Soviet scientist Trofim D. Lysenko, who had Stalin's support for his idea that animals and plants were able to transmit characteristics acquired from their environment. Muller proposed a more detached, scientific idea of inheritance, but the entire field of genetics was all but abolished in the USSR before his eyes during the 1930s.

Muller stayed in Scotland until 1940. He then returned to the United States and spent the rest of World War II at Amherst College in the biology department. In 1945 he accepted a professorship at Indiana University, Bloomington, which he held for almost twenty years. That year he was one of three scientists at the university who received a $95,000 grant from the Rockefeller Foundation for a six-year genetics research program.

Muller continued to watch the developments in Soviet science with great interest. Lysenkoism continued its reign, and in protest Muller resigned his membership in the Academy of Sciences of the Soviet Union in 1948. Subsequently, he was denounced as a scientist who betrayed "the real interests of science." Ironically, at the same time it was announced that Lysenko had received the prestigious Order of Lenin for his work.

When Muller retired from his teaching duties at Indiana University in 1964 he remained on the faculty as professor emeritus. He also served as a member of the Institute for Advanced Learning in Medical Sciences at City of Hope Medical Center in Duarte, California (1964–1965) and as visiting professor in the departments of zoology and genetics at the University of Wisconsin (1965–1966).

In the late 1950s and 1960s Muller turned his efforts to the idea of selective breeding by proposing that the sperm of notable men be frozen and kept in sperm banks for future use. Although critics said this was tantamount to breeding people like animals, Muller countered with the optimistic opinion that if war, dictatorship, overpopulation, and fascism could be avoided, humanity could take the information it had gained from genetics and apply it to yield greater capabilities and richer human lives. Frozen sperm, collected early in life, could also be used for procreation, avoiding the negative effects of radiation, including developmental defects in the offspring of affected men.

Muller campaigned throughout the 1950s and 1960s for a ban on nuclear weapons and greater awareness of the negative effects of a hydrogen bomb explosion. He also warned that X rays were capable of causing mutations that might not show up in the patient but might affect his or her descendants. This was not a universally accepted view at the time. In 1955 Muller was barred by the Atomic Energy Commission from presenting a paper at a conference that addressed the idea of genetic damage produced by radiation.

Muller was a prolific author, with more than 370 papers to his credit, as well as a number of books, including *Mechanism of Heredity* (1915, 1922) and *Out of the Night: A Biologist's View of the Future* (1935). He coauthored *Genetics, Medicine and Man* (1947) and *Studies in Genetics* (1962).

The most notable award Muller received was the 1946 Nobel Prize in physiology and medicine for his work on heredity and mutations created by X-ray manipulation. He was also the corecipient, with William E. Castle of Harvard University, of the first Kimber Genetics Award, presented by the National Academy of Sciences in 1955. He received the Darwin Medal in 1959 and the Alexander Hamilton Award in 1960.

Among Muller's professional memberships were those in the American Academy of Arts and Sciences, American Genetic Association, American Philosophical Society, American Society of Zoologists, Society for Experimental Biology and Medicine, and American Humanist Association; he served as president of the last from 1955 to 1959. He was voted an honorary life membership in the American Institute of Biological Sciences in 1961. He was also a member of the Royal Danish and Royal Swedish academies of science, the Royal Society in London, Genetical Society of Japan, Japan Academy, National Institute of Sciences in India, and World Academy. Muller died in Bloomington, Indiana.

The year Muller received the Nobel Prize, an editorial in the *New York Times* (3 Nov. 1946) noted, "Professor Muller did as much as any single man, William Bateson and Thomas Hunt Morgan not excepted, to raise genetics, or the science of heredity, from its humble beginnings to its present position. Biologists will rejoice that such brilliant work has been fittingly recognized."

• Most of Muller's papers are at the Lilly Library at Indiana University, Bloomington; additional material is at the American Philosophical Library, Philadelphia, Pa. Muller's views of Soviet science are highlighted in his autobiographical account, *Out of the Night* (1935). In addition to the works cited in this article, he contributed to *Bibliography on the Genetics of Drosophila* (1939) and *The Modern Concept of Nature: Essays on Theoretical Biology and Evolution* (1973). A complete bibliography of Muller's writings is in G. Pontecorvo, ed., *Biographical Memoirs of Fellows of the Royal Society* 14 (1968). See Mark B. Adam, "Eugenics in Russia," in *The Wellborn Science* (1990). Other comments by Muller on the Soviet system can be found in "Observations of Biological Science in Russia," *Scientific Monthly* 16 (1923), and "Resignation of Professor Muller from Academy of Sciences of the USSR," *Science* 108 (1948), as well as in "Science under Soviet Totalitarianism," in *Totalitarianism*, ed. Carl J. Friedrich (1954). Elof Axel Carlson wrote a biography of Muller, *Genes, Radiation and Society: The Life and Work of J. H. Muller* (1981). Carlson also edited *Man's Future Birthright: Essays on Science and Humanity* (1973), which includes some of Muller's ideas. His obituary is in the *New York Times*, 6 Apr. 1967.

MARIANNE FEDUNKIW STEVENS

MULLETT, Alfred Bult (8 Apr. 1834–20 Oct. 1890), architect, was born in Taunton, Somerset, England, the son of Augustin Aish Mullett, a draper, and Hannah Bult. The family moved to Glendale, Ohio, near Cincinnati, in 1845. The Mulletts became farmers, and Alfred attended Farmer's College, now the University of Cincinnati, from 1852 to 1854. By 1857 he had entered the architectural office of Isaiah Rogers in Cincinnati, and he became a partner in 1859 or 1860; little else is known of his life or work until he visited Europe in 1860. Most of Mullett's diaries were destroyed, but a detailed itinerary from 13 October to 7 December 1860 lists the countries and cities he visited and the buildings he saw. After returning to the United States, Mullett held a minor position in the Treasury Department during 1861; he was transferred to the Bureau of Construction within the department at the behest of Salmon P. Chase, secretary of the treasury, in 1863. Chase had appointed Isaiah Rogers head of the bureau in 1862 and supervising architect of the department the following year. Mullett succeeded Rogers, who resigned in 1865, and he served as supervising architect of the Treasury Department until 1874, during which time he designed and constructed $50 million worth of federal buildings in the boom years following the Civil War. Also in 1865, Mullett married Pacific Pearl Myrick; they had six children.

Mullett designed thirty-five federal buildings, of which eighteen were extant as of 1992. They include a marine hospital, an assay office, and two branch mints. For the U.S. Customs service in Philadelphia (1867–1871) and San Francisco (1874–1881), he designed two huge appraiser's stores, each occupying a whole city block; the remainder of Mullett's designs are for combined postal services, custom facilities, and federal courts. His later buildings range from small domestic-scale brick structures in Wiscasset (1868–1872) and Machias (1871–1872), Maine, to the elaborate New York Courthouse and Post Office (1869–1880), which cost over $8.5 million. All of his designs are of classical derivation, the most significant being the mid-sized buildings costing $300,000–$400,000; they were designed in the Renaissance revival idiom, following the tradition of Ammi B. Young and the immense expensive structures inspired by buildings in Second Empire France.

Two of Mullett's Renaissance revival buildings remain extant in Columbia, South Carolina, and Knoxville, Tennessee (both 1871–1874). Each building is three stories high, with string courses at each floor level, along with a wide overhanging cornice at the eaves, pedimented windows, and quoins at the corners of the building. The Knoxville building is constructed of load-bearing Knox County marble and, like most of Mullett's designs, utilizes fireproof construction with cast-iron columns and wrought-iron beams and includes innovative ventilation and heating systems.

Mullett's designs in the Second Empire style include the Sub-Treasury and Post Office in Boston (1869–1874); custom houses and post offices in Cincinnati (1874–1885), Philadelphia (1874–1884), New York (1869–1880), and St. Louis (1873–1884); and the $10 million State, War, and Navy (now the Executive Office) Building in Washington, D.C.; all but the last

two have been demolished. These buildings displayed a profusion of classical detailing and sculpture, including clusters of columns, almost to the exclusion of wall surfaces. Bulbous concave and convex high-pitched roofs above decorative cornices capped the buildings. Mullett rarely deviated from the Renaissance and Second Empire styles, except for occasional experiments with the less decorative neoclassical or Greek revival modes, the latter seen in the extant San Francisco Branch Mint (1869–1874).

Corruption during the President Grant era was rife, especially with regard to building projects for the federal government. Because his office was responsible for so much money and because so many federal employees were corrupt, Mullett himself was highly suspect, but five separate investigations indicated he was innocent of any wrongdoing. During the fall of 1874, however, Mullett was again unjustifiably but publicly accused of corruption. He immediately offered his resignation, which was accepted and which he later regretted; he officially left the Treasury on 31 December 1874.

Mullett was thereafter involved in a number of enterprises, including the patenting of many building elements and component parts relating to fireproof construction. He trained his two eldest sons, Thomas and Frederick, in the practice of architecture, and between 1884 and 1889 Mullett was given forty building permits in Washington, amounting to almost $750,000 worth of work. He rebuilt a theater and designed houses, a bank, and the 120-foot-high *Baltimore Sun* Building at 1315-17 F Street NW in Washington (1885–1887), which was as structurally innovative and inventive as Mullett's earlier work, even though it was based on the design of the *New York Tribune* Building (1873–1875) by Richard Morris Hunt.

After 1874, Mullett encountered problems collecting fees from clients and the federal government, and he filed claims against both. Plagued by financial difficulties and failing health, he took his own life, shooting himself at his home.

Mullett's most significant creations were his buildings for the federal government in the decade following the Civil War. His designs were comparable to those by John McArthur, Jr. (1823–1890), in Philadelphia and by Arthur Gilman and G. J. F. Bryant in Boston. Together, the major works of this small group of architects produced a rich and highly variegated style, evocative of the Renaissance revival and the French Second Empire, that peaked in popularity at the time of Grant's presidency and declined soon afterward.

• The National Archives (Record Group 121) holds correspondence and drawings of all federal constructions by Mullett. Progress information on these projects is in "Reports of the Supervising Architect," *U.S. Treasury Reports* (1865–1874). See also Daisy M. Smith, ed., *A. B. Mullett Diaries & c.: Annotated Documents, Research & Reminiscence Regarding a Federal Architect Engineer (1834–1890)* (1985), and Smith, ed., *A. B. Mullett: His Relevance in American Architecture and Historic Preservation* (1990), which contains essays contributed by Lawrence Wodehouse, Charles Hosmer, Robert Dunning, Theodore Turak, and John Dawson. Mullett is treated extensively in Wodehouse, "Alfred B. Mullett and his French Style Government Buildings," *Journal of the Society of Architectural Historians* 31 (Mar. 1972): 22–37.

LAWRENCE WODEHOUSE

MULLICAN, Moon (29 Mar. 1909–1 Jan. 1967), honky-tonk pianist and vocalist, was born Aubrey Wilson Mullican in Corrigan, Texas, the son of Oscar Luther Mullican, a farmer, and Virginia (maiden name unknown). Oscar Mullican raised cotton, corn, and peas on ground that Mullican, who was noted for his colorful speech, later characterized as "so poor, it would take two mad Irishmen and a gallon of whisky just to raise a fuss on it." Mullican learned the rudiments of guitar from an African-American farmhand, Joe Jones, who worked for his father. Oscar Mullican bought a pump organ in 1917 so that the children could learn how to play religious music. In 1923 Mullican played his first dance as leader of a trio, and by the time he was fourteen, he was slipping into Lufkin, Texas, at nights to play piano in bars for tips. At age sixteen, he left home after an altercation with his father and went to Houston. By that point he had developed a distinctive style on the piano that was rooted in barrelhouse and boogie-woogie styles. He also had a good mastery of the popular songs of the day that he had acquired from a neighbor's phonograph.

By the time Mullican left home, he had acquired the nickname "Moon," a truncation of "Moonshine." His first job after leaving home was at the Brass Rail in Houston, where he played from 6:00 P.M. until 6:00 A.M. The first professional group that Mullican joined was probably the Blue Ridge Playboys, with whom he recorded for Vocalion in 1936. He joined western swing fiddler Cliff Bruner's Texas Wanderers in 1937 and recorded with them during the late 1930s as well as with Buddy Jones, the Sunshine Boys, Jimmie Davis, and the Modern Mountaineers. Mullican later asserted that he made over one hundred recordings (as a sideman) during one year, probably in the early 1940s. No one has attempted a complete discography of all the sessions on which Mullican was a sideman, though. He also appeared in the movie *Village Barn Dance* in 1939.

Between 1940 and 1946 Mullican led a band called the Showboys with Cliff Bruner, and around 1943 he first settled in the Beaumont, Texas, area. While he was there, he played regularly on radio station KPBX. He owned nightclubs in and around Beaumont, as well as in Odessa in west Texas. Describing his music in the late 1940s, Mullican called it "Texas Socko" or "East Texas Sock." "Technically," he said, "it is two-four rhythm with accent on the second beat—and when we say accent we mean accent." Mullican asserted that the style had originated in Houston a decade earlier.

In 1946 Mullican signed with King Records, which would become his most significant recording affiliation. King was a Cincinnati-based independent label

that had been in business since 1943. An announcement in *Billboard* magazine in 1946 states that Mullican had recorded twelve sides for the Houston-based Gulf label, although these were never issued, leading to speculation that Sydney Nathan, president of King Records, had bought the Gulf masters together with Mullican's contract.

In late 1946 Mullican recorded "New Pretty Blonde," a nonsense version of a cajun song, "Jole Blon," then a hit for cajun fiddle player Harry Choates. It became his first charted record the following year. After that point, Mullican became a very successful recording artist and scored several more major hits on King Records, including "Sweeter Than the Flowers," "I'll Sail My Ship Alone," as well as country versions of the pop hits "Mona Lisa" and "Goodnight Irene." Mullican's records adapted particularly well to the exigencies of the jukebox trade, which then accounted for well over half of all country records sold.

Mullican asserted that Hank Williams was responsible for bringing him to the Grand Ole Opry in Nashville in June 1951. By then, Mullican was billing himself "King of the Hillbilly Piano Players." Shortly after he joined the Grand Ole Opry, he and Hank Williams collaborated on "Jambalaya (On the Bayou)," which became one of Williams's biggest hits and later became a big pop hit for Jo Stafford. Mullican recorded it at the same time as Williams for King Records, although his version failed to register on the charts.

In 1955 Mullican left Nashville and returned to East Texas. He started his own club in Beaumont, but he remained under contract to King Records until 1958. His last major charted hit, "Cherokee Boogie," was in 1954. After his King contract expired, Mullican was signed to the Coral division of Decca Records by pianist-producer Owen Bradley, himself an admirer of Mullican (Bradley was occasionally known as "Half Moon"). At that time, Bradley was assistant to Decca's New York–based chief of country repertoire, Paul Cohen, but by the time Mullican was signed, the face of country music had been altered by the advent of rock 'n' roll. Mullican had incorporated elements of blues and boogie-woogie into his style as far back as the late 1920s and felt able to compete in the new market conditions. However, his recordings for Coral, made between April 1958 and October 1959, failed to find favor with the teen-slanted radio programmers and he was dropped from the label.

Bradley recalled the dilemma he faced in producing Mullican in an interview with Rich Kienzle: "Moon wasn't rock 'n' roll at all. He'd written a lot of good songs and was a great performer in person. . . . Trying to find a formula for him was hard and [it was hard] to find something to get him a great big record. . . . We were trying what *we* liked, what *musicians* might like, instead of what the public liked."

After being dropped by Coral, Mullican was signed to Starday Records, a Nashville-based independent label, and he recorded his last hit, a version of "Ragged but Right," for them in 1961. Mullican's contract was taken over by Jack Clement, who had produced Johnny Cash and others for Sun Records but was then operating as an independent producer, songwriter, and music publisher in Beaumont. Clement brought Mullican onto Hallway Records, owned by Beaumont promoter Bill Hall, with whom he was associated. Between 1962 and 1964 Mullican made his last recordings for Hallway, recordings that were later leased to New York–based Kapp Records in 1969 for an album titled *The Moon Mullican Showcase*.

Mullican's health began failing in the early 1960s. He had a heart attack on stage in Kansas City in 1962, although he recovered and played a showdate there in 1963 as a "make good" that was recorded and later issued as a live album. Mullican had another heart attack shortly after midnight on New Year's Day 1967, and he died two hours later in Beaumont, Texas.

Mullican was a maverick performer in country music. However, he was not a true country musician; his style incorporated elements of jazz, blues, boogie-woogie, western swing, pop, and cajun music. Very few artists tried to imitate him even when he was at his commercial peak. Perhaps the most notable Moon Mullican disciple was Jerry Lee Lewis, who paid a spoken tribute to Mullican on his *More of the Greatest Live Show on Earth* LP, recorded at Panther Hall in Fort Worth, Texas, in September 1966 when Mullican was ailing. Mullican's songs, particularly "Cherokee Boogie" and "I'll Sail My Ship Alone," are still performed, as, of course, is "Jambalaya" (although credited solely to Hank Williams, Mullican was—for a time at least—receiving royalties from the song).

• It was probably Mullican's widow, Eunice, who provided the basic biographical data found in Linnell Gentry, *A History and Encyclopaedia of Country, Western, and Gospel Music* (1969). The longest interview with Mullican was conducted by Gordon Baxter, reprinted under the headline "Pop Never Wanted Me to Be a Musician" in *Music City News*, Feb. 1967, pp. 16–17. Other published sources include two sets of liner notes: Rich Kienzle, for *Moon's Rock*, Vollersode, Germany: Bear Family Records, BCD 15607 (1992) and Phil Tricker, for *Moonshine Jamboree*, London, England: Ace Records, CDCHD 458 (1993). Mullican himself and his then-manager distributed a promotional folio titled *King of the Hillbilly Piano Players: Souvenir Album* (undated), and an undated issue of the King Records house magazine (probably from early 1947) recounts what is probably a fanciful version of the story behind Mullican's hit recording of "New Pretty Blonde." Both are located in the King Records/IMG files.

COLIN ESCOTT

MULLIKEN, Robert Sanderson (7 June 1896–31 Oct. 1986), chemical physicist, was born in Newburyport, Massachusetts, the son of Samuel Parsons Mulliken, a renowned organic chemist, and Katherine Wilmarth Mulliken, a distant relative of his father. Mulliken was a quiet and well-behaved child who attended public schools.

In 1913, the year of Danish physicist Niels Bohr's publication of a new hybrid model of the atom, Mulliken presented at his high school graduation ceremony the essay "Electrons: What They Are and What They Do." The elucidation of the role played by electrons in the structure and spectra of molecules would be a recurrent theme in his future scientific research. Mulliken studied chemistry at the Massachusetts Institute of Technology, from which he graduated in 1917. After graduation he accepted a wartime job as a junior chemical engineer for the U.S. Bureau of Mines and conducted research on poison gases at the American University in Washington, D.C. After the war he worked as a chemist for the New Jersey Zinc Company.

In 1919, attracted by the work on the separation of isotopes done by the physical chemist William Draper Harkins, Mulliken entered the graduate program in chemistry at the University of Chicago. There he earned his Ph.D. in 1921 with a dissertation on the partial separation of mercury isotopes by evaporation and other processes. He stayed one more year at the university, where he worked as a National Research Council postdoctoral Fellow on an extension of his former research to obtain bigger isotope separations with mercury by using improved equipments and methods. In the process, he built the first "isotope factory," an apparatus based on the different behavior of isotopes under the processes of evaporation and diffusion through a membrane.

Still a National Research Council Fellow, Mulliken moved in 1923 to the Jefferson Physical Laboratory at Harvard University. Through discussions with physicists Edwin Crawford Kemble and Raymond Thayer Birge, he assisted in their preparation of the 1926 comprehensive report on the spectra of diatomic molecules for the NRC. The spectra of molecules, then known as band spectra, were at that time a hot topic in American physics. More complicated than the spectra of elements, band spectra were classified on the basis of three types of contributions associated with the three different components of the energy of a molecule: one the result of nuclear rotations, another of nuclear vibrations, and the last of electronic motions. By implication, the detection of the presence of different isotopes in molecular spectra (isotope effect) could be considered the result of three contributions—rotational, vibrational, and electronic. Mulliken began by looking for evidence of vibrational contributions to the isotope effect in visible and ultraviolet spectra. His experimental work enabled him to identify a new molecular fragment—boron monoxide (BO)—and pointed to the existence in molecules of an energy at a temperature of zero degrees Kelvin (zero point energy), a concept that was soon to find a safe place in the framework of the new quantum mechanics. He then shifted to the consideration of the electronic distribution in molecules and found evidence for analogies in the spectroscopic behavior of diatomic molecules with the same number of electrons (isoelectronic molecules) and the element in the periodic table with the same number of electrons. This analogy, which occurred in one form or another to other scientists such as Rudolf Mecke and Hertha Sponer in Germany and Birge in the United States, was the starting point for the classification of diatomic molecules into different families and the suggestion that similar electronic structures were associated with corresponding systems of energy levels.

In 1926 Mulliken became an assistant professor of physics at New York University. An active research group soon gathered around Mulliken. This extremely productive period coincided with the recognition of Mulliken as an international leader on the diagnosis of band spectra. In the meantime, matrix and wave mechanics were being created in Europe. During this period Mulliken began a longtime friendship with Friedrich Hund, the German theoretical physicist who introduced quantum mechanics into the study of molecular structure. Formerly, molecular rotations and vibrations had been studied in the framework of the old quantum theory. Hund used quantum mechanics to show that the electronic quantum states of a diatomic molecule could be interpolated between two limiting cases: the situation in which the two atoms are separated and the opposite situation, in which the two nuclei are thought to be united into one. Hund's work gave theoretical support to Mulliken's former hypothesis that electronic quantum numbers could change drastically in the process of molecule formation and to his subsequent successful attempt to assign individual quantum numbers to electrons in molecules.

In 1928 Mulliken moved to the University of Chicago as an associate professor of physics. The following year he married Mary Helen Von Noé; they had two daughters.

Mulliken's work on the interpretation of the spectra of diatomic molecules came to an end with the preparation of three classic review articles in which he introduced the famous correlation diagrams that related the state of the molecule with the separated atoms and the united atom descriptions. In an influential 1935 review article on the quantum theory of valence, physicists John Hasbrouck Van Vleck and Albert Sherman claimed that the correlation diagrams play a role relative to diatomic molecules that is equivalent to that played by the periodic table of Mendeleev for atoms. In 1930 Mulliken worked successfully toward securing an international agreement on notation for diatomic molecules and in 1955 he did the same for polyatomic molecules. He then shifted to the study of polyatomic molecules and to valence-related questions.

The assignment of quantum numbers to electrons in molecules led Mulliken to suggest in 1932 an entirely new approach to the question of molecule formation and chemical bonding. This approach dispensed altogether with the conceptual framework of classical valence theory—abandoning the notions of chemical bonds and valence—and replaced it with a theory in which molecule formation was analyzed in terms of the motions of each electron in the field of two or more nuclei and that of other electrons, in what he called "molecular orbitals." To counteract the received view of a molecule as an aggregate of atoms, Mulliken contended that "a molecule is a molecule is a molecule." Mulliken's new approach to valence theory, which came to be known as the molecular orbital theory, re-

sulted from a painstaking analysis of band spectral data. It was a largely phenomenological theory based on the extension of Bohr's building-up principle to molecules, according to which the molecules were pictured as being formed by feeding electrons into orbits (or orbitals) that encircled all of the nuclei. Mulliken was joined by Hund, Erich Hückel, Gerhardt Herzberg, John Lennard-Jones, Charles Coulson, and others in developing the molecular orbital theory. Lennard-Jones, for instance, suggested in 1929 that molecular orbitals be represented by a linear combination of atomic orbitals.

Mulliken's extension of the idea of molecular orbitals to small polyatomic molecules (1932–1935) brought about several important new results. After physicist John Clarke Slater's effective proof that the analysis of atomic spectra could be carried out successfully without recourse to group theory, Mulliken showed that, when dealing with polyatomic molecules, group theory was not an unnecessary mathematical invention. He argued that group theory enabled one to obtain qualitative information on individual molecular orbitals and properties from the symmetry of the molecule. As the symmetry of the molecule can be different in different electronic states, group theoretical methods proved to be an indispensable tool in the classification of the states of highly symmetrical molecules like benzene. Mulliken also developed a quantum theory of the double bond along the lines suggested by Hückel and introduced a scale of absolute electronegativities. Formerly defined as the tendency of atoms in molecules to attract electrons to themselves, Mulliken now suggested calculating the electronegativity of an atom as the average of the ionization potential (the energy required to remove an electron from an atom) and the electron affinity (the energy released when an atom gains an electron and becomes a negative ion) of each atom. This new scale was intended as a reply to chemist Linus Pauling's scale of relative electronegativities.

In the meantime, Pauling had developed an alternative method to study molecular structure and chemical bonding. Originating in the work of German physicists Walter Heitler and Fritz London on the hydrogen molecule, the method was extended to other molecules by Slater and, especially, by Pauling, who based his semi-empirical approach in the ideas of hybridization of bond orbitals and resonance among several valence-bond structures. Pauling came to believe that bonds are formed as a result of the overlapping of two atomic orbitals and that the stronger bond is formed by the atomic orbital that can overlap the most with a certain atomic orbital in the other atom. The bond direction is the direction in which the concentration of individual bond orbitals is highest. The strength and directional character of bonds is thus explained as a result of the overlapping of individual bond orbitals, which is itself a reflection of a greater density of charge concentrated along that particular direction. Pauling further realized that under certain conditions atomic orbitals were altered during bond formation. In these cases atomic orbitals must be combined together to form the original state, and the new hybridized orbitals, which were formed as linear combinations of atomic s, p, and d orbitals, were particularly suited for bond formation. Furthermore, in those compounds for which no single structure seemed to represent adequately all of its properties, Pauling suggested that the actual bonding in the molecule could be regarded as a hybrid of two or more conventional forms of the molecule, which led to a phenomenon that he called "resonance among several valence-bond structures." Contrary to Mulliken's approach, Pauling's resonance theory of the chemical bond was an extension of classical structural theory, and thus envisioned molecules as aggregates of atoms bonded together along privileged directions.

While working on the structure and spectra of polyatomic molecules, Mulliken became full professor in 1931 and was elected a member of the National Academy of Sciences in 1936. On U.S. entry into World War II Mulliken stopped his research temporarily to serve as director of the Information Division of the Plutonium Project (part of the Manhattan Project) at the Metallurgical Laboratory of the University of Chicago.

After the war Mulliken resumed his former work. Supported first by the Rockefeller Foundation and then by the Office of Naval Research and other granting agencies, Mulliken's group, named after 1952 the Laboratory of Molecular Structure and Spectra, continued to produce high-quality work on the experimental and theoretical study of molecular structure and spectra. Among Mulliken's postwar contributions were the development of the charge-transfer interpretation of spectra of donor-acceptor molecular complexes; the calculation of spectral intensities and the explanation of the selection rules that characterize transitions in molecular spectra; the theory of hyperconjugation (pseudo-triple bond) in organic molecules; the "magic formula," an attempt to quantify Pauling's criterion of maximum overlapping by defining bond strength in terms of the overlap integral (the integral over all space of the product of two atomic orbitals, each coming from different atoms); and the concept of population analysis, in which the concept of overlap population (the electron population between atoms) was put forth as the best measure of the strength of a chemical bond. With the appearance of the first digital computers in the mid-1940s Mulliken's group moved away from semi-empirical calculations—in which the computation of molecular properties was carried out by setting up a theoretical framework and then, at certain points, integrals that were difficult to compute were substituted by experimentally determined quantities—and toward wholly theoretical ("ab initio") calculations. The use of computers to calculate the time-consuming integrals of the molecular orbital method opened the way to the investigation of molecules that were otherwise inaccessible to experimentation.

In 1955 Mulliken worked for one year in London as scientific attaché of the U.S. embassy. From 1956 to 1961 he was Ernst Dewitt Burton Distinguished Service Professor of Physics and from 1961 to 1985 Distinguished Service Professor of Physics and Chemistry at the University of Chicago. From 1964 to 1971 Mulliken was also Distinguished Research Professor of Chemical Physics at Florida State University. Mulliken's recognition came late in his career. In the 1960s he received five awards from the American Chemical Society, the G. N. Lewis Gold Medal, the Theodore William Richards Gold Medal, the Peter Debye Award, the John Gamble Kirkwood Award, and the J. Willard Gibbs Medal. In 1966 he was awarded the Nobel Prize in chemistry for his "fundamental work concerning chemical bonds and the electronic structure of molecules by the molecular orbital method." He received the award in chemistry rather than in physics, because the study of molecular structure and spectra had migrated during Mulliken's career from physics to chemistry. He died in Alexandria, Virginia.

Mulliken was instrumental in the definition of the basic concepts and methods used to study molecular structure, in developing its notation and shaping its language. He built a career in the boundary between experiment and theory, and between chemistry and physics.

• Mulliken's papers, correspondence, and other manuscript materials are in the Joseph Regenstein Library of the University of Chicago. Some letters as well as an interview with Mulliken conducted by Thomas S. Kuhn in 1964 are deposited in the Archives for the History of Quantum Physics in the American Institute of Physics, and in the American Philosophical Society. A collection of Mulliken's most important papers on molecular structure and spectra is *Selected Papers of Robert S. Mulliken*, ed. D. A. Ramsay and J. Hinze (1975). Mulliken's autobiography, *Robert S. Mulliken: Life of a Scientist, An Autobiographical Account of the Development of Molecular Orbital Theory with an Introductory Memoir by Friedrich Hund*, was edited posthumously by Bernard J. Ransil (1989). Mulliken's earlier recollections include "Molecular Scientists and Molecular Science: Some Reminiscences," *Journal of Chemical Physics* 43 (1965): S2–S11; his Nobel Lecture of 1966, "Spectroscopy, Molecular Orbitals, and Chemical Bonding," *Nobel Lectures in Chemistry 1963–1970* (1972); "Spectroscopy, Quantum Chemistry, and Molecular Physics," *Physics Today* 21, no. 4 (1968): 52–57; and "The Path to Molecular Orbital Theory," *Pure and Applied Chemistry* 24 (1970): 203–15. An assessment of Mulliken's contributions to quantum chemistry is Per-Olov Löwdin and Bernard Pullman, *Molecular Orbitals in Chemistry, Physics, and Biology: A Tribute to R. S. Mulliken* (1964).

ANA SIMÕES

MULLIN, Willard Harlan (14 Sept. 1902–21 Dec. 1978), cartoonist, was born in Franklin, Ohio, the son of Milo Mayberry Mullin and Edna Marie Ballard, dairy farmers. The Mullins moved to California in 1906, and very early in life, young Willard resolved to become a sports cartoonist. After graduating from Los Angeles High School in 1920, he took a job in the sign department of Bullock's department store, where he perfected his lettering technique while waiting for an opportunity to enter the newspaper field as an artist. On 1 January 1923 he joined the four-man art department of the *Los Angeles Herald*, where he worked until 1934 except for two brief sojourns in Texas on the staffs of other Hearst papers. Early in 1924, he spent several months doing promotional cartoons to drum up circulation for the *San Antonio Light*; and for most of 1925, he ran the art staff of the *Fort Worth Record*, returning to Los Angeles when the Texas paper folded. At the *Herald*, he began by performing routine art chores during regular working hours (lettering headlines, retouching photographs, doing layouts) while volunteering for evening assignments sketching sporting events, boxing particularly. Over the years, his sports cartoons appeared more and more frequently, but Mullin remained a general assignment artist rather than a sports specialist. He married Helen Tousley in 1929; they had one child.

In the fall of 1934, Mullin heard that the *New York World Telegram* was looking for a sports cartoonist; he submitted samples and was hired. He remained with the paper until it collapsed in 1967, the casualty of a disastrous succession of printers' strikes that crippled New York newspapers in the mid-1960s. He settled his family first in Jackson Heights, moving in 1939 to Plandome, Long Island, and retiring, in 1971, to Pointe Verde Beach, Florida.

For most of his 33-year career with the *World Telegram*, Mullin's cartoon ran large across the top of the first page in the sports section, five or six columns wide on an eight-column format, six days a week. Just as his cartoon dominated his paper's sports section, so did Mullin tower over his profession: his distinctive style soon set the fashion for all sports cartoonists. He conceived his cartoons as if he were writing a sports column. Typically, he declared his subject for the day with a large realistically rendered portrait of an athlete; he then developed his story—an observation or comment on the athlete's most recent accomplishment—in a series of small figures (sometimes called "Goomies"), often caricatures of the principal subject, in topical vignettes that surrounded the large picture. Sometimes the large drawing depicted generic athletes of a particular sport, and Mullin's commentary explored the state of that sport or some aspect of the news about it. Sometimes his cartoon took shape as a series of narrative pictures in comic strip form. Always, he hoped to make a point or cover the news of some sporting event or provoke a laugh; on a good day, he did all three.

Mullin was a passionate sports fan, and his passion showed in the vigor of his drawings. To preserve the energy of the creative act itself, he worked from preliminary sketch to final drawing on the same piece of art paper. In his drawings, he tried to capture the feel rather than just the appearance of the action. To this end, he exaggerated both anatomy and motion, enlisting the entire figure in his expression of an idea. "You start with the thought and feeling of the action," he said. "A few lines will give you the sweep of the runner's legs and forward thrust of his body." A football player running for a touchdown did not simply run; he bent forward at the waist and again at the ankles, assuming a charging, jutting off-balance posture that however impossible in actuality was vivid in suggesting the velocity and determination of his progress.

Mullin's athletes were bony and muscular caricatures of their breed; supple in motion, loose-limbed and sinewy rather than muscle-bound, they captured perfectly the pure physicality of sport. The large pictures in his cartoons were rendered in matchless fluid line with a brush; the smaller action figures, with a delicate penline. Mullin usually gave the large drawing a soft, gray tone by shading pebble-finish art paper with a crayon; the small pictures he embellished with strategically placed solid blacks.

During his last seventeen years with the *World Telegram*, Mullin worked at home in Plandome. When he finished his cartoon, he took it a hundred yards down the street to the Long Island Railroad station and handed it to a conductor on the Manhattan-bound train; the conductor then passed it along to a messenger at Penn Station to take to the paper's office. In addition to drawing his daily cartoon, Mullin illustrated hundreds of advertisements, books, and articles in such magazines as *Life*, *Saturday Evening Post*, *Look*, *Time*, and *Newsweek*.

Mullin's pictures became virtually synonymous with sports; his symbols, their visual lexicon. Football teams were represented by their mascots (usually animals), basketball players were skinny and awkward, and boxers were wide-eyed innocents. The New York Giants he depicted as a huge, amiable lout with huge feet and a tiny head; the Milwaukee Brave was beer-bellied (in recognition of the brew for which the city was famed); St. Louis Swifty, a Mississippi riverboat gambler, was a "card" sharp (evoking the nickname for the Cardinals); the New York Yankees were somewhat snooty city slickers in pinstripe uniforms. Mullin's prized creation, however, was the Bum who stood for the Brooklyn Dodgers. The beloved tramp was born one day in the late 1930s just after the underdog Dodgers lost another one at Ebbets Field. Mullin was taking the cab back to the newspaper office, and the driver asked him, "How'd our bums do today?" The next day, the woebegone hobo debuted in the paper.

Mullin enjoyed saloon life, consuming both food and drink with appreciative gusto, and was close friends with many sports celebrities, newspaper and magazine reporters as well as athletes. Sports columnist Red Smith wrote, "For approximately forever, Mullin did a daily cartoon. . . . The National Cartoonists Society saluted him as Sports Cartoonist of the Century, an understatement. He was the sports cartoonist of the eras, including the Paleozoic, because there never was another who combined such news sense and wit and perception with such a comic pen." Mullin died of cancer while visiting his daughter in Corpus Christi, Texas.

• According to Mullin, the only substantial collection of his original art is held in the manuscript collection of the Bird Library at Syracuse University. Mullin told the story of his life to Dave Camerer in *A Hand in Sport* (1958), a notable volume, consisting of thirty pages of autobiographical text and 190 pages of cartoons reprinted from every period of Mullin's career with his running commentary underneath each picture. His work appears in few books, most of which he illustrated for others, *Menke's Encyclopedia of Sports* (1944), John Lardner's *It Beats Working* (1947), and Red Smith's *Out of the Red* (1950). He also edited and illustrated *The Junior Illustrated Encyclopedia of Sports* (1960), with Herbert Kamm, and wrote and illustrated Lesson 23 of the Famous Artists Cartoon Course (c. 1955) in which he explains in graphic detail how he composed his cartoons. More about his working methods and attitudes can be found in an interview conducted by Jud Hurd in *Cartoonist PROfiles 39* (Sept. 1978). The obituary in the *New York Times*, 22 Dec. 1978, rehashes the major events in Mullin's life.

ROBERT C. HARVEY

MULLINS, Edgar Young (5 Jan. 1860–23 Nov. 1928), theologian and president of the Southern Baptist Theological Seminary, was born in Franklin County, Mississippi, the son of Seth Granberry Mullins, a minister, and Cornelia Blair Tillman. At eight years of age, Mullins moved with his family to Corsicana, Texas, where his father purchased land, organized a school, and founded a church. His father, a master of arts graduate of Mississippi College, was insistent that all nine of his children should receive college educations. However, Edgar, who was fourth in line, was forced to seek employment to help out with his older sisters' school expenses. Therefore, at one time or another, he was a newspaper boy, printer's devil, typesetter, printer, messenger boy, and telegrapher. At fifteen years of age, he was employed full-time as a telegrapher.

Finally Mullins's turn came, and he entered Texas Agriculture and Mechanical College (now University), from which he graduated in 1879. He then began to study law, but the course of his life was changed by his conversion during a revival meeting in Dallas under the preaching of William Evander Penn, a lawyer turned evangelist. A few weeks later, on 7 November 1880, Mullins was baptized by his minister father. A short time later he gave up his plans to become a lawyer in order to prepare for the gospel ministry. He entered the Southern Baptist Theological Seminary, Louisville, Kentucky, in 1881 and graduated four years later. Shortly after graduation he was ordained and began his first pastorate at Harrodsburg, Kentucky. In 1886 he married Isla May Hawley, who became truly a partner in the ministry of her husband. They had two children who died young.

Although Mullins longed to serve as a missionary, his health was poor, and his physician advised him to give up his commitment to missionary service in Brazil. He remained at Harrodsburg until accepting the call in 1888 to the Lee Street Baptist Church, an inner-city church in Baltimore, Maryland, which he served with increasing acclaim until 1895. At that time his dream of missionary service led him to accept the position of assistant secretary of the Foreign Mission Board of the Southern Baptist Convention in Richmond, Virginia. In spite of his devotion to foreign mis-

sions, he felt himself unsuited for the task. While in the process of attempting to develop an educational program for the board in colleges and churches, Mullins received an unsolicited call to the Baptist church of Newton Center, Massachusetts. He served there from 1895 until 1899, when he was elected president of the Southern Baptist Seminary, which was in the throes of the Whitsitt controversy, during which seminary president William Heth Whitsitt was attacked by Baptist leaders for challenging the belief that Baptist practice could be traced in an unbroken line back to apostolic times.

Mullins was unusually prepared for his latest challenge. He had taken advantage of opportunities in Baltimore for further study at Johns Hopkins University as well as the numerous opportunities afforded by his three years in the Boston environment. Once at the seminary, he was also made professor of theology, which in turn made possible his many articles and books (1899–1929). Under his skillful leadership, the controversy that had led to the forced resignation of his predecessor, Whitsitt, was soon under control. He vastly increased the endowment for the seminary and moved it in 1926 from the downtown property to a spacious new campus adjacent to Cherokee Park. Mullins also led the Southern Baptist Convention safely past a fundamentalist attempt to take over the denomination through adoption of revision of the New Hampshire Confession of Faith.

Recognition of Mullins's scholarship and stature as a leading spokesman for Baptists was symbolized by his election as president of the Southern Baptist Convention, 1921–1924, and of the Baptist World Alliance, 1923–1928. Of his more than fifteen books, *The Axioms of the Christian Religion* (1908) and *The Christian Religion in Its Doctrinal Expression* (1917) were the most important. *The Axioms of the Christian Religion*, a vigorous apologetic for the uniqueness of the Christian faith in its basic theological concepts, was widely read. It was a textbook in systematic theology for seminary students until the publication of *The Christian Religion in Its Doctrinal Expression*, which became the major textbook in systematic theology and remained so for more than thirty years. His most widely circulated sermon was "The Baptist Conception of Religious Liberty," which was delivered in 1923 before a congress of the Baptist World Alliance in Stockholm, Sweden. Mullins died in Louisville, Kentucky.

• Mullins wrote *Baptist Life in the World's Life* (n.d.) and *Why Is Christianity True?* (1905). A biography by his wife is Isla May Mullins, *Edgar Young Mullins: An Intimate Biography* (1929). Other helpful sources are Walter B. Shurden, ed., *The Life of Baptists in the Life of the World: 80 Years of the Baptist World Alliance* (1985); Faculty of the Southern Baptist Theological Seminary, *Edgar Young Mullins: A Study in Christian Character* (1929); Douglas Clyde Walker III, *The Doctrine of Salvation in the Thought of James Petigru Boyce, Edgar Young Mullins, and Dale Moody* (1986); Russell H. Dilday, Jr., *The Apologetic Method of E. Y. Mullins* (1960); and Norman Wade Cox and Judson Boyce Allen, eds., *Encyclopedia of Southern Baptists*, vol. 2 (1958).

W. R. ESTEP

MULRY, Thomas Maurice (13 Feb. 1855–10 Mar. 1916), charities leader, was born in the city of New York, the son of Thomas Mulry, a successful contractor, and Parthenia Crolius. Mulry was raised in a deeply Roman Catholic family. Of the fourteen Mulry siblings, four brothers entered the Society of Jesus (Jesuits) and a sister joined the Sisters of Charity. Mulry was educated at Catholic parochial schools, De LaSalle Academy, and Cooper Union. In 1872, at the age of seventeen, he entered the family excavating business, Mulry and Son, located in lower Manhattan. That same year he joined the St. Vincent de Paul Society, a voluntary association of lay Catholic men dedicated to charitable works. Mulry's association with the Vincentians was characterized by extraordinary energy, probity, and geniality, and it earned him local and national leadership positions in the emerging area of charity administration.

In 1901 Mulry was elected a trustee of the Emigrant Industrial Savings Bank of New York and served as its president from 1906 until his death in 1916. Founded by refugees from the Irish rebellion of 1798, by the early twentieth "the Emigrant" was the largest savings bank in the world and a vital institution in the development of the city's immigrant communities. During his presidency the bank's assets increased 60 percent and he served as a member and/or director of the boards of numerous companies and professional associations, including the Mutual Life Insurance Company, the Advisory Council of Real Estate Interests, the Prudential Real Estate Corporation, and the United States Title Guaranty Company.

Mulry's most important contributions, however, resulted from his leadership among charity workers. He became a member of the superior council of the New York conference of the St. Vincent de Paul Society in 1885 and president in 1905. Under his direction the society was reorganized into a national organization, which he served as president until his death. Religious charitable and correctional institutions of the time often had to compete both for the souls of the poor as well as for politicized public funding. Because the overwhelming number of the city's destitute children were Catholics, there was great suspicion on the part of many that disproportionate public funds were being spent on their relief. Mulry, whose honesty and tact enabled him to cooperate with many of his non-Catholic peers, was able to persuade religious and nonreligious organizations of their common cause and to prevail upon public authorities to continue to fund private, religious charities.

With the full support of the ecclesiastical authorities, Mulry secured the cooperation of a variety of Catholic charitable organizations in New York. On a national level this process culminated in the creation of the National Conference of Catholic Charities in Washington, D.C., in 1910. Mulry was responsible as well for adapting several non-Catholic initiatives to Catholic purposes, such as youth "fresh air" summer programs and "day nurseries" for working mothers. In 1908 he was made a Knight of St. Gregory by Pope Pius X and in 1912 was awarded the Laetare Medal by the University of Notre Dame as the outstanding Catholic layperson of the year. In 1915 he was made an honorary Doctor of Laws by the Catholic University of America.

In his attempts to coordinate religious and public relief efforts, Mulry worked with a number of influential figures in the emerging field of social work, including Josephine Shaw Lowell, Homer Folks, James E. West, Edward T. Devine, and Seth Low. He was also an officer of many nondenominational religious and public charitable organizations, such as the New York City Conference of Charities and Corrections, the New York State Conference of Charities and Corrections (president in 1903), and the National Council of Charities and Corrections (president in 1908). In 1909, at the invitation of Theodore Roosevelt, he served, along with Folks and West, as a vice president of the first White House Conference on the Care of Dependent Children. The conference placed child welfare at the top of the Progressive party agenda, and its recommendations resulted in the creation of the federal Children's Bureau in 1912.

Mulry's career spanned a transitional time in the development of American welfare policy. While he worked to keep private, religious organizations at the center of publicly-funded welfare efforts, it is likely that this position facilitated the assumption by the public of what had been private charity. While working for the placement of orphaned, abandoned, and neglected children in foster homes, Mulry vigorously defended the necessity of large institutions, recognizing, better than most, the Sisyphean task of finding individual placements for the thousands of such children in New York. From its inception in 1899 until his death in 1916, the Catholic Home Bureau placed only about three thousand of the roughly one hundred and fifty thousand children who passed through Catholic institutions during that period.

Unlike many of his more secular- and professionally oriented peers, Mulry was unwavering in his conviction that the influence of religion was crucial to effective charity, and he defended the prerogative of religious organizations in dispensing it. It was his attempts to protect the autonomy of religious organizations that led to Mulry's only political office, as a delegate to the 1915 Convention to Revise the Constitution of the State of New York. His task was to defend the various religious charities he represented, particularly the Catholic ones, against a gathering storm of criticism. Later that same year John A. Kingsbury, reform mayor John Purroy Mitchel's commissioner of charities, issued a report charging malfeasance and incompetence on the part of the directors of many Catholic institutions and recommending that the governor investigate the state board of charities. Amid hyperbolic press accounts of Catholic mismanagement and greed, Mulry sensed the undercurrent of nativist prejudice he had struggled to overcome: "the same old arguments, dressed up, perhaps, in a little newer form" (quoted in Meehan, p. 146).

Within a few weeks of testifying before a hostile commission chaired by prominent New York attorney Charles S. Strong in January 1916—a result of Kingsbury's report—Mulry was struck with pneumonia and died suddenly in the city of New York. The timing of his death in the midst of the controversy led Auxiliary Bishop Patrick Hayes to tell several thousand mourners at St. Patrick's Cathedral that Mulry had died "a martyr to charity." Had he lived he would have seen the commission recommend the very changes in welfare policy that he had resisted: greater supervision of charities by the state board and further professionalization in the administration of private charities.

Mulry left behind as large and as religious a family as the one in which he was raised. In 1880 he had married Mary Elizabeth Gallagher, with whom he had thirteen children; of the ten who survived infancy, three became priests and one a Sister of Charity. In 1920 the area in front of the Mulry home at 10 Perry Street was dedicated as Mulry Square in an elaborate celebration featuring Mayor John Hylan and Archbishop Patrick Hayes.

Mulry led Catholic and non-Catholic institutions through a period of dramatic change in American welfare policy. Although autonomous, private, and volunteer religious institutions were eventually superseded by professional and public welfare agencies, Mulry's mission helped lay the foundation for many developments in American social work. He played a leadership role in establishing standards for social services, and he helped found several college programs of social work, including the Fordham University School of Sociology and Social Service, the New York School of Social Work, and the Catholic University School of Social Work. His efforts on behalf of poor New Yorkers were instrumental in helping tens of thousands of immigrant families adapt to the harsh realities and take advantage of the multiple opportunities of American life.

• Eulogistic summaries of Mulry's life and work can be found in two sources written shortly after his death: William J. Kerby, "The Late Thomas Maurice Mulry," *Catholic World*, July 1916, and Thomas F. Meehan, *Thomas Maurice Mulry* (1917); the latter contains numerous testimonials from contemporaries and texts of several of Mulry's principal speeches. A respectful documentation of Mulry's work from the point of view of academic social work can be found in Joseph W. Helmes, *Thomas M. Mulry: A Volunteer's Contribution to Social Work* (1938). A more analytical, if brief, critical perspective placing Mulry in the context of the politics of charity is Elizabeth McKeown and Dorothy M. Brown, "Saving New York's Children," *U.S. Catholic Historian* 13 (Summer 1995): 77–95. His obituary in the *New York Times*, 11 Mar. 1916, is filled with fanciful biographic inventions but gives a sense of the impact of his sudden death.

JOSEPH M. MURPHY

MUMFORD, James Gregory (2 Dec. 1863–19 Oct. 1914), surgeon and medical writer, was born in Rochester, New York, the son of George Elihu Mumford, a lawyer and banker, and Julia Emma Hills. As a child, Mumford suffered an attack of rheumatic fever and later was incapacitated many times during his life from heart disease. Educated at the St. Paul's School in Concord, New Hampshire, he entered Harvard College in 1880 and graduated with the class of 1885. He afterward matriculated at the Harvard Medical School, graduating in 1890 and in his senior year serving as house officer at the Massachusetts General Hospital. After further training at the Boston Lying-in Hospital and in some of the hospitals in Europe, he was appointed in 1892 to the staff of the Carney Hospital in Boston. That same year he married Helen Sherwood Ford; they had no children. In 1894 Mumford received the appointment of surgeon to outpatients at the Massachusetts General Hospital, the institution he was closely associated with for the next eighteen years. In 1892 and 1893 Mumford served as surgeon to the Naval Brigade, Massachusetts Volunteer Militia, and later was commissioned in the Medical Corps of the U.S. Army.

Despite his recurring heart disease, Mumford maintained an active practice and a teaching career at the Harvard Medical School. From 1896 to 1903 he held the appointment of assistant in clinical surgery; between 1900 and 1903 he was assistant in operative surgery; and from 1903 to 1909 he served as instructor in surgery. Mumford was a religious man possessed of a social conscience. Unlike most surgeons of his day, he was interested in seeing that surgical patients received good medical services as well. In 1910 Richard Clark Cabot related, in an appreciation of Mumford delivered to the Boston Society of Medical Improvement in early 1915 and subsequently published in the *Boston Medical and Surgical Journal* (172, no. 13 [1 Apr. 1915]: 470–73), that Mumford had proposed purchasing the Emergency Hospital in Boston, then on the market, in an attempt to bring good medical and surgical services within the economic reach of everyone; here, he hoped, patients could receive good medical care at a low price, while yet providing good salaries for the staff. The plan fell through, however, for lack of funds. For twelve years between 1894 and 1906, Mumford spent his summers at nearby Nahant, and for half of each year he carried on a general family practice that included, in his early years, very little surgery.

Twice in Mumford's later years his health gave way under the strain of his many activities. In 1912 he accepted the directorship of the Clifton Sanitarium in Clifton Springs, New York, partly for health reasons and partly to carry out his idea of cooperative medical and surgical practice. He made good strides in invigorating the institution and in turning it into a model medical and surgical practice. However, a difference in opinion over policy between Mumford and financial directors of the sanitarium led to his resignation a short time before his death, which was brought about by a sudden heart attack from which he died three hours later in Clifton Springs.

A highly gifted writer, Mumford was described by Cabot as one of the three or four American medical writers who seriously tried to write good English. In between his professional activities as hospital surgeon, teacher, and private practitioner, he found time to write about doctors, past and present, as well as timely medical essays and, every two years or so, a substantial book. Within twelve years, eight books, aggregating nearly 3,500 pages, came from his hand, and during a slightly longer period sixty of his articles appeared in medical journals. His books were: *Mumford Memoirs* (1900), a family history and genealogy; *A Narrative of Medicine in America* (1903); *Clinical Talks on Minor Surgery* (1903); *Surgical Aspects of Digestive Disorders* (1905); *Surgical Memoirs and Other Essays* (1908); *The Practice of Surgery* (1910); *One Hundred Surgical Problems* (1911); and *A Doctor's Table Talk* (1912). He was also author of the lengthy introductory article, "Narrative of Surgery; a Historical Sketch," in W. W. Keen's *Surgery: Its Principles and Practice* (1906–1913), and coauthor, with Thomas Francis Harrington, of *The Harvard Medical School, 1782–1905: A History, Narrative and Documentary* (1905), a work that, despite its poor organization and lack of an index, is still useful because of its inclusion of biographies of all graduates to that time.

Mumford's interest in medical history brought him into close friendship with renowned physician William Osler and neurosurgery pioneer Harvey Cushing, the latter referring to Mumford's work at the Clifton Springs sanitarium as done "in the face of physical incapacitation that signified extraordinary heroism." Mumford's talent as a medical historian and as an entertaining essayist earned him a wide reputation in medical circles throughout the United States and the British Isles.

• The most extensive biographical record of Mumford is Richard C. Cabot's 1915 appreciation of him, cited above. Obituaries are in the *Journal of the American Medical Association* 63, no. 17 (24 Oct. 1914): 1493; *Lancet* 2 (14 Nov. 1914): 1170; and the British *Medical Journal* 2 (24 Oct. 1914): 906.

RICHARD J. WOLFE

MUMFORD, Lawrence Quincy (11 Dec. 1903–15 Aug. 1982), eleventh librarian of Congress, was born on a farm near Ayden in Pitt County, North Carolina, the son of Jacob Edward Mumford and Emma Luvenia Stocks. Mumford worked on the family tobacco farm while attending grammar school and high school. He attended Duke University, receiving his A.B. in 1925. The 1925 Duke yearbook reported, "He doesn't make much noise, but he is always doing something." In 1928 he received an M.A. in English from Duke. As an undergraduate, Mumford was a student assistant in the Duke University Library. He worked full-time in the library from 1926 to 1928 while pursuing graduate studies. In the fall of 1928 he enrolled in the Columbia University School of Library Science, receiving his B.S. degree in 1929.

Mumford then accepted a job offer from Keyes D. Metcalf at the New York Public Library, beginning a career and a personal relationship that lasted a life-time. Mumford spent sixteen years in positions of increasing responsibility at the New York Public Library. Soon after he joined the staff, he met Permelia Catherine "Pam" Stevens, a children's librarian. They were married in 1930 and had one child. Permelia Mumford died in 1961, and in 1969 Mumford married Betsy Perrin Fox.

Mumford's career at the New York Public Library was interrupted between September 1940 and August 1941, when he was asked to analyze the Library of Congress's cataloging operations and make recommendations for their improvement. After the committee report was issued, Archibald MacLeish, the librarian of Congress, persuaded Mumford to take a leave of absence from the New York Public Library to organize the new processing department at the Library of Congress and serve as its director. In his 1941 annual report, MacLeish said Mumford performed "a minor—perhaps a major—miracle" during his year there.

In 1945 Mumford became assistant director at the Cleveland Public Library and director in 1950. At Cleveland, Mumford won consistent gains in the library's budget, skillfully dealing with city officials and business leaders. He served as president of the Ohio Library Association (1947–1948) and chaired several committees of the American Library Association (ALA) between 1941 and 1953. He was elected president of the ALA for 1954–1955.

On 22 April 1954 President Dwight D. Eisenhower nominated Mumford to become librarian of Congress; after being confirmed by the Senate, he became the first professionally trained librarian to be appointed librarian of Congress. In 1939 the ALA had opposed President Franklin D. Roosevelt's nomination of writer and poet Archibald MacLeish because he was not a trained librarian. Luther H. Evans, Mumford's immediate predecessor, was a political scientist. Relations between the Congress and the library had deteriorated during the Evans administration. Speaking in the House of Representatives in favor of Mumford's nomination, Congresswoman Frances P. Bolton of Ohio said the Library of Congress was "in need of a very real housecleaning. . . . [it] has fallen into patterns of inefficient and unwise operations."

Mumford immediately learned about congressional unhappiness with his predecessors. At the library's 1954 budget hearings he was told, "The new Librarian should be mindful that the Library is the instrument and the creature of Congress." At his confirmation hearings that July, he heard complaints about Evans's frequent absences from Washington and learned that some members of Congress thought the library should consider "withdrawing" or at least "de-emphasizing" many of its national services. Mumford promised to be a full-time librarian, to strengthen the library's services to Congress, and to consider all the questions raised by members of Congress and their staffs. But he stood his ground against a diminution of the library's national role, maintaining that its vast resources should be available both to Congress and to the nation at large.

Working to overcome the atmosphere of distrust he had inherited, Mumford politely explained and justified each budget request. Consultation with Congress was frequent, and the library's budget slowly increased, as did its staff and the size of its collections. Further expansion was on the horizon: in 1957 Mumford initiated planning for a third major Library of Congress building. The James Madison Memorial Building, the largest library building in the world, was authorized in 1965. Construction began in 1971 and was finally completed in 1980. Mumford shared this accomplishment with an important ally in Congress, Senator B. Everett Jordan of North Carolina.

Mumford's cautious philosophy worked with Congress, but it made others impatient and uncomfortable. University librarians felt that Mumford, whose experience was primarily in public libraries, was not exercising the national leadership that research libraries expected from the Library of Congress. In 1962, at the request of Senator Claiborne Pell of the Joint Committee on the Library, Harvard University Library associate director Douglas W. Bryant prepared a memorandum on "what the Library of Congress does and ought to do for the Government and the Nation generally." Bryant urged expansion of the library's national activities and services, recommending that the Library of Congress be officially recognized as the National Library and that it be transferred to the executive branch of government where, he felt, it would receive more generous funding.

Mumford and his senior advisers, chief assistant librarian Rutherford D. Rogers and assistant librarian for public affairs Elizabeth Hamer, decided to rebut the Bryant memorandum, and Senator Jordan inserted Mumford's reply in the *Congressional Record* for 2 October 1962. He strongly defended the library's position in the legislative branch of government, asserting that it performed "more national functions than any other national library in the world." The Bryant memorandum and Mumford's reply were both published in the library's 1962 annual report. The library's forceful response signaled a new confidence. The Madison Building had been authorized, and more federal funds for education were becoming available. For the Library of Congress, this translated immediately into promising new acquisitions and cataloging programs.

Expansion of the library's overseas acquisitions and cataloging programs was built on initiatives that had been taken by Evans. In 1958 the library was authorized to use U.S.-owned foreign currencies (under the Agricultural Trade Development and Assistance Act) to acquire books for itself and other U.S. libraries and to establish acquisitions offices in foreign countries. Passage of the Higher Education Act of 1965, through Title II-C, also was significant for the Library of Congress as well as for academic and research libraries, providing funds to the library for the ambitious purpose of acquiring and cataloging, insofar as possible, all current library materials of value to scholarship published throughout the world.

The successful introduction of automation to the library's cataloging procedures in the mid-1960s was an achievement of great importance for libraries and scholarship, particularly the 1965 inauguration of the MARC (Machine-Readable Cataloging) system for distributing cataloging information in machine-readable form. Other expansions of the library's national role during the Mumford administration included the publication of bibliographic tools such as the *National Union Catalog of Manuscript Collections* and the *Pre-1956 National Union Catalog* and the expansion of the National Books for the Blind program to include the physically handicapped.

The Legislative Reorganization Act of 1970 redesignated the Legislative Reference Service, the department that works directly for the Congress, as the Congressional Research Service (CRS); the act also broadened its responsibilities, provided for the rapid expansion of its staff, and gave the CRS a new independence within the library's administrative structure. There was an internal cost, however: a split between CRS and the rest of the library that became increasingly difficult for Mumford and his senior officers to bridge.

The last years of the Mumford administration were troublesome for other reasons as well. Final approval from Congress for the use of the Madison Building as a Library of Congress building did not occur until 1971; in the meantime, the library's two other buildings became increasingly overcrowded. Employee groups accused the library of racial discrimination in the areas of recruitment, training, and promotion practices, charges that led to two decades of controversy and lawsuits. Mumford, a shy man, became increasingly remote, and his health suffered. He retired on 31 December 1974. He died in Washington, D.C.

While the twenty-year Mumford administration may have ended unhappily for the librarian personally, his librarianship was one of the most productive periods in the library's history. The growth of the library under Mumford's leadership was unprecedented. In two decades, the size of the library's annual appropriation increased tenfold, from $9.4 million to $96.7 million; the number of staff members nearly tripled, from 1,564 to 4,250; and the number of items in the collections more than doubled, from approximately thirty-three million to seventy-four million.

Mumford was fortunate to head the Library of Congress during a period of economic stability and, as part of President Lyndon B. Johnson's Great Society, increased federal expenditure and involvement in education and research. But Mumford also created his own opportunities. The rapprochement he reached with Congress between 1954 and the early 1960s was his most important accomplishment.

• Mumford's official correspondence is in the Integrated Support Services Office in the Library of Congress. A small collection of his personal papers is in the Library of Congress Archives in the Manuscript Division. The Senate hearings on his nomination are important: U.S. Congress. Senate. Committee on Rules and Administration. *Nomination of Lawrence Quincy Mumford to Be Librarian of Congress.* 83d Cong., 2d sess., 1954. The most concise statement of his philosophy as librarian of Congress is in "The Bryant Memorandum and the Librarian's Report on It to the Joint Committee on the Library," *Annual Report of the Librarian of Congress for the Fiscal Year Ending June 30, 1962,* pp. 89–111. Two useful biographical articles are Rutherford D. Rogers, "LQM of LC," *Bulletin of Bibliography* 25 (Sept.–Dec. 1968): 161–65, and Benjamin E. Powell, "Lawrence Quincy Mumford: Twenty Years of Progress," *Quarterly Journal of the Library of Congress* 33 (July 1976): 239–57. Mumford's contributions to the Library of Congress are summarized in John Y. Cole, *Jefferson's Legacy: A Brief History of the Library of Congress* (1993). An obituary is in the *Washington Post,* 17 Aug. 1982.

JOHN Y. COLE

MUMFORD, Lewis (9 Oct. 1895–26 Jan. 1990), urban historian and cultural critic, was born in Flushing, New York, the illegitimate son of Lewis Charles Mack, a Jewish businessman from New Jersey, and Elvina Conradina Baron Mumford, a German Protestant. Mumford never knew his father, learning his identity only in 1942. He grew up in a lower middle-class environment in Manhattan and in 1912 graduated from Stuyvesant High School, where he was chiefly interested in science and technology. New York's museums and libraries contributed much to his education. Beginning in 1912 Mumford studied at City College, Columbia University, New York University, and the New School for Social Research. He earned enough credits for a degree but never graduated. Between 1914 and 1918 Mumford suffered from what he then regarded as incipient tuberculosis but which he later believed to have been a thyroid problem. He served in the U.S. Navy from 1918 to 1919. Having begun his career as a freelance writer, Mumford joined the staff of *The Dial* in 1919.

In 1915 he had discovered the works of his "master," Patrick Geddes, the Scottish biologist, sociologist, and urban planner, and Geddes invited him to London in 1920 to serve as editor of the *Sociological Review.* Mumford returned to America the same year, marrying Sophia Wittenberg in 1921. They had a daughter and a son who was killed in World War II, deeply affecting Mumford and making his work more pessimistic. During the 1920s Mumford established himself as a polymathic writer. After residing in Sunnyside, Queens, between 1925 and 1936, he and his family settled permanently in a rustic house in Amenia, New York.

Mumford was a visiting professor at Dartmouth, Stanford, the University of California at Berkeley, the University of Pennsylvania, Wesleyan, and the Massachusetts Institute of Technology. He received honorary degrees from the universities of Edinburgh (1965) and Rome (1967), the 1961 National Book Award (for *The City in History*), the Presidential Medal of Freedom (1964), the Emerson-Thoreau Medal (1965), the National Medal for Literature (1972), and the National Medal of Arts (1986).

Seen in American context, Mumford is one of a number of progressive thinkers, including Thorstein Veblen, John Dewey, Van Wyck Brooks, and Waldo Frank, who sought to renew American culture after World War I. They hoped to counteract capitalist materialism, the division of labor, the decline of local communities, and the divorce between high and low culture. Although Mumford during the 1930s called himself a communist, radical, and revolutionary, and although he inclined toward technocratic, bureaucratic, and collectivist values, he opposed both Bolshevism and the American Communist party and was on the whole a democratic socialist. He rejected Marxism, centrism, class warfare, and revolution in favor of class cooperation and a participatory reformist program aimed at a more equitable distribution and humane use of social wealth.

Mumford's interdisciplinary methods, his organic philosophy, and his interest in cities and regions all reveal Geddes's influence. His appreciation of self-reliant individualism derived from Ralph Waldo Emerson, while John Ruskin nourished his craft values and his concept of a non-pecuniary "life-economy." William Morris inspired his hopes for social and economic devolution to an intimate local level. He was indebted to Veblen's puritanical work ethic, praise of the neolithic village, technocratic values, and attack on the culture of money and conspicuous consumption. Ebenezer Howard's concept of the Garden City informed his urbanism and regionalism.

Mumford opposed economic determinism in arguing for the predominant influence of values or ideology in human life. The key to his thought is the Coleridgean antithesis between static mechanism, identified as the imposition *ab extra* of an abstract form or plan on living matter, and the organic form or plan that shapes itself from within, at once adapting to and mastering its environment. Mumford conceived of nature ecologically, as a complex system of balances and interdependences; following Geddes, he stressed the importance of balance and limitation in organic and social life. Just as the individual was ideally a harmonious union of diverse aptitudes, so human societies should strive for balance among their internal functions and for ecological harmony with nature. Accordingly, argued Mumford, cities must limit their growth, avoiding formless, destructive expansion into surrounding rural societies and the natural environment upon which their own vitality depends.

Fascinated with the idea of defining and shaping an organic society, Mumford analyzed utopian writing in his first book, *The Story of Utopias* (1922). Surveying ideal societies from Plato to William Morris, he criticized the vast majority as examples of closed planning, rigid blueprints for totalitarian uniformity and regimentation. According to Mumford, among nineteenth-century utopian works only Morris's *News from Nowhere* avoided these errors by accommodating the human need for artistic expression, craft production, guild organization, and an intimate village society in harmony with nature. Yet for all his suspicion of utopias and of closed or centralized planning, Mumford's *Technics and Civilization* (1934) and *The Culture of Cities* (1938) charted a "neotechnic" utopia, placing great faith in machinery, efficiency, technocracy, and centralized control. Only in the 1960s did Mumford decisively repudiate utopianism as inherently repressive, conformist, and inorganic.

The Culture of Cities and *The City in History* (1961) established Mumford as the foremost historian of the city in the English-speaking world. He conceived of the city not just as a physical container or commercial center but as a setting for vivid social drama, art, symbolism, ritual, and social interaction. Developing ideally according to an "open" or organic plan, the city must maintain a limited size and population as well as a coherent functional form, for which the preservation of neighborhoods is essential. A city must also strike a healthy balance with its natural environment and local and regional societies. *The Culture of Cities* and *The City in History* contrasted ancient Greek and medieval cities with ancient Rome and modern commercial and industrial metropolises. The former, according to Mumford, were small, culturally unified, intimate, and comparatively well balanced socially, economically, and environmentally; the latter were politically centralized, overplanned, regimented, excessively large, fragmented, alienating, and destructive of neighborhoods and regions. These historical works coincided with and contributed to Mumford's efforts in urban and regional planning.

Throughout his career Mumford advocated garden cities as a means of restoring urban life to a more human scale and a more natural environment. He was a founder in 1923 of the Regional Planning Association of America, which aimed to transplant metropolitan residents to smaller cities, to promote economic balance between cities and regions, and to create self-sufficient regions. Mumford helped to plan Radburn, in Fair Lawn, New Jersey, in 1928 and after 1938 served as an urban planning adviser in Hawaii and Britain. He admired the Tennessee Valley Authority yet believed that the federal government should have acted more vigorously in regional recovery. In 1948 he opposed the city planner Robert Moses's Stuyvesant Town, a Manhattan housing project, and in 1958 he helped to obstruct Moses's plan to eviscerate Washington Square for the sake of urban traffic. Mumford was also a fervent critic of Moses's plan to extend highways into the heart of New York City, arguing, correctly, that this would result not only in the destruction of thriving neighborhoods and the displacement of their residents but in a massive buildup of traffic in the urban core. Mumford's *The Urban Prospect* (1968) pessimistically surveyed America's failed urbanism, lamenting the increasing congestion, expansion, and formless suburbanization of the modern metropolis— a confirmation of Mumford's worst fears in *The Culture of Cities*.

Mumford was a founder of the history of technology, his major works in this field being *Technics and Civilization* and the two volumes of *The Myth of the Machine: Technics and Human Development* (1967) and *The Pentagon of Power* (1970). *Technics and Civilization* attempted to explain why Western Europe and America "surrendered" to the machine and tried to restore broader, more humane, and more vital values to an imbalanced, overly technological civilization.

Mumford charted three phases of Western technological development: the "eotechnic" era, characterized by dispersed power sources and nonmonopolizable fuels such as wind and water, which encouraged political decentralization and ecological harmony; the "paleotechnic" era, dominated by iron, coal, industrialism, mining, and railroads, which contributed to political and economic centralization and environmental destruction; and the twentieth-century "neotechnic" era, typified by electricity, the dynamo, light synthetic metals, cars, and airplanes, which afford the possibility of local and regional autonomy and a healthy natural environment. In *The Transformations of Man* (1956) Mumford acknowledged that his neotechnic utopia never materialized; yet instead of rejecting technology per se, he continued to blame its failures on its abuse by capitalism and the state.

In *Art and Technics* (1952), *The City in History*, and *The Myth of the Machine*, Mumford opposed the identification of human beings as essentially toolmakers, arguing that human development owed less to tools and machines than to the symbolic forms of art, language, drama, ritual, and dream—the educational province of the humanities. In *The Pentagon of Power* Mumford traced the overmechanization and overorganization of modern civilization to the mechanical and quantitative outlook of Galileo and Descartes. He contended that modern society was dominated by the "megamachine," an immense organizational and militaristic apparatus consisting of physical and human parts and having as its primary purpose the expansion of bureaucratic, centralized control over humanity and nature.

Many consider Mumford to be the twentieth century's greatest American architectural critic. His architectural criticism appears in *Sticks and Stones* (1924), *The Brown Decades* (1931), *The Culture of Cities*, *The South in Architecture* (1941), *From the Ground Up* (1956), *The Highway and the City* (1963), and numerous articles. From 1931 to 1963 he wrote the *New Yorker*'s "Sky Line" column. An architectural "organicist," Mumford rejected universal rules in favor of the open plan, thus accommodating the diversity and peculiarity of human functions, social and regional differences, and symbolic necessities. The work of architecture was to create a worthy human environment and to express the dominant values of its age. It should make use of contemporary materials and technologies in order to achieve a period style encompassing all building forms, from the civic to the domestic to the commercial. It should also harmonize with its social and regional environment while providing a setting for expressive ornament and social symbolism.

Mumford's writings on architecture aimed to unite the romantic and the utilitarian: functional buildings should satisfy emotionally, symbolically, and ecologically. Like Ruskin, Mumford deplored the formalism and uniformity of Renaissance architecture, much preferring Gothic, and castigated the rampant jerry-building of urban and suburban land speculators. Mumford found the architectural eclecticism of the nineteenth century to be a poor substitute for a genuine style. Although Mumford admired handicraft, in the 1930s he saw great possibilities in architectural functionalism, characterized by mass production, standardized forms, and austere geometrical design. Mumford's favorite modern American architects were Henry Hobson Richardson, Louis Sullivan, and especially Frank Lloyd Wright, all of whose buildings combine the functional use of machinery with ornamentation, symbolism, and a powerful feeling for local landscape. By the late 1940s Mumford had become a bitter critic of functionalism and the international style that embodied it, charging that Le Corbusier, Mies Van der Rohe, and their followers, in their worship of technology and automatic application of steel, glass, and other standardized forms, had created an inhumane architecture devoid of ornament and symbolism and ill-adapted to real human functions.

It is less well known that Mumford helped to found American studies in this country. In *The Golden Day* (1926), Mumford, inspired by his friend Van Wyck Brooks's 1918 *Dial* essay "On Creating a Usable Past," joined with Brooks in attempting to reclaim America's largely forgotten cultural legacy as an essential step toward cultural renewal. While *The Golden Day* shared Brooks's disapproval of the Puritans for their distrust of art and vitality, it also celebrated seventeenth- and eighteenth-century American society for its localism, village scale, ecological harmony, comparative egalitarianism, craft-based rather than commercial or industrial economy, and cultural unity. This culture was threatened by the rapacious, exploitative pioneer mentality and by the rise of capitalism in the nineteenth century. Like Brooks, Mumford admired Emerson, Henry David Thoreau, Nathaniel Hawthorne, Herman Melville, and Walt Whitman for preserving spiritual and cultural values in an increasingly commercial and practical society. Mumford contended, however, that after the Civil War America declined into a "pragmatic acquiescence," the idolatry of utilitarian and business success. In *The Brown Decades*, Mumford modified this bleak picture of late nineteenth-century American culture, resurrecting the "buried" tradition of neglected American artists such as Albert Pinkham Ryder, Frederick Law Olmsted, Thomas Eakins, Richardson, Sullivan, and Wright. Mumford's *Herman Melville* (1929), a biography and critical study, helped to make Melville a canonical writer.

Mumford must be seen not simply as a scholar and critic but as a moralist and public intellectual. Frequently messianic and apocalyptic in tone, he assumed the mantle of prophet from Victorian critics such as Thomas Carlyle and Ruskin. He often exhorted his readers to resist or withdraw from the technological power complex in order to develop balanced personalities as the basis for a new "organic synthesis." During the late 1930s he denounced American appeasement of Hitler, charging that bland progressivist optimism and worship of technological solutions had blinded the United States to the evil of nazism. After World War II Mumford campaigned against atomic weaponry and was one of the first intellectuals to oppose the war in Vietnam. Although Mumford's work routine and disciplined style of life oddly consorted with his romantic appreciation for spontaneity and variety, he largely practiced what he preached, enjoying rural and urban life in nearly equal measure while attempting as much as possible to live outside the "megamachine." He loved gardening, finding in it a sense of harmony with nature. He never learned to drive and for most of his life did not own a television. He died in Amenia, New York.

• Mumford's papers, including manuscripts, notes, and correspondence, are in the Lewis Mumford Collection, University of Pennsylvania. Some of his correspondence and manuscripts are in the Yale University Library, Dartmouth College Library, Princeton University Library, Cleveland Public Library, and the State Historical Society of Wisconsin Library, Madison. Of major importance are *The Van Wyck Brooks–Lewis Mumford Letters: The Record of a Literary Friendship, 1921–1963*, ed. Robert E. Spiller (1970); and *The Letters of Lewis Mumford and Frederick J. Osborn: A Transatlantic Dialogue, 1938–70*, ed. Michael Hughes (1971). Mumford's autobiography is *Sketches from Life: The Autobiography of Lewis Mumford; the Early Years* (1982); he completed only the first of a projected two volumes. A bibliography can be found in Elmer S. Newman, *Lewis Mumford: A Bibliography, 1914–1970* (1971). The standard biography is Donald L. Miller, *Lewis Mumford: A Life* (1989). The journal *Salmagundi* (Summer 1980) contains important essays on Mumford. An obituary is in the *New York Times*, 28 Jan. 1990.

ROBERT CASILLO

MUNCH, Charles (26 Sept. 1891–6 Nov. 1968), orchestral conductor, was born Charles Münch in Strasbourg, Alsace, the son of Ernest Münch, a professor of music at the Strasbourg Conservatory and an organist at the cathedral, and Célestine Simon. His close-knit family enjoyed home concerts, sometimes joined by Albert Schweitzer, the noted French humanitarian, theologian, and Bach scholar. Munch first studied violin at the Strasbourg Conservatory. After further study with the violin pedagogue Carl Flesch in Berlin, he moved to Paris in 1912 to study with French violinist Lucien Capet. He also took up the study of medicine for a short period of time.

As a native of the then German Alsace Munch was conscripted into the German army in World War I, during which he was gassed at Peronne and wounded at Verdun. With cession of Alsace to France, he became a French citizen in 1919. That same year he auditioned successfully for the post of concertmaster in the Strasbourg orchestra, and he joined the faculty of the Strasbourg Conservatory under composer and conductor Guy Ropartz, who became a lifelong friend. In 1926 Munch succeeded in a competition for the post of concertmaster of the Leipzig Gewandhaus Orchestra under Wilhelm Furtwängler. During his service in Leipzig Munch nervously but successfully conducted his first orchestra at the famous Thomaskirche, at which Johann Sebastian Bach had served as cantor.

With the rise of Adolf Hitler in Germany, Munch left for Paris in 1933, at which time he dropped the umlaut from his surname. There he conducted the Straram, Lamoureux, and other orchestras, rising quickly to the first rank of French conductors. He was named director of the Société philharmonique de Paris in 1935, became a professor at the École normale de musique in 1936, and served as principal conductor of the Société des concerts du conservatoire as well as a professor at the Paris Conservatoire from 1938 to 1946. Munch was admired for his sensitivity to musical timbres and coloristic effects as well as for his warm personality. He championed new French music by such composers as Florent Schmitt and Olivier Messiaen in his capacity as professor at the École normale de musique. In 1934 he married Genevieve Maury.

During the four years of French occupation during World War II Munch remained director of the Conservatoire orchestra, but he turned over most of his fees to the French Resistance movement and courageously prevented the removal of Jewish and other "undesirable" members of the conservatory by the Nazis and their French collaborators. For these and other actions he was awarded the Legion of Honor (red ribbon) in 1945 and the title of commander in 1952.

After having made guest appearances with the BBC and London symphonies Munch made his debut with the Boston Symphony Orchestra (BSO) as guest conductor on 27 December 1946, followed by a transcontinental tour of the United States with the French Orchestre national de la radiodiffusion français. He moved to the United States in 1949 when he was appointed to succeed Serge Koussevitzky as conductor of the BSO. This position placed Munch at the head of one of the world's great orchestras and centers of musical activity. The writer of his obituary in the *New York Times* likened Munch's task to "follow[ing] Thomas Alva Edison as an inventor." Munch was very different in character from the stern and uncompromising Koussevitzky; according to his obituary, he ended his introductory speech to the BSO players by saying, "Now, let's work, gentlemen. You know very well I am nothing without you." However, he "sustained the orchestra's brilliance and discipline" (Slonimsky) by his musicianship and his special personal touch with tone color and with French music, in which he was "all but unapproachable" (Schonberg). Less preoccupied with technical perfection and minutiae than Koussevitzky, Munch disliked intensive rehearsals. He was far more approachable than was his predecessor, especially by musicians, whose company he enjoyed.

Munch's European charm, coupled with his sensitivity and humility, endeared him to all but a few critics. He maintained an inflexible rule of never replying to criticism because he believed that one could never win an argument with the media. In an article published after Munch's death, *New York Times* critic Harold Schonberg observed that Munch conducted the music of Bach, Haydn, and Mozart in much the same way as did nineteenth-century conductors, neglecting implications of musicological research into eighteenth-century performance practice. Schonberg's criticism was ahead of its time in presaging the 1970s and 1980s boom in "period instrument" performance. But some writers in the 1990s, such as Peter Kivy, have pointed out disadvantages in "authentic" performance, asserting that the period instrument approach inherently poses problems in conveying the immediacy and inspiration of earlier works to general audiences. Thus in the future a "living tradition" performance style such as Munch employed for older music may once again become "modern."

Although he was known for championing contemporary French music, Munch nevertheless acknowledged the limits of audiences' abilities to absorb experimental contemporary music. In the approximately 500 works he programmed during his first five years at the BSO, Munch tended to avoid radically avant-garde pieces and even minimized his personal conducting of non-French contemporary compositions. Most of the works by such non-French twentieth-century composers as Bela Bartok and Igor Stravinsky were led by guest conductors. Although Munch introduced compositions by Roy Harris, Lucas Foss, Walter Piston, William Schuman, and Roger Sessions, the number of American compositions performed was modest.

Munch left the orchestra in 1962 and returned to France, where he founded the Orchestre national de Paris, effectively the French national orchestra, at the request of Andre Malraux, the French minister of culture. He was on tour with this orchestra in the United States when he suffered a heart attack and died in Richmond, Virginia.

Probably the best summation of Munch's artistic philosophy is contained in the final paragraph of his autobiography: "In the end it is the public who writes our history. . . . There is only one valid, certain, effective way to keep its favor: to practice our art with frankness and joy, and to love music more than anything else in the world" (p. 104). Munch was highly respected during a time of charismatic conductors such as Arturo Toscanini, Leopold Stokowski, Wilhelm Furtwängler, and Serge Koussevitzky. His reputation in English-speaking countries, however, has not been as lasting as in France.

• The most comprehensive source of information on Munch is his autobiography, *I Am a Conductor*, trans. Leonard Burkat (1955). A chronological and annotated volume of Munch's correspondence from 1912 to 1968 is *Charles Munch, un chef d'orchestre dans le siecle: Correspondance présentée par Genevieve Honegger* (1992). See also the entry on Munch in *Baker's Biographical Dictionary of Musicians*, 8th ed., rev. Nicolas Slonimsky (1991); Harold Schonberg, "Munch's Ideals: Clarity and Perception," *New York Times*, 7 Nov. 1968; Harry Ellis Dickson, *Gentlemen, More Dolce, Please: An Irreverent Memoir of Thirty Years in the Boston*

Symphony Orchestra (1969); and Peter Kivy, *Authenticities: Philosophical Reflections on Musical Performance* (1995). An obituary is in the *New York Times*, 7 Nov. 1968.

FRANK T. MANHEIM

MUNDAY, Richard (?–1739), carpenter and architect, first appears in the historical record on 29 November 1713, when he married Martha Simons in Newport, Rhode Island. His parentage, as well as the date and place of his birth, are unknown. In April 1719 Munday renewed his license to keep an inn, but in 1721 he purchased land in Newport and is referred to as a house carpenter in the deed. The following year he was given the privileges of full citizenship of the town.

The building with which Munday's name is first associated is Trinity Church in Newport. In 1723 Reverend James Honyman and the members of the vestry, with the support of the British Society for the Propagation of the Gospel, embarked on a campaign to replace a small church originally built about 1698. By 1725 the interior was under construction, but it was not until 1733 that the church was finally dedicated. None of the surviving documents (many from the period in question have disappeared) specifies Munday as the master builder, architect, or artisan. The extant papers, however, do indicate that whenever there was a question concerning the physical fabric, the church authorities asked Munday for advice, and on at least one occasion they paid him for that advice. The building's appearance suggests a familiarity with both high-style London church design and Christ Church in Boston. Originally the nave of Trinity Church was six bays long and did not include a projecting apse at the east end. Inside the nave, two rows of superimposed columns carried the galleries over the side aisles, a support system employed both at Christ Church and by Christopher Wren in his London parish churches. Rebuilt in 1763, the steeple at the west end of Trinity Church also seems to be derived from the Boston precedent and Wren's work. The handling of certain ornamental details, especially the pediments over the north doors, reveal not so much an archaic or provincial stylization of classicism, but a knowledge of the more exaggerated scale of some English baroque architecture. The attempted sophistication of the design and Munday's ongoing role in construction suggest that he had experience in earlier significant building projects.

The Seventh Day Baptist Meetinghouse in Newport, begun in late 1729, has also been credited to Munday. Construction was directed by a two-member building committee. One member was Henry Collins, a London-educated, wealthy merchant who commissioned paintings from John Smibert and Robert Feke. Collins's involvement may account for the contrast between the high-style interior ornamentation and the relatively unpretentious and essentially domestic exterior of the meetinghouse. The design of portions of the pulpit paneling repeats forms used at Trinity, and close examination of some of the molding profiles indicates that the same tools were employed at Trinity

Church. It is this physical evidence rather than documentary proof that has been the basis for considering Munday's involvement.

By 1731 Munday had moved to Bristol, Rhode Island, perhaps to build galleries for St. Michael's, an Episcopalian church that was destroyed by fire in the late eighteenth century. While in Bristol Munday's first wife, with whom he was childless, died, and in 1732 he married Elizabeth Hubbard, daughter of the wealthy landowner Nathaniel Hubbard and great-granddaughter of the seventeenth-century New England historian William Hubbard. Five children were born to the couple between 1733 and 1738. A mason's account records suggest that in 1738 Munday was building a house for himself in Newport.

In February 1739 the general assembly of Rhode Island passed an act for the erection of a new seat of colonial government. The design of the Colony House has been attributed to Munday because not only did he draw the plan but, as his widow stated in a 1743 petition, he advised and supervised the initial phase of construction. Munday's rectangular Colony House followed certain conventions of northern European town halls and earlier New England statehouses in that he placed one large space on the first floor and several meeting rooms above. The exterior of the brick building was ornamented with a richly carved balconied entrance and with rusticated sandstone quoins, window surrounds, and a beltcourse. The coloristic and textural effects recall the stylistic features of English baroque architecture.

In May 1739 Munday and Benjamin Wyatt signed a contract for the construction of a dwelling for Daniel Ayrault, a wealthy ship-owning merchant who was also a vestryman of Trinity Church. The surviving contract indicates that fashionable ornamental details such as a modillioned cornice, a shell-hooded doorway, and symmetrical planning features, including a central passage, were gradually challenging New England vernacular traditions. A plan for Ayrault's house, which served as a model for the house as built, also survives and is thought to be by the hand of Wyatt. Both the Colony House and the Ayrault House were incomplete at the time of Munday's death.

In his will, presented in court on 5 November 1739, Munday speaks of himself simply as a housewright, but his inventory shows that he had prospered in his profession. The partially obliterated inventory includes not only a chest of carpenter's tools but twenty-five books, gold and silver jewelry, and a female African-American slave.

Richard Munday, whose career presages the advancement of the architect in England and America from skilled craftsman to design professional, came to the Newport building scene at an opportune moment. His knowledge of English academic architecture and his ability to transfer those features successfully to colonial building types corresponded with Newport's emergence as one of the most prosperous urban centers in colonial America. Munday's architectural success would not have been possible without the commercial maritime wealth of the town's merchants, whose economic activities put them in contact with the wider British Empire, and for whom social ambitions, artistic and intellectual achievements, and civic improvement were all worthy pursuits.

• The Ayrault plan and contract are published in several secondary sources. The basic chronology of Munday's life can be established by consulting the primary sources reprinted in James N. Arnold, *Vital Records of Rhode Island, 1630–1850*, vols. 4 and 6 (1894), and the original probate records in the Newport Town Council Records, 1735–1741, vol. 8, at the Newport Historical Society. The most complete biography is Norman M. Isham, *Trinity Church in Newport, Rhode Island: A History of the Fabric* (1936). Further details concerning Munday's individual works appear in George Champlin Mason, *Annals of Trinity Church, Newport, Rhode Island, 1698–1821* (1890); Don A. Sanford, "The History of the Seventh Day Baptists in Newport," *Newport History* 66 (Summer 1994): 1–48; and Isham, "The Colony House at Newport, Rhode Island," *Old Time New England* 8 (Dec. 1917): 2–22. A general overview and a discussion of other possible Munday buildings are in Antoinette F. Downing, *Early Homes of Rhode Island* (1937); and Downing and Vincent J. Scully, Jr., *The Architectural Heritage of Newport, Rhode Island*, 2d ed. (1967).

BARBARA BURLISON MOONEY

MUNDELEIN, George William (2 July 1872–2 Oct. 1939), Catholic archbishop of Chicago, was born in New York City, the son of Francis Mundelein, a laborer, and Mary Goetz. Mundelein was educated at Catholic elementary and secondary schools and at Manhattan College in New York, from which he received his B.A. degree in 1889. He pursued his seminary studies at St. Vincent's Archabbey in Latrobe, Pennsylvania, then at the Urban College of the Propaganda in Rome. He was ordained to the priesthood in Rome on 8 June 1895 and served first in the diocese of Brooklyn. He received rapid promotion from his bishop, Charles McDonnell, becoming chancellor of the diocese after just two years as a priest, a monsignor at age thirty-four, and an auxiliary bishop at thirty-seven. At one time he simultaneously held ten different positions in the Brooklyn diocese.

On 9 December 1915 Pope Benedict XV appointed Mundelein third archbishop of Chicago. He was installed in that city on 9 February 1916, the youngest Catholic archbishop in the United States at that time, and remained there until his death. Chicago was an important archdiocese, with the largest Catholic population in the United States, but it had a record of uncertain episcopal leadership and a rebellious clergy. Mundelein's assignment in Chicago was to assert papal and episcopal authority, discipline the clergy, centralize the administration, and increase fundraising. He succeeded in all these tasks and was widely noted for his business skills. One businessman remarked to him, "There was a great mistake in making you a Bishop instead of a financier, for in the latter case Mr. [J. P.] Morgan [1867–1943] would not be without a rival in Wall Street" (Kantowicz, "Cardinal Mundelein," p. 54).

Though a striking individual, Mundelein was also typical of a whole generation of Catholic bishops in the United States early in the twentieth century. In the years surrounding World War I, a number of American-born but Roman-trained bishops came to power in the largest urban dioceses of the United States. These men, including William O'Connell in Boston and Dennis Dougherty in Philadelphia, were consolidating bishops who, like their counterparts in American business and government, were searching for order in the administrations they headed. Simultaneously, they attempted to gain new respect for the American Catholic church both in Rome, where their financial support became the mainstay of the Vatican, and in the United States, where their business ability and political influence bolstered the self-image of their religious communities and earned a sometimes grudging respect from non-Catholics.

Mundelein pursued a number of building projects, most notably Quigley Preparatory Seminary in downtown Chicago, completed in 1918, and St. Mary of the Lake major seminary in a rural location about forty miles north of the city. St. Mary of the Lake typifies Mundelein's attempt to make Catholic institutions first-class in their fields. At a time when most Catholic seminaries were ramshackle affairs, Mundelein's architect laid out a lavish, thousand-acre campus surrounding a small lake. All the buildings were of Early American design, with the main chapel a copy of a Congregational meetinghouse in Old Lyme, Connecticut, and the bishop's own residence modeled on George Washington's "Mount Vernon." Mundelein attempted to show in brick and mortar that his church could be both truly Catholic and truly American.

In 1924 Pope Pius XI named Mundelein to the College of Cardinals, the first American cardinal from a city west of the Appalachians. Two years later Cardinal Mundelein hosted the Twenty-eighth International Eucharistic Congress in Chicago. First held in France in 1881, the biannual congress had become a massive pilgrimage of priests, prelates, and laypeople. This devotional gathering had come to the Western Hemisphere only once before, to Montreal in 1910, and never to the United States. Over 800,000 people attended the final day's procession on the grounds of St. Mary of the Lake seminary. This once-in-a-lifetime event is a good example of how Mundelein attracted favorable publicity to the Catholic church of Chicago. Boosterism and civic pride overcame any anti-Catholic feelings on the part of non-Catholic Chicagoans, who took pride in the media attention lavished on their city.

Though Mundelein was similar to the other consolidating bishops in his financial prowess and his quest for publicity, he was more politically and socially liberal than most. His auxiliary bishop, Bernard J. Sheil, the founder of the Catholic Youth Organization, exercised considerable influence on Mundelein, and together they gave Chicago a reputation as a stronghold of liberal Catholicism. Mundelein reorganized and expanded the work of Catholic charities in

Chicago, encouraged Sheil in his wide-ranging social work projects, and appointed a liberal intellectual priest as rector of St. Mary's seminary. Mundelein supported industrial union organizing at the time of the sit-down strikes in Detroit's auto plants, and Bishop Sheil addressed a rally of Chicago packing house workers in person.

Mundelein became a friend and supporter of President Franklin D. Roosevelt. The two met about a dozen times between 1933 and the cardinal's death, and they kept in close contact through personal couriers, most notably Roosevelt aide Thomas Corcoran. (By chance, Corcoran happened to be at the cardinal's seminary residence north of Chicago the night Mundelein died.) Mundelein hosted Roosevelt himself in Chicago on 8 October 1937 after the president delivered his "quarantine address" on foreign policy. The Mundelein-Roosevelt relationship was a useful one for both parties. The cardinal's support helped neutralize Catholic suspicions that the New Deal was radical or communistic, and Roosevelt's friendship gave Catholics a feeling of pride and self-confidence.

Mundelein was a consolidating bishop who centralized the administration of his archdiocese and set it on a firm financial footing, while tying it more closely to Rome. It was often remarked that he "put the Catholic church in Chicago on the map." Though the Catholic church was the largest religious denomination in the United States as early as 1850, it lacked status and respect. The leadership of Cardinal Mundelein and his generation of big-city bishops raised the prestige of American Catholics, giving them clout both at home and in the Vatican.

• Mundelein's papers, consisting mostly of official administrative documents, are at the archives of the archdiocese of Chicago. A selection of Mundelein's speeches from his first two years in Chicago were published as *Two Crowded Years* (1918); and an official biography by Paul R. Martin, *The First Cardinal of the West* (1934), was written to commemorate his twenty-fifth anniversary as a bishop. Edward R. Kantowicz, "Cardinal Mundelein of Chicago and the Shaping of Twentieth-Century American Catholicism," *Journal of American History* 68 (1981): 52–68, assesses Mundelein's significance; and Kantowicz, *Corporation Sole: Cardinal Mundelein and Chicago Catholicism* (1983), provides a comprehensive study of his administration in Chicago. Other historical studies that contain considerable information about Mundelein include: James W. Sanders, *The Education of an Urban Minority: Catholics in Chicago, 1833–1965* (1977); Charles Shanabruch, *Chicago's Catholics: The Evolution of an American Identity* (1981); Joseph John Parot, *Polish Catholics in Chicago, 1850–1920* (1981); and Steven Avella, *This Confident Church* (1992).

EDWARD R. KANTOWICZ

MUNDT, Karl Earl (3 June 1900–16 Aug. 1974), U.S. congressman and senator, was born in Humboldt, South Dakota, the son of Ferdinand J. Mundt, a hardware merchant, and Rose E. Schneider. Mundt graduated from Carleton College in Northfield, Minnesota, where he met and married Mary Moses in 1924; they did not have children. He then taught high school speech and social science in Bryant, South Dakota, also serving from 1924 to 1927 as the town's superintendent of schools. After earning a master's degree in education at Columbia University in 1927, his wife also earning the same degree, he chaired the speech department at Beadle State Teachers College in Madison, South Dakota. From 1927 to 1936 he worked with his father in the Mundt Loan and Investment Company.

Mundt's interest in conservation led him to enter politics, beginning with election in 1927 as state president of the conservation-oriented Izaak Walton League. He then served a six-year term on the South Dakota State Game and Fish Commission. In 1936 he ran unsuccessfully as a Republican for a U.S. House seat, but another bid in 1938 resulted in victory.

Prior to the attack on Pearl Harbor, Mundt earned a reputation as a bedrock Republican and isolationist, opposing both the Selective Service Act (1940) and Lend-Lease (1941). Appointed to the Special House Committee on Un-American Activities (the Dies Committee) in 1943, he served on the subcommittee that briefly investigated the internment of Japanese Americans. Incredibly, the subcommittee concluded, among other things, that the civil and military authorities pampered the interned Japanese, making them the best-fed civilians in the country.

After the war and Mundt's appointment to the Dies Committee's successor (HUAC), his staunch anticommunism flourished. In a 17 May 1946 speech on the House floor, he said that "the extreme privilege of free press and free speech" would not stop the committee from exposing anyone "engaged in actions which are un-American even though their activities are legal." Nevertheless, Mundt's career defied stereotype. He was a consistent environmentalist and in 1946 helped create the United Nations Educational, Scientific and Cultural Organization (UNESCO).

Mundt was involved in the HUAC's highly publicized 1948 hearings involving Alger Hiss, the former State Department official whom ex-Communist Whittaker Chambers accused of being a member of a Communist cell while employed in the New Deal Agriculture Department during the mid-1930s. Although Mundt's contribution to the Hiss-Chambers case was secondary to that of freshman congressman Richard M. Nixon, but his involvement led to controversy. Four months after the case broke, Laurence Duggan, also a former State Department official, died after a fall from the sixteenth floor of a midtown New York City office building. Within hours of the apparent suicide, Mundt, with Nixon's concurrence, told newspaper reporters that Duggan's name had appeared alongside Hiss's on the seven-name list of former Communists that Chambers had supplied. Asked when the committee would release the other five names, Mundt said, "We'll name them as they jump out of windows," a remark that led to bitter criticism. Mundt and Nixon issued a public apology and announced rules of fair play that the committee would follow in investigating future subjects.

In 1949 Mundt was elected to the Senate, where his principal legislative legacy was the Internal Security Act of 1950, particularly the sections requiring the registration of domestic Communists. Having favored registration since his days in the House, he achieved some fame in promoting that cause. He also served on Joseph R. McCarthy's Permanent Subcommittee on Investigations, chairing the 1954 televised U.S. Army hearings that led to McCarthy's downfall. The hearings focused on McCarthy's charge that the army had blocked his earlier efforts to probe subversion at the Signal Corps research center at Fort Monmouth, New Jersey. This assignment could have been the turning point in Mundt's political career, but years of speech and debate training failed to prepare him to handle either McCarthy or McCarthy's principal adversary, U.S. Army counsel Joseph N. Welch, and he completely lost control of the hearings.

Mundt never again gained the limelight, although in the 1960s his criticisms of Vietnam peace activists and of normalizing relations with China attracted some attention. After he suffered a debilitating stroke in 1969, the Senate Republican leadership in 1972 took the unprecedented step of stripping him of seniority and key committee assignments. Mundt resigned his post, and in November Democrat James G. Abourezk took over his Senate seat. He died at Georgetown University Hospital in Washington, D.C.

• Mundt's papers, including correspondence with FBI director J. Edgar Hoover, are at the Karl E. Mundt Library in Madison, S. Dak. Some fifty unpublished research papers on various aspects of Mundt's career are also on file in the Mundt Library, ranging from Gerald Lange, "Americanism over Radicalism: Mundt's First Election" (1973), to Douglas T. Leon, "Karl Mundt: The Whooping Crane and the Conservation Ethic" (1979). The only biography is Scott Heidepriem, *A Fair Chance for a Free People: A Biography of Karl E. Mundt, United States Senator* (1988). An obituary is in the *New York Times*, 17 Aug. 1974.

KENNETH O'REILLY

MUNFORD, Robert, III (1737?–Dec. 1783?), dramatist, was born in colonial Virginia, probably in Prince George County, the son of the plantation owner Robert Munford II and Anna Bland. Following his father's death when Munford was eight, he was taken into the Essex County plantation home of his uncle William Beverley, the father of the cousin he would later marry. In 1750 Munford went with the Beverley family to England, where he enjoyed a private-school training under the very able classics master John Clarke. This education equipped him to undertake the translation of Ovid's *Metamorphoses*, which, although he had finished only the first book, his son would publish in 1798.

When Beverley died in 1756 without making provision for his nephew in his will, Munford returned to Virginia and began studying law in the office of his second cousin, Peyton Randolph. His training was interrupted by the French and Indian War, in which he served as a captain-lieutenant chiefly entrusted with recruiting duties; although he took part in the campaign to capture Fort Duquesne, he saw little combat. Soon after resuming his law studies, he came into possession of his father's former lands and, in 1760 or 1761, married Anna Beverley, who brought to their union a large dowry and land holdings that appeared to assure them the leisured life of southern Virginia plantation owners. They would be the parents of three children.

In the next years Munford rose through a series of local offices to election to the House of Burgesses in 1765, and he represented his county there or in its successor body, the House of Delegates, for twelve of the next fifteen years. He very early joined Patrick Henry and others in pleading the colony's grievances against Parliament. As the war neared, Munford joined in the resistance to Governor Dunmore, but he felt his conservative sympathies severely tried by many of his fellow Virginians' increasing militancy. Early in 1775 he wrote of these colonists' want of "a due Sense of the obligations both of Duty & allegiance that bind them to their Sovereign & to the preservation of civil order," but in time he sided with the American revolutionaries.

During the first years of the war Munford led a retired life, and it was probably during this time that he wrote his most artistically successful drama, *The Candidates; or, the Humours of a Virginia Election.* Internal evidence shows that it was written sometime after mid-October of 1770, and it was almost certainly a product of the following decade. Despite the description of the play as a comedy on the title page of its 1798 first printing, the author's son William more aptly classified it as a farce. Although its plotting was taken from English comic drama, Munford's varied characterization and social commentary invested *The Candidates* with local appeal. Beneath its slapstick and other elements of burlesque the play implies a critique of the responsibilities and dangers inherent in democracy. Political types familiar in colonial Virginia elections engage in such accepted practices as "treating," or supplying the voters with free alcohol; circulating rumors to undermine opposing candidates' reputations; and making extravagant campaign promises. In the end, the play demonstrates the truth of one of its patricians' declarations that "in order to secure a seat in our august senate, 'tis necessary a man should either be a slave or a fool; a slave to the people for the privilege of serving them, and a fool himself, for thus begging a troublesome and expensive employment." Although written to be staged, *The Candidates* was almost certainly not performed during its author's lifetime.

Following his election to the House of Delegates in 1779, Munford was appointed to responsible legislative positions, but his influence declined when his committee was found to have neglected the funding of needed defensive measures. In February 1781 he was named commanding colonel of the combined militias of Lunenberg, Mecklenburg, and Brunswick counties. After leading his forces into North Carolina, he took part in the battle of Guilford Courthouse before an attack of gout forced him to return home. Public records of the last two years of Munford's life tell of his being repeatedly accused of public intoxication and disorderly conduct, charges that seem to have forced him from the local offices he still held. At the same time, he was plagued by actions for indebtedness that may have hastened his death.

While no certain date can be assigned *The Patriots*, internal evidence suggests that it was written in the two years following the spring of 1777; there is no record of its ever having been produced. (The 1776 Philadelphia printing that is sometimes cited is a ghost edition; the play did not appear in print before the 1798 collection of his writings edited by his son.) The drama, although heavy with many of the farcical elements of *The Candidates*, would have had topical appeal for its caricature of personalities readily identifiable in southern Virginia public life. Much in the play derives from contemporary English drama, and it is like the earlier work in playing upon Virginia political life. In its satire of the popular mania for testing true loyalty, the play portrays the rivalry between early American ethnic groups and shows how justice was sometimes surrendered to partisanship. When one of the suspect American Scots demands proof of the disloyalty he is charged with, his accuser answers, "Proof, sir! we have proof enough. We suspect any Scotchman: suspicion is proof, sir." In portraying the local inquisitorial committee's vigilante mentality and the widespread intolerance of Scottish merchants and alleged Tories, Munford could draw upon attitudes he had known in Mecklenburg County, where his stepfather had been just the kind of enterprising Scot who suffered the animosity of the region's English settlers.

Munford's reputation as a playwright is entirely posthumous. There is no evidence that either of his plays was staged in his lifetime; their first recorded performance was a 1949 production of *The Candidates* in Williamsburg. Not even the 1798 collection of Munford's writings brought recognition to one who had thought of himself as "Virginia's first and only comic son." For almost fifty years Munford's literary efforts went totally unremarked, and until the first analyses of his plays appeared at the end of the nineteenth century, they were ignored as the slight diversions of a leisured gentleman. Since they first attracted serious study, Munford's stage satires have come to be seen as interesting pieces of stagecraft that derive their humor from two sources; they draw upon such sophisticated comedies as George Farquhar's *The Recruiting Officer* and Richard Sheridan's *The Rivals* while converting the frequently absurd and even scandalous practices of early Virginia—especially its politics—into lively theater. They continue to be of historical interest for preserving the style of late eighteenth-century Virginia's political life, and their idiom of broad humor is a measure of early American taste in drama.

• The principal collections of Munford's papers are in the libraries of the Virginia Historical Society, Duke University, and the College of William and Mary. Munford's writings were first published as *A Collection of Plays and Poems, by the Late Colonel Robert Munford, of Mecklenburg, in the State of Virginia* (1798). The texts of the plays and background material are given in Jay B. Hubbell and Douglass Adair, "Robert Munford's *The Candidates*," *William and Mary Quarterly*, 3d ser., 5 (Apr. 1948): 217–57, and Courtlandt Canby, "Robert Munford's *The Patriots*," *William and Mary Quarterly*, 3d ser., 6 (July 1949): 437–503. Rodney M. Baine, *Robert Munford: America's First Comic Dramatist* (1967), is the standard study of the plays. Jay B. Hubbell briefly assesses Munford's literary importance in *The South in American Literature, 1607–1900* (1954), pp. 142–48. A biographical-critical sketch by Homer D. Kemp appears in James A. Lavernier and Douglas R. Wilmes, *American Writers before 1800: A Biographical and Critical Dictionary* (1983). Political culture in *The Candidates* is the subject of Richard R. Beeman, "Robert Munford and the Political Culture of Frontier Virginia," *Journal of American Studies* 12 (Aug. 1978): 169–83.

HUGH J. DAWSON

MUNFORD, William (15 Aug. 1775–21 June 1825), court reporter, poet, and politician, was born in Mecklenburg County, Virginia, the son of Robert Munford, a planter, playwright, and poet, and Anne Beverley. William began his education at the grammar school at William and Mary, then attended the college. His talents and intelligence impressed his teachers, including George Wythe, America's first professor of law. Munford was one of a special group of students Wythe invited to live in his home in Williamsburg. When Wythe gave up his professorship to accept a position as the head of the Virginia Court of Chancery, Munford continued his legal studies with Wythe's successor, St. George Tucker, before he returned to Mecklenburg County in 1794 to begin practicing law.

It was not long before Munford entered politics. He represented Mecklenburg County in the Virginia House of Delegates, from 1797 to 1798 and 1800 to 1802, when he was elected to the state senate. After representing his district until 1806, he was elected by the legislature to the council of state (that advised and assisted the governor), where he served until 1811. Munford was rumored to be a member of a political club, or cabal, called the Richmond Junto, that supposedly ran the Republican party, which in turn ran the state. Despite its assumed omnipotence, the junto's membership was shadowy, and, in fact, the group probably did not exist.

In 1802 Munford married Sarah Radford. The couple had eight children. After his election to the council of state, Munford moved his family to Richmond.

Munford had no desire to try to lead the life of a country gentleman. Nor did he wish to continue his career in the law and politics. His inclination and talents led him to literature, the love of which he acquired from his father. He had done well in poetry, drama, and the classics in college, and he published a collection of poems, a play, and political addresses in *Poems and Compositions in Prose on Several Occasions* (1798). But he saw that he was not going to make money as a creative writer so he turned his talents elsewhere. In addition to supplementing his income handsomely, he made a significant contribution as a compiler, editor, and translator.

In 1806 Munford joined William Waller Hening in printing the Virginia Court Reports. Their four volumes, known as "Hening and Munford," reported the cases decided by the Virginia Supreme Court of Appeals. Needing to support his growing family, Munford increasingly took on clerical and editing positions. In 1811 he became clerk of the House of Delegates. After Hening withdrew as a reporter of the cases of the court of appeals in 1809, Munford continued to compile the opinions by the judges and prepared the volumes of case reports known as "Munford 1–6."

By 1819 Munford had simply taken on too many projects. Desperate to make money in publishing, he had taken a position assisting Hening and Benjamin Watkins Leigh in compiling *The Revised Code of the Laws of Virginia*, which was published in 1819. He was still clerk of the House of Delegates and reporting the opinions of the court of appeals, and he was preparing a two-volume work, *A General Index to the Virginia Law Authorities*, to assist lawyers, judges, and students of Virginia law. At the same time, he was pursuing a goal he had probably decided on in studying the classics at William and Mary: a translation of Homer's *Iliad*.

Unable to carry on all of these projects, he got increasingly behind in reporting the opinions of the court of appeals. Despite its connection with the alleged junto and Munford's assumed membership in same, in December 1819 the court of appeals asked the legislature to remedy the situation, complaining that there was a three-years' backlog of unpublished reports and that they were inaccessible, locked up in Munford's office. The court requested that the legislature allow the appointment of a person capable of publishing the reports soon after the decisions were made. In 1820 the legislature so authorized, and the court appointed Francis Walker Gilmer to be the official court reporter.

Munford did publish the first volume of his *Index*, in 1819, but failed to get the second volume published. He finished his translation of the *Iliad* but died in Richmond before he could secure its publication. His translation was eventually published in 1846, and Munford won some posthumous acclaim. Although the *Southern Literary Messenger* (Richmond) proclaimed that Munford's name was "destined to stand high among the literary men of Virginia," he would be remembered for the volumes of court reports he compiled.

Munford perhaps could have accomplished more in literature or the law if he had pursued one to the exclusion of the other. What makes him unusual among his fellow lawyers and politicians in Virginia, however, was his combination of the two.

• A collection of Munford's correspondence is in the Virginia Historical Society. See Pamela I. Gordon's biographical essay in *The Virginia Law Reporters before 1880*, ed. William Hamilton Bryson (1977), and Earl G. Swem and John Williams, *A Register of the General Assembly of Virginia 1776–1918, and of the Constitutional Conventions* (1911).

F. THORNTON MILLER

MUNGER, Theodore Thornton (5 Mar. 1830–11 Jan. 1910), Congregationalist clergyman, was born in Bainbridge, New York, the son of Ebenezer Munger, a physician and farmer, and Cynthia Selden. When he was six years old the family moved to Homer, New York, and Munger received his schooling at the village academy. After spending a year at Western Reserve College in Ohio, he matriculated at Yale in 1847 and graduated four years later. Graduating also from his alma mater's divinity school (1855), he pursued a brief term of postgraduate study at Andover Theological School.

In 1856 Munger was ordained and became minister of the Village Congregational Church in Dorchester, Massachusetts. Leaving there in 1860, he preached in churches around Boston, notably at Jamaica Plain and on Nantucket. In 1863 he accepted an invitation from the Centre Church in Haverhill; thereafter he held pastorates in Providence, Rhode Island (1869–1871), Lawrence, Massachusetts (1871–1875), San Jose, California (1875–1876), East Hartford, Connecticut (1876–1877), and North Adams, Massachusetts (1877–1885). In 1885 Munger became minister of the United Congregational Church in New Haven, Connecticut, where he served until retirement in 1901, remaining pastor emeritus until his death. In 1864 he married Elizabeth Kinsman Duncan; they had four children. Three years after her death in 1886, he married Harriet King Osgood.

A large part of Munger's historical significance derives from his identification with New Theology, but his activity along that line was the product of many years of slow maturation and sermon preparation. He was not considered a popular preacher, and most of his pulpit appearances failed to entertain large audiences, but in these thoughtful, restrained messages Munger based his ideas on practical experience and offered sound advice about coping with everyday dilemmas. His first book, *On the Threshold* (1881), a collection of addresses to young people, did not appear until he was more than fifty years old. Readers appreciated its realistic suggestions regarding moral choices and soon pushed sales to more than 25,000 copies. The volume was reissued as part of the Cambridge Classics series. His second book, *Freedom of Faith* (1883), was also widely read in the United States and England; some consider this appeal for open-mindedness in formulating religious affirmations to be his most important publication. Munger's lifelong attempt to clarify religious questions and answers, to grasp proper procedures and criteria, produced in him a facility for clear thinking and straightforward explanations. His readable prose made theology understandable to the masses.

Munger called for a reconstruction of religious thought, and seminal essays in *Freedom of Faith* have since been regarded as a manifesto of the New Theology, a liberal movement he endorsed. He called for an appreciation of spiritual truth that was discerned by human experience, not dry discussions of intellectual propositions shaped into arid systems. His sermons and articles appealed to laypeople and clerics alike because he explained New Theology to those unacquainted with esoteric scholarship and to those bewildered by the accusations of conservative critics. While admitting that he wanted to revise traditional conceptions in the Calvinist body of ideas, Munger insisted that he did not wish to demolish them entirely. He simply wanted to reach a broader range of realities in religious topics. Like many thinkers before him, he wanted to state in contemporary language the spiritual truths suggested and validated by human experience. This perspective also involved an attitude about biblical authority that conservatives found unacceptable. Espousing a "natural interpretation" of the Bible, Munger and other liberals viewed authors of Scripture as inspired writers who were nonetheless limited by their historical contexts.

Another broad principle in New Theology that Munger defended with literary flair was that there was no fundamental antagonism between revelation and science, faith and natural processes, sacred and secular. In his view of reality, spiritual impulses blended with material developments, and kingdoms of this world evolved into the kingdom of Jesus Christ. This was not secularizing theology, it focused instead on a wider study of man, showing a concern for real people who faced real problems. Religion could thus be a moral influence in all of life, rather than a magical force applied in only a few circumstances.

Munger proclaimed that divine revelation was embodied in the growth of human society, and he expected to discern additional validation of Christianity as culture became progressively richer. He saw the new emphasis to be on God's perseverance in saving humankind, not on threats of punishment or eternal damnation. Traditional categories such as divine sovereignty, incarnation, and resurrection were still relevant in his revised version of a heritage that stemmed from sixteenth-century Geneva; but he understood them respectively as the affirmation that the divine dwelled in human consciousness, the introduction of a redeeming force into human experience, and the continuation of human spirit and personality beyond this life. With these emphases Munger did much to free theology from the bonds of abstract logic. His ardent faith and gentle spirit gave liberal thought an air of dignity. He died in New Haven.

• Munger's papers, which include correspondence, sermons, and research materials, are housed in Yale University Library. In addition to works cited in the text, he wrote *Lamps and Paths* (1884), *Character through Inspiration, and Other Papers* (1897), *Horace Bushnell: Preacher and Theologian* (1899), *The Message of Christ to Mankind* (1899), and *Essays for the Day* (1904). Biographical information is in Benjamin W. Bacon, *Theodore Thornton Munger: New England Minister* (1913). Obituaries are in the *New Haven Evening Register*, 12 Jan. 1910, and *Congregational and Christian World*, 22 Jan. 1910.

HENRY WARNER BOWDEN

MUNI, Paul (22 Sept. 1895–25 Aug. 1967), actor, was born Mehilem "Muni" Weisenfreund in Lemberg, Austria (now Lvov, Ukraine), the son of Nachum Farel Weisenfreund and Salche Fischler (they later anglicized their names to Nathan Philip and Sally), touring Yiddish actors. The family came to the United States in 1901 and settled in New York's Lower East Side. In 1908 Muni joined a Yiddish-language stock company in Cleveland, Ohio, and made his acting debut in *Two Corpses at Breakfast*. He performed and toured with his parents in Yiddish vaudeville and theater until 1913; he then toured in the Midwest (1914–1917) and performed in Philadelphia (1917–1918). In 1921 he married Bella Finkel, an actress; they had no children.

Muni became a member of Maurice Schwartz's famed Yiddish Art Theatre in 1918 and stayed with the company as a leading performer until 1926. Among the productions he appeared in were *Hard to Be a Jew, Anathema, The Inspector General, Middle Class People,* and *Wolves*. He performed with the company in London in 1924 in *Sabbetai Zvi*. Muni was frequently singled out for praise by reviewers; the *New York Times* critic in the 1923 review of *Anathema* remarked, "There are several excellent individual performances—notably . . . Muni Weisenfreund as the poor, bewildered, heart-sick Jew."

Muni made his English-language debut in the Broadway production *We Americans* in 1926, playing an aged Orthodox Jewish father. In 1929 he was signed to a film contract by Fox, which renamed him Paul Muni. He was nominated that year for an Academy Award for his first movie, *The Valiant*. Unhappy with his second movie, *Seven Faces*, in which he performed seven roles, he returned to the Broadway stage, appearing in *This One Man* (1930) and *Rock Me, Julie* (1931). His greatest early success came in Elmer Rice's *Counsellor-at-Law*, which opened on Broadway on 6 November 1931; it was revived a year later and again in 1942. Brooks Atkinson, in his *New York Times* review wrote, "Mr. Muni gives one of those forceful and inventive performances that renew faith in the theatre" (7 Nov. 1931).

Muni went on to a number of stage roles, including Maxwell Anderson's *Key Largo* (1939), for which he received a Drama League award, and *Yesterday's Magic* (1942). He performed in two theatrical pageants that dealt with the plight of Europe's Jews during the Holocaust, playing the principal narrator in *We Will Never Die* (1943), a mass memorial for Europe's Jewish dead staged at Madison Square Garden, and a Holocaust survivor hoping to settle in a new Jewish state in *A Flag Is Born* (1946). Later in the decade, he appeared in a revival of *They Knew What They Wanted* (1949), and as Willy Loman in the 1949 London premiere of *Death of a Salesman*.

Muni's most successful later role was in the Broadway production of *Inherit the Wind* (1955–1956), in which he played the Clarence Darrow–like attorney Henry Drummond, and for which he won the Tony Award. Muni had to leave the show in the summer of 1955 because a malignant tumor required that his eye be removed; he was replaced by Melvyn Douglas, who gave way to Muni when he recovered. He performed in only one more stage production, *At the Grand*, a musical adaptation of *Grand Hotel*, which was presented on the West Coast in 1958 but never made it to Broadway.

Muni is probably best known to the public through his twenty-three film roles. He returned to movies in 1932 in *Scarface* and *I Am a Fugitive from a Chain Gang*. With the sucess of these films, he signed a long-term contract with Warner Bros.; it gave him the unusual prerogative of script approval and freed him to appear on stage between films. He scored triumphs in biographical films, receiving an Academy Award for *The Story of Louis Pasteur* (1936), the New York Film Critics' Award for *The Life of Emile Zola* (1937), and critical praise for *Juarez* (1939). Among his other films were *The Good Earth* (1937), *We Are Not Alone* (1939), *Hudson's Bay* (1940), *The Commandos Strike at Dawn* (1942), *Counter-Attack* (1945), *A Song to Remember* (1945), *Angel on My Shoulder* (1946), and *Stranger on the Prowl* (1953). His last critically-acclaimed film performance was *The Last Angry Man* (1959), in which he portrayed Sam Abelman, a physician who worked in a Brooklyn slum for almost half a century; for this performance he was nominated for an Academy Award.

Muni also appeared several times on television. In 1953 he starred in the *Ford Theatre* courtroom drama "The People vs. Johnson." He played an aging senator in "A Letter from the Queen," aired on *General Electric Theatre*. He appeared in a live *Playhouse 90* courtroom drama, "The Last Clear Chance," and was nominated for an Emmy Award for this performance. Muni's last appearance as an actor was as a guest on the series *Saints and Sinners* in 1962. During these last appearances, he had difficulty remembering lines.

Suffering from degenerating health and eyesight, Muni retired for the last few years of his life. He died at his home in Santa Barbara, California.

Muni was noted as a technically-skilled character actor who could transform himself through the use of vocal and physical techniques as well as with makeup. He researched his roles intensely and stayed in character even when he left the studio. Even as a young actor in the Yiddish theatre, he made his reputation playing older characters. At the peak of his film career, he was noted for biographical roles in which he captured the essence of historical personalities. A *New York Times* review of *Inherit the Wind* captures the technical brilliance of his acting, "Not a detail has been overlooked as he gets inside the character—the shuffling gait, the unpressed suit, the ruffled gray hair, the grimace in amazement, the cunning of the trial attorney, the booming, stentorian voice of the lawyer rushing in for the kill" (22 Apr. 1955). His obituary in *Newsweek* (4

Sept. 1967) called Muni "the greatest character actor of his day."

• Book-length works on Muni include Jerome Lawrence, *Actor: The Life and Times of Paul Muni* (1974), and Michael B. Druxman, *Paul Muni: His Life and His Films* (1974). A filmography is in Ephraim Katz, *The Film Encyclopedia*, 2d ed. (1994). Articles on Muni appear in several later twentieth-century standard references on the theater and film. A review of his performance in *Anathema* is in the *New York Times*, 9 Feb. 1923. Useful articles include Jerome Beatty, "The Man Who Is," *American Magazine*, Feb. 1938, pp. 42–43, 86–89, and Murray Schumach, "Muni's Second Fling with Fame," *New York Times Magazine*, 22 May 1955, pp. 17, 78. Obituaries are in *Variety Obituaries* (1988) and *Newsweek*, 4 Sept. 1967.

ALVIN GOLDFARB

MUNN, Biggie (11 Sept. 1908–18 Mar. 1975), college athlete, coach, and administrator, was born Clarence Lester Munn in Grow Township, Minnesota, the son of H. B. Munn and Jessie (maiden name unknown), farmers. Munn's father died when he was eight years old, and his mother moved the family to Minneapolis, where Munn attended first Jordan and then Minneapolis North high schools. Even though he had to work before-school and evening jobs in order to help the family, Munn was a three-sport high school star. An All-City fullback from 1925 to 1927, Munn was the captain of the football team in his senior year. He won varsity letters in basketball three years, and as the captain of the track and field team he performed superbly in field and running events, including the javelin and shotput, long jump, discus, relays, and 100-yard dash. In five track meets during his senior year, he averaged four first places in his six events, set state records in the javelin and shotput, and was undefeated in the 100-yard dash, which he ran in 10 seconds. At North High School Munn gained his nickname "Biggie" due to his almost-six-foot height, stocky build, and well over 200-pound weight.

Munn followed another remarkable high school athlete, Bronco Nagurski, to the University of Minnesota, where they played together on the 1929 Golden Gophers football team and became lifelong friends. In his three years of varsity football, Munn played for Coach Herbert Orin "Fritz" Crisler, earning All-America recognition as a guard in the 1930 and 1931 seasons and serving as team captain in his senior year. He was utilized as a punter and was a double-threat with his reliable kicking and his ability to run from punt formation. Munn also threw the shotput for the University of Minnesota track-and-field team, setting records for the Western Conference and in the Penn Relays, when he threw for 48'7⅝". He also won the Western Conference award for outstanding performance in athletics and academics. He adopted the motto, "the difference between good and great is a little extra effort," and it became his trademark philosophy later as a coach.

After his graduation in 1932, Munn became an assistant to Bernie Bierman, who was in his first year as head football coach at Minnesota. Under Bierman,

Munn learned the fundamentals of coaching and saw Coach Bierman build Minnesota in just three years to a national champion team in the 1934 season with a perfect 8–0–0 season. From Bierman Munn learned that effective line play was the key to offensive success, with blocking schemes, quick-pulling guards, and endurance conditioning being central features.

In 1935 and 1936 Munn served as athletic director and three-sport coach (football, basketball, and track) at Albright College in Reading, Pennsylvania, where his football teams won thirteen games, lost two, and tied one. During the 1937 season Munn served as line coach under Ossie Solem at Syracuse University.

In 1938 Munn joined Crisler's coaching staff at the University of Michigan. For eight years Munn developed the powerful Wolverine lines that made the explosive offense one of the most frequently high-scoring and consistently winning teams in the country. He drove his players to be fierce blockers with an emphasis on agility, speed, and sound fundamentals. Three of the guards that Munn coached at Michigan gained recognition on Grantland Rice's All American teams. In 1946 Munn was called back to Syracuse to succeed Ossie Solem as head coach and was given a three-year contract. However, after experiencing a disappointing 4–5 season and realizing that the football team lacked alumni and institutional support, Munn canceled his contract.

In December 1946 Munn was hired as head coach at Michigan State College and given the opportunity to rebuild its program and transform a school with a "cow college" image into a national football powerhouse. In the first game of the 1947 season, Munn's Michigan State team was humiliated by the University of Michigan 55–0 at Ann Arbor, but the team recovered to post a 7–2 season record. Munn's teams lost three consecutive games to Michigan until the 1950 team won at Ann Arbor, and in each of the last four years of Munn's tenure as head coach, the Spartans beat their Wolverine rivals. After three winning seasons under Munn, Michigan State began playing a partial Big Ten Conference schedule, beating three Big Ten teams and posting an 8–1 season record in 1950. They lost only to Maryland, in the third game of the schedule, and gained an eighth-place national ranking. In the 1951 season Munn's team went undefeated in nine games and were ranked second nationally behind Tennessee with a 10–1 record. In 1952 Munn's team gained the national recognition it deserved when it posted a second undefeated season with another 9–0 record and claimed a national championship. The Football Coaches Association voted him Coach of the Year by a wide margin in 1952. The 1952 team played under the cloud of a one-year probation from the Big Ten Conference, but the national championship more than dispelled any questions about the school's future as a powerhouse. Michigan State was first qualified for the conference championship in the 1953 season and lost only to Purdue, winning the conference and beating the University of California at Los Angeles in the Rose Bowl to climax a 9–1 season. In his seven years as head coach, Munn's teams were 54–9–2.

As head coach, Munn was known for being a tough and demanding disciplinarian who was respected by his players. His remarkable success as a coach can also be attributed to his effective recruitment program, which featured the development of new areas of recruitment in Hawaii and Pennsylvania, as well as the utilization of talented black American athletes such as Leroy Bolden, Ellis Duckett, and Don Coleman. Munn also developed a versatile multiple offense system that utilized the single-wing and variations of the T formation. His offense was built around a simplified system that could be quickly taught and understood by his players. His 1953 book titled *Michigan State Multiple Offense* detailed the successful system he developed and became a textbook studied by coaches at all levels. He recruited linemen who were quick and agile and who could execute a variety of specialized blocks essential to a multiple offense, and his backfields were noted for their quickness in hitting open holes and their speed to the outside. His teams were noted for their stamina gained from demanding conditioning and for their mastery of the basic techniques and mechanics of blocking and tackling. The two-platoon system allowed Munn to use a large number of players and to substitute freely in order to keep his teams fresh. In his system Munn taught players to learn their specialized roles on offense and defense while fostering a sense of team spirit and unity. To Munn, the intangible qualities of "heart and desire" were more important than physical attributes of height and weight.

In 1953, at the height of his success, Munn turned over the head coaching job to one of his assistants, Hugh Duffy Daugherty, whom Munn had hired in 1947. The next year Munn became director of Health, Physical Education, Recreation for Men and Women and Athletics. As director, he oversaw the construction of the Men's Intramural Building, improvements of the Women's Intramural Building, the construction of an ice arena, and the football stadium's expansions and improvements. An active and highly visible person off campus, Munn was president, board director, and honorary trustee of the Fellowship of Christian Athletes. He belonged to and was active in many organizations such as the Red Cross, Boy Scouts, Rotary, and Shriners, and he served on the U.S. Olympic Committee and belonged to the American Football Coaches Association. He was known statewide for his coaching clinics and his innumerable appearances as a guest speaker for banquets and lectures. A dynamic and forceful speaker, he was an effective proponent of competitive sports and the values of team pride, teamwork, and campus spirit fostered by football. He believed in physical conditioning and activity for all students and built a fifteen-sport varsity program and an active and diverse intramural program. He was also the co-originator, with Lansing, Michigan, journalist George Alderton, of the State of Michigan Sports Hall of Fame.

In October 1971 Munn suffered a stroke that left him partially paralyzed and curtailed his work, forcing him to retire on 1 September 1973. Numerous honors were accorded Munn, including inclusion in the Minnesota Sports Hall of Fame as player and coach, in the Michigan Sports Hall of Fame as coach in 1961, and in the National Football Foundation Hall of Fame in 1959. On 1 November 1974 the Munn Ice Arena on the Michigan State University campus was dedicated. On 10 March 1975 Munn suffered a second stroke. He died in a Lansing, Michigan, hospital. He was survived by his wife, Vera Jean Wattles, and by their two children.

Munn's legacy to Michigan State University was the establishment of a successful national football program that coincided with the development and expansion of the institution into prominence during the post–World War II period. His teams and their success brought pride and spirit to a growing institution. Munn also directed the development of a full varsity sports program and an intramural and recreational program for students.

• The John A. Hannah Papers in the Michigan State University Archives and Historical Collections, East Lansing, Mich., contain many documents related to Munn's tenure as coach and as director of Health, Physical Education, Recreation for Men and Women and Athletics. Munn's *Michigan State Multiple Offense* (1953), while largely a technical how-to book on football, does contain some autobiographical material and an enunciation of his philosophy of coaching and his observations on the value of intercollegiate athletics. For Munn's career in college football, see Fred W. Stabley, *The Spartans: A Story of Michigan State Football* (1975), and Tom Perrin, *Football: A College History* (1987). For the background of Munn's being hired in 1947, see Beth J. Shapiro, "John Hannah and the Growth of Big-Time Intercollegiate Athletics at Michigan State University," *Journal of Sport History* 10 (Winter 1983): 26–40. Duffy Daugherty (with Dave Diles), *Duffy: An Autobiography* (1974), contains valuable information on Munn as a head coach and on the transition from Munn to Daugherty. Valuable newspaper obituaries include those in the *New York Times* and the *Lansing State Journal*, both 19 Mar. 1975.

DOUGLAS A. NOVERR

MUÑOZ MARÍN, Luis (18 Feb. 1898–30 Apr. 1980), Puerto Rican political leader and author, was born in San Juan, Puerto Rico, the only son of Luis Muñoz Rivera, a political leader who won from Spain the island's first measure of autonomy, and Amalia Marín. Born only five months before the island became a U.S. possession, he spent many of his formative years in New York City and Washington, D.C. He completed elementary school in San Juan but graduated high school from Georgetown University's preparatory school, which he attended between 1911 and 1915 while his father served in Congress as resident commissioner for Puerto Rico. Upon graduation, Muñoz studied law for one year at Georgetown University law school.

Following the death of his father, Muñoz left the university and became secretary to the new resident commissioner from Puerto Rico, Félix Córdova Dávila. During this time (1916–1918) Muñoz organized his father's papers and poems for publication and contributed articles to the *Baltimore Sun* and various national magazines. In 1917 he published two books of essays, *Borrones* and *Madre Haraposa*.

To pursue his career as a writer, Muñoz moved in 1918 from Washington, D.C., to New York City, where he founded *La Revista de Indias (The Review of the Indies)*, a magazine devoted to Latin American culture, and worked as a freelance writer for various journals. In July 1919 he married the Mississippi-born translator Muna Lee.

Except for several brief visits to Puerto Rico during the 1920s, Muñoz remained in New York City until 1931, when he returned permanently to San Juan with his wife and two children. In San Juan he became editor of the newspaper *La Democracia* and joined a group of ex–Union Party members in forming the Liberal party (1932). The new party recognized political independence as part of its platform, a position Muñoz shared at the time.

Although the Liberal party lost the 1932 election to the opposition, the coalition of the Socialist and the Republican parties, Muñoz won his first elected office, as senator in the insular legislature.

He used his time in office to promote social justice and economic reform for the islanders by conveying news of the plight of economically depressed Puerto Rico to the Franklin D. Roosevelt administration. In December 1933 Muñoz was invited to tea at the White House by Eleanor Roosevelt. The story he painted of the island's despair brought Mrs. Roosevelt and several government officials to San Juan the following March.

The next two years were spent drafting and putting into effect an economic recovery plan, known locally as the Chardón Plan (named after Dr. Carlos Chardón, chancellor of the University of Puerto Rico) and in Washington as the Puerto Rico Reconstruction Administration. Over $70 million were appropriated for this project by the U.S. government. One essential piece of the project was to provide homesteads to the landless rural population through a land reform.

The years 1936 to 1938 were difficult for Muñoz. His marriage to Muna Lee ended in separation (and divorce in 1940). Differences with the Liberal party leadership over the island's future political status led to his ouster from the party in 1937. Muñoz no longer believed that independence was the best formula for Puerto Rico.

A born leader, Muñoz rallied his forces and began his political comeback. Convinced that the political future of any insular party rested with the rural masses, Muñoz founded the Partido Popular Democrático (Popular Democratic Party) (PDP), with the profile of the *jíbaro* (peasant) as the party's symbol. The slogan of the new party was simply Bread, Land, and Liberty, for Muñoz claimed to have learned from the peasants that the island's unresolved political status was not the issue.

His campaign among the rural and urban poor for land reform, medical attention, electricity, and other social reforms led to an astounding victory for the PDP in 1940. Muñoz became president of the senate, a position that permitted his party to launch the promised reforms. A law passed in 1941 created a land authority with power to acquire land and to subdivide it among the landless. Other legislation to provide the poor with electricity, water, and accessible schools and clinics also followed. The result was a landslide victory for the PDP in 1944, followed by successive victories during the next five elections.

With the end of World War II, Muñoz and the leaders of the PDP impressed upon Washington the need to reform Puerto Rico's political structure. They demanded, and obtained, the right to elect their own governor (1947) and the right to draft a constitution of their own choosing (1950).

In 1948 Muñoz became the first elected governor of Puerto Rico. That year he also married Inés Mendoza, a schoolteacher, with whom he had two children.

No longer convinced that independence was the best political solution for the colony, Muñoz proposed autonomy as a third alternative to the standard options of statehood and independence. His plan called for an autonomous Puerto Rico, in association with the U.S. government, held together by a solemn compact or union between two equally sovereign states.

Between 1950 and 1952, Muñoz and the PDP, working with the people of Puerto Rico, the U.S. Congress, and the president of the United States, altered the colonial structure by providing the island with a constitutional, autonomous government, called the Commonwealth of Puerto Rico, which was recognized by the international community at the United Nations in 1953. Under commonwealth status, residents of Puerto Rico pay no federal income taxes but do not vote in presidential elections or have voting representation in Congress, except for one resident commissioner. The island qualifies for all federal grant programs, and the United States represents Puerto Rico in foreign affairs and protects it militarily.

Faced with growing opposition from the pro-statehood and pro-independence movements during the 1950s, Muñoz proposed to President John F. Kennedy in 1962 the idea of a plebiscite in which the people of Puerto Rico could decide, once and for all, their preference. Once the idea was accepted, Muñoz declined his party's nomination in 1964 for a fifth term as governor, suggesting his friend and colleague, the secretary of state, Roberto Sánchez Vilella for the job. In order to give his attention to the upcoming plebiscite, scheduled for July 1967, Muñoz returned to the senate.

The plebiscite was a success for Muñoz's position on status, as 60 percent of the voters demonstrated their preference for the commonwealth formula, although with some revisions in the scope of the federal powers Washington still held over the island. Despite the electoral victory, the terms of the plebiscite were never implemented because Washington was no long-er interested, and the PDP government itself was ousted from office by the pro-statehood party in the 1968 elections and several times after that.

Elected to the senate in 1968, Muñoz only served two years of his four-year term before resigning in May 1970. He set out on a voluntary exile to Italy that year, to write his memoirs. He returned to Puerto Rico in 1972 to a massive welcome of his compatriots. His work on behalf of the PDP helped it to win the 1972 gubernatorial elections.

In his thirty years in power, Muñoz made many changes in Puerto Rico, even though his dreams remained unfulfilled at the time of his death in San Juan. In his quest for social justice, he transformed Puerto Rico from a backward, agricultural country into a modern nation, dependent on industry and commerce. Yet he was unable to eliminate poverty and inequality. Politically he led the colony into a new, autonomous relationship with the United States but was unable to resolve the island's fundamental political question. Consequently the debate over commonwealth, statehood, or independence continued unabated.

When he retired from active politics in 1975, Muñoz was still considered an unequaled statesman, recognized internationally for his political genius, the mentor of his party, and the beloved father figure of hundreds of thousands of Puerto Ricans.

• The papers of Luis Muñoz Marín, from his essays and poetry to his political speeches, are housed in the *Fundación Luis Muñoz Marín* in San Juan, Puerto Rico. The Documents and Archival Collection of the New York Public Library has copies of Muñoz's correspondence dating to 1927 and 1928. Muñoz's personal *Memorias, 1898–1940* (1982) offer valuable insight into his motivations for his political career.

The best three biographies on Muñoz are Thomas Aitken, Jr., *Poet in the Fortress* (1964); Thomas Mathews, *Luis Muñoz Marín: A Concise Biography* (1967); and Carmelo Rosario Natal, *La Juventud de Luis Muñoz Marín: Vida y Pensamiento, 1898–1932* (1989). The biography of Manuel de Heredia, *Luis Muñoz Marín: Biografía Abierta* (1973), contains valuable excerpts of a taped interview with Muñoz but is generally a poor work. Of interest to young readers are the shorter, popular accounts published by Marianna Norris, *Father and Son for Freedom: The Story of Puerto Rico's Luis Muñoz Rivera and Luis Muñoz Marín* (1968), and Philip Sterling and María Brau, *The Quiet Rebels: Four Puerto Rican Leaders* (1968). For details on his career consult the Puerto Rican newspapers *El Mundo, El Imparcial,* and *La Democracia* as well as the *New York Times* and the *Washington Post* indexes. A front-page obituary is in the *New York Times,* 1 May 1980; see also the related editorial in the *New York Times,* 2 May 1980.

OLGA JIMÉNEZ WAGENHEIM

MUÑOZ RIVERA, Luis (17 July 1859–15 Nov. 1916), resident commissioner for Puerto Rico in Washington, D.C., writer, and newspaper editor, was born in Barranquitas, Puerto Rico, the son of Luis Ramón Muñoz Barrios, a merchant and landowner, and Monserrate Rivera Vásquez. Inhabitants of a small town in the mountainous interior of Puerto Rico, Muñoz Rivera's parents sent him at age six to the only local school. At age ten he had gone beyond what formal education could be offered there and studied with private tutors. His father taught him the rudiments of bookkeeping and basic business practices, and Muñoz Rivera became a modestly successful businessman. His father was mayor of Barranquitas and a member of the pro-Spanish Conservative party, and his uncle Vicente was a member of the Liberal party, So Luis grew up listening to the political discussions that agitated the Spanish colony in the 1860s and 1870s. At issue was local autonomy versus control by Spanish-appointed governors and their hand-picked advisory councils. The issue continued to agitate Puerto Ricans despite a change of colonial masters after the Spanish-American War in 1898.

Despite his father's ties to the Conservatives, Muñoz Rivera joined the Liberal party in 1883 and was elected to the town council of Barranquitas. He became a representative to the convention that created the Autonomist party in 1887. Reacting to the move toward autonomy, Governor Romualdo Palacio, supported by fearful Conservatives, unleashed a wave of repression and terror, the componte, against the Autonomists. Hundreds were arrested, tortured, and killed, and others fled into exile. While short-lived, the government terror left the Autonomists in disarray but still alive as a party. In 1889 Muñoz Rivera ran for a seat in the provincial assembly and was declared the winner, but the election was contested. By the time the courts decided in his favor, his term had expired. At this juncture, Muñoz Rivera sold his share in a general store, borrowed money, and went into the newspaper business in the southern town of Ponce. The first issue of La Democracia appeared on 1 July 1890, and the Autonomist politician combined his journalism with his political activities for much of the rest of his life. In 1893 he married Amalia Marín. They had one son, Luis Muñoz Marín, who became Puerto Rico's first elected governor in 1948 and a founder of the Commonwealth of Puerto Rico.

Through La Democracia Muñoz Rivera argued for autonomy or self-government within the Spanish empire. Owing to the weakness of the Autonomist party, he urged an alliance with the Spanish Liberal Fusion party led by Práxedes Mateo Sagasta. Republicans in his own party, finding an alliance with Spanish monarchists repugnant, opposed the idea. A trip to Spain in 1895 convinced Muñoz Rivera that, without such an alliance, Puerto Rican Autonomists would continue to flounder and hopes for insular self-government would dim. He persuaded the Autonomists to reorganize as the Liberal party, and with Muñoz Rivera as president, they united with Sagasta. Sagasta became prime minister in August 1897. Inheriting a war with Cuban insurrectionaries and fearing the loss of Puerto Rico if promised concessions were not made, he granted the island its Charter of Autonomy in November.

No sooner had Puerto Rico won home rule and Muñoz Rivera become president of the Council of Secretaries and secretary of state, the United States, now at war with Spain, invaded the island and took posses-

sion of it as a prize of war. Muñoz Rivera was a Puerto Rican nationalist and patriot but also a realist and political moderate. Saddened by the turn of events, he devoted the rest of his life to the struggle for greater home rule for his beloved island. It was an uphill battle that inspired him to write one of his more memorable poems, in which he compared himself and his country to the Greek legend of Sisyphus, eternally doomed to push a boulder up the side of a steep mountain only to have it roll to the bottom before reaching the top. The United States put its new possession under martial law but prevailed on Muñoz Rivera and his colleagues to remain in office. When General Guy V. Henry assumed command, however, Muñoz Rivera found him impossible to work with and resigned early in 1899.

U.S. control sent Puerto Rico's economy into decline. Blocked from their traditional market by Spanish tariffs imposed on the primary exports of coffee, tobacco, and sugar, growers faced similar exclusion from the U.S. market. Representing the island's sugar planters, Muñoz Rivera went to Washington in 1899 to urge a free trade agreement. The Foraker Act of 1900 established a civil government on the island but delayed free trade for two years and gave all executive and judicial power over Puerto Rico to Congress. Puerto Rican voices were heard only in a house of delegates that was elected by the people but held no power over education or public safety. Upon his return from the United States, Muñoz Rivera moved to San Juan, where he opened a new newspaper, El Diario de Puerto Rico, and founded the Federal party to oppose the Foraker Act and press for home rule. On one occasion he was wrongfully brought before a judge for armed assault. Asked by the judge if he had ever been charged with breaking the law, he replied, "Forty-two times, and every time it was for wanting to make a free country out of what others want to turn into a slave colony." He was acquitted.

Joining with disaffected Republicans, Muñoz Rivera's Federal party in early 1904 formed the Unionist party. The new party elected him to the house of delegates, where he served from 1906 to 1910. In 1910 the house of delegates sent him as resident commissioner for Puerto Rico to the U.S. House of Representatives, where he had no vote and usually no voice. Nevertheless, he privately informed congressmen of Puerto Rican needs and aspirations. In 1901 he had established in New York a Spanish-English newspaper, the Puerto Rico Herald, and he continued to write for that paper as well as for La Democracia. Both journals conveyed his party's beliefs about the proper U.S.–Puerto Rican relationship. For example, in the Herald he wrote, "We affirm the right of Puerto Rico to assert its own personality, either through statehood or independence. If the United States continues to humiliate and shame us, we can forget about statehood and support independence, with or without U.S. protection."

Muñoz Rivera, Unionists, and Republicans hoped that, when the U.S. Democrats took power in 1913, they would overturn the hated Foraker Act. Unfortunately, it took World War I and the fear of German influence in the Caribbean to move Congress to heed Puerto Rican complaints. Congress crafted the Organic Act for Puerto Rico, known as the Jones Bill, in January 1916 to replace the Foraker Act. The Jones Bill made the island a U.S. territory, granted its population U.S. citizenship (with all civil rights except trial by jury), set up a legislature that was an elected body (though subject to a presidential veto), and organized tax collections paid into the local treasury for use in Puerto Rico, among other provisions. It perpetuated a colonial status for the island while at the same time bestowing blanket U.S. citizenship—albeit with limitations—on a people whom Muñoz Rivera did not think wanted it. Despite its shortcomings, Muñoz Rivera argued in its favor, giving several significant speeches in the House of Representatives. On 5 May 1916 he demanded:

Give us now the field of experiment which we ask of you. . . . It is easy for us to set up a stable republican government with all possible guarantees for all possible interests. And afterwards, when you . . . give us our independence . . . you will stand before humanity as a great creator of new nationalities and a great liberator of oppressed people.

Exhausted and in ill health, the poet, editor, and statesman returned to Puerto Rico and an outpouring of gratitude from his people. He died from liver disease in Santurce, a suburb of San Juan, more than four months before the Jones Bill became law in March 1917. While his private correspondence reveals that Muñoz Rivera deeply desired Puerto Rican independence as his long-term goal, his knowledge of the United States told him that the most he could hope for in his lifetime was a limited form of home rule as spelled out in the Jones Bill. Besides his importance as a politician and statesman who continually championed greater home rule for Puerto Rico and a clearer definition of its relationship to the United States, Muñoz Rivera is noted in Puerto Rico for his nationalistic poetry and his political writings.

• Muñoz Rivera's writings have been collected into *Obras Completas*, ed. Lidio Cruz Monclova (8 vols., 1968); and *Campañas Políticas*, ed. Luis Muñoz Marín (3 vols., 1925). His poetry was published as *Poesías* (1961). A solid biography dealing with the earlier part of his political career is Cruz Monclova, *Luis Muñoz Rivera: Diez Años de su Vida Política* (1959). Frederick E. Kidder, "The Political Concepts of Luis Muñoz Rivera (1859–1916)" (Ph.D. diss., Univ. of Florida, 1965), studies his political philosophy of Puerto Rican autonomy and demonstrates its importance for future political developments. Arturo Morales Carrión, *Puerto Rico: A Political and Cultural History* (1983), is useful for placing Muñoz Rivera in the context of Puerto Rican history. Also see Frank Otto Gatell, "The Art of the Possible: Luis Muñoz Rivera and the Puerto Rican Jones Bill," *The Americas* 17 (July 1960–Apr. 1961): 1–20. Obituaries are in the *Puerto Rico Illustrado*, 18 and 25 Nov. and 7 Dec. 1916.

ERROL D. JONES

MUNROE, Charles Edward (24 May 1849–7 Dec. 1938), chemist, was born in East Cambridge, Massachusetts, the son of Enoch Munroe, an instrument maker, and Emeline Elizabeth Russell. He pursued his boyhood interest in chemistry as a student at the Lawrence Scientific School of Harvard University, from which he received a bachelor of science degree summa cum laude in 1871. Remaining there as an assistant in chemistry for another three years, he established both a course in chemical technology, the nineteenth-century beginnings of present-day chemical engineering, and a successful summer school in chemistry, the first of its kind in the country. These were two educational innovations of which he remained especially proud.

After being named professor of chemistry at the U.S. Naval Academy in 1874, Munroe began his investigations into explosives, for which he gained worldwide recognition. In 1886 he moved to the Naval Torpedo Station and War College at Newport, Rhode Island, where he developed a smokeless gunpowder in response to announcements that France had adopted such a powder for military use in 1887. All the smokeless powders developed in Europe were mixtures of cellulose nitrates with various other compounds, but Munroe's goal was to produce one consisting of a single, chemically pure, highly nitrated cellulose. Although the resulting "indurite" was hailed by President Benjamin Harrison as "one of the greatest achievements of my administration," it was not used by the U.S. military because of technical problems in its large-scale production.

From his work on smokeless powder, Munroe discovered the so-called Munroe effect, in which the detonation of guncotton transfers a raised or relief design onto an adjacent metal plate. The study of this phenomenon not only increased understanding of explosions themselves, but also led to important developments in armor-piercing shells and other munitions based on "hollow," or "shaped," charges, which concentrate the explosive force at a particular point.

In 1892 Munroe moved to Washington, D.C., to become professor of chemistry and dean of the Corcoran Scientific School at Columbian University (renamed George Washington University in 1904). The following year he became dean of the graduate school, which he had helped to establish. His former student and colleague Nevil Monroe Hopkins credited Munroe with providing the "reputation, hard work, and energy" needed to transform Columbian into "a flourishing and progressive university." Munroe was awarded honorary Ph.D. (1894) and LL.D. (1912) degrees in recognition of his exemplary service to the university, with which he maintained an active association long after his formal retirement in 1917.

Throughout his life Munroe served as a consultant to many private organizations and volunteered his expertise to many government agencies, including the Census Bureau, National Research Council, and Bureau of Mines. In 1900 the Swedish Academy of Sciences selected him to nominate individuals for Nobel prizes in chemistry, and he himself received several awards from foreign governments. At the time of his death, Munroe was the last of the original group of chemists who had established the chemistry subsection, which later became Section C, of the American Association for the Advancement of Science, as well as the sole surviving charter member of the American Chemical Society, which he served in numerous capacities, including that of president (1898). A member of American and foreign scientific societies, he was elected fellow of both the American Association for the Advancement of Science (1874) and the Chemical Society of London (1888).

Munroe married Mary Louise Barker, the daughter of chemist and physicist George F. Barker, in 1883. They had five children. Munroe died at his country home in Forest Glen, Maryland. He retained his striking appearance—including the snow-white hair that he had since his early twenties—until the end of his life. Although most often remembered for his scientific and technological accomplishments in the field of explosives, his leadership roles in professional scientific societies, and his unfailing service to the U.S. government, Munroe was also a popular and inspiring teacher for nearly half a century. A man of jovial temperament and delightful wit, he made lasting friendships among his colleagues and students, including many from his early days at Harvard and Annapolis, where the midshipmen had always affectionately referred to him as "Munzie."

• Monroe donated his personal papers to the Gelman Library at George Washington University. Popular reviews by Munroe on explosives, including some of his own work, appear in *Scribner's Magazine* 3 (1888): 563–76; *Journal of the American Chemical Society* 18 (1896): 819–46, and *Popular Science Monthly* 56 (1900): 300–312, 444–55. Tributes to Munroe are by Harvey W. Wiley, *Industrial and Engineering Chemistry* 15 (1923): 648–49, and J. N. Taylor, *General Science Quarterly* 10 (1926): 480–88. For a more recent application of the Munroe effect, see Volta Torrey, "The Bazooka's Grandfather," *Popular Science*, Feb. 1945, pp. 65–69 ff. An obituary appears in the *Washington Post*, 8 Dec. 1938; longer posthumous tributes are in *The Chemist* 15 (1938): 385–89, and by Charles A. Browne, *Journal of the American Chemical Society* 61 (1939): 1301–16 (with a bibliography of Munroe's publications compiled by J. N. Taylor).

RICHARD E. RICE

MUNSELL, Joel (14 Apr. 1808–15 Jan. 1880), printer and publisher, was born in Northfield, Massachusetts, the son of Joel Munsell, a wagon- and plowmaker, and Cynthia Paine. Munsell attended the local elementary school and worked with his father for three years. In 1825 he went to Greenfield, Massachusetts, where he became an apprentice in a printing shop and continued his education by reading widely and studying Latin, French, and Spanish. He left for Albany, New York, in 1827 and for six years held a variety of jobs there. He amassed volumes of scrapbooks on literary, historical, and typographic subjects and continued to do so all of his life.

On 1 May 1834, with a partner, Munsell bought the *Microscope*, a newspaper on which he had worked, and its printing office. He had carefully saved for this purpose. At the same time he was busily engaged in preparation for his marriage to Jane Bigelow on 17 June. His wife died exactly twenty years later, on 17 June 1854, leaving him with three children. Mary Ann Reid, a recent arrival from Canada, had been called in to help during his wife's illness. She continued to take care of the children after their mother's death. Munsell married her in 1856. Six more children were born of this union.

Munsell bought another printing plant in 1836 and for the next decade and a half was busily engaged as a practical printer who aimed to do his job well and increase the size of his business. By circular and advertisement he solicited printing of every type, including calling cards, newspapers, circulars and handbills, programs and show bills for concerts, and auction bills. Books and pamphlets in English, French, German, Greek, and Latin were offered, as were sermons, lectures, and addresses. By 1848 the press had issued eighty-one separate items and employed from forty to sixty workers.

A significant change in the press occurred after 1850 as the average annual output of books and pamphlets more than doubled. Although Munsell continued to print calling cards, to-let notices, letterheads, and circulars, his personality as a printer emerged clearly. He was now an antiquarian in the type of material he printed and in the manner of his typography, and more of his attention was focused on the writing, editing, and printing of works relating to American history, genealogy, and the history of printing and paper making. He also sold the books of fellow publishers. He established himself as a full-fledged publisher and bookseller.

To provide for his growing business, Munsell purchased up-to-date equipment, including new steam-powered presses, and to the stock of copper and steel engravings he added the work of wood engravers and lithographers. He began printing on stereotype plates as well as directly from type, and he acquired cylindrical presses. A small bindery was established, which he later spun off as a separate business under his son Charles.

Commercial printing of items such as popular tales, annual reports of religious associations, sermons, hymns, poetry, textbooks, and legal reports continued to be a source of income for the firm. Beginning in 1842 and until his death in Albany, Munsell annually printed *Webster's Calendar or Albany Almanac*. In addition, he attempted several short-lived newspapers.

In 1850 when Isaac Q. Leake undertook to publish his father-in-law's *Memoir of the Life and Times of General John Lamb* and had insufficient funds to pay for it, Munsell assumed a large share of the cost, thus in effect becoming the publisher. Subsequently he helped subsidize other volumes of American history that he deemed worthy of publication, sending out circulars to prospective purchasers. *Commissary Wilson's Order-*

ly Book; *Expedition of the British and Provincial Army under Maj. Gen. Jeffrey Amherst, against Ticonderoga and Crown Point, 1759* became the first volume of Munsell's historical series. Although he frequently had to use his own money and had on occasion to act as editor, ten volumes of his series were published by 1862. Although many volumes were printed at a loss, he continued to solicit and produce more volumes of his series.

With the publication of Winslow C. Watson's *Pioneer History of the Champlain Valley* in 1863, Munsell launched his Series of Local American History. Twelve volumes were published by 1877. His interest in local history was further manifested in his publication of the *Annals of Albany*; ten volumes appeared from 1850 to 1860. They contained more varied materials from manuscript and printed sources: court records; baptismal records and historical accounts of every church, school, and public institution; biographical accounts of leading citizens; and descriptions of Albany by American and foreign visitors. The *Annals* sold well, and the first four volumes were reprinted. A new series, *Collections on the History of Albany*, was printed more sumptuously in royal octavo (a larger-sized paper) in an edition of 400 copies between 1865 and 1871.

The Munsell press printed its first genealogy in 1847, and others soon followed. Between 1860 and 1870 thirty family histories were mentioned in *Bibliotheca Munselliana*, his volume listing his imprints. In 1862 his firm issued William H. Whitmore's *A Handbook of American Genealogy*, an enlarged edition of which was issued in 1868. In the same year Munsell also published Daniel Steele Durrie's *Bibliographia Genealogica Americana*, which was reissued in 1878.

The work of publishing brought Munsell into the business of bookselling. Catalogs were issued periodically. He contributed countless copies of his historical publications to historical societies from New England to the Midwest. He was pleased to record the names of seventeen historical associations that honored him with membership.

Munsell investigated the historical traditions of his craft. He introduced the use of two colors, red and black, on some of his title pages, following the tradition of Johann Fust and Peter Schoeffer, Gutenberg's successors. Books in the early half of the nineteenth century were printed in "modern" typefaces with sharp distinctions between thick and thin parts of letters and hairline serifs. The first book printed in the nineteenth-century revival in Caslon "oldstyle" type appeared in England in 1844. Munsell imported a font of type from the Caslon foundry and in 1854 issued *Papers Relating to the Island of Nantucket*, the first book printed in the United States in the oldstyle revival. Following the style of the English publisher, he adopted, for his title pages, the printer's mark of Adlus Manutius, a dolphin twined around an anchor with the words "Aldi Albaniensis Discipulus," the Albany disciple of Aldus. Eighteen of Munsell's thirty-eight existing scrapbooks contain typographic extracts.

They were culled for his publication, *Typographical Miscellany*, which he issued in 1850. He was the first American to publish material on paper and papermaking, which he issued in 1856 as *A Chronology of Paper and Paper Making*. Revised and augmented editions appeared in 1857, 1864, 1870, and 1876.

Munsell also compiled the most extensive list of imprints ever published by an American printer with his *Bibliotheca Munselliana*, issued in 1872, listing more than 2,000 items. A current revision, compiled by Henry Bannister, has more than doubled that number.

Joel Munsell principally became the greatest printer of his era because of his contributions to the art of typography, his work in printing history, and the voluminous output of his press, which included almost every type of reading material available in his day. Although much of the printing was undistinguished due to the necessity of containing costs to meet competition, he nevertheless established an outstanding reputation. H. O. Houghton of the Riverside Press referred to the Albany printer as "one whose name is already celebrated as a master of the typographic art, and who has besides done so much for the cause of good letters."

• Joel Munsell's Diary, vols. 1 to 4 (vol. 3 is missing), is in the New-York Historical Society; his Journal (1849–1878) is in the Albany Institute of History and Art. Manuscript collections of letters are in the New-York Historical Society, the New York State Library, the American Antiquarian Society, the Massachusetts Historical Society, the Library of Congress, the Essex Institute, the Boston Public Library, the Long Island Historical Society, the State Historical Society of Wisconsin, Harvard University, and the New York Public Library. A full-length biography by David S. Edelstein, *Joel Munsell: Printer and Antiquarian* (1950), has a complete bibliography. Obituary notices are in the *Albany Evening Journal*, 22 Jan. 1880; *Albany Institute Minutes*, 16, 20 Jan. 1880; *New York Genealogical and Biographical Record* 9 (Apr. 1880): 53–62; and *New England Historical and Genealogical Record* 34 (July 1880): 232–46.

DAVID S. EDELSTEIN

MUNSEY, Frank Andrew (21 Aug. 1854–22 Dec. 1925), author and publisher, was born near Mercer, Maine, the son of Andrew Chauncey Munsey, a carpenter and farmer, and Mary Jane Merritt Hopkins. Aside from a few months enrolled at Poughkeepsie Business College in 1881, Munsey gained his business education through experience. As a boy, working at a grocery in Lisbon Falls, Maine, he taught himself telegraphy, eventually leaving to become a telegraph operator at several hotels in New England. His proficiency led to his appointment as manager of the Western Union office in the state capital, Augusta.

From this position, and from his residence in Augusta House, a gathering place for politicians, Munsey was able to observe what became his two lifelong passions, politics and publishing. Augusta was the home of Republican Senator James G. Blaine, a presidential hopeful, and the site of a sizeable magazine publishing industry. The magazines were cheap tabloids serving primarily as carriers of advertising, but they also were quite profitable.

With the city's leading publisher as a mentor, Munsey soon learned the business and decided to go to New York to publish his own periodical, a youth magazine to be titled *Golden Argosy*. With his personal savings of $500 and a $3,500 investment by two others, he began to acquire manuscripts, including Horatio Alger, Jr.'s "Do or Dare; or, A Brave Boy's Fight for Fortune."

By the time Munsey reached New York City in September 1882, he had only $40 left and a set of manuscripts. When his major investor withdrew soon after his arrival, Munsey released the other from any further obligation. He subsequently forged a deal with a printer, who served as both his publisher and his employer. Ten weeks after his arrival in New York, 2 December 1882, Munsey published his initial weekly issue of *Golden Argosy* (dated 9 Dec. 1882), and never missed a deadline thereafter. When his employer and publisher went bankrupt five months later, Munsey took total control of his magazine and became the publisher. Aided by a $300 loan from an Augusta banker, he managed to make his magazine succeed. Because he could not afford to pay for new material, Munsey resorted to writing his own. His first effort was a serialized novel, *Under Fire*, in 1885. This was followed by *Afloat in the Great City* in 1887, *The Boy Broker* in 1889, *Derringforth* in 1894, and *A Tragedy of Errors* in 1899.

When Senator Blaine received the Republican presidential nomination in 1884 and set up his headquarters in New York, Munsey joined the campaign and began a new, party-endorsed magazine, *Munsey's Illustrated Weekly*. Despite receiving no financial help from the Republicans, Munsey managed to publish the magazine through the campaign, ending up with a large subscription list and enough debt to force his creditors to carry him.

Although Munsey was making $1,500 per week with *Golden Argosy* in 1887, he tried to expand his profits and circulation by tinkering with it; he tried to change nearly everything, including the title, which was shortened to *Argosy*. None of the changes seemed to help his expansion efforts.

Subsequently, he began a new publication, the comic *Munsey's Weekly*, in 1889. A failure, it was made a monthly in 1891 and retitled *Munsey's Magazine*. Munsey also took an option on a newspaper, the New York *Star*, changing the title to the *Daily Continent* and converting it to a tabloid, but released his option only four months later.

In 1893 Munsey made a decision that was fateful not only for his life, but also for magazine publishing in the United States. To encourage subscriptions from a larger mass audience, he reduced the price of *Munsey's Magazine* from the then-standard quarter to a dime, and then formed his own distribution company, Red Star News, to combat a boycott by other distributors who were upset by his reduced price. Munsey also be-

gan to heavily advertise his publications, which eventually enabled him to claim the largest magazine circulation in the world in 1898. Because the advertisers could not afford to ignore his circulation, the profits became enormous. Addressing the Sphinx Club in 1898, Munsey declared, "There was never anything deader in this world than the old idea of big profits and small volume."

Munsey next branched out by constructing a printing plant in New London, Connecticut, in 1895. He subsequently changed it to the Mohican Hotel, then to a department store, and finally to a huge grocery, the beginnings of his interstate chain of Mohican grocery stores. In this, he was following the same technique that he used in his publishing enterprises: "I keep on experimenting, creating and killing, till I happen to hit the public's taste."

Munsey continued refashioning his publication empire through the creation, purchase, recombination, and, sometimes, destruction of a variety of magazines: *Peterson's Magazine, Scrap Book* (1895), *Quaker* and *Puritan* (1897), *Junior Munsey* (1900), *Godey's Ladies Book* (1898), *Woman* and *Scrapbook* (1906), *Ocean* (1907), *Live Wire* (1908), *Railroad Man's Magazine* (1906), *Cavalier* (1908), and *Railroad* (1919). However risky his method may have seemed, his focus was on making a profit, and in this he was remarkably successful. In 1907 he was able to claim that he had earned $9 million in twenty-five years of publishing. His total circulation in 1901, he claimed, was twice that of *Harper's, Scribner's,* and *Century* combined.

Munsey reentered the newspaper business for the first time in a decade in 1901, with the purchase of the New York *Daily News* and the Washington *Times*. Here, the methods he was using with his magazine empire proved less successful, leading him to kill the *Daily News* in 1904 and sell the *Times* in 1917. He picked up the *Boston Journal* in 1902 but dropped the evening edition in 1903, replacing it with the *Evening News*, which also was dropped after a year's trial. The morning edition of the *Journal* was sold off in 1913. Munsey's papers always looked better because of improved graphics, but his constant tinkering never let his changes settle in with the public.

Imitating the big business barons he saw as his peers, Munsey dreamed of operating a huge trust. In a speech to the Merchants' Club of Boston in 1902, he advised:

I think I shall be able to make good by the power of organization and by applying the methods that are now employed by our great business combinations, popularly known as trusts. In my judgment it will not be many years . . . before the publishing business in this country will be done by a few concerns, three or four at the most. There will be a line of newspapers representing each of the two great political parties, and another chain independent of politics. . . . This is an age of organization and of consolidation.

Munsey's ideal trust was not limited to publishing, but included all other forms of business enterprise, efficiently and profitably articulated.

In an attempt to realize his scheme, Munsey founded, bought, merged, killed, and sold a variety of metropolitan newspapers: the Philadelphia *Times* and *Baltimore News* (1908); *New York Press* (1912); *New York Sun* (1916); New York *Herald*, New York *Evening Telegram*, *Baltimore American*, *Baltimore News*, and Baltimore *Star* (1920); New York *Globe* (1923); and the New York *Evening Mail* (1924). In the end, he owned only the New York *Evening Telegram* and the New York *Evening Sun*, and his dream of being master of a giant trust lay in ruins. Although many of the papers needed improvement, and some were so moribund as to be beyond resuscitation, Munsey's efforts consequently earned him from journalists everywhere a determined hatred that would dog his reputation for decades. Each newspaper merged and/or folded was another journalistic voice stilled and another set of jobs lost. In an obituary, William Allen White charged him with having "succeeded in transforming a once-noble profession into an 8-percent security."

Munsey's political aspirations were similarly frustrated. Having strenuously supported Republicans all his life, and Warren G. Harding in particular, Munsey fully expected to be named ambassador to England when Harding became president in 1920; he was totally ignored, however, and soon retreated from any further political activity.

In some aspects, Munsey argued, his life was a failure:

I have no heirs. I am disappointed in my friendships. And I have no clear views on religious problems. Today I have forty million dollars, but what has it brought me? Not happiness. Where can I leave it? I have made up my mind to leave it where I made it—in New York City, and where I can get its equivalent in value.

Never married, Munsey died nearly alone in New York City, accompanied by only a few acquaintances and employees. No surviving family members had visited him in the hospital, nor were any present at his death. Most of his estate was willed to the Metropolitan Museum, of which he apparently knew little except that it was approved by the strata of wealthy people he most admired.

Though Munsey was in many ways a man of his time, he was far ahead in imagining the future of mass communications in the United States, foreseeing large conglomerates run by businessmen purely as businesses and communications content primarily as a carrier of advertisements. Arthur Brisbane wrote of him: "Munsey was a very even, rather cold, extremely intelligent BUSINESS man and—so far as his friends could see—ONLY a business man. He displayed no more imagination than any inanimate object. In fact, he didn't believe in imagination." As even Brisbane admitted, some of the publications Munsey killed "needed strangling" for the good of others; yet there is often something bloodless about economic efficiency that is humanly unsatisfying, as Munsey himself recognized when he evaluated his life.

Much of Munsey's prediction about the direction that the newspaper industry would take, in terms of financial support and inclusion in conglomerates, was accurate; although he could not have foreseen its application to other, later-developed communication industries, such as broadcasting, he would not likely have been surprised. Today, however, the path he trod is far more remembered than the pathfinder.

• Munsey wrote *The Founding and Development of the Munsey Publishing House* (1907). He also contributed the pamphlets *Getting On in Journalism* (1898), *A Great Event for the Argosy* (1907), *The Daily Newspaper; Its Relation to the Public* (1910), *Starve the Railroads and We Starve Ourselves* (1914), and *Militant American Journalism* (1922).
George Britt, *Forty Years—Forty Millions: The Career of Frank A. Munsey* (1935), is the most complete biographical source. Evaluations of Munsey's professional career are included in Louis Filler, *Crusaders for American Liberalism* (1939); Allen Churchill, *Park Row* (1958); Frank Luther Mott, *American Journalism* (1950) and *A History of American Magazines* (1957); and Oswald Garrison Villard, *Some Newspapers and Newspaper-Men* (1923). At Munsey's request, D.O.S. Lowell wrote *A Munsey-Hopkins Genealogy, Being the Ancestry of Andrew Chauncey Munsey and Mary Jane Merritt Hopkins* (1920). Personal statements about Munsey are to be found in Robert L. Duffus, "Mr. Munsey," *American Mercury*, 2 July 1924, pp. 297–304; Erman Jesse Ridgeway, "*Frank A. Munsey: An Appreciation*" (privately printed, 1926); and R. H. Titherington, "In Memoriam: Frank A. Munsey," *Munsey's Magazine*, Mar. 1926, pp. 189–93. Obituaries are in the *New York Times*, 12 Dec. 1925 and 10 Jan. 1926, and in the New York *Sun*, 22 Dec. 1925.

JACK H. COLLDEWEIH

MUNSON, Aeneas (13 June 1734–16 June 1826), physician, was born in New Haven, Connecticut, the son of Benjamin Munson, a respected schoolmaster, and Abigail Punderson. Munson attended the Hopkins Grammar School and entered Yale College in 1749. Following graduation he studied divinity with Ezra Stiles, who was then a tutor at Yale. Munson received a license to preach, was chaplain to Lord Gardiner, and was stationed on Long Island in 1755 during the French and Indian War.

After only a few years, which included a brief term as a teacher, Munson changed careers from the ministry to medicine. According to his student, protégé, and lifelong friend Eli Ives, Munson had made the changes because "the close application to study and the wont of exercise of the ministry produced dyspepsia and hypochondria." Munson studied medicine with practitioners in East Hampton and Gardiner's Island and briefly practiced in Bedford, New York. In 1760 he opened his medical practice in New Haven and rapidly attained wide public and professional recognition. In 1761 he married Susanna Howell; they had nine children before her death in 1803. In 1804 Munson married a widow, Sarah Perit, with whom he had no children.

Munson was regarded as a committed member of the Whig party and was a leader in the patriotic movement. He was a justice of the peace at New Haven in

1776 and served in the Connecticut legislature from 1778 to 1781. Between 1780 and 1783, Munson served as a surgeon's mate in the American revolutionary armed forces. He was present at the siege and surrender of British general Charles Cornwallis at Yorktown. Munson was said to have dined with General George Washington as a guest in the home of the Connecticut statesman Roger Sherman. Munson maintained numerous contacts with Yale College over the years and was a close friend of patriot Nathan Hale during Hale's college years.

An active and prominent member of the Connecticut medical community, Munson had a large practice and was loved by his many patients. He was one of the organizers of the Medical Society of New Haven County in 1784. He was also active in the formation of the Connecticut Medical Society in 1792 and served as its first vice president and, for seven successive years (1794–1801), as its president. The society was empowered by the state legislature to award the M.D., and in 1794 Munson became the third physician to receive this honor.

Munson received regional and national recognition as an expert in materia medica and botanical remedies. In 1813 he was one of four founding professors of the Medical Institution of Yale College and was appointed professor of materia medica and botany there. As the most respected physician in Connecticut, his name added luster and credibility to the new school. However, because of his advanced age, he was not expected to lecture or to perform other academic duties. Munson's student and friend Eli Ives was appointed adjunct professor and assumed all of the teaching responsibilities of his mentor's position. Munson attained emeritus professor status in 1820. He died at his home in New Haven.

Munson was famous not only for his encyclopedic medical knowledge but also for his dry and sometimes biting wit. Munson considered his wit to be an "infirmity" that he could not suppress. A number of examples of his humor are recorded. Munson was dining with the Yale Corporation and its president, Timothy Dwight, in the Commons. Dwight was a noted trencherman who also fancied himself to be an authority on nutrition. During the meal, Dwight announced to those in the room: "You will observe, gentlemen, that I eat a great deal of bread with my meat." Munson instantly replied: "Yes, and we notice that you also eat much meat with your bread." On another occasion, when a woman with a very large mouth threw open her jaws to have a tooth extracted, Munson quipped: "Madam, you need not open your mouth so wide; I shall stand outside."

Munson was an expert in materia medica and a skillful clinician. He was very active in the organization of county and state medical societies in Connecticut. His great professional stature was important in the successful founding of the Yale Medical School, only the fifth medical institution in the United States at that time.

• Documents referring to Munson are preserved at the New Haven Colony Historical Society, New Haven, Conn. Information regarding his life and career is also available in M. A. Munson, *The Munson Record: A Genealogical and Biographical Account of Capt. Thomas Munson and His Descendants*, vol. 2 (1896), pp. 765, 768–83, and Eli Ives, "Historical Sketch of the Medical Society of New Haven County," *New Haven Morning Journal and Courier*, 26 Oct. 1852.

HOWARD A. PEARSON

MUNSON, Gorham Bert (26 May 1896–15 Aug. 1969), literary journalist and editor, was born in Amityville, New York, the son of Hubert Barney Munson, a Methodist minister, and Carrie Louise Morrow. Munson dated the beginning of his intellectual life to his senior year at Wesleyan University, in Middletown, Connecticut. There he thrilled to the call of the "Young American" critics—Van Wyck Brooks, Lewis Mumford, Randolph Bourne, and particularly Waldo Frank—for a new, native-born American art. By the spring of 1919 Munson was living in Greenwich Village, writing poetry and book reviews and scraping together a living.

Munson eagerly embraced the avant-garde literary scene of New York and Paris in the 1920s. He is noted in part for his early friendship with the poet Hart Crane. The two young, aspiring writers became fast friends in 1919, and for the next few years Munson functioned as an important and sympathetic critic of Crane's early poetry. In 1921 Munson married Elizabeth Delza, a professional dancer; in July of that year they traveled to France. Inspired in part by a Malcolm Cowley essay on the newest generation of writers, Munson, in collaboration with Matthew Josephson and Kenneth Burke, established a magazine for experimental writers. *Secession* (1922–1924) became one of the most important avant-garde literary publications of the period, promoting the writing of Crane, Frank, Cowley, Burke, Josephson, Wallace Stevens, William Carlos Williams, Marianne Moore, Slater Brown, and Yvor Winters. Munson viewed *Secession* not only as a platform for pugnacious assaults on inferior art but also as a "group-organ," a medium by which the best and most farsighted writers would formulate a common program and direction.

Josephson, another young American writer in Europe at the time, was vital to the founding of *Secession*, and Munson's tempestuous relationship with him constitutes a dramatic, if minor, episode in American literary history. Josephson joined enthusiastically in Munson's plans for a new magazine, supplying much of the early material. When Munson returned to the United States early in 1922, Josephson handled the magazine's publication in Europe. Josephson, however, disdained Munson's intellectual abilities. Both he and Cowley valued Munson more for his political skills than his critical perspective and envisioned *Secession* less as a journal of serious criticism than as a place for polemics and stunts. In one issue, for example, they cut a hapless contributor's poem to the final two lines. Unamused, Munson considered Josephson and Cowley to have sabotaged his magazine. Their feud reached its apex in the fall of 1923 when, at a dinner meant to rally modernist writers in New York, Cowley's burlesque reading of a letter from the absent Munson, which accused Josephson of being an intellectual "fakir," led to dissension and bickering. Josephson and Munson later engaged in a fistfight.

A solemn and serious young man, Munson did not fit in bohemia. Although he had rejected his father's Methodism, he still demanded spiritual illumination from the passing intellectual fads of the day. In *Destinations*, a collection of critical essays published in 1928, he stated that modernity had caused Americans to be "blown into chaos" and that they had become spiritually rudderless and consumed with shallow ideals. He insistently called upon artists to achieve a greater rigor in their art and to formulate an artistic direction. They must he believed, heed the destinations to which they were leading Americans. In Munson's view, the aim of art was the articulation of intellectual "certitude."

Throughout the 1920s Munson was attracted to individuals or groups who promised a revelatory insight into the absolute. His most curious and long-lasting commitment was to Alfred Richard Orage, a British critic and former editor of *New Age* who arrived in New York City in December 1923 preaching the wisdom of the Greco-Armenian mystic George Ivanovitch Gurdjieff. The "Gurdjieff system" was a rigorous discipline of the mind and body informed by Eastern spirituality. Munson not only dove eagerly into the mysticism of Gurdjieff but also adopted Orage's views on political economy. This entailed the advocacy of Social Credit, a strain of underconsumptionist economic theory associated with another Englishman, Major C. H. Douglas, that called on the government to circumvent the private banking elite and provide credit directly to consumers.

By the end of the 1920s Munson was attracted to the conservative New Humanism of Irving Babbitt and Paul Elmer More, who preached the social efficacy of classical ideals and didactic art. For Munson, Humanism represented another school of rigorous self-discipline. As modern men and women we are all liberated from social conventions, established authorities, and religious dogma, he argued in *The Dilemma of the Liberated* (1930). The satisfaction of our natural desires does not lead to happiness, he stated; modern liberation results in a vapid and shallow life. In the end, Munson felt that the Humanists failed to solve this dilemma. They provided sensible instruction on the nature of character but failed to arrive at a way to know the self. The religious spirit, Munson declared, teaches that true freedom comes only at the risk of great sacrifice. In the "fiery light" of the religious spirit, "we liberated ones perceive that we are in truth only pseudo-liberated. We have put the weight on being free from something, but the real question is, free from what?" (*Dilemma of the Liberated*, pp. 281–82).

Munson had a long career as a teacher and editor after the 1920s and served intermittently as an editor at various publishing houses through 1960. He edited *New Democracy*, the chief organ of the Social Credit movement in America, from 1933 to 1939, and he served for a time in the New Deal Works Progress Administration, although he later became an outspoken critic of liberal Keynesianism. In addition to publishing books on propaganda, economics, and even a travelogue of the Penobscot area of Maine, which he loved, he also taught writing, most notably from 1927 to 1969 at the New School of Social Research in New York City, where his students included William Styron and Jack Kerouac. But his historical significance lies mainly in his critical engagement with the intellectual currents of the 1920s and the intellectual record he left of a tortuous but ever-hopeful search for spiritual enlightenment in a decade of cultural liberation.

• Munson lost much of his correspondence when his literary effects, stored in a warehouse, were illegally sold at auction. He left no major collection of papers; his own outgoing correspondence is scattered through numerous collections. Near the end of his life he wrote *The Awakening Twenties: A Memoir-History of a Literary Period* (1985), which was published posthumously. For his relationship to Hart Crane, see John Unterecker, *Voyager: A Life of Hart Crane* (1969), and Philip Horton, *Hart Crane: The Life of an American Poet* (1957). For the controversies surrounding *Secession*, see Munson's memoir and Gorham Munson, "The Fledgling Years, 1916–1924," *Sewanee Review* 40 (Jan.–Mar. 1932): 24–54; Matthew Josephson, *Life among the Surrealists* (1962); Malcolm Cowley, *Exile's Return: A Literary Odyssey of the 1920's* (1934); Hans Bak, *Malcolm Cowley: The Formative Years* (1993); and Frederick J. Hoffman et al., *The Little Magazine: A History and Bibliography* (1946). An account informed by the perspective of John Wheelright is Alvin H. Rosenfeld, "John Wheelright, Gorham Munson, and the 'Wars of Secession,'" *Michigan Quarterly Review* 14 (Winter 1975): 13–40. Important writings by Munson not mentioned above include *Waldo Frank: A Study* (1923), *Robert Frost: A Study in Sensibility and Good Sense* (1927), *Aladdin's Lamp: The Wealth of the American People* (1945), and *Penobscot: Down East Paradise* (1959). Obituaries are in *Variety*, 27 Aug. 1969, and *Publishers Weekly*, 8 Sept. 1969.

PAUL V. MURPHY

MUNSON, Thurman Lee (7 June 1947–2 Aug. 1979), baseball player, was born in Akron, Ohio, the son of Darrell Munson, a farm laborer, and Ruth (maiden name unknown). The family moved in 1955 to Canton, Ohio, where Munson's father became a truck driver. Munson graduated from Canton-Lehman High School in 1964, garnering All-State baseball, football, and basketball honors. On an athletic scholarship, he attended Kent State University, where from 1964 to 1968 he excelled as a football linebacker and All-America baseball catcher; he did not graduate.

The New York Yankees baseball club selected Munson in the first round in the 1968 free-agent draft. Scout Gene Woodling signed the 5'11", 190-pound right-handed catcher in June 1968 for a $75,000 bonus. Munson began his professional baseball career with Binghamton, New York, of the Class AA Eastern League. After spending the 1969 season with Syracuse, New York, of the Class AAA International League, he joined the New York Yankees in September. In 1968 he married Diane Lynn Dominick; they had three children.

The Yankees experienced a rebirth in the 1970s with Munson, who continued the rich tradition of such outstanding catchers as Bill Dickey, Yogi Berra, and Elston Howard. In 1970 Munson batted .302 to win American League Rookie of the Year honors and help catapult the Yankees from fifth to second place in the American League East. His .998 mark in 1971 equaled a club mark for best fielding percentage by a catcher. In 1973 Munson hit .301 with 20 home runs and sparkled behind the plate with the first of three straight Gold Glove Awards. He adeptly handled Yankee pitchers and possessed arguably the junior circuit's quickest release in throwing out base stealers. Fans, however, voted Carlton Fisk the starting American League catcher in the 1973 All-Star Game, although Munson had outperformed the Boston Red Sox star in every offensive statistical category except home runs. From 1974 to 1976 Munson started for the American League in the All-Star Game. His pinnacle was reached in 1975, when he ranked third among American League batters with a stellar .318 mark and knocked in more runs (102) than any Yankee in over a decade.

Before the 1976 season, New York manager Billy Martin designated Munson the first Yankee captain since Lou Gehrig. That season New York won its first American League title since 1964, with Munson batting .302 with 17 home runs and 105 runs batted in and garnering the American League Most Valuable Player Award. Munson, a phenomenal postseason performer, batted .435 in the American League Championship Series against the Kansas City Royals. His eight singles established a five-game Championship Series record. In the World Series against the Cincinnati Reds, Munson batted .529 with nine hits. He also set three records for a four-game World Series, including most singles (eight), most assists by a catcher (seven), and most runners caught stealing (five). Nevertheless, the powerful Reds vanquished the Yankees in four games. New York owner George Steinbrenner's November 1976 acquisition of free-agent slugger Reggie Jackson chagrined Munson. Jackson's arrival challenged Munson's leadership and relegated his salary to third highest of the Yankees, causing the catcher to seek renegotiation of his contract. Jackson, who claimed to be "the straw that stirred the drink," boasted that he, not Munson, was the team leader. Jackson solidified those claims as the hero of the 1977 and 1978 World Series.

Munson continued to excel offensively in 1977, batting .308, belting 18 roundtrippers, and knocking in 100 runs. New York again bested Kansas City in the American League Championship Series and captured its first World Series title since 1962. Munson helped the Yankees conquer the Los Angeles Dodgers in the 1977 World Series, recording a .320 batting average, eight hits, one home run, and three runs batted in.

Early in 1978 he and Steinbrenner finally came to terms over a contract giving Munson about $420,000 each of the next four years. Arm troubles, tendinitis, and weak knees diminished his 1978 power production, but he still batted .297. The Yankees eliminated the Boston Red Sox in a dramatic East Division playoff game and defeated the Kansas City Royals in the American League Championship Series. Munson batted .320 with eight hits and seven runs batted in to help New York vanquish the Los Angeles Dodgers again in the 1978 World Series. His memoir, *Thurman Munson: An Autobiography*, was issued the same year.

Munson died in an August 1979 crash while attempting to land his Cessna Citation twin engine jet plane at Akron-Canton Airport in Ohio. A licensed pilot since 1977, he frequently had flown his plane between New York and his Canton home near Cleveland. Flying had enabled him to spend more time with his family. The Yankees posthumously retired Munson's uniform number, 15.

Munson joined Fisk and Johnny Bench in earning recognition as the best major league catchers of the 1970s. The seven-time American League All-Star (1971, 1973–1978) compiled a .292 career batting average, belted 113 home runs, and knocked in 701 runs in 1,423 games. Munson, the only Yankee to receive both American League Rookie of the Year and Most Valuable Player honors, hit over .300 five seasons and drove in at least 100 runs three campaigns. Besides helping the Yankees secure three American League pennants, he batted .339 and knocked in 10 runs in American League Championship Series. In 16 World Series games, he batted .373 with 25 hits and 12 runs batted in and helped spark the Yankees to two World Series crowns.

Over the course of his career, the curt, sullen, moody Munson often clashed with fans, the media, and Yankee management. He craved respect more than love and bristled at being overshadowed by more popular, less productive players. His peers, nevertheless, respected him as a reliable, industrious, and bold leader who hit clutch line drives, exhibited competitive desire, and performed even when injured.

• For Munson's reminiscences, see Thurman Munson and Martin Appel, *Thurman Munson: An Autobiography* (1978). The National Baseball Hall of Fame, Cooperstown, N.Y., has a clippings file. Bill Libby, *Thurman Munson: Pressure Player* (1978), and Bill Gutman, *At Bat: Carew, Garvey, Munson, Brock*, rev. ed. (1978), also review the catcher's career. Shorter biographical accounts include *Sports Illustrated*, 13 Sept. 1976, pp. 24 ff. and *Sport* 66 (June 1978): 72–78. See also, Steve Jacobsen, *The Best Team Money Can Buy: The Turmoils and Triumphs of the 1977 New York Yankees* (1978), Philip Baske, *Dog Days: The New York Yankees—1964–1976* (1994), and especially Bill Madden and Moss Klein, *Damned Yankees* (1990). For Munson's career record, see *The Baseball Encyclopedia*, 9th ed. (1993). Obituaries are in the *New York Times*, 3 Aug. 1979; *Newsweek*, *Sports Illustrated*, and *Time*, all 13 Aug. 1979; and the *Sporting News*, 18 Aug. 1979.

DAVID L. PORTER

MÜNSTERBERG, Hugo (1 June 1863–16 Dec. 1916), psychologist, was born in Danzig, Germany, the son of Moritz Münsterberg, a lumber merchant, and Minna Anna Bernhardi, an artist and homemaker. After several years of private school he entered the Gymnasium in Danzig where he excelled, passing the state-sponsored examination on graduation in 1881, an accomplishment achieved by not even one in one hundred German students. Münsterberg entered the University of Leipzig in 1882 to study medicine, but he switched to psychology in the summer of 1883 after taking a course from Wilhelm Wundt, whose Leipzig laboratory, founded in 1879, is commonly associated with the beginnings of scientific psychology. Münsterberg worked in the experimental psychology of the laboratory, principally on questions of the will. He completed his Ph.D. with Wundt in 1885, writing as his dissertation a critical evaluation of contemporary theories of evolution. As a student, Münsterberg converted from Judaism to Lutheranism, a not uncommon act for German Jews who wanted to pursue an academic career. In 1887, after receiving an M.D. at the University of Heidelberg, with a research topic on the visual perception of space, he accepted a position at the University of Freiburg. There he married Selma Oppler in 1887; they had two children.

Münsterberg quickly established a reputation based on his opposition to Wundt's ideas about voluntary action, arguing that the will was not directly experienced, but the result of the perception of changes in muscles, joints, and tendons. His research gained considerable attention within German psychology circles and led to Münsterberg's promotion to associate professor in 1892. His work was also known outside of Germany and was particularly admired by American psychologist William James, who had met him in 1889 and whose ideas on the experience of emotion bore a similarity to Münsterberg's views on the experience of will. James invited him to take a three-year appointment as director of Harvard University's psychology laboratory.

Münsterberg's years at Harvard, from 1892 to 1895, were most successful. An especially popular teacher, he was also well regarded by his colleagues, although some were dismayed at his flamboyancy and dogmatism. Harvard offered him a permanent position; because, however, his goal was a chair in psychology in Germany, he took a two-year leave of absence from Harvard and returned in 1895 to Freiburg, indicating that he would decide between America and Germany in that time. When a professorship in Germany was not forthcoming, Münsterberg returned in 1897 to Harvard, where he spent the rest of his life. He reasoned that if he could not live his life in Germany, then he would bring the best of Germany to America. What America needed was Germany's social idealism, and he would make that his lifelong project. Toward that end, he began his dual career of psychologist and popular writer.

Münsterberg's first book in English, published shortly after his return to Harvard, was titled *Psychology and Life* (1899) and consisted of six essays, four of which had already been published in the popular press. He described the purpose of this book as "a scientific synthesis of the ethical idealism with the physiological psychology of our days." The book was well received and established Münsterberg as a psychological expert with the public. Invitations for public lectures, inquiries from the press, and consulting opportunities in business and industry increasingly came his way. Though initially disparaging of applied psychology, Münsterberg became one of its chief promoters, publishing a series of groundbreaking applied books: *On the Witness Stand* (1908), *Psychotherapy* (1909), *Psychology and the Teacher* (1909), *Psychology and Industrial Efficiency* (1913), *Psychology and Social Sanity* (1914), and *Business Psychology* (1915).

In addition to pursuing his goals in applied psychology, Münsterberg sought to inform his native Germany of the strength of America's virtues, which he saw as an idealistic commitment to self-fulfillment. These virtues were described in his best-known book, *Die Amerikaner* (1904), which, translated into English, established him as the chief interpreter of American culture to the Germans. As noted earlier, however, Münsterberg remained principally interested in bringing America the advantages of German *Kultur*. After his return from Germany in 1897, he devoted considerable energy to this task through his writing for newspapers and popular magazines, public speeches, liaisons with political figures, and leadership within the German-American community. As tensions in Europe grew in the early twentieth century, Münsterberg became more outspoken on behalf of Germany. He spent a year in Berlin in 1910–1911 to organize and direct the Amerika Institut, an entity of the Prussian Ministry of Education that had been founded to improve cultural relations between Germany and the United States but had an obvious political agenda given the growing tensions between Germany and England.

Münsterberg's actions on behalf of Germany caused serious problems for him with his Harvard colleagues as early as 1907 (although he had been accused of being a secret agent for Germany as early as 1901). Those difficulties escalated yearly. When war broke out in 1914, Münsterberg increased his political efforts on behalf of Germany but reduced his writing in the popular press. His views alienated many of his psychology colleagues and angered much of the American public, causing groups to call for his deportation. One Harvard alumnus threatened to withdraw a promised gift to Harvard of $10 million unless Münsterberg was dismissed from the faculty.

The last few years of Münsterberg's life were exceptionally stressful; ostracized by many of his colleagues, he withdrew from most campus life and devoted himself to his work on the psychology of motion pictures (published in 1916 as *The Photoplay*). On a cold December day he walked from his home to Radcliffe College, where he was to teach a class. During the lecture he suffered a heart attack and died.

According to biographer Matthew Hale, Jr., when Münsterberg died, "he was arguably the best-known psychologist in America and the most prominent member of America's largest minority, the German-Americans." Those two roles—psychologist and spokesperson for Germany—defined Münsterberg's life in the United States. As a professor at Harvard University, his considerable and controversial reputation was built on work in applied psychology and his popular writings, both on psychology and on the value of German *Kultur*. In his life, his politics overshadowed his psychology.

Münsterberg's reputation in psychology today stems from the historical importance of his applied work. He is regarded as a pioneer in the field of industrial/organizational (I/O) psychology, and his 1913 book, which treats many of the topics of contemporary I/O psychology and vocational guidance, is recognized as a defining text for those fields. His book *On the Witness Stand* and related writings deal with topics such as the reliability of eyewitness testimony, the behavior of juries, and lie detection, and are recognized as the earliest contributions to the modern fields of law psychology and forensic psychology.

Like others of the twentieth century, Münsterberg recognized the role of science in social engineering, and that recognition undergirded his career in applied research. Despite public criticism of him in the last years of his life and the revisionist treatment of his psychological contributions after his death, this pioneer applied psychologist represented a significant force in the growing professionalization of psychology in the early part of the twentieth century.

• Münsterberg's papers, which contain more than 6,000 letters, can be found in the Department of Rare Books and Manuscripts of the Boston Public Library. Significant correspondence also exists in various collections at Widener Library of Harvard University. Full-length biographies include one written by his daughter Margaret Münsterberg, *Hugo Münsterberg: His Life and Work* (1922), and Matthew Hale, Jr., *Human Science and Social Order: Hugo Münsterberg and the Origins of Applied Psychology* (1980). An extensive account of Münsterberg's activities as a German in America is in Phyllis Keller, *States of Belonging: German-American Intellectuals and the First World War* (1979), pp. 5–118. See also Jutta Spillmann and Lothar Spillmann, "The Rise and Fall of Hugo Münsterberg," *Journal of the History of the Behavioral Sciences* 29 (1993): 322–38. Obituaries are in *Journal of Applied Psychology* 1 (1917): 186–88, and the *New York Times*, 17 Dec. 1916.

LUDY T. BENJAMIN, JR.

MURAT, Achille (21 Jan. 1801–15 Apr. 1847), writer, was born in Paris, France, the son of Joachim Murat and Caroline Bonaparte, Napoleon's youngest sister. In 1808 Achille traveled with his family to Naples, where his father was made king and he became crown prince of Naples. His father's stormy reign ended with his defeat by the Austrians at Tolentino on 3 May 1815, after which Joachim became a fugitive. His wife sent Achille and the other children to Gaeta, surrendered Naples on 20 May 1815, and rejoined her children. Under the protection of the Austrian government, they were sent to Trieste, then to Hainburg near Vienna, and eventually to Frohsdorf, Austria. Since they were Bonapartes, the Austrians kept the family under close scrutiny, but Achille received an excellent private education at Frohsdorf with the help of exiled French historian Count Antoine Thibaudeau.

After Napoleon's death in 1821, strictures on family members relaxed, and Achille acquired permission to travel to America—as long as he agreed not to return to Europe without official permission. After arriving in New York on 19 May 1823, Murat spent time with Joseph Bonaparte, brother of Napoleon, at Point Breeze, New Jersey, but before long he learned of the Spanish uprising against Ferdinand VII and returned to Europe, violating his agreement and endangering his family. In Gibraltar, he may have written a political pamphlet encouraging the Spanish revolt, but if so, no copies survive. Murat could do little in Spain to encourage the doomed revolt, and he soon returned to America and renewed his application for citizenship.

In 1824 Murat visited Washington, where he met Florida's congressional representative, Richard Keith Call, who convinced him to settle in the Florida Territory. Murat left Washington and traveled through the South to St. Augustine, keenly observing American manners, customs, government, and institutions in the southern cities along the way. His observations would form the basis of his most important writings. Two months after arriving in Florida, he purchased a nearby plantation, which he named "Parthenope." Life as a Florida planter was a relaxing change from Europe's political disorder. Most evenings, Murat admitted, he would "stretch out, light a cigar . . . and read the *Commentaries* of Blackstone until I feel the happy influence of common law stealing over me, when I fall asleep" (quoted in Hanna, p. 80). In 1825 middle Florida was opened for settlement, and Murat sold Parthenope to acquire land near Tallahassee. He entered into a partnership with James Gadsden, and together they purchased the "Wascissa" plantation. Within a year Murat had cleared a separate portion of Wascissa for himself, naming it "Lipona," an anagram of Naples (Napoli). On 12 July 1826 he wed Catharine Daingerfield Willis Gray, a great-grandniece of George Washington. They had no children.

During the early days at the new plantation, Murat recorded his observations on America in four letters to Count Thibaudeau. The first two, dated June and July 1826, were written from Wascissa. The second two, dated July 1826 and February 1827, were written from Lipona. The letters appeared anonymously in the Paris periodical *Revue trimestrielle* (1828) and separately as *Lettre sur les États-Unis* (1830). Murat also published a review essay of several works concerning Florida exploration and settlement in the *American Quarterly Review* (1827). His entrance into America's world of letters was furthered when he came to know Ralph Waldo Emerson during the nine-day passage from St. Augustine to Charleston in the spring of 1827. While

Emerson disagreed with Murat's atheism, he was impressed with the Frenchman's active mind. Emerson described Murat as a man "with as ardent a love of truth as that which animates me, with a mind surpassing mine in the variety of its research, & sharpened & strengthened to an energy for *action*" (*Journals*, vol. 3, p. 77).

In 1828 Murat became a naturalized citizen and was admitted to the Florida bar, but his new country and profession could not keep him away from Europe after the July 1830 French revolt against Charles X. Murat reached London before year's end, and he crossed into Belgium the following year. King Leopold made Murat a colonel and authorized him to recruit a foreign legion, but the Austrians pressured Leopold to rescind his kindnesses to the young Bonaparte, and Murat's fledgling army was disbanded. His European visit subsequently evolved into a restful sojourn in London and Brussels. Murat took advantage of the leisure and wrote extensively. His writings reveal that these European experiences had only solidified his American identity. Using his four earlier letters to Count Thibaudeau as a basis, Murat added six more and published the collection as *Esquisse morale et politique des États-Unis de l'Amérique du Nord* (1832). Murat greatly criticized religion, supported slavery, and argued that the principles of self-government within the United States elevated the country well above Europe. Overall, he found the independence of Americans their distinguishing characteristic. The work was soon translated into Dutch, English, and German. The English translation appeared as *A Moral and Political Sketch of the United States of North America* (1833), and it included an antislavery essay by William Bridges Adams tempering Murat's proslavery position. The work was later translated by H. J. S. Bradfield as *America and the Americans* (1849). During his European sojourn, Murat also wrote *Exposition des principes du gouvernement républicain, tel qu'il a été perfectionné en Amérique* (1833), a discourse concerning the American form of government directed to the French and German people. While Murat lacked de Tocqueville's contemplative insight, his dramatic depictions of American manners and customs make his writings a worthwhile resource for understanding the antebellum South.

In 1833 he returned to Florida, where he lived out his days as a planter. His inherited wealth had been long since exhausted; many speculative business deals had failed; and Murat lived a modest life at his plantation. Six years later, a visitor to Lipona wrote in the *New Yorker* that "he might be met in the woods, on a lean horse, dressed in the common homespun of the country, with a long whip in his hand, hunting cattle, with the outward style of what is known in that country as a *Georgia cracker*." Murat died in Tallahassee. While an outside observer may have scorned Murat's descent from crown prince to cracker, Murat never perceived his new life as a descent. Only in America could he live out the enlightened democratic principles he so ardently admired.

• The most thorough treatment of Murat's life is A. J. Hanna, *A Prince in Their Midst: The Adventurous Life of Achille Murat on the American Frontier* (1946). Hanna lists manuscript material within his thorough bibliography, but another large cache of Murat letters unavailable to Hanna has since been acquired from a private collector by the Stanford University Library. Other useful information can be found in *Journals and Miscellaneous Notebooks of Ralph Waldo Emerson*, ed. William H. Gilman et al., vols. 3 and 4, and *New Yorker*, 3 Aug. 1839, p. 319. Murat is the subject of Steve Glassman's *Blood on the Moon* (1990), a historical novel.

KEVIN J. HAYES

MURCHISON, Clint, Jr. (12 Sept. 1923–30 Mar. 1987), businessman, was born Clinton Williams Murchison, Jr., in Dallas, Texas, the son of Clinton Williams Murchison, Sr., a Texas oil wildcatter, and Anne Morris. His father amassed a large fortune during the oil boom of the 1920s and founded a company that later became Southern Union Gas. Murchison, Jr., was a Phi Beta Kappa graduate of Duke University in 1945 with a degree in electrical engineering. He married Jane Catherine Coleman that same year; the couple had four children. After World War II Murchison earned a master's degree in mathematics at the Massachusetts Institute of Technology. In 1942 his father had started a company, which in 1950 was turned over to Murchison and his brother John and named Murchison Brothers. The partnership would eventually hold interests in more than 100 companies, including real estate, construction, insurance, banking, oil and gas, airlines, and publishing.

In the 1950s Murchison became interested in the idea of owning a professional football team. The National Football League (NFL) had decided to expand into Dallas, and Murchison paid $600,000 for the franchise and players in January 1960. Along with general manager Texas E. "Tex" Schramm and head coach Tom Landry, Murchison formed what would become known as "America's team," one of the most popular and profitable sports franchises in the world. The Dallas Cowboys and their trademarks, such as their Lone Star logo and voluptuous cheerleaders, became famous around the globe, and the team's brash, successful style eventually would draw equal measures of acclaim and disdain.

The team's early days, however, were anything but impressive, as it finished its inaugural season without a win. The Cowboys steadily improved, both on the field and in the ticket office; the team played in the NFL championship games in 1966 and 1967 and in the Super Bowl after the 1970 season. Murchison built the team a new stadium in Irving, Texas, just outside of Dallas, and the team began to play there in 1971.

On the business front, Murchison Brothers was busy in the early 1960s, winning a major proxy battle for control of Alleghany Corp., exploring for oil in Australia, and acquiring and developing real estate in Texas and California. In so doing the brothers continued the practice passed down from their father, that of borrowing great sums of money and "spreading it around like manure." Murchison invested in high-risk deals that often fell through and insisted on personally guaranteeing loans. According to a former secretary, "Clint would have a group of businessmen in his office, and one of the men in the meeting would say, 'Oh, Clint, that'll never work,' at which point a big grin would come across Clint's face and you could almost see the wheels turning in his head. . . . Nine times out of ten he'd go ahead with a deal that everyone else said couldn't possibly work" (quoted in Wolfe, p. 356). Murchison's marriage to Jane ended in divorce in 1973, and in 1975 he married Anne Ferrell Brandt.

In the 1970s the fortunes of Murchison Brothers began to decline as rising interest rates combined with falling land values in the Dallas area, forcing the overextended partnership to borrow even more. After Murchison had spent more than $50 million on his brainchild, Optimum Systems Inc. (OSI)—which had been created to help the Cowboys assess and draft players—his brother John refused to allow the investing of further partnership funds in the company. To protect his family from bankruptcy, John decided to part ways with his free-spending brother. The dissolution agreement signed in 1978 stipulated that John would be removed from OSI debt and that the partnership would be dissolved by October 1981.

Murchison was hit on another front at this time, from another generation within the family. Decades before, his father had started trust funds for his grandchildren, and the funds had grown to more than $150 million in assets by the mid-1970s. In 1971 the brothers had begun pledging the trusts' assets as collateral on their loans; as a result, when the grandchildren came of age to receive the funds, that money was not made available by the brothers. Murchison's nephew John Murchison, Jr., did not keep his dissatisfaction quiet. After John, Sr., died of a heart attack in 1979, John, Jr., pressed for dissolution of the partnership and access to his trust fund. John eventually sued his uncle, and the same action was threatened by John, Sr.'s widow, Lupe, in an effort to speed dissolution of the partnership.

The drop in oil prices in the 1980s exacerbated Murchison's financial problems. Banks began to foreclose on Murchison-backed projects, such as a housing development in Beverly Hills, California, and a golf-condominium development in Key West, Florida. When interest rates hit 20 percent, Murchison was paying $80 million annually to service the interest on his debt.

In 1983 the partnership was finally liquidated, and John Murchison, Jr., received his full trust fund. Meanwhile, Murchison's health had begun to suffer, and late that year he was diagnosed with olivopontine cerebellar atrophy, a rare degenerative nerve disease that gradually robbed him of mobility and speech. His financial straits forced him to sell off his prized Cowboys in 1984. Various banks filed multimillion-dollar claims against him, and he retreated into bankruptcy in 1985. With debt calculated at more than $500 mil-

lion, Murchison's bankruptcy was one of the largest in American history.

Murchison spent the short remainder of his life essentially bedridden and unable to speak. He died in a Dallas hospital of complications caused by pneumonia. His passing ended a life marked by excesses, a lavish and at times reckless existence. Had his brilliant mind been wedded with a more temperate business style, like that of his brother John, Murchison's fortune would likely have continued to grow. Although the end of Murchison's life brought great losses, the Dallas Cowboys—one of his creations and perhaps his proudest achievement—have continued a legacy of success, with, fittingly, an air of immoderation.

• The best account of Murchison's life and business dealings is Jane Wolfe, *The Murchisons: The Rise and Fall of a Texas Dynasty* (1989). See also Sam Blair, *Dallas Cowboys: Pro or Con?* (1970), and Jim Donovan et al., *The Dallas Cowboys Encyclopedia: The Ultimate Guide to America's Team* (1996), for details on Murchison's reign as the Cowboys' owner. An obituary is in the *New York Times*, 1 Apr. 1987.

PETER J. HOFFMANN

MURCHISON, Clinton Williams (11 Apr. 1895–20 June 1969), oil executive and industrialist, was born in Tyler, Texas, the son of John Weldon Murchison, a banker, and Clara Williams. Murchison attended public schools in Athens, Texas, and briefly attended Trinity University, then located in Waxahachie, Texas. In 1916 he began working as a teller at the First National Bank of Athens, where his father was president. With the entrance of the United States into the First World War in 1917, Murchison enlisted in the U.S. Army and attended Officer's Training School at Camp Pike, Arkansas. The war ended before Murchison left the country, and he ended his stint in the army in Flint, Michigan, in 1918.

Returning to Texas in 1919, Murchison joined with his old friend Sid Richardson in trading oil leases in Wichita Falls. In a time before the emerging scientific field of geological exploration became important, Murchison and Richardson operated on rumor and chance to find oil. They met with much success in purchasing oil leases surrounding prospective oil fields in and around Burkburnett, near Wichita Falls, and then selling their leases for significant profits when a field began to produce. They often retained an interest in the producing oil wells they had sold or leased. In 1920 Murchison married Anne Morris. They had three sons, one of whom died in childhood. In 1921 Murchison formed a partnership with Ernest Fain, a shoe salesman in Wichita Falls, to drill for oil in northwest Texas. Murchison-Fain became one of the first oil companies, other than the majors, to hire and make use of geological scientists in oil exploration. The fortunes of Murchison, Fain, and Richardson (who was unofficially tied to the firm) waned when the price of oil fell from $3.50 to $1 per barrel in 1921, a result of flush production encouraged by the development of the oil fields in the Los Angeles Basin. In 1925, however, Murchison-Fain struck a highly lucrative deal with the Magnolia Oil Company (an affiliate of Standard–New Jersey) to sell their oil-producing properties near Holliday, Texas. Murchison himself realized $1.6 million from the deal. With Murchison wishing to expand operations throughout Texas and Fain wanting to remain in the Wichita Falls area, the partners decided to split the company. Murchison left the partnership with $5 million in financial and physical assets, including oil properties in the Permian Basin area of West Texas. In 1927, after the death of his wife the previous year, Murchison returned to the business of oil exploration in Texas, basing his operations in Dallas. He proved willing to engage in creative financing schemes and risky production ventures. He purchased properties by promising payment after prospective wells had begun producing and sold them retaining the right to half the proceeds once the purchaser had earned back his investment. Murchison continued his golden touch, amassing an industrial and financial empire. In 1928 he established the Murchison Oil Company (again based in Dallas), engaging in oil exploration in West Texas.

Murchison was one of the earliest proponents of tapping the market for the natural gas segment of the petroleum industry. Many of his oil wells also produced significant amounts of natural gas. The standard practice of the industry in its earliest years was to "flare," or burn, natural gas off as an unnecessary byproduct of crude oil production. Murchison was one of the first to depart from the practice and actively consider natural gas as an energy source. In 1929 he founded the Southwest Drilling Company to service the West Texas community of Wink, itself an overnight oil boomtown that lacked the gas pipeline infrastructure that Murchison could provide. With the market for natural gas rapidly expanding because of the post–World War I population boom, Murchison in 1929 established the Southern Union Gas Company, based in Dallas, with his brother Frank Murchison and brother in-law Ernest Closuit. Electrical power utility companies also proving a potentially great market for natural gas, Southern Union Gas helped to provide power and energy to communities in Texas, Oklahoma, New Mexico, Colorado, and Arkansas. Murchison was also one of the first to explore for oil and gas in Canada.

Murchison was an outspoken critic of oil prorationing, which entailed governmental limitation of oil production to meet market demand in order to prevent prices from collapsing during the economic depression of the 1930s. When the highly prolific East Texas field came into production in late 1930, Murchison pressed his partners in Southern Union to undertake operations there. In the midst of the depression, however, with the oil market characterized by extreme overproduction and severe price deflation, Murchison's partners in Southern Union balked. Thus in 1931 Murchison left to form, with Dudley Golding, a drilling and production company, Golding and Murchison Production, also based in Dallas. Murchison's corporate goals, however, clashed with the policy of prorationing, which was gaining wide acceptance by Texas and federal officials and the major oil companies. Such governmental restrictions were anathema to Murchison—he contended the policy was a violation of the constitutional rights of private property and personal liberty. In a symbolic statement of his entrepreneurial philosophy—and his stance toward prorationing—Murchison renamed Golding and Murchison Production the American Liberty Oil Company. On a more tangible basis, Murchison became a leading producer of "hot" oil, produced in excess of state quotas, and hot oil became a significant source of profits. While Murchison's views were shared by many others in the industry (and his actions imitated by more than a few) the battle against government prorationing of oil was lost with the passage of the Interstate Oil Compact of 1935, which empowered the federal government to join with the oil-producing states in policing hot oil. Murchison continued to produce hot oil, however, until the 1940s, when wartime demand for oil made all-out production, rather than production restrictions, the most pressing national need. He married Virginia Long in 1942. They had no children.

In the postwar era, Murchison continued to explore for petroleum. In 1948 he purchased enough stock to gain control of the Delhi Oil Corporation, a subsidiary of Southern Union whose main purpose was exploration. In 1955 Delhi merged with the Taylor Refining Company, creating the Delhi-Taylor Oil Corporation. With Murchison serving as its president, Delhi-Taylor became a fully integrated concern, with assets exceeding $71 million. He continued as president until 1964, when the firm's assets were sold to Tenneco, a natural gas pipeline corporation. Early in the 1950s Murchison became interested in the petroleum reserves of western Canada, being especially attracted by the large reserves of natural gas in the province of Alberta. In 1950 he created Canadian-Delhi to tap the Canadian gas reserves and the following year created a subsidiary organization, the Trans-Canada Pipe Lines, to bring the gas to market. Nationalist opposition to foreign ownership of the pipeline project delayed completion and led to Murchison's practical withdrawal from the project. Beginning in 1952 Murchison expanded his oil operations in Venezuela.

A one-man conglomerate, Murchison ultimately became one of the wealthiest men in America. Since the 1930s he had been diversifying his holdings by acquiring a handful of insurance companies, consolidating them in 1955 into Life Companies, Inc., based in Dallas. In this era of prosperity, Murchison continued to accumulate diverse holdings, including controlling interests in banking, chemicals, transportation, publishing, sporting goods, and toys. In all of these vast holdings, Murchison took a passive role and retained existing personnel and infrastructure. Only in the petroleum-related activities did Murchison actively take part, always having a controlling influence in those corporations. At one time, he owned more than 100 companies simultaneously, with properties and assets throughout the Western hemisphere, ranging from

Venezuela, throughout the continental United States, and into Canada. In 1954 Murchison appeared on the cover of *Time* magazine with the subheading "a big wheeler dealer."

During his adult life, Murchison was active in philanthropy for juvenile delinquents, owning for a short time the Del Mar (Calif.) Turf Club, a racetrack whose profits he largely allocated to boys' programs. Murchison also liked to spend time hunting, fishing, and raising cattle at his 76,000-acre ranch in the Sierra Madre of Mexico and his 2,000-acre ranch near Athens, Texas. A Presbyterian, Murchison was an ardently conservative southern Democrat, opposing both Presidents Franklin Roosevelt and Harry Truman and contributing monies to Republicans such as Senator Joseph McCarthy. When he retired in 1964, his personal fortune was estimated to be $500 million, making him one of the world's wealthiest persons. In 1965 Murchison suffered a series of debilitating strokes. He died in Athens, Texas, four years later.

Murchison will be best remembered for his role in the dramatic growth of the Texas oil industry, whose producing reserves made the state the leading oil province in the world for most of the twentieth century. His risk-taking entrepreneurial style epitomized the hallowed American tradition of economic individualism. He was one of the pioneers in the development of the natural gas industry, was one of the early boosters of Dallas, and was a key figure in establishing that city as an oil town and major metropolis. He was also a pioneer in tapping the prolific oil reserves of the West Texas Permian Basin. Both Murchison and his son Clinton William Murchison, Jr., were instrumental in the establishment of the Dallas Cowboys franchise of the National Football League in 1960.

• There are no Murchison papers. Information on Murchison can be found in the *New York Times*, which reported extensively on his business dealings. Other sources include Ferdinand Lundberg, *The Rich and the Super Rich: A Study in the Power of Money Today* (1969); F. Lincoln, "Big Wheeler-Dealer from Dallas," *Fortune*, Jan. 1953, pp. 116–20, and Feb. 1959, pp. 152–54; "New Athenians," *Time*, 24 May 1954, pp. 90–94; "Murchisons and Allan Kirby," *Life*, 28 Apr. 1961, pp. 74B–79; C. Amory, "Oil Folks at Home," *Holiday*, Feb. 1957, pp. 52–57; James Presley, *A Saga of Wealth: The Rise of the Texas Oilmen* (1978); and Jane Wolfe, *The Murchisons: The Rise and Fall of a Texas Dynasty* (1989). Obituaries are in the *New York Times* and on the front page of the *Dallas Morning News*, both 21 June 1969.

BRUCE ANDRE BEAUBOUEF

MURDOCH, James Edward (25 Jan. 1811–19 May 1893), actor, was born in Philadelphia, Pennsylvania, the son of Thomas Murdoch, a bookbinder, and Elizabeth Keel (or Keely). With only a few years of formal education, he was apprenticed to his father in the family business. However, he soon became interested in acting. He joined an amateur acting group and began private study in elocution under Lemuel G. White, who had tutored Edwin Forrest. Although Murdoch's father hoped his son would follow the family trade, he was persuaded to engage the Arch Street Theatre and the whole company then in residence for the night of 13 October 1829 to permit eighteen-year-old James to make his stage debut as Frederick in *Lovers' Vows.* Charles Durang remarked, "We did not see the whole of this performance, but it was the best first appearance we ever saw" (2d ser., chap. 48). Writing in the 1850s, Durang recalled that "it was then prophesied that this gentleman would rapidly rise in the profession" and noted that this prophecy was "amply fulfilled" as Murdoch became recognized as "the best general actor of our day."

Murdoch advanced steadily in his chosen profession, but not without encountering difficulties. After his successful debut he was invited to act, without pay, in some additional productions at the Arch and then took a paid engagement to play in Halifax, Nova Scotia, in the spring of 1830. But the company went bankrupt, and Murdoch's father had to provide money for his return home. The next season he joined the company of Vincent De Camp, acting in South Carolina and Georgia; but that engagement too ended with financial difficulties. Returning to Philadelphia, he was just starting to emerge as an important actor in his native city when, in 1832, he mistakenly took arsenic for medicine. This accident permanently damaged his health; thereafter he was never strong enough to withstand the fatigue of long engagements and had to spend a good deal of time during his most active years in rest and retirement. In this early period, as he rose to a leading position in light comedy and juvenile tragedy, the well-built young actor, who "possessed a strong, full-toned, clear voice" and "manly and well-defined features, capable of varied and unlimited expression" (Ludlow, p. 643), performed intermittently throughout the East and on the southern circuit, often in second roles to Edwin Forrest or Junius Brutus Booth. Although playing widely and achieving a national reputation, Murdoch acted most often in Philadelphia where for ten years, beginning in 1832, he was a regular member of the company at the Chestnut Street Theatre and also appeared occasionally at the Arch and Walnut Street theaters. He first appeared in New York on 16 July 1836 at Mrs. Hamblin's Theatre as Jaffier in *Venice Preserved*. In June 1838 he acted for the first time at the Park Theatre, New York, in a particularly successful engagement playing opposite Ellen Tree in *Much Ado About Nothing* and *The Lady of Lyons* and opposite Charlotte Cushman in *Wild Oats* and *The School for Scandal*. In 1840–1841 he became stage manager of the Chestnut Street Theatre and shortly thereafter served as stage manager of the National Theatre of Boston.

Although he had little formal education, in 1842, while still in the successful management of the National, Murdoch decided to withdraw from the stage to devote himself to intensive study. In particular, he studied the anatomy of the vocal organs, and he studied rhetoric with William Russell of Boston, with whom he collaborated on a book, *Orthophony: Or, Vocal Culture in Elocution* (1845). In this period he also taught elocution to law and divinity students and lectured on "The Uses and Abuses of the Stage" and on Shakespeare's principal characters.

On 20 October 1845 Murdoch returned to the stage to play Hamlet at the Park Theatre. This performance began a period lasting until the Civil War in which he reached the zenith of his career. Acting leading roles in comedy and tragedy in all the principal cities of the East, South, Midwest, and in 1853 in California, he won great popularity and established his place as one of the foremost American actors of the nineteenth century. The noted actor and manager Joseph Jefferson, writing in the late 1880s, remarked, "I do not remember any actor who excelled him in those parts that he seemed to make especially his own" (*Autobiography*, p. 153). Jefferson praised his versatility and especially his originality. Recalling how Murdoch as Charles Surface won highest honors among a particularly powerful cast playing in *The School for Scandal* in Washington in 1853, Jefferson lauded the "finish and picturesque style of Murdoch's acting." Jefferson observed further that "there was a manliness about his light comedy that gave it more dignity than the flippant style in which it was usually played" and made him especially effective in the roles of old English comedy (p. 153). Murdoch, who acted frequently in Smith-Ludlow theaters in New Orleans, Mobile, and St. Louis, was praised too by Noah Ludlow for his comic roles: "Any character in comedy depending on the good delivery of fine sentiments," he "could give more effect to than any actor I have ever seen" (*Dramatic Life*, p. 643). Ludlow, however, reserved highest honors for Murdoch's Hamlet. Recalling Murdoch's performances in St. Louis in 1846, he declared them "the best representation of the Danish prince I have ever seen; his readings, his action, his appearance—in short, his *tout-ensemble* was my *beau idéal* of the character." Noting that "the pervading quality of the performance was grace and propriety of conception and delivery: relieved by electrical flashes on passages of a more elevated character," the critic for the *Spirit of the Times* (25 Oct. 1845) similarly called Murdoch's Hamlet "the best in the country."

In 1856, during the height of his popularity in the United States, Murdoch was able to fulfill "a longcherished desire to appear upon the London boards" (*The Stage*, p. 359). While in England on a vacation, he was engaged by John Buckstone to appear at the Haymarket Theatre. Murdoch's opening on 22 September in *The Inconstant* met with unbridled applause. Of his success in London, Jefferson observed, "The public was surprised to see comely old English manners so conspicuous in an American actor, and he gained its sympathy at once" (*Autobiography*, pp. 153–54). The enthusiastic reception accorded him as young Maribel led to Murdoch's continuing at the Haymarket for 110 nights, the longest consecutive list of performances he ever played. After appearing in *The School for Scandal*, *Wild Oats*, *The Wonder*, and *The Dramatist*, Murdoch went on to Liverpool, where he won similar acclaim. There, in addition to his comic

roles, he played Hamlet and was compared favorably with Kean and Macready and was said to resemble Charles Young. However, ill health forced him to cut short this engagement. After returning to the United States he spent much time, when not acting, on his grape farm near Cincinnati, which he had purchased three years earlier.

During the Civil War Murdoch gave up acting and devoted himself to the Union cause. He won acclaim for his patriotic readings in all the major cities of the North, in army hospitals, in the camps, and according to J. Bunting, "wherever there was money to be raised or fainting courage to be cheered" (*The Stage*, p. 23). After the war he acted rather infrequently. He gave lectures on the drama and very popular dramatic readings of patriotic poems and of scenes from Shakespeare. In 1880 he published a book of reminiscences, *The Stage, or, Recollections of Actors and Acting from an Experience of Fifty Years*. On 22 May 1889, nearly sixty years after his debut, he returned to the stage for a farewell at the Academy of Music in Philadelphia.

As a pioneer of the American stage, Murdoch never achieved the acclaim of the tragedian Edwin Forrest, five years his elder, but he was certainly the leading performer of high comedy in his era and was probably the best American-born representative of Hamlet until the advent of Edwin Booth. In private life, Murdoch was much respected and admired for his "high-bred courtesy, genial companionship, unfailing good humor, and ready wit" (Ainsworth R. Spofford, cited by Edwin A. Lee). He and his English-born wife, Eliza Mary Middlecott, whom he had married in 1831, had six children who survived infancy. Murdoch died on his farm in suburban Cincinnati.

• A "Biographical Sketch of the Author" by J. Bunting is prefaced to Murdoch's *The Stage*. Information on Murdoch's appearances in the South and Midwest is in Noah Ludlow, *Dramatic Life as I Found It* (1880; repr. 1966), and in Sol Smith, *Theatrical Management in the West and South for Thirty Years* (1868), and on his appearances in New York in Joseph N. Ireland, *Records of the New York Stage*, vol. 2 (1867), and George C. D. Odell, *Annals of the New York Stage*, vols. 4–8 (1928–1936). Joseph Jefferson, who acted with Murdoch and was stage manager for a production of *The School for Scandal* in which both appeared, provides a significant evaluation of his fellow performer in his *Autobiography* (1889). In *Twenty-six Years of the Life of an Actor and Manager*, Francis Courtney Wemyss offers recollections of Murdoch's early career in Pittsburgh and Philadelphia. Charles Durang, *The Philadelphia Stage from 1749 to 1855*, published in three series in the *Philadelphia Sunday Dispatch* beginning with the issue of 7 May 1854 and available complete in bound volumes in the Pennsylvania Historical Society and University of Pennsylvania libraries, offers the fullest account of Murdoch's career in his native city. Edwin A. Lee, "Sheridan's Ride and the Men Who Made It Famous," *New York Dramatic Mirror*, 19 Dec. 1903, pp. 18–19, provides an account of Murdoch's activities during the Civil War and of his patriotic readings as well as a biographical sketch. There are numerous theatrical reviews of Murdoch's performances in the newspapers of the various cities in which he acted. Obituaries are in the *New York Dramatic Mirror*, 27 May 1893, and the *Cincinnati Commercial Gazette*, 20 May 1893.

JANE WILLIAMSON

MURDOCK, George Peter (11 May 1897–29 Mar. 1985), anthropologist, "totemic ancestor" of cross-cultural research, and university professor, was born near Meriden, Connecticut, the son of George Bronson Murdock and Harriett Elizabeth Graves, farmers. As an adult, Murdock enjoyed telling how his boyhood experience behind an ox-driven plow had prepared him for the study of subsistence techniques in his career in anthropology. He received an A.B. with honors in history from Yale University in 1919, after a tour of duty in World War I as an army first lieutenant in field artillery, and he competed that same year in the national Forest Hills tennis tournament. Admitted to Harvard Law School and influenced by undergraduate courses with sociologist Albert G. Keller, he undertook a year-long trip through Asia and Europe and decided on a more adventurous career in anthropology. When ethnologist Franz Boas denied him admission at Columbia University because of his "sociological" orientation, Murdock completed the "science of society" Ph.D. program in anthropology and sociology at Yale in 1925. There he acquired his cross-cultural orientation, in a tradition established by William Graham Sumner and continued by Murdock's graduate adviser, Keller. Murdock's dissertation, a critical translation of Julius Lippert's *The Evolution of Culture*, was published in 1931.

In 1925 Murdock married Carmen Swanson, a Yale graduate student in biochemistry, who became his lifelong companion and scientific reader/critic; they had one child. After a brief teaching job at the University of Maryland, he returned as an assistant professor to Keller's department at Yale in 1928, where he taught until 1960, reaching emeritus status. He helped Edward Sapir found the anthropology department in 1931 and served as its chair from 1937 to 1943 and from 1953 to 1957.

Murdock undertook field work among the Haida in 1932 and among the Tenino in the summers of 1934 and 1935, reconstructing their traditional cultures. His first major comparative ethnographic publication, which set the tone for later work, was *Our Primitive Contemporaries* (1934). Instrumental in shaping his work were the interdisciplinary human behavior orientations of Yale's Institute of Human Relations. There he joined psychologists Clark L. Hull and Neal Miller, sociologist John Dollard, Freudian psychoanalysts, and others, and cofounded in 1937 the Cross-Cultural Survey that systematized the Sumner-Keller comparative tradition by using E. B. Tylor's and Murdock's own comparative work as a model. Murdock broke with Keller's evolutionism but kept the conviction that a science of society required systematic comparative study. He helped to introduce sampling procedures and statistical testing. In 1937 he published newly coded data on the sexual division of labor and

the first demonstrations of the synthesis of a new cross-cultural approach. He also organized the survey's regional bibliographies and classifications of ethnographic materials, both by regional similarities and by subject matter, as in his *Outline of Cultural Materials* (1938). There followed a spate of articles such as his "Cross-Cultural Survey" and "Double Descent" (1940). Although interrupted by the start of World War II, he and his colleagues had established the basis for the organization in 1946 of the Human Relations Area Files and for the emergence of disciplinary interest in cross-cultural studies that followed. In February 1943 he arranged for the Cross-Cultural Survey on Micronesia to be taken over by the navy, where he was a reserve officer.

Commissioned in April 1943 a lieutenant commander in the Naval Office of Occupied Areas (research unit for the islands of Micronesia), Murdock and junior officers Clellan S. Ford and John W. M. Whiting, whom he had enlisted, prepared a series of handbooks on the Marshall, Caroline, Marianas, Izu, Bonin, and Ryukyu islands. Murdock's influence in promoting the relevance of social science research in the wartime and postwar contexts gave rise to navy proposals of annexation of Micronesian Trust Territories as the alternative to postwar administration by the United Nations with the goal of granting them early independence. These proposals and Murdock's overall Pacific research plans, while initially opposed at the time by members of the Pacific Science Association with a more Boasian (culture-historical) and less utilitarian approach to anthropology, were the source of compromises in 1946 both in terms of research priorities and policy settlement of Micronesian trusteeships. The navy named Murdock field director of the 1947–1948 Coordinated Investigation of Micronesian Anthropology, which employed forty-two anthropologists from twenty institutions. He himself worked in 1947–1948 with five Yale anthropologists and linguists on Truk in the Carolines, publishing with Ward H. Goodenough his first study of a fully functioning non-Western culture, "Social Organization of Truk." He helped to found and was president in 1947 of the Society for Applied Anthropology and received the Viking Medal in 1949. In 1951 he helped Alexander Spoehr reorganize the Bishop Museum in Honolulu; they founded with Yale and the University of Hawaii the Tri-Institutional Pacific Program that funded more than twenty field projects over ten years. He and Harold Coolidge organized the Pacific Science Board of the National Research Council, of which Murdock became a member and chairman (1953–1957), helping to further research in the region for decades and to include anthropologists through the 1950s on the administrative staffs of the Trust Territories. He was elected president of the American Ethnological Society in 1952 and of the American Anthropological Association in 1955.

Murdock's chief interests were in social organization and the regulation of sexual behavior. Among his many publications were comparative articles on "Bifurcate Merging" and "Family Universals" in 1947, "North American Indian Social Organization" (1955), and "Cultural Correlates of the Regulation of Premarital Sexual Behavior (1964). His landmark work, *Social Structure* (1949), brought conceptual clarity to the study of family and kinship organization by testing an integrated set of human behavioral principles against the cultural variation found in a sample of 250 societies that he coded on features of kinship organization. The book stimulated recognition of new problems, such as cognatic descent groups, that Murdock explored with others, as in his 1960 edited volume, *Social Structure in Southeast Asia*, and classic articles on "Cognatic Forms of Social Organization" (1960) and "The Kindred" (1964). His ethnographic reading was prodigious, and he demanded that students master the regional ethnographies of their chosen areas of study. His highly influential comparative study, *Africa: Its Peoples and Their Culture History* (1959), embodied his teaching principles concerning regional cultures. *Explorations in Cultural Anthropology* (1964), a festschrift edited by Goodenough, shows the range of scholarly and scientific problems undertaken by his students.

Although in 1960 he faced the pleasant prospect of emeritus status at Yale, Murdock accepted instead an offer from University of Pittsburgh dean of social sciences John P. Gillin to become a Mellon Professor. At Pittsburgh, Murdock launched a new anthropology department and, with the backing of the university, founded the journal *Ethnology* as an outlet for descriptive ethnographic articles and cross-cultural studies as well as for the issue of his *Ethnographic Atlas* (1967, also published by installments) of coded comparative ethnographic data. In 1964 he was elected to the National Academy of Sciences; he received the Herbert E. Gregory Medal in Tokyo in 1966 and the Wilbur Lucius Cross Medal in 1967. Reprints of his essays appeared in 1965 as *Culture and Society*. Between 1964 and 1968 he was called on to help organize the Division of Behavioral Sciences of the National Research Council. By 1970 his atlas had grown to include 1,270 cases coded from his ethnographic readings. He and Douglas R. White selected and annotated 186 cross-culturally representative societies from Murdock's database to establish a Standard Cross-Cultural Sample (1969) for the comparative research community. With funding from the National Science Foundation, they planned and codirected Pittsburgh's Cross-Cultural Cumulative Coding Center, which hired and supervised coders to compile and publish, mostly with Murdock's coauthorship, systematic data sets on the standard sample. Murdock continued to publish extensively on methodology in cross-cultural studies. The cases in his atlas were further culled in the *Atlas of World Cultures* (1981), a unique tool for cross-cultural studies. The cumulative "Focused Ethnographic Bibliography for the Standard Cross-Cultural Sample" was published in *Behavior Science Research* (23 [1988]: 1–145).

Murdock received the Huxley Memorial Medal in London in 1971. His Huxley lecture on "Anthropology's Mythology" (*Proceedings 1971* [1972]: 17–24), debunked "culture" and "social system" as grand explanations for human behavior. He argued instead for rebuilding a behavioral approach to anthropology in terms of operational concepts. In 1976 Marshall Sahlins's *Culture and Practical Reason* described two of the main paradigms of anthropological theory and identified Murdock with "praxis theories" of individual behaviors, interacting to shape culture, as opposed to "culturological theories." He described Murdock as anthropology's Robespierre for announcing the "demise" of culture as an explanatory concept in its own right.

Following retirement in 1973, Murdock resettled outside Philadelphia to be near his son's family and his former student Goodenough. His penultimate and last substantive book, *Theories of Illness: A World Survey* (1980), showed a comparative behavioral approach to supernatural projections that was still creatively evolving even in his eighty-third year. He died at home in Devon, Pennsylvania.

Murdock's detractors viewed his cross-cultural approach as too mechanical and connected with a classification system that now appears outdated and an artifact of Western civilization. His regional comparative studies, however, and the work of his later years, starting with the Standard Cross-Cultural Sample, was concerned with reintegrating a more Boasian culture-historical approach into comparative studies. While his descriptive comparative categories allowed theories of his day to be tested, he encouraged novel approaches and developments in cross-cultural research that would supercede his own.

Murdock's long career spanned both the coming of age of American anthropology and the emergence of controversial divisions over the nature of anthropology's subject matter. Many of Murdock's contributions enter into late twentieth-century debates in anthropology and methodology, and his cross-cultural samples and databases (also republished in *World Cultures* electronic journal, vols. 1, 2, and 4) continue in wide use, even if they are much reworked and reinterpreted through later analyses. The Standard Cross-Cultural Sample has been used in hundreds of published cross-cultural studies (such as those cited in *Behavior Science Research* 25 [1991]: 79–140), each of which also contributes to a cumulative cross-cultural database. Debates that his comparative studies stimulated, especially over "etic" concepts used in description or comparison versus "emic" concepts of specific cultures, continue alongside efforts to contextualize cross-cultural materials through the networks of observed behaviors and historical linkages that connect the elements of cultural systems.

A modest but feisty man, whom Cambridge anthropologist Edmund Leach dubbed "Six-gun Pete," Murdock abhorred pomposity in any form and was continually open to new ideas and projects. Goodenough wrote that Murdock "did not see anthropology as an arena in which people competed for recognition and status or in which the object was to impose some ideological version of truth on the treatment of its subject matter. He saw it, rather, as a cooperative undertaking toward improving our understanding of what goes on in the human world and the processes that give it shape." In the fifty years between his first publication in 1931 and his last in 1981, Murdock played both controversial and leading roles in anthropology's growth and development.

• The journal *Ethnology* 24 (1985): 307–17, published Alexander Spoehr's review of Murdock's contributions and his complete bibliography. The *American Anthropologist* 88 (1986): 682–86, carried an assessment of his life's work by John W. M. Whiting. *Behavior Science Research* 22 (1988): 1–9, a special issue devoted to a retrospective assessment of Murdock, included a review of his contributions by Ward H. Goodenough and separate reviews of his contributions to the Human Relations Area Files, the *Ethnographic Atlas*, and the study of North American Indians, Africa, and kinship and social structure. John A. Barnes's *Three Styles in the Study of Kinship* (1971) reviews Murdock's approach in contrast to others.

DOUGLAS R. WHITE

MURDOCK, Victor (18 Mar. 1871–7 July 1945), journalist, congressman, and editor, was born in Burlingame, Kansas, the son of Marshall Mortimer Murdock, an editor and publisher, and Victoria Mayberry. In 1872 Murdock's father founded the *Wichita Eagle*. Victor attended public schools and Lewis Academy in Wichita. As a boy, he learned to operate a linetype at the *Eagle*, one of his few mechanical achievements. In 1890 he married Mary Pearl Allen; they would have two daughters. In a news story during the 1890 congressional campaign he jokingly dubbed Populist Jeremiah Simpson "Sockless Jerry." Not taking affront, the rustic but learned Simpson capitalized on this, and despite their political differences, he became a lifelong friend of Murdock.

In 1892 he moved to Chicago and became a reporter for the *Chicago Inter Ocean*. Not knowing professional baseball language, he enlivened his stories by changing such expressions as "a two-base hit" to "swatted a two-bagger." This led to slang and provincialisms being used widely by other sports writers. In 1893 he covered William McKinley's Ohio gubernatorial reelection. Murdock returned to Wichita in December 1893 to work as managing editor of the *Eagle*.

In 1903, when Seventh District congressman Chester I. Long was selected for the Senate, Murdock was elected to the House of Representatives as a Republican. He was assigned to the Post Office and Post Roads Committee. He voted for Joseph G. "Uncle Joe" Cannon for Speaker, and his early bills called largely for Union Civil War pensions. In 1906 Murdock was elected to the Executive Committee of the Kansas Square Deal Club, which promoted reform legislation. He was disappointed when Governor Edward W. Hoch bypassed him as a replacement for ousted senator J. Ralph Burton. He failed also in a 1907 senatorial bid.

Murdock's bright red hair, snapping eyes, and booming voice caught and held attention. He became angered when Speaker Cannon failed to return a morning greeting. Cannon's habitual rudeness and rigid control of bills sent to committee hardened into insurgency in 1907, when Cannon blocked Murdock's "divisor" amendment that would have prevented railroads from overcharging for carrying mail. As insurgent publicity chairman, Murdock generated negative publicity for Cannon and received a great deal of press coverage for himself. Although George W. Norris's parliamentary maneuver of 19 March 1910 brought Cannon's removal as chairman of the Rules Committee, Robert S. La Forte observed "In the long run, public scorn defeated Cannon, and Murdock played the premier role." House colleagues, envious of the attention given Murdock, caused him to receive only minor committee assignments.

Murdock praised the Postal Savings Depositories Act (1910) for encouraging thrift and hailed the Mann-Elkins Act (1910) for bringing fairer freight rates to small towns. With his own reelection assured in 1910, Murdock's campaigning helped defeat four of six standpat Republican Kansas congressmen. In 1911–1912 he supported Senator Robert M. La Follette's presidential ambition within the Republican party and then Theodore Roosevelt's Progressive party candidacy. As a Republican, Murdock was reelected to Congress, but five Kansas Democrats won House seats, and Woodrow Wilson carried the state and nation for president. Murdock was not enthusiastic about Wilson's "New Freedom." He did not back the Clayton Antitrust Act (1914) nor the Federal Trade Commission Act (1914), asserting that Roosevelt's industrial commission would have better regulated big business. He held that the Federal Reserve Act (1913) handed over control of banking to Wall Street.

In 1914 William Allen White persuaded Murdock to run for the Senate as a Progressive. Murdock carried only three of Kansas's 105 counties. In 1915 he became chairman of the National Progressive Committee. When Roosevelt refused the Progressive nomination, discontent followed Bainbridge Colby's nomination of the fiery Murdock. The Progressive campaign met no success. At St. Louis in 1917 Murdock chaired the last Progressive convention, held in conjunction with the Prohibition party. Although Murdock did not campaign for Wilson in 1916, the *Eagle* supported Wilson as a peace president.

In 1917 Murdock declared himself a Democrat and was named to the Federal Trade Commission (FTC). He led a vigorous probe into food speculation and later joined two others to report on exorbitant executive salaries and wartime profiteering on such items as flour milling, coal, oil, metals, and processed foods. This report was available to government control agencies, such as the War Industries Board (WIB), the Food Administration, and the Fuel Administration. He resigned as FTC chairman in 1924 and returned to Wichita as editor in chief of the *Eagle*. His brother,

Marcellus Murdock, had kept the paper running while Victor Murdock pursued his political career.

For the next twenty years Murdock's articles and editorials became models of style, accuracy, and substance. Murdock, who earlier had found the lyceum and Chautauqua circuits lucrative, spoke thousands of times without pay to clubs, commencements, luncheons, and dinners. An ardent Wichita booster, he welcomed new firms and extolled civic improvements. He owned farmlands, encouraged dam construction, and promoted sugar beets and soybeans as new crops. He invested personally in the developing local aircraft industry.

Politically, Murdock remained a Democrat, but in 1924 he supported White's losing bid as an independent for governor against the Ku Klux Klan and in 1928 supported the anti-Klan Republican Clyde M. Reed, who became governor. In 1936 Murdock upheld New Deal agricultural relief measures as useful and constitutional and, although personally friendly, did not back Alf M. Landon's presidential bid.

Murdock was the author of several books: *China the Mysterious and Marvellous* (1920); *Folks* (1921), comprising fifty-one vignettes about prominent and otherwise notable Kansans; *Constantinople* (1926); and the posthumously published *"It May Chance of Wheat"* (1965), which discoursed expertly on the staple's history, germination, adaptability, milling, and complex marketing.

Ill for nearly a year, Murdock died in Wichita. Versatile, courageous, ubiquitous, he remains a dominant figure of the Progressive Era. A tribute in his newspaper held, "The *Eagle*, Wichita, and the Southwest will not be the same without him" (9 July 1945).

• Murdock's papers are in the Library of Congress. Newspaper clippings and related materials are at the Kansas State Historical Society, Topeka, and the public libraries of Wichita; Kansas City, Kans.; and Kansas City, Mo. Works that discuss Murdock's political career include Anna Marie Edwards, "The Congressional Career of Victor Murdock, 1903–1909" (Master's thesis, Univ. of Kansas, 1947); Lillian Tuttle, "The Congressional Career of Victor Murdock, 1909–1911" (Master's thesis, Univ. of Kansas, 1948); Lenis Boswell, "The Political Career of Victor Murdock, 1911–1917" (Master's thesis, Univ. of Kansas, 1949); Leland Paul Moore, "A Critical Study of the Progressive Movement in Kansas Politics from 1908 to 1936" (Master's thesis, Univ. of Southern California, 1937); Marvin A. Harder, "Some Aspects of Republican and Democratic Party Factionalism in Kansas" (Ph.D. diss., Columbia Univ., 1959); Thomas C. Blaisdell, *The Federal Trade Commission* (1932; repr. 1967); Blair Bolles, *Truant from Illinois* (1951); O. Gene Clanton, *Kansas Populism* (1969); Pendleton Herring, *Federal Commissioners: A Study of Their Careers and Qualifications* (1936); Kenneth W. Hechler, *Insurgency: Personalities and Politics of the Taft Era* (1940); Bliss Isely and W. M. Richards, *Four Centuries in Kansas* (1944); Robert M. La Follette. *La Follette's Autobiography* (1960); Arthur S. Link, *Woodrow Wilson and the Progressive Era* (1954); Robert S. La Forte, *Leaders of Reform: Progressive Republicans in Kansas, 1900–1916* (1974); Donald R. McCoy, *Landon of Kansas* (1966); Craig Miner, *Wichita, the Magic City* (1988); George E. Mowry, *Theodore Roosevelt and the Progressive Movement* (1960); George W. Norris, *Fighting Liberal: The Autobiography of George W. Norris* (1961); Russell B. Nye, *Midwestern Progressive Politics* (1951); Robert W. Richmond, *Kansas* (1974); A. Bower Sageser, *Joseph L. Bristow, Kansas Progressive* (1968); Francis W. Schruben, *Kansas in Turmoil* (1969); Homer E. Socolofsky, *Arthur Capper: Publisher, Politician, and Philanthropist* (1962); William Allen White, *The Autobiography of William Allen White* (1946); William Zornow, *Kansas: A History of the Jayhawk State* (1957). Obituaries are in the Wichita Morning Eagle, 7 July 1945, and the *Kansas City Times*, 11 July 1945.

FRANCIS W. SCHRUBEN

MURFREE, Mary Noailles (24 Jan. 1850–31 July 1922), novelist and short-story writer, was born at "Grantland," a thriving plantation near Murfreesboro, Tennessee, the daughter of William Law Murfree, a successful planter and lawyer, and Fanny Priscilla Dickinson. Mary's great-grandfather, Colonel Hardy Murfree, had been an officer in the Continental army, distinguishing himself at the capture of Stony Point, New York, where he commanded the North Carolina revolutionary troops. Moving to middle Tennessee in 1807, he gave his name to Murfreesboro and founded as well a distinguished line of successful planters and lawyers, which included Mary's father.

Mary's childhood at Grantland, and later Nashville, was idyllic, marred only by a fever when she was four that left her partially paralyzed for the remainder of her life. Possibly as a result of this lameness, she became an avid student, reading history and English literature and later studying French, Italian, and Latin as well as reading law under her father's tutelage. Her parents provided the best possible education available to a young southern lady, including a French governess, a private academy in Nashville, and, after the war, an exclusive French finishing school, Chegary, which she and her only sister, Fanny, attended between 1867 and 1869 in Philadelphia.

The Civil War destroyed both Grantland and the Murfree family prosperity, although Mary's father moved the family safely back to Nashville early in the conflict. Life in federally occupied Nashville was not easy, but the Murfree family avoided being caught in the great battle at Murfreesboro (31 Dec. 1862–3 Jan. 1863) that was fought over and destroyed Grantland. Murfree drew upon these wartime experiences in two later works of historical fiction, *Where the Battle Was Fought* (1884) and *The Storm Centre* (1905). In her later fiction, however, she was primarily concerned with the physical destruction of the war and its impact on individual lives; she never attempted to exonerate either the Confederacy or the lifestyle of the southern aristocracy she knew so well.

Encouraged by her family to write stories, Murfree began her literary career by publishing two stories in *Lippincott's Magazine* under the pseudonym R. Emmett Dembry. "Flirts and Their Ways" (May 1874) and "My Daughter's Admirers" (July 1875) were both satirical sketches of polite society. Although mildly amusing, neither showed particular insight into the manners or customs of postwar society, and Murfree soon abandoned further examination of the upper class in Victorian America. Earlier critics have suggested that in so doing she missed her best opportunity to develop her talents, but these stories are too superficial and glib, even by nineteenth-century standards, to really justify such expectations.

Instead she soon turned to the mother lode she eventually mined to exhaustion—the mountains and mountaineers of Tennessee. During her childhood Murfree spent many summers at the popular resort of Beersheba Springs in the Cumberland Mountains of middle Tennessee. Here at this fashionable resort for wealthy southerners she observed the native mountaineers carefully, but always from a safe distance. During the 1870s the family also visited the Great Smoky Mountains in eastern Tennessee, and Murfree later fused in her fiction the mountaineers of the Cumberlands with the more rugged mountain scenery of the Great Smokies, mentioning by name specific places such as Cades and Tuckaleechee coves, Thunderhead, and Gregory's Bald. The first of these stories, "The Dancin' Party at Harrison's Cove," appeared in 1878 in the *Atlantic* under her new pen name, Charles Egbert Craddock, which she took, in part, from a minor character in an unpublished manuscript.

When this story was published along with seven others on the same theme in 1884, the resulting volume, *In the Tennessee Mountains*, was an immediate critical and popular success. Many of Murfree's novels employed elements popular in the local color school: a unique geographic setting, dialect, strange characters idealized or romanticized, and the innate cultural superiority of the narrator, which permitted innumerable satiric comments on the contrast between the peculiar local ways and mainstream America. These novels about the Tennessee mountains formed the bulk of Murfree's critical reputation and widespread popularity during the last two decades of the nineteenth century: *Down the Ravine* (1885), *The Prophet of the Great Smoky Mountains* (1885), *In the Clouds* (1886), *The Story of Keedon Bluffs* (1888), *The Despot of Broomsedge Cove* (1889), *In the "Stranger Peoples'" Country* (1891), *His Vanished Star* (1894), *The Phantoms of the Footbridge and Other Stories* (1895), *The Mystery of Witch-Face Mountain and Other Stories* (1895), *The Juggler* (1897), and *The Young Mountaineers* (1897). *In the Tennessee Mountains* was an instant success. Fourteen editions were published in two years, including one in England. *The Prophet of the Great Smoky Mountains*, her finest novel, also was immensely popular and well received in England as well as the United States.

Departure from the Tennessee mountain theme usually met with indifference from Murfree's otherwise enthusiastic public, as evidenced when she explored the colonial history of the Old Southwest in *The Story of Old Fort Loudon* (1899), *A Spectre of Power* (1903), *The Frontiersmen* (1904), and *The Amulet* (1906). Murfree's explorations of antebellum southern plantation life, in *The Fair Mississippian* (1908) and *The Story of Duciehurst* (1914), were similarly unsuccessful.

Even at the height of Murfree's popularity in the 1880s, critics lamented her episodic plots, overelaborate descriptions of mountain scenery, and stock characters—such as the beautiful maiden, scolding old woman, and tyrannical infant—who reoccur with monotonous regularity in her writing. Her own brother complained that her characters were bereft of common humanity and represented types of personalities rather than individuals. Yet ironically at the same time critics were decrying Murfree's skill as a creative artist, they praised her portraits of Tennessee mountaineers as authentic. Such critics believed that Murfree's literary sins should be partially overlooked because she accurately portrayed the Tennessee mountain community before it was forever changed by modern industrialism.

Scholars in the late twentieth century, however, have vigorously denied the very authenticity of the fictional world upon which Murfree's reputation rests. Linguists who studied the mountain regions of the southern Appalachians have unequivocally denied the accuracy of her dialect. Far more pernicious, however, was Murfree's underlying assumption that the Tennessee mountaineers were so culturally backward and inherently inferior that they could never hope to become part of mainstream America. Her mountaineers were occasionally noble savages, but never an integral part of the human family. They could never be successful in the outer world, nor were mixed marriages ever permitted between mountaineers and outsiders of Murfree's own class. Quite unconsciously Murfree imposed a subtle form of bigotry on her fictional subjects; however well-intentioned, her patronizing depiction of them contributed to their separate but unequal status in mainstream America.

Despite her growing popularity, Murfree earned only a modest income from her writing; even during her most productive years, she continued to live with her family. The years after the Civil War also brought continuing financial problems to Murfree's father, who never recovered the wealth based on land and slaves accumulated before 1861. In 1872 the family moved back to "New Grantland," a modest, one-and-a-half-story cottage on their former plantation. In 1881 William Law Murfree moved his family to St. Louis, Missouri, to be closer to his son, Willie. Although Murfree's law practice briefly revived in St. Louis, in 1890 the family once again returned to New Grantland. Mary's family circle steadily shrank as her father died in 1892, and both her only brother Willie and her mother died in 1902. Her sister Fanny, who also never married, remained her only companion in her later years.

Shy and retiring, Murfree occasionally visited her publisher in Boston, but her relationship with Houghton Mifflin became increasingly strained as she continued to demand advances for her books before submitting them. Ironically her writing career, begun as a hobby, was the major source of income for Murfree and her sister after 1900. Yet at the same time, public taste was moving toward realism in literature, and

Murfree's books declined in popularity at the very point she was most desperate for income. Despite her intelligence and education, Murfree's awareness of the changing realities of publishing was always minimal, and her correspondence with her publishers shows both obstinacy and manipulativeness. In 1912 she was elected state regent of the Tennessee Daughters of the American Revolution, the only public ceremonial role she seemed to enjoy. After suffering from failing eyesight, which prevented her from much writing during her last years, she died in Murfreesboro.

Long before her death, Murfree's novels and short stories no longer engaged the attention of the American public. Unfortunately, her portrayal of the southern mountaineer, accepted as authentic in her own lifetime, perpetuated a grotesque but durable stereotype in the American consciousness. For decades after her popularity ended, historian Henry D. Shapiro argues, her writings "remained the principal text used to understand the peculiarities of mountain life." The stereotype she helped create continues to haunt both Appalachian fiction and scholarship, hindering understanding of the complex realities of southern mountain life and perpetuating Appalachia's low self-image. In a tragic sense, Murfree's fictional southern mountaineers are the spiritual ancestors of *Li'l Abner* and *Snuffy Smith*. If Appalachians continue to be unable to see themselves in the American national mirror, Murfree's enduring fictional distortions must bear major responsibility.

• A major source is the Mary Noailles Murfree Collection at Emory University, although Murfree family papers and letters are scattered in various collections at Harvard, Bowdoin, the Chicago Historical Society, Princeton, the Tennessee State Library and Archives, the University of Virginia, and the University of North Carolina at Chapel Hill. Early biographers, such as Sue Mooney, "An Intimate Study of Mary Noailles Murfree, Charles Egbert Craddock" (M.A. thesis, George Peabody College for Teachers, 1928); Eleanor B. Spence, "Collected Reminiscences of Mary N. Murfree" (M.A. thesis, George Peabody College for Teachers, 1928); and Edd Winfield Parks, *Charles Egbert Craddock (Mary Noailles Murfree)* (1941), all had the advantage of interviewing Mary's sister, Fanny Murfree, after Mary's death, but these accounts are necessarily sympathetic because Fanny insisted on approving each study before publication. Richard Cary, *Mary N. Murfree* (1967), is more critical but not as detailed. The best recent biography is Alice Fay Taylor, "Mary Noailles Murfree: Southern Woman Writer" (Ph.D. diss., Emory Univ., 1988).

The best critical appraisal of Murfree's impact is in Henry D. Shapiro, *Appalachia on Our Mind: The Southern Mountains and Mountaineers in the American Consciousness, 1870–1920* (1978). See also Durwood Dunn, *Cades Cove: The Life and Death of a Southern Appalachian Community, 1818–1937* (1988); Cratis D. Williams, "The Southern Mountaineer in Fact and Fiction" (Ph.D. diss., New York Univ., 1961); Robert Love Taylor, Jr., "Mainstreams of Mountain Thought: Attitudes of Selected Figures in the Heart of the Appalachian South, 1877–1903" (Ph.D. diss., Univ. of Tennessee, 1971); and Joseph S. Hall, *The Phonetics of Great Smoky Mountain Speech* (1942).

DURWOOD DUNN

MURIE, James Rolfe (1862–18 Nov. 1921), teacher, farmer, and ethnographer, was born in Grand Island, Nebraska, the son of a Skiri Pawnee—the other Pawnee bands were the Pitahawirata, Kitkahahki, and Chawi—only known as Anna Marie. Shortly thereafter he was abandoned by his father, James Murie, a Scot captain in Major Frank North's U.S. Army Pawnee scout battalion.

Murie and his mother moved in with her brother, who "lived like a white man" (Parks [1978], p. 76) near the Pawnee Indian Agency in Genoa, Nebraska. In 1874 the Pawnees relocated to a new reservation in Indian Territory. Formerly bison hunters, horticulturalists, and raiders, they began farming and laboring in a cash economy. Murie spent the next two years attending day and boarding schools at the agency, where he learned enough English to serve as the agent's interpreter. In October 1879 Murie was selected to attend Hampton Normal and Agricultural Institute in Virginia; he graduated in 1883 and returned home the first Pawnee to receive a higher education.

Following a brief stint as a store clerk and bookkeeper at the Mattock and Bishop agency store, Murie became assistant teacher at the new Pawnee agency boarding school in the fall of 1883. His goal was the betterment of his people through education. A year later, Murie took twenty-one children to Haskell Institute in Kansas, where he was appointed assistant disciplinarian and drillmaster on 1 January 1885. Two years later, Murie resigned and traveled east, where he lobbied the Indian commissioner to appoint him as a teacher at the Pawnee school. Denied the position by the agent, Murie settled down among the Skiri and began farming. In 1887 he married Pawnee tribal member Mary Esau; they had eight children, four of whom lived to adulthood. In 1890 Murie was cultivating twelve acres and preparing the Pawnee for impending land allotment following the Dawes General Allotment Act of 1887. Within a couple of years, he moved into a log cabin at the Pawnee agency, where he remained active in tribal politics. When allotment finally occurred in 1893, and the agency became the town of Pawnee, Murie served as interpreter and census taker for the tribe. Between 1896 and 1916 Murie intermittently worked as a bank clerk in Pawnee.

Murie is best known for his ethnographic work with the Pawnee while serving as tribal consultant for Alice C. Fletcher, George A. Dorsey, and Clark Wissler. Fletcher, a Smithsonian Institution Bureau of American Ethnology anthropologist who knew Murie from his school days at Hampton Institute, began ethnographic fieldwork with the Pawnee in the mid-1890s and solicited Murie's assistance during her three field trips. Although Murie was never given proper credit for his work as interpreter, collaborator, and liaison with the Pawnee people, Fletcher did spark his interest in recording the lifeways of his people. While in residence in Washington, D.C., between 1898 and 1902, Fletcher corresponded with Murie, who also visited her when in town for tribal business.

From 1902 to 1906 Murie worked full time for Dorsey, the curator of anthropology at the Field Museum of Natural History in Chicago. Dorsey had begun work with the Pawnee in 1899 as part of a larger project studying the myths and rituals of the Caddoan peoples. Murie collected the bulk of the Pawnee materials that were published by Dorsey and subsequently spent the summers of 1903 and 1905 working in North Dakota with his linguistic cousins, the Arikara. The standard procedure was for Murie to collect ethnographic texts that were then edited and typed by Dorsey. Some of these data were published, but the majority of the materials pertaining to culture history and ceremonies remain housed in manuscript form at the Field Museum. Murie also recorded Pawnee and Arikara songs on cylinders and collected items of material culture, including medicine bundles. Today, the Field Museum has among the largest collections of Pawnee materials, matched perhaps only by the collections at the American Museum of Natural History. At times, Murie and his family lived in Chicago while he worked at the Field Museum, but the majority of his time was spent in Pawnee collecting texts and material culture. Between 1906 and 1909 Murie divided his time between working for Dorsey and working at the Pawnee bank as cashier and interpreter.

In 1910 Murie was hired part time by the Bureau of American Ethnology at the Smithsonian Institution. Equipped with a camera, typewriter, graphophone, and tents and given a stipend, Murie was awarded a five-year commission to chronicle Pawnee ceremonies. For the first time in his ethnographic career, Murie was working freelance. His field notes and cylinder recordings were deposited at the bureau.

In 1912, while working for the bureau, Murie was approached by Clark Wissler, the curator of anthropology at the American Museum of Natural History, who was in the process of amassing data on Plains warrior societies. Wissler asked the bureau director, F. W. Hodge, if he could commission Murie to fill gaps in the Pawnee data. Robert Lowie, who also worked for the American Museum, visited Murie in the summer of 1912 to solicit his help for the project. In 1913, working concomitantly for the American Museum and the bureau, Murie collected data concerning the history and ceremonial song and dance of the Pawnee societies. He sent his field notes to Wissler for editing and revisions. Research culminated in 1914 with the publication of Murie's only solo article, "Pawnee Indian Societies" (*Anthropological Papers* 11 [1914]: 543–644).

In 1919 Murie divorced his first wife and married another Pawnee, Josephine Walking Sun; they had two children, one of whom lived to adulthood. He was active in tribal affairs and often accompanied the tribal delegations that visited Washington, D.C. A member of the Episcopal church, he was also president of the local Indian Farmer's Institute and had memberships at the Masonic Lodge and the Mystic Shrine in Tulsa, Oklahoma.

After publication of "Pawnee Indian Societies," Murie commenced a comprehensive study of Pawnee ceremonialism. The project was jointly sponsored by the American Museum and the bureau and again was directed by Wissler. At its completion in 1921, Murie's magnum opus totaled almost 1,600 pages and was divided into two parts: Skiri ceremonialism and ceremonies of the Pawnee South Bands (Chawi, Pitahawirata, and Kitkahahki). Before Murie could travel east to begin a lecture series on his work, he died suddenly of apoplexy as he chopped wood in his front yard in Pawnee.

Although of Pawney descent, Murie maintained the non-Indian values imposed on him in the government schools; his standard attire was a suit, and he was a firm believer in the Episcopal faith. Anthropologically speaking, his observations of Pawnee culture were derived from a Euro-American point of view, but he was undoubtedly empathic with Pawnee culture. His ability to record ethnographic and linguistic texts in his native tongue and the fact that he gained rapport with the priests and medicine men of his tribe enabled Murie to write about his people from an insider's perspective. Murie spent over thirty years collecting information about his Pawnee people and spent two summers with the Arikara. His fieldwork is important because of its high degree of ethnographic and linguistic accuracy. Although Murie did not analyze his data, subsequent students of Pawnee and Arikara cultures have relied heavily on his work.

• Two unpublished works by Murie are housed in the Anthropological Archives at the Field Museum of Natural History: "Pawnee Ethnographic and Linguistic Notes" (1902) and "Arikara Ethnographic Notes" (1902). His magnum opus, *Ceremonies of the Pawnee*, was edited by Douglas R. Parks (1981, repr. 1989). As Alice Fletcher's assistant, Murie provided information for her book *The Hako: A Pawnee Ceremony* (1904), and for several minor articles. With Murie's assistance, George Dorsey published nine works on the Pawnee and Arikara, including *Traditions of the Skidi Pawnee* (1904), *Traditions of the Arikara* (1904), and *The Pawnee: Mythology* (1906). Together, Murie and Dorsey published an article for the Field Museum, edited by Alexander Spoehr, "Notes on Skidi Pawnee Society," *Anthropological Series* 27 (1940): 67–119. Biographical information is found in Murie's *Ceremonies of the Pawnee* (1989), pp. vii–x; Parks, "James R. Murie: Pawnee Ethnographer," in *American Indian Intellectuals*, ed. Margot Liberty (1978), pp. 74–89; and Von Del Chamberlain, *When Stars Came Down to Earth: Cosmology of the Skidi Pawnee Indians of North America* (1982), pp. 33–41.
BENJAMIN R. KRACHT

MURIETA, Joaquín (1829?–1853), folk hero in Hispanic and California popular culture, was born most probably in Sonora, Mexico. The story of Murieta has been told in many versions, all based on John Rollin Ridge's 1854 account, *The Life and Adventures of Joaquín Murieta, the Celebrated California Bandit*. Ridge's tale covers the years from 1850 to 1853, when California was in the throes of the gold rush. Whether Ridge based his character on a historical figure or a composite of bandit chieftains described in the California press has been widely discussed by novelists, California historians, and Murieta's Mexican and Chilean biographers. Works on Murieta, both avowedly fictional and purportedly biographical, suggest that he was likely a creature of Ridge's imagination.

According to Ridge, Murieta was about eighteen when he appeared in California in 1850 seeking his fortune in the gold rush. Accompanied by his girlfriend, Rosita, and a half brother, he proceeded to stake his claim in the area of Murphy's Diggings (near Columbia, Calif.). He and his family encountered discrimination and cruel treatment at the hands of the newly arrived American miners, who resented the Mexicans, Chileans, Chinese, and even the native Californios. Exorbitant taxes were imposed on these "foreigners," who were beaten and forbidden to file any claim to a gold deposit. According to Ridge, Murieta was driven off his claim, his half brother was lynched, and Murieta suffered a humiliating flogging. After such treatment, Murieta embarked on a vendetta of banditry and killing. In 1854 several newspaper accounts described the decapitation of a bandit named Joaquín by a California ranger, Harry Love, who subsequently displayed the bandit's head throughout the state. Shortly after this incident, Ridge published his story. In 1859 the *California Police Gazette* retold Ridge's tale in serial form in ten installments, claiming that its version was the true one. The anonymous writer elaborated with dramatic flair on episodes included in Ridge's story and added others that enhanced Murieta's image of daring. Several chapters with a story-within-a-story structure gave more depth to Ridge's straightforward narrative. The life of the bandits at their camp, down to the lyrics of songs, is described in colorful detail.

As early as 1862 the *Gazette* version was translated into French by Robert Hyenne as *Un bandit californien (Joaquín Murieta)* and in 1906 from French into Spanish by the Chilean Carlos Morla Vicuña as *El bandido chileno Joaquín Murieta en California*. The Spanish translation indicates Murieta's birthplace as Santiago de Chile. In 1908 Ireneo Paz wrote a version in Spanish, *Vida y adventuras del más célebre bandido sonorense*, reasserting that Mexico was Murieta's country of birth. Then in 1926 Ignacio Herrera published *Joaquín Murieta, el bandido chileno en California*, which follows the Morla Vicuña translation almost verbatim. Research conducted in 1985 and 1986 presents evidence that Murieta may have been born in Sonora, Mexico, because several Murrieta (with a double *r*) families still living in Sonora believe they may be related to him. This research, however, fails to discover any conclusive evidence that Murieta was a historical figure.

In the 1920s, 1930s, and early 1940s, western pulp magazines included in every issue a short novel featuring a Robin Hood outlaw. One of these novels was *The Fighting Sheriff* (1929), by Charles H. Snow, which closely followed the Ridge and *California Police Gazette* versions. Also during these years several western novels devoted to Murieta were published. Of these,

Walter Noble Burns's 1932 book, *The Robin Hood of El Dorado*, encompasses the Ridge story and elaborates on it with eyewitness accounts, detailed portrayals of historical figures, and realistic descriptions of the customs and environment in the mining camps. Because Burns had a reputation as a California historian, his work was accorded greater credence and authority than any other. The 1936 film *Robin Hood of El Dorado*, starring Warner Baxter, Bruce Cabot, Ann Loring, and Margo, was based on Burns's novel. It portrays a Murieta who rises to fight for justice; greedy American miners and discriminatory treatment of Mexicans are vividly portrayed.

Murieta also has been the protagonist of plays, poems, and ballads. One of the better-known works is Pablo Neruda's *Fulgor y muerte de Joaquín Murieta* (1966), a dramatized ballad presenting the bandit as a defender of the oppressed.

The enduring presence of Murieta in both American and Hispanic culture has been sustained and nourished by western pulp stories, novels, films, and plays. In the 1980s the nineteenth-century Robin Hood became a historical icon reminding Mexican-Americans that discrimination against them has been prevalent in California since after the Mexican-American War.

• Historical information on Murieta and the gold rush can be found in Theodore H. Hittell, *History of California* (4 vols., 1885–1897); Joseph Henry Jackson, "Joaquin Murieta," *Bad Company* (1949), and introduction to John Rollin Ridge, *The Life and Adventures of Joaquín Murieta* (1955); Remi A. Nadeau, *The Real Joaquín Murrieta: Robin Hood Hero or Gold Rush Gangster?* (1974). Biographical information on Ridge is available in Franklin Dickerson Walker, "The Fifties," *San Francisco's Literary Frontier* (1939).

Other fiction based on Ridge's book and the *California Police Gazette* account includes Ernest Klette, *The Crimson Trail of Joaquín Murieta* (1928); Dane Coolidge, *Gringo Gold, a Story of Joaquín Murieta, the Bandit* (1939); and Samuel Anthony Peeples, *The Dream Ends in Fury: A Novel Based on the Life of Joaquín Murrieta* (1949).

Works relating Murieta to Mexican Americans and the Chicano movement in California include Alberto Huerta, "Murieta y los californios: Odisea de una cultura," *Religión y Cultura* 29 (1983): 615–50; Celso Aguirre Bernal, *Joaquín Murrieta: raíz y razón del movimiento chicano: un enfoque histórico* (1985); and Manuel Rojas, *Joaquín Murrieta, el Patrio: el "Far West" del México cercenado* (1986).

LYDIA D. HAZERA

MURNAGHAN, Francis Dominic (4 Aug. 1893–24 Mar. 1976), applied mathematician, was born in Omagh County, Tyrone, Ireland, the son of George Murnaghan, a sometime Irish member of the House of Commons, and Angela Mooney. The young Murnaghan received his early education at the Christian Brothers School in Omagh and later studied at University College at the National University of Ireland in Dublin, where he received his B.A. in 1913 and M.A. in 1914. There he was a student of Arthur W. Conway in applied mathematics. In 1914 he won a traveling studentship in mathematical physics and, on Conway's advice, went to the United States to study with

Harry Bateman at Johns Hopkins University. There in 1916 he obtained his Ph.D. in mathematics with a dissertation titled "The Lines of Electric Force Due to a Moving Electron."

After two years as an instructor at the Rice Institute, Murnaghan returned to Johns Hopkins as an associate (1918–1921), associate professor (1921–1928), and finally as professor of applied mathematics and head of the mathematics department (1928–1948). In 1919 he married Ada May Kimbell; they had a son and a daughter. Murnaghan became a naturalized U.S. citizen in 1928, but he never lost his Irish heritage or deep feeling for Ireland. From 1930 to 1948 he served as an editor of the *American Journal of Mathematics*. He held visiting positions at Rutgers (1926), Chicago (1928, 1930), Pennsylvania (1929), the Institute for Advanced Study (1936–1937), Duke (1941), Brown (1943–1944), and the Dublin Institute for Advanced Studies (1948, 1956). Awarded a D.Sc. in 1940 by the National University of Ireland, he was elected a member of the Royal Irish Academy the same year, the National Academy of Sciences in 1942, and later the Academia Brasileira de Ciencias. In 1948 a quarrel with the university president caused Murnaghan to retire from Johns Hopkins and begin a new career in Brazil at the Instituto Tecnológico de Aeronáutico and the Centro Brasileiro de Pesquisas Fisicas in Rio de Janeiro. Remaining there intermittently until 1960, he was also a consultant at the David Taylor Model Basin of the U.S. Navy in Bethesda, Maryland (1955–1963).

Murnaghan's research naturally falls into three distinct areas of activity, each of which includes some noteworthy contributions. From 1916 to 1936 he was actively engaged in mathematical physics, including electrodynamics, relativity, tensor analysis, dynamics, elasticity, fluid dynamics (primarily aerodynamics), quantum mechanics, differential equations, and celestial mechanics. His most significant work of this time was reported in three books. The first of these, *Vector Analysis and the Theory of Relativity* (1922), was based on his Johns Hopkins lectures in the summer of 1920. This was one of the first books by an American author to offer a technical discussion of Albert Einstein's theory. Although well received, it offered more of a careful exposition of the theory than new results of lasting importance. His next book, *Theoretical Mechanics: An Introduction to Mathematical Physics* (1929), coauthored with Joseph S. Ames, was very successful and remained in print for more than twenty years. Finally, in collaboration with Harry Bateman and Hugh L. Dryden, he produced the monumental National Research Council report *Hydrodynamics* (1932), which remains one of the definitive reference works on hydrodynamic theory.

In 1937 Murnaghan's interests took a dramatic turn with the appearance of his first major papers on elasticity theory and group representations. The former, pursued until 1953, centered on the problem of formulating a theory of elasticity without appeal to the usual assumptions of small deformations, or that the material is stress-free and isotropic. In particular, he suc-

ceeded in deriving a new version of Hooke's law valid for large deformations and high pressures. Although much of this work was controversial and not entirely successful, it was nevertheless important in showing that such a theory was possible and was summarized in a small book, *Finite Deformations of an Elastic Solid* (1951). Murnaghan's research on group theory was a more substantial endeavor and arguably his most significant mathematical contribution. Almost immediately after the birth of modern quantum theory in the heroic period of 1925–1929, physicists recognized the theory of groups as an important mathematical discipline. However, it was not widely understood, and many of the people attempting to use it were puzzled by how to do group-theoretic calculations. Murnaghan's interests were specifically directed to making group theory a convenient and practical mathematical tool for both mathematicians and physicists. His efforts resulted in a treatise, *Theory of Group Representations* (1938), which gave an essentially self-contained account of the subject. The first book in English explicitly devoted to this topic, it was widely read and very influential. Murnaghan's fascination with group theory never faded, and for the next three decades he continued to perfect and polish his methodology with the aim of making it more accessible to a general audience.

Murnaghan was a born teacher who had a seemingly insatiable desire to communicate his enthusiasm and love for mathematics. His publications include some eighty research papers and seventeen books based on his lecturing experience. The latter included three textbooks written in Portuguese while in Brazil. His classic *Introduction to Applied Mathematics* (1948) is especially noteworthy for its modern approach and rigor. All of his books display an unusual lucidity, originality of thought, and characteristic charm. Although much of his work dealt with physical topics, he never compromised on mathematical issues and always maintained that being a mathematician was an indispensable requirement for doing applied mathematics. Through his personal influence and professional writing, Murnaghan did much to raise the standards of applied mathematics and to make it a respectable part of the American mathematical community. He died in Baltimore.

• The archives at Johns Hopkins contain a collection of Murnaghan's papers. Murnaghan served as a consulting editor for *Webster's New International Dictionary*, 2d ed. (1958), and his definitions of mathematical terms given there provide a vivid illustration of his penchant for precision. His views on pedagogy and research emerge from his textbooks but are clearly elucidated in his articles "On the Teaching of Mathematics," *Science* 100 (1 Dec. 1944): 482–86, and "The Evolution of the Concept of Number," *Science Magazine* 68 (Apr. 1949): 262–69. There is an interesting autobiographical sketch in *McGraw Hill Modern Scientists and Engineers*, vol. 2 (1980). Obituary notices are in the *Baltimore Sun*, 25 Mar. 1976, and the *Year Book of the American Philosophical Society for 1976*.

JOSEPH D. ZUND

MURPHY, Audie (20 June 1924–28 May 1971), soldier and film actor, was born Audie Leon Murphy in Hunt County, Texas, the son of Emmett Murphy and Josie Bell Killian, tenant farmers. Murphy was reared in the rural poverty familiar to Texas sharecropping families in the 1920s and 1930s. With barely a fifth-grade education, he left home at fifteen, facing what looked to be a bleak future. Then came Pearl Harbor, and, just after his eighteenth birthday in June 1942, he enlisted in the army. Shorter, thinner, and younger than the average GI, Murphy as an infantryman capitalized on his hunting skills and, from Sicily, through Italy and France, and into Germany, exhibited uncommon aggressiveness against the enemy. His prowess and initiative in combat earned him a battlefield commission and his country's highest decorations, including the Congressional Medal of Honor for his daring standoff (firing a machine gun atop a burning tank destroyer) against a German counterattack at the Colmar Pocket in Alsace in January 1945.

A cover photo story in *Life* (16 July 1945) rendered the freckled, baby-faced war hero a national celebrity. At the invitation of actor James Cagney, Murphy visited Hollywood and was attracted by the prospects of making money in the movie business. His starring debut as a juvenile delinquent in *Bad Boy* (1949) coincided with the publication of his autobiographical bestseller, *To Hell and Back* (much of the text contributed by publicity writer and friend David "Spec" McClure). Beginning with his portrayal of Billy the Kid in *The Kid from Texas* (1950), Murphy carved out a niche for himself in the western, often playing a frontier variation of his original "bad boy" role.

Murphy's biggest hit was the 1955 film adaptation of *To Hell and Back*. From the outset of his film career Murphy had resisted having his military heroics exploited on screen. "War is a nasty business," he once wrote, "not the sort of job that deserves medals." His apprehensions about filming *To Hell and Back* proved correct as commercial considerations resulted in a sanitized image of the war and a glorification of his role in it.

Thereafter, Murphy's screen popularity began to ebb. He had already become self-deprecating about being typecast in westerns ("All I am required to do is ride a horse, shoot straight, and look somber") and credited John Huston as the one director who could ever get him to act. Unfortunately, neither of his films for Huston (*Red Badge of Courage* in 1951 and *The Unforgiven in* 1960) nor most of his nonwesterns (notably, *The Quiet American* in 1958) were commercially successful. Murphy fell back on low-budget westerns until even their marketability dissipated in the mid-sixties. His one attempt at a television series, *Whispering Smith* (1961), failed after twenty-five episodes. One bright spot in an otherwise declining career was his cowriting of lyrics to country and western songs, six of which were recorded.

By the time of his last screen appearance, a cameo role as Jesse James in *A Time for Dying* (1969), Murphy was bankrupt as a result of heavy gambling debts and failed investments. In the judgment of one biographer, Murphy's penchant for ruinous gambling, womanizing, crude practical jokes, carrying guns, and accompanying police officers on patrols and raids suggest the troubled underside of a personality otherwise characterized by generosity, loyalty to friends, and a sense of professional responsibility in both soldiering and acting. Plagued since the war with nightmares and other symptoms of what was later called post-traumatic stress syndrome, Murphy also experienced an unstable domestic life. His highly publicized marriage to starlet Wanda Hendrix in 1949 ended in divorce two years later. His marriage to Pamela Archer in 1951 produced two children but, especially as his career declined, became increasingly strained with frequent separations.

Killed in a plane crash, Murphy was buried at Arlington Cemetery. Numerous eulogies and memorials resurrected the memory of Murphy the soldier-hero, with only a passing nod to a screen career that spanned nearly two decades and more than forty films.

• The most comprehensive scholarly biography, which also lists major archival sources, is Don B. Graham, *No Name on the Bullet: A Biography of Audie Murphy* (1989). See also Harold B. Simpson, *Audie Murphy, American Soldier* (1975); Graham, "Audie Murphy: Kid with a Gun," in *Shooting Stars*, ed. Archie P. McDonald (1987); and John H. Lenihan, "The Kid from Texas: The Movie Heroism of Audie Murphy," *New Mexico Historical Review* 61 (Oct. 1986).

JOHN H. LENIHAN

MURPHY, Charles Francis (20 June 1858–25 Apr. 1924), Tammany Hall political boss, was born in New York City, the son of Dennis Murphy and Mary Prendergrass (or Prendergrast), Irish immigrants. Throughout his life Murphy lived and worked on Manhattan's Lower East Side, known as the Eighteenth Assembly District or Gas House District, which was the bastion of his political strength. At age fourteen he quit public school and took his first job at Roaches Shipyard. Two years later he became a driver for the Crosstown Blue Lines Horsecar Co., which transversed the district. In 1878, using $500 that he had saved, he purchased the first of his four saloons and named it Charlie's Place. The saloon, which did not serve women, was a gathering place for local dock workers and laborers. The second floor of the building housed the Sylvan Social Club for young men ages fifteen to twenty, whose baseball team Murphy had organized in 1875. With the saloon, club, and baseball team as his anchors, Murphy began to emerge as a political figure.

In 1883, when the district's assemblyman Edward Hagan, Murphy's friend and political benefactor, did not get the Tammany Hall nomination for reelection, Murphy managed Hagan's successful independent campaign. That was the only time that Murphy broke with the Democratic party. Two years later he supported Francis Spinola, the person whom he had defeated, for state senate, and in 1886 he was instrumental in helping Spinola get elected to Congress. That year Murphy also opened two more saloons, one of which became the headquarters for the Anawanda Club, the Eighteenth Assembly District Tammany club. In 1892 Murphy, who by then owned four prosperous saloons, succeeded Hagan as the Democratic district leader and became a member of the Executive Committee of Tammany Hall.

In 1897 Murphy was appointed commissioner of docks, his only paid official position. He was proud of the position and retained the title "Commissioner" as his preferred form of address for the rest of his life. During his tenure in office he set up a system of dock leasing that greatly benefited the party coffers. In 1901, with his brother and several friends, Murphy organized the New York Contracting and Trucking Company, which rented space on the docks. In the years when Tammany was in power the company did a lucrative business. Later, when various commissions investigated the company for corruption, Murphy denied that he retained a financial interest in it, and the investigators were never able to prove otherwise.

For Murphy 1902 was an important turning point. That year he married Margaret J. Graham. They had no children, and Murphy adopted Margaret's child from her previous marriage. Also in 1902 Richard Croker, the corrupt boss of Tammany Hall, was driven from his position. Within the year Murphy won the power struggle to succeed him and by a resolution of Tammany's governing body was appointed chief, a position he never relinquished.

Known as a man of few words, Murphy had gained control of a fragmented and severely weakened Tammany Hall. His first task was to consolidate his position and reestablish Tammany's base. To do this he had to cleanse Tammany of the aura of corruption and give it a facade of respectability. Although the insider contracts and land speculation, the bread and butter of the machine, never stopped, Murphy did try to select competent leaders and had his people support much of the progressive legislation of the period. Among the leaders who emerged through Tammany ranks were Al Smith, two-time governor of New York and the Democratic party's 1928 candidate for president, and Robert Wagner, who rose to preeminence in the U.S. Senate during the New Deal.

In the tradition of the machine politician, Murphy was known as a generous man to all who were in need. He realized that, to maintain its dominance, Tammany needed to be inclusive and bring the growing immigrant Jewish community under its wing. Although in one to one relationships problems often developed between the Irish leaders and the Jews, Tammany, under Murphy's leadership, did win Jewish support by standing up against anti-Semitism.

Murphy also extended Tammany Hall's political influence, first over the other borough party organizations, then to the state level, and finally to the national level. He was responsible for the election of three New York City mayors and three New York State governors. He was also responsible for the impeachment of Governor William Sulzer, whom he had helped to

elect in 1912. At the time of his death Murphy was preparing to go to the 1924 Democratic National Convention and was expected to nominate Smith for president.

A few years before his death, Murphy justified his career, saying:

I have lived in this City all my life. My neighbors know me. It is the fate of political leaders to be reviled. If one is too thin skinned to stand it he should never take the job. History shows the better and more successful the organization and the leader the more bitter the attacks. Success is always a target.

When Tammany can elect its candidates so often in a city of 6,000,000 inhabitants, in a city of intelligence, in a city dotted all over by the church spire and the schoolhouse, it seems silly to use the time worn campaign cry that there is nothing good and everything corrupt in Tammany. (*New York Times*, 26 Apr. 1924)

At the time of Murphy's death, a *New York Times* editorial on 26 April 1924 called his stewardship of Tammany "comparatively mild." The editorial went on to say:

[Murphy] did not openly affront the moral sense of the citizen. He was reticent in speech and had admirable traits which bound his friends to him. But nothing of this should make us forget he was the exemplar and beneficiary of the system which without official responsibility degrades our official life, and which condemns New York City to suffer from maladministration and the lowest moral standards in public office.

Murphy died suddenly in New York City while he was at the height of his political powers.

• The Edwin P. Kilroe Collection of Tammaniana in the special collections of the Columbia University Libraries in New York has material on Murphy. Nancy Joan Weiss, *Charles Francis Murphy, 1858–1924: Respectability and Responsibility in Tammany Politics* (1968), is a book-length monograph; and "Murphy Steadily Advanced to Power," *New York Times*, 26 Apr. 1924, provides a chronology of Murphy's political career.

NEDDA C. ALLBRAY

MURPHY, Edgar Gardner (31 Aug. 1869–23 June 1913), Episcopal clergyman and social reformer, was born near Fort Smith, Arkansas, the son of Samuel W. Murphy and Janie Gardner. When her husband, whose occupation is unknown, abandoned the family in 1874, Janie Gardner Murphy moved her children to San Antonio, Texas, where she earned a modest living by running a boardinghouse. Befriended by the local Episcopal priest, Walter Richardson, young Murphy chose to prepare for the ministry by entering the University of the South at Sewanee, Tennessee, in 1885. There he was deeply influenced by the philosophical theology of William Porcher Du Bose. After his graduation in 1889 and a year of study at New York's General Theological Seminary and Columbia University, Murphy returned to San Antonio to assist his childhood mentor. He was ordained a deacon in 1890. A year later he married Maude King, a schoolteacher from New England who boarded at his mother's house. They had two sons; one, Gardner Murphy, became a noted psychologist.

In 1893 Murphy accepted a parish in Laredo, Texas, where he was ordained a priest. In his first year there he organized a protest against the burning of a black man accused of raping and murdering a white girl. From 1894 to 1898 he served Episcopal parishes in Chillicothe, Ohio, and Kingston, New York. His first books, *Words for the Church* (1897) and *The Larger Life* (1897), espoused a broad doctrine of the church and a liberal Christian theology for a conservative social gospel. Only by recognizing "that the home of truth is not individual but social," he argued in *Words for the Church*, could human beings do the work of Christ in the world.

In 1899 Murphy moved to St. John's Episcopal Church in Montgomery, Alabama, where he tried to address the social problems of the New South from the vantage of a thoughtful conservative. He organized the Alabama Child Labor Committee in 1901 to lobby for protective legislation, and, two years later, he was a founder of the National Child Labor Committee. But he opposed a national child labor law; this led to his resignation from the committee in 1907. Because of his interest in the child labor question, Murphy resigned from the pastorate at St. John's and, in 1903, from the priesthood altogether to serve as executive secretary of the newly organized Southern Education Board. In that capacity he helped mobilize local efforts to strengthen public schools throughout the South. Education, he believed, was a "safe" reform, binding the chaotic into the coherent and the irresponsible into the responsible.

Murphy treated social issues, primarily race relations, in his two most important books, *Problems of the Present South* (1904) and *The Basis of Ascendancy* (1909). In 1900 he had organized the Southern Society for the Promotion of the Study of Race Conditions and Problems in the South. Until his death, Murphy was the white South's most sophisticated spokesman for racial segregation. It was the institutional requirement of his belief that the two races must develop separate cultural forms if each was to achieve its highest fulfillment. "It is just because I profoundly believe in the Negro's destiny that I beg him to follow, not those who would turn him into a white man," Murphy told the American Academy of Political and Social Science, "but those who would turn him into the worthier and finer possibilities of his own nature." Opposed to both the harsh extreme of radical white racism and the egalitarian hopes of black and white racial assimilationists, Murphy gave racial separatism a gentle voice. He died in New York of heart failure, traceable to a severe bout with rheumatic fever in 1893.

• The Edgar Gardner Murphy Papers are in the Southern Historical Collection at the University of North Carolina, Chapel Hill. Other collections, such as the Silas McBee and Southern Education papers in the Southern Historical Collection, the Robert C. Ogden and Booker T. Washington papers at the Library of Congress, and the William Porcher Du Bose, Silas McBee, and Benjamin Lawton Wiggens papers at the University of the South, include important correspondence. Hugh C. Bailey, *Edgar Gardner Murphy* (1968), is the standard biography, but see also Stephen C. Compton, "Edgar Gardner Murphy and the Child Labor Movement," *Historical Magazine of the Protestant Episcopal Church* 52 (1983): 181–94, and Ralph E. Luker, *A Southern Tradition in Theology and Social Criticism* (1984).

RALPH E. LUKER

MURPHY, Frank (13 Apr. 1890–19 July 1949), politician and Supreme Court justice, was baptized William Francis Murphy in what is now Harbor Beach, Michigan, the son of John F. Murphy, a Canadian-born attorney, and Mary Brennan. He was deeply attached to his mother, who died in 1924, and his chief biographer believes that this attachment probably accounted for his not marrying. Educated in the public schools, Murphy received an LL.B. from the University of Michigan in 1914. After graduation he joined a Detroit law firm that was counsel to the city's employer association. He also taught in a night school for immigrants, which, he later wrote, gave him an insight into the problems of "the submerged majority," and beginning law classes at the University of Detroit, his one direct connection with American Catholic education. Soon after the United States declared war on Germany in 1917, Murphy attended a Reserve Officers Training Camp, was commissioned a first lieutenant, served with the American Expeditionary Forces (AEF) in France without seeing combat, did occupation duty in Germany, and under the army's postarmistice educational program, studied law briefly at Lincoln's Inn, London, and Trinity College, Dublin. He sailed for home in July 1919 and was discharged as a captain the next month. While in France in August 1918 he had received but declined a Democratic nomination for Congress, and before he returned to the United States, he was named first assistant U.S. attorney for Michigan's Eastern District.

Murphy was an exceedingly able prosecutor who, in two and a half years as a federal attorney, apparently won all but one of the cases he prosecuted, and that one resulted in a hung jury. Although by 1927 he was highly critical of the government's methods during the first "red scare" of 1919–1920, at the time he not only participated in the prosecution of radicals but was a supporter of A. Mitchell Palmer's failed presidential candidacy. Murphy accepted the Democratic nomination for Congress in 1920 from Michigan's First District and was badly defeated. He resigned as a federal prosecutor early in 1922 and formed a successful and financially rewarding law partnership. He also resumed teaching law at both the University of Detroit and at the nighttime Detroit College of Law.

In 1923 Murphy won a seat on Detroit's "nonpartisan" Recorder's Court and was reelected in 1929. He soon achieved local popularity and national standing as a progressive, innovative judge noted for a friendly attitude toward labor. His most famous cases were the two murder trials of Dr. Ossian Sweet and ten other persons. Sweet was a black physician who, having bought a home in a white neighborhood, defended it from a white mob with the help of some friends. One white man was shot to death and another wounded. The National Association for the Advancement of Colored People participated in the successful defense and brought in Clarence Darrow as lead attorney. Murphy's unprejudiced handling of the case drew favorable national comment and won him the support of Detroit's growing black community. Although it was not publicly known until 1975, Murphy received illegal retainers from the Chrysler Corporation while on the bench, in addition to insider tips on the market from one of its executives, although there is no evidence that these in any way influenced his decisions.

In 1930, as Detroit began to feel the brunt of the Great Depression, Murphy won election as mayor, gaining 31 percent of the vote in a five-man field; the incumbent mayor, who had lost a recall election, came in second. As had been true of his races for the Recorder's Court, Murphy ran best in black and ethnic wards, worst in those that had a high percentage of native whites of native white parentage. He was reelected in 1931 with 64 percent of the vote. An estimated 100,000 workers were unemployed in Detroit when Murphy first took office, and responses to the depression were the leitmotiv of his administration. He soon became the spokesperson for the nation's mayors in their struggle for federal relief funds and was a founding father and the first president of the U.S. Conference of Mayors. Although Detroit then elected its mayors in nonpartisan elections, Murphy was an early supporter of Franklin Delano Roosevelt. After Roosevelt was nominated for president, Murphy, an excellent speaker, campaigned for him throughout Michigan. He hankered after an appointment as U.S. attorney general or governor general of the Philippines, but these posts were slated to go to Thomas J. Walsh and Homer S. Cummings. Walsh's preinauguration death and Cummings's appointment as attorney general left the Philippines for Murphy. He served there from 1933 to 1936.

An unusual colonial proconsul, Murphy brought his liberal notions with him and tried to put them into practice. Thus he helped Filipino women achieve suffrage and oversaw reforms in the administration of justice. His greatest service to the Filipino people was in assisting their independence campaign. Unlike many American colonial administrators, he reported to Washington that the people of the islands were ready for self-government and helped Manuel Quezon and other Filipino leaders in the negotiations that produced the 1934 Tydings-McDuffie Act, which provided for a ten-year period as a commonwealth to be followed by independence. When the commonwealth period began in 1935, Murphy became the first high commissioner.

In 1936, with the continuation of the New Deal seemingly in jeopardy, Murphy returned to seek Michigan's governorship, partially in response to a direct request from Roosevelt. As it turned out, Murphy needed Roosevelt's coattails, since the president carried Michigan with 56.3 percent of the vote while Murphy won with only 51 percent.

When Murphy became governor on 1 January 1937, the General Motors sit-down strikes had already begun. True to his prolabor principles, he refused to allow Michigan's National Guard to be used to break the strike, although he did send in troops to maintain order after violence occurred in Flint. He played a crucial role in helping to mediate the GM sit-downs and similar disputes during the 1937 strike wave, a role that gained him both widespread praise as a champion of labor's right to strike and heavy criticism for failing to enforce court injunctions for strikers to evacuate the plants. After this dramatic beginning, the remainder of his two-year term was prosaic and similar to those of other New Deal governors who had to contend with legislatures less liberal and reform-minded than themselves. Although Murphy presided over a progressive and efficient administration highlighted by a liberal unemployment compensation law, an expanded old-age assistance law, and a whole host of other New Deal–type reforms, he failed to win reelection in 1938, losing to the Republican he had defeated in 1936 and garnering only 47 percent of the vote. His defeat opened the way for his federal career: his appointment as attorney general of the United States was announced on the day his successor took office.

Murphy's one-year tenure as attorney general was energetic and successful. In line with his liberal convictions, he established the first civil liberties unit within the department and asked Congress to create a system of federal public defenders, but his enthusiastic support of attempts to suppress espionage and seditious activity—what Leo Ribuffo has called the "brown scare"—seemed to some to threaten civil liberty. He was very much a "law and order" attorney general and significantly improved the administration of the Department of Justice. In common with his immediate predecessors and successors, however, he failed adequately to supervise the Federal Bureau of Investigation (FBI) director, J. Edgar Hoover, and assisted him in expanding his power over the gathering of counterintelligence.

Murphy's year in the department was followed by an appointment as associate justice of the Supreme Court of the United States. With his appointment, the fifth made by Roosevelt, the Court truly became "the Roosevelt Court." Murphy was the first of Roosevelt's appointees to have judicial experience and the only one of the nine men Roosevelt named to positions on the Court who had been a trial judge. Murphy's appointment to the Court, although greeted with great public approval, was felt to be inappropriate by many legal insiders, chief of whom was his vitriolic fellow justice, Felix Frankfurter, who may have coined the canard about "tempering justice with Murphy" and predicted, quite erroneously, that Murphy would swing to the conservative side after a few years on the bench. Some of the objections to Murphy, who was clearly not a legal scholar, came from distaste for his fervent and florid Catholicism. Harvard's Thomas Reed Powell sneered that Murphy would bring with him as colleagues "Father, Son, and Holy Ghost." A more reasoned later criticism by Archibald Cox held that Murphy's opinion in *Thornhill v. Alabama* (1940), which identified peaceful picketing with free speech, was "more concerned with speaking out against intolerance and oppression than with legal craftsmanship," although Cox argued that the benefits of *Thornhill* outweighed its disadvantages.

Murphy's performance as a justice was commendable. He carried his share of the Court's work load, and his decisions and dissents are particularly notable in the fields of civil liberties and labor legislation. Many of his finest opinions were eloquent and evoked both natural and constitutional law. While concurring in the Court's decision voiding a deportation order for labor leader Harry R. Bridges, he wrote in *Bridges v. Wixon* (1945):

The record in this case will stand forever as a monument to man's intolerance for man. Seldom if ever in the history of the nation has there been such a concentrated and relentless crusade to deport an individual because he dared to exercise the freedom that belongs to him as a human being and that is guaranteed to him by the Constitution.

He went on to argue that the Immigration Act of 1918 was invalid, because it was based on guilt by association, a position that, had the rest of his brethren adopted it, would have made many of the prosecutions of the second "red scare" at least more difficult.

What many consider Murphy's finest hour as a civil libertarian came in the now infamous Japanese-American cases of 1943–1944, which sanctioned the mass roundup of native-born American citizens of Japanese ancestry and their incarceration in concentration camps. Murphy had originally written a dissent in the first of the cases, *Hirabayashi v. United States* (1943), which involved a curfew rather than incarceration. Collegial pressure and wartime patriotism caused him to modify it slightly into a concurrence, warning that what the Court justified bore "a melancholy resemblance to the treatment accorded to members of the Jewish race in Germany" and "goes to the very brink of constitutional power." (The original draft had said "over the brink.") The next year Murphy dissented, with two others, in *Korematsu v. United States* (1944), which did entail complete loss of liberty, and insisted that the majority decision was a "legalization of racism." Murphy also tried to protect the rights of conscientious objectors, religious dissidents, and American Indians and even wished to apply constitutional standards to the proceedings in the Tokyo War Crimes Trials. He was also concerned with the rights of defendants in ordinary criminal trials, and some of his dissents in such cases prefigure the criminal law decisions of the Warren Court (1953–1968). Had he lived to serve on that Court, Murphy would no doubt have been comfortable with most of its innovations.

That was not to be. Murphy began to experience heart disease in 1943 and from 1946 on was hospitalized periodically with a number of illnesses. He died of a coronary thrombosis in Detroit.

• Murphy's papers and some of those of his family and associates are in the Michigan Historical Collection, University of Michigan. The massive three-volume life and times by Sidney Fine, *Frank Murphy: The Detroit Years, Frank Murphy: The New Deal Years,* and *Frank Murphy: The Washington Years* (1975–1984), is copiously documented, and each volume contains a multipage bibliographical note. An obituary is in the *Detroit Times,* 20 July 1949.

ROGER DANIELS

MURPHY, Gardner (8 July 1895–18 Mar. 1979), psychologist, was born in Chillicothe, Ohio, the son of southern reformer Edgar Gardner Murphy and author Maud King. In 1902 Murphy moved with his mother to Massachusetts while his father continued his social reform work in Montgomery, Alabama. Deeply influenced by his maternal grandfather, George Augustus King, who worked with Ralph Waldo Emerson in developing the Concord Free Library, Murphy spent much time at the library between the ages of seven and thirteen. He received an A.B. at Yale University in 1916, an M.A. at Harvard University in 1917, and a Ph.D. at Columbia University in 1923.

After the May 1917 passage of a U.S. conscription law, Murphy enlisted as a private in the Yale Hospital Unit of the U.S. Army Expeditionary Forces. Sent to France after training, he was a second lieutenant in the Army Corps of Interpreters in 1918–1919 and received an honorable discharge on 7 July 1919. His war experiences fostered a lifetime of peace efforts, which included lectures, articles, service on postwar planning committees during World War II, financial and moral support of politicians George McGovern and Hubert Humphrey, and working with nuclear scientist Leo Szilard toward total disarmament.

While studying at Columbia after his discharge, Murphy deeply impressed Robert S. Woodworth (psychology chairman) with a distinguished seminar report and in 1921 was invited to teach social psychology. This led subsequently to the publication of his pioneering *Experimental Social Psychology* (1931; 2d ed., 1937), for which he received the prestigious Nicholas Murray Butler Award in 1932. Counter to contemporary arguments over the relative importance of heredity and environment, Murphy said and wrote that "human development is both biological and social." He did not join those seeking to analyze motives; he saw tissue needs as the source of motives. By helping to bring social psychology into the mainstream of experimental psychology, Murphy's *Experimental Social Psychology* set a new empirical trend and spurred the rapid development of social psychology texts.

In 1923 Murphy introduced an innovative course on the history of psychology and wrote *An Historical Introduction to Modern Psychology* (1929; 1949; 1972 with

J. Kovach). This work, which integrated classical thought from Plato and Aristotle with modern psychological concepts, became a "bible" for graduate students. Among other distinctive features, it included a chapter on psychoanalysis at a time when the work of Sigmund Freud was not frequently mentioned by academic psychologists. Murphy also devoted a chapter to William James, which along with later articles, such as "William James on the Will" (*Journal of the History of Behavioral Science* 7 [1971]: 249–70), and his book with R. O. Ballou, *William James on Psychical Research* (1960), contributed to his identification with the James tradition. In 1926 he married Lois Margerie Barclay; they had two children, one of whom was adopted.

At Columbia Murphy also supported dissertations on such topics as the experience of African-American children in segregated schools; this research led to Kenneth and Mamie Clark's study of the self-image of black children and ultimately to Kenneth Clark's decisive contribution to the brief for the U.S. Supreme Court's 1954 decision in *Brown v. Board of Education* to abolish segregation in public schools. Reflecting his intense commitment to human betterment in general, Murphy, at a conference of the American Psychological Association (APA) held in 1943 to revise the APA constitution, passionately supported the addition of the phrase "as a means of promoting human welfare" to the sentence "the object of the APA shall be to advance psychological science." The revised version was accepted by the APA membership in 1945.

Having been an enthusiastic participant in the formation of the Society for Psychological Study of Social Issues (SPSSI) in 1936, Murphy served as its second president in 1937 and was selected toward the end of World War II to prepare *Human Nature and Enduring Peace* (1945). This work included the Psychologists' Manifesto on Human Nature and Peace, signed by over 2,000 psychologists, stating that human nature is not preoccupied by war, that it is primarily interested in peace.

In 1940 Murphy created an independent psychology department at City College of New York, which had previously included psychology with philosophy. In subsequent years, more students from that department pursued advanced degrees in psychology than from any other college or university. Murphy's effect on his students was profound; one colleague later wrote that Murphy's "lectures held generations of students spellbound." Another commented that Murphy had "a natural talent for bringing the most unexpected types and views together . . . with the flair of a great orchestra conductor."

Murphy's course on personality (which students called a "course of life") drew faculty and students from other departments by providing a famous "alternative to Marxism" at a time when many intellectuals were sympathetic to communism. But during World War II, as a result of his support for the scientific work of a known Communist teacher, Murphy's security clearance was withdrawn and he acceded to the request for his withdrawal from the Emergency Committee in Psychology of the National Research Council. His course on teaching personality also led to the comprehensive *Personality: A Biosocial Approach to Origins and Structure* (1947), in which he drew on everyday experience, on the lives of scientists and people in the arts, and on empirical scientific evidence, reaching the conclusion that personality is both biological and social.

In 1940 Murphy began innovative experiments on the relation of affect to perception. With Harold Proshansky he published "The Effects of Reward and Punishment on Perception" (*Journal of Psychology* 13 [1942]: 282–93).

As an active participant in the American Society for Psychical Research, he served the society as an administrator, critic, theoretician, communicator, member of the board of trustees, and chairman of the Research Committee, in which role he demanded adherence to the highest scientific standards. Together with the work of J. B. Rhine at Duke University, Murphy's work led to the establishment of courses in psychical research and parapsychology at a number of universities.

In 1950 Murphy spent six months in India as a United Nations Educational, Scientific, and Cultural Organization (UNESCO) consultant to Indian psychologists, studying tensions between Moslems and Hindus, between castes, and between labor and management. His report to UNESCO was followed by a book for the public, *In The Minds Of Men* (1953). This work stimulated Indian psychologists to undertake research on social problems they had not hitherto been studying.

As director of research at the Menninger Foundation from 1952 to 1967, Murphy initially addressed the trustees with an ambitious approach to research: the major objectives were to develop a sense of the importance of research as an integral aspect of diagnosis, therapy, and training and to coordinate research efforts at Menninger, Topeka State Hospital, and the local Veterans Administration Hospital. He encouraged ongoing research, located funding resources, and supervised, edited, and arranged for publication of reports. He was especially interested in projects comparing the results of supportive psychotherapy with those of psychoanalysis, studies of perception and cognitive styles, and studies of subconscious perception. Murphy's own research, which extended his City College studies on the influence of affect on perception, resulted in *Development of the Perceptual World*, with Charles Solley (1960); *Encounter with Reality*, with Herbert Spohn (1968); and *Outgrowing Self-Deception*, with Morton Leeds (1975).

In the 1960s Murphy hired Elmer Green, a biopsychologist, to develop biofeedback as a research and therapy resource; it has since come into widespread use. Murphy's deep interest in community problems led him to join William Key in a study of two groups of families: one was relocated as part of urban renewal work; the other, to make way for Highway 70. Both groups were more satisfied than were families moved into high-rise city apartments; a major factor was the freedom of *choice* provided to the Topeka families.

After his retirement in 1967, Murphy was professor of psychology at George Washington University (1968–1973). In 1972 he received the Gold Medal Award of the American Psychological Foundation, which recognized him as "a peerless teacher, a felicitous writer, an eclectic psychologist of limitless range, [who] seeks to bring the whole human experience to bear in understanding behavior."

In addition to serving as president of SPSSI, Murphy was president of the Eastern, the Kansas, the Southwestern, and the American Psychological Associations, the Society for Psychical Research (London), and the American Society for Psychical Research. The American Academy of Arts and Sciences elected him as a fellow, as did the New York Academy of Sciences and the American Association for the Advancement of Science.

In his spare time, Murphy climbed mountains in New Hampshire, Colorado, Canada, and India; played the piano, improvising and remembering what he had heard at concerts and operas; sang all the words of scores of songs; wrote limericks about friends and places he loved; played baseball and other games with his children; and read poetry and classical novels. He died at home in Washington, D.C.

Basic to his integrative and expanding contributions to psychology were Murphy's early experiences of life in both the North and the South, his emphasis on Greek and Latin in high school, and his education in modern science at Yale. His humanistic contributions to psychology had their roots in his early exposure to William James, and his literary finesse owed much to the literary legacy of his maternal grandfather and his parents. Gardner Murphy's permanent contributions include taking social psychology out of the arm chair and making it scientific, setting psychology to work on human problems, developing a comprehensive theory of personality, and bringing parapsychology into science, as well as showing the relation of feelings to perception; all of these have remained stable aspects of psychology.

• Murphy's papers are in the Archives of the History of American Psychology at Akron University, Akron, Ohio; the archives of the Menninger Foundation, Topeka, Kans.; and the Concord Free Library, Concord, Mass. Autobiographical chapters appear in *A History of Psychology in Autobiography*, vol. 5, ed. E. G. Boring and Gardner Lindzey (1967), and in P. Krawiec, *The Psychologists*, vol. 2 (1974). See also Murphy's "Notes for a Parapsychological Autobiography," *Journal of Parapsychology* 21 (Sept. 1957): 165–78. A comprehensive biography is Lois Barclay Murphy, *Gardner Murphy: Integrating, Expanding and Humanizing Psychology* (1990). A nearly complete bibliography of his writings is included in Murphy, *There Is More Beyond* (1989). An account of his teaching is contained in J. Peatman and E. I. Hartley, eds., *Festschrift for Gardner Murphy* (1960).

LOIS BARCLAY MURPHY

MURPHY, George (4 July 1902–3 May 1992), actor, dancer, and politician, was born George Lloyd Murphy in New Haven, Connecticut, the son of Michael Murphy, a university and olympic track coach, and Nora Long. In his autobiography Murphy called his family "close-knit" and "dominated by a loving father who constantly demanded the best of us." His father died in 1913 and in 1917, at the age of fifteen he ran away from home after his mother's death with the intention of joining the navy in order to serve in World War I. He returned shortly after, finished high school, and attended Yale University. Discontented with school, Murphy left Yale in his junior year and worked in a number of occupations from toolmaking to coal loading before his girlfriend, Julie Johnson (real name Juliette Henkel), taught him to dance.

Murphy worked as a dancer in cocktail lounges, nightclubs, and restaurants. He and Johnson formed a dance act and performed on what was left of the vaudeville circuit. They were married in 1926 and by 1927 had found success on Broadway. Murphy made his Broadway debut in the chorus of *Good News* (1927). Murphy and Johnson had their big break on Broadway in 1929 when they took over the lead roles in the successful musical *Hold Everything*. Murphy then began a successful solo career in revues and musical comedies, including *Of Thee I Sing* (1933) and *Roberta* (1934).

During the 1930s Murphy moved from the stage to the screen. His first movie role was as Eddie Cantor's younger brother in *Kid Millions* (1934), and he appeared in over forty films in his career. Murphy capitalized on the popularity of movie musicals in such films as *After the Dance* (1935); *Top of the Town* and *You're a Sweetheart* (1937); *Little Miss Broadway*, with Shirley Temple, and *Hold That Co-ed* (1938); *Broadway Melody of 1940*, with Fred Astaire, *Public Deb No. 1*, and *Little Nellie Kelly*, with Judy Garland (1940); *A Girl, a Guy, and a Gob* and *Rise and Shine* (1941); *For Me and My Gal*, which also starred Judy Garland and Gene Kelly (1942); and *Show Business* and *Step Lively* (1944).

Murphy also appeared in nonmusical movies, including *Jealousy* (1934), *Public Menace* (1935), *London by Night* (1937), *Risky Business* (1939), *Ringside Maisie* (1941), *The Navy Comes Through* (1942), *Having Wonderful Crime* (1945), *The Arnelo Affair* (1947), *Big City* (1948), *Border Incident* and *Battleground* (1949), *It's a Big Country*, *Walk East on Bacon*, and *Talk about a Stranger* (1952).

In 1939 Murphy and his wife, Julie, had a son; a daughter followed in 1943. During this time Murphy joined the Republican party and became active in politics and in the business side of the film industry. As a founding member of the Screen Actors Guild, Murphy helped unionize the actors, who through the guild created better working conditions and support for the working actor. Murphy played a role in the guild's fight against racketeering in the 1930s and the Communist party takeover in the 1940s. He served on the guild board from 1937 to 1939, as vice president from

1940 to 1943, and as president from 1944 to 1945. In 1940 and 1947 he helped found Hollywood Republican Committees. He received a Special Academy Award in 1951 "for services in interpreting the film industry to the country at large." Murphy retired from acting after 1952 and served as public relations spokesman for Metro-Goldwyn-Mayer. He resigned in 1958 and joined Desi Arnaz and Lucille Ball at Desilu Productions as a vice president. He then moved to Technicolor Studios as vice president and director of operations in 1960.

Murphy continued to be active in politics. He was chair of the state central committee of the California Republican party in 1952, directed the entertainment for the 1953 and 1957 inaugurations, and coordinated the programming for the 1952 and 1956 Republican National Conventions. In 1964, an underdog Murphy was elected the U.S. senator from California. Dismissively dubbed by the opposing party as the "Ziegfeld of the Republican Party," Murphy battled against those who saw him as merely a "song and dance man" rather than a serious politician. Through his knowledge and integrity Murphy changed the minds of his fellow senators. During his term in office he developed throat cancer, which left his voice a mere whisper. In 1970 Murphy ran for a second term in the Senate, but he lost to John Tunney. He nevertheless remained active in politics and worked as a partner in a public relations firm.

In his autobiography Murphy quotes President Richard Nixon as saying, "For over twenty years I have known and respected Senator Murphy, both as a loyal friend and supporter and as a strong and effective spokesman for the principles of the Republican Party. All Californians can be proud and thankful for the job George Murphy is doing for the state and the nation" (p. 428). The autobiography also quotes Governor Ronald Reagan on the friendship and professional relationship he shared with Murphy, "It is paying daily dividends in progress for California. It's good to know that when I call on Washington, Senator Murphy is there to answer . . . and to help" (p. 428).

In 1973, after the death of his wife, Murphy retired to Florida where he wrote his autobiography. He married socialite Betty Blandi in 1982. Murphy died of leukemia in Palm Beach, Florida.

Murphy has been called "a screen natural with limited range but considerable personality" (Maltin, p. 640). His personality coupled with his boyish looks led him to play primarily "good guy" roles. Child star Shirley Temple, who later became prominent in Republican politics, remembered Murphy as someone who "was calm, [had] no temper, and always knew his lines. He had a natural sense of rhythm" (New York Times, 5 May 1992). His real importance to the theater and film industry, however, lay in his off-screen roles in public relations and politics. Murphy's founding and development of the film actor's union and his outspoken support of the entertainment industry changed it for the better as the Screen Actors Guild continues to provide protection and support to film actors and performers.

• Murphy's autobiography, written with Victor Lasky, Say . . . Didn't You Used to Be George Murphy? (1970), contains the most detail about Murphy's life. He is also included in The Illustrated Who's Who of the Cinema (1983), Ephraim Katz's Film Encyclopedia (1994), and Leonard Maltin's Movie Encyclopedia (1994). See also David F. Prindle, The Politics of Glamour: Ideology and Democracy in the Screen Actors Guild (1988). An obituary appears in the New York Times, 5 May 1992.

MELISSA VICKERY-BAREFORD

MURPHY, Gerald Cleary (26 Mar. 1888–17 Oct. 1964), painter, businessman, and friend to artists and writers, was born in Boston, Massachusetts, the son of Patrick Francis Murphy, the owner of an upper-scale leather goods store, and Anna Elizabeth Ryan. Patrick Murphy moved his business, the Mark Cross Company, and his family to New York City in 1892. Gerald's father was a strict disciplinarian who expected his son to receive a sound education and join the family business. His mother was such a devout Catholic that she changed Gerald's birthdate from 26 March to 25 March, the Feast of the Annunciation. Murphy resisted his parents' business and religious pressures, although he temporarily joined Mark Cross after graduating from Yale in 1912.

Murphy enjoyed social success at Yale and was admitted into Skull and Bones, a socially exclusive secret society. However, he found the Yale atmosphere uncongenial to the arts and excessively oriented toward athletics. In subsequent years, he steadfastly refused any relationship with his alma mater.

In 1915 Murphy married Sara Sherman Wiborg, daughter of Frank B. Wiborg, a cofounder of the successful printing-ink company Ault and Wiborg. The couple had three children. During World War I Murphy received aviation training in the U.S. Signal Corps at Kelly Field in San Antonio, Texas, and at Roosevelt Field on Long Island, but the war ended before he was to sail for England. Murphy left Mark Cross in the fall of 1919 to study landscape architecture at Harvard, and in June 1921 he departed for Europe with his family to study the famous landscape gardens of England.

Murphy's career as a painter began and ended in Europe during the 1920s. Inspired by Braque, Picasso, and Juan Gris, Murphy studied art with Natalia Goncharova, a Russian artist and set designer for the Diaghilev ballet in Paris. He quickly developed a style combining realism with abstraction on large canvases. The first Murphy painting to be exhibited was his Razor in 1923, at the Salon des Indépendants in Paris. The painter Fernand Léger, who became a lifelong friend of Murphy's, was quick to acclaim the American's originality. The Indépendants exhibit of 1924 included Murphy's 12' by 18' Boatdeck, Cunarder, and the 1925 exhibit featured his Watch, a large-scale depiction, on a 6½' square canvas, of the internal workings of a watch. The Galerie Georges Bernheim in Paris sponsored a one-man show of Murphy's paintings in 1928.

A slow and meticulous painter, Murphy, by most estimates, had completed only ten paintings by the fall of 1929, when his youngest child, nine-year-old Patrick, was diagnosed with tuberculosis. At that time, Murphy permanently abandoned painting. Patrick died in 1937, two years after the unexpected death from meningitis of his older son, Baoth. When asked why he stopped painting, Murphy would say that the world had too many mediocre painters. The real reason appears to be that when his first son fell ill and the two boys later died, an aspect of his creative spirit vanished from his life. He continued to express his aesthetic sense in gardening and decorating the Murphy homes, but he never returned to painting, which perhaps was too much associated in his mind with the period of his sons' youth and health.

A revival of interest in Murphy's paintings began with a brief discussion of his accomplishments in Rudi Blesh's *Modern Art USA* in 1956 and with the decision by Douglas MacAgy, director of the Dallas Museum for Contemporary Arts, to include five Murphy paintings in a 1960 exhibit of five forgotten American painters. MacAgy's article about the paintings in *Art in America* (1963) gave the revival added impetus, and the Museum of Modern Art, New York, acquired Murphy's *Wasp and Pear* in 1964 from another Murphy friend, Archibald MacLeish. The revival was solidified by a one-man show at the Museum of Modern Art in April 1974, followed in August by a showing at the Dallas Museum of Fine Arts, which had merged with the Dallas Museum for Contemporary Arts.

Only six of Murphy's paintings are known still to exist: *Wasp and Pear, Razor, Watch* (the last two in the Dallas Museum of Fine Arts), *Bibliothèque, Doves,* and *Cocktail.* Despite the small number of paintings that Murphy produced, he is recognized as an important and innovative painter who reacted more to the intellectual climate of Europe in the 1920s than to the styles and methods of his contemporaries. His attention to scale and his interest in machinery (represented in three of his paintings—*Engine Room, Roulement à Billes* [Ball Bearing], and *Watch,* the first two of which have been lost) prefigure pop art and make him appear strikingly modern.

Murphy is perhaps even better known as a friend to many of the greatest artists and writers of his time. Murphy first visited Antibes on the Riviera in the summer of 1923; in 1925 the Murphys took up residence there in the renovated Villa America, where they entertained such luminaries as Ernest Hemingway, F. Scott and Zelda Fitzgerald, Picasso, John Dos Passos, and Cole Porter.

Famous as a gracious host, Murphy combined his own painting with a determination to meld life into a continuous work of art that consisted of exquisitely prepared food (often a mixture of French and American cuisine), music (including Murphy's collection of the latest jazz records), swimming on the beach that he personally had cleared of seaweed, and fine conversa-

tion. It was Murphy the genteel host, rather than the painter, after whom Fitzgerald fashioned his protagonist Dick Diver in *Tender Is the Night.*

Murphy lived a similar lifestyle in the United States after he returned in 1932 to take up his duties with the Mark Cross Company. He became president of Mark Cross in 1934 and merged the company with the Drake America Corporation in 1947, remaining as president until his retirement in 1956.

Writing to Fitzgerald in December 1935 after Baoth's death, Murphy offered his conviction that "only the invented part" of his life, "the unreal part," had any "scheme" or beauty (Miller, p. 151). Murphy's attitude toward life also may be reflected in a Spanish proverb, "Living well is the best revenge," that he quoted frequently and that Calvin Tomkins used as the title of his book about the Murphys. During their decades in the United States, the Murphys lived in New York City at Snedens Landing, overlooking the Hudson River, and at East Hampton, where Murphy died.

• Murphy's letters, along with photographs and other related materials, are in the Honoria Murphy Donnelly Collection in East Hampton, N.Y. A selection of the letters appears in *Letters from the Lost Generation: Gerald and Sara Murphy and Friends,* ed. Linda Patterson Miller (1991). The earliest biographical study of Murphy (and Sara) is Calvin Tomkins, *Living Well Is the Best Revenge* (1962; repr. 1978). A more personal account is Honoria Murphy Donnelly with Richard N. Billings, *Sara and Gerald* (1982). Examinations of Murphy's painting appear in Rudi Blesh, *Modern Art USA: Men, Rebellion, Conquest, 1900–1956* (1956); Douglas MacAgy, "Gerald Murphy: 'New Realist' of the Twenties," *Art in America* 51, no. 2 (1963): 49–57; and William Rubin, *The Paintings of Gerald Murphy* (1974), which accompanied the 1974 exhibition at the Museum of Modern Art, New York. Elizabeth Hutton Turner, *Americans in Paris (1921–1931): Man Ray, Gerald Murphy, Stuart Davis, Alexander Calder* (1996), accompanied the 1996 exhibition at the Phillips Collection, Washington, D.C., and includes essays by Elizabeth Garrity Ellis and Guy Davenport, color reproductions of Murphy's surviving paintings, and an overview of his life and work. Comments on Murphy by his friends and acquaintances are found in the correspondence of Hemingway, Fitzgerald, and other contemporaries, as well as in such memoirs as John Dos Passos, *The Best Times: An Informal Memoir* (1966), and Archibald MacLeish, *Riders on the Earth: Essays and Recollections* (1978). An obituary is in the *New York Times,* 18 Oct. 1964.

EDWARD J. RIELLY

MURPHY, Henry Cruse (5 July 1810–1 Dec. 1882), lawyer, U.S. congressman, and historical scholar, was born in Brooklyn, New York, the son of John G. Murphy, a skilled mechanic, and Clarissa Runyon. Murphy attended Columbia University, graduating in 1830, and studied law. In 1833 he married Amelia Greenwood; they had two children.

In 1834 Murphy became city attorney of Brooklyn, and in 1835 he joined in a partnership with John A. Lott. John Vanderbilt joined the firm, which had a long and successful practice in Brooklyn. The three attorneys were active in local politics and dominated the

Brooklyn Democratic party from the formation of the firm through the 1850s. In 1841 Murphy became one of the owners of the *Daily Eagle*, later the *Brooklyn Eagle*. Although the owners intended the newspaper to be a Democratic party organ, it soon developed an independent reputation. Walt Whitman was briefly editor of the paper from 1846 to 1848.

In 1842 Murphy was elected mayor of Brooklyn, in which post he worked for improvements in the waterfront and warehouse district. That same year he was also elected as a Democrat to the Twenty-eighth Congress. He ran unsuccessfully for reelection in 1844 but was elected again to the Thirtieth Congress, serving from March 1847 to March 1849. He also served in the New York State constitutional convention of 1846. He was considered as a candidate for the presidency of the United States in the Democratic convention of 1852 by the delegation from Virginia, which finally settled on Franklin Pierce to resolve the convention deadlock.

From early in his career, Murphy was interested both in Brooklyn civic affairs and in writing political and historical commentary centered around the city and New York generally. He gathered rare editions of early Dutch works describing exploration and colonization of the area, building a rich library of over 4,000 volumes. He contributed articles to the *United States Magazine and Democratic Review*, the *North American Review*, and New England and New York historical journals. He also edited and translated historical documents and wrote historical monographs. He was a founder of the Long Island Historical Society and the Brooklyn City Library.

In 1857 the James Buchanan administration appointed Murphy minister to Holland, where he served four years. While there he purchased several important additions to his library and published some of his studies on early Dutch exploration. Although a Democrat, he was supportive of the Federal position in the Civil War and communicated the Union's position to the Dutch government in 1861. He was recalled by Abraham Lincoln, and in 1861 he ran and was elected as state senator in New York. He served in the New York upper house from 1861 to 1873. In the 1868 Democratic National Convention, he served as chairman of the Committee on Resolutions. In 1868 he contested the nomination of the Tammany supported candidate for governor of New York. He was a candidate before the state legislature for the U.S. Senate in both 1867 and 1869.

Murphy invested in local real estate and remained active in Brooklyn affairs. He became president of the Flatbush and Coney Island Railroad and obtained the passage of the state legislation necessary to the building of the Brooklyn Bridge while state senator in 1867. He was president of the Brooklyn Bridge Corporation.

Murphy is remembered as one of the leading citizens of Brooklyn in the mid-nineteenth century and as a scholar and politician whose interests focused around those of his city. He died in Brooklyn.

• Murphy wrote *Henry Hudson in Holland: An Inquiry into the Origin and Objects of the Voyage Which Led to the Discovery of the Hudson River* (1859), *The Voyage of Verrazzano* (1875), and *A Celebration at Tammany Hall* (1863). He compiled and edited *The Charters of the City of Brooklyn* (1857), *Old Dutch Burying Grounds* (1862), and *Anthology of New Netherland* (1865). He translated and edited *The Representation of New Netherland*, by Adriaen Van der Donck (1849); *Broad Advice to the United Netherland Provinces*, attributed to Cornelis Melyn (1857); *Voyages from Holland to America* (1857); *Journal of a Voyage to New York and a Tour in Several of the American Colonies in 1679–80 by Jasper Danckaerts and Peter Sluyter* (1867); and *The First Minister of the Reformed Protestant Dutch Church in North America* (1880). He wrote the preface to *Jacob Steendam, noch vaster: A Memoir of the First Poet in New Netherland* (1861). His *Catalogue of an American Library, Chronologically Arranged*, which described his book collection, was published in 1853. See also Raymond A. Schroth, S.J., *The "Eagle" and Brooklyn: A Community Newspaper, 1841–1955* (1974), and David McCullough, *The Great Bridge* (1972). Obituaries are in the *Brooklyn Eagle* and the *New York Times*, both 2 Dec. 1882.

RODNEY P. CARLISLE

MURPHY, Isaac (16 Oct. 1799–8 Sept. 1882), lawyer and politician, was born outside of Pittsburgh, Pennsylvania, the son of Hugh Murphy, a paper manufacturer, and Jane Williams. He was raised in the Pittsburgh area and attended nearby Washington College. He studied law and was admitted to the bar in Allegheny County, Pennsylvania in 1825. In 1830 he moved to Clarksville, Tennessee, where he taught school and practiced law. That same year he married Angelina Lockhart. The couple had six daughters.

Murphy and his wife moved to Washington County in the Arkansas Territory in 1834 and settled near Fayetteville. He taught at several schools and in 1844 helped found Far West Seminary, a short-lived college that tried to attract Indian students. He also practiced law after being admitted to the Arkansas bar in 1835; in 1841 he was Master in Chancery in Washington County. Murphy obtained additional income helping survey public lands in Franklin County in 1837–1838. He was active in the local Democratic party, serving as county treasurer, 1836–1838, and as a member of the General Assembly in 1846 and 1848. As a legislator he opposed his party's handling of the affairs of the Arkansas Real Estate Bank and the Arkansas State Bank. He supported plans for public schools. He joined the California gold rush in 1849 but returned to Fayetteville in 1851. In 1854 he settled in Huntsville, in Madison County, where he continued to practice law, headed the Huntsville High School, and backed his two oldest daughters in establishing the Huntsville Female Seminary as a Democrat. In 1856 he was elected to the state senate as a Democrat.

Murphy opposed secession in 1861 and was elected as a Unionist delegate to the state convention that spring. In the second session of the convention, on 6 May, the delegates passed a secession resolution. Alone among the delegates, Murphy refused to change his vote to make the resolution unanimous. He returned to Huntsville for a while, but, leaving his daughters at home (his wife had died in 1860), he fled his neighbors' hostility for Union lines in 1862. He joined the staff of Union general Samuel R. Curtis in April 1862, although he received no formal rank. He accompanied General Frederick Steele's force that captured Little Rock in September 1863.

Following the Federal occupation, Murphy became involved in Unionist politics at Little Rock and participated in a convention in October 1863 that affirmed the loyalty of Arkansas and asked President Abraham Lincoln to permit the state's return to the Union. In January 1864 a convention at Little Rock adopted a new constitution revising that of 1836 and chose Murphy as provisional governor. President Lincoln abandoned his own plans for a loyal government, deciding to cooperate with the Murphy government instead. An election in March 1864 ratified the proposed constitution and made Murphy, who ran without opposition, governor. During the remaining year of the war, Murphy's two major goals were to secure Arkansas's readmission to the Union and to obtain federal military protection for Unionists in the state. But conflict between Lincoln and the Congress delayed and ultimately blocked re-admission, and without recognition from Congress, Murphy had little leverage with the army for securing policies that helped local Unionists.

At the end of the war President Andrew Johnson treated the Murphy government as the legitimate state government. Furthermore, it was generally accepted by the people, even though it was not recognized by Congress. The legislature elected in 1866 ultimately helped to doom Murphy's efforts to obtain congressional recognition. Ignoring his pleas for actions that would not anger northerners, the newly elected Conservative-Democratic majority rejected the Fourteenth Amendment, enacted black codes severely restricting the rights of freedmen, and passed pro-Confederate bills, including one that established pensions for Confederate veterans. Such actions by Arkansas and other southern states led Congress to reject congressmen elected there in 1866 and to impose a new Reconstruction program on the South in March 1867.

Murphy remained in office following the inauguration of congressional Reconstruction, although General E. O. C. Ord, commander of the Fourth Military District, dissolved the General Assembly. Murphy's government did little however, beyond assisting the military in registering voters and preparing for a new constitutional convention. Murphy, unlike many other white Unionists, did not become active in the new state Republican party, and in fact he refrained from all political activity. On 2 July 1868 he left office following the election and inauguration of Republican governor Powell Clayton. He returned to Huntsville, where he renewed his law practice and also farmed. He died at Huntsville.

• There are no major collections of Murphy papers, although a few letters written by him as governor are in the Murphy/Berry Family Collection, Arkansas History Commission, Little Rock. The best biographies are John I. Smith, *The Cour-*age of a Southern Unionist: A Biography of Isaac Murphy, Governor of Arkansas, 1864–68* (1979), and William L. Shea, "Isaac Murphy," in *The Governors of Arkansas*, ed. Timothy P. Donovan and Williard B. Gatewood, Jr. (1981); an obituary is in the Little Rock *Daily Arkansas Gazette*, 12 Sept. 1882.

CARL H. MONEYHON

MURPHY, Isaac (16 Apr. 1861–12 Feb. 1896), jockey, was born Isaac Burns on a farm near Frankfort, Kentucky, the son of James Burns, a bricklayer, and a mother (name unknown) who worked as a laundrywoman. During the Civil War his father, a free black, joined the Union army and died in a Confederate prisoner-of-war camp. Upon the death of his father, his widowed mother moved with her family to Lexington, Kentucky, to live with her father, Green Murphy, a bell ringer and auction crier. Accompanying his mother to work at the Richard and Owings Racing Stable, the diminutive Isaac was noticed by the black trainer Eli Jordan, who had him suited up for his first race at age fourteen. His first winning race was aboard the two-year-old filly Glentina on 15 September 1875 at the Lexington Crab Orchard. Standing five feet tall and weighing only seventy-four pounds, Murphy had by the end of 1876 ridden eleven horses to victory at Lexington's Kentucky Association track.

Since colonial times, African Americans had been involved in the care and training of horses, particularly on antebellum and post–Civil War farms and plantations in the South. They had also ridden them as jockeys, an occupation once considered beneath the dignity of white men. At the inaugural Kentucky Derby in 1875, fourteen of the fifteen jockeys were black. Blacks triumphed in fifteen of the first twenty-eight derbies. In his first Kentucky Derby in 1877, Murphy (who had adopted his grandfather's surname as a tribute) placed fourth aboard Vera Cruz. He later rode the same horse to victory in another major stakes race and tallied nineteen first-place finishes that year. Two years later, Murphy signed with J. W. Hunt Reynolds and came in second in the Kentucky Derby with the moneymaker Falsetto. Among Murphy's numerous victories between 1879 and 1884 (the year he signed with Ed Corrigan of New York) were the Clark Handicap in Louisville, Kentucky; the Distillers Stakes in Lexington, Kentucky; the Saratoga Cup in New York; the Brewers Cup in St. Louis, Missouri; and the first American Derby in Chicago, Illinois. Incredibly, he posted wins in forty-nine of the fifty-one races he entered at Saratoga in 1882. His first Kentucky Derby win at Churchill Downs, on 27 May 1884 aboard Modesty, was clocked at 2 minutes, 40.25 seconds, two lengths ahead of his nearest rival. It was the first of three such conquests there; the other two occurred successively in 1890 and 1891, with the mounts Riley and Kingman, respectively.

Renowned for his adept manipulation of his mounts via intuitive, precise pacing, Murphy rarely employed stirrups or the whip except to please the crowd, and his trademark come-from-behind finishes became known as "Murfinshes." It was his habit to lay on the horse's neck to coax it to the finish line. At a time when jockeys customarily wagered on the outcome of races, Murphy, a devout Baptist, enjoyed a reputation for scrupulous honesty and integrity. A mild-mannered, gracious man who never swore, he married Lucy Osborn in 1882; they had no children. Murphy and his wife resided in a mansion at 143 North Eastern Avenue in Lexington, overlooking the backstretch of a nearby racetrack. At the peek of his career, his yearly salary ranged from $10,000 to $20,000 excluding bonuses, making him the highest-paid jockey in the nation. His income befitted a man who rode nearly every premier horse of the era to victory at all the major racing events except the Futurity. It is believed that Murphy was the first black American to own a racehorse—he owned several, in fact—and he invested his winnings in racehorses and real estate. He spent extravagantly on clothes and soirees at his home and was attended to at the track by his personal valet.

Several writers have asserted that Murphy's most memorable and exciting race was that which occurred at Sheepshead Bay in New York on 25 June 1890. It matched him against the heralded white jockey Ed "Snapper" Garrison and attempted to settle the long-standing debate as to who was the better professional. The event had pronounced racial overtones that in certain respects prefigured the Jack Johnson versus Jim Jeffries boxing match twenty years later. Murphy, riding Salvador, edged out Garrison, aboard Tenny, by half a head in one of the most publicized races of the century.

Ironically, just two months later Murphy's popularity was tarnished and his career began to unravel when he fell off of his mount at the end of the running of the Monmouth Handicap. He maintained that he suffered from chronic dieting and that he may even have been drugged. Nonetheless, he was charged with drunkenness and suspended. The press, including the *New York Times* (27 Aug. 1890), was quite baffled by such uncharacteristic behavior from the gentlemanly Murphy and roundly chastised him. Although he continued to rack up victories at the track the following year (1891), his penchant for champagne and the struggle to hold down his weight, which had risen to 140 pounds, eventually took their toll. In 1892 he won six races, the next year four races, and in 1894, the year he was suspended for a second time for being drunk at the track, he failed to win a race. Retirement was forced upon him in November 1895. Within three months Murphy died in Lexington, the ravages of alcohol and dieting having weakened his resistance to pneumonia. He left $30,000 to his wife, but this sum was hardly enough to satisfy his creditors and she died a pauper.

Murphy, arguably the most influential and widely respected African-American athlete of the nineteenth century, was curiously ignored for many years by historians and journalists. Half a century after his death, an article filled with anecdotes and quotations pertaining to his career appeared in the *Negro Digest* (Nov. 1950). Its title bemoaned, "No Memorial for Isaac Murphy." In 1967, through the efforts of Lexington sportswriter Frank Borries, Jr., Murphy's remains were transported from their ignominious location in the city's decrepit No. 2 Cemetery and reinterred in Man o' War Park. In 1977 the remains of both the jockey and the famed thoroughbred (whom Murphy never rode) were moved to hallowed ground near one another at the Kentucky Horse Park outside of Lexington. In 1955 he was the first jockey inducted into the National Museum of Racing Hall of Fame, and in 1956 he was also enshrined in the National Jockey's Hall of Fame at Pimlico, Maryland.

Murphy's three Kentucky Derby wins were later exceeded by Eddie Arcaro (five), Bill Hartack (five), and Bill Shoemaker (four); his back-to-back Kentucky Derby wins were later equaled by African-American Jimmy Winkfield (1901 and 1902), Ron Tucotte (1972 and 1973), and Eddie Delahoussaye (1982 and 1983). To his recollection, he was victorious in 44 percent of his contests, winning 628 of 1,412 mounts; but according to other sources, Murphy's winning percentage was closer to 33 percent. In any event, 33 percent represented the best winning record of any jockey in American turf history. The annual Isaac Murphy Award was established in 1993 by the National Turf Writers' Association to honor the jockey with the best win-loss record. The Isaac Murphy Stakes (formerly the American Derby, which Murphy won on four occasions) was initiated in 1997 at Chicago's Arlington International Racecourse.

• For further information on Murphy's life and career, see Betty Borries, *Isaac Murphy: Kentucky's Record Jockey* (1988), and Stephen P. Savage, "Isaac Murphy: Black Hero in Nineteenth Century American Sport, 1861–1896," *Canadian Journal of History and Physical Education* 10 (1979): 15–32. Other useful sources include a well-researched magazine article by Jim Bolus, "Honest Isaac's Legacy," *Sports Illustrated*, 29 Apr. 1996. See also Arthur R. Ashe, *A Hard Road to Glory: A History of the African-American Athlete, 1619–1918* (1988); Rick Cushing, "Isaac Murphy: A Pioneer Who's Had Few Followers," *Louisville Courier-Journal*, 30 Apr. 1990; L. P. Tarelton, "A Memorial," *Thoroughbred Record*, 21 Mar. 1896, p. 136; and Frank T. Phelps, "The Nearest Perfect Jockey," *Thoroughbred Record*, 13 May 1967, pp. 1245–48.

ROBERT FIKES, JR.

MURPHY, James Bumgardner (4 Aug. 1884–24 Aug. 1950), experimental pathologist, was born in Morganton, North Carolina, the son of Patrick Livingston Murphy, a psychiatrist and director of the Western North Carolina Insane Asylum (now the Broughton Hospital), and Bettie Waddell Bumgardner. Murphy had an "intimate, personal and, in fact, clinical interest" in animals during his childhood. This inclination and his military preparatory school experiences at the Horner School in Morganton were significant factors in his skill at dissection and observation and in his appreciation for discipline. These talents helped attract the attention of people important in the development of his career and eventually brought him to prominence.

Murphy's college education began in 1901 at the University of North Carolina, where he earned a B.S. in 1905. He entered the Johns Hopkins Medical School the same year, graduating in 1909 with an M.D. His years as a medical student presaged a career in research rather than practice; within a few weeks of starting his freshman year his skill at dissection and drawing gained the attention of Harvey Cushing, the famous neurosurgeon. In 1907 his father died, and Murphy found himself without the money needed to continue in medical school. As he was preparing to leave, Henry M. Hurd, director of the Johns Hopkins Hospital, became aware of Murphy's financial straits and helped him to complete his course of study. Murphy later repaid Hurd's generosity by quietly giving financial and other support to young people during their medical school years.

For the two years following his graduation Murphy worked in psychiatry in New York with Adolf Meyer, an early leader of international stature in U.S. psychiatry, and was invited to go as resident when Meyer moved to Johns Hopkins in 1911. Heeding the advice of Florence Sabin, an instructor of anatomy, Murphy chose instead to assist Peyton Rous at the Rockefeller Institute. Aside from service as a major in the Army Medical Corps in World War I, he spent the rest of his life at the institute. Rous, later to win the Nobel Prize for his work, had recently shown that a malignant tumor of fowls could be transmitted by a filterable agent. Murphy's skill with his hands and his imagination quickly proved valuable; he showed that the transmissible agent was still active after freezing and drying, and that it, and grafts of mammalian tumors, could be grown in chick embryos. Murphy recognized that the embryo does not reject transplanted tissue as does the adult animal. This original observation supported later efforts to use embryonic tissues in transplantation.

These early successes were followed by elegant experiments that showed the importance of lymphocytes in graft rejection, tuberculosis, and resistance to cancer. The field of immunology, however, was at that time concerned not with cells like lymphocytes but with proteins—antibodies—in the blood plasma. This was a result of the success achieved by vaccines against such diseases as tetanus, in which antibodies were central. Interest in the cells involved in immune reactions later assumed major importance, however. Murphy's 1916 description of how grafted lymphocytes affected chick embryos was rediscovered in 1957. His work did not interest the immunologists of early years and was not useful to clinicians of that day; it required other developments before it could be seen as prescient and be fitted into medical practice.

Murphy's organizational and administrative talents complemented his scientific accomplishments. In his early years cancer was considered something of a disgrace; it was not to be mentioned on the radio, for example. Murphy was active in the organizations impor-

tant in bringing it out of the shadows. He served on the board and executive committee of what is now the American Cancer Society for sixteen years, the advisory council of the National Cancer Institute when the Cancer Act of 1937 was passed, and the Committee on Growth of the National Research Council. His service on the board of the Memorial Hospital in New York was a particular help to its director, James Ewing, a kindred spirit; Murphy was also a board member of Memorial's associated Sloan-Kettering Institute for Cancer Research. He was commissioner of the New York State Board of Charities and a member of the boards of the New York State Institute for the Study of Malignant Diseases and the Roswell Park Memorial Institute in Buffalo.

In 1919 Murphy married Ray Slater, a Bostonian who was working as secretary to diplomat William Bullitt in Washington when Murphy was in the army there. The elder of their two children, James Slater Murphy, graduated in medicine from Johns Hopkins and became a research virologist at the Rockefeller Institute. Summers on Mount Desert Island in Maine were a long-standing pleasure to Murphy and his family. He served on the Mount Desert Island Hospital and as vice president of the Jackson Memorial Laboratory in Bar Harbor. Murphy died in Bar Harbor the year he retired from the Rockefeller Institute.

• Murphy's papers are at the University of North Carolina at Chapel Hill and the Rockefeller Archives in New York. The best appraisal of Murphy's work is found in Ilana Löwy, "Biomedical Research and the Constraints of Medical Practice: James Bumgardner Murphy and the Early Discovery of the Role of Lymphocytes in Immune Reactions," *Bulletin of the History of Medicine* 63 (1989): 356–91. An excellent memoir, with a complete bibliography of Murphy's writing, is in Clarence C. Little, "James Bumgardner Murphy," National Academy of Sciences, *Biographical Memoirs* 34 (1960): 183–203; Little, a distinguished geneticist, was Murphy's close friend and colleague.

ROBERT W. PRICHARD

MURPHY, John Benjamin (21 Dec. 1857–11 Aug. 1916), surgeon, was born in Appleton, Wisconsin, the son of Michael Murphy and Ann Grimes, farmers. He completed his secondary education in 1876 and then taught in the local school for two terms before taking up the study of medicine with H. W. Reilly, an Appleton physician. He matriculated at Rush Medical College in Chicago, Illinois, in 1878, receiving his M.D. degree two years later. After completing a one-year internship at Chicago's Cook County Hospital, he entered private practice as the associate of Edward W. Lee, a Chicago physician. In 1882, having decided to pursue a career as a surgeon, he went to Europe to study the latest surgical techniques at the Allgemeines Krankenhaus in Vienna, Austria, and at the universities of Berlin and Heidelberg in Germany.

In 1884 Murphy returned to Chicago and resumed his partnership with Lee. Later that year he also became a lecturer in surgery at Rush and an attending surgeon at Cook. In 1885 he married Jeannette Plamondon, with whom he had five children. He was the first physician to arrive at the police station where over sixty wounded policemen had been carried after the Haymarket Riot of 1886; his ability to take charge of the chaotic medical situation at the station and then perform emergency surgery for more than twelve hours nonstop gained him a citywide reputation that helped him to open his own surgical practice the following year.

Murphy developed an intense interest in abdominal surgery, partly because of the Haymarket experience and partly because recent advances in antisepsis and anesthesia had greatly increased the odds of a patient surviving a complicated internal operation. He began performing experimental surgery on dogs and immersed himself in the contemporary surgical literature. In 1889, shortly after reading an article by the British pathologist Reginald Fitz that attributed most inflammation of the lower right abdomen to an infected appendix and urged its earliest possible removal, he performed the first successful appendectomy in the United States. Over the next fourteen years he campaigned assiduously among his fellow surgeons concerning the utter necessity of this surgical procedure. He himself performed more than two thousand appendectomies, often on the patient's kitchen table in order to save precious time. Largely owing to his efforts, appendectomies eventually became accepted, routine procedures.

In 1892 Murphy left Rush to become professor of clinical surgery at Chicago's College of Physicians and Surgeons. That same year he revolutionized abdominal surgery by inventing the Murphy button, a mechanical device that greatly facilitated the reconnection of the severed ends of the intestine after a portion had been surgically removed. The device consisted of two bowl-headed metallic cylinders; after each bowl was stitched to the inside of one of the intestine ends, the two cylinders were fitted together to form a ball-shaped mechanical union, which was passed in a stool when the intestine grew back together. The Murphy button transformed what had been a difficult, dangerous procedure requiring hours to complete into a simple operation that any competent surgeon could perform in minutes, and thus made possible a whole range of abdominal surgical procedures.

In 1895 Murphy assumed the additional duties of chief of the surgical staff at Mercy Hospital and began experimenting with a number of surgical procedures not related to the abdomen. In 1896 he was the first surgeon to remove part of an artery and then suture together the two ends. Two years later he was one of the first surgeons to use nitrogen gas to collapse and splint an abscessed tuberculous lung. His surgical studies of the spinal cord and its related nerves informed some of the earliest neurosurgical procedures. He performed breakthrough operations involving bones, joints, and tendons, as well as the prostate gland. Meanwhile he continued his pioneering work in abdominal surgery by developing a method for administering saline solution rectally for the treatment of

peritonitis. He also became the first American physician to recognize *Actinomycosis hominis*, a fungal infection of the gastrointestinal tract occasionally communicated to humans from animals.

In 1901 Murphy became professor of surgery at Northwestern University Medical School, but he left four years later to return to Rush as cochairman of the surgery department. In 1908 he returned to Northwestern as chairman of the surgery department, a position he held until his death. The notes from Murphy's clinical presentations were in great demand by surgeons across the United States. To satisfy this demand he published *The Surgical Clinics of John B. Murphy, M.D., at Mercy Hospital, Chicago* (5 vols., 1912–1916), one of the most important surgical reference works of the day.

Murphy served as president of the Chicago Surgical Society (1904), the Chicago Medical Society (1904–1905), the American Medical Association (1911–1912), and the Clinical Congress of Surgeons (1914–1915). He was awarded Notre Dame University's Laetare Medal in 1904, and in 1916 Pope Benedict XV made him a knight commander in the Order of St. Gregory the Great. In 1921 a Chicago hospital was named after him, and in 1926 the American College of Surgeons, which he cofounded in 1913, named its newly constructed headquarters in Chicago in his honor. He died in Mackinac Island, Michigan.

Murphy possessed a missionary's zeal as well as supreme confidence in his own ideas and abilities. These traits frequently resulted in intemperate remarks at the expense of colleagues, who responded by accusing him throughout his career of stealing patients and ideas, charging exorbitant fees, and thrusting himself into the public spotlight—charges that were not without foundation. Nevertheless, he was one of the foremost surgeons of his day. He contributed to the advance of surgery by demonstrating the critical importance of appendectomies and by developing many of the first techniques and apparatus for performing a variety of surgical procedures.

• Murphy's papers are at Northwestern University's Galter Library. A biography is Loyal Davis, *J. B. Murphy: Stormy Petrel of Surgery* (1938). An obituary is in the *Chicago Daily Tribune*, 12 Aug. 1916.

CHARLES W. CAREY, JR.

MURPHY, John Henry, Sr. (25 Dec. 1840–5 Apr. 1922), newspaper publisher, was born in Baltimore, Maryland, the only son of Benjamin Murphy, Jr., a whitewasher, and Susan Coby. Murphy was born a slave. The Baltimore *Afro-American*, the newspaper he would guide to prominence during the first two decades of the twentieth century, described Murphy's educational attainment as "limited." A short man, he walked with a limp, the result of a childhood horseback riding incident that left one leg longer than the other. Freedom for the Murphys came via the Maryland Emancipation Act of 1863.

Despite his limp, Murphy answered Abraham Lincoln's call for troops and joined the Union army during the Civil War. He enlisted as a private in Company G of the mostly black Thirtieth Regiment of the Maryland Volunteers—an infantry unit—on 18 March 1864. During his twenty-one months in uniform he served under General Ulysses S. Grant in Virginia and General William T. Sherman in North Carolina. He left the army in December 1865 as a sergeant.

After his discharge, Murphy returned to Baltimore. On his first day back home he met Martha Elizabeth Howard, daughter of a well-to-do Montgomery County, Maryland, farmer. Howard's family had been born slaves, but her father, Enoch George Howard, had purchased his freedom and later that of his wife and children and eventually even bought his former master's property. It took two years for Murphy to convince Howard's father that he was sincere about marriage. The couple were married in 1868; they would have eleven children.

To support his growing clan, Murphy worked at various jobs over the next twenty years. He followed his father as a whitewasher for a time, until the use of wallpaper became widespread. Murphy later used his veteran's status to get a political patronage job with the U.S. Post Office, but he lost that when the Democrats came to power with the 1884 election of Grover Cleveland as president. Subsequent jobs included being a porter, a janitor, and a feed store manager. (Neither Murphy nor others who have written about him cite dates or lengths of time that he stayed at his various jobs.)

Murphy was in his forties when he decided to become a printer, as he described himself. Active in local organizations, particularly the African Methodist Episcopal (AME) church, in the 1880s Murphy became superintendent of Sunday schools for the Hagerstown (Md.) AME Church District. For years Murphy had wanted to structure black church schools into some type of organization, and he saw a newspaper as a means of achieving this goal. His initial publication, designed to generate more community interest in Sunday school work, was the *Sunday School Helper*, which he began in the late 1880s in the basement of his home. Murphy's competition came from publications started by other local black church groups. The *Afro-American*, which, under the leadership of the Reverend William Alexander, carried a combination of church and community news, was the Baptists' publication. The *Ledger*, edited by the Reverend George F. Bragg, was allied with the Episcopal church. (Initial publication dates have yet to be established for any of these weekly publications.)

The *Afro-American*'s parent company was the Northwestern Family Supply Company, a Reverend Alexander enterprise that operated a dry goods store. When Alexander's larger business failed and was auctioned off, in 1896 Murphy acquired, with $200 borrowed from his wife, the *Afro-American*, then a one-page weekly with a circulation of 250. Murphy merged the two publications and dropped the *Sunday School*

Helper name but retained the church and community news content. As time passed, Murphy brought his children into the enterprise by assigning them various editorial, printing, and circulation tasks. Between 1900 and 1901 the *Afro-American* merged with the *Ledger* and was known for a time as the *Afro-American Ledger* (1901–1916), when it was published semiweekly. Under this arrangement, Murphy became the publisher, and Bragg became the editor. Murphy eventually obtained control and returned the newspaper to its former—and current—name, the *Afro-American*. During the last three decades of his life, Murphy guided the operation as it became one of the premier black newspapers of all time. In the process he not only achieved success, fame, and financial reward; he laid the foundation for a venerable publishing concern that would be headed by generations of Murphys for nearly a century.

Murphy said he wanted to publish a newspaper that would "render service to the whole community." Like many of his black newspaper executive contemporaries, he was a Republican, but he vowed not to let the *Afro-American* be a newspaper "tied to the apron strings of any political party, fraternal organization or religious denomination." He established the paper's motto of "Independent in All Things, Neutral in Nothing." Murphy credited two characteristics for his success: faith and industry. He said he had "faith in the ability of the black man to succeed in this civilization, faith in myself and faith in God. Then, too, I believe in just plain, everyday, hard work."

Murphy had hoped to live to be 100 years old and on his eightieth birthday wrote a letter to be opened on Christmas Day 1940. A reflection on his life and a statement of the philosophy that made him one of the most respected "race" men of his time, the letter reads in part:

I measure a newspaper not in buildings, equipment and employees—those are trimmings. A newspaper succeeds because its management believes in itself, in God and in the present generation. It must always ask itself whether it has kept faith with the common people; whether it has no other goal except to see that their liberties are preserved and their future assured; whether it is fighting to get rid of slums, to provide jobs for everybody; whether it stays out of politics except to expose corruption and condemn injustice, race prejudice or the cowardice of compromise. . . . [The *Afro-American*] has always had a loyal constituency who believed it honest, decent and progressive. It is that kind of newspaper now and I hope it never changes.

Murphy remained active until shortly before his death in Baltimore. Tributes poured in. The one from the Negro (later National) Newspaper Publishers Association (NNPA), the black newspaper publishers trade organization, was a fitting epitaph. To his peers, it said, Murphy was "a noble Roman of the fourth estate and . . . an inspiration to future generations of black men."

By the time he died, Murphy had managed to establish a newspaper with an extensive readership outside the city that was once called "the graveyard of black newspapers." The *Afro-American*'s circulation of 14,000 at the time of his death made it one of the ten largest black newspapers in the United States. As the number of black newspapers grew, with the migration of blacks to the North the *Afro-American* became one of the "Big Five" black newspapers of the first half of the twentieth century. Although Murphy did not start the *Afro-American*, he was the driving force that transformed the publication from a local newspaper into one of the most significant and influential black journals in the nation. John Henry Murphy was a man of perseverance and vision, and his life indicates that one is never too old to succeed.

• The *Afro-American* Archives are located at Bowie State College, Bowie, Md. An additional primary source is a letter by John H. Murphy, "Sergeant Murphy: Story of a Civil War Veteran," dated 25 Dec. 1920, Schomburg Center for the Study of Black Culture Clipping File 3003, 362–1. See also "John Henry Murphy," *Afro-American*, 7 Apr. 1922, p. 7 (obituary); "John Henry Murphy, Sr., 1840–1922," *Afro-American* (magazine section), 9 Jan. 1957, p. 4; and "Letters and Telegrams Eulogize John H. Murphy," *Afro-American*," 14 Apr. 1922, p. 7. An important source on the influence of the *Afro-American* is Roland E. Wolseley, *The Black Press: U.S.A.*, 2d ed. (1990).

JAMES PHILLIP JETER

MURPHY, Michael Charles (26 Feb. 1861–4 June 1913), athletic trainer and track and field coach, was born in Westboro, Massachusetts; little is known about his parents and his early life, except that he was educated in the local primary and secondary schools in Westboro. After finishing high school, Murphy joined the volunteer fire department. As a fireman he demonstrated great athletic ability, especially running speed and endurance. In the late 1870s he profited from these skills in track and field as a sprinter and as a long distance walker in six-day pedestrian contests. Murphy also played on local minor league baseball teams and fought in bareknuckle prize fights.

In 1886 Murphy retired from athletic competition and opened his own athletic training camp in Westboro. Although one of the first athletes to use his facility was John L. Sullivan, who held the world heavyweight boxing title from 1882 to 1892, Murphy specialized in the preparation of runners and walkers. In 1887 Yale University hired him to coach the track and field team, with the sole purpose of defeating Harvard University in the Intercollegiate Association of Amateur Athletes of America (IC4A) championships. Since the establishment of the IC4A as the governing organization of intercollegiate track and field in 1876, Harvard had dominated the championships, winning the title each year from 1880 to 1886. Murphy served as the track and field coach at Yale from 1887 to 1890 and led the university to the IC4A championship in 1887 and 1889. His leading performer was Charles H. Sherrill, who captured IC4A titles in the 100-yard

dash from 1887 to 1890 and the 220-yard dash from 1888 to 1890 as well as the 100-yard dash in the National Association of Amateur Athletes of America championships in 1887. Murphy instructed Sherrill to start from a crouching rather than a conventional standing position, and Sherrill became the first national champion sprinter to successfully employ the crouch start. In 1890 Murphy resigned from Yale and joined the Detroit Athletic Club in Detroit, Michigan. There he developed John Owen into the first sprinter to break the 10-second mark for 100 yards. Owen accomplished the feat in defending his Amateur Athletic Union title in 9.8 seconds in 1890.

Murphy coached the Detroit Athletic Club until 1893, when he returned to Yale and led the university to three consecutive IC4A championships. In 1895 he also served as the coach of the New York Athletic Club and prepared athletes for the first track and field meet between the United States and Great Britain. Held that year in New York City, the meet featured athletes predominantly from the New York and London Athletic Clubs, although athletes from other nations also participated in the event. Murphy's star performer in the meet was Bernard J. Wefers, who equaled the world record of 9.8 seconds in the 100-yard dash and established a world record of 21.2 seconds in the 220-yard dash.

In 1896 Murphy became the track and field coach at the University of Pennsylvania, and he led the Quakers to IC4A titles from 1897 to 1900. His leading performers during this time were John W. B. Tewksbury and Alvin C. Kraenzlein. Tewksbury won the IC4A 100- and 220-yard dash titles in 1898 and 1899. Kraenzlein, who perfected the straight lead-leg hurdling technique under Murphy, won IC4A tiles in the 100-yard dash in 1900, the 120-yard high hurdles and the 220-yard low hurdles from 1898 to 1900, and the long jump in 1899. In 1900 Murphy coached the U.S. Olympic track and field team, which included athletes from Pennsylvania and other Ivy League universities. His team won 19 of 20 events, led by victories in the 200 meters and 400-meter hurdles by Tewksbury, and in the 60-meter dash, the 110 and 200 hurdles, and the long jump by Kraenzlein.

In 1901 Murphy returned to Yale and, from 1902 to 1904, again won three consecutive IC4A team championships. He returned to the University of Pennsylvania in 1905 and led Penn to three more IC4A titles in 1910, 1912, and 1913. Murphy also coached the U.S. Olympic track and field teams in 1908 and 1912. Shortly after Penn's 1913 IC4A triumph, Murphy died at his home in Philadelphia after a lengthy illness. His wife was Nora B. Long.

Sport historians recognize Murphy as one of the first systematic track and field coaches and sports conditioning specialists in the United States. His *Athletic Training*, published posthumously in 1914, reflected his thirty years of experience in developing track and field athletes. Murphy, who had completed a two-year medical course at the University of Pennsylvania, understood the mechanics and physiology of the human body as well as any physician. However, he claimed that his success in developing world-class track and field athletes came not from science but from the observation and refinement of techniques. These techniques, more than any other factor, led to wins and record-setting performances. In this regard Murphy revolutionized track and field by perfecting the crouch start through Sherrill and straight lead-leg hurdling through Kraenzlein. Furthermore, he helped to establish the United States as a twentieth-century international track and field power through his successful coaching of U.S. Olympic teams.

• A biographical file on Murphy is at the University of Pennsylvania Archives and Records Center, Philadelphia. For the role of Murphy in the development of collegiate track and field, see Ronald A. Smith, *Sports and Freedom: The Rise of Big-Time College Athletics* (1988). See Roberta J. Park, "Athletes and Their Training in Britain and America, 1800–1914," in *Sport and Exercise Science: Essays in the History of Sports Medicine*, ed. Jack W. Berryman and Roberta J. Park (1992) for analysis of Murphy's training methods and interest in medicine and physiology. For statistical information on Murphy's record as a track coach, see Frank G. Menke, *The Encyclopedia of Sports*, 4th rev. ed. (1969). For the history of track and field in general, consult Roberto L. Quercetani, *A World History of Track and Field Athletics* (1964). An obituary is in the *New York Times*, 5 June 1913.

ADAM R. HORNBUCKLE

MURPHY, Robert Cushman (29 Apr. 1887–20 Mar. 1973), ornithologist, was born in Brooklyn, New York, the son of Thomas D. Murphy, a secondary-school official, and Augusta Cushman. In his early years the family moved to a rural part of Long Island, New York, where the boy, encouraged by his parents, took an interest in the local wildlife. He enjoyed going out with a local fisherman for bluefish, and he identified local birds. In 1906 he met Frank Michier Chapman, curator of birds at the American Museum of Natural History, who hired him for a short time to proofread the galleys of his own book on warblers.

Murphy attended Brown University, where he received a Ph.B. in 1911. Earlier he had become acquainted with Frederic Augustus Lucas, then curator of the museums of the Brooklyn Institute of Arts and Sciences. Lucas appointed Murphy curator of birds and mammals at the institute in 1911 and arranged for him to sail, in 1912, as naturalist on a New Bedford whaling ship, *Daisy*, to the subantarctic. Murphy married Grace Emeline Barstow shortly before that one-year trip; the couple had three children.

The whaling trip gave Murphy an opportunity to observe and collect oceanic birds. During its stop of almost four months for elephant seals on South Georgia Island, he obtained specimens of penguins, other birds, marine mammals, and plants, which were all to be deposited in the American Museum of Natural History.

On his return Murphy continued at the Brooklyn Institute, where he became head of the Department of Natural History in 1917. That year he also received an

M.A. in zoology from Columbia University. In 1919–1920 he visited Peru for several months to observe the guano-producing birds of the offshore islands.

In 1921 Murphy became associate curator at the American Museum of Natural History, advanced to curator of oceanic birds in 1926, in 1942 became chairman of the Department of Birds, and in 1949 was named Lamont Curator of Birds. His first book was *Bird Islands of Peru* (1925). He organized an expedition to collect oceanic and coastal birds under the leadership of Rollo H. Beck. Murphy's next scientific book was on these large collections, *The Oceanic Birds of South America* (2 vols., 1936), which his biographer Dean Amadon calls "noteworthy for its remarkably readable style." The scholarly treatise included the effects of climate, currents, and land masses on the distribution of oceanic birds, as well as general natural history and a detailed account of each bird species and its habits, illustrated with photographs, color plates, and maps. The book was awarded the John Burroughs Medal for excellence in natural history writing and the Brewster Medal of the American Ornithologists Union.

In 1932 Murphy, assisted by his wife, cataloged and shipped to the United States the very large collection of birds (280,000 specimens) accumulated by Lionel Walter Rothschild in England; it had been sold to the American Museum of Natural History in 1931. Many details about the collection were known only by Rothschild, so compiling the 740-page catalog and the packing took the couple four months. Murphy was general manager of the Whitney South Sea Expedition that operated for about a decade from 1935 on the schooner *France*, although he was never able to join it himself. He was under pressure at the museum to study the new collections quickly, and he was much aided in this by biologist Ernst Mayr, a scientist destined for great eminence.

The family of philanthropist Harry Payne Whitney donated funds for a new wing of the museum for the growing collections of birds. Murphy was extensively involved with the supervision and construction of the Whitney Memorial Hall of Oceanic Birds. He often helped create other exhibits for the museum and as a popular lecturer there contributed to a rising interest in conservation. In addition he traveled extensively: to Baja California, Mexico, Peru, and Ecuador three times, the western Mediterranean, the archipelago of Las Perlas off Panama, New Zealand, and the subantarctic region three times, and the Caribbean area several times. He obtained many new specimens and considerable scientific information on habits and habitats of birds. According to Mayr, "With iron self-discipline, no matter how strenuous the day, he recorded his daily experiences in considerable detail in a diary, an extraordinarily valuable record considering the drastic changes all of these places have experienced since then."

After retiring from the American Museum of Natural History in 1955, Murphy maintained an office there for some years in an emeritus capacity. In 1960 he was representative of the National Science Foundation and biologist on the icebreaker *Glacier* in the Antarctic, and in 1970 he revisited South Georgia Island, which he had last seen in 1912.

Through the years he published nearly 600 articles in scientific journals and in popular magazines, including *Natural History*, *National Geographic*, and *Scientific Monthly*. In 1947 he published an account of his 1912 whaling voyage as *Logbook for Grace*, derived from his original diary and letters to his wife. Well written, it primarily represents Murphy's acceptance of the already declining whaling industry and his own enthusiasm for gathering information on subantarctic birds and mammals. In *A Dead Whale or a Stove Boat* (1967) he presented photographs of whaling that he had taken and developed during the 1912 trip.

Murphy was an early conservationist who concentrated his continuing efforts on Long Island, New York, where he and his family lived for many years. He was the first president of the Long Island chapter of the Nature Conservancy, which obtained natural habitat locally for preservation, and he was an adviser on the Fire Island National Seashore. His book on the region, *Fish Shape Paumanok: Nature and Man on Long Island*, was published in 1964. Having become well aware of the decline in whale populations through the years, he also participated in efforts to save them.

Murphy received the Daniel Giraud Elliot Medal of the National Academy of Sciences in 1943 and other scientific honors. He died on Long Island.

• Murphy deposited his diaries and considerable other material with the American Philosophical Society of Philadelphia; this was later supplemented by his widow and daughter. Among his many publications were about fifty memorial accounts or tributes of his colleagues. He also published "John James Audubon (1785–1851): An Evaluation of the Man and His Work," *New-York Historical Society Quarterly*, Oct. 1956, pp. 315–50. Biographies of Murphy are by Ernst Mayr, *Yearbook of American Philosophical Society of Philadelphia for 1973* (1974): 131–35, and by Dean Amadon, *The Auk* 91 (1974): 1–9. Historical information on the American Museum of Natural History, including Murphy's role, is in Geoffrey Hellman, *Bankers, Bones and Beetles* (1968), and in Douglas J. Preston, *Dinosaurs in the Attic* (1986).

ELIZABETH NOBLE SHOR

MURPHY, Robert Daniel (28 Oct. 1894–9 Jan. 1978), diplomat, was born in Milwaukee, Wisconsin, the son of Francis Patrick Murphy, a railroad worker, and Catherine Louise Schmitz. Of Irish Roman Catholic and immigrant German stock, Murphy obtained a scholarship to Marquette Academy and later worked at the Treasury Department while earning a law degree from George Washington University (LL.B., 1920).

Murphy joined the foreign service in 1921 and was assigned a post as vice consul in Zurich. In that year he married Mildred Taylor; they had three daughters. Transferred to Munich, Germany, later in 1921, he remained a vice consul until 1925. Then, after a short period as consul in Seville, he served in the State De-

partment from 1926 to 1930, meanwhile earning his LL.M. degree from George Washington University (1928). In 1930 he was assigned to Paris, where Ambassador William Bullitt made the hard-working Murphy counselor of embassy in 1939. His affable personality and excellent French enabled him to make a wide range of contacts that helped the embassy produce accurate analyses of prewar political conditions.

In May 1940, after the Nazi invasion of France and Bullitt's return to the United States, Murphy was assigned to Vichy, the capital of Marshal Philippe Pétain's collaborationist government. As chargé d'affaires, he headed the embassy until Ambassador William Leahy arrived in January 1941 with instructions to strengthen American relations with Pétain. While Murphy did not formulate this "Vichy Gamble" policy, he became closely identified with it.

Early in 1941 President Franklin D. Roosevelt named Murphy his personal representative and sent him to North Africa to stiffen the resistance of French administrators. In February, Murphy negotiated an agreement with General Maxime Weygand providing American nonmilitary supplies to North Africa. American vice consuls were to verify the shipments.

After Pearl Harbor, Murphy continued to keep in touch with Vichy administrators. In July 1942 the Allies decided to invade North Africa (Operation TORCH) in early November. With only three months to D day, and having failed to obtain the approval of French officials in North Africa, Murphy turned to General Henri Giraud and Admiral François Darlan (the Vichy commander in chief) for cooperation. When the landings took place on 8 November 1942, Darlan happened to be in Algiers, and in cooperation with the Allies, helped obtain a French surrender. Murphy and General Mark Clark then negotiated the Clark-Darlan Agreement, which left Vichy administrators in office but gave the Allies control of French facilities. Roosevelt and General Dwight Eisenhower upheld the agreement, but much of the press in the United States and Great Britain criticized Murphy for making the Darlan deal. Nevertheless, at the Casablanca conference in January 1943, Murphy helped Giraud persuade American military authorities to rearm the French colonial forces in North Africa.

Murphy's influence on French affairs waned as Charles de Gaulle and the Free French replaced the "Giraudists," but by late 1943 the Italian surrender had shifted Allied strategic attention to the European mainland. As political adviser to Eisenhower, Murphy helped in the surrender negotiations. While serving on the Allied Advisory Council for Italy, he came into contact with two Communist leaders: Andrei Vyshinsky, whom he escorted during a tour of Italy, and Marshal Josip Tito, from whom he learned about the determination of the Yugoslavs to regain control of their country and to expand in the direction of Trieste.

In the fall of 1944 Murphy again became political adviser to Eisenhower, now supreme allied commander. Certain inadequacies in the plans being made for the occupation of Germany disturbed him. There was no guaranteed access to Berlin and no clear-cut policy regarding France. After Germany's defeat, Murphy attended the Potsdam conference (July 1945). From 1945 to 1949 Murphy remained in Germany with the rank of ambassador, and he served as political adviser to General Lucius Clay, the head of the military government in Germany. He took part in the talks leading to Bizonia, the fusion of the British and American occupation zones, and he supported the decision to introduce a new currency. When the Soviet Union threatened to blockade Berlin, Murphy advocated a strong response and came close to resigning when Washington decided to supply Berlin only by air. Murphy left Germany in February 1949, at the height of the Berlin airlift, to become director of the State Department's Office of German and Austrian Affairs in Washington.

In September 1949 Murphy was appointed ambassador to Belgium, a post he held for two years. In the spring of 1952, after the Japanese peace treaty was finally signed, he became the first postwar American ambassador to Japan. Japan was rapidly moving into self-government, and the Korean cease-fire talks were proceeding at Panmunjom under the supervision of General Clark. When Eisenhower became president in 1953 and named a new ambassador to Japan, Murphy stayed on as Clark's adviser. The armistice in Korea was finally signed in July 1953, and Secretary of State John Foster Dulles made Murphy assistant secretary of state for United Nations affairs.

In November 1953 Murphy was advanced to the post of deputy under secretary for political affairs, becoming under secretary for political affairs in August 1959—the third ranking position in the State Department and the highest available to a career officer. In Murphy's words: "The work was grueling, but it concerned the entire sweep of American foreign policy and diplomacy and it provided my most satisfying years." In 1956 he received the rank of "career ambassador," a rank held by only three other foreign service officers.

When the negotiations between Italy and Yugoslavia over Trieste reached a standstill in 1954, Eisenhower sent Murphy to Belgrade, where his acquaintance with Tito opened the way for compromise and settlement. In 1955 another trip to Belgrade paved the way for better military and economic cooperation between Yugoslavia and the United States.

In 1956 Murphy headed a mission to sway British prime minister Anthony Eden from using force during the Suez crisis. In 1958 he helped negotiate an agreement between Tunisia and France that anticipated the independence of France's African colonies. Murphy also served as Eisenhower's troubleshooter in mid-1958 when the president sent marines to Lebanon. His negotiations paved the way for General Fuad Chehab to succeed Camille Chamoun as president. During a month-long sojourn in the Middle East Murphy emphasized in talks with Gamal Abdel Nasser, Hussein I, and Karim Kassem, the new dictator in Iraq, that the

United States had no intention of keeping its troops in Lebanon.

During his last year in office, Murphy orchestrated a plan whereby Nikita Khrushchev would visit the United States, to be followed by an Eisenhower tour of the Soviet Union. Khrushchev did visit the United States, but because of the U-2 incident Eisenhower's visit was canceled.

After his retirement in 1959, Murphy was elected to the board of directors of Corning Glass Works and became president of Corning International. For the next eighteen years he remained associated with Corning, becoming chairman of the board in 1964 and honorary chairman of Corning International in 1971. During these years he wrote his memoirs, carried on extensive correspondence, and served on a number of special boards, including the president's Foreign Intelligence Advisory Board (1961, 1965); the Intelligence Oversight Board (chairman, 1976); an ad hoc advisory group on Vietnam (Mar. 1968); and the Commission on the Organization of the Government for the Conduct of Foreign Policy (1973–1974). Murphy died in New York City.

Having devoted most of his professional life to implementing official policies, Murphy felt strongly that "a professional diplomat understands when he accepts government service that he is obedient to official policy, no matter how repugnant a particular line may be to him personally." Murphy was thorough and dependable, giving the impression of open-mindedness and of reaching conclusions only after careful examination. Harold Macmillan said of him: "there is no man with whom I had a more pleasant relationship, often in difficult and baffling circumstances, and whose character I grew so quickly both to appreciate and admire." A poor boy who worked his way to positions of the highest responsibility, Murphy exemplified the tradition of Horatio Alger. He circulated with ease among diplomats and generals, smoothing ruffled feelings and locating acceptable compromises. He was the consummate diplomat.

• Murphy's papers, deposited in the Hoover Institution, Stanford, Calif., comprise 146 boxes mostly devoted to correspondence with some 1,000 individuals and 24 boxes of speeches and writings. They have been catalogued by Grace M. Hawes in *Robert D. Murphy: A Register of His Papers in the Hoover Institution Archives* (1989). There is no book-length biography, but Murphy's memoirs, *Diplomat among Warriors* (1964), which covers his life in considerable detail from childhood to retirement, is accurate and well balanced. See also Kenneth Pendar, *Adventure in Diplomacy* (1945); Dwight Eisenhower, *Crusade in Europe* (1948) and *Waging Peace* (1965); William Langer, *Our Vichy Gamble* (1947); William Leahy, *I Was There* (1950); and Harold Macmillan, *The Blast of War* (1967). An obituary is in the *New York Times*, 11 Jan. 1978.

ARTHUR L. FUNK

MURPHY, Turk (16 Dec. 1915–30 May 1987), jazz trombonist and bandleader, was born Melvin Edward Alton Murphy in Palermo, California, the son of Alton

E. Murphy, a ragtime trumpet player and drummer, and Mildred G. Pickering. After beginning on cornet, at age twelve Murphy switched to trombone, and upon entering high school in Williams, California, in 1929 he studied privately with Joe Pardee, a jazz trumpeter. Murphy played trombone in the school and town bands and earned the nickname "the Terrible Turk" for his aggressive football playing. Following graduation in 1933 Murphy left home to join Merle Howard's orchestra, where he met saxophonist Bob Helm, later a close musical associate. With Howard, Murphy and Helm toured the western states for almost a year, playing with trumpeter Bob Scobey at a jam session in Seattle.

In 1935 Murphy worked in El Paso, Texas, with Val Bender's band and then with Will Osborne, with whom he spent about a year touring hotels throughout the Midwest and South; he repeated that itinerary with Mal Hallett's band through late 1936, when he quit the road and settled in Oakland, California. Yearning to play jazz instead of commercial music, Murphy formed a band with Helm, who had since switched to clarinet, trumpeter Byron Berry, drummer Bill Dart, and three others. Sharing an apartment with Helm and Berry, Murphy worked as an automobile mechanic and studied jazz records from the 1920s, particularly the Louis Armstrong Hot Fives and Sevens with trombonist Kid Ory. Because of his limited exposure to formal compositional techniques and classically based rules of voice leading, Murphy also began studying theory and composition with Berkeley instructor Walter Scott. Starting in January 1938 Murphy and Helm played at jam sessions with ragtime pianist Paul Lingle in Redwood Canyon, where a frequent participant was trumpeter Lu Watters, an enthusiast of King Oliver, Jelly Roll Morton, and Louis Armstrong.

In 1940 Watters, aiming for the sound of King Oliver's Creole Jazz Band, set about rehearsing a New Orleans–style group that included Murphy. Initially there was no work in sight for a band playing that kind of music, but by the summer the band, which by this time included Murphy, Helm, Scobey, Berry, Dart, ragtime specialist Wally Rose on piano, and banjoist Clancy Hayes, was playing at concerts staged at the Dawn Club in downtown San Francisco. The Yerba Buena Jazz Band (YBJB) had been born.

With Ellis Horne replacing Helm on clarinet, the addition of banjoist Russ Bennett, and Dick Lammi on tuba, the band made its first recordings for the Jazz Man label in December 1941, thereby sparking the New Orleans Revival, which in turn sparked a major controversy in the world of jazz. Only hard-core collectors of classic 1920s jazz were prepared for what they heard, and even these were amazed at the fidelity with which these young men captured the spirit of their models. Equally impressive was their repertoire, consisting entirely of authentic stomps and blues and, even more surprisingly, ragtime pieces that had not been played since the pre-jazz era. Harking back to the improvised counterpoint of Oliver but with a heavier texture and more pronounced ragtime rhythms, the YBJB's ensemble sound was like nothing else extant in jazz. The band played at excessive volume, with little or no dynamic shading, and with a wanton disregard for proper intonation, thus fueling a controversy that remained unabated for the rest of the century. It obviously had little in common with the polished dixieland of the Bob Crosby band and even less with the increasingly popular jam session approach of Muggsy Spanier and Eddie Condon. With the powerful but sober trumpets of Watters and Scobey maintaining a forceful lead, Murphy's lusty trombone providing an oaken link between the horns and the rhythm section, and Horne's beautifully intoned contrapuntal figures weaving in and out of the ensemble, the band literally created its own niche in the jazz scene. Although another, more ambitious recording date took place in March 1942, with the advent of World War II the men dispersed. While they wanted to enlist en masse and continue playing together while in service, all but Watters and Murphy were rejected, the latter entering the navy in June. In the service Murphy received special permission to participate in several San Francisco concerts featuring legendary New Orleans trumpeter Bunk Johnson. Recordings of that band, which also included Horne, Hayes, pianist Burt Bales, banjoist Pat Patton, and bassist Squire Girsback, were made in early 1944.

In November 1945 Murphy was discharged, and after Watters reassembled the Yerba Buena Jazz Band in January 1946, they opened at the Dawn Club in March, this time with Helm on clarinet and banjoist Harry Mordecai taking the place of Hayes and Bennett. Many more recordings on the West Coast label and weekly broadcasts over KGO followed through 1946, but on New Year's Day 1947 the Dawn Club closed. Watters found a new location in El Cerrito across the bay, and in June the band opened at the renamed Hambone Kelly's.

While still a member of the Watters band, on 31 December 1947, Murphy recorded his first leader date, using a pared down personnel of Scobey, Helm, Bales, and Mordecai. This session appeared on the Jazz Man label and was later reissued on Good Time Jazz, the company for which Murphy continued to record through July 1951. The Watters band, which had been struggling throughout 1948 and 1949, finally disbanded on New Year's Eve, and from January 1950 on Murphy took over leadership. Although he continued to use Scobey and others from the Watters band, in January 1950 he replaced Helm with the gifted young clarinetist Bill Napier, whose liquid tone and smooth manner of phrasing provided a perfect contrast to Murphy's purposefully rugged style. More personnel changes followed in 1950, the most significant being that of Don Kinch for Scobey, who had recently left Watters to form his own band. During the spring and summer the band worked in Los Angeles, broadcasting from the Garden of Allah three times a week. Live performances from the Cinegrill were later issued on the Fairmont label. The band also played in San Diego, Denver, and Reno and in late August began a six-month run at Las Vegas's Last Frontier Hotel. In February 1951 the band returned to San Francisco, but work was scarce, and Murphy took a temporary job in a steel mill. In May, however, he reassembled the band—now with Kinch, Helm, Patton, and three others—for a job in Los Angeles and in July recorded his fifth session for Good Time Jazz. With Watters's retirement from music in early 1951, Helm and Rose went with Murphy permanently.

Beginning in August 1951 Murphy's band played in Sacramento, Denver, and Los Angeles. Returning to San Francisco, Murphy disbanded temporarily, working as a sideman in a house band. In January 1952 he took over the Venetian Room in San Francisco's Italian Village, and, with a band including Bob Short on cornet and tuba, Helm, Rose, Lammi, and blues vocalist Claire Austin, maintained a successful residency for two years, after which the band played in New Orleans and New York. From January 1953 through March 1956 the Murphy band recorded extensively for Columbia and in July 1957 appeared at the Newport Jazz Festival, where they were recorded by Verve. Murphy recorded two more albums for Verve, in 1957 and 1958, while his contemporaneous broadcasts from San Francisco's Easy Street were later released on the Dawn Club label. With constantly varying personnel, from 1959 through 1986 the band's performances appeared on labels such as Roulette, Victor, Atlantic, GHB, and Merry Makers.

In September 1960 Murphy and his pianist, Pete Clute, took over a waterfront saloon in San Francisco; under the name of Earthquake McGoon's it remained active through 1984, albeit in different locations over the years. During this period the band also played at Disneyland, toured Australia and Europe in 1974, and in 1977 appeared at the St. Louis Ragtime Festival. In 1981 the band performed at the Breda Jazz Festival in Holland and after the closing of McGoon's worked regularly at the Fairmont Hotel in San Francisco. In early 1987 Murphy appeared at a tribute concert at Carnegie Hall before returning to San Francisco, where he continued to play until a month before his death there.

The recorded performances of the YBJB remain definitive examples of latter-day, New Orleans–style polyphony, with solos only being used for timbral variety and pacing. Murphy largely followed this approach in his own groups, but he also featured his own undistinguished vocals, a distinct departure from the austere Watters concept of uncompromised orchestral jazz. As a composer, Murphy was responsible for at least two staples in the Watters canon, the virtuosic "Trombone Rag" and "Minstrels of Annie Street," and for his own group he composed instrumentals such as "Brother Lowdown," "Turk's Blues," "Little John's Rag," "Bay City," and "Mesa 'Round." Regardless of personnel, the Murphy band always had its own distinct sound, characterized by the leader's brash, assertive, Ory-styled trombone, itself an inspiration to scores of younger, like-minded players the world over.

• Murphy's early life and his career through the late 1950s are treated thoroughly in Lester Koenig, "The Turk Murphy Story," notes to *Turk Murphy's Jazz Band: Favorites* (Good Time Jazz FCD-60-011; 1986). Of equal importance is the 51-page booklet accompanying the four-disc complete collection, *Lu Watters' Yerba Buena Jazz Band* (Good Time Jazz 4GTJCD-4409-2; 1993). See also Jim Goggin and Peter Clute, *The Great Jazz Revival: A Pictorial Celebration of Traditional Jazz* (1994). An obituary is in the *New York Times*, 1 June 1987.

JACK SOHMER

MURRAH, Pendleton (1826–4 Aug. 1865), governor of Texas, was born probably near Maplesville, Chilton County, Alabama. His mother, whose last name was Murrah, was unmarried at the time of his birth, and he was placed in a home for orphans supported by a charitable society of the Baptist church. He received his early education at the orphanage, then the society financed his college education at Brown University in Providence, Rhode Island. He graduated in 1848. He moved first to Plantersville, in Dallas County, Alabama, where he was admitted to the bar and practiced law. He was ashamed of his mother and his birth, yet although he shunned his mother after he moved back into central Alabama, he provided her with money. He developed tuberculosis and in 1850 left for Texas, seeking a healthier climate. He settled in Harrison County, where he established a law practice. In October of that year he married Sue Ellen Taylor.

Active in politics during the 1850s, Murrah was connected primarily with the Democratic party and opposed to Sam Houston. He ran unsuccessfully for Congress in 1855. In 1857 he was elected as a representative to the state legislature from Harrison County. By 1858 he was an important enough member of the Democratic party that he became a member of the state executive committee. In 1860 Murrah was an alternate John C. Breckinridge elector.

Murrah's health worsened at the outbreak of the Civil War, and his career appeared to be at an end. The Texas secession convention considered him when they named representatives to the provisional Congress of the Confederacy, but Murrah's health forced him to withdraw his name. He also joined the Fourteenth Texas Infantry as quartermaster, but he was unable to serve in the field. Finally, he received an appointment in the Quartermaster's Department of the Confederate States Army in 1862.

In 1863, despite his earlier problems, Murrah ran for governor. He was supported by most of the regular Democratic leadership against Thomas J. Chambers, who had been a critic of the administration of President Jefferson Davis. Murrah won the election on 2 November 1863 by a vote of 17,486 to 12,254, and he took office three days later.

As governor, Murrah generally supported the Davis government but found himself in constant conflict with local military officials. Like other Confederate governors, Murrah struggled with the difficulties of financing state government in the face of growing inflation and inadequate resources. The state and the military became engaged in a battle for manpower, supplies, and money as the war progressed. Questions concerning the impressment of slaves by the army and numerous other issues tainted the relationship between civilians and the military.

Among all of the conflicts, however, Murrah's efforts to keep troops within the state and to raise money through the purchase of cotton were the most troublesome. He and other political leaders in the Trans-Mississippi had seen Confederate troops stripped from the region for service in the East. Murrah argued for keeping Texas state forces within the state to protect the frontier, and he opposed their conscription. Ultimately General Edmund Kirby Smith, commander of the Trans-Mississippi Department, allowed some military organizations to remain under state control. Keeping Texas troops on the frontier led to abuses, however, and Murrah vigorously tried to keep deserters and draft dodgers from taking advantage of the frontier service. This fight over states' rights persisted throughout the rest of the war.

Murrah and Smith also had a stormy relationship on the question of the Texas cotton bureau. To fund the state's government and military operations, the Texas military board authorized the governor to purchase cotton and export it. Planters who sold half their cotton to the state were allowed to export the rest to Mexico. The state cotton board operated in direct conflict with a similar organization authorized by Smith. Smith resolved this particular conflict by authorizing the impressment of cotton, driving the Texas bureau from the market in the summer of 1864.

Although he tried to protect Texas and its people with his various policies, Murrah was not a popular governor, nor was he particularly effective. Rumors circulated that he was involved personally and financially in the trade of cotton for supplies across the Mexican border, and, whether true or not, the accusations undercut his authority. In the last year of the war, because of his illness, he was unable personally to play an active role in public affairs.

When defeat appeared inevitable, Murrah pursued a fruitless attempt to negotiate peace terms with the victorious Federal authorities and prevent military occupation. He sent William P. Ballinger and Ashbel Smith to New Orleans on 24 May 1865 to confer with General E. R. S. Canby. In addition he called a special session of the Tenth Texas Legislature and proclaimed an election for a state constitutional convention to reorganize the government. Federal authorities prevented that from taking place and refused to accept Murrah's terms of surrender.

At the end of the war, Murrah fled Austin on 11 June 1865, escaping to Mexico with other Confederate officials. Conditions on the trail and persisting tuberculosis ended his life within two months. He died at Monterrey, Mexico, where he was buried in an unmarked grave.

• Murrah's gubernatorial papers are in the Texas State Archives, Austin. The Pendleton Murrah vertical file in the Center for American History, University of Texas at Austin, contains family information on his private life. Standard studies include Benny E. Deuson, "Pendleton Murrah," in *Ten Texans in Gray*, ed. W. C. Nunn (1968), and Ralph A. Wooster, "Texas," in *The Confederate Governors*, ed. W. Buck Yearns (1985).

CARL H. MONEYHON

MURRAY, Alexander (12 July 1755–6 Oct. 1821), naval officer, was born in Chestertown, Maryland, the son of William Murray, a physician, and Ann Smith. He went to sea in his early youth and at age eighteen commanded a merchant ship in the European trade. When the revolutionary war commenced, he wanted a commission in the Continental navy but discovered that the navy had too few fighting ships to offer him such an opportunity. Hence, in 1776 he joined the First Maryland Regiment of the Continental army as a lieutenant and campaigned under General George Washington at New York City. Severely wounded by a bursting cannon, he recovered to take part in the battle of White Plains, 28 October 1776. Promoted to captain, he was with Washington in the ensuing patriot retreat across New Jersey. In 1777 he applied for a naval commission, but although he was promised one by various congressmen, it was not forthcoming. He accepted command of a privateer, the *General Mercer*, at the end of 1777 and began raiding British shipping. In 1778 he commanded the *Saratoga*, which he surrendered to the enemy. After being released from captivity, he took command of the *Columbus*, then the *Revenge*, and was once again seized.

Released a second time, Murray at last received his much-coveted commission as lieutenant in the Continental navy on 20 July 1781. Serving on the frigate *Trumbull*, he was wounded and captured when the British frigate *Isis* battered his ship into submission. After his third release, in 1782 he married Mary Miller, with whom he had one child. He returned to privateer service, commanding the *Prosperity* on a voyage to the West Indies and capturing a more powerful enemy privateer in an unequal fight. He then joined in a successful foray against New Providence, Bahamas, with a combined American-Spanish force. Appointed a navy lieutenant on the frigate *Alliance*, the last Continental warship in active service, he held that position until *Alliance* was decommissioned in August 1785. Thereupon he left the navy, settled with his wife in Philadelphia, and became a prosperous merchant. In 1794 he sought command of one of six frigates being built for operations against the Barbary pirates but was not successful.

Murray's hopes for naval service improved in the late 1790s, when tense relations between the United States and France were aggravated by French depredations against American shipping on the high seas. In 1798 Congress responded by abrogating the Franco-American treaty of 1778, appropriating money to expand both the army and the navy, and commencing undeclared naval war with France. On 1 July 1798 Murray, whom Benjamin Stoddert, secretary of the navy, described as "a Man of good temper—good sense—honor and Bravery," was commissioned captain in the U.S. Navy and given command of the corvette *Montezuma*, twenty guns. In October Murray sailed for the West Indies in command of a squadron of three small ships with orders to seize and destroy French commerce and protect American trade. Misfortune struck his weak and undergunned squadron off Guadeloupe on 20 November, when the French frigate *L'Insurgente*, forty guns, captured one of his ships, *Retaliation*, fourteen guns, Lieutenant William Bainbridge commanding, and almost seized the others as well. Although Murray was not blamed by President John Adams and Bainbridge for this French success, he was censured by his colleague, Captain Thomas Truxtun, commander of the frigate *Constellation*, who declared that Murray possessed "the soul of a purser rather than an officer." On 9 March 1799 Murray captured one prize, the brig *Les Amis*, then sailed for home, reaching Philadelphia on 11 May.

Murray was struck down by yellow fever later that month and compelled to surrender command of the *Montezuma*, but he was promised a frigate by Stoddert as soon as he recovered. Consequently, on 13 June 1799 Murray took command of the newly commissioned *Insurgente*, captured five months before by the *Constellation*, and ordered to sail in European waters, showing the flag and seizing prizes, before returning to the West Indies. He left Chesapeake Bay on 14 August, visited Lisbon, Cádiz, Gibraltar, Madeira, and Tenerife, then set a course for Cayenne, French Guiana, which he reached on 31 October. In all this sailing, to his "very sensible mortification," he had not captured a single French vessel, a situation he attributed to the "crazy state" of his masts and spars. Repairing his ship in British Antigua during January 1800, he partially redeemed his cruise by taking two small prizes later that month in the Leeward Islands. In February he visited Jamaica and Havana, then sailed into Baltimore on 13 March. Despite his lack of success with *Insurgente*, he was appointed commander of the *Constellation* on 19 April and sent to Santo Domingo. There he captured two more prizes and on 25 July assumed command of the Santo Domingo Station when Captain Silas Talbot, commander of the frigate *Constitution*, went home. Murray returned to the United States in October, quickly refitted, and sailed on one more voyage to the West Indies before the war ended.

When the navy was reduced in 1801, Murray retained his commission in the peacetime establishment as commander of a completely refurbished *Constellation*. In 1802 he was ordered as part of a four-ship squadron to the Mediterranean Sea to make war on Tripoli by blockading the port. Murray was hampered by a ship that was too large for its assigned duty. Also, he was timid in executing his orders; he performed over the next few months, according to Midshipman Henry Wadsworth, like an "old woman." In September Murray reached a nadir when he allowed the *Franklin* to be seized by Tripolitan corsairs without firing a shot. Returning to the United States on 15 March 1802, he did not go to sea again until late 1805, when he commanded the frigate *Adams* on a commerce-protecting cruise in the North Atlantic. Thereafter, he served off the Carolina coast.

On 4 January 1808 Murray was part of a court that examined American officers who had surrendered the *Chesapeake* to the British ship *Leopard*, finding them guilty of various levels of negligence, dismissing one from service, and suspending one for five years. He assumed command of naval facilities at Philadelphia in 1808 and three years later became ranking officer in the navy by seniority. He served at Philadelphia until he died at his home near the city.

• Primary sources on Murray's role in the undeclared war with France and against the Tripolitans are in Dudley Knox, ed., *Naval Documents Related to the Quasi-War between the United States and France, 1797–1801* (7 vols., 1935–1938), and Knox, ed., *Naval Documents Related to the United States Wars with the Barbary Powers* (6 vols., 1939–1944). Information on his service in the American Revolution and general background is in Charles O. Paullin, *The Navy of the American Revolution* (1906); Gardner W. Allen, *The Naval History of the American Revolution* (2 vols., 1913); and William M. Fowler, Jr., *Rebels under Sail: The American Navy during the Revolution* (1976). His roles in the undeclared wars with France and with the Tripolitans are delineated by Allen, *Our Naval War with France* (1909) and *Our Navy and the Barbary Corsairs* (1905); Glenn Tucker, *Dawn like Thunder: The Barbary Wars and the Birth of the U.S. Navy* (1963); Howard P. Nash, *The Forgotten Wars: The Role of the U.S. Navy in the Quasi-War with France and the Barbary Wars, 1798–1805* (1968); and Fowler, *Jack Tars and Commodores: The American Navy, 1783–1815* (1984). An obituary is in *Poulson's American Daily Advertiser*, 8 Oct. 1821.

PAUL DAVID NELSON

MURRAY, Arthur (4 Apr. 1895–3 Mar. 1991), ballroom dancing teacher, was born Arthur Teichman in New York City, the son of Abraham Teichman and Sarah Schor, Austrian immigrant bakers. He quit high school to work at a succession of menial jobs, while studying architectural drafting at Cooper Union. His dancing, which began as a weekend hobby, blossomed into an ambition when he won the waltz contest at a local settlement house in 1912. He followed this triumph with a prize from the Grand Central Palace, a taxi dance hall, and he was promptly hired as a dance teacher. He also worked in a small studio for G. Hepburn Wilson.

Murray resolved to seek training with the renowned Irene and Vernon Castle. In 1914, for the grand sum of $200, he enrolled in their teacher's course at Castle House in New York, where he mastered the elegant Castle Walk and Hesitation Waltz, although he continued to oversee the bumptious turkey trot at the Palace. That summer the Castles employed him at their Marblehead, Massachusetts, studio.

A ballroom dancer called Baroness de Cuddleston, whom Murray had met at Castle House, engaged the teenager as her partner for the season at an Asheville,

North Carolina, resort. At her suggestion, he dropped his family name, Teichman. Immediately he became the favorite dancing partner of Mrs. George Vanderbilt and taught fashionable dances to her daughter at the Biltmore estate. He angrily confronted the baroness because she pocketed $47.50 for these lessons and gave him only $2.50. His revenge came soon, however, when he replaced her as the hotel social director. For several years he would return home during the slow winter season to try such odd jobs as reporter, photographer's apprentice, and salesman.

Seeking further education, Murray enrolled for two years in Georgia Tech in 1919, majoring in business administration. In the evenings he taught dancing at the Georgian Terrace Hotel in Atlanta, where he established Le Club de Vingt for prominent social families. Within a year more than 1,000 youngsters enrolled. He opened his first real dance studio in 1920, and on 27 March broadcast the first of many dance music programs over the radio. He continued to experiment with ways to reach new students through correspondence courses. At first he invested in Kinetescopes (rapidly moving pictures of dancers), but then he opted for simplified diagrams with footprints and dotted lines to indicate the dancers' pathway. Although popularly called "the man with the footprints," this device was not original to him.

Murray pioneered in the style of advertising that promised to share the secrets of "How I Became Popular Overnight," which drew from his own memories of being a "first-class failure." One of his first advertisements, placed in *True Story Magazine*, drew 40,000 responses, and another in the *New York Times* produced similar results. He followed these up with ads that depicted a man with beautiful women clinging to either elbow and a caption that boasted, "Thirty Days Ago They Laughed at Me!"

Murray's mail-order business was so successful that he returned in 1924 to New York, where he established an elegant studio on Forty-third Street. From a peak of ninety clerks employed to open mail, the decline was so noticeable by 1928 that he phased out correspondence courses and concentrated on a national system of franchises.

In teaching, Murray viewed five steps as fundamental to ballroom dance: walk, side-step, balance, pivot, and waltz. These could be easily depicted through his footprint charts that were a staple of the more than fifteen books credited to him. He also used radio to broadcast directions for dance steps (as well as to publicize his books) from the 1920s through the 1940s. After he married Kathryn Kohnfelder in 1925, she took over the preparation of dance books and articles, including *How to Become a Good Dancer* (1938). They had twin daughters who also became dancers. From 1950 and for almost ten years on and off, Kathryn was the star of "The Arthur Murray Party" on major networks for television, while he remained out of the spotlight. His indefatigable search for new dances led him in 1960 to the Peppermint Lounge, where he promised that, despite his personal dislike of the

dance, anyone "can become a Twist expert in six easy lessons" at his studio.

By 1943 Murray operated studios in forty-seven American cities, and by 1952 he ran an international franchise system that boasted more than 200 studios with an advertising bill of $3 million. When he sold his business in 1965, there were 350 franchised studios (fifty in foreign countries) and an annual volume of $25 to $30 million. Such phenomenal growth was not achieved without some missteps. In 1946, aggrieved by his autocratic ways and a multitude of petty rules with fines for infractions, Murray's instructors went on strike for better pay and working conditions. In 1960 the Federal Trade Commission ordered the company to cease high-pressure sales tactics. In 1964 Murray was arrested as a reluctant witness and made to testify before a Minneapolis grand jury investigating reports of other dance schools' fraudulent business practices. Two months later he announced his resignation as president and sold all his stock in the company, but he remained a consultant. In retirement he pursued art collecting and stock market investing. He died at his home in Honolulu, Hawaii.

Arthur Murray's name was a household word by the 1940s. The movie *The Fleet's In* (1942) featured a Johnny Mercer song with the catchy refrain, "Arthur Murray taught me dancing in a hurry." Despite his enormous success in life, Murray never forgot that he had once been so "painfully self-conscious" that he was fired from ten jobs in six months. In "How I Overcame an Inferiority Complex," from his book *Let's Dance!*, Murray describes how dance "liberated" him from low self-esteem. "I can well testify," he wrote in *Arthur Murray's Dance Book*, "to the therapeutic value of dancing." This insight inspired him to set up dances for troubled teenagers at New York's Psychiatric Hospital during the 1950s. He even volunteered to teach the lessons. Murray was able to use his own feelings of insecurity as a way of selling his product to others who suffered as he did, which explains why Lesson One in his earliest correspondence course (1923) was entitled "How to Gain Confidence." His ad copy "They Laughed at Me!" and self-serving confessions in many of his books intimated to eager subscribers that dance was the pathway to instant popularity.

• Arthur Murray's papers are in the Dance Collection at the New York Public Library for the Performing Arts, Lincoln Center. Murray's books on dance include *The Modern Dances: An Introductory Course* (1922; rev. ed., 1923); *Social Dancing, Part II* (192?); *The Modern Dances* (1925); *Arthur Murray Shows You How to Master Dancing* (c. 1930); *How to Become a Good Dancer* (1938; rev. ed., 1941, 1942, 1947; revised in 1954 and 1959 with the subtitle *With Dance Secrets by Kathryn Murray*); *The Arthur Murrays' Dance Secrets* (1946); *Dance Instructions with Music for Every Type of Social Dancing* (c. 1946); *Arthur Murray's Dance Book* (1942); *Let's Learn to Dance* (1951); *Let's Dance* (1953 and 1955); *Ballroom Dancing* (1953 and 1959); and *The Dance Book of Arthur Murray* (n.d.). Kathryn Murray, with Betty Hannah Hoffman, wrote an insouciant but informative biography, *My Husband, Arthur Murray* (1960). An early description of his New York activities is in Milton MacKaye, "Profiles: The Wallflower's Friend," *New Yorker*, 6 Jan. 1934, pp. 27–30. See also Sylvia Dannett and Frank Rachel, *Down Memory Lane: Arthur Murray's Picture Story of Social Dancing* (1954).

MAUREEN NEEDHAM

MURRAY, David (15 Oct. 1830–6 Mar. 1905), professor and educational administrator, was born in Bovina, Delaware County, New York, the son of William Murray and Jean Black, farmers. When he was five years old, Murray severely injured his leg in an accident and spent more than a year confined to bed. While recovering, he was given a biography of George Washington, which he read avidly and considered his lifelong guide. He completed his education at Delaware Academy and Fergusonville Academy and entered Union College, where he graduated with honors in 1852.

He accepted a position as a teacher and assistant principal at Albany Academy in New York, and in 1856 he became its principal. In 1863 Murray accepted a position as professor of mathematics and astronomy at Rutgers College in New Brunswick, New Jersey, where he quickly earned a reputation as an excellent teacher and efficient administrator. He also played an influential role as a civic and church leader in the city of New Brunswick. In 1867 Murray married Martha Nielsen; they had three children.

During these years Murray became a mentor to the first Japanese students in the United States, who had been sent to Rutgers in 1866 under the auspices of the Dutch Reformed church. His experience with these students marked the beginning of his lifelong interest in Japan and the education of its people. Following the Meiji Restoration of 1869, the new Japanese leaders recognized the crucial role that education would play in their attempts to modernize their country, and they looked abroad for both advice and models to emulate. In 1872 Arinori Mori, the Japanese chargé d'affaires and acting minister to the United States, sought the opinions of a number of prominent American educators about the future direction of Japan's public school system. Murray's long response to Mori's request, in which he stressed the need to adapt the new educational system to the national culture and avoid radical changes that were not harmonious with Japanese traditions, led to an invitation to Japan as an adviser to the Ministry of Education and national superintendent of Educational Affairs.

Murray and his family arrived in Tokyo in June 1873, and during his five-and-one-half-year tenure he reported directly to the minister of education, Fujimaro Tanaka. His work included a wide range of responsibilities, including inspecting educational conditions in the various prefectures, advising on the training of teachers, choosing and supervising the purchase of equipment, recommending curricular revisions, introducing foreign textbooks and teacher manuals, and advising on the construction and furnishing of new school buildings.

As a ranking adviser he was charged with implementing the important Education Order of 1872, which envisioned a modern, comprehensive school system based on the principles of universality and compulsory attendance. Modeled on the French Napoleonic model of centralized authority, it allowed considerable decentralization in financial matters. The government favored compulsory education but as a result of limited financial resources argued that, since local areas would benefit, they should pay the bulk of the cost. Because of the country's political and economic realities, the plan was never fully implemented.

Murray played a key role in creating Japan's first kindergarten and in the establishment of educational museums. He was especially interested in the newly organized Tokyo University, drawing up the plans and recommending the adoption of a system of university degrees and graduation modeled on those in American and British universities.

Among Murray's important long-term contributions to Japanese education was his advocacy of women's education. From his perspective, the principle of universal education assumed that women, no less than men, should attend school and be equally trained. Murray stressed not only the individual's right to an equal education, but also the advantages accruing to society. It was, he argued, "cheaper to educate the people than to govern the uneducated." In the case of women, he stressed the value of a good education because "the care and supervision of children naturally fall into her hands during their most impressionable years."

In addition to his day-to-day responsibilities, Murray was named a commissioner for Japan's participation in the 1876 Centennial Exposition held in Philadelphia, and he was responsible for organizing the Japanese education exhibition, which won widespread praise. It was during this visit to the United States that he began collecting materials for an educational museum in Japan.

Before leaving Japan, Murray was honored with a letter of praise from the minister of education and was awarded the Order of the Rising Sun by the emperor in recognition of his many contributions to the nation's educational advancement. An often overlooked accomplishment of Murray was his work in persuading the American government to return, in 1883, its portion ($750,000) of the Shimonoseki Indemnity Fund imposed by the western powers in retaliation for Japanese attacks on western vessels in 1863.

Soon after returning from Japan, in early 1880, Murray was appointed secretary of the board of regents of the State University of New York, where his work, including a history of the board of regents, was widely praised. In his final years, Murray served on the Rutgers board of trustees and maintained close ties with the New Brunswick Theological Seminary.

Upon his resignation because of poor health in 1889, he retired to New Brunswick, New Jersey, where he produced a number of historical works, including a *History of Education in New Jersey* (1889),

The Story of Japan (1894, 1906), and *Delaware County, New York: History of the Century, 1797–1897* (1897). His other publications include *Outline of Japanese Education* (1876), the first book on this specialized subject in English.

Of the numerous foreigners who served in Japan during the late nineteenth-century, none did so with greater distinction than Murray, who died in New Brunswick.

• Some of Murray's papers can be found in the archives of Rutgers University; the rest are in the Library of Congress. Other useful sources are Arinori, *Education in Japan: A Series of Letters* (1873); W. I. Chamberlain, *In Memoriam: David Murray* (1915); and Tadashi Kaneko, "Contributions of David Murray to the Modernization of School Administration in Japan," in *The Modernizers: Overseas Students, Foreign Employees, and Meiji Japan,* ed. Ardath W. Burks (1985).

EDWARD R. BEAUCHAMP

MURRAY, Henry Alexander, Jr. (13 May 1893–23 June 1988), biochemist, clinical psychologist, and Melville scholar, was born in New York City, the son of Henry Alexander Murray, Sr., a Scotsman who rose from impoverished circumstances to become a successful investor, and Fannie Morris Babcock, a New York socialite and daughter of eminent financier Samuel Denison Babcock, the founder of the Guaranty Trust Company. Spending the school year in Manhattan and summers on Long Island, Murray grew up in quiet and well-to-do circumstances as the middle of three children. The only apparent anomalies of his youth were an inordinate attachment to his mother, a mild stutter, and strabismus, or slight crossing of the eyes, a condition only partially corrected through a dramatic and somewhat spontaneous operation by a physician on the family dining room table while he was still a boy.

Murray prepared at the Craegie School and Groton Academy before entering in 1911 Harvard University, where he once said wryly that he majored in "rowing, rum, and romanticism." In 1916 he married Josephine Rantoul, a Radcliffe graduate from a prominent Boston family; they had one child.

In 1915 Murray entered the Columbia College of Physicians and Surgeons in New York, where an influential instructor, George Draper, instilled in him the importance of psychological factors in physical illness. After receiving an M.D. in 1919, Murray earned an M.A. in biology (Columbia, 1920) and then returned to Harvard, where he undertook empirical confirmation of the Hasselbach-Henderson equation under the physical chemist L. J. Henderson. This research involved the simultaneous measurement of different variables in a sample of blood, Henderson's success at which led to the subsequent development of blood plasma by other researchers. Murray would later adapt Henderson's blood-grid model to the multivariate study of personality in the 1930s.

From 1920 to 1922 Murray worked as a surgical intern at Presbyterian Hospital in New York. He then accepted a fellowship at the Rockefeller Institute for Medical Research, where he embarked on the study of aging in chick embryos. Beginning in 1924 he also attended at intervals Cambridge University, from which he received a Ph.D. in biochemistry in 1927.

By the mid-1920s Murray's scientific career had begun to change dramatically. His reading in 1923 of the works of Swiss psychiatrist Carl Jung had introduced him to depth psychology. The two met in 1925 and established a lifelong friendship. Within two decades, Murray would become world famous, himself, as a personality theorist and clinical psychologist.

Shortly after being introduced to Jung's ideas, Murray embarked on a forty-year relationship with Christiana Morgan, who became his paramour, confidante, professional working partner, and spiritual companion. Their experiment in the religion of the dyad, although ending tragically with Morgan's suicide in 1967, was meant as a universal prototype for the highest goal of individuation and transcendence envisioned in Jung's system.

Finally, through a series of fortuitous accidents during this period, Murray chanced upon the works of author Herman Melville. Eventually, Melville became a case study for Murray's new theory of personality and the subject of an ambitious biography by Murray. While the work itself was never published, its existence became well known, and its influence loomed large over several decades of Melville scholarship. As Murray's ideas began to appear in various articles and book chapters, he came to be seen as a pioneer in the application of depth psychology to modern literary criticism.

Then in 1927, through the influence of Henderson, Murray returned to Harvard as assistant to eminent psychopathologist Morton Prince, a specialist in hypnosis and multiple personality. In 1926 Prince had endowed the Harvard Psychological Clinic, an experimental research facility in abnormal psychology, in order to unite clinical and experimental psychology in an academic rather than a medical setting. Murray succeeded to the directorship when Prince died in 1929 and, instead of pursuing Prince's interests in dissociation and hypnosis, immediately made the clinic a haven for Freudian and Jungian analysis in Boston. Along with the Harvard neuropsychiatrist Stanley Cobb, who shared this emphasis, Murray colluded to introduce psychoanalysis into the university curriculum and to develop his scientific studies of personality, which he called personology.

Murray's method, bucking the trend in psychology toward large-scale statistical measurements of rat behavior, involved the intensive study of a single human being at many different levels of complexity, using an interdisciplinary team of researchers. Out of these endeavors he developed, with Morgan, the Thematic Apperception Test, still one of the most widely used tools in clinical psychology, and published, with his colleagues at the Harvard Psychological Clinic, *Explorations in Personality* (1938), a groundbreaking textbook in personality research that became the bible of personality theorists for decades and remained in print fifty years later. He followed this with a small monograph on personality, *A Clinical Study of Sentiments*, with Christiana Morgan (1945).

Adapting his knowledge of personality assessment to the war effort, Murray entered the army in 1943 and was commissioned as a major to head up the personnel selection program for the Office of Strategic Services under William "Wild Bill" Donovan. Murray went on to train agents in the United States, England, Europe, and China before his discharge as a lieutenant colonel. For his outstanding contributions he was awarded the Legion of Merit by the War Department in 1946. He was discharged in 1948.

After his return to Harvard University, Murray produced a final report on his work for the OSS, *Assessment of Men* (1948). Then, joining Gordon Allport, Clyde Kluckhohn, and Talcott Parsons in the newly formed Department of Social Relations, he embarked on a 25-year program to study personality in a social context. He launched the personality and culture movement with Kluckhohn (*Personality in Nature, Society, and Culture* [1948]); he studied the dynamics of mythology, both personal and societal (*Myth and Mythmaking* [1970]); and with a new cohort of young investigators he began the experimental assessment of personality in the context of the dyadic encounter. "Aspects of Personality," a report of this work and the sequel to *Explorations*, remained incomplete at the time of his retirement in 1962.

Like Melville's career one hundred years earlier, Murray's meteoric rise during the 1930s was superseded by a period of silence so long that when he died at age ninety-five, barely a single undergraduate in psychology remembered his name. A wide international circle of older associates, however, continued to remember him as witty and urbane, with a grace befitting his privileged station in life, a giant intellect to the end. An avid environmentalist and advocate of world government, he was also fervently antinuclear and a keen supporter of the Democratic party. After the death of his wife in 1962, Murray married Caroline Chandler Fish, who had five children of her own. He died in Cambridge, Massachusetts.

Of Murray's many unfinished projects and unrealized hopes, one can only surmise that each was an aspect of a larger, unfinished life vision. In the eyes of contemporary historians he may have been the American Icarus, who had flown too high. In his own opinion, however, he followed Melville: "If after all these fearful fainting trances, the verdict be, the golden heaven is not gained;—yet, in bold quest thereof, better to sink in boundless deeps, than float on vulgar shoals; and give me, ye Gods, an utter wreck, if wreck I do."

• Murray's papers are at the Harvard University Archives and the Henry A. Murray Research Center for the Study of Lives at Radcliffe College. Murray prepared an introduction to *Pierre; or, The Ambiguities* for Herman Melville's Complete Works series, vol. 7 (1949). His bibliography and a fine collection of papers appear in Edwin S. Schneidman, ed., *Endeavors in Psychology: Selections from the Personology of Henry A. Murray* (1981). A biography emphasizing Murray's relationship with Christiana Morgan is Forrest G. Robinson, *Love's Story Told: A Life of Henry A. Murray* (1992), but a better account is Claire Douglas, *Translate This Darkness: The Life of Christiana Morgan* (1993). Assessments of Murray's contributions to psychology appear in R. W. White, "Exploring Personality the Long Way: The Study of Lives," in *Further Explorations in Personality*, ed. A. I. Rabin et al. (1981), pp. 3–19; Salvatore R. Maddi and Paul T. Costa, *Humanism in Personology: Allport, Maslow, and Murray* (1972); and Calvin S. Hall and Gardner Lindzey, *Theories of Personality* (1957).

EUGENE TAYLOR

MURRAY, James Edward (3 May 1876–23 Mar. 1961), lawyer and U.S. senator, was born near St. Thomas, Ontario, Canada, the son of Andrew James Murray, a farmer and railroad employee, and Anna Mary Cooley. When James was five, his father moved the family from their farm into St. Thomas, where he began working for the Michigan Central Railroad, and James enrolled in a parochial school. When James was still a child his father died, leaving the care of the family to the boy's uncle, James A. Murray, who lived in Butte, Montana. A former prospector, Murray's uncle at the time was a wealthy mine owner, and he saw to it that Murray was educated and employed. Murray attended St. Jerome's College in Berlin (now Kitchener), Ontario. There is conflicting evidence as to whether he graduated in 1895 or 1897.

In 1897 Murray, with his mother and a sister, moved to Butte, where his uncle felt it would be a good experience for Murray to work in one of his mines. After a few months of mining, Murray in 1898 enrolled in New York University's School of Law, where he received his LL.B. degree in 1900 and his LL.M. in 1901. While in New York, Murray was exposed to the Democratic party and joined Tammany Hall, and he also became a naturalized citizen of the United States.

After law school, Murray returned to Butte to practice law. In 1905 he married Viola Edna Horgan: they had six sons. In 1906 Murray's connections helped him win election as Silver Bow County attorney. As county attorney, he sometimes came into conflict with local powers and was even ordered by a judge to spend a night in jail after publicly disparaging the judge's lack of decisiveness in a courtroom. After his two-year term Murray did not seek reelection but resumed private law practice and the management of some of his uncle's business interests. By 1915 he was prosperous enough to purchase the 26-room mansion originally owned by the son of one of Butte's "copper kings," William Andrews Clark.

Murray watched as Butte became a company town, its politics no longer leavened by the wars of the copper kings. The miners' union was crushed in successive stages by the New York owners of the Anaconda Copper Company. Murray continued his interest in politics and worked to elect Thomas J. Walsh U.S. senator in 1913 and worked for William W. McDowell in his unsuccessful bid for governor in 1920. He financed the miners' newspaper, the *Butte Bulletin*, during a brief but failed reemergence of unionism in 1917.

In 1921 Murray's uncle died and left his estate, valued at between $10 and $15 million, to his widow and Murray as the main beneficiaries. Murray inherited the majority of shares in the Monidah Trust Company, a private corporation that controlled most of his uncle's mining and real estate holdings. In May 1922 Murray's intense interest in the Irish independence movement led to his election as the president of the American Association for the Recognition of the Irish Republic. When civil war broke out in Ireland he split with the rest of the leadership, refusing to take sides, and resigned his presidency. He spent the remainder of the twenties looking after the business holdings he had inherited.

With the coming of depression in the 1930s, Murray reentered politics as the chairman of the Democratic Central Committee of Silver Bow County. During the year before the 1932 national convention he worked for the nomination of Franklin D. Roosevelt. After winning election, President Roosevelt appointed Murray to the state advisory board for the Public Works Administration. While in that position, Murray worked to gain federal assistance for the hard-hit farmers of eastern Montana.

A chain of events ensued that led to Murray's decision to run for the U.S. Senate. In 1933 Roosevelt appointed Montana senator Walsh as his attorney general, but Walsh died of a heart attack before taking office. Montana's Democratic governor John Erickson was to appoint a successor to fill out Walsh's term. With the blessing of Montana's other senator, Burton K. Wheeler, Erickson resigned as governor, and Lieutenant Governor Frank H. Cooney, when he became governor, appointed Erickson to the Senate. Because of this deal, and the fact that Erickson did not distinguish himself in office, Butte Democratic leaders persuaded Murray to challenge Erickson in the Democratic primary for the U.S. Senate in 1934. Murray won by fewer than 1,500 votes, aided by the plurality of more than 4,000 votes he polled in Silver Bow County. He won in the general election, pledging "one hundred per-cent support" of President Roosevelt.

In the Senate, Murray served on the Education and Labor Committee and the Foreign Relations Committee, quietly carried out his campaign pledge to support the New Deal, and secured almost $12 million for water projects in his home state through federal grants and loans. He occasionally came into conflict with Montana's senior senator Wheeler over such issues as the direction of the Works Progress Administration (WPA) in Montana and Roosevelt's 1938 Court-packing plan, which Wheeler opposed. Murray also became concerned with issues of employment and relief.

In foreign affairs, Murray was an isolationist during the 1930's, as were his constituents and most of his colleagues, but he shifted toward support of Roosevelt in foreign affairs as well, specifically the president's efforts in 1941 on behalf of the Allies through neutrality revision and lend-lease. This again was a break with Wheeler, and Murray risked the opposition of his own constituents. Although he favored helping the Allies, he opposed the Selective Service Act of 1940. In early 1941 he began concentrating on the problem of small businesses and government contracts as chair of the Senate Small Business Committee. In 1942 he introduced the Murray-Patman Act to mobilize small businesses in the war effort by creating the Smaller War Plants Corporation in the War Production Board. After the war, when congressional reorganization in 1947 limited senators to no more than two standing committees, Murray preferred membership on the Interior and Labor committees and resigned from Foreign Relations.

From the war years until his retirement in 1960, Murray promoted a variety of liberal issues. In a magazine article in January 1946, he used the metaphor of war for his efforts on behalf of liberal domestic programs, saying: "We must . . . campaign on many fronts. . . . There is a great war to be won, the war against depression and poverty." In the areas of jobs and health care, he sponsored a full employment bill in 1945, which passed in diluted form as the Employment Act of 1946. The act did not recognize a federal role in guaranteeing jobs as Murray had wanted, but it did create the Council of Economic Advisers and ensured a greater federal role in directing the economy. Murray also worked for an expanded Social Security measure, the Wagner-Murray-Dingall Bill, a section of which provided for payment of doctor and hospital bills. This bill never came to a vote, and Murray's plans for national health insurance died with it. Another of his unsuccessful bills during the Roosevelt-Truman period would have established a Missouri Valley Authority with federal government direction of water projects in the West patterned after the Tennessee Valley Authority. Instead Congress adopted the Pick-Sloan Plan and flood control by the Army Corps of Engineers, the Bureau of Reclamation, and private development. Murray also unsuccessfully pressed for congressional passage of legislation for medical care for the aged, federal aid to education, federal support for American Indians and national wilderness bills. He remained an ardent supporter of labor, unsuccessfully opposing postwar attempts to change the Wagner Labor Relations Act through such measures as the Taft-Hartley Bill, which became law. As Chairman of the Interior and Insular Affairs Committee in the 1950s, Murray promoted federal development of hydroelectric power through large dams in the West. Although his health was failing, Senator Murray intended to seek reelection to the Senate in 1960 at age eighty-four; he finally decided not to run again. He died in Butte.

• Murray's papers are in the archives of the Maureen and Mike Mansfield Library at the University of Montana in Missoula. A good biography is Donald F. Spritzer, *Senator James E. Murray and the Limits of Post-War Liberalism* (1985). Articles include William B. Evans, "Senator James E. Murray: A Voice of the People in Foreign Affairs," *Montana*, Winter

1982; Spritzer, "B. K. Wheeler and Jim Murray: Senators in Conflict," *Montana*, Apr. 1973; and Forrest Davis, "Millionaire Moses," *Saturday Evening Post*, Dec. 1945. An obituary is in *New York Times*, 24 Mar. 1961.

ROBERT T. BRUNS

MURRAY, John (1730 or 1732–25 Feb. 1809), fourth earl of Dunmore and royal governor of New York, Virginia, and the Bahamas, was born probably at Taymount Castle, Perthshire, Scotland, the son of William Murray, the third earl of Dunmore, and Catherine Nairne. Although William supported the Stuart pretender in 1745, the influence of his brother John, the second earl, one of George II's generals, preserved the title for the family. William succeeded in 1752 and his son John four years later. John had joined his uncle's regiment, the Third Foot Guards, in 1749 and served during the Seven Years' War but participated in no major action. In February 1759 he married Charlotte Stewart, daughter of the earl of Galloway, and the next year resigned his captaincy to embark on a parliamentary career as a Scottish representative peer, an office that he held except when in America until 1790. Notwithstanding extensive estates near Edinburgh and mining interests in the west of Scotland, the expense of London society and the gradual increase of his family to eleven children left Dunmore relatively poor for his station.

Dunmore's search for additional preferment remained unsuccessful until Lady Dunmore's brother-in-law Earl Gower rose in favor in Lord North's ministry. In 1770 Dunmore received appointment as governor of New York. He arrived at his post in October, leaving his family behind until he assessed the climate and social scene. Politically he gravitated toward frontier leaders like Sir William Johnson (1715–1774), who could help him obtain land grants. His energy in pressing New York's claims against New Hampshire in the area of modern Vermont won favor with the legislature, and in the process he secured 51,000 acres for himself on the shore of Lake Champlain. Without consulting him, Gower arranged his transfer to Virginia within the year because the income was greater. Despite that advantage, Dunmore vociferously protested in view of his success in New York and because the Virginia climate would further delay his family's coming. They did not join him until February 1774. Dunmore arrived in Williamsburg in September 1771. Initially many Virginians found him to their taste. A cultivated courtier, he brought with him a 1,300-volume library, one of the largest in the colonies, three organs, a harpsichord, and a piano as well as a small art collection. Occasionally George Washington joined him at the Williamsburg theater.

Dunmore again drew support from the land interest, among them Washington, who sought grants for veterans of the last war. Although British policy since 1763 restricted settlements beyond the crest of the Appalachian Mountains, Dunmore's willingness to stretch the rules to favor Virginia's claims in present West Virginia and the region around modern Pittsburgh—including his own claim of 100,000 acres for his sons—eventually brought a reprimand from his superiors. The contest with Pennsylvania exposed a buccaneering side to Dunmore. When Pennsylvania arrested his ally, Dr. John Connolly (1743–1813), Connolly escaped, seized Fort Pitt, and renamed it for the governor in January 1774. Meanwhile, the Shawnee, whom both white factions attacked, reasserted their rights in the area, precipitating a conflict known as Dunmore's War. In July 1774 the governor set out from Williamsburg to raise western militia ostensibly to subdue the natives, but his patent intention also to strengthen Virginia's claims against Pennsylvania led the colonial secretary to warn him against "exerting a Military Force . . . in Matters of Civil Dispute between the Subjects of the same State" (from Lord Dartmouth, 6 July 1774). In October Colonel Andrew Lewis's decisive victory at Point Pleasant on the Great Kanawha River forced the Shawnee to withdraw north of the Ohio River. Dunmore's return to the capital in December was triumphal. The birth of his eleventh child, Virginia, a few days before brought his popularity to its zenith at a ball celebrating the child's christening in January 1775.

The West, in fact, distracted Dunmore from broader imperial issues. Since July he had sent London only a few understated reports about developing resistance to enforcement of parliamentary taxes. Yet just weeks before his departure for the West, he had dissolved the General Assembly because the House of Burgesses designated a fast day to protest Parliament's closing of the port of Boston in retaliation for the Boston Tea Party in December 1773. While he was away, the first Virginia Convention met in Williamsburg and embargoed British trade, towns and counties formed extralegal committees and recruited volunteer companies for defense, and Virginia representatives attended the First Continental Congress in Philadelphia.

Perhaps misled by the popularity of his success in the West, Dunmore never swayed from his conviction that most Virginians remained loyal and that he could easily put down the handful of troublemakers with a few reinforcements. To the contrary, virtually his every act in the spring of 1775 persuaded the majority of white Virginians of his involvement in a conspiracy at the highest levels of government to suppress their liberties. In the end, no other royal governor was as reviled. Although Dunmore acted on his own, his seizure of the powder in the public magazine in Williamsburg on 21 April seemed a twin of General Thomas Gage's attack on Concord and Lexington in Massachusetts two days before, and when Virginians protested, Dunmore's threats to raise the slaves against them confirmed their suspicions. Publication of the report that he finally sent to London on his return from the West revealed that he called for a blockade of the Chesapeake like the one of Boston. His reconvening of the assembly on 1 June 1775 at the behest of the ministry to consider Lord North's peace proposal proved disastrous. With no confidence that the meeting would be effective, Dunmore had rigged a shotgun in the Williamsburg magazine that youths breaking in a few days after the session began triggered and barely escaped serious injury. With the gunshot, the litany of offenses by the governor so outraged white Virginians that some mentioned assassination.

Fearful for his safety, Dunmore fled from the capital with his family and aides early on the morning of 8 June. With a few reinforcements from the British Fourteenth Regiment, he gathered a small fleet at Norfolk and recruited the Queen's Own Loyal Regiment and, from among runaway slaves, Lord Dunmore's Ethiopian Regiment. Through the fall, while the convention trained a force to oppose him, he raided river plantations and captured munitions the rebels might have used. Flush with these victories, on 15 November he issued his Emancipation Proclamation, which he had already signed on the seventh, promising freedom to any slave who joined him but carefully confining the offer to males of fighting age whose masters were rebels. Several hundred runaways answered the call. Although many succumbed to smallpox in British ranks, others participated in the highly successful raids for rebel arms in Hampton Roads, and a detachment helped to defend the only overland approach to Norfolk at Great Bridge until the main rebel force arrived. Then, at the battle of Great Bridge on 9 December 1775, Dunmore suffered a catastrophic loss when he foolishly sent his regular troops to attack the Virginians across a narrow causeway that rebel riflemen easily raked. The Virginia commander, Colonel William Woodford, exalted, "This was a second Bunker's Hill affair, in miniature, with this difference, that we kept our post . . . " (to the Virginia Convention, 10 Dec. 1775). Dunmore immediately withdrew from Norfolk to his ships, allowing the Virginians, now with North Carolina reinforcements, to occupy the town. When the British commenced a bombardment on New Year's Day to cover some landing parties, the Americans easily drove off the invaders and for three days burned and looted the town, which they considered a nest of Tories. It was headquarters for the Scottish mercantile community, and several of the more prominent Scots had become Dunmore's lieutenants. Contemporaries, however, blamed the destruction on the governor, creating in Washington's phrase a "flaming" argument for independence (to Joseph Reed, 31 Jan. 1776). The correct account remained buried in the records until the twentieth century.

Dunmore's fleet of ninety-odd vessels crammed with Loyalists rode off Norfolk in anticipation of reinforcements throughout the spring. When General Henry Clinton arrived in February, however, Dunmore discovered to his "inexpressible Mortification" that Clinton's destination was Carolina (to Lord Dartmouth, 13 Feb. 1776). In late May Dunmore withdrew from Norfolk waters to Gwynn's Island at the mouth of the Piankatank River, where he suffered another defeat in July. When Clinton, having failed to take Charleston, retired to New York instead of returning to Virginia, Dunmore finally abandoned hope

of reinforcement and sailed from Chesapeake Bay on 7 August. About 300 soldiers of the Ethiopian Regiment accompanied him. Dunmore's departure at last relieved the fears of Virginia and Continental leaders that he might open a second front. Had his superiors supported him as he implored them, he might have seriously divided the colonial war effort. Now the manpower and foodstuffs of Virginia began to flow northward to Washington's army.

Returning to Britain after a short stay in New York, Dunmore reentered Parliament until 1781 when he received orders to recruit a Loyalist force to reinstate himself as governor after General Lord Cornwallis subdued Virginia. Dunmore reached Charleston with two transports of artillery and supplies before he learned of Cornwallis's defeat at Yorktown. During the following winter Dunmore advocated recruiting slaves and establishing a Loyalist refuge on the Gulf of Mexico, but finding little support, returned to Britain in the spring. He worked diligently for compensation to Loyalists and counseled fellow refugees before the Loyalist Commission after its creation in 1783.

In 1786 Dunmore became governor of the Bahamas, where many former Loyalists had emigrated. His alignment with the newcomers alienated older inhabitants, and his dealings with the legislature over the construction of grandiose fortifications that almost bankrupted the colony became as stormy as in Virginia. He established some of the Bahamas as free ports to exploit the lucrative Caribbean trade and joined the Maryland Loyalist William Augustus Bowles in contesting control of the Indian trade along the Gulf Coast with the white chief of the Creeks, Alexander McGillivray. Eventually Dunmore fell from favor at court when his daughter Augusta married a younger son of George III in violation of the Royal Marriage Act, and the king dismissed him from office in 1796. He retired to Ramsgate, Kent, where he died.

• Dunmore's papers are at Register House, Edinburgh, and a small revolutionary war collection is at the Earl Gregg Swem Library, College of William and Mary. His gubernatorial correspondence is in the Public Record Office, Admiralty, Colonial Office, and War Office series, and his petition to the Loyalist Commission is in the Audit Office. Material on Dunmore's War from the Draper collection, Wisconsin Historical Society, is in Reuben G. Thwaites and Louise P. Kellogg, eds., *Documentary History of Dunmore's War, 1774* (1905). The most complete study is Percy B. Caley, "Dunmore: Colonial Governor of New York and Virginia, 1770–1782" (Ph.D. diss., Univ. of Pittsburgh, 1939). A shorter study is John E. Selby, *Dunmore* (1977). Obituaries for Dunmore and his wife are in *Gentleman's Magazine* (1809), pt. 1, p. 587, and (1818), pt. 2, p. 640, respectively.

JOHN E. SELBY

MURRAY, John (1737–11 Oct. 1808), Quaker merchant, was born on Swatara Creek, near Lancaster, Pennsylvania, the son of John Murray, who had emigrated from Scotland in 1732. His mother's name is unknown. Murray worked with his older brother Robert Murray in the operation of a flour mill on Swatara

Creek. In 1753 the two brothers moved together to New York City, where they formed a mercantile partnership. Within fifteen years, the Murray brothers had become the largest shipowners in the thirteen colonies, and their enterprise had become the largest import-export business in New York City, bolstered by the contract demands of provisioning soldiers and sailors during the Seven Years' War in North America. In 1766 Murray married Hannah Lindley.

When Robert Murray went to England in 1767 and remained there until early 1775, John Murray took responsibility for the "American" side of the business. He was therefore present in New York City during the crucial ten-year period (1765–1775) in which the colonies moved toward outright rebellion against Great Britain. His personal feelings on the matter are unknown, although one would suspect that a man of his wealth and prominence would have leaned toward the Loyalist side of the political fence.

Early in 1775 the Murray brothers came under suspicion from the patriotic Committee of Sixty in New York. John and Robert Murray appear to have attempted to unload goods from the ship *Beulah* at a secret location off Sandy Hook in violation of the nonimportation agreement that was in effect at that time. The act was discovered, and the brothers were taken before the Committee of Sixty. After offering profuse apologies for their behavior, they were released and allowed to resume their normal business affairs.

The start of the Revolution in 1775 impelled Murray to keep a low profile in patriotic New York. Never clearly defined as either a Loyalist or a patriot, he remained close to his home during the years 1775–1776. Following the British capture of New York City and the subsequent occupation by British troops (Sept. 1776–Sept. 1783), Murray and other members of the city chamber of commerce at times managed the internal affairs of the city. This was an important time in Murray's life and in the business of New York City, which briefly had an opportunity to demonstrate whether an American city could indeed manage its own affairs during a military occupation. As events turned out, a feud between British generals James Roberston and Henry Clinton prevented the civil affairs of the city from functioning smoothly. Murray and his colleagues were much less responsible for this failure than were their British counterparts.

Following the war, the chamber of commerce received a new charter from the state. Murray was admitted to the new chamber on 13 February 1787, and he served as president of the organization from 1798 until 1806. Continuously active in the civic affairs of the city, he directed the Bank of New York for several years and contributed handsomely to philanthropic enterprises. He served on a commission that unsuccessfully attempted to build one of the state prisons in New York City (1796), and in association with Thomas Eddy, he issued a call for a meeting in 1805 to provide the means for what became the Free School for Poor Children. Murray was the first vice president of the Free School Association. He also worked with Eddy on relief for the poverty-stricken Oneida Indians, one of the six Iroquois nations that had been devastated by the events of the American Revolution, in upstate New York. He was a director of the Humane Society in New York, and he organized relief for prisoners in debtors' jail. Murray died in New York City. It is estimated that at the time of his death his estate was worth in the neighborhood of $500,000, a very large sum for that time.

Murray was an important member of a true merchant elite that flourished in British North America in the years prior to the Revolution and then to some extent managed to preserve its influence in the era that followed. Fortunate in that he managed to ride the political fence as one of those whom historian Michael Kammen has labeled "trimming neutrals" (Kammen, p. 365), Murray never suffered the loss of property or even prestige that many other semi-Loyalists did. He made a noteworthy effort to preserve the civil powers and liberties of New York City during its occupation. His failure to maintain that arrangement with the British occupying forces was his most salient defeat. Nevertheless, he emerged in the aftermath of the Revolution as a respected businessman who maintained his personal prosperity and gave much of himself to improve conditions for the poor in the city.

• Few sources exist for a full study of Murray's life and career. The basic and lasting sources are Arthur Schlesinger, Sr., *The Colonial Merchants and the American Revolution, 1763–1776* (1917); Joseph Alfred Scoville, *The Old Merchants of New York City* (1863); and Virginia D. Harrington, *The New York Merchant on the Eve of the Revolution* (1935). The best recent source for understanding Murray's time period is Michael Kammen, *Colonial New York: A History* (1975).

SAMUEL WILLARD CROMPTON

MURRAY, John (10 Dec. 1741–3 Sept. 1815), founder of organized Universalism in the United States, was born in Alton, Hampshire, England. Murray's father was a stern Calvinistic Anglican who apparently was successful in business; the family name of his gentler Presbyterian mother was Rolt. Murray, who had some formal schooling, later complained that during his childhood his father's constant harping about the "endless misery" of the damned "threw a cloud over every innocent enjoyment." When Murray was ten his family moved to Ireland, settling near Cork and his paternal grandmother, who was "in easy circumstances" and helped them out financially two years later when their home burned. His father refused an offer to prepare Murray for college, securing for him instead a place in business when his own health declined.

Murray accompanied his father, who was on friendly terms with John Wesley, into Methodism. Attracted especially by its hymn singing, he became an enthusiastic "class-leader of forty boys." Without his father's knowledge, Murray's constant diet of religious books was replaced with secular ones when a wealthy neighbor named Little opened his library to him. Becoming head of the family in his late teens after his father's death, Murray continued his father's strict disciplinary practices and faced a revolt from his eight siblings. Nevertheless, he left them and his mother in financial security after arguing successfully in court to recover three houses that had been fraudulently deeded to others by his mother's stepfather.

Murray moved in with his neighbors, the Littles, after their own sons had died. He began honing his preaching talents before increasingly wider audiences and became convinced that God planned for him "a life of wandering." En route to London, with a handkerchief filled with gold guineas from the Littles, Murray heard George Whitefield, an itinerant Calvinistic minister without allegiance to any sect, whose animated style and copious use of illustrations Murray later emulated. Hearing Whitefield made Murray determined to abandon Wesleyanism to follow him, but once in London he entered a more secular period. Describing himself as being "alternately serious, and wild, but never very moderate in anything" and having used up his gold guineas, Murray contemplated suicide. He found refuge in Whitefield's "Tabernacle" and employment in jobs that convinced him he "was never designed for a man of business."

In addition to Whitefield's services, Murray attended other religious meetings in London, where he made numerous friends, often delivered prayers, and turned down offers to preach. When he was about eighteen, he married Eliza Neale, who shared his interest in religion and whose grandfather had cut her out of his will because of her belief in Whitefield's teachings. The couple had one child. In 1760, after he was asked by the Methodist church, of which he was still a member, to reason with a young woman who had become an "unwavering believer of universal redemption," Murray himself became a convert to that doctrine. It was taught by James Relly, a much-maligned, zealous London preacher who had broken with Whitefield about 1750 and whose ideas Murray followed throughout the remainder of his life.

In the late 1760s life became a nightmare for Murray. He was thrown out of Whitefield's congregation, arrested for debt (from which his brother-in-law rescued him), his young son died, then his wife and four of his siblings died. Refusing Relly's suggestion that he preach Universalism, Murray again contemplated suicide, but, after meeting "a gentleman from America," decided to go there "to pass through life . . . as though I ne'er had been."

With his mind "suspended between two worlds," Murray sailed for America on 21 July 1770. After the brig *Hand-in-Hand*, on which he was a passenger, ran aground off the southern New Jersey coast, Murray was put in charge of its goods, which had been transferred to a sloop to lighten its load. When the wind changed the next day and the sloop was stranded, he went ashore to obtain provisions. There he was welcomed by Thomas Potter, a deeply religious Universalist farmer. He was convinced that Murray had been sent by God to preach in the little church that he had built on his property, whose pulpit Murray did fill on 30 September 1770. His preaching attracted larger and

larger audiences. A powerfully effective speaker with a vigorous intellect and a retentive memory, he preached in many places, including Philadelphia, New York City, Newport, Boston, and Portsmouth, New Hampshire, but kept his headquarters at Potter's farm in Good Luck, New Jersey, for the next four years. Those against his message (the union with Christ of all souls, not merely the elect, as Calvinists insisted) challenged him for "preaching damnable doctrines" and for lacking official credentials.

Seeking to avoid controversy, Murray responded to questions by simply quoting from Scripture, until in Gloucester, Massachusetts, in late 1774 he met a group versed in the writings of Relly. There his open discussions, becoming more positive and aggressive, brought even stronger opposition. In 1775 the Rhode Island Brigade of the Continental army, which was besieging Boston, asked Murray to be its chaplain; though other chaplains objected, George Washington, whose friend he had become, confirmed his appointment in September. When Murray recovered from the severe illness that ended his military career after eight months' service, he solicited relief money primarily from Washington and his officers to aid about a thousand people in Gloucester who were in need during "the worst winter they . . . experienced through the war" because of the disruption of commerce. Despite this patriotic work and Murray's intimate friendship with both John Hancock (first signer of the Declaration of Independence) and General Nathanael Greene, opposers of Murray's religious teachings accused him of being disloyal to the American Revolution because he was a native-born Englishman. Their accusations caused "curses, anathemas, and sometimes stones" to follow "his steps as he walked the streets."

Remaining in Gloucester, on 25 December 1780 Murray preached at the dedication service of the first edifice in America built specifically for a Universalist church as its full-time pastor. He was in the midst of the legal battle that resulted when possessions were seized belonging to members of his church who had refused to support with their taxes the established church from which they had separated. The court decision, which was favorable to the Universalists, was not reached until 1786. It was the first time a court exempted from taxpaying any denomination or sect regardless of whether it was incorporated. After an early 1788 visit to England, where he was described as "the most popular preacher in the United States," Murray married Judith Sargent Stevens in Salem that October. An "intelligent and gifted woman" of literary ability who anticipated "a new era in female history," she was the widowed daughter of Winthrop Sargent, a leading citizen of Gloucester and a prominent worker for the Universalist cause. One of their two children grew to adulthood.

In 1793 Murray became the settled pastor of a Universalist group in Boston, where he lived the rest of his life. In spite of his growing prominence, persecution of him and other Universalists continued. At a Boston service, he was challenged by John Bacon, pastor of the Old South Church. Finding that the audience responded favorably to his responses, some of Bacon's supporters pelted Murray with eggs. A master of "sarcasm and satiric wit," Murray quipped, "These are moving arguments, but I must own at the same time, I have never been so fully treated to Bacon and eggs" (Miller, vol. 1, p. 31).

With "the sentiments of the Universalists" becoming "every day more respectable," calls for Murray to preach increased. Next to Gloucester and Boston, his influence was greatest in Philadelphia, then the nation's capital. While there on a 1799 visit, he dined with President John Adams every week. During a reception, while introducing Murray to Secretary of War James McHenry, Adams remarked, "This gentleman has performed . . . next to a miracle; he has drawn the Vice President [Thomas Jefferson] to a place of worship" (Eddy, vol. 1, p. 512).

On 19 October 1809 Murray suffered a paralytic stroke that left him an invalid. Aided by an assistant pastor, he continued work with his church, sitting in the pulpit during the infrequent times he preached. After he died at his home in Boston, prominent Universalists participated in his funeral service, among them Hosea Ballou, who unlike Murray had leaned toward Unitarianism and had long been his chief theological adversary within Universalism. Although not an original thinker, Murray laid a foundation on which his successors could build. Rather than dooming to destruction all but a handful of the "elect," his message offered salvation not only to those who believed in Christ but even to nonbelievers (who could be redeemed through suffering after death). This message of hope attracted an "ever-expanding body of believers from all ranks of life." In tune with the optimistic republicanism and democratic outlook of their new nation, these believers spread Universalism and its message that all would ultimately partake of salvation.

• Although Murray and his wife left a valuable collection of correspondence, manuscripts, and papers, including his diaries (on which their writings were based), these papers did not survive storage by their daughter, Julia Maria Bingamon, in an unoccupied building at "Fatherland," the Mississippi plantation belonging to her husband's family. The Massachusetts Historical Society, however, has many important manuscripts associated with Murray and his work, including records of his Boston church from 1792 to 1815. Murray's own writings include *Records of the Life of the Rev. John Murray, Written by Himself, with a Continuation by Mrs. Judith Sargent Murray* (1816); *Letters, and Sketches of Sermons* (3 vols., 1812–1813); *Some Hints Relative to the Forming of a Christian Church* (1791); and *Universalism Vindicated* (1798), a 96-page collection of sermons. Many of Murray's sermons were published in pamphlet form, the earliest of which is *The Substance of a Thanksgiving Sermon Delivered at the Universal [sic] Meeting House in Boston, Feb. 19, 1795* (1795). The best source on Murray is Russell E. Miller, *The Larger Hope: The First Century of the Universalist Church in America, 1770–1870* (2 vols., 1971–1985). Other useful sources include Charles A. Howe, "How Human an Enterprise: The Story of the First Universalist Society in Boston during John Murray's Ministry," *Proceedings of the Unitarian Universalist Historical Socie-*

ty, 1990–1991 22: 19–34; Joseph Henry Allen and Richard Eddy, *A History of the Unitarians and the Universalists in the United States* (1894), vol. 10 in the American Church History Series; and Eddy, *Universalism in America: A History* (2 vols., 1886). An obituary is in the *Columbian Centinel*, 6 Sept. 1815.

OLIVE HOOGENBOOM

MURRAY, John Courtney (12 Sept. 1904–16 Aug. 1967), Jesuit theologian, was born in New York City, the son of Michael John Murray, a lawyer, and Margaret Courtney. Murray entered the New York province of the Society of Jesus in 1920. After completing courses in classical and philosophical studies at Weston College, with degrees conferred by Boston College (B.A. 1926, M.A. 1927), he taught Latin and English literature at the Ateneo de Manila, Philippines. He returned to the United States for theological studies at Woodstock College, Maryland (1930–1934, S.T.L.), was ordained a Roman Catholic priest in 1933, then pursued further studies at the Gregorian University (Rome). In 1937 he completed a doctorate in sacred theology (S.T.D.) with a specialization in the doctrines of grace and the Trinity. Returning to Woodstock, he taught Catholic trinitarian theology and, in 1941, assumed editorship of the Jesuit journal, *Theological Studies*. He held both positions until his death in Queens, New York.

Despite the heavily theoretical bent of his training and teaching, Murray was drawn into the intricate religious tensions of American public life. As a representative of the U.S. Catholic bishops, he helped draft and promote the 1943 "Declaration on World Peace," an interfaith statement of principles for postwar reconstruction, which led to his study of lay religious education and social action. In 1950, as a consultant to the religious affairs section of the Allied High Commission, Murray successfully recommended a close constitutional arrangement between the restored German state and churches, including the dispersal of state-collected taxes to German churches. After a lectureship in medieval philosophy and culture at Yale University (1951–1952), he collaborated with Robert M. MacIver of Columbia University in a project on academic freedom and religious education in public universities, during which he deepened his own understanding of American Constitutional law, arguing for tax aid to private schools and for ultimately sympathetic exposure to the faiths of the American people within public schools. Throughout his public life, several bishops consulted Murray on legal issues, such as censorship and birth control, leading him to recommend against coercive Catholic boycotts of pornographic literature and against Catholic opposition to the repeal of a Massachusetts law that had outlawed the sale or use of artificial contraceptives. In each case, Murray argued that participation in substantive public arguments offered a better school of public virtue than did simple appeals to civic coercion. In the submitting of moral opinions to public argument, he maintained, Americans might both deepen their moral commitments and preserve the "genius" of American freedoms. From 1958 through 1962 he participated in projects for the Center for the Study of Democratic Institutions, during which he applied just war criteria to Soviet-U.S. relations, arguing for a policy of nuclear deterrence and even for the moral possibility of limited nuclear war—arguing in this case that only a state of war is possible, given the total lack of shared values between the East and the West. After the election of John F. Kennedy, a Catholic, as president, Murray was celebrated on the 12 December 1960 cover story of *Time* magazine for his contributions to American domestic and foreign policy debates and for his sympathetic if critical understanding of religion in American public life. In 1966 he served on a presidential commission, prompted by the Vietnam war, that reviewed Selective Service classifications, agreeing with a minority that supported the allowance of a classification for those opposed on moral grounds to some, though not all, wars—a recommendation not accepted by the Selective Service Administration.

Two sets of Catholic doctrines complicated Murray's public involvement. First, Catholics claimed that there was no salvation outside the church and that Catholic teaching was socially necessary. In 1940 Murray himself had argued that America could "rescue from its deep abasement the essential idea upon which a democratic culture must be erected—the idea of the dignity of human nature and of man's spiritual freedom"—only by adopting the doctrines of the incarnation, the Trinity, and the cross. By 1944, however, he allowed that agreement on philosophical premises and natural theism (prescinding from revealed religious truths) would be sufficient for cooperation in the immense task of postwar reconstruction. His endorsement of full cooperation with other theists led to Catholic complaints that he was endangering American Catholic faith. At the time, many Catholics recommended minimal cooperation with non-Catholics for fear that lay Catholic faith would be weakened.

Second, Catholic doctrine on church/state relations also encouraged public distrust of a growing American Catholic minority. During centuries of European religious conflict, the church urged Catholics, if they could, to establish Catholicism as their sole, state-sponsored religion (establishment) and to suppress public expressions of non-Catholic and atheistic beliefs (political intolerance). Played out against America's prejudice toward Catholic immigrants, Catholic magisterial commitments to establishment did little to secure public trust, reaching a vitriolic climax during the 1928 presidential candidacy of Catholic Alfred E. Smith. At the insistence of several American bishops, Murray took up the issue of religious freedom as defined and protected by the First Amendment of the U.S. Constitution.

Murray eventually argued that Catholic teaching on church/state relations was inadequate to the moral functioning of contemporary peoples. The Anglo-American West, he claimed, had developed a fuller truth about human dignity, namely the responsibility of all citizens to assume moral control over their own religious beliefs, wresting control from paternalistic states. For Murray this truth was an "intention of nature" or a new dictate of natural law philosophy. Murray's claim that a new moral truth had emerged outside the church led to conflict with Augustus Cardinal Ottaviani (prefect of the Vatican Holy Office) and the eventual Vatican demand, in 1954, that Murray cease writing on religious freedom and stop publication of his two latest articles on the issue.

Murray continued to submit religious liberty manuscripts privately to Rome, all of which were rejected. When finally invited to the second (though not the first) session of Vatican Council II (1963), he drafted the third and fourth versions of what eventually became the conciliar endorsement of religious freedom, *Dignitatis humanae personae* (1965). After the council he continued writing on the issue, stating that the arguments offered by the final decree were inadequate, though the affirmation of religious freedom was unequivocal.

At that time Murray turned to questions of how his church might arrive at new theological doctrines. He argued that, if Catholics were to arrive at new truths about God, they would have to do so in conversation "on a footing of equality" with non-Catholics and atheists. He suggested restructuring his church, which over the last two centuries had developed its notion of authority at the expense of the bonds of love (secured in ongoing conversation) that more foundationally ought to define Christian living.

Since his death, writers have appealed to Murray's work for its theory of law and its insistence on a closer interplay between America's religious commitments and civic life. Amid fears of cultural anarchy, attention has focused on his mid-1960s claim that diverse religious communities can and must begin in appreciation of the good found in each community. That Murray drew from his own Catholic tradition a consistent basis for an appreciation of God's action beyond the Catholic community suggests to both Catholic and non-Catholic scholars the possibility of constructively bringing diverse, rich theological sources to public debates.

• Murray's collected papers are in Special Collections, Lauenger Library, Georgetown University. *We Hold These Truths: Catholic Reflections on the American Proposition* (1960) is a collection of thirteen of Murray's essays written between 1950 and 1960. Murray's *The Problem of God, Yesterday and Today* (1964) is a trinitarian analysis carried into a dialectic with atheistic existentialism and Marxism. *The Problem of Religious Freedom* (1965) was published during Vatican Council II and is included, with suppressed and late religious liberty articles, in *Religious Liberty: Catholic Struggles with Pluralism* (1993). Early and late Murray essays are collected in *Bridging the Sacred and the Secular: Selected Writings of John Courtney Murray* (1994). Recent works on Murray include Dominique Gonnet, S.J., *La Liberté Religieuse à Vatican II: La Contribution de John Courtney Murray, S.J.* (1994); Thomas P. Ferguson, *Catholic and American: The Political Theology of John Courtney Murray* (1993); J. Leon Hooper, S.J., *The Ethics of Discourse: The Social Philosophy of John Courtney Murray* (1986); D. Thomas Hughson, S.J., *The Be-*

liever as Citizen: John Courtney Murray in a New Context (1993); Robert McElroy, *The Search for an American Public Theology: The Contribution of John Courtney Murray* (1989); Keith J. Pavlischek, *John Courtney Murray and the Dilemma of Religious Toleration* (1994); Donald E. Pelotte, *John Courtney Murray: Theologian in Conflict* (1976); and George S. Weigel, *Tranquillitas Ordinis: The Present and Future Promise of American Catholic Thought on War and Peace* (1985). Obituaries include Walter J. Burghardt, "A Eulogy," *Woodstock Letters* 96 (Fall 1967): 416–20, and Emmet John Hughes, "A Man for Our Season," *The Priest* 25 (July–Aug. 1969): 389–402.

J. LEON HOOPER

MURRAY, Joseph (1694–28 Apr. 1757), lawyer, was born in Queen's (now Laoighis) County, Ireland, the son of Thomas Murray, a gentleman. Little else is known about his parentage or early life. Murray was in New York and practicing law before the Mayor's Court in 1718, but it is not clear where or when he acquired his legal training. In 1725 the Middle Temple granted him membership, but like a number of other successful colonial attorneys, he apparently had his name simply added to the rolls without studying at the Inns of Court. Nevertheless, Murray became widely celebrated for his erudite knowledge of the law and over the years assembled one of the best legal libraries in the colony. In 1728 the Common Council of New York City bestowed upon him the freedom of the city, describing him as a "zealous Assertor of the Rights and Privileges of this Corporation."

In 1731 Murray drafted the Montgomerie Charter for New York City, so named because it was patented during the tenure of Governor John Montgomerie (1728–1731). In response, the Common Council thanked Murray and praised "his great Learning Ability and Integrity" and "his Regard to this Corporation." Building an extensive and lucrative practice, Murray regularly appeared before the Mayor's Court and proved himself remarkably adept in both the common and civil law. By the mid-1730s he had earned the respect of his peers and was the senior member of the New York bar.

Especially known for his expertise in real estate law, Murray defended New York City in litigation with Harlem over land claims and with Brooklyn over ferry rights. In fact, he served as arbitrator or counsel in most of the important land disputes in both New York and New Jersey. As early as 1731 Murray's reputation in handling property cases led a business associate of Henry Lloyd, whose boundary dispute with the town of Huntington on Long Island was likely to go to trial, to advise the latter that Murray should be put under a retainer "rather than riske a Lawyer of his influence & Capacity's being against you" (Barck, vol. 1, p. 312). Later on Murray represented the East Jersey proprietors and the proprietors of the extensive Oblong or Equivalent Patent along New York's border with Connecticut. In 1754 he served on the commission appointed to settle the boundary between New York and Massachusetts and also reported to the provincial council on New York's disputed boundary with New Jersey.

A defender of New York City's commercial interests, Murray moved easily into provincial politics. He become an important ally of Adolph Philipse and later James DeLancey, both of whom were political leaders from the city's merchant community. In 1734 Murray sided with Governor William Cosby, who claimed gubernatorial prerogative when ordering the New York Supreme Court to sit as a court of exchequer, insisting that statutory approval from the provincial assembly was not necessary. This dispute escalated into a test of strength between the landed interest in the assembly, led by Chief Justice Lewis Morris, and the trading interests in the city, led by Philipse. After Cosby summarily dismissed Morris as chief justice and appointed the young James DeLancey in his place, Murray and William Smith, Sr., another prominent attorney who opposed Cosby, presented two perspectives on the court of exchequer in a rousing debate before the assembly. Murray's "Opinion Relating to the Courts of Justice in the Colony of New York" was appended to Smith's similarly titled *Opinion*, published as a pamphlet later in 1734. Murray based his argument on the premise that English common law was as fully in force in the British colonies as in England itself and that "fundamental courts" were part of English common law. Therefore, the royal governor, as the king's representative, did not need the assembly to pass a bill establishing what was basically a prerogative court in England.

Countering Smith's portrayal of the assembly as the guardian of popular liberties, Murray cited numerous cases in equity before 1730 in which the New York Supreme Court of Judicature had acted as a court of exchequer. As to "the Liberties and Privileges of the People," he concluded:

I would beg Leave only to propound this one Question, who is he that argues most in Favor of the Liberties of the People? He who affirms and proves, that they are entitled to those Liberties and Privileges, Laws and Customs of *England*, and the good old original Courts, that are by those Laws, without an Act? or, he who argues and says, we are not entitled to them, until an Act is passed to establish them? I suppose the Answer would be given, without Hesitation, in Favour of the former. (Smith, vol. 1, p. 264)

In 1735 Governor Cosby himself drew heavily from Murray's published opinion in defending the court of chancery. The issue itself became less important after Cosby's death in 1736. The following year, in the disputed assembly election between Garret Van Horne and Philipse, Murray and Smith once again debated before the assembly. Smith insisted that Jews, who were prohibited from voting in England, could not vote in New York, whereas Murray emphasized they could because provincial law did not specifically exclude them. Smith prevailed at the time, and Jewish votes were thrown out, although Philipse won the election anyway. Thereafter, Jewish votes were not disputed, and the evidence is that Jews regularly voted in city elections.

Through his marriage to Grace Cosby Freeman in 1738, Murray strengthened his political influence. His wife was the widowed daughter of Governor Cosby and was also related through her mother to the politically influential Duke of Newcastle and Earl of Halifax.

Murray played a prominent role in prosecuting both whites and blacks implicated in the slave conspiracy of 1741 in New York City. He argued for the acceptance of slave testimony against other slaves, even though the promise of leniency for those who confessed obviously made such evidence dubious at best. Two of his own five slaves, Jack and Adam, were accused of plotting the murder of Murray, his wife, his servants, and the three other slaves in his household. Jack and Adam were among the thirty-one slaves executed along with four whites. More than seventy other slaves charged in the conspiracy were transported from New York and sold in the West Indies.

Appointed to the provincial council in 1744, Murray broke with Governor George Clinton and joined the opposition led by Chief Justice Delancey, who shortly received appointment as lieutenant governor and rallied the council and the assembly against Clinton's plans for waging war against the French and American Indians. In 1753 Clinton's replacement as governor, Sir Danvers Osborne, having just arrived and still despondent over the death of his wife, hanged himself while staying as a guest with the Murrays. Upon Osborne's death, DeLancey succeeded to the governorship, and Murray became his trusted adviser, serving as a delegate to the Albany Congress in 1754. Murray remained on the provincial council until his death.

Murray's efforts on behalf of King's College (later Columbia University) reflected his twin commitments to education and religion. He was especially concerned with legal education, joining James Alexander, William Smith, Sr., and other lawyers in urging the supreme court to mandate minimum years for clerks or apprenticeship before they could qualify as lawyers. His surviving form books suggest both his own scrupulous regard for writing legal instruments properly and his concern that professional standards be maintained. His legal reputation and his extensive library of law books made clerkships in his office highly prized.

Murray was a founding trustee of the New York Library Society and strongly supported the early efforts for the College of New Jersey (later Princeton University). However, as a devout Anglican and vestryman of Trinity Church, Murray wanted the proposed college for New York to be affiliated with the Church of England. Like his colleague in the law and fellow Trinity vestryman, John Chambers, Murray began working toward the establishment of a college in New York City in the 1740s. More willing to compromise with New York dissenters than Chambers, Murray played a major role in winning Dutch support in 1754 for the charter granted King's College, to whose board of governors he was appointed. Upon his death in New York City, he and his wife having no children, Murray left his extensive library and the residual of his estate, amounting to more than £10,000, to King's College, the single largest gift bestowed upon any colonial college. Unfortunately, most of the volumes in the Joseph Murray Collection were destroyed or lost either in the great fire of 1776 or in the subsequent British occupation of New York City during the American Revolution.

Always supportive of New York City's mercantile interests, Murray became a recognized authority in contract law, played a significant role in provincial politics, and was much involved in both professional and civic efforts. His obituary in the *New York Gazette, or the Weekly Post-Boy* (2 May 1757) praised him as an "eminent attorney" who had proved "himself a Gentleman of the strictest Integrity, Fidelity and Honour." Its concluding description was particularly apt: "By Principle, he was a steady and hearty Friend to the National Constitution, both of Church and State, and frequent in his Attendance to the publick Offices and Ordinances of Religion." Friend and foe alike would have surely agreed.

• Relatively few Murray papers have survived. Miscellaneous correspondence is in the James Alexander Papers, M.S.S., V, New-York Historical Society Library. Some of his legal papers, including pleadings, are in the Office of the Commissioner of Records, New York City. His form book is in the Columbia Law Library, and the receipt book of Murray's estate is in the Museum of the City of New York. Highlights of Murray's career may be traced through the chronology in Isaac Newton Phelps Stokes, *The Iconography of Manhattan Island*, vol. 4 (6 vols., 1915–1928). References to his law practice are in Dorothy C. Barck, ed., *Papers of the Lloyd Family* (2 vols., 1927); *The Letters and Papers of Cadwallader Colden, 1711–1775*, vols. 2–3 (9 vols., 1918–1936); Thomas Jones, *History of New York during the Revolutionary War* (1879); and E. A. Jones, *American Members of the Inns of Court* (1924). Murray's involvement in the 1741 slave conspiracy is documented in Daniel J. Horsmanden, *The New York Conspiracy* (1971), and is discussed in Thomas J. Davis, *A Rumor of Revolt: The "Great Negro Plot" in Colonial New York* (1985). On Murray's politics, see William Smith, Jr., *The History of the Province of New-York*, ed. Michael Kammen (1972). Murray's efforts in civic affairs, especially the founding of King's College, are discussed by David C. Humphrey, *From King's College to Columbia University, 1746–1800* (1976).

RONALD HOWARD

MURRAY, Judith Sargent Stevens (1 May 1751–6 July 1820), writer, was born in Gloucester, Massachusetts, the first of the eight children of Winthrop Sargent and Judith Saunders, a well-established shipowning merchant family. She received an unusually extensive education, sharing her brother Winthrop's tutor, minister John Rogers, as Winthrop prepared for admission to Harvard College. She married sea captain and trader John Stevens on 3 October 1769; they had no children. Judith and John Stevens lived in the Sargent-Murray-Gilman-Hough House, which was probably built for the young couple by Winthrop Sargent. They made no secret of their patriot politics during the American Revolution. Influenced by the preaching of itinerant minister John Murray, the Sargent and Stevens families converted from Congregationalism to Universalism during or soon after the Revolution (the exact date of the change is uncertain). Murray was so appreciative of their support for his liberal theology that he made Gloucester his home base.

Financial reverses forced John Stevens out of the United States in 1786 to avoid debtor's prison; he died shortly after his arrival in the West Indies. In October 1788 widow Judith Stevens married the Reverend John Murray; they had two children, though only one survived infancy. In 1793 Judith and John Murray moved from Gloucester to Boston to establish the first Universalist congregation there. Both continued to be active in support of Universalist causes, though financial difficulties and John Murray's failing health forced Judith to attempt to supplement their income through her well-established writing career. John was paralyzed by a stroke in 1809, but when daughter Julia Maria married Adam Louis Bingamon, a wealthy planter from the Mississippi Territory, in 1812, the Murrays' financial struggles ended. Judith Murray remained in Boston until her husband's death in 1815 and then moved to Natchez, Mississippi, where she lived with her daughter. She died there a few years later, leaving the extensive manuscript record of her long writing career to the ravages of humidity.

These sketchy details of Murray's life provide a context for her lifelong literary pursuits. Her earliest dated work still extant is the prose "Reflections in the Manner of Hervey—Occasioned by the Death of an Infant Sister," which was written in October 1775, though not published until 1794. It was apparently Murray's ambition even as a young woman both to write and to publish her work: she reports (through a persona) that she was "seized with a violent desire to become a writer." She goes on to detail the high standards she set for herself:

I would be Cesar, or I would be nothing. The smoothness of Addison's page, the purity, strength and correctness of Swift, the magic numbers of Pope—these must all veil to me. The Homers and Vergils of antiquity, I would rival; and, audacious as I am, from the Philenias [Sarah Wentworth Morton] of the present age, I would arrogantly snatch the bays. (*The Gleaner*, vol. 1, pp. 14–15)

Like her literary models, Murray went on to pursue an eclectic writing career, widely various in subject matter and genre.

Murray's earliest writing was mostly poetry. She worked within the neoclassical aesthetic of her contemporaries, developing a rationalist perspective and employing heroic couplets. Often her poems prefaced her essays. Murray's poetry appeared between 1782 and 1803 in such periodicals as *Gentleman and Lady's Town and Country Magazine*, *Boston Magazine*, *Massachusetts Magazine*, *Universal Asylum and Columbian Magazine*, and *Boston Weekly Magazine*. Publishing under the pseudonym "Constantia" and later as "Honora-Martesia" or simply "Honora," she developed religious, moral, political, and literary materials. The poem prefacing Essay 19 on religious sentiments in her *Gleaner* series, for example, outlined the individual autonomy important to the liberal theology of Universalism:

Say, who is authoriz'd to probe my breast,
Of whatsoever latent faith possess'd;
. . . .
Religion is 'twixt God and my own soul,
Nor saint, nor sage, can boundless thought control.

Other poems explore the uncertainties of the revolutionary war, create epilogues and prologues to contemporary plays, plead for educational reform, extol the intellectual abilities of women, celebrate a spirit of political and literary nationalism, and mourn the death of her son George, who died in infancy.

The same variety that marks Murray's poetry is evident in her much better known prose works. A regular essayist for the *Massachusetts Magazine* in the early 1790s, she developed two popular series, "The Gleaner" and "The Repository." Though she ranged widely in subject matter for these and other essays, Murray's purposes were didactic and political. She apparently hoped to influence the development of public practice and policy on education for women in particular. Her essays "On the Equality of the Sexes" (written in 1779, published in 1790) and "Desultory Thoughts upon the Utility of Encouraging a Degree of Self-Complacency, Especially in Female Bosoms" (1784) describe the cruel sense of inferiority women are heir to as a result of their inadequate educations. Like Mary Wollstonecraft, whose work she knew, Murray argued that women should have greater access to a more comprehensive education. Her arguments went further than those of supportive American contemporaries like Benjamin Rush since they maintained that women should not only be educated as fit companions for men but also for economic self-sufficiency. Murray returned to this theme repeatedly, noting that American women "only contend for the capability of the female mind to become possessed of any attainment within the reach of masculine exertion" (*The Gleaner*, vol. 3, pp. 217).

In 1798 Murray's three-volume collection *The Gleaner* gathered together one hundred of her essays. Published by subscription in an attempt to alleviate Murray's financial distress at the time, these volumes contain much (though not all) of her periodical work and document concerns that move well beyond women's education. They include a sentimental serial novel, conduct literature for women, comments on such neoclassical preoccupations as justice and virtue, trenchant pro-Federalist observations on the state of contemporary politics, moral reflections, discussions of religion, and support for the development of American drama. In addition to essays and poems, *The Gleaner* contains Murray's two plays, *The Medium, or*

Virtue Triumphant and *The Traveller Returned*, both of which had been produced at Boston's Federal Street Theatre, in 1795 and 1796 respectively. Neither production was well received.

In her later years Murray attended more to editorial work than to her own writing. To support the spread of Universalist ideas, she prepared a three-volume edition of her husband's *Letters and Sketches of Sermons* (1812–1813). She also finished his autobiography, *Records of the Life of the Rev. John Murray* (1816), after his death.

Murray was well known to readers in late eighteenth-century New England and beyond. Despite her use of pseudonyms, her identity as a writer was well established. Subscribers to *The Gleaner*, Murray's collected works, included such notables as President John Adams, Martha and George Washington, and writers Sarah Wentworth Morton and Susanna Rowson. Although Murray all but disappeared from literary history for much of the nineteenth and twentieth centuries, she excited a good deal of attention among late twentieth-century historians of the American literary essay and feminist historians reconstructing political and literary traditions.

• The Sargent-Murray-Gilman-Hough House Association has collected materials relating to Murray's life, including a portrait by Copley. They are preserved in the Sargent House Museum in Gloucester, Mass., Murray's residence until 1793. Her letterbooks, containing more than 2,000 letters, can be found in the Judith Sargent Murray Papers at the Mississippi Department of Archives and History in Jackson.

The earliest full bibliography of her works is available in Vena Field, *Constantia: A Study of the Life and Works of Judith Sargent Murray 1751–1820* (1931), though it should be supplemented with the poetry checklist from Pattie Cowell, *Women Poets in Pre-Revolutionary America, 1650–1775* (1981). A listing of secondary sources on Murray's fiction has been provided by Patricia L. Parker in *Early American Fiction: A Reference Guide* (1984). Most of Murray's work has been out of print for many decades, but recent recovery efforts by feminist historians and literary scholars have resulted in two important book-length editions: Nina Baym introduces a reprint of *The Gleaner* (1992), and Sharon M. Harris has edited the *Selected Writings of Judith Sargent Murray* (1995). Both editions include Murray's two plays, her serial novel, and a generous selection of her prose essays. Harris includes selected letters as well. Cowell's *Women Poets* reprints a brief selection of poems.

Field's *Constantia* provides a reliable account of Murray's life. Sharon M. Harris's profile of "Judith Sargent Murray" in *Legacy: A Journal of American Women Writers* 11 (1994): 152–59 furnishes a useful briefer sketch. Chester E. Jorgenson, "Gleanings from Judith Sargent Murray," *American Literature* 12 (Mar. 1940): 73–78, reconstructs her neoclassical aesthetic and concept of liberty. Mary Beth Norton, *Liberty's Daughters: The Revolutionary Experience of American Women, 1750–1800* (1980), uses many examples drawn from Murray's life and works to support her analysis. Bruce Granger takes up Murray's "Story of Margaretta" in *American Essay Serials From Franklin to Irving* (1978), as does Madelon Jacoba in "The Early Novella as Political Message: The Margaretta Story by Judith Sargent Murray," *Studies in the Humanities* 18 (1991): 146–64. Mary Anne Schofield discusses Murray as "the first native-born woman dramatist to have her plays professionally produced" in "'Quitting the Loom and Distaff': Eighteenth-Century American Women Dramatists," in *Curtain Calls: British and American Women and the Theater, 1660–1820*, ed. Mary Anne Schofield and Cecilia Macheski (1991). Kirstin Wilcox discusses Murray's male persona and genre masquerades in "The Scribblings of a Plain Man and the Temerity of a Woman: Gender and Genre in Judith Sargent Murray's *The Gleaner*," *Early American Literature* 30 (1995): 121–44.

PATTIE COWELL

MURRAY, Lindley (22 Apr. 1745–16 Jan. 1826), grammarian and Quaker moralist, was born in Swetara, near Lancaster, Pennsylvania, the son of Mary Lindley and Robert Murray. His father's success as a merchant took the family from North Carolina to New York City. Lindley and his brother, John Murray, Jr., were sent to the Friends School in Philadelphia but were then summoned as apprentices in their father's firm, Murray, Sansom & Co., which became the largest New York shipowners. To assert his independence, Lindley ran away to school, to the Quaker Academy in Burlington, New Jersey. Discovered by his uncle John Murray in New York as he delivered a letter, he was prodigally welcomed back by his father, who arranged for him a private tutor in classical and English literature, as well as law studies, alongside John Jay, under noted law counsellor Benjamin Kissam.

Murray joined a debating society and began import trading on his own. His marriage by a clergyman to Hannah Dobson in 1767 caused his "disownment" as a Quaker until he "acknowledged his fault" three months later before the Meeting.

His father's health took his whole family to England in 1771. On their return Lindley prospered both in law and trade until prevented by the beginning of "the Troubles" (the War of Independence) in 1775. In 1774 he was a member of the "Patriot" Committee of Sixty to resist British taxation, and he did not resign when asked to so so by the New York Quakers' "Meeting for Sufferings." When the English army landed, his parents stayed in Manhattan, but Lindley retired to a farm at Islip on the Long Island bays, where for four years he produced salt, sailed a boat, and may also have settled black freedmen, until he could return to the city as an importer and lawyer. He was the leader in the setting up of the Friends Seminary in New York and in choosing its headmasters. He felt ready to retire in 1783 to the estate he then bought at Bellevue on the East River, later used by Quaker-led committees on which he served as a Refuge for Juvenile Delinquents and as a New York city hospital.

Before settling at Bellevue he had the first severe attack of a lifelong neurological illness, perhaps myasthenia gravis. When local trips to cooler resorts did not lead to permanent cure, he decided to move with his wife in 1784 to York, England. Two miles away they found a large house, where with only three servants he lived with resolute cheerfulness and piety, as an increasingly helpless invalid for the final forty years of his life. During this period he was eagerly visited by children and scientists such as Benjamin Silliman of Yale and the Quaker John Griscom. Ingenious gadgetry freed him to write, eat, visit, and oversee his famous botanical garden in the years when he could no longer stand. His first book, *The Power of Religion on the Mind, in Retirement, Affliction and the Approach of Death* (1787), reflected his experience by using examples from other men's lives and was given free to fellow citizens of York and by his will to Quaker youth of New York through the Lindley Murray Fund.

The Friends who welcomed the Murrays to York were William and Esther Tuke, whom Murray helped to design and support the first modern mental hospital, The Retreat, which he also persuaded the New York Friends to copy. Murray's second book was *Some Account of the Life and Labours of Sarah [Tuke] Grubb* (1792), the story of a woman who founded a school in Ireland modeled on Esther Tuke's Quaker girls' school at York (later called the Mount). Three teachers there, Ann and Mabel Tuke and Martha Fletcher, came out for long evenings to the Murrays' house to ask how to teach English grammar. The outcome was a third book, *English Grammar, Adapted to the Different Classes of Learners* (1795), which used varied fonts and an appendix to separate lessons and rules for children and principles for their teachers. The popularity of this book led to subsequent new editions.

Murray followed this book with several others, including *English Exercises* and *A Key to the Exercises* (1797), *Abridgement of the English Grammar* (only the children's text, 1797), *English Reader* (1799), *Sequel* (1800), and *Introduction to the English Reader* (1801). He went on to publish *English Spelling Book* (1804) and *First Book for Children* (1805), as well as French textbooks for English students, *Lecteur François* and *Introduction au Lecteur François* (1802). Printed with good typefonts (Lincoln read his *Reader* by firelight) on good paper in leatherbound volumes of 100 to 300 pages (though a revised *English Grammar* ran to two volumes), these books became enormously popular.

The books were first published in York and London (where Darton & Harvey arranged the copyrights), and the Murrays oversaw the printing of American editions by the Quaker printers Isaac Collins in New York and the Johnsons in Philadelphia. Each press reprinted them in annual editions of 10,000, making no effort to stop other printers from "pirating": Harvard Library's roster of 123 editions of the *Abridgement* includes only one of the 132 British or Quaker editions but includes the eighth Baltimore edition, the fifth from Canandaigua, four from Worcester, three from Pittsburgh, the third from Hallowell, Maine, sixteen editions from nine towns in New Hampshire and Vermont, and twenty-four from Boston. His secretary Elizabeth Frank thought a million copies of the *Grammar* were sold. Murray himself was content with receiving fees of £100 to £700 from the printer for all editions of each book, giving the money to Quaker schools and charities, while his brother John handled his investments.

Murray died in York. He made no claims of originality as a grammarian and was told so by outstripped rivals such as Noah Webster. He meant his rules to be memorized, to be understood only by teachers and advanced classes but applied in daily exercises in syntax and parsing sentence structures. Yet his terms were clear and simple (for example, using "noun" for "substantive") and were based on spoken English rather than written Latin. The phrases he quoted to show grammar and his selections for his *Reader*, which were based on his own constant reading, have struck most modern—and many earlier—readers as pedantic, but they appealed for half a century to teachers and parents for their moral tone and style, as well as their examples of virtue and courage.

• Murray outlined his own life in six "Letters" to his secretary Elizabeth Frank, to which she added accounts of his last days for his *Memoirs* (1827). Murray's *Compendium of Religious Faith* (1817) for young Quakers was shaped by the *Principles of Religion* (1805) by Henry Tuke, whose biography Murray wrote in 1816. His other books written specifically for Quakers made little mark. The definitive biography, Stephen Allott, *Lindley Murray, 1745–1826* (1991), is supplemented in Hugh Barbour et al., *Quaker Crosscurrents* (1995). See also Mary R. Glover, *The Retreat, York* (1984); Michael Belok, "The Most Successful Grammar," *Educational Forum* 21, no. 1 (Nov. 1966): 107–11, and "Lindley Murray's English Readers," *Education* 87 (1966–67): 496, 501. Peter Davis's unpublished paper is in the Haverford College Quaker Collection. Twenty-one letters from Lindley Murray to John Murray, Jr., are in the Haviland Records Room of New York Yearly Meeting.

HUGH BARBOUR

MURRAY, Mae (10 May 1889–23 Mar. 1965), dancer and motion picture star, was born Marie Adrienne Koenig in Portsmouth, Virginia, the daughter of immigrant parents not named in biographical sources. Her Austrian-born father was an artist who died when she was four. Her mother was from Belgium and returned there after her husband's death, leaving Murray in New York City with a grandmother, who put the child in a convent school and then in a boarding school near Chicago when Murray was nine. A few years later she ran away from the school and found work as a dancer in a touring show.

At age fourteen Murray found herself an adult in show business, without having had any real childhood or adolescence. She was a dancer who never had a lesson but was an extremely quick study who could pick up steps almost at once. She appeared first under the name of Mae Murray in a traveling revue, *About Town* (1906). From 1907 through 1913 she appeared on Broadway as a dancer in musical shows, including two editions of the Ziegfeld *Follies* (1908, 1909). In 1909 she married William A. Schwenker, a millionaire's son, but the marriage ended in 1910 after his father disinherited him.

When the craze for modern ballroom dancing began in the United States, Murray spent all of her savings to get to Paris. In twelve days spent haunting places of entertainment she learned a repertoire of the newest dances, from the maxixe to the tango. Back in New York, she quickly became an attraction as a ballroom dancer in cabarets. Murray achieved fame when she replaced the ailing Irene Castle as Vernon Castle's dance partner in the revue *Watch Your Step* (1914) on four hours' notice, having learned all the dances in that time. In 1915 she was back in the Ziegfeld *Follies*. Soon after she signed a Hollywood contract with the Lasky Feature Play Company.

In Murray's first film, *To Have and to Hold* (1916), she was cast as a sweet ingenue, but in later films director Robert Z. Leonard recognized that her unique screen quality was that of a vibrant and sensuous dancer. Socialite J. Jay O'Brien swept her into a second marriage on the set of a 1917 film, but divorce followed quickly. Meanwhile, Leonard and Murray began to create her star persona in a succession of films. In 1918 Murray wed Leonard. Murray's director-husband tailored her vehicles to avoid things she could not do and to emphasize what she could do well: dance, wear lavish costumes, and cast come-hither-but-not-too-close gazes at leading men. The plots of her films were basically all the same: Cinderella as dancing girl.

Before long the Leonard-Murray team had their own production unit to turn out her films, first at Universal, then at Metro (soon to become Metro-Goldwyn-Mayer). According to film historian DeWitt Bodeen, her three films directed by George Fitzmaurice, *On with the Dance*, *The Right to Love*, and *Idols of Clay* (all 1920), were her best.

In the years 1921 to 1925 Murray rose steadily to the peak of movie stardom. She starred in films whose titles suggest their nature: *The Gilded Lily* (1921), *Peacock Alley* (1922), *Jazzmania* (1923), and *Circe the Enchantress* (1924). She did not dance in silence; her films were always sent out with musical scores written for any type of accompaniment available in theaters of the day, from a pit orchestra to a pianist.

Some reviewers complained that Murray's perpetual movement in all scenes was distracting. In the films of these years she became more and more the unattainable love idol, both more and less than human, and more and more mannered, with her frizzed hair, half-shut eyes, pouting lips, and head tilting back. Gradually she began displaying her screen personality in real life. Writer Adela Rogers St. John observed in 1924 that "on or off [screen], unconsciously she dramatizes herself" (p. 43). Murray, with a salary of $7,500 a week (at a time when a middle-class family could be comfortable on $5,000 a year), lived as extravagantly as any princess on the silver screen. Enshrined as Metro's top star by 1924, she separated from Leonard that year and divorced him in 1925.

In 1925 Murray began work on her next movie, *The Merry Widow*. The operetta story had been rewritten to make her a glamorous musical comedy performer from America rather than a wealthy European widow. However, the haughty director, Erich Von Stroheim, wanted to make the picture a revelation of Europe's debauched aristocracy. Their battles on the set were epic. Protecting their star, MGM edited out Von Stroheim's influence and tailored the film to Murray's romantic style, allowing her "Merry Widow Waltz" to remain the climactic point of the film. The result was the smash hit of 1925, both with critics and the public.

But then Murray, giddy with her success, started to flout studio head Louis B. Mayer, earning his lasting dislike. Her next few pictures, made by directors who gave in to her whims, declined in quality. Disaster came in 1926 when she met David Mdivani, a reputed "prince" from Russian Georgia. He was one of three brothers known as "the marrying Mdivanis," who sought out wealthy women to be their wives. Three weeks after Murray met Mdivani, she married him.

In three years of high living, Mdivani went through Murray's entire $3 million fortune. He induced her to break her contract with MGM, which, combined with Mayer's enmity, left her unemployable in Hollywood. Mdivani gave her a son, whom she concealed for sixteen months, fearing the effect of motherhood on her screen image. Worse, she was off the screen in the years when talking pictures captured the public. When she returned, her "high . . . [but never] shrill" voice (*Variety*, 10 Nov. 1937) did not match her visual image, and she had aged. The three talking pictures she made at a minor studio in 1930–1931 were wretched failures.

The remainder of Murray's life was a nightmare ending to the Hollywood dream years. She declared bankruptcy in 1934, a year after she filed for divorce from Mdivani. She tried vaudeville, then a stage role in *The Milky Way* (1934), then some radio work and traveling shows. Her demands to be treated as a supreme star alienated those who hired her. After a long court battle in 1939–1940, she lost custody of her son to a surgeon who had operated on him and eventually adopted him.

By 1941 Murray was doing her "Merry Widow Waltz" at Billy Rose's Diamond Horseshoe in a nostalgic revue of silent screen has-beens. The engagement ended when she walked out, her demands unmet, and then sued Rose. In 1946 she declared bankruptcy again. In one last appearance, she successfully reprised her "Merry Widow Waltz" at Hollywood's Mocambo nightclub in 1950.

Murray's increasingly eccentric behavior, as she sank ever deeper into the delusion that she was still a great star, was recognized in Hollywood circles by everyone but herself. She was losing touch with reality, even while she made penurious cross-country bus trips to New York seeking "comeback" work. Dressed youthfully, her face framed by a picture hat, she became a garish caricature of a star. In 1959 a biography of her by Jane Ardmore appeared, titled *The Self-Enchanted*. Murray scurried around to Los Angeles bookstores to ink out her birth name reported there. She wanted to be entirely the star persona she had created. The book's small sales were painful evidence that she was now forgotten.

In 1960 Murray suffered a stroke in her small Los Angeles apartment and was taken to the home operated by the Motion Picture Actors' Relief Fund. At least once more, however, she made a cross-country bus trip. In 1964 she was found dazed and penniless in a St. Louis Salvation Army shelter under the delusion that she was in New York to publicize her "recent" biography. She was sent back to Los Angeles and the Motion Picture Actors' Home, and she died there the next year.

Murray's significance in film history is an unusual one. She is an outstanding example, though far from the only one, of how stardom can destroy a fragile personality. She is a major figure behind the stories of the self-destructiveness of stars presented in two of Hollywood's classic films about Hollywood. The story is told tragically in the character of Norma Desmond in *Sunset Boulevard* (1950) and comically in the figure of Lina Lamont in *Singin' in the Rain* (1952). Murray has become a Hollywood legend as a prototype that is the inspiration for such a character. It is enduring stardom of a sort, which is all Murray ever wanted.

• Materials on the life and career of Mae Murray are in the Billy Rose Theatre Collection at the New York Public Library for the Performing Arts, Lincoln Center. Jane Ardmore's biography, *The Self-Enchanted*, gives no dates for any events and relies on Murray's memories, which are often highly dramatized and distorted. Colorfully written biographical sketches are in Norman Zierold, *Sex Goddesses of the Silent Screen* (1973), and Ethan Mordden, *Movie Star: A Look at the Women Who Made Hollywood* (1983), and useful comments are in Richard Griffith, *The Movies* (1981), and Richard Schickel, *The Stars* (1964). DeWitt Bodeen's "Mae Murray 1889–1965," *Films in Review*, Dec. 1975, surveys her films and contains a filmography and numerous portraits and production photographs. A list of her stage appearances in musicals is in Roger D. Kinkle, *Complete Encyclopedia of Popular Music and Jazz* (1974). Informative articles written during Murray's period of fame are I. S. Sayford, "Talking All around Mae Murray," *Photoplay*, Oct. 1916; Alfred A. Cohn, "The Girl with the Bee-Stung Lips," *Photoplay*, Nov. 1917; Alice Bennett, "Mae Murray Makes-Believe," *Motion Picture Classic*, Feb. 1919; Delight Evans, "The Truth about Mae Murray," *Photoplay*, Aug. 1920; and Adela Rogers St. John, "Mae Murray—A Study in Contradictions," *Photoplay*, July 1924. An account of her stage beginnings, purportedly by a longtime friend, is Mary Morgan, "Secrets of Mae Murray's Success," *Photoplay*, Jan. 1922. All the articles include portraits and production photographs. Obituaries are in the *New York Times* and the *New York Herald Tribune*, both 24 Mar. 1965, and *Variety*, 31 Mar. 1965.

WILLIAM STEPHENSON

MURRAY, Orson S. (23 Oct. 1806–14 June 1885), Baptist minister, editor, and radical reformer, was born in Orwell, Vermont, the son of Jonathan Murray and Rosalinda Bascom, farmers. Murray grew up impoverished on a hardscrabble farm in Orwell, obtaining only a few years of schooling. His parents were devout Free Will Baptists, and as a teenager Murray felt called to the Baptist ministry. In 1828 he married Catherine Maria Higgins; the couple had nine children. Determined to have a classical education, he returned to school at the Shoreham and Castleton academies, completing his studies in 1832.

The turning point of Murray's life came in 1832, with his discovery of William Lloyd Garrison's journal the *Liberator* and Garrison's *Thoughts on African Colonization* (1832). Garrison's writing converted Murray to the cause of the immediate abolition of slavery. In 1833 he became the New England Anti-Slavery Society's agent for Vermont. Although facing considerable hostility, he achieved some success, organizing twenty local antislavery societies in one year. In December 1833 Murray attended the meeting that organized the American Anti-Slavery Society. In the next year he was a leading figure in the organization of the Vermont Anti-Slavery Society and was appointed its secretary and agent. In this role, he again embarked on the course of organizing local antislavery societies. He encountered more hostility than ever, including mobs on several occasions.

Murray did not give up his commitment to the Baptist church. In 1837 he was licensed as a Baptist preacher. Two years earlier he had purchased the controlling interest in the state's Baptist newspaper, the *Vermont Telegraph*, and had moved to Brandon to edit it. Since the paper had been under the control of the state Baptist convention, Murray apparently did not arouse too much fear in its membership.

Murray made the *Telegraph* into a reform organ far more radical than anyone anticipated. It advocated abolition, taking the Garrisonian side in the split that developed in the American Anti-Slavery Society late in the 1830s. Murray also became committed to nonresistance. When the Vermont Peace Society was formed in 1838 as an auxiliary of the American Peace Society, Murray was the leader of the minority faction that argued that a commitment to peace involved renouncing all use of coercive force and instead looking to the arrival of the government of God on earth. He applauded the formation of the New England Non-Resistance Society later that same year. Nonresistance became a regular feature of the *Telegraph*. These changes made the paper increasingly controversial, and by 1840 Murray was losing many subscribers.

Murray's final break with his past came early in the 1840s, when he lost his Christian faith and became an atheist or, in his own description, a freethinker. Murray repudiated conventional religion when he became convinced that it had become corrupted by creedalism and established churches and that it was hostile to truth and reform. This was too much for Vermont Baptists, who repudiated the *Telegraph* and suspended Murray's ministerial license in 1842.

Murray gave up publishing the *Telegraph* in the fall of 1843. He determined instead to move to New York City and publish a new reform journal, the *Regenerator*. Murray put out only a few issues before deciding to leave New York for Ohio. Murray had established ties with the Society for Universal Inquiry and Reform, a radical nonresistant group that included reformers John A. Collins and John O. Wattles, who intended to use the group to establish a series of utopian communities that would usher in the government of God. Murray planned to make his home in one of the communities, Prairie Home near West Liberty, Ohio, and publish the *Regenerator* there. By the time he arrived in the fall of 1844 after being shipwrecked on Lake Erie, Prairie Home had collapsed. Murray instead purchased a farm in Warren County, Ohio, that he named "Fruit Hills."

Murray spent the rest of his life at Fruit Hills. For a time he and about twenty others tried to form a community on the farm, but within a year the attempt failed. In April 1845 he resumed publication of the *Regenerator*. In it he, with considerable vehemence, supported diet and health reform, women's rights, nonresistance, and communitarianism, and attacked slavery, capitalism, and organized religion. Circulation was limited, and Murray depended on his children to do most of the work on the paper. In 1856 it ceased operation. After that, Murray faded from public view, although he held to many of his radical beliefs. As he lay dying, perhaps to prevent rumors of a deathbed return to Christianity, he dictated a last repudiation of religion. He died at Fruit Hills.

• There is no collection of Murray papers. A good account of his early life and the attempt to found a community at Fruit Hills is in the A. J. MacDonald Collection, Beinecke Library, Yale University. Murray's only published works are his journals, the *Vermont Telegraph*, and the *Regenerator*. Basic sources for his life can be found in the autobiography of his son, *Some of the Work of Charles B. Murray* (1914); and a lengthy obituary, probably by Charles B. Murray, in the Valentine Nicholson Papers in the Indiana Historical Society. Secondary works treating Murray include David M. Ludlum, *Social Ferment in Vermont, 1791–1850* (1939); Albert Post, *Popular Free Thought in America, 1825–1850* (1943); John Myers, "The Beginning of Antislavery Agencies in Vermont, 1832–1836," *Vermont History* 36 (Summer 1968): 126–41; and Thomas D. Hamm, *God's Government Begun: The Society for Universal Inquiry and Reform, 1842–1846* (1995).

THOMAS D. HAMM

MURRAY, Pauli (20 Nov. 1910–1 July 1985), lawyer, writer, and minister, was born Anna Pauline Murray in Baltimore, Maryland, the daughter of William Henry Murray, a public school teacher, and Agnes Fitzgerald, a nurse. Triracial, she had African, European, and Native American ancestry. Her parents both died when she was a child (her mother had a cerebral hemorrhage in March 1914; her father was murdered in a state hospital in June 1923), and she grew up from age three in North Carolina with her maternal grandparents and her mother's oldest sister, Pauline Fitzgerald Dame, a public school teacher who adopted her.

Murray graduated in 1926 from Hillside High School (which went only through grade eleven) in Durham, North Carolina, and then lived with relatives in New York City and graduated in 1927 from Richmond Hill High School. After working for a year in Durham for a black newspaper and a black insurance company, she returned to New York and entered Hunter College in 1928. She changed her name to Pauli, and, after time out for work and for what proved only a brief marriage (1930; later annulled),

earned a B.A. in English in 1933. She spent a year as field representative for *Opportunity* magazine, the voice of the National Urban League. She worked for four years (1935–1939) with the Works Progress Administration as a remedial reading teacher and then with the Workers' Education Project. Wishing to return home, she applied in 1938 for graduate study at the University of North Carolina, where her white great-grandfather had studied and his father had been a trustee, but that school rejected her because of her race.

Murray was active in civil rights in the 1940s. The first time was unintended, when she found herself arrested for "disorderly conduct" in March 1940 in Petersburg, Virginia, while taking a bus south to visit her family in North Carolina. Determined to implement what she understood of Gandhi's *Satyagraha* (nonviolent direct action)—despite what she later termed her "urge toward kamikaze defiance of Jim Crow"—she challenged the constitutionality of segregating interstate bus passengers. She courteously demanded fair treatment in jail while awaiting trial; returning to jail rather than pay the fine when she was convicted, she nonetheless learned that "creative nonviolent resistance could be a powerful weapon in the struggle for human dignity." In 1940–1942 she worked with the Workers Defense League in a coast-to-coast campaign for a new trial for Odell Waller, a black sharecropper who, convicted by an all-white jury of men who had paid their poll taxes, was eventually executed for the murder of his landlord in Pittsylvania County in Virginia.

Murray's involvement in the Waller case led to her decision to attend law school, and she entered Howard University in 1941 "with the single-minded intention of destroying Jim Crow." During her time at Howard, she planned and participated in student sit-ins in 1943–1944 designed to achieve the desegregation of drugstores and cafeterias in the nation's capital. She earned a law degree at Howard University in 1944, graduating cum laude and first in her class.

Deciding to obtain a graduate degree so that she could return to teach law at Howard, she applied to Harvard Law School, but that school rejected her because of her gender. She went instead to Boalt Hall at the University of California at Berkeley, where she earned an LL.M. in 1945 with a thesis titled "The Right to Equal Opportunity in Employment." Years later, she attended Yale University Law School, where she earned a J.D.S. in 1965 with a dissertation titled "Roots of the Racial Crisis: Prologue to Policy." She abandoned her plans to teach at Howard when her mentor there, Leon A. Ransom, was bypassed in 1946 for the deanship. Between her studies at Berkeley and Yale, she worked briefly as deputy attorney general in California and for the American Jewish Congress's Commission on Law and Social Action in New York, passed the bar exams in California and New York, ran as a Liberal party candidate for a seat on the City Council from Brooklyn in 1949, and from 1946 to 1960 spent much of her time in private practice in New

York, eventually (1956–1960) in the law firm of Paul, Weiss, Rifkind, Wharton, and Garrison.

Race, Murray had learned, was not the only major obstacle to a black woman's educational and professional advancement. She contributed to the theory of litigation against the constitutionality of discrimination on grounds of either race or sex. She served on the President's Commission on the Status of Women (1962–1963), and she contributed to passage of the 1964 Civil Rights Act with a ban on sex discrimination in employment. In 1966 she was a founding member of the National Organization for Women, established as a feminist counterpart to the National Association for the Advancement of Colored People. And she conceived her last major work, *Song in a Weary Throat: An American Pilgrimage* (1987), as "an autobiographical book on Jim Crow and Jane Crow" alike, on the costs of and struggles against segregation and discrimination by gender as well as by race.

As she made her political and spiritual pilgrimage through the twentieth century, Murray changed professions from time to time. Leaving her position with the New York law firm, she taught in West Africa at the Ghana Law School in Accra (1960–1961) and, after her studies at Yale, she served as vice president at Benedict College, a black school in South Carolina (1967–1968). In 1968 she accepted a temporary position at Brandeis University. Five years later she relinquished a tenured position there as the Louis Stulberg Professor of Law and Politics in the American Studies department, for she felt called to the Episcopal ministry, and in 1976 she earned an M.Div. from the General Theological Seminary in New York City. That year the Episcopal church changed its policy to permit the ordination of women priests, and in January 1977 at the National Cathedral in Washington, D.C., she was ordained and consecrated one of the church's first female priests and the first who was black. From 1977 to 1984 she served churches in Washington, D.C., and Baltimore, Maryland.

An accomplished writer as well as lawyer, educator, and minister, Murray gave the term "confrontation by typewriter" to the use of her talents in seeking change by writing letters to newspapers and public officials. She published essays and articles in progressive magazines and in law and theology journals, compiled *States' Laws on Race and Color* (1951), and coauthored *The Constitution and Government of Ghana* (1961). She wrote an account of her North Carolina family and childhood, *Proud Shoes: The Story of an American Family* (1956), a volume of poetry, *Dark Testament and Other Poems* (1970), and her posthumously published, award-winning *Song in a Weary Throat*, which was republished as *Pauli Murray: The Autobiography of a Black Activist, Feminist, Lawyer, Priest, and Poet* (1989).

At the forefront of social change in the United States from the 1940s to the 1980s, Murray achieved prominence as a lawyer, poet, educator, and minister. She worked to promote the rights of workers during the New Deal, of African Americans, notably in the 1940s, and of women, especially in the 1960s, as she demonstrated her commitment to "consciousness combined with action" and "reconciliation as well as liberation." By the 1970s she could note with some pleasure that, though she routinely lost her legal challenges in the 1930s and 1940s, the Supreme Court eventually decided cases the way she had hoped, and she had "lived to see my lost causes found." And yet she looked in vain for "a truly integrated society," and she entered the ministry in part because, she realized, "we had reached a point where law could not give us the answers." In an afterword to her autobiography, a friend, historian Caroline F. Ware, wrote of "the tremendous energy that drove her to achieve excellence in everything she undertook." The recipient of honorary degrees and other awards, Murray retired in 1984 and died in Pittsburgh, Pennsylvania.

• The Pauli Murray Papers are in the Schlesinger Library, Radcliffe College. A lengthy interview she gave Genna Rae McNeil in 1976 is in the Southern Historical Collection, Wilson Library, University of North Carolina, Chapel Hill. The fullest study of Murray's life is her autobiography. Charles Kuralt televised, on his CBS series "On the Road," Murray's first Holy Eucharist, on 13 Feb. 1977, at Chapel Hill, N.C. In an interview (1970) published in *Open Secrets: Ninety-four Women in Touch with Our Time*, ed. Barbaralee Diamonstein (1972), Murray avows her commitment to civil rights. Obituaries are in the *Washington Post* and the *New York Times*, both 4 July 1985, and in *Jet*, 22 July 1985.

PETER WALLENSTEIN

MURRAY, Peter Marshall (9 June 1888–19 Dec. 1969), physician, was born in Houma, Louisiana, the son of John L. Murray, a longshoreman, and Louvinia Smith, a laundress and practical nurse. Murray received his B.A. from Dillard University in 1910. His medical degree, awarded by Howard University in 1914, was one early sign of his drive and talent, bolstered by solid preparation. Like many Howard students, he financed his medical education by working a full-time government job, in his case a clerical post in the census bureau. But his responsibilities went beyond his own wants. His ailing mother in Louisiana also needed help, so he took a second job, a night watchman position; its sole advantage was that it gave him some time for study. After receiving his degree he remained in Washington, first as an intern at Freedmen's Hospital and then as a Howard instructor in surgery. In 1917 he married Charlotte Wallace, the daughter of a Colored Methodist Episcopal minister; the couple had one child.

By 1920, his preparation over, Murray was ready to make his own way. The path he took was that of hundreds of talented young blacks. Their destination was New York City and Harlem, and the influence Murray would exert—in the 1920s and until his death there a half-century later—in opening medicine and surgery to blacks made him as much a part of the Harlem Renaissance as Jean Toomer or Langston Hughes. By the mid-1920s he had performed surgery and won staff privileges in a number of New York and New Jersey hospitals, whose staffs were previously all white, including in 1928 the prestigious Harlem Hospital (where Murray was the second black physician admitted to practice and where he served until his retirement in 1953). In 1930 he was the first black physician to be board-certified in gynecology. In 1949, as a member of the Medical Society of the County of New York, the nation's largest affiliate of the American Medical Association, Murray became the first black to gain a seat in the AMA House of Delegates. From that position he pushed the AMA to officially repudiate the segregation practices of southern medical societies. Though the AMA took no action that year, Murray sensed a growing readiness, and in 1950, aided by pressure from the National Association for the Advancement of Colored People (NAACP) and from National Medical Association editor Montegue Cobb (who like Murray had been battling AMA exclusion for years), Murray won the passage of an AMA resolution urging segregated affiliates to eliminate racial restrictions. Leaving the pace of change up to the southern societies, the AMA appeal brought no immediate change, but it did put segregation under a cloud. By the mid-1950s, owing to pushing by black doctors at the local level, every southern state organization but two had integrated. Now, the way lay open for black doctors not just to mingle professionally with white physicians but also—and more important—to gain staff privileges at southern hospitals. In addition they were able to become part of the medical referral system and win appointment to state and local boards of health—all relevant to professional success and all contingent on membership in local AMA affiliates. In 1954, in recognition of Murray's achievements, his New York medical society elected him its first black president.

Murray's success in breeching white barriers was draped in irony, however. He built it not by militantly challenging white discrimination but by going along with medical segregation, to the extent of publicly acknowledging white medical superiority and black professional dependence. Had Booker T. Washington been alive in the pre–World War II era, he surely would have applauded Murray's strategy, for it seemed to bear out his own faith that the route to black inclusion in white society lay in hard work and accommodation to segregation.

One memorial to Murray's racial conservatism was his long campaign as leader of the all-black National Medical Association (which he served as president-elect in 1931, president in 1932, and chairman of its publications committee from 1943 to 1957) to improve black hospitals—a crusade that aimed to improve opportunities for black physicians and patients alike. That campaign also exposed the sharp division within the black medical community between those who, like Murray, supported accommodation and a minority that insisted on integration as the only moral course.

In 1932, for example, spokesmen for the latter strategy—a group led by a combative New York doctor, Louis Wright—strongly opposed the creation of a new, all-black Veterans Administration hospital in the city on the ground that it would transplant segregation to a region where it had not yet taken root. To Murray, who favored the VA facility, Wright's position was not only misguided but also demagogic. Admittedly, he told the National Medical Association (in his 1932 presidential address), demanding "our full rights" instead of half a loaf "might send a thrill down your spines." But when the issues were the welfare of thousands of black veterans and the professional needs of hundreds of black doctors, Murray felt, as did one professional correspondent, that "'we must look to practical results rather than resort to cowardly cant.'" Discrimination was objectionable, but "'we must not be so everlastingly afraid of so-called segregation that we rule ourselves out of . . . opportunities. It is not the ideal America that we are dealing with. . . . It is a prejudiced America.'"

Although the VA hospital project collapsed, Murray persevered in what he saw as the more realistic approach to "prejudiced America." One critical need of black Americans was better hospital care. Not only were available facilities shockingly deficient, but their physicians were poorly prepared and professionally torpid. To Murray the surest way to address those problems was by improving black hospitals. Usually that meant providing white directors; blacks, he lamented in 1932, simply were not capable of running their own facilities.

But black physicians would ultimately benefit. One defect of black medical education was a lack of accredited internships (a shortfall of about twenty per year). Although 1,400 approved posts went unfilled in white hospitals each year, Murray's preferred solution was not to try to open any of them to blacks but to create accredited internships by making black hospitals better. Although his foes protested, Murray's segregationist strategy usually prevailed in the councils of white foundations (such as the Duke Endowment and the Rosenwald Fund) because they found it philosophically preferable to integration. Probably Murray owed his own rise in establishment medicine to the same cause: whites liked him because he was safe, a man unlikely to make an issue of segregation.

To his credit, however, once he was inside white gates, Murray tried to push them open to other blacks—witness his effort against AMA segregation. Moreover, where black professional gains clearly depended on forcing open the doors of white institutions, Murray did not hang back. Thus, early on he lined up the NMA behind the desegregation of health department staffs, medical schools, and internships in tax-supported hospitals. Integrationists like Louis Wright might have finally won the day, but until desegregation occurred, conservative realists like Murray pushed black medicine steadily ahead via the segregated road.

In the annals of African-American history, the career of Peter Marshall Murray is in a way comparable to those of Phillis Wheatley, Matthew Henson, Julian Bond, and Edward Brooke. Just as those individuals registered important "firsts"—the first black published poet, polar explorer, major party vice presidential nominee, and modern U.S. senator—Murray, too, was a breaker of color bars, in medicine and public health. He died in New York City.

• Murray's papers are in the Moorland-Spingarn Research Collection at Howard University. His major scientific writings in gynecology are cited in Rayford Logan and Michael Winston, eds., *Dictionary of American Negro Biography* (1982). His professional agenda and racial philosophy are laid out in detail in his NMA presidential address found in the *Journal of the N.M.A.* 24 (Nov. 1932): 1–8. Treatment of his long connection with Howard (he was a trustee from 1926 to 1961) is found in Logan, *Howard University: The First 100 Years, 1867–1967* (1969). His lifelong campaign against medical discrimination is detailed in E. H. Beardsley, *A History of Neglect: Health Care for Blacks and Mill Workers in the Twentieth Century South* (1987). A lengthy discussion and assessment of Murray's career by long-time professional associate Montegue Cobb, a man who differed sharply with Murray on the segregation-integration issue, is in the *Journal of the N.M.A.* 59 (Jan. 1967): 71–74, 80. An obituary is in the *New York Times*, 21 Dec. 1969.

E. H. BEARDSLEY

MURRAY, Philip (25 May 1886–9 Nov. 1952), labor leader, was born in New Glasgow, Scotland, the son of William Murray, a miner, and Rose Ann Layden. His parents were Irish Catholics who had recently immigrated to Scotland. His father was head of the local coal miners' union, and Murray himself began working in the mines at age ten. After the family immigrated to the United States in 1902, both father and son found work in the coal fields near Pittsburgh, Pennsylvania. In 1904, at age eighteen, Murray precipitated a strike when he accused the checkweighman of cheating him. The strike was unsuccessful, but Murray was elected president of the United Mine Workers of America (UMWA) local and thereafter rose quickly through the ranks. In 1910 he married Elizabeth Lavery; they adopted one child, a son.

Murray was elected a member of the international executive board of the UMWA in 1912, became president of District 5, which included Pittsburgh, in 1916, and was appointed vice president of the international union by John L. Lewis when the latter became president in 1920. Murray's convivial and egalitarian style, considerable personal charisma, and ability to settle disputes through persuasion facilitated his rise, as did his intense personal loyalty to Lewis. In the 1920s he helped Lewis in his campaigns to purge radicals and socialists from the UMWA and to centralize power within the union. Murray's comprehensive knowledge of the local industry was an important aid in his negotiations with representatives of the coal companies, and it helped him to formulate the Kelley-Davis bill of 1925. Though never enacted, the plan to regulate the coal industry foreshadowed both the industry-stabilization measures of the New Deal and the strategies of government-supervised labor-management cooperation that Murray would pursue as head of the CIO.

In the 1930s Murray was active in the UMWA's organizing drives, taking advantage of provision 7(a) of the National Industrial Recovery Act, which facilitated union organization. At the 1935 convention of the American Federation of Labor (AFL), he argued that workers should be organized in industrial unions like the UMWA, which represent every worker in a plant, regardless of the worker's particular skill. Many of the skilled workers in the AFL, however, were still committed to organizing unions by craft. When the AFL declined to follow the UMWA's lead, Lewis and Murray led the UMWA and seven other industrially inclined unions out of the AFL to form the Committee for Industrial Organization (CIO, later Congress of Industrial Organizations). In May 1936 Murray was appointed chair of the CIO's Steel Workers' Organizing Committee (SWOC), which met with early success when in 1937 the country's largest steel corporation, U.S. Steel, recognized the union and signed a contract. The so-called Little Steel corporations, however, refused to recognize the union, and this led to a series of bloody strikes. The bloodiest was the "Memorial Day Massacre" in South Chicago, when police opened fire on unarmed strikers, killing ten and injuring many others. Although the strikes against Little Steel in 1937 were unsuccessful, SWOC continued to organize, and to seek legal sanctions against Little Steel through the National Labor Relations Board. In 1941 Little Steel finally capitulated.

In 1940 Lewis resigned as president of the CIO, as he had said he would if President Franklin D. Roosevelt was reelected for a third term, and Murray was elected to take his place. Murray's longtime friendship with Lewis was strained by the tension between Murray's pro-Roosevelt, prowar policy as CIO president and Lewis's defiant attitude toward government. The two men broke in 1942, when Lewis led the UMWA out of the CIO, and that same year the SWOC became the United Steelworkers of America.

Before and during World War II Murray led the CIO in an internationalist direction, urging support for the European powers fighting fascism and, after Pearl Harbor, agreeing to a "no-strike pledge" for the duration of the war. Murray urged CIO participation in the National War Labor Board (NWLB), partly out of the conviction that the industrywide stabilization and coordination required by the war effort would benefit the CIO and partly out of the realization that labor would be compelled to cooperate with the federal government if it did not do so voluntarily. The CIO did indeed grow under the NWLB but also lost a great deal of freedom of action.

Murray saw clearly that the fortunes of the CIO were tied to the support it received from the Democratic administration in Washington. In 1943 he organized the CIO's Political Action Committee, which organized voter registration drives and produced publications urging worker support of broad liberal political goals. He worked with both the Roosevelt and Truman administrations on New Deal legislation, organizing production during the war and settling labor disputes in the postwar period. Although he advocated labor's cooperation with government, he did not preach subordination. When a Republican Congress passed the Taft-Hartley Act over President Harry S. Truman's veto in 1947, Murray defied it by refusing to sign the anticommunist affidavit it required of union officials. As a consequence, the United Steelworkers of America was deprived of the services of the National Labor Relations Board for two years, until Murray relented in 1949.

Under Murray's leadership, the CIO participated in the formation in 1945 of the World Federation of Trade Unions (WFTU), an organization the AFL refused to join. Because the WFTU included Soviet trade unions, the CIO drew much criticism domestically for its participation, especially after the WFTU condemned the Marshall Plan for European recovery. Increasing criticism of the CIO's lukewarm attitude toward anti-Soviet foreign policy, combined with the decision of the CIO's communist-led unions to support independent progressive candidate Henry Wallace against Truman in the 1948 election, led to Murray's decision to expel ten of these unions from the CIO in 1949–1950 and to formally recognize the fact that the largest communist-led union, the United Electrical, Radio and Machine Workers of America (UE), had left the CIO in 1948. The loss of nearly a million members was eventually recouped, but CIO efforts to reorganize these workers into anticommunist unions were not always as easy or as successful as many hoped, and the rivalry between communist and anticommunist unions weakened the CIO and the American labor movement.

Murray died in San Francisco shortly after the 1952 presidential election. He had campaigned energetically for Adlai Stevenson and warned that a victory for Dwight D. Eisenhower, who owed little to organized labor, would be a setback for American unions. Murray was central to the development of industrial unionism in the United States, having played a crucial role in building both the UMWA and the CIO. He led the CIO for ten of its twenty years of independent existence and steered it toward the government-based, cooperative strategies that were to define American labor relations for decades after his death.

• Murray's papers are at Pennsylvania State University, but few scholars have found them of interest. Murray developed his ideas about cooperative "industrial democracy" in Morris Cooke and Philip Murray, *Organized Labor and Production* (1940). The best biographical treatment of Murray is Ronald Schatz, "Philip Murray and the Subordination of the Industrial Unions to the United States Government," in *Labor Leaders in America*, ed. Melvyn Dubofsky and Warren van Tine (1987). For broader perspectives on the movements in which Murray was involved, see Robert Zieger, *The CIO 1935–1955* (1995), and Irving Bernstein, *Turbulent Years* (1970), on the history of the CIO; and Paul F. Clark et al., eds., *Forging a Union of Steel* (1987), on the history of the United Steelworkers. Nelson Lichtenstein, *Labor's War at Home* (1982), and Melvyn Dubofsky, *The State and Labor in*

Modern America (1994), provide contrasting interpretations of the origins and consequences of the government-based approach to labor relations that Murray followed.

JONATHAN KISSAM

MURRAY, Robert (1721–22 July 1786), Quaker merchant, was born in Scotland, the son of John Murray. His mother's name is unknown. He immigrated with his father to the colony of Pennsylvania in 1732. As he grew to adulthood, he operated a small flour mill on Swatara Creek, in present-day Dauphin County, Pennsylvania. In 1744 he married Mary Lindley, with whom he had twelve children. He went on trading voyages to the West Indies and lived in North Carolina from 1750 to 1753. During these early years, he refined his merchant skills. In 1753 he and his younger brother John Murray went to New York City and began a merchant partnership.

The start of the French and Indian War was a fortunate period for mercantile enterprise. It brought shipping and supply contracts to many merchants in the colonies but especially to those in towns such as New York. Over the next ten years the Murray brothers rose to the height of success in the New York commercial world. The end of the war, however, initiated a mild economic depression in New York in the early 1760s. The Murray brothers suffered, as did many merchants engaged in the import-export trade.

Murray went to England in 1767 and remained there until early 1775, taking charge of his business affairs. He was therefore not present during the crucial period when colonial resistance to British taxes and duties led toward rebellion. Although surely aware of the rift between the colonies and the mother country, Murray appeared to take little notice of the import of the matter. On his return to New York City, he and his younger brother endeavored to have the ship *Beulah* unloaded from a secret position off Sandy Hook, to evade the watchful eyes of New York patriots enforcing the nonimportation agreement of October 1774. The *Beulah* was discovered, and both brothers were hauled before the Committee of Sixty, formed the previous year to enforce nonimportation. The Murray brothers promptly confessed their role and begged forgiveness. They were released after apologizing for the "trouble and uneasiness" they had caused.

In May 1775 the Murray brothers petitioned the Continental Congress to restore their former trade privileges. The fact that they found it necessary to do so indicates the strength that the patriot faction had gained in the politics of New York. However, the start of the American Revolution imperiled Murray's fortunes and those of many New York merchants. On 15 September 1776 British forces led by General Henry Clinton landed at Kip's Bay, Manhattan, and threatened to cut off the retreat of 3,500 American Continental soldiers led by General Israel Putnam. Murray's wife entertained the British officers, her hospitality delaying their pursuit by nearly two hours. Nearly all of Putnam's men were able to evade the British and to reach safety. A legend soon sprang up in the American forces that "Mrs. Murray saved this part of the Continental Army" (Thacher, p. 59). Subsequent studies of the matter have confirmed that the entertainment took place and that the two hours were quite significant, but it is extremely unlikely that Mary Murray acted intentionally to save the American troops.

Murray's own allegiance was never established clearly. In November 1776 he signed the Loyalist Declaration of Dependence that affirmed the authority of King George III and the British Parliament over the colonies. It is also significant that his shipping interests were not molested during the period of the British occupation of New York City (1776–1783). However, given his mild demeanor and the lack of any direct evidence to establish him as a firm Loyalist, Murray probably belonged to that third of New York merchants who have been characterized as "trimming neutrals" (Kammen, p. 365) during the American Revolution. Murray died in New York City three years after the end of the war.

Murray's merchant activities stand forth as the most significant aspect of his life and career. The ups and downs of his fortunes in the mercantile business indicate the boom and bust cycles in colonial America, a result in particular of the influence of the colonial wars. In his apparent obliviousness to the development of American revolutionary sentiment, Murray was typical of many New York merchants. Like many of his fellows, Murray saw no compelling reason to risk his hard-won fortune in the defense of a cause that seemed to him unnecessary in many respects, injurious to the conduct of business in general, and hazardous to his life, reputation, and fortune. He managed to steer a middle course during the years of the British occupation of New York City. If he was no firm patriot and no firm Loyalist, he belongs instead to that little-studied and little-understood group, the one-third of the American people whom even John Adams was to label as indifferent to the Revolution's success or failure.

• Few sources exist to study Murray's life and career. Arthur Schlesinger, Sr., *The Colonial Merchants and the American Revolution, 1763–1776* (1917), J. A. Scoville, *The Old Merchants of New York City* (1863), Leopold S. Launitz-Schurer, Jr., *Loyal Whigs and Revolutionaries: The Making of the Revolution in New York, 1765–1776* (1980), and Virginia D. Harrington, *The New York Merchant on the Eve of the American Revolution* (1935), all mention Murray at least in passing but none identifies him as a noteworthy Loyalist or patriot. One of the best sources for understanding the period in which Murray lived and worked is Michael Kammen, *Colonial New York: A History* (1975). For information about the incident involving Mary Murray and the battle of Kip's Bay see James Thacher, *Military Tour of the American Revolution* (1862), and William Cutter, *The Life of Israel Putnam, Major-General in the Army of the American Revolution* (1847). See also R. W. G. Vail, "The Loyalist Declaration of Dependence of November 28, 1776," New-York Historical Society, *Quarterly* 31, no. 1 (1947): 68–71.

SAMUEL WILLARD CROMPTON

MURRAY, Thomas Edward (20 June 1891–26 May 1961), engineer-inventor and Atomic Energy Commission member, was born in Albany, New York, the son of Thomas Edward Murray, a prominent engineer-businessman, and Catherine Bradley. Raised in Brooklyn and educated in the Catholic schools of New York City, Murray attended the Sheffield Scientific School of Yale University (B.S., 1911), where he studied mechanical engineering. In 1917 he married Marie Brady, with whom he had eleven children. Reflecting the devout religious atmosphere of his household, two of his sons became Catholic priests.

After graduating from college, Murray became a partner in businesses established by his father to develop and market inventions and to design electrical power plants. Following his father's death in 1929, he became chief executive of the enterprises. By 1950 he personally held 200 patents. During the 1930s he was receiver and chief operating officer of the bankrupt Interborough Rapid Transit subway line.

During World War II, Murray invented new designs for the manufacture of mortar shells, winning a distinguished service citation and a letter of appreciation from President Franklin D. Roosevelt. He also was a successful arbitrator in two important New York area labor disputes. A noted public figure, in 1945 he unsuccessfully sought support for the Democratic nomination for mayor of New York. In 1947 President Harry S. Truman appointed him the presiding officer of a three-person board of trustees to administer the health and welfare fund of the United Mine Workers. He resigned the following year, frustrated by a deadlock between the labor and management trustees.

In 1950 Truman named Murray to fill out the unexpired term of David E. Lilienthal on the Atomic Energy Commission (AEC) and appointed him to a full five-year term in 1952. Although McCarthyism was beginning to affect almost every area of American politics related to defense, Murray encountered no appreciable opposition, thanks to his status as a leading Catholic layman and successful businessman.

During his seven years on the AEC, Murray did not fit neatly into a liberal or conservative mold. His strong religious faith (he proposed beginning meetings with a prayer) shaded naturally into intense anti-Communism. He was the commission's strongest advocate of military priorities. In 1954 he voted with the majority to deny a security clearance to J. Robert Oppenheimer, declaring that, although not a betrayer of secrets, Oppenheimer had disregarded security regulations recklessly and thus might be considered "disloyal."

Despite his vote on Oppenheimer, Murray was a vocal critic of the Republicans during Dwight D. Eisenhower's presidency and frequently at odds with Lewis Strauss, Eisenhower's AEC chairman. Murray argued against private development of nuclear power plants, criticized the Dixon-Yates contract (an attempt to block expansion of the Tennessee Valley Authority), and advocated more openness about the hazards of radiation. He opposed hydrogen bomb tests and the development of larger thermonuclear devices, arguing that nuclear weapons were already large enough to destroy civilization. Far from being a disarmer, however, he favored the manufacture of thousands of tactical nuclear weapons for battlefield situations.

In 1957 President Eisenhower declined to reappoint him to the AEC, and thereupon the Democratic majority of the Congressional Joint Committee on Atomic Energy retained Murray as a part-time consultant. In 1958 he ran unsuccessfully for the Democratic nomination for a U.S. Senate seat in New York.

Murray devoted the balance of his life to business, religious, and charitable interests. Among his honors were the papal titles of Knight of St. Gregory and Knight of Malta. His career was in many ways representative of the rise of Irish Catholics in American society and politics. He died in New York City.

• No personal papers of Murray have been deposited in a research institution. He authored a book, *Nuclear Energy for War and Peace* (1960). A brief interview regarding his service on the AEC is in the Harry S. Truman Papers, *Memoirs* File, Harry S. Truman Library, Independence, Mo. The *New York Times* is a readily accessible source for highlights of his public career, especially his explanation of his vote against Oppenheimer, 30 June 1954, and his try for the Senate in 1958, 7–27 Aug. 1958. He receives occasional mention in *The Journals of David E. Lilienthal*, vols. 3–4 (1966, 1969). Richard G. Hewlett and Oscar Anderson, *A History of the United States Atomic Energy Commission*, vol. 2 (1969), mentions him and establishes the context for his early years on the AEC. An obituary is in the *New York Times*, 27 May 1961.

ALONZO L. HAMBY

MURRAY, William Davidson (17 July 1858–20 Nov. 1939), author and youth leader, was born in New York City, the son of John W. Murray and Mary Strothers Davidson. A few years after his birth the family moved to Plainfield, New Jersey, where Murray graduated from Plainfield High School in 1875. After receiving an A.B. in 1880 from Yale University, where he joined the Phi Upsilon fraternity, Murray entered the Columbia University Law School, where he completed his LL.B. degree in 1882. Afterward he opened his law practice in New York. In 1893 he married Mary E. Mosher; they had one child.

Even before his marriage, while still in his twenties, Murray had begun his long association with the Young Men's Christian Association (YMCA) through its student volunteer movement for foreign missions, begun in 1886. For fifty-one years he served on the organization's New Jersey State Board and made several trips to Europe to help promote its student mission work. He also made a successful organizational tour of Japan in 1892. From 1894 to 1925 he served as chairman of the YMCA's foreign work committee. During this time period he was also a trustee of the National YMCA Board, a board member of the Silver Bay Association for Christian Conference and Training, and a trustee of the committee on the work of John R. Mott, long-time general secretary of the YMCA's International Committee and founder-chairman of its World's Student Christian Federation. For twenty years Murray also served as a vice chairman of the International Committee and treasurer of the World's Christian Student Federation trustees. During World War I, Murray headed the YMCA war work at Camp Dix, New Jersey, and served on the YMCA's National War Work Council. After the war he conducted more extensive travels to Eastern Europe, Turkey, and the Orient on behalf of the YMCA's Committee on Promotion of Friendship between America and the Far East.

It was through his association with Edgar M. Robinson and other area YMCA leaders that Murray became involved with the formation of the Boy Scouts of America (BSA) in 1910 and served on the BSA's editorial board. As a delegate on its first National Council, he was the administrator of the BSA's first experimental camp at Silver Bay, New York. Largely as a result of that camp, Murray, along with the majority of the BSA executives, including Colin H. Livingstone and James E. West, came to favor Robert S. S. Baden-Powell's more cohesive military approach to scouting, as opposed to Ernest Thompson Seton's liberal, democratic approach characteristic of the latter's woodcraft Indian movement. Thus, from 1910 to 1926, Murray served faithfully on the BSA executive committee in good standing. In 1926 he was among the first recipients of the Silver Buffalo, the BSA's highest award "for distinguished service to boyhood."

From 1927 to 1930 Murray headed the committee that started the BSA's Cub Scout program for younger boys. In 1935 he headed the Boy Scout delegation that presented the five-millionth copy of the organization's *Handbook for Boys* to President Franklin D. Roosevelt at the White House. Then in 1937 he published *The History of the Boy Scouts of America*. Although that book was biased and served to rekindle the long-simmering controversy with Dan Beard and Ernest Thompson Seton over the degree of militarism in scouting and who had actually started the BSA program, it won him praise from chief scout executive James West, who declared Murray's service to the BSA to be "outstanding and indeed unequalled."

As an elder of Plainfield's Crescent Avenue Presbyterian Church, Murray taught a Bible class and served forty-one years as superintendent of the church's primary department. In addition to his 1929 autobiography, *As He Journeyed*, his writings included *The Life and Works of Jesus* (1910), *Bible Stories to Tell Children* (1910), *My Three Keys* (1920), *Fun with Paper Folding* (1928), *What Manner of Man Is This?* (1930), *The Message of the Twelve Prophets* (1931), and *The Teaching of Bible Classes* (1932). He also published several articles in *Boys' Life*, the BSA's organ that he helped purchase and launch in 1912; his last article, "Swimmin' Holes and Circuses," which depicted his boyhood memories of outdoor activities, appeared in the December 1939 issue.

In all, Murray practiced law for fifty-seven years until failing health forced him into semiretirement. He died at his Plainfield home.

• Papers relating to Murray's life and youth work may be found in the Plainfield City Library and the YMCA Historical Library in New York City. See also C. Howard Hopkins, *A History of the YMCA in North America* (1951); John Henry Wadland, *Ernest Thompson Seton: Man in Nature and the Progressive Era, 1880–1915* (1978); and *Who Was Who in America*, vol. 1 (1897–1943), p. 884. His obituary is in the *New York Times*, 21 Nov. 1939.

H. ALLEN ANDERSON

MURRAY, William Henry David (21 Nov. 1869–15 Oct. 1956), politician and agricultural advocate, was born in Toadsuck, Texas, near Collinsville, the son of Uriah Dow Thomas Murray and Bertha Elizabeth Jones, poor farmers. He grew up in north central Texas, running away from home at the age of twelve. For the next seven years he worked as an agricultural laborer, attending public schools sporadically. After matriculating at College Hill Institute, a secondary school at Springtown, he became a public school teacher in Parker County. There he became an activist in the Farmers' Alliance.

Joining the faction of the Democratic party led by James Stephen Hogg, Murray campaigned actively when Hogg sought the governorship. Endowed with a talent for oratory, Murray spoke widely in opposition to the Peoples or Populist party. A reformist Democrat, more moderate than his Populist opponents, Hogg favored regulation of the railroads, insurance companies, and the petroleum industry. In 1894, having established himself as a leader in the alliance and the Democratic party, Murray moved to the larger community of Corsicana, where he founded a newspaper, the *Corsicana Daily News*, and served as editor and publisher. He ran for the state senate in 1892 and 1894 but was defeated. When the newspaper failed financially, Murray moved in 1897 to Fort Worth, where, having read widely in legal texts, he entered the practice of law. Although Murray was admitted to the bar on 10 April 1897, his practice did not flourish, and in March 1898 he departed for Indian Territory.

Murray settled in Tishomingo, the capital of the Chickasaw Nation, establishing ties to the leaders of that tribe. His law practice proved lucrative, especially after he married Mary Alice Hearrell, niece of the Chickasaw governor, on 19 July 1899. They had five children. His relationship to the tribal leaders made him a prominent figure in the Chickasaw Nation, and he became deeply involved in Chickasaw politics. In 1905, when a major effort was made to obtain statehood for Indian Territory, Murray helped to write the constitution for the proposed state of Sequoyah. Although that effort failed, his role at the constitutional convention and his frequent speaking engagements made him a territorial leader. He spoke extensively in support of the Democratic party and for diversified agriculture. His eloquent speeches in favor of the cultivation of alfalfa led to his sobriquet, "Alfalfa Bill."

When the movement for separate statehood for Indian Territory failed, a joint statehood convention with Oklahoma Territory was held in Guthrie, Oklahoma Territory, in 1906, and Murray dominated the meeting. Supported by delegates from Indian Territory and by alliance members, he was elected president of the convention. Murray wrote major sections of the constitution, using his authority as presiding officer to win inclusion of his ideas. He opposed alien and corporate ownership of farm land and advocated safety and health inspections of coal mines, the eight-hour day for railroad workers and in public works, maximum freight rates on common carriers, and a 1 percent gross-receipts tax on coal, petroleum, and transportation companies. Voters in the territories approved the document, and on 16 November 1907 Oklahoma was admitted to the union. Although conservative politicians such as William Howard Taft denounced Murray's handiwork, the Oklahoma constitution included numerous examples of the reforms advocated nationally by progressives, among them the initiative and referendum processes and prohibition.

Murray won election to the Oklahoma House of Representatives in the first state legislature, and his colleagues made him Speaker of the House. For two years he fought for legislation to curb business excesses, such as a bank-guarantee law, and bills to enhance agricultural education. Murray constantly defended "the boys at the fork of the creek." Defeated for the Democratic nomination for governor in 1910, two years later he sought election to the U.S. House of Representatives and won an at-large seat. After congressional reapportionment, he ran successfully in the new Fourth District in 1914. During his four years in Congress Murray made few contributions to the legislative process, but he championed President Woodrow Wilson's preparedness program. A wave of isolationist enthusiasm in his district swept Murray out of Congress in 1916, and he again failed to win the gubernatorial nomination two years later. His strong support in sections of rural Oklahoma could not overcome the opposition his platforms engendered in the towns and cities.

Discouraged by successive defeats, Murray abandoned the United States throughout much of the 1920s, laboring instead to create an agricultural colony in southern Bolivia with his sons, and their spouses, and neighbors from Tishomingo. They suffered serious hardships as the promises of support from the Bolivian government failed to materialize, and the harshness of living conditions demoralized the settlers. When the colony failed, Murray returned in 1929 to Oklahoma, where he found political and economic chaos.

Although Oklahoma enjoyed unprecedented prosperity in the 1920s, the fabric of the state's government was rent by the rise of the Ku Klux Klan, the impeachment of two governors, and the rapid ascendancy of the previously moribund Republican party. The collapse of agricultural prices and catastrophic reverses in the petroleum industry because of overproduction created economic disaster by 1930. Murray found that his brand of reformist ideas and agrarianism now appealed to the voters.

In 1930 he ran for governor on a reform platform, and his fiery oratory swamped a prominent oilman who opposed him in the Democratic primary. Murray campaigned for greater regulation of business, reform of the State School Land Commission, an extensive highway construction program, and economy in the state government. Despite the strenuous efforts of the metropolitan press, he won an overwhelming victory in the general election. As governor Murray proved irascible, controversial, and colorful. He lambasted the administrations of the state's colleges and universities, and he planted crops on the lawn of the governor's mansion to feed the hungry. When free bridges were constructed over the Red River, a controversy broke out between the owners of toll bridges and the state, and Murray dispatched the National Guard to open the toll-free bridges. The National Guard was on duty throughout the Murray administration, as it was also sent into the oil fields to halt the production of illegal or "hot" oil. The governor advocated proration or limits on output to raise prices, and he appealed to the governors of other oil-producing states to curtail the flow of petroleum. In one of his few legislative triumphs, Murray successfully fought for the creation of the Oklahoma Tax Commission, the equalization of property taxes across the state, an income tax on upper incomes, and a corporate income tax.

In 1932 Murray sought the Democratic nomination for president. He campaigned across the country speaking on his platform "Bread, Butter, Bacon and Beans." He won only one delegate outside of Oklahoma, and his opposition to Franklin D. Roosevelt earned him the enmity of the New Dealers. After March 1933 Murray fought with federal agencies over relief funds and their administration. In addition to his personal animus toward Roosevelt, Murray was determined that relief funds would be administered by the state without interference from Washington. Becoming a vehement critic of Roosevelt and the New Deal, Murray caused Oklahoma to lose federal money, and he limited the impact of many relief programs and agencies. His often eccentric behavior continued to generate newspaper stories, but his support faded because of his refusal to cooperate with Washington.

When his gubernatorial term ended in 1935, Murray returned to his farm and began to publish books and pamphlets attacking the New Deal and Roosevelt. As Murray aged, his racism and anti-Semitism became more virulent when he defended segregation and condemned urbanization and industrialization. Defeat in the gubernatorial primary in 1938 was Murray's last political hurrah. He campaigned against Roosevelt in 1940, but the shaky, disheveled old man had lost his following. Only in 1950 when his son Johnston Murray was elected governor was the elder Murray to return to the governor's mansion. Throughout his life he championed agriculture and the family farm, often stating his firm belief that "civilization begins and ends with the plow." Murray died in Oklahoma City.

• Personal papers of William H. Murray are located in the Western History Collections at the University of Oklahoma and at the Oklahoma Historical Society. Additional materials about Murray are found in the Charles N. Haskell and Robert L. Williams collections at the Oklahoma Historical Society, and the gubernatorial records can be found at the Oklahoma State Library. Extensive records for the 1930s are in the Franklin D. Roosevelt Library at Hyde Park, N.Y. The "Murray Colony" File 824.52 in the Diplomatic, Legal and Fiscal Branch, National Archives, Washington, D.C., contains materials on the Bolivian fiasco. Murray's three-volume memoirs, *Memoirs of Governor Murray and True History of Oklahoma* (1945), must be used with great caution. His *Rights of Americans* (1937), *Uncle Sam Needs a Doctor* (1940), *Palestine* (1947), and *The Negro's Place in Call of Race* (1948) reveal his rapid plunge into racism and anti-Semitism. The standard biography is Keith L. Bryant, Jr., *Alfalfa Bill Murray* (1968). The best survey, which places Murray's career within the context of Oklahoma's political history, is James R. Scales and Danney Goble, *Oklahoma Politics: A History* (1982). An obituary is in the Oklahoma City *Daily Oklahoman*, 16 Oct. 1956.

KEITH L. BRYANT, JR.

MURRAY, William Vans (9 Feb. 1760–11 Dec. 1803), congressman and diplomat, was born in Cambridge, Maryland, the son of Henry Murray, a prosperous physician and commercial investor, and Rebecca Orrick. Murray's family supported the patriot cause during the American Revolution, although poor health prevented William from serving in the military. He was educated in Maryland and studied law at the Inns of Court (Middle Temple) in England from 1784 to 1787, during which time he also met and courted Charlotte Hughens (or Hughins). The two were married in Cambridge, Maryland, in 1789; they had no children.

While in London Murray befriended John Adams and his son John Quincy Adams, and with the elder Adams's support and guidance he wrote a series of essays, published anonymously as *Political Sketches* (1787). In these essays, Murray defended American political institutions against their critics, particularly Gabriel Bonnot de Mably and other French *philosophes*. He argued that liberty and republican government depended not on the absence of "luxury" and diversity, but on comprehensive laws, a relative equality of rights, and representative assemblies dedicated to preserving those rights. He also asserted that American strength depended on the absence of domestic political factions and on the country's distance from European conflicts. While the *Sketches* received a poor review in Britain, Murray himself sought to uphold their liberal, semi-isolationist precepts in his later career.

Upon his return to Maryland in 1787, Murray began practicing law, although within a year he won a seat in the Maryland House of Delegates and began his public career. In 1790 he successfully stood for election to the U.S. House of Representatives. During his three terms in Congress (1791–1797) Murray was a faithful but moderate supporter of the Federalist party and its goals. He attempted to block the Giles Resolutions (1793), which called for an audit of Alexander Hamilton's Treasury Department, and he opposed James Madison's 1794 resolution calling for discriminatory tariff rates on British shipping. He was a strong supporter of Jay's Treaty, and in March 1796 he denounced Edward Livingston's demand for all executive papers relating to the treaty, calling the motion "a deadly poison to both the Constitution and the character of the nation for honor and good faith" (speech of 23 Mar. 1796, *Annals of Congress*, vol. 5, p. 697). He insisted that any treaty negotiated in accordance with international law and ratified by the Senate was legally binding on the entire nation and that the House, which was bound to honor and enforce the nation's agreements, had no constitutional right to interfere with them.

Murray actively supported John Adams's presidential candidacy later that year and wrote a series of letters and essays in the press celebrating Adams's achievements and defending him against both Federalist and Republican critics. He planned to retire from public service shortly thereafter, but in February 1797 President George Washington appointed him minister to the Batavian Republic—the satellite state that France had established in the Dutch Netherlands—and Murray gratefully accepted the office and its responsibilities. His subsequent residence at The Hague was not without its setbacks; in April 1798, for example, Secretary of State Timothy Pickering severely reprimanded Murray for his hasty recognition of the Batavian Radicals following their January coup d'etat. But Murray also scored a few successes. He pressured the Batavian government into banning French privateering raids off the Dutch coast, thus relieving American shipping of a heavy burden, and obtained a favorable settlement for the owners of the *Wilmington Packet*, an American merchant vessel seized by a Dutch privateer in 1793. Moreover, in the absence of an official American representative in Paris, Murray served as one of the State Department's principal sources of information on the French government and its activities.

While Murray felt considerable distaste for the French Republic, he maintained a flexible attitude toward it, and in the wake of the XYZ affair and the beginning of the Quasi-War with France, he was selected by French foreign minister Charles Maurice de Talleyrand as the recipient of French peace overtures. In June 1798 Talleyrand dispatched Louis-André Pichon, former secretary to the French legation in Philadelphia, to The Hague to extend the olive branch. After three months of informal conferences with Pichon, Murray received official assurance from Talleyrand that France would respectfully receive any future minister sent by the U.S. government. He forwarded Talleyrand's letter to Philadelphia, where it helped convince President John Adams to begin formal peace negotiations.

On 18 February 1799 Adams asked the Senate to confirm Murray as minister to the French Republic. The Senate was stunned by Adams's abrupt shift from war preparations to reconciliation, but it eventually

granted his request. However, a group of High Federalist senators who doubted Murray's party loyalty convinced Adams to add Oliver Ellsworth and William Davie to the peace mission and to make Murray its junior member. Murray accepted his demotion with good humor and joined his fellow commissioners in Paris in March 1800, four months after Napoleon's coup and the liquidation of the French Republic.

The American commissioners and their French counterparts—Joseph Bonaparte, Charles-Pierre Claret Fleurieu, and Pierre-Louis Roederer—spent the next seven months in tedious, frequently deadlocked negotiations before reaching a compromise in September. The Convention of Mortfontaine (3 Oct. 1800), as modified by the U.S. Senate and ratified by both countries the following year, ended hostilities between the United States and France and released the former from its 1778 treaty obligations respecting military aid to France. In exchange, the U.S. government agreed to indemnify American merchants for damages inflicted by French privateers. At the request of the Thomas Jefferson administration, Murray returned to Paris in May 1801 to conduct the final ratification negotiations. He received word of his recall from The Hague shortly thereafter and returned to the United States in December. He spent the last two years of his life in Cambridge rebuilding his house (which had been destroyed by fire) and his law practice. Murray died at his estate in Dorchester County, near Cambridge.

John Quincy Adams, Murray's longtime friend and correspondent, eulogized his comrade as "one of the brightest characters which has arisen in the American Union since the establishment of its independence" (*Portfolio*, 7 Jan. 1804). Murray was more modest about his life and accomplishments, but his genial disposition, personal flexibility, and moderate political views made him a natural diplomat, and the negotiations he conducted between 1798 and 1801 prevented a dangerous and costly war between the United States and France. Ironically, these same negotiations, by splitting the Federalist party and ensuring Jefferson's presidential victory in 1800, helped end Murray's own political career. It was a fate that Murray accepted with little complaint.

• Murray's diaries and papers are at the Library of Congress, the Princeton University Library, and the Pierpont Morgan Library in New York City. His diplomatic correspondence can be found in the General Records of the Department of State, National Archives RG 59 (especially vols. 2–4 of "Despatches from the Netherlands"), and in the Timothy Pickering Papers at the Massachusetts Historical Society in Boston. Murray's correspondence with John Quincy Adams (1797–1803) is reprinted in *Annual Report of the American Historical Association for 1912*, ed. Worthington Ford (1914), as was Adams's 1804 obituary. Much of Murray's correspondence with James McHenry is reprinted in Bernard Steiner, *Life and Correspondence of James McHenry* (1907). His congressional speeches can be followed in Joseph Gales and William Seaton, comps., *The Annals of Congress* (1834–1856), while many of his laudatory essays on John Adams can be found in the *Gazette of the United States*, ed. John Fenno (1796). The best modern biography is Peter Hill, *William*

Vans Murray: Federalist Diplomat (1971). Shorter works include two articles by Alexander DeConde, "William Vans Murray and the Diplomacy of Peace," *Maryland Historical Magazine* 48 (Mar. 1953), and "William Vans Murray's *Political Sketches*," *Mississippi Valley Historical Review* 41, no. 4 (Mar. 1955). A complete account of contemporary Franco-American diplomacy can be found in DeConde, *The Quasi-War* (1966). For a solid overview of American politics and diplomacy in the 1790s, see Stanley Elkins and Eric McKitrick, *The Age of Federalism* (1993). An obituary is in *Poulson's American Daily Advertiser* (Philadelphia), 17 Dec. 1803.

DAVID NICHOLS

MURRELL, John Andrews (1806?–1 Nov. 1844), archcriminal according to legend but in reality a minor thief, was born in Lunenburg County, Virginia, and raised from infancy in Williamson County, Tennessee, the son of Jeffrey Murrell and Zilpha Andrews, farmers. He was the third of eight children; his three brothers also became felons, and at least one sister married a criminal. The reasons for this moral collapse are obscure. Jeffrey Murrell was a respectable, hard-working farmer who owned 146 acres and as many as three slaves. His estate, however, was frittered away in court costs, confiscated bail money, and other expenses connected to the villainy of his sons. Shortly after his death in 1824 the family was reduced to penury.

Nothing is known of Murrell's education, but he was literate and wrote in a fine copperplate script. He first ran afoul of the law at the age of sixteen and was in and out of difficulty thereafter. By the age of twenty-one he had already served three years in jail for stealing a horse, for which he was also whipped at the public pillory and ordered branded on the thumb. In 1829 he married Elizabeth Mangham from a neighboring farm family, and they had two children. By 1831, after first moving to Wayne County, Murrell had shifted residence to Madison County near the tiny hamlet of Denmark in western Tennessee, where he claimed to be a farmer but seems to have continued to excel as a wastrel. There is good reason to believe that he was an occasional counterfeiter, but it was for the crime of slave stealing that he was sentenced to ten years hard labor in 1834. After one attempt to escape he settled down and became a model prisoner at the Nashville penitentiary, where it was reported that he found Jesus, learned the blacksmith's trade, and contracted tuberculosis (not necessarily in that order). He died of tuberculosis, and his body was interred at Pikeville, Tennessee, where he had worked quietly as a blacksmith during the six months between his release and his death. According to one story, his body was dug up after burial, the head removed for use as a carnival exhibit, and the remainder left to be eaten by hogs.

This historical Murrell bears little resemblance to the legendary figure who has occupied a place in standard reference works and been the subject of several popular histories and novels. The legendary Murrell was a demonic figure who, after he was whipped and jailed as a youth, swore vengeance against respectable society. He traveled widely, murdering, stealing, and making the acquaintance of desperate men like himself all over the South. Eventually, the legend continued, he presided over a criminal conspiracy that stretched from Maryland to Louisiana, the Mystic Clan of the Confederacy, whose members were bound together by horrid oaths. The clan's purpose was to provoke slave uprisings throughout the region. Taking advantage of the chaos, Murrell and a band of followers would steal as much money as possible and then escape as troops marched from the North to suppress the rebellion.

The legendary—and bogus—Murrell was the creation of Virgil A. Stewart, an informer (possibly Murrell's confederate) whose testimony had sent Murrell to prison for slave stealing. Shortly after the trial, a small pamphlet appeared; the author's name, Augustus Q. Walton, appears to have been a pseudonym for Stewart. It described the conspiracy of the Mystic Clan in lurid detail, promoted Murrell to the status of master criminal—"the Great Western Land Pirate"—and presented Stewart as the savior of the South because he had been instrumental in ending Murrell's career before the conspiracy had had a chance to develop (at great personal risk—the pamphlet described several harrowing attempts on Stewart's life by furious henchmen). Although Stewart's motives are obscure, they certainly included, in descending importance, large measures of self-justification, self-aggrandizement, and the hope of monetary gain.

The pamphlet was greeted with derision in west Tennessee, where Murrell was seen as a thieving nuisance but singularly ill-suited for the grandiose role of archfiend. It found a more receptive audience in the Delta region of Hinds and especially Madison County, Mississippi, where Stewart began hawking the pamphlet in June 1835. Cotton lands had been recently brought under cultivation by large gangs of slaves, plantations were scattered, settlements were few, and the white population, outnumbered and fearful, was particularly susceptible to tales of an insurrection conspiracy. Convinced that Murrell's henchmen were determined to go ahead with the scheme despite their ringleader's imprisonment, whites in the area around Beattie's Bluff and Livingston in Madison County began an inquisition of slaves already identified as troublemakers. Under torture they implicated white men, virtually all of them outsiders or men of low status. So-called committees of safety were formed, and whippings and hangings began in earnest. Panic spread into neighboring counties and west to Louisiana, and patrols were stepped up over much of the South. Most of the killing occurred in Mississippi; seven white men were hanged by the committees of safety, and at least as many were murdered by spontaneous mobs. Several dozen were whipped and banished. The number of blacks who were hanged or otherwise killed can only be estimated but may have exceeded fifty. Gamblers, viewed as rootless and disreputable, also fell under suspicion. In Vicksburg five were hanged, and the rest were expelled; as July progressed, towns along the Mississippi River, from Cincinnati to New Orleans, were purged of the gaming fraternity.

Stewart claimed that Murrell had often expressed antislavery views as a way of gaining the confidence of slaves he intended to kidnap and then sell in other parts. The ruse acquired significance later in July 1835 when the Anti-Slavery Society began flooding the South with antislavery tracts. The entire regions responded as if threatened by foreign invasion. The mobbing of individuals who circulated the tracts and the mobbing of "Murelites" merged in the public mind, and Murrell acquired his true infamy. His career seemed to confirm the southern view that abolitionism was fraudulent while at the same time undermining the superior moral claims of antislavery proponents.

Little is known of Virgil A. Stewart, but his handiwork inspired one of the most bizarre outbreaks of mob violence in American history. Stewart's vogue was brief; even in the Mississippi Delta he was widely considered to be a charlatan a decade after the panic of the summer of 1835 had subsided. His creation, however, has lived on in popular histories and novels and standard reference works, including the *Dictionary of American Biography*.

• The view of Murrell as an archcriminal originated in August Q. Walton, Esq., *A History of the Detection, Conviction, Life and Designs of John A. Murel, the Great Western Land Pirate* (1835), written by Virgil A. Stewart or by a ghost-writer acting for Stewart; in either case, Walton is a pseudonym. Stewart was also responsible for H. R. Howard, comp., *The History of Virgil A. Stewart and His Adventure* (1836), which contains the Walton pamphlet, revised to reflect events of the panic of 1835; in it Murrell is made to express more explicit antislavery views. Two works that contributed additional details to the legend are *National Police Gazette*, eds., *The Life and Adventures of John A. Murrell, the Great Western Land Pirate* (1847), and Robert M. Coates, *The Outlaw Years: The History of the Land Pirates of the Natchez Trace* (1930). Coates as well as writers before and after him made uncritical use of Stewart's pamphlet and the *National Police Gazette* account as their main sources. The only scholarly treatment to date is James L. Penick, *The Great Western Land Pirate: John A. Murrell in Legend and History* (1981).

JAMES L. PENICK

MURRIETA, Joseph. *See* Murieta, Joaquin.

MURROW, Edward R. (25 Apr. 1908–27 Apr. 1965), broadcast journalist, was born Egbert Roscoe Murrow in Polecat Creek, near Greensboro, North Carolina, the son of Roscoe Murrow, a farmer and later an engineer on a logging railroad, and Ethel Lamb, a teacher. The Murrow family soon traveled to the state of Washington, which was still thought of as a frontier, full of labor strikes and conflicts over free speech, trade unionism, and legislative reform.

Ed, as he liked to be called, grew up in Skagit Valley, near Blanchard, and the year after high school worked in the lumber camps on the rugged Olympic Peninsula as a compassman. He then worked his way through Washington State College (now University), where he majored in speech and changed his name to Edward. A natural leader both in high school and college, Murrow was elected president of the National Student Federation in 1929. He moved to New York City after graduation to lead that organization for two years before going to the Columbia Broadcasting System (CBS), one of the two major radio networks.

Murrow began his broadcast career as a CBS director of talks and education in 1935 and was sent to Europe in 1937, not as a reporter, but to coordinate cultural broadcasts. When Adolph Hitler took over Austria, Murrow made the first of the more than 5,000 broadcasts of his career. He reported not just the compelling facts about the war but gave vivid descriptions that conveyed the mood and feelings of the time. He also developed a unique style of delivery, prompted by his former speech professor, Ida Lou Anderson, who suggested that Murrow pause when he began his account, "This . . . is London."

During the battle of Britain in 1940, Murrow reported, "Christmas Day began in London nearly an hour ago. The churchbells did not ring at midnight. When they ring again, it will be to announce invasion." A *Time* magazine writer observed the urgency of his reports: "Murrow made you feel about the possible defeat of Britain in World War II as personally, as you would about the death of a child."

Murrow hired the best he could find—Murrow's boys, who covered the rise of Nazism and the war fronts. They included Charles Collingwood, Eric Sevareid, William Shirer, Howard K. Smith, Richard C. Hottelet, and Bill Downs. In the postwar era, he hired Alexander Kendrick, David Schoenbrun, and George Polk. He hired print journalists because, as he once said, "I'm hiring reporters, not announcers."

To add power to their reporting, Murrow emphasized a vivid but simple style. He advised, "Never sound excited. Imagine yourself at a dinner table back in the United States, with the local editor, a banker and a professor, talking over coffee. You try to tell what it was like, while the maid's boyfriend, a truck driver, listens from the kitchen. Talk to be understood by the truck driver while not insulting the professor's intelligence." He instructed Mary Marvin Breckinridge, one of the "boys" for nearly a year, "When you report the invasion of Holland . . . understate the situation. Don't say the streets are rivers of blood. Say that the little policeman I usually say hello to every morning is not there today."

Murrow's art was natural; he had an ear for the cadence of pauses and the rhythm of the language. He also had a gift for effective terseness. For a "See It Now" Korean War segment, Murrow edited "This is a flight line of Mustang Fighters" to read "These are Mustang Fighters." He rewrote "Once fast fighter planes, but no longer a match against Russian built MIGS" to assert "Fast fighter planes in an earlier war—but no match for Russian built MIGS."

Murrow's stature was so great because of his World War II coverage that both the British Broadcasting Corporation (BBC) and CBS offered him leadership positions. In 1946 he was appointed the first vice president for CBS's news operations, a position he grew to hate. By 1947 he returned to his first love, reporting the news. "Edward R. Murrow with the News" was carried by 125 network stations to an audience of several million people every weeknight for thirteen years. Unlike most news anchors or commentators, he refused to allow sponsors to break into the news with a middle commercial. To hold his audience after the closing commercial, Murrow would come back at the end with a brief "Word for Today," usually a quotation appropriate to the latest news. His signature sign-off was "Good night and good luck."

With the advent of television, Murrow became one of the few major radio news reporters to make the switch successfully. While he grumbled that he wished television had never been invented, he told his audience, "This is an old team trying to learn a new trade," and, pointing to the two monitors showing respectively the Brooklyn Bridge and San Francisco's Golden Gate, said, "We are rather impressed with this new technology."

In "Person to Person," which ran from 1953 to 1959, Murrow, ever holding his trademark cigarette, interviewed well-known figures such as Eleanor Roosevelt, actresses Lauren Bacall and Marilyn Monroe, and newly wedded Senator John F. Kennedy and Jacqueline Bouvier in their homes. Critics complained that he politely leaned over backward in respecting a person's privacy. He retorted, "I could hardly expect to ring the doorbell, step inside and proceed to ask my host and hostess embarrassing questions."

Murrow and his coproducer, Fred W. Friendly, examined the Missouri River flood and other natural disasters, profiled the era's people, such as poet and writer Carl Sandburg and Robert Oppenheimer, father of the atomic bomb, and explored issues, such as statehood for Alaska and Hawaii and the dangers of smoking. "See It Now" (1951–1958) covered the Cold War topics of guilt by association, the McCarthyism of the era, and the character of then senator Joseph McCarthy.

These neophyte television programs pioneered many formats still in use today: the in-depth feature, the newsmagazine, and the investigative report. In fact, as biographer Ann Sperber recounted, "There's hardly a news program that isn't beholden in some way to Murrow and his partner, Fred Friendly."

In the 9 March 1954 broadcast of "See It Now," which featured a report on McCarthy, Murrow began, "This is no time for those who oppose Senator McCarthy's methods to keep silent," and they did not. He displayed McCarthy's methods by allowing him to speak in his own words, albeit excerpted. The impact was tremendous. CBS received 100,000 letters and affiliate stations were flooded with telephone calls. The McCarthy program worked because, as Murrow said later, "The timing was right and the instrument powerful." Although Murrow's broadcast occurred after numerous print attacks on the senator had already appeared, he was the first to employ the power of this new medium in critiquing McCarthy.

Yet Murrow lost. The McCarthy show made enemies, and Murrow's broadcast autonomy was too controversial. The critics and the public may have loved Murrow, but the sponsors did not. In fact, for several of the Cold War reports, including the McCarthy program, Murrow and Friendly paid for the promotion advertisements out of their own pockets. A year later Murrow lost his time slot to a quiz show. By 1958 "See It Now" had been taken off the air. There were no sponsors, and network owner William Paley could not take "the stomach aches each week." Such public affairs programs risked CBS's soaring profits as the network moved more and more of its energies into the entertainment division.

At the 1958 convention of radio and TV news directors, an angry Murrow gave a shocking address. He said that television's greatness grew out of talent and responsibility, not greater and greater profits. He pointed out, "I can find nothing in the Bill of Rights, or the Communications Act, which says they must increase their net profits each year, lest the Republic collapse." He asked that the networks donate one or two of their regularly scheduled programs for public affairs programming for "a most exciting adventure, an exposure to ideas." He summarized the power of television: "This instrument can teach, it can illuminate; yes, and it can even inspire. But it can do so only to the extent that humans are determined to use it to those ends. Otherwise it is merely wires and lights in a box."

Murrow then took a year's leave of absence from CBS. To replace "See It Now" the network offered "CBS Reports" with Murrow's authority greatly reduced. Murrow did occasional interviews with the international "Small World," where he brought together world leaders by remote telecasting and moderated their discussions. His last hurrah came when "CBS Reports" presented "Harvest of Shame" the day after Thanksgiving in 1960. An idea begun in 1959, this chilling documentary reported on U.S. exploitation of migrant farm laborers to keep the nation's larders stocked. In his tailpiece, Murrow pleaded for action, "The people you have seen have the strength to harvest your fruits and vegetables. They do not have the strength to influence legislation. Maybe we do."

Murrow's own strength was now at issue. He had followed his mother's dictum, "It is better to wear out than rust out," and he was about to wear out. In 1961, depressed and with a sense of purposelessness after his long struggles with management, he accepted an offer to become the director of the U.S. Information Agency (USIA). Ever controversial, his well-known independence caused him trouble when he enraged some members of Congress with the agency's uncompromising coverage of the civil rights struggle. He also hired back a man whom McCarthy had scapegoated out of the State Department, Reed Harris.

As the USIA director, Murrow emphasized plain speaking and straightforward reporting of the nation's international messages. He told agency writers to report the facts in perspective, including the bad as well as the good. Yet his experience as a reporter came into public conflict with his position as the country's propagandist when he asked the BBC to stop the showing of "Harvest of Shame." He resigned in 1964 after a lung operation for cancer. He died at his home in Pawling, New York. In 1934 Murrow had married Janet Huntington Brewster, who also did broadcasts from London during World War II and filled in for him on his popular interview series "Person to Person"; they had one son, Charles Casey Murrow.

Murrow was awarded the Presidential Medal of Freedom in 1964 and received an honorary knighthood posthumously from Great Britain in 1965. He had won four Peabody Awards for Excellence in Broadcasting in the 1950s. Upon receiving the 1962 distinguished alumnus award from Washington State University, Murrow explained his success, "A man is a product of his education, his work, his travel, his reading, all of his experience." Who he was and what he did left a legacy of professional excellence and integrity. A plaque found in the CBS network lobby tells it all. Underneath the face of Murrow, it reads, "He set standards of excellence that remain unsurpassed."

Many honors bear his name, and when American television journalists are asked to rank broadcasters, Edward R. Murrow's name is always first. He achieved international acclaim in his almost 25-year career. With each development of broadcasting from radio through television and during major international events, Murrow was there. He once said that he had "a front row seat for some of the greatest news events of history."

• The Edward R. Murrow Papers, 1927–1965, roughly cataloged, including his correspondence, speeches, and broadcast transcripts, are at the Fletcher School of Law and Diplomacy, Tufts University. They are available on microfilm. For broadcast selections that give some sense of the dimension of Murrow's more than 5,000 broadcasts in both radio and television, see *In Search of Light, the Broadcasts of Edward R. Murrow, 1938–1961*, ed. Edward Bliss, Jr. (1967). The definitive biography is A. M. (Ann) Sperber's precise and compelling *Murrow, His Life and Times* (1986). Others include Alexander Kendrick, *Prime Time, the Life of Edward R. Murrow* (1969), and Joseph E. Perisico, *Edward R. Murrow, an American Original* (1988). For personal accounts, see Joseph Wershba, "The Murrow I Knew," *Television Quarterly* 1 (1990), and Edward Bliss, "Remembering Edward R. Murrow," *Saturday Review*, 31 May 1975. For other topical insights, see the CBS section in David Halberstam, *The Powers That Be* (1979); R. Franklin Smith, *Edward R. Murrow, The War Years* (1978); Stanley Cloud and Lynne Olson, *The Murrow Boys, Pioneers on the Front Lines of Broadcast Journalism* (1996); and Betty Houchin Winfield and Lois B. DeFleur, *The Edward R. Murrow Heritage* (1986).

BETTY HOUCHIN WINFIELD

MURTAUGH, Danny (8 Oct. 1917–2 Dec. 1976), baseball player, coach, and manager, was born Daniel Edward Murtaugh in Chester, Pennsylvania, the son of a shipyard worker (parents' names unknown). As a teenager, Murtaugh became a scrappy infielder, playing sandlot and semiprofessional baseball. After graduating from Chester High School in 1935 he took a series of low-paying jobs in the local shipyards and in a cereal factory. A strong performance at a tryout session in 1937 led to a contract with the St. Louis Cardinals, for which he began his minor league career with the Cambridge, Maryland, team of the Eastern Shore League. He broke into the major leagues with the Philadelphia Phillies in 1941, leading the league with eighteen stolen bases in only eighty-five games. After that season he married Kathleen Patricia Clark, also a native of Chester, and they had three children.

Short in stature and a light hitter at the major league level, Murtaugh lasted as a player until 1951 because of his spirited and competitive nature. Mostly a second baseman, his lifetime batting average in 767 games was .254. His nine seasons included tours with the Phillies (1941–1943, 1946), Boston Braves (1947), and Pittsburgh Pirates (1948–1951). He missed the 1944 and 1945 seasons because of service in the army infantry, in which he saw combat in Europe and survived a German sniper attack near a farmhouse in Czechoslovakia.

Murtaugh's career as a manager began with mixed success in the minor leagues, but it ended with glory and two world championships at the helm of the Pittsburgh Pirates. After completing the 1951 season as a player, Murtaugh persuaded Branch Rickey, then the general manager of the Pirates, to assign him to a minor league post with the Pelicans of the Southern Association. Released after 1954, he found another job with the independent Charleston, West Virginia, team in the same league, but he was fired in mid-1955. The following year Joe L. Brown, a son of the comedian Joe E. Brown and the Pirates' new general manager, offered Murtaugh a job as manager of the Williamsport, Pennsylvania, farm club. But before the season began, Pirates' manager Bobby Bragan selected Murtaugh as one of his coaches. In August 1957, as the Pirates were suffering through a dismal season, Brown fired Bragan, and after another coach turned down the job, he offered the manager's post to Murtaugh.

The fortunes of both Murtaugh and the Pirates improved dramatically over the next few years. A second-place finish in 1958 earned Murtaugh a manager-of-the-year award. In 1960 Bill Mazeroski's dramatic home run against the New York Yankees won a World Series for the Pirates, and again Murtaugh received manager-of-the-year honors. A heart attack forced his retirement after the 1964 season, but he returned as interim manager in mid-1967. For the next two years he held a front office position, but in 1970 he managed the Pirates to a National League Eastern Division championship. For a third time he was named manager of the year. In May 1971, despite chest pains, he was still able to lead the Pirates to another world championship, this time over the Baltimore Orioles. He then resigned, but that retirement lasted only until late in 1973 when he started his fourth and final tour of duty as the Pirates' manager. His teams won two more Eastern Division titles (1974 and 1975) and finished second in 1976. He died in Chester, Pennsylvania, just two months after announcing his fourth retirement.

Murtaugh was a mild-mannered skipper, whose success came from his skill in handling a variety of personalities on his ball clubs. His players remembered him as a grandfatherly figure who took a quiet, steady approach to baseball. Somewhat paunchy, he had deep-set hazel eyes, a hawk nose, a jutting jaw, and thick black eyebrows. A total abstainer from alcohol, he toasted his team's victories with glasses of milk. But he loved to chew tobacco during games, and he smoked eight to ten cigars a day. He also enjoyed entertaining sportswriters and other listeners with stories of his misadventures and narrow escapes from serious injury or death as a young factory worker and as a soldier during World War II.

A mediocre performer during his playing days, he earned fame as a shrewd manager blessed with talented teams that won two world championships and three National League Eastern Division titles. Over his fifteen-year managing career, his teams won 1,115 games and lost 950 for a winning percentage of .540. That record places him among the top managers of the second half of the twentieth century.

• There is a clipping file on Murtaugh at the National Baseball Library, Cooperstown, N.Y. No biography of Murtaugh exists, but for details and anecdotes of his life, see Dick Groat and Bill Surface, *The World Champion Pittsburgh Pirates* (1961), and Bob Smizik, *The Pittsburgh Pirates: An Illustrated History* (1990). An obituary is in the *New York Times*, 3 Dec. 1976.

GEORGE B. KIRSCH

MUSE, Clarence E. (7 Oct. 1889–13 Oct. 1979), actor, producer, and writer of plays and films, was born in Baltimore, Maryland, the son of Alexander Muse and Mary Sales. He was educated at Dickinson College in Carlisle, Pennsylvania, where he became interested in music and participated in choral groups; although he graduated with a bachelor's degree in international law in 1911, he immediately embarked on a musical and theatrical career. In 1907 he married Frieda Belle Moore; the marriage was apparently dissolved soon after the birth of their son in 1910.

Muse sang with a hotel employees' quartet in Palm Beach, Florida, for one season. In 1912 he helped organize the Freeman-Harper-Muse Stock Company at the Globe Theatre in Jacksonville, in partnership with comedian George Freeman and choreographer Leonard Harper. The company toured in *Stranded in Africa* in 1912, starring Muse in the role of King Gazu.

By 1914 Muse was married to and performing in vaudeville on the East Coast with Ophelia (maiden name unknown), billed as the team of Muse and Muse. They settled in Harlem, New York, where they established the Muse and Pugh Stock Company (in partnership with another vaudevillian) at the Franklin Theatre. They had two children before their marriage ended. They soon moved their company to the Crescent Theatre, where they produced several plays during their brief residence, including *Another Man's Wife*, starring the two Muses. The company moved

again to a better venue, the Lincoln Theatre, where it merged with the Lincoln Players, a newly formed stock company already in residence. In mid-1916 the group joined the Lafayette Players, who were just beginning to establish a name for themselves at the Lafayette Theatre.

Muse soon became the leading dramatic actor of the Lafayette Players. For the next six years he was featured in a variety of plays, such as *The Master Mind*, *A Servant in the House*, and *Dr. Jekyll and Mr. Hyde*; in the last he played in whiteface makeup, creating a sensation. The Muses' last performance together was in 1922.

In 1920 Muse became one of the founding directors of the Delsarte Film Corporation in New York City, a black independent film company, for which he wrote, produced, and starred in several films (1920–1921), including *Toussaint L'Ouverture* and *The Sport of Gods*, based on a story by Paul Laurence Dunbar. He was supported in these films by members of the Lafayette Players.

After this film venture Muse moved to Chicago, where he became associated with the Royal Gardens Theatre, owned by an African-American businessman. There he produced and directed shows such as *Hoola Boola* (1922), *Rambling Around* (1923), *The Charleston Dandies* (1926, 1927), *The Chicago Plantation Revue* (1927), and *Miss Bandana* (1927). These shows toured the South on the newly organized black Theatre Owners Booking Association (TOBA) circuit. He also directed and supervised the production of the opera *Thais*, which was performed in Chicago and St. Louis with a cast of nearly 200 singers and actors.

In 1929 Muse went to Hollywood at the invitation of the Fox Film Corporation, to portray the ninety-year-old leading character, Uncle Napus, in an all-black musical of plantation life, *Hearts in Dixie* (1929), under a twelve-month contract at a reported salary of $1,250 per week. British film historian Peter Noble praised Muse's "charming performance, fine dignity, grand voice and noble bearing" (*Anthology of the American Negro in the Theatre*, comp. Lindsay Patterson [1967], p. 248).

Muse remained in Hollywood for the rest of his career. He became the protégé of director Frank Capra, who used him in several films; the most notable was *Broadway Bill* (1934), a horse-racing film in which Muse played the black companion and alter ego of Warner Baxter, the white star, while observing the distance in rank and station that the color barriers of the time required. Although Muse was a subservient domestic in this and most of his other Hollywood films, he managed to maintain a dignity in his carriage and manner that was unusual for black house servants in these early films. Capra treated him with great sensitivity and respect, and when he remade *Broadway Bill* with Bing Crosby, as *Riding High* (1950), Muse reprised his original role.

Other notable films that Muse made in his fifty-year stay in Hollywood were *Huckleberry Finn* (as Jim, 1931); *The Count of Monte Cristo* (as a deaf-mute,

1934); *So Red the Rose* (as Cato, a rebellious slave, 1935); *Show Boat* (1936); *Spirit of Youth* (1937); *Way Down South*, for which he co-wrote the story, screenplay, and songs with Langston Hughes, and played the part of Uncle Caton (1939); *Broken Strings*, his finest screen role, in an independent black film in which he starred as a concert violinist (1940); *Porgy and Bess* (1959); *Buck and the Preacher* (1972); *The World's Greatest Athlete* (1973); *Car Wash* (1976); and *The Black Stallion*, his last film (1979).

While making films, Muse also starred in *Porgy* and in a new production of *Dr. Jekyll and Mr. Hyde* presented by the Lafayette Players, who were transplanted to the Lincoln Theatre in Los Angeles after they left New York in 1928. He also directed the WPA's Federal Theatre production of Hall Johnson's *Run, Little Chillun*, presented in Los Angeles and Hollywood in 1938–1939. He is credited as co-writer of a number of songs, including "When It's Sleepy Time Down South."

At some point Muse married Willabella Marchbanks, with whom he had one child before they divorced in 1949. His final marriage, in 1954, was to Irene Claire Kellman.

Muse was elected to the Black Filmmakers Hall of Fame in 1973. He died on his ranch in Perris, California, a week after his ninetieth birthday.

• Documents relating to Muse are in the Schomburg Center for Research in Black Culture at the New York Public Library. Muse's publications include *Way Down South* (1932), not to be confused with his film by the same title, written with David Arlen, a chronicle of Muse's theatrical career, telling of his experiences on the TOBA circuit. He also wrote a pamphlet, *The Dilemma of the Negro Actor* (1934). For descriptions of Muse's films, consult Donald Bogle, *Toms, Coons, Mulattoes, Mammies, and Bucks: An Interpretive History of Blacks in American Films* (1973), and his *Blacks in American Films and Television: An Illustrated Encyclopedia* (1988); and Daniel J. Leab, *From Sambo to Superspade: The Black Experience in Motion Pictures* (1988). His screen works are described in Bernard L. Peterson, Jr., *Early Black American Playwrights and Dramatic Writers: A Biographical Directory and Catalog of Plays, Films, and Broadcasting Scripts* (1990), and Henry T. Sampson, *Blacks in Black and White: A Source Book on Black Films* (1977). His musical shows are described in Peterson, *A Century of Musicals in Black and White: An Encyclopedia of Musical Stage Works by, about, or Involving Black Americans* (1993), and Sampson, *Blacks in Blackface: A Source Book on Early Black Musical Shows* (1980). On the theatrical companies with which Muse was associated, see Peterson, *The African American Theatre Directory, 1816–1960* (1997).

BERNARD L. PETERSON, JR.

MUSGROVE, Mary (c. 1700–c. 1766), interpreter and liaison between early Georgians and the native Indians, whose Creek name was Coosaponakeesa, was the daughter of an English trader and an Indian mother, although her exact parentage and birthplace are unknown. Her later claims of "royal" Indian kinship have been questioned, but she did have powerful connections and standing among the Creeks. Details of her childhood are sketchy; it is known, however, that she spent time in each culture and spoke both languages. As early as 1716–1717 she married trader John Musgrove and established a trading post on the Savannah River at Yamacraw Bluff. None of their children survived to adulthood, and John Musgrove died in 1735.

Mary Musgrove's importance to the history of Georgia began with the founding of the colony. From the arrival of the first settlers in 1733, she served the colony in many capacities. Georgia officials often used her as an interpreter and, as colonial secretary William Stephens wrote, Georgia trustee James Oglethorpe " . . . would advise with her in Many Things, for his better dealing with the Indians." In 1737 Mary Musgrove was married a second time, to Jacob Matthews, a captain of twenty rangers. In 1738 or 1739 the couple established a trading post about 150 miles up the Altamaha River. From there Mary worked for good English-Indians relations and thwarted any designs of the Spanish or French. Her efforts were particularly important during the War of Jenkins' Ear (1739–1742), when she rallied the Creeks to the British effort. She suffered several losses during that war, including her trading post, which was destroyed by the Yamassees, Indian allies of the Spanish. Her plantation on the Savannah River also suffered when her overseer left to join the war effort. In the midst of these problems, Jacob Matthews died of an illness in 1742. When Oglethorpe left for England in 1743 he gratefully recognized Mary's service, giving her a diamond ring and £200 with a promise of additional payment. In 1744 she married Thomas Bosomworth, who outlived her.

Mary also assisted Oglethorpe's military successors, sending Indians when needed for war and quieting problems between the English and the Indians when necessary. In 1744 Major William Horton wrote, "The Indians since Mrs. Bosomworth's Arrival Seems [*sic*] very well Satisfyed. Before she came I was harrassed to death." Horton's successor, Colonel Alexander Heron, wrote to Mary in 1747, "I am no stranger to your good Inclinations towards the Inhabitants of this Colony nor to your humane disposition." She had founded a second trading post on the Altamaha in 1745 and from there offered her own supplies in diplomatic endeavors. In 1747–1748 she dispensed presents to the Indians at her own expense. In 1758 she helped avert French efforts to win Creek friendship and as late as 1760 continued as interpreter at Indian conferences. Her influence throughout these years in maintaining friendly relations with the Indians was undisputed.

More controversial in her own day and subsequently among historians were Mary's claims for land and compensation. Her requests began during her marriage to Jacob Matthews, the person many believed was the troublemaker behind the claims. At a 1737 barbecue, the Yamacraw chief Tomochichi granted Mary a parcel of Indian land near Savannah. British officials did not recognize grants from Indians to individuals, and the claim remained unsettled when Mary married Bosomworth in 1744. The Bosomworths subsequently received a grant of three Indian-owned sea islands—Ossabaw, Sapelo, and St. Catherine's—from Malatche, mico (principal chief) of the Lower Creeks, who asserted that he was the "rightful prince and emperor of the Creeks."

The Bosomworths pursued the claims for years. While the Savannah authorities continuously opposed Mary's claims, those in the southern and frontier areas supported her. *The Colonial Records of Georgia* include letters of support from Colonel Alexander Heron, from officers of Oglethorpe's regiment, and from southern inhabitants of the colony. In 1749 the Bosomworths, accompanied by over two hundred Indians, visited Savannah to force the issue. Receiving no satisfaction, the Bosomworths left Georgia in 1752 to present their case in England. Delayed in South Carolina while she performed diplomatic services with the Creeks on behalf of Governor James Glen of South Carolina, Mary arrived in London in 1754, presenting to the Board of Trade a memorial explaining her case and reiterating her services to the colony. Other memorials corroborated her version. The Board of Trade eventually referred the claims to the Georgia courts.

During Mary's absence the status of the land she claimed had changed, as had the Georgia government, which was now under royal control. Governor John Reynolds had sympathy with the justice of Mary's claims, saying in a 1756 letter to the Board of Trade, " . . . it is therefore my opinion that Mr. Bosomworth and his Wife have been very Ill used by that Court of President and Assistants, who I think acted in a very Injudicious, Unwarrantable, and Arbitrary Manner." The attorney general delayed Georgia court action, hoping for a change of opinion from a new governor.

But the second royal governor, Henry Ellis, sought a compromise, and his proposal was ultimately accepted by all parties. In agreeing to the settlement, the Privy Council in England said that while the Georgia courts offered the best way to settle, no jury in Georgia would render a verdict against the Bosomworths. In 1760 Mary received St. Catherine's Island (6,200 acres), where she lived. She relinquished any claim to Sapelo and Ossabaw but received £2,100 from the sale of those two islands to compensate her for goods she had supplied in 1747–1748 and as back salary for her years of service. She died on St. Catherine's, the land for which she had struggled so long.

Mary Musgrove's conflict with British officials reflects several major colonial issues, including differences in land ownership concepts between British and Indian cultures, British attitudes toward Native Americans, and growing tensions between Savannah and other areas of the colony. In spite of the controversy, Musgrove's contributions to Georgia were considerable. Her services as an interpreter were valuable, and her diplomatic efforts between the Indians and the colonists were crucial in a period when three great powers competed for the Indian friendship necessary in empire building. With French and Spanish intrigue so near the fledgling frontier colony of Georgia, the good relationship with the Indians meant survival. In this way, Mary Musgrove Matthews Bosomworth was a significant contributor to early Georgia.

• The primary sources related to Mary Musgrove—including letters, memorials, claims, and counterclaims—are found throughout Allen D. Candler, comp., *Colonial Records of the State of Georgia* (1904–1910); in Kenneth Colemen and Milton Ready, eds., *Colonial Records of the State of Georgia*, vols. 20 and 27–29; and in K. Coleman, ed., *Colonial Records of the State of Georgia*, vols. 30–32. Early Georgia historian William Bacon Stevens, *A History of Georgia*, vol. 1 (1847–1859; repr. 1972), pp. 224–41, attempted to unravel the complex "Bosomworth Affair." E. Merton Coulter, "Mary Musgrove, 'Queen of the Creeks': A Chapter of Early Georgia Troubles," *Georgia Historical Quarterly* 11 (Mar. 1927): 1–30; John P. Corry, *Indian Affairs in Georgia, 1732–1756* (1936); and J. P. Corry, "Some New Light on the Bosomworth Claims," *Georgia Historical Quarterly* 25 (Sept. 1941): 196–224, debate Mary Musgrove's role in early Georgia. A complete modern treatment with primary documents is John T. Juricek, ed., *Georgia Treaties, 1733–1763* (1989), vol. 11 of *Early American Indian Documents: Treaties and Laws, 1607–1789*, ed. Alden T. Vaughn (1989). Juricek, using some previously unpublished documents, discusses Indian affairs with great clarity; he asserts that Mary's father was trader Edward Griffin and her mother the sister of Brims and Chigelli, important Creek micos. See also Doris Fisher, "Mary Musgrove: Creek Englishwomen" (Ph.D. diss., Emory Univ., 1990). Rodney M. Baine, "Myths of Mary Musgrove," *Georgia Historical Quarterly* 76 (Summer 1992): 428–35, discusses Mary Musgrove's Indian kinships, also arguing that her father was trader Edward Griffin but that her mother was a Tuckabatchee Creek, " . . . whom Griffin evidently never married and may have subsequently abandoned." He makes a case for dating Mary's birth to 1708 and her first marriage to about 1725, although previous historians had argued earlier dates for both.

LEE ANN CALDWELL

MUSHALATUBBE (c. 1760–30 Aug. 1838), Choctaw chief, emerged from historical obscurity early in the nineteenth century. Said to be a member of the Haiyup Atukla clan, in 1809 he succeeded Homastubbee as hereditary chief of the Northeastern District, one of three comprising the old Choctaw Nation. Little is known about his antecedents, birthplace, or early life. However, his name, translated "the one who perseveres and kills," supports the tradition that he was among those Choctaws who regularly journeyed to present-day Arkansas, Oklahoma, and Texas to hunt game and challenge Osage warriors. He had perhaps three daughters and four sons with his two wives (names unknown), whom he maintained in separate homes in present-day Noxubee County, Mississippi, near Mashulaville and Brooksville. Wealthy in horses, cattle, and hogs, his family lived well, incorporating Anglo-American goods into a traditional Choctaw household. Anglo-American travelers as well as Choctaws found the portly, dignified, but surprisingly bald chief hospitable and generous.

Mushalatubbe's career reflected the confusion and hardship that resulted as Choctaws attempted to protect their nationhood while adjusting to rapid changes in the nineteenth century. In 1811 Shawnee chief Tecumseh, recruiting Indian tribes to his anti-American confederacy, conferred with the Choctaws at Mushalatubbe's home. Although Mushalatubbe found him persuasive, he eventually agreed with fellow district chief Pushmataha that attacking the United States was unwise. Instead, Mushalatubbe led Choctaw warriors in support of General Andrew Jackson against Tecumseh's Red Stick Creek allies. Thereafter he took great pleasure in Jackson's friendship, wearing his gift, a blue uniform, with pride. Nevertheless, in 1818 he opposed Jackson's proposal that the Choctaws exchange their traditional homeland for a new reservation west of the Mississippi River. But as Anglo-American pressure for the removal of all the eastern tribes mounted, in 1820 Mushalatubbe reluctantly signed the Treaty of Doak's Stand, whereby the Choctaws received title to a vast new western estate in exchange for some of their eastern lands.

This arrangement was not enough for land-hungry neighbors in Mississippi and Alabama, and the question of further land cessions began to undermine traditional Choctaw government following 1820. Mushalatubbe, Pushmataha, and Apukshunnubbee—the three hereditary district chiefs—retained considerable strength, especially among traditional Choctaws, but a new generation of literate, ambitious mixed-blood leaders threatened to unseat them. In his own district Mushalatubbe found support among the family of his nephew and potential heir Peter Pitchlynn; opposition centered on David Folsom and his relatives. Mushalatubbe and the Pitchlynns took a moderate position on removal, agreeing that it was preferable to complete dispossession, but Folsom, an ardent Choctaw nationalist, refused to consider it. His response to pressure for removal lay in adoption of constitutional republican government, Christian values, and the education offered by Christian missionaries. In 1824 the three district chiefs headed a party of Choctaws on a diplomatic mission to Washington, D.C. When both Pushmataha and Apukshunnubbee died in the course of the mission, Folsom and his reformers filled the resulting power vacuum. Folsom charged Mushalatubbe with misconduct and intemperance as the first stage in a political revolution in the Choctaw Nation. Although Mushalatubbe refused to abdicate, he did agree to a democratic election in 1826. At the next council he lost his office to the eloquent, energetic Folsom. The other two district chieftaincies soon similarly changed hands.

Deposed, Mushalatubbe and the Pitchlynn family then became leaders of the opposition "Republican" faction against Folsom's "Christian" party. Mushalatubbe, reacting to missionary support of Folsom, became antimissionary. He charged that the evangelists had propagated their religion at the expense of promised English education for Choctaw children. To prepare the Choctaws for eventual resettlement, he advocated exploration of the new lands beyond the Mississippi River. To federal officials he protested that he had been illegitimately ousted. But by 1830 Choctaw government had become a dead issue, as Mississippi and Alabama extended their laws over the Indian na-

tions within their boundaries. Folsom resigned rather than face state prosecution for filling his duties as district chief.

With Folsom removed, Mushalatubbe was reinstated amid a national crisis. Civil war threatened between supporters and opponents of removal, followers of Mushalatubbe and Folsom, antimissionary elements and Choctaw Christians. In 1830 disheartened Choctaws avoided bloodshed and signed the Treaty of Dancing Rabbit Creek, by which they agreed to immigrate to their new estate in present-day Oklahoma. With other Choctaw leaders, Mushalatubbe received sections of land and considerations for signing, favored treatment they accepted as their due. Unfortunately, Mushalatubbe, under constant criticism from Folsom, presided over a district in which half the people were disaffected. So deep was the division that when removal actually began, the factions chose to resettle in different areas of the new homeland. Mushalatubbe's people crossed the Mississippi River at Memphis on 3 November 1832 and marched forty-two miles through standing water sometimes up to their waists. Weakened by cholera, the survivors struggled on through winter weather to Fort Smith, Arkansas, and then southwest into a new northeastern district.

Mushalatubbe guided his supporters to the northern, Skullyville area, while Folsom led his followers south to the Red River Valley. Mushalatubbe, hoping for a new beginning for the Choctaws, settled on the prairie near Sugar Loaf Mountain in present-day Le-Flore County, Oklahoma. Elected in 1834 chief of the new northeastern district, he signed the Camp Holmes Agreement making peace between the native and immigrating tribes. In 1838 the immigrating Chickasaws brought smallpox to the new Choctaw Nation. It spread through the country, killing 500 Choctaws, among them perhaps Mushalatubbe.

Mushalatubbe, last of the hereditary district chiefs, favored adoption of necessary Anglo-American innovations while preserving traditional Choctaw culture as much as possible. Choctaws honored him, Apukshunnubbe, and Pushmataha by giving their names to the three divisions of the new homeland. The three arrows in the bow in the Great Seal of the Choctaw Nation preserve their memory.

• Mushalatubbe's dictated letters and other documents are in early federal records. Some material is available at the Oklahoma Historical Society, Oklahoma City. His role in Choctaw history is briefly covered in Angie Debo's classic *The Rise and Fall of the Choctaw Republic* (1934) and in Grant Foreman, *The Five Civilized Tribes: Cherokee, Chickasaw, Choctaw, Creek, Seminole* (1934). Early works in *Publications of the Mississippi Historical Society* 7 (1903) based on first-person reminiscences of Mushalatubbe are William A. Love, "Mingo Moshulitubbe's Prairie Village," pp. 373–78, and H. S. Halbert, "Origin of Mashulaville," pp. 389–97. Mushalatubbe's removal experience is described in Carolyn Thomas Foreman, "The Armstrongs of Indian Territory, Part II," *Chronicles of Oklahoma* 30 (Winter 1952–1953): 420–53. Perhaps his career is best seen in studies of his contemporaries: W. David Baird, *Peter Pitchlynn: Chief of the Choctaws*

(1972); Anna Lewis, *Chief Pushmataha: The Story of the Choctaws' Struggle for Survival* (1959); and Barry Eugene Thorne, "David Folsom and the Emergence of Choctaw Nationalism" (master's thesis, Oklahoma State Univ., 1988).

MARY JANE WARDE

MUSICA, Philip Mariano Fausto (12 May 1884–16 Dec. 1938), swindler, alias William Johnson and Frank Donald Coster, was born in New York City, the son of Antonio Musica, a barber, and Assunta Mauro, both recent immigrants from Naples, Italy. Musica attended public schools on the Lower East Side of Manhattan, where he was reportedly a good student with a somewhat depressive nature. After one or two years of attending high school, he left to help his father operate a modest grocery store.

As A. Musica and Son, the small business began importing fine cheeses—a venture Philip promoted in hopes of earning large profits. Unwilling to wait for the family to accumulate enough wealth to live comfortably, the younger Musica began bribing New York customs agents to lessen the duties the business paid on its imports. In 1909 New York officials began conducting routine, periodic investigations of the customs offices, and Musica's fraudulent activities were discovered. He pleaded guilty in court in order to protect his father from prosecution; he served five months of a one-year sentence at the Elmira Reformatory before family friends (including the Italian ambassador to the United States) pressured President William Howard Taft to commute the sentence.

Released from jail, Musica soon established the United States Hair Company, a firm that utilized his father's expertise as a barber. The company imported human hair, mainly from Italy and China, for use in the elaborate hair designs that were popular for women at the time. Musica's firm proved prosperous, and he took to dressing elegantly and to frequenting New York's best nightspots, particularly the Metropolitan Opera.

During the summer of 1912 Assunta Musica and her three youngest children visited Italy, where she collected poor-quality pieces of hair (chiefly barbers' scraps) and sent them to Philip in New York. By borrowing money against these fraudulent assets, Philip Musica generated huge profits for his family, amassing enough wealth to enter the United States Hair Company on the New York Stock Exchange (a dream of Philip's) in October 1912. However, in March 1913 another investigation at the New York customs offices revealed that the Musicas were guilty of falsifying their importing records.

Several days before investigators arrived on 17 March, the six family members living in the United States attempted to flee to Honduras, where extradition was difficult, if not impossible. Burns Detective agent Dan Lehon followed the Musicas to New Orleans, where they were apprehended with close to $70,000 in cash and $20,000 in jewels. The men were charged with grand larceny and tried on 11 April 1913; only Philip pleaded guilty, so that his father and brothers could go free. Philip Musica had in fact swindled some twenty-two New York–area banks out of $600,000 by repeatedly borrowing money against the fraudulent hair shipments from Italy.

Musica spent the next three years years awaiting sentencing at the Tombs in New York, where he became valuable to police authorities. He was found to be a careful and hardworking spy who reported on other prisoners' activities, including their conversations with their lawyers. When Musica was freed in March 1916, his entire family was reunited in a lavish home in the Bay Ridge section of Brooklyn. Soon thereafter, Musica began work as an investigator for the New York district attorney's office. He worked under the name William Johnson, uncovering acts of sedition and sabotage perpetrated by German spies in New York. The job came to an end in March, however, when Musica was found to have induced a witness to commit perjury in a trial concerning the murder of Barnet Baff. Musica jumped bail and spread a rumor that he had fled to South America, where he was killed; in reality, he continued to reside in New York.

In 1920, as Frank Costa, Musica opened the Adelphi Pharmaceutical Manufacturing Company of Brooklyn with $8,000 borrowed from his mother, who mortgaged her property and pawned her jewels. The company purported to manufacture furniture polish and hair tonics, but it was primarily a bootleg liquor supplier. Musica's two partners in the firm were Mary and Guiseppe Brandino, a brother and sister who used rough business tactics and who blackmailed Musica for the remainder of his life (he paid them to conceal his true identity). In 1922 the Adelphi Company was closed when federal officials discovered that it was bootlegging liquor; it is believed that Musica anonymously turned in the company to dissolve his troubled partnership with the Brandinos.

Early in 1923 Musica, alias Frank D. Coster, began Girard and Company, a drug manufacturing firm in Mount Vernon, New York. Besides hiring a legitimate chemist with a Ph.D. from the University of Heidelberg, Musica also employed his brothers George and Robert. The company sold drugs legally and liquor illegally, reporting sales of $2 million in 1925. Musica hired Price, Waterhouse and Company as the firm's accountants, and he studied their reporting methods closely. He noted particularly that accountants checked company inventories only on paper, almost never entering warehouses; Musica later employed this knowledge in his most grandiose case of swindling.

By the spring of 1925, Musica was using the name F. Donald Coster and claiming to have earned a Ph.D. and an M.D. from the University of Heidelberg. He solicited the advice of an investment banker, Julian F. Thompson, and asked that Thompson show him how to build up Girard and Company's assets so that it could be listed on the New York Stock Exchange. Thompson, who worked for Musica's company (first as an adviser, later as an employee) for the rest of his life, was impressed with Musica's dedication, diligence, and ingenious intelligence. In late 1925 Musica, with the aid of equally impressed bankers in Bridgeport, Connecticut, purchased a large abandoned factory in Fairfield, Connecticut, and moved Girard and Company there so that he could more easily bootleg liquor into New England. In the spring of 1926 Musica bought out the prestigious and well-respected drug manufacturing firm of McKesson & Robbins and merged the company with Girard and Company. Again, bankers in Bridgeport, as well as in Waterbury, helped Musica with the necessary loans, some even investing their personal funds. Also in 1926, Musica, as Coster, married Carol Jenkins Hubbard; they had no children.

Under the respectable guise provided by the McKesson & Robbins name, Musica ran legitimate drug wholesaling activities as well as illegitimate ventures. He retained his brothers George and Robert as employees, renaming them George and Robert Dietrich and giving them high-ranking positions; George became the assistant treasurer of the firm. Musica and George ran the crude drug department from Fairfield. This division of McKesson & Robbins bought large quantities of exotic raw materials from around the world to use in the production of drugs. In order to increase the firm's assets and his own financial worth, Musica began falsifying the quantities of crude drugs actually purchased and held in warehouses (reportedly all in Canada) for McKesson & Robbins. Musica devised an ingenious, elaborate scheme to prevent the Price, Waterhouse accountants from questioning the validity of the drug firm's purchases. The firm's common stock value rose steadily with Musica in control, and as a 10 percent shareholder, he prospered. Musica hired a third brother, Arthur, alias George Vernard, to aid the scheme; he fronted a bank that acted as a clearinghouse for Musica's falsified financial records.

Musica's illegal dealings proceeded smoothly until early 1937, when the company treasurer, Julian F. Thompson, requested that the crude drug department sell off some of its assets to help the less successful departments in McKesson & Robbins. Musica promised to do so but actually did the opposite, amassing more false inventories for his section of the firm. Thompson then became suspicious for the first time and began a private inquiry into Musica's department. Thompson pursued his investigation from March to late November 1938, when he confronted Musica with his complaints. The two men discussed the matter, and Musica, confessing nothing, placed the company in receivership on 5 December 1938, one day before Thompson and the board of directors had threatened to do so.

The ensuing investigation of fraudulent activities in the crude drug department led to the arrests of Musica and his three brothers. The charge was grand larceny, and federal authorities prosecuted the case because mail fraud was involved. On 11 December a New York district attorney's employee (and former colleague of Musica's in that office) recognized a newspaper picture of F. Donald Coster as being Philip Musi-

ca. On 15 December a positive identification was made by New York authorities using Coster's fingerprints.

During the proceedings Musica, free on bail, remained at his Fairfield home, obviously distraught. Shortly after noon on 16 December, as federal authorities stood on his doorstep waiting to rearrest him as Philip Musica, Musica shot himself in the head in his upstairs bathroom. A suicide note was found, pleading his innocence. Although Musica had earned more than $3 million from his reworking of the inventories at McKesson & Robbins, he had spent most of it by 1938—some on local charities, some on his manor-like home, and much to pay off relatives and blackmailers.

Philip Musica was temporarily successful at concocting and deploying one of the most elaborate corporate frauds in U.S. history. While posing as Frank Donald Coster he was admitted into the highest social circles of Fairfield County, Connecticut, and enjoyed a most comfortable life until his illegal activities were discovered.

• The most complete report on the personal life and business career of Musica is Robert Shaplen, "The Metamorphosis of Philip Musica," *New Yorker*, 22 and 29 Oct. 1955. "McKesson & Robbins: Its Fall and Rise," *Fortune*, Mar. 1940, pp. 72–75, focuses primarily on Musica's years there. The Dec. 1938 issues of the *New York Times* cover in detail the last events of his life. An obituary is in the *New York Times*, 17 Dec. 1938.

PATRICIA E. SWEENEY

MUSIN, Ovide (22 Sept. 1854–24 Nov. 1929), violinist, was born in Nandrin (near Liège), Belgium, the son of Jacques Musin, an engineer, and Louise de Milles. His earliest musical memory was of hearing a hurdy-gurdy, and he began playing the violin at age six. He entered the Liège Conservatory in 1863 at age nine, studying first under Heynberg and then, starting in 1870, with the celebrated Belgian violinist Hubert (sometimes referred to as "Henri") Léonard. Musin won first prize at the conservatory in 1868 and the gold medal for violin and quartet playing in 1869. In 1872 he followed Léonard to the Paris Conservatory where he completed his studies.

As a student at Liège, Musin played in the orchestra for one of Henri Vieuxtemps's last concerts, and at age thirteen he was co-winner of the Vieuxtemps Prize with the nine-year-old Eugène Ysaÿe. Later, after Vieuxtemps became paralyzed from a stroke, Musin frequented his home in Paris. At Liège Musin also played for Henryk Wieniawski, his idol. Musin presented one of his own compositions, the Caprice de Concert no. 1, to Wieniawski, who later played it on his last European tour. When Wieniawski fell ill in 1873, Musin replaced him with less than twenty-four hours' notice and proceeded to make his first tour of France.

In 1875 Musin organized a string quartet called the Quartette Moderne, which was designed to play new works by modern composers. the quartet gave the Paris premieres of several of Brahms's chamber works, including his string and piano quartets, two sextettes, and his quintette in C minor. When Musin traveled to Vienna in 1880 to play the Beethoven concerto with Hans Richter and the Vienna Philharmonic, he met with Brahms, whose *Academic Festival* Overture received its world premiere at the same concert. While in Vienna he also met with the composer Karl Goldmark.

Musin had close ties with other composers. At the Paris Conservatory he became good friends with the composers Gabriel Fauré and Camille Saint-Saëns, and he attended rehearsals for the ill-fated world premiere of Georges Bizet's *Carmen* with the composer. Musin performed often with Fauré, and he fingered and bowed Fauré's Berceuse for publication. Saint-Saëns wrote his Concertstück for Musin and dedicated it to him when it was published. In 1878 Musin organized five Saint-Saëns concerts at Steinway Hall in London, playing—among other things—Saint-Saëns's piano quintet with the composer at the piano. On another occasion Musin played Saint-Saëns' Introduction and Rondo Capriccioso at London's Royal Albert Hall with the composer conducting the orchestra of Covent Garden. At the same concert the great soprano Adelina Patti sang Charles Gounod's "Ave Maria" with Gounod at the piano, Saint-Saëns at the organ, and Musin playing violin obbligato. He also appeared in concert with Edvard Grieg conducting.

Musin toured extensively in Europe from 1873 through 1876, and he made his London debut in 1877, settling there for five years. In 1882 Musin toured Russia and Germany, where he appeared with the great conductor Hans von Bülow. He returned to Russia in 1884 and made his U.S. debut the same year playing the Mendelssohn concerto with the New York Symphony under Leopold Damrosch. In keeping with his commitment to modern music, Musin played Damrosch's own violin concerto at the Metropolitan Opera House with Leopold's son Walter conducting and gave the U.S. premiere of the Benjamin Godard concerto with the New York Philharmonic under the direction of Theodore Thomas. In 1891 Musin married Annie Louise Hodges-Tanner, a coloratura soprano from Wisconsin. The two frequently performed together in concert until her death in 1921.

Between 1892 and 1897 Musin made two world tours, including concerts in Mexico, New Zealand, Hawaii, Japan, China, Java, Australia, the United States, and Europe. He then returned to Belgium, where he joined the faculty of the Liège Conservatory in 1897, succeeding César Thompson as violin professor there the following year. He held that post until 1908, when he resigned to create his own music school, the Belgian Conservatory of Music, in Brooklyn, New York. He remained director of the conservatory until his death in Brooklyn.

Though never achieving the degree of fame of his compatriot Eugène Ysaÿe, Musin was an important exponent of the Belgian school of violin playing. He wrote numerous compositions for the violin, two sets of violin methods, and an autobiography. He also made six very rare recordings in New York, including performances of his own compositions.

• A good source for biographical information on Musin is his autobiography, *My Memories* (1920). A brief biographical sketch is in Alberto Bachmann, *An Encylopedia of the Violin* (1925). For Musin's approach to violin playing, see his *System of Daily Practice* (1899) and *The Belgian School of Violin Playing* (4 vols., 1916), in which he incorporated his teacher Léonard's method. See also Musin, "A Review of Violinistic Conditions," *The Violinist* (Jan. 1914): 32–34.

JOHN ANTHONY MALTESE

MUSMANNO, Michael Angelo (7 Apr. 1897–12 Oct. 1968), legislator, judge, and author, was born in the town of McKees Rocks in Stowe Township, Pennsylvania, the son of Antonio Musmanno, a railroad worker and coal miner, and Maddelena Castellucci. The son of Italian immigrants, Musmanno grew up in a working-class family and neighborhood. It is said that at the age of twelve, after offering a strong and successful defense against corporal punishment following a fight with a classmate, Musmanno was encouraged by his school principal to consider a career as a lawyer. When he was only fourteen years old, Musmanno began working as a coal loader. Growing up in the Pittsburgh area, he continued to work throughout high school in the coal industry and also held a job as a waterboy for the steel workers. Musmanno then attended evening classes while he continued to labor during the day.

After high school, Musmanno enrolled at Georgetown University in 1915 and began working on a Bachelor of Law degree. The entry of the United States into World War I temporarily halted Musmanno's studies at Georgetown. He served in the U.S. Army as an infantryman. On his return from duty, he resumed his studies at Georgetown, earning a Bachelor of Law degree in 1918. He then enrolled at George Washington University, where he earned both Bachelor of Arts and Master of Arts degrees. He then enrolled at National University (Washington, D.C.) and earned both a Master of Laws degree and a Master of Patent Laws degree.

In 1923 Musmanno was admitted to the Pennsylvania bar. He found employment as a legal assistant with the firm of John R. K. Scott, a successful and prominent Philadelphia lawyer. The first case that he was asked to try was one that pitted him against a very experienced and able lawyer. Musmanno was defending a woman against her doctor who was suing her for nonpayment of a $50 bill that she claimed she had already paid. When Musmanno realized that he was being outgunned by the experienced lawyer and articulate doctor, he appealed to the jury's sentiment. He asked the jury not to hold against his client the fact that he was trying his first case and appeared inexperienced compared to the doctor's lawyer. By asking them to focus on the evidence rather than the lawyers and return a just and fair verdict, he won this case, the first of forty-two cases in a row that he would win before losing his first case.

Throughout his career, Musmanno was a defender of those least able to defend themselves. After losing five of his last twenty-three cases, Musmanno became very discouraged and disappointed with his performance. He greatly admired and looked up to Scott, the man who had first given him a chance to practice law. Musmanno felt he was failing Scott whenever he lost a case. He resigned his position in 1924 and escaped to Europe in an effort to reexamine the direction of his life.

While visiting Europe, Musmanno decided to study Roman law at the University of Rome. While there, he earned his seventh degree, a Doctor of Jurisprudence (earlier, he had earned his sixth degree, a Doctor of Juristic Science from the American University in Washington, D.C.). In 1925 he returned to Pittsburgh and opened up a private law practice. During this time, the case of Nicola Sacco and Bartolomeo Vanzetti had been unfolding and had caught the attention of not only the legal world, but the general public as well. It was a controversial case in which two Italian immigrants had been tried and convicted of murder. Many people felt that their convictions were based more on anti-immigrant and political sentiments than on the evidence and the law. In his book *Verdict! The Adventures of the Young Lawyer in the Brown Suit* (1958), Musmanno relates what had attracted him to the most personally impacting case of his career: "The shoemaker and fish peddler were not clients of mine—and yet in some way I felt they were. They were clients of every lawyer devoted to the ideal of universal justice" (p. 268).

Contacting the chief counsel for Sacco and Vanzetti, Musmanno made arrangements to meet the two accused and condemned men. He then personally contacted several U.S. Supreme Court justices and begged them for a postponement of the execution at least until their case could be heard by the Court. Despite the unceasing efforts of Musmanno, the appeals team of which he had become an integral part was unsuccessful, and the two accused were put to death in the electric chair in 1927. He later authored a book, *After Twelve Years* (1939), in which he made a powerful case that Sacco and Vanzetti were unjustly convicted and executed.

In 1926, at the age of twenty-nine, Musmanno ran for a seat in the Pennsylvania legislature. He was unsuccessful but not deterred from trying again two years later. In 1928 he won election to the Pennsylvania House of Representatives and in 1930 was reelected to a second term. During this second term he fought for the protection of coal and iron workers. The law allowed companies to employ private police forces, which were used to keep workers in line and break up any union organizing. These police became notorious for their strong-armed tactics. Musmanno succeeded in getting a law to abolish these police forces passed by the legislature, but it was vetoed by the governor. Nevertheless, Musmanno successfully brought public attention to the problem of the mining police laws, which were revoked in 1935.

Musmanno became a judge in 1932, when he was elected to serve on the Allegheny County court. In 1934 he was elected to the Pennsylvania Common Pleas Court in Pittsburgh. Musmanno issued one of his most memorable opinions from this bench in December 1935. This opinion, *In re Legality and Authenticity of Santa Clause*, declared Santa Claus a reality recognizable by law and protected "against all insinuations to the contrary." At the outbreak of World War II he was commissioned as a lieutenant commander in the navy. By the end of his service, he held the rank of rear-admiral. At the close of the war, he served on the navy team that investigated whether Adolf Hitler had died or escaped the final battle in Berlin. It was in this capacity that Musmanno conducted interviews with many of Hitler's close associates. He was later appointed by President Harry S. Truman to serve as a judge at the Nuremberg Trials.

In 1951 Musmanno was elected to a 21-year term on the Pennsylvania Supreme Court. In his first five years on the court he wrote more dissenting opinions than all other justices combined had written in fifty years, and he was known for the strong and colorful language he used in these dissents. One of his most memorable dissents came in *Commonwealth v. Robin* (1966), in which a majority of the court held that applying Pennsylvania's obscenity statutes to prohibit circulation of Henry Miller's book *Tropic of Cancer* violated the U.S. Constitution. He wrote that "the defendants say that 'Cancer' is entitled to immunity . . . because court decisions have declared that only worthless trash may be proscribed as obscene. To say that 'Cancer' is worthless trash is to pay it a compliment. . . . It is a cesspool, an open sewer, a pit of putrefaction, a slimy gathering of all that is rotten in the debris of human depravity. And in the center of all this waste and stench . . . cavorts and wallows a bifurcated specimen that responds to the name of Henry Miller." While he was a frequent defender of the underprivileged in society, he was also an ardent anticommunist. His anticommunist zeal led him to serve as a coauthor of the Communist Control Act of 1954.

In 1961, because of his extensive contact with Nazis he had interviewed following the war and his firsthand judicial experience at the Nuremberg Trials, Musmanno was asked to be a prosecution witness in the trial of Adolf Eichmann, who had been the chief architect and operations officer of the Nazis' "final solution of the Jewish problem," in Israel. Following his deep convictions about the importance of such a trial, he went to Israel and testified. His testimony is believed to have been one of the key components of the trial that resulted in Eichmann's conviction.

One of the last battles that Musmanno fought was not in the courtroom. It was in academic institutions and the media, where people were questioning whether Christopher Columbus was the first to discover America. In 1965 the discovery of what became known as the Vinland Map led some scholars to declare that Leif Ericsson was the first to discover America. In reaction, Musmanno produced *Columbus WAS*

First (1966), in an attempt to preserve what he saw as the rightful place that this most famous Italian had held for so long in American minds. Ironically, Musmanno died on Columbus Day in Pittsburgh, where he would have served as grand marshal in the Columbus Day parade had he not been incapacitated by a stroke one day earlier. He was buried at Arlington National Cemetery, a short distance away from the gravesite of President John F. Kennedy, near whom Musmanno requested to be buried in his will.

Immensely competent and zealous in all his work, Musmanno, who never married, seemed driven by his unwavering commitment to justice (especially for the more vulnerable in society), a deep American patriotism, and a strong pride in his Italian heritage.

• The Justice Michael A. Musmanno Collection, which includes his personal library, private papers, and correspondence and artifacts taken from Musmanno's chambers and apartment, is in the Rare and Special Book Collections of Duquesne University Library in Pittsburgh, Pa. See also *Ten Days to Die* (1950), an account of Hitler's last days based on interviews of surviving intimates of Hitler conducted by Musmanno. For a fuller account of his life, see Gaeton Fonzi, "Musmanno Rides Again," *Greater Philadelphia Magazine*, Apr. 1964. See also Sally Stephenson, "Michael A. Musmanno: A Symbolic Leader" (Ph.D. diss., Carnegie Mellon Univ., 1981), which examines Musmanno's life in the context of the historical and social forces that were central to its shaping. An obituary is in the *New York Times*, 13 Oct. 1968.

JAMES N. GIORDANO

MUSSEY, Ellen Spencer (13 May 1850–21 Apr. 1936), social reformer and attorney, was born in Geneva, Ohio, the daughter of Platt Rogers Spencer, an abolitionist, farmer and temperance advocate, and Persis Duty. Mussey's father volunteered time to the underground railroad and was the inventor of Spencerian script, the standard form of handwriting employed in the United States at the end of the nineteenth century.

The Musseys lived on an isolated farmstead near Lake Erie until 1859, when they moved to Oberlin, Ohio. There Ellen attended grammar school for two years until her mother became ill and the family once again retreated to the farm, hoping that she would recover her health. When her mother died in 1862, Ellen's stern father required her to take full responsibility for the household and to teach handwriting in his school. Disasters multiplied, and two years later her father died; her younger sister died soon thereafter. These deaths, coupled with great responsibility at a young age, occasioned a physical breakdown. Mussey then migrated from one sibling to another over the course of the next four years, studying briefly at Rice's Young Ladies' Seminary in Poughkeepsie, New York, Lake Erie Seminary in Painesville, Ohio, and the Reformist Seminary in Illinois. After attending a business law course, she was invited to read law, but, when her sister died, she was unable to do so.

Moving to Washington, D.C., in 1869, Mussey lived with her brother Henry and his wife Sara Andrews Spencer, a leading suffragist. While working as an administrator for her brother's school, the Spencerian Business College, Mussey established an excellent reputation in Washington circles. In 1871 she left the Business College to marry Rueben Delavan Mussey, an attorney and retired brigadier general who was seventeen years her senior. He had two daughters from a previous marriage, and they had two sons together.

In 1876 her husband became ill with malaria, and Mussey assumed responsibility of his law office. Despite his rapid recovery, Mussey worked with her husband for over a dozen years. She then encountered a quick succession of deaths; in the course of ten years, from the early 1880s to the early 1890s, she lost her sister, her eldest son, her brother, and her husband. Alone and with a son to educate, she decided to practice law on her own. However, at that time no law school considered a woman to be capable of handling law study, and she was rejected by National University as well as Columbian College (later George Washington University) based on her sex. After numerous appeals, Mussey attained a special waiver in the form of an oral exam, due to the grief she was suffering over her recently deceased relatives; through this procedure, she qualified for the Washington, D.C., bar in 1893.

Aside from two brief partnerships, Mussey practiced mostly alone, specializing mainly in commercial, international, and probate law, although she represented the Norwegian and Swedish delegations for twenty-five years. In 1894 Mussey chaired the legislative committee of the District of Columbia's Federation of Women's Clubs and successfully campaigned for the Married Women's Property Rights Bill. In 1896 her efforts resulted in a bill passed through Congress that allowed women equal rights to child custody. Mussey also secured for women the right to conduct business and retain earnings. The following year she was a delegate and speaker at the second convention of the National Council of Women. She was also a member of the Legion of Loyal Women, serving two terms as president, and the Daughters of American Revolution, serving as vice president general from 1907 through 1909.

Mussey became certified to practice law before the Supreme Court in 1896, and a year later she became the first woman to qualify before the U.S. Court of Claims. A prolific writer, she contributed numerous articles to legal publications; she also worked as an attorney and executive committee member for the American Red Cross. An avid women's rights advocate, Mussey teamed with Emma Gillett, another Washington attorney, to found a law course for women. Because several of their students were rejected for admission to law school on the basis of their sex, Mussey and Gillett decided to found a law school for women; in 1898 the Washington College of Law (later attached to American University) opened to both females and males. Mussey taught classes, led the fundraising campaign, recruited volunteer instructors, and continually presented students for admission to the

Supreme Court bar. In addition, as the first dean of the institution, Mussey was the first woman to hold such a position in a law school. In 1899 and 1927 she received honorary LL.M. and LL.D. degrees from Washington College.

Mussey exhibited a keen interest in educational reform. In 1898 she led a successful crusade for public kindergartens, and as a member of the Board of Education (1906–1912) she helped secure funding for the schools. Throughout this period Mussey used her office to fight for passage of the Teachers' Retirement and Pension Bill, helped establish the District of Columbia's juvenile courts, founded a school for mentally challenged children, and garnered support for compulsory education.

During a trip to Scandinavia, Mussey became impressed by the enfranchisement of Norwegian women; as a result, in 1909 she joined the American suffrage movement. Affiliated with the National American Women's Suffrage Association, she represented the council at the 1911 International Council of Women in Stockholm, Sweden. Poor health forced a temporary setback in 1912, but by the following spring she joined 10,000 women in a suffrage march on Washington, leading an assemblage of lawyers.

The 1912 parade marked a turning point for Mussey. Harassed by onlookers, the parade turned into a riot and Mussey suffered a stroke. Her health deteriorated rapidly, and in August 1913 she relinquished her duties as dean of Washington College. Thereafter she was an honorary dean, although she still worked on legal and educational affairs. In 1917 Mussey chaired the National Council of Women's Committee on the Legal Status of Women, drafting the bill that would protect women's citizenship rights after marriage to foreign nationals; with suffragist Maud Wood Park making important contributions to this effort, the bill passed Congress in 1922 as the Cable Act. A founding member of the National Association of Women Lawyers and a charter member of the District of Columbia's Women's Bar Association, Mussey served as president of the latter organization from 1917 to 1919. Another medical crisis in 1930 temporarily stalled her reform efforts, but she continued her fundraising endeavors for Washington College and practiced law for an additional six years until her death in Washington.

Mussey's resolution to fight for equality for women emerged in every aspect of her career and civic life. A tireless worker, despite her illnesses, Mussey exemplified the liberal-legalist strain in American feminism that ultimately secured political and economic parity for women, using dogged determination and case-by-case litigation and law reform.

• A complete biography of Mussey is Grace Hathaway, *Fate Rides a Tortoise* (1937). For brief sketches, see Susan B. Anthony and Ida Husted, *History of Woman Suffrage*, vols. 4–6 (1902–1922); and Jane C. Croly, *History of the Woman's Club Movement in America* (1891). See also *Women Lawyers Journal* (1913–1939) and *Woman's Tribune* (1897–1902). An informative obituary is in the *Washington Post*, 22 Apr. 1936.

ELIF Ö. ERGINER

MUSSEY, Reuben Dimond (23 June 1780–21 June 1866), surgeon and medical educator, was born in Pelham, Rockingham County, New Hampshire, the son of John Mussey, a country doctor, and Beulah Butler. When Mussey was nine years old, his family moved to Amherst, New Hampshire, where he later studied at Aurean Academy. He graduated from Dartmouth College in 1803, having been admitted as a junior. While teaching in neighboring schools parts of each winter, Mussey studied with Nathan Smith, the founder of Dartmouth Medical College and its earliest teacher, and earned a bachelor of medicine degree from Dartmouth in 1805. That same year Mussey began three years of medical practice in Ipswich, which became part of Essex, Massachusetts. In 1805 he married Mary Sewall, who died, childless, in May 1807. In 1813 he married Mehitable "Hetty" Osgood, who "was blest with a . . . cheerful hope" that balanced his "somewhat anxious and despondent" temperament; they had nine children.

In 1809 Mussey earned an M.D. from the University of Pennsylvania, after studying there for nine months. Three years later he received the same degree from Dartmouth. While at the University of Pennsylvania, he "established for himself a high reputation as an original observer" by proving that Benjamin Rush, the school's premier teacher and America's most famous physician, was wrong in insisting that the skin did not absorb. In an experiment for his inaugural thesis, Mussey immersed himself in water containing three pounds of madder, a plant dye, and noted that with the addition of alcohol his urine was red for two days. Later, hoping to pass ink, he damaged his health by immersing his body for three hours in a solution of nutgall (containing tannic acid) and immediately after in sulphate of iron for the same period of time.

After receiving his first M.D., Mussey practiced for six years in Salem, Massachusetts, with Daniel Oliver. Although he distinguished himself as a surgeon, Mussey worked primarily as an obstetrician during these years, averaging more than three cases in that field each week during his last three years in Salem. From 1812 to 1838 he held the chair of anatomy and surgery at Dartmouth. Beginning in 1814 he also held the chair of medical theory and practice. In 1829 he spent ten months visiting hospitals and consulting with distinguished physicians in Paris and London. He took a specimen to Sir Astley Cooper, a famous English surgeon, to demonstrate that, contrary to what was generally believed, bones could heal after an intracapsular fracture, but Cooper refused to believe the evidence. From 1831 to 1835 Mussey was also professor of anatomy and surgery at Bowdoin College, and in 1836 he lectured at the Fairfield (N.Y.) Medical College.

In 1837 Mussey began teaching at the Medical College of Ohio (Cincinnati), where he was in charge of the Marine Hospital and "the acknowledged head of the surgical fraternity in the West." In 1850 he was elected president of the American Medical Association. In 1852 he founded the Miami Medical College (Ohio), where he lectured on surgery and was in charge of the surgical wards of St. John's Hospital. He maintained his childlike eagerness for experimentation and observation. When in 1856 Alexis St. Martin, famous in medical circles because an opening in his stomach enabled important experiments to be made, was presented at the school, Mussey was the only one in the medical audience who "was not satisfied to see and smell the excretion from the man's stomach but insisted upon tasting it" (Juettner, p. 322). After his retirement in 1857, Mussey moved to Boston.

Mussey's colleagues agreed that his accomplishments came through "indomitable industry," rather than through "natural talents." As a lecturer his "words came forth tardily," and he was "deficient in power of expression, in animation, and in grace of manner." Despite these drawbacks his students respected him, for his classes were instructive and practical. In operating he was also "painfully slow," and his hand "was tremulous. In watching its movements," surgeon Samuel D. Gross "almost felt inclined to seize the knife, and either run away with it, or do the cutting" himself. Despite his lack of dexterity, Mussey attained a national reputation as a surgeon. He was especially skillful in the mechanics of surgery and boldly assumed "any legitimate responsibility." He was also knowledgeable about hygiene and prepared his patients with care and personally superintended their after-treatment. Before an important operation, Mussey, a devout Christian, would pray with a patient, "the better to secure his confidence, and to inspire him with hopes of safety."

As Gross stated, Mussey's "surgical exploits were of a brilliant and fearless character." One of his operations was the "first recorded instance" of both arteries to the head being tied (twelve days apart) before removing "a large ulcerated and bleeding" vascular tumor from the head of a patient, who then had a "perfect" recovery. Mussey also surgically closed a lesion between the bladder and the vagina (suffered in childbirth) before James Marion Sims (who is credited with pioneering this surgical procedure) and successfully removed an ovarian tumor when the operation had been done only a few times in the world. Forty-nine times he removed stones from patients' bladders, with only four fatalities. He operated for strangulated hernias forty times, with eight fatalities. In 1848 he reported his early use of chloroform in sixteen operations "without its being followed by a single unpleasant symptom." His medical writings were mostly reports of his surgical operations.

Bothered by indigestion and headaches early in his career, Mussey turned to a vegetarian diet and gradually gave up wine and later quit drinking coffee and tea. He found that these changes helped calm his excitable nerves and made his hand steadier during surgical operations. He shared these ideas through publications such as *The Effects of Alcoholic Liquors in Health and Disease* (1855), showing an understanding of the toxic effects of alcohol remarkable for that time, and *Health: Its Friends and Its Foes* (1862). At the age of eighty-four he wrote "What Shall I Drink?" a short tract against stimulants and tobacco. He died in Boston with "his mind . . . still on the problems of science."

• Mussey's own writings include *Experiments and Observations on Cutaneous Absorption* (1809), "Animalcula in the Atmosphere of Cholera" (1849), "Aneurysmal Tumours on the Ear Successfully Treated by Ligation of Both Carotids" (1853), and various publications on drink and tobacco. For short biographies of Mussey, see Howard A. Kelly and Walter L. Burrage, eds., *American Medical Biographies* (1920); A. B. Crosby, "Eulogy on Reuben Dimond Mussey, M.D., LL.D.," *Transactions of the New Hampshire Medical Society* (1869): 61–81; Samuel D. Gross, *Autobiography of Samuel D. Gross, M.D., with Sketches of His Contemporaries*, vol. 2 (1887; repr. 1972), pp. 312–19; and John B. Hamilton, "Life and Times of Doctor Reuben D. Mussey," *Journal of the American Medical Association* 26 (4 Apr. 1896): 649–52. Additional biographical details are in Emmet Field Horine, *Daniel Drake (1785–1852): Pioneer Physician of the Midwest* (1961), and Otto Juettner, *Daniel Drake and His Followers: Historical and Biographical Sketches* (1909). An obituary is in the *Boston Transcript*, 25 June 1866.

OLIVE HOOGENBOOM

MUSSO, Vido William (13 Jan. 1913–9 Jan. 1982), jazz tenor saxophonist, was born in Carrini, Sicily. Details of his parents are unknown. Raised in Detroit from the age of seven, he first played clarinet. After moving to Los Angeles in 1930, he played saxophone and clarinet with Stan Kenton in local bands from 1932 and also led his own big band in 1935. Around 1933 he married Rose; her maiden name and further details of their marriage are unknown. He joined Gus Arnheim's orchestra in April 1936 but left in mid-August to become a featured soloist in Benny Goodman's big band. His style as a tenor saxophonist was founded upon the most emotive aspects of Coleman Hawkins's playing; this may be heard in a solo that follows the theme of "Jam Session," recorded by Goodman in 1936, and at the midpoints of take two (the master version) of Goodman's huge hit "Sing, Sing, Sing" (1937), in which the droning, hypnotic accompaniment provides an eminently suitable point of departure for Musso to develop an improvisation. During his tenure with Goodman, which lasted until 8 December 1937, he also recorded with fellow sidemen Lionel Hampton and Teddy Wilson, with Wilson's sessions devoted to accompanying singers, including Billie Holiday. On "Can't Help Lovin' Dat Man" (1937), Musso plays a quiet, pretty solo, without the characteristic timbral growl, just before Holiday begins to sing.

Musso joined the new big band of Goodman's former sideman Gene Krupa in April 1938 but left in June. Although he continued to record with Krupa into the fall, by August he and Kenton were forming a big band sponsored by broadcaster Al Jarvis of the radio show "Make Believe Ballroom." Musso's eccentricities made him a potentially delightful show-business personality. Easton recounts that he mangled the English language in hilarious ways: "References to boats that drowned and Cadillac conversibles kept his fellow band members entertained. Once when on the road with Harry James, he remarked, 'If somebody don't open a window on this bus, we'll all get sophisticated!'" (p. 51). She also recounts stories of his remarkable, often uncontrolled strength, of which he was somewhat unaware: shaking hands, he broke a man's arm and then was so upset with himself that he put his fist through the roof of the band bus. In many other ways he was too crude and irresponsible to handle the requirements of bandleading: he had disgusting habits (combing his hair and then dropping loose hairs while people were dining, for example), he got into fights with customers, he was easily distracted from the details of directing a band, he could not be trusted with money, and he was not dedicated to the rigors of booking engagements. Hence the band's music and finances were managed by Kenton, and after a few months of intermittent work the band itself was transferred from Musso to the comedian, trumpeter, and singer Johnny "Scat" Davis, without Kenton's continuing participation.

Musso briefly worked with Goodman again in October 1939 before joining James, yet another of the clarinetist's former sidemen, from January 1940 to April 1941. Recorded solos with James include "Jeffries' Blues." Musso failed again as a bandleader before replacing Georgie Auld in Goodman's band when Auld left to join Artie Shaw in June 1941. One year later Bunny Berigan died, and Musso left Goodman to lead Berigan's big band through its remaining contracted jobs. He was in Woody Herman's big band from late 1942 to October 1943. He then served in the U.S. Marine Corps and worked at a defense plant before returning to big bands as a soloist with Tommy Dorsey in the spring of 1945. Despite success with Dorsey, Musso feared flying, the leader's preferred mode of travel, and so he left to join Kenton's big band in October 1945. After an engagement in Los Angeles in August 1946, Musso left to start yet another band, but this too failed, and he rejoined Kenton late in January, only to have the band break up in April 1947 when Kenton became ill. While with Kenton he recorded his finest solos, including "Painted Rhythm," "Artistry Jumps," and "Intermission Riff," which present typically gruff, fluid, tuneful, swinging improvisations, and "Come Back to Sorrento," a pretentious slow ballad that nonetheless features Musso throughout, playing bright-toned, growling, sentimental melodies and bursting into a passage of moderately fast swing. With the fame that these accomplishments brought, Musso found himself in an all-star septet for a concert in Hollywood organized by Gene Norman in February 1947, but the resultant recordings show him to be overmatched by fellow tenor saxophonist Wardell Gray.

After leaving Kenton, Musso led bands in Los Angeles and Las Vegas, without reentering the national spotlight. In 1960 he settled in Las Vegas to focus on a lounge show band. After a hip operation in 1975 he went into semiretirement, moving to Palm Springs but continuing to perform on occasion locally and in Las Vegas. He died in Rancho Mirage, California.

With his command of a rather limited stylistic package, Musso was one of the "hottest" soloists in white big bands of the 1930s and 1940s, and in particular his manner of playing straight from the heart provided a much-needed contrast to the pretensions of Kenton's big band.

• Jim Burns, "Swing Tenors," *Jazz Journal* 19 (Dec. 1966): 13, 16, summarizes Musso's recorded work. Anecdotes about his years with Kenton appear in Carol Easton, *Straight Ahead: The Story of Stan Kenton* (1973), pp. 51–52, 70, 100–101, 103–5. A more detailed account of their association may be found in William F. Lee, *Stan Kenton: Artistry in Rhythm* (1980). For a full chronology of Musso's years with Goodman, see D. Russell Connor, *Benny Goodman: Listen to His Legacy* (1988). An obituary is in the *Los Angeles Times*, 25 Jan. 1982.

BARRY KERNFELD

MUSTE, Abraham Johannes (8 Jan. 1885–11 Feb. 1967), labor and peace activist, was born in Zierikzee, the Netherlands, the son of Martin Muste, a coachman and teamster, and Adriana Jonker. The family immigrated to the United States in January 1891, landing at Ellis Island and settling amid the Dutch community of Grand Rapids, Michigan. Muste attended Hope Preparatory School and Hope College, institutions sponsored by the Dutch Reformed Church of America, and graduated in 1905. He spent a year teaching Greek and Latin at Northwestern Classical Academy in Orange City, Iowa, before matriculating at the theological seminary of the Dutch Reformed Church in New Brunswick, New Jersey.

Graduating in 1909, Muste was licensed and ordained to the Dutch Reformed ministry. He became minister to the Fort Washington Collegiate Church in Washington Heights, receiving an exceptional salary for a young minister. In the same year, he married Anna Huizenga, the attractive and well-educated daughter of a prosperous Dutch Reformed minister and farmer. They had three children. Muste was poised for a comfortable career, and there is little in his stern Dutch background that would predict his future as a world-renowned activist. However, from 1909 to 1913, he attended Union Theological Seminary, where he was exposed to a more liberal and socially conscious theology, and received a bachelor of divinity degree in 1913. In 1914 Muste resigned his Fort Washington ministry because he no longer accepted Calvinist dogma or believed in the literal inspiration of the Bible.

Muste moved to Newtonville, Massachusetts, a suburb of Boston, to assume the ministry of the Central Congregational Church. His intelligence won him the respect of Boston's religious leaders and theologians, but in 1915 he became embroiled in the growing controversy over World War I. Muste began reading the works of Christian mystics, the Quaker scholar Rufus Jones, and others such as Leo Tolstoy, Ralph Waldo Emerson, and Henry David Thoreau. He was deeply moved by the pacifist strain in Christian mysticism, and as pressures mounted for American intervention in World War I, he announced abruptly that he was a confirmed pacifist. Muste's pacifism placed him at odds with his own congregation, and he again resigned his ministry, in December 1917.

Muste next moved his family to Providence, Rhode Island, where he was befriended by a Quaker Meeting and enrolled as a minister of the Society of Friends. His confidence in the organized churches as agents of peace and social change was shaken when most of them supported America's entry into war. Consequently, his activities were to gradually shift toward the militant labor movement over the next two decades.

In 1918 Muste returned to Boston to work as a mediator for the Fellowship of Reconciliation (FOR), a nondenominational peace organization seeking to promote nonviolent conciliation in labor disputes and other social conflicts. In this capacity, he became a leader of the Lawrence textile strike of 1919 and was elected general secretary of the Amalgamated Textile Workers of America. Muste was active in organizational drives and textile strikes throughout the East and Midwest, but his efforts met with little success. Thus in 1921 he accepted an invitation to become the chairman of the faculty of Brookwood Labor College.

Brookwood was a residential college in Katonah, New York, created to educate adult workers in the social sciences, labor history, and trade union strategy and tactics. Top leaders of the American Federation of Labor (AFL) harbored suspicions about the college, because its faculty promoted the organization of industrial unions and called for the formation of an independent labor party. Nevertheless, Muste was elected a vice president of the American Federation of Teachers in 1923, and the college received extensive financial support from state and local AFL affiliates. Many of its graduates during this period assumed leadership roles in the AFL; others became organizers for the Congress of Industrial Organizations during the 1930s. Muste's adherence to Trotskyist ideas, however, made him increasingly unpopular with the AFL.

The AFL's hostility, along with financial difficulties created by the Great Depression, sent Brookwood into decline by the early 1930s. The faculty was also torn by disputes concerning whether the college should emphasize labor activism over scholarship. As always, Muste preferred activism to scholarship, but he was in a minority at Brookwood and left the college in 1933.

In the late 1920s Muste had begun reading the works of Marx, Lenin, and Trotsky. He was soon convinced that revolutionary action by the working class, including violence under the leadership of a vanguard party, might be necessary to bring about the creation of a just social order. In 1929 he became founder and chairman of the Conference for Progressive Labor Action (CPLA). The "Musteites," as they were soon called, were most successful at organizing Unemployed Leagues in the early depression, and on this foundation Muste formed the American Workers Party in 1933. He agreed to merge the party with Trotskyist elements in 1934, but his leadership was over-

turned by them the following year. After his loss of the party chairmanship, Muste traveled to Europe, where he experienced a "reconversion" to pacifism while visiting the St. Sulpice cathedral in Paris. Although he remained a socialist throughout his life, the conversion at St. Sulpice convinced him that labor and radical movements were being defeated throughout the world because of their spiritual and ethical shortcomings. In 1936 Muste returned to the United States as industrial secretary of the FOR, and in 1937 he became director of the Presbyterian Labor Temple in New York City.

Muste continued to believe that major social disruption was necessary to achieve a just society, but he now believed that peaceful and nonviolent revolution, rather than class struggle, was the proper course of action. He concluded that a radical spiritual change must take place within individuals before any meaningful alteration of economic or political institutions was possible. In his writings, Muste argued that nonviolent action could succeed as a form of social struggle by tapping the reservoirs of moral force that bind a society to common values. Accordingly, he shifted his activism from the labor to the peace movement.

In 1940 Muste became the FOR's executive secretary, a post he held until his nominal retirement in 1953. Over the next three decades, he wielded extensive moral influence in three areas: the civil rights movements, the antinuclear movement, and the anti–Vietnam War movement. He encouraged FOR field workers to promote racial integration wherever possible, and as an offshoot of these efforts FOR staffers founded the Congress of Racial Equality (CORE) in 1942. Serving on CORE's National Advisory Board until his death, Muste helped to organize several desegregation marches in the South. He and his followers were influential in bringing a philosophy of nonviolent action to the burgeoning civil rights movement. Martin Luther King, a member of the FOR, acknowledged the considerable influence that Muste wielded in the early civil rights movement and in his own philosophical development.

Muste's role in the nascent antinuclear movement after World War II became increasingly prominent. He organized campaigns against the payment of taxes that supported the nuclear buildup, against the Selective Service and conscription, against nuclear testing, against civil defense, and against the deployment of new weapons. At the center of many antinuclear demonstrations both at home and abroad, Muste was often arrested and did much to draw international attention to his causes. Following his retirement from the FOR in 1953 and his wife's death in 1954, the absence of administrative and family responsibilities left Muste free to devote his energies entirely to organizing peace demonstrations and other direct action projects.

To support his many direct action projects, Muste organized the Committee for Nonviolent Action (CNVA) in 1957, serving as its national chairman. Muste protégés also helped organize the National Committee for a Sane Nuclear Policy (SANE), which evolved into a leading antinuclear organization during the 1950s and 1960s. Muste personally devoted considerable energy to mobilizing demonstrations to protest the threat of nuclear war, to oppose testing and manufacture of nuclear weapons, and to call for unilateral nuclear disarmament. One of the lasting images of his antinuclear activism is a 1959 wire-service photograph of an aging Muste scaling a barbed-wire fence to enter the Mead Air Force Base outside Omaha, Nebraska, a protest that led to his arrest by military authorities and imprisonment for eight days.

Muste was an early opponent of U.S. military intervention in Vietnam, and following the escalation of U.S. involvement in 1964, he stepped up his antiwar activities. The CNVA and the War Resisters League, also a Muste offshoot of the FOR, organized some of the first demonstrations against the Vietnam War. Eventually, Muste proposed merging the civil rights movement, the antinuclear movement, and the growing anti–Vietnam War movement into a single mass movement for nonviolent revolution seeking world peace and equality for all. Muste did succeed in forging a broad antiwar coalition that included all of these groups, as well as new student and countercultural groups, elements from the New Left, and the labor movement, in the National Mobilization Committee to End the War in Vietnam.

Though crucial to initiating the anti–Vietnam War movement, Muste did not live to see its culmination. He was organizing a mass demonstration against the war when he died in New York. Muste was a tireless activist and, despite his Trotskyist interlude, he is remembered mainly as "America's No. 1 Pacifist" and has often been called the "American Gandhi."

• Muste's association with Brookwood Labor College, the Conference for Progressive Labor Action, and the American Workers Party are well documented in the collection on Brookwood Labor College at the Walter Reuther Archives, Wayne State University, and in the microfilm collection on the Socialist Workers Party held by the State Historical Society of Wisconsin. Muste's personal papers and those of the Fellowship of Reconciliation are part of the Swarthmore College Peace Collection. Additional papers are included in the Labor Temple Collection of the Presbyterian Historical Society in Philadelphia.

Muste authored numerous essays and pamphlets. His most systematic and influential analyses of nonviolent direct action are *Non-Violence in an Aggressive World* (1940) and *Not by Might* (1947). "Sketches for an Autobiography" is the most important of his autobiographical essays; it is included in the only published collection of his writings, *The Essays of A. J. Muste*, ed. Nat Hentoff (1967). Muste published his recollections of the 1930s in Rita J. Simon, ed., *As We Saw the Thirties* (1967), and in the 1950s he recorded a memoir (no. 509) for the Columbia University Oral History Project. Hentoff, *Peace Agitator: The Story of A. J. Muste* (1963), provides an enthusiastic narrative of Muste's life. Jo Ann Ooiman Robinson, *Abraham Went Out: A Biography of A. J. Muste* (1981), is a richly documented biography that includes an excellent bibliographic essay.

Secondary sources relevant to Muste's involvement in the labor movement of the 1920s and 1930s are James O. Morris, *Conflict within the AFL* (1958); Charles F. Howlett, "Organizing the Unorganized: Brookwood Labor College, 1921–

1937," *Labor Studies Journal* 6 (Fall 1981): 165–79; Richard J. Altenbaugh, *Education for Struggle* (1990); and Roy Rosenzweig, "Radicals and the Jobless: The Musteites and the Unemployed Leagues, 1932–1936," *Labor History* 16 (Winter 1975): 52–77. On the context of Muste's peace activities, see Lawrence S. Wittner, *Rebels against War* (1969). Other useful sources are Robinson, *A. J. Muste, Pacifist and Prophet: His Relation to the Society of Friends* (1981), as well as numerous recollections of Muste published by former associates, including Paul Goodman, "On A. J. Muste," *New York Review of Books*, 28 Nov. 1963; John Nevin Sayre, "Fighting Reconciler: A. J. Muste As I Knew Him," *Fellowship*, Mar. 1967; and Nat Hentoff, "A. J. Muste, 1885–1967," *Saturday Review*, 8 Apr. 1967. Obituaries are in the *New York Times*, 12 Feb. 1967, and the *Village Voice*, 23 Feb. 1967.

CLYDE W. BARROW

MUYBRIDGE, Eadweard (9 Apr. 1830–8 May 1904), photographer of animal locomotion and inventor of the first theatrical motion picture projector, was born Edward James Muggeridge in Kingston-on-Thames, England, the son of John Muggeridge, a corn chandler, and Susannah (maiden name uncertain). Little is recorded about Muybridge's childhood and his education in Kingston, but there are numerous, partially conflicting accounts of his activities and accomplishments later in life. As a young man, he changed his name to what he thought represented its original Anglo-Saxon form. In the afterglow of the 1849 Gold Rush, Muybridge emigrated to California in 1852.

Muybridge arrived in the United States in his early twenties, obtained a position as a clerk, and while working at that job determined that he would devote the rest of his life to photography. After accepting a commission from the U.S. Coast and Geodetic Survey, he directed several photographic surveys of the Pacific Coast. Muybridge remained relatively unknown to the public until 1868, when exhibitions of his large and composite photographs of California's Yosemite Valley made him internationally famous as a photographer of the American West. In that year he also visited and photographed Alaska on a U.S. photographic expedition under a commission issued by Major General Henry Halleck.

Muybridge's expertise as a landscape photographer and his experience in photographing moving objects for the U.S. government came to the attention of Leland Stanford, a former governor of California, future U.S. senator, patron of higher education, railroad magnate, and avid sportsman. Stanford asked Muybridge to apply his photographic skills to help settle a controversy regarding whether a trotting horse, at any phase of its stride, had all four feet off the ground. The conventional wisdom was that at least one foot was always in contact with the earth's surface. Stanford and his friend and fellow horse-lover, Frederick MacCrellish, had taken opposite positions on the issue, and a $25,000 wager between the two men rested on the outcome of Muybridge's work.

With Stanford's financial support, in May 1872 Muybridge and John Isaacs (a train engineer on Stanford's Central Pacific railroad) used a set of wet-plate, still cameras actuated by trip lines to photograph Occident, a celebrated horse, trotting past their cameras at about 25 miles per hour. Owing to the limitations of the photographic equipment available at the time (principally, low shutter and film speed), the results were deemed incomplete because consecutive phases of the horse's stride were not captured on film; nonetheless, the photographs seemed to show that the horse's feet had at times all left the ground simultaneously.

In 1874 this project was interrupted by a startling event: Muybridge murdered his wife's lover. At the conclusion of the ensuing trial, the court case against him was dismissed with a ruling of justifiable homicide. Perhaps to escape the public eye for a time, and with financial backing once more provided by Stanford, Muybridge embarked on a photographic expedition to Mexico and Central America to take publicity photographs for the Union Pacific Railroad, owned by Stanford. He returned to the United States in 1877.

In 1878 Stanford commissioned Muybridge to photograph his fast mare, Sallie Gardner, at his thoroughbred racing stables in Palo Alto, California. There Muybridge set up a large number of still cameras parallel to a white background along a race course, which was partially covered with rubber matting in order to prevent dust from clouding the exposures. He ultimately used shutters actuated by an electrical timer to obtain a sequential record of the horse's running motion in photographs taken at equal time intervals, as described in the *Proceedings of the Royal Institution of Great Britain* (13 Mar. 1882). His best photograph series, taken at $1/25$ second intervals on dry plates while Sallie Gardner ran past his cameras at about 36 miles per hour, showed conclusively that a galloping horse's feet are, at times, all in the air.

In 1879 Muybridge invented a machine called a "zoopraxiscope" in order to project his serial photographic images (albeit somewhat altered) of animal locomotion on a large screen so that the animals appeared to move. It was widely used to show such events as racing horses, somersaulting athletes, battling gladiators, and flying flocks of birds by rapidly projecting serial photos printed on rotating glass disks. In 1880 Muybridge gave the world's first motion-picture presentation at a meeting of the San Francisco Art Association. While his zoopraxiscope was admittedly an extension of the principles employed in the zoetrope—a children's toy invented in 1833—and in the magic lantern projector, Muybridge's machine was the first capable of large-scale, theatrical photographic projection. Because of this, it was featured in an exhibit hall built expressly for it at the 1893 World's Columbian Exhibition in Chicago, Illinois; this Zooproxographical Hall was hailed as the world's first motion-picture theater.

On a European tour, Muybridge's projected work was seen by large audiences, and it was praised by both scientists and artists. The dilation of time made possible by his serial photography and moving-picture presentations both amazed and intellectually stimulated his spectators. In fact, Jean Louis Ernest Meissonier, a French painter engaged in a controversy over the position of horses in his pictures, actually employed the zoopraxiscope and Muybridge's images to convince his opponents he had portrayed horses' gaits correctly.

Largely owing to the advocacy of the esteemed artist and faculty member Thomas Eakins, Muybridge was engaged to conduct a series of locomotion studies at the University of Pennsylvania from 1884 to 1885. There he exposed more than 100,000 photographic plates in locomotion studies of men, women, children, beasts, and birds. The initial publication of this work in 1887 was comprehensive but prohibitively expensive. In 1899 the most important plates were republished in London as *Animals in Motion*.

Muybridge's equine motion studies inspired a French chronophotographer educated as a biologist, Etienne-Jules Marey, to develop his own photographic method of studying animal locomotion even more scientifically; Marey decomposed motion into overlapping images captured on a single photographic plate, instead of on separate plates as Muybridge had done. Building on Marey's work in the twentieth-century, Massachusetts Institute of Technology electrical engineering professor Harold Edgerton constructed a high-speed electronic stroboscope and extended the photographic study of animal locomotion to even smaller time intervals using the multiflash approach.

Muybridge returned to England in 1895 and settled in 1900 in Kingston-on-Thames, where he died. He bequeathed £3,000 to the Kingston Public Library, stipulating that the income be applied to purchase reference works. In addition, the library received a set of his lantern slides, a zoopraxiscope, and a selection of the photographic plates from his book, *Animal Locomotion*.

• The Eastman House Museum of Photography, Rochester, N.Y., and the Bancroft Library, University of California, Berkeley, as well as the Kingston Public Library, hold important resources. Accessible reprints of Muybridge's publications include *The Human Figure in Motion: An Electro-Photographic Investigation of Consecutive Phases of Muscular Actions*, with introduction by Robert Taft (1901; repr. 1955), and *Animals in Motion: An Electro-Photographic Investigation of Consecutive Phases of Animal Locomotion*, with introduction by A. V. Mozley (repr. 1979). Some useful studies of his work and related topics include W. D. Marks et al., *Animal Locomotion: The Muybridge Work at the University of Pennsylvania* (1888); A. V. Mozley, ed., *Eadweard Muybridge: The Stanford Years, 1872–1882* (1972); K. MacDonnell, *Eadweard Muybridge: The Man Who Invented the Moving Picture* (1972); G. Hendricks, *Eadweard Muybridge: The Father of Motion Pictures* (1975); R. B. Hass, *Muybridge: Man in Motion* (1976); J. Darius, *Beyond Vision* (1984); E. Jussim and G. Kayafas, *Stopping Time: The Photographs of Harold Edgerton* (1987); L. Monk, *Photographs That Changed the World* (1989); and M. Braun, *Picturing Time: The Work of Etienne-Jules Marey (1830–1904)* (1992).

JAMES H. WANDERSEE

MUZZEY, David Saville (9 Oct. 1870–14 Apr. 1965), historian and educator, was born in Lexington, Massachusetts, the son of David W. Muzzey, a real estate broker, and Anne W. Saville. After completing his undergraduate studies in classics at Harvard University in 1893, Muzzey spent the 1893–1894 academic year teaching mathematics at Robert College in Constantinople. In 1894 he enrolled in Union Theological Seminary in New York City, intending to prepare for a religious vocation. In 1897 he received a B.D. from Union and a seminary fellowship to study in Europe until 1899. He spent his first fellowship at the University of Berlin and the second at the Sorbonne. Looking back a half-century later, he pointed to his year in Berlin as the time when "I decided that I wanted to teach and not go into the ministry." In 1900 Muzzey married Ina Jeannette Bullis; they had two children. After Muzzey's first wife died in 1934, he married J. Emilie Young in 1937.

Muzzey's career after 1899 followed a path that was representative of the transition in America from the Protestant piety of the nineteenth century to the more secular culture of modern times. His first three books, which appeared between 1900 and 1905, focused on topics in religious history and were addressed to theological audiences. *The Spiritual Franciscans* (1904) won the American Historical Association's Herbert Baxter Adams Prize for 1905. The fashion in which Muzzey documented the history of this religious order reflected his developing interest in ethical culture. By 1899 Muzzey had begun to teach at the New York City Ethical Culture School, where he would lecture on classics and history for nearly a half-century. This commitment to the ethical culture movement eventually led him to serve as chair of the board of leaders of the New York Society. Throughout his professional life, Muzzey traveled across the nation speaking on ethical culture. By the 1930s and 1940s many of his talks were carried on local radio in New York. In these broadcasts Muzzey wrestled with the dilemmas of morality and pacifism in an age of total war and genocide.

The progressive historian James Harvey Robinson, who was influential in Muzzey's intellectual and professional development, secured a position for Muzzey on the Barnard College faculty in 1905. In 1907 Muzzey received a Ph.D. in history under Robinson at Columbia. He continued to teach undergraduate history courses at Barnard until 1922, when he joined Columbia's graduate history department. Muzzey remained at Columbia, where he became Gouverneur Morris Professor of American History in 1938, until his retirement in 1940. In his years at Columbia, Muzzey worked closely with many of the great intellectuals of the early twentieth century, such as the historian Charles Beard and the democratic philosopher John Dewey. During his academic career, Muzzey lectured widely, with especially noteworthy visits to the University of London in 1921 and to the University of California campuses at Berkeley and at Los Angeles in the late 1930s and early 1940s.

At Columbia Muzzey published two biographies. *Thomas Jefferson* (1918), was an unremarkable attempt at writing an objective history of the founding father. Amid the patriotic hysteria of World War I, his evenhanded account was a departure from more traditional hagiographies. Muzzey's second biography, *James G. Blaine: A Political Idol of Other Days* (1934), received greater acclaim, earning an honorable mention for biography from the Pulitzer Prize Board in 1935. Still holding to the virtue of objectivity, Muzzey rejected the traditional views of Blaine as either "a corrupt politician" or a "paragon of virtue" (p. 5). His pursuit of balance became a hallmark of his scholarship; he ended *James G. Blaine* by asserting that "it is the duty of the biographer of a public man, abjuring equally the spirit of adulation and denigration, to portray the facts of his life with as complete fidelity as possible to the record" (p. 493). In his study of Blaine's life, Muzzey locates much to be admired in the Gilded Age politician, but in the end he laments his subject's essential partisanship. Such a passion for objectivity would carry over to Muzzey's most important work, his series of American history textbooks.

First published in 1911 as *An American History* and later as *A History of Our Country*, Muzzey's textbooks dominated the field for fifty years. Generations of American high school and college students learned American history from Muzzey's New England–centered perspective. So great was the popularity of these works that, on his death, the *New York Times* assigned him "perhaps as much influence as any modern writer on the American conception of history." A 1979 survey of American history textbooks found that "even now . . . no American-history text has come anywhere near its popularity or anywhere near its sales relative to other textbooks" (FitzGerald, p. 69).

Built around a series of dramatic scenes in our nation's development, the Muzzey textbooks displayed a fine narrative style and a sharp sense of the importance of the individual actor. Though attempting to achieve a balanced portrait of the American past, his works paid little attention to the history of African Americans or to issues of expansion and foreign policy.

During the 1920s Muzzey's high school textbooks created great controversy. Amid the Red Scare and Americanization campaigns of the postwar decade, opponents accused the historian of slighting important figures in the national past. He was alleged to harbor pro-British sympathies. Muzzey's antagonists ranged from the Washington, D.C., Board of Education to Chicago Mayor Bill Thompson to the *New York Journal American*. Cartoons on the pages of Hearst newspapers across the nation regularly depicted Muzzey as a rat. For the decade that led up to the Great Depression, he was among the most recognizable and controversial academics in America. Informed by the controversies of the 1920s, Muzzey fought to maintain his voice as a public intellectual while he strove to achieve scientific objectivity in his scholarship. He died in Yonkers, New York.

• Some of Muzzey's personal papers are in the New York Society for Ethical Culture Papers at the New-York Historical Society. Some of his correspondence is preserved in the Columbia University Library's Collection of Faculty and Administration Correspondence. Among Muzzey's works that have not already been mentioned are *The Rise of the New Testament* (1900); *Readings in American History* (1915); *The United States of America* (1922); *The American Adventure* (1927); *Our Country's History* (1957); and, with Arthur S. Link, *Our American Republic* (1963). The Muzzey oral history at the Columbia University Oral History Project is the best source of information on his life. Frances FitzGerald, *America Revised* (1979), explores Muzzey's importance as a textbook author. An obituary is in the *New York Times*, 15 Apr. 1965.

DAVID QUIGLEY

MYER, Albert James (20 Sept. 1828–24 Aug. 1880), army officer, first chief signal officer, and first head of the National Weather Service, was born in Newburgh, New York, the son of Henry Beeckman Myer and Eleanor Pope McClanahan. After his mother's death in 1835, Albert lived with his aunt, Serena Nixon McClanahan, in Buffalo, New York. Myer learned telegraphy as a boy. He graduated from Geneva (now Hobart) College in 1847.

After graduation Myer worked for telegraph offices in Buffalo, studied medicine privately, and took a course of lectures at the University of Buffalo. In 1851 he received his M.D. from Buffalo Medical College, writing his thesis on "A New Sign Language for Deaf Mutes" that employed the Bain telegraphic alphabet. Geneva College also awarded him an M.A.

Myer hoped to become an army doctor, but for health reasons he spent two years in the South: in Stateburg, South Carolina, as a tutor and in Monticello, Florida, where he practiced medicine for a year. His health improved, he passed the army medical board examination in 1854 and was appointed assistant surgeon assigned to Forts Duncan and Davis in Texas near the Rio Grande. In addition to his regular medical duties, he served as post treasurer, supervised the diet of the troops, and reported weather observations to the surgeon general. Myer was seriously ill in 1855, by his own diagnosis with remittent fever and scurvy, but he recovered in several months.

Myer married Catherine Walden in 1857. The couple had six children. Soon after their marriage Catherine's father, Ebenezer Walden, passed away, leaving them financially secure.

In 1859 Myer's proposal for a comprehensive system of military and naval signals was reviewed favorably by a panel of officers headed by Lieutenant Colonel Robert E. Lee, and the system underwent successful field tests. (An earlier proposal had been shelved by Secretary of War Jefferson Davis in 1856.) Myer's signaling system, later known as "wig-wag," employed flags by day and torches by night, enabling military units to communicate in the field within a theater of operations. In 1860, with congressional approval, Myer became the army's signal officer with the rank of major. He was assigned to the Navajo Expedition of 1860–1861 in New Mexico under Major E. R. S. Canby.

In May 1861 Myer was called to establish a signal system for the Union army. He served as an aide to General Irvin McDowell at the first battle of Manassas (Bull Run) and then under General George B. McClellan as chief signal officer of the Army of the Potomac. He coordinated training in wig-wag and telegraphy for officers and enlisted men detached to him from various departments of the Union army. He also introduced the Beardslee telegraph, the army's first electrical communications equipment that was portable enough for tactical use.

At Myer's urging, Congress passed an act in 1863 providing for a separate Signal Corps for the duration of the war. Myer was appointed its chief signal officer with the rank of colonel. Misfortune befell him, however, late in 1863, when by attempting to recruit skilled telegraphers for commissions in the Signal Corps without approval of Secretary of War Edwin M. Stanton, Myer came into conflict with the U.S. Military Telegraph, which used civilian telegraphers. Stanton relieved Myer of his position, denied him access to the electric telegraph, and exiled him to the Memphis-Cairo area. Further misfortune struck in 1864, when the Senate failed to confirm his position. His appointment as the army's chief signal officer was formally revoked, his rank reverted to major, Signal Corps, and he was placed on inactive duty. He was befriended, however, by General Canby, who used him as signal officer for the Military Division of the West Mississippi; by President Andrew Johnson, who in 1866, after a long campaign by Myer, ordered Stanton to reinstate him as chief signal officer with rank of colonel; and by U.S. Grant in 1867, who as secretary of war reversed Stanton's decision of 1863 and recommended Myer for promotion to the ranks of brevet lieutenant colonel and colonel (retroactive to 1862) and brevet brigadier general (retroactive to 1865).

Myer returned to active duty in 1867. With his position restored, his promotion in hand, and his reputation intact, he now faced the task of rebuilding the Signal Corps and redefining its mission for peacetime service. He convinced the military academies at West Point and Annapolis to teach his system of military signaling and to adopt his book, *A Manual of Signals for the Use of Signal Officers in the Field and for Military and Naval Students, Military Schools, Etc.*, printed in 1864 during his exile and subsequently expanded and reissued several times. He also established his own camp of instruction near Washington, D.C., first at Fort Greble and then at Fort Whipple, and conducted other training courses for the Corps of Engineers. Because the U.S. Military Telegraph was no longer in existence, Myer was now also responsible for electric telegraphy. He argued that in peacetime the Signal Corps should be involved in military intelligence and surveillance of potential enemies. Still, there was no legislative authorization for a separate Signal Corps, and his modest budget request for 1869 was cut in half.

Myer suggested that the Signal Corps use telegraphy to monitor and predict the movement of destructive storms, an enemy of commerce. Congress was persuaded by Myer's zeal and signaling expertise and the promise of military discipline in the system. In 1870, with generous appropriations from Congress, the first National Weather Service was established in the War Department under the direction of the chief signal officer.

Because of his access to commercial telegraph lines, an aggressive construction program of military telegraph lines along the eastern seacoast and into the Southwest and Northwest frontiers, and during national emergencies, a direct line to the White House, Myer soon found himself at the center of an electric intelligence network spanning the nation. The men of his command served both as meteorological observers and at times as Secret Service agents, reporting to him on "peacetime enemies," such as striking workers in the rail strikes of 1877, American Indian uprisings in the Southwest, and natural hazards to commerce and agriculture. Signal service observers reported on the hatching and migration of locust swarms, on frost and drought in agricultural regions, on hazards to shipping along the coast, on floods and droughts affecting major waterways, and on washed-out bridges and heavy snowfalls along rail lines.

Myer represented the United States at the first International Meteorological Congress in Vienna in 1873 and at the second conference in Rome in 1879. He established the *Bulletin of International Meteorological Observations*, published by the Signal Office from 1875 to 1889. His office also issued the *Monthly Weather Review*, begun by Cleveland Abbe in 1872 and still published today.

Permanent status for the Signal Corps came late in Myer's life. It became a bureau of the War Department in 1875 and received a permanent enlisted force in 1878. An act of 24 February 1880 established the rank of the chief signal officer as brigadier general. Myer received that rank on 16 June 1880. Suffering from cardiovascular congestion and kidney disease, he died two months later in Buffalo, New York. The funeral was reported to the nation by telegraphy. In 1881 Fort Whipple, Virginia, was renamed Fort Myer.

• Myer's personal papers, many of which are available on four reels of microfilm, are located at the U.S. Army Military History Institute, Carlisle Barracks, Pa., and in the Manuscripts Division, Library of Congress. The Library of Congress collection also includes printed material relating to Myer's role in the Signal Corps, the National Weather Service, and the North Polar Expedition of 1871–1873. Myer's military service records and most of his official papers as chief signal officer (RG-111) and head of the National Weather Service (RG-27) are in the National Archives and Records Administration. He also issued an *Annual Report of the Chief Signal Officer*, published in the congressional documents series, 1861–1863 and 1867–1880.

On Myer's life see Paul J. Scheips, "Albert James Myer, Founder of the Army Signal Corps: A Biographical Study" (Ph.D. diss., American Univ., 1966). There is a brief entry for Myer in William H. Powell, comp., *List of Officers of the Army of the United States from 1779 to 1900* (1900; repr. 1967). Also by Scheips are "Albert James Myer: An Army Doctor in Texas, 1854–1857," *Southwestern Historical Quarterly* 82 (July 1978): 1–24, and "Union Signal Communications: Innovation and Conflict," *Civil War History* 9 (1963): 399–421. Documents on military signaling in the Civil War era are printed in Scheips, ed., *Military Signal Communications* (2 vols., 1980).

On Myer's meteorological work see Scheips, "'Old Probabilities': A. J. Myer and the Signal Corps Weather Service," *Arlington Historical Magazine* 5 (1974): 29–43; and George M. Kober, "General Albert J. Myer and the United States Weather Bureau," *Military Surgeon* 65 (1929): 65–83. On the origin and functions of the Weather Service see James Rodger Fleming, *Meteorology in America, 1800–1870* (1990), and Joseph M. Hawes, "The Signal Corps and Its Weather Service, 1870–1890," *Military Affairs* 30 (1966): 68–76. An obituary is in the *New York Times*, 25 Aug. 1880.

JAMES RODGER FLEMING

MYER, Dillon Seymour (4 Sept. 1891–21 Oct. 1982), government official, was born on a 135-acre farm in Licking County, Ohio, the son of John Hyson Myer and Harriet Estella Seymour. A 1914 graduate of Ohio State University, Myer was an instructor in agronomy at the University of Kentucky for two years before becoming the agricultural demonstration agent of Vanderburgh County, Indiana, in 1916 as part of the county agent system created by the federal Smith-Lever Act of 1914. The next year Myer became assistant county agent leader in the extension service of Purdue University; in 1920 he moved back to Ohio as the agricultural agent of Franklin County and two years later became the district supervisor of his alma mater's extension service. He remained in that post until 1934 with two years off for study at Columbia University, which awarded him an M.A. in education in 1926. In 1924 he married Jenness Wirt, who was then a home economics specialist at Ohio State. They had three children.

Myer, who had served as an Ohio supervisor of the Agricultural Adjustment Administration in 1933, joined the Washington, D.C., staff of the AAA in 1934. In 1935 he moved to the Soil Conservation Service of the Department of Agriculture, becoming its assistant chief in 1938. World War II changed what would, almost certainly, have been a lifetime career in the Department of Agriculture. The War Relocation Authority (WRA) was created in March 1942 to supervise the incarceration of the West Coast Japanese; it later also supervised the temporary haven at Fort Oswego, New York, for nearly a thousand European refugees. Milton S. Eisenhower, the first director of the WRA, had been Myer's superior in the Department of Agriculture and had asked Myer to help him select the original WRA staff. When Eisenhower resigned, President Franklin D. Roosevelt, at Eisenhower's behest, named Myer as his successor in June 1942.

Myer remained director until the WRA's termination in 1946. As was the case with most of the New Dealers who administered the agency, he believed that most Japanese Americans were loyal and wanted to see them reestablished in civil society. At the same time, however, he and his colleagues believed that "disloyal" Japanese-American inmates should be segregated from the "loyal," and they devised loyalty tests to facilitate that segregation. Myer, like his predecessor, thought that the relocation was unfortunate, but both men (and most WRA staffers) denied vehemently that their "relocation centers" were "concentration camps." Much of the wartime criticism of Myer came from persons such as Senator Albert B. Chandler (D.-Ky.), who thought that he and his agency were "too soft" on Japanese. Many contemporary scholars criticized Myer's policies as overly authoritarian, although most 1940s New Deal liberals thought that he and his agency had done a good job. He was thus considered by Democratic administrations for a number of bureaucratic positions in other areas in which he also had no expertise.

President Harry S. Truman awarded Myer the Medal of Merit and offered him the governorship of Puerto Rico, which he turned down. He became, instead, commissioner of the nation's Public Housing Authority in August 1946 because he wanted to do something about the slums that he had observed in connection with the urban resettlement of Japanese Americans. Congressional refusal to appropriate adequate funds for housing led him to leave that agency in 1947. Between 1948 and 1950 Myer was president of the Institute of Inter-American Affairs, an adjunct of the Pan American Union, with time out for a brief mission to the Middle East for the United Nations.

His nearly three-year tenure as commissioner of Indian affairs, from May 1950 to March 1953, has been described by Felix Cohen as a "regressive era in federal Indian policy," and he was attacked by the chief architects of the Indian New Deal: his former boss Harold L. Ickes, who had recommended him for the Medal of Merit, now described him as "a Hitler and Mussolini rolled into one," and John Collier, his predecessor as commissioner of Indian affairs, publicly called for his replacement. Myer appointed a number of administrators from the WRA to key positions in the Bureau of Indian Affairs (BIA). He reasoned that because he and his colleagues had been successful in running the WRA without significant prior knowledge of Japanese Americans, they need not have knowledge about American Indians to administer their affairs. Myer focused his efforts toward putting the BIA "out of business as quickly as possible but . . . with honor," a policy known officially as termination. Termination essentially reversed New Deal policies designed to perpetuate Indian culture under federal auspices and substituted a laissez-faire policy. Although Myer was replaced early in the Dwight D. Eisenhower administration, his policy of termination was continued.

For the next eleven years Myer filled various administrative positions in and out of government. Between 1953 and 1958 he was executive director of the Group Health Association, an insurance industry trade group; in 1959–1960 he returned to UN service as a senior expert in public administration, based in Caracas; and then he lectured for a term in the Graduate School of Public and International Affairs at the University of Pittsburgh. He joined the John F. Kennedy administration for two months in 1961 as temporary director of the Cuban Refugee Program. From then until his retirement at age 73 he served as a personnel consultant to several government agencies and the Brookings Institution.

In the last months of his life he was again involved in public controversy. The establishment of the Commission on the Wartime Relocation and Internment of Civilians (CWRIC) in late 1980 refocused public attention on the wartime incarceration of Japanese Americans. Too ill to appear at the CWRIC's Washington hearings, he authorized the commission's most vociferous critic, Lillian Baker, to read a statement opposing the idea of an apology. He died in Silver Spring, Maryland, just months before the CWRIC's report denounced both the decision to incarcerate and the process by which the WRA kept Japanese Americans imprisoned.

• Myer papers are in the records of the War Relocation Authority and the Bureau of Indian Affairs in the National Archives and in the Special Collections of the University of Arizona. There are three separate autobiographical interviews and other relevant materials created between 1969 and 1973 by the Regional Oral History Office, Bancroft Library, University of California, Berkeley. Myer's own account of the Japanese-American incarceration is *Uprooted Americans: The Japanese Americans and the War Relocation Authority during World War II* (1971), and his tenure at the BIA is detailed in *The Program of the Bureau of Indian Affairs* (1952?). Richard Drinnon, *Keeper of Concentration Camps: Dillon S. Myer and American Racism* (1987), is a hostile scholarly study of Myer's WRA and BIA years. There is no satisfactory published study of the War Relocation Authority; the best account of an individual camp is Sandra C. Taylor, *Jewel of the Desert: Japanese American Internment at Topaz* (1993). An account of Myer as BIA commissioner by Patricia K. Ourada is in Robert M. Kvasnicka and Herman J. Viola, eds., *The Commissioners of Indian Affairs* (1979), pp. 293–99. Felix S. Cohen, "The Erosion of Indian Rights, 1950–1953: A Case Study in Bureaucracy," *Yale Law Review* 62 (1953): 348–90, is a devastating contemporary critique by an acknowledged expert. Ickes's attacks may be seen in two columns in the *New Republic*, 3 and 24 Sept. 1951. An obituary is in the *Washington Post*, 25 Oct. 1982.

ROGER DANIELS

MYERS, Abraham Charles (May 1811–20 June 1889), army officer, was born in Georgetown, South Carolina, the son of Abraham Myers, a lawyer. Admitted to the U.S. Military Academy at West Point in 1828, his poor academic performance prolonged his stay to five years rather than the customary four, and he graduated in 1833. Commissioned a brevet second lieutenant, he was stationed in Baton Rouge, Louisiana. In 1836 he was transferred to Florida to take part in the First Seminole War (1836–1838). The year after the war he received a commission as captain in the Quartermaster Corps, the staff bureau of the army charged with providing the field forces with clothing, shoes, accouterments, wagons, cavalry horses, and draft animals—essentially everything in the soldier's life except his weapons, ammunition, and food. The remainder of Myers's military career was to be served in this branch.

In 1841 war broke out again with the Seminoles, and Myers served another two-year tour with the troops fighting them in Florida. The Mexican War brought more action and even the opportunity for combat recognition for this quartermaster officer. Myers was stationed on the Texas-Mexico border with part of Zachary Taylor's army, which fought the war's first battles in 1846. For gallantry at Palo Alto and Resaca de la Palma, Myers was brevetted major. When a shift in American strategy sent Brevet Lieutenant General Winfield Scott with an American army on a direct drive toward Mexico City, Myers, along with many of the regular army troops with Taylor, was transferred to Scott's newly created force. Once again his heroics attracted attention as he won a brevet to the rank of colonel for his conduct at the battle of Churubusco. At the same time he apparently did not neglect his staff duties, serving as chief quartermaster of Scott's army from April to June 1848. Between the Mexican War and the Civil War he performed quartermaster duties at various posts in the South and married Marion Twiggs, daughter of Department of Texas commander Brigadier General David E. Twiggs.

By 1861 Myers considered himself a Louisianan. When, on 28 January, officials of that state demanded the surrender of the quartermaster and commissary supplies in his charge, he readily complied, resigning his commission in the U.S. Army the same day. This action brought a sharp rebuke from U.S. adjutant general Samuel Cooper (1798–1876), who characterized it as showing "anything but a commendable spirit." Myers responded with a harsh letter of his own. However, within a few weeks the two men shared the same uniform and, for a time, even the same quarters, when both joined the Confederate army. Myers was commissioned a lieutenant colonel in the Quartermaster Department on 16 March. Nine days later he was named acting quartermaster general, and that December the position was made official. As quartermaster general, Myers presented the spectacle of a conscientious small-time bureaucrat thrust into a position far above his level of competence. He was quickly drawn into controversy when, in the late summer of 1861, General P. G. T. Beauregard blamed a lack of quartermaster and commissary supplies for the failure of the Confederate army in Virginia to follow up its success at the first battle of Bull Run (First Manassas). While commissary general Lucius B. Northrop entered into acrimonious exchanges on such subjects, Myers replied courteously and sought Beauregard's suggestions for improvement.

Still, the Quartermaster Department remained inadequate for the task before it, partially through the Confederacy's lack of industrial resources (such as facilities for manufacturing shoes), partially through the failure of the Confederate Treasury to provide anything like adequate funds, and partially through Myers's own inability to find creative solutions to novel problems or to exercise the strong administrative leadership needed in a far-flung organization. Nevertheless, Myers was promoted to full colonel on 15 February 1862. By the summer of 1863, criticism of Myers was becoming endemic in the Confederacy. He had the further misfortune to lose the good will of the touchy president Jefferson Davis through the loose tongue of his wife. Marion Myers seems to have characterized Varina Davis as "a squaw," and of course the comment was repeated until it reached the first family. On 7 August 1863 Davis, citing the need for greater efficiency in the department, relieved Myers as quartermaster general, replacing him with Brigadier General Alexander R. Lawton. Myers and his friends fought back and, on 26 January 1864, succeeded in getting the Confederate Senate to resolve that, as Lawton's name had not yet been sent to that body for confirmation, Myers was still legally quartermaster general. Not to be so easily outdone, Davis responded by submitting Lawton's nomination and obtaining its confirmation by the senate. Irreconcilable and unwilling to serve under Lawton, Myers was dismissed from the army.

A civilian again for the first time in thirty-four years, Myers settled in Georgia and lived for some time in poverty there. The decade after the war (1866 to 1877) he spent traveling in Europe, though with what financial means remains unclear. Returning to the United States, he resided for a time in Roland Lake, Maryland, before moving to Washington, D.C., where he died.

• Fory further information on Myers see William C. Davis, "*A Government of Our Own*" (1994); Richard D. Goff, *Confederate Supply* (1969); U.S. War Department, *The War of the Rebellion: A Compilation of the Official Records of the Union and Confederate Armies* (128 vols., 1880–1901); and Steven E. Woodworth, *Davis and Lee at War* (1995).

STEVEN E. WOODWORTH

MYERS, Ethel (23 Aug. 1881–24 May 1960), genre sculptor, was born Lillian Cochran in Brooklyn, New York. Orphaned at age three or four, she was adopted by Michael Klinck, a real estate broker, and Alfrata Orr; she was renamed May Ethel Klinck. Trained to be a concert pianist, Klinck turned to painting in her late teens. From 1898 to 1904 she attended Chase School of Art (renamed New York School of Art in 1898) in New York City, studying with William Merritt Chase, Robert Henri, Kenneth Hayes Miller, and others. She worked her way through schools as a monitor of the summer sessions and eventually became the school's assistant director. She also taught painting and ceramics.

Klinck began her career as a painter, following the progressive ideas of her teacher Henri, who had exhorted his students to go out into the city and sketch life around them. Klinck was sketching and painting the people of the Lower East Side of New York in an exuberant style as early as 1904. Because her art shared the principles of the Ash Can artists, she became interested in meeting painter Jerome Myers. They married in 1905, against her mother's wishes, and the following year their only child was born. Feeling that their studio was too small for two painters, or perhaps not wanting to compete with her husband, Myers abandoned painting for sculpture.

In New York Myers lived near or was friends with Mahonri Young, Abastenia St. Leger Eberle, and others who constituted a small group of radical artists revolutionizing American sculpture by departing from traditional themes to specialize in genre. Delineating contemporary urban life, she created individual figures that related to her paintings. Unlike Eberle, Myers preferred middle-class subject matter. She occasionally created commissioned portraits of society women, such as Mrs. Aldolph Lewisohn (1912, private collection, Los Angeles), and theatrical performers, such as Florence Reed (1920, Sheldon Memorial Art Gallery, University of Nebraska, Lincoln). Usually delineating single figures of women, she focused on types as expressed through attire, gesture, and activity. Her sculptures were small (usually under twelve inches) but conveyed in cogent terms strong personalities, often with a biting humor that verged on caricature. Her most memorable figures were of well-dressed matrons, whose fashionable clothing seemed somewhat ludicrous. Realistic in style, her sculptures have loosely modeled, somewhat expressionist surfaces that underscore the vitality of her themes. She often created her sculptures in polychrome plaster rather than bronze to save money.

At the time of her 1912 solo exhibition at the Folsom Galleries in New York, critics compared her sculptures to Tanagra figurines. In the spirit of Honoré Daumier, whose sculpture Myers admired, her works were considered social satire, and writers associated them with the dress reform movement of the early twentieth century. Other critics noted that Myers was depicting the new modern woman. Myers exhibited nine sculptures at the Armory Show of 1913 to considerable acclaim; she and Jerome were instrumental in the early phases of organizing that landmark exhibition. John Quinn purchased four of her statuettes from an exhibition she had the following year at the Martin Birnbaum gallery.

Possibly as a result of the modern art they encountered at the Armory Show, the Myerses traveled to Europe after the exhibition. But the outbreak of World War I disrupted their studies in France. After they returned home, Ethel's career suffered the fate of that of many married women artists: she largely gave up her art for her family. She helped with financial support working as a clothing designer for celebrities, opening her own shop, while also promoting her husband's art, raising a daughter, and promoting her child's dance career. Although she sculpted sporadically, in a somewhat more exuberant, abstract handling of form, the sculptures she exhibited—every few years at the Na-

tional Academy of Design annuals—were exclusively pre-1920 examples. She was one of only three sculptors who were members of the New York Society of Women Artists, established in 1925, and served as the society's treasurer.

In 1930 Myers resumed her career more seriously. She worked mainly in glazed, polychrome terra-cotta. She owned her own kiln and taught ceramics in her studio in Carnegie Hall. For a decade beginning in 1949 she directed the fine arts and ceramics department of Christodora House in New York. She was also a member of the New York Ceramic Society and exhibited at their annual shows.

After her husband's death in 1940, Myers stopped sculpting again, this time permanently, to devote her life to the promotion of her husband's paintings, organizing exhibitions and presenting lectures. At age sixty she studied creative writing at Columbia University, probably to improve her writing skills for the articles that she was devoting to Jerome's art. She died in Carmel, New York.

As Myers could not afford to cast her sculptures in bronze, most of the known bronzes by her are posthumous productions, produced in the 1960s by her estate. Small posthumous exhibitions of her art were held in 1963 at the Schoelkopf Gallery, New York, and Portland Art Museum, Maine.

• Myers's papers, including artist's reminiscences c. 1958, correspondence, newspaper and magazine clippings, and published catalogs, are in a private collection in New York City; a microfilm copy is in the Archives of American Art, Smithsonian Institution. Paula Ann Snorf, "The Sculpture of Ethel Myers" (1967; unpublished paper in Myers's papers), offers insight into the artist's oeuvre. The most important articles are "Notes of General Interest, at the Folsom Galleries," *Craftsman* 23 (Mar. 1913): 724–26, and Florence Barlow Ruthrauff, "Psychology of Clothes as Shown in the Art of Ethel Myers," *Arts and Decoration* 4 (July 1914): 350–51. *Ethel Myers* (1963, 1966), two catalogs published by Robert Schoelkopf gallery, New York, offer additional insight. See also Charlotte Streifer Rubinstein, *American Women Sculptors: A History of Women Working in Three Dimensions* (1990), pp. 211, 217–20. Ilene Susan Fort et al., *The Figure in American Sculpture: A Question of Modernity* (1995), places Myers's art in a larger social, artistic, and gender context. An obituary is in the *New York Times*, 25 May 1960.

ILENE SUSAN FORT

MYERS, Gustavus (20 Mar. 1872–7 Dec. 1942), historian, was born in Trenton, New Jersey, the son of Abram Myers and Julia Hillman. Desperately poor as a child, he was shunted off to public institutions and seldom saw his parents after the age of seven. Such experiences had, he later wrote, "a profound awakening influence in early life in shaping my sympathy for the underdog and clearing my vision in youthful years to the effects of oppressive environment and social injustice in general" (Kunitz and Haycraft, p. 1004). A voracious reader, Myers acquired from lectures and libraries the education many reformers received in college. Whether because of personality or contrasting experiences, Myers developed an early sense of superiority over those fellow "muckrakers" to whom wealth and public recognition came easily. By contrast, Myers regarded his poverty and difficulty in procuring publishers as personal badges of honor.

Reporting for the *Philadelphia Record* at eighteen or nineteen, Myers moved a year later to a variety of investigative reporting jobs with different newspapers in New York City. A Populist at first, Myers became attracted to socialism as a result of his membership in the Social Reform Club of New York City. He was a member of the Socialist party from 1907 to 1912. His first major publication, "History of the Public Franchises in New York City," appearing in the reform journal *Municipal Affairs* (Mar. 1900), launched his career as a muckraking historian. Yet, neither this piece nor his next, the self-published *History of Tammany Hall* (1901), elicited much popular or critical interest. Reflecting the passion and amateur methods of their author, the two publications read more like lawyers' briefs than critical examinations of the context of urban corruption. Their one novel feature (for the time) was the author's use of sources hitherto underutilized in scholarship and investigative reporting: journalistic investigations, municipal records, legislative proceedings, and court documents. But the real importance of his first two publications lay in their exposure of the author to, as he wrote, "the corrupt foundations of a number of great fortunes, which in many a eulogistic book had been represented as the rewards of ability, enterprise and thrift" (Kunitz and Haycraft, p. 1005). Myers would make his reputation attempting a wholesale revision of this representation.

Myers's attitude toward his native land was at its most jaundiced during the decade before World War I, ironically a formative time for him personally and professionally. In 1904 he married Genevieve Whitney, with whom he had two children. He spent the better part of this period fruitlessly seeking a publisher for what would become his most famous book, *History of the Great American Fortunes*. Finally, in 1909–1910, the socialist Kerr publishing house in Chicago released it in three volumes. Coldly received, the book gave Myers a reputation as a "fact-worshipping reporter" (*Time*, 27 Nov. 1939, p. 84). In 1911 he published a critical *History of the Supreme Court* (1911).

Myers resigned from the Socialist party in 1912, decrying it as materialistic and hostile to individualism. Partly impressed by Progressive gains, partly shocked by the much greater corruption he perceived overseas, Myers underwent a near total conversion during the First World War in his attitude toward his own country. His boosteristic writings cheered the nation as it became embattled first by war and then by postwar self-doubt. After turning his fire abroad with *History of Canadian Wealth* (1914), Myers fanned the flames of patriotism during World War I, serving the Committee on Public Information and writing *The German Myth: The Falsity of Germany's "Social Progress" Claims* (1918). His patriotic posture continued into the 1920s with the publication of *History of American Idealism* (1925), a book that disingenuously declared

complete and victorious America's crusade to end favoritism and unequal opportunity.

Because of the trajectory of Myers's career, the interwar years cast him in the uncharacteristic role of a man whose time had come. In the decade described by John Higham as "the tribal Twenties," a predictably positive reception greeted his history of American efforts to legislate morality, *Ye Olden Blue Laws* (1921). During the Great Depression, mass scorn for the venality of the heretofore-lionized economic elite made Myers seem like something of a seer. *Great American Fortunes* was republished in 1936 to scholarly praise by a mainstream press. A warm supporter of the New Deal, Myers was equally popular when he defended his country from British criticism. Here, in *America Strikes Back* (1935), he objected to the view that America was "a nation sodden with materialism." Myers's stance reached its logical culmination in *The Ending of Hereditary Fortunes* (1939), which hailed Progressivism and the New Deal for almost completely righting the wrongs he had identified thirty years earlier.

Myers's final book, conceived in 1925 but completed only three months before his death, was a sprawling *History of Bigotry in the United States* (1942). A Guggenheim Fellowship in 1941 and 1942 helped him complete the project, which represented a synthesis of his earliest and most recent writings. Debunking the popular American notion that home-grown bigotry was "spasmodic . . . and in nowise significant," he nevertheless identified its origins in large part as "a reflex of conditions in Europe." The book, Myers's most popular, went through four printings soon after its publication. The author failed to witness its success, dying shortly after its release, in New York City.

• In addition to the books already mentioned, Myers wrote *Beyond the Borderline of Life* (1910). An autobiographical account is in Stanley J. Kunitz and Howard Haycraft, eds., *Twentieth Century Authors: A Biographical Dictionary of Modern Literature* (1942). Useful biographical vignettes are in John Chamberlain, *Farewell to Reform* (1931); Louis H. Filler, *Crusaders for American Liberalism* (1939); and Vernon L. Parrington, *Main Currents in American Thought* (1927–1930). An obituary is in the *New York Times*, 9 Dec. 1942.

RICHARD A. REIMAN

MYERS, Isaac (13 Jan. 1835–26 Jan. 1891), labor leader, was born in Baltimore, Maryland, the son of free African-American parents, whose names and occupations are unknown. Myers was barred from public education, but he did attend a private day school run by a local clergyman. Leaving school at sixteen, he served an apprenticeship with a leading black ship caulker and then entered the trade himself, becoming by the age of twenty a supervisor, responsible for caulking some of Baltimore's largest clipper ships. During this period he married Emma V.; neither the precise year nor her full maiden name is known. They had three children, the first born in 1859.

Myers worked as a porter and shipping clerk for a wholesale grocer from 1860 to 1864, ran his own store for a year, and then went back to ship caulking. Soon after he returned to this trade, however, the city's white caulkers went on strike, demanding that all black caulkers be fired. With the support of the city government and the police, more than 1,000 black workers were driven from their jobs. In response, Myers proposed that the ousted men establish their own shipyard. Canvassing the local black churches, he managed to raise $10,000 in five-dollar shares. With another $30,000 borrowed from a ship captain, the group bought a shipyard and railway and in the winter of 1866 established the Chesapeake Marine Railway and Dry Dock Company. Within six months the firm was providing work for more than 250 African Americans. The business grew rapidly, virtually dominating the local shipbuilding industry and winning a major government contract against the bids of shipbuilders in several cities. Soon whites too joined the workforce, while the mortgage—scheduled to run six years—was paid off in five.

Myers's first wife having died in 1868, he married Sarah E. Deaver; they had no children. The following year Myers helped organize a statewide union of "colored mechanics," with representatives from every trade. About the same time, he was elected head of Baltimore's Colored Caulkers' Trades Union Society. Segregation was still the rule in the labor movement, but the relatively harmonious cooperation between these black unions and their white counterparts led Myers to think that it might be possible to achieve the same kind of relationship on a larger scale—a national union of African Americans working in tandem with the leading white labor organizations.

White leaders were having similar thoughts, and in August 1869 the National Labor Union (NLU) for the first time opened its convention to African Americans and women. Myers, who attended with nine other blacks (four from Maryland), galvanized the convention with a speech hailing biracial cooperation. "Silent, but powerful and far-reaching," he said, "is the revolution inaugurated by your act in taking the colored laborer by the hand and telling him that his interest is common with yours." The speech was warmly received, and although little integration occurred within individual unions, the convention did agree to admit black unions as affiliates.

At their own national labor convention that December, 214 African-American delegates from eighteen states established the Colored National Labor Union, with Myers as president. A few months later he set out on a nationwide tour, promoting the CNLU gospel of public education, apprentice training, unionism, and cooperative business ventures. Speaking to audiences of both black and white workers, Myers reiterated that they must work together, but he stressed that black unity was the necessary first step. Unions and cooperative associations were the key to black prosperity.

By this time, Myers had left the shipyard to become a messenger to the collector of customs in Baltimore, a position that made him only the second African American in Maryland history to receive a federal appointment. In 1870, with support from both white and black Republicans, Myers became a special agent of the Post Office Department. Returning to the NLU that summer (this time as one of five black delegates), Myers found his political loyalties put to the test, since many of those present had decided that labor should abandon the Republicans and form a new party dedicated to labor reform. The black delegates strongly disagreed. Though acknowledging the Republicans' flaws, they felt it would be foolish to abandon the party that had emancipated their race for an untested alliance with the white workers, who had so often excluded them in the past. When Myers urged the convention to stick with the Republicans, he aroused such intense hostility that he was almost assaulted. The Labor Reform party was endorsed in a landslide vote, and black delegates attended no more NLU conventions.

Five months later, Myers ended his presidential term at the Colored National Labor Union. Progress had been made in organizing black workers, he reported, but not as much as had been hoped, and the union faced severe financial difficulties. Calling for the creation of more black unions, Myers urged members to avoid politics and concentrate on "the business interests of the people." He closed by stressing again the need for solidarity among black workers as a necessary prelude to cooperation among workers of all races. The CNLU survived only one more year, disbanding soon after its third and final convention in 1871.

Myers worked as a detective in the Post Office Department from 1872 until his retirement in 1879, after which he operated a coal yard in Baltimore and then held another federal appointment as a gauger (1882–1887). He organized and directed the Maryland Colored State Industrial Fair Association in 1888, founded the Colored Business Men's Association of Baltimore and the Colored Building and Loan Association, and was an active member of the African Methodist Episcopal church. He died from paralysis at his home in Baltimore.

"If American citizenship means anything at all," Myers told the NLU convention in 1869, "It means the freedom of labor, as broad and universal as the freedom of the ballot." While the larger institutions with which Myers worked—the white labor movement and the Republican party—proved less staunch than he had hoped in defending those two freedoms, he held to his conviction that black workers could, by their own energy and talent, achieve the status they sought. Although he suffered many disappointments in pursuing that vision, his career represents an important milestone in the history of the African-American labor movement.

• As far as is known, Myers left no papers. For discussions of his career, see Philip S. Foner, *History of the Labor Movement in the United States*, vol. 1 (1947); Foner and Ronald L. Lewis, *The Black Worker: A Documentary History*, vol. 1 (1978), as well as the introduction to the abridged version, *Black Workers: A Documentary History* (1989); Foner, *Organized Labor and the Black Worker, 1679–1973* (1974); David Montgomery, "William H. Sylvis and the Search for Working-

Class Citizenship," in *Labor Leaders in America*, ed. Melvyn Dubofsky and Warren Van Tine (1987); Bruce Laurie, *Artisans into Workers: Labor in Nineteenth-Century America* (1989); and Felix James, "The Civil and Political Activities of George A. Myers," *Journal of Negro History* 58 (Apr. 1973): 166–78.

SANDRA OPDYCKE

MYERS, Lon (16 Feb. 1858–15 Feb. 1899), track athlete, was born Lawrence Eugene Myers in Richmond, Virginia, the son of Solomon H. Myers, a businessman. His mother (whose name is unknown) died when Lon was an infant. A Jewish family, the Myers' roots went back to the colonial seventeenth century when Myer Myers was a prosperous silversmith in New York City. A member of the first graduating class at Richmond High School (1875), Lon was a fragile, sickly boy of less than 100 pounds who was encouraged by his physician to take up running. He suffered frequent bouts of illness throughout his short life. During the 1880s, however, he was hailed in North America and Great Britain as the greatest foot racer of all time.

In 1876 the family moved to New York City. Lon Myers became a bookkeeper and joined the Manhattan Athletic Club, where he began an extraordinary decade of successful athletic competitions on two continents. Myers then weighed 114 pounds, stood just under 5′8″, and had long, slender legs. A clipping from the contemporary Manchester (England) *Athletic News* stated that "there never was a man more naturally cut out for running than L. E. Myers . . . possessing the most perfect action I ever saw exhibited by any pedestrian." The earl of Crawford said of Myers: "There is the only real runner I have ever seen" (*Rowing and Track Athletics*, p. 325). Despite poor health, Myers placed himself in the hands of a professional coach, John Fraser, whose wife exclaimed: "John, that boy has consumption; and if you undertake to train him it will kill him, and we'll be blamed" (*Lippincott's*, p. 221).

Running tracks of the nineteenth century, composed of dirt or cinder, were slower than the artificial surfaces of the late twentieth century. On 20 September 1879 in New York City, Myers ran 22¾ seconds for 220 yards (an American record), followed by 49⅕ seconds for the quarter-mile (440 yards), a world record and the first time that the distance had been run under fifty seconds. At the national championships that year he won the 220, the 440, and the half-mile (880 yards). In 1880 Myers won the 300, the 600 in American record time, and set a world record (2 minutes, 18.2 seconds) for 1,000 yards. At the 1880 American championships, his victories at 100, 220, 440, and 880 yards—all in one day—led Olympic champion Hugh Baxter, writing in 1931, to say, "If Lon Myers were running today, no one could touch him at distances 300 yards through the 1000." One expert eyewitness at the 1880 feat said of Myers: "His is the most perfect action I ever saw."

Myers traveled in 1881 to England, the historic home of track and field athletics, only to be met by skepticism after the experts saw his fragile build and listened to his persistent consumptive cough. Crowds in excess of 10,000 saw the American run to world records in the 440 (48.6) and half-mile (1:55.8). He was astonishing, wrote one journalist, "a running pair of legs consuming ground, his torso seemingly superfluous, scarcely articulating with those legs" (Peter Lovesey, *Athletics Weekly* [1968], p. 20). Returning to New York City, Myers ran world record times of 2:13.0 (1,000 yards) and 1:55.2 (880 yards) on 10 August 1881 and 16 September 1882, respectively.

During 1882 Myers again traveled to England and raced Walter Goodall George, world record holder for the mile and distances through ten miles. Massive crowds watched the two amateur champions: Myers won the 880, and George took the three-quarters-of-a-mile as well as the mile run. From 1883 through the running season of 1884 Myers won scores of races, canceled dozens of others due to illness, and faced persistent accusations of professionalism. His friendly rival, George, had already become a professional in 1884, and Myers joined him in 1886. The two raced each other that year before immense crowds, the American winning all three confrontations, and in so doing they made foot racing or "pedestrianism," as it was called then, one of the nation's most popular professional sports. Myers spent eighteen months in Australia (1887–1889), raced and won scores of races, defeated George at 1,000 and 1,500 yards, made a great deal of money, and returned home to his final retirement.

Myers could run no more by 1890; he was gravely ill and found great difficulty in his daily existence. He had run 5½ seconds for 50 yards (a record), and he had covered a mile in 4:27, with record runs at almost every distance in between, an unprecedented accomplishment. Myers died in New York City from a relapse following an attack of pneumonia. He had never married. A quarter-century later, Archie Hahn wrote, "There appears little likelihood that his equal will ever be seen again" (*How to Sprint*, p. 217).

• The most detailed biography of Myers is Don H. Potts, *Lon* (1993). Next in importance is J. D. Willis and R. G. Wettan, "L. E. Myers, World's Greatest Runner," *Journal of Sport History* 2 (Fall 1975): 93–111. See also Hugh Baxter, "Lon Myers . . . ," *Winged Foot*, May 1931, pp. 18–19, 48; Archie Hahn, "Lawrence E. Myers," in his *How to Sprint* (1925), pp. 213–19; [anon.], "Athletics in America," *Saturday Review*, 11 Oct. 1884, pp. 464–65; *Athletic Records of Wendell Baker* (scrapbook in Harvard University's Widener Library); André Cherrier, "George and Myers," *Éducation Physique et Sport* 31 (June 1956): 11; Thomas I. Lee, "The Record Breakers," *Munsey's Magazine*, July 1901, pp. 472–81; Walter Camp, "Track Athletics," *Century Magazine*, June 1910, pp. 270–79; [anon.], "Lawrence E. Myers in England," *Outing*, Nov. 1885, pp. 215–16; James S. Mitchel, "Athletic Giants of the Past," *Outing*, Sept. 1901, pp. 269–71; [anon.], "Lawrence Eugene Myers," London *Sporting Mirror*, July 1881, pp. 196–99; G. D. Goodrich, "Walter George v. Lon Myers," *Athletics Weekly*, 26 Jan. 1974, pp. 10–11, and 2

Feb. 1974, pp. 24–25; and Peter Lovesey, "He Made the Timekeeps Look Twice—Lon Myers," *Athletics Weekly* (1968, month not listed), pp. 19–31. For Myers's autobiography, "Confessions of a Champion Athlete," see *Lippincott's Monthly Magazine*, Aug. 1886, pp. 220–24. For additional information see S. Crowthers and A. Ruhl, *Rowing and Track Athletics* (1905), p. 325, and Ellery H. Clarke, *Reminiscences of an Athlete* (1911), pp. 24–25. An obituary is in the *New York Times*, 17 Feb. 1899.

JOHN LUCAS

MYERS, Myer (1723–12 Dec. 1795), silversmith, was born in New York City, the son of Solomon Myers, a shopkeeper, and Judith (maiden name unknown), who had emigrated from Holland at an earlier, unknown date. The Myers family belonged to Congregation Shearith Israel, commonly known as the Spanish and Portuguese Synagogue, in New York, and Myer probably received his earliest education there.

Myers became a freeman of the city of New York on 29 April 1746. It is not known with whom Myers served his apprenticeship, although it undoubtedly was with one of the prominent early eighteenth-century silversmiths in New York City. In the early 1750s he married Elkalah Cohen, with whom he had five children. She died in 1765, and in 1767 he married Joyce Mears, with whom he had eight children. Myers began to advertise in New York newspapers in 1753, and his career can be followed for the next forty years in scattered and fragmentary documents. He was a very active and respected member of Congregation Shearith Israel, serving as president in 1759 and 1770, and he was senior warden of King David's Masonic Lodge in 1769. As early as 1755 his family and religious connections led to a business relationship with patrons in Philadelphia. In 1763 and 1764 he formed a brief partnership with either Benjamin or Matthias Halstead; they advertised in the 10 November 1763 edition of the *New-York Gazette or the Weekly Post-Boy* that they "continue to make, all kinds of work, in gold and silver, and have to sell, a neat assortment of ready made plate, chased and plain; diamond rings, garnet hoops, and broaches [*sic*] in gold, crystal buttons and earrings, in ditto, silver, ivory, and wood etwees, tooth pick cases, and smelling bottles; cases of silver handled knives and forks, best spare blades for ditto, glasses for silver salts, cut cruets for table equipages, and an assortment of tools, for watch and clock makers." In 1763 and 1765 he purchased land in New Hampshire and Connecticut, respectively.

During the British occupation of New York during the Revolution, Myers fled with his family to Norwalk, Connecticut, where he stayed from 1775 until about 1781. In 1779 a British raid on Norwalk destroyed most of Myers's tools and those of his brother Asher, a well-known brazier. By 1782 Myers had gone to Philadelphia, where he was a member of and contributor to Congregation Mikveh Israel. By late 1783, at the end of hostilities, he returned to New York, where he remained for the rest of his life. Beginning about 1779 Myers trained or employed John Burger,

who advertised on 1 January 1784 in the *New-York Packet and the American Advertiser* that he had recently "had five years experience with that noted and proficient mechanic Mr. Myer Myers."

Myers was one of the master silversmiths of colonial America, and he is the only one recorded as being Jewish. His stature in the field is reflected by his position as chairman of the Gold and Silver Smiths' Society of New York in 1786. Myers's oeuvre includes more than 175 surviving objects made between the 1750s and early 1790s. His earliest works, such as tankards and porringers, are in a restrained baroque style. Beginning in the late 1750s he produced some of the most ambitious rococo objects in American silver, including a unique dish ring of c. 1755–1775 reflecting Irish influence, a dish cross, a snuffers and stand (all Yale University Art Gallery), and sets of rare cast candlesticks (Metropolitan Museum of Art and Yale University Art Gallery). Stylish coffeepots, ale jugs, cans, salvers, and sauceboats are among his other works made for wealthy and successful New York patrons, including Samuel and Susannah Cornell, Peter and Sarah Van Brugh, Robert and Mary Livingston, the Schuylers, and the Philipses. Myers's work is known especially for its pierced (*ajoure*) decoration, a difficult and specialized technique rarely encountered in American silver, as on a basket and fish slice (both Metropolitan Museum of Art) and other forms. Like the fine engraving found on much silver bearing Myers's mark, the piercing may have been the work of a London-trained specialist working in his shop. In 1753, for example, Myers advertised that Lewis Mears, "a jeweller by trade, [who] can engrave," had run away from his shop, where he was working as an English indentured servant (*New-York Gazette or the Weekly Post-Boy*, 9 Apr. 1753).

Perhaps Myers's most important commissions, undoubtedly the result of his religious connections, are five sets of *rimonim* (scroll ornaments, sometimes called Torah bells), the only eighteenth-century American examples known, made between 1765 and 1775 for Touro Synagogue, Newport, Rhode Island; Congregation Shearith Israel, New York City; and Congregation Mikveh Israel, Philadelphia. He also made church silver for Presbyterian congregations in New York. His latest objects, although not as ambitious as his earlier work, are in the neoclassical style, suggesting that Myers continued to work until his death in New York City. He was buried in the Shearith Israel cemetery, but his gravesite cannot be located today.

• The standard biography of Myers is Jeannette W. Rosenbaum, *Myer Myers, Goldsmith, 1723–1795* (1954), which contains illustrations of and technical notes on Myers's silver by Kathryn C. Buhler, a transcription of newspaper notices mentioning Myers, a genealogy, and a list of references to Myers in colonial court records. Several exhibitions have focused on Myers's work: the Brooklyn Museum (1954), and Tom Freudenheim, "Myer Myers, American Silversmith" (Jewish Museum, N.Y., 1965). Jane Bortman Larus, *Myer Myers, Silversmith, 1723–1795* (Klutznick Exhibit Hall, B'nai

B'rith Building, Washington, D.C., 1964), is a catalog of the Bortman-Larus collection of Myers's silver, which has since been dispersed. Myers's work is featured prominently in Morrison H. Heckscher and Leslie Greene Bowman, *American Rococo, 1750–1775: Elegance in Ornament* (1992), and Charles F. Montgomery and Patricia E. Kane, *American Art, 1750–1800: Towards Independence* (1976). Significant monographs include Guido Schoenberger, "The Ritual Silver Made by Myer Myers," *Publication of the American Jewish Historical Society* 43 (Sept. 1953): 1–9, and John D. Kernan, "Some New York Silver of Exceptional Interest: Johnson Silver by Myer Myers," *Antiques* 80 (Oct. 1961): 338–39. Myers's work is in many public and private collections, including the Yale University Art Gallery and the Metropolitan Museum of Art; see Buhler and Graham Hood, *American Silver, Garvan and Other Collections in the Yale University Art Gallery* (1970), and Frances Gruber Safford, *Colonial Silver in the American Wing* (1983).

GERALD W. R. WARD

MYERSON, Abraham (23 Nov. 1881–3 Sept. 1948), psychiatrist and neurologist, was born in the ghetto village of Yanova, Lithuania (then part of Russia), the son of Morris Joseph Myerson, a schoolteacher of socialist leanings who became a peddler, then a junk dealer, after emigrating to the United States in 1885, and Sophie Segal. The family first settled in New Britain, Connecticut, moving in 1892 to Boston's South End, where Myerson grew up in poverty. Following his graduation from Boston's English High School in 1898, he worked for seven years in his brother's shop, where he cut pipe.

Myerson never attended college, and, after completing a year at Columbia University's medical school, was forced back to manual labor. Following another year at Columbia, he transferred to Tufts University, where he studied psychology with Morton Prince and from which he received his M.D. in 1908. After graduating, he spent two and a half years at Boston City Hospital, following which he assumed a position as resident physician at the Alexian Brothers Hospital in St. Louis, Missouri. In 1910 he met Dorothy Marion Loman and proposed to her within forty-eight hours. Married in 1913, the couple had three children; their two sons became psychiatrists and their daughter a psychiatric social worker. Myerson returned to Boston in 1912 to join the first group of residents at the city's new psychopathic hospital. From 1913 through 1917 he was clinical director and pathologist at the Taunton State Hospital, and from 1918 through 1920 director of the Boston Psychopathic Hospital outpatient department.

Myerson joined the Tufts faculty in 1918 as assistant professor of neurology and was made full professor in 1921, holding the chair in neurology that had been Prince's. He held a number of other positions in the Boston area, including that of clinical professor of psychiatry at Harvard Medical School, a position he assumed in 1935. Myerson had opened a private practice in neurology and psychiatry in Boston in 1917. During his long career as one of the country's most distinguished psychiatrists, he saw some 25,000 patients.

Myerson was a member of the generation of young, ambitious, and talented physicians who remade the discipline of psychiatry in the early years of the twentieth century, bringing it out of the asylum and into the public eye. A great popularizer as well as a respected scientist, he published at least ten books and more than 150 articles. *The Nervous Housewife* (1920), an incisive, witty, and sophisticated analysis of women's social role and its limitations, enjoyed the widest circulation. Myerson's fiercely anti-Victorian iconoclasm structured the book, an attack on prior and existing gender arrangements and an argument for limited equality between the sexes. Among his other popular works were *The Terrible Jews, by One of Them* (1922), a reply to Henry Ford's anti-Semitic ravings; *When Life Loses Its Zest* (1925); and *The Psychology of Mental Disorders* (1927), a lucid summary of current psychiatric thinking that frankly acknowledged how little was known concerning mental disease. In a review of his last book, *Speaking of Man* (1950), Ashley Montague applauded Myerson's humane and unfailingly interesting approach and noted that he "wrote with such force and clarity that even a platitude sounds like an epigram" (*Saturday Review*, 9 June 1951).

Myerson's first research interests lay in the fields of eugenics and psychiatric genetics. Finding that 10 percent of Taunton State Hospital patients had relatives who had been hospitalized themselves, his interest in the hereditary transmission of mental disease, which had been sparked by his association in St. Louis with the neurologist William Washington Graves, intensified. He oversaw a large-scale study of the institutionalized feebleminded in Massachusetts and concluded, more temperately than most engaged in similar research, that while some feeblemindedness was traceable to environment and some to heredity, most was of unknown origin. Although he was an early advocate of limited sterilization for eugenical purposes, as an immigrant Jew he was alert to the eugenicists' racist assumptions and intentions, and he became a vigorous and informed critic of their movement. He published widely in the field; his books on the topic include *The Inheritance of Mental Diseases* (1925) and *Eugenical Sterilization—A Reorientation of the Problem* (1936). Something of his characteristic wit and polemical skill can be glimpsed in a dry, scholarly caricature (coauthored with Rosalie D. Boyle) of the eugenicists' modus operandi published in 1941, in which he suggested that manic-depressive insanity was rife among members of Boston's Brahmin caste. Noting that had the forebears of the state's chief justices and governors, its poets, philosophers, and psychologists, whose families were tainted by insanity, been sterilized, as eugenicists were proposing the defective should be, he darkly suggested that "the 'Who's Who' of American development" would look entirely different. It would have been clear to many that the James and Holmes families were among those to which he was referring.

A lifelong opponent of psychoanalysis, Myerson was throughout his life a proponent more of physical than of psychological therapies. He was an enthusiastic advocate of shock therapy, using it regularly and teaching others how to do the same. Convinced that there existed a biological basis for mental illness, he devoted much of his energy to identifying it. Although yielding little of significance with respect to the cerebral metabolism responsible for schizophrenia, he considered his development of a technique for obtaining blood from the internal jugular vein and the internal carotid artery his most important scientific contribution.

His laboratory interests notwithstanding, Myerson's arena was the wider world and the varieties of human behavior it sustained. He wrote on criminality and alcoholism, and despite his eugenical interests, saw the roots of both not in individual psychopathology but in social conditions. Known as an expert witness, he testified in several famous trials, including that of Sacco and Vanzetti, whom he examined at length and thought innocent and legally sane. Known as a skilled clinician, a brilliant diagnostician, inspiring teacher, and popular lecturer, Myerson was a member of many scientific organizations and president of the American Psychopathological Society in 1938–1939. He died in Brookline, Massachusetts.

• The Biographical Note to Myerson's *Speaking of Man* (1950) by his daughter-in-law Mildred Ann Myerson remains the best account of Myerson's life. His son Paul Myerson's tribute, "Abraham Myerson," in *Psychoanalysis, Psychotherapy and the New England Medical Scene, 1894–1944*, ed. George E. Gifford (1978), contains additional personal details. Myerson also figures prominently in Elizabeth Lunbeck, *The Psychiatric Persuasion: Knowledge, Gender, and Power in Modern America* (1994). An obituary is in the *New York Times*, 4 Sept. 1948.

ELIZABETH LUNBECK

MYLES, John (1621–3 Feb. 1683), Baptist minister, was born in Newton, Herefordshire, England, the son of Walter Myles, whose occupation is unknown; his mother's name is also unknown. Myles first appeared in the historical record when he entered Brasenose College, Oxford University, in March 1636. He sided with the Puritans against Charles I in the English Civil War, and about 1645 he became a Baptist minister, preaching for several years in Glamorganshire, Wales. On 1 October 1649, with Thomas Proud, he founded one of the first Baptist churches in Wales, at Ilston (near Swansea). Myles became the pastor and emerged as a popular and active leader among Welsh Baptists.

In 1649 Myles was appointed a trier in Wales for Cromwell's Independent National church, a position that required him to judge the moral and religious qualifications of those seeking ordination or other church positions. Myles, like many other English Baptists at this time, willingly worshiped with English and Welsh men and women of various persuasions. He helped form an association of Welsh Baptist churches, which sent him to London in 1651 as a delegate to a meeting of Baptist ministers.

When the Stuarts were restored to the English Crown in 1660, the government removed him as pastor. He left Wales for New England in 1662 or 1663, fearing persecution for his support of the Protectorate.

Myles arrived in Rehoboth in Plymouth Colony in 1663 or shortly thereafter and found several settlers who already were sympathetic to the Baptist cause; Obadiah Holmes had founded a short-lived Baptist church there in 1649. When Holmes's Puritan ministerial opponent in that venture, the Reverend Samuel Newman, died in July 1663 and was succeeded by an elderly, ill minister, Myles had a golden opportunity to reestablish the Baptist presence. In 1663 he and a fellow Welsh parishioner founded the first Baptist church in the English colonies to last any length of time. The church would later play a major role in the Baptists' battle for tax exemption in Massachusetts, from 1692 to 1734, and the congregation was still in existence in the late twentieth century. By 1664 Myles had married Ann Humphreys; the couple would have two children.

Myles proved as popular in the New World as he had been in the Old. He continued to follow a liberal church admission policy, even being willing to "hold communion with all such [as] by judgment of charity we conceive to be fellow-members with us in our Head, Christ Jesus, though differing from us in such controversial points as are not absolutely and essentially necessary to salvation," that is, baptism (McLoughlin, p. 131). The ministers and government of the Massachusetts Bay colony, however, reeling under the impact of growing numbers of Baptists entering the colony, protested to the Plymouth government (as they had earlier done against Holmes) about Myles and his fellow Baptists' presence, and the Pilgrim leaders began to investigate the fledgling parish. In July 1667 the Plymouth Court of Assistants levied a fine of £5 on Myles and another Baptist for establishing a public meeting without the court's approval, and they ordered him to leave Rehoboth within a month. However, the court also implied that if he moved his church closer to the Rhode Island border it would not bother him.

Several members of Myles's parish migrated to Barrington, Rhode Island. The court granted him and the remaining members land at Wannamoisett and incorporated the town as Swansea. Myles and his parishioners quickly constructed a new meetinghouse in 1667. The Plymouth government, contrary to its regular practice, exerted no control over the establishment of the town and its church, probably due to the presence of several influential colonists in the congregation and the sympathetic support of two local Congregationalists. Instead, five settlers (three Baptists and two Congregationalists) established the basic rules for admission to the town, and the church approved them. Only "erroneous persons," "men of evil behavior," and anyone who might "become a charge to the place" would be denied admission as inhabitants.

The exclusions were designed to convince Massachusetts and Plymouth authorities that the Baptists were equally hostile to heretics like Quakers and that they were different from their Puritan brothers and sisters only in their beliefs on nonessential points (in their view) like infant baptism. However, Swansea used the provisions only twice—to keep out a man who refused to sign the articles and in 1707 to eject a "contentious" minister. And though the town quickly established a reputation as a special haven for Baptists, Myles's well-known policy of toleration attracted several prominent Congregationalists. These individuals were interested mostly in obtaining land and several became town proprietors, but they were also more sympathetic to Baptists than many others and attended services in Myles's church.

Swansea's town covenant stated that ministers should be paid, but it did not stipulate whether this should be done voluntarily or through taxes. In 1673, when Myles was the only minister, the town voted him the substantial sum of £40 from town taxes to serve as schoolmaster. The town also voted that the positions of minister and schoolmaster would remain united as long as the minister would accept only weekly contributions for "ministerial maintenance." In 1675 the town explicitly voted that the pay was for both positions, though there seems to have been no punishment for those who refused to pay the school rate. The town also awarded Myles a minister's lot, a town-built house, and the use of and income from ministry and school lots.

Swansea's Baptist congregation was broken up when the church was burned in 1675 during King Philip's War. Myles moved to Boston, where he became pastor of the First Baptist Church, established in 1665 by Thomas Gould. There he served from 1676 to 1678, though the parish lacked a meetinghouse and members worshipped in a private home. He was apparently as popular in Boston as he had been in Rehoboth and Swansea. The church grew and even spawned a second church near Woburn. Myles himself, however, returned to Swansea in 1678 when the reorganized church offered him a salary of £60 to serve again as both minister and schoolmaster. He finished his life there as pastor.

Myles was a tolerant, humane, and generous man, loved and respected by those who followed and worshipped with him, Baptists and Puritans alike. Even Cotton Mather, while objecting to his religious opinions, described him in the *Magnalia Christi Americana* (1702) as a man of great piety and admirable character.

• The records of the First Baptist Church in Swansea, Special Collections, Brown University Library, include information from the period of Myles's tenure. The best source of information on Myles's life and career is William McLoughlin, *New England Dissent, 1630–1833: The Baptists and the Separation of Church and State*, vol. 1 (1971). Also see John M. Bumsted, "The Pilgrim's Progress" (Ph.D. diss., Brown Univ. 1965) and "A Well-Bounded Toleration: Church and State in the Plymouth Colony," *Church and State* 10 (Spring 1968): 265–79; and Herbert M. King, *Rev. John Myles and the Founding of the First Baptist Church in Massachusetts* (1905), which also contains several useful documents.

RONALD P. DUFOUR

MYRDAL, Gunnar Karl (6 Dec. 1898–17 May 1987), social scientist and author, was born in Gustafs, Sweden, the son of Carl Adolf Pettersson, a building contractor, and Anna Sofia Karlsson. In 1924 he married Alva Reimer; they had three children. Ambitious, brilliant, and fiercely independent, Myrdal received a law degree in 1923 and a doctorate in economics in 1927, both from the University of Stockholm. By 1933 the university had hired him as the distinguished Lars Hjerta Professor of Economics.

Influenced by the Great Depression and his wife's passion for social equality, Myrdal joined the Social Democratic party and became a leading member. He served in the Swedish Parliament from 1936 to 1938 and again from 1944 to 1947, also holding other government posts. Advocates of social engineering and moral reform, he and Alva (a corecipient of the 1982 Nobel Peace Prize) helped shape the policies of Sweden's welfare state in the 1930s and 1940s.

In the United States, Myrdal achieved wide recognition for authoring *An American Dilemma: The Negro Problem and Modern Democracy*, a landmark study of race relations commissioned by the Carnegie Corporation during the Great Depression and published in 1944. The corporation had worked hard to find an "unbiased" social scientist—one whose country had no direct involvement with imperialism—to direct this major study of the status of African Americans in the United States. In 1938 they chose Myrdal, who hoped to fashion U.S. public policy on race relations, to supervise this project, employing forty-eight academics and reformers. Totaling more than 1,500 pages, *An American Dilemma* became the most comprehensive social science study of race relations of its time, and its thesis reigned as the predominant interpretation for twenty years.

The volume's main point was that whites lived with a profound moral and psychological conflict because of the inconsistency between their belief in equality (what Myrdal called the "American Creed") and the scandalous way they treated African Americans. According to Myrdal, "The American Negro problem is a problem in the heart of the American. It is there that the interracial tension has its focus. It is there that the decisive struggle goes on" (*American Dilemma*, p. xlvii). Myrdal laid the blame for one of America's most vexing problems squarely on whites. Although he concluded that racism pervaded the United States, Myrdal, an integrationist, believed that whites would eventually change and live up to the principles of the American Creed. The substantial gains African Americans made toward equality during and after World War II partly confirmed Myrdal's optimism.

Shaped by changing race relations during the Second World War, *An American Dilemma* also influenced the development of civil rights in the postwar era. In the landmark 1954 case of *Brown v. Board of Education of Topeka*, which overturned federally sanctioned segregation, Chief Justice Earl Warren, speaking for a unanimous Supreme Court, cited Myrdal's *An American Dilemma* as evidence that segregated schools psychologically damaged African-American children. Throughout the 1950s and early 1960s, scholars, civil rights organizations and leaders, presidents, Congress, and policy makers endorsed the main ideas of *An American Dilemma*.

Yet Myrdal's *An American Dilemma* fell out of favor as the African-American freedom struggle turned toward nationalism and as whites backpedaled on civil rights in the wake of urban riots during the late 1960s. In an age of cultural pluralism, scholars have criticized Myrdal for misunderstanding African-American culture and for advocating assimilation. Moreover, some critics have argued that white supremacy is part and parcel of the American Creed. Although scholars have rejected some of Myrdal's conclusions, *An American Dilemma* continues to be required reading for anyone interested in the study of twentieth-century race relations in the United States.

After the publication of *An American Dilemma*, Myrdal worked vigorously from 1947 until 1957 as secretary-general of the United Nations Economic Commission for Europe, planning the reconstruction of that war-torn continent and advocating détente between the United States and the Soviet Union. His involvement with the United Nations piqued his interest in Africa and Asia, and Myrdal moved to New Delhi, India, in 1957 to be with his wife and to conduct research. After ten years of work, he published *Asian Drama: An Inquiry into the Poverty of Nations* (1968) and *The Challenge of World Poverty: A World Anti-Poverty Program in Outline* (1970). Reflecting his international vision of equality, Myrdal argued in these books that prosperity in the nations of the third world depended upon the establishment of welfare states.

Myrdal devoted his life to attacking some of the most serious human problems. He made a special plea to the United States, his "second homeland," to eliminate poverty by expanding the welfare state and to fulfill their democratic principles, publishing *Beyond the Welfare State* (1960), *Challenge to Affluence* (1963), and *Against the Stream* (1973). As he reached his seventies, Myrdal set out to write a sequel to *An American Dilemma*, "An American Dilemma Revisited," in an effort to answer his critics of the past thirty years. Returning with Alva to the United States in 1973 as a visiting scholar, Myrdal hoped to complete much of this project, spending half of his time in America and half in Stockholm during the 1970s. In 1974 he was a corecipient of the Nobel Prize in economics.

In Myrdal's last years, he returned with Alva to Stockholm to finish "An American Dilemma Revisited," although Parkinson's disease and the infirmities of old age prevented him from completing it. In 1984 neurosurgery for aphasia hospitalized Alva; she died on 1 February 1986, devastating Myrdal. He died in Stockholm on the thirty-third anniversary of the Supreme Court's *Brown v. Board of Education* decision.

• Important correspondence of Myrdal's can be found in the Arbetarrorelsens Arkiv (Archive of the Labor Movement) in Stockholm, Sweden. For insights into the making of *American Dilemma*, the Carnegie Corporation of New York has two reels of microfilmed materials. A near exhaustive bibliography of Myrdal's writings is Harald Bohrn and Kerstin Assarsson-Rizzi, *Gunnar Myrdal: A Bibliography, 1919–1981* (1981). Excellent treatments of Myrdal and the impact of his ideas are Walter A. Jackson, *Gunnar Myrdal and America's Conscience: Social Engineering and Racial Liberalism, 1938–1987* (1990), and David Southern, *Gunnar Myrdal and Black-White Relations: The Use and Abuse of "An American Dilemma," 1944–1969* (1987).

MILLER H. KARNES

MYRICK, Herbert (20 Aug. 1860–6 July 1927), author, editor, and publisher, was born in Arlington, Massachusetts, the son of Henry Lewis Myrick, a Unitarian minister who later entered the Episcopal clergy, and Lucy Caroline Whittemore. The young Myrick's interest in agricultural publishing began in secondary school through part-time work at *The Standard*, a local newspaper purchased by his father in Fort Collins, Colorado, after the senior Myrick had accepted a position as chaplain in the state prison in 1874. With his family's return to Massachusetts in 1877, Myrick combined his interests in agriculture and publishing to finance his collegiate education at Massachusetts Agricultural College and Boston University (B.S., 1882) by working in various capacities for the *New England Homestead*, published by Phelps Publishing Company of Springfield, Massachusetts. He married Elvira Lawrence Kenson of San Francisco in 1885; they had three children.

After graduation Myrick embarked on a highly successful career as an editor and publisher of periodicals for farmers and homemakers. He acquired a one-twelfth interest in the Phelps Publishing Company in 1882. Myrick's clear expository style, positive tone, and sensitivity to issues of general interest to his readership were abiding qualities that sustained his long, successful career. His talent was initially reflected in the growth of the *New England Homestead* from a circulation of 12,000 to 70,000 during his tenure as editor. In 1883 he helped to launch the monthly *Farm and Home*, which eventually attained a readership of more than 350,000. In 1891 he was appointed president of Phelps Publishing's subsidiary in New York, Orange Judd Publishing Company, Inc., which produced a specialized line of agricultural periodicals, including the *American Agriculturist* and *Orange Judd Farmer*. Under Myrick's leadership, the subsidiary broadened its line of publications by introducing in 1910 specialized vocational journals, such as *School Agriculture*, *Domestic Science*, and *Manual Training*. This was followed by two regional agricultural periodicals, the *Orange Judd Northwest Farmstead* and *Orange Judd Southern Farming*, in 1910 and 1912, respectively. Another successful venture was the acquisition in 1900 of the struggling *Good Housekeeping* magazine, whose initial circulation of 3,000 was increased a hundredfold when it was later sold to William R. Hearst in 1911. Concurrently the Good Housekeeping Institute was established, which served as a testing laboratory to evaluate products that sought to advertise in the magazine. Independently, in 1907 Myrick formed the Educational Press, which published *Current Events* for public schools, and the Bushnell Company, which sponsored another agricultural journal, *Dakota Farmer*.

Myrick was also a leader and publicist for many efforts to improve the condition of American agriculture. The central principle that guided this activism he termed "cooperation." An early aspect of this agrarian progressivism was the promotion of farmers' cooperatives that sought to assist their members by bolstering their efficiency and by increasing their market power. In 1878 he helped to launch the first cooperative creamery in the United States at Hatfield, Massachusetts. Later, he played a key role in the formation of producers' cooperatives for milk, tobacco, and plants in New England.

Myrick also sought to enlist the assistance of the federal government to improve economic conditions in American agriculture. In 1885 he formed the U.S. Postal Improvement Association, which successfully lobbied for the establishment of parcel post, rural free delivery service, and lower postal rates on plants and seed stock. Two years later he actively supported passage of the Hatch Act, which authorized the establishment of agricultural experimentation centers, federal demonstration training of improved farming techniques, and the imposition of pure food requirements. Later in 1901 Myrick founded the Farmers' Political League, a forerunner of the Farm Bloc. Myrick also worked to protect domestic agriculture from foreign competition by helping to found the League of Domestic Producers, an association that tried to influence tariff legislation on commodities, including cotton, fruit, nuts, sugar, tobacco, and wool. In spite of this support of protectionism, Myrick believed that much could be achieved through international cooperation in agricultural research and called for the establishment of a world institute, an idea that was eventually implemented by the king of Italy in Rome.

The principle of cooperation also guided his efforts to establish innovative banking institutions that could mobilize capital in small, rural communities for local business and farming interests. Although he was a proponent of Massachusetts's credit union law, he became disenchanted with this type of organization when it failed to have much effect on local finance. Instead, he became a convert to the various types of "people's" banks that were common in small towns in Continental Europe, particularly Germany and Italy. He explained this concept in his book *Co-operative Finance* (1912).

Many of Myrick's ideas about farm finance were implemented by the passage of the Federal Farm Loan Act on 17 July 1916, which established a five-member Federal Farm Board, chaired by the secretary of the treasury. The Board monitored the activities of twelve regional Federal Farm Loan Banks as well as several private, joint-stock land banks. Under this system, regional Federal Farm Loan Banks largely financed their activities by issuing bonds backed by farm mortgages that collateralized loans to farm loan associations. Because of the leading role he played in helping to launch these institutions, Myrick was appointed director of the Springfield, Massachusetts, regional branch.

By 1923 the Federal Land Banks were beginning to experience financial pressure because of the postwar collapse of prices both for agricultural land and products. This induced Myrick, now serving also as the representative of the American Farm Bureau Federation, to play an active role in the passage of the Agricultural Credits Act of 1923, which authorized the formation of the Federal Intermediate Credit Bank. This latter institution made loans through a network of regional branches to corporations or cooperatives but not to individuals. Unlike the Land Banks, their equity was financed solely by the Treasury Department, and their pool of credit was further augmented by the issuance of collateral trust debentures backed by loans on warehouse receipts held by producer associations. Myrick also served as a director of the Springfield regional branch of this bank.

Neither of these banking institutions in whose development Myrick had played a central role, however, was capable of surmounting the severe economic problems that began to beset American agriculture in the 1920s. With the advent of the New Deal administration of President Franklin D. Roosevelt, both banks were revived through their absorption into the Farm Credit Administration established by the Agricultural Adjustment Act of May 1933.

In addition to these primary interests, Myrick invented machinery for drawing cotton fiber, which he began to manufacture in 1891 through the Metallic Drawing Roll Company, of which he was president until 1923. Myrick died at Bad Nauheim, Germany, while in residence for medical treatment.

• Some of Myrick's correspondence can be found in the correspondence of Robert John Bulkley at the Western Reserve Historical Society in Cleveland, Ohio. Myrick was a prolific author. His works include *New Methods in Education* (1890); *How to Co-operate* (1891); *The Crisis in Agriculture* (1900); *A National View of Southern Development* (1912); *The Federal Farm Loan System* (1916); *Rural Credits System for the United States* (1922); and a book of poems mainly written with his mother, *Ode to the Organ and Other Poems by Mother and Son* (1926). Obituaries are in the *New York Times* and the *Springfield (Mass.) Republican*, both 7 July 1927, and the *New England Homestead*, 16 July 1927.

PAUL J. MIRANTI

N

NABOKOV, Nicolas (17 Apr. 1903–6 Apr. 1978), composer, teacher, and music promoter, was born in Lubcha, Novogrudok, in the Minsk region of Belorussia, the son of Dimitri Dimitrievich Nabokov, a court chamberlain and justice of the peace, and Lydia Falz-Fein. In 1911 his family moved to St. Petersburg, and from 1913 to 1920 Nabokov studied composition privately with Vladimir Ivanovich Rebikov. He spent the 1920s and early 1930s in Germany and France, first at the Stuttgart Conservatory (1920–1922) and then at the Berlin Hochschule für Musik (1922–1923), where he studied with Paul Juon and Ferruccio Busoni. From 1923 to 1926 he attended the Sorbonne in Paris, from which he earned the degree of License ès lettres. Following graduation, Nabokov worked until 1933 in both Paris and Germany as a private teacher of languages, composition, and literature. During this period he got his first important break as a composer, a commission from Sergei Diaghilev (partly as a result of Stravinsky's endorsement) for the ballet-oratorio *Ode* (1928); Diaghilev subsequently produced the work in London, Paris, and Berlin.

In 1933 Nabokov was invited to the United States by the Barnes Foundation (Albert C. Barnes Gallery of Merion, Pa.) to present a lecture series on European musical traditions. He became a U.S. citizen in 1939. From the mid-1930s through the early 1950s Nabokov held a series of teaching positions, first as head of the music department at Wells College in Aurora, New York (1936–1941), then at St. John's College in Annapolis, Maryland (1941–1942), and at the Peabody Conservatory in Baltimore (1943–1945 and 1947–1951). Between 1945 and 1947 he worked for the U.S. military government in Berlin as an assistant in charge of film, theater, and music, and as adviser for cultural affairs to the American ambassador. In 1947–1948 he served as editor in chief of the Russian section of the "Voice of America," which he had helped to establish. Paris was Nabokov's primary residence from the 1950s on, but he was active as a composer and a promoter of music festivals all over the world. In 1951 he became secretary-general of the Congress for Cultural Freedom, and in this position he organized three large and very influential music festivals: "Masterpieces of the Twentieth Century" (Paris, 1952), "Music in Our Time" (Rome, 1954), and "East-West Music Encounter" (Tokyo, 1961). Unbeknownst to Nabokov, the congress was funded primarily for propaganda purposes by the CIA, which hid the source of the monies by channeling them through various American foundations.

From 1963 to 1968 Nabokov served as director of the Berlin Music Festival, and he acted as cultural adviser to the West German chancellor Willy Brandt from 1963 to 1966. In 1968 Nabokov taught as a visiting professor of humanities at the Graduate Center of the City University of New York. The last official position Nabokov held was as composer in residence at the Aspen Institute for Humanistic Studies from 1970 to 1973. He was elected to the National Institute of Arts and Letters in 1970. Nabokov spent the last several years of his life in Paris and New York; at the time of his death in New York City he was making plans for a large Stravinsky festival that was to be held in Venice in 1980.

As a composer, Nabokov is best known for his dance music. His most renowned composition, *Don Quixote* (1964–1965), is a full-length ballet written for George Balanchine and first performed by the New York City Ballet in 1965. Altogether Nabokov wrote five ballets, including *La vie de Polichinelle* (1934), *Union Pacific* (1934), *The Last Flower* (after Thurber, 1941), and *The Wanderer* (1966). *Union Pacific*, which was written for the Ballets Russes (to a libretto by Archibald MacLeish), commemorates the completion of the transcontinental railroad and utilizes popular nineteenth-century American tunes; Nabokov claimed that it was "the first truly American ballet," conveniently ignoring earlier works such as John Alden Carpenter's *Krazy Kat* (1921) and *Sky Scrapers* (1923–1924).

Nabokov, a cousin of author Vladimir Nabokov, was married four times, to Natalie Shakhovskoy (1928), Constance Holladay (1939), Patricia Blake (1948), and Dominique Cibiel (1970). The first three marriages ended in divorce, and he had a total of three children.

Nabokov's music is basically lyrical, with strong dramatic elements. In addition to dance works, he wrote operas, three symphonies, incidental music, choral and vocal works, concert pieces for voice and orchestra, concertos, and various other instrumental compositions. He wrote two books of memoirs, *Old Friends and New Music* (1951) and *Bagázh: Memoirs of a Russian Cosmopolitan* (1975), and was working on a third at the time of his death. In addition, he wrote a biography of Igor Stravinsky (1964), edited a four-volume series titled *Twentieth-Century Composers* (1971), and contributed many articles—mainly on Russian music and musicians—to periodicals such as the *Atlantic Monthly*, *Harper's*, *Musical America*, *New Republic*, and *Partisan Review*. Nabokov was a cosmopolite, fluent in four languages and familiar with many leading figures in the arts. In the *New York Times* obituary, Arthur Schlesinger, Jr., is quoted as describing his close friend as "one of the more remarkable men of the age—[a] gifted composer, vivid writer, organizer of memorable artistic festivals, courageous champion of humane and liberal values, brilliant conversationalist, the most generous of friends, a true citizen of the world."

• There is no known collection of Nabokov's manuscripts or letters in repositories in the United States. Nabokov's two autobiographical accounts are entertaining and chatty; *Bagázh*, to a certain extent, was an expansion of *Old Friends and New Music* and was written, according to the author, as a "storyteller's and story-maker's book." Much information about the composer's career can be gleaned from the later memoir, although he deliberately omits personal information such as the dates of marriages.

There are surprisingly few other sources of information about Nabokov; most are in biographical dictionaries, including entries by John Vinton in *Dictionary of Contemporary Music* (1974), David Ewen in *American Composers: A Biographical Dictionary* (1982), Peggy Glanville-Hicks and Bruce Carr in *New Grove* (1980), Carr and Katherine Preston in *New Grove American* (1986), and Richard Taruskin in *Opera Grove* (1992). An obituary is in the *New York Times*, 7 Apr. 1978.

KATHERINE K. PRESTON

NABOKOV, Vladimir (23 Apr. 1899–2 July 1977), novelist in two languages, was born in St. Petersburg, Russia, to Vladimir Dimitrievich Nabokov, a prominent aristocratic politician, and Elena Ivanovna Rukavishnikov, also of wealthy and educated upbringing. Nabokov's grandfather served as minister of justice under Czars Alexander II and III, while his father led the Constitutional Democratic party in pre-Revolutionary Russia and edited an influential literary journal. Nabokov grew up in spacious St. Petersburg apartments and on large country estates, learning English and French at the same time as Russian from a succession of governesses and tutors. He later attended St. Petersburg's most prestigious school, the Tenishev Academy.

As White Russians, even liberal ones who had struggled for reforms under the Czar, the Nabokovs were in danger in Soviet Russia, and in 1917 the family first fled to the Crimea, then sailed hastily to London in 1919, and settled finally, in 1920, in Berlin. Here Nabokov's father founded an influential émigré journal, *Rul* (*The Rudder*), which catered to the large and literate Berlin community of exiled White Russians, and continued writing polemics for the Constitutional Democratic party and serving as unofficial head of Berlin's émigré colony. Meanwhile, a string of Elena Nabokov's pearls, smuggled out of Russia in a can of powder, paid for her son's first two years at Cambridge. At Trinity College (1919–1922), Nabokov earned distinction in French and Russian.

At a political speech in Berlin in 1922, two would-be assassins rushed the stage, firing at Paul Milyukov, the featured speaker. Nabokov's father interposed himself in defense of Milyukov, and was killed on the spot. Nabokov, home from Cambridge for Easter, was summoned by telephone to the scene of his father's assassination. A number of critics have identified in this experience the origin of the so-called "wrong man murdered" theme that recurs in several of Nabokov's novels, especially *Pale Fire* (1962).

By 1921, while he was still at Cambridge, Vladimir Nabokov had begun to publish poems and sketches in Russian in *Rul*, using the pseudonym "Sirin" (a fabled Russian bird of paradise) to distinguish himself from the father (and editor) whose name he shared. The early poetry, metrically rigorous and complex, shows a particular concern with mortality ("Angels" is such a sequence) and an almost scientific, minute observation of nature.

In Berlin following his father's murder, Nabokov graduated from the literary magazines and began to write novels. In *Mashen'ka* (1926; translated as *Mary* in 1970) Nabokov re-creates the Russian émigré world of Berlin to tell of Ganin's love for a woman from whom he had to part in Russia, and who subsequently reappears in Berlin married to another man. This wistful story of first love asserts how richly one's memories may endow a barren present.

Prominent in the lively literary community of Russian Berlin, Nabokov had many romantic involvements, and chose in 1925 to marry Véra Evseevna Slonim, a twenty-three-year-old Russian Jewish émigrée whom he had first met at a masked charity ball. As if suddenly relieved of distractions, the married writer now wrote prolifically. In the course of a brilliant and twofold career, Nabokov published seventeen novels and scores of short stories as well as several volumes of verse, scholarly articles in lepidoptery, translations, plays and screenplays, chess problems, and lectures on literature. As "Sirin," Nabokov wrote his first seven novels in Russian, to a generally warm reception in the émigré community. After *Mary* came *King, Queen, Knave* (1928), concerning an adulterous triangle that turns to murder; *The Defense* (1930), a novel about a chess master's fatal obsession; *The Eye* (1930), told by an apparent suicide; *Glory* (1932); *Laughter in the Dark* (1933); *Despair* (1936); and *Invitation to a Beheading* (1938), a Kafkaesque fable where totalitarian terrors yield to barbs of irony.

While living in Paris, Nabokov wrote *The Real Life of Sebastian Knight* (1941), his first novel composed in English. The narrator endeavors to compile an accurate biography of his mysterious brother, but by novel's end, in what would become a Nabokov trademark, the narrator comes to suspect that he is himself an invented character caught inside a fiction. Nabokov next wrote *Bend Sinister* in English (1947), and then published his last and most ambitious novel in Russian, *The Gift* (1952), in some ways the author's grateful farewell to the Russian language as an artistic medium. His remaining eight novels were written in English.

Nabokov, his wife Véra, and their six-year-old son had fled to America by ship to escape the Nazi terror in 1940, and Nabokov assumed teaching positions at several American colleges and universities, notably at Harvard, Wellesley, and Cornell. Following the tumultuous commercial success of *Lolita* (1955), Nabokov was able to quit teaching, as his witty and wry story of a middle-aged European intellectual's obsession with a twelve-year-old American "nymphet" made the suddenly best-selling author a household name. "I never imagined that I should be able to live by my writing," he said, "but now I am kept by a little girl named Lolita."

Pnin (1957), his most accessible novel, tells of the comic experiences of a Russian émigré professor somewhat overwhelmed by American campus politics. *Pale Fire* (1962), hailed by Mary McCarthy as "one of the very great works of art of this century," pairs a long poem about mortality with a comically erroneous annotation, and so inaugurates what would later be recognized as a general postmodern theme of literary criticism *as* fiction. *Ada* (1969), a massive family chronicle centering on an incestuous love triangle, is Nabokov's most ambitious novel in English, while *Transparent Things* (1972) and *Look at the Harlequins!* (1974) are slighter and more distinctly valedictory works. The English versions of his short stories appeared in four volumes: *Nabokov's Dozen* (1958); *A Russian Beauty* (1973); *Tyrants Destroyed* (1975); and *Details of a Sunset* (1976).

Nabokov's fiction is characterized by the assumption that art is a game, rather than a lesson; his esthetic strategies involve game-playing, rather than didacticism or mimesis. His works have been called "writerly" in their concern for the medium of language and their deliberate betrayals of artifice. They are frequently self-conscious; they indulge in puns and translingual wordplay while telling stories of passion, murder, obsession, and death. The triumphant paradox of Nabokov's artistry is that even as he revealed the strings binding his characters to the puppeteer's hand, he managed to pluck readers' heartstrings as well. John Hawkes has said that "Nabokov is the writer who nourishes and sustains us," and an entire generation of postmodernists, including William Gass, Don DeLillo, and Donald Barthelme, have cited *Pale Fire* as an important influence on their work. Nabokov, who considered himself an American, died of an unidentified viral ailment in Montreux, Switzerland (where he had lived with his wife in the Palace Hotel since 1959), and was widely eulogized as one of the major writers of the twentieth century.

• Nabokov's papers are divided between the Vladimir Nabokov Archive in Montreux, Switzerland, and the Library of Congress in Washington, D.C. Other collections exist in the archives of Cambridge, Cornell, Harvard, and Stanford Universities and at Wellesley College. A fair sampling of his correspondence appears in *Selected Letters 1940–1977* (1989). His poetry, both Russian and English, has been published in several collections. His Russian plays have been collected in a U.S. edition (1987). His nonfiction includes a biography of Gogol (1944; rev. ed., 1961), essays and interviews, lectures on literature, and an autobiography, *Conclusive Evidence* (1951), which he revised as *Speak, Memory* (1966). He also published translations, into both Russian and English, of others' work.

The definitive biography is Brian Boyd, *Vladimir Nabokov: The Russian Years* (1990) and *Vladimir Nabokov: The American Years* (1991). The standard bibliography is Michael Juliar, *Vladimir Nabokov: A Descriptive Bibliography* (1986), updated annually in the journal the *Nabokovian*. An annotated bibliography of Nabokov criticism appears in Samuel Schuman, *Vladimir Nabokov: A Reference Guide* (1979). Important critical work includes Alfred Appel, Jr., and Charles Newman, eds., *Nabokov: Criticism, Reminiscences, Translations and Tributes* (1970); Julia Bader, *Crystal Land: Artifice in Nabokov's English Novels* (1972); L. S. Dembo, *Nabokov: The Man and His Work* (1967); Norman Page, ed., *Nabokov: The Critical Heritage* (1982); Carl R. Proffer, ed., *A Book of Things about Vladimir Nabokov* (1974); Peter Quennell, ed., *Vladimir Nabokov: A Tribute* (1980); Brian Stonehill, *The Self-Conscious Novel: Artifice in Fiction from Joyce to Pynchon* (1988); and Brian Boyd, *Nabokov's Ada: The Place of Consciousness* (1985). Obituaries appeared in the *New York Times* and the *Washington Post*, 5 July 1977, and in *Time*, *Newsweek*, and *Publishers Weekly*, 18 July 1977.

BRIAN STONEHILL

NACHMANSOHN, David (17 Mar. 1899–2 Nov. 1983), biochemist, was born in Jekaterinoslav (now Dnepropetrovsk), Ukraine, the son of Moses Nachmansohn and Regina Klinkowstein. Nachmansohn's family moved before he reached school age to Berlin, Germany, where he received his early education. In 1918 Nachmansohn graduated from the Gymnasium in Berlin and entered Berlin University. Although his interest had been largely in the humanities and philosophy, because of the unsettled political and bleak economic conditions existing in Germany at that time, his family urged him to study medicine. He passed the medical board in the winter of 1923–1924. He then became interested in the study of biology and joined the laboratory of Peter Rona, director of the biochemical laboratory of the pathology department of the University of Berlin. As a part of the indoctrination to his laboratory, Rona familiarized his fellows with the exciting work then being carried out by Otto Warburg, Otto Meyerhof, and Carl Neuberg. This and his acquaintance with Hans H. Weber had a great influence on the future work of Nachmansohn. Nachmansohn's first experiments were on distinguishing the independence of protein hydration from protein ionization. This work, carried out in 1925–1926 while he was a fellow at the University of Berlin, gave Nachmansohn a solid background in both physical and protein chemistry as well an ability to critically analyze experimental problems.

Through Weber's advice, Nachmansohn went to work in Meyerhof's laboratory at the time Grace and Philip Eggelston discovered a phosphate compound in muscle (named phosphagen) that broke down on muscle contraction. Fisk and Subbarow shortly thereafter discovered the compound was a phosphate linked with creatine by a phosphoramide bond. Meyerhof found phosphagen had a very high heat of hydrolysis (10,000 to 12,000 cal/mole). Nachmansohn was fascinated by this work, and he took on the problem of finding the relationship between phosphocreatine breakdown, lactic acid formation, and the tension developed in muscle. Nachmansohn found that rapidly contracting muscle contained more phosphocreatine than slowly contracting muscle: information that foretold the role of phosphocreatine in muscle contraction.

While a fellow working in Meyerhof's laboratory in the Kaiser Wilhelm Institute in Dahlem (a suburb of

Berlin) in 1926–1927, Nachmansohn was stimulated by the great scientists of the faculty of Berlin University as well as those of the surrounding Kaiser Wilhelm Institutes. The Haber Colloquia particularly impressed Nachmansohn, for these conferences showed the importance and interrelationship of the various fields of science.

Nachmansohn began working on acetylcholine in 1936 while he was in Paris working at the Sorbonne between the years 1933 and 1939. His first significant finding was that acetylcholine esterase was present in large amounts in excitable tissues (muscles and nerves) and hardly measurable in such organs as the liver and kidney. From the work of J. Lindhard he learned that the electric organ of the ray Torpedo was a modified muscle fiber with structures comparable to the motor end plate. He measured the concentration of acetylcholine esterase in the electric tissues and found it exceedingly high. This finding opened the path for the elucidation of the generation of bioelectricity. Nachmansohn purified acetylcholine esterase from the electric organ and presented the first unequivocal evidence for the electrogenic activity of acetylcholine. Subsequent work with the electric organ of the ray Torpedo resulted in the purification and crystallization of acetylcholine esterase.

After moving in 1939 to Yale University, where he remained until 1942, and continuing at Columbia University, Nachmansohn carried out studies on the mechanism of generation of electricity by the electric cell. He found not only that the electric organ contained phosphocreatine and ATP in high concentrations, but that there was also breakdown of phosphocreatine on electric discharge. This was the first evidence that biochemical generation of electricity derived its energy from the same source as muscle contraction: ATP, phosphocreatine, lactic acid formation, and oxidation of carbohydrate. Next Nachmansohn investigated whether the electric tissue contained the enzymes capable of using the energy of ATP for the acetylation of choline. These studies demonstrated the existence of the enzyme choline acetylase: the first demonstration that ATP could participate in energy-building reactions other than phosphorylation. Acetylation was found to result from the coupling of two reactions: first, ATP + Acetate + CoA $\rightarrow$AMP + inorganic phosphate + acetyl CoA, and second, Acetyl CoA + Choline (or sulfonamide) $\rightarrow$CoA + Acetylcholine (or acetylsulfonamide). Subsequent work on the localization of acetylcholine esterase indicated it was present in all excitable tissue—not only in the axon but also in the membrane of the axon and conducting fibers. In his 1953 Harvey Lecture, Nachmansohn advanced the theory that acetylcholine acts as a signal recognized within the membrane by an acetylcholine receptor protein that produces a conformation change that increases the permeability of the membrane to ions, resulting in membrane depolarization, which generates an action potential. Ernest Shoffeniels, in Nachmansohn's laboratory, subsequently isolated the electroplax, the single-cell elementary unit of electric

tissue, which opened a new approach to neurophysiology and pharmacology. Nachmansohn's work on the acetylcholine receptor contributed to its being the first receptor molecule to be characterized biochemically.

Nachmansohn summarized his result by developing a theory in which acetylcholine played a principal role in generating the nerve impulse. This theory was not readily accepted by scientists and remains controversial, although many experiments have since nullified objections to the theory. In the 1950s the Department of Defense provided support for Nachmansohn's work, which was considered to have the potential to provide a defense against nerve gas.

Nachmansohn retired in 1967 but continued to work to extend the knowledge of the action of acetylcholine as well as travel and lecture. Being a Zionist, he made many trips to Israel and through articles supported the Hebrew University and the Chaim Weizmann Institute. He was a believer in the world fraternity of science and was among the first scientists of German-Jewish origin to return to Germany after World War II. Nachmansohn devoted a great deal of time to studying the contributions of German Jews to science in the first third of the twentieth century. The results of these studies were summarized in his *German Jewish Pioneers in Science: 1900–1933* (1979).

Nachmansohn married Edith Berger in 1929; they had one daughter. Nachmansohn was a stimulating conversationalist and an avid traveler. He was a scholar and a lover of art and antiquities. Although he had strong convictions, he never let his scientific opinions interfere with his enjoyment of life. With his friends he was always kind and understanding. Nachmansohn died in New York City.

• Nachmansohn provides an autobiographical account in "Biochemistry as Part of My Life," *Annual Review of Biochemistry* 41 (1972): 1–28. See also Severo Ochoa, "David Nachmansohn—March 17, 1899–November 2, 1983," National Academy of Sciences, *Biographical Memoirs* 58 (1989): 356–404.

DAVID Y. COOPER

NADELMAN, Elie (20 Feb. 1882–28 Dec. 1946), sculptor, was born in Warsaw, Poland, the son of Philip Nadelman, a jeweler, and Hannah Arnstam. After studying at the Warsaw Gymnasium, the High School of Liberal Arts, and briefly at the Warsaw Academy of Arts, Nadelman joined the Imperial Russian Army in 1900. A year later he returned to the Warsaw Academy and soon won the annual competition for a tribute to Frédéric Chopin from *Sztuka*, a journal published by the Polish artistic community in Paris. In 1904, during a six-month visit to Munich, Germany, Nadelman came in contact with two powerful influences on his work—Archaic Greek sculpture at the Glyptothek and eighteenth- and nineteenth-century dolls at the Bayerisches Nationalmuseum. While in Munich he was drawn to the German Romantics and the Jugendstil or art nouveau style.

In 1904 Nadelman went to Paris, where his eclectic tastes embraced neoclassicism, mannerism, the sculpture of Rodin, and the paintings of Seurat. From 1905 to 1908 he exhibited at the Salon d'Automne and Salon des Indépendants. During this period, he dedicated himself to the analysis of the interrelationship of form and space, labeling his pen and ink studies "Rapport des Formes" or "Recherches des Volumes." It was during these years that he met Gertrude and Leo Stein. The handsome and articulate artist soon was a sensation among the Parisian avant-garde.

Although Nadelman was considered by critics to be a progressive in his analysis of abstract form, few scholars have thoroughly assessed his artistic influence on other artists of the period. Athena T. Spear, who dated his early works and isolated his drawing and carving styles, suggests that Nadelman was one of the first to look at African masks. According to her, his early heads may have inspired such artists as Brancusi and Modigliani. Picasso saw Nadelman's plaster head of 1908 (now lost) before creating his cubist *Head* of the following year. Although Nadelman claimed to have been an early cubist, his approach to form was different from that of the analytical cubists. Using curves, he abstracted the human body; however, he neither abandoned nor fractured natural form. His biographer, Lincoln Kirstein, states that as the son of a jeweler, Nadelman became a meticulous craftsman whether he worked in marble, wood, bronze, terracotta, or ceramic, which may have broadened his definition of "fine art" to include varied forms of sculptural expression.

In 1909 a successful showing of Nadelman's standing nudes, figurines, heads, reliefs, and drawings held at the Galerie Druet in Paris drew considerable critical attention including that of André Gide and Bernard Berenson. Whether classified as proto-cubist, mannerist, or baroque, the works recalled ancient Greek sculpture—simplified, exaggerated, and stylized. By 1910 Nadelman further reduced his figures to supple contours and swelling forms, generally labeled as tubular style, involving simplification, surface refinement, grace of movement, style, and elegance.

By the summer of 1910 Alfred Stieglitz sent for several of Nadelman's drawings and that fall published the artist's philosophy in *Camera Work*, in which he stated:

I employ no other line than the curve, which possesses freshness and force. I compose these curves so as to bring them in accord or opposition to one another. In that way I obtain the life of form, i.e., harmony. In that way I intend the life of the work should come from within itself. The subject of any work of art is for me nothing but a pretext for creating significant form, relations of forms which create a new life that has nothing to do with life in nature, a life from which art is born, and from which spring style and unity.

A year later two more successful exhibitions were held, one in Barcelona and another in Paterson's Gallery in London. Upon seeing his work in London,

Helena Rubinstein (Princess Gourielli-Tchkonia) purchased the entire exhibition, which she later displayed in her international beauty salons.

The sculptor was represented in the Armory Show in New York City in 1913 with his famous proto-cubist plaster head and twelve drawings. The following year saw the publication of André Salmon's article on Nadelman in *L'Art Decoratif*, another exhibition at the Galerie Druet, a showing in Berlin, and the preparation of *Vers L'Unité Plastique*, a portfolio of fifty facsimiles of drawings published in Paris in 1914 and reissued in New York as *Vers la Beauté Plastique* in 1921.

With the outbreak of World War I, Nadelman immigrated to the United States. At this time, American sculpture was in dire need of rejuvenation, and as both a theorist and a European modernist, Nadelman was eagerly accepted among New York's avant-garde. The influential critic Martin Birnbaum arranged for a showing of his work at Scott and Fowles Gallery and published an article on his work in *The International Studio* in 1915. The Rhode Island School of Design Museum soon became the recipient of one of his marble heads, and thereafter his sculpture entered the collections of the nation's leading art museums including the Detroit Art Institute, the Brooklyn Museum, and the Cleveland Museum of Art.

In 1915 Stieglitz gave Nadelman a solo exhibition at his Photo Secession Gallery "291." Included was a plaster rendition of *Man in the Open Air* (a bronze rendition is in the Sculpture Garden, Museum of Modern Art). The figure, in contemporary dress—merely suggested by his bowler hat and a whimsical bow tied on his chest—became a twentieth-century Apollo, an icon of urban sophistication. Nadelman's interest in simplified form, craft, and caricature drew him naturally to American folk art. From 1916 to 1920 there appeared, among his neoclassical nudes and idealized portrait busts, small figures that celebrated American culture. *Tango* (Whitney Museum of American Art), *Host* (Hirshhorn Museum), *Woman at the Piano* (Museum of Modern Art), *The Orchestra Conductor* (Amon Carter Museum, Fort Worth, Tex.), and *Dancer* (Jewish Museum, New York), created in cherry wood, gessoed, and painted, evoking earlier crafts, were decidedly witty statements on the contemporary New York scene.

The year 1917 saw another highly successful exhibition at Scott and Fowles Galleries. Despite some controversy over his stylish and satiric pieces, Nadelman became an integral part of New York's artistic life. As a member of the Penguin Club, an adviser to leading painters and sculptors, and a friend of Gertrude Whitney, Carl Van Vechten, Henry McBride, and Florine Stettheimer, he was one of the most influential artists of his time and an instrumental agent in making New York City an art center. He opened a worship and, with the help of three assistants, turned out numerous replicas of his sculpture in various media.

In 1919 Nadelman married Viola Flannery, a wealthy widow and an expert on handmade textiles;

they had one son. Together the couple assembled European and American handicrafts including figureheads, weathervanes, and chalkware. They eventually built an enormous collection that was housed in a separate building on the grounds of "Alderbrook," their country home at Riverdale-on-Hudson, New York. In 1926 they opened the collection to the public as the Museum of Folk and Peasant Arts, later called the Museum of Folk Arts.

In the 1920s Nadelman explored a new medium—galvano-plastique, metal over plaster—both enlarging his figures and focusing on vague contours, seeming weightlessness, and gesture. With the stock market crash of 1929 the Nadelmans lost their entire fortune. The following year he was given his last solo exhibition in Paris. He also received two architectural commissions—an overdoor for the Fuller Building on Fifty-Seventh Street and a figure of Aquarius for the Bank of the Manhattan Company on Wall Street, both in New York City. After that, he all but stopped exhibiting and associated less with former colleagues. With the loss of his studio, the accidental destruction of many of his works, and the eventual sale of his folk art collection to the New York Historical Society in 1937, the artist further secluded himself. At this time his work took a different and far more expressive turn exemplified by an almost five-foot papier-maché statue of two female nudes. The figures, having the monumentality of ancient earth mothers and the innocence of oversized dolls, meld into one form, with features and details blurred. These figures were later cast in bronze and enlarged in marble (State Theater at Lincoln Center, New York). Most of the creations of his later years, aside from a portrait head, *Charles Baudelaire* (Hirshhorn Museum and Sculpture Garden, Smithsonian), were figures in various poses created in inexpensive materials for popular consumption. As specters from the past, they summon both Greek Tanagra figurines and Pennsylvania chalkware and represent the culmination of Nadelman's lifelong pursuit of form manifested in both traditional and popular expression.

During World War II, although in ill health, Nadelman served as an air-raid warden in Riverdale, New York. His final achievement was the instruction of wounded veterans in ceramics and modeling as occupational therapy in the Bronx Veterans' Hospital. He died in Riverdale. Two years later the Museum of Modern Art, the Institute of Contemporary Art, Boston, and the Baltimore Museum of Art gave a major retrospective exhibition of his work, and in 1975–1976 another retrospective was given at the Whitney Museum of American Art and the Hirshhorn Museum and Sculpture Garden, Smithsonian Institution.

• The bulk of Nadelman's papers are held by his son E. Jan Nadelman and granddaughter Cynthia J. Nadelman. Drawings and personal papers are also in the Archives of American Art in New York City. For analysis of the artist's work, bibliography, and chronology, see Lincoln Kirstein, *Elie Nadelman* (1973); *The Sculpture of Elie Nadelman* (exhibition catalog, Museum of Modern Art, 1948); *Elie Nadelman Drawings* (1949); and John I. H. Baur, *The Sculpture and Drawing of Elie Nadelman* (exhibition catalog, Whitney Museum of American Art, 1975). For an excellent analysis of his early work, see Athena T. Spear, "Elie Nadelman's Early Heads (1905–1911)," *Allen Memorial Art Museum Bulletin* 28, no. 3 (Spring 1971), and "The Multiple Styles of Elie Nadelman: Drawings and Figure Sculptures ca. 1905–12," *Allen Memorial Art Museum Bulletin* 31, no. 1 (1973–1974). For an overview of Nadelman's early years in New York, see Roberta K. Tarbell, "Figurative Interpretations of Vanguard Concepts," *Vanguard American Sculpture 1913–1939* (exhibition catalog, Rutgers University Art Gallery, 1979). For his folk art collection, see Christine I. Oaklander, "Elie & Viola Nadelman: Pioneers in Folk Art Collecting," *Folk Art* 17 (Fall 1992), and Elizabeth Stillinger, "Elie and Viola Nadelman's Unprecedented Museum of Folk Arts," *Magazine Antiques* 146 (Oct. 1994). See also Cynthia J. Nadelman, "Elie Nadelman's Beauport Drawings," *Drawing* 7, no. 4 (Dec. 1985); Jeanne L. Wasserman, *Three American Sculptors and the Female Nude: Lachaise, Nadelman Archipenko* (exhibition catalog, Fogg Art Museum, 1980); and Klaus Kertess, "Child's Play: The Late Work of Elie Nadelman," *Artforum* 23, no. 7 (Mar. 1985).

SYLVIA LAHVIS

NAGEL, Ernest (16 Nov. 1901–20 Sept. 1985), philosopher of science, was born in Bohemia, in what is now part of the Czech Republic. His parents' names are unknown. When he was ten years old, he immigrated to the United States. In 1919 he became a U.S. citizen. He was educated in New York City, receiving his Ph.D. in philosophy from Columbia University in 1931. In 1935 he married Edith Alexandria Haggstrom; they had two children

Nagel wrote his dissertation on measurement and continued to be interested in the conceptual nature of measurement throughout his career. Examples and discussion are to be found in many of his later articles. He wrote in the tradition of German mathematician Hermann von Helmholtz and German physicist and physiologist Otto Hölder, who had begun the formal work on the foundations of measurement in the nineteenth century. Those foundations are closely connected to the nineteenth-century history of geometry, a subject of interest to Nagel throughout his career. In a major historical analysis published in 1939, *The Formation of Modern Conceptions of Formal Logic in the Development of Geometry*, Nagel traced the importance of the introduction of projective geometry in the nineteenth century for later developments in the foundations of mathematics. He also later devoted one chapter and parts of other chapters to geometry in *The Structure of Science: Problems in the Logic of Scientific Explanation* (1961). The widely disseminated conventional views of geometry that were advocated by Jules-Henri Poincaré came under Nagel's scrutiny and received from him a close, detailed critique.

With "Principles of the Theory of Probability" (1939), published in the first volume of the *International Encyclopedia of Unified Science*, Nagel defended the frequency interpretation of probability. He made, however, a sustained effort to survey the various alternatives and to deal with many of the problems that have been raised about the frequency interpretation. He was perhaps the first American philosopher to call serious attention to the important method of arbitrary functions in probability theory that began with Poincaré and was extended by Eberhard Hopf, George D. Birkhoff and others. This approach, based on relatively straightforward principles of physical symmetry, as in the case of roulette or coin-flipping, provided a detailed account of observed probabilistic phenomena as recorded in relative frequencies.

Among his generation of philosophers of science, Nagel was especially intent on critically examining the foundational claims made about quantum mechanics, particularly in relation to questions of causality. Characteristic of Nagel's analysis was his emphasis on the deterministic elements that remained in quantum mechanics, given the deterministic solutions of the Schrödinger equation, the fundamental equation of quantum mechanics. In "The Meaning of Reduction in the Natural Sciences" (1949), Nagel concentrated on another central topic in the foundations of physics: the possibility of reducing one physical theory to another. Using as his example the most important case within classical physics of such reduction, Nagel offered a detailed conceptual analysis of the attempts to reduce thermodynamics to statistical mechanics. Only toward the end of the twentieth century did much more extensive philosophical analyses begin to appear. Nagel's analysis broke new ground by showing how complex any real case of reduction is as opposed to the speculative generalities often to be found in philosophy.

But the full scope and intensity of Nagel's critical faculties as a philosopher were more fully displayed in his discussions of theories of induction proposed during his lifetime, especially by Rudolph Carnap and Hans Reichenbach. Both Carnap and Reichenbach advanced general theories of induction that in principle were meant to apply to scientific theories and their comprehensive use and assimilation of empirical evidence. Although Nagel saw merits in Carnap's and Reichenbach's different proposals, he doubted that an actual working scheme for the general quantitative confirmation of scientific theories could be developed. Typical of his philosophy was his detailed critique of the difficulties of philosophical schemes that seemed too grand in conception. Looking at the literature much later, it is easy enough to see that his general view is correct, even though Carnap's approach retains some currency in the conceptual framework of subjective probability. In any case, later philosophy has sustained Nagel's skepticism; no one expects to encounter the kind of formulation that would reduce a genuinely important scientific theory to Carnap's framework.

Nagel wrote about a wide range of issues in the philosophy of science, and it is not possible here to survey them all in detail. His most important book, *The Structure of Science*, remains perhaps the most detailed and authoritative exposition of the different kinds of explanations advanced in different parts of science. Characteristic of Nagel's critical approach to philosophy is his unwillingness to give any unified account of the nature of scientific explanations or the nature of scientific laws.

The nature of teleological explanations in biology became the focus of the John Dewey Lectures that Nagel gave at Columbia in 1977 and published in 1979 as *Teleology Revisited and Other Essays in the Philosophy and History of Science*. In some of the most detailed studies of alternative approaches to teleological explanations still to be found in the philosophical literature, he contends that the analysis of goal-directed processes in biology is in principle similar to the analysis of the structure of physical processes. Integral to his general philosophical outlook is the idea that goal-directed behavior of biological organisms forms as much a part of the natural world as the physical processes treated in classical and modern physics.

Nagel also wrote a great deal about the social sciences and tangled with many of the main issues that have been raised concerning their status. He was perhaps most concerned about the thesis that the social sciences are not sciences in the sense that the natural sciences are. The object of his criticism, the so-called *Verstehen* view of the matter has as a premise that empathetic understanding is required in any fully developed social science. Characteristically skeptical and critical, Nagel remarked that one need not be a psychotic in order to be a scientifically successful psychiatrist studying paranoia. While he did not lay down any methodological rules for arriving at scientific results in the social sciences, he argued that the same general standards characteristic of the other sciences be imported and used in the social sciences as well. In this connection he was especially persuasive in defending a probabilistic concept of causality and the reliance on statistical methods in the social sciences.

In the final chapter of the *Structure of Science*, Nagel defends the thesis that the same general critical apparatus of evidence and argument can be used in historical inquiry as in the scientific disciplines. Rather than an identity of method, the two fields share identity of general philosophical viewpoint toward acquiring knowledge about the world. Consistent with his other philosophical views, Nagel was critical of those historians who have tried to establish, on a speculative basis, general historical laws. In contrast, he was sympathetic with historians who attempt to propose tentative but intricate explanations of important historical events such as the French Revolution. Properly skeptical of finding a final and fully satisfactory explanation of complex historical phenomena, Nagel was nevertheless confident that good scholarship and thoughtful analysis can vastly increase our understanding of historical phenomena from an objective standpoint.

Almost all of Nagel's teaching career was spent at Columbia, where he was on the faculty from 1931 to 1970. From 1967 until his retirement in 1970, he held the position of University Professor at Columbia, where he continued to teach after his retirement. He received many honors from various institutions. He was among the most prominent philosophers of science in the United States of his generation. In 1977 he was elected to the National Academy of Sciences, an honor conferred on very few philosophers. He died in New York City.

• The works of Nagel include "The Formation of Modern Conceptions of Formal Logic in the Development of Geometry," *Osiris* 7 (1939): 142–224, "The Meaning of Reduction in the Natural Sciences," in *Science and Civilization*, ed. Robert C. Stouffer (1949), *Teleology Revisited and Other Essays in the Philosophy and History of Science* (1979), *An Introduction to Logic and Scientific Method*, with Morris R. Cohen (1934), *Sovereign Reason, and Other Studies in the Philosophy of Science* (1954), and *Logic without Metaphysics, and Other Essays in the Philosophy of Science* (1957). For an exposition of Nagel's approach to logic and scientific method, see Patrick Suppes, "Nagel's Lectures on Dewey's Logic," in *Philosophy, Science and Method: Essays in Honor of Ernest Nagel*, ed. Sidney Morgenbesser et al. (1969).

PATRICK SUPPES

NAGURSKI, Bronko (3 Nov. 1908–7 Jan. 1990), college and professional football player, was born Bronislau Nagurski in Rainy River, Ontario, Canada, the son of Ukranian immigrants Nicholas Nagurski, a grocer, and Michelina Nagurski. While growing up in International Falls, Minnesota, where he had moved with his family in November 1912, Nagurski established a reputation as an all-around athlete. He began playing football with neighborhood children as early as kindergarten, and he had played sandlot football by the time he entered International Falls High School. He played both basketball and football (as a tackle and fullback) at International Falls, although the football team did not win a single game in the two years he was there. Nagurski completed his senior year at Bemidji, Minnesota, High School, where he was prohibited from taking part in football because he lived outside the school district.

University of Minnesota head football coach Clarence W. Spears convinced Nagurski to attend Minnesota on the recommendation of an alumnus who had seen him play. At the time that Nagurski entered the university in the autumn of 1926, he weighed 185 pounds. The Gophers went 6–0–2 in his first year with the team, including a 7–7 tie in South Bend that ended Notre Dame's twenty-season home win streak against intercollegiate opponents. Nagurski gained All-America honors at both offensive fullback and defensive tackle in 1928 and 1929. He helped the Gophers amass an 18–4–2 record from 1927 to 1929, the four losses coming by a total of five points.

After graduating from Minnesota with a B.A. in 1930, and by this time standing 6'2" and weighing 225 pounds, Nagurski signed to play with the Chicago Bears of the National Football League. Playing on both sides of the ball (fullback and tackle on offense and defensive linebacker), he joined a team that included the famed Harold "Red" Grange at halfback. In Nagurski's nine years with them, the Bears compiled a 79–20–12 record and won NFL championships in 1932, 1933, and 1943.

For that era, Nagurski was one of the largest men in professional football. He had a size 19 neck, and his huge hands required a size 19½ championship ring. A fullback on offense, he not only was a threat to run, but he also was a great blocker, and, because of one play, he is credited with revolutionizing the rules and thereby encouraging the passing game. In 1932, with the Bears playing the Portsmouth Spartans for the NFL championship, he broke a scoreless tie in the fourth quarter by faking a line plunge, jumping higher than players at the scrimmage line, and completing a pass to Grange for the game's lone touchdown. Portsmouth protested under the rule that prohibited forward passes within five yards of the line of scrimmage, but the protest failed, and the next year the NFL changed the rule to allow a forward pass from anywhere behind the scrimmage line.

Over the next five seasons Nagurski played a major role in the Bears' success while attaining personal honors. In 1933, after the NFL split into Eastern and Western divisions, the Nagurski-led Bears won the Western Division championship and went on to defeat the New York Giants in the first NFL championship under the new league alignment. He was selected all-pro at fullback from 1932 to 1934, leading his team to the title game again in 1934 but this time losing to the Giants. That same year he began a lucrative career as a professional wrestler that lasted until 1960.

In 1936 he married his high school sweetheart, Eileen Kane. They had six children.

The Bears were in the championship game once more in 1937, losing to the Washington Redskins. Nagurski retired following the 1937 season when the Bears would not meet his demand for a $6,000 annual contract. In 1943, when a shortage of players threatened the NFL during World War II, he was persuaded to play one more season. At age thirty-five and having been inactive for six years, he nevertheless scored a touchdown in the Bears' victory over the Redskins in the championship game.

Considered by sportswriter Grantland Rice, among others, as one of the greatest players in football history, Nagurski in nine NFL seasons gained 4,031 yards rushing as the Bears' fullback. His 4.6 yards per carry average places him among the league's career rushing leaders. He was inducted into the National Football Foundation Hall of Fame in 1951, and twelve years later he became a charter member of the Professional Football Hall of Fame.

In 1960 Nagurski retired to International Falls, where he owned and managed a service station. Racked with arthritis and forced to use canes or a wheelchair, he spent the last years of his life as a recluse. He died in International Falls.

• Biographical files on Nagurski at the Pro Football Hall of Fame, Canton, Ohio, and at the sports information office of the University of Minnesota contain various newspaper clippings and sketches. Although no full-scale biography of

Nagurski has been published, information on him appears in Arthur Daley, *Pro Football's Hall of Fame* (1963); Norman Katkov, "Bronko the Great," *Sport*, Nov. 1954, pp. 51–59; *Biographical Dictionary of American Sports: Football* (1987); and *The Encyclopedia of Football*, 16th rev. ed. (1979). An obituary is in the *New York Times*, 9 Jan. 1990.

BRIAN S. BUTLER

NAIL, John E. (22 Aug. 1883–6 Mar. 1947), real estate entrepreneur, was born in New London, Connecticut, the son of John Bennett Nail, a businessman, and Elizabeth (maiden name unknown). Nail was raised in New York City and was graduated from a New York City public high school. His father was the role model on which he based his own business career. The elder Nail was an entrepreneur who prospered from the growth of Harlem and its inflated real estate market. He was one of several blacks who prior to the turn of the century recognized the potential of Harlem's housing market and profited from his prescience. Nail, known to friends and family as Jack, worked for a time in his father's business, where he first entered into the real estate profession in the 1900s. After a brief stint as a self-employed real estate agent in his own Bronx office, Nail accepted employment with Philip A. Payton, Jr., whose Afro-American Realty Company was one of the most successful black-owned real estate firms in New York at the time.

Payton, a real estate trailblazer like Nail's father, had also seized on the opportunity to invest in the Harlem real estate market. Between 1890 and 1914 southern blacks flooded into New York City in pursuit of social and economic betterment. Many gravitated to Harlem, where a sizable black settlement had taken shape as a result of earlier migration. By 1910 there were 91,709 blacks living in New York City, 60,534 of whom were southern born. This mass migration of blacks placed an unforeseen pressure on the city. Racial antagonism and violence intensified as did social and residential segregation. Areas formerly open to blacks became restricted, and blacks found themselves relegated to an increasingly crowded Harlem. Nail saw his opportunity in this evolving situation. Following Payton's example he educated himself on the intricacies of New York City's segregated housing market. In 1907, when Payton's company suffered financial setbacks (it went bankrupt in 1908), Nail and a colleague, Henry C. Parker, resigned their sales positions and founded the real estate firm of Nail & Parker, Inc. In 1910 Nail married Grace Fairfax; they had no children.

Nail was the moving force in Nail & Parker. He served as president, and Parker acted as secretary-treasurer. The firm had modest beginnings that, with the implementation of an aggressive advertising campaign, developed into a full-service company that offered mortgages to blacks, bought, sold, managed, and appraised properties, and collected rents. Nail recognized the need for black property ownership as a way to counter the discriminatory real estate practices of white lending institutions and white landlords. He urged blacks to invest in Harlem property to secure the future of the black community there. The firm engineered a significant coup when it successfully broke the deeply entrenched unwritten "covenant" that maintained that certain Harlem blocks were to remain white; blacks could neither own nor rent property in these areas. Furthermore, the covenant established restrictions in an attempt to prevent black real estate agents from controlling the Harlem housing market. It was a difficult battle to combat, but ultimately Nail & Parker were victorious in their efforts to dismantle the system.

In 1911 Nail & Parker, Inc., negotiated a million-dollar deal. Working as agents for St. Philip's Episcopal Church, of which Nail was a member, the real estate firm figured prominently in the transaction in which the church purchased several properties in Harlem for $1,070,000. The annual rents collected on these investments amounted to $25,000. The church, the real estate agents, and the black community all benefited from this transaction. Nail & Parker aggressively pursued other Harlem properties not only to increase the company's revenues but also to provide housing and stability for the community. The firm also sold a $200,000 property to Madame C. J. Walker, who had amassed a fortune developing hair-care products. In 1929 the firm was granted management responsibilities of the largest and finest apartment building in Harlem, which was owned by the Metropolitan Life Insurance Company. As their client list expanded and their transactions multiplied, Parker and Nail established respectable reputations both for themselves and for their business. Nail, particularly, earned respect from members of the white and black communities alike, and emerged as an authority on property condemnation. Even the city of New York sought his expertise.

Despite his status, black tenants claimed that Nail was an exploitive landlord who overcharged his tenants. The threat of a mass exodus from Harlem during the 1920s and early 1930s in response to exceedingly high rentals was quelled when the company reluctantly reduced some rents. In his own defense, Nail cited the high rentals elsewhere in the city. Nail's philosophy reflected that of Booker T. Washington, who emphasized the importance of establishing an economic foundation on which blacks could build a stronger and more stable community and compete more directly with the white power structure.

Although Nail & Parker temporarily weathered the depression, the firm collapsed in 1933, at which time Parker and Nail divided forty-five shares of the company apiece, and the remaining ten shares were apportioned to Isador D. Brokow, their silent white partner. Parker and Nail parted company, and that same year Nail established a new real estate venture, the John E. Nail Company, Inc., with Nail as president and David B. Peskin, a white real estate agent, as secretary and treasurer. The firm was active in several large real estate transactions, including as broker in a deal whereby the St. Philip's Church leased to Louis B. Lipman ten six-story apartment houses for an aggregate rental of $1 million.

Nail's reputation earned him a place as the first black member of the Real Estate Board of New York, and he became the only black member of the Housing Committee of New York and was a member of the Harlem Board of Commerce. News of his accomplishments extended beyond New York's boundaries; he acted as consultant for President Herbert Hoover's Committee on Housing during the depression.

Nail's interests were not confined to housing. He and a coterie of influential cohorts, including Robert Abbott, publisher of the *Chicago Defender*, and Harry Pace, a respected entrepreneur, engineered a campaign to discredit race leader Marcus Garvey. Garvey's rise to prominence threatened this elite core group who accused Garvey and his black nationalism philosophy of inciting hatred between the races. Nail and this self-styled Committee of Eight had nurtured a careful relationship with the white community, and they believed Garvey's rhetoric undermined their efforts to balance race relations. The battle between Garvey, who charged his attackers with being "Uncle Tom Negroes," and the members of the committee represented a broader split between an elite group of blacks and the masses of lower-income blacks who supported Garvey's celebration of African culture and his philosophy of self-help. Ironically, the two opposing factions shared a belief in the importance of economic development.

Nail's deep commitment to the black community is reflected in his role in the development of the Colored Merchant's Association, created to advance race solidarity and economic stability. Unfortunately, the first Harlem CMA cooperative, established in 1930, failed to attract black consumers, who complained of high prices during a time when survival was their chief concern. Nail was also concerned with the overall plight of urban blacks and held the position of vice president of the New York Urban League for a time. He was chair of the Finance Committee of the 135th Street Branch of the YMCA, which was located in the heart of Harlem, and was involved with the NAACP. Nail died in New York City.

• There are no personal papers of John E. Nail. However, included in the papers of his brother-in-law, James Weldon Johnson, held at Yale University's Beinecke Rare Book and Manuscript Library, is the John E. Nail Scrapbook. The most comprehensive biography of Nail is in John N. Ingham and Lynne B. Feldman, *African-American Business Leaders: A Biographical Dictionary* (1994), which also includes a detailed bibliography. A useful biography of Nail appears in the *Dictionary of Negro Biography* (1982). Gilbert Osofsky, *Harlem: The Making of a Ghetto* (1966), offers general information about Harlem real estate, specific data on Nail & Parker, and a brief biographical sketch of Nail. Additional valuable information pertaining to Harlem real estate can be found in the papers of the Works Progress Administration in the Schomburg Center for Research in Black Culture, New York City Public Library.

LYNNE B. FELDMAN

NAIRNE, Thomas (?–c. 18 Apr. 1715), South Carolina political leader and explorer of the colonial Southeast, was a native Scot who emigrated to South Carolina prior to 1695. At Charles Town Nairne married Elizabeth Edwards Quintyne (b. 1658), a Scot and widow of Richard Quintyne, a Barbadian settler of Carolina. Through land grants and his wife's inheritance Nairne established a plantation on St. Helena Island, south of Charles Town. In addition to his political and planting activities, Nairne was a magistrate, surveyor, admiralty judge, and provincial Indian agent. In 1702 he led neighboring Yamasee Indians on a slave-catching raid to Florida. He then sold captured Indians in Charles Town.

A member of South Carolina's Commons House of Assembly, Nairne opposed the policies of the governor, Sir Nathaniel Johnson. Johnson, a High Church Anglican, sponsored laws in 1704 to exclude Nonconformists from political office and to establish the Church of England in the province. In addition Johnson was deeply involved in the province's lucrative, unregulated Indian trade. Although nominally Anglican, Nairne opposed the establishment because it was a dangerous source of political and social discord (Johnson sought to exclude Dissenters from holding public office). With his firsthand knowledge of Indian affairs, Nairne also opposed Johnson's Indian policy, believing the policy unwise and dangerous to the security of South Carolina. Nairne sponsored legislation in 1707 to regulate the Indian trade and to curb traders' abuses of the Indians. The 1707 law appointed a provincial Indian agent, and Nairne was the first to hold that office. As part of his agent's duties and in the role of frontier diplomat during Queen Anne's War (1702–1713), Nairne and Thomas Welch, an Indian trader, traveled from Charles Town overland to the Mississippi River. On their journey they visited the Chickasaws, Tallapoosas, Choctaws, and other regional Indian tribes to strengthen diplomatic alliances with these tribes against the French colonies in the Southeast. While among these tribes Nairne wrote a series of dispatches that contained considerable ethnohistorical data on southern Muskhogean life. He also gathered geographical and strategic information from which he composed "A Map of South Carolina Shewing the Settlements of the English, French & Indian Nations from Charles Town to the Mississippi." Published in London in 1711 as part of Edward Crisp's "A Compleat Description of the Province of Carolina in 3 Parts," Nairne's map was an important source of information for eighteenth-century cartographers.

Nairne's opposition to Governor Johnson led to his arrest in June 1708 on a charge of treason against the Crown. Johnson procured two witnesses, characterized by Nairne as "lewd fellows . . . one being a Lunatick and the other a meer Villain," who deposed that he had disparaged Queen Anne's claim to the English Crown and avowed his support for James Edward Stuart, the exiled former Prince of Wales. Nairne was lodged in the Charles Town jail for the remainder of 1708. While in prison he was elected to the Commons

House of Assembly to represent Colleton County. He also composed a memorial, dated 10 July 1708, to Charles Spencer, earl of Sunderland, the British secretary of state. That memorial outlined a visionary strategy to wrest southern North America from the French and Spanish and to secure it for the nascent British American empire.

Nairne was released on bond in December 1708 or January 1709 to face a Commons House investigation of his conduct as Indian agent. He summarily jumped bail and fled to London where he presented his case directly to the Carolina proprietors and to the Crown. There he vindicated himself and was appointed admiralty judge of South Carolina. He also arranged to publish his map and, more significantly, *A Letter from South-Carolina; Giving an Account of the Soil, Air, Product, Trade, Government, Laws, Religion, People, Military Strength, &c. of that Province. Together with the Manner and Necessary Charges of Settling a Plantation there, and the Annual Profit it will produce. Written by a Swiss Gentleman, to his Friend at Bern* (1710). The pamphlet is a lengthy promotional tract, but it nonetheless presents an objective account of the history and political economy of the province.

Nairne returned to Charles Town in 1711 and, with Governor Johnson out of office, resumed his public career. He served briefly in the Commons House and then took up his former post as Indian agent. Again, Nairne sought to regulate Indian trade (licensing traders, setting bonds, establishing standard rates) and to reduce exploitation of Indians by white traders. He failed in that endeavor and was unable to avert the catastrophe of an Indian war.

Called the Yamasee War (1715–1717), the conflict was in fact a war between South Carolinians and a confederation of southeastern tribes that included the Ochese, Tallapoosa, Yamasee, and remnants of smaller tribes in the region. Nairne was one of the first casualties of the Yamasee War. Hearing rumors of a planned uprising he traveled from his St. Helena plantation to Pocotaligo, a nearby Yamasee town, to calm the situation. But he was too late. On Good Friday, 15 April 1715, the uprising began simultaneously throughout the Southeast. Nairne and two companions were captured. The two were killed outright, but Nairne suffered torture by fire. According to one report he survived three days as he was slowly burned to death. His plantation was destroyed by Indians, as were most white settlements on the frontier. Nairne was survived by his wife and their son, Thomas Nairne, Jr. (d. 1718).

In his *Letter from South-Carolina* and other writings, Nairne revealed himself to be a man of education with an active, curious intelligence. He was a close observer of Indian societies, comparing and contrasting them with European society objectively and with admiration for the former. As an imperial strategist Nairne foresaw the successful British conquest of North America.

• A manuscript of "Capt. Thomas Nairne's Journalls to the Chicasaws and Talapoosies" is in the British Library, Additional Manuscript 42559; and a holograph, partial manuscript of Nairne's *Letter from South-Carolina* (1710), titled "Description of Carolina," is in the John Carter Brown Library, Providence, R.I. Letters and documents of Thomas Nairne are found in the Great Britain Public Record Office, and in the records of the Society for the Propagation of the Gospel in Foreign Parts, London, England. Another manuscript collection, Documents Relating to the Treason Trial of Thomas Nairne, is in the Henry E. Huntington Library and Art Gallery, San Marino, Calif. His "Journalls to the Chicasaws and Talapoosies" is published as *Nairne's Muskhogean Journals: The 1708 Expedition to the Mississippi River*, ed. Alexander Moore (1988); Nairne's 10 July 1708 memorial is printed as an appendix. *A Letter from South-Carolina* (1710; repr. 1718, 1732) is reprinted in Jack P. Greene, ed., *Selling a New World: Two Colonial South Carolina Promotional Pamphlets* (1989). Thomas Nairne's "Map of South Carolina" and a discussion of its provenance is reproduced in William P. Cumming, *The Southeast in Early Maps* (1962). Verner W. Crane, *The Southern Frontier, 1670–1732* (1928), describes Nairne's political career and the context of his imperialism. The sketch of Nairne in *Biographical Directory of the South Carolina House of Representatives*, ed. Walter B. Edgar and N. Louise Bailey, vol. 2 (1977), pp. 491–92, elucidates his career as a Commons House member.

ALEXANDER MOORE

NAISMITH, James (6 Nov. 1861–28 Nov. 1939), inventor of basketball, was born in Almonte, Ontario, the son of John Naismith, a lumberman and carpenter, and Margaret Young. In 1870 both of Naismith's parents died in a typhoid epidemic, leaving him to be raised by a religiously strict grandmother and then by a bachelor uncle. His schooling was interrupted by five years' work in a logging camp, but in 1883 he entered McGill University, intending to study for the ministry. After receiving his A.B. in 1887, he studied theology for three years at a Presbyterian seminary affiliated with McGill; during his last year he directed undergraduate gymnastics classes. Having excelled athletically in school, he decided that rather than become a clergyman he could do good more effectively by combining sport and religion in the teaching and promotion of physical education. In 1890 he enrolled in a two-year course for Young Men's Christian Association (YMCA) physical directors at a new training college in Springfield, Massachusetts.

At Springfield, Naismith distinguished himself on the football field as well as in the classroom. Much lighter than his opponents, who included players on the era's football powers Yale and Harvard, he aggressively played center under the captaincy of Amos Alonzo Stagg, who became a highly renowned college football coach.

More important, at Springfield, Naismith invented basketball as the only major modern sport without ancient roots to originate in the United States. His mentor, Luther Gulick, keenly felt the need for some indoor competitive game that would be more attractive than gymnastic exercises, filling out the calendar between autumn football and spring baseball. In response to Gulick's assignment, Naismith devised thirteen simple rules prohibiting the roughness of football and diminishing the usual bunching of players around soccer and ice hockey nets. His innovation featured the tossing of a soccer ball into peach baskets suspended from balcony railings at each end of a gymnasium. In a class of eighteen, nine men played on each team for the first basketball game in December 1891.

This simple, fast-paced game quickly became popular. Within a decade its rules and style of play were streamlined, with Naismith himself serving on several of the rules committees that made changes. His original version merely called for passing the ball before taking a shot. Soon dribbling (bouncing the ball) was permitted, and the size of teams became standardized at five players (six for women) on the court. From Springfield, basketball immediately spread throughout North America and around the world by means of YMCA literature and Springfield-trained personnel. In addition to the YMCA, colleges and high schools promoted it.

Yet Naismith's invention brought him no immediate fame and never any fortune. From 1891 until 1895 he remained at Springfield, supervising the college's physical education programs. In 1894 he married a local girl, Maude Evelyn Sherman; they had five children. In 1895 they moved to Colorado, where he directed the physical exercise program at the Denver YMCA while studying at the Gross Medical School. Receiving a medical degree in 1898, he accepted an appointment as the first instructor of physical education at the University of Kansas. He coached the basketball and track teams there until 1905, but he largely lost touch with his own invention as it expanded and became more competitive in the early years of the century. Basketball, he insisted, should be played and enjoyed recreationally, not coached and taken too seriously.

Primarily interested in health and exercise science, at the University of Kansas Naismith gave more attention to intramural programs than to varsity sport. He attended most home basketball games, but he put his energy into creating a comprehensive student health service. For almost forty years he conducted physical exams and established medical records for all new male undergraduates. The effects of competitive athletics on physiological and cardiovascular development especially claimed his attention. He examined campus intramural squads and Kansas high school teams before and after basketball tournaments, and on the basis of X rays and urine tests he concluded that most players were in better, not worse, physical condition after periods of intense competition.

To the end of his days, Naismith remained a muscular Christian moralist, primarily concerned with sport's contribution toward a healthy body and soul. "With him, questions of physical development inevitably led to questions of moral development, and vice versa," recalled one of his students. Moral principles informed all of his essays in various physical education journals, a chapter on athletics in *The Modern High School* (1916), and a pamphlet, *The Basis of Clean Living* (1919). For several years he directed daily chapel

services at Kansas. In 1916 he was ordained as a Presbyterian minister, and in that same year he spent four months as chaplain and chief hygienic officer for the First Kansas Regiment (National Guard) stationed on the Mexican border. From 1917 until 1919 he served in a similar dual capacity for the YMCA. First at army bases in the United States and then for nineteen months in France, he attempted to raise the morale and protect the morals of American servicemen by means of exhortation, hygienic instruction, and competitive athletics. French and Italian army teams vigorously competed against Americans at the Inter-Allied Games of 1919.

Naturalized as a U.S. citizen in 1925, Naismith might have lived out his life as an obscure midwestern college professor had not one of his former students, Forrest "Phog" Allen, campaigned to make basketball an Olympic sport. Allen, an energetic, highly successful coach at Kansas, finally succeeded in getting basketball put on the program for the 1936 Berlin games; he insisted that Naismith should be the event's honorary guest. The National Association of Basketball Coaches agreed, urging colleges and universities to charge an extra penny to each of their 1935–1936 games to raise enough money to send Naismith to Berlin. According to one estimate, the fund amounted to $1,000 or so. Ironically, Berlin rain made the outdoor basketball games much like the passing, low-scoring style that Naismith created almost a half-century earlier. Canadian and American teams appropriately reached the finals, with the Americans winning individual gold medals by the modest score of 19–8.

Naismith returned home stooped and tired. In 1937 he retired from teaching. Within the year, his wife died. Two years later he married a widow friend, Florence Mae Kincaid. Naismith died in Lawrence.

By 1939 virtually every American high school and college sponsored a basketball team. Far more than Naismith ever anticipated, the college game thrived. In its rules and in the speed, agility, and skill required of participants, it vastly differed from the game first played in that small gym in Springfield, but the rudiments remained the same. Naismith would have appreciated the eulogy from the *Journal of Health and Physical Education*, which praised him as "an athlete who could practice medicine and preach a sermon," as "a physician who encouraged healthful living through participation in vigorous activities," and as a builder of "character in the hearts of young men." Whatever the later commercial developments of basketball, Naismith's invention of the game for purposes of moral and physical health fulfilled both his ministerial and medical callings. Enshrining him as a charter member in 1959, the Naismith Memorial Basketball Hall of Fame in Springfield is named in his honor.

• The bulk of Naismith's papers are in the private possession of his descendants, but several dozen pieces of correspondence and notes reside in the University of Kansas archives in Lawrence. Naismith's own posthumously published *Basketball: Its Origin and Development* (1941) is more of a personal memoir than the title suggests, especially for his early years. The only full biography, Bernice Larson Webb, *The Basketball Man: James Naismith* (1973), was reprinted with a helpful afterword by Steven Jansen (1994). John Dewar's "The Life and Professional Contributions of James Naismith" (D.Ed. diss., Florida State Univ., 1965) is immensely useful. See also R. Tait McKenzie, "Reminiscences of James Naismith," *Journal of Health and Physical Education*, Jan. 1933, pp. 21, 55; M. Whitcomb Hess, "The Man Who Invented Basketball," *American Scholar*, Jan. 1949, pp. 87–92; and Grace Naismith, "Father Basketball," *Sports Illustrated*, 31 Jan. 1955, pp. 64–65. An obituary is in the *New York Times*, 28 Nov. 1939.

WILLIAM J. BAKER

NAKIAN, Reuben (10 Aug. 1897–4 Dec. 1986), sculptor, was born in College Point, Long Island, New York, the son of Armenian immigrants George Nakian, a factory worker and weaver, and Mary Malakian. His family moved to New York City when he was nine and later to suburban New Jersey. Visiting the Metropolitan Museum of Art as a young boy, he was impressed by the antique plaster casts of Greek and Roman sculpture. At age thirteen, encouraged by his parents, he took drawing lessons at an academy in Jersey City, where he copied eighteenth- and nineteenth-century German engravings. Soon after, he began modeling heads and figures in clay. Nakian left school in 1912; he never attended high school. However, he studied for a brief period at the Art Students League in New York while working at the Philip Morris advertising agency. From 1913 to 1915 he did lettering and design work for *Century Magazine*, where he met many artists, including John Sloan, George Bellows, and Everett Shinn. In the evenings during 1915, he studied life drawing with Homer Boss and A. S. Baylinson at the Independent Art School directed by painter Robert Henri and clay modeling at the Beaux-Arts Institute of Design (now the National Institute for Architectural Education) in New York.

Nakian's mother died in 1911, and his father and only surviving brother died in 1916. In search of experience as an apprentice he contacted the sculptor and medalist James Earle Fraser, who recommended that he work with the sculptor Paul Manship. Nakian served a three-year apprenticeship to Manship, who was impressed by his red-chalk drawings, and to Manship's chief assistant, Gaston Lachaise. Nakian learned the fundamentals of sculpture, including carving, plaster casting, and bronze patination and made drawings and sculptures of animals. One of his first sculptures was a plaster bank representing a cow, made in 1917, of which replicas were made for the "Free Milk for France" campaign. In 1919 he was awarded a Louis Comfort Tiffany Foundation Farm Fellowship and spent a summer on Long Island making studies of farm animals.

In the early 1920s Nakian shared a New York studio with Lachaise and was influenced by his images of female nudes. He then acquired his own studio in New Jersey, and later Greenwich Village, through an award and stipend given by Gertrude Vanderbilt Whitney

for a period lasting about six years. In 1926 in the galleries of the Whitney Studio Club, he had his first solo exhibition of smoothly stylized animal sculptures. He became friends with sculptors William Zorach and Constantin Brancusi, whose 1926 American exhibition Nakian helped install. In 1930 he was included in the new-talent show at the Museum of Modern Art. Awarded a Guggenheim Fellowship in 1931, he traveled to Italy and France, where he visited Brancusi. While in Europe he was impressed by ancient Roman portraiture and images from classical mythology; the latter, especially, would fascinate him and provide subject matter for much of his career. He later said that throughout his stay in Europe he was "dying to get back. I wanted to make American art."

In 1932–1933 he modeled two series of realistic portrait busts: one of nine fellow New York artists, including painters Raphael Soyer and Peggy Bacon and sculptors Lachaise and Concetta Scaravaglione, and the other of President Franklin D. Roosevelt and members of his staff and cabinet. The portraits were shown at the Downtown Gallery in New York in 1933 and 1935, respectively, and the latter series was also seen in Washington, D.C., at the Corcoran Gallery of Art. Nakian gained further national recognition in 1934 for an eight-foot-high plaster sculpture of the baseball hero Babe Ruth that was never cast in bronze and is now lost.

In 1934 Nakian married Rose St. John; they had two sons. In 1936 they moved to Staten Island, where they raised vegetables, flowers, goats, and olive trees. Nakian also completed several Works Progress Administration art projects. During their ten years there, Nakian produced little sculpture but made many ink drawings. He became friends with Arshile Gorky, a painter also of Armenian descent, and other abstract artists such as Willem de Kooning and Stuart Davis, who introduced him to European modernism. After a period of soul-searching, he emerged with an interest in abstract expressionism. His portrait bust of Marcel Duchamp from 1943 illustrates his shift to abstract expressionism, with its dramatic surface modeled in a cubist style. The influences of Paul Cézanne and Brancusi are seen in the Duchamp bust, considered to be one of Nakian's masterpieces.

Most often Nakian chose to depict pairs of goddesses, nymphs, cupids, and animals from classical mythology, such as Leda and the swan, and Europa and the bull. He stated, "I live with the Greek gods in spirit." His Mediterranean ancestry and keen awareness of the art of the past prompted this kinship. Nakian believed that artists must measure themselves against the masters: "Art that's going to live has to be part of tradition. It has to be part of Titian, Rubens, Rembrandt and Cézanne. It has to be part of Greek sculpture and the caveman drawings. Art comes out of art."

In about 1945 Nakian moved his family to Stamford, Connecticut, although he kept a New York studio until 1948. In 1949 he had his first solo exhibition in fourteen years, at Egan Gallery in New York. From

1946 to 1951 he taught at the Newark School of Fine and Industrial Arts, where he had access to a large kiln and made terra-cotta reliefs with incised images, often of nude goddesses, that he called "stone drawings" and are reminiscent of work by Pablo Picasso.

From 1952 to 1954 Nakian was an instructor at Pratt Institute in Brooklyn, New York. Beginning in the mid-1950s, he made large-scale free-form sculptures using a technique he devised where layers of plaster were spread over cloth and then attached to an armature of steel pipes and wire mesh that could be cast in bronze. In 1958 he received a Ford Foundation Fellowship, and in 1961 he represented the United States with fifty-eight works at the São Paulo Bienal in Brazil.

In the 1960s Nakian executed commissions for monumental abstract metal sculptures: *Birds in Flight* for the façade of the Loeb Student Center at New York University, and *Voyage to Crete* for the foyer of the New York State Theater at Lincoln Center. They were cast in aluminum and bronze, respectively. In 1966 the Museum of Modern Art organized a major retrospective that included over 160 of his works. The Philadelphia College of Art (now the University of the Arts) awarded him the Gold Medal for Excellence in 1967. The next year, ten of his monumental works, including the *Judgment of Paris* series and *The Goddess with the Golden Thighs*, represented the United States in the thirty-fourth Venice Biennale. From 1972 to 1974 he taught at the New York Studio School.

His work is in many public institutions, including the Museum of Modern Art (*Seal* [1920], *"Pop" Hart* [1932], *Young Calf* [1927], study for *The Rape of Lucrece* [1958], *Hiroshima* [1965–1966]), the Whitney Museum of American Art (*The Lap Dog* [1927], *Seal* [1930], *Pastorale* [1950], *Olympia* [1961]), the Metropolitan Museum of Art (*Garden of the Gods I* [1979–1980]), and Saint Vartan Armenian Cathedral (*Descent from the Cross* [1970–1972]), all in New York; the Hirshhorn Museum and Sculpture Garden in Washington, D.C. (*Venus with Goat* [1952], *Rape of Lucrece* [1955–1958], *Olympia* [1960–1962], *The Goddess with the Golden Thighs* [1964–1965], *Europa and the Bull* [1949–1950]); the Milwaukee Art Museum (*Dikran Kelekian* [1942], *Voyage to Crete* [1949], *Judgment of Paris: Minerva* [1963–1966]); the Detroit Institute of Arts (*The Goddess with the Golden Thighs* [1964–1965]); and Walker Art Center in Minneapolis, Minnesota (*The Goddess with the Golden Thighs* [1964–1965]).

Nakian had a long and distinguished career in the passionate pursuit of his art. "To be a good artist takes years. You can't be in a hurry. You've got to pay the price," he advised. He worked continuously until his death, often exploring new media, such as printmaking and styrofoam carving, or returning to earlier media, such as red-chalk drawing. In 1985, the year before his death, retrospective exhibitions were organized by the DiLaurenti Gallery in New York and the Milwaukee Art Museum in Wisconsin, which traveled to the Stamford Museum and Nature Center in Stamford, Connecticut. Nakian died in Stamford.

• Nakian's papers and an oral biography are in the Archives of American Art, Smithsonian Institution, Washington, D.C. "Apprentice to the Gods: Reuben Nakian," a half-hour television documentary film that features an interview with the artist was produced by the National Museum of American Art's documentaries unit with the assistance of the Smithsonian Institution Office of Telecommunications and made available on videotape in 1985. An unpublished chronology with Nakian quotations, compiled by Marguerite Strop in 1988 and updated by the Nakian Estate, is very helpful. See also Avis Berman, "When Artists Grow Old," *Art News* 82 (Dec. 1983): 77–83, and Anne G. Terhune, "The Sculpture of Reuben Nakian from 1920 to 1965" (master's thesis, Institute of Fine Arts, New York Univ., 1967). Two of Nakian's many exhibition catalogs include: the Museum of Modern Art, *Nakian* (1966), with an essay by Frank O'Hara; and the Milwaukee Art Museum, *Reuben Nakian: Sculpture and Drawings* (1985), with an essay by Gerald Nordland. An obituary is in the *New York Times*, 5 Dec. 1986.

SUSAN JAMES-GADZINSKI

NAMPEYO (c.1859–20 July 1942), Native American potter, was born in Tewa Village (Hano), First Mesa, Hopi reservation, Arizona, the daughter of Qotsvema, a Hopi farmer from Walpi, and Qotcakao of the Corn Clan at Hano. She was named Tcumana (Snake Girl) by her paternal grandmother because her father was of the Snake Clan; however, her Tewa name, Numpayu ("Snake that does not bite"), was more commonly used because she lived at Hano.

Little is known of Nampeyo's early life, but she spent considerable time at Walpi with her Hopi grandmother, a potter who encouraged Nampeyo to take up the art. Nampeyo learned quickly and by early adulthood had earned a reputation as one of the finest First Mesa potters. Although Hano women at this time produced only undecorated utility wares, Walpi potters thickly slipped and painted their vessels. Termed "crackle ware" in the "decadent" Hopi style, the pottery incorporated a number of Zuni designs. Nampeyo showed exceptional skill in designing, shaping, and decorating the vessels.

In 1875 Thomas Keam established Keams Canyon Trading Post, twelve miles east of First Mesa. Before this time non-native goods were rare in the area; now such items were available in exchange for Hopi handicrafts, and Nampeyo found a ready market for her ceramics. Having this outlet, she made an effort to improve upon the already fine quality of her work. A member of the Hayden Survey party lodged with her brother in 1875 reported that Nampeyo was a gracious hostess of exceptional natural beauty. Her beauty reputedly ended her first marriage in 1879 to Kwivoya; he refused to live with his bride, fearing that another man would steal her away from him. Nampeyo's second marriage to Lesso from Walpi in 1881 appears to have been stable. They had at least five children.

Lesso took an active interest in Nampeyo's pottery and assisted in the work. By 1890 she was producing crackle-wear vessels of outstanding quality, which drew on Hopi designs as well as adaptations from Zuni and suggestions of some elements from the Rio Grande Tewa pueblos. Most important, a few vessels bore the yellow surface color and designs derived from prehistoric Sikyatki pottery. Although 1892 has been suggested as the beginning date for her collection of Sikyatki potsherds as models, her use of the designs appears to have occurred before this date. In 1895 J. W. Fewkes excavated the Pueblo IV ruin of Sikyatki and unearthed almost five hundred mortuary vessels, which he permitted Nampeyo and Lesso to copy. However, the common assertion in the literature that he was responsible for the Sikyatki Revival in 1895 is erroneous.

The complete revival of the Sikyatki style brought about a renaissance in Hopi ceramics. Nampeyo experimented with various clays until the yellow firing Sikyatki clay was located; she also experimented with paints and duplicated them as well as the surface characteristics and graceful shapes. Although the early vessels bore a very close resemblance to the original Sikyatki designs, perhaps with some copying, Nampeyo gradually developed complete freedom of design. In 1896 Walter Hough, who had accompanied Fewkes, secured several early revival pieces from Nampeyo for the U.S. National Museum.

The immediate success of the revival brought with it jealousy from other First Mesa potters and Nampeyo began to teach a number of interested women who were then able to raise their economic level. She continued to grow in her mastery of the style, and Lesso continued to search for potsherds (and Sikyatki vessels) at many ruins on the reservation. Nampeyo's sense of freedom—a flowing quality—and the use of open space are particularly noteworthy.

Although Nampeyo was unable to speak, read, or write English, she demonstrated her ceramic abilities to non-Indians and posed for many photographs. The Santa Fe Railroad and Fred Harvey Company used Nampeyo as the Hopi culture photo-symbol to attract travelers to the Southwest. On three occasions the Fred Harvey Company arranged for Nampeyo and members of her family to demonstrate ceramics, twice at Hopi House, Grand Canyon (1905, 1907), and once in Chicago at the U.S. Land and Irrigation Exposition (1910). During this period Nampeyo was described as "the greatest maker of Indian pottery alive" and Lesso as a "famous Indian dancer." By 1910 Nampeyo's reputation was well established in both the United States and Europe. She was visited by untold numbers of people while at home. Her prodigious ceramic production could not keep up with the demand for her work, which made it necessary for her to produce smaller vessels that took less time and involved other members of the family who painted the formed vessels.

World War I ushered in a period of little domestic travel, and by the time tourists and others returned when the war was over, Nampeyo was aging and had great difficulty with her sight. Reported to be totally blind at times, she never completely lost her sight. In the 1920s she continued to form vessels but could not decorate them. The painting was done by Lesso, who had mastered the style and reputedly could rival the decorative ability of his wife. Following his death in 1932, her daughter Fannie painted the designs for Nampeyo, and it is quite likely that her other daughters, Annie and Nellie, assisted because they, too, were adept in the style.

Nampeyo was cared for by her children during her final years. She taught her granddaughters to make pottery and continued to mold vessels almost to the day of her death. She died at her home in Idaho.

Even though Nampeyo gained an international reputation for creating a renaissance in Hopi pottery, she participated fully in such traditional activities as ceremonies, food exchanges, and work parties. Other Hopis viewed her as a typical resident of the mesa. By teaching her art to many other First Mesa women, she made an immeasurable contribution to her people, one that continues through the generations to this day.

• Robert Ashton, Jr., provides many color photos of vessels in "Nampeyo and Lesou," *American Indian Art* 1 (Summer 1976): 24–33. Ruth L. Bunzel's classic study, *The Pueblo Potter: A Study of Creative Imagination in Primitive Art* (1929), includes material derived from interviews with Nampeyo. See also M. R. Colton and H. S. Colton, "An Appreciation of the Art of Nampeyo and Her Influence on Hopi Pottery," *Plateau* 15 (1943): 43–45, and in the same issue an obituary by E. Nequatewa, a Hopi, "Nampeyo, Famous Hopi Potter (1859? to 1942)," pp. 40–42; F. H. Douglas, "The Age of Nampeyo the Potter," *Masterkey for Indian Lore and History* 16 (1943): 223; and T. R. Frisbie, "The Influence of J. Walter Fewkes on Nampeyo: Fact or Fancy?," in *The Changing Ways of Southwestern Indians*, ed. A. H. Schroeder (1973). Barbara Kramer corrects the spelling of Lesso's name (from Lesou) in "Nampeyo, Hopi House, and the Chicago Land Show," *American Indian Art* 14 (Winter 1988): 46-53. Muckenthaler Cultural Center, *Nampeyo, Hopi Potter: Her Artistry And Her Legacy* (1974), is an exhibit catalog that provides interviews with family members. Maxwell Museum of Anthropology, *Seven Families in Pueblo Pottery* (1974), is a catalog that features Nampeyo and her descendants. K. A. Sikorski, *Modern Hopi Pottery* (1968), includes a number of Nampeyo's descendants. Lois E. Jacka, *Beyond Tradition: Contemporary Indian Art and Its Evolution* (1988), shows the evolution of Indian art from Nampeyo's Sikyatki Revival to the 1990s.

THEODORE R. FRISBIE

NANCE, Ray Willis (10 Dec. 1913–28 Jan. 1976), jazz musician, was born in Chicago, Illinois. (His parents' names and occupations are unknown.) Nance displayed musical ability early. At age six he took piano lessons from his mother, and at nine he began five years of violin study with a private teacher. By his fourteenth birthday he was accepted at the Chicago College of Music. At first, his study of the violin was meant to please his mother, he said. "But after a time, I got to like it." He continued instruction with Max Fischel, the college's best teacher, for seven more years while he attended public school.

Nance's high school, Wendell Phillips, had an excellent music program. There, he learned to play trumpet, mainly on his own. He played in the school band, and he also learned to twirl the baton, becoming, he claimed, "the shortest drum major anyone ever saw." (His full adult height was 5′4″.) In addition, he played violin with the school's symphony, although he was not yet a match for an older student, Milt Hinton, who became a leading jazz bassist.

After graduating (around 1930), Nance attended Lane College in Jackson, Tennessee, intending to start his own band. Instead, he was expelled after a single semester for a firecracker prank. After returning to Chicago he formed a sextet, which soon became a staple at Dave's Cafe on the South Side, playing for dancing, performing novelty vocal numbers, and improvising enough for Nance to develop jazz skills.

Nance's chief influence was trumpeter Louis Armstrong, although some of his early recorded solos also show the influence of Harry James (without James's characteristic vibrato). Nance also listened to the best jazz violinists of the era: Joe Venuti, whose technique he "appreciated"; Stuff Smith, who aroused his greatest enthusiasm; and the classically trained Eddie South, whose playing was closest to his own later style.

After several years at Dave's Cafe, Nance's sextet moved to the Midnite Club in 1935 for an extended stay. In February 1937, by which time the group had disbanded, Nance was ready to join the Earl Hines orchestra at Chicago's Grand Terrace ballroom. With Hines he played trumpet, not violin. He remained with the band for almost two years, gaining "a world of experience" during engagements in California and New York City. He recorded his first novelty vocal while with Hines, the precursor of many more.

Information is sketchy, but Nance probably married at some point in the later 1930s (his wife's first name was Gloria). When the Hines band prepared for another road trip, Nance stayed behind and joined Horace Henderson's band at Swingland in January 1939. Nance and Emmett Berry were the band's trumpet soloists, and Nance resumed playing violin. He recorded one of his best string solos with Henderson, two 32-bar choruses of "Kitty on Toast," which composer-critic Gunther Schuller describes as displaying "a level of skill . . . beyond most 'jazz' violinists of the period."

When Henderson made travel plans in March 1940, Nance again chose to remain in Chicago. Working as a single at a musical variety club, he added tap and acrobatic dancing to his repertoire. In recognition of his diverse talents, a bandmate nicknamed him "Floorshow."

In November 1940, when veteran trumpeter Cootie Williams left the Duke Ellington band to join Benny Goodman, Ellington surprised many by hiring Nance to replace him. Nance proved equal to the challenge. He learned the "growl" technique, an Ellington trademark, initiated by Bubber Miley and closely identified with Williams. The style was more than "just a matter of blowing with the mute," Nance explained. "You've

got to concentrate to produce a certain sound. . . . It has great descriptive quality."

On pianist-composer Billy Strayhorn's "Take the A-Train," his first recorded Ellington feature in February 1941, Nance played what was quickly recognized as a classic trumpet solo. With mute, then open horn, he created subtly inflected phrases memorable in themselves, yet naturally coalescing. Ellington soon made full use of his violin as well. In June 1941 Nance recorded his initial string solo with the band, "Bakiff," and seven months later he recorded one of his most celebrated violin solos on "Moon Mist."

In 1944 Nance took a leave of absence from the band for nine months of work-a-night jobs. By early 1945 he was happy to come back to the Ellington fold. Ellington immediately featured Nance's violin on recordings of "Prelude to a Kiss," "Caravan," and "Black Beauty." Nance continued as a band regular for the next eighteen years.

Some of Nance's best work on Ellington recordings include his solos on various versions of some of the longer Ellington compositions and collaborations with Strayhorn, among them the symphonic suites *Black, Brown and Beige* (1943) and *Liberian Suite* (1947) and the songs "Perfume Suite" (1945) and "Suite Thursday" (1960). Also noteworthy are his contributions to such albums as *Historically Speaking—The Duke* (1956), *Blues in Orbit* (1959), *Anatomy of a Murder* (1959), *Afro-Bossa* (1963), and *Duke Ellington's Jazz Violin Session* (1964).

An incident in February 1961 stunned Ellington's public. During a Las Vegas engagement, Nance, tenor saxophonist Paul Gonsalves, and two other band members were arrested on marijuana possession charges. At trial, Gonsalves was acquitted, but Nance was discovered to have been convicted on drug charges in New York five years earlier; he received a sixty-day jail sentence.

Ellington accepted him back with the band on his release, and by all accounts Nance's conduct as a performer was untainted over the next two years. Then, during a government-sponsored tour of the Near East in September 1963, Nance and the recently returned Cootie Williams became involved in a mounting dispute. At a concert in Amman, Jordan, Nance refused to stand during national anthem ceremonies. A minor diplomatic scandal may have been headed off because senior band members persuaded Ellington that Nance's erratic behavior made him unfit to remain with the orchestra, and Ellington fired him.

Although Nance was heard on Ellington recordings from 1965 until 1971, he never officially rejoined the band. He led his own group in 1964, worked with a studio orchestra at the New York World's Fair in the mid-1960s, was with clarinetist Sol Yaged's group for six years until 1971, played with pianist Brooks Kerr in 1973, and took part in Chris Barber's tour of England in 1974. He made albums under his own name and with Gonsalves. He died in New York City.

Ellington in his characteristically formal way once said that, musically, "Raymond has perfect taste."

Whether or not that was actually the case, Nance was an important and affecting jazz soloist and an integral part of the Ellington orchestra for many years. He seldom reached the heights of the great jazz soloists, but he left an indelible personal mark on the music's history.

• Many books and articles on Ellington also discuss varied facets of Nance's contribution. Among the better sources are Stanley Dance, *The World of Duke Ellington* (1971); Duke Ellington, *Music Is My Mistress* (1973); L. MacMillan, "Don't You Dare Sing No Sad Songs for Ray Nance," *Coda*, July 1976, pp. 6–7; Mercer Ellington, with Dance, *Duke Ellington in Person: An Intimate Memoir* (1978); John Edward Hasse, *Beyond Category: The Life and Genius of Duke Ellington* (1993); and Mark Tucker, *The Duke Ellington Reader* (1993). An informal interview with Nance in Dance, *The World of Duke Ellington* (pp. 131–40) is anecdotal and especially helpful. An obituary is in the *New York Times*, 30 Jan. 1976.

ROBERT MIRANDON

NANTON, Joe "Tricky Sam" (1 Feb. 1904–20 July 1946), jazz trombonist, was born Joseph N. Irish in New York City, of West Indian parentage. Details of his upbringing are unknown. Nanton first worked professionally in the early 1920s with pianist Cliff Jackson. He held obscure jobs in Harlem, playing at Leroy's Club with pianist Fat Smitty and drummer Crip and then for about two years at another club with pianist Earl Frazier, banjoist Seminole, and Crip. In 1925 he rejoined Jackson's group, then called the Westerners, at the Nest Club.

In 1926 Nanton joined Duke Ellington's big band at the Kentucky Club. To this point he had been known as Joe Nanton. Fellow Ellington alto saxophonist Otto Hardwick explained, "I nicknamed Tricky Sam, too. He could always do with one hand what someone else did with two. Anything to save himself trouble" (Dance, p. 61). Nanton immediately became one of Ellington's featured soloists. He remained with the band throughout its years in residency at the Cotton Club (1927–1931) and subsequent incessant touring, except for a period in October 1937 when he had pneumonia. Late in 1945 he suffered a stroke. He was well enough to resume touring with Ellington around May 1946 but died soon afterward while in San Francisco with the band. He was survived by his wife Marion; her maiden name and details of the marriage are unknown.

Nothing more is known of Nanton's life, but his colleague in Ellington's band, cornetist Rex Stewart, gave a sense of his personality:

Before he got the nickname Tricky Sam, Joe was sometimes called the Professor, because he knew something about almost everything. . . . He was well acquainted with such erudite and diverse subjects as astronomy, how to make home brew, and how to use a slide rule. He could recite poetry by ancient poets that most of us never knew existed, and he knew Shakespeare. . . . [He was] a fierce nationalist and devoted follower of Marcus Garvey back in the thirties (when political awareness was unheard of in a musician).

Nanton was one of the most distinctive soloists in jazz. Emulating Ellington's trumpeter Bubber Miley, he adapted Miley's "growl and plunger" technique to the trombone, combining vocalizing with a muted sound to achieve an almost human and conversational instrumental sound. A famous and characteristic solo may be heard on "Ko-Ko" (1940): focusing on a little two-note motif, Nanton effectively "speaks" the syllables "ya-ya" through his trombone over and over again, each time altering fine details of the motif's rhythm and pitch—instrumental jazz is often alleged to "tell a story," and here it almost does. Hundreds of excellent recorded examples survive, including several versions each of "East St. Louis Toodle-Oo" (1926–1927) and "Black and Tan Fantasy" (1927); "The Blues I Love to Sing" (1927); several versions of "Jubilee Stomp" (1928); "Yellow Dog Blues" (1928); "Harlem Flat Blues" (1929); "Hot Feet" (1929); "Stevedore Stomp" (1929), on which Ellington uncharacteristically featured Nanton playing open rather than muted trombone; several versions each of "Old Man Blues" and "Ring Dem Bells" (both 1930); "Mood Indigo" (1930); "It Don't Mean a Thing If It Ain't Got That Swing" (1932); "Slap Happy" (1938); "Blue Serge" (1941); "Just a-Settin' and a'Rockin'" (1941); and "Main Stem" (1942). Additionally, Nanton appears in the Amos and Andy movie *Check and Double Check* (1930) and Ellington's film shorts *Black and Tan* (1929), *Symphony in Black* (1934), and *Duke Ellington and His Orchestra* (1943).

• An interview by Inez M. Cavanaugh, "Reminiscing in Tempo: Tricky Sam Goes over the Great Times He Had with Duke, Bubber, Freddie Jenkins," *Metronome* 61 (Feb. 1945): 17, 26, is reprinted in *The Duke Ellington Reader*, ed. Mark Tucker (1993). Surveys and tributes are by Barry McRae, "Joe 'Tricky Sam' Nanton," *Jazz Journal* 13 (June 1960): 14–16; Rex Stewart, *Jazz Masters of the Thirties* (1972; repr. 1982); Duke Ellington, *Music Is My Mistress* (1973); Dick M. Bakker, *Duke Ellington on Microgroove*, vol. 1: *1923–1936* (1977), identifies Nanton's early recorded solos. For musical analysis, see Gunther Schuller, *Early Jazz: Its Roots and Musical Development* (1968); Kurt Robert Dietrich, "Joe 'Tricky Sam' Nanton, Juan Tizol and Lawrence Brown: Duke Ellington's Great Trombonists, 1926–1951" (Ph.D. diss., Univ. of Wisc., 1989); Schuller, *The Swing Era: The Development of Jazz, 1930–1945* (1989); Tucker, *Ellington: The Early Years* (1991); Dietrich, *Duke's 'Bones: Ellington's Great Trombonists* (1995); and Barry Kernfeld, *What to Listen for in Jazz* (1995). See also Stanley Dance, *The World of Duke Ellington* (1970; repr. 1981); Albert McCarthy, *Big Band Jazz* (1974); and John Chilton, *Who's Who of Jazz: Storyville to Swing Street*, 4th ed. (1985). An obituary is in *Down Beat*, 12 Aug. 1946, p. 9.

BARRY KERNFELD

NAPIER, James Carroll (9 June 1845–21 Apr. 1940), politician, attorney, and businessman, was born on the western outskirts of Nashville, Tennessee. His parents, William C. Napier and Jane E., were slaves at the time of his birth but were freed in 1848. After manumission and a brief residency in Ohio, William Napier moved his family to Nashville, where he established a livery stable business. James attended the black elementary and secondary schools of Nashville before entering Wilberforce University (1864–1866) and Oberlin College (1866–1868), both in Ohio.

James Napier began his career as a race leader and politician during the Reconstruction era in Tennessee as Davidson County commissioner of refugees and abandoned lands in the Freedmen's Bureau. In 1870 he led a delegation of black Tennesseans to petition President Ulysses S. Grant and Congress for relief from politically motivated violence aimed at nullifying black voting strength, for removal of the state's conservative government, and for rejection of the state's 1870 constitution. Unsuccessful in this effort, Napier and his delegation urged the president and Congress to establish a national school system and to enforce the Fifteenth Amendment in their home state. Napier subsequently received a position as a Treasury Department clerk in Washington, D.C., possibly the first African American to hold such a post. Under the tutelage of John Mercer Langston, the prominent black politician and acting president of Howard University, Napier entered the institution's law school in the District of Columbia. After obtaining a law degree in 1872, he returned to Nashville to begin a practice and in 1878 married Langston's only surviving daughter, Nettie Langston. Theirs was a childless union that lasted sixty years.

Under Presidents Rutherford B. Hayes, James A. Garfield, and Chester A. Arthur, Napier held patronage appointments in the Nashville offices of the Internal Revenue Service, serving as a gauger (1879–1881), clerk (1883–1884), and deputy collector (1885). Owing to his business, legal, and political acumen, Napier emerged as the ranking African-American politician in Tennessee in the two decades after the Civil War. He served on the Nashville City Council from 1878 to 1889 and the state Republican party executive committee, was a delegate to six Republican national conventions, and made an unsuccessful bid for election to the Fifth District congressional seat in 1898. As a city councilman Napier led successful efforts for the hiring of the first African-American schoolteachers in Nashville, the establishment of the city's first modern schools (including high school training) for black Americans, and the employment of the city's first black firefighters. In the 1890s, however, the rise to power of the "lily whites," dedicated to the removal of blacks from political participation in the South, and the emergence of more outspoken, younger African-American leaders such as Robert R. Church, Jr., of Memphis curtailed Napier's influence in state and local politics.

Napier still remained a force to be reckoned with, however, due to his dignified manner, political connections, and behind-the-scenes approach to getting things done. His friendship and alliance with the educator Booker T. Washington in 1891 kept him in the inner circles of federal politics. He became a member of the so-called "black cabinet" that advised Republican presidents. Offered positions as consul to Bahia, Brazil, and as consul-general for Liberia in 1906 and 1910, respectively, Napier refused both appointments. A recommendation from Washington led to Napier's appointment in 1911 as register of the U.S. Treasury, the most prestigious and highest federal position then available to an African American. Napier acquitted himself well in this position. Presiding over a staff of seventy-three, in addition to his official duties accounting for the receipt and expenditure of all public money, Napier found time to press for the continued development of the African-American community. He testified before Congress in 1912 for passage of the Page Bill for equitable distribution of funds (set aside in the Morrill Acts of 1863 and 1890) for African-American land-grant southern colleges. Napier's efforts were to no avail. He resigned from his post two years later to protest President Woodrow Wilson's sanctioning of segregation in federal office facilities. After 1913 Napier retreated from involvement in national politics to focus more exclusively on economic self-help in the black community.

Napier used his influence as lawyer, lecturer, businessman, head of the Nashville Board of Trade, and organizer of a branch of the National Negro Business League (NNBL) to promote economic and educational development among African Americans. Aware of the collapse of the Freedmen's Bank and the resulting economic dislocation in the African-American community during Reconstruction, Napier entered the banking business to provide saving, credit, and investment opportunities to blacks and to demonstrate the advantages, both personal and collective, of entrepreneurial endeavors. He utilized his own estate as collateral for funds to underwrite the first year's operation of the Nashville One-Cent Savings Bank in 1903. He went without salary as the cashier of the bank to ensure its success and development. He and Richard Henry Boyd, the founding president of the enterprise (later renamed the Citizens Savings Bank) steered it toward ultraconservative fiscal policies in lending and investment to guarantee the bank's financial success so that it might serve as a model for other black businessmen and bankers. The bank was founded to inspire "systematic saving among our people," according to Napier. From its opening on 6 January 1904 (with deposits of $6,392 from 145 individuals), deposits of the Citizens Savings Bank reached a high of $209,942 within thirty-five years.

Napier supported larger cooperative black capitalist endeavors by joining Booker T. Washington's NNBL, which first convened in Boston in 1900. This organization was designed to bring black businessmen from around the nation to annual meetings to discuss entrepreneurship as a means to individual and collective uplift in the black community. The 1903 annual NNBL meeting was held in Nashville, under the aegis of Napier, one of the vice presidents of the organization. Napier inherited and held the NNBL presidential mantle after Washington's death in 1915, serving until 1919. He attended the upstate New York Amenia Conference of 1916 and was one of the ranking Bookerites to effect a successful but short-lived modus vivendi between the Washington and W. E. B. Du Bois–NAACP factions vying for controlling leadership of the black community.

Napier continued to promote the idea of industrial development and training as an economic strategy to provide jobs and entrepreneurial opportunities for blacks as one of the founders of Nashville's Tennessee Agricultural and Industrial State Normal School for Negroes (now Tennessee State University). Serving as a trustee of Meharry Medical College, Fisk College, and Howard University, Napier also took a keen interest in higher education and publicly extolled the virtues of both higher and industrial education in preparing African Americans for "all the duties and responsibilities of life." As trustee of the Anna T. Jeanes Fund, which supported educational opportunities for black southerners, Napier was instrumental in obtaining more than $75,965 between 1909 and 1926 for Tennessee and establishing the organization's presence in twenty-eight counties in the state. Napier lectured frequently on medical jurisprudence at Meharry. In the 1920s he served as a member of the southern regional Commission on Interracial Cooperation established to prevent violence and conflict between blacks and whites. Two years before his death in Nashville, Napier was appointed to the city's housing authority at age ninety-three. He was reported shortly after 1900 to have amassed personal wealth of more than $100,000; the value of his real estate was assessed at $43,016 at the time of his death.

Napier eschewed confrontational politics in favor of cooperative efforts to further African-American organizational and institutional development within a segregated society. He was clearly in the cadre of elite African-American leaders in the first half of the twentieth century.

• Atlanta University's Woodruff Library, Special Collections, has a vertical file of clippings on Napier. A collection of Napier papers is at Fisk University. A significant essay on him is Herbert L. Clark, "James Carroll Napier: National Negro Leader," *Tennessee Historical Quarterly* 49 (1990): 243–52. For other profiles, see Louis Harlan, *The Booker T. Washington Papers*, vol. 4 (1975), pp. 453–54; Lester Crawford Lamon, *Blacks in Tennessee, 1791–1970* (1981) and *Black Tennesseans, 1900–1930* (1977); and Cordell Hull Williams, "The Life of James Carroll Napier from 1845 to 1940" (M.A. thesis, Tennessee State Univ., 1954). Obituaries are in the *Journal of Negro History* (July 1940): 400–401, and the *Nashville Banner*, 23 Apr. 1940.

MACEO CRENSHAW DAILEY, JR.

NAPOLEON, Phil (2 Sept. 1901–30 Sept. 1990), jazz trumpeter and bandleader, was born Filippo Napoli in Boston, Massachusetts. Details of his parents are unknown, but Napoleon clearly came from a musical family; four brothers and two nephews became professional musicians. He secretly borrowed his brother's cornet at age four and taught himself to play. In about a year his parents were presenting him in vaudeville and classical concerts as a curly-haired boy prodigy.

Napoleon ran away from home at age eleven. He played in circuses and tent shows, traveling to New Orleans and then to the West Coast, where, by one unconfirmed account, he married at age fifteen. He returned east, to New York City. In the summer of 1917 he cofounded the Original Memphis Five for an engagement at the Harvard Inn, a dance hall on Coney Island. Modeled after the popular Original Dixieland Jazz Band, the Original Memphis Five included Napoleon, pianist Frank Signorelli, trombonist Miff Mole, clarinetist Jimmy Lytell, and drummer Jack Roth. In later life both Napoleon and Signorelli claimed sole credit for founding the band.

After a season at the Ritz in Brooklyn, the Original Memphis Five toured in vaudeville from 1918 to 1919. The band broke up because of personal disputes, with Napoleon and Mole joining Sam Lanin's dance orchestra at the Roseland Ballroom on Broadway in 1920. By 1921 a reconstituted Original Memphis Five held a residency at Healy's Balconades, a restaurant in New York.

Napoleon's most important work was in the studio, where he contributed to hundreds of jazz and jazz-flavored recordings during the 1920s. Using musicians and an instrumentation drawn from the Original Memphis Five, he recorded from July 1921 to mid-decade as a member of Lanin's Southern Serenaders, similarly from August onward with Ladd's Black Aces, and from December onward in another band under Lanin's direction, Bailey's Lucky Seven. Ladd's Black Aces was the first of his several pseudonymous groups of white musicians whose recordings were blatantly meant to be sold as "race records," a marketing category that had just emerged. The first Black Aces session that August produced versions of "Aunt Hagar's Children Blues" and "Shake It and Break It" performed by Napoleon, trombonist Moe Grappell, clarinetist Doc Behrendson, pianist (and comic) Jimmy Durante, and Roth, with Lanin singing on the latter title.

In April 1922 the original group—Napoleon, Mole, Lytell, Signorelli, and Roth—masqueraded as the Original Dixieland Jazz Band on recordings of "Gypsy Blues" and "My Honey's Lovin' Arms." From that same month through September they made a few sessions as Jazzbo's Carolina Serenaders, with Lanin, Sidney Arodin, or Lytell on clarinet and an alto saxophone added for the titles made in April. Then, beginning with "Lonesome Mama Blues" in May, the Original Memphis Five recorded extensively under its own name, with Mole and Charlie Panelli alternating as trombonist. Further pseudonymous activities in 1922 included versions of "I Wish I Could Shimmy Like My Sister Kate" and "Got to Cool My Doggies Now," recorded in September as a seven-piece faux African-American band, the Cotton Pickers, as well as sessions by McMurray's California Thumpers and the Southland Six.

Napoleon had considerable technical control of the trumpet, which later in life made him well suited to the diverse and immediate demands facing a staff musician in recording and radio studios. He recalled meeting young cornetist Bix Beiderbecke in November 1922: "Bix—well, he liked what I did. I'd take him aside and show him what I was doing. He used to come around and ask me if he could come along to the studios with us. What the hell, there was nothing wrong with that. And we showed him how we did things" (quoted in Sudhalter and Evans, pp. 83–84).

For a few recordings with blues singers early in 1923, the Original Memphis Five were billed as the Nubian Five with Lena Wilson; they were credited under their own name for Alberta Hunter's discs, including "'Tain't Nobody's Business." Later that year they recorded in an enlarged group, the Tennessee Ten. Napoleon may be heard to advantage on many of their subsequent recordings under the name of the Original Memphis Five, including "Farewell Blues," "Memphis Glide," "Who's Sorry Now?" (all from 1923), "Static Strut," and "Off to Buffalo" (both in 1926).

Napoleon married Victoria (maiden name unknown) around 1926. Little is known of their family life. Late that year he organized a big band that made a few insignificant recordings into 1927 and found no success outside the Rosemont Ballroom in Brooklyn. He became a staff trumpeter at NBC. In June 1928 a new Original Memphis Five, including trombonist Tommy Dorsey, reed player Jimmy Dorsey, and Signorelli, recorded "I'm More Than Satisfied." In May 1929 he led two sessions by Napoleon's Emperors, whose membership included violinist Joe Venuti, the Dorseys, Signorelli, and guitarist Eddie Lang; his nephew Teddy Napoleon served as drummer on the second session. During the late 1920s and early 1930s Napoleon also recorded as a sideman with numerous groups, including the Charleston Chasers, Miff Mole's Molers ("After You've Gone" [1929]), the New Orleans Black Birds, and the Dorsey Brothers Orchestra. He recorded yet again with the Dorseys and Signorelli on the final session by the Original Memphis Five, including "Jazz Me Blues," in November 1931.

Napoleon left NBC in 1936. In 1937 he once again tried his hand at leading a big band. He then resumed work as a studio musician, apart from a period with Jimmy Dorsey's big band in 1943. Reunited with Signorelli, and with Tony Spargo (Sbarbaro) of the Original Dixieland Jazz Band as drummer, he recorded four Dixieland sessions for the Mercury label in 1946. Later that decade he worked in the musical instrument business, his duties unknown.

In May 1949 Napoleon established a new Memphis Five at Nick's club in New York. Signorelli played in the group briefly. Napoleon recorded a dozen titles in 1950, including "When the Saints Go Marching In" from a session in March; his nephew Marty Napoleon served as his pianist in June. In 1954, still at Nick's, the six-piece Memphis Five consisted of Napoleon, clarinetist Gail Curtis, trombonist Harry Di Vito, pianist Johnny Varro, bassist Pete Rogers, and drummer Lew Koppelman.

In June 1956 Napoleon brought his group to Miami, Florida, where he settled. Thereafter he occasionally appeared on television shows. He also performed at the Newport (R.I.) Jazz Festival in July 1959, and in October he recorded the album *Phil Napoleon and His Memphis Five* with Di Vito, Varro, and Rogers still in the group. In 1966 he opened his own club, Phil Napoleon's Retreat, near Miami, and led the band there. He died in Miami. He had been inactive for some years, and hence his death seems not to have received any immediate publicity.

Passionately devoted to Dixieland jazz, Napoleon had mixed feelings about big band jazz, and he expressed a deep distaste for bebop during the early 1950s, when he reinitiated his career as a keeper of the early jazz flame. He was a politely lyrical soloist, accomplished in the technique of interweaving collective improvisation that characterizes the Dixieland jazz style and fluent in the characteristic "hot licks" and muted sounds of early jazz trumpeting. Although not among the most imaginative, innovative, or inspired of these trumpeters, and not a familiar name to many listeners, Napoleon nevertheless played a considerable role in shaping America's conception of jazz via his hundreds of recordings as the lead melody instrumentalist with the Original Memphis Five and related groups.

• Useful sources include George T. Simon, "The Napoleonic Revolution," in *Simon Says: The Sights and Sounds of the Swing Era, 1935–1955* (1971), pp. 415–17; "Dixieland Revisited," *Time*, 30 June 1952, pp. 69–70; Rex Rengaw, "Mister Dixieland," *PIC*, June 1954, pp. 39–41; Simon, *The Big Bands*, 4th ed. (1981), pp. 471–72; Samuel B. Charters and Leonard Kunstadt, *Jazz: A History of the New York Scene* (1962; repr. 1981), p. 125; Gunther Schuller, *Early Jazz: Its Roots and Musical Development* (1968), pp. 185–86; Richard M. Sudhalter and Philip R. Evans, with William Dean-Myatt, *Bix: Man and Legend* (1974), pp. 82–84; and James Lincoln Collier, "The First Hot Bands," in *The Blackwell Guide to Recorded Jazz*, ed. Barry Kernfeld (rev. and expanded 2d ed., 1995), pp. 11–14. An obituary is in *Jazz Journal International*, Oct. 1991, p. 18.

BARRY KERNFELD

NARVÁEZ, Pánfilo de (1478?–1528), Spanish conquistador and accidental explorer of Florida, was born in Valladolid, Spain, the son of noble parents. Nothing is known of his youth. He sailed to the Caribbean in about 1500 and served in the conquests of Jamaica and Cuba. As a reward for his service in Cuba, he received grants of land and *encomiendas*, to which he added by marrying a widow, María de Valenzuela. They are not known to have had any children. Governor Diego Velázquez appointed him accountant (*contador*) and during the years 1515–1518 used him as a special agent (*procurador*) in Spain.

In 1520 Narváez's career took a new turn. Outraged by Hernán Cortés's seizure of control of the expedition that Velázquez had prepared for the conquest of Mexico, Velázquez appointed Narváez captain-general of the Mexican Conquest and commander of a new expedition Velázquez was sending to seize Cortés and Mexico. Narváez sailed from Cuba with 900 Spaniards, an undisclosed number of Indians, and as many as nineteen ships. After landing at Veracruz, he was surprised and defeated by Cortés on 23 May. Narváez lost an eye in the fighting and was held prisoner until 1523. After traveling in Mexico and returning to Santiago de Cuba (1525), Narváez sailed to Spain to seek a reward for his services to the Crown.

On 11 December 1526 Charles V granted Narváez the right to conquer Francisco de Garay's grant, Amichel, and Juan Ponce de Leon's grant, Florida; that is, the entire coast of the Gulf of Mexico from the Soto la Marina River (called the Río de las Palmas in the contract) to Cape Sabel and northward on the Atlantic coast of Florida to Ponce de Leon Inlet. Narváez also obtained the titles of *alcalde mayor* (district judge), governor, captain-general, and *adelantado* for himself and his heirs along with various economic privileges.

Narváez and his expedition of some 600 soldiers, colonists, secular priests, African slaves, a few women, and Franciscan friars sailed from San Lucar on 17 June 1527 in five ships. Alvar Núñez Cabeza de Vaca was treasurer. Arriving at Santo Domingo, the fleet stayed forty-five days, during which Narváez acquired horses and 140 men deserted. Sailing to Trinidad, Cuba, for supplies, the fleet was struck by a tropical storm that sank the two ships that had entered Trinidad's harbor, drowning sixty men and twenty horses. To prevent further losses and prepare supplies, the expedition wintered at Xagua (now Jagua), Cuba.

On 20 February 1528 Narváez sailed for Havana with five ships, 400 men, and eighty horses. He planned to resupply there before crossing the Gulf of Mexico, evidently for Amichel, since he had hired Diego de Miruelo, a pilot who claimed to have been to the Río de las Palmas. Dogged by bad luck, as the fleet rounded Cape San Antonio it was struck by strong winds that drove it northward into the gulf. Because the fleet's supply casks were nearly empty, Narváez ordered a landing on the coast of Florida. The lookouts sighted land on 12 April 1528; two days later, while on a southward course, they saw a pass. The fleet dropped anchor and a party went ashore (14 Apr. 1528). Although claims have been entered for ports from Charlotte Harbor on the south to Pensacola Bay on the northwest, the most likely landing spot is the mainland inside of Johns Pass, today part of St. Petersburg, Florida.

Exploring parties sent overland to the north and northeast both discovered a great bay (Tampa Bay) and remarked that there seemed to be few Indian villages. The pilots, according to Cabeza de Vaca, claimed they were south of the great bay (Tampa Bay) discovered by Alonso Alvarez de Pineda in 1519. Narváez decided to send the ships north to seek the bay while he marched the army overland in the same direction. The route chosen was close to the coast, across miles of sandhills and pine flatwoods where the only food was hearts of palmettos.

Fifteen days after the march began on 2 May, the 300 men in the shore party crossed the Withlacoochee River, defeated 200 Indians from a nearby village, and occupied it. Scouting parties sent downstream to the sea did not find the bay they were seeking. Departing the Withlacoochee River on about 23 May, the Spaniards moved north and inland, apparently bypassing the Ocale settlements. On 17 June a chief and his retinue met them and conducted them to a river that likely was the Suwanee. By this point in the journey, the Spaniards were aiming to reach Apalachee and had picked up Indian trails that may have been used by Hernando de Soto eleven years later.

Once across the Suwanee, the Spaniards camped at the village of their host, Dulchanchellin, but awoke the next day to find themselves alone. Pushing on to the north and northwest, the army captured guides, who led them into difficult terrain and occasional skirmishes with Indians. Finally, on 25 June their guides informed them that they were at "Apalachee." Cabeza de Vaca's description of the place suggests that it was not one of the principal towns of that people. By clever guiding, the town's residents kept the Spaniards from discovering any other towns during the twenty-five days they camped there. Their unwilling hosts did tell them that the chiefdom of Aute, to the southwest, had abundant foods.

Narváez and his army departed "Apalachee" on 20 July. Eight or nine days later, after marching through initially difficult terrain of thick forests and swamps and crossing the St. Marks River, the Spaniards came out onto the coastal plain at Aute, probably just east of the Ochlockonee River. Here they camped and built five barges, killing the horses for food and for their hides (used for water bottles) and manes (used for cordage).

The barges were put to sea on 22 September with 240 men. Rowing with sweeps and using small sails, they spent a month moving steadily westward along the Gulf Coast and passed the freshwater outpouring of the mouths of the Mississippi River. Once west of the Mississippi, the barges began to separate. A week later, four of them were cast ashore in a storm, while the fifth, with Narváez in it, was swept to sea and disappeared, evidently swamped by waves. This was south of modern Galveston, Texas, although the exact location is disputed.

Narváez was tall with blond hair with some intermixed red hair. He was described by contemporaries as cultivated in speech and habits but not very prudent or cautious and a man who did better under orders than giving them. The events of his life fully support those judgments.

• Narváez's early career is described in documents printed in *Colección de Documentos inéditos . . . de las antiguas posesiones Españolas . . .* , 1st ser. (42 vols., 1864–1884), vols. 1, 3, 11, 12, 14, 16, 22, 26, 35; 2d ser. (21 vols., 1885–1928), vols. 1, 18, 20; and in Antonio de Herrera y Tordesillas, *Historia general de los hechos de los Castellanos en las islas y tierra firme del Mar Oceano* (1726; repr. 10 vols., 1945), vol. 3, pp. 201–3, 226–33, 256–59, 310–33. His trip to Florida is described in

Alvar Núñez Cabeza de Vaca, *La Relación o Naufragios de Alvar Núñez Cabeza de Vaca* (1555; repr. 1986); and Fanny Bandelier, trans., *The Journey of Cabeza de Vaca* (1904; repr. 1922). Other accounts are Cyclone Covey, *Cabeza de Vaca's Adventures in the Unknown Interior of America* (1961), and Gonzalo Fernández de Oviedo, *Historia General de las Indias* (4 vols., 1851–1855), vol. 3, pp. 579–618, published in English as *The Journey of the Vaca Party*, trans. Basil C. Hedrick and Carroll L. Riley (1974). Secondary studies are Morris Bishop, *The Odyssey of Cabeza de Vaca* (1933); Cleve Hallenbeck, *Alvar Núñez Cabeza de Vaca: The Journey and Route of the First European to Cross the Continent of North America, 1534–1536* (1940; repr. 1971); and Robert Weddle, *Spanish Sea: The Gulf of Mexico in North American Discovery, 1500–1685* (1985).

PAUL E. HOFFMAN

NASBY, Petroleum Vesuvius. *See* Locke, David Ross.

NASH, Abner (c. 1740–2 Dec. 1786), revolutionary state governor, was born in that part of Amelia County, Virginia, that became Prince Edward County, the son of John Nash and Ann Owen, who were originally from Wales and had established a large plantation on the Appomattox River. Abner Nash became an attorney in Prince Edward County in 1757 and was elected to the Virginia House of Burgesses in 1761 and 1762. He and his brother Francis Nash, later a general in the North Carolina Continental Line, migrated to North Carolina in late 1762 or early 1763, settling first in Hillsborough, where they acquired property and erected a mill. A year later Abner Nash moved to Halifax and began practicing law. He was elected to the lower house of the North Carolina General Assembly in 1764, 1765, and 1770–1771 from Halifax. During the back-country Regulator uprising, Nash served as the brigade major in the 1768 militia muster at Hillsborough that temporarily suppressed the Regulators.

In Halifax Nash married Justina Davis Dobbs, the widow of royal governor Arthur Dobbs, who died in 1765. They had three children. He represented his wife in a suit to recover her late husband's bequest, which had been withheld by her Irish stepson. Nash's effort to attach the Dobbs family's North Carolina property to ensure payment—a form of legal attachment prohibited by the Crown—contributed to the controversy between royal governor Josiah Martin and the provincial assembly over the attachment clause in the court law. This confrontation forced the closure of the colony's higher courts for several years and fueled the growing revolutionary crisis. Following the death of his first wife in 1771, Nash left Halifax for New Bern, and within a year he married Mary Whiting Jones. They had five children. The Nashes established a plantation seat, "Pembroke," on the Trent River.

Nash was an early participant in the revolutionary movement, attending as a delegate from New Bern all five of the Provincial Congresses from 1774 to 1776. He was described in this period by his antagonist, royal governor Martin, as "an eminent lawyer, but an unprincipled character" who was committed "to promote sedition and rebellion here." Nash's leadership of the revolutionary New Bern Committee of Safety led to his confrontation with Martin on 23 May 1775 at the governor's residence over the disposition of the palace signal cannon. This encounter convinced Martin just six days later to flee the capital for refuge on a British warship in the Cape Fear River, and royal authority was virtually ended in the province. Martin again singled out Nash as one of four patriots who stood "foremost among the patrons of revolt and anarchy." Nash was elected to the provincial council, which exercised the executive authority in the province in 1775 and 1776. At the fourth Provincial Congress in April 1776 Nash served on the committee that drafted the Halifax Resolves, the first official action for independence by any province. He also was named to the committee that drafted the first state constitution. When the new state government convened in 1777 Nash was elected to the House of Commons from New Bern and was elected the state's first Speaker of the house. He returned to the house the next year, and then in 1779 he was elected from the newly formed Jones County to the state senate, where he served as Speaker of the senate.

During a dismal period in the Revolution, Nash was elected governor of the state in April 1780 and served until June 1781. In 1780 the British completed the conquest of South Carolina, destroyed the army of General Horatio Gates at Camden in August, and first invaded North Carolina in incursions by Lord Cornwallis at Charlotte and by Major Patrick Ferguson in the west. The disheartened state government was in such shambles that Nash proposed a Board of War to be granted extraordinary power to assist him in preparing the nearly prostrate state to resist the enemy advances. The divided executive authority exacerbated governmental divisions, contributing to continued weakness in the state government. The full-scale British invasion by Lord Cornwallis in early 1781 encouraged a Loyalist rising that nearly brought an end to the state government. The strategic success of General Nathanael Greene's campaign freed the state from the British by the end of the year, but Nash had declined to run for a second term as governor. His plantation home was burned by Major James Craig's British raid on New Bern in August 1781. Despite the severe hardships of this period and his declining health, Nash remained in public life by service in the House of Commons in 1782, 1784, and 1785. He was first elected to the Continental Congress in 1778 but did not serve until his election in 1782. Although he was reelected to Congress in both 1783 and 1785, he did not attend. While preparing to take his seat in Congress, he died of consumption in New York City.

Nash's career in the revolutionary era, while short, was significant. He held many civil posts in the early state government and rose to prominence in all of the legislative bodies in which he served. His leadership in the revolutionary movement cost Nash his home, his fortune, his health, and finally his life; but once committed, he never wavered in his devotion to the cause of forging a new state and nation.

• There are a few papers of Nash in collections in the North Carolina State Archives, Raleigh. His public papers are published in William L. Saunders, ed., *The Colonial Records of North Carolina*, vols. 6–10 (1888–1890), and Walter J. Clark, ed., *The State Records of North Carolina*, vols. 11–25 (1896–1900). Biographical sketches are J. G. deRoulhac Hamilton, *Presentation of the Portrait of Governor Abner Nash to the State of North Carolina* (1909), and Frank Nash, "Governor Abner Nash," *North Carolina Booklet* 22 (1923): 3–11. Useful for background are Hugh F. Rankin, *The North Carolina Continentals* (1971), and David T. Morgan and William J. Schmidt, *North Carolinians in the Continental Congress* (1976).

LINDLEY S. BUTLER

NASH, Arthur (26 June 1870–30 Oct. 1927), men's clothing manufacturer, was born in Tipton County, Indiana, the son of Evermont Nash (occupation unknown) and Rachel Mitchel. Nash's parents were devoted Seventh-day Adventists, and he received a strict religious upbringing in that faith. After attending local Indiana schools, he began a course of study at the theological school of the Seventh-day Adventists in Battle Creek, Michigan. He proved to be a stellar student and upon graduation became an instructor at a Seventh-day Adventist school for ministers and missionaries in Detroit. He was ordained in 1894. Soon thereafter he experienced a crisis of faith when he refused to accept that a kindly and charitable woman, who ran a home for discharged prisoners, could not be saved because she had rejected the tenets of the Adventists. After an angry confrontation with church elders, he resigned his position and withdrew from the church.

For the next five years, Nash wandered through the Middle West doing laboring and construction jobs and reading widely in atheistic literature. Upon returning to Detroit, in 1899 he married Maud Lena Southwell, a superintendent of a Young Women's Christian Association boarding school; they had three children. Having rediscovered religion, in 1900 Nash became a minister in a Disciples of Christ church in Bluffton, Ohio. But he once again questioned why a virtuous and yet nonreligious man could not be saved, and church officials asked for his resignation. Nash then began to sell clothing in Ohio farm communities. Proving quite adept at this, in 1909 he decided to begin manufacturing men's clothing in Columbus, Ohio. His business prospered until a devastating flood in 1913 practically wiped him out.

Nash then moved to Cincinnati and in 1916 opened the A. Nash Company, a small firm that cut goods before sending them out to a contractor. At this time, after delivering a sermon titled "What Is the Matter with Christianity," Nash also began to develop the Golden Rule philosophy, which he hoped could Christianize industry. Following the conclusion of World War I, Nash bought out his contractor and upon discovering how poorly his new employees had been paid, he immediately raised their wages. In 1919 the firm moved into a new plant and benefiting from the postwar boom began a period of rapid expansion. By 1925, the A. Nash Company was worth more than $20 million and employed more than 3,000 workers.

Nash proved to be an innovator in the ways that he organized his business and in his management of the work force. Unlike most clothing firms that produced ready-to-wear suits in bulk, Nash employed more than 2,000 part-time salesmen who, after displaying samples, took orders in small towns and cities throughout the Middle West. These salesmen then sent the measurements to the firm's cutters, who cut each garment separately. After being cut, the goods were then assembled in a manner similar to that used by the large ready-to-wear manufacturers. The success of this unique "tailor-to-trade" system depended on Nash's ability to assemble a large number of local sales agents who might be tailors, barbers, or even ministers but who required no expense accounts and who did the firm's advertising on their own.

Nash developed his national reputation, though, because of the unique way in which he organized his work force. Desiring to create what he termed the "Golden Rule Family," Nash forbade the use of time clocks anywhere in the plant, instituted a forty-hour week, stabilized employment, banned the use of fines, and eliminated piecework except for the cutters. Despite his earlier dislike for the idea, in 1924 Nash developed a profit-sharing plan and distributed over $600,000 in dividends and stock to his employees. Disdaining any use of a formal system of representative government, Nash periodically addressed and exhorted his employees in "town meetings" and mass meetings. In the early 1920s, a number of national periodicals publicized his efforts to bring the "Kingdom of God" to his shop, and Nash became known to the larger public as "Golden Rule Nash." An extrovert, Nash also made numerous speeches in which he enthusiastically expounded on how the teachings of Jesus could be applied to the everyday business world. His ideas also became widely known through his autobiography, *The Golden Rule in Business* (1923; rev. ed., 1930).

During the early 1920s, neither the Amalgamated Clothing Workers of American (ACWA) nor the United Garment Workers had any success in their efforts to organize Nash's plant. As a result, antiunion advocates of the open shop began to cite Nash's firm as an example of the benefits of operating nonunion. This bothered Nash, who in 1923 commented: "The fact that the A. Nash Company is not a union shop seems terribly significant to some employers, until they learn that it isn't an antiunion shop. What right would I have to object if fellow workers want to join a union?" Nevertheless, the firm remained unorganized until 1925 when Celestine Goddard, a progressive-minded social worker, convinced a group of liberal ministers to condemn Nash for operating on a nonunion basis. Stung by this criticism, Nash approached the ACWA's president Sidney Hillman with the idea of organizing his employees. Besides desiring to show his concern for his workers, Nash had pragmatic motives for contacting the union: the ACWA's technical expertise could prove useful in organizing aspects of his business.

The employer-led union organizing drive represents a unique chapter in American labor history. Much to the dismay of his middle managers and foremen, Nash tried to convince his employees that he now believed unions to be an essential way to reach true brotherhood. At one meeting he asked them to reject identification with "avaricious organizations of capital" and to join with labor "to undo the heavy burdens, to let the oppressed go free and to break every yoke." He invited Hillman to Cincinnati to address his workers and finally in December 1925, Nash employees voted to join the ACWA. A great Cincinnati civic meeting on 11 December 1925 honored Nash and Hillman for their contributions to labor peace and employee/employer cooperation.

Because he was such a maverick both in the ways that he ran his business and managed his employees, Nash never had any significant impact on the men's clothing industry or on the larger business world. His ideas on labor also did not generally comport with the welfare capitalist movement initiated by employers who sought to discourage unionization by building bonds between employers and employees. Nash's ability to work closely with the ACWA is significant in that it demonstrates that despite its radical reputation, the union recognized the need to work closely with employers to improve employees' efficiency and craftsmanship. With Nash's encouragement, the ACWA even placed a union representative on the firm's executive board. Nash died of heart disease in Cincinnati. His death occurred before many of the new and innovative ideas concerning labor and management cooperation could be fully carried out.

• Nash did not leave any personal papers. His autobiography contains reprints of articles dealing with his ideas and their implementation. See also Arthur Nash, "A Bible Text That Worked a Business Miracle," *The American Magazine*, Oct. 1921, pp. 37, 112–17; Charles W. Wood, "Yes, He Has No Common Sense," *Colliers*, 28 July 1923, pp. 14, 20; Robert W. Bruère, "Golden Rule Nash," *The Nation*, 6 Jan. 1926, pp. 9–10; Silas Bent, "A Path to Peace in Industry," *Century Magazine*, Oct. 1926, pp. 677–87; and Bruère, "The Golden Rule through Union Eyes," *The Survey*, 1 Mar. 1927, pp. 147–50. An obituary is in the *New York Times*, 31 Oct. 1927.
DAVID J. GOLDBERG

NASH, Charles Edmund (23 May 1844–21 June 1913), Reconstruction politician, was born in Opelousas, Louisiana, the son of free parents Richard Nash and Masie Cecile. The first African-American congressman from Louisiana, Nash received little public school education. As a young man, he worked as a bricklayer in New Orleans.

In 1863 the nineteen-year-old Nash joined the Tenth Regiment of the Corps d'Afrique, later renamed the Eighty-second United States Colored Infantry. He joined the army as a private but was soon promoted to the rank of sergeant major. Nash's regiment fought at the Battle of Port Hudson, Louisiana, and was involved in the last infantry battle of the Civil War, the Battle of Fort Blakely, Alabama, in April 1865. While storming Fort Blakely, Nash received wounds that cost him most of his right leg and earned him an honorable discharge. Apparently, about ten days before his discharge he received promotion to first lieutenant, but it was not approved. His leg wounds pained him for many years, and he may have been adjusting to life during the years 1865 to 1869, when there is little information about him.

In 1869 Nash returned to Louisiana, where his military record and his political affiliations with the Republican party earned him a position as a night inspector in a politically influential New Orleans Custom House. In 1874 this association allowed him a triumphant nomination as the Republican candidate from the Sixth Congressional District in Louisiana. Nash won the election and took his seat in 1975, assigned to the Committee of Education and Labor. Nash's tenure in Congress was short and the only bill that he introduced, a bayou survey in his district, was swiftly quashed. Sometime after his election to Congress, he married Martha Ann Wycoff. They had no children.

As a freshman congressman, Nash found it difficult to get the floor to speak. Finally, on 7 June 1876, he made a significant address on political affairs in his state. Nash consistently supported the Fourteenth Amendment and criticized the efforts of white southern Democrats to suppress native Republicans and plead for racial peace. He urged national reconciliation on the part of all Americans, pledged his loyalty to the Republican party, pleaded for decency in the treatment of southern blacks, and emphasized the importance of education for black and white Americans. In his speech Nash warned of the perils of unfair election practices and inadequate education, citing "the ignorance of the masses" as Louisiana's gravest danger and most injurious obstacle to harmony. "The race issue is the issue of ignorance," he argued. In his prescription for a healthy southern society, Nash explained that "education dispels narrow prejudices as the sun dispels the noxious vapors of the night. The South needs more and better schools." Furthermore, he insisted on the importance of "equal rights before the law, and . . . participation in the elective franchise" for all male citizens. Nash concluded with a call to northerners and southerners, and black and white Americans, to strive for these goals together. Referring to the ending of the Civil War, he exhorted: "The battle-cry is no longer sounded; war's thunder-clouds have rolled muttering away, and the skies are bright after the storm. The heroes of one side are sleeping side by side with those whom they withstood in battle . . . this country is our joint inheritance, this flag has always been our joint banner. The glories of our past belong to both of us . . . Let there be peace between us, that these swords which we have learned to use so well, may if used again strike only at a common foe."

Nash received the Republican nomination for a second term in the House of Representatives, but his bid for reelection was defeated in 1876 when he lost to a white Democrat opposed to Reconstruction reforms. Nash's impassioned speech had gone over well on the floor of Congress, but not so well in his home state. The election of 1876, commonly cited as the end of Reconstruction, marked the end of Nash's political career. He returned to Louisiana in March 1877. In 1882 he served briefly as the postmaster of the coastal town of Washington, Louisiana, before moving back to Opelousas, where his first wife died two years later. Nash then moved to New Orleans, where he took a job making cigars and married a French woman named Julia Lacy Montplaisir in February 1905. Nash died in New Orleans.

In many ways Nash typifies the experiences of politically active African Americans during the Civil War and Reconstruction. He supported the Union during the war and espoused patriotism, reconciliation, and political involvement after the war. During Reconstruction he gained access to the government that would have been impossible before the Civil War. A byproduct of the New Orleans Custom House political "machine," Nash never distinguished himself as a congressman. His incredibly brief tenure did not encourage his independence in Congress, and he never made a notable political impact.

• Nash's speech is in the *Congressional Record*, 44th Cong., 1876–1877. For biographical details about Nash, see Eric Foner, *Freedom's Lawmakers: A Directory of Black Officeholders During Reconstruction* (1996); *The Afro-American Encyclopedia*, vol. 6 (1974); and Charles Lanman, *Biographical Annals of the Civil Government of the United States, during Its First Century* (1876). See also Samuel D. Smith, *The Negro in Congress* (1940). For additional information on military accounts of the Civil War, see George H. Hepworth, *The Whip, Hoe, and Sword, or the Gulf Department in '63* (1864). Also see J. J. Pipkin, *The Story of a Rising Race* (1902), where Nash's military experiences are treated. For the unique context of Reconstruction politics in Louisiana, see Joe Gray Taylor, *Louisiana Reconstructed 1863–1877* (1974).

CHANDRA MILLER

NASH, Charles W. (28 Jan. 1864–6 June 1948), automobile manufacturer, was born in DeKalb County, Illinois, the son of David L. Nash and Anna Caldwell. The family moved to a farm near Flint, Michigan, while Charles was still an infant, and when his parents separated, the seven-year-old was bound out to a local farmer. Nash worked for the farmer until he was twelve, while acquiring a minimal grade school education. Eventually escaping from servitude, Nash labored as a farm hand, apprentice carpenter, hay presser, farm foreman, and grocery clerk. Extraordinarily ambitious and frugal, Nash used his savings to purchase sheep, eventually owning eighty of them. His youth, Nash later recalled, was characterized by "sheep, books, and hard work." In 1884 he married Jessie Halleck, the daughter of a local farmer; the couple had three children.

Seven years later, at the age of twenty-seven, Nash became an upholstery trimmer for the Flint Road Cart Company, owned by William C. Durant and Josiah D. Dort. Rising rapidly through the firm's ranks, Nash had become a vice president and director of the revamped Durant-Dort Carriage Company by 1895. His introduction of the conveyor belt assembly line helped establish Durant-Dort as the leading carriage manufacturer in the world, turning out 56,000 carriages during its peak year of 1906. Four years later Nash became president and general manager of the financially insolvent Buick Motor Company, a subsidiary of the General Motors Corporation founded by Durant. Nash was so successful at reorganizing Buick and placing it on a solid financial footing that he was elected unanimously as the president of the nearly bankrupt General Motors in 1912. Within three years Nash doubled production, divested the company of several unprofitable subsidiaries, came close to doubling the annual gross sales revenue, and quadrupled net profits, catapulting General Motors to the status of industrial giant.

At odds with Durant, in 1916 Nash borrowed capital from eastern investors and purchased the Thomas B. Jeffrey Motor Car Company of Kenosha, Wisconsin, transforming it into Nash Motors. Conservative and pragmatic, Nash set out to build a "simple car" for the "average man," working sixteen to eighteen hours a day to design a new model, retool the assembly line, train the workers, and establish retail outlets. In 1917 the new company sold 18,553 cars and 3,800 trucks before converting to wartime production. Characteristically, Nash threw himself into the war effort at home and, at the request of President Woodrow Wilson, supervised aircraft production for the U.S. Army. Returning to Kenosha immediately following the armistice of November 1918, Nash positioned his company to compete in the automobile boom of the 1920s by proclaiming "no radical changes in design; no sweeping departures." He tailored his strategy toward "the great middle-class" by building a "medium-priced and moderate-sized car," and by inventing methods of creative financing. Operating on this philosophy between 1920 and 1928, Nash Motors increased its production from 38,000 to 138,000 automobiles, its gross sales from $57 million to $123 million, and its profits from $7 million to $29 million.

A benevolent despot in dealing with his workforce, Nash nevertheless expected them to work long, hard hours for lower than the prevailing wage and under less than safe and healthy conditions. Like his rival Henry Ford, however, Nash established numerous financial aid, recreation, and education programs for his workers and their families, most notably the Ke-Nash-A Club, a social and benevolent association. He also sponsored frequent social events for his workers, culminating in the annual company picnic and Christmas bonuses for members of his business "family." He gave large donations to the Boy Scouts, the YMCA, and the Kenosha Youth Foundation. A conservative Republican in politics, Nash greatly admired Presidents Calvin Coolidge and Herbert Hoover, opposed government intervention in the economy, and urged reliance on private charity for social welfare.

With his policy of never making a car that had not already been sold, Nash had a minimum inventory on hand when the Great Depression hit. Consequently he cut production drastically, put his money in government bonds, and laid off a large segment of his workforce. Between 1929 and 1933 Nash production was cut from 116,633 to 14,973. Although generally opposed to the New Deal, Nash cooperated with the National Recovery Administration, achieving a short-lived resurgence in 1934. Philosophically opposed to unionization, Nash experienced a series of clashes with the burgeoning labor movement, denouncing its leaders as "communists" and vowing to "close the plant and throw the key in Lake Michigan" before he would extend recognition to a union. A series of confrontations, strikes, and lockouts, combined with financial setbacks and family difficulties, motivated Nash to resign as company president in 1932.

Although continuing as chairman of the board, Nash spent much of his time in Beverly Hills, California. The merger of Nash with Kelvinator in 1937 turned Nash largely into an absentee owner. When he died in Beverly Hills, Nash's personal fortune was estimated at $44 million in cash, stocks, and bonds, plus 62,900 shares of Nash Kelvinator stock. Many observers praised him as the epitome of the self-made man and the personification of the American Dream. One former worker who later became a union leader still remembered him as "a hard nosed, tight fisted boss" who "could make a damn fine car."

• The most detailed treatment of Nash's life and one that places him squarely within the context of the development of the American automobile industry is Thomas J. Noer, "Charles W. Nash: Self-Made Man" in *Kenosha Retrospective: A Biographical Approach*, ed. Nicholas C. Burckel and John A. Neuenschwander (1981). Nash's contributions to the development of the automobile industry are discussed in James J. Flink, *The Car Culture* (1975); Stephen W. Sears, *The American Heritage History of the Automobile in America* (1977); and John B. Rae, *The American Automobile* (1965). The outcome of the Nash-Kelvinator merger is profiled in Keith Hutchinson, "Success Story," *Nation*, 4 Jan. 1941, pp. 19–20, while the corporation's labor policies are discussed in "Drift to Draft: Nash-Kelvinator Finds Way to Protect Essential Labor," *Business Week*, 19 Sept. 1942, pp. 90–96. Obituaries are in the *New York Times* and the *Kenosha Telegraph-Courier*, both 7 June 1948.

JOHN D. BUENKER

NASH, John Henry (12 Mar. 1871–24 May 1947), printer, bibliophile, and typographer, was born in Woodbridge, Ontario, Canada, the son of John Marvin Nash, a mechanical engineer, and Catherine Cain. Though withdrawn from public school at age sixteen to begin his practical education by learning his father's trade, Nash insisted on becoming a printer. He began his career in 1888 with an apprenticeship at James Murray and Company, a Toronto printing firm. Despite his thorough training and seeming determination to become a printer, Nash left the business after a few years and embarked on the life of a bicycle racer. A major fad in the 1890s, bicycle racing offered the opportunity for wealth and fame, and both appealed to him. He traveled the racing circuit from around 1890 to 1892, when his passion for the sport waned and he decided to go back to printing. Nash returned to Toronto to work for Brough and Caswell and then for Milne-Burgham Company, where he remained until 1894. In the winter of 1894 he left Toronto to work for App-Stotts in Denver, Colorado; he stayed there a mere four months, after which he relocated to San Francisco.

The artistic and intellectual atmosphere of the Bay area appealed to Nash. More important, San Francisco was an established center of fine printing. He first worked for Hicks-Judd Company as a compositor, then in 1898 left to work for the Stanley-Taylor Company, a nationally recognized firm. He was soon promoted from compositor to foreman, a position that allowed him to express his views about printing and book design. Nash helped design the first two issues of Stanley-Taylor's *Western Printer* (1901), a well-received publication, and for the first time was widely recognized for his work. In 1900 he married Mary Henrietta Ford, with whom he had one child.

Nash was never completely satisfied working for someone else, and he spent much of his life flitting from one job to another. He left Stanley-Taylor to become superintendent of the Sunset Press, subsequently went back to Stanley-Taylor, left that firm again, then returned once more. Frustrated, and believing that his pay and position were incommensurate with the quality of his work, in 1902 Nash entered into a partnership with Bruce Brough to form the Twentieth Century Press. The firm's chief clients were Paul Elder and Morgan Shepard, owners of an art shop that carried stylish books. Like Nash, Elder regarded books as works of art, and this mutual appreciation afforded Nash the luxury of experimenting with different papers and ink, elaborate colophons, and exotic bindings.

After the disastrous 1906 earthquake, Elder relocated to New York City. Nash joined him and moved his family to Flatbush. Nash's career gained momentum in New York. Among his significant achievements was a four-volume set of Western classics that comprised works by Bret Harte, W. H. Rhodes, Robert Louis Stevenson, and Ambrose Bierce. Also while in New York, he made connections with Theodore DeVinne, the best-known printer of the time, and Henry Lewis Bullen, director of the Typographical Library and Museum of American Type Founders Company.

By 1909, San Francisco had recovered, and Nash accompanied Paul Elder and Company on its return to the Bay area. Soon dissatisfied, however, he left Elder's company and went back to Stanley-Taylor, which was renamed Taylor, Nash, and Taylor. Nash, assured a regular salary, was appointed vice president and allowed complete control over the Fine Work Department. His most-notable accomplishments included editions of Charles Dickens's *What Christmas Is as We Grow Older* (1912) and John Galen Howard's *Brunelleschi* (1913). The firm's reputation peaked in 1914–1915 when it published *TNT Imprint*, its house organ.

After another period of discontent and resettlement, Nash started his own business, the John Henry Nash Fine Arts Press. Despite a lack of capital, inadequate equipment, and insufficient supplies, Nash's good reputation and connections kept him in business. His book work was supported by wealthy mining operator William Andrews Clark, Jr., and other commissions derived from Nash's previous associations. His most expensive commission—$40,000—was from William Randolph Hearst, who along with Clark, made Nash the most generously patronized fine printer of his time. Books were Nash's specialty, but other printing work sustained him both in this early period and later. Though not wealthy, he was financially stable.

The 1920s was a prosperous time for San Francisco and for Nash. It was a period of great demand for fine printing, and although there were other reputable printers in the area, Nash was considered one of the best. He was especially well recognized for his books, such as his four-volume edition of Dante's *Divine Comedy* (1929). Nash's goal in embarking on the project had been to create "a monument alike to [Dante], to his translator, and to the printing art" (Blumenthal, p. 101), and the many accolades that the edition received attest to his success. Also in this period he established the library and typographical museum in San Francisco, probably his proudest achievement. The library contained about 3,000 items, including Nash's and others' imprints, stationery, business papers, and early editions of the Bible and Chaucer. The collections were open to the public.

By 1933–1934 the depression had taken its toll. William Andrews Clark had ceased to order printing and business in general had declined. Nash's health also had deteriorated. He retired in 1936, at the age of sixty-five, but was back at work six months later, after his health had improved. Despite limited success, such as his much-acclaimed edition of Ralph Waldo Emerson's *Composition* (1937), he closed his business and in 1938 set his sights on Eugene, Oregon, where the University of Oregon (with which he had been affiliated for roughly a decade) offered him eager students, a home for his library, and an ideal setting for the John Henry Nash Fine Arts Press. Over the next few years, however, the university's enthusiasm waned, and in 1942 Nash returned to California, where he found a permanent home for his library at the University of California, Berkeley. He died shortly thereafter at his home in Berkeley.

Biographer Robert D. Harlan rightly described Nash as a "technician, artist, salesman, and educator" (p. 117). Although he was criticized for restricting himself to archaic typographical styles, his near technical perfection and his use of various typefaces, ornaments, and high-quality materials were esteemed by those who appreciated the craftsmanship involved in such work. Moreover, the ambitious Nash was well received by businessmen who found him to be as interesting as he was likable. A master promoter, he became the clear leader of his profession in the San Francisco area and thereby helped elevate fine printing to an art form.

• Nash's library, papers, and correspondence are collected as the John Henry Nash Archives at the University of California, Berkeley. The best published work is Robert D. Harlan, *John Henry Nash: The Biography of a Career* (1970). Also see Joseph FauntLeRoy, *John Henry Nash, Printer* (1948). In addition to entries in the standard biographical reference works, a biographical sketch can be found in Joseph Blumenthal, *The Printed Book in America* (1989). An obituary is in the *New York Times*, 25 May 1947.

STEPHEN L. LEVINE

NASH, Norman Burdett (5 June 1888–3 Jan. 1963), Episcopal bishop, was born in Bangor, Maine, the son of Henry Sylvester Nash, an Episcopal priest, and Bessie Keffler Curtis. He grew up in Cambridge, Massachusetts, where his father was a professor at the Episcopal Theological School. Nash graduated from Harvard in 1909 and for the next two years studied at the Harvard Law School. He then entered the Episcopal Theological School and received his B.D. in 1915. He was ordained deacon on 27 May 1915, and in 1915–1916 he studied in England at Cambridge University. He was ordained a priest on 4 October 1916 and joined the faculty of the Episcopal Theological School, where he taught New Testament.

In October 1917 Nash married Marian Noble; they had three children. At that time, he began work with the Y.M.C.A., serving with the French army until February 1918. He then became chaplain and a first lieutenant of the 150th Field Artillery in the Rainbow Division of the U.S. Army, serving in that capacity until the spring of 1919. In 1919 he returned to Cambridge as assistant professor of New Testament at the Episcopal Theological School. He also served as rector of St. Ann's Church in South Lincoln, Massachusetts (1916–1923).

Nash studied abroad in 1924. In 1925 he became assistant professor of Christian social ethics and lecturer in New Testament. "This combination of sound New Testament scholarship with a growing knowledge of Sociology proved a particularly happy one, and Nash's courses were among the most stimulating in the School, as was his playing of touch-football with the students the most vigorous and volcanic" (Muller, p. 192). In 1927 he became professor of Christian social ethics, serving in that position until 1939. He then left the Episcopal Theological School to become the rector of St. Paul's School in Concord, New Hampshire (1939–1947). In an address at St. Paul's, he said, "Education is to master the wisdom of the good life in fellowship, and to aid students in the life-long study and practice of the art of handling life" ("Memorial to Norman B. Nash," p. 2).

On 11 December 1946 Nash was elected bishop coadjutor of the diocese of Massachusetts and was consecrated at Trinity Church in Boston on 14 February 1947. He served as bishop coadjutor until 1 June 1947, when he became the tenth bishop of Massachusetts, serving until October 1956.

During his episcopate, Nash concentrated on several themes. He was especially concerned about the life of the Christian family. He insisted that the task of the church is to teach the principles of Christian family life and to mediate the help of God so that more homes would be filled with the spirit of mutual consideration and service, and with that peace that keeps people steadfast in the face of a dangerous and insecure world. He supported the remarriage of divorced persons in the church and wanted persons otherwise remarried to have communicant status in the church. He claimed that this change in the marriage canons of the Episcopal church was intended as relief for Christians, and not a concession to American polygamy.

Nash was also deeply committed to the ecumenical movement both within the Anglican communion and among world denominational bodies. He attended the Lambeth Conference of 1948 and was struck by how international and multiracial the Anglican communion had become. He noted that the word "Anglican," that is, English, for this particular church was historically accurate, but as a descriptive name it had become an anachronism. The Lambeth conference made him aware of the wide Anglican range of doctrine, ethics, and ceremonial. He insisted that diversity and unity were the hallmarks of Anglicanism.

Nash was also deeply impressed by and committed to the formation and work of the World Council of Churches (WCC), which held its organizational meeting at Amsterdam in 1948. For him the birth of the WCC was a much greater event than the Lambeth Conference. The significance of the formation of the WCC was that it gave the churches a new opportunity to enter into a living spiritual contact with each other and to reconstitute the fellowship that had been broken. The launching of the WCC meant that in principle the churches agreed to listen and to speak to each other.

As bishop, Nash also continued his interest in and work for the social implications of the gospel, a theme that dominated his teaching at Cambridge. He was an advocate for displaced persons following World War II and urged each parish and mission in the diocese to adopt one family. He also urged the people of the diocese to give generously for world relief, pointing out that almsgiving is a part of the Christian's worship. He was also very much concerned about the anti-Communist movements of the 1950s. At a time when the country was in turmoil over the threat of Communism, he appealed in a letter to President Dwight D. Eisenhower for executive clemency for eleven Communists who were convicted under the Alien Registration Act, known as the Smith Act, which made the advocacy of the violent overthrow of the United States government unlawful. Nash argued the violation of liberty was more a threat than eleven Communists watched by the FBI.

From 1956 until 1959 Nash served as the bishop in charge of the American churches in Europe.

A leading educator and proponent of social justice, he was a Stalwart leader of ecumenism in Massachusetts. He died in Cambridge.

• Nash's papers are in the Archives of the Diocese of Massachusetts and the Archives of the Episcopal Divinity School, Cambridge, Mass. He published very little, and there has been no study done of his life and work. His time at the Episcopal Theological School is discussed briefly in James Muller, *The Episcopal Theological School, 1867–1943* (1943), and in George L. Blackman, *Faith and Freedom: A Study of Theological Education and the Episcopal Theological School* (1967). See also "Memorial to Norman B. Nash (1888–1963)," an unpublished paper given at the annual meeting of the Headmasters Association, Rye, N.Y., 14–15 Feb. 1963. An obituary is John H. Fenton, "The Lord Taketh Away," *Church Militant* 66 (Feb. 1963): 2, 5.

DONALD S. ARMENTROUT

NASH, Ogden (19 Aug. 1902–19 May 1971), writer, was born Frederick Ogden Nash in Rye, New York, the son of Edmund Strudwick Nash, importer and exporter of naval stores, and Mattie Chenault. Nash's formal education at St. George's School in Newport, Rhode Island (1917–1920), was made possible by his father's four-year struggle to recoup losses suffered in a financial setback in 1913. In the fall of 1920 Nash enrolled at Harvard, but a second reversal of his father's fortunes prevented him from continuing beyond his first year. Returning to Newport, Nash taught French at St. George's School before leaving town and taking up a succession of jobs in New York. Beginning in 1921, he worked in the mail room of a brokerage firm and attempted to sell bonds, remaining for a year and a half. He also worked briefly as a salesman before he found a job writing streetcar ads for an advertising franchise, a position he kept until 1925.

In New York Nash shared an apartment with five men, including Joseph Alger, with whom Nash collaborated in writing a children's book, *The Cricket of Carador* (1925). Although the book was not a success—Nash claimed that it sold fewer copies "than you could count on the thumbs of one hand"—its publication by Doubleday, Page & Co. resulted in Nash's meeting Dan Longwell, Doubleday's advertising manager, who soon hired Nash as an assistant.

Nash's duties at Doubleday did little to provide an outlet for his desire to write poetry. His first, unsuccessful efforts, written as a youth and as a student at St. George's, were imitations of the Victorian poets, but in 1930 he began to emphasize the "ludicrous side" of these first "attempts at serious poetry." In discovering this knack for writing verse, Nash acknowledged a debt to Julia Moore, "the Sweet Singer of Michigan," but credited Samuel Hoffenstein for the "slightly cynical . . . approach which opened the doors wide for me."

Deciding in the early 1930s "that it would be better to be 'a good bad poet than a bad good poet,'" Nash rose to sudden prominence as a humorous poet when the eccentric verses he had begun composing at his desk at Doubleday started appearing regularly in the *New Yorker*. His fractured rhymes, seemingly interminable lines, and irreverent attitude—expressed, for example, in a desire to live "in nonchalance and insouciance" but for the necessity of "making a living, which is rather a nouicance"—quickly became his trademark and the inspiration for a host of imitators.

Nash left Doubleday in late 1930 to become managing editor of the *New Yorker* for what turned out to be a brief, three-month stint—"the usual period of tenure at the time," according to Nash. During this period his first collection of poems, *Hard Lines*, was published. The book enjoyed a phenomenal success, selling more than 20,000 copies in just six weeks. It was the first of several events that made 1931 an important year, personally and professionally, in Nash's life. In the same year, he married Frances Rider Leonard, became an associate editor at the book publishing firm of Farrar & Rinehart, and published his second book of verse, *Free Wheeling*.

Despite the economic depression, or perhaps because of it, Nash found a wide audience for his humorous poems in newspapers and periodicals such as the *New York Journal American* and the *Saturday Evening Post*. At the time, markets for humor were plentiful, emboldening Nash to leave his editorial post in 1933 for the freedom of freelance writing. This career move bore fruit with the publication of *The Primrose Path* in 1935 and *The Bad Parents' Garden of Verse* in 1936, the latter work inspired in part by the birth of the Nash's two children, in 1932 and 1933. Described by his daughter as "gentle, unassuming," Nash protected his privacy, discouraging personal inquiries with a quip as terse as his best poems, "I have no private life and no personality." In truth, however, his personal passions—the quiet domesticity of family life, odd but lovable animals, and sports (especially horse racing and baseball)—are all publicly displayed in his poems, as is his desire to reap financial reward.

Lured by the possibility of a different kind of success as well as a lucrative salary, Nash set off in 1936 for Hollywood and the studios of MGM. He remained there for two unhappy years, producing little work of his own, although 1938 would see the publication of *I'm a Stranger Here Myself*, one of his most popular books. Nash would make another unsuccessful effort at writing for the screen in 1940 before finally returning east to Baltimore. Once established there, however, Nash set out again, this time on a lecture tour, the first of many he would make over the next twenty years to supplement his income.

With the U.S. entry into World War II in 1941, Nash volunteered for military service, but he was rejected because of poor eyesight. Instead, he served as an air-raid warden and wrote war bond jingles for the Treasury Department. He also continued his regular writing of poetry, publishing *Good Intentions* in 1942. The following year, Nash collaborated with S. J. Perelman and Kurt Weill in producing the hit Broadway musical *One Touch of Venus*. Nash spent the next thir-

teen years trying to duplicate this success, writing lyrics for *Sweet Bye and Bye* (1946), *Two's Company* (1952), and *The Littlest Revue* (1956). *Two's Company*, the most successful of the three efforts, opened on Broadway, but when Bette Davis's voice "gave out," the show closed after four weeks.

Meanwhile, Nash continued to dominate the light-verse market with a continuous stream of popular books, between 1949 and the end of the next decade publishing five new volumes of poetry as well as an anthology representing thirty years of work, *Verses from 1929 On* (1959). Starting in the late 1950s Nash increasingly turned to the writing of books for children. Among his most notable efforts are *Custard the Dragon* (1959), *The Adventures of Isabel* (1963), and *The Cruise of the Aardvark* (1967).

By the 1960s many of the markets for humor (for example, the *New York Journal American*) that had sustained Nash during the early days of his career had disappeared. During that turbulent decade, a period of personal self-doubt during which Nash questioned the "relevance" of his writing, many of his verses, nostalgic in tone, failed to attract the large audiences he had once enjoyed. Still, he continued to write, publishing *Marriage Lines: Notes of a Student Husband* (1964), *There's Always Another Windmill* (1968), *Bed Riddance: A Posy for the Indisposed* (1970), and *The Old Dog Barks Backwards*, which appeared in 1972 after his death in Baltimore.

Dismissed by many critics for his lack of seriousness, Nash nevertheless enjoyed a tremendous popular appeal. Among American poets, Nash is remembered for his distinctive voice. His wry observations about human nature, expressed in poems such as "Reflections on Ice-Breaking," are the indelible mark that he leaves on American literature.

• Manuscripts and letters of Ogden Nash are in the Ogden Nash Collection in the Harry Ransom Humanities Research Center at the University of Texas, Austin. A selection of Nash's letters is collected in *Loving Letters from Ogden Nash: A Family Album* (1991), introduced and selected by Linell Nash Smith. Nash's published works include *Happy Days* (1933), *One Touch of Venus* (1944), *Many Long Years Ago* (1945), *Ogden Nash's Musical Zoo* (1947), *Versus* (1949), *Family Reunion* (1950), *Parents Keep Out: Elderly Poems for Youngerly Readers* (1951), *The Private Dining Room and Other New Verses* (1953), *You Can't Get There from Here* (1957), *Custard the Dragon and the Wicked Knight* (1961), *The New Nutcracker Suite and Other Innocent Verses* (1962), *Everyone But Thee and Me* (1962), and (selected by Linell Smith and Isabel Eberstadt, with an introduction by Archibald MacLeish) *I Wouldn't Have Missed It: Selected Poems of Ogden Nash* (1975). Bibliographical works include George W. Crandell, *Ogden Nash: A Descriptive Bibliography* (1991), and Lavonne Axford, *An Index to the Poems of Ogden Nash* (1972). A biography of Nash is David Stuart, *Ogden Nash: A Biography* (1987). An important interview can be found in Roy Newquist, *Conversations* (1967). For biographical information, see also *The Dictionary of Literary Biography*, vol. 11: *American Humorists, 1800–1950*, pt. 2 (1982). Obituaries are in the *New York Times* and the London *Times*, 20 May 1971.

GEORGE W. CRANDELL

NASH, Philleo (25 Oct. 1909–12 Oct. 1987), educator, federal administrator, and lieutenant governor of Wisconsin, was born in Wisconsin Rapids, Wisconsin, the son of Guy Nash, a cranberry grower, and Florence Philleo. He attended elementary and high schools in Wisconsin Rapids, followed by a brief period of study at the Curtis Institute of Music in Philadelphia. In the fall of 1927 Nash enrolled in Alexander Meiklejohn's Experimental College at the University of Wisconsin in Madison. Later he studied anthropology at the University of Wisconsin, receiving an A.B. in 1932. He then entered the University of Chicago for graduate training.

In 1935 Nash married Edith Rosenfels, a fellow anthropology student, who accompanied him to Oregon, where they jointly conducted research among the Klamath Indians. The couple had two children. Following receipt of his Ph.D. in 1937, Nash joined the faculty of the University of Toronto as a lecturer in anthropology and assistant keeper of the ethnological collections of the Royal Ontario Museum. He gave up this position in 1941 and, with his wife and children, returned to Wisconsin to assist with management of the family cranberry business.

After U.S. entry into World War II, Nash began working in the Office of War Information, where in 1942 he assumed the duties of special assistant to the director. Three years later he and his wife helped establish the Georgetown Day School in Washington, D.C., and Nash served as president of the school's board of directors from 1945 until 1952.

In 1946 Nash joined President Harry S. Truman's staff as special assistant for minority affairs. In this capacity, he helped to write the final report of the President's Committee on Fair Employment Practices and to develop the policies that prohibited racial discrimination in the military and civil service. Near the end of his White House career, Nash became the target of an attack by Wisconsin senator Joseph R. McCarthy, who charged him with being a Communist. Nash called this accusation a "contemptible lie" and received strong support from President Truman in disavowing the senator's claim.

In 1953, following the inauguration of President Dwight D. Eisenhower, Nash resumed management of the family business in Wisconsin. He also involved himself in the affairs of the Democratic party, and voters from his native state chose him in 1958 as their lieutenant governor, a post he held until 1960.

Returning to Washington in 1961 as commissioner of Indian affairs in the Department of the Interior, Nash promoted the idea of self-sufficiency for Native-American communities through greater educational opportunities, including increased federal funding for college scholarships, decreased emphasis on off-reservation boarding schools, and the construction of more schools close to the homes of Indian families, and he supported the attraction of industry to reservations and nearby areas.

After leaving the Bureau of Indian Affairs in 1966, Nash remained in Washington, where he served as a consultant to the Phillips Petroleum Company, while his wife continued as director of the Georgetown Day School. During this period the Nashes—at the invitation of Ambassador Chester Bowles—spent six weeks in India lecturing and consulting with university and government officials concerning economic development programs on American Indian reservations.

In 1969 Nash joined the faculty of the American University as a professor of anthropology and in 1973 became director of the university's Learning Center, an experimental department that developed the skills of students whose test scores were not sufficiently high to admit them into regular programs and directed them toward eventual degree programs. From 1977 until his death ten years later, Nash lived in Wisconsin Rapids, where he was manager and president of the Biron Cranberry Company.

Honors accorded Nash by his colleagues in the anthropology profession included the distinguished service award of the American Anthropological Association (1984) and the Bronislaw Malinowski Award of the Society for Applied Anthropology (1986). He was treasurer of the association from 1968 to 1970 and was president of the society in 1970–1971. He also was secretary of the anthropology section of the American Association for the Advancement of Science, from 1974 to 1978, and president of the Anthropological Society of Washington, D.C., in 1975–1976. At its annual meeting in Tampa in the spring of 1988, the Society for Applied Anthropology devoted a special session to Nash and his work; in 1989 the National Association for the Practice of Anthropology published a book including some of the papers read at that session.

• Nash's government papers are in the Harry S. Truman Library in Independence, Mo. Three interview tapes that concern his government service are in the John F. Kennedy Memorial Library in Boston. Documents related to his work as commissioner of Indian affairs are in the Stewart Udall Archives at the University of Arizona. Field notes and other materials, including photos, from Nash's anthropological research are in the anthropological archive of the Smithsonian Institution in Washington, D.C. Nash's more important publications include "The Place of Religious Revivalism in the Formation of the Intercultural Community of Klamath Reservation," in *Social Anthropology of North American Tribes: Essays in Social Organization, Law, and Religion*, ed. Fred Eggan (1937); "An Introduction to the Problem of Racial Tensions," in *The North American Indian Today*, ed. C. T. Loram and T. F. McIlwraith (1943); "Research in American Indian Education," in *Proceedings of the National Research Conference on American Indian Education* (1967); "Applied Anthropology and the Concept of Guided Acculturation," *Indian Historian* 6, no. 23 (1973): 23–35; "Anthropologist in the White House," *Practicing Anthropology* 1, no. 3 (1979): 3, 23–24; "Science, Politics, and Human Values, A Memoir," *Human Organization* 45, no. 3 (1986): 189–201; and "Twentieth Century Government Agencies" in *Handbook of North American Indians*, vol. 4, ed. Wilcomb E. Washburn (1988). For a complete bibliography of Nash's published works, see Ruth H. Landman and Katherine Spencer Halpern, eds., *Applied Anthropology and Public Servant: The Life and Work of Philleo Nash* (1989), pp. 45–50. An obituary is in *American Anthropologist* 90, no. 4 (1988).

JAMES E. OFFICER

NASSI, Thomas (2 Mar. 1892–21 Dec. 1964), musician and pioneering music educator, was born Thoma Nashi (Nasji) in Dardha, Albania, the son of Gaqo Nashi. His mother's name is not yet known. A member of the educated Albanian Orthodox minority, Nassi's father had moved the family to the mountain community of Dardha, near Korça, Albania, in order to escape domination by the Ottoman Turks. The Korça region of southeastern Albania was a center of Albanian Orthodox church and nationalist activity and has been the place of origin of most Albanian immigrants to the United States. The elder Nassi abandoned his family when Thomas was six years old, after which the boy was sent to the care of an uncle in Athens, Greece. There he received a lyceum education and training in music. His first instrument was violin, followed by flute after a wrist injury.

Immigrating to the United States in 1914 under the Hellenicized name Thomas G. Nassis (changed to Nassi after 1918), he worked for the Great Northern Paper Co. in Millinocket, Maine. He next moved to Boston to study at the New England Conservatory (NEC). Between admission (1916) and graduation (1918) Nassi first displayed the extraordinary gifts and accomplishments in educating and organizing music performance groups on a large scale that characterized most of his life. While still a student he organized the first Albanian-American (Vatra) Band in Worcester, Massachusetts (Dec. 1916). Commuting by train from his residence in Boston, he personally trained many of the factory workers who made up the ensemble. *Vatra*, meaning *hearth* in Albanian, was the name of a then recently organized Pan Albanian movement. He simultaneously organized the first choirs in the Albanian Orthodox parishes in Boston, Southbridge, and Worcester. He also served as a substitute flutist in the Boston Symphony under Karl Muck and Pierre Monteux. During this period he met his future wife, Olympia Berishi Tsika, who had chanced to emigrate to the United States from the same town (Dardha) in Albania as Nassi. They were married in 1918, and their lifelong musical partnership produced three musically active children.

After leaving the U.S. Army Nassi, now a naturalized U.S. citizen, remobilized the Vatra Band and in 1920 headed a group of forty Albanian-American musicians who volunteered to go to Albania to support Albanian independence. At considerable risk the Vatra Band did much to sustain public morale during the nationalists' effort in 1920 to keep Albania from being partitioned and annexed by Greece and Italy. Nassi adapted the Albanian national anthem, originally composed by a well-known Romanian musician, Cyprian Porumbescu. Nassi's songs, especially "Vlora Vlora" (celebrating the defense of Vlora against the Italian army) evoked a sense of national pride and solidarity and became popular throughout the country. Nassi and the Vatra Band toured all the major towns in Albania and introduced many Albanians to Western music, including Wagner and Handel's *Messiah*. Nassi translated solo and orchestral excerpts of the latter work into Albanian for performance by newly formed local ensembles. During the six years he and his wife spent in Albania Nassi organized the country's school music system, taught in high schools and the French Lycée, and organized bands and choral societies. He found time to compose a mass, two rhapsodies, and two operettas. In addition to his work in music he served as representative of the American Red Cross, the Veterans' Bureau, and the American Legion and as an adviser to the League of Nations. He also helped organize the first YMCA in Albania.

In 1924 the Yugoslav-assisted forces of Ahmed Zoglu overcame the democratically oriented government led by Bishop Fan S. Noli. Although Nassi continued to enjoy the support of President Zoglu, the latter's increasingly autocratic tendencies (he assumed the title of King Zog in 1928) disillusioned Nassi, and he returned to the United States in 1926. Settling in Boston, he joined the music staff of the local school system, while founding the Nassi music school and music publishing enterprise in Brockton. He reassumed leadership of the choirs of the Albanian Orthodox churches in Boston, Worcester, and Southbridge that he had founded earlier, and he introduced Western liturgical music and notation systems to the choir in the new church in Natick.

In 1929 Nassi and his family moved to Chatham, in Cape Cod, and in 1934 to Orleans, where he remained until his death. Until his retirement in 1949 Nassi and his wife, Olympia, supervised virtually the entire musical education of the rather isolated communities in the Lower Cape, comprising Provincetown, Truro, Wellfleet, Chatham, Eastham, Harwich, and Orleans. In addition to providing training from elementary school students on up, Nassi founded school musical ensembles, the regional Monomauset (high school) Orchestra (1930), the Cape Cod Community and Junior Community bands, choral societies and glee clubs, and the Cape Cod Philharmonic Orchestra, now named the Cape Cod Symphony. He directed regional Cape and New England youth festival orchestras and bands. He also established a publishing concern in Orleans for his original compositions and arrangements of music relating to Albania, including folk music he had collected in the Albanian countryside. He died in Orleans.

Nassi played a dual role as a music educator and popularizer in Albania and in the United States. He may be considered the father of the introduction of Western music to Albania after it gained its independence from Turkey in 1912. The one hundredth anniversary of his birth was celebrated nationally in Albania in 1992. Having pioneered music development in the Albanian-American community in Massachusetts (leaving a unique resource of musical compositions and arrangements), he and his family became the principal leaders and organizers of classical and community music activities in Cape Cod, Massachusetts. Nassi was at home in orchestral, choral, band, and folk music, in performance as well as in composition. His influence continues to be felt through the Cape Cod

Symphony. He had special gifts in the phenomenally efficient development of musical organizations.

• Nassi donated his papers and music to the Albanian National Archives before returning to the United States in 1926; the Albanian-American weekly newspaper, *Dielli*, is available in the Boston Public Library and Harvard University Library. Biographical information was provided by Carmen Nassi Bartlett, Nassi's daughter; the Very Reverend Arthur T. Liolin, chancellor of the Albanian Orthodox Archdiocese in America; and Eno Koço, London, England. Nassi's available published music includes (for voice and piano): *Hymni Flamurit* (The Flag Hymn), by Kristo Floqit, Cyprian Porumbescu, and Nassi (1918; 2d printing 1947); *Prapë Ardhi* (A Love Song), by Floqit and Nassi; *Malesore* (To the Mountain Girl), for tenor and male trio, by Floqit and Nassi; *Ender Dashurie*, by Nick Kreshpani and Nassi; *Kënga e Mullirit* (The Miller's Song), vocal quartet, by Remzi Qyteza and Nassi; and *O Moj Ti Me Syt'e Zinj* (Your Eyes Enchant Me), by Asdreni (Aleksander Stavre Drenova) and Nassi; (for flute [violin] and piano, based on folk songs collected and arranged by Nassi): *Fyelli i Bariut* (Shepherd's Flute); *Bilbili* (The Nightingale); *Katrë Valle: Salushe, Baraçe, E Hequr, Gajdë* (A Suite of Albanian Folk Dances); and *E Qarë* (Albanian Lament).

For biographical information see Thomas Nassi and Olympia Nassi, "Music on Lower Cape Cod," in program notes for the Central and Lower Cape School Symphony Orchestra Concert (the last under Nassi's direction) (1949); T. G. Nassi, speech delivered to Drita, the Albanian-American student organization at Harvard University, in 1960; repr. in *Dielli* 74, no. 7 (1983); E. Van Buren, "Looking Back: The First 25 Years, Part I: 1962–1982," in program notes for Cape Cod Symphony (1987); Ramadan Sokoli, *Shekuj* (Albanian Encyclopedia of the Arts), vol. 16 (1994); and M. W. Royse and Frank Manuell, eds., *The Albanian Struggle in the Old World and New* (1939). An obituary is in the *Cape Cod Standard Times*, 25 Dec. 1964; remembrances are reprinted in *Dielli* 74, no. 7 (1983).

FRANK T. MANHEIM

NAST, Condé (26 Mar. 1873–19 Sept. 1942), magazine publisher, was born Condé Montrose Nast in New York City, the son of William Frederick Nast, a speculator-inventor who never made much money, and Esther Ariadne Benoist. The family moved to St. Louis, his mother's birthplace, where Nast grew up attending public schools. A rich aunt favorably impressed by Nast financed his college education at Georgetown University in Washington, D.C. There he gained public relations experience raising money for the school's sports teams as the student president of the athletic association. He also became friends with Robert Collier, whose father was a New York publisher.

Nast completed his B.A. in 1894 and his M.A. in 1895, both at Georgetown University. In 1898 he earned a law degree at the St. Louis Law School of Washington University. Instead of pursuing a career in law, Nast worked for a time at improving the profitability of a printing press, a family investment that had not done well until Nast joined the venture. Success in this endeavor inspired his friend Collier, now chief of operations at *Collier's Weekly*, to offer Nast a job as advertising manager in 1900. Nast's strategies at *Collier's*

included ads aimed at affluent audiences and the use of color illustrations, and his work earned him a salary of $12 per week. Advertising income at *Collier's* grew from a few thousand dollars to more than a million dollars annually in 1905, at which time Nast was promoted to business manager. At the age of thirty-five he made $50,000 per year, an extravagant sum in those days.

Nast nevertheless resigned from his post at *Collier's* in 1907 to concentrate on another business he had cofounded, the Home Pattern Company, where he began convincing advertisers to include ads with dress patterns. This enterprise led Nast to believe there was a market for fashion news. In 1909 he purchased *Vogue*, a 24-page magazine that had been published with little success since 1892. Although the magazine was barely surviving at the time, its stockholders were among the wealthiest people in the nation. Nast hoped to use those connections to create a publication that would offer fashion advice to wealthy women. On 24 June 1909 *Vogue* began publication with Nast listed as president. Within fourteen years Nast turned *Vogue* into one of the world's leading fashion magazines.

Nast's success as a publisher was due in part to his wise choice of editors. He appointed Edna Woolman Chase to run *Vogue*, and the two were soon controlling fashions among rich women in the United States. Nast's goal of making a magazine that would appeal to the wealthy, instead of trying to attract a mass audience, was a success. His readership was comparatively small (in the 1920s circulation was approximately 137,000), but because they were so well-to-do, Nast could ask nearly five times the usual advertising rates. In spite of his success at *Vogue*, Nast felt a compulsion to expand his holdings. In 1913 he purchased two more magazines, *Dress* and *Vanity Fair*, combining the two and installing the creative and innovative Frank Crowninshield as editor of the new *Dress and Vanity Fair*. This sophisticated monthly, with the title soon shortened to *Vanity Fair*, focused on art, entertainment, literature, and society stories and introduced readers to avant-garde movements in art and literature.

Nast extended his holdings rapidly. In 1914 he opened the Vogue Pattern Company, and in 1915 he acquired *House and Garden* magazine, where he hired yet another very talented editor, Richardson Wright. During the next ten years the magazine doubled its audience. Nast created British and French editions of *Vogue* in 1916 and 1920, respectively. In 1921 he published *Jardin des Modes*, which was aimed at a less affluent, larger audience. Other foreign language versions of *Vogue* failed to pan out in South America and Germany. He had a printing plant constructed in 1921 at Greenwich, Connecticut, naming it Condé Nast Press, and by 1922 all of his companies were combined into Condé Nast Publications, Inc.

By the end of the 1920s Nast had invested heavily both in his publishing empire and in the stock market, so that when the stock market crashed in 1929 and the ensuing depression hit, his financial situation was seriously undermined. In addition to losses on investments in the stock market, annual income for Nast's publications fell from $10 million to practically half that amount between 1930 and 1933, and profits became significant losses. The value of his company's stock fell from more than $90 to less than $5 a share.

Thanks to assistance from Lord Camrose, a British press owner, Nast was able to continue operation of his company, but he never fully recovered financially. Nast was nevertheless still a leader in the magazine publishing business, introducing the use of color photography in his magazines in 1931. *Vanity Fair* became a casualty of the depression, however, as Nast was forced in 1936 to end publication of that magazine, which because Crowninshield put a higher priority on artistic quality than on appealing to advertisers had never been profitable. Some features of *Vanity Fairy* soon became part of *Vogue*. In 1939 Nast introduced *Glamour of Hollywood*, the only magazine he actually created from scratch. *Glamour* targeted young working women and was instantly popular.

Nast's personal life included some setbacks also, as both of his marriages ended in divorce. In 1902 he had married Jeanne Clarisse Coudert. Although they had two children, the couple separated in 1906. Still on friendly terms for many years, they formally ended the relationship with divorce in 1925. In 1928 Nast married Leslie Foster, who had worked for a time at *Vogue*; they had one daughter. Nast became increasingly uncomfortable in a marriage to a woman young enough to be his daughter, and within five years he sought another divorce.

One of Nast's great passions was entertaining, and his social life was highly publicized. He lived in a thirty-room Park Avenue penthouse, where he could entertain as many as 350 people simultaneously at three different parties. His social gatherings attracted some of the most wealthy and famous people of the day, including the Astors, Vanderbilts, and entertainer Groucho Marx. Paradoxically, while Nast loved these parties, he would seem aloof among his guests. However, his fondness for these events is demonstrated by the fact that even in the face of his financial troubles during the depression, he refused to give up his lavish penthouse and parties.

The strain of the struggle to repair his finances while maintaining his expensive social activities increasingly took a toll on Nast. He became more and more difficult to work with. Even long-term employees like Chase, editor of *Vogue* for years, found his temperamental behavior hard to endure. His health deteriorated, but although he suffered from a heart condition and a series of heart attacks he would not slow down his working schedule. In the fall of 1942, while visiting his twelve-year-old daughter at camp in Vermont, he hiked up a hill with her and suffered a serious heart attack. He died two weeks later in his New York City penthouse. After his death, *Time* commented on Nast's influence on the nation's culture, writing that Nast had turned an obscure fashion magazine purchased for nearly nothing into "a feminine bible of taste," so that "the best-dressed women in all U.S. towns were *Vogue* subscribers (28 Sept. 1942). Although he was still deeply in debt when he died, the magazines he made successful thrived long after his passing.

• Nast's papers are located at the Condé Nast Archives, at Condé Nast Publications, Inc., in New York City. Two book-length works about Nast and his publications are Caroline Seebohm, *The Man Who Was Vogue: The Life and Times of Condé Nast* (1982), and Edna Woolman Chase and Ilka Chase, *Always in Vogue* (1954). Edna Chase brings to this book the many years of personal experience with her employer. Edna Chase, "Fifty Years of *Vogue*," appeared in *Vogue*, 15 Nov. 1943, the year after Nast's death. Obituaries are in the *New York Times* and the *New York Herald Tribune*, both 20 Sept. 1942, and *Time*, 28 Sept. 1942.

ALAN KELLY

NAST, Thomas (30 Sept. 1840–7 Dec. 1902), political cartoonist, was born in Landau, Bavaria (now Germany), the son of Thomas Nast, a musician, and Apellonia Apres. In 1846 the family immigrated to the United States, settling in New York City. There Nast displayed sufficient artistic talent and potential to merit studying under Theodore Kaufman, a fellow German émigré who specialized in painting historical scenes. Impressed with Nast's work, Henry Carter (a.k.a. Frank Leslie) hired him as a staff artist for *Frank Leslie's Illustrated Newspaper* in 1855; there Nast developed the craft and style of using art as political and social commentary, both by illustrating stories and with cartoons. By 1858 he had become a freelance artist for *Harper's Weekly* and the *New York Illustrated News*; for the latter he prepared drawings of New York tenements and the funeral of John Brown, the martyred abolitionist. He traveled to Europe in 1860 on assignment for *Leslie's*, providing coverage of boxing in England and Garibaldi's campaigns in Italy. His work won him great renown. Upon his return to New York in 1861 he married Sarah Edwards, a cousin of the author James Parton. They had five children.

At the beginning of the Civil War, Nast provided sketches for the *News*, then for *Leslie's*. In 1862 he joined the staff of *Harper's Weekly*. Although the paper hoped to draw upon his experiences in Italy to prepare realistic portrayals of battle, Nast proved far more successful in presenting abstract images of the political issues at stake and the experience of the common soldier. Among his favorite subjects was Christmas in camp; Santa Claus made his inaugural appearance wearing the stars and stripes of the Union cause. Other illustrations connected campfires and home fires, playing upon domestic images. Abraham Lincoln remarked on Nast's effectiveness in inspiring readers to support the war effort. As Parton put it, "From a roving lad with a swift pencil for sale, he had become a patriot artist, burning with the enthusiasm of the time." Ulysses S. Grant went further, declaring: "He did as much as any man to preserve the Union and bring the war to an end" (Keller, p. 13).

Peace in 1865 did not still Nast's pen. His commentaries on Reconstruction advocated justice for blacks and questioned the wisdom of Andrew Johnson's leniency to former Confederates. By 1866 he had come out foursquare against the president. The following year he illustrated David Ross Locke's satirical commentaries on Johnson and the Democrats through the character Petroleum V. Nasby. In this work as well as in his contributions to *Harper's* he began to develop his talents as a caricaturist. In 1868 he turned his talents to electing Grant. The Republican Convention featured a painted Nast cartoon contrasting an empty "Democratic Podium" with Grant at the "Republican Podium." The caption "Match him!" served as the party's rallying cry during the campaign. In another particularly pointed cartoon, he contrasted the Union war hero with his opponent, Democrat Horatio Seymour, who as governor of New York had addressed draft rioters as "my friends."

Yet it was Nast's campaign against the Tweed Ring in New York City that won him the most notice as a cartoonist. Disgusted with the activities of William Marcy Tweed and his Democratic associates of Tammany Hall, Nast did much to publicize the extensive web of corruption, kickbacks, and abuse of power and public trust that sustained the ring. Tweed testified to Nast's effectiveness when he observed that while many of his constituents could not read, they could still understand "those damn pictures!" Failing to buy off Nast with the promise of a European tour, Tweed threatened to deny Harper & Bros. access to the lucrative textbook market, but the artist persisted. Fearing for his safety and that of his family, Nast moved to Morristown, New Jersey. With the defeat of the Tweed Ring in 1871, Nast tasted success. His portrayals of Tweed proved so vivid that when the boss sought exile in Spain, local authorities, interpreting a Nast cartoon of Tweed as evidence that he was wanted for kidnapping, arrested and extradited him to the United States in 1876.

Nast long supported the Republican party. His cartoons endorsing the Grant administration portrayed the president as a strong man devoted to the public good. His attacks on Grant's opponents, especially Carl Schurtz and Charles Sumner, proved so savagely effective that at one point the editor of *Harper's Weekly*, George William Curtis, asked him to ease up. Perhaps most devastating, however, was a series of cartoons attacking Horace Greeley, the Democratic candidate for president in 1872. Nast represented his running mate, B. Gratz Brown, as a tag hanging from Greeley's coat; other cartoons showed Greeley consorting with a host of tawdry and corrupt Democrats. Grant's opponent was led to remark that he was not sure whether he was running for president or for the penitentiary; his death not long after the election lent a bittersweet note to Nast's efforts. While other northerners retreated from Reconstruction, Nast reaffirmed the necessity of federal intervention to stop white supremacist terrorism in the South. He opposed inflationary monetary policy and the income tax while endorsing a strong national defense. Elsewhere he assailed the Catholic church, which he saw as attempting to violate the separation of church and state by using public funds to support sectarian schools and questioned the loyalty of Catholics to American institutions. These themes stood in marked contrast to his efforts to present the claims of Native Americans and Chinese immigrants to fair treatment.

The end of Reconstruction and the Grant presidency marked the beginning of Nast's declining influence. His disputes with the management of *Harper's* increased in frequency and intensity; rival cartoonists such as Joseph Keppler, whose works appeared in color in *Puck*, proved challenging competition. Deprived of the emotional issues of war and Reconstruction, Nast did what he could with the economic issues of the 1870s and 1880s, but they, like his commentary on presidents and major politicians, lacked punch and passion. Only in 1884, when the Republicans nominated James G. Blaine for president, did Nast rouse himself for one last effort, breaking with the party as he highlighted charges that Blaine was beholden to corrupt railroad interests.

Among Nast's most notable contributions to American popular art was his creation of lasting symbols. The best known was Santa Claus, who first appeared in 1862. Nast's Santa, a genial, rotund elf who distributed presents and good cheer, differed from the thin, ascetic precursors in European folklore, such as Père Noël or, in Bavaria, Pelze-Nicol. He became one of Nast's favorite subjects. To represent Tammany Hall, Nast seized upon the tiger's head used by Tweed and his associates as their emblem. In 1870 he devised the donkey to designate the Democrats, followed in 1874 with an elephant as the symbol of the Republican party.

Nast left *Harper's Weekly* in 1886. His efforts to establish his own weekly journal foundered in 1892. Financial troubles dogged him for several years after he lost his savings in the collapse of Grant and Ward in 1884. Cartooning gave way to oil painting, including a deeply researched portrayal of Robert E. Lee's surrender to Grant at the McLean parlor at Appomattox Court House. After veering toward the Democratic party in 1884, Nast returned to Republican ranks eight years later. In 1902 Theodore Roosevelt appointed him to a consulship in Guayaquil, Ecuador; not long after Nast arrived, he contracted yellow fever, died, and was buried there.

Nast's work marked an important transformation of political cartooning. Before the Civil War, cartoonists' work relied on dialogue rather than imagery. To Nast, the picture became the message: text commonly was relegated to a caption or appeared in the picture as a broadside. Many historians call him the father of modern American political cartooning. His work remains in the first rank of that genre, expressive and passionate.

• There is no central collection of Nast's papers. His work is available in runs of *Harper's Weekly* (1858–1886) and *Frank*

Leslie's Illustrated Newspaper (1855–1858). The New York Public Library contains three volumes of a "scrapbook" containing valuable material, as well as the "Catalogue of Thomas Nast's Grand Caricaturama." Albert Bigelow Paine, *Th. Nast: His Period and His Pictures* (1904), is an appreciative biography accompanied by wonderful illustrations, while J. Chal Vinson provides a more modern appraisal in *Thomas Nast: Political Cartoonist* (1967). Extremely useful are Morton Keller, *The Art and Politics of Thomas Nast* (1968), and Thomas Nast St. Hill, *Thomas Nast: Cartoons & Illustrations* (1974); both contain a good selection of Nast's work. Adam Gopnik, "The Man Who Invented Santa Claus," *New Yorker*, 15 Dec. 1997, pp. 84–102, is an informative account of Nast's life and career.

BROOKS D. SIMPSON

NAST, William (15 Jan. 1807–16 May 1899), Methodist clergyman and editor, was born in Stuttgart, Württemberg (now Germany), the son of Elizabeth Magdalene Ludovika Böhm and Johann Wilhelm Nast, merchants. He was baptized in the Lutheran church five days after birth, receiving his father's full name, but most historical references have Anglicized his name to William. Orphaned at the age of seventeen, he lived with his eldest sister, who had married a theologian, and it was assumed that he would pursue a ministerial career. After attending schools in Stuttgart and Baihingen-an-der-Enz, Nast began seminary studies in 1821 in Blaubeuren. Up to that point he had been strongly influenced by German Pietists and periodically experienced a deep sense of sin together with strong hopes for salvation. At the seminary, however, influences of a rationalistic, skeptical sort awaited him in the form of his roommate, David Friedrich Strauss. Wrestling with unresolved tensions between faith and reason, Nast turned away from the ministry and for a time (1825–1827) studied at the University of Tübingen. Thereafter, on the advice of his brother-in-law, he sought relief by traveling to the New World for a change of scene.

Nast arrived in the United States in 1828, still plagued with doubts and inner struggles over his spiritual condition. For several years he functioned as a private tutor near Harrisburg, Pennsylvania. In 1832 he became librarian and instructor in German at the U.S. Military Academy. Then, after a brief sojourn at the Lutheran College in Gettysburg, Pennsylvania, he worked in a commune run by fellow Württembergers, followers of George Rapp, in the town of Economy, situated in the same state. In 1835, with the aid of bishop Charles P. McIlvaine, he was appointed professor of Greek and Hebrew at Kenyon College in Gambier, Ohio. That same year he accompanied a friend to the local Methodist quarterly meeting and there finally experienced such a strong sense of religious uplift that he once again thought seriously of becoming a clergyman.

The German population was growing rapidly in Ohio, and Methodist leaders were eager to win the Germans to their church. So in 1835 the Methodists admitted Nast on trial as "missionary among the German immigrants in and near Cincinnati." This inaugurated a clerical career that flourished for a full six decades. In 1836 Nast married Margaret Eliza McDowell, forming a union that produced five children and lasted until Eliza's death sixty-two years later. Nast threw himself into evangelical activity, targeting German-speaking audiences as his special concern. He traveled an average of 300 miles per month, and his activities eventually took him from Ohio to Kentucky, Wisconsin, Illinois, Missouri, and Iowa. Nast preached, organized, and offered nurturing moral support to his flocks. The cumulative results of his missionary itinerancy qualified him for the title "Father of German Methodism."

The educational aspects of Methodist piety did not escape Nast's attention. In 1839 he began publishing *Der Christliche Apologete*, a German church paper that he edited for more than five decades, until 1892. Through this medium Nast influenced tens of thousands of German-Americans, keeping before them the issues of Teutonic culture in a new country, evangelical Christian experiences, and vigorous church life. From German sources he translated general introductions to Bible study, exegetical commentaries, and a defense of orthodox Christology. His own writings in German included a biography of John Wesley and his principal aides, songbooks for worship in his native tongue, and a catechism for basic doctrinal instruction. Some point to these efforts and call Nast the founder of German Methodist Christian literature in America. His concern for building churches and providing for elementary religious education reached a new level in 1863, when he helped establish German Wallace College in Berea, Ohio. He served as the first president of this institution, which originally existed as a department of Baldwin University, and remained nominal president for the rest of his life. In 1913 the two merged to form Baldwin-Wallace College. As the years progressed Nast continued to preach the certainty of salvation and faith, sometimes as much to reassure himself as to win over the uncommitted. This vital and persistent elder statesman maintained his efforts of both outreach and consolidation until his death at home in Cincinnati.

• One of Nast's titles in English indicates his main interest in publishing: *A Commentary of the Gospels of Matthew and Mark, Critical, Doctrinal, and Homiletical, Embodying for Popular Use and Edification the Results of German and English Exegetical Literature, and Designed to Meet the Difficulties of Modern Skepticism* (1864); another title is *The Gospel Records: Their Genuineness, Authenticity, Historical Verity, and Inspiration, with Some Preliminary Remarks on the Gospel History* (1866). Nast's biography of John Wesley is *Das Leben und Wirken des Johannes Wesley und seiner Haupt-Mitarbeiter* (1852). A useful biography is Carl F. Wittke, *William Nast: Patriarch of German Methodism* (1959). An obituary is in the *Cincinnati Enquirer*, 17 May 1899.

HENRY WARNER BOWDEN

NATHAN, George Jean (14 Feb. 1882–8 Apr. 1958), drama critic and editor, was born in Fort Wayne, Indiana, the son of Charles Narét-Nathan, a landowner and businessman, and Ella Nirdlinger. Nathan was raised in a well-to-do family with international connections and social prominence; his father, a world-traveler, had prominent relatives in Belgium and France, where he owned vineyards; his mother's family were among the founders of Fort Wayne. Members of the extended family had interests in the theater and journalism. After graduating from high school in Cleveland, Ohio, where the family had moved in 1888, Nathan attended Cornell (1900–1904). There he attained prominence of his own as editor of the campus newspaper and literary magazine and as an award-winning fencer. His midwestern upbringing was leavened with frequent summer excursions to Europe, and following his graduation he spent a year at the University of Bologna.

In 1905 Nathan's uncle Charles Frederic Nirdlinger, drama critic for the *New York Herald*, helped him become a reporter on the paper. He later served as third-string theater reviewer but was temperamentally unsuited to being either a reporter (he found fact-gathering tiresome and sometimes made up details and stories) or a daily reviewer. He particularly bridled at editors who encouraged only favorable reviews in order not to jeopardize advertising revenue. When the opportunity arose in 1906 to write for magazines, Nathan began what eventually became a fifty-year career during which he contributed to more than thirty periodicals, including *Harper's Weekly* (1908–1923), *Puck* (1912–1929), *Judge* (1922–1935), *Vanity Fair* (1930–1935), and *Esquire* (1935–1946). In the last decade of his life he returned to reviewing on the *New York Journal-American*.

In 1908 Nathan began an association with the *Smart Set*, the magazine with which his name is most closely connected, and his partnership with H. L. Mencken, another young critic recently hired to breathe life into the self-styled "magazine of cleverness." In 1914, after several changes in the editorship, Nathan was offered the job by the *Smart Set*'s new publisher, Eltinge F. Warner, but Nathan agreed only if he could share the position with Mencken. Between 1914 and 1923, the coeditors turned the perpetually struggling magazine into a *succès d'estime*, publishing writers who were to define the literary sensibility of the next generation including F. Scott Fitzgerald, Eugene O'Neill, Ben Hecht, and James Joyce. Not every issue of the *Smart Set* could boast of two of Joyce's *Dubliners* stories or one-act plays by O'Neill. In fact, the editors recognized the mediocrity of many of the contributions, but in its style and tone, set by Mencken, and Nathan's reviews and features pillorying the philistine taste of Americans, the magazine was influential beyond its modest circulation. During World War I Nathan and Mencken often went unpaid by the magazine's owner, but by launching several racy publications (*Parisienne*, *Saucy Stories*, and *Black Mask*) and selling their interests in them, they did well financially. Despite the work of editing several magazines simultaneously and contributing to other periodicals, both Mencken and Nathan pursued other projects individually and in col-

laboration. At the time he and Mencken left the *Smart Set* in 1923, Nathan had published nine collections of criticism.

By the early twenties, Mencken was looking to move beyond the *Smart Set* formula. With Alfred Knopf, he planned the launch of a new magazine that would be more socially and politically oriented. Nathan did not share Mencken's interest in politics but went along out of friendship and ultimately came up with the name for the new venture: the *American Mercury*. Like the *Smart Set*, the *Mercury* was a critical and cultural success, defining the tone of the 1920s by puncturing the pretensions of the "booboisie" in its relentless attack on puritanism and sham. It made its literary mark as well; but Nathan quickly tired of the politics, and Mencken became impatient with what he felt was Nathan's unwillingness to do his share of the editorial labors. Nathan resigned the editorship in late 1924 but continued as the regular drama critic until he sold his financial interest to Knopf and Mencken in 1929. The parting of the longtime collaborators was not amicable, and Mencken, according to one of his biographers, took petty revenge on Nathan by moving his desk into Knopf's secretarial pool and removing his name from the building directory.

Nathan's departure from the editorship of the *Mercury* did not hamper his reputation. His steady stream of critical essays and books continued, and he was at the height of his power as critic. With his elegant suits and his collection of overcoats (forty-eight by his count) and his walking stick, he was a flamboyant figure on the New York social scene, although he claimed not to care for society much. His abrupt departures from plays not to his liking became legendary, as did his verbal virtuosity and wit in skewering the mediocre and bad performances of many a popular play.

Nathan was one of the most prominent and prolific critics and editors of his time, known as much for his flamboyant personal style and acid wit as the content of what he wrote. Fellow critic John Mason Brown wrote that Nathan was "a dazzling showman, and what he wrote was often more entertaining than what he wrote about." Although his mode of "destructive criticism" was resented by many, he labored indefatigably to promote serious drama and expand the range of the American theater. His championing of Eugene O'Neill (whose mother was a school friend of Nathan's mother), J. M. Synge, Sean O'Casey, and William Saroyan as well as his encouragement of experimental theater were among his lasting accomplishments. The theater, for all of his unhappiness with the quality of much that was being produced, continued to fascinate and attract him, and he admitted to less than a highbrow taste in popular entertainment (although he despised movies). Some of his judgments have not held up well (he predicted that Noel Coward would suffer the fate of famous turn-of-the-century dramatist Clyde Fitch), but overall his essays and reviews were founded on a critical common sense and a firm belief in excellence; they bear rereading not only for their style but also for their picture of the American theater in the early to middle years of the twentieth century. His social commentary, as exemplified by *Autobiography of an Attitude* (1925) and *The New American Credo* (1927), reflects the tone and style of his association with Mencken and has not aged well.

The lure of magazine editing attracted Nathan to a new venture in the 1930s. As the *Mercury* slipped in prestige during the Great Depression, Nathan along with O'Neill, Theodore Dreiser, Ernest Boyd, and James Branch Cabell launched the *American Spectator*, a monthly "literary newspaper" designed to recapture the spirit of mockery and high spirits that the editors felt the *Mercury* had lost, but with more emphasis on the literary. Nathan and Boyd seem to have done the bulk of the work, and Dreiser, who soon dropped out, was replaced by Sherwood Anderson. An eclectic mixture of styles and subjects, the *Spectator* was dedicated to the "untrammeled expression of individual opinion," and the editors asserted that its lack of dogmatism and taboos convinced its opponents that the magazine championed "whatever cause they oppose." By 1935 Nathan announced that the fun of running a magazine had gone out of the enterprise, and he and his coeditors gave it up despite their claims of success. The magazine reappeared several months later, but after two changes of editors and format, it ceased publication in 1937.

In the 1940s Nathan resumed his association with the *Mercury* under the ownership of Lawrence Spivack (1941) and also launched a series of annuals under the general title *Theater Book of the Year*, which continued publication until 1951, when the onset of ill health began to reduce his capacity for work. A longtime bachelor, Nathan had many relationships with women, including a romance with Lillian Gish. He married actress Julie Haydon in 1955. For most of his life Nathan seems to have been troubled by his Jewish lineage, and he was a public skeptic about religion in general. He nonetheless accepted communion in the Roman Catholic Church shortly after his marriage and a few years before his death in his suite at the Royalton Hotel in New York, where he had lived for fifty years.

• Nathan's personal papers are in the Cornell University Library, and some of his letters are among the Mencken papers in the New York Public Library. The Billy Rose Theater Research Collection of the New York Public Library contains extensive files of clippings on Nathan. Biographical details can be found in two books of appreciation published during his life: Isaac Goldberg, *The Theater of George Jean Nathan* (1926), and Constance Frick, *The Dramatic Criticism of George Jean Nathan* (1943). Further details can be found in A. L. Lazarus's introduction to *A George Jean Nathan Reader* (1990) and in Carl Bode's *Mencken* (1969). Many of Nathan's forty books were reprinted by Fairleigh Dickinson University Press, which also published several collections of his correspondence with O'Neill and O'Casey. In addition to Lazarus's selection of pieces (which includes some of Nathan's correspondence), Alfred A. Knopf published *The World of George Jean Nathan*, ed. Charles Angoff (1952). Following his death, he was the subject of many appreciations by fellow critics and journalists; these include two in the *New York Times*, by John Mason Brown on 13 Apr. 1958 and by Brooks Atkinson on 27 Apr. 1958.

MARTIN GREEN

NATHAN, Maud (20 Oct. 1862–15 Dec. 1946), activist in Jewish and community organizations, was born in New York City, the daughter of Robert Weeks Nathan, a businessman, and Anne Augusta Florance. Maud grew up in an orthodox Sephardic Jewish environment. Prominent members of New York City's Spanish-Portuguese Jewish community, her father's family proudly dated its arrival to the colonies in 1773. Maud was educated in private schools until, at the age of twelve, her father suffered business reverses and the family moved to Green Bay, Wisconsin, where she completed public high school. In 1880 she married her cousin Frederick Nathan, a stockbroker; they had one child, who died at age eight. The couple settled in New York City.

By the 1880s, the New York City Jewish community had established an array of social service organizations, some of which addressed the problems facing the newly arriving Eastern European Jewish immigrants, while others served the established community's needs. During this period, Nathan volunteered to teach English to young immigrants at the Hebrew Free School Association and served as a director of Mount Sinai Hospital's Nursing School. When the National Council of Jewish Women was formed by Chicagoan Hannah G. Solomon in 1893, Nathan became an active member of the local chapter. Also, after her synagogue, Congregation Shearith Israel, created its sisterhood in New York City, Nathan became its president.

In her autobiography, *Once Upon a Time and Today* (1933), Nathan attributed her commitment to fighting for social justice and to active work in the community to her religious upbringing. Having grown up in a family that observed the Jewish Sabbath and the holiday rituals, she embraced Jewish principles, particularly the teachings of the prophets that emphasized social justice. Ever mindful of being a Jew in a Christian world, she believed that the Jewish commitment to righteousness blended well with the Christian emphasis on charity and social obligation. Therefore, it seemed perfectly appropriate to her to work in both the Jewish and Gentile communities for the social good.

Toward that end, Nathan also became one of the first members of New York City's Consumers' League, formed in 1891 to promote better conditions for workers. In 1897 she became the chapter president, remaining in that office for twenty-one years, and in 1898 she was elected to the National Consumers' League executive board. The league functioned as an educational group, creating a "white list" of merchants who treated workers well, and it engaged in legislative lobbying to improve wages and working conditions for women. In 1926 she published *Story of an*

Epoch-Making Movement, an account of the activities of the Consumers' League.

As a result of her observations of working conditions for women and children, Nathan also became an avid supporter of woman suffrage. She led the woman suffrage campaign of New York City's Fifteenth Assembly District and became a delegate to the 1913 convention of the International Women's Suffrage Alliance in Budapest. Besides urging all women to join the suffrage cause, she often spoke directly to Jewish women. At a 1915 symposium, she asked Jewish women to speak for women's right to vote, as the U.S. government was "the one government that gives to the Jew the equal chance. . . . There are thousands of Jewish women in the industrial world, [and] all of them should have something to say in the making of the laws that govern them."

Nathan was a very effective speaker and enjoyed the public forum. She also effectively used publicity stunts to convey her message; for example, she gave twenty-four speeches in one day from the backseat of an automobile during a woman suffrage campaign. Her work within the Jewish community prepared her for undertaking other organizational efforts by teaching her organizational skills, public speaking, grassroots organizing, and fundraising. She also drew upon her extensive contacts in the Jewish community to gain financial assistance for her work on behalf of Jewish organizations, the Consumers' League, and woman suffrage.

In all of her work, she remained committed to good works and to the view that women's volunteer activities can make a substantial difference. She also firmly believed in the ability of Jews and Christians to work together for the common good. She retired from active social work in the 1920s and lived comfortably into old age. She died in New York City.

• Nathan's papers can be found at the Schlesinger Library, Radcliffe College, Cambridge, Mass. For her role in the Consumers' League of New York City, see the league papers at Cornell University. For her role in the Jewish community, see Jacob Rader Marcus, *The American Jewish Woman: A Documentary History* (1981), and Linda Gordon Kuzmack, *Woman's Cause: The Jewish Woman's Movement in England and the United States, 1881–1933* (1990). An obituary is in the *New York Times*, 16 Dec. 1946.

JUNE SOCHEN

NATHAN, Robert Gruntal (2 Jan. 1894–25 May 1985), novelist, was born in New York City, the son of Harold Nathan and Sarah Gruntal. From a prominent New York family, his aunts were Annie Nathan Meyer, founder of Barnard College, and Maud Nathan, founder of the Consumer's League. Nathan attended public and private schools in the United States and Switzerland before entering Harvard University in 1912. There he was an editor of *Harvard Monthly*, in which his first stories and poems appeared.

In 1915 Nathan left Harvard before graduating to support himself and his new wife, Dorothy Michaels. They had one child (Nathan's only child) before divorcing in 1922. In 1930 he married Nancy Wilson; they divorced after six years. In 1936 he married Lucy Lee Hall Skelding; this marriage ended in divorce, as did one to Janet McMillen Bingham (1940) and one to Clara May Blum Burns (1951). In 1955 he married Shirley Keeland. After her death he married Joan Boniface Winnifrith (actress Anna Lee) in 1970.

Nathan concentrated on writing throughout his life, from his first novel *Peter Kindred*, a semiautobiographical, unsuccessful novel that came out in 1919, to *Heaven and Hell and the Megas Factor*, which appeared in 1975. The only two nonwriting jobs he held were as solicitor for a New York advertising firm from 1916 to 1918 and as a lecturer at the New York University School of Journalism (1924–1925). From 1943 to 1949 he worked as a screenwriter for Metro-Goldwyn-Mayer Studios writing screenplays for *The White Cliffs of Dover* (1944), *The Clock* (1945), and *Pagan Love Song* (1950). Four of his novels were also made into films, *The Enchanted Voyage* as *Wake Up and Dream* (1946), *The Bishop's Wife* (1947), *Portrait of Jennie* (1948), and *One More Spring* (1950).

Nathan served as vice president of the National Institute of Arts and Letters (1939); as a charter member and president of PEN (1940–1943); as chancellor of the Academy of American Poets; and as a board member of the Huntington Hartford Foundation. He received the Award of Honor from the California Writer's Guild. During World War II he held an appointment to the Advisory Council of the Writers War Board and received a silver medal from the U.S. Treasury Department.

In addition to novels and screenplays, Nathan also wrote poetry and music, often in collaboration with Walter Damrosch, director of the New York Symphony. Their chorale for baritone, male chorus and orchestra, *Dunkirk*, was first performed on 2 May 1943. Other works by Nathan are *Violin Sonata* and musical settings to the poems of Walt Whitman and A. E. Housman. Many of Nathan's own poems were set to music by collaborators such as Richard Hageman and Phillip James. Nathan also contributed short stories and poems to *New Yorker*, *Atlantic*, *Harper's*, *Scribner's*, *Century*, *Redbook*, and *Cosmopolitan*.

Nathan's best known work is *Portrait of Jennie*, a short fantasy about two lovers. The male is an artist who lives in a world of regular chronology, while the female's life moves on an entirely different plane. When they first magically meet, she is a young girl not from the artist's own time but from almost thirty years earlier. In the little over a year of their acquaintance, she ages rapidly to become nearly the same age as he.

Nathan's later works changed from light pastoral fantasies to darker, more biting satires. *Sir Henry* (1955) satirizes the knightly ideal, while *The Weans* (1960), a mock archaeological treatise, attacks American arrogance. The subject matter of *A Star in the Wind* (1962), a nonfantastic story about a young journalist covering the birth of the state of Israel, reflects Nathan's thinking about his own Jewish heritage. In *Stonecliff* (1967), an aging novelist manipulates a young critic to use him as a character in his current book. The novelist's attitude and methods strongly resemble Nathan's own creative approaches, yet they do not escape his satire.

Nathan's best work is known for its quiet, melancholic mood and its recurring theme of the power of love and faith to transcend differences, even those of time and space—as the artist and Jennie come together despite the different time periods in which they live in *Portrait of Jennie*. Influences on Nathan's work include James Branch Cabell, H. G. Wells, Jonathan Swift, Cervantes, and Anatole France. Stephen Vincent Benet, a friend of Nathan's from Greenwich Village days in the 1920s, called Nathan "one of our most individual and scrupulous artists." Because of its gentle spoofing, Nathan's work has often been called "whimsical," a term Nathan rejected because he felt it neglected the satire in his work: "I'm about as whimsical as a scorpion." Although at times his works slip into sentimentality, the best are works of fragile beauty which stir the heart. Nathan stated his own aims, "I have tried . . . to be a comforter in the world . . . to suggest the mystery and the magic."

Nathan died in his Hollywood, California, home of kidney failure.

• Nathan's personal papers and manuscripts are in the Beinecke Library at Yale University, which also has Dan H. Laurence's collection of Nathan materials. Clarence Kenneth Sandelin, *Robert Nathan* (1968), has some biographical information but is mainly a discussion of Nathan's work up until 1967. Dan H. Laurence, "Robert Nathan: Master of Fantasy," *Yale University Library Gazette* 37 (1962): 1–7; Pat Magarick, "The Sane and Gentle Novels of Robert Nathan," *American Book Collector* 23, no. 4 (1937): 15–17; and Francis Roberts, "Robert Nathan: Master of Fantasy and Fable," *Prairie Schooner* 40 (Winter 1966): 348–61. Nathan's obituary appeared in the *Los Angeles Times*, 26 May 1985.

ANN W. ENGAR

NATION, Carry (25 Nov. 1846–9 June 1911), temperance reformer, was born Carry Amelia Moore in Garrard County, Kentucky, the daughter of George Moore, a planter and stock trader, and Mary Campbell. Carry's mother was mentally unstable, refused to provide conventional parenting, and instead focused the family's attention on indulging her regal fantasies. This left Carry's father as the principal parental figure in her life, but devotion to her father produced its own tensions since George Moore was a slaveholder, the owner of the women and children among whom and in whose care Carry spent much of her childhood. When the Civil War broke out, Moore moved his slaves from Missouri to Texas to prolong their bondage for as long as possible. As a result of the conflict between her feelings for her father and her ties to his slaves, Nation developed a deep ambivalence on racial issues. She said she "never want[ed] to live where there are none of the negro [sic] race. I would feel lonesome without them." Nevertheless, Nation persisted in viewing her father as the kindest of slaveholders and advised African Americans against striving for social equality with

whites. This ambivalence no doubt contributed to her belief that "whiskey . . . is a worse evil than chattel slavery" (*The Use and Need of the Life of Carry A. Nation*, rev. ed. [1905], p. 29).

From bitter personal experience Nation came early to a realization of whiskey's dire effects. In 1867 she married Charles Gloyd, a physician who had boarded with her family. Having spent much of her early life as a semi-invalid because of a lingering intestinal disorder, Nation had had little formal education, and she was consequently much impressed by the apparent learning and cultivation of Dr. Gloyd. Gloyd, however, was a habitual drunkard and died within two years of their marriage, leaving Nation with an infant daughter; she also assumed responsibility for support of Gloyd's widowed mother. For a time she supported her daughter and mother-in-law through work as a teacher in Holden, Missouri. After being discharged from her position, the victim of a trustee's nepotism, she married (in 1877) David Nation, a lawyer, editor, and minister. The Nations, however, had little in common, and although the marriage lasted for years, it was apparently a loveless match, which finally ended when Carry's public career led her to neglect her wifely duties; David sued for divorce on grounds of desertion. They had no children. Carry's daughter by Gloyd, Charlien, during the 1880s developed a disfiguring illness whose treatment preoccupied her mother. Carry attributed her daughter's infirmities to Gloyd's excessive drinking.

After periods spent in Missouri and Texas, the Nations moved during the 1890s to Medicine Lodge, Kansas. There Carry Nation became active in the Woman's Christian Temperance Union (WCTU). Kansas had adopted prohibition in 1880 by constitutional amendment, but by the 1890s enforcement of prohibitory law was lagging. With the aid of other women Nation forced the saloons of Medicine Lodge to close through public demonstrations and social pressure. Such methods had been used by American temperance women in their communities since at least the 1850s, most notably during the great Women's Crusade of 1873–1874, which gave birth to the WCTU. Temperance women had less often employed violence; when they had, both their goals and the impact of their attacks had always been local. Either before or shortly after she began her onslaught against saloons, Nation conceived a more ambitious strategy that depended on the publicity that could be generated by even a short but sustained campaign of antisaloon violence. She later explained her rationale: "The smashing in Kansas was to arouse the people. If some ordinary means had been used, people would have heard and forgotten, but the 'strange act' demanded an explanation and the people wanted that, and they never will stop talking about this until the question is settled" (*Use and Need of the Life*, rev. ed. [1905], p. 126). In May 1900 she drove to Kiowa, Kansas, with a collection of stones wrapped in rags. These she used to attack three "joints." She then confronted the crowd attracted by her violence with the contradiction represented by the existence of the joints in a prohibition state. "I have destroyed three of your places of business," she said, "and if I have broken a statute of Kansas, put me in jail; if I am not a law-breaker your mayor and councilmen are" (*Use and Need of the Life*, rev. ed. [1905], p. 72). Returning unmolested to Medicine Lodge, she once again publicly explained her actions.

In December 1900 she launched her most famous attack, upon the opulent Hotel Carey bar in Wichita. She was jailed, but upon her release, undaunted, she advanced on the state capital. Through a confrontation with the governor, attacks on Topeka saloons, and an appearance before the state temperance convention, Nation galvanized Kansas's dry forces. Other women began to raid saloons across Kansas, while renewed prohibitionist pressure convinced state lawmakers first to defeat an antiprohibitionist offensive and then to tighten prohibitory legislation.

Nation's actions placed American prohibitionists in a potentially awkward position. Not only had most temperance folk long since put their faith in the power of law, but also both of the leading prohibitionist organizations, the Prohibition party and the Anti-Saloon League, had since the mid-1890s devoted their efforts to cultivating socially conservative adherents of the evangelical Protestant denominations. Civil disobedience such as Nation's exposed prohibitionists both to charges of hypocrisy in their professions of devotion to legal means and to accusations of hooliganism. Another important element affecting prohibitionists' situation was the death in 1898 of their subtle, ingenious, and charismatic leader, Frances Willard. With Willard gone, male prohibitionists were reevaluating the support for women's rights that the WCTU under her leadership had extracted from them. Nation justified her forays against saloons not only on the grounds of their illegality, but also as a response to women's sufferings from the operation of the liquor traffic. Furthermore, she was acutely conscious of the politics of gender. Addressing the Kansas legislature, she stated: "You refused me the vote and I had to use a rock" (quoted in Bader, p. 147). The antiprohibitionist press moved swiftly to distort Nation's image into a combination of deranged virago and hayseed outlaw, the former a standard journalistic treatment for suffragists, the latter drawing on the caricatures of the Populists that had been elaborated by conservative newspapers only a few years before. Employed at a time when the prohibition movement was weak, the strategy worked to alienate Nation from her potential allies. Nation's sense of divine mission, which often made her intolerant of differing views, only increased the distance created by the conservative press between Nation and other prohibitionists. Although she received occasional rhetorical approval and formed brief local alliances, her dream of a new, more militant, determined, and inclusive women's temperance movement attracted little support.

Lost in the newspaper cartoons was another Carry Nation. She was described by a prohibitionist colleague:

She fears no man, counts no cost, asks no quarter and gives none to friend or foe; always in a good humor, never unhinged or nonplussed. She relies on God for her strength. She has no plans or schemes. She is simple as a child, yet well educated and thoroughly posted in the Bible and most all questions of the day. The flash of her dark brown eyes, the beaming smile that generally plays over her countenance, the sweet, musical, soft voice, with the peculiar southern accent and the bright fire of zeal and deep earnestness, when once warmed up on her favorite subjects, all have an overmastering influence over men and women, whether privately or publicly, that no artist can paint nor pen describe (*Northwestern Mail* [Madison, Wis.], 28 Feb. 1901).

During the remaining years before her death, she supported herself by lecture tours, selling her autobiography and small souvenir hatchets commemorative of one of the weapons used in her attacks on saloons. Eventually she took her temperance and antismoking lectures to the vaudeville circuit, justifying her appearances there as an attempt to reach an audience, even a hostile one, wherever it might be found. She lived frugally and spent part of what she earned on the lecture circuit to build in Kansas City, Missouri, a home for drunkards' wives and mothers. In 1905 she moved to Guthrie, Oklahoma Territory, and in 1909 to Boone County, Arkansas. Two years later she collapsed during a lecture and died at a hospital in Leavenworth, Kansas.

Carry Nation's efforts helped to maintain prohibition in Kansas and later to bring Oklahoma into statehood under prohibition. In the end, however, Nation's enemies probably benefited more than her friends from her brief, spectacular appearance on the public scene. The image of Carry Nation created by the conservative press provided a means of marginalizing the issues Nation championed. When the prohibition movement revived, it did so under Anti-Saloon League leadership as a single-issue, hierarchically organized political lobby controlled by men. Such a movement had little interest in challenging the representation of women's grass-roots temperance activity as emotionally driven, explosive, and violent. Although it has been rebutted by historians, that stereotype survives in the popular mind.

• The Kansas State Historical Society in Topeka holds a collection containing clippings, correspondence, and a bibliography. The best source is Carry Nation's autobiography, *The Use and Need of the Life of Carry A. Nation,* first published in 1904 and then in subsequent editions. Copies are extant of two of the three newspapers she edited, the *Smasher's Mail* and the *Hatchet.* Nation has been the subject of three biographies: Herbert Asbury, *Carry Nation* (1929); Carleton Beals, *Cyclone Carry* (1962); and Robert Lewis Taylor, *Vessel of Wrath* (1966). All are popular treatments that emphasize the dramatic events of her life, and none evinces sympathy or places her career in an appropriate historical context. The best recent interpretation is in Robert Bader, *Prohibition in Kansas* (1986).

JACK S. BLOCKER, JR.

NATWICK, Grim (16 Aug. 1890–7 Oct. 1990), film animator, was born Myron Natwick in Wisconsin Rapids, Wisconsin. He earned his nickname for his solemnity and the determination he brought to his work. Natwick studied art at the Chicago Institute of Art and the National Academy of Design in New York. A friend from art school introduced him to animation, and his first job was at the William Randolph Hearst Studio, working under the supervision of Gregory La Cava. After one year of this work, Natwick quit and moved to Vienna to study at the Vienna National Academy. He studied in Vienna from 1925 to 1928; there his style was heavily influenced by Gustav Klimt and Egon Schiele. He had gone to Vienna to become a serious artist, but after receiving his certificate, Natwick returned to New York, where he was hired by the Fleisher studio to do animated films. His early animations include "Krazy Kat," with Bill Nolan, and "Song Car-Tunes."

The hit song "Boop-Boop-A-Doop," by Helen Kane, inspired one of Natwick's most famous creations, the musical cartoon character, Betty Boop. First appearing in 1930 as movies with sound began to appear, Boop was instantly immensely popular. Her miniskirt, appearing decades before the fashion became a vogue, and her suggestive sexual persona made her the first cartoon character to be censored by Hollywood. Natwick described her evolution from a dog into a girl: "She started out as a little dog with long ears, but the rest of her was extremely feminine and she did a rather swinging dance in the first picture which no dog could have done, so after a few pictures the long ears developed into earrings and she was nothing but a cute little girl" (Canemaker, p. 58). Boop later reappeared in the 1988 hit movie *Who Framed Roger Rabbit?* After a three-year stint working at Ub Iwerks studio, Natwick was hired by Walt Disney in 1934. His early work with Disney included segments of the movies *Mickey's Fire Brigade* (1935), *Musicland* (1935), *Cookie Carnival* (1935), *Alpine Climbers* (1936), *Mickey's Polo Game* (1936), and *Mother Goose Goes Hollywood* (1938). The art classes that Disney sponsored for its animators, which included talks by Rico LeBrun, Jean Charlotte, and Frank Churchill, further refined Natwick's technical skill. Natwick was largely responsible for the character of Snow White in the Disney movie of the same title, animating eighty-four scenes, or roughly one-tenth of the entire film. After four years at Disney, Natwick returned to Fleisher studios. There he worked on one of the first feature-length cartoons, *Gulliver's Travels* (1939), animating the character of Princess Glory.

After World War II, Natwick joined the newly formed United Productions of America (UPA), a small group of former Disney artists. His work at UPA includes *Trouble Indemnity* (1950), *Willie the Kid* (1952), *Gerald McBoing Boing* (1950), and *Rooty Toot-Toot* (1952), which featured Natwick's creation, the curvaceous Nelly Bly. Natwick retired in 1968, intending to return to oil painting. However, he came out of retirement in 1973 to deliver a lecture series on animation at Dick Williams's London studio. While there he became interested in Williams's current project, the feature cartoon *The Cobbler and the Thief* (1981), and he took on responsibility for the animation of one of its characters, the Mad Holy Old Witch. Natwick never married but had one daughter. He died in Santa Monica, California.

One of the most innovative and important American film animators, Natwick is remarkable both for his range of inventiveness and the sheer volume of work he produced. His animations are noted for the fluidity of their movements. Natwick attributed this to his interest in sports: "I notice that, among animators, there are either former athletes or athletic devotees. There's a physical feeling in animation. When I animate a scene I feel I know it perfectly. When I make one drawing I know exactly how that figure feels. I know exactly how it feels to stretch that leg forward and then I know how those 'in-betweens' are going to feel" (Canemaker, p. 58). He was also especially noted for his skill in drawing female characters, the best known of which were Betty Boop, Snow White, and Princess Glory.

• Little biographical information on Natwick exists, but articles on the animator appear in John Canemaker, "Grim Natwick," *Film Comment* (Jan. 1975) and *Annual Obituary*, 1990.

ELIZABETH ZOE VICARY

NAVARRE, Pierre (28 Mar. 1790?–20 Mar. 1874), fur trader and military scout, was born in Detroit, Michigan, the son of François Utreau Navarre and Marie Louise Godet. Pierre (also known as Peter) was of French descent. His grandfather Robert Navarre, an officer in the French army, was a pioneer settler of Detroit and author of "Journal of the Conspiracy of Pontiac" (later published as *Journal of Pontiac's Conspiracy 1763*, ed. R. Clyde Ford [1910]), which has provided historians with valuable insights into the 1763 Indian uprisings. The Navarre family resettled on the River Raisin south of Detroit during Pierre's childhood. He moved in 1807 to the mouth of the Maumee River, where he built, with his brother Robert, a cabin near an Ottawa village where the widow and son of Pontiac resided. As a young man, Navarre, fluent in Potawatomi and conversant in several other Indian dialects, made his living as a fur trader. His trading activities in the early years of his career were centered around Fort Wayne. His brothers also entered the Indian trade. The treaty signed by the Ottawa and the federal government in 1833 included a provision allocating 800 acres of former Ottawa land to the Navarre family, with the explanation that "the said Jacques, Robert, Peter, Antoine, Francis and Alexis Navarre have long resided among these Aborigines, intermarried with them, and been valuable friends."

As a trader, Navarre formed a close association with the Miami chief Little Turtle. After the outbreak of hostilities between the United States and England in 1812, he sought to arrange an alliance between the Miami and the United States but was rebuffed by General

William Hull. The Miami fought on the British side. With three of his brothers—Robert, Alexis, and Jacques—Navarre joined Hull's army. The brothers were taken prisoner when Hull surrendered Detroit but were later paroled. They broke their paroles by volunteering as scouts in General James Winchester's army. It is said that the British commander, General Henry Proctor, placed a £200 bounty on Navarre's head. Navarre provided invaluable service to the American cause as a courier for General William Henry Harrison. On 5 August 1813 he carried a message from Admiral Oliver Hazard Perry at Port Clinton to Harrison at Fort Meigs that led to the crucial reinforcement of Perry's forces. On 9 September, disguised as an Indian, Navarre crossed the British lines to deliver a fateful message to Perry from Harrison that impelled the latter to engage the enemy in the battle of Lake Erie. Navarre also participated in the battle of the Thames and later claimed to be Tecumseh's killer.

After the war, Navarre resumed his work as a fur trader, but he quarreled with his employers and took up farming at his cabin on the Maumee. Navarre was married three times. With his first wife, Catherine Susor, he had one child. In 1825 Navarre, probably a widower, married Geneveva Robert; they had one child who lived only two days. Geneveva died in 1827. Navarre's third wife was Catherine Bourdeau, with whom he had two sons. Property and tax records suggest the Navarres were not particularly prosperous, but he did enjoy the esteem of his fellow Toledans. Greatly in demand as a raconteur, Navarre's vivid stories of his military service were a mainstay of the meetings of the Maumee Valley Pioneer Association, an organization that he headed for several years. While Navarre particularly enjoyed recounting his heroic nighttime trek in a torrential downpour from Fort Meigs to Fort Stephenson and back bearing dispatches for General Harrison, the greatest historical interest attaches to his eyewitness account of the death of Tecumseh. Navarre insisted that Richard Mentor Johnson did not kill the chief; in some versions he claimed that he had fired the fatal shot to protect Johnson. In 1863 Navarre told historian Lyman C. Draper that, at the time of his death, Tecumseh "was standing behind a tree that had been blown down, and was killed by a ball that past diagonally through his chest. After his death he was shot several times, but otherwise his body was not mutilated in the least, being buried in his regimentals, as the old chief desired, by myself and a companion, at the command of General Harrison. All statements that he was scalped are absolutely false." Historians have ridiculed Navarre's claim that Tecumseh was buried in British regimental garb, doubt his boast that he was Tecumseh's killer, generally accept his testimony about the state of Tecumseh's corpse, and do not know whether he was part of a burial party or not. Navarre's credibility is undermined by his patently false assertion that he was closely acquainted with Tecumseh.

A colorful character, immortalized in W. H. Machen's often reproduced portrait that shows Navarre in the garb of a forest scout, this pioneer son of the frontier spent his waning years embellishing his memories of a heroic youth. He may have exaggerated his age, for while he claimed to have been born in 1785, other evidence suggests that he was five years younger. Originally denied a military pension because of the absence of documentary evidence of his enlistment, Navarre was granted a stipend of eight dollars a month for life by special act of Congress in 1864. Impoverished in his old age, Navarre died in Toledo and was buried in an unmarked grave at Mount Carmel Cemetery. A monument honoring Peter and Robert Navarre was erected at Navarre Park in East Toledo in 1914. A cabin built by Navarre's sons late in his life also became his monument. Moved to Navarre Park in 1922, it was twice relocated, first to the Toledo Zoo in 1957, and more recently it was installed as part of a frontier life exhibit at the Toledo Botanical Gardens. The Navarres are still remembered and honored as early Toledo pioneers.

• Navarre's account of the death of Tecumseh is in the Draper manuscripts, State Historical Society of Wisconsin. On his family background, see Christian Denissen, *Navarre; or, Researches after the Descendants of Robert Navarre* (1879) and *Genealogy of the French Families of the Detroit River Region* (1987). On Navarre's career, the following are useful: H. L. Hosmer, *Early History of the Maumee Valley* (1858); Clark Waggoner, *History of the City of Toledo and Lucas County, Ohio* (1888); Charles Elihu Slocum, *History of the Maumee River Basin* (1905); John Sugden, *Tecumseh's Last Stand* (1985); and Larry R. Michaels, *East Side Story: People and Places in the History of East Toledo* (1993).

ALFRED A. CAVE

NAVARRO, Fats (24 Sept. 1923–7 July 1950), jazz trumpeter, was born Theodore Navarro in Key West, Florida. Little is known of his parents, though reference is made to the fact that his father was a barber and to his Cuban, African-American, and Chinese antecedents. As a child, Navarro had piano lessons, but then switched to trumpet and tenor saxophone. While still in high school in Key West he began to play professionally on the tenor saxophone, before switching definitively to trumpet. On his graduation in 1941, he joined Sol Allbright's band on the road, traveling north to Cincinnati, where he took some formal lessons on trumpet. Later that year he joined Snookum Russell's band in Indianapolis, with whom he traveled around the Midwest for almost two years. His main influences on trumpet until that time had been his third cousin Charlie Shavers and then, more significantly, Roy Eldridge, the harmonic link between Louis Armstrong and the beboppers of the 1940s.

In late 1943 Navarro joined Andy Kirk's band, and the presence of Howard McGhee in the trumpet section brought a bebop influence to his playing. His first recordings were with Kirk, but they included no solos of note. In 1944, while the Kirk band was in New York, Navarro sat in at Minton's (sometimes referred to as "the bebop laboratory") and was noted by at least one critic (Leonard Feather) for his solo work with the band at the Apollo Theater. In January 1945 he replaced Dizzy Gillespie, who was by then a significant influence on him, in Billy Eckstine's band. At that time this was the most modern and influential big band, having had several notable members besides Gillespie, including Charlie Parker, Dexter Gordon, and Art Blakey.

In June 1946 Navarro left Eckstine, choosing to spend the remainder of his brief career in small groups (except for a brief stint with Lionel Hampton in 1948) primarily in the New York area. He acquired the nickname "Fats" or "Fat Girl" because of his weight, cherubic face, and high voice. Navarro married Rena Clark sometime in the late 1940s and had one daughter. He died in New York City, of tuberculosis complicated by heroin addiction.

A few recorded solos with the Eckstine band exist, but most of Navarro's work is in the small-band format favored by the beboppers; he made more than 100 recordings primarily as a sideman with groups led by Bud Powell, Charlie Parker, Tadd Dameron, Kenny Clarke, Coleman Hawkins, and Dexter Gordon, among others. A small number of these recordings are compositions by Navarro himself.

Navarro had a highly individual style, and was, along with Gillespie, one of the leading bebop trumpeters of the 1940s. He had a big, beautiful sound, quite different from Gillespie's, and though he had a wide range (concert Fs above high C appear regularly in his solos), he exploited the upper register less than Gillespie. Very long, clearly articulated phrases and a strong sense of swing characterize his style. In these respects and in his general fluency Navarro was a significant influence on, most importantly, Clifford Brown, among many others. According to Gillespie himself quoted in an obituary by George Simon in *Metronome* (Oct. 1950), Navarro was "the best all-around trumpeter of them all. He had everything a trumpeter should have: tone, ideas, execution, and reading ability."

• Navarro can be heard to good advantage on *The Fabulous Fats Navarro* (2 vols., 1947–1949); "Wail" (Bud Powell Quintet, 1949), with its long phrases and evidence of the influence of Charlie Parker; "Lady Bird" (Tadd Dameron Septet, 1948); *One Night in Birdland* (1950?); and live with Parker on "Street Beat" (1950?). No full-length biography exists, though there is a discography by M. Ruppli in *Discographical Forum* (c. 1979–1982): no. 42, pp. 4–6; no. 43, pp. 7–8; no. 44, pp. 3–6; and no. 45, pp. 11–13. An early appreciation by B. Ulanov, *Metronome*, Nov. 1947, pp. 19, 38–39; and articles by G. Hoefer, *Down Beat*, 27 Jan. 1966, p. 16, J. Burns, *Jazz Journal* (May 1968): 12, R. Russell, *Down Beat*, 19 Feb. 1970, pp. 14–16, 33, and W. Balliett, *New Yorker*, 12 June 1978, pp. 116–19. See also I. Gitler, *Jazz Masters of the Forties* (1966), pp. 97–102.

HOWARD BROFSKY

NAVIN, Frank (18 Apr. 1871–13 Nov. 1935), baseball team owner, was born Francis Navin in Adrian, Michigan, the son of Thomas Mack Navin and Eliza Crotty. His Irish-born father, who worked as a carpenter before becoming a railroad worker, instilled a strict moral code. Navin never smoked or drank, but he acquired a lifelong passion for gambling. While visiting in Detroit in 1887, Navin was swept up in baseball enthusiasm as the Detroit Wolverines, the city's National League team, won a championship. He became a passionate fan and retained his interest in baseball even after 1889, when Detroit lost its National League franchise.

Influenced by his brother Thomas, he settled in Detroit and studied law, graduating from the Detroit College of Law in 1897, but he chose not to become an attorney. In 1898 he married Grace M. Shaw; they did not have children. Thomas, a prominent Michigan Republican, persuaded him to run in Detroit for justice of the peace. His defeat at the polls and his brother's subsequent imprisonment for embezzlement drove Navin out of politics. He found employment in a gambling establishment, where he worked evenings. During the day he was an accountant for Sam Angus, who owned an insurance company and was principle stock holder in the Detroit Tigers, a franchise in the fledgling American League. Navin became the accountant for the baseball team.

In 1904, when Angus went bankrupt, Navin persuaded William Yawkey, scion of a wealthy Michigan family, to purchase the Tigers. Navin acquired $5,000 worth of stock in the team. Some shares he bought with money won in a card game; the remainder was given to him by Yawkey. Navin believed that the ball club should be a profitable affair and clashed with Ed Barrow, the manager and general manager, who wanted to spend Yawkey's money lavishly to build a winning team. Navin gained Yawkey's confidence, forced Barrow to resign at the end of the 1904 season, and assumed his responsibilities as general manager. Navin gave gifts of money to sportswriters and expected them to write favorably about the Tigers; they also were expected "to paste" players who made unreasonable contract demands. By resisting pressure to trade the tempestuous, young Ty Cobb, and by hiring Hughie Jennings as manager, Navin was the architect of the pennant-winning teams of 1907, 1908, and 1909.

During the pennant years a grateful Yawkey gave half the club to Navin, and later sold 25 percent to John Kelsey, an automotive executive. Despite the Tigers' success on the field, the club was only marginally profitable because the city did not allow Sunday baseball. In 1903, while working as a bookmaker in a gambling establishment, Navin took a $500 bet on a horse, which won, at 3 to 1 odds. When Frank Croul, who had placed the bet, went to collect his $1,500 winnings, which equaled the annual salary of a star baseball player, Navin returned the $500 wager, claiming that the bet was made too late. Croul was a politically prominent figure, and knowing that Sunday baseball would be a financial windfall for Navin he used his influence to prohibit it. Croul became police commissioner in 1909 and in 1910 obliged Navin to make substantial contributions to Detroit charities in return for Sunday baseball. As a result of the restriction being lifted, attendance improved, and Navin tore down the wooden Bennett Park and built Navin Field, a steel-and-concrete structure that was completed in 1912. Some Detroiters resented the new stadium being named after a professional gambler with a shady reputation. The ballpark, however, continued to bear his name until a few years after his death, when it became Briggs Stadium.

In 1920 Yawkey died, and Walter Briggs, a Detroit industrialist, purchased Yawkey's 25 percent of the club. Attendance during the sports boom of the generally prosperous 1920s skyrocketed, rising to more than one million fans in 1924. Detroit became one of the best franchises in baseball, but during the twenties the Tigers did not win a championship. Navin, who became rich from the ball club, was reluctant to allow games to be broadcast on radio. He relented when Malcolm Bingay, a prominent local journalist, convinced him that it would help attendance. Critics blamed Navin's frugal policies and Ty Cobb's inept field management for the team's also-ran finishes. Navin enjoyed a good salary and substantial profits while he kept players' salaries low. His disputes with Cobb over salary were long-running and acrimonious. In 1908 Navin resisted demands for a contract that guaranteed Cobb's salary in case of injury. At the end of his career, in 1926, Cobb claimed that Navin cheated him out of a $10,000 bonus.

From 1921 to 1935 Navin was the chief adviser to Kenesaw Mountain Landis, the commissioner of baseball. He also was one of Detroit's most prominent citizens and supported many charities. He knew many industrialists and belonged to eight clubs. He went horseback riding every day and owned six race horses.

In 1931 Navin was nearly ruined by the depression and by losing bets on horse races. He lacked funds to take the team to spring training. Briggs, who had acquired Kelsey's interest, purchased some of Navin's shares and became majority stockholder. Unlike Navin, he drew no salary and took no money from the profits. Spending liberally, he built the championship teams of 1934 and 1935 and helped restore Navin's finances. Navin died in Detroit a month after the Tigers won its first world series in 1935.

Navin, who developed a poker face while working as a croupier, was generally considered cold and calculating. His letters to players, despite some good advice about fast living, were cynical. He liked "to let them know where to get off." His intimate friends, however, saw a compassionate man with a fine sense of humor and a genuine instinct for generosity.

• Navin's letters are in the *Detroit Baseball Club Letterbooks* (12 vols., 1900–1912), Ernie Harwell Collection, Detroit Public Library. For accounts of Navin and the Tigers, see Malcolm Wallace Bingay, *Detroit Is My Home Town* (1951) and *Of Me I Sing* (1949); *Detroit News*, 1905–1935, especially 13 Nov. 1935; Frederick G. Lieb, *The Detroit Tigers* (1946); John L. Lodge, *I Remember Detroit* (1949); Hank Greenberg, *Hank Greenberg—The Story of My Life*, ed. Ira Berkow

(1989); and Ty Cobb with Al Stump, *My Life in Baseball: The True Record* (1961). For family background, see *Browns' City Directory of Adrian, Michigan* (1870).

ANTHONY J. PAPALAS

NAZIMOVA, Alla (4 June 1878–13 July 1945), actress, was born in Yalta, Russian Crimea, daughter of Jewish parents Jacob Leventon, a pharmacist, and Sophia Harvit. After a boarding school education, at seventeen she entered the dramatic academy of the Philharmonic Society of Moscow. Upon graduation in 1898, she studied with Stanislavsky as an apprentice at the Moscow Art Theatre. A marriage at the age of twenty to fellow actor Sergei Golovin did not endure but could not be ended because there was no divorce law in prerevolutionary Russia. They had no children.

The young actress took the stage name of Nazimova. Ambitious to become a leading actress, she decided to forego years of small parts with the Moscow Art Theatre; instead, she went to provincial companies where she could play more important parts. In the next few seasons, she played dozens of roles, advancing to leads in St. Petersburg. For the 1903–1904 season she joined the company of Pavel Orlienieff, a well-known actor-manager later known in the United States as Paul Orleneff. It was a time of political tension in Russia. When Orleneff's production of *The Chosen People*, a pro-Jewish play, was interdicted by government censors, he decided to take a company of Russian actors abroad, where the play could be staged. Nazimova, by this time involved personally with Orleneff to the point that it was assumed they were married, went with him.

After appearances in London and Berlin, Nazimova played Lia in *The Chosen People* in New York in March 1905. The troupe, playing in Russian at a theater far from Broadway, was well received critically; financially the engagement was not a success, and Orleneff decided to return with his troupe to Russia. Nazimova's powerful stage personality had, however, gained the attention of the Shuberts, New York producers who saw her as a potential star. She elected to stay in New York, signed with the Shuberts, and by intense study learned English well enough that in November 1906 she could appear in an English-language production of *Hedda Gabler*.

Other actresses had played Hedda in New York previously, but Nazimova brought to the role a new interpretation on the basis of her Stanislavskian training in naturalistic acting. The *New York Dramatic News* said, "Her conception of the heroine was so entirely contrary to the treatment given by Mrs. Campbell, Mrs. Fiske and others that it was almost like witnessing a new play" (24 Nov. 1906). The effect on the audience was electric: "many of the professional stars in the audience sat up straight and glared at the woman with such astonishment as to make all of us believe that here was a revelation." Nazimova next appeared as Nora in *A Doll's House* (1907), and admiring audiences could hardly believe this was the same woman who had portrayed Hedda. At that time, major dramatic actresses had a style and image that they maintained from play to play. Such versatility as Nazimova showed was a sensation in that day. Almost overnight she became a major star, referred to as "Mme. Nazimova" or simply "Nazimova."

Nazimova's career suffered from the lack of any government-sponsored art theater in the United States to underwrite productions of classic dramas for a discerning, if limited, audience. The Shuberts, facing the realities of a commercial theater, put her into vehicles of broader commercial appeal to mass audiences, with titles like *The Comtesse Coquette*. In such roles as these, she toured for several years, alternating them with appearances in various Ibsen plays. In 1911 she went under the management of leading producer Charles Frohman, in hopes of better luck as an artist with him, but with no better results. He starred her in *Bella Donna* (1912), a lurid melodrama of a husband poisoner. In 1912 she announced her marriage to Charles Bryant, an actor in the *Bella Donna* company.

By that time, Nazimova's reputation as an actress of high art was sadly tarnished by the exaggerated performances such starring vehicles called for. Her extreme bodily postures (which a *Green Book* writer in March 1912 called "draping herself over the parlor furniture"), her exotic airs, and her heavily accented declamations, were derided. Her tour in *Bella Donna*, though commercially successful, gained critical sneers: "[Her performance was] in some ways on the worst level of American dramatic art . . . It is heartbreaking to compare the Nazimova of today with the Nazimova of six years ago" (*Boston Transcript*, 25 Nov. 1913); and "What she gives us are the externals of her art, without any of the enlivening spirit which made notable some of her past roles" (*Philadelphia Inquirer*, 13 Dec. 1913).

Like other dimming stars of the time, Nazimova next went into vaudeville in dramatic sketches. One of these, a one-act drama titled *War Brides* (1915), was a great success, and its expanded film version (1916) opened to her a new career in motion pictures. In a highly emotional portrayal, she played a European war widow who sees other women of her family and village being widowed and kills herself as a protest against the endless toll of war. It fit precisely with the antiwar, anti-German sentiment of the United States at the time and won high praise both for its message and its art. It showed, furthermore, that here was a stage star who could play to the camera. The *New York Times* review noted: "Her marvelously mobile face, capable of indicating varying shades of emotion, especially those of sorrow, is a priceless asset for the dumb show of the screen" (13 Nov. 1916).

After returning to Broadway in a dual role in *'Ception Shoals* (1917) and performing in a repertory of Ibsen and Chekhov plays in 1918, Nazimova entered into a motion picture contract with the Metro Company. In Dewitt Bodeen's words, "It was an extraordinary contract which allowed her her own production unit as well as approval of all stories, directors, and casts." That meant that she could use Charles Bryant

recurrently as leading man or director. Also, it paid her $13,000 a week. But the studio was paying for the actress of the commercial theatrical vehicles, the exotic and emotionally intense woman with the air of a femme fatale, not for the superb actress of classic European dramas. Bodeen notes that "the studio [in the contract] allowed itself loopholes which would curtail her doing Ibsen and Chekhov on the screen."

Nazimova's years in Hollywood might be called a gilded imprisonment. She lived splendidly on an estate she called "The Garden of Alla." (It later became a chic Hollywood hotel called The Garden of Allah.) She entertained the notables who flocked to the film capital. But the artistic cost was high. Metro wanted her in films she considered hokum, however much she showed her versatility in them by such means as playing dual roles. She gained a Hollywood reputation for being temperamental and haughty, while her public popularity declined. By August 1921 *Photoplay* was printing "An Open Letter to Mme. Alla Nazimova" in which the anonymous writer deplored the "pap" of her films, calling them "an insult . . . to a public which has exalted and enriched her." The writer placed the responsibility for the trashy films squarely with Nazimova, since she had so much control over her pictures.

In 1922 Nazimova used her own money to make three films that would show her as an artist. One, *A Doll's House*, gained respectful reviews though the drama was judged to be unsuited to the silent screen. The other two, highly stylized versions of *Camille* and *Salome*, were critically assailed as being not art but arty; the public, bewildered or repelled, would have nothing to do with them. They cost the actress her popularity with movie audiences and the fortune she had made in the movies. She returned to the stage in two unsuccessful plays, one in 1923 and the other in 1927, with vaudeville tours in between. Her relationship with Charles Bryant deteriorated, and in 1925 he made public that they were not wed, then married another woman.

From 1928 to 1936 Nazimova reclaimed her stature as a superb stage actress by appearances with two groups more interested in true theater art than in the box office. One was Eva Le Gallienne's Civic Repertory Group, with which she appeared outstandingly as Mme. Ranevsky in *The Cherry Orchard* (1928). The other was the Theatre Guild, which presented her to highest critical acclaim as Natalia Petrovna in *A Month in the Country* (1930) and as Christine Mannon in *Mourning Becomes Electra* (1931). In 1935 she had a great success in *Ghosts*, playing Mrs. Alving, on Broadway and on tour. In 1936, three decades after she first played the role, she appeared in *Hedda Gabler* once again and was hailed as "an actress of extraordinary powers" (*New York Times*, 17 Nov. 1936). She also directed both *Ghosts* and *Hedda Gabler*.

After a final stage appearance in *The Mother* (1939), Nazimova's last years were spent in Hollywood, where her nephew Val Lewton was a director. Sound film appearances in supporting roles included *Escape* (1940) and *Since You Went Away* (1944). She died of a heart attack in Hollywood, California.

• Materials on the life and career of Nazimova are in the Billy Rose Theatre Collection at the New York Public Library for the Performing Arts, Lincoln Center. Useful biographical information is in Clifford Ashby, "Alla Nazimova and the Advent of the New Acting in America," *Quarterly Journal of Speech* (Apr. 1959). A list of her stage appearances is in *Who Was Who in the American Theatre 1912–1976* (1978). Her comments on her preparation for a role are in Morton Eustis, *Players at Work* (1969). Her film career is discussed in Dewitt Bodeen, "Nazimova," *Films in Review* (Dec. 1972), which also includes a filmography. Her vaudeville appearances are discussed in Anthony Slide, *Encyclopedia of Vaudeville* (1994). Portraits and production photographs are in Daniel C. Blum, *Great Stars of the American Stage* (1952), *A Pictorial History of the American Theatre* (1960), *A Pictorial History of the Silent Screen* (1953), and *A Pictorial History of the Talkies* (1968). Obituaries are in the *New York Times* and the *New York Herald Tribune*, both 14 July 1945.

WILLIAM STEPHENSON

NEAGLE, John (4 Nov. 1796–17 Sept. 1865), portrait painter, was born in Boston, Massachusetts, the son of Maurice Neagle, a native of Doneraile, County Cork, Ireland, and Susannah Taylor, the daughter of a New Jersey farmer. His father died in 1800. Neagle attended grammar school in Philadelphia and briefly studied art with the drawing master and artist Pietro Ancora. He worked in his stepfather Lawrence Ennis's grocery and liquor store until the age of fifteen, when he entered into an apprenticeship contract with a local coach decorator named Thomas Wilson. When Wilson began to take painting lessons from Bass Otis, Neagle was impressed with the likenesses he saw in the artist's studio, and resolved to become a portraitist. He studied with Otis for about two months, then enthusiastically embarked on an independent but rigorous study of art. By 1815 Neagle had begun to paint small oil sketches, which he sold for five dollars apiece. Neagle was further inspired when Otis introduced him to Philadelphia's most distinguished painter, Thomas Sully. Tired from the drudgery of decorating coaches and encouraged by the successful results of his early efforts, Neagle left Wilson and set up a modest practice. In 1818 he sought greater professional opportunities in Lexington, Kentucky, but was frustrated by competition from Matthew Harris Jouett, a successful portrait painter already established in the city. Neagle proceeded to New Orleans, where prospects for a portraitist were equally bleak, and promptly returned to Philadelphia.

From 1821 on, Neagle exhibited regularly at the Pennsylvania Academy of the Fine Arts in Philadelphia. His notebooks reveal that by 1824 Sully had become his mentor. In the summer of 1825 Neagle made an important journey to Boston, where he studied with Gilbert Stuart and met Washington Allston. In May 1826 he married Sully's stepdaughter Mary Chester Sully and departed immediately for New York City. The exact number of their children is unknown. There he executed portraits of noted actors, which later appeared as engraved illustrations in a series of books titled *The Acting American Theatre*. In 1827 Neagle exhibited his most famous work, the full-length *Pat Lyon at the Forge* (Museum of Fine Arts, Boston). He painted a second version of it in 1829 (Pennsylvania Academy of the Fine Arts, Philadelphia); these were exceptionally innovative portraits because Neagle represented his proletarian patron in the Grand Manner style that had hitherto been reserved for aristocratic or distinguished patrons.

Throughout the 1830s Neagle painted prominent Philadelphia doctors, lawyers, businessmen, and clergymen of various denominations. In 1833 he completed his most technically accomplished portrait, *Dr. William Potts Dewees* (University of Pennsylvania School of Medicine, Philadelphia). In 1834 he applied unsuccessfully for the position of drawing instructor at West Point Military Academy. An active participant in art organizations, in 1835 Neagle was elected first president of the Artists Fund Society, a group of dissident artists who seceded from the Pennsylvania Academy because they felt that the administration there did not adequately represent their interests.

Although born a Roman Catholic, Neagle and his family converted to the Episcopal faith in 1840. In the early autumn of 1842 a group of Philadelphia's prominent Whig citizens commissioned him to paint the full-length *Henry Clay* (The Union League of Philadelphia), a portrait that served as a political icon for the Germantown Clay Club during the statesman's bid for the presidency of the United States in 1844. Neagle traveled to Clay's farm "Ashland" in Lexington, Kentucky, and remained in the state, painting portraits of prominent people until early 1843.

The Clay portrait was Neagle's last important work. Depressed by the death of his beloved wife in 1845, he retreated from society. With few exceptions, his artistic creativity waned, and his activity as a professional portraitist gradually diminished. He continued to paint portraits until the late 1850s, when he suffered a severe stroke and died in Philadelphia.

Neagle was a scrupulously polite, serious, hardworking individual with a wide range of intellectual and philanthropic interests. Second only to his father-in-law Sully, he was Philadelphia's leading portraitist and exponent of the romantic British-influenced painterly style of Sir Thomas Lawrence. His portraits are often remarkable for the iconographic devices he used to explicate his subjects' professions, accomplishments, or significant experiences in their lives. As a member of the academy and as president of the Artists Fund Society, he was untiring in his efforts to promote the fine arts in the United States.

• Neagle's diaries, scrapbooks, notebooks, and correspondence are preserved in the American Philosophical Society and the Historical Society of Pennsylvania in Philadelphia. For the most comprehensive survey of Neagle's career, with a detailed bibliography of primary and secondary sources, see Robert W. Torchia, *John Neagle: Philadelphia Portrait Painter* (1989). See also William Dunlap, *A History of the Rise and Progress of the Arts of Design in the United States* (1834);

Thomas Fitzgerald, "John Neagle, the Artist," *Lippincott's Magazine*, May 1868, pp. 477–91; Mantle Fielding, *Exhibition of Portraits by John Neagle* (1925); Marguerite Lynch, "John Neagle's 'Diary,'" *Art in America* 37 (Apr. 1949): 79–99; Ransom R. Patrick, "John Neagle, Portrait Painter, and Pat Lyon, Blacksmith," *Art Bulletin* 33 (Sept. 1951): 187–92; and Bruce W. Chambers, "The Pythagorean Puzzle of Pat Lyon," *Art Bulletin* 58 (June 1976): 225–33.

ROBERT WILSON TORCHIA

NEAL, Alice B. *See* Haven, Emily Bradley Neal.

NEAL, David Dalhoff (20 Oct. 1838–2 May 1915), artist, was born in Lowell, Massachusetts, the son of Stephen B. Neal, a businessman, and Mary M. Dalhoff. He attended public schools in Lowell until the age of fourteen, when his father died. Young Neal was forced to make his own way in the world, and at the suggestion of friends he traveled to New Orleans, where he secured a position as clerk with a firm that imported wood. In his spare time Neal devoted himself to studying art, an interest he had developed at a young age, but he made little progress because there were no art schools or museums in New Orleans. In 1853, after less than a year in New Orleans, Neal traveled to San Francisco in hopes of furthering his studies of art. He was apprenticed to a wood engraver, and he soon became a successful draftsman on wood. In addition to engraving, Neal occasionally painted portraits and worked for the police sketching the likenesses of criminals.

After two years working in San Francisco, Neal returned to New England and enrolled in a private school in Andover, New Hampshire, to continue his education. He remained there until his funds ran out and then returned to San Francisco, where he made the acquaintance of the German painter Charles Nahl. Nahl encouraged Neal's interest in art and provided him with his first formal instruction in painting.

In 1861 Neal met S. P. Dewey, a wealthy Californian who became interested in Neal's artistic career. Dewey offered to finance a trip to Europe for Neal and to support him for several years while he studied abroad. Neal set off for Munich immediately, enrolling at the Bavarian Royal Academy, where he drew and painted from antique casts. After two years Neal entered the studio of Chevalier Maximilian Ainmüller. Neal had married Ainmüller's daughter, Marie, in 1862; they had two children. Ainmüller specialized in architectural studies and interiors at the Royal Academy and was superintendent of the Royal Manufactory of Stained Glass of Bavaria. Under Ainmüller's tutelage Neal began lessons in oil painting.

Neal followed Ainmüller's advice and devoted himself to painting interiors of ecclesiastical architecture. These early paintings sold quickly and helped establish Neal's reputation in Munich as a painter. Although Neal found success with his architectural paintings, his main goal was to devote himself to figure painting. In 1869 Neal met Karl von Piloty, who was impressed with the young artist and advised him to be-

gin immediately studying figure painting from live models. Within a year Neal had entered Piloty's studio, and soon after he completed his first elaborate figure composition, a painting representing James Watt, the modern inventor of the steam-powered engine.

In 1875, while working in Piloty's atelier, Neal began his most important painting, *The First Meeting of Mary Stuart and Rizzio* (private collection), which was praised for its composition and handling of color as being equal or superior to Piloty's. In 1876 Neal first exhibited the painting at the Bavarian Royal Academy in Munich and was honored with the gold medal, the academy's highest honor; Neal was the first American on whom it was bestowed. After the exhibition at the academy the painting was shown at the Munich Art Union and in London, Boston, Chicago, and elsewhere in the United States before being acquired by D. O. Mills, the president of the Bank of California in San Francisco.

The success of *The First Meeting of Mary Stuart and Rizzio* established Neal's reputation in Europe as well as in the United States as a painter of historical subjects. Dr. Förster, the art critic for the *Wartburg* journal, wrote in 1876 that Neal was a "highly gifted artist," and that the painting "is excellently well conceived and represented in a most masterly manner: the characters, particularly those of the principal personages, are well carried out with equally as much knowledge of the times, as well as a love and feeling for the subject" (no. 9, 1876). The *Chicago Tribune* exclaimed "This is high art!" after Neal's *The First Meeting of Mary Stuart and Rizzio* was exhibited in Chicago (24 Mar. 1878).

Neal went on to have great success with historical paintings in the manner of the Munich school; these include *Cromwell Visiting Milton* (1883), *Nuns at Prayer*, and *The Burgomaster*. He also became an accomplished portraitist, during his later years devoting himself almost exclusively to portrait painting, dividing his time between Munich and the United States while executing portrait commissions of wealthy Americans. His subjects included Whitelaw Reid, Mrs. W. C. Whitney, Charles Crocker of San Francisco, Robert Garret of Baltimore, and Professor Samuel Green of Princeton University, among others. Neal's portrait paintings were described as having "a distinct value as works of art, and as such are calculated to be treasured by posterity long after the affectionate interest of friends and family in the originals has passed away. They bear . . . the impress of the study of Van Dyck, although perhaps more at second than at first hand—the works . . . of Franz Lenbach" (John R. Tait, "David Neal," *Magazine of Art* 9 [1885–1886]: 95–101).

Neal was one of the first American artists in Munich to achieve prominence. The skillful painting technique and impressive realism that Neal learned from Piloty is evident in his historical paintings as well as his portraits. Many of the young American artists who came to Munich in the 1870s such as Toby Rosenthal and Charles Henry Miller, looked to Neal as a model, and for a time Neal was influential as a teacher at his own school. Although Neal was an American by birth, he died at home in Munich.

• Contemporary references on Neal include S. G. W. Benjamin, *Our American Artists* (1879). Twentieth-century sources on Neal include Ilene Susan Fort and Michael Quick, *American Art: A Catalogue of the Los Angeles County Museum of Art Collection* (1991); Sona K. Johnston, *American Paintings, 1750–1900, from the Collection of the Baltimore Museum of Art* (1983); Michael Quick, *American Expatriate Painters of the Late Nineteenth Century* (1976); and an obituary, "David Neal," *American Art News* 13, no. 33 (12 June 1915): 5.

ANNE R. NORCROSS

NEAL, John (25 Aug. 1793–20 June 1876), author and women's rights activist, was born in Falmouth (now Portland), Maine. His father, a Quaker schoolmaster of the same name, died a month after the birth of Neal and his twin sister, leaving Neal's mother, Rachel Hall, the difficult task of raising them in precarious financial circumstances. He attended several Quaker schools, the town school, and Portland Academy until age twelve. Combative and rebellious from early childhood, Neal, in 1808, left his native village and a job as shopkeeper's apprentice for an itinerant career as writing master, schoolmaster, and portrait sketcher. During the War of 1812, he became a partner in the dry-goods business of John Pierpont and Joseph Lord, managing a branch store in Baltimore. Their venture collapsed during the postwar recession. Pierpont went on to a career in the ministry—and to become the grandfather of John Pierpont Morgan. Neal turned to the study of law (and to an intensive program of self-education in languages and literature), determined to finance his studies through professional authorship.

Between 1816 and 1823, Neal wrote five novels, *Keep Cool* (1817), *Logan* (1822), *Seventy-Six* (1823), *Randolph* (1823), and *Errata, or the Works of Will Adams* (1823); a book of poetry, *The Battle of Niagara* (1818); a five-act tragedy, *Otho* (1819); and hundreds of articles for magazines and newspapers. He also helped ghostwrite Paul Allen's *History of the American Revolution* (1819). In addition, by 1823, he had secured admission to the bar and established a flourishing practice.

Neal's novels created something of a sensation. These semiautobiographical works included a thinly veiled account of an amorous involvement with Pierpont's young sister-in-law and a caustic criticism of William Pinkney, a prominent Baltimore lawyer and statesman. A break with Pierpont and a challenge to a duel by Edward Coote Pinkney, the statesman's son, contributed to Neal's decision, in late 1823, to leave Baltimore and pursue his literary career in England. He was determined, too, to campaign against the patronizing attitude of cultured Britain toward American writers—an attitude epitomized by Sydney Smith's scornful question, posed in 1820 in the *Edinburgh Review*: "In the four quarters of the globe, who reads an American book?"

During three and a half years in England, Neal wrote numerous articles about American life and literature for British journals—most notably *Blackwood's Edinburgh Magazine*, to which he contributed an extraordinary series (in five installments) on about 130 American writers, living and dead (including himself). William Blackwood also published Neal's *Brother Jonathan* (1825), a sprawling, three-volume work that featured scenes of New England life and the revolutionary war. Its prose-poetic sweep and vivid colloquialism anticipates, as do few other novels of its time, the racy exuberance and immediacy of Herman Melville. This excerpt describes New York just before the battle of Brooklyn Heights:

The city of New York is built upon the south extremity of New York Island. It was chiefly remarkable, in the time of our story, for great opulence; narrow, crooked, abominable streets, like the flues of a furnace; rat holes; or the subterranean passages through London *city*; high, Dutch (not hoch Deutsch) buildings; badly contrived; irregular; not only, out of shape, in every case; but, half the time, without any shape at all—unwholesome—top-heavy, and crowded; huge warehouses; three cornered shops; with an occasional habitation, quite princely. (3:78–79)

The novel, however, was a financial failure and marked the beginning of the end of Neal's British campaign.

Returning to the United States in late 1827, Neal encountered bitterness and hostility in his native Portland because of his revelatory and controversial writings. With characteristic defiance, he abruptly abandoned his intention to live in New York and settled down to practice law in Portland. The following year, he married his cousin Eleanor Hall, with whom he had five children. In 1828 he founded and edited the *Yankee*, a short-lived but influential literary journal that promoted Jeremy Bentham's utilitarian ideas (Neal had lived in the Bentham household toward the end of his stay in England). He also encouraged the early literary efforts of John Greenleaf Whittier, Nathaniel Hawthorne, and Edgar Allan Poe.

In the following years, Neal produced three more novels—*Rachel Dyer* (1828), *Authorship* (1830), *The Down-Easters* (1833)—and several short stories, three of which, "Otter-Bag" (1829), "David Whicher" (1832) and "Idiosyncrasies" (1835), anticipate the psychological insights of Poe, Hawthorne, and Melville, as well as Mark Twain's witty and ironic colloquialism. Neal edited the *New England Galaxy* in 1835 and the journal *Brother Jonathan* in 1843, while contributing essays, poems, and stories to such magazines as *Godey's*, *Graham's*, *Harper's*, and the *Atlantic Monthly*. Later books included a religious treatise, *One Word More* (1854); a novel, *True Womanhood* (1859); three dime novels for the House of Beadle; and a collection of witty (sometimes subversive) sayings of children, *Great Mysteries and Little Plagues* (1870). His pride in his native town—along with his awareness of its problems—was summed up in *Portland Illustrated* (1874), received by most of his townsmen as a routine guidebook. Two years later John Neal died in Portland, his earlier eminence largely forgotten.

In the half-century he lived in Portland, Neal was an active participant in several crusades, most notably as an advocate of health reform and as a pioneer champion of women's rights. While in London, he had become so enthused about the value of exercise for people of studious habits that he wrote to Thomas Jefferson urging him to make "a gymnastick school quite an indispensable part" of the newly established University of Virginia. Soon after his return to Portland, he initiated and directed gymnastic classes and was invited to establish Bowdoin College's first gymnasium in 1828. He was dismayed, however, when his attempts to integrate blacks into his Portland classes were rejected by their classmates. "This, I acknowledge, went far to dishearten me; for what was bodily training? what a system of gymnastics, weighed against humanity and consistency?"

As a member of the London Debating Society, Neal had defended the proposition "that the intellectual powers of the two sexes are equal" and wrote an article for *Blackwood's*, "Men and Women" (1824), supporting this view. He featured numerous articles on women's rights in the *Yankee*. Neal's 1843 address to the Broadway Tabernacle of New York, on "Rights of Women," was a devastating indictment of democratic America's hypocrisy concerning the status of women.

Though an enemy of racial prejudice, Neal had little sympathy for abolitionism and actively supported the American colonizationist movement in the decades before the Civil War. Other crusades involved phrenology, spiritualism, temperance, and civic improvements. The cause of women's rights was an overriding and lifelong concern.

Neal wrote hastily and voluminously, and many of his works are formless and chaotic. But Whittier, in 1830, summed up the reasons for his hold on readers: "Critics may talk as they please, but for ourselves we *do* like the bold, vigorous and erratic style of Neal." Poe wrote in his *Marginalia* that he was "inclined to rank John Neal first, or at all events second, among our men of indisputable *genius*." Neal's pioneering efforts led the way to the great language experiments of Melville, Walt Whitman, and Mark Twain—efforts and achievements increasingly recognized in our time.

• Letters from Neal are in the John Neal Papers and the Henry Wadsworth Longfellow Papers in the Houghton Library of Harvard University; the John Pierpont Papers in the Pierpont Morgan Library; and the Blackwood papers in the National Library of Scotland. His autobiography is *Wandering Recollections of a Somewhat Busy Life* (1869). For an anthology of his fiction, criticism, and writings on women's rights, see Benjamin Lease and Hans-Joachim Lang, eds., *The Genius of John Neal: Selections from His Writings* (1978). See also Fred Lewis Pattee, ed., *American Writers: A Series of Papers Contributed to Blackwood's Magazine (1824–1825) by John Neal* (1937), and Harold Edward Dickson, ed., *Observations on American Art: Selections from the Writings of John Neal (1793–1876)* (1943). A chronology of his life and a set of annotated bibliographies, primary and secondary, can be found in Donald A. Sears, *John Neal* (1978). For a more recent set of bibliographies, primary and secondary, see Francesca Orestano, *Dal Neoclassico al Classico: John Neal e la Coscienza Letteraria Americana* (1990). See also Benjamin Lease, *That Wild Fellow John Neal and the American Literary Revolution* (1972), and *Anglo-American Encounters: England and the Rise of American Literature* (1981); and Fritz Fleischmann, *A Right View of the Subject: Feminism in the Works of Charles Brockden Brown and John Neal* (1983).

BENJAMIN LEASE

NEAL, Josephine Bicknell (10 Oct. 1880–19 Mar. 1955), physician, was born in Belmont, Maine, the daughter of Alton J. Neal and Mary Alexander. She graduated from Bates College in Lewiston, Maine, in 1901, receiving a bachelor's degree in physics with honors. She taught school in Maine until she had saved enough money to begin her study of medicine. She told a *New York Herald Tribune* reporter many years later (17 Jan. 1938), "I studied medicine just because I always wanted to."

Neal completed her medical education in 1910, receiving her M.D., again with honors, from Cornell University Medical College. She obtained her New York State medical license in 1913. From 1910 to 1914 she worked for the New York City Department of Health in the meningitis division of its research laboratories. From 1914 to 1920 she taught medicine at her alma mater.

By 1922 Neal had begun her lifelong affiliation with Columbia University's College of Physicians and Surgeons. She worked as an assistant in the department of medicine and as an attending physician in the pediatric tuberculosis section of the Vanderbilt Clinic.

From 1927 to 1929 Neal was director of the William J. Matheson Survey of Epidemic Encephalitis. In 1928 she went abroad to carry on her research work on behalf of that group. Following her directorship, Neal became executive secretary of the William J. Matheson Commission for Encephalitis Research. *Encephalitis: A Clinical Study* (1942) incorporated the findings of the commission; Neal wrote four of its nine chapters, in collaboration with six colleagues. In addition to the approximately 75 articles she wrote for medical journals, she contributed to two of the classic medical textbooks of her time. She wrote the chapter on meningitis in Frederick Tice's *Practice of Medicine* (1922) and the chapter on epidemic meningitis in Isaac Arthur Abt's *Pediatrics* (1923, 1926).

In addition to her contributions to the encephalitis study, Neal was "field marshal" of the New York City Department of Health's campaign against infantile paralysis or poliomyelitis, then a much-feared and common disease. She and another physician, Helen Harrington, became involved with the effort against this disease as a result of their association at Willard Parker Hospital, where they both served during infantile paralysis epidemics; their experience with the devastation it caused to patients and parents led to their desire to prevent as well as cure it. Neal served as secretary of the International Commission for the Study of Infantile Paralysis from 1929 to 1932. In 1934 W. H. Park, director of the Bureau of Laboratories of New York City, Henry Wirt Jackson, an associate, and Neal herself were inoculated with a vaccine prepared by Maurice Brodie of New York University. It was hoped that this vaccine could be used to immunize people against infantile paralysis, and Neal and her colleagues wanted to study the antibodies activated by the virus in the vaccine. In January 1938 announcement was made of the new Foundation for Infantile Paralysis, to be financed by funds raised at celebrations of Franklin Delano Roosevelt's birthday on 29 January.

Neal told *New York Herald Tribune* reporter Emma Bugbee on 17 January 1938:

The most important development since I began studying infantile paralysis . . . is the discovery that in many cases there is no actual paralysis at all. This should be a great comfort to parents. When an epidemic sweeps a city, there need not be the panic of earlier years, when every case seemed doomed to permanent paralysis. Unfortunately there is as yet no way of telling in advance just which persons are susceptible to the disease in its most serious form; nor is it possible to prevent its assuming the paralyzing form even when diagnosed. However, we now believe that of every 100 stricken only about twenty-five will be paralyzed.

The most constructive work has been that of the orthopedists in the after-care of paralyzed victims. We cannot yet prevent the disease, nor have we found a cure, but we do know a great deal about treating the victims so they will not be permanently crippled . . . I certainly hope that some of the funds of this new foundation will be devoted to orthopedic work.

From 1929 to 1944 Neal was clinical professor of neurology at Columbia University's College of Physicians and Surgeons. She also served on the staff of the Neurological Institute as a consultant in neurology (1932–1935), attending neurologist (1936–1938), consultant (1938–1939), and assistant attending neurologist, from 1939 until her retirement. In 1936 she became certified by the American Board of Psychiatry and Neurology as a specialist in neurology. She also served on the attending medical staffs of the Willard Parker Hospital, St. Vincent's Hospital, and the New York Infirmary.

Neal received various honors and awards throughout her life. She was awarded the John Metcalfe Polk Prize by Cornell University. In 1926 her first alma mater, Bates College, made her an honorary doctor of science; Russell Sage College did the same in June 1937. In 1931 she was elected a fellow of the American College of Physicians.

Neal was a member of the Women's Political Union and worked in the cause of woman suffrage. She died in New York.

• Newspaper accounts of Neal's work on infantile paralysis include "Dr. Josephine B. Neal Marshals City's Infantile Paralysis Fight," *New York Herald Tribune*, 17 Jan. 1938, p. 4;

and "Two Women Hailed in Paralysis Fight," *New York Times*, 16 Jan. 1938. An obituary is in the *New York Times*, 20 Mar. 1955.

H. CLAIRE JACKSON

NEAL, Marie Catherine (7 Dec. 1889–6 June 1965), botanist and author, was born in Southington, Connecticut, the daughter of Linus B. Neal, a banker, and Eva W. Chedney. As a girl, she went on hunting and fishing excursions with her father, discovering in nature her future life's work. Neal's interest in plant life was heightened by her first course in botany at Smith College, from which she graduated in 1912 with a B.A. degree. She had worked in college as a secretary for Travelers Insurance Company and the Connecticut Children's Aid Society. Upon graduation, she became a secretary in the geology department at Yale, working for Herbert E. Gregory. She moved to Honolulu, Hawaii, in 1920 to continue her work for Gregory, after his appointment as director of the Bishop Museum. Neal was placed as research assistant in the museum's conchology department in the division devoted to the study of mollusks, as there were no museum openings in botany. She worked there for ten years from 1920 to 1930. In 1923 Neal cataloged 200,000 terrestrial mollusks and in 1928 coauthored with Henry A. Pilsbry and C. Montague Cooke, Jr., a monograph titled "Land Snails from Hawaii, Christmas Island and Samoa." While completing these tasks, she continued to pursue her botany studies, made an extensive botanical collecting trip to New Zealand, and completed her master's thesis in marine algae of Hawaii, obtaining her master's degree from Yale in 1925. Her articles written in this period for the *Paradise of the Pacific* magazine on Hawaii's cultivated plants popularized her name and field.

Her first major book, *In Honolulu Gardens*, coauthored with Berta Metzger, was published in 1928. This book contained scientific descriptions and illustrations of over eighty families of Hawaiian plants. Her book was intended as "a floral guide of Honolulu" with "the commonest and most conspicuous herbs, vines, shrubs, and trees that are seen in gardens and parks and along roadsides described." *In Honolulu Gardens* offered a kaleidoscope of scientific information; in addition, it included many plants and Hawaiian legends as to the plants' origins and uses. Neal compiled information from botany, ethnology, folklore, and literature, while Metzger contributed legends drawn from published and unpublished Bishop Museum sources, including a manuscript on Hawaiian proverbs. Neal produced the illustrations, often from living plants and a few from museum photographs. The book was well received by scholars and laymen alike.

In 1930 Neal was appointed botanist at Bishop Museum and took charge of the herbarium, which later was named after her. She earned an international reputation for her outstanding scholarship and at the same time was pleased to aid schoolchildren on tour of the museum identify Hawaii's plants and their uses.

She handled countless inquiries about Hawaiian plants and those of the Pacific in general from scholars around the world and from laymen. Neal greatly expanded the museum herbarium's collections, establishing 175,000 sheets of specimens as plant varieties found throughout the Pacific area excluding mainland America and continental Asia. As a scientific scholar of note she guided the growth of the herbarium collection—identifying, mounting, preserving, and filing botanical specimens—and aided many others in the use of the collection for their own scientific work. As her reputation grew, she was able to attract grants to the museum from various government agencies and eleemosynary foundations. Outmoded museum facilities were replaced with the most up-to-date equipment, and the space allocated to the herbarium was greatly enlarged.

During vacations she toured the outer islands of the Hawaiian chain seeking new plants and conducting research for her books or scientific journal articles. On a trip to Mauna Kea supported by the Hawaiian Academy of Science, Neal and her friend and colleague Constance Hartt, who taught at the University of Hawaii, found several new species of moss. Their discoveries led to a joint publication titled "The Plant Ecology of Mauna Kea," which appeared in *Ecology*. One of the new moss species was named after Neal: *Mielichoferia nealiae* Bartr. An orchid, a tree fern, and a shell were also named after Neal, a testimony to her varied research and vast expertise.

Neal enjoyed gathering plant life from tide pools and coastal areas in secluded and undisturbed offshore islets. She collected mosses and lichens for a special shade garden at her home. For Neal, botanical research was a continuous outdoor adventure to which she devoted her keen mind, strong will, great physical stamina, and intellectual energy. After she grew slightly deaf, however, she avoided large groups and declined opportunities to speak or read papers at scientific meetings. But she always enjoyed the children's visits to the museum and would help them identify the flowers and seeds that they wanted to use for making leis. On 1 May, Hawaii's Lei Day, she worked in the museum's booth at Kapiolani Park so that she could dispense accurate scientific names for all the materials used in the lei exhibit and could encourage the public to visit the herbarium.

Her monumental work was *In Gardens of Hawaii*, published in 1948 and revised in 1965. An expansion of *In Honolulu Gardens*, it described more than 2,000 botanic species, of which 600 were illustrated. "The enormous task of compiling detailed information of the variety included by Miss Neal," wrote then museum director Roland W. Force, "could only have been achieved by one who possessed both Miss Neal's botanical competence and her conscientious dedication to accuracy and completeness." Besides its wealth of modern scientific information, her book was an archive of ancient Hawaiian knowledge about plants and how they were used in construction, as food, medicines, decorations, and adornments, and in religious

sacrifice. She labored to preserve the richness of her adopted culture.

Neal was a fellow of the American Association for the Advancement of Science and a member of the Hawaiian Botanical Society, the Hawaiian Academy of Sciences, the Hawaiian Botanical Gardens Foundation, Friends of Foster Gardens, the Audubon Society, the Wilderness Society, and the scientific honorary Sigma Xi. For her outstanding scientific contributions, she was recognized as Friend of the Year in 1964 by the Friends of Foster Gardens in Honolulu. The following year she died in Honolulu. Neal will be remembered as a pioneer botanist who contributed greatly to the ever-enlarging scientific reputation of the Bishop Museum in Hawaii and for her humanitarian efforts to spread her knowledge of Hawaii's culture and ecology to the community.

• The scientific papers and books of Marie Neal are located in Bishop Museum, Honolulu, Hawaii, and the Records of the Herbarium Pacific should be especially consulted. Neal's numerous popular articles are best represented in the *Paradise of the Pacific* magazine. A brief biography of Neal appears in Barbara Bennett Peterson, ed., *Notable Women of Hawaii* (1984). The best sources for her scholarship are found in *Bishop Museum Bulletin* 67 (1930): 1–84 and 126 (1934): 39–49, and in the publications discussed above. Neal's work is mentioned in Thomas G. Thrum, *Hawaiian Almanac and Annual* 55 (1928): 49–61 and 57 (1930): 74–79. Otto Degener and Irma Degener, in the *New Illustrated Flora of the Hawaiian Islands*, 25 January 1968, have a commemorative piece on Neal. An obituary is in the *Honolulu Advertiser*, 7 June 1965.

BARBARA BENNETT PETERSON

NEALE, Alfred Earle (5 Nov. 1891–2 Nov. 1973), college and professional athlete and coach, was born in Parkersburg, West Virginia, the son of William Henry Neale, a wholesale produce operator, and Irene T. Fairfax. Called "Greasy" as a retort by a childhood friend whom Neale had called "Dirty," the nickname stuck, and Neale enjoyed its use by all who knew him throughout his life. At the age of ten Neale went to work setting pins in a bowling alley and selling newspapers. After the eighth grade he left school and took a job with the Parkersburg Iron & Steel Co. He resumed his education in high school two years later and became a star in football, even coaching the team during his sophomore year. During the summers he played on neighborhood and then semiprofessional baseball teams; he was offered his first professional contract in the summer of 1912. He played briefly with Altoona, Pennsylvania, in the Tri-State League and then with two Ontario clubs in the Canadian League before enrolling at West Virginia Wesleyan in the fall of that year. There he became a three-sport athlete, starring as an end in football and helping his team defeat rival West Virginia University in 1912 and 1913. In college Neale met two people who would play important roles in his life: John Kellison, a football teammate who became his closest long-term friend and who served as his assistant coach on five different football teams, and

Genevieve Horner, a coed at Wesleyan whom he married during the summer of 1915. They had no children.

After playing with two different baseball teams in two different leagues during the summer of 1915, Neale accepted his first college coaching job at Muskingum College in New Concord, Ohio, where he coached basketball and football. In 1916, after only two summers (1912 and 1915) of professional baseball with five different minor league teams in four leagues, Neale made the jump to major league ball with the Cincinnati Reds. For five seasons (1916–1920) he was a regular in the Cincinnati lineup, his best overall season being in 1917, when he hit .294 in 121 games with 25 stolen bases. In the 1919 World Series he played in all eight games against the Chicago White Sox, hit .357 with ten hits to lead Reds' starters in batting, and played a solid game in the outfield. He had hits in six of the eight Series games, two of them three-hit games. Four of his ten hits in the "Black Sox" Series came off the two White Sox pitchers involved in the fix. Neale was convinced that all of the Series games, except for the first one, were honest because the players involved in the scheme were not given their payoff after the initial game. After starting the 1921 season with the Philadelphia Phillies, Neale returned to the Reds, but he saw only limited play during two remaining seasons. His batting average for eight major league seasons was .259.

Neale's college coaching career continued during his major league playing days. In 1916 he went back to West Virginia Wesleyan and coached football and basketball for two seasons. He played one season of professional football in 1917 for the Canton Bulldogs, coached by Jim Thorpe. He then held a series of college coaching jobs at Marietta College (1919–1920), Washington and Jefferson College (1921–1922), and the University of Virginia (1923–1928). His 1919 team at Marietta, after losing its opener, 61–0, won all of its remaining games. Neale's younger brother played for Marietta in 1919 and 1920. Neale's 1922 Washington and Jefferson team went undefeated, and in a battle of unbeatens it tied the highly favored University of California in the Rose Bowl, 0–0. Neale's approach to coaching college football, he said, was to "instill confidence in the team" and "to scare them if they're overconfident." He was an innovator of offensive plays that provided surprise and control of the ball, was a master strategist who could quickly size up an opponent's strengths and weaknesses, and could inspire a winning attitude in a team.

After returning to professional baseball as a coach for the St. Louis Cardinals in 1929, Neale became the head coach at West Virginia University, but he left there in 1934 to become the backfield coach under Raymond Pond at Yale University, where he remained until 1940. His favorite coaching jobs were at the University of Virginia and at Yale, where less pressure was exerted to recruit and subsidize athletes and where the university presidents supported a strong tradition of student-athletes. However, he was not against subsidizing athletes in order to win.

In 1941 Neale became head coach of the Philadelphia Eagles in the National Football League. After winning only two games in each of his first two seasons, and after the merger of the Eagles and Pittsburgh Steelers in 1943, Neale took the Eagles to second-place finishes in the NFL's Eastern Division in 1944, 1945, and 1946 and then to division championships from 1947 through 1949. In 1948 and 1949 the Eagles won the NFL championship games, with the 1949 team posting an 11–1–0 season record and scoring 364 points to its opponents' 134. Neale's high-scoring and exciting Eagles teams contributed significantly to the growing success and popularity of professional football in the immediate postwar period, and he became nationally recognized as a coaching genius and strategist. After a disappointing 6–6 record in 1950, and after the Eagles were sold to a syndicate, Neale was fired, to the surprise of many. In his career with the Eagles, from 1941 through 1950, his teams compiled a 63–43–5 record, and Neale's coaching introduced innovations such as the man-to-man pass defense, the triple reverse, and the fake reverse. He achieved remarkable results through intelligent coaching, effective use of talent, and expert psychology that encouraged confidence, professional pride, and satisfaction in his teams.

From 1951 until his death in Lake Worth, Florida, Neale led an active life. His first wife died in 1950, and he married Ola Gettys in 1963; they lived in New York City and in Florida. Neale's coaching career was recognized by his induction into the National Football Foundation College Football Hall of Fame in 1967 and the Pro Football Hall of Fame in 1969. He was recognized, as well, as a man who truly enjoyed competitive sports and the friendships and associations they fostered and strengthened.

• The Research Library at the Pro Football Hall of Fame in Canton, Ohio, has an extensive clipping file on Neale's career. Biographical information can be found in Neale's autobiography, written with Tom Meany, published in three parts under the title "Football Is My Life," *Collier's*, 3, 10, and 17 Nov. 1951. For his career in college football, Allison Danzig's *The History of American Football: Its Great Teams, Players, and Coaches* (1956) and Tom Perrin's *Football: A College History* (1987) are essential. For Neale's professional career, see Denis J. Harrington's *The Pro Football Hall of Fame: Players, Coaches, Team Owners and League Officials, 1963–1991* (1991). Information on Neale's career with the Cincinnati Reds and his skills as an outfielder can be found in Eugene Murdock's interview with Hall of Fame center fielder Edd Roush in Murdock's *Baseball between the Wars: Memories of the Game by the Men Who Played It* (1992). Gerald Holland's "Greasy Neale: Nothing to Prove, Nothing to Ask," *Sports Illustrated*, 24 Aug. 1964, is informative and revealing. Personal information was provided by a nephew of Neale's, Tom Neale, of Parkersburg, West Virginia. An obituary is in the *New York Times*, 3 Nov. 1973.

DOUGLAS A. NOVERR

NEALE, Leonard (15 Oct. 1746–18 June 1817), archbishop of Baltimore, was born at Port Tobacco, Charles County, Maryland, the son of William Neale, a prosperous planter, and Anne Brooke. In 1758 he was sent to St. Omer's College in French Flanders, where five of his brothers also would be enrolled. On 7 September 1767 he entered the Jesuit novitiate at nearby Watten. After completing the study of philosophy and theology at the English College at Liège, he was ordained 5 June 1773, about a month before the suppression of the Society of Jesus. From 1773 to 1779 Neale was engaged in pastoral work in England and from 1779 to 1783 in Demerara, British Guiana. Returning to his native land, he labored near his ancestral home until 1793, when he was appointed pastor of St. Mary's Church in Philadelphia and vicar general of Bishop John Carroll of Baltimore.

When the priest elected to be Carroll's coadjutor with right of succession died unexpectedly, Neale was chosen, probably also by an election of the clergy, to fill the position. It is doubtful that he was Carroll's choice. Although he was appointed coadjutor in Rome in 1795, the Napoleonic wars delayed the arrival of the papal briefs for five years. When on 7 December 1800 Neale was raised to the episcopacy by Bishop Carroll, he became the first Catholic bishop ordained in the United States. In 1802–1805 Neale joined Carroll in effecting a restoration of the Society of Jesus in the United States by an affiliation of former members with the Jesuit remnant in Russia. Neale's brothers Charles and Francis Ignatius joined the society and played important roles in the early years of its revival.

Carroll had in 1799 named Leonard Neale president of Georgetown College but soon judged his regulations too monastic for a democratic society and in 1806 replaced him. As coadjutor Neale proved to be a disappointment. Even after Carroll's elevation to the archbishopric of Baltimore in 1808 with four suffragan bishops, he entrusted Neale with few responsibilities. As a consequence Neale had greater leisure to pursue what he considered his greatest achievement, the creation of a sisterhood, the first founded in the United States. From Philadelphia he had brought a group of pious women to Georgetown and chose for them the rule of a cloistered order in Europe, the Visitation nuns. In Georgetown they opened a successful convent school. As soon as he became archbishop, Neale obtained for the order the official approval of the Holy See.

On the death of Carroll on 3 December 1815 Neale became the second archbishop of Baltimore. Despite the misgivings of many he proved to be a decisive administrator, moving immediately to remedy a number of abuses Carroll had tolerated. He imposed a strict discipline upon the clergy. When he replaced three priests as pastors, however, he provoked acts of rebellion in Norfolk, Virginia, and Charleston, South Carolina, still parts of the archdiocese, and in the Virgin Islands, whose care had been entrusted to Carroll in 1804. In all three places Neale had assigned French priests over largely Irish congregations. While it was never his intention to arouse ethnic antagonisms, he harbored a strong aversion to "that pernicious system," the trustee arrangement that Carroll had sanctioned for the administration of church property. In a *Letter to the Most Reverend Leonard Neale* (1816) the trustees of Norfolk published a lengthy defense of their position and of the rights of trustees in general. When the aggrieved priests or trustees of the three trouble spots complained to the Holy See, some in person, Neale was, in effect, rebuked by the Roman authorities. In one of the strongest letters from an American bishop to the pope, Neale remonstrated that he could "scarcely believe that such an order emanated from the Holy See," an order by which "the door is opened to every rebellion in this distant country." Rome reversed itself, but by the time its decision arrived Neale was dead. In an effort to provide worthy pastors, Neale negotiated in 1816 a concordat with the Jesuits that gave them control of forty of the some fifty congregations in Maryland.

As a result of his labors in South America and a bout with yellow fever in Philadelphia, Neale's health was seriously impaired, a condition that was not recognized until after his appointment as coadjutor. As soon as he became archbishop, Neale requested a coadjutor of his own, but news of the latter's appointment did not arrive until after his death. As a bishop Neale led an almost eremitical life, residing in austere apartments in Georgetown, where he died largely unmourned. He visited his see city only two or three times in the year and a half he was archbishop of Baltimore. Although his tenure as archbishop was brief, it had far-reaching consequences in the ethnic discord it generated and the trustee crises it set in motion in the Catholic church in the United States.

• Archbishop Neale's papers are in the archives of the archdiocese of Baltimore. His only scholarly biography is M. Bernetta Brislen, "The Episcopacy of Leonard Neale, Second Archbishop of Baltimore," *Historical Records and Studies* 34 (1945): 20–111. See also Peter Guilday, *The Life and Times of John Carroll: Archbishop of Baltimore (1735–1815)* (1922); Thomas W. Spalding, *The Premier See: A History of the Archdiocese of Baltimore, 1789–1989* (1989); and Joseph B. Code, *Dictionary of the American Hierarchy (1789–1964)* (1964).

THOMAS W. SPALDING

NEARING, Scott (6 Aug. 1883–24 Aug. 1983), economist and social reformer, was born in Morris Run, Pennsylvania, the son of Louis Nearing, an engineer, and Minnie Zabriskie. During his youth, a central influence on Nearing's life was his grandfather, Winfield Scott Nearing, the superintendent of the Morris Run Coal Mining Company. His grandfather embodied the contradictions of the elite in their exercise of authority for the benefit of the common good as well as their abuse of power for preserving wealth and status. Nearing attended the University of Pennsylvania beginning in 1901, earning a doctorate in economics from the university's Wharton School in 1909 under the tutelage of progressive economist Simon Nelson Patten. Between 1906 and 1915 Nearing became involved in progressive social causes in Philadelphia, serving as secretary of the Pennsylvania Child Labor Committee while teaching sociology at Temple University and economics at Swarthmore College and at the Wharton School. Beginning in 1913 he taught at the Rand School in New York City and lectured on social science at the Chautauqau, New York, summer school. During this time he spent his summers and weekends at Arden, Delaware, a single-tax community based on Henry George's antimonopolist critique of industrial capitalism.

Nearing's economic writings focused on the unequal distribution of wealth in American society and the concepts of earned and unearned income as a way of understanding the U.S. economy. His outspoken views on social reform directly challenged the local manufacturing interests, including some university trustees who owned manufacturing plants that hired child labor. In 1915 Nearing was fired from his position as an assistant professor of economics at the Wharton School in one of the first major academic freedom cases of the twentieth century. His case was investigated by the newly formed American Association of University Professors, which concluded that Nearing's academic freedom had been violated. From 1915 to 1917 Nearing was professor of social science and dean of the College of Arts and Sciences at the University of Toledo, Ohio. In April 1917 he was fired from this position for his opposition to American preparedness and involvement in World War I. Following his firing he became chairman of the antiwar People's Council for Democracy and Peace and joined the Socialist party. In March 1918 Nearing was indicted by the federal government under the Espionage Act for writing an antiwar pamphlet, *The Great Madness: A Victory for American Plutocracy*, published by the American Socialist Society. While under indictment, he ran for U.S. Congress in the fourteenth congressional district of New York City as the Socialist party candidate, losing to the incumbent, Fiorello La Guardia. In February 1919 Nearing was tried and acquitted.

Nearing continued his political involvement in left-wing politics during the 1920s, drifting away from the Socialist party and joining the Communist party in 1927. He remained active in radical causes, establishing an alternative press service, the Federated Press; serving as a trustee for the American Fund for Public Service, a fund established to support radical and labor causes; and traveling to Mexico, Canada, China, and the Soviet Union. By January 1930 Nearing's independent radicalism led to his expulsion from the Communist party, which was announced in the *Daily Worker*. All the while he lived a life of strenuous simplicity. Joseph Freeman, in his autobiography, *An American Testament* (1938), noted that Nearing "liked physical labor on his Jersey farm, and often prepared his own meals, consisting chiefly of raw fruits and vegetables." Nearing, wrote Freeman, "lived his life literally, renouncing all personal comforts, and preaching the gospel of the new world with the intensity of a Savonarola."

Nearing married Nellie Seeds in 1908. They had one child and later adopted another. Nearing became estranged from his wife during the 1920s, and in 1929 he met Helen Knothe, of Ridgewood, New Jersey. Helen and Scott bought a farm in 1932 in Jamaica, Vermont, to begin a subsistence lifestyle living off the land. Helen and Scott were married in 1947, the year Nellie died.

During the course of his life, Nearing wrote fifty books and numerous pamphlets and articles. His most enduring writing is a book published with Helen in 1954, *Living the Good Life: How to Live Sanely and Simply in a Troubled World*, the writing of which coincided with a renewal of their homesteading experiment with a move to Harborside, Maine. *Living the Good Life* was immediately compared with Henry David Thoreau's *Walden*, published a century before, as an account of an act of deliberate liberation through an alternative way of life. When *Living the Good Life* was reprinted in 1970, it became a bestselling bible of the countercultural back-to-the-land movement. He died on his farm at Harborside, Maine.

Nearing exemplifies the independence of American radicalism and a tradition of dissent that fuels social activism. In a profile of Nearing from *World Tomorrow* (1930), Roger Baldwin wrote that "there have always been native sons in each generation to voice the old revolt against privilege and power. Scott Nearing is not merely one of them, he is doubtless the best known of them, both at home and abroad." Nearing appeared as a "witness" to an American century captured in the 1982 film *Reds* about his friend and comrade John Reed. In the 100 years that spanned his life, he shared the political journey to the left with many of his radical contemporaries, but he was a rare case in that he remained on the left, becoming a major figure in the socialist movement of the 1910s and the counterculture of the 1970s and 1980s.

• Nearing's papers are located at Boston University and at Swarthmore College. Stephen J. Whitfield, *Scott Nearing: Apostle of American Radicalism* (1974), is a social biography that followed the publication of Nearing's autobiography, *The Making of a Radical: A Political Autobiography* (1972). John Saltmarsh, *Scott Nearing: An Intellectual Biography* (1991), assesses Nearing's activism and his contribution to twentieth-century American social and cultural criticism.

JOHN A. SALTMARSH

NEEF, Francis Joseph Nicholas (6 Dec. 1770–8 Apr. 1854), educator and author, was born in Soultz, Alsace, France, the son of Francis Joseph Neef, the town miller, and Anastasia Ackerman. Neef studied for the Roman Catholic priesthood at the abbey school at Murbach, where he became proficient in Latin and Greek. Inspired by the French Revolution, however, he abandoned his clerical studies to serve in the French army. Attaining the rank of noncommissioned adjutant suboffice, he was seriously wounded at the battle of Arcole during the Italian campaign of 1796 when an Austrian round lodged between his right eye and nose. The injury brought him an honorable discharge and lifelong health problems, including recurrent headaches, fainting spells, and temporary blindness.

While recuperating from his wound, Neef read the published writings of the Swiss educational reformer Johann Heinrich Pestalozzi (1746–1827) who argued that all instruction should be based on sensation and organized into lessons that focused on the form, number, and names of objects in the child's environment. Rejecting the current school practices of rote learning, religious indoctrination, and corporal punishment, Pestalozzi advised that schools should offer children emotional security.

In 1800 Neef became an instructor of foreign languages and physical education at Pestalozzi's new institute in Burgdorf, Switzerland. There, Neef deepened his understanding of Pestalozzian pedagogy. In 1803 Neef married Eloisa Buss (1784–1846), who was to become a major collaborator in his educational activities.

In 1802 Neef established at Pestalozzi's request an orphan's school in Paris modeled on Pestalozzian principles, and in 1804 the school was visited by William Maclure (1763–1840), the American philanthropist. Maclure persuaded Neef to immigrate to the United States and establish similar schools there.

Subsidized by Maclure, Neef and his family immigrated to the United States in 1806. Settling near Philadelphia, the center of Maclure's scientific and educational circle, Neef spent two years studying English and writing his *Sketch of a Plan and Method of Education* (1808). The *Sketch* was designed to familiarize Americans with Pestalozzian methods and to serve as a prospectus for his school near the Falls of the Schuykill, five miles from Philadelphia. Neef's school at the Falls, operating from 1809 to 1812, enrolled a total of seventy-five students over time. Using object lessons and field studies, Neef's students enjoyed a relaxed learning situation free from corporal punishment and psychological coercion. Languages were taught by conversation and mathematics by the manipulation of physical objects and the practical application of computational skills. Neef's teaching of the natural sciences, in particular, emphasized direct interaction with the environment. The curriculum also featured physical education exercises, sports, and military drill.

In a book published a year after the *Sketch*, *Logic of Condillac, Translated by Joseph Neef, as an Illustration of the Plan of Education Established at His School Near Philadelphia*, Neef demonstrated his tendency to infuse his method of instruction with empiricism. Like John Locke, Étienne Bonnot de Condillac asserted that the source of human knowledge lay in the sensory perception of objects. Condillac's epistemology aligned nicely with the Pestalozzian emphasis on object teaching. Neef's emphasis on direct experience rather than authority and tradition is also evident in a volume he published in 1813, *The Method of Instruct-ing Children Rationally in the Arts of Writing and Reading*.

In 1813 Neef moved the school to Village Green, Pennsylvania, but there he became embroiled in religious controversies because of his views as a freethinker. Declining enrollments and financial losses prompted Neef to close the school in 1815 and move to Louisville, Kentucky. After an unsuccessful attempt to open another school, Neef temporarily left education. In 1821 he turned to farming near Louisville.

Five years later, at Maclure's request, Neef joined Robert Owen's communitarian socialist experiment at New Harmony, Indiana. Here, he ran a Pestalozzian school that enrolled approximately 200 students over time, ranging in age from five through twelve. Besides reading, writing, natural sciences, and mathematics, Neef's curriculum included a wide range of vocational activities that reflected Maclure's emphasis on utilitarian as opposed to classical studies. At New Harmony, Neef became a member of Maclure's Education Society, which was responsible for organizing and conducting the community's schools. Neef also sided with Paul Brown's "democratic" faction in its opposition to Owen's alleged paternalism. When the Owenite community dissolved in 1827, Neef moved to Cincinnati where he tried unsuccessfully to establish a Pestalozzian school. His efforts in 1828 to establish a seminary for the instruction of youth in Steubenville, Ohio, also failed. From 1830 to 1834 Neef resided at Jeffersonville, Indiana. He returned in 1835 to New Harmony where he was involved in several of the residues of Maclure's educational efforts, particularly the School Press of the Workingmen's Institute. Living in semiretirement, Neef remained in New Harmony until his death.

Neef was part of the emigration of intellectuals, scientists, and educators from Europe to America in the early nineteenth century. He is significant in the history of American education for his pioneering efforts to introduce Pestalozzian educational theory and practice to the United States. Directly trained by Pestalozzi, Neef's rendition of Pestalozzian principles, in his *Sketch* and *Method of Instructing Children*, closely followed the Swiss educator's philosophy and method. Neef, however, adapted Pestalozzianism to the milieu of the U.S. early national period by emphasizing republican civic education. With Maclure's financial support, Neef's schools represented an educational alternative to the conventional denominational schools or district schools that existed in the United States before the common school movement of the 1830s and 1840s. Neef's curriculum and instructional method, which emphasized the importance of children's direct experience in the educational process, anticipated the progressive practices of the late nineteenth and early twentieth centuries. Neef is also significant for his attraction to Owenism at New Harmony and his efforts to link Pestalozzianism to communitarianism.

• Letters and other documents relating to Neef are in the Joseph Neef Papers (1799–1849) in the Illinois State Historical

Survey of the University of Illinois at Urbana-Champaign and in the papers of William Maclure, Joseph Neef, and others in the Workingmen's Institute at New Harmony, Indiana. For Neef's educational theory and work in the United States, see Gerald L. Gutek, *Joseph Neef: The Americanization of Pestalozzianism* (1978). A biography of Neef is Charles W. Hackensmith, *Biography of Joseph Neef, Educator in the Ohio Valley, 1809–1854* (1973). Also, see George B. Lockwood, *The New Harmony Movement* (1905); Thomas A. Barlow, *Pestalozzi and American Education* (1977); Arthur Bestor, *Backwoods Utopias: The Sectarian and Owenite Phases of Communitarian Socialism in America: 1663–1829* (1950); and John F. C. Harrison, *Quest for the New Moral World: Robert Owen and the Owenites in Britain and America* (1969). There is a section on the American Pestalozzians in Kate Silber, *Pestalozzi: The Man and His Work* (1960).

GERALD L. GUTEK

NEEL, Alice Hartley (28 Jan. 1900–13 Oct. 1984), painter, was born in Merion Square, Pennsylvania, the daughter of Alice Concross Hartley and George Washington Neel, a clerk for the Pennsylvania Railroad. To please her family, she trained first to be a secretary but enrolled in the Philadelphia School of Design for Women (now Moore College of Art) in November 1921, telling her parents that she was studying commercial design. She graduated with a traditional training for a career as a figure painter in May 1925, and that same year she married Carlos Enriquez, a Cuban whom she had met at the Chester Springs Summer School of the Pennsylvania Academy of Fine Arts in 1924. In 1926 they moved to Havana, where she had her first exhibition at a small gallery. Instead of portraying the upper-class surroundings of her in-laws, Neel showed pictures of the poor, already revealing her social conscience and strong sense of identification with the disadvantaged.

In May 1927 Neel returned to Philadelphia with her daughter, Santillana, born six months earlier. In the fall her husband joined them in New York. Santillana died of diphtheria that winter, a tragedy commemorated in two later paintings (*Requiem*, 1928; *Futility of Effort*, 1930). A second daughter was born in November 1928. Neel's husband returned to Havana in May 1930, taking their daughter with him, but Neel remained in New York. The depression had, however, made it impossible to launch a career as an artist, and the combination of professional difficulties and loneliness resulted in a nervous breakdown. Neel spent a year in hospitals or at home in Philadelphia, gradually recovering. She began drawing again (*Suicidal Ward, Philadelphia General Hospital*, 1931), and by the fall of 1932 she was well enough to move back to New York. She lived for a year with Kenneth Doolittle, a sailor according to Neel, until, in a fit of jealousy, he vandalized most of her work. Her husband visited her with their daughter that summer, but she never saw him again. She never remarried but later had two sons by different companions. Neel raised them alone. Her many portraits of them and their families inspired some of her finest work.

Neel joined the Public Works of Art Project (PWAP) in 1933, earning $30 a week; from 1935 she was in the Works Progress Administration, which gave her $27 a week in return for producing a painting every six weeks. She exhibited in Philadelphia in a group show and received her first review (by Arthur B. Carles) in the *Philadelphia Inquirer*. Throughout the 1930s, Neel's work revealed both compassion for the poor and an awareness of current political developments (*Investigation of Poverty at the Russell Sage Foundation*, 1933; *West 17th Street*, 1935; *Nazis Murder Jews*, 1936). The majority of her paintings were, however, as they would continue to be for the rest of her life, pictures of friends and acquaintances whose physiognomy and personality appealed to her: poets, musicians, writers, political radicals, her neighbors in Spanish Harlem, and an occasional eccentric. Her career, like that of Pablo Picasso, cannot be understood without close knowledge of her family and friends, for her work is a visual diary of the people she encountered throughout her life who affected her deeply, even in a brief encounter. Her picture of an early "beatnik," Joe Gould, in the nude has a certain notoriety, but the forceful drawing, sober color, and intensity of her portrayals of Kenneth Fearing (1935, Museum of Modern Art, N.Y.) and Pat Whalen reading the *Daily Worker* (1935, Whitney Museum of American Art, N.Y.) are more typical of her work in that decade.

One of Neel's finest paintings from this period is *T. B. Harlem* (1940, National Museum of Women in the Arts, Washington, D.C.), which shows a young Puerto Rican in a hospital bed recovering from surgery for tuberculosis that collapsed a lung and removed eleven ribs. Typical of Neel is the choice of a vulnerable human being at a vulnerable moment and her willingness to exploit that moment while also empathizing deeply with the trauma of her subject. Her drawing is full of expressive distortions that have reminded critics of German Expressionism, a movement about which she claimed little firsthand knowledge. Her technique may look slapdash, but her compositions are always artfully calculated to emphasize significant gestures and thus project the character of each individual as powerfully as possible.

The support of the WPA ended in 1943, a time when Neel had two small children to support and only intermittent help from friends. She rarely sold anything and felt increasingly isolated in the 1950s as nonfigurative styles were promoted by New York galleries, and the human figure, even in her unsentimental form, was ignored by dealers, critics, and patrons. As she once wrote, "When I go to a show today of modern work I feel that my world has been swept away—and yet I do not think it can be so that the human creature will be forever *verboten*" (honorary doctorate address, Moore College of Art, 1971). Only in the 1960s did Neel begin to emerge from obscurity, receive some critical attention, and become better known. In December 1960 her portrait of Frank O'Hara (*Frank O'Hara, No. 2*, 1960) appeared in *Art News*. In 1962 three of her portraits were shown at the Kornblee Gallery in New York with work by Milton Avery, Elaine de Kooning, Larry Rivers, and others. That year she was awarded the Longview Foundation Prize by Dillard University, New Orleans, which acquired her picture of Stewart Mott, and she was profiled in *Art News* by Hubert Crehan. She was represented by the Graham Gallery for the first time in 1963, showing regularly with them until 1983, when she joined the Robert Miller Gallery.

Neel's work was by now well known in New York's art community. She painted many artists in the 1960s and 1970s (Robert Smithson, Benny and Mary Ellen Andrews, Isabel Bishop, Duane Hanson, Andy Warhol, the Soyer brothers [the last two paintings are in the Whitney Museum of American Art]), and other members of the New York art world (the composer Virgil Thompson [National Portrait Gallery, Washington, D.C.], critics such as John Perrault, John Gruen and his family, David Bourdon and Gregory Battcock [University of Texas at Austin], the art historian Linda Nochlin with her daughter Daisy [Boston Museum of Fine Arts], the scientist Linus Pauling [National Portrait Gallery], curator Jack Bauer, and filmmaker Michel Auder). She also continued to paint people she encountered in her daily life—a door-to-door salesman (*Fuller Brush Man*, 1965), the picture framer who reminded her of Marcel Proust (*Dennis Florio*, 1978), and, always, members of her own family. Of these, Neel responded most powerfully to Nancy Neel, her daughter-in-law, who was also in effect her private secretary and assistant, seeing in her a metaphor for the tensions between women's many roles in modern America and even a female Everyman facing the stress of daily life. Hating her own appearance, Neel never depicted herself until she was eighty, when she painted herself in the nude (National Portrait Gallery). A limited retrospective of Neel's work at the Whitney Museum in 1974 was followed by a more extensive survey organized by the Georgia Museum of Art in Athens in 1975. Many smaller shows followed at college and university museums and Neel became a popular speaker, known for pungent one-liners and irreverent comments about the people she had met and painted and the obstacles she had faced. She still rarely sold her work, rarely painted on commission, and continued to live modestly in the apartment she had moved to in 1962 on Broadway and 107th Street. Despite cataracts and failing health, she continued to paint until a few months before her death in New York.

Neel disliked the term "portrait" applied to her work, and her paintings are not conventional portraits. She nearly always painted people at her request, not theirs, and few of them could have afforded to buy her pictures. Her sitters came to her house, sat in her chairs, and were painted by Neel as she saw them, not as they wanted to be seen. Thus she inverted the usual relationship between artist and patron and revelled in the freedom that this situation gave her to "capture souls," rather than cater to bourgeois egos, and to expose some aspect of each human personality that moved her rather than following the bland neutrality of traditional portraiture. Neel's paintings became for the artist an extended portrait of the American psyche in the twentieth century. Few figurative painters of specific individuals, and certainly no American painters, have portrayed such a broad cast of human characters, especially those at the lower end of the economic and social scale. Neel forged her own immensely democratic form of portraiture whose integrity and compassion have been best understood by other artists.

The "human creature" was Neel's favorite and most frequent subject, but she also produced occasional landscapes and still lifes. These works record her spontaneous response to a visual encounter that sometimes also seemed to have metaphorical significance. The shadow of a building passing across the wall of a house on the street opposite her studio seemed a symbol of death approaching and so became the subject of one of her most powerful cityscapes (*107th and Broadway*, 1976). *Falling Tree* of 1958, which shows a forked tree trunk leaning across a summer landscape full of foreboding dark shadows, invites a similar reading to explain its expressive power. Neel also loved to paint flowers—velvety gloxinias brought by a visitor, Roses of Sharon gathered from the hedges of her modest summer house at Spring Lake, New Jersey, or lilacs bought to celebrate the arrival of warm weather. In these works, her pleasure in the sensation of sight and her ability to capture her joy in paint without the anxiety that permeated almost everything else she depicted makes them her most immediately appealing images. They are utterly without sentimental prettiness. She captures the visual character of each plant with her usual rough virtuosity and never lingers over fussy detail. In these works those who never met Neel can sense her energy and joie de vivre, for she was wonderful company and thoroughly enjoyed life away from the easel.

• Few of Neel's paintings can be seen in public collections; most of her work still belongs to her family. In addition to the museums and institutions mentioned above, there are paintings or drawings by her in the following public collections: Akron Museum of Art; Baltimore Museum of Art; Brooklyn Museum, N.Y.; Hirshhorn Museum and Sculpture Garden, Washington, D.C.; Honolulu Academy of Art; Hood Art Museum, Dartmouth College; Metropolitan Museum of Art, N.Y.; National Gallery of Art, Washington, D.C.; and Yale University Art Gallery. The Robert Miller Gallery in New York handles her estate. The best sources on Neel are Patricia Hills's *Alice Neel* (1983) and the essay by Cindy Nemser in *Alice Neel: The Woman and Her Work* (1975), a catalog for an exhibition at the Georgia Museum of Art, Athens. An obituary is in the *New York Times*, 15 Oct. 1984.

ANN SUTHERLAND HARRIS

NEF, John Ulric (14 June 1862–13 Aug. 1915), chemist and professor, was born in Herisau, Appenzell, Switzerland, the son of Johann Ulric Nef, a textile worker, and Anna Mock. His father immigrated to the United States in 1864 and worked at a textile mill in Housatonic, Massachusetts, where his family joined him in 1868. Nef was encouraged by his father to enjoy music, to work hard in school and at farm chores, and to cultivate sports. Nef played baseball, swam, and in later life was a vigorous hiker, mountain climber, and tennis player. As an undergraduate at Harvard, he became fascinated by chemistry and gave up his original plan to study medicine. He received scholarships to pay his way and graduated near the top of his class in 1884. He was awarded a Kirkland scholarship, which allowed him to spend three years of graduate work in Adolf von Baeyer's laboratory in Munich, then a leading center of research in organic chemistry. Nef's thesis was on quinone carboxylic acids, a topic suggested by Baeyer, who regarded him as one of his most brilliant students. He received his Ph.D. in 1886, summa cum laude. In Munich he indulged his life-long interest in music.

After an additional year of research, at Munich, he returned to a teaching position at Purdue (1887–1889), followed by three years at Clark University in Worcester, Massachusetts. Nef carried out the extended investigations with his own hands in these years. The resulting publications established his research reputation and led to his appointment as associate professor at the new University of Chicago, where he stayed for the rest of his life. Chicago rapidly became a leading university, and Nef's work established it as a center of chemical research and teaching.

Nef was a bold and prolific experimentalist, a good trainer of researchers (although a poor lecturer), and a dogmatic and doctrinaire thinker. He was convinced that reactions of organic compounds proceeded through divalent intermediates (methylenes), and he presented this view with great persistence and emphasis. Although methylene intermediates have not proved to be as widespread as Nef supposed, the concept is used to explain reactions where a methylene group ("carbene") gives additional reactions. Nef also studied the action of alkali on simple sugars, which results in isomerization and breakdown of the sugar chain in some cases. His hope that this work might lead to an understanding of the fermentation of sugars proved to be illusory, although the research did increase knowledge of the chemistry of simple sugars. Nef developed the use of acetylenes in synthesis—an important step, particularly with compounds related to vitamin A.

Nef told William Rainey Harper, president of the University of Chicago, that it should be possible to establish at Chicago a school of chemistry equal in quality to the good German universities. He succeeded in this, but his aim to imitate the administrative structure of European universities failed. Nef's own rather authoritarian personality was at home in the European professorial system, where the professor was the complete autocrat of his department or institute, controlling if he wished all research and teaching activity. Such a system never flourished in the egalitarian society of American chemistry. In his later years at Chicago, Nef unsuccessfully tried to raise money to support a personal research institute, which would free him from teaching and administrative responsibilities.

Nef married Louise Bates Comstock in 1898; one son was born. This very happy marriage was a bright spot in the record of personal strain—resulting from work and his mother's poor health—which had characterized Nef's life. His wife's untimely death in 1909 was a great blow. His years of very hard, driving work produced serious physical breakdowns in 1903 and 1911. He died suddenly of a heart attack in Carmel, California.

The twenty-eight doctoral students and eight research associates supervised by Nef during his years at Chicago published their research without his name, though he directed their research in detail. A number of his students reached responsible positions in academia and research institutions, including H. A. Spoehr, who became an expert on photosynthesis at the Carnegie Institution.

• The two boxes of Nef papers at the University of Chicago contain *inter alia* letters, mainly from his Chicago years, a manuscript biography of Nef by his son, and hundreds of pages of handwritten laboratory notes. The biography by M. L. Wolfrom in *National Academy of Sciences Biographical Memoirs* 34 (1960): 204–27, has a complete bibliography of his publications and a list of publications by his collaborators, based on research done under his direction. L. W. Jones, *Proceedings of the American Chemical Society* (1917): 44–72, gives a detailed if uncritical account of Nef's scientific work.

D. STANLEY TARBELL

NEGRI, Pola (31 Dec. 1899?–1 Aug. 1987), silent screen actress, was born Barbara Apolonia Chalupiec in Lipno or Janowa, Poland, the daughter of Jerzy Mathias-Chalupiec, a Slovak immigrant, and Eleanora de Kielczeska. The facts of Negri's life, especially her early years, have been obscured by romanticized memory and successive coats of studio publicity. Her year of birth has been reported as any from 1894 to 1899; her father's occupation has ranged from count to violinist to tin master; her autobiography declares that her mother came from "impoverished nobility." In any case, she claimed that her father was taken away by Russian czarist authorities in 1905 and that she and her mother subsequently moved to Warsaw.

While still very young, Negri enrolled in the Imperial Ballet School in Warsaw and attracted enough attention to be considered later for the Warsaw Imperial Academy of Dramatic Arts. Appearing in productions of Henrik Ibsen's *The Wild Duck* and Gerhart Hauptmann's *Hanele*, she eventually caught the eye of Polish film pioneer Aleksander Hertz. As Pola Negri—her last name adopted from her favorite writer, Italian poet Ada Negri—she had already made her film debut in one of Poland's earliest motion pictures, *Niewolnica Zmyslow* (A slave to her senses, aka Slave of sin; 1914). With Hertz, she made seven films between 1915 and 1916 and became a star of the fledgling Polish film scene. She also kept her place on stage, where her part in the Polish version of Max Reinhardt's pantomime play *Sumurun* brought her the chance to work with the great theater director in Berlin.

Among Reinhardt's circle, she met comic actor and director Ernst Lubitsch, with whom she formed a strong friendship and collaboration that resulted in several successful films between 1918 and 1922. Especially popular were their historical costume films made for the German film studio PAGU and distributed by UFA: *Carmen* (1918), *Madame Du Barry* (1919), and the film version of *Sumurun* (1920). She played her roles with a lusty abandon that won her many fans on both sides of the Atlantic, making her one of the most popular stars of the German cinema. *Madame Du Barry* was released in the United States as *Passion* in 1920 to such acclaim that she and Lubitsch won contracts with Paramount in 1923.

The collaboration with Lubitsch was not to continue, however; they made only one film together in the United States (*Forbidden Paradise*, 1924). Instead, the studio carved a niche for Negri as the duplicitous vamp she had played in two of her German films, *The Eyes of the Mummy* (1918) and *Carmen*. Her first films in the United States—*Bella Donna*, *The Cheat*, and *The Spanish Dancer*—quickly cast her as the quintessential femme fatale. She struggled against this typecasting throughout her six years in Hollywood and later protested, "I was never the vamp. I was the great dramatic actress. Would you call the chambermaid I played in *Hotel Imperial* a vamp? Or the peasant in *Barbed Wire* a vamp? Definitely not. As far as I'm concerned, vamps went down the drain with the market in 1929" (quoted in Rosen, p. 111). Still, while her performance in *Hotel Imperial* (1927) was one of the best of silent cinema, her American career never matched the critical success she had enjoyed in Germany.

In fact, it was Negri's off-screen persona that kept her in the public eye and earned her reputed $10,000-a-week salary. Like most big stars, she was the object of many publicity stunts. From the very beginning, Paramount made much of a supposed rivalry between Negri and the other diva of the studio, Gloria Swanson. Studio publicists also eagerly played up her arguments with producers and directors. Her legendary affairs and marriages helped keep the publicity fires burning; Charlie Chaplin, Rod La Rocque, and Rudolph Valentino could be counted among her flames. She claimed Valentino to be the one great love of her life and her histrionics at his funeral are the stuff of Hollywood myth. She married Prince Serge Mdivani on the rebound in 1927 (she had been married from 1919 to 1923 to Polish army officer Count Eugene Dambski; neither marriage resulted in children), and she blamed her eventual decline at the box office on the Valentino cult: "They wanted me to remain faithful to Rudy's legend. I refused" (*Los Angeles Times*, 9 Aug. 1987). Her flamboyance expressed itself in her clothes as well; she was responsible for many of the fashions that we now associate with the Roaring Twenties: turbans, leather boots for women, and leopards on leash.

The stock market crash and, as Negri would later write, her husband's mismanagement of her financial affairs led to the loss of a large part of her considerable fortune and to her divorce from Mdivani in 1931. After the critical and box-office failure of her first talkie, *A Woman Commands* (1932), she left Hollywood for Germany, where she made several films before the outbreak of World War II. Among them, *Mazurka* (1935) was said to be Adolf Hitler's favorite, and newspapers in Europe and the United States printed reports of a romance between Negri and the Führer. She struck back with a lawsuit against the French magazine that started the rumor and won a 10,000-franc judgment.

Negri returned to the United States in 1941, her fortune depleted, but she had trouble finding work. Her only film of the 1940s was the inconspicuous comedy *Hi Diddle Diddle* (1943). Her luck turned when she met and befriended Margaret West, a wealthy Texas woman who shared her fondness for travel and invited Negri to share her Texas and California homes. Negri retired from the screen and became an American citizen in 1951. The two women were devoted, yet platonic, companions (as Negri stressed in her biography) until West's death in 1963. Negri made a comeback that year in Walt Disney's *The Moonspinners*. She later admitted that she took the part only to forget West's death. Negri spent her later years active in philanthropical, cultural, and religious endeavors until her death in San Antonio, Texas.

• Clippings on Negri can be found in the Academy of Motion Picture Arts and Sciences Center for Motion Picture Study in Beverly Hills, Calif. Her autobiography is titled *Memoirs of a Star* (1970). See also Marjorie Rosen, *Popcorn Venus: Women, Movies, and the American Dream* (1973). Obituaries are in the *Los Angeles Times* and the *New York Times*, 3 Aug. 1987.

SCOTT CURTIS

NEIGHBORS, Robert Simpson (3 Nov. 1815–14 Sept. 1859), explorer and Indian agent, was born in Charlotte County, Virginia, the son of William Neighbours, a college professor, and Elizabeth Elam. Both parents died of pneumonia when Robert was four months old. Robert, the last of seven children, spent his youth with court-appointed guardian Samuel Hamner. Before Neighbors left Virginia, he received at least one year and nine months of formal schooling paid for by Hamner. Christened Samuel Robertson Neighbours, the nineteen-year-old youth reworked his name when he traveled to Louisiana. While working as a clerk Neighbors heard about the fall of the Alamo. He volunteered and arrived in Texas in the spring of 1836, fighting in the battle of San Jacinto in Captain Hayden Arnold's company. Back in Louisiana he joined the Masonic Lodge at St. Albans.

In 1838 Neighbors wrote his name in the visitors' log at the Houston Masonic Lodge. Settling there, he obtained a job as a store clerk, but his army connections propelled him into a career in politics. Several important Texas Republic figures were fellow Masons, and on 30 January 1839 Texas president Mirabeau B. Lamar appointed him a Texas army first lieutenant. A year later as a major he took command of Galveston Island's Fort Travis. Reassigned army quartermaster by president Lamar, Neighbors languished for the next three years until he joined Captain John Coffee Hays's Ranger company in July 1842. Neighbors and forty men were left behind to guard a session of the Texas Western District Court when Mexican general Adrian Woll attacked Texas. At dawn on 15 September 1842 Woll and 1,600 soldiers surrounded San Antonio. After a short fight on the foggy public square, Neighbors asked for terms. Fifty-two men, including Neighbors, Samuel Maverick, and the entire Texas court system, were marched in chains to Mexico. After three grueling months, the prisoners stopped at the foot of the fortress of San Carlos de Peroté, a seventy-year-old former Spanish prison.

Ragged and starved, Neighbors and his men were thrown into the dungeon. For two years the Texans suffered captivity until Mexican president Antonio López de Santa Anna released them on 24 March 1844. Neighbors stepped ashore at Galveston from the brig *Neptune* in April.

After his return, Neighbors spent three years as a Texas Indian agent. He explored the source of the Red River and helped arrange the important 1847 Meusebach-Comanche Treaty as a "special representative" of the first Texas governor, James Pinckney Henderson. Neighbors accompanied German noble, John O. Meusebach, the commissioner-general of the Adelsverein German immigration company, when he met the San Saba Comanches, still "antagonized" by Dr. F. A. Schubert's expedition of 1846. The treaty talks were held at Council Springs, Robinson County, and included Caddoes and other peoples. The agreement permitted German settlers to travel unharmed in Comanche territory and offered mutual reports of wrongful acts. Neighbors was instrumental later that year heading off a confrontation with the Penateka Comanches, which permitted Germans to settle on parts of the country. Historian Rupert N. Richardson said Neighbors "instituted a field system of Indian contact. Instead of waiting for the Indians to come to him, as was the common practice, Neighbors visited them in their camps. He had greater influence with Indians than any other agent in Texas."

With the election of President Zachary Taylor, Neighbors lost his federal patronage job and turned to state politics. Neighbors took time in July 1850 to marry Elizabeth Ann Mays from Seguin, Guadalupe County; they had four children. That fall Neighbors and Maverick were elected representatives to the Fourth Texas Congress. Neighbors submitted a law that established Indian reservations. At the national convention in 1852 he helped nominate Franklin Pierce.

On 9 May 1853 President Pierce appointed him supervising Indian agent for Texas. Since the Texas government retained ownership of its land after statehood, the federal government could not set aside land in Texas. Agent Neighbors argued for both a "homeland" for the Penateka Comanches and a refuge for the more friendly Indians. After two years of exploring West Texas with Randolph B. Marcy, Neighbors persuaded the Penateka Comanches to settle in the north. He camped them along the Brazos Clear Fork in unorganized Throckmorton County. Seventy miles east, other tribes moved onto the Lower Brazos Reservation. Neighbors set up his headquarters at Fort Belknap in Young County and sent a fellow Texas legislator, John Robert Baylor, to run the Upper Reservation.

Neighbors's troubles increased when Secretary of War Jefferson Davis ordered the Second U.S. Cavalry Regiment to Texas, ostensibly to guard the Indian reservations. Davis, however, planned for the Texas frontier to be a training ground for Confederate generals. When Robert E. Lee arrived in December 1855, he led sixteen junior officers destined for general rank. That April Lee established Camp Cooper near the Comanches.

Lee submitted Neighbors a negative report on Baylor, and Neighbors fired the agent for corruption. The infuriated former agent established a base of operations in Buchanan County from which he could retaliate against his enemies. For three years the ranch served as headquarters for a band of vigilantes called the Old Law Mob. Baylor also edited a rabid Jacksboro newspaper called the *White Man*. For two years the newspaper incited hatred and fear against Neighbors and the Indians.

In May 1859 Baylor and 300 armed settlers attacked the Lower Reservation but were chased away by the Indians. Unfortunately the incident convinced the Texas state government that the reservation experiment had failed.

On 26 June the Texas governor ordered Neighbors to move the angry, confused, and fearful bands of Indians to the Leased District in Indian Territory. Bitter, Neighbors collected his wards and led them north on 30 July, settling several groups of Indians, including the Penateka Comanches near Fort Cobb in the middle of August. On 12 September he returned to Fort Belknap to conclude his affairs. Two days later, on the town's street, Patrick Murphy stepped out and, without provocation, drew his pistol. Neighbors tried to talk to the man, but Murphy's brother-in-law Ed Cornett shot Neighbors in the back. Mortally wounded, Neighbors died within a few minutes. The townspeople buried Neighbors in the town cemetery. County authorities charged Baylor as an accomplice in Neighbors's murder, but a trial was never held. A year later the Young County sheriff tracked down Cornett on another charge and killed him for resisting arrest.

• To examine Neighbors's life story through original documents, see the U.S. government's "Commissioner of Indian Affairs Documents" (microfilm). Also see "Texas Ranger Papers" and "Neighbors' Papers," including the letter of Mrs. Catherine Mays Darden, 20 Sept. 1910, in the Archives Division of the Texas State Library in Austin. Valuable information is in Anna Muckleroy, "The Indian Policy of the Republic of Texas," *Southwestern Historical Quarterly* 25–26 (1921–1923); and Lena Clara Kock, "The Federal Indian Policy in Texas," *Southwestern Historical Quarterly* 28–29 (1924–1926). Neighbors's exploring partner Randolph B. Marcy wrote *Thirty Years of Army Life on the Border* (1866; repr. 1963). For a recent biography, see Kenneth Neighbours, *Robert S. Neighbors on the Frontier of Texas, 1835–1859* (1975). Brief sketches can be found in Walter Prescott Webb, ed., *Handbook of Texas* (2 vols., 1952), and Dan L. Thrapp, *Encyclopedia of Frontier History* (1995).

VERNON R. MADDUX

NEIHARDT, John Gneisenau (8 Jan. 1881–4 Nov. 1973), poet laureate of Nebraska, was born John Greenleaf Neihardt near Sharpsburg, Illinois, the son of Nicholas Neihardt, who had several unskilled occupations, and Alice Culler. Neihardt's father was a man with intellectual yearnings, if little education. Neihardt recalled that his father told him of Charles Darwin and Thomas Huxley, for example, before he was ten years old. In naming his son after the poet John Greenleaf Whittier, Nicholas Neihardt gave his son "the most precious name he knew," according to John Neihardt's autobiography, *All Is but a Beginning* (1972, p. 6). However, Neihardt did not wish to be named for another poet and so he changed his middle name to honor the Prussian field marshal August Graf von Gneisenau. All too soon Nicholas deserted his family, and so Alice Neihardt moved her children to the prairies of Kansas and Nebraska, where she worked as a dressmaker. Neihardt went to school, did farm work, and had, as he remembered it, a happy childhood.

Neihardt was eleven when he gave up the development of a steam turbine of his own design for poetry. As he tells the story, a dream in a time of illness inspired him to make this change. In his dream the world spun, there was darkness, and the boy Neihardt found himself flying face down through a starry vastness. "There was a dreadful speed. . . . A great Voice . . . drove me on." This dream came upon him six times. Eventually he understood the dream to be calling him to abandon himself to "the costly rewards of spiritual striving" (*All Is but a Beginning*, p. 48). Neihardt did not dawdle in his newfound poetic vocation. When he was fifteen he wrote and published (in a local newspaper) a mock epic, *The Tentiad*, about the collapse of a revivalist's tent in a windstorm. At sixteen he wrote a long poem influenced by Hindu mysticism, *The Divine Enchantment* (1900), but this volume met with little success.

Neihardt earned his bread in many ways in these early years. He had graduated from Nebraska Normal School in 1896, and so he was a qualified teacher. He taught for a time in Hoskins, Nebraska, but he was seldom able to find such work. He did farm work, day labor, marble polishing, and janitorial work. In 1900 he worked briefly as a reporter for the *Omaha Daily News* and then as a clerk for J. J. Elkin, an Indian trader on the Omaha reservation. In 1903 he became editor of the *Bancroft Blade*. But throughout these years he continued to write lyric love poetry and poems of love, and of the yearning for love's spiritual fulfillment. In 1907 some of these poems were published in New York as *A Bundle of Myrrh*.

This book was an immediate success, praised by many critics, including those of the *New York Times*. But his most ardent reader was surely Mona Martinsen, the daughter of Rudolph Martinsen, sometime president of the Missouri, Kansas & Texas Railroad. Mona Martinsen was recently returned to New York from Paris, where she had studied sculpture with Rodin. She wrote the poet a letter, and he replied. After six months of amorous correspondence, she boarded a train to Omaha, where Neihardt met her at the station with a marriage license in hand. Thus in 1908 Martinsen went from a life of moneyed ease to a cottage without running water or electricity. She soon added the art of homemaking to her other accomplishments, and by all accounts theirs was a loving marriage until her death in 1958. They had four children. Neihardt published two more volumes of lyric poetry, *Man-Song* (1909) and *The Stranger at the Gate* (1912). In these poems Neihardt gave expression to his conception of ideal love: mature, married love. H. L. Mencken was among those who praised these poems.

In 1912 Neihardt determined not to write further lyrics and short stories. He was ready to pass on to the less personal labor of the mature poet: writing epics. He was thus thinking of himself as a participant in a lofty and venerable tradition much like Virgil, Edmund Spenser, and John Milton, who wrote epics in their maturity. That Neihardt should think of himself in such company is a measure of his poetic ambition. Eventually Neihardt's epic took the form of five "songs," each in heroic couplets. Neihardt's heroes were the fur trappers, mountain men, Indians, and other courageous common men. Together these songs tell in tragic terms the history of the westward expansion, from the time of the mountain men to the end of the Indian wars. In chronological order they are *The Song of Three Friends* (1919), *The Song of Hugh Glass* (1915), *The Song of the Indian Wars* (1925), *The Song of the Messiah* (1935), and *The Song of Jed Smith* (1941); these were published together as *A Cycle of the West* (1949). The *Songs* were well received; from 1919 to 1928 school editions of *Three Friends*, *Hugh Glass*, and *Indian Wars* were published, complete with explanatory notes and a preface by Julius House.

Neihardt's best-known work, however, is *Black Elk Speaks* (1932), the as-told-to autobiography of an Oglala Sioux medicine man. At the heart of this book is Black Elk's Great Vision, which shaped Black Elk's life and gave him the powers and the purpose of his calling. *Black Elk Speaks* has achieved the status of scripture for some American Indians; the book has been published in numerous editions and has been translated into eight languages. It is one of the most widely read books about American Indians. One of the things that drew Black Elk to Neihardt was his sense that Neihardt took visions and spiritual powers seriously, as indeed Neihardt did, from the time of his own vision at age eleven to his founding of a Society for Research in Rapport and Telekinesis in 1961.

In 1948 Neihardt moved to a farm near Columbia, Missouri, and joined the faculty of the University of Missouri. He was at work on *Patterns and Coincidences: A Sequel to* All Is but a Beginning (1978), the second volume of his autobiography, when he died in Lincoln, Nebraska.

• Neihardt's papers are widely scattered. Most are in the Western Historical Manuscript Collection in the Ellis Library, University of Missouri at Columbia; the Seymour Library, Knox College; the Henry E. Huntington Library, San Marino, Calif.; and the Bancroft Library, University of Calif. at Berkeley. For biographies of Neihardt, see Julius T. House, *John G. Neihardt* (1920); Blair Whitney, *John G. Neihardt* (1976); and Lucile Aly, *John G. Neihardt* (1977). For a bibliography, including listings of Neihardt papers, letters, and manuscripts and listings of films and audiotapes of Neihardt, see John T. Richards, *Rawhide Laureate: John G. Neihardt: A Selected, Annotated Bibliography* (1983). For Neihardt's psychic experiments, see John T. Richards, *SORRAT: A History of the Neihardt Psychokinesis Experiments* (1982). For literary criticism, see Paul Olson, "*Black Elk Speaks* as Epic and Ritual Attempt to Reverse History," in *Vision and Refuge: Essays on the Literature of the Great Plains*, ed. F. C. Luebke and V. Faulkner (1982): 3–30, and Vine Deloria, Jr., ed., *Essays in Memory of John G. Neihardt* (1984). An obituary is in the *New York Times*, 4 Nov. 1973.

H. DAVID BRUMBLE

NEILSON, Nellie (5 Apr. 1873–26 May 1947), historian, was born in Philadelphia, the daughter of William George Neilson, a mining engineer and a founder of Standard Steel works, and Mary Louise Cunningham. One of six children, Neilson attended private schools in Philadelphia and received all of her academic training at Bryn Mawr College (a B.A. in 1893, an M.A. in 1894, and a Ph.D. in history in 1899). Her dissertation, "Economic Conditions on the Manors of Ramsey Abbey," was a study of an entire estate, rather than just an individual manor, combining economic and legal history; it was published upon its completion. The best known among women who had received the doctorate in history before 1900, Neilson also was the first woman to publish in the *American Historical Review*; her article, "The Boon Services on the Estates of Ramsey Abbey," appeared in 1897, two years before she received the doctorate.

In 1900 Neilson became a reader in English at Bryn Mawr, and in 1902 she joined the history faculty at Mount Holyoke College, where she taught until 1939. At Mount Holyoke, she was promoted to full professor and chairperson of the Department of History in 1905, a position that she held until retirement. Neilson inspired dozens of Mount Holyoke undergraduates to seek advanced training in medieval history, many of whom followed in her footsteps and attended Bryn Mawr.

Neilson spent many summers in England, where she studied at Cambridge and Oxford, and conducted research in the British Library and Museum. Having worked at Bryn Mawr under the direction of Charles McLean Andrews, a historian of colonial America, she also studied in 1897–1898 at the London School of Economics with Paul Vinograff and Frederick William Maitland, pioneers in the field of British medieval history. Her major scholarly contribution, the illumination of the diversity of land use and customary rites in England, emphasized the influence of local customs on the development of the common law. She published "Customary Rents" in *Oxford Studies in Social and Legal History* in 1910 and *A Terrier of Fleet, Lincolnshire* in 1920. During the 1920s, Neilson's most productive years, she published three edited collections of documentary source materials and two pathbreaking articles: "Custom and the Common Law in Kent," *Harvard Law Review* (1925), and "The Cartulary of Bilsington, Kent," *British Academy Record of Social and Economic History* (1928). Throughout the 1930s and early 1940s she continued to publish articles on British medieval economic and legal history in such journals as *Harvard Law Review, Toronto Law Journal, American Economic Review, Economic History Review*, and *Speculum*.

Active in the American Historical Association from its early years, Neilson had served on several committees as well as the Executive Council and was elected to the editorial board of the *American Historical Review* in 1935. Serving on the board until 1940, she not only enhanced her own credentials but was also able to assist more women in getting articles published in the *AHR*. Although she probably would not have labeled herself a feminist, she believed that women scholars should be judged by the same standards as their male colleagues and should be awarded the same recognition.

A campaign, which began in 1932, to elect her the first woman president of the AHA took almost ten years of lobbying by women historians and their male allies to succeed. Having finally earned the respect of men in her field, who recognized her superior scholarship and teaching skills, Neilson was elected the third vice president of the association in 1940. She took office as president in 1943, when she was seventy years old. Suffering from near-blindness and a heart condition as she advanced in age, Neilson could not effectively serve in the office of president. Her presidential address, "The Early Pattern of the Common Law," dealt with the themes that had preoccupied her throughout her scholarly career.

Neilson achieved international recognition as a medievalist and became a member of the Selden Society and the Institute of Historical Research. She was a founding member of the Medieval Academy of America in 1847 and a founder of its journal *Speculum*. Elected the academy's president, she was for many years its only female fellow. The British Royal Historical Society named her a fellow.

Neilson continued to live in South Hadley, Massachusetts, after her retirement, and died at her home there. She never married. Neilson's major contribution was as a teacher and scholar. In her work she showed the influence of local custom on the development of the common law in medieval England. As a teacher she inspired many young women to pursue graduate training in history.

• Mount Holyoke College Archives contains the records of the Department of History, which provide insight into Neilson's work as the chairperson. Her colleague Viola Barnes provided an oral history that discusses her relations with Neilson, which can be found at the College Archives under Barnes's name. Neilson's correspondence may be found in the records of the American Historical Association, in the papers of J. Franklin Jameson in the Manuscript Division of the Library of Congress, and in the M. Cary Thomas Papers at Bryn Mawr College Archives. The best biographical treatment is Penina Migdall Glazer and Miriam Slater, *Unequal Colleagues: The Entrance of Women into the Professions, 1880–1940* (1987).

JACQUELINE GOGGIN

NEILSON, William Allan (28 Mar. 1869–13 Feb. 1946), college president, was born in Doune, Perthshire, Scotland, the son of David Neilson, master of the Free Church School, and Mary Allen. He was educated at the University of Edinburgh, where he took a master's in philosophy in 1891 and then moved to Canada, where he taught English at Upper Canada College (1891–1895), a preparatory school for boys in Toronto.

Neilson then entered the graduate program in English literature at Harvard University, arriving just at the time when the development of graduate education was gaining momentum under the leadership of President Charles W. Eliot. Neilson worked with two distinguished scholars, Francis J. Child and George L. Kittredge, who were particularly dedicated to advancing rigorous notions of scholarship in the academic profession. He received his Ph.D. in 1898.

Neilson's first teaching position was at Bryn Mawr College, where the president, M. Carey Thomas, was committed to developing a women's college with the highest academic standards. Although he did not have a satisfactory relationship with President Thomas and left after two years, it was his first experience teaching women students and an early indicator of his later commitment to first-rate education for women undergraduates. His mentor, Kittredge, invited him to return to Harvard, where he became a successful member of the English department. Neilson's major scholarly contribution was as the editor of the Cambridge edition of William Shakespeare's *Complete Dramatic and Poetic Works* (1906; rev. ed. 1942). Except for a brief interlude at Columbia University from 1904 to 1906, Neilson spent all of his teaching career at Harvard until 1917, when he was offered the presidency of Smith College.

A colleague from Harvard who had joined the Smith faculty, Sidney Fay, nominated Neilson to be the third president of Smith College. President Eliot and other Harvard colleagues encouraged Neilson to stay at Harvard. They believed that a professorship at Harvard held far greater significance and promise for a contri-

bution to American education than the presidency of a women's college. Neilson himself was ambivalent about leaving a distinguished faculty position and undertaking an administrative position with fundraising responsibilities. After much deliberation, Neilson accepted the position and moved to Northampton, Massachusetts, in September 1917. In part he was influenced by the fact that the Smith trustees emphasized their desire to appoint a scholar-president for the first time. Neilson also had had fifteen years of experience in teaching women at two other important women's colleges, Radcliffe and Barnard, during his tenure at Harvard and Columbia. From those experiences he had developed much sympathy for the educational mission of the women's colleges.

Neilson's twenty-two years at Smith were crucial in developing the reputation of that institution as one of the outstanding liberal arts colleges in the country for women. He developed a faculty of teacher-scholars when many had not yet accepted that ideal for the small women's schools. He used every device possible, from raising salaries to reorganizing the class schedule to allow faculty more research time, in order to attract a distinguished faculty of men and women. He recognized that the most outstanding men would eventually be lured to larger universities and that the women, having fewer opportunities, would more likely spend their entire career at Smith.

During Neilson's tenure, he oversaw the construction of dormitories so that the campus could become fully residential. He was responsible for the building of a music building, a gymnasium, and an art gallery. All of these reflected avant-garde ideas about the necessity of including music, art, and physical education in the curriculum, not as frills for the finishing education of young ladies, but as disciplines to be treated with rigor equal to other departments. He played a crucial role in the development of a graduate program in the newly emerging field of psychiatric social work.

Outside of Smith, Neilson was well known for his devotion to liberal causes. He was an outspoken defender of academic freedom during the 1920s when there was considerable Red-baiting on campuses. He actively defended several controversial members of his faculty against the wishes of a small vocal group of alumnae. He also urged the United States to join the League of Nations, advocated recognition of the Soviet Union, served on the board of the National Association for the Advancement of Colored People from 1930 to 1946, and joined in the efforts to overturn the conviction of Sacco and Vanzetti. During the 1930s Neilson made special efforts to appoint academics who were refugees from Germany and encouraged colleagues at other institutions to do the same. In addition, he served as president of the Modern Language Association in 1924.

After his retirement in 1939 Neilson continued to be active in a variety of liberal organizations and undertook to write a history of Smith College. He died in Northampton just before the completion of this work. Neilson was married in 1906 to Elisabeth Muser; they had three children, one of whom died at age seventeen.

• All of Neilson's papers are in the archives at Smith College. The most complete biography is Margaret Farrand Thorp, *Neilson of Smith* (1956). An obituary is in the *New York Times*, 14 Feb. 1946.

PENINA MIGDAL GLAZER

NELL, William Cooper (20 Dec. 1816–25 May 1874), abolitionist and historian, was born in Boston, Massachusetts, the son of William Guion Nell, a tailor, and Louisa (maiden name unknown). His father, a prominent figure in the small but influential African-American community in Boston's West End during the 1820s, was a next-door neighbor and close associate of the controversial black abolitionist David Walker. Nell studied at the all-black Smith School, which met in the basement of Boston's African Meeting House. Although he was an excellent student, in 1829 he was denied honors given to outstanding pupils by the local school board because of his race. This and similar humiliations prompted him to dedicate his life to eliminating racial barriers. To better accomplish that task, Nell read law in the office of local abolitionist William I. Bowditch in the early 1830s. Although he never practiced, his legal skills and knowledge proved valuable in the antislavery and civil rights struggles of his era.

Nell naturally gravitated toward the emerging abolitionist crusade. In 1831 he became an errand boy for the *Liberator*, the leading antislavery journal, beginning a long and close relationship with its editor, William Lloyd Garrison. His talents were quickly recognized, and he was soon made a printer's apprentice, then a clerk in the paper's operations. In the latter position, which he assumed in 1840, he wrote articles, supervised the paper's Negro Employment Office, arranged meetings, corresponded with other abolitionists, and represented Garrison at various antislavery functions. The pay was low, so he was forced to supplement his income by advertising his services as a bookkeeper and copyist. But he remained one of Garrison's most ardent supporters, even as the Boston abolitionist grew increasingly controversial because of his singular devotion to moral rather than political means and his embrace of a wide variety of reforms.

After the antislavery movement divided into two hostile camps in 1840 over questions of appropriate tactics and women's role, Nell vehemently criticized those black abolitionists who parted company with Garrison. He moved to Rochester, New York, in 1848 and helped Frederick Douglass publish the *North Star*. But when growing conflict between Garrison and Douglass forced him to choose sides, he returned to Boston and the *Liberator*. In 1856 Nell traveled through lower Canada West (now Ontario) and the Midwest, visiting black communities, attending antislavery meetings, and submitting regular reports to the *Liberator*. His accounts of this journey are a useful record of African-American life in those areas at the time.

Nell was perhaps the most outspoken and consistent advocate of racial integration in the antebellum United States. He worked closely with white reformers and regularly pressed other blacks to abandon "all separate action, and becom[e] part and parcel of the general community" (quoted in Smith, p. 184). Nell participated in a statewide campaign to end segregated "Jim Crow" cars on Massachusetts railroads in the early 1840s. He used the antislavery press as a vehicle to attack black exclusion from or segregation in churches, schools and colleges, restaurants, hotels, militia units, theaters, and other places of entertainment.

From 1840 to 1855 Nell led a successful petition campaign to integrate the public schools of Boston, which ended when the Massachusetts legislature outlawed racially separate education in the state. He even opposed the existence of voluntary separatism among African Americans. In 1843 he represented Boston at the National Convention of Colored Citizens in Buffalo and used that forum as a vehicle to speak out against exclusive black gatherings and activism. An outspoken critic of the black churches, he often attended the predominantly white Memorial Meeting House in West Roxbury.

But Nell supported separate black organizations when they met needs not performed by integrated ones. For example, in 1842 he helped establish the Freedom Association, a local black group founded to aid and protect fugitive slaves. He remained active in this group for four years until the interracial Boston Vigilance Committee was founded for the same purpose. Although he established numerous cultural and literary societies—most notably the Adelphic Union and the Boston Young Men's Literary Society—among Boston blacks after 1830, these were always open to individuals of every race and class.

Nell tempered his opposition to politics and exclusive black activism in the early 1850s. He was nominated by the Free-Soil party for the Massachusetts legislature in 1850. After the Fugitive Slave Act of 1850 was passed, he stepped up his role in local underground railroad activities until illness forced his temporary retirement from the antislavery stage.

About this time Nell began extensive research on the African-American experience in the United States. He perceived that black history and memory would help shape the identity of his race and advance the struggle against slavery and racial prejudice. His research resulted in the publication of *Services of Colored Americans in the Wars of 1776 and 1812* (1851), *Colored Patriots of the American Revolution* (1855), and dozens of articles and pamphlets. The careful scholarship and innovative use of oral sources in Nell's works, which were far broader than their titles suggest, made them the most useful and important histories of African Americans written in the Civil War era.

Nell's historical activism also took a more popular turn. In 1858 he organized the first of seven annual Crispus Attucks Day celebrations in Boston to honor

African-American heroes of the American Revolution. Held the fifth day of every March in Faneuil Hall, the festivities consisted of speeches, martial music, displays of revolutionary war relics, and the recollections of aged black veterans. These gatherings symbolically rejected the decision of the U.S. Supreme Court in *Dred Scott v. Sandford* (1857), which unequivocally denied black claims to American citizenship. Nell also petitioned the Massachusetts state legislature on numerous occasions for an Attucks monument in Boston.

When the Civil War came, Nell embraced the Union cause, anticipating the end of slavery and racial inequality in American life. His hopes were buoyed in 1861, when he was employed as a postal clerk in the Boston post office. This made him the first African American appointed to a position in the U.S. government, and he held the job until his death. He was further encouraged by the Emancipation Proclamation and the decision to enlist black troops in the Union army.

The end of the war brought a series of personal changes for Nell. When the *Liberator* ceased operations in December 1865, it marked the denouement of Nell's lengthy career in reform journalism. But it did not mean the abandonment of activism; during the late 1860s he waged a successful campaign to end racial discrimination in theaters and other public places in Boston. Nell married Frances A. Amers of New Hampshire in 1869; they had two sons. He spent the remainder of his life completing a study of African-American troops in the Civil War. It was apparently unfinished when he died in Boston of "paralysis of the brain."

• Most of Nell's published letters and editorials can be found in the *Liberator* (Boston) and the *North Star* (Rochester). These and many manuscript letters are available in the microfilm edition of the *Black Abolitionist Papers* (1981). Brief biographies of Nell are in C. Peter Ripley et al., eds., *The Black Abolitionist Papers*, vol. 3 (1991), and James O. Horton, "Generations of Protest: Black Families and Social Reform in Ante-Bellum Boston," *New England Quarterly* 94 (1976): 242–56. Longer studies include Robert P. Smith, "William Cooper Nell: Crusading Black Abolitionist," *Journal of Negro History* 55 (1970): 182–99; Dorothy Porter Wesley, "Integration versus Separatism: William Cooper Nell's Role in the Struggle for Equality," in *Courage and Conscience: Black and White Abolitionists in Boston*, ed. Donald M. Jacobs (1993), pp. 207–24; and James O. Horton and Lois E. Horton, *Black Bostonians: Family Life and Community Struggle in the Antebellum North* (1979). An informative obituary is in the *Pacific Appeal* (San Francisco), 18 July 1874.

ROY E. FINKENBINE

NELSON, Benjamin (11 Feb. 1911–17 Sept. 1977), sociologist and historian, was born in New York City, the son of Marks Nelson, a small-store owner and later a real estate businessman, and Mary Finesmith, a poet who wrote in both English and Yiddish. Both of his parents immigrated to the United States from Russia in 1906. After graduating from the City College of New York in 1931, Benjamin Nelson went to Columbia University where he earned a doctorate in medie-

val history in 1944. The subject of his dissertation, "The Restitution of Usury in Late Medieval Ecclesiastical Law," and all its religious, social, and legal ramifications was a significant point of reference in his major writings, especially *The Idea of Usury: From Tribal Brotherhood to Universal Otherhood* (1949). In 1945 he was appointed to the social science faculty of the University of Chicago, where he served until 1948, when he moved to the University of Minnesota. In 1944 he was awarded a Guggenheim fellowship.

Nelson's book on usury was recognized at once as a classic contribution to the great debate about the influence of religion on economic development that had begun with the publication of *The Protestant Ethic and the Spirit of Capitalism* (1904–1905) by the German sociologist Max Weber. However, due to Nelson's stress on the many interconnections between the idea of conscience, ethical theory, and psychology—what he called "systems of spiritual direction"—and other areas of life, he contributed new dimensions to the debate.

When Nelson moved back to New York in 1952, he simultaneously explored modes of psychotherapy, new ideas relating to art and literature, and the problematics of sociological and psychoanalytic theory. His return to New York coincided with the ending of his first (childless) marriage to Eleanor Rackow, whom he had married in 1945. In New York he gave public lectures and wrote essays on Freud and his influence. Several of the essays were included in *Freud and the Twentieth Century* (1957) and *Sigmund Freud on Creativity and the Unconscious* (1958). Nelson served as a major series editor at Harper Torchbooks, where he brought out several dozen books on religion, literature, philosophy, the arts, and sciences. These included works written by or about thinkers such as Adler, Bainton, Bentham, Burkhardt, Cassirer, Durkheim, Eliade, and Feuerbach, the philosophers Hegel, Kant, Kierkegaard, and Santayana, the historian Tawney, the medievalist Henry Lea, the historian of science Alexander Koyré, the theologian Schleiermacher, and many others. Throughout his career Nelson strove to integrate the social sciences into a comprehensive study of all the experiences and expressions of humankind. He took Goethe's famous phrase "let nothing human be foreign to me" seriously as can be seen in his editor's note to the Torchbook edition of Ludwig Feuerbach's *The Essence of Christianity*: "Every generation needs access to the entire spectrum of the human spirit: that is its inalienable right and unavoidable responsibility."

In 1956 Nelson became chair of the sociology department and coordinator of the social science program at Hofstra University. He also married Marie Coleman at this time; they had no children. In 1959 he was appointed professor of sociology and history as well as chair of the Department of Sociology and Anthropology at the State University of New York at Stony Brook (originally located at Oyster Bay). In 1966 he joined the graduate faculty of the New School for Social Research, where he held the title of professor of history and sociology until his death, serving at the same time as chair of a new master of arts program in liberal studies.

Nelson's continuing interest in and expansion of Max Weber's work resulted in an invitation to join the centenary celebration of Weber's life and work in Heidelberg in 1964. In 1972 and 1973 he received invitations to address two international symposia celebrating the 500th anniversary of the birth of Copernicus. Nelson was one of those very rare academics who could move with ease from canon law and religious history to psychoanalysis, to art and literature, to sociological theory, and then to the philosophy, history, and sociology of science. In the mid-1960s he was a major figure in the reestablishment of the International Society for the Comparative Study of Civilizations, which he served as president from 1971 to 1977. He was also a leader in establishing the Society for the Scientific Study of Religion, of which he became vice president in 1968 and again in 1976.

In the last decade of his life Nelson was as actively exploring the history of Europe as of China and the Middle East. He was very much influenced by the implications of Joseph Needham's grand project, designed to explain why modern science arose only in the West and not in China. During the last five years of his life, he was absorbed by what he called "Needham's challenge." In Nelson's view, the resolution of this intellectual problem was even more central to world history than was Weber's intent to explain the unique Western origins of modern capitalism. At the heart of Nelson's thought was concern for systems of spiritual direction and the legal and social processes by which universal standards are fashioned to encompass ever-larger segments of humanity. This theme was first set out in *The Idea of Usury*. According to Nelson, John Calvin's abolition of the prohibition against usury paved the way for a "universal otherhood" joining Christians and Jews together as equal partners in trade and commerce. In place of the Deuteronomic dualistic ethic of allowing only Jews to lend money at interest to gentiles (but not to fellow Jews), Calvin proposed that Christians and Jews alike could earn profit on loans provided that they follow the universal law of justice. This theme of universal participation and fraternization found reinforcement in Needham's idea of "ecumenical science," that is, the idea that scientific truths do indeed have a universal appeal and applicability. According to Nelson the issue was not whether a particular people made an advance over the Greeks in specialized fields such as optics, astronomy, or mathematics, but whether or not they accomplished "a comprehensive breakthrough in the moralities of thought and in the logics of decision which open out the possibility of creative advance in the direction of wider universalities of discourse and participation" (*On the Roads to Modernity*, p. 98). Nelson died on a train in Germany before he could fully apply this framework to the history of both Arabic and Chinese science as he had planned. Toby E. Huff, one of Nelson's students with whom a collaborative study had

been planned, furthered the thesis in *The Rise of Early Modern Science: Islam, China and the West* (1993).

The significance of Nelson's work is marked by its translation into many foreign languages, including German, Italian, and Portuguese. Talcott Parsons called *The Idea of Usury* "a classic essay," and it was greatly admired by the intellectual historian George Boas. A selection of Nelson's seminal essays on the origins of modernity and on modern philosophy, science, and the analysis of civilizations was translated into German and published under the title *Der Ursprung der Moderne. Vergleichende Studien zum Zivilisationsprozess* (1977). As Bryan R. Wilson of Oxford University put it, "Nothing that [Nelson] wrote was trivial, and none of the themes that he addressed was of less than first-rank importance."

• The Benjamin Nelson Papers are in the archives of Columbia University. They contain a vast array of correspondence with virtually all of the major thinkers of American intellectual life of the middle half of the century. An interview with Nelson that illuminates his intellectual development is in "Systems of Spiritual Direction," *Criterion* 11, no. 3 (1972): 13–17. This interview is reprinted in E. V. Walter et al., eds., *Civilizations East and West: A Memorial Volume for Benjamin Nelson* (1985). A very useful collection of Nelson's important ideas covering the last decade of his life is *On the Roads to Modernity: Conscience, Science, and Civilizations: Selected Writings by Benjamin Nelson*, ed. Toby E. Huff (1981). The book contains a complete bibliography of Nelson's writings and further biographical details. See also another memorial tribute to Nelson, "Sociology and Psychoanalysis in Civilizational Perspective: A Memorial for Benjamin Nelson," *Comparative Civilizations Review*, no. 8 (1982). Both memorial volumes contain assessments of Nelson's work. Other assessments, along with Nelson's response, are in "A Symposium on Civilizational Complexes and Intercivilizational Encounters," *Sociological Analysis: A Journal in the Sociology of Religion* 35, no. 2 (1974). Obituaries are in the *New York Times*, 20 Sept. 1977, and *ASA* [American Sociological Association] *Footnotes* (Dec. 1977): 6.

TOBY E. HUFF

NELSON, Donald Marr (17 Nov. 1888–29 Sept. 1959), business executive and government official, was born in Hannibal, Missouri, the son of Quincy Marr Nelson, a locomotive engineer, and Mary Ann MacDonald. He studied chemical engineering at the University of Missouri, graduating with a B.S. degree in 1911. Shortly thereafter he married Estelle Lord, who died in 1923. In 1926 he married Helen Wishart; they separated in 1940 and were divorced in January 1945. The following month Nelson married his secretary, Marguerite S. Coulbourn; twenty-six years old at the time, she died only two years later, in February 1947. In November 1947 Nelson married Edna May Rowell, but the marriage ended in divorce. He married Lena Peters Schunzel in February 1959. He had no children.

In 1912 Nelson began work as a chemist for Sears, Roebuck and Company. In a highly successful thirty-year career with the company, he moved steadily up the executive ladder. In 1927 he became head of merchandising, and in 1939 he was appointed executive vice president and chairman of the executive committee. At a time when most business executives bitterly opposed Franklin D. Roosevelt's New Deal, Nelson's public statements earned him a reputation as a liberal, a friend of organized labor, and a champion of small business.

Consequently, Roosevelt offered Nelson a series of key roles in the agencies set up to mobilize the nation's economy for the coming of war. Nelson headed the National Defense Advisory Committee (June 1940), the Division of Purchases of the Office of Production Management (January 1941), and the Supply, Priorities, and Allocations Board (July 1941). In January 1942, after the United States entered the war, Roosevelt named Nelson head of the War Production Board (WPB). Created to "exercise general responsibility" over the nation's economy, the WPB was involved in every aspect of economic mobilization, from the conversion of industry to a wartime footing to the allocation of steel, aluminum, and copper. Although Nelson was an able administrator, he was criticized for lacking decisiveness and for permitting the army and navy to exert control over military procurement.

In 1944 Nelson and military officials fought a battle over industrial reconversion that became known as "the war within a war." Nelson favored the gradual resumption of civilian production, even while the war continued, so as to maintain full employment. The military, however, fearing that workers would desert war plants for permanent, peacetime jobs, opposed early reconversion. Nelson recognized that early steps to resume civilian production would enable small businesses to compete more successfully in the postwar market, a prospect that was not at all appealing to executives of large corporations with large war orders. Defending his policies to President Roosevelt, Nelson argued that he had gotten along just fine with the public, farmers, workers, management, and Congress. Since his only difficulties were with the military, he added, the military must be at fault.

In any event, the president decided that Nelson had outlived his usefulness. In August 1944 Roosevelt relieved him of his WPB post and sent him on a factfinding mission to China and the Soviet Union. Following the war, Nelson left government service. He served as president of the Society of Independent Motion Picture Producers from 1945 to 1947. He was elected chairman of the board of Electronized Chemicals in 1948 and president of Consolidated Caribou Silver Mines in 1950. He died in Los Angeles.

• There is a small collection of Nelson's correspondence in the Henry E. Huntington Library, San Marino, Calif. Other relevant correspondence may be found in the Franklin D. Roosevelt Library, Hyde Park, N.Y. The papers of the War Production Board are located in the National Archives. *Arsenal of Democracy* (1946) provides Nelson's own account of his work with the WPB. There is no biography of Nelson, nor is there a modern, scholarly account of the War Production Board. An obituary is in the *New York Times*, 30 Sept. 1959.

RICHARD POLENBERG

NELSON, Edward William (8 May 1855–19 May 1934), naturalist and government official, was born in Amoskeag, New Hampshire, the son of William Nelson, a butcher, and Nancy Martha Wells. Nelson's father enlisted in the Union army and was killed near the end of the Civil War. Nelson lived with his maternal grandparents in upstate New York while his mother served as an army nurse in Baltimore. For several years the Nelson brothers worked on their grandfather's farm while Edward began learning something of the natural history of the area. Following the war, Nelson's mother became a dressmaker in Chicago. Her sons attended the local public schools, and Edward began collecting bird and insect specimens. His mother lost all of her possessions in the Chicago Fire of April 1871, but she found temporary housing and gradually rebuilt her business.

An older friend taught Nelson how to prepare birdskins, and he entered the Cook County Normal School in the spring of 1872, hoping to continue his formal education. An unusual case of blood poisoning brought about by his working with some decaying bird specimens made him very ill. A doctor recommended that he spend some months in the dry uplands of the Rocky Mountains while recovering. Nelson and a school friend joined Samuel Garman, a zoologist at Harvard's Museum of Comparative Zoology, who was going west in the summer of 1872 to work with the paleontologist Edward Drinker Cope. Nelson, a volunteer paying his own expenses, collected fossils and birds for Cope for some weeks. Following an argument between Cope and Garman, the latter decided to do his own collecting around the Great Salt Lake, and although Cope urged Nelson to remain, the two younger men felt obliged to stay with Garman. For the rest of the year Nelson collected birds and some mammals in Utah, Nevada, and California. Early in 1873 he returned to his studies in Chicago, selling his western collections to the Normal School, which used them to establish a museum.

Nelson completed his studies at the Normal School in 1875, while in the meantime he began new collections of birds and fish. He enrolled at Northwestern University in the fall of 1875, but he left before the end of the semester and began teaching in Dalton, Illinois. By the following spring he had decided to leave teaching and seek employment as a naturalist. On the suggestion of Henry W. Henshaw, a naturalist with the Wheeler Survey, Nelson sought employment with the Smithsonian Institution but found there were no immediate openings. He took a course in zoology at Johns Hopkins University in Baltimore while waiting for an opportunity to develop.

In the spring of 1877 Spencer F. Baird, the Smithsonian's assistant secretary, advised Nelson of an opening as a weather observer in Alaska for the U.S. Army Signal Corps. Since this would provide some opportunity for collecting animals, Nelson enlisted in the army as a private; underwent a month of training at Fort Myer, Virginia, learning his basic duties as weather observer; and then spent four years at St. Michael, Alaska. Between the end of June and the end of October 1881 he served as naturalist on the revenue ship *Corwin*, exploring parts of the Alaskan and Siberian coasts and investigating the rapid decline of Eskimos on St. Lawrence Island. The results of his natural history and ethnological investigations and collections were published in 1887. Some years were spent in Washington preparing this report, but pneumonia, followed by a critical case of tuberculosis, compelled him to seek recovery in the montains of Arizona. There his mother slowly nursed him back to health, but not until 1890 was he again able to work in sustained fashion.

Nelson then began an association with the U.S. Biological Survey that would last four decades. From November 1890 until the fall of 1891 he was a member of the survey's Death Valley Expedition, collecting vertebrate and plant specimens. In 1891 he began a lifelong friendship and professional association with Edward A. Goldman, a young Californian then in his late teens. Following several months in the coastal region of California, during which Nelson taught Goldman the basic essentials of field natural history, Nelson was ordered to begin a brief biological reconnaissance in the Mexican state of Colima. This turned into a fourteen-year effort (1892–1906), during which the two men collected biogeographical data and specimens from every part of that country. There were periodic interruptions for business and vacation trips to the United States.

Beginning in 1907, however, Nelson's growing administrative responsibilities with the Biological Survey brought an end to most of his field work. He published *Lower California and Its Natural Resources* (1921) on the basis of work he and Goldman had done there in 1905 and 1906. However, apart from Goldman's published account of their fourteen-year itinerary and an outline of their biogeographical findings, the latter of which was outdated (1951), no comprensive faunal study based on their Mexican investigations was ever completed. Named chief field naturalist of the Biological Survey in 1907, Nelson was placed in charge of biological investigations in 1913 and became assistant chief of the survey in 1914. In 1916 he began an eleven-year tenure as third chief of the Biological Survey. For two more years (1927–1929) he was principal biologist with the survey, after which he was engaged in his own writing and research until his death. In 1930 he was appointed a research associate with the Smithsonian Institution.

As chief of the survey, Nelson essentially became the nation's first wildlife and conservation administrator. The Biological Survey's traditional research programs continued but at a much slower tempo than previously. Nelson had oversight of those provisions of the Migratory Bird Treaty with Canada (1916) affecting the United States, and he took pleasure in the passage of the Migratory Bird Conservation Act, signed on the eve of his retirement. His interest in Alaskan game management was instrumental in the passage of the Alaska Game Law of 1925, but he failed in his ef-

forts to secure enactment of public shooting grounds game refuge legislation. This was passed several times by one house of Congress or the other, but no final action was taken. Nelson was also obliged to continue with the trapping, shooting, and poisoning of predatory mammals and noxious rodents, begun under his predecessors by congressional mandate. This program, conducted principally in the western states, was highly controversial and brought the survey much obloquy. Nelson authored a number of technical faunal papers on mammals and birds; his monographic *Rabbits of North America* (1909) was generally accounted his best. Nelson's "The Larger North American Mammals" (1916) and "The Smaller Mammals of North America" (1918) were popular studies published as special issues of *National Geographic Magazine*. Combined in one volume as *Wild Animals of North America* (1918), the studies were published in a revised edition in 1930.

Nelson never married, having concluded that the heart condition resulting from his near-fatal bout with tuberculosis mitigated against his taking that step. An able naturalist and effective administrator, he was considered brusque and imperious by some subordinates. Nelson was the second president of the American Society of Mammalogists from 1921 to 1923. He was awarded an honorary M.A. degree by Yale University and an honorary doctorate of science by George Washington University, both in 1920. More than 100 genera and species of animals and plants were named in his honor, together with an island and lagoon in Alaska, and a small mountain range in California. He died in Washington, D.C.

• The Mexican field notebooks of both men are in the Smithsonian Institution Archives. There are holograph letters of Nelson's in the papers of Albert Kenrick Fisher, and a brief assessment of Nelson in the papers of Waldo Lee McAtee, both in the Manuscript Division, Library of Congress. Both men were longtime staff members of the Biological Survey who knew and worked with Nelson. See also Records of the United States Fish and Wildlife Service, National Archives and Records Administration, Washington. Nelson and Goldman jointly authored a short popular summary of Mexican biogeography in *Naturalist's Guide to the Americas*, ed. V. E. Shelford (1926). A very useful biographical sketch is Edward A. Goldman, "Edward William Nelson—Naturalist," *Auk* 3 (Apr. 1935), by Nelson's longtime friend and associate. See also Walter P. Taylor, "Edward A. Goldman," *Journal of Mammalogy* 28 (1947); M. Lantis, "Edward William Nelson," *Anthropological Papers of the University of Alaska* (1954); Jenks Cameron, *The Bureau of Biological Survey: Its History, Activities, and Organization* (1929); Keir B. Sterling, *Last of the Naturalists: The Career of C. Hart Merriam*, rev. ed. (1977); and Sterling, "Two Pioneering American Mammalogists in Mexico: The Field Investigations of Edward William Nelson and Edward Alphonso Goldman, 1892–1906," in *Latin American Mammalogy: History, Biodiversity, and Conservation*, ed. Michael A. Mares and David J. Schmidly (1991). An obituary is in the *(Washington D.C.) Evening Star*, 19 May 1934.

KEIR B. STERLING

NELSON, Hugh (30 Sept. 1768–18 Mar. 1836), congressman, diplomat, and jurist, was born in Yorktown, Virginia, the son of Thomas Nelson, a merchant and governor of Virginia, and Lucy Grymes. The great event of his childhood was the American Revolution, in which his father played a prominent role. He graduated from the College of William and Mary in 1790 and shortly thereafter moved to Albemarle County, Virginia. Nelson married Eliza Kinloch in 1799; they had nine children who survived to maturity. Nelson and his family lived at "Belvoir," an Albemarle County estate acquired from his father-in-law.

An attorney by profession, Nelson spent most of his adult life in public service. He was a delegate to the Virginia Assembly, 1805–1809. In 1807 and again in 1808 he was elected Speaker of the Virginia House of Delegates. In 1809 he accepted an appointment as judge of the General Court of Virginia, a position he held until his election to the U.S. Congress in 1811.

Nelson served six consecutive terms in Congress. Throughout his political career he was a supporter and confidant of the Republican leadership from Virginia, especially of his Albemarle neighbors Thomas Jefferson and James Monroe. His relationship with James Madison was not as close as it was with Jefferson or Monroe, but Nelson was a presidential elector for Madison in 1808 and was one of the president's leading supporters in Congress. Although his term in Congress was not distinguished, Nelson was an able spokesperson for the Republican administrations, and Monroe in particular depended on his support and friendship. Jefferson, living in retirement at "Monticello," relied on Nelson for information on the proceedings in Congress. Nelson's influence within the House of Representatives is evidenced by his three appointments as chairman of the Judiciary Committee (1815–1817, 1817–1819, and 1821–1823). He resigned his seat in Congress in March 1823 to accept an appointment as U.S. minister to Spain.

When President Monroe needed a trustworthy lieutenant to serve as minister to Spain in the stormy years immediately following the independence of the South American republics, he turned to this old friend and supporter. Monroe and Secretary of State John Quincy Adams preferred to manage the nation's foreign affairs from Washington; nevertheless, they considered Nelson's mission to be one of great importance. Upon Nelson's departure for Spain, Adams presented him with seventy-one handwritten pages of instructions relating to a variety of matters, including the suppression of piracy, the nontransfer of Cuba, trade agreements, and implementation of the Adams-Onis Treaty of 1819. Nelson arrived at Gibraltar in late July but, because of the war raging in Spain, was not able to present his credentials to the royal court at Madrid until December. Nelson proved to be a reliable representative at the Spanish court, keeping Monroe and Adams informed about the tumultuous events occurring in Spain and establishing good personal rapport with the Spanish court and its ministers. Nelson was unable to persuade Spain to return to the negotiating table to resolve the issues referred to in his instructions, but he was able to create an aura of friendly relations between the two countries. In early 1825 he asked Monroe to relieve him of this assignment; President Adams issued the recall orders in April of that year, and Nelson left Spain in July.

Nelson returned to Albemarle County, where he lived in retirement except for one term in the house of delegates (1828–1829). He was active in the affairs of the Episcopal church, serving as a vestryman for his parish and frequently as a delegate to both state and national Episcopal conventions. He maintained close ties with his alma mater, holding a seat on the Board of Visitors of the College of William and Mary. Nelson died at Belvoir.

• The Manuscript Division of the Library of Congress has a small collection of Nelson's papers. The extensive correspondence relating to his mission to Spain can be found in the diplomatic correspondence of the Records of the Department of State (RG 59) at the National Archives. *Annals of Congress* offers brief references to his congressional service. For a biographical sketch and genealogical background, see R. C. M. Page, *Genealogy of the Page Family in Virginia* (1893). The bicentennial edition of the *Biographical Directory of the United States Congress* (1989) confuses this Hugh Nelson with his uncle of the same name (1750–1800).

DANIEL PRESTON

NELSON, John (1653?–16 Nov. 1734), colonial entrepreneur, was born in England, the son of Robert Nelson, a London lawyer and member of Gray's Inn, and Mary Temple. In the late 1660s he came to Boston as the protégé of his mother's brother, Sir Thomas Temple, the proprietor and governor of Nova Scotia. Appointed deputy governor of Nova Scotia in 1670, Nelson's first task was to surrender its scattered outposts back to the French. Temple's death in 1674 left Nelson with little more than his uncle's uncertain title to what was now French Acadia, but he soon emerged as a leading trader with the region, exchanging its fish, furs, and feathers for cargoes of food, cloth, and hardware. Several of the French army officers commanding garrisons there became his lifelong friends. In 1682 he traveled to Quebec on behalf of the Massachusetts government to negotiate for terms by which English vessels could fish in Acadian waters. Soon afterward, he married Elizabeth Tailer, the niece of Massachusetts magistrate William Stoughton; the couple had six children.

London's creation of a royally governed Dominion of New England in 1686 seemed to offer Nelson, English born and Anglican in religion, new opportunities for advancement. But his continued trading with French contacts in Acadia soon brought him into conflict with royal governor Sir Edmund Andros. In April 1689 Nelson helped lead Boston's militia in an uprising that overthrew Andros's government. He served briefly in a council of safety but withdrew in the face of popular demand for a restoration of old-line Puritan rule. He then proposed an expedition against Port Royal in Acadia, only to have its leadership assumed by Sir William Phips. After Phips had plundered and abandoned Port Royal, Nelson organized and helped lead a smaller venture to establish a garrison and trading post there. But in September 1691 he and his companions were captured by a French frigate at the mouth of the St. John River, and he was taken overland to Quebec to begin four years of French imprisonment and seven years away from his family in Boston.

In Canada, Nelson continued the series of exploits that made his name famous among the French. Hearing of a Canadian plan to attack New England, he persuaded two French deserters to convey a warning to Boston. But Phips, now governor of Massachusetts, deliberately betrayed his rival's espionage to the French by sending the deserters on a doomed mission to Acadia to assassinate one of Nelson's French trading partners, Jean-Vincent d'Abbadie de Saint-Castin. With his scheme exposed, Nelson was shipped off to France, to Rochefort, and then to the inland fortress of Angoulême. There he languished for two years, smuggling out letters to French and English friends pleading for his release. Ultimately, in August 1695, he was transferred to the Bastille in Paris to meet with French officials as part of a plan to reactivate a treaty providing for America's neutrality in the war raging between France and England. Nelson was released on parole and reached London early in 1696, only to find little interest in Whitehall for either the French proposals or his own schemes for a conquest of Canada. Not until he had made a dramatic dash back to France in mid-1697 (for which contact with the enemy he was briefly charged with high treason in England upon his return) could he free himself from the bond that enforced his parole.

Before returning to Boston in the summer of 1698, Nelson submitted a variety of memorials to England's Board of Trade on the boundaries of Acadia, the poor state of the fisheries, the need for a consolidation of the northern English colonies, and the value of better relations with the Indians. These memorials provided information that the board would use in formulating many later policies, but Nelson played no part in their execution. Back in Massachusetts he settled down to a quiet family life in his home on Long Island in Boston Harbor, trading with Acadia upon occasion and maintaining a friendly correspondence with Governor Philippe de Rigaud de Vaudreuil and other officials of French Canada. For several years after 1717 Nelson drew upon his family ties to members of the powerful Temple clan in England, first to advance the career of his brother-in-law, Colonel William Tailer, who served as lieutenant governor of Massachusetts, and then to help his second son, Paschal Nelson, assert the family's claim to lands in what had again become English Nova Scotia. But the claim failed, and Nelson finally conveyed his title to Samuel Waldo in 1729 for a mere one hundred pounds. A more enduring legacy of the family's long-standing involvement with eastern New England was the extensive land speculation around the Kennebec River launched by Robert Temple, the husband of Nelson's daughter Mehitable.

Nelson died at Robert Temple's house on Noddle's Island in Boston Harbor, three weeks after his wife, Elizabeth. In his last years he lamented the losses he had suffered from being, in his words, "crusht between the two Crownes" of France and England. Too incorrigibly independent, and too loyal to his own personal alliances to satisfy either Whitehall's officials or Puritan leaders in Boston, he never amassed a fortune or held high office. But his adventurous career sheds light on the role of the roving entrepreneurs who worked within the overlapping fringes of European settlement in America. Nelson's trading and his highly personal diplomacy linked old and New England with France and New France and helped to shape the more formal conflict of empires that followed in eighteenth-century America.

• Nelson's papers as preserved by his family, mostly documents relating to his imprisonment and his claim to Acadia, are in the Temple-Nelson papers, Houghton Library, Harvard University. A number of family letters from Nelson's later years are printed from the Lloyd papers in *Collections of the New-York Historical Society* 59 (1927). Memorials authored by Nelson are in the British Library and the Public Record Office, London, and the Massachusetts Archives, Boston. Fuller references, particularly to the many French sources for Nelson's life, are given in the only modern biography, Richard R. Johnson, *John Nelson, Merchant Adventurer: A Life between Empires* (1991).

RICHARD R. JOHNSON

NELSON, Knute (2 Feb. 1843–28 Apr. 1923), congressman, U.S. senator, and governor of Minnesota, was born in Evanger, Voss, Norway, the illegitimate son of Helge Knudtson and Ingeborg Kuilekval Johanson, probably farmers. His mother brought him to the United States in 1849. After a brief sojourn in Chicago, the two moved to La Grange, Wisconsin, where Ingeborg married Norwegian immigrant farmer Nels Nelson, whose surname was taken by young Knute. Removing to Deerfield, Wisconsin, near Madison, the young man labored on his stepfather's farm and attended the local common school and Albion Academy, where he worked for the principal to earn tuition and room and board.

After teaching in a district school during the winter of 1860–1861, Nelson enlisted in the Fourth Wisconsin Infantry and served from 1861 to 1863, rising to the rank of corporal. He participated in the operations against New Orleans and Vicksburg under Generals Benjamin Butler and William Tecumseh Sherman, respectively, and was wounded and taken prisoner for a month during the siege of Port Hudson. Returning to Wisconsin at the completion of his enlistment, Nelson reentered Albion Academy and completed his Ph.B. in 1865. After reading law with future U.S. senator William F. Vilas in Madison for two years, he was admitted to the state bar in 1867 and practiced in Cambridge, Wisconsin. During his four years there, Nelson served a term in the state legislature, launching a political career that was to span over a half-century. In 1869 he married Nicoline Jacobson; they had six children, of whom only two survived into adulthood.

In 1871 Nelson relocated to Alexandria, Minnesota, a frontier county seat, where he served as county attorney, state senator, and University of Minnesota regent during the next decade. In addition, he homesteaded on government land and practiced law, managing "to get on one side or the other of about every case of importance in the six or seven counties in my part of the country." Elected to Congress as a Republican in 1882 after a bitter nomination battle that split the party, he served three terms, declining a fourth in 1888. Representing a new rural, agricultural district consisting of twenty-nine northern counties that were heavily Norwegian and Swedish, Nelson, the first immigrant from either of these countries to serve in the Congress, was something less than a heavily partisan Republican congressman. He favored lower tariff rates and railroad regulation while seeking to open American Indian lands to white settlement and to construct a canal linking Lake Superior to interior waters. After practicing law for four years, Nelson was nominated by his party for governor in an effort to prevent Norwegian-American defections to the burgeoning People's party. As chief executive, he strove to co-opt and moderate Populist proposals, favoring state inspection and ownership of grain elevators and a tax on the gross earnings of corporations. Elected governor in 1892 and 1894, he resigned in 1895 after being chosen for the U.S. Senate, a position he held until his death.

Independent, forthright, and politically astute, Nelson generally succeeded in remaining in the good graces of both regular and insurgent Republicans during the titanic struggle that rent the party in two during the height of the Progressive Era. A member of the committees on Indian Affairs and Public Lands and eventual chairman of the Judiciary Committee, he diligently pursued the interests of midwestern farmers and merchants while steering a middle course on the divisive issues of the period. Although generally voting with the regular Republicans on economic matters, Nelson supported tariff reduction, the federal income tax amendment, strengthening the Interstate Commerce Commission, and enforcement of the Sherman Anti-Trust Act. He authored the Nelson Bankruptcy Act of 1898 to permit debtors to achieve solvency and the legislation establishing the Department of Commerce and Labor in 1902. He also led the unsuccessful opposition to the adoption of the Adamson Act, providing for an eight-hour day for railroad employees, because he opposed the growing power of the Railway Brotherhoods and saw the act as a possible step toward nationalization. True to his Scandinavian Protestant roots and those of much of his constituency, Nelson strongly advocated the national Prohibition amendment and the Volstead joint federal-state enforcement legislation. A "mild reservationist," Nelson generally backed Democratic president Woodrow Wilson during the bitter struggle over the Versailles treaty and the League of Nations and was the only Re-

publican to oppose the Knox Resolution, which would have allowed the United States to retain "all the advantages accruing to it" upon ratifying either the treaty or the league charter. Dubbed "the Grand Old Man of Minnesota" and the "hardest working man on the Hill" by journalists, Nelson was so unassuming that he frequently signed his name "K. Nelson, farmer." At home in Minnesota, he generally donned boots and overalls to work with the hired men on his farm and insisted on being called "Uncle Knute" rather than "Senator" or "Governor." He died on a train near Timonium, Maryland, en route to his home in Alexandria, Minnesota.

• All previous writings on Nelson's life and career are superseded by Millard L. Gieske and Steven J. Keillor, *Norwegian Moses: Knute Nelson and the Failure of American Politics, 1860–1923* (1995). This biography is firmly grounded in materials found in the seventy-nine boxes of Nelson's personal papers housed in the Archives Division of the Minnesota Historical Society. It greatly expands on Gieske's "The Politics of Knute Nelson, 1912–1920" (Ph.D. diss., Univ. of Minnesota, 1965), which concentrates heavily on Nelson's role in the political conflict over U.S. involvement in World War I and the ratification of the Treaty of Versailles. The earliest biography, Martin W. Odland, *The Life of Knute Nelson* (1926), is generally uncritical but useful for its reproduction of numerous letters by and about Nelson. While Rolfsrud Erling Nicolai, *Scandinavian Moses: The Story of Knute Nelson* (1986), stresses Nelson's skillful practice of ethnocultural politics, it provides little scholarly analysis. A laudatory contemporary account is "Knute Nelson," *Minnesota Historical Society Bulletin* 5 (1924): 329–47. Nelson's obituary is in the *St. Paul Pioneer Press*, 29 and 30 Apr. 1923.

JOHN D. BUENKER

NELSON, Nels Christian (9 Apr. 1875–5 Mar. 1964), archaeologist, was born near Fredericia, Denmark, the son of Soren Nelson, a farmer, and Anne Kirstine Larsdatter. Nelson emigrated to the United States in 1892 to work on an uncle's farm in Minnesota. He learned English and worked his way through high school.

Nelson first enrolled at Stanford University with a concentration in philosophy and subsequently transferred to the University of California at Berkeley where he majored in anthropology and archaeology and was awarded the B.L. (1907) and M.L. (1908) degrees. He was married in 1911 to Ethelyn G. Field. After receiving his master's degree, he briefly worked for the U.S. Geological Survey and the Museum of Anthropology of the University of California before assuming a position in 1912 at the American Museum of Natural History as assistant curator of anthropology. He remained at the American Museum for the rest of his professional career, rising in the ranks until he was appointed curator of prehistoric archaeology in 1928. Although he retired formally in 1943, he maintained his connection with the museum until his death, which occurred in New York City.

Nelson's archaeological experiences were quite broad. He undertook archaeological fieldwork in various parts of the United States such as the Ellis Landing

Shellmound in California (1906–1908), a number of southwestern sites during the mid-1910s, and Mammoth Cave in Kentucky (1916); and in European sites such as Castillo Cave in Spain (in 1913). During the mid-1920s he accompanied the famous paleontologist Roy Chapman Andrews to East Asia, where he was able to uncover important archaeological materials and information at sites in Inner and Outer Mongolia, Yunnan, Szechuan, and the Yangtze River gorges.

Nelson was highly regarded in the anthropological and archaeological professions and was elected to the presidencies of the American Ethnological Society (1929), the American Anthropological Association (1937), and the Society for American Archaeology (1942–1943).

Of all Nelson's varied accomplishments, he is best known for his landmark research in the American Southwest and particularly for his pioneering use of stratigraphic field techniques. Although the practice, borrowed from geology, of excavating archaeological sites by stratigraphic levels had spread through Europe in the late nineteenth century, it had been applied only sporadically in the Americas prior to World War I. But in 1911, the Mexican anthropologist Manuel Gamio had stratigraphically excavated a site in the Basin of Mexico that allowed him to define a chronological sequence for Central Mexico. However, the significance of this achievement had gone unrecognized at that time. Just three years later, Nelson, in his third field season in the Galisteo Basin of New Mexico, stratigraphically excavated a ten-foot-deep deposit of refuse at Pueblo San Cristobal in one-foot levels. Nelson had learned about the stratigraphic method in particular from his participation in excavations at Castillo Cave as well as from his knowledge of the research of the German archaeologist Max Uhle on a shellmound site in the San Francisco Bay area.

Separating and counting the different ceramic sherds from each of the ten arbitrary levels in the Galisteo Basin, with the lowest level being the earliest and the top one the latest, Nelson found that the principal ceramic types had normal distribution frequencies: relatively small numbers of sherds in early times, then growing frequencies, and finally reductions in numbers until the types died out. Nelson's research was soon published in "Pueblo Ruins of the Galisteo Basin, New Mexico" (*Anthropological Papers of the American Museum of Natural History* 15, pt. 1 [1914]: 1–124) and "Chronology of the Tano Ruins, New Mexico" (*American Anthropologist* 18, no. 2 [1916]: 159–80). The important 1914 excavation at Pueblo San Cristobal is discussed in the latter work. His writings were widely read and had considerable influence on his colleagues in the American Southwest and on archaeologists throughout the western hemisphere. In particular, Nelson's strategy of excavation in arbitrary one-foot levels became common practice in many parts of North America where the natural strata were not clearly visible.

Nelson's personal warmth and his wide-ranging, careful scholarship attracted many friends and garnered him deep, well-deserved professional respect in the archaeological community.

• The basic facts in this biographical sketch are taken from J. Alden Mason's obituary of Nelson, which appeared in *American Antiquity* 31, no. 3 (1966): 393–97. A full listing of Nelson's publications can be found in this obituary. Additional biographical information is provided by D. R. Barton in "Mud, Stones, and History: the Rise of N. C. Nelson from Danish Farm Boy to One of America's Outstanding Chroniclers of the Life and Times of Prehistoric Man," *Natural History* 47, no. 5 (1941): 293–96, 303, and the biographical article by Adele Hast in the *Dictionary of American Biography*. Supplement 7 (1961–1965): 569–71 (1981). An obituary is in the *New York Times*, 6 Mar. 1964. Discussions of the significance of Nelson's pioneering stratigraphic research are featured in Leslie Spier, "N. C. Nelson's Stratigraphic Technique in the Reconstruction of Prehistoric Sequences in Southwestern America," in *Methods in Social Science*, ed. S. A. Rice (1931) pp. 275–83; Richard B. Woodbury, "Nels C. Nelson and Chronological Archaeology," *American Antiquity* 25, no. 3 (1960): 400–401, and "Nelson's Stratigraphy," *American Antiquity* 26, no. 1 (1960): 98–99; and Gordon R. Willey and Jeremy A. Sabloff, *A History of American Archaeology* 3d ed. (1993), pp. 97–108.

JEREMY A. SABLOFF

NELSON, Ozzie (20 Mar. 1906–3 June 1975), television actor/director and bandleader, and **Harriet Nelson** (18 July 1909–2 Oct. 1994), television actress and singer, were icons of American middle-class culture of the baby-boom era following World War II. They were universally recognized as "Ozzie and Harriet," which was the title of their popular television sitcom. Ozzie was born Oswald George Nelson in Jersey City, New Jersey, the son of George Waldemar Nelson and Ethel Orr. He grew up in nearby Ridgefield Park, New Jersey, where his banker father was active in civic organizations. George Nelson was also interested in amateur theatricals, bringing the whole family in on the act, so that from an early age young Oswald sang and acted for the public. His work never entirely lost its original amateur orientation.

Ozzie Nelson was always an overachiever. The youngest Eagle scout on record at age thirteen, he was the pride of the Rutgers University class of 1927. In college he made good grades, drew cartoons, played football, boxed, and even got in a few games of lacrosse. In his spare time he continued to lead a band he had formed in high school. After college he continued the same pattern at New Jersey Law School, but the band (by then an orchestra) took up increasing chunks of his time. By the time he graduated in 1930, the orchestra had flourished, and he never bothered to take the bar exam.

In 1932 Nelson decided to boost his band's popularity by adding a girl singer. He had seen perky, attractive Harriet Hilliard in a short Paramount film, then heard her sing in New York and decided to hire her. Harriet was born Peggy Lou Snyder in Des Moines, Iowa, the daughter of Roy Snyder, a theatrical director, and Hazel McNutt, an actress. (Both parents used the surname "Hilliard" on stage.) At the age of six weeks she made her stage debut, and she had her first speaking role at age three. She attended public schools and St. Agnes Academy in Kansas City, Missouri. She brought Nelson the little extra something his band needed, and according to his memoirs their summer 1932 engagement at Glen Island Casino put the Ozzie Nelson Orchestra on the map. As they toured the country in a bus with the band, Nelson busied himself writing duets for the two of them—boy-girl numbers, often humorous, that proved popular. The pair married in 1935.

Harriet Nelson soon began commuting to Hollywood to sing and act in films. Her best known role was that of the ingenue in *Follow the Fleet* (1936), a Fred Astaire–Ginger Rogers vehicle. Meanwhile, her husband continued touring with the band but worked increasingly in radio. In 1941 both Ozzie and Harriet joined Red Skelton in Los Angeles for what proved to be one of the most popular offerings on the airwaves. The Nelsons brought with them to Hollywood their band, their belongings, and their two sons: David Ozzie Nelson (born in 1936) and Eric Hilliard Nelson, nicknamed Ricky (born in 1940).

When Skelton was drafted in 1944, Nelson immediately proposed that the couple come up with a radio show of their very own—a show in which they would play themselves, to be titled "The Adventures of Ozzie and Harriet." The International Silver Company agreed to sponsor the program, and the Nelsons began a relationship with the American airwaves that was to last twenty-two years.

The program purportedly depicted day-to-day life in the Nelson home in humorous fashion. David and Ricky, at first portrayed by actors, began to play themselves in 1949. In that same year, the Nelsons negotiated a new contract for their show, which gave ABC "The Adventures of Ozzie and Harriet" for its radio network, with an option to move the program to television after two years. Ozzie Nelson served as the program's head writer, director, and star.

The televised version of "The Adventures of Ozzie and Harriet" premiered in the fall of 1952 and provided ABC with an immediate, family-oriented hit. Over the years, "Ozzie and Harriet" has come to symbolize the idealized "normal" American home of the 1950s—white, middle class, and suburban. In fact, the program was not all sweetness and light; the bumbling version of himself Ozzie Nelson portrayed was a portrait of masculinity in crisis. Nevertheless, the family's dilemmas were always resolved in the space of a half hour, and the Nelson boys—who drew many of the program's fans—never rebelled against their all-knowing parents.

In 1957 the show achieved renewed popularity by allowing Ricky to sing and play the guitar on the air. The teenager, carefully managed by his father, soon became one of the nation's most popular singers. Ozzie Nelson continued to direct his family on-screen and off until 1966. When the boys married in the early 1960s, their wives joined the cast of "Ozzie and Harriet" on television as well as in life, enhancing the program's claims to realism. In fact, it diverged more and more from reality as the years went by; on-screen, both boys went to college and law school, while their offscreen counterparts barely finished high school.

By 1966 "The Adventures of Ozzie and Harriet" had played itself out and was canceled. In their retirement, Ozzie and Harriet Nelson enjoyed performing in plays at state fairs and dinner theaters. They invariably portrayed married couples and played off their earlier televisual personas. They also did well on the television talk-show circuit.

The always productive Ozzie Nelson churned out his autobiography in 1973. In this book, titled simply *Ozzie*, he set his authorial seal on his life and marriage, rewriting his personal history to sound like a television program. Throughout he maintained the wholesomely humorous, conversational tone that had typified the televised "Adventures." He characterized himself as a lucky amateur. In fact, he was a shrewd entrepreneur who captured and retained the attention of the American public by marketing "normal" family life in an era in which the family was a prominent cultural symbol.

The Nelsons made one final foray into televisual fiction, re-creating the on-screen Nelson home for a syndicated program titled "Ozzie's Girls," which debuted in the fall of 1973. Ozzie Nelson came down with liver cancer and had to discontinue production after one season. He died at his home on a tree-lined drive in Hollywood, surrounded by his family.

After Ozzie's death, Harriet Nelson occasionally appeared on television in movies and in miniseries. She died in Laguna Beach, California.

• The Billy Rose Theatre Collection of the New York Public Library for the Performing Arts, Lincoln Center, includes several clipping files about Ozzie and Harriet Nelson. In addition, the best sources about Ozzie Nelson's life are his autobiography and the 1949 *Current Biography* listing about him and Harriet Hilliard. The Nelsons' status as cultural icons is probed in Sara Davidson, "Those Happy, Happy, Happy Nelsons," *Esquire*, June 1971, pp. 97–101ff, and in Tinky "Dakota" Weisblat's "What Ozzie Did for a Living," in the *Velvet Light Trap*, no. 33 (Spring 1994): 14–23. Ozzie's obituary is in the *New York Times*, 4 June 1975, while Harriet's appeared in the same paper, 4 Oct. 1994.

TINKY "DAKOTA" WEISBLAT

NELSON, Rick (8 May 1940–31 Dec. 1985), singer and actor, was born Eric Hilliard Nelson in Teaneck, New Jersey, the son of Ozzie Nelson and Harriet Hilliard Nelson (née Peggy Lou Snyder), radio and television stars who did much to define the situation comedy. Nelson made his first professional appearance on radio in 1949 on "The Adventures of Ozzie and Harriet." He played the smart-aleck little brother to David Nelson, and his wisecracks were used as laugh-winning punch lines. Moving with his family to television, Rick used the medium to debut as a rock star in the early days of that musical form (1957), recording a cover version of Fats Domino's "I'm Walkin'," reportedly to impress a girl. The record sold more than 1 million copies in two weeks, highlighting the fact that the white treatment of rhythm and blues, called rock and roll, could sell, particularly if the singer were photogenic and nonthreatening, or at least not black.

Sales of his several rock hits, primarily ballads, from 1957 until 1962 have been estimated at 35 million records. A large part of his success was due to the quality of musicians in his backup group: James Burton and Glen Campbell on guitars, for instance. In 1967, in the midst of the do-your-own-thing 1960s, Nelson put together a country rock band, which provided a calming music in contrast to psychedelic and hard-driving electric blues.

Along with this new direction in music, Nelson also played rock revival concerts. A particularly nostalgic crowd at Madison Square Garden in 1971 inspired him to write "Garden Party." The tune gave a perceptive description of celebrity adulation as seen through the eyes of one whose popularity had crested. Part of the song's lyrics proclaim that if memories were all Rick had to sell, he would rather drive a truck.

Despite the legal problems he often encountered in the record business (such as attempting to get out of contracts with inordinately long commitments, failure by the company to release recordings, and recording companies being bought out by other companies who were not interested in a musician's development), Nelson continued to record albums. Reviews were mixed, however, and the singer and his Stone Canyon Band continued to perform at local fairs, nightclubs, and college campuses until his death.

On New Year's Eve 1985 the band was flying to a gig in Dallas, Texas, after leaving Guntersville, Alabama. According to the National Transportation Safety Board, a fire ignited in the right aft section of the aircraft. The plane crashed and burned in a field near DeKalb, Texas. Though the pilot and copilot survived, Rick Nelson, his fiancée, and all five members of Nelson's Stone Canyon Band died. The cause of the fire was not determined, but the February 1988 issue of *Flying* reported that it appeared the pilot did not adhere to emergency procedures for an in-flight fire.

At the time of his death Nelson was divorced from Kristin Harmon, whom he had married in 1964. They had four children, two of whom, twin sons Matthew and Gunnar, achieved some success in the rock arena in the early 1990s performing as Nelson. A daughter, Tracy Nelson, became an accomplished television and film actress.

Rick Nelson's legacy is similar to that of many other early performers in rock music: he made the new music more accessible, if not completely acceptable, to mainstream America. In addition, his covers of songs by black rhythm-and-blues artists allowed recognition and increased record sales by those performers.

Like several musicians who were playing rock at the beginning of the turbulent 1960s, Nelson turned to country music as that decade came to a close. This was not merely a strategy to remain popular. The roots of rock and roll contain the work of early country artists, such as the Callahan Brothers, Jimmie Rodgers, and other purveyors of white blues.

Rick Nelson began his career as an entertainer on radio and then television. He used the latter new medium to change his image from a child of wry pronouncements to a teen capable of demonstrative song. The rock music that he performed with finesse, and his ballads and up-tempo assertions of self-reliance—the teen ideal—endeared him to America's youth. Their parents could learn how to react to this new phenomenon from Ozzie and Harriet, examples of a true, loving mother and father, who took his musical aspirations in their stride.

• Two biographies on Nelson are Joel Selvin, *Ricky Nelson: Idol for a Generation* (1990), and Philip Bashe, *Teenage Idol, Travelin' Man: The Complete Biography of Rick Nelson* (1992). Nelson's recordings, both early and late, are available on *The Ricky Nelson Singles Album* (United Artists, 1979) and *The Ricky Nelson Singles Album, 1963–1976* (MCA Coral, 1977) as well as on albums of Rick Nelson and the Stone Canyon Band. Obituaries are in *Newsweek*, 13 Jan. 1986; *People Weekly*, 20 Jan. 1986; and *Rolling Stone*, 13 Feb. 1986.

PATRICK JOSEPH O'CONNOR

NELSON, Samuel (10 Nov. 1792–13 Dec. 1873), U.S. Supreme Court justice, was born in Hebron, Washington County, New York, the son of John Rogers Nelson and Jean McArthur, farmers. (Some sources give his mother's maiden name as "Jane McCarter.") Nelson attended the local school, Washington Academy, in Salem, New York, and Granville Academy. He graduated from Middlebury College in Vermont in 1813 and began working as a clerk at the law firm of Savage & Woods. The partnership split in 1815, and Nelson followed Woods from Salem to Madison County, where the two became partners in a new firm. After being admitted to the bar in 1817, he moved to Cortland, New York, and opened his own law practice. In 1819 Nelson married Pamela Woods, the daughter of his former partner. (Some sources give her name as Pamilla.) They had one child before her death in 1822.

In 1820, after his law practice had proved a financial success, Nelson entered politics, serving as a presidential elector for James Monroe. That same year he was elected postmaster of Cortland. Attending the New York constitutional convention of 1821, he supported the extension of suffrage to male citizens without property. In 1823 he became a judge on the state's sixth circuit, responsible for nine New York counties. He married Catherine Ann Russell, the daughter of another judge, in 1825; they had three children. After eight years on the sixth circuit, he was promoted to associate justice on the New York Supreme Court. He became chief justice in 1837. He achieved widespread respect for his leadership of the court, and the opinions written during his tenure were widely cited in other states. Resigning as chief justice in 1845, Nelson ran for the U.S. Senate as a Democrat but lost by a narrow margin. He served at the state constitutional convention the following year.

In February 1845 Nelson was nominated by President John Tyler to be an associate justice on the U.S. Supreme Court. The nomination had been offered to many candidates before Nelson, all of whom had either declined or been refused by the Senate. Because of the difficulty in filling the post and because Nelson was easily the best qualified nomination yet made, the Senate quickly approved his nomination in March 1845.

Nelson's career on the bench was marked by an interest in technical cases rather than in the better-known constitutional issues. Specializing in admiralty and maritime law, patent law, equity, international law, and the conflict of laws, he gained a reputation as a diligent, reliable, fair-minded, and apolitical judge.

Nelson's opinion in the Dred Scott case illustrates his lack of political bias. The slave Dred Scott sued for freedom after his master took him into a territory Congress declared "free" in the Missouri Compromise of 1820. The first question to be settled was whether Scott was a U.S. citizen. Precedent dictated that in these cases citizenship status was determined by the law of the state in which the suit was brought, and under Missouri law Scott remained a slave and therefore was not a citizen. Nelson therefore voted that the Court should not hear the case. Other, more politically motivated members of the court voted to hear the case. In the final court decision, Nelson agreed with the majority that Scott must remain a slave, but he submitted an independent opinion.

In the tense circumstances leading up to the Civil War, Nelson urged compromise and conciliatory policies. Although he did not oppose the war, his lack of enthusiasm led some critics to call him unpatriotic. His court decisions also reflected his antipathy toward the war. He dissented from the majority in the *Prize Cases* (1863), which concerned ships that in attempting to break the economic blockade against the South were seized by Union forces. Nelson wrote that since Congress had not issued an official declaration of war, there was no legal war blockade to enforce. He voted with the unanimous majority in the *Milligan* case (1866), overturning the military tribunal's conviction of Lambdin P. Milligan, who had been charged with aiding the Confederacy, conspiring to free Confederate prisoners, and inciting insurrection in a military court set up under President Abraham Lincoln's authority. Nelson argued that the president had no authority to set up a military tribunal in secure areas where civil courts were functioning.

Nelson was a member of the 1871 Joint High Commission that investigated the *Alabama* Claims, a dispute between the United States and Britain over the Confederate cruiser *Alabama*, which had been built privately in England and sold to the Confederacy despite official British neutrality. The United States wanted Britain to pay reparations for the damages caused in battle by the ship. The final ruling on the case decreed that countries must use "due diligence" in preventing the sale of military weapons to the enemy of a country with which the first nation is at peace, and it awarded the United States more than $15 million. Nelson resigned from the Supreme Court in No-

vember 1872, just before completing fifty years on the bench. He died in Cooperstown, New York.

• Two good sources for biographical details and Nelson's judicial decisions are Frank Otto Gatell, "Samuel Nelson," in *The Justices of the United States Supreme Court*, vol. 2, ed. Leon Friedman (1969), and Clare Cushman, ed., *The Supreme Court Justices: Illustrated Biographies, 1789–1993* (1993). For further information, see Edwin Countryman, "Samuel Nelson," in *Green Bag* (June 1907), and Richard H. Leach, "The Rediscovery of Samuel Nelson," *New York History* 34 (1953): 64 ff. See also Henry J. Abraham, *Justices and Presidents: A Political History of Appointments to the Supreme Court* (1985). For details of Nelson's role in the Dred Scott case, see Don E. Fehrenbacher, *The Dred Scott Case: Its Significance in American Law and Politics* (1978).

ELIZABETH ZOE VICARY

NELSON, Thomas (26 Dec. 1738–4 Jan. 1789), merchant-planter and public official, was born in Yorktown, Virginia, the son of William Nelson (1711–1772), a prosperous merchant-planter, and Elizabeth Burwell. Educated first at home and then at a private school in Gloucester County, Nelson was sent to England in 1753. There, under the care of London merchant Edward Hunt, he attended grammar school at Hackney, near London, followed by three years at Christ College, Cambridge. Returning home in 1761, he married Lucy Grymes the following year. The union produced thirteen children, eleven of whom lived to maturity.

William Nelson, ambitious for his son, almost certainly paved the way for Thomas's election to the House of Burgesses from York County in 1761 as well as his appointment as justice of the peace and colonel of the militia. Nelson did not emerge as a political leader until the late 1760s, devoting most of his energy to the mercantile business. He also acquired the characteristic common among the Virginia elite of not being able to live within his income. It was reported in 1768 that "Colonel Nelson" lived "like a Prince." His debts were substantial. When his father died in 1772, he inherited 20,000 acres of land and more than 400 slaves. The mercantile firm was left to him and his brother Hugh Nelson. Difficult political and economic times as well as the inexperience of the brothers resulted in the rapid deterioration of the once-prosperous business, and Nelson remained heavily in debt for the rest of his life.

Beginning in the late 1760s, Nelson took on a steadily increasing political role in opposition to Britain's policies toward the American colonies. Regularly elected to the House of Burgesses, he supported nonimportation in response to the Townshend Duties and condemned the Intolerable Acts. In July 1774 he called for suspension of trade with Britain and chaired a York County committee to enforce such a policy. In the fall of 1775 members of the committee boarded a British merchant vessel, and Nelson personally dumped its tea into the York River. Governor John Murray, earl of Dunmore, described him as being "as violent as any . . . Patriot of them all." The preceding summer Nelson was chosen by an extralegal convention meeting in Richmond to command one of the three Virginia regiments that were being formed, but he declined when he was elected to the Second Continental Congress. From that point on he moved quickly in support of a movement for independence. Frustrated by the slow progress toward that goal, he returned to Virginia in the late winter of 1776, continuing his efforts. In May, when another convention met in Williamsburg, Nelson played a major role in framing resolutions instructing Virginia's delegates to Congress to propose to that body that the "United Colonies" be "free and independent states." Nelson delivered Virginia's resolutions to Philadelphia, and in July he was one of the signers of the Declaration of Independence.

Periodically in ill health from 1776 on, Nelson nevertheless continued in the Continental Congress until the spring of 1777 and returned briefly in 1779. He also continued to serve in the Virginia legislature throughout the war; commanded the state's militia in 1777; was a brigade commander in 1780–1781; and played a significant part in the state's loan drives of 1780, sometimes pledging his own private security. In June 1781 he replaced Thomas Jefferson as governor. Nelson's leadership infused new energy into Virginia's war effort. He sometimes exceeded his authority, but he was able to provide crucial support for the allied forces up to the victory at Yorktown on 19 October. Illness then forced him to resign his post in November.

Nelson worked for the remainder of his life to reestablish his mercantile business. But heavy prewar debts, neglect of private affairs during the war, and the state's failure to reimburse him for the loans he had guaranteed in 1780 thwarted his efforts. During these postwar years he served periodically in the legislature and was a trustee of the towns of Williamsburg and Yorktown, a director of the insane asylum in Williamsburg, and a member of the Board of Visitors of the College of William and Mary. With his health worsening and his business affairs in disarray, he declined to represent Virginia at the Constitutional Convention in Philadelphia in May 1787. Nelson ultimately opposed the ratification of the proposed constitution.

At the time of Nelson's death his fortune, which had been described "as inferior to very few," was dissipated. His family, with its economic underpinnings gone, never regained its former status. Even so, no Virginia patriot made as great a sacrifice of his ease and wealth as did Nelson. He died at his plantation "Montair" in Hanover County.

• There is no central collection of Nelson family papers. A large body of manuscripts did not survive the nineteenth century. The only substantial group of Nelson letters is in the William and Thomas Nelson Letterbook, 1766–1775, at the Virginia State Library. Other collections of private papers that contain Nelson material can be found at the Virginia Historical Society; the University of Virginia; the College of William and Mary; the Research Library of the Colonial Williamsburg Foundation; and the Manuscripts Division of the Library of Congress. Nelson's governorship can be followed in *Official Letters of the Governors of the State of Virginia*, ed. H. R. McIlwaine (1926–1927). Other published works that include Nelson letters are *The Papers of Thomas Jefferson*, ed. Julian P. Boyd et al. (1952–); *Writings of George Washington*, ed. John C. Fitzpatrick (1933–1944); *The Papers of James Madison*, ed. William T. Hutchinson et al. (1962–); and *The Letters and Papers of Edmund Pendleton*, ed. David J. Mays (1967). The standard biography of Nelson is Emory G. Evans, *Thomas Nelson of Yorktown: Revolutionary Virginian* (1975).

EMORY G. EVANS

NELSON, Thomas Henry (12 Aug. 1824–14 Mar. 1896), lawyer and diplomat, was born in Mason County, Kentucky, the son of Thomas W. Nelson, a physician, and Frances Doniphan, both members of prominent Kentucky families. Nelson attended the Mayville schools before moving to Rockville, Indiana, where he studied and practiced law for six years in Indiana and eastern Illinois. In 1844 he married Elizabeth Key, the daughter of Colonel Marshall Key, a Kentucky political leader; the couple had six children. In the early 1850s he settled permanently in Terre Haute, Indiana. In 1855 he took his first law partner, Abram Adams Hammond, who later became governor of Indiana. In 1856 he formed a second partnership with Isaac N. Pierce. Occasionally he faced Abraham Lincoln as a legal opponent, but they became friends. Nelson, who became a leader in the Whig party, was also one of the founders of the Republican party in the Midwest. He ran unsuccessfully for the U.S. Congress in 1860.

President Lincoln appointed Nelson minister resident to Chile on 1 June 1861. He labored with considerable success to win Chilean amity even during claims negotiations and settlements. Nelson and other North Americans acted heroically and with determination during the fire at the Church of Campañía in Santiago on 8 December 1863. About 2,000 people died in the fire. Santiagoans honored him with a 4 July 1864 celebration for his role in saving people during the fire. This goodwill did not last, however. In 1864 hostilities broke out between Peru and Spain over the Spanish seizure of the Chincha Islands. The Chilean government quickly came to the support of Peru, but it also expected U.S. military support. It was disappointed and resentful of Nelson's efforts to end the conflict through peaceful negotiations. After his recall on 12 March 1866, Nelson worked hard for the adoption of the Fourteenth Amendment.

On 16 April 1869 Nelson was appointed minister resident to Mexico. He reported soon after his arrival that Mexico's foreign trade was in the hands of British, French, and German merchants. Beginning in 1869 he conducted talks and negotiations with the Mexican government over raids by the Kickapoos, Lipans, and Mescaleros from northern Mexico against U.S. settlements and citizens. The Mexicans responded that the Indians had only crossed the border into Mexico after the U.S. forces had driven them off their traditional land. The Mexican government also argued that the Indians caused more damage and loss of life in Mexico than north of the border. Though the government of Mexico finally agreed to respond speedily to U.S. requests for permission to pursue the Indians into Mexican territory, it refused to grant a general permission for U.S. forces to cross the Rio Grande. In 1870 Nelson presented to Mexico the complaints of U.S. officials and Texans when Juan N. Cortina, considered a bandit and renegade in Texas, was appointed military commandant at Tamaulipas; these complaints persuaded Mexico to replace Cortina in late 1870. In 1871 Nelson contended with a considerable surge of anti-Americanism fueled by rumors of U.S. annexationist sentiment and the alleged willingness of Mexican president Benito Juárez to sell parts of northern Mexico to the United States. In 1872 and 1873 Nelson unsuccessfully negotiated for formal protection of the railroad and canal rights of U.S. concessionaires. However, the Mexican government treated the railroad entrepreneurs favorably, signing a concession in mid-1873 for the International Railroad Company of Texas to build a railroad from Mexico City to the Pacific coast.

After his recall from Mexico on 16 June 1873, Nelson returned to practice law and to engage in politics in Terre Haute until his death there. He served the Republican party well and demonstrated tact, patience, and intelligence while serving several Republican administrations as a diplomat in Chile and Mexico.

• Some of Nelson's private papers are in the Manuscript Division, Library of Congress. The Porter Cornelius Bliss Papers in the Latin American Library, Tulane University, contain useful material because Bliss was the secretary of legation during Nelson's service in Mexico. The U.S. State Department's microfilmed records contain his official correspondence from Chile (microfilm M10, reels 17–23) and from Mexico (microfilm M97, reels 36–49). Some of his official correspondence was published in the U.S. State Department, *Papers Relating to the Foreign Relations of the United States 1863–1864* and *1870–1873* (1864–1875).

A biography of Nelson has yet to be published. His career in Chile is described in Jay Kinsbruner, *Chile: A Historical Interpretation* (1973), and Henry Clay Evans, *Chile and Its Relations with the United States* (1927); his service in Mexico is described in James Morton Callahan, *American Foreign Policy in Mexican Relations* (1932), and Luis G. Zorrilla, *Historia de las Relaciones entre México y los Estados Unidos de América, 1800–1958* (2 vols., 1965). An obituary is in the Indianapolis *Sunday Journal*, 15 Mar. 1896.

THOMAS SCHOONOVER

NELSON, William (1711–19 Nov. 1772), merchant, planter, and public official, was born in Yorktown, Virginia, the son of Thomas Nelson, a merchant, and Margaret Reade. His father sent him to England for his education in 1722. Part of his time in England was spent in Penrith, Cumberland, but the details of his education are not known. Clearly the stay was a long one; the first indication that he was back in Virginia was in 1732 when he was appointed to the York County Court as a justice of the peace. Nelson then entered the family mercantile firm, a flourishing business that included periodic involvement in the slave trade. By

this time he was being described as "a young Gentleman of merit and fortune." In 1738 he married Elizabeth Carter Burwell from an old and distinguished Virginia family; they had six sons. (The eldest son, Thomas Nelson, attended Christ's College, Cambridge, and was a signer of the Declaration of Independence.)

Nelson's father died in 1745 and left him the bulk of the estate. The size of the inheritance is not clear, but cash bequests, apart from what he received, amounted to £10,000, which suggests that it was substantial. It included the mercantile concern and 3,270 acres of land in Hanover County. Nelson was, over time, to accumulate nearly 30,000 acres of land and build the business into one of the most prosperous Virginia-owned firms. He regularly dealt with eight or ten British companies, located in London, Bristol, Liverpool, and Whitehaven, which provided him with goods for an extensive wholesale and retail trade. This trade extended throughout the colony, and his contacts ranged as far afield as Philadelphia and New York City. After 1765 his annual volume of business was, at a minimum, between £5,000 and £10,000. At one time Nelson owned a one-half interest in one or perhaps two merchant vessels, and in the absence of banks he also carried on an extensive banking business, lending considerable sums of money. On his numerous acres he produced large amounts of tobacco, frequently described as the best in Virginia. In Hanover County his property was so extensive that in addition to overseers he retained two farm managers. He managed plantation and mercantile concerns with careful attention. Whether it was planting clover to restore the fertility of his lands or collecting unpaid debts, he let no detail escape him. And in Virginia, which was noted for the heavy indebtedness of its citizens, Nelson was able to keep himself free of the burden. Among Virginians of Nelson's class this was an exceptional action, which gives some insight into his character and success.

The wealth Nelson accumulated from planting and mercantile activity provided the underpinning for what was an immensely successful career as a public servant. After ten years of seasoning on the county court, he was elected to the House of Burgesses from York County and quickly emerged as an important member of that body. In 1745 Nelson was appointed to the Council of State, the highest post a Virginian could hope to attain. It served as an advisory body to the governor, the court of highest appeal in the colony, and the upper house of the legislature. He remained a member until his death. Nelson was joined on the council by his brother Thomas in 1749, and over the middle decades of the eighteenth century they represented perhaps the strongest single family influence in Virginia's governmental affairs. As early as 1756 Nelson was described as being, with the exception of the governor, "the greatest man in the Country." Neither governors nor John Blair, the president of the council through most of these years, did much without consulting him. In 1770, when Governor Lord Botetourt died, Nelson, as the senior member of the council, served as acting governor until the arrival of Lord Dunmore in 1771.

Nelson, as a member of the council, did not express himself publicly on the emerging contest with the mother country in the 1760s. Privately, he was a strong defender of Virginia's "rights" within the empire. Despite the repeal of the Stamp Act, he remained restive under the Navigation Acts which, he said, placed "cruel Impositions and clogs on our trade." English politics, he charged, were corrupt, and it was a farce for the English people to consider themselves "the Freest people on Earth." In contrast, America was the land of hope where "brave men" came during "the usurpation of the last century" and "laid the Foundation of what may in future ages become a mighty Empire." During the crisis over the Townshend Acts, he charged that the question was whether Americans were "to be Slaves or Freemen." He reduced his imports by about 50 percent, and he and his son Thomas wore suits, shirts, shoes, hose, buckles, wigs, and hats of Virginia manufacture exclusively.

Nelson died in Yorktown, Virginia, after a "tedious and painful Illness." "The Chief ornament of the Country is gone," wrote one commentator, while another stated that "no man amongst us better understood & no one was more strenuous in promoting the true Interest of his Country, whether view'd in a political or commercial light."

• The only substantial group of Nelson letters that remain are in the William and Thomas Nelson Letterbook, 1766–1775, at the Library of Virginia in Richmond. Nelson letters can also be found in collections of private papers at the University of Virginia in Charlottesville; the Virginia Historical Society and the Library of Virginia in Richmond; the College of William and Mary and the Research Library of the Colonial Williamsburg Foundation in Williamsburg; and the Manuscripts Division of the Library of Congress in Washington, D.C. Nelson's public career can be followed in H. R. McIlwaine and John P. Kennedy, eds., *Journals of the House of Burgesses, 1619–1776* (1905–1915); McIlwaine, ed., *Legislative Journals of the Council of State*, 2d ed. (1979); McIlwaine, et al., eds., *Executive Journals of the Council of Colonial Virginia* (1925–1966); and John C. Van Horne, ed., *The Correspondence of William Nelson As Acting Governor of Virginia, 1770–1771* (1975). There are also a few Nelson items in W. W. Abbot et al., eds., *The Papers of George Washington, Colonial Series* (1983–1995), and in George Reese, ed., *The Official Papers of Francis Fauquier: Lieutenant Governor of Virginia, 1758–1768* (1980). See also Jack P. Greene, "A Mirror of Virtue for a Declining Land: John Camm's Funeral Sermon for William Nelson," in *Essays in Early Virginia Literature Honoring Richard Beale Davis*, ed. J. A. Leo Lemay (1977). For other information concerning Nelson see Emory G. Evans, "The Nelsons: A Biographical Study of a Virginia Family in the Eighteenth Century" (Ph.D. diss., Univ. of Virginia, 1957), and Evans, *Thomas Nelson of Yorktown: Revolutionary Virginian* (1975).

EMORY G. EVANS

NELSON, William (27 Sept. 1824–29 Sept. 1862), naval and army officer, was born near Maysville, Kentucky, the son of Thomas W. Nelson, a physician, and Frances Doniphan. He attended Norwich Academy in Ver-mont from 1837 to 1839 and was appointed midshipman in the U.S. Navy on 28 January 1840. He served with the fleet that supported General Winfield Scott's landing at Veracruz (9–29 Mar. 1847) during the Mexican War. In 1855 he was promoted to lieutenant, a relatively advanced grade in the navy of that day. Standing 6'5" and weighing 300 pounds, Lieutenant Nelson was an imposing figure, and he had the personality to match. A fellow officer described him as "ardent, loud-mouthed, and violent."

A staunch Unionist, Nelson visited Kentucky several times during the spring of 1861, reporting his findings directly to Abraham Lincoln. Anxious to further the Union cause in Kentucky—a vitally strategic state that at the moment was professing a policy of strict neutrality—Lincoln sent Nelson back to the state with orders to begin recruiting a pro-Union home guard to counter the secessionist-dominated state militia. Back in his home state, Nelson established Camp Dick Robinson in Garrard County and over the weeks that followed enlisted and armed at least 10,000 loyal Kentuckians. That fall he was given the rank to go with his position, being commissioned brigadier general of volunteers (16 Sept. 1861). On 5 November he led Union forces in occupying Prestonsburg, Kentucky.

In December Nelson was given a division command in General Don Carlos Buell's Army of the Ohio. In April Confederates under General Albert Sidney Johnston moved to attack the Union army of General Ulysses S. Grant at Pittsburg Landing (Shiloh), Tennessee, before Buell could join forces with Grant. The Confederates launched their attack (6 Apr. 1862) barely twelve hours before Buell's arrival. That evening Nelson, commanding the lead division of Buell's army, had his troops ferried across the Tennessee River and entered Grant's lines just as Union troops were bracing for the expected final Confederate assault aimed at driving them into the river. Appalled at the sight of large numbers of skulkers cowering under the bluffs near the river, Nelson tried to rally them and, failing that, sought permission to open fire on them (it was not granted). The presence of Nelson's division was enormously welcome, though Confederate general P. G. T. Beauregard, commanding in place of the fallen Johnston, recalled his troops well before darkness fell. The next morning Nelson's and the other divisions of Buell's army joined the survivors of Grant's in driving the Confederates back.

After Shiloh, Union department commander Henry W. Halleck took personal command of both armies and, drawing together other troops from the department as well, began a glacially slow advance to the vital rail junction of Corinth, Mississippi. Nelson participated in this campaign, which culminated in the capture of Corinth on 30 May 1862. That summer he was rewarded for his services thus far in the war with two promotions. On 16 July his naval rank was advanced to lieutenant commander, and the next day he was promoted to major general of volunteers.

In mid-August Confederate general Edmund Kirby Smith led his force northward from East Tennessee, through the Cumberland Mountains, and toward central Kentucky. He was the harbinger of a major Confederate invasion, as Braxton Bragg's Confederate army was to follow him within a few weeks. On 19 August Nelson was assigned to draw together various newly recruited units in Kentucky to form an army to oppose Smith. The rebels allowed him little time. On 30 August news reached his Lexington headquarters that his inexperienced subordinates had chosen to offer battle to Smith's advancing veterans at Richmond, some twenty miles to the southeast. Nelson rode all morning to reach the battlefield, arriving that afternoon as his troops (some 7,000 raw recruits) were breaking for the rear. He strove to rally them under heavy fire. "If they can't hit me," he shouted, gesturing toward the furiously firing Confederates, "they can't hit anything!" He shortly received two flesh wounds, and his troops continued their hasty trek toward safer regions. With losses that day of 206 killed, 844 wounded, and 4,303 captured, his forces were all but annihilated. Smith used but 7,000 of his own men, lost a mere 451 of them, and subsequently marched unopposed into Lexington.

Nelson went to Louisville, where Buell had repaired with his army and was trying to organize a defense of the state. Both men took rooms at the Galt House Hotel. Also present in Louisville was Brigadier General Jefferson C. Davis, on leave from his unit west of the Mississippi. Davis volunteered his services for the present emergency. A difference of opinion occurred between Davis and Nelson and resulted in Nelson insulting Davis and ordering him out of the department. Several days later Davis, accompanied by his friend, Indiana governor Oliver P. Morton, arrived at the Galt House. Davis demanded satisfaction. Nelson called him an "insolent puppy." Davis threw a wadded up calling card into Nelson's face, and Nelson knocked the brigadier to the floor with a slap across the face. Nelson then went up the stairs toward Buell's room, still referring to Davis as an "insolent scoundrel" and promising to "teach him a lesson." Meanwhile, Davis was importuning bystanders for a pistol. Obtaining one, he dashed after Nelson and accosted him in front of Buell's door. Nelson turned on him. Davis warned, "Not another step closer!" Then he shot Nelson in the chest at a range of about eight feet. Nelson collapsed and asked for a clergyman. Within thirty minutes he was dead. In the confusion attending the Confederate invasion, Davis, aided by his powerful political friend Morton, was never brought to trial. Nelson was buried in Maysville.

• For further information on Nelson see Shelby Foote, *The Civil War: A Narrative* (3 vols., 1958–1974); Robert U. Johnson and Clarence C. Buel, eds., *Battles and Leaders of the Civil War* (4 vols., 1884–1887); E. B. Long and Barbara Long, *The Civil War Day by Day: An Almanac, 1861–1865* (1971); U.S. War Department, *The War of the Rebellion: A Compilation of the Official Records of the Union and Confederate Armies* (128 vols., 1880–1901); and Ezra J. Warner, *Generals in Blue: The Lives of the Union Commanders* (1964).

STEVEN E. WOODWORTH

NELSON, William Rockhill (7 Mar. 1841–13 Apr. 1915), newspaper publisher, was born in Fort Wayne, Indiana, the son of Isaac DeGroff Nelson, a businessman and politician, and Elizabeth Rockhill, the daughter of an Indiana lawmaker and congressman. Nelson grew up in a cultured, prominent family. He was an avid reader from age five but had no interest in formal education. Ordered by his parents in 1856 to attend the University of Notre Dame, the willful and mischievous young man was sent home after two undisciplined years of study. His father, then the clerk of Allen County (Ind.) Circuit Court, hired Nelson as his deputy. He studied law while working for his father and was a member of the bar at age twenty-one.

Dissuaded from volunteering for the Union army by his parents, Nelson spent the Civil War practicing law in Fort Wayne. Over the next fifteen years, Nelson was a cotton speculator, merchant, construction contractor, real estate developer, bridge builder, and Democratic party worker. Construction projects had earned him $200,000 by 1876, but he lost the fortune to debts incurred by a partner in a failed general store.

One asset Nelson retained was a share of the Fort Wayne *Sentinel*, a Democratic newspaper his father had owned from 1840 to 1842. Nelson and Samuel E. Morss, an experienced Fort Wayne journalist, bought out other shareholders in the *Sentinel* in 1879. Determined to attract readers, they undercut their competitors by selling issues for two cents. Under their leadership, the *Sentinel* advocated civic improvements, including better roads and a water works. The slow growth of Fort Wayne soon led Nelson and Morss to look for a booming city in which they could publish a newspaper. The Missouri River town of Kansas City was ripe for commercial development. Still a rugged cow town, Kansas City had grown from 32,000 to 56,000 residents over ten years. Yet streets and sidewalks were unpaved and lined with bars and brothels.

Nelson and Morss sold the *Sentinel* in 1880 and moved to Kansas City. Although four newspapers already were being published there, Nelson and Morss established the Kansas City *Evening Star*, its first issue appearing on 18 September 1880. As they had in Fort Wayne, the publishers appealed to readers with a 2-cent paper that emphasized local news. Nelson handled business affairs while Morss directed the editorial side until 1882 when Morss, in ill health, sold his interest to Nelson and left for Europe.

In complete control of the *Star*, Nelson had a clear vision of the kind of newspaper he sought to publish. He rarely, if ever, wrote for publication. Instead, he hired able journalists to carry out his orders and spent many hours each day directing the staff, often planning stories and outlining editorials. Nelson refused to promote himself, allowing the *Star* rather than its publisher to become an entity. His 1881 marriage in Chicago to Ida Houston, a physician's daughter from Champaign, Illinois, was one of the rare occasions his name appeared in the *Star*. The couple had one child.

Nelson was a staunch supporter of whatever he thought was good for Kansas City. He routinely refused appointments to committees or public posts, believing it was important that the newspaper and its staff retain an independent voice. He supported both Republicans and Democrats, judging candidates and issues by how they would affect the community. Under Nelson's guidance, the *Star* did not merely support public policy; it crusaded for action. "Anybody can print news," Nelson said, "but the *Star* tries to build things up. That is what a newspaper is for." Seldom was the *Star* not crusading for or against an issue of public concern, such as honest municipal government and community beautification. Nelson was often successful in bringing about reforms. For example, Kansas City's parks and boulevard system stemmed from his unending demands for community improvements. Other campaigns waged by the *Star* included those favoring a commission form of municipal government, a city auditorium, a Federal Reserve Bank in Kansas City, a city-owned water system, flood protection, and a public defender's office. The *Star* crusaded against voter fraud, the general property tax, liquor at amusement parks, and saloons (banning liquor advertisements cost the paper an estimated $100,000 a year). The *Star*'s unrelenting focus on the community won over readers. Circulation rose from 3,000 in 1880 to 10,000 in 1883 and to 25,000 in 1886. By 1893 its circulation of 50,000 was double that of its closest competitor.

Nelson believed that reporters were the most important part of the *Star* staff. "They are the fellows whose work determines whether the paper shall attract readers or repel them," he wrote. Although he paid miserly wages, he gave reporters unusual freedom to express their points of view in stories. Like the publisher, the reporters had to remain independent of forces outside the *Star*. Nelson's newspaper became a respected training ground for prominent journalists, including William Allen White, Alfred Henry Lewis, and Eugene C. Pulliam.

Through the years the *Star* remained conservative in its coverage and presentation of news. Nelson rejected the sensationalism that Joseph Pulitzer, William Randolph Hearst, and other contemporaries used to build circulation. Headlines were small, and illustrations were used instead of half-tone photographs. Comic strips were banned because Nelson thought they cheapened a paper. He reprinted articles from a variety of publications, believing that his paper was the main reading material for many families.

In 1890 Nelson created a weekly edition of the *Star* to be sold in rural areas for twenty-five cents a year. He established the Sunday *Star* in 1894 and bought the morning *Times* in 1901 but did not increase subscription prices. Instead, he continued to charge merchants and other businessmen high rates to advertise. By 1900 the *Star*'s daily circulation reached 87,000, and the rural edition sold 150,000 copies a week. Circulation of the *Star* rose to 170,000 by 1911.

Nelson was earning an estimated $1 million annually at the time of his death in Kansas City. Thereafter, his wife and daughter assumed control of the *Star* and the *Times*, until his daughter's death in 1926, when the papers were sold to employees for $11 million. Money from the sale was used to establish an art museum on the site of the Nelson estate.

In thirty-five years of publishing the *Star*, Nelson retained readers and advertisers with strong coverage of local affairs. His commitment to the community showed how a newspaper could be a leader yet remain independent. In an era of press sensationalism, Nelson was among the nation's few prominent editors who developed community spirit and responsibility through journalism.

• Early studies of Nelson include a book by the staff of the Kansas City *Star, William Rockhill Nelson: The Story of a Man, a Newspaper and a City* (1915), and Icie F. Johnson, *William Rockhill Nelson and the Kansas City Star* (1925). Modern assessments include three unpublished dissertations, Charles Elkins Rogers, "William Rockhill Nelson: Independent Editor and Crusading Liberal" (Univ. of Minnesota, 1948); William Jackson Bell, "A Historical Study of the Kansas City Star Since the Death of William Rockhill Nelson, 1915–1949" (Univ. of Missouri, 1949); and William L. McCorkle, "Nelson's Star and Kansas City, 1880–1898" (Univ. of Texas, 1968). For a personal view of Nelson, see William Allen White, "The Man Who Made the Star," repr. in Edwin H. Ford and Edwin Emery, *Highlights in the History of the American Press: A Book of Readings* (1954). A lengthy obituary is in the Kansas City *Star*, 13 Apr. 1915.

DOUGLASS K. DANIEL

NEMEROV, Howard (1 Mar. 1920–5 July 1991), poet and novelist, was born in New York City, the son of David Nemerov and Gertrude Russek. Benefiting from an affluent family background, he graduated from Harvard University with an A.B. in 1941. He married Margaret Russell in 1944; they had three children. After serving in the Royal Canadian Air Force between 1942 and 1944, Nemerov continued his war effort as a member of the U.S. Army Air Forces in 1944–1945. He was discharged as a first lieutenant. Nemerov began his lengthy teaching career as an English instructor at Hamilton College in Clinton, New York, in 1946.

In 1947 Nemerov published his first volume of poetry, *The Image and the Law*, a collection that typifies much of the poet's verse. Nemerov wrote about what both he and critics would characterize as a schism between sly, ironic wit and quite serious, even pessimistic philosophizing. As F. C. Golffing noted in a review of this book, "Nemerov tells us that he dichotomizes the 'poetry of eye' and the 'poetry of the mind,' and that he attempts to exhibit in his verse the 'everpresent dispute between the two ways of looking at the world'" (*Poetry*, Nov. 1947, pp. 96–97). The success of this first volume was due in part to Nemerov's ability to fuse these apparent differences in the poems. Critics also noted in Nemerov's poetry echoes of the modernist poets Wallace Stevens, T. S. Eliot, W. H. Auden, and William Butler Yeats. Such comparisons were made again with the appearance of Nemerov's second volume of poetry, *Guide to the Ruins* (1950).

While some critics condemned Nemerov as an imitator, others praised his attention to the moral dilemmas of the modern sensibility.

Written at the same time as *Guide to the Ruins*, Nemerov's first novel, *The Melodramatists*, was actually published the previous year, in 1949. Like *Ruins*, the novel addresses "a satiric view of certain phases of contemporary civilization" (Herbert Barrows, *New York Times*, 3 Apr. 1949). Simultaneously humorous and biting, *The Melodramatists* established Nemerov's reputation as a serious writer with talents in multiple genres. At this time Nemerov also was associate editor of the literary magazine *Furioso* (1946–1951), and he began writing what would become a considerable body of criticism.

Nemerov's next major publication was a second novel, *Federigo; or, The Power of Love* (1954); it was followed by another volume of verse, *The Salt Garden* (1955), which many critics felt marked Nemerov's maturation as a poet. *Salt Garden* balanced philosophical skepticism and social satire, voiced with lyrical sadness. This volume also revealed Nemerov's deep interest in nature, and his verse now drew comparisons with the work of Robert Frost. Over the next decade Nemerov continued to demonstrate his ability to bring his keen eye for foible and philosophy to a variety of genres, publishing the novel *The Homecoming Game* (1957), poems in *Mirrors and Windows* (1958) and *New and Selected Poems* (1960), short stories in *A Commodity of Dreams* (1959), verse and plays in *The Next Room of the Dream* (1962), and several volumes of combined essays, verse, and fiction.

In 1969 Nemerov became a professor of English at Washington University in St. Louis, Missouri, which he would make his primary residence for the rest of his life. With the poems in *Gnomes and Occasions* (1973), Nemerov's insightful cynicism was perceived to have mellowed in comparison to earlier works, yet the poems of this volume retain their philosophical bearing on a modern lifestyle that is often teetering on the edge of absurdity. Critical recognition of the importance and seriousness of Nemerov's poetic vision reached fruition with his induction into the American Academy and Institute of Arts and Letters in 1977 and with his publication of *Collected Poems* (1978), which included verse from previous years and new additions. *Collected Poems* won both the Pulitzer Prize and the National Book Award. Nemerov mainly wrote verse in subsequent years, publishing two major volumes, *Sentences* (1980) and *Inside the Onion* (1984). He became poet laureate of the United States in 1988, a post he retained until his death in St. Louis.

After a rather quiet early career Nemerov emerged ultimately as a major poet. Although his early verse was occasionally accused of being more imitative than original, he developed a strong, independent voice that became influential and respected. Throughout his career Nemerov conveyed a moral vision of a society that was fragmenting even as it aspired to wholeness; his writings maintain a sense of humor in the face of what is depicted as a potentially bleak moral landscape.

• A substantial collection of Nemerov's papers resides at Washington University in St. Louis, Mo. M. L. Rosenthal discusses a number of Nemerov's poems in *The Modern Poets* (1960). The first extended discussion of Nemerov's work was Peter Meinke's 45-page pamphlet *Howard Nemerov* (1968). Julia A. Bartholomay, *The Shield of Perseus: The Vision and Imagination of Howard Nemerov* (1972), is a second substantial work that draws heavily on Freudian thought. William Mills, *The Stillness in Moving Things: The World of Howard Nemerov* (1975), is a significant work that examines Nemerov's philosophical positions, linking him to German phenomenology. In *Howard Nemerov* (1980), Ross Labrie presents an insightful variety of biographical and critical information. The two major bibliographies of Nemerov's work are Bowie Duncan, *The Critical Reception of Howard Nemerov: A Selection of Essays and a Bibliography* (1971), and Diana E. Wyllie, *Elizabeth Bishop and Howard Nemerov: A Reference Guide* (1983). An obituary is in *Annual Obituary* (1991).

PAUL WAYNE RODNEY

NEOLIN (fl. 1762–1763), Native American religious leader whose prophecies inspired the participants in the Indian war of 1763, was also known as "The Delaware Prophet." Nothing is known of the life of Neolin, "The Enlightened," other than that he was a member of the Delaware (Lenni Lenape) tribe, before he became known as a religious prophet. Toward the end of the French and Indian War, the victorious British placed garrisons of soldiers in the formerly French forts in Indian country in New York and Pennsylvania and to the west in the Ohio Valley and around the Great Lakes. They also instituted a niggardly trade policy that restricted Indian access to European goods. Native American resentment was widespread, and efforts were under way to organize pan-Indian military resistance.

It was in the midst of this turmoil that Neolin, in 1761 or 1762, experienced a religious vision. In his vision, after a miraculous journey he was introduced to the Master of Life. This supreme being gave him a series of instructions that he and the other Indians were to obey and a prayer that they should repeat morning and evening. In a later vision he was shown a map, which he was told to reproduce on parchment and sell to every household, that would serve as a visual reminder of the main points of the message of the Master of Life.

The teachings of Neolin included some innovative religious ideas, foreign to traditional Native American belief and probably derived from exposure to Christian doctrine. The map showed a path to Heaven, where the Master of Life resided, and another to Hell, presided over by a Devil. New rituals required the use of emetics, fasting, and sexual abstinence. But the social gospel Neolin taught was the inspiring part of his message. The Master of Life, he said, required the Indians to give up drinking alcoholic beverages to the point of drunkenness, to cease interpersonal and intertribal fighting, and to live in faithful monogamous marriages. Most important of all, they were to return to the virtuous ways of their ancestors, live by the bow and arrow, give up their dependence on European trade goods, and drive the redcoats—the British soldiers—out of Indian territory. Inoffensive white men—like the friendly French habitants—might remain.

Neolin's teachings spread like wildfire, borne by other prophets who carried with them copies of the map that showed how the traditional Indian way of life led to Heaven, and the white man's way led Indians to Hell. Pontiac, an Ottawa leader who sparked the revolt against the British in 1763, personally became a follower, and no doubt his message declaring the possibility of a revitalization of traditional native cultures along nativistic lines gave confidence to many others. But, after temporary successes, the failure of Pontiac to capture the British fort at Detroit led to a disintegration of the Indian campaign, and by 1764 the "war" was over. Indian preachers continued to display their maps and promulgate the gospel according to Neolin for several years thereafter, but they were eventually discredited, according to Christian missionary reports, for failing to observe the code of conduct they were recommending to their followers.

• Neolin's teachings and their historical context are reviewed in Howard H. Peckham, *Pontiac and the Indian Uprising* (1947), and Anthony F. C. Wallace, *The Death and Rebirth of the Seneca* (1970). His doctrine was first published in Henry R. Schoolcraft, *Algic Researches*, vol. 1 (1839), pp. 239–48, translated from the diary of a French resident of Detroit, Robert Navarre, during the uprising. The document was preserved by Lewis Cass, former governor of Michigan Territory, and a copy was later transmitted by him to Francis Parkman for use in the writing of *The Conspiracy of Pontiac* (1851). See also Charles Hunter, "The Delaware Nativistic Revival of the Mid-Eighteenth Century," *Ethnohistory* 18 (1971): 39–49.

ANTHONY F. C. WALLACE

NERINCKX, Charles (2 Oct. 1761–12 Aug. 1824), Catholic missionary, was born in Herffelingen in Brabant, Belgium, the son of Sebastian Nerinckx, a physician, and Petronilla Landgendries. The eldest of fourteen children, Charles was one of several of his siblings who entered Catholic religious orders.

Following seminary studies at Enghien, Gheel, and Louvain, Nerinckx was ordained a Catholic priest in November 1785. After ten years as a priest at Mechlin and Meerbeek, he went into hiding to escape the invading anti-Catholic forces unleashed by the revolution in France. Deciding that his clerical skills could not be effectively used at home, he made his way to Amsterdam in 1804 and there took ship for America.

Nerinckx offered his services to the man who was then the only Catholic bishop in the United States, John Carroll in Baltimore. After studies in English at Georgetown College, the 44-year-old Nerinckx was assigned by Carroll in 1805 to the missions in frontier Kentucky. There he would spend almost the entirety of his remaining nineteen years.

At that first major center of Catholicism in the West, Nerinckx joined Stephen Badin, another priest-exile from the French Revolution. Together they would be the leading figures in the Catholic community until the arrival in 1811 of the first bishop of the West, Benedict Joseph Flaget, yet another French émigré.

Nerinckx was a man of immense frame and energy who often assisted physically in the building of churches in the wilderness. He was responsible for the construction of fourteen churches. In 1812 he was instrumental in founding and fostering the first religious community of Catholic women in America not directly linked to European forebears: the Sisters of Loretto. He also made attempts to establish other religious communities—a brotherhood of men and a sisterhood of black women—that did not meet with such success.

Like other Catholic and Protestant missionaries, Nerinckx spent much of his time on horseback visiting far-flung frontier settlements. A typical day might begin with the hearing of confessions, followed by the recitation of the rosary, the celebration of mass with a lengthy sermon, and religious instruction. Next would come any burials, marriages, or baptisms needed by the community. Nerinckx became especially known for his tender care and teaching of the children of the frontier settlements.

Many early priests of Kentucky, Nerinckx included, were often considered by their parishioners as stern in their moral sensitivities. Dancing and the reading of novels were heavily discouraged. In part, the resulting tensions reflected the difference between the pieties of the French-trained clerics and the laity who were largely from British Maryland stock. A key to Nerinckx's disposition is revealed in his private notebooks. There he wrote: "Your heart must be of three kinds: 1. Childlike with God. 2. Motherly toward others. 3. Stern toward yourself."

Disagreement with his bishop—who found Nerinckx's rules for the Sisters of Loretto too severe—resulted in Nerinckx's departure from Kentucky in 1824. He journeyed to Missouri where he proposed to work among American Indians, but there death overtook him. His remains were later returned to the Motherhouse of Loretto in 1833.

An early Kentucky Catholic historian who had known Nerinckx personally, Martin John Spalding, noted that Nerinckx could be "disagreeable" in his preaching and that he seldom laughed or smiled. But he was among that hardy group Spalding called "an iron race of pioneers." Nerinckx, Spalding insisted, "feared no difficulties and was appalled by no dangers" (*Sketches of the Early Catholic Missions of Kentucky* [1844]). A man of rectitude and complexity, Nerinckx set a tone for discipline and survival in a frontier society while bringing to it the messages of compassion and justice that he found in the Gospel texts.

• Copies of Nerinckx's notebooks are at the Loretto Motherhouse Archives at Nerinx [*sic*], Ky. The earliest biography of

Nerinckx is Camillus P. Maes, *The Life of Rev. Charles Ne-rinckx* (1880), which was followed by William J. Howlett, *The Life of Rev. Charles Nerinckx* (1915). A somewhat novel-istic treatment of his life is Helene Magaret, *Giant in the Wil-derness* (1952). A careful account of Nerinckx's work is Herman Schauinger, *Cathedrals in the Wilderness* (1952). A carefully researched monograph by Florence Wolff, archivist of the Sisters of Loretto, is *With Captain Dogwood: The Life and Spirit of Reverend Charles Nerinckx as Related by His Con-temporaries* (1986).

CLYDE F. CREWS

NESBIT, Evelyn Florence (25 Dec. 1884–17 Jan. 1967), model and showgirl, was born in Tarentum, Pennsyl-vania, the daughter of Winfield Scott Nesbit, a lawyer, and Elizabeth (maiden name unknown). While her early childhood was moderately comfortable, Evelyn, along with her mother and younger brother, endured considerable financial hardship following the sudden death of her father in 1893. The family moved first to Pittsburgh, and later to Philadelphia, where Nesbit's mother struggled to earn a living in a variety of posi-tions—from boardinghouse keeper to sales clerk—while her children attended elementary school. Eve-lyn's secondary education was interrupted when she began working as a stockgirl in Philadelphia's Wana-maker's department store; although she returned to her studies briefly in her later teens, she never re-ceived a high school diploma.

Within months of the family's arrival in Philadel-phia, Nesbit had drawn the attention of a number of prominent visual artists for whom she was asked to pose; before long, modeling became her full-time oc-cupation. Always considered an unusually attractive child, by the age of fifteen it had become clear that Nesbit's physical attributes were a marketable com-modity, garnering her considerable public notice and the promise of substantial earnings. Eager to enhance her career prospects, Nesbit and her mother moved to New York City in 1900. Shortly thereafter, Nesbit found work as a model, posing for such renowned art-ists and photographers as Carroll Beckwith, Frederick Church, and Herbert Morgan. As her professional reputation grew, she was invited to serve as the model for George Grey Barnard's sculpture *Innocence*, now in the Metropolitan Museum of Art, and Charles Dana Gibson's sketch "The Eternal Question," originally published in *Collier's*, as well as a series of now classic photographs by Rudolf Eickemeyer and Gertrude Kasebier. More lucrative than any of these ventures were the many advertisements in which Nesbit was featured around the turn of the century, when newspa-pers had just begun printing commercial photographs.

By 1901 her widely publicized likenesses had helped earn Nesbit a small role in the Broadway musi-cal *Floradora*. Like all of the "Floradora Girls," as the show's dancers were popularly known, Nesbit cap-tured the attention of numerous wealthy, male theater-goers interested in becoming acquainted with its glam-orous young stars. Among her many admirers was the internationally renowned architect Stanford White,

with whom she developed an intimate relationship. It was also during this time that Nesbit was introduced to her future husband, Harry K. Thaw, the wealthy and eccentric son of a prominent Pittsburgh family who was later to become notorious as the murderer of Stan-ford White. Thaw's intense animosity for White, whom he saw at once as a despicable rake and a daunt-ing rival for Nesbit's affections, provided the focal point for the severe emotional and physical abuse he inflicted upon her as their relationship evolved. Over the next few years, however, Nesbit persisted in her efforts to establish a stage career, performing in a number of short-lived musical comedies, including *The Wild Rose*, *Tommy Rot*, and *The Girl from Dixie*.

In spite of the conflicts plaguing their relationship, Nesbit and Thaw were married in 1905. After a short honeymoon in the western United States, they stayed briefly at "Lyndhurst," the Thaw family's opulent Pittsburgh estate. Thereafter, they traveled, often in-dependently, to various European and American cit-ies. In the early summer of 1906 Nesbit and Thaw to-gether went to New York City for an extended visit. On the evening of 25 June they attended the premiere of a new musical, *Mamzelle Champagne*, at Madison Square Garden's rooftop theater. As it happened, Stanford White was also in attendance. Toward the end of the performance, Thaw approached White's ta-ble and shot him in the head three times, killing him instantly.

Throughout the months leading up to Thaw's 1907 trial, Nesbit remained outwardly loyal to her husband, visiting him regularly in prison and supporting him in public statements. Her poignant testimony concerning her youthful "seduction" at the hands of Stanford White—by far the most sensational aspect of the tri-al—was likewise tailored to assist in Thaw's defense. When the first jury deadlocked, Thaw was retried the following year and found not guilty by reason of tem-porary insanity. During this period Nesbit's relations with Thaw and his family deteriorated significantly. Thaw divorced Nesbit in 1916, denying paternity of the child to whom she had given birth while he was confined to a state mental hospital.

When it became evident that the Thaw family was unwilling to provide for her support, Nesbit resumed her performing career. In 1913 she traveled to Europe, where she appeared in the musical *Hello Ragtime* with Jack Clifford (formerly Virgil Montani). Nesbit and Clifford, who were married in 1916, spent several years touring the vaudeville circuit. When they di-vorced in 1919, Nesbit continued to perform her caba-ret act with a new partner. In 1914 Nesbit starred in her first motion picture, *Threads of Destiny*. This was followed by appearances in a number of minor films, such as *Redemption* (1917), *Her Mistake* (1918), *Wom-an, Woman* (1919), *A Fallen Idol* (1919), and *My Little Sister* (1919). During this time Nesbit also published the first of her two autobiographies, *The Story of My Life* (1914). The second, *Prodigal Days*, was published twenty years later.

Plagued by persistent drug problems, Nesbit's mental, physical, and financial circumstances declined steadily thereafter. In an attempt to support herself and her child, she embarked upon a number of ventures, opening a tea room near Broadway in 1921, performing in various nightclub acts, and establishing several speakeasies—none of which proved successful. Impoverished and increasingly removed from her former lifestyle, Nesbit tried in 1922 to end her life by ingesting poison. Four years later, she again attempted suicide.

Her fortunes improved somewhat in the 1930s, when Nesbit performed with some regularity in various burlesque and cabaret acts. She was unable by this point to command either the audiences or the wages that she had earlier in her career. In the 1940s Nesbit lived in Hollywood, where she was supported by her only child, Russell Thaw. In 1955 she served as technical adviser for the film version of *The Girl in the Red Velvet Swing*, based on her affair with Stanford White. She devoted a great deal of time to sculpting and painting in the last years of her life, even taking on some pupils. She died in Santa Monica, California.

• Primary source materials dealing with Evelyn Nesbit's life and work are not archived in a single location. Selected documents relevant to her theatrical career are held at the Shubert Archives and the Billy Rose Theatre Collection at the New York Public Library for the Performing Arts, Lincoln Center, both in New York City. Information concerning Nesbit's motion picture performances may be found at the William Fox Research Library in Los Angeles as well as the National Archives film collection in Washington, D.C. A concise overview of Nesbit's life is provided by Richard Ketcham in "Faces from the Past," *American Heritage* (June 1969). Most of the secondary writing on Nesbit focuses on her relationship with Stanford White and the subsequent trials of Harry K. Thaw for his murder. Among these works, Paul Baker, *Stanny: The Gilded Life of Stanford White* (1989), is by far the strongest. Phyllis Abramson, *Sob Sister Journalism* (1990); Kevin Brownlow, *Behind the Mask of Innocence* (1991); Gerald Langford, *The Murder of Stanford White* (1962); Suzannah Lessard, *The Architect of Desire: Beauty and Danger in the Stanford White Family* (1996); and Michael Mooney, *Evelyn Nesbit and Stanford White: Love and Death in the Gilded Age* (1976), also contain useful information about Nesbit's experiences during those years. For a fictionalized account of this era, see E. L. Doctorow's acclaimed novel *Ragtime* (1972), from which both film (1981) and musical (1997) versions have been adapted. See also Charles Samuels, *The Girl in the Red Velvet Swing* (1953), and the 1955 film by the same name. Obituaries are in the *New York Times*, 19 Jan. 1967, and *Newsweek*, 30 Jan. 1967.

LISA CARDYN

NESTLE, Charles (2 May 1872–22 Jan. 1951), creator of permanent waving devices for human hair, was born Karl Ludwig Nessler, in Todtnau, Bavaria, the son of Bartholomew Nessler, a shoemaker, and Rosina Laitner. For some unknown reason, the vagaries of hair fascinated Nestle as a young man. He invested long hours in the study of its properties. This youthful interest led Nestle to work briefly in a neighboring village as a barber's apprentice. Not long after, he traversed the border into nearby Switzerland to work successive jobs in small electric appliance and watch parts firms. Although he developed solid knowledge of simple mechanics and electric motors and equipment, Nestle soon tired of factory work and followed his early interest in hair to salons, where he learned to cut it and wave it, while closely studying its properties.

In 1899 Nestle moved to Paris to study the Marcel wave—the leading technique of the time that utilized heated tongs to wave hair—developed by Henri Marcel. Eventually he secured a position in an exclusive Paris salon where he could observe and utilize the Marcel method, and there he began developing his own permanent-waving system. Because of his growing skill and reputation as a Marcel wave hairdresser, he was asked by a wealthy English customer to take his talents and the hair-waving devices with which he was experimenting to London.

It was after he arrived in London about 1900 that he took the name Charles Nestle. In 1901 he married a co-worker from his days at the salon in Paris, Katherine Laible; they had four children. After opening his own London hairdressing shop he organized a series of public lectures to demonstrate his new approach to hair waving. Nestle discovered after many hours of analysis and experimentation that dampening the hair augmented its curl-holding tendencies significantly. He also found that applying a borax paste followed by winding the hair on heated curlers made it porous enough to draw additional moisture from the atmosphere, thus enabling the stylist to set a curl more permanently.

Because customers were initially reluctant to accept his new waving system, Nestle had to manufacture and market false eyelashes and eyebrows to remain in business. Eventually, however, through a successful advertising campaign he overcame customers' reluctance to trying the "Nestle-wave." In the meantime he continued to improve his equipment. In 1909, for example, he began using electric heaters instead of gas, and in 1912 he developed a mechanized curling device that sped up the process that originally took twelve hours to complete.

Following the start of World War I, because he had remained a German citizen Nestle was declared an enemy alien in his adopted city, forcing him to depart for the United States in 1915 without his family. Once in New York he learned to his dismay that over 600 hairdressers were using waving systems that copied his. Demonstrating the same resourcefulness he had in London, Nestle opened a salon in Manhattan and soon was able to show that his machinery produced a longer-lasting "permanent" wave. By the time his family joined him in 1919, Nestle had founded the Nestle Company, which manufactured and distributed beauty salon equipment and hairdressing supplies. He also was operating a large and attractive salon on Fifth Avenue, and had established a beauty salon supply factory on Long Island.

Nestle continued to modify his hair-waving equipment. By the mid-1920s he had secured patents on various curling devices, waving solutions, and hair-testing machines. In 1927 he opened on Broadway what was then the largest beauty salon in the world. There he personally handled and waved the hair of leading actresses of stage and screen. He also purchased an office building in midtown that became headquarters of the worldwide operations of the Nestle Company.

Nestle was involved in the affairs of various hairdressing associations, and in 1926, as Master Hair Dressers Association president, he spoke out against the new and increasingly popular bobbed hairstyle of the flapper era. In 1928 Nestle published *The Story of Hair*, which continued his attack on short hairstyles for women and included an analysis of the properties of human hair, with recommendations for hair care and treatment, curling and dyeing methodology, and "cures" for male baldness. *The Story of Hair* not only culminated Nestle's lifelong examination of hair from the hairdresser's viewpoint, but it also contained a pseudoscientific account of the relationship of human psychology and physiology to hair. Nestle maintained that his experiments and analysis in Europe and New York showed that hair growth was related to "nervous energy," that thick hair producers tended toward obesity, and that criminals had more hair than the rest of the population.

Nestle began negotiations with the LeMur beauty parlor supply firm of Cleveland in 1928, and the next year a merger was completed. Initially Nestle was active in the affairs of the new company, but eventually became less involved with Nestle-LeMur because of poor health. The company, which would later become one of the dominating manufacturers of permanent wave supplies and hair-care products, showed a profit in 1929 but experienced significant losses during the depression. It regained profitability in 1939 and was successful for many years thereafter. Nestle, however, lost most of his sizable fortune through failed investments in skin-care products that were marketed separately from Nestle-LeMur.

Nestle continued to analyze hair and to develop and introduce to the marketplace new health-care products until he died in Harrington Park, New Jersey. The international growth of the beauty parlor and hair-care industries that followed Nestle owe their advance to his unswerving dedication to experimentation and analysis and to his invention of the successful permanent waving device that remains an essential element of hair care.

• For a more detailed examination of Nestle's career, see Hans Lehmberg, *Karl Ludwig Nessler, die Lebensgeschichte eines Friseurs und Erfinders* (n.d.); on permanent waving see J. Stevens Cox, *An Illustrated Dictionary of Hairdressing and Wigmaking* (rev. 1984). Nestle's *The Story of Hair* (1928), in addition to touching on his life and work, is an excellent example of the widespread 1920s fascination with human psychology ("pop" or otherwise) and race-based anatomical analysis. Photographs of Nestle and some of his original waving machines, plus information on his career, are in *Life*, 5 Feb. 1951. For a general outline of Nestle's career, see obituaries in *Time*, 5 Feb. 1951, and the *New York Times*, 24 Jan. 1951.

ROY HAYWOOD LOPATA

NESTOR, Agnes (24 June 1880–28 Dec. 1948), labor leader, was born in Grand Rapids, Michigan, the daughter of Thomas Nestor and Anna McEwen. Her father, who owned a grocery store at the time of her birth, built a successful career in local politics and maintained his family in considerable comfort during the first ten years of Nestor's life. However, after he sold his store and was defeated in an election for sheriff in the mid-1890s, he found it difficult to find work in the depressed economy and moved to Chicago in 1896. The family joined him a few months later, but he became ill and could find employment only sporadically. Soon Nestor, who was in the eighth grade, had to leave school and go to work. For her, as she later recalled in her autobiography, "childhood was over."

Nestor got a job at the Eisendrath Glove Company, but she had never been physically strong and found the sixty-hour weeks exhausting. Moreover, glove operators had to buy their own needles and machine oil and pay "rent" for the machines they used, all out of the small wages they earned. The male cutters in the shop, who had recently formed a union, urged the women to join them. Nestor spoke up decisively in favor of union action, and in 1898 she led the women in a strike. After just ten days of picketing the employers succumbed, raising the lowest wages, ending machine rent, and allowing a union shop.

In 1902 Nestor helped organize a female glove workers' local. She later wrote that "where the women have locals of their own, greater interest is shown because they have full responsibility for their own affairs." As president, Nestor represented the local at the founding convention of the International Glove Workers Union (IGWU) later that year, and the following year she was elected an IGWU vice president. She served until 1906, when she was elected to a paid full-time position as IGWU secretary-treasurer shortly after giving up factory work because of her chronic respiratory problems. Her new assignment, she later said, "changed the whole course of my life." After serving three years, she was elected as president, becoming the first woman to head an international union; she held the office until 1915.

Despite Nestor's commitment to the glove workers' union, she knew that working women in every occupation needed help, and that legal protection was needed as well as labor organization. In 1904 she found an institution that shared her concerns: the new National Women's Trade Union League. Nestor became a national league board member in 1907, and in 1913 she became the first working woman to serve as the president of the Chicago League; she held both positions for the rest of her life. On behalf of the league, she worked to organize women in a wide variety of occupations, ranging from milliners to stockyard workers. She also helped lead numerous strikes (including the historic garment workers' strikes of 1909 and 1910–1911), directed fieldwork for the league's Training School for Women Organizers, and lectured frequently to middle-class audiences.

Through the league, Nestor developed friendships with leading Chicago reformers, including Jane Addams, Mary McDowell, and Margaret Dreier Robins. With their support, she joined the fight for state laws to protect working women. Although Nestor's figure was slight and her style low-key, she was a courageous and persistent lobbyist. She was also pragmatic: she was deeply committed, for instance, to the eight-hour workday for women, but when she concluded that that goal was not politically attainable, she played a major role in persuading the state legislature to pass the Ten-Hour-Day Law (covering female factory workers) in 1909. This was followed by a second law in 1911 extending the coverage to women in retail and clerical jobs. She also fought for child-labor laws, minimum wages for women, federal health programs for mothers and infants, and the creation of a public employment service and a Women's Bureau in the U.S. Department of Labor.

Nestor was on the National Commission on Vocational Education in 1914, and during World War I she served on a labor mission to England and France, the Woman's Committee of the U.S. Council of National Defense, and the Illinois Industrial Survey Commission. In 1928 she ran against the incumbent for the Democratic nomination to the Illinois state legislature. Labor and women's groups were supportive, but neither Nestor's call for welfare legislation nor her status as a temperance-minded feminist proved appealing to the broader electorate, and her "wet" opponent defeated her decisively.

During the depression, Nestor served on a variety of state and municipal boards having to do with labor issues. She also played a key role in finally winning the eight-hour workday for women in 1937. That year, her lifelong commitment to the IGWU faced a test, when many members began leaving for a rival union affiliated with the Congress of Industrial Organizations. Despite her progressive associations, Nestor remained loyal to the IGWU and worked with the American Federation of Labor (AFL) to restore the union to its former strength. She became the director of research and education for the union in 1938 and served until her death. During World War II, Nestor lobbied—just as she had during World War I—for strict standards of worker safety and well-being despite the pressures of wartime production. She also wrote *Brief History of the International Glove Workers Union of America* (1942) and served on an AFL postwar planning committee. She died in Chicago just a few months after being appointed to the Illinois Displaced Persons Commission.

Nestor's contribution to working women can be measured in the institutions she shaped, including her own local, the IGWU, the National Women's Trade Union League, and dozens of public and private boards. It can also be measured in the lives she changed—through the laws she fought for, the labor conditions she worked to improve, and the vivid example of her own life. Yet reviewing Nestor's career illuminates not only how much she gave to the labor movement but also how much it gave to her. The work was often difficult and frustrating; as late as 1936 she wistfully quoted to a colleague: "'We shall not travel by the roads we make.'" Nevertheless, not many women who experienced either a comfortable childhood or a harsh factory life had as much opportunity for challenge, service, recognition, and achievement as Nestor found in the labor movement.

• Nestor's papers are at the Chicago Historical Society; they are also included in Edward T. James, ed., *Papers of the Women's Trade Union League and Its Principal Leaders* (1979; microfilm). Correspondence with her appears in the papers of Mary Anderson at the Radcliffe College Women's Archives in Cambridge, Mass. Her own account of her life is *Woman's Labor Leader: An Autobiography* (1954). See also Colette Hyman, "Labor Organization and Female Institution Building," in *Women, Work, and Protest: A Century of U.S. Women's Labor History*, ed. Ruth Milkman (1985); Alice Kessler-Harris, "Problems of Coalition-Building," in Milkman (1985); S. M. Franklin, "Agnes Nestor of the Glove Workers," *Life and Labor* 3 (Dec. 1913): 325–28; Joyce Maupin, *Labor Heroines: Ten Women Who Led the Struggle* (1974); Gladys Boone, *The Women's Trade Union Leagues in Great Britain and the United States of America* (1968); and Allen F. Davis, *Spearheads of Reform* (1967). Obituaries are in *Life and Labor* 99 (Feb. 1949): 1–2; the *New York Times*, 29 Dec. 1948; and the *Chicago Tribune*, 29 Dec. 1948.

SANDRA OPDYCKE

NETSVETOV, Jacob (1804–26 July 1864), Native American Orthodox priest and missionary in Alaska, was born Iakov Igorovich Netsvetov, the son of Igor Netsvetov, a Russian fur trader, and Maria Alekseeva, an Unangan Aleut from the island of Atka in the Aleutian chain. Hence he was a creole, of Native American and Russian blood. His birthplace was either Atka or the island of Saint George in the Bering Sea, but he was raised on the latter island, where his father worked for the Russian-American Company, becoming a company manager there in 1818. Jacob was educated at home in his early years. In 1823 he entered the seminary in Irkutsk, Siberia. Two years later he married a Siberian creole woman, Anna Simeonovna; they had no children. In 1826 he graduated from the seminary with certificates in history and theology. On 4 March 1828, while still in Irkutsk, he was ordained to the priesthood in the Russian Orthodox church, making him the first Native American Orthodox priest.

Netsvetov was immediately assigned to be the first resident pastor for the Unangan Aleuts living on Atka Island and the other islands of the western Aleutian archipelago. He and his wife reached Atka in June 1829. He soon discovered that most of the islanders had been previously introduced to Orthodox Christianity and had been baptized by laymen from Siberia associated with the extensive fur-trading operations in Russian America. By the end of 1829 he had completed the baptism of hundreds of Aleuts through the administration of the sacrament of chrismation (anointing with holy oil).

For the next fifteen years Netsvetov labored to strengthen and spread Christianity throughout the western Aleutian Islands, and he even made two trips to the Kurile Islands north of Japan. His parish stretched from Atka Island to Attu Island, a distance of about 700 miles. For his frequent trips among the islands, he traveled by kayak or on one of the Russian-American Company's sailing vessels, and wherever necessary he held services in a portable "church-tent" that he constructed. In 1831 Netsvetov reorganized and began teaching in a bilingual (Russian and Aleut) boarding school on Atka Island, which graduated dozens of Aleut and creole students during his time there. He adapted for use among the Atkan Aleuts the translations of scriptural and liturgical texts done by Father John Veniaminov (who later became Saint Innocent) in the Unalaskan dialect of the Unangan language, since the Atkans spoke a different dialect of this language. Other scriptural, liturgical, and secular texts he translated directly into the Aleutian dialect, including the entire Gospel of Matthew. He also compiled a comprehensive dictionary for the Unangan language.

In 1844 Netsvetov, who had become a widower in 1836, was assigned by Bishop Innocent Veniaminov to the Kuskokwim–Lower Yukon River region of the southwestern mainland of Alaska. Although settling on the coast of the Bering Sea would have given him considerably more access to the outside world, he gained permission from Bishop Innocent to set up his headquarters in the village of Ikogmiut (now known as Russian Mission), on the Yukon River about 150 miles inland, in order to have more contact with the tribal peoples of the interior. He was only the second priest ever to minister to the Yup'ik Eskimos and the Athabascan Indians of this area. Through his efforts during the next eighteen years, Orthodox Christianity became firmly established as the faith of these peoples, which greatly helped to bring an end to the previous recurrent hostilities between the Yup'iks and the Athabascans.

Netsvetov's daily journals from this period, which he kept meticulously and faithfully, give detailed descriptions of his extensive missionary work in this vast wilderness of roughly 30,000 square miles. He learned the Yup'ik language and made the first translations of scriptural and liturgical texts into this tongue. When he ministered to the various Athabascan groups, he relied on creole interpreters. From his base in Russian Mission, in most years he made three round trips: in the spring, downriver and up the seacoast by kayak to Saint Michael's Redoubt; in the fall, up the Yukon and Innoko rivers; and in the winter, overland by dogsled to the Kuskokwim River. During these journeys nomadic tribal men, women, and children gathered in the scattered villages along the rivers on hearing of Netsvetov's approach. In this way he proclaimed the Christian faith to and baptized hundreds of Native Americans and ministered regularly to them. He and

his assistant, Constantine Lukin, a creole from Kodiak Island, vaccinated and dispensed medicine to the natives of this area, which helped them to resist the smallpox that ravaged other parts of Alaska.

Netsvetov's journals also record his various ethnographic observations, which provide the first detailed view of the traditional Alaskan Eskimo culture. While in the Aleutians, he prepared specimens of various fish and other forms of marine life for the museums of natural history in Saint Petersburg and Moscow.

His extensive missionary accomplishments are all the more noteworthy in light of the exceedingly rigorous and often dangerous climatic conditions in which he traveled and labored. Partly because of the bitter cold of the winters and partly because of undernourishment from occasional food shortages in the Alaskan interior, Netsvetov suffered from various debilitating chronic illnesses, beginning in 1848. Yet he carried on, even when the pain was virtually unbearable, for as he once wrote in his journal, "I was again bothered in increased degree by my illness in the cold. If it had not been for the natives, I probably would not have dared to celebrate [the church services]. It is for them that it was necessary to make the decision to celebrate."

In 1863, severely crippled by arthritis, nearly blind, and exhausted from his years of illness and exposure to the harsh climate of the Alaskan interior, Netsvetov—an archpriest since 1848 (a singular honor at that time)—moved to Sitka (near Juneau), where he spent his last year serving the chapel for the Tlingit Indians. Long regarded as a saint by the peoples whom he served, in October 1994 this distinguished teacher, linguist, and missionary priest was officially canonized as a saint by the Orthodox church in America, in a ceremony held in the cathedral in Anchorage. He is revered as Saint Jacob, Enlightener of the Peoples of Alaska.

• Netsvetov's journals have been published as *The Journals of Iakov Netsvetov*, trans. Lydia T. Black (2 vols., 1980 and 1984). For more on Netsvetov's mission and on Orthodox Christianity in Alaska, see Michael Oleksa, *Alaskan Missionary Spirituality* (1987); Oleksa, *Orthodox Alaska: A Theology of Mission* (1992); and Barbara S. Smith, *Orthodoxy and Native Americans: The Alaskan Mission* (1980).

DAVID C. FORD

NETTLETON, Alvred Bayard (14 Nov. 1838–10 Aug. 1911), journalist, was born in Berlin township, Ohio, the son of Hiram Nettleton and Lavinia Janes, farmers. After working with a leading mercantile and lumbering firm at Lexinton, Michigan, Nettleton entered Oberlin College in 1859. While at college, he worked on the *Oberlin News*, the campus paper.

The Civil War interrupted Nettleton's studies. He enlisted as a private in Company H of the Second Ohio Volunteer Cavalry in September 1861. He was subsequently elected first lieutenant. In June 1865 he was mustered out of the service after participating in more than seventy battles and minor engagements in more than a dozen states and territories. He was appointed colonel and breveted brigadier general on the recommendation of General George A. Custer for gallant and meritorious services in the Shenandoah Valley Campaign. During the war, in 1863, he married Melissa R. Tenney; they had three children.

While away from Oberlin, Nettleton was awarded degrees (A.B. 1863, A.M. 1866) from the college and studied law in New York. In 1866 he became the editor of the *Sandusky Daily Commercial Register*; during his tenure at the *Register* Nettleton became acquainted with financier Jay Cooke and published Cooke's views about the national banking system and the resumption of specie payments. While editing the paper, Nettleton served as Cooke's sounding board for Ohio senator John Sherman.

In 1868 Nettleton became financial editor of the *Chicago Advance* and continued to spread Cooke's message. A 2 September 1869 article, "Why, When and How to Resume," served as a mouthpiece for Cooke's views. After his stint at the *Advance*, Nettleton went to work directly for Cooke; when Cooke took over the Northern Pacific Railroad project, he asked Nettleton to take charge of the publicity for marketing the securities of the railroad. Nettleton assumed the project with great enthusiasm, traversing the proposed route in Minnesota and the Dakota Territory. Despite the struggles of the Northern Pacific, Cooke retained Nettleton to work out a plan of reorganization that was satisfactory to the bondholders of the railroad. He continued to serve as Cooke's mouthpiece; in early 1870 he carried out a mission demanding and receiving the resignation of the head of the Northern Pacific Railroad for Cooke.

Also in 1870, Nettleton became a trustee of Oberlin College, a position he would hold until 1892. He continued his newspaper work in 1875 when he became managing editor for the *Philadelphia Inquirer*. This assignment lasted for about a year; afterward, he became active in mining and manufacturing. In March 1880 he settled in Minneapolis after having purchased a half interest in the *Daily Tribune*. While working with this paper, he was also a member of the Anti-Saloon National Committee of the Republican party. He sold his interest in the *Tribune* in 1890.

After leaving the *Daily Tribune*, Nettleton served as the Minneapolis representative of sundry eastern banks and capitalists, placing mortgage loans and dealing in investments generally. In 1890 President Benjamin Harrison appointed him assistant secretary of the treasury, a position that made him director of the U.S. Immigration Bureau. While assistant secretary, Nettleton supervised the enlarging and rebuilding of the facilities at Ellis Island; for a brief period after the death of Secretary William Windom, he served as acting secretary of the treasury.

Nettleton remained in Washington after his tenure as assistant secretary in order to serve on the World's Columbian Exposition Commission and to work on other projects. In 1899 he returned to Chicago, where he lived for the rest of his life. While there, he worked on various business enterprises and occasional journalistic and magazine work. In 1900 he wrote *Trusts or Competition?* and was responsible for many pamphlets and magazine articles. He died in Chicago.

Nettleton was a Congregationalist, a member of the Grand Army of the Republic, a member of the Military Order of the Loyal Legion of the United States (in 1887 he presented a paper, "How the Day Was Saved at the Battle of Cedar Creek," before the Minnesota Commandery), and chairman of the National Association of Surviving United States Volunteer Officers of the Civil War. He enjoyed a successful career as soldier and journalist; his association with Jay Cooke made him a significant regional actor in the debate over larger financial questions that the nation faced after the Civil War.

• The scant published material on Nettleton includes brief character sketches in G. E. Warner and C. M. Foote, *History of Hennepin County and the City of Minneapolis* (1881), and Henrietta Larson, *Jay Cooke: Private Banker* (1936). A broad commentary on his life can be found in the Military Order of the Loyal Legion of the United States, Minnesota Commandery, *In Memoriam: Companion Brevet Brigadier A. B. Nettleton* (Circular No. 12, whole number 444, 1912). Ellis Paxson Oberholtzer, *Jay Cooke: Financier of the Civil War* (1907), contains a valuable discussion of his relationship to Cooke; a very brief discussion of his military career is in William Marvel, comp., *Biographical Sketches of the Contributors to the Military Order of the Loyal Legion of the United States* (1995). An obituary is in the *Minneapolis Morning Tribune*, 12 Aug. 1911.

JONATHAN M. BERKEY

NETTLETON, Asahel (21 Apr. 1783–16 May 1844), Congregational minister and evangelist, was born in North Killingworth, Connecticut, the son of Samuel Nettleton and Ann Kelsey, farmers. At the age of eighteen, Nettleton experienced a powerful conversion during a local revival and was inspired to become a foreign missionary. After graduating from Yale (B.A., 1809), he moved to Milford, Connecticut, where he studied theology with Rev. Bezaleel Pinneo and was ordained to preach in 1811.

While at Yale, Nettleton met Samuel J. Mills, a leader in the nascent American foreign missions movement. In 1812, when the first contingent of Congregational missionaries was commissioned by the American Board of Commissioners for Foreign Missions, Mills urged that Nettleton be included in the group, but debts incurred to attend college prevented him from accepting Mills's offer.

Determined to go abroad as soon as possible, Nettleton preached in area churches on a temporary basis, spurning all offers of permanent employment. Wherever he went, people responded to his plain, low-key preaching style. So successful was he at his craft that Nettleton abandoned his dream of becoming a missionary and dedicated his life to evangelistic work. From 1817 to 1822 Nettleton served the Consociation of Litchfield County, Connecticut, as an evangelist to the backwoods areas of eastern Connecticut and parts of New York and Massachusetts. In 1822 Nettleton was stricken with typhus and was forced to temporarily withdraw from his work as an evangelist. While recuperating, he published his only book, a hymnal entitled *Village Hymns for Social Worship, Selected and Original* (1824). After 1824, he resumed preaching but was forced to spend winters in the South or abroad due to his weakened health.

Nettleton was best known for his active opposition to the "new measures" of Charles G. Finney and his followers. Finney's practice of publicly praying for the conversion of individuals in attendance, his use of "protracted" or week-long meetings, and his claim that conversion could be produced with the use of the right means rankled conservatives like Nettleton who viewed salvation as a divine act. In the fall of 1826 Nettleton wrote a critical review of Finney's sermon, "Can Two Walk Together except They Be Agreed," and the controversy between the "New Lights" and "Old Lights" was begun. In the summer of 1827 Nettleton, Lyman Beecher, and a number of other conservative Massachusetts clerics called a meeting to discuss their differences with the revivalists of western New York. At the New Lebanon Conference (18–26 July 1827), both sides presented their theological views and traded charges and countercharges before finally concluding with a vaguely worded compromise resolution (which claimed that revivals were the work of God accomplished through human means) that both sides could claim as an exoneration of their positions. Finney emerged from the meeting unscathed, his reputation enhanced, not diminished, while Nettleton left the meeting embittered by the lack of support from his more moderate New England brethren.

Feeling betrayed by Beecher and the moderates at the conference, Nettleton began to drift toward the more extreme, conservative branch of Congregationalism. In 1828 he backed the "revolt of the conservatives," during which the strict Calvinists attacked the moderates for the liberalizing tendencies of the New Haven Theology promulgated at Yale by Beecher's friend and ally, Nathaniel William Taylor. The controversy continued until 1834, when the conservatives withdrew their support from Yale as a training post for the ministry and established the Theological Institute of Connecticut (later known as Hartford Theological Seminary). Nettleton declined an invitation to serve as professor of pastoral theology, but he settled, in 1832, at East Windsor Hill, preaching on occasion and giving lectures at the seminary. He died at East Windsor Hill.

In the final analysis Nettleton must be viewed as a tragic figure. An inadvertent pioneer of professional evangelism, Nettleton made possible the rise of theological innovators such as Finney, whom he later denounced.

• Nettleton's letters, diaries, and sermons are in the Hartford Theological Seminary Library. There are a number of accounts of Nettleton's life. One of the first, Bennet Tyler, ed., *Memoir of the Life and Character of Rev. Asahel Nettleton* (1844), also contains some primary materials. Regarding the New Lebanon Conference see [Lyman Beecher], *Letters of the Rev. Dr. Beecher and Rev. Mr. Nettleton, on the "New Measures" in Conducting Revivals of Religion, with a Review of a Sermon by Novanglus* (1828). The only published biography is John F. Thornbury, *God Sent Revival: The Story of Asahel Nettleton and the Second Great Awakening* (1977). See also Sherry P. May, "Asahel Nettleton" (Ph.D. diss., Drew Univ., 1969), and George H. Birney, "The Life and Letters of Asahel Nettleton, 1783–1844" (Ph.D. diss., Hartford Theological Seminary, 1943). For a historical perspective on Nettleton's place in the Second Great Awakening, see Keith J. Hardman, *Charles Grandison Finney, 1792–1875* (1987); Bernard A. Weisberger, *They Gathered at the River* (1958); and Charles C. Cole, *The Social Ideas of the Northern Evangelists, 1826–1860* (1954).

DAVID B. RAYMOND

NEUBERGER, Richard Lewis (26 Dec. 1912–9 Mar. 1960), journalist and politician, was born in Portland, Oregon, the son of Isaac Neuberger, a restaurant owner, and Ruth Lewis. He grew up in relatively comfortable circumstances within the small Jewish community in Portland and attended local schools, graduating from Lincoln High School in 1930. While covering sports for the school newspaper, he met Lair H. Gregory, sports editor for the *Oregonian*, the major city newspaper. Under Gregory's tutelage, Neuberger decided to become a reporter.

Neuberger entered the University of Oregon in 1931 to study journalism and soon had a prominent place on the *Daily Emerald*, the campus paper. He was named the *Emerald*'s editor in his sophomore year, an unprecedented honor. Beginning as a political conservative, by 1933 Neuberger had moved to the left, and his editorials took a more reformist stance on campus and political issues. He opposed mandatory student fees and attacked fraternities. During the summer of 1933 he traveled in Germany. His 1933 article "The New Germany" in the *Nation* marked his debut in magazines and warned eloquently of the dangers that Nazism posed. "One of the major premises of the Nazi movement is intense preparation for a war of aggression" (Neal, p. 10). Successful as a writer from then on, Neuberger studied law during 1933–1934 at the University of Oregon and then took up writing full time. Neuberger became embroiled in a cheating episode during his law school career, and his difficulties with the dean, Wayne Morse, laid the basis for their later feud in the Senate.

For the next six years, Neuberger published at the prolific rate that marked his public career. Nearly one hundred articles appeared in journals such as *Harpers*, the *New Republic*, and *Current History*. Named in 1936 by the *New York Times* as a correspondent for the Pacific Northwest, Neuberger also wrote or coauthored three books, *An Army of the Aged* (1936), which was critical of the Townsend Plan for old-age assistance; *Integrity* (1937), a biography of Senator George William Norris, and *Our Promised Land* (1938), an overview of his home region of the Pacific Northwest.

In 1940 Neuberger won a seat in the Oregon House of Representatives as a Democrat. He developed an interest in forestry and conservation issues that marked his subsequent political career. He resigned his seat in 1942 to enter the army. As a second lieutenant, he served on the staff of General James A. O'Connor, who directed construction of the Alaska Highway. It was, Neuberger told Secretary of the Interior Harold Ickes, "quite an assignment but the deep wilderness on the Highway gets pretty lonesome at times" (Ickes Papers). First sent to Washington in 1944, he also attended the San Francisco Conference in 1945 shortly before he left the military. There he met Adlai Stevenson (1900–1965), whom Neuberger ardently supported as a presidential candidate in 1952 and 1956. He married Maurine Brown in 1945; they had no children.

Neuberger resumed his writing after the war, but politics occupied more of his energies. Losing a race for the state senate in 1946, he was victorious two years later. His wife won election to the Oregon house as its only woman member in 1950. The Neubergers became the first married couple to serve in a state legislature at the same time. They remained popular vote getters in their districts in 1952 despite the appeal of Dwight D. Eisenhower and the Republican ticket. By then Neuberger had ambitions for national office.

In the 1954 election, the incumbent Republican senator, Guy Cordon, proved vulnerable to Neuberger's hard-hitting attacks. Neuberger described Cordon as an enemy of conservation who had given away natural resources in and out of Oregon. The over-confident senator did not take Neuberger's challenge seriously since the state had not elected a Democrat to the Senate in four decades. Neuberger, however, pulled off a stunning upset that helped the Democrats regain control of the Senate.

Neuberger's single term was very productive. He endorsed statehood for Alaska and worked hard to preserve the Oregon Dunes and the Klamath Basin. He was a strong supporter of the Hells Canyon Dam in Idaho and also pushed hard for the regulation of billboards and outdoor advertising. Unlike his Democratic colleague, Wayne Morse, Neuberger cooperated with the Senate leadership, including the Democratic Majority Leader, Lyndon Johnson. Relations with Morse, which had been patched up since their college days, deteriorated over the resulting favorable publicity that Neuberger was receiving, and a celebrated political feud ensued. Personality conflicts lay at the root of the discord. On a number of key issues of the late 1950s, including the civil rights bill of 1957, Neuberger became a major legislative player. He also worked closely with Mary Lasker, a philanthropist and health advocate, to promote greater congressional funding for cancer research. In 1958 Neuberger himself was diagnosed with cancer following a regular physical checkup. After radiation therapy, he believed that his treatment was "progressing favorably" (letter at Center for American History, Univ. of Texas). He prepared to run for a second term in 1960 and was regarded as

certain to be reelected until his sudden death in Portland, Oregon, after a cerebral hemorrhage. His wife succeeded him in the Senate and was elected to his seat in 1960.

Neuberger was one of the more interesting and intelligent of the liberal Democrats who came to national prominence during the period after World War II. He combined electoral appeal with legislative skill and had the promise of a brilliant career in the Senate when he died. Wayne Morse dubbed him "Mr. Conservation" for his many legislative accomplishments in his one-term Senate career. An influential author and journalist, he left behind illuminating writings about the issues he championed and the people he knew. When Johnson spoke of his "probing mind and great heart" (Johnson Library), his assessment reflected the judgment of Neuberger's Senate colleagues and several generations of national Democrats.

• Neuberger's extensive and well-organized papers are located at the University of Oregon, Eugene, as are the papers of his wife, Senator Maurine Neuberger. The same library has the papers of Neuberger's teacher, senatorial colleague, and intraparty adversary, Wayne Morse. The Lyndon B. Johnson Library, Austin, Tex., has numerous letters relating to his senatorial service. Other Neuberger letters are in the Harold Ickes Papers, Manuscript Division, Library of Congress. Among Neuberger's extensive books and writings, the most autobiographical is *Adventures in Politics: We Go to the Legislature* (1954), which recounts his political partnership with his wife. Important for his later differences with Morse are Neuberger's articles "Wayne Morse: Republican Gadfly," *American Mercury* 65 (July 1947): 14–16, and "Morse versus Morse," *Nation*, 14 Jan. 1950, pp. 29–30. Steve Neal, ed., *They Never Go Back to Pocatello: The Selected Essays of Richard Neuberger* (1988), is a selection from Neuberger's 200 published articles along with the editor's excellent biographical essay. Robert E. Burton, *Democrats of Oregon: The Pattern of Minority Politics, 1900–1956* (1970), considers the context within which Neuberger rose to prominence. Lee Wilkins, *Wayne Morse: A Bio-Bibliography* (1985), has some comments on the Neuberger-Morse relationship. Mason Drukman, "Oregon's Most Famous Feud: Wayne Morse versus Richard Neuberger," *Oregon Historical Quarterly* 95 (Fall 1994): 300–367, is an extended examination of the Morse-Neuberger rivalry that is critical of Neuberger. Neuberger's wife supplied some very helpful information about her husband's political career. The *New York Times*, 10 Mar. 1960, has a full obituary.

LEWIS L. GOULD

NEUENDORFF, Adolph Heinrich Anton Magnus (13 June 1843–4 Dec. 1897), conductor, composer, and administrator, was born in Hamburg, Germany. He came to the United States with his parents (names unknown) in 1854 in the first wave of German immigrants. The family settled in New York, where his father was employed as a bookkeeper. Neuendorff studied violin with George Matzka, a violist in the New York Philharmonic and its emergency conductor in 1876, and with Joseph Weinlich. His principal piano teacher was Gustav Schilling, who also taught him composition and theory. Schilling was noted for writing a six-volume encyclopedia of music, the *Enzyk-*

lopädie der gesamten musikalischen Wissenschaften oder Universallexikon der Tonkunst (1835–1838), and such esoteric books as *Versuch einer Philosophie des Schönen in der Musik oder Ästhetik der Tonkunst* (1838). Neuendorff also studied theory and composition with Karl Anschütz, the conductor of the Ullman-Strakosch opera troupe, formed by Bernard Ullman and Maurice Strakosch, who joined forces briefly (1857–1860) presenting opera at the Academy of Music in New York and touring in the eastern United States.

Neuendorff's debut as a pianist took place in 1859 at Dodworth Hall in lower Manhattan. It was his talent as a violinist, however, that launched his career as a professional musician. In 1860 he became concertmaster of the orchestra at the old Stadt Theater and subsequently performed in South America as a violinist from 1861 to 1863. During the 1864–1865 season Neuendorff served as the musical director of the German Theater in Milwaukee, Wisconsin, where there was a large German population. The following year he returned to New York and served as chorus master for Anschutz at the new Stadt Theater, succeeding Anschutz as conductor and music director in 1867. Neuendorff conducted Wagner's *Tannhäuser* in 1870. During his final season at the theater he imported a German company and produced the first complete American performance of Wagner's *Lohengrin* on 3 April 1871. A reviewer for the *New York Times* (4 Apr. 1871) commented that "the performance . . . was creditable to the artists and management, though by no means as illustrative vocally or scenically of the work as the partisans of Mr. Wagner might reasonably desire." For the 1871–1872 season Neuendorff joined forces with Carl Rosa, the German impresario, violinist, and conductor, and Theodor Wachtel, the great German tenor, to mount a season of Italian opera at the Academy of Music. In 1872 Neuendorff became manager of the Germania Theatre, located near Tammany Hall. He held the position for eleven years, during which he brought many European actors and singers to the United States.

Neuendorff presented a season of German opera at the Academy of Music in 1875 that starred Wachtel and soprano Eugenie Pappenheim. After conducting Beethoven Festival performances at the academy in 1876, he covered the opening of the Festspielhaus, a theater designed by Wagner with excellent acoustics, and the first performance of *Der Ring des Nibelungen* at Bayreuth in Germany for the *New Yorker Staats-Zeitung*, an important German-language newspaper. Neuendorff returned from the trip with copies of the score and Wagner's suggestions concerning performances in the United States. This inspired Wagner festivals in New York and Boston the following year that included the American premiere of *Die Walküre* on 2 April 1877 at the academy.

When in 1878 Theodore Thomas relinquished the directorship of the New York Philharmonic to become the head of the new College of Music in Cincinnati, the members of the orchestra elected Neuendorff over Leopold Damrosch by a vote of forty-six to twenty-nine.

Damrosch had been the concertmaster in Liszt's orchestra in the court at Weimar before coming to New York in 1871 to conduct the Männergesangverein Arion, an important German men's chorus formed in 1854. During the 1878–1879 season Neuendorff conducted the first New York performances of Tchaikovsky's symphonic fantasia *Francesca da Rimini*, op. 32, and his Symphony no. 3 in D Major, op. 29. The reviews found the fantasia "wild and disconnected" and the symphony "worthy of the consideration of all thoughtful lovers of music." The orchestra was praised but Neuendorff's contribution grudgingly acknowledged. The Philharmonic Society's ticket receipts fell from $12,499 under Thomas to $7,158 under Neuendorff, the lowest figure in sixteen years, and the individual Society players, who elected their conductor, took home a proportionately small dividend. As a result, Neuendorff proved unable to successfully compete with Thomas for the Society's favor; Thomas was reinstated as director for the 1879–1880 season, and the receipts went back up to $18,736. Nonetheless, during the 1880 season Neuendorff conducted the Materna concerts.

In 1881 Neuendorff moved the Germania Theatre to Broadway and 13th Street and renamed it the German Theater. Following the financial failure of the theater in 1883, he moved to Boston and became the first conductor of the Music Hall Promenade Concerts (1885–1889), known after 1900 as the Boston "Pops." Fashioned after European models, these concerts inspired other "pops" orchestras. Boston critics responded enthusiastically: "Mr. Neuendorff is a conductor par excellence. He is a great organizer, and has the secret of getting from his men the best work of which they are capable" (*Boston Evening Record*, 6 June 1885). Neuendorff did not, however, sever his New York connections entirely. In the summer of 1886 he led the "Popular Summernight Concerts" in the New Central Park Garden. He also directed concerts featuring eleven-year-old piano prodigy Josef Hofmann, beginning with his celebrated debut at the Metropolitan Opera House in November 1887. While in Boston, Neuendorff assumed leadership of the Emma Juch Grand Opera Company (1889–1891), which was salvaged from what had been the American and National opera companies. The ensemble toured the United States, Canada, and Mexico; their presentations of Wagner operas, the first of their kind in Mexico, met with considerable success. During the summer of 1892 Neuendorff led a summer series at the Lennox Lyceum, unusual for its location away from Broadway, at Fifty-ninth Street and Madison Avenue, and for its polygonal layout. Later that year he returned to New York to conduct the English Grand Opera, which was managed by Oscar Hammerstein.

From 1893 to 1895 Neuendorff conducted performances in Vienna at the Imperial Opera, where his wife, the Austrian soprano Georgine von Januschowsky, was one of the prima donnas. They were married around 1890; they had one child. In 1896 he returned to New York and became the director of music at

Temple Emmanu-El. He conducted the Metropolitan Opera in their 1896 spring tour of Chicago, St. Louis, Cincinnati, and Cleveland—six operas in twenty-nine performances, all sung in German, including Gounod's *Faust*. Neuendorff succeeded Anton Seidl as conductor of the permanent orchestra of the Metropolitan Opera House. He made his final public appearances, with that orchestra, at the Madison Square Roof Garden concerts in the summer of 1897. He died in New York City.

Neuendorff's life was a continuous flurry of entrepreneurial and musical activity. In addition to conducting and composing, he produced about forty operas. His compositions show facile craftsmanship; though pleasant, they are largely predictable and undistinguished. His works include four comic operas: *Der Rattenfänger von Hameln* (1880), *Don Quixote* (1882), *Prince Waldmeister* (1887), and *The Minstrel* (1892); two operettas: *Kadettenlaunen* (n.d.) and *Der Schalk von Aberdeen* (1892); two symphonies (1878 and 1880), overtures, cantatas, choruses, songs, and piano pieces, including the "Marie Waltzes" (1881). Neuendorff was also active as church organist and choral society conductor through much of his career. He apparently possessed a "kindly nature," and an unsigned obituary in the *Musical Courier* cites Neuendorff as the person "who probably did more to bring the German drama up to its present high standard in New York than any other one man" (8 Dec. 1897). The *New York Times* obituary states that "he had frequently been styled by his musical friends the original American Wagnerian" (5 Dec. 1897). Although well known and well respected in musical circles, Neuendorff left no permanent musical legacy that bears his name. His most important contributions include his efforts to promote the music of Wagner and other contemporary composers, his many concert performances, and his work in theater management.

• A promotional flier put out by Neuendorff's manager Max Bachert, titled "Neuendorff's Boston Popular Concert Orchestra" (n.d.), sheds light on his reception in Boston through newspaper quotations. Reviews and articles in the *New York Times* (1878–1897) sketch his New York activity; see especially reviews dated 4 Apr. 1871, 22 Dec. 1878, 9 Feb. 1879, 6 Apr. 1879, 10 Jan. 1882, and 10 June 1892. See also *New York Times* articles "Breaking the Contract," 7 Feb. 1882; "Grand Opera in English," 25 Nov. 1892, and "Famous Conductors," 12 Sept. 1897. Gerald Fitzgerald, ed., *Annals of the Metropolitan Opera* (1989), provides details concerning his tenure with that company. John H. Mueller, *The American Symphony Orchestra: A Social History of Musical Taste* (1951), and Howard Shanet, *Philharmonic: A History of New York's Orchestra* (1975), both discuss Neuendorff's connection to the New York Philharmonic. Other than those cited in the text, an obituary is in the New York *Sun*, 30 June 1898.

FRANCIS P. BRANCALEONE

NEUGEBAUER, Otto Eduard (26 May 1899–19 Feb. 1990), mathematician, was born in Innsbruck, Austria, the son of Rudolf Neugebauer, a railway engineer. His mother's name is unknown. His parents having died

when he was a child, he was raised by an uncle. He attended Gymnasium in Graz and, upon graduating in 1917, served in the Austrian army as an artillery lieutenant. After World War I he spent a year in an Italian prisoner-of-war camp, where he shared a pencil with fellow internee Ludwig Wittgenstein. From 1919 to 1921 he studied electrical engineering and physics at the University of Graz. By then his inheritance, placed in government bonds, had completely eroded. He transferred to the University of Munich, where he studied with physicist Arnold Sommerfeld and mathematician Arthur Rosenthal. On Sommerfeld's advice, he moved to the University of Göttingen in 1922. His manifest brilliance resulted in his becoming amanuensis to mathematician Richard Courant and superintendent of the famous mathematical reading room. Neugebauer designed Göttingen's new mathematical institute, built with Rockefeller money in 1929. Widely perceived as the most brilliant mathematics student at Göttingen in the 1920s, Neugebauer decided to specialize in the history of mathematics. He completed a doctorate on Egyptian fractions in 1926 and the *venia legendi* (which qualified him to lecture as a *Privatdozent*) in 1927. He then married fellow mathematics student Grete Bruck; they had a son and a daughter. Ancient mathematics dominated the rest of his life.

In the late 1920s Neugebauer set out to organize the study of ancient mathematics. He learned Akkadian and made epoch-making discoveries in Babylonian algebra and algebraic geometry—notably the preclassical knowledge of higher-order polynomial equations and the Pythagorean relation. He undertook to inventory all known Babylonian mathematical texts on clay tablets; these he published, in facsimile and with commentary, in his three-volume work, *Mathematische Keilschrift-Texte* (1935–1937). A torrent of specialized works, commentary, and book reviews issued from his pen. Appointed associate professor (*extraordinarius*) in 1932, Neugebauer turned down a call to become full professor at the Darmstadt Institute of Technology to remain at Göttingen. He was able to do so financially because the publishing house of Springer had confided editorship of two mathematical periodicals and a monograph series to him. One of the periodicals became the premier mathematics abstracting journal of the twentieth century, the *Zentralblatt für Mathematik und ihre Grenzgebiete*, which appeared for the first time in 1931.

Neugebauer's scholarship took place under the growing shadow of National Socialism in Germany. In April 1933 the Nazi regime fired Courant, a Jewish veteran of World War I, as director of the Göttingen mathematical institute. Courant named Neugebauer, a nominally Christian veteran, as acting director. But with remarkable strength of character, Neugebauer refused to take an oath of loyalty to the Nazi regime. For this transgression he was fired by the university dean. Then Danish mathematician Harald Bohr, with grants from the Rask-Oersted Foundation and the Rockefeller Foundation, arranged for Neugebauer to become professor at the University of Copenhagen. Neugebauer retained this post until 1939, continuing to publish the *Zentralblatt* in Germany. The racial laws forced him to give up editing the journal. Mathematicians in the United States, who had been angling for Neugebauer for a number of years, used this opportunity to bring Neugebauer and his journal to Brown University. Neugebauer took up his new post in 1939, and he brought with him Olaf Schmidt as an assistant. The *Zentralblatt* took new life as *Mathematical Reviews*, funded by the Rockefeller and Carnegie foundations and overseen by the American Mathematical Society. Neugebauer remained associated with the journal until 1948, after which time he devoted his life exclusively to history of the exact sciences—that is, the sciences based on computation and precise observation.

Monographs and studies of special topics paved the way for his introductory lectures, *The Exact Sciences in Antiquity* (1951, 1970), and then for his magisterial, three-volume *History of Ancient Mathematical Astronomy* (1975). Neugebauer belongs to a tradition of intensive scholarly publishing more at home in Europe than in America. His writings are technically demanding, assuming that the reader is familiar with ancient and modern languages as well as the secondary literature. Neugebauer, an independent thinker who in his youth was a partisan of left-wing politics, flew no ideological flag in his scholarly work. He strove mightily to avoid the signal affliction of scholarship—tedium. His work sparkles with original insight and energetic prose. Near the end of his long career, Neugebauer published, in collaboration with his former student Noel Swerdlow, a definitive account of Nicolaus Copernicus's epoch-making book on heliocentrism, *Mathematical Astronomy in Copernicus's 'De Revolutionibus'* (1984).

Beginning in the 1940s, Neugebauer split his time between Brown and the Institute for Advanced Study in Princeton, where he was a "member with long-term appointment." He retired from Brown in 1969; from 1980 until his death in Princeton, New Jersey, he held a permanent appointment at the Princeton Institute. Neugebauer was a member of the Royal Danish Academy, the Royal Belgian Academy, the Austrian Academy, the British Academy, the Irish Academy, the National Academy of Sciences, and the Académie des Inscriptions et Belles-Lettres, among other learned corporations. He received numerous awards of great distinction, notably the Franklin Medal of the American Philosophical Society (1987) and the Balzan Prize (1986).

Under Neugebauer's distinguished direction, the Department of the History of Mathematics at Brown became the world's preeminent center for the study of the exact sciences in the period up to the Renaissance. The permanent professors included Abraham Sachs, Richard Parker, Gerald Toomer, and David Pingree; the visiting professors included Olaf Schmidt (who had a position at the University of Copenhagen) and Edward S. Kennedy (with a position at the American University in Beirut). Neugebauer's enterprise completely transformed our understanding of antiquity. It qualifies as one of the major cultural achievements of the twentieth century.

• On Neugebauer's instructions, his personal papers were destroyed after his death. Material relating to his career in the United States is found in the Brown University Archives and the Archives of the Institute for Advanced Study in Princeton. Neugebauer's annotated collection of his own reprints is in the Rosenwald Collection at the Historical Library of the Princeton Institute. A treatment of Neugebauer's contributions to the history of mathematics and his methodology is Lewis Pyenson, "Inventory as a Route to Understanding: Sarton, Neugebauer, and Sources," *History of Science* 33 (1995): 253–82. J. Sachs and G. J. Toomer's inventory, "Otto Neugebauer, Bibliography, 1925–1979," *Centaurus* 22 (1979): 257–80, covers his productive years. Noel Swerdlow wrote a persuasive commemorative article in *Proceedings of the American Philosophical Society* 137 (1993): 139–65.

LEWIS PYENSON

NEUMANN, Franz Leopold (23 May 1900–2 Sept. 1954), lawyer and political theorist, was born in Kattowitz, Upper Silesia (later Katowice, Poland), the son of Josef Neumann, a salesman of leather goods, and Gertrud Gutherz. Neumann served in the German army during World War I. In late 1918 and early 1919 he was a member of the radical soldiers council during the period of the unsuccessful Spartacist Revolution. After the war he studied at the Universities of Breslau, Leipzig, Rostock and Frankfurt am Main. At Frankfurt he was a student of the distinguished jurist Hugo Sinzheimer. Neumann received his law degree in 1923 and was accepted as a member of the Berlin bar in 1927.

In the later 1920s Neumann served as a legal adviser for the Social Democratic Party, wrote regularly for socialist publications such as *Die Arbeiter* and *Die Gesellschaft*, and taught at the capital's progressive institution of higher learning, the Deutsche Hochschule für Politik. As legal adviser to the Social Democratic Party he took part in the momentous appeals case before the German Supreme Court at Leipzig that followed the July 1932 seizure of the Social Democratic government of Prussia by the right-wing national government of Franz von Papen. Neumann joined other distinguished lawyers and defenders of the republic, such as Hermann Heller, in challenging the legality of Papen's actions, which had been carried out under an edict signed by President Hindenburg. In this legal battle he struggled against Papen's chief lawyer and one of the leading critics of Weimar parliamentary government, Carl Schmitt. The conflict with Schmitt, whom Neumann viewed as the most intelligent of the antidemocratic and later pro-Nazi thinkers, would be a continuing theme of Neumann's work.

In 1933 Neumann was briefly imprisoned by the Gestapo, and in May he was able to flee from Germany to London. In London he studied political science at the London School of Economics with the distinguished democratic socialist and pluralist Harold Laski and received a Ph.D. in 1936. While in England

Neumann came to the conclusion that the Nazi regime, which he detested, would not be destroyed by resistance within Germany and would have to be destroyed from the outside. Although England would play a part in that destruction and offer him safe haven, he came to feel that "one could never quite become an Englishman." He was then invited to work at the Institute of Social Research, which was associated with Columbia University, and took this opportunity to emigrate to the United States. The institute, based in Frankfurt until the Nazi takeover in 1933, had been invited to relocate to Columbia by the university's president, Nicholas Butler Murray, and its members had come to New York from their exile in Geneva. In joining the institute, Neumann became the colleague of scholars such as Max Horkheimer, Herbert Marcuse, Theodor Adorno, Otto Kirchheimer, Erich Fromm, and Frederick Pollack. A common theory of history bound the members of the school together. Related to those of Hegel and Marx, the theory judged historical developments against the growth of freedom and the development of human potential and was used to interpret social phenomena. In 1937, shortly after joining the institute, Neumann married Inge S. Weiner, who had emigrated from Magdeburg; the couple had two children.

At the institute Neumann concentrated on the study of Nazism. He was particularly interested in the role that German industrialists and financiers had played in the rise of Hitler to power and the question of whether Nazism was the product of a crisis stage of monopoly capitalism. His work, which was of a high scholarly caliber, reflected a clear political position that placed him within the ranks of Marxist interpreters. The prominent historian of twentieth-century Europe H. Stuart Hughes said of Neumann that "even more strenuously than [Max] Weber, he argued the intellectual's obligation to take a stand." In 1942 Neumann became a consultant with the Board of Economic Warfare, and in 1943 he joined the Office of Strategic Services, the intelligence-gathering, analytic, and espionage agency that was the ancestor of the Central Intelligence Agency.

Working against Nazism in his writing as well, he published his major work, *Behemoth: The Structure and Practice of National Socialism*, in 1942. In this study he depicted Nazism's main theme as the assertion

that all traditional doctrines and values must be rejected, whether they stem from French Rationalism or German idealism, from English empiricism or American pragmatism, whether liberal or absolutist, democratic or socialist, they are hostile to the fundamental goals of National Socialism: the resolution by imperialistic war of the discrepancy between the potentialities of Germany's industrial apparatus and the actuality that existed and continued to exist.

In agreement with his close friend Herbert Marcuse, he concluded that Nazi Germany was not a state in the Hegelian sense of a rational entity. He also attacked German intellectuals who had betrayed their traditions by endorsing this new form of barbarism, being particularly critical of his old enemy Carl Schmitt. Neumann's book placed him squarely within the major school of left-wing refugee intellectuals in its analysis of Nazism. Still concerned with monopoly capitalism when he wrote *Behemoth*, Neumann did begin, however, to evidence an awareness of anti-Semitism and psychological anxiety among the masses as contributors to the success of Nazism. This major work proved to be a valuable analytical tool in understanding the nature of Nazism. In 1945 Neumann became the head of German research for the State Department, and in 1947 he became a professor of government within the graduate program at Columbia University. In the later 1940s and early 1950s he served as American liaison with the Free University of Berlin and worked to establish an institute of political science in West Berlin. He established contacts with the German trade unions and the Social Democratic Party and was concerned with German progress toward the creation of a viable democratic society. In his own scholarly work he moved away from a primary reliance on Marxist analysis to a more multifaceted approach to political analysis that considered, in addition to economic factors, the role of long-standing prejudices and aspects of human behavior in motivating political action. Reflecting the influence of his American experience, Neumann's later work took the less ideological and dogmatic approach to scholarship of the American scholarly tradition. While in Switzerland in 1954 he was killed in an automobile accident.

In the preface to a collection of Neumann's posthumously published essays, *The Democratic and the Authoritarian State: Essays in Political and Legal Theory* (1954), Marcuse said of his friend and colleague, "He was in a rare sense a political scholar. From the beginning, his theoretical work was animated by a political interest: for him politics was a life element, and he consistently tried to fuse his academic work with practical activity."

• Some of Neumann's papers are at Houghton Library at Harvard University. The principle sources on Neumann's work, Martin Jay, *The Dialectical Imagination: A History of the Frankfurt School and the Institute of Social Research, 1935–1950* (1973), and H. Stuart Hughes, *The Sea Change: The Migration of Social Thought, 1930–1965* (1975), put Neumann in the context of his colleagues and intellectual allies and provide information about his life, his work, and the importance of the American experience to his development. Obituaries appear in the *New York Times*, 13 Sept. 1954, and in the *American Political Science Review* 48 (1954): 1239.

PAUL BOOKBINDER

NEUMANN, John Nepomucene (28 Mar. 1811–5 Jan. 1860), canonized saint and Roman Catholic bishop, was born in Prachatitz, Bohemia, the son of Philip Neumann, a stocking factory operator, and Agnes Lebis. Reared in a pious household of moderate means, John attended the diocesan seminary of Budweis (1831–1833) and Prague's archiepiscopal seminary

(1833–1835). In addition to his ecclesiastical courses, he studied English to prepare himself for the American missions. When ordination to his own overstaffed diocese was postponed, he emigrated to the United States. Shortly after his arrival, Bishop John DuBois of New York welcomed him, ordaining him for his diocese on 25 June 1836. There, for four years, Neumann labored among the impoverished immigrants scattered throughout the Buffalo-Rochester area.

Drawn to community life, Neumann entered the Congregation of the Most Holy Redeemer in 1840. He took vows in St. James Church, Baltimore, on 16 January 1842, the first Redemptorist professed in America. Neumann continued to travel widely to minister in areas where there were heavy concentrations of Germans. He became the Redemptorists' vice regent in 1847, then vice provincial the following year.

In 1852, despite the misgivings of several American prelates about his suitability for a prestigious see, Neumann was named bishop of Philadelphia, the largest diocese in the country. Though Germans were underrepresented in the hierarchy, some other Catholics resented his foreign birth, customs, and reserved demeanor. The humble Neumann himself tried to avoid the ecclesiastical honor, finally accepting it out of obedience. On 28 March he was consecrated in Baltimore by Archbishop Francis Patrick Kenrick, one of Neumann's spiritual advisees and his staunchest supporter for the office.

Neumann's episcopal style proved markedly personal, enhanced by his facility with six modern languages to which, out of pastoral solicitude, he added Gaelic. For the beleaguered Italians, he opened their first national parish. Yearly the bishop journeyed to the more populous areas of his 35,000-square-mile jurisdiction; the other districts he visited biannually. "He travels throughout the diocese like a shining light and with indefatigable labor promotes the piety of the people," Kenrick approvingly informed Rome (Rush [1977], p. 56). In time many came to esteem Neumann for his holiness and learning, still his debt-burdened episcopacy was never free from controversy. Several times he petitioned Rome that his vast see be divided and that he be given the newer and poorer territory. Instead, in 1857 James Wood, a native-born Unitarian convert, was appointed coadjutor bishop of Philadelphia with the right to succession. Mistakenly, he expected that Neumann would resign the Philadelphia see. Rather, Neumann entrusted Wood with the diocesan finances and continued his own unflagging spiritual ministry. This arrangement proved less than satisfactory to Wood.

In 1860 the "little bishop" as some affectionately called him, died at the age of forty-nine. Apoplexy unexpectedly struck him down while on an errand in Old Philadelphia. Neumann left an impressive legacy. In the midst of his pressing duties as a missionary priest, he had prepared a popular catechism, *Katholischer Katechismus*, that continued to be published in German and in English even after his death. In 1849 *Biblische Geschichte des Alten und Neuen Testamentes zum Gebrauch der katholischen Schulen*, his study of the Bible, had appeared. He had traveled to Rome for the promulgation of the doctrine of the Immaculate Conception (1854), participated in three councils in Baltimore, and conducted three diocesan synods. He had written learned articles in the field of theology and frequently contributed articles, some unsigned, to Catholic periodicals and newspapers. He had been a staunch defender of the rights of the church, going to the civil courts when necessary.

Neumann's more enduring accomplishments were the institution of the Forty Hours Devotion on a diocesan basis and the establishment of a unified parochial school system. Always concerned for the spiritual welfare of his people, the bishop regularly joined the faithful, parish by parish, in the Forty Hours ceremonies. He established almost a dozen new churches a year. To promote Catholic education, he reopened closed schools and built new ones. He recruited seven additional religious orders to staff the schools and founded a new community, the Sisters of the Third Order of St. Francis of Philadelphia. Thanks to his efforts, a community of black women, the Oblate Sisters of Providence, was saved from dissolution in 1847. Though he built an orphanage especially for the German poor, he also took a lively interest in the private Catholic academies patronized by the more affluent youth. In a church plagued with a scarcity of native priests, he fostered the vocations of the students at St. Charles Borromeo seminary, where he had improved the standards. To nurture even younger candidates, Neumann opened a preparatory seminary at Glen Riddle, Pennsylvania, the year before he died.

In accord with his wishes, Philadelphia's fourth bishop was buried with his Redemptorist confreres, entombed at St. Peter the Apostle Church, Fifth Street and Girard Avenue. Considered a saint by many even before he died, stories of Neumann's hidden virtues, even miracles granted through his intercession, quickly circulated after his death. When they persisted, a diocesan investigation of his life was instituted in 1885. On 11 December 1921 Pope Benedict XV declared that Neumann's Christian virtues were of heroic degree. He had, the pope said, performed his duty "with constant perfection in the midst of inevitable difficulties" (Curley, p. 399). On 13 October 1963 Pope Paul VI proclaimed him Blessed. That same pontiff, on 19 June 1977, declared Neumann a canonized saint, the first male citizen of the United States so honored.

• Neumann's writings also include *Manuale Devotionis Quadraginta Horarum in usum Sacerdotum Dioceseos Philadelphiensis* (1855), which became the model for other dioceses as they established the Forty Hours Devotion. The first biography of Neumann is *Leben und Wirken des hochseligen Johannes Nep. Neumann* (1883) by his nephew and frequent traveling companion, the Redemptorist John Berger. It contains valuable material on Neumann's early life and identifies and evaluates all primary source material in American and European archives. Greatly amplifying Neumann's Redemptorist and episcopal periods, Michael J. Curley, *Venerable John Neu-*

mann, C.SS.R: Fourth Bishop of Philadelphia (1952), is the definitive study. For a frank discussion of the uncomfortable relationship between Neumann and Wood, see Alfred C. Rush and Thomas J. Donaghy, "The Saintly John Neumann and his Coadjutor Archbishop Wood," in *The History of the Archdiocese of Philadelphia*, ed. James F. Connelly (1976), pp. 209–52. Neumann's canonization precipitated a spate of devotional publications, among them *The Autobiography of St. John Neumann, C.SS.R.*, ed. and trans. Alfred C. Rush (1977). See Robert H. Wilson, *St. John Neumann (1811–1860): Fourth Bishop of Philadelphia* (1977), pp. 72–74, for a brief description of the miraculous cures attributed to Neumann's intercession and accepted by Rome in his canonization process. The *Philadelphia Daily News*, 10 Jan. 1860, and Philadelphia's *Catholic Herald*, 14 Jan. 1860, carry obituary notices.

MARGARET MARY REHER

NEUMANN, John Von. *See* Von Neumann, John Louis.

NEUMARK, David (3 Aug. 1866–15 Dec. 1924), rabbi, Jewish philosopher, and Hebraist, was born in Szczerzec, Galicia, the son of Solomon Neumark, a shopkeeper, and Schifrah Scheutz. He received a traditional Jewish education and attended *cheder* (a communal Jewish elementary school) at a very young age while simultaneously receiving supplemental Hebraic instruction from his father who was himself a learned Jew. When his father died, Neumark's mother ran the family store on her own so that her seven-year-old son would be able to continue his Jewish education. After finishing *cheder*, he attended the local *bet midrash* (Hebrew academy) as well as the community school in his home town. At this time, he began reading modern Hebrew literature, which gave him exposure to both Jewish Enlightenment thinkers and to critical scholarship.

Contrary to his mother's desire, Neumark traveled to Lemberg in 1887 to pursue secular studies with the goal of enrolling in both a university and a liberal rabbinical seminary. He graduated from the local *Obergymnasium* (a German language state institution) in 1892 and began studying simultaneously at the University of Berlin and the Hochschule für die Wissenschaft des Judentums. During this period, the Hebrew and Yiddish author Reuben Brainin urged him to compose a Hebrew essay on the German philosopher Friedrich Nietzsche, which he promised to publish in his influential but short-lived journal, *Mi-mizrakh u-mi-ma' arav* (From East to West). He accepted the assignment and subsequently wrote "Introduction to the Theory of the Superman," which was his first Hebrew publication as well as the first article on Nietzsche in Hebrew.

Neumark received a Ph.D. in philosophy and Semitic languages and literature in 1896. He was ordained a rabbi by the Hochschule in 1897. His first pulpit was in the Bohemian town of Rokonitz, near Prague. In 1899 he married Dora Turnheim; they had three children. In 1904, after having been considered for the post of *rabbino maggiore* (chief rabbi) of Rome,

Neumark returned to Berlin to become an editor of the *Hebrew Encyclopedia (Otzar Ha-yahadut)*, which was being published by the Hebrew literary society known as "Achiasaf." Through his association with Achiasaf, Neumark met the Hebrew essayist and Zionist thinker Ahad Ha-Am (Asher Ginsberg) and became a frequent contributor to Ahad Ha-Am's Hebrew monthly, *Hashilo'ah* (The Messenger).

While editing the *Hebrew Encyclopedia*, Neumark taught in Berlin's Central Jewish Congregation. Unsuccessful in his bid to become the congregation's rabbi, in 1906, he subsequently accepted an offer from Kaufmann Kohler to become professor of Jewish philosophy at Hebrew Union College in Cincinnati, Ohio, where he taught until his death.

Neumark's many erudite publications distinguished him as one of the leading students of Jewish philosophy in his day. His doctoral dissertation, *Die Freiheitslehre bei Kant und Schopenhauer* (published in 1896), identified him as a promising young scholar. "Judah Hallevi's Philosophy in Its Principles," his first publication in English, was published in the *Catalogue* of the Hebrew Union College in 1908, and an article titled "Crescas and Spinoza" appeared the following year in the *CCAR Yearbook* (1909). He published the balance of his scholarship in the field of Jewish philosophy in an English volume, *The Philosophy of the Bible* (1918), and two German volumes titled *Geschichte der jüdischen Philosophie des Mittelalters* (1907–1928). Neumark's untimely death prevented him from completing eight additional volumes that he planned to publish on the history of Jewish philosophy. A revised edition of his *Geschichte* was published in Hebrew under the more encompassing title *Toldot Ha-Pilosofyah Be-Yisrael* (1921, 1929).

Neumark devoted a great deal of scholarly attention to the topic of dogma in Judaism. In opposition to Moses Mendelssohn, he argued that Judaism possessed a system of dogmas and that some of the most pivotal sections of the Pentateuch adumbrated Judaism's fundamental dogmas. He published a two-volume history of Jewish dogma in Hebrew, titled *Toldot Ha-Ikkarim be-Yisrael* (1912–1919). He also contributed a wide variety of essays and book reviews to Hebrew, German, and English periodicals. His Hebrew essays on Jewish philosophy often contained neologisms of his own invention that were later employed by scholars in need of nomenclature to convey various philosophic concepts in the Hebrew idiom.

In 1919 Neumark began editing a scholarly quarterly titled *Journal of Jewish Lore and Philosophy*, which, after four issues, became the *Hebrew Union College Annual* (HUCA), the college's annual journal of learned articles. He served as a member of the HUCA's board of editors from its inception until his death. A number of his articles on Jewish philosophy were published posthumously by the Central Conference of American Rabbis under the title *Essays in Jewish Philosophy by David Neumark* (1929).

Neumark rejected the notion that Jewish philosophy could verify the existence of God by means of logical or physical proofs. In his view, the primary function of Jewish philosophy was to express the spiritual relationship that linked human existence to the world and the infinite. "The world as viewed by religion," wrote Neumark, "is incomparably richer than the world perceived by our senses, that world where the inexorable laws of nature rule supreme" (Brainin, p. 244).

Neumark was also an active participant in the Zionist movement. Like his mentor Ahad Ha-Am, he opposed a "Hebrew nationalism" that was devoid of religion. Neumark believed that a true national restoration could only derive from the process of spiritual renewal. Afflicted with a chronic and acute case of diabetes, Neumark died in Cincinnati.

To date, the impact of Neumark's career as a modern scholar and a leading exponent of Reform Judaism has not been fully evaluated. He represents a small but significant group of European scholars who brought a unique blend of traditional rabbinic scholarship and modern academic discipline to America. This unique synthesis of traditional Jewish learning, Hebraic thought, and modern academic proficiency enabled Neumark to become a seminal figure in the development of modern Jewish scholarship in North America.

• The most complete collection of Neumark's papers is in the Jacob Rader Marcus Center for the American Jewish Archives, Cincinnati, Ohio. A helpful source is Anthony D. Holz, in *Reform Judaism in America: A Biographical Dictionary and Sourcebook* (1993). For additional biographical information and a listing of Neumark's publications, see two issues of the *Hebrew Union College Monthly* that were dedicated to him, Jan. 1924 and Feb. 1924. For synopses of his philosophical work, see Meyer Waxman, *Dr. David Neumark: Philosopher and Historian of Jewish Philosophy and Dogmatist* (1925), and Waxman, *History of Jewish Literature*, vol. 4 (1960), pp. 927–33. See also Abba Hillel Silver, "David Neumark: A Tribute," *Hebrew Union College Monthly*, 29 May 1926, pp. 2–6; "Congratulations, Dr. Neumark!" *Hebrew Union College Monthly*, Dec. 1923, pp. 1–2; Jacob Rader Marcus, "David Neumark," *Hebrew Union College Annual* 37 (1966); and Michael A. Meyer, *Hebrew Union College–Jewish Institute of Religion: A Centennial History, 1875–1975* (rev. ed., 1992), pp. 68–9. An obituary is in *CCAR Yearbook* 35 (1925): 240–42.

GARY P. ZOLA

NEUTRA, Richard Joseph (8 Apr. 1892–16 Apr. 1970), architect, was born in Vienna, Austria, the son of Samuel Neutra, the owner and designer of a metal foundry, and Elizabeth Glazer. During Richard Neutra's early life, Vienna enjoyed an impressive renaissance in music, literature, art, and architecture. In these pre–World War I years the architectural figures who most directly influenced him were Otto Wagner, Josef Hoffmann, and Adolf Loos. What caught Neutra's imagination about the works of these Austrian designers was their abstract simplicity, coupled with a Viennese sense of restraint and refined elegance. Though he never studied or worked for Hoffmann,

Neutra's mature work as a designer comes closest to this Viennese master in his concern for elegant, polished details.

As happened with his slightly older friend, Rudolph M. Schindler, Neutra was encouraged to immigrate to the United States both by Loos's admiration for American architecture and by the 1910 publication in Berlin of Frank Lloyd Wright's famous *Ausgeführte Bauten und Entwürte*, often called the Wasmuth portfolio. Perhaps because of his father's fondness for machines, Neutra as a young man did not study architecture at the Vienna Academy of Fine Arts but at the Technische Hochschule, which he entered in 1911. As a reserve officer, he was called to active duty in the Austrian army in 1914. Because of ill health he was granted a leave, during which he completed his degree at the Hochschule in 1918. In 1919 he went to Zurich, Switzerland, where he worked in Otto Froebel's nursery. There, under the direction of the horticulturist and landscape designer Gustav Ammann, he developed what was to become a hallmark of his approach to design: the treatment of the landscape and the building as a single entity through a union of interior and exterior space. While in Switzerland he met Dione Niedermann; they were married in Germany in 1922 and had three children.

In 1921 Neutra obtained the position of city architect in the small town of Luckenwalde, near Berlin. Later in the same year he entered the Berlin office of Eric Mendelsohn, where he remained through the fall of 1923. What part Neutra played in Mendelsohn's designs of these years remains conjectural. One can assume that Neutra probably did contribute to the design of such buildings as the 1921–1923 additions to the Berliner Tageblatt (later altered), but the basic concept of this design and others is purely Mendelsohn's.

In 1923, with Schindler's help and encouragement, Neutra did come to the United States. Arriving in New York, he worked briefly for several architects before he went to Chicago, where he hoped to realize one of his goals in America: to meet Louis H. Sullivan and, above all, Frank Lloyd Wright. In Chicago he obtained a position with the large and prestigious commercial firm of Holabird and Roche. He met Sullivan, but their acquaintance was brief because the Chicago master died in April 1924. At Sullivan's funeral he finally met Wright and in the fall of 1924 went to live and work with him at "Taliesin" in Wisconsin. In January 1925 Neutra arrived in California with his wife and first child, who had joined him in Chicago the year before. They lived with Schindler and his wife Pauline at their Hollywood house on Kings Road.

Schindler provided Neutra with opportunities to collaborate as a landscape architect on several projects. Especially important for him were his garden designs for the 1925 Howe house in the Silver Lake district of Los Angeles and the 1922–1926 Lovell house at Newport Beach. Eventually Neutra, Schindler, and the planner Carol Aronovici formed a design team to pursue large projects; they called themselves the Architectural Group for Industry and Commerce (AGIC). The best-known project of this collaboration was their entry in the League of Nations Building Competition of 1926; it was among those selected for inclusion in the exhibition that traveled through Europe.

While working with Schindler and Aronovici, Neutra further developed his vision of architecture and city planning in his ideal urban plan, which he satirically called "Rush City Reformed." In this homage to the machine and modernist solution to the chaos and rush of city life, he projected a science-fiction city of the future, which drew on much earlier urban designs—the visual implication of speed of the futurist Antonio Sant'Elia, the rationalist city of Charles Garnier, and the city of skyscrapers of Le Corbusier.

Neutra established his reputation as America's foremost modernist with his 1929 steel-frame design for the Lovell house in Los Angeles. As was the case with Le Corbusier's Villa Savoye at Posey (1929–1930), the Lovell house became internationally known via photographs published in newspapers, magazines, and books throughout Europe and the United States. The Lovell house was one of the few American examples included in Henry-Russell Hitchcock and Philip Johnson's modernist 1932 exhibition, *The International Style: Architecture since 1922*, which was held at the newly opened Museum of Modern Art in New York City.

When the Lovell house was finished, Neutra went on a world tour, lecturing in Japan and in Europe. Although American building activities were dramatically reduced during the depression years of the 1930s, Neutra was able to enhance his worldwide reputation through a remarkable array of small-scaled buildings, mostly single-family houses and small apartment buildings. His admiration for the machine was displayed in such designs as his own 1932 Los Angeles house (the VDL Research house), the prefabricated metal Beard house (Altadena, 1934), the Plywood Model House (Los Angeles, 1936), and above all his streamline moderne Von Sternberg house (Northridge, 1936), which suggested a beached ocean-liner. All of these houses, as well as his other designs of this decade, reveal Neutra's efforts toward a fusion of the landscape with the building.

As was true of many other exponents of the modern, a number of Neutra's houses of the late 1930s and early 1940s were less insistently committed to the image of the machine. This is especially evident in such designs as the brick-and-wood-clad Nesbitt house (Brentwood, 1942) and in the extensive wartime housing he designed for the Channel Heights project in San Pedro in 1942. In the years after World War II, Neutra's designs continued to reflect his dualism, sometimes epitomizing the machine aesthetic, as in his Kaufmann house of 1946 in Palm Springs, and at other times exhibiting a more easygoing and milder modernism, as in his Treweek house of 1949, overlooking Silver Lake in Los Angeles.

In 1949 Neutra formed a partnership that lasted eleven years with the much younger planner and architect Robert Alexander. He hoped that through such a partnership he would at last obtain large-scale planning and architectural commissions. This goal was realized in part with such structures as the U.S. Embassy in Karachi, West Pakistan (1959), and the Los Angeles County Hall of Records, Los Angeles (1962). Generally, though, his larger-scaled late buildings are a disappointment, especially compared to his earlier work of the 1930s. Exceptions to the general blandness of his late commercial and institutional work were his small residential commissions, many of which continued to maintain the design quality of his previous work.

During the last years of his life Neutra joined in architectural practice with his son and continued to design, write, and lecture until his death in Wuppertal, Germany. Although his stature as a preeminent modernist was somewhat diminished in the 1960s, his reputation as an exponent of modernism continues as strong as in the 1930s.

• Most of Neutra's drawings are housed in the library at the University of California, Los Angeles. Neutra wrote extensively during his life. His most important writings are *Wie baut Amerika?* (1927), *Neues Bauen in der Welt* (1929), *The Architecture of Social Concern in Regions of Mild Climate* (1948), *Mysteries and Realities of the Site* (1951), *Survival through Design* (1954), *Life and Shape* (1962), and *Nature Near: Late Essays of Richard Neutra*, ed. William Marlin (1989). For his diaries and correspondence see *Richard Neutra, Promise and Fulfillment, 1919–1932*, comp. and trans. Dione Neutra (1985). The best accounts of Neutra and his architecture are Esther McCoy, *Richard Neutra* (1960) and *Vienna to Los Angeles: Two Journeys* (1979), and Thomas Hines, *Richard Neutra and the Search for Modern Architecture* (1982). Neutra's work was published in three volumes by Willy Boesiger, ed., *Richard Neutra, Buildings and Projects* (1951–1966). Obituaries are in the *New York Times*, 18 Apr. 1970, *Journal of the American Institute of Architects* 53 (June 1970): 6, 20, and *Progressive Architecture* 51 (June 1970): 57.

DAVID GEBHARD

NEVE, Felipe de (1727–21 Aug. 1784), military officer and colonial administrator, was born in Bailén, Spain, the son of Felipe de Neve and María (maiden name unknown). His father, a Sevillian by birth, reached the rank of captain in the king's army. His mother was also born in Seville. The family formed part of the old aristocracy of Andalusia. Neve married María Nicolasa of Seville. There were no children.

By 1774 Neve had become a major in Spain's Queretero regiment of cavalry. The next year he crossed the Atlantic, unaccompanied by his wife, to become governor of the Californias, with headquarters in the Baja California capital of Loreto, where he arrived on 4 March 1775. He was to spend less than two years governing from Loreto.

Neve was next appointed to serve as the governor of the Californias in Alta California. He arrived at its capital, Monterey, on 3 February 1777 to carry on Spain's last colonization effort in the new world and served in that post until 12 July 1782. Neve found Upper California in miserable shape. Only 146 soldiers, who lacked horses, arms, and equipment, guarded the whole of the province against Indians and intruders. His orders came from the viceroy in Mexico City, who constantly stressed the need to strengthen the province in every way possible. Neve, therefore, proceeded to establish a series of outposts at key points in the province. In 1777 he founded San Jose, California's first civic pueblo, along the banks of the Guadalupe River. Civic pueblos differed from the mission-pueblos, which were established around California's religious outposts.

On 4 September 1781 Neve established another tiny community, at Los Angeles. This became the province's second civic pueblo. The founding of that pueblo was surely his most important achievement. The governor had authorized the recruiting of its first residents in Sonora, Mexico. To govern these forty-four persons he drew up a *reglamento*, or code of laws. Derived from Spain's "Laws of the Indies," the decree laid down the rules that residents of the new community were required to follow. The *reglamento* was Los Angeles's initial charter as well as California's first written constitution. Neve also authorized establishment of a pueblo near the Presidio of Santa Barbara, to the north of Los Angeles.

Neve may well have been the best of California's eleven Spanish governors. Like his predecessors, he was a soldier, but he possessed a a statesman's mind. He demonstrated considerable tact in dealing with California's Franciscan missionaries, who were already in California before his arrival. The celebrated mission-founder, Fray Junipero Serra, did not like him. A clash of authority between the military and religious representatives of Spain had proven to be inevitable—the age-old conflict of church and state had been transported overseas. Neve objected to the harsh discipline practiced by the padres against their Indian charges at California's missions. The governor considered the missions to be state agencies serving a civil purpose—to remold the Indian population as a community and to instill in them work habits that would aid the Crown's colonizations plans. The padres did not favor the arrival of colonists, who would disrupt nearby mission life. Ultimately the missions were to become secular bodies, a notion fiercely resisted by the missionaries.

Neve faced other challenges as well. In 1782 he led a punitive expedition against the Yuma Indians along the Colorado River after they had revolted, massacring soldiers, a priest, and settlers. During that year Antonio Bucareli, viceroy of Mexico, appointed Neve, by then a brigadier, the commander-inspector of New Spain's (Mexico's) *Provincias Internas*, the northernmost provinces. Because he had proved to be a strong guardian of Spain's remote province in North America, Neve was ultimately placed in charge of the entire frontier of New Spain from the Sabine River in Texas to San Francisco (then Yerba Buena) in California. His salary of 8,000 pesos per year was then a substantial sum. In 1782 he was also awarded one of the great honors of the Spanish kingdom, the Cross of the Order of San Carlos.

On 15 February 1783, when his immediate superior, Teodoro de Croix, became viceroy of Peru, Neve took over the post of comandante general of the *Provincias Internas*. On 17 June 1784 Neve set out from Arispe in Mexico, the capital of the interior provinces, for a journey of inspection to Chihuahua. He was unwell, and the heavy rains he encountered, in addition to oppressive heat, drained his strength. He was forced to rest along the way but found that he could go no further than the Hacienda de Nuestra Señora del Carmen de Pena Blanca, today's Colonia Ricardo Flores Magón. Weak and exhausted by dysentery, Neve died there, alone and away from his family in Spain.

• Neve's Spanish records are in the Archivo General de Indias in Seville. His provincial documents are in the Archivo General de Indias, Audiencia de Guadalajara, Mexico. The correspondence of his superior, Teodoro de Croix, is in five volumes at the Bancroft Library, the University of California, Berkeley. Neve's 1779 regulations for the governance of California's pueblos have been published as *Reglamento para el Gobierno de la Provincia de Californias* (1929). A complete biography is Edwin A. Beilharz, *Felipe de Neve: First Governor of California* (1971). Also see Orra Eugene Monnette's slight *Don Felipe de Neve* (1930).

ANDREW ROLLE

NEVELSON, Louise (23 Sept. 1899–17 Apr. 1988), sculptor, was born Louise Berliawsky in Kiev, Russia, the daughter of Isaac Berliawsky, a contractor, and Minna Ziesel Smolerank. In 1902 her father immigrated to the United States, and three years later the Berliawsky family left Russia to join him in Rockland, Maine. Isaac Berliawsky owned a lumberyard and became a building contractor. Nevelson recalled that at age six she was assembling scraps of wood that she found in her father's lumberyard. She attended elementary school and high school in Rockland. In 1918, shortly after her graduation from Rockland High School, she became engaged to Charles Nevelson, a wealthy shipowner from New York. They were married in 1920 and had one child. Nevelson moved to New York City after her marriage, and during the 1920s she studied painting and drawing there with Theresa Bernstein and William Meyerowitz. She also took drama classes and private voice instruction.

Nevelson attended the Art Students League beginning in 1929, and she studied there with Kenneth Hayes Miller and Kimon Nicolaides. In 1931 she separated from her husband and left for Munich, where she planned to study with Hans Hofmann. Her travels included Berlin, Vienna, and Paris, where she was impressed with the Musée de Louvre and seriously studied primitive art at the Musée de l'Homme. After her return to New York City, she studied briefly with Hofmann at the Art Students League in 1932. The following year she served as an assistant to Mexican muralist Diego Rivera.

Louise Nevelson's first works of art were exhibited in New York galleries as early as 1933. These stone, terra-cotta, plaster, and wood sculptures were influenced by cubism and pre-Columbian art. By 1937 she was employed by the Works Progress Administration, and she taught sculpture at the Educational Alliance School. In 1941, the year her divorce was finalized, Nevelson had a solo exhibition of her paintings and sculpture at the Nierendorf Gallery. She remained with the gallery and Karl Nierendorf, with whom she had an intimate relationship, for the next seven years. She introduced found objects into her sculpture in 1942. In these sculptures the inspiration of Native American art joined with her interest in cubist sculptural forms. The links between the volumetric forms found in African and pre-Columbian sculpture and the works of European artists such as Constantin Brancusi and Jacques Lipchitz provided a point of departure for her work, as they had for other Americans experimenting with carving. For Nevelson the ancient art and architecture of Mexico and Central America opened a world of primitive mystery and heroic form in which art and myth were joined. Nevelson's carvings are reminiscent of the sculptures of Henry Moore, because he often chose to model reclining figures and was obviously influenced by primitive sources.

By 1943 Nevelson had shown her first exhibition installation organized around a specific theme: The Circus: The Clown in the Center of His World, which was shown at the Norlyst Gallery simultaneously with a solo exhibition of paintings and drawings at the Nierendorf Gallery. After these shows Nevelson destroyed about 200 paintings and sculpture, apparently for lack of storage space. She purchased a four-story townhouse on East Thirtieth Street in 1943, and she lived there for the following sixteen years. The house was frequently a gathering place for artists and organizational meetings of the Sculptors' Guild and the Federation of Modern Painters and Sculptors. Beginning in 1944 Nevelson showed abstract wood assemblages, Sculpture Montages, at the Nierendorf Gallery.

By 1946 Nevelson's work had been selected for the annual exhibition at the Whitney Museum of American Art, and she was frequently included in Whitney Annuals (later Biennials) thereafter. In 1947 she began working to produce a series of etchings at Atelier 17, a printmaking studio established by Stanley William Hayter that was modeled after a similar workshop in Paris. After her father's death in 1946 and Nierendorf's death in 1947, Nevelson, to relieve her grief and depression, traveled to England, France, and Italy, and she also visited Central America. After her return to New York City in 1949, she began working at the Sculpture Center and changed from assembling wood pieces to working in terra-cotta or marble. Two years later she had a brief sojourn in Mexico City, which was followed by another trip to Central America, where she visited Mayan sites on the Yucatan peninsula. In 1952 Nevelson exhibited in the annual exhibition of the National Association of Women Artists and was included in its group shows thereafter. Having returned to Atelier 17 in 1953, she completed a series of prints she had begun six years earlier, and she produced thirty editions in all.

Nevelson's Ancient Games and Ancient Places was an exhibition held at Grand Central Moderns gallery in 1955 with examples of her etchings and sculpture. Colette Roberts at Grand Central Moderns continued to represent Nevelson until 1958.

Nevelson's wood sculptures of the early 1950s, such as Black Majesty (1956, Whitney Museum of American Art), can be compared to works by Louise Bourgeois, who was her friend in these years. Both women created organic abstractions in wood that seem indebted to surrealist imagery. Totemic forms like First Personage (1956) parallel totems found among Native American peoples. In shows such as the Royal Voyage (of the King and Queen of the Sea) at Grand Central Moderns in 1956 Nevelson illustrated her personal fantasy of belonging to a royal family with her abstract imagery. An iconoclast with a flair for the theatrical, she wore flamboyant clothing and expressed her opinions freely.

Nevelson's signature works are the large "walls," such as Sky Cathedral (1958), which was made for her brother's Thorndike Hotel in Rockland, Maine. These walls feature stacked boxes and crates that make an architectonic "environment." In Moon Garden Plus One, her 1958 show at Grand Central Moderns, Nevelson created her first environmental exhibition, a theatrical triumph featuring blue lighting for the solid black wall constructions. Each of the separate boxes was displayed with an open front and was filled with furniture fragments, wooden scraps, and architectural ornaments. Nevelson painted the entire construction black to unify her composition and to minimize the identification of each found object. By placing small objects in covered spaces she created a complex interplay of light and shadow, contrasting the individuality of elements with their uniformity as an overall composition. Later she introduced all-white constructions and gold constructions, for which she supplied titles such as Royal Tide (1961). In an autobiographical context, these works refer to her own tendencies to view herself as royalty; she often wore expensive or exotic jewelry and clothing, creating her personal legend.

Installations, which began in the late 1950s, were another type of trademark work for Nevelson. In these, she combined individual constructions into a unified installation. In Nevelson's view, production of the work and its presentation were related creative activities. She viewed the exhibition as a useful venue for exploring new architectural formats and introducing improvisational effects. Although never closely identified with artists of the New York School (she did not attend meetings of the club or participate in key exhibitions), Nevelson's constructions are contemporary with the works of the abstract expressionists and share some characteristics with that style. Her walls have no center or focus and can be described as "overall" compositions. Her working method incorporated improvisation because she built constructions of found objects assembled without any models or preliminary drawings.

For her constructions, which are architectural in scale, Nevelson may have been inspired by commercial window displays. A fashion-conscious woman, she admired the window decorations of Bergdorf Goodman and other fashionable stores in New York City. In addition, the elaborate installations and "decors" designed by Frederick Kiesler for Peggy Guggenheim's Art of this Century Gallery and other surrealist-related installations may have inspired her. Many of Nevelson's environments have personal associations: an ensemble titled *Dawn's Wedding Feast* (1959) is a drama of white-on-white, featuring a sixteen-foot wedding chapel and wedding cake. This work suggests her ambivalence about marriage and her commitment to her artistic career rather than a personal relationship. In 1959 she became president of the New York chapter of Artists Equity.

After 1960 Nevelson introduced new materials and methods into her sculpture. From Plexiglas, Formica, and enamel, she created both large-scale environments and smaller relief constructions. Seemingly in response to the minimalism of the 1960s, her constructions introduced clean, sharp edges and geometric structure. In these works she traded using ragged wood fragments for the anonymity of manufacture and the perfection of surface. To achieve these smoother surfaces she hired a fabricator to make finely crafted boxes to order.

For the Venice XXXI Biennale in 1962, Nevelson was one of four artists selected to represent the United States. She constructed black, white, and gold environments for installation in the United States Pavilion in Venice. A political activist as well as an ambitious artist, Nevelson was the first woman to be elected national president of Artists Equity (1963).

In 1962 Nevelson joined the Sidney Janis Gallery as the first woman artist and the first American sculptor to be represented there. A Ford Foundation grant in 1963 enabled her to go to the Tamarind Lithography Workshop in Los Angeles, where she produced twenty-six editions of lithographs. In 1964 Nevelson began to show at Pace Gallery, which still represented the artist at the time of her death. In 1966 her first sculptures fabricated in aluminum were produced, and in the following year she made small Plexiglas sculptures and produced multiples in bronze, wood, polyester resin, and black Plexiglas.

Nevelson was given her first major retrospective exhibition in 1967 at the Whitney Museum of American Art. In the 1970s, when Nevelson was in her eighties, she was awarded commissions for sculpture on public sites. The majority of these sculptures were fabricated steel. For example, Princeton University commissioned *Atmosphere and Environment X* in 1969, and it was her first large-scale sculpture in corten steel. *Nightsphere-Light* (1969) is a 47-foot-wide wall constructed in wood for the Juilliard School of Music at Lincoln Center in New York City. Concurrently, Nevelson received considerable attention in Western Europe with solo exhibitions in Holland, Italy, and France.

Nevelson's later public commissions included an outdoor corten steel construction titled *Night Presence IV* on Park Avenue in New York City and *Atmosphere and Environment XIII: Windows to the West*, commissioned by the city of Scottsdale, Arizona, in 1972. In 1977 Nevelson designed the Chapel of the Good Shepherd for St. Peter's Lutheran Church at the Citicorp complex in Manhattan. The dazzling white interior includes wooden constructions on the walls, mobile wooden columns, and altar, and it is the first chapel to be entirely designed by an American artist. In 1980 retrospective exhibitions were arranged at the Phoenix Art Museum in Arizona and at the Whitney Museum. She died in New York City. Her lifelong interest in the arts and her creation of art forms can be viewed as a drama of the psyche finding three-dimensional realization.

• Nevelson's papers and her personal archive of 21,000 items, including original essays, statements by the artist, correspondence, clippings, catalogs, and press releases, are in the Archives of American Art, Washington, D.C. Her autobiography is *Dawns Plus Dusks* (1976). See also Laurie Wilson, *Louise Nevelson: Iconography and Sources* (1981); Jean Lipman, *Nevelson's World* (1983); and Laurie Lisle, *Louise Nevelson: A Passionate Life* (1990). Obituaries are in the *New York Times*, 18 Apr. 1988, and *Time* and *Newsweek*, both 2 May 1988.

JOAN MARTER

NEVERS, Ernie (11 June 1903–3 May 1976), football player and coach, was born Ernest Alonzo Nevers in Willow River, Minnesota, the son of George Nevers and Mary (last name unknown), innkeepers. Nevers attended high school in Superior, Wisconsin, and won local acclaim as a basketball player. When his parents moved to Santa Rosa, California, he enrolled at Stanford University, where he earned 11 athletic letters in football, basketball, and baseball.

Nevers played fullback in Coach Glenn "Pop" Warner's double-wing offense, handling most of his team's running, passing, and kicking. In 1924, his junior year, Nevers suffered two broken ankles and missed most of the regular football season. Stanford was invited to play in the 1925 Rose Bowl against Notre Dame's undefeated team, led by the fabled Four Horsemen. Although the Irish won 27–10, Nevers was named the game's outstanding player and received national attention for his 114 yards rushing in 34 attempts while playing the full 60 minutes on specially bandaged ankles. Warner, who had coached Jim Thorpe during his All-America seasons, said, "Nevers can do everything Thorpe could do and he always tries harder. Ernie gives 60 minutes of himself every game."

As a senior in 1925, Nevers was a near-unanimous All-America and second only to Red Grange of Illinois as the most publicized football player in the country. Following the season, he received $25,000 to turn pro, opposing Grange and the Chicago Bears in a series of

Florida-to-California exhibition games that helped popularize pro football.

After playing professional basketball in Chicago that winter, he pitched for the St. Louis Browns during the 1926 baseball season.

Blond, handsome, articulate, modest, and talented, Nevers was a prototypical American sports hero—and the key to the survival of the National Football League in 1926. In the fall of that year, Grange and his personal manager, C. C. Pyle, launched the American Football League in opposition to the then seven-year-old NFL. The AFL placed teams in several major NFL cities, including New York, Chicago, and Philadelphia. One NFL team, the Rock Island Independents, actually jumped to the AFL. In addition to Grange, the new league signed a number of star players, and some preseason observers predicted it would exceed the NFL in popularity.

Nevers turned down an AFL offer and cast his lot with the NFL, signing to play and coach for the Duluth Eskimos for $15,000. He immediately became the NFL's top drawing card. The team was renamed the Ernie Nevers Eskimos for publicity purposes. It played all but its opening game on the road so that most of the then-21 other NFL teams could boost their attendance with Nevers's popularity.

He played all but 27 minutes of his team's 14 regular-season and 15 nonleague games. The 6-foot, 200-pound fullback contributed almost all of his team's offense. Although he lacked the breakaway speed of Grange, he excelled at line-plunging and could seldom be stopped by a single defender. A strong punter and accurate placekicker, he also was rated as one of the league's better passers at a time when the air game was only an infrequent weapon. On defense, he backed up the line and was regarded as a superior tackler. Moreover, he played with a fervor that inspired his team. Despite the backbreaking schedule that often saw them play several games a week, the Eskimos finished with a winning NFL record of 6–5–3. Nevers scored 71 points, second in the league, and was named on every all-pro team. Reportedly, he earned $60,000 for playing three professional sports that year.

He continued his baseball and football careers in 1927. His pitching was undistinguished except that he gave up two of Babe Ruth's 60 home runs. In football, the AFL had gone bankrupt, making Nevers's drawing power less important to the NFL. Nevertheless, the Eskimos continued as a road team, although with less success than before. Often behind in games, Nevers passed more often. Unofficial statistics show he completed 45 percent of his throws, an unusually high percentage for the time. He was again chosen all-NFL.

He pitched his final season for the Browns in 1928, finishing with a career record of 6–12. Because of a back injury, he temporarily retired from the NFL to assist Coach Warner at Stanford that fall.

In 1929 he returned to pro football as player-coach of the Chicago Cardinals, one of the weaker NFL teams. Almost single-handedly, he improved them to a .500 record. He led the league in scoring with 85 points, a total that would not be exceeded for 11 seasons. More than two-thirds of his total came in two games. On November 24 he scored all 19 points in the Cardinals' victory over Dayton. Four days later, in a Thanksgiving Day game at Comiskey Park, he set an NFL record by scoring all of his team's points in a 40–7 rout of the Chicago Bears. His six touchdowns for the game also marked a league record, though twice tied since.

He played for the Cardinals through 1931 when a broken wrist suffered in a postseason all-star game ended his playing career. During Nevers's tenure as player-coach he was chosen all-league each year as the Cardinals compiled a respectable 16–16–3 record. In his five NFL seasons he scored 301 points.

Nevers returned to Stanford as backfield coach for four years, served as head coach at Lafayette College in 1936, and then assisted at the University of Iowa in 1937–1938. In 1939 the perennially weak Cardinals brought him back as head coach, but he was unable to inspire his team from the sideline as he once had on the field. The Cards stumbled to a 1–10 record.

Nevers married twice. Mary Elizabeth Heagerty, whom he wed in 1926, died of pneumonia in 1943. In 1947 he married Margery Luxem; they had one child. During World War II he served in the South Pacific with the U.S. Marine Corps as a captain of aviation ordnance. Following the war he became a public relations man for a wholesale liquor distributor in California. He died in San Rafael, California.

Besides being chosen to several college and pro all-time teams, Nevers was elected a charter member of the Stanford Hall of Fame, the Helms Athletic Foundation (Citizens Savings Bank) Hall of Fame, the National Football Foundation Hall of Fame, and the Pro Football Hall of Fame. Of all the enshrinees in the Pro Football Hall, he had the shortest career—five seasons—but he is also the only player ever chosen to the all-league team every year he played.

• A biography by Jim Scott, *Ernie Nevers, Football Hero,* was published in 1969, and many short biographical articles within larger works are available. Among the most authoritative are those by Don R. Smith in *Pro Football Hall of Fame All-Time Greats* (1988), Arthur Daley in *Pro Football's Hall of Fame* (1963), Jack Hand in *Great Running Backs of the NFL* (1966), and L. Robert Davids in *Biographical Dictionary of American Sports: Football* (1987). Unofficial pro rushing, passing, and kicking statistics culled from newspaper accounts are available in David S. Neft and Richard M. Cohen, *The Football Encyclopedia* (1991). The Pro Football Hall of Fame in Canton, Ohio, has an extensive clipping file on Nevers. Obituaries are in the *Chicago Tribune* and the *New York Times,* 4 May 1976.

BOB CARROLL

NEVILLE, Wendell Cushing (12 May 1870–8 July 1930), Marine Corps officer, was born in Portsmouth, Virginia, the son of Willis Henry Neville, a ship's carpenter, and Mary Elizabeth Cushing. His parents raised him as a Methodist. After his father's death in 1883, an older brother provided for Neville's education, and he graduated from Norfolk Academy in 1885. Choosing an option not unusual for the sons of poor southern families of the era, Neville took an appointment to one of the service academies, reporting to Annapolis in the fall of 1886. Although a rather poor student, Neville survived the rigorous demands of the institution to graduate in 1890. After completing the postgraduation cruise in 1892, he and his classmates returned for further examinations and assignment to the fleet. Because of his low academic standing, Neville did not qualify for a commission in the navy, and he accepted a second lieutenant's vacancy in the Marine Corps. Years later he claimed it to be his first choice because of a hearty dislike for standing watches at sea.

For almost the next decade and a half, Neville performed duties typical of Marine Corps officers in the age of sail. His tours alternated between assignments at various navy yards and in command of Marines serving in the ships of the fleet. As a junior officer, Neville served in the *Raleigh*, the *Cincinnati*, and the *Texas* and at the barracks at navy yards in New York, Boston, and Washington. While stationed in the nation's capital, he married Frances Adelphia Howell, the daughter of Rear Admiral John Adams Howell, in 1898. They had one child.

Neville saw action ashore three times as a junior officer: first as a member of Robert W. Huntington's battalion that deployed in 1898 to Guantánamo Bay, Cuba, early in the Spanish-American War; next with Littleton W. T. Waller's battalion ordered to China in 1900 during the Boxer Rebellion; and finally in command of his own battalion, formed from ships of the fleet, sent ashore to subdue rebellious Cubans in 1906. For his conduct at Guantánamo Bay and in China, he received mention in dispatches and was advanced in rank by brevet. By 1914 Neville had risen in rank to lieutenant colonel and had earned a reputation throughout his branch of the naval services as a resolute and capable campaigner. Friends called him "Buck," a nickname that he carried throughout his adult life.

While commanding the Marine Barracks, Charleston, South Carolina, Neville formed and led a battalion that deployed with a brigade to the Caribbean in response to the conflict between the United States and Mexico in 1913–1914. Assuming command of the Second Regiment of Marines, Neville earned the Medal of Honor at Veracruz for "conspicuous courage, coolness, and skill in the conduct of the fighting." The citation added that "his responsibilities were great and he met them in a manner worthy of commendation."

From 1915 to 1917 Neville commanded the Legation Guard in Beijing (Peking); during that time, he was promoted to colonel. Returning home just as the United States entered World War I, Neville sailed to France with the Fifth Marines and led this regiment through the battles of Belleau Wood and Soissons, during which he earned an army citation, two regimental citations, a Croix de Guerre, and the Legion of Honor. Promoted to brigadier general, Neville commanded the Fourth Brigade (Marine), Second Division, American Expeditionary Forces, and led it for the remainder of the war and during the occupation of Germany. Under his leadership, the brigade participated in the St.-Mihiel, Blanc Mont, and Meuse-Argonne offensives. To his other decorations, Neville added both the Army and Navy Distinguished Service Medals and two additional Croix de Guerre. He earned a reputation for forceful and decisive leadership on the western front.

A year after Neville returned home, Secretary of the Navy Josephus Daniels ordered him promoted to major general. For the next decade, Neville served at Headquarters Marine Corps in Washington, then in command of the Department of the Pacific in San Francisco, and finally at Quantico. When Major General Commandant John Archer Lejeune stepped down from the Marine Corps's highest post in 1929, he recommended Neville as his successor. Both President Herbert Hoover and Secretary of the Navy Charles Francis Adams agreed to Neville's appointment. During his short tenure in command of the Marines, Neville pursued several goals: refurbishing the aging physical plant of his service; gaining congressional passage of an efficient means of officer promotion; and enhancement of the amphibious assault mission as the raison d'être for the smaller of the naval services. The first two goals failed to reach fruition, but Neville's emphasis on professionalism and combat readiness in support of the fleet prevailed. His Marines continued to serve in the navy's ships, and large formations manned deployments to Haiti, Nicaragua, and China.

Plagued by chronic hypertension, Neville suffered a debilitating stroke in March 1930 that left him partially paralyzed. He died in Edgewater Beach near Annapolis, Maryland. Known for his gruff exterior and personal dynamism, Neville led by good-natured directness and honesty. An obituary in the *Washington Post* reflects what most Marines felt upon hearing of his passing: "An indomitable will, a sense of humor and conspicuous courage were joined with personal magnetism to make [Neville] a soldier of heroic mold" (9 July 1930).

• What few personal papers Neville retained are at the Marine Corps Historical Center, Washington Navy Yard. His name may be found in the correspondence of both Lejeune and Daniels, Manuscripts Division, Library of Congress; in a collection of the papers of James G. Harbord, New-York Historical Society; and in the Herbert Hoover Papers, Hoover Presidential Library, West Branch, Iowa. At the National Archives and Records Administration, Washington, RG 127 (U.S. Marine Corps) is useful for any study of Neville's entire career along with RG 120 (American Expeditionary Forces) for his duty in World War I. Neville's fitness reports may be found either in his Officers Qualification Record at Headquarters Marine Corps, Washington, or in the Records of Marine Corps Examining Boards, Entry 62, Records of the Navy Judge Advocate General, RG 130, Federal Records Center, Suitland, Md. Printed sources useful in further study of Neville's life and times include Jack Shulimson, *The Marine Corps' Search for a Mission, 1880–1898* (1993); and biographies of two important contemporaries, Merrill L. Bartlett, *Lejeune: A Marine's Life* (1991), and Hans Schmidt, *Maverick Marine: General Smedley D. Butler and the Contradictions of American Military History* (1987). Philip N. Pierce, "The Whispering Commandant," *Leatherneck* 67 (Apr. 1984): 36–51, is also helpful.

MERRILL L. BARTLETT

NEVIN, Ethelbert Woodbridge (25 Nov. 1862–17 Feb. 1901), composer and pianist, was born at "Vineacre," the family's estate at Edgeworth near Pittsburgh, Pennsylvania, the son of Robert Peebles Nevin, an author, poet, and newspaper publisher, and Elizabeth Duncan Oliphant, a pianist for whom the first grand piano had been carried across the Allegheny Mountains to western Pennsylvania. Ethelbert was the fifth of eight children. His youngest sibling, Arthur, also was a composer and musician.

He received musical training at home and by six could sing and play his own accompaniments at the piano. His life was devoted to music; he studied piano and composition with teachers in Pittsburgh, and at eleven his first work, "Lilian Polka" (written for his sister), was published. During a family year abroad he studied piano with Franz Böhme in Dresden. He attended Western University of Pennsylvania for one year but in 1881 took up music full-time. He moved to Boston to study piano with Benjamin J. Lang and harmony with Stephen A. Emery and supported himself by teaching piano students. He returned to Pittsburgh in 1883 to teach and to perform recitals, often including his own songs, chamber works, and piano pieces.

From 1884 to 1886 Nevin went to Berlin to study piano with Karl Klindworth and theory and composition with Carl Bial, with additional lessons in composition from Otto Tiersch and piano from Hans Von Bülow. He returned to Pittsburgh for his debut, then established himself in Boston as a concert pianist and piano teacher. He married Anne Paul in January 1888; their son Paul was born later that year. *The Sketch Book* (1888), a collection of ten songs and ten piano pieces, was one of the first such publications by an American composer. Nevin, fluent in French and German, often chose poems in those languages for his songs, including "Lehn' deine Wang an meine Wang" by Heinrich Heine for *The Sketch Book*. In 1889 his brother Arthur joined them in Boston to begin his musical studies.

Nevin divided his time between composing and practicing piano, still planning a career as a virtuoso pianist. In 1890 he gave concerts in Boston, New York, and Philadelphia and published four Sacred Songs, as well as one of his greatest successes, *Water Scenes*, which included "Narcissus." In spring 1891 the family returned to Berlin, then to Paris, where he took students, composed, gave lecture recitals on Wagner, and attended many concerts. He composed quickly, often writing a song in an afternoon. Early in 1892 he returned to Berlin to study and compose. That year his daughter Dorothy was born, and the family returned to America in December. He finished his Opus 20 songs, which won praise for their "moving charm" and simplicity—of these "Dites-moi" and "Every Night My Prayers I Say" gained renown. About these songs Philip Hale wrote, "You find first of all a melody apparently spontaneous; . . . harmonies that support, enrich, but do not call the attention away from the singer; and the results of faithful technical study do not obtrude. The appeal is direct; there is no attempt to create merely a *Stimmung*" (quoted in Thompson, p. 136). And Rupert Hughes offered a refined opinion: "Nevin's songs have lyrical contour, lyrical impulses; they come forward in graceful curves like waves. . . . I know of no other American composer who has so much essentially of the song spirit that made Franz Schubert popular among both the masses and the classes" (quoted in Thompson, p. 136).

Nevin struggled throughout his life against ill health. Back in Boston he taught and performed recitals but suffered a nervous breakdown and took an extended voyage in 1894 to recover. The following year he spent less time performing and increasingly programmed his own compositions. Seeking serenity, he took his family to Italy, where he wrote his piano suites *Maggio in Toscana* and *A Day in Venice* and where they withstood a series of earthquakes in Florence and Montepiano and spent 1896 in Venice. They returned to New York in the fall. On one concert he shared the program with Isadora Duncan, who illustrated in classic dances his songs "Narcissus," "Ophelia," and "Water Nymph." And there, in one day in 1897, he wrote perhaps his best known song, "The Rosary," to a poem by Robert Cameron Rogers.

After his mother, to whom he was devoted, died, Nevin moved back to Vineacre in 1898. Willa Cather described "An Evening at Vineacre" in an 1899 article for the *Courier*. Nevin wrote his last successful songs there, including "Mighty Lak' a Rose" and "At Rest," and "The Quest," which was unfinished but later scored by Horatio Parker. He spent the winter of 1900–1901 in New Haven, Connecticut, where he died.

Nevin was a miniaturist who avoided large musical forms. He wrote some fifty-five piano pieces, eighty-five songs, twenty choral works, and miscellaneous pieces. Cather quoted his father as saying, "We are all creatures of sentiment, we live and die by it, dispute it as we will, and it is the strongest force there is"; this, she remarked, "explains Ethelbert Nevin and his music" (quoted in Thompson, pp. 206f). An obituary summed up his gentle spirit: "The notes of deep passion, of tragedy, or breadth and force, were not within his gamut. He spoke in a charming idiom. . . . His fancy played lightly on April breezes; he felt and expressed the blitheness, the changing sunshine and shadow of life" (*New York Mail & Express*, 18 Feb. 1901).

His widow, Anne Paul Nevin, helped achieve passage of the Copyright Act of 1909, which protected composers' claims to their works.

• The Ethelbert Nevin Collection in the University of Pittsburgh Music Library holds most of his extant manuscripts, correspondence, photographs, programs, and artifacts; a catalog was compiled by Yin-fen Wang (1987). Vance Thompson, a lifelong friend, wrote *The Life of Ethelbert Nevin from His Letters and His Wife's Memories* (1913). For a definitive biography, see John Tasker Howard, *Ethelbert Nevin* (1935). The most extensive musical study is Hui-ling Liu, "The Piano Music of Ethelbert Nevin" (master's thesis, Univ. of Florida, 1995). An obituary is in the *New York Times*, 18 Feb. 1901.

DEANE L. ROOT

NEVIN, John Williamson (20 Feb. 1803–6 June 1886), religious thinker and educator, was born near Shippensburg, Pennsylvania, the son of John Nevin and Martha McCracken, farmers. His father was what was called a "Latin farmer," educated at Dickinson College and able to teach his children Latin, Greek, and other subjects. John Williamson was the eldest of nine children, all of whom had, or were associated by marriage with, distinguished careers in education, the clergy, banking, or journalism. The Nevins were Presbyterians of the classical Reformed tradition, which provided careful religious instruction and catechetical training, allied to a system in which the church was the essential medium of salvation.

After attending a parochial school associated with the Middle Spring Presbyterian Church, John Williamson was prepared for college by his father. At fourteen years of age he went to Union College in Schenectady, New York. Union was an institution representing an alliance of Protestant denominations, all of which seemed more committed to revivalistic experience than to sacramental piety. While at Union Nevin was "converted" during a series of meetings in which students anxiously explored their spiritual condition. This conversion, he observed later, was based on the principle that the experience "lay outside of the Church, had nothing to do with baptism and Christian education, required rather a looking away from all this as more of a bar than a help to the process." The issue raised here reappeared in his later theology.

Having graduated from Union in his nineteenth year, Nevin returned to the Cumberland valley to consider his professional future. For two years he plowed and harrowed his father's acres and contemplated studying theology at Princeton. In 1823 he entered Princeton and, while there, spent more time in biblical and language study than he had intended. He finally discovered that he did not wish to serve as pastor of a congregation. However, when the famous Charles Hodge took leave from his professorship for two years of study in Europe, the school offered Nevin his place.

When Hodge came back from Europe in 1828, Nevin returned home. He studied political economy on his own and preached in the Presbytery of Carlisle before accepting a position in 1830 as professor of biblical literature at the new Western Theological Seminary in Allegheny City, near Pittsburgh, Pennsylvania. During his ten years in this position, he also preached in Presbyterian churches and addressed various ecclesiastical meetings and literary societies. He married Martha Jenkins of Lancaster County in 1835.

During this period, Nevin supported an evangelical moralism that condemned the use of "ardent spirits," maintained a solemn view of anything frivolous, and opposed the "desecration" of the Christian Sabbath. He later took exception to the individualism and subjectivism of American religion, referring to them as the "Puritanism and Methodism" of our public and religious life. He never escaped the confines of his earlier moralism, however, and never perceived the discrepancy between it and his mature theological vision.

While in Pittsburgh, he mastered German and began reading Johann August Neander's church history as well as other works in theology and philosophy. German scholarship had a profound effect on his thought; when he was called to a theological professorship at the theological seminary of the German Reformed church in Mercersburg, Pennsylvania, in 1840, he had already entered an intellectual realm that was in harmony neither with the spirit of his Old School Presbyterianism nor with the revivalism of New School Presbyterianism. In 1841 Nevin also became acting president of Marshall College, the Reformed collegiate institution in the same town.

Nevin had concluded that the prevailing American religious spirit was inadequate to the task of maintaining the public spirit of the nation. In 1843 he published a tract entitled *The Anxious Bench*. In little more than a hundred pages, Nevin set the tone for much of his later thought. The tract attacked the new measures revivalism associated with Charles Grandison Finney. These measures were based upon the assumption that Christianity was primarily an experience of "getting religion," or being converted. Nevin saw this assumption as destructive of a profound Christian faith and out of keeping with the historical understanding of Christianity he had discovered in Neander. He criticized the conventional American Protestant exaltation of "Bible and Private Judgment" as the solitary norms of theological truth. In *The Anxious Bench* he objected to the assumption that Christianity was primarily about extending a message of salvation to the masses. This was a mechanical principle, against which he proposed extending the Church's organic life from within through catechetical instruction and sacramental nurture.

After a young Swiss scholar, Phillip Schaff, joined Nevin at Mercersburg in 1844 and delivered his inaugural lecture on *The Principle of Protestantism*, the two professors began to formulate a view of historical development that made a place for both Catholicism and Protestantism. Thus was born the Mercersburg theology, and Nevin was its principal theologian. In 1846 Nevin published a work on the Eucharist, entitled *The Mystical Presence*, which stressed a doctrine of real presence that he maintained avoided the peculiarities of Lutheran and Roman Catholic interpretations of the Eucharist while opposing the Puritan and rationalistic notions of a simple memorial supper.

Nevin's ideas seemed to many within the German Reformed church to be soft on Catholicism at a time when American nativism led to the formation of the Know-Nothing party and the emergence of anti-Romanist activities. His thought was controversial because it ran counter to the evangelical Protestant spirit of the American nation. It was churchly and sacramental among a people who valued the immediate experience of the individual and maintained loyalty, at least in principle, to a simple life unadorned by ritual behavior. Nevin's was a historical and philosophical mind in a nation inclined to an anti-intellectualism that affected religion, education, and politics. Nevin was a prolific writer. Many of his ideas were developed in response to books and major political, religious, and theological events and movements.

Outside the German Reformed church, Nevin's theology brought him recognition as an intellectual. Inside the church, however, Nevin and Schaff met with considerable resistance. Schaff managed to direct his intellectual and scholarly interests into more congenial environments, becoming more and more interested in ecumenical matters and eventually leaving Mercersburg for Union Theological Seminary in New York City. Nevin, however, tried to maintain the integrity of his position within the church. He left Mercersburg for early retirement when Marshall College moved to Lancaster in 1853. For a time his dissatisfaction with the prevailing Protestantism led him to consider Roman Catholicism. He was instrumental in the design and promotion of a liturgy in keeping with his theology, but he retired from much official duty because he did not wish to be a disruptive force in the educational life of the Church. In 1866, however, he was pressed back into service as president of Franklin and Marshall College, where he served until a final retirement in 1876. He died in Lancaster, Pennsylvania.

Nevin's thought deserves far greater attention than it has received; he was one of the seminal religious thinkers of nineteenth-century America.

• Most of Nevin's works and papers are to be found in the archives of the Evangelical and Reformed Church Historical Society, located on the campus of Lancaster Theological Seminary in Pennsylvania. The Brownson Collection at the University of Notre Dame Archives contains some correspondence between John Nevin and Orestes Brownson. The archives of the Episcopal Diocese of Maryland include five letters of Nevin to William Rollinson Whittingham, a high church Episcopalian sympathetic to the Oxford Movement. In addition to works cited in the text, Nevin also published *History and Genius of the Heidelberg Catechism* (1847). Much of his work appears in volumes of the *Mercersburg Review* and the *Reformed Church Messenger*. Theodore Appel, *The Life and Work of John Williamson Nevin* (1889), is the only published biography of Nevin. However, information on Nevin's life and evaluations of his work may be found in James Hastings Nichols, *Romanticism in American Theology: Nevin and Schaff at Mercersburg* (1961); Luther J. Binkley, *The Mercersburg Theology* (1953); and Hugh T. Kerr, ed., *Sons of the Prophets: Leaders in Protestantism from Princeton Seminary*

(1963). Compare Richard E. Wentz, "The World of Mercersburg Theology," in *The Mystical Presence*, by Rev. John W. Nevin, D.D. (1963), pp. IX–XXIII.

RICHARD E. WENTZ

NEVINS, Allan (20 May 1890–5 Mar. 1971), journalist and historian, was born Joseph Allan Nevins on a farm near Camp Point, Illinois, the son of Joseph Allan Nevins, a farmer, and Emma Stahl, a former schoolteacher. Although he attended the local country school, Nevins received his most meaningful education at home from his parents. A sober-minded Calvinist, whose extensive personal library of 500 volumes lacked novels and poetry, Nevins's father required his children to spend their spare hours performing farm chores. At the age of eighteen, Nevins escaped farm drudgery by enrolling at the University of Illinois, where, studying the works that had been denied him as a child, he majored in English literature. His ceaseless industry was a matter of concern for his mentor, Professor Stuart Sherman, who repeatedly warned his star pupil: "You are still working too hard. I seriously urge you to cultivate a little leisure and gaiety. . . . It is not indispensable for you to achieve immortal fame before you are twenty-five" (quoted in Tingley, p. 180). But Nevins's self-imposed pace never slowed.

Graduating in 1912, Nevins remained for another year at Urbana, where he taught freshman English and worked on a master's degree in history. His thesis, a biography of Robert Rogers, the notorious Loyalist raider during the Revolution, was published in 1914. In 1913 he accepted a position as editorial writer for the *New York Evening Post*. He did not, however, regard this move as an abandonment of his consuming interest in history. He always insisted that journalism provided the best training for a historian: it demanded clear, lively writing, related current events to their historical antecedents, emphasized the role of the individual in affecting those events, and, not least important, taught the writer to respect the sanctity of deadlines. Nevins applied this training to his engagement in historical scholarship while still grinding out his daily editorials. In 1916 he married Mary Fleming Richardson; they had two children. In 1922 he published a history of the *Evening Post*. After serving briefly as literary editor of the *New York Sun* from 1924 to 1925, he moved in 1925 to the *New York World*, where he returned to writing editorials.

During these years, Nevins produced two major historical studies, *The American States During and After the Revolution, 1775–1789* (1924), the pioneer study of a hitherto largely ignored aspect of the revolutionary period; and *The Emergence of Modern America, 1865–1878* (1927), which gave needed emphasis to the historical significance of American industrialization. These two books attracted the attention of academia, and in 1927 he was appointed associate professor of history at Cornell University. One year later, having published *Frémont, the West's Greatest Adventurer* (1928), he was invited to join the Columbia University faculty as an assistant professor of history. He accepted this demotion in rank in order to return to the city that he would always regard as the intellectual capital of the United States.

Nevins divided his time between the editorial office of the *World* and the classrooms at Columbia until 1931, when he was given the DeWitt Clinton Chair in American history and finally abandoned his career in journalism. In 1932 he published *Grover Cleveland: A Study in Courage*, for which he won his first Pulitzer Prize in biography. Four years later he again was awarded the Pulitzer for *Hamilton Fish* (1936), his monumental biography of the distinguished member of President Ulysses S. Grant's cabinet.

As occupant of a chair at one of America's most respected universities and twice recipient of the most prestigious prize in historical scholarship, Nevins had made a rapid transition from editorial writing to preeminence in his chosen professional field. He approached the study and teaching of history almost reverentially: "To Allan Nevins," wrote his protégé Ray Billington, "knowledge of the past was mankind's most precious asset," and offered the best hope for salvation from self-destruction. The lectern was his pulpit, from which he delivered sermons on "American Political History, 1865 to the Present," "American Social History" and "Great Literature of American History" to hundreds of undergraduate and graduate students for over a quarter of a century.

Nevins's lectures were written with meticulous care and revised each year to accommodate new information, interpretations, and concerns that affected the vision of the past. Never a skilled orator, he delivered his lectures in rapid tempo to an audience that feverishly attempted to take down each precious minutia offered up. He spoke in a strained, gravelly voice which always seemed on the verge of breaking but never quite did.

His graduate seminars, which often contained as many as thirty students, were dedicated to the training of scholars and teachers who, having acquired their advanced degrees, could go out to spread his gospel of the importance of history. Nevins had only contempt for the narrow pedant who wrote dull monographs on arcane subjects only to impress a chosen few, who were themselves engaged in the same sterile exercise. In his presidential inaugural address to the American Historical Association in 1959, he spelled out the four "fundamental requirements" for historical works: that history encompass "every need, taste and mood," that it be "written with gusto" and "a delight that communicates itself to style," that it be "assimilable to current needs," and that it give "due emphasis to personal motivation and initiative" (*American Historical Review* 65 [1960]: 258–59).

Determined to also get his message to the general public, Nevins strove to write the kind of books that his "broad democratic public" would enjoy reading and to explain in simple, layman terms what history should be and what historians should do. This he did in many articles for popular journals and in his aptly named book, *The Gateway to History* (1938; repr. 1962). He was the moving force in the founding of the Society of American Historians, which was organized to honor those historians who were, in his words, dedicated "to the object of making sound historical writing more artistic, and bringing it more closely home to the American people." This select society of some two hundred historians was the only professional organization to which Nevins was ever truly committed. He rarely attended the annual meetings of the major historical associations, and he deplored their journals for doing little to extend an appreciation of history to a nonprofessional audience. As early as the 1930s, he campaigned for a different type of historical journal, one containing articles of sound history but profusely illustrated and written in a style that excited interest. In 1949 this dream became a reality with the publication of *American Heritage*. Although many professionals regarded this venture as pandering to the lowest common denominator of the history-reading public, the magazine enjoyed great success. By 1967, its circulation of 330,000 far exceeded the number of subscribers to any of the major professional journals.

Never satisfied with the primary source material available for research, Nevins constantly sought out untapped resources. He decried the ubiquitous telephone, which was making letter writing obsolete. Even sadder to him was the knowledge that many notable figures had never taken the time to keep diaries, preserve their correspondence, or write their memoirs. He said he often wept over the *New York Times* obituary page, not so much for the death of the individual as for the great store of history that that person had carried unreported to the grave. This sense of loss inspired what Nevins would regard as his greatest contribution to the profession—the establishment of the Oral History Research Office at Columbia in 1948. Although the concept of oral history was at least as old as Herodotus, Nevins was the first to conceive of a great archival center that would contain the recollections of those who had played a role in the history of their time, gained through interviews by trained historians, recorded by the most advanced technology available, and transcribed into manuscript form. Because such an undertaking required more funding than the university could provide, for years Nevins and his colleague Henry Steele Commager urged the independently wealthy historian Frederic Bancroft to make the school a substantial gift. Upon his death in 1945, Bancroft bequeathed $2 million to Columbia for the promotion of the study of American history, and a portion of this bequest enabled Nevins to establish the Oral History Research Office. Starting with a small staff that was headed by Nevins himself the Oral History Research Office became one of the university's most successful projects and was widely emulated by other institutions. At the time of Nevins's death, the collection consisted of 340,000 pages of manuscript collected from more than 2,500 persons whose stories might otherwise have never been told.

In addition to being a successful fundraiser for his beloved university, Nevins also proved to be a significant fund provider. In 1965 he astounded his colleagues by giving to Columbia $500,000 to establish a chair in American economic history. When asked how someone who had never received more than a $12,000 annual salary could possibly have accumulated funds for such a gift, Nevins replied laconically, "By frugal living." Nevins had, in fact, set aside a portion of his income from royalties for this benefaction.

While writing over fifty books, editing scores more, publishing more articles and reviews than anyone ever attempted to count, and overseeing the work of more than one hundred doctoral candidates, Nevins found time for public service. He served as a special representative of the Office of War Information in Australia and New Zealand during World War II and as chief public affairs officer for the American embassy in London during 1945–1946. In 1961 he took over as chairman of the floundering Civil War Centennial Commission and turned that observance into a memorable nationwide commemoration. Nevins's record of activity raised questions about the ability of one individual to achieve as much as he had. Some historians believed that he must have a corps of researchers and writers who in assembly-line fashion turned out the material that bore his name. The students and colleagues who were familiar with his work habits, however, never doubted the authenticity of his authorship.

In addition to his two Pulitzer prizes, Nevins received in 1947 the Scribner's Centenary Prize and the Bancroft Prize in history for the first two volumes of his Civil War history; and received Gold Medals for history from the National Institute of Arts and Letters in 1957 and from the New York Historical Society in 1958. He was given the Alexander Hamilton Award from Columbia University in 1968 and received honorary degrees from twenty-seven colleges and universities. He also held two appointments as Harmsworth Professor of History at Oxford (1940–1941; 1964–1965), and visiting professorships at the California Institute of Technology (1937–1938) and Hebrew University in Jerusalem (1952).

In spite of the international recognition that he received as a historian, Nevins always felt somewhat alienated from his profession. He once said, "I never received a Ph.D. degree in history, and I don't write articles for the professional journals. I doubt very much that I could get a tenure-track position at any university in America if I were now seeking one." Throughout his career he was generally in opposition to the mainstream of historical scholarship and remained faithful to his concept of history as being narrative in form and literary in style—an art, not a science. At a time when many of his fellow historians were insisting that only great, irresistible and impersonal forces, not individual pilots, determined the course of history, he continued to be a critic of all ideologues, be they Marxists or theologues, who used deductive reasoning to prove a preconceived thesis. In time, he became more tolerant of those who used soci-

ological methodology and quantifiable data. He even urged his students to take advantage of whatever insights could be gained from sociologists, economists, and psychologists to make the past more understandable, but, for Nevins, history could never be a part of what he regarded as an oxymoron—the so-called "social sciences."

During the 1940s, when those who called themselves consensus historians dominated the profession, Nevins felt more in tune with the prevailing current of historical interpretation. Although he had always believed the history of the United States to be a history of commonly shared ideals and objectives, no matter how diverse the population, Nevins undertook as his magnum opus a study of the American Civil War, the period in which conflict most dramatically and bloodily prevailed over consensus. This study preoccupied him for the remainder of his life.

Having reached the mandatory age for retirement at Columbia in 1958, Nevins was appointed senior research associate at the Huntington Library in San Marino, California. Obliged to leave the city and the university that had been the centers of his adult life, Nevins sold his home in Bronxville and moved with his wife to San Marino. Relinquishing only his teaching duties, he continued his work on the Civil War and completed his three-volume history, *Ford: The Times, the Man, the Company* (1963).

With this work, which amplified the same theme of consensus expressed in his earlier biographical studies of Abram S. Hewitt (1935), Peter Cooper (1935), and John D. Rockefeller (1953), Nevins found himself out of step with the prevailing sentiment of his profession. The brief era of consensus history had ended with McCarthyism in the 1950s and the rise of the civil rights movement in the early 1960s. American history was once again being presented as a continuing epic of conflict between labor and capital, between blacks and whites, between plutocracy and democracy. Nevins had scorned the economic determinists who accepted Charles Beard as their master in the 1920s, and the debunkers, like Matthew Josephson and W. E. Woodward, who shot down American hero worship in the 1930s. Now, a generation later, he had no patience with his young colleagues who denied that there had ever been a consensus in America as to either ideals or goals. Nevins's last two biographies, *Herbert Lehman and His Era* (1963), and *James Truslow Adams: Historian of the American Dream* (1968), reinforced his consensus theme. Attacking the validity of the robber baron thesis, he argued that the great entrepreneurs—Rockefeller, Carnegie, and Ford—were "industrial statesmen," and that the industrial revolution that they had fostered in the United States "came none too soon and none too fast." He encouraged his fellow historians to give the industrial era "an interpretation of exalted character" because these builders had given America the tools for "winning the First World War, the Second World War, and the ensuing struggle against Communist tyranny" ("New Lamps for Old in History," repr. in Billington, pp. 56–67). Such an interpretation was not likely to be adopted in the 1960s, a decade beset with conflicts over race relations, the Vietnam War, and the "imperial presidency."

In June 1967 Nevins suffered a major stroke, which affected his sight and made reading and typing difficult. During the ensuing months, only what close associate Mort Lewis called "Nevins's triumph of will," enabled him to pursue the completion of the last two volumes of *Ordeal of the Union*. A remarkable recovery enabled him to teach a short graduate seminar at Claremont College in the spring of 1969, but a second stroke in June 1970 necessitated his being moved to a nursing home in Menlo Park, California, where he died nine months later.

• Nevins's papers are in the Columbia University Library. He never wrote an autobiography but did supply a taped interview to the Columbia Oral History Research archives. No full-length biography of him has been published, but short biographical articles include Donald F. Tingley, "Allan Nevins: A Reminiscence," *Journal of the Illinois State Historical Society* 66 (1973): 177–86; Mort R. Lewis, "Allan Nevins' Triumph of Will," *American History Illustrated* 11 (1977): 26–33, which deals with the last years of Nevins's life; and Henry Steele Commager, "Allan Nevins," *American Historical Review* 77 (1972): 869–70. *Allan Nevins on History*, compiled and introduced by Ray Allen Billington (1975), is a valuable collection of articles and speeches by Nevins, many hitherto unpublished, that give his views on the purpose and methodology of history as a discipline. Billington's prefatory essay is an affectionate appraisal of Nevins as journalist, teacher, and scholar. C. Vann Woodward's review of Billington's book in *Reviews in American History* 4 (1976): 25–26, gives a less laudatory evaluation of Nevins as a historian. *Essays in American Historiography*, ed. Donald Sheehan and Harold C. Syrett (1960), contains papers presented by former students at the time of Nevins's retirement from Columbia. On the establishment and development of the Columbia Oral History Research Office, see Forrest Pogue, "Louis Starr: A Remembrance," *Oral History Review* (1980): 93–97, and Michael D. Gibson, "A Methodological Overview of Oral History," *Annals of Iowa* 44 (1979): 639–57. An excellent obituary is in the *New York Times*, 6 Mar. 1971.

JOSEPH FRAZIER WALL

NEVIUS, John Livingstone (4 Mar. 1829–19 Oct. 1893), missionary to China, was born in Ovid, New York, the son of Benjamin Hageman Nevius, a farmer, and Mary Denton. He attended Ovid Academy and then Union College, graduating in 1848. After college, he taught school in Georgia for a year before entering Princeton Theological Seminary. About 1850 he decided on a career as a missionary, and by the time of his graduation in 1853 he received appointment from the Presbyterian Board to go to China. A month after he was ordained by the Presbytery of New Brunswick in May 1853, he married Helen Sanford Coan. In September they sailed for China; they disembarked at Ningpo.

Nevius spent the first few years in China preaching at a church in Ningpo and doing evangelistic work in San-Poh. In 1857 his wife returned to the United States because of ill health, but she later rejoined him. They pioneered a mission station in Hangchow in 1859; political unrest, however, forced them out. After spending some months in Japan, they returned to China, relocating to Tengchow, Shantung. There, Nevius aided fellow missionaries Calvin Mateer and Hunter Corbett in the establishment of the first American Presbyterian Mission for that province.

Nevius spent his years in Shantung involved in various projects. In 1862 he translated Acts and the Gospel of Mark for the Delegates Version of the Bible. He also produced many other written works in both Chinese and English, including *China and the Chinese* (1869), which was meant to better acquaint the West with "our next neighbor." In the preface to this book, Nevius wrote that American "ignorance of other countries is truly remarkable" and that even "educated men in the United States" had trouble believing that the Chinese were capable of "intellectual and moral perceptions" and could become "true and reliable Christians." Not only did he believe they could become true Christians; he saw missionaries as temporary workers and thought that the indigenous Christians should assume responsibility for their churches as soon as possible. Accordingly, he opposed the establishment of schools and hospitals that required the continuing presence of Westerners as teachers and doctors. Known as the "Nevius Method," these ideas became a part of the preparation for missionary candidates.

A strong believer in Christian unity, Nevius, along with Mateer, developed the idea for an all-China Christian conference. The realization of this concept, however, was years in the making as denominational and regional jealousies interfered with a joint Protestant effort. However, because the Chefoo-Tengchow area was a popular spot for missionaries in the summer months, Nevius and Mateer, the resident hosts, were in a strategic position to push their idea. Talks first took place on a casual basis in the late 1860s, but by the mid-1870s support grew. Nevius, known as a mobilizer, led things the first year, but by 1875 Mateer headed the effort. Finally, in May 1877 the first General Conference of Protestant Missionaries was held at Shanghai; it marked "an organizational milestone in the China missions story" (Hyatt, p. 175).

Nevius worked in Shantung for more than thirty years. He thrived on itinerating in the countryside, engaging in such evangelistic work throughout his career. His thoughts on the role of missionaries in China were progressive for his time, and his faith in the converted indigenous people to control their own churches, schools, and hospitals was unconditional. Nevius died suddenly at Chefoo, apparently of a heart attack after a brief illness. A paper he had prepared, "The Attitude of the Native Church to the Government," was read at the Shantung Missionary Conference held six weeks after his death.

• Nevius's papers and diaries disappeared after his wife, Helen C. Nevius, used them to write *The Life of John Nevius* (1895), which remains the standard biography. In addition to *China and the Chinese* (1869), Nevius wrote *The Truth Manifested* (n.d.) and *Methods and Mission Work* (1886), and coauthored the *Nevius-Mateer Hymnal* (1877); his *Demon Possession and Allied Themes* was published posthumously in 1894. See also Irwin Hyatt, *Our Ordered Lives Confess* (1976); H. P. Beach, *Princely Men in the Heavenly Kingdom* (1903); and C. A. Clark, *The Korean Church and the Nevius Method*. Articles of interest include F. F. Ellinwood, "Rev. John L. Nevius, D.D.," *Church at Home and Abroad*, Feb. 1894, and Gilbert Reid, "The Rev. John L. Nevius, D.D.," *Missionary Review of the World*, May 1894.

THE EDITORS

NEW, Harry Stewart (31 Dec. 1858–9 May 1937), U.S. senator and postmaster general, was born in Indianapolis, Indiana, the son of John C. New, a banker and newspaper publisher, and Melissa Beeler. He grew up amid Gilded Age Indiana's Republican politics: his father was financial assistant to the state's wartime governor, Oliver P. Morton, treasurer of the United States under President Ulysses S. Grant and assistant treasurer under President Chester A. Arthur, and director of Benjamin Harrison's 1888 presidential campaign.

Harry New's youth was spent in Indianapolis, where his lifelong friend Booth Tarkington would set the "Penrod" stories. He attended public school but in 1873 at age fifteen began three years of travel in Europe, often on his own, with letters of introduction from the then Senator Morton. Thereafter he attended Butler University in Indianapolis for a year. He began work in 1878 as police reporter on the Indianapolis *Journal*, which his father purchased in 1880, and from the outset he benefited from his father's prominence. The *Journal* experience seems to have been pleasant. In later years, he loved to recall "the busiest and most exciting four hours in my twenty five years as a news gatherer," the Sunday night he unmasked a plot to disguise the imminent failure of an Indianapolis bank. Soon he was into politics, where he assisted his father in the Harrison campaign and may have done more than that: Harrison narrowly carried pivotal Indiana, and on election day Harry was arrested for interfering with precinct marshals. After Harrison's victory New's father became consul-general in London, and during part of this assignment the son accompanied him.

By the mid-1890s Harry S. New was a man with a future, "an American of affairs . . . and one knew at once that he would make a rattling fight to arrive where he was going," so Tarkington described a newspaperman character based on his friend in *The Gentleman from Indiana* (1899). New inevitably was elected to office, first serving as a state senator (1896–1900). During the Spanish-American War he was a captain of volunteers but saw no combat. Afterward he became a national Republican committeeman, from 1900 to 1912. In 1907–1908 he served as national party chairman for William H. Taft, and in 1912 he directed Taft's Indiana campaign.

In 1916 New ran for the U.S. Senate and won Indiana's first primary and then direct election under the Seventeenth Amendment. Tarkington endorsed him as from "the old Hoosier stock that stood for cool level-headedness, for common sense and kindness . . . and when he acts something happens." New was appointed to the committee on military affairs, with responsibility for aviation; a month later, April 1917, the country was at war. When British and Italian aviators came to Washington, New became the first congressman to fly, taking off from the Potomac Park polo field. His subcommittee reviewed the lack of aviation preparedness, and he coauthored its report.

As a senator New did not stand out. Other senators, including California's progressive Hiram Johnson, thought him "pleasant" but one of the "dark-age politicians," a member of the Republican old guard. The major issue he faced was the Treaty of Versailles, including President Woodrow Wilson's plan for the League of Nations. New and his poker friend Senator Warren G. Harding of Ohio were "strong reservationists" rather than "irreconcilables"; they particularly opposed Article X's implication that American troops might come under League control. As a member of the committee on foreign relations, New joined Henry Cabot Lodge of Massachusetts to demand revisions that President Wilson could not accept rather than counseling rejection outright.

New did not play a role in the 1920 Republican convention, despite his friendship with Harding. He was not present in George Harvey's "smoke-filled room," and he supported General Leonard Wood until the ninth ballot, when several states broke the impasse between Wood and Frank Lowden. New then switched to Harding, who won on the tenth ballot. During the campaign Harding and party chairman Will H. Hays, also from Indiana, prevailed upon New to direct the campaign speakers' bureau in Chicago. In the 1922 Republican primary, he and his opponent, former senator Albert J. Beveridge, publicly agreed on the issues, leaving the latter to allege that New was spending lavishly on the campaign. New was innovative in using radio to address voters in Indianapolis from Washington. The contest came down to the personalities of the stalwart incumbent and the former Bull Moose challenger. Beveridge's victory was nationally interpreted as a repudiation of President Harding, as was Beveridge's loss to Democrat Samuel Ralston in the fall election.

When New's term expired in 1923, Harding appointed him postmaster general, an office he held through the subsequent administration of Calvin Coolidge. He admitted to the newspapers that the appointment was based on friendship with Harding and his own political reputation. In 1927 his political instincts led him to tell Coolidge that the federal government should bring the famed aviator Charles A. Lindbergh directly to Washington from Europe for a national welcome. When Lindbergh stepped ashore at the Washington Navy Yard from the cruiser *Memphis*, the postmaster general greeted him and escorted him through the cheering crowds along Pennsylvania Avenue. As postmaster general New developed government-owned fleets of delivery vehicles in many cities.

He believed his greatest accomplishment was establishing the air-mail service as a government-supported demonstration of aviation's commercial potential as well as its military necessity. He encouraged construction of lighted airports, all-hour operations, and emergency landing fields. In 1923 he organized daily full air-mail service from New York to San Francisco in twenty-eight hours, and by 1929 the post office had contracted for air routes between major cities and to Latin America.

President Herbert Hoover in 1932 appointed New to his last public position, U.S. commissioner for the forthcoming Century of Progress Exposition in Chicago; in the depression's deepest summer his annual salary was $10,000. During the campaign he made radio speeches critical of the Democratic candidate, Franklin D. Roosevelt. Just prior to the election, Hoover quietly enlisted New to persuade former President Coolidge to make a major political address, which the candidate thought would turn the tide. New secretly traveled to Vermont, but Coolidge's poor health did not allow him to make the speech.

In 1880 New had married Kathleen Milligan, who died in 1883; from this union was born one child, dead in infancy. An illegitimate son, Harry S. New, Jr., was born in Indianapolis in 1887, and New virtually admitted paternity when, in 1919, the son was arrested in California for murder. The senator acknowledged that he knew the boy's mother when he was unmarried and that there were circumstances "which I did not care to dispute which resulted in my doing everything in my power to make amends then and later." The matter did not surface during the 1922 primary contest. New married Catherine M. Brown in 1891; his second marriage was childless. The former senator and postmaster general spent his last years at his estate, "Hemlock Hedge," in Bethesda, Maryland. He died in Baltimore and was buried in Indianapolis.

His Senate colleague Hiram Johnson aptly summarized New's political career: "New of Indiana, is the type of Indiana politician, pleasant and affable, whose mind is ever dealing, with . . . negotiations, and manipulations." The Indianan's life was not touched by financial scandal, that bane of Gilded Age politics, probably because his father had made financial striving unnecessary. As for political and administrative accomplishments, they appear to have been minor, as behooved an exemplar of the conservatism of his time.

• Harry New's papers (Indiana State Library) contain few letters. Useful articles are Howard F. McMains, "Booth Tarkington and the League of Nations, Advice for Senator Harry S. New," *Indiana Magazine of History* 84 (1988): 343–52, "The Guest of the Nation, Charles Lindbergh's Return to the United States in 1927," *New York History* 66 (1985): 263–80, and "Harry New's Secret Visit to Calvin Coolidge: A 1932 Election Memoir," *Vermont History* 53 (1985): 221–30. For Hiram Johnson's comments, see *The Diary Letters of Hiram Johnson*, ed. Robert E. Burke (7 vols., 1983). Obituaries are in the *New York Times* and the *Indianapolis Star*, both 10 May 1937.

HOWARD F. MCMAINS

NEWBERRY, John Strong (22 Dec. 1822–7 Dec. 1892), geologist and paleontologist, was born in Windsor, Connecticut, the son of Henry Newberry, an entrepreneur, and Elizabeth Strong. In 1824 the Newberrys moved to inherited property south of Cleveland in the Western Reserve. In Ohio, Henry Newberry built mills, opened quarries, and developed some of the state's initial coal mines, whose well-preserved plants of Pennsylvanian age fascinated his son John. While growing up in Cuyahoga Falls, John Newberry collected widely in natural history and compiled a list of Ohio's flora. In 1841 Newberry guided James Hall, then one of New York's state geologists, to local mines and outcrops. Hall encouraged Newberry's interests in geology and paleontology, as did Samuel St. John, professor of natural history at the Western Reserve College, from which Newberry graduated in 1846. Newberry then followed the route of physician to professional work in natural history. In 1848 he graduated from the Cleveland Medical School, whose faculty included St. John and physician-naturalist Jared Kirtland, and married Sarah Brownell Gaylord; they had seven children. The Newberrys traveled to Paris, where John continued his medical training and studied with Adolphe Brongniart and other members of the Jardin des Plantes, and they visited noted fossil sites in Europe. Newberry returned to the United States in 1851, the year he published in Kirtland's *Family Visitor* a study of the Eocene quarries and fish on Italy's Monte Bolca, became a member of the American Association for the Advancement of Science, and began to practice medicine. He and Kirtland trained Ferdinand Hayden, before sending Hayden on to employment with Hall, and aided immigrant paleobotanist Leo Lesquereux.

In 1855 Newberry exchanged his private practice for a government appointment. During the next five years, he served as a surgeon-naturalist with three of the many reconnaissances for railroad, riverine, and wagon-road routes in the Southwest sponsored by the U.S. Army Corps of Topographic Engineers (CTE) as part of its responsibilities since 1838 for determining transportation lines and assessing natural resources in the trans-Mississippi region. During the intervals between these expeditions, Newberry worked up his collections at the Smithsonian Institution in Washington, D.C. There he compared his specimens to those returned by Hayden and other geologists from CTE reconnaissances in the Great Plains, northern Rocky Mountains, and the Pacific Northwest, and prepared three major reports for publication. In 1856–1857 Newberry also served as professor of chemistry and natural history at the Columbian College (later George Washington University). In these reports (the last of which did not appear until 1876) and separate articles, Newberry established initial stratigraphic sections for the Colorado Plateau and the Grand Canyon, promoted for the latter an origin by fluvial erosion, linked his stratigraphic work to the results of the equally pioneering efforts further north by Hayden and Fielding Meek, championed the Cretaceous age of lignitic floras on both sides of the Cretaceous-Tertiary boundary (Lesquereux thought them all of Tertiary age), and suggested the Rocky Mountains had been elevated between Cretaceous and Miocene times.

After 1865 Newberry extended his studies to include the Paleozoic rocks of the Mississippi Valley. In 1874 he proposed, as had Amos Eaton, Hall, Sterry Hunt, and Andrew Ramsay before him, that sequences of similar sedimentary strata represented "circles of deposition" produced by cycles of marine transgression, deposition, and withdrawal. A year later Grove Karl Gilbert, whom Newberry had helped to train as a geologist, advanced his mentor's work by applying formal names to a more detailed Grand Canyon stratigraphy and by providing a greater understanding of the geologic structure and history of the Colorado Plateau and Basin-Range provinces.

Newberry left science in June 1861 to help the Union armies in the Civil War. He joined the U.S. Sanitary Commission, a religious-military organization approved by President Abraham Lincoln and patterned after the reform agency established in Great Britain during the Crimean War. As secretary of the commission's Western Department, Newberry directed, principally from Louisville, its benevolent work for Union wounded and sick throughout the Mississippi Valley. After the war he returned to work at the Smithsonian.

During the late 1860s Newberry began a dual career as a university teacher and a government scientist, twice drawing full salaries from both sources. In 1866 he accepted the newly created professorship of geology and paleontology at Columbia University's School of Mines, which he had helped to found two years earlier, and joined the Century Club. In 1869 Ohio governor Rutherford B. Hayes chose Newberry to lead the state's revived geological survey. In New York and Ohio, Newberry helped to train two of his sons, as well as Arthur Hollick, James Kemp, and others as scientists and engineers. Meek and Edward Orton, Sr., served as officers of the Ohio survey; Edward Cope, Gilbert, Hall, O. C. Marsh, John Stevenson, and other geologists and paleontologists were among its collaborators. In 1870 Newberry's survey published a preliminary, thirteen-color geologic map of Ohio, at a scale of eighteen miles to the inch (1:1,104,480) but failed to issue promptly the promised assessment of the state's mineral resources. Ohio's legislators, also influenced by the growing economic depression and external critiques of the survey, ended funding in 1874. Newberry continued to publish final reports, partly at his own expense. By 1882, when Orton succeeded Newberry, the Ohio survey had issued six such volumes—three on geology, two on paleontology, and one on zoology—and a thirteen-color, six-sheet geological map of the state at four miles to the inch (1:253,440). Between 1884 and 1888 Orton published the reports on the state's coals, coke, petroleum, natural gas, iron ore, and clays.

In the 1870s Newberry also completed vital paleontological and stratigraphical studies for the federal geological and geographical surveys of the territories led by Hayden and by John Powell, as well as for Amos Worthen's Geological Survey of Illinois. Newberry's disputes with Hayden and Lesquereux, now Hayden's paleobotanist, over practice, results, and publication, particularly about the ages of the paleofloras involved in dating the "Laramie Formation" rocks astride the Cretaceous-Tertiary boundary, caused permanent estrangement. As a charter member of the National Academy of Sciences, Newberry served on the academy's committee (chaired by Marsh) that Congress requested in 1878 to plan for increased economy, efficiency, harmony, and utility in mapping and assessing the lands and resources of the public domain. When U.S. president Rutherford Hayes asked Newberry in 1879 to recommend a leader for the newly created U.S. Geological Survey, Newberry strongly backed Clarence King, who contributed directly to the politico-scientific reforms, rather than Hayden, who opposed them. Powell, King's successor as USGS director, made Newberry a part-time employee in 1884 to prepare reports in stratigraphic paleontology as part of Powell's expanded program in general geology. In subsequent years Newberry agreed with his USGS colleague Lester Ward that some of the disputed Cretaceous-Tertiary floras in the West were of Tertiary age. Newberry's four USGS monographs—on North America's Paleozoic and Triassic fish and its Mesozoic-Cenozoic floras—appeared between 1888 and 1898, the last two volumes posthumously under Hollick's editorship.

Before Newberry suffered a stroke in December 1890, his continued efforts for and awards from varied scientific and social groups reflected his wide-ranging interests and expertise. He helped to reinvigorate the Lyceum of Natural History (later the New York Academy of Sciences) and served as its president from 1868, a year after he led the AAAS, until his death. Experience gained before and during the 1876 Centennial Exposition led Newberry to gather statistics on quarries and building stone for the Tenth Decennial Census of 1880. He led the Torrey Botanical Club from 1880 to 1890. The Geological Society of London elected Newberry a foreign member in 1883 and awarded him its Murchison Medal five years later. In 1888 Newberry helped to found the Geological Society of America and acted as its vice president. He chaired the Committee of Organization for the Fifth International Geological Congress, planned for Washington, D.C., in 1891, but his declining health prevented active service as the meeting's president. He died in New Haven, Connecticut.

More than 200 volumes and articles by Newberry record his interest in a wide range of topics in natural history; his USGS colleague Charles White believed that "few men have worked in so many different fields or worked so well in them" (White, p. 14). More than 80 percent of Newberry's publications, however, treat topics in the general and economic geology, paleobotany, and vertebrate paleontology of North America. He is best known for his contributions to the knowledge of Paleozoic and Mesozoic fish, Mesozoic and Cenozoic floras, and the geology of the American Southwest. Cope and Ward agreed that Newberry was a better paleontologist than a neontologist and more interested in stratigraphic applications than systematics (Fairchild, pp. 162–64). Some thirty taxa are named for him, and and the Newberry Professorship of Geology in Columbia's Department of Geological Sciences honors his contributions to science through education and research.

• Record Groups 57 (Geological Survey) and 77 (Corps of Engineers) at the National Archives and Records Administration contain documents relating to Newberry's work for the federal government. Other manuscript materials are held by the Butler and Low Libraries at Columbia University, the New York Academy of Sciences, the New York Botanical Garden, and the Ohio Historical Society. *U.S. Geological Survey Bulletin* 746 (1923): 775–80 lists Newberry's principal publications in the earth sciences; these data also are available on CD-ROM as part of the American Geological Institute's "GeoRef" online bibliographical database. Newberry recorded his Civil War stewardship in *The U.S. Sanitary Commission in the Valley of the Mississippi, during the War of the Rebellion, 1861–1866* (1871); also see Charles J. Stillé, *History of the United States Sanitary Commission* (1866), and George W. Adams, *Doctors in Blue: The Medical History of the Union Army in the Civil War* (1952).

Among the major memorials by Newberry's contemporaries are those by Herman L. Fairchild in *New York Academy of Sciences Transactions* 12 (1893): 152–86; John J. Stevenson in *American Geologist* 12 (1893): 1–25; and Charles A. White in National Academy of Sciences, *Biographical Memoirs* 6 (1909): 1–24. William H. Goetzmann, *Army Exploration in the American West 1803–1863* (1959); Goetzmann, *Exploration and Empire: The Explorer and the Scientist in the Winning of the American West* (1966); and Mary C. Rabbitt, *Minerals, Lands, and Geology for the Common Defense and General Welfare*, vol. 1: *Before 1879* and vol. 2: *1879–1904* (1979, 1980), place Newberry's work in the context of federally sponsored geology; also see Frank N. Schubert, *Vanguard of Expansion: Army Engineers in the Trans-Mississippi West 1819–1879* (1980). Michael C. Hansen and Horace R. Collins evaluate the Newberry-Orton survey in the *Ohio Journal of Science* 79 (1979): 3–14.

RENÉE M. JAUSSAUD
CLIFFORD M. NELSON

NEWBERRY, Truman Handy (5 Nov. 1864–3 Oct. 1945), businessman and senator, was born in Detroit, Michigan, the son of John Stoughton Newberry, a lawyer, congressman, and manufacturer who founded the Michigan Car Company, and Helen Parmelee Handy. Newberry attended Michigan Military Academy in Orchard Lake, Charlier Institute in New York City, and Reed's School in Lakeville, Connecticut. He graduated with a Ph.B. from the Sheffield Scientific School at Yale College in 1885. Newberry began his business career as a staff member of the Detroit, Bay City, and Alpena Railroad, of which he became superintendent of construction. After his father's death in 1887, Newberry assumed total control of the family's business enterprises, including the presidency of the Detroit Steel and Spring Company. He also engaged

in various other manufacturing activities. In 1888 he married Harriet Josephine Barnes, with whom he had a daughter and twin sons.

Having carefully managed the fortune he inherited, Newberry became a multimillionaire and one of the leaders of established Michigan society in Detroit and Grosse Pointe. Among his business interests were directorships in the Michigan Bell Telephone Company, Cleveland-Cliffs Iron Company, Parke Davis and Company, Union Guardian Trust Company of Detroit, People's State Bank, and Detroit and Cleveland Navigation Company. The advent of the automobile especially attracted his attention. Along with other Detroit investors, including Henry B. Joy and Russell A. Alger, Newberry provided the capital and impetus in 1903 to move the Packard Motor Car Company from Warren, Ohio, to Detroit, thereby making Detroit the center of the nation's automotive industry. Approximately 200 cars were manufactured in 1904 in this successful venture.

Newberry had a varied career in business and politics. In 1893 he assisted in organizing the Michigan State Naval Brigade. A navy lieutenant stationed on the cruiser *Yosemite*, he saw action off the Cuban coast in the Spanish-American War of 1898. Newberry was colonel and aide-de-camp to Michigan governor Hazen S. Pingree in 1899. After serving as assistant secretary of the navy from 1905 to 1908 under President Theodore Roosevelt, Newberry was promoted to secretary of the navy in December 1908, serving until the end of Roosevelt's presidency in March 1909. In this role he sought to overhaul and improve the administrative machinery of the navy and in the process became identified with the Progressive movement. During World War I he was a lieutenant commander in the U.S. Naval Fleet Reserve and assistant to the commandant of New York City's Third Naval District until 1919.

A member of Michigan's orthodox Republican society, Newberry, in a spirited primary contest in 1918, successfully challenged former governor Chase S. Osborn, William G. Simpson, and Henry Ford for the Republican senatorial nomination. Michigan's open primary law enabled Ford, a nominal Republican, to run in both party primaries. Ford won without opposition the Democratic nomination for U.S. senator, commanding the support of President Woodrow Wilson. Newberry's friends, who condemned Ford for his pacifism, poured over $200,000 into the campaign, far exceeding the $3,750 maximum amount allowed under Michigan law for senatorial contributions and expenditures. Newberry, ensconced at his naval post in New York, denied knowledge of his committee's financial activities. In the November election, Newberry, backed by former presidents Theodore Roosevelt and William Howard Taft, narrowly defeated Ford by a vote of 220,054 to 212,487 in a state normally classified as Republican. The widespread assumption was that Newberry had bought his victory, and an incensed Ford challenged the outcome. In 1920, after a seven-week trial, Newberry was convicted of violating the Federal Corrupt Practices Act, fined $10,000, and sentenced to two years in prison. Court appeals kept him out of jail until the U.S. Supreme Court, on 2 May 1921, ruled in a five to four decision that the law under which Newberry had been convicted was unconstitutional, because Congress lacked the power to regulate primary elections.

Although he had nominally served in the upper chamber since 4 March 1919, Newberry formally took his seat in the Senate on 12 January 1922. In 1919 he signed the resolution sponsored by Republican senator Henry Cabot Lodge of Massachusetts opposing the covenant of the League of Nations. In a postwar Senate controlled by Republicans, Newberry should have enjoyed political advantages, but the stigma of his controversial election and trial overshadowed his record and proved detrimental to his career. Senator Atlee Pomerene, an Ohio Democrat, continued the attacks on Newberry, contending, as did many newspaper editorials, that the Senate itself was on trial. Repudiated in his own state by the election of former governor Woodbridge N. Ferris, a Democrat from Big Rapids, and confronted with a majority of the Senate pledged to unseat him, Newberry resigned on 18 November 1922. He chose to save his party further embarrassment and to avoid endangering his supporters in the Senate by stepping aside. Newberry was replaced by James Couzens, a former associate in the Ford Motor Company. After his resignation, Newberry devoted the rest of his life to business matters.

One of Michigan's leading industrialists, Newberry gained national attention for his business acumen. He also earned a good reputation for his performance in the appointive political offices he held, but the 1918 election scandal proved to be insurmountable and resulted in the ruination of his political career. The Newberry affair, however, led to the Corrupt Practices Act of 1925. Moreover, the citizens of a small village in Luce County were willing to overlook political indiscretions and renamed their town, originally called Grant Corner, in honor of the Detroit industrialist. Newberry died at his home in Grosse Point Farms, Michigan.

• The Newberry papers are in the Burton History Collection at the Detroit Public Library. Some of Newberry's letters pertinent to his career are in the papers of George Dewey, Theodore Roosevelt, and William Howard Taft in the Manuscripts Division of the Library of Congress. The papers of Roy D. Chapin, Edwin Denby, and Henry B. Joy in the Michigan Historical Collections at the University of Michigan at Ann Arbor also contain valuable materials relating to Newberry. Two studies of the senatorial campaign and outcome are Alfred E. Lucking, *Ford-Newberry Election Contest* (1921), and Spencer Ervin, *Henry Ford vs. Truman H. Newberry: The Famous Senate Election Contest* (1935; repr. 1974). See also Seward W. Livermore, *Politics Is Adjourned: Woodrow Wilson and the War Congress, 1916–1918* (1966). An obituary is in the *New York Times*, 4 Oct. 1945.

LEONARD SCHLUP

NEWBERRY, Walter Loomis (18 Sept. 1804–6 Nov. 1868), real estate investor, was born in East (now South) Windsor, Connecticut, the son of Amasa Newberry and Ruth Warner, wealthy farmers. When Newberry was less than a year old, the family moved to Oneida County, New York, and he attended school in nearby Clinton. His mother died when he was eleven, but he managed to complete his secondary education. After graduation he received an appointment to West Point but failed the physical and returned home. Newberry went to work for his brother, Oliver, a shipbuilder and merchant in Buffalo, New York. Oliver also owned a dry-goods store in Detroit, where his younger brother went to work in 1830. Two years later voters elected Walter Newberry to the Detroit City Council, but a fire destroyed the store that same year and the brothers moved to Chicago in 1833.

The Newberrys arrived in Chicago when its population was little more than 100; it doubled in size within a year and by 1837 had more than 4,000 residents. Walter began buying and selling property in Wisconsin, northern Michigan, and northern Illinois and became wealthy very quickly. The brothers also invested in railroad development and helped finance construction of the first railroad to enter the city, the Galena & Chicago Union Railroad. This road came in from western Illinois, the site of several rich iron mines. Walter Newberry sat on the board of directors of the Chicago Union and would serve as company president for a brief period just before the Civil War.

Along with William B. Ogden, another wealthy real estate dealer and the first president of the Chicago Union, Newberry organized the Whig party in Illinois and helped Ogden become Chicago's first mayor. In 1842 Newberry married Julia B. Clapp of Oxford, New York, with whom he had six children, three of whom died in infancy. The couple moved into a large home on Chicago's North Side that would burn to the ground during the Great Chicago Fire in 1871. Always active in local affairs, Newberry was president of Chicago's first Young Men's Library Association, a member of the city's board of health, a five-year member of the board of education, and a major financial contributor to St. Paul's Evangelical Church.

Newberry's investments in railroads and real estate made him a millionaire by 1850, when he was selected to serve as a vice president of the Merchant's Loan and Trust Company. North Side voters elected him city comptroller for one term in 1851, and he became acting mayor for a brief time that same year after the elected mayor left town suffering from nervous exhaustion. An antislavery man, Newberry joined the Republican party in 1855 and supported Abraham Lincoln for the Senate in 1858 and for the presidency in 1860. His continued contributions to the city included money donations to the Orphans Benevolent Association and helping to found the Chicago Historical Society in 1857.

Beginning in 1857, Newberry became afflicted with a mysterious illness that no one seemed able to diagnose. Local doctors were unable even to treat him, so he visited Europe for the first time after hearing that a French doctor had discovered a cure. His business and political activities diminished greatly after he became ill. He would return to France every winter for treatment. Perhaps realizing that this illness was threatening his life, Newberry discussed his estate in 1866 with a lawyer who pointed out that Chicago had no free public library. Newberry, who had been involved in several real estate deals with William B. Astor, the son of John Jacob Astor, the financier whose $400,000 bequest helped fund the New York Public Library, decided to contribute one-half of his estate to founding a public library in Chicago.

Newberry died at sea while crossing the Atlantic to visit his doctor in Paris and to join his family in France. His wishes were carried out and eventually $2.1 million and some prime city property were donated by his family to endow the Newberry Library, which soon became one of the world's great research libraries. The railroad he had helped to develop later became part of the Chicago and Northwestern railroad system. Newberry's contributions to philanthropic projects were many and his work for charity and public education helped make Chicago a more humane city.

• Very little information about Newberry is available. The most significant details of his life are in a manuscript written in 1990 by Ralph H. Halvorsen, "The Newberrys," and in the also unpublished George B. Utley, "Walter Loomis Newberry: Pioneer" (1935), both in the Newberry Library. Other scattered papers at the library mostly concern business details. See also Alfred T. Andreas, *History of Chicago* (1886), and Edwin O. Gale, *Reminiscences of Early Chicago* (1902). An obituary is in the *Chicago Tribune*, 20 Nov. 1868.

LESLIE V. TISCHAUSER

NEWBOLD, William Romaine (20 Nov. 1865–26 Sept. 1926), philosopher, was born in Wilmington, Delaware, the son of William Allibone Newbold, an Episcopal clergyman, and Martha Smith Baily. As a youngster Newbold was already attracted to the study of ancient languages. He entered the University of Pennsylvania as a sophomore in 1884; there he organized and taught an informal class in biblical Hebrew. He studied Sanskrit for two years and acquired an excellent knowledge of Greek and Latin. After graduating with a B.A. in 1887, with prizes in Latin and philosophy, he taught Latin for two years at Cheltenham Military Academy, near Philadelphia, while working toward his doctorate in philosophy (awarded 1891) at the University of Pennsylvania. After a period of study in Berlin, Newbold returned to the University of Pennsylvania as instructor in philosophy (1892–1894), assistant professor (1894–1903), professor (1903–1907), and Adam Seybert Professor of Intellectual and Moral Philosophy (1907–1926). He served as dean of the graduate school (1896–1904) and worked to raise the standards for admission to graduate work and to improve the school's administration.

Between 1892 and 1902 Newbold read widely in the psychology of religion and published a series of papers and reviews on subjects such as hypnosis, hallucination, trance, telepathy, and schizophrenia. He became a corresponding member of the Society for Psychical Research (London) and later served as psychology editor (1895–1896) for the *American Naturalist*. He was also a member of the Seybert Commission for the Investigation of Spiritualism, which was established under the will of philanthropist Henry Seybert to investigate claims of psychic phenomena and spiritualism. Subsequently he turned his attention to Greek philosophy, preparing translations of works by Aristotle and Plotinus and publishing a well-received essay on Philolaus (1905). Newbold wrote a book on the Greek theory of sound, but as with his translations he never submitted it for publication. Some years later he became interested in the influence of Greek philosophical thought on Oriental Christianity and published papers on Syriac religious poetry (1911, 1918).

During the First World War Newbold lectured on the political and historical causes of the war to the Reserve Officer Training Corps at the University of Pennsylvania. In 1920 he delivered a series of lectures on Valentinian Gnosticism in Philadelphia for the Bohlen Foundation; however, these were never published. Throughout these years Newbold acquired such expert knowledge of early Christian theology that he was offered but declined a chair in ecclesiastical history at the Episcopal Theological Seminary in New York, an unusual honor for a layman. His last major religious inquiry was a study of the symbolism of the chalice of Antioch (1925), believed by some to have been the cup used at the Last Supper.

Newbold was interested in puzzles, codes, and cryptography and is said to have done some cryptographic work for the U.S. government before World War I. This led him to the last major undertakings of his mature years, on which his reputation rested even during his lifetime. The first was his attempt to decipher five inscriptions from Rome and Pompeii, for which no convincing interpretation had then yet been offered. Newbold claimed in 1926 that they were Aramaic, written in Latin and Greek characters. Although he argued his ingenious proposal with erudition, his work was philologically ill-founded, sometimes mixing features of more than one dialect of the language in one reconstructed sentence. The resulting translations were improbable, even bizarre. For example, Newbold rendered one graffito "A strange mind has driven A. and he has pressed in among the Christians who make a man a prisoner as a laughing-stock." This he took to refer to a "disturbance of mind imposed by magic from without." None of his Aramaic "decipherments" was plausible.

Newbold's last undertaking was an attempt to decipher a manuscript in the possession of Wilfrid Voynich, a bookseller. Written in what appeared to be cipher, it contained a seventeenth-century inscription noting that a previous owner believed it might have been written by the thirteenth-century English philosopher Roger Bacon. This manuscript received considerable publicity in its time (*Illustrated London News*,

20 May 1920; John M. Manly, "The Most Mysterious Manuscript in the World," *Harper's*, July 1921). Newbold assumed that it was written by Bacon during a period of imprisonment with the deliberate intention of deceiving a reader into thinking words or symbols might mean one thing when they actually meant something else. He conjectured that the purpose was to guard esoteric knowledge that set Bacon apart from all other scholars of his time. Newbold also assumed that Bacon had access to optical aids, unknown in the thirteenth century, such that the letters of the manuscript when examined microscopically were "really perfect nests of tiny characters," Newbold said. When these microscopic characters were arranged in sequence, they still did not spell anything, so Newbold devoted years of labor to rearranging them in sequences, assigning the letters secondary values, and then trying to read any resulting text. At a public demonstration of his decipherment offered at the University of Pennsylvania in 1921, a chemist produced copper using a formula Newbold had derived from his decipherment.

Newbold's research was left unfinished at the time of his death in Philadelphia, but his partial decipherment of the Voynich manuscript was published posthumously as *The Cipher of Roger Bacon* (1928). George Sarton, the historian of science, wrote of this work, "When a man is as utterly devoid of critical sense as Newbold proved himself to be, there is no limit to the eccentricities which his mind may conceive. I do not doubt a moment his honesty, but he was undoubtedly, to put it as gently as possible, a self-deceived enthusiast" (*Isis* 11 [1928]: 144). Later scholarship on Bacon did not include the Voynich manuscript among his works and took no account of Newbold's book. Newbold's efforts were a curious modern reversion to the legend of Bacon's miraculous powers, which found wide currency in scholastic circles in Europe after his death (Sarton, *Introduction to the History of Science*, vol. 2, pt. 2, p. 967).

In 1896 Newbold had married Ethel Sprague Kent Packard of Boston. They had no children. Newbold was a short, slight man of studious habits and intense spirituality. Despite his recondite interests, he was warm and approachable and a gifted teacher with a wide circle of admiring students and colleagues. He had the ability to communicate his interests and enthusiasms to others and to convince them of their value. His remarkable research capacity led him in many directions, while his linguistic abilities and scholarly attainments earned him a reputation for brilliance among his contemporaries, although they often expressed regret that he published so little in his primary field of expertise, ancient philosophy. In private life he carried out extensive genealogical research and was a competent sailor.

Newbold was a member of the American Oriental Society, American Psychological Association, American Philosophical Association, American Philosophical Society, American Society for Psychical Research, Society for Biblical Literature, British Society of Franciscan Studies, Oriental Club of Philadelphia, and Phi Beta Kappa.

• Newbold's scholarly papers and correspondence are in the archives of the University of Pennsylvania, Philadelphia. Some family papers of genealogical interest are in the manuscripts department of the Bryn Mawr College Library, Bryn Mawr, Pa. A bibliography of Newbold's writings was published in Roland G. Kent, ed., *Newbold Memorial Meeting* (1927), together with a biographical sketch; a portion of this publication also appeared in the University of Pennsylvania, *General Magazine and Historical Chronicle* (Jan. 1927): 185–203. Personal and family data are in F. A. Virkus, *The Abridged Compendium of American Genealogy*, vol. 1 (1925), p. 946. Assessment of Newbold's work in Aramaic is based on a private communication (1994) of Franz Rosenthal, Sterling Professor Emeritus, Yale University. A more sympathetic appraisal of Newbold's decipherment of the Voynich manuscript is Raoul Carter, "Le Chiffre de Roger Bacon," *Revue d'histoire de la philosophie* 3 (1929): 31–66, 165–79. Obituaries and appreciations are in the *American Journal of Archaeology* 31 (1927): 101; the *Journal of the American Oriental Society* 47 (1927): 345; and the *Philadelphia Public Ledger*, 27 Sept. 1926.

BENJAMIN R. FOSTER

NEWBORN, Phineas, Jr. (14 Dec. 1931–26 May 1989), jazz pianist, was born in Whiteville, Tennessee, the son of Phineas Newborn, Sr., a drummer, and Rosie Lee Murphy. While the senior Newborn led a band at the Flamingo Club on Beale Street in Memphis, the six-year-old Newborn, Jr., commenced jazz and classical studies with Georgia Woodruff, his first-grade teacher. He later studied arranging with Onzie Horne.

Newborn learned to play trumpet, baritone horn, French horn, and tuba in high school, but he began his professional career in 1945 as a pianist. Prodigiously gifted, he was inspired by the great jazz pianists of the 1930s, above all the virtuoso Art Tatum. Yet he also spent years accompanying rhythm and blues and urban blues musicians, with whom he toured the South during school vacations. Newborn began playing with his father's band by the age of fifteen and was a regular member from 1948 to 1950. He also joined the band of electric guitarist and singer Saunders King in 1947, and he was on electric guitarist and singer B. B. King's first recordings in 1949. These experiences gave his style an earthy lyricism generally lacking in Tatum's work.

After graduating from high school, Newborn taught himself to play vibraphone. While majoring in music at Tennessee Agricultural and Industrial State University in Nashville from 1950 to 1951, he learned to play still more instruments: alto, tenor, and baritone saxophone. He left Tennessee A & I in 1952 when his father refused to let him transfer to Juilliard School in Manhattan. Newborn also studied at Lemoyne College in Memphis from 1952 to 1953. He worked with vibraphonist Lionel Hampton's band in 1950 and 1952, and he was a member of rhythm and blues tenor saxophonist Willis Jackson's band in 1953. Also in the early 1950s he toured with B. B. King and Jackie Brenston and did session work in Memphis.

After serving in the army from 1953 to 1955, Newborn spent ten months as a sideman in his father's group; he also worked with his brother, guitarist Calvin Newborn. Phineas then formed his own quartet, including Calvin. The Willard Alexander Agency convinced them to leave Tennessee and come north, initially to perform in Philadelphia at Pep's nightclub late in 1955. Following the advice of Count Basie, who had heard Phineas play in Memphis in 1952, writers and promoters John Hammond and Leonard Feather went to hear him in Philadelphia and were deeply impressed. Hammond secured jobs for the quartet in New York. With Calvin, fellow Memphis bassist Jamil Nasser (known at that time as George Joyner), and drummer Kenny Clarke, Newborn debuted at the club Basin Street and began recording in the spring of 1956. Oscar Pettiford replaced Joyner for Newborn's first recording session, and several drummers, including Philly Joe Jones, Denzil Best, and Roy Haynes, played with Newborn in his first years of international exposure.

In February 1958 Newborn performed with poet Langston Hughes and bassist Charles Mingus at the Village Vanguard. He then worked with Mingus on the soundtrack of John Cassavetes's film *Shadows*. In 1958 he recorded the albums *Fabulous Phineas* and *We Three*, worked with drummer Roy Haynes at Birdland in New York, toured Europe with a Jazz from Carnegie Hall package in October, and performed with Haynes at the Five Spot club in New York toward year's end. He briefly toured Italy in April 1959.

Hammond and Feather had touted Newborn as the next major jazz sensation, but even while admiring his technical facility, other critics disparaged his musical content as shallow and accused him of overplaying. Touring proved grueling for Newborn, and he suffered personal and health problems. He temporarily stopped performing but reemerged in 1961 in Los Angeles, where he recorded with tenor saxophonist Teddy Edwards and trumpeter Howard McGhee. He also made two outstanding albums of his own, *A World of Piano!* and *The Great Jazz Piano of Phineas Newborn* for Contemporary. In October 1962 Newborn's trio performed on television in the "Jazz Scene" series, but he remained in California, declining the tours that would have followed the success of his albums.

In the late 1950s Newborn married Dorothy Stewart; they had two daughters. The failure of this marriage, which ended in divorce, business problems, the death of his father, and his difficulty in handling responsibility led to a nervous breakdown sometime around 1960. Newborn was intermittently confined to Camarillo State Hospital, while restricting his performances to local clubs in southern California. He made only a few additional recordings, including the albums *The Newborn Touch* (1964) and *Please Send Me Someone to Love* (1969). He later fathered a son with another woman.

Newborn returned to Memphis in 1971 to live with his mother. Further episodes of mental instability plagued him. In 1974 he recorded the album *Solo Piano*. At this time he was mugged and badly beaten; although several of his fingers were broken, he recovered and resumed playing. He recorded *Solo* (1975); *Back Home*, with Ray Brown and Elvin Jones (Sept. 1976); and *Look Out . . . Phineas Is Back!* with Brown and Jimmy Smith (Dec. 1976). A tour of solo concerts began in 1975 at Shrine Auditorium in Los Angeles. That year he also performed at the nightclub Keystone Korner in San Francisco, and he made the first of several Japanese tours, during one of which he recorded *Phineas Is Genius* with a trio in concert (1977). In 1978 he was again in Japan, and he returned to New York for the first time, performing at the Village Gate. In July 1979 Newborn starred at the Montreux Jazz Festival in piano duets with Jay McShann, Hank Jones, and John Lewis, in a piano trio with Herbie Hancock and Chick Corea, and in a trio with bassist Ray Brown and drummer Dannie Richmond. Throughout the 1980s he occasionally made brief annual performances in New York City, usually at the club Sweet Basil. In the 1980s he frequently played in Memphis clubs. Newborn died in Memphis. The cause was not disclosed, but his agent Irvin Salky reported that x-rays had recently revealed a growth on one lung.

Newborn's most personal signature was the perfectly coordinated doubling of swift melodies in the right and left hands, separated by two octaves. He articulated fast bop melodies in a hard, cutting, precise manner, but he also ranged into more lyrical areas of jazz, presenting blues-tinged pop themes, inserting passages of harmonized melody in two-handed block chords and passages of old-fashioned "oom-pah" striding in the left hand, and replacing the general restlessness of bop with a willingness to repeat ideas.

• For a detailed biography of Newborn and his family see Stanley Booth, *Rythm Oil: Journey through the Music of the American South* (1992). Useful interviews and surveys on Newborn are David C. Hunt, "Phineas Newborn, Jr.: Problems of a Virtuoso," *Jazz & Pop* 9 (June 1970): 22–24; Len Lyons, "Phineas Newborn: A Jazz Self Portrait," *Contemporary Keyboard* 2 (May–June 1976): 16, 44; Robert Palmer, "Once and Future Piano Wizard," *New York Times*, 21 Apr. 1978; and Leonard Feather, "Piano Giants of Jazz: Phineas Newborn, Jr.," *Contemporary Keyboard* 5 (Aug. 1979): 62–63. See also Richard Palmer, "Piano in the Background," *Jazz Journal International* 37 (Nov. 1984): 17; and Ken Hodges, "The Forgotten Ones: Phineas Newborn," *Jazz Journal International* 39 (Sept. 1986): 22–23. Obituaries are in the *New York Times*, 28 May and 29 May 1989, and *Jazz Journal International* 42 (July 1989): 23.

BARRY KERNFELD

NEWCOMB, Charles King (16 Feb. 1820–1894), Transcendentalist author, was born in Newport, Rhode Island, the son of Lieutenant Henry S. Newcomb of the American navy and Rhoda Mardenborough. His father died in a shipwreck in 1825, and his mother, who was comfortably well off, moved the family to Providence, where Charles grew up, graduating from Brown University in 1837. Although originally wanting to follow in his father's footsteps in the navy, he decided instead to enter the ministry and so enrolled in the Episcopal seminary in Alexandria, D.C. (now Va.), in September 1837. He returned to Providence in a year after deciding he was not a sectarian.

His mother was an active member of the Providence literary and social world and a friend of many of the New England Transcendentalists, a group of young writers and thinkers centered in Concord and Boston, among them Ralph Waldo Emerson and Margaret Fuller, to whom she introduced her son. But she was a demanding mother who insisted that her children's prime duty in life was to look after her and assure her continued happiness. In May 1841, probably in part at least to escape her domineering, Charles joined the Transcendentalist Brook Farm community established that year by Rev. George Ripley and his friends in West Roxbury, Massachusetts, to encourage literary and artistic efforts. Newcomb was not an active member, but a boarder who joined in the intellectual life of the community but not the labor. Nonetheless, he was popular with all the communitarians, who were both puzzled and amused by his eccentricities, which included maintaining an altar in his bedroom decorated with portraits of Jesus, various Roman Catholic saints, and Fanny Ellsler, the then-popular dancer.

While Newcomb was at Brook Farm he wrote the only work published in his lifetime, "The Two Dolons," which appeared in the July 1842 issue of the Transcendentalist *Dial*. Its main theme seems to be the closeness between children, nature, and the ideal, but it frequently violates the standard rules of grammar and at times is unintelligible. Emerson spoke of it as "native gold," but it was more often the butt of critics. Apparently Newcomb conceived of it as the first in a series, for it appeared in the *Dial* as "The Two Dolons: from the Ms. Symphony of Dolon. The First Dolon"; but no further installments ever appeared, and it is not known if any were ever written.

In 1845 Newcomb abandoned Brook Farm and returned to live with his mother in Providence, devoting his time chiefly to reading, long walks, and occasional visits with his Transcendentalist friends. He started keeping a journal, which eventually filled twenty-seven manuscript volumes. He gave the journal the all-inclusive title "Principles of Life, illustrated in thoughts on Nature, Scholarship, Shakspear, Government, the war of the great American Rebellion, & Morals & Man in general." Among its more interesting passages are his criticisms of Shakespeare and particularly of *Hamlet*. He was more concerned with Shakespeare as a moralist than as a dramatist. He also included 1,015 "Songs of Love," strange, erotic, doggerel poems, only a few of which have ever been published even though they give some remarkable insights not only into Newcomb's personal life, but also into some of the hidden sexual mores of his time. He is the only one of the Transcendentalists known to have created a significant body of erotic literature, a subject about which most of them were exceedingly reticent. The journal also records his great enthusiasm for professional baseball, one of the earliest such accounts.

In 1862 he served for three months in the defense of Washington in the Tenth Rhode Island Volunteer Infantry. After his mother's death in 1865, he abandoned Providence and lived alone in a rooming house in Philadelphia. In 1871 his vast journal came to an end, or at least no later volumes have been found. He moved to London in that year and then later to Paris, where he died. Almost nothing is known of these later years of his life.

When Emerson was at the height of his career, he was constantly discovering what he liked to call "so many promising youths" of whom he expected great literary achievement—men such as Jones Very, Ellery Channing, and Christopher Pearse Cranch—all of whom seemed to fade in their abilities as they grew older. Newcomb was perhaps chief among these. Emerson first hailed him as "my brightest star," but, sadly, as with the others, Newcomb's promise was never fulfilled, and he is remembered primarily as the most disappointing of all those once-bright stars. However, the vastness of his manuscripts leaves open for students of Transcendentalism a great opportunity for further study of the workings of the minds and personalities of its adherents.

• Newcomb's manuscripts, including his journal and his family papers, are in the Brown University Library. The Houghton Library at Harvard University has his letters to the Emerson family and to Caroline Sturgis. *The Journals of Charles King Newcomb*, ed. Judith Kennedy Johnson (1946), which prints roughly a fortieth of the three-million-word manuscript, includes the only extended biographical sketch. The only two critical articles on Newcomb are Richard Lee Francis, "Charles King Newcomb: Transcendental Hamlet," *Emerson Society Quarterly* 57 (1969): 46–51, which is devoted chiefly to his Shakespearean criticism, and Thomas Altherr, "'The Most Summery, Bold, Free & Spacious Game': Charles King Newcomb and Philadelphia Baseball, 1866–1871," *Pennsylvania History* 54 (Apr. 1987): 69–83. Brief biographical sketches may be found in George Willis Cooke, *An Historical and Biographical Introduction to Accompany the Dial* (1902), and in Joel Myerson, *The Transcendentalists* (1984).

WALTER HARDING

NEWCOMB, Harvey (2 Sept. 1803–30 Aug. 1863), editor, clergyman, and children's author, was born in Thetford, Vermont, the son of Simon Newcomb, a farmer and mechanic, and Hannah Curtis. After moving with his family to Alfred, New York, in 1818, he taught school for eight years. In 1826 he became the editor and publisher of the *Westfield Western Star*; in 1828 he moved to Buffalo, New York, and edited the anti-Masonic *Buffalo Patriot* for nearly two years. In 1830 he married Alithea Wells; they had four children.

Moving to Pittsburgh in 1830 to edit the *Christian Herald*, a children's paper, he discovered an aptitude for writing on religious and moral themes for children. He left the *Christian Herald* in 1831 and for the next ten years wrote books for children and youth and contributed to such periodicals as the *Youth's Companion and Sabbath School Reader*. Many of the books were published by the Massachusetts Sabbath School Society for use in Sunday school libraries and classes. His books for children, some of which were published anonymously, may have numbered as many as 100. Most were fairly brief in length, and many were dialogues, often between a mother and her children. Among them were fourteen volumes on the history of the Christian Church, including the *History of the Waldenses* (1835); volumes on the Bible, such as *The Benjamite King: or, The History of Saul* (1839); books excoriating such bad behavior as avarice, lying, and intemperance; books encouraging missions and evangelical conversion, such as *The Wyandot Chief; or, The History of Barnet, a Converted Indian* (1835) and *The Tract Distributor* (1833); and many Sunday school "question books" on different parts of the Bible. *The Sabbath School Teacher's Aid* (1840) was a collection of anecdotes used by Sunday school teachers to supplement their lessons; it emphasized the importance of strictly observing Sunday as the Sabbath. His work, *A Practical Directory for Young Christian Females* (1833), went through at least ten editions.

Newcomb directed other writings to an adult audience. *The Negro Pew* (1837; repr. 1971) was a vehement appeal for the abandonment of racial exclusion and segregation in religious meetings. Newcomb argued that persons should be judged solely on the basis of their moral and intellectual worth, not on their skin color. He thought that the natural capacities of blacks were "in no respect inferior to whites" and that Africans had made important contributions to ancient civilization. He cited later examples of significant achievements by those with black skin, concluding that "there never was a more . . . despicable sentiment than the prevailing prejudice against color." His children's books on the American Indians expressed indignation about the way in which native Americans had been oppressed and deprived of their rights.

Another of Newcomb's books directed at adults was *Newcomb's Manual for Maternal Associations* (1840), in which he encouraged women with children to form associations so that they could more faithfully and effectively fulfill their role as Christian mothers and gave directions for the organization and maintenance of such groups.

In February 1840 Newcomb was licensed to preach by the Middlesex South Association of the Congregational Church, even though he had no college or seminary education. He served as a supply preacher for the Congregational Church of West Roxbury, Massachusetts, in 1841–1842. In October 1842 he was ordained the pastor of the West Needham, Massachusetts (later Wellesley) Congregational Church. Newcomb's attempt to increase and systematize his congregation's benevolences for missionary work created tensions that led to his dismissal; he and some supporters who seceded from the West Needham church in July 1846 formed the Orthodox Congregational Church of Grantville, Massachusetts (later renamed the First Congregational Church of Wellesley Hills).

Newcomb left that pastorate in November 1849 and served as an assistant editor of the *Boston Traveller*, a general newspaper that was proud of its high moral tone, for approximately one year and of the *New York Observer*, a Presbyterian weekly, for two years. From 1852 to 1859 he lived in Brooklyn, New York, establishing mission Sunday schools and preaching at the Park Street Mission Church. For part of this time he also led a private school for young women. In October 1859 he was installed as the pastor of the Congregational Church in Hancock, Pennsylvania, where he remained until poor health necessitated his retirement. After retiring, he returned to Brooklyn.

Throughout the 1840s and 1850s Newcomb had continued to write. In 1842 he published *The Four Pillars*, a treatise on the evidences of Christianity. His manuals for the direction of young people—*The Young Lady's Guide to the Harmonious Development of Christian Character* (1839; fifteen editions by 1857), *How to Be a Man: A Book for Boys* (1846; fifteen editions by 1862), and *How to Be a Lady: A Book for Girls* (1846; fifteen editions by 1857)—gave advice on successful living and matters of morality, religion, health, conversation, and reading. (He believed that reading novels was dangerous for young women as it leads to an overexcited imagination that is injurious to their health.)

In 1854 Newcomb published the *Cyclopedia of Missions*, which contained maps and statistical tables and was widely consulted for several generations. It provided information on the history of Christian missions and current missions of all denominations around the world, and included the stories of individual missionaries. Newcomb edited the work and wrote a substantial part of it, soliciting contributions from various experts for the rest. It was revised and corrected through its fifth edition in 1860.

Newcomb's activities as a minister, editor, and writer for children and adults reveal his commitment to revivalism and his support for such causes as foreign missions, Sunday schools, temperance, and antislavery. With little formal education, he emerged as an effective and skillful popularizer of the values and outlook of many antebellum northern evangelicals. He was particularly committed to the dissemination of knowledge and piety to the young, recognizing the need to adapt his various messages to their capacity. He was also a prolific contributor to the advice literature of the early republic.

• Manuscript correspondence between Newcomb and the Quaker merchant and abolitionist Lyman A. Spalding is located in the Cornell University Library. Brief narratives of Newcomb's life are in the *Congregational Quarterly* 5 (Oct. 1863): 352–53, and John B. Newcomb, *Genealogical Memoir of the Newcomb Family* (1874). The latter makes reference to a manuscript autobiography left by Newcomb. Details on his pastorates are given in Edward H. Chandler, *The History of the Wellesley Congregational Church* (1898), and George Kuhn Clarke, *History of Needham, Massachusetts, 1711–1911* (1912). An obituary is in the *New York Observer*, 3 Sept. 1863.

DEWEY D. WALLACE, JR.

NEWCOMB, Simon (12 Mar. 1835–11 July 1909), mathematical astronomer and political economist, was born in Wallace, Nova Scotia, the son of John Burton Newcomb, an itinerant schoolteacher, and Emily Prince. Through reading and home instruction, young Newcomb gained a solid, basic education, though he spent long hours working on neighboring farms. At age sixteen he became an apprentice to a New Brunswick herbal "doctor." Increasingly disillusioned with the herbalist, he ended the agreement after two years by fleeing to the United States. (Descended from New Englanders, he became a naturalized U.S. citizen in 1864.)

In 1854 Newcomb began a series of jobs as a teacher and tutor in rural Maryland while continuing to develop his interests in political economics, religion, and especially mathematical astronomy. Drawing on the resources of the nearby Smithsonian Institution, he came to know its director, physicist Joseph Henry. In late 1856 one of Henry's scientific contacts arranged for Newcomb to join the staff at the Nautical Almanac Office in Cambridge, Massachusetts, to assist in creating astronomical tables for use in navigation. There he engaged in regular philosophical discussion with coworker Chauncey Wright and enrolled in his spare time as a student of mathematics at Harvard's Lawrence Scientific School, where he studied primarily under mathematical astronomer Benjamin Peirce. After receiving a B.S. in 1858, he remained at Harvard as a "resident graduate" while continuing to do computations at the Almanac Office.

Beginning also to engage in independent research, Newcomb analyzed the orbital motions of the asteroids and argued that they could not have originated from the break-up of a single planet between Mars and Jupiter. In 1860 he traveled to a remote region of the upper Saskatchewan River on a solar eclipse expedition, and the following year he accepted an appointment as professor of mathematics at the U.S. Naval Observatory in Washington. In 1863 he married Mary C. Hassler; they had three children.

Newcomb soon took the lead in streamlining the Naval Observatory's methods and, with a new transit instrument, began to reveal systematic errors in accepted values for the right ascensions (celestial longitudes) of stars. He also undertook theoretical studies of planetary and lunar positions. Formulating complex mathematical expressions to calculate orbital irregularities caused by the gravitational perturbations of interacting celestial bodies, and then constructing positional tables that would allow comparisons with properly rectified observational data, became the focus of his career. Through the late 1860s he concentrated on the planets Uranus and Neptune and on the motion of Earth's moon (the latter analysis became a lifelong passion, grounded on old lunar records that he resurrected in Paris while on an 1870 solar eclipse expedition). These planetary and lunar studies earned him the 1874 Gold Medal of London's Royal Astronomical Society. About this time, Newcomb also took charge of the Naval Observatory's new telescope, the nation's largest refractor, and mounted an expedition to observe the transit of Venus across the solar disk.

Wanting a position with more authority and with a computational rather than observational emphasis, Newcomb successfully arranged in 1877 to be appointed superintendent of the U.S. Navy's Almanac Office, now located in Washington. He proved to be an effective leader, not only revitalizing the office's publication of navigational tables but also charting an associated course of basic research. "The programme of work which I mapped out," he explained in his autobiography, *The Reminiscences of an Astronomer* (1903), involved, as one branch of it, a discussion of all the observations of value on the positions of the sun, moon, and planets, and, incidentally, on the bright fixed stars, made at the leading observatories of the world since 1750. One might almost say it involved repeating, in a space of ten or fifteen years, an important part of the world's work in astronomy for more than a century past. . . . The other branches of the work were . . . the computation of the formulae for the perturbation of the various planets by each other.

By the mid-1890s, with the help of associates such as George W. Hill, he had accomplished most of this ambitious program; he published his "preliminary results" in *The Elements of the Four Inner Planets and the Fundamental Constants of Astronomy* (1895). Although he stepped down from the Almanac Office in 1897, at the mandatory naval retirement age of sixty-two, support from the Carnegie Institution enabled him to continue working on this comprehensive project, particularly an elusive fluctuation in the moon's motion. At about the time of his retirement, he parlayed his planetary studies into an international project to bring order to the different national ephemerides through the adoption of uniform constants and consistent positional data. By the turn of the century, many of Newcomb's new constants, tables, and theories were becoming the norm in positional astronomy, a status that they retained through the mid-twentieth century. Newcomb received the Copley Medal of the Royal Society of London in 1890 and became one of eight foreign associates of the Paris Academy of Sciences in 1895. His widely reprinted and translated *Popular Astronomy* (1878) and other writings also spawned a large following among the public.

By the time of his retirement, Newcomb also had developed a solid reputation as a political economist. Through a steady stream of books, articles, and speeches that began in the 1860s, he sought to provide a dispassionate analysis of issues such as finance, trade, taxation, currency, and labor by providing a more logical, mathematical, and scientific formulation. In 1885 Newcomb assembled his ideas into a textbook, *Principles of Political Economy*. Though the main chapters reflected the influence of classical political economists, especially the liberalism of John Stuart Mill, Newcomb elaborated his own views on tying the value of the dollar to the average price of commodities and developed a mathematical equation for the circulation of money in society. The ways in which Newcomb marshaled the language of scientific method in response to social, cultural, and intellectual issues linked him to the nascent pragmatic movement in the United States, whose better-known members, especially Chauncey Wright but also Charles S. Peirce and William James, he knew personally.

Beginning in the 1870s Newcomb supplemented his jobs at the Naval Observatory and Almanac Office by teaching at Johns Hopkins University and Columbian (later George Washington) University. In 1877 he served as president of the American Association for the Advancement of Science and from 1883 to 1889 was vice president of the National Academy of Sciences. He also edited the *American Journal of Mathematics* for much of the period between 1885 and 1900, published a series of mathematical textbooks during the 1880s, and in 1892 helped reform secondary-school curricula by chairing the mathematics subcommittee of the National Educational Association's influential "Committee of Ten." In 1899 he became the first president of the Astronomical and Astrophysical Society of America (later the American Astronomical Society). In his later years, Newcomb wrote a science fiction novel, *His Wisdom the Defender* (1900). He died in Washington, D.C.

Although Newcomb's name slipped from prominence after his death—a consequence of his lack of a truly dramatic discovery and of the coming of a new style of spectroscopic and relativistic astronomy—Newcomb was the most celebrated and vocal American scientist of the late nineteenth century. As early as 1898, the president of the Astronomical Society of the Pacific, in awarding the group's first Bruce Medal to Newcomb, could speak of "the undoubted fact, that he has done more than any other American since Franklin to make American Science respected and honored throughout the entire world" (W. Alvord, *Publications of the Astronomical Society of the Pacific* 10 [1898]: 56). Later, Albert Einstein called Newcomb "the last of the great masters" of classical, perturbational astronomy (E. F. Brasch, *Science* 69 [1929]: 248–49). Economist John Maynard Keynes described Newcomb's *Principles* as "one of those original works which a fresh scientific mind, not perverted by having read too much of the orthodox stuff, is able to produce from time to time in a half-formed subject like Economics" (Hutchison, p. 269, n. 1).

• The Library of Congress houses the Simon Newcomb Papers. In addition to Newcomb's writings already mentioned in the text, see his *Sidelights on Astronomy and Kindred Fields of Popular Science: Essays and Addresses* (1906). For an annotated bibliography of his extensive writings and early articles about him, see Raymond C. Archibald's list in *Memoirs of the National Academy of Sciences* 17, 1st mem. (1924): 19–69; this same issue of *Memoirs* (pp. 1–18) contains a brief but comprehensive biography by W. W. Campbell, including a list of Newcomb's awards. Archibald also compiled chronological "synoptic notes" on Newcomb's career in *Science*, n.s., 44 (1916): 871–78. For more personal recollections, refer to Charles K. Wead et al., "Simon Newcomb: Memorial Addresses," *Bulletin of the Philosophical Society of Washington* 15 (1910): 133–67; and an appraisal by Newcomb's sister, Sara Newcomb Merrick, "John and Simon Newcomb: The Story of a Father and Son," *McClure's*, Oct. 1910, pp. 677–87. Arthur L. Norberg offers historical commentary in "Simon Newcomb and Nineteenth-Century Positional Astronomy" (Ph.D. diss., Univ. of Wisconsin, 1974); "Simon Newcomb's Early Astronomical Career," *Isis* 69 (1978): 209–25; and "Simon Newcomb's Role in the Astronomical Revolution of the Early Nineteen Hundreds," in *Sky with Ocean Joined: Proceedings of the Sesquicentennial Symposia of the U.S. Naval Observatory* (1983): 74–88. For additional analysis, see Carolyn Eisele, "The Charles S. Peirce–Simon Newcomb Correspondence," *Proceedings of the American Philosophical Society* 101 (1957): 409–33; T. W. Hutchison, *A Review of Economic Doctrines: 1870–1929* (1962), pp. 269–78; Loretta M. Dunphy, "Simon Newcomb: His Contributions to Economic Thought" (Ph.D. diss., Catholic Univ. of America, 1956); and Herbert C. Winnik, "The Role of Personality in the Science and the Social Attitudes of Five American Men of Science, 1876–1916" (Ph.D. diss., Univ. of Wisconsin, 1968). The only book-length study of Newcomb's life and thought is Albert E. Moyer, *A Scientist's Voice in American Culture: Simon Newcomb and the Rhetoric of Scientific Method* (1992).

ALBERT E. MOYER

NEWCOMB, Theodore Mead (24 July 1903–28 Dec. 1984), social psychologist, was born in Rock Creek, Ohio, the son of Ozro Robinson Newcomb, an itinerant Congregational minister, and Cora Mead, a teacher. The second of three children, Newcomb was raised in an atmosphere rich in academic interest and "informed social morality." As a youth, Newcomb readily identified with his parents' values. In high school, he was class valedictorian, and at his commencement oration he attacked the decision by the New York State Legislature to bar two duly elected members of the Socialist party. In 1920 Newcomb entered Oberlin College with a view to becoming a Christian missionary.

Newcomb's college years were intellectually uneventful, and he graduated from Oberlin (B.A., 1924) with his missionary ambitions intact. To pay off a college loan, he taught in a high school for a year and then decided to further his religious education by enrolling at Union Theological Seminary in New York City. At Union, Newcomb was influenced by the religious liberalism of Harrison Elliot and the Christian socialism of Harry F. Ward. Courses offered at nearby Columbia University by progressive educator William H. Kilpatrick and personality psychologist Goodwin Watson also left a noticeable mark on his intellectual outlook. Under the influence of these scholars, Newcomb's ethical interests were intensified and secularized. He abandoned his plans to become a missionary, and in 1927 he transferred to Columbia to pursue graduate studies in psychology, a field that Newcomb regarded as the modern means of religious endeavor. At Columbia, he worked closely with psychologist Gardner Murphy and with Watson, who served as his advisor on a dissertation that examined behavioral consistency in a group of young men (*The Consistency of Certain Extrovert-Introvert Behavior Patterns in 51 College Boys* [1929]).

After receiving his doctorate in 1929, Newcomb taught at Lehigh University (Bethlehem, Pa.) for one year before accepting a position in the Department of Psychology at Case Western Reserve University in Cleveland. While at Case, he worked with Gardner and Lois Murphy on a revision of their *Experimental Social Psychology* (1931), a landmark text that helped shift the methodological emphasis in social psychology from philosophical interpretation to experimentation. Newcomb contributed two lengthy sections on attitude and personality measurement to the revised version (1937). In 1934 Newcomb moved to Bennington College in Vermont where he continued his research on attitudes. At Bennington, his attention turned increasingly to the socioeconomic upheavals caused by the depression. He was a vocal supporter of the Spanish Loyalists, and he helped form Bennington's first Teachers Union and a local of the Textile Workers Organization.

Newcomb's progressivism was reflected in his psychological research. Political concern is particularly apparent in *Personality and Social Change: Attitude Formation in a Student Community* (1943), a study of student attitudes toward the New Deal, focusing on the psychological and sociological processes through which attitudinal changes occur. His most-significant published work, the book developed into a standard reference in the field of attitude formation. Its importance derives not only from its status as one of the first studies of attitude formation conducted by a psychologist but also from its emphasis on the interdependence of theory and observation and of theory and application.

Political interest also lay at the heart of Newcomb's other major professional project of the depression era: his involvement with the Society for the Psychological Study of Social Issues. The society was formed in 1936 to facilitate social change by encouraging socially relevant psychological research. Its success in this respect was limited, but the society helped to legitimize social psychology within the discipline of psychology. Newcomb was a charter member of the society, and he played a decisive role in the organization's early history. He served terms as secretary treasurer (1942–1944) and as president (1945–1946), and he coedited the society's first published book, *Industrial Conflict* (1939). Newcomb also served as senior editor of the society's *Reading in Social Psychology* (1947), a widely used collection of articles that helped bring together a rapidly developing field.

In 1941 Newcomb left Bennington for the University of Michigan in Ann Arbor. His appointment was in sociology rather than psychology, an indication of the still-marginal status of social psychology within many psychology departments. Shortly after arriving in Michigan, Newcomb accepted a position with the Foreign Broadcast Intelligence Service in Washington, and in 1943 he was appointed head of the service. Newcomb returned to the University of Michigan in 1945 to discover that a number of important changes had taken place. The most significant development was the appointment of Donald Marquis as chair of the psychology department. Marquis supported social psychology, and he encouraged its development at Michigan. With his support, Newcomb obtained a cross-appointment in the psychology department and a mandate to develop an interdisciplinary social psychology. In 1947 an interdepartmental doctoral program in social psychology was established with Newcomb as chair. Under his leadership, the program developed into the leading center of social psychological research in the United States.

The 1950s and 1960s constituted a period of heavy administrative responsibility for Newcomb. He served as chair of Michigan's program in social psychology from 1947 to 1963, he was president of the American Psychological Association in 1955, and he was editor of the prestigious *Psychological Review* from 1954 to 1959. In the 1960s Newcomb also worked to concretize the social psychological principles he had spent his life studying. He suggested that the undergraduate learning environment at the University of Michigan be redesigned in order to integrate students' personal and intellectual lives. The university administration accepted the idea, and in the late 1960s a "residential college" was opened with Newcomb as an associate director. Throughout this period Newcomb maintained an active program of social psychological research. His 1950 textbook, *Social Psychology*, was the first introductory text to fuse psychological research on attitudes and group processes with the sociological tradition of symbolic interactionism and role theory. This text was followed by *The Acquaintance Process* (1961) and *Persistence and Change: Bennington College and Its Students after 25 Years* (1967), a follow-up to his Bennington study. Newcomb retired from the University of Michigan in 1972, but he continued to lecture and to conduct research until his death in Ann Arbor.

Newcomb's numerous contributions to social psychology earned him a number of honors, including election to the National Academy of Sciences (1974), the Kurt Lewin Award from the Society for the Psychological Study of Social Issues (1962), and a Distinguished Scientific Contribution award from the American Psychological Association (1976). Colleagues described him as a friendly, generous man, with a quick wit and a passionate commitment to social justice. Throughout his career he maintained a close personal and intellectual relationship with his wife, Mary Shipherd; the two were married in the early 1930s and had three children.

Newcomb stood at the forefront of two important trends in the history of American psychology: scientific precision and disciplinary expansion. He was a pioneer in the movement to transform the methodological orientation of social psychology from philosophy to experimental science. He also played an important role in the postwar campaign to diversify the subject matter of psychology and to extend its professional reach. His scholarly and administrative accomplishments helped propel social psychology into the mainstream of American psychology.

• Newcomb's professional papers, correspondence, and personal photographs are in the University of Michigan Archives. Correspondence can also be found in the papers of Gordon W. Allport (Harvard Univ.), Richard Boys (Univ. of Michigan), and the Society for the Psychological Study of Social Issues (Univ. of Akron). The best biographical source is Newcomb's autobiography in *A History of Psychology in Autobiography*, vol. 6, ed. Gardner Lindzey (1974); see also the shorter autobiography, "The Love of Ideas," *Society* 17 (1980): 76–82. On his work with the Society for the Psychological Study of Social Issues, see articles by Harris, Finison, and Capshew in "Fifty Years of the Psychology of Social Issues," *Journal of Social Issues* 42 (1986). Reminiscences of Newcomb by his colleagues can be found in *American Psychologist* 41 (Dec. 1986): 1380–81, and the *American Journal of Psychology* 99 (Summer 1986): 293–98. An obituary is in the *New York Times*, 31 Dec. 1984.

IAN NICHOLSON

NEWCOMER, Christian (1 Feb. 1749–12 Mar. 1830), carpenter and clergyman, was born in Lancaster County, Pennsylvania, the son of Wolfgang Newcomer, a carpenter, and Elizabeth Weller, a midwife. One of eight children, he was educated in a Mennonite elementary school and trained in carpentry and farming by his father, a German-speaking Swiss immigrant. These occupations supported him and his family in Pennsylvania and on the farm he purchased in 1775 at Frederick (later Washington) County, Maryland, near Hagerstown at Beaver Creek. He married Elizabeth Baer in 1770, and to this union four children were born.

Newcomer's early life was marked by conflicting emotions of faith and doubt, by intense religious experiences, including his conversion at about age seventeen, and by a protracted inner struggle of uncertainty over a call to the ministry. He also faced numerous hardships for being a conscientious objector during the American Revolution. These psychologically stressful emotions and experiences culminated in his withdrawal from the Mennonite church in 1777 and were resolved by his entrance into the work of the ministry. He joined an association of German Reformed revivalistic preachers, often referred to as "Dutch Methodists," under the leadership of Philip William Otterbein and George Adam Geeting of Baltimore.

As early as 1766, Otterbein had organized pastors to extend the prerevolutionary war revival, begun by Jonathan Edwards, George Whitefield, and others, to the frontier German population of Pennsylvania, Maryland, and Virginia who were unchurched and lacked pastoral leadership. The war interrupted their efforts, but in 1789 these clergy convened a conference in Baltimore; by 1800 the need for cohesion and a better-defined organization led to the founding of the Church of the United Brethren in Christ. Newcomer actively participated in these early conferences and between meetings traveled and preached in local congregations and at great meetings (*grosse Versammlungen*). The great meetings featured love feasts, administration of communion, clerical discipline, singing, praying, preaching, and exhorting. Persons converted under Newcomer's evangelistic preaching were formed into classes or small societies, marked by lay leadership, where members pledged themselves to a pietistic lifestyle of prayer, Bible study, and moral conduct.

By 1795, fully mature and confident of his clerical abilities, Newcomer began devoting all his time and energies to the work of the ministry. He felt the need to extend United Brethren work to the western frontier and traveled extensively to establish churches in central and western Pennsylvania, Ohio, Kentucky, Indiana and north into parts of Canada. He had attained a proficiency in English that equipped him to establish important contacts and friendships with the leaders of the postrevolutionary revival, particularly with Methodist leaders such as bishops Francis Asbury, Richard Whatcoat, and William McKendree. These relationships, coupled with his considerable organizational and leadership skills, motivated Newcomer to promote the adoption of a discipline, or book of church order, for the United Brethren and to advocate closer ties with the Methodists. His abilities and these initiatives were recognized by his election and ordination to the office of bishop in 1813, a position he held for life.

Newcomer's journal, published posthumously, covers the last thirty-five years of his life (1795–1830) and provides an intimate portrait of a circuit rider's life and ministry on the western frontier. At times he faced opposition, as when he "had an appointment to preach at the 10 mile meeting house. On our arriving we were refused admittance, so I preached to the people from under the shelter of an oak tree and the canopy of heaven." After riding long days on horseback over primitive trails and roads, he sometimes found it difficult to secure food and lodging: "We rode all day over mountains [in western Pennsylvania]; stopped at several houses to refresh ourselves and horses, but could not procure anything for love or money." His reward for the difficult work lay in meeting spiritual needs. In 1810, on his way home from a trip to Ohio, he remarked, "My heart gave uncommon gratitude to my heavenly Father for his benevolent protection, and for the good health which I had enjoyed on this long journey, but more especially for the assistance continuously bestowed on his unworthy servant, in declaring His counsel and preaching the gospel of free salvation to lost sinners." He died at his farm in Frederick County, Maryland.

Newcomer's accomplishments include his leadership in establishing and organizing the Church of the United Brethren in Christ. He was a member and/or delegate to all the general conferences of the church from 1789 to 1829, organized annual conferences, coauthored the first book of discipline, and served as the third bishop of the church. His tireless service as a circuit rider helped expand the postrevolutionary war revival and the spread of United Brethren work. His mastery of English enabled him to assist German-speaking citizens, particularly the Pennsylvania Dutch, in assimilating into American society. It also enabled him to recruit young men for the ministry and equip the new denomination to take its rightful place in national life as an indigenous American church. His promotion of closer cooperation, together with his proposals for union with other denominations, particularly with the Methodists and the Evangelicals led by Jacob Albright, mark him as one of American Protestantism's pioneer ecumenists. His proposals established historical precedent for the union in 1946 of the United Brethren and the Evangelical church to form the Evangelical United Brethren church and, in 1968, the union of that body with the Methodist church to form the United Methodist church.

Possessed of native intelligence, shrewd leadership skills, and an entrepreneurial outlook, Newcomer helped inspire a German-American sectarian community to form an indigenous denomination that took its place in the broader spectrum of national life, an influence that continues to the present.

• Newcomer's journal, the most important document on his life and career, was published as *The Life and Journal of the Revd. Christian Newcomer, Late Bishop of the Church of the United Brethren in Christ, Written by Himself. Containing His Travels and Labours in the Gospel from 1795 to 1830, a Period of Thirty-Five Years*, ed. John Hildt (1834). Ira D. Landis added historical and genealogical notes to Hildt's translation and republished the years 1795–1815 serially in the *Mennonite Research Journal* 6–17 (Apr. 1965–July 1977). The most complete modern assessment is John Dallas Robertson, "Christian Newcomer (1749–1830), Pioneer of Church Discipline and Union among the United Brethren in Christ, the Evangelical Association, and the Methodist Episcopal Church" (Ph.D. diss., George Washington Univ., 1973). See also Paul Rodes Koontz, "Christian Newcomer," in *The Bishops: Church of the United Brethren in Christ*, vol. 1 (1950). Daryl M. Elliott, "Entire Sanctification and the Church of the United Brethren in Christ to 1860," *Methodist History* 25 (1987): 203–21, includes Newcomer's doctrinal views on Christian perfection. A good account of Mennonite and Newcomer's involvement with revivalism is Sem C. Sutter, "Mennonites and the Pennsylvania German Revival," *Mennonite Quarterly Review* 50 (Jan. 1976): 37–57. J. Bruce Behney and Paul H. Eller, *History of the Evangelical United Brethren Church* (1979), provides the best contemporary account of Newcomer's contribution to denominational history.

ELMER O'BRIEN

NEWELL, Edward Theodore (15 Jan. 1886–18 Feb. 1941), numismatist, was born in Kenosha, Wisconsin, the son of Frederick Seth Newell, a business executive, and Frances Cecelia Bain. Newell came from an affluent family whose wealth was derived from lumber interests and the Bain Wagon Company, Kenosha's most extensive manufacturing enterprise. Consequently, he had the opportunity to travel and pursue his collecting interests early in life, attending sales of coins at the Hotel Drouot in Paris at the age of fifteen. He received his early education at the Harvard School in Chicago and from private tutors, after which he received his B.A. (1907) and M.A. (1909) from Yale University. Having demonstrated his abilities as a numismatist while an undergraduate, he was in 1905 elected a fellow of the Royal Numismatic Society and

appointed assistant curator at the American Numismatic Society in New York, where he now resided. In 1909 he married Adra Nelson Marshall of Jersey City, New Jersey; they had no children. The American Numismatic Society elected him to its council in 1910 and to its presidency in 1916, a position he held until his death. During World War I he served in the Military Intelligence Division of the army as a first lieutenant.

Newell possessed a thorough background in ancient history, literature, and Oriental cultures, as well as an intense interest in the coinage of Alexander the Great and his Hellenistic successors. His acute observations on this coinage culminated in his most distinguished contributions to scholarship. Newell intended a complete survey of the coinage and progressed toward that end with a series of detailed studies of relevant coin hoards and the issues of specific mints and kings. In 1911 he published "Reattribution of Certain Tetradrachms of Alexander the Great," a study of tetradrachm coins from a hoard found at Demanhur, Egypt, in 1905. Newell's findings forced a complete reappraisal of the previously accepted conclusions reached by Carl Ludwig Müller in his work *Numismatique d'Alexandre le Grand*, published in 1855. Müller had maintained that symbols on the coin reverses indicated the issuing mints. Newell, employing new data and die linkages, demonstrated that many of the symbols on the coins did not relate to the issuing mint cities but to the magistrates responsible for their issue. He proved that tetradrachms that Müller assigned to widely distant mints had actually been struck from the same obverse die. Newell's overall conclusions, published in the "Reattribution" and a later work on the same hoard, provided the basis for attribution of the greater part of Alexander's coins to their issuing mints.

Newell applied his methodology in subsequent publications, which included *The Dated Alexander Coinage of Sidon and Ake* (1916); "The Seleucid Mint of Antioch" (1917) and "Tarsos under Alexander" (1918) in the *American Journal of Numismatics*; and *The Coinages of Demetrius Poliorcetes* (1927). In *The Coinage of the Eastern Seleucid Mints* (1938) and *The Coinage of the Western Seleucid Mints* (1941), he established the chronology and mint designations of the coinage of the first six Seleucid kings. Altogether, Newell published some sixty titles, most of which bore the imprint of the American Numismatic Society.

Newell's scholarship, administrative abilities, and benefactions had a profound influence on the society. In his first presidential address, he spoke of the need to improve the society's financial situation and expand programs and facilities. In building the collections, he led by example, presenting his collection of 5,000 Islamic coins to the society in 1917. He also purchased important collections of Islamic and Indian coins, which he donated. His initiatives established an impressive core of Oriental holdings and attracted donations from others. His efforts to establish a publication fund were realized in 1920, when funding was obtained for a new series, Numismatic Notes and Monographs, to be devoted to original scholarship. Newell would eventually write eighteen of the monographs in this series and oversee the introduction of another large-format series in 1937, Numismatic Studies, to which he contributed his studies of the eastern and western Seleucid mints.

Newell established relationships with American institutions conducting excavations abroad and offered the society's facilities for study of the coins found and publication of the results. He prepared the reports of coins discovered in Anatolia by the expedition of the Oriental Institute of the University of Chicago, and his cooperation with the Yale scholars conducting excavations at the Syrian site of Dura-Europus resulted in publications on five coin hoards in Numismatic Notes and Monographs, one by Newell himself. Assistance was also offered to the sponsors of excavations at Seleucia-on-Tigris and Corinth.

Within ten years of assuming the society's presidency, Newell had successfully addressed its financial and program needs. He enjoyed similar success in rallying support for expansion of the physical facilities, and in 1929 construction began on a new building, which opened to the public in November 1930. The expansion was much needed, for under Newell's direction the collections were to grow from something over 50,000 items to some 200,000 items.

After his death, Newell's collection of 87,000 coins, which included 60,000 Greek and 23,000 Roman coins, was donated to the American Numismatic Society, placing it among the world's foremost collections of ancient coins. The Newell collection, along with his manuscripts, notes, and casts, continues to provide source material for ongoing scholarly research. His published works remain the point of departure for most research on the coins of Alexander and his successors and—though some of his attributions and chronology have been modified—the basic edifice that he constructed remains intact. In addition to his knowledge of the coinages of classical antiquity, he was an authority on Islamic, Sassanian, and Indian coinage as well as oriental seals. His direction of the American Numismatic Society greatly enhanced that institution's reputation and led, in 1937, to its being elected to membership in the American Council of Learned Societies.

In recognition of his scholarship, Newell was the first recipient of the Archer M. Huntington Medal, awarded in 1918 by the American Numismatic Society. Among other distinctions, he was awarded the medal of the Royal Numismatic Society (1925) and the Prix Allier d'Hauteroche of the Académie des Inscriptions et Belles-Lettres (1929). He was a trustee of the American Schools of Oriental Research (1922–1941) and a member of numerous numismatic and other learned societies.

Newell died of heart failure in New York City.

• Newell's papers, including correspondence, manuscripts, and notes, are at the American Numismatic Society in New York City. For early family photographs and history, consult the Kenosha County (Wis.) Historical Society & Museum. His "Reattribution of Certain Tetradrachms of Alexander the Great" was published in seven installments in the *American Journal of Numismatics*: 45, no. 1 (1911): 1–10; 45, no. 2 (1911): 37–45; 45, no. 3 (1911): 113–25; 45, no. 4 (1911): 194–200; 46, no. 1 (1912): 22–24; 46, no. 2 (1912): 37–49; and 46, no. 3 (1912): 109–16. The American Numismatic Society reprinted it as a monograph in 1912. For a complete bibliography, see American Numismatic Society, *Dictionary Catalogue of the Library of the American Numismatic Society* (1962); if the former is unavailable, see Paul A. Clement, "A Bibliography of the Writings of Edward T. Newell," *American Journal of Philology* 68 (Oct. 1947): 427–32. Events of his career may be found in Howard L. Adelson, *The American Numismatic Society, 1858–1958* (1958), and can be gleaned from *Proceedings of the American Numismatic Society*, 47th–87th Annual Meetings (1905–1945). See also obituaries in the *Numismatist*, Apr. 1941, pp. 267–69; *Coin Collector's Journal*, Apr. 1941, p. 50; and *Yale University Obituary Record of Graduates Deceased during the Year Ending July 1, 1941* (1942), pp. 114–15.

FRANCIS D. CAMPBELL

NEWELL, Frederick Haynes (5 Mar. 1862–5 July 1932), engineer, was born in Bradford, Pennsylvania, the son of Augustus William Newell and Annie Maria Haynes. His mother died while he was a child, and he was raised by unmarried aunts in Newton, Massachusetts, where he completed high school. In 1885 he graduated from the Massachusetts Institute of Technology with a B.S. in mining engineering. He married Effie Josephine Mackintosh in 1890; the couple had three children.

Newell worked for several years after graduation on a variety of land and railroad surveys in northern Pennsylvania. In 1888 he was appointed assistant hydraulic engineer for the U.S. Geological Survey, where he assisted John Wesley Powell in administering the Irrigation Survey of western rivers, potential reservoir sites, and irrigable lands. He became the USGS's chief hydrographer in the early 1890s, with responsibility for recording the flow of American rivers. When Congress passed the National Reclamation Act in 1902, creating a Reclamation Service within the USGS, Newell was appointed chief engineer. He served as the service's director from 1907 to 1914, when he resigned under pressure.

During this period Newell, along with Gifford Pinchot of the U.S. Forest Service, was a leader in the conservation movement. He shared the movement's emphasis on the efficient use of natural resources and on government's role in encouraging it. In his 1902 book, *Irrigation in the United States*, Newell foresaw a West settled by yeoman farmers on arid lands that had been irrigated by sensible, efficient government works. During his tenure the Reclamation Service undertook irrigation projects that served almost 1.5 million acres of land, costing almost $100 million. Although a number of notable dams and other projects were built, these activities sparked considerable controversy. Newell's resignation in 1914 was linked, in part, to complaints from farmers, whom the law obliged to repay the cost of these projects, and to criticism of the cost overruns that plagued the service from its inception.

Following his resignation, Newell served as head of the Department of Civil Engineering at the University of Illinois from 1915 to 1920, when he returned to Washington, D.C. At the same time, he became involved in a growing social movement within the American engineering profession that sought to foster greater unity among engineers, to raise engineering's status, and to involve engineers in social reform activities. This complex movement brought together a variety of concerns, including the feeling of many engineers that they were badly underpaid and some engineers' belief that the engineering profession was not accorded sufficient respect. The latter group argued that engineers should be given additional power to allow them to lead society out of the impasse created by what they regarded as the selfish conflict between capital and labor. Building on his earlier efforts to make technology a public resource, Newell sought to create a strong, independent engineering profession; he was critical of the national engineering societies, which he saw as too conservative and too closely tied to business to be effective vehicles. Instead, he and other engineering reformers sought to create a federation of local and regional engineering societies. To this end, Newell helped organize and was an active participant in three conferences on engineering cooperation between 1915 and 1917 at which plans for engineering unity were debated.

These conferences were badly divided, however, and did not succeed in presenting a plan for unifying the engineering profession. Newell therefore turned his attention to another potential vehicle for accomplishing this end: the fledgling American Association of Engineers (AAE), which had been founded in 1915 by a group of young Chicago-area engineers. He had not been directly involved in the organization's creation and initially regarded it largely as representative of "younger men" who, in many cases, had not yet reached "professional" rank. But, the failure of engineering cooperation led him to become actively involved in the association; he eventually became its president in 1919. As its leader, Newell sought to fuse younger engineers' discontent about their material situation with engineering reformers' desire to unify the profession, raise its status, and encourage social reform. Although he opposed the idea of engineering unions, he helped build support for the AAE by moving it in a more militant direction, including supporting the idea of engineering licensing (which, it was hoped, would help to enhance engineering incomes). But Newell was unable and unwilling to satisfy younger engineers' desire for aggressive action to improve their material situation. From the point of view of younger engineers, Newell and other engineering reformers focused too much on engineering unity and the status of the engineering profession and were too sensitive to pressure from the more conservative engineering societies. By 1921 the AAE's membership and its leaders had begun to drift apart, and the organization fell into decline. Although Newell continued to participate in the association well into the 1920s, he became much less active; his position as director of field services, which he took up after his presidency ended, was abolished in 1921 as part of an insurgency within the AAE.

In 1924 Newell and A. B. McDaniel founded the Research Service, an organization of engineering consultants in various fields of engineering and construction. He served as its president and remained actively involved in consulting and engineering affairs until his death in Washington, D.C.

Newell's career was of central importance to the early twentieth-century conservation movement, especially to its efforts to fuse government and technology into an effective developer of American natural resources. Although western water projects have been criticized by some for their cost, for their environmental consequences, and for favoring larger landowners, there is general agreement that Newell and the other leaders of the Reclamation Service left a permanent mark on the American West. He was less successful in his efforts to forge an independent American engineering profession; his failure in this area reflects the deep social divisions that characterize engineering in the United States.

• Newell's papers are in the Manuscript Division of the Library of Congress. His major works include *Hydrography of the Arid Regions* (1891); *The Public Lands of the United States and Their Water Supply* (1895); *Principles of Irrigation Engineering* (1913), with D. W. Murphy; *Irrigation Management* (1916); and *Water Resources, Present and Future Uses* (1920). He was joint editor of *Engineering as a Career* (1916) and editor of *Planning and Building the City of Washington* (1932). The best account of Newell's role in the U.S. Geological Survey and the Reclamation Service is Donald C. Jackson, "Engineering in the Progressive Era: A New Look at Frederick Haynes Newell and the U.S. Reclamation Service," *Technology and Culture* 34, no. 3 (1993): 539–74. His career as an engineering reformer and with the American Association of Engineers is discussed in Edwin T. Layton, Jr., *The Revolt of the Engineers* (1971); Layton, "Frederick Haynes Newell and the Revolt of the Engineers," *Midcontinent American Studies Journal* 3, no. 2 (1962): 17–26; and Peter Meiksins, "Professionalism and Conflict: The Case of the American Association of Engineers, *Journal of Social History* 19, no. 3 (1986): 403–21. An obituary is in the *New York Times*, 8 July 1932.

PETER MEIKSINS

NEWELL, Harriet Atwood (10 Oct. 1793–30 Nov. 1812), American missionary to India, was born in Haverhill, Massachusetts, the daughter of Moses Atwood, an entrepreneur, and Mary Tenney. One of nine children, she was educated from 1807 to 1810 at Bradford Academy under the principalship of Abraham Burnham, a Dartmouth graduate and Congregationalist minister. Burnham held that religious experience was required for an effective Christian life and promoted religious awakening among his students at the academy. Each student also read widely in Christian writers like John Bunyan, Joseph Bellamy, and the Puritans.

In 1806 Burnham spearheaded a revival in Bradford, and several of his students were caught up in the enthusiasm, including Harriet and her older friend Ann Hasseltine. Her childhood journal and letters reveal a spiritual devotion characteristic of New England Puritans: she wrestled with sermons she heard and read, and personal illnesses were her teacher. She suffered from a weak constitution and frequent headaches but learned to rely upon her religious faith. Beginning in 1810 she observed with great interest the developing romance between her friend Ann and Adoniram Judson, an aspiring overseas missionary, who subsequently married. Through Judson in 1810, Harriet met Samuel Newell, a graduate of Harvard College and Andover Theological Seminary, who was also preparing for missionary service under Congregationalist sponsorship. Although she was not as overtly enthusiastic about missionary service as her friend Ann, she was impressed with Samuel's sense of calling. Both Harriet and Samuel were described as "shy and introspective." The couple was married at Haverhill on 9 February 1812, following a widely attended commissioning service for America's first overseas missionaries at Salem Tabernacle three days earlier.

Although physically frail and considered a poor prospect for travel, Harriet joined her husband and the Judsons and sailed on the ship *Caravan* on 19 February bound for India. She relied heavily upon the personal support and fortitude of her childhood friend Ann. Harriet's correspondence with her mother covered careful details of the voyage to India, during most of which she was sick, in part due to her being pregnant. After initial permits were issued at Calcutta, the Newells arrived in Serampore on 17 June 1812. There they accepted the invitation of William Carey, the English Baptist missionary, to stay at his home. Harriet was much impressed with the evangelical work of the Baptist missionaries and the organization of their home and compound.

After six weeks at Serampore, the Newells were forced to withdraw from India, owing to the East India Company's colonial monopoly and the impending military hostilities between Britain and the United States. Samuel Newell negotiated a plan to organize a mission on the Isle of France (Mauritius), which required an additional sea voyage across the Indian Ocean. Her strength weakened from a heavy visitation schedule and a hasty departure from Serampore, Harriet became ill during the voyage with a fever and intestinal symptoms, at length giving birth to a daughter. To complicate matters, the ship *Gillespie*, in which they were traveling, sprang a leak and was forced to secure repairs at Coringa on the Coromandel coast, delaying Harriet's need for medical assistance. On the final stage of the voyage, a violent storm drenched the passengers, leaving Harriet and her child sick from exposure. The child died on 13 October, and Harriet succumbed to consumption less than two weeks later.

Harriet Newell was buried in the Port Louis Cemetery on the Isle of France. At a little over nineteen years old, she was among the first American missionaries and the first one to die overseas. Her posthumously published journal, plus Ann Judson's published affection for her, created the first hagiographic model for American women missionaries. Because of her early death, however, some critics questioned the American Protestant missionary enterprise and the role of women in particular.

• Not much documentation exists concerning Newell, owing to her short career. There are miscellaneous papers at the American Baptist Historical Society in Rochester, N.Y., and Andover Newton Theological School in Newton Centre, Mass. Of major published material is Leonard Woods, *The Memoir of Mrs. Harriet Newell, Wife of Rev. Samuel Newell* (1831), which the American Tract Society published; *Life and Writings of Mrs. Harriet Newell* (1831); and Frances C. Longstroth, *Harriet Atwood Newell: A Sketch* (1913). Newell's alma mater dedicated a portrait of her later in the century and published addresses of appreciation for her life: Bradford Academy, *In Memoriam: Rufus Anderson, Harriet Newell, and Ann H. Judson* (1884). The best modern account of Newell's career is in Courtney Anderson, *To The Golden Shore: The Life of Adoniram Judson* (1956).

WILLIAM H. BRACKNEY

NEWELL, Peter (5 Mar. 1862–15 Jan. 1924), cartoonist, illustrator, and humorous poet, was born Peter Sheaf Hersey Newell in McDonough County, Illinois, near the small town of Bushnell, the son of George Frederick Newell, a wagon maker, and Louisa Dodge. Named for his father's business partner and relative Peter Sheaf Hersey, Newell showed an early taste for drawing and was encouraged in it by his family. While in high school, he did a large oil painting, *The Good Samaritan*, which his father proudly framed and submitted to the annual Bushnell County Fair and which won a blue ribbon. Newell caricatured his classmates and teachers throughout high school, from which he graduated in 1880, but, seeing no prospects for a career in art, took a job in a cigar factory in Bushnell.

After three months at this unsatisfying work, Newell was given a job at the City Photography Gallery in nearby Jacksonville, Illinois, where he helped with the developing, printing, and mounting and worked at an easel making large crayon portraits from photographs. At night he produced humorous sketches, which he sent to magazines. His first submission, to *Harper's Bazar*, met with an ambiguous response: He had accompanied the cartoon with a letter asking if his work showed talent, and the editor answered, "No talent indicated," but sent a check. Soon Newell's work began appearing in a number of periodicals and brought him enough money to go to New York in 1883. He studied at the Art Students League but found the training incompatible with his own antic fancy and left after one term, convinced, according to Mabel Hall Goltra, "that the originality of his work would be destroyed by formalized, academic training" (p. 137).

Newell returned to work for the City Photographic Gallery in 1884, but in the fall of that year he opened a studio of his own in Springfield. In 1885 he married Leona Dow Ashcraft, a childhood sweetheart. The couple had three children. His studio was not a success, and the Newells spent the winter of 1885–1886 in New York. They then traveled through the Midwest for three years, living briefly in Nebraska, Colorado, and Chicago, while the artist tried to establish himself as a freelancer. Success arrived gradually after the family moved back to New York City in 1888 and Newell began working in the flat-tone technique that was beginning to replace line drawings in book and magazine illustration. He sold cartoons, often accompanied by humorous verse, to many national periodicals, including *Scribner's*, *Godey's*, the *Saturday Evening Post*, *Judge*, and *St. Nicholas*, and became a regular contributor to the various *Harper's* publications. His cartoons of African Americans, a popular subject of graphic humor at the time, were especially successful. In 1893 he achieved national fame with a half-tone cartoon published in the August issue of *Harper's Weekly*, showing a gentleman comforting a frightened little girl. The caption, which was to become one of the most widely quoted pieces of doggerel in the country, read:

"Of what are you afraid, my child?" inquired the kindly teacher.
"Oh, sir, the flowers, they are wild," replied the timid creature.

That same year Newell covered the World's Columbian Exposition in Chicago for *Harper's* and also published his first book, *Topsys and Turvys*. Inspired by the sight of one of his children examining a picture book upside down, it was a collection of illustrated verses whose pictures could be reversed top to bottom to form others, with inventive couplets to explain the double images. A second volume of *Topsys and Turvys* appeared the next year. In 1896 Newell published *A Shadow Show*, containing seventy-two droll silhouettes. In 1899 a collection of Newell's work, *Pictures and Rhymes*, appeared, with the still-popular "Wild Flowers" as its frontispiece, followed in 1909 by *Jungle Jangle*, a collection of illustrated nonsense verse about animals. A particularly ingenious novelty volume by Newell was *The Hole Book* (1908), produced with an actual hole through the center of the pages and illustrating the path of a bullet shot off by a naughty boy. In 1912 Newell repeated the device with *The Rocket Book*, detailing the career of a rocket set off in the basement of an apartment house as it passed through each of the floors. Even more innovative was his 1910 volume *The Slant Book*, bound in the shape of a rhomboid and recounting the hilarious effects of a baby carriage rolling down a hill.

Harper's Weekly sent Newell to cover the Paris Exposition in 1900 and both the Republican and Democratic presidential conventions in 1912. He continued to produce cartoons and advertising art for magazines, and in 1905 the *New York Sunday Herald* ran his comic strip, *The Naps of Polly Sleepyhead*, an engaging fantasy series inspired by Winsor McCay's *Little Nemo in Slumberland*. Newell became best known, however, as an illustrator, earning praise for both his fidelity to the spirit of the works he illustrated and the high degree of imagination he brought to them. He provided art for more than fifty books besides his own eight, including Steven Crane's *Whilomville Stories* (1900), six titles by Mark Twain, and seven by John Kendrick Bangs. He considered his illustrations for Bangs's *Mr. Munchausen* (1901) the most successful of his artistic creations, but it was for his controversial illustrations of the work of Lewis Carroll (*Alice's Adventures in Wonderland* [1901]; *Through the Looking Glass* [1902]; and *The Hunting of the Snark* [1903]) that he became most famous. Criticized for presuming to compete with the original engravings by Sir John Tenniel, Newell published a spirited defense of his own pictorial interpretations in *Harper's* ("*Alice's Adventures in Wonderland* from an Artist's Standpoint," Oct. 1901, pp. 713–17).

Newell's gentle humor, which Albert Lee called "as demure as a Quaker's smile and as guileless" (p. 335), won him the respect and affection of a wide public. In 1893 the Newells moved to Leonia, New Jersey, where the genial artist was an exceptionally popular citizen, participating widely in civic affairs and singing in his local church choir. Described by Charles Battell Loomis as "over six feet tall, with a whimsical face [and] shaggy eyebrows acting as awnings over the kindest blue eyes" (p. 51), he was known to his neighbors as "Uncle Peter." In his later years he devoted himself to "serious" painting, on which he worked conscientiously until his death in Little Neck, Long Island. His conventional art work was exhibited at the New York Academy of Design and the Philadelphia Academy of Fine Arts, but it is for the whimsical charm of his distinctive humorous drawings that he is likely to be remembered.

• Critical and biographical material on Newell is in Albert Lee, "Book Illustrators, XXII: Peter Newell," *Book Buyer*, July 1896, pp. 348–50; Regina Armstrong, "The New Leaders in American Illustration, V: The Humorous Men: Newell, Kemble, Sullivant, Zimmerman and Hamilton," *Bookman*, June 1900, pp. 334–41; Louise Morgan Sill, "Mr. Newell's Latest Drawings," *Harper's Bazar*, Sept. 1902, pp. 779–83; Charles Battell Loomis, "Interesting People: Peter Newell," *American Magazine*, May 1911, pp. 48–51; Joyce Kilmer, "Peter Newell Says Domestication Helps Artists," *New York Times Sunday Magazine*, 17 Sept. 1916, p. 12; Philip Hofer, "Peter Newell's Pictures and Rhymes," *Colophon*, Dec. 1931; Mabel Hall Goltra, "Peter S. Newell, Cartoonist," *Illinois State Historical Society Journal* 41 (June 1948): 134–45; and Michael Patrick Hearn, "Peter Newell, American Comic Illustrator," *American Book Collector*, July–Aug. 1983, pp. 3–11. An obituary is in the *New York Times*, 16 Jan. 1924.

DENNIS WEPMAN

NEWELL, Robert (30 Mar. 1807–Nov. 1869), Oregon pioneer, was born in Muskingum County, Ohio. Nothing is known about his family or his early years, except that his education was sporadic. In his teens he became apprenticed to a saddlemaker in Cincinnati and worked in that occupation until March 1829, when he joined a trapping party in St. Louis and headed west. On this journey he met another trapper named Joseph L. Meek, who became his lifelong friend. Meek later became one of the Old West's most famous trappers.

Newell worked as a trapper in the Rockies throughout the 1830s. During that time he acquired the nickname "Doc," presumably because he treated the minor injuries of fellow trappers. Newell may have become fairly knowledgeable about local remedies derived from Indian lore, for his trapping activities drew him into close contact with area tribes, in particular the Nez Percé. That association was strengthened by his marriage to a Nez Percé woman in 1833.

In 1840 Newell, along with Joseph Meek, their families, and two other men, set out for the Oregon country in a three-wagon caravan from Fort Hall, on the Snake River in present-day Idaho. The group settled in the Willamette Valley, near what is now Hillsboro, Oregon, where they earned a living as farmers. Newell became an active participant in area politics, and in May 1843 he met with other American settlers at nearby Champoeg to organize a provisional government. There he served on the legislative committee that drafted a constitution, which was ratified in July.

Soon afterward Newell became a member of the provisional government's house of representatives, and the following year he and his family moved to the Champoeg area. He served in the house until Oregon Territory was organized in 1848; during that time he was also house speaker for two terms. He was one of three peace commissioners who helped bring an end to the 1848 Cayuse uprising. In the mid-1840s Newell built and operated two keelboats on the upper Willamette River; they are believed to have been the first such boats running on that part of the river.

Newell's first wife died in December 1845, and several months later he married Rebecca Newman. They subsequently had children, although the exact number is not known. The gold rush drew Newell, along with other Oregonians, to California in the winter of 1848–1849. After achieving modest prosperity there, he returned to his home in Oregon in the fall of 1850 and became a merchant. When Indians threatened the area in 1855–1856, Newell led a company of scouts to defend the settlers. Four years later he was elected to the newly established state legislature, where he served several terms.

After floods destroyed much of his Champoeg property in December 1861, Newell and his family moved to Lapwai, in present-day Idaho, the site of a U.S. Army post and Indian agency. There he served for six years as an interpreter and a special commissioner, encouraging the Indians to adopt white practices. Newell's second wife died in the spring of 1867; he married his third wife, Jane M. Ward, in June 1869.

In 1868 Newell accompanied Nez Percé chiefs to Washington, D.C., where he successfully lobbied for the post of Indian agent of the Nez Percé reservation at Lapwai. He was replaced in this post the following July because of a new policy dictating that Indian agents should be army officers, but he was considered by the Nez Percé to have been a good agent, and the first who spoke their language. Suffering from heart disease, Newell moved to Lewiston, where he died four months later. His third wife and several children from his second marriage reportedly survived him.

Newell is remembered for his contributions to the early Oregon community as a political leader, entrepreneur, and public-spirited businessman. In private life he was active in both the Episcopal church and the Masons.

• Some primary material is published in *Robert Newell's Memoranda*, ed. Dorothy O. Johansen (1959). An unpublished diary of Newell's 1868 Washington trip with some details of his family is quoted in Alvin M. Joseph, Jr., *The Nez Percé Indians and the Opening of the Northwest* (1965), and Clifford M. Drury, *Chief Lawyer of the Nez Percé Indians, 1796–1875* (1979). The diary is privately held. Biographical information on Robert Newell can be found in T. C. Elliott, "'Doctor' Robert Newell: Pioneer," *Oregon Historical Society Quarterly*, June 1908, pp. 103–26. See also H. W. Scott, *History of the Oregon Country* (6 vols., 1924), and C. H. Carey, *History of Oregon* (1922).

ANN T. KEENE

NEWELL, William Augustus (5 Sept. 1817–8 Aug. 1901), governor of New Jersey, U.S. representative, and physician, was born in Franklin, Ohio, the son of James Hugh Newell, a civil engineer and cartographer, and Eliza D. Hankinson. Newell's parents were longtime New Jerseyans, but Newell was born while his parents were on an extended visit in Ohio. In 1819 his family returned to Freehold, New Jersey, where Newell attended the public schools. He graduated from Rutgers College in 1836, and he earned a degree in medicine from the University of Pennsylvania in 1839. He first practiced under the tutelage of his uncle in Manahawkin before establishing his own practice in Imlaystown. In 1844 he moved to Allentown, which would be his permanent New Jersey residence. He married Joanna Van Deursen (c. 1837); they had three children.

In 1846 Newell won election to Congress from the Second District as a Whig, and he was reelected two years later. His most prominent achievement in Congress came in the area of marine safety. After witnessing an offshore shipwreck that cost the lives of thirteen people, he began experimenting with lifesaving devices, and in 1848 he authored the legislation that created the U.S. Life Saving Service. That year he sponsored a $10,000 appropriation toward the erection of lighthouse stations along an especially treacherous portion of the New Jersey coastline. Each station was equipped with a cannon capable of shooting a line to wrecked ships, along which a car could be transported to retrieve passengers. After this innovation saved the lives of more than 200 people aboard the Scottish brig *Ayrshire* in 1850, Congress extended its use along the entire Atlantic Coast.

The acclaim Newell won for these efforts did not immediately enhance his political career. He opposed the creation of the Utah and New Mexico territories on a popular sovereignty basis, thus allowing for the possibility of slavery within their borders, which formed part of the overwhelmingly popular Compromise of 1850. In the face of that support for the compromise, he and every other New Jersey Whig congressman refused to run for reelection that year. The passage of the unpopular Kansas-Nebraska Act of 1854, together with an upsurge in animosity toward Catholic immigrants, revived Newell's career. He joined the nativist American party in 1855, but one year later the Republican party challenged the Americans for leadership of the state's anti-Democratic forces. Although Republicans and Americans ran different presidential candidates in 1856, both parties' conventions chose Newell to head an "opposition" ticket as their gubernatorial candidate, despite some Republicans' disdain for Newell's nativism. Newell squeaked out a victory, receiving 51 percent of the votes cast, over Democrat William C. Alexander.

Limited by the state constitution to one three-year term as governor, Newell advocated restrictions on both the sale of liquor and the voting rights of naturalized citizens as well as the strict enforcement of naturalization laws. He suggested that the legislature pass resolutions requesting Congress to lengthen the naturalization period and denouncing sectional (especially prosouthern) extremists. Democrats, however, controlled at least one branch of the legislature throughout Newell's term, and hence his partisan agenda had no chance of adoption. Newell's patronage allocation, despite some dissatisfaction, did help weld the Republican and American factions into a single, if not entirely cohesive, party.

As governor, Newell presided over the state's eight-man court of pardons, and his vote in 1857 against commuting the death sentence of James P. Donnelly, a Catholic Irish-American convicted of murder by a Protestant jury on the basis of questionable evidence, would plague his political career in years to come. Although Newell cast just one of six negative votes, Donnelly singled him out for abuse in a two-hour speech prior to his execution.

During the Civil War, Newell served as Abraham Lincoln's superintendent of the Life Saving Service in New Jersey, as a surgeon for the federal draft board in the state, and as Lincoln's personal physician. A delegate to the Republican National Convention and a congressional candidate from the Second District in 1864, Newell defeated incumbent Democrat George Middleton with 51.6 percent of the votes cast. As a congressman, Newell supported congressional Reconstruction efforts, voting in favor of the Civil Rights Act of 1866 and the act extending the life of the Freedmen's Bureau. Renominated in 1866, Newell narrowly lost (with 49.4 percent of the votes cast) the election to Charles Haight. During the campaign, Democrats distributed in German the nativist recommendations Newell had made as governor and chastised him for his role in the Donnelly affair.

After resuming his career in medicine, Newell unsuccessfully sought a Republican congressional nomination in 1868. Two years later he won the nomination but lost the election (with 49.3 percent of the votes cast) to Democrat Samuel Forker. If Newell's anti-immigrant reputation hindered him somewhat in his home congressional district, it proved to be a major handicap in 1877 after he won the Republican gubernatorial nomination. Democrats selected Civil War general George McClellan as their candidate and blasted Newell's nativistic prejudice. The insurgent Prohibition and Greenback parties attacked the Republican party's alleged vacillation on prohibition and the division in the party over the resumption of paper money in specie. Newell won only 45 percent of the votes cast, the poorest showing of any gubernatorial candidate in fifteen years.

Despite his political setbacks, Newell continued to play a role in government. Appointed president of the New Jersey State Board of Agriculture in 1875, he promoted the establishment of a federal Department of Agriculture. Five years later, President Rutherford Hayes appointed Newell as the governor of Washington Territory, a position he held until 1884. He advocated temperance and Sabbatarian legislation, an upgraded lifesaving service on the Pacific Coast, and measures to assimilate forcibly the territory's American Indians. A federal American Indian inspector for one year, Newell afterward resumed his medical practice in Washington.

After the death of his wife in 1899, Newell returned to New Jersey, where he spent the last two years of his life writing papers for the Monmouth County Historical Society. He died probably in Allentown.

• There is no known repository of Newell papers. Douglas V. Shaw's essay on Newell in *The Governors of New Jersey, 1664–1974: Biographical Essays*, ed. Paul A. Stellhorn and Michael J. Birkner (1982), is the most detailed treatment of his life. See also William Gillette, *Jersey Blue: New Jersey Politics in the Civil War Era, 1854–1865* (1995); and William Nelson, ed., *The New Jersey Coast in Three Centuries* (1902). For details of Newell's career in the 1850s, see the obituary by Alanson A. Vance, "A Political Reminiscence" (Morristown) *Jerseyman*, 12, 19, 26 Nov. and 3, 10, 17 Dec. 1901.

LEX RENDA

NEWHOUSE, Samuel Irving (24 May 1895–29 Aug. 1979), newspaper publisher and media mogul, was born Solomon Irving Newhaus in New York City, the son of Meier Neuhaus, a garment worker, and Rose Arenfeldt. His father, an immigrant from near Vitebsk in Russia, did not fare well in the United States and eventually left his wife and eight children to seek a healthier climate in Arizona. As the eldest child, Samuel became the head of the household.

Newhouse's first job, at age twelve, was as an office boy for Bayonne, New Jersey, judge Hyman Lazarus. Within four years the judge gave the industrious teenager a man-size order to take over a sickly daily he owned, the *Bayonne Times*. Newhouse almost immediately halted the drain on the *Times* by improving home delivery and increasing circulation and advertising. Simultaneously, he attended evening classes at the New Jersey Law School and earned a law degree in 1916.

He lost his first court case and never practiced law again.

Instead, Newhouse began a career as a purchaser of newspapers, his first acquisition being a Fitchburg, Massachusetts, daily with an attractive newsprint contract. After shifting the newsprint to the *Bayonne Times*, Newhouse sold the Fitchburg property for a 50 percent profit. In 1922 he bought the *Staten Island Advance* and, for a brief time, uncharacteristically wrote stories, chiefly to save a reporter's salary. On 8 May 1924 Newhouse married Mitzi Epstein, a fashion design student; the couple raised two sons.

By the 1930s Newhouse planned his wide-ranging media empire, rooting it in the immediate New York City area. He bought, merged, suspended, or created five newspapers on Long Island during the next decade; the first of these was the *Long Island Daily Press*, 51 percent of which he purchased in 1932. From the outset the Newhouse pattern was to seek controlling, if not full, interest in all properties that he bought. Other traits for which Newhouse became known were already in place by the early 1930s. His resistance to organized labor was evident when the newly formed American Newspaper Guild voted to strike against both the *Long Island Daily Press* and the *Staten Island Advance* in 1934. Other Newhouse dailies, at least in Newark; Long Island; St. Louis, Missouri; and Portland, Oregon, figured prominently in Guild strike history. Newhouse's penchant for sniffing out weakened newspapers, the victims of financial downturns, family owners' feuds, libel suits, or labor unrest, surfaced when he bought the ailing *Newark Ledger* in 1935.

As increased costs and taxes afflicted American newspapers, Newhouse saw opportunities to add to his chain. From a seventeen-month period in 1937–1939, he emerged with new and strengthened papers in Newark (*Star-Ledger*), Long Island (*Star-Journal*), and upstate New York (*Syracuse Herald-Journal*). He also became known for burying dailies (four in this period alone) while absorbing their circulations and disemploying their staffs. The Syracuse purchase was executed in a shroud of silence, as were later transactions in Harrisburg, Pennsylvania; Portland; and Denver, Colorado. Newhouse rationalized that it was good business to operate secretly, catching arch enemies—especially the Guild—off guard and allowing him to buy up remaining stock. Such a maneuver also covered up outright deception, as when Newhouse used a strawman to buy two Harrisburg dailies from their publisher's widow, who would not have sold directly to Newhouse.

In the post–World War II period, Newhouse entered broadcasting for the first time with his purchase of WSYR in Syracuse. From then on he often assumed control of the radio and television stations of the newspapers he bought; this occurred in St. Louis, Portland, and Birmingham, Alabama. After a bitter six-year court battle, he succeeded in getting full control of the *Jersey Journal* in 1945; six years later he bought the sickly *Jersey Observer* and merged it with the *Journal*. In 1950 he extended his media combine nation-

wide, picking up the Portland *Oregonian*. Newhouse, who had become famous for his philosophy of editorial autonomy, was sought by the *Oregonian* publishers when they decided to sell.

Taking the stand that he did not care what his newspapers advocated as long as they made profits, Newhouse was roundly criticized. His local autonomy principle was attacked as not being genuine, secured as it was by relatives and friends who headed various media. At least sixty-four cousins, nephews, and in-laws, as well as his sons, brothers, and sisters, were employed by Newhouse. His newspapers themselves were described as yielders of great profits, not great truths, and as dispassionate, flat, and lacking in forceful editorial control.

Newhouse's acquisitions in the 1950s and 1960s came swiftly, characterized by big-money deals and at times long court battles. In 1955 he bought the 103-year-old *St. Louis Globe-Democrat*, then at death's door, and for a while made it highly competitive, using his proven formula of reduced staffs, merged elements, and waste elimination. That same year he paid the highest newspaper price in U.S. history, $18.7 million, for the Birmingham News Company, *Huntsville Times*, four Alabama broadcast stations, and a motor freight line.

In 1960 Newhouse made two more purchases, much to his later regret. Heirs and employees of the *Denver Post* kept him in court for thirteen years and ultimately prevented him from increasing his original 15 percent investment; in Springfield, Massachusetts, the Bowles family did the same thing, limiting him to a 40 percent stake. Over the years, Newhouse attempted unsuccessfully to buy the *New York Times*, *Washington Post*, *Baltimore Sun*, *Philadelphia Inquirer*, the Thomson newspapers, and numerous other dailies in Wichita, Kansas; Detroit, Michigan; Houston, Texas; Nashville, Tennessee; Omaha, Nebraska; Buffalo, New York; Boston, Massachusetts; and Rome, Italy. In the midst of the long and violent Portland newspaper strike, he bought the *Oregon Journal* (1961) to monopolize that city's dailies.

By 1963, after paying another record price ($42 million) for the two New Orleans, Louisiana, dailies, Newhouse led U.S. publishers in number of properties, owning outright twenty-six newspaper units in eleven cities as well as parts of five others. Part of his success was attributed to his ability to make quick decisions, which in turn resulted from his large financial reserves and his encyclopedic knowledge of newspaper ledger sheets.

Newhouse's ventures in magazine publishing began in 1959, when he purchased Condé-Nast, consisting of *Vogue*, *Glamour*, *Bride's Magazine*, *Home and Garden*, *Vogue Pattern Book*, and *Jeune Mariée*. His gaining all the stock in major rival Street and Smith (*Mademoiselle*, *Charm*, and seven other periodicals) a short time later placed him second to Hearst Publications among newspaper publishers bringing out magazines.

Newhouse, however, retained his primary interest in newspapers as he continued to add to his chain, paying $15–20 million in 1966 for control of three Mobile, Alabama, and two Pascagoula, Mississippi, newspapers; a record $54.2 million in 1967 for the *Cleveland Plain Dealer*; and still another record-breaking $305 million in 1976 for eight Booth newspapers in Michigan and *Parade* magazine. In 1966 he bought back *Bayonne Times* and merged it with the *Jersey Journal*. That same year he bought the *Newark Evening News* and shut it down, leaving his *Star-Ledger* as Newark's only daily and the largest newspaper in New Jersey.

Besides one of the nation's largest and most profitable media empires, Newhouse left two other legacies when he died. His donations of more than $15 million to Syracuse University built a living memorial to him—the S. I. Newhouse School of Public Communications; while his ingenious way of calculating his taxes left his family with the dubious distinction of owing the largest tax bill in Internal Revenue Service (IRS) history—more than $1 billion. However, the beehive-type business charter that he had created and amended many times also gave the family the means to defeat the IRS and pay less than one-twentieth of the amount owed. After Newhouse's death in New York City, his sons expanded the company to include Random Books, the *New Yorker*, *Gentleman's Quarterly*, *Self*, *Vanity Fair*, and Fawcett Books.

Newhouse was one of the great success stories of the business world. Between the 1950s and 1960s he quickly came out of relative obscurity to lead a new breed of publishers, motivated by bottom-line economics rather than journalistic motives or the public welfare.

• Because the Newhouse family has been very private and secretive, shying from interviews and either bringing or threatening lawsuits against Newhouse's two biographers, there are no publicly available repositories of primary documents. The two biographies were done almost a generation apart: John A. Lent, *Newhouse, Newspapers, Nuisances* (1966), and Richard H. Meeker, *Newspaperman: S. I. Newhouse and the Business of News* (1983). A third book on Newhouse's son S. I. Newhouse, Jr., Thomas Maier's *Newhouse: All the Glitter, Power, and Glory of America's Richest Media Empire and the Secretive Man Behind It* (1994), has sections on the career of the elder Newhouse. Newhouse, with the help of David Jacobs, related the story of his life and career in *A Memo for the Children from S. I. Newhouse* (1980). Newhouse's obituary is in the *New York Times*, 30 Aug. 1979.

JOHN A. LENT

NEWLANDS, Francis Griffith (28 Aug. 1848–24 Dec. 1917), representative and senator, was born in Natchez, Mississippi, the son of James Birney Newlands, a physician, and Jessie Barland. Both parents were Scottish immigrants. Soon after his birth the family moved to Quincy, Illinois, where his father sought to overcome the alcoholism that brought ruin to his medical career. Newlands's father died in 1851, and Newlands's mother married Ebeneezer Moore, a well-situated businessman, banker, and ex-mayor. Moore's financial setbacks in the panic of 1857 placed the family in strained circumstances, causing them to move to

Chicago then to Washington, D.C., where Moore received a minor political appointment in 1863. In this same year Newlands entered Yale College at the young age of fifteen, but he withdrew in March 1866 because of financial problems that were further complicated by the death of his stepfather in October 1866. His "shortest, gladdest years" came quickly to an end. Upon returning to Washington, D.C., he studied law at Columbian College (now George Washington University) and, after admission to the bar, departed for San Francisco in 1870 to seek his fortune and offer support to his struggling family.

In San Francisco Newlands began a law practice and a social life that soon saw his name associated with some of the most prominent families in the city. By the fall of 1874 the San Francisco press buzzed with news of his courtship and impending marriage to Clara Adelaide Sharon, daughter of the Comstock and Bank of California magnate, William Sharon. The marriage took place in November 1874 after the legislative elections in Nevada, which assured Sharon a U.S. Senate seat. The Newlands had three children. Clara Newlands died in childbirth in 1882, leaving Sharon's entire estate of nearly $30 million under Newlands's trusteeship after Sharon's death in 1885. It fell to Newlands to defend the estate in a messy divorce trial growing out of an alleged common law marriage between Sharon and Sarah Althea Hill. While handling this "wretched case," he also sought the office of U.S. senator from California, but he was shut out of the running by the senatorial ambitions of fellow Democrat George Hearst and because of his unpopular support of U.S. Supreme Court justice Stephen J. Field's presidential candidacy. Newlands's own ambitions then turned to Nevada where the Sharon estate held numerous properties. He married again in 1888 to Edith McAllister, the daughter of San Francisco lawyer Hall McAllister. The two children of this marriage did not survive infancy. Newlands's arrival in Nevada in late 1888 caused political rumors to fly in the state's press about his plans to spend freely and capture a U.S. Senate seat from Nevada. He prudently chose not to press his advantages of wealth in the manner of William Sharon, but rather he sought support by announcing plans for a vast irrigation scheme in Nevada to free the state from the grips of a mining depression that it had suffered since the failure of the Comstock.

What Newlands had hoped would be an immediate springboard into the Senate proved to be the beginning of a lengthy apprenticeship for that office—ten years as Nevada's lone U.S. congressman from 1893 to 1903. During that time he became first a Republican, then a spokesman for the Silver party, and finally in 1896 came back to the Democratic party when it embraced the silver cause. The silver issue dominated Nevada politics when Nevadans believed that the coinage of silver money would raise silver prices and revive mining in the state. After the silver money issue failed in the 1896 presidential election, Newlands emerged as a vocal western Democrat in support of national action on irrigation and one of the principals responsible for the passage of the National Reclamation Act in 1902, known in Democratic party circles as the Newlands Reclamation Act. Under national reclamation the federal government built selected irrigation projects in the West financed by western lands sales with settlers committed to long-term paybacks for water supplied. His reputation secured by this regional aid package from the federal government to the arid states, Newlands won his U.S. senatorship in 1903. In foreign affairs after the Spanish-American War he was anti-imperialist but did support territorial acquisitions if they could be considered for eventual statehood. In his view Cuba qualified but not the Philippines.

As a leading western progressive senator, Newlands worked for the conversion or "modernization" of the Democratic party from its states' rights traditions into a "national action party." Ironically, his brand of progressivism resembled Republican Theodore Roosevelt's (1858–1919) New Nationalism that welcomed expansion of national governmental power. In Nevada Newlands had early advocated community and state aid to irrigation projects, but local sources were too poor to undertake the larger projects that Nevada's extreme aridity demanded, prompting him to look to the national government. He stood for a National Incorporation Act but settled for the creation of a Bureau of Corporations and ultimately the Federal Trade Commission to oversee corporate activities. He supported the establishment of the Children's Bureau to nationalize standards for the protection of childrens' welfare and advocated a never-achieved Federal Bureau of Fine Arts to promote art and beauty in American life. For western public land he backed the federally managed scientific conservation movement of that era. Finally and most comprehensively, he fought for a Rivers and Harbors Commission to develop and control the waterways of the country for irrigation, flood control, electrical power, and transportation. Although generally approved by 1917, it never achieved the powers he envisioned. He clearly supported the delegation of congressional authority to commissions and boards of experts, such as the Forest Service and the Reclamation Service, to carry out the many complicated functions of government.

The issue of race attracted Newlands's interest, reflecting a West Coast politician's concern about Asians and also his unreconstructed Civil War Democratic party views about African Americans. Above all he believed racial issues should be addressed and established by federal policies. Asian immigration should be stopped by Congress, and African Americans should be resettled in lands "scientifically prepared" outside of the United States, possibly in Cuba. He became a vocal advocate of repealing the Fifteenth Amendment to the Constitution to enable states to disenfranchise the African-American population. Participation of these people in politics, he believed, promoted racial strife that unnecessarily disrupted and paralyzed American government and politics. By 1910 some press sources hailed him as a possible Democratic presidential nominee who might unite the West and the South in an all-white-America policy that reserved the full privileges of citizenship for whites alone, excluding Asian and African Americans.

Newlands easily won reelection to the Senate in 1908, but he barely retained his Senate office from the Republicans in the fiercely contested 1914 election, when the Socialist party candidate won large numbers of Democratic votes. Newlands sought to build "a model commonwealth" in the midst of a far-flung desert, mountainous environment by supporting the direct democracy measures of referendum, initiative, recall, and popular election of U.S. senators. Economic regulatory commissions such as public service commissions to oversee the charges of private utilities commanded his support, as did the prohibition of gambling and prostitution and restrictions on the saloon in Nevada's frontier society. He envisioned irrigated farms fostering commerce and ultimately industry. To achieve all of these he believed in community, state, and especially national government action.

Senator Newlands took much satisfaction in seeing Democratic president Woodrow Wilson move toward a greater assertion of national power during his administrations and away from the limited government concepts espoused in his New Freedom campaign of 1912. The emergency of World War I provided the opportunity for the implementation of much of this strong central government action, including federal control of railroads. Newlands's senatorial career was often more devoted to larger national policies than to the everyday functions of a politician from a small state seeking favors for his constituents. For this latter oversight he was often criticized by Nevadans, but others admired the national reputation he achieved during the Progressive Era. Newlands died in Washington, D.C.

• Yale University's Sterling Library holds the large collection of Newlands papers. See also A. B. Darling, ed., *The Public Papers of Francis G. Newlands* (2 vols., 1932); H. H. Bancroft, *Chronicles of the Builders of the Commonwealth*, vol. 4 (1892); M. F. Hudson, comp., *Senator Francis G. Newlands; His Work* (1914); *Francis Griffith Newlands . . . Memorial Addresses . . . in the Senate* (1920); and the obituary in the Washington, D.C., *Evening Star*, 25 Dec. 1917. An assessment of his state and national contributions is William D. Rowley, "Francis G. Newlands and the Promises of American Life," *Nevada Historical Society Quarterly* 32 (Fall 1989).

WILLIAM D. ROWLEY

NEWMAN, Alfred (17 Mar. 1901–17 Feb. 1970), conductor and film composer, was born in New Haven, Connecticut, the son of Michael Nemirovsky (later Newman), a Russian immigrant and struggling produce dealer, and Luba Koskoff, a cantor's daughter who instilled a love for piano in young Alfred. By age eight Newman had become a gifted pianist and soon was performing classical repertory. At age ten, thanks to society matron Ella Wheeler Wilcox, he studied on scholarship at New York's Von Ende School with Sigismund Stojowski, and at age eleven he soloed with the New Haven Symphony.

In 1913 his family moved to New York City, and by age sixteen, with money from recitals in New York, Boston, and Philadelphia, Newman became their sole support. He won numerous Von Ende awards and medals. He took a job accompanying vaudeville comedienne Grace La Rue for her 1918 revue, *Hitchy-Koo*. Music director William Daly, influential in George Gershwin's career, taught Newman the baton technique of conducting. On shows such as *The Greenwich Village Follies* (1919) and *George White's Scandals of 1920*, he was billed as "the youngest music director in the country." He was involved in works by legends Richard Rodgers and Lorenz Hart, Jerome Kern, Otto Harbach, and George and Ira Gershwin.

At age twenty-six Newman was invited by Fritz Reiner to conduct the Cincinnati Orchestra, then Irving Berlin convinced Samuel Goldwyn to bring him to Hollywood as music director for a romantic comedy, *Reaching for the Moon* (1930), for which he composed a song. Goldwyn signed him to a three-month contract and quickly assigned to him *Whoopee!* (1930), starring Eddie Cantor, with choreography by Busby Berkeley. For the next nine years he worked with Goldwyn and the independent United Artists. His first original score was for the musical comedy *One Heavenly Night* (1930). That year he also composed another eight scores, working twenty-hour days, seven days a week.

Early scores by Newman included three classics, *Dodsworth* (1936), *Stella Dallas* (1937), and *Gunga Din* (1939). In 1939 he joined fledgling Fox Studios and was nominated for Academy Awards for *The Hunchback of Notre Dame*, *The Rains Came*, *Wuthering Heights*, and *They Shall Have Music*.

In Hollywood, where he studied briefly (and later recorded) with Arnold Schoenberg, Newman fine-tuned the art of film scoring with immense musical variety, using mood underscoring throughout a film instead of merely punctuating a dramatic action or moment. He and United Artists music director Charles Dunwart developed what came to be known as "the Newman System," an upgrading of film music synchronization.

From 1939 to 1960 Newman was head of 20th Century–Fox's music department, and he propelled it to prominence. Though scores for low-budget programs were composed assembly-line fashion in two to three days (by other house music staff), Newman's philosophy on "A" films was "to achieve total perfection and don't settle for anything less."

Newman associate, choral director, and record producer Ken Darby said, "He had a marvelous gift of innate and acquired good taste . . . a swift, analytical mind . . . and a pair of fantastically accurate ears. He knew where to put a microphone to obtain optimum results." Darby reported that when Newman's reach for perfection outstripped technical facilities available, he invented his own.

Among Newman's best scores is his epic treatment, with an orchestra of 128 musicians, for *Captain from Castile* (1947). It was nominated for an Academy Award. Film music historian Tony Thomas noted that the film "had everything—love, death, pomp, circumstance, action, scenery, and the Church . . . grandeur [that] inspired the use of the complete orchestral palette in the grand manner." The score's key phrases, the twelve-bar "Conquistador" theme and its offshoot, "Conquest," found their place in concert repertory.

Newman's expertise is reflected in forty-five Academy Award nominations and nine wins. His most heard piece, however, is the 1953 20th Century–Fox fanfare. Newman was self-critical, and, associates revealed, his most successful scores were written at times of self-doubt. According to Thomas, Newman's greatest gift was his ability "to musically comment on the gamut of human experience"—whether it was the swashbuckler saving a king in *The Prisoner of Zenda* (1937), the harsh life of Welsh miners in *How Green Was My Valley* (1941), Deep South racial prejudice in *Pinky* (1949), the doomed romantics of *Wuthering Heights* (1939), or conveying faith and strength against great disbelief in *The Song of Bernadette* (1943), which he researched for a year and which won the Academy Award for best score.

Newman's score for *The Robe* (1953) combined sanctity, sensuality, passion, and Near East scales into an eight-measure phrase for the "main title," variations of which he used throughout the film. Film writer Page Cook observed, "Newman's music not only prepares the viewer for the dramatic events that follow but establishes the harmonic character of the entire work."

During Newman's prodigious career, he scored 255 films, including *The Hurricane* (1937), *The Razor's Edge* (1946), *Gentleman's Agreement* (1947), *Mother Wore Tights* (1947), *The Snake Pit* (1948), *A Letter to Three Wives* (1949), *All about Eve* (1950), *Love Is a Many-Splendored Thing* (1955), *Anastasia* (1956), and *How the West Was Won* (1963). His compositions for *Street Scene* (1931) were used in four films.

In 1960, as Fox undertook cost cutting in the face of shrinking movie attendance and the aftermath of a musicians strike, Newman retired with a salary of $104,000. Freelancing again, he was never without work. His health declined in 1964 during scoring of *The Greatest Story Ever Told* (1965). He died in Los Angeles. Newman was married three times to actresses Beth Meakins (1931, divorced 1940; one child); Mary Lou Dix (1940, divorced 1943; one child); and his widow, Martha Montgomery (1947; five children).

• The 20th Century–Fox research library and the Academy of Motion Picture Arts and Sciences maintain extensive files on Newman. The composer's bound scores, recordings, and career memorabilia are housed in the Alfred Newman Library, University of Southern California, Los Angeles. Fred Steiner, "The Making of an American Film Composer: A Study of Alfred Newman's Music in the First Decade of Sound" (Ph.D. diss., Univ. of Southern California, 1981), is the best single study of Newman's life and work. Fred Karlin, *Listening to Movies: The Film Lover's Guide to Film Music* (1994); Tony Thomas, *Film Score: The Art and Craft of Movie Music*, rev. ed. (1991); and Thomas, *Music for the Movies* (1973), provide excellent overviews of Hollywood's film composers. Newman's music can be sampled on compact disc; see, for example, *The Classic Music of Alfred Newman* (Varese Sarabande Records, 1992), conducted by Newman; and *Captain from Castile: The Classic Film Scores of Alfred Newman* (RCA Records, 1973), National Philharmonic Orchestra conducted by Charles Gerhardt. Newman also recorded pop music collections for Majestic (later Mercury) and Decca Records beginning in the 1940s. His work and film scoring philosophy are featured in the video series *Music for the Movies*, "The Hollywood Sound" (Sony, 1995). All contain extensive notations. An obituary is in the *New York Times*, 19 Feb. 1970.

ELLIS NASSOUR

NEWMAN, Angelia French (4 Dec. 1837–15 Apr. 1910), church worker, reformer, and lecturer, was born Angelia Louise French Thurston in Montpelier, Vermont, the daughter of Daniel Sylvester Thurston, a farmer and tanner, and Matilda Benjamin. When "Angie," as she was commonly known, was about age seven, her mother died. Her father remarried shortly thereafter. Angie attended the local academy, and later briefly taught school until around 1852, when her family moved to Wisconsin. In 1856, soon after her eighteenth birthday, she married Frank Kilgore, the son of a Methodist minister from Madison. The marriage was childless, and he died within a year. She subsequently worked as a teacher at Central Public School in Madison and spent one term (1857–1858) at Lawrence University in Appleton. In 1859 she married David Newman, a dry goods merchant; they would have two children.

In 1871 the Newmans moved to the new city of Lincoln, Nebraska, where they joined St. Paul Methodist Episcopal Church, and he became a successful real estate and insurance agent. A staid, nonsmoking teetotaler and Sunday school superintendent, David Newman encouraged his wife, who had been raised as a Methodist, to become more actively involved in church work and associated causes. Despite a chronic debilitating condition known as "pulmonary weakness" and occasional bouts of invalidism, Angie Newman served for a decade as a leader in the denomination's Woman's Foreign Missionary Society, formed in 1869 to generate funds and mobilize lay talent to pursue "women's work for women." Echoing this popular phrase, Newman served as organizer, correspondent, and secretary of the St. Louis (later the Western) Branch of the society. Her frequent accounts in the society's magazine, the *Heathen Woman's Friend*, reported on her organizing trips—one into frontier western Nebraska, where she survived a train wreck and a grasshopper plague—as well as a succession of fundraising missionary fairs and children's auxiliaries and the ever-present selling of life memberships and missionaries' portraits. Newman was honored—and money was raised—by having an infant in a Methodist foundling home in India named for her and by the designation of Angie F. Newman Hall at Lucknow, a girls' school. She received tributes for her "thorough preparation" as hostess of the 1877 meeting of the Western Branch in Lincoln, where she made one of her characteristically strong emotional appeals; "the heathen at home," her epithet for those who opposed the mission cause, became the title of her well-received pamphlet published in 1878.

Like many leading missionary advocates. Newman turned after 1880 to the newly formed Woman's Home Missionary Society and chose as her chief concern the status of women, both "gentile" and Mormon, in Utah Territory. A trip to Salt Lake City (for health reasons) during the summer of 1876 had convinced her that Utah was akin to the Far East as a missionary field: "Salt Lake is to all intents 'foreign.'" She soon began to travel throughout the Midwest and the Northeast, where she was introduced to the audiences who came to hear her as a "brilliant speaker" and an "earnest advocate of reform." She would then proceed to lecture on the evils of Mormonism—a nonreligion in her view—and in particular the practice of polygamy, which she saw as a threat to all Christian women. So potentially injurious was it thought to be that Newman and her supporters sacrificed a cherished secular cause, woman suffrage, to hit at polygamy. They argued that suffrage was a ruse in Utah, as plural wives would be expected to vote as instructed by their husbands, thus helping to perpetuate the status quo. Although the "abomination" of polygamy had been outlawed by Congress since 1862, the Mormon church did not prohibit the practice until 1890. In the interim Newman applied as much pressure as she could. As founding secretary of the Mormon Bureau of the Woman's Home Missionary Society (formed in 1883 in response to one of her lectures) and as the first superintendent of the Mormon Department of the Woman's Christian Temperance Union (formed in 1886), she worked to collect a quarter of a million signatures on a petition urging Congress to override the Utah Territory's grant of the vote to women. Congress responded in 1887 by passing the Edmunds-Tucker Act, which further moved against plural marriage and revoked woman suffrage in Utah.

To Newman's credit, she was sensitive to the social upheaval that would result from the suspension of polygamy; to assist the women and children whose lives would be disrupted by it, she also worked to establish a place in Salt Lake City where abandoned wives could go for assistance in redirecting their lives. A frequent witness before the Senate Education and Labor Committee between 1885 and 1891, she played a critical role in having the Industrial Christian Home Association in Utah Territory incorporated in 1886 and in getting Congress to allocate $40,000 for the founding of the Industrial Home for refugee wives. Congress continued to appropriate funds for the home (a few thousand dollars per year) until 1893, when the effort was abandoned; too few wives and children had been served. Newman blamed political interference.

Newman's anti-Mormon activity helped bring her a special distinction in September 1887, when she became the first woman to be selected as a lay delegate to the Methodist General Conference. (Four other women delegates were selected that same year, but Nebraskan Methodists met early; thus she has the distinction of being "first.") In May 1888 Newman proudly took her seat at the legislative body's opening session held in the Metropolitan Opera House in New York City. Her expectations were premature, however. The male delegates, laymen as well as clergy, voted not to permit Newman and the other women to be seated, asserting that their sex made them ineligible to serve as delegates. Newman and the others, by continuing to support church causes, no doubt aided in the eventual seating of women delegates at the General Conference held in 1904.

David Newman's death in a railroad accident in 1893 hardly slowed his widow's pace. Newman held leadership positions in the Woman's Relief Corps of the Grand Army of the Republic, the Daughters of the American Revolution, the National Council of Women, and the National Conference of Charities and Corrections; for a decade she was appointed by successive governors of her state to serve as a delegate to the NCCC. She continued to lecture widely, primarily for the WCTU, extolling the virtues of abstaining from alcohol and remaining socially pure. Near the turn of the century she spent time in Hawaii and wrote with her accustomed enthusiasm about the islands' special opportunities for missionary service. She later boasted of having been a hospital inspector in Hawaii around the time of the Spanish-American War. An ardent Republican and enthusiastic supporter of President William McKinley and his foreign and domestic policies, after his assassination in 1901 she wrote *McKinley Carnations of Memory: The McKinley Button of Two Campaigns*; privately printed in 1904, it is a blending of her political and religious sentiments. She died several years later in Lincoln.

Newman's life combined both intense struggle and eventual economic security, and her career typifies the strengths and the weaknesses of American Protestantism in the last third of its great missionary century. A descendant of the nation's Puritan establishment, she embraced the moral certitude of her church and her country and strove to bring dissident interests in line with that vision. Her willingness to impose her will on others—by force if necessary—would, at the end of the twentieth century, likely be viewed by mainstream Protestants as arrogant and mean-spirited; her causes, quaint and intolerant. Yet for her era, she was a beacon of moral assurance and progressive social reform, a credit to her sex as well as to her church and class.

• Sketches of Newman's life are in Frances E. Willard and Mary A. Livermore, eds., *A Woman of the Century. Fourteen Hundred Seventy Biographical Sketches Accompanied by Portraits of Leading American Women in All Walks of Life* (1893), and Ernest H. Cherrington, ed., *Standard Encyclopedia of the Alcohol Problem*, vol. 4 (1928). For details of family and early life, see Brown Thurston, *Thurston Genealogies* (1880); Reuben Gold Thwaites, *Historical Sketch of the Public Schools of Madison, Wisconsin, 1838–1885* (1886); and Lawrence University, *Annual Catalogue* (1857–1858). For Newman's church and reform work, see issues of the *Heathen Woman's Friend*, Boston (1869–1880); *Woman's Home Missions*, Delaware, Ohio (1884–1901); and the *Christian Advocate*, New York City (1886–1901); also see Laura E. Tomkinson, *Twenty Years' History of the Woman's Home Missionary Society of the Methodist Episcopal Church, 1880–1900* (1903). For Newman and the 1888 General Conference, see Methodist Episcopal Church General Conference, *Journal* (1888); James M. Buckley, *Constitutional and Parliamentary History of the Methodist Episcopal Church* (1912); and the *New York Times*, 29 Apr.–8 May 1888. An obituary is in the *Nebraska State Journal* (Lincoln), 16 Apr. 1910.

THEODORE L. AGNEW

NEWMAN, Barnett (29 Jan. 1905–4 July 1970), painter and sculptor, was born in New York City, the son of Abraham Newman, a manufacturer of men's clothes, and Anna Steinberg. The Newmans were emigrants from Lomza in Russian Poland and named their first son Baruch, which they Americanized to Barnett. Newman attended the National Hebrew School (of which his father, an ardent Zionist, was a founding trustee) and DeWitt Clinton High School, both in the Bronx. Cutting classes in high school, Newman would visit the Metropolitan Museum of Art. In an interview not long before his death he commented, "Growing up in New York, the word 'museum,' for me, meant the Metropolitan" ("In Front of the Real Thing," *ARTNews*, Jan. 1970, p. 60).

In 1922, with the permission of his mother, Newman began attending classes at the Art Students League, where he became friends with artist Adolph Gottlieb. Newman's parents, particularly his father, persuaded him to go to college, and he duly enrolled in City College of New York in 1923, graduating with a bachelor's degree in philosophy in 1927. Though Newman wished to begin an artistic career, his father induced him to join the A. Newman Company, the family garment business. He promised Barnett that if after two to three years he disliked the clothes trade the elder Newman would bankroll his son's career in the arts.

Preparing to take up his father's offer and leave the apparel industry, Newman saw his plans dashed by the stock market crash and the start of the Great Depression, which wiped out the prosperous Newman firm. Abraham Newman was devastated by the failure of his business, and Barnett took over the day-to-day operation of the company.

Newman proved to be an able businessman and ran the business until 1937, when he liquidated it soon after his father died of a heart attack. While still in the garment industry, Newman took an interest in municipal politics and ran for mayor (with writer Alexander Borodulin as the candidate for comptroller) on the "artists-writers" ticket in 1933. Journalist A. J. Liebling wrote in the *New York World-Telegram* (4 Nov.

1933) that the two "aesthetes" were running because "the forces of self-expression should express themselves by the ballot." Never losing interest in his artistic career, Newman also worked from 1931 through 1939 as a substitute art teacher in New York City public schools. (Ironically, Newman, like a number of other well-known artists, never passed the New York City certification exam for art teachers and thus could never be employed as a full-time instructor.) It was at a teachers' meeting in 1934 that Newman met fellow instructor Annalee Greenhouse. The two married in June 1936; they had no children. Newman refused to join any of the government-sponsored artist relief programs of the 1930s. He later gave two reasons for avoiding the Works Progress Administration arts projects: first, that he earned more money as a substitute art teacher, and second, that he did not want to compromise his work by taking handouts from the government.

Becoming dissatisfied with his art, Newman stopped painting in 1939–1940 and began to question the basic suppositions underlying the artistic milieu of the late 1930s. He and his compatriots found no satisfaction in either the pictorial figurativism of the social-realist school ascendant in the United States at this time or in the plethora of abstract "isms" coming out of Europe. He said in an interview with Emile de Antonio and Mitch Tuchman shortly before his death that during this period, "for me painting was dead" (*Painters Painting* [1984], p. 41). When the United States entered the Second World War, Newman applied for conscientious objector status, but he was exempted in 1942 from military service on physical grounds.

Newman wrote several essays on the nature of art to clarify his own thinking. These unpublished "monologues" (as he termed them) had titles such as "The Plasmic Image," "The Problem of Subject Matter," and "Prologue for a New Esthethic," in which he states that "my paintings are concerned neither with the manipulation of space nor with the image, but with the sensation of time" (quoted in Thomas Hess, *Barnett Newman* [1971], p. 73). Newman felt his work embodied an essential spirituality. The belief, an outgrowth of his philosophy, was influenced by the Jewish mystical writings of the Kabbalist literature. Newman's view was that the artist was a metaphysical-religious figure whose role was not merely to be a depicter of the world but a creator. Ironically, though an intense theorist on the nature of art throughout his life, Newman would also say that "aesthetics is for artists what ornithology is for the birds."

Newman took up painting and drawing again between 1941 and 1945, but he destroyed nearly all his work from this period. As he began to paint again, he continued with his intensely personal theorizing and went public with his ideas in catalog essays on pre-Columbian and Northwest Coast Indian art for exhibitions in 1944 at the Wakefield Gallery and in 1946 at the Betty Parsons Gallery. His increasing confidence in his work culminated in 1946 when he began a series of vertically striped works, the first of which was *Eu-clidian Abyss* (1946–1947). From 1946 through 1949 Newman took part in a number of group shows at the Betty Parsons Gallery, helped to establish the gallery, and encouraged younger artists such as Jackson Pollock and Hans Hoffman. Writing for *Tiger's Eye*, a small but influential magazine of art, literature, and criticism, he began to be a presence in the New York art scene.

By the beginning of 1948 Newman had come to terms with his aesthetic, and it was on his birthday that year that he began the painting *Onement I* that would be the trademark stripe or, as he called it, "zip" painting. Invigorated, he completed twenty large paintings between October 1948 and December 1949. Newman's first one-man show opened in January 1950 at the Parsons Gallery. Consisting of his large mural-size canvases, the show received a favorable review in the *New York Times* by Aline Louchheim Saarinen but was a critical failure with the rest of the art press as well as with the artists coalescing into the New York school of abstract expressionism. His second solo show at the Parsons Gallery (Apr. 1951) was equally ill received, and over the next seven years Newman rarely exhibited. The New York art world divided into two camps, with Newman associated with the "intellectual" group of "uptown" painters (including Gottlieb, Mark Rothko, Clyfford Still, Robert Motherwell, and Ad Reinhardt), who showed at the Parsons Gallery. In contrast to this group were the "bohemian" artists (Pollock, Arshile Gorky, Willem de Kooning, Franz Kline, and David Smith), who lived in Greenwich Village, affected a more "workerlike" air, and were shown at the Egan Gallery.

This stratification and lack of acceptance made the 1950s a dark time for Newman. Though abstract expressionism had come into vogue, Newman's own work was languishing unseen. Construction work forced him and his wife out of their apartment in Manhattan, and the couple moved to Brooklyn. He withdrew from painting and created no new works in 1956 or 1957. In November 1957 he suffered a heart attack, and after a period of recuperation took up painting again in 1958.

A few hopeful signs did appear. Critic Clement Greenberg praised Newman's work in his article "American-type Painting" in the *Partisan Review* (22, no. 2 [Spring 1955]: 179–96). As the decade drew to a close, Newman's career began to take off. In 1958 his work was selected for the Museum of Modern Art's "New American Painting" exhibition, which toured Europe. Later that year he was given an important retrospective at Bennington College in Vermont. Increasingly, his work was shown throughout the United States and Europe. In his large, color-dominated canvases, in which abstraction was totally divorced from figurative representation, a new generation of minimalist and conceptual artists saw precedent for their own work.

The last ten years of his life saw Newman move from being an outcast of the art world to becoming one of its stars. His paintings began not only to sell but to command high prices (upwards of $5,000 each). In 1964 he made his first trip to Europe, and in 1965 he represented the United States at the São Paulo (Brazil) VIII Bienal. His major series of fourteen paintings, *Stations of the Cross: Lema Sabachthani*, which he had begun in the late 1950s, was completed in 1966 and was the subject of an exhibition at the Guggenheim Museum in April of that year. Newman also experimented with sculpture, completing the monumental *Broken Obelisk* in 1967.

Encouraging younger painters and attending the exhibitions of other artists wearing his ever-present monocle, Newman became, in the words of *Time* magazine, the "father confessor" of the art world, possessing "seigniorial poise" (18 Oct. 1971) and the look of a "celebrated raconteur" (20 July 1970). He did not, however, neglect his painting to partake of the art world's social whirl. He turned to printmaking, completing eighteen lithographs that he entitled the *Canto* series. The last half of the 1960s also found Newman completing a number of large-scale canvases, including *Who's Afraid of Red, Yellow and Blue I, II, III* (1966–1967), *Shimmer Bright* (1968), and *Be I* (1970).

In 1969 the Knoedler Gallery in New York City held a large show of Newman's recent work; in the same year a major retrospective exhibition of his work was organized by the Stedelijk Museum in Amsterdam and traveled to the Museum of Modern Art in New York and the Tate Gallery, London. Lauded as one of America's most important painters, Newman died in New York City.

Newman's reputation increased after his death, and his work has been the subject of numerous exhibitions. It soared in price throughout the 1980s, and in 1986 the National Gallery of Art in Washington, D.C., acquired the *Stations of the Cross* series at a cost of $4 million.

• Significant examples of Newman's work are represented in the collections of the Museum of Modern Art (New York City), the Tate Gallery (London), the National Gallery of Art (Washington, D.C.), the Hirshhorn Museum and Sculpture Garden (Smithsonian Institution, Washington, D.C.), and the Stedelijk Museum (Amsterdam). A complete biographical essay by Thomas B. Hess is included in the Tate Gallery exhibition catalog, *Barnett Newman* (1972). *Barnett Newman: Selected Writings and Interviews*, ed. John P. O'Neill (1990), collects Newman's statements on his aesthetic. An important profile by Harold Rosenberg, "The Art World: Icon Maker," appeared in the *New Yorker*, 19 Apr. 1969, pp. 136, 138, 140, 142. Betty Parsons, in taped interviews at the Archives of American Art (Smithsonian Institution), discusses Newman's association with her gallery. Obituaries are in the *New York Times*, 5 July 1970, and *Time*, 20 July 1970.

MARTIN R. KALFATOVIC

NEWMAN, Frances (13 Sept. 1883–22 Oct. 1928), author, was born in Atlanta, Georgia, the daughter of William Truslow Newman, a federal district judge, and Frances Percy Alexander. She attended private schools in Atlanta and nearby Decatur, Georgia, and finishing schools in New York and Washington, D.C.

In 1910 she made the first of several trips to Europe. Newman studied Italian and Greek at the University of Tennessee's Summer School of the South in 1911 and graduated from a one-year library science program at the Atlanta Carnegie Library in 1912.

After a year as a librarian at Florida State College for Women in Tallahassee, the homesick Newman returned to Atlanta to work at the Carnegie Library. She never married, but she established a household with her orphaned nephew and with "Mammy" Susan Long, who had attended at her birth. Newman said that Long told disturbing stories about slavery times and "must be mostly responsible for my lack of a southern lady's traditional illusions" (*Letters*, p. 273). Newman's writing career began at the Atlanta library, where, as head of the lending department, she described recent acquisitions and literary trends in the *Carnegie Library Bulletin*. Soon the *Atlanta Journal* and the *Atlanta Constitution* were printing her outspoken reviews and "Library Literary Notes," which caught the attention of novelist James Branch Cabell and critic and editor H. L. Mencken.

Newman's first publication outside Atlanta was "The Allegory of the Young Intellectuals" (1921), the first of many essays she wrote for the *Reviewer*, a well-known "little magazine" edited by Emily Clark in Richmond, Virginia. Subsequently her articles and reviews appeared in the *Bookman*, the *Freeman*, *Saturday Review of Literature*, and the major New York newspapers. Newman preferred the work of D. H. Lawrence, Virginia Woolf, James Joyce, Compton Mackenzie, Katherine Mansfield, Luigi Pirandello, and other British and Continental writers to most American literature, though she did praise the fiction of Cabell, Joseph Hergesheimer, Sherwood Anderson, Ring Lardner, Elinor Wylie, and especially Henry James. Her comments on Willa Cather, F. Scott Fitzgerald, Sinclair Lewis, Eugene O'Neill, and several other contemporaries were so harsh, though, that Clark said a "prismatic, malicious wit" was "really Frances's heart and soul" (Clark, p. 194). At the same time Clark observed that Newman was "surely, in speech and print, of all women most articulate" (p. 210).

Although she completed a novel, "The Gold-Fish Bowl," in 1921, Newman did not publish this comedy of manners about a clever young librarian named Anne Delane. Late in 1922 she resigned from the Carnegie Library and in 1923 traveled to France, where she studied French literature, history, and the history of ideas at the Sorbonne and with a private tutor. Newman's first published book, *The Short Story's Mutations: From Petronius to Paul Morand* (1924), displays her skills as a translator, anthologist, and literary critic. In more than sixty pages of commentary, she explains how each of the sixteen authors represented in the volume is "the creator of a new epoch in his art."

Newman's own first short story, "Rachel and Her Children" (1924), was published by Mencken in *American Mercury*. Ironically the story won an O. Henry Memorial Award, though Newman said she did not "admire either O. Henry or his Memorial" (*Letters*, p. 150). Her only other short story, "Atlanta Biltmore," was written in 1924 but remained unpublished until 1989. Newman became a librarian at the Georgia School of Technology early in 1925, but she took a long leave of absence later that year and thereafter spent most of her time writing. She worked especially well at the MacDowell Colony in New Hampshire during the summers of 1926 and 1927. From 1924 to 1928 Newman's articles for the *Atlanta Journal Magazine* included the weekly "Elizabeth Bennet's Gossip," named after Jane Austen's *Pride and Prejudice* heroine. Newman told Emily Clark she was "not proud of such chatter, but I need the money and it's so easy" (*Letters*, p. 121).

With the publication of *The Hard-Boiled Virgin* in 1926, Newman herself became a major subject of Atlanta gossip. Banned in Boston, the book was a national bestseller. A story about the sexual and literary development of Katharine Faraday, an upper-class southern girl, *The Hard-Boiled Virgin* refers to menstruation, childbirth, naked bodies, venereal disease, abortion, and birth control, but the references are glimpsed through the cover of Newman's highly experimental prose. A strong modernist influence is apparent in the long sentences, repetitive syntax, absence of dialogue, abundance of allusions, and ironic tone. In each chapter or "episode" (Newman's term), the narrator shows how preoccupied Katharine Faraday is with protecting her virginity, even though "she knew that in Georgia no lady was supposed to know she was a virgin until she had ceased to be one, and that she was supposed to find the adjective's application to Mary the mother of Jesus as mysterious as the incarnation and its application to Elizabeth as mysterious as the reasons why a royal lady with so many suitors had never taken a husband." Katharine finally has an affair, but—hard-boiled to the end—she continues to erect barriers against men.

In *Dead Lovers Are Faithful Lovers* (1928) Newman developed a two-part structure to contrast two very different types of southern women, both of them "idiotically in love" with the same man (*Letters*, p. 309). Evelyn Page Cunningham, whose father describes her as "probably the last of the Virginia belles," is the central consciousness for the first half of the book. In a transitional scene that Newman calls the "modulation," the point of view slides to the mind of Isabel Ramsay, an unmarried librarian who begins an unconsummated affair with Evelyn's husband. Evelyn's fear that Charlton Cunningham might be unfaithful is alleviated only by his sudden death. Newman, who characteristically wore purple dresses and wrote with purple ink, asked that the book be "bound in violet, not only because I like violet, but because it suits the triumphant widow idea of the book and of the title" (*Letters*, p. 298).

Newman's death in a New York hotel was first ascribed to a brain hemorrhage, complicated by pneumonia, but an assistant medical examiner implicated the barbiturate Veronal, which Newman had been tak-ing for severe pain behind her right eye. Suicide seems unlikely (see Wade, pp. 42–49). Newman's final work, *Six Moral Tales from Jules Laforgue* (1928), the first translation of Laforgue by an American, was published posthumously. James Branch Cabell said that "had some five years more of living been accorded to Frances Newman she would have stayed remembered, not merely as unique, but as supreme among the women writers of America" (Cabell, p. 30). Controversial during her lifetime for her bold fiction and her caustic assessments of other writers, Newman was neglected for almost a half century after her death. Reprints of her novels in 1977 and 1980 led to studies by literary critics and cultural historians, who were especially interested in her portrayal of southern women in the early modern era.

• The most extensive archives are the Frances Newman Collection at the Atlanta–Fulton County Public Library and the Frances Newman Papers at Georgia Institute of Technology. A large number of Newman's essays and book reviews are gathered and annotated in Emory Reginald Abbott, "Purple Prejudices: The Critical Writings of Frances Newman" (Ph.D. diss., Vanderbilt Univ., 1992); Abbott's bibliography includes all of Newman's known critical work. Another important dissertation is Margaret Manning Duggan, "'The Gold-Fish Bowl': Miss Newman's Five-Finger Exercise" (Univ. of South Carolina, 1985), a critical edition of Newman's unpublished first novel. Duggan's preface includes a detailed biographical discussion. Hansell Baugh edited selected correspondence in *Frances Newman's Letters* (1929). Barbara Ann Wade, "Frances Newman: Southern Feminist and Literary Experimenter of the 1920's" (Ph.D. diss., Univ. of Washington, 1989), is the most comprehensive treatment of Newman's fiction and her life. For chapters on Newman by her contemporaries, see James Branch Cabell, *Some of Us: An Essay in Epitaphs* (1930), and Emily Clark, *Innocence Abroad* (1931). Chapters on Newman's resistance to southern tradition appear in Anne Goodwyn Jones, *Tomorrow Is Another Day: The Woman Writer in the South, 1859–1936* (1981), and Kathryn Lee Seidel, *The Southern Belle in the American Novel* (1985). On aestheticism and artistry in Newman's most famous novel, see Abbott, "A Southern Lady Still: A Reinterpretation of Frances Percy [*sic*, for Alexander] Newman's *The Hard-Boiled Virgin*," *Southern Quarterly* 27, no. 4 (1989): 49–70. An obituary is in the *New York Times*, 23 Oct. 1928.

JOAN WYLIE HALL

NEWMAN, Henry Roderick (Mar. 1843–Dec. 1917), watercolorist and painter, was born in Easton, New York, the son of Roderick B. Newman, a physician and surgeon, and Mary (maiden name unknown). His family moved to New York City when he was two years old. His father insisted that he study medicine, but his own inclinations were for art. At his father's death about 1861, Newman persuaded his mother to allow him to pursue painting for a year, and he retreated to Stockbridge, Massachusetts, to sketch directly from nature. He began exhibiting his work at the National Academy of Design in New York in 1861. His earliest pictures of landscapes and outdoor flower studies indicate that Newman from the first subscribed closely to the artistic philosophy of John Ruskin, the champion of the Pre-Raphaelites in England. Ruskin preached a literal imitation of nature, which Newman took to heart in his earliest known pictures, which are hard and brilliant in effect. The surviving correspondence from Newman to Thomas Charles Farrer, a founder of the American Pre-Raphaelite movement, indicates a mentor-pupil relationship comparable to that between Ruskin and the British Pre-Raphaelite landscape painter John Brett, who took careful advice from Ruskin on the imaging of landscape and the selection of subjects. In 1864 Newman was elected to the Association for the Advancement of Truth in Art, the American expression of the Pre-Raphaelite Brotherhood in England, and in 1867 he was admitted to the newly founded American Watercolor Society. He became a regular exhibitor at the National Academy and at the Brooklyn Art Association; through Farrer, he obtained a teaching position at the Free School of Art for Women at the Cooper Union in New York.

Considerations of both his health and the tepid reception of Pre-Raphaelitism in America motivated Newman to sail for Europe in 1870, where, except for an occasional brief trip back, he became a permanent resident. He stayed briefly in France, but moved on to Venice and Florence, where he established his home and studio in the Piazza dei Rossi. In Italy he continued to render exquisite flower compositions—anemones and roses were among his favored types to paint—in which his style increased somewhat in luminosity and airiness. In landscape his preference shifted from the view paintings of his early work to architectural studies, sometimes even to compositions of flowers and architecture based on sites in Florence and on the Gulf of La Spezia. A portrait of the façade and piazza of Santa Maria Novella in Florence, shown to Ruskin by Newman's American colleague Charles Herbert Moore, stirred Ruskin to begin a correspondence and friendship with the artist. Newman certainly met Ruskin no later than 1880, when he stopped at Ruskin's home in Coniston, England, en route to America and sold him several of his drawings. Ruskin's first known letter to Newman already reveals his advising the painter on the selection of subjects. Ultimately, Ruskin acquired at least nine of Newman's watercolors for St. George's Guild (Ruskin Museum) in Sheffield.

In June 1883 Newman married Mary Watson Willis, an Englishwoman. During this time, he involved himself in the international effort to eliminate American duties on artworks imported into the United States. He traveled regularly with his wife, chiefly to Egypt in deference to his delicate health, beginning in the late 1880s. A decade later he visited Japan. Ancient Egyptian architecture, notably at Philae and Abu Simbel, constituted his principal subjects from the 1890s to about 1907. His activity seems to have been curtailed after this time, for there is little if any dated work known from the last decade of his life.

Given his lifelong devotion to Pre-Raphaelitism, Newman had strong Anglophilic sympathies. "His conversation, which showed habits of independent thought and a fine sense of humor, was carried on in a low, melodious voice, which might have been that of a highly cultured Englishman moving in the best circles of society," said an acquaintance (Forman, p. 525). A collector of Italian illuminated manuscripts, Newman's work habits were somewhat monkish, despite the frequent necessity of working outdoors in front of his subjects. Laboring over an architectural subject in the streets of Florence for days on end, he was said to secrete himself amid market stalls so as not to be disturbed by onlookers. A witness of Newman at work in Egypt said that he painted his watercolors "by the inch and can tell before hand just how many days one will take him, say six weeks [of] mornings for [a picture of] about ten by fourteen, near an hour to the square inch. And he does his inch, finishing it in each hour" (Wilbour). Much of his mature work may be described as at once gorgeous and insubstantial. The transparent stippled watercolor technique of Pre-Raphaelite landscape artists imparts a wonderfully sun-saturated effect to motifs but simultaneously can deny them the sense of mass and weight. Moreover, the painstaking, myopic application of pigment frequently undermines the integrity of design. Depending on one's taste, such faults either detract from or stimulate one's appreciation for the artist's precious perception of the received world and his sincere devotion to his craft.

• The most comprehensive account of Newman is Kent Ahrens, "Pioneer Abroad, Henry R. Newman (1843–1917): Watercolorist and a Friend of Ruskin," *American Art Journal* (Nov. 1976): 85–98; the best contemporary description is H. Buxton Forman, "An American Studio in Florence," *Manhattan* 3, no. 6 (June 1884): 525–39; Newman's life and examples of his work are perceptively treated in Linda S. Ferber and William H. Gerdts, *The New Path; Ruskin and the American Pre-Raphaelites* (1985); the artist's working methods are criticized in Charles Edwin Wilbour, *Travels in Egypt* (1936). See also Royal W. Leith, *A Quiet Devotion: The Life and Work of Henry Roderick Newman* (1996). An obituary is in the *New York Times*, 31 Jan. 1918.

KEVIN J. AVERY

NEWMAN, Isidore (28 Feb. 1837–30 Nov. 1909), financier and philanthropist, was born Isidore Neumond in Kaiserslautern, Rhenish Bavaria (now the German state of Rheinland Pfalz), the son of Jacob Neumond, a merchant, and Clara Kahn. His family had been merchants in the area of Kaiserslautern for generations. In 1808, when the Emperor Napoleon Bonaparte required all of the Jews in his Empire to take permanent family names, Isidore's family adopted the name Neumond, which means "new moon." Isidore Newman arrived in New Orleans on 18 November 1853 in steerage on a sailing ship, a penniless Jew sixteen years old. He was met by his uncle, Charles Newman, who had arrived in New Orleans in 1828 and set himself up, along with his sons Edward, Jacob, Louis, and Morris, in the money-changing business, probably changing money for sailors who had just docked in the port of New Orleans. Young Isidore had blond hair, blue eyes, a heavy German accent, a love of music, and a wardrobe consisting of one suit hand-sewn by his mother.

Newman's education included a year (1850–1851) in the trades school (*Gewerbeschule*) of Kaiserslautern, and he had worked as a horse merchant (*Pferdekaufmann*) there. Charles helped him to make his way to Harrisonburg, Catahoula Parish, Louisiana, where he clerked in a general store. Despite his low wage, he saved money, bought land, helped to pay the passage to bring his two younger brothers, Henry and Charles, from Kaiserslautern, and established the Newman Brothers cotton brokerage. The Civil War ended this shaky, overly leveraged venture. He would never again be caught short of cash, and he would never again fail in business.

Newman returned to New Orleans and worked as a bookkeeper for Henry Stern, the husband of his first cousin, Annette Newman, the only daughter of his uncle, Charles Newman. Henry Stern owned a wholesale shoe business at the foot of Canal Street near the Mississippi River. In 1868 Isidore and his brother, Henry, established their own banking and brokerage business, Isidore Newman and Brother, at 27 Camp Street, close to where his Uncle Charles and his sons had established their brokerage business at 19 Camp Street. On 24 June 1868 Newman married Rebecca Kiefer of Port Gibson, Mississippi. They had eight children.

During the crash of 1873, Newman helped keep Louisiana and New Orleans afloat by cashing the scrip that the bankrupt state and city had paid to their employees. That year he was elected to the board of directors of the New Orleans Association for the Relief of Jewish Widows and Orphans, an organization that he and his family would continue to support. In 1877 he became a founding member of the New Orleans Stock Exchange, serving as its first treasurer and later, from 1880 to 1885 and in 1890–1891, as its president. He helped Louisiana, New Orleans, and other southern cities and states to recover from the Civil War by issuing soundly financed bonds. After the Louisiana Constitutional Convention of 1879, he helped to put the state's debt on a solid basis. The following year he proposed the ten-year bond issue that stabilized New Orleans' finances. He also helped to finance bonds to construct levees throughout Louisiana.

In 1882, when 173 refugees from pogroms in Russia landed in New Orleans, Isidore and Henry Newman offered them land near Harrisonburg in Catahoula Parish, Louisiana. The immigrants were led by Hermann Rosenthal, whom Rabbi Max Heller of Temple Sinai, New Orleans, called "a man of means, distinguished scholar and writer" (*Jubilee Souvenir of Temple Sinai, [New Orleans], 1872–1922* [1922], p. 69). In December 1882, after celebrating Hanukkah with a serenade in front of the houses of the Newman brothers in New Orleans, seventy-three men from the group boarded steamers and sailed to the new settlement, which was called "Sicily Island." Rosenthal wrote in a letter of 21 December: "We have nowhere found such

generous men . . . as our coreligionists of New Orleans." The colonists fenced in 450 acres, plowed 200 acres, dug wells, and planted fruit trees, even though they had only two mules and two yoke of cattle in the colony. Weeds, malaria, and a flood of the Mississippi River in April 1883 wrecked their hopes, and Rosenthal, speaking in New York on 24 May, said: "In the paradise promised, [we] only found serpents." The survivors of the Sicily Island experiment were relocated. But valuable lessons were learned, and two decades later Jews were being settled successfully on farms by the Baron de Hirsch Fund in 1901 and by Jacob Schiff in 1907. Also in 1882 Isidore Newman's donation of more than $30,000 saved the Touro Infirmary from bankruptcy.

Newman's generosity was overlooked in an ugly article in the *New Orleans Times Democrat* on 23 June 1890, in which an "eyewitness" reported that Newman had colluded with a rival bidder for the Louisiana Lottery in order to keep the price low. The eyewitness told Newman that the Louisiana legislature would vote against his syndicate even if he made the highest bid because "you have done nothing for relief of the suffering people. You have made no movement for their welfare at any time." Newman replied the next day in a letter to the paper, explaining that he had attempted to combine with his rivals in order to keep the bids from becoming "ruinous." He said nothing about his charity, which involved an annual pre-Christmas search for charitable institutions listed in the New Orleans directory followed by a gift to many of them accompanied by a four-word note: "Inclosed Please Find Check." Newman did not seem stung by the attack, nor did he talk about his donations. Just before his death, he estimated his wealth at less than $4 million, and his charitable donations were said to have been at least $2 million. He was, according to one authority, the leading philanthropist in the city.

In the early 1890s came two seminal events in Newman's life. In 1890 Professor G. Bamberger of Chicago spoke to the directors of the New Orleans Jewish Orphans' Home about a training and industrial school, and in February 1893 Newman bought the entire issue of $350,000 in 6 percent bonds of the New Orleans and Carrollton Railway. Newman, who had himself attended a trade school in Rhenish Bavaria when he was thirteen, realized that if the American South were to prosper it must industrialize, and that to industrialize it must have a trained labor force. In addition, it would have to electrify its cities and improve urban public transportation. Newman's business investments and his charitable donations, while remaining broadly eclectic, would henceforth focus on these goals.

Newman bought nearly all of the streetcar lines in New Orleans, and around 1893 he purchased the Edison Electric Company so that he could electrify them. He followed the same pattern in Birmingham, Alabama; Little Rock, Arkansas; Nashville, Knoxville, and Memphis, Tennessee; and Houston, Texas. He merged all but the Nashville operation into the American Cities Railway and Light Company, a holding corporation capitalized at $17 million. As Newman's power grew, so did his frustration with his city, and in May 1903 he said: "Perhaps there is no city of its magnitude in the civilized world that has progressed less than New Orleans. . . . This is to be attributed, to a great extent, to the want of factories and skilled labor of all kinds." Remembering Bamburger's speech and, perhaps, his own schooling, Newman donated the money for a manual training school for the Jewish Orphans' Home. By the time the Isidore Newman Manual Training School opened in October 1904, he had given approximately $75,000.

Newman stipulated that the school should be coeducational, and that in addition to the Jewish orphans of the six-state area of B'nai B'rith No. 7 (Louisiana, Mississippi, Texas, Alabama, Arkansas, and Florida), 100 pupils from New Orleans would be admitted without regard to creed. There would be no uniforms; Newman did not want anything to distinguish the orphans from the tuition-paying students. All students would receive a well-rounded liberal education in addition to instruction in manual training for boys and domestic education for girls. Classes in music (Newman's eldest son paid for the band instruments), art, and citizenship would also be required, and physical education would be offered in the first school gymnasium in the city. For founding this school, Newman was awarded the New Orleans *Daily Picayune* Loving Cup in 1903 as "the Citizen of New Orleans Whose Individual Act Contributes Most to the Welfare of the Community."

If Newman had been stung by the *Times Democrat's* attack of 1890, he was now vindicated. When in 1907 the school and community honored him on his seventieth birthday, he said:

For years it has been the desire of my heart to do something for this city and State which have made me what I am. I have my reward in this school. . . . I have one more wish in life . . . to see practical results from this school, to see the children trained here started in life, to give them a helping hand, to help them with my advice, to lend them funds, if necessary, to start them in business. I want to see an alumni of this school of which I can be proud.

A friend said: "During the last years of his life, he just lived for that school."

Newman's business interests continued to expand. In 1909 the Maison Blanche Department Store in New Orleans, which he owned, opened its new building. He also had large holdings in land, whose value appreciated as New Orleans grew. He gave money to many charities, but only to those that were open to all religions, such as the National Jewish Hospital for Consumptives, which opened in Denver in 1899. Newman served on its board of managers. A lover of music, he gave about $2,000 each season to finance free summer concerts in Audubon Park, New Orleans, and he erected an outdoor bandstand there in 1904. In 1909 the national executive committee of B'nai B'rith, at its meeting in New York, unanimously reelected him to that committee. When Newman died in New Orleans, the New Orleans Stock Exchange hung up wreaths of black crepe as a sign of mourning, and it closed early so that members could attend his funeral. In his will Newman bequeathed equal amounts to the Young Men's Hebrew Association and the Young Men's Christian Association, and he also left money to the German Protestant Home, the (Roman Catholic) Little Sisters of the Poor, the Lafon Home for Old Folks (colored), and Tulane University (all in New Orleans), and for the poor of Kaiserslautern, Germany. In his will he mentioned twenty-eight charities of all kinds in many places. His life, with its vision, triumphs, and frustrations, had been a mirror of the post-Reconstruction South.

• For information on Newman see the index in the Louisiana Collection of the New Orleans Public Library (which gives references to articles in the New Orleans newspapers); the New Orleans Notarial Archives; the New Orleans Conveyance Office; the family research center of the Church of Latter Day Saints in Salt Lake City; and the archives of Kaiserslautern, Rheinland Pfalz, Germany. There are some family papers in the possession of Edwin A. Neugass III of Annandale, Va. Also see Joseph Magner, *The Story of the Jewish Orphans Home of New Orleans* (1905); Glenn R. Conrad, ed., *A Dictionary of Louisiana Biography*, vol. 2 (1988); Edwin Adams Davis, *The Story of Louisiana*, vol. 2 (1960); Alcée Fortier, *The History of Louisiana* (1904); Leo Shpall, *The Jews in Louisiana* (1936); Anon., *The Israelites of Louisiana* (1904); and Bobbie Malone, *Rabbi Max Heller, Reformer, Zionist, Southerner* (1997). James Neugass, *Rain of Ashes* (1949), is a *roman à clef* about Newman's family.

EDGAR LEON NEWMAN
HERMAN KOHLMEYER, JR.
EDWIN A. NEUGASS III

NEWMAN, Pauline (18 Oct. 1893?–8 Apr. 1986), labor organizer, was born in Lithuania, the daughter of Meyer Newman and Tillie (maiden name unknown). In Lithuania at that time, only landowners' children received schooling, and since Pauline's parents were poor and owned no land she obtained no formal education. She did go to a secular Sunday school, however, where she learned to sing Russian folk songs and recite poetry. After her father died, her brother, who was living in the United States, sent for Pauline, her mother, and her two sisters. They emigrated in 1901.

Although Pauline was a child and unable to qualify for working papers, she went to work at the Triangle Shirtwaist Company, cutting loose threads off of finished blouses. She worked long hours, was not allowed to talk or sing, and received a salary of $1.50 for a seven-day week—with little apple pies for overtime. When inspectors arrived to search for child laborers, she hid with the other girls in wooden boxes.

Newman's initiation as a strike leader came in 1907, when the landlord in her tenement building announced a raise in the rent. Gathering tenants from the buildings, Pauline convinced them not to pay the rent and to demand that the landlord install toilets on each floor. A local newspaper printed the story of Newman's strike. The landlord, not wishing notoriety and needing his rent, agreed not to raise the rent, although he refused to install the toilets.

Wishing to master English and regretting her lack of education, Pauline joined the Socialist Literary Society; she attended meetings twice a week and listened to a professor who taught English literature. She began reading Charles Dickens, George Eliot, and poetry, which improved her language skills and made her a lifelong avid reader. Her interest in socialism also grew, giving meaning and relevance to her life. Through socialism she saw that change might occur, and she wanted "to be part of making that change." In 1908 she actively campaigned for Eugene V. Debs, the Socialist party candidate for president, riding the rails on his Red Special "whistle-stop train."

After returning to New York, Newman joined with other workers in November 1909 in the "Uprising of the Twenty Thousand," during which garment workers walked out of 500 New York shirtwaist shops. Newman solicited donations on behalf of strikers and the Women's Trade Union League (WTUL), traveling throughout New York and New England. Her very first speech merited front-page newspaper coverage (the article included her photograph). She spoke before audiences at women's clubs, colleges, and union hall meetings, raising over $6,000 in support of the strikers.

Newman's oratorical skills, ability to speak Yiddish, and identification with fellow Jewish workers compelled her to leave her job at the factory following the strike and become the first organizer for the International Ladies' Garment Workers' Union (ILGWU), a position she held from 1909 to 1913. Much of her time was spent traveling to cities such as Philadelphia and Cleveland to promote unionism. She had an uneasy relationship with male union officials during this time because they sometimes belittled her efforts. Nevertheless, she once remarked that the job as organizer saved her life because she had not been at the Triangle factory when a fire broke out on 25 March 1911, killing 146 women workers.

In addition to her duties as organizer, Newman served as an inspector for the Joint Board of Sanitary Control for the women's garment industry in New York from 1912 to 1918. The ILGWU sometimes allowed Newman to speak for other groups, such as the Socialist party and the Federation of Jewish Philanthropies, for whom she canvassed funds. From 1913 to 1915, for instance, she went on a lecture tour throughout the Northeast as a Socialist speaker. A fervent believer in women's right to vote, she campaigned and was a full-time organizer for "Votes for Women" in 1915 and was a Socialist candidate for Congress in New York's Eighteenth Congressional District.

A member of the WTUL since 1909, Newman helped establish a Philadelphia branch in 1915, serving as president from 1918 to 1923. As a WTUL speaker, she sought to bring Philadelphia women candy makers, textile workers, and small-tool workers into unions. She also led strikes of the Philadelphia waistmakers and the Kalamazoo corsetmakers.

In 1923 Newman was appointed as a delegate for the WTUL to the International Congress of Working Women held in Vienna, Austria, and she traveled throughout Europe for a year. Upon returning to New York City, she took an appointment as the educational director of the ILGWU Health Center, which she had helped found in 1913. Newman educated the public about the risks and prevention of disease. But as health services expanded and costs soared, Newman soon took on the duties of fundraising. The ILGWU fully funded the health center in 1934, enabling it to expand its medical services and building facilities. Throughout her career with the health center, Newman acted as a liaison between medical personnel and local unions.

Devoted to aiding union women and the community, Newman took additional assignments while serving the health center. She was appointed by the mayor as a member of the New York State Minimum Wage Law Commission, which established minimum wages for various industries; in this capacity she studied the taxicab industry in the 1930s. In 1938 she joined the organizing committee to oppose the Equal Rights Amendment, fearing that protective legislation for women would be hurt by the amendment's enforcement. Newman frequently wrote for the *American Hebrew*, *Labor Age*, the *Progressive Woman*, *Justice*, and the *Jewish Daily Forward*. She never retired from the health center and in the later years of her life focused mainly on disease prevention. At age ninety Newman continued to walk to the health center, write, and give lectures. She died in New York City, having never married. (She believed that while single Jewish women could be independent, a married one dedicated herself to home and hearth.) She compensated for a lonely life on the road by maintaining countless friendships with other women.

A fiery speaker, Newman carried her soapbox with her when she went to speaking engagements and got on it even amid jeering. She never minded heckling; she often used it to her advantage, answering back and getting the crowd to side with her. Maida Springer Kemp, a fellow union member, said of Newman that "she was one of the giants, determined, articulate, volatile about workers' dignity, and the pursuit of excellence" (interview by Elizabeth Balanoff, 4 Jan. 1977, Roosevelt University). Although she sometimes felt "thrown about like a wave" and exhausted from dealing with class and feminist differences, Newman never stopped fighting for higher standards for women in the workplace.

• The most authoritative source of information on Newman's personal life is her oral history in Joan Morrison and Charlotte Fox Zabusky, comps., *American Mosaic: The Immigrant Experience in the Words of Those Who Lived It* (1980). Articles authored by her that illuminate women's union experiences are "How Women Forged Early Unions," *Allied Industrial Worker*, Aug. 1976, and "We Needed Hope More," *GBBA Horizons*, Sept. 1976. Information on her life and labor activities is in Gladys Boone, *The Women's Trade Union Leagues in Great Britain and the United States of America* (1942); Mary E. Dreier, *Margaret Dreier Robins: Her Life, Letters, and Work* (1950); Rose Schneiderman, *All for One* (1967); Cecyle S. Neidle, *America's Immigrant Women* (1975); Alice Kessler-Harris, "Organizing the Unorganizable: Three Jewish Women and Their Union," *Labor History* 17 (Winter 1976): 5–23; and Barbara Mayer Wertheimer, *We Were There: The Story of Working Women in America* (1977). Also see Nancy Schrom Dye, *As Equals and as Sisters* (1980); Nancy MacLean, *The Culture of Resistance: Female Institution Building in the International Ladies' Garment Workers Union, 1905–1925*, Michigan Occasional Paper, no. 31 (Winter 1982); and Gus Tyler, *Look for the Union Label: A History of the International Ladies' Garment Workers' Union* (1995). An obituary is in the *New York Times*, 10 Apr. 1986.

MARILYN ELIZABETH PERRY

NEWPORT, Christopher (1561–Aug. 1617), privateer and sea captain, was christened at Harwich, England, on 29 December 1561, the son of Christopher Newport, a shipmaster, and Jane (maiden name unknown). Young Christopher presumably served a North Sea apprenticeship before venturing into oceanic waters. He was serving on the *Minion* of London in 1580 when he jumped ship at Bahia, Brazil, rather than face the irate master. By 1584, however, he was back in England, where on 19 October he married Katherine Procter.

The Spanish seizure of English shipping in 1585 led to privateering reprisals by merchants who had suffered losses, and by 1587 Newport was one of their privateers. In 1587 he was master's mate on John Watts's *Drake* at the attack on Cadiz. In 1589 he was master of the *Margaret* of London, owned by Robert Cobb and others. In 1590, his wife having died, Newport married Ellen Ade. He returned to the service of John Watts in that year, was promoted to captain (of the *Little John*), made his first Caribbean privateering voyage, and lost his right arm during an attack on two Spanish treasureships off Cuba. In 1591, as captain of Cobb's *Margaret*, he combined Barbary trade with Caribbean privateering, but in 1592–1595, when captaining the *Golden Dragon*, belonging to Cobb's partner John More, Newport was active only in the West Indies. In 1592 came evidence of his increasing reputation: in that year he was given command of a flotilla of privateers and apparently pioneered privateer attacks on the towns of the Spanish Caribbean. In his return, off the Azores, he also helped capture the vastly rich *Madre de Dios* and had the honor of sailing it back to England.

Between 1587 and 1595 Newport had been merely an employee, however successful, of leading London merchants; in 1595 his status changed. In that year he married Elizabeth Glanville, a London goldsmith's daughter, and thereafter was a partner with two Glanvilles and three others, owning one-sixth of the heavily armed *Neptune*. In it he raided the Spanish Caribbean almost annually until 1603. Peace was signed in 1604, and in 1604 and 1605 he returned there to trade, in the latter year bringing back live from Hispaniola two

young "crocodiles" and a wild boar, which he presented to the king.

From these frequent voyages Newport gained an unrivaled knowledge of Caribbean waters, and thus, in 1606, command of the Virginia Company's first fleet. His formal instructions are dated 10 December 1606, but he was already in command of the chartered *Susan Constant*, for on 23 November, the *Susan Constant* collided with the *Philip and Francis*. A resulting lawsuit delayed the *Susan Constant*, the *Goodspeed* (Captain Bartholomew Gosnold), and *Discovery* (Captain John Ratcliffe) less than a month. They sailed on 20 December and after delays entered Chesapeake Bay on 26 April 1607.

Here Newport's sole command ended. Sealed instructions brought from London appointed a council of seven: Newport, Gosnold, and Ratcliffe were balanced by four landsmen, Edward Maria Wingfield, Captain John Smith, John Martin, and George Kendall. Moving up the River James, the expedition on 12 May rejected Archer's Hope as a site for the colony "because the ships could not ride neere the shoare," and two days later chose Jamestown. Here the council chose Wingfield as its president.

Newport had been instructed, once the council was active, to spend two months exploring the region but to return to England, "if God Permit," by May. Delays had made this timetable impossible; Newport could afford only a week. On 21 May he sailed upriver seeking the source of the James but went only to the falls. He was back at Jamestown on 27 May, the day after a major Indian attack on the settlement. Fortification was a matter of haste, and Newport lent sailors for the task. Within the fort—according to Gabriel Archer—Newport played the peacemaker, persuading the council on 10 June to heed the complaints of the discontented and admit Smith to the board. Wingfield, however, suggests that inadvertently Newport exacerbated Archer's and Gosnold's distrust for Wingfield.

On 22 June Newport sailed for England in the *Susan Constant*, promising to be back in November. He wrote enthusiastically to Lord Salisbury from Plymouth on 29 July about the gold ore he was carrying, and by 12 August he was in London with his cargo. To the disappointment of investors, the ore was worthless; he promised, however, to bring better on his next voyage. Making a fast turnaround, he reached Jamestown in the *John and Francis* on 2 January 1608 to find only half the colonists alive. He resumed his place on the council and apparently took over as president. The key to the colony's survival was Powhatan, and to him Newport and Smith made a successful visit, returning to Jamestown on 9 March laden with provisions. After spending the next four weeks refining ore and reforming matters in the colony, Newport sailed to England on 10 April.

Another fast crossing brought him into the Thames on 21 May. Again he wasted no time. In the fall he was back in the colony, bringing the second supply, with seventy colonists and ceremonial gifts for Powhatan and with orders to find Ralegh's lost colony or the Pacific or gold. By now Smith was president; he still disliked the generosity of Newport's methods in handling Powhatan, the latter's "coronation," and Newport's vain expedition upriver to Monacan occurring against Smith's better judgment. Again Newport did not stay long, reaching England by mid-January 1609.

That year the Virginia Company was reformed. A second royal charter, which named Newport among its hundreds of adventurers, altered the form of government, and in May a fleet of nine vessels was dispatched to the colony. Sir Thomas Gates, a veteran of the Dutch wars, went as deputy governor. Sir George Somers was admiral and William Strachey secretary. Though ordered to cross in separate vessels, Newport carried all three in the *Sea Adventure*. The fleet was to pass west of the Canaries and "steere away directly for Virginia without touching at the West Indies." This new shorter route produced disaster for the fleet. It was scattered by a storm on 24 July and the *Sea Adventure* driven onto the Bermudas, though without loss of life. The islands enabled the survivors to endure the winter of 1609–1610 easily. An early attempt to reach Virginia failed, but on 10 May a second attempt succeeded. On 23 May Gates arrived to find Jamestown "so full of misery and misgovernment" that he decided to evacuate the settlement and retreat to Newfoundland, but the governor, Lord De La Warr, arrived and halted this evacuation. Appointing his council, he named Newport vice admiral of Virginia. Newport nevertheless returned to England by early September. In 1611 he made his last voyage to Virginia, carrying Sir Thomas Dale to the colony, which he reached on 12 May. Newport spent about three months in the colony, being charged by Dale with the building of a "bridge" or quay at Jamestown. He probably left about 20 August and reached England in late October 1611.

The Virginia Company showed its appreciation of Newport's services by granting him thirty-two shares worth £400, and after Newport's death the company agreed to turn them into land. The grant would have equaled 1,600 acres, with 300 more for six men sent out by Mrs. Newport in 1619, and may well have been assigned at Newport News, which commemorated the captain.

In 1606, before his involvement with Virginia, Newport was granted in reversion a post as a master of the Royal Navy; in 1612, after his involvement ended, he succeeded to the post. Thereafter, Newport served the East India Company, undertaking three voyages to Bantam. Before his last voyage for the company, Newport on 16 November 1616 made his will, "being to go with the next wind and weather, captain of the Hope, to sail into the East Indies, a long and dangerous voyage." With him as master's mate went his son Christopher. By 16 May 1617 they were in Saldanha Bay (north of Capetown) and on 15 August at Bantam. "Shortly after" his arrival there Newport died.

• The wills of Newport and his son are in the Prerogative Court of Canterbury, 85 and 92 Meade. Family records are in the parish registers of Stepney, of which Limehouse formed part in Newport's lifetime. *Calendar of State Papers, Colonial, East Indies, 1513–1616* and *1617–1621* has primary material on Newport. Kenneth R. Andrews is indispensable on Newport's privateering: "Christopher Newport of Limehouse, Mariner," *William and Mary Quarterly*, 3d ser., 11 (1954): 28–41; *Elizabethan Privateering . . . 1585–1603* (1964); and *Trade, Plunder and Settlement . . . 1480–1630* (1984). Newport's Virginia phase is discussed in Philip L. Barbour, *The Jamestown Voyages under the First Charter, 1606–1609*, Hakluyt Society ser. 2, nos. 136 and 137 (1969); David B. Quinn, Alison M. Quinn, and Susan Hillier, *New American World*, vols. 3 and 5 (1979); Alexander Brown, *The Genesis of the United States* (2 vols., 1890); and Susan M. Kingsbury, *The Records of the Virginia Company of London* (1906–1935). For Newport's last years the sources are scattered: Sir William Foster, *The Embassy of Sir Thomas Roe to the Court of the Great Mogul, 1615–1619*, vol. 1, Hakluyt Society ser. 2, no. 1 (1899); Foster, *The Voyage of Thomas Best to the East Indies, 1612–14*, Hakluyt Society ser. 2, no. 75 (1934); Foster, *The Voyage of Nicholas Downton to the East Indies, 1614–15*, Hakluyt Society ser. 2, no. 82 (1939); and Michael Strachan, *Sir Thomas Roe, 1581–1644* (1989).

DAVID R. RANSOME

NEWSOME, Joseph Thomas (2 June 1869–8 Mar. 1942), lawyer and editor, was born in Sussex County, Virginia, the son of Joseph Newsom and Ann (maiden name unknown), former slaves. He graduated from Virginia Normal and Collegiate Institute (later Virginia State University) in 1894 and, after teaching for a time in Sussex County, graduated from Howard University Law School in 1899. He joined the Virginia bar in 1899, moved to Phoebus (near Hampton), and then settled in Newport News. He married Mary B. Winfield, an 1892 graduate of Virginia Normal, in 1900; they had one daughter.

Newsome—or "Lawyer Newsome," as he was known—practiced for four decades in the Newport News area. Active in politics, he served as the assistant sergeant at arms at the 1920 Republican National Convention in Chicago. Yet, bridling at the "lily-white" practices that his party displayed, he ran in 1921 for the office of attorney general on a state ticket that the Lily-Black party mounted that year. In the 1928 presidential campaign, as some leading black Virginians contemplated breaking with the Republican party to back Democrat Al Smith, Newsome brokered a compromise agreement that the leaders would not pledge collectively to support either candidate but rather would decide for themselves individually. He helped found and lead the Warwick County Colored Voters League, which lobbied for schools, community improvement, and voter registration. Newsome's efforts led to the establishment during World War I of Huntington High School for black residents of Newport News. He was one of two black attorneys who made a successful appeal to the state supreme court in 1931 of a case, *Davis v. Allen*, that originated in Hampton and in which black residents were routinely rebuffed in their efforts to register to vote.

Newsome and the black church were important to each other throughout his life. He taught Sunday school for many years, first in Sussex County and then in the Trinity Baptist Church in Newport News until 1923. He also served Trinity Baptist as a Sunday school superintendent, a member of the board of trustees, a choir member, and an usher. Afterward he served at Carver Memorial Presbyterian Church. He spoke of his commitment to "the Cause," which he associated with the religious concerns of his fellow black Virginians. Newsome could have—and may have—applied the term as readily to the civic improvement and political empowerment of black Virginians in the Tidewater area. His home was a community center from the time he purchased it in 1906 until his death, and Booker T. Washington met there on occasion with local leaders.

Newsome edited the *Newport News Star*, a black newspaper, from the late 1920s after its founder, Natt N. Lewis, died. He stepped down as editor after the newspaper was taken over in the late 1930s by the *Journal and Guide*, the black voice of neighboring Norfolk. That newspaper subsequently issued a Peninsula edition that for a time was called the *Norfolk Journal and Guide and Newport News Star*. During the last few years of his life, Newsome contributed a column titled "In the Drift of the Current" to the *Journal and Guide*.

A noted criminal lawyer, Newsome was involved in some famous cases in eastern Virginia. In 1939, for example, when Newsome defended June Clark against the charge that she had murdered her stepson in her home, he convinced the jury to acquit her on the grounds of self-defense. Similarly, in 1941 Lindsay Smith went on trial on the charge that he had murdered a white soldier stationed at Fort Eustis. The soldier had invaded Smith's home after an argument that originated with the white soldier's refusal to stop harassing young black women. Newsome convinced the jury that Smith had the right to protect his home, by force if necessary, if convinced that his life was in danger.

Even in his seventies, Newsome remained an active participant in public affairs. Early in World War II, Governor James H. Price appointed Newsome to the Hampton Roads Regional Defense Council, and Newport News mayor T. Parker Host named him to a local committee for the organization of a civilian defense police force. In 1940 Judge Herbert G. Smith of the Newport News Corporation Court appointed Newsome as a commissioner of chancery. At the time of his death, Newsome was serving as the president of the Old Dominion Bar Association, recently established as a black counterpart to the Virginia State Bar Association.

Newsome died at his home in Newport News. Appropriations in the late 1980s of $125,000 from the Newport News City Council and $150,000 from the Virginia legislature made it possible for his home to be restored and converted into a black history museum and community center, called "Newsome House."

• Various materials on Newsome can be found at the Newsome House, including letters, newspaper items, photographs, and a permanent exhibit on his life. Andrew Buni, *The Negro in Virginia Politics, 1902–1965* (1967), touches on his public life. Obituaries are in the *Norfolk Journal and Guide* and the *Richmond Afro American*, 14 Mar. 1942.

PETER WALLENSTEIN

NEWTON, Frankie (4 Jan. 1906–11 Mar. 1954), jazz trumpeter, was born William Frank Newton in Emory, Virginia. Nothing is known of his parents, childhood, or musical training, but his first professional work was with the Cincinnati-based band of Clarence Paige, with whom he began playing several years before 1926. In early 1927, while in Lexington, Kentucky, he joined Lloyd Scott's Symphonic Syncopators, then on tour. When Lloyd and his brother Cecil Scott returned home to work in Ohio, Newton settled in Harlem, where he played trumpet during the summer of 1927 in Elmer Snowden's band at the Nest Club. In the fall he went on another tour with the Scotts, and in December the band took up residency at the Savoy Ballroom in Harlem.

Newton remained at the Savoy through the next two years, making his first records with Cecil Scott's Bright Boys in November 1929. After their return to the Savoy following a June 1930 tour, the Bright Boys quit en masse after a falling out over unpaid back earnings. Now freelancing and based in Harlem, from mid-1930 through 1931 Newton played with Chick Webb at the Savoy, Charlie Johnson at Small's Paradise, Snowden at the Nest Club, Bobby Neal at the Strand Ballroom, and Fats Waller at Connie's Inn. In 1932 he played briefly with pianist Garland Wilson on radio station WEVD and then joined the Sam Wooding orchestra for residencies at the Arcadia Ballroom and the Pelham Heath Inn.

In September 1933 Newton returned to the Johnson band, and in November he accompanied Bessie Smith on her last recording date. In late 1935 he left Johnson for medical reasons but returned to the band briefly in early 1936. Starting in the spring of 1936 he spent a year in Teddy Hill's band, leaving in May 1937 when he suffered from complications following a tonsillectomy. He had also appeared on records by Teddy Wilson, Art Karle, and Mezz Mezzrow in 1936 and by Teddy Hill in 1936 and 1937. From July through September 1937 he worked at the Onyx Club in New York City with Buster Bailey, Pete Brown, Don Frye, and John Kirby, who was soon appointed leader of the group. In August Newton and Kirby recorded a session with Charlie Barnet's otherwise all-white band, while in surrounding months the nucleus of the Kirby group participated in recording dates led by Bailey, Willie "The Lion" Smith, and singers Jerry Kruger, Maxine Sullivan, and Midge Williams. Using essentially the same men, but with the addition of Cecil Scott and with Edmond Hall in place of Bailey, Newton also recorded sessions under his own name in March, April, and July 1937. In November and December 1937 Newton played in Mezzrow's short-lived

14 Disciples of Swing at both the Harlem Uproar House on Fifty-second Street and the Savoy, but the public proved unwilling to accept the racially mixed group, and Mezzrow soon dissolved the band. From December 1937 through February 1938 Newton worked with the Mills Blue Rhythm Band, under the leadership of Lucky Millinder.

Starting in December 1938 Newton led his own octet at Café Society Downtown, and, except for an absence in February due to illness, he remained there through 1939, recording sessions with that band in April and August. A few days before the first of these dates he recorded some of his best blues work in a group called the Port of Harlem Jazzmen, and later that month he provided the muted trumpet on Billie Holiday's famous recording of "Strange Fruit" for Commodore. The following June the Port of Harlem group returned to the Blue Note studios, this time with the addition of Sidney Bechet. In February 1940 Newton took a racially mixed band, including tenor saxophonist Joe "Flip" Phillips, into Kelly's Stable in New York, and the group remained there through the summer. He played later engagements at various vacation resorts in the spring of 1941, Harlem's Mimo Club in the fall, and returned to Kelly's Stable that winter. In a revealing departure from his usual working environs, Newton spent the summer of 1941 in Bechet's quintet at the leftist-oriented Camp Unity in Wingdale, New York.

From November 1942 through February 1943 Newton led a sextet in Boston. In April he took this group, with trombonist Vic Dickenson, into Café Society. In June 1944 he worked at George's in New York and from August through December he was at the Pied Piper in Greenwich Village with James P. Johnson, the celebrated stride pianist with whom he had recorded an exceptional session the previous June. During the next two years he led his own group at several locations in Boston and New York City and made a number of recordings with Mary Lou Williams, Buck Ram, Miss Rhapsody, Hank D'Amico, Joe Turner, and Stella Brooks, on whose date he was once again reunited with Bechet. The Brooks session would be his last studio effort.

In early 1947 Newton worked at Fifty-second Street's Downbeat Club in Sid Catlett's quartet, but from the spring through the fall he was inactive because of illness. In late 1947 he worked with Ted Goddard's band at the Savoy in Boston, but in the summer of 1948 he lost his home and trumpet in a fire. By early 1949 he was freelancing in Boston and that summer played in several concerts and appeared with Edmond Hall's band. In May 1950 he again had his own band at the Savoy, but by 1951 his playing was limited to occasional Friday night appearances at the Stuyvesant Casino in Lower Manhattan. By this time Newton had settled in Greenwich Village, where he devoted himself primarily to politics, social work, and painting. His decision to stop playing may have been prompted by failing health and by resentment toward the lack of opportunities for jazz performers of his generation to work in the bop-dominated scene of the day. A long-standing spokesman for racial and economic equality, in the 1930s Newton had become attracted to Marxist philosophy and left-wing causes, an interest that he shared with the equally literate and politically conscious Edmond Hall. Newton died, reportedly of acute gastritis, in New York City. On 26 April 1954 a memorial concert was held in his behalf at New York's Basin Street, featuring the bands of Eddie Condon, Red Allen, Jimmy McPartland, and Bob Wilber as well as soloists Pee Wee Russell, Flip Phillips, Willie "The Lion" Smith, Buck Clayton, and Pete Brown.

Though not as influential as Red Allen, Rex Stewart, Roy Eldridge, Bunny Berigan, Cootie Williams, or Buck Clayton, Frankie Newton was nevertheless one of the better trumpet players of the Swing Era. Obviously inspired by Louis Armstrong, he had a full, broad tone that was equally compelling with or without a mute, and he could improvise with great originality. Apart from his playing on many of the records under his own name, as well as most by the Port of Harlem groups, his better solos are found on Cecil Scott's "In A Corner," Art Karle's "Lights Out," Mezz Mezzrow's "The Panic Is On," Teddy Wilson's "All My Life," Teddy Hill's "Blue Rhythm Fantasy" and "China Boy," Charlie Barnet's "Emperor Jones," Jerry Kruger's "So You Won't Sing," Buster Bailey's "Dizzy Debutante" and "Chained to a Dream," and Midge Williams's "An Old Flame" and "The One Rose." Of the few records he made in the 1940s the sessions with James P. Johnson and Joe Turner, Miss Rhapsody's "Sweet Man" and Hank D'Amico's "Gone at Dawn" serve as prime examples of his inventiveness.

• A general source of information dealing with Newton's early associations is Albert McCarthy, *Big Band Jazz* (1974), while somewhat more detailed coverage can be found in books written by or about a few of his colleagues. Dicky Wells, *The Night People: The Jazz Life of Dicky Wells*, as told to Stanley Dance (1991), and Bill Coleman, *Trumpet Story* (1990), discuss Newton during his time with Cecil Scott's band. A brief discussion of his playing is on the Port of Harlem Jazzmen records in John Chilton, *Sidney Bechet: The Wizard of Jazz* (1987), and mention of his activities in Boston is in Manfred Selchow, *Profoundly Blue: A Bio-Discographical Scrapbook on Edmond Hall* (1988). Thorough discographical treatment is in Brian Rust, *Jazz Records, 1897–1942* (1982), and Walter Bruyninckx, *Traditional Jazz Discography, 1897–1988* (5 vols.) and *Swing Discography, 1920–1988* (13 vols.). A brief career chronology is in John Chilton, *Who's Who Of Jazz* (1985).

JACK SOHMER

NEWTON, Hubert Anson (19 Mar. 1830–12 Aug. 1896), astronomer and mathematician, was born in Sherburne, New York, the son of William Newton, a railroad and canal engineer, and Lois Butler. Newton graduated from Yale College in 1850 with a special interest in mathematics, although he had also studied astronomy there under Denison Olmsted. Newton pursued his mathematical studies privately from 1850 to 1853, when, at the death of Yale's professor of mathematics, Anthony D. Stanley, he was named tutor in mathematics and essentially given complete charge of the college's mathematical instruction. In 1855 he was appointed professor of mathematics to succeed Stanley and immediately asked for and received a year's leave of absence for study abroad to prepare himself for his new post.

Newton spent the 1855–1856 academic year in Paris, where the lectures of the distinguished geometer Michel Chasles left a particularly strong impression on him. After his return to New Haven, Newton, whose teaching duties occupied between fifteen and twenty hours per week, also devoted time to original geometrical researches. In particular, he published a paper, titled "To Describe a Circle Tangent to Three Given Circles" (*Mathematical Monthly* 1 [1859]: 239–44), which reflected the instruction he had received under Chasles.

After 1861, when Newton's interests shifted permanently from mathematics to astronomy, he made an effort to keep himself apprised of the latest developments in mathematical research. This left him reasonably well suited to guide and advise his two best-known students: the mathematician Eliakim Hastings Moore and the physicist-chemist-mathematician Josiah Willard Gibbs. Newton counseled Gibbs as an undergraduate and influenced his decision to study in Paris and Germany. He served as the director of Moore's dissertation research (on a topic in geometry) from 1883 to 1885. At a time when Yale College had not yet adopted the research ethic, which characterized not only the best German universities but also newly founded American institutions like Johns Hopkins University (opened in 1876), Newton encouraged his most talented students in this direction and thereby prepared them for the then rapidly changing academic environment in the United States.

The circumstance that appears to have turned Newton toward astronomy was the formation in 1861 by the Connecticut Academy of Arts and Sciences of a committee to coordinate observations of the meteor showers that regularly occur in August and November. As a member of this committee Newton played a particularly active role in making personal observations and in gathering, collating, and analyzing the data collected by other observers in various locales. This research activity resulted in a series of papers on meteors—their paths, their altitudes, their velocities, their periods, etc.—in the 1860s. Most notable among these works are "Altitudes of Shooting Stars Observed on the Night of Nov. 13–14th, 1863, at Washington, Haverford College, Germantown, Philadelphia and Other Places" (*American Journal of Science* 40 [1865]: 250–53), and "On Shooting Stars" (*Memoirs of the National Academy of Sciences* 1 [1866]: 291–312). In the latter paper Newton tried to systematize the properties not of one particular shower but of meteor showers in general, using the statistical methods then recently put forth by the British physicist James Clerk Maxwell. Newton cautiously concluded, on the basis of his velocity analysis of the especially large and bright mete-

ors he dubbed "meteoroids," that their orbits were not approximately circular but rather were elliptical of relatively large eccentricity, like cometary orbits. The British astronomer John Couch Adams later confirmed this conclusion mathematically. The phenomenon of meteor showers thus became part of the long-standing study of comets.

Newton's role in this discovery not only earned him international recognition but also quite naturally led to his work on comets themselves. In an 1878 paper titled "On the Origin of Comets" (*American Journal of Science* 16 [1878]: 165–79), Newton used a statistical analysis of both the aphelia and the inclinations of the orbits of known comets to test the conflicting hypotheses on cometary formation of Immanuel Kant and Pierre Simon de Laplace. He concluded, in agreement with Laplace, that comets formed independently of the formation of our solar system. Newton also devoted his last substantial work, "On the Capture of Comets by Planets, Especially Their Capture by Jupiter" (*American Journal of Science* 42 [1891]: 183–99 and 482–91), to a statistical analysis of the behavior of comets.

Newton married Anna C. Stiles in 1859, and the couple had two children. A quiet, modest, and retiring man, Newton poured most of his energies into his classroom teaching throughout his career. He never sought notoriety for the research he also managed to do, and yet he received recognition both at home and abroad for his achievements. He was named as one of the original members of the National Academy of Sciences in 1863; was elected to the presidency of the American Association for the Advancement of Science in 1885 and to the vice presidency of the American Mathematical Society (1894–1896); and was made a foreign member of the Royal Society of London in 1892. Newton also served the broader American scientific community as an editor of the *American Journal of Science* beginning in 1864. Moreover, he was an energetic proponent of the metric system and prepared the table of equivalents between metric and nonmetric units that formed part of the act passed in 1866 that legalized the use of the metric system in the United States. He further satisfied his strong sense of civic duty by serving a term as an elected alderman to the city council of New Haven.

Newton's work on the theory of meteors and comets was significant, although not seminal. His contributions lay principally in his supporting role in the establishment of a scientific community in America in the last half of the nineteenth century and in his enlightened attitudes toward the relationship between teaching and research at a Yale College that only slowly adopted the production of original research as part of its institutional mission. Newton died in New Haven.

• The most comprehensive published source on Newton's life is J. Willard Gibbs, "Hubert Anson Newton," *American Journal of Science* 3 (1897): 358–78, which also contains a complete bibliography of Newton's works. See also "Biographical Sketch of the President of the Association," *Science* 6 (1885): 161–62, and A. W. Phillips, "Hubert Anson Newton," *Bulletin of the American Mathematical Society* 3 (1896): 169–73. Newton's place in the development of mathematics in the United States is discussed in David Eugene Smith and Jekuthiel Ginsburg, *A History of Mathematics in America before 1900* (1934; repr. 1980), and in Karen Hunger Parshall and David E. Rowe, *The Emergence of the American Mathematical Research Community 1876–1900: J. J. Sylvester, Felix Klein, and E. H. Moore* (1994).

KAREN HUNGER PARSHALL

NEWTON, Huey P. (17 Feb. 1942–22 Aug. 1989), leader of the Black Panther Party, was born Huey Percy Newton in Monroe, Louisiana, the son of Amelia Johnson Newton and Walter Newton, a sharecropper and Baptist preacher. Walter Newton so admired Louisiana's populist governor Huey P. Long that he named his seventh and youngest son after him. A proud, powerful man, Newton defied the regional convention that forced most black women into domestic service and never allowed his wife to work outside the home. He always juggled several jobs to support his large family. Like thousands of black southerners drawn to employment in the war industries, the Newtons migrated to California during the 1940s. Settling in Oakland, the close-knit family struggled to shelter young Huey but could not stop the mores of the ghetto from shaping his life. Years later, those same ghetto neighborhoods became the springboard of the Black Panther Party that thrust Newton into national prominence.

While attending Oakland's Merritt College, Newton met Bobby Seale, a married student recently discharged from the army, when they became involved in developing a black studies curriculum. Discovering that they both felt impatient with student activism in the face of blatant discrimination and police violence, the two formed a new organization in October 1966. Adopting the symbol of the all-black political party in Lowndes County, Alabama, that Black Power spokesman Stokely Carmichael had helped organize, they named their organization the Black Panther Party for Self-Defense.

Seale and Newton wrote out a ten-point platform and program for the group, demanding as its first point "power to determine the destiny of our black community." The program outlined aspirations for better housing, education, and employment opportunities and called for an end to police brutality. It insisted that blacks be tried by juries of their peers, that all black prisoners be released because none had received fair trials, and that blacks be exempted from military service. It concluded with a quotation from the Declaration of Independence asserting the right to revolution.

Initiating patrols to prevent abusive behavior by local police, the disciplined, uniformly dressed young Panthers immediately attracted attention. Wearing black leather jackets and black berets, the men and women openly carried weapons on their patrols. These acts were legal under the gun laws then in force, but

the California legislature swiftly acted to prohibit the patrols in July 1967.

The Black Panthers were buoyed along by the current of dissent and protest surging through black communities. As in other urban areas, Oakland's black families felt a deep sense of injustice at the treatment meted out by the police, and the Black Panther Party continued to attract members. In October 1967 Newton was wounded following a late-night traffic stop in which Oakland police officer John Frey was killed. Upon his arrest, the startling news that the minister of defense of the Black Panther Party was accused of killing a white policeman was broadcast nationally. Police killings of black youths had triggered numerous riots and urban uprisings, but in all the previous incidents no policemen had been killed. Newton's indictment for murdering Frey threw a spotlight over Oakland's Black Panther Party. Soon, Charles R. Garry, a prominent San Francisco trial attorney, took up Newton's legal defense, and the Black Panther's minister of information, the writer Eldridge Cleaver, initiated the "Free Huey" movement that made Newton internationally famous.

Newton's case became the centerpiece of a massive mobilization campaign advocating the Black Panther Party program. Membership soared. During the murder trial in the summer of 1968, a fateful year marked by the assassinations of the Reverend Martin Luther King, Jr., and U.S. senator and presidential candidate Robert Kennedy, thousands of supporters flocked to rallies outside the Oakland courthouse. The international effort in defense of Newton succeeded in blocking his conviction (and execution) for murder, but the jury found him guilty of manslaughter.

Newton openly advocated revolutionary changes in the relationship between poor blacks and the larger white society and concentrated on the untapped potential of what he called the urban "lumpen proletariat" to forge a vanguard party. The "Free Huey" movement galvanized blacks, resulting in phenomenal growth and the development of a national Black Panther Party buoyed by the rallying cry "All Power to the People!" The Panthers advocated self-determination to replace the racist, economic subjugation of blacks they viewed as "colonialism." By the time Newton was released following a successful appeal in 1970, the Black Panther Party had offices in more than thirty cities, including New York, Philadelphia, Chicago, and Los Angeles. It had established an international section in Algeria and inspired the creation of similar organizations in Israel, the West Indies, and India.

As were numerous leaders and members of the Black Panther Party, Newton was subjected to nearly constant surveillance, police harassment, frequent arrests, and a barrage of politically inspired invasions of privacy. He faced two retrials on the manslaughter charge but was never again convicted of killing Frey (both trials ended in hung juries). In the meantime, Panther leaders in Los Angeles and Chicago were shot to death in 1969 under circumstances in which special police units worked secretly with federal intelligence agents—many of the criminal charges brought against Panthers resulted from clandestine police–FBI collaborations engineered by COINTELPRO (the U.S. government's counterintelligence program). Between 1968 and 1973, thousands of Panthers were arrested, hundreds were tried and imprisoned, while thirty-four were killed in police raids, shoot-outs, or internal conflicts.

Newton's symbolic appeal to young blacks was powerful, especially because of the defiant resistance to police authority he represented. Such conduct had never been so central to any previous black leader, and it shocked many who were accustomed to a more restrained demeanor. Newton, who often expressed the belief that it was crucial "to capture the peoples' imagination" in order to build a successful revolutionary movement, was more effective as a catalyst than as a traditional leader. Newton was not an especially captivating speaker or skilled political organizer; rather his talent lay in inspiring a small group of exceptionally talented individuals, directing their energies, and eliciting a loyalty so profound that they were willing to risk their lives building the revolutionary organization he founded.

The unique way the Black Panther Party fused conflicting elements within one organization paid tribute to Newton's vision. Free breakfasts for schoolchildren and other programs provided community service, but unlike other reformers, they also simultaneously engaged in electoral politics and challenged the imperialist domination of blacks—all with a flamboyant bravado. While the traditional civil rights organizations sought "first-class citizenship," the Panthers viewed the legacy of slavery, segregation, and racism as a form of colonialism in which blacks were subjects, not citizens of the United States; instead of seeking integration, the Panthers identified with the struggles of other colonized African and Asians, and sought black liberation.

The Black Panthers were not ideologically consistent over time; the party moved from a nationalism inspired by Malcolm X to a Marxist anti-imperialism influenced by Franz Fanon, Che Guevara, and Mao Tse Tung and finally into a synthesis that Newton called "intercommunalism," which he claimed was required by the collapse of the nation state within the global economy. Although the Panthers remained an all-black organization, it forged coalitions with other radical groups involving whites, Asians, and Latinos. The volatile mixture of external repression, internal dissension, and an escalating use of purges led to several highly publicized expulsions that divided the governing central committee.

Precipitated by Newton's denunciation and expulsion of Eldridge Cleaver and the entire International Section in February 1971, the Black Panther Party broke into rival factions, a division the press named the "Newton-Cleaver split." The factions were loosely defined by ideological differences. Whereas the Newton-controlled portion of the party abruptly backtracked and began to advocate moderate solutions to

black oppression—and ceased to attract new members—those opposing Newton escalated their devotion to revolutionary tactics and coalesced around a network of freedom fighters who eventually formed the underground Black Liberation Army.

An increasingly paranoid Newton took bold steps to consolidate his personal supremacy over the volatile organization, and as chapters dwindled or were closed, he introduced the "survival pending revolution" program. While the Panthers publicly engaged in conventional political and economic activities, Newton, who had become heavily addicted to cocaine, led the organization into subterranean criminal activities. Following indictments brought against him for assaulting several Oakland residents, including a prostitute who later died, Newton fled to Cuba in 1974. He left behind an organization virtually in shambles, saddled with an Internal Revenue Service investigation into its finances, and dwindling numbers of supporters. Even party chairman Bobby Seale repudiated the unsavory developments and left the organization.

En route to Cuba, Newton married his secretary, Gwen Fontaine. Following his return in 1976, Newton was tried on assault and murder charges but was not convicted. He then enrolled in the History of Consciousness program on the Santa Cruz campus of the University of California. He received his Ph.D. from that program in 1980, by which time the Black Panther Party had virtually disbanded. Although a small retinue of supporters continued to be drawn to Newton's strong personal magnetism, he ceased to function as the leader of a revolutionary movement. By 1982 his marriage had ended in divorce and the last vestige of the Black Panther Party, its Youth Institute, had closed for lack of funds.

Newton married Frederika Slaughter of Oakland in 1984. His repeated efforts to overcome alcohol and cocaine addiction were not successful, and he briefly spent time in prison in 1987 for a probation violation. Early on the morning of 22 August 1989 Newton was shot and killed in Oakland by a 25-year-old crack dealer whom he had insisted give him drugs free because of who he was. Newton's flamboyance, vision, and passion came to symbolize an entire era, yet in the end, the same demons that ravaged the community he had sought to transform destroyed him as well.

• Huey P. Newton's papers, which include a significant amount of legal material, are housed at the Department of Special Collections, Stanford University Library. A collection of Newton's writings, many of which initially appeared in the *Black Panther* newspaper, was published as *To Die for the People* (1972). Following his release from prison, his autobiography, *Revolutionary Suicide* (1973), was released; it was republished in 1995. *In Search of Common Ground* (1973), by Erik Erikson and Huey Newton, presents two lengthy discussions between the renowned psychiatrist and Newton that took place at Yale University and in Oakland. *War against the Panthers: A Study of Repression in America* (1996) is the published version of Newton's Ph.D. dissertation.

Black Panther trials, including Newton's murder case, have generated a voluminous literature. One example is

White Justice: Black Experience Today in America's Court-rooms, ed. Sara Blackburn, with an introduction by Haywood Burns (1971). Several books have been devoted exclusively to Newton's first murder trial, including Edward M. Keating, *Free Huey* (1970), and Ann Fagan Ginger, ed., *Minimizing Racism in Jury Trials: The Voir Dire Conducted by Charles R. Garry in People of California v. Huey P. Newton* (1969). Federal government investigations of the Black Panther Party produced an enormous amount of documents, including published volumes of hearings and congressional reports, such as the report of the House Committee on Internal Security, *Gun Barrel Politics: The Black Panther Party* (1971). The U.S. Senate Select Committee to Study Governmental Operations with Respect to Intelligence Activities, Final Report, Book 3 (1976), explicitly covers the COINTELPRO activities directed against the Black Panther Party.

Newton is the central character in the film *Panther*, directed by Mario Van Peebles, who also coauthored, with Ula Y. Taylor and J. Tarika Lewis, a pictorial history of the Black Panthers and the story behind the film book, also entitled *Panther* (1995). An obituary is in the *New York Times*, 23 Aug. 1989.

KATHLEEN N. CLEAVER

NEWTON, Isaac (31 Mar. 1800–19 June 1867), farmer and first commissioner of agriculture, was born in Burlington County, New Jersey, the son of Isaac Newton and Mary Newton, farmers. Following his father's early demise, the infant Isaac and his mother lived in Burlington County with his paternal grandfather, a well-established farmer. There Newton learned the agricultural trade.

After completing a common school education, Newton chose to follow in the footsteps of both his father and grandfather, becoming a farmer. After his marriage in 1821 to Dorothy Burdsall, Newton ran several farms in Delaware County, Pennsylvania. (The number of their children, if any, is unknown.) His farms produced well, and he expanded into the production of ice cream and confections in Philadelphia. He also carried on a successful butter trade, even selling to the White House. A member of the Pennsylvania State Agricultural Society and the U.S. Agricultural Society, he campaigned actively for the establishment of a federal department of agriculture.

In 1861 Newton obtained his first governmental position in the U.S. Patent Office, where he was the superintendent of its agricultural division. This office, established in 1839, was responsible for the collection and distribution of seeds, the dissemination of information to farmers, the collection of agricultural statistics, and "other agricultural purposes." Operating on the most minimal of budgets, it was the precursor to the modern Department of Agriculture.

On 15 May 1862 President Abraham Lincoln signed the bill creating the U.S. Department of Agriculture. It had narrowly missed becoming a bureau of agriculture within the Department of the Interior. On 1 July 1862 Lincoln appointed Newton the first commissioner of agriculture. Newton envisioned a Department of Agriculture with duties far beyond those carried out formerly by the Patent Office. He planned for his department to systematically collect and publish information about agriculture, to introduce new plants and animals to the United States, and to address questions from farmers. He also hoped that the department would test implements, carry out chemical analyses of soils and plants, and help establish within the department professorships in entomology and botany. He planned for the creation of an agricultural library and museum. In all of these objectives, Newton was successful.

Newton was particularly careful about establishing statistical studies of American agriculture. Beginning in the summer of 1863, the department published regular reports, detailing crop and weather conditions. Monthly crop reports, including acreage, yields, and production, began in 1863, and the department's yearly reports, started in 1861, have continued ever since. In his 1864 annual report, Newton advocated that the federal government issue daily weather reports; these recommendations led to the organization of the Weather Bureau.

Because the department was founded at the beginning of the Civil War, Newton was also responsible for aiding in the Union's war effort. The government established a garden in Washington, D.C., where the Department of Agriculture attempted to grow cotton and find substitutes for products, such as cane sugar, flax, and hemp, normally grown in the southern states. Some of these experiments were successful, others were not. At the war's conclusion, Newton hoped for a speedy reunification, without which the United States was unlikely to be agriculturally self-sufficient. In 1866 he sent Oliver H. Kelley, a clerk, to the southern states to see what could be done to assist southern farmers damaged by the war.

One of Newton's chief accomplishments as head of the Department of Agriculture was bringing high-quality personnel into the department. Although Newton himself was not highly educated, during his years in office a nucleus of scholarly college- and university-trained men came to work for him, including botanist William Saunders, who was responsible both for laying out many of the parks in Washington, D.C., and for the introduction of the navel orange to the United States, and clerk Kelley, who was a founder of the Grange. Newton set a standard that was maintained by the department long after his years as commissioner.

Newton died before the Department of Agriculture's new office building could be completed. The cause of his death officially was sunstroke, suffered in the line of duty. The previous July Newton had heard a storm approaching and went to one of the department's experimental farms to make sure that wheat samples being harvested were protected from the rain. He vigorously attended to these duties while wearing a high silk hat and a frock coat. Overcome by heat and exertion, he never recovered, dying eleven months later. The location of his death is unknown.

As the first commissioner of the Department of Agriculture, Newton established the priorities of the agency. He envisioned his department as a scientific institution, gathering information that would make farmers more productive and keep the United States self-sufficient. He created a firm foundation for the department, giving it a separate identity, including its own office building, library, and museum. Although he did not envision the Department of Agriculture as the advocacy agency for farmers that it would become, he was influential in establishing many of its long-term functions and goals.

• For more information see Willard W. Cochrane, *The Development of American Agriculture: A Historical Analysis* (1979) p. 96; J. W. Stokes, "Death of Hon. Isaac Newton," *Monthly Report of the Agricultural Department*, May–June 1867; and U.S. Department of Agriculture, *After a Hundred Years: The Yearbook of Agriculture, 1962* (1962), and *Century of Service: The First 100 Years of the United States Department of Agriculture* (1963).

PAMELA RINEY-KEHRBERG

NEWTON, John (24 Aug. 1822–1 May 1895), soldier and engineer, was born in Norfolk, Virginia, the son of Thomas Newton, a U.S. congressman, and Margaret Jordan Pool. Newton attended West Point, where he graduated 1 July 1842, second in a class of fifty-six. Following graduation he was commissioned a second lieutenant and posted to the engineers. He served as assistant to the Board of Engineers until 1843 then as an instructor of engineering at West Point until 1846. Subsequently assigned to duties of increasing responsibility in fortification, river, harbor, and lighthouse work, he was the superintending engineer of construction of Forts Wayne, Michigan; and Porter, Niagara, and Ontario, New York. He married Anna M. Starr in 1848; they had six children. In 1858 he served as the chief engineer of the Mormon Expedition, his only field service prior to the Civil War.

At the outbreak of the war, Newton was a captain in the Corps of Engineers, serving as superintending engineer of Fort Delaware and engineer of repairs to Fort Mifflin in Delaware Bay. He was posted to the position of chief engineer of the Departments of Pennsylvania and the Shenandoah. On 6 August 1861 he was promoted to major in the Corps of Engineers and was assigned on 28 August to be assistant engineer in the construction of the defenses of Washington, D.C. He supervised the building of Fort Lyon, one of the capital's largest works. On 23 September 1861 he was promoted to brigadier general of volunteers and in October was assigned to command of an infantry brigade in William B. Franklin's division. However, he remained active in the construction of the capital's fortifications until the Peninsula campaign in March 1862. During this campaign, Newton participated in the engagement at West Point, Virginia, 7 May 1862, where Franklin reported he displayed "great judgment in handling his regiments under fire"; he was also at Gaines' Mill and Glendale.

In the Maryland campaign in September 1862, Newton saw action at Crampton's Gap and Antietam. At Crampton's Gap Newton was slow to bring his brigade into action. Nevertheless, Sixth Corps commander (and fellow engineer) Franklin recommended Newton's promotion to major general for "his conspicuous gallantry and important services" in the battle. In the reorganization of the Sixth Corps after Antietam, Newton was placed in command of the Third Division. He saw limited action at Fredericksburg, following which he and other federal generals openly criticized army commander Ambrose E. Burnside. Newton carried his criticism personally to the president. Burnside retaliated by seeking Newton's and other officers' dismissal from the service. Newton's indiscretion in this affair and his subsequent testimony to the Committee on the Conduct of the War later damaged his career. However, there were no immediate repercussions, and he was promoted to major general of volunteers on 30 March 1863. He participated in the successful storming of Marye's Heights during the Chancellorsville campaign, where his division lost over 1,000 men.

On the first day of the battle of Gettysburg, Newton was selected by General George G. Meade to take command of the First Corps following the death of General John F. Reynolds. Newton proved unimpressive as a corps commander. His chief of artillery, Colonel Charles Wainwright, complained that Newton "knows enough theoretically at any rate, but is intensely lazy." In another instance Wainwright wrote, "This way [Newton] has of indulging himself and not considering the comfort of his men is outrageous." In a visit to Newton's headquarters, Colonel Theodore Lyman (1833–1897) of Meade's staff wrote that Newton "produced a huge variety of liquids which I had to refuse. . . . They come from all sides and in great variety, even champagne!" In the reorganization of the Army of the Potomac in March 1864, Newton was relieved of command. Despite his apparent inefficiency as a corps commander, General Meade tried to retain Newton as a division commander but was unsuccessful. On 18 April 1864 his promotion to major general of volunteers failed to be confirmed, likely a result of his activities against Burnside during the winter of 1862. Newton was transferred to command of the Second Division, Fourth Corps, in the Army of the Cumberland. He led this division through the Atlanta campaign and participated in the battles of Rocky Face Ridge, Dallas, Kennesaw Mountain, Peach Tree Creek, Jonesborough, and Lovejoy's Station. His division was particularly effective at Peach Tree Creek, and Newton's performance in the campaign was praised by his corps commander, General David S. Stanley, who recommended his promotion. Newton was instead reassigned in October 1864 to a minor command embracing the District of Key West and Tortugas, Florida, where he remained to the end of the war. In March 1865 he was brevetted major general of both volunteers and the regular army for his services during the war.

Following the war, Newton was assigned to be superintending engineer of fortification, river, and harbor work in the general vicinity of New York harbor. He gained distinction in this position for supervising the removal of several major obstacles to navigation in New York's East River, including Flood Rock, a nine-acre reef in Hell Gate. He used 200,000 pounds of dynamite to remove this reef, and the detonation, on 10 October 1885, sent tremors that were recorded 183 miles away. Newton was promoted to colonel on 30 June 1879 and to brigadier general and chief of engineers on 6 March 1884. He was retired at his own request on 27 August 1886 to accept the position of commissioner of public works of New York City. In 1888 he took the position of president of the Panama Railroad Company and held this post until his death in New York City. Although Newton's record as a leader of troops in the Civil War was uneven, he was an excellent engineer and made his greatest contributions in that field.

• For official Civil War correspondence by and about Newton, see *The War of the Rebellion: A Compilation of the Official Records of the Union and Confederate Armies* (128 vols., 1880–1901). A sketch of Newton's professional career is in G. W. Cullum, *Biographical Register of the Officers and Graduates of the United States Military Academy*, vol. 2, 3d ed. (1891). Also see Lewis Randolph Hamersly, *Records of Living Officers of the United States Army* (1884), and *National Academy of Science Biographical Memoirs*, vol. 4 (1902). For a contemporary perspective of Newton as a corps commander, see Allan Nevins, ed., *A Diary of Battle: The Personal Journals of Colonel Charles S. Wainwright 1861–1865* (1962). An obituary is in the *New York Times*, 2 May 1895.

D. SCOTT HARTWIG

NEWTON, Joseph Fort (21 July 1876–24 Jan. 1950), Baptist, Universalist, and Episcopal minister, lecturer, and author, was born in Decatur, Texas, the son of Lee Newton, a Baptist minister and lawyer, and Sue Green Battle. Raised according to the rigid doctrinal standards and strict moral code in place among Texas Baptists at the turn of this century, much of Newton's life was a pilgrimage in search of gentler, more open-ended religious insight. Largely self-educated, he learned classical languages and literature with his mother's help, and in 1895 he was ordained a Baptist minister. Later that year he entered Southern Baptist Theological Seminary in Louisville, Kentucky, where his predilection for a liberalized religious perspective became more intensified. He read widely, learning more from poets and critical essayists than from the formal syllabus prescribed for divinity students. Newton searched for a faith that could satisfy the mind while it sanctified the heart. He grew increasingly dissatisfied with theological tenets that separated churches, and in 1897 he left both the seminary and the denomination because he found sectarian exclusiveness to be absurd and reactionary dogmas embarrassing.

In 1900 Newton married Jennie Mai Deatherage; the couple had two children. That same year he began serving as associate minister of the Nonsectarian Church in St. Louis, Missouri, a post that appealed to him because the group imposed no creedal or ritual tests for membership. Between 1903 and 1908 he led the People's Church in Dixon, Illinois, a congregation organized on similar principles. During this time Newton also became active in the Masonic order, publishing books on its importance and eventually rising to a 33d degree Mason himself. For eight years, beginning in 1908, he was pastor of the Liberal Christian Church in Cedar Rapids, Iowa. There he expanded his theological position to a universalist one, preaching what he called salvation available to everyone instead of merely a salvage operation for damaged souls. He believed religion was for improved daily living, not just to rescue souls from future punishment. A local newspaper printed his weekly sermons, which were collected into monthly pamphlets and issued annually in book form. With simple, lucid English prose this preacher of God's love emphasized the good in human nature, hoping to facilitate the blessings in life and faith that people could experience.

Such buoyant, romantic optimism made Newton increasingly well known. By 1915 his fame had spread to England, leading to an invitation to fill the pulpit at London's City Temple, often regarded as "the Cathedral of British Nonconformity." Newton drew thousands of listeners there each week during the wartime years of 1916 to 1919. As always, lectures on various cultural topics (ideas, heroes, saints, modern literature) together with sermons and devotional works poured from his prolific pen. In 1919 he returned to the United States as minister of the Church of the Divine Paternity, a Universalist congregation in New York City. There for the next six years he continued preaching, lecturing at colleges and cultural organizations, and publishing. He also began editing the *Master Mason*, a monthly magazine that furthered the cause of freemasonry. Now in the mature years of his pastoral life, he produced countless versions of a single affirmation: the love of God is the origin and end of human life; it fills daily experience with tenderness, tenacity, and final triumph.

All of these positive feelings, plus his rejection of all obstacles to cooperative human fellowship, made Newton a paragon of ecumenism in the first half of this century. This inclusive attitude influenced his decision in 1925 to accept the invitation of the Episcopal bishop of Pennsylvania to enter that communion. His move may have been another sign of his continual theological development, too, since he said that he regarded Episcopalianism as the median between arid liberalism and acrid literalism, being respectful of tradition but tolerant of contemporary innovations. He served first as lay reader, then as deacon, and in 1926 as ordained priest at the Memorial Church of St. Paul in Overbrook, Pennsylvania. In 1930 he was transferred to Philadelphia to become co-rector for five years at St. James's Church. Between 1935 and 1938 he tried as "special preacher" to combine St. James's with another congregation, calling the experiment "the Associated Churches." The attempt failed due to parochial jealousy, however, and beginning in 1938 Newton served until his death in Philadelphia as rector at the alternative parish, the Church of St. Luke and the Epiphany.

During all these years, writings of many sorts continued to appear in abundance. Between 1932 and 1944 Newton wrote a syndicated newspaper column called "Everyday Living." He was an associate editor of the *Christian Century*, adviser to the Federal Council of Churches, and lecturer at the College of Preachers in Washington, D.C. In 1939 a poll querying 25,000 clergy declared Newton to be one of the five most prominent ministers in the country. His pulpit eloquence, widely distributed publications, and the confidence-inspiring tone of his message made him a figure to be reckoned with in popular religious culture. In all these different ways he tried to celebrate the worth of human life, to find meaning and purpose in every aspect of daily experience, and to promote that in religion which could sustain people through their sufferings and bear them to victory.

• A prolific author, Newton produced over fifty books, edited more than thirty others, and issued hundreds of his speeches in pamphlet form. A small sampling of his volumes include *What Have the Saints to Teach Us?* (1914); *The Sword of the Spirit: Britain and America in the Great War* (1918); *The New Preaching: A Little Book about a Great Art* (1930); *His Cross and Ours* (1941); *The One Great Church: Adventures of Faith* (1948); and *River of Years: An Autobiography* (1946). An obituary is in the *New York Times*, 26 Jan. 1950.

HENRY WARNER BOWDEN

NEWTON, Richard Heber (31 Oct. 1840–19 Dec. 1914), Episcopal clergyman, was born in Philadelphia, Pennsylvania, the son of Richard Newton, an Episcopal clergyman, and Lydia Greatorex. Newton received his A.B. from the University of Pennsylvania in 1861 and studied at the Philadelphia Divinity School in 1862–1863. Bishop Alonzo Potter of Pennsylvania ordained him deacon on 19 January 1862. Also in 1862–1863 Newton was assistant minister at St. Paul's Church, Philadelphia, where his father was the rector, and in 1863–1864 he was assistant minister at the Church of the Epiphany, Philadelphia. In 1864 Newton married Mary Elizabeth Lewis, with whom he had four children. From 1864 to 1866 Newton was minister-in-charge of Trinity Church, Sharon Springs, New York. Bishop William Henry Odenheimer of New Jersey ordained him priest on 15 July 1866. When his father became rector of the Church of the Epiphany, Philadelphia, in 1866, Newton became rector of St. Paul's, a position he held until 1869. His most significant ministry was as rector of All Souls' Church, New York City (1869–1902), where he gained a reputation as a leading liberal preacher in the Episcopal church. In 1903 he became the preacher at Stanford University in California. His retirement years were spent at East Hampton, Long Island, where he died.

Newton was an advocate of the principles of biblical higher criticism, the critical study of the literary methods and sources used by the authors of the books of the New Testament, and especially the Old Testament, in an attempt to determine the literary form, date, authorship, and purpose of a given text. In 1883 Newton published *The Right and Wrong Uses of the Bible*, a widely read book that popularized the results of higher criticism, among them that Moses was not the author of the Pentateuch, and that defended the critical and historical study of the Bible, which, like any other book, was subject to interpretation. Newton argued that there was nothing to fear in the scholarly criticism of the Bible and that higher criticism would not damage the Bible but enhance its message and meaning. Furthermore, he asserted, the revelation of God should not be identified with the words of the Bible. In Newton's view an improper (wrong) use of the Bible would be to try to make it answer scientific questions; a proper (right) use would be to treat it as a human book containing the progressive revelation of God, a revelation that, in the Christian view, is more complete in the New Testament than in the Old Testament.

Newton was also a leader in the Social Gospel movement led by Washington Gladden and Walter Rauschenbusch. This movement insisted that the teachings of Jesus and the total message of Christian salvation should be applied to society, social institutions, and economic life as well as to the individual. Newton's views on this subject were the focus of one of his earliest and most significant books, *The Morals of Trade*. Published in 1876, it comprised a series of addresses on business ethics delivered to his All Souls' congregation. Reflecting the influences of leaders of British Christian social thought such as Frederick Denison Maurice and Frederick W. Robertson, it argued that Christian ethical standards should be applied to business and that laissez-faire should be restricted by government intervention. Because the church had emphasized spirituality rather than morality, it had concentrated on saving a few individuals rather than the regeneration of the world. For the Kingdom of God to be realized, Newton wrote, the church must become the "conscience-guide" of business and insist that cooperation replace competition. Newton's record as a social reformer was distinguished, but he was never a radical; he opposed street demonstrations and all revolutionary doctrines. Newton also supported Henry George and his single tax movement. His book *Womanhood: Lectures on a Woman's Work in the World* (1881) acknowledged the contributions of women in the workplace.

As a Broad Churchman, Newton supported the ecumenical activities of the Episcopal church and was committed to the unity of the churches in the United States. The term "Broad Church" had been coined by the contributors to *Essays and Reviews*, published in England in 1860. Broad Churchmen opposed the High Church belief that the Episcopal church was the one true American church, and they invited non-Episcopalians to preach in Episcopal churches. Newton, a major figure in the movement, participated in the church congresses of the Episcopal church, which constituted the primary forum for Broad Churchmen and which advocated liturgical openness, commitment to social ministry, and a broad toleration for diversity of thought.

On his seventieth birthday in 1910 the executive committee of the Conference of Religion wrote in a letter to him: "We honor you for your work during many years for the displacing of error by truth, of superstition by reason, of dogmatic sectarianism by religious solidarity, a formal religionism by vital religion and of conventional morals by moral ideals" (*A Service*, p. 38).

• There is no known repository of Newton's papers. His other books include *The Children's Church: A Service Book and Hymnal* (1872), *Studies of Jesus* (1880), *The Book of the Beginnings: A Study of Genesis with an Introduction to the Pentateuch* (1884), *Philistinism: Plain Words concerning Certain Forms of Modern Skepticism* (1885), *The Present Aspect of the Labor Problem* (1886), *Social Studies* (1887), *Church and Creed* (1891), *Christian Science: The Truths of Spiritual Healing and Their Contribution to the Growth of Orthodoxy* (1898), *Parsifal: An Ethical and Spiritual Interpretation* (1904), *The Mysticism of Music* (1915), and *Catholicity: A Treatise on the Unity of Religions* (1918). Some tributes to Newton are in *A Service to Honor the Memory of the Rev. R. Heber Newton, D.D., and to Perpetuate the Ideals to Which His Life Was Dedicated. Church of the Ascension, Fifth Avenue and Tenth Street, New York City, February the Seventh, 1915* (1915). Obituaries are in the *New York Times*, 22 Dec. 1914, and *Churchman*, 23 Jan. 1915.

DONALD S. ARMENTROUT

NEWTON, Robert Safford (16 Dec. 1818–9 Oct. 1881), physician, was born near Gallipolis, Ohio, the son of John Newton and Lydia Safford, farmers. Newton's early education was at the common school because his father planned for him to go into farming and deemed that sufficient for a farmer. Desiring more education, Newton persuaded his father to allow him to attend an academy in Lewisburg, Virginia, for one year (1833–1834). He farmed and taught school until 1837, when he left the farm and began his medical studies with Edward Naret in Gallipolis. While studying with Naret he was tutored in Greek, Latin, philosophy, and mathematics by the principal of the Gallipolis Academy and the pastor of the Methodist church. In 1839 he attended the Medical University of Louisville, Kentucky (a traditional, or allopathic, school of medicine), obtaining his medical degree in March 1841. He returned to Gallipolis and began practice. Two years later he married Mary M. Hoy. In 1845 they moved to Cincinnati, Ohio. At least one son survived childhood.

Newton soon broke with traditional medicine and took up the eclectic cause, of which he was an American pioneer. Eclecticism was a movement opposed to the excesses of prevailing medical practice, such as bloodletting and the indiscriminate use of the heavy metal-containing drug calomel. The eclectics arose out of a number of disparate "botanic" groups who, among other beliefs, supported a doctrine that every region of the earth produces indigenous medicinal plants that are ample for the cure of local diseases—that Nature provides equally for disease and its remedy.

From 1845 to 1849 Newton carried on a successful medical practice in Cincinnati. In 1849 he was appointed to the chair in surgery at the Memphis Institute, an eclectic school. The business affairs of the Cincinnati Eclectic Medical Institute became precarious following the death of Thomas Vaughn Morrow, its founder, and Newton was invited by the trustees to return to Cincinnati and take over the management of the institute. In 1850 Newton, along with the entire Memphis faculty, moved to Cincinnati. Newton assumed the chair of surgical practice and operative surgery. In December 1852 the board of the institute appointed him treasurer. Because clinical facilities in the city were closed to eclectic practitioners owing to the intense rivalry between medical factions, Newton began a clinical institute that provided medical services to the community and a training ground for the students of the eclectic school. He thus enlarged the scope of influence of the school as well as his own standing within the community.

In spite of the efforts of the trustees, financial difficulty continued. By 1856 matters were so bad that the faculty were not paid, despite good attendance and tuition payments. To compound the problem, there were factions within the faculty resulting in considerable rancor. In April the majority of the faculty voted to remove Newton as secretary, over the objections of the trustees; they also attempted to seize control of the board by the unlawful issuance of new stock. The Superior Court of Ohio issued an injunction against this group. When legal maneuvers failed, the rebellious faction resorted to force, which was answered in kind by Newton and a group of his supporters. The resultant confrontation lasted for one night and one day, with the deployment of barricades, knives, pistols, and other weapons. When a six-pound cannon appeared, the mayor and city police intervened.

By 1857 the courts had settled the issue in favor of Newton and the existing board. Newton continued at the institute as head of clinical medicine (1854–1858) and then of clinical surgery and operative gynecology (1858–1861). In spite of his rivals' efforts to unseat him, he continued to edit the *Eclectic Journal of Medicine* until 1862; he had started the journal in 1851.

Newton left Cincinnati in 1863 for New York City, where he organized the State Eclectic Medical Society and served as its president for three terms. He assisted in establishing the Eclectic Medical College of New York City, which was chartered in 1865. For seven years (1865–1872) he assisted in editing the *Eclectic Medical Review*, and with Alexander Wilder he began the *Medical Eclectic* (1865–1874). His publications were not as an author but as an editor: *The Eclectic Dispensatory of the United States* (with John King, 1852), *Chapman on Ulcers* (1853), *Physiological Botany* (1853), *The Eclectic Practice of Medicine* (with W. Byrd Powell, 1854), *An Eclectic Treatise on Diseases of Children* (1854), *Syme's Surgery* (1856), and *Pathology of Inflammation and Fevers* (1856). In his editorial efforts Newton championed the cause of eclectic medicine, but in his surgical practice, Newton's procedures followed contemporary norms. There was little divergence of opinion on surgery among eclectics and other practitioners, including homeopaths and allopaths. In his medical practice, however, Newton was an ardent practitioner of eclectic methods: he gave no harsh medications and disavowed bleeding. He became a supporter of the new "eclectic concentrates," herbal tinctures that could be standardized and were relatively stable compared to the individually-prepared prescriptions that generally prevailed. These concentrated fluid medicines began the commercial manufacture of medicinals by companies such as W. S. Merrell. Newton also supported notions concerning psychological influences on disease, particularly mesmerism and phrenology.

Newton was described in an editorial in the *Eclectic Medical Gleaner* of July 1905 as a large, portly man who was independent of thought, a good surgeon, an impressive lecturer, and generally indifferent to business affairs. "His best work," according to Otto Juettner, "was done in the columns of the *Eclectic Medical Journal.*" Newton was an important spokesman for the eclectic cause, which raised serious questions regarding practices in mainstream medicine. Through his edited publications, his lectures to professional and lay publics, his educational and organizational efforts, his individual clinical practice, and the clinical institutions he headed, he emphasized less harsh methods of treatment, supported the introduction of a variety of herbals into the pharmacopoeia, particularly as concentrates, and espoused psychological factors as a component in the course of disease. He was one of many voices, but an important voice in his time. He died in New York City.

• The most complete archives of eclectic medicine, including material on Newton, are at the Lloyd Library in Cincinnati, Ohio. Important sources include Harvey Wickes Felter, *History of the Eclectic Medical Institute, Cincinnati, Ohio, 1845–1902* (1902); Otto Juettner, *Daniel Drake and His Followers: Historical and Biographical Sketches* (1909); and John S. Haller, Jr., *Medical Protestants: The Eclectics in American Medicine, 1825–1939* (1994). Biographical sketches include those by Harvey Wickes Felter in the *Eclectic Medical Gleaner*, July 1905, and by John Uri and C. G. Lloyd in the *Bulletin of the Lloyd Library of Botany, Pharmacy and Materia Medica* (1910).

STANLEY L. BLOCK

NEWTON, William Wilberforce (4 Nov. 1843–25 June 1914), Episcopal clergyman, was born in Philadelphia, Pennsylvania, the son of Richard Newton, an Episcopal clergyman, and Lydia Greatorex. He was the younger brother of Richard Heber Newton, who also became an Episcopal clergyman. He attended the Episcopal Academy in Philadelphia and graduated from the University of Pennsylvania in 1865. He graduated from the Philadelphia Divinity School of the Protestant Episcopal church in 1868 and was ordained deacon by Bishop William Bacon Stevens of Pennsylvania on 19 June 1868. Bishop Stevens ordained him priest on 19 February 1869. In 1869–1870 he served as an assistant to his father at the Church of the Epiphany in Philadelphia. He married Emily Stevenson Cooke

in 1870; they had three children. He was the rector of St. Paul's Church in Brookline, Massachusetts (1870–1875), Trinity Church in Newark, New Jersey (1875–1877), St. Paul's Church in Boston, Massachusetts (1877–1881), and St. Stephen's Church in Pittsfield, Massachusetts (1881–1900). In 1903–1904 he served as chaplain of the English Church at Dinan, Brittany, and in 1905–1906 he was rector of the Church of the Ascension in Wakefield, Rhode Island.

Newton was active in numerous religious and civic organizations. In 1884 he organized the American Congress of Churches, an effort to promote interdenominational cooperation among the churches; the congress met at Hartford, Connecticut, in 1885 and at Cleveland, Ohio, in 1886, and he served as its secretary until 1888. Newton was a member of the school boards of Brookline and Pittsfield, the World's Red Cross Society, the Society for the Prevention of Cruelty to Animals, and the English Society for the Elevation and Purification of the Stage. He edited his father's writings and was one of the editors of the *Pennsylvania Monthly* (1875–1880), a secular magazine. From 1885 to 1906 he was editor of the *American Church Sunday School Magazine*. He died in Boston.

Richard Newton had been known as "the prince of preachers to children," and William Newton continued that tradition. He published *The Gate of the Temple, or Prayers for Children* (1875) and six volumes of sermons for the Pilgrim Series of Sermons for Children (1877–1890). He also wrote several novels, including *The Priest and the Man; or, Abelard and Heloise* (1883).

Newton was raised in the evangelical tradition of the Episcopal church, which emphasized the severity of sin, justification by grace, and the atoning death of Jesus Christ. In his book *Yesterday with the Fathers* (1910), he wrote: "The keynote to all this radical theology of the Evangelical party was found in the word 'satisfaction.' The divine nature was satisfied by the Atonement of Jesus Christ. This was enough; more than this could not be desired or expected" (p. 191).

Newton identified himself with the Broad church party of the Episcopal church, a movement that began in England and was inspired by Frederick Denison Maurice, although Maurice did not consider himself a Broad churchman. Along with Phillips Brooks and William Reed Huntington, Newton was one of the American leaders. Like them he interpreted the Christian faith in its broadest and most inclusive terms. Committed to the unity of the Church and to cooperation among the diverse American denominations, Newton was opposed to any expression of dogmatic sectarianism. With other Broad churchmen he affirmed the Christian creeds but asserted that they must be reinterpreted by each generation. He called for the church to be open to the intellectual and social trends of the day and to appropriate the truths of evolution and science. Newton was unconcerned about ritualistic issues and thus the issues that divided supporters of high church and low church. Like other Broad church leaders he urged toleration of a variety of theological views. The Episcopal church of present was shaped by the Broad church party.

- Some of Newton's other books are *Essays of Today: Religious and Theological* (1879); *The Voice of St. John and Other Poems* (1881); *Coming to Confirmation* (1881); *The Legend of St. Telemachus* (1882); *Summer Sermons from a Berkshire Pulpit* (1885); *The Vine Out of Egypt* (1887); *Dr. Muhlenberg* (1890), a life of William Augustus Muhlenberg; *The Child and the Bishop Together with Certain Memorabilia of the Rt. Rev. Phillips Brooks* (1894); *A Run through Russia: The Story of a Visit to Count Tolstoi* (1894); and *The Abiding Value of First Principles* (n.d.). His *Yesterday with the Fathers* has some autobiographical material.

DONALD S. ARMENTROUT

NEYLAND, Robert Reese, Jr. (17 Feb. 1892–28 Mar. 1962), football coach, was born in Greenville, Texas, the son of Robert Reese Neyland, a lawyer, and Pauline Lewis. A schoolboy star in football, basketball and baseball, Neyland (which he pronounced Knee-land) attended Burleson Junior College (Tex.), where he captained the football and baseball teams, from 1909 to 1910. He briefly played varsity football and baseball at Texas A & M (1910–1911) before he accepted an appointment to the U.S. Military Academy at West Point. There he starred as an end on the 1914 and 1915 football teams. He was also heavyweight boxing champion at West Point from 1914 through 1916 and was even better known as a baseball pitcher with a career record of 35 wins and 5 losses. When he graduated in 1916, he shared the coveted Golden Saber for "Best Athlete in the Senior Class" award, and the newspaper cartoonist Robert Ripley's "Believe It or Not" feature hailed him as "probably the most remarkable athlete since Jim Thorpe."

Spurning professional baseball offers from John McGraw of the New York Giants and Connie Mack of the Philadelphia Athletics, Neyland began his military career on 13 June 1916, as a second lieutenant in the U.S. Army Corps of Engineers. He served briefly on the Mexican border before being sent to France from 1917 to 1918.

After the war, he entered Massachusetts Institute of Technology, receiving a B.S. degree in civil engineering in 1921. He then accepted an appointment to teach at West Point, where he was an aide-de-camp to the young superintendent, General Douglas MacArthur, whom Neyland later called "unquestionably the greatest officer and man I ever knew." MacArthur believed that physical exercise as well as intramural and intercollegiate athletics were essential for future officers' training, and Neyland played a part as assistant coach of the football and boxing teams and head coach of the baseball team from 1921 until 1924. He recalled these years as some of the happiest of his life. In 1923 he married Ada Fitch of Grand Rapids, Michigan, with whom he had two children.

In 1925 the University of Tennessee appointed Neyland head of its Reserve Officers' Training Corps program and assistant football coach. Within a year the head football coach, M. Beal Banks, became ill, and

Neyland took over from him. He soon established Tennessee as a major power in the Southern Conference. Over the next nine seasons his teams had 76 wins, 7 losses, and 5 ties, with undefeated strings of 33 and 28 games, winning conference championships in 1927 and 1932.

During the next decade Neyland combined his football and military careers. While continuing to teach military science at the university, he served as an engineer on what became part of the Norris Dam and Tennessee Valley Authority projects. In 1935 he was required as an officer in the Regular Army to serve overseas. But after one unhappy year away from football in Panama, he retired from active military duty to return to Tennessee. Although he worked part-time as an engineer on the Tennessee and Cumberland River projects in the late 1930s, coaching football was now his life. As head coach (and athletic director after 1938), he led Tennessee to a record of 43 wins, 7 losses, and 3 ties over the next five seasons. The team was undefeated and won Southeastern Conference titles in 1938, 1939, and 1940; the 1939 team set a NCAA record of not being scored on in the regular season. Neyland was less successful in bowl games during these years, losing to Southern California in the 1940 Rose Bowl and to Boston College in the 1941 Sugar Bowl.

He returned to active army duty in May 1941 and served in the United States for several years as an engineer. He also reluctantly coached a college all-star football team that beat the professional New York Giants and Brooklyn Dodgers before losing by one touchdown to the Chicago Bears in charity games. In early 1944 he was sent to the China-Burma-India theater to work with troops supplying American forces in the region. He also found time there to develop a competitive sports program to help maintain the morale of troops in Calcutta. He received numerous honors for his services, including the Distinguished Service Medal, the Legion of Merit with Oak Leaf Cluster, the Order of the British Empire, and the Chinese Order of Cloud and Banner.

Retiring from active service as a brigadier general in 1946, Neyland returned to Tennessee to find collegiate football changed. It was now a more wide-open offensive game, using the T formation and unlimited substitution. Yet he eschewed what he called "rat race football" and retained his traditional single-wing offense and a solid defense. Over the next seven seasons his teams won 54, lost 17, and had 4 ties, winning Southeastern Conference championships in 1951 and 1956, a national championship in 1951, and appearing in three bowl games (beating Texas in the 1951 Cotton Bowl and losing to Maryland in the 1952 Sugar Bowl and to Texas in the 1953 Cotton Bowl). He was forced by a kidney and liver illness to retire from coaching at the end of the 1952 season after achieving an overall record at Tennessee of 173 wins, 31 losses, and 12 ties.

Neyland was an innovative force in the development of modern college football. He rarely wrote of his theories of the game or became involved in coaching clinics, but he fulfilled an early promise that he was going to "develop good football coaches as well as good football teams." More than 100 of his former players (Murray Warmath, Harvey Robinson, Bob Woodruff, Bowden Wyatt, Herman Hickman, Bobby Dodd, Billy Barnes, and Johnny Majors, among others) went into coaching and carried on his legacy. Neyland was one of the first to take movies of both practices and games to study tactical situations and an individual player's techniques. Staff meetings with his assistant coaches were held in which all aspects of game preparation were carefully planned. He also introduced tearaway jerseys, lightweight pads, and low-cut shoes, and he was one of the first to use a cover to protect the field's grass surface before game days. Contemporaries recall his innovative placement of an assistant in a tall building near the stadium to communicate directly during a game with coaches on the bench. He was not given to locker-room histrionics and said that victory came from proper preparation, a simple game plan, and superior execution on the field.

Neyland never abandoned his military background in approaching the game. Following in the footsteps of his mentor at West Point, Charles Daly, he saw football as a "war game," and his personal papers are full of references to military-football principles and metaphors. The head coach, he said, was to be commander in chief and was to create a "unity of command" in order to organize the training and preparation to achieve victory. He thought in terms of recognized military principles such as "mass," "economy of force," "maneuver," the element of surprise, and strategic and tactical simplicity of both offensive and defensive plans. All aspects of the game, including leadership (he designated a player as the "field general"), techniques for each position, the equipment, the locker room, and even the playing field ("the field of battle"), were given careful attention.

At times, alumni and fans were critical of Neyland's commitment to an older style of football. But while he did reluctantly accept the two-platoon system of substitution, he never abandoned the single wing for the T formation. His system of power football was built around a strong running attack, although on occasion he used the forward pass. Characteristically, he studied the problems of the passing game, focusing on protection of the passer and precise timing between passer and receivers. On defense he used multiple formations, aggressive pursuit of the ball, and to execute his plans the recruitment of smaller, more agile players.

Although he was somewhat aloof from other coaches, they held him in high esteem. Knute Rockne called him the best defensive coach in the country. Describing him as a "master of defensive football," Ray Graves said Neyland's "pass defense and theory have stood through the years and are still the basis of most football coaching techniques." Neyland was chosen Southeastern Conference coach of the year in 1936, received the Amos Alonzo Stagg Award in 1955, and was inducted into both the Helms Hall of Fame and the National Football Hall of Fame in 1956. Elected to the prestigious NCAA football rules committee in 1951, he served as its chairman for the last few years of his life. His star players received many SEC awards and national recognition, and a number of them were elected to the National Football Hall of Fame. The University of Tennessee's old Shields Watkins football stadium (upgraded over the years) was dedicated to Neyland on 20 October 1961.

A power on the University of Tennessee campus, Neyland worked closely with the faculty chairman of athletics and made friends with many prominent alumni and state political leaders. He worked to develop grant-in-aid programs for SEC athletes, but at the same time he helped establish scholarship funds at Tennessee to "help good Tennessee boys go to school." He also was instrumental in the building of a new basketball arena. A private, taciturn man of stern, military bearing, he was respectfully called "the Major," by his players in the early years, who both feared and revered him. To his close friends, he was a genial host and an avid fisherman and bridge player. He died in New Orleans and was buried in Knoxville.

• This article is based in part on personal interviews and correspondence with some of Neyland's former players and university associates. Neyland's papers are in the hands of his family and unavailable to scholars. The Sports Information Office at the University of Tennessee contains an extensive file, including newspaper clippings. Also see R. Neyland, "The Best Player I Ever Coached (Gene McEver)," *Saturday Evening Post*, 17 Nov. 1951; Arthur Daley, "Neyland's Imprint," *Chattanooga Times*, 18 Apr. 1962; and Tom Siler, *Tennessee: Football's Greatest Dynasty* (1960) and *Tennessee's Dazzling Decade, 1960–1970* (1970). Also see Andrew Kozar, "Football as a War Game: General Robert Reese Neyland's Application of Basic Military Principles to Coaching," *Proceedings and Newsletter* of the North American Society for Sport History (1990), pp. 19–20. An obituary is in the *New York Times*, 29 Mar. 1962.

DANIEL R. GILBERT

NEYMAN, Jerzy (16 Apr. 1894–5 Aug. 1981), statistician, was born in Bendery, Moldavia, the son of Polish parents, Czeslaw Neyman, a judge, and Kazimiera Lutoslawska. Shortly after Neyman's birth, the family moved several times, including to Simferopol in the Crimea, where Neyman began his schooling. After his father's death in 1906, they moved to Kharkov, where Neyman excelled in the Gymnasium and entered the University of Kharkov (now Maxim Gorki University) in 1912. Neyman was known by different names over this period; called Jurek as a boy, he was Yuri Czeslawovich Neyman at the University of Kharkov, and for a time in the 1920s he published under the name Jerzy Splawa-Neyman, adopting his Polish grandfather's old heraldic or *Herb* prefix Splawa (signifying the family coat-of-arms, a shield depicting two rivers).

At university, Neyman studied mathematics; his thesis on Lebesgue's theory of integration was awarded a gold medal in 1916. He remained at the University of Kharkov until 1921, teaching and studying probability and mathematical statistics with S. N.

Bernstein, including the application of probability to experimental problems in agriculture. In 1920 he married a Russian, Olga Solodovnikova; they had one child, born in 1936. The couple separated in the early 1950s but remained married until her death in 1979.

In 1920 Neyman was arrested and held for several weeks as a Pole during the Russian-Polish War. In 1921, hearing that he was about to be arrested for a second time by the Bolsheviks, Neyman and his family departed for Poland, where he worked first as a senior statistical assistant at the National Agricultural Institute in Bydgoszcz, and then at the State Meteorological Institute and as an assistant at the University of Warsaw. He received his Ph.D. in mathematics there in 1924 with a dissertation on the application of probability to agricultural experimentation. The dissertation was a careful, rigorous mathematical treatment of problems in estimation, with particular attention to the concept of a "true value," an early attempt to formulate a mathematical model for causal inference. But this work was written in ignorance of the recent developments in England, especially in the work of R. A. Fisher, and it was consequently limited in scope.

Neyman had encountered Karl Pearson's *Grammar of Science* as a student in 1916 and knew of the work of Pearson's Biometric Laboratory at University College London. In fall 1925 Neyman, with support from Warsaw, traveled to London for a year's visit to study in Pearson's laboratory. There he met William S. Gosset and Fisher and became familiar with English statistical work. He also met Pearson's son Egon, who initiated a collaboration that would between 1928 and 1938 produce ten papers on mathematical statistics, some of them fundamental to later development of the field, and would change the direction of Neyman's career.

Neyman spent 1926–1927 in Paris on a Rockefeller Fellowship. He then returned to Warsaw but kept in contact with Egon through correspondence, visits, and mutual vacation trips. The initial fruits of this collaboration, published between 1928 and 1931, were primarily inspired by an idea of Egon Pearson's that the likelihood ratio (the ratio of the probability of the data under two competing hypotheses) could be adopted as a principle that, with due attention to alternative hypotheses, could provide a unifying device for the derivation of tests of significance. In 1933 Neyman took an important step further, proving what has come to be known as the Neyman-Pearson Fundamental Lemma. The Lemma showed that the likelihood ratio was more than an intuitively attractive principle: under some regularity conditions it was the optimum procedure in the sense that, subject to controlling the probability of Type I Errors (false negatives), it would provide the smallest possible probability of Type II Errors (false positives).

In December 1933 Neyman accepted an offer from Egon Pearson to join him at University College London. The position was initially that of visiting assistant professor, but by 1935 he was appointed reader. During these years Neyman independently produced two other works of lasting significance, a paper on the

foundation of sampling (1934) and his theory of confidence intervals (1937).

During 1934–1935 Neyman's relationship with Fisher became increasingly contentious. The break flared in 1935 when Neyman read a paper to the Royal Statistical Society claiming that Fisher's test for the analysis of randomized experiments employed a biased estimate of variance, and again in 1937 when Fisher refused to accept Neyman's confidence intervals as a formalization of his own concept of fiducial inference. Toward the end of his life, Neyman wrote of the dispute several times in terms that, however tempered, hinted at a bewildered resentment that Fisher, who had inspired much of his early work, should have rejected him and his approach so emphatically. Modern statistics bears the indelible mark of both men's work.

In 1937 Neyman visited the United States for six weeks, speaking at several universities and giving a series of lectures organized by W. Edwards Deming at the U.S. Department of Agriculture. The lectures were an immense success, and they were quite influential in developing interest in mathematical statistics in the United States. Even before the printed version was issued (in mimeograph form in 1938), Neyman accepted an offer from the University of California at Berkeley to join its mathematics department and start a statistical laboratory to help empirical scientists in other departments. Neyman was eager to accept, particularly because he would be unconstrained by previously established programs such as he had encountered everywhere else he had worked. He set to work energetically, but the Second World War was a serious distraction to academic work everywhere.

During the war Neyman was largely absorbed in military research, particularly on bomb sights and targeting problems. In 1946 Deming, working with the Department of State, arranged for a group of statisticians including Neyman to travel to Greece to serve as neutral observers during an election hotly contested between the royalists and the communists. A few weeks after their arrival Neyman was effectively dismissed and sent home for insubordination. He had evidently spent too much time in the villages and camps of the opposition to the royalists, and his continued presence was considered detrimental to the perception of the observers as a neutral group.

Neyman continued work on mathematical statistics after the war, including on applications to astronomy, to meteorology, and to biostatistics. But his great achievement of the postwar years was his success in building the Berkeley program into the foremost mathematical statistics program in the world. Already in the spring of 1945, when the end of the war was in sight, he made plans for the first of what would become an influential series of quinquennial Berkeley Symposia in Mathematical Statistics and Probability, held in August 1945. From then and for the next decade or so he was tireless in inviting the best statisticians and probabilists in the world to Berkeley; some for visits, some to stay. He developed an energetic teaching program, pestered the university administration without cease for resources, and overcame all manner of obstacles, including an extremely divisive controversy between the university and its board of regents over a loyalty oath that had been imposed upon the faculty.

Neyman's great success in creating both a program and a school was due to two factors. The first was the force of his personality; the second was the character of his intellectual agenda. Neyman was polite and generous, but he was insistent and unyielding with respect to his view of what was best for his program. In 1954 Neyman finally succeeded in obtaining agreement to the formation of a separate Department of Statistics with himself as chairman. A contemporary memo by the assistant to the university president gives an apt summary: "Here, a willful, persistent and distinguished director has succeeded, step by step over a fifteen year period, against the original wish of his department chairman and dean, in converting a small 'laboratory' or institute into, in terms of numbers of students taught, an enormously expensive unit; and he then argues that the unit should be renamed a 'department' because no additional expense will be incurred" (Reid, p. 239).

Neyman's success went far beyond a single institution. His work of the 1930s on the mathematics of optimal statistical procedures proved ideal for the foundation of an extremely influential school of thought (now known as the Neyman-Pearson School, or even the Berkeley School). The theory attracted a phenomenal group of students in the postwar era, who in turn expanded on it to make it the dominant approach to academic statistics in much of the world for an academic generation. Several of his students remained at Berkeley, including Erich Lehmann, Lucien Le Cam, Joseph Hodges, and Elizabeth Scott. Scott, one of his earliest recruits as a student in 1938, was his constant companion over much of the last three decades of his life. Neyman's own work in his last decades focused primarily on applications of statistics, particularly in meteorology and medicine. In 1969 Neyman received the U.S. National Medal of Science. He actively taught and wrote up until his death in Berkeley, California.

• Neyman's personal papers are in the Bancroft Library at Berkeley. A portion of Neyman's doctoral dissertation was translated, with commentary by T. P. Speed and D. B. Rubin, in *Statistical Science* 5 (1990): 463–80. His most important papers are collected in *A Selection of Early Statistical Papers of J. Neyman* (1967) and *Joint Statistical Papers of J. Neyman and E. S. Pearson* (1966). The best treatment of his life and character is Constance Reid, *Neyman—from Life* (1982), based in large part on Neyman's own recollections in the last years of his life. Biographical articles include those by D. G. Kendall et al., in *Biographical Memoirs of Fellows of the Royal Society* 28 (1982): 378–412, which includes a complete bibliography; by E. L. Lehmann in National Academy of Sciences, *Biographical Memoirs* 63 (1994): 394–420; by E. L. Scott in *Encyclopedia of Statistical Sciences*, ed. S. Kotz and N. L. Johnson, vol. 6 (1985), pp. 215–23; and by L. Le Cam in *International Encyclopedia of the Social Sciences*, vol. 18 (1979), pp. 587–90.

STEPHEN M. STIGLER

NIBLACK, Albert Parker (25 July 1859–20 Aug. 1929), naval officer, was born in Vincennes, Indiana, the son of William Ellis Niblack, a member of Congress and an Indiana Supreme Court judge, and Eliza Ann Sherman. Appointed to the U.S. Naval Academy from Indiana in September 1876, Niblack graduated in June 1880 and, after the required two years of sea duty (served in the screw sloop *Lackawanna*), received his ensign's commission in June 1882.

After brief service in the screw gunboat *Yantic*, Niblack was detailed to the Smithsonian Institution in November 1882. Promoted to ensign, junior grade, in March 1883, he served with the U.S. Coast and Geodetic Survey (July 1884–Feb. 1888). During the summers of 1885, 1886, and 1887, he explored the Pacific Northwest, later publishing his findings in *The Coast Indians of Southern Alaska and Northern British Columbia* (1890). He also earned praise for his part in the rescue of the crew of the stranded American merchantman *Ocean King* in May 1887.

Following ordnance and torpedo instruction at the Washington Navy Yard (Feb.–July 1888), another stint at the Smithsonian, and a tour at sea in the cruiser *Chicago* (Mar. 1889–Apr. 1892), Niblack served in Washington in the Bureau of Navigation. Promoted to lieutenant, junior grade, in March 1893, he returned to survey work in the Coast Survey vessel *Patterson* (Mar.–Oct. 1893).

Niblack returned to the Bureau of Navigation in November 1893 and then served in the dispatch boat *Dolphin*. He joined the armored cruiser *New York* to serve as flag lieutenant for Rear Admiral Richard W. Meade, commander in chief, North Atlantic Station (Aug. 1894–May 1895). Washington duty again followed, in the office of the assistant secretary of the navy (June 1895–Aug. 1896).

Service as naval attaché in Rome, Berlin, and Vienna (Jan. 1897–May 1898) followed, and Niblack was promoted to lieutenant in November 1897. Returning to the United States, he was assigned to the gunboat *Topeka*, which operated on the blockade of Havana during the Spanish-American War. After a brief tour of duty in command of the torpedo boat *Winslow* (Aug.–Dec. 1898), he went to the gunboat *Concord* and served in that ship until May 1899, though he served for one month as acting navigator in the cruiser *Boston*, commanding that warship's landing force in support of the occupation of Ilo Ilo, Philippines. After service in the battleship *Oregon* (May 1899–Jan. 1900) and in the gunboat *Castine* (Jan.–Dec. 1900), he served in a succession of ships over the next several months—armored cruiser *Brooklyn*, battleship *Kentucky*, and storeships *Manila* and *Culgoa*—before he reported to the Bureau of Navigation in October 1901 as inspector of target practice. Despite changes Niblack instituted in the navy's system of gunnery training, however, the fleet's shooting failed to improve appreciably during his tour.

Promoted to lieutenant commander in July 1902, Niblack participated in the deliberations of the Olongapo Board (Nov. 1902–Jan. 1903) concerning potential naval station sites before he traveled to San Francisco, California, and thence to Honolulu, assuming command of the naval station at Pearl Harbor in August 1903. The following November Niblack wed Mary Augusta Harrington, daughter of California pioneer William Pierce Harrington; the couple had no children. Placed in charge of the establishment of lighthouses for the territory of Hawaii (Jan. 1904), he was given additional duties commanding the converted tug *Iroquois* in February and as inspector of customs at Midway and adjacent islands the following month. He returned to the cruiser *Chicago* in May 1906 as executive officer and subsequently served on the Navy Department Board considering Honolulu land boundaries (June–Oct. 1907). He received promotion to commander in July 1907.

Niblack commanded a succession of ships as officer in charge of ships on the Naval Academy Station—*Severn*, *Hartford*, *Olympia*, and *Chicago*—and later the gunboat *Tacoma* (June 1909–May 1910). He returned to naval attaché duty at Buenos Aires, Argentina; Rio de Janeiro, Brazil; and Santiago, Chile. Promoted to captain in May 1911, he served as naval attaché in Berlin, Germany, and The Hague, Netherlands, between December 1911 and July 1913. After brief tours of temporary duty in the Office of Naval Intelligence (ONI) and the Naval War College, he commanded the battleship *Michigan* (Dec. 1913–Nov. 1915), participating in the occupation of Veracruz, Mexico, in April 1914. After the *Michigan* ran aground, Niblack was "found guilty [Jan. 1915] of suffering a vessel of the Navy to be stranded," but the mishap does not appear to have adversely affected his attainment of flag rank.

After instruction at the Naval War College, Niblack sat on the General Board—the U.S. Navy's highest policy advisory body—from December 1916 to April 1917. Given command of Division One of the Atlantic Fleet in April 1917 as the navy mobilized for war, his broad pennant in the battleship *Alabama*, he received promotion to flag rank in August 1917. Soon thereafter Niblack broke his flag in the gunboat *Nashville* in November 1917 at Gibraltar as commander of Squadron Two, Patrol Force (later, Patrol Squadrons Based on Gibraltar). Ships under the admiral's direction not only escorted convoys, thus ensuring the safe passage of men and matériel on board transports and cargo vessels, but actively patrolled to seek and destroy the enemy submarines that menaced the Allies' main logistical lifeline through the Straits of Gibraltar. He remained in this important post, which Secretary of the Navy Josephus Daniels considered "the gateway through which passed one-fourth of all shipping of the Allies," for the remainder of hostilities. Daniels rewarded Niblack's "fine judgment and ability" with the Distinguished Service Medal and lauded Niblack and his force as a "tower of strength in that region."

After commanding U.S. naval forces in the eastern Mediterranean (Jan.–Mar. 1919), Niblack directed the ONI (May 1919–Aug. 1920) and served as naval attaché in London (Sept. 1920–Jan. 1921) before becoming commander of U.S. naval forces operating in European waters, with the rank of vice admiral, in January 1921. Completing his naval career as commandant of the Sixth Naval District (July 1922–July 1923), Niblack, who held decorations from not only his own government but several foreign powers, was transferred to the retired list on 25 July 1923.

Subsequently representing the United States in the International Hydrographic Bureau in Monaco in 1924, Niblack was elected its president in 1927. He died in Monte Carlo. Regarded by contemporaries as clever and witty, zealous and enthusiastic, Niblack, an able author, penned *The History and Aims of the Office of Naval Intelligence* (1920), *Why Wars Come* (1922), *Summary of Data on Coastal Signals, with Proposals for Their Unification* (1926), and numerous articles in the *U.S. Naval Institute Proceedings*, twice earning its prize essay award.

• A small collection of Albert Parker Niblack Papers (167 items) is in the Indiana Historical Society Library in Indianapolis. Letters concerning his service in Europe during World War I are in the William Sowden Sims Papers in the Library of Congress Manuscript Division. Biographical material is in the Ship Name and Sponsor File for the destroyer *Niblack* (DD-424), which was named in his honor in 1937, in the Ships' Histories Branch of the Naval Historical Center. His testimony in the post–World War I controversy over the navy's preparedness for the conflict is in U.S. Congress, *Hearings before the Subcommittee of the Committee on Naval Affairs, United States Senate*, vol. 1, pt. 2, 66th Cong., 2d sess., 1921. The *U.S. Naval Institute Proceedings* index lists twenty-three articles by Niblack published during the course of his career. An obituary is in the *New York Times*, 21 Aug. 1929.

ROBERT JAMES CRESSMAN

NIBLO, William (1789–21 Aug. 1878), restaurateur and theater manager, was born in Ireland. Nothing is known of his father or mother, and little is known of his childhood. Niblo came to the United States at a young age and apprenticed to the proprietor of a coffee house at Forty-three Pine Street in New York City. After rising to a position of responsibility, he married Martha King, the owner's daughter, and eventually acquired his father-in-law's business. Niblo's establishment, which he named the Bank Coffee House, became known for its culinary excellence and genial atmosphere, making it a popular meeting place for merchants.

In 1823, deciding that a restaurant and concert garden venture could prove profitable, the entrepreneur leased land at the corner of Broadway and Pine Street. Niblo developed the property, part of which had been the site of a circus, renovating the circus into an arena for light entertainments, which he named Sans Souci, and building a restaurant and public concert garden nearby. He built a new theater one year later and transformed the Sans Souci into a concert hall. The new facility, a large, three-story building with a smooth facade, sported expansive corridors that contained rich shrubbery, pleasant paths, and a ceiling lined with numerous rows of colored lights. He named the entire complex Niblo's Garden and Theatre, and in order to assure proper patronage he provided stage coach service from the distant Battery, where his audiences lived, to the uptown location of his establishment. Niblo's Garden, as it was identified by the public, instantly became the amusement facility for fashionable New Yorkers, and the Niblo name became synonymous with fine entertainment.

At first summer programs consisting of concerts, fireworks, and rope dancers made the place popular, but by 1838 Niblo's became associated with topnotch stage actors and plays. Along with introducing the Ravels, a famous acrobatic group, Niblo's Garden featured the elder Joseph Jefferson's variety troupe, the National Theatre Company with George Vandenhoff and George Hill, Charles Kean in *Hamlet* and *Macbeth*, Edwin Forrest in *Richelieu* and *Macbeth*, Charlotte Cushman as Meg Merrilies in *Guy Mannering*, and J. H. Hackett his New York City debut as Falstaff in *The Merry Wives of Windsor*. Other important performers who played at Niblo's included William Florence, Fornasari in *The Barber of Seville*, Anna Cora Mowatt, E. L. Davenport, Dion Boucicault, and Adelina Patti.

Over the years the theater owner employed various expert managers to run his enterprise, including John Sefton, Henry Palmer, and James J. Wallack, with Niblo functioning mainly as lessee. Although he apparently had little to do with the actual running of the theater, the association of the Niblo name with good taste and fine quality led people to attribute the venture's success to him.

During its existence Niblo's Garden underwent various transformations. In 1846, when the theater burned down, Niblo considered retirement but was persuaded to erect a new building. In 1849 the new Niblo's Garden opened and was thought to be superior to its predecessor. In 1851, when his wife died, the owner closed the theater's doors for a season. The next year, when the Metropolitan Hotel was built on the land adjacent to the auditorium, audiences entered Niblo's through the hotel lobby.

By 1861 Niblo had retired permanently, and William Wheatley, who would introduce the famous extravaganza leg-show the *Black Crook* (1866) on Niblo's stage, succeeded him. Over the years as his affluence increased, Niblo became self-schooled in art and literature; he also turned to collecting. Known as a charitable man, he gave freely to churches and art institutions, and he purchased the American history library of Francis Lister Hawks, following the latter's death, and donated the collection to the New-York Historical Society. As a member of the Calvary Protestant Episcopal Church, he was credited with building its chapel.

Niblo died in New York. For some years Niblo's Gardens continued to be an important theatrical forum. In 1872, after another fire destroyed the theater, it was rebuilt. But by this time the theatrical center of New York had moved further uptown, and Niblo's never regained its popularity or prominence. When it was demolished in 1895, New York lost its oldest playhouse.

During his lifetime Niblo provided entertainment for discriminating audiences and a respected forum for fine entertainers. With his good taste, business acumen, and individual vision, he created a venture that encouraged the enjoyment and development of theater and culture in nineteenth-century New York.

• There is no known collection of Niblo's papers, and little information is available on him. Two early twentieth-century works that touch on Niblo are T. A. Brown, *The History of the New York Stage*, vol. 1 (1903); and G. C. D. Odell, *Annals of the New York Stage*, vols. 3–7 (1928–1931). An obituary is in the *New York Times*, 22 Aug. 1878.

PAUL MROCZKA

NICE, Margaret Morse (6 Dec. 1883–26 June 1974), ornithologist, was born in Amherst, Massachusetts, the daughter of Anson Daniel Morse, a professor of history at Amherst College, and Margaret Duncan Ely. In her youth, she developed a strong love of nature. At Mount Holyoke College, from which she received an A.B. in 1906, she studied languages and the natural sciences. Attracted by the prospect of being able to study living animals, she enrolled in 1907 as a graduate student at Clark University, where she worked with the biologist Clifton F. Hodge and the distinguished developmental psychologist and university president G. Stanley Hall.

In 1909 Margaret Morse married a fellow graduate student, Leonard Blaine Nice. Before her marriage she had conducted research on the food of the bobwhite and had considered turning this work into a doctoral dissertation, but as she later recounted in her autobiography: "Instead of raising bobwhites, I was married; instead of working for a Ph.D., I kept house. Sometimes I rather regretted that I had not gone ahead and obtained this degree. . . . But no one had ever encouraged me to study for a doctor's degree; all the propaganda had been against it. My parents were more than happy to have me give up thoughts of a career and take up home-making" (p. 33). The first of the Nices' five daughters was born in 1910. Blaine Nice's career as an academic physiologist took the family to Boston in 1911 and then successively to Norman, Oklahoma, in 1913; Columbus, Ohio, in 1927; and Chicago, Illinois, in 1936. The roles of housewife and mother initially left Margaret Nice with little time for research, but she made the most of her circumstances. Based on observations of her first child, she published in 1915 a paper on early childhood vocabulary development. Eleven years later Clark University counted this publication as a master's thesis and awarded Nice an A.M. in psychology "as of 1915."

In 1919 Nice began studying the bird life of Oklahoma. Her early studies ranged from close examinations of the nesting behavior of birds to censuses of local bird populations. This work culminated in *The Birds of Oklahoma* (1924), a monograph she coauthored with her husband. It was in Ohio, however, that she conducted her most significant ornithological work. Exploiting the relatively new technique of placing distinctive bands on the legs of birds as a means of identifying individuals in the field, she in 1928 trapped and banded her first song sparrow (*Melospiza melodia*). The following year she conducted an intensive study of two song sparrow pairs. She subsequently expanded her efforts, making a census of all the song sparrows in a forty-acre flood plain near her Columbus home. By 1935 she had banded a total of 870 song sparrows. She recorded the behavior of individual birds throughout their lives, kept track of family lineages, located the territories that individual birds occupied from year to year, and studied the birds' mating, migration, and song production. Prominent among her concerns was the idea that males occupy and defend territories, an idea made current by the English ornithologist H. Eliot Howard in his *Territory in Bird Life* (1920). Nice's study of the song sparrow, focusing as it did on the detailed life histories of all the individuals in a local population, was virtually unprecedented.

As a regular participant at the meetings of ornithological societies in the United States and later in Europe, Nice made contact with the world's leading ornithologists and eventually took her place amongst them. In 1931 she met the young German ornithologist Ernst Mayr, who was working at the American Museum of Natural History in New York. Mayr put her in touch with Erwin Stresemann, the editor of the prestigious German *Journal für Ornithologie*, in which Nice's first extended account of her song sparrow work was published in 1933–1934. She further described her research in later articles and in two important monographs published as "Studies in the Life History of the Song Sparrow" in the *Transactions of the Linnaean Society of New York* in 1937 and 1943.

Nice's scientific contacts, her own work as a field ornithologist, and her facility with modern languages enabled her to gain a broad view of contemporary advances in ornithology. In 1934 she began reviewing current ornithological literature on bird behavior, ecology, and life histories for the journal *Bird-Banding*. From then until 1942, when ill health caused her to cut back her efforts, she wrote hundreds of abstracts on the latest work in the field. Nice, as much as anyone, signaled to American ornithologists the importance of the work of the young Austrian naturalist Konrad Lorenz. She in turn had an influence on Lorenz's thinking, at least indirectly, by putting Lorenz in contact with the American zoologist Wallace Craig, whose ideas profoundly affected Lorenz's understanding of instinct. Concluding that the work of Lorenz and his Dutch colleague, Nikolaas Tinbergen, provided the most promising foundation for studying wild birds under natural or seminatural conditions, Nice spent a month in 1938 in Lorenz's home in Austria learning how to raise altricial birds. The second volume of her song sparrow study, focusing on behavioral questions, reflects her commitment to the views of the European ethologists.

Nice's most important contributions to ornithology were primarily in matters of scientific practice rather than in matters of theory. She is noteworthy for the remarkable life-history studies she conducted and also for the major role she played in the network of communication among twentieth-century ornithologists interested in field studies and behavior. In 1938–1939 she became the first woman president of a major American ornithological society, the Wilson Ornithological Club. She was also during the course of her career a forceful spokesperson for conservation. She died in Chicago at the age of ninety, a woman who throughout her life had sought "to open the eyes of the unseeing to the beauty and wonder of the earth and its wild life" (Nice [1979], p. 264).

• The bulk of Nice's papers are at the Cornell University Library. Additional items relating to her editorial work for *Bird-Banding* and the *Wilson Bulletin* are held by the Wilson Ornithological Society. Among Nice's publications, in addition to those cited above, are "The Theory of Territorialism and Its Development," in *Fifty Years Progress of American Ornithology (1883–1933)*, ed. American Ornithologists' Union (1933), pp. 89–100; and "Development of Behavior in Precocial Birds," *Transactions of the Linnaean Society of New York* 8 (1962): 1–211. See also her popular book, *The Watcher at the Nest* (1939). The most important source of biographical information is Nice's own autobiography, *Research Is a Passion with Me* (1979), which includes a selected bibliography of her scientific writings. See also Milton B. Trautman, "In Memoriam: Margaret Morse Nice," *Auk* 94 (1977): 430–41. Nice's career is discussed in Marianne Gosztonyi Ainley, "Field Work and Family: North American Women Ornithologists, 1900–1950," in *Uneasy Careers and Intimate Lives*, ed. Pnina G. Abir-Am and Dorinda Outram (1987), pp. 60–76; and Gregg Mitman and Richard W. Burkhardt, Jr., "Struggling for Identity: The Study of Animal Behavior in America, 1930–1945," in *The Expansion of American Biology*, ed. Keith Benson et al. (1991), pp. 164–94. Nice's contribution to American ornithology is discussed in Ernst Mayr, "Epilogue: Materials for a History of American Ornithology," in Erwin Stresemann, *Ornithology from Aristotle to the Present* (1975), pp. 365–96.

RICHARD W. BURKHARDT, JR.

NICHOLAS, Albert (27 May 1900–3 Sept. 1973), jazz clarinetist and saxophonist also known as "Nick," was born in New Orleans, Louisiana. Although his parents' names and occupations are unknown, it is known that he was the nephew of the New Orleans clarinetist and trumpeter Wooden Joe Nicholas, from whom he received his first training on the clarinet in 1910. At age thirteen he started studying with the famed soloist and teacher Lorenzo Tio, Jr., whose other clarinet students included Johnny Dodds, Jimmie Noone, Albert Burbank, Omer Simeon, and Barney Bigard. By age fifteen Nicholas was playing with cornetists Manuel

Perez, King Oliver, and Buddy Petit as well as working with Oak Gaspard's Maple Leaf Orchestra. In November 1916 he enlisted in the navy, and while based in Cuba and Gibraltar aboard the convoy ship USS *Olympia*, he played clarinet in the ship's otherwise all-white band.

Shortly after his discharge in December 1919, Nicholas resumed his professional career in New Orleans by joining first Petit and then Gaspard's orchestra. By September 1921 he was playing at the Cadillac Club with Arnold De Pass's band, which at that time included the young Panamanian pianist Luis Russell. The following spring he worked with Perez's quartet at the Oasis and later that year began a lengthy engagement at Tom Anderson's cabaret leading a six-piece band comprising, among others, Russell, saxophonist Barney Bigard, and drummer Paul Barbarin. In May 1924 Nicholas turned the group over to Russell so that he could take Buster Bailey's place in King Oliver's Creole Jazz Band for a week at Chicago's Grand Theatre and on a six-week tour of one-night stands in Pennsylvania, Illinois, and Indiana. He was back in New Orleans by the summer and resumed leadership of his band until December 1924, after which he returned to Chicago to play in Oliver's newly formed Dixie Syncopators at the Plantation Cafe. After appearing on several exceptional recordings with Oliver and fellow New Orleanian Richard M. Jones, Nicholas left the Syncopators in August 1926 for a prestigious job at the Plaza Hotel in Shanghai, China, with drummer Jack Carter, whose band also included pianist Teddy Weatherford and the trumpeter and singer Valaida Snow.

Nicholas left Carter in October 1927 and with banjoist Frank Ethridge traveled widely throughout Asia with stops at Hong Kong, Manila, Singapore (where they played at the famed Raffles Hotel), Sumatra, Java, and India. In December they moved on to Egypt, where they were asked to add their talents to the local dance bands at Cairo's Fantasio and Alexandria's plush Casino San Stefano. After a brief stopover in Paris, where he reunited with his old friend Sidney Bechet, Nicholas returned home in October 1928. A short time later he joined Russell's new band in New York City at Club Harlem, followed by back-to-back bookings at the Savoy Ballroom, the Roseland, the Saratoga Club, and Connie's Inn. During 1929 and 1930 he and other Russell bandsmen used their layoff time to work and record with Jelly Roll Morton, an experience Nicholas repeated in 1939 and 1940. After his departure from the Russell band in December 1933 he played at the Savoy with Chick Webb's band, the Cotton Club in Philadelphia with Sam Wooding, and on radio in New York with a novelty group called the Blue Chips. In December 1934 he joined guitarist Bernard Addison's jazz group at Adrian's Tap Room, a midtown Manhattan club run by famed jazzman Adrian Rollini, and stayed on when bassist John Kirby assumed leadership of the band for the duration of the job.

In the spring of 1937 Nicholas rejoined the Russell band, now serving as background to star trumpeter and singer Louis Armstrong, but because of minimal opportunities for creative expression he left Armstrong after two years to join drummer Zutty Singleton's trio, with pianist Clyde Hart, at Nick's Tavern in Greenwich Village. They opened in December 1939, and from February to May 1940 they alternated sets with Bechet's quintet. Nicholas remained at this venue until June, when the trio, now with pianist Eddie Heywood and then Don Frye, moved into the neighboring Village Vanguard. Nicholas's career took a downward curve shortly after the termination of the Vanguard job in October 1940. He worked in white trumpeter Bobby Burnet's all-black sextet at Café Society between February and March 1941, occasionally substituted for Bailey in John Kirby's popular sextet, and continued participating in the Sunday jam sessions at Jimmy Ryan's on Fifty-second Street, but by the summer of 1941 he felt compelled to find regular employment outside of music.

Nicholas first took a job as a subway guard on New York's Eighth Avenue line, and then for the duration of the war worked for the government in Washington, D.C. In late 1945, however, pianist Art Hodes hired him for the group he was bringing into New York's Stuyvesant Casino, Nicholas's first steady job as a musician in five years. He started recording again as a featured soloist with Bechet, Baby Dodds, Mutt Carey, and Wild Bill Davison, as well as with his own quartet in June 1947, the first time he led a recording session in over two decades as an artist. He also appeared with Bunk Johnson in concert around this time, worked with Kid Ory in Los Angeles in February 1946, led his own group at Jimmy Ryan's the following September, and from January through August 1947 was heard regularly on the historic "This Is Jazz" radio series. He left the show after a dispute with producer and host Rudi Blesh.

In 1948 Nicholas played at the Barrel in St. Louis in a trio with pianist Ralph Sutton and drummer Art Trappier; between 1949 and 1953 he led his own groups in and around Los Angeles and San Francisco, recorded with Bob Scobey's Frisco Band (in 1950), and appeared at several prestigious jazz concerts. Around June 1953 he worked with cornetist Rex Stewart's band at Boston's Savoy Café and also recorded with that group. Acting on Bechet's suggestion, he moved to Paris in October 1953, and with the exception of a few American sojourns between 1959 and 1970, he remained in Europe until his death in Basel, Switzerland. During his 1959 visit he recorded with Minneapolis cornetist Doc Evans and Art Hodes's Chicago-based All-Star Stompers. Now at the peak of his musical powers, Nicholas's concert appearances and recording activities skyrocketed as never before, and he was the object of adulation all over the continent, second only to his lifetime friend Bechet. He spent the last twenty years of his life delighting in his hard-won fame.

As did most clarinetists of his generation, Nicholas started out playing the older Albert-system clarinet, but while in Egypt he purchased a Boehm-system instrument to facilitate his mastery of the difficult classical parts he sometimes had to play. Indeed, all of his best records, beginning with the 1929 sessions with Russell and Morton, were performed on this technically improved model. Nicholas's warm and woody tone, a characteristic shared by other Tio students, is linked directly to the delicacy and grace of the French approach to classical clarinet playing, a heritage indigenous to the New Orleans–born Creoles. But there was more to Nicholas than his tone. He was also a highly imaginative and thrilling improviser, a masterful technician, and an ensemble player of the greatest sensitivity. He could handle his instrument with flawless control even at the fastest tempos, yet he was also capable of playing slow blues with passion and conviction. There is no question that as a consummate jazz clarinetist his seat on the pantheon of the giants is rightfully deserved.

• It is unfortunate that Nicholas, a reflective and voluble speaker, never took the time to write his autobiography, but his oral reminiscences, as documented on a British album, *Albert Nicholas Quartet, Double-Up DUO 114*, recorded in the spring of 1973, reveal him to be a man of considerable wit and vitality and the possessor of an excellent memory. His career ran parallel with the development of jazz in the United States and saw this music's dissemination to the far reaches of the globe. Brief references to Nicholas are in Samuel Charters and Leonard Kunstadt, *Jazz: A History of the New York Scene* (1962), and Arnold Shaw, *52nd St.: The Street of Jazz* (1971), but these citations are invariably in reference to the bandleaders with whom he was most closely associated. They offer little that cannot also be found in the standard discographies: Laurie Wright, *King Oliver* (1987), Brian Rust, *Jazz Records, 1897–1942* (1982), and Walter Bruyninckx, *Traditional Jazz Discography, 1897–1988* (6 vols., 1985–1989) and *Swing Discography, 1920–1988* (12 vols., 1985–1989). Al Rose and Edmond Souchon, *New Orleans Jazz: A Family Album* (1978), is helpful in detailing the facts of Nicholas's early activities, but the best overall guide, however succinct, is John Chilton, *Who's Who of Jazz* (1985), which also offers entries on other artists and further supportive information. See also Ian Carr et al., *Jazz: The Essential Companion* (1987), and Richard Cook and Brian Morton, *The Penguin Guide to Jazz on CD, LP, and Cassette* (1992). A particularly rewarding interview is in *Storyville* 57 (Feb.–Mar. 1975): 86–96.

JACK SOHMER

NICHOLAS, George (c. 1754–25 July 1799), lawyer, was born in Williamsburg, Virginia, the son of Robert Carter Nicholas, a planter and treasurer of the colony of Virginia, and Anne Cary. He devoted his life to the perpetuation of a social and political order dominated by gentlemen such as himself. A descendant of the Carters, one of the wealthiest and most influential families in colonial Virginia, he grew up expecting to command the attention of his peers and the deference of everyone else. His education, which prepared him for a life as the independent master of his household and his county, climaxed with the study of law at the College of William and Mary. The first thing most people noticed about him, even as a young man, was his large, bald head and his great bulk. James Madison (1751–1836) reportedly laughed till he cried when someone described Nicholas as "a plum pudding with legs to it." But within the pudding was a formidable and ambitious intellect that worked to maintain the power of traditional leaders in a period of immense social upheaval.

With the outbreak of the American Revolution, Nicholas enlisted in the patriot cause, determined to protect the independence of his state from the alleged efforts of the British government to reduce its gentlemen to little more than slaves. In 1777 he attained the rank of lieutenant colonel, an honor that recognized his social status rather than military skill. Indeed, Nicholas seems to have spent little time in the service. He spent 1778 in Baltimore, where he courted and married Mary Smith. The couple had thirteen children. Sometime in the early 1780s Nicholas moved his growing family to Charlottesville, Virginia, where the practice of law seemed especially promising.

Nicholas began his career in public service with his 1781 election to the Virginia House of Delegates from Hanover County. In 1783, and again from 1786 to 1788, he represented Albemarle County in the Virginia House. During those years Nicholas became friends with James Madison and acquired a reputation as a man of sharp intelligence and well-honed political skills. He put those assets to good use in 1788 when he ably advocated the ratification of the federal Constitution in the Virginia convention.

At about the same time, Nicholas became interested in relocating to Kentucky. The financial and political prospects in Virginia's western county were too much for ambitious young men to resist. Shortly after the 1788 convention, Nicholas and his household migrated across the Appalachians. He had a brick house built in Lexington, but his true home was a large plantation about five miles from Danville, where he tried to reestablish the world of the landed gentry he had left behind. Nicholas profited from the enormous number of legal squabbles created by the chaotic nature of landholdings in Kentucky. He also speculated in land and invested in a cotton factory and an iron furnace, both of which failed. Still, the foundation of his reputation was his legal achievements, which led to his appointment as the first chair of law at Transylvania University in Lexington some time in the 1790s.

Given his talents and experience, it is hardly surprising that Nicholas became a leading political figure. He particularly dominated the 1792 Kentucky constitutional convention. Among other things, he staunchly supported a legal guarantee of slavery, arguing that the institution would attract immigrants while abolition would degrade whites through cultural and sexual miscegenation. He was also responsible for provisions that centralized political authority. Increasingly distrustful of popular government in a revolutionary society in which ordinary men claimed the right to act like gentlemen, Nicholas came to believe that public service led the better sort of men "to spend your time and money to no purpose, in serving people who think they confer a favor on you by permitting you to do so." His acerbic style made him a controversial figure, as a brief stint as Kentucky's first attorney general demonstrated. Unable to accommodate himself fully to democratic government, he moved away from seeking public office, remarking that he "never intend[ed] to have any hand in the game of government but wish[ed] to know how the *hands* are managed."

For a few years after his arrival in Kentucky, Nicholas wrote astute letters to Madison and Thomas Jefferson, which were read by them and by George Washington as barometers of western public opinion. Like that of other prominent Kentuckians, Nicholas's loyalty to particular governments appears fickle in retrospect. A strong Federalist in 1788, Nicholas supported Kentucky statehood in 1792, flirted with the Spanish in the mid-1790s, and by the end of the decade was a critic of the Adams administration. The consistent theme after his arrival in Kentucky was his search for a government powerful enough to defeat the American Indians who threatened the state from the north and the south, open the Mississippi River to trade by Americans, and generally do those things necessary to preserve the hegemony of planters and lawyers like himself. In the end, his loyalty was not simply to his own interests, but to the hierarchical social order to which he was committed by both education and temperament. Nicholas died suddenly in Lexington.

• There are small collections of Nicholas papers in the University of Virginia library, the Kentucky Historical Society, the Library of Congress, the University of Kentucky library, the Filson Club in Louisville, and the University of Chicago. Significant correspondence can also be found in William T. Hutchinson et al., eds., *The Papers of James Madison* (17 vols., 1962–), and Julian P. Boyd et al., eds., *The Papers of Thomas Jefferson* (23 vols., 1950–). Biographical sketches include Hugh Blair Grigsby, *The History of the Virginia Federal Convention of 1788* (2 vols., 1890), pp. 281–98; an untitled manuscript by Wilson Cary Nicholas, Thomas Jefferson Papers, Massachusetts Historical Society; Matilda Nicholas Barrett, "George Nicholas, a Biographical Sketch" (1887), Bennett Young Collection, Filson Club; Huntley Dupre, "The Political Ideas of George Nicholas," *Register of the Kentucky Historical Society* 39 (1941): 201–23; and Richard H. Caldemeyer, "The Career of George Nicholas" (Ph.D. diss., Indiana Univ., 1951). See also Joan Wells Coward, *Kentucky in the New Republic: The Process of Constitution Making* (1979); Mary K. Bonsteel Tachau, *Federal Courts in the Early Republic: Kentucky, 1789–1816* (1978); and Patricia Watlington, *The Partisan Spirit: Kentucky Politics, 1779–1792* (1972).

ANDREW CAYTON

NICHOLAS, John Spangler (10 Mar. 1895–11 Sept. 1963), embryologist, was born in Allegheny, Pennsylvania, the son of Samuel Trauger Nicholas, a Lutheran minister, and Elizabeth Ellen Spangler. Because his father changed parishes every few years, he grew up in a number of small Pennsylvania communities, graduating from the public high school in Middle-

town. In 1912 he matriculated at Pennsylvania (now Gettysburg) College with the intention of becoming a physician, but he soon developed an interest in biology. He spent the summer of 1915 studying botany and bacteriology and taught these subjects as an assistant during his senior year. He received his B.S. degree in 1916 and remained at the college as an assistant and graduate student while also teaching Latin, Greek, and English at Gettysburg Academy. After receiving his M.S. degree in 1917, he enrolled in the graduate zoology program at Yale University but left a year later to enlist in the U.S. Army Medical Corps as a private. He spent World War I at the Army Medical School in Washington, D.C., testing and preparing typhoid vaccines.

Nicholas returned to Yale after being discharged in 1919. He became interested in embryology and determined that the development of a salamander's forelimb bud into either a right or left limb is controlled in large part by the narrow ring of tissue surrounding the bud and not by the development of the salamander as a whole; in 1924 he showed that the development of forelimb buds is also dependent to a certain degree on the development of the skeletal limb girdle. He received his Ph.D. degree in zoology in 1921, the same year he married Helen Benton Brown, with whom he had no children.

After graduation, Nicholas accepted a position as instructor of anatomy at the University of Pittsburgh School of Medicine; he was promoted to assistant professor in 1922. He participated in a wide range of zoological experiments that were probably intended to investigate the German zoologist Hans Spemann's theory of embryonic induction, which postulated that in each developmental sequence the tissue induced by the previous sequence somehow induced the further development of tissue in the following sequence. In 1923 Nicholas and W. W. Swingle showed that the removal of a cat's parathyroid gland always results in the animal's death; in 1925 he demonstrated that rat fetuses in the late stages of development lack the ability to regenerate extirpated limbs. In 1927, the year after he returned to Yale as an assistant professor of zoology, he demonstrated that rat embryos cannot regenerate sections of the spinal cord. These experiments were followed by ones in which he transplanted rat fetal tissue to locations outside the mother's uterus; in 1931 he demonstrated that such tissue continued to differentiate into specialized cells, albeit at an altered rate. Although these results helped settle several minor controversies, they neither proved nor disproved the validity of Spemann's theory.

In 1927 Nicholas became a member of the Scientific Advisory Committee at Cold Spring Harbor Laboratory on Long Island, where he studied the embryological development of the common minnow. Very little was known about the embryology of this or any other teleost (bony) fish because no method had been devised to remove the chorion, the teleost egg's hard shell, without breaking the egg. Nicholas solved this problem in 1927 by modifying scissors used by eye surgeons. This technique permitted the study of most fish embryos; however, because Nicholas did not fully publish the facts surrounding his modification of iridectomy scissors until 1942, he never received sufficient credit.

In 1932 Nicholas was promoted to associate professor of comparative anatomy. In 1935 he became Bronson Professor of Comparative Anatomy, a chair he relinquished in 1939 to become Sterling Professor of Biology. In a series of experiments conducted during the 1940s, he made an important contribution to the understanding of cellular movement during embryonic development. It was known that the blastula, a hollow ball of cells that forms from the fertilized egg, realigns itself drastically during gastrulation into three germinal layers, which in turn develop into the various organ systems. By experimenting with salamander eggs, Nicholas showed that significant cell realignment also takes place in the endoderm, the innermost germinal layer, during pregastrulation. This finding prompted other researchers to study cellular movement during the blastular stage. Meanwhile, his work with rat embryos continued, stimulated by his invention in 1937 of a special glass "uterus" that permitted the close observation of fetal development. In 1942 he demonstrated for the first time that cells isolated from a mammalian embryo as early as the two-cell stage and transplanted into a uterus continue the process of embryonic development, a result in keeping with similar results conducted on the embryos of nonmammals.

In 1946 Nicholas became chairman of the Department of Zoology and the next year director of the Osborn Zoological Laboratory, positions he held until 1956. He retired in 1963 and died in New Haven, Connecticut.

Nicholas was a gifted tinkerer: he turned a foot pedal from a sewing machine into a focusing device for a microscope, and he invented the Nicholas illuminator, a microscope lamp that focuses cool bright light within a restricted field. He loved to work in the laboratory so much that he often put off writing up the results of his research for years, which occasionally resulted in someone else receiving credit for his discoveries. He served as president of the American Biology Society in 1945 and of the U.S. Scientific Manpower Commission from 1956 to 1958; he was managing editor of the *Journal of Experimental Zoology* from 1947 to 1963. In 1948 he helped found the American Institute of Biological Sciences, remaining active in its affairs until his death. He chaired the National Research Council's Division of Biology and Agriculture in 1948 and the National Academy of Sciences' Anatomy and Zoology Section from 1955 to 1958. He was elected to the National Academy of Sciences in 1949.

Nicholas's work with amphibian, fish, and mammalian embryos contributed significantly to the development of experimental embryology in the United States. His most important experiments demonstrated that mammalian embryonic development is almost as flexible as that of the lower vertebrates.

• Nicholas's papers are located in the Archives Collection of the Sterling Library, Yale University. He contributed chapters to Arthur K. Parpart, ed., *The Chemistry and Physiology of Growth* (1949); Edmond J. Farris and John Q. Griffith, eds., *The Rat in Laboratory Investigation* (1942; 1949); and Benjamin H. Willier et al., eds., *Analysis of Development* (1955). A biography, including a bibliography, is Jane M. Oppenheimer, "John Spangler Nicholas," National Academy of Sciences, *Biographical Memoirs* 40 (1969): 239–89. Obituaries are in the *New York Times*, 12 Sept. 1963, and *Journal of Experimental Zoology*, Oct. 1963.

CHARLES W. CAREY, JR.

NICHOLAS, Robert Carter (28 Jan. 1729–8 Sept. 1780), treasurer of Virginia and revolutionary leader, was born probably in Williamsburg, Virginia, the son of George Nicholas, an immigrant physician who was ambitious to establish his place in the Virginia elite, and Elizabeth Carter Burwell, the widowed daughter of Robert "King" Carter, one of the wealthiest and most powerful members of the Virginia gentry at the end of the seventeenth century and in the first decades of the eighteenth. Carter at first disapproved of the marriage, but in time he provided generously from his estate for his young grandson Robert Carter Nicholas. In 1751 Nicholas married Anne Cary, forming a link with another prominent Virginia family. They would have five sons and two daughters. By then he had already been chosen, at the age of twenty-one, as a member of the Common Council of Williamsburg. He became a vestryman of Bruton Parish Church in 1754.

Two years later Nicholas won a seat in the Virginia House of Burgesses as a representative of York County. He served through 1761, when he failed to return. In that relatively brief period he emerged as an influential member of the house, serving on important committees, including the Committee of Correspondence with the colony's agent in England, and taking an active role in the financial affairs of the colony during the French and Indian War.

During his absence from the legislature for some five years, Nicholas was absorbed in a busy legal practice. He was one of the most successful of the small group of attorneys admitted to practice before the General Court, the highest court of the colony. From 1758 to 1772 he served, too, as a member of the examining committee for admission of new attorneys to the Virginia bar, approving the applications, among others, of Thomas Jefferson and Patrick Henry.

In 1766 Nicholas actively reentered provincial politics with his election to the House of Burgesses from James City County. In the same year he also became treasurer of Virginia upon the death of John Robinson, who had for many years jointly held the two most prestigious offices in the gift of the lower house of the legislature, its Speakership and the office of treasurer. Upon his death, irregularities, which some had long suspected, were found in his treasury accounts as a consequence of illegal loans to many important Virginians. Nicholas sought and received from the governor an interim appointment as treasurer until the legislature could fill both positions permanently. The debate over the disposition of the two offices provoked an unusually bitter struggle within the small elite who dominated provincial politics. Nicholas, a man esteemed by many for his piety, conservative temperament, and sense of probity, wished to retain the post of treasurer, while his strongest opponent, Attorney General Peyton Randolph, a longtime ally of Robinson, sought election to both offices. In the end Nicholas was elected treasurer, continuing in the office until 1776, and Randolph became the new Speaker.

In succeeding years Nicholas gave almost his full attention to the duties of the treasurer and the politics of the developing imperial crisis, at first restricting his law practice and then discontinuing it altogether. Although decidedly among the more conservative of the Virginia patriots, he played a central role in the revolutionary movement. He helped frame a series of addresses adopted by the 1768 session of the Burgesses that protested British policies and supported more pointed resolutions adopted the following year that led to the dissolution of the assembly by the governor. Nicholas also signed both the nonimportation agreement of May 1769 and the revised agreement of June 1770 and served as a member of the provincial Committee of Correspondence created in 1773.

When the leaders of the revolutionary movement in Virginia turned in mid-1774 to a series of extralegal conventions to advance their cause and challenge royal authority, Nicholas played a prominent role in all of the sessions. At the suggestion of Jefferson, who thought Nicholas's widely recognized piety made him the best choice, he successfully introduced in the House of Burgesses a resolution for a day of fasting and prayer on 1 June 1774, the date on which the British ordered the port of Boston closed as a consequence of that city's famous Tea Party. When John Randolph, the attorney general of the colony and a staunch defender of imperial policy, published a pamphlet attacking the Virginia action and ridiculing the fast day, Nicholas answered in an anonymously published pamphlet, *Considerations on the Present State of Virginia Examined* (1774), the lengthiest statement of the moderate but ultimately uncompromising position he took throughout the conflict.

From 1773 to 1775 Nicholas became deeply involved in a local religious dispute that pitted him once more against Peyton Randolph. On this occasion the focus of the controversy between the two prominent vestrymen of Bruton Parish Church was an effort by Randolph and his supporters to choose Samuel Henley, professor of moral philosophy at the College of William and Mary, as the new rector and then lecturer of the parish. Henley was an ordained Anglican minister but an outspoken critic of the religious establishment in the colony and an exponent of theological views that to Nicholas seemed distinctly heterodox. Nicholas won the battle within the vestry, but the lengthy and open dispute, fought in the newspaper as much as in the church, contrasted the treasurer's traditional beliefs with the more tolerant and Enlightenment-tinged positions of Randolph and Henley and revealed the religious tensions in Virginia, much as the earlier contest over the treasurership had opened up political fissures.

As the revolutionary crisis moved toward independence, Nicholas continued as an active member of the Virginia conventions, undertaking in his capacity as treasurer to purchase and import military supplies for the colony. The climactic convention of May 1776, which adopted a resolution for independence and drafted a new state constitution and a Declaration of Rights, momentarily seemed to isolate the cautious Nicholas. He was the last delegate to stand against separation from Britain, and the opening article in the Declaration of Rights, declaring all men to be free and equal, aroused his concern lest it bring about the emancipation of slaves or civil unrest. The convention adopted qualifying language to answer his fears. He was likewise among those who fought to protect the Anglican church against the rising demand for its disestablishment. Ultimately he acceded to the new order and continued to sit for James City County in the new state legislature, although he failed in an effort to win election as Speaker of the House of Delegates. In 1779 he received an appointment as a judge of the new High Court of Chancery of Virginia, but he did not live long enough to exert a strong influence on its development. He died at "The Retreat," his estate in Hanover County, Virginia.

Nicholas was the founder of a political dynasty. Four of his sons carved out political or judicial careers at the state or national levels the most illustrious of them being Wilson Cary Nicholas, a key supporter and ally of Jefferson. A daughter, Elizabeth, married Edmund Randolph, attorney general in the presidency of George Washington. Nicholas in many respects typified a large group of leaders of conservative temperament at the state level who might have been expected to have hesitated at so unsettling and drastic a change as the Revolution but who nonetheless cast their lot with the American cause.

• Some Robert Carter Nicholas Papers are in the Alderman Library, University of Virginia, but for the most part information on Nicholas's career must be extracted from a variety of Virginia records of the revolutionary era. Victor Dennis Golladay, "The Nicholas Family of Virginia, 1722–1820" (Ph.D. diss., Univ. of Virginia, 1973), provides a good account of Nicholas. See also William J. Lescure, "The Early Political Career of Robert Carter Nicholas, 1728–1769" (M.A. thesis, College of William and Mary, 1961). Scattered but frequent references to Nicholas are in David J. Mays, *Edmund Pendleton, 1721–1803: A Biography* (2 vols., 1952), effectively describe his political and judicial career, while Rhys Isaac, *The Transformation of Virginia, 1740–1790*, chap. 10 (1982), contains a perceptive discussion of Nicholas's role in the fight over the rectorship of Bruton Parish.

THAD W. TATE

NICHOLAS, Wilson Cary (31 Jan. 1761–10 Oct. 1820), Jeffersonian political lieutenant and governor of Virginia, was born in Williamsburg, Virginia, the son of Robert Carter Nicholas, the last treasurer of the Colony of Virginia, and Anne Cary, the daughter of a wealthy Tidewater planter. A resident of Williamsburg for most of his youth, Nicholas briefly attended the College of William and Mary in 1779 but earned no degree. Too young to become involved in the early stages of the American Revolution, he commanded Virginia volunteer units from the fall of 1780 until the following fall, but there is no evidence that he was actually involved in battlefield action.

Following the death of Nicholas's father in September 1780 and Cornwallis's devastation of the family's Hanover County plantation in the spring of 1781, the Nicholases moved to Albemarle County, where the family owned extensive property. There Nicholas took up the life of a planter and built a home that he named "Mt. Warren." In 1785 he married Margaret Smith, the daughter of a prominent Baltimore merchant and sister of Mary Smith, who had married Nicholas's elder brother George in 1778. The couple had twelve children, nine surviving childhood.

As befit his family's status, Nicholas quickly assumed positions in local and state leadership. He served as a justice of the peace on the Albemarle County Court from 1786 to 1800 and after 1789 as county lieutenant of the local militia unit, with the rank of colonel. From 1784 to 1786 he succeeded his brother George as a member of the Virginia House of Delegates for Albemarle County. During his years in the Virginia House, Nicholas allied with James Madison on almost all issues, including Madison's successful 1785–1786 battle for legislative approval of Thomas Jefferson's reintroduced 1778 bill for religious liberty. Nicholas and his brother George were elected as Albemarle's representatives to the Virginia ratification convention of the proposed federal Constitution in 1788; Wilson Nicholas was described by his brother-in-law Edmund Randolph as a "warm friend of the Constitution without the alteration of a letter."

Following another term in the Virginia House in 1788–1789, Nicholas temporarily retired from politics to his Mt. Warren farm. Unfortunately, he also began his disastrous forays into land speculation in southwestern Virginia. Although claims to more than one million acres passed through his hands and those of his various partners, he realized only losses, which along with other debts—some inherited and some from his efforts to assist equally debt-ridden family members—eventually drove him to financial ruin.

From 1794 to 1799 Nicholas once again sat for Albemarle in the Virginia House of Delegates. Voting consistently with the emerging Republican party, he became a trusted Jeffersonian lieutenant and played a key role in the strategies that led to the adoption of the Virginia and Kentucky Resolutions of 1798. His reward was election to the U.S. Senate in 1799. More a moderate Republican than an ardent ideologue, Nicholas continued his loyal support of Jefferson as a behind-the-scenes leader rather than a vocal spokesman on the floor. His "silent influence in Legislative bodies" and his generally moderate views proved very effective in rounding up the votes for measures such as the repeal of the Judiciary Act of 1801 and the Louisiana Purchase in 1803.

Believing a salaried office might be a partial solution to his mounting debts, Nicholas resigned his Senate seat at the conclusion of the 1803–1804 session and accepted a post as collector of U.S. customs for the port of Norfolk, Virginia. The appointment brought Nicholas little financial relief and led to public criticism that he had accepted a "pecuniary office." In April 1805, after less than a year in office, he quit the post and returned to Mt. Warren.

Nicholas's second retirement from political office proved to be even shorter than his first. Jefferson, besieged both by Federalists and "schismatics" in his own party, pressed Nicholas to return to Congress. Eventually heeding the entreaties of his neighbor from "Monticello," Nicholas successfully stood for election to the federal House of Representatives during the winter of 1807–1808, in time to assist in the passage of the Embargo Act and to help orchestrate the presidential nomination of James Madison. His style of leadership led his political enemies to view him as "the arch-magician who pulls the strings and makes the political puppets dance."

Concluding that the embargo was causing more harm than good and fearful that erosion of support could lead to the breakup of the Republican party, Nicholas introduced a bill for repeal that included a provision for letters of marque and reprisal against the vessels of England and France unless those nations ceased their violations of American maritime rights. Following the defeat of his bill, Nicholas accepted the Non-Intercourse Act of 1809 as the best that could be gained at the moment, but he clearly viewed it as no real solution in the face of continued British depredations against American commerce and honor. Increasingly frustrated with what he saw as Madison's irresolution, and suffering from bouts of rheumatism, he resigned his House seat in November 1809.

Ever the man behind the scenes, Nicholas had been careful not to make his disenchantment with Madison public. Due to the efforts of Jefferson, Madison and Nicholas reconciled, and when Nicholas succeeded James Barbour as governor of Virginia late in 1814, he saw it as his duty to help the president bring the War of 1812 to a proper conclusion. After the war ended Nicholas sounded a nationalist note in his call for a strong navy and federal encouragement of manufacturing. On the state level he advocated a bold program of statewide public education, based largely on Jefferson's suggestions, and a comprehensive state network of canals and turnpikes. The legislature authorized the creation of a permanent reserve for the funding of transportation improvements, and it also assigned a portion of the debt owed to the state by the federal government for expenditures during the War of 1812 to the Literary Fund to finance the education of the children of the poor. Little else of the grand plans survived, except legislative permission allowing the nascent Albemarle Academy to change its name to Central College; it later became the University of Virginia.

At the conclusion of his two terms as governor in 1816, Nicholas spoke wistfully of returning to Mt. Warren, but the pressure of his ever-present debts again led him to seek an appointment with a salary, this time as the president of the Richmond branch of the Second Bank of the United States. As ill suited for banking as he was skillful in politics, Nicholas promoted policies of easy credit and generous terms for his fellow Virginians. When the parent bank began its policy of contraction in 1819, the Richmond branch did not have the resources to withstand the pressure, and it collapsed in August of that year. Disgraced and blamed by many for the bank's failure, Nicholas resigned and turned over his entire estate to trustees charged with settling his oppressive debts. Part of those debts involved two notes, totaling $20,000, that had been endorsed by his friend at Monticello, an obligation that eventually helped drive Jefferson's estate into bankruptcy.

A ruined and broken man with no unencumbered property to call his own, Nicholas died at "Tufton," the home of his son-in-law (and Jefferson's grandson), Thomas Jefferson Randolph. In a characteristic move of kindness and generosity, Jefferson had the remains of his old friend buried in the family graveyard at Monticello. In doing so, Jefferson put to rest the body of a man who in Nicholas's own words had never "possessed any shining talents or imagination" but who had provided valuable service to his state, his nation, and the party of Jefferson in the formative years of the new republic.

• The great bulk of Nicholas's papers are in the Alderman Library, University of Virginia, in the Wilson Cary Nicholas Papers, the Randolph Family Papers, especially that part of the collection entered as the Edgehill-Randolph Papers, and the Thomas Jefferson Papers. The Library of Congress has its own collection of Wilson Cary Nicholas Papers, and a smaller collection of Wilson Cary Nicholas Papers resides in the Walter R. Perkins Library, Duke University. The fullest accounts of his life may be found in Dennis Golladay, "The Nicholas Family of Virginia, 1722–1820" (Ph.D. diss., Univ. of Virginia, 1973), and Elinor Janet Weeder, "Wilson Cary Nicholas, Jefferson's Lieutenant" (M.A. thesis, Univ. of Virginia, 1946). Also see Golladay, "The Nicholas Family and Albemarle County Political Leadership, 1782–1790," *Magazine of Albemarle County History* 36 (1978): 124–56, and David N. Mayer, ed., "Of Principles and Men: The Correspondence of John Taylor of Caroline with Wilson Cary Nicholas, 1806–1808," *Virginia Magazine of History and Biography* 96 (1988): 345–88. The six volumes of Dumas Malone's monumental *Jefferson and His Time* (1948–1981) trace Jefferson's personal, political, and financial connections with Nicholas. Also see Daniel P. Jordan, *Political Leadership in Jefferson's Virginia* (1983).

DENNIS GOLLADAY

NICHOLLS, Francis Redding Tillou (20 Aug. 1834–4 Jan. 1912), Louisiana governor and jurist, was born in Donaldsonville, Louisiana, the son of Judge Thomas Clark Nicholls, a state legislator and district court judge, and Louise Hannah Drake. He graduated from the United States Military Academy at West Point in 1855 and was commissioned a brevet second lieutenant. After serving in Florida and California, he resigned his commission and returned in 1856 to Louisiana, where he studied law at the University of Louisiana (now Tulane University). He passed the bar examination without earning a degree and began a successful law practice with his brother Lawrence in Napoleonville. In April 1860 he married Caroline Zilpha Guion; they had one son and five daughters.

Although reluctant to support secession, Nicholls had a distinguished career serving the Confederacy. He and his brother Lawrence raised an infantry company, the Phoenix Guards, in which he served as captain. He later served as the commander of the Eighth Louisiana Regiment, participating in the first battle of Manassas and in Stonewall Jackson's Valley Campaign. He lost his left arm from a wound received at the battle of Winchester in May 1862 and his left foot at the battle of Chancellorsville in May 1863. By this time he had risen to the rank of brigadier general. Although his wounds forced him to retire from the field, Nicholls served the Confederacy as superintendent of the conscript bureau of the Trans-Mississippi department until the end of the war, when he returned to his law practice in Napoleonville.

Nicholls became governor of Louisiana in 1877 after a hotly contested election in which both sides manipulated the vote count. Nicholls's supporters, the Bourbon Democrats, prevented blacks from voting in the country parishes where they were a majority and padded the voting rolls in New Orleans with thousands of deceased persons. Both Nicholls and his opponent claimed victory and organized governments, but a promise that Nicholls would be recognized as governor was part of the Compromise of 1877. Nicholls immediately appointed new justices to the Supreme Court of Louisiana to replace those appointed by his Republican predecessors and sent a force of state police to capture the building that housed the court. Nicholls's justices were installed, giving his administration power and authority. Neither President Ulysses S. Grant nor President Rutherford B. Hayes challenged the legitimacy of the new court. The Bourbon Democrats had chosen "all that was left" of Nicholls as their candidate because he was a wounded Confederate hero and appeared honest. Nicholls soon lost control of his party, which was determined to maintain control of state government by lies, intimidation, and fraud, and found himself surrounded by crooks. Enraged by his outspoken criticism of violence against blacks, tax fraud, and the corrupt Louisiana lottery, the Bourbon Democrats succeeded in calling a constitutional convention that reapportioned the legislature, lowered taxes, and called a special election, which cut Nicholls's term short by one year when Louisianians ratified it in 1879. The Democratic administrations that followed Nicholls's were so blatantly corrupt that party leaders passed over the incumbent, Samuel D. "McLottery" McEnery, and turned again to the "Maimed Brigadier" as their candidate for governor in 1887. Nicholls won after a bitter campaign and placated the disgruntled McEnery by appointing him to the Louisiana Supreme Court.

Nicholls's second term was mainly a crusade against the corrupt Louisiana lottery. Officials of the lottery offered to pay an annual fee of $1.25 million into the state treasury if the legislature would renew its charter for another twenty-five years. Lottery officials also made it clear that pliant legislators would be generously rewarded from the lottery's "slush fund." Although the Louisiana legislature passed a resolution to submit a constitutional amendment to the state constitution to recharter the lottery, Nicholls vetoed the bill. Lottery supporters asserted that, under the state constitution, Nicholls did not have the authority to veto a proposed constitutional amendment. In *State ex rel. Morris v. Mason* (1891), the Louisiana Supreme Court ruled that the resolution was not subject to veto, a decision concurred in by the court's newest justice "McLottery" McEnery. Louisianians, however, were so disgusted with the lottery's corruption that they voted overwhelmingly against the recharter amendment. Nicholls later said his veto of the lottery's recharter stemmed from a belief that he would not "permit one of my hands to aid in degrading what the other was lost in seeking to uphold . . . the honor of my native state."

Although Nicholls was opposed to the lottery's corrupt influence over state politics, his record is not without flaws. He allowed himself to be used by less-than-upright politicians to win the 1876 election, and he appointed former governor McEnery to the Supreme Court to gain his office in 1887. He also made no attempt to stop his party from its wholesale disenfranchisement of blacks, and he sanctioned such meager support for the state public schools that several generations of African Americans in Louisiana had no opportunity for a decent education. Nicholls also has the dubious distinction of supporting and signing the state's first "Jim Crow" segregation law in 1890. The constitutionality of this law, which mandated segregated railroad cars, was upheld by the U.S. Supreme Court's decision in *Plessy v. Ferguson* (1896). Nicholls's successor, Murphy J. Foster, appointed him chief justice of the Louisiana Supreme Court in 1892. He continued in that office until 1904, at which time a provision in the new Louisiana Constitution of 1898 caused him to become an associate justice. He served the court in that capacity until ill health forced him to seek retirement in 1911. Nicholls died at Ridgefield Plantation in Thibodeaux, Louisiana.

• There is no known collection of Nicholls's papers, nor is there a full-length biography except C. Howard Nichols, "Francis Tillou Nicholls, Bourbon Democrat," (Master's thesis, Louisiana State Univ., 1959). Barnes F. Lathrop edited an autobiography of a portion of Nicholls's life as a brief article, "An Autobiography of Francis T. Nicholls, 1834–1881," *Louisiana Historical Quarterly* 17 (1934): 246–67. Other articles include Berthold C. Alwes, "The History of the Louisiana State Lottery Company," *Louisiana Historical Quarterly* 27 (1944): 964–1118, and Hilda McDaniel, "Francis T. Nicholls and the End of Reconstruction," *Louisiana Historical Quarterly* 32 (1949): 357–509. Books dealing with aspects of Nicholls's career include Joseph G. Dawson III, *Army Generals and Reconstruction Louisiana, 1862–1877* (1982); Joseph G. Dawson III, ed., *The Louisiana Governors: From Iberville to Edwards* (1991); William I. Hair, *Bourbonism and Agrarian Protest: Louisiana Politics, 1877–1900* (1969); Garnie W. McGinty, *Louisiana Redeemed: The Overthrow of Carpetbag Rule, 1876–1880* (1941); and Joe Gray Taylor, *Louisiana Reconstructed, 1863–1877* (1974). The Louisiana Supreme Court case involving the lottery recharter can be found in 43 La. Ann. 590 #10,794 (1891). An obituary is in the New Orleans *Times-Picayune*, 5 Jan. 1912.

JUDITH K. SCHAFER

NICHOLS, Anne (26 Nov. 1891?–15 Sept. 1966), playwright and producer, was born in Dale's (or Dales) Mills, Georgia, the daughter of George Nichols, a lawyer, and Julia Bates. Nichols spent a great deal of her early life moving from town to town. When Nichols reached the age of ten, her family finally moved from Dale's Mills permanently to Philadelphia, Pennsylvania, but did not settle down anywhere. Rather, the family moved around the Philadelphia area. When she was fifteen, her parents placed her in Ogontz, a girls' seminary near Philadelphia. At age sixteen Nichols ran away from the school to New York City to pursue a career as an actress.

Nichols landed her first part in a production of *The Shepherd King* as a chorus girl. The show opened in Boston in 1911 and then moved to New York, where Nichols left the production, figuring it would take too long to reach leading lady status if she continued playing such small parts. She then began working in motion pictures; her first jobs were with the Vitagraph company on movies in Texas and California.

After a year and a half, preferring the presence of a live audience, Nichols returned to the theater. Soon she began writing sketches for vaudeville. Her first, *Humanity* (1915), was a hit when it went on in a small New Jersey town. Following this success Nichols continued writing and performing sketches for vaudeville. She wrote her first full-length play, *Heart's Desire*, in collaboration with Adelaide Matthews in 1916 as part of Fiske O'Hara's touring company. She wrote a total of seven plays for O'Hara's company, and this led to her being "employed as a sort of 'tailor' of plays. [She] would be sent out to see an actor, study his type and style, and then write a play to fit him" (Mullett, p. 171). Over the next few years Nichols wrote several other plays, including *The Guilded Cage* (1920) and *Love Dreams* (1921), a musical, in collaboration with Walter Jansen.

Nichols's most successful play, and one of the most successful in history, was *Abie's Irish Rose*, which she wrote in 1919. Nichols got the idea for this comedy about the marriage of a Jewish boy to an Irish Catholic girl from a story O'Hara told her one night over dinner. Nichols began writing the play immediately after hearing the story and completed it in three days. After several failed attempts to get *Abie* produced, Nichols found success in 1922. Nichols noted that despite the first production's popular success in New York City (it also ran forty-two weeks in Los Angeles), it was "bad"

(Schmidt, p. 134). She even walked out on the play's first night in New York. However, Nichols contended that she "really never lost faith in the play" despite the New York public's indifference to it. The fact that Nichols put up her own money to keep the play in production evidences this faith. Legend would have it that Nichols and *Abie* battled an army of bad reviews, but, in fact, some very important reviewers found at least some merit in the play. While *New York Times* critic William B. Chase noted that some scenes "sagged," he also noted that the audience's uproarious laughter indicated a favorite with the public (24 May 1924). After two months of lukewarm reviews, *Abie* caught on with the public and never let go. Over a period of five years the play ran for 2,327 consecutive performances (a record at the time). It broke engagement records in numerous U.S. cities and was performed in Canada, Europe, Australia, and China. Nichols ascribed the success of *Abie* to her sense of audience, her knowledge of the Jewish and Irish cultures, and the "human and genuine" element of the play. Nichols noted that the "emotions [the play's characters] experience are common to us all" (Mullett, p. 171).

Nichols continued writing, producing, and directing other plays, including *Just Married* (1921) and *Pre-Honeymoon* (1936), which she wrote and staged with Alfred Van Ronkel. However, retaining ownership of the successful *Abie* prevented Nichols from devoting as much time as she would have liked to writing and producing. She constantly had to deal with the business side of producing the play. In 1927 Harper and Brothers published *Abie's Irish Rose* as a novel. *Abie* was made into a motion picture in 1928 and again in 1946. In 1929 Nichols sued the Universal Picture Corporation, alleging that the company had stolen the idea for the motion picture *The Cohens and the Kelleys* from *Abie's Irish Rose*. The judge ruled against Nichols, declaring that the theme of parents foiling young lovers was so old it belonged to the public domain. *Abie* saw a revival on the stage in 1937 as well as 1954. In 1942 the play was broadcast on NBC radio.

Later in her life Nichols had to go into seclusion in order to find peace from the public that so loved *Abie's Irish Rose*. In 1962, to mark the fortieth anniversary of *Abie*, she gave an interview from an undisclosed location in Cape Cod, Massachusetts. The interview ended with a plea by Nichols to be allowed to remain in seclusion.

Nichols was married to Henry Duffey (in certain sources spelled Duffy), a producer. There is a discrepancy as to the year of their marriage. Some sources date it 1914; others, 1915. Nichols and Duffey were divorced in 1924. They had one son.

At the time of her death, Nichols was working on her autobiography, titled "Such Is Fame." She died in Cliff House Nursing Home in Englewood Cliffs, New Jersey.

Abie's Irish Rose so overwhelmed Nichols's career that later in life she noted, "People think it's the only thing I ever did" (*New York Times*, 21 May 1962). This was and still is true. However, rather than being remembered as merely the author of the play, Nichols should be considered the parent of the play, who loved and supported it from its conception through its decline. She was known for her strong belief in the play and her bravery in supporting it. Benjamin De Casseres noted, "It was . . . the consciousness in the mind of Anne Nichols that she had incarnated her idea perfectly that gave her the indomitable courage and will to persist in her enterprise" (p. 7).

• Nichols's unfinished autobiography has not been published. Important biographical sources are Mary Braggiotti, "Abie's Rose Grows an Olive Leaf," *New York Post*, 26 June 1943; Arthur Gelb, "Author of *Abie's Irish Rose* Reviews 40 Years," *New York Times*, 21 May 1962 (this article notes that Nichols was sixty-six at the time of the interview, which would make her year of birth 1896); Jean Meegan, "Old Man Abie, He Just Goes Rolling," *Milwaukee Journal*, 3 Oct. 1943; Mary B. Mullett, "The Story of Anne Nichols and Her $5,000,000 Play," *American Magazine*, May 1924, pp. 18–19, 170–72; Karl Schmidt, "The Play Is the Thing," *Ladies' Home Journal*, July 1924, pp. 32, 134, 137; Anne Nichols, "The Million Dollar Hit," *Theatre Arts Magazine*, July 1924, pp. 19, 54. See also Doris Abramson and Laurilyn Harris, "Anne Nichols: $1,000,000 Playwright," in *Women of the American Theatre*, ed. Helen Krich Chinoy and Linda Walsh Jenkins (1981). A thorough list of Nichols's career activities appears in *The Biographical Encyclopedia and Who's Who of the American Theatre* (1966). An obituary is in the *New York Times*, 16 Sept. 1966 (this entry notes that Nichols was seventy-five when she died, which would make her year of birth 1891.

JESSICA LEXIE HOLLIS

NICHOLS, Charles Henry (19 Oct. 1820–16 Dec. 1889), psychiatrist and mental hospital administrator, was born and raised in Vassalboro, Maine, the only son of Caleb Nichols and Eunice Kelly, farmers. His parents were prominent Quakers. Nichols was educated at the public schools and academy of the town and at the Friends' School in Providence, Rhode Island. There his tutor was Pliny Earle (1809–1892), who later became a pioneer of mental medicine. After teaching school for several years, Nichols turned to the study of medicine, first at the University of the City of New York and then at the University of Pennsylvania, where he obtained an M.D. in 1843.

Nichols practiced medicine in Lynn, Massachusetts, until 1847. He then became assistant physician to Amariah Brigham (founder and editor of the *American Journal of Insanity*) at the New York State Lunatic Asylum in Utica. In 1849 Nichols succeeded Pliny Earle as resident physician of the Bloomingdale Asylum, in New York City, where he proved especially skillful in improving sanitary facilities. In the spring of 1852, he resigned after a series of disputes with the hospital board.

In the fall of 1852, President Millard Fillmore appointed him first medical superintendent of the Government Hospital for the Insane (now St. Elizabeths Hospital), in Washington, D.C. In this post, which Nichols retained for twenty-five years, he became one of the most influential leaders of his profession, and

St. Elizabeths became a national model for asylum construction and management. Nichols and social reformer Dorothea Dix, who had helped found the hospital and who recommended his appointment, selected the 185-acre site for the hospital and drafted the law for its organization. Nichols designed the institution's first structures, including the 250-bed Center Building, in consultation with Thomas U. Walter, Architect of the Capitol.

The Center Building was an early example of the Kirkbride linear plan named for Thomas Story Kirkbride, who claimed it enhanced medical supervision and promoted a therapeutic relationship between patients and hospital employees. Nichols modified the linear plan by making sections of the hospital wings recede according to what he termed an echelon arrangement, which brought more light and air into the wards. He also developed new methods of heating, ventilation, and sanitation. The design of the Center Building was reproduced in several state mental hospitals, as well as in Canadian and Australian asylums. In 1856 Nichols built the first of two separate lodges for blacks, which he considered to be "the first and only special provision for the suitable care of the insane African in any part of the world."

Nichols married Ellen G. Maury (daughter of John W. Maury, a former mayor of Washington) in 1857; they had two children, one of whom died in childhood. His wife died in 1865; his second marriage, in 1872, was to Mrs. Sarah Lathrop Garlick.

During the Civil War he conducted a general hospital for volunteer soldiers that operated out of the east wing of the Center Building, and he served as a volunteer surgeon at the first battle of Manassas.

In 1873 Nichols was elected president of the Association of Medical Superintendents of American Institutions for the Insane (now the American Psychiatric Association) and served for six years. In an 1876 speech before the International Medical Congress in Philadelphia, he called for a more liberal stance on the size and physical layout of hospitals. Owing to an accumulating number of chronic cases, he recommended revising the standard capacity of mental hospitals from 250 to 600 beds, preferably providing separate hospitals for males and females under one medical superintendent. Earlier, at the 1866 annual meeting of medical superintendents, his colleagues had endorsed a similar proposal by Nichols. He also acquired a reputation in forensic psychiatry, most notably in his testimony for the defense in the trial of Charles Guiteau for the assassination of President James A. Garfield.

Nichols enjoyed the social and political life of the capital, and he played a prominent role in local affairs and organizations. He served as president of the first board of school commissioners, the metropolitan police board, and the levy court of Washington County. He was also a trustee of the Columbia Hospital for Women and Lying-in Asylum and Columbian University (now George Washington University). He was a member of the Washington National Monument Society and a "life director" of the American Colonization Society, both headquartered in the capital. His imperious bearing and political alliances with men such as Alexander "Boss" Shepherd made him a number of enemies and were factors in several investigations into his management of St. Elizabeths. The most serious investigation occurred in 1876 as part of a Congressional probe into corruption and fiscal extravagance in the administration of President Ulysses S. Grant. For three months Congress conducted public hearings on charges that Nichols was guilty of misappropriating funds, abusing patients, and mismanaging the hospital farm. He was cleared of the charges.

In 1877 Nichols resigned from St. Elizabeths to become superintendent of the Bloomingdale Asylum in New York City, which offered him a higher salary and a free hand in guiding expected renovations and construction. In 1889, in preparation for removing to White Plains and building a new hospital there, he was sent on a four-month tour of European hospitals. Shortly after his return, he died (in New York City) before having a chance to implement his plans. But his extensive notes on European hospitals were published, and many of his recommendations were incorporated by architect James Brown Lord in the design of the new Bloomingdale, now the New York Hospital–Cornell Medical Center/Westchester Division.

• Although Nichols left no body of personal papers, much of his correspondence survives as part of the records of St. Elizabeths Hospital, at the National Archives, and in the archives of the New York Hospital–Cornell Medical Center. Letters revealing his close relationship and consultations with Dorothea Dix are in her papers at the Houghton Library, Harvard; a small sample of his Civil War correspondence is at the Library of Congress manuscript division. His only writings were "On the Best Mode of Providing for the Subjects of Chronic Insanity," *Transactions of the International Medical Congress* (Philadelphia: Centennial Medical Commission of Philadelphia, 1876), and the 100-page, posthumously published "Notes on Hospitals for the Insane Abroad," ed. Samuel B. Lyon, in *Proceedings of the Forty-fourth Annual Meeting of the Association of Medical Superintendents of American Institutions for the Insane* (1890). Information on his career can be found in Winfred Overholser, ed., *Centennial Papers, Saint Elizabeths Hospital, 1855–1955* (1956), and William L. Russell, *The New York Hospital: A History of the Psychiatric Service, 1771–1936* (1945). There are two articles on different aspects of his career: Frank Rives Millikan, "St. Elizabeths Hospital: End of the Cathedral Era," *Washington History* 1 (Fall 1989): 26–41; and Allen D. Spiegel, "Temporary Insanity and Premenstrual Syndrome: Medical Testimony in an 1865 Murder Trial," *New York State Journal of Medicine* 88 (Sept. 1988): 482–92.

FRANK RIVES MILLIKAN

NICHOLS, Dudley (6 Apr. 1895–4 Jan. 1960), screenwriter, was born in Wapakoneta, Ohio, the son of Grant Byron Nichols, a doctor, and Mary Means. He attended the University of Michigan, where he studied engineering. After service in the navy during World War I, Nichols worked as a journalist for the *New*

York Evening Post and later the *New York World*. In 1924 he married Esta Varez Gooch-Collins; they had no children.

As a journalist, Nichols specialized in covering trials, and many of the screenplays that he would later write end with trial sequences, such as *This Land Is Mine* (1943) and *Pinky* (1949). He also wrote about the theater, reviewing the opening night in 1928 of Eugene O'Neill's *Strange Interlude*. Nichols would subsequently write two scripts based on O'Neill's plays *The Long Voyage Home* (1940) and *Mourning Becomes Electra* (1947).

In 1929 Nichols went to Hollywood to work at the Fox Film Corporation. He told his boss the only film he remembered seeing was director John Ford's 1924 *The Iron Horse*, so he was put together with Ford on a submarine film, *Men without Women* (1930). It was the first of fourteen films the pair did, becoming one of the most famous writer-director collaborations in American film history. Nichols brought an appreciation of literature and drama to Ford's work, helping to increase Ford's reputation for serious filmmaking in the thirties. In return, Ford pushed Nichols to put less emphasis on dialogue and more on visual elements. The two men usually collaborated on a script. Dan Ford, Ford's grandson, described them as "an ideal team. Dudley Nichols was the butterfly, John the bull. John was bursting with enthusiasm and energy while Nichols was subtler, more controlled. His were the Athenian qualities of logic and grace."

Their fourth film, *The Lost Patrol* (1934), was an intense drama of a British army patrol in the Mesopotamian desert in 1916 being killed off one at a time by unseen Arab soldiers. Their next film, *The Informer* (1935), was highly acclaimed in its time for its German-Expressionist atmosphere. Based on a novel by Liam O'Flaherty, the film tells the story of Gypo Nolan, who betrays his Irish revolutionary friend Frankie to British soldiers for the reward. The overly obvious symbolism of the "wanted" poster for Frankie that follows Gypo wherever he goes has dated the film badly.

Four years later, Nichols and Ford collaborated on *Stagecoach* (1939), considered one of the classic westerns. As in many of his scripts (and not only those for Ford) Nichols takes a group of characters and isolates them, here in a stagecoach crossing Indian country. The characters are vivid, if clichéd, and the scenes, as in many of Nichols's scripts, are supremely playable. Structurally, the film is weakened by telling two stories. One, about an Indian uprising, begins at the film's start and ends twenty minutes before the end; the second, about the outlaw, the Ringo Kid, begins fifteen minutes into the film and continues to the final scene.

Perhaps the best Nichols-Ford collaboration came the following year with *The Long Voyage Home*. Nichols took four of O'Neill's one-act plays about life on board a freighter and wove them into a single striking film. Ford's visuals and Nichols's sense of drama were in excellent balance. Their last collaboration was *The Fugitive*, a 1947 adaptation of Graham Greene's novel *The Power and the Glory*. Ford departed greatly from Nichols's script, and the resulting rift between the two men never healed.

Although much of his most notable work was done with Ford, Nichols worked with many other major directors. In 1935 he was one of several writers on Cecil B. DeMille's spectacle *The Crusades*, and in 1938 he was cowriter of one of the great screwball comedies of the thirties, *Bringing Up Baby*, directed by Howard Hawks. In 1943 Nichols wrote the entertaining, if propagandistic, *Air Force* for Hawks. In this film, the group of men is a bomber crew, and the film takes place mostly on the plane. In 1941 Nichols had written the political thriller *Man Hunt* for Fritz Lang to direct, and in 1945 he wrote Lang's *Scarlet Street*. Nichols wrote the first drafts of the race-relations drama *Pinky*, directed by Elia Kazan, and although thematic changes were made in subsequent drafts by screenwriter Philip Dunne, Dunne noted that he kept most of Nichols's structure. Nichols directed three films in the forties, but they were not successful, and Nichols later admitted he did not have the personality to direct.

Nichols was admired by other writers not only for his screenwriting skills and the substance of the subject matter of his films but also for his often vocal support of the craft of screenwriting. At a time when many writers, including screenwriters, looked down on the craft, Nichols spoke and wrote about contributions writers made to the art of the film. Nichols was a founding member of the Screen Writers Guild in 1933 and served as its president in 1938–1939. When the Guild was fighting to stop the Motion Picture Academy from turning it into a company union, Nichols refused to accept the Academy Award given to him for *The Informer* as a statement of solidarity with other writers.

Nichols's reputation has suffered since his death. His seriousness as a writer in his films of the thirties and forties is now seen as part of a turgid style that has dated badly, and the victories he won for more intelligent subject matter have been overshadowed by later changes in the issues that movies deal with. A growing number of film historians, however, have begun to admire his later, lighter, less self-consciously "important" pictures, such as his last one, the 1960 comic western *Heller in Pink Tights*, and Nichols's reputation as an early fighter for recognition for the screenwriter still stands. He died in Hollywood.

• Nichols's papers are in the Special Collections of the Library of the University of California at Los Angeles, along with studio files from RKO and Fox, where he spent much of his creative life. There is as yet no biography of Nichols. Paul Jensen's "The Career of Dudley Nichols" (*Film Comment*, Winter 1970–1971, pp. 56–63, reprinted in Richard Corliss, ed., *The Hollywood Screenwriters* [1972]), is a detailed look at Nichols's work and career from a later perspective. Nichols is occasionally referred to in books about his directorial collaborators, but his contribution to their work is often downplayed, as in Tag Gallagher's *John Ford: The Man and His Films* (1986).

TOM STEMPEL

NICHOLS, Edward Leamington (14 Sept. 1854–10 Nov. 1937), physicist, was born in Leamington, England, the only son of Edward W. Nichols, an artist, and Maria Watkinson, a teacher. Originally from New England, Nichols's parents spent long periods abroad in places suitable for artwork and study. Several years after Nichols was born, the family returned to the United States and settled first in New Jersey and later in New York, where Nichols attended the Peekskill Military Academy. In 1871 he entered Cornell, where he became interested in chemistry. He changed his plans after studying physics with the innovative and dynamic teacher William A. Anthony. While at Cornell, he met Ida Preston, his future wife.

After he received the B.S. in 1875, Nichols continued his education in Germany, which led the world in physics research and the new electrical technologies. He studied under many prominent physicists, including both Gustav and Eilhard Wiedemann at the University of Leipzig (1875–1876); Hermann Helmholtz, Gustav Kirchhoff, Emil Du Bois–Reymond, and Heinrich W. Dove at the University of Berlin (1876–1878); and J. B. Listing at the University of Göttingen. Nichols was impressed with the German idea of the research university, which he later promoted in the United States.

In 1859 Kirchhoff had derived a relationship for radiation that involved an unknown mathematical function of wavelength and temperature. Determining this function was desirable for both theoretical and practical reasons. Working under Helmholtz, Nichols made careful spectrophotometric measurements of radiation from an incandescent platinum wire, hoping to elucidate Kirchhoff's function. This research ("Über das von glühenden Platin ausgestrahlte Licht") was accepted in 1879 for the Ph.D. at Göttingen. Nichols later published several papers based on his thesis and other researches done in Germany.

After returning to the United States, Nichols received a fellowship from Johns Hopkins University. He worked with H. A. Rowland on electromagnetic problems for a year and then joined Thomas A. Edison's Menlo Park Laboratory. There Nichols developed photometric methods for incandescent lights while consolidating and extending the foundations in illumination science that he had acquired in Germany. In 1881 he married Ida; they had two children. That same year he was appointed professor of physics and chemistry at Central University in Kentucky, where he studied super-heated liquids and questions related to agricultural concerns. As professor of physics and astronomy at the University of Kansas from 1883 to 1887, he published papers on color vision, spectrophotometric studies of pigments and the sky, the senses of taste and smell, chemical behavior of iron in a magnetic field, and other topics in electrotechnology and electromagnetic theory.

In 1887 Nichols returned to Cornell as head of the physics department. With his experience in German universities forming his ideal, Nichols instituted seminars and improved laboratory instruction. Enrollment increased rapidly both because of his influence and because of broad economic and social changes in the United States. During his career at Cornell Nichols became a major figure in American physics through his researches, his leadership, and his educational roles.

Nichols's researches at Cornell developed the major themes begun earlier: electricity and magnetism, measurement and instrumentation, but above all, light. Perhaps his early exposure to art and to natural vistas influenced his passion for the study of light's multifarious aspects and applications. Many of his early papers at Cornell dealt with the analysis and measurement of artificial light sources. He continued his interests in pigments and color vision. In 1901, prompted by the controversial work of physicists Wilhelm Wien, Max Planck, and others, Nichols revisited his thesis problem, the general radiation function. His main interest was not in abstract theory but in finding relationships "for actual surfaces" (*Physical Review* 13: 68). A few years later he published a survey article for the *Physical Review* on energy distribution in incandescent sources. In 1904 he began an extended collaboration with his colleague and former student Ernest Merritt on the puzzling phenomena of phosphorescence and fluorescence. This topic occupied Nichols for the rest of his career.

"Cold light" was interesting for both theoretical and practical reasons, yet its complexities and its practical limitations deterred many researchers. Perhaps unaware of all the experimental difficulties, Nichols and Merritt began their quantitative researches with the controverted question of Stokes's law of fluorescence, an empirical relationship between the wavelengths of fluorescent light and the light that produced it. In spite of criticism by a leading German spectroscopist for their "relatively crude" methods, Nichols and Merritt's results were frequently cited. With significant support from the Carnegie Foundation, Nichols and Merritt wrote more than two dozen papers and monographs together on optical luminescence. Over a period of thirteen years they used a spectrophotometer to examine the luminescence of zinc sulfate and to determine fluorescence spectra of organic dyes and uranium compounds. They analyzed relations of luminescence to absorption, exciting wavelength, and electrical conduction; the effects of temperature and of the method of producing luminescence; energy distribution in fluorescence spectra; and phosphorescence's rate of decay. Nichols and Merritt became recognized as leading authorities in this area.

For Nichols his retirement in 1919 meant more time for the research he loved. As Nichols's successor, Merritt became increasingly occupied with administrative duties and was unable to continue the collaboration. Working alone and with students and other researchers, Nichols continued research on luminescence and related phenomena for another seventeen years. Approximately one-fourth of his papers were published during his retirement. As an experimental physicist inclined toward applications, Nichols did not spend much time on theoretical problems, believing it was more important to acquire useful data.

Nichols was a pivotal figure in the professionalization of physics in the United States, not only because of his research contributions, but also through his vision and leadership. At a time when research was not considered an important function of the university, Nichols advocated and embodied the ideal of educator as researcher. Both at Cornell and as a public spokesman for the profession, Nichols publicized the practical value of research and supported changes that would encourage it. He developed a photometric laboratory at Cornell that was useful for problems in illumination engineering. The Illumination Engineering Society later elected him their second honorary member (the first was Edison). In 1893 Nichols founded the *Physical Review*, the first physics journal in the United States, which he edited for twenty years. During this period he contributed numerous book reviews and biographical articles for the benefit of the profession. Nichols was one of the founding members of the American Physical Society in 1899, acting as president during 1907–1909. Although he disliked administrative work, he served Cornell as dean of the College of Arts and Sciences and as faculty representative to the university's board of trustees.

Nichols used his leadership skills in many other organizations. He acted as secretary for Section B, vice president, and president of the American Association for the Advancement of Science, vice president of the American Institute of Electrical Engineers, and president of the Kansas Academy of Science and of Sigma Xi. He served on the Bureau of Standards visiting committee and as secretary for the Chamber of Delegates to the 1893 Electrical Congress in Chicago.

Although a strong proponent of academic research, Nichols was keenly interested in teaching. An outstanding teacher whose enthusiasm for his subject was contagious, his experimental lectures attracted many students and were even attended by faculty members. The son and husband of intellectual women, Nichols was supportive of women in science, and many women did research in his department. Nichols wrote and collaborated on textbooks and a laboratory manual, and he was interested in secondary school physics education. He was highly esteemed by students and colleagues, who found him a sympathetic and helpful mentor and friend. His influence as an educator extended far beyond Cornell. When he retired his former students were occupying educational, industrial, and government positions throughout the United States, including thirty-five department chairs.

Nichols received many honors, including the Cresson Medal of the Franklin Institute, the Rumford Medal of the American Academy of Arts and Sciences, and the Ives Medal of the Optical Society. He was elected a member of the National Academy of Sciences and an honorary member of the Optical Society of America, the National Electric Light Association, and the Association des Ingénieurs de l'Éclairage, Paris, as well as a fellow of the American Association for the Advancement of Science and associate fellow of the American Academy of Science.

Intellectual interests from his mother and artistic sensibilities from his father coalesced in Nichols, who was an amateur violinist as well as a scholar. He was greatly influenced by his cosmopolitan upbringing, choosing to travel abroad frequently and eventually visiting all six continents. Nichols maintained a love for scenic places and became an avid fisherman. No narrow academic, he edited Johnson's *Encyclopedia* and Webster's *Dictionary* for several years. Nichols balanced his wide interests in his professional and personal life. He was an active Episcopalian who saw science as supportive of and complementary to religious faith and values. Calm and dignified in manner, principled and tolerant, Nichols combined "perseverance in seeking new knowledge with a conservative regard for old ideals and approved traditions" (*Cornell Alumni News*, 1945, p. 369). He died in West Palm Beach, Florida.

• Nichols's papers at Cornell's Department of Manuscripts and University Archives include correspondence, administrative records, laboratory notebooks, records from his study in Germany, and biographical material. Nichols's joint research with Merritt was published in the *Physical Review* between 1904 and 1917. Much of his work on luminescence is in *Studies in Luminescence* (1912), with Merritt; *Fluorescence of the Uranyl Salts* (1919), with H. L. Howes, Merritt, and others; *Selected Topics in the Field of Luminescence* (1923), with Merritt and C. D. Child; and *Cathodo-Luminescence and the Luminescence of Incandescent Solids* (1928), with Howes and D. T. Wilber. He wrote several textbooks, including *A Laboratory Manual of Physics and Applied Electricity* (2 vols., 1895), with other authors; *The Elements of Physics* (3 vols., 1896), with W. S. Franklin; and *The Outlines of Physics, an Elementary Textbook* (1898). Biographical articles that have bibliographies are F. K. Richtmyer, *Journal of the Optical Society of America* 20 (Apr. 1930): 161–72; and Ernest Merritt, National Academy of Sciences, *Biographical Memoirs* 22 (1940): 343–66. Obituaries are in the *New York Times*, 11 Nov. 1937; *Science* 86 (Nov. 1937): 483–85; *Physical Review* 53 (1 Jan. 1938): 1–2; *Journal of the Optical Society of America* 28 (Jan. 1938): 31–32; *Nature* 14 (8 Jan. 1938): 66–67; and *Proceedings of the American Academy of Arts and Sciences* 72 (1936–1937): 374–76.

MARJORIE C. MALLEY

NICHOLS, Ernest Fox (1 June 1869–29 Apr. 1924), physicist and university president, was born in Leavenworth, Kansas, the son of Alonzo Curtis Nichols, a photographer, and Sophronia Fox. Nichols, described as a frail and delicate youth, was schooled at home. His parents died when he was in his teens, and in 1884 he went to live with his maternal uncle, General Simeon M. Fox of Manhattan, Kansas. Shortly after his arrival he was accepted into Kansas State Agricultural College in Manhattan.

Nichols received his B.Sc. in 1888 and stayed on at the college for one year as an assistant in chemistry. He enrolled at Cornell in 1889, a decision influenced by Cornell physicist Edward Leamington Nichols (no relation), who visited Manhattan in 1885 to give a talk on experimental physics. Nichols studied under E. L. Nichols at Cornell, doing research on infrared radiation and gaining expertise in the construction and use of sensitive instruments such as the weak field galvanometer. The results of his research appeared as the first article published in the journal *Physical Review* (ed. E. L. Nichols).

In 1892 Nichols completed his studies at Cornell (he received his M.Sc. the following year) and became professor of physics and astronomy at Colgate University. While there, he met and in 1894 married Katherine Williams West; they had one daughter. Also in 1894 Nichols obtained a leave of absence to study at the University of Berlin's Physical Institute. There he worked closely with Heinrich Rubens on the study of infrared radiation. Nichols's initial assignment was to perfect a new instrument, later known as the Nichols radiometer, which would be sensitive to the long-wavelength radiation under scrutiny. Nichols's radiometer was based on the earlier device designed by Sir William Crookes and on improvements suggested by Ernst Pringsheim.

Nichols and Rubens concentrated their infrared research on quartz and fluorite, which share the property of producing practically monochrome radiation in response to successive reflections from their surfaces. Using this method of "residual rays," they detected radiation with an estimated wavelength of fifty micrometers, ten times longer than the longest previously observed infrared wavelength. Not only did they extend the known infrared spectrum, but they also experimentally confirmed that infrared was a form of electromagnetic radiation.

Nichols returned to Colgate University in 1897. At this time he completed the requirements for his Ph.D. from Cornell, which was awarded that year. In 1898 he became professor of physics at Dartmouth College, taking part in the final design and equipping of the new Wilder Physical Laboratory, which opened the following year.

Nichols entered the field of astrophysics research because of a chance meeting in 1897 with George Ellery Hale, director of the University of Chicago's Yerkes Observatory. Hale wanted to study the Sun's corona but was prevented from doing so regularly because the corona was visible only during rare total solar eclipses. Sensing the possibility of detecting the corona's infrared radiation at other times, Hale tried to enlist Nichols and his new radiometer. Nichols professed some interest in this research, but what really intrigued him was trying to detect the extremely faint infrared radiation from the stars and planets. Hale invited him to do that at Yerkes, and Nichols brought his radiometer there in the summers of 1898 and 1900 to measure the heat from the stars and planets. While he could not provide absolute measurements of their heat, he could reliably detect infrared radiation from Jupiter, Saturn, and the bright stars Arcturus and Vega. He never had the time to repeat his Yerkes experiments, but they provided the impetus for the later work of William W. Coblentz and Carl O. Lampland

at Lowell Observatory, and of Edison Petit, Seth B. Nicholson, and Charles G. Abbot at Mount Wilson Observatory.

Nichols's most significant work at Dartmouth was done in collaboration with Gordon F. Hull and concerned the pressure of electromagnetic radiation. As early as 1873 James Clerk Maxwell had predicted that light, as a form of electromagnetic radiation, would exert pressure on any obstacle it encountered. Nichols thought that his radiometer, suitably modified, could finally detect the minuscule pressure of light. Nichols and Hull were able to announce in 1901 that they had detected the pressure of light and verified the predicted equivalence of the pressure to the energy of the incident radiation. Simultaneously, their results were independently confirmed by Peter Lebedev, who had been working on the same problem in Moscow.

Nichols left Dartmouth in 1903 to become professor of physics at Columbia University. There he continued his research into long-wavelength infrared radiation. He spent the winter of 1904–1905 at the Cavendish Laboratory at Cambridge University and the summer of 1906 at Hale's new observatory on Mount Wilson, California.

Nichols's career underwent a major change in 1909, when he became president of Dartmouth College. In his seven years in this position he did a great deal of work improving the level of scholarship and the financial solvency of the institution, but his scientific research suffered from neglect.

Nichols resigned as president of Dartmouth in 1916 and took a position as professor of physics at Yale University. When the United States entered World War I the next year, he worked with the Department of Naval Ordnance through the National Research Council. After the war he returned to Yale, but in 1920 he resigned to become director of research in pure science at General Electric's Nela Park Laboratory in Cleveland, Ohio. He had barely settled into his new position when he was offered the presidency of the Massachusetts Institute of Technology in 1921. He accepted, but his health became so poor that he was quickly forced to resign. He returned to Nela Park, where he worked for the remainder of his life.

At Nela Park Nichols worked with James D. Tear in an attempt to fill in the gap in the electromagnetic spectrum between the infrared and radio waves. Up to 1920 the longest detected infrared radiation had a wavelength of 0.4 millimeters, and the shortest radio waves were seven millimeters long. Together Nichols and Tear constructed a device that produced radio waves down to 0.22 millimeters. They then isolated infrared radiation from a mercury arc with a wavelength of 0.42 millimeters, effectively bridging the two extremes of the electromagnetic spectrum. Nichols announced the results of this landmark research at the spring 1924 meeting of the National Academy of Sciences in Washington, D.C. He collapsed on the stage in the midst of his presentation; colleagues rushed to his assistance, but he died before an ambulance arrived.

Nichols was respected as an experimental physicist and was one of the leading figures in American infrared research in the first two decades of the twentieth century. His great patience and dexterity enabled him to succeed in constructing and refining his delicate radiometer. He has also been lauded for his ability to construct new and innovative experimental methods. Although his colleagues were dismayed when he left research to become president of Dartmouth, he left the school in much-improved condition. Ironically, he is best remembered for his dramatic death, prompting some to write that his passing could not have been done better if it had been planned that way.

• Nichols's papers as president of Dartmouth are at that institution's archives, and there are a handful of letters from Joseph Larmor, with Nichols's notebooks from Larmor's lectures, in the Colgate University archives. Correspondence between George Ellery Hale and Nichols is in the director's papers at the Yerkes Observatory archives. The best account of Nichols's scientific career is Edward L. Nichols, "Ernest Fox Nichols 1869–1924," National Academy of Sciences, *Biographical Memoirs* 12 (1929): 97–131; it contains a complete bibliography of Nichols's papers as well as reprinted newspaper and magazine accounts of his death. See also Philip Fox, "Ernest Fox Nichols," *Astrophysical Journal* 51 (1925): 1–16, which contains remembrances of Nichols by family members and colleagues. An obituary is in the *New York Times*, 30 Apr. 1924.

RONALD BRASHEAR

NICHOLS, Herbie (3 Dec. 1919–12 Apr. 1963), composer and musician, was born Herbert Horatio Nichols in New York City, the son of Joel Nichols, a building supervisor, and Ida (maiden name unknown). His parents, originally from Trinidad and St. Kitts, had moved to New York in 1910. Nichols first lived at Sixty-first Street and Eleventh Avenue, in the area known at the time as "San Juan Hill." The family moved to Harlem when Nichols was seven. When he was not practicing or winning at chess, checkers, or marbles, the young Nichols spent much time in the public library. From age seven to age fourteen he took lessons in classical piano and general music instruction with Charles L. Beck. An intelligent and motivated youngster, Nichols attended DeWitt Clinton High School and began study at City College of New York at age fifteen.

While still in high school, Nichols, who was introduced to jazz piano by Roy Testamark, formed an impressive small combo. In 1937 he joined the Royal Baron Orchestra, led by Freddie Williams, which included noted musicians such as bassist George Duvivier, drummer Rip Harewood, and arranger Billy Moore, Jr. Nichols wrote several arrangements for the group so challenging that he himself was afraid to sight-read them. In 1938 he became house pianist at Monroe's Uptown House for rhythm and blues alto saxophonist Floyd "Horsecollar" Williams. There in the late 1930s Nichols participated in the jam sessions that were instrumental in the evolution of an emerging style called bop, playing with Lester Young, Kenny Kersey, and Dizzy Gillespie.

Drafted into the army in September 1941, Nichols went overseas with the Twenty-fourth Infantry Regiment of the Ninety-second Division on standby in the Pacific. During this time he read widely, wrote over fifty poems, and composed a number of tunes. Later in his tour of duty, he was assigned to an army band, first playing drums and then piano. Nichols maintained a strong fondness for the drum. He valued its acoustical properties and African heritage and scored for drums melodically as well as rhythmically.

After his discharge in August 1943, Nichols returned to New York City and attempted to create a forum for his own music with little success. He landed meager work accompanying dancers and singers and learned to play multiple styles during this period, a skill that would allow him to remain a viable working musician for the rest of his life. In 1945 he worked for six months in Harlem with a bop combo featuring alto and baritone saxophonist Sahib Shihab. He recorded with Danny Barker for Apollo records (c. 1946) and worked with swing leader Hal Singer in Brooklyn and Dixieland drummer Freddie Moore at the Village Vanguard. During this time Nichols discovered Thelonious Monk, who had not yet recorded for Blue Note. The two pianists became colleagues, sharing each other's philosophies and insights, and in 1946 Nichols wrote an article for *Music Dial*, one of the earliest known writings about Monk, in which he recognized Monk's unique style and touted his innovative approach.

Nichols traveled the eastern and midwestern dance circuit during late 1946 and early 1947 with a relatively advanced swing band that included noted trombonist J. J. Johnson, tenor saxophonist Illinois Jacquet, and his brother Russell Jacquet on trumpet and vocals. In an unsuccessful attempt to promote his own style, Nichols worked in New York as a freelance pianist and leader later in 1947. He procured several dance jobs in New York City as leader in 1948. He also worked with blues drummer Johnny Felton and supplemented his income by teaching piano privately. At the end of the 1940s he toured the Midwest with John Kirby's band.

Although Nichols was unable to obtain work playing his music in 1950, he recorded as a sideman in swing and rhythm and blues styles for the Mercury, Decca, and Abbey labels. Composer and band leader Edgar Sampson hired Nichols as a sideman at the Club 845 in the Bronx, and during that time he became versed in Latin music styles, particularly the mambo. He also worked with saxophonist Lucky Thompson. For a short time Nichols pursued commercial musical avenues with limited success, writing arrangements for vaudeville acts.

Thelonious Monk introduced Nichols's music to composer and pianist Mary Lou Williams in 1951. Nichols played from his songbook for Williams, who admired Nichols's style. Williams recorded several of his songs, including "The Bebop Waltz" (as "Mary's Waltz"), "Stennel" (as "Opus 2"), and "At Da Function" on her Atlantic recording, *Mary Lou Williams Trio*. This break for Nichols sparked limited interest in his music among audiences previously unfamiliar with his work, and during 1952 in New York he recorded for the first time as a leader with his own quartet for Hi-Lo. An unrehearsed, impromptu effort, the 78 RPM included "S'Wonderful" on one side and Nichols's "Whose Blues" on the flipside. Although the album received a favorable review in *Down Beat*, the only work he landed for the remainder of the year was as a sideman performing Dixieland and blues along the East Coast.

Little changed for Nichols during the next three years. Traveling throughout the East, he worked mostly as a sideman, performing music that diverged from his own style. However, he occasionally had rewarding performance opportunities with musicians such as Sonny Stitt, Rex Stewart, Arnett Cobb, Big Nick Nicholas, and Wilbur de Paris. While he continued to promote his own music to record companies and clubs, Nichols studied classical music, jazz, and music from both Africa and the Caribbean.

Nichols's persistence paid off in 1955 when Al Lion of Blue Note Records, persuaded by Charles Mingus and Teddy Kotick, signed Nichols to record his own original trio compositions. The four dates between May 1955 and April 1956 included drummers Art Blakey and Max Roach and bassists Al McKibbon and Teddy Kotick. The sessions, originally slated for twenty-four compositions, yielded twenty-nine original titles, many of which were distributed over two ten-inch albums titled *The Prophetic Herbie Nichols, Volumes 1 and 2*, released in 1955. Although critically acclaimed on their release, the recordings received scant revenue from sales. Regardless of the previous lack of financial success, Blue Note released additional titles in the twelve-inch album *The Herbie Nichols Trio* the next year.

Nichols continued to perform his own music occasionally in New York City from 1955 to 1958; in November 1955 he performed solo piano sets, sandwiched between sets of Blakey's Jazz Messengers, at the Cafe Bohemia. In 1957 he performed at Basin Street South with a trio including Billy Phillips and G. T. Wilson. Nichols played in the house band at the Page 3, accompanying performers such as the singer Sheila Jordan. Nichols's colleagues, including Thelonious Monk, Randy Weston, and Cecil Taylor, regularly heard him at the club and recognized the distinction of his style. Nichols also recorded his last sessions as a leader for Bethlehem. Seven of these twelve titles were released first as *Love, Gloom, Cash, Love*, later titled *The Bethlehem Sessions*, in 1957.

However, Nichols continued to work more with Dixieland, blues, and swing musicians for his remaining years. During his later years his most regular job was with a revivalist Dixieland band at the Riviera in Greenwich Village, a trendy hangout for Ivy Leaguers. The creative outlets for Nichols's own music were limited to concerts on cruise ships, in concert halls, and at universities. Many of these performances

served as apprentice opportunities for younger musicians. Steve Swallow played alongside Nichols during a shortened tour on a cruise ship in the spring of 1960. Buell Neidlinger first performed with Nichols during one of many Dixieland appearances Nichols made at Jimmy Ryan's. Roswell Rudd performed alongside Nichols and saxophonist Tina Brooks in the fall of 1960 during a jam at a college party at Yale University. Rudd and Neidlinger, both students at Yale University, studied with Nichols during this period. Nichols returned to Yale in the spring of 1961 along with Rudd and Billy Higgins as part of an NAACP benefit concert featuring John Lee Hooker, Paul Bley, and Cecil Taylor.

Nichols's final documented performance of contemporary jazz was a loft concert in 1962 with hard bop and avant-garde saxophonist Archie Shepp and hard bop bassist Ahmad Abdul Malik. Nichols briefly toured Scandinavia during 1962 with a mixed group of Dixieland and apprentice musicians; though he mostly accompanied the larger group, he also had the opportunity to lecture on his own music and to play some trio selections. One of his final appearances was in 1963 in Harlem accompanying the rhythm-and-blues tenor saxophonist Hal "Cornbread" Singer, one of the first musicians ever to employ Nichols. Four months after returning to New York City from a lengthy gig during the fall of 1962 at a Newfoundland air force base, Nichols checked into Kingsbridge VA Hospital, where he was diagnosed with acute myelocytic leukemia. He died several days later. He was never married.

Nichols was an intellectual and serious composer who read widely and wrote nearly fifty poems. His sources of musical inspiration included painting, sculpture, architecture, literature, boxing, and dancing. He was an ardent student of both classical and jazz composers, equally fascinated with works by Bela Bartok, Igor Stravinsky, Johann Sebastian Bach, Ludwig van Beethoven, Frédéric Chopin, Heitor Villa-Lobos, Jelly Roll Morton, Duke Ellington, John Lewis, and Art Tatum. He was also influenced by contemporary musicians and composers like conductor Dmitri Mitropoulos and composers Paul Hindemith, Dmitri Shostakovitch, and Walter Piston. A particular focus upon orchestral literature reflected Nichols's vision of a larger medium for his works that went beyond his trios, including larger sections of winds and brass.

Nichols maintained a detailed personal catalog of his own works, dating from 1939 to 1961. It included approximately 170 titles, twenty-nine recorded by Blue Note and twelve recorded by Bethlehem. Mary Lou Williams recorded four of his titles on Atlantic, and "Lady Sings the Blues" was written for and recorded by Billie Holiday in June 1956. Over half the listed titles included lyrics, and a wide variety of styles were indicated throughout, including ballad, march, stomp, shuffle, blues, waltz, calypso, mambo, tango, swing, and rag.

In addition to western European classical music, Nichols's efforts emphasized constant study of African music and culture. His emphasis on these areas in his music anticipated the contributions of the Association for the Advancement of Creative Musicians and many other musicians of the middle to late 1960s. He commented on the beauty of African village singing and attributed special significance to the drum as a melodic instrument in jazz, with its specific tuning in fifths as a highly desirable quality. His compositions often featured drum parts integrated in a way that was critical to their success. Nichols observed how drummers for bop musicians such as Dizzy Gillespie and Charlie Parker would "drop bombs" at critical points in the structure of a chart, and he stated in an interview with A. B. Spellman, "Each 'bomb' created a newly rich and wholly unexpected series of overtones, beginning in the lower registers. These rich syncopations were fitting accompaniments to the supplemental overtones played by the horns in the higher registers. That is why the pianists became so percussive with their left hands" (Spellman, p. 175). Specific jazz drummers influencing Nichols were Art Blakey, Denzil Best, and Sonny Greer.

Nichols's advanced level of education created a rift between himself and other musicians that was perceived by jazz audiences at large. He felt incompatible with the competitive jazz scene, which he saw as laden with Uncle Toms and drug addicts. His strong, highly personal philosophy about his own compositions and performance was original to jazz musicians of his time. Versed in vastly differing musical idioms, Nichols developed an amalgamated musical style that, although meagerly acknowledged, was unique among his contemporaries.

Roswell Rudd and Buell Neidlinger both recorded Nichols tribute albums, most notably Rudd's 1983 *Regeneration* album for Soul Note. Another tribute is a 1985 album from Soul Note titled *Change of Season*.

• A. B. Spellman, in *Four Lives in the Bebop Business: Black Music, Four Lives* (1966/1970), extensively details Nichols's career. Good information on Nichols is in the liner notes to *The Complete Blue Note Recordings of Herbie Nichols* (Mosaic MR5-118), written by Roswell Rudd, which offers specific biographical information, detailed discographical data, and interviews with several of Herbie's colleagues. See also John Litweiler, *The Freedom Principle: Jazz after 1958* (1984), for stylistic and contextual analysis, and Gary Giddins, *Rhythm-a-ning* (1985), for a discussion of Rudd's tribute album.

DAVID E. SPIES

NICHOLS, Kid (14 Sept. 1869–11 Apr. 1953), baseball player, was born Charles Augustin Nichols in Madison, Wisconsin, the son of Robert James Livingston Nichols, a butcher of Dutch descent, and Christina Skinner. In 1881 the family moved to Kansas City, Missouri, where young Nichols attended school and played sandlot baseball. In 1886 the sixteen-year-old Nichols, after starring for the amateur Blue Avenue team of Kansas City, brashly sought tryouts with three major league teams. Spurned by all three, he began his professional career as a pitcher for the Kansas City club of the minor Western League. The Kansas City fans and newspapers nicknamed him "Kid." After spending two seasons with that club, in 1889 Nichols joined manager Frank Selee's Omaha, Nebraska, team of the Western League, where he compiled a brilliant 36–12 record with 357 strikeouts.

In 1890 Nichols married Jane Curtain of Kansas City, and they would have one daughter. That same year the slim, 5'10½" Nichols was sold to the Boston Beaneaters of the National League for $3,000. Selee, who by then was managing the Boston team, arranged the deal that began Nichols's major league career. Because Boston, like most National League teams in 1890, had lost several players to the rival Players League, the twenty-year-old Nichols became a starting pitcher. Tutored by a pair of veterans, pitcher John Clarkson and catcher Charley Bennett, Nichols made an impressive debut. Relying on an overhand motion to deliver fastballs, curves, and change-ups, and displaying excellent control, Nichols posted a 27–19 record with a league-best seven shutouts.

The following year the Boston team was bolstered by returning veterans from the defunct Players League, and Nichols's 30 victories contributed to the Beaneaters' first league championship since 1883. For Nichols, it was the first of four consecutive seasons during which he won at least 30 games. In two of those seasons, 1892 and 1893, Nichols's combined 69 victories helped Boston win the league championship both years. Indeed, while most pitchers were adversely affected by the 1893 ruling that extended the pitching distance to 60'6", the adaptable Nichols posted a 34–13 record that year. In mastering the new distance Nichols credited his conditioning and control, adding that he always used the same motion for each delivery. The following year, in a season dominated by hitting, Nichols produced a 32–13 record.

Although the Beaneaters finished behind the dominant Baltimore Orioles from 1894 through 1896, Nichols ranked with Amos Rusie and Cy Young as the league's ablest pitchers. After compiling a 26–16 record in 1895, Nichols won 92 games over the following three years to lead all National League pitchers and helped Boston win consecutive pennants in 1897 and 1898.

After Nichols posted a 21–19 mark in 1899, arm trouble contributed to his only losing season at Boston. Nevertheless, in recording his 300th major league victory in 1900, he became the youngest major league pitcher to achieve that lofty goal. For his success Nichols credited his pitching style and his conditioning regimen, both of which enabled him to shoulder a heavy workload. He averaged 426 innings of pitching during each of his first five seasons and 370 a season over the next five.

After finishing the 1901 season with a 19–16 mark, Nichols obtained his release from Boston. His earnings during his 12 seasons with the Beaneaters were limited by the league's prevailing salary cap policy. Most years he received the maximum annual salary of $2,400, but bonuses and expense allowances occasionally augmented his earnings.

In 1902 Nichols rejoined the Kansas City club of the minor Western League as a player-manager. Over the next two seasons he won 48 games and lost 19. However, his hopes of becoming part owner of the team vanished when the club was sold at the end of the 1903 season.

Still an effective pitcher, in 1904 Nichols accepted an offer from owner Frank D. Robison to become player-manager of the St. Louis Cardinals of the National League. In staging a successful comeback to the major-league level, Nichols posted a 21–13 pitching mark and directed a lackluster club to a fifth-place finish. But when the 1905 Cardinals foundered in the early going, the team's co-owner, Stanley Robison, replaced Nichols as manager and later released him as a player. Nichols then joined the National League Philadelphia Phillies and finished the season with an 11–11 pitching record. He rejoined the Phillies in 1906, but, weakened by pleurisy, he lost his only decision and voluntarily ended his major league career.

During his 15-year major league career Nichols appeared in 620 games, starting 561 and completing 531, and pitched a total of 5,056 innings. He compiled a 361–208 record, and his total victories and innings pitched ranked him seventh among major league hurlers; only three pitchers completed more games. Nichols's feat of winning 30 or more games in a season seven times remains unsurpassed. He compiled a lifetime earned run average of 2.95, pitched 48 shutout games, and struck out a total of 1,868 batters while walking only 1,268. In recognition of these achievements, Nichols was voted into the National Baseball Hall of Fame in 1949.

Following his retirement Nichols managed a minor league team in 1908, coached the Missouri Valley College team for several years, and coached and sponsored amateur teams in Kansas City. In 1913 he patented an electric scoreboard that was used for reconstructing games until it was outmoded by radio broadcasts. Nichols also sold insurance, real estate, and automobiles, and he booked movies for a local theater. In his later years he managed a Kansas City bowling establishment. An avid bowler and golfer, he won city championships in both sports. Widowed in 1933, Nichols resided with his daughter in Kansas City, where he died.

• The National Baseball Library in Cooperstown, N.Y., contains a file on Nichols as well as two unpublished manuscripts touching on his career: George V. Tuohey and Tim Murnane, comps., "Boston Base Ball, 1871–1897"; and Tuohey and Murnane, "Charles Augustin Nichols." Nichols's place in baseball history is covered in David Q. Voigt, *American Baseball* (1983); Ira Smith, *Baseball's Famous Pitchers* (1954); and Paul McFarlane, ed., *Hall of Fame Fact Book* (1983). Articles include "'Charlie' Nichols Shows Ambitious Pitchers How to Puzzle Heavy Batsmen," *Boston Post*, 24 Mar. 1901; Randy Linthurst, "When Rusie Opposed Kid Nichols," *Baseball Research Journal* (1976): 112–14; and John J. O'Malley, "Nichols Youngest to Win 300," *Baseball Research Journal* (1975): 95–99. For Nichols's major league statistics, see John Thorn and Pete Palmer, eds., *Total Baseball*, 3d ed. (1993). An obituary is in the *Sporting News*, 11 Apr. 1953.

DAVID Q. VOIGT

NICHOLS, Mary Gove (10 Aug. 1810–30 May 1884), reformer and author, was born Mary Sargeant Neal in Goffstown, New Hampshire, the daughter of William A. Neal and Rebecca R. Neal. Although Mary's formal education was limited, with encouragement from her freethinking father she was reading by the age of six. Her father treated her like a son, and the two often engaged in "intellectual sparring." Despite her abilities, Mary was a shy and lonely child who never felt equal to her siblings.

The family moved to Vermont when Mary was twelve. For two years she was seriously ill and at one time contemplated suicide. At the age of fifteen she became a Quaker. She studied French and Latin and secretly read her brother's medical books. While waiting for a teaching position, she submitted stories, essays, and poems for publication. After her brother hid his books, she obtained medical books through her editor.

On 5 March 1831 she married Hiram Gove, a hatter from New Hampshire. From the first she realized that the marriage was a mistake and referred to it as "martyrdom." When her husband failed financially, a constantly ill and unhappy Mary supported the family with her sewing. The couple had one daughter who survived infancy. But when four subsequent pregnancies resulted in miscarriages or stillbirths Mary sought ways to improve her health. As early as 1832 she used cold-water treatments on herself and neighborhood women. These treatments, consisting of various methods using cold water to bathe and douche, were believed to have a healing effect on the body.

In 1837 the Goves moved to Lynn, Massachusetts, where Gove opened a girls' school. Her health improved when she followed Sylvester Graham's natural system of nutrition, exercise, and daily baths. She joined the lecture circuit in 1838 as the first woman to speak to women publicly about anatomy, hygiene, and physiology. As she presented her material to large audiences she became confident that a woman's awareness of her body and health gave her greater freedom over her own destiny. Her twelve different lectures included the need for improvement in women's status. Some praised the information she presented while others criticized her for moving "out of her sphere."

In addition to lecturing, in 1839 Gove published a pamphlet, "Solitary Vice: An Address to Parents and Those Who Have Care of Children," and articles in the *Boston Medical and Surgical Journal*. In 1840 recurring tuberculosis prevented her from lecturing, and she assumed the editorship of the new *Health Journal and Advocate of Physiological Reform*. When the journal was unsuccessful she returned to lecturing. In 1842 she published *Lectures to Ladies on Anatomy and Physiology*.

Physically and mentally drained from the effects of her troubled marriage Gove left her husband in the early 1840s and returned to her parents' home with her daughter. In 1842 she met Englishman Henry Gardiner Wright, mystic, writer, and teacher, who had come to the United States to establish a utopian community. A mutual attraction developed between the pair, and Gove declared that she was "living love." She began the *Health Journal and Independent Magazine* in 1843, but it quickly failed. In 1845 her husband kidnapped her daughter and she had the child re-kidnapped. She claimed that the stress from the incident caused her to lose much of her hair and to have blurred vision. Tragedy struck her again when Wright had a tumor removed, returned to England, and died in 1846.

Wright had introduced Gove to hydropathy treatments, and when she moved to New York City in 1845 she opened a water-cure establishment where patients followed a cycle of various bathing and sweating treatments. Becoming "one of the American water-cure 'giants,'" she published *Experience in Water-Cure* in 1849. She rejoined the lecture circuit and wrote for the *American Review*, *Godey's Lady's Book*, and the *Water-Cure Journal*. In 1846 she published a novel, *Uncle John*, using the pseudonym Mary Orme. The novel's women characters were representative of the prejudices against women who wandered outside of what society deemed normal behavior.

Wanting to "emancipate women from the needless terrors of childbirth," Gove devised a four-step program that included good health, a woman's discovery of her own body, bathing, and erasing negative thoughts about childbirth. She offered an individualized mail service. Women sent their complete medical history to her, and she replied with the best treatment for an initial fee of $5 and a subsequent fee of $1.

Many intellectuals, Fourierists, and socialists gathered at Gove's home to debate issues of the day. As a member of the New York literati she "moved in the circles of advanced male thinkers." On 29 July 1848, after she was divorced, Gove wed Thomas Low Nichols, a journalist who advocated women's rights. Married by a Swedenborgian clergyman, she made Nichols promise that their relationship would be companionate, and she stated that she "resign[ed] no rights to my soul." The couple had one daughter.

Because women were not allowed into medical school, Mary Nichols's husband attended school for her, teaching her what he learned. After his graduation the couple opened the first college to train students as water-cure physicians in 1851. At the American Hydropathic Institute, located in New York City, they devised "one harmonious system" of lectures. Although successful at first, the school closed because of Thomas Nichols's outspokenness on matters of intimacy and his advocacy of free love. In 1853 they started the *Nichols' Journal of Health, Water-Cure, and Human Progress*, in which they freely advocated their reforms. They failed to receive funding to open a new school intended to teach women about their bodies, control childbearing, and find careers for women that would pay what men earned. Nichols's views were fur-

ther espoused in her autobiographical *Mary Lyndon* (1855) and in a book coauthored with her husband, *Marriage: Its History, Character and Results* (1854).

For a brief period in 1854 Nichols became a Spiritualist. In 1856 "spirits" directed her and her husband to move to Cincinnati, where they opened Memnonia Institute, which they called "a school of health, progress, and harmony." Free love was replaced with chastity, purity of spirit, diet, and self, and no criticism of others. In 1857 during a seance Nichols and her husband were directed by spirits of Jesuits to become baptized in the Catholic faith. After converting to Catholicism, they abandoned their home and institute. Nichols found her "mission" in life by visiting convents and instructing nuns on cleanliness and the "natural laws of health." Travel took a toll on her delicate health, and she stopped touring in 1860.

In 1861 the Nicholses, opposed to the Civil War, left for England. They turned to writing as a means of support, and Nichols published *Uncle Angus*, a novel, in 1864. In the same year the couple moved to Malvern, where they operated a water-cure establishment from 1867 to 1875. Nichols published two pamphlets in 1869, *Vital Law* and *Despotism*, which called for better health standards for children and an elevation in women's status. Two eye surgeries performed in 1875 restored her vision after she nearly went blind. In 1875 the couple opened a health food and water-cure store in London, where Nichols died.

Because of her fragile health, Mary Gove Nichols constantly sought methods to improve the health of women. Outspoken on the issues of women's property rights, temperance, vegetarianism, free love, dress reform, and the right of women to make decisions about their own bodies, Nichols's multifaceted reforms made her a forerunner in the women's rights movement.

• In addition to her works mentioned above, Nichols's writings include three novels, *Agnes Morris; or, The Heroine of Domestic Life* (1849) and *The Two Loves; or, Eros and Anteros* (1849), which were published anonymously, and *Jerry; a Novel of Yankee American Life* (1872). Nichols's articles in the *Water-Cure Journal* include "Mrs. Gove's Experience in Water-Cure" 8 (1849): 98–100; "Maternity, and the Water-Cure of Infants" 11 (1851): 57–59; "A Lecture on Woman's Dresses" 12 (1851): 34–36; and "Woman the Physician" 12 (1851): 73–75. An important account of Mary Gove Nichols is in Janet Hubly Noever, "Passionate Rebel: The Life of Mary Gove Nichols, 1810–1884" (Ph.D. diss., Univ. of Oklahoma, 1983). See also Bertha-Monica Stearns, "Two Forgotten New England Reformers," *New England Quarterly* 6 (Mar. 1933): 59–84; "Memnonia: The Launching of a Utopia," *New England Quarterly* 15 (June 1942): 280–95; Helen Beal Woodward, "Brown Bread, Cold Water, and Sex: Mary Gove-Nichols," in *The Bold Women* (1953); and John B. Blake, "Mary Gove Nichols, Prophetess of Health," *Proceedings of the American Philosophical Society* 3 (June 1962): 219–34. For further background on Nichols's ideas on free love, see John C. Spurlock, *Free Love: Marriage and Middle-Class Radicalism in America, 1825–1860* (1988).

MARILYN ELIZABETH PERRY

NICHOLS, Minerva Parker (14 May 1861?–17 Nov. 1949), architect, was born near Peoria, Illinois, the daughter of John Wesley Parker, a schoolteacher who died serving in the Civil War, and Amanda Melvina Doane, an architect-builder's assistant, a seamstress, and a boardinghouse manager. The first ten years of her life Nichols lived in central Illinois near her grandfather, Seth Brown Doane, an architect-builder, who was assisted by his daughter. As Nichols later recalled, her mother was familiar with "the plane and the saw as well as the compass and T square" (*Philadelphia Real Estate Record and Builders' Guide*, 26 Mar. 1890). In 1876, after a brief residence in Chicago, during which time her mother married a local physician, Samuel Maxwell, Nichols, then fifteen, moved to Philadelphia with her family.

Nichols's higher education was devoted to preparing for a career in architecture, before academic training for the profession became available in Philadelphia. She first obtained a teachers' certificate for drawing from the Philadelphia Normal Art School (1879–1882) and then a certificate upon completion of a full course in architectural drawing at the Franklin Institute (1886). She continued her studies at the Pennsylvania Museum and School of Industrial Arts (1888–1889) during her first year of active practice. The *Philadelphia Real Estate Record and Builders' Guide* (*PRERBG*) (14 Aug. 1889) welcomed Minerva Parker as the only female architect practicing in Philadelphia and one "fully prepared" by her studies in art schools and through practical experience working in architects' offices to practice as an equal of the men in her profession. Nichols probably served her apprenticeship with Edwin W. Thorne, a prolific suburban residential architect, rather than the oft-cited Frederick G. Thorn, a designer of industrial structures for Wilson Brothers. Thorne and Nichols both worked out of 14 South Broad Street in 1888–1889. After Thorne moved, Nichols advertised herself for the first time as an architect in the 1890 Philadelphia city directory and maintained her solo practice at that address until 1894.

The *PRERBG* promoted Nichols's career with a prominent photograph and front-page article on 26 March 1890. Nichols was the fifth individual singled out for this honor, the first and only architect, and the sole woman. Quotations stressed that she believed proper architectural training and licensing were essential regardless of gender to ensure the high quality of the profession. Eleven specific residential commissions were cited, and Nichols affirmed that domestic architecture was her specialty. Her brief six-year career was prolific and diverse. Forty-five of the fifty-three commissions listed in the *PRERBG* between 1888 and 1893 were residential. In addition, she provided designs for an inn, two churches, a school, a store, a foundry, and a spaghetti factory. Although her work was concentrated in the Philadelphia suburbs, she provided designs for clients as far afield as Dr. Ida V. Stambach in Santa Barbara, California. From the outset Nichols worked for men in the building industry, for whom she designed personal dwellings as well as series of houses for their speculative developments.

Ten of her forty-five residences were designed for women, many of whom were professionals. Rachel Foster Avery, a prominent suffragist leader and close friend of Susan B. Anthony, commissioned Nichols to design her house in Somerton, Pennsylvania (1890). Nichols's commitment to the equality of the sexes aligned her with the suffragists and may have been pivotal in her selection in the summer of 1890 by the Queen Isabella Society to design their proposed pavilion at the 1893 Chicago World's Columbian Exposition. Her Spanish design remained unexecuted because of the political differences between the Isabellas and the Board of Lady Managers, especially the president, Bertha Honore Palmer. Publicity accompanying this commission spread Nichols's reputation as a pioneer woman architect. Subsequently she was selected to design the New Century Clubs for Women in Philadelphia (1891) and Wilmington (1892); the latter club still stands. In 1891 she became an instructor of architecture and historic ornament at the Philadelphia School of Design for Women. She also began to receive recognition in professional journals and books. Her design for a house in Cynwyd, Pennsylvania, was published in the leading architectural journal, the *American Architect and Building News* (11 Feb. 1893), and an interior hall view appeared in *Northwestern Architect* (Apr. 1893). Nichols was one of only two architects included in the 1893 volume *A Woman of the Century: Fourteen Hundred-Seventy Biographical Sketches Accompanied by Portraits of Leading American Women in All Walks of Life*, by Frances E. Willard and Mary A. Livermore, and she was the featured "Representative Woman" in *Woman's Progress* (May 1893), which included her essay "Architecture, Architect and Client." The introduction professed that Nichols's femininity never prevented her from supervising the construction of her designs, noting that she "seems to be as much at home on joists and ladders as the ordinary woman is in her parlor," thus refuting an issue often raised by men as to why women could not be coequals as architects. Nichols encouraged her clients to "be familiar with architectural styles," elaborating that "different rooms, with their several uses, can be finished in the various styles with splendid effect. We love the simple classic in a reception room, or the warmth of the East in a library. England gladden[s] our dining-rooms and halls with dark carvings and crackling hearths." Stylistically Nichols has been linked by recent historians to the "Philadelphia Eclectics." In house designs she favored Queen Anne, Shingle, and Colonial Revival styles, whereas her public buildings were designed in the more formal Renaissance, Spanish, and Georgian revivals.

A longtime Unitarian, Minerva Parker married the Reverend William Ichabod Nichols, pastor of the Spring Garden Unitarian Church, Philadelphia, in December 1891. She continued her active architectural practice for two years until 1894, when the first of their four children was born. During that year she moved her office into her home and provided the designs for the Browne and Nichols School in Cambridge, Massachusetts, a school cofounded by her husband's brother. In 1896 she moved with her husband to Brooklyn, where he took up his new position as general secretary of the Brooklyn Bureau of Charities. Throughout her life Nichols maintained her keen interest in architecture. She worked on the Hackley School in Tarrytown, New York, and restored the Unitarian Church in Deerfield, Massachusetts (1913), when her husband became its rector. After her husband's death in 1917, she designed several houses in Westport, Connecticut, where she resided until she died.

Minerva Parker Nichols was the second American woman architect to receive recognition. Unlike Louise Blanchard Bethune, who took her husband as her partner shortly after opening her Buffalo office in 1881, Nichols established the first successful American architectural practice run by a woman working alone, without the assistance or partnership of a man. She was brought into national prominence by her design for the Queen Isabella Society. Her most significant public buildings were the New Century Clubs and the Browne and Nichols School.

• Nichols's drawings are located at the Schlesinger Library, Radcliffe College, in Cambridge, Mass.; at the Delaware Historical Society in Wilmington, Del.; and in the private collection of Caroline Nichols Baker, Racine, Wisc. The most important primary source is the *Philadelphia Real Estate Record and Builders' Guide* for the years 1887 to 1894, especially 19 Dec. 1887, p. 598; 14 Aug. 1889, p. 378; and 26 Mar. 1890, p. 1. Her earliest drawings were published in *Carpentry and Building* 9 (Oct. 1887): 196–97. Articles by her appeared in the *American Architect and Building News*, 10 Dec. 1891, p. 170, and *Woman's Progress* 1 (May 1893): 56–62. An early biographical sketch is in A. A. Doane, *The Doane Family* (1902). Other pertinent sources are Janice C. Croly, *History of the Women's Club Movement in America* (1898); Sandra L. Tatman and Roger W. Moss, *Biographical Dictionary of Philadelphia Architects, 1700–1930* (1985); Susanna Torre, *Women in American Architecture: A Historic and Contemporary Perspective* (1977); Jeanne Madeline Weimann, *The Fair Women* (1981); and Ellen Perry Berkeley, ed., *Architecture: A Place for Women* (1989), pp. 27–40. A photograph of a "House in Germantown, Pa, by Mrs. Minerva Parker Nichols, Architect, Philadelphia" appears in Philip G. Hubert, Jr., "Occupations for Women," *The Woman's Book*, vol. 1 (1894), p. 20. An obituary is in the *New York Times*, 20 Nov. 1949.

KATHLEEN SINCLAIR WOOD

NICHOLS, Red (8 May 1905–28 June 1965), jazz cornetist, was born Ernest Loring Nichols in Ogden, Utah, the son of Ernest W. Nichols, a music teacher and conductor. His mother's name is unknown. Nichols started on the bugle and violin at age three. A year later he was playing cornet in his father's youth band, and by age six he was a soloist. He began playing for dances at age twelve and soon was copying the style of Nick LaRocca, a cornetist with the newly popular Original Dixieland Jazz Band. Although his father considered jazz vulgar, Nichols persisted, winning a

scholarship to Culver Military Academy in Culver, Indiana, where he enrolled in December 1919. Intensely involved in musical activities, he organized the Culver Jazz Band but was expelled in September 1920 for academic deficiencies and minor infractions of school rules.

In 1921 Nichols was back in Ogden, working with his father three nights a week in a theater pit band and sitting in with clarinetist Boyd Senter's band in Salt Lake City, Utah, on his nights off. He left home in March 1922 to join a dance band in Piqua, Ohio. In August of that year, he joined the Syncopating Five, which performed in Indianapolis, Indiana, and in November recorded as the Syncopating Seven in Richmond, Indiana. Renamed the Royal Palms Orchestra, the group then performed in Atlantic City, New Jersey. Nichols joined Johnny Johnson's orchestra in Asbury Park, New Jersey, in September 1923, and when Johnson accepted a more lucrative job in Miami Florida, Nichols took over leadership of the band. In 1924 he led a group that included violinist Joe Venuti at the Pelham Heath Inn, a speakeasy on Pelham Parkway in Westchester County, New York. From 1924 through 1926 he was busy performing with the California Ramblers, Sam Lanin's orchestra, and the Cliquot Club Eskimos. Concurrently he began recording with small studio groups for different record labels under different group names, including the Arkansas Travelers, Lanin's Red Heads, the Hottentots, the Red Heads, and We Three. In this setting his colleagues often included trombonist Miff Mole, drummer and tympanist Vic Berton, and, beginning in 1925, clarinetist and alto saxophonist Jimmy Dorsey. Nichols stated that he often used trumpet rather than cornet because of its more piercing quality, but nothing is known of the details of this distinction in his recorded work.

By 1925 Nichols was also playing in Broadway pit orchestras. In October of that year he recorded "Rhythm of the Day" as a member of Ross Gorman and his Earl Carroll Orchestra, while performing in the *Second Earl Carroll's Vanities*, where he met a dancer, Barbara "Bobbie" Meredith. Late in April 1927 Nichols joined Paul Whiteman's orchestra. While playing at Whiteman's club, as well as in the pit band for the musical *Lucky*, he married Meredith in New York on 4 May 1927. Although Whiteman was the best man at the wedding, Nichols disliked his music and quit his band within a month.

In November 1926, before joining Whiteman, Nichols had signed a presumably exclusive recording contract with the Brunswick company. For the forthcoming recordings, Berton suggested the punning name Red Nichols and his Five Pennies, although in fact the group size ranged from five to twenty pieces over the next five years. During this time the list of Nichols's sidemen—in the Pennies, in Red Nichols' Stompers, in his Captivators, and under other names—reads like a who was who of white jazz. The most important jazz recordings are from the first Pennies sessions of December 1926 to January 1927, which yielded "Washboard Blues," "That's No Bargain," "Buddy's Habits," "Boneyard Shuffle," "Alabama Stomp," and "Hurricane." These recordings present small groups, including Mole, Dorsey, and Berton, playing an amalgamation of solos, carefully arranged passages, and improvised Dixieland counterpoint. Here the Pennies' tone quality is fundamentally in the tradition of the Original Dixieland Jazz Band and is similarly top-heavy, owing to the absence of a bass instrument. Nevertheless, Eddie Lang's guitar and Berton's eccentric tympani drumming added to the traditional mix. Venuti was added for "Bugle Call Rag" (Mar. 1927), and bass saxophonist Adrian Rollini (Nichols's colleague from the California Ramblers) was called in for the sessions of June 1927 that produced "Cornfed" and "Mean Dog Blues."

Over the fifteen years until his wartime retirement, Nichols seemingly tried to follow the winds of jazz fashion without giving up his love of the Dixieland style. After leaving Whiteman he gathered together a larger group, including Pee Wee Russell on clarinet, for recordings of "Eccentric" and "Feelin' No Pain" (Aug 1927). "Eccentric" shows evidence of the Dixieland style giving way to big band jazz in whole passages of block harmonies arranged for the ensemble. That same session produced "Ida, Sweet as Apple Cider," which sold a million copies. This recording starts with a smarmy chorus of reeds playing the harmonized melody, thus carrying the Pennies' style away from jazz and into a mainstream pop tradition that led from Whiteman to Guy Lombardo. By the time of "Alice Blue Gown" (Feb. 1929), Nichols's band showed that it could make substantial steps toward achieving a smooth and relaxed swing rhythm, but this was not characteristic of the Pennies' output. In April 1929 trombonist Glenn Miller arranged "Indiana" for a big band of Pennies including trombonist Jack Teagarden, clarinetist Benny Goodman, and drummer Gene Krupa.

Despite the "exclusive" contract, Nichols continued recording prolifically for other labels during these years. He made discs by Red and Miff's Stompers and Miff Mole's Molers, including another version of "Feelin' No Pain," as well as "Honolulu Blues" (1927) and "Shim-Me-Sha-Wabble" (1928), the last selection involving Chicago-style jazzmen: clarinetist Frank Teschemacher, pianist Joe Sullivan, guitarist Eddie Condon, and Krupa. Nichols also made further recordings by the Arkansas Travelers and Red Heads, and he initiated new pseudonyms: the Charleston Chasers, Six Hottentots, Alabama Red Peppers, Wabash Dance Orchestra, Midnight Airedales, and Louisiana Rhythm Kings, this final name joining together Teagarden, Russell, Sullivan, tenor saxophonist Bud Freeman, and drummer Dave Tough in 1930.

Nichols's dominance of the recording studio temporarily extended into Broadway as well. In 1929 and 1930 Teagarden, Miller, Goodman, Dorsey, and Krupa worked under his direction in the pit orchestra of George Gershwin's musical *Strike Up the Band*, and he then led the band for Gershwin's *Girl Crazy* in 1930

and 1931. In summer 1931 clarinetist Artie Shaw also worked with Nichols.

During the mid-1930s Nichols became a studio musician for CBS radio, directing music for the "Ruth Etting Show" (1934–1935) and, following a tour as bandleader, the "Atlantic Family Program" (1935), which featured Bob Hope. Nichols also directed the "Kellogg Prom Show" (1935–1936).

In the late 1930s Nichols led a big band based as much in Dixieland jazz as in the swing style. The group stayed together with many interruptions and changes in personnel until spring 1942, when Nichols sold the band and settled temporarily in San Leandro, California. In 1943 his only child was stricken by polio, encephalitis, and spinal meningitis, ultimately paralyzed from the waist down. To earn money for her care, Nichols abandoned music and worked as a welder at the Pacific Bridge shipyards in Alameda, California. He then resumed playing, spending the first half of 1944 in Glen Gray's orchestra. In May, while he was in New York with Gray, his wife moved the family to Los Angeles in the hope that warm weather would be better for their daughter. By adulthood she was fully recovered.

Nichols re-formed the Pennies in September 1944, and they began recording for producer Dave Dexter on the Capitol label. In a bizarre situation, the evidently old-fashioned Dexter attempted to have Nichols replace trumpeter Howard McGhee for Coleman Hawkins's sextet session early in 1945, although Nichols couldn't play the music and McGhee could. The Pennies were mainly active in southern California at the El Morocco Club from 1945 to 1948, the Hangover Club from 1948 to 1951, the Playroom from 1951 to 1953, and Marineland, but they also performed in San Francisco, Phoenix, Reno, and Las Vegas. Nichols also worked in studio orchestras. After an article in *Reader's Digest* called attention to the drama of his interrupted career, he became the subject of a somewhat fictionalized Hollywood film biography, *The Five Pennies* (1959), starring Danny Kaye as Nichols. Consequently, he began to tour more widely, including a stand at the Roundtable in New York in 1959, a State Department tour to the Near East in 1960, and another overseas tour in 1964. After further jobs in California and Nevada, he died in Las Vegas.

Like most jazz musicians, Nichols adamantly claimed to have achieved an individual style of his own. The recordings speak otherwise, exhibiting a deep debt to Bix Beiderbecke's restrained and elegant soloing but without Beiderbecke's melodic perfection and emotional impact. Nichols was nonetheless a fine cornetist whose work is characterized by consistency, a pretty timbre, precise technique, and organization. Certainly he does not deserve the vicious remarks about him that have circulated in the jazz literature, remarks stemming probably from friction caused by his dominance of the field rather than from a levelheaded assessment of his jazz-making. Writer Rockey Spicer maintains that, to the college crowd, Nichols's ever-changing mid-1920s studio group was "the best jazz band in the country." His recordings were critical in the dissemination of the music, and "he, perhaps as much as anyone, made jazz socially acceptable" (Spicer, pp. 44–46).

• Nichols's papers, including music, are held at the University of Oregon, Eugene; his record collection is at the University of Kansas, Lawrence. Additional unpublished notes from Rockey Spicer's interview with Nichols are in the files of the Institute of Jazz Studies, Newark, N.J. For specific biographical information see Stephen M. Stroff, *Red Head: A Chronological Survey of Red Nichols and His Five Pennies* (1996). Another contemporary assessment is Stanley Hester, *The Red Nichols Story: After Intermission, 1942–1965* (1986). For more information on Nichols, see Grady Johnson, *The Five Pennies: The Biography of Jazz Band Leader Red Nichols* (1959), and Horst L. Lange, *Loring "Red" Nichols: Ein Porträt* (1960). Interviews are by Charles Emge, "Jazz Hit Its Highest Peak to Date on My Mid-'20s Records: Nichols," *Down Beat* 18 (7 Sept. 1951): 2–4, 16, and Rockey Spicer, "Nichols' Worth of Music," *Westways* 66 (Aug. 1974): 44–47, 70, 73. Wally Backensto surveys Nichols's career and catalogs his recordings in "The Red Nichols Story," *Record Research* 2 (Apr.–May 1957): 3–11, and "Red Nichols Memorial Issue," *Record Research*, no. 96/97 (Apr. 1969): 2–17, including corrections to the imaginary portions of Johnson's pulp biography. Three articles on Nichols are collected in *Down Beat* 26 (9 July 1959): 19–23. Further catalogs of recordings by John R. T. Davies appeared in *Storyville* from Feb./Mar. 1978 through Apr./May 1979. See also Otis Ferguson, "The Five Pennies," in *Jazzmen*, ed. Frederic Ramsey, Jr., and Charles Edward Smith (1939; repr. 1977). Obituaries are in the *New York Times*, 29 June 1965, and *Down Beat* 32 (12 Aug. 1965): 10.

BARRY KERNFELD

NICHOLS, Ruth Rowland (23 Feb. 1901–25 Sept. 1960), aviation pioneer, was born in New York City, the daughter of Erickson Norman Nichols and Edith Corlis Haines. Nichols's father was a member of the New York Stock Exchange and sent his daughter to exclusive private schools. She graduated from Miss Masters' School at Dobbs Ferry, New York, and from Wellesley College in 1924. An average student, Nichols was interested in athletics and other strenuous activities. She was encouraged in these endeavors by her father, who had an adventurous spirit himself, having joined the Rough Riders under Theodore Roosevelt (1858–1919) and trying other stunts with varying degrees of danger thereafter.

Nichols first fell in love with airplanes when her father took her to an air show at Atlantic City, New Jersey, in 1919 as a reward for her graduation from Miss Masters' School. When she visited Florida during a break from Wellesley in 1922, she took flying lessons from Harry Rogers and received the first hydroplane pilot's license issued to a woman by the Federation Aeronautique Internationale. From then on she was hooked, and although she worked for a time in a New York City bank, she quickly turned to aviation as her life's work. "I felt as if my soul were completely freed from my earthly body," she later recalled.

Nichols first gained notice as the co-pilot for Harry Rogers during a nonstop flight from New York to Miami in 1928, being called by the press, to her horror, the "Debutante Aviatrix." Almost immediately thereafter she permanently left her bank job to sell aircraft for the Fairchild Aviation Corporation. Moderately successful, in 1929 she traveled throughout the United States in a Curtiss "Fledgling" aircraft to establish a chain of aviation country clubs for sports fliers. Most, however, did not survive long after the stock market crash of October 1929. At essentially the same time, Nichols and Amelia Earhart formed a pilots' organization for women, the "Ninety-Nines," which for years advanced equality for women in aviation.

Throughout the 1930s Nichols engaged in several aviation activities ranging from work for Fairchild Aviation and other aircraft companies to making record-setting flights. In 1930 she set a cross-country flight record of 13 hours and 21 minutes, shaving an hour off a mark set by Charles A. Lindbergh on a Los Angeles to New York flight. On 6 March 1931 she set a women's world altitude record of 28,743 feet, and the next month she set the women's world speed record of 210.754 miles per hour. She later set records in a Lockheed Vega, named *Akita*, a single-engine, high-wing monoplane of monocoque wood construction. The Vega would become her trademark throughout the decade.

Soon thereafter Nichols toyed with the idea of flying around the world in the Vega, but pilot Clarence Chamberlin suggested instead that she make a solo transatlantic flight, the first woman to do so. Following up on the suggestion, Nichols took off from Floyd Bennett Field, New York, on 22 June 1931, amid great fanfare. The attempt soon failed, however, because Nichols crashed at St. John, New Brunswick, the result of a mechanical failure. The crash effectively ended her attempt—she went to the hospital with five cracked vertebrae—but weather and lack of funds also prevented her from trying again. Nichols was philosophical about her crash. She commented that "when a person loves flying and understands it and knows the reason for an accident, there is no fear. I could hardly wait to be in the air again. That's just natural."

By 25 October 1931 Nichols had recovered sufficiently to attempt another flight record. This time, supported by a special steel brace for her back, she set a women's distance record of 1,977 miles in 14 hours during a flight from Oakland, California, to Louisville, Kentucky. On 17 February 1932 Nichols set another record, the diesel engine altitude record for men and women, with a flight to 19,928 feet. On 29 December 1932 she set another record, perhaps more significant in the long run, as the first woman pilot for a passenger airline by flying for New York and New England Airways. This airline, operated by Chamberlin, failed within a few months because of the depression.

Through most of the rest of the 1930s Nichols engaged in a series of varied aviation activities. She participated in air shows and races, lectured at universities and civic gatherings, and did some barnstorming. She recalled that during these years most pilots seemed to mark time because there was little money for what she called "big-time aviation." Among other things, Nichols and Chamberlin flew Condor transports all over New England, giving rides to people for a dollar a head. Disaster struck Nichols's barnstorming on 21 October 1935, when she was flying as a co-pilot for a Condor just as it left Try, New York, bound for another engagement. Harry Hublitz, in the pilot's seat as one engine exploded, crash-landed the aircraft. Passengers were injured only slightly, but Nichols, who was thrown clear of the aircraft, suffered numerous broken bones, cuts, and burns. Hublitz died of his wounds a few hours later.

For nearly a year Nichols recuperated, and by the summer of 1936 she was able to walk with a cane. Excited by the prospects of women pilots winning the Bendix Trophy for cross-country racing, a first for the time, Nichols decided to get back into flying, this time with the Emergency Peace Campaign. Working out of the organization's headquarters in Philadelphia, she found that the Quaker-dominated effort provided her with an emotional boost she had not felt in years. Flying throughout the Northeast and Midwest on behalf of the organization, Nichols tried to alert Americans to the immediacy of war and to organize efforts to promote peace.

With the coming of war in Europe in 1939, Nichols organized a flying school at Garden City, New York, training pilots as part of the Civilian Pilot Training Program sponsored by the Civil Aeronautics Authority. The next year she became a director of the newly organized Relief Wings, a humanitarian effort to join private planes and airports in coordinating and carrying out emergency and relief efforts. Nichols also worked with the Civil Air Patrol during the war and with the White Plains, New York, Hospital from 1945 to 1947. She did work for the United Nations International Children's Emergency Fund (UNICEF) and in July 1949 made a round-the-world flight on its behalf.

In 1952 Nichols became the director of women's activities for the Save the Children Federation in New York City, serving until 1954. Then she became director of the women's division of the United Hospital Fund, and in 1958 she took over as field director for the National Nephrosis Foundation. In every case Nichols mixed her humanitarian activities with her love of flying, using her celebrity status and airplane to raise funds and increase recognition for the cause. She also successfully lobbied for permission from the air force to fly a supersonic jet. In 1958, at age fifty-seven, she co-piloted a jet to a speed of 1,000 miles per hour and an altitude of 51,000 feet, the highest altitude achieved by any woman to that date. In 1960 Nichols was suffering from deep depression and was placed in a doctor's care. After an overdose of barbiturates she died in New York City.

Her death put to rest the warring elements of Ruth Nichols's life. As she explained in her autobiography, she had inherited two important conflicting attitudes, an adventurous nature with a certain self-destructiveness that came from her father and a deeply spiritual commitment to the welfare of others that came from her mother's Quaker ancestry. She played these themes out throughout her life, blending them more effectively after her near-fatal 1935 crash. Yet she believed that the love of speed and danger was not entirely reconcilable with the spiritual perfection of humanity. Regardless of her personal dilemma, Nichols was a leading member of a single generation of pilots who brought to most Americans a fundamental shift in the way in which they approached travel, prodding them from land and sea to air transport.

• There is no formal collection of Nichols's papers, but some materials are held by the Ninety-Nines at Oklahoma City. Material by and about her can be found in scattered collections at the National Air and Space Museum, Smithsonian Institution. The Oral History Collection's Aviation Project at Columbia University has an oral history with Nichols completed not long before her death. Her autobiography is *Wings for Life*, ed. Dorothy Roe Lewis (1957). Short sketches of her career can be found in Cecil R. Roseberry, *The Challenging Skies: The Colorful Story of Aviation's Most Exciting Years, 1919–1939* (1966), and Jean Adams et al., *Heroines of the Sky* (1970). An obituary is in the *New York Times*, 26 Sept. 1960.
ROGER D. LAUNIUS

NICHOLS, Thomas Low (1815–1901), hydrotherapist, health educator, and writer, was born in Orford, New Hampshire. His parents, whose names are unknown, were probably farmers. After growing up in New England, he enrolled in Dartmouth Medical College in 1834, only to drop out without earning a degree. Over the next six years he pursued journalism, submitting columns to the *New York Herald* and writing for newspapers in Lowell, Massachusetts, and Buffalo, New York. In Buffalo he helped found and write for a political magazine, the *Buffalonian*. His contributions to it resulted in a four-month imprisonment for libel, the story of which he self-righteously related in his first book, *Journal in Jail* (1840). After his liberation from Buffalo, Nichols moved to New York City, where he continued to write fiction and nonfiction. He developed an interest in communal living arrangements and studied the work of Josiah Warren, Charles Fourier, and John Noyes.

In 1848 Nichols married a hydrotherapist and popular health lecturer, Mary S. Gove, with whom he had one child. Together they opened a water-cure house in New York City that provided an alternative approach to healing—relying on baths, wet-sheet packs, fresh air, exercise, a healthy diet, and abstinence from tobacco, alcohol, medication, and most invasive medical procedures. From 1849 to 1852 he was a regular contributor to the *Water-Cure Journal and Herald of Reforms* and the *American Vegetarian and Health Journal*, writing on vegetarianism, preservation of health, and management of specific illnesses. The *Water-Cure Journal* later refused his work in response to his advocacy of free love, the philosophy that "passional affinities" rather than legal contracts should guide a person's love life. Nichols argued especially for women's right to refuse sexual relationships devoid of love, even in marriage. These writings were widely misinterpreted and abused as supporting promiscuity. Always in pursuit of an audience and never shying from controversy, the Nicholses founded their own hydropathic journal, *Nichols' Journal of Health, Water-Cure, and Human Progress*, in which Thomas Nichols defined the conditions of health as "a sound constitution, a pure nutrition, and a free exercise of all the organs of the body, and all the faculties and passions of the soul" (May 1853).

Thomas Nichols's more significant works of this period include *Woman in All Ages and Nations* (1849), *The Curse Removed* (1850), and *Introduction to Water-Cure* (1850). In the last he charged, "The whole system of allopathy [orthodox medicine] is one of weakening and poisoning. Every good it gains, is the infliction of some mischief." In 1851, one year after he earned his medical degree from the University of the City of New York and was elected secretary of the American Hygienic and Hydropathic Association of Physicians and Surgeons, Nichols and his wife established the nation's first hydropathic medical school, the coeducational American Hydropathic Institute. In 1852 they moved their school to Port Chester, New York.

The following year Nichols published a widely read and sexually explicit physiology textbook, *Esoteric Anthropology*, followed in 1854 by *Marriage: Its History, Character, and Results*, coauthored with his wife. A central thesis of these texts was that a woman should determine when and whether she would have children, and who the father of those children would be. Efforts to found an "Institute of Life" called "Desarrollo" adjacent to the Long Island commune "Modern Times" were stymied by members' hostility toward the Nicholses' free-love dogmatism.

Distanced from the water-cure leadership in New York and increasingly interested in spiritualism, the Nicholses moved in 1855 to Cincinnati, where they published *The Nichols' Monthly*. Separately, Thomas Nichols published *Religions of the World*, a comparative textbook. The following year the couple established a short-lived "School of Life," the Memnonia Institute, in Yellow Springs, Ohio, only to abandon the project suddenly in 1857 when the family somewhat mysteriously converted to Catholicism. The Nicholses described their conversion as inspired by a visiting spirit who, during a spiritualist séance, instructed them to adopt Catholicism. For several years the Nicholses continued to lecture on health and hygiene at a variety of Catholic institutions, recanting prior teachings and writings that were at odds with the church.

The couple returned to New York City in 1861 but felt unable to pursue their writing and lecturing in the tense and politically restrictive atmosphere preceding the Civil War. Nichols wrote, "The Union lost all charm for me when it was no longer the free choice of the people, and had to be imposed by arms upon even a single State" (*Forty Years of American Life* [1864], p. 5). The Nicholses therefore emigrated permanently to England later that same year.

Before establishing a new water-cure facility in Malvern in 1867, the Nicholses supported themselves as journalists and writers of short fiction. Thomas Nichols wrote for *Chambers' Encyclopedia* and *All the Year Round*, was a correspondent for the *New York Times*, and briefly published the *Nichols' Journal of Sanitary and Social Science*. His two-volume text, *Forty Years of American Life* (1864), playfully and vividly describes the geography and mannerisms of Americans; it was reprinted well into the twentieth century. In 1875 he began editing and publishing the *London Herald of Health*, continuing his life's work as an advocate of health reform and vegetarianism.

Mary Nichols died in 1884; three years later Nichols published a moving tribute to her, *Nichols' Health Manual, Being Also a Memorial to the Life and Work of Mary S. Gove Nichols*. This devoted book quotes his wife's diaries and published writings at length and recounts much of their life together.

Writing ceaselessly on topics that would become some of the next century's most pressing health concerns—reproductive rights, domestic violence, second-hand smoke, fatty diets, and the importance of good hygiene and regular exercise—Nichols led in the belief that health reform should be the foundation of social reform. The popular health movement represented one among many nineteenth-century reform initiatives, including abolitionism, temperance, women's rights, dress reform, the free-love movement, and Fourierism. As a health advocate considered radical even by fellow reformers, Nichols viewed medical knowledge as a means of individual empowerment. He died in Chaumont-en-Venzin, France.

• Many of Nichols's publications are held at the American Antiquarian Society in Worcester, Mass., and at the library of the British Museum. Additional books by Nichols include *Ellen Ramsay* (1843), *Lady in Black* (1844), *Raffle for a Wife* (1845), *Nichols' Medical Miscellanies* (1856), *Esperanza* (1860), *Father Larkin's Mission in Jonesville* (1860), *Biography of the Brothers Davenport* (1864), *How to Live on Sixpence a Day* (1871), *Human Physiology, the Basis of Sanitary and Social Science* (1872), *How to Behave* (1873), *How to Cook* (1873), *Eating to Live* (1881), *Dyspepsia* (1884), and *Social Life: A Manual of Morals and Good Behaviour* (1895). See Susan Cayleff, *Wash and Be Healed* (1987), and Jane Donegan, *"Hydropathic Highway to Health": Women and Water-Cure in Antebellum America* (1986), on his relationship to the water-cure community; Roger Wunderlich, *Low Living and High Thinking at Modern Times, New York* (1992), on his involvement with the free-love community; Philip Gleason, "From Free-Love to Catholicism: Dr. and Mrs. Thomas L. Nichols at Yellow Springs," *Ohio Quarterly* 70 (1961): 283–307, on his conversion; and Bertha-Monica Stearns, "Two Forgotten New England Reformers," *New England Quarterly* 6 (1933): 59–84, on his other writings.

JEAN SILVER-ISENSTADT

NICHOLS, William (? 1780–12 Dec. 1853), architect, was probably born in Bath, England, likely the son of Samuel Nichols, a carpenter builder who also served as surveyor to the city of Bath. He acquired competence in the rudiments of standard construction in brick and wood, surveying, planning, and drafting, before emigrating to the United States around 1800. He was probably also familiar with the era's major architectural books, including James Stuart and Nicholas Revett's *Antiquities of Athens* (1762–1805). He later acquired George Richardson's *New Vitruvius Britannicus* (1802), Peter Nicholson's *Architectural Dictionary* (1819), and Minard Lafever's *The Beauties of Modern Architecture* (1839). Their engravings represented the essential currency of contemporary architectural discourse and the means by which the Greek Revival became the first modern international style—the profiles of ancient edifices used as the design for construction. The scant documents associated with Nichols's career record that he eventually owned an extensive library and collection of prints.

He first practiced in North Carolina, in the towns of New Bern and Edenton, where addition of a spire to St. Paul's Church (1806–1809) established him as "Architect and House Joiner." His choice of that region might have been encouraged by the prior presence of William Tatham, another emigrant from his native west country of England who was active in the coastal survey of North Carolina (1805–1806). There he established the stylistic constituents of his work applying to traditional Palladian formal compositions classic revival motifs drawn from the publications and their interpretation in Britain just prior to his emigration. The New Bern Academy, for example, is fronted by a curved portico probably inspired by the domestic architecture of John Soane. In smaller commissions such as the Skinner Law Office in Edenton (attribution), he neatly dignified the typical frame box with a Greek anta (square column) portico, displaying both his adaptability and that of Greek forms as replicated in engravings to vernacular wood construction. This pragmatic historicism seems to have brought a series of domestic commissions culminating in "Hayes," the plantation house for James C. Johnston near Edenton (1814–1817). He used the Tuscan Doric hexastyle fullheight portico to span the main central block, effectively transposing British high-style architecture to Southern planter society.

Nichols evidently accepted the racial and political prejudices of the plantocracy and also accommodated himself to the coalescing of pan-state nationalism attendant upon the War of 1812. He became a U.S. citizen in 1813. After a brief visit to New York in 1817, he was appointed state architect of North Carolina (1817–1825); in 1818 the title changed to superintendent of public works. He refurbished the existing State House (by Rodham Atkins) in Raleigh, adding a handsome engaged entrance portico and Greek detailing. He also included space in the rotunda for Antonio Canova's statue of George Washington, installed under Nichols's supervision in 1821. When the building burned, however, Nichols was replaced by the New York firm of Ithiel Town and Andrew J. Davis for work on the new capitol. He then worked on his own. He made an addition to the "Governor's Palace" (1820–1824) in Raleigh and built the New Chapel (now Gerrard Hall) at the University of North Carolina (1824–1826).

Nichols visited New York in 1824, Washington, D.C., and Tennessee (surveying property owned by the University of North Carolina). He moved to Alabama, becoming state architect (1827–1831) and state engineer (1831–1833). He typified the peripatetic career patterns of architects in the early Republic. The apparent durability of the ancient architectural vocabulary that Nichols wielded so adeptly clearly resonated among the new settler communities. His Ionic-projected portico and rotunda of the State Capitol at Tuscaloosa (1827–1831, replaced in 1847) manifested stability. Nichols also designed several two-story or full-height porticoed plantation houses, notably those for James Dearing, General Dennis Dent, and Samuel Meek in Tuscaloosa (1828–1834). Each house reflects his ability to recast current design conventions, as also represented by his use of the double distyle-in-antis portico of Christ Church in Tuscaloosa (1829–1831) and by his revision of the Jeffersonian model for the Rotunda at the University of Alabama he designed in the same period.

During most of this period Nichols resided with his second wife, Sarah Simons, whom he had married in 1815, some two years after the death of his first wife of eight years, Mary Rew. His third marriage, to Lydia Lucinda Smith, was solemnized in 1836 and continued to his death.

Nichols completed surveys for the proposed Tennessee Canal and a proposed railroad between the Tennessee and Alabama rivers in 1832–1833. He applied, unsuccessfully, for the post of state architect of Mississippi in 1835 on the grounds that he "had more experience in the construction of State Capitols than any individual in the Union—and from being well versed in the vicious prices and modes of building in the Southern country . . . could bring with [him] a fund of information which would result in producing an Edifice not surpassed for Elegance, Convenience, Stability, and Economy of Expenditure by any building of similar Character of the Union" (quoted in Peatross, p. 23).

Nichols served as assistant state engineer, then as assistant state architect in Louisiana (1833–1835). He adapted Benjamin H. Latrobe's Charity Hospital in New Orleans for the Louisiana Legislature (1835) and designed the state penitentiary at Baton Rouge (1836–1841). By contrast, Nichols's Mississippi State Capitol in Jackson (1835) translated the national Capitol of Charles Bulfinch into the disciplined classicism of metropolitan Greek Revival. Equally sophisticated is his temple-fronted Lyceum at the University of Mississippi, Oxford (1845–1848), where he planned the octagonal campus and completed other buildings including two fine faculty houses. He also designed the elegant Corinthian-pilastered and semicircular porticoed Governor's Mansion in Jackson (c. 1836–1842) and dabbled in revivalist styles of the Gothic for the Mississippi State Penitentiary in Jackson (1836–1841) and the Italianate for Colonel J. M. Dyer's "Terry-

Stone" in Lexington (c. 1853). But his courthouse in Yazoo, Mississippi (1849–1850, demolished), and the Lexington Female Academy in Lexington, erected in the year of his death, are in his Greek Revival style. Both testify to his adept adaptation of ancient models to modern American conditions and cultural aspirations. Also notable was his nurturance of higher levels of design, craft, and construction, particularly as a teacher of the North Carolina architect John Berry. Nichols contributed substantially to the fabric of the pre–Civil War South, and if less innovative than such other British émigrés as William Jay and John Haviland, he had a sure sense of proportion and symbolism.

• Reference to Nichols's public work exists in the archives of the states for which he worked as architect or engineer: North Carolina, Alabama, Louisiana, and Mississippi. Other material is preserved in special collections at the libraries of Tulane University, the University of Mississippi, Mississippi State University and at the Louisiana Room of Louisiana State University, Historic New Orleans Collection, and the Southern Historical Collection and North Carolina Room at the University of North Carolina at Chapel Hill.

The major written study, albeit relatively brief as a result of the dearth of archival records, is C. Ford Peatross, *William Nichols, Architect*, compiled to coincide with an exhibition at the University of Alabama Art Gallery in 1979. It includes an appendix by Robert O. Mellown rejecting the traditional attribution to Nichols of the President's Mansion at the University of Alabama. Besides considerably extending and illustrating the architect's oeuvre, Peatross corrects misinformation in the scant preceding literature while acknowledging the early scholarly recognition accorded to Nichols by Talbot Hamlin in his seminal *Greek Revival Architecture in America* (1944) and Cecil D. Elliot's articles on the North Carolina Capitol published in the *Southern Architect* in 1958.

RHODRI WINDSOR LISCOMBE

NICHOLS, William Henry (9 Jan. 1852–21 Feb. 1930), industrial chemist and entrepreneur, was born in Brooklyn, New York, the son of George Henry Nichols and Sarah Elizabeth Harris, a Quaker. He attended the Polytechnic Institute of Brooklyn from 1865 to 1868, when it was still effectively a preparatory school and where he was first exposed to and fascinated by the study of chemistry. After several months at Cornell University, he was asked to leave when he refused to reveal the names of his cohorts in allegedly placing a team of horses and a cart on a dormitory roof. Nichols moved in 1869 to New York University, where John W. Draper, one of the leading chemists of the day, became his mentor. An obviously bright student, Nichols received a B.S. from New York University in 1870 and earned an M.S. from that institution in 1873. That same year he married Hannah Wright Bensel of Brooklyn; they had three children.

In 1870 Nichols and his friend Charles W. Walter founded Walter and Nichols, a manufacturer of acids. Because of Nichols's youth, his father assumed financial responsibility of and gave his name to the company, which was incorporated a year later as G. H. Nich-

ols & Co. After Walter's untimely death in about 1875, Nichols hired Francis J. B. Herreshoff as factory manager. Herreshoff's scientific and technical capabilities would later prove invaluable to the young firm's subsequent growth in the chemical industry.

A primary product of the Nichols firm was sulfuric acid of a higher concentration than standard industry grade. Objecting to Nichols's insistence on manufacturing the higher-strength acid, his competitors sought to take his business by undercutting the price. But because acid refining of petroleum, which required the stronger acid, was just at that time beginning to emerge, Nichols's firm was flooded with orders.

Nichols acquired a Canadian copper pyrites mine to serve as an alternative source to Sicilian sulfur, which though almost pure was expensive. With the invention of a special water-jacket smelting furnace developed by Herreshoff, the company extended its product range through the sale of copper matte, an intermediary by-product. Nichols himself later developed an electrolytic method for the production of copper. As the metallurgical business expanded, the company became increasingly profitable through not only the production of copper but also the recovery of gold and silver. In 1890 the company was reorganized into Nichols Chemical Co. and Nichols Copper Co.; Nichols served as president of both.

In 1899 Nichols Chemical Co. joined with eleven other firms to form the first heavy chemicals consolidation, General Chemical Co. Nichols was named president, and in 1907, when he became chairman of the concern, his son William H., Jr., was appointed president. Nichols's other son, Charles, was named a director of the company. (In this consolidation the Nichols copper business was kept separate.) The new company initially produced products that were largely dependent on the production of sulfuric acid (still the company's most important line), but new compounds and derivatives were quickly added, which brought the total number of products to over 300.

At this time most sulfuric acid was produced through the chamber process, by which it was difficult to attain stronger pure concentrations of the acid. Development of a contact or catalytic process in Europe in 1901 led Nichols and Herreshoff to experiment successfully with a nonpatent-infringing process suitable to American conditions. After acquiring the necessary European patents, General Chemical plants adopted the contact process by 1905. This process facilitated the production of oleum, which was used in the production of petroleum products, munitions, and dyestuffs.

Nichols subsequently became interested in using catalysis to synthesize ammonia through atmospheric nitrogen fixation. Announcement of the German Haber process (named after the German chemist Fritz Haber, who developed an ammonia synthesis process by the direct catalytic combination of nitrogen and hydrogen) led Nichols and his colleague Frederick W. de Jahn to begin work in 1911 on a similar process, which was in experimental use by 1916. The process was offered to the U.S. government, and although a full-scale plant, U.S. Nitrate Plant #1, had been completed by the time of the armistice, it was not yet in commercial operation. In 1919 Nichols formed a subsidiary, Atmospheric Nitrogen Co., to manufacture ammonia.

In 1910 General Chemical, in conjunction with Barrett Manufacturing Co. and Semet-Solvay Co., had organized Benzol Products Co. to produce aniline oil and salts used as dye intermediates, but Germany continued to dominate the dye industry until World War I. In 1917 Benzol Products joined with National Aniline, Schoellkopf Aniline and Chemical Works, and Beckers Aniline and Chemical Works to form National Aniline and Chemical Co., with Nichols as its first chairman. Within several years this new company was producing 55 to 60 percent of America's domestic dyes and exporting an amount larger than the total of prewar German imports.

In December 1920 Nichols engineered his final and largest merger when he brought together Barrett, General Chemical, National Aniline and Chemical, Semet-Solvay, and Solvay Process to form Allied Chemical and Dye Co. as a holding company of which he became chairman, a position he held until his death.

In Nichols were combined the skills of the professionally trained scientist and the perceptive industrialist. Alert to the changing nature of the chemical industry and its increasing reliance on scientific and technical development, he was a lifelong advocate of research and scientific education. The Nichols Medal, which he created for the American Chemical Society (ACS) in 1902, was established to recognize original work that would stimulate chemical research. In his 1908 address on the award of the Perkin Medal to Herreshoff, he emphasized that he had hired Herreshoff because of his formal training and without concern about his lack of practical experience. This theme of the importance of scientific training and research was also echoed in Nichols's 1919 presidential address for the American Chemical Society.

Active in many professional and industrial areas, Nichols was founding member in 1876 of the ACS and served as its president in 1918–1919. He also played a role in founding the Chemists' Club of New York in 1898, and he was president of the Society of Chemical Industry in London in 1904–1905, one of only four Americans at that time to have been so honored. During World War I he served as chairman of the Committee on Chemicals of the Council of National Defense and later as an incorporator of the Chemical Alliance, a private body of industrial executives, which in effect took over coordination of the nation's wartime needs for chemical production and pricing. Between Nichols was a director and vice president of both the Corn Exchange Bank and the Title Guarantee and Trust. He was also a member of the American Association for the Advancement of Science, the Canadian Mining Institution, the American Electro-Chemical Society, the Franklin Institute, and Phi Beta Kappa.

Nichols was acknowledged as having played an important role in the formation of the modern chemical industry, both as a chemist and an industrial entrepreneur. His colleagues regularly referred to him as "Doctor" in recognition of his many pioneering scientific accomplishments, which included contributing to the development of processes for the catalytic manufacture of sulfuric acid, the electrolytic refining of copper, and the production of synthetic ammonia. He also played a key role in the organization of the modern chemical industry by coordinating its first large-scale merger, which resulted in the formation of General Chemical and subsequently of Allied Chemical and Dye Co., which at the time of his death was one of the largest chemical concerns in the United States. He died in Honolulu, Hawaii.

• Nichols left no known collection of personal papers. Among his most important published essays are "The Chemist and Reconstruction," *Journal of Industrial and Engineering Chemistry* 11 (May 1919): 399–400; "Chemistry at New York University—A Retrospect," *Journal of Chemical Education* 5 (Apr. 1928): 448–51; "The Efficiency and Deficiencies of the College-Trained Chemist, When Tested in the Chemical Field," *Journal of Industrial and Engineering Chemistry* 1 (Feb. 1909): 102–5; "The Future of the American Dye Industry," *Journal of Industrial and Engineering Chemistry* 11 (Jan. 1919): 53–55; "The Management of a Chemical Industrial Organization," *Journal of the Society of Chemical Industry* 24 (15 July 1905): 707–12; and "Research and Application," *Journal of Industrial and Engineering Chemistry* 11 (Oct. 1919): 917–21. While no biography is available, William Haynes, *American Chemical Industry*, vol. 2 (1945) and vol. 6 (1949), is helpful for understanding the chemical industry of the period. See also a biographical sketch by Daniel P. Jones and Robert F. Gould in *American Chemists and Chemical Engineers*, ed. Wyndham Miles (1976), pp. 363–65, and two contemporary sketches, one by James F. Norris in *Industrial and Engineering Chemistry* 18 (Mar. 1926): 317–19 and the other by Charles Robinson Smith in *Industrial and Engineering Chemistry* 15 (Apr. 1923): 424–25. Obituaries are in *Industrial and Engineering Chemistry* 22 (Apr. 1930): 394; *Proceedings of the American Chemical Society* (1930): 46–50; and *Science* 71 (23 May 1930): 528.

STEPHEN H. CUTCLIFFE

NICHOLSON, Eliza Jane Poitevent Holbrook (11 Mar. 1849–15 Feb. 1896), newspaper publisher and poet, was born in Gainesville, Hancock County, Mississippi, the daughter of Captain William J. Poitevent, a builder-owner of steamboats and a lumber manufacturer, and Mary A. Russ. Because of her mother's ill health, Eliza Poitevent spent much of her youth at the farm of her uncle and aunt, Mr. and Mrs. Leonard Kimball, some twenty miles from her birthplace. In 1867 she graduated from the Amite (La.) Female Seminary. She would later describe her time there as "useless education," given the academic instructions imposed on "intellectual women" in that era. She began writing poems during her early teens. However, it was not until after her graduation that her first published efforts appeared in the *South* under the name Pearl Rivers, a pseudonym she chose after the river near her home. Later her poems appeared in New York periodicals, including the *Home Journal* and *Ledger*. The *South* has been described as "a little sheet" whose editor, J. W. Overall, encouraged her writing. Her life on her relatives' farm exposed her to the outdoor life, and reflections of her experiences appeared in her works.

By 1870 her poems had appeared in the New Orleans *Picayune*, whose editor, Colonel Alva M. Holbrook, had read her literary efforts in other periodicals. At $25 a week she became the new literary editor. In 1872 she and Holbrook were married.

In 1873 her poems were collected in a book titled *Lyrics by Pearl Rivers* (she died before her second collection could be published). It was reported that her first volume was "warmly received" in the *Picayune* and praised by other critics as well, including Paul Hamilton Hayne. James A. Renshaw noted in a tribute to her that "there is a charm about these youthful productions, so simple, so sweet, a something akin to the whistle of the birds and the drum of the locusts of which she writes." In her more mature years she wrote *Hagar*, described as "a more pretentious poem," which received favorable comment. *Leah* was the second of her later, long dramatic monologues. These two poems were published in *Cosmopolitan* in 1893 and 1894, thus reaching a wider audience than she had with the *Picayune*. About her dramatic monologues, one writer noted, "The sincerity of her emotions is usually evident, though sometimes obscured by inadequate technique and expression." Yet apparently her writing appealed to many readers. Three pamphlets also appeared, apparently including all of the nearly fifty poems she wrote.

Colonel Holbrook lost control of the *Picayune* briefly in early 1872 when it was acquired by a group of local businessmen, but he regained control in late 1874. When he died in early 1876, the newspaper had a debt of $80,000 and faced strong competition. George Nicholson acquired an interest in the publication after he moved to the United States from England in 1842 and was at this time the business manager. On 27 June 1878 he and Eliza Holbrook were married. They had two children.

Eliza Nicholson carried on as publisher of the newspaper and introduced changes such as the wider use of fiction, fashion articles, art, and other material. Such contents made the paper more attractive to the entire family, especially to women and children. Such contents also helped increase circulation, thus attracting more advertisers. According to some sources, she became the first woman publisher in the Deep South. Thomas Ewing Dabney, whose history of the *Times-Picayune* is the major source for background on this newspaper, wrote that "she edited and created with the careful attention to detail and the rare discrimination which were later to leave a lasting influence on journalism." During her career, personal journalism was much in vogue across the nation. She continued to write poems, which frequently appeared on page one.

Nicholson "invaded the privacy of the New Orleans social life" and introduced society stories to the *Picayune*. She termed this project "a gossipy little creature," titled the "Society Bee," which early shocked the city. As James A. Renshaw noted, "The 'Bee' was supposed to buzz its way through open door or window into the homes of society folk, gathering as its sweets the details of this or that entertainment for the next Sunday's feast"—certainly a pioneer approach for that era. Three years after Nicholson's death, Dorothy Dix (Elizabeth M. Gilmer) began her advice column in the *Picayune*, which prepared the way for the many how-to columns in today's publications.

Nicholson's instincts proved accurate; soon the society section was the largest unit of the Sunday edition. She added a weather cartoon, a department for young people, and hints for the home along with menus and medical advice, elements common in today's newspapers but innovative for her era. Pithy comments by one of her columnists, Nat Burbank, were copied by newspapers across the nation. These humorous items became known as "Picayunes."

Involvement in publishing left little time for Pearl Rivers to write poems. No doubt her literary efforts were more directed toward her prose for the *Picayune*, some written anonymously. Her more creative efforts generally were signed.

George Nicholson died on 4 February 1896, and on 15 February his widow died, during an influenza epidemic. In 1932 a lagoon in City Park in New Orleans was dedicated as the Pearl Rivers Memorial.

Eliza Nicholson deserves recognition because of her major contributions to the newspaper industry. As a trailblazer she expanded the appeal of a large city daily newspaper to include not only the business leaders of her area, but members of their families as well. Obviously she was able to gauge her potential audience.

• Additional information on Eliza Nicholson can be found in Thomas Ewing Dabney, *One Hundred Great Years: The Story of the Times-Picayune from Its Founding to 1940* (1944), and James A. Renshaw, "Eliza Jane Poitevent Nicholson: A Bit of a Tribute," *Louisiana Historical Quarterly* 6 (Oct. 1923): 580–84.

WILLIAM H. TAFT

NICHOLSON, Francis (12 Nov. 1655–5 Mar. 1728), colonial governor and soldier, was born in the parish of Downholme, in Yorkshire, England. While his parentage and early years remain obscure, a supposition developed among his contemporaries that he was the illegitimate son of Charles Paulet, who bore the titles of Lord St. John and, later, duke of Bolton and who became his patron. From Nicholson's writings it is known that he had some local schooling, probably prior to becoming a page to Lady St. John during his teenage years. At twenty-three he joined the King's Holland Regiment as an ensign and served in Flanders. By July 1680 Nicholson was in Tangier, a lieutenant in the King's Own Regiment. There he developed a reputation for being a strict drillmaster and loyal adherent to King Charles II. Appointed an aide-de-camp to Colonel Percy Kirke, deputy governor of Tangier, he served as an envoy to the emperor of Morocco and as a courier. For exemplary service, he was brevetted captain.

With Tangier's abandonment in February 1684, Nicholson returned to England. Two years later he was ordered to Boston, Massachusetts, as captain of a regiment to serve with Edmund Andros, who was seeking to place the colonies of Massachusetts, Plymouth, Connecticut, and Rhode Island under coordinated royal control and thereby establish the Dominion of New England (the dominion was later intended to include New York and New Jersey as well). Nicholson's first task was to seek the surrender of Connecticut's colonial charter. Unsuccessful in that endeavor, he was then dispatched to French-occupied Nova Scotia to obtain the return of a fishing vessel held by authorities. He failed again but appears to have returned to Boston with military intelligence. This so pleased Andros that he named Nicholson to the dominion's council.

In 1688 Nicholson became lieutenant governor, serving in New York. His military background led him to give serious attention to bolstering militia strength along the colony's long border with French Canada. Nicholson's allegiances to Crown and church were sorely tested when news reached New York in March 1689 that King James II had been deposed by his daughter Mary and her husband, William of Orange. While Nicholson as a military officer had sworn loyalty to James, a Catholic, he was at the same time a staunch supporter of the Church of England. Until the situation was clarified, Nicholson urged New Yorkers to follow his lead and maintain law and order. The colonists, however, had resented Nicholson's intrusions into their affairs, as well as the favors he had shown to a number of prominent Dutch and English merchants. A distinct lack of tact on Nicholson's part further inflamed the situation. When New Yorkers heard of the April uprising in Boston against Andros, Jacob Leisler, a local militia officer, challenged Nicholson, who had hesitated in naming the Protestant William and Mary as the rightful monarchs. With the support of the militia in the city, Leisler seized control. Nicholson abandoned New York and sailed for England.

Despite his having left a military post, Nicholson was appointed lieutenant governor—in effect, acting governor—of Virginia in 1690, partly as a result of the efforts of his patron, the duke of Bolton. Intercolonial defense had become a chief concern of Nicholson's, and among his first orders of business on arriving in Virginia in May 1690 was to examine frontier fortifications not only in that colony but also in North Carolina and Maryland. Despite Nicholson's reputation for being difficult to deal with and for having a violent temper, he appears to have quickly developed a working relationship with the House of Burgesses and the Virginia councillors. He proved especially supportive of the efforts of Scottish minister James Blair, the newly appointed commissary of Virginia, to establish the College of William and Mary. At the same time, Nicholson encouraged an expansion in the activities of Anglican ministers.

Feeling secure in his relations with leading Virginians, Nicholson looked forward to being named governor. Such hopes were dashed when he received word in February 1692 that Andros had instead received the honor. Nicholson became lieutenant governor of Maryland, a proprietary colony that he in earlier reports had accused of being mismanaged. Dissatisfied, he returned to England and solicited additional political and church support for a better appointment. His efforts were rewarded by his being named governor of Maryland in 1694. Nicholson immediately moved to encourage Anglicanism in Maryland by advocating the creation of additional parishes and construction of dwellings for clergymen. He also offered financial support for a free public school. Nicholson moved the provincial capital from St. Mary's, created by a Catholic proprietor and none too well situated geographically, to a more convenient location, Annapolis, named for a Protestant member of the royal family. Nicholson's resentment of his former colleague Andros was exacerbated by the latter providing protection for some Maryland Catholic refugees of the 1689 revolutions and for some Protestant dissenters who had fought the Anglican ecclesiastical courts that Nicholson established. Acting as a trustee of the College of William and Mary, Nicholson, in collusion with James Blair, sought to engineer Andros's ouster. In 1698 Nicholson was finally rewarded with appointment as captain general and governor in chief of Virginia. On his appointment, Nicholson was warned by the archbishop of Canterbury, who had been apprised of his bad temper, to avoid future outbursts. Blair carried the archbishop's message to Nicholson, leading to a coolness between the two men that would have fateful results.

As in Maryland, an immediate issue confronting Nicholson involved the location of the provincial capital. He liked the idea of bringing the seat of government near his beloved college, William and Mary. The new capital was named Williamsburg in honor of the king. Nicholson remained concerned with intercolonial cooperation in military and economic affairs, as he had been during his first stint in Virginia. He organized a meeting in New York in 1700 with the governors of New York, New Jersey, and Pennsylvania for discussion of such mutual concerns as control of pirates and postal service. As war approached between England and France in 1701, Nicholson sought increased expenditures for military protection and for military aid to the northern colonies. As his requests for monetary support continued, he increasingly antagonized both the council and the burgesses. For his part, Nicholson had become convinced that native born Americans, whom he dubbed "Creoles," were too provincial in their concerns, warranting strengthened imperial control. He called for the appointment of non-native officials, believed the colonies should be governed by a viceroy, and recommended a standing army be quartered in America at the colonists' expense.

Nicholson's differences with the Virginians on these issues bespoke more immediate political problems. Nicholson could be a relentless foe, pursuing his adversaries with executive decrees and court actions and treating criticism as sedition. In order to enforce his authority, Nicholson had created a new militia with well-trained, handpicked officers. Although he remained on friendly terms with many of the leading landowners and clergy, his relations with Blair worsened. In 1702 Blair complained to the archbishop of Canterbury that Nicholson ruled over Virginians as "a company of galley slaves by continual roaring and thundering, cursing and swearing, base, abusive, billingsgate language to that degree that is utterly incredible to those who have not been the spectators to it" (Morton, vol. 1, p. 381). Blair had close political and family connections with powerful council members and created a group in opposition to the governor. By 1703 Blair and his allies on the council were making a concerted effort to obtain the governor's ouster, complaining that he was intruding on their prerogatives. In the meantime, Nicholson organized his supporters among the council and House of Burgesses. After political shifts in Britain, the matter came to a head. In 1705 Nicholson was replaced by George Hamilton, earl of Orkney.

After his return to England, Nicholson was called on to serve as a consultant to the Board of Trade and was extremely active in the Society for the Propagation of the Gospel in Foreign Parts. With warfare against France continuing, Nicholson in 1709 became involved in a scheme to conquer Canada and was named commander of the English force of New York, New Jersey, and Connecticut. The effort, however, had to be abandoned when adequate land and sea support failed to appear, supplies dwindled, and desertions mounted. Nicholson sailed home and in March 1710 was named to lead the effort to reconquer Acadia (Nova Scotia). Successful in this venture, he again returned to England, where he learned that he had been elevated to the rank of lieutenant general and ordered back to America for another attempt on Canada. This, too, had to be called off when a supporting fleet ran aground.

In October 1712 Nicholson was appointed governor of Nova Scotia. He spent very little time there, turning over most of his responsibilities to a lieutenant governor. Having also been commissioned to audit colonial finances and investigate an assortment of other official matters, he ended up alienating various of his fellow officeholders both in Nova Scotia and elsewhere in the northern colonies. He returned to Britain in 1714.

Nicholson received his last assignment, as the first royal governor of South Carolina, in 1720. Again he concentrated on building colonial defenses against Indians and rival European powers, strengthening Anglicanism, and furthering education. He angered merchants, however, by acquiescing to a flood of paper money. He left the colony in 1725 and died in London three years later.

During his long career, Nicholson sailed across the Atlantic sixteen times and served as both an administrative and military representative of royal authority. In the process he alienated scores of men with his vanity, erratic nature, and sometimes violent behavior. At the same time, he won loyal adherents through his official support of, and personal generosity toward, the Anglican church and its ministers as well as the causes of education and science.

• The Colonial Williamsburg Research Library contains two important manuscript collections, the papers of Francis Nicholson and of William Blathwayt. Nicholson's colonial career can be traced in such published documentary collections as W. N. Sainsbury et. al., eds., *Calendar of State Papers, Colonial Series, America and West Indies, 1685–1721* (1899–1953); E. B. O'Callaghan and B. Fernow, eds., *Documents Relative to the Colonial History of New York* (15 vols., 1853–1887); H. R. McIlwaine, ed., *Journals of the House of Burgesses of Virginia, 1659/60–1693* (1914); McIlwaine, ed., *Executive Journals of the Council of Colonial Virginia*, vols. 1–3 (1925–1928); and *Proceedings of the Council of Maryland, 1636–1770* (11 vols., 1885–1912). Nicholson himself published *Journal of an Expedition for the Reduction of Port Royal* (1711), reprinted in *Reports and Collections of the Nova Scotia Historical Society*, vol. 1 (1879), and *An Apology or Vindication of F. Nicholson, His Majesty's Governor of South-Carolina, from the Unjust Aspersions Cast on Him by Some of the Members of the Bahama-Company* (1724). Biographical treatments include Stephen S. Webb, "The Strange Career of Francis Nicholson," *William and Mary Quarterly*, 3d ser., 23 (1966): 513–48; Bruce T. McCully, "From the North Riding to Morocco: The Early Years of Governor Francis Nicholson, 1655–1686," *William and Mary Quarterly*, 3d ser., 19 (1962): 534–36; and Bruce T. McCully, "Governor Francis Nicholson, Patron *Par Excellence* of Religion and Learning in Colonial America," *William and Mary Quarterly*, 3d ser., 39 (1982): 310–33. On other aspects of his career, see also Richard L. Morton, *Colonial Virginia: The Tidewater Period 1607–1710* (1960); Warren M. Billings et al., *Colonial Virginia: A History* (1986); and David S. Lovejoy, *The Glorious Revolution in America* (1972).

JACOB JUDD

NICHOLSON, James (c. 1736–2 Sept. 1804), naval officer, was born in Chestertown, Maryland, the son of Joseph Nicholson and Hannah Smith. Even though he came from a distinguished family, little is known of his early years except that he was educated in England. He joined the Royal Navy and was present at the British fleet's siege of Havana in 1762 at the end of the Seven Years' War (known in America as the French and Indian War). In 1763 he married Frances Witter, and the couple moved to New York City. They had eight children. Little is known of his activities between 1763 and 1775.

Nicholson moved to the Eastern Shore of Maryland by 1775. When the Revolution began, he offered his services to Maryland and was appointed captain of the ship *Defence*. Commanding that ship, he managed to block the British ship *Otter* from advancing up the Chesapeake Bay, and he captured several British prizes. In recognition of these services, Nicholson was appointed a captain of the new Continental navy on 6 June 1776, and he was placed at the top of the list, ahead of twenty-three other officers. His appointment was attributable to his service with the Royal Navy, his success in command of the *Defence*, and the fact that the Marine Commission of the Continental navy wanted to ensure that each state was well represented. Nicholson, as a member of a notable southern family, was needed to balance the predominance of northern captains.

Nicholson was named to command the frigate *Virginia*, which was to be built in the Baltimore shipyard of George Wells. Nicholson arrived in Baltimore, recruited men, and was nearly ready to put to sea when he was ordered by the Marine Commission to proceed to Philadelphia to rescue ships there from possible capture by the British during the fall of 1776. Only the ship *Randolph* was seaworthy, and Nicholson returned to Baltimore. In the spring of 1777 he resorted to the British system of impressment to fill out his crew, and for this he was reprimanded by Congress and was suspended from his command for five months. He was reinstated in October 1777, and in early 1778 he sailed from Baltimore.

The first and last cruise of the *Virginia* under an American flag was both tragic and comic. Nicholson sailed on 30 March and evaded the two British blockading vessels during the night. His ship was almost free when it struck a sandy shoal off Cape Charles on the southern side of the Chesapeake Bay. The ship's rudder was broken, and it began to take on water. When three British frigates approached the *Virginia* the next morning (1 Apr.), Nicholson had his barge lowered, and he escaped to the shore, leaving his ship to be surrendered. This shameful episode caused consternation in Congress, but Nicholson was never tested by a court of inquiry, most likely for the same reasons that had given him first place on the captain's list.

Following fifteen months of inactivity, Nicholson was given command of the *Trumbull* in New London, Connecticut. He sailed in mid-May 1780 with a green crew, and 250 miles north of Bermuda he fought an engagement with the HMS *Watt* for two and a half hours. The battle was one of the fiercest of the entire war. Six Americans died and thirty-two were wounded, while the British suffered about ninety casualties in total. Both ships limped away to refit. Nicholson reached Boston, and the British went to New York.

Following a series of undistinguished cruises off the capes of Delaware, in the summer of 1781 Nicholson sailed the *Trumbull* from Boston, heading for Havana. He was overtaken by the British ship *Iris*, and the majority of his crew refused to fight. Nicholson and a handful of faithful men fought heroically for an hour and a half before they were forced to surrender. He was paroled and returned to the United States, but he held no other significant command during the war. A court of inquiry on 29 November 1781 determined that no neglect of duty or cowardice could be attributed to the captain.

Nicholson moved to New York City and remained on active duty in the much-reduced postrevolutionary navy. In April 1785 he asked Congress for a leave of absence from the navy, which was granted. He sailed for a time in the merchant service, and following that, he emerged as a reputable leader of the Republican faction in New York City. His house on William Street became a meeting place for followers of Aaron Burr and Thomas Jefferson, and Nicholson became a political broker. In April 1789 he commanded the barge that took George Washington from New Jersey to New York City prior to Washington's inauguration. In 1801, when the Republican party came into its own with the election of Jefferson, Nicholson sought and obtained from the new president the post of commissioner of loans for New York City. He held that post until his death.

It is difficult to evaluate Nicholson's career. Within his own time he was viewed as a pariah by some of his naval colleagues for having left his ship prior to its surrender in 1778. Historian William Fowler has noted that, as a captain in the Continental navy, Nicholson never captured nor defeated a single enemy ship. His conflicts with the Marine Commission and Congress exemplify his attitude toward his superiors. His conduct in the loss of the *Virginia* was unpardonable, and clearly the system for making appointments in the navy was flawed. He redeemed himself to some extent while in command of the *Trumbull* and ended the war exactly where he had begun, at the top of the captain's list. To some extent Nicholson played in the navy a role analogous to that of General Charles Lee in the Continental army. Both men had been trained in the British armed forces, and both gave average to poor performances in the service of the new United States.

• The best sources for Nicholson's life are the volumes written about the Continental navy, especially William M. Fowler, Jr., *Rebels under Sail: The American Navy during the Revolution* (1976); Nathan Miller, *Sea of Glory: A Naval History of the American Revolution* (1974); and John A. McManemin, *Captains of the Continental Navy* (1982). See also Fowler, "James Nicholson and the Continental Frigate *Virginia*," *American Neptune* 34, no. 2 (1973): 135–41.

SAMUEL WILLARD CROMPTON

NICHOLSON, James William Augustus (10 Mar. 1821–28 Oct. 1887), naval officer, was born in Dedham, Massachusetts, the son of Nathaniel Dowse Nicholson, a naval officer during the War of 1812, and Hannah Gray. He was the grandson of Samuel Nicholson (1743–1811), a prominent naval officer of the American Revolution and senior officer in the U.S. Navy from 1803 to 1811. He married Mary Heap; they had one child.

Nicholson entered the U.S. Navy as a midshipman in 1838, a month before his seventeenth birthday. He served in both the West India and Mediterranean squadrons and in 1844 was assigned to the screw steamer *Princeton*, though too late to witness the explosion of the "Peacemaker" in February of that year. A decade later, as a lieutenant on board the *Vandalia*,

Nicholson participated in Matthew C. Perry's historic visit to Japan in 1853. When the Civil War broke out in 1861, Nicholson had just completed a three-year tour on the *Vincennes* (1857–1860) off the coast of West Africa. In April 1861 he volunteered to participate in the expedition to relieve Fort Sumter in Charleston harbor on board the *Pocahontas*, but the expedition arrived too late to prevent the fort's capitulation.

During 1861–1862 Nicholson commanded the steamer *Isaac Smith* in the South Atlantic Blockading Squadron, participating in the capture of Port Royal Sound (7 Nov. 1861) and the seizure of Jacksonville and St. Augustine (Mar. 1862). At St. Augustine, which post he commanded briefly, he got into a heated discussion with a local minister for preaching against the government of the United States. His commanding officer, Rear Admiral Samuel F. Du Pont, confided to his wife that Nicholson was "not exactly a pleasant person, but a capital officer."

Promoted to commander (16 July 1862), Nicholson obtained command of the new monitor *Manhattan* and was assigned to the West Gulf Blockading Squadron under Rear Admiral David G. Farragut. He participated in the naval assault on Mobile Bay (5 Aug. 1864) and dueled the Confederate ironclad ram *Tennessee*. During that fight, Nicholson risked double charging his fifteen-inch guns, and the risk paid off when his shots were the only ones to penetrate the *Tennessee*'s armor plating. Following this battle, Nicholson and the *Manhattan* spent the rest of the war on the Mississippi River.

After the war, Nicholson served in the Pacific Squadron as commanding officer of the iron-hulled double-ender *Mohongo*, and he witnessed the Spanish bombardment of Valparaiso, Chile, in April 1866. Later that summer he received the Hawaiian monarch Kamehameha V on board during a visit to those islands. Promoted to captain (15 July 1866), Nicholson commanded the experimental warship *Wampanoag* during its sea trials in 1867. He commanded the *Lancaster*, flagship of the Brazil Squadron, during 1871–1872 and later served as commandant of the New York Navy Yard (1876–1880). In 1881 he was promoted to acting rear admiral and assigned to command the European Squadron. In June 1882 he played an important role in protecting American lives and property, as well as the citizens of several neutral powers, during the British attack on Alexandria. For this he received official commendation from the Navy Department and from several foreign governments. Nicholson retired as a rear admiral on 10 March 1883; he died in New York City.

• Little work has been done on Nicholson's career. The elements of his Civil War career can be pieced together from *The Official Records of the Union and Confederate Navies in the War of the Rebellion* (30 vols., 1894–1922), especially vols. 12, 13, and 21. See also the entries for *Isaac Smith*, *Manhattan*, and *Mohongo* in the *Dictionary of American Naval Fighting Ships*. Nicholson is mentioned briefly in John D. Hayes, ed., *Samuel Francis Du Pont: A Selection from His Civil War Letters* (3 vols., 1969).

CRAIG L. SYMONDS

NICHOLSON, John (1757–5 Dec. 1800), land speculator, financier, and entrepreneur, was born in Wales, the son of William Nicholson and Sarah (maiden name unknown), farmers. John Nicholson emigrated from Wales with his family and settled in Chamberstown (now Chambersburg), Pennsylvania. Nicholson enlisted in the Continental army after the revolutionary war began and served as sergeant of the Pennsylvania Line. He had no formal education but was apparently astute in finances; in October 1778 he was appointed clerk in the Chamber of Accounts of the Board of Treasury of the Continental Congress. It was during this period that he met Robert Morris, "the Financier of the Revolution," and began a twenty-year friendship and business association.

After the Revolution, Nicholson was appointed auditor (1781) and then comptroller general (1782–1794) of the Commonwealth of Pennsylvania. He used his role of comptroller general to gain control of vast land holdings in Pennsylvania and, from this base, eventual control over twelve million acres in seven states and territories. Nicholson was able to use his official position for personal gain because he used fictitious names when land warrants were taken out. Many of the land office surveyors were his agents, and prominent Pennsylvanians such as Daniel Brodhead, surveyor general of Pennsylvania, and the governor of the commonwealth, Thomas Mifflin, were his business partners. Governor Mifflin in 1792 exclaimed that "the operations of the land office . . . may be regarded with the most sanguine expectations of benefit and emolument."

Nicholson's Pennsylvania holdings were amassed through several means, not the least of which was his office's supervision of the Donation and Depreciation Lands that were set aside to pay the soldiers of the Pennsylvania Line for their efforts during the Revolution. In addition, he was the officer responsible for the purchase by Pennsylvania of the Erie Triangle from the federal government in 1792. He preempted, with the help of Mifflin, Brodhead, and others, almost all of the 202,000-acre tract and incorporated it as part of his Pennsylvania Population Company in 1792, the first of several land companies he formed to promote the sale of his holdings.

In addition to the Pennsylvania Population Company, Nicholson engaged in several other major speculative land schemes. In 1794 he and Robert Morris formed the Asylum Company, consisting of one million acres in north-central Pennsylvania, to sell lands to refugees of the French Revolution. Queen Marie Antoinette was to be one of the occupants, but events in France precluded that. Prince Talleyrand and a future king of France, Louis Philippe, did visit the place, but there were never enough émigrés to make the venture profitable. Almost all who did settle returned to their homeland in 1800 when Napoleon declared amnesty.

Undaunted, Nicholson and Morris moved onto the speculative path created by the development of the new capital of the republic—the Federal City, now

Washington, D.C. In 1793, when public sale of building lots at auction failed to produce enough buyers or revenue for erection of the public buildings, Nicholson and Morris formed a partnership with James Greenleaf, merchant, financier, and land speculator from New England. Together they approached George Washington and the Congress and purchased 6,000 of the 15,000 lots available. All of the purchases were credit arrangements and when financiers could not be found to support the purchases, the partnership disintegrated in acrimony in 1797, with Greenleaf being blamed by Nicholson and Morris for the failure. Nevertheless, their venture motivated other investment in the new city, and President Washington praised Nicholson for his efforts in furthering the development of the capital. The government was able to carry out its intended move to the new capital in 1800; six hundred buildings stood ready, and work was proceeding on the president's house and the Capitol building. This would not have been possible without the efforts of Nicholson and his partners.

Nicholson's final major land speculation venture was the North American Land Company, begun in 1795 in partnership with Morris and Greenleaf. The company was a giant consolidation of the scattered lands of the partners encompassing six million acres in seven states and territories. Like his other ventures, most of the land was secured on credit; when enough buyers did not materialize, the project collapsed in 1798.

It was not for lack of effort that these land speculation schemes failed. The wars of the French Revolution were raging in Europe and thus diverted capital from investing in land and other speculative ventures in America; immigration also was thwarted.

Another contributing factor to Nicholson's failure was his propensity to engage in many simultaneous ventures hoping that the next one would be the fortune-saver. Unfortunately, overextension and credit exhaustion were the results. While his land speculations were unfolding, he engaged in establishing iron, textile, glass, and button manufactories; lead, copper, and silver mines; canals (Delaware and Susquehanna); road projects (Lancaster Turnpike); and steamboat development (he sponsored James Fitch and James Rumsey). Morris warned him that all of these ventures would "consume your time, pick your pocket, suck your blood, make complaints and never will retribute one shilling for a pound. Therefore cast them off and save thyself." Nicholson did not abandon these projects, but he had to sacrifice all of them and his land holdings to pay his creditors. When he could not pay, legal suits were brought against him.

Morris, his friend and partner, suffered the same fate. Morris entered Prince Street Debtors' Prison in Philadelphia on 16 February 1798. Nicholson joined him there in late 1799. Entrepreneurial to the end, Nicholson published a paper from prison called "The Supporter" or "Daily Repast" to try to pay expenses, but even that failed.

Nicholson died in the Philadelphia debtors' prison a year later, leaving a wife and eight children. Some of the legacies he left were an astounding debt totaling $12 million, more than four million acres of land subject to state liens, the development of Washington, D.C., building lots, inventors whom he sponsored, internal improvement projects, some land settlements, and deteriorating manufactories.

Like many of his contemporaries, Nicholson was a speculator caught up in the promotion of the new nation and himself. And like many others, he was brought down by too much faith in the rapid growth of that new nation.

• Nicholson's papers, including his notebooks, letterbooks, and journals, can be found in the Pennsylvania Historical and Museum Commission, Public Records Division, William Penn Memorial Archives, Harrisburg. Other important manuscript sources are the Robert Morris Letterbooks and Diary in the Library of Congress Manuscript Division; the Pennsylvania Population Company Papers in the Erie Public Museum Manuscript Collections; John Nicholson Correspondence and Letterbooks in the Historical Society of Pennsylvania; and the Reverend David Croft Papers, Tioga Point Museum Collections, Athens, Pa. Primary public documents of note are Edmund Hogan, *The Pennsylvania State Trials* (1794); Hann Jan Hindekoper, "Remarks on the Late Proceedings of the Nicholson Commissioner," Historical Museum, Meadville, Pa; and John Nicholson, "An Address to the People of Pennsylvania," in *Early American Imprints*, ed. D. Evans (1792).
The best secondary sources are Robert Arbuckle, *Pennsylvania Speculator and Patriot: The Entrepreneurial John Nicholson* (1975); Allen Clark, *Greenleaf and Law in the Federal City* (1901); and Howard Swiggett, *The Forgotten Leaders of the Revolution* (1955). Also of value are Nelson Hale, "The Pennsylvania Population Company," *Pennsylvania History* 16 (1949): 122–30, and Normal B. Wilkinson, "Land Policy and Speculation in Pennsylvania, 1779–1800" (Ph.D. diss., Univ. of Pennsylvania, 1958).

ROBERT D. ARBUCKLE

NICHOLSON, Meredith (9 Dec. 1866–21 Dec. 1947), author and diplomat, was born in Crawfordsville, Indiana, the son of Edward Willis Nicholson, a farmer and a Union officer in the Civil War, and Emily Meredith, a Civil War nurse. The family moved to Indianapolis when Meredith was six, and he remained there most of his life but still retained a close relationship with Crawfordsville. He attended the Indianapolis schools but quit at age fifteen, taking various jobs. He began sending his verses to newspapers and at age nineteen started to study law but soon deserted law for journalism, serving with the *Indianapolis Sentinel* and then the *Indianapolis News*. He succeeded in educating himself by home study, learning various languages and reading many types of books. His first book was mediocre, a group of poems titled *Short Flights* (1891), which in spite of clichés brought him an honorary A.M. from Wabash College in Crawfordsville in 1897. A second publication, *Poems* (1906), was of the same quality and was known mostly for his prefatory poem, "To James Whitcomb Riley," but Nicholson could see that poetry was really not his field.

In 1896 Nicholson and Eugenie Kountze, an educated, wealthy young woman from Omaha, Nebraska, were married; the couple had three children. After a frustrating year as a stockbroker, he lived unhappily in Denver for three years as the treasurer and auditor of a coal-mining company. Missing Indiana, he wrote his well-known study, *The Hoosiers* (1900), which was considered one of the best discussions of Indiana culture and literature and prompted the award of a doctor of literature degree from Wabash College. In 1901 the Nicholsons returned to Indianapolis, where Meredith decided to see whether he could make a career of writing. His first novel, *The Main Chance* (1903), a bestseller, was set in Omaha and was a criticism of big business with its doubtful legal methods, blackmail, and finally violence. Yet, instead of being a realistic protest against injustice, it is mostly a love story.

Having proved that he could be successful in writing, he published a novel almost yearly until 1929. *Zelda Dameron* (1904) was set in Indianapolis and attempted to link the pre–Civil War city with contemporary times. Next came his greatest success, *The House of a Thousand Candles* (1905), a thrilling plot story. In a written note (a copy is in the Indiana State Library) he said, "At this time there was a deluge of tales in imitation of Anthony Hope's 'Prisoner of Zenda.' It occurred to me to show if possible that a romantic tale could be written, without an 'imaginary kingdom,' with the scene in our own Indiana." More than 250,000 copies of the book were sold in the United States, and it was translated into five languages. A drama adapted from the novel played in three foreign countries, and two motion pictures were made from it.

Nicholson now found himself internationally famous. He produced a less successful novel in *The Port of Missing Men* (1907), in which he again attempted to place romantic adventure in America, this time in the hills of Virginia, with the involvement of the Hapsburgs. *The Lords of High Decision* (1909) was a tale of Pittsburgh's coal barons, and it illustrated his concept of humor, cheer, and hope utilized to relieve realism. *A Hoosier Chronicle* (1912), considered by many critics his best novel, is semiautobiographical, depicting the early history of Wabash College and providing a realistic glimpse of Indiana politics, but it often includes through authorial intrusion praise of his native state and does not have the appeal of *The House of a Thousand Candles*. Additional romances increased Nicholson's popularity—eight novels were bestsellers from 1903 to 1916—rather than his stature as a man of letters; probably the best known of these is *The Poet* (1914), a fictional biography of James Whitcomb Riley that included a tribute to the poet. A hybrid of romanticism and realism was *The Proof of the Pudding* (1916), a presentation of early Indianapolis and its changing morals, which was spoiled by the usual happy conclusion.

Nicholson also tried other forms such as a three-act comedy coauthored by Kenyon Nicholson (no relative), *Honor Bright* (1923), and a book of short stories and familiar essays, *Best Laid Schemes* (1922). Some novels were realistic in part, but he could not permit the behavior of his characters to lead to the conclusions that his readers expected, and he always entered the story, disposing of the evil characters and showering happiness on the deserving. His usual novel allowed young love to triumph over difficulties and featured good living and the essential worth of people. His last novel, *The Cavalier of Tennessee* (1928), is a romantic treatment of Andrew Jackson.

Nicholson's sincerity is seen best in his collections of essays, which had been published previously in periodicals: *The Provincial American and Other Papers* (1912), *The Valley of Democracy* (1918), *The Man in the Street: Papers on American Topics* (1921), and *Old Familiar Faces* (1929). The pieces differ in style—some are narratives, some are familiar essays—but most are effective because of Nicholson's good sense of timing. Throughout, the reader discovers his tolerance, sentimentality, humor, his belief in "folks" as the core of the democratic process, the continuous desire for strong self-government, and three main ideas: the necessity for all to participate in a good democracy, the value of separating partisan politics and municipal government, and the desirability of decentralizing government. Actually, Nicholson preferred to be remembered as an essayist rather than a novelist. He tried to practice what he preached as a moderate leader in the Democratic party, as a "reform" city councilman, 1928–1930, and as a leader against the Ku Klux Klan. Although he was not a provincial, in all his works he manifests his love of Indiana, both of the city and the small town, and his belief despite his travels that his home state was superior. He said that he was an "incurable hick."

Nicholson was now famous, and he enjoyed his fame. Affable and personable, he was a joiner of organizations and a very popular public speaker. He was elected to the National Institute of Arts and Letters and to honorary membership in many organizations. His literary endeavors declined in the 1920s and ended with the death of his wife in 1931. Nicholson entered diplomatic service as the American envoy to Paraguay (1933–1934) and served in Venezuela (1935–1938) and in Nicaragua (1938–1941). He and Dorothy Wolfe Lannon were married in 1933 but were divorced in 1943.

Nicholson is recognized as one of the "big four" of Indiana literature before World War II along with the poet James Whitcomb Riley, the humorist and satirist George Ade, and the novelist Booth Tarkington. Probably, however, he wrote less that was substantial than the other three, and much of his work, such as articles, speeches, and introductions to books, is dated; his fame has endured mostly as a romantic novelist. He died in Indianapolis.

• The Indiana State Library, Indianapolis, holds letters by Nicholson in its manuscript collection and many newspaper clippings about him in its Indiana Biography Series. See also Nicholson's "Without Benefit of College," in his *Old Familiar Faces* (1929). Dorothy Ritter Russo and Thelma Lois Sullivan, *Bibliographical Studies of Seven Authors of Crawfordsville, Indiana* (1952), gives a chronology of his books and pamphlets, biographical references, an exhaustive list of first editions—books, ephemera, contributions—and periodicals containing first appearances along with information about many of his publications. Jacob P. Dunn, *Indiana and Indianans* (1919), and *Meredith Nicholson: American Man of Letters*, published anonymously by Scribners, n.d. [1925?], are early appreciations. Unfavorable assessments are in Russell E. Smith, "The Play Boy of the Wabash," *Bookman* 52 (Oct. 1920): 133–36, and Randolph S. Bourne, *History of a Literary Radical* (1920). R. E. Banta, *Indiana Authors and Their Books, 1816–1916* (1949), gives a brief but adequate treatment. Jean Sanders, "Meredith Nicholson: Hoosier Cavalier" (master's thesis, DePauw Univ., 1952), is valuable, and a detailed discussion of the entire body of Nicholson's work is in Arthur W. Shumaker, *A History of Indiana Literature* (1962). An obituary appears in the *Indianapolis Star*, 22 Dec. 1947.

ARTHUR W. SHUMAKER

NICHOLSON, Samuel (1743–29 Dec. 1811), naval officer, was born in Maryland, the son of Joseph Nicholson and Hannah Smith. He went to sea at an early age and rose in the merchant marine prior to the start of the Revolution. He became an active patriot by 1775, and he went to Europe on business during 1775–1776. While visiting Paris, he met with Benjamin Franklin and sought to obtain a commission in the navy of the United States, unaware that the Continental Congress had in fact commissioned him a captain in the Continental navy as of 10 December 1776. Working with Franklin, Nicholson developed a plan to enter naval service. He went to Dover, England, and purchased a cutter, the *Dolphin*. He then took the vessel to Calais, France, where he outfitted it for action. Nicholson worked with fellow Marylander, Captain Joseph Hynson, during the purchase, not suspecting that Hynson, a double agent, was reporting his every move to the British secret service.

On 18 May 1777 Nicholson sailed aboard the *Dolphin* as part of an American raiding group commanded by Captain Lambert Wickes. After a cruise in the Irish Sea, during which the Americans took at least a dozen prizes (some reports say as many as twenty-five), Nicholson brought the *Dolphin* to anchor in Saint-Malo. He later sailed it up the Loire to Nantes, where it was seized by French authorities, ending its career.

In the spring of 1778 Nicholson sailed for America aboard the 34-gun frigate *Deane*, which had been built in Nantes for the American cause. Continuing as captain of the *Deane* until September 1782, Nicholson led two cruises in 1779, in the course of which he captured a number of prizes. He had less success on two cruises in 1780 and 1781. In 1780 he married Mary Dowse. They had four children who became naval officers.

During March through May 1782 Nicholson cruised in the West Indies. He captured the HMS *Jackal* and two British privateers, the *Swallow* and the *Elizabeth*. When he returned to Boston in May, he was charged on four counts brought by Lieutenant Michael Knies, who cited Nicholson's "Tyranny and Oppression." Nicholson faced a court of inquiry in August 1782 and was judged guilty in a finding that exceeded the powers of the court. He faced a true court-martial in Boston during 12–19 September 1783. He was acquitted, but a definite taint on his career had been established.

Little is known of his life and career for the next decade. On 4 June 1794 he was commissioned a captain in the new U.S. Navy and was given the important position in Boston Harbor as superintendent of the construction of a new frigate, the USS *Constitution*. The ship was launched on 21 October 1797 after three years of construction and a total cost of $302,718.84. On the day of the launch, Nicholson intended to hoist the American flag over the ship for the first time; instead, a caulker named Samuel Bentley hoisted the flag before Nicholson came on board that day. Although symbolic, this reflected some of the frustrations and vexations that Nicholson suffered during his career.

On 22 July 1798 Nicholson led the USS *Constitution* out of Boston Harbor, making sail for the first time. He captained the first two cruises of the ship (22 July–10 Nov. 1798, 29 Dec. 1798–14 Apr. 1799) and suffered both personal tragedy and professional disappointment. His son, Samuel Nicholson, Jr., a midshipman, died during the first cruise, and Nicholson's capture of two French ships (the *Niger* and the *Spencer*) led to trouble with Benjamin Stoddert, the secretary of the navy. When the ship returned to Nantasket Roads outside of Boston on 14 April 1799, Nicholson's active career had come to an end. Nonetheless, he was retained in the navy during the naval reforms of the Thomas Jefferson administration, and he served as the first superintendent of the naval yard at Charlestown, Massachusetts. He was the senior officer in the naval service from 1803 until his death in Boston, Massachusetts.

Nicholson led an unusual life and suffered through the vagaries of a somewhat tormented career. He was one of the generation of early American naval officers who won their stripes during the period of the Continental navy (1775–1783). As a rule, these individuals tended to be freebooters and reckless, like John Paul Jones, rather than exhibiting the type of careful and correct behavior of a later generation. In 1794, commissioned in the new U.S. Navy, Nicholson found himself out of his element. Conscious perhaps of his earlier service, he may have looked down upon the younger men under his command, and certainly they did not bear him any great good will. Despite the difficulties of moving from one generation of naval officers to a second, Nicholson cannot be easily absolved of error. He became suspicious and cantankerous in his later years of service. To his credit, he was the first captain of what would become the most successful ship in the history of the U.S. Navy, "Old Ironsides."

• An important article is Stephen Tallichet Powers, "Robert Morris and the Courts-Martial of Captains Samuel Nicholson and John Manley of the Continental Navy," *Military Affairs* 44, no. 1 (1980): 13–17. See also Tyrone G. Martin, *A Most Fortunate Ship: A Narrative History of "Old Ironsides"* (1980); William M. Fowler, Jr., *Rebels under Sail* (1976); and Leonard F. Guttridge and Jay D. Smith, *The Commodores: The U.S. Navy in the Age of Sail* (1969).

SAMUEL WILLARD CROMPTON

NICHOLSON, Seth Barnes (12 Nov. 1891–2 July 1963), astronomer, was born in Springfield, Illinois, the son of William Franklin Nicholson, an educator and farmer, and Martha Ames. Despite the rigors of farm life, Nicholson's early interest in science was encouraged by his father, who had earned a master's degree in geology from Cornell University. His father's background in natural history led Nicholson to an early focus on geology and botany, although the young scientist also pursued topics in electricity and owned a small telescope. Nicholson's interest in astronomy flourished after he enrolled in Drake College (Des Moines, Iowa) in 1908. He soon came under the tutelage of D. W. Morehouse, who had recently discovered the unusually bright comet that would later be named after him.

Nicholson proved to be a gifted astronomy student at Drake. He took several photographs of Halley's Comet during its 1910 appearance and, with fellow student Alma Stotts, computed the orbit of the minor planet discovered in 1909 by noted astronomer Joel Hastings Metcalf. The two students persuaded Metcalf to name the asteroid Ekard (Drake spelled backward) and in 1911 published the details of its orbit in *Popular Astronomy*. After graduation in 1912, Nicholson and Stotts both entered the astronomy program at the University of California and were married in 1913. Three children were born to the couple between 1915 and 1921.

Nicholson held a fellowship in astronomy during his first year at Berkeley but accepted an instructorship beginning in the fall of 1913. For the next two years, he taught astronomy while serving as an assistant at the Lick Observatory, where he began his observations of the satellites of Jupiter. In 1914 Nicholson was instructed to make photographs of the eighth satellite of Jupiter, discovered six years earlier, with the 36-inch Crossley reflector. His analysis of these long-exposure plates led to the discovery of a ninth satellite of the planet, which possessed the same period, distance, and retrograde motion as Jupiter VIII. Nicholson's finding was particularly noteworthy, as the new satellite was at the limit of detection with the equipment available to him. The discovery of the satellite and the calculation of its orbital characteristics became the subject of Nicholson's doctoral dissertation, leading to his Ph.D. in 1915.

Nicholson then joined the staff of Mount Wilson Observatory in southern California and soon began contributing to the observatory's solar research program directed by George Ellery Hale. Nicholson observed and reported sunspot activity and made various records of solar surface and magnetic data. His solar investigations continued until his retirement in 1957, providing many series of long-term observations that were crucial to the expansion of solar astronomy. Nicholson was also involved with stellar and galactic research at Mount Wilson. He worked with Harlow Shapley on the spectral characteristics of Cepheid variable stars, which were increasingly important for the determination of astronomical distances. He later joined Walter Baade and Edwin Hubble in a project to measure various spiral galaxies, adding significant support for the conclusion that these phenomena were "island universes" at great distances. During the 1920s and 1930s, Nicholson collaborated with Edison Pettit to apply the vacuum thermocouple to astronomical research. Temperature measurements made in 1927 showed that the lunar surface cooled rapidly during eclipse conditions, providing important insight concerning the surface characteristics of the Moon. Later thermocouple studies disclosed the high surface temperature of Mercury, the low density of the Martian atmosphere, and the relatively low temperatures of sunspots as compared with those of the solar surface.

Nicholson remained interested, however, in the smaller bodies of the solar system, including minor planets and planetary satellites. In 1938 he began exposing a large number of photographic plates with the 100-inch Hooker Telescope on Mount Wilson to examine more completely the nine known moons of Jupiter and to search for other faint Jovian satellites. Nicholson's observations led to the discovery of two new satellites. In 1951, while pursuing more detailed observations of the tenth moon of Jupiter, Nicholson discovered yet another satellite, thus joining Galileo as the only astronomer to discover four companions of the giant planet. Nine years later he announced the discovery of a new Trojan asteroid, Menelaus. Nicholson was also active in other Mount Wilson projects, including solar eclipse expeditions in 1925, 1930, and 1932, as well as investigations of the connection between geomagnetic and solar activity. He published 267 articles on a wide range of topics in various scientific periodicals.

While pursuing his research projects, Nicholson remained involved in scientific organizations. He was twice elected president of the Astronomical Society of the Pacific (1935, 1960) and served as editor of the organization's *Publications* from 1940 to 1955. He chaired the astronomy section of the American Association for the Advancement of Science in 1944 and was an active member of the American Astronomical Society and the International Astronomical Union.

Nicholson also devoted much time to public and community service. He was very popular as a public lecturer, displaying an ability to present astronomical concepts and discoveries to lay audiences. After his retirement in 1957, Nicholson became western region coordinator for the visiting professors program of the American Astronomical Society and the National Science Foundation. In addition to his administrative contributions, Nicholson gave forty-five lectures over the next five years in the central and western states as part of this program. His community service also included various activities with the Boy Scouts of America beginning in the 1920s and important participation in the administration of the Altadena (Calif.) Library Board during the 1950s and early 1960s.

Nicholson's research and other contributions led to many honors and awards. He was elected to the National Academy of Sciences in 1937. On 13 June 1963 the Astronomical Society of the Pacific presented Nicholson with its prestigious Catherine Bruce Gold Medal in recognition of his lifetime contributions to astronomy. Unfortunately, Nicholson was confined to a Los Angeles hospital room at the time and could only listen to the award ceremony via a special telephone link with the San Diego meeting. He died less than three weeks later.

• A small collection of Nicholson's papers and correspondence is available in the Carnegie Observatories Collection at the Huntington Library, San Marino, Calif. Nicholson's most significant publications include "The Application of Vacuum Thermocouples to Problems in Astrophysics," *Astrophysical Journal* 56 (1922): 295–317 (with Edison Pettit); "Lunar Radiation and Temperatures," *Astrophysical Journal* 71 (1930): 102–35 (with Edison Pettit); "The Satellites of Jupiter," *Publications of the Astronomical Society of the Pacific* 51 (1939): 85–95; and "Solar Flares and Moderate Geomagnetic Activity," *Publications of the Astronomical Society of the Pacific* 62 (1950): 202–10 (with Oliver R. Wulf). A useful biographical sketch, with complete bibliography, is Paul Herget, "Seth Barnes Nicholson," National Academy of Sciences, *Biographical Memoirs* 42 (1971): 200–227. An obituary is in the *New York Times*, 3 July 1963.

GEORGE E. WEBB

NICHOLSON, Timothy (2 Nov. 1828–15 Sept. 1924), Quaker reformer and printer, was born in Perquimans County, North Carolina, the son of Josiah Nicholson, a teacher and farmer, and Anna White. Both parents came from families long prominent in Quaker affairs in North Carolina, and by Timothy Nicholson's own account, their influence and that of Quaker neighbors was such that he never questioned Quaker teachings. He was educated in the Quaker Belvidere Academy in Perquimans County and at the Friends Boarding School (now Moses Brown School) in Providence, Rhode Island. He married twice, first in 1853 to Sarah N. White, who died in 1865, and then in 1868 to her sister, Mary White. There were six children by the first marriage and two by the second.

After finishing his course at Providence in 1848, Nicholson returned to Perquimans County and took charge of the Belvidere Academy, which had been on the verge of collapse. Under his direction it again became a flourishing institution, attracting Quaker students from all over eastern North Carolina. In 1855 Nicholson became the head teacher of the Preparatory Department of Haverford College, a Quaker school outside Philadelphia. Four years later he was promoted to superintendent of the college, in charge of the

institution's buildings and grounds and business affairs.

In 1861 Nicholson moved his family to Richmond, Indiana, which was largely populated by Quakers who had come from North Carolina. He became partner with his brother John in a bookstore that eventually became the largest book and printing business in the city.

After his arrival in Richmond, Nicholson became a leader in reform and philanthropic causes, especially traditional Quaker concerns. In the 1860s he played an important role in collecting funds for Quaker educational and relief work among the freed slaves in the South. He was an uncompromising advocate of Prohibition but always opposed the Prohibition party, working instead through the Republicans. He was active in various peace causes, especially in the effort to secure the exemption of Friends from military service.

Nicholson was best known, however, as a prison reformer, another traditional Quaker concern. In 1867 the Indiana Yearly Meeting appointed Nicholson to a committee to seek improvements in the Indiana prison system, where conditions were scandalously bad. Nicholson became the committee's leading member, and Quaker work was critical in bringing about change. In 1870 the state established a reform school for boys to take them out of the adult prison system, and a separate prison for women and girls. In 1889 Nicholson became a charter member of the Indiana Board of State Charities, charged with investigating and making recommendations about all jails, prisons, public hospitals, and asylums; he served until 1908. His work gave him a national reputation as a prison reformer, which was crowned by his election in 1901 to the presidency of the National Conference of Charities and Corrections.

After 1860 Nicholson also established himself as a leader among American Quakers. In the first half of the nineteenth century, the American Friends had been badly divided by a series of schisms. In the 1820s they had split into Orthodox and Hicksite factions. The former emphasized views of the centrality of Christ and the authority of the Bible that were similar to those of evangelical Protestants; the latter placed more emphasis on the Quaker doctrine of Inner Light. In the 1840s and 1850s the Orthodox, in turn, had divided into Gurneyite and Wilburite parties. The Wilburites, taking their name from the New England Quaker minister John Wilbur, were unyielding primitivists, skeptical of all religious innovation. The Gurneyites, influenced by the English Quaker minister Joseph John Gurney, were more open to influences from other religious groups, especially the evangelical denominations, and to ties with them in good works such as reform causes. After 1870 many Gurneyites abandoned most of the traditional peculiarities of Quakerism, embracing revivals, music, and pastoral ministry, and giving up plainness of speech and dress. They instead embraced a radical Wesleyan holiness theology.

Between 1860 and 1900, the Indiana Yearly Meeting of Friends was the largest in the world, and Nicholson was one of its most influential members. As the clerk, or presiding officer, of the yearly meeting of ministers and elders, he was a crucial figure in moderating the revivals within the Indiana Yearly Meeting. He was a critic of the holiness theology and premillennialism of the revivalists. He was especially active in combating attempts to introduce water baptism among Friends and in helping to curb the power and influence of the emerging pastoral class. He played a central role in the 1887 conference of the Gurneyite yearly meetings in Richmond that produced the Richmond Declaration of Faith, one of the defining documents of Gurneyite Quakerism, and in the subsequent series of conferences that led to the formation of a national organization of Friends, the Five Years Meeting, in 1902. In large part because of his influence and leadership, the Indiana Yearly Meeting achieved a reputation for balancing innovation and tradition in these years.

After 1900 Nicholson remained active in Quaker affairs. A trustee of the Quaker Earlham College in Richmond from 1865 to 1914, he was firm in defending the school's freedom to teach Darwinian evolution and modernist Bible scholarship against attacks from Quakers who sympathized with the emerging fundamentalist movement. He served as clerk, or presiding officer, of the Indiana Yearly Meeting from 1904 until 1911. He also continued to be active in the Five Years Meeting, attending and playing a leading role in its 1922 session, when he was ninety-three. He became well known in his last years for holding to many traditional Quaker peculiarities; for instance, he adamantly refused to use titles, opening a letter to President Woodrow Wilson with simply "Dear Woodrow." Nicholson died in Richmond.

• Nicholson's only published writings were articles and letters in newspapers and Quaker journals. There is a small collection of Nicholson papers in the Friends Collection at Earlham College. A number of letters from Nicholson between 1875 and 1895, important for his role in Quaker affairs, are in the Joel Bean Papers at Friends Historical Library of Swarthmore College. A biography is Walter C. Woodward, *Timothy Nicholson: Master Quaker* (1927). See also Thomas D. Hamm, *The Transformation of American Quakerism: Orthodox Friends, 1800–1907* (1988).

THOMAS D. HAMM

NICOLAY, John George (26 Feb. 1832–26 Sept. 1901), journalist and private secretary and biographer of Abraham Lincoln, was born in Essingen, Bavaria, the son of John Jacob Nicolay, a farmer and barrelmaker, and Helena (maiden name unknown). The Nicolay family emigrated to the United States when John was a small boy, arriving in New Orleans in 1838. From there the family moved frequently, living in Ohio, Indiana, and Missouri, before settling in Pike County, Illinois, where John's father and brothers operated a flour mill. Nicolay clerked for a year in a store in White Hall, Illinois, before going to work as a typesetter at the *Free Press*, a newspaper published in Pittsfield, Illinois. In 1851 Nicolay became acquainted with John Hay, who had come to Pittsfield from Indiana to study at the local academy. Nicolay, who had pursued self-education during his time at the *Free Press*, became editor and proprietor of the paper in 1854. In 1856 he sold the *Free Press* and moved to Springfield, Illinois, where he went to work as a clerk in the office of the Illinois secretary of state.

Nicolay became active in Republican party politics and soon became a political lieutenant for one of the capital's leading citizens, Abraham Lincoln. When Lincoln was nominated by the Republican party for the presidency in 1860, he named Nicolay his private secretary. John Hay had by this time graduated from Brown University and had returned to study law in the office of his uncle in Springfield. He resumed his friendship with Nicolay, who obtained Hay's appointment as Lincoln's assistant secretary.

Nicolay and Hay went to Washington with Lincoln in 1861. The two men shared a room at the White House and had an exceptionally close relationship with Lincoln, though they stood somewhat in awe of the president. Lincoln and his two secretaries had a good deal of mutual affection: Lincoln called Nicolay and Hay "the boys," and they called him, between themselves, "the Ancient" or "the Tycoon." This intimacy did not extend to Mary Todd Lincoln, whom the two men did not like. Nicolay and Hay were quite different. Nicolay was solemn and meticulous, and Hay cheerful and witty. They served Lincoln for four years, performing a wide variety of political and personal duties and remaining close friends throughout, a working friendship that became the foundation for an important literary collaboration in later years. After Lincoln won reelection in 1864, Nicolay served as American consul in Paris, remaining in that post until 1869. In 1872 Nicolay became marshal of the U.S. Supreme Court, a position he held until 1887. During much of his time as marshal, Nicolay worked with Hay on a ten-volume biography entitled *Abraham Lincoln: A History*, eventually published in 1890; it was this biography that brought them lasting fame.

Nicolay and Hay had considered the idea of a biography early in Lincoln's first term, and Hay had kept a diary with this project in mind. Nicolay had also saved important papers and kept careful notes of conversations. The book took about fifteen years to produce. Both men were convinced the project could succeed only if they had access to the president's papers, now in the possession of Lincoln's son Robert Todd Lincoln. He agreed to lend his father's papers to them on the condition he be allowed to review the manuscript prior to the book's publication. In 1885 the two authors circulated manuscripts of their biography, already more than half a million words long, to leading publishers. The *Century* magazine outbid its rivals, offering Nicolay and Hay the astonishing sum of $50,000 for the book's serial rights, plus royalties on book sales. The magazine began publishing abridgements of the book in November 1886, continuing through February 1890. When the ten-volume set appeared in 1890, it sold roughly 7,000 copies, even though thousands had read the abridgements in the *Century*. Nicolay continued after 1890 to make Lincoln scholarship his lifework. In 1901 he wrote a one-volume abridged edition of the *History* that sold 35,000 copies.

The Nicolay-Hay biography has had lasting historical significance. Both Hay and Nicolay were partisan Republicans, writing under the watchful eye of the martyred president's son in a period when the ideal of historical objectivity had yet to be fully established. In delivering the manuscript to Robert Todd Lincoln, Hay and Nicolay assured him that "every line has been written in the spirit of reverence and regard." Nevertheless, the biography is useful, because while the authors' conclusions are predictable, they are generally grounded in documentary sources and historical records. Additionally, they provide important eyewitness evidence of Lincoln's shifting moods and anxieties, particularly his gloom over the uncertain outcome of the 1864 election. There is no question that the Nicolay-Hay biography reflected the partisanship of the period and has a strong pro-Lincoln bias. It contains intense criticism of General McClellan, the Copperheads, and the Radical Republicans, and it depicts Lincoln as a grand, almost mythical figure. Nevertheless, the biography made an important contribution to Lincoln scholarship. While far too admiring, Nicolay and Hay were the only biographers to have access to Lincoln's papers for more than fifty years. The biography also played an important role in the Civil War historiography of the late nineteenth century, shaping interpretations and prompting attacks by other biographers, such as William Herndon and Jesse W. Weik. Together Nicolay and Hay also edited Lincoln's writings, which were published in two volumes in 1894 and later enlarged to twelve volumes.

On 15 June 1865 Nicolay married Therena Bates of Pittsfield, Illinois; they had a son, who died in infancy, and a daughter. Nicolay produced other books on Lincoln, including *A Short Life of Abraham Lincoln* (1902), and he wrote the article on Lincoln for the ninth edition of the *Encyclopaedia Britannica* (1882). He also wrote on the history of the Civil War more generally; his other works include *The Outbreak of Rebellion* (1881), and the Civil War chapters in the *Cambridge Modern History* (1903). Nicolay died in Washington, D.C.

• Nicolay's voluminous papers are held in the Library of Congress. Books that include evaluations of the Nicolay-Hay biography include Benjamin P. Thomas, *Portrait for Posterity: Lincoln and his Biographers* (1947); Merrill D. Peterson, *Lincoln in American Memory* (1994); David Donald, *Lincoln Reconsidered* (1956); and Mark Neely, *Abraham Lincoln Encyclopedia* (1982). For general treatments of Nicolay's life, see Helen Nicolay, *Lincoln's Secretary, A Biography of John G. Nicolay* (1949); W. R. Thayer, *The Life and Letters of John Hay* (2 vols., 1915); *Letters of John Hay and Extracts from Diary* (3 vols., 1908); Helen Nicolay, *Personal Traits of Abraham Lincoln* (1912); and obituaries in the *Washington Post* and *Evening Star*, 27 Sept. 1901.

DANIEL HAMILTON

NICOLLET, Joseph Nicolas (29 July 1786–11 Sept. 1843), explorer, astronomer, and mathematician, was born in Cluses, a small town in the duchy of Savoy in the Alpine region of eastern France, the son of Francois Nicollet, an artisan and watch finisher, and Marie Dussaugey. He began his education in the local school where his godfather, Nicolas Berthoud, was schoolmaster. Through the Abbé Ressiat who taught him Latin he was sent to the neighboring town of Samoens to attend the Latin school there, the Manor Berouse. Since his family was impoverished after the French invasion of 1792, he tutored younger children to earn his tuition, distinguishing himself as an excellent student, particularly in mathematics. He also developed as a fine violinist. As Napoleon restricted religious schools, in 1804 Nicollet left the Manor Berouse to attend a secular institution. This was L'École Normale in Chambéry, a larger, more cosmopolitan town and the capital of the French Department of Mont Blanc. He received further training in mathematics and the natural sciences but longed to study in Paris with some of the great scholars of the age. In 1809 his school principal, George Marie Raymond, facilitated his admission to L'École Normale in Paris, where he prepared for a teaching career. Meanwhile, he became a part-time instructor at the Lycée Imperial, specializing in astronomy and mathematics. He also began to publish scholarly papers and wrote encyclopedia articles to support himself. By 1817 he had attracted the attention of the Marquis de Pierre Simon Laplace, one of the eminent astronomers of the day, who was also a professor of mathematics at the École Militaire. Laplace was impressed by Nicollet and appointed him secretary of the observatory at the institution.

Within a few years Nicollet made his mark as an astronomer, but he experienced problems in advancing his career. A gentle man of undistinguished background, he found it difficult to attract needed patrons or to best the cutthroat competition for status and position that was characteristic of post-Napoleonic France. He had discovered a comet in the constellation of Pegasus in 1821 and had made significant astronomical observations in southern France, which won him a solid reputation. But friction with the ambitious observatory director, Dominique Francois Arago, as well as the political and economic turmoil of the revolution of 1830 impeded his success. In that year he had been involved in disastrous stock market speculations that left him and friends for whom he had made investments virtually penniless. In December 1831 he decided to emigrate to America.

He arrived in New Orleans in 1832 and quickly searched out contacts with leaders of the French community there. A small, intense man of considerable polish and sophistication, he moved easily in the best social circles. He particularly sought out members of the Chouteau family, who were among the wealthiest in the city. The Chouteaus were already preeminent in controlling the fur trade of the Mississippi Valley, with operations extending northward into the Illinois country. In view of Nicollet's background and experience they persuaded him to join them in expeditions they were sending into the St. Louis region. Nicollet embarked on the first of these explorations in 1836, searching for the source of the Mississippi River. In this quest he came into contact with the Chippewa Indians and reported his findings on their language, customs, religious practices, relations with other tribes, and attitudes toward American settlers to U.S. Army officers stationed at Fort Snelling, at the juncture of the Mississippi and Minnesota rivers, the site of present-day Minneapolis.

Nicollet impressed his new American friends in the U.S. Army. As a result of their recommendations Secretary of War Joel Poinsett invited him to Washington, D.C., and gave him various assignments. One of these in 1838 was a commission to conduct a survey of the upper Missouri country, accompanied by Lieutenant John C. Frémont. In the following year he continued the survey by steamboat and also explored the sources of the Red River and the North Dakota country. When he returned to Washington, D.C., in 1840, he prepared some of the first accurate maps of the region northwest of the Mississippi River. In these projects he worked closely with the eminent Swiss émigré Ferdinand Hassler, chief of the U.S. Coast Survey. He was at work on this major undertaking when he died in a Washington, D.C., boardinghouse. He had been a lifelong bachelor.

The significance of Nicollet's life in the United States was as an explorer and mapmaker. A scientist of note, he was one of the illustrious circle of talented, adventurous, and highly skilled men who gathered around Hassler. That group developed the first accurate scientific data about the still-unknown regions of the Mississippi Valley. In his brief career as a pioneer explorer he contributed much to westward expansion in the nineteenth century and to more accurate knowledge of the Native Americans in that area.

• The Nicollet manuscripts are in the Library of Congress. Additional manuscript materials are in the National Archives and the Minnesota Historical Society. Published documents are Martha Coleman Bray, ed., *The Journals of Joseph N. Nicollet: A Scientist on the Mississippi Headwaters with Notes on Indian Life, 1836–37* (1970), and *Joseph N. Nicollet on the Plains and Prairies: The Expeditions of 1838–39 with Journals, Letters, and Notes on the Dakota Indians*, translated from the French and edited by Edmund C. Bray and Martha Coleman Bray (1976). The best biography is Martha Coleman Bray, *Joseph Nicollet and His Map* (1980). Martha Coleman Bray, "Joseph Nicolas Nicollet, Geographer," in *Frenchmen and French Ways in the Mississippi Valley*, ed. John Francis McDermott (1969), and Martha Coleman Bray, "Joseph Nicolas Nicollet, Geologist," American Philosophical Society, *Proceedings* 114 (Feb. 1970): 37–59, are useful. The *Daily Globe* (Washington, D.C.), 11 Sept. 1843, has an obituary.

GERALD D. NASH

NICOLLS, Matthias (1626–c. July 1693), New York government official and jurist, was born in Plymouth, England, and baptized on 29 March 1626, the son of Matthias Nicolls, a minister of the Church of England, and Martha Oakes. The Reverend Mr. Nicolls, who was from the landed gentry, died in 1631. Martha Nicolls moved to Plympton with her son, who in time studied law in London at two Inns of Court, Inner Temple and Lincoln's Inn. He was admitted to the bar at Lincoln's Inn in 1649 and for the next fifteen years was a barrister in London. During this period he married Abigail Johns; they had at least four children.

In 1663 King Charles II appointed Nicolls secretary to the royal commission being sent to conquer New Netherland and granted him also the military rank of captain. The appointment was made on the recommendation of one of the commissioners, Massachusetts merchant Samuel Maverick, who was informed that Nicolls "hath beene bred a scholar."

Nicolls sailed with his family on the flagship *Guyny* (Guinea), arriving at Boston in July 1664 and at Manhattan in August. Following the surrender of New Netherland, Richard Nicolls, who was not related to Matthias Nicolls, became governor of New York. Matthias Nicolls was appointed provincial secretary, president of the court of assizes (the colony's highest court), and served on special courts of oyer and terminer (for major crimes), courts of admiralty, and courts-martial. He undoubtedly was the principal framer of the "Duke's Laws" (they replaced the colony's Roman-Dutch law; drawing on legal codes of other English colonies, they were based on Anglo-Saxon law) by which the colony thereafter was regulated. He was also a member of the provincial council and for ten years served in the New York City Common Council, eight years as alderman and two as mayor. He served also as commander of cavalry in the Long Island militia.

In 1673 New York was recaptured by a Dutch military and naval force and held for fifteen months, during which time Nicolls oversaw the duke of York's interests from Connecticut. While moving from Fairfield to New Haven, he and his family were shipwrecked, and three of his children drowned.

In 1674, when New York returned to English rule, Governor Edmund Andros reappointed Nicolls as provincial secretary, member of council, and mayor of New York City. In 1677 he was also granted the lucrative position of New York City vendue master (a government official in charge of public auctions).

Nicolls returned to England in January 1681 to testify on behalf of Andros, who had been charged with malfeasance. He met with the duke of York and undoubtedly also with the Board of Trade, which oversaw colonial affairs. After a long period of separation from his family, who had remained in America, Nicolls returned to New York in August 1683, just before the arrival of Governor Thomas Dongan.

Dongan brought with him instructions to reorganize the courts, establish county governments, and create an elected assembly. Over the next few months Nicolls was commissioned a judge of the court of oyer and terminer, the court of admiralty, and Queens County tax collector. He was elected to the General Assembly, his first elective office, and was chosen Speaker.

After word was received in 1689 that King James II had been deposed by William of Orange, New York's government collapsed. Following a period of anarchy, Jacob Leisler took control, strengthening his position by dismissing all officials holding commissions under Governors Andros and Dongan. Matthias Nicolls retired to Cow Neck (now Manhasset), Long Island, where he had a large estate.

Governor Henry Sloughter arrived from England in 1691 to take control of New York's government. Although the Lords of Trade and Plantations had decided not to reappoint Nicolls to the council because of his age, he petitioned the council for the position of provincial vendue master, which was granted him on 28 November 1692. He died not long thereafter, his widow petitioning for and receiving letters of administration on 22 July 1693.

Little is known of Matthias Nicolls's private life, although occasional glimpses are afforded by personal notes, a couple of scraps referring to New Year's Eve and Valentine's Day festivities. Among his close friends was Fitz-John Winthrop (1638–1707), son of Governor John Winthrop (1606–1676) of Connecticut; some engaging letters survive. In one, Nicolls describes a newlywed colleague bouncing around the office and makes some wry comments on the pleasures of marriage. Connecticut official John Allyn found Nicolls to be "a sweet natured gentleman."

Matthias Nicolls served the king, the duke, several governors, and the colony of New York in every branch of government, providing a unity and continuity for the fledgling government for a quarter of a century. As author of the Duke's Laws, which derive from Anglo-Saxon law, and as chief judge, whereby he interpreted those laws and established precedent, he virtually created the legal system under which New York operates to the present day.

• No body of Nicolls's private papers seems to exist. The Winthrop Family Papers at the Massachusetts Historical Society include a few letters relating to him, some of which are published in the society's *Collections*, 5th ser., 8 (1882), and 6th ser., 3 (1889). The New York State Archives contains records from his public career, most of which have been published in the series *New York Historical Manuscripts* (1977–). Most of the relevant material in the Public Record Office in London has been microfilmed as Great Britain, Colonial Office, *New York Records, 1664–1781* (1975), and some has been published in *Documents Relative to the Colonial History of the State of New York* (1853–1887). A genealogical work on the family is Rosalie Fellows Bailey, *The Nicoll Family and Islip Grange* (1940). See also Peter R. Christoph, "Matthias Nicolls: Sixth and Eighth Mayor of New York," *New York Genealogical and Biographical Record*, vol. 120 (1989).

PETER R. CHRISTOPH

NICOLLS, Richard (1624–28 May 1672), the first English governor of New York, was born in Ampthill, Bedfordshire, England, the son of Francis Nicolls, a lawyer, and Margaret Bruce. His father, one of the squires of the bath to Sir Edward Bruce, died the year Nicolls was born. Amply provided for, the family continued to live at Ampthill Great Park, a royal chase. With the outbreak of the civil war when he was eighteen, Nicolls fought on the royal side against the forces of Oliver Cromwell, commanding a troop of horse. In 1648 Nicolls went into exile with the Stuarts in France, where he served in the household of James, the duke of York. Four years later, in the spring of 1652, he and the duke fought in the army of Marshall Turenne in the war of the Fronde. In 1660, when the monarchy was restored in England under Charles II, the duke, who was the king's brother, named Nicolls a groom of his bedchamber.

Nicolls was well educated. He read Latin and Greek and was fluent in Dutch and German. He studied at Oxford, where he received a doctor of civil law degree in 1663. The following year, in March, Charles II gave to his brother, the duke of York, the territory in North America occupied by the Dutch, New Netherlands. The duke then gave Nicolls command of a force whose mission was to gain control of the Dutch province. Nicolls, now a colonel, headed a commission that included Sir Robert Carr, George Cartwright, and Samuel Maverick. He was commanded by the duke "to use such force as could not be avoided for their [the Dutch] reduction."

With a force of 300 soldiers and four frigates, Nicolls sailed from Portsmouth, England, in June 1664, arriving in Boston, Massachusetts, on 27 July. Although Boston had agreed to supply him with 200 men, its help was unnecessary. New Amsterdam and the province of New Netherlands were militarily unprepared. The Dutch West India Company, which administered the colony, had treated it solely as a commercial venture. New Amsterdam, a city of about 1,500 people, was indefensible and virtually helpless. Peter Stuyvesant, known as "Peg Leg Pete," the director general of the colony since 1647, remonstrated with the burghers to fight but to no avail. They were indifferent to the threat and refused to organize. As a consequence, Stuyvesant capitulated and on 27 August 1664 surrendered New Amsterdam and the colony to the English without a shot being fired. The duke of York named Nicolls governor of all his newly conquered territories, now called New York. Three-quarters of the inhabitants of the city were Dutch, and the remainder were French, Swedes, Finns, Portuguese, and some blacks, mainly from Brazil, a Portuguese territory. Although the burghers offered no resistance, according to Washington Irving, in a private meeting they "unanimously determined never to ask any of their conquerers to dinner."

Nicolls's first task was to give some structure to the city and province. When he arrived, livestock wandered freely throughout the city, causing disputes over ownership. He ordered that the cows and pigs be branded. He moved slowly, respecting the customs that had evolved, and he did not confiscate any property. In February 1665, having completed their terms, the eight burgher masters named their successors, who in turn were confirmed by Nicolls.

The following June, however, under instructions from the duke of York, Nicolls created an English municipal form of local government, comprising a mayor, alderman, and sheriff with one-year terms, appointed by him. The first mayor of New York, Thomas Willett, had little power. Nicolls and his governor's council, which he also appointed, had the power to impose taxes and make laws and also acted as the court of assizes, the highest tribunal of the vast province. In Albany, where he had allowed the Dutch officials to stay in power, his representative was accused of treating the people in an arbitrary manner. Nicolls acted swiftly, appointing a three-man commission, two members of which were Dutch, to investigate the charges. He accepted their report and removed the official.

In October 1665 Nicolls called a meeting of representatives from Westchester and the townships of Long Island at Hempstead, Queens County. Remembering the English civil war, he was reluctant to devolve any power to the localities, which had under Stuyvesant enjoyed some independence. He thus presented to them a code of laws, civil and criminal, known as the Duke's Laws, which had been mainly devised by his secretary Mathias Nicolls (no relation) and were based on English, Massachusetts, Dutch, and Roman law as well as local customs. Although Albany and much of the Hudson River valley were allowed to retain some elements of their local Dutch institutions, under the statutes the townships of Westchester and Long Island lost self-government and the right to impose taxes. Death was the penalty for murder, treason, kidnapping, striking one's parent, and denying the one true God. Unorganized and unprepared, the thirty-four representatives of the communities agreed. In November Nicolls submitted the code to the duke of York for approval, writing, "My endeavors have not been wanting to put the whole government into one form and policy, and now the most factious republicans can not but acknowledge themselves fully satisfied with the way and method they are in."

In addition to a new form of government, the English introduced into the colony fine horses of a different strain from the heavy Dutch type used for farmwork. Nicolls encouraged horse racing, and in Hempstead on the flat lands of Long Island he had a racetrack built that he called Newmarket Course, named for the track near London, England. His intention was to encourage the "bettering of the breed of horses."

During Nicolls's tenure two witchcraft trials revealed the prudent manner in which he exercised his authority. In late 1665 Ralph Hall and Mary Hall were accused of murdering George Wood and his baby by means of witchcraft. The court of assizes heard the case and found no evidence to warrant their execution for the charge of murder. In another instance two years later the court found no evidence against Katherine Harrison, who was accused by her Westchester neighbors of being "a person lying under the suspicion of witchcraft."

The Second Anglo-Dutch War began in 1665. England was unable to give any assistance to its new colony, and the Dutch seized several ships owned by New Yorkers and interrupted commerce. Out of his own funds, Nicolls paid for the few troops he had. In July 1667 hostilities ended with the Peace of Breda, and New York remained English. Shortly after, Nicolls, now in debt, requested the duke of York to relieve him of his command. The duke finally granted his petition, replacing him with Colonel Francis Lovelace, who arrived in the spring of 1668.

The colonists were sad to see Nicolls leave. Mayor Cornelius Steenwyck gave a farewell dinner in his honor, and the Dutch burghers signed a letter calling him "a wise and intelligent governor." Accompanied to the ship by a large procession, Nicolls departed for England on 28 August 1668. The New York he left had only about 400 houses, and the entire province had only about 6,000 people.

When war broke out with the Dutch again in 1672, Nicolls volunteered, along with the duke of York and the earl of Sandwich, to serve on a ship as part of the lord high admiral's household. In a sea engagement at Sole Bay, England, Nicolls was killed when the ship he was on was hit.

Good natured and genial, Nicolls, who never married, cut a tall and erect figure. He was honest and fair, and he remained so when entrusted with virtually absolute authority over the vast colony of New York. As such he earned the respect of the people.

• See Charles Wooley, "A Two Years Journal in New York" (1860), in Gowans's *Bibliotheca Americana* (5 vols., 1845–1869). For life in England in the 1660s, see Samuel Pepys's *Diary*. For the Dutch in America see Oliver A. Rink, *Holland on the Hudson: An Economic and Social History of Dutch New York* (1986), and Arnold J. F. Van Laer, ed., *Correspondence of Maria van Rensselaer, 1669–1689* (1985). A whimsical history of early N.Y. is Washington Irving, *Diedrich Knickerbocker: A History of New York* (1838). An interesting and readable history is Edward R. Ellis, *The Epic of New York City* (1966).

GEOFFREY GNEUHS

NIEBUHR, H. Richard (3 Sept. 1894–5 July 1962), theologian and educator, was born Helmut Richard Niebuhr in Wright City, Missouri, the son of Gustav Niebuhr, a German immigrant and clergyman in the German Evangelical Synod of North America, and Lydia Hosto. He was the brother of Reinhold Niebuhr, professor of applied Christianity at Union Theological Seminary, New York.

The religious milieu of the Niebuhr family combined a piety and theology derived from both the Lutheran and Reformed legacies of Protestantism together with influences of pietism. The family also shared a deep interest in music, literature, and art. The conservation of the language and other aspects of German culture was strongly defended by many members of the Evangelical Synod; the Niebuhr family were leaders in efforts to bring its educational institutions and other aspects of its life and practices into the mainstream of American Protestantism and culture. Their efforts included the cultivation of a sense of social responsibility that marked the careers of both Reinhold and H. Richard, and the introduction of aspects of critical biblical scholarship and more liberal theology into Eden Theological Seminary, in Webster Groves, Missouri, where the denomination trained its ministers. The combination of faithfulness to the best in the historical identity of his denomination with leadership to change it was a critical aspect of Niebuhr's personal, ecclesiastical, and scholarly life during the early decades of his career.

In 1908 Niebuhr enrolled in his denomination's Elmhurst College in Illinois, at that time a school similar to a German Gymnasium. It provided him with solid exposure to the classics, but little to the physical and social sciences. He graduated in 1912, but at that time Elmhurst did not confer a bachelor's degree. He then enrolled in the Eden Seminary, graduating in 1915, again with no degree. He was ordained in 1916 and served as minister of the Walnut Park Evangelical Church in St. Louis, still a German-language congregation. Niebuhr received an M.A. from Washington University, St. Louis, in 1917. In 1919 Eden Seminary called him to its faculty, and the following year he married Florence Marie Mittendorf. They had two children.

Over the next few years Niebuhr broadened his education by periods of study at Union Theological Seminary, a prestigious center of liberal theology, and at Columbia University in New York; by studies of sociology at Washington University; and by summer sessions at the University of Michigan and the University of Chicago. These studies of social science and philosophy were decisive in directing Niebuhr's early publications, and they had a continuing influence throughout his career. In 1922 he engaged in full-time theological studies at Yale, where he earned his B.D. (1923) and his Ph.D. (1924). His dissertation was on Ernst Troeltsch's philosophy of religion. Troeltsch's combination of historical, sociological, ethical, philosophical, and theological scholarship informed both the agenda and the content of Niebuhr's future work.

During his studies at Yale Niebuhr served as pastor of the Clinton, Connecticut, Congregational Church. Upon completion of his Ph.D. he became president of Elmhurst College, where he developed programs to bring the college's faculty and curriculum up to the accepted standards of American higher education, to admit women and attract students from a variety of backgrounds, and to improve its financial basis and physical facilities.

Exhausted by his multiple duties as college president, Niebuhr returned to Eden Seminary in 1927 to teach theology. During that tenure he wrote *The Social Sources of Denominationalism* (1929), a classic study of the historical sociology of American Protestantism; a moral and theological critique of the ethnic, class, and racial barriers to Christian unity; and an idealistic pro-

posal for overcoming them. The theme of Christian unity recurred throughout his career in his participation in denominational mergers and in the ecumenical movement. The book also signaled his persistent concern for the relations of the church to the "world," a concern that took different forms under altering political, social, and theological circumstances. It also illustrates the multidisciplinary matrix within and from which his constructive theological proposals developed.

In 1930 Niebuhr studied in Germany and traveled briefly in the Soviet Union. He astutely observed the near-despair of the spiritual and political situation in Germany, the church's weak efforts to relate to the working classes, and the tensions between Lutheran Orthodoxy and its liberal theological critics. Upon his return to the United States he translated Paul Tillich's *Die Religiöse Lage der Gegenwart* (*The Religious Situation* [1932]), which introduced Tillich's thought to American readers. After Hitler's rise to power Niebuhr supported the Confessing Church's opposition to Nazism. In the Soviet Union the commitment to the idea of equality appealed to him, and for some years he was impressed by an affinity between some aspects of Marxism and Christianity, for example, Marxism's recognition that history was driven by forces beyond human control and its hopeful view of the future.

In 1931 Niebuhr joined the faculty of Yale Divinity School, where he served until his death; he was promoted to professor in 1938 and in 1954 was named Sterling Professor of Theology and Christian Ethics. During his tenure his theological, historical, and ethical scholarship came to fruition; his passionate wrestling in lectures with theological and ethical issues deeply affected countless students for the ministry, and his erudition and critical analytic acumen deeply marked the work of scores of doctoral students. With the contributions of his colleagues Robert L. Calhoun, Roland Bainton, and others, Yale Divinity School achieved an eminence in American theological education rivaled only by Union Theological Seminary, where Reinhold Niebuhr and Paul Tillich taught.

During his Yale tenure Niebuhr also contributed to ecumenical activity by his support for the union of his Evangelical Synod with the German Reformed Church in 1934—forming the Evangelical and Reformed Church—and for the subsequent union of that new denomination with the Congregational Christian churches to form the United Church of Christ. He also participated in the Federal Council of Churches Commission on "The Relation of the Church to War in the Light of the Christian Faith" (1944) and in the World Council of Churches Commission on "Christ and the Church." In 1954 and 1955 he directed a study of Protestant theological schools in the United States and Canada that deeply influenced theological education in both countries.

During the 1930s, political, international, and theological factors shaped Niebuhr's theological work in a way that differed from his earlier career. He and Reinhold responded to Japanese aggression in China in different ways. Reinhold favored American intervention to resist the aggression; H. Richard turned the issue more to judgment on America, arguing that imperialistic greed motivated U.S. policy and that self-righteousness was a danger. His thought was turning from liberal Protestantism to a deeper appreciation of themes of divine judgment in, and the limits of human control over, historical events. Increasingly he warned the Christian churches against the temptations of various political and social movements of both the Left and the Right.

Contributing to this direction in Niebuhr's work was the growing influence of the European theology known as "neo-orthodoxy." He was active in a theological discussion group that included such shapers of Protestant theology as his brother Reinhold, Paul Tillich (who had immigrated from Germany), Wilhelm Pauck, John C. Bennett, Walter M. Horton, and Robert L. Calhoun. He studied the writings of the Danish theologian Søren Kierkegaard and the Russian novelist Fyodor Dostoyevsky, as well as the theological and biblical scholarship of such contemporary Europeans as Karl Barth, Rudolf Bultmann, and Emil Brunner. He shared in the "moral realism" that found reigning views of the human and society to be shallowly optimistic, in the new appropriation of biblical theological themes as central to Christian theology, and in the sense that the church had to find its identity over against the world that threatened to subsume it.

A milestone in Niebuhr's work came out of the milieu: his coauthorship with Wilhelm Pauck and Francis Pickens Miller of *The Church against the World* (1935). He put the question of the book starkly. "The question of the church, seen from the inside, is not how it can measure up to the expectations of society nor what it must do to become a savior of civilization, but rather how it can be true to itself: that is to its Head [Christ]. What must it do to be saved?" (p. 4). Niebuhr's essay, "Toward the Independence of the Church," rejected "ascetic and romantic" flights from the world while charging the church with bondage to capitalism, nationalism, and anthropocentrism. The church must reject these idols and be active in social reform but also guard against identification with secular reform movements. Its loyalty must be to God and Christ; it must repent of its failure to fulfill its main task: "understanding, proclaiming and preparing for the divine revolution in human life" (p. 154). The tension between maintaining both historic Christian identity and engagement in political and cultural transformation continued throughout his career.

Niebuhr also concentrated on the history of American Protestantism and its theologies. This issued in *The Kingdom of God in America* (1935), a work he explicitly differentiated from *The Social Sources of Denominationalism*. The sociological approach of the latter "helped to explain why the religious stream flowed in these particular channels but it did not account for the force of the stream itself"; "it did not explain the Christian movement that produced" the socially conditioned institutions; it accounted for the diversity but not the unity to be found within American Christianity; and it did not explain the independent, aggressive faith "which molds culture instead of being molded by it" (pp. vii–viii).

Just as the sociological interpretation of *The Social Sources* finally was in the service of Niebuhr's religious and moral critique, so also the religious and theological interpretation of *The Kingdom of God* was in the service of his developing constructive theology. He isolated three themes in the history of the American Protestant movement. In the early period the Kingdom of God meant the sovereignty of God; in the period of revivals it meant the reign of Christ in individual lives; and in the recent period, the kingdom of God on earth. He criticized progressive liberalism for teaching innocuously that "a God without wrath brought men without sin into a kingdom without judgment through the ministration of a Christ without a cross" (p. 193). Niebuhr's interest in the sovereignty of God as central to Christian theology, a theme of Jonathan Edwards (1703–1758) (whose influence on him was great), was advanced in this book, which also became a landmark historical study of American Christianity.

During the thirties and forties Niebuhr was developing another emphasis: the relational view of the self and of knowledge, which grounded his theological method and his view of ethics. He was also occupied with the relations of value theory and theology. Influenced by the American pragmatic tradition, especially by the work of George Herbert Mead, he argued against "objective" and "subjective" theories of value in favor of a "relational" view, that values occur in the relations of beings to one another. During this period he was also deeply influenced by the writings of the Jewish philosopher and religious thinker Martin Buber. He creatively combined strands from Mead and Buber in his interpretation of moral experience.

In *The Meaning of Revelation* (1941), Niebuhr creatively combined the work of Ernst Troeltsch and Karl Barth. Like Troeltsch, he contended that no theology could escape from historical relativism. Revelation was not, as had been argued in many traditional sources, objective knowledge of the external facts of the Christ event. Rather, the Christ event provided the "inner history" of the Christian community by forming and shaping the meaning of its common life. Persons who participated in the community were informed and directed in their interpretation and understanding of their personal lives, the events of their lives in the world, and their relation to the sovereign God by the Christian story. The narratives of Christ's life, death, and resurrection provided "reasons of the heart" for their way of life and were the source of "a permanent revolution" in forms of human religion.

A series of articles published in the *Christian Century* in 1942 and 1943 are the best examples in print of Niebuhr's "applied theology": "War as the Judgment of God," "Is God in the War?" and "War as Crucifixion." He interpreted World War II theologically, not only ethically, as an occurrence in which prideful and self-aggrandizing societies discovered their limits, discerned their complicity in evil, and encountered a sovereign and inscrutable power that they could not control.

Niebuhr recovered from a deep depression in 1944 to continue his influential career as teacher and scholar. In 1951 he published what became a classic typological study of positions taken in the history of Christian ethics, *Christ and Culture*. He distinguished five types: Christ against culture, the Christ of culture, Christ above culture, Christ and culture in paradox, and Christ the transformer of culture. In analyzing the weaknesses and strengths of each type, he came to an argued preference for the last. This marked a somewhat different emphasis from "The Church against the World" espoused fifteen years before.

Indications of Niebuhr's differences from some neo-orthodox themes became clearer in the last decade of his life. Against an exclusive Christocentric theology he argued that Jesus bore witness not to himself but to God, that the church was instrumental to the love of God and neighbor and not an end in itself, and that the Bible was only a means to the end of acknowledging God. These criticisms are made forcefully in *The Purpose of the Church and Its Ministry* (1956), one of three books that issued from his study of theological education in North America.

Three important themes of Niebuhr's work are highlighted in *Radical Monotheism and Western Culture* (1960) and in two books published posthumously, *The Responsible Self* (1963) and *Faith on Earth* (1989).

One is his account of faith and its role not only in religious life and theology, but also in many other spheres of human experience and activity. He works from the Latin *fides*, *fiducia*, and *fidelitas*, to distinguish faith as believing, as trust or confidence, and as loyalty or fidelity. These activities or forms of faith can be seen in interpersonal experience, in intellectual activity in the sciences and other scholarship, in public life, and in professional roles as well as in religious life. One effect of this account is to demystify faith and to lay a basis for understanding religious life as both continuous with and different from other activities. All forms of faith have "objects," people believe *in*, have confidence *in*, are loyal *to* someone or something. Theology functions critically to assess the objects of faith and shows the limits and perversions of various movements, for example, nationalism; or ways of knowing, for example, science; when their objects become absolutized. Niebuhr in this way shows a strong Protestant sensitivity to all idolatries. Theology functions constructively by making a case not for blind leaps of subjective certitude, but for an object of believing, trust, and loyalty that transcends partial objects: the God of monotheism.

He thus brought to fuller clarity the second important theme anticipated in earlier writings, of "radical monotheism." In contrast to such "faiths" as henotheism, which elevated one finite principle to authority over others, as in nationalism; and polytheism, which maintained faith in many sources of value, radical monotheism made its center of faith and value the principle of being itself, the One beyond the many from which the many are derived and in which they participate. Influenced by Jonathan Edwards, Niebuhr identified the principles of being and value: he described the Creator and the God of grace as one. Thus theology issued in a universal confidence and a universal loyalty; it "dethroned" all absolutes short of the principle of being and yet reverenced relative beings.

The Responsible Self, based on Niebuhr's Robertson Lectures at the University of Glasgow in 1960, was drawn from his influential lectures on Christian ethics. The subtitle is significant, "An Essay in Christian Moral Philosophy." Its framework was not authorized by biblical theology, but by an account of the character of human experience, particularly moral experience. "All life has the character of responsiveness, I maintain" (p. 46). The relational, or interactional, view of the self with other selves and with God, present in earlier publications, assumed special prominence here.

He used the distinction made by philosophers between teleological ethics, "man the maker," seeking to attain good ends; and deontological ethics, "man the citizen," obliged to give right obedience to law; as a basis for a third ideal-type, *cathekontic* ethics: "man the answerer," responding to other persons and events. He viewed our human action as response to action upon us. "What is going on?" is a question prior to "What ought we to do?" The action upon us has to be interpreted, and we respond accountably to that interpretation in the context of our social solidarity. Our actions are to be a fitting response, then, to the events in which we participate. Thus far we have a moral philosophy. What makes it Christian are the themes and symbols used in interpretation—such themes as absolute dependence, sin, and salvation. These refer us to God, who is not only the principle of being, but an active agent. "Responsibility affirms: 'God is acting in all actions upon you. So respond to all actions upon you as to respond to [God's] action'" (p. 126). In this moral philosophy, Christ is the paradigm of responsible action, and in this sense exemplary; but Christ is also the Christian's source of confidence that God is not indifferent to creation, but affirms and seeks the good of creatures.

Niebuhr died in Greenfield, Massachusetts. More than thirty years after his death, his work continues to receive attention by scholars and students. His publications, like his lectures, reflected broad and deep erudition. But he was less given to detailed critical analysis of the thought of others than to creatively synthesizing their contributions in his own theological and ethical thinking. He combined deep religious and moral passion with learning and intellectual acumen; theology and ethics were keys to understanding profound aspects of human experience in their ambiguities and tragedies, as well as their possibilities for human good.

• Niebuhr's literary remains are housed in the Andover-Harvard Theological Library at Harvard University, Cambridge, Mass. In addition to the books mentioned in the text, he coauthored with Daniel Day Williams and James M. Gustafson, *The Advancement of Theological Education* (1957), and coedited with Daniel Day Williams, *The Ministry in Historical Perspectives* (1956). *H. Richard Niebuhr: A Lifetime of Reflections on the Church and the World* (1986), by Jon Diefenthaler, is the most biographical of secondary works. Paul Ramsey, ed., *Faith and Ethics: The Theology of H. Richard Niebuhr*, a festschrift published in 1957, contains a bibliography of his publications, as do Libertus A. Hoedemaker, *The Theology of H. Richard Niebuhr* (1970), and James W. Fowler, *To See the Kingdom: The Theological Vision of H. Richard Niebuhr* (1974). See also Donald E. Fadner, *The Responsible God* (1975); John D. Godsey, *The Promise of H. Richard Niebuhr* (1970); C. David Grant, *God—The Center of Value* (1984); Jerry A. Irish, *The Religious Thought of H. Richard Niebuhr* (1983); Lonnie D. Kliever, *H. Richard Niebuhr* (1977); Douglas F. Ottati, *Meaning and Method in H. Richard Niebuhr's Theology* (1982); Melvin R. Keiser, *Recovering the Personal* (1988); Charles Schriven, *The Transformation of Culture* (1988); Martin L. Cook, *The Open Circle* (1991); and Ronald F. Thiemann, ed., *The Legacy of H. Richard Niebuhr* (1991). An obituary is in the *New York Times*, 6 July 1962.

JAMES M. GUSTAFSON

NIEBUHR, Reinhold (21 June 1892–1 June 1971), theologian and political journalist, was born Karl Paul Reinhold Niebuhr in Wright City, Missouri, the son of Gustav Niebuhr, a German immigrant preacher, and Lydia Hosto, his parish assistant and organist. Reinhold grew up in Missouri and Illinois, where his father, a minister of the German Evangelical Synod of North America, had a series of parishes. From age ten he lived in Lincoln, Illinois, a heavily first- and second-generation German-American town, where his family lived, he later recalled, in "genteel poverty." One of four children (and three sons), he was the apple of his father's eye and decided as a boy to follow his father into the ministry. At age fifteen, having finished the ninth grade at Lincoln High School, he left for three years of boarding school at the Synod's proseminary, Elmhurst College, outside of Chicago. In later years he much regretted having missed a solid high school education. Neither did he ever attend an undergraduate college. His lack of a B.A. degree, and his poor schooling in English, modern history, and the sciences, led him to condemn his church for giving only lip service to education. At age eighteen he enrolled at the Synod's Eden Theological Seminary, outside of St. Louis, where he starred in debate and worked hard on his English writing skills. In 1913 he received the bachelor of divinity degree and was ordained a minister.

Gustav Niebuhr died suddenly in the same spring, and after graduation Reinhold served as interim pastor of his father's church prior to leaving in the fall to attend Yale Divinity School. There he hoped to remedy some of his scholarly deficiencies before taking a congregation of his own. He spent two years at Yale, receiving a second B.D. in 1914 and an M.A. in 1915. At Yale his theological liberalism deepened. At Eden he had already come to an "evangelical liberal" standpoint, which depreciated dogma and stressed the centrality of love in personal and social life. At Yale he was influenced by a more fully "modernist liberal" Protestantism that rejected supernaturalism altogether and deemphasized the Bible as a timeless source of authority. His professors urged him to remain at Yale for a Ph.D., but although he was excited by ideas and yearned to express himself in writing, he thought the scholarly life was too passive. He wanted to immerse himself in the world of social and political affairs as well as the world of ideas, and he believed that a base in the ministry would permit him to combine his practical and intellectual interests.

His first and only congregation was the Bethel Evangelical Church in Detroit, a middle-class parish that grew from sixty-five members when he arrived in 1915 to over 600 when he departed for a professorship at Union Theological Seminary in 1928. In his first years at Bethel, World War I was bloodying Europe, and he struggled to Americanize his mostly German congregation by introducing more English-language services. He was appalled at the extent of the pro-German, anti-British sentiment both at Bethel and in the wider Synod. Once his widowed mother arrived to take over much of the parish work in 1916, he embarked on a campaign to rid the Synod of pro-German feeling. Appointed executive secretary of the Synod's War Welfare Commission in 1917, he spearheaded a crusade against "disloyalty" within the church: the word "German" was dropped from the Synod's name, and the German language was dropped from many Synod churches. At Bethel, German-language services were suspended, at his urging, for the duration of the war, and in 1919 they were stopped once and for all.

During the 1920s Niebuhr became well known nationally as a liberal Protestant speaker and writer. His forceful preaching attracted new members as well as many visitors to Bethel. He had a gift for rapid-fire, stirring sermons that were as emotional as they were intellectual. His listeners were awed by his quickness of mind. Through the years, believers and nonbelievers alike were riveted by his command of pulpit and platform. If he used notes at all he would outline the sermon or talk on a single sheet of paper, then undam a river of bold assertions, vivid anecdotes, humorous asides, and philosophical ruminations. His words cascaded with such energy that sentences were sometimes abandoned halfway through in order to make room for those that followed.

Niebuhr was a great orator at a time when great oratory was dying out, but many members of his audiences still recognized and flocked to it. Many called him a prophet in the biblical sense, and though he was very aware of the danger of pride, he also felt called to bring down God's judgment on human pretensions. His constant theme was that of Amos: God was not interested in solemn assemblies and burnt offerings; He wanted justice to roll down like waters and righteousness like an everlasting stream. Niebuhr insisted on the reality of sin at a time when many liberal ministers stressed instead the unbounded human potential for growth and fellowship. And he avoided merely accusing others of sin: it was not him judging others, but God judging everyone, including him. Human beings were inveterate self-aggrandizers, but God showed mercy by offering forgiveness as well as judgment. Niebuhr always provided a moment of reassurance after finding fault.

Having written many articles for Synod publications during and after the war, Niebuhr became in 1922 an editorialist for and contributor to the *Christian Century*, the Chicago weekly at the forefront of liberal Protestantism. He ranged broadly from domestic and foreign politics to social, religious, and cultural affairs. His writing for the *Century* was informed by a consistent, liberal vision of the crisis confronting the United States and Europe after World War I. In the wake of the Versailles Treaty many secular liberals had concluded that idealism about world brotherhood and social justice was misguided. But many religious liberals like Niebuhr thought that liberalism had merely failed to develop an adequate spiritual energy to carry it toward those still valid goals.

Niebuhr wanted to help build a politically potent labor party (on the model of the British Labour party of Ramsay MacDonald), and he believed that only a religious movement could supply the requisite motive force: an emotional power capable of sparking militant action while also keeping such action under ethical judgment. Where socially concerned liberal churchpeople in the late nineteenth and early twentieth centuries had seen the church as a neutral mediator between the warring camps of labor and capital, Niebuhr urged liberals to take the side of labor. In 1922 he joined the Fellowship for a Christian Social Order, founded after the war by wealthy layman Sherwood Eddy and his right-hand man, pacifist Kirby Page, and in 1923 he became its traveling secretary. Eddy paid for an assistant pastor for Bethel Church, and Niebuhr spoke all over the East and Midwest about the political and religious crisis.

He also took a leading role in social battles in Detroit itself. When the Ku Klux Klan tried to influence the mayoral race in 1925, Niebuhr spoke out forcefully against the Protestant candidate who had received Klan funding. The victorious Catholic candidate, John Smith, then appointed Niebuhr to head an interracial committee charged with investigating race relations in Detroit, a city to which southern African Americans had been streaming ever since the war. Data turned up by the committee helped Niebuhr conduct a campaign against Henry Ford's industrial policy. Ford posed as the workers' benefactor, Niebuhr argued, but meanwhile the wages of the average Ford worker were dropping, while the assembly line was speeding up.

The campaign against Ford, himself a self-proclaimed Christian idealist, confirmed Niebuhr in his growing belief that liberalism was fatally weakened by its sentimental faith in the power of reason and good will to bring about social justice. Standing up to capitalists such as Ford required a determination of the sort that only a dynamic labor movement, sparked by the churches, could muster. Reason was of course indispensable for analyzing social or political situations, but many liberals mistakenly considered it a transformative force as well as a tool. Niebuhr believed that social movements could not be built by appeals to reason alone, just as God could not be found through a rational act of mind. Religious belief and political action both required faith and will as much as knowledge and education.

As early as 1926 Niebuhr began arguing for the abolition of private property in major industries, but it was only in 1929, after moving to New York City to become an editor of the Socialist *World Tomorrow* and an associate professor of ethics at Union Theological Seminary, that he joined the Socialist party. It was a personal struggle for him to embrace socialism, since, like Marxism, it was usually premised on the notion that society was ruled by force, not brotherly love. Niebuhr knew that moral idealism was impotent to change capitalism—industrialists such as Ford would not voluntarily surrender their power—yet he remained wedded to the liberal Christian view that love had to be the fundamental principle of both individual and social life. But since the Socialist party in the 1920s was increasingly dominated by non-Marxists like Norman Thomas, himself a Protestant minister, Niebuhr found it possible to jump into party activities without resolving his theoretical dilemma.

In 1930 he was the Socialist candidate for the New York state senate from the Upper West Side of Manhattan and received a disappointing 1,500 votes out of more than 30,000 ballots cast. In 1932, a presidential election year in which Socialist hopes were high because of the depression, he ran for Congress from the same district and did no better; again he received just under 5 percent of the vote. The message from the voters nationwide was clear: the Socialist party was not to be a vehicle for a mass democratic movement in the United States. Niebuhr remained a Socialist for the rest of the decade, but after 1932 he did not take the same active role in party affairs.

His important book *Moral Man and Immoral Society*, published just after the 1932 election, revealed that he had finally resolved his dilemma about how to preach both love and justice. It also revealed that he had been preparing even before the 1932 election to part political company with his liberal and Socialist friends, who believed, as he had, that the ultimate goal of religious and political action was to convert society into a vast fellowship. *Moral Man* mocked and belittled the long-standing liberal Protestant quest to construct a community of love on earth. Niebuhr insisted that society comprised power blocs that were to be rearranged in the interest of justice. It was not like a garden to be weeded and replanted. "The dream of perpetual peace and brotherhood—will never be fully realized," he wrote, as society is "in a perpetual state of war." Love might still be the fundamental rule of life for individuals—inspired "saints" really could sacrifice self-interest to the interests of others—but the highest ethical ideal that larger groups could embrace was justice.

Between the Socialist defeat of 1932 and World War II, Niebuhr devoted himself increasingly to religious rather than secular organizations. He was the leader of the Fellowship of Socialist Christians (FSC), founded in 1931, and became the editor of its journal *Radical Religion*, begun in 1935 after the collapse of the *World Tomorrow*. In 1934, at his urging, the FSC took measures to ensure that it was more than a radical discussion club: it enacted a "discipline" for its members in the form of a tax on their salaries to provide contributions for the unemployed.

In 1933 Niebuhr also began to take more interest in theological study, partly in response to some vociferous critiques of *Moral Man*. Such critics as his brother H. Richard Niebuhr, himself a professor of ethics, at Yale Divinity School, pointed out that the book failed to deliver any message of hope in its relentless analysis of perpetual social conflict. Niebuhr got to work on a project of reflection that would ultimately produce such major works as *Beyond Tragedy* (1937) and *The Nature and Destiny of Man* (2 vols., 1941, 1943). He was assisted by his wife, Ursula Keppel-Compton, a theology student from England, whom he had married in 1931 and with whom he had two children.

His theological work was also aided by the arrival at Union Seminary in 1933 of German theologian Paul Tillich. Tillich offered Niebuhr a way to extend himself from ethics, on which liberals tended to focus, to theology but without embracing the neo-orthodoxy of Swiss theologian Karl Barth, which Niebuhr regarded as excessively "Lutheran" in its disinterest in history and social transformation. By centering on the notion of myth, Tillich tried to show how Christianity was a form of knowledge, not just an ethical imperative. Niebuhr's *An Interpretation of Christian Ethics* (1935) followed Tillich closely in analyzing the two central Christian "myths": the stories of the Creation and the Fall. The power of Christianity as an ethical force stemmed from its commitment to the idea of a Creator who loved people but also judged them, and to the idea that human beings are responsible for their own sin.

In the late 1930s his theological work was influenced by, and also interrupted by, the growing threat of European fascism. Niebuhr was one of the first radical American Christians to argue that the class struggle had to take a back seat to the "united front" effort to stop Hitler and Mussolini. Reflecting on the course of European history deepened Niebuhr's sense that Christian theology provided a correct account of the tangled mix of creativity, pretension, and delusion in human nature. He immersed himself in European affairs, secular and religious. In 1937 he was a major speaker at the Oxford (England) Conference on Church, Community, and State, where he argued that the world crisis was not just the result of economic conditions or class oppression, but of human nature itself. In his view Communists and liberals were equal-

ly deluded: the former thought that a new system of property relations would foster a new social harmony; the latter thought that the human self was a benign force for good that merely needed training and education to reach its potential. Christians knew the truth, he said: the self was divided against itself, capable of selfless action but always liable to puff itself up and mistake its parochial interests for the universal good. Original Sin was the Christian doctrine that humanists found the most unbelievable, but it was ironically the one doctrine, Niebuhr suggested, that was empirically verified day after day.

In 1939 he delivered his Gifford Lectures, titled "The Nature and Destiny of Man," at the University of Edinburgh. He was only the fifth American to be chosen as Gifford Lecturer since 1888, and he astonished his audience with his extemporaneous delivery from notes. In the middle of one of his lectures in October, Edinburgh was bombed by the Nazis. The audience grew alarmed at the sound of antiaircraft guns a few miles away, but Niebuhr did not notice, and they remained in their seats. He was worried not about German planes, but about whether his lectures were scholarly enough, a sign of his lingering doubts about his academic credentials. But the publication of the lectures in two volumes in 1941 and 1943 established him as a major Christian thinker and a major American cultural figure.

The completion of *The Nature and Destiny of Man* was delayed by Niebuhr's wartime activities, which included his founding and editing of *Christianity and Crisis* and his chairmanship of the Union for Democratic Action (UDA), both founded in 1941. *Christianity and Crisis* was designed as an "interventionist" alternative to the pacifist *Christian Century*, and it brought together former Socialists such as Niebuhr (who resigned from the party in 1940) and respected pillars of the establishment like Henry Sloane Coffin, president of Union Seminary. The UDA emerged directly from the Socialist party when interventionists in its ranks lost patience with the party's isolationism. It was a non-Communist, prolabor, antifascist lobbying and educational group.

As chairman of the UDA, Niebuhr spoke widely and testified before congressional committees in support of Lend-Lease and other measures to defend Britain. He conceded that such a stance might lead to American participation in the war, but he insisted that a Nazi victory would be an intolerable blow to Western civilization as a whole, not just to Europe. After Pearl Harbor, Niebuhr was active on many fronts. He traveled to Britain for the Office of War Information to address the British public as well as Allied troops. He tried to mobilize support for German democrats inside and outside of Germany by chairing the American Friends of German Freedom, based in New York. He tried to get the Roosevelt administration to facilitate European Jewish emigration to the United States. Niebuhr was one of only a handful of American intellectuals to publicize the plight of the Jews during the war.

In 1944 he published *The Children of Light and the Children of Darkness*, an application of the ideas in *The Nature and Destiny of Man* to the realm of democratic theory. Democracy was vindicated, he thought, because it accorded so well with the Christian doctrine of human nature, a doctrine that matched the facts of human experience better than any other philosophy did. "Man's capacity for justice makes democracy possible," he wrote, "but man's inclination to injustice makes democracy necessary." In a stark reversal from *Moral Man and Immoral Society*, he now regarded bourgeois democracy not as a system of inequality to be transcended through social struggle, but as a system of equality. The oligarchies that had troubled him in the earlier work now were "kept fluid" by "pressure from below." Democratic society was self-correcting because of its "openness" and its free marketplace of ideas.

The Children of Light provided an ideological foundation for a new political party to which Niebuhr lent his considerable prestige in 1944: the Liberal party of New York. It grew out of a split in the American Labor party, a pro–New Deal group based in the New York garment trades, and Niebuhr was elected vice chairman. He remained active in the Liberal party in the postwar period. *The Children of Light* also expressed the founding philosophy of the Americans for Democratic Action (ADA), which emerged out of the UDA in 1947. Niebuhr co-chaired the meeting that established the ADA and served on its board, but he always devoted much more of his political energy to the Liberal party in New York than he did to the Washington-based ADA.

After the war Niebuhr remained a dominant figure in religious as well as political affairs. He was a key participant at the Amsterdam Assembly of the World Council of Churches in 1948, and he made speaking tours of England, Holland, and Scandinavia. In 1946 he was a member of a government delegation to Germany, and in 1949 he was an official American delegate to the UNESCO conference in Paris. He also participated from time to time in the deliberations of the State Department's policy planning staff.

His last significant book, *The Irony of American History*, based on lectures given between 1949 and 1951, appeared in 1952. It resembled *The Children of Light* in its vindication of pragmatic democracy. But it went further in combining political theory with his longstanding interest in the moral and religious underpinnings of political life. He hoped to provide a motive force for pragmatic democracy by seeing the American experience as ironic, not tragic or pathetic. His ironic view of American history stressed that Americans were responsible for their fate even though they were not fully in control of that fate. Historical action did not lend itself to completely conscious mastery, but neither were human beings at the mercy of forces beyond their power to shape. The ironic view underscored the ability of a people to mobilize themselves for action while cautioning them against inflated hopes. An ironic sensibility was essential for the moral life, since it encouraged a person to find fault with unjust conditions or institutions but also promoted both criticism of oneself and forgiveness of those who did wrong.

Niebuhr's life changed dramatically in early 1952, when a series of strokes left him partially paralyzed in one arm, made it more difficult for him to speak, and sent him into periodic depressions. His teaching at Union Seminary, always the center of his activities since 1928, now became even more important since he traveled less and less frequently. He still wrote a great deal on both politics and religion and was himself a cultural figure of great stature. Like other ADA liberals he attacked Joseph R. McCarthy for weakening the anti-Communist cause with his scattershot accusations. Like other Eurocentric observers he argued against committing American military forces to the fight against communism in Asia because it might tempt the Soviets to aggression in Europe. Like other Protestant liberals he bemoaned the resurgence of religious fundamentalism in the person of Billy Graham. In 1959 the American Academy of Arts and Sciences signaled his stature by admitting him to its fifty-member inner circle.

After his retirement in 1960, he had teaching stints at Harvard and Princeton, and he continued to write on international affairs and domestic politics until the mid-1960s, when his health declined considerably. In 1964, after *Christianity and Crisis* endorsed Lyndon Johnson (the first presidential endorsement in the magazine's history), Johnson chose Niebuhr to receive the Medal of Freedom, the nation's highest civilian honor. After Johnson escalated the war in 1965, Niebuhr became one of his leading critics. His writings of the 1960s were dominated by his antiwar editorials, though he also voiced increasing skepticism about the doctrine of nuclear deterrence, of which he had earlier been a zealous exponent. He died at his summer home in Stockbridge, Massachusetts.

Niebuhr was a uniquely gifted individual. His journalistic and oratorical talents were combined with a very unusual depth of mind. He was one of the last great liberal Protestant preachers and among twentieth-century preachers was matched only by Martin Luther King, Jr. It is fitting that the single work of Reinhold Niebuhr's that has had the greatest impact on American culture is a prayer, even though not many people know that he wrote it, during the 1940s. It is the Serenity Prayer made famous by Alcoholics Anonymous. Niebuhr made slight variations in it from time to time, but in one common form it reads: "God, give us the serenity to accept what cannot be changed; give us the courage to change what should be changed; give us the wisdom to distinguish one from the other."

• The major collection of Niebuhr's papers is at the Library of Congress. Other noteworthy works by Niebuhr include *Does Civilization Need Religion?* (1927), *Leaves from the Notebook of a Tamed Cynic* (1929), *Reflections on the End of an Era* (1934), *Faith and History* (1949), *The Self and the Dramas of History* (1955), *The Structure of Nations and Empires* (1959), and *Man's Nature and His Communities* (1965). A complete bibliography of his published writings is D. B. Robertson, ed., *Reinhold Niebuhr's Works: A Bibliography* (1954; rev. ed., 1983). The first complete biography is Richard Wightman Fox, *Reinhold Niebuhr: A Biography* (1985). June Bingham, *Courage to Change* (1961), offers an account of Niebuhr's life to that point by a close personal friend, and Paul Merkley, *Reinhold Niebuhr: A Political Account* (1975), is a good introduction to his political views. An excellent treatment of his early political thought is in Donald B. Meyer's two chapters on Niebuhr in *The Protestant Search for Political Realism, 1919–1941* (1960). Useful older works on Niebuhr's theology are Gordon Harland, *The Thought of Reinhold Niebuhr* (1960), and Hans Hofmann, *The Theology of Reinhold Niebuhr* (1956); a significant, more recent interpretation is Dennis McCann, *Christian Realism and Liberation Theology* (1981). A compelling feminist critique of Niebuhrian theology, which argues that pride may be man's cardinal sin but not woman's, is Judith Plaskow, *Sex, Sin, and Grace* (1980). Ursula M. Niebuhr has published some letters to and from her and Reinhold in *Remembering Reinhold Niebuhr* (1991), which also includes some fragmentary reminiscences of her own. A lengthy front-page obituary is in the *New York Times*, 2 June 1971.

RICHARD WIGHTMAN FOX

NIEHAUS, Charles Henry (24 Jan. 1855–19 June 1935), sculptor, was born in Cincinnati, Ohio, the son of John Conrad Niehaus and Sophia Block, German immigrants. As a youth he practiced wood engraving, stonecutting, and marble carving. He studied at the McMicken School of Design in Cincinnati before traveling to Munich in 1877 and enrolling in the Royal Academy, where classical art was the focus of the curriculum. Before graduating from the academy at age twenty-two he became the first American to win a medal there. He also studied in Rome before returning to Ohio in 1881.

Following his return, the state of Ohio commissioned him to create a marble statue of President James A. Garfield (1885), who had just been assassinated, for Statuary Hall in the U.S. Capitol. He also received a commission for a bronze statue of Garfield (1885) for Cincinnati (funded by public subscription) and a state contract for a heroic-scale marble figure of Senator William Allen (1887) to represent Ohio in Statuary Hall. Like many successful sculptors of his day, he chose to work on these commissions in Rome, where from 1883 to 1885 he enjoyed the benefit of inspiration from antique and Renaissance art and proximity to Italian artisans and marble.

Both of the statues for the Capitol exhibit a rather dry naturalism made more pedestrian by hip-high marble "props" (a tree trunk for Allen, a podium for Garfield) that were commonly used as structural supports for the ponderous weight of marble figures' torsos. A hint of lifelessness often found in American figurative sculpture executed in marble in the third quarter of the nineteenth century—when neoclassicism reigned as the sculptural style of the day—pervades these statues and much of Niehaus's work.

Yet Niehaus imbued the bronze *Garfield* with vitality in a masterful fashion. He depicted the statesman in a rhetorical pose. Dressed in formal attire with an unbuttoned knee-length cloak, he holds his speech in his right hand while gesturing effectively with his left. Garfield's noble head is contrasted admirably by the voluminous folds and various textures of his clothing. The pose is natural, and the figure is animated. The statue conveys Garfield's appearance as well as his character. In many ways Niehaus never surpassed this early work, despite numerous commissions for monumental portraits of politicians, soldiers, and other heroes.

While in Rome the sculptor modeled three small figures inspired by classical antiquity: *Silenus*, *Athlete with a Strigil* (1883), and *Caestus* (1883). The *Caestus* depicts a nude boxer who wraps his fists with leather straps as did the ancient Roman pugilists. The *Athlete with a Strigil* scrapes the oil and sand from his youthful body after exercise in the palestra. It won medals at the World's Columbian Exposition (Chicago) in 1893 and the Pan-American Exposition (Buffalo) in 1901 as well as four other exhibitions. These ideal and mythological subjects stand out from the portraiture that constitutes the bulk of Niehaus's oeuvre. Yet they indicate his affection for the antique and anticipate two idealized, colossal male nudes produced later in his career: the *Orpheus* on the Francis Scott Key Memorial in Baltimore (1922), and the *Driller* on the Edwin Drake Monument in Titusville, Pennsylvania (1901), commemorating the first oil well drilled in that state.

After his stay in Rome, Niehaus moved to New York City. Commissions for portraits, architectural sculpture, and monuments soon followed. In 1888 he married Letitia Gorman; the couple had one child. His second-place finish behind Karl Bitter in the 1891 competition for the Astor Memorial Doors for Trinity Church in New York earned him the contract for the south doors (1894). He also completed the *Triumph of Law* pediment of the Appellate Courthouse (1896–1900) in that city, and he executed a carved oak tympanum and portraits of Moses and Edward Gibbon for the Library of Congress (1897). His bust of Vice President Daniel Tompkins (1891) and his statue of Senator Oliver Morton (1899) entered the U.S. Capitol collection. He showed his ability to design and model in the animated French Beaux-Arts style with sculpture for the Pan-American Exposition and the Dewey Memorial Arch (New York City, 1899). In 1900 Niehaus married Regina Armstrong, an art critic, whom he divorced in 1906.

Before the turn of the century Niehaus submitted a model for a memorial to Samuel Hahnemann in a competition organized with the assistance of the National Sculpture Society. The jury, composed of Daniel Chester French, Olin Levi Warner, George Bissell, Thomas Hastings, and Russell Sturgis, reviewed twenty-five models from the United States and abroad before awarding the commission to Niehaus. The sculptor's design to memorialize the German physician who founded the science of homeopathy features a seated figure at the center of an elaborate stone exedrae, which is adorned with two large bronze historical reliefs. The model won a gold medal at the Pan-American Exposition and was shown at the Louisiana Purchase Exposition (1903). Niehaus was noted for such masterful maquettes. In his *History of American Sculpture* (1924), Lorado Taft acknowledged Niehaus "could scarcely make a bad sketch. The finished work may prove a disappointment, but the little model is generally irresistible, not alone for the fine detail which beguiles all committees alike, but for the rarer and more precious qualities of good composition and artistic grasp of the material." In 1913 the critic Charles Caffin called the *Hahnemann* the sculptor's "finest work . . . equalled by few others in the country."

Yet few works by Niehaus matched the brilliance of his early bronze *Garfield* for Cincinnati or his *Hahnemann*. This was perhaps due to the sheer volume of statuary he created over the half century he worked. In addition to the sculpture already discussed, his oeuvre includes the John Paul Jones Monument in Washington (1912), statues for the U.S. Capitol (*John Ingalls*, 1904; *Zachariah Chandler*, 1912; *Henry Clay*, 1928; and *Ephraim McDowell*, 1928), figures of Thomas Hooker and John Davenport for the statehouse in Hartford, Connecticut, two statues of Governor William Goebel at Frankfort, Kentucky, as well as the Kentucky statehouse pediment (1907), *Benjamin Harrison* in Indianapolis, and *Admiral Perry* (1916) and *Abraham Lincoln*, both for Buffalo, New York. A seated *Lincoln* (1900) is in Muskegon, Michigan, as is his *Admiral Farragut* (1900) and standing *McKinley* (1902). A variation of *McKinley* (1907) is at his tomb in Canton, Ohio. Niehaus also executed equestrian monuments to Saint Louis (1903), Confederate general Nathan Bedford Forrest in Memphis, Tennessee (1904), and Ulysses S. Grant for New York City. In New Jersey, World War I memorials by Niehaus are located in Hoboken (1922), Newark (1923), and Hackensack (c. 1923).

Niehaus never experimented with abstract or nonrepresentational art. His style remained academic, traditional, and figurative. German neoclassicism outweighed French naturalism as influences, yet Niehaus could animate his figures—particularly his studies and maquettes—like those of the best French and French-trained artists of his time. In his *History* Taft called Niehaus "a veteran of vast achievement and solid worth . . . winner of numberless competitions and indefatigable builder of monuments."

Niehaus worked until the final year of his life, when failing health forced him from his studio behind his home in Grantwood, New Jersey. He died in Cliffside Park, New Jersey, where he lived with his daughter.

• About fifty items regarding Niehaus's work and the National Institute of Arts and Letters are in the library of the American Academy of Arts and Letters. The most complete study of Niehaus is Wayne Craven, *Sculpture in America* (1984). Lorado Taft, *History of American Sculpture* (1903; rev. ed. 1924), also discusses the sculptor at length. Charles Caffin, *American Masters of Sculpture* (1913), included Niehaus among the eleven artists featured in his book. Beatrice Proske, *Brookgreen Gardens Sculpture* (1943), wrote about his work at Brookgreen Gardens, and James Goode, *Outdoor Sculpture of Washington, D.C.* (1974), documented his Hahnemann and John Paul Jones memorials. *Art in the United States Capitol* (1978) illustrates ten portraits. Obituaries are in the *New York Times*, the *New York Herald-Tribune*, and the *American*, all 20 June 1935.

MICHAEL W. PANHORST

NIELSEN, A. C. (5 Sept. 1897–1 June 1980), market research engineer and business executive, was born Arthur Charles Nielsen in Chicago, Illinois, the son of Danish immigrant Rasmus Nielsen, a business executive, and Harriet Burr Gunn, a teacher. He received his early education at the grammar school in Berwyn and Morton High School in Cicero. He went on to the University of Wisconsin, where in 1918 he obtained a B.S. in electrical engineering, delivering the valedictory address and graduating with the highest grades a student had ever achieved there. In 1918 he also married Gertrude B. Smith; they had five children. That year he enlisted in the U.S. Naval Reserve as an ensign and served during World War I on the USS *Manchuria*.

After returning to Chicago in 1919, Nielsen first plied his engineering skills at a number of firms. Anxious to branch off on his own, he turned to his former fraternity brothers to raise $45,000, and the A. C. Nielsen Company opened its doors in 1923. The company did performance surveys of industrial equipment and provided manufacturers of industrial goods with product evaluation reports. By 1930 the company's annual sales had reached $205,854. But as the depression continued, sales declined 75 percent and the staff fell from forty-five to six. With only one prospect on the horizon, Nielsen persuaded his fourteen-year-old son, Arthur, Jr., to invest his life savings of $54 in the company. The funds enabled Nielsen to travel to New York City, where he made the sale. His son learned an important lesson in capitalism and recovered his investment many times over, eventually stepping into his father's shoes as CEO.

With industrial manufacturing in a slump, Nielsen launched the Nielsen Food and Drug Index, a research service that recorded the retail flow of grocery and drug brands by regular audits of carefully selected samples of stores. Using this information, food and drug manufacturers could measure the sales of their products against their competitors' and establish what Nielsen called "share of market"—which, Nielsen believed, could provide the facts upon which to base business decisions. He also believed that these data could be obtained from small samples, which, if systematically and continuously collected, would provide a "moving picture" of a market. Most executives of the 1920s and 1930s, however, were unfamiliar with statistical methods and viewed his work with skepticism.

Nielsen remained undaunted. In 1936 he learned of the existence of the Audimeter—a mechanical device that made a minute-by-minute record of when a radio was on and where its dial was set—that was being developed by Massachusetts Institute of Technology professors Robert Elder and Louis Woodruff. Always the engineer, Nielsen acquired the invention in 1936, and after some technical modifications he patented it under his company name two years later.

After a four-year pilot project with Audimeters installed in 200 midwestern homes, the company added 800 homes on the East Coast and began offering the Nielsen Radio Index (NRI) on a commercial basis. However, customer response to the NRI was slow. Broadcasters, publishers, and advertisers disparaged the service, believing that since radio signals were intangible there could be no empirical means of verifying the accuracy of Nielsen's ratings. They preferred the cheaper services of the Cooperative Analysis of Broadcasting (Crossley ratings) and C. E. Hooper (Hooperatings), both of which used telephone calls and door-to-door interviews. Yet statistics prevailed: Crossley folded in 1946 and Nielsen bought Hooper's assets in 1950. That year, with 1,500 Audimeters in place representing 97 percent of the United States in coverage area, Nielsen emerged the undisputed ratings champion.

A true visionary, Nielsen then took a chance on a device that fifty years later would prove to be an essential household appliance and business tool—the computer. His son Arthur, Jr., stationed at the army's Aberdeen Proving Grounds during World War II, was assigned to the detail responsible for constructing a building that would house ENIAC, the thirty-ton archetypal computer designed to calculate ballistic problems for large weaponry. Arthur, Jr., sensed that the machine could prove useful for business applications. He persuaded its inventors, J. Presper Eckert, Jr., and John W. Mauchly, to call upon his father after the war. In 1946 they signed a contract to deliver a prototype in twelve months for the princely sum of $150,000. After four years of cash problems and delays, Eckert and Mauchly sold out to Remington Rand. Undeterred, Nielsen arranged with Thomas Watson, Jr., the son of IBM icon Thomas Watson, Sr., to complete the development work. Univac I, the world's first electronic computer, was finally delivered to Nielsen in 1955, and it enabled the Nielsen Company to produce its reports faster, more cheaply, and more comprehensively.

In the early 1950s the Nielsen Company adapted its Audimeter methodology to television, finally abandoning radio ratings in 1964. The company, which was acquired by Dun and Bradstreet for $1.3 billion in 1984, had earned a position as the premier TV ratings service.

Nielsen did more than develop market research tools. He created services that reduced the cost of distribution—marketing, sales, and advertising—involved in moving goods from factory to consumer. According to his son Arthur's oral history, "His services caused essential goods to be priced lower than would otherwise be possible, resulting in higher standards of living through the world."

Later in life Nielsen turned to philanthropic activities, including support for hospitals, medical research, and organizations devoted to education in economics and political economy. His son noted that Nielsen "gave much of his wealth away" to those "born in poverty with no chance to rise on that account," while withholding his money from those he believed "could have wrecked their lives by not having to work." Although a series of strokes in the 1970s led him to hand over the reigns of the company to his son, Nielsen never officially retired. He died in Chicago.

• Books, magazines, newspaper stories, and journal articles on the history of market research or broadcast and cable ratings cover the contributions of Nielsen. Articles in *Business Week* and *Newsweek* address the history of Nielsen's corporate success and the challenges that the company has faced. A folksy oral history by Arthur C. Nielsen, Jr., is available at corporate headquarters in Chicago. An obituary is in the *New York Times*, 4 June 1980.

CARON SCHWARTZ ELLIS

NIEMANN, Carl George (6 July 1908–29 Apr. 1964), organic chemist, was born in St. Louis, Missouri, the son of Julius Henry Niemann, a salesman for a brewery, and Ella Louise Danner. Niemann initially enrolled in the manual training program at Cleveland High School in St. Louis. He changed to a college preparatory program after taking high school chemistry, a course that also led him to build a chemistry laboratory in the basement of the family home. His uncle George Danner helped him get chemicals and arranged a job for Niemann as a chemist at Monsanto Chemical Company after his graduation from high school. While working at Monsanto, Niemann also attended evening classes at Washington University and continued his experiments in his personal laboratory on weekends.

In 1926 Niemann enrolled at the University of Wisconsin. His college education was interrupted when his father died in 1928. An only child, he returned to St. Louis to help his mother, working for an additional year at Monsanto. When he returned to his studies at Wisconsin (earning a B.S. in 1931), he began research with Karl Paul Link on carbohydrates, work that he continued at Wisconsin for his Ph.D. (1934). Niemann published his first research paper at the age of twenty-two, in the *Journal of the American Chemical Society* (52 [1930]: 2474–80). He married Mary Grant Parkhurst in 1934; they had two daughters.

After a short period of postdoctoral research with Link, Niemann moved to the Rockefeller Institute in New York City in 1935 for two years of postdoctoral research on proteins with Max Bergmann. Niemann regarded Bergmann as the main influence on his later research. His experimental skill is demonstrated in thirteen research papers with Link and seven with Bergmann.

After a year in London as Rockefeller Foundation Fellow at the University College Hospital Medical School, Niemann became in 1938 an assistant professor at the California Institute of Technology, where he spent the rest of his life. In 1939 Niemann published his first independent paper (on secretin) and a collaborative paper with Linus Pauling on protein structure (*Journal of the American Chemical Society* 61 [1939]: 1860–67), a paper of historical significance in view of Pauling's later contributions to the structure of proteins. However, Niemann's primary research field in his early years at Caltech involved the synthesis and activity of compounds related to thyroxine, the thyroid hormone.

During World War II, in collaboration with Ernest H. Swift, Niemann worked for the National Defense Research Council, developing methods for rapid identification of compounds that might be used in chemical warfare. In 1944 he traveled in the Pacific war zone as a consultant to the General Headquarters Staff in the Southwest Pacific. He was awarded a Presidential Certificate of Merit for his contributions.

After the war, Niemann's main research interest was the mechanism of action of the enzyme alpha-chymotrypsin, which functions in digestion of proteins. This research resulted in many publications over fifteen years, culminating in a review published in *Science* only about a month before his sudden death. Niemann and his students investigated a large number of factors that affected the rates of catalysis by alpha-chymotrypsin, including salts, non-aqueous solvents, inhibitors, and dimerization and adsorption of the enzyme. Their principal effort, however, was built on Niemann's prowess as a synthetic chemist: he and his students synthesized new substrates and determined the relationship between structure of the substrate and enzyme activity. Niemann hoped to deduce information about the active site of the enzyme by its response to substrate structure. Returning to Emil Fischer's description of enzyme and substrate as "lock and key," Niemann's research had the objective of understanding the structure and operation of the lock by using various keys as probes. In 1960 his research group found the surprising result that some substrates with the unnatural D stereochemistry were better substrates than the L isomers for alpha-chymotrypsin. Although he was a leader in this era of research on enzyme mechanisms, Niemann recognized in his 1964 review that he and his colleagues had only begun to understand the mechanism of action of this enzyme. Later crystallographic determination of the structure of enzymes and enzyme derivatives achieved many of Niemann's objectives.

Niemann was elected to the National Academy of Sciences in 1952 and served for the two years before his death as chairman of the Chemistry Section. For ten years, he was a member of the editorial board of *Organic Reactions*, an annual review devoted to detailed articles on various important synthetic reactions. He had been chairman of the faculty of Caltech.

Niemann was a highly independent scientist, noted for his abilities in synthetic chemistry, and a craftsman in his scientific writing. He was a quiet, unpretentious man who was polite but did not waste words. His colleagues found him highly effective but independent and reluctant to take time away from his research and writing. His main administrative position at Caltech, as chairman of the Divisional Graduate Committee, enabled him to work independently and minimize time away from research. He frequently visited his students in the laboratory and discussed the progress of their research. Outside of chemistry, Niemann was an enthusiastic birdwatcher and reader, with specialized interest in the Civil War.

Although Niemann was known mainly for his later work on chymotrypsin (summarized in *Science* 143 [1964]: 1287–96), he published considerable research in other areas: on the synthesis of amino acid and thyroxine analogues, on blood group substances, on hydrazides, and on ionization constants. He also produced a number of papers on analytical methods and experimental techniques including semimicro methods. At the beginning of a trip to Europe, Niemann suffered a heart attack and died in Philadelphia, Pennsylvania.

• Because Niemann discarded correspondence after it was completed, no personal papers have survived. His colleague at Caltech, J. D. Roberts, wrote a memoir that includes a list of Niemann's more than 250 research publications in National Academy of Sciences, *Biographical Memoirs* 40 (1969): 290–319. An obituary is in *Engineering and Science* (May 1964): 17.

PAUL HAAKE

NIES, Konrad (17 Oct. 1861–10 Aug. 1921), writer, was born in Alzey in Rheinhessen, Germany, the son of Franz Nies, a prosperous baker, and Katharina Margarethe Breyer. After attending public school in Alzey, Nies served as an apprentice to a dry-goods merchant for two years. However, theater was his early passion, and he entered an actors' training school in Leipzig when he was seventeen. As a teenager he gave recitations from Goethe's *Faust* and other works on the public stage and appeared in several performances with H. Curschman, a leading German actor of the time. At age twenty-one he played Hamlet before directing and starring in his own work, a monodrama titled *Konradin von Hohenstaufen*. The work itself and Nies's acting received only moderately favorable reviews, and Nies decided to emigrate to the United States to further his studies and to try performing on the German stage in America.

Nies arrived in the United States in August 1883. He settled in Ohio, where he lived briefly with his brother Philip, and restaged *Konradin von Hohenstaufen*. During the mid-1880s Nies also attended Duane Academy, a branch of Denison University in Ohio, and performed on various German-American stages in Wisconsin and Nebraska. As restless in America as he had been in Germany, Nies accepted a job as a representative of the Freidenker Publication Company. While traveling in this capacity throughout the Midwest he met Elisabeth Waldvogel, whom he married in 1887. They had two children. Also in 1887 Nies published a novel titled *Die Volkersfiedel*.

In April 1888 Nies began one of the most significant projects of his career, a periodical titled *Deutsch-Amerikanische Dichtung*, designed to cultivate interest in German and German-American literature. However, due to the rather narrow scope of the journal, which was devoted almost exclusively to creative writing, and limited financial support from the German-American community, the project failed, leaving Nies financially destitute but still devoted to the cause of promoting German-American literature, particularly German poetry. Nies supported himself by teaching high school German in Newark, Ohio, and later directed a private school for girls in St. Louis, Missouri. His first book of poetry, *Funken*, was published in Leipzig in 1891. In addition to teaching and pursuing his own writing, he lectured widely in several American and German cities.

During the early 1890s Nies suffered from asthma and exhaustion and developed tuberculosis of the larynx; nevertheless, he continued to write. Between the years 1900 and 1905 he published four verse-dramas (*Deutsche Gaben*, *Rosen im Schnee*, Im Zeichen der Freiheit, and *Die herrlichen Drei*) and his second volume of poetry, *Aus Westlichen Weiten*. While on a combined rest and lecture tour throughout Europe, Nies engaged in an extramarital affair with Olga Khripunowa, a Russian noblewoman. He returned from his trip abroad in 1907 nearly bankrupt and facing a costly divorce suit. Confronted by debt, Nies accepted a position editing the *Denver Demokrat*; he returned to editing several years later to become editor in chief of the *Colorado Herold* in 1916–1917. Continuing his efforts to acquaint Americans with German literature, he spent the year 1913–1914 touring a number of German-populated American cities.

Nies turned to spiritualism near the end of his life, reconciling with his wife in 1909 and retreating in solitude to a home overlooking San Francisco Bay, which he called "Waldnest." American involvement against Germany in World War I distressed him greatly, and he turned to writing war poetry. He composed his first war poem in 1914 and continued to speak out against the war, publishing "Zum Rettungswerk," a poem sympathetic to his defeated homeland, in 1918.

Nies died in San Francisco's German Hospital of complications following an appendectomy. The poems in his last volume of poetry, *Welt und Wildnis* (1921), show increased pessimism, engendered largely by the war between his two countries, and a fear of old age. Many scholars, however, consider this work to be Nies's most sophisticated.

According to Robert E. Ward, "[t]he life of Konrad Nies mirrors the tragedy of the German-American who so desperately sought to retain his cultural heritage in a foreign environment." Nies is considered one of the most prolific and versatile German-American writers. His work reflects his German identity, and the zeal with which he promoted German literature reflects a love of America that was deep enough to compel him to share his culture. However, Nies arrived in the United States just as the popularity that German literature had enjoyed during the period from 1830 to 1880 began to wane, and his maturation as a poet unfortunately coincided with the anti-German sentiment surrounding World War I.

His themes, however, are universal: love of country, friendship, nature. Formally, his work is conservative rather than experimental; in particular, his later poetry demonstrates sophisticated command of the sonnet form. Today his work contributes to our understanding of American life from the perspective of a German American at the turn of the century.

• There is no known repository of Nies's papers. Robert E. Ward gives a complete account of his life and work in "Konrad Nies: German-American Literary Knight," *German-American Studies* 3 (1971): 7–11, reprinted in *German-American Literature*, ed. Don Heinrich Tolzmann (1977). An overview by Ernst Rose, "German-American Literature" in *Cassell's Encyclopedia of Literature*, 2d ed. (1970), places Nies within the context of the German contribution to American letters. See also C. R. Walther-Thomas, "Konrad Nies, ein deutsche Dichter in Amerika" (Ph.D. diss., Univ. of Pennsylvania, 1933). An obituary is in the *San Francisco Chronicle*, 12 Aug. 1921.

ELIZABETH ANN BEAULIEU

NIEUWLAND, Julius Arthur (14 Feb. 1878–11 June 1936), organic chemist and botanist, was born in Hansbeke, Belgium, the son of Jean Baptiste Nieuwland, a laborer, and Philomena Van Hoecke. In 1880 the family moved to South Bend, Indiana, where Flemish immigrants had established a community. At age fourteen Nieuwland decided to become a priest and entered Holy Cross Seminary at the University of Notre Dame. He received a bachelor's degree in classical studies from the university in 1899. The Holy Cross order sent him to its college at Catholic University in Washington, D.C., to continue studies for the priesthood and to undertake work in science, his interest in science having become evident at Notre Dame. In 1903 he was ordained as a Holy Cross Father, and in 1904 he earned a doctorate in chemistry with a minor in botany.

Nieuwland was professor of botany at Notre Dame from 1904 to 1918 and professor of chemistry from 1918 to 1936. As a botanist, he published about 100 papers in plant taxonomy and anatomy. On becoming a chemistry professor, he continued his botanical work during the summer only. His botanical contributions consisted largely of a taxonomic record of the flora of several regions, especially of Indiana and Michigan.

There was no convenient outlet for the publication of papers on the biota of the Midwest. In 1909 Nieuwland founded the *American Midland Naturalist* and was its editor until 1932. The high quality of this journal, devoted to the natural history of the prairie states, gained it worldwide distribution. With his plant collection he founded the university herbarium. He also collected rare botanical books, an interest that led him to publish reprints of scarce writings by botanists, including North American naturalists, as supplements to the journal.

During his years as botany professor Nieuwland sporadically pursued chemical studies. His doctoral dissertation foreshadowed his career in chemistry. Its subject was the reactions of acetylene, and it displays an overpowering interest in reactions rather than in compounds and synthesis. His aim was to discover new reactions and extend old ones. This research resulted in the invention of new catalysts and reactions that greatly expanded knowledge of the chemistry of acetylene. These acetylene reactions produced both innocuous compounds and highly toxic and explosive ones. The reaction of acetylene with arsenic chloride yielded an exceptionally hazardous substance. He refused to do further research on it, but Winford Lee Lewis of the Chemical Warfare Service later developed it into "Lewisite," the most potent poison gas made during World War I.

In 1906 Nieuwland resumed his study of the reaction of acetylene and a mixture of copper and alkali metal chlorides. He noted a peculiar odor but was unable to identify the source. Fourteen years later he substituted ammonium chloride for the alkali metal chloride and obtained a new gas and a new liquid. In 1921 he identified these as monovinylacetylene and divinylacetylene, a dimer and trimer of acetylene. After further research, he presented his findings in 1925 at a conference in New York at which Du Pont chemists were present. In the 1920s, with the American automobile industry burgeoning and the price of natural rubber controlled by foreign monopolies, Du Pont was seeking a substitute for rubber. Nieuwland's new gas and liquid impressed the company's chemists as possible sources for polymerization into a synthetic rubber. Du Pont proposed to Nieuwland a collaborative research program in which it would finance his research and the company would develop practical products from his compounds. The proposal agreed on with Notre Dame provided the university with a share of profits made under any patents that might result and a royalty based on polymer sold over the life of the patents.

The collaboration proceeded slowly at first, but in 1929 Nieuwland discovered the direct addition of hydrogen chloride to monovinylacetylene to form 2-chlorobutadiene, an analogue of isoprene, the basic unit in natural rubber. Known as "chloroprene," it polymerized into an elastic substance. Du Pont developed the process and used it to market the first commercially successful synthetic rubber, "neoprene," in 1931. Neoprene remains the most versatile and widely applicable of all synthetic rubbers. Nieuwland stayed close to the progress at Du Pont and was proud of his contribution to it.

Nieuwland remained active in chemical research until his death, which occurred following a heart attack in a laboratory at Catholic University where he had gone to do summer research. Many honors came his way in his last years. In 1935 the Chemical Foundation of New York established the Nieuwland Foundation for Chemistry at Notre Dame. He was especially pleased with the Gregor Mendel Medal awarded him by Villanova University in 1936 because botany was his favorite science. He was a quiet-mannered priest and scholar who shunned personal publicity and was never happier than in a marsh or meadow considering all its botanical specimens.

Nieuwland's collaboration with Du Pont benefited both the company and his university. The collaboration represents both one of the first and also one of the most outstanding examples of successful interaction between academic and industrial research. The nation also benefited by getting a head start in developing a strong synthetic rubber industry, a development of major importance during World War II.

• Nieuwland's papers are in the University of Notre Dame Archives and include his correspondence, manuscripts, patents, and lecture notes. The July 1936 issue of *American Midland Naturalist* contains a bibliography of his publications. A manuscript incomplete at his death appeared in 1945 as *The Chemistry of Acetylene*, with Richard R. Vogt as coauthor; it became the standard work on the subject. He traced the development that led to the discovery of neoprene in "The Story of Synthetic Rubber," *Proceedings of the Indiana Academy of Science* 44 (1935): 17–21. The most informative studies of his scientific career are by William S. Calcott, "Father Nieuwland, the Chemist," and Marcus Lyon, "Father Nieuwland, the Botanist," both in a special edition of the Notre Dame publication *Catalyzer* (Feb. 1937): 39–44. See Hermann E. Schroeder, "Nieuwland and Neoprene: A Retrospective Reassessment," *Rubber World* 181 (Mar. 1980): 39–42, and 182 (Apr. 1980): 40–42, for the collaboration between Nieuwland and Du Pont. An obituary is in the *New York Times*, 12 June 1936.

ALBERT B. COSTA

NIGGER ADD (1845?–24 Mar. 1926), cowboy, roper, and bronc rider, also known as Negro Add or Old Add, was born Addison Jones, reportedly in Gonzales County, Texas; his father and mother are unknown. The early life of Add is clouded in conjecture. He may have been a slave on the George W. Littlefield plantation in Panola County, Mississippi, and relocated with the Littlefields when they settled in Gonzales County, Texas, in 1850. It is also possible that he was born in Gonzales County and was purchased by the Littlefields after they arrived. There is no record of his youth and early adulthood.

There are many stories about Add in cowboy memoirs and biographies, but the only name given is Nigger Add or Old Negro Add. It apparently seemed of little consequence in cowboy country that Add had a last name. Everyone who spoke or wrote about Add agreed, however, that he was an outstanding cowboy and bronc buster. Vivian H. Whitlock, who cowboyed with Add for several years on the LFD ranch in Texas and eastern New Mexico, called him "the most famous Negro cowpuncher of the Old West." J. Evetts Haley, biographer of George W. Littlefield, called him "the most noted Negro cowboy that ever 'topped off' a horse."

Add's reputation with horses was due to his ability, as he used to say, "to look a horse square in the eye and almost tell what it was thinking" and to ride every horse he saddled, with one exception. Add is reported to have been thrown only by a bronc named Whistling Bullet. In typical cowboy fashion Add tried Whistling Bullet again, and according to Pat Boone, a district judge in Littlefield, Texas, he was the only man to ride him.

While the work of "taking the first pitch out of a bronc" often fell to black cowboys, Add performed this task with a special skill, daring, and raw nerve. Several cowboys commented that they saw Add perform this feat on various occasions. According to Haley,

He would tie a rope hard and fast around his hips, hem a horse up in the corner of a corral or in the open pasture, rope him around the neck as he went past at full speed, and where another man would have been dragged to death, Add would, by sheer skill and power on the end of a rope, invariably flatten the horse out on the ground. (P. 184)

As was the custom of the day, cowboys from neighboring ranches often worked round-ups together, and Add, who was known and respected by ranchers and cowboys of eastern New Mexico and West Texas, was a familiar sight. N. Howard "Jack" Thorp, noted cowboy song collector and songwriter, spoke of camping with Add and a group of black cowhands from South Texas in March 1889 at the beginning of his first song-hunting trek. Later Thorp helped to ensure Add's place in history by writing a cowboy song titled "Whose Old Cow?" that in a humorous fashion recognized Add's ability to identify earmarks and brands.

As cowboys gained experience in the cattle business, they rose from the rank of tenderfoot to top hand or even range boss or foreman. Thorp, in fact, referred to Add as the LFD outfit's range boss. West Texas black cowboys, however, had little chance to pass cowboy status, as was suggested by Whitlock: "He [Add] was a good cowhand, but because of the custom in those days, never became what was known as a 'top' hand." There also was a certain unwritten yet generally understood deference black cowboys were expected to extend to their white counterparts. This situation was the legacy of slavery, which crossed the frontier with the settlers, ranchers, and cowboys. A black cowboy who challenged those traditions did so at his peril.

Add at various times came up to that line and sometimes crossed it. One white cowboy, Mat Jones, said that Add was "a privileged character." This may have referred to the fact that he was well liked or even protected by LFD officials. Jones told a story that became legend on the LFD about Cliff Robertson, a white cowboy who came from a neighboring ranch as a "rep," or representative. Ranches often sent reps who were seasoned cowboys to other ranches during round-ups to make sure that their stock was identified, properly branded, and returned to home ranch. Add rode up to change his horse and said to Robertson, "What horse do you want, lint?" The term "lint" was a derisive one that referred to a young, inexperienced cowboy from East Texas with cotton lint still in his hair. Robertson tried to catch his own horse and threw a lasso and missed. Add then threw his rope and caught the horse and began to drag it out. Robertson, feeling insulted and embarrassed, came after Add with his rope doubled, or, as some cowboys said, with a knife to cut the rope. At this point Bud Wilkerson, the LFD's range wagon boss, rode between them and said to Add, "Drag the horse out, and I will tend to the lint." Robertson was so angered by the experience that he cut out his horses and went back to his home ranch.

Add, like many cowboys, traveled to other ranches where he could not depend on the protection and goodwill of the LFD. Jones related another story when Add was the LFD rep at the Hat ranch and breached the proper etiquette for a black cowboy. Add went to drink from a water bucket and, finding it empty, followed a standard cowboy procedure that he apparently used on the LFD without thought. He began to siphon water through a hose attached to a large water tank. To get the water started, Add used a method referred to as "sucking the gut." As Add was in the process of starting the water, a white cowboy named Tom Ogles picked up a neck yoke and hit him on the back of the neck, knocking him out. Add, who was reported to have knocked out a black man from a neighboring town with one punch and was described by everyone as stocky, short, and very powerfully built, did nothing. When he regained consciousness, he waited for the remuda to arrive, got his horse, and rode home. This incident provided ample evidence that Add recognized the limitations that society had placed on him.

Add's reputation as a roper also gained him respect and renown. He was able, according to some of his fellow cowboys, to go into a corral and rope any horse with uncanny accuracy. One roping story told by Whitlock attests to Add's roping talents as well as his sense of cowboy humor. One day Add was sitting on his horse in front of the Grand Central Hotel in Roswell, New Mexico, when a runaway team of horses pulling a milk wagon came racing down the street. He made a big loop in his lariat, rode alongside the team, threw it around the horses' heads, and allowed the slack to drape over the wagon. He then turned his horse off in a steer-roping style and caused the wagon, horses, and milk bottles to crash and scatter all over the street. After Add retrieved his rope, he was reported to have said, "Them hosses sure would've torn things up if I hadn't caught them."

Addison Jones was more fortunate than many black cowboys west of the Pecos in that he found someone locally to marry. It was not uncommon for black men in West Texas either to travel back to East Texas to find a wife or to remain single. In 1899 Add and Rosa Haskins were married by Rev. George W. Read. Add gave his age as fifty-four, while his bride was listed as thirty-six. Haskins, who was a cook and domestic for a number of prominent Roswell families, came to New Mexico from Texas sixteen years before she married Add. There is very little to indicate whether the couple enjoyed marital bliss, but according to Thorp, the announcement of the wedding to a few friends prompted ranchers throughout the Pecos valley to send wedding gifts to Old Add. The lack of a wedding registry and communications may have been the reason that Add and Rosa found nineteen cookstoves at the freight office in Roswell when they came to pick up their wedding presents.

Add's life was lived and ended, according to former Texas and New Mexico sheriff Bob Beverly, the way an old cowboy's life should be:

Add . . . realized his work was over. He had ridden the most dangerous trails and had conquered the wildest horses. He had always been thoroughly loyal to the Littlefields and the Whites. He was at the end of his road and he laid down and died knowing full well that his efforts had been recognized and appreciated by the really great cowmen of Texas and New Mexico. (Bonney, p. 141)

Addison Jones died in Roswell and, according to Elvis Fleming, suffered a final double indignity of having his name misspelled and the improper birth data carved into his tombstone. The name on Add's grave is Allison Jones, with a birth date of 24 March 1856, rather than 1845. Old Add lived an ordinary yet extraordinary life as a black cowboy in West Texas and New Mexico. He succeeded in living a life worth remembering, which was something few cowboys, black or white, were able to achieve.

• Elvis E. Fleming, "Addison Jones, Famous Black Cowboy of the Old West," in *Treasures of History III*, Historical Society for Southeast New Mexico (1995), pp. 34–46, is the best and most comprehensive account of Addison Jones to date. J. Evetts Haley, *George W. Littlefield, Texan* (1943), is a very readable sketch of Add's experiences on the LFD and draws from cowboy memories of him. See Cecil Bonney, *Looking over My Shoulder: Seventy-five Years in the Pecos Valley* (1971); Mat E. Jones, *Fiddlefooted* (1966); Eugene H. Price, *Open Range Ranching on the South Plains in the 1890s* (1967); Vivian H. Whitlock, *Cowboy Life on the Llano Estacado* (1970); and N. Howard "Jack" Thorp, *Songs of the Cowboys* (1921; repr. 1966) and "Banjo in the Cow Camps," *Atlantic Monthly*, Aug. 1940, for personal experiences of cowboys who worked with Add. Addison Jones's full name was revealed in print for the first time in Connie Brooks, *The Last Cowboys: Closing the Open Range in Southeastern New Mexico, 1890s–1920s* (1993).

MICHAEL N. SEARLES

NIGHTHAWK, Robert (30 Nov. 1909–5 Nov. 1967), blues artist, was born Robert Lee McCullum (or McCollum) in Helena, Arkansas. Almost nothing is known of his parents except his father's surname, McCullum, his mother's maiden name, McCoy, and that they were sharecroppers. When still in his teens, Robert left home to travel and work. He began his musical career as a harmonica player but switched to guitar around 1930 when he and a cousin, Houston Stackhouse, were working on a farm at Murphy's Bayou, Mississippi. Stackhouse, who had traveled with and learned from Delta blues legend Tommy Johnson, recalled that he taught McCullum to play guitar, passing along much of the Johnson repertoire. At the same

time, McCullum taught his brother Percy to play harmonica, and the three began playing locally, eventually branching out to such Mississippi venues as Crystal Springs and Jackson.

After a mid-1930s altercation, supposedly involving a shooting, McCullum left Mississippi and settled in St. Louis, then the urban blues capital of the country. Through a connection with Walter Davis, a St. Louis pianist and part-time talent scout, McCullum was brought to the attention of Bluebird records. On 5 May 1937 he was one of five St. Louis artists who participated in a marathon recording session for Bluebird in Aurora, Illinois. McCullum played as a duo with Big Joe Williams and in a trio format with Williams on guitar and Sonny Boy Williamson on harmonica, an early foreshadowing of the 1950s Chicago band sound. At that session McCullum waxed six sides as a featured artist, among them "Prowling Nighthawk," the inspiration for the name by which he later became best known. On those first recordings, though, he used his mother's maiden name and called himself Robert Lee McCoy, possibly still fearing repercussions from the earlier trouble in Mississippi.

Proving himself competent on both guitar and harmonica, McCullum worked as a house musician for Bluebird from 1937 to 1940, the most prolific recording period of his career. A 1938 session with Williamson and Speckled Red yielded eight sides, this time issued under the name "Rambling Bob." A switch to Decca in 1940 found him using the alias "Peetie's Boy," in deference to Decca star Peetie Wheatstraw. That same year he married washboard player Anne (or Amanda) Sortier.

By 1942 McCullum had switched to electric guitar, transforming techniques he had picked up from guitarist Tampa Red (Hudson Whittaker) into an exciting slide style that eventually influenced such artists as Earl Hooker, Muddy Waters, and Elmore James. Now playing as Robert Nighthawk, he began using radio to promote his band, create a reputation, and acquaint countless aspiring blues artists with his distinctive instrumental sound. Beginning with station KFFA in his birthplace, he gained fame, if not fortune, via the airwaves. As one band member, pianist Pinetop Perkins, recalled, "We weren't making any money, we were just advertising the band." Indeed, radio exposure made Nighthawk a celebrity, ensuring attendance at his band's many regional appearances.

Although leading the life of a musical celebrity in the South, Nighthawk traveled to Chicago sporadically. In 1948 Muddy Waters, at whose wedding reception Nighthawk had played in 1932, brought him to the attention of the Chess brothers, Leonard and Phil, owners of the Chess record label. A 1949 session for Chess resulted in a two-sided classic, "Black Angel Blues" and "Annie Lee Blues," two electric-slide blues drawn from the repertoire of Tampa Red. Nevertheless, Chess appeared to lose interest in Nighthawk after 1950.

Sessions for the United label in 1951 and its subsidiary label, States, in 1953 produced other classics in the

Delta blues tradition, among them "The Moon Is Rising" and Tommy Johnson's "Maggie Campbell." The recordings were poorly distributed and promoted, however, and did little to further Nighthawk's career.

Nighthawk returned south to play around Helena and nearby Friar's Point, Mississippi. He visited Chicago in 1960 to work with Kansas City Red and again in 1964 to work with a band called the Flames of Rhythm that played in the Maxwell Street market district, a magnet for blues artists. Also in 1964 he recorded several cuts for a British album, recorded an album for the Testament label, and appeared at the Chicago Folk Festival. After this brief flirtation with the mushrooming folk/blues revival audience, Nighthawk once again returned south to play clubs in Jackson and Lula, Mississippi. In 1965 he took over KFFA's "King Biscuit Time" after the death of the show's long-time star, Sonny Boy Williamson No. 2 (Aleck Miller).

By 1967, his own health failing, Nighthawk reunited with his cousin and first teacher, Stackhouse, for a final Testament recording. He died of congestive heart failure at Helena Hospital.

Nighthawk's limited recording activity in the 1950s and early 1960s, the heyday of his peers, led later critics to label him "overlooked" and "underappreciated." Described by many who knew him as introverted, he made little impact during the blues revival. Instead, he remained true to his roots, returning again and again to the audiences that had supported him throughout his life.

Remembered by history as a 1930s recording artist and influential guitar stylist, Nighthawk actually made his deepest impression through radio and live performances, which were warmly recalled by the southern black audiences whose culture and traditions he embraced. Unlike artists who moved to Chicago, he preferred his familiar southern venues; his southern audiences likewise appreciated his art, as did his fellow blues musicians. As guitarist/mandolinist Johnny Young put it: "Nighthawk was a hell of a good musician. . . . He was so good he almost made me cry." Robert Nighthawk was inducted into the Blues Foundation Hall of Fame in 1983.

• For general information see Sheldon Harris, *Blues Who's Who: A Biographical Dictionary of Blues Singers* (1979; repr. 1989); and Jim O'Neal, "Living Blues Interview: Houston Stackhouse," *Living Blues*, no. 17 (Summer 1974): 20–36. For samples of his guitar playing, listen to *Lake Michigan Blues 1934–1941*, Nighthawk Records 105; *Robert Nighthawk: Bricks in My Pillow*, Pearl, PL-11; and *Robert Nighthawk and His Flames of Rhythm: Live on Maxwell Street*, Rounder Records, 2022.

BARRY LEE PEARSON
BILL McCULLOCH

NIJINSKA, Bronislava (8 Jan. 1891–21 Feb. 1972), ballet dancer and choreographer, was born in Minsk, Russia, the third child of the Polish dancers Tomasz Nijiński (Russ., Foma Nizhinsky) and Eleonora Bereda. Although Bronislava Nijinska is often identified as the sister of the celebrated Vaslav Nijinsky, she was a major artist in her own right and a key figure in the development of twentieth-century ballet. Most of her work was done in Europe, but she spent more than a third of her life in the United States and obtained citizenship in 1949.

Nijinska made her stage debut when she was just three years old, dancing with her two brothers, Stanislav (born in 1886) and Vaslav (born in 1889), in a Christmas pageant in Nizhni Novgorod. Two years later, the Nijinsky family moved to Saint Petersburg, and soon afterward her parents separated. Seeking to create a stable environment for her children, Eleonora Nijinsky took Vaslav and Bronislava to audition for the Imperial Theater School, the state academy of dance attached to the Maryinsky Theater. They were accepted as ballet students in 1898 and 1900, respectively.

Nijinska's principal teachers at the Imperial School were Enrico Cecchetti, Nikolai Legat, and Michel Fokine. During the summer holidays she was taught by her brother Vaslav, to whom she remained extremely close during her childhood. As his pupil, she became the first person to know and be influenced by his radically new ideas regarding the dance and his desire to substitute a rigorously stylized form of movement for the classical ballet tradition. When Nijinska graduated in 1908, she was given the First Award based on her superior marks in both academics and dancing. Like her brother, she was hired as an artist of the Imperial Theaters and was thereby assured a secure and privileged life in Saint Petersburg.

The following year, in spring 1909, the Russian impresario Serge Diaghilev assembled a troupe of dancers organized around the Maryinsky's summer recess. In its first Paris season at the Théâtre du Châtelet, the company—in which Nijinsky was a principal dancer and Nijinska a member of the corps de ballet—introduced Russian ballet to the West, and a new concept of performance that integrated dance, music, choreography, and visual design. A second Paris season was presented by Diaghilev in 1910. The following year Nijinska submitted her resignation to the Imperial Theaters and with her brother joined Diaghilev as a member of his newly formed Ballets Russes, a permanent touring company whose base of operation centered in both Paris and Monte Carlo.

Between 1911 and 1913, Nijinska emerged as a strong and talented dancer. It was also during these years that she assisted her brother as he choreographed his first ballets, *L'Après-midi d'un Faune*, *Jeux*, and *Le Sacre du Printemps*. In 1914 Nijinska helped Vaslav to organize a company of his own in London. In spite of their efforts, the debut season of the Saison Nijinsky was canceled after a two-week run at the Palace Theatre.

Shortly after the outbreak of World War I, Nijinska returned to Petrograd (formerly Saint Petersburg) with her first husband, Aleksandr Kochetovsky, whom she had married in 1912, and their daughter Irina. Husband and wife were engaged as leading dancers by the Petrograd Private Opera Theater in 1915. It was in that year as well that Nijinska presented her first choreography—the solos *La Poupée* and *Autumn Song*—at the Narodny Dom Theater. The following year the couple went to Kiev and worked together staging divertissements and ballets at the State Opera Theater, where Kochetovsky had been appointed ballet master.

Beginning in 1917, Nijinska taught at a variety of institutions, including the State Conservatory of Music, the Central State Ballet Studio, the Yiddish Cultural Center Drama Studio, and the Ukrainian Drama School. Just after the October Revolution, she took a brief trip to Moscow, where she began work on a choreographic treatise titled "On Movement and the School of Movement." It is in this essay that she documents her search for a new means of expression based on the extension of the classical vocabulary of dance steps.

After returning to Kiev, Nijinska resumed teaching, and on 10 February 1919, only three weeks after the birth of her son, Léon, she opened a dance studio that she called the École de Mouvement. Under its aegis, she presented a solo concert that included her first plotless ballet compositions—*Mephisto Valse* (1919) and *Twelfth Rhapsody* (1920)—which may well stand as the first abstract ballets in the history of twentieth-century dance.

In mid-1920, after learning of Nijinsky's tragic mental illness, Nijinska determined that she would leave Russia in order to join him in Vienna. In May 1921 she placed an advanced student in charge of her school and undertook a six-week journey to Austria with her mother and two children. While in Vienna, in September 1921, Nijinska was invited by Diaghilev to rejoin the Ballets Russes in London. In addition to dancing with the company and conducting rehearsals, she arranged several new dance sequences for *The Sleeping Princess* and thus began her tenure as the company's first and only female choreographer.

Between 1922 and 1924, Nijinska served as principal dancer, ballet mistress, and choreographer for the Ballets Russes. During this period she choreographed seven major ballets—*Le Mariage d'Aurore*, *Le Renard*, *Les Noces* (The Wedding), *Les Tentations de la Bergère*, *Les Biches*, *Les Fâcheux*, and *Le Train Bleu*. Among her collaborators were the composers Igor Stravinsky, Francis Poulenc, Georges Auric, and Darius Milhaud, and the visual artists Mikhail Larionov, Natalia Goncharova, Marie Laurencin, Juan Gris, Georges Braque, Henri Laurens, and Pablo Picasso. In addition to demonstrating her versatility as a choreographer, Nijinska performed leading roles in many Ballets Russes productions.

Nijinska and Kochetovsky separated in 1919 and divorced in 1924. That same year she married Nicholas Singaevsky, a former pupil and dancer with Diaghilev's Ballets Russes; they had no children. The next year, owing to disagreements with Diaghilev over her ideas for abstract ballets, Nijinska resigned from the Ballets Russes and formed her own company, the Théâtre Choréographique Nijinska. For this troupe of eleven dancers she created six short ballets—*Holy Etudes*, *The Sports and Touring Ballet Revue*, *Savage Jazz*, *On the Road*, *Le Guignol Humoresque*, and *A Night on a Bald Mountain*—that were presented during a summer tour of English resorts, with a selection performed afterward in Paris. Nijinska invited the Russian avant-garde painter Alexandra Exter to design the costumes for these ballets.

From her home in Paris, Nijinska continued to work on a variety of projects. She returned briefly to the Ballets Russes in 1926 to choreograph a modern version of *Romeo and Juliet*, with sets and costumes by the surrealist painters Max Ernst and Joan Miró. The same year she was engaged by the Teatro Colón in Buenos Aires as choreographic director and principal dancer, an association that lasted until 1946.

In Paris, in the summer of 1928, Nijinska was invited to organize and direct the Ida Rubinstein Ballet. She created seven new ballets for the company, including *Le Baiser de la Fée*, to Stravinsky, and *Boléro* and *La Valse*, both to the music of Maurice Ravel. The Russian stage designer Alexandre Benois designed the sets and costumes for all these productions. The Rubinstein Ballet dissolved a year after its founding but was reactivated in 1931 and 1934, with Nijinska's works retained in repertory.

During this period, Nijinska also staged dances for the Opéra Russe in Paris as well as for Max Reinhardt in Berlin. In January 1932 she again founded her own company, which she called the Théâtre de la Danse Nijinska, and which proved to be, in size and repertory, her most ambitious undertaking. This 32-member touring company was in existence from 1932 to 1934 and performed choreography by Nijinska in France, Spain, Italy, and Monte Carlo. Her husband served as the company's business manager.

Although an injured Achilles tendon suffered in 1933 precipitated the end of Nijinska's performance career, she continued to gain recognition as a choreographer and teacher. In 1934 she was awarded the medal of the Archives Internationales de la Danse in Paris for twenty-five years of artistic activity. The following year, working as a guest choreographer, Nijinska created *Les Cent Baisers* for Colonel W. de Basil's Ballets Russes de Monte Carlo, and she was invited to the United States to stage the dance sequences in Reinhardt's feature film *A Midsummer Night's Dream*. Sadly, it was also during this year that she and her family were involved in an automobile accident in which her son Léon was killed and her daughter Irina critically injured.

During the second half of the 1930s, Nijinska was associated with two companies, the Markova-Dolin Ballet, for which she worked as ballet mistress and choreographer, and the Polish Ballet, for which she served as artistic director and choreographer from 1937 to 1938. For the Polish Ballet she created five new works, including *Chopin Concerto*, an abstract ballet conceived in a neoclassical style. On the basis of her work for the company, Nijinska received the

Grand Prix for choreography at the 1937 Exposition Internationale in Paris, and her company received the Grand Prix for performance.

With the outbreak of World War II, Nijinska (under contract to de Basil) left Europe and traveled with her family to the United States. Although she was to have continued on to Australia, the contract allowed her to accept an invitation from Lucia Chase in New York to stage her own version of *La Fille Mal Gardée* for the inaugural season of Ballet Theatre (later renamed American Ballet Theatre). The following year Nijinska settled in Hollywood, where she opened the Bronislava Nijinska–Hollywood Ballet School in 1941.

Throughout the ensuing decade, Nijinska continued to choreograph works for companies in Europe— Sergei Denham's Ballet Russe de Monte Carlo, the Markova-Dolin Ballet, and the Grand Ballet de Monte Carlo. In America she choreographed new productions for Ballet Theatre, Ballet Repertory, Chicago, and Ballet International. Nijinska opened a new studio in Beverly Hills in 1951 where, as before, she frequently left her daughter Irina Nijinska in charge while she fulfilled her choreographic engagements. The studio was closed in 1955 after Nijinska moved to Pacific Palisades, but she continued to teach in nearby Brentwood and Pasadena.

During the last decade of her life, Nijinska began to compose her long-planned memoirs. Her work was interrupted in the 1960s when Sir Frederick Ashton, artistic director of Britain's Royal Ballet, asked her to restage *Les Biches* and *Les Noces*. The revival of these two acknowledged masterpieces assured their survival and the continuance of Nijinska's legacy.

After the death of Nijinska's husband in 1968, her daughter became her mother's full-time associate, accompanying her on all artistic engagements. Between 1968 and 1972, Nijinska restaged *Les Biches*, *Les Noces*, *Brahms Variations*, *Le Mariage d'Aurore*, and *Chopin Concerto* for ballet companies in the United States and Europe. While working on her memoirs, with contracts to restage her ballets pending, Nijinska died in Pacific Palisades, California.

Bronislava Nijinska's remarkable achievements in the world of dance have yet to be fully acknowledged. As one of twentieth-century ballet's great innovators, she transformed the art form and helped move ballet from the nineteenth-century realm of Romantic ballerinas, costumed as swans and sylphs, into contemporary sensibility. By subtly altering classical ballet steps, she extended the line of the dancer's body and introduced a new kind of athleticism and verve to the ballet. In the more than eighty works she created, she revealed an authentic individuality of style, and her repertoire introduced a new classicism that made dance a medium of modern art expression. As the twentieth century drew to a close, the contemporary relevance of Nijinska's work was confirmed by the numerous companies—the Dance Theater of Harlem, the Joffrey Ballet, the Oakland Ballet, and the Paris Opera Ballet, among others—that preserved and performed her choreography.

• The Bronislava Nijinska Archives are in Pacific Palisades, Calif. *Bronislava Nijinska: Early Memoirs*, translated and co-edited by her daughter Irina Nijinska and Jean Rawlinson, was published posthumously (1981; repr. 1993). Biographical treatments include Nancy Van Norman Baer, *Bronislava Nijinska: A Dancer's Legacy* (1986); Jack Anderson, "The Fabulous Career of Bronislava Nijinska," *Dance Magazine*, Aug. 1963, pp. 40–46; Peter Williams, "Nijinsky/Nijinska," *Dance Gazette*, July 1984, pp. 16–19; and Gunhild Schuller, "Bronislava Nijinska: Eine Monographie" (Ph.D. diss., Univ. of Vienna, 1976). Discussions of Nijinska can be found in several works focusing on Diaghilev, among them Richard Buckle, *Diaghilev* (1979); Lynn Garafola, *Diaghilev's Ballets Russes* (1989); and Serge L. Grigoriev, *The Diaghilev Ballet, 1909–1929* (1953). On Nijinska's choreography see her own "On Movement and the School of Movement," *Ballet Review* 13 (Winter 1986): 75–81, and Garafola, "Choreography by Nijinska," *Ballet Review* 20 (Winter 1992): 64–71. Also see A. V. Coton, *A Prejudice for Ballet* (1938), and Arnold L. Haskell, *Ballet—To Poland* (1940).

NANCY VAN NORMAN BAER

NIKANDER, Juho Kustaa (3 Sept. 1855–13 Jan. 1919), Lutheran clergyman, was born in Lammi, Finland, the son of Johann Kustaa Nikander, a carpenter, and Hedwig Maria Metsämaa, the operator of a bakery business after her husband's death in 1867. Following his father's wish, Nikander entered the University of Helsinki in the fall of 1874 to study for the ministry of the Church of Finland. He completed his academic program with honors in 1879 and was ordained that year in the diocese of Porvoo. After a few years of parish service in Finland, Nikander accepted a call to become the pastor of three Finnish congregations in Michigan. Accompanied by his sister, Wilhelmina, he left his homeland in December 1884 and arrived in Hancock, Michigan, on 3 January 1885. He soon broadened his field of activity to include other Finnish settlements throughout the United States and Canada. In 1890 Nikander helped to found the Suomi Synod, a Finnish-Lutheran church body that he served as president from 1890 to 1898 and again from 1902 until his death. Although many Church of Finland pastors served Suomi Synod parishes during Nikander's lifetime, no formal ties existed between the two bodies, and he was unable to persuade the Church of Finland to endorse the synod as its own missionary extension in North America.

The first years of the Suomi Synod were marred by controversy. Many Finnish Americans criticized Nikander and his colleagues for the constitutional authority they invested in the synod and the clergy as over against individual congregations and the laity. Constitutional changes made during the 1890s ameliorated the situation. Nikander proved to be a capable president, sensitive to the circumstances of American democracy. "Now my first concern," he had written upon his arrival in Hancock, "is to organize the care of these congregations into an order that is feasible for this land of freedom" (R. Wargelin, p. 5). Further controversy stemmed from the rise of the socialist labor movement in the decades surrounding the turn of the century. Many Finnish Americans who settled as workers in the industrial regions of the upper Midwest embraced socialism and subscribed to the socialist charge that churches and clergy were aligned with capitalists against the interests of workers. Nikander and other synod leaders lended credence to this charge by opposing labor strikes, which in turn prompted angry denunciations of the synod and led to the disaffection of Finnish workers.

Despite these problems, the Suomi Synod became the largest single organization of Finnish Americans, growing from 2,100 members in nine congregations at its founding to more than 28,000 members in 135 congregations a quarter-century later. In 1915 the synod counted congregations in eighteen states, from New England to the Pacific coast, as well as in Canada. Although it never claimed more than 13 percent of all Finnish Americans, the synod successfully maintained a thriving church life among its constituents until 1962, when it merged with three other church bodies to form the Lutheran Church in America (succeeded in 1988 by the Evangelical Lutheran Church in America).

Nikander labored ceaselessly until his death to promote the interests of the synod. One of his major activities was to help author, edit, produce, and distribute a variety of synod publications. As he wrote to a colleague in Finland in 1889, Nikander disapproved of the "foolish and useless" materials his countrymen were reading, and he believed it was his responsibility "to awaken the minds of these people to spiritual things" (R. Wargelin, p. 67). His most-enduring contribution, however, was as founder and president of the academy that became Suomi College in Hancock. From the outset of his arrival in America Nikander had perceived a need for trained pastors to care for the scattered Finnish settlements, and the Suomi Synod was organized in part to meet that need. The synod opened a school of higher education in 1896 and began to graduate its own ministers ten years later. Nikander served as president of the school from its founding until his death.

Nikander displayed single-minded devotion to the purely religious mission of the Suomi Synod. For example, although he was a teetotaler in personal practice, he nevertheless resisted the temperance movement because he believed it distracted the church from its true purpose. In another letter to Finland he wrote, "Temperance work here and there seems to have a moderating and uplifting effect upon our countrymen," but in response to those who questioned his decision not to participate in it, "I have replied that I have sufficient work to do as a preacher of the Gospel and cannot find time for anything else" (R. Wargelin, p. 54). One of Nikander's students and subsequent successors to the presidency of the synod and the college remembered him as "a saintly man" who "had only one ambition: to further the work of the Kingdom of God"; that same person, however, remembered him also as a stern man whose discipline "seemed unnatural to us in some respects" (J. Wargelin, p. 37).

In 1902, at the age of forty-seven, Nikander married Sanna Kristiina Rajala, with whom he had three children; the eldest, Viljo Kustaa Nikander, became a pastor of the Suomi Synod and served as president of Suomi College from 1937 to 1947. He later recalled that sometimes when the family walked to church on Sunday morning they would have to make their way past numerous loggers and miners who, having imbibed most of a month's wages the night before, were trying to sleep it off. "No criticisms from father. He simply was determined to get us to church" (Jalkanen, p. 320). Nikander died in Hancock.

• Nikander's papers, including writings in Finland before his arrival in America, are housed in the archives of Suomi College in Hancock, Mich. The Finnish-American Heritage Center at Suomi College houses other useful items, including a manuscript history of the Suomi Synod, "Blades, Ear and Corn," written by Heikki Kangas. Most of Nikander's writings were intended for publications of the Suomi Synod; these include *Paimen Sanomia*, a religious periodical that first appeared in 1889; *Lehti Lapsille ja Kuviakin*, a religious journal for children, started in 1892; *Amerikan Suometar*, a Finnish-language newspaper begun in 1899; and *Kirkollinen Kalenteri*, the Suomi Synod yearbook. His other works include hymns and curricular material for the synod, such as a Bible history and a biography of Martin Luther. Unfortunately, the bulk of his vast correspondence as president of the Suomi Synod and Suomi College has been lost. Some of the letters he wrote to a contact in the Church of Finland have been translated and edited by Raymond W. Wargelin in *Dear Uncle: Letters by J. K. Nikander and Other Pioneer Pastors* (1984).

The 1920 edition of *Kirkollinen Kalenteri* includes approximately fifty pages (pp. 52–172) of material on Nikander's life, most of it in Finnish, prepared in memoriam. Biographical material can also be found in John Wargelin, *A Highway to America* (1967); Ralph J. Jalkanen, ed., *The Faith of the Finns: Historical Perspectives on the Finnish Lutheran Church in America* (1972); and Jacob W. Heikkinen, *The Story of the Suomi Synod: The Finnish Evangelical Lutheran Church of America, 1890–1962* (1986).

PAUL A. BAGLYOS

NIKOLAIS, Alwin (25 Nov. 1910–8 May 1993), choreographer, designer, and composer, was born in Southington, Connecticut, the son of John Nikolais and Martha Heinrich. From an early age he studied music. During his high school years he was an organ accompanist for silent films at the Westport Movie House. In 1929 he graduated from Lewis High School in Southington.

In 1933, after attending a performance by the German expressionist dancer Mary Wigman, Nikolais became interested in studying percussion and approached Truda Kaschmann, a former Wigman student teaching in Hartford, who persuaded him to study dance. While a dance student, Nikolais also directed the Hartford Parks Marionette Theatre from 1935 to 1937. In 1937 he began teaching, dancing, and choreographing for his own dance company and school in Hartford.

From 1938 to 1940 Nikolais spent summers at the Bennington School of Dance in Vermont, where he was influenced particularly by Hanya Holm, another Wigman student. He collaborated with Kaschmann in his first fully commissioned professional work as a dancer and choreographer, *Eight Column Line*, which premiered in Hartford in May 1939. From 1940 to 1942 and from 1946 to 1949 he directed the dance department of the Hartt School of Music in Hartford.

During World War II Nikolais served with the U.S. Army's Criminal Investigation Department. After he was discharged, he studied and taught with Holm in New York City and in summer dance workshops at Colorado College in Colorado Springs, where, in 1949, he met his long-time lead dancer and associate, Murray Louis. In 1948 Nikolais began teaching at the Henry Street Settlement, a neighborhood center devoted to social work on the Lower East Side of Manhattan. In the following year he became artistic director of the Henry Street Playhouse, which he established as a leading dance school and theater.

Nikolais retired as a performer in the early 1950s and devoted himself fully to teaching, choreographing, designing, and composing. In 1951 he formed a resident Henry Street Settlement performing group, the Playhouse Dance Company, which would later change its name to the Alwin Nikolais Dance Company. The group provided regular concerts and children's shows but was not solely a performance ensemble. Nikolais also emphasized training in dance composition and teaching, extending the dancer's aesthetic and professional responsibilities.

Nikolais became recognized for his integral use of percussion training for teachers and dancers, for his own original system of movement notation, Choroscript, and for his experimental projects featuring mixed-media spectacle and electronic music. A *Dance Magazine* (July 1993) retrospective notes that Nikolais's 1950s choreography introduced dance to the era of modern multimedia theater. During those years Nikolais and his ensemble gave master classes and performances on university campuses across the United States, and they also performed at the 348-seat Henry Street Playhouse with little technical support. Nikolais designed and often made costumes, constructed props, set lighting, hand painted slides, composed the music, and operated or cued the technical effects for each performance. Special exits and entrances were choreographed to enable the dancers themselves to switch slides, make technical changes, or provide musical accompaniment.

Masks, Props, and Mobiles (1953), the first of Nikolais's major innovative works, was presented in separate parts, or movements. The piece introduced his characteristic depiction of figures in motion, blending and interacting with a stage environment of projected colors and patterns. This dance also introduced his integral use of tent- or cocoon-style stretch fabric costumes that continuously resculpt and extend the dancer's shape. His stated intention was to have the dancer's motion create and control linear designs and sculptural shapes without revealing his or her own physical body.

Nikolais's Henry Street projects represented an ongoing effort to broaden the dancer's medium. *Kaleidoscope* (1956), according to Nikolais himself, further explored the use of props and costume as a "means of extending the body as an abstract protagonist" (*Dance Magazine*, Feb. 1961, p. 31). In *Prism* (1956), he first used an electronic score and consciously designed lighting to determine the appearance of figures in motion. His two contrasting pieces, *Tower* (1965) and *Tent* (1968), each presented dancers creating a material construction and becoming the living parts of the evolving dominant image.

Other important Nikolais dance compositions from this period include *Village of Whispers* (1955), *The Bewitched* (1957), *Cantos* (1957), *Mirrors* (1958), *Allegory* (1959), *Totem* (1959), *Imago* (1963), *Sanctum* (1964), *Galaxy* (1965), *Vaudeville of the Elements* (1966), *Première* (1967), and *Fusion* (1967). Selections from his 1950s dance concerts were televised by the Ford Foundation and the Canadian Broadcasting Corporation, and his music was recorded by Hanover-Signature. Some principal compositions of the 1960s were collaborations with avant-garde filmmaker Ed Emshwiller.

Through the 1960s Nikolais established a reputation for theatrical displays of sculptured movement of diversified human shapes abstracted by lighting and design, occasionally presented with entertaining wit and humor. During the 1970s, however, his multimedia style was dismissed by some New York reviewers as a dated innovation. The same reviewers questioned the ambiguity of many of his newer pieces, such as *Tribe* (1975), *Triad* (1976), *Styx* (1976), and *Arporisms* (1977), which featured undisguisedly human figures who could be seen within the context of mythical or otherwise recognizable themes.

Since his first intercontinental tour in 1968, Nikolais had cultivated a strong popularity abroad, which may have drawn him away from his long-time role as a community-based artist and teacher. In 1970 he moved from the Henry Street Playhouse to larger studio and office facilities in lower Manhattan, which thereafter housed both the Nikolais Dance Theatre and the Murray Louis Dance Company. The two companies and their founders were closely allied, and Louis often took on the local direction of both companies while Nikolais toured more extensively. By the late 1970s Nikolais's international commitments made it difficult for him to reserve uninterrupted time for developing new works in his New York studio. He also adapted to the demands of taking performances on tour and began to choreograph pieces that could be staged on portable or collapsible sets, which he designed in order to control freight expenses.

From 1979 to 1981 Nikolais was engaged in a yearly teaching residency at the Centre Nationale de Danse Contemporaine in Angers, France, where he was asked to create a national contemporary dance company. Hoping to establish a core group of artists who would ultimately choreograph their own performances, Nikolais considered the dancers' technical ability a secondary concern and chose to work with those dancers who displayed the most creative potential. Through the 1980s he continued to tour worldwide and create new works, including *Schema* (1980, for the Paris Opera Ballet), *Pond* (1982), *Graph* (1984), and *Crucible* (1985).

Nikolais died in New York City. His honors include the Dance Magazine Award (1967), the Grand Prix de la Ville de Paris (1969), the Capezio Award (1982), the Scripps American Dance Festival Award (1985), two Guggenheim fellowships, the French government's bestowal of the titles of commander of the Order of Arts and Letters (1982) and knight of the Legion of Honor (1985), Kennedy Center honors (1987), and the National Medal of Arts (1987).

Regarded as the pioneer of multimedia dance theater, Nikolais, nonetheless, has been criticized for eclipsing the human expressiveness of his dancers in his innovative staging. His illusionist designs were later compared unfavorably to more extravagant developments in multimedia performance. His proponents, however, have recognized that his dance works elicit the kind of emotion inherent in the discovery of form and allow dancers to realize their expressive potential as aware participants in a greater design. As Nikolais explained in a 1979 interview, "Rather than dominate, the dances join the grace of all the elements that surround the dancers and of which they are also a part" (Rogosin, p. 78).

Along with his uncompromising devotion to the intricacies of form, Nikolais was known for his geniality and disinclination to tyrannize his audiences, students, or dancers. In his dance compositions, he attempted to create stimulating images without taking away the privilege of the spectator's own reactions. In his teaching abroad, his stated goal was not to choreograph or impose his own artistry but rather to train independent choreographers by sharing his aesthetic theories. Moreover, he respected his dancers' creativity, maintaining that physical technique is the means toward an end but useless if that end is not understood.

• An extensive holding of reviews and audiovisual materials is in the Dance Collection of the New York Public Library for the Performing Arts. Murray Louis's preservation project of twelve works of Nikolais is chronicled in Joseph H. Mazo, "Nikolais Works Are Preserved on Video," *Dance Magazine*, Feb. 1995, p. 22. Significant remarks by Nikolais are recorded in Elinor Rogosin, *The Dance Makers: Conversations with American Choreographers* (1980); Marcia B. Siegal, ed., "Nik: A Documentary," *Dance Perspectives* 48 (Winter 1971); "No Man from Mars," in Selma Jeanne Cohen, *The Modern Dance: Seven Statements of Belief* (1966); and "Growth of a Theme," *Dance Magazine*, Feb. 1961, pp. 30–34. Studies include Jana Mermel Feinman, "Alwin Nikolais: A New Philosophy of Dance: The Process and the Product" (Ed.D. diss., Temple Univ., 1995); Sue Ann Straits, "The Alwin Nikolais Artist-in-Residence Program at the University of Wisconsin-Madison: An Ethnography of Dance Curriculum-in-Use" (Ph.D. diss., Univ. of Wisconsin, Madison, 1980); Nancy Thornhill Zupp, "An Analysis and Comparison of the Choreographic Processes of Alwin Nikolais, Murray Louis, and Phyllis Lamhut" (Ed.D. diss., Univ. of North Carolina, Greensboro, 1978); and Winston Grant Gray, "The Dance Theatre of Alwin Nikolais" (Ph.D. diss., Univ. of Utah, 1967).

Other important commentary is in Deborah Jowitt, "Portrait of the Artist as Survivor," in her *The Dance in Mind: Profiles and Reviews 1976–83* (1985), pp. 288–92; Richard Lorber, "Toward an Aesthetics of Videodance," *Arts in Society* 13, no. 2 (Summer–Fall 1976): 242–53; and Barbara E. Nickolich, "The Nikolais Dance Theater's Uses of Light," *Drama Review* 17, no. 2 (June 1973): 1–12. Notable articles in *Dance Magazine* include Mazo, "Alwin Nikolais (1910–93): The Nik of Time," July 1993, pp. 28–31; Stephen Greco, "Nikolais and Louis on the Road," Nov. 1985, pp. 64–66; Joseph Gale, "The Grand Tours: A Year with Murray and Nik," Feb. 1973, pp. 36–39; Tobi Tobias, "Nikolais and Louis: A New Space," Feb. 1971, pp. 46–53; Murray Louis and Ruth E. Grauvet, "Alwin Nikolais's Total Theater," Dec. 1966, pp. 56–69; and Walter Sorell, "The Henry Street Playhouse Produces a Major Dance School, Workshops and Company," Jan. 1958, pp. 49–52. An obituary is in the *New York Times*, 10 May 1993.

TED BAIN

NILES, David K. (23 Nov. 1890–28 Sept. 1952), liberal activist and government official, was born David K. Neyhus in Boston, Massachusetts, the son of Russian-Jewish immigrants Asher Kohen Neyhus, a tailor, and Sophie Berlin. Although he never legally changed his name, he probably began using the name "Niles" when he entered politics. Niles graduated from Boston Latin School but was too poor to go to college. Instead, he went to work in a department store. In search of intellectual stimulation, Niles began to attend Sunday lectures at Boston's Ford Hall Forum. There he attracted the attention of its director, George W. Coleman, who invited the young man to become his assistant. During World War I, Coleman went to Washington to run the Information Office of the U.S. Department of Labor and took Niles along as an aide. Afterward Niles resumed his affiliation with the Ford Hall Forum, which he eventually headed.

In 1924 Niles ventured into reform politics, running the speakers' bureau of the Progressive party and campaigning for its presidential nominee, Robert La Follette. As a result, Niles established close relations with leading progressives, such as George William Norris and Burton K. Wheeler, and later he often served as go-between for them and President Franklin D. Roosevelt. In 1926 and 1927 Niles devoted himself to the effort to win a new trial for Nicola Sacco and Bartolomeo Vanzetti, the anarchists who had been sentenced to death for robbery and murder. In this endeavor Niles worked with later Supreme Court justice Felix Frankfurter, and the pair established a lasting political friendship. In 1928 Niles divided his time between the Ford Hall Forum and leading the National Committee of Independent Voters for Democratic presidential nominee Alfred E. Smith. During the 1928 campaign, Niles met Roosevelt and Harry Hopkins. Four years later Niles and Senator Norris were codirecting the National Progressive League for Roosevelt's presidential campaign.

In 1933 President Roosevelt and his Federal Emergency Relief administrator, Hopkins, brought Niles into government, appointing him chairman of the National Recovery Administration's Adjustment Board for Massachusetts and head of that state's Federal Emergency Relief Administration (FERA). After the Works Progress Administration (WPA) replaced the FERA in 1935, Hopkins summoned Niles to Washington to serve successively as WPA consultant, director of information, and administrative assistant. Under whichever title, Niles's main responsibilities included troubleshooting, public relations, and liaison to organized labor. He was so successful at labor relations that it was rumored he convinced labor leader John L. Lewis to contribute $500,000 to Roosevelt's 1936 campaign.

Niles and Hopkins belonged to the group of New Dealers who convinced the president to resume spending to combat the "Roosevelt recession" of 1937 and to attempt to purge antiadministration Democrats in the 1938 elections. These activities led disapproving journalists to refer to the "ubiquitous Dave Niles" as "sword bearer" for the liberals and Hopkins's "confidential agent." When Hopkins became secretary of commerce in 1939, Niles accompanied him as assistant, and both resigned together in 1940. That summer Niles helped to maneuver the Democratic convention's third-term draft of Roosevelt. Subsequently, Niles, New York mayor Fiorello La Guardia, and Senator Norris organized the Independent Citizens Committee for Roosevelt.

Following the president's reelection, Hopkins again drew Niles into the inner circle of New Dealers. In 1941 and 1942 Niles acted as labor consultant for the Office of Production Management and its successor, the War Production Board. Hopkins had long valued Niles's intelligence, loyalty, discretion, and lack of personal ambition. In August 1942 Roosevelt, appreciating these same qualities, appointed Niles one of his six administrative assistants. Niles's duties covered advising the president on politics and maintaining friendly contacts with labor, independent progressives, and minorities. In the 1944 elections close collaboration with Sidney Hillman and the Congress of Industrial Organizations (CIO) Political Action Committee brought out the labor and liberal vote for Roosevelt.

When Harry S. Truman became president in 1945, Niles was one of the few Roosevelt assistants he retained. The former senator from Missouri distrusted and little understood New York and northeastern liberal, ethnic, and labor politics. He depended on Niles as guide to and liaison with these groups. Truman also grew quite fond of Niles. On Niles's advice, Truman fought for a permanent Fair Employment Practices Commission and established the President's Committee on Civil Rights. However, Niles's greatest influence lay in helping to convince Truman to support opening Palestine to Jewish refugees and creating a Jewish state there.

Though not originally a Zionist, Niles became a passionate advocate of a Jewish homeland because of the Holocaust, the woeful plight of the displaced survivors, and the anti-Semitism he bitterly observed even in parts of the U.S. government, including the State Department. Niles, sometimes bursting into tears while discussing the issue, persuaded the president of both the justice and domestic political advantage in embracing the Zionist cause and countered the pro-Arab bias of such State and Defense department officials as Loy Henderson and James Forrestal, who largely blamed Niles for Truman's pro-Israel stance. When on 14 May 1948 the White House announced U.S. recognition of the newborn state of Israel, Niles was the first person Truman informed, because the president knew how much it meant to his assistant.

Assessing how much power Niles exercised in either the Roosevelt or Truman White House is difficult, because this extremely secretive, self-effacing official usually met with the president alone, committed little to writing, and celebrated each new year by stripping his office files. Niles himself claimed, "I am a man of no importance."

Niles, who never married, was wholly devoted to the presidents for whom he worked and the causes in which he believed. Illness forced him to resign as administrative assistant in May 1951. When he died in a Boston hospital, Truman said of him: "Presidents have been served by many able men, but seldom by one so truly selfless. His passion for anonymity was matched only by his sense of public responsibility. David Niles' quick mind and warm heart were always in the service of humanity."

• The David K. Niles Papers are in the Harry S. Truman Library in Independence, Mo. Some Niles correspondence and other papers are at Brandeis University and at the Franklin D. Roosevelt Library at Hyde Park, N.Y., especially in the papers of Harry Hopkins, Samuel Rosenman, and Isador Lubin. The fullest journalistic sketch of Niles's life and career is Alfred Steinberg, "Mr. Truman's Mystery Man," *Saturday Evening Post*, 24 Dec. 1949, pp. 24, 69–70. For Niles's role in the Roosevelt administration, see Joseph P. Lash, *Dreamers and Dealers* (1988); Jonathan Daniels, *White House Witness, 1942–1945* (1975); and Joseph Alsop and Robert Kintner, "We Shall Make America Over: The New Dealers in Action," *Saturday Evening Post*, 19 Nov. 1938, pp. 14–15, 86. Descriptions of Niles and his activities in the Truman administration are in David McCullough, *Truman* (1992); the reminiscences of Niles's assistant, Philleo Nash, in *The Truman White House: The Administration of the Presidency, 1945–1953*, ed. Francis H. Heller (1980); and Robert S. Allen and William V. Shannon, *The Truman Merry-Go-Round* (1950). On Niles's role in gaining U.S. support for the creation and recognition of the state of Israel, see Michael J. Cohen, *Truman and Israel* (1990); Zvi Ganin, *Truman, American Jewry, and Israel, 1945–1948* (1979); and John Snetsinger, *Truman, the Jewish Vote, and the Creation of Israel* (1974). Obituaries are in the *New York Times*, 29 Sept. 1952, and *Time*, 6 Oct. 1952.

BARBARA BLUMBERG

NILES, Hezekiah (10 Oct. 1777–2 Aug. 1839), journalist and historical documentarian, was born near Chadds Ford in Chester County, Pennsylvania, the son of Hezekiah Niles, a carpenter, and Mary Way. Two months before his birth, his Quaker family had fled their home in Wilmington, Delaware, to escape invading British soldiers. Niles's father was killed shortly before the boy's fourteenth birthday when a signpost fell on him as he was leaving his carpentry shop. Niles was probably educated at the Friends School in Wilmington before becoming apprenticed at the age of seventeen to Benjamin Johnson, a printer, bookbinder, and bookseller. Johnson was a surrogate father, affording the eager boy continuing education by giving him free access to his library. Niles rose early each morning to read before going to work, where he was just as diligent, achieving while still young a reputation as the quickest, most efficient typesetter in America.

Niles's first wife, Ann Ogden, died in 1824. The couple had twelve children, seven of whom survived infancy. Niles's second marriage, to Sally Ann Warner in 1826, produced eight children, all of whom survived their father.

In 1805 Niles started a short-lived literary magazine, then moved to Baltimore, buying and editing the *Baltimore Evening Post* for five and a half years. Then, on 11 September 1811, he produced the first issue of *Niles' Weekly Register*, which was later renamed *Niles' National Register* but is more often referred to simply as *Niles' Register*. It was an idealistic, ambitious project and remains one of the most vital reference tools for scholars of nineteenth-century political history. Less a newspaper than America's first national news magazine, the *Register* printed official reports, significant documents, facts, and statistics of national interest for nearly forty years and was read in every state and in many foreign countries. Even in size it resembled a modern news magazine: 6⅛″ by 9⅝″, it normally ran sixteen pages, though he often expanded it to twenty-four pages in the 1830s and a few times doubled it to thirty-two pages. By 1825 it was being mailed to 700–800 post offices. Among its avid readers were Thomas Jefferson, James Madison, and Andrew Jackson. Congress received ten copies weekly for its members.

Niles was a passionate nationalist who favored political isolationism, capitalist democracy, and a steep tariff to encourage economic growth. "Protect the manufacturers for the present, and in a little time, they will protect themselves and us," he wrote. He opposed states' rights, sectionalism, and nullification, yet his editorial treatment of these issues was remarkably even-handed, for he reprinted editorials and documents from the southern states advocating these issues. He saw editorial bias as contrary to his mission to be an authoritative historical documentarian for the future. The *Register's* prospectus, published 24 June 1811, vowed the publication would be a "Book of Reference, a Fund of Reading," and its motto, adopted in 1817, was "The Past—the Present—for the Future."

So eager was Niles to fulfill that mission that by 1828 three days of his working week were consumed poring over official reports for material useful to future historians as well as his contemporaries. So determined was he to be objective and thorough in his task that he scorned influence from politicians, endorsed no individual political candidates, rejected all advertisements, and refused all anonymous materials. So successful was he in promoting national communication that he correctly congratulated himself on doing as much as any contemporary to create a definable "national character."

Niles was less successful with two book-length collections of the *Register*, losing $25,000 on the first and less but still a considerable amount on the second. However, pamphlet reprints of his essays did well, with *Politics for the Farmer*, which provided information on political mobilization and encouraged themes of protective tariffs and nationalism, alone selling 90,000 copies.

Niles was elected clerk of Baltimore and served on two national tariff committees but was defeated as a candidate for official printer to Congress in the mid-1820s and again when he ran for state legislator in 1831. Fiercely opposed to the charter of the Bank of the United States in his youth, he reversed himself in the late 1820s, believing bank president Nicholas Biddle had brought caution and stability to the bank following mismanagement and the financial panic of 1819. But in 1832, with Andrew Jackson's presidential victory and pledge to veto the bank's re-charter, Niles's political labors effectively ended, and he turned the *Register* more than ever in the direction of an objective reference book.

In October 1835 Niles was thrown to the ground and injured when the horses drawing a carriage in which he was riding bolted. He never regained his health and nine months later suffered a stroke that paralyzed his right side. Unable to continue his work, he turned the *Register* over to his son William Ogden Niles. Six months after his death in Wilmington, Delaware, his heirs sold the periodical, and it was finally dissolved on 28 September 1849.

Numerous newspapers wrote glowing accounts of Niles's career. The *Baltimore Sun*, in particular, paid reverent homage: "Such a man is a true patriot, and as long as the United States shall preserve its independence, so long shall the name of Hezekiah Niles . . . be quoted as an example for imitation, by all who desire to obtain that noblest and highest title: a good and honest man, in private life; in public, a pure disinterested patriot." During his lifetime, he was honored by two cities taking his name: Niles, Ohio, and Niles, Michigan.

• The Library of Congress houses the Hezekiah Niles Papers as well as a large selection of his letters in the William Darlington Papers. Numerous libraries have partial collections of the *Register*, though some have nearly complete sets. Richard Gabriel Stone, *Hezekiah Niles as an Economist* (1933), is outdated, but four of its five chapters offer studies in Niles's economics theories. An excellent biography of both Niles and his *Register* is Norval Neil Luxon, *Niles' Weekly Register: News Magazine of the Nineteenth Century* (1947), which includes an exhaustive but outdated bibliography. Dickson J. Preston, *Newspapers of Maryland's Eastern Shore* (1987), is a superb study of that region's history and its newspapers. More general but still useful are the numerous accounts of America's press in Niles's era, such as Thomas C. Leonard, *The Power of the Press: The Birth of American Political Reporting* (1986), and Frank Luthor Mott, *American Journalism: A History of Newspapers in the United States through 250 Years, 1690 to 1940* (1941).

STEPHEN M. ZEIGLER

NILES, John Jacob (28 Apr. 1892–1 Mar. 1980), balladeer and composer, was born in Louisville, Kentucky, the son of John Thomas Niles and Louise Sarah Reisch. Through oral tradition, John Jacob learned "old timey" music from his father, a folksinger and square dance caller. From his mother, a pianist and church organist, he gained the more formal elements of theory and note-reading skills. When Niles was twelve, his family moved to rural Jefferson County, Kentucky, where Niles began collecting folk music under his mother's tutelage. By 1907 Niles had composed his first important song, "Go 'Way from My Window," based on a single line of text collected from an African-American worker on his father's farm.

Upon graduation from DuPont Manual Training High School in 1909, Niles began work as a mechanic for the Burroughs Adding Machine Company. This job required him to make frequent service calls in eastern Kentucky, trips that also afforded him an opportunity to collect traditional Appalachian music. World War I intervened, however, and Niles left the Burroughs company in 1917 to enlist as a cadet in the aviation section of the Army Signal Corps. Before traveling overseas in 1918, Niles married Roberta Voorhies of Louisville, who died that same year of influenza.

Niles served as a reconnaissance and taxi pilot, eventually attaining the rank of lieutenant. Niles also used his wartime experience as yet another opportunity to record people's songs and stories. Ten years later his extensive notes and diaries were transformed into two volumes of wartime songs, *Singing Soldiers* (1927) and *Songs My Mother Never Taught Me* (1929), and a biography of the Lafayette Escadrille flyer Bert Hall titled *One Man's War* (1929).

In October 1918 Niles crashed while flying from Boulogne to Paris and until 1925 was partially paralyzed. Recuperating from his injuries, he remained in France after the armistice and studied at the Schola Cantorum in Paris (Dec. 1918) and the Université de Lyon (May 1919). At Lyon he completed the popular song "Venezuela," based on a fragment of work chant collected from the singing of dock workers at Boulogne.

Upon returning to the United States, Niles entered the Cincinnati Conservatory, where he continued his musical studies in voice, theory, and opera. Three years later he moved to Chicago and spent six months attending U.S. Veterans' Music School and singing part time with the Lyric Opera. While in Chicago he also performed on early radio programs broadcast by the Westinghouse Company. In 1921 he married Helene Babbitt of Des Moines, Iowa; their childless marriage ended in divorce in 1931.

Displeased with the progress of his operatic career, Niles moved to New York City in 1925 and took a succession of jobs such as serving as emcee at nightclubs, including the Silver Slipper. At the same time, he published a series of colorful essays for *Scribner's* magazine, including "Hillbillies" (1927), "In Defense of the Backwoods" (1928), "The Sixth Hangar" (1928), and "The Passing of the Street Cry" (1929). Niles also published his first musical collection, an arrangement of eight African-American spirituals titled *Impressions of a Negro Camp Meeting* (1925). Subsequent successful works in this vein included *Seven Kentucky Mountain Songs* (1928) and *Seven Negro Exaltations* (1929).

In 1928 Niles commenced a five-year partnership with singer Marion Kerby. Niles (piano, tenor) and Kerby (contralto) toured successfully throughout the United States and Europe, performing a concert repertoire consisting entirely of arrangements of folk material interspersed with original compositions such as "Black Is the Color of My True Love's Hair" and "Jesus, Jesus, Rest Your Head." These concerts were noteworthy for their popularization of folk music in an art music setting.

During this period, Niles also developed a business and personal relationship with noted photographer Doris Ulmann. Between 1928 and 1933 they made four trips into the southern Appalachian Mountains, where Niles assisted Ulmann with her photography and expanded his collection of traditional mountain music. Much of the material gathered in these trips was later reflected in published collections such as *Songs of the Hill Folk* (1934), *Ballads, Carols, Tragic Legends* (1937), and, ultimately, *The Ballad Book* (1961).

In 1936, after a brief tenure as musical director at the John C. Campbell School in Brasstown, North Carolina, Niles married journalist Rena Lipetz. Following travel in Europe, the couple moved to Lexington, Kentucky. One year later, they settled on a farm in Clark County, Kentucky, and started a family that would eventually include two children.

At this point Niles was at the zenith of his solo concert career. He was presenting over fifty concerts annually and was invited to perform twice at the White House for President Franklin D. Roosevelt. Niles also made his first commercial recordings, releasing *Early American Ballads* (1938) and *Early American Carols and Folksongs* (1940) for RCA Victor's Red Seal label. His popularity was well documented in articles, such as Roger Butterfield's extensive *Life* magazine feature (Sept. 1943).

This public recognition also subjected him to a certain amount of scrutiny and even litigation concerning his appropriation of folk material. However, several lawsuits summarily established Niles's claims of ownership and confirmed the copyrights to his material.

Nelson Stevens, writing in the *Arizona Quarterly* (Autumn 1948), addressed the criticism of Niles's use of folk music: "One hears stories going around to the effect that John Jacob Niles, emulating Johannes Brahms, has quietly put some of his own inventions among his folk songs. If so, he is a genius."

Niles maintained an active concert and recording career during the 1950s and 1960s, but increasingly he turned his attention to the composition of art music. During this period he wrote hundreds of solo songs as well as works in more extended forms such as the oratorio (*Lamentation* [1951]) and the cantata (*Mary the Rose* [1955]). The capstone of this final period of composition was the *Niles Merton Songs* composed between 1967 and 1970. This cycle of twenty-two songs for solo voice and piano was based on poetry of the Trappist monk Thomas Merton.

At age eighty-six Niles finally retired from the concert stage and spent his remaining days working on an autobiography (unpublished) and completing a volume of poetry published as *Brickdust and Buttermilk* (1977). Niles died at his farm in Kentucky.

John Jacob Niles was a charismatic performer whose concerts, recordings, and musical publications introduced a large audience to the American folk repertoire. However, Niles's background and distinctive performance practice characterize him as a "singer of folksongs" rather than a traditional folksinger. His choice of song and style were pragmatically designed to appeal to an audience rather than a community of scholars.

As a composer, Niles was always most successful writing for the solo voice. His early works in the style of folk music have an enduring place in the standard literature, and the *Niles Merton Songs* merit further consideration. Niles was instrumental in preserving and disseminating an American heritage, but he also enriched the art song repertoire through a unique compositional approach that married traditional and originally composed material.

• Most of Niles's manuscripts, recordings, letters, concert programs, publications, photographs, musical instruments, and other memorabilia are contained in the John Jacob Niles Collection of the Special Collections and Archives Department of the Margaret I. King Libraries of the University of Kentucky, Lexington. A catalog to this collection was compiled by Jamie Odle Hamon and Anne G. Campbell for the University of Kentucky Libraries. Niles's recordings for Tradition (1957–1960) have been reissued as *The John Jacob Niles Collection* on Gift Horse Records (G4-10008). A representative sampling of Niles's compositions is contained in *The Songs of John Jacob Niles* (1990). An initial biography, discussion of the works, and complete descriptive thematic catalog are found in Ronald Pen, "The Biography and Works of John Jacob Niles" (Ph.D. diss., Univ. of Kentucky, 1987). A short biographical sketch is also in David F. Burg, "John Jacob Niles," *Kentucky Review* 2 (1980): 3–10. The most noteworthy obituary is in *Sing Out* 28 (Jan.–Feb. 1980).

RON PEN

NILES, Nathaniel (3 Apr. 1741–31 Oct. 1828), politician, theologian, and inventor, was born in South Kingston, Rhode Island, the son of Samuel Niles and Sarah Niles (occupations unknown). Plagued by poor health as a youth, Nathaniel spent one year at Harvard before illness forced him to drop out of school. When his health returned, he entered the College of New Jersey and graduated in 1766. Following graduation Niles made a start at several careers, teaching school in New York City, studying medicine and law, and finally taking up theology under the tutelage of Joseph Bellamy. Although never ordained, he preached at Congregational churches throughout southern New England and published several sermons in the early 1770s. Around 1773 he settled in Norwich, Connecticut, where he worked in the factory of Elijah Lathrop and continued to preach in local pulpits. Applying his talents to mechanical improvements, Niles invented a water-powered process for drawing wire from bar iron and manufactured an improved wool-carding machine of his own design. Sometime in the mid-1770s he married Nancy Lathrop, his employer's daughter, a union that produced four children before her death c. 1781.

When the American Revolution began in 1775, Niles enthusiastically supported the war against England. "The American Hero," his "Sapphic Ode" in commemoration of the Battle of Bunker Hill, became a popular song among New England soldiers and militiamen inspired by stanzas such as "Fame and dear Freedom lure me on to battle; / While a fell despot, grimmer than a death's head, / Stings me with serpents, fiercer than Medusa, / to the encounter." From 1779 to 1781 Niles represented Norwich in the Connecticut legislature, but near the end of the Revolution he decided to leave southern New England and relocate on the northern frontier. He purchased land in the sparsely settled town of Fairlee, Vermont, and around 1781 led a group of several Norwich families to the upper Connecticut River valley. The acknowledged town father and largest landowner of Fairlee, Nile was pressed into frequent local service as a preacher and physician, and quickly rose to prominence in Green Mountain State political circles as well. In 1784 and 1785 he represented Fairlee in the lower house of the state legislature, where his colleagues elected him Speaker in both sessions. Between 1785 and 1790 he also served three terms on the Governor's Council, the 13-man forerunner to Vermont's state senate and the dominant branch of Vermont government during its existence as a virtually independent republic between 1777 and 1791. The October 1784 session of the legislature named him as one of three delegates to Congress to "transact and negotiate business of this state with that body," and also elected him to the state supreme court, where he served until 1788. While playing these several key roles in independent Vermont's government, Niles found time in his late forties to start a new family as well, marrying Elizabeth Watson of Plymouth, Massachusetts, in 1787 and later fathering five children.

As Vermont's population grew and the national government stabilized under the new Constitution in the late 1780s, an increasing majority of Vermonters favored their state's official admission into the federal union. Niles was a strong advocate of statehood; at the convention that met in Bennington in January 1791 to decide Vermont's course he teamed with Nathaniel Chipman to persuade the delegates to ratify the Constitution and clear the way for Vermont to become the fourteenth American state. His political reward was election later that year to Congress, where he served two terms and aligned himself with the emerging Jeffersonian faction in the House of Representatives. Closer to home, from 1793 to 1820 he was a trustee of Dartmouth College, clashing with president John Wheelock in the early 1800s and siding with the Federalist majority on the Dartmouth board that removed Wheelock from office in 1815 and launched the controversy that culminated in Daniel Webster's famous speech before the U.S. Supreme Court three years later.

After his two terms in Congress, Niles returned to leadership in state and local affairs. He represented Fairlee six times in the Vermont House between 1800 and 1814, sat on the Governor's Council again from 1803 to 1808, served as a presidential elector in 1804 and 1812, and participated in the 1814 convention that revised Vermont's state constitution. In the legislature he was an influential member of the Jeffersonian democratic faction, a strong opponent of state banks, and a vocal advocate of a national constitutional amendment to end the importation of slaves. He supported the Jefferson and Madison administrations during the Embargo and the War of 1812, expressing strong public criticism of Governor Martin Chittenden's 1813 attempt to keep Vermont troops from serving outside the state's borders. In 1814 he helped persuade his fellow legislators not to appoint Vermont delegates to the Hartford Convention, the notorious gathering of New England Federalists. After the war he retired to West Fairlee, where farming, the study of Latin and theology, and the writing of poetry, sermons, and philosophical essays filled his remaining years. He died in West Fairlee.

• There is no substantial archive of Niles manuscripts; several folders of correspondence, financial records, and essays at the Vermont Historical Society constitute the only known collection that has survived. Copies of Niles's published sermons and pamphlets are in the libraries of the Vermont Historical Society and the University of Vermont. There is no detailed biography of Niles; among the brief published sketches are Abby M. Hemenway, ed., *The Vermont Historical Gazetteer*, vol. 2 (1867–1891), pp. 907–12; Prentiss C. Dodge, ed., *Encyclopedia Vermont Biography* (1912), pp. 63–64; Jacob G. Ullery, comp., *Men of Vermont* (1894), pp. 127–29; Walter H. Crockett, *Vermont: The Green Mountain State*, vol. 5 (1921–1923), pp. 56–57; John W. Stedman, comp., *The Norwich Jubilee* (1859), pp. 83–86; and Frances M. Caulkins, *History of Norwich, Connecticut* (1874), pp. 470–71. An obituary is in the (Montpelier) *Vermont Watchman and State Gazette*, 18 Nov. 1828.

J. KEVIN GRAFFAGNINO

NIMHAM, Daniel (1726–31 Aug. 1778), chief of the Wappinger band of Mohicans, lived at a village called Wickapee in the New York Highlands near the present-day line of Dutchess and Putnam counties. A son of a chief or shaman called Nimham (various spellings) (his mother's name is unknown), Daniel first appears in the records around 1756 when he and about 225 Wappingers relocated among their Mohican brethren at the mission town of Stockbridge, Massachusetts, at the onset of the French and Indian War. It is uncertain whether he received his Christian first name here or had it previously. From this point forward his identity and interests were connected with the Indian residents there.

The Nimhams, like other Hudson River Indians, had lived in amicable proximity to colonial New Yorkers long enough that their culture was a mixture of native and colonial customs. Although still living in wigwams and hunting and planting in traditional ways, many tribe members supported themselves in good measure by selling crafts such as baskets and brooms or by hiring themselves out as laborers for the large agricultural estates along the river. During his tenure at Stockbridge, Nimham held some town offices and was involved with the Stockbridge Indians in defending their land rights in western Massachusetts. He was also allotted land within Stockbridge itself without some of the restrictions placed on other Indians who relocated there.

Nimham, his fellow tribesmen, and the Stockbridge Indians served with the English during the French and Indian War. Nimham held the rank of captain, the usual designation for principal Indian military leaders. His influence among Mohicans was such that he apparently persuaded those at Stockbridge to curtail their service in 1757. His reasons may have involved irresolution of a dispute concerning the alleged killing of some tribe members by whites near Fishkill, New York, or the Mohicans' growing uneasiness over land issues east of the Hudson.

Following the war Nimham gained fame—or notoriety, depending on who was doing the reporting—when he sought restoration of tribal claims to about 200,000 acres, including the territory occupied by the Wappingers before they relocated to Stockbridge. According to them and their colonial supporters, upon their return from the war they found their land occupied by tenants installed during their absence by land barons Roger Morris, Philip Philipse, and Beverley Robinson. Nimham reacted by seeking support from several New England men who saw an opportunity to carve parcels of land from the estates by allying their interests with those of the Wappingers. To represent his claims before the New York government, Nimham engaged as a tribal guardian a Connecticut man whose own farm was threatened by the land barons. Although able to speak English, Nimham was illiterate and needed assistance to negotiate the legal complexities the challenge required. He and his partners, in the meantime, began issuing their own leases to willing tenants, including some of the large landholders' own tenants.

After failing to win the case at a hearing before Cadwallader Colden and the governor's council in 1765, Nimham's guardian was thrown into jail. Nimham and his allies, however, merely turned to an alternative plan of appealing their case before King George III. Through a combination of money-raising schemes in exchange for promises of future land grants, Nimham joined three other prominent Stockbridge Mohican chiefs in 1766 for a trip to London. They were chaperoned by a Massachusetts lawyer who was promised an extensive tract of land for 999 years should his efforts prove successful.

Nimham and his fellow chiefs were well received by London society and officialdom, and they quickly became attractions at fashionable gathering places. The lords of trade and the king sympathized with their plight and sent instructions for both William Johnson and New York's governor to reconsider their case with less prejudice. During the Indians' absence, and in large part because of their trip, the landlord-tenant tensions had increased with violence on both sides. When Nimham and the others returned from England, they added fuel to the fire by turning out tenants who held leases under the landlords, who the Indians now felt would be overruled. A second hearing held by royal governor Henry Moore and the council, however, was essentially comprised of the same interests that ruled in the first. After three days of hearings in early March 1767, Nimham left without a decision, only to learn later that the governor and council had ruled against him. Neither Nimham nor his fellow Stockbridge chiefs ever received land or compensation for their New York claims, and ironically the Stockbridge Mohicans lost considerable Massachusetts land repaying the obligations incurred by the pursuit. Nimham and his fellow Stockbridges lived on the fringes of outright destitution for the next decade.

When the Revolution began, the Indians at Stockbridge joined the patriotic fervor of their townsmen, most of whom were now non-Indian. An Indian militia arrived in Cambridge a week after the skirmish at Lexington to help maintain the rebel siege at Boston. Nimham arrived in June, and the Stockbridges reconnoitered and harassed the British throughout the summer. Nimham and especially his son, Abraham, continued to be active on the American side. They were together in a Stockbridge Indian company of about fifty tribesmen at White Plains, New York, in the summer of 1778. They and rebel allies skirmished occasionally with British contingents under the command of John Simcoe. After attacking a Loyalist corps and causing it to retreat on 30 August, the Indians fell into a trap laid the next afternoon by Simcoe. About 500 rangers, Loyalists, and cavalry flanked a road traveled by the Indian company within present-day Van Cortlandt Park. When the Nimhams and their warriors discovered and engaged the Loyalists on one side of the road, Simcoe and his men fell on the Indians' flank and rear. The Indians fired on their new pursuers, and

Simcoe credited Nimham with wounding him. Nimham reportedly cried out to his tribesmen to flee, saying that he was old and would die there. Simcoe's orderly fulfilled Nimham's prophecy by shooting and mortally wounding him. Abraham Nimham was also killed, as were at least half the Stockbridge company in an intense skirmish that lasted into the evening. A tradition handed down through the family on whose land the battle was fought maintained that several farmers later found Daniel Nimham's body, partially devoured by farm dogs. They buried him and piled stones to prevent further attacks.

Besides his contributions as a fighter in both the French and Indian War and the Revolution, Nimham's significance lay in his willingness to challenge the claims of the rich and powerful landholders up and down the Hudson River Valley at a time when Indians in his area were largely viewed with pity or contempt. Although it cannot be certain whether it was Nimham's initiative or that of his colonial neighbors that started the challenge, his is the name that gave it recognition. The challenge publicly exposed on both sides of the Atlantic the questionable claim of the land barons' expansive holdings, and it precipitated the sometimes violent landlord-tenant disputes that lasted several years.

• The most complete account of Nimham with bibliographical references is in Patrick Frazier, *The Mohicans of Stockbridge* (1992). Other references are scattered throughout numerous published and unpublished manuscript sources, including *The Papers of William Johnson* (13 vols., 1921–1962), various land records in the New-York Historical Society, and records in the Stockbridge, Mass., Town Hall and the Stockbridge Library Historical Room. Contemporary accounts of the New York land controversy appear in "Statement of a Controversy between Daniel Nimham et al. and Philipse Heirs, March 9th, 1765," in the New-York Historical Society's Philipse-Gouverneur Land Titles, folio 13, no. 45, and "A Geographical, Historical Narrative or Summary of the Present Controversy between Daniel Nimham and . . . Frederick Philipse . . . ," Lansdowne Mss., vol. 707, folios 24–51, British Museum Library. The latter version was also published in an article edited by Oscar Handlin and Irving Mark in *Ethnohistory* 11, no. 3 (1964): 193–246. The main accounts of Nimham's battle and death in the Revolution are found in John G. Simcoe, *Simcoe's Military Journal* (1844), and Thomas F. Devoe, "The Massacre of the Stockbridge Indians, 1778," *Magazine of American History* 5, no. 3 (1880): 187–94.

PATRICK FRAZIER

NIMITZ, Chester William (24 Feb. 1885–20 Feb. 1966), admiral, was born in Fredericksburg, Texas, the son of Chester Bernard Nimitz, a cattle drover, and Anna Henke. Born nearly five months after his father died from a rheumatic heart, Nimitz was brought up by his mother, assisted in various ways by several relatives. In 1890 Anna Nimitz married her late husband's brother William. Despite a move to nearby Kerrville where the Nimitzes managed a small hotel, the family struggled financially. From the age of eight Chester Nimitz began working after school and on weekends as a delivery boy for a meat market and later as a desk clerk and handyman at the hotel. He hoped to attend the U.S. Military Academy, but when informed that no appointment would soon be available he entered the Naval Academy instead. He graduated seventh in the class of 1905.

After two years of service in East Asian waters on the battleship *Ohio* and on various small craft, Nimitz was commissioned an ensign and remained in the Far East until late 1908 when he returned to the United States and began duty in submarines. He became a lieutenant in 1910. While stationed in the Boston area in 1913 Nimitz married Catherine Freeman; the couple had four children.

During his four years with the Submarine Force, Nimitz gained extensive knowledge of the diesel engines that the navy had recently adopted for surface propulsion for submarines and in 1913 was selected to head a small mission to further study diesel technology in Germany. Nimitz was then ordered to the navy yard in Brooklyn, New York, to supervise the building and installation of large diesels in the new fleet oiler *Maumee*. He went to sea in the *Maumee* as executive officer and chief engineer. Nimitz was on board when the United States entered World War I and helped devise plans that allowed the *Maumee* to refuel destroyers while underway at sea, a procedure never before used by the U.S. Navy.

In August 1917 Nimitz was promoted to lieutenant commander and named engineering aide and then chief of staff to Captain Samuel Robison, commander Submarine Force, Atlantic Fleet. Nimitz's expertise in diesels had been recognized in the navy (and by business where he turned down a financially rewarding career), but being stereotyped as an engineering specialist could be detrimental for a line officer who aspired to high command. In the words of his most informed biographer, Nimitz became "concerned less with machinery than with people, less with construction and maintenance than with organization, and thus he found his true vocation" (Potter, *Nimitz*, p. 130).

Between 1918 and 1922 Nimitz had short tours in the office of the chief of naval operations and as executive officer of the battleship *South Carolina*. He spent two years at Pearl Harbor where he supervised the construction of the first submarine base there. Following a rewarding year as a student at the Naval War College, he rejoined Robison (now an admiral and commander in chief, Battle Fleet) as aide and assistant chief of staff.

In 1926 Nimitz reported to the University of California at Berkeley to organize and direct its first Naval Reserve Officers Training Corps program. He was promoted to captain in 1927. Nimitz then spent four years at San Diego (1929–1933) where his principal duty was to command the tender *Rigel* and the deactivated destroyers whose maintenance was carried out by personnel from the *Rigel*. Next he commanded the cruiser *Augusta* in Far Eastern waters (1934–1935) before serving as assistant chief of the Bureau of Navigation, the agency that handled personnel matters, including promotion, assignment, recruiting, and training.

With his promotion to rear admiral in 1938, Nimitz spent a year in command of Battleship Division One based at Long Beach, California. His flagship was the *Arizona*. He was then ordered to Washington as chief of the Bureau of Navigation where the effects of a new program of ship construction necessitated accelerated recruitment and training. The V-7 program, which brought college graduates into the naval reserves as ensigns after a seven-week training course, was instituted during Nimitz's tenure as bureau head.

On 16 December 1941 Secretary of the Navy Frank Knox advised Nimitz that he would become commander in chief of the Pacific Fleet (CinCPac). President Franklin D. Roosevelt, who had had frequent conferences with Nimitz about personnel questions during the previous three years, had already come to recognize Nimitz's qualifications for a major fleet command and had in fact asked Nimitz if he wished to command the Pacific Fleet (then named United States Fleet) when Admiral James O. Richardson was relieved in January 1941. Nimitz declined, believing it would be inappropriate to move ahead of some four dozen more senior officers to accept this prized command. Admiral Husband Kimmel, whom Nimitz had long known and respected, received the appointment. However, after Pearl Harbor, when Roosevelt and Knox decided to replace Kimmel and agreed to offer Nimitz the position a second time, he accepted it as his wartime duty.

When Nimitz began his tenure as CinCPac on 31 December 1941, his principal assets were three aircraft carriers and the various cruisers and destroyers that had come through the Japanese attack on Pearl Harbor unscathed. He also had under his command many submarines, but defective torpedoes would hamper their effectiveness for over a year. Since the Japanese had neglected to attack the oil storage depot and other shore installations, Pacific Fleet warships could continue to use Pearl Harbor as their operating base.

Nimitz's major strategic responsibilities were to guard the supply lines between the United States and the Hawaiian Islands (including the outpost of Midway Island) as well as the South Pacific route between the United States and Australia, whose defense was considered an American priority. The only offensive actions Nimitz's command could undertake were hit-and-run raids on scattered Japanese bases. (None was more heartening than the raid on Tokyo carried out by air force bombers operating from the carrier *Hornet* in April 1942.)

At the end of March 1942 Nimitz was given the additional title of commander in chief Pacific Ocean Area. In a decision many historians later criticized, the Combined Chiefs of Staff divided the Pacific into two areas: the Southwest Pacific, which included Australia, New Guinea, and the Philippine Islands (then almost entirely in Japanese control); and the Pacific Ocean Area, which included everything else save for the coastal waters of Central and South America. Within the Pacific Ocean Area Nimitz had command of the Pacific Fleet as well as all Allied ground and air forces based in the region. If the situation required, he could order units of the Pacific Fleet to operate in the Southwest Pacific, which was under the direction of General Douglas MacArthur. The Joint Chiefs of Staff in Washington decided overall matters of policy and communicated with Nimitz through the chief of naval operations, Admiral Ernest J. King, who represented the navy on the JCS. King and Nimitz conferred several times a year, ordinarily in San Francisco.

With the exception of the Tokyo raid, Japanese forces retained the initiative in the Pacific throughout 1942. Relying on timely information provided by his intelligence experts, Nimitz ordered carrier task forces to the Coral Sea in May and to the vicinity of Midway in June to thwart Japanese plans to occupy Port Moresby, New Guinea, and Midway Island. Beginning in August 1942, the struggle for Guadalcanal in the Solomon Islands dominated events in the Pacific.

Nimitz's responsibilities required that he command from shore where he would have available appropriate communications facilities and immediate access to intelligence analysts. Effective senior commanders, Nimitz believed, needed to choose competent subordinates, define their objectives, and provide them with the means necessary to meet these goals. They should not interfere with the conduct of any individual operation since the commander on the scene would know best what tactical measures to take. At Midway, as historian Dean Allard has pointed out, Nimitz did just that. He gave his chief task force commanders the strongest forces he could muster and told them to engage the enemy under the principle of calculated risk, defined as avoiding "exposure of your force to attack . . . without good prospect of inflicting . . . greater damage on the enemy."

Nimitz did believe in seeing things for himself, however. He visited Midway in May 1942 to ascertain the needs of the key outpost, and in September he went to Guadalcanal when the operation there appeared to be in jeopardy. His evaluation of the Guadalcanal campaign and the South Pacific headquarters led him to replace the area commander, longtime friend Robert L. Ghormley, with the aggressive Admiral William Halsey. As the war continued Nimitz visited Tarawa and Okinawa among other places and in 1944 moved his own headquarters to Guam to be nearer the scene of combat.

Calm and affable, Nimitz got on well with both admirals and younger staff officers. His concern for enlisted personnel is amply documented. Nimitz loved a good story, but he also used his collection of tales, frequently described as "salty" or "Lincolnesque," for serious purposes. Although reporters compared CinCPac conferences to college seminars where ideas were freely exchanged, the planning sessions at which he presided sometimes grew argumentative. Then Nimitz usually had an appropriate anecdote that eased tensions. Cautious in his strategic thinking, he often had good reason to be so. For instance, because two of the Pacific Fleet's four carriers had been sunk during the Guadalcanal campaign and the remaining two damaged, Nimitz believed that any subsequent operation would have to take place within 300 miles of his nearest air bases.

By the last half of 1943, the combined air groups from the new carriers that Nimitz had available numbered some 700 planes, enough to give his forces air superiority in any operation they undertook. The bold steps that King had been urging Nimitz to pursue could finally be undertaken. While American troops continued to advance in New Guinea and the Solomon Islands, Nimitz's air and amphibious forces began a devastating new Central Pacific campaign that seized those Japanese bases that promised to be useful in future American operations and bypassed the remainder. Among those taken by American forces were Tarawa in the Gilberts, Kwajalein and Eniwetok in the Marshalls, and Saipan, Tinian, and Guam in the Marianas.

Planners in Pearl Harbor and Washington agreed on taking Leyte in the Philippines after the conclusion of the Marianas operation, but King then wanted to seize Formosa while Generals George C. Marshall and MacArthur favored a return to Luzon, the northernmost of the major Philippine Islands. Nimitz and most of his senior officers believed that invading Formosa as King proposed would be too ambitious and that landings on Luzon followed by assaults upon Iwo Jima and Okinawa would require fewer personnel while also providing the steppingstones for the invasion of Japan. MacArthur would have control of the Luzon campaign and Nimitz of the Iwo Jima and Okinawa operations. King, who had been adamant about invading the Marianas, deferred to Nimitz's reasoning in this instance. The capture of Okinawa in the spring of 1945 turned out to be the last of the great amphibious operations undertaken by Nimitz's forces.

After the Japanese surrender Nimitz, who had been promoted to the five-star rank of Fleet Admiral in 1944, began a two-year appointment as chief of naval operations (CNO). His term was dominated by four primary concerns: overseeing the demobilization of the wartime navy; assessing the material and personnel needs of the service in the postwar years; assisting Secretary of the Navy James Forrestal in developing an appropriate position for the navy in regard to the unification of the armed services; and formulating a mission for the navy in opposing the Soviet Union, the only great-power adversary the United States might have to face in the foreseeable future. Since the Soviet Union, unlike Japan, was primarily a land power, the navy's role was defined accordingly. Deciding how the navy could best use atomic energy was a closely related matter. Eager to see nuclear power developed for use by submarines, Nimitz also supported the inclusion of atomic weaponry in the navy's arsenal.

Led by Admiral Forrest Sherman, Nimitz's chief wartime planner, strategists assumed that in the event of a Soviet attack the Red army would make major gains in Western Europe. However, they anticipated that planes operating from carrier task forces in the Mediterranean could defend oil resources in the Middle East, bomb accessible targets in the Soviet Union, help to seize and defend bases that would enable the United States and its allies to gain the strategic initiative. Keeping open the Atlantic sea lanes would also be essential.

Nimitz reached mandatory retirement age in 1947. He rejected many lucrative business opportunities to lead a much anticipated life of leisure in Berkeley but soon grew restless. He became involved in public service, chiefly as a roving goodwill ambassador for the United Nations and then as a regent at the University of California. Mindful of the fact that his daughter Nancy had difficulty securing a government job because of her involvement in radical causes during the 1930s, Nimitz spoke firmly against McCarthyism when freedom of speech became an issue at Berkeley. He died in the naval hospital on Yerba Buena Island, California.

Nimitz's place in history rests primarily on his command of the Pacific Fleet and the Pacific Ocean Area during the Second World War. For almost four decades after the end of the war historians treated him kindly, but thereafter they raised questions about his grasp of strategy, his knowledge of logistics, and his proclivity to compromise on issues of planning and on personnel assignments. While some of these criticisms have merit, in the largest sense Nimitz was a superior leader. One of the three Americans to command a theater of operations in World War II (the others were Generals Dwight Eisenhower and MacArthur), Nimitz had to take over a command that was in shambles and far inferior to the enemy. Furthermore, like most naval officers of his generation, he had spent much of his professional life expecting that the next great naval war would produce another Jutland. Yet the self-effacing Nimitz had the requisite leadership skills and flexibility to rebuild the Pacific Fleet and to reorient operations around powerful carrier task forces in which battleships played only supporting roles. While American submarines devastated Japanese merchant shipping, the mobility and striking power of the carriers made possible the island-hopping campaigns in which Nimitz's forces seized positions that put Japan itself in striking distance and that would have provided essential forward bases had an invasion of Japan been necessary.

• The most important papers relating to Nimitz can be found in various collections at the Naval Historical Division, Navy Yard, Washington, D.C. The Nimitz Museum in Fredericksburg, Tex., has other items of interest. Nimitz did not write a memoir but did participate in the preparation of E. B. Potter and Fleet Admiral Chester Nimitz, *Triumph in the Pacific: The Navy's Struggle against Japan* (1963). Biographies of Nimitz are E. B. Potter, *Nimitz* (1976), and Frank A. Driskill and Dede W. Casad, *Chester W. Nimitz, Admiral of the Hills* (1983). Virtually every book about World War II in the Pacific will have some materials about Nimitz, but among the most important are Samuel Eliot Morison, *The Two-Ocean War: A Short History of the United States Navy in the Second World War* (1963); Clark G. Reynolds, *The Fast Carriers: The Forging of an Air Navy* (1968); Reynolds, *Admiral John H. Towers* (1991); Edwin P. Hoyt, *How They Won the War in the Pacific: Nimitz and His Admirals* (1970); Ronald Spector, *Eagle against the Sun: The American War with Japan* (1985); Dan Van der Vat, *The Pacific Campaign* (1991); and Robert W. Love, Jr., *The History of the U.S. Navy*, vol. 2, *1942–1991* (1992). For insight into Nimitz's leadership as recorded in contemporary magazine articles see, for example, Stanley High, "Nimitz Fires When He Is Ready," the *Rotarian*, Apr. 1943, 29–30, 56; Joseph Driscoll, "Admiral of the Reopened Sea," *Saturday Evening Post*, 8 Apr. 1944, pp. 24–25, 36–39; and Fletcher Pratt, "Nimitz and His Admirals," *Harper's*, Feb. 1945, pp. 209–17. Dean C. Allard, "Nimitz and Spruance: A Naval Style of Command," in *Military Leadership and Command: The John Biggs Cincinnati Lectures, 1988,* ed. Henry S. Bausum (1989), is essential. On issues that arose during Nimitz's tenure as CNO, Steven T. Ross, "Chester William Nimitz," in *The Chiefs of Naval Operations,* ed. Robert William Love, Jr. (1980); Michael A. Palmer, *Origins of the Maritime Strategy: American Naval Strategy in the First Postwar Decade* (1988); Edward Sheehy, *The U.S. Navy, the Mediterranean, and the Cold War, 1945–1947* (1992); and Townsend Hoopes and Douglas Brinkley, *Driven Patriot: The Life and Times of James Forrestal* (1992), are especially useful. An obituary is in the *New York Times*, 21 Feb. 1966.

LLOYD J. GRAYBAR

NIN, Anaïs (21 Feb. 1903–14 Jan. 1977), writer, was born in Paris, France, the daughter of Joaquin Nin, a Spanish composer and pianist, and Rosa Culmell, a singer. Nin's handsome father was a concert pianist, and Nin's early life was spent traveling around Europe with her parents. She was exposed to the world of art and artists as well as the stormy relationship between her parents.

Nin began writing her diary, for which she is best known, on her journey to New York with her mother and two brothers in 1914, after the family was abandoned by her father. She writes that she wanted "to record everything for my father. It was really a letter, so he could follow us into a strange land." From 1914 to 1922 Nin lived with her mother and brothers in New York, dropping out of school at sixteen. She married a banker, Hugh P. Guiler, in Cuba in 1923 after working as a Spanish dancer and artist's model in New York; they had no children.

Nin's return to Paris with her husband in 1931 opened an important period in her creative life, as she met a number of other contemporary writers such as Antonin Artaud and Lawrence Durrell who were attempting to explore varieties of form, the subconscious, and the irrational in their work. She also became acquainted with Henry Miller and June Miller while waiting for the publication of her first book, *D. H. Lawrence: An Unprofessional Study* (1932). It was during this time in Paris that she began psychotherapy, first with Dr. René Allendy and later with Otto Rank. Her first novel was published in Paris in 1936 (*The House of Incest*), followed by a collection of three novelettes, *Winter of Artifice*, in 1939. Both were well-received in Europe.

Nin returned to New York at the beginning of World War II, continued writing her diary as well as fiction, and began to print and publish her own work under the imprint Gemor Press, since finding an American publisher for her work was difficult. Between 1939 and 1945 she wrote and self-published a collection of short stories, *Under a Glass Bell* (1944), and a novel, *This Hunger* (1945), and printed limited editions of *The House of Incest* and *Winter of Artifice*. In 1939 the influential critic Edmund Wilson reviewed *Under a Glass Bell* favorably and helped Nin find an American publisher. The next twenty years of her life were spent writing, acting, and continuing psychoanalysis. In 1961 she moved to Los Angeles, and the first of her diaries was published in 1966. At this time, she began to give speeches and lectures around the country, and she was elected to the National Institute of Arts and Letters in 1974. She died in Los Angeles.

Nin's fiction explores the female psyche in a style most critics describe as surreal; Nin uses dreams and dream states, stream of consciousness, and disjointed narrative to suggest the isolation and fragmentation of her characters. Certain motifs such as enclosures, doubles, mirrors, windows, webs, the labyrinth, and division permeate her work, providing clues to her major themes. Bettina Knapp writes, "Nin's works are quests. Her goal was to explore the woman and artist living within her." The fiction is an extension of her diary; often whole passages from the diary appear in the novels and short stories. Taken together, they provide a collage of a woman struggling to become known to herself and to record her growth as an artist. Critics agree, however, that Nin's reputation will ultimately rest on her diary; often quoted is Henry Miller's early evaluation, in 1937, that the diary would stand "beside the revelations of St. Augustine, Petronius, Abélard, Rousseau, Proust, and others."

For over sixty years, from age eleven until her death, Anaïs Nin created herself through language, primarily in her diary. "Yes, my life flows into ink!" Nin wrote at eighteen, a statement that her lifework supports. Understanding this complex woman and her work involves sifting through an immense amount of material; her diary alone is over 35,000 pages in 200 manuscript volumes. Even with the pages of the published diary before us, it is difficult to know what was real and what was constructed, since she certainly edited and to some extent revised the diary over time. As Nancy Scholar points out, "Attempting to set out the 'facts' of Anaïs Nin's life is a hazardous enterprise. Nin made an art out of her life, and made her life the subject of her art." Because no authoritative biography has been published, the "facts" of her life emerge slowly and in a fragmented form, much as she structured her writing. Her body of work, however, reveals a woman searching for a way to express, in her words, "feelings, instincts, emotions, and intuitions; . . . the hardest language to gain." Nin writes not just her life, but the often unwritten and unspoken lives of many women, as she struggles to express, to understand, and to become a whole being.

Since 1985, information has become available that makes a reconsideration of Nin's life necessary. Volumes 1 through 7 and the early diary were all published before the death of Nin's husband in 1985, and because of Guiler's request that he be left out of the diary, many other events were deleted. After his death, however, two unexpurgated versions of the diary were published that are much more explicit. The material now available details Nin's relationship with Henry Miller and June Miller (*Henry and June: From the Unexpurgated Diary of Anaïs Nin*, 1986) and with her father (*Incest: From "A Journal of Love:" The Unexpurgated Diary of Anaïs Nin*, 1992).

Nin's relationship with Henry Miller and June Miller in Paris in 1931–1932 influenced her professionally and personally; as a writer, Nin wanted to explore the inner being, identity formation, and sexuality. Henry Miller, a struggling writer, was interested in similar ideas, and he and Nin encouraged each other artistically. Nin and Henry Miller became lovers, and while there seems to be some question about the exact nature of Nin's relationship with June Miller, it is clear from the diary that she was infatuated with June, calling her "the most beautiful woman on earth." *Incest* removes the cloudy language of volume 1 of the diary that explores Nin's meeting with her father after a twenty-year separation. She was reunited with her father in 1933 and evidently became his lover. As further unexpurgated material from her writings appear, the process of understanding Nin's life and work will continue.

Nin's legacy to contemporary women writers is a mixed one, as is the critical assessment of her work. Her emphasis on the necessity to discover the self, to journey into the interior, to experiment, and to write have given women a strong model; the sheer quantity of her literary work is both remarkable and inspiring. With other modernist writers, Nin's work provides innovative forms for communicating the psychology of self and the search for meaning and wholeness, but from a staunchly female perspective. Yet Nin's work is problematic for many writers and critics because her life so often overshadows her art. Her blending of the genres of diary, autobiography, and fiction makes distinguishing between her life and her art difficult. Nin's fierce commitment to her writing throughout her life stands side by side with the image of Nin as a young writer giving her only typewriter to Henry Miller so he could write. Not surprisingly, feminist scholars continue to be divided on Nin's work and how to evaluate it; the erotica in particular has been both praised and condemned. Without doubt, however, Nin's work will continue to offer writers and scholars a complex perspective on one woman's life and, by extension, on the lives of many women.

• Nin's handwritten journals are housed in the Special Collections Department of the University of California, Los Angeles. Nin edited her diaries for publication in seven volumes, and since her death additional unexpurgated versions have appeared. *Cities of the Interior* (1959) is Nin's most critically acclaimed novel, originally published in five parts: *Ladders to Fire* (1946), *Children of the Albatross* (1947), *The Four-Chambered Heart* (1950), *A Spy in the House of Love* (1954), and *Solar Barque* (1958), published in expanded form as *Seduction of the Minotaur* (1961). Her most famous works besides her diaries are her erotica, *Delta of Venus: Erotica* (1977) and *Little Birds: Erotica* (1979). Her nonfiction work includes her observations on the novel in *The Novel of the Future* (1968), and a collection of essays, *In Favor of the Sensitive Man and Other Essays* (1976). Benjamin Franklin, *Anaïs Nin: A Bibliography* (1974), is particularly helpful in following the publishing history of Nin's work, which is complicated; another helpful bibliography is Rose Marie Cutting, *Anaïs Nin: A Reference Guide* (1978). Bettina L. Knapp, *Anaïs Nin* (1978), Nancy Scholar, *Anaïs Nin* (1984), and Deirdre Bair, *Anaïs Nin: A Biography* (1995) provide overviews of Nin's life and work. Scholarly studies of Nin's work include Evelyn J. Hinz, *The Mirror and the Garden: Realism and Reality in the Writings of Anaïs Nin* (1971); Evelyn J. Hinz and Fraser Wayne, *World of Anaïs Nin: Critical and Cultural Perspectives* (1978); and Sharon Spencer, *Collage of Dreams: The Writings of Anaïs Nin* (1981). Two collections of critical essays on Nin's work are Sharon Spencer, ed., *Anaïs, Art, and Artists: A Collection of Essays* (1986); and Robert Zaller, ed., *A Casebook on Anaïs Nin* (1974). Two journals are devoted to Nin and her work, *Anaïs: An International Journal* (1983-) and *Under the Sign of Pisces: Anaïs Nin and Her Circle* (1970–1981).

SHERRYL HOLWICK BOOTH

NISBET, Eugenius Aristides (7 Dec. 1803–18 Mar. 1871), congressman and Georgia Supreme Court judge, was born in Greene County, Georgia, the son of James Nisbet, a physician and planter, and Penelope Cooper. Growing up on a plantation near present-day Union Point, Nisbet was exposed early to politics and government by his father, a delegate to the 1798 Georgia constitutional convention and for twelve years a member of the Board of Trustees of the University of Georgia. Beginning his education at Powelton Academy in neighboring Hancock County, Nisbet attended the College of South Carolina, then transferred to the University of Georgia, where he graduated with highest honors in 1821. Preparing for his chosen profession in the manner typical of the day, he remained in Athens for two years, reading law in the office of Augustin Smith Clayton, a distinguished judge and politician. A desire for more formal training led him in 1823 to Litchfield, Connecticut, where he attended the famous law school operated by Tapping Reeve and James Gould. Returning to Georgia later that year, Nisbet was ready to practice law but was under the legal age. In an unusual and controversial move, the state general assembly admitted him to the bar by special action. Capitalizing on the attendant notoriety, he opened an office in Madison and quickly established a lucrative practice in the Ocmulgee Judicial Circuit among some of the state's most notable lawyers. In 1825 he married Amanda Battle, a childhood friend; they had twelve children, five boys and seven girls.

At age twenty-four Nisbet was elected to the state legislature, where he served as representative from 1827 to 1829 and as senator from 1830 to 1835. He distinguished himself in the state house by chairing a committee that dealt successfully with reform of the state penitentiary amid calls for its abolition. In the state senate, he championed an increase in appropriations for higher education and was an unsuccessful advocate of the creation of a state supreme court. Nisbet was a member of the Troup faction in Georgia politics, one of two parties at the time. As that group dissolved, Nisbet joined a majority of the Troupites in creating the "State Rights" party in opposition to Andrew Jackson and the nationalism he represented. This group later became allied with the Whig party. Sensing greater political and professional opportunities in the growing city of Macon, Nisbet left Madison for the larger town in 1837. Elected to Congress on the Whig ticket in 1838 and reelected in 1840, he supported the national Whig positions in favor of the tariff and the national bank. His career in Washington was cut short, however, when he resigned to deal with a large debt for which his firm had become liable as a surety. Discharging this debt proved a strain on him for many years.

In 1845 Nisbet again left his private practice to accept appointment to the newly created Supreme Court of Georgia, an institution he had long advocated. With careful legal scholarship and a commitment to justice during the court's crucial first eight years, he and his colleagues Joseph Henry Lumpkin and Hiram Warner overcame the distrust that had prevented the establishment of such a body during the state's first seventy years. Nisbet's opinions were regarded by his contemporaries as clear, precise, and learned. Establishing new precedents at the time, their impact was largely confined to the nineteenth century. The Georgia General Assembly completely revised the law on divorce in response to his holding in *Head v. Head* that abandonment was insufficient to support a divorce decree under the common law. Two of his opinions were well regarded as eloquent tributes to those in the legal profession and enunciations of the high standards they were called to uphold. In *Mitchum v. the State* Nisbet wrote, "Where learning and character, and practiced skill, and eloquence, and enthusiasm, chastened by discretion, are enlisted in behalf of the litigant, he may rest assured that he holds in his counsel the very best guarantee against all forms of wrong and oppression in the administration of the law." In *Moody v. Davis* he elaborated on the dual role of a lawyer as both the representative of a party and an officer of the court and the diligence required of a judge to know and apply the law in his efforts to ascertain the truth.

In 1853 Nisbet's political opponents prevented his reelection to the court by the legislature, so he returned to practicing law. He continued to be politically active, joining Benjamin Harvey Hill as a leader of the state's Know Nothing party, but he identified with the Democratic party on the national level and was a delegate to the Democratic National Convention of 1860. Although he had been known as a Union man, at the Georgia secession convention of 1861 he unexpectedly assumed leadership of those supporting withdrawal from the Union. On 18 January he introduced a resolution authorizing the appointment of a committee to draft an ordinance of secession. Although opposed by Herschel V. Johnson, Hill, and Alexander H. Stephens, the resolution passed. Nisbet was named chairman and drafted the Articles of Secession, which were adopted the following day by a vote of 208 to 89. Nisbet was also chosen as a delegate to the convention in Montgomery that organized the Confederate States of America. Later that year he ran for governor against Joseph E. Brown, who was seeking an unprecedented third term. The electorate sent a majority of Nisbet men to the legislature, but Brown was reelected decisively in spite of opposition from almost every major newspaper in the state. After this defeat, Nisbet took no active role in politics during the Civil War or Reconstruction but continued his law practice in Macon until his death there.

During his lifetime, Nisbet was known for his support of education and as an outstanding orator and literary critic. In 1850 he presided over a convention of delegates elected by the counties to devise a plan for common schools. He was offered the chair of belles-lettres at both the University of Georgia and Oglethorpe College but declined. He did serve as a trustee of the University of Georgia and as president of the Board of Trustees of Oglethorpe. Nisbet was a popular speaker and writer, delivering addresses before many literary groups, such as the Literary Society of the State University and the Georgia Historical Society, and contributing to several popular magazines of the day. His most lasting contributions were as a jurist, helping to firmly establish the Georgia Supreme Court as an institution in a state that had for many years resisted centralized legal authority.

• Principal sources on Nisbet are the Nisbet Family Papers in the Southern Historical Collection at the University of North Carolina at Chapel Hill; the Eugenius A. Nisbet Papers at the Duke University Library, Durham, N.C., and the Eugenius A. Nisbet Papers in the University of Georgia Libraries, Athens. Biographical sketches are in George White, *Historical Collections of the State of Georgia* (1854); by J. R. Lamar in *Great American Lawyers*, vol. 4, ed. W. D. Lewis (1908); and by Bernard Suttler in *Men of Mark in Georgia*, vol. 3, ed. William J. Northern (1907). Useful information is in several tributes by contemporary lawyers and jurists published after his death in *Georgia Reports*, vol. 43 (1871). Additional materials are in I. W. Avery, *The History of the State of Georgia* (1881); Walter B. Hill, "The Supreme Court of Georgia," *Green Bag* 4 (1892); and U. B. Phillips, *Georgia and State Rights* (1902). Two works on Nisbet's life are John M. Sheftall, "Eugenius Aristides Nisbet: Georgia Jurist" (honors thesis, Univ. of Georgia, 1980), and Malcom D. Jones, "Life and Times of Eugenius A. Nisbet," (MS, Washington Memorial Library, Macon, Ga., n.d.).

JAMES K. REAP

NISSEN, Greta (30 Jan. 1905?–15 May 1988), dancer and actress, was born Grethe Ruzt-Nissen in Kristiania (Oslo), Norway, the daughter of Carl Andreas Franz Nissen, an agent, and Agnes Magdalene Larsen, a cashier. In 1908 Grethe's mother divorced her improvident husband and relocated in Copenhagen with Grethe and her younger brother. Grethe was coached for a dance career from early childhood. Queen Maud reputedly accepted her as a protégé in 1911, and that same year her mother may have falsified her actual age by one year to enroll her in the Laeseskole for Balletelever (Reading School for Ballet Students) of Det kongelige Teater in Copenhagen.

In Denmark, Nissen first danced with the Royal Theatre's famous corps de ballet on 1 January 1914 in Ludwig Heiberg's play *Alferne*, as choreographed by Gustav Uhlendorf. There she was taught the intricate series of steps that were an integral part of the school of August Bournonville. In May 1918 the great Michel Fokine was appointed guest artist at Det kongelige Teater. This led to a confrontation between Fokine's naturalistic choreographic innovations and the more artificial Bournonville school. Until his immigration to the United States in 1919 Fokine was Nissen's teacher.

Nissen attained celebrity in the early 1920s. At the age of seventeen she was a popular ballerina in Norway. Then, in 1923, she played the role of an ingenue in two Danish silent films, *Daarskab, Dyd og Driverter* and *Lille Lise Let-paa-Taa*. She made her Oslo debut as a solo artist at the Nationaltheatret on 17 May 1922 to music by Chopin, Brahms, and Borodin. Critics praised her for her expressive use of her body and her sensitive interpretations of the music using Fokine's concepts. She gave forty-two Fokine programs across Norway.

Nissen enjoyed a splendid New York debut on 12 February 1924 as the Crown Princess in "A Kiss in Xanadu," Winthrop Ames and Deems Taylor's cameo musical interlude for George S. Kaufman and Marc Connelly's *Beggar on Horseback*. Critics hailed her as "a pantomimist of exotic charm and rich allure" and favorably compared her dance to the principals' dramatic performances. Jesse Lasky soon signed the dancer-actress to a Paramount movie contract at a reported salary of $75 a week, which over the next two years climbed to $1,500. Before leaving for California, she played King Serge's mistress in *The King on Main Street*, filmed partly on location by Monta Bell and costarring Adolphe Menjou and Bessie Love. In Hollywood she was publicized as the "Viking's Daughter," but her compelling "Norskdom" was initially squandered by studio bosses amid a succession of roles as mistresses, princesses, and biblical temptresses. Her fine-tuned dancer's art was obscured beneath dark, frizzy wigs and behind harem costumes.

Between 1924 and 1927 Nissen acted in nine silent films for Paramount and one for Universal. In *Blonde or Brunette?* critics acclaimed her performance as a young bride who alternates between the fast life of a jazz baby and an absurdly fastidious and domesticated wife. In 1926 she returned to the New York stage as a costar in the Oriental pantomime "Mlle. Bluebeard" of Florenz Ziegfeld's lavish revue *No Foolin'*.

Nissen had learned English in Oslo, but she still spoke it with a Norwegian inflection, and by 1927 the first sound films had appeared. Her appearances in *Fazil*, which had music and sound effects, but no dialogue, and the silent film *The Butter and Egg Man*, both released in 1928, had little appeal or impact. She went to Rochester, New York, to immerse herself in English lessons and appear in two comedies. During June and July 1928 she played Aura Nomi in Gladys Ungar's Hollywood satire *Double Exposures* and the Actress in Ferenc Molnar's *The Guardsman*. Reviewers were friendly, and Howard Hughes assigned her the role of Helen in *Hell's Angels*, his World War I air-combat epic. His decision to make the film as a full talking feature meant reshooting scenes with dialogue. Nissen (reportedly being paid $2,500 a week) was replaced by the neophyte Jean Harlow (at $125 a week). But Nissen won praise for her roles in twelve Hollywood talkies for Fox, Columbia, RKO/Radio, and other studios between 1931 and 1934. On 30 March 1932 she eloped with actor Weldon Heyburn (Weldon H. Franks); they divorced amicably on 23 September.

Nissen soon renewed her dance and theater career in England, where she appeared in five lucrative, unspectacular films. She made her London stage debut at the Palace Theatre on 24 April 1934 in the revue *Why Not To-night*, acting, singing, and, notably, dancing in Agnes de Mille's landmark ballet "Three Virgins and a Devil." In December 1934, as the costar of *Hi-Diddle-Diddle* at the Comedy Theatre, she was the principal dancer in "Navarra," to music by Isaac Albéniz, and sang, danced, and acted in several revue sketches and musical numbers.

She toured, commencing in August 1935, in Edward Sheldon's *Romance*; starred in Lewis Wallace's comedy-drama *Borrow the Moon* during June–July 1937; and made her West End acting debut on 28 September 1937, opposite Cyril Ritchard, in Arthur Reid's comedy *People in Love*. Reviewers praised Nissen as "vivacious and charming, with a fluent command of English" but added that she "mistakes an arch and kittenish manner for the mischief with style . . . proper to a very light comedy."

On the eve of World War II Nissen returned to the United States and married Los Angeles manufacturer Stuart D. Eckert in June 1940. They had one son, and she retired from show business. She died in Montecito, a suburb of Santa Barbara.

Near the end of her life Nissen confessed that her silent-screen career playing stereotypical vamps and exotic princesses was enjoyable and exciting. At the same time she achieved artistic success as a dancer on the stages of New York and London.

• DeWitt Bodeen, "Greta Nissen," *Films in Review* 32 (Jan. 1981): 25–35, is the pioneer biographical essay and definitive filmography. Pat M. Ryan, "'A Dancer Must Be Perfect All Over': Greta Nissen on Stage and Screen," *Dance Chronicle* 22, no. 2 (1989): 285–322, also gives accounts of Nissen family history, Danish dance training and performance, the Norwegian "Fokine evenings," and Palladium filmography; documents the various Scandinavian, U.S., and English phases of Nissen's stage and screen careers; and discloses pervasive myths and fabrications. Ryan also lists articles on Nissen in fan magazines. See also articles and interviews in 1927 and 1928 issues of *Norgesposten* (Brooklyn) and James Watters, *Return Engagement* (1984). The Nissen sketches in the *New York Times*, 9 Mar. 1924, and in Hal C. Herman, *How I Broke Into the Movies* (1930), are untrustworthy. Obituaries are in the *Santa Barbara News-Press*, 15 July 1988, and *Variety*, 17 Aug. 1988.

PAT M. RYAN

NISSEN, Henry Wieghorst (5 Feb. 1901–27 Apr. 1958), psychobiologist, was born in Chicago, Illinois, the son of parents who had immigrated from Germany; their names are unknown. His father was a bookkeeper for the Pabst Chemical Company. Nissen studied at the University of Illinois, where he read widely in German and English literature and received a B.A. in English in 1923. For the next three years Nissen worked in Chicago and New York as a correspondent and statistician for the Pupman Thurlow Company. In 1924 Nissen enrolled in night courses at Columbia University to begin study for an M.A. he also started working as an assistant in the psychology department of Barnard College. His interest and aptitude for psychology was noted by Dr. C. J. Warden, a professor of comparative psychology at Columbia, who encouraged Nissen to pursue a Ph.D. and enroll in graduate school full time. In 1927 Nissen married Jane Marion Stowby. They had two children, but later separated. Many years later Nissen married Kathy Hayes, coauthor of *The Ape in Our House*, but they separated as well.

Nissen's first formal contribution to the field of psychology, a paper coauthored by Warden on the obstruction method of testing animal drives, was published by the *Journal of Comparative Psychology* in 1928. One year later Nissen's dissertation, titled "The Effects of Gonadectomy, Vasotomy, and Injections of Placental and Orchic Extracts on the Sex Behavior of the White Rat," was published as a *Genetic Psychology Monograph*. These works, as well as Nissen's student presentation at the American Psychological Association, impressed Robert Yerkes, an authority in the field of primate psychobiology and professor at Yale University. Through Yerkes, Nissen was offered a position as research assistant with rank of assistant professor at Yale, which he accepted upon conferral of his Ph.D. In the fall of 1929 Nissen traveled to Africa to observe free-ranging chimpanzees in French Guinea on an expedition organized by Yerkes and funded with the aid of the Pasteur Institute. Nissen's report, "A Field Study of the Chimpanzee: Observations of Chimpanzee Behavior and Environment in Western French Guinea," was published as a *Comparative Psychology Monograph* in 1931. Nissen returned from this expedition with eighteen chimpanzees destined to serve as laboratory subjects in New Haven and Florida.

In 1933 Nissen was promoted to research associate at the level of associate professor of psychobiology at Yale, and in 1939 he moved to Florida as the assistant director of Yale laboratories in Orange Park, a location chosen by Yerkes as highly suitable for the establishment and maintenance of a chimpanzee colony. Nissen began this colony with several animals from Western French Guinea and continued to study and supervise its growth for over twenty-five years. He was especially interested in the psychobiology and daily life patterns of chimpanzees, and he carefully recorded observations of all aspects of chimp life in the colony, including infancy, youth, reproduction, disease, diet, and general medical, dental, and surgical care. Not only Nissen's own research, but all publications of the Yale Laboratories for Primate Biology produced during his time there were affected by his work with the colony.

Following Yerkes's retirement in 1941, Nissen became assistant director of the Yale Laboratories. In 1944 he was promoted to research associate with rank of professor at Yale, a position he would hold for the subsequent twelve years. In 1946 Nissen left Orange Park to serve as the director of research in biopsychology at the Rockland State Hospital in New York for one year. Upon his return, Nissen began a comparative infant study program at the colony in order to discern the ideal environment for chimp development and possibly extend his conclusions to the development of human children. He was elected to the National Academy of Sciences in 1953 and promoted to director of the Yale Laboratory of Primate Biology, recently renamed after Yerkes, in 1955. During these years Nissen studied the cognitive function of chimpanzees; specifically, he was interested in possible motivations for what were often classified as innate animal behaviors. In this venue, Nissen created a popular schema of drive behavior in animals and collaborated with A. H. Reisen on a series of studies concerning the psychological and anatomical development of chimpanzees, especially the processes of bone ossification and dentition. Though he was an avid boater, fisherman, and table tennis enthusiast, Nissen was plagued by health problems. During his career Nissen suffered a ruptured appendix, a critical case of pneumonia, and an advanced case of emphysema that was aggravated by his addiction to smoking.

Throughout the early 1950s Nissen conducted hundreds of research projects in psychology, medicine, physiology, neurology, and endocrinology and was considered the leading authority on the biology of the chimpanzee. He served as a consultant to the Psychiatric Institute and Hospital of New York City, as president of the Florida Psychological Association, and as a member of the American Psychological Association, the Society of Experimental Psychologists, and the American Society of Naturalists. In 1956 the Yerkes Laboratories were transferred from Yale to Emory University in Atlanta, Georgia, and in 1957 Nissen's title changed to professor of psychobiology at Emory. At the time of his death, Nissen had authored or coauthored fifty-seven papers on the social interaction, stimulus response, cognitive development, mating behavior, anatomical development, and problem-solving behaviors of chimpanzees. He had enjoyed the support of numerous organizations and private donors, including the Carnegie, Rockefeller, and Ford Foundations, as well as the National Institutes of Health, the Atomic Energy Commission, and the National Science Foundation. Nissen firmly believed that mental processes could be understood only upon consideration of both genetics and environment. He used this outlook to create innovative and highly influential studies of the sensory perceptions, drives, motivations, and socially-determined behaviors of chimpanzees, that affected the field of psychobiology for years to come.

• Nissen's papers have not been archived, and not many especially informative or accessible articles were written about him in the years following his death. A substantial source of information is the collection of Robert Yerkes's papers at Yale University. A good biographical source is Leonard Carmichael, "Henry Wieghorst Nissen," *Biographical Memoirs of the National Academy of Sciences* 38 (1970). For further discussion of Nissen's views on the importance of genetics in understanding and studying psychological processes, see his chapter titled "Phylogenetic Comparison" in *The Handbook of Experimental Psychology*, ed. S. S. Stevens (1951). The secrecy that surrounded Nissen's life and work is mentioned in his obituary in the *New York Times*, 30 Apr. 1958, and may account for the dearth of sources.

KRISTIN M. BUNIN

NITCHIE, Edward Bartlett (18 Nov. 1876–5 Oct. 1917), special educator and author, was born in Brooklyn, New York, the son of Henry Evertson Nitchie and Elizabeth Woods Dunklee. His life underwent a complete change when at the age of fourteen he became almost totally deaf. In spite of this handicap, he completed his preparatory education at the Adelphi Academy and Brooklyn Latin School (both in Brooklyn, New York) and the Betts Academy of Stamford, Connecticut. Forced by his hearing loss to make adaptations in order to benefit from his teachers' lectures, Nitchie habitually sat in the front row of the classroom, made extensive use of an ear trumpet, and conducted post-class interviews with his instructors. Using these methods he made excellent grades, and he entered Amherst College in 1895 at the age of nineteen. While at Amherst Nitchie continued to use his adoptive measures effectively; he not only achieved academic success (named Phi Beta Kappa during his junior year, he graduated magna cum laude in 1899), but he also served as the class "Ivy Poet" at commencement, as well as the editor of the *Amherst Literary Magazine*.

Graduation proved to be a bittersweet experience for Nitchie; despite his promising record, he could not find employment. Forced to abandon his original plans of becoming a minister, he moved to New York City in 1900 and began the study of lip-reading (now called speechreading) with John Dutton Wright. A fellow Amherst graduate, Wright had been teaching deaf students in New York using the lip-reading method for a dozen years prior to Nitchie's arrival. Convinced by his own experience that the art of lip-reading was largely self-taught, he published the results of his studies, titled *Self-Instructor in Lip-Reading*, in 1902. With the encouragement of Wright and Alexander Graham Bell (who, in addition to inventing the telephone, was a leading figure in the so-called oral method of deaf instruction), Nitchie then opened the New York School for the Hard-of-Hearing in 1903.

Nitchie entered the field of deaf education at a time when the profession was badly divided over the question of instructional methods. The controversy, which was both widespread and bitterly personal in character, centered on the two main pedagogical schools of thought regarding the instruction of deaf students in communication skills: the so-called combined method (that included the use of sign language) favored by deaf educators such as Thomas Hopkins and Edward Miner Gallaudet, and the "oralist" school that was promoted by men like Bell. The "oral" school was clearly in the ascendancy at the time of Nitchie's entrance into the field, and under the influence of its leaders, Nitchie took an active role in its promotion. As the head of the New York School until his death, Nitchie taught 1,100 students, 117 of whom later became deaf educators themselves. Constantly improving and refining his instructional methods, he published *Lessons in Lip-Reading for Self Instruction* in 1905, with a revised edition appearing in 1909. He also published *Lip-Reading Simplified* (n.d.) and in 1912 produced *Lip-Reading Principles and Practice*. The latter was his most successful book and soon became the standard text in most schools using the oralist methods. Nitchie took time from his many activities to marry Elizabeth Logan Helm of New York in June 1908; they had one son.

Remembering well his own difficulties in adapting to a hearing world, Nitchie actively promoted the Nitchie Alumni Association upon its founding in 1910. Created to encourage social interaction between students and their peers as well as to provide financial assistance to needy students, the organization continued to expand in its scope and became the Nitchie Service League in 1912. In its new incarnation, the group provided educational, recreational, and employment assistance to its members; it became (at Nitchie's suggestion) the New York League for the Hard-of-Hearing in 1914. Nitchie's organization served as a model for similar groups in cities throughout both the United States and Canada, and it helped to break down established prejudices against deaf employees.

Nitchie was plagued by poor health for a number of years prior to his death, which occurred in New York City. While his early demise cut short what promised to be a long and fruitful career in the field of deaf education, he still deserves to be remembered for his role in advancing educational, occupational, and social opportunities for deaf individuals in the early years of the twentieth century.

• Nitchie's papers do not appear to have survived, and information about his life and career is scarce. The best sources remain a series of articles that appeared in the *Volta Review* following his death: Juliet Douglas Clark, "Edward Bartlett Nitchie: An Appreciation" (Nov. 1917): 617–18; Alice N. Trask, "Edward Bartlett Nitchie" (Dec. 1917): 647–48; and Elizabeth Brand, "Aftermath: A Tribute to Edward B. Nitchie" (Dec. 1917): 648–50. While it ignores Nitchie and his contributions to the field, Richard Winefield's *Never the Twain Shall Meet: Bell, Gallaudet, and the Communications Debate* (1987) provides an excellent overview of the educational controversies that swirled around him. A brief obituary is in the *New York Times*, 6 Oct. 1917.

EDWARD L. LACH, JR.

NIVEN, David (1 Mar. 1910–29 July 1983), actor and author, was born in London, England, the son of William E. G. Niven, an inheritor of extensive landholdings, and Henrietta de Gacher. He sometimes named as his birthplace the more arresting locale of Kirriemuir, Scotland, where his father had an estate. William Niven served as a naval lieutenant during World War I and died at Gallipoli in 1915. Finding herself in reduced financial circumstances because of her husband's gambling, Henrietta Niven made a second marriage in 1917 to a man who remained distant from her four children. Niven's rootless childhood was spent in a series of boarding schools, ending at Stowe House. During these years he showed a budding interest in amateur dramatics and writing but not in serious study. He was known as the school clown of Stowe, a born entertainer whose devil-may-care charm got him in and out of various scrapes. In 1927 he entered the Royal Military College at Sandhurst. He continued to appear in amateur dramatic productions there and also during his army service as a junior officer in the Highland Light Infantry from 1929 through 1933.

Niven found army life increasingly distasteful compared to the social whirl of London that opened to him when his regiment was posted back from Malta to Dover. Besides making friends and attending parties where he honed his talents as an amusing raconteur, he appeared as an extra in two British films, one in 1932 and another in 1933. A Christmas trip to New York in 1932, as the guest of heiress Barbara Hutton, made him think of leaving the army to seek a more exciting, lucrative career in the United States. He resigned his commission in the summer of 1933, returned to New York, and found several short-lived jobs there. Meanwhile his British accent, polish, and flashing smile made him a desirable "extra man" at social events, bringing him an increasing circle of friends. One of these, professional party-giver Elsa Maxwell, suggested in 1934 that he seek his fortune in Hollywood, where a number of British actors had done well in films.

Niven arrived in Hollywood in September 1934, innocent of professional acting experience. He registered at Central Casting for extra work, categorized as "Anglo-Saxon Type No. 2008," but soon moved on to a long-term contract with Samuel Goldwyn. He also began a three-year romantic involvement with movie star Merle Oberon, whom he had first met in London several years before. She promoted Niven for small parts in screen productions, as did other friends he charmed on the Hollywood social circuit, and she helped him master film acting technique. From one-line bit parts in 1935, Niven progressed to larger roles in 1936, showing skill that year as a romantic figure in *Dodsworth*, as a light comedian in *Thank You, Jeeves*, and as a man of action in *The Charge of the Light Brigade* and *Beloved Enemy*. In 1937 he stood out in a swashbuckling featured role in *The Prisoner of Zenda*, as he did in the comedy *Bluebeard's Eighth Wife* (1938) and as a British flying officer in *Dawn Patrol* (1938). He achieved costarring status in a series of 1939 films ranging from the drama *Wuthering Heights* to the romantic comedy *Bachelor Mother*. That year full stardom came to him as a gentlemanly burglar in *Raffles*. His publicity, meanwhile, pictured him as a lovable scamp of a playboy.

The outbreak of World War II in 1939 brought a sudden halt to the upward trajectory of Niven's career. As soon as *Raffles* was completed he left Hollywood for Great Britain to join up and in 1940 entered army service once more as a subaltern in the Rifle Brigade. In 1940 he married Primula Rollo; the couple had two sons. After serving as a captain of commandos, Niven volunteered to serve with the secret Phantom "A" Squadron (a reconnaissance or counter-invasion unit) and was promoted to major. As a motion picture star, much of his time in the war years went to morale-building appearances, including three British films, but he also served in Normandy in 1945. He left the army as a lieutenant colonel at war's end and was awarded the American Legion of Merit.

Niven re-entered commercial filmmaking with a British picture, titled in the United States *Stairway to Heaven* (1945). In 1946 he returned to Hollywood, needing to rebuild his career there from the bottom up, only to discover that his screen persona of the suave, debonair British gentleman was no longer in demand. A personal tragedy came a few weeks after his return: his wife was killed when she fell down a flight of stone basement stairs at a Hollywood party. Niven had to struggle out of deep depression to continue working. His films for the rest of the decade were largely undistinguished. While in London in 1948 to play the title role in a British production, *Bonnie Prince Charlie*, he met Swedish model Hjordis Tersmeden and married her ten days later.

By 1950 Niven's screen career was faltering badly, and he received only third billing in *The Toast of New Orleans*. That year he began work on a novel, somewhat autobiographical, about a young British actor's romantic and professional misadventures in Hollywood. It was published in 1951 as *Once Over Lightly* (in Britain titled *Round the Rugged Rocks*) to mildly favorable reviews. In 1951 and 1952 he began appearing on television. Together with Hollywood veterans Charles Boyer and Dick Powell, he formed a television production company in 1952 and rotated starring appearances with them and others in the successful dramatic series "Four Star Playhouse."

Although a Broadway stage role in *Nina* (1951) was not a success, Niven had better luck in the San Francisco stage production of the Broadway hit comedy *The Moon Is Blue* in 1952. He repeated his role in the play's film version (1953). The film, which defied the Motion Picture Production Code by using words like "seduce" and "virgin," was a scandalous success; Niven's accomplished comic performance won him the Golden Globe award and began to revive public interest in him as a screen personality. His status as a star was firmly re-established by his winning performance as Phileas Fogg, the central role in a tremendous hit, *Around the World in Eighty Days* (1956). For his portrayal of a shabby retired British colonel in *Separate Tables* (1958), Niven received an Academy Award for best actor.

In 1960, for tax benefits and also because both husband and wife remained European in outlook, Niven relocated his family to a new home in Switzerland. The couple adopted two daughters over the next few years. On screen he maintained his versatility, playing with equal success a dramatic role in *The Guns of Navarone* (1961) and a comic role in *The Pink Panther* (1964). On television he starred in the series "The Rogues" (1964–1965). Many other screen appearances through the 1960s and 1970s were in forgettable productions, and film acting in one or two films a year became simply a means for him to earn money. He worked hard only on his two books of the decade, *The Moon's a Balloon* (1970) and *Bring on the Empty Horses* (1975). The unprecedented success of these two volumes of Hollywood memoirs, which sold millions of copies, was immensely gratifying to him.

In 1981 Niven published a second novel, *Go Slowly, Come Back Quickly*, another tale of glamorous Hollywood figures and another bestseller for him. While on a book tour to publicize the work, he began to experience symptoms of the wasting muscular condition known as Lou Gehrig's disease. Though both speech and movement became increasingly difficult, he continued to act and to work on a novel. It remained unfinished when he died at his home near Gstaad, Switzerland.

Niven always professed to be amazed at his success as an actor whose career spanned nearly fifty years. He zealously maintained his publicity image as a playboy adventurer who parlayed a dazzling smile, irresistible personal charm, and gifts as a raconteur into international fame. The range of his roles and the skill of some performances revealed a more serious professional side, however, and his personal history had its dark, even tragic, aspects. In the words of Sheridan Morley, his longtime friend and biographer, "The Niven of the films and autobiographies—the cheerfully grinning but stiff-upper-lipped storyteller—[hid] a much darker, more complex and intriguing figure behind the clenched mask of the grin and tonic man" (p. 2).

• Materials on Niven's life and career are in the Billy Rose Theatre Collection at the New York Public Library for the

Performing Arts, Lincoln Center. His life story is told in Sheridan Morley, *The Other Side of the Moon* (1985). Karin J. Fowler, *David Niven: A Bio-Bibliography* (1995), contains a biographical section; a chronology of his life; a filmography with plot summaries and review excerpts; listings of stage, radio, and television appearances; an annotated bibliography of books and other publications concerned with Niven; and a bibliography of other references to him in print. Obituaries are in the *New York Times*, 30 July 1983, and *Variety*, 3 Aug. 1983.

WILLIAM STEPHENSON

NIXON, Edgar Daniel (12 July 1899–25 Feb. 1987), Alabama civil rights leader, was born in Robinson Springs, Alabama, near Montgomery, the son of Wesley Nixon, a tenant farmer and, in later years, a Primitive Baptist preacher, and Susan Chappell. Nixon's mother died when he was nine, and thereafter he was reared in Montgomery by a paternal aunt, Winnie Bates, a laundress. Nixon attained only an elementary education, and at thirteen began full-time work, first in a meat-packing plant, then on construction crews, and in 1918 as a baggage handler at the Montgomery railway station. As a result of friendships that he made in this last job, he managed in 1923 to become a Pullman car porter, a position he would hold until his retirement in 1964. In 1927 he was married to Alleas Curry, a schoolteacher. The couple soon separated, but they had Nixon's only child. In 1934 he married Arlet Campbell.

Exposed by his railroad travels to the world beyond Montgomery, Nixon grew increasingly to hate racial segregation. He became a devoted follower of A. Philip Randolph, who was attempting in the late 1920s and early 1930s to unionize the all-black Pullman porters. In 1938 Nixon was chosen as president of the new union's Montgomery local. In 1943 he organized the Alabama Voters League to support a campaign to obtain voter registration for Montgomery's blacks. The effort produced a vigorous white counterattack, but Nixon himself was registered in 1945.

Montgomery's blacks were sharply divided between a middle-class professional community centered around the campus of Alabama State College for Negroes and the working-class blacks who lived on the city's west side. The Montgomery branch of the National Association for the Advancement of Colored People (NAACP) was dominated by college-area professionals and failed to support Nixon's voter registration drive actively. Nixon therefore began organizing the poorer blacks of west Montgomery, where he resided, to attempt a takeover of the branch. He was defeated for branch president in 1944 but was elected in 1945 and reelected in 1946 in bitterly contentious races. In 1947 he was elected president of the Alabama Conference of NAACP Branches, ousting the incumbent, Birmingham newspaper editor Emory O. Jackson. But national NAACP officials, who were hostile to his lack of education, quietly arranged for Nixon's defeat for reelection to the state post in 1949. And in 1950 he also lost the presidency of the Montgomery

branch to the same man he had beaten in 1945. Nevertheless, in 1952 he won election as president of the Montgomery chapter of the Progressive Democratic Association, an organization of Alabama's black Democrats. And in 1954 he created consternation among Montgomery's whites by becoming a candidate to represent his precinct on the county Democratic Executive Committee. Though he was unsuccessful, he thus became the first black to seek public office in the city in the twentieth century.

During his years with the NAACP, Nixon had become a friend of Rosa L. Parks, the branch secretary during much of this period. When Parks was arrested on the afternoon of 1 December 1955 for violating Montgomery's ordinance requiring racially segregated seating on buses, she called Nixon for help. After he bailed her out of jail, he began telephoning other black leaders to suggest a boycott of the buses on the day of Parks's trial, 5 December, to demonstrate support for her. The proposal was one that black leaders had frequently discussed in the past, and it was greeted enthusiastically by many of them. The black Women's Political Council circulated leaflets urging the action, and a meeting of black ministers gave it their approval. The boycott on 5 December was so complete that black leaders decided to continue it until the city and the bus company agreed to adopt the plan of seating segregation in use in Mobile, under which passengers already seated could not be unseated. The Montgomery Improvement Association was formed to run this extended boycott, and Nixon became its treasurer.

Nixon, however, became increasingly antagonistic toward the association's president, the Reverend Martin Luther King, Jr. Nixon viewed King as an ally of the Alabama State College professionals, and he believed that King's growing fame was depriving him, and the poorer blacks whom he represented, of due credit for the boycott's success. After King moved to Atlanta in 1960, Nixon engaged in a protracted struggle for leadership of Montgomery's blacks with funeral director Rufus A. Lewis, the most prominent figure among his rivals in the middle-class Alabama State community. The contest culminated in the 1968 presidential election, when Nixon and Lewis served on alternative slates of electors, each of which was pledged to Hubert H. Humphrey. The Lewis slate defeated the Nixon slate handily in Montgomery. Nixon thereafter slipped into a deeply embittered obscurity. He accepted a job organizing recreational activities for young people in one of Montgomery's poorest public housing projects, a position he held until just before his death in Montgomery.

• The Library of Alabama State University, Montgomery, holds several scrapbooks of clippings and other material related to Nixon. Numerous scholars conducted interviews with him before his death; representative transcripts may be seen at Alabama State University; the Martin Luther King Center, Atlanta; and Howard University, Washington, D.C. The struggles within the Montgomery NAACP branch may be traced in the Branch Correspondence, NAACP Papers, Library of Congress. Note, however, that Lewis V. Baldwin and Aprille V. Woodson, *Freedom Is Never Free: A Biographical Portrait of Edgar Daniel Nixon, Sr.* (1992), is unreliable. On Nixon's role in the Montgomery bus boycott, see J. Mills Thornton III, "Challenge and Response in the Montgomery Bus Boycott of 1955–1956," *Alabama Review* 33 (July 1980): 163–235. On his relationship with King see David J. Garrow, *Bearing the Cross: Martin Luther King, Jr., and the Southern Christian Leadership Conference* (1986). A not entirely accurate obituary appeared in the *New York Times*, 27 Feb. 1987.

J. MILLS THORNTON III

NIXON, John Thompson (31 Aug. 1820–28 Sept. 1889), jurist, was born in Fairton, Cumberland County, New Jersey, the son of Jeremiah S. Nixon, a timber company operator and later a shipbuilder, and Mary Shaw. Shortly after his birth the family moved to the county seat of Bridgeton, where Nixon spent his childhood. When he was nine years old the family moved to Delaware. In 1837 he entered the College of New Jersey (now Princeton University). After graduating in 1841 he spent two more years in Princeton teaching classical languages. Nixon's association with the school continued throughout his lifetime. He served as a trustee of the college from 1864 until his death.

In 1843 Nixon moved to Staunton, Virginia, to tutor the children of Isaac S. Pennybacker, a U.S. judge for the western district of Virginia. Nixon read law under Pennybacker and was admitted to the Virginia bar in 1844. Pennybacker invited Nixon to form a law partnership; Nixon was to oversee their law office while the judge attended his duties as a newly elected U.S. senator, but Pennybacker's untimely death in 1845 ended those plans. Nixon returned to Bridgeton to join the practice of Charles E. Elmer, the cousin of Lucius Q. C. Elmer, who was best known as the author of a leading treatise on New Jersey statutory law. In 1851 Nixon married Lucius Elmer's daughter, Mary H. Elmer, with whom he had three children.

After establishing a successful legal practice Nixon turned his attention to politics. In 1848 he was elected as a Whig to the general assembly of New Jersey and the following year he served as Speaker. From 1859 to 1863 he served in the U.S. House of Representatives, first as a member of the American, or Know Nothing, party, then as a Republican. During his first term, when partisan disagreement over the slavery issue thwarted the selection of a Speaker of the House, Nixon was instrumental in forging a compromise by promoting William Pennington, a former governor of New Jersey, for the post. After the outbreak of the Civil War, Nixon diligently supported President Abraham Lincoln's war policies.

Between his service in the general assembly and in Congress, Nixon made his first significant contribution to New Jersey jurisprudence by updating his father-in-law's digest, which had been in need of revision since the adoption of a new state constitution in 1844. Nixon published the second edition of Elmer's *Digest of the Laws of New Jersey* in 1855, then issued two subsequent revisions in 1861 and 1868. Although Elmer's name continued to appear on the title page,

the book became universally known among New Jersey bar members as "Nixon's Digest."

Nixon decided not to seek reelection to Congress in 1862, hoping instead to be named to a vacancy on the federal district court in New Jersey. President Lincoln passed over Nixon in favor of Richard S. Field, a New Jersey senator, and Nixon returned to his law practice in Bridgeton. During the 1860s he assumed a leading role in Presbyterian church government that continued throughout his life. In 1877 he represented the American congregations at the meeting of the Presbyterian Alliance in Scotland. In 1883 he was named to the board of directors of the Princeton Theological Seminary, a leading institution for the training of Presbyterian ministers.

In 1870, following the death of Field, President Ulysses S. Grant nominated Nixon to the federal court for the district of New Jersey. While the New Jersey court was not considered a particularly prestigious appointment, Nixon's nomination came at a propitious moment in the history of the federal judiciary. The necessity of resolving the troublesome constitutional dilemmas of Reconstruction and the increased national character of economic activity enhanced the power of the federal judiciary and led to the expansion of federal jurisdiction in areas such as criminal law, bankruptcy, and patents. Especially in the area of patents, Nixon quickly earned a reputation for delivering impartial and speedy justice, something that federal courts in neighboring states could not promise. Of his 338 published opinions, approximately one-third dealt with the complex and highly technical area of patents. Throughout his career he consistently ranked among the nation's busiest patent judges, and his cases were frequently discussed in the leading treatises on patent law.

Nixon's jurisprudence was guided by three principles: deference to Congress, a belief in economic development through individual entrepreneurship, and a devotion to Presbyterian religious principles. His devotion to Republican nationalism led him to strictly enforce congressional legislation that promoted national economic development and political participation for the freed slaves. At the same time he distrusted large concentrations of wealth, favoring instead individual enterprise as a means to economic and social improvement. This preference was most apparent in his patent opinions. His decision in *Webster v. New Brunswick Carpet Company* (1874), for example, decried the "old story of poor inventors patiently waiting at the door of rich capitalists." Finally, especially in his later years, Nixon based his decisions on moral concepts nurtured by a life as a devout Presbyterian. Nixon not only enforced his ethical beliefs in cases as diverse as contracts, bankruptcy, and criminal law, but he also demanded moral behavior from the witnesses, jurors, and attorneys who appeared in his courtroom. "The chicanery, arts and cunning devices of what the world denominates as the sharp lawyer," recalled his colleague A. Q. Keasbey, "never received a moment's countenance from him." Occasionally these guiding principles came into conflict, prompting the Supreme Court to overturn his decisions when they placed moral considerations over statutory requirements or legal precedent. Nixon refused to adopt the formalistic, rule-bound jurisprudence characteristic of other jurists at the end of the nineteenth century, however, preferring instead to meet the needs of public policy by rewarding self-reliance and moral conduct.

As Nixon's reputation attracted more litigants to his courtroom, the increasing workload took its toll. During his final years on the bench his health and eyesight began to fail until virtual blindness forced him to curtail his activities. Nixon planned to retire at the age of seventy, but with less than a year remaining he died in Stockbridge, Massachusetts, while returning to New Jersey from a vacation in Maine.

• Nixon left no papers, but records pertaining to his work on the federal district court are available in the National Archives–New York Region in Bayonne, N.J. His published opinions appear throughout the *Federal Cases* (1894–1897) and in the *Federal Reporter* (1880–1889). Nixon's *Address Delivered before the Cliosophic and American Whig Societies of the College of New Jersey* (1863) is a clear statement of his moral philosophy. The most complete account of Nixon's life is A. Q. Keasbey, "John T. Nixon," *Proceedings of the New Jersey Historical Society*, 2d ser., 11 (1890): 39–51. For an excellent analysis of Nixon's work on the bench see Stephen B. Presser, "Judicial Ajax: John Thompson Nixon and the Federal Courts of New Jersey in the Late Nineteenth Century," *Northwestern University Law Review* 76 (1981): 423–86. An informative obituary is in the *New Jersey Law Journal*, Oct. 1889, pp. 322–23.

ERIC W. RISE

NIXON, Pat (16 Mar. 1912–22 June 1993), first lady, was born Thelma Catherine Ryan in Ely, Nevada, the daughter of William Ryan and Katarina "Kate" Halberstadt. Her father called his youngest child his "St. Patrick's babe in the morn" because she just missed being born on St. Patrick's Day. Throughout her life she was known as "Pat," and after her father's death she began using the name Patricia as a tribute to him. William Ryan was a miner until he decided to try truck farming in Artesia (now Cerritos), California. Pat remembered hard times but close family ties as the Ryans worked to make the farm a financial success. Life became more difficult when Kate Ryan succumbed to cancer when Pat was fourteen years old. William Ryan died of silicosis just prior to Pat's graduation from high school, making his daughter and two sons orphans.

Determined to better herself, Pat attended Fullerton Junior College, supporting herself by working in a bank and cleaning houses. When an elderly couple offered her a job chauffeuring them to New York in their car Pat jumped at the chance to earn some money and see the country. When she reached New York, she found employment as an X-ray technician at Seton Hospital and remained there for two years. She returned to California and enrolled at the University of

Southern California. To help defray expenses she worked as a movie extra and at a variety of other jobs. She graduated cum laude in 1937 with a degree in marketing and a teaching certificate.

It was impossible to find a job at the nadir of the Great Depression, thus Pat took a job teaching business subjects at Whittier (Calif.) High School. At that time teachers were expected to have some community involvement, and Pat auditioned for a part in the local theater group's production of *The Dark Tower*. During the audition she met another young thespian, attorney Richard Nixon, who was attracted to the lovely young teacher. He proposed marriage that first evening; Pat turned him down.

Richard was persistent, and eventually the two began to date; they were married in 1940. He accepted a job with the Office of Price Administration (OPA) in Washington, D.C.; they lived there until he enlisted in the navy. Pat Nixon returned to California to work as a price analyst for OPA.

After Richard Nixon returned safely from the service he decided to run for election to the U.S. House of Representatives from California's Twelfth Congressional District. Financed with receipts from the sale of Pat's parents' house, Richard conducted his initial foray into politics. Though pregnant, Pat accompanied her husband to all his speeches and meetings. She met female voters at teas and coffees. She made phone calls, stuffed envelopes, and recruited volunteers. Despite limited funds, Richard Nixon was elected to the House. The Nixon family grew to include Patricia (born in 1945 and named for her mother, but always known as Tricia) and Julie (born in 1947). When they moved to Washington, Pat ran her husband's congressional office, receiving no salary for her efforts. Richard was reelected to the House in 1948.

The year 1950 saw Richard and Pat Nixon engaged in another political campaign. After a bitter and hard-fought race he won election to the U.S. Senate. His electoral successes and the Alger Hiss case brought Richard to the attention of national Republican officials, and he was chosen for vice president on the 1952 Republican ticket behind Dwight Eisenhower.

Richard Nixon's political career almost ended inauspiciously when he was accused of having an $18,000 slush fund that had been established for him by wealthy Republican contributors. In an attempt to prove his innocence to Eisenhower and to set the record straight, Richard gave an unprecedented public accounting of his personal finances and an explanation of the fund. His speech was televised nationally, and Pat was immortalized when her husband spoke of his wife's "good Republican cloth coat."

While Richard was successful in remaining on the ticket, the experience left Pat disillusioned with the electoral process. Even though he and Eisenhower swept to victory, Pat had watched her husband humiliated on national television. She never felt the same about politics and lost her zest for it.

The vice presidential years were busy for Pat and Richard Nixon as they traveled around the world performing official duties. Pat maintained her own schedule on trips and visited hospitals, orphanages, and public works projects. At home, the second lady occasionally presided at social events to aid First Lady Mamie Eisenhower.

Richard Nixon ran against John F. Kennedy in 1960, narrowly losing the presidency. In 1962, against his wife's wishes and advice, he waged a campaign for governor of California and suffered another demoralizing loss. The Nixons then moved to New York City, where Richard Nixon joined a law firm. For the first time in many years Pat was truly happy. She and her husband were out of the limelight, and she had time to spend with her children. The good times were short lived, however, as Richard returned to national politics and was elected president in 1968.

When Pat Nixon entered the White House, she announced that her project would be volunteerism. She encouraged Americans to get involved in projects and volunteer their time helping others. She gave speeches and visited the volunteer projects and locations that were especially successful. In addition, she continued the restoration of the White House begun by Jacqueline Kennedy and expanded the fine arts and furniture collection.

Pat Nixon was perhaps the most hospitable first lady to live in the White House. She welcomed thousands to her official home, the greatest number to visit the executive mansion to that time. Those who felt that she was cool and distant with large crowds saw an animated and warm woman in one-on-one contacts.

Pat Nixon believed that anyone who took the time to write to her deserved a response, and she personally signed thousands of letters, sometimes spending four hours per day at the task. She traveled extensively, visiting American troops in Vietnam (becoming the first first lady to visit a war zone since Eleanor Roosevelt) and also heading a U.S. mission to an earthquake-devastated region in Peru, bringing food, clothing, and medical supplies.

In June 1972 the newspapers reported a break-in at the Watergate complex in Washington, D.C. Most people believed it was a botched robbery attempt, but a succession of congressional committees and special prosecutors worked to establish a link between the break-in, the Committee to Re-Elect the President, and President Nixon.

Pat Nixon proclaimed her husband's innocence of Watergate-related charges and urged him not to fight impending impeachment charges. As she traveled to various volunteer projects she heard the jeers of demonstrators demanding her husband's resignation. Eventually she limited and then almost stopped traveling entirely because of the constant presence of protesters.

In August 1974 President Nixon acknowledged that he had lost support in Congress and resigned from office. The Nixons returned to their home in San Clemente, California. Shortly after their return, Richard Nixon developed phlebitis and required surgery. In 1976 Pat suffered a stroke that left her partially paralyzed. She had another stroke in the early 1980s but fully recovered from the effects of both strokes. The Nixons moved to northern New Jersey in 1980. Richard wrote a number of books and began the rehabilitation of his reputation. The great joy of the Nixons' later years was their grandchildren, whom they saw frequently.

Pat Nixon became increasingly frail as she approached her eightieth birthday. She was diagnosed with and treated for emphysema. She died of lung cancer at home in Park Ridge, New Jersey. Richard Nixon died ten months later.

Early in his career, Pat Nixon served her husband as speech critic, editor, and office assistant. She was a constant but silent presence by his side as he conducted campaigns for state and national office. While she did not seek to be nor was she consulted on policy matters, she was a good judge of character and advised her husband on personnel matters. She brought no major changes to the office of first lady but was considered to be the human side of her husband's administration as she faithfully fulfilled her responsibilities and continued the tradition of the first lady working on a project while in the White House.

• Pat Nixon's papers may be found in three locations. Her pre– and post–White House materials are housed at the Richard Nixon Presidential Library and Birthplace, Yorba Linda, Calif. These materials have not been processed and are not yet available for research. White House textual materials, Special Files, the President's Personal Files, and the White House Central Files all have information pertaining to Pat Nixon and are open to research at the Nixon Presidential Materials Project in College Park, Md. Material relative to Pat Nixon is also available in the Richard M. Nixon Project at the California State University, Fullerton Library. The best primary source on Pat Nixon is daughter Julie Nixon Eisenhower's biography, *Pat Nixon: The Untold Story* (1986). Other useful sources include Richard Nixon, *In the Arena: A Memoir of Victory, Defeat and Renewal* (1990) and *RN: The Memoirs of Richard Nixon* (2 vols., 1978). A number of secondary sources deserve mention: Lester David, *The Lonely Lady of San Clemente: The Story of Pat Nixon* (1978), presents a sympathetic but superficial portrait of the former first lady. Judith Viorst wrote an enlightening piece about her, "Pat Nixon Is the Ultimate Good Sport," *New York Times Magazine*, Sept. 1970. Pat Nixon's tenure as first lady is also analyzed in the following: Carl Sferrazza Anthony's "Patricia Nixon" in *American First Ladies: Their Lives and the Legacies*, ed. Lewis L. Gould (1996); Betty Boyd Caroli, *First Ladies*, 2d ed. (1995); Myra G. Gutin, *The President's Partner: The First Lady in the Twentieth Century* (1989); and Gil Troy, *Affairs of State* (1997). An obituary is in the *New York Times*, 23 June 1993.

MYRA G. GUTIN

NIXON, Pat Ireland (29 Nov. 1883–18 Nov. 1965), physician and historian, was born at Old Nixon in Guadalupe County, Texas, the son of Robert Thomas, a farmer and stockman, and Frances Amanda Andrews. Nixon received a bachelor's degree from the University of Texas in 1905 and a medical degree from the Johns Hopkins University School of Medicine in 1909.

After postgraduate training at the Johns Hopkins Hospital, mostly in gynecology, Nixon began a general practice in San Antonio, Texas, in October 1911. He attended patients for more than fifty years and served on the staffs of three San Antonio hospitals: Baptist Memorial, Nix Memorial, and Santa Rosa.

Nixon was a devoted member of several professional societies. He served as president of the Bexar County Medical Society in 1926 and of the Texas Surgical Society in 1956. As a founder of the Bexar County Medical Library Association, Nixon orchestrated the acquisition of more than 2,000 volumes of rare medical books, which eventually formed the basis of the P. I. Nixon Medical Historical Library at the University of Texas Health Science Center at San Antonio. Nixon also edited *Southwest Texas Medicine*, the journal of the Southwest Texas District Medical Society and the Bexar County Medical Society, from 1934 to 1938.

Nixon crusaded for improvements in city government and for better public health programs in San Antonio. Appointed a member of the San Antonio Board of Health in 1928, he served on city and city-county health boards for two decades. Nixon lobbied fearlessly for a council-manager form of government, because he felt the entrenched commissioner form of city government had no built-in checks and balances against cronyism and corrupt forms of patronage. He also encouraged successful efforts to eliminate shameful slums as an effective way to control the incidence of communicable diseases, especially tuberculosis, in the city.

Nixon became the first scholar to write extensively about the history of medicine in Texas, completing twenty articles and three books. In *A Century of Medicine in San Antonio* (1936), Nixon chronicled "the evolution of medicine from a few straw beds on the adobe floor of the Alamo with one doctor to modern, thoroughly equipped hospitals of three hundred beds" (p. ix). Believing that "the medical annals of Texas" were an "inseparable part" of its cultural history and could not be "lightly dismissed," Nixon consulted early Texas newspapers, the Bexar Archives, and the Nacogdoches Archives, to produce his 507-page *The Medical Story of Early Texas (1528–1853)* (1946). In this book he provides extraordinary details about diseases, physicians, and medical care from the year that Spanish explorer Cabeza de Vaca treated Indians living on the Gulf Coast of Texas (1528) until a small group of physicians organized the State Medical Association of Texas in January 1853. Nixon celebrated the accomplishments of this organization in *A History of the Texas Medical Association 1853–1953* (1953). This chronicle of the evolution of a professional society over 100 years relied especially on the *Proceedings* and *Transactions* of the association and its serial, the *Texas State Journal of Medicine*, founded in 1905. Esteemed by colleagues, Nixon served as president of three major cultural organizations: the San Antonio Historical Association (1941), the Texas State Historical Association (1946–1949), and the Philosophical Society of Texas (1946).

Nixon married Olive Gray Read in 1912; they had four sons. A devout Methodist, he also wrote articles and books about his church and family. In 1963 the Nixons donated 12,000 books about Texas to the Trinity University Library in San Antonio. He died in San Antonio.

Although Nixon was not trained as a professional historian, his book-length contributions to the medical historiography of Texas are still extraordinary documents because they are the earliest monographs on medicine in Texas that are grounded in an exhaustive analysis of primary sources and also because they are well organized, readable, and interesting. Throughout his career, Nixon demonstrated the richness and power of his belief in the intimate connection between medical practice and the social and cultural contexts of that practice, realizing that physicians should actively support efforts to improve the quality of life for the communities in which they practice. Herbert Lang, professor of history at Texas A&M University, believed Nixon symbolized the ideal physician: "sensitive to the needs of his patients, congenial in his relations with colleagues, active in the affairs of his community, and concerned for the future of his profession" (Lang, p. 47).

• Nixon's letters, speeches, and research notes are in the Pat Ireland Nixon Papers, housed in the library of the University of Texas Health Science Center at San Antonio. This library also holds an oral history interview with Mrs. A. G. (Nathalie) Grum, a librarian at the Bexar County Medical Society who worked closely with him. Nixon provides details about his family in *The Early Nixons of Texas* (1956) and *In Memoriam: Olive Read Nixon 1886–1964* (1965). A bibliography of Nixon's writings is included in Herbert Lang's edition of Nixon's autobiography, *Pat Nixon of Texas: Autobiography of a Doctor by Pat Ireland Nixon*, ed. Herbert H. Lang (1979). Lang provides a thoughtful assessment in his introduction to this book. An obituary is in the *San Antonio Express*, 19 Nov. 1965.

CHESTER BURNS

NIXON, Richard Milhous (9 Jan. 1913–22 Apr. 1994), thirty-seventh president of the United States, was born in Yorba Linda, California, on the outskirts of Los Angeles, the second of five sons born to Frank Nixon, who ran a grocery store in Whittier, California, and Hannah Milhous. His mother's Quaker views and emotional restraint countered to a degree his father's combative and volatile nature: as an adult Nixon exhibited both characteristics. Hard work came naturally to him. He succeeded through perseverance rather than brilliance. A good student because he applied himself, Nixon excelled scholastically at both Whittier High School and Whittier College. His special talent was debating, although he doggedly tried to make "first string" on his high school and college football teams. These interests helped him develop skills he later used as a politician: perseverance and rhetorical attack. They also reinforced his combative, aggressive personality.

Nixon won a scholarship to Duke Law School in 1934, and graduated third in his class in 1937. After failing to receive an offer from a prestigious eastern law firm, Nixon practiced in Whittier from 1937 until 1942. During that time he courted and married Thelma Catherine Patricia "Pat" Ryan, whom he met during the rehearsal of a play after she moved to Whittier to teach high school commercial subjects. Even though as a young, successful lawyer he was one of Whittier's most eligible bachelors, they did not become engaged or married until three years later in 1940. They had two children.

In 1942 Pat and Richard Nixon moved to Washington, where Nixon first worked in the Office of Price Administration. Disillusioned by the red tape of the federal bureaucracy, he obtained a commission in the navy, serving in the South Pacific from 1942 to 1946, and left with the rank of lieutenant commander.

Nixon's years as a politician before becoming president were peppered with controversy. Under the direction of Murray Chotiner, a campaign consultant for such Republican luminaries as Earl Warren and William Knowland, Nixon used Hollywood media campaigns and political packaging techniques (now considered commonplace) complete with innuendos about his opponents' presumed Communist sympathies. Such tactics proved successful in 1946, when he defeated five-term liberal Democratic Congressman Jerry Voorhis, and again in 1950, when he ran against the equally liberal Democrat Helen Gahagan Douglas for a U.S. Senate seat. These early congressional and senate races earned Nixon the reputation among Democrats as an opportunistic product of the Cold War, a "political polarizer" who would do anything to win an election.

In 1948 he proposed the Mundt-Nixon bill, which would have required individual Communists and Communist organizations to register with the federal government. In that same year, Nixon, as a member of the House Un-American Activities Committee, initiated the successful attempt to discredit Alger Hiss by exposing his subversive connections with the Communist party in the 1930s. Ex-Communist Whittaker Chambers had claimed that he had known Hiss to be a Communist agent, accusations that Hiss emphatically denied. Nixon's painstaking and publicity-seeking tactics contributed to Hiss's indictment and subsequent conviction for perjury on 21 January 1950. The episode catapulted Nixon to national prominence and earned him the undying enmity of many liberals and partisan Democrats.

National attention over the Hiss case brought Nixon to the attention of Dwight Eisenhower, the Republican candidate for president in 1952, and won Nixon the vice presidential nomination. But almost immediately Nixon found himself in trouble when it was charged that he had created a slush fund of around $18,000 to further his political career. By going on nationwide television on 23 September, Nixon successfully defended himself and forced Eisenhower to keep him on the Republican ticket. In this broadcast he presented embarrassingly detailed information about his family's finances, including the fact that his wife Pat did not own a fur coat but only "a respectable Republican cloth coat." The speech is probably best remembered, however, because of his maudlin declaration that his children would keep a dog named Checkers, even though the cocker spaniel had been a political gift. The "Checkers" speech has been so satirized and condemned that it is often forgotten that it marked Nixon's debut as a successful television personality. Although what he said was denounced for its emotionalism, its illogical assertions, and implicit attacks on Democrats, he had already tried out much of it before live audiences with good results. In its uncut version, it still makes for powerful television and shows Nixon at his debating best—looking directly into the camera and delivering an effective, engaging, and emotional speech.

During his years as Eisenhower's vice president, from 1953 until 1960, Nixon campaigned widely for Republican candidates and in the process obtained the unenviable reputation of being the party hatchet man, especially because of his attacks on Adlai Stevenson, twice Eisenhower's Democratic opponent. As a result, elements within the press, many academics, and liberals in general found it easier to criticize the conservatism of the Eisenhower administration by forgoing attacks on a popular president and concentrating instead on the personality and campaign tactics of his vice president. In the process they overlooked Nixon's consistent support for educational reform and civil rights.

Nixon's apprenticeship under Eisenhower left him with strong impressions about how the cabinet in general and the National Security Council should be run. At the time, however, he remained outside President Eisenhower's private group of advisers. Occasionally humiliated by Ike in public, Nixon bided his time and mended his own political fences by courting both moderate and conservative Republicans and creating a "centrist" image of himself among supporters within his own party, which ensured his presidential nomination in 1960. By his own efforts, Nixon upgraded the office of vice president and gave it a much more meaningful and institutionalized role than his predecessors had. Nixon's public image as a leader benefited when Eisenhower suffered a heart attack in 1955, a bout with ileitis in 1956, and a stroke in 1957. Throughout these illnesses, Nixon handled himself with considerable tact, presiding over nineteen cabinet sessions and twenty-six meetings of the National Security Council. Following his stroke, Eisenhower worked out a plan with Nixon, Secretary of State John Foster Dulles, and Attorney General William Rogers to create the office of acting president in the event he became incapacitated from illness. This formal agreement substituted under Presidents Eisenhower and Kennedy for a constitutional amendment (not ratified until 1967) granting the vice president full authority to govern when the president could not discharge the powers and duties of his office. Nixon's stature was further enhanced by several well-publicized trips abroad on behalf of the president. In 1958 he traveled to Latin America; in Caracas anti-American protesters stoned his car. The next year Nixon confronted Soviet leader Nikita Khruschev in an impromptu and much-noticed "kitchen" debate in Moscow.

Nixon's unsuccessful campaign for the presidency against John F. Kennedy in 1960 was fraught with ironies and political lessons he never forgot. Repeatedly the press described Kennedy as a "youthful front runner" representing a new generation, even though Nixon was only four years older than his 43-year-old opponent. In the course of the campaign, Kennedy successfully projected an image since found wanting: that of a devoted father and family man in robust health, an intellectual who was seemingly less of a cold warrior than Nixon. The fact that Nixon's congressional and vice presidential records on social issues, especially civil rights, and foreign policy were more liberal than Kennedy's were lost in the Democrats' media blitz.

During the 1960 campaign, Nixon learned the hard way the significant role that television could have in forming impressions and shaping opinion. In his television debates with Kennedy, Nixon won the rhetorical points, but Kennedy won the hearts of the American people. The election proved the closest in U.S. history since Grover Cleveland defeated James G. Blaine in 1884. To his credit Nixon did not challenge this 1960 election that he lost by only 112,000 popular votes, even though such luminaries of the Republican party as Bryce Harlow, Herbert Klein, Len Hall, Thurston Morton, and even Eisenhower, all urged Nixon to contest the results. Many question whether the Democratic candidate legally won Illinois or Texas, whose combined electoral college tally tipped the election in Kennedy's favor, 303 to 219. Moreover, there were confused returns from Alabama, and the closeness of the vote in Missouri, New Mexico, Nevada, and Hawaii meant that a shift of less than 12,000 votes would have given Nixon a majority in the electoral college.

Temporarily retiring to private life, Nixon wrote his first book, the bestseller *Six Crises* (1961). He decided with great reluctance to run for governor of California in 1962, and his defeat prompted his much-quoted remark to reporters that they would not "have Nixon to kick around anymore." Defeat also spurred him to move to New York, where he joined a prestigious law firm. Most important, however, he continued to build bridges between moderate and conservative factions within the Republican party, especially after the Republican nominee Barry Goldwater's overwhelming defeat by Lyndon B. Johnson in the 1964 presidential election. In the ensuing years, Nixon earned a reputation as a party healer and foreign policy specialist, which resulted in his nomination as the Republican presidential candidate in 1968.

Nixon became his party's standard bearer because of his political moderation, not his extremism. In contrast to the 1960 campaign, circumstances were very much in his favor. The Democratic party was hopelessly divided over the Vietnam War and haplessly led by Hubert H. Humphrey in the wake of Johnson's unexpected refusal to run again, Robert Kennedy's assassination, and George C. Wallace's strong, racially explosive third-party bid. Had President Johnson halted the bombing of North Vietnam and renewed the Paris peace talks before the end of October, Humphrey might have been able to squeeze by Nixon, for the election results proved to be almost as close as they had been in 1960, with Nixon winning by 500,000 popular votes and receiving 301 electoral votes, compared to 191 for Humphrey and 46 for Wallace. Contributing to Nixon's success in 1968 was the sharp decline in Democratic strength in the South; from that point on, Republicans could increasingly count on the region for support.

During his first term Nixon set a fast pace on both domestic and foreign policies. He initiated environmental legislation, attempted reform of both welfare and health care, undertook significant government reorganization, and strengthened the civil rights of African Americans, Native Americans, and women. At first, the Nixon administration outpaced Congress on environmental legislation because it relied on the permit authority in the Refuse Act of 1899 to begin to clean up water supplies before either house formulated comprehensive water pollution enforcement mechanisms. Nixon's Family Assistance Plan (FAP) for drastically reforming welfare—defeated by a combination of liberals and conservatives—was at the time the most progressive put forward by any president since Franklin D. Roosevelt. It would have redirected welfare in the United States from the service-oriented program of Aid to Families of Dependent Children (AFDC) to an income-maintenance system for working and nonworking poor families. FAP constituted a negative income tax or guaranteed annual income for all poor households, including those headed by single women.

His administration also compiled an impressive civil rights record through such affirmative action programs as "set-asides" in government contracts and through financing the Equal Employment Opportunity Commission's enforcement of civil rights acts and guidelines. As president, Nixon only reluctantly undertook desegregation of southern schools after several Supreme Court decisions left him no recourse. Despite his continued opposition to school busing, by the end of 1972 his administration had reduced the number of African-American children attending all-black schools in the South to 8 percent. Nixon's New Economic Policy, moreover, was unprecedented (since World War II) in establishing wage and price controls to curb inflation, and he daringly "floated" the dollar on international currency markets.

At the time the president's significant domestic reforms took a back seat in the public mind to his seemingly dazzling foreign policy accomplishments. Much to the surprise of many who considered him an inveterate cold warrior was his administration's accommodation with the two major Communist powers, the People's Republic of China and the Soviet Union. His broad geopolitical and structural approaches to U.S. diplomacy ushered in a transition period marked by the end of the bipartisan Cold War consensus in Congress. Nixon took advantage of this opportunity to fight the Cold War by other than traditional containment policies. He was the first president to deliver annual State of the World Addresses to Congress.

To effect his "grand design" for the world, Nixon chose Henry Kissinger, a Harvard professor whom he scarcely knew, as his special assistant to the president on national security affairs. They soon established so close a relationship that conflicts between Secretary of State William P. Rogers and Kissinger usually ended in favor of the latter. Rogers finally resigned in September 1973, and Kissinger replaced him while retaining his original post.

Shortly after Nixon and Kissinger joined forces, they reorganized the National Security Council, ensuring a White House–centered model for decision-making in foreign policy. The NSC was turned into a series of interdepartmental groups all subjected to review committees headed by Kissinger. This design undercut the preeminence of the State Department by placing the formulation of foreign policy in the White House. Advice from the NSC was not always consistent. In the spring of 1969 it approved the secret bombing of Cambodia, but it recommended no U.S. military response in the EC-121 incident, involving the shooting down of a U.S. Navy plane by North Korea. Nixon also consulted the NSC on ways to keep Taiwan in the United Nations with a "two China" policy; to conduct secret incursions into Cambodia and Laos; to negotiate the détente agreements with the Soviet Union; and to determine Middle Eastern policy as well as policy in Angola and southern Africa in general.

Nixon's successes in improving relations with the People's Republic of China and the Soviet Union are often cited as his presidency's most important diplomatic achievements. Both were important components of his grand geopolitical design. Since 1949 the United States had refused to recognize Communist China. Nixon reversed this standard Cold War policy by first ordering a number of unilateral gestures of reconciliation. Normalization of U.S. relations with China was designed to bring this giant Communist segment of the world into the ranks of "civilized" nations. The obvious importance and success of rapprochement were symbolized by the president's trip to the People's Republic in February 1972 with its attendant joint "Shanghai Communiqué." Rapproachment with China laid the foundation for formal diplomatic recognition in 1979 under the Carter administration.

Nixon's attempts to achieve détente with the Soviet Union proved more problematic because it entailed complex changes in established Cold War political and economic policies. Among the motives guiding such changes were the anxiety of avoiding nuclear war, the desirability of building a network of mutually advantageous relationships, and the wish to modify Soviet behavior by ensuring de facto acceptance of international cooperation and competition (sometimes referred to as "competitive coexistence"). Nixon's underlying assumption was that international stability would be enhanced by according the Soviet Union a greater stake in the existing status quo. To a lesser degree détente was a response to the domestic and international economic problems that the United States faced as result of the Vietnamese war. The one thing détente did not represent under the Nixon administration was a continuation of the traditional Cold War policy of containment.

The success of détente depended on the personal interactions among several powerful individuals—and their perceptions of their respective nations' relative strength and the tangible benefits accruing from "relaxed tensions." In May 1972 Nixon traveled to Moscow and signed ten formal agreements with Soviet leaders. They provided for the prevention of military incidents at sea and in the air; scholarly cooperation and exchange in the fields of science and technology; cooperation in health research; cooperation in environmental matters; cooperation in the exploration of outer space; and facilitation of commercial and economic relations. The most controversial agreements, however, consisted of an Anti-Ballistic Missile Treaty, an Interim Agreement on the Limitations on Strategic Arms (a continuation of SALT I), and a statement called the Basic Principles of U.S.-Soviet Relations. Earlier Strategic Arms Limitation Talks (SALT I) held in Helsinki in 1969 and Vienna in 1970 had led to the two arms-control documents at the 1972 Moscow summit. One limited the deployment of antiballistic missile systems (ABMs) to two for each country, and another froze the number of offensive intercontinental ballistic missiles (ICBMs) at the level of those then under production or deployed. Unlike SALT I, the ABM Treaty was of "unlimited duration . . . and not open to material unilateral revision." Until the Strategic Defense Initiative (SDI) in the last half of the 1980s, the ABM Treaty essentially succeeded in relegating deployment of conventional ballistic missile defense systems to minor strategic significance.

SALT I, on the other hand, was an agreement of limited, five-year duration and attempted to establish a rough balance or parity between the offensive nuclear arsenals of the two superpowers, despite ongoing "missile gaps" related to specific weapons. SALT I did not stop the nuclear arms race; it recognized that unregulated weapons competition between the two superpowers could no longer be rationally condoned. Freezing further missile buildup, SALT I ensured that when SALT II was signed in 1979 the total American-Soviet missile strength would remain essentially unchanged.

Détente with the USSR soon floundered after Nixon left office. Of equally debatable value was the Nixon Doctrine, issued in 1969, according to which the United States would no longer commit troops to East Asia (and implicitly in other parts of the world). In fact, subsequent administrations engaged in unprecedented arms sales to foreign nations and continued to deploy American troops abroad.

Although Nixon came to office committed to negotiating a quick settlement of the Vietnam War, he ended up expanding and prolonging the conflict in the name of "peace with honor." While gradually withdrawing U.S. combat troops from Vietnam under the policy of so-called Vietnamization, the president allowed Kissinger to initiate secret negotiations with the North Vietnamese. Begun in August 1969, they were largely unproductive by the time they were made public—over Kissinger's protests—in January 1972. Only marginally better terms were reached in 1973: North Vietnam agreed to allow the greatly weakened South Vietnamese president Nguyen Van Thieu to remain in power in return for the North's being able to keep troops in place below its border. Whatever gain the United States could claim as a result of that agreement paled beside the loss of an additional 20,552 American lives during the three-year negotiation period. The fatal weakness of the diplomatic arrangement reached in 1973 was evident two years later, in April 1975, when President Gerald Ford was compelled to order the emergency evacuation of the last remaining U.S. troops from Saigon.

Neither Nixon nor Kissinger ever admitted that their policies destabilized most of Indochina, leading—in addition to the collapse of South Vietnam—to the massive loss of life and defeat of non-Communist regimes in Laos and Cambodia. With the exception of ending the draft, creating an all-volunteer army, and finally publicly endorsing the return of U.S. POWs as a major condition of peace, practically every action taken by Nixon with respect to Vietnam created resentment, suspicion, and protest from those who opposed the war. Following Lyndon Johnson's presidency, the antiwar movement had grown in intensity rather than diminished. In this polarized atmosphere, Nixon made support of American involvement in the war a matter of patriotism, which he considered to be the attitude of the "silent majority," while antiwar protestors vilified and demonized him.

In general, Nixon's foreign policy did not succeed in the Third World. Both his and Kissinger's indifference and geopolitical calculations resulted in policies that often failed to take into account the economic and social realities of individual nations. For example, U.S. relations with India deteriorated because Pakistan served as the conduit to China in the early secret stages of rapprochement. In turn, this led to Pakistan's suppression of Bangladesh's independence and to India's decision to develop nuclear weapons—all because Nixon and Kissinger decided that the United States "could not let an American/Chinese friend (Pakistan) get screwed in a confrontation" while the Soviets seemed to be allying themselves with India. In his foreign economic policy, Nixon employed far fewer questionable tactics (with the exception of the economic warfare his administration conducted against Salvador Allende's government in Chile in 1971–1973) and followed the counsel of a much broader group of advisers than he did with respect to other aspects of diplomacy.

Improved public relations tactics, along with economic policies that brought the nation out of a recession, progressive domestic programs, and some personal foreign policy achievements (except for Vietnam) ensured Nixon's reelection in 1972. By choosing the staunchly liberal, antiwar candidate George McGovern, the badly divided Democratic party turned the contest into a rout. To most voters Nixon simply seemed the safest candidate. In fact, Nixon seemed to have achieved the goal of his first inaugural address when he said: "We cannot learn from one another until we stop shouting at one another." He won by a stunning landslide: 520 electoral votes to 17 for McGovern and a margin of almost 18 million popular votes.

During his truncated second term, Nixon undertook few domestic policy initiatives, and most of his efforts in foreign affairs were not successful. In the Middle East, in particular, he and Kissinger pursued a policy that seemed to negate itself: that of stalemate. Early in Nixon's first term, Secretary of State William Rogers and the assistant secretary of state responsible for Middle Eastern affairs, Joseph Sisco, had hammered out a plan that called for a more neutral stance toward Israel and the Arab nations and substantial Israeli withdrawal from occupied territory in return for a contractual peace brokered by the United States and the USSR. Although the Rogers Plan was meant as a realistic proposal to the Soviets, Kissinger met separately with the Soviet ambassador to the United States, Anatoly Dobrynin, and told him that the White House was not in fact interested in pursuing the proposal. In October 1969 the Soviet Union officially rejected the Rogers Plan, leaving the Nixon administration with no apparent positive alternative until the aftermath of the October War of 1973, when Israel, with belated U.S. support, devastatingly turned back its enemies and took additional territory. Kissinger at that point undertook what was popularly known as "shuttle diplomacy," traveling back and forth among the Arab nations and Israel. By then, however, the years of stalemate had cost the United States more than Kissinger could ever gain back. Relations with even the best of American friends among the Arab states were further worsened when the Organization of Petroleum Exporting Countries (OPEC) embargoed oil exports to the United States in retaliation for American support of Israel during the October War. Domestic consequences followed: during the first months of 1974 the decreased, intermittent availability of car fuel led to long lines at gas stations and public anger at the Arabs.

Meanwhile, a cloud was forming over the Nixon presidency that would eventually overshadow everything else in which the White House was involved. The Watergate affair had its origins in a second break-in, on 17 June 1972, of the Democratic National Committee (DNC) headquarters at the Watergate complex along the Potomac in Washington, D.C. The culprits, caught by Washington metropolitan police, were on the payroll of the president's reelection campaign and ostensibly were seeking to steal or photograph files in an effort to uncover and deflect DNC strategies directed against Nixon. In all, twenty individuals with ties to the president or to his reelection campaign were indicted for crimes related to the break-in and the subsequent attempts to cover up any links to the White House. The cover-up resulted in criminal convictions of some of the president's closest advisers, including his two chief aides, H. R. Haldeman and John Erlichman; the counsel to the president, John W. Dean III; a special assistant to the president, Charles Colson; and the president's former attorney general, John Mitchell, Jr. Also implicated were prominent Republican party officials. The men actually involved in the break-in, the "Plumbers" as they were called, were largely under Erlichman's supervision and had engaged in previous break-ins. Several of the Plumbers—such as E. Howard Hunt, James McCord, and G. Gordon Liddy—were former CIA or FBI agents specifically employed by the White House and paid with Nixon campaign funds to carry out political espionage. They, in turn, hired the four Cubans arrested in the Watergate complex.

Despite multiple investigations by public officials and private individuals, many factual questions about the Watergate incident remain unanswered, and its historical significance is still disputed by scholars. For example, the true reason for the original break-ins at the Watergate office complex remains unknown. Conventional wisdom holds that the burglars were after political intelligence to use against the Democrats in the presidential campaign, even though the DNC had moved its central operation from Washington, D.C., to facilitate organizing its nominating convention in Florida. The scheme of bugging the offices apparently originated with Liddy. The original bugs, however, were not placed in or near the office of the chair of the DNC, Lawrence O'Brien. Instead, they were put in outer offices that had been designated for the work of state party chairmen and the Young Democrats—but were often unoccupied. Strong circumstantial evidence indicates that a call-girl service operated out of these offices and that John Dean indirectly ordered the break-ins to discover whether the name of his future wife might be on a telephone list of prostitutes. Neither this nor any other theory has been satisfactorily documented.

The Watergate affair, however, encompasses a host of illegalities and unconstitutional acts associated with the Nixon administration, including bribes offered to indicted defendants, the solicitation of illicit campaign contributions, and the compilation of an "enemies list" (with the aim of taking revenge on party or administration figures deemed to be disloyal as well as on outsiders opposed to the president, especially antiwar protesters). Possibly none of the crimes and misdemeanors brought out by the affair would have resulted in the impeachment of the president had not his closest aides and Nixon himself engaged in a cover-up. The charge of obstruction of justice was based on the destruction of incriminating evidence and interference in federal investigations. Even the obstruction charge might not have led to impeachment if the "smoking gun" tape of 23 June 1973 had remained undiscovered; on the tape the president can be heard approving a plan to direct the CIA to request that the FBI halt its investigation into the source of the cash possessed by the Watergate burglars and into the "silence" money promised them by the administration. The tape for 20 June 1973 is equally famous because of a gap of eighteen and a half minutes during which Nixon first discussed Watergate with Haldeman. Although the president's personal secretary was blamed for the erasure, the evidence of her culpability is not conclusive. The recorded conversations between the president and his aides came from 4,000 hours of secret, voice-activated tapes made, at Nixon's behest, in the Oval Office, the Cabinet Room, the Old Executive Office building, and Camp David between February 1971 and July 1973.

After the existence of the tapes came to light, the first of several serious constitutional issues arising out of Watergate surfaced. Instead of destroying the tapes, Nixon tried to assert his control over them by claiming executive privilege when Congress and the first Watergate special prosecutor, Archibald Cox, requested the originals or unedited transcripts. On 24 July 1974 the Supreme Court ruled in *United States v. Nixon* that the president could not retain possession, thus significantly limiting executive privilege with regard to presidential documents. By the time the decision was handed down, Nixon had fired Cox in the so-called Saturday Night Massacre of 20 October 1973, over which Attorney General Elliot Richardson and Deputy Attorney General William Ruckelshaus resigned.

The second constitutional question arising from Watergate concerned the grounds for impeachment. After those directly involved in the 1 June 1972 break-in that launched the affair were convicted on 30 January 1973, they were threatened with extremely heavy sentences by Judge John J. Sirica; one of those convicted, John McCord, then sent the judge a letter, released on 23 March, implicating the Committee for the Re-election of the President (often derogatorily called CREEP) and the White House. By June, when John Dean, who technically had been investigating Watergate for the president, decided to testify before the Select Committee on Presidential Campaign Activities, headed by Senator Sam Ervin (D-N.C.), the president's closest advisers—including Haldeman, Erlichman, and Dean himself—had already resigned. Once Dean began testifying, the "stonewalling" started to crumble. Constitutional responsibility for sorting through the mounting evidence against the president and his top aides ultimately fell to the House Judiciary Committee, chaired by Peter W. Rodino (D-N.J.). In the wake of the Cox firing, it took the House of Representatives until 6 February 1974 to approve an official impeachment inquiry into the president's conduct.

The heart of the case rested on the report of the second Watergate special prosecutor, Leon Jaworski, which stated that "beginning no later than March 21, 1973, the President joined an ongoing criminal conspiracy to obstruct justice, obstruct a criminal investigation, and commit perjury (which included payment of cash to Watergate defendants to influence their testimony)." In addition, a federal grand jury secretly named Nixon an unindicted co-conspirator because Jaworski had recommended that there be no formal indictment of a sitting president. Most of the other charges against Nixon and his administration, except for questionable campaign contributions and antitrust suits, were not pursued by the Watergate Special Prosecution Force. The WSPF concluded that there was "insufficient evidence and/or substantial legal problems mitigating against . . . bringing . . . criminal charges" for the misuse of federal agencies or mistreatment of antiwar protesters. It also found that the Ervin committee had "exaggerated" the use of federal agencies, such as the Internal Revenue Service, for or against the president's friends and enemies. And the Rodino Committee voted against potential impeachment issues such as the secret bombing of Cambodia and the impoundment of funds appropriated by Congress.

Despite the spectacular revelations at nationally televised hearings of the preceding year, the Senate dragged its feet in attempting to resolve the intensely debated question of impeachment into the summer of 1974. Until just before his hand was finally forced, Nixon could still take solace in his popularity ratings. But on 9 August 1974, following the disclosure of the "smoking gun" tape, the president chose to resign rather than face certain impeachment, despite his assertion that he had been acting in the interests of national security. His claim was that he had wanted to avoid exposing various subversive activities sponsored by the United States against Cuba, activities that several Republican and Democratic administrations had promoted. The extraordinary scene of Richard M. Nixon departing one last time with his family from the White House grounds by helicopter was watched by millions on television. The ex-president, the first to resign from office, maintained a determined smile and at the top of the stairway leading into the craft gave a victory salute to those in attendance.

The constitutional crisis brought about by Watergate precipitated demands for accountability on the part of government officials and for greater access to government information. Congress was soon to act on bills designed to open up the executive branch to public scrutiny and to reform elections and the financing of political campaigns. Hastily drafted and passed, much of the supposedly ameliorative legislation either failed or was ignored by Nixon's successors, as in the case of the War Powers Act, or had unintended negative consequences, as happened with the campaign finance reform measures that led to the creation of political action committees (PACs) and unlimited "soft-money" contributions. As time went by, even the special prosecutor system initiated with Watergate was called into question because of what was perceived as the waste of money on dubious investigations into the conduct of subsequent administrations.

In an effort to put the Watergate affair to rest, at least as it was related to the president who had resigned in disgrace, Nixon's successor, Gerald Ford, gave him an unconditional pardon on 8 September 1974. Nixon had appointed Ford in October 1973 to be his vice president as the result of another, unrelated scandal that had forced the resignation of Spiro T. Agnew, Nixon's running mate in both 1968 and 1972. (Agnew was found to have accepted money for political favors when he was governor of Maryland.) Freed from any federal criminal or civil liability connected to Watergate, Nixon did not hide in private life. He wrote several books and traveled extensively. Abroad, he remained widely respected for his foreign-policy views; at home, his rehabilitation proceeded slowly. Pat Nixon, his wife of more than four decades, died in 1993.

The following year, Richard Nixon succumbed to a stroke in New York City, his family having honored his living will that extraordinary measures not be taken if he were to suffer a catastrophic disability. At his funeral, prominent Republicans and Democrats alike eulogized him as an elder statesman respected for his expertise in foreign affairs. In popular opinion, however, his name remained synonymous with the Watergate affair and all of its murky, myriad meanings.

• The Nixon Presidential Materials located in the National Archives facility in College Park, Md., include 40 million pages of documents, 4,000 hours of secretly recorded conversations, 5,312 microforms, 2.2 million feet of film, and 2,000 pages of oral history. With the passage of time, portions of this material have been released; once all are available to scholars, the Nixon presidency will be the best documented in the nation's history. Stanley I. Kutler, *The Abuse of Power: The New Nixon Tapes* (1997), provides transcripts of tapes made from June 1971 to July 1973. Various kinds of nonpresidential papers are housed at the Richard M. Nixon Library in Yorba Linda, Calif.

Following his resignation from office, Nixon published *RN: The Memoirs of Richard Nixon* (1978), *The Real War* (1980), *Real Peace: A Strategy for the West* (1983), *No More Vietnams* (1985), *Defeat and Renewal* (1990), and *Beyond Peace* (1994).

The large number of biographies, memoirs by aides and associates, and published histories related to Nixon's political career vary considerably in quality and objectivity. The most sophisticated psychoanalytical accounts include David Abrahamsen, *Nixon vs. Nixon: An Emotional Tragedy* (1977); Leo Rangell, *The Mind of Watergate: An Exploration of the Compromise of Integrity* (1980); and Fawn Brodie, *Nixon: The Shaping of His Character* (1980). As his papers became available in the 1990s, less psychoanalytical and more balanced biographies began to appear: Stephen E. Ambrose, *Nixon* (3 vols., 1987–1991); Roger Morris, *Richard Milhous Nixon: The Rise of an American Politician* (1990); Herbert Parmet, *Richard Nixon and His America* (1990); Tom Wicker, *One of Us: Richard Nixon and the American Dream* (1991); Jonathan Aitken, *Nixon: A Life* (1993); and Joan Hoff, *Nixon Reconsidered* (1994).

Accounts of the Watergate affair have been colored by journalistic accounts, such as the two bestsellers by Bob

Woodward and Carl Bernstein, *All the President's Men* (1974) and *The Final Days* (1976). The best early study of the affair in terms of documentation is J. Anthony Lukas, *Nightmare: The Underside of the Nixon Years* (1976). Concerning the various congressional investigations of Watergate-related events, see Stanley I. Kutler, *The Wars of Watergate: The Last Crisis of Richard Nixon* (1990); Fred Emery, *Watergate: The Corruption of American Politics and the Fall of Richard Nixon* (1994), contains a wealth of details about all aspects of the affair. The most controversial study is Len Colodny and Robert Gettlin, *Silent Coup: The Removal of a President* (1991), which posits that John Dean probably was the mastermind of both the break-ins and the cover-up. All the major figures indicted and convicted of Watergate crimes, except John Mitchell, published personal accounts. A culled version of H. R. Haldeman's dictated and written diaries were published as an edited book, *The Haldeman Diaries: Inside the Nixon White House* (1994); a complete version is on CD-ROM. A good review of the Watergate literature is Ruth P. Morgan, "Nixon, Watergate, and the Study of the Presidency," *Presidential Studies Quarterly* 26, no. 1 (Winter 1996): 217–38.

JOAN HOFF

NIZA, Marcos de (c. 1495–25 Mar. 1558), missionary and explorer, was probably born in Nice, Duchy of Savoy (now in France), of French parentage; little else is known about his parents. Niza arrived in the New World at Santo Domingo in 1531, professing his final vows as a Franciscan friar in the same year. Niza arrived in Peru with Pedro Alvarado in January 1534; although many sources claim he witnessed the execution of the famous Inca leader Atahualpa on 29 August 1533, he probably did not. He arrived at Santiago, Guatemala, on 25 September 1536 and wrote a report of Alvarado's Peruvian expedition. Bishop Fray Juan de Zumárraga, to whom he wrote about experiences in Peru, spoke highly of him, stating that he was "reliable, of approved virtue and fine religious zeal."

By April 1537 Niza arrived in Mexico. He was asked by New Spain's viceroy Antonio de Mendoza to seek out and report the facts about the northern border of New Spain, what is now known as New Mexico. Rumors had circulated about great cities of wealth to the north as early as 1526 from Tejo, a slave of Nuño de Guzmán, the latter a slave trader and first governor of Nueva Galicia. Alvar Núñez Cabeza de Vaca in 1536 and his three companions (Andrés Dorantes, Alonso Castillo Maldonado, and Esteban) arrived in Mexico City after their failed expedition with Pánfilo de Narváez in 1527 to Pascua Florida with their own tempting tales of cities to the north. The wealth harvested from the Peruvian Inca and the Aztecs in Tènochtitlán fueled a flurry of speculation about the north as another plunder-rich Mexico.

In order to organize the expedition, Mendoza sent Esteban and Niza north to explore and report on Cabeza de Vaca's account. On 17 April 1538 Holy Roman Emperor Charles V gave his permission for the expedition. Niza was to watch for signs that the South and North seas (Pacific and Atlantic oceans) were joined, to take formal possession of all that he crossed, and to inform the natives of the one true God. As the expedition drew nearer, Niza assumed a position of promi-nence in New Spain, commanding the respect of those who knew him for his Peruvian travels and narratives. By 1539 Niza became vice commissary of his order, and the following year he was elected provincial. By early March 1539 Fray Marcos left Culiacán with Esteban and a small host of others. By 23 March Esteban had grown impatient and was allowed to hurry on ahead with a small contingent of Indian allies. As Niza plodded along behind, he began to hear stories from informants that indicated that indeed great villages lay ahead, several stories high, "and on the doors of the principal houses there were many decorations composed of turquoise stones, of which there was a great abundance in that land" (Bolton, p. 28). Esteban sent back to Fray Marcos a cross, as required, to indicate a "discovery." The cross was as tall as a man, symbolizing a great find. Before Niza could catch up to Esteban, however, an informant from Esteban's entourage returned and reported that Esteban had been killed by the villagers. Zuni oral tradition states that Esteban came with a gourd that was not "of our people," that Esteban demanded food, riches, and probably women. The Zuni placed him in a secured room, and when Esteban tried to escape, they killed him. Niza, instilled with fear but also a driving curiosity, allegedly forged ahead and looked over a mesa to see the village. As the sun set on the village of stone, mud, and straw, however, it might have appeared to him as a city of gold. He claimed he constructed a stone mound, with a cross at its zenith, and took possession of the city he saw, and all those out of view, and "named them the New Kingdom of San Francisco." He returned to Mexico City and on 2 September 1539 reported to the viceroy what he had seen and heard. Niza reported that this village, Cíbola (Zuni village of Háwikuh), was a walled city guarded by gates, its people were rich, women wore belts of gold, and throughout the country great industry existed. On 2 September 1539 Fray Marcos authenticated his *Relación* in Mexico City.

Viceroy Mendoza knew that Niza had a penchant for dramatization, but he believed Niza had seen something truly great. After all, Friar Antonio de Ciudad Rodrigo, father provincial of the Franciscans in New Spain, stated on 26 August 1539 that Niza was "skilled in cosmography and in the arts of the sea, as well as in theology." Niza had seen the riches of Peru and Mexico; he certainly would not be quickly excited without cause. It was not long before the news of this great "discovery" was the talk of Mexico City and its surrounding communities. Interest in the north increased as people embellished the stories with each retelling. The Spanish Crown's policy of carefully issued contracts for "discovery" meant that Mendoza would carefully choose an individual to lead the Crown-approved expedition. Marcos de Niza agreed to assist the expedition. The king's sanction of Francisco Vásquez de Coronado's expedition arrived on 6 January 1540, and the expedition set out the following month. Niza returned with Coronado to the land of Cíbola, reaching Háwikuh on 7 July 1540. Pedro de Castañeda, a soldier and chronicler of the Coronado expedition, cursed Niza, for in Coronado's own words, "I can assure you he has not told the truth in a single thing he has said." Niza, embarrassed, ill, and embittered, turned south by August 1540 and headed to Mexico City, with soldiers Melchor Gallegos and Juan Díaz. The Coronado expedition would not return until 1542.

Although criticized by Castañeda and by many future historians, Niza nevertheless still commanded some respect in New Spain. He was made father provincial of the Franciscan Order, a position he held until 1542. Although not much is known about his final years, Augustin de Vetancurt (1971) reports that he retired, crippled, to Jalapa in hopes of regaining strength. He resided at a monastery in Xochimilco, a suburb of Mexico City. His fantastic adventures, which led him across the Atlantic to Santo Domingo, Guatemala, Peru, New Spain, and Cíbola, ended with his death in Mexico City.

• Few monographs about Fray Marcos de Niza include his entire life. One monograph that includes much of Niza's life is Fray Angelico Chavez, O.F.M., *Coronado's Friars* (1968). Descriptions of Niza's travels in New Mexico are in Herbert Eugene Bolton, *Coronado, Knight of Pueblos and Plains* (1949; repr. 1992); Augustin de Vetancurt, *Teatro mexicano; descripción breve de los sucesos ejemplares, históricos y religiosos del Nuevo Mundo de las Indias* (1971); John Francis Bannon, *The Spanish Borderlands Frontier, 1513–1821* (1974); and George P. Hammond, *Coronado's Seven Cities* (1940). More specifically illustrating Niza's time in New Mexico are George P. Hammond and Agapito Rey, trans. and eds., *The Gallegos Relation of the Rodríguez Expedition to New Mexico* (1927), and *Narratives of the Coronado Expedition* (1940); Cleve Hallenbeck, *The Journey of Fray Marcos de Niza* (1949); Frederick Webb Hodge, *History of Hawikuh, New Mexico: One of the So-Called Cities of Cíbola* (1937); and George Undreiner, "Fray Marcos de Niza and His Journey to Cíbola," *The Americas* 3 (Apr. 1947): 415–86. More critical of Niza's career is Henry R. Wagner, "Fray Marcos de Niza," *New Mexico Historical Review* 9, no. 2 (Apr. 1934): 184–227. Of some assistance placing Niza within historical context are John Wesley Powell, *Fourteenth Annual Report of the Bureau of Ethnology to the Secretary of the Smithsonian Institution, 1892–1893* (1896); and Stewart Udall, *To the Inland Empire: Coronado and Our Spanish Legacy* (1987). And finally, an overview of Niza's career in Peru is Fr. Antonine Tibesar, *Franciscan Beginnings in Colonial Peru* (1953).

SANDRA K. MATHEWS-LAMB

NOAH, Mordecai Manuel (19? July 1785–22 Mar. 1851), politician, playwright, and Jewish communal leader, was born in Philadelphia, Pennsylvania, the son of Manuel Mordecai Noah, a failed businessman, and Zipporah Phillips. He was orphaned at the age of seven and was raised by his grandparents Jonas and Rebecca (Machado) Phillips. In his youth, first in Philadelphia and later in Charleston, South Carolina, he published journalistic pieces, a political pamphlet, a critique of Shakespeare (*Shakspeare* [sic] *Illustrated* [1809]), and two plays (*The Fortress of Sorrento* [1809], never produced, and *Paul and Alexis, or the Orphans of the Rhine* [1812], later produced as *The Wandering Boys*).

Thanks in part to recommendations from influential American Jews, he won appointment in 1811 as America's first consul to Riga. War intervened, and he never assumed this post; instead, in 1813 he became U.S. consul to Tunis. The government hoped that he would be able to forge special ties with influential Jews in North Africa and entrusted him with an additional secret mission: to devise a "means for the liberation" of eleven captive American seamen in Algiers.

Noah's efforts to free American captives were mostly unsuccessful. Only two seamen were released, the ransom paid was excessive, and the secret agent Noah appointed, Richard R. Keene, turned out to have an unsavory past. Although Noah carried out his other consular duties successfully and also established ties with local Tunis Jews, Secretary of State James Monroe recalled him in 1815, ostensibly on religious grounds. In fact, the failed secret mission really precipitated the recall.

In the wake of the recall, Noah published *Correspondence and Documents* (1816) in his own defense, followed by *Travels in England, France, Spain and the Barbary States in the Years 1813–14 and 15* (1819), his most important book. It describes his experiences abroad and contains valuable information on early nineteenth-century Tunisian Jewry.

Back in New York City, Noah resumed his career in political journalism. He edited the *National Advocate* and, later, important New York newspapers such as the *New York Enquirer*, the *Evening Star*, and the *Sunday Times and Noah's Weekly Messenger*. In return for his editorial support, he also held a variety of appointive political posts, serving as sheriff of New York (1821–1822), grand sachem of the Tammany Society (1824), surveyor and inspector of the New York port (1829–1832), and judge in the New York Court of Sessions (1841–1842). In his spare time he returned to the theater, earning a reputation through his reviews as "the finest theatrical critic of the day in America" (Henry D. Stone, *Personal Recollections* [1873], p. 81). He also wrote several plays, notably *She Would Be a Soldier* (1819).

Noah's prominence propelled him to leadership within the Jewish community. As early as 1818 he delivered the main address at the consecration of the Second Mill Street Synagogue of New York's Congregation Shearith Israel. He used the occasion to instruct Jews concerning their own history and condition, traced Jewish rights in every country, and then concluded, patriotically, that "OUR COUNTRY [is] the bright example of universal tolerance, of liberality, true religion, and good faith." To his mind, America was the Jewish people's "chosen country"—at least until Jews could "recover their ancient rights and dominions, and take their rank among the governments of the earth."

Two years later, on 16 January 1820, Noah laid before the New York legislature a petition requesting that it survey, value, and sell him Grand Island in the Niagara River to serve as a colony for the Jews of the world. The petition was tabled. Five years later, however, an investor acting on Noah's behalf purchased 2,555 choice acres on the eastern shore of the island, and on 15 September 1825 Noah staged an elaborate dedication ceremony for a colony to be called Ararat, a refuge for persecuted Jews around the world.

Titling himself Judge of Israel and dressed in a regal costume, Noah issued a proclamation complete with a series of decrees. Among other things, he called on Jews to remain loyal to governments that protected them, to undertake a worldwide census, to abolish polygamy (practiced by Jews in Muslim lands), and to learn how to read and write. He also levied a three-shekel head tax "upon each Jew throughout the world." In a lengthy address, he then explained the details of his colonization plan, including its implications for America and for ultimate Jewish restoration to Palestine. Here, as in so many of his other pronouncements on Jewish affairs, he sought to prove that he could be a good citizen as well as a good Jew, helping his people and his country at the same time.

Although Ararat attracted attention throughout much of the Jewish world, it proved a complete failure: it never progressed beyond the original cornerstone. Still, Noah remained active in Jewish affairs, playing a particularly effective role vis-à-vis the non-Jewish community, where he was greatly respected. He explained Jewish practices in his newspapers, defended Jews whenever he saw them attacked, and promoted Jewish charities. He also delivered celebrated addresses on Jewish themes, including one, in 1837, arguing that the Indians were descendants of the lost ten tribes of Israel and another, in 1845, seeking Christian help in promoting restoration of the Jews to Palestine.

Noah died in New York from the effects of a paralyzing stroke. His funeral, attended by Jews and non-Jews alike, was probably the largest funeral of any Jew in America to that time.

• Papers of Mordecai Noah are scattered. The best collection, including photocopies of letters found elsewhere, is in the American Jewish Archives, Cincinnati, Ohio. Other letters, including valuable family letters, are found at the American Jewish Historical Society on the campus of Brandeis University, Waltham, Mass. Jacob Blanck, *Bibliography of American Literature*, vol. 6 (1973), offers the most complete bibliography of Noah's writings. For corrections and additions, as well as a complete list of secondary sources, see the bibliographical essay found in the biography by Jonathan D. Sarna, *Jacksonian Jew: The Two Worlds of Mordecai Noah* (1981). An earlier biographical study is Isaac Goldberg, *Major Noah: American Jewish Pioneer* (1938).

JONATHAN D. SARNA

NOAILLES, Louis Marie (17 Apr. 1756–7 Jan. 1804), soldier, known by his title, the vicomte de Noailles, was born in Paris, France, the son of Philippe, a marshal and duc de Mouchy, and Anne d'Arpajon. At age twelve he was inducted into the king's personal guard. At fifteen he was breveted sous-aide major of the Noailles regiment and two years later assumed the rank of captain. In 1773 he married his cousin Louise de No-ailles, sister of the future wife of the marquis de Lafayette; the couple had three children who survived infancy. Noailles carried the title chevalier d'Arpajon until 1775. At nineteen he became a serious student of military science and academics.

Noailles desired to go to America with Lafayette and wrote to Jean-Frédéric Phelypeaux, the comte de Maurepas and Louis XVI's chief minister, to that effect, but his family discouraged him from pursuing the idea. He served in the French army as aide to the quartermaster and supernumerary in Brittany and Normandy in June 1778. He was promoted to the rank of mêtre de camp en second in the regiment of the colonel general of Hussards in 1779. He served in the West Indies campaign, distinguishing himself at the siege of Grenada on 4 July 1779. D'Estaing wrote to his father, "The vicomte has acted like a lieutenant general. . . . I cherish him and esteem him." At the siege of Savannah with d'Estaing, Noailles covered the French rear guard in its withdrawal in October. D'Estaing this time predicted, "He will do the greatest things." On 20 January 1780 he was awarded the chevalier de Saint-Louis and on 8 March 1780 was named mêtre de camp en second of the Soissonnais regiment.

Noailles returned to America with Rochambeau's army in July 1780. With the French army inactive at Newport, Rhode Island, Noailles offered his services to the Americans but withdrew the request when Lafayette predicted that Rochambeau would not assent. After distinguishing himself notably at the siege of Yorktown in October 1781, he was the French army representative at the surrender of Charles, Lord Cornwallis. He returned to France with Lafayette and was promoted to mêtre de camp and commandant of the regiment of the King's Dragoons on 27 January 1782, then he transferred to the regiment of Chasseurs of Alsace in March 1788.

Noailles returned to France from the American Revolution filled with its liberal ideas. He served in the Assembly of Notables in 1787, and on 16 March 1789 he became a deputy to the Estates General for the nobility of the bailliage of Nemours. On 13 June he proposed to the majority of his order that they join the commoners of the Third Estate, and along with Lafayette, he went on 25 June to join others in forming the National Assembly. On the night of 4 August Noailles proposed the abolition of the privileges of nobility before the National Assembly, and on 19 June 1790 he proposed the abolition of noble titles. On 26 February 1791 he was elected president of the Constituent Assembly. He became maréchal de camp in the Army of the North on 28 November 1791 but resigned his commission in May 1792 to protest the lack of military discipline. Though he was obliged to flee from France to England in the summer of 1792 as the revolution radicalized, his wife remained in France and was guillotined on 22 July 1794.

Noailles sailed to the United States in April 1793. Settling in Philadelphia, he prospered in business ventures with William Bingham, Robert Morris (1734–1806), and John Nicholson. Among their projects was the establishment of a French émigré community known as Asylum, near Pittsburgh. Although the French National Convention had declared the death penalty for all émigrés in 1792, Napoleon began removing the restrictions in 1800. His French legal status was restored to him on 1 March 1800, and Noailles went to Saint Domingue in November 1802, initially as a business venture to supply foodstuffs to the French military expedition there under the command of Napoleon Bonaparte's brother-in-law Charles-Victor-Emmanuel Leclerc. Once there he accepted the rank of provisional général de brigade under Leclerc's successor Rochambeau, the son of Noailles's commander in the American Revolution. In August 1803 Noailles took command of the French forces at Môle Saint Nicholas against a large outfit of freed slaves and a British blockade. Escaping with a few men to Baracoa, Cuba, in early December, Noailles there chartered three vessels with the escort schooner *Courrier*. On 31 December 1803 he encountered the English corvette *Hazard* and did battle with it, taking it as a prize. Unfortunately he received a grave chest wound in the encounter and died in Havana. His body was buried in nearby Nuebitas, but his heart was returned to France, buried in the church of Poix at Somme, and later removed to the family plot at Corrèze. His name is inscribed on the Arc de Triomphe in Paris.

Noailles reflected those qualities of charm and valor that were characteristic of many of his colleagues in the French army in the American Revolution. Along with a few, such as Lafayette, he also displayed a genuine interest in some of the principles of the American Revolution and supported the movement for liberal change in France that eventually led to the French Revolution.

• Noailles's correspondence is widely scattered. His military file is at the Service Historique de l'Armée de Terre, 1st ser., dossier 3822, at Vincennes. Useful portions of his correspondence are in the P. S. du Pont de Nemours Papers at the Hagley Museum and Library, Wilmington, Del., and in the Newport (R.I.) Historical Society. His papers confiscated during the French Revolution are in the Archives Nationales, Paris, T 11083. The best brief study of his importance is Maurice Gaignaire, "Le glorieux destin d'un gentilhomme contestaire: Le vicomte de Noailles 1756–1803," *Revue historique des Armées*, no. 149 (1982): 52–67. On his popularity with the Newport community during the American Revolution, see Anna Wharton Wood, ed., "The Robinson Family and Their Correspondence with the Vicomte and Vicomtesse de Noailles," *Bulletin of the Newport Historical Society*, no. 42 (1922): 1–35. Noailles is also treated in the Marquis de Castellane, *Gentilhommes démocrates: Le vicomte de Noailles, les deux La Rochefoucauld, Clermont-Tonnerre, le comte de Castellane, le comte de Virieux* (1891). His career in the American Revolution is covered unevenly in Thomas Balch, *The French in America during the War of Independence of the United States, 1777–1783* (2 vols., 1891–1895). See also Amblard Marie Raymond Amédée, vicomte de Noailles, *Marins et soldats français en Amérique pendant la guerre de l'indépendance des Etats-Unis 1778–1783* (1903).

ROBERT RHODES CROUT

NOBLE, James (16 Dec. 1783–26 Feb. 1831), U.S. senator from Indiana, was born near Berryville, Clarke County, Virginia, the son of Thomas Noble, a physician, and Elizabeth Claire Sedgwick. During the 1790s the Noble family settled in Campbell County, Kentucky, where Noble was educated in the pioneer schools of the day. On 7 April 1803 he married Mary Lindsay of Newport, Kentucky; they had six children. Shortly after his marriage Noble began the study of law under the tutelage of Richard Southgate, a lawyer in Newport.

After completing his legal studies and being admitted to the bar, Noble moved to Brookville in the Indiana Territory. Like his contemporaries David Wallace and James Brown Ray, both future governors of Indiana, Noble was known throughout the territory for his eloquent public speaking, a skill he used to sway juries to his way of thinking in many trials. Jacob B. Julian of Indianapolis remembered that, as a youth, he was taken by his older brother to hear Noble address a jury in a murder case held in Centerville, Indiana. Noble's arguments on behalf of the accused, Hampshire Pitt, were so loud, and his denunciations of the prosecution so intense, that the young Julian became alarmed and demanded to be taken home. Noble used his legal talents for the prosecution in the trial of four white men accused of murdering nine Miami and Seneca trappers, including three women and four children, near Markelville, Indiana, in the spring of 1824. The team of Noble, Harvey Gregg, and Phillips Sweetzer, Noble's son-in-law, won guilty verdicts, and three of the men were executed—reputedly the first time in the United States that whites had been punished in such a way for killing Native Americans. The incident would be the basis for Jessamyn West's bestselling historical novel *The Massacre at Fall Creek* (1975).

Noble's younger brothers, Noah (Indiana's governor from 1831 to 1837) and Lazarus (adjutant general of Indiana during the Civil War), followed him to Indiana, and the family became heavily involved in Hoosier politics. Noble served as prosecuting attorney for Wayne, Franklin, and Switzerland counties. Clerk of the territory's house of representatives in 1810 and 1813, he served as a representative in 1813 and 1814. On 25 May 1815, following the death of Elijah Sparks, Noble was appointed by Indiana territorial governor Thomas Posey to serve as judge for the Third Judicial Circuit.

Along with his legal and political duties, Noble operated a ferry on the Ohio River near his home in Switzerland County. He also was commissioned a lieutenant colonel in the Seventh Regiment of the Indiana militia on 22 April 1811 and was promoted to colonel the following year. In 1820 Noble joined the Vincennes Bank as director of its office in Brookville.

Described by contemporaries as a large man with black hair and dark eyes, Noble played an important part in the development of Indiana's constitution as one of five men—the others being James Brownlee, William H. Eads, Robert Hanna, and Enoch McCarty—to serve as Franklin County's representatives to the state constitutional convention. In this capacity Noble headed the committee responsible for drafting the legislative branch portion of the constitution, served on the committee that wrote the provisions for the judicial branch of government, chaired the panel on banks and banking companies, and served as a member of the committees on the militia and school lands. Upon the constitution's completion, Noble was elected to serve as a member of the house of representatives at the first Indiana General Assembly. In the early years of Indiana, Noble was one of three men, the others being Jonathan Jennings and William Hendricks, who dominated the state's politics. This "Hoosier Triumvirate" had no regular party apparatus but depended on their personal popularity to gain victories at the ballot box.

Indiana's first state government met on 4 November 1816 at Corydon. Four days later the general assembly selected Noble to be one of Indiana's first two U.S. senators, along with Waller Taylor. He was reelected to the post in 1821 and again in 1827. During his years in the Senate, Noble, a Democratic Republican, served as chairman of the Committee on Pensions and the Committee on the Militia. A tireless advocate on behalf of internal improvements, Noble also was the driving force behind legislation in Congress to allow the sale of public lands in quarter sections and to extend the Cumberland road from Wheeling, West Virginia, to the Mississippi River. Noble died at his Washington, D.C., boardinghouse.

• Noble's life and career are highlighted in Nina K. Reid, "James Noble," *Indiana Magazine of History*, Mar. 1913, and W. W. Woollen, *Biographical and Historical Sketches of Early Indiana* (1883). Indiana's early politics and Noble's role in it are highlighted in Logan Esarey, "Pioneer Politics in Indiana," *Indiana Magazine of History*, June 1917. Noble's role in the formation of Indiana's early government is explored in John D. Barnhart and Dorothy L. Riker, *Indiana to 1816: The Colonial Period* (1971), and Gayle Thornbrough and Dorothy L. Riker, eds., *Journals of the General Assembly of Indiana Territory, 1805–1815* (1950). Brief biographical information on Noble can also be found in *A Biographical Directory of the Indiana General Assembly*, vol. 1: *1816–1899* (1980), and *Biographical Directory of the United States Congress, 1774–1989* (1989).

RAY E. BOOMHOWER

NOBLE, John Willock (26 Oct. 1831–22 Mar. 1912), secretary of the interior, was born in Lancaster, Ohio, the son of John Noble and Catherine McDill. Noble spent three years at Miami College before transferring in 1851 to Yale College, where he graduated with honors the same year. He graduated from Cincinnati Law School a year later and studied in the law offices of Henry Stanbery and his brother, Henry C. Noble, before his admission to the Ohio bar in 1853. Deciding his fortunes lay in the West, he moved to St. Louis in 1855. Unsuccessful, and possibly finding the proslavery atmosphere distasteful to his Republican and Free Soiler beliefs, he moved the following year to Keokuk, Iowa. There he quickly rose to prominence. He built a successful practice and shared leadership of the state bar with Samuel Freeman Miller, a future U.S. Supreme Court justice. Noble served as city attorney from 1859 to 1861.

At the outbreak of the Civil War, Noble fought in the battle of Athens, Missouri, before he enlisted in the Union army in August 1861. He joined the Third Iowa Cavalry as a lieutenant and rose through the ranks while seeing action in several western campaigns and in southern cavalry raids. He served with distinction in every grade from lieutenant to colonel and was brevetted brigadier general for service in the field on 13 March 1865. During the war he also served as judge advocate general of the Army of the Southwest and the Department of Missouri. In February 1864 he had married Lisabeth Halsted. They had no children.

After the war, Noble returned to St. Louis to establish a law practice. In 1867, at the recommendation of Stanbery, now President Andrew Johnson's attorney general, he was appointed U.S. district attorney for eastern Missouri. After three years of remarkable success enforcing internal revenue laws against the corrupt whiskey and tobacco interests, he returned to his lucrative practice as a railroad lawyer. His success as district attorney brought him to the attention of President Ulysses S. Grant, who offered him the position of solicitor general in 1872. Noble declined, even though he knew it might lead to becoming attorney general. While in private practice, he argued successfully numerous times in front of both the state courts and the U.S. Supreme Court. His reputation as an outstanding lawyer and an incorruptible man as well as his active support of the 1888 Republican presidential candidate led to his appointment as secretary of the interior by his college friend, President-elect Benjamin Harrison, in 1889.

Noble was uniquely qualified to handle the department's two most sensitive issues, the public domain and Civil War pensions. In the 1880s and 1890s pensions were an important political issue, because Union veterans were a sizable voting block in several key states. Corporal James Tanner, a popular war veteran, ardent Harrison supporter in 1888, and leading advocate of pensions for all who served, was appointed commissioner of pensions. Relations between the commissioner and secretary, a respected veteran in his own right, rapidly deteriorated because of Tanner's controversial position on pensions and his poor administrative skills. When highly irregular and illegal administrative activities by Tanner's staff came to light, including re-rating some pensioners who were employees of the bureau and upgrading others, Noble ordered Tanner to follow proper procedures. Tanner pointedly refused, claiming the secretary had only limited power over him. With President Harrison's support, Noble forced Tanner's resignation six months after Tanner was appointed.

The public domain was the Interior Department's largest area of responsibility in the late nineteenth century. The department oversaw the dispersal of land grants and the settlement of land claims, a job for which this railroad lawyer was well suited. Noble's most notable achievement as secretary came from his involvement in the creation and passage of Section 24 of the Land Revision Act of 1891, now known as the Forest Reserve Act. In the spring of 1890, after separate meetings with the Law Committee of the American Forestry Congress, both Harrison and Noble were convinced of the need for setting aside western forests for watershed protection. Nearly a year later, during the final days of the Fifty-first Congress, a bill aimed at repealing timber-culture laws was under consideration by a joint conference committee. One of the members added a new clause, Section 24, before submitting it for a vote. The amendment called for granting the president power to set apart and reserve public land as public reservations, but it failed to spell out why the land should be set aside or how the land should be managed. Nevertheless, with little debate, both houses quickly approved the bill. When informed of the law's existence, Noble recognized its importance and potential. The Forest Reserve Act, as it became known, was the genesis of the national forest system. By bringing the law to the president's attention, Noble helped initiate the federal government's involvement in resource management. Gifford Pinchot later praised the law as "the most important legislation in the history of Forestry in America . . . [and] the beginning and basis of our whole National Forest system."

At the end of the Harrison administration, Noble retired from political life and returned to his practice in St. Louis. He initially found it difficult to regain his practice, and his time in Washington had left him financially strapped. He soon developed lucrative mining interests that made up for the losses while he was in Washington. He died in St. Louis.

Noble was a talented lawyer whose political connections led to his appointment to public office and to his most notable achievement. The legislation Noble helped draft started the federal government's involvement in natural resource conservation while permanently altering the federal government's handling of public lands.

• Noble's papers have not been located. The Department of the Interior Papers are in the National Archives, and Noble appears in the Benjamin Harrison Papers in the Library of Congress. The one surviving document from Noble discussing his own participation in the creation of the forest bill is his 1908 speech in the Harrison papers. Printed documents are limited to the *Annual Report of the Secretary of the Interior* (1889–1893); *Letter from the Commissioner of Pensions to the Secretary of the Interior Showing the Total Number of Cases Allowed by the Bureau of Pensions, and the Total Value of the First Payments in Said Cases, from March 1, 1889, to December 31, 1892, Inclusive, as Well as the Condition of the Pending and Completed Files of the Bureau and the State of the Pension Roll, December 31, 1892* (1893); and *Reports of the Secretary of the Interior Relative to Yosemite Park, 1892* (1893). Secondary sources deal with the issues Noble faced as secretary as well as Harrison's presidency. Harry J. Sievers offers a brief comparison of Harrison's and Noble's early years, in *Benjamin Harrison, Hoosier Statesman: From the Civil War to the White House, 1865–1888* (1959) and *Benjamin Harrison,*

Hoosier President: The White House and After (1968). More recent scholarship on his presidency is Homer E. Socolofsky and Allan B. Spetter, *The Presidency of Benjamin Harrison* (1987), which is the best source on the domestic issues Noble faced as secretary. Donald L. McMurry examines the pension issue in "The Political Significance of the Pension Question, 1885–1897," *Mississippi Valley Historical Review* 9 (June 1922): 19–36, and "The Bureau of Pensions during the Administration of President Harrison," *Mississippi Valley Historical Review* 13 (Dec. 1926): 343–64. See also Mary R. Dearing, *Veterans in Politics: The Story of the G.A.R.* (1952); and William H. Glasson, *Federal Military Pensions in the United States* (1918).

The history of public land management and legislation has been thoroughly covered in several general histories of the topic. Ron Arnold, "Congressman William Holman of Indiana: Unknown Founder of the National Forests," in *The Origins of the National Forests*, ed. Harold K. Steen (1991), pp. 301–13, examines the literature on who originated the Forest Reserve Act and offers a concise history of the bill. Steen's book is the best place to start for this topic. An obituary is in the *New York Times*, 23 Mar. 1912.

JAMES G. LEWIS

NOCK, Albert Jay (13 Oct. 1870–19 Aug. 1945), critic and writer, was born in Scranton, Pennsylvania, the son of the Reverend Joseph Albert Nock, an Episcopal minister, and Emma Sheldon Jay. When Nock was ten, he moved with his family to Alpena, a lumbering town in Michigan, where his parents provided books and respect for learning. The family then moved to Brooklyn, New York, and Nock was educated at home until age fourteen, then attended a boarding school in Illinois before entering St. Stephen's College (later Bard College) in 1887. Nock received his B.A. in 1892, then spent several years studying in graduate school, including Berkeley Divinity School, then located in Middletown, Connecticut. He may have played semiprofessional baseball during these years as well. He did not earn a graduate degree but entered the Episcopal ministry in 1897, a profession he pursued until 1909, working in several parishes in Pennsylvania, Virginia, and Michigan. In 1900 Nock married Agnes Grumbine, a native of Titusville, Pennsylvania. They had two children.

This early, quiet career as a minister ended abruptly in 1909, when Nock left the ministry, his wife, and his children to take up journalism. From 1910 to 1914 he wrote for the muckraker journal *American Magazine*, where he worked with Lincoln Steffens and John Reed, among others. Nock was also associated with progressive politician Brand Whitlock, mayor of Toledo, whom he persuaded to write an autobiography. During this period Nock, a pacifist, supported Woodrow Wilson's campaign for president. He may have worked in the State Department of this Democratic administration for a time, but when Wilson took the United States into World War I, Nock became disillusioned with politics. This disillusionment was an important milestone in his philosophical development, for never again did he trust politics and politicians. Indeed, Nock became a philosophical anarchist, and his criticism of the politics of his day paved the way for future critiques of collectivism and the state. In 1919 he wrote for a short time for Oswald Garrison Villard's magazine, the *Nation*. He then entered a publishing venture with British single-taxer Francis Neilson, whose wife's inherited fortune paid for the launching of the *Freeman* in 1920.

Nock's lofty, formal writing style, acerbic wit, and cosmopolitan interests soon won him a name as a social critic. The critic's function was to do "Isaiah's Job," preaching publicly, assessing culture with "no account of optimism or pessimism." Those who cared to would stop and listen, while the rest of society would pass the critic by. Nock's views combined libertarian notions of politics and social relations with elitist longings for "civilization" and ranged from commentary on elections to literary criticism to attacks on the materialistic bent of American economics. He agreed with Matthew Arnold, from whom he adopted his ideas about a "remnant" of "civilized" individuals who would somehow keep culture and excellence alive. The remnant would consist of people who were able to transcend the materialism and politics of modern society.

Nock was also an admirer of Thomas Jefferson, whose agrarianism and political philosophy were important parts of his own thought. He was also influenced by Herbert Spencer, and for a time he was a supporter of Henry George's single-tax reforms. His attack on the state was further bolstered by the work of anthropologist Franz Oppenheimer, from which he drew his notions of government as the organized plunder and exploitation of society by the ruling class. Nock's critique of the state was derived, then, from nineteenth-century liberalism, and his individualist-anarchism bridged the years when the philosophy of freedom was at its lowest ebb, making him the link between liberalism and the libertarian/conservative movement of the post–World War II era. He was a noninterventionist in foreign policy, but his cosmopolitanism separated him from the popular image of isolationists as provincial populists. He supported women's rights, wrote reports on the education system, and attacked the idea of progress as an impossible myth. Nock's wide-ranging interests included biography, and he wrote biographies of Jefferson and of François Rabelais, as well as numerous biographical essays. This inclination also led to his own autobiography, *Memoirs of a Superfluous Man*, which was published in 1943 and remains his most influential work.

Throughout his later years Nock became increasingly disillusioned with the world around him but refused to give up his hope that the remnant would find him and heed his jeremiads in time to save civilization from decadence and destruction. Nock died in the home of a friend in Wakefield, Rhode Island. His influence has been recognized by the postwar conservative movement, but his contributions to literary criticism, education, and the genre of the essay have been largely ignored. His broad interests and often quirky intellectual musings make Nock an elusive figure whose true place is among the iconoclasts of American literature, a man with whom it is difficult to agree all of the time but impossible to read without being stimulated to thought.

• The Albert Jay Nock Papers are in the Library of Congress, and Yale University possesses an Albert Jay Nock Collection. Nock's writings, sources for understanding his life, include *A Journal of These Days: June 1932–December 1933* (1934); *Journal of Forgotten Days: May 1934–October 1935* (1948); *Letters from Albert Jay Nock, 1924–1945, to Edmund C. Evans, Mrs. Edmund C. Evans, and Ellen Winsor*, ed. Frank W. Garrison (1949); and *Selected Letters of Albert Jay Nock*, ed. Francis Jay Nock (1962). For collections of Nock's important works, see *The State of the Union: Essays in Social Criticism* (1991) and *Our Enemy the State* (1935; repr. 1994). Other editions of his essays include *The Freeman* (1920), *The Myth of a Guilty Nation* (1922), *On Doing the Right Thing and Other Essays* (1928), *The Book of Journeyman: Essays from the New Freeman* (1930), *Free Speech and Plain Language* (1937), *Snoring as a Fine Art and Twelve Other Essays* (1958), and *Cogitations from Albert Jay Nock* (1970). For Nock's work as a biographer and historian, see *Jefferson* (1926), *Francis Rabelais: The Man and His Work* (with Catherine R. Wilson, 1929), *A Journey into Rabelais's France* (1934), and *Henry George: An Essay* (1939). Other works edited or coedited by Nock include *Selected Works of Artemus Ward* (1924) and *The Urquhart–Le Motteux Translation of the Works of Francis Rabelais* (1931). The best source on Nock himself remains his autobiography. Other important biographical accounts include Van Wyck Brooks, *Days of the Phoenix* (1957); Frank Chodorov, *Out of Step* (1962); Robert M. Crunden, *The Mind and Art of Albert Jay Nock* (1964); J. Sandor Cziraky, "The Evolution of the Social Philosophy of Albert Jay Nock" (Ph.D. diss., Univ. of Pennsylvania, 1959); and Michael Wreszin, *The Superfluous Anarchist: Albert Jay Nock* (1971).

A. JAMES FULLER

NOCK, Arthur Darby (21 Feb. 1902–11 Jan. 1963), historian of religion and classical scholar, was born at Portsmouth, England, the son of Cornelius Nock and Alice Mary Ann Page. He attended Trinity College, Cambridge, the college of William Robertson Smith and James G. Frazer, from which he received his B.A. in 1922 and his M.A. in 1926. He was Fellow of Clare College, Cambridge, 1923–1930, University Lecturer in Classics at Cambridge, 1926–1930, and visiting lecturer in the history of religions at Harvard, 1929–1930, having probably obtained the latter position on the recommendation of Gilbert Murray to A. L. Lowell. In 1930 he decided to leave England permanently and became Frothingham Professor of the History of Religions at Harvard, a post he held until his death. This allowed him to teach the subjects of his research rather than undergraduate composition. He took American citizenship in 1936. He was editor of the *Harvard Theological Review* from 1930 to 1963 and editor for Greek and Roman religion of the widely used *Oxford Classical Dictionary* (1949). He held the prestigious Gifford Lectureship at Aberdeen, Scotland, in 1939–1940 and 1946–1947 but published the resulting lectures on Hellenistic religion only in part.

By his own admission, his reading of Gilbert Murray's *Four Stages of Greek Religion* (1912) as a schoolboy left on him "a permanent impress and impulse."

He never fully abandoned the Anglo-Catholicism that allowed him to see the importance of religion and ritual in a way that many could not. Although he later called himself a historian, he began his scholarly career as a philologist, editing, after a suggestion of Murray, Sallustius's *Concerning the Gods and the Universe* (1926). The subject matter confirmed his subsequent inclinations. His editing (1945 ff.) with A. J. Festugière of the *Corpus Hermeticum* further demonstrated the philological expertise that was already evident in the remarkable familiarity with Greek, Latin, and German that he displayed as a precocious undergraduate. He knew Hebrew and Oriental sources only in translation, however. The historian Edwyn Bevan recommended him at age twenty-two to A. E. J. Rawlinson, later bishop of Derby, who invited Nock to contribute his great essay, "Early Gentile Christianity and Its Hellenistic Background," to Rawlinson's *Essays on the Trinity and the Incarnation* (1928). This paper first won him international acclaim.

He published his Donnellan Lectures, originally given in 1931 at Trinity College, Dublin, and later delivered as the Lowell Lectures in King's Chapel, Boston, as *Conversion: The Old and the New in Religion from Alexander the Great to Augustine of Hippo* (1933). In this widely admired book he sought the pagan origin of conversion and repentance in the Greek philosophical tradition rather than in cult. His short *St. Paul* (1939) was sound rather than innovative. His most enduring contributions were made in erudite articles and influential reviews, which have been collected as *Essays on Religion and the Ancient World*, edited by Zeph Stewart (2 vols., 1972). Here one finds oft-cited papers on central subjects, including eunuchs in ancient religion, the Augustan Restoration, astrology, Orphism, Christianity and classical culture, Zoroaster, Poseidonius, Gnosticism, and—the topic of one of Nock's most famous essays—the "Religious Attitudes of the Ancient Greeks." All are written by a historian in full command of the primary sources and secondary literature and no friend of theory or indeed philosophy.

Nock's middle-class origin, his Germanic professionalism, and his passion to understand antiquity as a whole (which separated him from the dilettantism of Sir John Sheppard or the dry textual criticism of A. E. Housman at Cambridge) did not hinder an American career. He worked closely with scholars of a sort not found at Cambridge, such as Campbell Bonner in Michigan, William S. Ferguson at Harvard, and Michael I. Rostovtzeff at Yale. A confirmed bachelor, he remained the eccentric English don living amid Harvard undergraduates at Eliot House. His college lectures on the history of religion and his graduate seminars on Greek and Roman religion and on *Acts* taught three generations of Harvard men the centrality of religion in the ancient world. His great student, the Columbia historian of religion Morton Smith called him "a great classical scholar with a mind enormously learned, outstandingly accurate, cautious, balanced, conservative." The conviction of this "lonely and vulnerable man" that scholarship mattered above all else permanently altered the careers of students willing to understand him. He died in Boston.

• Published sources for Nock's life are Crane Brinton et al., *Harvard Studies in Classical Philology* 68 (1964): ix–xii; William M. Calder III, *The Classical Outlook* 70 (Fall 1992): 8–9; E. R. Dodds and Henry Chadwick, *Journal of Roman Studies* 53 (1963): 168–69; Martin P. Nilsson, *Gnomon* 35 (1963): 318–19; and Morton Smith, *The Secret Gospel* (1973), pp. 24–25. There is a full bibliography of his writings (over 400 items) in Stewart, ed., *Essays on Religion and the Ancient World*, vol. 2, pp. 966–86. His principal publications have all been mentioned above.

WILLIAM M. CALDER III

NODA, Alice Sae Teshima (28 July 1894–25 July 1964), businesswoman, was the daughter of Yasuke Teshima and Eki Kurauchi, plantation immigrant laborers to Hawaii from Fukuoka, Japan. The Teshimas arrived in 1899, labored on a plantation near Wahiawa, and by 1904 had saved enough to become independent pineapple growers. Alice Sae Teshima graduated from McKinley High School. In December 1912 she married Steere Gikaku Noda, whose parents also had immigrated as plantation laborers to Hawaii, in 1891. She had met her future husband while they both were attending the Hawaii Japanese Language School. He took a post as deputy-collector for the federal Internal Revenue Service in Honolulu and, later, as an interpreter-clerk for the District Court of Honolulu until, after studying law, he served as court practitioner after 1930. The Nodas had four children. After the birth of their last child, she returned to school, attending the Honolulu Dental Infirmary, and upon graduation in 1922 she worked as a dental hygienist for the Department of Public Instruction, teaching children dental care. By 1924, through her effort, competence, skills, and leadership, she became the head of the Honolulu Dental Hygiene School. By 1925 she was a recognized community leader, serving as president of the Dental Hygienists' Association.

From her early concerns with health and hygiene, Alice Noda became interested in developing a second career in "beauty culture," or cosmetics and hair care, which she pursued part-time while still a hygienist. She attended the McDonald Beauty Specialist's School of Los Angeles and upon certification opened the Cherry Beauty Salon in Honolulu on Fort Street in 1923, the first of four salons she would develop into a chain. Noda became known as a beauty specialist and enjoyed an ever-widening circle of patrons. In March 1925 when Princess Asaka of Japan toured Hawaii, Noda acted as her official guide and interpreter. When Noda was asked by the princess to make up her face, Noda complied and was presented with silver candlesticks in appreciation of her assistance and advice during the state visit.

Noda entered the cosmetology business at a time when beauty "secrets" were becoming democratized and shared with the masses and were no longer the secreted monopoly of the wealthy. Cosmetics and hair care came to be seen as necessities rather than luxuries through the efforts of individuals like Noda. To keep up with her new profession's advances, Noda studied in New York in 1927 under Charles Nestle, inventor of the permanent wave, at the Nestle Institute of Hair Dyeing and under Emile Shoree at his School of Facial Beauty Culture. Upon returning to Honolulu, Noda introduced the mainland's beauty secrets of the 1920s flapper age into the islands, and women flocked to her salons. Reaching again the highest positions in her profession, she became the first examiner of the Territorial Board of Beauty Culture, which licensed other practitioners, and president of the Honolulu Hairdressers and Cosmetologists Association in 1930. Professional success and financial security had been attained, and with fame came responsibilities. In 1931 she served as vice chairman of the League of Women Voters in Honolulu and was also active in the administration of the Girl Scouts of Honolulu. The effects of the depression did not diminish her business fortunes, and in 1933 Noda assisted, through her development of codes of fair practice for the cosmetology industry, in putting the National Recovery Act into effect in Hawaii.

In 1936 she expanded to Tokyo, Japan, and upon the opening of her beauty salon in the Ginza, a Japanese newspaper wrote that Alice Sae Teshima Noda "has been making a place for herself in this city of keen competition in every line of business activity." Her salon on the sixth floor of the Kyobunkwan Building gained a wide following. A reporter on Tokyo wrote that "so far as the strong trend toward permanent waves and other styles of foreign-style hair dressing in Japan is concerned, one has only to take a stroll on the Ginza and see the large number of women converts to the feminine art that had been unknown in this country a few years back." In Japan she also introduced the art of skin peeling, which she had studied in Los Angeles under Madame Nell Anderson. Japanese actresses and foreign embassy women of all nationalities frequented Noda's Ginza salon. She gained further recognition through a beauty column she wrote for syndicated Japanese newspapers. After a year, appointing capable administrators for her Ginza salon, she returned to Honolulu to speak on her beauty secrets before numerous women's groups, lecture at the University of Hawaii, and write articles for distribution to shipboard passengers on the luxury liners coming through Honolulu. As a beauty expert Noda enjoyed considerable prestige and renown, as the heroines of the 1920s and 1930s were movie stars who made a fetish of beauty. There was also the desire among her Oriental female clients in Hawaii to become Americanized and viewed as modern, to ensure upward social mobility, and to leave the plantation laborers' image behind. Noda sold the Tokyo salon in 1941 because of the growing problems between the United States and Japan, which culminated in U.S. involvement in the Second World War.

In 1954 Noda was elected the first president of the newly reconstituted Japanese Women's Society (JWS) in Honolulu. Before 1941 the organization had always been headed by the Japanese consul general's wife. During the war, it had been disbanded, its assets frozen. The JWS was reorganized with Noda at its head; its funds were restored, and, after expenses were paid, the funds were donated to the Oriental library at the University of Hawaii. During Noda's presidency, the JWS began plans to build a care-home facility, Hale Pulama Mau (House of Cherishing Care), for elderly Japanese; it was completed in 1980. Noda died in Honolulu, a respected leader of the community because of her business knowledge, administrative talents, managerial style, international contacts, poise as a speaker, considerable charm, and radiant beauty. She was a successful role model for young women moving off Hawaii's plantations in search of urban careers, and she exemplified business acumen on an international scale.

• Alice Noda's papers and documents are in the possession of her daughter, Lillian Yajima, in Honolulu, Hawaii. Various Honolulu newspapers carried articles on Noda's salons and beauty practices in both Japanese and English: *Nippu Jiji*, 25 Sept. 1933; *Japan Times*, 8 Mar. 1936; *Chugai Shogyo Sinpo*, 30 July 1936; *Honolulu Star-Bulletin*, 19 Sept. 1921, 21 Mar. 1931, 16 Jan. 1932, 20 July 1954, 26 Feb. 1961; *Honolulu Advertiser*, 28 May 1922, 14 Feb. 1932, 17 Jan. 1933, and 27 Jan. 1937.

BARBARA BENNETT PETERSON

NOGUCHI, Hideyo (24 Nov. 1876–21 May 1928), bacteriologist, was born Seisaku Noguchi in Inawashiro, Japan, the son of Sayosuke Kobiyama, a gambler, woodcarver, and odd job man, and Shika Noguchi, a farmer. Shika was the last of the Noguchi family and adopted her husband, according to Japanese custom, to preserve the name. When Seisaku was only two, he fell into a fire and badly burned and crippled his left hand. The family was desperately poor, but a teacher and school examiner, Sakae Kobayashi, sponsored young Seisaku's education and found a surgeon who operated on the injured hand. The boy became the surgeon's assistant and, with the aid of his patrons, passed the national medical examinations in 1897. Although he still had little use of his left hand, his ability, industry, and eagerness to learn impressed others, and he continued to find sponsors throughout his career. Humble in manner, he harbored great ambitions, expressed in his choice of an adult name, Hideyo, "great man of the world."

Young Noguchi was briefly employed as medical librarian at Juntendo Hospital before obtaining a similar position with the prominent bacteriologist, Shibasaburu Kitasato, at the Government Institute of Infectious Diseases, in September 1898. In early 1899 a medical commission from Johns Hopkins Medical School, which included Simon Flexner, visited the institute on its way to study dysentery in the Philippine Islands. Noguchi met Flexner and expressed his wish to come to the United States. Flexner responded with friendly courtesy and did not take the young man's inquiry, nor two letters he later received from Noguchi, seriously. Noguchi, however, solicited friends to pay his passage and to look after his mother and, within a few months, startled Flexner by appearing in his office at the University of Pennsylvania, announcing that he had come to work with "the Professor."

The nonplussed Flexner nevertheless helped Noguchi to find an American sponsor, the distinguished physician Silas Weir Mitchell, who secured funding for Noguchi to study the action of snake venoms and the development of antitoxins under Flexner's direction. Although his English was very limited and his knowledge of immunology and snake venom even more so, Noguchi applied himself to research with fierce energy and determination and, over the next several years, became a competent bacteriologist. In 1903–1904 he studied in Copenhagen and then returned to the United States to join Flexner, who had become the first director of the newly founded Rockefeller Institute of Medical Research.

As an associate at the Rockefeller, Noguchi dedicated himself to his work, his approach to which colleague Paul Franklin Clark described as "multiple experiments now and always." Noguchi continued his research on snake venoms, publishing in 1909 *The Action of Snake Venoms upon Cold-Blooded Animals*. He also researched and published from 1911 to 1928 on many other problems, including complement fixation, spirochetes, syphilis and its diagnosis, trachoma, poliomyelitis, Oroya fever, yellow fever, rabies, and tuberculosis.

Noguchi's most noted achievement was his culturing in 1911 of the spirochete *Treponema pallidum*, which had been identified as the etiologic agent of syphilis in 1905. He developed a method of passing through rabbit testicles and growing in pure culture spirochetes that produced lesion in monkeys, although others were unable to duplicate his results. He also improved on August von Wassermann's diagnostic test for antibody formation in blood or spinal fluid and developed a luetin skin test, neither of which were widely used. In 1913, working with J. W. Moore, he demonstrated the presence of *T. pallidum* in the cerebral cortex of paresis and tabes dorsalis patients, proving that these neurological diseases were the deadly final stages of syphilis infection. In another project in the same period, he and Flexner isolated "small globoid bodies" from the nervous systems of monkeys suffering from paralytic poliomyelitis; these were cultured and used to infect other animals. Noguchi and Flexner announced these globoid bodies to be the causative agent of polio in 1913.

These findings brought Noguchi fame. He was invited to speak in Vienna, visited Paul Ehrlich, the Nobel-winning bacteriologist and immunologist at the Royal Prussian Institute for Experimental Therapy in Frankfurt, and was summoned home to receive the Imperial Prize of the Japanese Academy in 1915; earlier he had been made a full member of the Rockefeller Institute. But other scientists had already questioned his polio research. Over the next few years, Noguchi applied his "special methods" of intensive culturing using hundreds of tubes to several diseases, including trachoma and Rocky Mountain spotted fever, in several cases proclaiming that he had found the causative agent. Many of his reported discoveries, including the "globoid bodies" implicated in polio, have since been refuted.

In spite of the fact that he lived in the United States for thirty years, Noguchi was never close to his American colleagues; although many of them were fond of him, others patronized or belittled him. Those who knew him best appreciated his glints of humor and generosity. He married an American, Mary Dardis, in 1911; they had no children. He remained most comfortable with, and often hosted in his home, other immigrant Japanese, with whom he relaxed by playing chess, writing haiku, and painting.

In June 1918 Noguchi went to Ecuador to investigate an outbreak of yellow fever. Working with specimens from victims there, from Peru and Mexico, and later from Brazil (1924), he isolated a spirochete, *Leptospira icteroides*, which he identified as the infective agent. Others thought this identical to the spirochete often found in infected guinea pigs, suggesting that it was an experimental artifact. In 1925 a yellow fever commission in Africa, led by Henry Beeuwkes, found no *Leptospira* and suggested a viral agent. Noguchi himself traveled to Accra (now in Ghana), where he confirmed these findings. He contracted the disease himself, as did several members of the expedition, and died in Accra in great distress over his failure.

• There is archival material on Noguchi at the Rockefeller Archive Center in Pocantico Hills, N.Y., in the Rockefeller University Archives in New York City, and in the Simon Flexner Papers at the American Philosophical Society Library in Philadelphia. Noguchi's death was commemorated in a series of obituary tributes, but as his scientific reputation declined in later years, more critical accounts appeared. A biography by Gustav Eckstein appearing soon after Noguchi's death, *Noguchi* (1931), includes translations of many of his letters to friends and relatives. A more recent work, Isabel R. Plesset's *Noguchi and His Patrons* (1980), is probably now the best source. There are also at least two biographies in Japanese and one in Spanish. Personal memoirs include Paul Franklin Clark, "Hideyo Noguchi, 1876–1928," *Bulletin of the History of Medicine* 33 (1959): 1–20, and the comments of Thomas M. Rivers in Saul Benison's oral history, *Tom Rivers: A Life in Medicine and Science* (1967), the latter unfortunately colored by racial bias. Later articles on Noguchi's work are S. S. Kantha, "Hideyo Noguchi's Research on Yellow Fever (1918–1928) in the Pre-Electron Microscope Era," *Kitasato Archives of Experimental Medicine* 62 (Apr. 1989): 1–9, and Susan E. Lederer, "Hideyo Noguchi's Luetin Experiment and the Antivivisectionists," *Isis* 76 (Mar. 1985): 31–48. An obituary by Simon Flexner is in *Science* 69 (1929): 653–60.

DANIEL M. FOX
MARCIA L. MELDRUM

NOGUCHI, Isamu (17 Nov. 1904–30 Dec. 1988), sculptor, was born out of wedlock in Los Angeles, California, the son of Yonejirō "Yone" Noguchi, a Japanese poet, and the American writer Leonie Gilmour. In

1904 Yone, who was well known for interpreting the East to the West through his poetry, returned to Japan to teach. Leonie and Isamu joined Yone in Tokyo in 1906. Isamu, who lived with his mother in Chigasaki from 1912 to 1916, attended Japanese and Jesuit schools and in July 1918 arrived at the Interlaken School in Rolling Prairie, Indiana. The school was converted to a military training camp shortly thereafter, so the school's founder, Edward Rumely, placed him in a public high school in Indiana (La Porte), where he graduated in 1922 as Isamu Gilmour. Rumely then arranged for him to work in Connecticut as the apprentice to Gutzon Borglum, the sculptor of Mount Rushmore. Borglum told Isamu that he would never be a sculptor, and that fall, funded by Rumely, Isamu enrolled as a premed student at Columbia University in New York.

In 1924, at his mother's urging, he began a sculpture class at the Leonardo da Vinci Art School. With the encouragement of the school's director, Onorio Ruotolo, he left Columbia and became a sculptor. He took the name Noguchi and with Rumely's help set up his first studio in New York and began to exhibit academic figurative sculpture. In 1926 Noguchi saw a Constantin Brancusi exhibition at the Brummer Gallery in New York and was impressed.

Awarded a John Simon Guggenheim Fellowship to travel to Paris and the Far East for 1927 to 1928, he only went to Paris, where he worked for several months as Brancusi's assistant, polishing his bronzes. Brancusi's influence lasted throughout Noguchi's career, particularly the emphasis on pure and simple shapes, the skill of carving stone and wood, and as Noguchi later said, a "respect for tools and materials." In the afternoons he drew at the Académie de la Grand Chaumière and the Académie Colarossi. After Noguchi left the older artist's studio, he began to create his first abstract stone, wood, and brass sheet metal sculpture and abstract gouache drawings. These were exhibited on his return to New York in 1929 in his first one-man show at the Eugene Schoen Gallery. He sold nothing.

Noguchi supported himself by making representational portrait sculpture, his subjects including the inventor R. Buckminster Fuller and the choreographer Martha Graham, both of whom were his friends. First exhibiting these works in 1930 at the Marie Sterner Gallery in New York, he continued to make portraits until the early 1940s.

Economic success enabled Noguchi to return to Paris for two months in 1930, followed by a trip via Moscow to Beijing, where he remained for seven months, studying ink-brush technique with Ch'i Pai-shih and creating a series of large figurative brush paintings. In 1931 he had a painful reunion with his father and was befriended by his uncle Totaro Takagi. He traveled from Tokyo to Kyoto, where he was impressed with the Zen gardens and ancient *haniwa*, pre-Buddhist mortuary figures. He worked in Jinmatsu Unō's pottery and exhibited his ceramic sculpture in Tokyo before returning to New York in October. In 1932 he exhibited his Beijing brush drawings and ceramic sculpture in New York. The aluminum *Miss Expanding Universe* (1932), the first sculpture that Noguchi made after his return to New York, is a futuristic interpretation of a *haniwa*.

A member of a circle of socially conscious artists, in 1933 Noguchi began designing his first large-scale public projects (all unrealized). "Play Mountain," his first playground design, was rejected in 1934 by Robert Moses, New York City parks commissioner, and Noguchi was excluded from the government Public Works of Art Project due to the nontraditional sculpture he presented for review. Noguchi later called "Play Mountain" "the kernel out of which have grown all my ideas relating sculpture to the earth" (*A Sculptor's World*, p. 22).

His 1935 design for *Frontier*, the first stage set used by Martha Graham, initiated an involvement with the theater that would last until 1966 and manifested Noguchi's interest in the relationship of objects to their environment. After leaving New York for California in 1935, he sculpted portrait heads in Hollywood in order to finance a trip that year to Mexico City, where he made a bas-relief mural called *History Mexico* for the Abelardo Rodriguez Market.

Noguchi returned to New York in 1937, the year he designed his first mass-produced product, the bakelite *Radio Nurse*, an intercom for Zenith Radio Corporation. In 1940 he installed a relief over the Associated Press Building entrance at Rockefeller Center—the largest stainless steel casting to that time. He designed his first fountain, constructed of magnesite, in 1938 for the Ford Motor Company Building at the New York World's Fair of 1939–1940 and his first playground equipment in 1939 (unrealized) for Ala Moana Park in Honolulu, at the invitation of Dole Pineapple. He also received his first commission to design a table, for A. Conger Goodyear, president of the Museum of Modern Art in New York; a modified version of this table would be put into production by the Herman Miller Furniture Company in 1947.

In 1941, after the New York City Parks Department rejected his "Contoured Playground" (1940) design for Central Park, Noguchi decided to begin a new life out west, and he drove to California with some friends, including the painter Arshile Gorky. Considered to be the last surrealist and the first abstract expressionist, Gorky provided Noguchi with an important link to both groups between 1942 and 1948.

In the wake of the Japanese attack on Pearl Harbor, the half-Japanese Noguchi suddenly was viewed as an alien threat. In January 1942 he organized the Nisei Writers and Artists Mobilization for Democracy, a group that hoped to stop the anti-Japanese hysteria by showing the patriotism of Japanese Americans. In March, believing he could help, Noguchi voluntarily submitted himself to a six-month internship in a Japanese-American relocation camp in Poston, Arizona. While there, he organized woodworking and ceramic projects and formulated a plan for a park and recreation areas and a cemetery—projects never realized.

Ironically, during his internment, Noguchi had his first one-man exhibition at the San Francisco Museum of Art.

Disillusioned with public projects, the artist returned to New York. After setting up a studio on Mac-Dougal Alley in Greenwich Village, he focused on studio sculpture and produced such works as *This Tortured Earth* (1943), *Monument to Heroes* (1943), and *Sculpture to Be Seen from Mars* (1947)—models for visionary environmental sculptures that directly respond to the detrimental effects of war. Also in this period he made a series of *Lunar* sculptures (1943–1948) that were lit internally by electricity. This series coincided with the development of his designs for freeform furniture and lamps.

In 1946 Noguchi was represented in the exhibition "Fourteen Americans" at the Museum of Modern Art in New York, where he showed his marble and slate interlocking-slab sculptures. These fragile, totemic, and biomorphic figures—for example, *Kouros* (1944–1945), now at the Metropolitan Museum of Art—exemplified the chaos following World War II. In the exhibition catalog, Noguchi asserted his belief that "it is the sculptor who orders and animates space, gives it meaning" and that "growth is the constant transfusion of human meaning into the encroaching void." In the 1940s Noguchi applied his view of the "sculpture of spaces" to the stage, collaborating intensively with choreographers Graham, Erick Hawkins, Merce Cunningham, and George Balanchine and with composer John Cage. In 1949 Noguchi had his first one-person show in New York since 1935 at the Charles Egan Gallery.

Awarded a Bollingen Foundation Fellowship to write a book on the "environments of leisure" (not completed), he traveled to see the important monuments and public sites in England, France, Spain, Egypt, Greece, Italy, India, Cambodia, and Indonesia and afterward arrived in Japan in May 1950. After 1952 he divided his time between Japan and New York. Major projects in Japan included his first monumental project, the design for the railings of two bridges into Peace Park at Hiroshima (1951–1952), his design of the garden for the new *Reader's Digest* Building in Tokyo (1951); his design for a memorial room and garden for his father, who died in 1947, at Keiō University (1951–1952), and his design for a large memorial to the Dead (1952) at Hiroshima (unrealized).

In 1951 Noguchi began collaborating with Japanese lantern makers in Gifu, Japan, manufacturing his Akari light sculptures ("light as illumination") using traditional paper and bamboo construction. Over three decades Noguchi would develop new designs, which initially were shown and sold in Japan but by 1954 were being exported and exhibited internationally and that continue to be produced by the original firm.

In 1952 Noguchi married actress Yoshiko "Shirley" Yamaguchi. The couple moved into a 200-year-old farmhouse owned by the potter Kitaoji Rosanjin in a rice valley in Kita Kamakura. Noguchi built a studio at the farmhouse and fired his pottery in Rosanjin's kiln. He sold some ceramics in Japan and sent the rest to the Stable Gallery in New York, where they were shown in 1954. He designed a United Nations playground in 1951 and his first plaza in 1951–1953, for the Lever House in New York (both unrealized). Subsequently separated by immigration difficulties, Noguchi and Yamaguchi divorced in 1957. The plaza project initiated his work with the architect Gordon Bunshaft of Skidmore, Owings & Merill.

Between 1956 and 1958 Noguchi designed his first major landscape project, the "Jardin Japonais" for the UNESCO headquarters in Paris, built by Marcel Breuer. For this project Noguchi brought gardeners, plantings, and eighty-eight tons of stone from Japan. In homage to Brancusi, who died in 1957, he made a series of Greek marble sculptures, including birds. In the late 1950s Noguchi worked with cast-iron (1956) and sheet aluminum (1958–1959) and created a series of balsawood pieces that were later cast in bronze (1959–1962).

In the 1960s Noguchi continued to create public environments and public sculpture, with his first plaza realized in 1961 at the First National City Bank Building in Fort Worth, Texas. Through his garden commission in 1956–1957 for the General Life Insurance Company in Bloomfield Hills, Connecticut, and his white marble sunken garden for the Beinecke Rare Book and Manuscript Library at Yale University in New Haven, Connecticut (1960–1964), he continued a relationship with his most important patron, Bunshaft. Other projects included the sunken garden for Chase Manhattan Bank Plaza in New York (1961–1964), where the placement of stones recalls Ryōanji, a Zen garden Noguchi had visited in Kyoto, Japan; and the Billy Rose sculpture garden at the Israel Museum in Jerusalem (1960–1965). In 1961 he moved to Long Island City. In 1974 he bought an old factory building across the street from his home and studio for display and storage of his sculpture; it opened as the Isamu Noguchi Garden Museum in 1985. Also in 1961, he began a five-year collaboration with the architect Louis Kahn on a series of models for "Riverside Drive Playground" in New York (not realized). His first realized playground was in Japan at Kodomo No Kuni (Children's Land) in Yokohama (1965–1966).

Beginning with his role as an artist-in-residence at the American Academy in Rome in 1962, Noguchi traveled back and forth to Italy for more than a decade, working from the stone quarries at Querceta and making banded marble sculptures (1968–1973). In the late 1960s he began working in basalt and granite. On the island of Shikoku, Japan, in 1966 he initiated a collaboration with the stone carver Matsatoshi Izumi that would last the rest of his career. He later established a studio in the village of Mure on the island. In 1968 his first retrospective was held in the United States at the Whitney Museum of American Art. The artist designed fountains, including those for Expo 70 in Osaka, Japan. His first playground realized in the United States was *Playscapes* (1975–1976), built in Piedmont

Park in Atlanta, Georgia. Other important commissions were his *Red Cube*, which was placed in front of a bank on Broadway in New York (1968), and his stainless steel *Monument to Ben Franklin*, erected in Philadelphia in 1984 from an original design of 1933.

In 1986 Noguchi represented the United States at the Venice Biennale, and in 1987 he received the National Medal of Arts from President Ronald Reagan. In 1988 he was awarded the Third Order of Sacred Treasure by the Japanese government and the Award for Distinction in Sculpture by the Sculpture Center in New York. Two of his public projects have yet to be completed: Bayfront Park in Miami (begun 1979) and a 400-acre park for Sapporo, Japan (begun 1988). Noguchi died at a New York hospital.

Noguchi achieved international fame for his work in many areas, including sculpture, public projects, dance sets, and design. He fused the aesthetics of two very different cultures—those of the United States and Japan—with the legacy of Brancusi and the surrealists. His apprenticeship with Brancusi, whose sculptures and pedestals blurred the boundary between art and furniture, helped Noguchi translate traditional Japanese aesthetics into a modern idiom and provided him with a precedent for the role of the sculptor as designer. The utopian philosophy of Fuller inspired Noguchi to move beyond sculpture, not only in his experimentation with new techniques and materials but particularly in his visionary environmental projects, which are the most inclusive of all of his works in their combination of sculptural form, design, and public space. Not restricting himself to working alone in his studio, Noguchi made collaboration an important part of his career. With his last works in basalt and granite, Noguchi continued to express a sensitivity to materials and nature.

• The papers of Isamu Noguchi, including photographs, early catalogs, newspaper clippings, and articles, are housed at the Isamu Noguchi Foundation, Long Island City, N.Y. His autobiography is *Isamu Noguchi: A Sculptor's World* (1968). Many of the artist's important writings are compiled in *Isamu Noguchi: Essays and Conversations*, ed. Diane Apostolos-Cappadona and Bruce Altshuler. The most up-to-date biography is Altshuler's *Isamu Noguchi* (1994). See Nancy Grove and Diane Botnick's catalogue raisonné *The Sculpture of Isamu Noguchi, 1924–1979* (1980) for the current locations of works mentioned in the text. See also Bert Winther, *Isamu Noguchi: Conflicts of Japanese Culture in the Early Postwar Years* (1993); Dore Ashton, *Noguchi: East and West* (1992); Grove's exhibition catalog *Isamu Noguchi: Portrait Sculpture* (1989); Grove, *Isamu Noguchi: A Study of the Sculpture* (1985); Martin Friedman's exhibition catalog *Noguchi's Imaginary Landscapes* (1978); and Sam Hunter, *Isamu Noguchi* (1978). Michael Brenson published a substantial, page one obituary in the *New York Times*, 31 Dec. 1988.

DEBORAH A. GOLDBERG

NOGUCHI, Yone (8 Dec. 1875–13 July 1947), poet and critic, was born in Tsushima, Aichi, Japan, the son of Dempei Noguchi, a landowner, and Kuki Ukai. Withdrawing from a middle school in Nagoya, Noguchi went to Tokyo, where at fifteen he began to read Vic-

torian writers such as Thomas Macauley, the kind of reading many literary hopefuls were doing in the United States. In 1891 he entered Keio, one of the oldest colleges in Japan, and studied Herbert Spencer and Thomas Carlyle. He also read works such as *Sketch Book* by Washington Irving and poetry by Oliver Goldsmith and Thomas Gray. He even tried translating these poems into Japanese. At the same time he was taken up with Japanese culture and tradition as well. He became interested in haiku and Zen at this time and began visiting Zen temples, a practice he later continued whenever he returned to Japan.

To realize his ambition of living and writing in an English-speaking country, he left college after two years and arrived almost penniless in San Francisco in 1893. He lived among Japanese immigrants in the city for two years and worked for nearly a year for a Japanese newspaper, translating news of the Sino-Japanese War. In late 1894 he was motivated by curiosity and interest to walk from San Francisco to Palo Alto, where he stayed at a prep school near Stanford University and read the poems of Edgar Allan Poe.

In 1896 Noguchi, aspiring to become an English-language poet, paid tribute to Western poet Joaquin Miller, who enjoyed Noguchi's youthful spirit. For the next three years Noguchi lived in Miller's isolated mountain hut in Oakland, leaving only to perform necessary errands in Los Angeles or to walk to San Francisco to see his publishers. Miller introduced him to poet Edwin Markham, British author Charles Warren Stoddard, and publishers Gelett Burgess and Porter Garnett.

During the first year of his association with Miller, Noguchi published some poems in *The Lark*, the *Chap Book*, and *The Philistine*. In 1897 he produced two collections of poetry, *Seen and Unseen; or, Monologues of a Homeless Snail* and *The Voice of the Valley*. All of these writings won critical praise. Willa Cather, for instance, wrote, "While Noguchi is by no means a great poet in the large, complicated modern sense of the word, he has more true inspiration, more melody from within than many a greater man" (Cather, p. 579). Like the wandering poet in his homeland, Noguchi spent much time roaming and reading in the countryside.

Noguchi visited Chicago, Boston, and New York. In New York he brought out *The American Diary of a Japanese Girl* (1901). Published under the pseudonym Miss Morning Glory, the novella recounts the life of a Japanese maid. Noguchi then traveled to England, where in 1903 he produced *From the Eastern Sea*, his third collection of poetry. Thomas Hardy and George Meredith were especially impressed with his work. "Your poems," Meredith wrote to Noguchi, "are another instance of the energy, mysteriousness, and poetical feeling of the Japanese, from whom we are receiving much instruction" (*Japan and America*, p. 111).

In 1904 Noguchi returned to Japan. That same year his son Isamu Noguchi was born in Los Angeles but remained with his mother, Leonie Gilmour, an American literary enthusiast. In 1906 Noguchi married Mat-suko Takeda, a Japanese woman with whom he had seven children. Also in 1906 he accepted a position as a professor of English at Keio University, the school he had left in 1893. In 1913 he returned to England to deliver a series of lectures at Oxford and in London. Back in Japan he influenced poets such as Tōson Shi-mazaki, Sakutarō Hagiwara, and Kotaro Takamura.

By 1915 Noguchi, a well-known bilingual poet, had published not only books of literary criticism widely read in England and America, such as *The Spirit of Japanese Poetry* (1914) and *Through the Torii* (1914), but several collections of his own English poems. Among his Western contemporaries, Noguchi's writings had a strong influence on Ezra Pound and other imagists. Much of Pound's early poetry and Noguchi's poetics thus reflect the imagist principles. Pound's fas-cination with haiku was matched by his interest in vor-ticism as it was manifested in the visual arts. Pound realized, for example, that great sculptors were able to intensify their art, not by polishing brass or stone sur-faces, but by relating form to the infinite. More direct-ly, however, Noguchi showed Pound that Japanese poets had used the same technique. Noguchi ex-plained how a great haiku poet such as Bashō was able to awaken to a vision of the infinite. The attempts of Pound and his contemporaries at haiku were uneven, with the most remarkable effort seen in Pound's hai-ku-like poems, such as "In a Station of the Metro" and "Alba."

In 1915 Noguchi published *The Spirit of Japanese Art*, the first of a lavishly illustrated, ten-volume series on traditional Japanese painters. The series included artists such as Hiroshige, Kōrin, Utamaro, Hokusai, and Harunobu and established Noguchi as the fore-most authority on Japanese visual art in the West in the 1920s and 1930s. William Butler Yeats, who be-came acquainted with the Nō play, the classic Japa-nese drama form, through Noguchi and others, was also fascinated by Noguchi's books on Japanese pain-ters. Yeats wrote to Noguchi in 1921, "Your 'Hiroshi-ge' has given me the greatest pleasure. I take more and more pleasure from oriental art; find more and more that it accords with what I aim at in my own work. The European painter of the last two or three hundred years grows strange to me as I grow older, begins to speak as if in a foreign tongue" (*English Letters*, p. 220).

Noguchi's growing renown as a poet and a critic was cut short by World War II. His connections to the West were severed, and after the war he wrote to his estranged son, sculptor Isamu Noguchi, of his sadness at the horrors the war had brought to Japan. He died in Tokyo. In half a century he published almost 100 books, about one-quarter of which were written in English and published in America, England, and Ja-pan. No other Japanese writer has written so much and so well in English as Yone Noguchi. His role as poet and interpreter of the cultures of East and West is unique in literary history. Noguchi's work brings to light not only Yone Noguchi the cross-cultural writer,

but the relationship between America and Japan in particular.

• Many of Noguchi's papers and manuscripts are in the Keio University Library, Tokyo. His poetry collections also in-clude *The Pilgrimage* (2 vols., 1908), *Japanese Hokkus* (1920), *The Ganges Calls Me: Book of Poems* (1938), and *Selected Eng-lish Writings of Yone Noguchi: An East-West Literary Assimila-tion*, vol. 1 (poetry), ed. Yoshinobu Hakutani (1990). No-guchi's autobiographical writings include *The Story of Yone Noguchi Told by Himself* (1914) and *Yone Noguchi: Collected English Letters*, ed. Ikuko Atsumi (1975). Noguchi's literary, cultural, and art criticisms are also in *Lafcadio Hearn in Ja-pan* (1918), *Hiroshige* (1921), *Japan and America* (1921), *Kō-rin* (1922), *Utamaro* (1923), *Hokusai* (1924), *Harunobu* (1927), *Emperor Shomu and the Shosoin* (1941), and *Selected English Writings of Yone Noguchi: An East-West Literary As-similation*, vol. 2 (prose), ed. Hakutani (1992).

For the earliest assessment, see Willa Cather, "Two Poets: Yone Noguchi and Bliss Carman," in *The World and the Par-ish: Willa Cather's Articles and Reviews, 1893–1902*, vol. 2 (1970). The earliest modern assessment is Kamei Shunsuke, *Yone Noguchi, an English Poet of Japan: An Essay* (1965). See also Isamu Noguchi, *A Sculptor's World* (1968). The recent assessment is in Hakutani, "Yone Noguchi's Poetry: From Whitman to Zen," *Comparative Literature Studies* 22 (1985): 67–79; " Father and Son: A Conversation with Isamu Nogu-chi," *Journal of Modern Literature* 17 (1990): 13–33; and "Ezra Pound, Yone Noguchi, and Imagism," *Modern Philolo-gy* 90 (1992): 46–69. For Noguchi's relationship with Yeats, see *Selected English Writings of Yone Noguchi*, ed. Hakutani, vol. 2.

YOSHINOBU HAKUTANI

NOLAN, Lloyd Benedict (11 Aug. 1902–27 Sept. 1985), film, stage, and television actor, was born in San Fran-cisco, California, the son of James Charles Nolan, a shoe manufacturer, and Elizabeth Shea, whose first name is given in some sources as Margaret. Nolan's mother at one time had herself hoped for an acting ca-reer, and her feelings for the theater may have influ-enced Nolan to join the drama group at Santa Clara Preparatory School, from which he graduated. His in-terest in the stage continued at Stanford University, where he majored in prelaw until he left school after his junior year to devote himself full time to acting.

At the Pasadena Playhouse in 1927, Nolan began his professional career, studying with drama coach Gil-more Brown and appearing in productions of Shake-speare and Ibsen. Within a year he traveled to Chicago in a road company of *The Front Page* (1928), remain-ing there for a seven-month engagement.

In those years every aspiring professional actor un-derstood that the next career step was to reach New York's Broadway. Nolan shared that dream, but ap-parently his acting résumé was still too skimpy for no-tice. Instead, he went to Dennis, Massachusetts, on Cape Cod, and found work with the backstage crew at the Dennis Theatre. He eventually reached New York as a chorus member in *The Cape Cod Follies* (1929), which played for eighty shows at Broadway's Bijou Theater. When the show's run ended, he remained in New York, but his only work was in two shows pre-sented outside Manhattan.

In 1931 Nolan finally made his Broadway debut in *Sweet Stranger*. He came close to finding his breakthrough part in a hit, *One Sunday Afternoon* (1933). During the play's 320-performance run he married Mary Mell Elfird, an actress, in May 1933; they had two children. Choice parts eluded him after his initial success, and he signed a contract with Paramount Pictures and set out for Hollywood.

For the next dozen years Nolan was among Hollywood's busiest actors, averaging five to six pictures each year. His first screen credit was for a forgettable and forgotten George Raft vehicle, *Stolen Harmony* (1934). However, better parts followed.

In 1935 Nolan was featured in four pictures, including the box-office hit *G-Men*, which spawned a flock of FBI pictures. He made seven films in 1936, six in 1937 (*Wells Fargo* the most notable), five in 1938, four in 1939, and ten in 1940. Among that avalanche of 1940 productions, at least several were "program pictures" in a Mike Shayne private detective series for 20th Century–Fox; through 1942 Nolan starred in a total of seven Shayne pictures. Nolan was featured in thirteen movies in 1941 and 1942; by 1943 the number fell to two. Both of those films, however, *Bataan* and *Guadalcanal Diary*, were among the most outstanding military action dramas of World War II. Following the war, in 1945, Nolan found two more of his best roles, both of them in commercially successful films. In *A Tree Grows in Brooklyn* he played the kindly neighborhood cop, while in *The House on 92nd Street* he assumed the role of another FBI agent, this time in an innovative semidocumentary shot on actual locations (relatively rare at the time).

During Nolan's first extended decade in films he played a strikingly wide range of parts in more than fifty features. Usually his name was the third, fourth, or fifth in a picture's opening credits. His acting was authoritative but unobtrusive, his characterizations immediately credible. One producer lauded him as "one of the most professional actors who ever worked in Hollywood."

With a decline in studio-produced motion pictures in the later 1940s and early 1950s, the number of Nolan's own screen roles fell off, too. As an alternative he returned part time to the stage and to the fledgling field of televised drama. In 1951 he starred at $250,000 a year in "Martin Kane, Private Eye" for NBC, but the pressures of coast-to-coast commuting and film-production scheduling forced him to temporarily withdraw from TV.

From 1946 through 1951 Nolan appeared in ten Hollywood pictures, including *Lady in the Lake*, *Somewhere in the Night* (both 1946), and *The Street with No Name* (1948). Then, in 1951, Herman Wouk's novel *The Caine Mutiny* was a major bestseller, and the 1954 film (with the same title) starring Humphrey Bogart was a huge success as well. In the brief interval between bestseller and movie hit, the novel's dramatic core was explored in *The Caine Mutiny Court-Martial*, for which Nolan was chosen in July 1953 to depict the paranoid Captain Queeg in the key role. Directed by Charles Laughton, the show toured for almost four months and visited more than sixty American cities.

Opening at New York's Plymouth Theatre in January 1954, *Court-Martial* met with instant success. Critical and audience response to Nolan as Captain Queeg was unanimous. Brooks Atkinson of the *New York Times* wrote, "Nolan's portrait of fear, desperation and panic is a stunning piece of work . . . because he has every detail . . . under control." The respected Walter Kerr of the *New York Herald Tribune* stated, "Nolan holds back nothing. . . . Yet there is no excess. . . . Though the character is wildly out of control, the actor continues to shape—and make meaningful—all his exhausting effects."

For his tour de force artistry Nolan received the Donaldson Award and the New York Drama Critics Award as the season's outstanding actor. The next year he repeated the part on television; for that presentation he won the Emmy Award. He starred in and directed the play in 1956 for a London production at the Hippodrome Theatre.

Returning to the more mundane world of feature film acting after that career-crowning success, Nolan appeared in another thirty theatrical and television movies, the best or best-known of which were *Peyton Place*, *A Hatful of Rain* (both 1957), *Sergeant Ryker* (1959), and *Airport* (1970). He also played the lead in "Special Agent 7" (1958–1959) on network television and costarred (1968–1971) with Diahann Carroll on "Julia," one of his rare stabs at comic acting.

Nolan's wife died in 1981. He remarried the following year (the surname of his second wife, Virginia, could not be ascertained for this entry).

In all, Nolan played important supporting roles in more than 100 motion pictures. He died in Los Angeles before Woody Allen's *Hannah and Her Sisters* (1986), his final film, was released.

• One of the best sources for Nolan's career is the article in *Current Biography 1956*, which, although entirely laudatory, is rich in details not found elsewhere. Around the time of his *Caine Mutiny Court-Martial* success, profiles were published in *Theatre Arts*, Oct. 1954, and the *New Yorker*, 27 Feb. 1954. Most standard film reference works contain useful articles. An obituary is in the *New York Times*, 28 Sept. 1985.

ROBERT MIRANDON

NOLAN, Philip (c. 1771–21 Mar. 1801), contraband trader, was born in Belfast, Ireland, the son of "Pedro" (Peter) Nolan and Ysabela Cassedy. Nothing is known of his early life or when he came to America, but judging from his letters, Nolan received a good education. He became associated with General James Wilkinson in Kentucky and followed him west. By 1788 Nolan served as Wilkinson's bookkeeper, living in his home and working for him until 1791.

During these years Nolan also represented Wilkinson's business interests at New Orleans, proceeding down river with several shipments of tobacco and other goods. It is fairly certain that Nolan was privy to his mentor's clandestine dealings with Spanish officials at

New Orleans. On more than one occasion Nolan received payment of Spanish silver for Wilkinson's efforts toward separating the "Western Country" from the United States, and he wrote bogus financial statements to mask these payments as the proceeds of tobacco sales.

At New Orleans Nolan learned of the opportunities for trade in the adjoining Spanish province of Texas, especially the plentiful herds of wild mustangs virtually free for the taking. In 1791, as Wilkinson's tobacco speculations began to collapse, Nolan used his mentor's influence to secure a passport from Governor Esteban Miró to enter Texas. His first trading venture there was unsuccessful because his goods were confiscated by suspicious officials. After living with the Indians for two years, Nolan reached New Orleans with fifty mustangs. He was greeted by the new governor of Louisiana, Francisco Luis Hector, baron de Carondelet, as a person "risen from the dead."

By June 1794 Nolan had returned to Nacogdoches armed with a passport from Carondelet authorizing him to obtain horses for the Louisiana militia regiment. He visited the provincial capital, San Antonio de Béxar, and met Governor Manuel Muñoz. Through Muñoz he was given permission to export horses to Louisiana, granted by the commandant general of the interior provinces, Pedro de Nava. By the end of 1795 Nolan was back in Natchez with 250 mustangs and eager to expand his operations. With the sanction of Spanish officials in both Louisiana and Texas, his prospects seemed bright.

During these two trips Nolan gained much information about the "unknown land" but not without arousing suspicions among the Spaniards as to his loyalties. These suspicions were intensified when Nolan, returning from a so-called mapping expedition up the Missouri River, arrived at Natchez with the party of Andrew Ellicott, boundary commissioner for the United States. Nolan attempted to mollify Manuel Gayoso de Lemos, governor of Natchez, by proposing a split of profits from a planned trading expedition. Going on to New Orleans he obtained another passport from Carondelet, dated 17 June 1797. Three days later Nolan drew up a will, leaving his worldly possessions to his father and making a businessman of New Orleans his executor. When he left for the third time for Texas in July, Nolan took a considerable load of trade goods, even though trade between Texas and Louisiana was strictly prohibited by the Spanish king because rampant smuggling nullified the benefits of legitimate commerce.

Nolan, however, was adept at bending the rules. He arrived at San Antonio in October 1797, presenting his credentials and claiming to have Carondelet's permission to visit Nuevo Santander (the modern state of Tamaulipas) in search of horses to fulfill his contract. Writing Nava on the subject, Nolan offered to supply his troops with guns of the latest design and to draw for him a map of the territory connecting Louisiana to New Spain. Nava seemed pleased with Nolan's good intentions; he ordered Muñoz to assist his horse-gathering operation and gave approval for Nolan to provide trade goods worth 2,000 pesos to defray his expenses.

Meanwhile, Manuel Gayoso had become disenchanted with Nolan, perhaps because of Wilkinson's duplicity. Gayoso, now captain-general of Louisiana, wrote letters to the viceroy of Mexico and to Commandant General Nava. In them he warned of foreigners (like Nolan) who were stirring up the Indians of Texas against Spanish authority. Nava tried to justify himself in condoning Nolan but nonetheless revoked the permission for him to introduce trade goods. Thinking that Nolan had left Texas in mid-1798, Nava became alarmed when he found him still there almost a year later. Governor Muñoz defended Nolan vigorously, claiming that his delays were unavoidable and that it would be unwise to alienate a man of such talent, whose usefulness to Spain could be great in the years ahead. Muñoz, in bad health, simply looked the other way, allowing Nolan to leave Texas with more than 1,200 mustangs. Toward the end of 1799 Nolan arrived in Natchez and learned of Gayoso's hostility toward him. That December he married Frances Lintot, daughter of a prominent Natchez planter.

Nolan intended to meet with Thomas Jefferson, who had written him concerning Texas and its innumerable wild horses, but apparently the meeting never took place. Instead, Nolan sold his horses and was soon making plans for another trip to Texas. He could not obtain a passport for this venture and knew that it would be a dangerous undertaking. José Vidal (formerly Gayoso's secretary at Natchez) watched Nolan's movements closely and attempted to deny him passage by going before the territorial court of Mississippi. Unable to stop Nolan, Vidal alerted officials in Spanish Texas of his forthcoming "invasion," terming it a military expedition with dire implications.

With twenty-odd well-armed men, Nolan left Natchez in October 1800 and made his way to the Texas plains by going north of Nacogdoches, despite a brush with the Ouachita militia en route. On a tributary of the Brazos River near present-day Waco he erected a small fortification, including some corrals, and began catching mustangs. Although he visited the Comanches and other northern Indians, there is no evidence he was trying to subvert them, as the Spaniards suspected. Five months later Nolan was killed in a battle at sunrise by troops from Nacogdoches sent to intercept him. A rival trader, William Barr, carried Nolan's papers and severed ears to the commandant general as proof that the intruder was dead and his purpose foiled. Nolan's men were captured, tried, and spent years in prison for their part in Nolan's final expedition, the precise nature of which is still something of a mystery.

Philip Nolan was survived only six months by his wife, who gave birth to their son, also named Philip. A daughter, María Josefa, had been born out of wedlock in 1798. According to the census of 1815, she was living with her mother, Gertrudis Quiñones, at Mission San José.

Because of his decade in Texas and his ties with Wilkinson, Nolan has traditionally been viewed as the first of a long line of filibusters who eventually made Texas free of Spanish and Mexican rule. The available evidence suggests, however, that he was motivated by personal profit and not by political considerations. Nonetheless, Philip Nolan opened the way for other Anglo-Americans who would later achieve Jefferson's dream of attaching Texas to the union.

• Documents relating to Philip Nolan are widely scattered across Mexico, Spain, and the United States. The most notable collections are the Archivo General de Indias, Seville; the Archivo General de la Nación, Mexico City; the Béxar Archives (University of Texas, Austin); and the Nacogdoches Archives (Texas State Archives, Austin). Nolan's will is among the Notarial Records of New Orleans, and many Nolan documents are housed at the Beinecke Library, Yale University. General Wilkinson published a few of Nolan's letters in his *Memoirs of My Own Times* (1816). E. E. Hale used Nolan's name for a fictional character in his *The Man without a Country* (1863), thereby creating much confusion about the real Nolan. See the treatments in John Edward Weems, *Men without Countries* (1969) and Noel M. Loomis, "Philip Nolan's Entry into Texas in 1800," in *The Spanish in the Mississippi Valley, 1762–1804* ed. John Francis McDermott (1974). The most complete study is Maurine T. Wilson and Jack Jackson, *Philip Nolan and Texas: Expeditions to the Unknown Land, 1791–1801* (1987), wherein the documentation for this article is fully cited.

JACK JACKSON

NOLDE, Otto Frederick (30 June 1899–17 June 1972), clergyman of the Lutheran Church in America and associate general secretary of the World Council of Churches (WCC), was born in Philadelphia, Pennsylvania. Nothing is known about his parents. After graduating from Muhlenberg College in Allentown, Pennsylvania, in 1920, he studied at the Lutheran Theological Seminary (LTS) in Philadelphia, from which he graduated in 1923. That year he was ordained into the Lutheran ministry by the Pennsylvania Ministerium, a constituent synod of the United Lutheran Church in America (ULCA). Also in 1923 he served as a "fellow" at LTS, and in 1925 he was elevated to faculty status, a position he retained to his retirement in 1968. From 1925 to 1943 he served on the faculty of the University of Pennsylvania. He earned a doctorate from the University of Pennsylvania in 1928, writing "The Department of Christian Education in the Theological Seminary: A Study of the Lutheran Theological Seminary at Philadelphia, Pennsylvania." From 1943 to 1962 he served as dean of the seminary's graduate school. Nolde's first marriage was to Ellen Jarden. They had three children before Ellen died in 1961. He later married Nancy Lawrence; they had no children.

Helping to engage Lutheranism in the broader ecumenical discussions characteristic of early twentieth-century American Christianity, Nolde's sphere of influence extended far beyond the bounds of the ULCA and its seminary in Philadelphia. He served as an associate consultant to the U.S. delegation to the meeting in San Francisco that led to the founding of the United Nations. Nolde's task was to address the religious freedom clause in the Declaration of Human Rights, and he provided the language that states: "All human beings are born free and equal in dignity and rights. They are endowed with reason and conscience and should act toward one another in a spirit of brotherhood" (*Free and Equal*, p. 3). The field of human rights was one Nolde adopted as his own. He is best known for his work with the WCC's Commission of the Churches on International Affairs (CCIA), serving as director from 1946 until 1969.

It was Nolde's task to act as a spokesperson for the WCC on matters of world affairs. While serving in this capacity he had the opportunity to redefine Lutheran doctrine and practice for the present. Significant in this regard was his application of the principles of biblical interpretation outlined by the German scholar Rudolf Bultmann to the realm of theological and academic affairs. In 1964 he outlined a series of six theses that applied Bultmann's principle of demythologizing to the ecumenical realm, arguing particularly that China should be brought out of isolation and into the world family; that disarmament should be a priority for the church and the world; that the United States and the Soviet Union should cooperate in space exploration generally and in moon exploration particularly; and especially that basic human rights, or equitable race relations and religious liberty, were matters of international rather than merely national concern.

Nolde was not content simply to formulate policy. He was always concerned that the policies and work of the CCIA impact human life in a very concrete way. Breaking significantly from traditional Lutheran theology, which held that the "Two Kingdoms" were separate in their spheres of influence, Nolde argued that it was precisely the task of the churches and not governments to assure that human rights were protected. "Let every nongovernmental organization in its worldwide contacts manifest its pledge to promote respect for, and observance of, human rights without discrimination. Honoring that pledge in its own life and action may mean more than the recommendations accepted by this conference and will certainly undergird them" (*The Churches and the Nations*, p. 169). For him no firm division existed between the two kingdoms. Rather, the two were closely intertwined, and it was the church's ministry to impact life in the world. In his own valedictory to the U.S. Conference for the WCC, the breadth of Nolde's concern in this regard comes through clearly. He struck what had become his characteristic themes, asserting that the United States should expand the antiballistic missile test-ban treaty to include all testing, keep the oceans and seabed from becoming a battleground for nationalistic expansion, include the Soviet Union in a partnership for peaceful space exploration, offer China a greater voice in world affairs, and look at the situation in Vietnam from the perspective of the whole rather than just the south.

Nolde's goal was to move the churches, especially the Lutheran church, which had theologically and practically isolated itself, into a positive role in influencing governmental policies regarding human rights. When he died in Wyndmoor, Pennsylvania, he remained committed to the axiom of action he had for so many years encouraged: "Whatever one's religion or belief, let a good conscience and an enlightened understanding impel each one of us to dedicated and continuing effort" (*The Churches and the Nations*, p. 169). In this he was a pioneering spirit. In 1988 his church body, the Lutheran Church in America, merged with the Association of Evangelical Lutheran Churches and the American Lutheran Church to form the Evangelical Lutheran Church in America. Many of the principles first articulated by Nolde found their way in the fabric of the new church body. His visionary efforts had finally found concrete expression in his own tradition.

• Nolde wrote *Toward World-Wide Christianity* (1946), *Freedom's Charter* (1949), *Free and Equal: Human Rights in Ecumenical Perspective* (1968), and *The Churches and the Nations* (1970). See also Betty Thompson, "Tribute to a Diplomat," *Christian Century* 86 (28 May 1969): 736. An obituary is in *Minutes of the Proceedings of the 1973 Convention of the Southeastern Pennsylvania Synod of the Lutheran Church in America* (1973), pp. 15–16.

LAWRENCE R. RAST

NOLEN, John (14 June 1869–18 Feb. 1937), city planner and landscape architect, was born in Philadelphia, Pennsylvania, the son of John Christopher Nolen, a carpenter, and Matilda Thomas. His father died when Nolen was less than a year old. When the boy reached the age of nine, his mother enrolled him in Girard College, a school for fatherless boys. The college imbued Nolen and his classmates with the precept of self-improvement through hard work, intellectual development, clean living, and physical exercise. After graduating with high honors at the age of fifteen, Nolen worked for the Girard Estate Trust Fund, seeking to save sufficient money to continue his education.

In 1890 he entered the Wharton School of Finance at the University of Pennsylvania as an economics and public administration major. During the summers from 1892 to 1894 Nolen worked as superintendent of Onteora Park, a private resort in the Catskill Mountains offering programs in drama, art, and music. He graduated from the university with a Ph.B. degree in 1893. After graduation Nolen served for ten years as executive secretary of the Society for the Extension of University Teaching, an outgrowth of the University of Pennsylvania that sought to promote adult education through lectures and night courses. Through this post he gained much administrative experience and developed his skills as a public speaker and advocate. Nolen married Barbara Schatte of Philadelphia in April 1896. She was a homemaker and talented gardener who supported Nolen's career and enthusiasm. The couple had four children.

In 1901 and 1902, during a year-long visit to Europe, Nolen observed many cities and villages that had been beautified through state-sponsored art, architecture, and landscape design. Upon returning, he decided to become a landscape architect. At age thirty-four he moved his family from Ardmore, Pennsylvania (near Philadelphia), to Cambridge, Massachusetts, and entered the newly created School of Landscape Architecture at Harvard University.

At Harvard Nolen studied with Frederick Law Olmsted (1870–1957) and other members of the pioneer landscape architecture firm, the Olmsted Brothers. The Harvard faculty strengthened his belief in the possibility of improving the quality of cities through application of the design arts. In 1905 Nolen received his A.M. degree and immediately opened a practice in Cambridge as a landscape architect. Although in his first decade of practice he spent much of his time designing parks, boulevard systems, and other staples of landscape architecture, Nolen also swiftly became a leader in the infant city-planning field. Between 1905 and 1910 he prepared replanning recommendations for Roanoke, Virginia; Savannah, Georgia; Reading, Pennsylvania; San Diego, California; and Madison, Wisconsin.

In 1909 Nolen was asked to serve as one of the principal speakers at the founding National Conference on City Planning in Washington, D.C. He defined the mandate of city planning as improving the quality of living for all classes of urban residents. During the following twenty-five years, Nolen tirelessly promoted this definition of planning and concentrated his energies on three aspects of improving the lives of urban dwellers: replanning the physical character of existing cities and towns, constructing affordable housing for working-class people, and building new towns outside existing cities. Drawing on his earlier career with the Society for Extension of University Teaching, Nolen spread his view of city planning through public speaking at countless conferences and business meetings and through a steady stream of magazine articles and several books. He also spread his message through some 400 planning and landscape architecture projects.

Although he prepared some fifty replanning studies for large- and medium-size cities between 1905 and 1932, Nolen increasingly became dissatisfied with the possibilities of solving the chief urban problems through replanning recommendations. Rigid existing urban layouts and high real estate values made reshaping the character of cities very difficult. Instead, Nolen became an advocate of planning and constructing new towns in the countryside. In such communities, urban beauty could be built into the site plans and the architecture from the start, proper distribution of public amenities could be achieved, and a mix of market-rate and low-cost workers' housing could be constructed. In his new-town advocacy, Nolen was influenced considerably by the ideas of the English Garden City movement, launched at the turn of the century by the utopian reformer Ebenezer Howard.

Nolen achieved a reputation as a new-town planner with the plans that he prepared for two communities in particular: Kingsport, Tennessee, an industrial city created between 1915 and 1920, and Mariemont, Ohio, a "garden suburb" of Cincinnati planned between 1920 and 1925. He also served as town planner for several communities constructed by industrial companies for their workers: Kistler Village, Pennsylvania (1916), and the Overlook Colony near Wilmington, Delaware (1917). During World War I he planned Union Park Gardens, New Jersey, a town constructed by the federal government for war industry workers. In the 1920s Nolen designed several resort communities in Florida, but few prospered after the Florida land boom bubble burst in 1927.

Nolen's planning practice, like those of most city-planning consultants, decreased markedly after the nation entered the Great Depression of the 1930s. He spent his last years writing and lecturing on city and regional planning and serving as a consultant to the National Planning Board, a New Deal agency. He died at his Cambridge home.

John Nolen helped create the field of city planning, and his chief contribution to its growth and vitality was as an energetic and effective advocate. He lectured about the values of planning to countless audiences across the United States and in many foreign countries. He also authored over 275 books, periodical articles, speeches, and unpublished manuscripts on planning topics. Nolen chose to keep his office staff small, to allow him time to spread the "gospel" of planning. Even so, his practice covered every region of the nation, and he traveled as many as 25,000 miles per year to visit the sites of his planning projects.

Nolen's peers repeatedly recognized his stature as one of the principal spokesmen for the planning profession. They elected him successively to serve as president of the National Conference on City Planning, the American City Planning Institute, and the International Federation for Housing and Town Planning. Nolen also influenced the field of city planning through the subsequent work of several designers who began their careers in his office. Justin R. Hartzog and Hale Walker, who served as Nolen's associates during the 1920s, later became town planners for two of the model greenbelt towns built by the Federal Resettlement Administration in the 1930s. Earle S. Draper, who started his career as an assistant to Nolen in the planning of Kingsport, Tennessee, proceeded to become planner of numerous textile towns across the South after World War I. In the 1930s he became the planner for Norris, Tennessee, the principal new town created by the Tennessee Valley Authority.

Nolen's own prominence waned in his last years, as city planning became institutionalized as a function of local governments and as advocates of low-cost housing and new towns turned for inspiration from Kingsport and Mariemont to Radburn, New Jersey, the model community planned in 1929 by architects Henry Wright (1878–1936) and Clarence Stein. His lasting monument is the field of city planning itself, spread throughout the United States in no small part by his promotion of its virtues. His son, John Nolen, Jr., adopted his father's profession and became a leader in the planning field through a long association with the National City Planning Commission in Washington, D.C.

• Nolen's papers from his planning practice and other interests were donated by John Nolen, Jr. to Cornell University, where they are housed in the Department of Manuscripts and Archives as the John Nolen Papers. His professional library was donated by his widow to the University of North Carolina at Chapel Hill, where it became the John Nolen Memorial Collection in City and Regional Planning. A comprehensive bibliography of Nolen's planning reports, periodical articles, and books is found in John L. Hancock, *John Nolen, Landscape Architect, Town, City, and Regional Planner: A Bibliographical Record of Achievement* (1976). Nolen's chief books include *Replanning Small Cities* (1912), *City Planning* (which he edited in 1916), *New Ideals in the Planning of Cities, Towns, and Villages* (1919), and *New Towns for Old* (1927). The only biographical study to date of Nolen's career is John L. Hancock, "John Nolen and the American City Planning Movement: A History of Culture Change and Community Response; 1900–1940" (Ph.D. diss., Univ. of Pennsylvania, 1964). For a comparative study of Nolen's planning of three new towns, see James A. Glass, "John Nolen and the Planning of New Towns: Three Case Studies" (M.A. thesis, Cornell Univ., 1984). Obituaries are in the *Planner's Journal* Jan.–Feb. 1937; *Planning and Civic Comment* Jan.–Mar. 1937; and *American Society of Planning Officials Newsletter*, Mar. 1937.

JAMES A. GLASS

NOLL, John Francis (25 Jan. 1875–31 July 1956), Catholic bishop, writer, and publisher, was born in Fort Wayne, Indiana, the son of John Noll, a businessman active in local politics, and Anna Ford. After preparatory seminary studies at St. Lawrence College, Mount Calvary, Wisconsin, he attended Mount Saint Mary's of the West Seminary at Cincinnati and was ordained a diocesan priest at Fort Wayne in 1898.

Noll was then assigned to a series of rural parishes in northern Indiana. In 1903, while pastor at Besancon, Indiana, he began publishing *Kind Words from Your Pastor* for parishioners whose previous pastor had alienated them. From this effort to explain church positions in a simple, straightforward style, he launched the periodical *Parish Monthly* for instruction and edification that was soon widely distributed and eventually became known as *Family Digest*. In 1911, while Noll was pastor of St. Mary Church, Huntington, Indiana, *The Menace*, a periodical containing lurid stories about Catholicism, began to circulate. To refute its assertions, Noll founded in 1912 the weekly *Our Sunday Visitor*. Published from Huntington, the "*Visitor*," sold at Catholic churches on Sundays, soon circulated nationally. It contained apologetical, instructional, and devotional articles written in a popular style to improve Catholics' knowledge of their religion. Noll also wrote pamphlets explaining Catholic beliefs. His book of instructions in the Catholic faith for adults, *Father Smith Instructs Jackson* (1913), eventually went through sixty printings and translations in six languages.

His reputation as an effective spokesman for Catholicism led to his appointment as fifth bishop of Fort Wayne in 1925. While remaining publisher of *Our Sunday Visitor*, he directed his energies to the administration of a diocese then comprising the northern half of Indiana. He established fifty-four parishes, founded a minor seminary, built Catholic high schools in several cities, and organized a diocesan office of Catholic charities. He founded the Missionary Sisters of Our Lady of Victory at Huntington to carry on catechetical work.

Noll also took an active part in national Catholic affairs as a founder of the Catholic Press Association, board member of the Catholic Extension Society, treasurer of the American Board of Catholic Missions, and secretary of the administrative committee of the National Catholic Welfare Conference at various times from 1930 to 1947. He also served on the Conference's Committees on Obscene Literature, Catholic Refugees, and the committee that founded the Legion of Decency to combat morality in motion pictures.

By the 1950s Noll's major interest was to restart construction—discontinued since 1932—of the National Shrine of the Immaculate Conception in Washington, D.C. Through advocacy in his publications and by chairing the bishops' committee for the National Shrine, Noll promoted fundraising so that construction resumed in 1954 and was completed in 1959 after his death. Pope Pius XII recognized Noll's contributions in 1953 by conferring on him the personal title of archbishop. Though Noll did not lead a major Catholic diocese, he gained wide influence among American Catholics through his national publications and the causes he promoted. He died in Fort Wayne.

• The *Our Sunday Visitor* Collection at the University of Notre Dame Archives includes Noll's papers. A limited number of his papers are in the Archives of the Diocese of Fort Wayne-South Bend in Fort Wayne. John Francis Noll, *The Diocese of Fort Wayne: Fragments of History* (1914), chronicles diocesan issues. Richard Ginder, *With Ink and Crozier: A Biography of John Francis Noll, Fifth Bishop of Fort Wayne and Founder of Our Sunday Visitor* (1950), is a popular biography. Clifford Stevens, "John Francis Noll: 1874–1956," *Homiletic and Pastoral Review* 75 (Apr. 1975): 21–32, is a sympathetic portrait.

JOSEPH M. WHITE

NOLTE, Vincent Otto (21 Nov. 1779?–19 Aug. 1856), merchant, was born in Livorno, Italy, the son of John Henry Nolte, a merchant. Little is known of his mother. He was educated privately in Germany and at age sixteen was apprenticed to the Livorno mercantile house of Otto Frank, managed by his uncle. There he rejected his uncle's authority, spent much of his time in idle pursuits, and as a result soon found himself back in Hamburg working in his father's counting-house. As he explains in his memoir, *Fifty Years in Both Hemispheres* (1853), his father's reproaches gave him the impetus he needed, and he quickly learned "the ABC's of the mercantile craft." With the gradual decline of his father's business over the next few years,

however, Nolte eventually decided to leave Germany and in 1804 took a position with the house of Labouchère and Trotreau at Nantes, France.

In July 1805 Nolte set sail for the United States to act as agent in a massive transfer of Mexican silver to Europe. He became an American citizen and lived in New Orleans for a short time, receiving large shipments of Spanish dollars and converting their value into trade goods to be shipped to England. Unfortunately, rising tensions between the United States and England soon put an end to the enterprise, and Nolte was forced to sail to Cuba to attempt to recover stranded assets. On his way back to New York, his ship ran aground in heavy seas off the coast of Florida, but after a day and night at sea he and his fellow passengers were rescued.

By 1809 Nolte was back in Europe, arranging financial support for his return to New Orleans as an independent merchant. Early in 1812 he arrived in New Orleans and began to establish his business when war broke out between England and the United States. Cut off from regular trade by a naval blockade, Nolte sold cotton to the English at Pensacola and engaged in several personal quarrels, one of which led to a duel. In December 1814 he joined the citizen militia under the command of General Andrew Jackson and participated in the battle of New Orleans as both soldier and reluctant supplier of the famed cotton bales that formed the American redoubts. After still another duel in 1815, he returned to Europe to reestablish business relationships in France and, while there, toured the recently contested battlefield of Waterloo.

In 1820 Nolte married Lisida Fevé; they had five children. For roughly ten years he ran a thriving mercantile house in New Orleans, specializing in large and risky speculations in cotton. By 1826, however, after a disastrous fall in cotton prices, he was forced to declare insolvency and sail again to Europe to negotiate debt payments with foreign creditors. After spending a weekend in the London debtors' prison and several months following his case in the Court of Chancery, he returned to New Orleans to oversee the cancellation of his company's remaining debts. In 1829 he left New Orleans for the last time and settled in France.

In Paris, with the help of General Lafayette, he undertook to supply the French National Guard with secondhand arms purchased from Prussia. The venture succeeded for a time, but by 1834 Nolte was again in financial trouble and without a regular income. Over the next two and a half years he attempted without success to obtain permission to publish a medal history of England using the recent invention of Nicholas Collas for making engraved copies of medallions. In 1837 he again found himself in debtors' prison, this time for more than three and a half months. The year 1839 saw his last trip to the United States, from which he was forced to flee by his creditors. Back in Europe one month later, Nolte searched for work in Venice and Trieste, eventually traveling to Odessa for the merchant house of Grant Brothers, & Co. and acting as correspondence secretary upon his return.

As early as 1814, Nolte had begun to write and publish in a variety of forms, ranging from personal attacks on New Orleans enemies to public reports on local finances. In 1828, during the presidential campaign of Andrew Jackson, he published a satirical description of the candidate's visit to New Orleans. During his final years he turned once again to writing and before his death produced a study of the "system of assurance and bottomry," several numbers of a Hamburg trade journal, and, of course, his memoir. He died in Paris.

Nolte might very well have been forgotten but for his autobiography, which provides a useful insider's view of nineteenth-century economics and history. His financial career demonstrates both the great opportunities and the enormous risks of early American commerce. In addition, his encounters with several significant historical figures—including Napoleon, John James Audubon, Lafayette, Jackson, and Queen Victoria, among others—afford intriguing glimpses into the lives of the period's major figures.

• Nolte's memoir is the major source of information about his life. His other works include *Wilhelm Benckes System Des See Assekuranz und Bodmerei Wesens* (1851–1852) and *Memorial of Facts Connected with the History of Medallic Engraving, and the Process of M. Collas* (1838). Thomas Shields's pamphlet *An Imposter Detected; or, An Exposure of the Calumnies and Falsehoods of Vincent Nolte on the Character of Thomas Shields, a Purser in the Navy of the United States* (1815) provides an opposing version of one of Nolte's New Orleans quarrels.

CLARK DAVIS

NOONE, Jimmie (23 Apr. 1895–19 Apr. 1944), jazz clarinetist, was born in Cut Off, Louisiana, the son of James Noone, a farmer, and Lucinda (maiden name unknown). Noone's full name is unknown; his first name has also been spelled *Jimmy*. Since the family's farm was ten miles outside New Orleans, Noone resided in Hammond while he attended school, returning home for vacations. At age ten he began to play guitar. In 1910 cornetist Freddie Keppard's Olympia Orchestra performed at a local dance hall, and Noone heard clarinetist Sidney Bechet.

Inspired to learn the instrument, Noone began taking informal lessons from Bechet when his family moved to New Orleans later that year. At a performance in 1913, at a time when Bechet's clarinet was being repaired, Noone was forced to fill in for him. His performance was so impressive that he remained a band member until Keppard left for California in 1914, at which point Noone and cornetist Buddy Petit formed the Young Olympia Band. Noone also led a trio in the summers of 1916 and 1917 and worked with trombonist Kid Ory and trumpeter Papa Celestin.

In 1917 Keppard invited Noone to Chicago to join the Original Creole Band, which after a residency there toured until it disbanded in the spring of 1918. In the fall, after further work in New Orleans, Noone returned to Chicago to join King Oliver in Bill Johnson's band at the Royal Gardens. Concurrently, he led a band after-hours.

In the summer of 1920 Noone joined Doc Cooke's orchestra as a clarinetist and soprano saxophonist. He began taking lessons from classical clarinetist Franz Schoepp, who had him play duets with fellow student Benny Goodman. Under Schoepp's direction, both men developed an unusual virtuosity. Also around this time, probably in 1922, Noone married Rita Thomas, a professional golfer; they had three children. While with Cooke, Noone also joined Mae Bradley's orchestra at the Dreamland Café and Ollie Powers's Harmony Syncopators, with which he made his first recordings in September 1923. The next month he appeared at one recording session as a substitute for Johnny Dodds in Oliver's Creole Jazz Band.

In the summer of 1926 Noone was playing at an after-hours club, the Nest; it is unclear whether he or Powers was the leader. Lavishly remodeled, the Nest became the Apex Club in the autumn of 1926, and Noone left Cooke's orchestra to concentrate on his most significant work as featured soloist and leader of the Apex Club Orchestra, an ensemble with the unusual pairing of clarinet (Noone) and alto saxophone (Doc Poston, who also played clarinet), together with a conventional rhythm section of piano, banjo or guitar, and drums (Powers, who remained in the band). Noone also returned to work with Cooke's orchestra in 1927.

Late that year Earl Hines was accompanying a singer at the Apex, and Noone's pianist was unable to appear; Hines sat in and held the job. Unfortunately, however, Noone was, according to Hines, jealous of anyone who received greater applause than he did. When the club management asked Hines to lead a band and the musicians' union then fined him for allegedly trying to steal Noone's job, Hines quit as soon as his contract expired. (Reed player Franz Jackson also described Noone as overly sensitive, although by other accounts Noone was admired for a kind and gentle nature.)

Despite the Apex Club's closing in the spring of 1928, Powers's death, and Hines's discontent, the orchestra between May and August 1928 made magnificent recordings documenting the stature of Hines and Noone as two of the finest improvisers in jazz. In their virtuosity, rhythmic feeling, and choice of repertory, they participated in the emerging swing style, but in keeping with the earlier New Orleans jazz style, Noone was devoted to improvising against an explicitly stated melody rather than soloing with only chords, bass, and percussion. In this context Noone wove clear, fluid, elaborate countermelodies on such tunes as "I Know That You Know," "Every Evening," and "A Monday Date." He favored the clarinet's luscious low- to mid-range and reserved high notes for climactic passages, not in a simpleminded way (i.e., start low, end high), but with a fine sense of musical architecture, the climaxes arriving in flowing succession. Noone was not a great blues player, but on "Apex Blues" he plays a solo distinguished by its warm, delicate lyricism. Another sort of melodic lyricism, heavy and sentimental, may be heard on versions of "Sweet

Lorraine," which achieved a popularity in jazz for some years after 1928, particularly in its association with Noone.

With further changes in personnel, the band kept working in Chicago; pianist Teddy Wilson joined for a period in 1933 and Budd Johnson played tenor sax and wrote arrangements sometime before May 1935. Noone also led a larger group at the Greystone Ballroom in Detroit, played for a month at the Savoy Ballroom in New York in mid-1931, and in mid-1935 made an unsuccessful attempt to establish the Vodvil Club in Harlem in partnership with bassist Wellman Braud. With the increasingly uninteresting recordings of the Apex Club Orchestra drawing to a close early in 1935, Noone the following year made four excellent sides in Chicago with his New Orleans Band, including "'Way Down Yonder in New Orleans" and "The Blues Jumped a Rabbit." At this time his band was regularly broadcasting on radio. While continuing to hold long residencies at clubs in Chicago, Noone also began touring the South and Midwest from 1938 into the 1940s.

The promising revival of New Orleans jazz on the West Coast enticed him to bring his family to Los Angeles in 1943. In the East End Kids' film *Block Busters* (1944) he performed "Apex Blues" and "Boogie Woogie." After joining Kid Ory's band, which broadcast on Orson Welles's radio series for Standard Oil, Noone was stricken by a fatal heart attack at home in Los Angeles. His son Jimmy (or Jimmie) Noone, Jr., developed an international following as a jazz clarinetist from around 1985 until his death in 1991.

Noone's recorded legacy is not the equal of Sidney Bechet's or Johnny Dodds's. Nonetheless, his best recordings remind us why, in his lifetime, these three men were mentioned in the same breath as the greatest of the New Orleans jazz clarinetists.

• The outstanding survey of Noone's life and recordings is by Albert J. McCarthy, "Jimmie Noone," *Jazz Monthly* 10, no. 4 (1964): 10–13; further information on his association with Cooke appears in McCarthy's *Big Band Jazz* (1974). Briefer surveys are by J. Lee Anderson, "Evolution of Jazz," *Down Beat*, 13 July 1951; Martin Williams, *Jazz Masters of New Orleans* (1967); and Barry McRae, "A. B. Basics, no. 36: Jimmie Noone," *Jazz Journal*, Dec. 1969, p. 16. Gunther Schuller analyzes Noone's style in *Early Jazz: Its Roots and Musical Development* (1968). William Howland Kenney III, "Jimmie Noone: Chicago's Classic Jazz Clarinetist," *American Music* 4 (1986): 145–58, summarizes his career and assesses his playing, with annotated examples. Revised and in many cases problematic details of his recordings as a leader are summarized in Laurie Wright's "Jimmie Noone," *Storyville*, no. 153 (1993): 84–86, and "Jimmie Noone (the Vocalion Recordings)," *Storyville*, no. 154 (1993): 124–28. Kid Ory, singer Tommy Brookins, clarinetist Joe Marsala, and Louis Armstrong recall Noone in Nat Shapiro and Nat Hentoff, eds., *Hear Me Talkin' to Ya: The Story of Jazz as Told by the Men Who Made It* (1955). Hines, Teddy Wilson, Budd Johnson, saxophonist Franz Jackson, and drummer Wallace Bishop discuss their associations with Noone in Stanley Dance, *The World of Earl Hines* (1977). Noone's brief periods with Oliver are described in *Walter C. Allen & Brian A. L. Rust's "King"*

Oliver, rev. Laurie Wright (1987). Information on his family comes from Stanley Dance, "Jimmie Noone Junior," *Jazz Journal International* 38, no. 7 (July 1985): 18–19, and Johnny Simmen, "A Note on Jimmy Noone," *Storyville*, no. 127 (1986): 19–22. An obituary by Vincent McHugh, "The Blues for Jimmy," appears in *Selections from the Gutter: Jazz Portraits from 'The Jazz Record,'* ed. Art Hodes and Chadwick Hansen (1977).

BARRY KERNFELD

NOPKEHE. *See* Hagler.

NORBECK, Peter (27 Aug. 1870–20 Dec. 1936), governor and senator, was born near Vermillion, Clay County, Dakota Territory, the son of Goran Person Kjostad, a Swedish immigrant who changed his name to George Norbeck, and Karen Larsdatter Kongsvig, an emigrant from Norway. Norbeck lived on his family's farm and attended local schools. The family moved to Charles Mix County in 1885. From his father, a Lutheran minister and legislator, Norbeck learned the fundamentals of politics. He attended the University of Dakota for two terms in the late 1880s but did not earn a degree. In 1892 he started working as an artesian well driller and six years later formed a partnership with Charles Nicholson and Oscar Nicholson. The company of Norbeck and Nicholson, located in Redfield, South Dakota, eventually became the leading artesian well drilling business in the state. In 1900 Norbeck married Lydia Anderson. The couple had four children.

Norbeck's political career began in the early years of the twentieth century. A member of the Redfield city council for two terms, he was elected state senator from Spink County for three consecutive terms, serving from 1909 to 1915. President of the Progressive Republican League of South Dakota in 1911, the year in which he formed the Siva Oil Company, Norbeck actively participated in national politics. In 1912 he at first favored Senator Robert M. La Follette of Wisconsin for the Republican presidential nomination. When La Follette's political strength declined, Norbeck switched his allegiance to former president Theodore Roosevelt, whom he greatly admired. Norbeck was one of the leaders in South Dakota of Roosevelt's Bull Moose party, which carried the state in the presidential election.

Norbeck's career in politics gained momentum after the Progressive campaign of 1912. He was elected lieutenant governor in 1914 and governor of South Dakota in 1916 and 1918, the first native South Dakotan to attain the latter office. As governor he outlined a program of governmental action and sponsored several measures designed to improve the social and economic welfare of the people. Foremost among these enactments was the plan for rural credits, which enabled the state to extend loans to farmers. Other proposals included a road-building program and creating the office of marketing commissioner, a highway department, and a workmen's compensation system. An industrial commission was among the five new departments established under Norbeck's guidance in 1917, when a busy legislative session enacted 376 laws. Amendments to South Dakota's constitution permitted the state to engage in certain business enterprises, such as packing, cement making, coal mining to establish hydroelectric plants, flour mills, terminal elevators, and providing hail insurance on crops. Public approval of these initiatives for reform was overwhelming. Norbeck had mastered the political scene. An advocate of conservation and preservation of natural resources, the governor secured passage of a law establishing the Custer State Park and Game Sanctuary in the Black Hills. He also favored old-age pensions for Native Americans, and for his efforts on their behalf, he was adopted by the Sioux tribe with the title of "Chief Charging Hawk." During the First World War, Norbeck delivered speeches in favor of the war effort.

The year 1920 was a turning point in Norbeck's political career. At the Republican National Convention that year in Chicago, Norbeck headed a delegation pledged to General Leonard Wood as the party's presidential standard-bearer. Later that year Norbeck was elected to the U.S. Senate, where he served until his death. A postwar depression in agriculture, deepened by a glutted market and a continuing decline in crop prices, hurt Norbeck financially and increased his determination to help farmers through legislative action. He endorsed the McNary-Haugen Farm Relief Bill, which would have sanctioned price fixing by a federal farm board. It was vetoed by President Calvin Coolidge, who viewed the measure as an improper use of the taxing power and as unwise legislation that would benefit special interests and lead to overproduction and profiteering. Under President Franklin D. Roosevelt, Norbeck supported the Agricultural Adjustment Act in 1933, a plan that sought to restore the producer's purchasing power by establishing parity prices for certain commodities and subsidies for acreage reduction. Later he sharply criticized the U.S. Supreme Court for its invalidation of this program.

In addition to supporting legislation to cope with agricultural distress and serving as a spokesman for farming interests, Norbeck was active in other areas. He pushed for the completion of the Mount Rushmore National Memorial, the enlargement of Yellowstone National Park, and the establishment of Grand Teton National Park and Badlands National Monument. He also introduced a bird sanctuary and migratory bill, which Congress passed. As chair of the Senate Banking and Currency Committee from 1927 to 1933, Norbeck investigated the operations of the New York Stock Exchange, blaming its manipulations for the Great Depression.

In the election of 1932, South Dakotans returned Norbeck to the Senate while voting for Franklin D. Roosevelt for president. Norbeck supported most New Deal measures. He endorsed Roosevelt for reelection in 1936, warning Republicans to offer more than mere criticism of Roosevelt and fears about subverting the Constitution and urging them to give progressives a voice in party affairs. His views often exasperated conservative Republicans, while those espousing more radical solutions charged him with being too conservative. Opposed to political radicalism, Norbeck embraced the moderate progressivism embodied by Theodore Roosevelt. Instead of growing more conservative in his later years, he steadfastly maintained his principles through Republican and Democratic administrations. He was a man of honesty and simplicity who never forgot his roots among the people of the northern plains. He died at his home in Redfield.

• Norbeck's papers are at the University of South Dakota Library in Vermillion. Some letters are in the manuscript collections of contemporaries, including those of Woodrow Wilson and Theodore Roosevelt at the Library of Congress. His speeches are in the *Congressional Record* from 1921 to 1936. The major work on Norbeck is Gilbert C. Fite, *Peter Norbeck: Prairie Statesman* (1948). See also Peter Norbeck and George Norbeck, *The Norbecks of South Dakota* (1938); Lydia Norbeck, "Recollections of the Years," ed. Nancy Tystad Koupal, *South Dakota Historical Collections* 39 (1978): 1–147; Gilbert C. Fite, "Peter Norbeck and the Defeat of the Non-Partisan League in South Dakota," *Mississippi Valley Historical Review* 33 (1946): 217–36; Fite, "South Dakota's Rural Credit System: A Venture in State Socialism, 1917–1946," *Agricultural History* 21 (1947): 239–49; and Fite, "The History of South Dakota's Rural Credit System," *South Dakota Historical Collections* 24 (1949): 220–75. An obituary is in the *New York Times*, 21 Dec. 1936.

LEONARD SCHLUP

NORDBERG, Bruno Victor (11 Apr. 1857–30 Oct. 1924), mechanical engineer, and inventor, was born in Björneborg, Finland, the son of Carl Victor Nordberg, a shipbuilder, and Dores Hinze. He became acquainted with mechanical processes at home. His father died while Nordberg was attending a Finnish preparatory school and was unable to influence his son's original career choice.

In school, Nordberg especially enjoyed classes in languages, history, and theology. When he matriculated at the University of Helsingfors, he realized his innate engineering ability and interest in technical problems. He worked closely with Professor Rudolf Kolster, a physicist at the university, who convinced him to pursue an engineering career. Nordberg enrolled in the basic science and mathematics classes that he had ignored while focusing on liberal arts. While establishing this theoretical foundation, he also took advanced engineering classes to finish with his class.

Nordberg graduated in 1878 and immigrated to the United States two years later, in either 1879 or 1880. He believed that he would have access to more opportunities in mechanical engineering in America than in Finland. He worked in Buffalo, New York, for four months and then accepted a position at the E. P. Allis Company in Milwaukee, Wisconsin. Nordberg's assignment was to detail Corliss engine parts, but when the designer who had been hired to build two large vertical blowing engines quit because he disliked the company's conditions, Nordberg offered to complete the task.

Wanting to improve the efficiency of the design, Nordberg designed a poppet valve governor to achieve an economy previously considered impossible. He stressed the advantages of a poppet valve for use in steam engines to improve steam distribution control. Such a device was crucial for machinery utilizing high steam pressures and functioning in super heats. When Nordberg seized the chance to design a blowing engine for Allis, he proved that he was an able engineer, advancing him professionally. In 1882 he married Helena Clara Hinze; they had two sons.

In 1886, bolstered by the financial support of friends, Nordberg established the Bruno V. Nordberg Company to manufacture governors. He rented a small shop on the third floor of a building and pursued mechanical design of heavy machinery, especially for mining applications. In nearby northern Michigan, copper mining was a booming business requiring a variety of equipment. Nordberg also skillfully invented and designed large air compressors and diesel engines, and as demand increased, he arranged for his engines to be built at the Wilkins Manufacturing Company in Milwaukee.

By 1890 Nordberg realized that he needed larger facilities to produce his machinery. He established the Nordberg Manufacturing Company, of which he was president and chief engineer until his death. He had filed for at least twenty patents by the second year of operation. He manufactured his specially designed governors for Corliss-valve and poppet-valve engines of various sizes and services and built other necessary items, including heaters, condensers, compressors, and pumps. Most of the products were enormous, complicated machines, many specially designed for clients' unique situations.

Nordberg was renowned for the mining hoists he created, both electric and steam-powered, to carry heavy loads from great depths at efficient speeds. He improved designs and invented new hoists used worldwide by metal mines. Nordberg's best-known hoists were owned by the Tamarack Mining Company and the Quincy Mining Company in Hancock, Michigan. For Tamarack, Nordberg designed a hoist drum in 1897 that was twenty-five feet in diameter, a record size until he built the "mammoth" hoist for the No. 2 Shaft at Quincy, which was the largest hoist in the world at that time. Most of Nordberg's hoists were steam powered and his compound-condensing reel hoist for the Homestead Mining Company and air and electric hoists were considered "unusual" but functional. Contemporary engineers considered the pneumatic hoisting system he built in 1908 for the Anaconda Copper Company in Butte, Montana, to be Nordberg's greatest engineering achievement.

Nordberg also built large compressors for mining companies. Both the Champion Copper Company's compressor at Painesdale, Michigan, and the pumps he designed for the Wildwood Water Works in Pennsylvania enabled the plants to achieve record outputs. Copper mining required stamping, and Nordberg's compound steam stamps used in the milling operation at Northern Michigan Copper Mines was considered fantastic. From the late nineteenth century and through the first half of the twentieth, the majority of copper ore in the United States was crushed and smelted by crushers designed and manufactured by Nordberg's company.

Nordberg focused on engines, building the first and largest Uniflow engine in the United States used for work with a rolling mill, which flattens strips of metals, such as copper, steel, and aluminum, into sheets or wires of a desired thickness. His design for winding engines conserved power, and he invented diesel engines of both two and four cycles, operating up to 12,000 horsepower. Realizing the advantages of diesel engines as early as 1912, Nordberg perfected a horizontal solid injection engine running at 50 and 100 horsepower per cylinder. He improved engines until his death, and the immense two-cycle Nordberg engines were the largest in America during his lifetime.

Nordberg created vacuum pumps and gas compressors of various sizes and pressures for the chemical industry. He constructed underground shovels, both crawler and rail-mounted types, that were compact for use in tunnels. Nordberg also designed railway machinery and power-driven tools to maintain railway tracks.

Capable of a tremendous volume of work, Nordberg acquired a professional reputation for consistently manufacturing reliable products and was admired for his ability to resolve difficult engineering problems. In 1890 the French Academy presented Nordberg with a gold medal for his "noteworthy inventions," which totaled at least seventy patents, ranging from cutoff gears for steam engines to steam pumps.

Nordberg had joined the American Society of Mechanical Engineers in 1893, participating in other engineering and scientific organizations. Many mechanical engineers claimed that Nordberg was influential in gaining the profession respect from other engineering branches. Journals such as *Engineering* regularly printed descriptions and blueprints of his designs.

By 1900 Nordberg had built a larger plant that eventually expanded to more than forty acres. He recruited talented engineers to work with him, realizing that their engineering abilities would complement his work. Nordberg respected his employees, nurturing their professional interests and convincing them to devote their careers to his work. Engineers filed for patents, assigning them to Nordberg's company. As he aged, he selected long-term employees to assume responsibility within the company.

Nordberg and his wife enjoyed family vacations on the Great Lakes where he sailed yachts that he designed for fun. Nordberg also enjoyed fashioning model boats, and these creations revealed his mechanical genius. In his home laboratory, he conducted electrical and chemical experiments, and he ensured that his children have college educations at the University of Wisconsin.

Nordberg died in Milwaukee. He had requested that his son, Bruno Victor Edward Nordberg, who had worked in the company as a draftsman, succeed him as executive engineer, and Rudolf Wintzer, who had been his assistant, as chief engineer. The Nordberg Manufacturing Company continued to grow, building and supplying heavy industrial machinery throughout the world and producing war materials for World War II.

• A technical summary of Nordberg's contributions is "Men Who Made the Industry," *Diesel Power* 25 (May 1947): 75. *The Symons Cone Crusher: Standard and Short Head Types for Fine Reduction Crushing*, Bulletin 66 of the Nordberg Manufacturing Co. (1937), is a brief pamphlet illustrating several types of machinery based on Nordberg's designs. Obituaries appear in *Mechanical Engineering* 46 (Dec. 1924): 934 and *Engineering*, 21 Nov. 1924, p. 706.

ELIZABETH D. SCHAFER

NORDBERG, William (31 Mar. 1930–3 Oct. 1976), physicist, was born in Fehring, Austria, the son of Hans Nordberg, and Sophie (maiden name unknown). Nordberg completed undergraduate work in physics at the University of Graz and received a Ph.D. in physics there in 1953.

Nordberg immigrated to the United States soon after graduating. His parents remained in Austria. The U.S. Army Signal Corps hired him as an atmospheric physicist. Nordberg conducted research for the meteorological division in the corps' engineering laboratories until 1959. During this time he also was project scientist for the International Geophysical Year Rocket Program and Vanguard 11 Meteorological Satellite at Fort Monmouth, New Jersey.

When a group of scientists were transferred from the army to the National Aeronautics and Space Administration (NASA), Nordberg accepted a position at the Goddard Space Flight Center in Greenbelt, Maryland. His first assignment was as head of the physical measurement section in the meteorology branch of the Satellite Applications Systems Division. Nordberg was promoted to administrative and management positions while conducting scientific research about the Earth's resources and meteorology. In January 1974 he was selected as director of applications at Goddard.

Nordberg gained international respect for his pioneering investigation of the Earth and its environment, using satellite-based, remote-sensing devices. A renowned space physicist, Nordberg studied the Earth's atmosphere with sounding rockets and satellites. He surveyed the Earth's environmental resources from space. The information enabled mapping of global conditions, including ocean currents, rainfall, and sea ice coverage. His research also helped weather forecasting. He refined highly accurate scientific instruments used in remote sensing.

Nordberg attended space science conferences around the world, sharing his uncommon experiences and encouraging other physicists to pursue similar work. He collaborated with physicists, meteorologists, and scientists from the U.S. Air Force Air Weather Service. The military provided jet aircraft for some of Nordberg's nonsatellite atmospheric investigations.

In his earliest work at Goddard, Nordberg analyzed how atmospheric conditions, such as rainfall and temperature, affected areas near Goddard. With Wendell Smith, he prepared a NASA publication, *Preliminary Measurements of Temperatures and Winds above 50 km over Wallops Island, Virginia*, in 1963. From this basic work, he developed more sophisticated research problems. Nordberg studied stratospheric temperature patterns using radiometric measurements collected by the TIROS VII satellite. The Nimbus I and II and ERTS-I satellites also made observations for him.

Nordberg's publications reflected the diverse studies he undertook with satellites. Using meteorological satellites, he interpreted radiation data. Nordberg compiled microwave maps of polar ice, revealing discrepancies in atlases. He stressed that "imaging thermally-emitted microwaves with satellites" was a "powerful tool" because entire regions could be viewed in one image, and cloud cover did not interfere with data collection. Nordberg used satellites to measure microwave emissions from the ocean and infrared emissions from the earth and to study interactions between the upper and lower atmospheres. He remarked that satellites enabled observation of both remote, unexplored areas and well-known regions and that they provided information to evaluate damage to the environment, such as strip mining and fires.

Often Nordberg's papers appeared first, or near the front, of the published proceedings of conventions and symposiums, revealing his importance within his profession. He returned to his native country to speak about the peaceful uses of space technology, emphasizing how atmospheric research could enable long-term weather forecasting. Nordberg represented NASA at conferences sponsored by the United Nations and in a joint Soviet-American symposium held in Leningrad on observations of the Bering Sea and experiments conducted on it.

In September 1975 Nordberg summarized his research and personal ambitions for space science at the Thirty-First Nobel Symposium, on the impact of space science on humanity, at Spatind, Norway. He presented "The Impact of Earth Resources Exploration from Space." He remarked that despite their use for weather forecasting and intercontinental communications for fifteen years, satellite surveys of global resources were in their fledgling stages. He told the audience that the LANDSAT system had been used since 1972 to transmit information about land forms, natural resources, and air quality. Satellites could observe the entire globe in a short time, recording data frequently and regularly. This method was more affordable and reliable than previous techniques, such as aircraft. Nordberg described how satellites provided consistency because "satellite observations are made everywhere by the same instruments under the same controlled conditions" to produce thematic maps.

Nordberg considered satellites as "the only economical and practical tool from which we may expect to obtain the kind and amount of information necessary for global management of earth resources and for protection of our life-sustaining environment." He outlined how satellites empowered humans to explore, protect, and improve their communities. He predicted that satellites would eventually enable scientists to acquire hydrodynamic information to evaluate currents for better shipping and navigation routes, to identify surging glaciers, and to distinguish geological hazards that might affect construction of bridges and other major structures. Seismic activity could also be monitored by satellites.

Nordberg explained that satellites enabled a "global assessment," in the present and future, which was "necessary to manage the extraction, distribution, conservation and renewal of these resources." Nordberg challenged his colleagues to assist each other in expanding usage and application of satellite-collected data. "I consider the achievement of such information transfer as a major challenge to the space programme of the next decade," Nordberg asserted. He concluded that scientists should foster "effective transfer of information from those who make the observations to those who are in need and in a position to apply this information to the solution of these problems."

Listed in *American Men and Women of Science*, Nordberg was a member of the American Association for the Advancement of Science, the American Geophysical Union, and the American Meteorological Society. He was honored for his scientific successes. NASA presented Nordberg the 1975 William T. Pecora Award, which was NASA's highest award. He also received NASA's Exceptional Science Achievement Award in 1965 and the Distinguished Service Medal for his contributions to and applications of remote sensing of Earth from spacecraft.

Nordberg married Beatrice Junek; they had no children. He was diagnosed with cancer in 1973 and died in Greenbelt, Maryland. The Committee on Space Research, the Israel Academy of Sciences and Humanities, and the International Association of Meteorology and Atmospheric Physics organized a 1977 symposium, the Contribution of Space Observations to Global Food Information Systems, as a memorial to Nordberg. A collection of papers presented at the symposium was edited by E. A. Godby and J. Otterman and published in 1978.

• Two important works of Nordberg's not mentioned in the text are "Geophysical Observations from Nimbus I," *Science* 150 (1965): 559–72; and, with James S. Kennedy, "Circulation Features of the Stratosphere Derived from Radiometric Temperature Measurements with Tiros VII Satellite," *Journal of the Atmospheric Science* 24 (Nov. 1967): 711–19. An obituary is in the *New York Times*, 7 Oct. 1976.

ELIZABETH D. SCHAFER

NORDEN, Carl Lukas (23 Apr. 1880–15 June 1965), mechanical engineer, was born in Semarang, Java, the son of Edward Norden, a prosperous merchant, and Cornelia Gersen. After his father's death in 1885, Carl returned with his family to the Netherlands. Norden

attended the Royal Art Academy at Dresden, Germany, from 1893 to 1896. In 1897 Norden became apprenticed to an instrument maker in Zurich, Switzerland. In 1900 he entered the Federal Polytechnic Institute in Zurich, from which he graduated four years later with a degree in mechanical engineering.

Norden emigrated to the United States in 1904. He worked for H. R. Worthington Pump and Machine Works and J. H. Lidgerwood Manufacturing Company, both of Brooklyn. In 1911 he was hired by Elmer Sperry, founder of the Sperry Gyroscope Company and head of that company's research and development staff, to help develop practical gyrostabilizers. He married Else Fehring, daughter of a wealthy German family, in 1907; they had two children.

Sperry and Norden sustained a stormy professional relationship for four years, during which time Norden quit repeatedly, only to return the next day. Norden's research at Sperry Gyroscope reduced the tendency of Sperry's gyroscopes to oscillate, making them more suitable for naval use. In recognition of Norden's achievement, Sperry offered him a $25-per-week raise, which Norden considered an insult. This caused Norden's final resignation in 1915, after which he established himself as a consultant. He continued to work as a paid consultant to Sperry Gyroscope on naval gyrostabilizers until 1917.

From 1918 to the end of World War II Norden worked closely with the U.S. Navy. Initially he worked on a stable gun platform and an "aerial torpedo," essentially a flying bomb similar to the later self-propelled German V-1. Launched by a catapult, the torpedo was built to guide itself to a preset target. Norden's project for the navy did not succeed, but his assistance to Sperry on a similar project for the U.S. Army helped lead to successful tests of a Sperry-guided torpedo in 1922. In the same year the navy's Bureau of Ordnance contracted with Norden to develop the Mk XI bombsight. This telescopic device was intended to improve bombing accuracy by providing a stable reference for a bombardier's use. Concerned that the project would be more than the solitary designer could manage, the navy proposed that he take on a partner, former army colonel, Theodore Barth, to provide the production engineering experience that Norden lacked. Captain Frederick I. Entwhistle from the Bureau of Ordnance joined them soon after. The navy accepted the team's design for the Mk XI in 1928 and negotiated with Norden and Barth to produce eighty sights. This led to the establishment of Carl L. Norden, Inc., of Brooklyn. This company, owned by Norden and Barth, was formed under an agreement that it would work at the exclusive direction of the navy's Bureau of Ordnance, undertaking no commercial or foreign business. This highly irregular arrangement later caused substantial friction with the U.S. Army.

As the Mk XI bombsight went into production, the navy contracted with Norden to design a new sight. Norden then went to Zurich, where he did much of his design work, returning in 1930 with the design for the Mk XV, which became the famous "Norden bombsight" of World War II. Far simpler to operate than his earlier design, Norden's new bombsight automatically provided true air speed, ground speed, wind speed, wind direction, and drift angle. Tests of the prototype at the Dahlgren Naval Proving Ground in 1931 demonstrated a circular error of less than 150 feet, although such accuracy was never achieved in operational use. Fleet exercises during the early 1930s showed that the sight was the most accurate available. It was brought to the army's attention in 1931 and, after negotiations among Norden, the army, and the navy, the army received its first Mk XV (in army usage, the M-1) in 1933 via the navy's Bureau of Ordnance. Because the Norden bombsight was designed for bombing from level flight, the navy did not use it during World War II. The exclusivity clause in the navy's contract with Carl L. Norden, Inc., however, prevented the army from contracting directly with the company; the army, therefore, had to obtain the bombsight through the navy. This prevented the army from obtaining needed modifications from Norden, and it was forced to have others modify its Norden-built bombsights.

The Norden Mk XV/M series bombsight was used by the U.S. Army Air Forces throughout World War II in both Europe and Japan. Its accuracy in combat never approached that which it attained in peacetime and varied greatly with circumstance. A circular error of 1,200 feet was frequently experienced in use of the device by the Eighth Air Force in Europe. A combination of high altitudes, anti-aircraft fire, and poor weather conditions rendered Norden's precision sight an imprecise weapon.

Norden designed other devices for the navy during the 1920s, including the catapults and arresting gear for aircraft carriers *Lexington* and *Saratoga* and the first hydraulically controlled aircraft landing gear. He considered himself to be a mechanical engineer and would not enter the field of electronics. In part, this was no doubt due to an inclination to follow his own talents—mechanics and hydraulics—but like Thomas Edison, Norden also did not believe in alternating current, which is an important part of electronics technologies. He also resisted mass production techniques, believing that precision equipment could not be made by machine. His company's bombsights were handmade, leading to a substantial production bottleneck during the war.

Norden remained a Dutch citizen, although he tried three times to become a naturalized U.S. citizen. At each attempt, a needed witness failed to appear. Outside of engineering, he pursued a youthful interest in art through painting and became a trustee of the Swedenborg Foundation of New York. He preferred a cloistered existence and made few public appearances. On accepting the American Society of Mechanical Engineers' Holley Medal in November 1944, he revealed that all his patent rights had been turned over to the U.S. government for $1 each. He retired after the war and died in Zurich, Switzerland.

• Articles relating to Norden's inventions are referenced in *Applied Science and Technology Index* and *Engineering Index*. The General Services Administration, National Archives and Records Service, has RG 74 (Ordnance), RG 72 (Bureau of Aeronautics), and RG 342 (Material Division), holding extensive documents on the Norden bombsight. Norden Systems, the descendant of Carl L. Norden, Inc., retains a few documents from its early years. Also see Thomas Parke Hughes, *Elmer Sperry: Inventor and Engineer* (1971), and Stephen L. McFarland, *America's Pursuit of Precision Bombing, 1910–1945* (1995). An obituary is in the *New York Times*, 16 June 1965.

ERIK M. CONWAY

NORDICA, Lillian (12 Dec. 1857–10 May 1914), the first American soprano to achieve top rank as a prima donna, was born Lillian Norton in Farmington, Maine, the daughter of Edwin Norton, a farmer and photographer, and Amanda Allen. (The year of her birth has mistakenly been given as 1859, and the date of her death as 12 May.) She studied voice from 1871 to 1876 with John O'Neill at the New England Conservatory of Music in Boston. On 30 September 1876 she made an impressive debut as soloist with Patrick Gilmore's Band at Madison Square Garden, New York, and she toured with that band for almost two years in the United States and Europe.

Lillian Norton's great ambition was for opera, and in 1878 she left the band to study voice and operatic roles, principally with Antonio Sangiovanni at the Milan Conservatory. She made her operatic debut in March 1879 as Donna Elvira in Mozart's *Don Giovanni*, at the Teatro Manzoni in Milan. Her debut as prima donna was in April 1879 at the Theatre Guillaume in Brescia, as Violetta in Verdi's *La Traviata*. ("Norton," said Sangiovanni, comes hard to the Italian tongue, so he changed her name to "Nordica" and Nordica it remained.) Over the next three decades the "Lily of the North" sang in many of the great opera houses and concert halls of Europe and the United States, from Russia to California. She sang Elsa in Bayreuth's first *Lohengrin* (1894), following exhaustive coaching by the Wagnerian high priestess, Cosima Wagner.

In New York, Nordica's appearances included four "firsts" that reflect her climb to stardom: (complete with her own private railway car) first operatic role in New York (26 Nov. 1883, as Marguerite in Gounod's *Faust* at the Academy of Music); first time at the Metropolitan but as part of a touring company (27 Mar. 1890, as Leonore in Verdi's *Il Trovatore*); first with the Metropolitan company but as a last-minute replacement for Emma Albani (18 Dec. 1891, as Valentine in Meyerbeer's *Les Huguenots*); and finally as a prima donna, in her own right, of the Metropolitan Opera from 1893 to 1907.

During this period Nordica was at her peak, both on the operatic stage and in concert halls, where her repertoire included operatic arias, popular ballads, and art songs in German, French, Italian, and English. Offstage, she was an ardent suffragist. When she died she was planning for "an American Bayreuth" and an

Institution of Music for Girls, both to be near her home at Ardsley-on-Hudson, New York. Nordica was married three times: in 1883, to Frederick Allen Gower, who died in 1885; in 1896, to Zoltan Döme, whom she divorced in 1904; and in 1909, to George W. Young. She once wrote that she was "just a poor picker of husbands."

Nordica last sang at the Metropolitan Opera on 8 December 1909, as Isolde (one of the seven Wagnerian roles for which she was famous), though she continued a strenuous schedule of opera and concerts elsewhere. Her last public performance was at Melbourne, Australia, 25 November 1913, near the beginning of an intended around-the-world tour. Fortune, however, deserted her: she sailed for Java on the Dutch ship *Tasman*, which struck a coral reef in Torres Strait. The ship eventually made land, but Nordica suffered from exposure and subsequent pneumonia. She died in Batavia (now Jakarta), Java. Her funeral was in London on 6 July, and her ashes were subsequently placed in the Jersey City plot of the Young family.

• The amplest source of information is the Nordica Memorial Association at Farmington, Maine. The association has many letters, photographs, and other documents of the Norton family, together with a collection of Nordica books and other materials. An excellent biography is Ira Glackens, *Yankee Diva: Lillian Nordica and the Golden Days of Opera* (1963), which also reprints Nordica's two small legacies to singers: "How to Sing a Ballad," *Musical Digest* 16 (Mar. 1931): 24–25, 44, 50; and "Lillian Nordica's Hints to Singers" (1922). A longtime friend of Nordica, William Armstrong, devotes to her a section of *The Romantic World of Music* (1922; repr. 1969), pp. 37–74. The Theater Collection, New York Public Library, has three scrapbooks containing clippings, correspondence, and photographs; also an autograph letter by Nordica.

WILLIAM LICHTENWANGER

NORDOFF, Paul (4 June 1909–18 Jan. 1977), composer and music therapist, was born Paul Norman Hof Bookmyer in Philadelphia, Pennsylvania, the son of Paul Hof Bookmyer, a printer, and Katherine Huntington, a pianist. Also prominent in his childhood was a grandmother from upstate Pennsylvania who helped raise him and who often recited poetry to him at bedtime. Paul's early musical instruction was with private local piano teachers. At the age of fourteen he entered the Philadelphia Conservatory, where he studied for four years with Hendrik Ezerman and thereafter with Olga Samaroff. It was Samaroff who persuaded him to find a more suitable surname for the concert pianist she expected he would become. "Nordoff" was formulated from "Norman" and "Hof" and became the name under which his reputation was established.

Nordoff received his bachelor of music degree in 1927 and for the next six years combined Samaroff's piano instruction with studies in composition at Juilliard under Rubin Goldmark. He earned his master's degree at the Philadelphia Conservatory in 1932 and graduated cum laude from Juilliard in 1933. Having by now demonstrated considerable promise as a vocal

and instrumental composer, he was awarded Guggenheim fellowships in 1933 and 1935, which gave him the opportunity to travel in Europe and to devote himself to composition. During this period, he wrote the *Secular Mass* for chorus and orchestra (1934), subsequently performed by Eugene Ormandy, and the Piano Concerto (1934), which was premiered in Holland and later played by Nordoff with the National Symphony under Hans Kindler (1938).

By the end of his Guggenheim years, Nordoff had made some important connections in Germany and was concertizing with a Munich singer. In 1937, however, with Hitler's political ambitions becoming an increasing threat, the composer left Germany after having arranged for the publication of twelve of his songs by Schott. Back in America, he began a five-year tenure (1938–1943) as head of the composition department at the Philadelphia Conservatory. He also organized a "Modern Chamber Music Concerts" series in Philadelphia, which in its first season (1937–1938) presented the première of his own Piano Quintet, written in 1936. On the basis of this work, Nordoff was awarded the Pulitzer Traveling Fellowship in 1940.

Nordoff's other important compositions of the thirties include the opera *Mr. Fortune* (1936–1937) and incidental music for Broadway productions of *Romeo and Juliet* (1935) and Shaw's *St. Joan* (1936), both starring Katherine Cornell. In 1939 Nordoff composed the music for Martha Graham's *Every Soul Is a Circus* (he later wrote scores on commission for Doris Humphrey and Agnes de Mille). A second opera, *The Masterpiece*, followed in 1940 and was produced in Philadelphia in 1941.

In 1944, inspired by the work of his future wife, Sabina Zay, a eurythmist, Nordoff composed *That Was the True Light That Lighteth Every Man That Comes into the World* for speakers, singers, eurythmy, and instruments. This was followed in 1945 by *The Sun*, a cantata with eurythmic ballet. Nordoff and Zay were married in that same year; they had three children.

Also in 1945, Nordoff became assistant professor of music at Michigan State University. Four years later, he left to join the faculty of Bard College at Annandale-on-Hudson, New York, where he was made a full professor in 1953. The years of Nordoff's academic appointments also saw continued growth in his reputation as a composer. In 1948 he composed the Concerto for Violin and Piano for Eugene List and Carroll Glenn. He began to receive orchestral commissions, and in 1949 wrote *Lost Summer*, for mezzo-soprano and orchestra, for the Louisville Orchestra. This was followed by *Lyric Sonata* (1952), for violin and piano, and *Dance Sonata* (1953), for flute and piano, as well as a number of songs and piano works. In 1954 Nordoff received recognition of his contributions to the academic and creative worlds of music in the form of a Ford Foundation Faculty Fellowship. Then came commissions for two more large works: *Winter Symphony* (1954) for the Louisville Orchestra and *Tranquil Symphony* (1955) for the New Orleans Symphony. He remained at Bard College until 1959.

Nordoff's growing success as a conventional composer and teacher was paralleled by his increasing interest in the spiritual teachings of Rudolph Steiner's anthroposophy and their practical application to the education of handicapped children. In 1960, after several years of training, he was awarded a bachelor's degree in music therapy by Combs College. He spent the rest of his life working with these children. Abandoning all his other former musical activities, he practiced in institutions throughout the United States and Europe, such as the Institute of Logopedics in Wichita, Kansas (1961–1962), the University of Pennsylvania Department of Psychiatry (1962–1965), and a number of treatment centers in Finland, Germany, and England.

Together with his collaborator, Clive Robbins, Nordoff wrote many articles and books describing their work with disabled children and music, notably *Music Therapy for Handicapped Children* (1971), *Music Therapy in Special Education* (1971), and *Creative Music Therapy: Individualized Treatment for the Handicapped Child* (1977). Nordoff and Robbins also produced several musical plays and many play-songs for use in the therapeutic situation, which were published by Theodore Presser. Nordoff viewed his work with handicapped children as "an experience of discovery—of the extent of the therapeutic possibilities of music" and expressed his joy in finding that regardless of whether the music was improvised or specially composed, it "communicates, engages, vitalizes, and—as a result—children change." Nordoff died in Herdecke, Germany.

Paul Nordoff's concert music, which was conservative, tonal, and consonant, largely fell out of fashion during the 1950s and 1960s, when the composing norm was serial, dissonant, and radically experimental. Late-twentieth-century neoromanticism, however, has brought about a renewed wave of interest in his strong lyrical gifts, particularly evident in his songs. As a music therapist, Nordoff fathered both theory and practice in this country, and the Nordoff-Robbins Music Therapy Clinic of New York University is but one of many training and treatment centers that perpetuate his work.

• Paul Nordoff's manuscripts are held in the Moldenhauer Archives in Spokane, Wash. A complete listing of his published and unpublished works is available from the American Society of Composers, Authors, and Publishers in New York City, and a selected listing is found in the *New Grove's Dictionary of Music and Musicians* (1980). For a comprehensive treatment of his life and work, see David Ewen, *American Composers* (1982). Also, see Ruth C. Friedberg, *American Art Song and American Poetry*, vol. 2 (1984), p. 181, for an in-depth discussion of Nordoff as a song composer. An obituary is in the *New York Times*, 19 Jan. 1977.

RUTH C. FRIEDBERG

NORELIUS, Eric (26 Oct. 1833–15 Mar. 1916), Lutheran pastor, editor, and church president, was born Erik Pehrson in Hassela, Hälsingland, Sweden, the son of Anders Pehrson and Elizabeth Jonsdotter, tenant farmers. Strongly influenced as a youth by the religious awakening in Sweden, he sought to become a pastor but lacked financial resources to pursue necessary basic studies. After two years of high school in Sweden, he emigrated to the United States at the age of seventeen, having chosen a new, Latinized name for himself. He was invited to enroll at Capital University in Columbus, Ohio, where he spent several years but did not graduate. Following preparatory and theological study at Capital (1851–1853 and 1854–1855), he was ordained by the Lutheran Synod of Northern Illinois in 1856. In 1855 he married Inga Charlotta Peterson; they had five children. Having visited Swedish settlements in Minnesota during the summer of 1854 while still a student, young Norelius welcomed the opportunity to return as a missionary pastor. He established his first congregations at Red Wing and Vasa (1856–1858). After a brief interlude in Attica, Indiana, he returned to Minnesota for the rest of his ministry, serving the parish in Vasa during three separate periods (1861–1881, 1884–1890, 1901–1905). He held a brief pastorate at Spring Garden (1882–1884) and maintained a continuous pastoral relationship with a small congregation in Goodhue, Minnesota, from 1869 to 1915.

Norelius was a facile writer and saw the Swedish church press as a vital force both in building the immigrant community and advancing his own church political causes. He edited several periodicals during his career, *Minnesota Posten* (1857–1858), *Hemlandet* (1859), *Svenska Lutherska Kyrkotidningen* (1877), and *Augustana* (1889–1890).

Norelius led the formation of the Swedish Lutheran Minnesota Conference in 1858 and was one of the founders of the Augustana Synod in 1860. Twice during his career the synod elected him as its president (1874–1881 and 1899–1911) and, after his retirement, named him president emeritus. In 1910 the king of Sweden made him a knight commander of the Order of the North Star.

During his sixty years of active ministry, Norelius exercised formative leadership in nearly every aspect of the life of the pioneer Swedish Lutheran church. Conservative in doctrine and practice, he contended against the tendency of many immigrant Lutheran clergy and lay persons to join other American religious groups, especially Methodists and Baptists. Although he was a cofounder of the Augustana Synod and later its president, he employed both press and pulpit to oppose centralization of synodical power at the expense of outlying districts, especially Minnesota.

Norelius was a pioneer in establishing educational and charitable institutions. To encourage young men to prepare for pastoral and teaching ministries on the frontier, he opened a school in his home that later developed into Gustavus Adolphus College in St. Peter, Minnesota. The first children's home of the Augustana Synod emerged from his initiative in caring for a family of four orphaned immigrant children. He organized relief for the victims of the Sioux Indian massacre of 1862, also known as Little Crow's War, in the Minnesota River valley.

The most enduring contributions of this patriarch of Swedish Lutheranism were mediated through his facility with the written word. Church historian G. Everett Arden noted that over the first fifty years of the life of the Augustana Synod, Norelius was a member of practically every important commission and committee that formulated the polity and policies of the synod, its conferences, and its institutions. Elected as official historian of the synod in 1869, Norelius also gathered records, minutes, and letters, upon which, together with his voluminous diaries, he based his two-volume history of early Swedish Lutheranism in America. The first volume, describing Swedish settlements, immigrant leaders, and Lutheran congregations before 1860 remains, in the judgment of its translator, Conrad Bergendoff, "an unparalleled source for the beginnings of Swedish immigration to America a century and a half ago." Norelius died in his home in Vasa, Minnesota.

• Collections of archival material, including Norelius's writings, mostly in Swedish, are in the libraries of Augustana College, Rock Island, Ill., and Gustavus Adolphus College, St. Peter, Minn. Portions of his *De Svenska Luterska Församlingarnas och Svenskarnes Historia i Amerika*, vol. 1 (1890), have been translated by Conrad Bergendoff and published as *Swedish Pioneer Settlements and Swedish Lutheran Churches in America, 1845–1860* (1984). Norelius's journals have been translated by Emeroy Johnson, *Early Life of Eric Norelius, 1833–1862* (1934), and by G. Everett Arden, *The Journals of Eric Norelius* (1967). Each of the published translations contains an evaluation of Norelius by the translator. A biography is Johnson, *Eric Norelius* (1954). An obituary is in the *Minneapolis Journal*, 16 Mar. 1916.

RICHARD W. SOLBERG

NORELIUS, Martha (20 Jan. 1910–23 Sept. 1955), swimmer, was born in Stockholm, Sweden, the daughter of Charles Norelius, a swimmer; her mother's name is unknown. Norelius was originally coached by her father, who swam for Sweden in the 1906 Olympics. After the Norelius family emigrated to the United States, however, Louis de Breda Handley took over as her coach, and Norelius soon made an impact in U.S. swimming circles as the top U.S. swimmer from 1924 to 1929, with her fame resting primarily on her Olympic accomplishments. She won the 400-meter freestyle event in 1924 at Paris, leading an American sweep in an Olympic record time of 6:02.2. In 1928 she defended that Olympic championship at Amsterdam, winning the final with a world record of 5:42.8. The mark broke the world record of 5:45.4, which she had set in winning her heat at the 1928 Olympics. Her 15-second victory margin in 1928 has remained the most dominant Olympic swim victory, as she was the only woman to have defended the 400-meter event at the Olympics. At the 1928 Olympics, Norelius won her third gold medal by participating on the 4 ×100-meter freestyle relay team.

Norelius won 11 individual Amateur Athletic Union (AAU) titles between 1925 and 1929, at distances ranging from 100 yards to 500 yards, and captured three consecutive outdoor titles at 440 yards from 1926 to 1928. Between 1925 and 1928 she set 19 world records and 30 American records. During her career she represented the Women's Swimming Association of New York and swam on three AAU national championship relay teams with that club. Her career best times were 2:40.6 for 200 meters/220 yards at Miami, Florida, on 28 February 1926; 5:42.8 for 400 meters at Amsterdam in 1928; 12:17.8 for 880 yards at Massapequa, Long Island, New York, on 31 July 1927; and 23:44.6 for 1,500 meters at Massapequa on 28 July 1927.

Norelius was considered the first woman to swim like a man, as previously most women swam low in the water with a two-beat kick. Her front crawl resembled that of Johnny Weissmuller, with a high head position, arched back, and six-beat kick, hydroplaning over the water. In marathons she used the same high elbow and long glide armstroke, but with almost no kick. Norelius received more publicity than any female swimmer before World War II, perhaps because she trained at her father's pools at the Greenbriar in White Sulphur Springs, West Virginia, and the Breakers in Palm Beach, Florida, where she was the darling of the social set. Norelius always swam with a cap and once won a national 500-yard race although starting late while putting on the cap.

In 1929 the AAU suspended Norelius for giving an exhibition in the same pool as some professionals. She then turned professional herself and won the $10,000 Wrigley Marathon in Toronto, Ontario, Canada. She met Joe Wright, one of Canada's greatest rowers. Wright had won an Olympic silver medal for Canada in the 1928 double sculls, three American national sculling titles, nine Canadian national sculling titles, and the 1928 Diamond Sculls at Henley. He also played professional football with the Toronto Argonauts of the Canadian Football League.

Norelius and Wright were married in the Prince of Wales Suite at the Greenbriar on 15 March 1930. They settled in Toronto, where they lived for eight years, until they divorced. Martha Norelius Wright returned to the United States and married twice more. She had five daughters, two by Wright, and three by her third husband, Alanson Brown, Jr. (The name of her second husband is unknown.) She settled in the St. Louis area, where she died.

• For more information on Norelius, see John Arlott, *The Oxford Companion to Sports and Games* (1976); Pat Besford, *Encyclopaedia of Swimming*, 2d ed. (1976); Bob Ferguson, *Who's Who in Canadian Sport*, 2d ed. (1985); Lord Killanin and John Rodda, eds., *The Olympic Games, 1984*, 3d ed. (1983); and Bill Mallon and Ian Buchanan, *Quest for Gold: The Encyclopaedia of American Olympians* (1984). For statistical information, see Spalding's Athletic Library, *Athletic Almanacs for 1926–30* (1926–1930); Swedish Olympic Committee, *Sverige och OS* (1987); and David Wallechinsky, *The Complete Book of the Olympics*, 3d ed. (1991).

BILL MALLON

NORMAND, Mabel (9 Nov. 1892–23 Feb. 1930), silent screen comedienne, was born in Staten Island, New York, the daughter of Claude G. Normand, a stage carpenter and pit pianist, and Mary Drury. Mabel was a backstage child, and there is no evidence that she received any formal education.

By the time Normand reached the age of sixteen her doe eyes, full lips, and other attributes brought her modeling opportunities with commercial illustrators and photographers. Famous artists Charles Gibson and James Montgomery Flagg featured her in their cover art for publications such as the *Saturday Evening Post*. Photographers posed her for hats, shoes, dresses, cold cream, and Coca-Cola. In spite of her mother's dislike of the movies and her desire for her daughter to remain a model, Normand moved to the fledgling New York motion picture industry, lured by a higher salary. Gradually she cut back her modeling to appear in one-reel films created by Biograph and Mack Sennett's Keystone studios. Her film debut was in 1910, with a short called *Over the Garden Wall*. Twelve movies later, in 1912, she joined Keystone with *The Water Nymph*.

Normand acted in more than a hundred comedies for Mack Sennett and, through her persistence and the confidence of Sennett, eventually achieved the status of writer-director-actor in her own films. Her biographer, Betty Harper Fussell, noted that "when women directors were unheard of, unless like [Mary] Pickford they were in a position to run the whole show, Mabel fought for and won the right to direct her own films" (pp. 72–73). Sennett's 1914 guarantee that Normand would thereafter "direct every picture she acts in" seems, in fact, to have allowed her to codirect with her male leads. She collaborated with Charlie Chaplin on the 1914 films *Mabel at the Wheel*, *Mabel's Busy Day*, and *Mabel's Married Life*, but Chaplin eventually persuaded Sennett to give him sole control over the writing and directing of his comedy shorts. In 1915 Normand was teamed with comedian Roscoe "Fatty" Arbuckle in seven shorts in which the pair equally contributed to writing and directing scenes. With Arbuckle, Normand did not experience the clash of egos she experienced when she codirected with Chaplin.

Normand exhibited a range of comic skills from the innocent, violated heroine in the 1913 one-reel *Barney Oldfield's Race for a Life* to the perky, sly, comic villainess in the feature-length *Tillie's Punctured Romance* (1914). When Mack Sennett established the Mabel Normand Feature Film Company in 1916, another dimension of her talent blossomed with the multireel, genteel comedy *Mickey*, a work directed by Sennett and released in 1918. Normand brought to the title role the sort of charm, warmth, and sentiment that audiences found fascinating in Mary Pickford films. She dressed in a baggy shirt and pants that muted her ample, 24-year-old figure. Gone was the usual broad slapstick of Normand's previous films as she portrayed a mistreated tomboy-orphan in rural mid-America. *Mickey* brought in millions for the financial backers, but Normand received little money for her efforts and her growing popularity.

Believing that Sennett rather than the backers of the film had slighted her, Mabel signed a contract with Samuel Goldwyn and starred in such films as *Molly O'* (1921) and *The Extra Girl* (1923). Unlike Mary Pickford, who was called "America's Sweetheart," Normand in her early Sennett films had the type of beauty and vivacity that suggested mature sexuality rather than the teenaged cuteness projected by Pickford. When Normand switched to genteel, sentimental features like *Mickey*, she lost that distinctive sensuality. However, even in these latter roles, Normand surpassed Mary Pickford in the vitality that she displayed onscreen.

In February 1922 the murder of director William Desmond Taylor, with whom she was romantically involved, brought about the downfall of Normand's career. Since she was the last one known to have seen Taylor before he was murdered, many people assumed that she was either an accomplice or the perpetrator of this still-unsolved crime.

With the rejection of a public that once adored her, Normand suffered both psychological and physical pain. Her high living, which included late hours, drugs, and alcohol, must have aggravated the tuberculosis that eventually took her life. Despite the negative and sensational journalistic accounts that plagued Normand, she struggled on, hoping to make a comeback even at the end of the decade that would signal the demise of the silent motion picture. She returned to Sennett in 1923 and moved to Hal Roach's studio in 1926, but she had no box office successes after the Taylor scandal. Her marriage in 1926 to actor Lew Cody, an alcoholic, did not give her the support she needed. They had no children. Until her death in Monrovia, California, Normand was haunted by the murder that ruined her career. On her deathbed she asked a friend, "Do you think God is going to let me die and not tell me who killed Bill Taylor?" (Fussell, p. 14).

Only when critics in the 1960s began reevaluating silent screen comedy was Normand's contribution fully appreciated. Her most broadly based slapstick films of the 1910s reveal that she was a natural comic actress with a stage presence that rivaled that of almost all the actors in her films with the exception of Charlie Chaplin, who could match and sometimes exceed her seeming spontaneity. She was, however, his equal in her spirit of play and overwhelming gaiety. Many critics now rank her as the greatest comedienne of the silent era.

• Many details about Normand's life are revealed in Betty Harper Fussell's *Mabel* (1982). Other works that mention Normand's career are John Montgomery, *Comedy Films* (1954); Mack Sennett (with Cameron Shipp), *King of Comedy* (1954); Gene Fowler, *Father Goose: The Story of Mack Sennett* (1934); and Theodore Huff, *Charlie Chaplin* (1951). Important articles are Stephen Normand, "Mabel Normand: Her Grandnephew's Memoir," *Films in Review*, 25, no. 7 (Aug.–Sept. 1974): 385–97, and Anthony Slide, "Forgotten

Women Directors," *Films in Review*, 25, no. 3 (Mar. 1974): 165–68, 192. An obituary is in the *New York Times*, 24 Feb. 1930.

DONALD W. MCCAFFREY

NORRIS, Charles Gilman Smith (23 Apr. 1881–25 July 1945), writer and editor, was born in Chicago, Illinois, the son of Benjamin Franklin Norris, a traveling jeweler, and Gertrude Glorvina Doggett, a former actress. His mother had hoped for a daughter, and her apparent indifference to her son troubled Charles Gilman Norris (the Smith was ultimately dropped) throughout his life as he sought to establish a literary name for himself apart from his more celebrated brother, Frank Norris, and his own wife, Kathleen Norris. In 1892 Norris's father deserted the family and on his death in 1900 left his entire estate to his new family. In his eleven novels Charles Norris utilized these themes of childhood rejection and financial deprivation.

Between the ages of three and six, Norris lived in San Francisco, but after the middle brother, Lester, died in 1887, the family moved to Paris to support Frank's artistic ambitions. The two surviving brothers were close, and in 1894, Charles and his mother followed Frank to Harvard for the year. Charles graduated from Lowell High School and entered Berkeley as a history major in 1899, joining Frank's fraternity. At Berkeley, where he was often visited by Frank and his family, Charles thrived on the social and artistic life. In October 1902 Frank died of peritonitis, just prior to Charles's 1903 graduation from Berkeley.

To distance himself from his family, Norris headed to New York to become the assistant editor of *Country Life in America*. Until 1905, Norris soaked up New York's social whirl, gathering material that he subsequently incorporated, along with aspects of Frank's life, into his first novel, *The Amateur* (1916). For the next three years Norris worked as the circulation manager of *Sunset* magazine in San Francisco, where he met Kathleen Thompson, whom he married in 1909 in New York City. They raised one natural son, one adopted son, a nephew, and two nieces. Between 1908 and 1914 Norris worked as art editor of *American Magazine* and then as assistant editor of the *Christian Herald* before resigning to devote himself full time to the management of his wife's writing career, his own writing, and the championing of other writers such as his brother, Frank. Norris's shrewd machinations within the publishing world ensured his brother's reputation as well as substantially increased his wife's popularity, making her one of the nation's highest-paid authors.

After the publication of *The Amateur*, Norris volunteered for the army, training troops at Camp Dix while writing a second novel. *Salt* (1918), an indictment of American education, provoked a letter of praise from F. Scott Fitzgerald, who declared that Lester Wagstaff (the protagonist's half brother), George Hurstwood, and Tom Buchanan were the three best characters in contemporary American literature. In 1919 Norris's mother died, precipitating a return to California, and

although Norris and his wife traveled extensively thereafter, California remained their home. Norris's third novel, *Brass* (1921), dealt with divorce and was made into a 1923 Warner Brothers film. Norris dedicated *Bread* (1923), an account of a married woman's struggle in the business world, to the "Working Women of America"; Sinclair Lewis admired this book, which was purchased by Metro Pictures. *Pig Iron* (1925), an Algeresque novel of a man's rise and fall, outsold *The Great Gatsby, Manhattan Transfer,* and *An American Tragedy*. In 1927, *Zelda Marsh*, a Cinderella backstage romance, was published. The August 1930 publication of *Seed*, with its theme of birth control, prompted high praise from Theodore Dreiser and was sold to Universal Pictures, as was *Zest* (1933). *Hands* (1935) chronicled three generations of a family, while *Bricks without Straw* (1938) explored the conflicts between parents and children. The publication of Norris's final novel, *Flint* (1944), a San Francisco novel of labor strife, preceded his first stroke, which kept him in a New York hospital for two months. After his wife accompanied him on a westward train journey, Norris died at his home in Palo Alto, California.

Norris and his wife entertained many prominent people of the stage, screen, political, and publishing worlds, such as Noel Coward, Frank Doubleday, Edna Ferber, Herbert Hoover, Fannie Hurst, Charles Lindbergh, Harpo Marx, Jack Reed, Harold Ross, Ida Tarbell, and Alexander Woollcott. Because of his ability to manipulate and coerce the publishing industry for the benefit of his literary friends and family members, Norris shaped the popular fiction of America for over thirty years. His wife Kathleen always maintained that while New York made her a writer, Norris made her successful. For the Norris family alone, he sold over one hundred book manuscripts and more than a thousand shorter pieces.

Norris's own novels detail middle- and upper-class life in New York and San Francisco between 1890 and 1945. Norris was not so much interested in language experimentation as in economic, political, and social issues and the ways in which his characters face daily problems such as jobs, bills, birth control, and divorce. Although his fiction harks back to the more traditional aspects of the late-nineteenth-century novel, in his best work Norris shares with his brother the ability to tell a good story marked by realism and careful historical research in a morally neutral world. Apart from his own writing, Norris's involvement in publishing a wide circle of writers attests to his influence on the evolution of American literature.

• Apart from those papers in the possession of friends and family, the bulk of unpublished Charles Gilman Norris materials is housed in the Bancroft Library of the University of California at Berkeley. Richard Allan Davison's *Charles G. Norris* (1983) is the only full-length book on Norris; it is both a well-researched biography and an insightful critical study. Kathleen Norris's two autobiographies, *Noon: An Autobiographical Sketch* (1925) and *Family Gathering, the Memoirs of Kathleen Norris* (1959), contain useful information on the early years of Charles and Kathleen Norris's marriage as well as photographs of Norris and his friends. Interesting material can also be found in an interview in the *New York Times Book Review*, 12 Mar. 1922, p. 17, entitled "The Norrises Discuss Marriage," and in an interview with Arnold Patrick in *Bookman*, July 1925, pp. 563–66. Franklin Walker's biography, *Frank Norris* (1932), contains early biographical material, as does a chapter on Frank Norris in Kenneth S. Lynn's *The Dream of Success* (1955). Arnold Goldsmith's article, "Charles and Frank Norris," *Western American Literature 2* (Spring 1967): 30–49, is a strong critical study of Charles Norris's work. Comparisons between Norris and his contemporaries can be found in Richard Allan Davison, "F. Scott Fitzgerald and Charles G. Norris," *Journal of Modern Literature* 10, no. 1 (1983), which presents a full discussion of the Fitzgerald-Norris relationship, and in Richard Allan Davison, "Charles G. Norris and John Steinbeck: Two More Tributes to *The Grapes of Wrath*," *Steinbeck Quarterly* 15 (Summer–Fall 1982): 90–97. Obituaries are in the *New York Times*, 26 July 1945; *Time* and *Newsweek*, both 6 Aug. 1945; and *Publishers Weekly* and the *Saturday Review of Literature*, both 11 Aug. 1945.

M. A. THOMPSON

NORRIS, Edward (c. 1584–20 Dec. 1659), Puritan clergyman, was born probably in Tetbury, Gloucestershire, England, the son of Edward Norris, the parish rector, although the identification is uncertain. His mother's name is unknown. He earned a B.A. from Magdalen Hall, Oxford, in 1607 and his M.A. in 1609. By 1624 he was rector at Anmer, Norfolk. From 1635 to 1638 he wrote three pamphlets debating John Traske, a London antinomian who held that the "True Gospel" freed believers from the constraints of the moral law in favor of individual, inspired conscience. His writings in England presaged his role in Massachusetts as a defender of non-Separatist Puritan orthodoxy. He married prior to emigration. All that is known of his wife is her first name, Eleanor. The couple had one son, Edward, who later became a schoolmaster at Salem.

In 1639 Norris and his family arrived in Boston, Massachusetts, where he and his wife joined the church in July. In September 1639, after trial sermons, he became the redoubtable Hugh Peter's colleague at Salem, thus beginning a pastorate that lasted in that town until his death. After Peter's departure for England in 1641, Norris generally followed his predecessor's policy of fostering religious and political stability and economic development by functioning as a mediator in disputes among the town's and colony's lay leaders and as an apologist for their collective interests. His concern for stability led him, for instance, to write a defense of a proposed "standing council," or a set of magistrates, presumably former governors and other notables, who would serve for life so as to counter democratic tendencies in the new Massachusetts government. This proposal failed but Norris had so alienated members of the newly separated lower house that the deputies refused to invite him to give the annual election sermon in 1645. However, he was given that honor in 1646 once tempers cooled.

His main interest was in developing and preserving the influence of the church and religion under pioneer conditions. Initially following a trend in Bay Colony churches of the 1640s, he, unlike Hugh Peter, rigorously applied the tests of conversion to prospective members in order to strengthen the prestige and élan of the congregation within the community. Yet by 1652 he was among the first to conclude, correctly in the case of Salem and similar towns, that this approach was failing and to advocate more inclusive standards for membership, some of which were later embodied in the Half-Way Covenant. However, his own church, while allowing him some latitude in individual cases, refused to adopt broader policies on baptism until after his death.

Similarly, as late as 1646 Norris refused to heed the call of the Massachusetts General Court for the Cambridge Synod to consider standardizing the organization and policies of the colony's churches because he feared that such synods might undermine both the autonomy of the churches and the close links between individual congregations and their communities. By 1652, however, he had decided that extreme local diversity was a more serious liability. That year he and the Salem church petitioned the general court for laws limiting the congregations' choices of ministers to those of "certain approval" so as to control separatist and transient preachers. The possibility of a government role, even a minor one, in licensing clergy remained a delicate issue throughout the colonial era in Massachusetts.

Norris was most noted among his peers for his doctrinal sophistication. Indeed, his well-known sensitivity to separatist and antinomian tendencies in Puritanism probably explains his initial appointment at Salem. Coping with local dissent was rarely easy. On one occasion in 1644 his rigor led to charges that "there was no love in the church and that they were biters and devourers," while his cultivation of close connections between religious and secular authority was interpreted cynically in the claim that "Mr. Norris said that men would change their judgment for a dish of meat." For the colony at large, he was chosen first among a committee of seven clergymen in 1647 to compose a confession of faith, despite his opposition to synods. In an even more telling sign of his reputation for theological clarity, he was assigned, along with John Cotton and John Norton, the task of convincing the powerful magistrate, William Pynchon, that his lay attempt at theology, *The Meritorious Price of Our Redemption* (1650), was heretical in a "Socinian" direction by stressing Christ's morality rather than his atonement as central to salvation.

In 1656, as Norris was in his seventies, the Salem church finally hired an assistant, John Whiting. In 1658 Norris suffered a stroke while in the pulpit. He died the following year in Salem. Thus, this staunch definer and defender of the New England Way played no major role in the Quaker controversy that was beginning to embroil his town and colony.

• Biographical information about Edward Norris can be gleaned from Sidney Perley, *History of Salem* (3 vols., 1924–

1927), and L. A. Morrison, *Lineage and Biographies of the Norris Family in America* (1892). Assessments of his role in the religious and political life of Massachusetts can be found in J. K. Hosmer, ed., *Winthrop's Journal* (2 vols., 1908); Richard P. Gildrie, *Salem, Massachusetts, 1626–1683: A Covenant Community* (1975); and Philip F. Gura, *A Glimpse of Sion's Glory: Puritan Radicalism in New England, 1620–1660* (1984).

RICHARD P. GILDRIE

NORRIS, Frank (5 Mar. 1870–25 Oct. 1902), novelist, was born Benjamin Franklin Norris in Chicago, Illinois, the son of Benjamin Franklin Norris, a prosperous jewelry merchant, and Gertrude Doggett, an actress and teacher. In 1884 the elder Norris moved the family to California to escape the cold and damp Chicago climate, which exacerbated the pain of his hip ailments. After a year in Oakland, the family moved to San Francisco, where they established themselves among the social elite of the city. The potential that young Frank exhibited for drawing while recovering from a fracture of his left arm convinced his parents of the need for formal training. In 1887 the family relocated to Paris, where Norris took art lessons at the Atelier Julien. There he developed a fascination for medieval culture and for literature, writing and illustrating an article on armor that appeared in the *San Francisco Chronicle* on 31 March 1889.

His father, who had returned the rest of the family to San Francisco in 1888, disapproved of Norris's literary aspirations and, wanting him to enter the jewelry business, called him home in 1889. The following year Norris entered the University of California at Berkeley as a limited-status student on account of his inability to pass the mathematics portion of the entrance examination. At Berkeley he took courses in English, French, history, and zoology with Joseph LeConte, whose attempts to reconcile evolution with religion greatly influenced Norris. He also read avidly the works of Rudyard Kipling, Robert Louis Stevenson, and Émile Zola, who served as models for his contributions in his college years to the San Francisco magazines *The Argonaut*, the *Overland Monthly*, and *The Wave*. In 1892 his father took a trip around the world by himself, returning to Chicago rather than San Francisco. His parents divorced in 1894, leaving Frank without financial support. That same year Norris left the university without attaining a degree and enrolled that fall in Harvard as a special student. In Cambridge Norris devoted most of his efforts to English 22, a popular composition course taught by Lewis E. Gates, where he worked on exercises that would appear in his novels *Vandover and the Brute*, *McTeague*, and *Blix*.

In the winter of 1895, with credentials from the *San Francisco Chronicle* that his mother had helped secure, Norris went to South Africa to cover the conflict between the Boers and the British. He arrived in Johannesburg in late December in time to witness the raid of Dr. Leander Starr Jameson to liberate the city from Boer control. He was arrested in the Boer counterattack and was ordered to leave the city, but a fever delayed his departure until January 1896. When he returned to San Francisco, he joined *The Wave* as an assistant editor, writing sketches, stories, and filler. His first novel, *Moran of the Lady Letty*, a romantic sea story of a young socialite kidnapped on the San Francisco waterfront and brought to manhood by the influence of the blond heroine Moran, was serialized in the magazine in 1898 and attracted the attention of S. S. McClure, who offered him a position in New York with the McClure syndicate and publishing firm. During the Spanish-American War Norris served as a reporter for *McClure's Magazine* in Cuba, where he covered the Santiago campaign and where he suffered a bout of malaria.

Norris came to national prominence in 1899 when his novel *McTeague*, which had been completed in 1897, was published. The novel was a graphic and compelling story of the degeneration of the title character, a dentist described by Norris as "a young giant, carrying his huge shock of blonde hair six feet three inches from the ground; moving his immense limbs, heavy with ropes of muscle, slowly, ponderously," suggesting "the draught horse, immensely strong, stupid, docile, obedient." McTeague's unsuccessful struggles with his elemental passions and with the impress of environment end with his murder of his wife and his own death in the alkali desert of California. The book's detailed portrayal of the lower-middle-class milieu of Polk Street in San Francisco, its exacting investigation of the nature of obsession, and its striking use of such vibrant images as the gilded tooth that hangs outside of McTeague's office and the caged canary were especially noteworthy departures. Critical opinion on the book was divided. The *Literary World* (1 Apr. 1899) took Norris to task for writing pages "for which there is absolutely no excuse" and labeled the book "false to the highest standards"; Willa Cather, on the other hand, commended Norris in the *Pittsburgh Leader* (31 Mar. 1899) for his use of "the only truthful literary method of dealing with that part of society which environment and heredity hedge about like the walls of a prison" to produce "a true story of people, courageous, dramatic, full of matter, and warm with life." Norris followed his success in September 1899 with *Blix*, the tale of how the love of the title character rejuvenated the life of the journalist Condy Rivers. *Blix* was a fictionalized account of Norris's courtship of Jeannette Black, whom he married in 1900 after a three-year acquaintance. The couple had one child. *A Man's Woman*, which Norris admitted was a poorly constructed novel in which a nurse's devotion to duty saves a fever-stricken Arctic explorer, appeared in early 1900. Norris supplemented his royalties with work as a reader of manuscripts for the firm of Doubleday and Page, which he joined in late 1899. In that position he discovered and recommended for publication Theodore Dreiser's *Sister Carrie*.

In 1901 Norris published the first novel of his proposed trilogy of the "Epic of Wheat," which was to follow wheat through its production, distribution, and consumption. The trilogy was to include *The Octopus*, the story of the struggles between wheat farmers in California's San Joaquin Valley and the Southern Pacific Railroad; *The Pit*, a tale of the Chicago Board of Trade; and *The Wolf*, a depiction of the relief of a famine in an Old World community. *The Octopus* has an epic sweep in which the travails and desires of the individual characters give way to the life-giving, impersonal power of the wheat. The poet Presley reflects at the end that good issued from the crisis that left the wheat ranchers ruined: "Falseness dies; injustice and oppression in the end of everything fade and vanish away. Greed, cruelty, selfishness, and inhumanity are short-lived; the individual suffers, but the race goes on." Although many critics found this ending unconvincing after the portrayal of the defeat of the farmers, many nonetheless applauded the scope, daring, and vibrancy of the novel.

Norris moved back to California in 1902, finding New York and Chicago difficult places in which to work. In the summer he had an attack of appendicitis. The acute pain necessitated an operation, which revealed gangrene and peritonitis. He died of peritonitis in San Francisco. His death ended research on *The Wolf*. Published posthumously in 1903 were *The Pit*, his most financially successful novel, and *The Responsibilities of the Novelist*, a collection of essays written for the periodical press on the art and business of fiction writing. *The Pit*, which centered on the romance of business in which the joy of competition rather than greed was seen to drive capitalists, was relatively limited in scope; the wheat, which had been his great theme in *The Octopus*, does not make an appearance. *Vandover and the Brute*, which publishers had rejected during Norris's lifetime for its shocking portrayal of the reversion of a socially prominent youth into an animal-like being, was published, with amendments by Norris's brother Charles, in 1914.

Norris intended his fiction to challenge the literary conventions of his day. Critical of the insistence that literature reveal the common and average range of human behavior in polite language, he argued in "A Plea for Romantic Fiction" (1901) that only by taking cognizance of variations could fiction penetrate below the surface of things to true life forces. It was necessary, he contended, to explore "the unplumbed depths of the human heart, and the mystery of sex, and the problems of life, and the black, unsearched penetralia of the soul of man." For much of the twentieth century critics have taken these injunctions as a valid description of Norris's own fiction, hailing *McTeague* and *The Octopus* as landmarks in a naturalistic fiction of degeneration, sordid environment, and operation of chance that challenged the prevailing complacency of polite letters in the nineteenth century. Typical is Ludwig Lewisohn's judgment in *Expression in America* (1932) that Norris "definitely and finally broke the genteel tradition." Criticism in the last third of the twentieth century has tended to modify or dispute this view, fastening on the predictable love stories in such works as *Blix*, *A Man's Woman*, and *The Pit*, his often adolescent and racialist prating, the conservative implications of his determinism of instincts and impulses, and the contradictions between Norris's stated conclusions and the action and character that he portrayed. If Norris's brand of naturalism did not fully sustain itself, his departures during his short career did provide paths for writers who followed him.

• Norris's papers, including extant manuscripts, are in the Bancroft Library of the University of California, Berkeley. Franklin Walker, ed., *The Letters of Frank Norris* (1956), and James D. Hart, ed., *A Novelist in the Making: A Collection of Student Themes and the Novels* Blix *and* Vandover and the Brute (1970), contain important published source material. Norris's short stories were collected in *The Third Circle* (1909) and vol. 10 of *The Collected Works* (1928). William Dean Howells, "Frank Norris," *North American Review* (Dec. 1902): 769–78, is the most complete contemporary retrospective of Norris's career. Franklin Walker, *Frank Norris: A Biography* (1932), has continued to be seen as the definitive biography. Maxwell Geismar, *Rebels and Ancestors: The American Novel, 1890–1915* (1953), contains an appreciation of Norris's influence on challenges to the Genteel Tradition. Donald Pizer, *The Novels of Frank Norris* (1966), is a thorough and complete analysis of his entire output, with a special emphasis on the sources from which Norris drew. Donald Graham, ed., *Critical Essays on Frank Norris* (1980), contains a variety of perspectives and is especially informative on the "lesser" fiction. Larzer Ziff, *The American 1890s: Life and Times of a Lost Generation* (1966), contains a valuable reevaluation of Norris's career and his symbolic meaning for his generation. Barbara Hochman, *The Art of Frank Norris, Storyteller* (1988), is an examination of the style of an author who claimed to reject any stylistic considerations. Modern-day reevaluations can be found in Walter Benn Michaels, *The Gold Standard and the Logic of Naturalism* (1987), and Lee Clark Mitchell, "Naturalism and the Languages of Determinism," in *The Columbia Literary History of the United States*, ed. Emory Elliott et al. (1988). Obituaries are in the *New York Times*, 26 Oct. 1902, *Current Literature* (Dec. 1902), and *The Critic* (Mar. 1903).

DANIEL H. BORUS

NORRIS, George William (11 July 1861–2 Sept. 1944), congressman and senator, was born in Sandusky County, Ohio, the son of Chauncey Norris and Mary Magdalene Mook, farmers. Three years old when his father died, "Willie" learned to do hard work while he was no more than a child. Graduating from Northern Indiana Normal School (later named Valparaiso University) in 1880 and from law school at Valparaiso, Norris was admitted to the bar in 1883. He taught school before moving west in 1885 to the Great Plains state of Nebraska, where he built a law practice first in Beaver City and later in McCook. Much of his legal practice involved mortgage-loan services for financial and insurance companies. In 1889 Norris married Pluma Lashley, the daughter of a prosperous businessman in Beaver City. The couple had three daughters. After Pluma's death in 1901, Norris married Ella Leonard, a McCook schoolteacher, in 1903. They had no children.

Hard times, a shortage of rain, declining prices for farm products, along with heavy mortgages and high interest rates led to agrarian protest movements on the

Great Plains. William Jennings Bryan, a Nebraska Democrat, made his political career by appealing to that agrarian discontent at the same time that Norris was getting started there. Though Norris observed those economic difficulties and later became a leading insurgent and progressive, he was a Republican politically and did not share Bryan's agrarian radicalism. In those troubled times Norris was quite conservative.

Norris became increasingly active politically, however, and in 1892 won election as county prosecuting attorney and, in 1895, as judge of the Fourteenth Judicial District. In 1902 he was elected to the U.S. House of Representatives from the Fifth District of Nebraska, a position he filled for five terms, until 1913. In 1912 he was elected U.S. senator from Nebraska, and he served in that capacity for thirty years.

In the House of Representatives, Norris initially did not identify particularly with the Progressive movement that was gaining momentum in those years. He quietly learned the essentials for legislative effectiveness, including a thorough knowledge of parliamentary procedures, mastery of details on legislative issues at hand, a talent for compromise, courage, and persistence. He sought ways to make democratic government more efficient. Throughout his career his greatest impact grew logically out of House and Senate committees on which he served and out of his concern for agriculture, labor, and small business. He first won national attention in 1910, when he played the central role in breaking the iron hand control that Speaker of the House Joseph G. Cannon had exercised over legislative matters in the House. He accomplished that through a coalition of insurgent Republicans and Democrats that deprived the Speaker of membership on the House Rules Committee, and by providing that members of that powerful committee would be chosen by the House rather than by the Speaker. Gradually Norris became more progressive on public issues. Others among western agrarian progressives were more colorful orators than he, but none surpassed him in legislative and parliamentary skills. He prided himself on his independence, honesty, courage, and integrity. Neither presidents nor party organizations controlled his positions on public issues.

Norris focused his attention largely on domestic matters, but he also gained prominence for positions he took on foreign affairs. He opposed American intervention in Latin American countries, worried about excessive expenditures on a big navy, and after World War I erupted in 1914, insisted that the United States should remain neutral and not become a belligerent in that European war. In April 1917 he was one of only six senators who voted against the American declaration of war on Germany and the Central Powers. In 1919–1920, after the war, he voted against the Versailles treaty and American membership in the League of Nations. He never repudiated the positions he took on those issues and was identified in the public mind with so-called "isolationism."

In the 1920s Senator Norris increasingly identified with insurgency against conservative Republican presidential policies, supporting Al Smith for president in 1928. Reflecting his background, his Nebraska constituency, and the hard times that farmers were suffering in that so-called "prosperity decade," Norris and other insurgents attacked the privileged positions of urban big business and finance and battled on behalf of western farmers. He supported variations of the McNary-Haugen farm bills that never successfully overcame presidential vetoes. The Herbert Hoover administration's Agriculture Marketing Act of 1929 fell short of the wishes of Norris and of the needs of hard-pressed farmers.

In the 1920s, however, Norris gained greatest attention for his long and persistent political efforts to convert the federal government's World War I Muscle Shoals facilities in Alabama into a public power and regional planning program. That brought him into direct confrontation with wealthy and powerful private utility companies as well as with presidential leadership in his own Republican party.

Though his efforts on behalf of the farmer and public power failed during the 1920s, Senator Norris successfully pushed through approval of the Norris–La Guardia Anti-Injunction Act of 1932 on behalf of organized labor and the Twentieth Amendment to the Constitution ending "lame-duck" sessions of Congress.

Through all of this Norris never really had a comfortable relationship with the presidency—whatever the party or circumstances. That all changed with the election of Franklin D. Roosevelt in 1932. Though Roosevelt was a Democrat and Norris a Republican, the two men saw eye to eye on most issues. Roosevelt courted the Nebraska senator, emphasizing particularly the public power issue. Norris did not agree with Roosevelt on all issues and Roosevelt might not have been his first choice, but he considered the New Yorker the best hope for those who sought progressive reforms in the United States. Norris endorsed Roosevelt for the presidency before the nominating convention in 1932 and campaigned actively for his election. Norris could have had a cabinet position if he had been willing to make himself available—which he did not. Throughout his years in the White House, Roosevelt conferred frequently with the Nebraska senator on policies and tactics.

Most importantly, President Roosevelt's support enabled Norris to accomplish his goal of converting the Muscle Shoals facilities into the Tennessee Valley Authority (TVA) to produce public power and implement regional economic planning. The Tennessee Valley Act was the first reform measure passed during the "One Hundred Days" special session called by Roosevelt after he took office in 1933. Consistent with his interest in public power and in rural America, Norris played a central role in the creation of the Rural Electrification Administration (REA) and in making it a permanent government program. With TVA in the background, Norris's persistent and skillful efforts also accomplished smaller but significant water and power projects in his home state of Nebraska. He also played a major role in winning approval for a one-house legislature in the state of Nebraska—the only state government to take that course.

Senator Norris voted for most of the New Deal legislation urged by the Roosevelt administration. Though most western progressives supported the greater part of Roosevelt's New Deal, their agrarian orientation, their distrust of eastern urban big business and finance, and their objections to big government and federal bureaucracy gave them emphases that differed in tone and substance from those of Roosevelt's New Deal liberals. Norris quietly made the transition from agrarian progressivism to New Deal liberalism more easily and comfortably than most of those "Old Progressives." And he did so without eroding the compassion and concern he always felt for the farmer, small business people, and ordinary people everywhere.

Though Norris was absorbed primarily with domestic issues and though he continued to want the United States to stay out of foreign wars and alliances, gradually he was won over to support for more active roles for the United States in world affairs. That gradual shift in his foreign policy views revealed itself when he spoke out in support of Roosevelt's proposal early in 1938 for enlarging and strengthening the American navy. He was particularly shocked and troubled by Japanese aggression and atrocities in China and East Asia. He opposed peacetime selective service legislation in 1940 and draft extension in 1941, but he supported most of President Roosevelt's proposals for extending aid short of war to the victims of Axis aggression—including the Lend Lease Act of March 1941. Norris was the only one of the leading Senate "isolationists" or noninterventionists who modified his foreign policy views and supported the president's aid-short-of-war policies before the Japanese attack on Pearl Harbor brought the United States into World War II.

Norris's political base in Nebraska seemed secure, as was his place in the Senate and his relationship with the popular president in the White House. As he grew older he gave thought to retirement, but urged on by friends and supporters (including President Roosevelt), he ran successfully for a fifth term in 1936 as an Independent Progressive—the first time he had not run as a Republican.

In 1942 he was eighty-one years old with fading strength and health; he preferred to retire. Reluctantly, he ran for a sixth term—again running as an Independent Progressive. He did very little active campaigning, however, and he lost the election. His support for President Roosevelt's foreign policies was consistent with national patterns but was less popular in small towns and rural areas across the Great Plains in Nebraska. Norris was shocked by the hostility directed against President Roosevelt and his policies by Nebraskans in both Republican and Democratic circles. Norris was saddened (really embittered) by what he saw as the lack of appreciation shown him in the 1942 election by farmers and townspeople for his ef-

forts on their behalf over the course of his forty years in Congress.

Though Roosevelt offered Norris various positions in his administration after his defeat, the old man declined them all. If his health and years had permitted, he would have welcomed an opportunity to share in planning the postwar peace. His thinking put particular priority on disarmament after the war. Norris spent his last months at his home in McCook writing his autobiography, which was published after his death there.

Despite his defeat in 1942, Norris was respected in and out of Congress for his political courage, legislative skills, integrity, honesty, and positive legislative accomplishments. In a nationwide poll, professional historians and political scientists across the country in 1957 ranked Norris as the greatest senator in American history, even ahead of such giants as Henry Clay and Daniel Webster. It was an impressive tribute to a man who had served his country and its people well through a long and honorable public career.

• Norris's papers are in the Manuscript Division of the Library of Congress, Washington, D.C., and are open for use by researchers. Norris's own autobiography, written in McCook, Nebr., without ready access to his correspondence files and when his health was failing, is George W. Norris, *Fighting Liberal: The Autobiography of George W. Norris* (1945). Though several biographies of him have been written, the most thoroughly researched and comprehensive is the three-volume work by Richard Lowitt, *George W. Norris: The Making of a Progressive, 1861–1912* (1963), *George W. Norris: The Persistence of a Progressive, 1913–1933* (1971), and *George W. Norris: The Triumph of a Progressive, 1933–1944* (1978). A briefer, more analytical study that takes a topical approach to Norris's views and actions is Norman L. Zucker, *George W. Norris: Gentle Knight of American Democracy* (1966).

WAYNE S. COLE

NORRIS, Isaac (26 July 1671–4 June 1735), Quaker politician, provincial Pennsylvania officeholder, and merchant, was born in Southwark, London, England, the son of Thomas Norris, a Quaker carpenter, and Mary Moore. About 1678 his family immigrated to Port Royal, Jamaica. The extent of his formal education is unknown, but in adulthood he was well read in both classical Latin authors and the best of contemporary English literature. He first visited Philadelphia on a trading voyage in 1692; during his absence his father was killed in the earthquake that destroyed Port Royal on 7 June 1692, and his brother and sister died shortly thereafter. Norris settled permanently in Philadelphia about 1693. He gained important political and commercial connections through his marriage in 1694 to Mary Lloyd, a daughter of Thomas Lloyd, a former deputy governor of the province. The couple had fourteen children, including Isaac Norris (1701–1766).

Norris was elected to the provincial assembly in the years 1699–1701, 1703, and 1705. He became close friends with William Penn during Penn's second visit to Pennsylvania. In 1706 Norris went to England, remaining there two years, during which time he was instrumental in negotiating a settlement of Penn's legal dispute with the heirs of his steward Philip Ford, to whom Penn had mortgaged Pennsylvania in 1696. After returning to Pennsylvania, Norris was a member of the governor's council from 1709 until his death. He was also elected to the assembly in the years 1710–1713, 1715–1716, and 1718–1720, serving as Speaker of the House in the assemblies of 1712 and 1720. In 1711 Penn appointed Norris one of his five commissioners of property, charged with overseeing the sale of Pennsylvania land to discharge Penn's debts; later Penn, in his will, made Norris one of the trustees of the province. Norris was an alderman of the city of Philadelphia from 1713 to 1727, and he was elected to a one-year term as mayor of the city in 1724. He was a justice of the Philadelphia County courts continuously from 1715 until his death, becoming president justice in 1726. After 1720 he also served several years as a master in Chancery court. In 1731 he declined appointment as chief justice of the Pennsylvania Supreme Court. Against his own inclination, he was elected to a final term in the assembly in 1734 because of his personal antipathy to Andrew Hamilton, who then dominated the political scene in Pennsylvania.

After his 1708 return from England, Norris was second only to James Logan, the provincial and proprietary secretary, as the chief representative of the Penn family's interests in Pennsylvania. He led the successful drive to oust the anti-Penn faction headed by David Lloyd from the colonial assembly at the election of 1710. This he accomplished, in part, by publishing an influential pamphlet, *Friendly Advice to the Inhabitants of Pennsylvania* (1710), which condemned the assemblies of the years 1706–1709 for failing to act in the best interests of the colony. Norris later became an implacable opponent of Sir William Keith, the last governor of Pennsylvania personally appointed by William Penn, who was in office from 1717 until his removal by the Penn family in 1726. Norris believed that Keith betrayed the Penns' trust by aiming to disrupt the colony in order to force the British Crown to take Pennsylvania away from the proprietary family and, presumably, install Keith himself as royal governor. Norris's transatlantic commercial interests led him to oppose Keith's populist program of emission of paper money by the Pennsylvania government as a remedy for the depressed colonial economy of the early 1720s. He denounced paper money as "Vile Bills of Credit[,] the contrivance & refuge of Bankrupts & designers" because the paper currency drove coin out of circulation, which complicated his exchanges with England (Norris Letterbook, 1716–1730, p. 395). He feared the consequences of the unrestricted immigration into Pennsylvania in the 1720s of thousands of German and Scots-Irish colonists, who might be made use of by Keith for political purposes as "an oblig'd & Engaged Army of Mirmydons" (Letterbook, 1716–1730, p. 422). At the same time, and for the same reason, he deeply resented Keith's involvement of working-class Philadelphians in the political process because they were, in Norris's view, "that Sort of People who . . . may be Truly call[e]d A Mob" (Letterbook, 1716–1730, p. 516).

Within ten years of his settlement in Philadelphia, Norris had become one of the most prosperous merchants in Pennsylvania. Involved to a limited extent in the export of furs and tobacco, he concentrated mainly on the overseas provision trade, shipping flour, bread, and other foodstuffs to the West Indies and Europe. His involvement in the provision trade led him to invest in shipping and in milling operations. He also invested heavily in real estate, both in and near Philadelphia and on the frontier. In 1704, in partnership with the merchant William Trent, Norris bought 7,500 acres on the Schuylkill River, including the site of present-day Norristown, from William Penn, Jr. He later bought Trent's share in this land; he also bought from Trent the Slate Roof House in Philadelphia, which had been William Penn's residence during his second visit to the colony.

Norris developed an estate, "Fairhill," in the Northern Liberties of Philadelphia, where he resided after 1717. A devoted but undogmatic Quaker, Norris was an active member of Philadelphia Monthly Meeting for nearly forty years, and he served eighteen years as clerk (chief officer) of Philadelphia Yearly Meeting. Norris suffered a stroke while attending a Quaker meeting in Germantown, Pennsylvania; he was taken to James Logan's home, where he died.

Despite his years of public service, Norris was a reluctant officeholder who wrestled with the problem of reconciling Quaker religious principles with participation in the civil government of a colony inhabited by both Quakers and individuals of other religious denominations who did not share Quaker scruples against the use of force and the taking of oaths. Conflict in both the civil and religious realms deeply disturbed him; he wrote to one correspondent, "I really Love peace and good will . . . to & w[i]th all good men" (Letterbook, 1709–1716, p. 517).

• The various Norris family manuscript collections, including eight volumes of Isaac Norris's letterbooks, in the Historical Society of Pennsylvania, constitute the most important source for Norris's life and career. Other Norris material can be found in the Penn and Logan manuscript collections at the historical society. Some important Norris material can be found in Richard S. Dunn and Mary Maples Dunn, eds., *Papers of William Penn* (5 vols., 1981–1987). Published sources for Norris's political career include the proceedings of the Pennsylvania Assembly in the *Pennsylvania Archives*, 8th ser., vols. 1–3 (1931), and the *Minutes of the Provincial Council*, Colonial Records, vols. 2 and 3 (1852). Minutes of the Quaker meetings in which Norris was active are found at the Friends Historical Library, Swarthmore College. An account of the Norris family appears in John W. Jordan, *Colonial and Revolutionary Families of Pennsylvania*, vol. 1 (1911; repr. 1978).

JEFFREY L. SCHEIB

NORRIS, Isaac (23 Oct. 1701–13 July 1766), Quaker political leader and Philadelphia merchant, was born in Philadelphia, the son of Isaac Norris and Mary Lloyd, who as members of the Society of Friends joined in William Penn's "Holy Experiment" and settled in Philadelphia in 1694. The junior Isaac Norris was educated at the Friends' School. In adulthood he was, like his father, devoted to books; as his biographer George Washington Norris wrote, Norris "might indeed be called learned; for, in addition to a knowledge of Hebrew, he wrote in Latin and French with ease, and his reading was extensive." By the time Norris came of age, his father had been for many years one of Philadelphia's most successful merchants. The family was prosperous enough to send Norris to England in 1722 for several months; he returned to England for a longer visit in 1734–1735, at which time he also traveled on the Continent. He managed the family firm, Norris and Company, during his father's later years and became the senior partner after his father died in 1735. Norris married Sarah Logan, James Logan's eldest daughter, on 6 June 1739; they had two daughters: Mary, later the wife of statesman John Dickinson, and Sarah.

Like his father before him, Norris entered politics while still in his twenties, serving as a member of the common council of Philadelphia from 1727 to 1730 and as an alderman from 1730 to 1742. He was chosen to represent Philadelphia County as a member of the Assembly of Pennsylvania in 1735, succeeding his late father. In 1742 Norris moved from his famous "Slateroof House" in Philadelphia to "Fairhill," the estate in the Northern Liberties of Philadelphia that his father had developed. He retired from active involvement in his business in 1743 to devote himself entirely to public affairs; his wife died the following year. During his tenure as an assemblyman, which lasted until 1766, he was for a long time the Speaker of the assembly (1751–1764), and he represented Pennsylvania at the Indian Conferences held it Albany, New York, in 1745 and 1754. Norris also participated in a variety of civic and charitable organizations, including the College and Academy of Philadelphia, which he served as a trustee from 1751 to 1755.

During Norris's first term as Speaker in 1751, the assembly had the statehouse enlarged by the addition of an entrance tower, which was to be topped by a bell manufactured in England. Norris's instructions, that the bell "be cast by the best workmen, and examined carefully before it is shipped," were plainly ignored, and the bell cracked on its arrival in Pennsylvania and later cracked again after being recast. The passage from Leviticus that Norris chose to adorn the bell, "Proclaim Liberty throughout the land, unto all the inhabitants thereof," was to hold deep significance for later generations. The text, originally chosen to honor Penn's proclamation of religious liberty fifty years earlier, took on new meaning after the Declaration of Independence was adopted in a room below the belfry in 1776. The Liberty Bell has symbolized the ideals proclaimed in that document ever since.

Norris's political career was shaped above all by the demographic transformation of mid-eighteenth-century Pennsylvania society, which had serious conse-quences for the social position of Friends and the political role they played. Norris led the Quaker party during a long transitional period in which it maintained its hegemony in the assembly even though Friends were increasingly becoming a minority in the colony's population. The party maintained control by gerrymandering Pennsylvania's electoral districts so as to underrepresent the colony's new counties, where fewer Quakers lived, and through the calculated allotment of political patronage. Under Norris's leadership, the Quakers in government stood united in their adherence to what historian Alan Tully has termed the "ideology of civil Quakerism." While other sects tended to dissolve in factionalism, the Quakers remained cohesive and disciplined.

The glue that held the disparate groups within the Quaker party together in Norris's day was their shared opposition to proprietary government. Norris, like almost all second-generation Quakers, took a much more critical view of William Penn's descendants than Quakers of Norris's father's generation had held of Penn himself. In particular, the Penns' refusal to pay any taxes on their vast proprietary estates aroused the Quaker party's concerted opposition. The dispute with the Penns was further complicated by the Quakers' unyielding pacifism. When Deputy Governor George Thomas asked the assembly to raise funds to provide for the defense of the colony against possible Spanish invasion, the Quakers refused, declaring that they would put their trust in God and the mother country rather than compromise their scruples. The assembly thus declined to appropriate moneys for military use or to raise a militia. The conflict persisted until the end of the French and Indian War in 1763. Norris, whose steadfast pacifist principles made him a hero to Quaker historians, was so conspicuous in this dispute that Pennsylvanians often referred to the Quaker majority in the assembly as the "Norris party." Norris was a particularly sharp thorn in the side of Deputy Governor Robert Hunter Morris, who once provoked Norris to rise from the Speaker's chair during an especially acrimonious debate, declaring, "No man shall ever stamp his foot on my grave and say, Curse him! here lies one who basely betrayed the liberties of his country."

Norris's opposition to the Penn family extended only so far, however. Although only ill health prevented Norris from traveling to England with Benjamin Franklin to represent the antiproprietary faction in 1757, he broke with Franklin and other more radical leaders of the Quaker party over the proposal to transform Pennsylvania from a proprietary to a royal colony. Norris resigned as Speaker on 20 May 1764 rather than subscribe his requisite signature to the petition for a royal colonial charter that the assembly had approved. (Historians differ as to whether Norris in fact resigned because of his poor health or because of his disapproval of the petition.) Franklin succeeded Norris as Speaker but lost his seat in the following fall election. Norris was once again elected Speaker in October, resigning, however, after only a few meetings of the assembly.

Norris retained his seat in the house, nevertheless, and was reelected in 1765. Then his health declined further, and he died the following year at Fairhill. Norris bequeathed his impressive library, built on the foundation of the carefully hoarded stock of books inherited from his father, to his son-in-law John Dickinson; Dickinson donated the collection to Dickinson College in Carlisle, Pennsylvania, in 1784.

• The papers of Isaac Norris and the Norris family are in the manuscript collections of the Historical Society of Pennsylvania in Philadelphia. The standard biography is George W. Norris, "Biography of Isaac Norris," *Pennsylvania Magazine of History and Biography* 1, 4 (1877): 449–54. Numerous works are available about the Norris era in Pennsylvania politics, including Gary B. Nash, *The Urban Crucible: Social Change, Political Consciousness, and the Origins of the American Revolution* (1979); Bruce C. Daniels, ed., *Power and Status: Officeholding in Colonial America* (1986); Alan Tully, *Forming American Politics: Ideals, Interests, and Institutions in Colonial New York and Pennsylvania* (1994); Milton Flower, *John Dickinson: Conservative Revolutionary* (1983); James Hutson, *Pennsylvania Politics, 1746–1770: The Movement for Royal Government and Its Consequences* (1972); and William S. Hanna, *Benjamin Franklin and Pennsylvania Politics* (1964).

GEORGE BOUDREAU

NORRIS, J. Frank (18 Sept. 1877–20 Aug. 1952), fundamentalist pastor, preacher, and evangelist, was born John Franklyn Norris at Dadeville, Alabama, the son of James Warren Norris and Mary Davis, poverty-stricken farmers. The family moved from Alabama to Hubbard, Texas, as sharecroppers when Norris was eleven years old. Converted at age thirteen during a brush arbor revival, he soon thereafter felt a call to the ministry. He was graduated from Baylor University (B.A.) in 1903 and from the Southern Baptist Theological Seminary (Th.M.) in 1905. While at Baylor he met and in 1902 married Lillian Gaddy, the daughter of the general missionary for the Texas Baptist General Convention. They became the parents of four children.

Norris's first full-time pastorate, from 1905 to 1908, was the McKinney Avenue Baptist Church in Dallas, where he built attendance from fewer than 100 to nearly 1,000 persons. He also served from 1906 to 1909 as the business manager and later as the editor of the *Baptist Standard*, the voice of the Southern Baptist Convention in Texas. As editor Norris successfully campaigned against racetrack gambling at the state fair, criticized denominational leaders for "centralizing" tendencies, and worked with B. H. Carroll to relocate the Southwestern Baptist Theological Seminary from Waco to Fort Worth. In 1909 he accepted a call to the First Baptist Church of Fort Worth, a congregation he served from 1909 to 1952. From 1934 to 1948 he was also the minister of the Temple Baptist Church in Detroit, commuting by train or airplane on alternate Sundays between these large preaching posts.

Norris claimed that he was minister of the largest number of people in the world under a single pastor's leadership, about 25,000. Many of Norris's members in Detroit were transplanted southerners drawn to that city by the automobile industry and attracted to Norris's church by his southern ways of expression. Norris's churches were defined by his fundamentalist theology (including emphasis on biblical inerrancy and the premillennial second coming of Jesus), colorful preaching, programs of home visitation, a well-organized Sunday school, wide publicity, and strident pronouncements on social and political issues. Norris also traveled extensively in the United States, conducting revivals in forty-six states and speaking as a debater and preacher on behalf of fundamentalist causes. His revivals in Houston and San Antonio in the 1920s drew numerous converts.

Norris edited his own tabloid newspaper known as the *Fence Rail* (1917–1921), *The Searchlight* (1921–1927), and *The Fundamentalist* (1927–1952). He used it to publish his flamboyant, hard-hitting sermons, to expose his understanding of sin in individuals and in society, and to bring his readers news of fundamentalism. Norris claimed for *The Fundamentalist*, which competed against the *Baptist Standard*, 80,000 readers. He was also a pioneer radio preacher, conducting at the peak of his ministry weekly broadcasts over twenty-seven stations, reaching most of the nation with dramatic rhetoric and ultraconservative theology.

When he was no longer welcomed by the Southern Baptist Convention, Norris founded in 1933 the Premillennial, Baptist, Missionary Fellowship, renamed in 1939 as the Fundamental Baptist Missionary Fellowship with Norris as its head. The fellowship supported foreign missions and the Bible Institute that met in Norris's church and was designed to prepare men for the ministry in the fellowship. In 1944 the institute was renamed the Bible Baptist Seminary. In 1950 the fellowship divided into the World Baptist Fellowship, which remained loyal to Norris's leadership, and the Baptist Bible Fellowship, which broke with him because of his domineering ways.

Norris's life was a story of storm and controversy. At Baylor he led a student revolt that helped force the resignation of the president. In the local church, he dismissed officials and boards almost at will, replacing them with individuals of his own choosing or not replacing them at all. He did not spare civic leaders. In 1911, in the midst of a campaign against alcohol, prostitution, and municipal corruption, Norris preached a sermon entitled "The Ten Biggest Devils in Fort Worth, Names Given." He invited them to dispute the charges, but the only one who responded was hooted off the platform. In 1926 Norris stirred up anti-Catholic feelings by accusing the Catholic mayor of Fort Worth of directing city funds to Catholic institutions and by attacking the mayor's personal character. In the midst of these charges and the tensions they created, Norris shot and killed in his study at the church an unarmed lumberman-friend of the mayor. Norris was indicted and charged with murder. His attorneys argued that he had shot in self-defense when a drunken stranger of unsavory reputation created an "apparent danger." After deliberating for forty minutes, the jury found Norris not guilty. The event, however, left Norris and his movement with a lifelong notoriety. In the presidential election of 1928 Norris campaigned arduously against the Catholic Alfred E. Smith on behalf of "that Christian gentleman and statesman, Herbert Hoover." Norris spoke 119 times in thirty cities over three and a half months and contributed to Smith's defeat and Hoover's Republican victory, even though the Democrats in Texas held a majority of more than 400,000 voters.

Norris's conflicts with denominations, especially the Southern Baptist Convention, were lengthy, bitter, and spectacular. He disliked the convention because it failed to respect the independence of the local church and because its leaders seemed to him too tolerant of theological liberalism. Norris's acerbic charges led to disciplinary action against him. The Pastor's Conference at Fort Worth expelled Norris in 1914; the Tarrant County Baptist Association excluded him in 1922; and the Baptist General Convention of Texas censured Norris in 1922, declined to recognize his delegate in 1923, and in 1924 ousted both minister and church from the state organization. Norris basked in the publicity of these controversies and reacted by declining to use denominational literature, withholding financial support, throwing his weight in the direction of fundamentalist organizations like the World's Christian Fundamentals Association and the Baptist Bible Union, and finally founding his own fellowship of churches. During his last decades, he crusaded against evolution, supported Zionism, and added a strident voice to anti–Russian Communist causes. In the 1930s one of Norris's sermons led to the conversion of John Birch, a student at Mercer University who followed Norris to Fort Worth, attended his institute, and became a missionary to China under his auspices. When Birch was killed in China, the John Birch Society, an anti-Communist organization, was named after him. Norris died while attending a youth rally in Keystone Heights, Florida. The funeral service in Fort Worth was attended by 5,000 people. Characteristically, Norris was buried in a red tie, a white shirt, and a blue suit.

Few people were neutral about Norris. His followers saw him as a courageous and undaunted spiritual leader with exceptional preaching ability, a persistent critic of personal and social wrongdoing, and an imaginative spokesperson for the disinherited, those to whom Norris referred as the "folks at the fork of the creek." Others viewed him as an independent, dogmatic, and militant dictator who maligned anyone who differed with him, divided churches, and disrupted denominations. He was one of three preachers who gave to first-generation fundamentalism its public image, the other two being John Roach Straton of New York and W. B. Riley of Minnesota. His extremism illustrated the diversity within the ranks of fundamentalist leaders. An integral figure in right-wing politics in the United States, Norris exemplified the vituperation and violence that occasionally marked both religion and politics in America.

• The papers of Norris from 1928 to 1952 are located at the Dargan-Carver Library of the Southern Baptist Convention, Nashville, Tenn. Primary sources may also be found in his newspapers. Norris wrote several books, although invariably these are collections of sermons and debates stenographically recorded. The most important is *Inside History of the First Baptist Church, Fort Worth; and Temple Baptist Church, Detroit, Life Story of J. Frank Norris* (n.d.). Two books written appreciatively about Norris by pastoral associates are Louis Entzminger, *The J. Frank Norris I Have Known for Thirty-four Years* (1946), and E. Ray Tatum, *Conquest or Failure? Biography of J. Frank Norris* (1966). A sympathetic treatment is also found in George W. Dollar, *A History of Fundamentalism in America* (1973). More critical studies include Clovis Gwin Morris, "He Changed Things: The Life and Thought of J. Frank Norris" (Ph.D. diss., Texas Tech Univ., 1973); C. Allyn Russell, "J. Frank Norris: Violent Fundamentalist," in *Voices of American Fundamentalism: Seven Biographical Studies* (1976); and R. G. Toulouse, "A Case Study in Schism: J. Frank Norris and the Southern Baptist Convention," *Foundations* 24 (Jan. 1981): 32–53.

C. ALLYN RUSSELL

NORRIS, Kathleen Thompson (16 July 1880–18 Jan. 1966), novelist, was born in San Francisco, California, the daughter of James Alden Thompson, a bank manager, and Josephine E. Moroney. The family lived for a few years in Mill Valley, northeast of San Francisco. Kathleen was tutored at home and studied in a Dominican convent school in San Rafael. The deaths in 1899 of both parents one month apart left Kathleen and her older brother to care for their four younger siblings and an invalid aunt as well. A small family legacy soon went to pay bills.

While her older brother worked for an electrical company and her sister Teresa taught in a private kindergarten, Kathleen worked in a hardware store. She studied creative writing at the University of California for one term (Fall 1903), but she had to quit to earn more money and became a librarian. She sold a short story to the *Argonaut* in 1904, sent sketches on the San Francisco earthquake and fire of 1906 to the *San Francisco Call*, and was hired to write society columns for the *Call* and for two other newspapers as well. She published more short stories. In 1908 she met Charles Gilman Norris, the younger brother of novelist Frank Norris. Charles Norris was art editor of the *American Magazine* in New York City, where he and Kathleen were married in 1909 and where they made their first home. She placed three short stories in the *New York Telegram*. Her first novel, *Mother*, was based on her own childhood experiences with her mother. Originally published as a short story in the *American Magazine* and expanded to triple its length, it became a runaway bestseller with more than 1.5 million copies in print. Three of her novels, all early ones—*Mother*, *The Heart of Rachael* (1916), and *Harriet and the Piper* (1920)—were on bestseller lists.

Norris was a prolific writer. Before 1920 she published eleven novels; in the 1920s, twenty-two more; in the 1930s, twenty-eight more; and so on. She published articles, short fiction, and serial installments of novels in *American Magazine, Collier's, Good Housekeeping, Ladies' Home Journal,* the *Saturday Evening Post,* and *Woman's Home Companion.* Typically, an item by Norris in a given magazine would boost its sales by as much as 100,000 copies. Edward Bok, editor of *Ladies' Home Journal,* was delighted when Norris let him serialize her novel *Mother* after it had appeared in book form.

Although Charles Norris himself wrote eleven novels and three plays between 1916 and 1944, he was even busier as his wife's mentor and literary agent. In 1920 they moved to San Francisco. Ultimately, she wrote eighty-one novels and seven other books, rang up sales totaling 10 million copies, earned $9 million, and was the highest-paid writer in the United States at the time. She and her husband had a son, who became a physician, and twin daughters, who died in infancy; they later adopted a second son. When her sister Teresa, who had married poet-critic William Rose Benét, died during the World War I influenza epidemic, the Norrises made a home for her three children as well. They also relished playing host and hostess to innumerable friends—not least among them Noël Coward, Herbert Hoover, Charles Lindbergh, Harpo Marx, and Theodore Roosevelt, Jr.—in their spacious, 200-acre ranch home near Saratoga, California. In addition, they traveled extensively.

Norris developed a writing method that was simple and obviously effective. She would play solitaire, think about various character combinations and incidents while doing so, and then effortlessly type out a single draft. She could write with children—and, later, grandchildren—playing around her desk. For a quarter of a century she also wrote for the Bell Newspaper Syndicate. In 1945 she wrote scripts for "Bright Horizons," a radio soap opera. She devoted much time and energy campaigning for women's rights and prohibition and against the death penalty, was committed to pacifism, worked with Lindbergh on the America First Committee before World War II began, and later argued for a ban on nuclear-weapons testing. Her novels were always too sentimental to admit of much moralizing, but they regularly featured strong female characters and occasionally included hints favoring pacifism.

Norris once explained that her formula for plots was to place a woman in trouble and then get her out of it. A given heroine would often be young, innocent, poor, and eager for life's delights; she would be drawn to a higher, and more dangerous, social level—one of opulence and conspicuous consumption—and be morally challenged. Norris could adeptly sketch the tempting glitter of riches and deftly describe the banquets, servants, country-club activities, and accoutrements of sporty idlers. She said that she aimed her works directly at her female readership, was never aware in her own psyche of any dark side that modern authors fretted over too often, and—given her Roman Catholic upbringing—steadfastly avoided the seamy and the vulgar. Her most ambitious novel was *Certain People of Importance* (1922), a 486-page, multigenerational history of a New England family migrating to the Midwest and then California. Titles of the following Norris novels suggest their contents: *The Foolish Virgin* (1928), *Mother and Son* (1929), *Second Hand Wife* (1932), *Wife for Sale* (1933), *Three Men and Diana* (1934), *Secret Marriage* (1936), *An Apple for Eve* (1942), *Mink Coat* (1946), and *Shadow Marriage* (1952). *Baker's Dozen* (1938) reprints thirteen popular Norris short stories, replete with household activities, marital difficulties, sorrows, loneliness, romance, tears, and joys.

After her husband's death in 1945, Norris wrote several more novels and enjoyed a rich family life and many friendships as she aged. She was hospitalized for severe arthritis from 1959 to 1963 and thereafter lived in her son's home in San Francisco, where she died. Over the years, reviewers of her novels either praised them for being sincere, honest, readable, and skillfully, meticulously composed, or else criticized them for being flat, dull, more of the same, and interminable. Popular and wholesome, Kathleen Thompson Norris has been accurately defined as the grandmother of the American sentimental, domestic novel.

• Norris's papers are at Stanford University and at the University of California at Los Angeles. *Who Was Who in America with World Notables,* vol. 4, *1961–1968* (1968), lists Norris's titles. Norris wrote two autobiographical books: *Noon* (1925), about her youth and early successes, and *Family Gathering* (1959, her last publication), concerning her husband, children, sister, cousins, and grandchildren. An extensive essay on Norris is in Grant Overton, *The Women Who Make Our Novels* (1928), pp. 227–42. Isabella Taves, *Successful Women and How They Attained Success* (1943), describes Norris's writing method. Details of her most popular novels are in Alice Payne Hackett and James Henry Bourke, *80 Years of Best Sellers: 1895–1975* (1977). Richard Allan Davison, *Charles G. Norris* (1983), includes valuable information about Kathleen. A detailed obituary is in the *New York Times,* 19 Jan. 1966.

ROBERT L. GALE

NORRIS, Mary Harriott (16 Mar. 1848–14 Sept. 1918), writer and educator, was born in Boonton, New Jersey, the daughter of Charles Bryan Norris and Mary Lyon Kerr. Her parents decided to send their daughter to Vassar even before its official opening. To prepare for college, Norris attended a private school where she learned Latin and chemistry, often the only girl in her class.

In her book *The Golden Age of Vassar,* first published in 1915, Norris remembers her college days. College life in Vassar's early years was fairly Spartan, filled with hard work, both physical and mental. However, the students established a strong sense of camaraderie and close ties to the faculty. Norris thoroughly enjoyed her college days and was appreciated in return, delivering the annual address at the Vassar commencement in 1872.

After graduating with an A.B. in 1870, Norris started to write novels. Her first book, *Fräulein Mina; or, Life in a North American German Family* (1872), achieved reasonable success. During her life she published more than a dozen novels, all of which received contemporary acclaim.

Her novels combined romantic tales with inspiring morality. Her aim in writing was always to be instructional. She wanted to persuade her readers, mostly young women, to remain virtuous and religious, and she was often explicit in these goals. In the preface to *Dorothy Delafield* (1886), she wrote, "The author presents *Dorothy Delafield* to the reader, hoping that earnest girls and Christian mothers will love her, and . . . will gain fresh inspiration." In addition to her novels, Norris edited a series of classic texts for use in schools, including works by Henry Wadsworth Longfellow, George Eliot, and Sir Walter Scott, and contributed to a number of periodicals.

Norris also had an active career in education. In 1880 she founded a private school in New York City, of which she remained principal for sixteen years. In 1898 she spent a year at Northwestern University as dean of women and assistant professor of English. She was the "first regularly elected Dean of Women of the University" (Wilde, p. 99). During that year she organized a students' self-governing association and created a library in the women's hall. Every Tuesday she gave a talk on religion in chapel, and on Thursday evenings her regular themes were personal hygiene, grooming, and etiquette. The class of 1899, which she supervised during her year, made her "greatly pleased" by electing her an honorary member.

After her year at Northwestern, Norris returned to her writing. She never married and spent her last years in Morristown, New Jersey, where she died. In a letter to the *New York Times* on 23 September 1918 her friend John Alfred Faulkner of Drew Theological Seminary paid her tribute when he mentioned "her gracious and noble spirit, her progressive outlook and sympathy with every right advance for women, her unconquerable diligence . . . , and her loving devotion to God and humanity."

• Norris's books include the *Ben and Bentie* series (1873–1876), *A Damsel of the Eighteenth Century* (1889), *Phebe* (1890), *Afterward* (1893), *The Nine Blessings* (1894), *John Applegate, Surgeon* (1894), *Lakewood* (1895), *The Gray House of the Quarries* (1898), *The Grapes of Wrath* (1901), *The Story of Christina* (1907), and *The Veil* (1907). Her editorial work includes *Silas Marner* (1890), *Marmion* (1891), *Evangeline* (1897), *Kenilworth* (1898), and *Quentin Durward* (1899). There is little biographical information on Mary Harriott Norris. For her college life, see her own book, *The Golden Age of Vassar*, and for her work at Northwestern University, see Arthur Herbert Wilde, *Northwestern University: A History* (1905). Many of her novels are rare and difficult to locate; however, in their introductions Norris gives considerable in-sight into her motivations and mission for writing. There is also some biographical information in the *New York Times* obituary and the letter from Faulkner on 23 Sept. 1918.

CLAIRE STROM

NORSTAD, Lauris (24 Mar. 1907–12 Sept. 1988), air force officer, was born in Minneapolis, Minnesota, the son of the Reverend Martin Norstad, a Norwegian Lutheran minister, and Marie Johnson. He grew up in Red Wing, Minnesota, and after high school received an appointment to the U.S. Military Academy, where he graduated in 1930, ranking 139 in a class of 241 students. He was commissioned into the cavalry, but in 1931 he transferred to the Air Corps, an option for young officers. Norstad's penchant for analysis as well as action, which had already been evident when he was at West Point, doubtless was a factor in his interest in a career in the Air Corps, then undergoing constant doctrinal debates as well as technological changes. During the 1930s he served as commander of the Eighteenth Pursuit Group at Schofield Barracks, Hawaii. In 1935 he married Isabelle Helen Jenkins; they had one daughter.

At the outset of World War II Norstad was assistant chief of staff for intelligence, Air Force Combat Command Headquarters at Langley Field, Virginia, and at Bolling Field, Washington, D.C. Thereafter, General Harold H. "Hap" Arnold, the commanding general of the army air forces, named Norstad to his advisory council, a body he had created to assist him in long-range planning. Arnold's purpose was to have available to him a distinctly Air Corps in-house "think tank" of bright young officers. Several months later, General Arnold assigned Norstad to the post of assistant chief of staff for operations, Twelfth Air Force. Norstad went to London to help plan the North African air campaign and then to North Africa when Operation Torch was launched. It was in the confusion of Torch—the first combined Anglo-American large-scale offensive operation of the war—that he came to the attention of General Dwight Eisenhower, who had been appointed supreme commander. In his wartime memoirs, *Crusade in Europe* (1948), Eisenhower recalled being "so impressed with his alertness, grasp of the problems and personality that I determined never to lose sight of him. He was and is one of those rare men whose capacity knows no limit" (p. 119).

In December 1943 Norstad became director of operations of the Mediterranean Allied Air Forces (MAAF), which gave him valuable experience in coalition warfare. Promoted to brigadier general in March 1943 at the age of thirty-six, he was below the age "zone" prescribed at that time. This required General George C. Marshall to request an exception to the policy from Congress. At MAAF, Norstad helped plan bombing missions against Axis forces and installations in the Balkans and in Italy. These activities helped open a second front in Europe, thus distracting German forces operating in the Soviet Union and bringing about the ultimate collapse of Italian forces and the capitulation of Italy.

In mid-1944 Norstad went to Washington, D.C., as chief of staff of the Twentieth Air Force, which was under the direct control of General Arnold. Chief of Staff Norstad assisted Arnold in planning B-29 missions against Japan that preceded the atomic bombing of Hiroshima and Nagasaki. Because of this experience, Norstad served on the Spaatz Board to study the effects of the atomic bomb on the employment, size, organization, and composition of the postwar air force, leading to the creation of the Strategic Air Command.

In 1945 Norstad became assistant chief of air staff, plans, and a year later he became director of the Plans and Operations Division, War Department General Staff, charged with planning the size and utilization of the postwar air force. In this connection, Norstad became the army's representative to work with the U.S. Senate subcommittee on legislation for unifying the armed forces under a Department of Defense. In his War Department general staff role, he was one of the four negotiators (the others being Secretary of the Navy James V. Forrestal, Assistant Secretary of War W. Stuart Symington, and Vice Admiral Forrest P. Sherman) who worked out the agreement that was embodied in the controversial Armed Forces Unification Act of 1947. From October 1947 to October 1950 Norstad was air force acting vice chief of staff for operations, responsible for implementing aerial defense and attack plans in an emergency.

When General Eisenhower was called out of retirement to become the first supreme allied commander, Europe (SACEUR) of the North Atlantic Treaty Organization (NATO), he tapped Norstad in October 1950 to become commanding general, U.S. Air Forces in Europe (USAFE). In April 1951 Norstad was named commander, Allied Air Forces, Central Europe (AFCENT), and in July 1952, at age forty-five, he became the youngest American officer to be promoted to full general (four stars). In July 1953 he became air deputy to the SACEUR, General Alfred Gruenther, and on Gruenther's retirement in 1956, Norstad became NATO's fourth SACEUR—the only air force officer to achieve this very high position, which he occupied until January 1963. At the same time, in September 1958, he was appointed commander in chief, U.S. European Command (CINCEUR).

As SACEUR, Norstad advocated using tactical nuclear weapons and giving NATO greater control over and latitude to use these weapons. He saw conventional forces as a "shield" or "tripwire," good only to serve as a means to establish the credibility of a Soviet attack, which would be met with a devastating nuclear response both in Europe and against the Soviet homeland. As he said on the CBS show, "The Twentieth Century," "If there is any question about our willingness or our ability to use these atomic weapons, it is my judgment that we have lost a great part of the deterrent effect, which is the important thing."

On Norstad's retirement on 2 January 1963 from NATO and also from the U.S. Air Force, he became president of the International Division of Owens-Corning Fiberglass and later chairman and chief executive officer of Owens-Corning Fiberglass Corporation and was also named a director. His major concern was in developing the international activities of the corporation, but he also instituted management reforms focused on planning and decentralized decision making. In the latter aspect of his duties, he encountered many of the same institutional problems associated with change that he knew so well from his military career. During the administration of President Richard Nixon, Norstad was able to continue his public service activities by serving on the President's Commission on an All-Volunteer Force and on the General Advisory Committee on Arms Control and Disarmament.

In an interview with the Cleveland *Plain Dealer* published on 28 May 1972, Norstad observed of his times and his contribution to them:

I would like to believe that in my time Americans have tried hard. Fearful wars were fought. Tyrannies were put down. Broken societies were repaired. Vast sections of mankind have found freedom. A world organization has been set to adjudicate the disputes of nations and to extend the rule of reason and of law. New alliances have been constructed to hold off the newest tyranny, and under this defensive shield we have prospered. That record, with all its imperfections, we add to our legacy to you, and without apology.

He died in Tucson, Arizona, and was buried in Arlington National Cemetery.

• General Norstad's papers are on deposit at the Eisenhower Library, Abilene, Kans. They are also on microfilm at the Air Force Historical Research Agency, Maxwell Air Force Base, Ala. His "U.S. Air Force Oral History Interview" is also on deposit at both libraries. Although General Norstad is mentioned in numerous works discussing events that occurred, in particular, after the end of World War II to his retirement in January 1963, no major biography has yet been published. Robert S. Jordan discusses General Norstad's NATO career in two books, *Political Leadership in NATO: A Study in Multinational Diplomacy* (1979) and *Generals in International Politics: NATO's Supreme Allied Commander, Europe* (1987). Other aspects of his career are discussed in Herman S. Wolk, *Planning and Organizing the Postwar Air Force, 1943–1947: The United States Air Force Official Histories* (1984); Michael S. Sherry, *The Rise of American Air Power: The Creation of Armageddon* (1987); Ronald Schaffer, *Wings of Judgment: American Bombing in World War II* (1985); and Perry McCoy Smith, *The Air Force Plans for Peace, 1943–1945* (1970). General Norstad first achieved national prominence when his picture appeared on the cover of *Life*, 1 Nov. 1948. An obituary is in the *New York Times*, 14 Sept. 1988.

ROBERT S. JORDAN

NORSWORTHY, Naomi (29 Sept. 1877–25 Dec. 1916), psychologist and educator, was born in New York City, the daughter of Samuel B. Norsworthy, a mechanical engineer, and Eve Ann Modridge. Norsworthy's parents had emigrated from England a few years before her birth. Her mother was a member of the Plymouth Brethren and instilled the values of simplicity, organization, discipline, and service in her children. Norsworthy, who never married, maintained a close relationship with her mother throughout her life.

Norsworthy had a spartan childhood, involving strict observation of religious practices and a highly disciplined approach to studies. Her most distinctive childhood memories centered on her resolve to become a teacher. At the age of fifteen, before completing high school, she entered Trenton Normal School to prepare for a teaching career. Upon completion of that training, she spent three years teaching third grade in Morristown, New Jersey.

In the fall of 1899 Norsworthy entered Teachers College of Columbia University to qualify to teach chemistry. There she attracted the attention of Edward L. Thorndike, a psychologist trained by William James and James McKeen Cattell, who recruited Norsworthy as his student assistant in psychology. In 1901 she completed a B.S. in psychology and entered Columbia's graduate program, completing her Ph.D. in 1904 with a dissertation on mental retardation in children. Thorndike's active support played a critical role in helping Norsworthy overcome opposition to the appointment and promotion of a female faculty member. Norsworthy was appointed instructor of psychology at Teachers College in 1905 and was promoted to associate professor of educational psychology in 1909. She offered Columbia's first course on the psychology of exceptional children in 1907.

Norsworthy was a hardworking and exceptionally effective teacher. Thorndike, who called her "the perfect teacher," attributed her success to "thorough, conscientious preparation" and "sympathetic insight into students' minds." She had large classes and frequently filled in for other faculty members. Despite fragile health, she supplemented her heavy teaching responsibilities with service as adviser to women and work with the Young Women's Christian Association and other social and religious organizations on campus. Norsworthy lived up to her belief that the "happiness that is abiding, calm and steady comes only through service" (Higgins, p. 212).

A well-deserved sabbatical leave in 1913 gave Norsworthy the opportunity to work on a child psychology text for teachers. She was soon forced to set this project aside in order to nurse her mother. After her mother's death in 1915, her own ill heath forestalled the completion of this work. Published posthumously with revisions and additions by her colleague Mary Theodora Whitley, *The Psychology of Childhood* (1918) presents a "descriptive study of children" organized according to Thorndike's classification of the basic instincts. Its emphasis on "the physiological basis of the tendencies" was tempered by Norsworthy's discussion of physiological plasticity and a full description of the molding, modifying power of habit. The moral and religious development of children was treated as thoroughly as their physical, intellectual, and social development. Two additional chapters—one on exceptionality in children and one on methods in child

psychology—served to make this text more comprehensive than others of the period.

A second text, *How to Teach* (1917), coauthored with colleague George Strayer, was completed in the final year of Norsworthy's life. Its central thesis was that the aim of education—"social efficiency"—is achieved by shaping each individual's abilities so they "become intelligently active for the common good." Norsworthy and Strayer's belief in the central role of individual differences led them to reject both G. Stanley Hall's recapitulation theory of development and the mental discipline approach to learning, with its emphasis on rote learning. However, they were also highly critical of the intensely individualistic attitude fostered by the overemphasis on competition in most schools. They argued that schools should provide opportunities for helpfulness, cooperation, and the development of ideals of service. Finally, they advocated the use of standardized tests to measure children's achievement, an approach that later became widespread.

Norsworthy's work in psychology earned her recognition beyond the confines of Columbia. She became a member of the American Psychological Association in 1905 and was listed in the first edition of *American Men of Science* (1906). Although she was offered other positions, she turned them down because she doubted her ability to handle increased physical exertion. The summer following her mother's death, Norsworthy was diagnosed with cancer. She died in New York City.

Norsworthy's death at the age of thirty-nine cut short her career as an educational psychologist. Her contributions were eclipsed by the reputation of Leta Stetter Hollingworth, who succeeded her at Teachers College. Nevertheless, Norsworthy was a pioneer in the study of exceptional children and in the mental testing movement. Her educational psychology, with its emphasis on active and cooperative learning and the development of social activism, anticipates much contemporary work.

• Frances Caldwell Higgins, *The Life of Naomi Norsworthy* (1918), provides a full account of Norsworthy's life; the work, however, is a tribute written by a close friend, not an authoritative biography. A cameo sketch of Norsworthy, based primarily on Higgins's work, is presented in Elizabeth Scarborough and Laurel Furumoto, *Untold Lives: The First Generation of American Women Psychologists* (1987).

DEBORAH JOHNSON

NORTH, Elisha (8 Jan. 1771–29 Dec. 1843), physician, was born in Goshen, Connecticut, the son of Joseph North, Jr., a part-time medical practitioner, and Lucy Cowles. Elisha served as an apprentice first for his father, a healer without academic medical training, and then for Lemuel Hopkins of Hartford. In 1793 the younger North began medical courses at the University of Pennsylvania. His leaving two years later without a degree was not unusual during an era when few had formal medical education. North married Hannah

Beach of Goshen in 1797; they had eight children. North returned to practice in his home town, beginning a career marked by an eclectic curiosity and a willingness to consider new ideas.

In 1800 North was one of the first in the United States to systematically carry out what he called "the business of vaccination" against smallpox. With fluid obtained from a person inoculated with smallpox in nearby New Haven, North injected a small number of patients with good success. He may have been the first in the United States to recognize a natural case of cowpox in a human and to exploit it as protection against smallpox at a time when the immunological cross-reactivity between cowpox and smallpox was still a new concept. As a result, North was able to refer a cowpox-vaccinated patient to the prominent physician and journal editor, Edward Miller of New York City. Genuine smallpox vaccine matter was unavailable in New York that winter, and Miller used fluid from North's patient to vaccinate others, praising North for opinions and practice "formed in the most judicious and accurate manner" in respect to cowpox (Bolton, p. 140). Although there was later some dispute over who first introduced cowpox vaccination to the United States, North must be ranked among the first to promote and practice the procedure.

When spotted fever arrived in Connecticut in 1807, North refused to accept the standard therapies of sweating and bleeding. His successful system-stimulating regimen included such medicaments as wine, camphor, opium, and oil of peppermint. That winter he treated sixty-five patients, losing only one. North's *A Treatise on a Malignant Epidemic, Commonly Called Spotted Fever* (1811) was the first American book written on the disease, which most likely was cerebrospinal meningitis. Fellow physicians gave North favorable reviews and even medical rivals provided him with published endorsements that later were included in a memoir of North by his grandson Henry Carrington Bolton.

In 1812 North moved his family to New London, Connecticut, where he joined the New London County Medical Society, in which he held several offices. Always concerned about the status and standards of medicine, North already was a member of the Medical Society of Litchfield County and the state medical association. In 1813 the state society awarded North an honorary M.D., making him one of the last to receive the degree at the discretion of the society, regardless of formal training.

During this period North gained considerable experience as a surgeon, especially of the eye. In the spring of 1817 he opened an eye infirmary in New London, the first in the United States. Although the infirmary was not financially successful, he wrote of it later in his *Outlines of the Science of Life*: "Our success, or exertions, probably hastened, in this country, the establishment of larger and better eye infirmaries." Little is known about North's eye infirmary, which apparently closed its doors sometime after 1829. Some historians have since argued that North may deserve more credit

for his contributions to ophthalmology than for his other achievements. In addition to his invention of a speculum oculi, North devised a method for performing lithotomy as well as other instruments such as an improved trephine, a trocar, and a new form of catheter.

North also devoted his often-witty pen and his scientific mind to issues outside his daily medical practice. In the 1820s he and his family lived for several years on a farm outside New Haven, where he experimented with peat as a fuel and reported his findings in the *American Journal of Science* (11 [1826]: 66). Opposed to a state law forbidding exhumation of bodies for the purpose of dissection, in 1829 North wrote several newspaper essays for the *Connecticut Gazette* defending the practice; including "The Rights of Anatomists Vindicated." In the 1830s North became interested in phrenology, again writing a number of newspaper articles on the topic, as well as *The Pilgrim's Progress in Phrenology* (1836) written under the name "Uncle Toby."

In 1829 North published *Outlines of the Science of Life . . .* , his broadest and most philosophical work. Topics ranged from atmospheric pressure to "the Evils of Great Cities" to "the Great First Cause, or God." Also included were William Beaumont's gastric juice studies, which Beaumont himself did not publish until 1833, the "Utility of the Medical Profession," and the poor training possessed by too many medical men. North's concept central to his views on physiology was that the vitality of the living body resided in the blood.

After North died in New London, an unidentified medical contemporary of his wrote that the multitalented physician had "exhibited a remarkable degree of caution, deliberation, and careful reflection" in his medical practice: "As a counseling physician he enjoyed the confidence and friendship of his brethren, and was much valued for his philosophical habits of mind in cases of difficulty and uncertainty" (Bolton, p. 148).

• No collection of North's papers is archived. The most comprehensive biographical account is a memoir written by North's grandson, Henry Carrington Bolton, "Memoir of Dr. Elisha North," in *Proceedings of the Connecticut Medical Society* n.s. 3 (1887): 135–60. It includes a list of North's publications as well as reprinted testimonies from his contemporaries. Other articles on North are Walter R. Steiner, "Dr. Elisha North, One of Connecticut's Most Eminent Medical Practitioners," *Johns Hopkins Hospital Bulletin* 19 (1908): 301–7; F. L. Pleadwell, "A New View of Elisha North and His Treatise on Spotted Fever," *Annals of Medical History* 6 (1924): 245–57; William Snow Miller, "William Beaumont and His Book; Elisha North and His Copy of Beaumont's Book," *Annals of Medical History* n.s. 1 (1929): 155–79; Sebastian R. Italia, "Elisha North: Experimentalist, Epidemiologist, Physician, 1771–1843," *Bulletin of the History of Medicine* 31 (1957): 505–36; and Daniel M. Albert and Marvin L. Sears, "Dr. Elisha North and the First Eye Infirmary in the United States," *American Journal of Ophthalmology* 71 (1971): 578–87.

DIANE D. EDWARDS
DANIEL M. ALBERT

NORTH, Frank Mason (3 Dec. 1850–17 Dec. 1935), Methodist Episcopal clergyman and ecumenical leader, was born in New York City, the son of Charles Carter North, a businessman, and Elizabeth Mason. He graduated with high honors in 1872 from Wesleyan College (Middletown, Conn.), where he also earned an M.A. in 1875.

North was married in 1874 to Fannie Laws Stewart; they had two sons, but she and their second son both died in 1878. Seven years later he married Louise Josephine McCoy, a member of the first graduating class (1879) of Wellesley College and a subsequent member of its faculty; they had one son. In 1892 the family moved to New York City and then in 1915 to Madison, New Jersey, where they made their home until North's death.

In 1873 North entered the ministry of the Methodist Episcopal Church and served six churches in the New York Conference and one from 1887 to 1892 in Middletown, Connecticut. From Middletown he was called to become corresponding secretary of the New York City Church Extension and Missionary Society, later the New York City Society. In that position he supervised or developed more than thirty missions and immigrant churches, including the Church of All Nations, one of the first interracial, cosmopolitan congregations. He also initiated and edited the *Christian City*, a journal serving not only the City Society but other metropolitan religious agencies locally and nationwide.

After his two decades as "home mission" executive in the New York urban area, the General Conference of the Methodist Episcopal Church elected North as corresponding secretary of its Board of Foreign Missions, a post he occupied from 1912 until his retirement in 1924. During that period, as one of an administrative triumvirate, he introduced the structure of Area secretaries (associates responsible for specific geographical regions), visited Methodist missions around the world from 1914 to 1915, and guided the church through the financial crisis of its postwar Centenary Fund, when many programs for postwar expansion and development had to be curtailed for lack of support.

Although he spent most of his life as a denominational executive, North gained greater stature as a pioneer leader of the ecumenical movement. As early as 1894 he joined with Washington Gladden, Josiah Strong, and others to form the Open and Institutional Church League for the purpose of nonsectarian evangelism and social service. This led to the establishment in 1901 of a National Federation of Churches and Christian Workers for ecumenical consultation and cooperation, an organization that was addressed the following year by President Theodore Roosevelt (1858–1919). In late 1908 many of the same church officers, who represented thirty-three denominations and seventeen million constituents, gathered to establish the Federal Council of the Churches of Christ in America. North was elected vice chairman of the Executive Committee and chairman of the Commission on the Church and Social Service for the first quadrennium, from 1908 to 1912. In the latter role he introduced a revised version of a report on "The Church and Modern Industry," which had been adopted earlier in 1908 by the Methodist Episcopal General Conference and which now became "The Social Creed of the Churches," a statement of economic, political, and humanitarian goals and principles for the wider ecumenical movement.

As chairman of the Executive Committee from 1912 to 1916 and president of the Federal Council from 1916 to 1920, North guided the churches of the nation not only in their quest for peace but also in their hope that the war would indeed "make the world safe for democracy" and create conditions for social justice and the realization of the Kingdom of God on earth.

North's commitment to social concerns had begun early. Coming from a Republican business family, he had written in college a treatise on socialism and during his pastoral ministry a major series of articles on "The Christianity of Socialism" and "The Socialism of Christianity," published in *Zion's Herald* in 1891. In all of these writings he emphasized the need for public policies of justice and social reform in addition to private charity, for cooperation instead of competition, and for the application of Christian principles to political and economic life.

North had few hobbies, but he wrote dozens of poems: for moments of personal sorrow or devotion, for missions, and for special occasions at Wesleyan or Drew University (a Methodist institution his father had helped to found and with which North was closely associated as trustee and Madison neighbor). A number of these verses appeared in the hymnals of various denominations and in several languages, but no other has remained such a favorite as "The City Hymn," first published in the *Christian City* in 1903 as "A Prayer for the Multitudes" but better known as "Where Cross the Crowded Ways of Life." Remembered as a Republican who wrote eloquently on Christian socialism and a preacher who insisted that faith be applied to poverty and injustice in the inner city, North gave impetus to the ecumenical movement and empowered millions of Christians around the world to sing a new song.

• Most of North's papers, both personal and professional, are in the library of Drew University, Madison, N.J. For further biographical information, see Creighton Lacy, *Frank Mason North: His Social and Ecumenical Mission* (1967), and *Frank Mason North* (prepared and published by friends, 1936). North's writings include his series on Christianity and socialism in *Zion's Herald* (14, 21, 28 Jan., 4 Feb. 1891); hymns in the *Christian City* (passim); and *Hymns and Other Verses* (privately published in 1931). See also Charles Howard Hopkins, *The Rise of the Social Gospel in American Protestantism, 1865–1915* (1940), and Samuel M. Cavert, *The American Churches in the Ecumenical Movement, 1900–1968* (1968).

CREIGHTON LACY

NORTH, John Ringling (14 Aug. 1903–4 June 1985), circus owner and producer, was born in Baraboo, Wisconsin, the son of Henry Whitestone North, a railroad engineer, and Ida Ringling, the only sister of the famed Ringling brothers whose circus he eventually came to control. North attended public schools in Baraboo, graduating from high school in 1921. He attended the University of Wisconsin and Yale but left the latter school in 1924 to marry Jane Connelly. They had no children and divorced in 1927. North worked briefly for an investment house on Wall Street and then as a real estate salesman in Sarasota, Florida, for John Ringling (his uncle and the man for whom he was named). When Ringling died in 1936, control of the Ringling Bros. and Barnum & Bailey Circus passed into the hands of creditors. Childless, Ringling left the bulk of his estate to the state of Florida, but in a codicil contested by other members of the family he named his nephew John Ringling North as executor. Using that position as leverage, North first convinced the other surviving members of the family, who owned a majority interest in the circus stock, to name him president of the circus corporation for the next five years. He then acquired a loan that allowed the family to pay off the circus's creditors and regain control. A labor dispute during 1938, the first year of his management, left the circus crippled and helpless in Scranton, Pennsylvania, and threatened to ruin North's chances of saving the circus. In response he took the Ringling show off the road for the remainder of the season and sent its acts out with another circus also owned by the corporation.

During the next five years North set about modernizing the circus and was often criticized by traditionalists for turning it into a Broadway revenue replete with dozens of show girls. Besides the many physical innovations he introduced through the designer Norman Bel Geddes, he also hired ballet master George Balanchine, composer Igor Stravinsky, and Broadway director John Murray Anderson to give the circus performance more appeal. His greatest piece of showmanship, however, was the acquisition and subsequent ballyhoo of the gorilla Gargantua, whose name became a household word between 1938 and 1949. During this period North also managed to retire all of the claims against his uncle's estate, including one from the Internal Revenue Service for unpaid taxes amounting to over $13 million. He also won the numerous lawsuits that challenged his position as executor. In 1940 he married Germaine Aussey. They had no children and divorced in 1943.

When his five-year term as circus president ended after the 1942 season, he was replaced by his cousin Robert Ringling. On 6 July 1944 the circus suffered a disastrous fire in Hartford, Connecticut, in which 168 persons died, placing the circus once more in chaos. Three years later John Ringling North emerged as the majority stockholder by buying his uncle's estate (exclusive of the art museum and its holdings) from the state of Florida and then just enough of the remaining stock from a disenchanted relative to give him 51 percent.

For the next several years the circus's fortunes soared as the performances grew ever more glittering and audiences more enthusiastic. North contributed to the circus's glamour by writing several songs for each new production. Although the show enjoyed huge profits during this period, most of the money went to pay off the liabilities incurred from the Hartford fire.

In 1951 the Cecil B. DeMille movie *The Greatest Show on Earth* was released, and royalties from it kept the show afloat financially for a few more years. Then declining business forced cutbacks in its size and lavishness.

North's own interest in the show also began to decline at this time, and he devoted himself increasingly to a hedonistic lifestyle he had modeled after his uncle. He celebrated through the night and slept all day. His name was linked romantically with dozens of women, but he remained a bachelor. Preferring Europe to the United States, he spent more of his time there, touring, eating in the very best restaurants, drinking to excess, and scouting circus acts, in that order. During his stays in the United States he lived aboard his private railroad car, the *Jomar*.

By 1956 an inescapable and overwhelming combination of circumstances—from changing tastes to union problems—forced North to end the circus season prematurely and announce that "the era of the tented circus is a thing of the past." From that time forward the Ringling circus played in enclosed arenas. The controversy that swirled around the innovations North brought to circus performances in the early 1940s was nothing compared with the criticism he took for packing in the big top. Determined to disprove his critics, among whom were his relatives who retained 49 percent interest in the operation, North struggled to revitalize the circus. Once the circus began making money again, his interest waned, and he finally sold the show to a consortium of businessmen, which included Irvin Feld, in 1967 for $8 million.

Free of the circus, North spent most of the rest of his life in Europe, maintaining the same habits he had pursued while young. In 1968 he became a citizen of Ireland. His headquarters, however, were in Zurich, Switzerland, where he maintained an apartment.

He had renounced his American citizenship after it became illegal for private citizens to hold gold. He had previously acquired a huge holding of the bullion after selling much of the property he had acquired when purchasing his uncle's estate. Included in the real estate holdings was the bulk of waterfront property on Long Boat Key in Florida. He also profited from the oil wells he continued to own (also acquired in the purchase of the estate). By the time of his death in Brussels he had accumulated three and a half tons of gold, most of it bought at about $35 an ounce. His total estate was valued at around $100 million.

Although his flamboyant life gave the circus plenty of free publicity and the circumstances surrounding its abandonment of the big top were ultimately inescapable, North's neglect brought the situation to a head sooner that it need have and thus put the show into considerable financial difficulty. Despite such mismanagement he gave the talented artists he brought to the circus the freedom to make it a viable entertainment that continues.

• The bulk of the papers relative to the management of Ringling Bros. and Barnum & Bailey Circus prior to its sale to the Felds, including some of John Ringling North's personal correspondence, has been deposited with the Circus World Museum and Research Library in Baraboo, Wis., North's boyhood home. In addition the Baraboo Public Library and the Circus World Museum have maintained files of newspaper clippings and other miscellanea relative to North and his years with the circus.

For a firsthand account of what it was like to grow up around a circus, *The Circus Kings* (1960), written by Henry Ringling North (John's brother) with Alden Hatch, is useful but sometimes gives the kind of public relations slant that characterizes circus publicity departments. Ernest Albrecht's biography of North, *A Ringling by Any Other Name* (1989), covers all aspects of the man's professional and personal life that often impinged on each other. *Billboard*, which until 1960 chronicled the outdoor entertainment business, is a reliable source for information regarding the circus's management under North's stewardship.

During the circus's climactic years under canvas, Michael Burke served as the owner's surrogate in the day-to-day dealings of the circus on tour. His autobiography, *Outrageous Good Fortune* (1984), is a revealing insider's account of that turbulent period and the role North played in it. Sarasota's two newspapers, the *News* and the *Herald Tribune*, published during the time of North's numerous and protracted legal battles, provide detailed accounts of the tangled mess of lawsuits North had to fight his way through. Some specific articles of interest are "North Again Heads Circus," *Sarasota Herald Tribune*, 16 Nov. 1947; "Ouster of Norths Asked in Lawsuit," *Sarasota Herald Tribune*, 7 Sept. 1957; and "Circus Ponders Shifting Winter Home," *Sarasota News*, 17 Nov. 1959. These and many other articles about North are available on microfilm at the Sarasota Public Library. An obituary is in the *New York Times*, 6 June 1985.

ERNEST ALBRECHT

NORTH, William (1755–3 Jan. 1836), army officer and U.S. senator, was born at Fort Frederic, Pemaquid, Maine, the son of Captain John North, a surveyor, militia officer, and local judge, and Elizabeth Pitson. After his father's death in 1763, North moved with his mother to Boston. He attended Boston Latin School, then took a position in a merchant's office, where he remained until the British closed the port of Boston in the fall of 1774. In May 1776 North was commissioned a second lieutenant in Colonel Henry Knox's artillery regiment of the Continental army. He was promoted the following year to captain in Colonel William Lee's regiment of the Massachusetts line, and he saw action in the battle of Monmouth in June 1778. In April 1779 Lee's regiment was consolidated with Henry Jackson's Additional Continental Regiment, and North continued as captain.

In May 1779 North was appointed aide-de-camp to Baron von Steuben, inspector general of the Continental army, an assignment that influenced the rest of his career. The bachelor Steuben developed an extraordinarily intense emotional relationship with North and another of his young aides, Captain Benjamin Walker,

treating them as surrogate sons. North traveled constantly with Steuben and mingled in prominent social circles; during 1780–1781 he was with the inspector general in Virginia, and he took part in the siege of Yorktown and capture of Lord Cornwallis's army. North's close friendship with his wartime commander continued until Steuben's death in 1794, and North and Walker served as executors of their mentor's estate and inherited his American property.

North remained in military service after the Peace of Paris, and in October 1783 he became inspector of the small body of troops retained from the Continental army. In June 1784, when Congress authorized a regiment of 700 men to push federal authority into the Northwest, North continued as inspector, though he lived mainly at Steuben's New York City residence and apparently visited the frontier garrisons on only one occasion. During the winter of 1786–1787, he served as a major in a Massachusetts infantry regiment, part of a force added temporarily to the army in response to the uprising of debtor farmers in western Massachusetts led by Daniel Shays. In October 1787 he married Mary Duane, the daughter of Mayor James Duane of New York City. They had six children.

North left the army soon after his marriage and settled as a gentleman farmer on an estate in Duanesburg, near Schenectady, New York. He served several terms in the state assembly and was Speaker during 1795 and 1796. In 1798 Governor John Jay appointed him to fill a seat in the U.S. Senate left vacant by the resignation of John S. Hobart. A staunch Federalist, North supported the Sedition Act, Alien Enemies Act, and other measures intended to check the Democratic-Republican opposition. He also helped push through Congress the Adams administration's controversial military program for the Quasi-war with France, which included dramatic increases of the army and navy, the formation of the marine corps, and authorization for a provisional army to be raised after a declaration of war. He left the Senate in August 1798, after the New York legislature elected James Watson as Hobart's regular replacement.

On 19 July 1798 President John Adams appointed North to the office of adjutant general of the army, a position that carried the rank of brigadier general. For the first eight months of his tenure, North remained on inactive duty. In March 1799, however, Congress added the role of assistant inspector general to the adjutant general's functions. At the request of Major General Alexander Hamilton, who was inspector general and de facto commander of the army during the Quasi-war, the administration called North to New York City to serve as Hamilton's chief of staff. For more than a year, North worked closely with Hamilton, supporting the inspector general's ambitious efforts to rationalize military administration, instill uniformity and discipline, improve officer training, and generally build the army into a permanent and solid pillar of the federal system. During the winter of 1799–1800, North began a basic revision of the army's general regulations. However, Democratic Republicans denounced the Federalist attempt to create a large standing army as a threat to liberty, and even Adams, resentful of Hamilton's challenge to his party leadership, withdrew his support. On 14 May 1800, after the administration had reached a diplomatic settlement with France, Congress drastically reduced the army and abolished many staff offices, including those of Hamilton and North.

Discharged in June 1800, North returned to his Duanesburg estate. He was a representative to the New York assembly in 1810 and again served as Speaker. Since the 1790s, North had promoted turnpike and canal projects in upstate New York, and he was a director of the Western Inland Lock Navigation Company, which attempted unsuccessfully to build a canal and river link between the Hudson River and Lakes Seneca and Ontario. In 1810 the New York legislature named him to the newly formed board of commissioners to survey a route for a canal connecting the Hudson with Lake Erie. During the years that followed, the commissioners' enthusiastic reports and energetic advocacy of the project convinced the state to launch the Erie Canal.

North lived mainly in Duanesburg during his later years and died in New York City. He was representative of many revolutionary war veterans who used their military service as a means to achieve financial security and political status in the postwar era. His most important role was his support, both as U.S. senator and adjutant general, of the controversial Federalist military program of the Quasi-war period.

• A collection of North's papers is preserved at the New York State Library (Albany). A biographical sketch and information on his family background are in James W. North, *The History of Augusta, from the Earliest Settlement to the Present Time* (1870). For his friendship with Steuben and excerpts from his correspondence, see Friedrich Kapp, *The Life of Frederick William von Steuben, Major General in the Revolutionary Army* (1859); and John M. Palmer, *General von Steuben* (1937). His Senate service may be traced in *Annals of the Congress of the United States, 1789–1824* (1834–1856). For his role as adjutant general during the Quasi-war, see Harold C. Syrett, ed., *The Papers of Alexander Hamilton*, vols. 22–24 (1961–1987). Data on his involvement in transportation projects and service on the N.Y. canal commission may be gleaned from Francis P. Kimball, *The Capital Region of New York State: Crossroads of Empire* (1942); and Ronald E. Shaw, *Erie Water West: A History of the Erie Canal, 1792–1854* (1966).

WILLIAM B. SKELTON

NORTHEN, William Jonathan (9 July 1835–25 Mar. 1913), politician and educator, was born in Jones County, Georgia, to Peter Northen, a planter, and Louisa Maria Davis. In 1840 the family moved to Penfield in Greene County, Georgia, where Peter Northen directed Mercer University's manual labor program and farmed a modest plantation. William Northen attended Mercer University, graduating with a B.A. in 1853. That same year he experienced Christian conversion, joined the Baptist church, and suffered his first emotional and physical breakdown. Like many driven individuals, Northen struggled with depression and exhaustion several times during his life.

William Northen began teaching at Mount Zion in Hancock County in 1854, and three years later became director of the prestigious Mount Zion Academy. In December 1860 he married Martha Moss Neel, with whom he had two children. When the Civil War began, Northen enlisted in the Thomas Stocks Guards, a company commanded by his father. In 1863 he suffered another breakdown, and spent the remainder of the war performing hospital service in Atlanta and Milledgeville.

After the war, Northen returned to teaching, but following a third breakdown in 1874 he retired to his plantation in Hancock County. He turned his farm into a showcase of scientific agriculture and diversified farming, gaining particular success in the breeding of fine livestock. Northen organized the Hancock County Farmer's Club, and soon thereafter entered politics as a Democrat, winning a seat in the Georgia House of Representatives of 1877–1878. Under the banners of temperance and educational reform, he won reelection to the state house of 1880–1882, and served as chairman of the Education Committee. There he promoted greater state support of the public schools, a longer school year, and technical training for students.

In 1884 Northen won election to the Georgia Senate, but in 1886 he left the senate to serve as president of the Georgia Agricultural Society, an organization made up largely of wealthy farmers interested in promoting scientific agriculture. Northen argued that farmers' problems of declining prices, debt, and eroding soil could be solved through thrift, hard work, and the techniques of scientific agriculture. Building on his statewide success as president of the Agricultural Society, in August 1889 Northen announced his candidacy for governor.

In 1887 the Southern Farmers' Alliance began organizing in Georgia, promoting cooperative solutions to farmers' problems of debts and prices. The Alliance also offered a powerful critique of American capitalism, calling for substantial reform to protect farmers from the power of corporate and financial interests. Northen joined the Alliance, but never really shared its radicalism. Aspects of Northen's gubernatorial platform—lower tariffs, better schools, and freed silver—appealed to members of the Alliance, but Northen's refusal to embrace the Alliance's subtreasury plan to create low-cost, federally subsidized loans for farmers turned some Alliancemen against him. Northen's only viable opponent in the 1890 election, however, left the race to run for Congress, allowing Northen to win the November election without opposition.

Governor Northen led a successful educational reform movement that increased the number of Georgia's public schools, doubled the length of the school term, and helped establish two new education colleges. Northen showed real concern for the plight of Georgia's black people, successfully supporting an increase in state funds for black public schools and the creation of Savannah State College. He opposed lynching, calling it an "outrage . . . absolutely without excuse or palliation," and unsuccessfully urged the passage of antilynching legislation, though he rejected any concept of social equality for black people.

In 1892 Northen ran for reelection. Populist opponents criticized his failure to bring meaningful agricultural reform, his ties to the railroads, and his intimacy with the business class of Atlanta. Northen, the Populists argued, did not really represent the interests of Georgia's farmers. In an acrimonious election highlighted by violence and fraud, Northen crushed his Populist opponent by more than 70,000 votes. The support of black voters provided much of Northen's margin of victory.

After leaving office in 1894, Northen served as head of the Georgia Immigrations and Investment Bureau working to attract settlers and money to Georgia. He also served as president of both the Georgia Baptist Convention and the Southern Baptist Convention. Northen sat on Mercer University's board of trustees from 1869 until his death at his home in Atlanta.

• Northen's papers are in the Georgia Department of Archives and History in Atlanta, Georgia. Though he edited seven volumes of biographical sketches titled *Men of Mark in Georgia* from 1907 to 1912, they reveal little about the editor himself. The best recent profile of Northen's career as governor is in Barton C. Shaw, *The Wool-Hat Boys: Georgia's Populist Party* (1984). Other sources include James Calvin Bonner, "The Gubernatorial Career of W. J. Northen" (M.A. thesis, Univ. of Georgia, 1936); C. Vann Woodward, *Tom Watson, Agrarian Rebel* (1938); and A. B. Caldwell, "William Jonathan Northen" in *Men of Mark in Georgia*, ed. William J. Northen, vol. 4 (1907–1912): 285–92. An obituary is in the (Atlanta) *Constitution*, 26 Mar. 1913.

JONATHAN M. BRYANT

NORTHROP, John Howard (5 July 1891–27 May 1987), biochemist, was born in Yonkers, New York, the son of John Isaiah Northrop and Alice Belle Rich, biologists. Northrop's father, a member of the Columbia College (now Columbia University) zoology department, was killed nine days before the birth of his son in an explosion at the university. Northrop's mother was a gifted naturalist whose efforts to introduce children to the wonders of nature culminated in the nature studies program in New York City schools. In 1919 she bought a farm near the Berkshire Mountains in order to give urban children a direct experience with nature. After her death in 1922 in an automobile accident, the farm became the "Alice Rich Northrop Memorial Farm" and provided summer nature programs for city schoolchildren.

Under his mother's influence Northrop gained a large fund of knowledge about science and the outdoors. He engaged in camping, sailing, and fishing throughout his life. After attending Yonkers public schools he enrolled at Columbia University, where he received three degrees in chemistry (B.S., 1912; M.A., 1913; Ph.D., 1915). He then became a research chemist at the Rockefeller Institute for Medical Research in New York.

In 1917 Northrop married Louise Walker, a Barnard College graduate whom he had met at the Woods Hole Marine Biological Laboratory; they had two children. In 1918 and 1919 he held a captain's commission in the U.S. Army Chemical Warfare Service. Because there existed a shortage of acetone, which was a component of some explosives, he developed a fermentation process for its production from potatoes.

After the war, Northrop returned to the Rockefeller Institute, where he served as an assistant to the physiologist Jacques Loeb. In 1924 he became a full member of the institute, a position that assured him a lifetime of research support. Because he loved the outdoors and disliked the long commute from his suburban home, he transferred in 1926 to the institute's branch in Princeton, New Jersey, where he lived on a lakeshore and walked to work. He also bought a farm in northern Maine, where his family spent summers, and often went on hunting and fishing trips to Canada. He sold the farm during the depression, purchased property on Cape Cod, and did his research in the summer months at nearby Woods Hole until 1949.

At Princeton, Northrop gathered together a small group of talented scientists to conduct research on enzymes, which had been the subject of his doctoral work. His Nobel Prize–winning work stemmed from the first isolation of an enzyme by James Sumner of Cornell University in 1926. Enzymes had never before been isolated in pure form, and their nature was a mystery. Scientists reacted to Sumner's work with skepticism, doubting that his concentrated substances were really pure. Northrop wanted to resolve the controversy by developing improved methods for the isolation and purification of enzymes from organic sources. He and his proficient research group crystallized seven enzymes, most between 1930 and 1935, and established their purity as homogeneous substances. The pure enzymes proved to be proteins.

Because enzymes were of such great scientific importance, being physiologically active catalysts with precise specificity in carrying out all the chemical reactions within organisms, Northrop's elucidation of the nature of enzymes resulted in the Nobel Prize in chemistry in 1946, an award he shared with Sumner and institute colleague Wendell Stanley. His research had made it possible to study and understand many of the specific chemical reactions that are characteristic of living cells.

By adapting Northrop's methods to viruses, Stanley isolated a virus for the first time in 1935. This feat inspired Northrop to study bacterial viruses, and in 1938 he isolated a bacteriophage, a virus that was active against the staphylococcus bacillus. He proved that it was a nucleoprotein, a protein-nucleic acid (DNA) combination. The isolation of the phage was also an important confirmation of a 1936 revelation by British scientists of the presence of nucleic acid in a virus.

Between 1940 and 1942 Northrop extended his studies to the isolation of antitoxins. World War II, however, interrupted his studies, and his group investigated the military uses of gases and their detection from 1942 to 1945. In 1947 the Rockefeller Institute announced the closing of its Princeton unit. Although Northrop had the opportunity to continue research at the New York center, he refused to return to the city. The institute agreed to support him in another capacity and funded a professorship for him at the University of California. The move to Berkeley meant the loss of his research group and a reduction in the scope of his research. In the postwar years he concentrated on phage viruses and made relatively modest experimental contributions to the field. In 1951, however, he introduced a concept of major importance by suggesting that nucleic acid was the essential part of a virus—the protein serving to protect the nucleic acid and promote its entry into a cell. A virus was, he theorized, little more than DNA in a protein shell. One year later experiments provided the first conclusive evidence that DNA was the hereditary substance, capable of replicating and producing genetic changes within cells.

In Berkeley Northrop suffered from frequent respiratory ailments, which he blamed on the damp Bay Area climate. After his retirement in 1970, he and his wife moved to the dry desert climate of Arizona and bought a small house near Wickenburg. Remaining active into his nineties, he rode horseback, played golf and tennis, shot skeet, and took fishing trips to Wyoming. To his dismay, his diminished eyesight weakened his marksmanship, and in his last years he relinquished his more strenuous activities. Although he still largely took care of himself (his wife had died in 1975), a Wickenburg woman visited him daily and did his shopping for him. She found Northrop dead in his home from a self-inflicted gunshot wound.

Among Northrop's many honors in addition to the Nobel Prize was his election to the National Academy of Sciences and to the American Philosophical Society. He valued privacy and seldom attended meetings of any professional society. Although warm and considerate to his scientific associates, he remained removed from the scientific community, partly because of his increasingly severe deafness. His closest friends were fishermen and hunters.

Northrop's isolation of enzymes and proof of their protein nature led to a proliferation of studies that unraveled the specific chemical reactions taking place in living cells and led to an understanding of catalysis in living systems. His virus work focused attention on the presence of nucleic acids in viruses and what role they might have in life processes.

• Northrop's papers are in the Rockefeller University Archives. He wrote an autobiographical article for *McGraw-Hill Modern Scientists and Engineers* (1980). The major exposition of his work and ideas on enzymes and phage viruses is his *Crystalline Enzymes* (1939). His Nobel lecture is in *Nobel Lectures: Chemistry, 1942–1962*, vol. 3 (1964), pp. 124–34. The most informative essay on his life is by his son-in-law, the Nobel laureate Frederick Robbins, in *Proceedings of the American Philosophical Society* 135 (1991): 313–20. For a detailed exposition of his scientific work see Roger Herriott, "A Biographical Sketch of John Howard Northrop," *Journal of General Physiology* 45 (1962): 1–16. An important source that includes a bibliography is Herriott, "John Howard Northrop," National Academy of Sciences, *Biographical Memoirs* 63 (1994): 423–50. An obituary is in the *New York Times*, 16 July 1987.

ALBERT B. COSTA

NORTHROP, John Knudsen (10 Nov. 1895–18 Feb. 1981), aircraft designer and manufacturer, was born in Newark, New Jersey, the son of Charles Wheeler Northrop and Helen C. Knudsen. Shortly after Northrop was born, his family moved to Nebraska, where his father worked as a salesman in a Lincoln department store. In 1904 Charles Northrop moved to California, where he took a job as a semi-skilled carpenter; his family followed him there, and for a time they lived in tents until their financial position improved. After graduating from Santa Barbara High School in 1913, Northrop worked first as a garage mechanic and then became an architectural draftsman. In 1916 he was hired by local aviation enthusiasts Allan and Malcolm Loughead, who were building a seaplane for exhibition flying. (The name was pronounced—and later spelled—Lockheed; see the entries on Allan Haines Lockheed and Malcolm Lockheed.) "The Lougheads' plane was just being built sort of by guess and by golly," Northrop recalled. "When I got there I was given the job of designing the wing struts. I hardly feel I was qualified, but at least the wings didn't come off " (quoted in Coleman, p. 11).

Northrop was drafted into the army in 1917, but because aeronautical skills were deemed essential to the war effort, he was released to return to the Loughead Aircraft Company, which had a contract to build Curtiss flying boats for the navy. In 1918 he married Inez M. Harmer, his high school sweetheart. They had three children before divorcing in 1948.

While at Loughead, Northrop helped to develop a process to make monocoque or single-shell fuselages. Whereas conventional fuselages derived their strength from internal bracing, the monocoque form enabled the outside skin of the fuselage to bear the load. This permitted a more aerodynamically efficient shape than conventional designs. Northrop used the monocoque fuselage in the design of his first airplane, the Loughead S-1 Sportsplane. Although a technological success, the S-1 found no buyers because the postwar market was saturated by war surplus aircraft. In 1920 the depressed market forced Loughead out of business. Northrop, unable to find other employment, worked for his father for the next three years, helping him design and build houses.

Northrop returned to the aviation industry in 1923 when he was hired as a draftsman by the Douglas Aircraft Company of Santa Monica. Donald W. Douglas soon recognized Northrop's talents and promoted him to designer and project engineer. In 1926 Northrop left Douglas and joined with Allan Loughead to form the Lockheed Aircraft Company. Northrop designed the Lockheed Vega for the new company. Featuring the smooth lines of a wooden monocoque fuselage and a single cantilevered wing, the four-passenger Vega first flew in July 1927. It went on to become the premier single-engine aircraft of its era, placing Northrop in the forefront of aircraft designers.

In search of aerodynamic efficiency and eager for the freedom to experiment, Northrop left Lockheed in June 1928 and persuaded George Randolph Hearst, eldest son of the newspaper publisher, to finance the Avion Corporation. The following year Northrop designed and tested a prototype flying wing. Although not a true flying wing because it used twin booms and a tail structure, this innovative design marked the beginning of Northrop's obsession with streamlining.

In 1929 the United Aircraft and Transport Corporation added the Avion Corporation to its expanding aeronautical complex and renamed it the Northrop Aircraft Corporation. Northrop turned to the commercial application of his experimentation and used the all-metal, stressed-skin multicellular technique he had pioneered for the prototype flying wing in the design of the Northrop Alpha, which appeared in March 1930. The first in a series of clean-lined, low-wing aircraft that included the Beta, Delta, and highly successful Gamma (with a production run of 347), the single-engine Alpha was the forerunner of modern transports and ranks as a major development in aircraft structural methods.

In 1931 after United combined the Northrop Aircraft Corporation with its Stearman division of Wichita, Kansas, Northrop resigned from the company because he preferred to remain in California. On 1 January 1932, following discussions with aircraft manufacturer Donald Douglas, he became president of a new Northrop Corporation, a subsidiary of the Douglas Aircraft Company. He resigned when the subsidiary was absorbed into the parent company in 1937. Two years later he organized and became president of Northrop Aircraft, Inc.

While producing commercial aircraft, Northrop never abandoned his search for aerodynamic perfection. In July 1940 the N-1M, Northrop's first true flying wing, took to the air. Extensive testing over the next sixteen months led to a contract with the army air forces for development of an intercontinental bomber that eventually would result in the YB-49.

Northrop had more immediate priorities, however. He manufactured 1,131 aircraft of his own design during World War II, including 674 copies of the P-61 "Black Widow," a twin-engine night fighter that became operational in the summer of 1944.

All the while, but on a low-priority basis, Northrop continued experimental work on the flying-wing bomber. The XB-35, with its 172-foot wing span, first flew in June 1946. Powered by four Pratt & Whitney Wasp Major engines that turned eight four-bladed contra-rotating propellers, the huge aircraft had just begun testing (and developing serious propeller and gearbox problems) when it was overtaken by the jet revolution. A modified jet version with eight General Electric jet engines, redesignated the YB-49, appeared in 1947. Despite major stability problems, the air force was sufficiently impressed by the tests of the flying wing to order thirty reconnaissance versions of the aircraft. In 1949, however, the government abruptly cancelled the contract and ordered the destruction of eleven partially completed aircraft. While air force officials cited continuing control problems with the YB-49s, Northrop always believed that his refusal to merge with the Consolidated Vultee Aircraft Corporation had caused the cancellation. In any event, it was a deeply saddened man who watched as his lovely flying wings were cut into scrap metal.

In 1950 Northrop married Margaret Batemen, his longtime secretary. Two years later the couple retired to Santa Barbara.

Prior to his retirement, Northrop worked on two final projects: the development of the Snark, an intercontinental cruise missile that was guided by an inertial navigation system (what Northrop termed "an automatic celestial navigation system"); and the design and production of the F-89 Scorpion, a twin-jet, all-weather fighter. Although Northrop received credit from air force officials for his pioneering work in the missile program, his Snark was never successful because of guidance and reliability problems. The F-89 turned out to be a greater success for his company, with a production run of 1,050 aircraft.

Northrop enjoyed the early years of his retirement. In the 1960s, however, he suffered heavy financial losses in real estate, which left him with limited funds. A wrenching family tragedy occurred in 1966, when his daughter Ynez, her husband, and their two children were killed in an automobile accident. In 1977 he lost his wife to illness. Six months before his death at Glendale, California, a measure of professional vindication came when the frail designer was taken on a visit to his old company and shown the plans for the new B-2 Stealth bomber—a flying wing.

Northrop was the most successful of the self-taught designers, and he had a major impact on the developing aircraft industry in the United States during the interwar years. As Donald Douglas commented in the 1940s, "Every major airplane in the skies today has some Jack Northrop in it." Later, the single-minded pursuit of aerodynamic efficiency would lead to the flying-wing design. Only after his death—and after computers were used to solve the control problems of tailless aircraft—would Northrop's dream become a reality.

• There is a small collection of biographical material on Northrop at the Western Museum of Flight, Hawthorne, Calif. Ted Coleman, *Jack Northrop and the Flying Wing* (1988), is an admiring biography that reprints Northrop's 35th Wilbur Wright Memorial Lecture, "The Development of All-Wing Aircraft" (1947). More critical views of Northrop can be found in Wayne Biddle, *Barons of the Sky: From Early Flight to Strategic Warfare—The Story of the American Aerospace Industry* (1991), and Michael E. Brown, *Flying Blind: The Politics of the U.S. Strategic Bomber Program* (1992). E. T. Wooldridge, *Winged Wonders: The Story of the Flying Wings* (1983), and Richard Sanders Allen, *The Northrop Story, 1929–1939* (1990), focus on the aircraft.

WILLIAM M. LEARY

NORTHROP, Lucius Bellinger (8 Sept. 1811–9 Feb. 1894), Confederate commissary general of subsistence, was born in Charleston, South Carolina, the son of Amos Bird Northrop, a native of Connecticut who read law and became a partner of Robert Y. Hayne, but who died when Lucius was a baby, and Claudia Margaret Bellinger, a member of an eminent and affluent Charleston family. Lucius Bellinger Northrop attended West Point, where he began an acquaintance with Jefferson Davis. Graduating in 1831, Northrop served in the dragoons. Stationed at Fort Gibson, Arkansas, he nurtured several close friendships, especially with Davis, and became known as a fun-loving but not especially able or conscientious young officer.

Northrop and Davis both got into serious scrapes and were court-martialed in January-February 1835. Davis was tried for failure to fulfill assigned duties and for exhibiting contemptuous conduct before a superior officer; Northrop's offenses were negligence of duty resulting from his attending a horse race instead of overseeing a work party and subsequently ignoring a disciplinary order. Each testified in the other's behalf. Both were found guilty of charges of lesser severity than the initial accusations, and neither suffered any long-term consequences. Already close to each other, this episode of mutual defense added another deeply special bond to their relationship. Davis remained Northrop's loyal and dogged friend for life.

As early as the age of twenty-three, Northrop commenced suffering chronic physical maladies. Apparently his immune system was dysfunctional, and he contracted a number of communicable, debilitating illnesses. Although he lived to be eighty-two years of age, he was sickly for the rest of his life and was probably a hypochondriac. Northrop's various maladies were exacerbated by a severe wound he sustained in 1839, when he accidentally shot himself in the knee while pursuing a Cherokee fugitive. There was no provision for retirement for soldiers disabled in the line of duty, so he was relieved from active service, but retained on the army rolls, on sick furlough. He spent several years recuperating at home in Charleston and subsequently studied medicine in Philadelphia. In the early 1840s, Northrop married Maria Euphenia Joanna de Bernabeu. The army dismissed him in January 1848 because he was practicing medicine on charity patients in Charleston, but his friend Jefferson Davis, then U.S. senator from Mississippi, and others induced President James K. Polk to reappoint Northrop in August of the same year. Northrop was then promoted to captain and resumed his practice of medicine. Northrop remained officially in the army, on sick leave, until 1861.

At the outset of the Civil War, Northrop offered his services to the Confederacy. One of President Davis's first appointments was to make Northrop a colonel in charge of the Commissary Department, the agency responsible for procurement, storage, and distribution of foodstuffs for the Confederate army. Always close to Davis, he and the president often took walks together and discussed the ponderous problems of the moment.

Holding his commissary post for nearly four years, Northrop encountered seemingly insurmountable difficulties. He had numerous clashes with Generals Joseph E. Johnston and P. G. T. Beauregard, who charged that lack of food and supplies hampered troop operations. Northrop's inability to solve supply problems, coupled with a personality that seemed offensive to many critics, reinforced ever-growing suspicions of his incompetence and caused many persons to demand his replacement. Northrop's problems were much intensified by the Confederacy's gradual loss of food-producing areas and by the deterioration of the southern rail transport system. Some of the employees in Northrop's department were dealing with dishonest speculators and were found to be corrupt. Northrop was charged with inefficiency and favoritism for failing to weed them out. But Davis obstinately supported Northrop until quite near the war's end. He nominated Northrop a brigadier general on 26 November 1864 but did not dare submit the nomination to the senate for confirmation, knowing that it surely would be rejected. Northrop was never actually fired but was made subordinate to an officer of superior rank, Isaac M. St. John, unofficially on 30 January 1863 and formally on 16 February 1865. The most careful student of Northrup's wartime career, Thomas R. Hay, concluded that in truth there really was rather little that Northrop could have done to alleviate the problems he faced, and, given the realities, it is not likely that any one else could have performed much better in his job.

Northrop fled with the government at war's end and was taken prisoner in North Carolina. Because conditions were so severe in Confederate military prisons, it was suspected that some incarcerated troopers had been deliberately starved. Northrop was held on suspicion of having been personally and willfully involved in this suspected atrocity, but the charges soon were dismissed as absurd. Released after four months, he moved to Charlottesville, Virginia, and there—at "Tudor Acres," the former home of Colonel John S. Mosby—Northrop farmed sporadically until 1890. He became paralyzed and lived thereafter at the Confederate home in Pikesville, Maryland, where he died. Having converted to Roman Catholicism, he was buried in the New Cathedral Cemetery, Baltimore, Maryland.

• The Lucius B. Northrop Papers are located at the New York Public Library. For a good sketch and all known wartime photographs of Northrop, see William C. Davis, ed., *The Confederate General*, vol. 4 (1991). A much fuller sketch is Thomas R. Hay, "Lucius B. Northrop; Commissary General of the Confederacy," *Civil War History* 9 (Mar. 1963). Hay completed a full-length study of Northrop but apparently failed to publish it. There is of course a great deal of official documentation concerning the Confederate Commissary Department in *War of the Rebellion: Official Records of the Union and Confederate Armies.*

HERMAN HATTAWAY

NORTHUP, Solomon (July 1808–1863?), author, was born in Minerva, New York, the son of Mintus Northup, a former slave from Rhode Island who had moved to New York with his master early in the 1800s and subsequently been manumitted. Though Solomon lived with both his parents and wrote fondly of both, he does not mention his mother's name or provide any details regarding her background, except to comment that she was a quadroon. She died during Solomon's captivity (1841–1853), whereas Mintus died on 22 November 1829, just as Solomon reached manhood. Mintus was manumitted upon the death of his master, and shortly thereafter he moved from Minerva to Granville in Washington County. There he and his wife raised Solomon and his brother Joseph, and for the rest of his life Mintus remained in that vicinity, working as an agricultural laborer in Sandy Hill and other villages. He acquired sufficient property to be registered as a voter—a notable accomplishment in those days for a former slave.

As a youth Solomon did farm labor alongside his father. Only a month after the death of Mintus, Solomon was married to Anne Hampton, and he soon began to do other kinds of work as well. He worked on repairing the Champlain Canal and was employed for several years as a raftsman on the waterways of upstate New York. During these years, 1830–1834, Anne and Solomon lived in Fort Edward and Kingsbury. In addition to his previous labors, Solomon began farming, and he also developed a substantial reputation as a fiddler, much in demand for dances. Anne, meanwhile, became well known as a cook in local taverns. They moved to Saratoga Springs in 1834, continuing in the same professions. They maintained their household there, which soon included three children, until 1841, when what had been a quite normal life took a dramatic turn for the worse.

In March of that year Solomon Northup met a pair of strangers in Saratoga who called themselves Merrill Brown and Abram Hamilton. Claiming to be members of a circus company, they persuaded him to accompany them for a series of performances until they rejoined their circus. As their terms seemed lucrative and Northup needed money, he agreed to join them as a fiddler. These con men, to secure Northup's trust, told him that he should obtain free papers before leaving New York, since they would be entering the slave territories of Maryland and Washington, D.C. They further lulled him by paying him a large sum of money. In Washington, however, Northup was drugged, chained, robbed, and sold to a notorious slave trader named James H. Burch.

Thus began Northup's twelve years as a slave. His narrative, *Twelve Years a Slave: Narrative of Solomon Northup*, far more than just a personal memoir, provides a detailed and fascinating portrait of the people, circumstances, and social practices he encountered. His account of the slave market, his fellow captives, and how they were all treated is especially vivid. Burch's confederate, Theophilus Freeman, transported Northup and the others by ship to New Orleans, where they were sold in a slave market. Northup was purchased by William Ford, a planter in the Red River region, and though Ford was only his first of several masters, Northup spent his entire period of captivity in this section of Louisiana.

Despite the heinous injustice of Northup's kidnapping and enslavement, he speaks quite favorably of the man who becomes his master: "In my opinion, there never was a more kind, noble, candid, Christian man than William Ford. The influences and associations that had always surrounded him, blinded him to the inherent wrong at the bottom of the system of Slavery" (*Puttin' on Old Massa*, ed. Osofsky, p. 270). This passage, distinguishing between Ford's personal character and environmental influences, reflects Northup's extraordinary fair-mindedness, a trait that makes his text especially compelling and persuasive. Nonetheless, Northup's respect for Ford did not reconcile him to accept his plight as a slave. Northup, called "Platt" while enslaved, made attempts as opportunities arose to escape and to notify his friends and family in New York of his situation. As his narrative shows, however, the constant surveillance and severe punishments of the slave system stifled such efforts. Even to obtain a few sheets of writing paper required waiting nine years. He feared to reveal his identity as a free man, lest he suffer extreme reprisals.

Northup's skills as a rafter brought him distinction along the Red River, but financial difficulties forced Ford to sell him in the winter of 1842 to John M. Tibeats, a crude, brutal, and violent neighbor. The choleric Tibeats compulsively worked, whipped, and abused his slaves. Eventually he attacked Northup with an ax, and in self-defense Northup drubbed him mercilessly, then fled to the swamps. Luckily, by a legal technicality, Ford retained partial ownership of Northup, and when the fugitive arrived back on Ford's plantation after several days of struggling through the swamps, Ford was able to shield him from Tibeats's wrath. New arrangements were made, which contracted Northup out to work for Edwin Epps, an alcoholic plantation owner in Bayou Boef, who remained Northup's master for the next decade. Northup's skills as a carpenter, a sugar cane cutter, and especially as a fiddler kept his services in demand, making him perhaps the most famous slave in the region—but, ironically, known by the false name Platt.

Northup's fortunes took a turn for the better in 1852 when a Canadian carpenter named Bass came to work on Epps's new house. A genial but passionate man, Bass was regarded as an eccentric in the community because of his outspoken antislavery views. Hearing him debate Epps on the topic, Northup decided that Bass was a white man worth trusting. The two became friends, and Bass promised to mail a letter for Northup. At Northup's direction, Bass composed a letter to

William Perry and Cephas Parker of Saratoga, New York, informing them of Northup's situation. When these men received the letter, they consulted Henry B. Northup, the son of Mintus Northup's former master. He, in turn, initiated a complicated series of arrangements that led to his being appointed by the governor of New York as a special agent charged to secure the rescue of Solomon Northup from slavery in Louisiana. Fortunately New York had enacted in 1840 a law designed to address cases like Solomon's, where New York citizens were kidnapped into slavery. The process, however, required obtaining proofs of citizenship and residence and various affidavits. Consequently it was the end of November before Henry Northup was empowered to act on behalf of the governor. Solomon, meanwhile, grew deeply depressed, having no way of knowing whether the letter had been delivered.

Nevertheless, Henry Northup acted with dispatch and arrived in Marksville on 1 January 1853 to seek out and liberate Solomon Northup. Unfortunately, though the local officials cooperated with his mission, no one knew a slave named Solomon Northup. A lucky inference by the local judge produced an encounter between Henry Northup and Bass, who revealed his authorship, the slave name, and the location of Solomon. Henry and the sheriff journeyed to the Epps plantation and laid claim to Solomon before the furious Epps could avoid a large financial loss by sending him away. After a brief formal proceeding, Solomon regained his freedom and returned northward with Henry.

They decided to stop in Washington and bring kidnapping charges against James Burch, which they filed on 17 January 1853. Due to various technicalities, Burch evaded conviction, but the case did serve the important purpose of bringing many facts into the public record, thereby confirming Solomon's own account. He arrived in Sandy Hill, New York, on 20 January and proceeded to Glens Falls, where he was reunited with his wife and children, who had grown to adulthood in his absence. The narrative ends at this point, and little is known of Northup's subsequent life, except that he contracted with David Wilson, a local lawyer and legislator, to write this memoir, which was published later in 1853. It sold quite well and resulted in the identification and arrest of Northup's kidnappers, whose real names were Alexander Merrill and Joseph Russell. Their trial opened 4 October 1854 and dragged on for nearly two years, snarled by technicalities over jurisdiction, which finally received a ruling by the state supreme court that returned the case to the lower courts, who in turn simply dropped it. Northup never received legal recompense for the crimes committed against him. The sale of his book earned him $3,000, which he used to purchase some property, and he returned to work as a carpenter. Nothing is known of his ensuing years. He apparently died in 1863, but scholars have not been able to confirm this. His narrative remains, however, one of the most detailed and realistic portraits of slave life.

• Much research on Northup was published by Sue Eakin and Joseph Logsdon in their introduction to the Louisiana State University edition of *Twelve Years a Slave* (1968). The most commonly available edition is included with narratives by Henry Bibb and William Wells Brown in *Puttin' on Ole Massa*, ed., Gilbert Osofsky (1969). Surprisingly, most of the growing body of scholarship on slave narratives since 1980 has ignored Northup's fine book. It has been discussed, however, by several historians, such as Ulrich Bonnell Phillips in *American Negro Slavery* (1918, 1966), Kenneth Stampp in *The Peculiar Institution* (1956), and, most notably, John Blassingame in *The Slave Community* (1972), which made Northup's book a central example in its very influential argument that slave narratives should be much more highly valued by historians of the African-American past.

DAVID LIONEL SMITH

NORTON, Alice Peloubet (25 Feb. 1860–23 Feb. 1928), home economics educator, was born Mary Alice Peloubet near Gloucester, Massachusetts, the daughters of Francis Nathan Peloubet, a Congregational minister, and Mary Abby Thaxter. During her youth the family moved to a succession of Massachusetts pastorates in Oakham, Attleboro, and Natick. Alice graduated from Smith College with an A.B. in 1882. In 1883 she married Lewis Mills Norton, a teacher of chemistry at the Massachusetts Institute of Technology (MIT).

At MIT Alice Norton met Ellen H. Richards, the first woman to graduate from MIT and the first to become a member of the faculty, as an instructor in sanitary chemistry. Norton joined the Sanitary Science Club Richards had set up under the auspices of the Association of Collegiate Alumnae, which Richards had founded with Marion Talbot in 1882. Norton assisted Richards and Talbot in the preparation of *Home Sanitation: A Manual for Housekeepers* (1887).

In 1893 Lewis Norton died, leaving his wife with five children to support. Turning to Richards for advice, Alice Norton embarked on a career in the developing field of domestic science or home economics. The home economics movement had originated in the 1880s to promote the application of science to daily life. In addition to educating young women in household skills, the movement also sought to provide careers in teaching and institutional management for women trained in the sciences who found themselves largely barred by sexual discrimination from positions in industry or academics.

With Richards's backing, Norton undertook a series of lectures on sanitary science as it applied to the home, speaking at various institutions, mostly in Massachusetts. At the same time she continued her education, enrolling at MIT for further study in sanitary chemistry (1894–1896) and at the Boston Normal School of Household Arts (1896). On the basis of her research on yeast, Smith College granted her an A.M. in 1897. From 1896 to 1900 Norton taught at Brookline High School, where she developed an innovative curriculum in domestic science, including classes on the family and a course for boys on camp cookery.

In 1900 Norton moved to Chicago to take a faculty position at the Chicago Institute, a new elementary and teacher-training school headed by the progressive educator Francis W. Parker. In 1901 the institute was absorbed by the University of Chicago, becoming its School of Education, and Norton was appointed assistant professor of the teaching of home economics. In 1904 Marion Talbot, who had come to the University of Chicago in 1892 and served as dean of women, became head of a new department of household administration. Norton worked with Talbot until 1913, when the appointment of a new dean of the School of Education led a number of faculty, including Norton, to resign because they disagreed with his narrow view of home economics as household skills. Talbot tried unsuccessfully to obtain a position for Norton in her department, but when that failed Norton spent a year as a dietitian in charge of Cook County's public institutions.

Norton took an active role in Chicago women's clubs. She belonged to the Illinois Federation of Women's Clubs and headed its household economics committee (1910–1912). She joined the Woman's City Club of Chicago (1911–1912) and chaired its food and market committee. She also administered, with Anna Barrows, the School of Domestic Science in Chautauqua, New York, where she taught summer courses intermittently (1899–1905, 1915–1917, and 1920). She published *Food and Dietetics* (1904), which went through several editions, and numerous articles on food and diet.

A charter member of the Lake Placid Conference on Home Economics, which met from 1899 to 1907, Norton worked closely with Ellen Richards to develop the field of home economics. When the Lake Placid Conference formed the American Home Economics Association (AHEA, renamed the American Association of Family and Consumer Sciences in 1994) in December of 1908, Norton became a councilor-at-large (1909–1913) and later served as secretary (1915–1918). Her most important contribution to the field came as editor of the *Journal of Home Economics* (1915–1921). She insisted that home economics be broadly defined, and during her editorship articles on the family shared the journal's pages with more technical articles on food preparation and home sanitation.

During World War I Norton served as editor for home economics in the Home Conservation Division of the United States Food Administration (1917–1918). She helped prepare the "Thrift Leaflets" distributed by the War Savings Division of the Treasury Department. Her interests remained wide. She was involved in the National Child Labor Committee, the Religious Education Association, the Immigrants' Protective Association, the pro-suffrage Political Equality League, the Foreign Policy Association, the Women's International League for Peace and Freedom, and Congregational church groups.

In 1921 the AHEA inaugurated a home economics department at the Constantinople Woman's College in Turkey. Norton accepted an appointment as department head and taught at the college until June 1923; she worked diplomatically to overcome traditional beliefs that housework should be left to menials. When she returned to the United States, she became acting head of the home economics department at Indiana University for one year (1924–1925). During the last years of her life, she worked at Smith College's Institute for the Coordination of Women's Interests, where she published *Cooked Food Supply Experiments in America* (1927) as an institute bulletin. She died in Northampton.

• An editorial and tribute to Alice Peloubet Norton appear in the *Journal of Home Economics*, Sept. 1928. For other mentions of Norton see Marion Talbot's autobiography, *More than Lore* (1936); Hazel Thompson Craig, *The History of Home Economics* (1945); and Caroline Hunt, *The Life of Ellen H. Richards* (1918). See also Sarah Stage and Virginia B. Vincenti, eds., *Rethinking Home Economics, Women and the History of a Profession* (1997).

SARAH STAGE

NORTON, Andrews (31 Dec. 1786–18 Sept. 1853), theological controversialist, biblical scholar, and man of letters, was born in Hingham, Massachusetts, the son of Samuel Norton, a shopkeeper, and Jane Andrews. He graduated from Harvard in 1804. Shy, fastidious, and bookish, Norton had gravitated to literary circles in college; afterward he remained at Harvard to study for the ministry with Henry Ware (1764–1845), a leader of the Congregationalist "Liberals" (anti-Calvinists), later called Unitarians. Norton's literary ambitions persisted, and from 1805 his poetry and criticism appeared in the *Monthly Anthology*. Increasing polish and learning did not cover his deficiencies as a preacher, however, and not until 1809 did Norton find a pulpit, in remote Augusta, Maine. Within months he abandoned it for a tutorship at tiny Bowdoin College. He returned to Cambridge, jobless, in the summer of 1810.

In January 1811 the faltering *Anthology* offered Norton its editorship, which he turned down to become a mathematics tutor at Harvard. The *Anthology* soon collapsed, whereupon Norton resigned the tutorship to launch, in January 1812, the *General Repository and Monthly Review*. Norton's polemics against Calvinism, particularly his "Defence of Liberal Christianity" (1812), were much noticed. But his acerbity distressed older Liberals, while his theological pedantry bored lay readers. In 1813 the *General Repository* sank.

Norton's career now took its crucial turning. In April 1813 Harvard nervously appointed him Dexter Lecturer on Biblical Criticism. Neither was Norton a biblical scholar at the time, nor did he immediately settle into the role. He continued to contribute to miscellaneous publications (as he would throughout his career, favoring the *North American Review* and the *Christian Examiner*) and tried in 1814 to secure a professorship of Greek. Yet by 1817 he had taught himself enough German to scout the so-called higher criticism.

Though his commitment to scholarship was deepening, Norton remained a polemicist who trained his guns chiefly on Calvinists. When the "Unitarian controversy" split the Massachusetts Congregational establishment after 1815, Norton emerged as the Liberals' intellectual heavyweight. His *Statement of Reasons for Not Believing the Doctrines of Trinitarians* (1819; much enlarged, 1833) became a Unitarian classic. Promoted to Dexter Professor of Sacred Literature in 1819, Norton dominated the new Harvard Divinity School. His pallid complexion, soft voice, short stature, and spare figure reinforced the image of the austere scholar. His rigid views shut out other perspectives, and his reserve made him seem chilly, despite his personal generosity and private wit. Students approached the "Unitarian Pope" with deference, even trepidation.

Marriage in 1821 to Catharine Eliot, daughter of a prominent merchant, brought Norton wealth, a Cambridge estate called "Shady Hill," and a seal on his rise into the Boston elite. Four of the couple's six children survived infancy, including the scholar and critic Charles Eliot Norton, and Andrews proved a devoted parent. Fame and family did not, however, improve his feeble health, his tendency to despondency, or his combative temperament. In the mid-1820s he battled the Harvard Corporation to gain greater independence and influence for the resident faculty. Losing, Norton retreated into his work at the divinity school. In the winter of 1827–1828, serious illness interrupted his teaching, and a summer in Britain failed to restore full health. In the spring of 1829, weakened in body and disillusioned with the Harvard administration, he resigned his professorship.

Retiring to the life of an independent scholar at Shady Hill, Norton concentrated on his major work, which he had begun in 1819. *Evidences of the Genuineness of the Gospels* (3 vols., 1837–1844), though soon outdated, helped to found biblical scholarship in the United States. Growing erudition altered neither Norton's basic exegetical stance (dependent on English rather than German antecedents) nor his Lockean epistemology. Against conservative Calvinists like Moses Stuart of Andover Seminary and Charles Hodge of Princeton, Norton insisted that the biblical text was a human document, subject to interpretation in the same way as any other ancient writings. Against radical Germans, he insisted that the Gospels dependably recorded a divine revelation, given in Jesus' teaching and proved by his miracles. These evidences of Christianity had for Norton "almost the force of mathematical demonstrations." He appreciated the philological achievements of the higher critics but loathed their "extravagant speculations" as tending to atheism.

Norton remained a power within Unitarianism and occasionally thundered in public. Most famously, his suspicion of "German metaphysicians" spawned an intemperate attack on the Transcendentalism of his former student Ralph Waldo Emerson (*Discourse on the Latest Form of Infidelity* [1839]). This episode has made Norton notorious among historians as a hidebound reactionary despite his later blast against the Fugitive Slave Law and his significant role in introducing European literature to Americans. He published editions of the English poet Felicia Hemans in the 1820s, translated Alessandro Manzoni's *I promessi sposi* (1834), advised Thomas William Parsons on his Dante translations, and in 1833–1834 edited with Charles Folsom the *Select Journal of Foreign Periodical Literature*. Deteriorating health curtailed his writing in the 1840s and from 1850 required summer residence at Newport, Rhode Island. There Norton died.

• The Andrews Norton Papers are in the Houghton Library, Harvard University. There is scattered correspondence in other collections at the Houghton (notably the Charles Eliot Norton Papers), in the Harvard University Archives, and in several other repositories. Absent a full biography, see Lilian Handlin, "*Babylon est delenda*—the Young Andrews Norton," in *American Unitarianism, 1805–1865*, ed. Conrad Edick Wright (1989); William Newell, "Biographical Notice," in Norton, *Statement of Reasons*, (3d ed., 1856); and Jerry Wayne Brown, *The Rise of Biblical Criticism in America, 1800–1870* (1969).

JAMES TURNER

NORTON, Charles Eliot (16 Nov. 1827–21 Oct. 1908), scholar and critic, was born at "Shady Hill," his family's estate in Cambridge, Massachusetts. His parents were Andrews Norton, biblical scholar and man of letters, and Catharine Eliot, daughter of a wealthy Boston merchant. Charles grew up in an academic household frequented by George Ticknor (his uncle), Henry Wadsworth Longfellow, and others of the literary elite of patrician Boston. The intellectual bent developed in this childhood grew more decided at Harvard College, where his closest friend was Francis J. Child, later famed for "Child's Ballads."

Upon graduation in 1846 Norton apprenticed himself in the East India trade. Mercantile duties by no means precluded other interests. He helped a new friend, Francis Parkman, prepare *The California and Oregon Trail* (1849) for the press. In 1847 appeared the first of Norton's own numerous publications, an article on Coleridge in the *North American Review* (followed in 1848 by one on William Tyndale and in 1849 by another on the Mound Builders: the miscellany was to be characteristic). In these years he also set up a night school for Irish immigrants, possibly the first such school in the United States.

In 1849 Norton sailed as supercargo to Madras and Calcutta. Fascinated by India, he sought out both British colonial officials and Indian leaders—an early sign of two of Norton's most consequential qualities, omnivorous curiosity and a capacity for friendship with diverse individuals. Commercial duties completed, he traveled across the subcontinent by boat and palanquin to investigate Indian culture and imperial rule. Confrontation with India sharpened Norton's budding sense of cultural evolution as well as his commitment to American republicanism. From Bombay

Norton sailed for Europe, visiting Alexandria, Smyrna, and Corfu en route.

His arrival in Venice in March 1850 marked an epoch in his life. The richness of European culture, appreciated before at second hand, overwhelmed him on direct experience. Norton crisscrossed Italy, France, Britain, Germany, Switzerland, and Austria by train, coach, boat, mule, and on foot, settling for weeks at a time in London, Paris, and Florence. He gained entry through his privileged connections to salons, clubs, ateliers, and private collections, dining with Scottish peers, English scientists, French painters, Swiss peasants, American expatriates. The friendships Norton formed initiated the network of British acquaintance that shaped his career, while the linguistic skills he solidified enabled his later scholarship.

He returned home in January 1851. A miscellany of philanthropic and literary activity filled his hours outside the countinghouse: teaching in the night school and, for several months, French at Harvard; writing and lecturing about his Indian experiences; erecting model tenements for the poor; editing two hymn books; and elaborating his conservative reformism in the anonymous *Considerations on Some Recent Social Theories* (1853). Summers in Newport, Rhode Island, in the 1850s expanded his circle to include many New York artists who summered there. Their acquaintance sharpened Norton's already lively appreciation of painting and drawing. During these years he developed the two friendships that were to matter most: those with George William Curtis (first encountered in Paris in 1850) and James Russell Lowell.

By 1853 Boston's India trade was rapidly declining, but not so rapidly as Norton's interest in it. Andrews Norton's death in that year left Charles in charge of the family's considerable wealth but uncertain of his own future. His literary and artistic bent (extending even to an appreciative review of *Leaves of Grass* in 1855) was obvious; what career it might lead to was not. Moreover, Norton's health, never sturdy, was growing shakier. The doctors advised Europe. In October Norton sailed, with his mother and two unmarried sisters.

For a sick man, Norton ingested Europe with a healthy appetite. A three-week tramp across Sicily by mule and foot with Lowell and an English friend in the spring of 1856 suggests at least one stretch of considerable vitality. But in general Norton's frenetic pace of 1850 settled down into long stays in a few cities—London, Paris, Florence, Venice, and, for a total of eight months, Rome—varied by shorter visits elsewhere. He looked at paintings and buildings with as much fascination as before but with a cooler, more practiced eye. He began seriously to translate Dante. His acquaintanceship from 1850 expanded into a broader and firmer network of lasting transatlantic friends, most of them artists and writers: the Brownings, Arthur Clough (first befriended in Boston), Dante Gabriel Rossetti, Elizabeth Gaskell, John Simon, William Morris, and, ultimately the closest, Edward and Georgiana Burne-Jones and John Ruskin. When Norton returned to Shady Hill in August 1857, he had not entirely recovered his health, but he had moved closer to a literary career.

Over the next few years, this vocation gained sharper focus. For the new *Atlantic Monthly* he wrote frequent articles and reviews, including the first American account of the discovery of the Roman catacombs and in 1859 his meticulously literal partial translation of Dante's *Vita Nuova* (privately printed later that year as a book). In the same year Norton published *Notes of Travel and Study in Italy*, which became a respected companion for the cultivated English or American tourist.

Meanwhile his personal life was assuming its mature form. Election to the Saturday Club in 1860 signaled his elevation into Boston's literary establishment and deepened into permanent friendships his acquaintance with Ralph Waldo Emerson, Oliver Wendell Holmes (1809–1894), and Samuel G. Ward. In May 1862 Norton brought home to Shady Hill a wife, Susan Ridley Sedgwick, the orphaned daughter of Theodore Sedgwick (1811–1859) and great-niece of the novelist Catharine M. Sedgwick. They had six children. In 1864 the Nortons took up what was to be a lifelong summer residence in Ashfield, a small town in western Massachusetts. Ashfield symbolized for Norton the honest life, simple manners, broad prosperity, and homogeneous population that he attributed to the early republic—qualities the loss of which, he came to believe, endangered republican democracy in America.

With the outbreak of the Civil War, Norton added occasional Union propaganda to his literary output. Early in 1863 he became editor of the New England Loyal Publication Society, which supplied newspapers with pro-Union boilerplate. In October 1863 Norton also took over, with his friend Lowell, the editorship of the *North American Review*. Lowell supplied prestige and frequent articles; Norton did the bulk of the editorial work and wrote some sixteen articles and many shorter reviews over the next four years. Two of the articles, "Religious Liberty" (1867) and "The Church and Religion" (1868), expressed Norton's growing heterodoxy. He enlivened the staid *North American*, publishing the first articles of writers such as Henry Brooks Adams and Henry James, Jr.

Norton used the *Review*, and the Loyal Publication Society to promote national and liberal principles. To infuse these more widely into American politics, in 1865 he helped Edwin L. Godkin to found the weekly *Nation* in New York. For the next three years Norton served the *Nation* as de facto chief editorial consultant and fund raiser, as well as writer of over twenty-five articles and reviews. He still found time to complete his translation of the *Vita Nuova* (1867). But Norton's health began again to crumble. Sheer pressure of work could explain the decline, but his letters also suggest restlessness with journalism, though no clear idea of another career.

In 1868 he resigned his editorship of the *Review*, left the *Nation* to Godkin, and in July sailed with wife, mother, sisters, and children to England. Most of the first year abroad was spent in England with old friends and new. Notable among the latter were Leslie Stephen, Dickens, Mill, Darwin, G. H. Lewes, and George Eliot. Many hours were passed with Ruskin, whose views on art powerfully influenced Norton. In May 1869 the Nortons left England, passing the summer near Vevey, Switzerland, then heading for Italy in October. For the next year and a half they rented palazzi in Florence, Siena, and Venice, finally settling in Dresden in September 1871.

During this nomadic interlude Norton introduced the *Rubaiyat* to American readers, sent home a first-hand account of the Vatican Council, and assailed England's class-ridden social order. He so despaired of the extremes of wealth and poverty in Europe that he welcomed the Paris Commune as helping to destroy a hopeless social order, to make way for the slow and painful evolution of a better; he cheered Italian unification as a small step in this evolution. News from home of political corruption soured his hope that the Civil War had regenerated the republican ideals of the American Revolution; and for the United States, too, he more and more pitched his hopes in the distant future. But for the most part Norton devoted himself to the study of medieval and Renaissance art and literature, burrowing in Italian archives and spending day after day in galleries. The translator of the *Vita Nuova* grew into a scholar of literature, the amateur of painting into an expert art historian. In this work Norton seemed to have no particular vocational aim in view, though he did toy with the idea of returning to Harvard—an institution, he thought, that could contribute a little to resisting the American slide from republican ideals into plutocracy. Meanwhile, his drift away from Christianity had in 1869 eventuated in agnosticism. He now found in art and in the slow progress of humanity the spiritual ideals and consolation once provided by religion.

This worldview was put to the test in February 1872, when Susan Norton died after childbirth. Shattered, Charles left Dresden and led his household gradually back to Paris for the summer, thence to London, where he passed a grim winter, spending his time chiefly with Ruskin, Leslie Stephen, and, surprisingly, Thomas Carlyle, forming a close friendship with the old man. The family returned to Shady Hill in May 1873.

Charles W. Eliot, the new president of Harvard and Norton's first cousin, invited him to join the faculty. Mostly to distract himself from the loss of his wife, Norton agreed. He began as an annual lecturer in the fall of 1874 and the next year became the first professor of art history in the United States. In teaching, Norton brought his faith in art to bear on his anxieties about the future of republican democracy. Exposure to great art and literature, Norton believed, built character and infused high ideals: an antidote for the creeping materialism and self-seeking that infected the leadership classes of the United States. His lectures mixed intellectual history and connoisseurship with denunciations of contemporary degeneracy. A slight man with a voice that students often had to strain to hear, Norton nonetheless attracted them in droves, liberally dispensing easy grades in order to do so.

He also carried his message outside Harvard College, reviewing scores of books on art and literature for the *Nation* and offering public lectures on subjects ranging from medieval architecture to Dante. He organized exhibitions (notably one in 1874 devoted to J. M. W. Turner, for whose work Norton was the great American advocate) and promoted mass reproduction of art. He popularized poetry through editions of individual poets and a widely reprinted newspaper column. He edited the *Heart of Oak* books (1894–1895), a series of anthologies for young readers. He advised American collectors of European art, most famously Isabella Stewart Gardner (the Gardner Museum in Boston ultimately resulting). Because of his close ties with Britain, he was perhaps the single most significant personal link between American and British intellectual life, introducing books and people from one side of the Atlantic to the other.

By the late 1880s Norton had become the most prominent cultural critic in the United States, though ill health from time to time stemmed his prodigious output. He urged improvement of aesthetic taste, education, and intellectual life, performing for Americans something like the function of Matthew Arnold in England. As in his teaching, Norton insisted that the fate of the republic depended on its moral tone; and he joined with his friend and Ashfield neighbor George W. Curtis in the campaign for civil service reform.

Though Norton's scholarship was rarely of enduring quality, he nevertheless had far-reaching influence on academic knowledge. His *Historical Studies of Church-Building in the Middle Ages: Venice, Siena, Florence* (1880) helped to found medieval studies in the United States. In 1879 Norton founded the Archaeological Institute of America, which became the major professional society for archaeologists in the United States; and through it for the next decade he was the chief organizer of American archaeology, establishing in 1882 the American School of Classical Studies at Athens and (overcoming his own classicist bias) underwriting the early work of Adolph Bandelier in the American Southwest. In the late 1870s Norton took over from Lowell the teaching of Dante at Harvard and in 1880 organized the Dante Society of America. Through his teaching, the Dante Society, and his critical writings, he established academic Dante studies in this country. His own prose translation of the *Divina Commedia* (1891–1892) was long standard. In later years he turned his attention to English and American poets. "The Text of Donne's Poems," published in 1896 in *[Harvard] Studies and Notes in Philology and Literature*, was seminal in modern Donne scholarship. Ambivalent about the professionalization of scholarship, Norton never directed a doctoral dissertation. But among students who felt his hand powerfully were the art historian Bernard Berenson, the critics George E. Woodberry and Irving Babbitt, the Dante scholar Charles H. Grandgent, and Arthur R.

Marsh, the first professor of comparative literature in the United States.

As his older friends died, their families often asked Norton to edit their literary remains. These editions, despite adherence to the conventions of Victorian editing, were standard resources for a long time; a few still are. Norton edited the *Philosophical Discussions* of Chauncey Wright in 1878 and the Emerson-Carlyle correspondence in 1883. After James A. Froude's intimate revelations of Carlyle, the latter's angry relatives turned to Norton; there resulted three volumes of Carlyle's letters (1886, 1887, 1888) and an edition of his *Reminiscences* (1887). Norton later published *Two Notebooks* of Carlyle (1898). He also edited letters (1893), lectures (1891), and poems (1895) of Lowell; the poems (1893) and Dante translations (1893) of Thomas W. Parsons; *Orations and Addresses* of Curtis (1894); Emerson's letters to Samuel G. Ward (1899); and Ruskin's letters to Norton himself (1904).

Norton retired from Harvard in 1898, characteristically provoking a national storm by using his last lecture to denounce the Spanish-American War as the knell for American republican ideals. For the next few years he sustained an active schedule of publication, including a revision of his *Divine Comedy* (1902). He died at Shady Hill.

• The Charles Eliot Norton Papers are in the Houghton Library, Harvard University. There is much correspondence in other collections at the Houghton, in the Harvard University Archives, and in some hundred other repositories in the United States and Europe. Pending the publication of a full modern biography, see Sara Norton and M. A. DeWolfe Howe, *Letters of Charles Eliot Norton with Biographical Comment* (2 vols., 1913); John Lewis Bradley and Ian Ousby, *The Correspondence of John Ruskin and Charles Eliot Norton* (1987); and Kermit Vanderbilt, *Charles Eliot Norton: Apostle of Culture in a Democracy* (1959); as well as the briefer assessment in Martin Green, *The Problem of Boston: Some Readings in Cultural History* (1966).

JAMES TURNER

NORTON, Charles Hotchkiss (23 Nov. 1851–27 Oct. 1942), mechanical engineer and inventor, was born in Plainville, Connecticut, the son of John Calvin Norton and Harriet Hotchkiss. His father was a cabinetmaker in the Whiting and Royce clock dial factory, and his mother worked there painting dials. Intensely curious about mechanical devices and processes, at the age of eight Norton suffered an accident while making a toy cannon out of molten lead on his mother's stove; pouring the lead into a mold containing some moisture resulted in an explosion and a scar on his forehead. He watched his grandmother work a loom in her attic, and he built waterwheels and small engines out of discarded spiceboxes. His parents and relatives encouraged these interests.

After attending public elementary school, Norton was employed at the Seth Thomas Clock Company in Thomaston, Connecticut, in 1866. Starting with general chores, he soon earned the position of machinist. He rapidly advanced to foreman, superintendent of machinery, and then to manager of the tower-clock department. He worked for Seth Thomas for twenty years, becoming familiar with the American system of manufacture, which relied on machine tools to achieve standardization and interchangeability of parts. At this firm Norton invented a mechanism by which the hands of a large public clock could be set back or forward without disturbing the clock's pendulum. He also developed a nonrecoiling hammer for striking the hours. Both these improvements were incorporated in a clock which he helped his uncle build for Independence Hall in Philadelphia. Even though engaged in an industry usually characterized by small and relatively precise parts, Norton had begun the process of enlarging the procedures to a massive scale with his work on tower clocks.

In 1873 Norton married Julia Eliza Bishop of Thomaston, Connecticut; they had two daughters. In 1886 he was hired as assistant engineer by the Brown and Sharpe Manufacturing Company of Providence, Rhode Island. This company had pioneered in the development of the single-thread sewing machine. Brown and Sharpe had also perfected a grinding machine attached to a lathe, which was used in the manufacture of small metal parts. Originally designed by Jacob R. Brown between 1864 and 1876, the machine had first been used for sharpening tools and finishing machined surfaces. It had evolved with Brown and Sharpe into a machine tool for the grinding of needle bars for sewing machines—potentially a metal-cutting machine for high-volume production. Norton redesigned the machine, giving it greater strength, and also designed a spindle which made internal grinding of parts much easier. While at Brown and Sharpe he also contributed to the development of the Westinghouse air brake, widely adopted in the railroad industry.

In 1890 Norton left Brown and Sharpe to help establish a new firm in Detroit, in partnership with Henry Martyn Leland and Robert C. Faulconer. Faulconer provided capital, Martyn served as general manager, and Norton was the designer of new machinery. He worked with the firm for five years, then returned to Brown and Sharpe. The small company he helped found in Detroit was later taken over by the Cadillac automotive company.

Back at Brown and Sharpe Norton began to perfect the application of cylindrical grinding to larger machinery, working out means by which a larger, wider grinding wheel could be employed with greater power, higher speed, and more rigid construction, to produce heavier cuts on a regular-volume basis. He suggested the ideas to Brown and Sharpe, but they did not care to risk the capital necessary to develop the heavier equipment, and Norton searched for a way to put his ideas into practice. Brown and Sharpe made small grinding equipment for a number of firms throughout New England and New York, so Norton was able to meet a wide variety of industrialists, making contacts which would prove valuable for the development of his concept, both in raising funds and in marketing his later innovations. After divorcing his first wife, he married Mary E. Tomlinson of Plainville on 16 June 1896.

In 1900 Norton founded his own company in Worcester, Massachusetts, with help from the Norton Emory Wheel Company. (Its owners were unrelated to him.) The Emory Wheel Company provided the funding so that Norton's venture into larger grinding wheels could be an independent business. He served the new company as chief engineer, establishing a new shop in the Worcester factory and producing his first massive cylindrical grinding machine in the first nine months of the company's existence. The new machine weighed six and one-half tons; it was eighteen by ninety-six inches and used a two-foot-diameter wheel, four times as large as any previous grinding wheel. Its cutting action was sixteen times more efficient than any other grinding machine then in use. Its accurate feed mechanism could serve as a micrometer, permitting excellent precision. The machine was first priced at $2,500, a heavy investment at the time. The first cylindrical grinding machine, produced in 1900, was sold to the R. H. Hoe company in New York, a manufacturer of newspaper printing presses; it remained in continuous operation for twenty-seven years. In 1928 it was presented for display at the Edison Institute of Technology in Dearborn, Michigan.

In a 1903 experiment Norton discovered that the crankshaft grinder could accomplish in fifteen minutes what previously took five hours of turning, filing, and polishing. Such demonstrations brought the machine to the attention of industrial engineers, especially those establishing automotive manufacture by the assembly-line process. In 1905 the first machine for grinding crankshafts and camshafts sold directly to the automobile industry was bought by the Locomobile Company. Over the next few years orders came in from Pope Hartford, Thomas Flyer, Haynes, and Clark Motors. Ford Motor Company placed an order for thirty-five of the machines for making the Model T at Henry Ford's Highland Park factory.

In the first decades of the twentieth century the Norton grinding machine became indispensable in automotive manufacture. Norton's personal fame derived from his developing it from an earlier special-purpose device. In this regard Norton's work can be seen as a crucial link between nineteenth-century and twentieth-century industrial practices. Procedures and equipment developed in armories and in bicycle, sewing-machine, and clock factories laid the groundwork for interchangeable parts and standardization. Later, as Ford and others took machine work out of independent machine shops and into factories with assembly-line production, Norton's grinding machine had direct impact on mass-production techniques. Norton continued to work to perfect the machine, aiming at reducing cost, increasing efficiency, and achieving ever-higher precision.

The Norton Grinding Company received national publicity with the grinding of the rollers for the Panama Canal emergency gates. It was known worldwide, both for its carborundum grinding wheels and for the grinding machines developed by the related but nominally independent Norton Grinding Machine company.

Norton's childhood memories of his parents' abolitionism and of the tragedies of the Civil War made him a lifelong opponent of war. However, like many American pacifists, he became an enthusiastic supporter of the U.S. effort in World War I. In 1914 he began designing equipment essential to the war effort, including a grinder for the crankshaft of the Liberty motor. He also designed machines to grind gun tubes, rifle barrels, bayonets, and machine guns. Other contributions of the firm included work on aircraft engines, field artillery, and munitions.

In 1915 Norton's second wife died. On 7 January 1917 he married Grace Harding of Spencer, Massachusetts. In 1917 Norton published a pamphlet, *Principles of Cylindrical Grinding*.

On 24 June 1919 the Norton Emory Wheel Company formally took over Norton's grinding-machine company. The merged company continued to supply the automotive industry with machine tools and equipment, although sales through the 1920s fluctuated widely. In 1930 at least 55 percent of the business of the Grinding Division (Norton's former firm) went to the auto trade, and cylindrical grinding machines represented 87 percent of the total sales of the parent Norton company. Norton himself stayed with the merged company until 1934, when he retired but remained an active consultant. He earned more than 100 patents related to the manufacture of grinding machines. He was the recipient of the John Scott Medal from the Franklin Institute in 1925. On his retirement he moved to Plainville, Connecticut, where he energetically took up oil painting at age seventy-four. He died at his home in Plainville.

• Some Norton Company records are available on microfilm at the Harvard University Library. Baker Library, Harvard Business School, has papers of the Manufacturers' Research Association, which includes Norton Company items. Norton wrote a personal memoir, *Etched in Memory* (1936). His career is detailed in two books focusing on his inventions: Mildred McClary Tymeson, *The Norton Story* (1953); and Robert S. Woodbury, *History of the Grinding Machine* (1959). An obituary is in the *New York Times*, 28 Oct. 1942.

RODNEY P. CARLISLE

NORTON, Elijah Hise (24 Nov. 1821–5 Aug. 1914), congressman and jurist, was born near Russellville, Kentucky, the son of William F. Norton, a farmer and salt merchant, and Mary Hise. He attended Centre College in Danville, Kentucky, before transferring to the law department of Transylvania University, where he graduated in 1841. He was admitted to the bar and returned to Russellville to establish his practice.

In January 1845 Norton moved to Platte City, Missouri, and formed a law partnership with S. P. S. McCurdy. He married Malinda C. Wilson in 1850, and they had seven children. She died in 1873, and in 1877 Norton married Missouri Marshall. They had no children.

A staunch Democrat, Norton sided with the anti-Benton wing of the party when the Missouri Democracy split over the issue of slavery extension and Thomas H. Benton's reelection to the Senate in 1850. Norton was appointed county attorney for Platte County in 1851 and the following year was elected circuit judge of the Platte Purchase District, consisting of seven counties. Reelected without opposition in 1857, he retained that post until 1860, when he was elected to Congress.

In the secession crisis that followed, Norton was chosen as a delegate to the 1861 state convention called to determine Missouri's course of action, and he strongly opposed secession. While fully supporting the war effort during his single term in Congress, Norton, himself a slaveowner, staunchly defended the institution of slavery. He opposed Abraham Lincoln's plan for compensated emancipation in the Border States in the spring of 1862 as well as a subsequent attempt in the spring of 1863 proposed by his colleague John W. Noell. In one of his final speeches in Congress, on 9 January 1863, Norton railed against the Emancipation Proclamation as "in direct violation of the Constitution and every principle professed by [Lincoln]." In addition, he spoke out against the attempt by Congress to give Lincoln control over the state militia. Out of tune with the changing mood of his war-racked constituents, he lost his bid for reelection in 1862 to Benjamin F. Loan, who ran on the Emancipation ticket.

Norton returned to Platte City and resumed the practice of law. While active in the revived Democratic party following the war, he made no move to seek public office during the period of Radical control in Missouri. In the wake of the Radical demise in 1870, he became more assertive and was elected a member of the Missouri Constitutional Convention of 1875. He served as chair of the Special Committee on Representation and Apportionment, where, in spite of urban opposition, he secured the retention of equal county representation in the lower house of the legislature. Norton was appointed by Governor Charles H. Hardin to fill a vacancy on the state supreme court in 1876 and was elected to a ten-year term two years later by a large plurality. His opinions from the bench were marked by "their exceeding vigor and plainness of expression, coupled with marvelous clarity of reasoning" (Wilson, p. 127). He was honored with an LL.D. in 1882 by William Jewell College, on whose board he had served since 1871. His declining years were marked by ill health. He died at his country home outside Platte City.

• No body of Norton papers is known to exist. A two-page autobiographical letter, written in July 1861, is in the Charles Lanman Collection in the Western Historical Manuscripts Collection at the University of Missouri–Columbia. Biographical sketches can be found in L. C. Krauthoff, *The Supreme Court of Missouri* (1891); A. J. D. Stewart, *The History of the Bench and Bar of Missouri* (1898); and J. C. Maple and R. P. Rider, *Missouri Baptist Biography*, vol. 3 (1918). The "Memorial Address" by Robert P. C. Wilson at the death of Norton is in the *Proceedings of the Missouri Bar Association* (1914), pp. 123–31.

WILLIAM E. PARRISH

NORTON, John (6 May 1606–5 Apr. 1663), Puritan minister, was born in Bishop's Stortford, Hertfordshire, England, the son of William Norton and Alice Browest. Little is known of his parents or his childhood. However, he entered Peterhouse College at Cambridge University at the age of fourteen, earning his B.A. in 1624 and his M.A. in 1627. After graduating, he became an usher at the grammar school and a curate at the church in Stortford. Norton was increasingly drawn to Puritanism, and as a result of his beliefs he declined a substantial beneficence from his uncle and a fellowship at Cambridge. Instead, he studied theology and became a chaplain in the house of Sir William Masham. Norton determined that he could best serve God in the New World. He and his recent bride (her name is unknown) prepared to sail to Massachusetts Bay in America with the Reverend Thomas Shepard. A severe storm thwarted their attempt to leave England in 1634. The next year the voyage succeeded, and in October 1635 Norton landed at Plymouth. He remained as minister at the church in Plymouth Colony throughout the winter, but in 1636 he settled in Massachusetts Bay.

Norton's arrival in Massachusetts coincided with the Antinomian crisis. In Puritan theology, God predestined certain people to be saved, and those so chosen were the elect. Election required belief in the grace of God. This "covenant of grace" was analogous to a contractual relationship with God. Antinomians, particularly Anne Hutchinson, argued that the ministers relied instead on a covenant of works to determine whether individuals were members of the elect. Thus, the Antinomians believed that the ministers erroneously judged the actions of people as a means of determining whether specific individuals were among the elect. Hutchinson went further to question the authority of the ministers, claiming that people could still receive revelations directly from God. Such beliefs threatened the foundation of Puritan theology, specifically the belief that God's will was no longer personally accessible and that revelation had ceased in biblical times.

Norton, as a staunch opponent of Antinomianism, became a member of the Massachusetts Synod of 1637, which was called by the colony's leadership to deal with the theological differences that arose from the controversy. In 1638 Norton was ordained as teacher of the church at Ipswich, and in 1648 he participated in the synod that wrote the Cambridge Platform, which was meant to provide structural guidelines for congregations in Massachusetts. John Cotton recommended that after his death Norton should succeed him as minister of the First Church at Boston. Cotton died in December 1652, and after a four-year controversy between the congregations of Boston and Ipswich, both of which desired Norton's service, Norton was ordained at the Boston church on 23 July 1656. On the same day Norton, whose first wife had died (date unknown), married a woman called Mary. There are no records of children from either marriage.

In 1662, after the Stuart Restoration, Norton and Governor Simon Bradstreet went to England as deputies of Massachusetts to petition King Charles II to reconfirm their charter and to answer questions concerning the colony's treatment of Quakers. Although successful in obtaining assurances from the king that the charter would remain intact, the conditions that were attached caused the colonists to feel that Norton and Bradstreet had surrendered the liberty of the colony. Since Massachusetts had previously governed itself like an independent colony, King Charles wanted to reestablish England's control over the colony's legal and religious practices. Thus, he required court proceedings to be held in the king's name, made property the voting qualification instead of church membership, enforced tolerance for religious dissenters, and implemented the Navigation Acts. Some claimed that Norton's anguish over his countrymen's unjust criticisms contributed to his death six months later, although there is little evidence to support such a claim. He died in Boston, apparently of a stroke suffered shortly after preaching the morning service.

Norton was one of the most prominent first-generation Puritans in Massachusetts. He was well known for his orthodoxy, his writings, and his persecution of Quakers. He supported the death penalty for Quakers who violated an order of banishment from the colony. He wrote official theological tracts for the General Court, and he participated actively in the church synods. While respected for his erudition and his oratory, Norton was unflinching in his animosity toward those who disagreed with him on matters of doctrine. Still, his influence on the community, through such documents as *The Heart of New England Rent at the Blasphemies of the Present Generation* (1659), an attack on Quakerism written at the request of the General Court of Massachusetts, cannot be dismissed. His treatise, *The Orthodox Evangelist* (1654), was a critical and technical explanation of Puritan theology, providing insight both into the state of Puritan faith and into Norton's own beliefs. His surviving works are a necessary and useful tool in the process of reconstructing the state of Puritan beliefs in early Massachusetts.

• None of Norton's personal papers or diaries have survived. His published works are in the Massachusetts Historical Society; the texts are also available on microfilm. Among Norton's published works are *Responsio ad Totam Questionum Syllogen . . . a Guilielmo Apollonio . . . Propositam. Ad Componendas Controversias . . . in Anglia . . .* (1648), the first Latin textbook written in the colonies; *A Discussion of the Sufferings of Christ* (1653); *Abel Being Dead Yet Speaketh: or The Life and Death of John Cotton* (1658); election sermons; and a catechism. He also left unfinished works, which are in the Massachusetts Historical Society. For a colorful chronology of Norton's life, see A. W. McClure, *The Lives of the Chief Fathers of New England*, vol. 2, *The Lives of John Wilson, John Norton, and John Davenport* (1846). See also W. B.

Sprague, *Annals of the American Pulpit*, vol. 1 (1856), for more on Norton's theological contributions. Cotton Mather, *Magnalia Christi Americana* (1702), and George Bishop, *New England Judged by the Spirit of the Lord* (1661), discuss Norton's life and death. Family genealogy can be found in W. H. Whitmore, *A Genealogy of the Norton Family* (1859). A recent assessment of Norton's concept of Providence is Michael P. Winship, "Encountering Providence in the Seventeenth Century: The Experiences of a Yeoman and a Minister," *Essex Institute Historical Collections* 126, no. 1 (Jan. 1990): 27–36.

JANICE DURBIN-DODD

NORTON, John Pitkin (19 July 1822–5 Sept. 1852), agricultural chemist, was born in Albany, New York, the son of John Treadwell Norton and Mary Hubbard Pitkin, prosperous farmers. The family had property in Farmington, Connecticut, to which they returned from Albany when John was thirteen. He decided to become a farmer, and his father required that he be educated in this work although, according to historian Louis I. Kuslan, "such education was almost unknown at that time" (p. 434). Norton studied in Albany, New York City, New Haven, Connecticut; and Boston, Massachusetts, working on his father's farm during the summer. He took an early interest in mineralogy and all other natural sciences. From 1840 to 1843 he attended the chemistry lectures of Benjamin Silliman, Sr., at Yale College, and in the winter of 1843–1844 he did research in the Analytical Laboratory at Yale under Benjamin Silliman, Jr., who had taken over that fee-supported facility from his father.

By arrangements made by the Sillimans, Norton went to Europe in 1844, where he studied agricultural chemistry with James F. W. Johnston at Edinburgh University for two years. There he carried out chemical studies on oats, in which he determined the variations and changes in the water and mineral composition in this plant during its growing period and tried to determine the relationship between the minerals of the plant and the soil. The Highland Agricultural Society (Scotland) awarded him a cash prize for his research. Impressed by the existence of an institution for chemical studies in agriculture in Scotland, Norton wrote to an American farming magazine, the *Cultivator*, in January 1845: "I may suggest . . . that in the formation of agricultural colleges on an extended scale, such as now seem to be projected in our country, with each should be connected a branch for the pursuit of *chemistry* as connected with agriculture, and for the dissemination of knowledge on that subject" (Kuslan, p. 435). Norton was possibly the author but at least a major participant with both Sillimans in the production of a document in the early 1840s titled "Proposals for Establishing a Chair of Agricultural Chemistry and Vegetable and Animal Physiology in Yale College."

While in Scotland Norton received an offer from Union College in New York to join its faculty, and he reported this to Silliman, Jr., who, with his father, pressured Yale to give a position to Norton. Soon after his return to the United States in 1846, Norton was appointed to a new professorship of agricultural chemistry at Yale—probably the first of its kind in the nation. The professorship was in a newly established program for "graduates and others not members of the undergraduate classes," according to the college's resolution. Norton spent nine months studying agricultural chemistry with Gerardus Johannes Mulder in Utrecht, the Netherlands, and then returned to the United States to take up his position. He married Elizabeth P. Marvin in 1847; they had two sons, but one died in infancy.

Simultaneous with Norton's appointment at Yale was that of Silliman, Jr., as professor of practical chemistry, but in spite of some fundraising efforts by the college neither appointment was secured by an endowment. Yale expanded the nonundergraduate program in 1847 into the Department of Philosophy and the Arts, which included the two professors of the new School of Applied Chemistry. The college provided the former house of Yale's president as a laboratory for chemistry but offered very little additional support, so Silliman, Jr., and Norton spent a considerable amount of their own money on equipment. Norton's first students included a number of farmers eager for professional advice as well as some students in chemistry. The laboratory carried out commercial chemical analyses for a fee, and students paid an annual fee for classes and laboratory instruction. Discouraged by not having been offered a paid appointment at Yale, Silliman, Jr., left in 1850 and took a position at the University of Louisville, which left Norton in sole charge of Yale's program in applied chemistry. When it was funded in 1852, Silliman, Jr., returned. That year the bachelor of philosophy degree was established separately from the traditional undergraduate bachelor's degree. Two years later the young establishment became the Yale Scientific School (in 1860 it was renamed the Sheffield Scientific School).

Norton is credited with establishing what became a major scientific teaching program at Yale and with pioneering scientific studies of agriculture in the United States. He published on the potato disease (1847) that had appeared in Ireland in 1845, but the identification of the fungus that caused it was not made until some years later. He wrote about proteins of peas and almonds and published on other farming subjects. In addition to scientific papers, he wrote popular articles on agriculture and always showed a sympathetic attitude toward farmers' problems. He was a strong believer in soil analysis for improving agriculture. His textbook *Elements of Scientific Agriculture*, perhaps the first in the field, was published in 1850.

Norton was considered an indefatigable worker who was keen on scientific studies in agriculture and who strongly desired to help humankind. He encouraged a plan to have a university established in Albany, New York, in which agricultural courses would be supported by the state. In 1851 he traveled to Albany twice a week to lecture while continuing to teach at Yale. He developed tuberculosis and died at his father's residence in Farmington, Connecticut.

• Norton's archival records, including diaries, correspondence, and lecture notes, are in Manuscripts and Archives of the Yale University Library. His published work includes "On the Analysis of the Oat," *American Journal of Science and Arts* 3 (May 1847); "The Potato Disease," *American Journal of Science and Arts* 3 (July 1847); and "Account of Some Researches on the Protein Bodies of Peas and Almonds, and a Body of Somewhat Similar Nature Existing in Oats," *American Journal of Science and Arts* 5 (May 1848). Considerable biographical material on Norton is in Louis I. Kuslan, "The Founding of the Yale School of Applied Chemistry," *Journal of History of Medicine and Allied Sciences* 24 (1969): 430–51. A brief unsigned memorial tribute to Norton is in the *American Journal of Science and Arts* (Nov. 1852): 448–49.

ELIZABETH NOBLE SHOR

NORTON, Mary Teresa Hopkins (7 Mar. 1875–2 Aug. 1959), congresswoman, was born in Jersey City, New Jersey, the daughter of Thomas Hopkins, a road construction contractor, and Maria Shea, a governess. Both parents were Irish immigrants. Mary Hopkins attended public and parochial schools in Jersey City but did not finish elementary school. After keeping house for her widowed father for several years, she graduated from Packard Business College in New York City in 1896. She worked as a secretary and stenographer until her marriage to Robert Francis Norton, a businessman, in 1909.

The death of Norton's only child, a son born in 1910, led to her commitment to promoting child welfare. In 1912 she became secretary, and then president, of the Queen's Daughters' Day Nursery, sponsored by Saint Joseph's Church in Jersey City, which continued its work until 1927. During World War I the nursery provided day care for the children of female workers on a nonsectarian basis.

Norton's visits to city hall to lobby for public funds brought her to the attention of Mayor Frank Hague of Jersey City, boss of a notorious Democratic political machine. After woman suffrage was ratified in 1920, he adopted her as his protégé to organize and represent women. Protesting "I know nothing of politics," she was nevertheless persuaded to enter politics by Hague, who replied, "Neither does any suffragist." Named the first woman member of the State Democratic Committee in 1920, she was elected to the Hudson County Board of Freeholders in 1923. She persuaded the board to finance the construction of a maternity hospital in Jersey City. In 1924 Norton was elected to Congress from the Twelfth Congressional District, which included Bayonne and part of Jersey City, a predominantly Catholic, working-class area. She thus became the first woman elected to Congress from the eastern United States and the first woman Democrat elected to Congress.

In the House, Norton introduced the first proposal to repeal Prohibition; she also proposed an amendment to exempt income under $5,000 a year from taxation. She was named head of the District of Columbia Committee in 1932, making her the first woman to chair a congressional committee. Under her guidance, the committee legalized boxing and liquor sales in

Washington, D.C., obtained a Public Works Administration grant for a tuberculosis hospital, and helped to improve conditions in the slums. She introduced a bill to crack down on prostitution as well but could not get it through Congress.

In 1937 Norton became chair of the House Labor Committee, charged with guiding the Fair Labor Standards Act through Congress. Franklin D. Roosevelt's bid to guarantee a permanent federal standard for wages and hours, the bill was opposed by a coalition of conservatives, southerners, and Republicans. After an initial defeat, Norton's committee rewrote the legislation, removing a clause that provided for a regional differential in the South, which had been criticized by *Time* magazine as a "concession to Southern industry's cherished conviction that climatic and racial conditions below the Mason & Dixon line entitle its workers to a lower wage scale" (16 May 1938). This final draft also eliminated wage differentials for women. Aided by the support of Roosevelt and the election of Claude Pepper in Florida, which the administration portrayed as a southern referendum on the legislation, Norton set a new congressional record by obtaining 218 signatures on a petition to release the bill from the Rules Committee in just over two hours. Robert Mouton of Louisiana, the final congressman to sign the petition, kissed Norton's hand, a gesture acknowledging the magnitude of her achievement. She also succeeded in raising the minimum wage from 40 to 75 cents an hour during her tenure on the Labor Committee. Beginning in 1944, she annually attempted to pass a bill establishing a permanent Fair Employment Practices Commission banning racial or religious discrimination in employment but was unable to get it out of committee.

Norton worked tirelessly in favor of legislation that would benefit working-class women. She did not support all legislation dealing with women's issues, however. She opposed passage of an Equal Rights Amendment to the Constitution, fearing that it would lead to the destruction of protective legislation for women. Her Catholic beliefs led her to attempt to block passage of the Gillett Bill, which exempted information about birth control from obscenity laws. However, she consistently supported the principle of equal pay for equal work and federal support for day care centers, particularly during World War II. In 1944 she predicted that women's economic position after the war would be "heartbreaking." Because "women won't vote for women," she feared, their representation in government would continue to be inadequate.

During the Truman administration, Norton continued her support of American labor. She attended the International Labor Organization Conference in Paris in 1945 as an adviser and alternate delegate. She opposed passage of the 1947 Taft-Hartley Act, an antilabor measure intended to curb the power of unions and inhibit strikes. After control of the Labor Committee passed to the Republicans in 1947, she resigned and joined the Administration Committee, which supervised finances for the House of Representatives, becoming chair in 1949.

Besides her service in Congress, as a member of the Hague machine, Norton was an effective political operative. She never lapsed in her support of Hague and denied that he had ever been corrupt in his dealings with her. Norton was either chairperson or vice chairperson of the New Jersey Democratic Committee from 1921 to 1944. She was the first woman state chairperson of either party, supervising the dispensing of federal patronage in New Jersey. Her designation as delegate-at-large to the 1924 Democratic National Convention introduced her to the national political scene. She was a member of the Alfred E. "Al" Smith wing of the party until Hague shifted his allegiance to Roosevelt early in the New Deal. At the 1944 Democratic convention, Norton cochaired the Platform and Resolutions Committee. From 1944 to 1952 she was a member of the Democratic National Committee. In 1950 she had enough political clout to ensure Hague's continuance on the New Jersey State Executive Committee after his fall from power.

Norton demonstrated that a woman could function as a conventional politician. She once remarked, "I'm no lady. I'm a member of Congress." Her husband supported her career until his death in 1934. The Women's National Press Club honored her with its Woman of Achievement Award in 1946; the next year Theta Phi Alpha named her Catholic Woman of the Year. Norton retired from Congress in 1951, after which she served as an adviser to the secretary of labor. She died in Greenwich, Connecticut.

• Norton's papers, including a typescript autobiography, are in the New Jersey Collection, Alexander Library, Rutgers University, which also houses "Summary of the Legislative Career of Representative Mary T. Norton," prepared in 1950 by the Legislative Reference Service, Library of Congress. There is no biography. The best account of Norton's career is in *Notable American Women: The Modern Period* (1980). Profiles of Norton appeared in *Collier's*, Aug. 1943; *Ladies' Home Journal*, May 1933; *New York Post Magazine*, 28 Nov. 1942; *Newsweek*, 26 June 1937; and *Time*, 16 May 1938. An obituary is in the *New York Times*, 3 Aug. 1959.

HELEN C. CAMP

NORTON, William Warder (17 Sept. 1891–7 Nov. 1945), book publisher, was born in Springfield, Ohio, the son of Percy Norton, a patent lawyer, and Emily Warder; his mother died when he was two years old. Norton attended local public schools and received his secondary education at St. Paul's School in Concord, New Hampshire. Upon graduation in 1909 he entered Ohio State University in Columbus, Ohio, to study mechanical engineering.

Norton left college after his junior year to become foreign sales manager of Kilbourne & Jacobs, a manufacturing company in Columbus. After several years there he moved to Philadelphia, where he became a manager at Harrisons & Crossfield, Ltd., a British-based export-import firm with offices in that city. In 1916 he moved to New York City to open and head a new company office there. During World War I Norton took a leave of absence to serve in New York City as a supply officer with the rank of ensign in the Naval Overseas Transport Service.

At war's end Norton returned to Harrisons, but he began pursuing other interests in his free time. He volunteered at a New York settlement house and served in 1921 as treasurer of the American Association of Social Workers. To further his education, he enrolled part-time at the New School for Social Research; he helped to organize a student support association there and served two years as its chairman. He also became a member of the board of trustees of the People's Institute, an adult-education school.

Norton became interested in establishing a publishing division of the People's Institute, and in 1923 he proposed to the school's director, Everett Dean Martin, that such a division publish a series of lectures sponsored by the institute and given as part of the Cooper Union Forum in New York City. Martin agreed to back the proposal, and that fall the People's Institute Publishing Company was formally established. The first book published was Martin's *Psychology*. This was followed by *Influencing Human Behavior*, by Harry A. Overstreet, and *Behaviorism*, by John Watson.

All three books originated as a series of weekly lectures that were taken down and transcribed by a stenographer. Norton, still at work as a businessman during the day, edited the lectures at night, and they were printed individually in pamphlets sold to subscribers. At the conclusion of each series the pamphlets were gathered into slipcases and sold in New York bookstores.

The enterprise was moderately successful, and the demands on Norton's time became more than he could handle on evenings and weekends. In 1926 he became a full-time publisher, changing the name of the firm to W.W. Norton & Company, Inc., and began publishing bound books. He also expanded the editorial list to include nonfiction works for the general educated public, written by scholars in the sciences, social sciences, and humanities. The firm became especially known for its psychology books as it added works by Sigmund Freud, Karen Horney, and Otto Fenichel to its list. Other early Norton authors included Edith Hamilton, Lancelot Hogben, Malvina Hoffman, Thomas Hunt Morgan, and Bertrand Russell.

In 1922 Norton married Mary Dows Herter; the couple had one daughter. Mary Norton was involved in her husband's firm from its inception as the People's Institute Publishing Company, and through her influence W.W. Norton began publishing books about music; offerings in this field grew until the company had one of the most extensive lists of music books in the English language. Mary Norton also encouraged her husband to publish fiction and poetry, and she herself translated some of the works, including Rainer Maria Rilke's poems.

W.W. Norton grew steadily and in the early 1930s established a college textbook department. As his firm prospered, Norton continued his support of adult education in New York City. He also became active in several professional organizations, serving as chairman of the Joint Board of Publishers and Booksellers, president of the National Association of Book Publishers, and president of the Publishers Lunch Club. During the Spanish Civil War he served as treasurer of the American Friends of Spanish Democracy, and during World War II he was chairman of the Council on Books in Wartime, a cooperative effort by various publishing companies that resulted in the distribution of 123 million books to armed forces personnel throughout the world.

Ill health forced Norton's resignation from the Council on Books in Wartime in November 1944, but he remained president of W.W. Norton. His health grew steadily worse, and he died in a New York City hospital a year later. Norton is remembered today as a pioneer in the promotion of adult educational publishing, and the company he founded continues to be a major publisher of quality trade books and textbooks.

• Many of Norton's personal and company papers are at the Columbia University Library. Biographical information on Norton can be found in the *Ohio State Monthly*, Oct. 1938; *Publishers Weekly*, 2 Dec. 1944; and Charles A. Madison, *Book Publishing in America* (1966). See also Robert O. Ballou, *A History of the Council on Books in Wartime* (1946), and John Jamieson, *Editions for the Armed Services, Inc.: A History* (1948). An obituary is in the *New York Times*, 9 Nov. 1945.

ANN T. KEENE

NORWOOD, Henry (1614–1689), royalist soldier, treasurer and auditor of Virginia, and lieutenant governor of Tangier, was born at or near Leckhampton, Gloucester, England, to a family with a "near affinity in blood" to the Berkeleys. His parents' names are unknown. Norwood entered the Inns of Court in 1637, but his legal studies were broken by the civil war. He followed his family into the royalist ranks, rose from volunteer to major, and was distinguished at the storm of Bristol, where he killed the parliamentary commander in single combat. In 1648, after the city was retaken by the parliamentarians, Norwood fled into Holland.

In September 1649, immediately after "the bloody and bitter stroke of the king's assassination" (Norwood, "Voyage," p. 3), Major Norwood took passage with other royalist officers, including Majors Philip Honywood, Francis Lovelace, and Francis Moryson, in the *Virginia Merchant* bound for the Old Dominion in search of employment under Norwood's cousin, the royal governor Sir William Berkeley. Norwood's account of the nightmare passage survives as a classic of early American literature. The ship was dismasted and swept clean of its upperworks; passing vessels refused help; the ship's company starved; and Norwood and his companions were marooned on the Eastern Shore of Maryland and reduced to cannibalism before they were rescued by the Accomacs, taken to Northampton County, and finally crossed the Chesapeake to Virginia in February 1650.

Berkeley named Norwood treasurer and quitrent receiver of Virginia. Norwood was central to the cavalier connection that came to dominate the colony. On behalf of the cavaliers, he recrossed the Atlantic in May 1650, found the exiled Charles II at Breda, and invited him to join his officers in America. The king gave Norwood a patent for his Virginia offices but employed him in the Netherlands and England as a secret agent, one of "the Sealed Knot." Norwood collected munitions for an uprising in England under the often-used cover of gathering arms for an American colony, here Virginia. Arrested in 1654, Norwood was personally interrogated by the dictator Oliver Cromwell, who consigned him to imprisonment in the Channel Islands. Norwood was not released until after Cromwell's death in September 1658.

In the spring of 1660 Norwood was instrumental in the negotiations with the military leaders who restored Charles II. Norwood was called to the bar, made captain of Sandowne (now Sandown) Castle, was esquire of the body at the coronation, and after disbanding Cromwellian regiments in England, took command of the Cromwellian conquest at Dunkirk until it was sold to the French in December 1662.

In 1663 Norwood was promoted to lieutenant colonel of the Second, or Queen's Royal, Regiment in garrison at Tangier, of which outpost Norwood was joint commander with Sir Tobias Bridge, of Bridgetown, Barbados, until the governor general, Andrew Rutherford, earl of Teviot in the peerage of Scotland, arrived. Under Teviot's command, Norwood distinguished himself in fighting with the Moors and in negotiating with their leaders. When Teviot was killed, Norwood succeeded as colonel of the Second and was commissioned lieutenant governor and commander in chief in February 1666. His term in command was marked by a dramatic upturn in trade at Tangier, including tobacco shipped to Norwood by his correspondents Berkeley and Colonel Richard Nicolls, governor of the newly conquered New York. Besides shares in ships, Norwood acquired house property in Tangier and quarreled with the first civil mayor of the town, John Bland, over the authority of the corporation. Bland's son Giles Bland would lead the opposition to Berkeley in Virginia.

In 1669 Norwood brought home wealth enough to purchase the family estate at Leckhampton, was commissioned justice of the peace, and in 1671 undertook to remodel the corporation of the city of Gloucester in the interest of royal authority. Encouraged by a royal grant of the Virginia quitrents for life, Norwood became a Gloucester alderman in 1672, mayor in 1673, and a member of Parliament in 1675, serving in the interest of the Protestant imperialist, Thomas Osborne, earl of Danby. Recognized as a loyalist, an imperial administrator, an expert on Virginia, and an enemy of independent jurisdictions, Colonel Norwood was consulted by the Crown when, early in 1676, news arrived of (Nathaniel) Bacon's Revolution in Virginia.

Norwood's analysis of the Virginia situation, dated 17 July 1676, damned the government of his cousin.

Norwood reported, "2 millions tobacco raised for building of forts at the heads of the rivers upon great men's new plantations and settlements" had gorged the Berkeleyan grandees but left Virginia frontiersmen unprotected from American Indian raids. "The great Injuries that is done in Courts by the Insinuation of some that make advantages by the governor's passion age or weakness" meant that elite injustice by Berkeley's cronies was the rule in Virginia. The worst failure of Berkeley's regime was not excessive taxation or legal injustice, however, but military weakness. That "which hath been the main cause of those tumults [was] the not tymely Suppressing the Incursions of these formidable savages whereby many men were Cut of and several plantations deserted." As auditor, Norwood could inform the Crown that Indian and civil war endangered no less than £100,000 per annum in royal customs revenue on tobacco. Thoroughly alarmed, the imperial authorities disapproved of the Berkeley government's request for a charter. Instead, the lord high admiral, the duke of York (afterward James II), dispatched a punitive expedition to put down the Indians, the revolutionaries, and the regime of Norwood's "cousen" Berkeley.

Despite the downfall of the cavaliers and the modernization of the Virginia government, Colonel Norwood retained claims on provincial quitrents and escheats until 1682. Then the growing royal and imperial authority to which Norwood had devoted his adult life displaced him from his first and last provincial offices. In the last public act of his life, Norwood pledged his support for a new king and queen with a handsome loan to William and Mary following the coup of 1688. That coup, "the Glorious Revolution," centered on Norwood's old regiment and his former subaltern, John Churchill. Norwood died at Leckhampton, ending a life coterminous with the creation of the modern English state and empire.

• Norwood's report is in Colonial Office 1 (General File), vol. 25, 156–58, British Public Record Office, misdated 17 July 1667 (should be 1676). This error is repeated in W. Noel Sainsbury et al., eds., *Calendar of State Papers Colonial, America and West Indies*, no. 1532, 1661–1668 (1860–1969). Norwood's commissions are in State Papers Domestic, 44 (Secretary of State's Entry Books), vol. 2, esp. 25, 98. For fiscal records, see Treasury Group 64, vol. 88, folios 8b–9a, 26b, 47b. Henry Norwood, "A Voyage to Virginia," was printed in *Tracts and Other Papers, Relating Principally to the Origin, Settlement, and Progress of the Colonies in North America*, comp. Peter Force, vol. 3, no. 10 (1836–1844). The best biographical account is P. H. Hardacre, "The Further Adventures of Henry Norwood," *Virginia Magazine of History and Biography* 67 (1959): 271–83. Norwood's military career is most fully treated in Lieutenant Colonel John Davis, *The History of the Second, Queen's Royal, Regiment . . .* (1887). Norwood's imperial governments in Virginia and Tangier are treated in Stephen Saunders Webb, *The Governors-General: The English Army and the Definition of the Empire, 1569–1681* (1979); *1676: The End of American Independence* (1984), and *Lord Churchill's Coup: The Anglo-American Empire and the Glorious Revolution Reconsidered* (1995). On the Berkeley-

Norwood connection, see Bernard Bailyn, "Politics and Social Structure in Virginia," in *Seventeenth-century America*, ed. James Morton Smith (1959).

STEPHEN SAUNDERS WEBB

NORWOOD, Rose Finkelstein (10 Sept. 1889–25 Sept. 1980), labor organizer and leader, was born in Kiev, Russia, the daughter of Henry Finkelstein, a distillery worker who aspired to be a rabbi, and Fanny Schafferman. When Rose Finkelstein was one year old, she emigrated with her parents and older sister to Boston, where her father became a tailor and her mother operated a small grocery store. During her grammar school years in largely Irish-American East Cambridge, Finkelstein was taunted by other children as a "Christ Killer" and was injured several times when they threw bricks at her. These assaults, the most searing memory of her childhood, forced the family to move to a Jewish neighborhood in Dorchester.

Leaving high school in her senior year (1908), Rose Finkelstein became an operator for the New England Telephone Company in Boston. Her father was a staunch trade unionist, and she absorbed from him a lifelong reverence for the labor movement. In 1912 she became a charter member of the Boston Telephone Operators' Union, organized by the International Brotherhood of Electrical Workers with major assistance from the Women's Trade Union League (WTUL). Finkelstein served on the union's executive board and was a leader of the 1919 New England telephone strike. Involving 8,000 operators, it was one of the largest strikes ever initiated and led by women. Lasting six days, it paralyzed telephone service in five New England states and was one of the few in the wave of postwar strikes to end on favorable terms for the workers.

In 1919 Finkelstein, whose educational desires had been frustrated by repeated moves throughout her childhood, and by her mother's indifference to the schooling of her daughters, began a long involvement with workers' education. She entered the Boston Trade Union College when it opened that year. Sponsored by the Boston Central Labor Union, the college recruited a distinguished faculty composed of professors from such schools as Harvard, MIT, Wellesley, Tufts, and Simmons to teach night classes to working people. Finkelstein studied economics, government, literature, history, psychology, and law there until the school closed in 1931. The Boston Trade Union College's governing board considered her one of the school's best students. In 1921 she was part of the first class to attend Bryn Mawr Summer School for Women Workers in Industry. To the consternation of Bryn Mawr's administration, she joined with other worker-students to demand that trade union hour standards be applied to the college's black maids and groundskeepers. She attended summer institutes at Brookwood Labor College in 1928 and 1935.

In December 1921 Finkelstein married Hyman Norwood, owner of a small tire and battery business and a former streetcar conductor and motorman who had participated in the Boston Elevated strike of 1912. Norwood was also a Russian Jew who had immigrated to the United States as a young child. An avid motorcycle racer, he met Finkelstein at a race in 1916. During the next several years the couple learned to pilot airplanes together. They had two children.

Although compelled by New England Telephone to resign as soon as she married, Rose Norwood remained active in the labor movement through the WTUL during the 1920s, serving as vice president of the Boston chapter and on its executive board. Influenced by childhood memories of her parents' discussions of the Dreyfus affair, she became deeply involved in the defense of Nicola Sacco and Bartolomeo Vanzetti between 1921 and their execution in 1927. She retained a strong emotional commitment to the Sacco-Vanzetti defense throughout her life, attending memorial meetings through the 1970s. Through the WTUL, she also became involved in the interwar peace movement and joined the Women's International League for Peace and Freedom. But, alarmed by the threat of fascism, she abandoned pacifism by 1939, and actively campaigned for lend-lease legislation in early 1941.

During the 1930s Norwood emerged as one of the nation's most prominent and energetic woman labor organizers. Her indefatigability on the picket line became legendary. Undeterred by police dogs, she continued to leaflet in the snow and bitter cold long after male organizers had retired. In 1933 she began work with the Commercial Telegraphers' Union and led a successful organizing drive at the Boston Postal Telegraph Company. Four years later she became business agent for the laundry workers' union, directing strikes in Boston, Watertown, and Somerville. Norwood demanded that management establish a guaranteed weekly wage in an industry where employment was notoriously irregular.

During the 1940s Norwood worked in Massachusetts as an organizer, first for the International Ladies' Garment Workers' Union (ILGWU) and then for the International Jewelry Workers' Union (1944–1949). Her work for the ILGWU included successful campaigns at a General Electric factory in Lowell, and at Vatco, a Boston company that made automobile seat covers. In 1944 she also organized the staff of the Boston Public Library for the American Federation of State, County, and Municipal Employees and worked for the boilermakers' union organizing workers in the shipyards at Portland, Maine.

Norwood became president of the Boston WTUL in 1941, serving until it disbanded in 1950. She championed women's causes in a labor movement that was largely hostile to them. In speeches and articles she vigorously defended the right of married women to hold jobs. In 1942 she spearheaded the unsuccessful effort to put the Massachusetts Federation of Labor on record as supporting the creation of public day care centers for the children of women war workers. Norwood also hosted a regular radio program on "Women and Labor" and sponsored talks by European women labor leaders. She held forums and wrote extensively to draw public attention to the plight of domestic workers, calling for their unionization and for them to be covered by government-funded insurance.

Norwood's involvement in organizing librarians led her to conceive of the "Books for Workers" program, through which public libraries supplied books to factories and union halls. During World War II she served on the Boston *Herald* Rumor Clinic, chaired by Gordon Allport and designed to combat anti-Semitic and racist prejudice as well as Nazi-inspired rumors intended to undermine the Allied war effort; she was its only woman member. She served on the Advisory Committee of the Boston Branch of the National Association for the Advancement of Colored People and was a member of the Massachusetts Committee for the Marshall Plan. She also became deeply attached to the Labor Zionist cause.

In 1949 Norwood became an organizer for the Retail Clerks' International Union, working in Boston, Pennsylvania, and New Hampshire. Repeatedly thrown off the premises of the Jordan Marsh department store in Boston, she became a master of disguises, continually returning hidden behind sunglasses. Norwood ended her career as an organizer for the Building Service Employees' International Union, retiring in the mid-1950s.

In her last years Norwood lamented labor's new quiescence. Although forgotten by the labor movement, she emerged as a prominent and outspoken advocate for Boston's senior citizens. Boston's mayor Kevin White appointed her to the advisory council to his Commission on the Affairs of the Elderly. She died in Boston, surviving her husband by twenty-three years.

For over four decades Rose Norwood was one of the nation's most prominent labor organizers; a relentless voice for women's causes in the labor movement; a leading advocate of workers' education; and a tireless crusader against fascism, anti-Semitism, and racism.

• The Rose Finkelstein Norwood Papers are in the Arthur and Elizabeth Schlesinger Library, Radcliffe College, Cambridge, Mass. Letters from Rose Norwood are also in the National Women's Trade Union League Papers in the Library of Congress, Washington, D.C. See also Stephen H. Norwood, *Labor's Flaming Youth: Telephone Operators and Worker Militancy, 1878–1923* (1990) and "Rose Finkelstein Norwood" in *Biographical Dictionary of American Labor*, ed. Gary Fink (1984). Obituaries are in the Boston *Globe*, 28 Sept. 1980, and in the Boston *Herald-American*, 27 Sept. 1980.

STEPHEN H. NORWOOD

NOTESTEIN, Wallace (16 Dec. 1878–2 Feb. 1969), historian and educator, was born in Wooster, Ohio, the son of Jonas O. Notestein, a professor of Latin, and Margaret Wallace. He received a B.A. from the College of Wooster in 1900 and an M.A. (1903) and Ph.D. (1908) from Yale.

Notestein began his teaching career at the University of Kansas in 1905, moving in 1908 to the University of Minnesota as a professor of history. In 1920 he went to Cornell University, where he held the Goldwyn Smith Chair in English History for eight years. In 1928 he returned to Yale University as the Sterling Professor of History, and he held that position until his retirement in 1947. His interests took him to Oxford University as an associate member of All Souls College (1931–1932) and as a fellow of Balliol College and the Eastman Professor at Oxford (1949–1950).

Notestein became one of the outstanding historians of seventeenth-century British culture and government of his era. His doctoral dissertation under George Burton Adams at Yale, "A History of Witchcraft in England, 1558–1718," established him as a leading seventeenth-century English historian. Early in his career he became interested in the origins of parliamentary law and political process, and he devoted much attention to discovering the sources of conflict in the English Parliament of the early modern era. He accumulated scores of parliamentary diaries, and he and his students edited and interpreted these primary sources as new data on the period. Notestein pioneered techniques and principles for editing this wideranging type of resource. The results of his labors were scholarly editions of the debates of the House of Commons in 1621 and 1629, as well as scores of articles in support of his scholarship. He made forty trips to Great Britain to conduct research or to teach.

Several important hypotheses were advanced in Notestein's work. In the Raleigh Lecture to the British Academy in 1924 (he was the first American invited to deliver this lecture), entitled "The Winning of the Initiative by the House of Commons," he presented his conclusion on the events that led to the English Civil War: the tactics of procedure were all-important in the rise to power of the Cromwell party. His classic work, *The English People on the Eve of Colonization* (1954), asserted that the seventeenth century in England was a time of differentiation, a transition from the Middle Ages to the birth of modern British institutions. That book became an authority for American colonial historians to understand the immediate context of English colonial expansion. In other works he introduced a literary technique of a short study that he called a "character." He used characters to illustrate paradigms in the seventeenth century, describing people, institutions, and types. His *English Folk: A Book of Characters* (1938) and *Four Worthies: John Chamberlain, Anne Clifford, John Taylor, Oliver Heywood* (1957) illustrate the use of this technique. His ancestry and love of Scottish literature led him to write *The Scot in History* (1946), a major survey of the subject.

Notestein's influence was felt in other than educational areas. During World War I he was a research historian for the U.S. Committee on Public Information and later for the U.S. Department of State in 1918. He was chosen by the Woodrow Wilson administration to serve on the U.S. Committee to Negotiate Peace at Paris in 1919. From that work he produced *Conquest and Kultur: The Aims of the Germans in Their Own Words* (1917). Later his reputation in working with parliamentary sources led to an appointment as a member of the British Committee Appointed by the Prime Minister on the Records of the House of Commons (1929–1932).

Notestein was remembered as a masterful conversationalist who epitomized the art of teaching history. He was respected as a scholar-teacher on both sides of the Atlantic, and he produced an amazing quantity of historical scholarship: seven original works and ninety-four articles or reviews. Notestein married Ada Louise Comstock in 1943 upon her retirement as the president of Radcliffe College; they had no children. He died in New Haven, Connecticut, having been professor emeritus at Yale from 1947 to 1969.

• The Yale University Library contains an extensive collection of Notestein's personal papers, spanning the period between 1899 and 1958. Other published works by Notestein not already mentioned include *Commons Debates* (1935), *The House of Commons, 1604–1610* (1971), and, of a different kind, *A Short Bibliography of American History* (1920). His dissertation was published as *The History of Witchcraft in England from 1558 to 1718* (1968). Biographical details are found in W. A. Aiken, ed., *Conflict in Stuart England: Essays in Honor of Wallace Notestein* (1960).

WILLIAM H. BRACKNEY

NOTMAN, John (22 July 1810–3 Mar. 1865), architect, was born in Liberton, near Edinburgh, Scotland, the son of David Notman, thought to have been a stonecutter and builder, and Mary Christie. He probably attended the parish school in Liberton, after which he was apprenticed to a builder and then worked as a draftsman in the office of architect William Henry Playfair.

Notman immigrated to Philadelphia in 1831 and most likely first worked as a carpenter. In 1836 a group developing Laurel Hill, a rural cemetery on the outskirts of the city, selected Notman's plan for a picturesque landscape and classical gatehouse. Over the next several years Notman also designed the cemetery's Gothic Revival chapel and the superintendent's residence (both since demolished), as well as a number of monuments. Laurel Hill Cemetery, much visited and publicized, secured Notman's reputation as a landscape architect. Among the important landscapes he subsequently designed are Hollywood Cemetery (1848) and Capitol Square Park (1851, altered), both in Richmond, Virginia.

The Laurel Hill project introduced Notman to the patrons who supported his first domestic works, Nathan Dunn's cottage *ornée* (1837–1838, altered) and Bishop George Washington Doane's Riverside (1839, demolished); the latter introduced to the United States the romantic villa, derived from Tuscan prototypes. Andrew Jackson Downing, the landscape architect who espoused and popularized picturesque landscapes and architecture in the United States, published both designs in his influential *A Treatise on the Theory and Practice of Landscape Gardening* (1841), referring to Notman, along with architect Alexander Jackson Davis, as the two "successful American architects" working in picturesque modes. Downing also published a Notman house in *Cottage Residences* (1842); over the next fifty years a number of houses were constructed based on this design, particularly in North Carolina.

The depression following the panic of 1837 was especially severe in the Delaware Valley. The early 1840s became a fallow period in Notman's career but were personally rewarding. In 1841 he married Martha Pullen; the newlyweds moved into a house at 1430 Spruce Street in Philadelphia, where the childless couple resided until their deaths.

The decade from 1845 to 1855 was Notman's most productive. In 1845 he had on his boards drawings for the enlargement and remodeling of the New Jersey State House (1845–1846, altered and largely destroyed by fire); the New Jersey State Lunatic Asylum (1845–1848, now known as Trenton Psychiatric Hospital, altered); the Chapel of the Holy Innocents in Burlington, New Jersey (1845–1847); and The Athenaeum of Philadelphia (1845–1847). The asylum was the first to implement fully the progressive ideas of Thomas S. Kirkbride for the treatment of the mentally ill. Kirkbride believed that mental hospitals should be located in pleasant suburban surroundings. The buildings would feature an administrative core, flanked by a system of wings and intersecting pavilions, which allowed for separation of the patients by sex and class of illness. Evidently, however, Kirkbride and Notman were not simpatico, perhaps because both publicly claimed credit for the plan of the New Jersey building.

Notman was more successful with the other building types. The Athenaeum introduced the Renaissance palazzo to the United States as a model for both libraries and gentlemen's clubs, a prototype that was followed for generations. After the English Ecclesiological Society praised the Chapel of the Holy Innocents, commissions followed from High Anglican congregations seeking a return to the "purer" building forms of English medieval churches. Notman's masterpiece in the Gothic mode sanctioned by the ecclesiologists, St. Mark's in Philadelphia (1847–1852), stresses form and materials over ornament. Other churches in the same vein include St. Peter's in Pittsburgh (1851–1852) and the Cathedral of St. John in Wilmington, Delaware (1857–1858). For Philadelphia's Low Church congregations and other denominations Notman adopted different styles: Romanesque for Holy Trinity (1856–1859) and St. Clement's (1855–1859), and Renaissance for the facade of the Catholic Cathedral of St. Peter and St. Paul (1851–1857).

Notman returned with great success to the Italianate villa, surviving examples of which are in New Jersey and include "Ellarslie" (c. 1848) in Trenton and the John P. Stockton House (1848–1849, now called Lowrie House), "Prospect" (1851–1852), and "Fieldwood" (1853?–1855, now Guernsey Hall), all in Princeton. In these houses he developed and refined the picturesque asymmetry and fluid spatial dynamics that he had introduced in Riverside. In his villas and other buildings Notman employed such technological advances as central heating, sophisticated ventilation systems, and indoor plumbing. When he rebuilt Nassau Hall in Princeton after a fire (1855–1859), he fitted it with rolled iron joists, making it one of the first half-dozen buildings in the United States to employ this form of construction. Rolled iron, a form of wrought iron, had great tensile strength, in contrast to cast iron, which performed well only in compression. Its use for horizontal members was a step toward the steel-framed construction that made skyscrapers feasible.

Like other transplanted British architects, Notman brought to his adopted country the latest stylistic modes and sophisticated approaches to design. His abilities were recognized by his peers. Thomas U. Walter, then architect of the U.S. Capitol, wrote to a prospective client, "You wish me to recommend some one to you in whose taste I have confidence. My own impression is that Mr. Notman . . . is the best Archt in Philada." (Walter letterbooks, 14 Apr. 1854, The Athenaeum of Philadelphia).

Notman's sense of professionalism was strong. He was a founding member in 1857 of the American Institute of Architects. His increasing insistence on payment of a percentage of building costs, reimbursement for construction supervision, and the return of competition drawings sometimes led to acrimonious exchanges with clients. Such attitudes may have led to the decline of his practice in the last decade of his life, although a fondness for alcohol may also have been a contributing factor. He died in Philadelphia.

• A large collection of Notman's drawings is at The Athenaeum of Philadelphia. An anonymous biographical sketch is in the manuscript collections of the Historical Society of Pennsylvania in Philadelphia. The most complete account of Notman's life and work is Constance M. Greiff, *John Notman, Architect* (1979). Master's theses by Jonathan F. Fairbanks, "John Notman: Church Architect" (Univ. of Delaware, 1961), and Keith W. Morgan, "The Landscape Gardening of John Notman" (Univ. of Delaware, 1973), at the Winterthur Library in Wilmington, Del., deal in more detail with his churches and landscapes, respectively. Some biographical information, including a list of works (not totally correct), is in Joseph Jackson, *Early Philadelphia Architects and Engineers* (1923); it was probably supplied by George W. Hewitt, who worked in Notman's office. See also Phoebe Stanton, *The Gothic Revival and American Church Architecture* (1968), for the context of Notman's work in this field.

CONSTANCE M. GREIFF

NOTT, Abraham (5 Feb. 1768–19 June 1830), judge and congressman, was born in Saybrook, Connecticut, the son of Josiah Nott, a farmer and deacon, and Zerviah Clark. His paternal grandfather was a well-known Congregational minister, and when Abraham entered Yale College it seemed likely that he, too, would become a minister. On his graduation from Yale in 1787, feeling no strong religious call and experiencing ill health, he decided to move to the South.

In 1788 Nott first settled in McIntosh County, Georgia, where he was temporarily employed as a tutor. In the following year, Nott moved to Camden, South Carolina, and read law with Daniel Brown. In May 1791 he was admitted to the bar in Charleston, South Carolina, and moved up-country to the Union District. He established himself at Union Court House and opened a law office in the house in which he was a boarder. In this area, which had a considerable settlement of Scotch-Irish Presbyterians, Nott quickly established a major local reputation. In 1794 Nott married Angelica Mitchell, with whom he moved to a plantation near Grindal Shoals on the Pacolet River. The couple had ten children.

Nott became a Hamiltonian in the early 1790s and in 1798 was elected to the U.S. Congress as a Federalist. He only served for two years, for he was in a region that deserted the Federalist party in the years after 1800. During his brief congressional service, he opposed the renewal of the Sedition Act in 1799, and in 1800, after first voting for Aaron Burr in the tied presidential election of 1800, eventually withdrew his support in the Federalist move that allowed Thomas Jefferson to be elected. (The initial Federalist support for Burr had helped alienate the southern electorate.)

Nott sought a judgeship in 1801 but was defeated. His reputation as a lawyer continued to grow, and by 1804 he had moved most of his practice to Columbia, the state capital. This was made possible when he invited one of his pupils, David Johnson, into partnership at Union Court House. Johnson later became governor of the state. Nott now kept up a home in Columbia as well as retaining his plantation on the Pacolet River.

After several years of the successful practice of law in Columbia, Nott was in 1810 elected as a judge. In Columbia he associated with the leading jurists, intellectuals, and politicians of South Carolina, and one of his sons was later described as belonging to "one of the most respectable families in our State." In 1807 Nott was elected as intendant (mayor) of Columbia.

From its foundation in 1805, Nott was associated with South Carolina College, later the University of South Carolina. He was a member of the board of trustees from that time until his death and was much involved with the committees concerned with college operations and the buildings. The college became controversial in the 1820s when the free-thinking Thomas Cooper was appointed as president. Nott, however, while raising free-thinking sons, remained closely connected with church affairs and was involved in the establishment of the Presbyterian church in Columbia.

Nott's reputation as a jurist continued to be extremely high, although in 1816 he caused a major controversy when he attacked an act of the state legislature with the phrase "that which was conceived in sin must be brought forth in iniquity." This paraphrase of a passage from the Bible for a secular use caused offense among many of the religious in South Carolina. Nott, however, weathered the storm and in 1824 became president of the South Carolina Court of Appeals. He held this position with great distinction until his death in the Fairfield District while on the way from Columbia to his plantation in the Union District.

It was said of Nott that he was a man of "very prepossessing manners and genial temperament" and that he "brought into the social circle the keen, shrewd, and flashing intellect which distinguished him on the bench." He was renowned for his legal learning, which was said to have been "much beyond that usually brought to the profession in America."

• There is no large collection of Nott papers, but there is material relating to Abraham Nott and the Nott family in the South Caroliniana Library of the University of South Carolina and in the South Carolina Department of Archives and History, both in Columbia. There is also manuscript material in the Historical Society of South Carolina in Charleston. Secondary sources relating to Nott are limited, but there is information in John B. O'Neall, *Biographical Sketches of the Bench and Bar of South Carolina* (2 vols., 1859); James D. Bailey, *History of Grindal Shoals and Some Early Adjacent Families* (1927); and Reginald Horsman, *Josiah Nott: Southerner, Physician, and Racial Theorist* (1987). There is an appreciation of Nott in the *Charleston Courier*, 30 June 1830.

REGINALD HORSMAN

NOTT, Eliphalet (25 June 1773–29 Jan. 1866), fourth president of Union College, was born in Ashford, Connecticut, the son of Stephen Nott and Deborah Selden, farmers. Nott was reared in New England Congregational society. His grandfather, Abraham Nott, was minister in the Second Congregational Church of Saybrook, Connecticut. The large inheritance he left was dissipated by Eliphalet's father in failed farming and business ventures. After his mother's death in 1788, Eliphalet lived with his brother Samuel, a Congregational minister in Franklin, Connecticut, with whom he prepared for college while teaching in a local school. After two years as principal of Plainfield Academy, Nott enrolled at Rhode Island College (now Brown University) in 1795. But after excelling in his entrance examination he was instructed to spend the summer preparing for a special examination. Passing that, he received an M.A. in the fall.

In 1796 Nott studied divinity with his brother and married Sarah Maria Benedict. He then accepted a missionary post as pastor of the Presbyterian Church at Cherry Valley in upstate New York. Within two years Nott had founded an academy, published the mathematics textbook *Federal Money,* and gained a reputation as a powerful preacher and orator. In 1798 Nott was named pastor of the prestigious First Presbyterian Church of Albany, New York, sometimes referred to as "the court church" because of the number of political leaders in the congregation. As his prestige grew, in 1800 Nott was named co-chaplain of the New York State legislature and a trustee of Union College in Schenectady. When college president Jonathan Edwards (1745–1801) the younger died in 1801, Nott helped elect his former teacher, Jonathan Maxcy, as third president of Union. When Maxcy left to become president of South Carolina College in 1804, Nott was offered the presidency. Having become a widower that same year, he moved with four small children to Schenectady.

Union College had had three presidents in the nine years after its founding in 1795 and was hampered by Columbia University partisans who blocked state aid and by internal conflicts between Dutch Reformed and Presbyterian supporters. Nott's appointment guaranteed Presbyterian dominance, and his influence in Albany brought legislative approval in 1805 of four lotteries, which eventually brought Union $76,000 in 1813. The next year he convinced the legislature to create the "Literature Lottery" with Union as the main beneficiary, although it did not produce a significant income until he took personal charge of its administration in the early 1820s.

In that year Union graduated the largest class in the United States and by 1829 had a total enrollment of 219, which only Harvard and Yale surpassed. In 1839 Union's 315 students made it second to only Yale. Nott moved the rapidly growing college from its original site to a spacious new site on the outskirts of Schenectady, using the dowry of his second wife (Gertrude Peebles Tibbits, whom he married in 1807) as collateral. In 1812 he hired a former European court architect, Joseph Jacques Ramée, to design a Roman classical campus reminiscent of Thomas Jefferson's University of Virginia. This design still dominates the center of the campus.

Nott soon became a champion of educational liberalism. Influenced by the Enlightenment and Scottish Common Sense Realism, Nott abandoned his traditional Calvinism for a more optimistic view of human nature. After a nearly disastrous student riot early in his presidency, he decided to permit much greater freedom to students. His tolerant attitude toward student activities made Union the home of the first three social fraternities in America: Kappa Alpha (1825), Sigma Phi (1827), and Delta Phi (1827). He also became a curricular innovator, increasing the courses in science and modern languages and offering one of the first scientific courses as an alternative to the classical curriculum. Under Nott, Union offered some of the first engineering and medical courses. Francis Wayland (1796–1865) (class of 1813), later an innovative president of Brown, studied under Nott.

Nott spoke out regularly on political issues, lending his oratorical skills to the antislavery, religious revival, and temperance movements. His temperance sermons, *The Lectures on the Use of Intoxicating Liquors* (1846), *Lectures on Temperance* (1847), and *Lectures on Biblical Temperance* (1863) were widely circulated. He was an active member of the American Association for the Advancement of Education, serving as its president in 1850. He was also a successful inventor, holding thirty patents, most notably one for the popular Nott Stove. Some of his other patents were for water-tube boilers and anthracite furnaces. He also promoted steamboats, including his own SS *Novelty.*

Nott's promotional schemes and his mixing of college and family finances created potential trouble. He had personally underwritten part of Union's growth, and by his figures the college owed him $366,177 by 1845. But some had a different view. In 1851 state senator James Beekman, a friend of a professor that Nott had fired, opened an investigation into the charge that Nott had pilfered $900,000 from the college. The charges were eventually squelched, but not until considerable damage had been done to Nott's reputation and to Union College.

Although he was eighty-one by the time the charges were cleared in 1854, Nott refused to step aside and tried to launch his "Grand Plan" to turn Union into a university with a three-year graduate course. But Nott's failing health and the financial controversies undercut fundraising. Nott's active career was ended by a paralytic stroke in 1859. He remained as the titular president until his death, having served a record sixty-two years. He died in Schenectady, survived by his third wife, Urania B. Sheldon, whom he had married in 1842, a year after his second wife's death.

The longest-serving president of an American College, Nott taught an extraordinary group of students, including one president (Chester A. Arthur), six cabinet members, fifteen senators, eighty congressmen, and fourteen governors. Nott's students served as the first presidents of six institutions of higher education: the universities of Illinois, Iowa, and Michigan; and Vassar, Smith, and Elmira colleges. Although his later years were tarnished, Nott was an educational trailblazer who helped shape American higher education in the early republican era. A man with extraordinary energy and ability to influence others, he turned a small frontier college into an educational leader that pioneered models of curriculum and student life that would be widely adopted after the Civil War.

• There is no collection of Nott papers; most did not survive. Some of his letters, sermons, memos, and patents are included in parts of the Union College Archives. An exhaustive biography is Codman Hislop, *Eliphalet Nott* (1971). On Union College during the Nott presidency see Andrew Van Vranken Raymond, ed., *Union University: Its History, Influence, Characteristics, and Equipment* (1907). For Nott's educational significance see frequent references in Frederick Rudolph, *The American College and University* (1962).

W. Bruce Leslie

NOTT, Josiah Clark (31 Mar. 1804–31 Mar. 1873), physician and racial theorist, was born in Columbia, South Carolina, the son of Abraham Nott, a U.S. Congressman, and Angelica Mitchell. Nott was brought up and educated in Columbia and on his father's plantation in Union District. He graduated from South Carolina College in 1824. While there, he was strongly influenced by its free-thinking president, Thomas Cooper. After a brief medical apprenticeship in Columbia, Nott attended the College of Physicians and Surgeons in New York in 1825–1826, and in the fall of 1826 he enrolled at the medical school of the University of Pennsylvania. He received his M.D. degree in March of 1827 and practiced medicine in Columbia for a few months before returning to Philadelphia as an intern at the Philadelphia Almshouse ("Old Blockley")

in the fall of 1827; in the following year he served as demonstrator in anatomy at the University of Pennsylvania medical school.

As a medical student, and in his first years as a physician, Nott was strongly attracted to the theories of the French physician François Broussais and the French school of physiological medicine. He was particularly attracted to their attack on the earlier metaphysical basis of medicine, and the emphasis on observation, analysis, and the pathology of disease. He later abandoned Broussais's theories but continued to stress the necessity of a scientific approach to medicine. Nott was a free-thinker, and he strongly opposed the attempts of clerics to influence scientific research and writing.

In the spring of 1829 Nott established what quickly became a successful practice in Columbia, and in 1832 he married Sarah Cantey Deas. Through her he was linked to some of the most important families in South Carolina. Of Nott's eight children, only one outlived the parents.

In 1835–1836 Nott went to Paris for an additional year of medical training. On his return, he settled in Mobile, Alabama. Over the next thirty years he established a very successful practice there and wrote extensively on medical matters. A Mobile visitor said of Nott in the 1850s that "He is at the head of the medical profession here; . . . a man of fine intellect, agreeable manners, and with the finished air of a thoroughbred and born gentleman" (J. H. Ingraham, ed., *The Sunny South . . .* 1860, pp. 513–14). Nott became particularly well known as an expert on yellow fever, a disease that killed four of his own children in one week in 1853. Although he never realized that the *Aëdes egypti* mosquito was the vector, he argued strongly that the disease was spread by "animalcules" rather than by some condition of the air.

Beginning in 1843 with the publication of his article on mulattoes as hybrids, Nott established a national and even international reputation as a writer on race. He became one of the group usually referred to as the American School of Ethnology, a group that looked for leadership to Dr. Samuel G. Morton of Philadelphia. In the 1840s and 1850s Nott frequently visited the North, became a friend and correspondent of most of the northern writers on race, including Louis Agassiz, and was regarded with great respect both throughout the United States and in Europe.

Nott believed that there were wide differences in innate capacity between the different races and that this difference was particularly marked between blacks and whites. He argued that whites and blacks belonged to separate species and that blacks were better off as slaves because free inferior races could not exist successfully in the presence of superior races. He believed that the American Indians, and probably many other colored races, were doomed to extinction. Superior races, he argued, brought all world progress, often by wars or conquests, and those concerned with progress should strive to keep the existing superior races pure.

In his abundant writings on race and on slavery, Nott often accompanied his defense of the existing social system in the South with an attack on the ways in which the clergy used their influence to stifle scientific progress. He was particularly anxious to refute the orthodox view, based on the Bible, that all human beings were descended from Adam and Eve. There had not been one creation, he argued, but many. Nott became the most vocal, and the best known, of those who defended polygenesis. His writings on race, although regarded as absurd by a later generation, were in the mainstream of American and European racial theory in the years before the Civil War. He caused greater controversy by his opposition to clerical interference with science, and by his attack on monogenesis, than he did by his views on superior and inferior races.

Nott wrote extensively on racial matters in pamphlets and articles, but his major work in this field was *Types of Mankind*, which was written jointly with George R. Gliddon and was published in 1854. This work was regarded as the standard account of racial origins in the 1850s, went through numerous editions in the next twenty years, and was overthrown only by the radical changes in the interpretation of racial origins produced by the work of Charles Darwin. The *Anthropological Review* of London commented in 1868 that Nott was "the most unflinching advocate of truths, however unpalatable themselves, which anthropology has had in the United States."

In the 1850s Nott became particularly interested in medical education. In 1857–1858 he served as professor of anatomy in the medical school of the University of Louisiana in New Orleans (later the Tulane School of Medicine), but he returned to Mobile in the latter year. For several years Nott had been urging the Alabama legislature to establish a medical school in Mobile, and largely as a result of his efforts this came into being in the fall of 1859. In the previous summer Nott had toured Europe and, with money donated by residents of Mobile, had bought apparatus and medical models for the new medical school. Nott continued his usual medical practice while also serving as professor of surgery in the new school, which later closed for several years because of the Civil War.

In the 1840s and 1850s Nott had become a vocal defender of southern rights, and he justified secession on the grounds that the North had denied the South its constitutional right to self-government. He threw himself enthusiastically into the Civil War, serving as a civilian volunteer surgeon at the first battle of Manassas. In October 1861 he enlisted as a surgeon in the medical department of the Confederacy. In the winter of 1861–1862 Nott was medical director of the Confederate General Army Hospital in Mobile, but he transferred to the medical staff of General Braxton Bragg and in that capacity served in the battle of Shiloh. After the battle, he continued on Bragg's staff and inspected the hospitals of the western army before joining Bragg at Chattanooga. In the late summer and fall of 1862 Nott accompanied Bragg's Army of Tennessee on its invasion of Kentucky. He then returned to Mo-

bile as medical inspector in the Department of the Gulf. In March 1863 Nott resigned from the Confederate medical service and returned to private practice, but he continued to operate in the Mobile military hospitals.

Nott was appalled at conditions in Mobile at the end of the war and could not come to terms with the freeing of the slaves. At first he continued to write on racial as well as medical matters, but he turned more exclusively to medical writings when in 1867 he left Mobile to settle in Baltimore. For the rest of his life he devoted himself to medicine rather than to racial questions. In Baltimore he began developing and writing about a new speciality in gynecology, and, on visiting New York, he was impressed by the work being accomplished in this field by Dr. J. Marion Sims and Dr. Thomas A. Emmet (1828–1919).

In May 1868 Nott moved to New York and established a general practice, but he continued his emphasis on gynecology. He was so successful in this field that by 1872 he had become president of the New York Obstetrical Society, and he also worked for a time at the Woman's Hospital. Late in 1872, after he had developed obvious signs of tuberculosis, Nott returned to Mobile, where he died the following year.

• Letters from Nott are scattered in a variety of archival collections. The most useful are the Samuel G. Morton papers in the Historical Society of Pennsylvania, the Joseph Leidy papers in the College of Physicians of Philadelphia and the Academy of Natural Sciences of Philadelphia, and the Ephraim G. Squier papers in the Library of Congress. Other manuscript collections and Nott's writings on medicine and race are cited in the fullest biography: Reginald Horsman, *Josiah Nott of Mobile: Southerner, Physician, and Racial Theorist* (1987). A brief but useful account by a colleague of Nott's is William H. Anderson, *Biographical Sketch of Dr. J. C. Nott* (1877). More recent contributions are provided by C. Loring Brace, "The 'Ethnology' of Josiah Clark Nott," *Bulletin of the New York Academy of Medicine*, 2d ser., 50 (1974): 509–28, and by William Stanton, *The Leopard's Spots: Scientific Attitudes Toward Race in America, 1815–59* (1960).

Nott's most famous racial work, written jointly with George R. Gliddon, was *Types of Mankind* (1854), but most of his written work was in the form of articles or pamphlets. Among the pamphlets his *Two Lectures on the Natural History of the Caucasian and Negro Races* (1844) was important in helping to build his national reputation. On medical matters, Nott frequently contributed to the *New Orleans Medical and Surgical Journal* and to other journals, most importantly on yellow fever but also on a variety of surgical procedures. As a result of his experience with gunshot wounds in the Civil War, he published *Contributions to Bone and Nerve Surgery* (1866).

REGINALD HORSMAN

NOVY, Frederick George (9 Dec. 1864–8 Aug. 1957), microbiologist, was born in Chicago, Illinois, the son of Joseph Novy, a master tailor, and Frances Janota, a milliner. Novy vividly remembered the Chicago fire of 1871, which started a few doors from their home. His love of science began early; while attending public high schools in Chicago, he held a part-time job at the public library to earn money for a microscope and a set of chemistry books. In his free time he read avidly in history and science, botanized, ran experiments in his home chemistry laboratory, and attended meetings of the Chicago Microscopical Club. In 1882 his parents moved to Ann Arbor to enable him to study chemistry with Albert B. Prescott at the University of Michigan. There the studious Novy excelled, taking every chemistry course the university offered and doing special projects. By his senior year he was substituting for the professor. In 1886 he received his B.S. degree and accepted a job at the university as an assistant in organic chemistry. The following year, he received his M.S. in chemistry for a thesis published as *Cocaine and Its Derivatives* (1887; 2d ed., 1890).

Victor C. Vaughan persuaded Novy to become an instructor in hygiene and physiological chemistry at the University of Michigan in 1887. The State Laboratory of Hygiene, with Vaughan as director, was to be housed in a new science building being constructed on the campus. In preparation, Vaughan and Novy spent the summer of 1888 studying bacteriology with Robert Koch and Carl Fraenkel at the Hygienic Institute in Berlin. They gave their first course in bacteriology, one of the earliest in the United States, in 1889. At a time when most bacteriologists were content to identify bacteria morphologically, Novy and Vaughan began research into food poisons and the toxic products of bacterial growth, coauthoring a book, *Ptomaines and Leucomaines, or the Putrefactive and Physiological Alkaloids* (1888); later editions were published under slightly different titles in 1891 and 1896 before the book was completely revised as *Cellular Toxins, or the Chemical Factors in the Causation of Disease* (1902). The Laboratory of Hygiene became widely recognized for their work on food toxicology.

Novy continued with his education as well, earning a Ph.D. in chemistry in 1890 and an M.D. in 1891. He married Grace Garwood in 1891; they had three sons, who all became physicians, and two daughters. When Vaughan was appointed dean of the medical school in 1891, Novy was promoted to assistant professor. He took over the operation of the department and the teaching of bacteriology, which had become a required course for medical and dental students. Novy taught the most rigorous bacteriology course in the United States: for twelve weeks, his students spent twenty-five hours a week in the laboratory. He published his teaching methods in *Laboratory Work in Bacteriology* (1894; 2d ed., 1899). Students recalled him as a thin, lanky man with unusual mannerisms; he was a strict disciplinarian but tempered his caustic criticism with wit and kindness.

During two summers Novy studied abroad, in 1894 at the Pathological Institute at Prague, and with Emile Roux at the Pasteur Institute in 1897. In 1902 he became professor and head of the newly created department of bacteriology and director of the hygienic laboratory, positions he held until his retirement in 1935. He served the medical school as chairman of its executive committee from 1930 to 1933, and as dean of medicine from 1933 to 1935.

Novy was the consummate researcher, often working late into the night. His chemistry skills made him particularly adept at the design of apparatus. The "Novy jar," a chamber he devised for cultivating anaerobic bacteria, became a standard piece of equipment. In 1894 he discovered an anaerobic bacillus that causes a fatal septicemia in animals, with symptoms of "malignant edema." Novy's methods and research on anaerobic bacteria by 1900 established him as one of the foremost bacteriologists in the country. His reputation earned him an appointment to the U.S. Commission to Investigate Plague in San Francisco in 1900, working with Simon Flexner of Philadelphia and Llewellys F. Barker of Chicago. They identified several cases of bubonic plague, proved the disease was endemic, and developed methods to prevent its spread.

Novy gained international fame for work he began in 1895 on the cultivation of the trypanosomes, with his student and colleague Ward J. MacNeal. They are thought to be the first to grow a pathogenic protozoan, *Trypanosoma brucei*, the agent of nagana, a South African livestock disease transmitted by the tsetse fly. Novy also created methods for growing spirochetes, a long-standing difficulty, by placing them in collodion sacs inside the peritoneal cavity of rats. With these methods, Novy and R. E. Knapp demonstrated that the relapsing fevers of different geographic regions were caused by different strains of spirochetes. Novy's careful technique enabled him to persuade Fritz Schaudinn, who had discovered the syphilis spirochete, that spirochetes were not transitional stages in the life cycle of trypanosomes but instead were independent life forms. Novy's colleagues nicknamed him "Spi" for his devotion to the study of spirochetes.

Novy's research on immunity to the trypanosomes led him to an interest in the problem of anaphylaxis, or shock caused by an allergic reaction. He and Paul De Kruif speculated that a poison caused the symptoms. Extensive studies in their lab and elsewhere failed to reveal the nature of the toxin, but their work laid much of the basis for the eventual discovery of the histamines. A few years later De Kruif advised Sinclair Lewis on the scientific background for his novel *Arrowsmith*, which had a character, Professor Max Gottleib, modeled partly on Novy.

In the 1920s Novy again drew on his genius with apparatus to do a series of studies on microbial respiration. With Malcolm H. Soule in 1925, he showed that the slow growth of tubercle bacilli in the body resulted from the low oxygen tension that slowed the microbe's rates of respiration and multiplication.

Opinions vary on which aspect of Novy's research was his most important, he was so widely admired for the excellence of his work. The National Academy of Sciences made him a member in 1924. In 1936 the American Association for the Advancement of Science unanimously selected him to receive the 250,000th microscope made by Bausch and Lomb Optical Company, an award for outstanding contributions to science through research with the microscope. When he died in Ann Arbor, alumni of the University of Michigan Medical School honored their beloved teacher by establishing the Frederick George Novy Fellowship for Research in Bacteriology.

Novy considered himself an old-fashioned bacteriologist, but his work was actually far broader. Over his seventy-year career he made pioneering contributions in chemistry, bacteriology, protozoology, immunology, and virology.

• A large collection of Novy's correspondence and research notebooks is at the Bentley Historical Library, University of Michigan, Ann Arbor. Among the biographical accounts, Ruth Good, "Dr. Frederick G. Novy: Biographical Sketch," *University of Michigan Medical Bulletin* 16 (1950): 257–68, best captures his personality. S. E. Gould, "Frederick George Novy, Microbiologist," *American Journal of Clinical Pathology* 29 (1958): 297–309, and Esmond R. Long, "Frederick George Novy," National Academy of Sciences, *Biographical Memoirs* 33 (1959): 326–50, place his science in context and include his bibliography. Novy published two laboratory manuals, *Directions for Laboratory Work in Urine Analysis* (1892), titled *Laboratory Work in Physiological Chemistry* in its second edition (1898), and *Directions for Laboratory Work in Bacteriology* (1894; 2d ed., 1898). On his methods and apparatus see "Laboratory Methods in Bacteriology," *Journal of Applied Microscopy* 1 (1898): 157–60, 190–92, 211–13, and 2 (1898): 235–40, 267–71. His research on trypanosomes is summarized in "On Trypanosomes," *Harvey Society Lectures* 1 (1906): 33–72. For his work on the spirochetes with R. E. Knapp, see "Relapsing Fevers and Spirochetes," *Transactions of the Association of American Physicians* 21 (1906): 456–64. His research with Paul de Kruif is found in "Anaphylatoxin and Anaphylaxis, parts 1–6," *Journal of Infectious Disease* 20 (1917): 499–656. "The Respiration of the Tubercle Bacillus," *Journal of Infectious Disease* 36 (1925): 168–232, is an example of his work on microbial respiration. See also his George M. Kober lecture, "Respiration of Microorganisms," *Journal of Laboratory and Clinical Medicine* 17 (1932): 731–47. An obituary is in the *New York Times*, 10 Aug. 1957.

PATRICIA GOSSEL

NOYCE, Robert Norton (12 Dec. 1927–3 June 1990), applied physicist and entrepreneur, was born in Burlington, Iowa, the son of the Reverend Ralph Noyce, a Congregational minister, and Harriet Norton. After serving in several parishes, in 1937 Rev. Noyce was appointed assistant superintendent of the Iowa Conference of Congregational Churches, whose offices were located on the campus of Grinnell College. The family lived on campus, and three of the four Noyce boys later attended the college. Noyce became valedictorian of his class at Grinnell High School. Known as the "Quiz Kid" for his ability to answer any question put to him, the precocious teenager took part in activities ranging from band and chorus, the Latin and science clubs, and drama to the High School Civil Air Patrol.

As a senior in high school, Noyce took the introductory physics course offered by Professor Grant Gale, a family friend, at Grinnell College. He then attended Grinnell from 1945 to 1949 with the half scholarship offered him as the son of a Congregational minister.

During a disciplinary expulsion in the summer and fall of 1948, imposed for stealing a pig for a campus luau, he worked in the actuarial department of the Equitable Life Assurance Society in New York City. During Noyce's absence, Gale learned by chance of the invention of the transistor at the Bell Telephone Laboratories; he immediately contacted Oliver Buckley, director of research there and a Grinnell graduate, and John Bardeen, one of the inventors and a family friend, in order to obtain the new device. When Noyce returned to Grinnell, he joined Gale in studying the transistor, a rare opportunity at that time. Noyce graduated from Grinnell in 1949 with a bachelor of science degree in physics and mathematics. Captivated by electronics—and by his transistor studies, in particular—he enrolled in the graduate program at the Massachusetts Institute of Technology, only to be disappointed there by the lack of opportunity to deepen his knowledge of transistor technology. In 1953 he completed a Ph.D. in physical electronics with a dissertation on the "Photoelectronic Study of Surface States on Insulators." Soon thereafter, in the same year, he married Elizabeth Bottomley; they would have a boy and three girls.

In 1953 Noyce's interest in transistor electronics pointed toward a research position in an industrial laboratory. He received job offers from several firms, including the Bell Telephone Laboratories. He chose to work for Philco, a relative newcomer to the field, reasoning that he would be a "necessary cog in the machine." Instead, Philco's lack of commitment to transistor research disappointed him, and after a few years he contacted William Shockley, who had led the transistor research team at Bell Laboratories. Shockley had recently founded the Shockley Semiconductor Laboratory in Mountain View, California, not far from the Stanford University campus in Palo Alto. In 1956 Shockley hired Noyce to join the fledgling research laboratory.

Initially, the Shockley Lab provided Noyce with an exhilarating taste of the single-minded dedication to transistor research he had been pursuing since his senior year at Grinnell. In November 1956 Shockley was awarded the Nobel Prize in physics for his part in the invention of the transistor, and the laboratory's future seemed bright. By the summer of 1957, technical differences, clashes with Shockley's managerial style, and the realization of entrepreneurial opportunities available in the nascent semiconductor industry led a group of seven researchers from the lab—Gordon E. Moore, Victor H. Grinich, Sheldon E. Roberts, Eugene Kleiner, Julius Blank, Jean Hoerni, and Jay Last—to break away and set up a new company, a move Noyce would later call an "in-house revolt." With the help of Arthur Rock at the investment firm of Hayden Stone, this group gained the financial backing of Fairchild Camera and Instrument Corporation for the new venture, but lacked a proven manager. Anticipating the demise of Shockley's laboratory after the defections, Noyce agreed to join the group, now dubbed the "Fairchild Eight," and became director of research of the new Fairchild Semiconductor Company. In 1959 he became its vice president and general manager.

Fairchild Semiconductor would become the seedbed for the growing wave of high-technology firms, startups, and spin-offs that defined the phenomenal growth of the region known after 1970 as "Silicon Valley." Noyce's new position moved him into a place of high visibility in the semiconductor industry. With the success of Fairchild Semiconductor, Fairchild Camera in 1959 fulfilled an agreement to buy out the shares of the eight founders, so that Noyce also became a wealthy man. However, his greatest achievement at Fairchild was technical, rather than entrepreneurial: his role in the invention of the integrated circuit, or IC.

Devised by Noyce in 1959 and patented in 1961, the IC built on Jean Hoerni's invention of the planar transistor, which had greatly improved the reliability of transistors by connecting together transistors and other electrical circuit elements on silicon. A conductive aluminum layer replaced wires to link the components, which became known as the "metal over oxide" process. In effect, Fairchild could now manufacture completed circuits, rather than cutting up silicon wafers to make transistors and then shipping them to customers, who would then assemble the circuits. The conceptual simplicity and resulting efficiency of this innovation led Noyce later to characterize it as arising out of his "own laziness." The IC reduced the complexity of circuit fabrication and made possible dramatic increases in the density of microcircuits. Although an independent version of the IC had been invented several months earlier by Jack Kilby at Texas Instruments, Noyce's scheme proved to be more easily manufactured; moreover, by virtue of his position at Fairchild, Noyce could promote the IC effectively, particularly through marketing. The IC, or "chip," became the foundation for the burgeoning semiconductor industry.

By 1968 Noyce held a dozen patents stemming from his work on transistors and integrated circuits at Fairchild. Yet, despite the quickly achieved commercial and technological success of the company, Noyce grew dissatisfied with its hierarchical, risk-averse management structure. In part, this was because tensions between the parent company in the East and the West Coast startup had begun to surface, but Noyce also believed that profit-sharing, which had been seen only a few years earlier as a creative management idea, now hampered technical innovation in the company by encouraging managers to squeeze every drop of profit out of established products. As a result of their conviction that it was time to start a smaller company along different lines, Noyce, Moore, and Andrew Grove left Fairchild in 1968 to found Intel Corporation (originally N. M. Electronics) in Santa Clara, California. Arthur Rock, who by then had become Silicon Valley's leading venture capitalist, provided financial backing and served as chairman of the board. Noyce was the first president and chief executive officer of Intel.

Initially, Intel focused on memory chips and avoided direct competition with Fairchild. The first major product was the 1103 Dynamic Random Access Memory, or DRAM, introduced in 1970 and based on the new metal-oxide semiconductor (MOS) fabrication process. In 1971 the company introduced erasable, programmable read-only memory (EPROM), invented by Dov Frohmann at Intel. With MOS fabrication and the EPROM, Intel established its identity as a company built to create and exploit technological advantages that it could maintain for years ahead of other companies. Late in 1971 Intel introduced the 4004 microprocessor, the first "computer on a chip," developed by a group led by Marcian E. "Ted" Hoff, Jr. Like the integrated circuit at Fairchild, the microprocessor inaugurated what Intel advertising called "a new era of integrated electronics" and within a few years led to the development of the first microcomputers. By then, Intel had honed the strategy of maintaining technological advantages, and it defended its leading position in the microprocessor market through successive generations of microcomputer technology. As president, Noyce built Intel from the ground up to create such competitive advantages by streamlining communication within the company, eliminating hierarchies, and encouraging risk-taking in research and development. He offered Intel employees stock options instead of profit-sharing, reasoning that the potential for increasing the share price better encouraged rapid moves to exploit technological innovations and develop new products.

Intel established itself quickly as one of the leading technology companies in Silicon Valley. By the mid-1970s, however, Noyce's role was changing. He divorced his first wife in 1974 and married Ann Bowers in 1975. They had no children. Also in 1975 he removed himself from the management of daily operations at Intel by stepping down as president and becoming chairman of the board, a position he held until 1979. He devoted much of his attention to industry-wide issues, such as the competitiveness of the U.S. semiconductor industry and technology policy. As an industry spokesman, particularly in the policy arena, he worked closely with the American Electronics Association and, in 1977, joined Wilfred Corrigan of LSI Logic, Jerry Sanders of Advanced Micro Devices, Charles Sporck of National Semiconductor, and John Welty of Motorola to found the Semiconductor Industry Association (SIA), which represented U.S. semiconductor manufacturers.

As an organization, the SIA recognized the importance of engineering education and research, including efforts to boost the competitiveness of U.S. electronics by stimulating cooperative projects linking firms, universities, and government. Noyce had served on the board of trustees of Grinnell College since 1962. He led the SIA in the founding of the Semiconductor Research Cooperative in 1981 and also served on advisory boards at MIT and Stanford. In 1982 he was appointed to the board of regents of the University of California, on which he served until

1988, including stints as vice chair of the board, chair of the Committee on Educational Policy, and chair of the Committee on Oversight of the Department of Energy Laboratories. His position as an industry leader at the height of the trade wars between the United States and Japan pushed Noyce into the forefront of the technological competitiveness debate during the second half of the 1980s; his many activities in this area included a seat on President Ronald Reagan's Commission on Competitiveness; a founding role in the California Legal Reform Project, which sought to reduce the litigation costs of companies; and the vice chairmanship of the Association for California Tort Reform.

In 1988 Noyce accepted the position of chief executive officer of a new research consortium, SEMATECH (Semiconductor Manufacturing Technology), located in Austin, Texas. SEMATECH came into being as a joint venture of state and federal government and a group of fourteen electronics companies, such as Intel, Hewlett-Packard, AT&T, IBM, and Texas Instruments. Its goal was to advance research and development in microelectronics and dispense the results to the members of the consortium. Noyce hoped that the new organization would create a united front in the U.S. semiconductor industry; this was a first step toward competing more effectively against countries that had been able to "utilize science and technology more effectively," as Noyce put it in his dedication speech for the SEMATECH facility in November 1988.

In May 1990 Noyce announced his decision to give up his position as CEO of SEMATECH by the end of that year. He felt that he had created a foundation for cooperation in the semiconductor industry, overcoming the resistance of companies and management who had been fierce competitors. The recovery of the domestic semiconductor industry was underway, with Intel taking the lead as one of the country's most profitable companies. With the addition of his role in the comeback of American semiconductor manufacturing, Noyce's career spanned the technological, industrial, and political development of American microelectronics from the early exploitation of the transistor through the integrated circuit, microprocessor, and personal computer. Awards recognizing Noyce's contributions included election to the National Academy of Engineering in 1969, the National Medal of Science given by President Jimmy Carter in 1979; the Faraday Medal of the IEEE in 1979; the National Medal of Technology given by President Ronald Reagan in 1987; and the first Charles Stark Draper Award (with Jack Kilby), the "Nobel Prize of Engineering," given by President George Bush in 1990. Noyce died in Austin, Texas.

• Noyce's personal papers have not yet been preserved. An important collection of company records and papers from Fairchild Semiconductor, including speeches, papers, and internal reports by Noyce, Gordon Moore, and others, is in the Department of Special Collections, Stanford University, which also holds records of the Shockley Semiconductor Laboratory, including some information about Noyce, in the William Shockley Papers. Materials relating to Noyce are also available through the historical program of Intel Corporation, including interviews with Noyce collected under the auspices of the Intel Oral History Program and an unpublished biographical paper, "Remembering Bob Noyce as a Student," prepared by Grant O. Gale in connection with the Noyce memorial service held in 1990. The most useful publications are Tom Wolfe, "The Tinkerings of Robert Noyce: How the Sun Rose on the Silicon Valley," *Esquire*, Dec. 1993, pp. 346–73; Robert E. Noyce and Marcian E. Hoff, Jr., "A History of Microprocessor Development at Intel," *IEEE Micro* 1 (Feb. 1981): 8–21; and Miller Bonner et al., eds., *Robert E. Noyce: 1927–1990* (1990?), a SEMATECH publication.

HENRY LOWOOD

NOYES, Arthur Amos (13 Sept. 1866–3 June 1936), chemist, was born in Newburyport, Massachusetts, the son of Amos Noyes, a lawyer, and Anna Page Andrews. Given to sailing, collecting bird eggs, and the study of railroad time tables as a boy, Noyes became interested in chemistry under the influence of a high school teacher in his native Newburyport. Supported in part by scholarship funds, Noyes took both bachelor's (1886) and master's (1887) degrees from the Massachusetts Institute of Technology, where he pursued the study of analytical and organic chemistry. Noyes remained at MIT as a teaching assistant the year after completing his master's degree; among his pupils was George Ellery Hale, an undergraduate who would later become one of America's leading astronomers and a partner with Noyes in the development of Caltech.

Like many American chemists of his generation, Noyes went to Germany for graduate study. He matriculated at the University of Leipzig in the fall of 1888, intending to polish his skills in organic and analytical chemistry. Disappointed, however, by the progress of his research and intrigued by the lively personality and stimulating lectures of Wilhelm Ostwald—Leipzig's newly appointed physical chemist—Noyes abandoned his plan and threw himself into the study of thermodynamics, mathematics, and a subject then at the core of physical chemistry: the behavior of aqueous solutions. Solutions were the site of numerous reactions of importance not just to academic chemists but also to biologists, geologists, and industrial chemists. An understanding of matter dissolved in water promised a revolution in the natural sciences comparable to that accomplished by Antoine-Laurent Lavoisier and his disciples when they had opened up the chemistry of gases, especially oxygen, a hundred years earlier. Physical chemists were beginning to develop such an understanding when Noyes arrived at Leipzig. When he received his doctorate in physical chemistry in 1890, Noyes became one of the first American practitioners of this new, and still controversial, specialty.

After his return in 1890 to the United States, Noyes was appointed instructor at MIT. During the next ten years he moved quickly through the ranks, teaching all branches of chemistry and building a significant record of publication in organic, analytical, and physical chemistry. An enduring interest in systematic methods of qualitative analysis, especially for the rare elements, dates from this decade. While teaching, writing textbooks, and pursuing research on a wide array of topics in basic science, Noyes also studied a number of problems of industrial importance. Together with another young chemist at MIT, Willis R. Whitney, Noyes perfected a process for recovering alcohol and ether vapors, and entered into a partnership with the American Aristotype Company of Jamestown, New York, for exploitation of this process in the production of photographic film. Income from this venture freed Noyes of financial concerns and allowed him to enlarge the scope of his research.

In 1903 Noyes entered with MIT into another sort of partnership. Promising to meet half of the operating expenses out of his own pocket, Noyes obtained approval from MIT to open a laboratory for research in physical chemistry. Staffed with young chemists of his own choosing, this laboratory quickly became internationally known for its exact measurements of the physical properties of aqueous solutions and contributed greatly to making MIT a center for graduate study in the basic sciences. Appointments at the laboratory carried light teaching obligations and served as crucial way stations for many of the leading American physical chemists of the early twentieth century, including G. N. Lewis and nearly a dozen other future members of the National Academy of Sciences.

In recognition of his work, Noyes was elected president of the American Chemical Society in 1904, made a member of the National Academy of Sciences in 1905, and was appointed acting president of MIT in 1907. Uncomfortable with the social obligations of MIT's presidency, Noyes returned to his laboratory after two years of service. He would later decline similar opportunities at other institutions. Although he held strong views on educational issues, Noyes preferred to exert influence through his large network of friends rather than to occupy positions of public prominence.

In 1913 Hale coaxed Noyes into assuming direction of the chemistry division of the Throop College of Technology in Pasadena, California. As a trustee of the small engineering school, Hale hoped to enhance the institution's science programs in order to complement the strengths of his observatory atop nearby Mount Wilson. For seven years, which were interrupted by his wartime service with the National Research Council, Noyes maintained his research laboratory at MIT while building a new laboratory and department at Throop. Dismayed by MIT's neglect of basic science and increasingly aggressive solicitation of industrially sponsored research, Noyes resigned his professorship at MIT at the end of 1919 and dedicated his full energies to Throop, which was renamed in 1920 at his suggestion, the California Institute of Technology.

In 1921 Noyes and Hale succeeded in bringing a third outstanding scientist to Pasadena, the Chicago physicist Robert A. Millikan, with whom both Noyes and Hale had worked during the war. A formidable team, Hale, Millikan, and Noyes together exercised great influence on American institutions of science during the 1920s and early 1930s. As members of the Executive Committee of Caltech, they were responsible for making Pasadena an international center for research in the natural sciences. As members of the National Research Council and advisers to philanthropic foundations, they helped devise innovations such as the Rockefeller-financed National Research Council Fellowship program, which would assist hundreds of American postdoctoral students to establish careers as productive investigators. Although criticized for their cozy relationships with the rich and powerful, their neglect of the social sciences, and their tendency to identify Caltech's interests with those of the national scientific community, they proved adept at mobilizing the resources through which the United States established traditions of excellence in the natural sciences.

Convinced that physics was the engine that propelled chemistry, Noyes ceded primacy at Caltech to the physics division of Millikan and encouraged chemistry students to study topics such as X-ray crystallography and quantum theory. This emphasis paid rich dividends in the accomplishments of the young faculty members and students whom Noyes assembled at Caltech and most especially in the work of Linus Pauling, whose career Noyes guided during the 1920s.

Although Noyes is not remembered for any particular contribution to science of outstanding importance, he left an enduring mark on American chemistry through his innovative textbooks, his creative institution building, and his remarkable eye for talent. He died, never having married, in Pasadena and left the bulk of his estate to Caltech.

• A small collection of Noyes's papers is in the California Institute of Technology Archives. The richest sources of his correspondence are the George Ellery Hale Papers at Caltech and the Harry Manley Goodwin Papers at MIT. A brief autobiographical sketch is in the National Academy of Sciences Archives. Noyes's most influential textbook, *A Course of Study in Chemical Principles*, with Miles Sherrill (1914), was designed to lead students to general equations through the solution of problems; it went through multiple editions until 1938. A bibliography of Noyes's publications is in Linus Pauling, "Arthur Amos Noyes," *Biographical Memoirs of the National Academy of Sciences* 31 (1958): 322–46. Other useful memoirs include those by Frederick G. Keyes, *Nucleus* (Oct. 1936): 11–16; Sherrill, *Proceedings of the American Academy of Arts and Sciences* 74 (1940): 150–55; and Charles A. Kraus, *Scientific Monthly* 43 (1936): 179–81. Noyes's career is treated in the context of the development of chemistry in America in John W. Servos, *Physical Chemistry from Ostwald to Pauling: The Making of a Science in America* (1990). On Noyes and Caltech, see Judith R. Goodstein, *Millikan's School: A History of the California Institute of Technology* (1991).

JOHN W. SERVOS

NOYES, Crosby Stuart (16 Feb. 1825–21 Feb. 1908), newspaper publisher, was born at Minot, Androscoggin County, Maine, the son of farmers. A frail man who did not respond well to the harsh Maine climate, Noyes worked various odd jobs in his youth. While attending high school in Minot, Noyes edited a weekly paper called the *Minot Notion* intended to promote "science, literature and the fine arts." He also wrote several stories, one of which was published in the *Boston Yankee Blade*. In 1847 Noyes moved to Washington, D.C., where he served as capital correspondent for several papers, including the *Lewiston* (Maine) *Evening Journal*, the *Yankee Blade*, and the *Philadelphia Saturday Evening Post*. Noyes also worked for bookseller Joseph Shillington and helped distribute the *Baltimore Sun*. In 1848 Noyes landed a full-time post as congressional reporter for the two-year-old weekly *Washington News*, where he worked for the next six years.

After a brief trip to Europe in 1855 recounted in the *Portland* (Maine) *Transcript*, Noyes was hired as a reporter by the struggling daily *Washington Evening Star*. Noyes wrote about sports, politics, religion, lectures, and congressional debates. Meanwhile, in 1856, Noyes married Elizabeth Selina Williams; the couple had three sons and two daughters. By the time of the Civil War, Noyes had been promoted to assistant editor, and he cultivated contacts with Secretary of War Edwin Stanton and other officials in the Lincoln administration. The *Star* was able to obtain Lincoln's 1861 inaugural address and publish it before other papers. Both Noyes and the *Star* were nonpartisan and independent politically. They supported Republican administrations in the 1860s, but based on patriotic loyalty rather than partisanship.

After the war ended, Washington's sharp decline in population and economic vitality influenced *Star* owner W. D. Wallach's decision to give up his paper. In 1867 Noyes joined Samuel H. Kauffmann, George W. Adams, Alexander R. Shepherd, and Clarence B. Baker in buying the *Star* from Wallach for $100,000. Noyes assumed the editorship and Kauffmann became president of the company. Shepherd and Baker sold their interests to the other three partners in a short time. Promising that the paper would be "independent, outspoken, honest," Noyes continued the *Star*'s focus on District of Columbia affairs yet did not ignore the fact that it was also the nation's capital.

Noyes became involved in district politics beginning in 1863 when he was elected as a Republican to a two-year term on the aldermanic board. City government became complicated after the Civil War, in part owing to the beginnings of black suffrage. The *Star* editorially supported the election of Sayles Bowen as mayor in the 1868 city elections. Yet Noyes and Shepherd became opponents of Bowen in the 1870 elections because Bowen became too closely tied to the Radical Republicans. Bowen was defeated with the help of the *Star*. Noyes then supported Shepherd's effort to change the city government to territorial rule with more control by the federal government. As the head of the Board of Public Works under the territorial government, Shepherd guided the city toward massive public improvements, including major paving contracts given to his friends, among them the *Star*. Both Noyes and partner Kauffmann were directors of the Metropolitan Paving Company run by Shepherd in 1872–1873 to spearhead the improvements. Charges of corruption led to two congressional investigations in 1872 and 1874. The reports, which criticized Shepherd, soon led to the termination of the territorial government and its replacement with a commission form. Although not entirely uncritical of Shepherd's methods, even after he sold his shares in the paper in 1873, Noyes and the *Star* justified the results of the improvements in Washington.

The *Star* continued to champion public works improvements in Washington and sought federal funding to that end. When a new form of government for the district was being debated in Congress in 1877, Noyes joined one hundred district citizens asking Congress to increase the funding of district expenses from 40 to 50 percent. Their appeal was successful when the final version was passed in 1878. As his tenure as editor in chief continued, Noyes consistently championed other public improvements in the district. Washington was a leader in the application of asphalt paving in American cities beginning in the late 1870s, a project endorsed by the *Star*. Noyes and the *Star* also prominently backed the creation of Rock Creek Park and Potomac Park. Noyes was an early member after the Civil War of the Union Club, which promoted civic improvements in Washington, and he served as a director of the club in the late 1860s and 1870s. He was also a member of the Board of Trade, founded in 1889 to advise Congress about economic and civic developments in the district. Noyes's middle son Frank became business manager of the *Star* in 1886, and his eldest son Theodore was named associate editor the same year.

Not noted for being gregarious, Crosby Noyes nonetheless presented two public addresses to major audiences: a paper on journalism to the World's Press Parliament in St. Louis in 1904, and another about the history of American journalism to the National Editorial Association in 1907 at Jamestown, Virginia. Henry Watterson learned his major lessons about the profession as a reporter for Noyes before becoming the noted editor of the *Louisville Courier Journal*. Noyes maintained significant friendships among leading national journalists, including Whitelaw Reid of the *New York Tribune*. Noyes died during a regular winter visit to Pasadena, California. Noyes's funeral in the District of Columbia was attended by Vice President Charles W. Fairbanks, Secretary of State Elihu Root, and Speaker of the House of Representatives Joseph B. Cannon.

The contribution of Crosby Stuart Noyes to American journalism arose from his belief that newspapers should serve first and foremost their local communities. He also understood the special significance of Washington as the nation's capital, and the *Star* gave thorough coverage to national news generated by the Congress and president. Noyes was part of an older journalistic tradition that practiced restraint in news and editorial accounts as well as marketing techniques. He was not at home in the new era of sensationalism.

• The bulk of the Noyes papers remain in family possession except for five Crosby S. Noyes letters from 1867–1870 deposited at the Library of Congress. The chief sources of biographical information include a pamphlet, Theodore Williams Noyes, comp., *Crosby Stuart Noyes, 1825–1908* (n.d.), which includes speeches along with biographical material; and grandson Newbold Noyes's memoir, *Crosby Stuart Noyes: His Life and Times* (1940). Related material about the *Washington Star* may be found in Samuel H. Kauffmann, *The Evening Star, 1852–1952: A Century at the Nation's Capital* (1952). See also James H. Whyte, *The Uncivil War: Washington during Reconstruction, 1865–1878* (1958). Obituaries are in the *Washington Evening Star* and *New York Tribune*, both 22 Feb. 1908.

DANIEL WEBSTER HOLLIS III

NOYES, Eliot Fette (12 Aug. 1910?–18 July 1977), designer and architect, was born in Boston, Massachusetts, the son of Atherton Noyes, an English professor. His mother's name is unknown. Noyes attended Phillips Andover Academy and Harvard University, where he majored in Greek and the classics. He withdrew from Harvard to spend two years in Iran on an archaeological expedition. He returned to the United States and in 1938 married Mary Duncan Weed; they had four children. That same year he graduated from the Harvard Graduate School of Design with a master's degree in architecture. He took his first job in Cambridge in the office of Walter Gropius and Marcel Breuer, the well-known proponents of the Bauhaus movement. In 1940, thanks in part to Gropius's recommendation, Noyes became director of the Department of Industrial Design at the Museum of Modern Art in New York.

During World War II Noyes enlisted in the U.S. Army Air Corps. He earned the rank of major and developed a lifelong appreciation for flying. Noyes returned to the Museum of Modern Art after the war but stayed for only a short while. He next took a position as design director at Norman Bel Geddes & Company. It was through Bel Geddes that Noyes made his first contact with undoubtedly his best-known client, International Business Machines. Bel Geddes had been a design consultant for IBM for a number of years (IBM had arranged for a design department as early as 1943). In 1947 IBM asked Bel Geddes to design the new Model A typewriter; Bel Geddes gave the job to Noyes. Later that same year Bel Geddes's company failed, but Noyes finished the design on his own and was held on retainer. It was, in fact, IBM's $400-a-month retainer that allowed him to begin his own company, Eliot Noyes and Associates, in New Canaan, Connecticut. It was during this period that Noyes designed a number of significant houses in and around the New Canaan area, including his own, "Noyes House" (1955).

Noyes's company broadened its scope and designed not only office equipment and industrial products but office buildings, houses, and schools. IBM continued to use Noyes as a consultant, and Noyes enjoyed such a close and productive relationship with then IBM director Thomas Watson, Jr., that in 1956 he was given the position of consultant director of design. It was then that IBM's corporate design began to emerge. Inspired a great deal by Olivetti, the Italian typewriter manufacturer, Noyes began to organize a coherent style for the company, including office spaces and machine products. He rejected annual product design changes that would, it was thought, please the customer; rather, Noyes sought fundamental design principles that would endure. IBM had professional standards to which it expected its employees to adhere, and Noyes tried to standardize the company's design aspects as well. He stated, "There must be consistent use of colour, detail and form—square corners and standard heights, kick-strips, bases and superstructures."

Noyes continued to design and was responsible for the IBM Model B electric typewriter of 1959 and the first Selectric of 1961. It has been said that both compare favorably with the classic typewriter styles of the 1950s by companies such as Nizzoli and Olivetti. He also was head of a team that designed one of the newer, smaller computer systems of the 1960s, the IBM System 360. The workstations especially were noted for their clear and user-friendly designs.

Noyes was in a very powerful position as design chief. All other internal design departments reported to him for review. His influence was not limited to IBM products, however; Noyes was also responsible for architectural works. Working closely with the Real Estate and Construction Division (RECD), Noyes himself was responsible for IBM branch office buildings in Arlington, Virginia, and Los Angeles (1961), the IBM Aerospace Building, Los Angeles (1965), and the IBM Management Development Center in Armonk, New York (1980). In addition, under his guidance IBM retained the services of other significant architects, including his former employer, Marcel Breuer, Mies van der Rohe, and Eero Saarinen.

Noyes's designs followed traditional Bauhaus notions of flat surfaces, crisp and clear lines, and simplicity. Good design was what the public would buy, he was convinced, no matter what consumer surveys revealed. He once stated that "good design is good business," and he held to that doctrine tenaciously. Noyes attempted to integrate design into industry, thus echoing the arts and crafts movement of the nineteenth century. But the design had to fit the product: he despised the idea that, for example, a modern radio should be housed in something looking like fine wood furniture—that is, like something it is not. He liked his designs clean and functional. "I prefer neatness," he once said.

In 1965 Noyes began work for Mobil Oil Corporation supervising company design. Of note is his design for Mobil's service stations with their unique cylindrical pumps. (He was not responsible for the blue Mobil logo with its red *o*, but he did hire Chermayeff, Geismar and Associates, the firm that was.) He also consulted for Westinghouse, working with Paul Rand (who designed both their and IBM's familiar logos). Noyes died in New Canaan, Connecticut.

Noyes's son Eliot, Jr., stated about his father, "He considered himself a bridge between the large corporations and the artistic sensibility. He believed the corporations needed someone to think about the impact of their products on the environment, human use, and esthetics."

• See Noyes's own *Organic Design in Home Furnishing* (1941). Peter Dormer, *Design since 1945* (1993), and John Heskett, *Industrial Design* (1980), both offer information on Noyes and good background data on design trends. Articles on Noyes include Scott Kelly, "Consultant Design: A Retrospective View," *Industrial Design* 13 (June 1966): 38–43; Ann Nydele, "Design for the Corporation," *Progressive Architecture* 56 (Oct. 1975): 80–85, and "Eliot F. Noyes (1910–1977)," *Industrial Design* 24 (Sept. 1977): 42–43. For more on Noyes's architecture see John Peter, *Masters of Modern Architecture* (1958), Ian McCallum, *Architecture USA* (1959), and Sherban Cantacuzino, *Modern Houses of the World* (1964). For a complete listing of Noyes's numerous awards and works, see Ann Lee Morgan and Colin Naylor, eds., *Contemporary Architects* (1994). An obituary is in the *New York Times*, 19 July 1977.

ROD A. MILLER

NOYES, George Rapall (6 Mar. 1798–3 June 1868), biblical scholar, professor, and Unitarian minister, was born in Newburyport, Massachusetts, the son of Nathaniel Noyes and Mary Rapall. His parents had intended him for the ministry but were unable to finance his education. With additional encouragement from his pastor, the Reverend Daniel Dana of First (Old South) Presbyterian Church, he entered Harvard College at age sixteen, supporting himself by teaching school. At Harvard, amid the liberalism of the nascent Unitarian movement, he began to question the religious orthodoxy of his childhood.

Graduating with an A.B. in 1818, Noyes taught for a year at Framingham (Mass.) Academy. In 1819 he entered Harvard's recently created Divinity School, where he came under the influence of the liberal biblical scholar Andrews Norton. Noyes received the A.M. in 1821 but spent an additional five years in biblical study, supporting himself as a tutor. Ordained a Unitarian minister in 1827, he served two parishes: Brookfield (1827–1834) and Petersham (1834–1840), both in Massachusetts. In 1828 he married Eliza Wheeler Buttrick; they had seven children, of whom five lived to adulthood.

During his pastorate, Noyes completed several biblical translations: *An Amended Version of the Book of Job* (1827), *A New Translation of the Book of Psalms* (1831), and *A New Translation of the Hebrew Prophets* (2 vols., 1833–1837). He considered the Book of Job one of history's most remarkable literary productions, summarizing it as a didactic poem upon "the providence of the one true God, and the duty of man."

Noyes first entered public theological debate on the pages of the Unitarian *Christian Examiner*, where in 1834 he published a lengthy refutation of *Christology of the Old Testament* by Ernst Wilhelm Hengstenberg, professor of theology at the University of Berlin. Against Hengstenberg, Noyes insisted that the Hebrew prophets possessed no miraculous foreknowledge of Jesus, and that the New Testament writers were incorrect in quoting Old Testament prophecies as literal predictions of Christ. He also denounced the doctrine of the plenary verbal inspiration of Scripture, calling it a millstone hung around the neck of Christianity. "It is true," Noyes wrote, "that the Bible contains the word of God. It contains also many things which have no claim to that appellation."

Following the appearance of Noyes's 1834 article, the Massachusetts attorney general, himself a Unitarian, threatened Noyes with indictment under an old blasphemy statute. But no charges were ever filed, and Noyes's reputation as a careful translator, biblical critic, and defender of liberal Christianity prompted Harvard to award him the doctor of sacred theology degree in 1839. The following year, upon the recommendation of Andrews Norton, Harvard appointed Noyes the Hancock Professor of Hebrew and Other Oriental Languages and Dexter Lecturer on Biblical Literature, a dual position he held for the remainder of his life.

At Harvard, Noyes continued to publish articles on biblical theology, opposing with particular vigor the Calvinist emphasis on substitutionary atonement, or the doctrine that God the Father demanded the sacrifice of his Son as propitiation for human sins. Moreover, like other Unitarians of the era, Noyes regarded the doctrine of the Trinity as a later metaphysical accretion that obscured the simple theism taught by Jesus in the Lord's Prayer.

Noyes typically buttressed his scholarly arguments with close linguistic analysis of Greek and Hebrew terminology. The Bible, he insisted, must be subjected to the same rigorous standards of interpretation applied to any other book. Foremost among interpretive criteria, in Noyes's estimation, was the meaning originally intended by the author. Noyes thus avoided allegorical or naturalistic explanations of biblical stories, advocating instead a "common sense" approach in which every biblical story had just one true meaning.

In 1846 Noyes published *A New Translation of the Proverbs, Ecclesiastes, and the Canticles*. But he is chiefly remembered for his translation of the New Testament, published posthumously by the American Unitarian Association in 1869. Noyes sought to preserve the "savor and spirit" of the familiar King James Bible, yet his translation, based upon the latest Greek text of Konstantin von Tischendorf, the German biblical scholar, represented the cutting edge of nineteenth-century biblical scholarship.

Noyes died in Cambridge, Massachusetts, a few days after correcting the final page proofs for his New Testament translation. Harvard colleague Andrew P. Peabody recalled him as a man whose liberal scholarly conclusions often seemed at odds with his essentially conservative religious temperament. Noyes himself wrote in 1847, "How can a true man, in his researches as a scholar, be more a conservative, than to aim to preserve all the truth at which, in the faithful exercise of his faculties, he can arrive? And how can he be less a radical, than to aim to eradicate all the error which falls in his way?" In maintaining a scientific skepticism toward the idea of prophecy fulfillment, Noyes appeared more radical than some of his Harvard Unitarian colleagues, including Henry Ware, Sr. Yet Noyes revealed a conservative side in his staunch defense of the miracles of Jesus, including the Resurrection, as the primary validation of Christianity. In arguing for the authenticity of New Testament miracles, Noyes opposed the transcendentalism of Emerson and the naturalism of German biblical critic David Friedrich Strauss. As Jerry Wayne Brown observed in 1969, Noyes's enduring confidence in the historical credibility of the Gospel narratives kept him from subjecting the New Testament to the same probing questions he used in judging the Hebrew Scriptures. Nevertheless, Noyes stands out as one of the greatest American biblical scholars and translators of the nineteenth century.

• Noyes's lectures are in the Harvard University Archives, with a microfilm copy at Princeton University. Noyes's correspondence with Andrews Norton is in the Norton papers at Harvard's Houghton Library. In addition to his Scripture translations, Noyes published numerous reviews of biblical scholarship, including "Hengstenberg's *Christology*," *Christian Examiner* 16 (1834): 321–64; "Stuart on the Old Testament," *Christian Examiner* 40 (1846): 69–77; "Porter's Principles of Textual Criticism," *Christian Examiner* 48 (1850): 26–40; "Davidson on Biblical Criticism," *Christian Examiner* 54 (1853): 419–27; "Professor Maurice and His Heresy," *Christian Examiner* 56 (1854): 260–97; and "The Scripture Doctrine of Sacrifice," *Christian Examiner* 59 (1855): 234–80. A broader statement of Noyes's theology is his "Discourse Delivered Before the Second Congregational Society in Brookfield" (1831) as well as the introduction to his edited volume, *A Collection of Theological Essays from Various Authors* (1856). Noyes assessed the state of American biblical studies in "Causes of the Decline of Interest in Critical Theology," *Christian Examiner* 43 (1847): 325–44. Biographical sketches of Noyes are found in the *Christian Examiner* 85 (1868): 76–81; an article by John C. Kimball in *Heralds of a Liberal Faith*, vol. 3, ed. Samuel A. Eliot (1910); and Andrew P. Peabody, *Harvard Reminiscences* (1888). The most important critical evaluation of Noyes's contribution to nineteenth-century biblical scholarship is Jerry Wayne Brown, *The Rise of Biblical Criticism in America, 1800–1870* (1969).

PETER J. THUESEN

NOYES, John Humphrey (3 Sept. 1811–13 Apr. 1886), religious and social reformer, was born in Brattleboro, Vermont, the son of John Noyes, an agnostic teacher, businessman, and member of the U.S. House of Representatives, and Polly Hayes, described by historians as "strong-willed" and "deeply religious." Noyes entered Dartmouth College at fifteen and graduated with high honors in 1830. After a year's study in the law office of his brother-in-law, Noyes experienced a relig-

ious conversion the day following a four-day revival in Putney, Vermont. As a consequence he decided to abandon law as a career and entered Andover Theological Seminary in 1831. Finding the conservative atmosphere unconducive to his particular kind of piety, he transferred to Yale Divinity School in 1832. There he felt free at first to explore his growing perfectionist convictions that humankind is not depraved and individual and social perfection can be achieved in this life. In 1833 Noyes received a license to preach and joined a free church that combined liberal theology with revivalist practices. In 1834 Noyes declared that he himself had reached a state of sinlessness, which he defined not as "perfection in externals" but as "purity of heart and the answer of a good conscience toward God." For this Noyes lost his preaching license and was dismissed from Yale and the free church. Noyes was convinced by this time that none of the established churches could support institutionally his radical version of perfectionism. He spent the next two years attempting to articulate his theology more clearly, formulating a social structure to undergird it, and seeking followers.

In 1836 Noyes returned to his home in Putney and with family and friends, most of them affluent and educated, formed a society of Bible communists. In 1837, in a letter proposing marriage to Harriet A. Holton, whom he married in 1838, Noyes put forth his view that complex marriage was a relationship between the sexes more compatible with his theology than traditional marriage. Excerpts of the letter were published without Noyes's knowledge in a free love newspaper, the *Battle-Axe and Weapons of War*. In the letter he claimed that "In a holy community there is no more reason why sexual intercourse should be restrained by law than why eating and drinking should be and there is as little occasion for shame in one as in the other." In such a system each adult male was considered the spouse of every adult female and vice versa, but these relationships, according to Noyes, needed to be regulated by both a theological rationale and a social structure.

By 1846 the community in Putney was actually practicing complex marriage. That and claims of miraculous healing so antagonized the neighborhood that Noyes was indicted for adultery in 1847 and departed to set up temporary headquarters in New York City. By 1848 the community was reestablished in Oneida, New York. There Noyes and his followers felt free to work out the intricacies of complex marriage. Members also practiced male continence, a form of birth control that historian Lawrence Foster has called "celibate intercourse" because it required that the male partner never ejaculate, either during or after intercourse. Noyes initiated this surprisingly successful form of birth control for several reasons: as a response to the stillbirths of four of his and Harriet Holton's first five children and their desire to prevent further pregnancies; as a means of regulating pregnancies among the community's multiple sexual partners; and as a way to live out Noyes's contention that sexual intercourse had "amative" as well as "propagative" functions. By 1869 the community was engaged in a form of eugenics called "stirpiculture," whereby certain couples were permitted to have children with the approval of a stirpiculture committee. Noyes's son Pierrepont, born to the communitarian Harriet Worden, was the son of such a union. Oneida's system of governance took the form of mutual criticism rather than written laws; individuals underwent scrutiny of their attitudes and behaviors by a committee or the whole community. The living and economic arrangements at Oneida were designed to further a new vision of family. Members lived together in the mansion, held property communally, shared in the raising of children as well as domestic and outdoor labor, and participated together in recreation and education. All of these practices emerged from Noyes's conviction that perfectionist theology must give rise to a radical restructuring of "family" that would in turn reform the broader society.

The Oneida community with Noyes as its leader persisted until 1879. At that time community leaders discontinued complex marriage because of internal dissatisfaction over the hierarchical nature of the "ascending" and "descending" fellowship on which stirpiculture matches were approved and because of external criticism of "immoralities." On 1 January 1881 the leaders divided and reorganized the communally held property. By this time Noyes, who had for many years spent much time in New York City and Wallingford, Connecticut, had left the community for good. After 1879 he lived with a small community of followers in Niagara Falls, Canada, where he died. He is buried at Oneida.

Noyes's significance lies not so much in the particularities of his perfectionist theology—his has been one among many in American religious history—but in the creativity of the social, economic, and sexual alternatives he constructed at Oneida. Historians, social scientists, and psychologists have acknowledged the ambiguities of Noyes's leadership. Communitarians submitted themselves to Noyes's ultimate authority, and members reported experiencing him as autocratic and paternalistic as well as flexible and accommodating. In sessions of mutual criticism Noyes could be cruelly direct and astutely affirming. In terms of gender roles, the community offered women advantages they did not enjoy in the wider society: freedom both from unwanted pregnancies and from total responsibility for childcare, full participation in the work and governance of the community, equal religious and sexual expression, and comfortable clothing and hairstyles. Yet Noyes asserted that women were spiritually inferior to men and needed to be governed by male authority. And even though men were considered spiritually superior in Noyes's perfectionist theory, they surrendered to him the autonomy they would have exercised outside the community in selection of work and spouse and custody of children. In spite of these ironies and contradictions, Noyes founded and led one of the longest-lasting and most successful utopian communities in nineteenth-century America. He offers students of religion, sociology, economics, psychology, gender roles, and family systems a subject for analysis that goes beyond the particular practices of the Oneida community and that has implications for understanding the viability and vulnerability of alternative social structures.

• The best primary sources for understanding John Humphrey Noyes's religious and social theories are his own writings, among them, *The Berean: A Manual for the Help of Those Who Seek the Faith of the Primitive Church* (1847), *Confessions of John H. Noyes. Part I: Confessions of Religious Experience, including a History of Modern Perfectionism* (1849), *History of American Socialisms* (1870), and *Male Continence* (1872). Other writings by Noyes are in George Wallingford Noyes, ed., *The Religious Experience of John Humphrey Noyes, Founder of the Oneida Community* (1923), and G. Noyes, ed., *John Humphrey Noyes: The Putney Community* (1931). Periodicals and other writings by Noyes and members of the community are listed in an annotated bibliography by Lester G. Wells, *The Oneida Community Collection in the Syracuse University Library*, microfilm ed. (1961). Secondary sources attest to the variety of interpretive perspectives elicited by Noyes and the Oneida community. Robert Allerton Parker, *A Yankee Saint: John Humphrey Noyes and the Oneida Community* (1935), remains the standard biography, amplified by a psychoanalytically oriented work by Robert David Thomas, *The Man Who Would Be Perfect: John Humphrey Noyes and the Utopian Impulse* (1977). Maren Lockwood Carden, *Oneida: Utopian Community to Modern Corporation* (1969), offers a sociological interpretation. Lawrence Foster, *Religion and Sexuality: Three American Communal Experiments of the Nineteenth Century* (1981) and *Women, Family, and Utopia: Communal Experiments of the Shakers, the Oneida Community, and the Mormons* (1991), treat Noyes and the Oneida community extensively and offer excellent bibliographies of primary and secondary sources. Ellen Wayland-Smith, "The Status and Self-Perception of Women in the Oneida Community," *Communal Societies* 8 (1988): 18–53, suggests the complexity of assessing the relative liberation or oppression of women's roles at Oneida in light of Noyes's autocratic leadership.

MARY FARRELL BEDNAROWSKI

NOYES, W. Albert, Jr. (18 Apr. 1898–25 Nov. 1980), chemist and educator, was born William Albert Noyes, Jr., in Terre Haute, Indiana, the son of William Albert Noyes, a chemistry professor and the future president of the American Chemical Society (ACS), and Flora Collier. His father was a deeply religious man who was active in the Congregational church and was a pacifist. Noyes, Jr., was raised in the old-fashioned, God-fearing New England tradition, against which he early rebelled. Although he never thereafter associated himself with any organized religion, he was upright, responsible, and ethical, exhibiting a great devotion to duty and an absolutely rigid integrity, along with great kindness and consideration for others and a total lack of meanness or pettiness.

Noyes attended the University of Illinois at Champaign-Urbana, where his father was chair of the Department of Chemistry, for a year (1916–1917) and then attended Grinnell College in Grinnell, Iowa, receiving his A.B. in 1919. During his undergraduate years he was a radio "ham" operator and took the commercial operators examination. When the United States entered World War I in April 1917, he enlisted in the U.S. Army Signal Corps Reserve. After a period as a shipboard radio operator, in June 1918 he was sent to France, where he served in the front lines until the armistice, rising in rank from sergeant to second lieutenant. Early in 1919 he arranged his discharge from the army in France rather than the customary discharge in the United States. He then enrolled in the Université de Paris à la Sorbonne, from which he received the *Docteur-ès-sciences* degree under the direction of renowned physical chemist Henri Le Châtelier in 1920. After studying at the Université de Genève (1920), in 1921 he married Sabine Onillon, whom he had met in Paris; they were married for almost sixty years and had one child.

Noyes became a teaching fellow at the University of California (1920–1921), an instructor (1922–1923) and assistant professor (1923–1929) at the University of Chicago, and an associate professor (1929–1935) and professor (1935–1938) at Brown University. He then spent twenty-five years at the University of Rochester, where he served as professor (1938–1963), chair of the chemistry department (1939–1955), dean of the graduate school (1952–1956), acting dean, then dean of the College of Arts and Sciences (1956–1958), and distinguished professor emeritus (1963). At Rochester he established what became one of the world's leading centers of photochemistry, attracting not only students and postdoctoral fellows but also numerous photochemical authorities as frequent visitors. Rochester's pioneering influence is still strongly felt by those working in this branch of physical chemistry.

In 1958 Noyes served as visiting lecturer at the University of Texas, Austin, where he became Ashbel Smith Professor of Chemistry (1963–1973) and Ashbel Smith Professor Emeritus (1973–1980). Known for giving direct and severe criticism if he felt that it would be constructive and well received, Noyes was endowed with a quick and ready sense of humor. He died in Austin.

Noyes carried out research on photochemistry, electrochemistry, discharge through gases, vapor pressures, thermal reactions, and the correlation between spectroscopy and photochemistry. In addition to his numerous scientific articles, he was the author of *Modern Alchemy*, with his father (1932); *Photochimie et Spectroscopie* (1937); *Photochemistry of Gases*, with Philip Albert Leighton (1941); *Traité de Chimie Physique*, with H. Weiss, a French translation of Edward Wight Washburn's text (1925); and *Spectroscopie et les Réactiées par la Lumière* (1938).

A consultant to various government agencies, during World War II Noyes served as section chair (1940–1942) and division chair (1942–1946) of the National Defense Research Committee, organizing and directing research groups at various universities. He was a member of the staff of the chief of the Technical Division of the U.S. Army Chemical Warfare Service

(1942–1946), chair of the Division of Chemistry and Chemical Technology of the National Research Council (1947–1953), and chair of the Committee on Chemical Warfare of the Research and Development Board (1948–1950). For his war work he was awarded the U.S. government's Medal for Merit (1948) and the King's Medal for Service in the Cause of Freedom from the United Kingdom (1948).

As adviser to the U.S. delegation of the first conference (1946) of the United Nations Educational, Scientific & Cultural Organization (UNESCO), he took part in drafting plans for that organization and served as a member of the U.S. Commission for UNESCO for six years. He took an active role in establishing sections of the International Union of Pure and Applied Chemistry and was vice president (1947–1951) and president (1959–1963) of the IUPAC. While vice president, he organized the IUPAC's Physical Chemistry Section. His bylaws were taken as a model by the other sections, and he served as interim president until a president was elected.

Like his father, Noyes managed to find time for a distinguished editorial career. He was editor of *Chemical Reviews* (1939–1949) and the *Journal of the American Chemical Society* (1950–1962), both of which his father had previously edited; the *Journal of Physical Chemistry* (1952–1964); and *Advances in Photochemistry*, volumes 1–8, with James Ninde Pitts and George Hammond (1963–1971). A longtime member of the National Academy of Sciences, he held many lectureships and received numerous domestic and foreign awards. His American Chemical Society awards included the Joseph Priestley Medal, the ACS's highest award (1954); the Chicago Section's J. Willard Gibbs Medal (1957); the Dayton, Ohio, Section's Austin M. Patterson Award (1963); and the Charles Lathrop Parsons Award for outstanding public service by an ACS member (1970). He was also chair of the ACS Committee on the Professional Training of Chemists and served as the ACS president in 1947. A member of many scientific societies, he was an honorary member of the Société Chimique de France and the Chemical Society of London. He was especially proud of his election as corresponding member of the French Académie des Sciences and as officer in the French Legion of Honor.

Like his illustrious father, Noyes was renowned not only as an educator and researcher but as a statesman-scientist who helped to promote peace through better international understanding, a reputation gained from his numerous national and international activities. In his own words, "No single person, no matter how gifted, can make great accomplishments in science or any other field. Ultimately his imprint will only be great if through relatives, friends, and colleagues, he obtains not only stimulation but sincere cooperation from them."

• Noyes's career is briefly summarized in "Four Americans on IUPAC Bureau," *Chemical and Engineering News*, 29 Aug. 1955, p. 3587. Marshall Gates's remarks at a memorial service for Noyes held on 2 Mar. 1981 are available as a typescript from the Department of Chemistry, University of Rochester. An obituary is in *Chemical and Engineering News*, 8 Dec. 1980, p. 8.

GEORGE B. KAUFFMAN

NOYES, William Albert (6 Nov. 1857–24 Oct. 1941), chemist, was born near Independence, Iowa, the son of Spencer W. Noyes and Mary Packard, farmers. Both parents encouraged intellectual pursuits and taught the children primarily at home. The boy became interested in chemistry from reading his father's copy of *Elements of Chemistry* (1831), by J. L. Comstock. He spent a few months of each year at a country school.

In 1874 Noyes attended an academy in Grinnell, Iowa, for a semester before entering Iowa College (later Grinnell College). To pay for college he taught at country schools during the winter and attended only the fall and spring college terms, but he studied the courses of the winter term in the evenings. Having also spent many evenings doing chemical analyses in the laboratory, he graduated in 1879 in both the classical course (A.B.) and the science course (B.S.).

Noyes then taught Greek and chemistry at the academy of Grinnell College and carried out chemical analyses commercially for a year. He was put in charge of the chemistry department of the college for a term when its one professor was on leave. In 1881 Noyes entered Johns Hopkins University, where his adviser in chemistry was Ira Remsen. He earned his expenses by conducting water analyses for pay, and in just a year and a half he received a Ph.D. (1882) in chemistry.

Noyes was hired as an instructor in chemistry at the University of Minnesota in 1882, and he carried out analyses for the Minnesota Geological Survey. The next year he became professor of chemistry at the University of Tennessee. In 1884 he married Flora Elizabeth Collier; only one of their three children survived to adulthood. Uncertain of the permanence of the Tennessee position, Noyes accepted an appointment in 1886 as professor of chemistry at Rose Polytechnic Institute in Terre Haute, Indiana. On leave for part of 1888–1889, he studied with organic chemist Adolf Johann Friedrich Wilhelm von Baeyer at the University of Munich in Germany. Noyes's wife died in 1900, and in 1902 he married Mattie Laura Elwell; they had one child.

In 1903 Noyes accepted the position of chief chemist of the newly established National Bureau of Standards in Washington, D.C. While overseeing the construction of the bureau's buildings in its first year, he also carried out researches in chemistry at Johns Hopkins University. In his new position, Noyes became known internationally. According to biographer Roger Adams, "His development of standard methods of analysis and standard specifications for chemicals established the base upon which the Bureau of Standards expanded to its present position of influence and prestige" (Adams, p. 185).

In 1907 Noyes became chairman of the department of chemistry at the University of Illinois at Champaign-Urbana, with the urging from the university president to build a strong graduate department. He greatly enlarged the teaching staff, and the number of papers published by members of the department increased considerably. Noyes's second wife died in 1914, and the next year he married Katharine Haworth Macy; they had two children.

From his earliest college days and throughout his career, Noyes carried out careful chemical studies and published more than 200 papers in both organic and inorganic chemistry. He determined the atomic weight of oxygen in 1889 with an accuracy greater than had previously been attained. In 1907 he obtained a value for the hydrogen-oxygen ratio, which is basic to the system of atomic weights. He also analyzed manganese, sulfur, and phosphorus in iron and steel, on which he wrote several significant papers from 1894 to 1902 that were published in the *Journal of the American Chemical Society*. For many years Noyes pursued studies of the molecular arrangements in camphor, a complex chemical derived from the camphor laurel tree, widely used in medicine and in various commercial products, including plastics. In 1902 he provided proof of the structure of camphoric acid that validated the formula proposed by German chemist Konrad Julius Bredt in 1893. From 1894 onward Noyes published more than forty articles on camphor. Beginning with a study of the formation of nitrogen trichloride from ammonium and chlorine in 1901, he was among the earliest chemists to determine that molecules of elements may ionize into positive and negative parts. This led him into studies of the electronic theory of valence. He carried out analyses of coal for a joint committee of the American Chemical Society and the American Society for Testing Materials in 1917.

Noyes's widely used textbooks, which went through several revisions, included *Elements of Qualitative Analysis* (1887), *Organic Chemistry for the Laboratory* (1897), *A Textbook of Organic Chemistry* (1903), and *A Textbook of Chemistry* (1913). His last book, for the layman, was *Modern Alchemy* (1932), coauthored with his son William Albert Noyes, Jr.

From 1902 to 1917 Noyes was editor of the *Journal of the American Chemical Society*, which under his direction became a very influential journal in its field. As a spin-off from it he founded in 1907 *Chemical Abstracts*, for which he obtained the help of almost thirty assistants to locate and summarize articles and books on chemistry. It has continued as an invaluable reference in its field. In 1919 Noyes became editor of the scientific monograph series of the American Chemical Society, and he served as the first editor of *Chemical Reviews*, from 1924 to 1926.

During his first trip to Europe in 1888, Noyes enjoyed getting acquainted with scientists of other nations. He traveled to Europe several times, and he was much dismayed by the First World War and the national animosities it provoked. Believing that scientists could contribute to world peace, he from 1920 to 1937 published pamphlets and articles on such topics as "Building for Peace," "International Understanding," and "Science in Place of War" and maintained correspondence with scientists of many nations.

Highly regarded by his students and colleagues, Noyes received a number of scientific honors, including election to the National Academy of Sciences in 1910 and the Priestley Medal of the American Chemical Society in 1935. In 1939 the University of Illinois rededicated its chemistry facility as the William Albert Noyes Laboratory of Chemistry. Noyes died in Urbana, Illinois.

• A considerable collection of Noyes's archival records is at the University of Illinois at Urbana-Champaign. Significant papers by Noyes include "Atomic Weight of Oxygen," *American Chemical Journal* 11 (1889): 155; "The Atomic Weight of Hydrogen," *Journal of the American Chemical Society* 29 (1907): 1718, and *Bulletin No. 4 of Bureau of Standards* (1908); "Camphoric Acid. XI. Confirmation of Bredt's Formula; Some Derivatives of Inactive Camphoric Acid," with Austin M. Patterson, *American Chemical Journal* 27 (1902): 425; "The Reaction between Chlorine and Ammonia," with Albert C. Lyon, *Journal of the American Chemical Society* 23 (1901): 460; and "Coal Analysis: Final Report of the Joint Committee of the American Society for Testing Materials and the American Chemical Society," *Industrial and Engineering Chemistry* 9 (1917): 100. Biographies are by Austin M. Patterson in *Science* 94 (1941): 477–79; B. S. Hopkins in *Journal of the American Chemical Society* 66 (1944): 1045–56, with bibliography; and Roger Adams in National Academy of Sciences, *Biographical Memoirs* 27 (1952): 178–208, with bibliography.

ELIZABETH NOBLE SHOR

NUGENT, Elliott (20 Sept. 1897?–9 Aug. 1980), actor, director, and playwright, was born in Dover, Ohio, the son of John Charles "J. C." Nugent, an actor and playwright, and Grace Fertig, an actress. Some sources indicate he was born in 1899. Nugent's early childhood was spent primarily at the home of his maternal grandfather in Dover, but he often accompanied his parents on vaudeville tours, occasionally performing as "Master Elliott, the Boy Monologist," and later, in an act with his sister, as "Master Elliott and Baby Ruth." When Nugent was thirteen years old his mother retired from show business and returned with her children to Dover. After graduating from Dover High School in 1915, Nugent, an excellent student and athlete, attended Ohio State University, where he began a lifelong friendship with classmate James Thurber, who would later become a well-known humorist and cartoonist. Nugent served in the U.S. Navy for several months in 1918 but returned to Ohio State in time to graduate with his class in the spring of 1919.

Immediately after graduating Nugent moved to New York City to commence a theatrical career and quickly landed a role in the road company of *Tillie: A Mennonite Maid*, starring Patricia Collinge. Nugent spent the summer of 1920 with the Stuart Walker Players in Indianapolis, Indiana, then participated in several productions that closed before reaching New York. An aspiring writer as well as an actor, during this period Nugent wrote a short story titled "Larry Pyramids," which was published in the *Smart Set* (Apr. 1921, p. 111).

Nugent made his Broadway debut in 1921 in a small role in the George S. Kaufman–Marc Connelly comedy *Dulcy*, starring Lynn Fontanne. That same year Nugent married actress Norma Lee, who also had a small role in *Dulcy*. The couple had three children. Nugent achieved recognition with *Kempy* (1922), a whimsical comedy that he coauthored with his father. Nugent starred as Kempy James, a naive young plumber who impulsively marries one of his customers. After participating in several failures, including *Dumb-Bell* (1923) and *The Rising Son* (1924), both cowritten with his father, Nugent returned successfully to Broadway in *The Poor Nut* (1925), yet another collaboration with his father. A collegiate comedy set at Nugent's alma mater, Ohio State, *The Poor Nut* starred Nugent as a shy botany student who becomes a big man on campus.

Tall, thin, and fair-haired, Nugent moved to Hollywood in 1929 to work in the motion picture industry. His first film was *So This Is College* (1929). He also appeared in *Not So Dumb* (1930), with Marion Davies; *Wise Girls* (1930), a retitled screen version of his stage success *Kempy*, for which he also wrote the screenplay; *The Virtuous Husband* (1931), with Jean Arthur; and *Life Begins* (1932), with Loretta Young (he is also credited with co-directing *Life Begins* with James Flood). Not content with acting and writing assignments, the ambitious Nugent began directing films on his own, beginning with *The Mouthpiece* (1932). He also directed *Three Cornered Moon* (1933), with Claudette Colbert; *She Loves Me Not* (1934), with Bing Crosby; *Love in Bloom* (1935), with George Burns and Gracie Allen; *Professor Beware* (1938), with Harold Lloyd; and *The Cat and the Canary* (1939), with Bob Hope.

Nugent made a memorable return to Broadway as an actor and playwright with *The Male Animal* (1940), coauthored by his old friend James Thurber. The play featured Nugent as a mild-mannered college professor who must simultaneously deal with two problems: a threat to his academic freedom and the return to campus of his wife's former beau, a handsome football hero. "When he retired to Hollywood some years ago Mr. Nugent had been long accustomed to playing timid young men who turn on their oppressors. Now, after his long cinema absence, he returns to a somewhat similar role and plays it even better than ever," said Richard Watts, Jr., in the *New York Herald Tribune* (10 Jan. 1940). Nugent also directed the screen version of *The Male Animal* (1942), which starred Henry Fonda in Nugent's stage role.

Rejected for military service during World War II, Nugent did his part by working in war-related stage and screen projects. In Philip Barry's play *Without Love*, he played the son of an Irish-American diplomat who believes Ireland must abandon its neutral status and align itself with England if the Axis powers are to be defeated. In the meantime he enters into a marriage of convenience with a wealthy young widow, played by Katharine Hepburn. A disappointing follow-up to the earlier Barry-Hepburn collaboration *The Philadelphia Story*, *Without Love* toured for a full season before opening at Broadway's St. James Theatre in November 1942 to mixed notices and moderate audience interest. Far more successful was John Van Druten's *The Voice of the Turtle*, a romantic comedy with Nugent and Margaret Sullavan as a soldier and an actress who are thrust together when the soldier is stood up by the actress's friend. *The Voice of the Turtle* (1943) eventually ran for 1,557 performances. "Mr. Nugent, playing with that down-to-earth naturalness that makes him seem hardly an actor, gives a perfect performance," wrote Louis Kronenberger in *PM* (9 Dec. 1943, p. 20). Nugent then directed James Gow and Arnaud d'Usseau's *Tomorrow the World* (1943), the story of a Nazi-inculcated German orphan who is adopted by an American family. Between theater assignments Nugent directed the musical film *Up in Arms* (1944), featuring Danny Kaye (in his first starring role) as a hypochondriac soldier on board a Pacific-bound troop ship.

After the war Nugent concentrated on directing Hollywood films, most notably *My Favorite Brunette* (1947), with Bob Hope; *The Great Gatsby* (1949), with Alan Ladd; *Mr. Belvedere Goes to College* (1949), with Clifton Webb; and *Just for You* (1952), with Bing Crosby. During these years Nugent experienced emotional problems and exhibited erratic behavior. He was hospitalized on several occasions and, with the help of psychiatry and religion, regained his mental health. An astute businessman with a wide variety of financial interests, Nugent produced several plays and for a time was involved in a production partnership with actor Robert Montgomery, a close friend from Nugent's early Hollywood days. His most successful venture as a theatrical producer was George Axelrod's comedy *The Seven Year Itch* (1952). Nugent also acted in live television, appearing on "Robert Montgomery Presents" and the "U.S. Steel Hour." He published a novel titled *Of Cheat and Charmer* (1962) and an autobiography titled *Events Leading Up to the Comedy* (1965). He died at his home in New York City.

• A collection of Nugent's papers, including manuscripts, programs, correspondence, and clippings, is at the Billy Rose Theatre Collection at the New York Public Library for the Performing Arts, Lincoln Center. For biographical information on Nugent, see "Also a Royal Family: A Few Notes on the Nugents, with Main Reference to Master Elliott," *New York Times*, 4 Aug. 1940; "A Bright Tyke Now Bosses His Father in Play," *New York Herald Tribune*, 18 Jan. 1942; "Varied Talents Make Nugent's Life a Busy One," *New York Herald Tribune*, 19 Dec. 1943; and Richard F. Shepard, "Elliott Nugent and Middle Age," *New York Times*, 11 Aug. 1957. See also Hermine Rich Isaacs, "Elliott Nugent," *Theatre Arts*, May 1944, pp. 280–84. An obituary is in the *New York Times*, 11 Aug. 1980.

MARY C. KALFATOVIC

NUGENT, Pete (16 July 1909–1973), tap dancer, was born in Washington, D.C., the son of Richard Nugent, a Howard University graduate and Pullman porter who later ran an elevator in the White House, and Pauline (maiden name unknown), who had attended Miner Teachers' College. Around 1920 the family moved to New York City, where he attended DeWitt Clinton High School. A poor student, Nugent was frequently tardy and truant; he quit school by the age of sixteen. He found work in the chorus of the TOBA circuit, the show-business circuit in the South and Midwest, headquartered in Nashville. This circuit was for black performers roughly what vaudeville houses were for whites, and it provided work for a number of black entertainers before it died out during the depression. The acronym stands for Theatre Owners' Booking Association, but because of the pitiful pay scale it was universally said to stand for "Tough On Black Ass." Many black acts got their starts on TOBA; if they were well received, they would move to Keith, another circuit, the peak of achievement for vaudeville performers, which did two or three shows a day in major cities.

In 1926 Nugent got a job working on Broadway in *Honeymoon Lane*, starring Kate Smith. Two years later, in 1928, he teamed up with Irving "Peaches" Beaman in Chicago; in 1931 Duke Miller was added to form a trio. In September of that year the team, "Pete, Peaches, and Duke," performed in New York City.

"Pete, Peaches, and Duke" was Nugent's big act, and one of the best of the era. Nugent was its leader and choreographer (though that word was unknown at the time). Offstage, Nugent walked in a much-imitated hip strut—his later partner Honi Coles once called it an "arrogant swagger"—that magically melted into angelic smoothness on the dance floor. He borrowed much from Eddie Rector, who was a key figure in the transformation of tap into a graceful and elegant stage craft. The acts he choreographed were marked by full use of the stage and by a unique interweaving of precisely synchronized ensemble and solo performances that was new to tap dancing. "Pete, Peaches, and Duke," according to jazz dance historian Marshall Stearns, was "the classic class act."

In 1937 Miller died of pneumonia and the act broke up. But "Pete, Peaches, and Duke" was much copied by both white and black acts (such as "The Dunhills," a white act whom Nugent coached, and "The Three Dukes," a black act).

In 1941 Nugent performed in *Jump for Joy* (to "Hickory Stick"), a short-lived musical by Duke Ellington that aimed to break through the stereotyped image of blacks that had been dominant in the theatrical world. Nugent choreographed a number for the Irving Berlin show *This Is the Army* for Warner Bros. (1943), dancing in the chorus line, and in 1944 he performed with Billy Eckstine's famous band, which included Dizzy Gillespie and Charlie Parker. In 1949 the Copacetics Club, an association of tap dancers, was formed in tribute to the late Bill "Bojangles" Robinson, with Nugent as an original member.

In 1952 Nugent quit the performing circuit at a time when tap dancing was losing its popularity. He was never able to play white nightclubs except in benefits, and he was tiring of low-down theaters and low, often unreliable, pay. He opened a studio with Honi Coles, with whom Nugent had been friends for many years. The studio, called Dancecraft, was located at 133 West Fifty-second Street in Manhattan. But because of problems with the building owners, the studio closed after about two years; still, a number of dancers who later became eminent studied there, including Brenda Buffalino.

When the studio closed, Coles went on the road again and later became production manager at the Apollo; Nugent became a business manager for a rock and roll group working for Motown. He also occasionally appeared at black clubs and at festivals, such as the 1962 Newport Jazz festival, at which he did Eddie Rector's routine. He also taught at Henry LeTang's studio. He never married, and he died in New York City.

• The most important source on the early history of tap is Marshall Stearns and Jean Stearns, *Jazz Dance* (1968; repr. 1994), as well as the interviews on which the book is based, available at the Institute for Jazz Studies at Rutgers University in New Jersey. The Dance Collection at the New York Public Library for the Performing Arts, Lincoln Center, also has an invaluable source of clippings, manuscripts, magazines, books, and films about tap dance and dancers.

ROBERT P. CREASE

NÚÑEZ CABEZA DE VACA, Alvar (c. 1490–c. 1559), soldier, explorer, and writer, was born in Jérez de la Frontera, Spain, the son of Francisco de Vera, a member of the municipal council, and Teresa Cabeza de Vaca, a noblewoman. Little is known about Núñez's early life. He chose to use his matrilineal surname to emphasize his relationship to Martín Alhaja, who was ennobled in 1212 with the name Cabeza de Vaca (Head of Cow) after directing the king's armies by marking their route with a cow's skull. Núñez's paternal grandfather, Pedro de Vera, was a conquistador and early Spanish governor in the Canary Islands. Núñez trained for a military career and by the time he left for the New World already had experience in battle.

In 1527 Núñez was appointed second in command for Pánfilo de Narváez's expedition to *la Florida* (the lands north of the Gulf of Mexico from the Florida peninsula to Mexico). From the very start Núñez and Narváez disagreed with one another concerning the best way to proceed. After landing on the Florida peninsula somewhere south of Tampa Bay, Narváez, against Núñez's advice, chose to send the ships north in search of a safe harbor while the main body of the expedition marched overland. Those on land never saw the fleet again. Instead, the expeditionaries, some four hundred in all, walked to Apalache (near modern-day Tallahassee) then to the *Bahía de Caballos* (Bay of Horses, perhaps Apalachicola Bay), so called because the party ate its horses to keep going. From April to September 1528, hoping to sail along the Gulf of Mexico to Spanish settlements in New Spain (modern-day Mexico) they built five makeshift boats, using their stirrups and armaments to forge nails and tools and their shirts to make sails. The 242 surviving men trav-

eled along the Gulf Coast until the flotilla was broken up in a storm off the Texas coast.

On or near Galveston Island, at a place the Spaniards named the *Isla de Malhado* (Island of Bad Luck), Núñez landed, but his boat was washed out to sea. Few other Spaniards survived the storm, and those who did were scattered throughout several Native-American villages in the region and held as slaves. Núñez worked the next six years as a trader between various coastal and inland tribes until September 1534, when, along with three others—Andrés Dorantes, Alonso del Castillo Maldonado, two of the Spanish leaders of the Narváez expedition, and Esteban, an African-born slave brought on the Narváez expedition by Dorantes—Núñez escaped and began a two-year trek across what is now the southwestern United States and northern Mexico.

At first, the four men suffered from starvation and exposure, at times unable to find either corn or the fruit of the prickly pear cactus, staples of the region's diet. As time went on, however, the four began to serve as faith healers among the Native Americans. Originally Núñez and the others were forced to participate in a Native-American shamanistic healing ritual. According to Núñez's account, though, he and the others called upon God, and in their minds they turned the event into a Christian laying on of hands ceremony. The sick man recovered, and as a result news of the four men's healing powers spread. An entourage formed, growing larger in each village they passed through, where people would bring the men food in exchange for their healing services. Finally reaching Spanish settlements in early 1536, Núñez returned to northern Mexico to convince the Native Americans there to stop hiding from slave traders and return to their homes. He did so by persuading them that if they would convert to Christianity, they would be safe.

In 1537 Núñez sailed back to Spain, where he hoped to be commissioned as the commander of his own expedition to *la Florida*, but Hernando de Soto had already been named the *adelantado* (military and civil governor) of these lands. At first Núñez remained silent about what he had found in the region, which made many people believe there were great riches there, inspiring them to accompany Soto. In time, on 18 March 1540, Núñez was named *adelantado* of the Rio de Plata region of South America; he arrived at Santa Catalina Island off the coast of Brazil in early 1541. From the mainland near there, Núñez led an expedition overland, finally arriving at Asunción, Paraguay, on 11 March 1542. The next summer he led an expedition up the Paraguay River. By early 1544, however, dissension had grown among Núñez's men, at least in part because of his liberal treatment of the native population, outlawing their enslavement. In April the colonists revolted, imprisoned Núñez for several months, then sent him back to Spain where he remained imprisoned from 1545 to 1551. In 1551 he was tried for malfeasance, found guilty, and exiled to Oran, Algeria, but in 1556 his sentence was reversed.

After being awarded a government pension, Núñez lived in Valladolid until his death.

Sometime between 1536 and 1541 Núñez wrote his *Relación* (1542), an account of his time in *la Florida*. Renamed *Naufragios* (*Shipwrecks*) when it was published in 1555 (along with an account of his years in South America, the *Comentarios*, by an author known simply as Pedro Hernández), Núñez's work is both an exciting adventure tale and an excellent ethnographic study. His sympathetic treatment of Native Americans makes his descriptions of them useful to modern scholars. In addition, *Naufragios* includes some of the earliest written references to the buffalo and the opossum. In many ways Núñez's importance lies as much in his role as a writer of ethnography, natural history, and literature as in his role as an explorer.

• English translations of Núñez's *Naufragios* vary in quality, but the extensive notes in the version by Cyclone Covey, *Cabeza de Vaca's Adventures in the Unknown Interior of America* (1961), make it quite useful to historians and anthropologists, though the placement of notes within the text interferes with the work's literary quality. The standard English-language biography is still Morris Bishop, *The Odyssey of Cabeza de Vaca* (1933), while the most recent Spanish-language biography is Bibiano Torres Ramirez, *Alvar Núñez Cabeza de Vaca* (1990).

E. THOMSON SHIELDS, JR.

NURSE, Rebecca (Feb. 1621–19 July 1692), victim of the Salem witchcraft trials, was born Rebecca Towne in Yarmouth, England, the daughter of William Towne and Joanna Blessing. She was baptized on 21 February 1621 in the Church of St. Nicholas. The family immigrated to the United States, settling in Topsfield, Massachusetts, when Rebecca was a young woman. At an unknown date she married Francis Nurse, a tray maker. The couple resided near the North River until they bought a 300-acre farm in Salem Village in 1678. Their eight children and their families lived on the property, and all farmed the land to make yearly mortgage payments. Rebecca Nurse contributed by tending to her productive flax garden and spinning the flax into thread.

According to some accounts, before the witch proceedings against Nurse, some townspeople may have been resentful of the Nurse family's success. But other factors such as previous lawsuits involving the boundaries between the Nurse property and that of the prestigious Putnam family may have added to the vindictiveness. Nevertheless, Nurse and her husband were considered prominent and respected members of the community. As a God-fearing Puritan, Nurse was a pious woman who read the Scriptures and raised her children according to tradition. Although not formerly dismissed from her membership at the First Church of Salem, Nurse attended the Reverend Samuel Parris's church in Salem Village.

Before the winter of 1691–1692 the belief in witches was common in New England, and over the years sporadic incidents involving witchcraft had occurred. At one time Nurse's mother was named a witch, and although she was never arrested this fact further enhanced the case against Nurse. The witchcraft furor began in the home of Parris. His daughter Betty, his niece Abigail, and their friends sometimes gathered in the kitchen with Tituba, their half-black, half–West Indian servant, who demonstrated tricks and practiced incantations. Reports filtered through the village that the girls, one of them Ann Putnam, were acting peculiar, crawling under chairs and stools and talking in nonsensical phrases. When they began to have visions a doctor verified that the girls had been bewitched.

Nurse took no particular notice when news of the girls' bewitchment first created a stir in the community, and curiosity seekers came from other villages to witness the phenomenon. Parris called a meeting of neighboring ministers to investigate the matter, and they quickly concurred that the girls had been possessed. Claiming she was not a witch, Tituba took measures to uncover the real witches. The girls, possibly fearing Tituba might expose their secret kitchen gatherings, named the servant. In turn Tituba became an accuser and named two other women as witches.

Villagers attended the examinations of the three women, but Nurse and her family objected to the proceedings and were not present, an act not looked on favorably by the congregation. The town divided into factions, and Nurse's husband was considered a member of the anti-Putnam group. On 13 March 1692 Ann Putnam claimed to have seen the apparition of the aged and nearly deaf Rebecca Nurse. A warrant for Nurse's arrest was issued on 23 March after she was named by Edward and Jonathan Putnam as "having committed sundry acts of witchcraft." The following day she was taken from her sickbed and examined by Parris at the meetinghouse. Four young girls accused her of afflicting them, one claiming that Nurse had bitten her and struck her with a chain. Nurse claimed her innocence, but when one of her accusers fell into convulsions, followed by the other three loudly screaming, the old woman was deemed guilty.

Nurse was taken to jail where she remained in deplorable conditions. Ministers came to pray and to cajole her into admitting guilt. Women arrived and examined her body and found a marking to prove that she was a witch. On 2 June she appeared before the grand jury, and four indictments were returned against her. A neighbor spoke out against her, charging that after an enraged Nurse had shouted at her husband when their pigs entered the Nurses' yard her husband had been "taken with strange and violent fits" and died.

Many villagers supported Nurse. When the court convened on 30 June family and friends, including Jonathan Putnam, signed a petition attesting to her piety and good character. When she was judged to be not guilty the four girls went into uncontrolled fits. The chief justice then asked the jurymen to reconsider their judgment. When the jury returned they asked Nurse to respond to a remark she had made. Commotion in the courtroom added to Nurse's anxiety and deafness, and she failed to answer their question. Her silence became the evidence needed to find her guilty and sentence her to be hanged. When Nurse learned of the circumstances, she and her family wrote an explanation to the governor who then granted a reprieve. The accusing girls complained that Nurse was still tormenting them. When the entire congregation of her original church voted for her excommunication, a sure sign of her expulsion from heaven, the governor rescinded the reprieve order.

On 19 July Rebecca Nurse was hanged on Gallows Hill and buried nearby in a shallow common grave. Family members later retrieved her body and buried it in a grave on the Nurse property. Two granite memorials were later erected, one for Nurse and another inscribed with the names of those who offered testimony in her favor. Over the years her family fought to clear Nurse's name and petitioned the courts. In 1706 Ann Putnam stood before the Nurse family and recanted her original testimony. In 1710 the General Court reversed the convictions of all the victims whose families had petitioned. In 1712 Nurse's excommunication from the First Church of Salem was revoked.

Nurse was an ordinary woman caught in the events of an extraordinary period of superstitious belief in witchcraft. Even her respected status was of no help when the community convinced itself with the help of its ministers that Nurse's body was the perfect one for the devil to inhabit and that Satan "may assume the shape of the innocent." The memory of Rebecca Nurse's travail survived because of those who believed in her and fought to clear her name.

• The proceedings of the Salem trials are in W. Elliot Woodward, *Records of Salem Witchcraft* (2 vols., 1864), and George L. Burr, ed., *Narratives of the Witchcraft Cases, 1648–1706* (1914). Other writings on the trials and Nurse are Charles Sutherland Tapley, *Rebecca Nurse: Saint But Witch Victim* (1930); Chadwick Hansen, *Witchcraft at Salem* (1969); Marion L. Starkey, *The Devil in Massachusetts: A Modern Inquiry into the Salem Witch Trials* (1949); Carol F. Karlsen, *The Devil in the Shape of a Woman: Witchcraft in Colonial New England* (1987); Elaine G. Breslaw, *Tituba, Reluctant Witch of Salem: Devilish Indians and Puritan Fantasies* (1996); Paul Boyer and Stephen Nissenbaum, eds., *Salem Village Witchcraft: A Documentary Record of Local Conflict in Colonial New England* (1972; repr. 1993); and Nissenbaum, *Salem Possessed* (1997).

MARILYN ELIZABETH PERRY

NUTHEAD, William (1654?–1695?), printer, was born probably in England. His parentage and background are unknown. He evidently served an apprenticeship in a printshop because records describe him as a printer from his first appearance in the colonies.

Nuthead arrived in Virginia, probably in late 1682, sponsored by John Buckner, a planter and merchant of Gloucester County. In February 1683 the Virginia governor Thomas, Lord Culpeper, ordered Buckner to appear before the council in Jamestown to answer charges that he had printed the acts of assembly of November 1682 and "several other papers" without first obtaining a license. Buckner claimed that Nuthead had only printed two sample sheets, "w[hi]ch were designed to be presented to his Excellency for his approbation of the print."

Buckner's explanation satisfied the governor and council, but they were determined to avoid "all troubles and inconveniences, that may be occasioned thorow [sic] the liberty of a presse." They therefore required Buckner and Nuthead to post a security bond for their good behavior and to refrain from printing anything else until the king's pleasure in the matter of a printing press for Virginia could be determined. In December 1683 the king dispatched a letter ordering the Virginia government to ensure "that no person be permitted to use any press for printing upon any occasion whatsoever" (*A History of Printing*, p. 2).

Thwarted in his attempt to establish a printing press in Virginia, Nuthead moved to St. Mary's City, the provincial capital of Maryland. The earliest evidence of Nuthead's Maryland press is a printed blank form, filled in with the name of two St. Mary's County residents and dated 31 August 1685. This form, printed several months earlier than the first known production of William Bradford's Philadelphia press, establishes Nuthead's precedence as the first person to operate a printing press in the English colonies south of Massachusetts.

Like most early colonial printers trying to establish a business, most of Nuthead's printing in Maryland consisted of blank forms used by government officials. Examples of four of these forms survive. Ranging from a 12-line bill to a 36-line administrator's bond, each form alternates typeset text with blank spaces for an official to fill in the details of a particular transaction. The small number of blank forms that survive belie the activity of Nuthead's press. At his death his estate listed over sixty accounts payable worth about £100 sterling from people in all parts of the province. Many of these debtors were provincial or local officials who probably owed Nuthead for blank forms they had acquired from him.

In July 1689 Maryland experienced its own version of England's Glorious Revolution when Protestants under John Coode overthrew the proprietary government. To explain their actions to the citizens of Maryland and the crown, the rebels drew up a manifesto entitled *The Declaration of the Reasons and Motives for the Present Appearing in Arms of their Majestyes Protestant Subjects in the Province of Maryland*. The Protestants shipped a manuscript copy of the document to England, but also had the manifesto printed by Nuthead on his St. Mary's press. No copy of Nuthead's printing of the declaration has been found, but a reprinting appeared in England in November 1689 with the colophon: "Maryland, Printed by William Nuthead at the City of St. Maries. Re-printed in London, and sold by Randal Taylor near Stationers Hall, 1689" (*Colophon*, p. 336). A month after printing the *Declaration*, Nuthead printed a broadside entitled *The Address of the Representatives of their Majestyes Protestant Subjects, in the Province of Mary-Land Assembled*. A single example of this broadside exists in the papers of the Lords of Trade in the Public Record Office in London.

In 1692 the English government installed Lionel Copley as Maryland's first royal governor and removed all authority from the proprietor, Charles, 3d Lord Baltimore, except the right to grant land. Nuthead successfully transferred his allegiance from the proprietary to the royal government and continued to supply blank forms to public officials. In October 1692 Richard Darnall, acting as the agent for the deposed proprietor, brought Nuthead a blank land warrant that included the proprietor's name as the issuer. Darnall asked Nuthead to print 500 copies immediately. Nuthead at first agreed, but must have later decided it might offend the royal government if he did work for an agent of the proprietor. When Darnall came to pick up the warrants Nuthead informed him "the Press & Letters were none of his and therefore [he] could not complye therewith without Order." Later in the month the council ordered Nuthead to print nothing but blank bills and bonds "without leave from his Ex[celle]ncy or the further Order of this Board" (*A History of Printing*, p. 9).

Nuthead's assertion that he did not own the "Press and letters" is puzzling. Perhaps it was simply a ruse to avoid a nasty confrontation with Darnall, or perhaps Nuthead in fact did not own the equipment in his printshop. The inventory of Nuthead's personal property taken in early April 1695 shortly after his death lists "a printing press, Letters & a parcell of Old Lumber" in the "Printeing house" worth £5, as well as some "printed papers" in an old trunk, together worth just five shillings (Prerogative Court Inventories and Accounts 12, MSA S 536, pp. 59–60, Maryland State Archives). Governor Lionel Copley died in September 1693, more than a year before Nuthead. Copley's inventory included thousands of blank forms of various types, as well as "1 printing press, Case, letters, box, etc." worth £15. Since there is no evidence that Copley ran a printshop, much of the printing equipment in Nuthead's St. Mary's printshop, as well as the inventory of unsold printed forms, appears to have been owned by the royal governor (Prerogative Court Inventories and Accounts 13A, MSA S 536, pp. 263–64, Maryland State Archives).

Nuthead had needed a patron in his abortive effort to establish a printing press in Virginia in the early 1680s. His business in Maryland, limited largely to printing blank legal forms, may not have been sufficiently profitable to enable him to furnish his printshop with his own equipment. Nuthead's small estate at the time of his death suggests that his survival as the colony's printer may have depended on having an investor like Governor Copley to help bear the expense of his printing operation. Nuthead had patented 300 acres of land in 1686 in Talbot County on Maryland's Eastern Shore, but unimproved and uncultivated land was worth little in seventeenth-century Maryland. His personal property, including the £5 worth of printing apparatus, totalled just £6.19.0. Nuthead died in St. Mary's City. He was survived by his wife Dinah (maiden name and marriage date unknown) and by two children.

• Virtually everything known about William Nuthead comes from the research and writing of Lawrence C. Wroth. Wroth documented Nuthead as Maryland's first printer in *A History of Printing in Colonial Maryland, 1686–1776* (1922), placed him in the context of printing in colonial America in *The Colonial Printer* (1931; repr., 1964), and established his precedence over William Bradford of Philadelphia as the first printer south of Massachusetts in "The St. Mary's City Press: A New Chronology of American Printing," *The Colophon*, n.s. 1, no. 3 (1936): 333–57.

GREGORY A. STIVERSON

NUTTALL, Thomas (5 Jan. 1786–10 Sept. 1859), naturalist, was born in Long Preston in the Craven District of western Yorkshire, England, the son of James Nuttall, of unknown occupation, and Margaret Hardacre. The family was not prosperous and had considerable financial difficulties. As a youth in Long Preston, Nuttall attended regularly the Church of England and went to school until age fourteen. His father having died in 1798, he then moved to Liverpool to serve from 1800 to 1807 as an apprentice in the printing business with his uncle Jonas Nuttall; in the evenings and on weekends he studied Latin, Greek, and French. With John Windsor, a young botanical friend, he explored the Craven Hills, and there was born his lifelong passion for studying plants in the field and his keen interest in geology and mineralogy. These interests were supplemented with other field experiences, gardening, visits to museums, and attendance at public lectures on botany.

By early 1807 Nuttall had become so dedicated to natural history that he wanted to pursue its study in North America, but his uncle considered such an adventure highly dangerous and financially worthless. Because of their differences, Nuttall relocated to London, where he nearly starved because no work was available in either natural history or printing. Through unknown means enough money became available for him to sail on the *Halcyon* from Liverpool to Philadelphia in 1808. Upon arrival he immediately began studying the plants and made his acquaintance with leading botanists and scientists of the area, foremost among them Professor Benjamin S. Barton at the University of Pennsylvania. Barton was writing a systematic treatise on the flora and fauna of known North America. His previous botanical assistant, Frederick Pursh, had left in 1807 so Barton hired the young and vigorous Nuttall to engage in field expeditions, primarily to collect living plants for botanical gardens, seeds for seedsmen and nurserymen, and dried plants for herbaria. When not traveling, Nuttall was headquartered at the Academy of Natural Sciences in Philadelphia, where he lectured on botany and published papers naming and describing plants that were new to science.

Financed by Barton, Nuttall's early travels were to Delaware (1809), Pennsylvania (1809), New York

(1809), the Great Lakes region (1810), up the Missouri River to Fort Mandon (1811), and down the Mississippi River to New Orleans (1811). When in the northern regions Nuttall sometimes traveled on boats of fur traders, and whenever the boat was ashore, Nuttall "hurriedly alighted in eager anticipation and lost himself in the vegetation. This habit occasioned exchange of witticisms among the voyageurs, who suspected the sanity of a person who dug up 'weeds' with such devotion and excitement" (Graustein, *Thomas Nuttall, Naturalist*, p. 52). From New Orleans he sailed to England in 1811 and was detained there during the War of 1812. Upon his second arrival in Philadelphia in 1815 Nuttall learned that Barton was in France. Without Barton's support, Nuttall financed his subsequent expeditions from his savings and the sale of plants and seeds to nurserymen. He explored the southeast coastal states in 1815–1816; upon his return to Philadelphia in February 1816, he learned of Barton's death in December 1815. Nuttall then explored the Ohio River, Kentucky, and the Carolinas in 1816–1817. While traveling, Nuttall encountered or sought out other botanists, among them English botanist John L. Bradbury in St. Louis, Dr. Charles W. Short in Kentucky, Dr. William Baldwin in Georgia, Stephen Elliott in South Carolina, and the Moravian botanist, Rev. David von Schweinitz in Bethlehem, Pennsylvania.

When Nuttall returned to Philadelphia in 1817 he set the type for his most noted publication, an excellent, accurately prepared now-classic book, *The Genera of North American Plants* . . . (2 vols., 1818). With technical descriptions in English rather than Latin, it was the first comprehensive work on plants of the Western Hemisphere published in the United States. Nuttall fully described 834 genera and all of the new species he proposed; in addition, he merely listed all previously named species, except those with new information. An amazing book for a young, self-taught botanist, it won him international acclaim, and shifted the publication of North American plant studies from the Eastern to the Western Hemisphere. Nuttall then undertook an expedition into the Arkansas Territory that extended from 1818 to 1820 and was financed by four of his friends from the American Philosophical Society, Zaccheus Collins, William MacClure, Correa da Serra, and John Vaughan. They later urged Nuttall to publish his observations on the region's natural history, resulting in a book, *A Journal of Travels into the Arkansa Territory* . . . (1821).

Nuttall's career turned to lecturing on botany at Yale College in the summer of 1822, followed by an appointment as curator of the Botanic Garden and instructor in natural history and botany at Harvard College in the autumn of that year. At Harvard until 1834, Nuttall worked diligently to improve the Botanic Garden and to receive its numerous visitors. He taught classes in botany and natural history, published papers on new species of plants, and wrote a textbook, *Introduction to Systematic and Physiological Botany* (1827; 2d ed., 1830). Students described him as not a brilliant teacher, but his dedication to plants elicited much interest, and he delighted his audience with a rich variety of scientific research. Harvard College conferred on Nuttall the honorary degree of master of arts in 1826. From 1826 to 1831 Nuttall engaged in intensive studies of birds and published two books, *A Manual of the Ornithology of the United States and Canada*, the first volume titled *Land Birds* (1832), the second *Water Birds* (1834); both volumes were revised and republished in 1840, 1891, 1896, and 1903. He asked for and was granted many leaves of absence from Harvard to conduct his scientific explorations, studying plants, birds, and minerals.

Nuttall was disappointed that, while on previous expeditions west of the Mississippi River in 1811 and 1818–1820, he never took or had the opportunity to cross the Rocky Mountains to the Pacific Coast. That opportunity came to him by accompanying his wealthy friend, Nathaniel J. Wyeth, who was planning his second transcontinental expedition. When Harvard College showed no interest in granting Nuttall a two-year leave with financial support, he reluctantly resigned his financially secure position in 1834 and joined Wyeth's expedition, which lasted until 1835. Returning again to Philadelphia, Nuttall published two papers on the plants he had obtained and worked out an agreement to name and describe the new species he discovered on his transcontinental journey in the first volume of John Torrey and Asa Gray's *Flora of North America* (1838, 1840). Nuttall's last book project in the United States was the preparation of a new edition of F. André Michaux's books on trees, published as *The North American Sylva*, . . . (3 vols., 1842–1849).

Although often described as shy, unsocial, or eccentric, Nuttall readily established acquaintanceships and had numerous lifelong friends. He made important contributions to botany, zoology, ornithology, geology, mineralogy, ecology, and horticulture through his pioneering scientific explorations in North America, work that has never been equaled in extent or productivity. He was not only a collector but also a thorough scholar who named and described numerous genera and hundreds of species of plants. Asa Gray, America's foremost botanist of the latter half of the nineteenth century, wrote: "No botanist has visited so large a portion of the United States, or made such an amount of observations in the field and forest. Probably few naturalists have ever excelled him in aptitude for such observations, in quickness of eye, tact, in discrimination and tenacity of memory" (*North American Review* 59 [1844]: 193).

Upon the death in 1841 of Nuttall's aunt Frances, widow of his uncle Jonas, Nuttall inherited "Nutgrove Hall," a country estate near Liverpool, England, with the proviso that he had to live there and could not be absent longer than three months during any calendar year. Nuttall, who never married, took up residence at Nutgrove Hall in 1842, but during the first year he suffered nostalgia to such an extent that his health became impaired. He made only one trip to the United States, staying six months by scheduling his trip to encompass three months of each of two calendar years (1847 and 1848). There he wrote his last paper on North American plants, *Descriptions of Plants Collected by William Gambel, M.D. . . .* (1848). Nuttall enabled his nephew Thomas J. Booth to participate in a botanical collecting expedition to Asia to obtain various species of Rhododendron that Nuttall grew in his garden. From these plants he named and described new species, as well as new species of other genera brought into cultivation. Nuttall interacted with the botanists of England until about a year before his death. He died at Nutgrove.

• The most extensive discussion of Nuttall's life is Jeannette Graustein, *Thomas Nuttall, Naturalist: Explorations in America 1808–1841* (1967). Also informative is Ronald L. Stuckey, "Biography of Thomas Nuttall; a Review with Bibliography," *Rhodora* 70 (1968): 429–38; and Frans A. Stafleu and Richard S. Cowan, "Thomas Nuttall," *Taxonomic Literature: A Selective Guide to Botanical Publications and Collections with Dates, Commentaries and Types*, vol. 3 (1981), pp. 781–87. Bibliographies of Nuttall's publications are in Ian MacPhail, *The Sterling Morton Library Bibliographies in Botany and Horticulture II* (1983); and C. Earl Smith, Jr., and John W. Thieret, "Thomas Nuttall (1786–1859): An Evaluation and Bibliography," *Leaflets of Western Botany* 9 (1959): 33–42. Critical analyses and supplementary information are in Joseph Ewan's introduction to the reprint of Nuttall's *The Genera of North American Plants* (1971) and Savoie Lottinville's introduction to the reprint of Nuttall's *A Journal of Travels into the Arkansa Territory during the Year 1819* (1980).

For original critical studies on Nuttall's travels, see Graustein, "Nuttall's Travels into the Old Northwest: An Unpublished 1810 Diary," *Chronica Botanica* 14 (1951): 1–88; Francis W. Pennell, "Travels and Scientific Collections of Thomas Nuttall," *Bartonia* 18 (1936): 1–51; Stuckey, "Thomas Nuttall's 1816 Ohio Valley Plant Collections Described in His 'Genera' of 1818," *Castanea* 31 (1966): 187–98; Stuckey, "The 'Lost' Plants of Thomas Nuttall's 1810 Expedition into the Old Northwest," *Michigan Botanist* 6 (1967): 81–94; and Robert Tatnall, "Nuttall's Plant Collections in Southern Delaware," *Bartonia* 20 (1940): 1–6. Selected biographical sketches written by Nuttall's contemporaries include (his nephew) Thomas Jonas Booth, "Mr. Thomas Nuttall, the Naturalist," *Settle Chronicle and North Ribblesdale Advertiser*, Jan.–Feb. 1861, reprinted in part by Pennell in *Bartonia* 19 (1938): 50–54; and [Elias Durand], "Biographical Sketch of the Late Thomas Nuttall," *Proceedings of the American Philosophical Society* 7 (1860): 297–315.

RONALD L. STUCKEY

NUTTALL, Zelia Maria Magdalena (6 Sept. 1857–12 Apr. 1933), ethnohistorian-archaeologist, was born in San Francisco, California, the daughter of Robert Kennedy Nuttall, a medical doctor, and Magdalena Parrott. At the age of eight she moved with her family to Europe, where she received an excellent, although largely informal, continental education that permitted her to speak, research, and publish in four languages throughout her long professional career.

When Nuttall was nineteen the family returned to San Francisco, where she met the young French ethnologist, Alphonse Louis Pinart, who was in the city on an ethnological mission for the French government. The couple married in 1880, and Zelia accompanied her new husband as he conducted further research in the West Indies, France, and Spain. The marriage ended in separation in 1881, probably shortly before the birth of their daughter in San Francisco. In an 1888 California divorce Zelia not only won the right to return to her maiden name but also the right of her daughter to be known henceforth by the name Nuttall.

In 1884, after her separation, Nuttall spent five months in Mexico, her mother's birthplace, with her comfortably wealthy family. There she became enchanted with Mexican history and archaeology, an interest that was to endure for the rest of her life. This exposure to Mexican culture and the ruins of Mexico's pre-contact cultures led to her first professional success, the publication of an article on the terracotta heads of Teotihuacán in 1886. In the article Nuttall convincingly argued for an earlier date for the effigies and for their use in funerary practices. Although she had no formal training in archaeology, an unexceptional fact for the time, the publication brought her to the attention of established professionals in the field and led to her acceptance into the prestigious Archaeological Institute of America and the equally acclaimed American Philosophical Society. Frederic Ward Putnam, the curator of the Peabody Museum at Harvard, was so impressed with her early publications that he named her special assistant in Mexican archaeology, a post she held for forty-seven years.

In 1886 Nuttall accompanied her brother to Europe, where she established her home in Dresden, Germany. For the next twelve years she searched the libraries and museum collections of Europe for clues to Mexican history and prehistory. During that period Nuttall made the discovery for which she is best known, a folding-screen pictorial book from pre-contact Mexico, now known as Codex Nuttall in her honor. For several years she traced this ancient document from Italy to England, where it was located in a private collection. She copied the document and hired an artist to make a faithful facsimile so that the codex would be available to scholars, and a few copies of the facsimile appeared in 1902. In 1903 she published on another archival discovery, the Codex Magliabecchiano, under the title *The Book of the Life of the Ancient Mexicans* with an introduction, translation, and commentary under her name. Although her claim of discovery was disputed by a European scholar who seems to have reported his find somewhat earlier, it was Nuttall who made this valuable document accessible to a wide circle of scholars.

In the centuries after the conquest of Mexico, these pictorial books had been regarded as of little significance. Their apparently primitive maps and drawings led some researchers to speculate that they were nothing more than children's books. Nuttall solidly proved otherwise, carefully documenting the historical significance of the two codices and thereby also establishing the historical value of several other codices then known to exist as well as others to be rediscovered over succeeding years.

Because of her social position and background, Nuttall had a wide circle of friends and acquaintances of wealth and position in Europe, the United States, and Mexico. She was often successful in convincing these wealthy individuals to underwrite anthropological projects in the days when most research was supported by private donations. On rare occasions she herself was awarded small grants for special projects, as for an archival research project she accomplished in 1896 in Russia, funded by her friend Phoebe Apperson Hearst. Her professional reputation and her long-standing friendship with Hearst resulted in Nuttall's being one of the five persons invited to meet to establish a department of anthropology at the University of California at Berkeley in September 1901.

In 1901 Nuttall published *The Fundamental Principles of Old and New World Civilizations*, in which she attempted to link the ancient civilizations of Mexico, Egypt, and the Middle East through the common use of symbols such as the swastika. Although not supported by subsequent research, her boldly stated conclusions generated much scholarly debate. In 1902 she purchased a colonial mansion in Coyoacán, Mexico, where she often entertained the rich and famous of the world. One such guest was D. H. Lawrence, who purportedly fashioned his character Mrs. Norris in *The Plumed Serpent* after Nuttall.

For many years Nuttall conducted archaeological research on her own property in Coyoacán and environs. Through this research she became one of the first to recognize an Archaic Level culture in the Valley of Mexico. At her estate she established an informal training site for young archaeologists from Mexico and the United States, and it was in her garden that the first complete study of Aztec pottery at a single site was carried out by Manuel Gamio, a Mexican archaeologist and one of several Nuttall protégés who later became leaders in Mexican archaeology.

Nuttall was active in Mexican archaeology for most of her long life and was instrumental in setting up the International School of American Archaeology and Ethnology in Mexico City. Her only attempt to direct a large archaeological project, on Isla de Sacrificios, Mexico, was thwarted before its start by Leopoldo Batres, Mexico's inspector of monuments. Having carried out preliminary research on the island, she was incensed when Batres appointed himself as director of her larger project after she had secured funding from the Mexican government. Not one to silently steal away to lick her wounds, Nuttall published a full account of the incident in the *American Anthropologist* in 1910.

Nuttall was often outspoken in her criticism of those who refused to treat her research with consideration and respect. She did not hesitate to engage in public feuds with several colleagues with whom she disagreed over interpretations of archaeological and historical data. The self-confident erudition of this Victorian-era woman did not endear her to many of the professionals in her field, virtually all of whom were men.

A significant archival find of her later years was the Drake manuscripts, uncovered in the National Archives of Mexico, and published in 1914. Her zeal to pursue research clues and leads discovered in old manuscripts was nowhere more evident than when she traveled by freighter to Alaska at the age of fifty-eight so that she could research firsthand Neah Bay, Washington, a place she was convinced was described by Drake as the "Bay of New Albion."

In her later years Nuttall made plans to establish her home as a Mexican center for science, where her extensive library and pre-Columbian artifact collection would be available for the use of scholars. The plans were not completed when she became ill and died in Mexico City, where she was buried in the American cemetery. Shortly after her death, all of her private papers were destroyed by heirs in accordance with her wishes.

• Letters by Nuttall are in the Frederic W. Putnam Papers, Harvard University Archives, and in the Franz Boas Papers, American Philosophical Society, Philadelphia. From 1886 until her death Nuttall published regularly. Her bibliography is as extensive as it is wide-ranging, covering subjects from "Coyote versus Long-tailed Bear," *Internationales Archiv für Ethnographie* 6 (1893): 95–97, to "Origin of the Maya Calendar," *Science* 45, supps. 12 and 14 (1927), and "The New Year of Tropical American Indigenes," *Boletín de la Unión Panamericana* 62 (1973): 67–73. The most informative source about Nuttall is Ross Parmenter, "Glimpses of a Friendship: Zelia Nuttall and Franz Boas," in *Pioneers of American Anthropology*, ed. June Helm (1966). See also Nancy O. Lurie, "Women in Early American Anthropology," in the same volume. An obituary by Alfred M. Tozzer in *American Anthropologist* 3 (1933): 475–82 includes the most nearly complete compilation of Nuttall's many publications. Two other obituaries deserve mention: Philip Ainsworth Means, "Zelia Nuttall: An Appreciation," *Hispanic-American Historical Review* 13 (1933): 487–89, and Doña Zelia Nuttall, Nota Bio-Bibliográfica," in *Boletín del Museo Nacional de México* 5 (1933): 115, 124.

BEVERLY NEWBOLD CHIÑAS

NUTTER, Gilbert Warren (10 March 1923–15 Jan. 1979), economist and political adviser, was born in Topeka, Kansas, the son of Coleman Evan Nutter, an electrical engineer, and Helen Rose Gilberg. Nutter was educated at the University of Chicago, where he was elected to Phi Beta Kappa in 1944. He received his B.A. in 1944, having already been inducted into the U.S. Army. Following his discharge from military service, for which he was awarded the Bronze Star with Oak Leaf Cluster, he spent the 1946–1947 academic year teaching at Lawrence College. He then returned to the University of Chicago, where he obtained an M.A. in 1948 and a Ph.D. in economics in 1949. In 1946 he married Jane Calvert Couch; they had four children.

Nutter's doctoral dissertation, published as *The Extent of Enterprise Monopoly in the United States, 1899–1939* (1951), typified Nutter's high standards of scholarship. Combining deep understanding of economic theory with meticulous empirical research, the study showed that industrial concentration had not increased during the period of study except in industries that operated under government control or supervision. The work was later updated through 1958 and published as *Enterprise Monopoly in the United States: Its Extent and Growth, 1899–1958*, with Henry Einhorn (1969). Questions of competition, monopoly, and related matters—a field known in the profession as industrial organization—remained central to Nutter's interests throughout his career.

Nutter spent the summer of 1949 with the RAND Corporation in Washington, D.C., after which he became a professor of economics at Yale University, where he remained until 1956. His appointment at Yale was interrupted by service in the Central Intelligence Agency during the Korean War. In 1956 he moved to the University of Virginia in Charlottesville, where he spent the remainder of his academic career. At the University of Virginia, he played a key role in building an exceptional faculty and in developing the approach to political economy that became widely known as the Virginia School. He was a cofounder of the Thomas Jefferson Center for Political Economy and for a number of years chairman of the economics department. He was named Paul Goodloe McIntyre Professor of Economics in 1967.

Nutter's work on monopoly and competition alone would have earned him a secure place as a scholar. He became best known, however, for his pioneering work on the economy of the Soviet Union. In 1953 he was named director of an ambitious project that was sponsored by the National Bureau of Economic Research to produce a comprehensive assessment of all aspects of the Soviet economy. Nutter himself produced *Growth of Industrial Production in the Soviet Union* (1962), a massive study of the growth of Soviet industrial output. At the time, industrial power and its growth formed the centerpiece of Soviet claims to economic strength. Through painstaking economic and statistical analysis, Nutter showed that Soviet industrial growth was not exceptional by relevant historical standards. He argued that forecasts of Soviet industrial growth would be better based on long-run average rates of growth than on the rapid rates seen in the interwar and immediate postwar periods. Many scholars consider the stagnation, decline, and ultimate collapse of the Soviet economy that began in the mid-1970s to substantiate Nutter's conclusions.

In addition to his career as a scholar, Nutter was deeply involved in public life. Early in his career, he worked as a speechwriter in Senator Barry Goldwater's 1964 presidential campaign. In 1969 President Richard M. Nixon appointed him assistant secretary of defense for international security affairs, a post that he held until 1973. This position engulfed him in a vast range of international security issues but perhaps none more demanding than those connected with the war in Vietnam. As the first high-level official in the Department of Defense to recognize the importance of creating a sound economic base for Vietnamese recovery, Nutter worked to that end on the basis of his deep understanding of market economic principles. He chaired the policy committee responsible for the POW/MIA issue, and he organized the Vietnam Task Force, which managed the immense organizational and logistical tasks of transferring responsibility for the conduct of the war to the Vietnamese, a step that the administration viewed as necessary for the withdrawal of U.S. troops. By the end of his term, although the Vietnamese army was combat ready, Nutter believed that because the necessary logistical support had not been provided, the army was left to be destroyed in the devastating war that followed.

After his service in the Defense Department, Nutter returned to academic life at the University of Virginia. His interests then turned to broader issues of political philosophy and the American nation, and he produced numerous writings and speeches on the history and promise of the United States. In a 1975 speech he said, "The American republic is to me the greatest wonder of all time, a system of representative government that has flourished for two hundred years despite the disastrous failure of every democracy in recorded history up to the founding of our republic."

Nutter's interest in human freedom and the dignity of the individual extended wherever people were oppressed. He was particularly concerned about the fate of the peoples of Central and Eastern Europe, who were at the time under Soviet domination. For almost two decades, he organized conferences and summer courses to educate westerners about the problems these people faced and to afford scholars from those countries opportunities to maintain external intellectual contacts. He remained a faithful friend to those in the Soviet bloc who demonstrated personal commitments to the ideals of the free society. A staunch defender of individual liberty, he was often critical of the actions of government and lamented its growth in the United States and elsewhere. He feared that government would come to dominate society and in the process would destroy the freedom that he believed was the heart of America's greatness. Applying his quantitative and analytical talents to measuring government's increase, he published *Growth of Government in the West* (1978).

Nutter was a member of the research staff of the National Bureau of Economic Research from 1955 until 1967. He served as vice president of the Southern Economic Association in 1966–1967 and was a member of the board of editors of the American Economic Association from 1969 to 1971. He became a member of the advisory committee to the Board of Visitors of the Citadel in 1975 and of the advisory committee on International Studies of the Hoover Institution in 1976. He served in both capacities until his death. He was also an adjunct scholar and member of the academic advisory committee of the American Enterprise Institute in Washington, D.C., from 1973 until he died. At both the American Enterprise Institute and the Hoover Institution, he played a key role in building institutions of great significance to public understanding and debate of the central issues of the time.

At the time of his death from cancer in Washington, D.C., his intellectual powers were at their peak and his wide experience most pertinent to the times. His contributions to understanding of the great issues of the time—the fundamental flaws of central economic planning, the dangers of the growth of government, the nature and extent of economic competition, and the nature and meaning of freedom in America—will remain as intellectual and moral landmarks.

• Nutter's scholarly and public service papers are in the archives of the Hoover Institution, Stanford, Calif. A comprehensive bibliography can be found in G. Warren Nutter, *Political Economy and Freedom*, ed. Jane Couch Nutter (1983). His works on the former Soviet Union include, in addition to those mentioned in the text, *Statistical Abstract of Industrial Output in the Soviet Union, 1913–1955* (1956); *Some Observations on Soviet Industrial Growth* (1957); "Industrial Growth in the Soviet Union," *American Economic Review* 49 (Sept. 1959): 695–701; and "The Structure and Growth of Soviet Industry: A Comparison with the United States," in U.S. Congress, Joint Economic Committee, *Planning of Growth and Economic Fluctuations in the Soviet Union*, pt. 1 (1959). He was cotranslator, with Marie-Christine MacAndrew, of Eugene Zaleski's *Planning Reforms in the Soviet Union, 1962–1966* (1967), and *Planning of Growth and Economic Fluctuations in the Soviet Union* (1971). Nutter's works on economic theory and industrial organization include "The Plateau Demand Curve and Economic Theory," *Journal of Political Economy* 63 (Dec. 1955): 525–28; "On Measuring Economic Growth," *Journal of Political Economy* 65 (Feb. 1957): 51–63; "Diminishing Returns and Linear Homogeneity," *American Economic Review* 53 (Dec. 1963): 1084–85; "Duopoly, Oligopoly, and Emerging Competition," *Southern Economic Journal* 30 (Apr. 1964): 342–52; "On Economic Size and Growth," *Journal of Law and Economics* 9 (Oct. 1966): 163–88; and, with John H. Moore, "A Theory of Competition," *Journal of Law and Economics* 19 (Apr. 1976): 39–65. He demonstrated the infeasibility of central economic planning in "Markets without Property: A Grand Illusion," in *Money, the Market, and the State* (1968). For examples of his writings on the American idea see "Economic Aspects of Freedom," in *Liberty under Law, Anarchy, Totalitarianism—This Is the Choice*, ed. American Bar Association (1969), and "Freedom in a Revolutionary Economy," in *The American Revolution: Three Views* (1975). An obituary is in the *New York Times*, 16 Jan. 1979.

JOHN H. MOORE

NUTTING, Mary Adelaide (1 Nov. 1858–3 Oct. 1948), nurse educator, was born in Quebec, Canada, the daughter of Vespasion Nutting, a county clerk of the circuit court, and Harriet Sophia Peasley (earlier Peaselee). Before her birth the Nutting family had moved from Massachusetts to Quebec, joining the other New England Loyalists who had relocated in Canada after the American Revolution.

After spending most of her childhood in Canada, Nutting traveled to the United States and lived with relatives in Lowell, Massachusetts, where she continued her studies in music and art, which she had begun in her teens at Bute House, a private school in Montre-

al. Her talent and training as a singer and pianist led to a teaching position in October 1882 at the church of England Cathedral School for Girls in St. Johns, Newfoundland. She was invited there by her sister Armine ("Minnie"), a teacher, who had gone there earlier in the year to "take charge" of the school. Failing to secure private music pupils and becoming a financial burden to her sister, she returned home to her mother in Ottawa in July 1883. Within a year her mother became seriously ill, and in November 1884 she died.

Nutting's mother's death, her sibling's subsequent marriages, and her grief-stricken father's inadequacy as a provider all contributed to her departure from home and another prolonged visit to her relatives in Massachusetts. In September 1889 she wrote to the Johns Hopkins Hospital applying for entrance to the newly opened school of nursing. In her application she described herself as "five feet five inches in height, weighing one hundred twenty nine pounds . . . not remarkably strong [but with] . . . a good deal of endurance." She maintained that she had no diseases or physical defects. At the time she had been living with her brother and his family for almost five years, and her eagerness to start a new life elsewhere is revealed in her application, which stated that she was "anxious to avoid suspense and also to begin . . . work at the earliest possible date." Accepted by return mail, Nutting began her student-nurse experience on the eve of her thirty-first birthday.

As a member of the first class at Hopkins, Nutting embarked on her lifelong career as a pioneer in nursing and nursing education. When she graduated in 1891, she became a head nurse at Hopkins and in 1893 was appointed assistant to Isabel Hampton, the superintendent of nurses and principal of the school. Within a year, Nutting replaced Hampton, who left the position after she married.

In 1895 Nutting submitted a plan to the trustees at Hopkins, calling for a three-year curriculum and an eight-hour day with no stipends for students. She believed that students should *not* be paid, for they were not employed, she argued, to work as servants might be but instead were to see themselves as students gaining entry into a profession through education. In addition, given nursing's importance, Nutting felt that the nursing students should hold the same status as other students preparing for professional roles and as such should proceed through the preliminary preparation course. In 1901 Nutting established the first preclinical course for nurses in the nation, giving students a six-month preliminary preparation before they embarked on the clinical care of patients. These initiatives were but a beginning to her ongoing mission to professionalize nursing. She was instrumental in the development of the Maryland State Association of Graduate Nurses and served as its first president in 1903; she helped draft the first legislation of nursing practice in Maryland in 1904. Nutting was also elected to a five-year term as chair and first president of the American Federation of Nurses, which was established in 1901.

Although she accomplished much during her six-year tenure at Hopkins, Nutting is remembered most for her many years of leadership in nursing education at Teachers College, Columbia University, which began in 1907. A firm believer in university-based education for nurses, she first taught part time at Teachers College from 1899 to 1907 while still at Hopkins. She assumed the duties of full professor in 1907, the first nurse to hold such an academic appointment anywhere. Beyond her many and varied contributions to nursing education, Nutting was instrumental in establishing standards for the practice of nursing and served in leadership positions as nursing organizations emerged. She was elected president of the newly formed American Society of Superintendents of Training Schools for Nurses in the United States and Canada in 1896 and 1909, elected as vice president in 1897, and served as secretary in 1903 and 1904. She was one of the founders of the *American Journal of Nursing* (1900). Nutting also wrote the first comprehensive four-volume history of nursing, with Lavinia Lloyd Dock, *A History of Nursing* (1907), and authored several other monographs, articles, and papers.

During World War I President Woodrow Wilson appointed her chair of the Committee on Nursing of the Council of National Defense. She was the recipient of many awards including the Liberty Service Medal from the Council of the National Institute of Social Sciences. A medal in her name was established for leadership in nursing education by the National League of Nursing Education (NLNE); she was its first recipient in 1944. Nutting served as honorary president of the Florence Nightingale International Foundation (1934), which she had first proposed as an international memorial to the founder of modern nursing. She was a member of the Equal Franchise Society and the Woman Suffrage party. A portrait of her by Cecilia Beaux commissioned by the Johns Hopkins alumnae in 1906 is at the Hopkins Hospital, and other painted by Stanislav Rembski in 1932 is at Teachers College.

Nutting retired from Teachers College in 1925. That same year, in a greeting in the souvenir program of the annual convention of the New York State Nurses' Association she wrote that "compassion may provide the motive, but knowledge is our only working power." She never married. Although she was not robust, she lived a long and productive life. She retained her Canadian citizenship but was recognized by those familiar with her words as a citizen of the world. Hopkins invested wisely in Nutting. She traveled widely in search of inspiration for her developing vision of the possibilities for nursing in general and the school in particular. The reforms and educational initiatives that she introduced became part of her lifelong pursuit to provide university-based education for nurses. Found among her papers and later shared in the pages of the *American Journal of Nursing* she helped to establish is the following brief note that reveals her universal and passionate pacifist beliefs: "This whole world is God's beautiful world, [and] we are first of all his chil-dren and only in a secondary way Americans or Canadians or British or of any other race. . . . Someday the mad ambition to dominate, which is a form of insanity wherever it is found, will be curbed" (58 [Nov. 1958]: 1529). One month shy of her ninetieth birthday, Nutting died after a long illness in White Plains, New York.

• Nutting's papers are at Teachers College, Columbia University. Some of her correspondence is also in the archives of the Johns Hopkins Hospital School of Nursing. For a complete bibliography of works by and about Nutting, see Helen E. Marshall, *Mary Adelaide Nutting: Pioneer of Modern Nursing* (1972). Obituaries and tributes are in the *New York Times*, 5 and 16 Oct. 1948; the *American Journal of Nursing* 48 (Nov. 1948); and the *Teachers College Record*, Dec. 1948.

OLGA MARANJIAN CHURCH

NUTTING, Wallace (17 Nov. 1861–19 July 1941), author, photographer, and antiquarian, was born in Marlborough, Massachusetts, the son of Albion Nutting, a farmer and manufacturer, and Elizabeth Sanborn Fifield. Following his father's death while serving in the Union army, Nutting grew up at the farm of an uncle in Maine. He dropped out of school in Augusta, Maine, because of poor health, then he worked and traveled for four years until he enrolled in Phillips Exeter Academy, from which he graduated in 1883. He studied at Harvard from 1883 until 1886, Hartford Theological Seminary from 1886 until 1887, and Union Theological Seminary in 1888. In 1888 he was ordained a Congregational minister. The same year Nutting married Mrs. Mariet Griswold Caswell of Colrain, Massachusetts; they had no children.

As a clergyman, Nutting served congregations in Newark, New Jersey (1888–1889); St. Paul, Minnesota (1899–1891); Seattle, Washington (1891–1894); and Providence, Rhode Island (1894–1904). He left the ministry in 1904 because he was suffering from a disturbance of the inner ear and related ailments that he described as a nervous breakdown.

Even before his retirement from the ministry Nutting had begun to experiment with photography. He taught himself the technical aspects of the art, and by 1898 he had published a magazine article on photographic technique. His photographs were published in *Harper's Monthly, Ladies' Home Journal*, and other popular magazines in 1902 and 1903, and he began selling prints through dealers near Providence. After leaving the ministry he devoted himself to establishing a photography business. He specialized in rural New England landscapes at first, then expanded his subject matter to interiors of old New England houses, sometimes with figures dressed in colonial costume. In 1905 he purchased an old house in Southbury, Connecticut, which he restored and used as a setting for many of his photographs. His distinctive "platinotype" prints were produced on high-quality platinum paper and were hand-tinted.

In 1906 Nutting set up a studio in his home, where he employed several young women full time as colorists. This photographic print enterprise proved very successful, and by 1912, when he moved the enterprise to Framingham, Massachusetts, he was employing more than one hundred colorists. Nutting later estimated that he had sold more than ten million prints by 1925.

Nutting's success in photography led him to publish collections of his work. His first book, which he published himself in 1913, was *Old New England Pictures*. Later books, also published by his Old America Company, included the States Beautiful series, with volumes on Vermont, Massachusetts, New Hampshire, Connecticut, Maine, Pennsylvania, New York, and Virginia; and the Country Beautiful series, which included volumes on Ireland and England. All of these volumes, published between 1922 and 1930, were mixtures of photographs and Nutting's own discursive commentary and opinions. A prolific author and lecturer, Nutting contributed articles to magazines and published *The Clock Book* in 1927 and *Photographic Art Secrets* in 1927.

The search for backgrounds for his photographs of colonial interiors led to Nutting's interest in antique furniture and ironware. He began collecting for his Southbury house, and in the process he educated himself about colonial furniture and accessories. He published a book on Windsor chairs in 1917 and *Furniture of the Pilgrim Century* in 1921, in which he hoped to foster an appreciation for old values, writing, "the strength and beauty of pilgrim furniture was an expression of pilgrim character." In the course of collecting he bought, restored, and furnished several old houses (the Webb house in Wethersfield, Conn.; the Wentworth-Gardner house in Portsmouth, N.H.; the Hazen Garrison house in Haverill, Mass.; the Cutler Bartlet house in Newburyport, Mass.; and the Iron Works house in Saugus, Mass.). He used the interiors of these houses as photographic backgrounds, calling them the "Wallace Nutting Chain of Colonial Houses." At the same time he opened the houses to the general public for an admission fee of twenty-five cents. He eventually sold the contents of three of those houses.

During the early 1920s Nutting assembled a second collection of antiques, which is now the core of the Wallace Nutting Collection in the Wadsworth Atheneum in Hartford, Connecticut. His *Furniture Treasury*, first published in 1928, is an encyclopedic photographic archive of early American furniture that continues to be an important reference work for collectors. Nutting also wrote articles and lectured widely on early American furniture.

Nutting's enthusiasm for collecting furniture of the colonial period included an interest in how the furniture was made. In 1917 he had opened a factory for making reproductions of colonial furniture, in which all of the pieces were handcrafted following the original processes. He also restored the eighteenth-century iron forge at Saugus, Massachusetts, and used it to manufacture reproductions of colonial hardware. Production in these factories was small, and prices were high; the photography business sustained the furniture and ironware operation. In 1922 Nutting sold the furniture reproduction company and with it the right to use his name on reproductions. He was dissatisfied with the quality of the new company's production however, and in 1924 he sold his own antique furniture collection to buy the company back.

In his photographs, books, lectures, collecting, and furniture reproductions, Nutting was an influential proponent of the colonial revival in American decorative arts. He was a tireless advocate of what he saw as a need to preserve the colonial crafts as physical manifestations of earlier, better values. This belief, combined with his diligent entrepreneurial activities, helped to foster an interest in early American decorative arts that has had an enduring effect on American popular taste.

• The Framingham (Mass.) Public Library holds a collection of Nutting's papers. He published an autobiography, *Wallace Nutting's Biography*, in 1936. Additional biographical information appeared in an interview with Marion T. Colley, "I Never Learned to Live until I Was Fifty," published in *American Magazine*, Jan. 1927, pp. 38–41. Louis M. MacKeil, *Wallace Nutting* (1984), is a short biography published by the Saugus Historical Society. For a thorough discussion of Nutting's photography see Joyce P. Barendsen, "Wallace Nutting, an American Tastemaker," *Winterthur Portfolio* 18 (1983): 187–212. His furniture collecting and reproductions are discussed in William L. Dulaney, "Wallace Nutting, Collector and Entrepreneur," *American Furniture and its Makers: Winterthur Portfolio* 13 (1979): 47–60. An assessment of Nutting's career as a collector appears in William N. Hosley, Jr., "The Wallace Nutting Collection at the Wadsworth Atheneum, Hartford, Connecticut," *Antiques* 126 (Oct. 1984): 860–74. Nutting's obituary is in the *New York Times*, 20 July 1941.

LINDA S. CHASE

NYE, Bill (25 Aug. 1850–22 Feb. 1896), American humorist and journalist, was born Edgar Wilson Nye in Shirley, Maine, the son of Franklin Nye, a lumberman, and Elizabeth Mitchell Loring. Nye actually grew up in Hudson, Wisconsin, where he "took [his] parents by the hand and gently led them" when he was but two, jested Nye years later. In Wisconsin he received nominal formal schooling. He tried his hand at farming, teaching, and studying law, but it was his interest in writing that developed most intensely and led him to write for small local newspapers. In fact, it was eventually his unsuccessful attempts to secure positions on Minneapolis and St. Paul newspapers that prompted Nye to leave the Midwest and head west in the spring of 1876.

Nye settled in Laramie City, Wyoming, where he rose to national fame during his two years as editor of the *Laramie Boomerang*, for which he wrote satiric and humorous editorials and features. In addition to his column in the daily paper, he collected in the weekly edition his best humorous observations for a whole page of fun and wit. These columns so bolstered the reputation of the *Boomerang* that Will M. Clemens said of Nye in 1882, he "has, during the past two years, written a larger quantity and a better quality of first-class, genuine humor, than any other funny man in America."

Irony, picturesque speech, and word play were mainstays of Nye's humor. He described a convict's hanging as his being "unanimously chosen by a convention of six property-holders of the county to jump from a new pine platform into the sweet subsequently." On another occasion, he made of the smell of codfish an unforgettable sensory experience: "Its chastened influence permeates the entire ranch. It steals into the parlor, like an unbidden guest, and flavors the costly curtains and the high-priced lambrequins. It enters the dark closet and dallies lovingly with your swallow-tail coat. It goes into your sleeping apartment, and makes its home in your glove box and your handkerchief case."

It was in Laramie City that Nye married Clara Frances "Fanny" Smith of Illinois in 1877, a marriage that was to produce seven children. There, he also served as U.S. postmaster (1882–1883); published his first two books of humorous essays and sketches, *Bill Nye and Boomerang* (1881) and *Forty Liars and Other Lies* (1882); and began preparation of a third, *Baled Hay*. In addition, he was president of the "Forty Liars Club," a group of homegrown wits who gathered to tell stories. However, financial and management troubles with the *Boomerang*, along with a severe attack of spinal meningitis, forced him to leave Laramie City in 1883. After a brief convalescence in Greeley, Colorado, he returned to Hudson, Wisconsin, where he published three collections of essays, stories, and sketches—*Baled Hay* (1884), *Boomerang Shots* (1884), and *Hits and Skits* (1884)—and, more important, began to deliver comic lectures on the stage. He lectured from 1885 until near his death, often sharing the platform with partners such as the Hoosier poet James Whitcomb Riley (the duo that was billed as the "Twins of Genius"). He became famous and much sought after as a humorous lecturer, rivaling if not equaling the reputation of Mark Twain. Lecturing as a part of the J. B. Pond Lyceum Bureau, Nye became a member of the esteemed "one-hundred-dollar-a-night" elite circle of major platform performers.

Nye continued to write prolifically while on the lecture circuit, publishing the humorous volumes of essays *Bill Nye's Remarks* (1887) and *Bill Nye's Thinks* (1888). He and Riley coauthored the popular *Nye and Riley's Railway Guide* (1888), a book that juxtaposed Nye's witty prose with Riley's homespun verses. Perhaps the major publishing breakthrough of his life, however, came in 1887 when Nye became a humorous Sunday columnist for the New York *World* newspaper. He moved to New York with his family in that year. His employment with the *World* continued until 1891, when his columns became widely syndicated. Nye's columns appeared in some seventy newspapers throughout the country until his death.

Never having fully recovered from the effects of the spinal meningitis contracted while in Laramie City, Nye was forced to leave New York in 1891 and relocate in a more temperate clime. He chose a location near Asheville, North Carolina, building a country home called "Buck Shoals" next to the property on which George W. Vanderbilt would soon erect "Biltmore." During the final six years of his life, Nye continued to write his syndicated Sunday columns, traveled the lecture circuit, experimented with gentleman farming, and boldly wrote two plays for the Broadway stage: *The Cadi* (1891) and *The Stag Party* (1895), the former of which ran for 125 performances. In the vein of his earlier counterpart Josh Billings (a.k.a. Henry Wheeler Shaw), he published a comic *Almanac for 1891*. He produced two highly popular volumes of burlesque history, *Bill Nye's History of the United States* (1894) and *Bill Nye's History of England from the Druids to the Reign of Henry VIII* (1896). He also wrote a final—and probably his best—book of humorous essays and sketches, *A Guest at the Ludlow* (posthumous, 1897), which covers a variety of subjects, reveals the richness of his late writing style, and is the most enjoyable for the modern reader.

Early in 1896 Nye's health began declining rapidly, culminating in a stroke that took his life. He died in his Buck Shoals home and was buried in nearby Fletcher, North Carolina.

Bill Nye was one of the most revered and widely read humorists of the last half of the nineteenth century. Though largely unheard of today, his was then a household name. His tall, angular, baldheaded figure was so well known that occasionally letters to him at the New York *World* would arrive with no other address than a caricature of his head and the words "New York *World*" on the envelope. He was a man of wide interests, and his columns touched on everything from places he visited during his travels to national political events. He could be genial but also caustic in his humor. Contemporary reviewers praised him for his originality of subject matter and uniqueness of delivery from the platform. Although tastes in humor change, much of Nye's writing is still funny. He avoided many of the stock comic devices of the other literary comedians of his times, the misspellings and grammatical distortions. His perspective and subject material are at times surprisingly modern, as is his use of irony and his sardonic tone. Historian T. A. Larson, in his book *Bill Nye's Western Humor*, has perhaps best summed up Nye's appeal when he states, "much that he wrote still transmits to the contemporary reader the whimsy and the idiocy that make people laugh."

• The most extensive body of materials on and by Nye is housed in the Bill Nye Collection at the University of Wyoming Library in Laramie. Libraries across the United States, however, have numerous letters and manuscripts (see J. Albert Robbins, ed., *American Literary Manuscripts*, 2d ed. [1977], p. 237). The best, most available published collections of Nye's humorous essays are *Bill Nye's Western Humor*, ed. T. A. Larson (1968), and *The Best of Bill Nye's Humor*, ed. Louis Hasley (1972). The only biography is Frank Wilson Nye, *Bill Nye: His Own Life Story* (1926). Book-length critical studies of Nye's career are Walter Blair, "The Background of Bill Nye in American Humor" (Ph.D. diss., Univ.

of Chicago, 1931), and David B. Kesterson, *Bill Nye* (1981) and *Bill Nye: The Western Writings* (1976). An obituary is in the *New York Times*, 23 Feb. 1896.

DAVID B. KESTERSON

NYE, Gerald Prentice (19 Dec. 1892–17 July 1971), U.S. senator, was born in Hortonville, Wisconsin, the son of Irwin Raymond Nye, a newspaper publisher, and Ella Prentice. Reared in Wittenberg, Wisconsin, young Nye and his father were followers of Robert M. La Follette's (1855–1925) progressive movement. He graduated from Wittenberg High School in 1911 and promptly began his fifteen-year career as a crusading small-town newspaper editor, first in Wisconsin and then in Iowa and North Dakota. Moving to North Dakota in 1916, he soon became active in the agrarian radical Non-Partisan League. In 1925 Governor A. G. Sorlie appointed Nye as a progressive Republican to fill a vacancy in the U.S. Senate caused by the death of the incumbent, Edwin F. Ladd. Nye won election and reelections to that seat in 1926, 1932, and 1938.

Nye's marriage in 1916 to Anna Margaret Munch, a nurse, produced three children and ended in divorce in 1940. Later that year he married an Iowa schoolteacher, Marguerite Johnson; they also had three children.

Both in his editorial capacities and as a U.S. senator, Nye spoke out aggressively for reforms beneficial to rural America. He considered the farmer the backbone of the land and disapproved of special privileges showered upon urban business interests. In his early years in the Senate Nye focused most of his energies on domestic issues, particularly those affecting western farmers. Critical of the conservative policies of his own Republican party, he voted for most of the New Deal measures enacted under the leadership of President Franklin D. Roosevelt, including the Agricultural Adjustment Act, the Social Security Act, and the Wagner Labor Relations Act. Foreign affairs generally did not play a prominent role in Nye's first eight years in the Senate or in his early relations with Roosevelt. Nonetheless, Nye's views of eastern urban business and financial interests extended into foreign affairs. Though he had supported American participation in World War I under President Woodrow Wilson in 1917–1918, he became critical of American involvement overseas after 1919, believing that foreign ventures were designed more to line the pockets of eastern business and financial interests than to guard American freedom.

Responding to public furor over the roles of munitions makers in provoking international conflict, in 1934 Nye became chair of a Senate special committee investigating the munitions industry. That investigation fit perfectly with the critical views of big business popular in those depression years, reflecting disillusionment with U.S. involvement in World War I. The so-called Nye Committee hearings won wide attention and sensational headlines. Under Nye's direction, the committee probed the business methods and profits of shipbuilders, munitions makers, and big financiers.

Based on its hearings and subpoenaed records, the Nye Committee became persuaded that businessmen had been more interested in profits than in national welfare. While the committee did not prove that munitions makers had dragged the United States into World War I, Nye and his associates were persuaded nonetheless that opportunities for economic gain had encouraged armament races and agitation that led to war.

The Senate probe also found that the executive branch of the government (especially the War, Navy, and State departments) shared with munitions makers in promoting armaments races and war. The committee sympathized with President Wilson in his efforts to keep the United States out of World War I, but it contended that the presidency needed help to resist war pressures. Nye publicly questioned the veracity of Wilson's assertion in 1919 that he had not known of the Allied secret treaties before the United States entered the war, precipitating heated Democratic denunciations of Nye and the committee investigation.

The Nye Committee failed to win enactment of any of the legislation it proposed. Nonetheless, the hearings highlighted difficulties in keeping the United States out of foreign wars and provided a catalyst for enactment of neutrality legislation. Senator Nye and others proposed legislation designed to keep the United States out of foreign wars by restraining the warmaking proclivities of both urban business and the executive branch of the government. The neutrality legislation enacted in 1935, 1936, and 1937 was neither so sweeping nor so mandatory as Nye wanted, but it was consistent with the determination of most Americans at that time to stay out of foreign wars. As chair of the Senate Munitions Committee and as a leading advocate of strong neutrality legislation, Senator Nye was at the pinnacle of his political career from 1934 to 1937.

President Roosevelt had gone along with the Nye Committee in its early phases but parted company as war abroad approached. Senator Nye first broke sharply with Roosevelt when he came out against the president's court-packing proposal in 1937. By 1939 Nye was one of the leading senators battling against President Roosevelt's efforts to repeal neutrality legislation and to extend all aid short of war to the victims of Axis aggression.

A powerful and persuasive orator, Nye reached thousands with his speeches and millions in his broadcasts. The senator became increasingly convinced after 1939 that Roosevelt's actions were not just "steps-short-of war" but actually "steps-to-war," motivated partly by the desire to cover up the failure of the New Deal to end the Great Depression.

In 1940 the America First Committee was organized with national headquarters in Chicago to oppose American entry into World War II. Throughout 1941 Senator Nye was one of the leading speakers addressing America First rallies all over the United States. On the afternoon of 7 December 1941, Senator Nye was addressing a large America First meeting in Pittsburgh, Pennsylvania, when he received news that the Japanese had attacked the United States at Pearl Harbor, Hawaii.

That news brought the noninterventionist efforts of Senator Nye and the America First Committee to an abrupt end. Like most noninterventionists, Nye supported the war effort against the Axis. He was a loyal and patriotic American, but he could never escape the stigma attached to the reputations of most who had opposed American entry into World War II before Pearl Harbor. The Japanese attack destroyed America First and essentially ended Senator Nye's public career. He went down to defeat the next time he faced North Dakota voters in 1944.

Nye subsequently headed a business consulting company in Washington, D.C., for some years and later worked on behalf of housing for the elderly under the Federal Housing Administration. He never again won election to public office. By the time he died in Washington he had faded from the memories of most, having become identified with an outdated agrarian society and with discredited foreign policies. The nation and the world had turned in directions that left him behind and forgotten.

• Senator Gerald P. Nye's papers are located at the Herbert Hoover Presidential Library, West Branch, Iowa. The records of the Nye Munitions Committee are in the National Archives, Washington, D.C., and the thirty-nine volumes of the committee's hearings and documents and the seven volumes of its reports have been published by the U.S. Government Printing Office. The fullest scholarly biography of Nye, focusing particularly on his role in foreign affairs and emphasizing agrarian bases for his views, is by Wayne S. Cole, *Senator Gerald P. Nye and American Foreign Relations* (1962). The best scholarly study of the munitions investigation is by John Edward Wiltz, *In Search of Peace: The Senate Munitions Inquiry, 1934–36* (1963). For a more concise study of Nye see John N. Schacht, ed., *Three Faces of Midwestern Isolationism: Gerald P. Nye, Robert E. Wood, John L. Lewis* (1981).

WAYNE S. COLE

NYE, James Warren (10 June 1814–25 Dec. 1876), governor of Nevada Territory and U.S. senator, was born at De Ruyter, New York, the son of James Nye and Thankful Crocker. His father's occupation is unknown. Although his family had very limited financial resources, James received a secondary education at Homer Academy and studied law in Hamilton, New York. He married Elsie Benson in Fabius, New York, and they had two children.

Eventually Nye drifted into the Democratic party, serving as a district attorney in 1839, as surrogate of Madison County from 1844 to 1847, and as a judge of the county court from 1847 to 1851. In 1848, he ran unsuccessfully for Congress on the Free-Soil ticket. After his defeat for Congress, Nye moved to Syracuse, New York, where he resided until 1857, when the Metropolitan Police Commission was created in New York City. At that time, Nye was appointed by the Tammany Hall organization as the first president of the Metropolitan Board of Police, a position he held until 1860.

Nye joined the Republican party in 1856, and according to his biographer, Effe Mona Mack, became a supporter and close friend of Abraham Lincoln, who later commissioned him brigadier general.

As a reward for his zealous support of the Republican party's ticket in New York State during the election of 1860, Nye was appointed territorial governor of Nevada in 1861. Nye arrived in Carson City, Nevada, on 8 July 1861 and immediately organized the territorial government. Samuel Clemens, who met Nye in Nevada at this time, described him as "a striking-looking man with long white hair, a friendly face and deep, lustrous dark eyes." Clemens went on to write that his tongue could express "every emotion. . . ." And "his eyes could out talk his tongue." Because of his stunning appearance, Nye was dubbed the "Gray Eagle" by his admirers.

At the first meeting of the territorial legislature, Nye unsuccessfully opposed laws that discriminated against blacks, declaring that such laws were behind the "spirit of the age." Furthermore, he emphasized the importance of establishing a system of common schools, noting that "the public have an interest in the instruction of every child . . . and as a matter of economy . . . it is much cheaper to furnish schoolhouses than prisons and keepers." The legislature listened politely and then voted against schools and for prisons.

During the Civil War, Nevada was important to Lincoln not only because it contained large gold and silver deposits, but also because an additional Republican state would expedite the ratification of the proposed amendment abolishing slavery. In March 1864 Congress passed an Enabling Act setting out the conditions under which Nevada would be admitted to the Union. Governor Nye promptly issued a proclamation calling for elections of delegates to a state constitutional convention, and by 31 October 1864 Nevada became a state.

In the presidential election of 1864, the Republican party carried Nevada, and in December 1864, the state legislature chose James Nye and William M. Stewart as senators, with Nye drawing the short term. Both senators hurried to Washington to vote in favor of the Thirteenth Amendment, which emancipated the slaves.

Nye served in the U.S. Senate until 1873. Adamantly opposed to President Andrew Johnson's plans for Reconstruction, he was a vociferous supporter of the Radical Republicans' Reconstruction program, though he did not sponsor any major legislation. After his defeat for reelection he returned East. While traveling with his daughter from Florida in 1875, Nye, confused and only partially dressed, stepped out of the train just as it left Richmond. Several hours later, he was found, half-naked, hiding in the Richmond depot. Shortly after this incident, he was committed to an insane asylum in White Plains, New York, where he died on Christmas day. His biographer reports that the contents of Nye's pockets at the time of his death included a handwritten note reading: "Dear General, Come up tonight and swap jokes.—signed—Lincoln." The note was a touching reminder of Nye's former prestige and influence.

• James W. Nye has not received much scholarly attention. Effe Mona Mack, "James Warren Nye: A Biography," *Nevada Historical Society Quarterly* 4 (July-Dec. 1961): 8–59, is the only biographical sketch presently available. The best summary of the territorial period from a political-constitutional standpoint is Eleanor Bushnell, *The Nevada Constitution: Origins and Growth*, rev. ed. (1968). Two useful general histories of Nevada that treat Nye are Elliott Russell, *History of Nevada*, 2d ed., with assistance of William D. Rowley (1987); and James W. Hulse, *The Nevada Adventure: A History*, 6th ed. (1990). An obituary is in the *New York Times*, 28 Dec. 1876. See also: *Daily Alta Californian*, 24, 27 May 1875, 29 Dec. 1876, 19 Jan. 1877; and *Biographical Directory of the American Congress*.

MARGARET HORSNELL

NYIREGYHÁZI, Ervin (19 Jan. 1903–13 Apr. 1987), romantic pianist and composer, was born in Budapest, Hungary, the son of Ignacz Nyiregyházi (pronounced NEAR-edge-hah-zee), a tenor in the chorus of the Royal Opera of Budapest, and Maria Borsodi, an amateur pianist. Ervin was a remarkable child prodigy who could sing before he could talk and who, by the age of three, was able to reproduce on a harmonica or piano any melody sung to him. He began formal piano lessons at the age of four and soon began composing music. In 1907 he performed his own compositions for the cellist David Popper and the composer Julius Erkel, both professors at the Budapest Academy of Music. By the age of five Ervin already possessed perfect pitch, a prodigious musical memory, and an extraordinary ability to transpose music into any key at sight. His precocity caught the attention of Géza Révész, the director of Amsterdam's Psychological Laboratory. Dr. Révész began a six-year study of the boy, which resulted in the publication of the book *Psychologische Analyse eines musikalisch hervorragenden Kindes* in 1916 (translated as *The Psychology of a Musical Prodigy* in 1925).

Ervin gave his first public recital in 1909 at the age of six. The next year he entered the Budapest Academy of Music, studying piano with István Tomán (a pupil of Franz Liszt) and Arnold Szekely. His fame spread quickly, and in 1911 Queen Mary of England invited him to play for her at Buckingham Palace. After his father died in 1914, Ervin, his younger brother, and his mother moved to Berlin. There he studied piano with Ernst von Dohnányi and made his orchestral debut playing the Beethoven third piano concerto with the Berlin Philharmonic under the direction of Max Fiedler, who was then Ervin's theory teacher. In 1916 Dohnányi moved to Budapest, and Ervin continued his piano studies with Frederic Lamond, another Liszt pupil. In 1917 the Nyiregyházi family returned to Budapest, and Ervin finished his studies with Dohnányi, graduating in 1918. He began an extensive period of touring throughout Europe, including performances with the legendary conductor Artur Nikisch in Berlin, and made his U.S. debut at Carnegie Hall on 18 October 1920.

He met with great success in the United States, settling in New York and touring under the management of R. E. Johnston. Then, in 1925, Nyiregyházi sued Johnston over a dispute about fees. Amid a torrent of adverse publicity, Nyiregyházi lost the suit. Blackballed by all major managements, he found himself unable to book appearances and was soon impoverished. He entered into a disastrous one-year marriage to Mary Kelen in 1926.

After divorcing Kelen in 1927, Nyiregyházi moved to California, where he went to work as a studio pianist for the motion picture company United Artists. He toured Europe in the 1930s and made a few U.S. appearances (including some for the Works Progress Administration during the Great Depression). The composer Arnold Schoenberg wrote to the conductor Otto Klemperer in 1935 that Nyiregyházi played with "unbelieveable newness, power and conviction" and said that he had "never heard such power of expression" (quoted in Benko), but the pianist gradually withdrew from public appearances and sank back into a life of poverty, alcohol, and a string of failed marriages (ten marriages in all, six ending in divorce, three ending in his wives' deaths, and the last ending with his death). He concertized briefly in Europe in 1959 but soon returned to Los Angeles and gave up performing altogether.

He sank into obscurity, living quietly in California for more than a decade. Then, in 1973, to earn money for the medical care of his ninth wife, Elsie, Nyiregyházi gave a few public concerts in San Francisco. A tape of one of these came into the hands of Gregor Benko, then president of the International Piano Archives (now affiliated with the University of Maryland). Benko was astounded by the playing, a throwback to the great romantic tradition of the nineteenth century, and arranged for Nyiregyházi to record an all-Liszt program for commercial release by the Archives. A Ford Foundation Grant led to a further series of recordings released by Columbia Records.

The recordings created a sensation. His highly individual—indeed, idiosyncratic—performances flew in the face of contemporary performance style, but devotees of romanticism were thrilled. And his extraordinary decline and reemergence made a great story. After a flurry of publicity in the 1970s, he again withdrew from the public eye, although he made a triumphant tour of Japan shortly before his death in Los Angeles.

Nyiregyházi spent most of his life composing. At the time of his death there were reportedly some 700 scores in the possession of his last wife, Doris, but they have never seen the light of day. He is best remembered, though, for his titanic piano playing. Harold C. Schonberg, the longtime music critic for the *New York Times*, wrote that Nyiregyházi's playing was "unique and has to be approached with no reference to any models" (13 Feb. 1978). His playing is "a kind of madness," Schonberg concluded, "but a divine madness."

• An early interview with Nyiregyházi by Harriet Brower can be found in *Musical America*, 11 Dec. 1920, p. 15. Robert J. Silverman, "A Candid Talk with Erwin Nyiregyházi," *Piano Quarterly* 117 (1982): 18–21, includes an extensive interview. Géza Révész, *The Psychology of a Musical Prodigy* (1925), is a thorough account of Nyiregyházi's prodigious talent as a child. For biographical information about Nyiregyházi, see Gregor Benko's comprehensive liner notes to the LP recording *Nyiregyházi Plays Liszt* (International Piano Archives 111), and Harold C. Schonberg, "The Case of the Vanishing Pianist," *New York Times*, 13 Feb. 1978. An extensive essay by Richard Kapp, "Recording with Ervin Nyiregyházi: A Chronicle," which details Nyiregyházi's 1978 recording sessions, can be found as an insert in the two-record LP album *Nyiregyházi* (Columbia M2 34598). An obituary is in the *New York Times*, 16 Apr. 1987.

JOHN ANTHONY MALTESE

NYSWANDER, Marie (13 Mar. 1919–20 Apr. 1986), psychiatrist and developer of methadone maintenance, was born Mary Elizabeth Nyswander in Reno, Nevada, the daughter of James Nyswander, a mathematics professor, and Dorothy Bird. In her teens she began calling herself Marie, the name she also used in her published work and by which she became professionally known. When Marie was two-and-a-half, her father divorced her mother. Dorothy Bird Nyswander took Marie to California and taught high school while completing doctoral work in psychology at the University of California at Berkeley. In 1926 Marie's mother moved to Salt Lake City to teach at the University of Utah, then in 1936 moved to New York City to begin a four-year research project on public school health services.

Her mother's independent, progressive outlook and the academic milieu in which she lived had a strong influence on Marie, who would later make her own contributions to health research. Marie's first experience of medicine was as a patient, however. When she was fifteen she spent a year in a tuberculosis sanatorium, where she immersed herself in the writings of Mann, Marx, and Engels. She became concerned with the plight of those less privileged than she and joined the Young Communist League, only to become disenchanted.

In 1937 Nyswander enrolled in Sarah Lawrence College, graduating in 1941. Although deeply interested in music and nature, she chose a career in medicine on practical grounds and enrolled in the Cornell University Medical School, from which she graduated in 1944. While in medical school she was briefly married (probably in 1943–1944) to Charles Berry, a young divorced anatomy instructor. After completing her surgical internship she joined the U.S. Navy in 1945, hoping to become an orthopedic surgeon. The navy did not want women surgeons, however, and she was posted to the Lexington Narcotic Hospital run by the U.S. Public Health Service.

At Lexington Nyswander saw addicts from all walks of life branded as psychopaths, ordered about, and subjected to racial slurs. She hated the institutional atmosphere, and in her subsequent work she strove to treat addicts more humanely, as individual patients. Initially she did so within the framework of psychoanalysis, which she began to study in the late 1940s at New York Medical College. She completed her analysis under Lewis Wolberg, founder of the Postgraduate Center for Mental Health, and in 1950 began her own psychiatric practice. In 1955 she helped to establish the Narcotic Addiction Research Project, a New York–based experimental outpatient program that provided addicts with intensive individual psychotherapy. In 1957, with the aid of the sociologist Charles Winick, she set up a musicians' clinic, which specialized in the treatment of jazz musicians addicted to heroin. During the early 1960s she also treated addicts in a storefront clinic under the auspices of the Narcotics Office of the East Harlem Protestant Parish.

Nyswander discussed her clinical experience in a book, *The Drug Addict as Patient* (1956). She never confined herself to treating addicts, however, and continued to see many types of patients in her private practice, including those with sexual and marital problems. They inspired her second book, *The Power of Sexual Surrender* (1959), which she published under the name Marie Nyswander Robinson. Leonard Robinson, Nyswander's second husband (to whom she had become engaged in 1953), was a lay psychoanalyst and writer who lent an editorial hand to both books. (The marriage, which was childless, ended in divorce in 1965.)

Nyswander's life and career took a dramatic turn during the mid-1960s. In 1962 Vincent Dole, a metabolic disease researcher at Rockefeller University, became interested in heroin addiction and chanced to read *The Drug Addict as Patient*. He invited Nyswander to collaborate in his research and arranged for her appointment to the staff of Rockefeller University.

Working with six male volunteers long addicted to heroin, Dole and Nyswander noticed that those who were given drugs like morphine remained preoccupied with getting high, constantly sought to increase their dosage, and experienced withdrawal symptoms if they did not inject themselves every few hours. Those who took methadone behaved differently. Experiencing neither craving nor intense euphoria, they were free from withdrawal symptoms for a full day and became more interested in work and school. Long-term methadone maintenance—legally stabilizing patients on a daily oral dose—seemed a promising strategy for breaking the cycle of heroin injection, reducing crime, and reintegrating addicts into society. Because methadone was itself an opiate, there was also less likelihood of relapse, the problem that had plagued Nyswander and others who had treated addicts through detoxification and talking therapy.

By 1965 Dole and Nyswander had data on twenty-two patients, some of whom had been maintained on methadone for fifteen months. They published their findings in the *Journal of the American Medical Association* and in several articles that followed. An important early supporter was Ray Trussell, the commissioner of New York City hospitals. Trussell helped them establish a research and demonstration project at the Manhattan General Hospital, then operated by Beth Israel Medical Center. The project was successful, and methadone maintenance, which received widespread and favorable publicity, continued to gain ground. The biggest surge came in the early 1970s, when methadone programs proliferated across the country. Robert Newman, another key ally, presided over dozens of new methadone clinics in New York City, home to roughly half of the nation's heroin addicts. Methadone maintenance eventually spread around the world, to countries as diverse as Australia, Hong Kong, Sweden, and Thailand.

Methadone maintenance also aroused considerable opposition. Agents of the Federal Bureau of Narcotics, opposed to all forms of drug maintenance and long suspicious of Nyswander's medical approach, tried to end the early methadone research through harassment and intimidation. They failed. More significant in the long run was the opposition of those who believed abstinence should be the ultimate goal of treatment. Methadone was still an addictive drug, they argued, on which patients remained dependent. Also controversial was Dole and Nyswander's thesis, published in 1967, that heroin addiction was a metabolic disease to which some people were neurologically susceptible. Those who argued that addiction was rooted in personality disorder—a position that Nyswander, despite her psychiatric training, had abandoned—criticized the metabolic hypothesis as unproven.

From 1974 until her death in New York City, Nyswander fought to preserve and consolidate the gains of the methadone revolution, which remained vulnerable to regulatory counterattack. Her influence was by no means confined to her writings. An attractive woman with an infectious smile, she impressed associates with her straightforward manner, her unsentimental compassion, and her easy rapport with patients. Vincent Dole, whom she had married in 1965, remarked that her secret was her ability to see the inner person. No other American psychiatrist of her generation affected the lives of so many addicted patients.

• Oral history interviews with Marie Nyswander (1981) and Vincent Dole (1982) are housed at the Columbia University Oral History Center. Portions of these interviews appear in David Courtwright et al., *Addicts Who Survived: An Oral History of Narcotic Use in America, 1926–1965* (1989), pp. 310–12 and 331–43. These sources were corroborated and supplemented by telephone interviews and by video recordings of eulogies at Nyswander's memorial service and dinner on 20 Oct. 1986. The video recordings are available through the Beth Israel Medical Center in New York City. In addition to her books Nyswander authored or coauthored numerous articles, among them "Withdrawal Treatment of Drug Addiction," *New England Journal of Medicine* 242 (1950): 128–30; "The Treatment of Drug Addicts as Voluntary Outpatients: A Progress Report," *American Journal of Orthopsychiatry* 28 (1958): 714–27; "Psychotherapy of Successful Musicians Who Are Drug Addicts," *American Journal of Orthopsychiatry* 31 (1961): 622–36; "A Medical Treatment for Diacetylmorphine (Heroin) Addiction," *Journal of the American Medical Association* 193 (1965): 646–50; and "Heroin Addiction—A Metabolic Disease," *Archives of Internal Medicine* 120 (1967): 19–24. Journalist Nat Hentoff profiled Nyswander in the *New Yorker*, 26 June and 3 July 1965, and subsequently in a book, *A Doctor among the Addicts* (1968). Briefer accounts are in *Vogue*, May 1968, pp. 210–11, 279, and the *New York Times Magazine*, 15 Oct. 1967, pp. 44–64. The most complete print obituary is in the *New York Times*, 21 Apr. 1986.

DAVID COURTWRIGHT

O

OAKES, George Washington Ochs (27 Oct. 1861–26 Oct. 1931), editor and publisher, was born George Washington Ochs in Cincinnati, Ohio, the second son of German immigrants Julius Ochs, a rabbi and unsuccessful drygoods merchant, and Bertha Levy. Both George and his older brother, Adolph Ochs, began their newspaper careers at early ages—Adolph was eleven, George was nine—by delivering the *Knoxville* (Tenn.) *Chronicle* to some fifty customers in the wee hours of the morning. Their pay envelopes were handed over, unopened, each week to their father, who in turn gave each boy a small allowance. While Adolph left school at age fifteen and became owner-publisher of the *Chattanooga Times* by age twenty, George continued to carry newspapers until his graduation in 1879 from the University of Tennessee at Knoxville.

As a university student, Oakes won highest class honors in math and Greek and was an influential member of Chi Delta, the campus debating society. Diploma in hand, Oakes left Knoxville to join his brother's paper in Chattanooga, first as a reporter and later as city editor, a position that almost cost him his life. In 1883, while copying divorce records that concerned a prominent Chattanoogan, Oakes was confronted by the man, who threatened to "shoot him full of holes" (Schuyler, p. 11). The man tried to make good his threat a few days later, but Oakes, quicker on the draw, wounded the man first. The brilliant intellectual was an excellent shot as well.

In 1896 Oakes became publisher of the Chattanooga paper when his brother went to New York City to run the newly purchased *Times*. Oakes served two terms as mayor of Chattanooga from 1893 to 1897, earning the animosity of state Democrats by refusing to support the free silver presidential candidacy of William Jennings Bryan. In 1900 he left the city to become editor of the *New York Times* Paris Exposition edition; while in Paris, he was awarded the Cross of the French Legion of Honor. He returned to the United States to publish the *Philadelphia Times*, purchased by his brother in 1901 and later merged with the *Philadelphia Public Ledger*. He served in that position until Adolph Ochs sold the paper to Cyrus Curtis in 1913. In 1907 Oakes married Bertie Gans, daughter of a wealthy Philadelphia banker and merchant. She died giving birth to their second son in 1913, and the boys were raised by Oakes's sister, Nannie.

The war years were difficult ones for Oakes. In 1915 he accepted a position from his brother as editor of *Current History*, a publication begun by the *Times* at the outbreak of World War I to chronicle the history of the war. He retained the editorship until 1925. The event that eventually precipitated U.S. entry into the war, the sinking of the *Lusitania*, so outraged Oakes

that he vowed that his two sons would no longer carry a surname of German origin. In 1917 the Philadelphia Court of Common Pleas granted his request to become George Washington Ochs Oakes, and his sons became John and George Oakes. The move saddened the Ochs family, but they later became reconciled to the change (Schuyler, p. 42).

Oakes spent his later years involved in the civic activities he loved. He had served as president of the Chattanooga Chamber of Commerce (1899–1901) and of the board of education (1897–1901). In New York City he was president of the Civitan Club (1925) and of the Tennessee Society of New York (1931). In 1925 he enrolled in Columbia University to pursue a doctorate and had earned all of his credits shortly before his death in New York City. He is buried at Mt. Sinai Cemetery in Frankford, Pennsylvania.

George, who built his career on the successes of Adolph, never forgot his debt to his brother. "His energy, his ability, his industry, his unselfish helpfulness to each member of the family, were an inspiration," Oakes wrote of Ochs. He was "an abiding influence in spurring their activities and molding their careers" (Schuyler, p. 47). Oakes, however, added his own intellectual stamp to the family fortunes. He complemented his brother's head for business with an intellect—and education—to match that of their brilliant and ineffectual father.

• The papers of George Washington Ochs Oakes are not centrally held by any one library. Many, however, are collected in *The Life and Letters of George Washington Ochs-Oakes*, ed. W. M. Schuyler, privately printed in 1933 (available at the University of Tennessee, Knoxville, library). Another useful reference, *A Memoir of Julius Ochs: An Autobiography*, privately printed (1960), is also available at the University of Tennessee, Knoxville, library. A definitive obituary is in the *New York Times*, 27 Oct. 1931.

SUSAN G. BARNES

OAKES, Urian (c. 1631–25? July 1681), Puritan clergyman and president of Harvard College, was born in England, possibly in London, the son of Edward Oakes and Jane (maiden name unknown). His parents brought Urian and his brother Edward to Cambridge, Massachusetts, about the year 1640. Although his occupation in England is unknown, Edward Oakes, Sr., in Massachusetts established himself as a respected member of the colony. Obtaining freeman status in 1642, he served as deputy to the General Court from Cambridge (1659–1682) and from Concord (1684–1686); he also was selectman (1643–1678) and a lieutenant in Metacomet's (King Philip's) War. Urian was sent to Harvard College, where he received a B.A. in 1649 and was then a fellow and tutor in the college from 1650 to 1653. Returning to England in 1654, while Cromwell was in power, Oakes obtained a living as rector of Tichfield in Hampshire County. He married Ruth Ames, daughter of the renowned theologian William Ames. The date of their marriage is unknown. They had two sons, both of whom would graduate from Harvard during their father's term as acting president. With the restoration of the Stuart monarchy and the passage of the Act of Uniformity in 1662, by which all clergy who did not conform to the Anglican order were ejected, Oakes lost his living at Tichfield. He was possibly employed as headmaster of the Grammar School in Southwark. Cotton Mather noted in *Magnalia Christi Americana* (1702) that Oakes returned to Tichfield as co-minister of a Congregational church "when the heat of persecution was a little abated."

In 1668 Jonathan Mitchell, minister of the Cambridge Church in Massachusetts, died, and Oakes was invited to be his successor. The illness and death of his wife in 1669, followed by his own protracted illness in 1670, delayed Oakes's acceptance of this position until the spring of 1671. He arrived in Massachusetts in July and was ordained on 8 November 1671. The next year he became a freeman of the colony and was also reinstated as a fellow of Harvard College. When Leonard Hoar was elected president of the college, however, Oakes and several other Fellows resigned in protest. The underlying causes of this controversy were never made explicit and remain obscure. Harvard historian Samuel Eliot Morison dismissed the possibility that the students and fellows were opposed to Hoar's plans to modernize the college curriculum; he speculates on "some fault in Hoar's character or conduct" (*Harvard College in the Seventeenth Century* [1936]). The Harvard overseers chose not to accept the resignations of Oakes and his colleague Thomas Shepard, and on 2 October 1673 they were "requested to continue their Assist[ance] to the College as Fellows according as they were formerly appointed thereto," as stated in the Harvard College Records. On 15 March, the day Hoar resigned as president, Oakes and Shepard accepted their reelection as Harvard fellows. Although there is no evidence that Oakes singularly instigated the movement against Hoar, he was squarely on the side of the president's antagonists, among whom were Increase Mather and Cotton Mather. Less than a month after Hoar's resignation, Oakes was asked by the Harvard overseers to be the acting president of Harvard College. Expressing a "deep sence [*sic*] of his unfitness," Oakes accepted the offer and served as acting president from 7 April 1675 until 9 February 1680, when he was elected president of Harvard College. He continued in this office until his death. Oakes presided over the college during a difficult period in its history, following the outbreak of King Philip's War. The student body was much reduced, and finances were under severe strain.

Oakes was praised by his contemporaries for his broad intellect and eloquence as preacher and author. He was moderator of the "reforming" synod of 1679, which promoted Increase Mather's plan to effect a revival of piety by means of covenant renewals, and he also was a censor of the Massachusetts press. His keen interest in providential history reflected Puritan sensibilities on both sides of the Atlantic. Oakes's first publication, *An Almanack for the Year of Our Lord 1650*, for example, was an inventive application of popular astrology to divine agency in church history. Together with daily astrological symbols, each month of the year (March to February) highlighted the events of one or more centuries of Christian history. February ended the calendar year with a synopsis of sixteenth-century Reformation: "The Gospell breaks out in Germany. . . . England happy under Queen Elizabeth."

Oakes was also a master of the jeremiad style, which characterized the preaching of second-generation New England clergy. His Artillery Election sermon of June 1672, "The Unconquerable, All-Conquering & More-than-Conquering Soldier," interwove the themes of apocalyptic warfare and salvation. The chilling statement, "This Earth shall be a continued Field and Stage of War till the last day," had immediacy for soldiers who were engaged in the recent outbreak of frontier warfare in Massachusetts. The experience of the frontier soldier became a metaphor for the overarching spiritual warfare between the legions of good and evil. "A Christian Man or Woman is by many degrees a better souldier than *Casar* or *Alexander*," Oakes declared in his Artillery Election sermon, because the battles of the Christian soul had the ultimate power of divine assistance. The sermon focused on the challenge of frontier warfare as an instrument of God's judgment against the declensions of his chosen people: "We live in Times of great Degeneracy, and in special of great Disaffection to the Ministers of Christ." Like his ministerial colleagues, Oakes's vision of reformation was one of restored social order: "Keep order. Fight every one in your own places where you are set. Be sure you keep Rank and File. Order is the Beauty of the World." His Election Sermon of May 1673 similarly balanced dire warnings of divine punishment with the promise of reward for communal reformation: "Whatever Dayes may come upon a sinful and secure world . . . yet it shall undoubtedly go well with the humble, waking, faithful Servants of God." The devastations of King Philip's War allowed Oakes to further develop the providential theme in two sermons posthumously published in 1682. In *A Seasonable Discourse* he pondered why God "hath waited and spared so long such an unworthy People." *The Sovereign Efficacy of Divine Providence* reviewed the ineffectual defense of New England's militias against Native American warriors. Here, as in the Artillery sermon of 1672, he warned against false confidence in military strength where spiritual defenses were weak: "it is a lesson God hath been teaching of us. . . . That the Battel is not to the strong. . . . Who sees not that God's Design is to humble proud New-England?"

Oakes is best remembered for *An Elegie upon the Death of the Reverend Mr. Thomas Shepard* (1677; repr. 1902). Here, too, he used the providential theme to frame Shepard's death in the context of divine judgment for communal sin: "Ah cursed sins! that strike at God, and kill His Servants, and the blood of Prophets spill." Historian Philip Gura notes that the *Elegie* "has rightly been praised as one of the best examples of Puritan incidental verse and displays Oakes's sympathetic knowledge of classical and Renaissance models."

Notwithstanding Oakes's prominence as an early president of Harvard College and the quality of his prose style that marks him as one of New England's best Puritan writers, surprisingly little has been written about him.

• The papers of Oakes are at the Harvard University Archives; documents relating to his Harvard career are published in the Harvard College Records, Colonial Society of Massachusetts, *Collections*, vol. 15. See also Oakes, *New England Pleaded With . . .* (1673). For background on the Oakes family consult Nathaniel B. Shurtleff, ed., *Records of the Governor and Company of Massachusetts Bay*, vols. 2–5 (1853). A comprehensive bibliography of Oakes's publications is in John L. Sibley, *Biographical Sketches of the Graduates of Harvard University*, vol. 1 (1873). For a contemporary and laudatory appraisal of Oakes's life and works see Cotton Mather, *Magnalia Christi Americana* (2 vols., repr. 1853), bk. 4, chap. 5, pp. 114–18; and his *Poem Dedicated to the Memory of . . . Urian Oakes* (1682).

A brief treatment of Oakes in the context of his intellectual and social world is in Perry Miller, *The New England Mind: The Seventeenth Century* (1936), and Samuel Eliot Morison, *Harvard College in the Seventeenth Century* (1936). More recent and specialized articles on Oakes are William J. Scheick, "Standing in the Gap: Urian Oakes's Elegy on Thomas Shepard," *Early American Literature* 9, no. 3 (Winter 1975): 301–6; and Philip Gura's brief note, "Urian Oakes," in *American Writers before 1800*, ed. James A. Levernier and Douglas R. Wilmes (1983).

BARBARA DAILEY

OAKLEY, Annie (13 Aug. 1860–3 Nov. 1926), shooter and Wild West star, was born Phoebe Ann Moses near Woodland, Ohio, the daughter of Jacob Moses and Susan Wise, farmers. Annie, as her sisters called her, grew up with poverty and hardship. Her father died when she was six, and in 1867 her mother married Daniel Brumbaugh, who died three years later. During this period, Annie began to work at the Darke County Infirmary. She also "hired out" to a farm family for two years but ran away after being overworked, beaten, and perhaps sexually abused. Annie returned to the infirmary and occasionally lived at home with her mother and her mother's third husband, Joseph Shaw.

Annie Moses gleaned minimal education but learned woodcraft thoroughly. While at home, she first trapped game, then taught herself to shoot her father's Kentucky hunting rifle. She supplied food for the family, sold surplus game to a shopkeeper, and helped pay off the mortgage. But her life changed dramatically when she won a match against stage-shooter Francis E. "Frank" Butler. The match occurred in 1875 or 1881; the six-year discrepancy may be a result of Wild West publicity that changed her birthdate to 1866.

After the match, Annie and Frank married, either in 1876 or 1882. When Frank's partner fell ill, Annie took his place. Annie soon chose the name Oakley, and the couple appeared in vaudeville and circuses as Butler and Oakley. In 1884, as they completed a season with the Sells Brothers Circus in New Orleans, William F. Cody's Wild West Exposition opened nearby. Butler, who now served more as Oakley's manager than partner, urged Cody to hire her. But Cody, who already employed several well-known shooting acts, refused.

In March 1885, when one of Cody's star acts resigned, Cody and his partner Nate Salsbury hired Oakley, the first Anglo woman to perform in the Wild West arena. She proved herself an excellent shot who could handle pistols, rifles, and shotguns with either hand. She traveled with Cody's Wild West in the United States and Europe for sixteen of the next seventeen seasons, missing only 1888 due to an unexplained spat between her and Cody.

During these years, Oakley and Butler developed an act and a persona for Oakley based on six themes: guns, horses, heroes, villains, Victorianism, and the American West. Oakley displayed amazing skill with both mainstays of western life, guns and horses. She also represented a hero, while explosions of fire and smoke convinced viewers that she could best all villains. Still, Oakley maintained Victorian modesty, claiming she wanted to be a "lady." Her demeanor, which included wearing skirts and riding sidesaddle, allowed all types of viewers to admire her. Oakley capped her image by adding to it the American West; she wore western style clothes, used western guns and tack, and made much of her friendship with Chief Sitting Bull.

In 1901, shortly after a train wreck that injured Oakley's back, Butler announced their departure from the Wild West. He had taken employment as a traveling representative for the Union Metallic Cartridge Company, while Oakley hoped to explore other interests, including hunting, match shooting, and giving charity exhibitions. Instead, she became embroiled in libel suits against newspapers that erroneously reported that she was a drug addict and a thief.

By 1910, Butler had resigned his position with UMC, and most of the trials had ended. Oakley decided to return to the arena. Between 1911 and 1913, she and Butler toured with Vernon Seavers's Young Buffalo Show. Here, they reinstituted their tested formula, billing Oakley as "Little Sure Shot" and the "Peerless Wing and Rifle Shot." Although most arena and rodeo cowgirls now wore trousers and rode astride, Annie persisted in wearing skirts and riding sidesaddle. She also continued to garner applause and rave reviews.

After Oakley retired from the Young Buffalo Show, she and Butler spent time shooting and hunting in Cambridge, Maryland; Pinehurst, North Carolina; and Leesburg, Florida. She continued to set records in matches and to give charity exhibitions, especially for orphans' homes. During World War I, Oakley and

Butler gave shooting exhibitions to American troops, while their dog, Dave, helped them raise money for the Red Cross by sniffing out money hidden by donors.

After the war's end, they returned to retirement. When, in 1922, an automobile accident crippled Oakley, she learned to shoot wearing a steel brace on her leg. Then, in 1923, Dave was killed in an automobile accident, a tragedy from which the couple, who were childless, never fully recovered. They soon returned to Ohio; a few years later Annie died in Greenville, Ohio. Days after her death, on 21 November, Frank, who was ten years older than Annie, died as well. They are buried side by side in a cemetery near Brock, Ohio.

In the years since Oakley's death, a growing number of children's and adults' books, stage plays, films, celebrations, and museum exhibits have honored her. The best known is *Annie Get Your Gun*, a musical that presents Oakley as a country girl who purposely lost her match with Butler. In truth, she was an intelligent and decisive woman. In the partnership of Oakley and Butler, she provided a driving force. Although some people found Oakley too "particular" and even obsessive, others admired her professionalism, for she trained daily and refused in arena appearances to use tricks and illusions. Others called her the most charming and generous woman they had ever known.

Today, most Americans remember Annie Oakley as a Wild West star, but she achieved far more than that. She was a consummate athlete who opened arena sports, including rodeo, to women. Oakley also campaigned for women as match shooters and hunters, giving free lessons and encouraging hundreds of women to follow her lead. She represented the best of the Old West, both to her era and subsequent ones. She came from humble beginnings, worked hard, and succeeded, yet she never lost her compassion for others. As the archetypal western woman, Oakley exhibited strength, courage, and skill combined with modesty, charm, and benevolence.

• Virtually no personal papers exist. The two best sources are Annie Oakley, "Autobiography" (undated) and *Powders I Have Used* (1914). Oakley and Butler also compiled invaluable scrapbooks of newspaper clippings, held by the Buffalo Bill Historical Society in Cody, Wyo. Biographies include Courtney Ryley Cooper, *Annie Oakley: Woman at Arms* (1927); Annie Fern Campbell Swartwout, *Missie: An Historical Biography of Annie Oakley* (1947); Walter Havighurst, *Annie Oakley of the Wild West* (1954); Isabelle S. Sayers, *The Rifle Queen: Annie Oakley* (1973) and *Annie Oakley and Buffalo Bill's Wild West* (1981); Shirl Kasper, *Annie Oakley* (1992); and Glenda Riley, *Annie Oakley and the Enduring West* (1994). Among articles are Claude R. Flory, "Annie Oakley in the South," *North Carolina Historical Review* 43, no. 3 (1966): 333–43; Louise Cheney, "Annie Oakley, Little Miss Sureshot," *Real West* 10 (Nov. 1967): 53–57; "Annie Oakley and the Wild West," special issue of *Cobblestone Magazine*, Jan. 1991; and R. Douglas Hurt, "Annie Oakley: An Enduring Western Legend," *True West* 36 (July 1989): 14–19.

GLENDA RILEY

OATES, William Calvin (30 Nov. 1833–9 Sept. 1910), military officer and politician, was born in Pike County, Alabama, the son of William Oates and Sarah Sellers, farmers. His family was impoverished, and Oates attended school intermittently during his childhood. He left home when he was seventeen and fled to Florida, convinced he had killed a man in a brawl.

For the next few years, Oates wandered throughout the Southwest, eventually making his way to Texas, where, as he admitted in an unpublished autobiography, he became "much addicted to gaming at cards" and his violent temper got him into trouble. His younger brother, John, who had been dispatched by the family, persuaded him to return to Alabama. Because a warrant for Oates's arrest (for assault, not murder) was still pending in Pike County, he avoided the authorities by settling down in a neighboring Alabama county, where he enrolled in an academy, taught school, and began to study law. By the late 1850s, Oates had successfully turned his life around, embracing a professional career as an attorney (he passed the bar in Oct. 1858) and the owner of a weekly newspaper in Abbeville, Alabama.

Oates argued against secession, but when Alabama left the Union, he decided to support his state and the Confederacy. In the spring of 1861 he was instrumental in raising a company of volunteers called the Henry Pioneers and was elected captain by the men in the ranks. The company was later incorporated into the newly formed Fifteenth Alabama Regiment, which served with General Robert E. Lee's Army of Northern Virginia. The regiment saw action in most of the noteworthy battles in the eastern theater of the war, including Gaines' Mill, Cedar Mountain, Second Manassas (Second Bull Run), Sharpsburg (Antietam), and Fredericksburg.

Oates was given command of the Fifteenth Alabama in the spring of 1863. His commission as a full colonel was delivered to Lee, but for reasons not known it was never confirmed by the Confederate Congress, which meant that technically Oates never achieved a rank higher than lieutenant colonel. Nevertheless, he claimed for himself the rank of colonel for the remainder of his service in the Confederate army. A rival, Alexander A. Lowther, supplanted Oates as regimental commander in July 1864. Shortly afterward Oates was given command of the Forty-eighth Alabama Regiment.

Nevertheless, the Fifteenth Alabama held Oates's loyalty and fondness, for, as he declared later in his life, "there was no better regiment in the Confederate army." At Gettysburg, on 2 July 1863, Oates was in command of his regiment for the first time in battle. On the slopes of Little Round Top, Oates and his Alabamians tried to dislodge the Union defenders of the hill, the Twentieth Maine Regiment under the command of Colonel Joshua Lawrence Chamberlain. After an hour of desperate fighting, some of it in hand-to-hand combat, Chamberlain led his troops in a bold bayonet charge that swept Oates's Confederates from the hillside. "We ran," Oates later confessed, "like a herd of wild cattle." In the rush of retreat, he had to leave behind his brother John, who had been mortally wounded in the fighting.

Although his men praised him as "a handsome and brave leader," some believed he was too aggressive and impetuous on the battlefield. He displayed those traits at the battle of Chickamauga in Georgia on 20 September 1863, when, after becoming separated from his brigade, he tried without proper authority to order South Carolina troops into battle.

Oates and his men were in the thick of the fighting in other battles, including Brown's Ferry and Lookout Valley near Chattanooga, the Wilderness, Spotsylvania, and Cold Harbor. He was wounded six times during the war, twice severely. On 16 August 1864, at Fussell's Mills (near Petersburg, Va.), Oates lost his right arm and was out of the war.

Oates resumed his law practice in Abbeville, Alabama, and he soon became involved in state and national politics. He served in 1868 as a delegate to the Democratic National Convention. From 1870 to 1872 he served in the Alabama House of Representatives. He took a seat in 1875 as a delegate to the state constitutional convention. In 1880 he was elected from Alabama's Third District to the U.S. House of Representatives, where he served seven consecutive terms. In 1882 he married Sarah "Sallie" Toney; they had one child. Oates resigned from Congress in 1894 and, running as "the one-armed hero from Henry County," won a hotly contested gubernatorial race against fusionist Reuben Kolb. Keeping a campaign promise, he served only a single two-year term as governor. His accomplishments as governor were not noteworthy. The state was mired in financial difficulties, and Oates's one term in office gave him little time to effect many changes.

In politics Oates was known as "a conservative among conservatives, and a party regular par excellence." He was a fierce opponent of immigration, organized labor, and free silver. Like other southern Democrats, he detested the Populists and approved the use of fraudulent tactics to defeat them at the polls. His racial views were typical of the patrician class in the South, despite his own humble background, and he fully believed that blacks were racially inferior to whites. Nevertheless, he asserted that "there are some white men who have no more right and no more business to vote than a Negro and not as much as some of them." He thought that conservative black leaders, such as Booker T. Washington, should provide a model for black self-improvement and personal advancement. At the Alabama constitutional convention of 1901, Oates served as a delegate and spoke out strongly against "grandfather clauses" and other measures that would disfranchise black voters exclusively. His most humanitarian appeal during the convention was made against lynchings of blacks and other acts of racial violence. The new Alabama constitution, however, effectively eliminated black suffrage in the state (and the votes of poor whites, too), and while Oates disliked the document, he decided not to oppose its ratification.

After leaving the governor's office, Oates hoped to run for the U.S. Senate, but he failed to win his party's nomination. Instead, the Spanish-American War gave him an opportunity to serve his country again. In 1898 he received a brigadier general's commission from President William McKinley, and he commanded three different brigades during the short war. "I am now a Yankee General, formerly a Rebel Colonel, and right each time!" he declared. However, his longing for a combat assignment went unfulfilled.

During the final years of his life, Oates practiced law and concentrated on his real estate ventures, an activity that had made him a wealthy man in the years after the Civil War. For all his remarkable experiences, the Civil War remained for Oates the pivotal event of his life, and his memories of Gettysburg were particularly vivid and anguished. In 1905 he published his magnum opus, *The War between the Union and the Confederacy and Its Lost Opportunities*, a massive book that combined a history of the entire war with an account of the Fifteenth Alabama and his own personal reminiscences. When he died in Montgomery, Alabama, he was remembered for his military and public service, but people who knew him well could not fail to recall something else about Oates. One newspaper obituary strikingly encapsulated in one sentence the essence of Oates, the man, "He was full of pluck."

• Oates's private papers, including some unfinished and unpublished autobiographies, letters, financial records, speeches, and news clippings, are in the possession of a descendant. At the National Archives in Washington, D.C., his military service records for both the Confederate and U.S. armies contain useful papers and correspondence. A bound book of manuscripts at the Gettysburg National Military Park contains extremely valuable documents, including copies of some direct correspondence exchanged between Oates and Chamberlain, related to a controversy over the erection of a monument to the Fifteenth Alabama on Little Round Top. Oates published several shorter pieces on Gettysburg and political topics, including "Gettysburg: The Battle on the Right," *Southern Historical Society Papers* 6 (1878): 172–82; "The Homestead Strike, A Congressional View," *North American Review* 155 (1892): 355–64; and "Industrial Development of the South," *North American Review* 161 (1895): 566–74. Reliable biographical information is in Robert K. Krick's introduction to Oates's *War between the Union and the Confederacy*, repr. ed. (1974), and the introduction to Glenn LaFantasie, ed., *Gettysburg: Colonel William C. Oates and Lieutenant Frank A. Haskell* (1992). An obituary is in the *Montgomery Advertiser*, 10 Sept. 1910.

GLENN W. LAFANTASIE

OATMAN, Johnson, Jr. (21 Apr. 1856–25 Sept. 1922), gospel hymn writer, was born near Medford, New Jersey, the son of Johnson Oatman, a merchant, and Rachel Ann Cline. Educated at Herbert's Academy, Vincetown, and the New Jersey Collegiate Institute, Bordentown, he was licensed and ordained as a local preacher in the Methodist Episcopal church but never held a pastorate. He married Wilhelmina Ried in

1878; they had three children. After working for many years with his father in Lumberton, New Jersey, he became associated with a life-insurance company in Mount Holly, New Jersey. In failing health in 1893, he retired to the seaside resort community of Ocean Grove, New Jersey. A "stronghold of Methodist Victorianism," Ocean Grove was a permanent site of carefully-regulated summer camp meetings patronized by urban middle-class evangelical Protestants in search of rest, wholesome recreation, and spiritual renewal (Jones, p. 33).

When Oatman's health improved, he devoted himself to another form of ministry—writing religious lyrics. In his day the production of gospel songs and hymns imbued with scriptural language was recognized as a worthy vocation. Convinced of the formative, expressive, and persuasive powers of the sung text, evangelical Protestants credited sacred songs with inculcating doctrine, precipitating conversions, and nurturing piety. The hymnist's divine "calling" was validated in such autobiographies as *Fanny Crosby's Life-Story, By Herself* (1903) and Ida L. Reed's *My Life Story* (1912). Hymnologists published sketches of hymnists, composers, and singing evangelists along with anecdotes attesting to hymns' inspiring and redemptive effects. The professions of creating, performing, and publishing gospel hymns (religious verses paired with tunes in the style of popular songs) were detailed in memoirs by successful individuals, including Ira D. Sankey's *My Life and Sacred Songs* (1906), Charles H. Gabriel's *Personal Memoirs* (1918), and George C. Stebbins's *Reminiscences and Gospel Hymn Stories* (1924).

Oatman, a singer from boyhood, was well suited and situated for his new career. Ocean Grove competed successfully with dozens of other religious vacation resorts and camp meetings founded in the postbellum United States, attracting thousands to associate with coreligionists, hear eminent preachers, and enjoy choral and congregational singing. Publicists cited a minister's advice to his congregation: go to the Ocean Grove camp meeting "to hear such singing as you can hear nowhere else this side of heaven" (Morris S. Daniels, *The Story of Ocean Grove* [1919], p. 158). Hymnists, composers, itinerant evangelists, settled clergymen, and hymnbook editors and publishers interacted at the "sacred grove."

Oatman's first hymn, "I Am Walking with My Savior," was written in 1892 and published in 1893 with a tune by John R. Sweney, then music director at Ocean Grove and other camp meetings. Oatman went on to write approximately 7,000 lyrics, selling many to prominent gospel-song composers and publishers for a dollar or two apiece. According to musician and hymnologist J. H. Hall, Oatman "constantly" had "more orders for songs than he [could] possibly fill" (p. 359).

Widely published and disseminated orally by evangelists and missionaries, several of Oatman's hymns entered the religious folk repertory. "No, Not One" ("There's not a friend like the lowly Jesus") was included in thirty-five collections within a year of its publication in 1895 and was translated into other languages. Well known in the United States, "Count Your Blessings" (1897) also became popular in England and Wales after being introduced by singing revivalist Rodney "Gipsy" Smith.

Written in 1898, "Higher Ground" ("I'm pressing on the upward way, New heights I'm gaining every day") was set to music by Charles H. Gabriel, a songleader at Ocean Grove and the compiler of numerous hymnbooks for Sunday schools and evangelistic services. This hymn of pilgrimage was favored by participants in the Holiness revival that stimulated the postbellum camp-meeting movement and exerted particularly strong influence at Ocean Grove. Citing the Bible as well as John Wesley's ideal of sanctification (also known as Christian perfection), advocates of Holiness laid claim to the joyous experience of immediate sanctification. Conversion regenerated the soul, but converts who proceeded to consecrate themselves wholly to God could receive the "second blessing" of entire sanctification—instantaneous cleansing from past transgressions and the disposition to willful sin. This purgation, often figured as a baptism by fire and equated with the indwelling of the Holy Spirit, enabled them to attain the "higher Christian life" of personal holiness, which in turn should generate reforms in church and society, ultimately purifying the world. Oatman's "How the Fire Fell" especially appealed to Holiness advocates because it testified that "the Lord sanctified me." "The Sanctifying Power" likewise articulated Holiness doctrine. Eight other texts by Oatman were included with tunes by Tali Esen Morgan in *Ocean Grove Christian Songs* (1902), a collection coedited by Morgan, who succeeded Sweney as Ocean Grove's music director.

Oatman's lyrics also had interdenominational appeal. Many of them employed first-person speakers voicing common emotions and religious experiences. These texts were readily learned because Oatman relied on regular four-line stanzas with exact rhyme. Often the initial stanza's fourth line is repeated in subsequent stanzas, sometimes with slight variation; that theme recurs also in the refrain. He used familiar images and phrases (Jordan River, the straight and narrow way) and traditional metaphors (the church as Christ's bride, life as journey, the Christian as pilgrim, heaven as home). Homer Rodeheaver, longtime music director for mass evangelist Billy Sunday, performed "No, Not One" and "Higher Ground" (*Twenty Years with Billy Sunday* [1936], pp. 130–31) and included the latter in hymnbooks published by his own company. Oatman's work remained widely popular long after he died at his daughter's home in Norman, Oklahoma.

Charles Gabriel, disgruntled by the late nineteenth-century proliferation of ephemeral gospel hymns, discovered in Oatman's texts "newness of thought, a freshness of contemplation and an originality . . . which is seldom found" (*The Singers and Their Songs* [1916], p. 22). Some of them appeared in mid-twentieth-century hymnbooks for use in evangelistic meetings. Oatman's hymns are accessible and, when mated with lilting tunes, conducive to energetic group singing.

• Fourteen hymns by Oatman are named in Jacob Henry Hall, *Biography of Gospel Song and Hymn Writers* (1914). Mel R. Wilhoit, "American Holiness Hymnody: Some Questions: A Methodology," *Wesleyan Theological Journal* 25 (Fall 1990): 39–63, identifies terminology associated with Holiness doctrine, places Oatman's work in the context of the Holiness movement, and cites major studies of gospel hymnody. See also Charles Edwin Jones, *Perfectionist Persuasion: The Holiness Movement and American Methodism, 1867–1936* (1974), and Melvin Easterday Dieter, *The Holiness Revival of the Nineteenth Century* (1980). Charles A. Parker surveys postbellum vacation resorts in "The Camp Meeting on the Frontier and the Methodist Religious Resort in the East—before 1900," *Methodist History* 18, no. 3 (Apr. 1980): 179–92. A broader cultural perspective is provided by Glenn Uminowicz, "Recreation in a Christian America: Ocean Grove and Asbury Park, New Jersey, 1869–1914," in *Hard at Play: Leisure in America, 1840–1940*, ed. Kathryn Grover (1992), pp. 9–38.

MARY DE JONG

OBERHOLSER, Harry Church (25 June 1870–25 Dec. 1963), ornithologist, was born in Brooklyn, New York, the son of Jacob Oberholser, a dry-goods merchant, and Lavera Church. The family name traced its origins to the hamlet of Oberholtz in northern Switzerland.

At the age of seven, Oberholser moved with his family to Newman Springs, Red Bank, New Jersey, where they lived on a farm near the Navesink River. In this rural environment, young Harry soon became interested in bird study, a hobby that grew into his life work. He enrolled at Columbia University in 1888, but in 1891 he was forced to abandon his education plans because of health problems. Meanwhile, his parents had relocated to Wooster, Ohio, to which Oberholser, after withdrawing from Columbia, moved and worked as a clerk in his father's store. Determined to become an ornithologist, Oberholser applied in 1894 for a government job with the Division of Economic Ornithology and Mammalogy in Washington, D.C. In February 1895 he accepted a position as clerk in that division, in the Department of Agriculture. The division became the Bureau of Biological Survey in 1896 and was merged with the U.S. Fish Commission in 1939 to create the Fish and Wildlife Service under the Department of the Interior. Oberholser was subsequently promoted to positions as assistant biologist in 1914, biologist in 1924, and senior biologist in 1928. While working for the government, he was able to complete his education at George Washington University, which granted him a B.A. and an M.S. in 1914 and a Ph.D. in 1916. Oberholser also served as a professor of zoology at American University from 1920 to 1935, and from 1904 to 1910 he spent a portion of each summer teaching zoology at the Biltmore Forest Summer School near Asheville, North Carolina. He married Mary Forrest Smith in 1914; they had no children.

During his initial fifteen years with the Agriculture Department, Oberholser worked under the direction of C. Hart Merriam, one of the leading authorities on the geographic distribution of plants and animals in North America. A proponent of the "life zones" concept, Merriam believed that many plant and animal species occurred in fairly distinct zones or belts that extended across the continent, a result in part of differences in temperature, elevation, and latitude. Oberholser's first assignment was to collate data and prepare range maps showing the geographical distribution and migration patterns of birds, based on published studies, museum skins, and the thousands of specimens being sent to the bureau. In this capacity, Oberholser soon emerged as one of the United States' preeminent experts on bird identification, and he frequently appeared as an expert witness to identify bird remains in trials for violation of federal game laws.

Oberholser gradually acquired an extraordinarily detailed knowledge of the geographic variation in plumage and morphology of North American birds. Under the influence of Robert Ridgway, renowned ornithologist at the U.S. National Museum, Oberholser devoted most of his scientific efforts to taxonomic research, which comprised a major portion of the nearly 900 publications he authored during his career. Known as a "splitter," Oberholser often described new subspecies based on very minute and subtle differences in morphology between various populations. He also supervised the government program to map the distribution of North American birds, initiated earlier by Wells W. Cooke. These data and maps were used to define bird ranges in the American Ornithologists' Union's *Checklist of North American Birds*. In 1920 Oberholser instigated the transfer of the North American bird banding program from the American Bird Banding Association to the Bureau of Biological Survey, and, beginning in 1928, he helped organize the national census studies that formed the basis of the government's management policies for waterfowl.

Although best known for his museum work, Oberholser was active during his early years as a field scientist, particularly in the period between 1895 and 1903. He took pride in having conducted field studies in almost every state in the Union, but he was particularly known for his lifelong interest in the aviafauna of Texas. During the period from 1900 to 1903, he explored and collected widely in Texas, where he was often accompanied by Vernon Bailey and bird artist Louis Agassiz Fuertes. Persistent medical problems forced Oberholser to abandon his field career in 1903, although he was able to make some brief studies in later years. He continued until well after retirement to labor over his manuscript on the birds of Texas, which remained unpublished at the time of his death. The three-million-word text was edited and condensed by Edgar B. Kinkaid, Jr., and subsequently published in 1974 as *The Bird Life of Texas*. Oberholser published his *Bird Life of Louisiana* in 1938 and assisted in the preparation of *South Carolina Bird Life* (1949) by Alexander Sprunt, Jr., and E. B. Chamberlain. After retiring from government service in June 1941, Oberholser became curator of ornithology at the Cleveland Museum of Natural History, where he remained until August 1947.

Oberholser was regarded as among the "most active and perceptive" scientists during the period when purely descriptive ornithology dominated the field. John W. Aldrich, his associate at the Department of the Interior, considered Oberholser's chief contribution to ornithology "his painstaking description of morphological differences between geographical populations" (Aldrich, p. 28). Based largely on his morphological work, Oberholser named eleven new families and subfamilies, ninety-nine genera and subgenera, and some 560 new species and subspecies of birds.

Oberholser was described as a "tall, gangling figure" with a "fantastic memory." Known for his strict self-discipline, attention to detail, and long work hours, Oberholser could be severe and demanding of his subordinates. He set detailed standards for his staff, who were expected to achieve a specified rate of production for specimens and labels every day. An ardent prohibitionist, he was nicknamed "H_2O" by his colleagues. Oberholser was an enthusiastic baseball fan, who faithfully attended the Washington Senators games, except on Sundays, when he taught one of the largest Sunday school classes in the District of Columbia, at the Washington Metropolitan Memorial Methodist-Episcopal Church. He actively followed financial and political affairs and enjoyed dramatics and group singing. A serious bibliophile, Oberholser sold his extensive ornithological library to the University of Illinois following his retirement. In 1939 Allan R. Phillips gave the species of bird known as the Dusky Flycatcher the name *Empidonax oberholseri* in his honor. Oberholser died in Cleveland, Ohio.

• Major archival repositories containing material by or relating to Oberholser include Oberholser's correspondence and the Waldo Lee McAtee Papers at the Manuscript Division of the Library of Congress, the Witmer Stone Papers and the American Ornithologists' Union Papers at the Academy of Natural Sciences in Philadelphia, the American Ornithologists' Union Papers at the Smithsonian Institution Archives, and the Western Reserve Historical Society Collection in Cleveland. Basic references on Oberholser include Barbara Mearns and Richard Mearns, *Audubon to Xantus* (1992), pp. 347–50, and John W. Aldrich, "In Memoriam: Harry Church Oberholser," *The Auk* 85 (1968): 25–29. Both sketches include photograph portraits of Oberholser. An obituary is in the *New York Times*, 26 Dec. 1963.

MARCUS B. SIMPSON, JR.

OBERHOLTZER, Sara Louisa Vickers (20 May 1841–2 Feb. 1930), author and social reformer, was born in Uwchlan Township, Chester County, Pennysylvania, the daughter of Paxson Vickers, a potter and manufacturer of earthenware, and Ann Thomas Lewis. The eldest of nine children, she attended Millersville State Normal School in Lancaster County, Pennsylvania, from 1858 through 1860. Oberholtzer became interested in reform movements early in life because of her Quaker upbringing and her family's active involvement in the abolition of slavery; her family's house was a refuge for escaping slaves.

In 1862 Sara Vickers married John Oberholtzer, a grain merchant; they had two sons. Although busy with domestic life in the early years of her marriage, Sara Oberholtzer wrote poetry, songs, and hymns. As a teenager, she had written to John Greenleaf Whittier and sent him some of her poems; their correspondence evolved into a friendship that lasted until his death. Her poetry appeared in such newspapers and magazines as *Godey's Lady's Book*, *Potter's American Monthly*, and *The Home Companion*. Collections of her verses were published in volumes titled *Violet Lee, and Other Poems* (1873), *Come for Arbutus, and Other Wild Bloom* (1882), *Daisies of Verse* (1886); *Souvenirs of Occasions* (1892), and *Here and There, Songs of the Land and the Sea That Came to Me* (1927). Many of her poems dealt with rural and domestic life, but some were written to commemorate historic events. One of her best known, written in 1879, was the burial ode for a fellow Chester Countian, author and world traveler Bayard Taylor. Her only novel, *Hope's Heart Bells* (1884), described Quaker life in southeastern Pennsylvania. Oberholtzer was also a correspondent for Philadelphia and Chester County newspapers, frequently writing about her extensive travels throughout the United States and Europe. She was the president of the Pennsylvania Woman's Press Association from 1903 to 1905.

Oberholtzer became a member of the Woman's Christian Temperance Union (WCTU) in 1886 upon formation of the local branch and was elected president on the local and county levels. As WCTU state superintendent of the Department of Narcotics, she wrote leaflets about the dangers of narcotics. Oberholtzer also formed the American Anti-Tobacco Society and, once her sons went to school, worked for the passage of legislation in Pennsylvania to prevent the sale of tobacco to boys.

Oberholtzer was an early advocate for the school savings banks movement in the United States. At a convention of the American Economic Association in Philadelphia in 1888, she first heard about the work of John H. Thiry, who had instituted savings bank programs in public schools in Long Island City, New York. The system, which had originated in France and was already established in several European countries, enabled children to make small weekly deposits through their schools. After corresponding with Thiry and visiting the Long Island City schools, Oberholtzer wrote to her local newspapers, schools, and teachers' organizations urging acceptance of the school savings plan. She also visited bank officials, convincing them to receive the children's modest deposits. With the establishment of local school savings bank programs, she expanded her efforts and promoted the concept nationally.

The National and World's WCTU adopted the school savings bank program as a department in 1891, with Oberholtzer as superintendent. It was one of forty departments created by the WCTU as part of its "Do Everything" policy, which encouraged its members to work on a broad range of reform issues. Oberholtzer believed that if children were taught thrift at an early age, they would be less likely to spend their money on alcohol and tobacco. The National WCTU provided Oberholtzer with an annual allocation to publicize the school savings program. She spoke on the topic throughout the United States before local branches of the WCTU, women's clubs, schools, and church groups. Oberholtzer addressed the World's Congress of Representative Women at the Columbian Exposition in May 1893. Her paper, "The Popular Inculcation of Economy," described the history, operation, and benefits of the school savings bank concept. Because the United States was in the midst of experiencing rapid economic growth, she wrote, "we are perhaps in the greatest need. Abundance begets extravagance; extravagance breeds vice and discontent. As an uplifting and leveling measure, as well as an educational safeguard, we need this teaching in the public schools" (p. 120).

Oberholtzer published and edited the quarterly periodical *Thrift Tidings* from 1907 through 1923, and she wrote thirty pamphlets on school savings banks, as well as numerous articles in magazines and newspapers. She regularly corresponded with school officials throughout the United States and in Europe and provided supplies such as roll books, envelopes, pupil cards, and deposit slips to schools involved in the program. Oberholtzer remained World WCTU school savings superintendent after the National WCTU ceased funding the program in 1916, but she did not receive financial assistance; however, she remained committed to the cause of school savings and funded *Thrift Tidings* herself. By 1929 the program had been introduced into nearly 15,600 schools in forty-six states, with more than 4 million depositors. Oberholtzer died at her home in Germantown, Philadelphia, Pennsylvania.

Oberholtzer's advocacy of school savings banks had its roots in the social reform tradition of the nineteenth century, and it extended through the Progressive era. Her involvement with the WCTU, an organization which encouraged women's activity in the public and political spheres, allowed Oberholtzer to promote two of her interests, temperance and thrift. Successful during her lifetime, the school savings program has continued after her death.

• Most of Oberholtzer's papers are in the Historical Society of Pennsylvania in Philadelphia; her correspondence and account books thoroughly document her involvement with the school savings bank movement. The Chester County Historical Society, West Chester, Pa., has several letters written by Oberholtzer, her manuscript copy of *Hope's Heart Bells*, and newspaper clipping files containing articles about her poetry and her work with the WCTU and school savings banks. Oberholtzer's best-known writing on the school savings bank program is "School Savings Banks," *Annals of the American Academy of Political and Social Science* 3 (1893): 14–29. Her address "The Popular Inculcation of Economy" is in May Wright Sewall, ed., *The World's Congress of Representative Women*, vol. 1 (1894), pp. 119–27. Biographical sketches of Oberholtzer appear in Gertrude Bosler Biddle and Sara Dickinson Lowrie, eds., *Notable Women of Pennsylvania* (1942), pp. 210–11, and in Janice H. McElroy, ed., *Our Hidden Heritage: Pennsylvania Women in History* (1983), pp. 195–96. Her obituary is in the *New York Times*, 4 Feb. 1930.

LYNN ANN CATANESE

OBERNDORF, Clarence Paul (16 Feb. 1882–30 May 1954), psychiatrist and psychoanalyst, was born in New York City, the son of Joseph Oberndorf, a prosperous merchant, and Augusta Hammerstein. Oberndorf's father, a scholarly man, had been a schoolteacher in Bavaria, but after immigrating to America at the age of thirteen he had established himself as a merchant in Selma, Alabama. Oberndorf first attended the Dallas Academy in Selma, then continued his education at Public School 69 in New York, having moved with his family to the city at age eleven following the death of his father from cancer. After living for a year in Munich, Germany, the family returned to New York, where the fifteen-year-old Oberndorf entered Mount Morris State High School in the Bronx. In high school Oberndorf began what he called his career as a "frustrated journalist" with regular contributions to the local newspaper about school activities.

After reading Balzac's *Country Doctor*, Oberndorf determined to become a doctor and eventually enrolled at Cornell University, with the support of a scholarship. He was editor of the *Cornell Era* in his junior year. Adolf Meyer's lectures at Cornell inspired Oberndorf's interest in psychiatry during his senior year. Upon graduating in 1906 with a medical degree, he took a two-year internship at Bellevue Hospital, followed by training in European psychiatric hospitals—first at the Charité Hospital in Berlin, then at Emil Kraepelin's clinic in Munich, where he first heard of the work of Sigmund Freud. He returned to America in 1909 and took up his first appointment as psychiatric resident at the Manhattan State Hospital on Ward's Island, where Meyer was director of the Psychopathological Institute and the new "dynamic psychiatry" (psychoanalysis as applied to psychiatric cases) had gained acceptance. within five months Oberndorf had opened a private practice devoted to dynamic psychiatry, and his lifelong career as a psychoanalyst began.

The young psychiatrist shared his enthusiasm for psychoanalysis with his friend and fellow psychiatrist Abraham A. Brill, and in 1911 they founded the New York Psychoanalytic Society, of which Oberndorf was president from 1917 to 1920. Convinced of the value of psychoanalysis for psychiatry in general, Oberndorf persuaded the directors of Mount Sinai Hospital to start an outpatient clinic for psychiatric disorders, where he successfully combined the services of psychiatrists and psychoanalysts in the psychiatric treatment of social problems. Oberndorf's clinic pioneered the practice of community psychiatry and was soon duplicated at other hospitals. During his time at Mount Sinai Hospital, Oberndorf helped establish, in 1919, the

Society for Mental Hygiene among Jews, which founded the Hillside Hospital on Long Island a few years later; Oberndorf remained a consulting psychiatrist and director of the hospital until his death. His interest in journalism met reward when, under the auspices of the International Psychoanalytic Association, he was made associate editor of the *International Journal of Psycho-Analysis*, a position he held from its founding in 1920 until his death. Having been analyzed by Freud during a five-month stay in Vienna in 1921, Oberndorf became responsible for teaching at the New York Psychoanalytic Society, where he organized the first formal psychoanalytic training program in America. To provide financial support for candidates, he and Brill established an educational trust fund that eventually became the American Psychoanalytic Foundation. In 1927, when the International Psychoanalytic Association sought to establish standard training procedures throughout its member societies, Oberndorf was among the American delegation that argued for the exclusion of nonmedical persons from training. As an opponent of so-called lay analysis, Oberndorf was one of those responsible for the strong connection between medicine and psychoanalysis in the United States.

Over the course of his life Oberndorf maintained a lively private practice and held many important administrative positions, including the presidencies of the American Psychoanalytic Association (1924 and 1936), the New York Society for Clinical Psychiatry (1938–1940), the New York Neurological Society (1943), and the American Psychopathological Society (1953–1954). In addition to his associate editorship of the *International Journal of Psychoanalysis*, Oberndorf helped to edit the *Psychoanalytic Review* from 1937, and the *American Journal of Psychiatry*, from 1948. His many publications include more than 120 clinical and historical papers on medicine and psychoanalysis and a detailed *History of Psychoanalysis in America* (1953). Oberndorf's psychoanalytic writings addressed a wide range of topics from depersonalization to the results of psychoanalytic psychotherapy. Although he recognized, through his research on therapeutic outcomes, that results depended more on the individual therapist than on the specific technique in which he or she was schooled, he remained an orthodox Freudian to the end. Oberndorf expressed his literary character through his writings on the psychiatric novels of Oliver Wendell Holmes and his own attempts at similar fictional work, including a collection of psychoanalytic short stories published in 1948. Known affectionately to his friends and colleagues as "Obey," Oberndorf had a reputation as a warm and kindly man. About his lifework in psychiatry he wrote, "The healing side of medicine, which is both a science and an art, has always absorbed my attention. It seems to me that above all the minister, the teacher and the physician are persons whose aim should be to alleviate suffering expeditiously and gently" (quoted in obituary, *Psychoanalytic Quarterly*, p. 428).

Oberndorf's contribution to psychoanalysis, though more organizational than scientific, cannot be underestimated. As one of the pioneers of psychoanalysis in America, as teacher, administrator, and editor, he promoted the cause of psychoanalysis as a special branch of psychiatry for more than fifty years. He never married and had no children. He died in New York City.

• Many of Oberndorf's papers concerning the early organization of psychoanalysis are in the archives at the Abraham A. Brill Library of the New York Psychoanalytic Institute. Among Oberndorf's own publications, the most significant is *A History of Psychoanalysis in America* (1953); a shorter essay, "Psychiatry at Ward's Island 40 Years Ago," *Psychiatric Quarterly* 24 (1950): 1–10, offers a detailed picture of a psychiatric hospital around 1910. His monograph *The Psychiatric Novels of Oliver Wendell Holmes* (1943) is complemented by his short stories collected in *Which Way Out* (1948). His autobiographical notes remain unpublished but are mentioned in a detailed obituary in *Psychoanalytic Quarterly* 23 (1954): 424–33, which includes a bibliography. Another obituary, in *International Journal of Psycho-Analysis* 36 (1955): 210–13, lists his many appointments.

GAIL DONALDSON

OBERON, Merle (19 Feb. 1911–23 Nov. 1979), actress, was born Estelle Merle O'Brien Thompson in Bombay, India, the daughter of Arthur Terrence O'Brien Thompson, a railway engineer, and Charlotte Constance Selby, a nurse's assistant. The truth about Oberon's origins and early life was not revealed until after her death. Throughout her lifetime, she steadfastly claimed to have been born into an aristocratic family in Tasmania. Ashamed of her dark-skinned mother and her poverty-stricken beginnings, she invented her own history when entering show business. She feared that the social prejudices of the day would have prevented her from becoming a star if it was known that she was half-caste. Michael Korda said in 1985, "Although I understand and sympathize with Merle, the childhood she really had must have been infinitely more interesting than the one she invented" (*Los Angeles Times*, 31 May 1985). Korda also stated that after years of deluding the public, she herself came to believe her own legend.

The young girl known as Queenie Thompson was raised in Bombay and Calcutta. She moved to England at seventeen, and worked as a dance-hall girl before landing work as an extra in a number of British films. Her exotic beauty brought her to the attention of Hungarian-born producer Alexander Korda, who was starting his own film studio, London Film Productions. Korda signed the unknown actress to a five-year contract and cast her in her first notable film role, as Anne Boleyn in *The Private Life of Henry VIII* (1933). Anne Boleyn, beheaded early in the film, was a small part, but Oberon made an indelible impression on moviegoers.

Still in England, Oberon starred in *Thunder in the East* (1934), *The Private Life of Don Juan* (1934), and *The Scarlet Pimpernel* (1935). In 1935 Korda sold half of Oberon's contract to producer Samuel Goldwyn, and her Hollywood career was launched. She debuted on American movie screens in *Folies Bergère* (1935). Before long, she emerged as one of the top-ranking actresses in the United States. She earned an Academy Award nomination for her role in *The Dark Angel* (1935) and subsequently starred in *Beloved Enemy* (1936), *These Three* (1936), and *The Cowboy and the Lady* (1938).

Oberon scored her greatest screen success with her portrayal of Cathy in the first film adaptation of Emily Brontë's classic novel, *Wuthering Heights* (1939). The film won widespread critical acclaim and made the prestigious "Ten Best" list in the *New York Times*. The *Times* reviewer said of Oberon: "She has perfectly caught the restless, changeling spirit of the Brontë heroine who knew she was not meant for heaven." Despite such glowing reviews, Oberon was not Oscar-nominated for her performance.

In a 1973 interview Oberon expressed her gratitude for her part in *Wuthering Heights*, the film for which she is best remembered, as she had come to appreciate the distinction that set her apart from a multitude of other performers. "[There have been] so many," she said, "the thousands who've been extras, the thousands who've played bit parts, the thousands who've maybe been leading ladies, and the thousands who've been 'stars', and [who] have never had a part to remember."

The caliber of Oberon's screen roles gradually declined in the 1940s. She appeared in two successive comedies that failed to click with audiences, *That Uncertain Feeling* (1941) and *Affectionately Yours* (1941), and then tackled the title role in Korda's romantic tale, *Lydia* (1941). She said at the time, "I never really acted before now. I just said those words and let it go at that. Korda makes me give out." Critics rated her performance a disappointment, however, and *Lydia* was a box office failure. She more successfully played George Sand in *A Song to Remember* (1945), a fictionalized account of the novelist's affair with Frederic Chopin.

Throughout her life, Oberon's personal affairs attracted more publicity than her professional endeavors. Gossip columnists delighted in reporting the romantic escapades of the glamorous imported star. After a broken engagement to United Artists head Joseph Schenck and several much publicized affairs (her paramours included actors Brian Aherne, David Niven, and Leslie Howard), Oberon married Alexander Korda in 1939. Korda was knighted in 1942, elevating Oberon to the status of Lady Korda.

Reviewers increasingly commented more on Oberon's beauty and physical attributes than on her acting ability in their critiques of her films. Commenting on her performance in the morose tearjerker *This Love of Ours* (1945), the *New York Herald Tribune* stated, "Though she is always poised and attractive, Miss Oberon's performance is accented on posing with her face, a white mask to cover her emotion, with very few changes of pace." By the mid-1950s, she had stepped

down to supporting roles, most notably in *Desiree* (1954) and *Deep in My Heart* (1954).

After her divorce from Korda in 1945, Oberon married cinematographer Lucien Ballard. They divorced in 1949. She married wealthy Italian industrialist Bruno Pagliai in 1957. They adopted two children in 1959. Until her divorce from Pagliai in 1973, Oberon resided with her family in Mexico, returning to Hollywood infrequently for television or film appearances. She became known less as an actress than as an international hostess, whose name was rarely out of the society columns.

Concurrent with her divorce from Pagliai was Oberon's final foray into films. She produced and starred in *Interval* (1973), a love story in which she was paired with a much younger man, played by Robert Wolders. The film was a commercial and critical failure, with the reviewer for the *New York Times* opining, "on the scale of awfulness, it is almost sublime" (16 June 1973). Oberon married Wolders, who was twenty-five years her junior, in 1975.

Six years after her death in Los Angeles, Oberon's life was the basis of a novel, *Queenie* (1985), by Michael Korda, once Oberon's nephew by her marriage to Alexander Korda. The novel was subsequently made into a television miniseries in 1987. The story of Oberon's life and the web of lies she strove so hard to protect have proven to be more memorable than any of her screen roles. Korda said of his former aunt, "Her greatest achievement was not in her roles, but herself, as Merle Oberon. She was her own work of art."

• The clipping file at the Academy of Motion Picture Arts and Sciences, Los Angeles, includes material on Oberon's career. Charles Higham and Roy Moseley, *Princess Merle: The Romantic Life of Merle Oberon* (1983), a full-length biography, contained the first published account of Oberon's true origins. James Robert Parish and Don E. Stanke, *The Glamour Girls* (1975), includes a lengthy chapter on Oberon, including a filmography and several photographs. Michael Korda wrote about his famous family in *Charmed Lives: A Family Romance* (1979). Oberon's remembrances of Laurence Olivier appear in Logan Gourlay's *Olivier* (1974). See also a lengthy interview in 1973 with Oberon by Al Kilgore and Roi Frumkes in *Films in Review*, Feb. 1982, pp. 76–95; Scott Berg, "Merle Oberon," *Architectural Digest*, Apr. 1990, pp. 208–11; "Green-eyed Legend Returns to Hollywood," *New York Times*, 19 Nov. 1972; "Merle Oberon: Her Life, Her Loves," *Los Angeles Times*, 10 June 1973; Robert Osborne, "Merle Oberon: A Touch of Class," *Los Angeles Times*, 9 Dec. 1979; Philip K. Scheuer, "Once a Lady," *Family Circle*, 7 Dec. 1945, pp. 10–11, 38; and Karen Winner, "Merle Oberon: Not at All What You'd Expect of Me," *Women's Wear Daily*, 8 Nov. 1972. Obituaries are in the *Los Angeles Times* and the *New York Times*, 24 Nov. 1979; *Newsweek* and *Time*, 3 Dec. 1979; and *Variety*, 28 Nov. 1979.

BRENDA SCOTT ROYCE

OBOLER, Arch (6 Dec. 1909–19 Mar. 1987), radio writer and dramatist, was born in Chicago, Illinois, the son of Leo Oboler and Clare Obeler (her maiden name was spelled slightly differently from her married name). As a boy he had a strong desire to be a naturalist and kept a sizable zoo of animals in his home, including frogs, turtles, salamanders, snakes, and scorpions. Drawing on his experiences with some of these animals, he sold his first story at age ten. He continued to write for the rest of his life.

He entered the University of Chicago with the intention of majoring in electrical engineering, but the writing habit soon swamped him, and he was finding little time for engineering. His attention was drawn to the possibilities of radio as a dramatic medium, and he sent a play called "Futuristic" to NBC. The network was sufficiently pleased with it to use it during the opening ceremonies for Radio City in 1932.

Around this time Oboler began working for the NBC affiliate in Chicago, where he wrote all kinds of material as needed. During his career, which spanned all of radio's golden age and beyond, he experimented with every kind of radio drama—fantasy, comedy, realism, satire, tragedy—although he seemed to have a special genius for the weird and macabre. He married a University of Chicago student, Eleanor Helfand (date unknown), and for their honeymoon they toured all the alleged haunted houses of New England. The couple had four sons.

By the mid-1930s Oboler was a major writer, having written radio sketches for, among others, Don Ameche, Joan Crawford, Edward G. Robinson, Rudy Vallee, and Walter Hampden. However, fame came to him as the principal writer of a program called "Lights Out," which had originated in 1936 in Chicago but shortly went out over the network. "Lights Out" was the creation not of Oboler but of another Chicago writer, Wyllis Cooper, but when Cooper went to the West Coast, Oboler, then writing a show called "Grand Hotel," was selected to take over in 1937.

"Lights Out" was originally a fifteen-minute show heard after midnight; it was intended to be eerie and spooky, a horror show. It began with the tolling of churchbells, a gong, and a chilling intonation by the announcer: "Lights out, Ev-rybody." There were sounds of howling winds and then the words, "This is the witching hour. . . . It is the hour when dogs howl and evil is let loose on the sleeping world. . . . Want to hear about it? . . . Then turn out your lights."

A good part of the effectiveness of "Lights Out" can be attributed to the use of the new techniques of radio sound effects, which were being raised to a high art. Human bones were broken by smashing spareribs with a pipe wrench. When people were electrocuted soundmen held frying bacon up to the microphone. Even more important, however, the stories made full use of the nonvisual but image-evoking qualities of radio. So overpowering were some of the scripts that a number of them are remembered vividly by people today. One episode, "Chicken Heart," was a story about a tiny organ that grew and grew until it consumed the whole world. The beating of the heart was rendered with a progressively louder thump-THUMP, thump-THUMP.

"Lights Out" attracted a huge listening audience and became a half-hour show during prime time, although complaints from listeners that children might listen in chased the program back to the after-midnight time slot. It continued to have a huge audience, however, and attracted major stars. Boris Karloff, then at the height of his career as a player of movie monsters, came to Chicago from southern California to appear in one of the most memorable episodes, "Cat Wife," about a man whose wife turns into a human-sized cat.

Oboler wrote "Lights Out" for two years and then, tired of trying to surpass his spooky effects week after week and also believing that it was limiting his range, withdrew from the program. "Lights Out" continued for a year after Oboler left, then died, although Oboler revived the show briefly during World War II. By this time the program had a number of successful competitors such as "Inner Sanctum Mysteries," "Suspense," and "The Hermit's Cave."

When Oboler moved to New York in 1938, radio drama was starting to be taken seriously. Orson Wells's famous broadcast of "The War of the Worlds" proved just how great an impact radio could have. Oboler was now at the high point of his creative energies and turned out all manner of plays over the next few years. (By 1940 he had written more than 400 radio plays). One of his plays, "Alter Ego," starring Bette Davis, won an award for the best radio play of 1938.

Oboler now had his own series, "Arch Oboler's Plays," in which he experimented with fantasy, serious drama, and other forms as well as some of his old "Lights Out" suspense material. As a writer of the shows, which drew all kinds of major stars from radio and the movies, Oboler introduced many new techniques to radio drama: monologues, a stream-of-consciousness technique, audio collage, the blending of voices, the filtering of certain sounds. By 1939 Oboler had become a nationally known individual in a medium where writers were invariably anonymous.

A short man, Rumpelstiltskin-like in appearance, Oboler usually directed his own plays standing on a table in the studio, not in the control booth like most directors. His overweening presence and high intensity managed to bring out electrifying performances from the actors.

"Arch Oboler's Plays" went off the air in 1940, and during the war years Oboler donated much of his time to producing propaganda plays for the government. In these years Oboler was the writer (and occasionally director) of programs such as "Everyman's Theatre," "Plays for Americans," "This Is Our America," "Free World Theatre," "Treasury Star Parade," and numerous others. In 1945 he won a Peabody award for radio drama.

His imaginative vision being particularly suited to radio, Arch Oboler did not make the transition to television with many other radio artists, but he continued to write for other media. In the waning years of radio he published some of his best radio plays in book-length anthologies and began a somewhat unsatisfactory career as a movie writer and director.

Oboler's first film was actually made in 1940 but not released until after the war; indeed it almost failed to be released entirely. This film was *Strange Holiday*, and it concerns a futuristic vision of a Nazi takeover of the United States. Also at war's end Oboler wrote and directed *Bewitched* (1945), adapted from one of his radio plays. It deals with a girl with two personalities who has her murderous side exorcised by a spiritualist. Film critic James Agee wrote of the film, "Oboler manages the first persuasive imitation of stream of consciousness I know of in a movie. Much more often he bores to desperation with the vulgarity and mere violence of his effects" (quoted in *Halliwell's Film Guide* [1994], p. 112).

Oboler received a certain amount of notoriety when he wrote and directed the first 3-D movie, *Bwana Devil* (1952). It was not critically well received, however. Critic Bosley Crowther found it hackneyed and old-fashioned. Oboler tended to garner a reputation for doing trite and gimmicky films. Other Oboler movies were *The Arnelo Affair* (1946), *Five* (1951), *The Twanky* (1953), *One Plus One* (1961), *The Kinsey Report* (1961), and *The Bubble* (1967).

Beginning in the 1960s radio stations around the country began "rediscovering" oldtime radio. Accordingly, many of Oboler's plays, including episodes of "Lights Out," have continued to be enjoyed. In some quarters Oboler remains an important cult figure of the popular culture, and he will be remembered as long as the art form known as radio drama comes to mind. He died in Westlake Village, California.

• Oboler wrote several screenplays and a novel, *House on Fire* (1969). Oboler's plays have been well anthologized since the 1940s. See, for example, *Fourteen Radio Plays* (1940), *Ivory Tower and Other Radio Plays* (1940), *Free World Theatre*, with an introduction by Thomas Mann (1944), and *Oboler Omnibus* (1945). A number of references are available. See the profile in "Genius's Hour," *Time*, 4 Sept. 1939, p. 30. Also see entries for Oboler in *Current Biography—1940*, *American Authors and Books*, and *Twentieth Century Authors*, all containing detailed reference material. See also Margaret Cuthbert, *Adventures in Radio* (1945), which contains radio plays by Oboler, Edna St. Vincent Millay, and Archibald MacLeish.

GEORGE H. DOUGLAS

OBOOKIAH, Henry. *See* Opukahaia.

O'BRIAN, John Lord (14 Oct. 1874–10 Apr. 1973), lawyer and politician, was born in Buffalo, New York, the son of John O'Brian, a real estate promoter and minor politician, and Elizabeth Lord. After attending public schools in Buffalo, he entered Harvard College, from which he received an A.B. degree in 1896. He then enrolled at University of Buffalo Law School. After receiving an LL.B. degree in 1898, O'Brian entered law practice in Buffalo. In 1902 he married Alma E. White; they had five children, all daughters.

While starting a practice and a family, O'Brian also taught insurance law as an unpaid instructor at Buffalo for fourteen years and gave lectures on medical jurisprudence at the university's medical school. In 1903 he became a trustee of the law school, remaining as a member of the university council until 1929 and chairing the committee that selected a new university chancellor in 1920. Elected a regent of the University of the State of New York in 1931, he served in that capacity until 1948. In 1974 the institution, by then known as the State University of New York at Buffalo, honored O'Brian by naming its new law school building after him.

O'Brian maintained a strong commitment to Harvard as well as Buffalo, serving as an overseer of his undergraduate alma mater from 1936 until 1945. In 1946 he became the lay chairman of a committee of distinguished theologians, appointed to determine whether Harvard's long-neglected divinity school should be closed. After the committee recommended revitalizing it instead, O'Brian headed up a successful effort to raise $5 million for that purpose. Harvard recognized his efforts by establishing the John Lord O'Brian Chair of Divinity. It was a fitting way to honor an active Christian, who had become a lay reader in the Episcopal church while still in law school and for many years served as chancellor of the Episcopal Diocese of Western New York.

In 1906, at the age of thirty-two, O'Brian entered public service, running successfully for a seat in the New York Assembly. A member of the ways and means and cities committees, he was a strong supporter of Progressive Republican governor Charles Evans Hughes. Although reelected in 1908, O'Brian resigned from the legislature in February 1909 to accept an appointment from President Theodore Roosevelt as U.S. attorney for the Western District of New York. He ventured back into electoral politics in 1913, losing a close race for mayor of Buffalo.

In 1914 Republican O'Brian, who had continued to serve as U.S. attorney into the administration of Democratic president Woodrow Wilson, returned to private practice in Buffalo. He soon became involved with the so-called Committee of Thirty-Nine, a group promoting wholesale revision of New York's constitution. In 1915 O'Brian won election as a delegate-at-large to a state constitutional convention. He chaired its rules committee and committee on county government. The voters rejected the constitution the convention produced, but while drafting it, O'Brian developed friendships with such prominent political figures as Elihu Root, Henry Stimson, Alfred E. Smith, Robert Wagner, and George W. Wickersham.

Two years later, Wilson's attorney general, Thomas Gregory, asked O'Brian to prosecute the Franz von Rintelen case. It involved a conspiracy to use German funds to persuade American labor leaders to call strikes against manufacturers of war material. O'Brian obtained seven convictions.

In the fall of 1917, after spending several months as chairman of the Draft Board of Appeals for western New York, O'Brian received an invitation from Gregory to move to Washington to head the Justice Department's new War Emergency Division. Its responsibilities included registering and interning enemy aliens and prosecuting espionage, sabotage, and other war-related cases. Despite the frenzied temper of the times, O'Brian pursued a moderate course, releasing well over half of the aliens arrested under presidential warrants. He issued instructions that the Espionage Act of 1917, which contained provisions directed at expression, was not to be made a "medium whereby efforts are made to suppress honest, legitimate criticism of the administration or discussion of governmental policies." Nevertheless, U.S. attorneys used that law and the Sedition Act of 1918 to prosecute much legitimate dissent. Ironically, when the Espionage Act was attacked as violative of the First Amendment, O'Brian successfully defended it before the U.S. Supreme Court in *Schenck v. United States* (1919). He inadvertently dealt another blow to civil liberties when he recruited into his division J. Edgar Hoover, who went on to become the antilibertarian director of the Federal Bureau of Investigation.

After World War I ended, O'Brian personally reviewed the files of every person who had been sentenced under wartime statutes and made recommendations concerning how much time each should serve. All of his recommendations were adopted without change by Gregory and Wilson. O'Brian then returned to private practice in Buffalo.

In 1926 he became vice chair of the Committee on the Reorganization of the New York State Government, which effected far-reaching reforms in the governmental structure of the Empire State. By 1929 he was back in Washington, having been appointed to head the Justice Department's Antitrust Division by President Herbert Hoover. As an assistant attorney general, O'Brian argued approximately twenty antitrust cases before the Supreme Court. In 1931 he was offered a federal district judgeship in Buffalo, but for unknown reasons he turned it down, just as he had declined earlier nominations to the New York Supreme Court, the New York Court of Appeals, the Court of Claims, and the Supreme Court of the District of Columbia.

Despite his prominent role in the Hoover administration and the fact that he had been a delegate to two Republican national conventions, when the New Deal's Tennessee Valley Authority found itself under legal attack, it turned to O'Brian for help. In *Ashwander v. Tennessee Valley Authority* (1935), he persuaded the Supreme Court that TVA had a constitutional right to sell the electric power generated by its dams. *Ashwander* was one of the New Deal's few successes in the Supreme Court prior to 1937. A grateful TVA board retained O'Brian to defend a suit brought by a number of utility companies, and in 1939 he won another victory before the Court.

While he was working on that case, the New York Republican party nominated him to run against incumbent Democratic senator Robert Wagner. Although unenthusiastic about the idea, O'Brian campaigned hard. He carried fifty-seven of sixty-one counties, but lost because of Wagner's strength in the New York City area.

O'Brian never again sought elective office. In late 1940, however, Roosevelt asked him to serve as general counsel of the organization that eventually became known as the War Production Board. Although leaving his lucrative private practice involved a huge reduction in income, O'Brian accepted the position. He assembled an outstanding legal staff at WPB and performed so well as general counsel that President Harry Truman awarded him the Presidential Medal of Merit for his service in that capacity.

After leaving the War Production Board in 1944, O'Brian became associated with the prestigious Washington law firm of Covington & Burling. He practiced there until his death twenty-nine years later. At Covington & Burling, O'Brian devoted much of his attention to international matters, advising clients such as the governments of Greece, Pakistan, and Denmark. In *Cors v. United States* (1949), he won another notable victory before the Supreme Court, persuading the justices that the government was wrong in contending that it did not have to pay full value for property it had seized for war purposes.

While at Covington & Burling, O'Brian continued to make occasional forays into public service. In 1948 he was appointed by Truman to chair a panel to deal with a threatened strike at the Oak Ridge, Tennessee, atomic energy plant, and during the Korean War he served on the National Advisory Board on Mobilization Policy. O'Brian also took a very public stand against the excesses of McCarthyism, arguing in a 1948 address to the New York State Bar Association, a speech at Columbia University, and the 1955 Godkin Lectures at Harvard that governmental measures designed to prevent the spread of subversive ideas were causing a dangerous erosion of human rights. The Godkin lectures, published as *National Security and Individual Freedom* (1955), received awards from both the Sidney Hillman Foundation and the National Conference of Christians and Jews.

By the time he died in Washington at the age of ninety-eight, O'Brian had distinguished himself not only as a politician and a public servant but also as a civil libertarian. He was best known, however, as an advocate, who had argued approximately fifty cases before the Supreme Court. "Few men in history have had a longer and more active practice before this court," Chief Justice Earl Warren observed of O'Brian in 1962. Warren's successor, Warren Burger, eulogized O'Brian as "the dean of the Supreme Court bar." As Burger noted, he "had a remarkable career in public service and in his profession."

• The Charles B. Sears Law Library in John Lord O'Brian Hall at the State University of New York at Buffalo houses O'Brian's personal and professional papers. This collection includes transcripts of a 1952 interview done by the Columbia University Oral History Research Office and a 1972 interview conducted by the Memphis State University Oral History Research Project on the Tennessee Valley Authority. The best source of information on him is the commemorative issue that the *Buffalo Law Review* published in 1974; "Remarks of Charles A. Horsky at the Dedication of John Lord O'Brian Hall," which appears at pp. 1–13, contains far more biographical data than any other article in that issue. The commemorative issue also includes selections from several of O'Brian's published works and a complete list of his speeches and publications. His most important published works are *National Security and Individual Freedom* (1955); "New Encroachments on Individual Freedom," *Harvard Law Review* 66 (1952): 1–27; "The Value of Constitutionalism Today," in *Government under Law*, ed. Arthur E. Sutherland (1957); and "Loyalty Tests and Guilt by Association," *Harvard Law Review* 61 (1948): 592–611. The basic facts of O'Brian's career are set forth in J. D. Hyman, "Dedication: John Lord O'Brian," *Buffalo Law Review* 20 (1971): 1–5, and in obituaries in the *New York Times* and the *Washington Post*, 11 Apr. 1973. Unfortunately, all of these articles, and the Horsky one as well, omit significant details concerning his personal life.

MICHAL R. BELKNAP

O'BRIEN, Davey (22 June 1917–18 Nov. 1977), college and professional football player, was born Robert David O'Brien in Dallas, Texas. (His parents' names are unknown.) In later years, O'Brien recalled having been a "problem child" with a "bad temper," but he credited the owner of a boys' camp where he spent his summers with getting him "on the right track." He insisted that a medal he earned there as best all-around camper meant more to him than any of his later awards.

O'Brien achieved early success on the gridiron as a pass-throwing all-state tailback for Woodrow Wilson High School. He entered Texas Christian University in 1935. One attraction was that, unlike most college football teams of the day, TCU under Coach Leo "Dutch" Meyer featured a wide-open passing attack. But in 1936, O'Brien's first season of varsity eligibility, he played only occasionally as a substitute for All-American "Slingin' Sammy" Baugh.

In his junior year in 1937, he succeeded Baugh as TCU tailback and led the nation in passing, completing 94 of 234 tosses for 969 yards while being named all-Southwest Conference. Although O'Brien was 5'7" and weighed barely 150 pounds, he ran from scrimmage 166 times and returned 66 kicks, exhibiting surprising durability.

In 1938 O'Brien was the most celebrated college football player in the country. He sparked the Horned Frogs to an undefeated season (11 wins), including a 15–7 Sugar Bowl victory over sixth-ranked Carnegie Tech. That year the Associated Press named TCU the national champions. In 1938 O'Brien again led the nation in passing, completing 93 of 167 attempts for 1,457 yards and 19 touchdowns. Only four of his passes were intercepted. In the Sugar Bowl he kicked a field goal and threw a 44-yard touchdown pass while completing 17 of 27 attempts for 225 yards. Coach Meyer called him "the greatest field general I ever saw." He was named to all major All-American teams and won virtually every individual award, including the Heisman Trophy, Walter Camp Memorial Trophy, Maxwell Memorial Trophy, and the Washington, D.C., Touchdown Club Award.

The Philadelphia Eagles of the National Football League made O'Brien the first choice of the 1939 college draft. None of the first three Heisman Trophy winners had chosen to play pro football, but O'Brien agreed to a contract for $12,000 plus a percentage of the gate. It is likely that only Baugh, who earned about $15,000 for the Washington Redskins, was paid more among NFL players. Because of O'Brien's slight physique, the Eagles insured him with Lloyds of London; Philadelphia was to receive $1,500 for each game he missed because of injury, but the team had no occasion to collect, as its star was never sidelined.

As a rookie in 1939, O'Brien was named quarterback on the official all-NFL team after completing 99 of 201 passes for a league-leading 1,324 yards. Despite his efforts, however, the weak Eagles were able to win only one of 11 games.

His passes constituted the bulk of Philadelphia's offense again in 1940 as the team rushed for a league low 298 yards in 11 games. Once more, the Eagles won only a single game, although O'Brien led the league in pass attempts with 277 and in completions with 124. His throws gained 1,290 yards, second only to Baugh's 1,367. At season's end, O'Brien was named to the all-NFL second team.

In his final game, O'Brien had perhaps the greatest day of any passer up to that time. On 7 December 1940, while the Eagles lost to Baugh and the Redskins, 13–7, O'Brien threw 60 passes, completed 33, and gained 315 yards, all league records. The completion record stood until 1948, and the attempt record was not surpassed until 1964.

The day after his last NFL game, O'Brien joined the Federal Bureau of Investigation at a salary of $3,200 per year. In 1951, after ten years with the FBI, he entered the Texas oil industry, eventually organizing his own drilling company. O'Brien married Florence Buster in 1940; they had two children.

O'Brien was named to the National Football Foundation College Football Hall of Fame in 1955 and the Texas Sports Hall of Fame in 1956. In 1960 he was one of the 25 players named to *Sports Illustrated*'s Silver Anniversary All-America team.

Starting in 1977, the year he died, the Davey O'Brien Educational and Charitable Trust of Fort Worth has presented a major college football award annually. During its first four years the honor was given to the outstanding college player in the Southwest and was called the O'Brien Memorial Trophy. In 1981 it was renamed the O'Brien Quarterback Trophy and awarded annually to the nation's top collegiate quarterback. O'Brien died in Fort Worth, Texas.

• A biographical article focusing on O'Brien's final game, "Wee Davey's Big Game," by Bob Carroll, is in *Sports Heritage*, July–Aug. 1987, pp. 48–51. Biographical sketches appear in John T. Brady, *The Heisman: Symbol of Excellence* (1984), pp. 44–47, and Dave Newhouse, *Heisman: After the Glory* (1985), pp. 289–90. Additional material may be found in Allison Danzig, *The History of American Football: Its Great Teams, Players, and Coaches* (1956); Bill Libby, *Champions of College Football* (1975); and Howard Roberts, *The Story of Pro Football* (1953). An obituary is in the *Washington Post*, 19 Nov. 1977.

BOB CARROLL

O'BRIEN, Edmond (10 Sept. 1915–9 May 1985), stage and film actor, was born in Brooklyn, New York. Nothing is known of his parents. One of his neighbors was magician Harry Houdini, who inspired in young Edmond a love for performing. O'Brien is reported to have said that Houdini "taught me a few of the easier tricks in his bag of magic" (*New York Times*, 10 May 1985). Nicknaming himself, around the neighborhood O'Brien became known as "Neirbo the Great." O'Brien attended Fordham University for a year in 1933 and then withdrew to accept a scholarship to attend the Neighborhood Playhouse School of Theatre. He supported himself by working as a bank teller and obtained stage roles in several major productions in and around New York. In 1937 he was cast in the great actor John Gielgud's American tour of *Hamlet*. He then received a feature role in the Broadway premiere of *Daughters of Atreus* at the Forty-fourth Street Theatre. It opened on 14 October 1936 but closed after only thirteen performances.

O'Brien's stage career continued with a role in the revival of *Parnell* in 1936 at the Forty-eighth Street Theatre. In 1937 he joined the Mercury Theatre, co-organized by Orson Welles, and appeared, in a small role, in Welles's much-discussed modern-dress production of *Julius Caesar*. O'Brien also performed in Welles's famous radio production of H. G. Wells's *War of the Worlds* (1938), which so vividly depicted an imaginary invasion by Martians that it caused panic in the northeastern United States. In 1939 he was a replacement actor in *Family Portrait*. That same year O'Brien went to Hollywood to play the poet Pierre Gringoire in the Twentieth Century–Fox production of *The Hunchback of Notre Dame*, in which Charles Laughton had the leading role. O'Brien then returned to New York to appear on stage in 1940 with Laurence Olivier and Vivien Leigh in a production of *Romeo and Juliet*.

O'Brien married actress Nancy Kelley in 1941; childless, they separated after only a year. He married Olga San Juan in 1948 (later divorced), and they had three children.

When World War II began O'Brien joined the U.S. Army and appeared in *Winged Victory*, Moss Hart's production about the air force. When Hart went to Hollywood to produce the movie version, O'Brien went with him to recreate his role. After the war O'Brien continued his film career. Over the next ten years he became a major film star, especially in film noir pictures. Of note are his roles in films such as *The Killers* (1947), George Cukor's *Double Life* (1949), Raoul Walsh's gangster movie *White Heat* (1949), which stars Jimmy Cagney, and *D.O.A.* (1950).

In 1952 O'Brien was given the role of Casca in Joseph L. Mankiewicz's star-studded production of *Julius Caesar* (1953). He followed that performance with a return to New York to appear in John Van Druten's *I've Got Sixpence* (1952). Brooks Atkinson, the theater critic for the *New York Times*, stated that O'Brien gave a "harsh and honest performance" (3 Dec. 1952).

O'Brien returned to Hollywood in 1954 to appear with Ava Gardner and Humphrey Bogart in Mankiewicz's production of *The Barefoot Contessa*. He received his only career Oscar as best supporting actor for that film. Later that year he appeared as Winston Smith in the film adaptation of George Orwell's *1984*. Atkinson, highly disappointed with the movie, wrote, "Mr. O'Brien wins genuine sympathy" (quoted in the *New York Times*, 10 May 1985).

After his success with Bogart and Gardner O'Brien teamed up with Howard Koch to direct the film *Shield for Murder* (1954). He also appeared in the film, playing the lead role of Barney Nolan. Of the film, an unidentified critic for the *New York Times* stated, "The story is intelligent and unstrained; qualities too rarely seen in films of this genre [gangster movies]" (28 Aug. 1954). In 1961 O'Brien returned to directing with the film *Man-Trap*, which Howard Thompson called "a second-rate melodrama" (*New York Times*, 30 Nov. 1961).

In 1962 O'Brien's career took a definitive turn to character roles. He played the part of Dutton Peabody, the rough-edged frontier editor in John Ford's classic film *The Man Who Shot Liberty Valance* (1962). He then had the wonderful opportunity to play the part of Raymond Clark, the old alcoholic senator, in *Seven Days in May* (1964). As a result of his excellent performance in that film he was nominated for a second Oscar for best supporting actor.

In the early sixties O'Brien tried acting for television but had very little success, so he returned to film. By 1969 he was playing rough, crusty old men, such as Sykes in Sam Peckinpah's movie *The Wild Bunch*. About this film, Vincent Canby of the *New York Times* wrote, "Mr. O'Brien is a special shock, looking like an evil Gabby Hayes, a foul-mouthed, cackling old man who is the only member of the Wild Bunch to survive" (26 June 1969). O'Brien's career virtually ended in 1974 with the film *99 and 44/100% Dead*, in which he had an almost insignificant role. He was reported as having failing vision and health. He later moved to a nursing facility in Inglewood, California, where he died.

O'Brien had the opportunity to work with many of the greatest actors in Hollywood history, such as Gardner, Bogart, Burt Lancaster, Raquel Welch, Donald Pleasence, Laughton, Maureen O'Hara, William Conrad, John Wayne, James Stewart, Cagney, William Holden, Robert Warren, and Andy Devine. O'Brien's filmography includes sixty-nine major motion pictures, eleven made-for-television movies, two television series, and six major theatrical stage plays. He is recognized as one of America's great character actors.

• Information on O'Brien is sketchy. Much is in reviews and articles published in the *New York Times*; see, for example, pieces by Brooks Atkinson (3 Dec. and 7 Dec. 1952), Bosley Crowther (20 July 1950, 2 Oct. 1950, 7 Oct. 1962, and 20 Feb. 1964), A. H. Weiler (13 Oct. 1950 and 24 May 1962), and Vincent Canby (26 June 1969). Brief biographical entries are in David Quinlan, *Quinlan's Illustrated Registry of Film Stars* (1991), and Ephraim Katz, *The Film Encyclopedia*, 2d ed. (1994). Obituaries appear in the *New York Times* and *New York Post*, both 10 May 1985.

HERBERT SENNETT

O'BRIEN, Edward Joseph Harrington (10 Dec. 1890–24 Feb. 1941), poet, editor, and anthologist, was born in Boston, Massachusetts, the son of Michael Francis O'Brien, a bookkeeper, and Minna Gertrude Hallahan. When he was seven years old, his father left the family home and was never heard of again. O'Brien and his younger brother were brought up in devout Catholic tradition by their mother and maternal grandmother.

O'Brien was educated at the Boston Latin School and Boston College. A deeply religious youth, he briefly contemplated, at the age of fifteen, entering the Jesuit order but decided that its restrictive regime would conflict with his desire to praise God through poetry and his determination to devote himself to an aesthetic, rather than an ascetic, way of life. He entered Harvard University in the autumn of 1908 but left of his own accord six months later, loftily declaring that he would not trust his education to the sterile teachings of professors but would educate himself "as long as life lasted."

Through his friendship with the poet William Stanley Braithwaite, he gained acceptance in the Boston literary world. In the autumn of 1908, about the time he entered Harvard, his essay on Francis Thompson was published in *Poet-Lore*, one of Boston's leading literary journals. It was a remarkable achievement for a youth of seventeen. From then on, there was no looking back. He became a book reviewer for the *Boston Transcript* and edited anthologies of the works of Francis Thompson and John Davidson. His articles and poetry appeared in the *Four Seas*, *Catholic World*, *Smart Set*, the *Little Review*, *Contemporary Verse*, *Others*, and the *Bookman*. In 1912 O'Brien announced the proposed publication in Boston of *Poetry*, a magazine that would be entirely devoted to verse and of which he would be editor. In Chicago, Harriet Monroe, who had already publicized her own forthcoming pioneer magazine bearing the same title, was scandalized, and she forestalled the usurper in establishing the title as her own by bringing forward the publication of her first issue, beating the Boston magazine—which was renamed the *Poetry Journal* and which did not appear until December 1912—by three months into the bookstores. The publishers of the *Poetry Journal*, impatient with O'Brien's uncharacteristic procrastination in setting up the magazine for publication, appointed a new editor, demoting him to assistant editor.

Braithwaite, who for some years had been editing a yearly *Anthology of Magazine Verse*, conceived the idea of founding a complementary volume of the best short stories appearing in magazines during the preceding twelve months. O'Brien helped Braithwaite with the reading and selecting of the stories and then, with Braithwaite's approval, took over the project himself, thus finding his central literary purpose in life. His first selection (of the best short stories of 1914) was published serially in the *Illustrated Sunday Magazine* during 1915. The first of the anthologies, *The Best Short Stories of 1915*, was published in April 1916 and contained twenty stories, including work by Maxwell Struthers Burt, Donn Byrne, Ben Hecht, Fannie Hurst, and Wilbur Daniel Steele. O'Brien's aim from the beginning was to ensure that, under his guidance, the American short story should free itself from its standing as a mere provincial off-shoot of the British short story and establish an independent character of its own. In his introduction to that first anthology, O'Brien bravely flew his battle standard, favorably comparing the contemporary American short story with its British counterpart (which he described as "cheap and meretricious") and predicting for it a potential development "as an art to the point where it may fairly claim a sustained superiority." In making his yearly selections, he eschewed the slick mechanical magazine story with its surprise O. Henry–type ending in favor of a more open form. In his introduction to the 1916 anthology, he wrote:

I am not at all interested in formulae, and organized criticism at its best would be nothing more than dead criticism, as all dogmatic interpretation of life is always dead. What has interested me, to the exclusion of other things, is the fresh living current of life which flows through the best of our work, and the psychological and imaginative reality that our writers have conferred upon the substance of it. No substance is of importance in fiction, unless it is organic substance. Inorganic fiction has been our curse in the past, and we are still surrounded by it in almost all of our magazines. The new impulse must find its own substance freshly, and interpret it naturally in new forms, rather than in the stereotyped utterances to which we have been so long accustomed.

O'Brien's attack had two results. Not only did he open doors, enabling writers, particularly the young unpublished writers he wished to encourage, to sense a promising new era of liberation, but, at the same time, even the most conservative of commercial editors began to respond to his lead. He accomplished his ends in a very simple and effective manner. At the back of each annual anthology he published a list of the "distinctive" short stories that had appeared during the year, awarding them one, two, or three asterisks in ascending order of distinction. He also included a section of "magazine averages," in which he listed in tabular form the names of the magazines that had published most short stories during the year, together with a breakdown of the *number* of distinctive stories appearing in each magazine, the magazine that had published the most distinctive stories heading the list with the other magazines following in descending order. Not content with that, O'Brien also offered a further table in which he recorded the *percentage* of distinctive stories out of the total number of stories published in each magazine.

Although the whole concept of these tables represented a somewhat dubious exercise, it proved to be a masterstroke. Magazine editors rose to the bait. With writers, already wooed by asterisks, beginning to produce and submit in ever-increasing numbers the sort of stories they knew O'Brien preferred and would consider for the anthologies, the editors found themselves, grudgingly at first, accepting these stories and publishing them, intent on making a better showing than their rivals in the O'Brien tables. If the "little magazines" of the day (such as the mimeographed *Gyroscope, Clay,* and *Story*) O'Brien wished to encourage were unable to compete with the commercial magazines in the number of stories they published, their editors invariably had the satisfaction of heading the percentage tables.

In 1919 O'Brien went to live in England, settling finally in Oxford, and from then on made his home either in England or on the Continent, only rarely returning to the United States. O'Brien began editing a companion anthology of British stories, the first of which, *The Best Short Stories of 1922,* was published in November 1922. In 1923 he married the English novelist Romer Wilson, with whom he had a son the following year. Romer was plagued by constant ill-health and eventually succumbed to cancer in January 1930. O'Brien remarried two years later, this time to a sixteen-year-old German schoolgirl, Ruth Gorgel. They had two daughters, born in 1935 and 1937. During the mid-1930s, the depression having savagely depleted his main source of income from the anthologies, he made several lecture tours in the United States. In 1937 he was engaged by Metro-Goldwyn-Mayer to act as its European story editor. This appointment, which necessitated that he move his family from Oxford to London, brought him comparative wealth for the first time in his life. There was, however, a price to pay. It was more than a full-time job. His duties entailed his supplying a large team of English writers (most of whom were indigent) with the latest novels so they could prepare plot outlines for his transmission to the MGM offices in Culver City and his giving fairly frequent lavish parties for visiting film personalities from Hollywood and the Continent. In addition, he had to cope with the inevitable hangers-on and refugees from Europe seeking work in England.

On the outbreak of war in September 1939, the O'Briens again moved, this time to Gerrards Cross, near to the MGM studios in Buckinghamshire. The U.S. lecture tours and his high-powered duties for MGM undoubtedly aggravated a long-standing heart condition, and he died suddenly in his sleep at the early age of fifty.

As Wilbur Schramm has written, O'Brien "was one of the great forces in American fiction although he spent little of his adult life in America and wrote no fiction. He was a poet who early ceased to write poetry, a critic who left hardly a sustained piece of distinguished criticism. He was simply a force." While it may not be true that he, and he alone, was responsible for the path the American short story took during the years 1915 through 1941, there is no doubt that his work played a considerable part in hastening the development of the genre to the high prestige it achieved and enjoyed during the two decades after World War I. Many of the writers he "discovered" and promoted at the beginning of their careers—including Sherwood Anderson, Ernest Hemingway, and William Saroyan—became eminent figures in the world of letters. As Saroyan himself has written, O'Brien was "the figurative, if not the literal, father of the American short story." If, as some feel, this is claiming too much, the list of the many writers who were encouraged and publicized by their appearance in his anthologies—among them Ring Lardner, Willa Cather, William Faulkner, Erskine Caldwell, James T. Farrell, F. Scott Fitzgerald, Thomas Wolfe, John Steinbeck, Richard Wright, Eudora Welty, and Jesse Stuart—does attest to his editorial acumen and the importance of the role he played in the American literary scene for more than a quarter-century.

• All extant collections of O'Brien's papers are in private hands. His poetry is collected in *White Fountains: Odes and Lyrics* (1917), *Distant Music* (1921), and *Hard Sayings* (1926). In Oxford, he edited with five coeditors the short story magazine *New Stories* (1934–1936). His criticism includes *The Advance of the American Short Story* (1923; rev. ed. 1931), *The Dance of the Machines: The American Short Story and the Industrial Age* (1929), and *The Short Story Case Book* (1935). His miscellaneous writings include *The World's History at a Glance: From 800 B.C. to 1913 A.D.* (1913), *Walks and Talks about Boston* (1916), *The Forgotten Threshold: A Journal of Arthur Middleton* (1919), *Son of the Morning: A Portrait of Friedrich Nietzsche* (1932), and *The Guest Book* (1935). Anthologies include *Poems of the Irish Revolutionary Brotherhood* [with Padraic Colum] (July 1916; new and enl. ed. Sept. 1916), *The Masque of Poets: A Collection of New Poems by Contemporary American Poets* (1918), *The Great Modern English Short Stories* (1919), *The Twenty-five Finest Short Stories* (1931), and *Elizabethan Tales* (1937). A good introduction to the work O'Brien did in his annual *Best Short Stories* is *50 Best American Short Stories 1915–1939* (1939). There is no published biography. The most complete modern assessments are Wilbur Schramm, "The Thousand and One Tales of Edward O'Brien," *American Prefaces* 7 (Autumn 1941): 3–17; Ruby Willoughby Phillips, "O'Brien's Magazines, O'Brien's Stories: A Table and an Index," *American Prefaces* 7 (Autumn 1941): 18–28; and Sister M. Joselyn, O.S.B., "Edward Joseph O'Brien and the American Short Story," *Studies in Short Fiction* (Fall 1965): 1–15. See also Robert Whitehand, "Edward J. O'Brien," *Prairie Schooner* 14 (Spring 1940): 1–12; and Roy Simmonds, "Edward J. O'Brien and *New Stories*," *London Magazine* 23 (Nov. 1983): 44–54, and "Ernest Hemingway and Edward J. O'Brien," *London Magazine* 28 (July 1988): 50–64.

ROY S. SIMMONDS

O'BRIEN, Jeremiah (1744–5 Sept. 1818), naval officer, was born in Kittery, Maine, the son of Mary Cain and Morris O'Brien, an Irish-born tailor, farmer, merchant, and sailor. Jeremiah received no formal education. In 1750 the family moved up the Maine coast to Scarboro, and when New England settlers were encouraged to move further north following the Treaty of Paris in 1763, the O'Briens relocated to a new settlement at Machias. There they entered the lumber business. Both father and sons prospered, and they eventually operated at least two sawmills. The O'Brien family became influential and decidedly Whiggish members of the community. When the town's first militia company was formed in 1769, Jeremiah O'Brien was among the first to join.

In May 1775, shortly after news arrived of the battles at Lexington and Concord, the people of Machias received copies of the Proclamation of the Provincial Congress of Massachusetts, "authorizing and requiring preparations and efforts incident to a state of hostility." O'Brien welcomed the news and with others set up a liberty pole at a prominent spot in the town. In early June three vessels—the sloops *Unity* and *Polly* and the armed British schooner *Margaretta*, commanded by Midshipman James Moore—arrived at Machias seeking lumber for use by British troops in Boston. When Moore spied the liberty pole, he insisted that were it not torn down he would open fire on the town. After heated discussion, Moore backed down, but his threat and his mission so incensed the townspeople that they determined to seize him and his schooner. On Sunday, 11 June, while the midshipman was in church, a group of Machias men stormed in to take Moore prisoner. Moore escaped to the *Margaretta*, cast off, and fell down the bay. The next morning Moore headed for the open sea, but a sudden gust jibed *Margaretta*, toppling a gaff and boom and forcing Moore to hove to for repairs. In hot pursuit aboard the two captured sloops, a party led by O'Brien came alongside the *Margaretta*. The Americans boarded, and in the melee Moore was mortally wounded. The Americans overwhelmed the British, and the *Margaretta* surrendered. Flushed with victory, O'Brien and his men returned to Machias escorting their prize, the first vessel of the Royal Navy to surrender to an American force. Some have labeled the event the first naval action of the Revolution.

O'Brien's fame spread quickly. The Machias Committee of Safety sent a full report of the battle to the Massachusetts Provincial Congress in Watertown, and on 26 June the congress passed a resolution praising the capture of the three vessels. The local Committee of Safety ordered that the *Unity* be given to O'Brien to cruise the waters off Machias. The armament from the *Margaretta* was transferred to the sloop, and the *Unity*'s name was changed to *Machias Liberty*. By early July 1775 O'Brien was cruising in the Bay of Fundy, accompanied by a schooner from East Machias commanded by Benjamin Foster. On 16 July they encountered the *Diligent* of eight guns and fifty men and the *Tatamagouche* armed with sixteen small swivel guns.

After a brief fight, O'Brien and Foster captured the two enemy vessels and brought them back to Machias. News of O'Brien's triumph reached the provincial congress, which rewarded him with the appointment "a captain of the Marine in the Colony." For the next year O'Brien and the *Machias Liberty*, accompanied by the *Diligent*, cruised the waters of the Gulf of Maine and nearby Bay of Fundy, harassing British trade in the region. His relationship with the Massachusetts Provincial Congress soured, however. He accused it of not providing support for his vessels and men and, in a moment of pique, actually threatened to sell the two vessels, despite the fact that he did not own them. After hearing of O'Brien's intemperate remarks, the congress decided in October 1776 to sell the *Machias Liberty*, leaving him without a command.

In the summer of 1777 O'Brien went to sea again, this time as a privateersman in command of the brig *Resolution* out of Newburyport. In September the *Resolution* captured the *Scarborough*, a provision vessel out of Cork bound for New York. Over the next two years O'Brien commanded the privateers *Cyrus*, *Little Vincent*, and *Tiger*. All cruised off New England. In 1780 O'Brien took the helm of the privateer *Hannibal*, twenty-four guns. While cruising off New York in 1780 the *Hannibal* was captured by two British frigates. O'Brien and his crew were held aboard the prison hulk *Jersey*, moored at Wallabout Bay. In July 1781 he was moved to Mill Prison in Plymouth, England, where he remained confined for nearly a year before managing to escape.

By October 1782 O'Brien was home in Machias. He never again went to sea. He returned to the lumbering business, remaining in Machias until his death there. He was active in local politics, and in 1811 President James Madison appointed him collector of customs for the District of Machias. Although some sources suggest he married a woman named Elizabeth Fitzpatrick, no evidence supports that claim.

• A biography of O'Brien is Andrew Sherman, *Life of Captain Jeremiah O'Brien* (1902). General accounts of the naval history of the Revolution include Gardner W. Allen, *A Naval History of the American Revolution* (2 vols., 1913), and William M. Fowler, Jr., *Rebels under Sail: The American Navy in the Revolution* (1976). O'Brien's death notice is in the *Boston Daily Advertiser*, 26 Sept. 1818.

WILLIAM M. FOWLER, JR.

O'BRIEN, John Joseph (4 Nov. 1888–9 Dec. 1967), business executive and sports administrator, was born in Brooklyn, New York, to John T. O'Brien, a construction superintendent, and Margaret Monohan. O'Brien's love for sports started early. He played football, basketball, and baseball at Commercial High School in Brooklyn and continued to play for YMCA and other teams while pursuing further education through night school and correspondence courses in law and accounting. In 1910 he began officiating basketball games, an avocation he engaged in over the next twenty years at high school, college, and professional levels.

O'Brien married Cecelia Regina Schwartz in 1913; the union produced four children. He also joined the Coverdale and Colpitts Company, an engineering firm, in New York City. By 1925 he was directing the company's day-to-day business, a job that he held until his retirement in 1958.

Noted for being well dressed, O'Brien changed clothes as often as four times a day to maintain an immaculate appearance. Indefatigable as well, he took on other jobs in addition to his work at Coverdale and Colpitts. In 1922 he became a trustee of the West Caddo Oil Syndicate, and in 1930 he was named vice president, secretary, and treasurer of the Pierce Oil Company. After his wife's death in 1934, he married Florence Gladys Comerford the following year; they had two children. By 1943 he had served as vice president, board member, and secretary of the Minneapolis & St. Louis Railroad. He also was secretary of the Friends of McGill University and president of the Catholic Club of Brooklyn.

O'Brien's real love, however, was basketball, and he devoted his considerable administrative abilities to organizing the game. In 1914 he helped initiate the Interstate League, an early professional circuit, and he served as its president from 1915 to 1917. From 1915 to 1930 he refereed games in the Eastern College Basketball Conference (today's Ivy League) as well as for other conferences. He officiated the first Army-Navy basketball game in 1920. The following year he formed the Brooklyn Arcadians and organized the Metropolitan professional league, acting as its president from 1922 until 1928.

In the 1920s both professional football and basketball were struggling to become established as popular alternatives to intercollegiate athletics. Although baseball players enjoyed popularity partly because of long-established and well-regulated leagues, athletes in other sports suffered from what was generally considered the taint of professionalism. Professional basketball's image was further tarnished when Jim Furey, owner of the famous Celtics, was imprisoned for embezzlement, although his crime was unrelated to the sport. In light of such problems, Joe Carr, head of the American Basketball League, opted for his other role as commissioner of the new National Football League. O'Brien stepped in to replace Carr for the 1927–1928 season and retained the presidency for the next twenty-five years.

During his tenure O'Brien brought respect and credibility to the league. He not only trained officials, but embarked on a program of expansion that extended franchises from New York to Chicago. What had been a regional league took on national dimensions. The depression curtailed such efforts, however, and O'Brien found it necessary to reorganize the league in 1933–1934. He did so successfully, maintaining operations as an eastern circuit until after World War II, when factionalism developed over teams' hiring of college stars who had been indicted in the point-shaving scandals of 1949–1951. At O'Brien's urging, the league disbanded in 1953.

In 1961 O'Brien was inducted into the Naismith Memorial Basketball Hall of Fame in Springfield, Massachusetts, cited for the new dignity and integrity his leadership brought to owners, players, officials, and the game. He died in Oceanside, New York.

• Information on O'Brien can be found in the O'Brien file at the Naismith Memorial Basketball Hall of Fame in Springfield, Mass. His obituary is in the *New York Times*, 11 Dec. 1967.

GERALD R. GEMS

O'BRIEN, Lawrence Francis, Jr. (7 July 1917–29 Sept. 1990), political strategist, was born in Springfield, Massachusetts, the son of Lawrence Francis O'Brien, a café owner and politician, and Myra Sweeney. He learned the rudiments of political organizing from his father, who spent a lifetime establishing a Democratic foothold in Republican-dominated western Massachusetts. An Irish immigrant, O'Brien, Sr., worked in politics as a means to combat nativism in the early twentieth century. The younger O'Brien remembered that his father "saw the Democratic Party as a means through which the Irish and other immigrant groups could fight back" and came to share his father's devotion to the party.

In addition to helping with his father's partisan activities, O'Brien worked in the family business while attending night school at Northeastern University in 1937. He completed his Bachelor of Laws degree in 1942, although he never became a lawyer. Soon thereafter, the army drafted O'Brien and assigned him to administrative duties at Camp Edwards, Massachusetts. While serving in the army, in 1944, he married Elva Brassard; they had one son.

Shortly after his discharge from the army in November 1945, O'Brien established his reputation as a skilled politician. He organized Foster Furcolo's successful campaign for the U.S. House of Representatives in 1948 and accompanied the congressman to Washington for two years. Congressman John F. Kennedy asked O'Brien to help run his senatorial campaign in 1952. Still a young and inexperienced politician, Kennedy hoped that an alliance with O'Brien would expand his political connections in western Massachusetts. Following Kennedy's victory, O'Brien declined an invitation to work as a senatorial aide in Washington, saying his hands were full running the family business. He did, however, maintain the senator's standing in his home state, keeping track of Kennedy supporters and financial backers.

Having shown his efficacy and loyalty in the 1952 race, O'Brien developed a close working relationship with Kennedy throughout the 1950s. Kennedy once boasted to *Newsweek* that O'Brien was "the best election man in the business" (27 June 1960). Indeed, O'Brien wrote two Democratic National Committee (DNC) standard campaign manuals, *Citizens for Ken-*

nedy and Johnson: Campaign Manual (1960) and *The Democratic Campaign Manual 1964* (1964). His greatest contribution to Kennedy's election was his talent for maximizing finite resources. In the West Virginia Democratic primary, for instance, he devised a scheme to use housewives to good effect. Realizing that these women were largely bound to the home during the day, he gave volunteers 300 names, supplied them with a short statement, and let them use their own time and phones to canvass voters. O'Brien later told *Newsweek*, "We called every voter in the state and it didn't cost us a nickel" (27 June 1960).

Kennedy recognized O'Brien's political usefulness and asked him to become a special assistant to the president for congressional relations. Although he did not draft any of Kennedy's New Frontier legislation, O'Brien became the primary executive branch liaison when a bill reached Congress. In much the same way that he maximized campaign assets, O'Brien increased presidential leverage with Congress. He reorganized and coordinated all White House relations with Capitol Hill under his personal leadership in the Office of Congressional Relations. Under his new centralized system, OCR kept close tabs on legislators and maintained detailed records about their backgrounds, districts, and pet projects. O'Brien's agency used its thorough intelligence network to direct patronage to cooperative members. Since OCR took credit for any presidential largess to politicians, this system forged valuable friendships between OCR and Democratic politicians over time.

Perhaps the greatest compliment to O'Brien's skill with Congress came when President Lyndon B. Johnson—a great parliamentarian himself—asked O'Brien to remain a presidential aide after Kennedy's assassination in November 1963. During his vice presidency, Johnson had little contact with legislative affairs; consequently, O'Brien's up-to-date organization helped him continue New Frontier efforts and advance the Great Society agenda. In 1965, for instance, O'Brien's extensive network on the Hill expedited the passage of the Higher Education Act. The bill spent an inordinate amount of time in committee, and O'Brien's relationship with congressional leaders helped the White House find a compromise among feuding legislators. By the end of 1965 O'Brien was ready to return to private life, but Johnson persuaded him to remain in the administration, offering him a cabinet position as postmaster general. As postmaster, O'Brien kept his office at the White House and continued his service to Johnson's legislative endeavors until April 1968.

Even though O'Brien was known as a "Kennedy man," he remained loyal to Johnson until the president decided against running for reelection in March 1968. Several days later both Senator Robert Francis Kennedy and Vice President Hubert Humphrey solicited his assistance, but O'Brien rejoined the Kennedy camp out of deference to the memory of John Kennedy. Following Robert Kennedy's assassination in California in June 1968, Humphrey again asked O'Brien to head his election efforts. The two men had become friends over the years, and O'Brien, a nonideological party loyalist, agreed to lead Humphrey's bid in the primary and general election.

After Humphrey's abortive campaign in 1968, O'Brien's main political role was his chairmanship of the DNC from 1970 to 1972. His office was a primary target of the Watergate burglars in 1972, so O'Brien resorted to using the public phones to make confidential phone calls. When the Democratic National Convention nominated Senator George McGovern, O'Brien resigned as chairman to assist the senator's unsuccessful campaign. Despite his official position as national campaign chairman, O'Brien's job was largely limited to liaison with Democratic officials and labor leaders.

The 1972 election was O'Brien's last major political assignment. He moved to New York City and turned his attention to his public relations firm, O'Brien Associates, which he had started in 1969. For the next several years he concentrated on building his business and completing his memoir, *No Final Victories: A Life in Politics—From John F. Kennedy to Watergate*, which he completed in 1974. In his final career move, he became the commissioner of the National Basketball Association, serving from 1 June 1975 until 1 February 1984. O'Brien was popular with the Players Association and helped the NBA's financial problems with policies like salary caps. Suffering from declining attendance, the NBA restored its popularity under O'Brien's leadership with timely reforms. An extensive substance-abuse policy enhanced the image of the athletes, and the three-point shot added a new dimension to the traditional game. In honor of his contributions to the NBA during these nine years, he was inducted into the Naismith Memorial Basketball Hall of Fame in 1991. O'Brien spent the last years of his life in New York City, where he died.

• The John F. Kennedy Presidential Library contains the earliest political papers for O'Brien in the Congressional Liaison Files. To a lesser extent, the library's Robert F. Kennedy and Theodore Sorensen papers contain documents pertinent to O'Brien. The Lyndon B. Johnson Library holds the Office Files of Lawrence F. O'Brien and of his principal staff members. His personal papers will be available in the JFK library for the years before November of 1963 and in the LBJ library in the years following that time. O'Brien's extensive oral history interviews with Michael Gillette are stored in both the Kennedy and Johnson libraries. Patrick Anderson wrote about O'Brien's role as presidential aide in *The President's Men: White House Assistants of Franklin D. Roosevelt, Harry S. Truman, Dwight D. Eisenhower, John F. Kennedy, and Lyndon B. Johnson* (1968). R. Scott Harris also covered his relationships with Kennedy and Johnson in "Lawrence F. O'Brien: Man behind the Presidents" (M.A. thesis, Univ. of Texas, 1993). Nigel Bowles, *The White House and Capitol Hill: The Politics of Presidential Persuasion* (1987), analyzes O'Brien's role in the growing influence of the modern presidency. For a description of O'Brien's role in the Watergate scandal, see Stanley I. Kutler, *The Wars of Watergate: The Last Crisis of Richard Nixon* (1990). An obituary is in the *New York Times*, 29 Sept. 1990.

R. SCOTT HARRIS

O'BRIEN, Morgan Joseph (28 Apr. 1852–16 June 1937), lawyer and jurist, was born in New York City, the son of Morgan Joseph O'Brien, a merchant, and Mary Ann Burke. O'Brien's father, an Irish immigrant, launched a series of mercantile ventures in New York City, principally a business in meats, and quickly prospered in the swiftly expanding economy of the 1840s and 1850s. Educated in the public schools, O'Brien received the A.B. degree from Fordham University (then St. Johns College) in 1872, the A.M. from St. Francis Xavier College the following year, and the LL.B. from Columbia College in 1875. In 1880 he married Rose M. Crimmins, the daughter of a prominent contractor; they had ten children.

O'Brien's legal career was divided into three distinct phases. During the first, he drew upon his father's mercantile associations and family friends, many from the rapidly growing Irish community, as well as the burgeoning entrepreneurial interests within the city to develop a highly successful and remunerative corporate practice. In particular, his career was advanced by the efforts of "Honest John" Kelly (1822–1886), a prominent Irish politician and Tammany leader from 1871 to 1886. His clients' concerns centered on the construction and expansion of the commercial infrastructure of the city—docks, warehouses, commercial properties, transportation facilities, and the like. Much of this work was intricate in nature, demanding substantial legal skill and detailed knowledge of municipal government.

As his legal reputation grew, O'Brien was drawn into numerous forms of public service, beginning a lifelong and increasingly prominent role in endeavors designed to improve life within and the governance of New York City. This public spiritedness led him, seemingly inevitably, into the second phase of his career—a long period of service in the state judiciary. In 1886 Mayor Abram S. Hewitt, recognizing O'Brien's extensive knowledge of the city and its government, appointed him as corporate counsel. The following year, at age thirty-five, he was elected an associate justice of the Supreme Court of the State of New York, where he served for eight years (1887–1895) before being elevated by Governor Levi P. Morton to the newly created appellate division. He served on this bench for eleven years (1895–1906), the last year, named by Governor Frank W. Higgins, as its presiding justice. The work of these courts reflected the issues of the times—the development of commerce and industry, emerging government regulation of the economy, public finance, and related matters. O'Brien wrote notable opinions concerning the issuance of bonds to finance public improvements and adjudicated the election cases of 1891 in a manner satisfactory to both the Democrats and Republicans.

In 1906 O'Brien extricated himself from the judiciary and entered upon the third, and most satisfying, phase of his career—the exciting and demanding challenges, as he regarded them, of high level corporate law and appellate practice. In later remembrances, he expressed a sense of opportunity lost while on the bench. He chafed under the limitations imposed upon the judiciary—he termed it a "treadmill"—and longed for the advocate's freedom to choose his clients, to champion their interests, and to take the lead in defining legal issues and applying legal principles. The deepest satisfactions for the lawyer derived, he believed, from the gladiator's contest and the "reputation" acquired through victory.

O'Brien and his close friend, Albert Barnes Boardman, formed the nucleus of a firm (originally O'Brien, Boardman, Platt & Dunning, later O'Brien, Boardman, Parker & Fox) that played a prominent role in the defense of large corporate interests—principally, banks and life insurance companies, construction, shipping and transportation interests, and industrial corporations—against the regulatory efforts of the developing positive government. Although never as influential as such giants of the early twentieth-century corporate bar as John G. Johnson and William D. Guthrie, "Judge O'Brien," as he was familiarly known, and Boardman were skilled counsel who enjoyed considerable success.

Hammer v. Dagenhart (1918) was probably their most important appellate litigation. Retained to protect southern textile manufacturers against federal child labor legislation, they fashioned a brief drawn largely from the familiar doctrines of constitutional laissez faire. In particular, they argued that the national commerce power was narrowly confined to manufacture and that its extension to interstate shipment would gravely impair American federalism. Although substantially derivative in character, this argument triumphed before the U.S. Supreme Court, a five-judge majority striking down the Keating-Owen Law in 1918.

While O'Brien's career at the bar was distinguished, his thought was conventional, essentially reflective of the world as he knew it. In public statements, he condemned undue legislative interference with private enterprise and subscribed to a kind of Christian humanism that minimized the harsh elements in the prevalent Social Darwinism. It was his person and his commitment to civic improvement that most deeply impressed those who knew him.

Beyond his work as counsel, O'Brien played a prominent role in business and professional activities, serving on the boards of many corporations, most notably as one of three trustees who mutualized the Equitable Life Assurance Society, and he took a leading part in the affairs of the New York City and State bar associations. He was active in Democratic party politics, working within New York City and State with such leaders as Grover Cleveland, Franklin D. Roosevelt, and a host of reform mayors and governors.

A genial individual, unfailingly courteous and conciliatory, who prized the making and holding of friends, O'Brien practiced in full measure what he recommended to others: namely, to consecrate "part of their lives at least unselfishly, disinterestedly and patriotically to service of their country and humanity." His life beyond the law was one of engagement, devoted to his family, his religious faith, the Irish in America and Ireland, and the improvement of society. At his death, he was memorialized as one of the first citizens of New York City and for "his primacy in things Irish and things Catholic." For sixty-five years, he gave unstintingly of his time, energy, and wealth to an extraordinary number of civic, charitable, educational, ethnic, humane, and religious causes. He led civil services, reform, and charter improvement campaigns in New York City, and he served as a trustee of the New York Public Library as well as of numerous other beneficent associations and educational foundations. An intimate friend of Cardinals John Murphy Farley and Patrick Joseph Hayes, he was knighted by the pope and honored for his services by foreign governments. A noted patron of Irish cultural organizations in America, he played a significant part in Ireland's efforts to gain independence.

O'Brien died in New York City.

• Neither a manuscript collection nor a biography exists for O'Brien. The nature of his thought is revealed in three of his articles: "Civilization of the Twentieth Century," private printing (1906); "The Making of Constitutions," New York State Bar Association (Jan. 1915); and "President's Address," New York State Bar Association (Jan. 1917). Sketches of his life appear in two memorial articles: Martin Conboy, "Morgan J. O'Brien," Memorial of the New York State Bar Association, *Bar Bulletin*, Mar. 1938, pp. 21–31; and J. C. Walsh, "Morgan J. O'Brien," *Journal of the American Irish Historical Society* 32 (1941): 78–84. An extended obituary appears in the *New York Times*, 17 June 1937.

STEPHEN B. WOOD

O'BRIEN, Pat (11 Nov. 1899–15 Oct. 1983), actor, was born William Joseph O'Brien in Milwaukee, Wisconsin, the son of William O'Brien, a dry-goods salesman, and Margaret McGovern. O'Brien later added Patrick to his name in honor of his paternal grandfather, a promising architect who had been shot to death trying to break up a barroom brawl.

O'Brien attended Marquette Academy, a private Catholic secondary school, where he befriended classmate Spencer Tracy, who shared his love of the theater. In 1918 both enlisted in the U.S. Navy, yet O'Brien never got beyond the Great Lakes Naval Training Center, where he played football. After the war he entered Marquette University's law school, and in a borrowed skirt he starred in a campus production of *Charlie's Aunt*.

During the summer of 1920 O'Brien tried to break into the Broadway stage, commuting from Jersey City where he lived with relatives. He wore "bright ties," appeared "neatly shabby," read theater notices, and appeared regularly at producers' and agents' offices. Finally he was hired as a chorus boy in *Adrienne*. His father's illness forced a return to Milwaukee, where he re-enrolled in law school, while keeping his hand in local amateur productions. Using a serviceman's entrance allowance, O'Brien, along with Tracy, returned to New York, where they enrolled in Sargent's School of Drama. Dining on pretzels and water to pinch pen-

nies, they were cast as robots at $15 a week in the Broadway play *R.U.R.* Next O'Brien got the part of a juvenile in the Plainfield (N.J.) stock company production of *Getting Gertie's Garter* at $50 a week.

O'Brien found two years of summer stock "brain tormenting, bone breaking and gratifying." Appearing in one and sometimes two plays a week, he thought he was ready for the big time by the fall of 1925. He played the role of the heavy in *A Man's Man* at the Fifty-second Street Theatre and toured with the production for six months. Good parts followed in *You Can't Win, Henry Behave*, and the Broadway version of *Getting Gertie's Garter*. While touring with *Broadway* in Chicago during December 1927 he met actress Eloise Taylor. They married in 1931 and would have four children.

When sound came to film, O'Brien headed for Hollywood, making *Fury of the Wild* (1929) and *The Freckled Rascal* (1929) for RKO before getting his big break on Broadway in the role of a bookie in the racetrack drama *The Up and Up*. Hollywood director Lewis Milestone saw the play and in December 1930 summoned O'Brien back to Hollywood for the role of Hildy Johnson in Howard Hughes's movie version of *The Front Page* (1931). The film was a smash, and O'Brien's fast-talking, hard-bitten reporter became a convention in early talking films. A personal services contract to Hughes kept O'Brien busily on loan out to other studios. In the best of these, *Air Mail* (1932), O'Brien worked with John Ford; in *American Madness* (1932), with Frank Capra; and in *Bombshell* (1933), with Victor Fleming.

O'Brien's agent, Myron Selznick, arranged for Warner Bros. to buy his contract from Hughes. What followed was a hectic seven-year stretch in which O'Brien came to personify, often as policeman or priest, the virtues of the social order in films with James Cagney and Humphrey Bogart. O'Brien's nine pictures with Cagney were big box office hits and established O'Brien's reputation as the one man in movies whom most American males were supposed to be like. As Father Jerry in *Angels with Dirty Faces* (1938) and Father Duffy in *The Fighting 69th* (1940), O'Brien had rarely been in better form in his portrayal of Irish Catholics. His underplaying magnified Cagney's self-certainty and became the basis for the biographical work for which O'Brien would be best known.

The role of Notre Dame's famous football coach in *Knute Rockne, All American* (1940), costarring future president Ronald Reagan, demonstrated O'Brien's ability to balance sentiment and spirit in a script worthy of his subtle acting. Released after the fall of France and during the battle for Britain, the film struck reviewers as "a timely and inspirational reminder of what this country stands for." O'Brien's success reflected his uncanny ability "to understand the human qualities" of his character. A quarter century after playing the part, O'Brien thought he had seen Rockne "clearer and closer" than any other character he had brought to the screen.

O'Brien's association with biographical parts continued while he was under contract to RKO. In *Bombardier* (1943), O'Brien played a real-life hero, Colonel Paddy Ryan, who trained bombardiers for action in World War II. *The Iron Major* (1943) saw him as Frank Cavanaugh, a college football coach eventually blinded by war wounds. In *Fighting Father Dunne* (1948), O'Brien is a St. Louis priest who rescues homeless newsboys in early twentieth-century America. O'Brien received recognition for "meritorious service" in leading USO shows overseas during the war. His annual position as leader of New York's St. Patrick's Day parade, beginning in 1946 before 1.5 million spectators, and his command performance before the king and queen of England later that year, seemed to confirm that Hollywood's Hibernian had become an American institution.

In the 1950s O'Brien returned to the stage with a nightclub act in which he recited poetry, sang songs, and told old Irish stories. He supported his old friend Spencer Tracy in two films, *The People against O'Hara* (1951) and *The Last Hurrah* (1958), where he was reunited with Irish director John Ford. He returned to Broadway in Nathanael West's *Miss Lonelyhearts* in 1957; did a wonderful bit in Billy Wilder's classic *Some Like It Hot* (1959), and starred in the television series "Harrigan and Son" on ABC the following year.

Throughout the 1960s and 1970s O'Brien and his wife toured the country's supper clubs and stages with new and old material made new by their enthusiastic performance. In 1973 the Catholic Actors Guild made O'Brien their man of the year. Heart problems did not prevent his honoring James Cagney at a Kennedy Center awards ceremony in 1980. When O'Brien died in Santa Monica, California, Cagney and Reagan were among the first to mourn publicly the passing of their favorite Irishman. Fourteen Catholic priests celebrated the last rites for an actor whose humor and humanity had captured the American ethos of decency over six decades.

• There is a collection of O'Brien materials at the State Historical Society of Wisconsin in Madison, which also has a collection of Warner Bros. materials. O'Brien's memoir, *The Wind at My Back* (1964), became a bestseller. Biographical articles appear in the *New York Times*, 21 Sept. 1930, and David Thomson, *A Biographical Dictionary of Film* (1994). O'Brien's career at Warner Bros. and inside the studio system is chronicled in Ted Sennett, *Warner Brothers Presents* (1971); Arthur Wilson, *The Warner Bros. Golden Anniversary Book* (1973); James Robert Parrish, *The Tough Guys* (1976); Rudy Behlmer, *Inside Warner Brothers, 1935–1951* (1987); and Robert Sklar, *City Boys* (1992). Critical reaction to his film work appears in *The New York Times Directory of the Film* (1971) and *Variety: International Showbusiness Reference* (1981). An obituary is in the *New York Times*, 16 Oct. 1983.

BRUCE J. EVENSEN

O'BRIEN, Willis Harold (2 Mar. 1886–8 Nov. 1962), movie special effects creator, was born in Oakland, California, the son of William Henry O'Brien, who ran a military academy and was an assistant district attorney, and Minnie Gregg. O'Brien ran away from home several times, starting at the age of ten or eleven, at about the time his family, previously well-off, suffered financial reversals. For nearly twenty years he held numerous jobs, including positions as factory worker, boxer, draftsman, and newspaper sports cartoonist. A period spent guiding scientists in search of fossils first acquainted him with prehistoric life.

In 1914 or 1915 while employed by a stone cutter in San Francisco, he sculpted a dinosaur and a cave man, layering clay on jointed skeletons, then filmed the models one frame at a time in various positions. When the footage was projected, the figures appeared to move on their own. This brief scene prompted a local film distributor, Herman Wobber, to finance a five-minute production in which humans interact with dinosaurs in mostly comic ways. O'Brien followed this with two other animated shorts.

The Edison Company purchased O'Brien's films and hired him to make more. He moved to New York and created six shorts for them. Released to theaters in 1917, these comic fantasies involved model humans and dinosaurs. The expressionless people were less interesting than the animals that sometimes had cute, if caricatured, personalities.

Financial difficulties led Edison to curtail production; O'Brien left in 1917. Around 1918 he married Hazel Ruth Collette, whom he had earlier courted in Oakland; they had two sons. Also around 1918 he made a short in which a man is chased by prehistoric monsters. Much of this film is live action, and the dinosaur scenes have smoother animation than O'Brien's prior efforts. Watterson R. Rothacker then hired O'Brien to make advertising shorts, but soon they decided to film Arthur Conan Doyle's 1912 novel *The Lost World*, about the discovery of prehistoric creatures in South America.

Rothacker arranged to have First National produce *The Lost World*, and O'Brien spent a year on the technical effects. The film, which premiered in February 1925, was a box-office success. O'Brien combined actors and animated models in the same image by exposing only part of the frame, then rewinding the film and exposing the other part. To create the impression of elaborate settings, he used the technique of painting on a pane of glass, then filming through it at the actual set.

O'Brien then began planning *Atlantis*, about people who live in underwater caverns, but First National lost interest. In 1929 he and Harry O. Hoyt, the director of *The Lost World*, developed *Creation*, in which occupants of a yacht are stranded on an island inhabited by prehistoric creatures. RKO agreed to back the project, and in 1930 O'Brien started work. In October 1931 RKO brought in Merian C. Cooper to evaluate the financial merits of all projects. Cooper disliked *Creation*'s story but saw in O'Brien's test scenes a way to make a film he had in mind about a gorilla. The result was *King Kong* (1933).

O'Brien's experience as a boxer can be seen in Kong's manner of fighting and, according to Cooper's assistant Archie Marshek, "We could see something of Obie showing through" in the ape's personality. O'Brien fully involves *Kong*'s humans in the animated action. To do so, he developed a process of projecting live-action footage onto little screens built into miniature sets, then refilming the images when animating the models. Many scenes are visually complex, incorporating in one shot miniature settings and animals, live-action segments, and several layers of glass paintings.

Kong opened on 2 March 1933 at two New York theaters and did exceptional business. RKO put a sequel into production in April, completed it in October, and released it in December. With such a short schedule, *Son of Kong* (1933) had much less animation and what there is, while impressive, reveals exaggeration and cuteness. O'Brien was emotionally detached from this production, perhaps due to the pressure of its short deadline.

O'Brien had separated from his wife in 1930, but he often visited their two sons. In early October 1933, his mentally unstable wife shot both boys, aged fourteen and thirteen, and then herself. Only his wife survived. "My husband is not to blame in any way," she said. "I just couldn't sleep and there was no one to leave the kids with." She died in November 1934.

Cooper made little use of O'Brien in the next years but did use his skill with miniatures and glass paintings to re-create a Roman city and a volcanic eruption in *The Last Days of Pompeii* (1935). During this period, around March 1934, O'Brien began dating Darlyne Prenett and on 17 November they married. The couple had no children. The film industry offered O'Brien little satisfaction. For various projects he made drawings and miniature settings, had models built, and shot test scenes, but these films were left uncompleted by their studios. During World War II he did miniature photography on documentaries for the military, and he also created some matte paintings for features.

Not until 1947 did he work on another major effects film, a new gorilla movie but one with a lighter tone than *Kong* and a happy ending. Because most of O'Brien's efforts were devoted to planning effects, young Ray Harryhausen did much of the animation. *Mighty Joe Young* (1949) is a technical achievement, with natural-looking animation and tightly knit combinations of live action and models. This charmingly sentimental film won O'Brien an Academy Award for special effects (the award didn't exist when *Kong* was released).

During the early 1950s, when Harryhausen started making low-budget films with animated creatures, O'Brien held out for work on a larger scale, but nothing resulted. Finally, O'Brien sold a story about cowboys and a dinosaur, expecting to animate *The Beast of Hollow Mountain* (1956), but others did it. Subsequently he was hired to supervise Harryhausen's animation for the prehistoric segment of the documentary *The Animal World* (1956).

After that, he and an associate did the effects for the low-budget *The Black Scorpion* (1957). Their efforts give the feature some impressive, frightening moments. Then, under even greater constraints, they provided a somewhat stiff but competently animated dinosaur for the British film *Behemoth the Sea Monster* (1959), which was titled *The Giant Behemoth* in the United States. O'Brien was approached to work on the remake of *The Lost World* (1960), but the producer decided to use live lizards instead of animated models. O'Brien's name is on the film, but his techniques and ideas were ignored by its makers.

Hope for a major production reappeared when O'Brien sold a story called *King Kong vs. Frankenstein*, but then he learned that it was being filmed in Japan as *King Kong vs. Godzilla*, with the monsters portrayed by men in suits. An English-dubbed version appeared in 1963. O'Brien died in Hollywood, California, frustrated at having another hope shattered.

Events failed to make him bitter. "He was a kid right up to the day he died," said his widow, "still a boy and a dreamer." O'Brien may not have been a complete artist, but he had imagination, sensitivity, and skill. With *King Kong*, in particular, he helped define the adventure-fantasy film. Unfortunately, O'Brien lived at a time when few producers shared his ambitions and visions, but even in cheap productions, his work stands out.

• O'Brien wrote "Miniature Effect Shots," *International Photographer*, Apr. 1933; reprinted as "Miniature Effects Shots" in *The Girl in the Hairy Paw*, ed. Ronald Gottesman and Harry Geduld (1976), pp. 183–84. Some of his stories and illustrations for unproduced projects appear in Steve Archer's *Willis O'Brien: Special Effects Genius* (1993). A key source of biographical information is Don Shay, "Willis O'Brien: Creator of the Impossible," *Cinefex*, Jan. 1982, pp. 4–71. Paul M. Jensen examines O'Brien's career in *The Men Who Made the Monsters* (1997). See also Jeff Rovin, *From the Land beyond Beyond: The Films of Willis O'Brien and Ray Harryhausen* (1977). Profiles of O'Brien appear in the *New York Times*, 25 June 1950, and 26 June 1955. An interview with Darlyne O'Brien is in *Classic Images*, May 1986, pp. 10–11. For a detailed look at O'Brien's production methods, see Orville Goldner and George E. Turner, *The Making of King Kong: The Story behind a Film Classic* (1975). An obituary appears in the *New York Times*, 12 Nov. 1962.

PAUL M. JENSEN

OCCOM, Samson (1723–14 July 1792), Methodist preacher and writer, was born into a Mohegan community near New London, Connecticut, the son of Joshua Occom and Sarah (maiden name unknown).

At seventeen Samson Occom was converted to Christianity by Rev. James Davenport during the "Great Awakening" (c. 1730–1740), when efforts to bring the gospel to New England Indians were rekindled by evangelists. In 1743 he enrolled in Eleazar Wheelock's private college preparatory school in Lebanon, Connecticut. During his four years there, he obtained a rudimentary education in English and theology. Occom's aspiration to attend college was thwarted by poor health and failing eyesight, but his progress as a scholar motivated Wheelock to realize his "Grand Design" and establish his famous Indian Charity School for the training of Indian missionaries in 1754.

The "Pious Mohegan," as Occom was sometimes called, devoted his life to the spiritual concerns of eastern Christian Indian communities. After leaving Wheelock's school he failed to find permanent employment until 1749, when he accepted a position as schoolmaster of the Montauk of Long Island, also serving as minister, scribe, and legal adviser until 1761. In 1751 he married Mary Fowler, a Montauk; they were said to have had ten children. In recognition of his missionizing efforts, he was examined by the Long Island Presbytery at Easthampton on 29 August 1759 and ordained the following day. Between 1761 and 1763 Occom undertook three missions to the Oneida of New York, but his endeavors there were halted by the outbreak of Pontiac's Rebellion in the spring of 1763. The Boston commissioners of the Society for the Propagation of the Gospel in New England, who had sponsored Occom's education, granted him a modest salary as minister to the Mohegan, the Niantic, and other Indian communities in New England late in 1764. That same year he was taken into service by the newly established Connecticut Board of Correspondents of the Scotch Society, headed by Wheelock.

Upon his return to Mohegan in 1764, Occom resumed a position of responsibility in the tribe, having been appointed one of its twelve councilors by sachem Ben Uncas II in 1742. Shortly after his return, he became embroiled in a long-standing dispute between a faction of the Mohegan and the Connecticut General Assembly over land ownership. Occom's taking sides with the Mohegan group demanding restitution in the so-called Mason Controversy met with the disapproval of colonial administrators and the Boston commissioners, who threatened to revoke his license if he continued to press the case. Occom was ultimately forced to withdraw from the issue and had to write a letter of apology to the commissioners for his "imprudent, rash, and offensive Conduct," but his relations with the commissioners were permanently impaired.

One of the highlights in Occom's career came in 1765 when he accompanied Rev. Nathaniel Whitaker on a trip to Great Britain to raise funds for Wheelock's Indian school. His presence in England and Scotland and the more than 300 sermons he delivered there created a public stir, resulting in the extraordinary collection of over £11,000 in donations. This success enabled Wheelock to move his school to New Hampshire where he ultimately expanded his "Grand Design" to found Dartmouth College in 1769.

Although Occom's public reputation was at its zenith after his return from England in 1768, his professional relations rapidly deteriorated. The Boston commissioners, who had opposed his journey to England because they suspected he might bring up the Mason Controversy there, refused to continue to employ him. Even his close relationship with Wheelock came to an abrupt end after Occom criticized the minister for supposedly failing to provide adequately for his family during his absence abroad and accused him of misappropriating the funds Occom had been instrumental in collecting for purposes other than training Indians. This charge proved well grounded as Wheelock abandoned his Indian missionary program and Dartmouth evolved into an institution for non-Indians. Occom also rejected Wheelock's plan to send him on a mission to the Tuscarora, preferring to remain among his own people. Wheelock interpreted Occom's progressive independence as arrogance resulting from the public attention he had been given in England. Although Occom still received some support from the Society in Scotland for Propagating Christian Knowledge, his subsequent missionary endeavors were beset with personal and, above all, financial problems.

In 1773 a disillusioned Occom and some of his relatives discussed plans for the establishment of Brothertown, an independent community of New England Christian Indians on a remote tract of land ceded to them by the Oneida in New York. However, the plan was interrupted temporarily by the American Revolution—during which Occom counseled his people to remain neutral—so he did not actually move with his family to Brothertown until 1789. Occom taught and ministered at Brothertown and the neighboring Indian community of New Stockbridge until his death.

Occom's writings include *A Sermon Preached at the Execution of Moses Paul, an Indian . . .* , which was published in 1772, the first monograph to be published by a North American Indian in English, and was printed in at least twenty editions, the last one by the Society for the Study of Native American Literature in 1982. Several of the hymns contained in his *Choice Collection of Hymns and Spiritual Songs* (1774) are believed to be of his creation and are still included in contemporary American hymnals. Occom also wrote an ethnographic study of the Montauk that was published posthumously in the *Massachusetts Historical Collections* (ser. 1, 10 (1809): 105–11), under the title "An Account of the Montauk Indians, on Long Island." Some of the herbal remedies recorded in his diary were reproduced in a pamphlet titled *Ten Indian Remedies* in 1954.

A harmonious relationship between Occom and his fellow American clergymen was essentially precluded by the latter's inability to surmount their overbearing, paternalistic attitude toward Indians. The fact that Wheelock and the missionary societies relegated him to a subordinate position in relation to white missionaries must have been a painful experience for a man of Occom's professional caliber. In England, where he was not in direct competition with white colleagues, his career was generally viewed more favorably, particularly by Rev. George Whitefield, one of the major exponents of the "Great Awakening." Among the Mohegan and the Montauk, however, Occom is still honored today as an elder who helped them survive through difficult times. On the recommendation of the Montauk Historical Society, "Samson Occom Day" was celebrated on Long Island in June of 1970.

• The bulk of Occom's writings, including letters, sermons, a diary from 6 Dec. 1743 to 6 Mar. 1790, and his autobiographical sketch, are in the Wheelock papers at the Dartmouth College Archives. Other writings, including a diary from 5 July to 6 Sept. 1787, are housed at the Connecticut Historical Society. Two detailed biographies are William DeLoss Love, *Samson Occom and the Christian Indians of New England* (1899), and Harold Blodgett, *Samson Occom* (1935). References to Occom can be found in Eleazar Wheelock, *A Plain and Faithful Narrative of the Original Design, Rise, Progress and Present State of the Indian Charity-School at Lebanon in Connecticut* (1763). Some of Occom's letters are reprinted in Leon B. Richardson, *An Indian Preacher in England* (1933). See also W. B. Sprague, "Samson Occom," *Annals of the American Pulpit* 3 (1858): 192–95; Belle M. Brain, "Samson Occom, the Famous Indian Preacher of New England," *Missionary Review of the World* 33 (1910): 913–19; Bernd C. Peyer, "Samson Occom: Mohegan Missionary and Writer of the Eighteenth Century," *American Indian Quarterly* 6 (1982): 208–17; and David Murray, "Christian Indians: Samson Occom and William Apes," chap. 2 in *Forked Tongues* (1991).

BERND C. PEYER

OCHS, Adolph Simon (12 Mar. 1858–8 Apr. 1935), publisher, was born in Cincinnati, Ohio, the son of Julius Ochs, a rabbi and unsuccessful dry-goods merchant, and Bertha Levy. Following the bankruptcy of Julius Ochs's dry-goods store, the family moved to Knoxville, Tennessee, in 1865. When Ochs was eleven he and his brother George became newsboys, rising at 3 A.M. each day to hand-fold copies of the *Knoxville Chronicle* for the fifty customers on their routes. Ochs's pay was $1.50 a week, most of which went to feed and house his near-destitute family.

Ochs continued on the newspaper route for two years until he moved to Providence, Rhode Island, as an apprentice in his uncle's grocery store. He proved unsuited to that trade and was soon back in Knoxville working as an office boy for the *Chronicle*. Because of his conscientious work habits, he was soon promoted to printer's devil and began a devotion to the physical appearance of the newspaper that became legendary in later years. If the paper was unreadable because of poor printing, Ochs maintained, the quality of the content was lost.

Though he became one of the most successful newspapermen of the twentieth century, Ochs never claimed to be a writer. A short stint as a reporter for the *Louisville Courier-Journal* led him back to Knoxville to serve as assistant to Franc M. Paul, the *Tribune*'s business manager. Impressed with Ochs's grim application to work, Paul invited the twenty-year-old to join him in Chattanooga as advertising manager for the struggling *Daily Dispatch*. The paper folded in just a few months, but Ochs remained to pay off the paper's debts by publishing Chattanooga's first city directory. Through contacts with the city's business leaders during production of the directory, Ochs was able to secure financing to purchase the *Chattanooga Times* in 1878. Ochs was soon able to turn a $1,500 debt into a $2,000 profit, and he quickly put another $10,000 into the paper. The *Times* owed allegiance to no political party and became a civic champion of the budding Chattanooga community.

In 1878 Ochs brought his still-impoverished family to Chattanooga; by 1882 he had installed them in a red-brick mansion. In 1883 he married Effie Miriam Wise of Cincinnati, daughter of the leader of the Reform Jewish movement in the United States. When their only surviving child, Iphigene, was born in 1892, life for Ochs seemed complete. However, he almost became a victim of his own success at promoting his adopted city. The newspaper had attracted new businesses and industries to the area, setting off a boom of land speculation in which Ochs himself invested. Only a mortgage on the *Times*'s handsome new building kept Ochs from bankruptcy when the 1893 crash came. With his cash flow stretched thin, Ochs went looking for a second paper to rejuvenate.

When negotiations fell through on the ailing *New York Mercury*, Ochs heard that the venerable *New York Times* might be for sale. Founded in 1851 by George Jones (1811–1891) and Henry Raymond, the *Times* had built its reputation on accurate Civil War reporting. The paper had begun to fade after Jones's death and in 1896 when Ochs came calling was nearly bankrupt. Using the connections he had made through his Chattanooga paper and mortgaging everything he had, Ochs came up with cash and investors to buy the *Times*. Circulation was sinking fast, but Ochs refused to lower the editorial standards of the paper to that of the "yellow press." Other newsmen laughed when Ochs introduced the "All the News That's Fit to Print" slogan, but the laughter stopped when they discovered he meant it. He refused to run comics in his paper, instituting instead a Sunday rotogravure section. He made book reviews a regular feature and gave letters to the editor a prominent place on his pages. More importantly, he refused $150,000 in advertising revenue from Tammany Hall.

The onslaught of the yellow press–inspired Spanish-American War threatened to wipe out the modest gains made by the *Times*. Ochs slashed the cost of his paper to match that of the penny press, and, as circulation rose (from 21,516 daily papers in 1896 to 82,106 daily papers in 1900), maintained that his success was "a vindication of the reader." By the beginning of World War I, the *New York Times* had become the "newspaper of record" for the English-speaking world, and Ochs was one of the country's leading citizens active in literary, charitable, and civic causes. His most notable civic activity, begun in 1911 and still active today, was the "Hundred Neediest Cases" charity, an appeal through the columns of the *Times* for New York's six most prominent charities. Ochs was an active member of the Tennessee Society in New York, and his $400,000 gift established the Julius and Bertha Ochs Memorial Temple in Chattanooga. Ochs chaired a $4 million fundraising campaign for Hebrew Union University in his native Cincinnati and was instrumental in founding the University of Chattanooga, now the University of Tennessee at Chattanooga.

As the prominence of the *Times* grew, Ochs was able to branch into other publishing ventures. As a member of the executive committee of the Associated Press, he was responsible for the wire service's expansion into Europe. His $500,000 investment resulted in the publication of the first *Dictionary of American Biography*. In 1901 he purchased the *Philadelphia Times*, merging it in 1902 with the *Public Ledger*, which he then sold in 1913 to Cyrus Curtis. For a time, Ochs also owned the *Nashville American*.

The anti-German backlash of World War I brought on bouts of depression that Ochs would battle the rest of his life. By 1925, he had begun to leave operation of the *Times* to his son-in-law, Arthur Hays Sulzberger. When Ochs died on a visit to Chattanooga, flags flew at half-mast, and the Associated Press wire fell silent worldwide for two minutes. Ochs's was a prototype "rags-to-riches" story. At age eleven, he was a paperboy delivering the *Knoxville Chronicle*; at fifteen he was a dropout from formal schooling. Five years later he was owner and publisher of his own newspaper in Chattanooga, and at thirty-eight he was the owner and publisher of the *New York Times*. Ochs took the once-respected but ailing *Times* and made it once again the newspaper for New York and the world, a newspaper for "intelligent, thoughtful people" in an age of screaming headlines and yellow journalism. A quarter-century later, the *New York Times* was not just a newspaper but an institution, one that had successfully separated news from opinion.

• The papers of Adolph Ochs are at the Hebrew Union University and the American Jewish Archives, Cincinnati, the University of Tennessee Library, and the Yale University Library. Biographies include G. W. Johnson, *An Honorable Titan* (1970) and *LXXV: Biography of Adolph S. Ochs at 75th Birthday* (1933). Histories of the *New York Times* include E. H. Davis, *History of the New York Times, 1851–1921* (1921); Meyer Berger, *The Story of the New York Times, 1851–1951* (1951); Gay Talese, *The Kingdom and the Power* (1969); and Harrison E. Salisbury, *Without Fear of Favor: The New York Times and Its Times* (1980). Other useful references are *A Memoir of Julius Ochs: An Autobiography* (no date), and W. M. Schuyler, ed., *The Life and Letters of George Washington Ochs-Oakes* (1933). A definitive obituary can be found in the *New York Times*, 9 Apr. 1935.

SUSAN G. BARNES

OCHS, George Washington. *See* Oakes, George Washington Ochs.

OCHS, Phil (19 Dec. 1940–8 Apr. 1976), folksinger and songwriter, was born Philip David Ochs in El Paso, Texas, the son of Jacob Ochs, a physician, and Gertrude Phinn. Ochs's earliest musical influences were country singers such as Hank Williams, Faron Young, and Johnny Cash, along with early rock and roll stars such as Buddy Holly and the Everly Brothers. In 1958 he attended the Ohio State University as a journalism major, where he became enamored of Cuban revolutionaries Fidel Castro and Che Guevara. After dropping out of school briefly to pursue a career as a singer, in the fall of 1959 he returned to Ohio State, where he became interested in the folk music of Woody Guthrie, Pete Seeger, and the Weavers while becoming more involved with leftist politics. There he honed his journalistic skills, writing both political commentaries and music criticism for the student newspaper, where he became known for his radical views. After being taught guitar by Jim Glover, his college roommate, Ochs joined with him to form a folk duo, the Singing Socialists, for which Ochs composed his first songs, often derived from newspaper accounts of current political stories. When the duo broke up, Ochs found some work as a soloist, performing mostly his own songs at local coffeehouses. During this period, he met the Chicago-based folksinger Bob Gibson, who encouraged Ochs to pursue his songwriting and with whom he coauthored some songs.

Angry at being passed over for the editorship of the student newspaper, Ochs left college in early 1962 before the completion of his senior year. Later that year he joined Glover in New York, writing a number of songs for the duo that Glover had formed with his fiancée. There, Ochs met Alice Skinner, whom he married in 1963. The couple had one child but separated within two years, remaining apart until Ochs's death.

Beginning in 1962 Ochs performed as a soloist in the Greenwich Village folk clubs and became a regular contributor and eventually an editor for *Broadside*, a new folk music journal. With Ochs's reputation as a performer rapidly growing on the East Coast, he was invited to perform at the prestigious Newport Folk Festival in 1963. Manager Albert Grossman, who had been instrumental in launching the career of Bob Dylan in 1961, became Ochs's manager, and his career began to blossom. He signed a recording contract with Elektra Records and in 1964 released his first of five albums for them, *All the News That's Fit to Sing*. Clearly influenced by Bob Dylan, the album contained a number of topical songs dealing with civil rights, the Cuban crisis, and the war with Vietnam, among other subjects. With this widely heralded first album and his next solo album, *I Ain't Marching Anymore*—which contained some of his most widely known and controversial songs, such as the title song, "Draft Dodger Rag," and "Here's to the State of Mississippi"—Ochs's reputation as one of the most important of the protest singers to emerge in Dylan's wake was confirmed. While his 1967 album for A&M Records, *Pleasures of the Harbor*, turned somewhat from the topical songs that had established his reputation toward more personal songs dealing with relationships, he retained his interest in liberal causes in the late 1960s and early 1970s, acting as an organizer and making appearances at political events that included a series of "War Is Over" rallies, a benefit concert for supporters of Chilean president Salvador Allende, and a widely publicized appearance at the student demonstrations during the 1968 Democratic National Convention in Chicago. Ochs also achieved notoriety as a witness for the defense in the trial of the "Chicago Eight" in the aftermath of the convention.

Following *Rehearsals for Retirement*, an autobiographical album released in 1969, Ochs, disappointed with his record sales and his inability to influence the larger youth audience, adopted Elvis Presley's stage persona for a series of appearances and recordings. Meeting a mixed reaction to his new image, Ochs returned to a more traditional posture. But by 1972 Ochs's career had slowed dramatically, and he began to lose confidence in his abilities as a songwriter and performer. In 1973 he visited Africa, where he was assaulted, with permanent damage done to his throat and vocal cords. Ochs suffered bouts of depression, and his public behavior became erratic. At age thirty-five he died by his own hand in Far Rockaway, New York, at the home of his sister.

At the height of his reputation in the mid-1960s, Ochs was widely celebrated as a socially committed folksinger whose songs combined directness of approach with colorful and insightful imagery. While his emphasis as a songwriter was on the meaning of the lyrics, his later songs were more distinctive in their melodic and harmonic content. He continues to be known as one of the foremost protest singers to emerge in the early 1960s.

• The most complete biographical source for Ochs is Marc Eliot, *Death of a Rebel* (1979). Important articles chronicling his career include Gary Friesen, "I Ain't Marching Anymore," *Sing Out!* 16 (1966): 3; Tom Nolan, "God Help the Troubadour: Pissing Away the Memories with Phil Ochs," *Rolling Stone*, 27 May 1971, p. 22; and Jeffrey Ressner, "Ochs by Penn," *Rolling Stone*, 1 Dec. 1988, p. 36. A more scholarly approach to Ochs's work is in Robert Niemi, "JFK as Jesus: The Politics of Myth in Phil Ochs' 'Crucifixion,'" *Journal of American Culture* 16 (1993): 35–40. An obituary is in the *New York Times*, 10 Apr. 1976.

TERENCE J. O'GRADY

OCHSNER, Alton (4 May 1896–24 Sept. 1981), surgeon, medical educator, and early crusader against cigarettes, was born Edward William Alton Ochsner in Kimball, South Dakota, the son of Edward Philip Ochsner, a retail merchant, and Clara Leda Shontz. The protégé of a distant cousin, Albert John Ochsner, Alton completed the two-year medical course offered by the University of South Dakota in 1918 and received his doctor of medicine degree from Washington University in St. Louis in 1920. He served his internship and a year of internal medicine residency at the Barnes Hospital in St. Louis before entering his residency in surgery under the tutelage of his cousin, chief surgeon at the Augustana Hospital in Chicago, the first Ochsner to establish an international reputation in medical circles. His mentor arranged for Alton to have a year of training at the Kantonsspital, University of Zurich, Switzerland, and another year at the Staedtisches Krankenhaus, University of Frankfurt, Frankfurt-am-Main, Germany. While in Switzerland Ochsner married Isabel Kathryn Lockwood of Chicago in 1923. He entered private practice at Chicago on 1 January 1925.

Ochsner accepted a 50 percent reduction in income in 1926 to join the medical faculty of the University of Wisconsin, because he wanted to do research and teach as well as perform surgery. At Wisconsin he developed a screening method for diagnosing the cold-weather lung disease bronchiectasis. His work attracted attention in the profession, and in 1927, at age thirty-one, he was appointed chairman of surgery at the Tulane University School of Medicine in New Orleans.

Although he often said he wanted to be remembered as a teacher, his skills as a surgeon and medical researcher were at least as important as his academic accomplishments in winning professional recognition for himself. Perhaps no other doctor ever has been elected to the presidencies of more national and international medical societies, including the American College of Surgeons, Society for Vascular Surgery, International Society of Surgery, American Cancer Society, and seven other similar associations.

Ochsner's estimate that he performed 20,000 surgical operations may be conservative. He flew to Buenos Aires to do a novocaine sympathetic ganglion block on Juan Peron, the Argentine president-dictator; to Panama City to save the life of former Panamanian president Tomas Gabriel Duque with a thyroid procedure; and to Paris to repair a hernia for motion picture actor Gary Cooper. Ochsner scored the first successful separation of pygopagus Siamese twins, the daughters of the mayor of Lafayette, Louisiana, who were joined at the sacrum, the bottom of the spine. In 1936 he became the first surgeon in the Deep South to excise a lung in treatment of cancer. According to one account it was the tenth pneumonectomy recorded in the world literature. His patient lived to survive Ochsner himself.

As early as his year of residence in Switzerland, Ochsner made his initial contribution in medical research. He and an associate, Karl Nather, reported a safe method of draining subphrenic abscesses in the area of the liver and right kidney. A seemingly tireless worker who could function on four hours of sleep, he found time to do experiments in the laboratory despite the demands of his operating and classroom duties. The result was nearly 600 published papers, many in collaboration with colleagues or his trainees.

Ochsner's interests were wide-ranging. He wrote about ulcers, skin cancers, varicose veins, blood clots, heart disease, and other subjects that aroused his interest in a career that spanned nearly fifty-five years. His coauthor in seventy-one papers, Michael E. DeBakey, is the only one of the scores of surgeons who trained under Ochsner who eventually equaled him in professional acclaim. Perhaps the most widely publicized surgeon in the last third of the twentieth century, DeBakey caught Ochsner's eye as a medical student at Tulane.

Ochsner moved to Tulane as the successor chairman to Rudolph Matas, a legendary figure in New Orleans medicine, the recipient of the first Distinguished Service Award of the American Medical Association. The new chairman quickly deemphasized textbooks in favor of journals, contending that much of the material in textbooks was already outdated. Drawing on techniques he had learned at Washington University from faculty members George Dock and Ernest Sachs, Ochsner inaugurated the so-called bull pen, an ordeal each senior student was required to undergo. Each student was given half an hour to examine a patient at the Charity Hospital of Louisiana; the students would then present their findings in an amphitheater crowded with students and faculty. Ochsner was depicted as a raging bull bent on goring the hapless toreador student, who was subjected to a barrage of searching questions. One student fainted under the onslaught. Medicine, Ochsner insisted, is a stressful profession, and the practitioner must learn to perform under pressure.

Ochsner quickly demonstrated his surgical prowess in the Charity Hospital, a sprawling institution to which the state provided funds for free care for impoverished citizens. It was Tulane's teaching hospital, where the faculty showed students how to treat patients. From Charity emanated legends about Ochsner's skills that started a demand for his surgical services that spread over the Deep South and into Latin America.

On 2 January 1942 four other surgeons at Tulane joined Ochsner in establishing the first full-scale group practice clinic in New Orleans, to the dismay of a community of solo practitioners who saw patients flocking to a facility where a variety of specialists offered treatment for a wide range of diseases. His associates chose the name Ochsner Clinic in recognition of the surgeon's reputation. Later the founders created the Alton Ochsner Medical Foundation, the largest independent (without university affiliation) health center in the South; it operates a hospital and conducts extensive medical research and educational programs.

The clinic never could have prospered had it depended on patient referrals from nonaffiliated New Orleans physicians and surgeons. Local anti-Ochsner sentiments eventually led to his dismissal from the chairmanship at Tulane after twenty-nine years. Joseph Merrick Jones, president of the university's board of administrators, masterminded the discharge on the claim that Ochsner was neglecting his responsibilities to the medical school in favor of his promotion of the clinic. Opposing the dismissal, the president of the university, Rufus C. Harris, said it was "one of the dirtiest deals I ever saw in my life." Harris insisted that Ochsner always did his job. Jones feared that Ochsner's membership on the faculty caused New Orleans doctors who were Tulane graduates to be less generous in their support of the medical school. Ochsner kept his appointment as clinical professor of surgery, and later supported what was an unsuccessful move to merge the school and the Ochsner Medical Institutions.

In his early years in New Orleans Ochsner survived a vengeful effort by Governor Huey P. Long to hurt him professionally. Through weird circumstances, there fell into Long's hands a copy of a letter Ochsner had written to a friend in which he criticized politicalization of the activities of Charity Hospital. In 1930 Long had Ochsner dismissed as chief visiting surgeon at the hospital, a post that he had inherited as chairman at Tulane. Since Ochsner's inability to demonstrate in the Charity operating rooms impeded his teaching opportunities, the Tulane board arranged for the chairman to operate in another hospital. After two years Ochsner was reinstated at Charity.

In 1939 Ochsner and DeBakey suggested in a published paper a connection between cigarette smoking and lung cancer. It marked the early stages of an obsession that occupied Ochsner for the rest of his life. In the years before the accumulation of scientific evidence of a link became overwhelming, his may have been the most authoritative voice in sounding a warning. He repeated his theme in countless speeches and in an even greater number of consultations with patients. Much of his late surgical activity was devoted to treating those who saw him after they were afflicted. He became in the 1950s and 1960s one of the world's busiest surgeons in the excision of whole lungs or lobes.

Ochsner received in 1948 the ultimate civic honor in New Orleans, ruling over the Mardi Gras celebration as the first medical doctor to be Rex, King of Carnival. He served as president of International House, a New Orleans institution for promoting world trade, and of the Metropolitan Crime Commission. He even found time to be active, as a conservative Republican, in political campaigns. An implacable foe of communism, he was president and later chairman of the Information Council of the Americas, which campaigned against Cuba's Fidel Castro and other Latin American Communists.

Ochsner and his wife were the parents of three medical doctor sons and an interior decorator daughter. The second son, John Lockwood Ochsner, succeeded his father as chairman of surgery at the Ochsner Clinic, and as a heart surgeon was widely recognized. After the death of Isabel Ochsner in 1968, he married Jane Kellogg Sturdy in 1970. Ochsner died in the Ochsner Foundation Hospital a few weeks after undergoing open heart surgery.

Ochsner lived long enough to enjoy the international prestige that he won for his accomplishments in surgery, research, and medical education. His income never approached the potential for a practitioner with his successes. "Anybody who gets rich in medicine either is doing too much or charging too much," he explained. His name is kept alive by the increasing activity of the institutions that bear it. A dozen years after his death 400 Ochsner doctors and 200 residents and interns were active in twelve facilities in South Louisiana. The annual number of doctor-patient encounters had reached 700,000.

• Ochsner's personal papers are housed in the Historic New Orleans Collection. For information on his life and career, see John Wilds, *Ochsner's: An Informal History of the South's Largest Private Medical Center* (1985), and Wilds and Ira Harkey, *Alton Ochsner: Surgeon of the South* (1990).

JOHN WILDS

OCKENGA, Harold John (6 July 1905–8 Feb. 1985), evangelical pastor and leader, was born in Chicago, Illinois, the son of Herman Ockenga, a Chicago Transit Authority employee, and Angie Tetzlaff. Ockenga was baptized in a Presbyterian church but regularly attended a Methodist congregation that he joined at age eleven. His Wesleyan upbringing and interest in becoming a minister informed his decision in 1923 to attend Taylor University, a Methodist institution in Indiana. After graduation in 1927 with a B.A. in English and history, Ockenga pursued theological training at Princeton Theological Seminary. The main attraction at the New Jersey institution was J. Gresham Machen, an accomplished New Testament scholar who had gained national notoriety during the modernist-fundamentalist controversy, thanks to his opposition to theological liberalism in the northern Presbyterian church. When Machen left Princeton in 1929 to found Westminster Seminary, Ockenga followed and in 1930 finished his theological education at the new Philadelphia school.

While at Westminster Ockenga came to know Clarence Macartney, a trustee at the seminary and a conservative Presbyterian minister who also combated theological modernism in the Presbyterian church. After pastoring two Methodist congregations in New Jersey, Ockenga accepted a call in 1931 to First Presbyterian Church, Pittsburgh, to be an assistant to Macartney. That same year Ockenga left his position under Macartney to become pastor of Point Breeze Presbyterian Church in suburban Pittsburgh. Concurrently, he enrolled part time at the University of Pittsburgh to pursue a Ph.D. in philosophy. While a student at Pittsburgh, Ockenga met Audrey Williamson, whom he married in 1935. They had three children.

Ockenga completed the Ph.D. program in 1939, writing his dissertation on the economic theories of liberalism and Marxism. But his later prominence stemmed chiefly from his gifts as a preacher and from his abilities as an organizer. Though Ockenga sympathized with the fundamentalists, he steered clear of ecclesiastical controversy, preferring the course of cooperation. His acceptance in 1936 of a call to Boston's Park Street Church, a traditionally conservative Congregationalist congregation in the heart of the city, reinforced Ockenga's mediating proclivities. Rather than advocating separation from the mainline denomination as many fundamentalists did, Ockenga chose to work alongside the existing structures of Protestantism. Under his leadership Park Street Church grew in size, programs blossomed, and contributions increased. Ockenga also gained a regional audience, with two of Boston's most powerful radio stations broadcasting the church's services each Sunday.

Ockenga's talents soon thrust him into the national spotlight. In 1929 J. Elwin Wright had founded the New England Fellowship, a regional association of conservative Protestants whose purpose was to foster greater cooperation and unity among area churches. Ockenga participated in and advocated the fellowship. Eventually it became the model for a national organization of conservatives. In 1942 at a meeting in St. Louis, the National Association of Evangelicals (NAE) was founded, and Ockenga became its first president, an office he held until 1944. While designed to foster unity and cooperation among conservatives nationwide, the NAE was also a rival to the Federal Council of Churches (now the National Council of Churches). Conservatives like Ockenga in mainline denominations sensed that they had no voice in the power structures of the Protestant establishment. The NAE was formed to fill that vacuum. Ockenga's outspoken opposition to communism, Roman Catholicism, and secularism in American life became important themes of the NAE's early identity, although the association rendered other less prominent but nonetheless influential services—from publishing Sunday School literature to posting conservative ministers as chaplains in the military.

Ockenga increased his visibility within the evangelical world when he accepted an invitation in 1947 to become the founding president of Fuller Theological Seminary in Pasadena, California. He wanted to retain his pastorate in Boston and thus served as president in absentia of Fuller from 1947 to 1954 and again from 1960 to 1963. Ockenga was largely responsible for charting the new seminary's course, while Harold Lindsell (the registrar) and the faculty managed the day-to-day operations. In his 1947 convocation address to the first thirty-nine seminarians at the opening of Fuller he summarized the seminary's aim and purpose as the rescue of western civilization generally and American culture specifically from barbarism and secularism by recovering the heritage of the Protestant Reformation, a heritage he thought responsible for shaping modern western society and to which evangelicals were the rightful heirs. It was in this same address, titled "The Challenge to the Christian Culture of the West," that Ockenga coined the phrase "new evangelicalism." This evangelicalism resembled fundamentalism in its conservative theological convictions. But unlike sectarian Protestants, who withdrew from the mainline churches and repudiated the secularism of the United States, new evangelicals believed it was their duty to develop a positive agenda for American culture and reestablish the Christian civilization that had once made the nation a haven for religious freedom and economic opportunity.

Ockenga provided valuable leadership to the new evangelical movement in various ways. His prolonged efforts to launch a revival in New England were finally realized in 1950 when he invited the young evangelist Billy Graham to hold a series of evangelistic meetings at Park Street Church. Graham's success in Boston—attendance quickly outran the church's facilities and the services were moved to the Boston Garden—led to an evangelistic crusade throughout New England featuring both Ockenga and Graham. Ockenga's partnership with Graham was crucial to the founding of *Christianity Today*, still the best-known evangelical publication in the United States. Graham established the magazine in 1956 as a voice for the new evangelical movement, and Ockenga served as chairman of *Christianity Today*'s board for its first twenty-five years.

Even after Ockenga retired as minister of Park Street in 1969, he continued to provide leadership and counsel to evangelicals in his role as president of Gordon College and Divinity School, located outside Boston. During his tenure at Gordon from 1969 to 1979 Ockenga presided over the merger of Gordon Divinity School and Conwell School of Theology (Philadelphia). He died at his home in suburban Boston. While many in New England remembered him as a great preacher and pastor, Ockenga left his most lasting mark as a successful organizer and leader of the institutions that gave conservative evangelical Protestants national identity and recognition.

• The bulk of Ockenga's papers, which have yet to be catalogued, are housed at Gordon-Conwell Theological Seminary, South Hamilton, Mass. Good guides to the themes and style of Ockenga's sermons may be found in many collections of sermons such as *These Religious Affections* (1937), *Everyone That Believeth* (1942), *Our Evangelical Faith* (1946), and *The Church in God* (1956). For assessments of Ockenga and his place in the post–World War II resurgence of conservative Protestantism, see George M. Marsden, *Reforming Fundamentalism: Fuller Seminary and the New Evangelicalism* (1987); Joel A. Carpenter, "Introduction," *Two Reformers of Fundamentalism* (1988); and Carpenter, "The Fundamentalist Leaven and the Rise of an Evangelical United Front," in *The Evangelical Tradition in America*, ed. Leonard I. Sweet (1984), pp. 257–88. Harold Lindsell, *Park Street Prophet* (1951), offers a hagiographical account of Ockenga's early career. H. Crosby Englizian, *Brimstone Corner* (1968), presents a positive perspective on Ockenga's efforts as pastor at Park Street Church. An obituary is in *Christianity Today* 29 (15 Mar. 1985).

D. G. HART

O'CONNELL, Denis (28 Jan. 1849–1 Jan. 1927), Roman Catholic bishop, was born in Donoughmore, County Cork, Ireland, the son of Michael O'Connell and Bridget O'Connell (also her maiden name), farmers. As an infant he moved with his family to Charleston, South Carolina, where three uncles and an aunt served as missionaries. The family relocated to Columbia in the mid-1850s and to Fort Mill in 1865. Three years later O'Connell enrolled in St. Charles College in Ellicott City, Maryland, to study for the priesthood. While there he met James Gibbons, the bishop of the newly created diocese of North Carolina, who became his lifelong mentor. In 1871 O'Connell was assigned to Gibbons's diocese and then immediately sent to Rome, Italy, to study at the Urban College of Propaganda. Six years later he received his doctorate in sacred theology and was ordained.

In 1877 O'Connell rejoined Gibbons, by now the bishop of Richmond, Virginia, and was made assistant pastor of St. Peter's, the diocesan cathedral. Shortly thereafter he returned to Rome, where he represented his mentor during the proceedings by which Gibbons was fully empowered to function as the archbishop of Baltimore. After serving in various positions under John J. Keane, Gibbons's replacement in Richmond, O'Connell in 1883 transferred to Baltimore, where he helped arrange the third plenary council of U.S. bishops called by Pope Leo XIII to settle several questions regarding canon law peculiar to the church in the United States. O'Connell served as a secretary during the council and as a member of the committee that went to Rome to gain the pope's formal approval for the council's decrees.

In 1885, two years before he was made a monsignor, O'Connell became rector of the North American College, which was essentially a residence hall for American seminarians studying in Rome. Over the next ten years he expanded its facilities and services while increasing the number of residents. This position placed him in close contact with all of the U.S. bishops, who called upon him to serve as their unofficial ambassador to the Vatican. As such he was on intimate terms with high-ranking church officials, including the pope. He used this position to gain Vatican support for the agenda of the more liberal bishops, such as Gibbons, whom he again represented during Gibbons's elevation to cardinal in 1886; Keane; and John Ireland, a close friend of Gibbons whose candidacy for archbishop of St. Paul, Minnesota, O'Connell successfully promoted. These prelates intended to strengthen Roman Catholicism in the United States by ridding it of all ethnic vestiges, allying it with the causes of the people instead of those of the state, and governing it without excessive Vatican interference. They were opposed by the conservative bishops on three main issues: church recognition for the Knights of Labor, a working-class organization, which the conservatives opposed because the Knights required members to take a secret oath; the prohibition of ethnic parishes, which the liberals believed would "Americanize" immigrants while the conservatives espoused the creation of new ethnic parishes as a means of ensuring immigrant loyalty to the Roman hierarchy; and negotiation with local school boards to pay the salaries of parochial school teachers while the parishes paid to build, maintain, and operate parochial schools, a development conservatives condemned because it relinquished control of church schools to secular authorities.

In 1895 the conservatives gained ascendency over the liberals and ousted O'Connell from the college because of his partisan support for the liberal cause. He remained in Rome for the next eight years as rector of Gibbons's titular church of Santa Maria in Trastevere and continued to serve as the liberal bishops' agent. Like Ireland and Keane, O'Connell was one of the foremost proponents of Americanism, which in his words meant "nothing else than that loyal devotion that Catholics in America bear to the principles on which their government is founded, and their conscientious conviction that these principles afford Catholics favorable opportunities for promoting the glory of

God" (Fogarty, p. 326). In an address before the International Catholic Scientific Congress in Fribourg, Switzerland, in 1897, he rejoiced that the separation of church and state in the United States allowed American Catholics to play a more active role in society, a role that was not possible in the stultifying atmosphere of church-state entanglement that permeated the Old World. Although he did not offer this role as a new model for the global church as Ireland did, he clearly saw it in these terms, and his address contributed to a growing debate in France, where liberal churchmen advocated the separation of church and state. The debate was squelched in 1899 when Leo, while applauding the patriotism and civic activities of American Catholics, condemned certain aspects of Americanism, such as its implied preference for divine inspiration over authority, its willingness to play down those dogmas that served as major stumbling blocks for Protestants who might otherwise convert, and its belief that the church could reshape society by adapting itself to modern culture.

In 1903 O'Connell was appointed rector of the Catholic University of America in Washington, D.C. When self-serving investments made by the school's lay treasurer resulted in the loss of almost two-thirds of the university's endowment fund the next year, O'Connell succeeded in implementing an annual collection in every Catholic church in the United States for the university's benefit. The success of the collection permitted the school to implement an undergraduate curriculum, bring the graduate curriculum up to the standards adhered to by secular universities, and enhance the credentials of the faculty. Leo's qualified condemnation of Americanism apparently induced O'Connell to retreat into bureaucracy and authoritarianism, because he refused to share power with the board of trustees or to consult with the faculty on a constructive basis. Consequently, he found himself without the much-needed support of the board and faculty during the financial crisis.

In 1908 O'Connell was made the auxiliary bishop of San Francisco, California, but he did not leave the university until the completion of the fall term. In 1912 he returned to the diocese of Richmond as bishop and served as a suffragan of Gibbons. He retired in 1926 and died in Richmond.

• O'Connell's papers are in the archives of the diocese of Richmond. A biography is Gerald P. Fogarty, *The Vatican and the Americanist Crisis: Denis J. O'Connell, American Agent in Rome, 1885–1903* (1974). An obituary is in the *New York Times*, 2 Jan. 1927.

CHARLES W. CAREY, JR.

O'CONNELL, Mary. *See* Anthony.

O'CONNELL, William Henry (8 Dec. 1859–22 Apr. 1944), Roman Catholic archbishop of Boston, was born in Lowell, Massachusetts, the youngest of the eleven children of John O'Connell, a textile mill laborer, and Bridget Farrelly. After an education in the public schools and a brief, homesick period at a Maryland seminary, he enrolled in Boston College, graduating in 1881. He then pursued clerical studies in Rome and was ordained to the priesthood in 1884. Returning home, he served in parishes in and around Boston, acquiring a reputation as a preacher.

His first significant advancement came in 1895 when he was appointed rector of his old seminary, the American College in Rome. The experience brought him to the attention of powerful Vatican officials, and it cultivated in him a lifelong spirit known as *Romanità*—"Roman-ness." At the time, the American church was divided between those who sought a distinctive national expression of Catholicism ("Americanists") and those who wanted a more complete reliance on the newly resurgent papacy ("ultramontanes"). O'Connell placed himself decidedly in the ultramontane camp, eagerly becoming an agent for the expansion of papal authority and influence within the church in the United States.

As a reward for his loyalty, O'Connell was made bishop of Portland, Maine, in 1901. Management of the affairs of this diocese, which was large in territory but small in population, demanded some effort, but most of O'Connell's time in Maine was spent campaigning for promotion to the more important archdiocese of Boston. Each of the two church factions sought to have one of its own chosen for this post, and O'Connell emerged early as the candidate who "stood for Rome." In January 1906, while O'Connell was in Rome after completing a diplomatic mission to Japan for the Vatican, he was designated coadjutor bishop, succeeding John J. Williams as Boston's archbishop in August 1907. He was elevated to the rank of cardinal in 1911, the first Bostonian and only the third American to have achieved that honor.

During his thirty-seven years as archbishop, O'Connell established a new, aggressive role for American Catholic churchmen. A large and imposing man, he rebuffed any slight against the church or its people, while simultaneously asserting Catholicism's vigor in defining and upholding moral standards. In his view, Catholics had taken over the responsibility, formerly entrusted to the Yankee Protestant elite, of protecting society and its values. "The Puritan has passed," he said in 1908, "the Catholic remains." He became a visible public figure, influential beyond his own church, with an impact that was not narrowly denominational but broadly moral. His relations with the rising group of local Irish politicians—including James M. Curley, John F. Fitzgerald, and David I. Walsh—were often stormy, as he competed with them for influence in the Catholic community. Even so, O'Connell had considerable political power. In 1924, for example, he helped defeat a referendum restricting child labor, believing the measure transferred to the state authority that properly resided with the church and the family.

Inside the church, O'Connell sought to expand the powers of his office, centralizing many archdiocesan activities. His hopes for wider influence in church affairs, however, never materialized. His aggressive personality and the polarizing circumstances under which he had been appointed archbishop ostracized him from other bishops. Worse, O'Connell was embarrassed by a scandal involving his own nephew, a priest and administrator in the Boston archdiocese who was secretly married and embezzling money from the church. O'Connell's reluctance to oust the nephew until forced by the Vatican damaged his reputation and prevented him from assuming the position of king-maker in the American church. The scandal never became public, but it was common knowledge among churchmen, and his influence with them ended.

Despite this troubled private life, O'Connell helped define a style for early twentieth-century American Catholicism characterized by confidence and self-assertion. Believing religion to be constantly at war with the modern world, O'Connell saw the church as an authoritative stronghold with both the right and the duty to restate unchanging values. In a world of turmoil and doubt, he proposed a clear, straightforward answer. Faith "settles our problems," he said in 1929; truth, articulated definitively by the church, was "so simple." (*Sermons and Addresses* 10:25) Religious styles have since changed, but for American Catholics of his era, emerging from poverty and nativist opposition into middle-class respectability, O'Connell provided a self-assured way of looking at themselves. He died at his residence in Brighton, a neighborhood that is part of the city of Boston.

• O'Connell's extensive papers, both personal and official, are preserved in the archives of the Archdiocese of Boston. He also left a substantial body of published writings, including an autobiography, *Recollections of Seventy Years* (1934), and eleven volumes of *Sermons and Addresses* (1911–1938). His published *Letters* (1915) have been demonstrated to be later falsifications rather than contemporary accounts. O'Connell's life and career are treated favorably and in detail in Robert Howard Lord et al., *History of the Archdiocese of Boston*, vol. 3 (1944), and Dorothy G. Wayman, *Cardinal O'Connell of Boston* (1955). The most complete recent treatment is James M. O'Toole, *Militant and Triumphant: William Henry O'Connell and the Catholic Church in Boston, 1859–1944* (1992).

JAMES M. O'TOOLE

O'CONNOR, Edwin Greene (29 July 1918–23 Mar. 1968), writer, was born in Providence, Rhode Island, the son of second-generation Irish Americans John Vincent O'Connor, a doctor, and Mary Greene. After attending public elementary schools and a Catholic high school (LaSalle Academy), O'Connor went to the University of Notre Dame. There, he met some Irish-American students whose families were involved in Chicago politics and began to develop an interest in his own ethnic identity, as well as the ambition to be a writer. He graduated in 1939 with a degree in literature and experience as a radio broadcaster. While honing his writing skills, he earned a living as a radio announcer in Providence, Palm Beach, Buffalo, and Hartford until he enlisted in the Coast Guard in 1942.

The most significant part of his military service occurred between 1943 and 1945, when he worked as a public information officer in Boston with Louis J. Brems, who had once been Boston's official greeter; O'Connor became fascinated by the city and remained there after the war.

In 1946 O'Connor stopped working in radio, determined to earn his living exclusively as a writer. He managed to get by doing freelance work and some teaching, but was not able to publish much fiction. In September 1947 the *Atlantic Monthly* printed O'Connor's short story "The Gentle, Perfect Knight" and, in April 1950, published a second story, "The Inner Self." That fall the *Yale Review* published another, "Parish Reunion." These stories are significant primarily because they mark the beginning of his career in fiction, for while O'Connor and the *Atlantic Monthly* had begun what would become a long relationship, most of the works he published in the magazine were essays. After two unsuccessful attempts to write novels during the 1940s (*Anthony Cantwell* and *Luther Sudworth*), O'Connor completed and published *The Oracle*, a satire about a radio commentator, in 1951. The book did not earn much critical or popular attention.

About a year later, O'Connor finished the manuscript of a novel entitled *A Young Man of Promise* and promptly abandoned the project. Around this time, he made his first visit to Ireland and turned to what would become his central literary preoccupation: chronicling the state of the Irish-American community as it became acculturated in the United States. He said he wanted "to do for the Irish in America what Faulkner did for the South" (quoted in Schlesinger, p. 11). Irish-American politics was his first subject, resulting in his most successful book up to that point, *The Last Hurrah*, which won the Atlantic Prize in 1955 and was published in February 1956. The protagonist of the novel, Mayor Frank Skeffington, is the political boss of an eastern city; the parallels between Skeffington and Boston's James Michael Curley are striking enough that many critics suggested the work was a roman à clef; indeed, when Curley read the book, he "referred it to his attorneys and was contemplating legal action" (Eliot, p. 28). Despite such a reaction, O'Connor claimed the book was not based on Curley's life. In addition to garnering critical attention, *The Last Hurrah* was welcomed by general readers. In less than a year, the hardback went through fifteen printings, making it the number two bestseller of the year; paperback sales ultimately exceeded a million copies; and Reader's Digest Condensed Books, the Book-of-the-Month Club, and other, smaller book clubs selected the novel for reprinting. In 1958 it was made into a movie, starring Spencer Tracy.

In 1957 O'Connor published a book for children entitled *Benjy: A Ferocious Fairy Tale*. Soon after, he began working on his next novel, which highlights the importance of religion to Irish Americans and examines the generation gap in an Irish-American context. The protagonist of *The Edge of Sadness* (1961), Father Hugh Kennedy, was praised by some critics as "one of the few realistic portrayals of a priest in American fiction" (Banks, p. 16). The priest's doubts about his vocation and his concerns with wavering faith epitomize the type of conflicts that were particularly acute for Irish-American Catholics at that time, and the sharp delineation of the evolving Irish-American character in the three generations of the Carmody family illustrates analogous social changes. The book was awarded the Pulitzer Prize in 1962.

In 1962 O'Connor married Veniette Caswell Weil, a divorced woman with a son; they had no children together. Although Roger Dooley criticized O'Connor's next novel, *I Was Dancing* (1964), in a *Saturday Review* article titled "The Womanless World of Edwin O'Connor" (21 Mar. 1964), it would be more accurate to say that women were being gradually introduced into O'Connor's fictional world—perhaps in part due to his own happy marriage. *I Was Dancing*, originally a play, concerns retired vaudevillian Daniel Considine, who does not want his son, Tom, to put him in a nursing home. Although Daniel is the central character, the son has a wife, Ellen, and Daniel has a sister, Delia. O'Connor's last published novel, *All in the Family* (1966), combines an attention to politics with a concern for family and focuses again on intergenerational conflict. Implicit is O'Connor's concern that the assimilationist impulse of third generation Irish Americans is pulling them away from the values and traditions of their parents and their heritage.

In his last two years, O'Connor wrote another play, *A Traveler from Brazil*, which he did not have the opportunity to polish; began two novels, *The Cardinal* and *The Boy*; and planned two more novels that he never started writing. The novel fragments—along with interesting comments by people who knew O'Connor—were published in *The Best and the Last of Edwin O'Connor* (1970), edited by Arthur M. Schlesinger, Jr. O'Connor died in Boston of a cerebral hemorrhage. Although he earned critical and popular recognition in his own time, this acclaim has not endured.

• The *Atlantic Monthly* and Little, Brown both have files on O'Connor. Robert David Banks, "The Irish-American Experience in the Fiction of Edwin O'Connor" (Ph.D. diss., Oklahoma State Univ., 1983), combines biographical information with critical readings of several of O'Connor's novels. Hugh Rank, *Edwin O'Connor* (1974), is a useful guide to his work. See also Thomas H. Eliot, "Robin Hood in Boston," *New Republic*, Mar. 1956, p. 28, and Richard A. Betts, "The 'Blackness of life': The Function of Edwin O'Connor's Comedy," *MELUS: Society for the Study of Multi-Ethnic Literature in the United States* 8, no. 1 (1981): 15–26. An obituary is in the *New York Times*, 24 Mar. 1968.

MARGOT ANNE KELLEY

O'CONNOR, Flannery (25 Mar. 1925–3 Aug. 1964), short-story writer and novelist, was born Mary Flannery O'Connor in Savannah, Georgia, the daughter of Edward Francis O'Connor, Jr., a real estate agent, and Regina Cline. In 1938 the family moved to Milledgeville, Georgia, which was to become the center of Flannery O'Connor's literary career. Edward O'Connor, who had been ill for some time, died of lupus erythematosus in 1941.

Flannery O'Connor (Mary was eventually dropped from her name) was brought up a Roman Catholic, which proved to have a crucial influence on her writing. She attended Peabody High School from 1938 to 1942 and received a bachelor's degree from Georgia State College for Women (now Georgia College) in June 1945. She took cartooning as seriously as writing during this period.

In the autumn of 1945 she left for the University of Iowa, scholarship in hand. After admission to Paul Engle's celebrated Writers' Workshop she began the apprenticeship of writing short stories, which determined the contours of the remainder of her life. The years at Iowa, which culminated in her receiving the master of fine arts degree in June 1947, began a five-year period away from her native Georgia. She spent parts of 1948 and 1949 at Yaddo, the artists' colony in upstate New York, then lived briefly in New York City before settling at Sally and Robert Fitzgerald's home in Ridgefield, Connecticut.

Ill health forced her return south in December 1950; after being hospitalized and treated for lupus, O'Connor and her mother retired to a farm outside Milledgeville, poetically named "Andalusia." Here she spent the remainder of her life, crafting her stories and novels. This sedentary existence permitted occasional lecture tours and visits and even a trip to Lourdes and Rome in the spring of 1958. She spoke with grim finality in a letter of 1 June of that year to the poet Elizabeth Bishop: "We went to Europe and I lived through it but my capacity for staying at home has now been perfected, sealed & is going to last me the rest of my life" (*The Habit of Being* [1979], p. 285).

O'Connor published "The Geranium" (the title story of her master's thesis at Iowa) in the summer 1946 *Accent*. This began a succession of appearances in distinguished quarterlies and monthlies such as *Sewanee Review*, *Kenyon Review*, *Partisan Review*, *Mademoiselle*, and *Harper's Bazaar*, which continued for the rest of her life. One other story in her master's thesis was revised to become the first chapter of her first novel, *Wise Blood*, published in 1952. This novel was some five years on the drawing board before O'Connor was willing to release it to Harcourt, Brace. She was committed to draft after draft of her stories and novels, often following circuitous routes on the way to final versions.

The hero of *Wise Blood*, Hazel Motes, whom O'Connor was to call "a Christian *malgré lui*" in her author's note to the 1962 second edition of the novel, sets the tone for the religiously displaced types that haunt her fiction. These unlikely creatures preach strange gospels, engage in rituals of drowning-baptism and "prayer healing" (burying morbid newspaper stories), have visions near "hog pens" and before figures of "artificial Negroes," and have heads of Byzantine Christs tattooed on their backs. Despite O'Connor's Roman Catholic upbringing and her ongoing commitment to its teachings, her characters tend mainly to be fundamentalist Protestants. These were the religious types she observed most frequently during her years in and around Milledgeville.

O'Connor brought out her first collection of short stories, *A Good Man Is Hard to Find*, in 1955. These ten stories reaffirm the fictional and religious agendas she advanced in *Wise Blood*; several won O. Henry awards and appeared in Martha Foley's annual *The Best American Short Stories*—as did a number of her later stories. Many O'Connor critics felt that her talents were more evident in the shorter form than in the novel; a typical response was Robert Drake's in his *Flannery O'Connor: A Critical Essay* (1966): "Her real *forte* is the short story."

Her second novel, *The Violent Bear It Away*, appeared in 1960. Its hero, Francis Marion Tarwater, goes through a typically American ritual of initiation, in the manner of Huckleberry Finn or William Faulkner's Ike McCaslin; the difference is that Tarwater finally has a vision of a burning bush and prepares for the unlikely career of a prophet. He is the most realized of those O'Connor characters capable of redemption.

O'Connor's final years were spent writing and revising the nine stories that comprise the posthumous collection *Everything That Rises Must Converge* (1965). She had also started a third novel, *Why Do the Heathen Rage?* (an excerpt of which appeared in the July 1963 *Esquire*), which remained unfinished at her death in Milledgeville.

The language of her fiction, whether she was writing novels or short stories, never markedly changed; it seemed to derive as much from an oral as from a written tradition. She used third-person discourse as unfailingly as Henry James (1843–1916) did. James was certainly one of two guides she had in respect to craft and technique; the other was Gustave Flaubert.

Few writers who left such a sparse literary inheritance—two novels and two collections of stories—have been the subject of so much postmortem editorial scrutiny. Sally and Robert Fitzgerald's collection of O'Connor's nonfiction prose, *Mystery and Manners*, appeared in 1969. Two years later all thirty-one of her stories, including early versions of chapters of *Wise Blood* and *The Violent Bear It Away* and the six stories that made up her master's thesis at Iowa, were made available as *The Complete Stories of Flannery O'Connor*. A volume of letters, edited by Sally Fitzgerald, appeared as *The Habit of Being* in 1979. Leo J. Zuber and Carter W. Martin brought together a less distinguished part of her oeuvre as *The Presence of Grace and Other Book Reviews by Flannery O'Connor* in 1983. Finally, in 1986, C. Ralph Stephens edited *The Correspondence of Flannery O'Connor and the Brainard Cheneys*. These posthumous volumes join the two collections of stories and the two novels to complete the canon of a writer who lived only thirty-nine years.

O'Connor's work has been translated into such languages as Czech, Dutch, French, German, Greek, Hungarian, Italian, Japanese, Norwegian, Polish, Spanish, and Swedish. Books and articles about her work continue to accumulate at an astonishing rate, especially given her modest output. The eulogies following her death have given way, on occasion, to some serious questionings of her habits of art; yet her intricately patterned fiction continues to attract critics who care about technique and craft. One of the most knowing comments about her career was made by writer Caroline Gordon, who was her close friend and mentor: "At any rate, she is already a rare phenomenon: a Catholic novelist with a real dramatic sense, one who relies more on her technique than her piety." Her place in American literature is probably next to another writer who became her friend, Katherine Anne Porter.

• The Ina Dillard Russell Library at Georgia College, Milledgeville, houses O'Connor's manuscripts; they are systematically described in Stephen G. Driggers and Robert J. Dunn, with Sarah Gordon, *The Manuscripts of Flannery O'Connor at Georgia College* (1989). The Russell Library also contains her collection of books, which numbers 712 items; Arthur F. Kinney went through them with scrupulous care and produced *Flannery O'Connor's Library: Resources of Being* (1985). The most complete source for biographical information is Sally Fitzgerald's "Chronology" in the Library of America, *Flannery O'Connor: Collected Works* (1988). For a collection of interviews, see Rosemary M. Magee, *Conversations with Flannery O'Connor* (1987). David Farmer's *Flannery O'Connor: A Descriptive Bibliography* (1981) "includes work published both in her lifetime and posthumously—from the early contributions to journals at Georgia State College for Women, through the stories and books that formed the bulk of the canon, to *The Habit of Being* of 1979" (p. xv). For an annotated bibliography of secondary material, see Robert E. Golden and Mary C. Sullivan, *Flannery O'Connor and Caroline Gordon: A Reference Guide* (1977).

Among the many critical books on O'Connor, which seem to average at least two a year since the mid-1970s, the following are the most useful: Martha Stephens, *The Question of Flannery O'Connor* (1973); Robert Coles, *Flannery O'Connor's South* (1980); and Frederick Asals, *Flannery O'Connor: The Imagination of Extremity* (1982). Two collections of essays that cover virtually all aspects of her career are Melvin J. Friedman and Lewis A. Lawson, eds., *The Added Dimension: The Art and Mind of Flannery O'Connor* (1966; 2d ed. 1977); and Melvin J. Friedman and Beverly Lyon Clark, eds., *Critical Essays on Flannery O'Connor* (1985). *Esprit: Journal of Thought and Opinion* (Univ. of Scranton) devoted its entire Winter 1964 number to Flannery O'Connor. Along with other material, it contains eulogies by such writers as Saul Bellow, Elizabeth Bishop, Kay Boyle, Caroline Gordon, and Robert Lowell.

MELVIN J. FRIEDMAN

O'CONNOR, Jessie Lloyd (14 Feb. 1904–24 Dec. 1988), journalist and social activist, was born in Winnetka, Illinois, the daughter of William Bross Lloyd, a writer and socialist, and Lola Maverick, a pacifist and founder of the U.S. section of the Women's International League for Peace and Freedom (WILPF). Jessie's grandfather was Henry Demarest Lloyd, muckraking journalist and author of *Wealth against Commonwealth* (1894), an exposé of Standard Oil. Her family's strong tradition of democratic socialism provided the foundation of a political education that was augmented by a constant stream of visiting radicals and reformers, including Jane Addams, Rosika Schwimmer, and John Reed. In 1915 she accompanied her mother to Europe aboard Henry Ford's Peace Ship.

After earning an A.B. in economics from Smith College in 1925, Lloyd visited London, where she witnessed a confrontation between police and strikers during the British General Strike. Inaccurate news reports of the incident confirmed her parents' contention that mainstream press accounts of the poor were untrustworthy. A short stint working in a Paris factory reinforced her desire to provide a corrective to slanted news coverage by reporting events herself.

Lloyd contributed stories to newspapers in the United States while working as a correspondent for the *Daily Herald* (London) in Geneva (1926) and Moscow (1926–1928). From Moscow she also sent stories to the Federated Press, a labor wire service in the United States.

From 1929 to 1935 Lloyd worked as a reporter for the Federated Press in the United States and was sent to Gastonia, North Carolina, in 1929 to cover the National Textile Workers Union's attempt to organize the Loray mill. She wrote a pamphlet on the strike, *Gastonia: A Graphic Chapter in Southern Organization* (1930).

Early in the depression Lloyd wrote stories about the unemployed in New York City. Her exposure to the plight of the jobless under capitalism and the activities of the Communist party on their behalf fostered in her an appreciation for Communists' courage and dedication. Over time she became disenchanted with the party, finding it doctrinaire and fraught with internecine battles, yet she never became part of the anticommunist camp within the American left. In 1957 she wrote of her accord with communist aims of "world peace, race brotherhood, [and] equality for women" but added that she "could not favor dictatorship of the proletariat or trust *anybody* with power, without guarantees of civil liberties for opponents."

In 1930 Jessie Lloyd married Harvey O'Connor, an editor for the Federated Press and a former logger, seaman, and member of the International Workers of the World. The O'Connors decided to open a bureau of the Federated Press in Pittsburgh, where the labor movement, in attempting to organize the steel mills and mining companies, was fighting its most bitter struggle. First they took a six-month trip to the Caribbean and Mexico, filing stories from each region they visited. The trip solidified a fruitful working relationship that would continue throughout the O'Connors' lives.

In 1931 the Federated Press sent Jessie O'Connor to replace a correspondent who had been shot while covering the coal miners' strike in Harlan County, Kentucky. Despite regular threats, she turned interviews with miners, their families, and members of the community into evocative stories carried in newspapers throughout the country. Her investigation of the murder of two men conducting a soup kitchen for the strikers led her to conclude in the O'Connors' 1987 memoir: "Class struggle is not something I want to preach. It is something that happens to people who try to resist or improve intolerable conditions."

After returning to Pittsburgh, O'Connor continued working for the Federated Press and helped revitalize the local ACLU. She also helped research and edit the first in a series of Harvey's exposés of American capitalism, *Mellon's Millions* (1933), a role she played for his subsequent books.

The O'Connors went to Moscow in 1932 to work for the English-language *Moscow Daily News*, but Jessie was troubled by the changes in Russia since 1928 and was unhappy translating dull stories of "socialist triumphs in new paper mills and state farms." When libel litigation over *Mellon's Millions* was resolved in 1933, the O'Connors returned to Pittsburgh where workers, guaranteed the right to organize by the National Recovery Act, were forming union locals throughout the steel industry. While reporting for the Federated Press from 1933 to 1935, O'Connor carried messages between organizers. During the Ambridge strike she narrowly escaped arrest and smuggled the main organizer out of town. During this period she also chaired the Pittsburgh chapter of the League against War and Fascism.

An heir to the *Chicago Tribune* fortune, her great-grandfather having been one of the paper's founders, O'Connor believed it was her duty to use her money to benefit radical causes. In 1934 she received publicity for demanding at a stockholders' meeting that U.S. Steel recognize a union of its employees. She helped fund many projects, from literacy and voting campaigns in the South to radical bookstores.

Although she continued to work periodically as a freelance journalist, in 1936 O'Connor turned her energies to volunteer work and later to caring for two children the O'Connors adopted in the early 1940s. From 1939 to 1944 they lived at Hull-House. While in Chicago, Jessie was general secretary of the League of Women Shoppers, working to organize buying power to improve workplace conditions and wages. For the Metropolitan Housing and Planning Council she made a film of housing conditions designed to convince her former Winnetka neighbors to finance improvements. She also worked for the Industrial Board of the Young Women's Christian Association (YWCA), the American Civil Liberties Union (ACLU), Spanish Refugee Relief, the American Committee for the Protection of the Foreign Born, WILPF, and the Campaign for World Government. O'Connor claimed she served on so many boards during this period that she did justice to none of them.

In 1945 the O'Connors moved to Fort Worth, Texas, where Harvey worked as publicity director for the Oil Workers International Union. In 1948 they settled in Little Compton, Rhode Island, where Harvey devoted himself to writing. Jessie was a member of the National Committee of the Progressive party from

1949 to 1952 and was a delegate to the People's World Constitutional Convention in 1950. During the 1950s Joseph McCarthy accused both O'Connors of being Communists. Harvey was called before the House Un-American Activities Committee (HUAC), and Jessie's passport was revoked. They joined with other activists to organize the National Committee to Abolish HUAC. From the 1960s on, Jessie demonstrated against the Vietnam War, was active in political campaigns, worked against construction of a local nuclear power plant, and traveled extensively.

For forty years, peace activists, union organizers, victims of McCarthy-era purges, novelists, and folk singers came to rest and recuperate at the O'Connor home in Little Compton. Beth Taylor, a friend who knew them in their last years, described them as "joyful, witty, accepting people" and noted that "anyone who came under their wing . . . felt their magnetism." Harvey died in 1987. Jessie died in Fall River, Massachusetts.

While Jessie's career received less public notice than Harvey's, she holds a significant place in the history of American radicalism. Beyond her career in labor journalism, she was part of an extensive network of radicals involved in every major social movement of the twentieth century. O'Connor's multiple interests and commitments probably diluted her impact in any single area, but her unwavering dedication to social justice was an example for all who shared her commitment.

• Jessie Lloyd O'Connor's papers are in the Sophia Smith Collection, Smith College, Northampton, Mass. The Smith College Archives holds a tape and transcript of an interview conducted for the Smith Centennial Study. Related manuscript collections are the Harvey O'Connor Papers at the Labor and Urban Affairs Archives, Wayne State University, and a smaller collection at the John Hay Library, Brown University; the Schwimmer-Lloyd Collection, including the papers of Lola Maverick Lloyd, William Bross Lloyd, and other family members at the New York Public Library; the Henry Demarest Lloyd Papers at the Wisconsin State Historical Society; and Federated Press Records at the Rare Book and Manuscript Library, Columbia University. Although she was not named coauthor of Harvey O'Connor's works, her contributions were such that they are listed as additional published works: *Steel—Dictator* (1935), *The Guggenheims* (1937), *The Astors* (1941), *The Empire of Oil* (1955), and *World Crisis in Oil* (1963). She is named as author of "One Woman's Resistance," an article about labor activist Louise Olivereau, in *Revolution in Seattle, a Memoir* (1964). The scant published sources on her life and work include the O'Connors' memoir written with Susan Bowler, *Harvey and Jessie: A Couple of Radicals* (1987); feature articles by Beth Taylor in the *Providence Sunday Journal*, 8 Feb. 1981, and *Ocean State Business*, 13–26 Feb. 1989; and an interview in *In These Times*, 19–25 Jan. 1977. The O'Connors are briefly discussed in the "Federated Press" entry in *Encyclopedia of the American Left* (1990). An obituary is in the *Providence Journal*, 27 Dec. 1988.

AMY HAGUE

O'CONNOR, Michael J. (27 Sept. 1810–18 Oct. 1872), Roman Catholic bishop, was born in Cork, Ireland, the son of Charles O'Connor and Ellen Kirk. He spent his early years in the nearby town of Glanny, where he proved to be an able student and a fervent Catholic. Irish bishop William Coppinger, seeking to cultivate a calling in the young altar boy, sent him to the Urban School of the Propaganda in Rome when O'Connor was fourteen. He completed studies for the priesthood when he was only twenty-three and because of his young age required a special dispensation to be ordained. The following year he received his doctorate in the fields of theology and sacred Scripture and quickly assumed the positions of vice rector of the Irish College and professor of sacred Scripture in the Propaganda.

In a very short time O'Connor's bishop called him back to Ireland, where he became curate of Fermoy and then chaplain of the convent of the Presentation in Doneraile. O'Connor wanted to continue his academic work, however, and began preparation for examination to fill the vacant chair of dogmatic theology at Maynooth College in 1838. In the meantime, Bishop Francis Kenrick of Philadelphia asked him to come to Philadelphia and teach at the St. Charles Borromeo Seminary. O'Connor had known Kenrick from their school days together in Rome and accepted the invitation. While rector of the seminary, he further strengthened his friendship with Bishop Kenrick, and Kenrick appointed him vicar-general of the western part of the Philadelphia diocese, centered in Pittsburgh. After the pope split the Philadelphia diocese in two in 1843, O'Connor seemed the inevitable choice to become the first bishop of the newly created Pittsburgh diocese, but O'Connor wanted to return to his academic pursuits and asked the pope to allow him instead to enter the Society of Jesus (Jesuits). Gregory XVI declined his request, however, and appointed him bishop of Pittsburgh.

The new diocese was geographically vast, extending from Lake Erie in the north to the West Virginia border in the south. O'Connor saw himself as a missionary bishop whose role was to establish the church throughout the area, so he immediately set about establishing parishes, recruiting priests and sisters from Europe to staff them, and building a seminary in Pittsburgh to train men for the priesthood locally. The Catholic population and institutional presence grew substantially under his initial tenure, but the diocese remained too large for one bishop to administer. O'Connor was successful in having it split in two, with nineteen northern counties becoming the Diocese of Erie. At the inception of the new diocese in 1853, O'Connor was assigned as bishop, but the Pittsburgh priests succeeded in having the pope reassign him to Pittsburgh after only four months at Erie.

O'Connor stood out among American bishops both for his constant yet tempered prodding of immigrant Catholics to assimilate to American culture and for his fervent defense of the church's right to participate in public discourse and to protect itself against nativist attacks. O'Connor's Americanist sentiments and actions alienated many among Pittsburgh's German Catholic population, who saw in his attitudes evidence of anti-German bias. His differences with the fledgling German Benedictine monastery of St. Vincent became especially strained, resulting in the loss of crucial financial support for the diocese from German missionary groups and at times spilling over to involve officials in Rome. At the same time, O'Connor was assailed by hostile Protestant politicians and nativist groups for his insistence that American culture allow for a strong Catholic voice. In his efforts to counter the charges leveled against the church by prominent nativists he founded in 1844 *The Pittsburgh Catholic*, the nation's second oldest Catholic weekly newspaper, and the oldest to be published without interruption. Tensions grew so great that at one time the nativist mayor of Pittsburgh had O'Connor arrested for building violations in connection with the construction of a Sisters of Mercy hospital in the city. O'Connor's difficulties with the German Catholic population stemmed in part from the immigrants' desire to maintain their language and culture in services and schools. O'Connor urged the German population to Americanize in part to ease his struggles with nativists, who saw in the German efforts a rejection of American values and culture.

Perhaps because of the highly stressful nature of these issues, O'Connor continued to seek a place in the academic world. He played a leading role in support of the establishment of an American college for seminarians in Rome. His health suffered under the strain of administering the diocese, and he took extended convalescent trips to Europe, Mexico, and the West Indies in the 1850s. His health continued to fail, his interest in academic work remained high, and finally he prevailed upon the pope to admit him to the Jesuit order and retire him as bishop of Pittsburgh. He had served seventeen years as Pittsburgh's first bishop when he officially resigned his position in May 1860.

After leaving Pittsburgh, O'Connor spent two years in Germany preparing to join the Jesuit order and then went to teach at Jesuit-run Boston College. The Jesuit Provincial in Baltimore, Maryland, soon appointed him as an assistant provincial because of O'Connor's extensive experience and connections in Rome. While in Baltimore, O'Connor revisited work with African Americans that had long held his interest. One of his earliest acts as bishop of Pittsburgh had been to establish a special chapel for African Americans. Nativist fears that he sought through this work to enslave blacks caused him to stop his efforts, but in Baltimore he returned to the cause. In 1863 O'Connor secured funds to establish the first African-American parish in the United States, St. Francis Xavier Church in Baltimore. He then persuaded a missionary order from London to come staff the parish; the order has since become known as the Josephites or Mill Hill missionaries.

At the time of O'Connor's death in Woodstock, Maryland, the Catholic church was growing rapidly in the United States. His ability to champion immigrant Catholic acculturation while simultaneously resisting native prejudice—all the while maintaining significant influence within the Vatican—made O'Connor a particularly powerful shaper of the nineteenth-century immigrant Catholic church in America. His later work among African Americans served as a catalyst for the growth of the church in the black community.

• The Michael O'Connor Papers form a small collection in the Archives of the Diocese of Pittsburgh. The best single source on O'Connor is Rev. Henry A. Szarnicki, *Michael O'Connor: First Catholic Bishop of Pittsburgh, 1843–1860* (1975). Brief biographies of O'Connor can be found in some of the histories of the Pittsburgh diocese. See especially Rev. Andrew Arnold Lambing, *Foundation Stones of a Great Diocese* (1914); Paul E. Campbell, ed., *Catholic Pittsburgh's One Hundred Years* (1943); and Monsignor Francis A. Glenn, *Shepherds of the Faith 1843–1993: A Brief History of the Catholic Diocese of Pittsburgh* (1993). O'Connor's work as a leader of the immigrant church is highlighted in Dolores Liptak, R.S.M., *Immigrants and Their Church* (1989). Stephen J. Ochs, *Desegregating the Altar: The Josephites and the Struggle for Black Priests, 1871–1960* (1990), highlights O'Connor's crucial role in initiating work among African-American Catholics.

TIMOTHY I. KELLY

O'CONNOR, William Douglas (2 Jan. 1832–9 May 1889), author and civil servant, was born in Boston, Massachusetts, the son of Peter D. O'Connor, a laborer (mother's name unknown). O'Connor left home at age eight, after an argument with his father. Except for that incident, nothing is known about his childhood or education. In the 1850s he came under the sway of the Providence, Rhode Island, poet Sarah Helen Whitman, one-time fiancée of Edgar Allan Poe, and published poems resembling but not approaching Poe's in quality. He also published several short stories in *Putnam's* and *Harper's* magazines. The best of these are "The Sword of Mauley" (1854), "Loss and Gain: A Tale of Lynn" (1854), "What Cheer?" (1855), and "The Ghost" (1856). His themes were romantic and sometimes mystical, featuring heroes that struck out for social justice; in style he often imitated the gothic sketches of Nathaniel Hawthorne and Poe.

In 1856 he married Ellen M. Tarr of Lowell, Massachusetts, with whom he had two children. They moved to Philadelphia, Pennsylvania, where he worked for the *Saturday Evening Post* for the next four years. During his tenure at the *Post* O'Connor published essays promoting Francis Bacon as the author of Shakespeare's works, especially in defense of Delia Bacon, whose *The Philosophy of the Plays of Shakespeare Unfolded* (1857) was one of the first treatises to raise this challenge. This interest eventually led to two volumes on the subject, *Hamlet's Notebook* (1886) and *Mr. Donnelly's Reviewers* (1889).

He resigned from his editorial post to write *Harrington: A Story of True Love* (1860), an antislavery novel published by the same Boston firm that issued the third edition of Walt Whitman's *Leaves of Grass* (1860). Had O'Connor's novel been issued earlier (the Civil War led almost immediately to the bankruptcy of his publisher), it might have enjoyed success. Paralleling the famous case of Anthony Burns, a slave who fled to Boston in 1854, it is remarkably passionate in its descriptions of the stark living conditions of the African-American community in Boston.

O'Connor, already an avid admirer of Whitman's poetry, befriended the poet in Boston in 1860, thus inaugurating a lifelong friendship and advocacy by O'Connor of the merits of *Leaves of Grass*. During the Civil War, both men worked as government employees in Washington, D.C. (O'Connor in the Treasury Department, Office of the Lighthouse Board). In June 1865 Whitman was summarily dismissed from his clerkship in the Bureau of Indian Affairs by Secretary of the Interior James Harlan. The firing was mainly part of the new secretary's efficiency program, but this former professor of mental and moral science may have also targeted Whitman for being the author of indecent poetry. In any event, the fiery O'Connor viewed the matter in those terms and (in spite of the fact that Whitman was hired by the attorney general's office the day after his dismissal) composed in the next nine weeks *The Good Gray Poet* (1866). The 46-page pamphlet extolled Whitman as America's greatest poet, condemned Harlan for the suppression of literature, and generally argued against the long tradition of literary censorship that had led in the nineteenth century to the expurgation of the Greek and Roman classics, Shakespeare, and the Bible.

Although *The Good Gray Poet* had little immediate impact on Whitman's critical reception, it marked the dividing line between the earlier Whitman of "nature without check" and the later, more avuncular poet of Love and Death, who had spent the war years (and "grown gray") ministering to the sick and wounded soldiers in Washington hospitals. This legend of the Christlike poet was further enhanced by O'Connor's 1868 short story "The Carpenter," published in *Putnam's*, which suggested Whitman's likeness to the Christian savior.

In 1872, however, O'Connor and Whitman quarreled over the merits of the Fifteenth Amendment, which gave voting rights to male freedmen. (The argument may have also involved Ellen O'Connor's brief infatuation with the poet.) O'Connor, who had harbored strong sentiments for the abolitionist movement, refused to speak to Whitman for the next decade—until the publication of the 1882 edition of *Leaves of Grass*, "banned in Boston" by the city's district attorney. O'Connor came to the poet's defense (as he had in 1876 when Whitman's book had come under attack, but the friendship was not renewed at that time), and their long estrangement came to an end. In the preface to O'Connor's posthumously published *Three Tales* (1892), which included "The Carpenter," Whitman testified that he had enjoyed "no better Friend. . . . He was a born sample of the flower and symbol of first-class knighthood here in the nineteenth century." O'Connor died in Washington, D.C.

Heroes of the Storm, O'Connor's selected accounts of rescue operations by the Life Saving Bureau (later the Coast Guard), was published in 1904. His widow married Albert Calder of Providence, Rhode Island, in 1902, and her reminiscences were a major source for one of the first reliable biographies of Walt Whitman, written by Bliss Perry and published in 1906.

• The bulk of the O'Connor papers are in the Henry W. and Albert A. Berg Collection, New York Public Library; the John Hay Collection, Brown University; and the Charles E. Feinberg Collection, Library of Congress. For biographical information, see Florence B. Freedman, *William Douglas O'Connor: Walt Whitman's Chosen Knight* (1985), and Jerome Loving, *Walt Whitman's Champion: William Douglas O'Connor* (1978). Obituaries are in the *Washington Post*, 12 May 1889, the *New York Daily Tribune*, 14 May 1889, and the *Springfield* (Ohio) *Republican* and the *Boston Transcript*, both 16 May 1889.

JEROME LOVING

O'CONOR, Charles (22 Jan. 1804–12 May 1884), lawyer and politician, was born in New York City, the son of Thomas O'Connor and Margaret O'Connor. O'Conor dropped the second *n* in his surname after a trip to Ireland led him to discover that this was the historic family spelling. His father had been involved in the Irish rebellion of 1798 and immigrated to New York, where he wrote editorials for the local papers. After his mother's death in 1816, O'Conor served as an apprentice to a tar and lampblack manufacturer. In 1817 he became an errand boy in a law office and later served as a clerk and law student in the office of Joseph D. Fay. He was admitted to the practice of law in 1824.

O'Conor's primary recognition came from the practice of law. In addition to his success in a number of highly publicized cases, O'Conor was an expert in wills, trusts, commercial law, and corporation law. In 1851 and 1852 he represented Catherine Sinclair Forrest against the tragedian Edwin Forrest in the New York courts when the two sued each other for divorce. The court granted the divorce, with alimony, to Catherine Sinclair Forrest. Benjamin R. Curtis, later a justice of the U.S. Supreme Court, said that O'Conor's representation was "the most remarkable exhibition of professional skill ever witnessed in this country."

In contrast to his success at the bar, O'Conor's political career brought him few honors. In 1846 he was elected to the New York Constitutional Convention, where he was prominent in opposing property rights for women. He was an unsuccessful candidate for lieutenant governor of New York in 1848. In 1853 President Franklin Pierce appointed him U.S. attorney for New York.

Before the Civil War O'Conor participated in two controversial cases in which he represented the interest of slaveholders maintaining that they could temporarily hold slaves in New York, *Jack v. Martin* (1834 and 1835) and *Lemmon v. the People* (1860). His opponents in the Lemmon case were William M. Evarts and Chester A. Arthur. *Lemmon* was thought by many to be a test case by which *Dred Scott* could be extended to protect the right of slaveholders to take slaves into free states.

In 1854 O'Conor married Cornelia Livingston McCracken, the widow of L. H. McCracken. They eventually separated.

On 19 December 1859, shortly after the hanging of John Brown, O'Conor gave a public speech at a "Union Meeting" of conservative men that was intended to assure the South of their repudiation of Brown's action. In that speech O'Conor defended slavery: "I insist that Negro slavery is not unjust. It is not only not unjust, it is just, wise, and beneficent." He represented Jefferson Davis after he was indicted for treason and, along with Horace Greeley and others, helped Davis obtain release on bail in 1867 by posting his bond. Davis was never brought to trial. O'Conor represented Georgia in its unsuccessful attempt to have the Supreme Court declare congressional reconstruction unconstitutional in *Georgia v. Stanton* (1868), and he was one of the counsel representing Governor Samuel Tilden in the Tilden-Hayes electoral contest before the electoral commission in 1877. In the latter case, the commissioners decided to award disputed votes to Rutherford B. Hayes, thereby electing him president.

Late in his life O'Conor also served a four-year term (1871–1875) as a special deputy attorney general for the state of New York. During that time he prosecuted the case against William M. "Boss" Tweed. The successful prosecution resulted in the demise of the "Tweed Ring." In 1867 the bar of New York presented a bust of O'Conor to the Supreme Court (trial court) of New York City, calling him "one of the greatest living advocates." After Chief Justice Salmon Chase's death some proposed O'Conor for chief justice, but legal historian Charles Fairman labeled that effort "a hopeless fantasy." In 1880 former Republican congressman and leading D.C. lawyer Albert Riddle described O'Conor as "the leader and Nestor of the New York Bar." In 1885 the Court of Claims referred to O'Conor as one of the "illustrious members of this bar" in *Carroll v. United States* (1885).

O'Conor was a leader of the Friends of Ireland. He was treasurer of the New York Law Institute for ten years and its president in 1869. He was an opponent of the codification movement (c. 1847–1882) led by David Dudley Field, which advocated reducing the common law writ system to a comprehensive code of procedure.

In 1872 O'Conor repudiated Horace Greeley, who had been nominated by the Liberal Republicans and the Democratic party, saying that the reelection of Grant would harm the Democrats less than compromising their principles by supporting longtime Republican Greeley. After repeated refusals to be a candidate, he ultimately accepted the nomination of the Straight-Out Democrats at their Louisville convention. With John W. Adams of Massachusetts as his vice presidential candidate, he ran unsuccessfully for president against Greeley and Grant in 1872. In an election with almost 6.5 million votes cast, O'Conor received fewer than 20,000 votes. O'Conor retired from the practice of law in 1881 and moved to Nantucket, Massachusetts, where he died.

• Some of O'Conor's legal papers are held by the New York Law Institute Library. Some of his correspondence is in the James Kent Collection and the Franklin Pierce Collection at the Library of Congress. A sketch of his life is John Bigelow, "Some Recollections of Charles O'Conor," *Century Magazine*, Mar. 1888, p. 725. The best analysis of the Lemmon case and its significance is in Paul Finkelman, *An Imperfect Union: Slavery, Federalism and Comity* (1981). See also Finkelman, *Slavery in the Courtroom* (1985). The leading account of the electoral commission is Charles Fairman, *Five Justices and the Electoral Commission* (1988). O'Conor's representation of Jefferson Davis is [Jefferson] Davis, 7 Fed. Cas. 63, no. 3, 621a (C.C.D. Va. 1867–1871). Contemporary accounts of O'Conor's repudiation of Greeley, the Louisville convention, and O'Conor's own nomination are in the *New York Times*, 14, 25, and 29 Aug. and 11, 13, 21, and 27 Sept. 1872. An obituary is in the *New York Times*, 17 May 1884.

RICHARD L. AYNES

OCONOSTOTA (1712?–1783?), Cherokee chief, was born probably at Chota (now Monroe County, Tenn.). His parents' names are unknown. He was not among the seven Cherokees who visited London in 1730. He first appears in the historical record in 1736 as a member of the Cherokee pro-French faction. According to traditional accounts, he became Great Warrior of Chota in 1738, which made him war leader of the "Overhill" Cherokee towns along the Little Tennessee and Hiwassee rivers. By 1753 his jurisdiction extended to the Cherokee towns in the Carolinas as well, thus encompassing the entire Cherokee nation.

Finding that the French could not adequately supply the Cherokees with trade goods, arms, and ammunition, Oconostota gradually warmed to the British. In 1753 he aided the pro-British Chickasaws in their war with the pro-French Choctaws by raiding Choctaw towns along the Tombigbee River. In 1755 he took five French prisoners during a campaign in the Illinois-Wabash region. That year he also led 500 Cherokees to a decisive victory over the Creeks at Taliwa, Georgia. When war broke out between Great Britain and France, Oconostota led an expedition against Fort Toulouse in the Alabama country, killing several Frenchmen and taking two prisoners. Later, he participated in an expedition against the French on the lower Ohio River.

In 1758 a group of Cherokees went to the Virginia and Pennsylvania frontiers to fight alongside the British against the French. There they frequently also clashed with backcountry settlers, which resulted in South Carolina's placing of an embargo on Cherokee trade. Since South Carolina had a virtual monopoly on trade with the Cherokees, Oconostota went to Charleston to negotiate the lifting of the embargo. There he and his retinue were held hostage and forced to accompany Governor William Lyttelton's army on a show of force into the Cherokee country. Oconostota gained his own release by agreeing, albeit insincerely, to surrender Cherokees who had killed settlers, but he made war on the British as soon as Lyttelton's army had returned to Charleston.

In February 1760 Oconostota appeared at Fort Prince George in upper South Carolina, demanding the release of the remaining Cherokee hostages. When the fort's commander, Lieutenant Richard Coytmore, appeared to parley, Oconostota signaled to concealed gunmen to fire, and Coytmore was mortally wounded. The garrison retaliated by killing all the Cherokee hostages.

Oconostota returned to the Overhill region and besieged Fort Loudoun, which the British had built along the Little Tennessee River in 1757. Leaving the conduct of the siege to Ostenaco (also known as Judd's Friend or by his title Outacite), his second-in-command and sometime rival, Oconostota then ambushed a relief expedition led by Colonel Archibald Montgomery on 27 June 1760. Montgomery's subsequent retreat ensured the fall of Fort Loudoun. The Fort's inhabitants were guaranteed safe passage to South Carolina, but on 9 August the Cherokees massacred many of them, probably on Oconostota's orders, to compensate for the Cherokee blood spilled at Fort Prince George.

Honor having been satisfied, Oconostota made peace overtures, but after news of the massacre reached Charleston, the British sought revenge. Oconostota went to New Orleans to solicit French assistance, but none was forthcoming. On 10 June 1761 Oconostota attacked a punitive expedition led by Colonel James Grant, but Grant had learned from Montgomery's mistakes, and Oconostota could not repeat his success. After he had burned most of the Cherokee towns, Grant demanded to negotiate with Oconostota, who would not, however, again entrust his person to the British. Consequently, the pro-British Cherokee leader Attakullakulla was recalled to power to negotiate a peace, which was concluded in the late summer of 1761 and ratified by the Cherokees on 13 October.

To rehabilitate himself with the British, he petitioned for permission to go to London to see the king. This was refused, but he had an opportunity of proving his loyalty in 1764 by his taking of eight scalps from Pontiac's Ottawa warriors, who were in revolt against the British. In 1767 he and Attakullakulla went, via Charleston and New York City, to Johnson Hall in the Mohawk River Valley of New York, where early in 1768 Sir William Johnson helped to negotiate a peace between the Cherokees and Iroquois. Oconostota was soundly defeated in a territorial dispute with the Chickasaws in 1773.

The Royal Proclamation of 1763 reserved the trans-Appalachian west for the Indians, but British authorities were unable to prevent the westward movement of colonists. Reluctantly, Oconostota agreed to the treaties of Hard Labor and Lochaber in 1768 and 1770, respectively, which formalized some white incursions beyond the Proclamation line. These did not stem the advance of the colonists, yet Oconostota declined to join the Indian confederacy that fought and lost the 1774 conflict known as Lord Dunmore's War. The practical effect of the colonists' victory was to open up Kentucky to settlement. Seeing that this was inevitable, in March 1775 Oconostota signed the Transylvania Purchase by which twenty million acres were conveyed to North Carolina land speculator Judge Richard Henderson. Oconostota hoped to deflect white settlement northward, away from the Overhill towns, but the younger warriors regarded the sale as appeasement of an aggressor. The resulting decline in Oconostota's prestige enabled them to persuade the Cherokee council, against his advice, that the split between the whites during the American Revolution was an opportunity not to be missed and that the Cherokees should make war against the American settlers. Oconostota was too old to participate in the mostly unsuccessful fighting, but he helped to make peace with the Americans in July 1777 at Long Island in the Holston River, and in Williamsburg he promised to support the American cause.

In 1780, encouraged by British successes in the South, the Cherokees resumed the conflict with the American colonists, whose land hunger they feared more than the remote British authorities. The attacks that Oconostota authorized were ineffective, and the fighting died out during 1781. In July 1782 Oconostota resigned as Great Warrior and spent that winter with Virginia's Indian agent, Joseph Martin, who accompanied him in the spring of 1783 to Chota, where he died and was buried in a canoe. His probable remains were discovered in the 1970s.

Joseph Martin described Oconostota in 1782 as "a very old man—had but little flesh, tho' very straight for a man of his age, very large-boned and from appearances must have been a man of extraordinary physical prowess." Oconostota said of himself, "I am no speaker and not much of a statesman." In 1772, Alexander Cameron, deputy southern Indian superintendent, wrote, "Oucconnastotah has not only vast sway with his own people but with other tribes." His military successes made him the leading Cherokee from 1760 to 1782. Despite the ultimate defeat of the Cherokees in the 1760–1761 conflict, Oconostota was associated with some of the most important victories won by Native Americans over Europeans—the defeat of Archibald Montgomery and of Fort Loudoun. In the early nineteenth century, Cherokees spoke of Oconostota as an almost superhuman figure from a heroic age.

• Oconostota's papers captured by the Americans during a 1781 raid by his forces are now housed at the National Archives and are reproduced in J. W. Hagy and Stanley J. Folmsbee, eds., "The Lost Archives of the Cherokee Nation, Part I, 1763–1772," and "The Lost Archives of the Cherokee Nation, Part II, 1772–1775," *Publication of the East Tennessee Historical Society* 43 (1971): 112–22, and 44 (1972): 114–25. The only biographical study is James C. Kelly, "Oconostota," *Journal of Cherokee Studies* 3 (Fall 1978): 221–38, which includes copious bibliographic notes; see also Kelly, "Attakullakulla," *Journal of Cherokee Studies* 3 (Winter 1978): 3–34. Good general accounts of Cherokee affairs, and of Oconostota's role, are found in John P. Brown, *Old Frontiers* (1938); David Corkran, *The Cherokee Frontier: Conflict and Survival, 1740–1762* (1962); and William MacDowell, ed. and intro., *Colonial Records of South Carolina*, ser. 2, *Documents Relating to Indian Affairs, 1754–1765* (1962), which is the best source of documents concerning Oconostota.

JAMES C. KELLY

O'DANIEL, Iron Mike (15 Feb. 1894–28 Mar. 1975), army officer, was born John Wilson O'Daniel in Newark, Delaware, the son of Amos O'Daniel, a dairy farmer, and Nora Wilson. He attended the University of Delaware and while there enlisted in the Delaware National Guard, serving as a sergeant with the First Infantry on the Mexican border in 1916. He graduated with a B.S. degree in 1917 and then began training at the Reserve Officers Training Camp at Fort Myer, Virginia, where he was commissioned a second lieutenant in the infantry reserves in October 1917. The army immediately gave him a regular commission and sent him to France with the 11th Infantry Regiment. His combat service during World War I at St. Mihiel and in the Meuse-Argonne earned him the Distinguished Service Cross and his nickname. Known as "Mike" in college, he became "Iron Mike" when he fought for twelve hours at St. Mihiel with a machine-gun wound in his face. Throughout his career he projected a toughness and tenacity consistent with the name. In 1920 he married Ruth Bowman; they had two children.

Between the world wars O'Daniel rotated frequently through a wide variety of military assignments at numerous locations. He served, for example, as an infantry instructor with the New Jersey National Guard from 1924 to 1927, as an executive officer with the Fort McClellan, Alabama, district of the Civilian Conservation Corps in 1936, and as a professor of military science in Augusta, Georgia, from 1936 to 1938. He was a battalion commander in the Twenty-fourth Infantry Division at Fort Benning, Georgia, when the United States entered World War II. His initial wartime assignments were as a training officer in Texas and Massachusetts. In July 1942 he took command of the American Invasion Training School in England. He led the 168th Infantry Regiment in the capture of Algiers in November 1942 and then organized the Fifth Army invasion training center in North Africa to prepare for landings in Sicily and Italy. For his contribution to the successful Allied assaults in Sicily and at Salerno, O'Daniel was made officer in charge of amphibious operations for the Fifth Army in October 1943. In December he became assistant commander of the Third Infantry Division, which landed at Anzio in January.

In February 1944 on the Anzio beachhead, O'Daniel assumed command of the Third Infantry Division and led that unit throughout the remainder of the war. After withstanding ferocious German counterattacks, the division broke out of the beachhead and joined the Fifth Army's push to Rome. The division then landed at St. Tropez in August 1944 and was a principal element in the Allied advance through the south of France in the winter of 1944–1945. O'Daniel's troops fought street by street, day and night, through the Colmar Pocket south of Strasbourg. In the spring of 1945 his men were part of the capture of Nuremburg and Munich, and in May 1945 they occupied Adolf Hitler's mountain retreat at Berchtesgaden, where O'Daniel accepted the surrender of German Field Marshal Albert Kesselring.

General Dwight D. Eisenhower later praised the five-foot-six-inch, square-jawed, outspoken O'Daniel as one of the United States's "outstanding combat soldiers." In appearance and demeanor, he reminded many of his contemporaries of General George S. Patton. Decorated many times for leadership and personal valor, O'Daniel, now a major general, was always near the front with his men. He would sometimes fly over their positions in a small plane and drop messages to the troops urging them onward. He was also a battlefield innovator. He invented a "battle sled," a steel tube on runners that could protect and transport a fully equipped infantryman. A tank could tow twelve sleds at a time.

After the war O'Daniel served as commanding general at Fort Benning, and from 1948 to 1950 he was U.S. military attaché in Moscow. Upon his return from the Soviet Union, he bluntly asserted in an article in *Collier's* magazine: "For all its advertised glory, Moscow impressed me as a vast slum." In July 1951 he was given command of the I Corps of the Eighth Army, and he led the unit through heavy fighting in Korea. In September 1952 he became commander of the U.S. Army in the Pacific.

In 1953 and 1954 the U.S. Joint Chiefs of Staff sent O'Daniel on three separate missions to Vietnam to evaluate France's chances for success in its war against the Communist-led Vietminh. O'Daniel urged General Henri Navarre, the French commander, to adopt a more aggressive strategy that included a plan to place a large French garrison at Dienbienphu in the mountains of northern Vietnam. O'Daniel sent Washington optimistic estimates of French prospects. Based in part on the general's calculations, U.S. aid to the French increased substantially, and in March 1954 O'Daniel became the head of the U.S. Military Assistance Advisory Group in Vietnam. Although his prediction of French success proved wrong and Navarre suffered a stunning defeat at Dienbienphu, O'Daniel remained convinced that, even after France agreed to a cease-fire and a north-south partition of Vietnam at the Geneva Conference of 1954, the southern part of Vietnam would maintain its independence from the Communist North. O'Daniel was the chief U.S. military officer in South Vietnam until his retirement from active duty in October 1955 with the rank of lieutenant general.

In retirement O'Daniel continued to be a strong advocate for U.S. support of South Vietnam. From 1956 to 1963 he served as chairman of a nonpartisan group known as the American Friends of Vietnam, and he lectured and published articles describing a bright future for the government in Saigon. After a visit to South Vietnam in July 1956, he announced that "Free Viet-Nam was now entirely pacified and secure." He published two books on Vietnam: *The Nation that Refused to Starve* (1960) and *Vietnam Today: The Challenge of a Divided Nation* (1966). His wife Ruth died in 1965, and in 1966 he married Gretchen Rufner Davies; they had no children. He died in San Diego, California.

O'Daniel was a hard-charging infantryman whose faith in his own and his soldiers' ability had served his nation well in World War I, World War II, and Korea. In Vietnam some U.S. officials found him impetuous and over-confident, but President Eisenhower found O'Daniel's spirit "refreshing." "'Iron Mike' O'Daniel," Eisenhower recalled in his presidential memoirs, "despite his nickname and his tough exterior, was a man of great ability and tact."

• O'Daniel's papers are in the archives of the U.S. Army Military History Institute, Carlisle Barracks, Pa. There are additional O'Daniel papers and transcripts of oral history interviews with him in the U.S. Army Center of Military History, Washington, D.C. For information on his combat commands in World War II, see Donald G. Taggart, ed., *History of the Third Infantry Division in World War II* (1947). His controversial comments on the Soviet Union are in his article "This Is Moscow Today," *Collier's*, 28 Apr. 1951, pp. 22–23. For analysis of O'Daniel's role in U.S.-Vietnam relations see Ronald H. Spector, *The United States Army in Vietnam: Advice and Support: The Early Years, 1941–1960* (1983); David L. Anderson, *Trapped by Success: The Eisenhower Administration and Vietnam, 1953–1961* (1991); and Joseph G. Morgan, *The Vietnam Lobby: The American Friends of Vietnam, 1955–1975* (1997). An obituary is in the *Washington Post*, 30 Mar. 1975.

DAVID L. ANDERSON

O'DANIEL, W. Lee (11 Mar. 1890–11 May 1969), Texas governor, U.S. senator, and radio performer, known as "Pappy," was born Wilbert Lee O'Daniel in Malta, Ohio, the son of William O'Daniel, a farmer and worker in a plow factory, and Alice Ann Thompson Earich, a seamstress and laundry woman. His father was accidentally killed working on a bridge construction project when O'Daniel was a baby, and he lived with his mother's third husband, Charles H. Baker, a farmer, outside of Arlington, Kansas, after 1895. O'Daniel attended local schools and then studied one year at a business college in Hutchinson, Kansas. Afterward he entered the flour milling business and worked at a variety of office jobs in Kansas towns. In 1916 he started the Independent Milling Company, and his firm soon operated into Texas. He married Merle Estella Butcher, with whom he would have three children, in 1917; the marriage exempted him from the draft in World War I.

O'Daniel's flour company was bought out in 1919, and he ran his own firm, United States Flour Mills Company, between 1921 and 1925 in New Orleans. He went to work for the Burrus Mill and Elevator Company in Fort Worth, Texas, in 1925. As a promotional technique, he started a radio program in 1930 with the "Light Crust Doughboys," a band led by fiddler Bob Wills. O'Daniel had a pleasing radio voice,

and he read poetry and performed his own songs over the air. "Beautiful Texas" became a statewide hit. By 1935, O'Daniel had formed his own Hillbilly Flour Company whose bags bore the slogan: "It tickles your feet, it tickles your tongue. Wherever you go its praises are sung." O'Daniel was already known as "Pappy" because of the flour's motto: "Please pass the biscuits, Pappy" (Douglas and Miller, p. 107). In contrast to his later claims that he came from a nonpolitical background, O'Daniel sent out Christmas cards in 1937 critical of Franklin D. Roosevelt and the New Deal for its welfare and spending policies.

In 1938 O'Daniel asked his listeners whether he should accept the many invitations he was receiving to run for governor in the Democratic primary. He soon reported that nearly 55,000 Texans had urged him to enter the race. O'Daniel's candidacy was not taken seriously within the Democratic party even though he was drawing bigger crowds than any of his dozen opponents. He had failed to pay the state poll tax and could not vote for himself, but even that lapse made no difference in the electorate's enthusiasm for him. He promised pensions for the elderly, observance of the Ten Commandments and the Golden Rule, and said that what Texas needed was "less Johnson grass and politicians; more smokestacks and businessmen" (Green, p. 23). By 1938, enthusiasm for the New Deal was waning in Texas, and there was a conservative tide among voters as the state's prosperity returned. Behind his rustic veneer, O'Daniel was receiving strong support from major corporations in Texas. He offered an attractive blend of media celebrity and simple answers to the state's problems.

O'Daniel easily defeated his opponents and won the Democratic primary without a runoff. He endorsed other Democratic candidates in their runoff elections, a tactic that irritated many in the party and foreshadowed the bickering that would mark his tenure in Austin. He had no serious Republican opposition in the general election. Once in office, however, O'Daniel found that his platitudes were difficult to translate into workable programs. He proposed a tax on all business transactions to pay for his pension program, but the legislature rejected the idea. O'Daniel's relations with the lawmakers were stormy all during 1939, and he based his reelection campaign in 1940 on the opposition he had encountered from the legislature. The governor also charged that Communist and Nazi activity permeated the state. O'Daniel easily won reelection from the adoring electorate.

During the early months of his second term, O'Daniel's administration attacked labor unions, appointed prohibitionists to the state's Liquor Control Board, and failed to resolve the revenue problems that confronted Texas. The death of U.S. Senator Morris Sheppard on 9 April 1941 opened the way for O'Daniel to advance politically. He appointed the 87-year-old son of Sam Houston to act as interim senator. In the general election that followed, O'Daniel defeated a crowded field of candidates, including Congressman Lyndon B. Johnson. Liquor lobbyists, eager to get O'Daniel out of the state, manipulated election returns to produce a narrow O'Daniel victory.

In the Senate, O'Daniel aligned with the conservative enemies of the New Deal. He sponsored legislation to outlaw strikes, to bar the union shop, and to end draft deferments for labor leaders. None of these laws ever passed. Facing the voters again for a six-year term in 1942, O'Daniel assailed his main rival, former governor James V. Allred, as an agent of "Communistic labor leader racketeers" and an ally of the Roosevelt administration (Green, p. 39). In the runoff election, O'Daniel defeated Allred by 18,000 votes.

When he moved to Washington, O'Daniel's career began a downward trend. Revealing his conservative views in their full intensity, he assailed the Roosevelt administration constantly and voted with the Republicans and conservative Democrats who attacked the president. O'Daniel's views were extreme even by the standards of Texas conservatism during the 1940s, and he seemed both shrill and ineffective. Personal errors compounded his political problems. He acquired an apartment house in Washington, evicted the tenants, and transformed the fourteen-room place into a family home. He also attacked his fellow lawmakers in 1947 as "Kremlin-hued" (*Austin American*, 12 Apr. 1947). By now, O'Daniel's actions seemed more like those of a buffoon than a genuine spokesman for the people of his state. Polls in 1947 showed him finishing third in a reelection race the following year. He announced on 20 May 1948 that he would not be a candidate for reelection. In his statement he said that there was only "slight hope of saving our nation from going entirely socialistic or communistic" (O'Daniel Biographical File).

After he left office, O'Daniel was a real estate broker in Washington, D.C., and then sold insurance in Dallas. He ran for governor of Texas in 1956 and 1958 and lost badly on both occasions. At the time of his death in Dallas, he was a largely forgotten figure in state politics.

O'Daniel was a meteoric phenomenon in the history of Texas. He won four statewide elections within as many years and for a time was as popular as anyone who has ever sought public office in Texas. His record as governor proved mediocre, and his performance as a U.S. Senator ranked even lower. O'Daniel's election began a trend of conservative governors in Texas that lasted into the 1980s. In retrospect, his victory in 1938 came to symbolize the end of the brief New Deal period in Texas politics and the emergence of a business-oriented "Establishment" that devoted only minimal attention to social welfare policies and the state's minority population.

• Records of the O'Daniel gubernatorial administration are housed in the Texas State Archives, Austin; the Center for American History, University of Texas at Austin, has a small collection of letters and clippings from his senatorial years as well as a biographical file with relevant documents. The Lyndon B. Johnson Library, Austin, and the Franklin D. Roosevelt Library, Hyde Park, N.Y., also have documents bearing on O'Daniel's public service. C. L. Douglas and Francis Miller, *The Life Story of W. Lee O'Daniel* (1938), was written just after his first campaign in 1938. Seth Shepard McKay, *W. Lee O'Daniel and Texas Politics, 1938–1942* (1944), is a good survey of newspaper coverage of O'Daniel's political career. John E. Ferling, "The First Administration of Governor W. Lee O'Daniel" (M.A. thesis, Baylor Univ., 1962), looks at O'Daniel's performance in office. R. Scott Harris, "Governor W. Lee 'Pappy' O'Daniel's Rise to Power" (honor's essay, Univ. of Texas at Austin, 1992), is a fresh appraisal of O'Daniel's career. The best general treatment of O'Daniel in the context of Texas politics is George N. Green, *The Establishment in Texas Politics, the Primitive Years, 1938–1957* (1979). A useful obituary is in the *Dallas Morning News*, 12 May 1969.

LEWIS L. GOULD

O'DAY, Caroline Love Goodwin (22 June 1875?–4 Jan. 1943), congresswoman, was born in Perry, Georgia, the daughter of Sidney Prior Goodwin, a businessman, and Elia Warren. Descended from a prominent Georgia family, well known within Confederate circles, Caroline attended private schools, graduating in 1886 from Lucy Cobb Institute in Athens, Georgia, a school attended also by her three sisters. Since according to the date she always listed as her birth year, 1875, she would have been only eleven years old at graduation, it is probable that her family was correct in estimating her birthdate at 1869.

Following graduation, Caroline Goodwin pursued her interest in art briefly at Cooper Union in New York City and then left for Paris, studying for a time with James McNeill Whistler. Because of her success she remained in Europe, studying and painting for eight years in Paris, Munich, and Amsterdam and deriving an income from magazine illustrations and costume design. In Paris she met Daniel T. O'Day, an independent oil company executive and Standard Oil Company officer. She returned to New York in 1901 and married O'Day. The couple lived in Rye, New York, and became the parents of one daughter and two sons.

After her husband's death in 1916, O'Day became involved in issues that had long concerned her. As a pacifist, she opposed United States entry into World War I and became a vice chairman of the Woman's International League for Peace and Freedom. During the war she developed an interest in social welfare and did volunteer work at a maternity center located on New York City's Lower East Side. Working with the New York Consumers' League, in the Women's Trade Union League, and as a board member of Lillian Wald's Henry Street Settlement acquainted O'Day with social issues that became the focus of her public life and drew her into Democratic party politics. An ardent suffragist, she went on to advance protective legislation for women, a more humane reception for Ellis Island immigrants, and improved working conditions for blue-collar laborers. Her Rye estate was often the site of trade union conferences, and she was a member of a state commission to set minimum-wage scales for laundry workers. At one time she was president of the Rye School Board. In 1923 Governor Alfred E. Smith appointed her to the State Board of Charities (later the State Board of Social Welfare). She remained in the post until 1935.

Meanwhile, O'Day became a stalwart in the women's division of the Democratic State Committee. In 1923 she replaced Harriet May Mills as chair of the women's division. Energized by O'Day and her new friends, Eleanor Roosevelt, Nancy Cook, and Marion Dickerman, New York women Democrats developed strong local units and emerged as an integral part of the party's organization. The quartet of activists traveled eight thousand miles by automobile throughout upstate New York, canvassing women Democrats in Republican strongholds, and led delegations of women to the state capital at Albany to prompt legislative action on Governor Smith's proposals. They lobbied for worker's compensation, removal of legal discriminations against women, and state implementation of federal programs for maternal and child health. Of the three friends, O'Day was closest to Dickerman. She often relaxed at "Val-Kill," Eleanor Roosevelt's personal cottage, and provided financial support for the furniture factory Cook and Roosevelt established there in the 1930s.

O'Day worked diligently in Smith's presidential campaign in 1928 and in Franklin D. Roosevelt's campaign in 1932. Both the president and the first lady aided O'Day in her successful bid in 1934 for New York's at-large seat in the U.S. House of Representatives in a campaign that drew eleven candidates. Not until O'Day's campaign had Eleanor Roosevelt left the White House to assist a candidate. O'Day's platform signified her political goals of higher wages and better working conditions for laborers, adequate relief for victims of the Great Depression at a reasonable cost to taxpayers, and wider opportunities for women in government. She was reelected for three more terms.

O'Day had once made a survey of conditions on Ellis Island for the New York State Industrial Commission, chaired by Frances Perkins. In the House, O'Day won membership on the Committee on Immigration and Naturalization and sponsored numerous bills for the relief of individual immigrants. She also served on the Committee on Insular Affairs, and from 1937 to 1942 she chaired the Committee on Election of President, Vice President, and Representatives in Congress. She was an ardent New Dealer, a friend to labor and to children. To curb child labor malpractices she helped amend the 1936 Walsh-Healy Government Contracts Act and the 1938 Fair Labor Standards Act. Her pacifism surfaced in her opposition to provisions of the Neutrality Act of 1939 allowing arms sales to nations at war against Nazi Germany. In 1940 she voted against the peacetime Selective Training and Service Act. She once asked editors of the women's *Democratic Digest,* "If down through the ages women had shared political power with men, would the world have become the armed camp that it is today?" Known as an advocate of women's causes, she nevertheless was the only congresswoman to oppose the Equal Rights Amendment. She feared the loss of protective legislation for working women.

O'Day was ill and bedridden early in 1942 but was advised by Democratic leaders not to resign from Congress. In the summer she suffered serious injuries in a fall at her home and never recovered. She died at her home one day after her congressional term ended in January 1943.

O'Day and New Jersey's Mary T. Norton were the best-known congresswomen in the 1930s. In spite of her great wealth, O'Day was known for her championship of the disadvantaged. Her reform impulse was tempered by a realistic sense of what was achievable under adverse conditions.

• There are no known O'Day papers. Sketches on her appear in successive editions of *Women in Congress,* in the *Biographical Directory of the United States Congress, 1774–1989,* and in *Current Biography* (1943). Her friend Marion Dickerman wrote a personal sketch in *Notable American Women,* vol. 2 (1971), that explains the discrepancy about O'Day's birthdate, and Hope Chamberlain included her in *A Minority of Members: Women in the U.S. Congress* (1973). She is the subject of an article, "She Represents New York," in *Independent Woman,* Dec. 1934, pp. 375 and 402, and a cover story in *Democratic Digest,* Jan. 1937, p. 9, a journal that contains frequent news notes on O'Day from 1934 to 1942. O'Day is mentioned in Susan Ware, *Beyond Suffrage* (1981); Joseph P. Lash, *Love, Eleanor: Eleanor Roosevelt and Her Friends* (1982); and Blanche Wiesen-Cook, *Eleanor Roosevelt, 1884–1933* (1992). O'Day's correspondence is in the microfilmed *Papers of Eleanor Roosevelt,* reel 14. The *New York Times* index points to news items on O'Day from 1923 to 1942 and to her obituary on 5 Jan. 1943.

MARTHA H. SWAIN

O'DAY, Molly (9 July 1923–5 Dec. 1987), musician, was born LaVerne Lois Williamson near McVeigh, Kentucky, the daughter of Joseph A. Williamson, a coalminer and farmer, and Hester Fleming. Two of her brothers were musicians, and she learned to play the guitar and banjo and to sing at an early age. Playing guitar, she accompanied her brothers fiddler Cecil ("Skeets") and banjoist Joe ("Duke") for local performances and at dances. In 1939 Skeets got a short-term job on Charleston radio, and Molly, then sixteen, followed him there, taking the name "Mountain Fern." They separately moved to smaller stations in West Virginia, their brother Duke rejoined them, and they briefly formed a trio.

In the fall of 1940 Molly traveled to Bluefield, West Virginia. Now using the name "Dixie Lee" Williamson, she met bandleader and guitarist Leonard "Lynn" Davis, who had his own western-flavored band, the Forty-Niners. She was hired as their lead singer and a year later married Davis. Over the next five years they moved from station to station, building a strong following on radio; sometime during this period she took her final stage name, Molly O'Day. It was also at this time she began dressing in pseudowestern attire, following the style of other female country performers, such as Patsy Montana and Texas Ruby. Davis and O'Day renamed the backing band the Cumberland

Mountain Folks, and O'Day's brother Skeets was often featured in the lineup. Future bluegrass and country vocalist Mac Wiseman played bass with the band beginning in 1946 and was featured on most of their Columbia recordings. While performing on radio in Alabama, the duo met a young guitarist and songwriter, Hank Williams, who taught them the song "Tramp on the Street," a tear-jerking ballad that would become one of O'Day's most popular tunes.

While performing on radio station WNOX out of Knoxville, Tennessee, in 1945 and 1946, the couple caught the attention of Nashville music publisher Fred Rose, who recommended them to Columbia Records. Rose, who represented Williams as a songwriter, urged Davis and O'Day to record Williams's material. In their early Columbia sessions (1946–1947), the band accompanied O'Day's strong vocals on "Tramp on the Street," the religious "Matthew 24," and the honky-tonk anthem "I Don't Care If Tomorrow Never Comes," written by Williams. Although O'Day's popularity was growing thanks to radio and recordings, she was increasingly nervous on stage and unhappy performing secular material. A 1949 session brought more classic performances, including her last hits, "Teardrops Falling on the Snow" and Hank Williams's composition "On the Evening Train," both quintessential tearjerkers.

O'Day apparently suffered an emotional breakdown sometime in late 1949 or early 1950 and was briefly hospitalized. She last recorded for Columbia in 1951, retiring from secular performances. She and Davis converted to the Church of God, and O'Day began singing exclusively in churches. Her big-lunged vocal style was influential on the next generation of female country singers, particularly Kitty Wells, who picked up O'Day's don't-mess-with-me attitude to score a big hit in 1952 with "It Wasn't God Who Made Honky Tonk Angels." Ironically, O'Day perhaps missed being the first female country music star by a year, as she abandoned the music just before it became acceptable for a woman to take such a gutsy approach.

O'Day and Davis settled near Huntington, West Virginia, and recorded sporadically for smaller labels, despite recurring heath problems for O'Day, who had contracted tuberculosis. The duo began a gospel radio show on WEMM in Huntington in 1974, which they hosted together for fourteen years until her death there.

• Ivan Tribe and John Morris have documented the duo's life and career in *Molly O'Day, Lynn Davis and the Cumberland Mountain Folks: A Bio-Discography* (JEMF Special Series, no. 7, 1975). Their complete Columbia recordings have been reissued on a two-CD set by Bear Family Records of Germany (15565).

RICHARD CARLIN

ODELL, George C. D. (19 Mar. 1866–17 Oct. 1949), theatrical scholar and college professor, was born George Clinton Densmore Odell in Newburgh, New York, the son of Benjamin Barker Odell, a business-

man who served as mayor of the town, and Ophelia Bookstaver. His older brother Benjamin Odell, Jr., served as governor of New York state from 1900 to 1904. George received his early education at Siglar Preparatory School in Newburgh and went to Columbia University, his choice of colleges being largely dictated by his desire to be close to the New York theater scene. He completed his B.A. in 1889, his M.A. in 1890, and his Ph.D. in 1893; both graduate degrees were in the field of literature. His study of English and Scottish ballads was published during the final year of work on his doctorate, and a little later he became the editor of school editions of *Julius Caesar* and *Henry V*.

Odell joined the teaching staff of the Columbia English department in 1895, advancing through various positions until he succeeded critic-playwright-scholar Brander Matthews in 1924 as professor of dramatic literature, the first such chair in an American university, which had been created for Matthews in 1902. Odell continued teaching until 1938. In 1920 he published *Shakespeare from Betterton to Irving*, a study of Shakespearean acting. Shortly thereafter he began work on the grand project that would happily occupy him for the rest of his life: *Annals of the New York Stage*, a fifteen-volume in-depth chronicle of the New York theater from its eighteenth-century beginnings to the final decade of the nineteenth century.

The design of the project involved a detailed chronicle of the New York stage, with commentary on houses, managers, playwrights, productions, and performers, as well as complete cast information for major productions. Similar studies of a more limited nature had been undertaken by Joseph N. Ireland, whose *Records of the New York Stage from 1750 to 1860* was published in two volumes in 1866–1867, and T. Allston Brown, whose *A History of the New York Stage: From the First Performance in 1732 to 1901* was published in three volumes in 1903. Odell adopted Brown's physical format for the presentation of his material but followed Ireland in offering a season-by-season account instead of summarizing the history of each theater in a single place. Like Ireland, he commented in detail on the careers of important playwrights, producers, and performers, but whereas Ireland confined his study to the offerings of the major houses, Odell undertook to cover all houses and types of stage performance, including opera, ballet, concerts, minstrel shows, and vaudeville. His commentaries were also more extended and personal in nature.

As a lifelong bachelor Odell was free to concentrate his entire attention on the one great passion of his life, the theater. A large, handsome man with a courtly bearing, he made his home at the Seymour Hotel on West Forty-fourth Street in the heart of the theatrical district, where he did his writing in the comfort of an old-fashioned, book-lined study.

The volumes were published two at a time from 1927 to 1947. He had hoped at one time to bring his study up to 1910 but was only able to complete it as far as 1894. Sales of the expensive series were never enough to bring him any financial royalties, but his reward came in the knowledge of an enormous undertaking splendidly fulfilled.

In 1942, at the time of the publication of the thirteenth and fourteenth volumes of the series, he gave a lengthy interview to Austin Stevens of the *New York Times*. Anticipating the use of an almost inevitable adjective with reference to his awesome scholarly achievement, he asked Stevens if he could avoid calling the *Annals* monumental, observing that it was not pleasant to have a work that had occupied most of his life described by a word that suggested a mausoleum. He summarized the aim of his project with no hint of false modesty: "I wanted to do a book on New York's theatre of which it could be said if you can't find it there you can't find it anywhere."

The strict regimen he adopted in pursuing his research goes far to make clear why he was able to accomplish so much. As he explained to Stevens, when he started the project he would finish his teaching responsibilities at Columbia about 2:00 P.M. on Fridays and would then go directly to the New York Public Library, arriving about 3:00 and working over the files until 10:00. By skipping lunch on Saturdays he could get in twelve hours. On Sundays he got in nine. This provided enough material for writing each evening through the following week. He did additional research at the New York and Long Island historical societies, the Columbia University Library, the Players, and the Harvard Theatre Collection, as well as digging into storage warehouses on the East Side and pursuing some material as far as the British Admiralty.

The *Annals* begin with a 500-page introductory volume that traces the early history of the New York theater to 1798. Each subsequent volume averages 700 pages and includes a substantial index. In 1942 it was estimated that the completed volumes contained about 4 million words, with the indexes running as high as 27,000 references.

The *Annals* are generously illustrated, with most of the pictures coming from Odell's extensive personal collection of theater memorabilia. As he explained in his introduction to the first volume, one of the objects of his work had been to justify—in his own eyes, at least—his lifelong habit of accumulating mementos of plays and players of other ages, adding, "Happy the man whose avocation merges finally into an absorbing vocation!"

The distinguishing characteristic of the *Annals* is Odell's engaging personal style. Throughout the long recital of physical facilities, personalities, and productions he maintains a contagious, zestful enthusiasm for each of his subjects. It is obviously a high adventure for him, and he makes it so for his readers with infinite personal charm. His enthusiasm breaks out charmingly at numerous points, such as in volume 7, where he interrupts a summary of hit productions with the declaration, "I hope the reader is beginning to love this season of 1859–60. How many rare successes which his longing eyes have strained through the printed page to see in actuality, have even so far passed before his vision!" And going on to speak of the premiere of

Dion Boucicault's *The Colleen Bawn*, he asserts, "The cast, as a whole, intoxicates the imaginative mind." Paying tribute to Joseph Jefferson, Odell says, "One sees out of how many fragments Jefferson built that noble, that matchless art of his later years—the most perfect, the most natural, the most simple (apparently) known to the theatre of all the days of my life."

His love of the high art of the theater did not blind Odell to the merits of plays that appealed to popular tastes. Writing about the 1890 rural melodrama hit *Blue Jeans*, he stated that in it "all elements combined to produce a splendid specimen of what drama critics of 1943 are clamouring for—'theatre,' that quality which draws the audience from its seats to become, as it were, sympathisers with the characters on the stage, vitally interested in their happiness and their sorrows."

Paying tribute to him at the time of his death in New York City, the *Herald Tribune* commented editorially,

Throughout his many years in the city, his towering figure and noble head were familiar sights in every theater. His knowledge of plays and their producers, of authors and actors was built on a solid foundation of personal observation. When he began to write his magnum opus, "Annals of the New York Stage," in the '20s, he had no need to learn matters of technique or terminology. That magic arch, which still charms and thrills as does no other approach to art, had become his own private doorway to life. . . . To do what one likes best, to hold one's mind single to a great task, to live to know accomplishment and to taste fame amid friendship and ease—such was the richly earned happiness of Professor Odell.

• The George Clinton Densmore Odell Papers, consisting of a large collection of theatrical memorabilia, clippings, photographs, and correspondence, are presently housed in the Rare Book and Manuscript Library of Columbia University. Information regarding Odell has been derived from the 18 Oct. 1949 obituary in the *New York Times* and clippings kindly furnished for this article by the Rare Book and Manuscript Library. The Austin Stevens interview will be found in the *Times* for 6 Sept. 1942.

ALBERT O. WEISSBERG

ODELL, Jonathan (25 Sept. 1737–25 Nov. 1818), Anglican clergyman, Loyalist, and poet, was born in Newark, New Jersey, the son of John Odell, a skilled carpenter, and Temperance Dickinson, the daughter of President Jonathan Dickinson of the College of New Jersey (later Princeton University). Odell's father provided in his will for a college education for his son. After graduating from the College of New Jersey in 1754, Odell conducted the college's grammar school, receiving in payment two-thirds of the school's proceeds. In 1756 he studied medicine and then joined a regiment of the British army, serving in the West Indies as an army surgeon. He received his A.M. from the College of New Jersey in 1757. During this period he decided to seek ordination as an Anglican clergyman, in spite of his family's historic ties to the Congregationalist church. While in England studying for the ministry, he taught at James Elphinston's Academy in Kensington and published his first poems. He met Benjamin Franklin, who recommended him to the Society for the Propagation of the Gospel and to his son William Franklin, governor of New Jersey, for appointment as an Anglican missionary in America.

Ordained in 1767, Odell immigrated to New Jersey where William Franklin inducted him as rector of St. Ann's Church, Burlington. He later added St. Andrew's, Mt. Holly, and St. James's across the Delaware River in Pennsylvania to congregations he served. In 1768 he was elected a member of the American Philosophical Society, for which he undertook translation of French treatises on silkworms. To augment his salary, Odell resumed the practice of medicine in 1771, and in 1774 he was elected to membership in the New Jersey Medical Society. In 1772 he married Anne de Cou of Burlington; they had two daughters and one son.

In 1775 Odell tried to remain neutral in the revolutionary upheaval, but private letters written to correspondents in England, which fell into the hands of the New Jersey Provincial Congress, revealed his disapproval of colonial resistance. His tenuous neutrality snapped in 1776, when he befriended captured British officers held in Burlington and entertained them with a poem written for the king's birthday on 4 June. The Burlington Committee of Safety retaliated by restricting Odell's movements. In December 1776, after patriot forces searched his house in search of Hessian troops, Odell slipped to the British garrison town in New York City. Late the next year he established himself in British-occupied Philadelphia, where he worked closely with his old friend Joseph Stansbury in publishing poetic political satire. He served as deputy chaplain to the British army and as chaplain to a battalion of Pennsylvania Loyalist troops, and he operated the British government's printing press and publication program. He persuaded Stansbury to moderate his harsh criticism of William Howe's Fabian strategy. When the British evacuated Philadelphia in May 1778, he returned to New York City; there he continued writing political poetry for garrison town newspapers that articulated the frustration felt by the Loyalist exiles with Howe's successor, Henry Clinton.

Odell sought to transform the Philadelphia and New York garrison towns into dynamic centers of metropolitan authority and stability. The most ambitious of all of the Loyalist poetic satirists, he produced in 1779 several long poems and a series of essays written with Samuel Seabury under the pseudonym "Britannicus," which sought to instill realism and zeal into the garrison town Loyalist populace and to discredit the Continental Congress. The French alliance was a prime target, as was the chaotic finances of the patriot regime. But unlike other garrison town partisans, Odell invited his readers to rethink the origins of the Revolution, acknowledge the mistakes the British made in the 1760s, and envision a new imperialism keyed to the self-interest of loyal colonists.

In 1779 Odell and Stansbury functioned as intermediaries between the American general Benedict Arnold and Henry Clinton by transmitting to Clinton Arnold's offer to defect to the British. Arnold entrusted his first written overture to Clinton to Stansbury, who in turn gave it to Odell. Hiding the letter in his clothing, Odell first let the letter get "damp," rendering half of the writing illegible. Thereafter, Major John André wrote in coded form Arnold's treasonous letters, which Odell then decoded for Clinton. When the negotiations between Arnold and Clinton went badly, Odell encouraged both sides to persevere. His modern biographer labels Odell's intrigues those of an "overanxious bungler" (Edelberg, p. 96).

In 1780 Odell published his major Loyalist poem, "The American Times," under the pseudonym "Camillo Querno," an allusion to the poet laureate and court jester to Pope Leo X and a veiled rebuke of George III for his failure to acknowledge Odell as the poetic voice of the king's friends in America. Here Odell wrote of "faction, pois'nous as the scorpion's sting" that "infects the people and insults the King," but he also diagnosed the British state as "rotten, rotten to the core/ 'tis all one bruise, one petrifying sore"—echoing Odell's experience as a physician (Edelberg, p. 119).

In May 1782 Odell joined the staff of Sir Guy Carleton—the last British commander in America—as chaplain to the King's American Dragoneers, and in July 1783 he became Carleton's assistant secretary. He encouraged Carleton's quixotic scheme of staying put in New York until Congress acknowledged a symbolic tie between America and the British Crown. He left New York with Carleton in December 1783 and went to London, where he sought compensation for his losses as a Loyalist. His reward was the lucrative post of New Brunswick provincial secretary. In that capacity Odell—now a slaveowner—tried to prevent black Loyalist exiles from re-emigrating to Sierra Leone. When the new Loyalist elite in New Brunswick demanded a degree of legislative autonomy from Britain, Odell scolded them for their failure to walk "peaceably within . . . sacred limits of religion and loyalty" (Edelberg, p. 158). He died in Fredericton, New Brunswick, Canada.

• Odell's papers are in the New Brunswick Museum, Saint John, New Brunswick, Canada. A modern biography is Cynthia D. Edelberg, *Jonathan Odell: Loyalist Poet of the American Revolution* (1987). On his early life, see James McLachlan, ed., *The Princetonians, 1748–1768* (1976); Winthrop Sargent, ed., *The Loyalist Poetry of the Revolution* (1858); and *The Loyal Verses of Joseph Stansbury and Doctor Jonathan Odell* (1860). On his New Brunswick years, see Ann G. Condon, *The Envy of the American States* (1984); and James W. St. G. Walker, *The Black Loyalists* (1976).

ROBERT M. CALHOON

ODETS, Clifford (18 July 1906–14 Aug. 1963), playwright, was born in Philadelphia, Pennsylvania, the son of eastern European immigrants Louis J. Odets, a printer, and Pearl Geisinger. Clifford was born into relative poverty, but Louis Odets was ambitious and by the time Clifford was in high school, Louis owned his own printing plant in the Bronx, where the family had moved when Clifford was six. Clifford was close to his aunt and uncle, Esther and Israel Rossman, from whom he imbibed much of the Jewish-American dialect, Yinglish, that lends ethnic authenticity to his early plays.

As the Odets family prospered, Clifford, an angry youth, became increasingly alienated from his parents and from his two younger sisters. The bourgeois status Louis sought appalled the young Odets, whose confrontations with his father were bitter and frequent. The animus between the two was heightened by Odets's failure at Morris High School. He dropped out in 1923. His early love of music and his voracious reading habits had a pronounced effect upon his later work. He became particularly enamored of Victor Hugo's *Les Misérables* (1862), a novel that celebrated the cause of the dispossessed, a theme Odets employed in his most influential plays.

Having left high school, Odets turned to elocution, the one thing he had succeeded at in high school. He joined the Moss Vaudeville Circuit, under its auspices reciting barroom ballads for three dollars a night plus whatever prizes his performances garnered. At Louis's insistence, Odets made an abortive attempt to be a copywriter in the printing plant, but he was an indifferent employee, leading Louis to the conclusion that his son would never amount to anything. Theater was in Clifford's blood; Louis considered this propensity the road to certain disaster. The young Odets drifted from one small acting company to another, serving apprenticeships with the Drawing-Room Players, Harry Kemp's Poets' Theatre, and Mae Desmond's Stock Company. He was associated with the Theatre Guild for a short time in 1929. He played bit roles and, although he could hardly be called successful, he gained considerable technical expertise in play production in the process.

A turning point in Odets's life occurred in 1931 when he became a charter member of the Group Theatre, recently formed by Harold Clurman, Cheryl Crawford, and Lee Strasberg. The Group Theatre was a collective acting company that aimed to bring a modicum of stability into the lives of young actors and playwrights during the darkest days of the Great Depression. Committed to the Stanislavsky method of acting, the Group Theatre set out to scuttle the star system, a hallmark of theater in the United States from its inception. The company staged new plays by promising young playwrights designed to give virtually equal parts to seven or eight actors. The plays the Group Theatre favored sometimes had a few minor roles, but the essential philosophy of the Group Theatre was to minimize such parts and to give a comparable number of lines to most of the actors in each play. Everyone in the company shared equally in its income. Stagehands, lighting technicians, actors, directors—all received equal compensation. This week's stage-

hand often had a significant role in next week's production.

Odets acted in the Group Theatre's plays but was busy simultaneously writing his own plays. He had completed an early version of *Awake and Sing!* (1935), variously entitled *9–10 Eden Street* and *I've Got the Blues*, at about the time New York's taxicab drivers went on strike. Moved by their demands, Odets closed himself in a Boston hotel room and, in three days, wrote *Waiting for Lefty* (1935). Much in need of money, he wrote the play in the fall of 1934 specifically for the *New Theatre–New Masses* theater contest. *Waiting for Lefty* won the first prize of fifty dollars. The production that followed on 5 January 1935 in a downtown meeting hall was a rousing success. The audience joined volubly in the play's final call for the cabbies to "Strike, strike, strike!" *Waiting for Lefty*, true to Group Theatre tradition, presented in positions of equivalent importance people from various walks of life who were eking out their existences as taxicab drivers.

The clamor surrounding the initial performance of *Waiting for Lefty* was so great that it was soon moved to Broadway. The play was too short, however, to be billed as a full evening's entertainment, so Odets quickly wrote a companion play, *Till the Day I Die* (1935), to complete the bill. This play deals with the situation of communists in Hitler's Germany. Because audiences were hungry for more Odets, the playwright hurriedly polished *Awake and Sing!*, which opened at the Belasco Theater in New York in February 1935. The play, which has been compared to the social dramas of Anton Chekhov, deals from a notably Marxist viewpoint with the social and economic problems of the depression as they affect three generations of the Jewish-American Berger family in the Bronx.

In autumn, another Odets play arrived on Broadway. *Paradise Lost* (1935) is a social drama about an upper-middle-class Jewish family caught in the grips of the depression. The play attacks many of the social ills that Odets, espousing idealistic communist sympathies, was convinced capitalism visits upon the masses. Odets, like many members of the Group Theatre, was more a liberal than a revolutionary. His early plays were, in their day, considered shocking tours de force, plays that the *New York Times* critic Brooks Atkinson labeled "fiercely dramatic in the theater." Michael Mendelsohn concludes, however, that Odets's agitprop plays read today seem "as dead as last year's newspaper." This contention is true up to a point, but in a 1985 television revival *Awake and Sing!* proved directly relevant to contemporary audiences.

In 1935 Odets was proclaimed the "great white hope" of American theater. His three-page monologue, *I Can't Sleep* (1935), performed by Morris Carnovsky, attacks the problems of poverty and the threat of homelessness, which pervaded his earlier plays. Odets, however, had begun, in *Golden Boy* (1937), to explore other social problems. The protagonist, Joe Bonaparte, is a boxer who, however unlikely as it may seem, is also a promising violinist. Every time he enters the ring, he risks damaging his sensitive hands. Financially strained, he confronts a basic conflict: economic necessity in a capitalist world makes devastating inroads on art. Bonaparte sees no alternative but to go for the money that boxing promises him. He wins the championship, but in so doing, he kills his opponent. His musician's hands now hopelessly compromised, Joe has the trappings of wealth, but they become his downfall. He gets into the high-powered Duesenberg his winnings have provided, but he wrecks it and dies in the crash. *Golden Boy* reveals personal conflicts that Odets was himself dealing with when the play was being written and Hollywood had made him generous offers to come to California and be a film writer.

Odets considered film writing a form of artistic prostitution, but the Group Theatre, which Odets looked upon as family, was foundering financially. He finally capitulated and went to Hollywood solely to earn money that he sent to the directors of the Group Theatre to keep afloat the institution that had given him his start and to which he was firmly committed. He produced a script for *The General Dies at Dawn* (1936), an undistinguished film, and during the next twenty-five years wrote several more film scripts, including *None But the Lonely Heart* (1944) and *The Sweet Smell of Success* (1957).

In 1937 Odets married the Austrian film star Luise Rainer. His world began to crumble shortly after his marriage. The period between *Golden Boy* and his next play, *Rocket to the Moon* (1938), was particularly difficult for him. He lost a great deal of his self-respect when he capitulated to Hollywood. He also became involved in an entangling romance with Frances Farmer, which led in 1941 to the dissolution of his marriage. *Rocket to the Moon*, produced by the Group Theatre, explores the questions of love and marriage that Odets was experiencing on a personal level.

His next play, *Night Music* (1940), also explores questions of love between men and women. He followed *Night Music* with *Clash by Night* (1941), the Group Theatre's last production before its dissolution. For Odets the breakup of the Group Theatre marked the end of the sort of family relationship that he had never been able to establish with his biological family. The production of *Clash by Night* also marked the end of an era for Odets. His last three plays, although they were stageworthy in many respects, disappointed audiences who asked the same question that critic Frank Nugent posed in his review of Odets's first film: "Odets, where is thy sting?" When the angry liberal of 1935 began to deal with themes whose chief focus was not the depression, audiences felt cheated and were incapable of judging his work in any context except that of their own expectations.

In 1943, settled in California, Odets married actress Betty Grayson. A seven-year hiatus occurred between *Clash by Night* and his next major drama, *The Big Knife* (1949), by any standards a strong script structurally, but not the play that audiences wanted from Odets. Admittedly, it was difficult to generate sympathy for a protagonist, Charlie Castle, who was being blackmailed by a Hollywood studio. The studio wanted Charlie to sign a multimillion-dollar contract and threatened, if he did not, to expose his role in a fatal automobile accident.

The Country Girl (1950), dealing with alcoholism, was more successful than *The Big Knife* and was made into an award-winning film starring Grace Kelly. The Odetses, who had a son and a daughter, divorced in 1952 shortly after *The Country Girl* closed. Odets's last play, *The Flowering Peach* (1954), is a warmly humane, often humorous redaction of the Noah story. In this play, Odets, who had begun a biblical exploration of his Jewish heritage, captures as well as he did in his earlier plays the authentic cadences of Jewish-American speech. The play, which favors resignation over revolution, was not commercially successful but continues to be well received in regional theaters.

The decade of the 1950s was a lonely and disenchanting one for Odets. Dissatisfied with the reception of his plays, scornful of the film writing that had made him wealthy, he became increasingly withdrawn. His disenchantment and self-hatred intensified after May 1952, when he was called to testify before the House Committee on Un-American Activities, at which time he admitted to his brief membership in the Communist party and identified other friends and associates in the theater who had a similar involvement during the 1930s. One year before his death in Los Angeles, he signed a contract to write four of the thirteen scripts for *The Richard Boone Show*, a television series, an arrangement he considered the ultimate prostitution of his talents. At the time of his death, he had completed three of these four scripts. A musical version of *Golden Boy* (1964), on which he had collaborated with William Gibson, was produced on Broadway the year after his death.

• The most substantial collection of Clifford Odets's papers is housed in the Billy Rose Collection of the New York Public Library at Lincoln Center. R. Baird Shuman's early study, *Clifford Odets* (1963), has been superseded by Gerald Weales's compact but thorough *Clifford Odets: Playwright* (1971), reprinted as *Odets: The Playwright* (1985; 1988). Margaret Brenman-Gibson, *Clifford Odets, American Playwright: The Years from 1906 to 1940* (1981), is the first volume of her projected two-volume biography of Odets, which, upon completion, will be the most comprehensive study of the playwright, although it is more psychoanalytical than literary. In *Clifford Odets: The Thirties and After* (1968), Edward Murray focuses on what happens to a playwright whose revolutionary cause disappears. Michael Mendelsohn, *Clifford Odets: Humane Dramatist* (1969), is an exhaustive and accurately detailed study, valuable for its discussion of Odets's film scripts. Harold Cantor, *Clifford Odets: Playwright-Poet* (1978), is among the best assessments of Odets's conscious artistry and use of language, which Ruby Cohn also discusses compellingly in *Dialogue in American Drama* (1971). Gabriel Miller, *Clifford Odets* (1989), views Odets's work in terms of its Chekhovian, romantic, tragic, melodramatic, and political visions. Miller's *Critical Essays of Clifford Odets* (1991) also is useful, as is William W. Demastes, *Clifford Odets: A Research and Production Handbook* (1991). Those interested in knowing more about Odets during the most difficult period of his creative life should consult *The Time Is Ripe: The 1940 Journal of Clifford Odets* (1988). Robert Cooperman, *Clifford Odets: An Annotated Bibliography of Criticism, 1935–1989* (1990), is thorough and accurate. William Gibson's introduction to Clifford Odets and William Gibson, *Golden Boy* (1965), and the preface to *Clifford Odets, American Playwright*, aforementioned, offer overall assessments of Odets and accounts of his final days. The two fullest obituaries are those in the *New York Times*, 16 Aug. 1963, and the *Los Angeles Times*, 15 Aug. 1963. A tribute by Harold Clurman appears in the *New York Times*, 25 Aug. 1994.

R. BAIRD SHUMAN

ODIN, Jean-Marie (25 Feb. 1800–25 May 1870), French Catholic missionary priest to the United States, first bishop of Galveston, Texas, and second archbishop of New Orleans, was born in Hauteville, France, the son of Jean Odin and Claudine-Marie Serol. The tiny village of Hauteville was a dependency of the Benedictine priory church of St. Martin d'Ambierle. Odin grew to maturity in a rural and devout Roman Catholic household, which helped him to develop a deep religious faith.

The Catholic church's educational and seminary system in the archdiocese of Lyon, under whose ecclesiastical jurisdiction St. Martin d'Ambierle church existed, was inadequate due to the dechristianization during the French Revolution. Initially this hampered Odin's education, but he eventually received normal seminary training. After attending several *petits seminaires* between 1814 and 1820, he entered the Sulpician *grande seminaire* of St. Irenaeus at Lyon.

In May 1822 Odin left France to serve as a missionary in the United States in the vast diocese of Louisiana and the Floridas, at that time under the ordinary authority of Sulpician bishop Louis William DuBourg. Odin attended the Vincentian seminary of the Barrens (now St. Mary's) at Perryville, Missouri, and was ordained there in 1823. Odin joined the Vincentians, taking his final vows in 1825.

Father Odin spent the next seventeen years headquartered at the Barrens seminary, laboring among the people of the Missouri-Arkansas area. In addition, Odin held several important positions at the seminary: professor of theology, treasurer, secretary to the rector, and eventually rector. For a few years Father Odin also acted as president of the lay college attached to the seminary.

During the years 1840 through 1861, Odin erected the base for the future of the Catholic church in Texas. He arrived in Texas on 13 July 1840 as a part of the Holy See's initiative to bolster Catholic evangelization in those lands north of the lower Rio Grande valley left unattended following the decline of the Franciscan missions. For the next two decades Father Odin struggled to serve the resident Catholic Mexicans, American Indians, and immigrants from the United States and Europe who had been entering Texas at an increasing rate since the 1820s.

Coming to Texas as vice prefect apostolic, Odin was named vicar apostolic and bishop of Claudiopolis on 16 July 1841. He was consecrated as such at St. Louis Cathedral in New Orleans on 6 March 1842, Bishop Antoine Blanc of New Orleans presiding. Bishop Odin became ordinary of the newly erected Diocese of Galveston on 21 May 1847. He recruited priests, brothers, and nuns from Europe, Canada, and the eastern United States to serve in his diocese; established churches, schools, a seminary, the first Catholic college in Texas (St. Mary's in 1852), hospitals, and other institutions; and personally carried out an exhausting missionizing schedule throughout Texas annually. In addition, Bishop Odin in 1858 convened the first Galveston diocesan synod, which planned the structure of the Catholic church in Texas for several decades to come.

In February 1861 the Holy See appointed Odin archbishop of New Orleans, the third oldest archdiocese in the United States. After serving in that capacity for nine years, Archbishop Odin traveled to Europe to attend the First Vatican Council, opened in 1869. In Rome he became ill and returned to France for recuperation at his boyhood home in Hauteville, where he died. Odin's greatest significance to the history of Roman Catholicism in the United States came from his efforts in strengthening the Catholic foundation in Texas.

• Archbishop Odin's letters up to 1861, as well as important documentation on him, are found in the De Andreis-Rosati Memorial Archives, Perryville, Mo. Similar correspondence and sources centering on his tenure as archbishop of New Orleans from 1861 through 1870 are on deposit in the Vincentian Collection of the Archives of the University of Notre Dame and the Archives of the Archdiocese of New Orleans. The Catholic Archives of Texas in Austin possess copies of most of these materials. The most important published works that focus either wholly or in part on Odin are Ralph Bayard, *Lone-Star Vanguard: The Catholic Re-Occupation of Texas (1945)*; Abbé Bony, *Vie de Mgr. Jean-Marie Odin, Missionaire Lazarist de la Nouvelle-Orleans par L'Auteur de L'Initiateur du Voeu National* (1896); John E. Rybolt, ed., *The American Vincentians: A Popular History of the Congregation of the Mission in the United States, 1815–1987* (1988); and Patrick Foley, "Jean-Marie Odin, C.M., Missionary Bishop Extraordinaire of Texas," *Journal of Texas Catholic History and Culture* (Mar. 1990): 42–60.

PATRICK FOLEY

ODLUM, Floyd Bostwick (30 Mar. 1892–17 June 1976), financier, was born in Union City, Michigan, the son of George A. Odlum, a Methodist minister, and Ellen Anderson. Odlum attended high school in Hillsdale, Michigan, graduating at the age of sixteen, at which time his family moved to Boulder, Colorado, where his mother sought to recuperate from tuberculosis. Odlum enrolled at the University of Colorado and studied journalism and law. In 1915 he received a Bachelor of Laws degree, and he later achieved the highest score on the Colorado state bar exam. Also in 1915 he married Hortense McQuarrie; they had two sons before divorcing in 1935.

Odlum struck out for Salt Lake City, where he found work as a legal clerk for Utah Power and Light, a subsidiary of the Electric Bond and Share Corporation, a utility holding company in New York City. In 1917 he moved to New York City to work for Electric Bond and Share's law firm, Simpson, Thacher and Bartlett. His work impressed his superiors, who transferred him to the offices of Electric Bond and Share, and in 1920 he became a vice president of the corporation. In 1926 he became vice chairman of Electric Bond and Share's foreign subsidiary, American and Foreign Power.

In 1923 Odlum, his friend George Howard, and their wives pooled $39,600 to buy utility stocks. Their pool grew quickly, so that by 1929 it had assets of $14 million and was called the Atlas Utilities Company. But in 1929 Odlum presciently sensed economic trouble ahead, leading him to convert his company's holdings into cash and its equivalent. Thus when the Great Depression struck, Odlum's money was safe and poised for new investments. As the economic slump deepened, he boldly bought up investment companies whose prices had fallen far below their true value. He then sold the liquid assets of these weak companies and used the profits to buy up more investment companies.

In 1932 Atlas Utilities Corporation changed its name to simply the Atlas Corporation, and Odlum began to concentrate on large-scale financing rather than on buying up more investment companies. By 1935 Atlas had assets of more than $100 million, and Odlum's deft dealings had brought him into control or management of a diverse array of businesses, including Greyhound Bus Lines; the Radio-Keith-Orpheum (RKO) and Paramount motion picture studios; the Hilton Hotels; the Bonwit Teller clothing store chain, of which his first wife became president; the Consolidated Vultee Aircraft (Convair) Corporation; Northeast Airlines; and the Madison Square Garden Corporation. In 1936 Odlum married Jacqueline Cochran, an airplane pilot who held numerous records for speed, distance, and altitude. They had no children. In 1940 the Atlas Corporation was divided into two parts. One continued large-scale financing, and the other merged with the U.S. Curtiss-Wright Corporation.

In the financial world Odlum became known as "Fifty Percent Odlum" because friends joked that "he buys everything for 50 cents on the dollar" (*Time*, 12 Sept. 1949). He combed the financial landscape in search of what he called "special situations," a company that seemed hopelessly downtrodden. If Odlum saw potential in the company's underlying value, he invested in the company, nursed it back to financial health by providing capital and good management, and then sold out at a large profit. For example, in 1934 he bought the RKO Corporation, reorganized it, promoted it with new publicity, and finally sold it to Howard Hughes in 1948, making a $17 million profit on his investment.

During the 1950s, especially after the lucrative 1953 sale of the Convair Corporation, Odlum invested heavily in uranium mining and spent a considerable amount of time on-site at mines in the Utah and Colorado hills. He also pushed for the development of the Atlas missile, which was later used in the Apollo missions to send American men to the Moon. When the government scaled back its funding for the Atlas missile, Odlum used Atlas Corporation funds to pay for its development for three years, until the government gave the missile higher priority.

In 1970 Odlum resigned as chairman of the Federal Resources Corporation, one of the myriad businesses he founded, and thereby cut his last formal tie to the corporate world. For much of his career he worked in New York City, where the Atlas Corporation was headquartered. He owned a Manhattan apartment that overlooked the East River, and at one time he also owned a home in Sands Point, Long Island. In 1947 Odlum bought a fifty-acre desert ranch at Indio, California, eighteen miles southeast of Palm Springs. Over the years he transformed it into a 723-acre farm, where he raised dates, grapes, and grapefruit. The ranch also contained the carefully preserved Eisenhower Cottage, where former president Dwight D. Eisenhower had spent nine years writing his memoirs. Odlum suffered from rheumatoid arthritis, and as the pain grew worse, crippling his hands and feet, he spent more time at his Indio ranch, often soaking in his Olympic-size swimming pool while conducting business with a long extension line telephone. After his retirement Odlum stayed year-round at the ranch. He founded the Arthritis and Rheumatic Foundation and served as its honorary chairman. He was also chairman of the Lovelace Foundation, which was involved in medical research and education.

Odlum was one of the few men in the United States who grew rich during the Great Depression. His keen financial timing enabled him to sense the right moment to buy or sell stock. He built the Atlas Corporation into one of the world's greatest investment corporations, controlling many companies in a vast array of industries. Odlum died in Indio.

• The Local History Files of the Palm Springs Public Library contain two articles on Odlum. For profiles of Odlum, see "Odlum's Midas Touch," *Newsweek*, 21 Mar. 1949, and "Rough Ride," *Time*, 12 Sept. 1949. "On the Trail of a Special Situation," *Business Week*, 28 May 1955, contains an article on Odlum's interest in uranium. "Mr. Odlum Gets the Business," *Fortune*, Sept. 1949, reports on Odlum's control of the Consolidated Vultee Aircraft Corporation of San Diego. An obituary is in the *New York Times*, 18 June 1976.

YANEK MIECZKOWSKI

O'DONNELL, Kenneth P. (4 Mar. 1924–9 Sept. 1977), politician, was born in Worcester, Massachusetts, the son of Cleo O'Donnell, a Holy Cross College football coach, and Alice M. Guerin. Christened Philip Kenneth, years later he changed his name to P. Kenneth and then to Kenneth P. Following high school graduation he enlisted in the U.S. Army Air Force. Commissioned a lieutenant, he had completed thirty bombing missions over Germany during World War II when he was shot down over Belgium and taken prisoner. Although severely wounded, he nevertheless soon escaped to England, where he required extensive hospitalization. A genuine war hero, he earned the Distinguished Flying Cross and the Air Medal with four clusters.

After the war O'Donnell entered Harvard (class of 1949), where he met and became close friends with Robert F. Kennedy, brother of the future president. He then held a variety of jobs in industry, mostly as a public relations consultant, while attending Boston College Law School. In 1948 he married Helen Sullivan; they had five children. He worked for John Kennedy and Robert Kennedy from 1952 until 1963, then for President Lyndon B. Johnson before returning to public relations work in Boston. In 1966 and 1970 he ran unsuccessfully for Massachusetts governor, the last time losing badly. He lacked finances, was unable to present a public image, and was relatively unknown. He turned to private affairs and ran his public relations and management consulting service.

Like so many young men of his generation, intense idealism coupled with a sense of duty suffused O'Donnell's character and principled his public actions. He found his fullest expression as an astute political aide, adviser, and friend of President Kennedy with a loyalty so intense and genuine that he subsumed his own aspirations in Kennedy's ideas and goals. O'Donnell's political career began with John Kennedy's 1946 run for Congress. At the behest of Robert Kennedy, he actively worked in a minor way on the campaign. In 1951 he joined John Kennedy's first campaign for senator, and his maturing knowledge and intense efforts were fundamental to JFK's victory over Republican Henry Cabot Lodge, Jr. Afterward he served as the senator's unpaid state representative. He slowly grew in stature and gradually earned Kennedy's full confidence, a tribute not only to O'Donnell's qualities but also to the astuteness of the rising senator as he pulled able and bright young men onto his staff. In 1957 O'Donnell moved to Washington, D.C., to work as assistant to Robert Kennedy, who was counsel of the Senate Rackets Committee. The next year O'Donnell joined John Kennedy's Washington staff as part of the close-knit inner circle of friends and advisers.

Upon election to the presidency, JFK appointed O'Donnell special assistant to the president, in which capacity he served as the White House appointments secretary, as major agent in political patronage, and as a principal political coordinator to the president. He was also in charge of the staff and of travel and advance men. Controlling who saw the president, he also acted as a political adviser, confidant, and sounding board for Kennedy's ideas, ranking next to Robert Kennedy in the president's trust, a position that had come slowly, only crystallizing in 1961. In these capacities, his friend and political associate Lawrence O'Brien remarked, he "played a major role in national politics and government" (*Boston Globe*, 10 Sept. 1977). O'Donnell, like so many of Kennedy's closest staff, was a liberal in politics and a progressive in social issues, suggesting the measure of the president reflected by his selection of closest aides. His devotion to Kennedy was complete; he had no political identity of his own.

O'Donnell carefully planned President Kennedy's November 1963 tour of Texas, an ordinary schedule with the usual careful security arrangements, concurred in by all agencies concerned. On 22 November, at Kennedy's order, O'Donnell had the nonbullet proof bubble top removed from the limousine. He and David Powers, another close friend and assistant of Kennedy, sat in the rear of the Secret Service's open top follow-up limousine just behind the president in the motorcade. They witnessed the assassination with clarity. Before the Warren Commission, O'Donnell affirmed the official conclusion that all shots had come from the rear, where the lone assassin allegedly had fired, but he later confided to his Massachusetts friend Speaker of the House Thomas "Tip" O'Neill a radically different story. From one of the best perches in the plaza, both men had actually "heard two shots that came from behind the fence" (O'Neill and Novak, p. 178). He alleged that respect for the feelings of Kennedy's widow kept them silent, an emotional rather than a logical decision. Local law notwithstanding, O'Donnell and other presidential aides had President Kennedy's body immediately transported to Washington for an autopsy, an act that unwittingly denied it a full and proper examination and put it into the hands of less qualified military prosecutors.

Among Kennedy's aides, O'Donnell remained on President Lyndon B. Johnson's staff the longest, serving as a presidential assistant for fourteen months. O'Donnell utilized his knowledge of urban politics, a great service to the new president, who lacked an urban, northern, and far western political grounding. His oral history of those years are remarkable for candor and trenchant insights on political affairs. In 1968 he helped convince New York senator Robert Kennedy to run for the presidency and later in the year worked on Hubert Humphrey's presidential campaign. After the June assassination of Kennedy, he worked unsuccessfully to place a peace plank in the Democratic party platform. In 1970, with Powers and ghost writer Joe McCarthy, he published *"Johnny, We Hardly Knew Ye": Memories of John Fitzgerald Kennedy*. This memoir repeated a point O'Donnell had made public earlier in a *Life* magazine article, that President Kennedy had planned to withdraw U.S. troops from Vietnam after he won the 1964 election. Although vigorously criticized by conservative columnists and politicians at the time, history has accorded his statement solid support.

The assassination of President Kennedy had profoundly stricken O'Donnell; the loss forever governed his life. His first wife died in January 1977. In April 1977 he married Hanna Helga Steinfatt, a German national working in the United States; they had no children. He died in Boston.

• Many of O'Donnell's papers were destroyed, and others have not been made public. The John F. Kennedy Library in

Boston contains some miscellaneous personal papers. An important oral history is in the Lyndon Baines Johnson Library. An article taken from his book appeared in "LBJ and the Kennedys: Excerpt," *Life*, 7 Aug. 1970, pp. 44–48. A well-researched biography is Daniel Charles Kenary, "The Political Education of Kenneth P. O'Donnell" (bachelor's honor thesis, Harvard Univ., 1982).

Discussions of O'Donnell are in Arthur M. Schlesinger, Jr., *A Thousand Days* (1965) and *Robert Kennedy and His Times* (1978). Patrick Anderson, *The President's Men* (1968), devotes a chapter to O'Donnell. See too Herbert S. Parmet, *Jack: The Struggles of John F. Kennedy* (1980), and James N. Giglio, *The Presidency of John F. Kennedy* (1991). Thomas P. O'Neill, Jr., and William Novak, *Man of the House: The Life & Political Memoirs of Speaker Tip O'Neill* (1987), recounts O'Donnell's comment on frontal shots at Kennedy. A discussion of Vietnam and President Kennedy is in John M. Newman, *JFK and Vietnam* (1992). The removal of Kennedy's body and the autopsy is discussed in Harold Weisberg, *Post Mortem* (1975) and *Never Again* (1995).

Obituaries are in the *Washington Post*, the *New York Times*, and the *Boston Globe*, all 10 Sept. 1977, with Mike Barnicle's appreciation, "Kenny O'Donnell: 'Casualty of History,' " in the same issue of the *Boston Globe*.

DAVID R. WRONE

O'DONOVAN, William Rudolf (28 Mar. 1844–20 Apr. 1920), sculptor and painter, was born in northern Augusta County, Virginia (now Preston County, W.Va.), the son of James Hayes O'Donovan, an itinerant tailor, and Mary Bryte. O'Donovan attended school in Virginia and later Greene Academy in Carmichaels, Pennsylvania. He left an apprenticeship with a marble cutter in Carmichaels in about 1859 to work in Virginia, before joining the Confederate army in 1861. O'Donovan served with the Staunton, Virginia, artillery in the Second Corps of the Army of Northern Virginia and surrendered with Robert E. Lee at Appomattox.

In about 1867 O'Donovan moved to New York City, where he established himself as a sculptor, although he had had no formal art training and never acknowledged any teacher. During his early years in New York O'Donovan shared a studio with the portrait sculptor James Wilson Alexander MacDonald, who became his close friend and mentor. In about 1871 O'Donovan began working with Maurice J. Power, a contractor who furnished American Revolution and Civil War sculptural monuments to civic commissions to mark hallowed sites and to memorialize historical events. O'Donovan assisted Power from 1871 to 1895 in this business by making three-dimensional figures and bas-relief tablets that were cast in bronze at the National Fine Art Foundry, which Power had founded in New York City in 1868.

O'Donovan created sculpture for the *Captor's Monument* (1880), Tarrytown, New York; the *Oriskany Monument* (1884), Oriskany, New York; the *Saratoga Battlefield Monument* (1885), Schuylerville, New York; the *Irish Brigade Monument* (1888), Gettysburg Battlefield; the *Soldiers' and Sailors' Monument* (1881), Lawrence, Massachusetts; the *Confederate Memorial Monument* (1872), Oakdale Cemetery, Wilmington,

North Carolina; and the *General John A. Wagener Monument* (n.d.; he was a German Confederate), Bethany Cemetery, Charleston, South Carolina. O'Donovan also modeled the statue of Archbishop John Hughes (1891), on the Fordham University campus, Bronx, New York; and figures of George Washington for the *Tower of Victory* (1887), Newburgh, New York; the *Trenton Battle Monument* (1892), Trenton, New Jersey; and *Plaza George Washington* (n.d.), Caracas, Venezuela.

O'Donovan first exhibited his documentary portrait busts of contemporaries in 1874 at the National Academy of Design. In 1876 he moved his studio to the Studio Building at 51 West Tenth Street, where he modeled painters William Page and Winslow Homer, who occupied studios near his own. O'Donovan formed a close friendship with Page and probably assimilated ideas about spirituality and physiognomy from him. Artists and collectors in the New York art community so admired O'Donovan's naturalistic bust of Page (1877) that they contributed funds toward a bronze casting of it for the National Academy of Design to honor Page for his past leadership of the academy. In 1878 the National Academy enhanced O'Donovan's reputation by electing him to associate membership, primarily to recognize his portrait of Page.

O'Donovan, along with Homer and others, receives credit for organizing the Tile Club in 1877, which arranged events and excursions for its membership, comprised of sculptors, painters, writers, and musicians. The remarks of some club members suggest that they considered O'Donovan a colorful individual. Writer and artist Earl Shinn in 1879 described him in a letter as "talented" and "an original if there ever was one." Similarly, O'Donovan's verbal wit and "eccentricity" impressed sculptor and illustrator James E. Kelly, who knew him at the foundry.

In 1879 the Society of American Artists invited O'Donovan into their membership, and with that group during the 1880s he exhibited his portrait busts and bas-relief portraits. His active interest in writing during that period culminated in publication of several articles: "A Statue of Shakespeare," *Lippincott's Monthly Magazine* (Jan. 1875); "Portraits of Washington," *The Independent* (22, 29 June 1876); "Rye and Round There," *Harper's New Monthly Magazine* (June 1879); and, later, with Samuel Parsons, "The Art of Landscape Gardening," *The Outlook* (Sept. 1906).

In 1891 O'Donovan spent some time working in Philadelphia at painter and sculptor Thomas Eakins's studio, where he modeled a bust of poet Walt Whitman. During his frequent visits to Whitman's home, O'Donovan cheered the ailing poet, who described O'Donovan as "a fine fellow, splendid magnetic fellow" (Whitman to John Johnston, 9 July 1891, Library of Congress).

O'Donovan's close association with Eakins from 1891 until about 1893 had begun with Eakins's acceptance of O'Donovan's invitation to collaborate on bas-relief equestrian portraits of Abraham Lincoln and Ulysses S. Grant for the monumental *Soldiers' and*

Sailors' Memorial Arch (1894) in Brooklyn. O'Donovan used death masks of Lincoln and Grant and images taken by photographer Mathew Brady as documentary sources for the faces and figures of the men. Eakins modeled the horses, a subject of special interest to him.

After 1895 O'Donovan modeled only a few works of sculpture; instead he created small pastel drawings and tempera paintings that often depict landscapes of suburban Westchester County. Contemporaries appreciated his painting style for its impressionistic brushwork, quiet mood, and harmonious color. The Macbeth Gallery and Cottier & Company presented his paintings in exhibitions in New York City during the decade prior to his death.

O'Donovan participated in civic affairs from 1898 to 1913 as a member of the jury to select the design of the *Maine Memorial* in New York City and from 1906 to 1909 as a member of the Decoration and Reviewing Stands Committee for the Hudson-Fulton Celebration Commission.

O'Donovan married a woman named Henderson (her given name is believed to be Henrietta), perhaps as early as 1882. They had one child before her death in 1887. In 1893 O'Donovan married Mary Corcoran, with whom he lived until his death in New York City. The couple had no children.

As a sculptor who helped to shape and refine the imagery of American Revolution and Civil War commemorative monuments to fulfill contract awards, O'Donovan integrated his aptitude and ability as a fine artist with the requirements of a commercial enterprise. He was always keenly interested in portraiture, and among his most successful portrayals are his subtly modeled bas-reliefs of artists and friends. Beyond recording the appearances of his sitters, O'Donovan affirmed the rich pictorial essence of the bas-relief medium. The current revival of interest in American figurative sculpture and initiatives being taken to inventory and restore the nation's outdoor sculpture may help to revive O'Donovan's reputation, which faltered when tastes in art shifted away from naturalism in favor of the abstractions of modernism.

• Institutions possessing sculpture by O'Donovan include the Brooklyn Museum, the Century Association (N.Y.C.), Columbia University, Cornell University, the Hirshhorn Museum and Sculpture Garden (Washington, D.C.), the Metropolitan Museum of Art, the National Academy of Design, the National Museum of American Art of the Smithsonian Institution, the Pennsylvania Academy of the Fine Arts, and Yale University. O'Donovan's papers, comprised of letters written to his family in western Pennsylvania between 1871 and 1880 are in the Historical Society of Pennsylvania. For an idea of his working methods and philosophy, see O'Donovan, "A Sculptor's Method of Work," *Art Journal* 5 (Feb. 1878): 62–63. See Joshua C. Taylor, *William Page: The American Titian* (1976), on his friendship with Page; Lloyd Goodrich, *Thomas Eakins* (1982), and William Innes Homer, *Thomas Eakins: His Life and Art* (1992), on his association with Eakins; Cleveland Moffett, "Grant and Lincoln in Bronze," *McClure's*, Oct. 1895, pp. 419–32, on the reliefs for *Soldiers' and Sailors' Memorial Arch*; and Walt Whitman, *The Correspondence*, vol. 5 (1969), on his Whitman bust. Obituaries are in the *New York Times*, 21 Apr. 1920, and *American Art News*, 24 Apr. 1920.

VIRGINIA B. KELLY

ODUM, Howard Washington (24 May 1884–8 Nov. 1954), sociologist, was born near Bethlehem, Georgia, the son of William Pleasants Odum and Mary Ann Thomas, farmers. At the age of thirteen Odum moved with his family to Oxford, Georgia. There he later attended Emory Academy and College, from which he received a B.A. in English and classics in 1904.

Odum remained in the South for almost all of his professional life. After teaching school for a year in Toccopola, Mississippi, he earned an M.A. in 1906 in classics at the University of Mississippi, where he began the study of social science under the psychologist Thomas Pierce Bailey, a graduate of Clark University. Odum himself then earned a Ph.D. in psychology from Clark in 1909, writing a thesis on folk songs of black migrant workers. He went to Columbia University to write a second, more theoretical dissertation under Franklin H. Giddings and in 1910 earned a Ph.D. in sociology; this dissertation was published as *Social and Mental Traits of the Negro* (1910). In December of that year Odum married Anna Louise Kranz, a fellow graduate student at Clark; they had three children.

After graduating from Columbia, Odum began his career as an applied social scientist. He researched and published a study on school hygiene for the Philadelphia Bureau of Municipal Research in 1912, then moved to the University of Georgia to teach educational sociology for the next seven years. He taught at Emory in 1919–1920, then accepted a post at the University of North Carolina at Chapel Hill, where he remained, apart from brief leaves, for the rest of his career. There he established a school of public welfare and directed it from 1920 until 1932, founded and began editing the *Journal of Social Forces* in 1922, and set up in 1924 the school's Institute for Research in the Social Sciences, which he directed until 1944. Especially in their support of the latter venture, several philanthropies associated with the Rockefeller Foundation helped Odum establish Chapel Hill as a regional center of sociological leadership.

Odum's many books of this period explored racial issues in the context of the problem-solving ideology quickly becoming characteristic of American social science. Maintaining his longtime interest in folk culture, he produced sociological texts (*The Negro and His Songs* [1925] and *Negro Workaday Songs* [1926]), the prose poem *An American Epoch* (1930), and a fictional trilogy based on a character named Left-Wing Gordon (*Rainbow Round My Shoulder* [1928], *Wings on My Feet* [1929], and *Cold Blue Moon* [1931]). Other works helped define social inquiry in terms of its possibilities for social change; among these, he authored *An Approach to Public Welfare and Social Work* (1926) and *Man's Quest for Social Guidance* (1927), and he edited *American Masters of Social Science* (1927).

In addition to vigorous publication of his views, Odum promoted his activist vision of social science in important institutional settings. Along with other leading figures in the Social Science Research Council, he served in the project leadership for President Herbert Hoover's investigation of *Recent Social Trends* (1933). A member of the Commission on Interracial Cooperation from 1919 to 1944, Odum resigned after he developed an integrationist framework that opposed the commission's emphasis on segregationist liberalism. He also attempted to bring social science exhibits into the mainstream of the plans for the 1933 Century of Progress exposition in Chicago before he quit in frustration in 1931. He spent the remainder of the 1930s and 1940s developing his ideas on regional identity that remain his most important intellectual contribution.

In conjunction with other advocates of regional planning such as Lewis Mumford, Odum attempted to conceive of the nation in terms of units large enough to support expensive public works projects yet small enough to retain distinctive identities. He theorized that natural resources, folk culture, and historical traditions could be binding forces within an area, and he resisted both homogenizing nationalism and provincial sectionalism. Some of his ideas were implemented within various New Deal agencies, but the regional ideal languished as federal bureaucracies and state governments struggled for primacy.

Odum's books *Southern Regions* (1936), and *American Regionalism*, with Harry E. Moore (1938), illustrate both the insights and the liabilities of his program. Neatly logical arguments for regional organization often underestimated the power of political actors' self-interest, and the prose, which both contemporaries and later generations found vague and slippery, confused and frustrated readers who sought specificity and careful argument. In *Southern Regions* he called regional planning "an extension and transubstantiation of the first great American experiment in social planning, namely, the Constitution," and claimed that regionalism "will utilize the full capacity of a social engineering competent to build not only new structures for the nation but to carry in the meantime the traffic of all the institutions in a transitional society and within these institutions to permit of orientation, spontaneity, flexibility" (pp. 579–80). Despite his efforts to advance the South while preserving its distinctiveness, he rarely moved beyond such abstractions and hyperbole.

After World War II, Odum sought to codify his outlook, but the terms that he favored—"technicways" and "stateways"—suffered from imprecision in contrast to the more widely accepted concept of folkways. His final books—*Understanding Society* (1947), *The Way of the South* (1947), and *American Sociology* (1951)—reflected his lifelong interests in folk culture, social improvement, and the fate of his region.

Odum became a fixture in Chapel Hill, where he was well liked and where he eventually died. His range of interests, vigorous pace of publication, and institutional interconnectedness made him an important figure in the growth of the modern South, but his intellectual legacy for students of race, region, and society remains unsystematic and uneven.

• The most extensive collection of Odum's papers is at the University of North Carolina in Chapel Hill, but Emory University also has some significant items. No complete biography has yet been published, but see Wayne D. Brazil, *Howard W. Odum: The Building Years, 1884–1930* (1988), a published but unrevised Ph.D. dissertation. A bibliography of Odum's writings is in Katherine Jocher et al., eds., *Folk, Region, and Society: Selected Papers of Howard W. Odum* (1964), pp. 455–69. On Odum and regionalism, see Allen Tullos, "The Politics of Regional Development: Lewis Mumford and Howard W. Odum," in *Lewis Mumford: Public Intellectual*, ed. Thomas P. Hughes and Agatha C. Hughes (1990), pp. 110–20. A recent study is Paul Challen, *A Sociological Analysis of Southern Regionalism: The Contributions of Howard W. Odum* (1992). On Odum's place in southern intellectual history, see Michael O'Brien, *The Idea of the American South, 1920–1941* (1979), and Daniel Joseph Singal, *The War Within: From Victorian to Modernist Thought in the South, 1919–1945* (1982). For a treatment of Odum's views on race and regionalism, see Morton Sosna, *In Search of the Silent South: Southern Liberals and the Race Issue* (1977). Odum's relation to the social science profession is discussed in John M. Jordan, *Machine-Age Ideology: Social Engineering and American Liberalism* (1994). An obituary is in the *New York Times*, 9 Nov. 1954.

JOHN M. JORDAN

O'DWYER, William (11 July 1890–24 Nov. 1964), mayor of New York City, was born in Bohola, County Mayo, Ireland, the son of Patrick O'Dwyer and Bridget McNicholas, schoolteachers. He attended Bohola National School and St. Nathays College in Roscommon. At the urging of his mother, who was convinced he had a vocation for the priesthood, O'Dwyer in 1907 enrolled at the University of Salamanca, a Jesuit seminary in Spain. Three years before graduating, however, he abandoned his studies and sailed for New York. Arriving in June 1910 with $25.35 in his pocket, O'Dwyer found work in a succession of unskilled positions. As a plasterer's apprentice, the future mayor helped in the construction of the Woolworth Building and several other Manhattan landmarks. At night O'Dwyer tended bar at the Vanderbilt Hotel, where he served (and came to detest) New York's Bohemian saloon set. In 1916 he married Catherine Lenihan, a telephone operator at the Vanderbilt. They remained together until her death in 1946 but had no children.

In July 1917 O'Dwyer joined the police force, walking Brooklyn's toughest waterfront beat. By 1924 he had become head of the department's legal bureau. During this time, he enrolled in evening classes at Fordham University Law School, receiving his LL.B. in 1923. After passing the New York bar in 1925, he resigned from the force and opened his own practice. Hoping to drum up business and establish a political base, O'Dwyer promoted Ireland's national soccer team's annual tours of the United States. His efforts made him a celebrity in the Irish-American community and helped him form close friendships with the reporters who covered the matches. This association paid off in 1932, when acting mayor Joseph V. McKee, at the suggestion of O'Dwyer's cronies in the press, appointed "Bill-O" a New York City magistrate. In 1935 Mayor Fiorello La Guardia named O'Dwyer the first judge of the Brooklyn Adolescent Court, where he presided until Governor Herbert Lehman chose him to fill a vacancy on the Kings County Court in December 1937. Though he won a full fourteen-year term the next year, O'Dwyer resigned in 1939 to run successfully for Brooklyn district attorney.

In this position, O'Dwyer gained national attention for his spectacular prosecutions of several professional killers, all members of organized crime's notorious enforcement team, Murder Inc. Less than three months after taking office, he announced the solution of fifty-six underworld-related homicides, resulting in the convictions and executions of seven of the ring's members. Though O'Dwyer declared triumphantly that he had "smashed" Murder Inc., his investigation never threatened the syndicate's top leaders. "All that happened was that the mob threw him some of the cowboys to take the heat off the bigshots," one critic later maintained. Others even claimed O'Dwyer may have been complicit in this process. In late 1941 a key witness, whose testimony could have led to the indictments of high-level figures such as Albert Anastasia, Frank Costello, and Benjamin "Bugsy" Siegel, mysteriously fell to his death from a hotel window while under heavy police guard. O'Dwyer labeled the death an accident, though the body landed twenty feet from the building. Subsequently, Anastasia's "wanted" cards and arrest sheets disappeared from police files. These irregularities did not undercut the affable district attorney's widespread popularity. He won the Democratic mayoral nomination in 1941 and came close to defeating the long-entrenched Republican mayor, La Guardia, in the general election.

Following the outbreak of World War II, O'Dwyer took a leave of absence to join the army. His work combating fraud in the U.S. Army Air Corps won him high praise from the Franklin Roosevelt administration. In 1944 President Roosevelt appointed him chief of the Economic Section of the Allied Commission, sending him to Italy as the president's personal representative to the Foreign Economic Administration. The next year O'Dwyer retired from the army at the rank of brigadier general and accepted an appointment as head of the War Refugee Board. Returning to New York after the end of the war, he resigned as district attorney—he had been reelected without opposition in 1943—and launched his second campaign for mayor.

Despite opponents' allegations that mob boss Costello had engineered his nomination, O'Dwyer won the election by a record majority of votes. Presenting himself as an "enlightened" Democrat, the mayor engaged in several highly publicized disputes with the leadership of the New York City Democratic machine, Tammany Hall, in hopes of demonstrating his independence and dedication to reform. O'Dwyer's attempts to clean up the party organization, however, had little lasting effect.

During his first term, O'Dwyer confronted numerous crises associated with the conversion to a peacetime economy and society. Since the war had delayed all new capital projects, O'Dwyer faced immediate demands for more schools, hospitals, subway cars, and other physical improvements. To solve this dilemma, the mayor relied heavily on the advice of Commissioner Robert Moses, appointing him to the newly created position of city construction coordinator. Moses soon negotiated an arrangement with New York state leaders that allowed O'Dwyer to raise revenue by levying new city taxes and increasing New York City's traditional nickel subway fare to a dime. Moses, however, directed most of this money toward slum clearance and building massive expressways—projects that ultimately transformed the landscape of the city. O'Dwyer settled a series of labor disputes, including tugboat and truck strikes, that threatened to cripple the city. He responded by establishing the Division of Labor Relations, which proved effective in restoring industrial peace. In 1948 the mayor led the successful campaign to bring the United Nations headquarters to New York. Well liked by most New Yorkers, he easily won reelection the following year. That December O'Dwyer married model Sloan Simpson. Childless, they divorced in 1953.

Meanwhile, a police corruption scandal in Brooklyn received wide publicity and exposure, linking the O'Dwyer campaign to illegal bookmakers and organized crime. Sensing that the tide had turned against him, O'Dwyer resigned on 1 August 1950, citing health reasons. Immediately thereafter, President Harry Truman appointed him ambassador to Mexico, a position he held until 1952. O'Dwyer returned briefly to the United States in 1951 to testify before the special Senate committee, chaired by Estes Kefauver, investigating police corruption and organized crime. Though no indictments were ever returned against the former mayor, he was periodically accused of associating with and accepting campaign contributions from known criminals, aiding crime while a New York official, and accepting a $10,000 bribe from the president of the Firemen's Association. When his term as ambassador ended with the election of Republican Dwight D. Eisenhower, O'Dwyer remained in Mexico. He practiced law in Mexico City until 1960, then returned to New York City, where he died.

"William O'Dwyer was a warm, gregarious, fallible human being who made real and lasting contributions to New York City. His rise was a flamboyant metropolitan success story," the *New York Times* editorialized at his death. Although his association with the underworld severely tarnished his reputation, O'Dwyer's love for his adopted city was sincere. For more than thirty years, he proved himself a tireless public servant, though one often victimized by men he had trusted.

• O'Dwyer's papers and correspondence are in the William Stiles Bennet Papers, Syracuse State Library; the William H. Allen Papers, Institute for Public Service, New York City; and the James P. O'Brien Papers, New York Public Library. U.S. Senate, *Report of the Special Committee to Investigate Organized Crime in Interstate Commerce*, 82d Cong., 1st sess., 1951, S. Exec. Doc. 725, contains a transcript of O'Dwyer's testimony to the Kefauver Committee. Though no biography has yet been published, Milton MacKaye, "The Ex-Cop Who Runs New York," *Saturday Evening Post*, 31 May 1947, pp. 18–19, 78–84, offers a thorough account of O'Dwyer's life through his first year as mayor. George Walsh, *Public Enemies: The Mayor, the Mob, and the Crime That Was* (1980), provides biographical information and a detailed account of O'Dwyer's association with organized crime. Burton Turkus (O'Dwyer's deputy district attorney) and Sid Feder, *Murder Inc.* (1951), includes an assessment of O'Dwyer's role in the case. Fred J. Cook and Gene Gleason, "The Men behind the Tiger," *Nation*, 31 Oct. 1959, pp. 265–69, recounts the mayor's relations with Tammany Hall and Costello, as does George Wolf and Joseph DiMona, *Frank Costello, Prime Minister of the Underworld* (1974). Robert Caro, *The Power Broker* (1974), and Joel Schwartz, *The New York Approach* (1993), examine the Moses-O'Dwyer relationship and Moses's role in formulating construction and revenue policies. Edward Robb Ellis, *The Epic of New York City* (1966), and Warren Moscow, *The Last of the Big-Time Bosses* (1971), have chapters on O'Dwyer and his administration. An obituary is in the *New York Times*, 25 Nov. 1964.

THOMAS W. DEVINE

O'FALLON, Benjamin (20 Sept. 1793–17 Dec. 1842), Indian agent, was born in Kentucky, the son of James O'Fallon, a physician, and Frances Eleanor Clark. He was sent, in his teens, to St. Louis to live with his maternal uncle, William Clark. Clark noted in a letter written to O'Fallon's brother John in 1809 that O'Fallon "has jenious but wants application." After dabbling in business, O'Fallon set off in 1816 for the St. Peters River to trade with the Sioux. His success convinced his uncle of his diplomatic skill, for in the following year Clark officially appointed him U.S. Indian agent (with the rank of major) to the Sioux. O'Fallon made his headquarters at Prairie du Chien, now in Wisconsin, where he quickly established a reputation among the St. Louis traders for the "rigor and firmness" with which he exercised his authority.

O'Fallon was equally strict with traders and Indians in enforcing Washington's policies and regulations. In his first year as agent, O'Fallon arrested a company of traders working for John Jacob Astor's American Fur Company for not having valid trading licenses. At the same time he liked to overawe the tribes with shows of military pomp and power, and the Sioux were much impressed by the troops. He reported to Clark of the Sioux in 1818, "Keep liquor away from them and they can be civilized." His strict enforcement of the government's control over the Indian trade led O'Fallon into inevitable conflict with the traders, who found government policies and regulations restrictive and unrealistic. But O'Fallon won and retained the respect of the tribes and succeeded in negotiating and keeping peace in his jurisdiction.

O'Fallon's knowledge of and experience with the "Indian character," bolstered by family and political connections, made him arrogant and overbearing, as his cocommissioner General Henry Atkinson was to discover when he appointed O'Fallon to treat with the Upper Missouri tribes in 1824. Atkinson had commanded the western frontier since 1819 and had jointly with O'Fallon held councils with the Upper Missouri tribes. Atkinson, at that time a novice at Indian relations, had committed some diplomatic blunders. "Unfortunately," Atkinson's biographer observed, "the Agent (O'Fallon) never explained the niceties of Indian diplomacy which might have helped Atkinson as the highest ranking military commander on the Mississippi-Missouri frontier" (Nichols, p. 65).

The Yellowstone expedition of 1825 was intended to pacify the tribes of the Upper Missouri, whose hostilities had culminated in a series of attacks against white trappers and traders in 1823. The immediate reaction of the U.S. government, a military expedition under the command of Colonel Leavenworth, had been hampered by indecision, ill luck, and ill will between Leavenworth and the military on one hand and the Indian subagent Joshua Pilcher and the traders on the other. General Atkinson, although more forceful and effective than Leavenworth in Indian affairs, was, however, like Leavenworth, unable to avoid quarreling with the resident Indian agent. O'Fallon, like his friend Joshua Pilcher before him, felt his qualifications to negotiate with the Indians vastly superior to those of the military, whose officers he relentlessly criticized in his correspondence.

The cocommissioners set out from St. Louis on 20 March 1825 and on 19 April arrived at Council Bluffs, now in Iowa, where they gathered their military escort of 476 troops. The tribes were treated to military pomp and some rockets, which "greatly impressed them." Treaties were then hastily concluded. So the expedition proceeded, arriving in July at the Arikara and Mandan villages, where treaties were concluded with the neighboring tribes. During a council with the Crow an altercation broke out between the Americans and a number of hostile Crow. O'Fallon lost his temper and struck a number of Crow in the head with his pistol. Atkinson, who had not been present when the fighting began, quelled the uproar by calling out and parading his troops.

Although there were no serious diplomatic repercussions, the episode manifested the underlying conflict between Atkinson and O'Fallon over the appropriate attitude to be adopted toward the tribes. O'Fallon was known for his severity; Atkinson was far more flexible (and humane, according to one St. Louis trader) in his attitudes toward the Indians, and he consistently sought to placate and appease them. The simmering tension between the two men finally erupted into violence one night in July. George Kennerly, O'Fallon's sutler, was present, and the following month he described the scene in a letter to his brother James:

What I had long expected has at last taken place, on the evening before last while at the supper table . . . they mutually seized, one a knife, the other a fork, and made the attempt to stab—fortunately I was sitting near, and threw myself between them running myself the risk of receiving the blows of one, or both. I stopped them at the time, they have not since spoke to each other, and how it will end God only knows. Family ties to O'Fallon notwithstanding, Kennerly blamed him for the quarrel, "as it is evident that he has provoked the General to this line of conduct, by his continual bad humor, and unnecessary interference with his duties as a military officer." O'Fallon's temper, a symptom of chronic ill health, Kennerly also attributed to "his extreme vanity, and want of liberality to do justice to any man, whom he thinks, in the opinion of others, stands as high as he does, in their judgement of the Indian character."

Despite the personal animosity between the cocommissioners, they maintained a united front in their councils with the tribes. After proceeding past the mouth of the Yellowstone River, the expedition returned to Council Bluffs in September and to St. Louis in October 1825. The expedition had taken seven months to complete and its results, twelve treaties concluded with sixteen Indian nations, mark the expedition on the whole as at least a diplomatic success.

O'Fallon had for a number of years complained of his health and had requested a leave of absence to visit some sulfur springs. He had been granted such a leave in 1824 but had postponed it in order to serve with Atkinson on the Yellowstone Expedition. The commission accomplished and the official report submitted, O'Fallon resigned his agency in December 1826, effective in March 1827. He returned to St. Louis, where he lived quietly for the remainder of his life. In 1835 he was suggested as a candidate for governor of Missouri but he did not run. He died at his residence, "the Cedars," in Jefferson County outside St. Louis.

• O'Fallon's papers are at the Missouri Historical Society, which has O'Fallon material in several other collections as well: the Chouteau Collection, Clark papers, Richard Graham Papers, Indians Papers, Kennerly diary and papers, Sibley papers, and Logan U. Reavis Papers. The Benjamin O'Fallon Letterbook is in the Yale University Western Americana Collection. Records of the Office of Indian Affairs and the Office of the Secretary of War at the National Archives contain O'Fallon material from his service with those agencies. O'Fallon receives significant mention in Roger Nichols, *General Henry Atkinson: A Western Military Career* (1965); John Sunder, *Joshua Pilcher: Fur Trader and Indian Agent* (1968); and Hiram Chittenden, *A History of the Fur Trade of the Far West* (1954).

PETER MICHEL

O'FALLON, James (11 Mar. 1749–c. Dec. 1793–Mar. 1794), physician, speculator, and adventurer, was born in Roscommon, western Ireland, the son of William Fallon and Anne Eagan. (O'Fallon added the prefix to his name about 1783.) He studied medicine for two years at the University of Edinburgh (1771–1773), did not graduate, but was licensed by that or another institution as a physician. Thereafter he visited Rome, perhaps in anticipation of entering the priesthood. Subsequently, however, he worked at a hospital in London. In Glasgow in 1774 he was advised by a doctor at the university to go to the colonies, where a revolt was in the making "in favour of Liberty." As his son John later wrote, "The strong spirit of freedom was already in James, and, (as a genuine Irishman) an hereditary aversion to British oppression" (Draper coll., 34J20).

After being shipwrecked off the coast of North Carolina, at Cape Hatteras, O'Fallon arrived at Edenton, North Carolina, in May 1774 and settled in Wilmington as a physician. "A genuine Irishman," according to his son's brief biographical note, O'Fallon was soon at odds with the local committee of safety for having written an "address" by "a Lawyer," critical of the committee. During January 1776 he was imprisoned. Despite this encounter, O'Fallon became an ardent patriot and was elected leader of a volunteer cavalry company. He supposedly fought at the battle of Moores Creek Bridge on 27 February 1776. During the war he served in the military hospital department, with assignments in Pennsylvania, Connecticut, and New York.

At war's end O'Fallon set up medical practice in Charleston, South Carolina. From 1783 to 1785 he was active in an antiloyalist movement, serving as secretary for the "Marine Anti-Britannic Society."

O'Fallon's historical significance rests on his role in grand schemes of frontier land speculation, which tied in with western separatism and involved U.S. relations with Spain, France, and Great Britain. In 1788 he unsuccessfully attempted to obtain Spanish backing for a colony of 5,000 families, mostly Irish Catholics, in northeastern Florida.

The South Carolina Yazoo Land Company, which received a huge tract of land by an act of the Georgia legislature on 21 December 1789, appointed O'Fallon as its general agent. O'Fallon was a shareholder in the company, along with some twenty prominent South Carolinians and several westerners, including John Sevier of Tennessee. The company instructed O'Fallon to take measures for occupying the grant, which consisted of ten million acres (at the cost of $66,964) in present southern Alabama and Mississippi. O'Fallon was also to establish an independent barrier state between the United States and Spanish Louisiana and to gain the friendship of the Spaniards and the Choctaw and Chickasaw Indians. In the spring of 1790, O'Fallon went to Kentucky to direct the company's enterprise. He told the governor of Louisiana, Esteban Rodríguez Miró, that he intended to settle about 2,000 families in the proposed state and that he would organize a government independent of the United States and in alliance with Spain. When the Spanish government balked at such an offer, O'Fallon declared to Miró that he would use force if necessary to achieve his purposes. He made military preparations, enrolling a battalion of 650 troops under Colonel John Molder; George Rogers Clark agreed to accept the overall military command. Frontier leaders Charles

Scott and James Wilkinson of Kentucky and John Sevier were to bring about 3,000 families to settle what is now Vicksburg. All three eventually backed out. Wilkinson was in the pay of Spain and kept the Spanish governor informed of O'Fallon's dealings. Wilkinson told Miró not to take O'Fallon, "a man of light character," seriously. The Nootka Sound Controversy of 1790, which brought Great Britain and Spain to the brink of war, caused O'Fallon to change his colonization plan into one of conquest of Spanish Louisiana and was a factor in Wilkinson turning against O'Fallon.

In September 1790 O'Fallon wrote President George Washington that he planned to establish a settlement on the Mississippi, by force if necessary, and that Charles Scott with 500 families and James Wilkinson with 1,000 families, would soon be setting out for Walnut Mills (Vicksburg); of course, there were no prospective settlers yet. Washington was aghast at O'Fallon's project, which he feared might lead to war with Spain, and in March 1791 he issued a proclamation calling upon westerners to refrain from participating in O'Fallon's treasonable scheme. The president also ordered the U.S. attorney in Kentucky to take action against O'Fallon. As the attorney was closely associated with Wilkinson, who himself was deeply involved in Spanish intrigue, nothing was done to apprehend O'Fallon. The Spanish Crown ordered O'Fallon arrested if he appeared in New Orleans.

This ended O'Fallon's scheme. The South Carolina Yazoo Company defaulted when Georgia insisted on payment in specie. O'Fallon then became involved with the plan of the French minister, Citizen Edmond Charles Genêt, to raise a force to attack Spanish Louisiana. George Rogers Clark was appointed commander of the proposed army. He and O'Fallon were friends, and O'Fallon married Clark's younger sister, Frances Eleanor Clark, in February 1791. Genêt's plans, however, never materialized.

O'Fallon's world was falling apart. The Yazoo Company and his Kentucky friends had abandoned him, and President Washington had denounced him. His wife left him, taking with her their two children, and O'Fallon had a serious altercation with Clark that ended their friendship. In 1792 O'Fallon advertised in Louisville that he would set up medical practice, providing there were enough subscribers to back him; in the fall of that year he was post physician at Fort Steuben (Wheeling, W. Va.).

The circumstances surrounding O'Fallon's death are mysterious; one tradition has it that he died from injuries suffered in a fight with Clark; another claims that he fell off his horse while making a trip eastward. The date of his death is uncertain but established by John Carl Parish, through court records, to have been anytime between December 1793 and March 1794. No obituaries appeared in the newspapers.

• The few papers of O'Fallon are scattered in various depositories, such as the Bancroft Library in Berkeley, California, the Library of Congress, the State Historical Society of Mis-

souri in Columbia, and the Draper Collection at the State Historical Society of Wisconsin in Madison. Particularly useful in the Draper Collection are the Clark papers and the Kentucky papers. A brief biography of O'Fallon's early years (furnished by his son, John) is found in Draper 34J20–23. A sketch of O'Fallon is found in the introduction to Louise P. Kellogg, "Letter to Thomas Paine, 1793," *American Historical Review* 29 (1923–1924): 501–5. Published letters are in *American State Papers* (38 vols., 1832–1861), *Indian Affairs* (vol. 1, 1832), and Charles Gayarré, *History of Louisiana* (vol. 3, 1903). For O'Fallon and the South Carolina Yazoo Company, see Charles H. Haskins, "The Yazoo Land Companies," *Papers of the American Historical Association* 5, no. 4 (1891): 395–437, and Arthur P. Whitaker, *The Spanish-American Frontier: 1783–1795* (1927). There is no full biography. A thoroughly researched life of O'Fallon, however, is John Carl Parish, "The Intrigues of Doctor James O'Fallon," *Mississippi Valley Historical Review* 17 (1930): 230–63.

HARRY M. WARD

OGBURN, William Fielding (29 June 1886–27 Apr. 1959), sociologist, was born in Butler, Georgia, the son of Charlton Ogburn, a merchant, and Irene Florence Wynn. After the death of his father in 1892, Ogburn led a penurious early life. At the age of sixteen he enrolled in Mercer University, from which he graduated in 1905. He then earned a doctorate in sociology at Columbia University in 1912 with a dissertation on "Progress and Uniformity in Child-Labor Legislation: A Study in Statistical Measurement," which was published as a monograph that same year.

After serving a year at Princeton University, Ogburn was called to Reed College in Portland, Oregon, where he taught from 1913 to 1917. He spent 1918 at the University of Washington and then returned to Columbia University, where he taught from 1919 to 1927. Ogburn's reputation quickly soared with the publication of *Social Change with Respect to Cultural and Original Nature* (1922), in which he set out his famous theory of "cultural lag"—the concept that changes in "material culture" invariably occur first with delayed, adaptive change in the "non-material culture." Although the term "technology" was not in vogue at that time, Ogburn's theory quickly became identified with a thesis about the ascendancy of technological change, the response of other aspects of cultural life, and the theoretical possibility of predicting future social changes based on the implications of technological discoveries and inventions already existing or currently in the patent process. Ogburn simultaneously published a study with Dorothy Thomas, "Are Inventions Inevitable: A Note on Social Evolution" (*Political Science Quarterly* 37 [1922]: 83–98), revealing that a great number of scientific discoveries had been made by multiple people, thereby suggesting that inventions are "inevitable."

From the outset of his career Ogburn was an avid researcher and prolific writer, who sought especially for ways to apply the new tools of statistical analysis to social phenomena. His early paper "How Women Vote" (*Political Science Quarterly* 34 [1919]: 413–33), represented one of the first uses of partial correlation statistical techniques in American social science. A social reformer at heart, Ogburn gave many lectures while at Reed and at Washington University in support of feminist and socialist causes. By the end of the 1920s Ogburn's reputation as a sociologist had solidified. From 1920 to 1926 he served as the managing editor of the *Journal of the American Statistical Association*. In 1929 he became president of the American Sociological Society and in 1931, the first (and only) sociologist to hold the presidency of the American Statistical Association. From 1937 to 1939 he was chair of the Social Science Research Council.

In 1927 Ogburn was recruited as professor of sociology to the University of Chicago, where he continued to serve until his retirement in 1951. In 1933 he was appointed Sewell L. Avery Distinguished Service Professor. As a result of Ogburn's command of sociology and statistical methods, he was chosen director of President Herbert Hoover's Research Committee on Recent Social Trends. This, the largest social science research project ever undertaken in the United States up to that time, was funded by the Rockefeller Foundation. Its landmark report, *Recent Social Trends* (2 vols., 1933), and Ogburn's follow-up reports on "Social Trends" provided the inspiration for the "social indicators" movement in the United States, an interdisciplinary effort to develop precise measures of social phenomena in order to track changes over time.

Ogburn's services as a social science consultant were sought on many occasions by the federal government at a time before this practice had been institutionalized on the federal level. In 1918 he acted as an examiner and head of the Cost of Living Department of the National War Labor Board. Under President Franklin D. Roosevelt he served in 1933 as director of the Consumer's Advisory Board of the National Recovery Administration. From 1935 to 1943 he served as a research consultant to the Science Committee of the National Resource Committee. He also directed the large national project "Technological Trends and National Policy"; the report was issued in 1937. Ogburn thus helped to institutionalize the routine employment of social scientists in the federal government.

Ogburn's wide-ranging research interests led him over the course of his career to publish studies on technology and the family; the demographics of cities; the influence of the business cycle on things such as unemployment, crime, divorce, suicide, and political elections; psychoanalysis and the social sciences; and, especially, the influence of technology on social change. His interest in psychoanalysis, which began in the 1910s, persisted after his move to Chicago, where he helped to establish the Chicago Psychoanalytic Institute in 1932. His textbook, *Sociology* (1940), with Meyer Nimkoff, became a leader in the field and went through four editions in the United States and five in Great Britain.

After his retirement from Chicago in 1951, Ogburn continued to be active, publishing, traveling, and serving on university faculties around the world. He died in Tallahassee, Florida. Considered one of the foremost sociologists of his time, Ogburn was a preeminent student of technology and social change and an early leader in bringing quantitative analysis into the mainstream of sociology and the social sciences.

• The William F. Ogburn Papers, on deposit at the University of Chicago, are extensive and provide important insights into the early relationships between social science research and the national government. The papers also contain personal diaries kept from 1942 to 1957, which were restricted until 1980. Ogburn's various research studies that provide early models of sociological research analysis, especially the use of quantitative techniques, include *American Marriage and Family Relationships*, with E. R. Groves (1928), *Social Characteristics of Cities* (1937), *The Social Effects of Aviation* (1946), and *Technology and the Changing Family*, with Meyer Nimkoff (1953). A useful selection of Ogburn's writings is *William F. Ogburn on Culture and Social Change*, ed. Otis Dudley Duncan (1964), which contains an extensive bibliography of Ogburn's writings. For Ogburn's theory of social change, see Toby E. Huff, "W. F. Ogburn on Culture, Technology and Social Change: Conflicts of Theoretical Rationales in the Development of Sociocultural Analysis—A Case Study (Ph.D. diss., New School for Social Research, 1971). For his role in the institutionalization of social science research in the federal government, see Barry D. Karl, "Presidential Planning and Social Science Research: Mr. Hoover's Experts," in *Perspectives in American History*, vol. 3 (1969). Obituaries are in the *New York Times*, 29 Apr. 1959, and the *Chicago Tribune*, 30 Apr. 1959.

TOBY E. HUFF

OGDEN, Aaron (3 Dec. 1756–19 Apr. 1839), soldier, public official, and entrepreneur, was born in Elizabethtown, New Jersey, the son of Robert Ogden II, a lawyer, and Phebe Hatfield. He attended the College of New Jersey (later Princeton University) and graduated with the class of 1773. Over the next three years he taught school, first in Princeton, then in Elizabethtown, but with the outbreak of hostilities between Great Britain and its American colonies, he was quickly drawn into the revolutionary confrontation.

Ogden's military career spanned the entire Revolution, from militia service in 1776, to the battle of Brandywine in 1777, through the Yorktown campaign of 1781. He rose from the rank of first lieutenant to that of major during the course of his service. Before being commissioned a lieutenant in the regular army in November 1776, Ogden had helped seize a British ship near Sandy Hook, New Jersey, and had served in the state militia. After the battle of Brandywine, he wintered at Valley Forge, fought at the battle of Monmouth Courthouse (June 1778), was wounded while on a scouting mission near Elizabethtown during the winter of 1778–1779, participated in John Sullivan's punitive expedition against New York and Pennsylvania Indians during the summer of 1779, served at the battle of Springfield (June 1780), and led an assault on British positions at Yorktown in the final major campaign of the war. Ogden also gave evidence in the court-martial of General Charles Lee, who was charged by George Washington with military incompetence at the battle of Monmouth Courthouse, and participated in the attempt to exchange Benedict Arnold, who had fled to the British, for Major John André, who had been captured and held as a spy by the Americans.

With the war over, Ogden prepared for the law under the tutelage of his brother, Robert, and in 1784 was admitted to the New Jersey bar. In 1787 he married Elizabeth Chetwood (daughter of Judge John Chetwood); the couple had seven children. While a lawyer, he became increasingly interested in politics; like many revolutionary officers who had left the service somewhat dissatisfied with the confederation government, he was drawn toward the Federalist camp of his friend and occasional legal associate Alexander Hamilton. As the Republicans rather than the Federalists generally held the upper hand in early nineteenth-century New Jersey politics, Ogden's political career initially consisted of honorific appointments, minor political offices, and electoral defeats. But the outbreak of an unpopular war with England in 1812 temporarily resurrected the Federalist party, and the legislature elected him governor in that year, a position he subsequently lost in the election of 1813 and failed to recapture in the 1814 election.

It is not for his military heroism or his political role, however, but for his involvement in the famous steamboat monopoly case, *Gibbons v. Ogden*, that Ogden is best remembered. Ever since the perfection of the steam engine in the mid-eighteenth century by Scottish engineer James Watt, entrepreneurs on both sides of the Atlantic had tried to utilize steam power for water travel. During the 1780s John Fitch became the first American to launch a truly successful steamboat, but it was Robert Livingston, a New York landowner and political leader, and Robert Fulton, an artist turned inventor, who initially realized the commercial potential of steamboat operations. In 1798 Livingston secured from New York a monopoly over all steamboat traffic in state waters in return for a promise to produce a steamboat that would go four miles an hour. By teaming up with Fulton, Livingston met the conditions in 1807, when their boat, the *Clermont*, steamed from New York City to Albany at five miles an hour. For the next decade, the partnership tried to fend off competitors, one of whom was Aaron Ogden.

Well before he became a steamboat proprietor, Ogden had been active in banking and transportation projects and land speculation. In one such venture, in 1800, he and Jonathan Dayton had initiated ferryboat operations between Elizabethtown and Manhattan. In 1804 Dayton sold his interest in the enterprise to Thomas Gibbons. Several years later the new partners built a steamboat, the *Seahorse*, to compete with the Livingston-Fulton monopoly for New York traffic. The rivalry was conducted in the waters of the Hudson as well as in the courts and legislative halls of both New Jersey and New York. In the end, the New York courts upheld the monopoly, and in 1815 Ogden reluctantly agreed to buy a license from John Livingston (Robert's brother, who, in turn, had a license from the

monopoly) to operate his steamboat on the New York run.

Within a year the Ogden-Gibbons partnership dissolved, primarily as a result of bitter personal differences. Gibbons began a rival steamboat line and hired young, resourceful Cornelius Vanderbilt to navigate his vessel. Both men turned to the courts. Ogden claimed that the New York monopoly gave him exclusive rights to run a steamboat from Elizabethtown to New York; Gibbons claimed that a state could not grant a valid monopoly for commercial traffic between states. Gibbons's claim was finally resolved by the U.S. Supreme Court in its 1824 decision, *Gibbons v. Ogden*. Siding with Gibbons, Chief Justice John Marshall used the occasion to define in the broadest possible terms "commerce" itself as well as congressional power over interstate traffic. He intimated that there was no concurrent state power to regulate commerce (which would have invalidated the monopoly) but then struck down the New York law on the grounds that it conflicted with a federal coastal licensing act.

The ruling was a crushing blow to Ogden. Badly in debt, he lost his home in Elizabethtown. In 1830 he was imprisoned in New York City. His old friend Aaron Burr (whom Ogden had helped avoid trial in 1807 for the dueling death of Alexander Hamilton) secured his release by convincing the New York legislature to end imprisonment for debt for revolutionary war veterans. Ogden was, however, able to support himself with a federal patronage position; having promoted Andrew Jackson's 1828 campaign for the presidency, he then applied successfully for a position as federal collector of customs in Jersey City, where he lived the remainder of his life.

In balance, Ogden's life was representative of many middle-state Federalists: comfortable, if not genteel, family background, college education, service as an officer in the revolutionary war, training as a lawyer, and involvement in politics and entrepreneurial undertakings. He moved in circles that included Washington, Hamilton, Burr, and the marquis de Lafayette (under whom he fought at Yorktown), but his claim for particular distinction rests on his involvement in the landmark case of *Gibbons v. Ogden*.

• The most significant collections of Ogden's papers are in the New Jersey Historical Society, Newark; Archibald S. Alexander Library, Rutgers, the State University of New Jersey, New Brunswick; and the Firestone Library, Princeton University. The pamphlet *A Narrative, Shewing the Promises Made to the Officers of the Line of the Continental Army . . .* (1826), presumed to have been written by Ogden, provides some evidence of his distressed financial state. Of the many court cases in which Gibbons was involved see, in particular, *Ogden v. Gibbons*, 4 Johnson Ch. 150 (1819), and *Gibbons v. Ogden*, 9 Wheaton 1 (1824).

By far the best treatment of Ogden's life is in Richard A. Harrison, *Princetonians, 1769–1775: A Biographical Dictionary* (1980), pp. 328–34; the essay is particularly valuable for its careful tracking of Ogden's extensive military service. See also the *Autobiography of Col. Aaron Ogden, of Elizabethtown* (1893), and William Ogden Wheeler, *The Ogden Family in America, Elizabethtown Branch, and Their English Ancestry*

(1907). Carl E. Prince et al., eds., *The Papers of William Livingston*, vol. 5 (1988), p. 573, contains a short sketch of Ogden's father that provides useful background on Aaron Ogden's career.

On Ogden's early legal interests, see Don C. Skemer, "The *Institutio legalis* and Legal Education in New Jersey: 1783–1817," *New Jersey History* 96 (1978): 123–34; on politics during the era, see Prince, *New Jersey's Jeffersonian Republicans: The Genesis of an Early Party Machine, 1789–1817* (1964); on his involvement in the steamboat case, see Maurice G. Baxter, *The Steamboat Monopoly: Gibbons v. Ogden, 1824* (1972).

PAUL G. E. CLEMENS

OGDEN, John Cosens (15 Nov. 1751–26 Sept. 1800), clergyman and Jeffersonian Republican propagandist, was born near Elizabethtown, New Jersey, the son of Moses Ogden and Mary Cozzens (also spelled Cosens and Cosins), artisans. Having graduated from the College of New Jersey (Princeton) in 1770, Ogden moved to New Haven, Connecticut, where he was employed by the collector of the port of New Haven, David Wooster. In 1774 he married Mary Wooster, his employer's daughter; they had three children. The year of independence marked a turning point in Ogden's life. Ogden developed an intense hatred of Connecticut's Congregational and political elite when, on the resignation of his father-in-law from the collectorship, Governor Jonathan Trumbull (1710–1785) refused to appoint Ogden to the post.

A strong-willed individual with an independent cast of mind, Ogden converted from the Presbyterian to the Protestant Episcopal church sometime during the revolutionary era. Ordained an Episcopal deacon in September 1786, he accepted the position of rector at Queen's Chapel in Portsmouth, New Hampshire. In March 1788 he was ordained a priest by Bishop Samuel Seabury (1729–1796) in what is said to have been the first Episcopal ordination conducted in Massachusetts. Ogden, blunt, contentious, and outspoken, did not shy from public controversy. Following a 1791 visit by Bishop Seabury to Portsmouth, a sharp conflict developed between Ogden and Congregational minister Samuel MacClintock over the Episcopal bishop's claims for the superiority of apostolic succession. Ogden's vehemence in defense of episcopacy, in which he branded MacClintock a liar and Congregationalists allies of the pope, so alienated his own congregation that he was forced, in January 1793, to resign and leave Portsmouth.

Ogden thereupon relocated to Hartland, Vermont, a town on the Connecticut River. Since no community in the region could support an Episcopal church, Ogden became a traveling missionary. A year later he wrote that he had "travelled five thousand miles" and had "preached in most parts of Vermont" as well as having visited New Hampshire and Canada. A knowledgeable parishioner, Philander Chase, described him as "a man of good talents and an excellent preacher."

Ogden had settled in Vermont largely in the expectation that glebe land, originally set aside to support the Anglican church, might be claimed by Episcopal ministers. In 1795, rebuffed by the Vermont legislature, an even more than usually embittered Ogden, unable to return to Connecticut where he could be jailed for a debt of $180, sent his family to live with his mother-in-law and moved to Troy, New York. He later complained that at this time he was reduced to "the necessity of travelling on foot with a wallet and staff" and that his annual income was "a pittance of less than one hundred dollars."

A decade of struggle and disappointment had by 1796 convinced Ogden that New England's Congregational and political establishments were in league to perpetuate each other's power and interests. Beginning in 1796 Ogden increasingly devoted his energy to exposing the nefarious designs of what he labeled New England's "Eastern Oligarchy." Although principally concerned with what he perceived to be Congregational religious intolerance and the influence of Yale College, Ogden was drawn into a small circle of New England Jeffersonian Republicans, including Connecticut Jeffersonian leader Ephraim Kirby and his own brother-in-law Pierpont Edwards.

Ogden's first political pamphlet, *An Appeal to the Candid, upon the Present State of Religion and Politics in Connecticut* (1796), was an attack on Yale and the Congregational establishment. It was followed by *A View of the New England Illuminati; Who Are Indefatigably Engaged in Destroying the Religion and Government of the United States, under a Feigned Regard for Their Safety—and under an Impious Abuse of True Religion* (1798). Three pamphlets with similar themes appeared in 1799.

In October 1798 Vermont congressman Matthew Lyon, a Jeffersonian Republican, was jailed by a Federalist judge for violating the Sedition Act by publishing a letter critical of President John Adams (1735–1826). Several thousand Vermont citizens signed petitions seeking a presidential pardon for their congressman, and Ogden, who both sympathized with Lyon's political views and thought of Lyon as a friend to the Episcopal church, agreed to carry the petitions to the president. Arriving in Philadelphia in December 1798, Ogden met with the president, only to be rebuffed by the remark that "penitence must precede pardon."

The *Aurora*, the nation's most influential Jeffersonian-Republican newspaper, was published in Philadelphia. Its editor, William Duane (1760–1835), was as eager for news of Lyon and of Federalist oppression as Ogden was to relate that news. From January 1799 until his death a little less than two years later, Ogden regularly contributed unsigned articles to the *Aurora*. It cannot be exactly established which contributions are his, but most of the material printed in the *Aurora* relating to New England during those years display the emotional style and vehement tone characteristic of Ogden's pamphleteering.

About the time he started writing for the *Aurora*, Ogden journeyed to Connecticut to supervise the printing of a nonpolitical work, *A Tour through Upper and Lower Canada*. At Litchfield he was seized and jailed, ostensibly for nonpayment of the $180 debt he owed to Secretary of the Treasury Oliver Wolcott, Jr. (1760–1833). In reality he was being punished for his politics. Ogden thus became for four months a minor Jeffersonian martyr.

In the fall of 1799 Ogden focused the attention of the *Aurora*'s readers on the group he had labeled the New England Illuminati. In the popular mind the Illuminati were a Jacobin-Freemason secret society that, having instigated the French Revolution, now plotted the destruction of all religion and government. Led by Jedidiah Morse, Timothy Dwight (1752–1817), and Theodore Dwight (1764–1846), members of the New England Congregational clergy had, during the 1790s, smeared Thomas Jefferson and his adherents with being the agents of "illuminatism in the United States." Ogden, who held to his own conspiratorial view of politics, and who understood the public relations value of a powerful image, endeavored through the *Aurora* to transfer the label "Illuminati," with all of its threatening conspiratorial connotations, from the Jeffersonians to the New England Congregational-Federalist oligarchy. Ogden's argument was picked up and spread by Jeffersonian newspapers throughout the nation during the presidential campaign of 1800. Ogden thus became one of the earliest successful practitioners of negative campaigning in an American presidential election. Hoping that his Jeffersonian notoriety might enable him to fill a pulpit in a southern state, Ogden journeyed into Virginia and Maryland during 1800. He died at Chestertown, Maryland, after a brief illness.

• A few dozen Ogden letters are in the Ephraim Kirby Manuscripts Collection, Duke University Library. A few letters are in the George Washington Collection of the Library of Congress. In addition to the pamphlets cited in the text, Ogden wrote *Friendly Remarks to the People of Connecticut upon Their College and Schools* (1799), *A Short History of Late Ecclesiastical Oppressions in New England and Vermont . . .* (1799), and *A View of the Calvinistic Clubs in the United States* (1799). His major nonpolitical work was *An Excursion into Bethlehem & Nazareth in Pennsylvania in the Year 1799* (1800).

Ogden's political influence is discussed in Alan V. Briceland, "John C. Ogden: Messenger and Propagandist for Matthew Lyon, 1798–1799," *Vermont History* 43 (1975): 103–21, and "The Philadelphia *Aurora*, the New England Illuminati, and the Election of 1800," *Pennsylvania Magazine of History and Biography* 100 (1976): 3–36. The entry on Ogden in *Princetonians: 1769–1775* (1980), pp. 93–97, gives special attention to religious issues. Genealogical information is in William O. Wheeler, *The Ogden Family in America* (1907), pp. 84, 140. Ogden's obituary is in the Philadelphia *Aurora*, 2 Oct. 1800.

ALAN V. BRICELAND

OGDEN, Peter Skene (12 Feb. 1790–27 Sept. 1854), fur trader and explorer, was born in Quebec City, Quebec, Canada, the son of Isaac Ogden, a jurist, and Sarah Hanson. The Ogden family had been prominent in the political affairs of colonial New Jersey since the 1660s. During the American Revolution, Isaac Ogden was a Loyalist; as a result, his properties were confiscated and he joined the Tory exodus to England in 1783.

In 1788 Isaac Ogden was appointed admiralty court judge in Quebec. Peter Ogden was born in that city, according to his biographer Gloria Griffen Cline, in 1790, not in 1794 as indicated in most previous accounts of his life. In 1796 Isaac Ogden received a judicial appointment to Montreal, a thriving fur trade entrepôt dominated by the North West Company. Although he received the beginnings of a legal education, Peter Ogden declined to follow his older brothers into the practice of law, instead joining the ranks of the North West Company at age twenty. He remained in the fur trade for the rest of his life.

Ogden, after a brief stint with the Montreal operations of the American Fur Company, gained a clerkship with the North West Company in 1810. His first wintering post was at Île-à-la-Crosse, in the lake country of northern Saskatchewan. Between 1810 and 1818 Ogden participated in the company's protracted struggle with the Hudson's Bay Company for supremacy in the Canadian fur trade. Implicated in several violent incidents involving Hudson's Bay employees, he was transferred to the distant Columbia River post, Spokane House, in 1818. In 1821, with the merger of the two firms, Ogden was one of three North West Company men refused employment in the new Hudson's Bay Company because of past actions. After traveling to London to plead his case, Ogden's experience and personal connections caused the company to reconsider; he was reassigned to Spokane House in 1823. He remained in the employ of the Hudson's Bay Company for the rest of his life.

The following year, Ogden took command of the Snake Country Brigade, the annual fur trapping foray into the territory south and east of the Columbia River. Between 1824 and 1830 chief trader Ogden led six consecutive Snake Country expeditions, a major object of which was to implement the company's scorched-earth "fur desert" policy, designed to blunt the penetration of American trappers into the Oregon country. Although his first expedition, in 1824–1825, ended in financial failure because of the desertion of many men to a party of Americans, Ogden's advance trappers may have been the first Euro-Americans to see Great Salt Lake. (Credit for the actual "discovery" remains in dispute among historians, with American trapper Jim Bridger usually given that honor; although some writers continue to misidentify Ogden as the lake's discoverer, it is clear from his journal that Ogden personally never saw Great Salt Lake on this trip.) Ogden's second (1825–1826) and fourth (1827–1828) brigades thoroughly explored the streams of the Snake River Plain and central Oregon. During the third expedition (1826–1827) Ogden was the first Euro-American to see northern California's Mount Shasta (although the mountain that he named "Mt. Sastise [Shasta]" was actually present-day Mount McLoughlin, in southern Oregon). On this trip, Ogden also explored the Klamath, Rogue, and Umpqua river drainages, thereby blazing the connecting route between his company's traditional territory in northwestern Oregon and new trapping areas in central California. Ogden's fifth expedition (1828–1829) led to the discovery of northern Nevada's Humboldt River. In 1829–1830 Ogden's final Snake Country Brigade (from which no journal survives) evidently reached south to the lower Colorado River and west across the Mohave Desert.

Ogden's later duties included post commands in southern Alaska and New Caledonia (interior British Columbia). He returned to the Columbia shortly before the 1846 American annexation of Oregon, after which Ogden served as chief factor at Fort Vancouver, the British company's venerable regional headquarters now on United States soil. This position called for tact and forcefulness, qualities Ogden successfully demonstrated during his negotiations with Cayuse Indians for the safe return of nearly fifty American women and children taken captive during the 1847 Whitman Massacre.

Ogden was a relatively short but burly man, renowned for his physical strength. Solicitous of his employee's welfare while exercising firm leadership, he held the respect of his French-Canadian and *meti* trappers. Like many of his fellow company officers, Ogden spoke French fluently and could converse in Chinook jargon and several Indian languages as well. Although his journals often reveal a dour, even cynical, outlook, many people who wrote of personal encounters with Ogden recall his affable and jocose character. Described in younger years by a contemporary as "humorous, honest, eccentric, law-defying . . . the terror of the Indians and the delight of all gay fellows," Ogden earned a somewhat similar assessment from Hudson's Bay Company Governor George Simpson in 1832: "A keen, sharp, off hand fellow of superior abilities . . . and not sparing of his personal labour. . . . Has been very Wild and thoughtless and is still fond of coarse practical jokes, but . . . he is a very cool calculating fellow who is capable of doing anything to gain his own ends." Ogden's private opinion of Indians, as revealed in his writings, was often cold and harsh, but he generally dealt equitably with the native inhabitants of the region. Ogden was married twice, first to an unidentified Cree woman while in Saskatchewan and later to a Nez Perce woman, Julia Rivet, with whom he spent the last thirty-five years of his life. Ogden fathered at least six children. He died at the home of his daughter and son-in-law in Oregon City, Oregon.

Ogden's tersely written Snake Country journals of the 1820s have yielded much valuable information about the Indians of the intermountain West. However, his role in extending geographic knowledge of the region during this period has proven to be his most significant legacy. Ogden's journals and field notes contributed directly to cartographic improvements by the Arrowsmiths, London cartographers whose maps of the region south of the Columbia corrected some of the major mapping errors of Lewis and Clark and others. In practical terms, Ogden's path over Siskiyou Pass subsequently became part of the main travel route between Oregon and California. His route along the Humboldt River similarly served as the major American emigrant trail across the Great Basin to California. In comparison to John Charles Frémont, who retraced some of Ogden's routes nearly twenty years later, Peter Ogden's reputation suffered during the nineteenth century from the neglect of American historians. In the twentieth century, Ogden came to be generally recognized as belonging to the front rank of the Far West's explorers.

• The Hudson's Bay Record Society, in Winnipeg, Manitoba, Canada, holds original copies of Ogden's journals (as transcribed by company clerks) as well as some of his official correspondence; some personal papers are held by the Oregon Historical Society. Verbatim versions of Ogden's *Snake Country Journals* were published by the Hudson's Bay Record Society in three volumes: 1824–1825 and 1825–1826 (1950), 1826–1827 (1861), and 1827–1828 and 1828–1829 (1971). All of these include excellent interpretive introductions. However, the 1961 interpretation of Ogden's 1926–1827 route through southern Oregon and northern California is erroneous; for a corrected interpretation of his third brigade's travels, see Jeff LaLande, *First over the Siskiyous: Peter Skene Ogden's 1826–1827 Journey through the Oregon-California Borderlands* (1987). Portions of Ogden's journals were first published in the *Oregon Historical Quarterly* (1909–1910), but these heavily abridged versions are not reliable. Ogden's anonymously published memoir, *Traits of American Indian Life and Character* (1853; repr. 1933), contains anecdotes and recollections from his fur trade career; this work is most valuable as evidence of Ogden's personal opinions on Indian culture. The standard biography of Ogden, an excellent life-and-times study, is Gloria Griffen Cline, *Peter Skene Ogden and the Hudson's Bay Company* (1974). A biography by Archie Binns, *Peter Skene Ogden, Fur Trader* (1967), is lively reading but takes excessive liberties with the historical record.

JEFF LaLANDE

OGDEN, Uzal (1744?–4 Nov. 1822), clergyman, was born in Newark, New Jersey, the son of Uzal Ogden, an iron manufacturer and county judge, and Elizabeth Charlotte Thébaut. Newark lacked a settled Anglican clergyman until the 1740s, when a group of lay persons raised funds for the construction of a building. In 1745 the Society for the Propagation of the Gospel in Foreign Parts (SPG) appointed Isaac Brown as the minister of congregation, which took the name Trinity Church. Members of the extended Ogden family were active. Colonel Josiah Ogden was one of the two organizers of the building program, and Uzal Ogden, Sr., later served as a warden of the parish. Uzal Ogden shared his family's interest in the Anglican church. His older brother Lewis graduated from Princeton in 1753. That same year, however, a religious revival at the institution led at least some members of the extended Ogden family to take a dislike to the college. Colonel Ogden's younger brother Isaac, for example, transferred to King's College (later Columbia) in New

York City. Whatever the cause, Uzal pursued his theological studies privately with the Reverend Thomas Bradbury Chandler of Elizabethtown.

Ogden began to publish pamphlets on religion in 1768 and in 1770 was appointed by the SPG to serve as a catechist for the Church of England in Sussex County, a position he held for two years. Toward the end of this period he published three catechetical pamphlets: "The Theological Preceptor," "An Address to the Youth of America," and "A Letter to a Master of a Family." After completing his term as a catechist, Ogden traveled to England, where he was ordained a deacon and, on 21 September 1773, a priest. Ogden returned to New Jersey by 1774 as a missionary for the SPG in Sussex, Morris, and Bergen counties. In 1776 he married Mary Gouverneur, with whom he would have four sons and three daughters.

The mid-1770s were difficult times for Anglican clergy in New Jersey. Most Anglicans were Loyalists, and many were driven into exile by patriots unhappy with their support of England. Chandler, with whom Ogden had prepared for ordination, left for England in 1775. Isaac Brown, the clergyman in Ogden's home parish in Newark, left New Jersey in 1777, first for New York and later for Nova Scotia. Ogden spent part of 1776 in New York but returned to New Jersey in the following year. For the next eleven years he divided his time between assisting Episcopal congregations that lacked clergy and visiting areas that had no Episcopal congregations. From 1784 to 1788 he also served as a part-time assistant at Trinity Church, New York, before accepting a call to become the rector of Trinity Church, Newark. He would serve in that capacity until 1805.

His relatives and Chandler disliked revivalism, but Ogden was one of a group of colonial Anglican clergy ordained in the 1760s and 1770s who were attracted to the revivalist ideas of George Whitefield and John Wesley. He imitated their methods in his own ministry, going on preaching tours, emphasizing personal conversion, arranging for the publication and distribution of his sermons, and organizing home meetings. Initially, at least, he did not distinguish between the Calvinist and the Arminian supporters of revival. He cooperated both with New Light Presbyterians, who subscribed to the former view, and with Methodist lay preachers, who held the latter. He regarded deism, rather than any particular brand of Christian theology, as his opponent. His longest published work, the two-volume *Antidote to Deism: The Deist Unmasked* (1795), would be devoted to refuting Thomas Paine's *Age of Reason*.

Ogden was a large man, about six feet tall and heavy in his old age. He was an impressive presence in the pulpit, preaching lengthy sermons, which on occasion were almost two hours long. He was popular in his early years and after the Revolution was a leader in the effort to reorganize disorganized Anglican parishes into the Protestant Episcopal church. He represented New Jersey at General Convention from 1785 to 1804, with the exception of 1795. In 1798 the New Jersey state convention selected him as bishop-elect. That same year, Princeton awarded him a doctor of divinity degree.

The selection of bishops was a two-step process, with both election by the state convention and approval by the General Convention of 1799 refused to grant consent to Ogden, citing irregularities in the election. A second New Jersey convention elected him later in the same year, but a trio of New Jersey Episcopalians that included Robert Morris (the brother-in-law of Presiding Bishop William White and perhaps the single most influential lay Episcopalian in the state) circulated a petition questioning his educational qualifications. The General Convention of 1801 again refused to consent to his consecration, and the diocesan convention allowed the matter to drop.

Two issues lay behind Ogden's dispute with his critics. Ogden's revivalist insistence that a change of heart mattered more than wealth or status made him popular with laypersons of modest means but made Morris and other members of the upper class uncomfortable. His prolix preaching style may have contributed to the second issue—intermittent loss of his voice, which caused problems as early as 1794. Opponents within his own parish cited both factors when they campaigned from 1802 to 1805 for his dismissal as rector of Trinity Church. Canon law, which granted life tenure to a clergyman, was on Ogden's side. His opponents, however, were able to convince the General Convention of 1804 to alter that provision, allowing a vestry to dismiss a rector, provided the ecclesiastical authority in the diocese (the bishop or the standing committee in a diocese without a bishop) consented. Ogden resisted both by appealing to the secular courts and by declaring that he would serve under the authority of the Bishop of London, but to no avail. In May 1805 the Standing Committee of New Jersey made his dismissal as rector final.

That October Ogden applied for admission as a presbyter to the Presbytery of New York. A subcommittee investigated his request, and Ogden appeared before the presbytery and agreed to the Confession of Faith and Form of Government in the Presbyterian church. He later commented to a friend that he did not believe that his embrace of the Presbyterian standards involved a change of conviction, for he believed that the Presbyterian confessions were consonant with the Anglican Thirty-nine Articles. Ogden was over sixty at the time he entered the Presbyterian church. He remained active in the presbytery and was a guest preacher at a number of churches but was never in charge of a congregation. He died in Newark. Because of inheritance from his family, Ogden was financially well off. Despite his long unemployment following his dismissal from Trinity Church in 1805, he left an estate large enough to include a bequest of $4,000 for poor orphans in Newark.

Ogden's early ministry helped to keep the Episcopal church alive in New Jersey in the difficult years during and after the American Revolution. The protracted fight that led to his dismissal resulted in a canonical change that would have significant impact on later Episcopal clergy: parish rectors lost the right of tenure enjoyed by their English counterparts. His conversion to the Presbyterian church came too late in his life for him to have significant impact on that denomination.

• John H. Norton, *The Life of Bishop Croes* (1859), has the most detailed account of the dispute between Ogden and his opponents in the Episcopal church. William Sprague, *Annals of the American Pulpit*, vol. 4 (1858), contains a profile of Ogden with excerpts from the records of the Diocese of New Jersey and the Presbytery of New York and three letters from men who knew him; Sprague's account notes, but does not identify, a journal prepared by a friend of Ogden's during a 1787 missionary tour of West Jersey and published in a Newark newspaper in 1819. Nelson Burr, *The Anglican Church in New Jersey* (1954), contains sketches of both Ogden and Trinity Church, Newark. Robert W. Prichard, *A History of the Protestant Episcopal Church* (1991), includes a description of the Anglican ordinands of the 1760s and 1770s who, like Ogden, supported revival.

ROBERT W. PRICHARD

OGG, Frederic Austin (8 Feb. 1878–23 Oct. 1951), historian and political scientist, was born in Solsberry, Indiana, the son of William R. Ogg and Sarah S. Law, farmers. The family later moved to Greencastle, Indiana, so that Ogg could attend college at DePauw University. He graduated in 1899 and earned a master's degree from Indiana University in 1900. Ogg began his teaching career in Indianapolis at the Manual Training High School. He married Emma Virginia Perry in 1903; they had no children. He completed his thesis, "Slave Property as an Issue in Anglo-American Diplomacy, 1782–1828," and received a Ph.D. in history from Harvard University in 1908.

Following brief appointments in history departments at Indiana University, Harvard University, and Boston University, Ogg served as an assistant professor of history at Simmons College in Boston from 1908 to 1914. His research and teaching interests shifted from political history to political science as the latter became established as a separate discipline. In 1914 Ogg accepted a post as an associate professor in the Department of Political Science at the University of Wisconsin in Madison. He was promoted to full professor in 1917, and he would remain at Wisconsin for the rest of his career.

Ogg's career at Wisconsin was marked by dedicated, professional service in political science. Ogg edited the Century Political Science Series, a collection of notable and influential books on history, government, and politics that included Andrew McLaughlin's Pulitzer Prize–winning book *A Constitutional History of the United States*. Ogg served as secretary-treasurer of the American Political Science Association from 1917 to 1925 and began coordinating news features for the organization's official journal, first published in 1906.

In 1926 Ogg became the managing editor of the *American Political Science Review* and continued in that capacity until 1949. Ogg was a tireless editor. He read and evaluated nearly every article submitted to the journal, typically making extensive editorial changes. Although most political scientists lauded Ogg's wisdom, patience, and tenacity during his twenty-four years as editor of the *Review*, he was also criticized for his dictatorial control over the profession's primary research outlet. During Ogg's management the emphasis on quality research articles increased, while a section on the news and notes regarding politics, government, and the profession was maintained and grew (this section would become a separate publication, *PS: Political Science and Politics*, in 1968). The annual length of the *Review* increased by one-third and circulation tripled during Ogg's tenure.

Ogg was also a prolific writer. His seventeen books include many classic works in history, biography, and political science. His first published work, "Jay's Treaty and the Slavery Interests of the United States," appeared in the American Historical Association's annual report for 1901. His first book, *The Opening of the Mississippi: A Struggle for Supremacy in the American Interior*, was published in 1904; this was followed in 1908 by an edited version of the personal narratives of Elias Pym Fordham, an early settler in the Midwest. Ogg's research covered American history (particularly early westward expansion), medieval history, and European social history and economic development, as well as government. His book *National Progress, 1907–1917* (1918) appeared as part of Albert Bushnell Hart's pioneering series, *The American Nation*.

Ogg coauthored with P. Orman Ray *Introduction to American Government and Politics*, a textbook commonly referred to as "Ogg and Ray." The work went through thirteen editions from 1922 to 1966 and was used by generations of students. This lengthy tome outlined the organizations, rules, and functions of the different levels of government and served as the model for future introductory American politics texts. A companion text, *Essentials of American Government*, also coauthored by Ogg and Ray, was published in 1932 and went through seven editions, with the last appearing in 1952. Ogg also wrote or cowrote several books on European and comparative politics. He collaborated with Walter Rice Sharp on *Economic Development of Modern Europe* (1917), Charles A. Beard on *National Governments and the World War* (1936), and Harold Zink on *Modern Foreign Governments* (1949). Many of his works were translated and revised through several editions.

Ogg oversaw development of the University of Wisconsin's increasingly prestigious political science department, serving as chairman of the department and of the graduate division of social sciences. He declined to teach large classes in the fields for which he wrote books and concentrated his efforts on instruction of graduate students, thereby effectively strengthening his role as a leader in the developing profession of political science.

Ogg retired from Wisconsin in 1948, although he continued to edit the *Review*. A Festschrift prepared by students and colleagues, *The Study of Comparative Government*, was released in 1949. It acknowledges

Ogg as "a leader in the growth and crystallization of the study of politics in the United States."

Ogg received an honorary LL.D. from DePauw University in 1928. He represented political science in the American Council of Learned Societies and authored its report *Research in the Humanistic and Social Sciences* (1928). Ogg was elected president of the American Political Science Association in 1941. President Harry Truman appointed Ogg to the seventh regional loyalty board of the Federal Civil Service Commission in 1948. He died at his home in Madison.

Although Ogg served a critical role in the development of a science of politics and oversaw its formation into a separate discipline, his works are seldom cited today. Nevertheless, the standards he established guided generations of political scientists and greatly enhanced the discipline. Unlike earlier scholars who focused on history and personalities in the study of politics and society, Ogg throughout his career advocated a scientific, systematic study of rules and institutions. He was the premier editor of political science research. Retrospective evaluations, such as Albert Somit and Joseph Tanenhaus's *American Political Science: A Profile of the Discipline* (1964), rank Ogg among the ten most influential founders of American political science.

• Ogg's papers were apparently destroyed after his death. For other influential historical works by Ogg, see *A Source Book of Medieval History: Documents Illustrative of European Life and Institutions from the German Invasion to the Renaissance* (1908), *Social Progress in Contemporary Europe* (1912), *The Life of Daniel Webster* (1914), *The Old Northwest: A Chronicle of the Ohio Valley and Beyond* (1919), *The Reign of Andrew Jackson* (1919), *Builders of the Republic* (1927), and *The Rise of Dictatorship in France* (1947). Assessments of Ogg's scholarship and career are in Harold Zink, "The Growth of the *American Political Science Review*," *American Political Science Review* 44 (1950): 257–65; the Wisconsin faculty's memorial resolution in the *American Political Science Review* 46 (1952): 289–91; Albert Somit and Joseph Tanenhaus, *The Development of American Political Science* (1982); and Valerie Martinez's brief biography in *American Political Scientists*, ed. Glenn H. Utter and Charles Lockhart (1993).

JAMES W. ENDERSBY

OGILVIE, John (1724–26 Nov. 1774), clergyman and missionary to the Mohawks, was of Scottish descent (parentage unknown) but was born probably in New York City, where he grew up. He attended Yale University, where he was influenced by Samuel Johnson, the prominent convert to Anglicanism who was then rector of a church in Stratford, Connecticut. Ogilvie served as a lay reader at Stratford and at the nearby towns of Norwalk and Ridgefield. At his graduation from Yale in 1748, the congregation at Norwalk wrote to the Society for the Propagation of the Gospel in Foreign Parts (SPG) asking that Ogilvie be ordained in England and sent to them as a missionary. Johnson and two other Connecticut Anglican clergymen supported the request.

Ogilvie did travel to England and was ordained by the bishop of London in 1749, but the SPG hired him as a missionary to St. Peter's Church in Albany and to the Mohawk Indians. The Reverend Henry Barclay, who had just left that post, had recommended Ogilvie, in part because the latter knew the Dutch language, which was widely used in Albany. Ogilvie returned to New York after a grueling ten-week voyage and recuperated at Barclay's home in the city, where he studied the Mohawk language. He also preached on occasion in Elizabeth Town, New Jersey, where he came to know Thomas Bradbury Chandler, another soon to be prominent Anglican clergyman. In the spring of 1750, he went to Albany. Ogilvie married Susanna Symes in 1752, and they had two children.

Ogilvie's ministry included the English colonists at Albany and the Mohawks located more than thirty miles away. The Indian ministry was centered at Fort Hunter, near the Lower Castle of the Mohawks, but included the Upper Castle at Canajoharie. His early letters to the SPG reflect some pessimism about the prospects of missionary work. Ogilvie believed that war and alcoholism had brutalized the Indians and that the behavior of the English Christians was a poor advertisement for their religion. Nonetheless, he seems to have been indefatigable: "I preach to the Indians twice every Sunday by the help of an Interpreter whom I hire for the purpose, & read most of our Liturgy to them myself in their own language." He also taught young Mohawks to read and write in English. Ogilvie was effective among his parishioners in Albany. The historian of St. Peter's Church claimed that "his culture, affability, judgment, varied knowledge and eloquence gave him at once a position in the community of which the memory long lingered in Albany" (Hooper, p. 88).

Ogilvie's world changed drastically as the Great War for Empire spread along the northern frontier. In June 1755 he attended a conference at Sir William Johnson's home in which the Indian commissioner enlisted the aid of the Six Nations for an expedition against Crown Point. Ogilvie later reported that half of the twelve Mohawk leaders who died in the ensuing battle at Lake George were Christians. In 1758 he wrote that "the Mohawk's River is a scene of all the Horrors of War," but he spent two months at Fort Hunter and preached elsewhere along the frontier as well as serving his parish in Albany. John Campbell, earl of Loudoun, appointed Ogilvie a chaplain to the Royal American Regiment in 1756 on the recommendation of Sir William Johnson, noting that the clergyman preached to the Mohawks in their own language and was very effective with them. Ogilvie accompanied British forces to Niagara in 1759 and to Montreal in 1760. He came back to Albany after the fall of Montreal but then returned at the request of General Jeffrey Amherst to provide religious services for the occupation forces until 1763.

In 1764 Ogilvie became assistant rector of Trinity Church in New York City; he held this position until his death. No longer an SPG missionary, he ceased to write letters to the society, and therefore little is known of his activities. He had ministered to blacks in Albany, however, and he continued to do so in Trinity Parish. *The Order for Morning and Evening Prayer . . . Collected and Translated into the Mohawk Language under the Direction of the Rev. Mr. William Andrews, the Late Rev. Dr. Henry Barclay and the Rev. Mr. John Oglivie* [sic] was published in 1769, probably reflecting substantial effort on Ogilvie's part. His first wife died in 1769, and Ogilvie later married Margaret Philipse, widow of Philip Philipse. Incapacitated by a stroke while in the pulpit in November 1774, Ogilvie died a few days later in New York City. Charles Inglis preached a eulogistic sermon, an anonymous writer published an elegy in *Rivington's New York Gazette*, and Ogilvie's likeness in mezzotint was offered for sale.

John Ogilvie carried on a successful ministry among the Mohawks, probably because he took the trouble to learn their language. He also was an effective spiritual leader for soldiers, for settlers in the frontier community of Albany, and for the urbane Anglicans of New York City. More flexible and energetic than many Church of England clergymen, he exemplifies the richness of colonial Anglicanism.

• Many of Ogilvie's letters are published in John Wolfe Lydekker, *The Faithful Mohawks* (1938), and Frank J. Klingberg, *Anglican Humanitarianism in Colonial New York* (1940). A brief but useful biography is contained in Dexter Franklin Bowditch, *Biographical Sketches of the Graduates of Yale College* (1885–1912). Other sources include Morgan Dix, *A History of the Parish of Trinity Church in the City of New York*, pt. 1 (1898); Joseph Hooper, *A History of St. Peter's Church in the City of Albany* (1900); *Collections of the New-York Historical Society . . . 1870* (1871); Stanley Pargellis, *Military Affairs in North America 1748–1765: Selected Documents from the Cumberland Papers in Windsor Castle* (1936; repr. 1969); and John C. Van Horne, ed., *Religious Philanthropy and Colonial Slavery: The American Correspondence of the Associates of Dr. Bray, 1717–1777* (1985).

S. CHARLES BOLTON

OGLE, Samuel (c. 1694–3 May 1752), governor of Maryland, was born in Northumberland County, England, the son of Samuel Ogle, a member of Parliament for Berwick, and Elizabeth Dawson, a widow. His mother died a few years after his birth, and his father remarried. Ogle probably spent part of his childhood in Ireland, where his stepmother had property and his father was commissioner of the revenue. His father was also a Crown commissioner for the colony of Maryland before his death in 1718. Little else is known of Ogle's life before his governorship, except that he was a cavalry captain.

Ogle was appointed governor of Maryland three times between 1731 and his death, the only colonial governor to hold the office three distinct times. His first appointment on 3 September 1731 brought Ogle to Maryland for the first time to replace the proprietor's brother, Benedict Leonard Calvert, who was too ill to continue in office. As the proprietor's administra-

tor and representative in Maryland, Ogle immediately faced controversy over the fees charged by various provincial officials and the clergy, the collection of the proprietor's quitrents on patented land, and the need for paper currency. Central to all these issues was the poor economic climate, caused primarily by the overproduction of tobacco and the inferior quality of the crops raised. Writing to the proprietor in 1731, Ogle said, "I can't promise to do everything to your lordships Content, but this I am sure of, that nobody in the world can set about your service with more Zeal and true Concern for your Prosperity than I shall do, so that I hope at least you will be perfectly satisfied with the Sincerity of my intentions."

When Ogle had been in office only a year, he was supplanted by the proprietor himself on his first visit to his province. Charles Calvert, fifth lord Baltimore and fourth proprietor of Maryland, assumed the governorship in December 1732. During the next six months and through one session of the assembly, Calvert established policies on the important issues of the day that would continue in their basic form until the Revolution. Perhaps overwhelmed by what was only the second time a proprietor had been present in the colony in Maryland's history, the lower house of the assembly passed or agreed to many solutions that it later regretted and attempted to override.

After serving as president of the council during the proprietor's visit, Ogle was again commissioned as governor in June 1733. It was his job to administer the new policies, often in the face of strong opposition by members of the lower house, who were known as the "country party" to distinguish them from the proprietor's adherents, known as the "court party."

Although the economy improved in the late 1730s and the paper currency emission of 1733 simplified financial transactions, payment of officers' fees and proprietary privileges continued to create dissension. Although the economy improved in the late 1730s and the paper currency emission of 1733 simplified financial transactions, dissension between the upper and lower houses continued, focusing on taxes and fees assessed to benefit the proprietor and his appointed officers of government. When a directive from the Crown required Ogle to ask the lower house for a continuation of the arms levy, the delegates countered with a request for the appointment of an agent to represent them before the Crown in protest to the proprietor's schedule of officers' fees and tonnage duty. The resulting stalemate forced Ogle to prorogue the assembly.

Although he was able to overcome the opposition long enough in 1740 to secure the money to pay volunteers for what turned out to be a disastrous expedition in the Caribbean during the War of Jenkins' Ear, Ogle's effectiveness as governor was severely diminished. In August 1742 the proprietor replaced Ogle with Thomas Bladen, a native Marylander who, while in London, had married Lady Baltimore's sister.

Bladen was even less effective at dealing with the lower house than Ogle had been, and Ogle succeeded him as governor in March 1747. Four months later the assembly passed the most significant piece of legislation of the entire Ogle governorship: the Tobacco Inspection Act, which would allow the export of only high-quality tobacco that had passed inspection at provincial inspection houses located on rivers up and down the Chesapeake Bay. At the same time, in anticipation of higher tobacco prices and increased revenues for the proprietor, officers' fees and certain other levies were reduced.

In July 1741 Ogle, then about forty-seven years old, married Anne Tasker, who was not yet eighteen years old and was the daughter of his friend and political colleague Benjamin Tasker. She had been reared in Maryland in a family of great political, economic, and social importance and brought to her marriage a dowry of £1,500 sterling. Samuel and Anne Ogle had five children, only three of whom survived infancy. Their son Benjamin Ogle (1749–1809) was governor of Maryland from 1798 to 1801.

During the hiatus of Bladen's governorship, the Ogles lived in London in a house on Saville Row, Westminster. A contemporary said, "I always believed Mr. Ogle's pride would not let him live in Maryland less than Gov'r" (Baltz, p. 16). While they were in England, Ogle charged his father-in-law with the building of a suitable country house on land Ogle owned in Prince George's County. The resulting mansion, named "Belair," remains today as an example of the Maryland five-part Georgian dwelling of the eighteenth-century wealthy planter class. Ogle participated in the pastimes of this class, especially encouraging thoroughbred horse breeding and racing. Among his own horses were two of the very finest stock, imported from England; he also owned a buffalo. He owned at least fifty slaves.

Ogle died in office, probably in Annapolis but possibly at Belair, after an illness of several months; he was buried at St. Anne's Church in Annapolis. At his death, incomplete inventories of his personal estate totaled over £2,500 in addition to bank stock in England valued at under £5,000. He owned over 2,500 acres of land in Prince George's and Anne Arundel counties, two lots in Annapolis, and the Saville Row house in England. His obituary in the Annapolis *Maryland Gazette* (7 May 1752) says, "His long Residence among us made him thoroughly acquainted with our Constitution and Interests, and his benevolent Disposition induced him invariably to exert all the Influence his Station, as Governor, gave him, and every Means which his own Good Sense could suggest, to promote the Public Good."

• Sir Henry A. Ogle, *Ogle and Bothal, or A History of the Baronies of Ogle, Bothal, and Hepple . . .* (1902), and Shirley Vlasak Baltz, *A Chronicle of Belair* (1984), provide family and personal information. Edward C. Papenfuse et al., eds., *A Biographical Dictionary of the Maryland Legislature, 1634–1789* (1979, 1985), and the files of the Legislative History Project at the Maryland State Archives in Annapolis detail Ogle's political and economic career and his relationships to other prominent Maryland families. For discussions of his effect on Maryland issues, see Aubrey C. Land, *Colonial Mary-*

land, a History (1981), and Charles Albro Barker, *The Background of the Revolution in Maryland* (1967), as well as the introductory material in the multivolume *Archives of Maryland* (1883–), see vols. 25, 28, and 37.

JANE WILSON McWILLIAMS

OGLESBY, Richard James (25 July 1824–24 Apr. 1899), soldier and politician, was born in Oldham County, Kentucky, the son of Jacob Oglesby, a merchant-farmer, and Isabella Watson. Oglesby's mother, father, two brothers, and a sister died in the cholera epidemic of 1833. The family's only slave, known to Richard as "Uncle Tim," was among the assets auctioned as part of the settlement of the meager estate, a scene that Oglesby later claimed made him an abolitionist. He was sent to live with relatives who migrated to Decatur, Illinois, in 1836. Oglesby received only a few months of formal schooling, but his oratorical skills attracted attention at an early age. In 1845 he read law in the office of Judge Silas Robbins, a prominent Springfield attorney, and he was admitted to the bar the same year. He practiced law in Sullivan and Decatur, a part of the Eighth Judicial Circuit, where he met and became an admirer of another ambitious, Kentucky-born Whig, Abraham Lincoln.

At the beginning of the Mexican War in 1846, Oglesby joined the Fourth Illinois Regiment and was elected first lieutenant. He fought in the battles of Veracruz and Cerro Gordo. He attended law school in Louisville, Kentucky, in the winter of 1848–1849, but he soon joined the gold rush to California with a party of Decatur residents. Oglesby returned to Decatur in 1851 with $5,000 in gold, which he parleyed into successful real estate development.

In 1856 Oglesby embarked on a twenty-month journey to Europe and the Holy Land in search of culture and faith, but the trip confirmed his disdain for monarchy and his religious skepticism. On a visit to the Tower of London, as a Swedish prince passed by, everyone except Oglesby bowed. The young American explained in his trip diary that "sovereigns pay little regard to princes" (26 June 1856). The opulence of the cathedrals and the commercialism of the Holy Land left him with "more doubt than faith," but he took the precaution of bottling Jordan River water "to carry home for baptism should I ever become a good Christian" (11 May 1857). Oglesby never joined a church, although he supported several.

After Oglesby returned to Decatur he began presenting what became quite popular speeches about his travels. The increased name recognition made him a viable Seventh District Republican congressional candidate in the 1858 Illinois election, which featured the Lincoln-Douglas debates. Both Lincoln and Oglesby lost their 1858 election bids, but the Illinois Republicans made a comeback in 1860, when Oglesby was elected to the state senate while contributing to Lincoln's successful campaign for president. It was Oglesby who devised the "rail-splitter" sobriquet for Lincoln at the Illinois state convention at Decatur.

When the Civil War began, Oglesby resigned his state senate seat and organized and commanded the Eighth Illinois Infantry Regiment. Colonel Oglesby was promoted to brigadier general after leading a brigade at Fort Donelson in Tennessee in February 1862 and to major general after receiving a near-fatal wound at Corinth, Mississippi, in October. After a brief stint in 1863 with the Sixteenth Army Corps in Tennessee, Oglesby was assigned to head the court-martial case against Surgeon General William Hammond in Washington, D.C. Before the trial was completed, Oglesby, with President Lincoln's assent, resigned his commission to run for governor of Illinois in 1864. As one of the best speakers in the West, he stumped for Lincoln's reelection and was himself elected.

Planning to lobby the federal government concerning state reimbursements and draft quotas and to visit the front, Oglesby arrived in Washington, D.C., on the afternoon of 14 April 1865 and was entertained by Lincoln, who read humorous stories to his delegation. Oglesby was awakened during the night with the news of Lincoln's assassination and was among those at Lincoln's deathbed. Oglesby helped persuade Mary Todd Lincoln that the body should be taken to Springfield, Illinois. He became president of the Lincoln National Monument Association, which built the tomb at Oak Ridge Cemetery. He delivered the major address at its formal dedication in 1874 in the presence of President Ulysses S. Grant and the cabinet.

During Governor Oglesby's administration (1865–1869), construction began on the new state capitol, and the legislature authorized new charitable, penal, and educational institutions. Oglesby opposed the lenient Reconstruction policies of President Andrew Johnson and helped form the Grand Army of the Republic, a powerful organization of Civil War veterans. At the end of his term, Oglesby was constitutionally ineligible for consecutive terms as governor, and he was frustrated because no U.S. Senate seat was available. In 1872, however, the Republican party again chose the popular politician as its gubernatorial candidate, with the apparent understanding that the legislature would choose him for the U.S. Senate should the GOP be successful in defeating the Liberal Republican party challenge. Oglesby won the popular election and, ten days after his inauguration, replaced the incumbent U.S. senator, Lyman Trumbull, who had sided with the Liberal Republican party. Oglesby served a rather undistinguished Senate term, which ended in 1879, when the more powerful former senator John A. Logan was chosen for the seat.

Oglesby again served as governor from 1885 to 1889, a term that involved violent railroad strikes and the labor strife that led to the Chicago Haymarket bombings of 1886. After the Illinois and U.S. Supreme courts refused to overturn the death penalty for the seven convicted "anarchists" accused of conspiracy in the bombing, Oglesby reduced the sentences of two who petitioned for mercy, but he refused, despite petitions from around the world, to commute the death sentences for the other five, who, protesting their innocence, preferred martyrdom to contrition.

Oglesby was married twice, first in 1859 to Anne Elizabeth White of Decatur; they had four children. Anne Oglesby died in the governor's mansion in 1868. Senator Oglesby then married the widow Emma Gillett Keyes, of the prominent Logan County Gillett family, in 1873; four children were born to their marriage. In 1889 Oglesby retired to a house he called "Oglehurst," in Elkhart, twenty miles north of Springfield, where he died.

• A massive collection of Oglesby papers is in the Illinois State Historical Library, Springfield. The collection includes his 1856–1857 trip diary. James T. Hickey, "Oglesby's Fence Rail Dealings and the 1860 Decatur Convention," *Journal of the Illinois State Historical Society* 54 (1961): 5–24, documents Oglesby's role in the "rail-splitter" campaign. The 1886 episode is covered in Mark A. Plummer, "Governor Richard J. Oglesby and the Haymarket Anarchists," in *Selected Papers in Illinois History, 1981*, ed. Bruce D. Cody (1982), pp. 50–59. A lengthy campaign biography, written by Franc B. Wilkie, *A Sketch of Richard J. Oglesby*, appeared in 1884. A brief biography is Plummer, "Richard J. Oglesby, Lincoln's Rail-Splitter," *Illinois Historical Journal* 80 (1987): 2–12. An obituary is in the *Chicago Tribune*, 25 Apr. 1899.

MARK A. PLUMMER

OGLETHORPE, James Edward (22 Dec. 1696–30 June 1785), founder of Georgia, philanthropist, and soldier, was born in London, England, the son of Theophilus Oglethorpe and Eleanor Wall. Having gone into exile with James II in 1688, the Oglethorpes named their last child for his son, James Edward Stuart. Even after Oglethorpe's father gave up on the Jacobite cause, his mother and sisters provided intelligence and courier services for efforts to restore the Stuarts. Their reputation shadowed Oglethorpe, for whom no overt adult Jacobitism is known.

Although young Oglethorpe's life was typical of his class and time, his intensity was not. He was educated at Corpus Christi College, Oxford, a Jacobite haven in which his classmates were other young men of the gentry; he also took the Grand Tour and fought the Turks. His active military career began immediately after the 1715 Jacobite revolt, when through the influence of exiled Scots he secured an appointment in the Austrian army of Prince Eugene of Savoy, who promoted Oglethorpe to lieutenant colonel. Oglethorpe followed his father and brothers into the House of Commons in 1722, representing the family borough of Haslemere.

Not surprisingly, in view of his family's Jacobite connections, Oglethorpe was no Whig. Nor did he follow a straight Tory line, although he was personally conservative and disdainful of the Whig leader Sir Robert Walpole. More diligent and purposeful than most of his fellow "Independents," he seems to have been a hardworking, abstemious, and sincere reformer with a military bent of mind, intent on improving England and on replicating the best attributes of England in America.

As the gap between rich and poor in England increased in the 1720s and 1730s, and as the numbers of unemployed poor multiplied, philanthropy became more fashionable and influential among England's ruling elite. Such philanthropists linked charity with public order and discipline. Enthusiasts supported more than one charitable cause, and circles of philanthropists overlapped and shifted. Young Oglethorpe was especially active in the group known as the Associates of Dr. Thomas Bray. Bray and his circle had championed prison reform for many years, but Oglethorpe's effort brought the abuses and neglect of English prisons vividly to public attention. He focused on prison reform following the death of a young friend in prison for debt. Directing a parliamentary investigation of prisons in 1729, Oglethorpe skillfully publicized his committee's findings and cemented ties among charitable groups. At age thirty-three he emerged as an effective coordinator, linking charitable, political, and military enthusiasts for a proposed colony at the southern tip of British settlement in North America.

For half a century before the founding of Georgia, British planners had envisaged a colony southwest of the Savannah River to secure the defense of the Carolinas and to challenge Spain and France in the southern interior. Their commitment and promotional efforts were effective by the time Oglethorpe and other philanthropists made public their goal of a settlement colony.

Oglethorpe and the other reformers who coordinated Georgia's political and financial support received a royal charter in June 1732 as the Trustees for Establishing the Colony of Georgia in America. Although Oglethorpe's promotional efforts had linked the colony with penal reform as a haven for released debtors, he and the other trustees allowed very few former prisoners to go to Georgia. Indeed, they screened applicants to avoid criminals and debtors. A high proportion of the English recruits were Londoners, not a promising background for frontier farmers. Oglethorpe and other trustees obtained Protestant settlers from Scotland, Ireland, the German lands, Switzerland, and Austria, both as indentured servants and as paying passengers.

Mercantilist economic goals were stock arguments in colonial promotions, but the Georgia Plan had ideological underpinnings that resulted in a degree of control over colonists unparalleled in British colonial experience. Oglethorpe and John Percival, the earl of Egmont, were chief architects of the Georgia Plan. As philanthropists concerned with public order and military security, they fashioned policies that have remained controversial. Oglethorpe and the other trustees saw the colony as a new start for the poor, who would begin on an equal landowning basis and would be protected from the competition and demoralizing example of slaveholding. The trustees' opposition to slavery was basic, and Oglethorpe's own commitment against slavery deepened with his years. Rum was forbidden, and the settlers could not sell their land. In particular Oglethorpe envisioned settlers as the sturdy yeomen of an older England, authenticating the nation's self-image while providing an effective militia. Meanwhile, bounties and subsidies would encourage settlers to produce goods for which Britain depended on Mediterranean sources, in particular silk, wine, and cochineal. Complaining of these restrictions, in particular the prohibition against slavery, many "malcontent" settlers abandoned Georgia. Other "malcontents" remained there to challenge openly the trustees' policies, for which Oglethorpe was the obvious symbol.

The trustees had a 21-year mandate to administer the colony, and they were barred from owning property there. Indeed, Oglethorpe was the only trustee to go to Georgia, and his function was more military than administrative. He took the first settlers there in 1733, founding the town of Savannah near their landing site at Yamacraw Bluff and forging an indispensable relationship with local Native Americans. The willingness of a group of these settlers to accompany Oglethorpe to England strengthened his campaign for the colony's funding and increased his fame. If Georgia was a peculiar colony, so was Oglethorpe as its most visible founder and its defender but never its governor. The trustees administered Georgia from London, without any governor; they relied on a secretary resident in Georgia, who was in his sixties and deferential toward Oglethorpe, for information and insights. Even so, the decisions Oglethorpe made in Georgia were sometimes at variance with what the other trustees had told the secretary. For example, when the London trustees decided to allow daughters to inherit land, a relaxation of the original "tail male" rule, the secretary made the news known, unaware that Oglethorpe had not yet received his packet from London. The consequences were damaging, for it appeared to the settlers that Oglethorpe in their midst was even more intransigent than the distant trustees. Requests for the changes had originated among the "malcontents." The episode drew a hard line between Oglethorpe and an increasingly volatile party of settlers.

Oglethorpe's administrative contribution to Georgia's success and to the growth of British power in the southern interior centered on his development of Augusta as a center for trade with distant Choctaws, Chickasaws, Uchees, and Cherokees as well as Creeks, his nearest and closest allies. Oglethorpe's scrupulous oversight of white traders and his full backing by the other trustees brought order and regulation from which European and indigenous traders benefited. Through this Oglethorpe outmaneuvered French trading and military rivals and, by his own account, surly South Carolina officials as well.

As Britain's relations with France and Spain deteriorated, Oglethorpe concentrated on defense. He built Fort Frederica on St. Simon's Island near the Spanish threat. After Anglo-Spanish hostilities erupted in the War of Jenkins's Ear, Oglethorpe prepared to attack St. Augustine. His campaign was thwarted, largely by the weather and sickness. When the Spanish attacked

Fort Frederica in 1742, Oglethorpe's preparations and discipline were vindicated with victory in the Battle of Bloody Marsh. Oglethorpe and his colony had fulfilled their military purpose of repelling the long expected Spanish attack on the British southern tier. On 16 November 1739 he had vowed to the other trustees: "The French have attacked the Carolina Indians and the Spaniards have invaded us. I wish it may not be resolved between them to root the English out of America. We here are resolved to die hard and will not lose one inch of ground without fighting" (quoted in Spalding and Jackson, eds., *Oglethorpe in Perspective*, p. 108). With Georgia safe, Oglethorpe left it for the last time in 1743. Returning to London, he was charged by a subordinate with mismanaging the Georgia campaign. A court-martial acquitted Oglethorpe in 1744. Later that year he married Elizabeth Wright, and they established their residence on her estate, "Cranham Hall" in Essex. The couple had no children.

During the 1745 Jacobite revolt, Oglethorpe's loyalty to the Crown was questioned, in effect ending his military career. Commanding a regiment in energetic pursuit of a Jacobite force, Oglethorpe drew back amid rumors of a French invasion and of vastly superior rebel strength. Whatever Oglethorpe's reason for halting his pursuit, his real or suspected Jacobite sympathies became an issue, apparently at the initiative of William Augustus, the duke of Cumberland. A son of George II, Cumberland delivered the death blow to the revolt—and to the Jacobite cause—at Culloden in 1746. In October of that year Oglethorpe faced charges that "he neglected his Orders and suffered the Rear of the Rebels . . . to escape" (British Public Records Office, War Office 71:7, pp. 195–284). The court-martial acquitted him "most honourably," a ruling confirmed by the king. With his name no longer listed in the Board of General Officers, the distinguishing mark of active army commissions, Oglethorpe in effect was honorably retired as lieutenant general. Out of favor at court and likely resentful of his humiliation, the old soldier took the opportunity afforded by the Seven Years' War to return to military life incognito. Pseudonyms and similar clues have indicated that a mysterious Englishman traveling in military circles on the continent during the years 1755–1760 was Oglethorpe, relieving his hurt, boredom, and inactivity, frequently in the company of Britain's ally Frederick the Great.

By tradition, a new reign offered closure. Whatever mixture of personal honor and Jacobite resentment Oglethorpe felt, the death of George II in 1760 eased its hold on him, and he resumed his quiet country life at Cranham. Near London, he continued to enjoy the company of its writers, particularly Samuel Johnson. He died at Cranham and was buried there in the Church of All Saints. The church was demolished and replaced, and the location of graves was lost. In 1923 research by Thornwell Jacobs of Georgia suggested the location of the Oglethorpe tomb, and excavation resulted in its ecclesiastical verification.

• Older useful treatments of Oglethorpe include Leslie F. Church, *Oglethorpe: A Study of Philanthropy in England and America* (1932), and Amos Aschbach Ettinger, *James Edward Oglethorpe: Imperial Idealist* (1936). More recent scholarship includes several works by B. Phinizy Spalding: *Oglethorpe in America* (1977); "James Edward Oglethorpe: A Biographical Survey," *Georgia Historical Quarterly* 56 (1972): 241–51; "Myths and the Man: James Edward Oglethorpe," *Georgia Review* 28 (1974): 52–57; "Oglethorpe and Johnson: A Cordial Connection," *Johnson Society Transactions, 1974* (1975), pp. 52–61; and "Profile of an Old Independent: Oglethorpe as Seen in the Papers of James Boswell," *Yale University Library Gazette* 53 (1979): 140–49. Two collections edited by Spalding and Harvey H. Jackson are useful: *Forty Years of Diversity* (1984), particularly the chapters by Spalding and Milton L. Ready; and *Oglethorpe in Perspective* (1989), especially the chapters by Betty Wood, Rodney M. Baine and Mary E. Williams, and Edward J. Cashin.

CAROLE WATTERSON TROXLER

O'GORMAN, Thomas (1 May 1843–18 Sept. 1921), second Roman Catholic bishop of Sioux Falls, South Dakota, was born in Boston, Massachusetts, the son of John O'Gorman and Margaret O'Keefe, recent Irish immigrants. The oldest of eight children, he moved with his family to Chicago and then, in 1852, to St. Paul, Minnesota Territory. In the autumn of 1853 O'Gorman, along with John Ireland, four years his senior, was sent to France by Joseph Cretin, first bishop of St. Paul, and enrolled in the preparatory seminary of Meximieux, near Lyons. He spent seven years there pursuing his classical studies. After five more years studying philosophy and theology at the Marist seminary at Montbel, near Toulon, he returned to St. Paul and, on 5 November 1865, was ordained to the priesthood by Cretin's successor, Thomas Langdon Grace. O'Gorman took away from this experience a fluency in written and spoken French, which was to be of great service to him in his career. The time in France also established his close relationship with Ireland, who would be his lifelong friend and patron.

Father O'Gorman's first assignment was the pastorate at Rochester, Minnesota, where he ministered for twelve years to the Catholics in that thriving community as well as to those in four mission stations in the surrounding countryside. He built churches and schools and performed the multitude of tasks required of a frontier priest. He was particularly noted for his pulpit and platform eloquence and for his devotion to the cause of Total Abstinence. That he stood high in the community was attested to by Dr. William Worrall Mayo, who, though not a Catholic, took pains to consult O'Gorman before deciding on the educational program for his sons Charles Horace Mayo and William James Mayo. The sons were destined to make Rochester one of the great medical centers in the world.

At the end of 1877 O'Gorman applied to Grace for a leave of absence in order to serve with the Congregation of St. Paul in New York City. The Paulists, founded by the charismatic Isaac Hecker as a distinctly American association of missionary priests, were devoted primarily to preaching and writing, activities O'Gorman fully and successfully participated.

Five years later O'Gorman returned to Minnesota and assumed the pastorate at the town of Faribault. Here too he won general esteem for his priestly work, though he also received much criticism for failures in the financial administration of the parish. In 1885 Ireland, now bishop of St. Paul, appointed O'Gorman first rector of St. Thomas Aquinas Seminary in St. Paul, which has since evolved into the University of St. Thomas. O'Gorman served in this post for two years without much distinction. After his removal from the rectorship he remained on the staff for three more years as professor of theology and history.

In 1890 O'Gorman was named professor of church history in the recently founded Catholic University of America in Washington, D.C. His academic duties in what was then a very small and exclusively clerical institution were slight. He took a leading role, however, in the struggle within the American Catholic hierarchy that dominated the 1890s and that pitted the liberal or Americanist bishops against those of a more conservative bent. The leader of the former group was Ireland, now archbishop of St. Paul, for whom O'Gorman, during his stay in Washington, acted as eastern agent. O'Gorman's exceedingly aggressive activities in behalf of the Americanist cause gained him as many enemies as it did friends, so much so that it was only in the teeth of powerful opposition that Ireland managed to secure from the Vatican, in 1896, his friend's appointment as bishop of Sioux Falls, South Dakota.

During his quarter-century episcopate, O'Gorman presided over the kind of remarkable growth characteristic of American Catholicism of that era. When he arrived, his diocese was coterminous with the state of South Dakota. Under his charge were about 30,000 Catholics served by sixty-four priests in 161 missions and stations. In 1902 the western half of the diocese was detached to form a separate jurisdiction. By the time O'Gorman died, that part of the original diocese left to his responsibility boasted a Catholic population of 70,000, with 140 priests ministering to 197 full-fledged parishes and missions, 116 nuns teaching nearly 5,000 children in thirty-one schools, and six hospitals staffed by men and women religious. O'Gorman also founded Columbia College, which survived, however, for only twenty years, and he directed the construction of a handsome cathedral.

Local preoccupations did not prevent the bishop of Sioux Falls from participating in activities of a wider scope. Most notable among these was the part he played as a member of the Taft Commission (1902), which successfully negotiated an agreement between the Vatican and the United States relative to church property in the Philippines. In this diplomatic venture he acted once more as agent for Archbishop Ireland, who had close ties to the Republican administration of Theodore Roosevelt (1858–1919). But O'Gorman's strenuous efforts to persuade two popes to award Ireland a cardinal's hat did not succeed. He died in Sioux Falls.

Thomas O'Gorman was a prelate of wit and cultivation who held many posts of responsibility during the time American Catholicism came of age. He was firm and forthright in his loyalties, and he readily identified the progress of his church with that of his country. He was widely admired for his literary gifts, best displayed in his sermons and in his *History of the Roman Catholic Church in the United States* (vol. 9 of the American Church History Series, 1895).

• The Archives of the Diocese of Sioux Falls contain some manuscripts in O'Gorman's hand, mostly sermons and lectures. A modest number of his letters may be found in the Archives of the Catholic Historical Society of St. Paul, the Archives of the Diocese of Richmond, and the Secret Vatican Archives in Rome. A short biographical study is Seraphica Marx, "The Life of Thomas O'Gorman, Bishop of Sioux Falls" (master's thesis, Univ. of South Dakota, 1959). An obituary is in the *New York Times*, 19 Sept. 1921.

MARVIN R. O'CONNELL

O'HANLON, Virginia (20 July 1889–13 May 1971), the girl to whom the phrase "Yes, Virginia, there is a Santa Claus . . . " was addressed, was born in New York City, the daughter of Dr. Philip F. O'Hanlon, a consulting surgeon for the New York police department, and Laura Virginia Plumb. Although her first name was Laura, she was known by her middle name. She attended Normal College of the City of New York (now Hunter College), where she received her B.A. in 1910, and Columbia University, where she received her master's degree in 1911. In 1912 she began teaching elementary school in the New York public schools. She married Malcolm Douglas, in 1915 had a daughter (also named Laura Virginia), and was soon widowed. By 1920 she was again living with her parents.

Later in life, Virginia returned to school and received her Ph.D. in 1930 from the Graduate School of Education at Fordham University. From grade school teacher she was promoted to junior principal. She worked in the New York City public school system for forty-seven years. For a number of years she was junior principal of P.S. Manhattan 31 on the Lower East Side, serving a diverse student body of Jewish, Puerto Rican, black, and Italian children, along with a special class of disabled students. She served the last three years of her career as junior principal of P.S. 401 in Brooklyn, which provided classes for chronically ill children in hospitals and institutions. She once spoke of the respect she felt children should be given: "Children are naturally so sincere and so serious about things that you feel you wouldn't want to disappoint them. In turn they give you a feeling of being young, and you enjoy all over again the things you had forgotten or thought you couldn't enjoy."

Virginia attained fame at the age of eight, when she was living at 115 West 95th Street. Like many eight-year-olds, she had come to question the existence of Santa Claus. It was a habit in her family to write to the Question and Answer column in the *New York Sun* when they had doubts about pronunciation or historical facts, and so her father suggested she write and ask about Santa Claus, which she did.

Dear Editor:

I am 8 years old. Some of my friends say there is no Santa Claus.

Papa says, "If you see it in The Sun, it's so."

Please tell me the truth; is there a Santa Claus?

Virginia O'Hanlon

"If you see it in *The Sun*, it's so" was an advertising slogan that appeared on the front page of the newspaper. Virginia checked the Question and Answer column for days with increasing disappointment. Then her father called from downtown and told her a whole editorial had been devoted to her letter. Charles A. Dana, the editor of the *Sun*, assigned Francis P. Church, an ex–Civil War correspondent who frequently wrote articles about controversial theological subjects, to pen the now-famous reply to her letter, which appeared Tuesday, 21 September 1897: "Yes, Virginia, there is a Santa Claus. He exists as certainly as love and generosity and devotion exist. . . . Alas! How dreary would be the world if there were no Santa Claus! It would be as dreary as if there were no Virginias."

Church, given to sardonic writings, was not generally known as the author of the reply (his own obituary did not mention it). Yet he showed the respect for children and joy in their youth of which Virginia later spoke. His editorial was so popular that the *Sun* reprinted it annually until 1949 when the paper was sold. It was translated into some twenty languages and circulated in innumerable reprintings.

Virginia took her childhood fame well; she frequently was called upon to read Church's reply at Christmastime and sent attractive copies printed by the New York School of Printing to those who requested any. She once remarked with good humor, "I am anonymous from January to November."

In failing health for several years, she died in a nursing home in Valatie, New York.

• Not much has been written about Virginia O'Hanlon other than the circumstances of her letter writing. A full obituary can be found in the *New York Times*, 14 May 1971, pp. 1 and 44. Shorter death notices appeared in *Newsweek*, 24 May 1971, p. 63, and *Time*, 24 May 1971, p. 71. *Parents' Magazine*, Dec. 1951, pp. 43 and 93–95, gives her story of the letter writing and a little about her experience as an educator.

ANN W. ENGAR

O'HARA, Edwin Vincent (6 Sept. 1881–11 Sept. 1956), Roman Catholic bishop and educator, was born on the family farm near Lanesboro, Minnesota, the son of Owen O'Hara and Margaret Nugent. After absorbing academic rudiments in public schools, O'Hara decided to enter the priesthood and in 1898 began study at St. Thomas College in St. Paul, Minnesota. Two years later he moved to the adjacent St. Paul Seminary for theological training and received ordination in 1905.

He was recruited for service farther west and served as assistant pastor from 1905 to 1911 and then pastor until 1920 of St. Mary's Cathedral in Portland, Oregon.

Early in his labors at St. Mary's, O'Hara disclosed an interest in education, organizing in 1907 both the Summer Institute for Teachers and the Catholic Education Association of Oregon. He also became deeply involved in questions of social justice and the rights of labor, combining Catholic doctrine regarding compassion for the poor with widespread humanitarian concerns that characterized the Progressive Era. Ill health dictated his release from clerical duties in 1910, and so the zealous priest pursued advanced studies at Catholic University in Washington, D.C., during a year of recovery. Returning to Oregon, O'Hara threw himself into social reform. By 1913 a committee he had formed was instrumental in lobbying the state to enact some of the country's earliest minimum-wage laws. Oregon's governor named O'Hara chair of the state's Industrial Welfare Commission. O'Hara's influence spread as California and Washington soon copied the trailblazing legislation verbatim. Those reformist laws were eventually sustained by the U.S. Supreme Court.

Duty called elsewhere in the aftermath of O'Hara's social involvements. He served as chaplain in the U.S. Army in 1918, studied a short while at the Catholic Institute in Paris, and in 1920 became pastor of St. Mary's Church in Eugene, Oregon. There he soon developed an abiding interest in Catholics who lived in rural districts. He approached the National Catholic Welfare Conference with concerns about people in farming areas and as a result helped create and lead its Rural Life Bureau. In 1921 O'Hara began publishing *St. Isidore's Plow* (renamed *Catholic Rural Life* in 1924), a journal that helped correlate the interests and pool the resources of Catholics involved in agriculture. In 1923 he convened the first National Catholic Rural Life Conference held in St. Louis, Missouri. Educational questions during those years revolved around Oregon's law that made attendance in public school compulsory. In 1925, as archdiocesan superintendent of schools, O'Hara spearheaded resistance to such a requirement and fought it through appeals all the way to the U.S. Supreme Court, where the legislation was declared unconstitutional. Leaving the pastorate for a transitional year in 1929–1930, O'Hara taught sociology classes at the Catholic University and in the summer at the University of Notre Dame. In November 1930 he became bishop of Great Falls, Montana.

Entering that higher level of ministry, Bishop O'Hara concentrated much of his energy on another aspect of sound Catholic education. He inaugurated the Confraternity of Christian Doctrine (CCD) in his diocese because he regarded it as the best means of expounding church teaching and moral values to all parishioners on a regular basis. By 1933 his advocacy had created a national headquarters for that educational institution in Washington, D.C., and in 1935 he convened the confraternity's first national congress. During this period he also succeeded in obtaining from Rome a policy statement requiring establishment of the CCD in every American diocese. Also in 1935 O'Hara became involved in committee work charged with revising the Baltimore Catechism, a document that had remained substantially unchanged since 1884. He helped coordinate the labors of the educational experts as well as bishops and theologians eventually to produce in 1941 revised instructional materials that combined accepted catechismal standards with efficient teaching techniques.

In 1939 O'Hara was transferred to a larger diocese centered in Kansas City, Missouri, where he continued activities, begun slightly earlier, that preoccupied him for the rest of his life. In 1935 he had helped form a committee of specialists to revise the Douai-Reims version of the English Bible. Under his leadership there followed the creation of the Catholic Biblical Association of America in 1936 and the appearance of the *Catholic Biblical Quarterly* in 1938. While no linguist himself, O'Hara provided effective administration to an unwieldy group of academicians. He also secured patronage from the American Catholic hierarchy for the project and felt no small sense of accomplishment when the first parts of the new translation were printed in 1952. Beginning in 1947 the bishop also played a central role in preparing an approved English version of all the church's sacred rituals. This concern placed him in the vanguard of twentieth-century liturgical reform that has touched church members in many meaningful ways. O'Hara was traveling to one such liturgical congress when he died suddenly in Milan, Italy.

• More than fifty boxes of O'Hara's materials are housed in the diocesan archives at Kansas City, Mo. In addition to writing many articles on social justice and rural problems, O'Hara produced two books, *Pioneer Catholic History of Oregon* (1911) and *The Church and the Country Community* (1927). The only full-length studies about the bishop are James G. Shaw, *Edwin Vincent O'Hara: American Prelate* (1957), and Timothy M. Dolan, *Some Seed Fell on Good Ground: The Life of Edwin Vincent O'Hara* (1992). An obituary is in the *New York Times*, 12 Sept. 1956.

HENRY WARNER BOWDEN

O'HARA, Frank (27 Mar. 1926–25 July 1966), poet, was born Francis Russell O'Hara in Baltimore, Maryland, the son of Russell Joseph O'Hara and Katherine Broderick, who both came from strict Irish-Catholic families. O'Hara always believed he was born 27 June 1926, but his parents apparently lied about his birthdate to hide the fact that he was conceived before their marriage. Shortly after their wedding in Grafton, Massachusetts, in September 1925, the couple moved to Baltimore, where their child was born six months later. They lived in Baltimore for eighteen months before being summoned back to Grafton so that Russell O'Hara could run the family farm for his ailing uncle.

In June 1944, shortly after his high school graduation, O'Hara enlisted in the U.S. Navy. He served as a sonarman third class on the destroyer USS *Nicholas*. After receiving an honorable discharge in 1946, O'Hara went to Harvard on the GI Bill. He took crea-

tive writing classes from John Ciardi and earned a B.A. in 1950. With Ciardi's recommendation, O'Hara was given a graduate fellowship in comparative literature at the University of Michigan, where he earned an M.A. in 1951. His collection of poems, "A Byzantine Place," and *Try! Try!*, a verse play, won O'Hara the Avery Hopwood Major Award in poetry.

O'Hara then moved to New York to join fellow poet John Ashbery, whom he had met at Harvard. Living at first on the money from the Hopwood, O'Hara wrote poetry and explored the city. In New York O'Hara was finally free to live openly as a homosexual and to indulge his interest in the arts. He worked briefly as an assistant to photographer Cecil Beaton, then looked for a more permanent job, preferably one that would allow him time to write. What he found was ideal. In December 1951 he was hired to work at the front desk of the Museum of Modern Art, selling postcards, publications, and tickets. He often wrote poems while he worked at the counter, and his friends in the art world frequently stopped by to visit. O'Hara began writing articles for *Art News* and in 1953 became an editorial associate. He continued to write for the publication when he returned to the Museum of Modern Art in 1955.

The abstract expressionism movement, whose major artists were Willem de Kooning, Franz Kline, and Jackson Pollock, was flourishing in New York, and O'Hara, along with John Ashbery and Kenneth Koch, became part of the avant-garde art scene. In 1952 O'Hara's *A City Winter and Other Poems* was published, a collection of thirteen poems with two drawings by Larry Rivers. The collection was the first of a series of books by poets with artists' drawings published by the Tibor de Nagy gallery. At this time O'Hara became involved with the Club, an artists' forum that had been established in the 1940s. Beginning in March 1952, O'Hara appeared on a series of panels to discuss art and poetry.

O'Hara's first collection of poetry to receive wide recognition was *Meditations in an Emergency* (1957). Even though early reviews were unenthusiastic, it became the collection for which he was primarily known during his lifetime. While *Meditations* was being prepared for publication, O'Hara was approached by a publisher about collaborating with artist Larry Rivers. The resulting project, a series of twelve lithographs titled *Stones*, was produced between 1957 and 1960. For the work, Rivers and O'Hara worked directly on the stones from which the lithographs were made. O'Hara had to write backward so the text would be readable in the finished lithograph. In 1960 O'Hara published the collections *Second Avenue* and *Odes*. Perhaps the most significant event in O'Hara's writing career occurred that year, when Donald Allen published *The New American Poetry: 1945–1960*. Allen classified the forty-four poets by groups: New York School, Beat Generation, San Francisco Renaissance, and Black Mountain. O'Hara, identified as part of the New York School, was a dominant poet in the anthology, with fifteen of his poems included. Two more collections were published during his lifetime: *Lunch Poems* (1964) and *Love Poems (Tentative Title)* (1965). Several more volumes of O'Hara's poems were published after his death, notably *The Collected Poems of Frank O'Hara* (1971), *The Selected Poems of Frank O'Hara* (1974), and *Poems Retrieved: 1950–1966* (1977).

O'Hara sought to capture in his poetry the immediacy of life, feeling that poetry should be "between two persons instead of two pages." He was inspired and energized by New York City as other poets have been inspired and energized by nature. In *Meditations* he wrote, "I can't even enjoy a blade of grass unless I know there's a subway handy, or a record store or some other sign that people do not totally *regret* life." He described his work as "I do this I do that" poetry because his poems often read like entries in a diary, as in this line from "The Day Lady Died": "it is 1959 and I go get a shoeshine."

O'Hara died of injuries he received when he was hit by a vehicle on the beach at Fire Island, on Long Island, New York.

• O'Hara's papers are in the Literary Archives, University of Connecticut Library, Storrs. Brad Gooch, *City Poet: The Life and Times of Frank O'Hara* (1993), is well researched and is the most comprehensive biography of O'Hara available. It also corrects inaccuracies in the newspaper reports of O'Hara's death. For a critical study of O'Hara's poetry, see Marjorie Perloff, *Frank O'Hara: Poet among Painters* (1977). A more concise study of O'Hara's life and work is Alan Feldman, *Frank O'Hara* (1979). Brief obituaries are in *Time*, 5 Aug. 1966, p. 76, and *Newsweek*, 8 Aug. 1966, p. 74.

CLAUDIA MILSTEAD

O'HARA, James (?1752–16 Dec. 1819), revolutionary war officer, businessman, and manufacturer, was born in County Mayo, Ireland, the son of Major John O'Hara. (His mother's name is not known.) The young O'Hara left Ireland in 1765 to attend the Jesuit College of St. Sulpice in Paris. In 1770 he briefly served in the Regiment of the British Coldstream Guards. The next year he resigned the ensign's commission granted to him by his relative, Lord Tyrawley, and briefly worked in a ship broker's office in Liverpool, acquiring business skills.

The ambitious O'Hara emigrated from England to Philadelphia in 1772 and settled in Pittsburgh the next year. Working for traders Devereaux Smith and Ephraim Douglas of Pittsburgh between 1773 and 1774, he conducted business with the Indians in western Pennsylvania and Virginia, acquired knowledge of their languages, and was appointed as an Indian government agent in 1774. Recognizing that wealth might be derived from trading with the Indians and from owning western lands, during these two years O'Hara began to purchase land tracts in western Pennsylvania.

During the American Revolution, O'Hara was a leader in western Pennsylvania. He enlisted in the Third Virginia Regiment as a private, spent his own money to maintain this regiment, and was elected captain. After briefly serving at Fort Pitt in 1777, O'Hara was sent the next year to Fort Kanawha to defend the American position against the Indians and to prevent them from helping British forces. In 1778 O'Hara's company served with George Rogers Clark during the expedition to Vincennes. By 1779 only twenty-nine soldiers from O'Hara's company at Fort Randolph still survived, and they were ordered to serve under General Daniel Brodhead, then commandant at Fort Pitt. In 1781 he served as commissary of the general hospital in Carlisle, Pennsylvania, and from 1781 to 1783 as assistant quartermaster under General Nathanael Greene. He appears to have been present at the battles of Cowpens, Guilford Courthouse, and Eutaw Springs. Also in 1783 O'Hara spent some time in Philadelphia and married Mary Carson, with whom he would have six children.

After the revolutionary war, O'Hara and his new wife went to Pittsburgh, and he became involved in the commercial, military, and political activities on the western Pennsylvania frontier. The O'Haras' home was known for its fine furniture and china and for the first carpets brought across the Allegheny Mountains. The neighbors, astonished to see them on the floor, called the carpets coverlets. In 1784 O'Hara started a general store, James O'Hara & Company, which sold dry goods and groceries, but he was forced to close it three years later, since many customers defaulted on their payments. Between 1784 and 1791 O'Hara served as a government contractor, providing Generals Josiah Harmar and Arthur St. Clair with supplies for their struggle against the Indians. He furnished American troops at Forts McIntosh, Defiance, Washington, and Hamilton with guns, food, and clothing. In 1789 he served as a presidential elector, casting his vote for George Washington as the first president of the United States.

In 1792 O'Hara was appointed by Washington as quartermaster of the U.S. Army. He was empowered to purchase supplies, to dispatch ships to troops situated on the western rivers, and to issue payments to American soldiers. O'Hara, who was with the forces of General Anthony Wayne in 1794, and whose home in Pittsburgh was then located in the exclusive neighborhood of Clapboard Row, was indirectly involved with the Whiskey Rebellion. When insurrectionists threatened to burn the home of Major Abraham Kirkpatrick, which was located next to that of O'Hara, the prominent attorney and writer Hugh Henry Brackenridge discouraged them, arguing that, if Kirkpatrick's home were burned down, O'Hara's house would suffer great damage. Demonstrating their respect for O'Hara, the rioters decided against malicious action. As the rebellion was being fought in Pittsburgh, O'Hara assumed an active role in General Wayne's expedition to suppress the Indians in the West. Selected as a negotiator, O'Hara used his knowledge of Indian languages to attempt to reach a compromise with them and in many instances was successful. More importantly, O'Hara traveled extensively, inspecting forts in Ohio, Michigan, Indiana, Kentucky, and Tennessee and purchasing food and clothing inexpensively, effective business techniques that helped to save Wayne's army and to bring about its victory. He resigned his position as quartermaster in 1796 but continued to serve as a government contractor until 1802.

During the late 1790s and the first two decades of the 1800s, O'Hara became the most prominent businessman and manufacturer in Pittsburgh. In partnership with Isaac Craig, he became one of the nation's pioneer glassmen, establishing the Pittsburgh Glassworks in 1795. He erected a building along the Monongahela River at the foot of Coal Hill for the production of glass in 1797 and hired the German chemist and glass cutter, William Peter Eichbaum, who had been working in Philadelphia, to superintend the new factory. One of the first of its kind to use coal as fuel for its furnaces, during the late 1790s the plant primarily produced green glass, especially windowpanes. After experimentation "at a cost of $30,000," the plant manufactured glass bottles. Buying out Craig in 1804, O'Hara introduced methods in the early 1800s for the manufacturing of white glass in his plant.

During the late 1790s O'Hara also was involved in the salt business. Recognizing the great expense of shipping salt from Baltimore to Pittsburgh, in 1795 he developed a system to bring salt from the Onondaga works in Salina, New York. He used wagons and boats to ship flour and other provisions in barrels to Salina then had these barrels unloaded, filled with salt, and returned to Pittsburgh. His efforts halved the price of salt in the Pittsburgh vicinity.

O'Hara contributed to the development of other businesses and industries in early Pittsburgh. In 1796 he built and operated a sawmill in Allegheny. Two years later he formed a partnership with John Reed to distill whiskey and in 1804 became a partner with John Coppinger in founding the Pittsburgh Point Brewery. Becoming involved in the shipbuilding business, he built ships to transport cotton to Liverpool and was a pioneer in this trade. Recognizing the potential importance of the iron industry, he invested in John Henry Hopkins's Ligonier ironworks in 1816 but lost in this industrial venture when the company closed the next year as a result of declining iron prices.

O'Hara's life was entwined with the development of Pittsburgh. Affiliated with the Federalist party, he ran unsuccessfully for Congress in 1802 but was named as a city burgess the following year. He held this position for only a brief time. Also prominent in local finance and speculation, in 1804 he was appointed as a director of the Pittsburgh Branch Bank of Pennsylvania and in 1815 became its president. O'Hara invested heavily in real estate in Pittsburgh and in Allegheny County, owning approximately $58,000 in land and buildings. In spite of his extensive land tracts in western Pennsylvania, Indiana, and Illinois, O'Hara found himself "land poor" during the crisis of 1817 and was presumedly saved from bankruptcy by his friend James Ross (1762–1847). An active member of the First Presbyterian Church of Pittsburgh, giving it a beautiful chandelier, O'Hara died at his home on Water Street.

O'Hara's career was important to the evolution of early Pittsburgh. With great incentive, he operated major businesses and industries during the inceptive years of Pittsburgh and was a precursor of the industrial leaders who arose during the last half of the nineteenth century.

• O'Hara's papers are housed in the archives of the Historical Society of Western Pennsylvania and reveal much about his career as an entrepreneur in the frontier society of Pittsburgh. Fine sketches of O'Hara's life are in Mary Carson Darlington, *Fort Pitt and Letters from the Frontier* (1892); *History of Allegheny County, PA.* (1889); and "The Founder of a Famous Pennsylvania Family," *American Historical Magazine* 4 (1909): 295–99. Susan Illis and Carolyn Schumacher, *General James O'Hara: Captain of Early Industry in Western Pennsylvania* (1993), contains profiles of O'Hara and his family. A stimulating assessment of his career as a Pittsburgh businessman and industrialist is by Leland Baldwin, *Pittsburgh: The Story of a City, 1750–1865* (1970). O'Hara's contributions to the glass industry are examined in Dorothy Daniel, "The First Glasshouse West of the Alleghenies," *Western Pennsylvania Historical Magazine* 32 (Sept.-Dec. 1949): 97–113, and in Solon J. Buck and Elizabeth H. Buck, *The Planting of Civilization in Western Pennsylvania* (1939). O'Hara's real estate activities are described in Charles Shetler, "James O'Hara's Landholdings in Allegheny County," *Western Pennsylvania Historical Magazine* 34 (Mar. 1951): 23–33.

WILLIAM WEISBERGER

O'HARA, James Edward (26 Feb. 1844–15 Sept. 1905), lawyer and politician, was born in New York City, the illegitimate son of an Irish merchant and a West Indian woman. Little is known of his early life, most of which he spent in the Danish West Indies. He returned to the United States as a teenager, visiting Union-occupied eastern North Carolina for the first time in 1862. At nineteen he became a teacher and operated freedmen's primary schools in the eastern North Carolina towns of New Bern and Goldsboro. He married Ann Marie Harris in 1864, but they separated in 1866, when he accepted the teaching post in Goldsboro. They later divorced.

With the advent of congressional Reconstruction, O'Hara began to participate in politics, serving as engrossing clerk at the state constitutional convention of 1868 and the subsequent session of the legislature. In 1869 he married Elizabeth Eleanor Harris; they had one son. O'Hara had earlier fathered an illegitimate son. O'Hara spent about two years in Washington, D.C., working as a clerk in the Treasury Department and studying at Howard University. Upon his return to North Carolina, he secured a license to practice law in 1873 and assumed a leading role in Republican politics. Hostile Democratic journalists soon noticed O'Hara, calling him "a bright mulatto, with cheek a plenty" and a man with "more than ordinary intelligence."

The young lawyer settled in Halifax County, one of the state's most important cotton-growing counties and the most populous county in the Second Congressional District, which had a strong black (and Republican) majority. Speaking at the Second District Republican Convention in 1874, O'Hara insisted to applause that "colored aspirants" should not be ruled out "on account of their color."

Though not nominated for Congress in 1874, O'Hara was elected to the Halifax County Board of Commissioners and served for the next four years as chairman of this powerful arm of local government. He was elected to the state constitutional convention in 1875. Nominated as a presidential elector in 1876, he withdrew after Democrats attempted to make an issue of his race.

It is difficult to assess O'Hara's tenure as county commissioner, especially in the light of repeated Democratic accusations that the board was corrupt and extravagant. The Republican commissioners were indeed indicted for malfeasance in office, although O'Hara claimed that the charges were politically motivated. The results of these court cases were inconclusive, and the state prosecutor dropped all charges after O'Hara and one associate pleaded nolo contendere and agreed to pay costs. The polemical language used by many of his opponents disguised their basic ideological difference with O'Hara about the role of local government in education and poor relief.

For five consecutive elections O'Hara pursued the Republican congressional nomination in the "Black Second." When he was first nominated to Congress in 1878, a host of enemies within the Republican party accused him of corruption and asserted that O'Hara, who had divorced his first wife a decade earlier, was actually guilty of bigamy. Three weeks before election day Republican leaders convened a new nominating convention and chose another candidate. Refusing to withdraw, O'Hara was victorious in the three-way general election until canvassing boards in three counties rejected hundreds of votes on flimsy technicalities and gave the victory to the Democratic nominee, William H. Kitchin. O'Hara contested the election but was unsuccessful.

O'Hara held no elective office between 1878 and 1883, though he was a significant leader in the statewide antiprohibition campaign of 1881, in the Liberal coalition between Republicans and dissident Democrats in 1882, and in organized black protests against Republican patronage policy. At another disorderly district convention in 1882 he claimed the Republican nomination for Congress and, after several months of conflict, secured the withdrawal of a competing Republican candidate, incumbent representative Orlando Hubbs. O'Hara easily won election and, backed by an unusually united party, won a second term two years later. He was then at the zenith of his political career, not only dominating his district but wielding considerable influence in the state and national party.

In 1886, however, O'Hara faced renewed opposition, as a divided Republican convention once again produced two "nominees." On election day O'Hara received three-quarters of the Republican votes, despite complaints that he had grown distant from his constituents, protests about the way he distributed patronage, and even negative comments about his complexion from an opponent proud to be "of unmixed African blood." But the election was lost to the youthful Democratic candidate, Furniford Simmons.

During his four years in Congress, with the Republican party in the minority, O'Hara found it difficult to shape significant legislation or influence debate. He proposed a constitutional amendment to fill the void left by the Supreme Court's nullification of the Civil Rights Act of 1875, advocated reimbursement for depositors in the failed Freedman's Savings and Trust Company, and sought federal aid for education, but these bills were ignored by the Democratic majority. His only success was securing the passage of seven private, pension, or relief bills. He made no lengthy speeches on the floor of the House, preferring instead to offer brief comments.

O'Hara's only significant national attention came in December 1884, when he offered a controversial amendment to the Reagan Interstate Commerce Bill providing that all railway passengers should "receive the same treatment and be afforded equal facilities . . . as are furnished all other persons holding tickets of the same class without discrimination." Supported by racially moderate northern Democrats, the amendment passed, although, after considerable debate, southern Democrats succeeded in tacking on another amendment making the point that equal could be separate.

O'Hara never held public office again after 1887, though he remained active in the Republican party into the twentieth century. He practiced law and briefly published a weekly newspaper, the Enfield *Progress*. He moved to New Bern, North Carolina, in 1890 and spent the last fifteen years of his life there.

Throughout his career O'Hara served as a convenient symbol for both friends and foes. For Republicans, this talented "carpetbagger" represented the aspirations of a small but increasing group of black professionals who demanded a greater voice in the party's awkward biracial alliance. For black voters, even impoverished landless laborers, he symbolized the hope that ex-slaves could participate in American democracy. For Democrats, especially the generation that ultimately chose to disfranchise blacks, O'Hara was a symbol of dangerous black assertiveness, though time and again they paid grudging compliments to his skill and resourcefulness.

• Most of O'Hara's personal papers have disappeared, though the Regenstein Library, University of Chicago, has a small collection that includes scrapbooks, photographs, and a significant biographical sketch by O'Hara's granddaughter, Vera Jean O'Hara Rivers. The minutes of the Halifax County Board of County Commissioners are available on microfilm at the North Carolina Division of Archives and History. One copy of the O'Hara newspaper, the Enfield *Progress*, is also available on microfilm there. For an example of O'Hara speaking for himself, see U.S. Cong., Senate, Exodus Committee, *Report and Testimony of the Select Committee of the United States Senate to Investigate the Causes of the Removal of Negroes from the Southern States to the Northern States*, 46th Cong., 2d sess. (1880), S. Rept. 693, pt. 1, pp. 49–71. O'Hara's congressional career is thoroughly discussed in Eric Anderson, *Race and Politics in North Carolina, 1872–1901:*

The Black Second (1981). For an analysis of his career in local politics, see Anderson, "James O'Hara of North Carolina: Black Leadership and Local Government," in *Southern Black Leaders of the Reconstruction Era*, ed. Howard N. Rabinowitz (1982). On O'Hara's contested election case, see U.S. Congress, House, *O'Hara v. Kitchin*, 46th Cong., 3d sess., H. Rept. 263; and U.S. Congress, House, *Papers in the Case of James E. O'Hara v. William H. Kitchin, Second District of North Carolina*, 46th Cong., 3d sess., H. Misc. Doc. 7.

ERIC ANDERSON

O'HARA, John Henry (31 Jan. 1905–11 Apr. 1970), novelist and short story writer, was born in Pottsville, Pennsylvania, the son of Patrick Henry O'Hara, a surgeon, and Katharine Elizabeth Delaney. The oldest of eight children, O'Hara had a strained relationship with his accomplished father, partly because of his dismissal from three schools—the Fordham Preparatory School, the Keystone State Normal School, and the Niagara Preparatory School. His discharge from Niagara in 1924 stemmed from a drinking problem, which led his father to secure him a job at the *Pottsville Journal* until he changed his behavior. O'Hara's plan to ultimately attend Yale was thwarted by his father's death the following year, forcing him to take various jobs as a steel worker, railway clerk, ship's steward, soda jerk, and gas meter reader.

O'Hara's writing career began in earnest in 1928 when he accepted a job as a reporter with the *New York Herald Tribune*. At various times thereafter, he was employed as a football writer, film critic, religion editor, and rewrite man for the *New York Morning Telegraph*, the *New York Daily Mirror*, the *New York*, and *Time*. He also served briefly as the managing editor of the *Pittsburgh Bulletin-Index*. O'Hara was fired from most of these jobs because of his penchant for alcohol. It was not in journalism, however, that his true writing talent could be found. In May of 1928 O'Hara had a short story published in the *New Yorker*. He continued writing stories and novels, and in 1933, following a divorce from first wife Helen Ritchie Petit, whom he had married in 1931, he attempted to quit drinking in order to devote himself full-time to writing fiction.

O'Hara's first major success was the novel *Appointment in Samarra*, published in 1934. He wrote the first 25,000 words of the book from a furnished room in New York City, using his bed as a desk. Down to his last three dollars, O'Hara sent letters to three publishing houses asking for money to complete the novel. Harcourt, Brace & Co., impressed by the unfinished manuscript, agreed to subsidize O'Hara's literary efforts for three months. The book, dealing with the last three days in the life of Julian English, a heavy-drinking, suicidal Cadillac salesman from the fictional town of Gibbsville, won O'Hara immediate fame and established him as an important literary figure.

In 1935 O'Hara published his first collection of short fiction, *The Doctor's Son and Other Stories*, and his second novel, *Butterfield 8*. The novel created something of a sensation because of its subject matter. It followed the life of Gloria, a young girl from a good family who nevertheless becomes an alcoholic juvenile delinquent with a predilection for nymphomania. One critic called it "a cruel and ugly story that will make you sick and bitter, yet hold you till its last venomous line."

In December 1937 O'Hara married his second wife, Belle Mulford Wylie; the couple had one child. In 1938 O'Hara's third novel, *Hope of Heaven*, about the unhappy relationship between a Hollywood writer and a bookshop clerk, met with mixed reviews. He had more success with one of his next efforts, *Pal Joey*. The character of Pal Joey, a reprehensible night club singer and dancer, first began appearing in O'Hara's short stories in the *New Yorker* in 1938. A compilation of the stories, published in 1940, was only moderately successful, but Joey's popularity soon increased when he came to life as part of a Broadway show. Noted composer Richard Rodgers, a friend of O'Hara's, convinced him that Joey would make a fine protagonist for a musical comedy. "He's a heel already," Rodgers said. "We'll make him the first hero of his kind." Rodgers, along with his partner Lorenz Hart, created the music and lyrics for the play, and O'Hara wrote the libretto. *Time* magazine said, "For those who can park their morals in the lobby, *Pal Joey* is a wow." Often described as the first American musical in which plot and music were integrated, the play became a standard of American musical theater.

O'Hara wrote other stage plays but never again made it to Broadway. His success as a novelist also brought him work as a screenwriter in Hollywood. He helped write the scripts for *I was an Adventuress* (1940), *On Our Merry Way* (1948), and *The Best Things in Life are Free* (1956), among others. Ironically, even though several of O'Hara's books were made into films—including *Pal Joey*, *Butterfield 8*, starring Elizabeth Taylor, and *From the Terrace*, with Paul Newman—he never worked on any of those screenplays because he did not consider writing for the movies to be a serious enough endeavor.

In the 1940s O'Hara traveled back and forth between New York and Hollywood. He began writing a column for *Newsweek* and completed two collections of short stories, *Pipe Night* (1945) and *Hellbox* (1947). The latter book was O'Hara's first for Random House, with whom he was associated for the remainder of his career. Random House's publisher Bennett Cerf considered O'Hara to be "one of the most underrated authors in America. He belongs right up there with William Faulkner and Ernest Hemingway" (*New York Times*, 12 Apr. 1970). In 1949 O'Hara wrote what many critics considered to be his first important work since *Appointment in Samarra*, the best-seller *A Rage to Live*, which examined the sexual relationships of the heroine Grace Caldwell Tate, a member of one of Pennsylvania's wealthiest families.

The 1950s were a time of great change in O'Hara's life, beginning with his vow early in the decade to stop writing short stories. The decision stemmed from a dispute he had with the *New Yorker*, which had given a bad review to *A Rage to Live*. In 1953 O'Hara gave up alcohol for good because of a stomach hemorrhage. In January 1954 his second wife passed away and he married for a third time in January 1955 to Katharine Barnes Bryan.

The third marriage coincided with O'Hara's most prolific period as an author. In 1955 he wrote *Ten North Frederick*, a book about a wealthy Gibbsville man who wants to be President of the United States. The novel earned O'Hara the National Book Award in 1956. He followed up that success with *From the Terrace* (1958). At 897 pages, it was O'Hara's longest novel and, according to him, his best. He closed out the five-year period with a third major work, *Ourselves to Know* (1960), a portrait of a man who murders his promiscuous younger wife.

During the 1960s O'Hara returned to short fiction, publishing thirteen books, seven of which were short stories or novellas. His short stories were generally considered of higher quality than his novels, and some critics regarded him as the consummate American short fiction writer of his time. O'Hara felt, however, that he had never been given the critical respect that his work merited. "It used to hurt never winning an award," he said. "I was okay for good notices when a book came out, but not good enough for an award. It used to hurt quite a bit" (*New York Times*, 12 Apr. 1970). He longed to win the Nobel Prize, which he never did, and would often lash out at the literary establishment for these perceived slights. "I've never been the pet of intellectuals, the eggheads," he said (*New York Times*, 12 Apr. 1970). "John was a thorny guy," admitted his publisher Cerf. "You never knew when you were offending him."

Whatever the critical response, O'Hara's work usually met with a high degree of commercial success. His stories, centering on the lives of wealthy people in small-town America and their preoccupations with sex, alcohol, money, and social status, seemed to touch a nerve with the public. O'Hara once said of himself, "Being a cheap, ordinary guy, I have an instinct for what an ordinary guy likes" (*Times*, 12 Apr. 1970).

O'Hara's books may have displayed that natural instinct, but they also contained the fruits of the tireless research he undertook to capture the speech, thought, and emotions of his characters. He would often examine the files of newspapers, magazines, old playbills, catalogues, and other documents so as to bring the right feel to his stories. In appraising his career, the *New York Times* reviewer Christopher Lehmann-Haupt wrote:

For John O'Hara the act of writing was not the agonizing search for new perceptions or novel modes of reality. It was getting down on paper what he knew best as clearly and economically as he knew how. And doing it was simply part of his day, as routine as the arrival of the commuter train and the highballs before dinner. . . . There are those who have observed that the writers whose work endures are not the pathfinders and experimenters, but rather those who stake out their territo-

ries and draw them so accurately as to give them lives of their own. If that is so, then John O'Hara's huge body of work may be around much longer than we had predicted. (12 Apr. 1970)

When Bennett Cerf turned seventy, he had a birthday party and invited only a few close friends. He didn't invite O'Hara because he didn't want him to have to make the long trip from his home in Princeton, New Jersey. "John was very huffy because I didn't invite him," Cerf said, "[but] [t]he next day I received 70 American Beauty roses, one for each year, and I cried with pleasure. That was John O'Hara, and we won't see his like for a long, long time" (*New York Times*, 12 Apr. 1970). O'Hara died in Princeton, survived by his third wife.

• O'Hara's papers are in the Pennsylvania State University Library. For a good biographical account of O'Hara's life, see Matthew J. Bruccoli, *The O'Hara Concern* (1975). See also Frank MacShane, *The Life of John O'Hara* (1980), and Finis Farr, *O'Hara: A Biography* (1973). Among critical studies are Robert Emmet Long, *John O'Hara* (1983); Charles C. Walcutt, *John O'Hara* (1969); Sheldon Norman Grebstein, *John O'Hara* (1966); and Edwin Russell Carson, *The Fiction of John O'Hara*. For a listing of O'Hara's published works, see the *New York Times*, 12 Apr. 1970, p. 88. Obituaries are in the *New York Times*, 12 and 13 Apr. 1970.

FRANCESCO L. NEPA

O'HARA, Mary (10 July 1885–14 Oct. 1980), author and composer, was born Mary O'Hara Alsop in Cape May Point, New Jersey, the daughter of Reese Fell Alsop, an Episcopal minister, and Mary Lee Spring. O'Hara spent her childhood in an upper-middle-class, privileged atmosphere in Brooklyn Heights, New York. She attended Ingleside finishing school and the Packer Institute, then studied music and languages for two years in Europe. After making her social debut in 1903, she married a third cousin, Elisha Kent Kane Parrot, in 1905; they had two children. The marriage estranged her from her father. In 1908 the couple moved to Los Angeles, where Parrot studied and eventually practiced law.

Parrot and O'Hara grew apart in Los Angeles, and the marriage ended in divorce within a few years. Although she tried composing music (an activity to which she would return throughout her life), O'Hara finally decided to write for the motion-picture industry. She landed a job at Metro-Goldwyn-Mayer, where she learned editing and title writing. Finally, at the time she adopted the pen name Mary O'Hara, she was allowed to write screenplays of her own.

In the 1920s O'Hara wrote extensively for the screen, first at MGM and later as a freelancer for Paramount, Warner Bros., and Universal Pictures. Among her credits are the screenplays for *Peg o' My Heart* (1922), *The Prisoner of Zenda* (1922), and *Scaramouche* (1923). While working in the film industry she met her second husband, Helge Sture-Vase, whom she married in 1922. Sture-Vase introduced himself to her, and to the film community, as a Swedish nobleman. Much later O'Hara discovered that he had misrepresented himself, however, although she never found out precisely what his family background was.

In the early 1930s Sture-Vase decided to try his luck as a sheep farmer, and he and O'Hara moved to Wyoming. There they bought a ranch but had little financial success with the venture. Trying to fight her loneliness and poverty, O'Hara began to write stories, focusing in particular on her environment. In 1940 she journeyed to New York City for a six-week writing course. One of the stories she presented to her professor at Columbia University, Whit Burnett, was the kernel for what would become the novel *My Friend Flicka*. Impressed with her talent and productivity, Burnett helped her publish some of her stories and negotiate with Lippincott on the publication of *My Friend Flicka* in 1941.

My Friend Flicka hit the bestseller list almost immediately. Set in Wyoming, the novel told the tale of a family coming together. Its hero, the ten-year-old Ken, was the son of a Wyoming rancher who learned to cope with his problems at home and at school through taking responsibility for a young horse named Flicka. Comparing the book to Marjorie Kinnan Rawlings's *The Yearling*, reviewer Marianne Hauser wrote in the *New York Times* (24 Aug. 1941):

To read this story is restful as well as adventurous, like viewing the countryside from the top of a hill. Miss O'Hara has a way of describing a landscape that makes you smell the grass and feel the coolness of the wind. Its face to the sun, the story moves with a firm, free stride. There is a fine, romantic aureole about it all, but it isn't "sweetness and light." It's rather the delightful, radiant touch of a fairy tale. And yet this is a very real book.

My Friend Flicka became a Twentieth Century-Fox film in 1943 and an ABC television series in 1957. Two of O'Hara's later books, *Thunderhead* (1943) and *The Green Grass of Wyoming* (1946), also were adapted for the screen.

Although none of O'Hara's later works matched the sales of *Flicka*, she continued to write profitably for the rest of her life. No longer financially stranded in Wyoming, she and Sture-Vase moved to Santa Barbara, California. Their marriage ended in divorce in 1947, however, and O'Hara resumed using her maiden name in her private life. In 1948 she moved to Connecticut, where she wrote industriously, eventually spending her winters in the warmer climes of Washington, D.C. She kept up her interest in music and in 1964 combined it with her love of the West by writing a folk musical, *The Catch Colt*, produced at Catholic University and at the Lincoln Theatre in Cheyenne, Wyoming. A hard worker throughout her life, O'Hara explained, "When asked the secret of my success, I translated the word *amateur*: 'I am motivated by love.'" She produced two autobiographies: *Novel in the Making* (1954) and *Flicka's Friend: The Autobiography of Mary O'Hara* (1982). She died in Chevy Chase, Maryland.

• Aside from the autobiographies listed in the text, good sources on Mary O'Hara Alsop are Anne Commire, ed., *Something about the Author*, vols. 2 (1971), 24 (1981), and 32 (1984); and Christine Nasso et al., eds., *Contemporary Authors*, new rev. ser., vol. 4 (1981). Obituaries are in *Time*, 27 Oct. 1980, and the *New York Times*, 16 Oct. 1980.

TINKY "DAKOTA" WEISBLAT

O'HARE, Kate Richards (26 Mar. 1876–10 Jan. 1948), socialist orator and columnist, was born Carrie Kathleen Richards in Ottawa County, Kansas, the daughter of Andrew Richards and Lucy Sullivan, homesteaders. In 1887 drought and financial reverses forced the Richards family to relocate to Kansas City, Missouri. Kate attended Pawnee City Academy in Nebraska in 1893–1894 but, after teaching school for one term, chose to work in her father's machine shop in Kansas City, becoming one of the first women to join the International Association of Machinists. Considering a ministry in the Disciples of Christ, she became a temperance worker and in 1896 joined the staff of the Florence Crittenton Mission in Kansas City, which sought to uplift prostitutes and alcoholics. Increasingly influenced by political tracts of social criticism to which her father had introduced her, she abandoned rescue efforts after hearing a talk by the famous militant union organizer "Mother" Mary Harris Jones. She turned to the growing socialist movement and, in 1901, enrolled in a school for organizers in Girard, Kansas. There she married a fellow student, Francis Patrick O'Hare of St. Louis in 1902. They combined marriage with careers as socialist agitators and organizers. The couple had four children.

The O'Hares lived in Kansas City, Kansas, where she wrote for the Socialist newspaper *Appeal to Reason*, published by one of her mentors, Julius A. Wayland. In 1904 the O'Hares became homesteaders in the Oklahoma Territories, during which time Kate O'Hare gained prominence. Drawing on her rural and religious background, she became especially popular as a speaker at the socialist summer encampments. When the O'Hares moved back to Kansas City, Kansas, in 1909, she assumed leadership in the state Socialist party and in 1910 was its unsuccessful candidate for the U.S. House of Representatives from the Second Congressional District. In 1911 the O'Hares moved to St. Louis where they both joined the staff of the *National Rip-Saw*, a socialist monthly with one of the largest subscription lists.

Kate O'Hare was second only to Eugene V. Debs in the number of speaking dates on the party's lecture circuit. She was elected to top party positions, served as a delegate to conventions, and sat on the national executive committee (1912–1913), the Woman's National Committee (1911–1912), and the Second International's executive body (1913–1914), the only woman other than Rosa Luxemburg to hold that position. She was a candidate for the party's vice presidential nomination in 1916 and that year became the first woman to run for the U.S. Senate. Contrary to her reputation, she was a revisionist socialist rather than an orthodox Marxist. Believing in the inevitability of socialism, she thought it would replace capitalism peacefully through reform, political action, and the education of workers. As a propagandist, she reached out to farmers and to women, recognizing varieties of exploited workers that others in her party did not see. O'Hare was instrumental in the party's adoption of an agricultural program. She cooperated with middle-class suffragists but always believed that the so-called "woman question" would be solved through socialism, and she did not consider herself a feminist.

From 1914 on, she campaigned constantly against American intervention in World War I, and she chaired the committee that issued an antiwar statement at the party's emergency convention when the United States entered the war in April 1917. That July, she was indicted for an antiwar speech she gave in Bowman, North Dakota, the same speech she had delivered dozens of times. After her conviction under the Espionage Act and following a lengthy legal struggle to avoid a prison term, she served fourteen months of a five-year sentence in Missouri State Penitentiary. When her sentence was commuted by President Woodrow Wilson in May 1920, she toured the country, demanding amnesty for political prisoners and also penal reform, especially opposing the prison contract labor system. In the 1920s she was instrumental in establishing Commonwealth College in Arkansas. An experiment in labor education, the college, which had been founded in Louisiana, was a long-standing interest of O'Hare's, and it operated in various places until 1940. With the decline of the Socialist party, she gradually ceased her work on its behalf.

She was divorced in 1928 and that same year married Charles C. Cunningham, an engineer, and settled in California. In the 1930s, still using the name O'Hare because of its public recognition, she joined Upton Sinclair's gubernatorial EPIC (End Poverty in California) campaign, served on the staff of Wisconsin progressive congressman Thomas R. Amlie (1937), and served briefly as assistant to the state director of the California Department of Penology (1939–1940). She died in Benicia, California.

• O'Hare's papers have not been collected. Her few extant letters are scattered in a variety of collections. The papers of Frank P. O'Hare at the Missouri Historical Society in St. Louis contain a number of her letters, including those from prison. Her published writings consist of columns in contemporary newspapers such as *The National Rip-Saw* (1911–) and its successors, *Social Revolution* (1917–1918) and *American Vanguard* (1922–1924), Socialist party pamphlets, and her writings on prisons, such as her *In Prison*, ed. Jack Holl (1977). There is one collection of her writings to date, *Kate Richards O'Hare: Selected Writings and Speeches*, ed. Philip S. Foner and Sally M. Miller (1982). Publications on O'Hare include Sally M. Miller, *Kate Richards O'Hare: A Life of Dissent* (1993); Miller, "Kate Richards O'Hare: Progression toward Feminism," *Kansas History* 7 (Winter 1984–1985): 263–179; Erling N. Sannes, "'Queen of the Lecture Platform': Kate Richards O'Hare and North Dakota Politics, 1917–1921," *North Dakota History* 58 (Fall 1991): 2–19; and Neil K. Basen, "Kate Richards O'Hare: The 'First Lady' of

American Socialism, 1901–1917," *Labor History* 21 (Spring 1980): 165–99. An obituary is in the *St. Louis Post-Dispatch*, 12 Jan. 1948.

SALLY M. MILLER

OHLY, John Hallowell (10 May 1911–9 Sept. 1990), government official and lawyer, was born in Brooklyn, New York, the son of John Henry Ohly, a surgeon, and Helen Hallowell. He graduated summa cum laude from Williams College in 1933 and magna cum laude from Harvard Law School in 1936. He spent another year at Harvard in a teaching and administrative position and from 1937 to 1940 practiced law in New York City. Ohly was married in 1937 to Elizabeth Congleton; they had three children.

In September 1940 Ohly joined the War Department in Washington, D.C., and spent the next six years working in the office of Under Secretary of War Robert P. Patterson as an attorney, labor relations adviser, and special assistant. His World War II service included organizing and overseeing the takeover by the War Department of the American railroad system, coal mines, and many industrial plants, involving hundreds of thousands of workers. The takeovers were a response to labor disputes and management noncompliance that had interrupted or threatened to interrupt production and services that were vital to the war effort. At the end of the war Ohly chose not to return to his law firm in New York. During the winter and spring of 1945–1946 he wrote a comprehensive but unpublished history of plant seizures during World War II. In 1946–1947 he served as executive secretary of the President's Advisory Commission on Universal Training and oversaw preparation of the commission's report. The report provided the main support for efforts, ultimately unsuccessful; to enact legislation providing for universal military training.

In September 1947 James Forrestal, the first secretary of defense, appointed Ohly as one of three statutory special assistants. Among his major responsibilities were functions later performed by the assistant secretary of defense for international security affairs. He handled matters that involved the White House, the National Security Council, the State Department, and foreign governments. Ohly thus played a top-level role in shaping and directing the growth of the Department of Defense and, indeed, of the whole national security establishment during the seminal Cold War years. In addition, he performed an astonishing variety of functions dealing with manpower, logistics, health affairs, intelligence, and administration of the department. "Jack Ohly was a secret weapon," another staff member said. "He could turn out more good work under great pressure than any man I have ever seen."

In October 1949 Ohly left the Department of Defense to become deputy director for mutual defense assistance. In this capacity he was responsible for the policies and overall direction of the entire U.S. economic and military assistance program for dozens of countries throughout the world, involving $5 billion in appropriations in 1951 and equivalent sums in subsequent years. During this period he also served as acting director and as special assistant to the secretary of state.

In 1951, at his own request, Ohly stepped down from deputy director to a position as assistant director that was physically and psychologically less demanding. For the next seven years he dealt primarily with overall planning in the successive agencies that administered the U.S. foreign aid program. This post involved general coordination and supervision of all elements of the multibillion-dollar foreign aid program and planning development of the annual program. Ohly's experience in dealing with other departments and with Congress made his service invaluable. Thereafter, until his retirement in 1968, Ohly worked for the International Cooperation Administration and its successor, the Agency for International Development. In 1961 he served as foreign aid adviser to Vice President Lyndon Johnson on his trip around the world.

In retirement Ohly displayed the same industry and energy that had marked all his endeavors. In particular, he devoted himself to the conservation of natural resources. Ohly's reverence for nature impelled him to deed to the National Park Service a large tract of land that provided access to one of the highest waterfalls in the state of Vermont. Ohly died in North Adams, Massachusetts.

The adjective most often applied to Ohly by his contemporaries was selflessness: he sought neither recognition nor monetary reward. Supreme Court justice William Brennan spoke of him as "that great man of public service." In his handling of plant seizures during World War II Ohly demonstrated the methodical and thorough inquiry and lucid oral and written argument and analysis characteristic of his work. Ohly's great acumen, indefatigable concentration, sincerity, and scrupulous honesty of purpose served him and the nation well in his frequent negotiations on economic and military assistance with representatives of countries from every continent. One of Ohly's favorite quotations, from the *Thoughts of Marcus Aurelius*, best describes him: "He had the power of readily accommodating himself to all, so that intercourse with him was more agreeable than any flattery; and at the same time he was most highly venerated by those who associated with him; and he had the faculty both of discovering and ordering, in an intelligent and methodical way, the principles necessary for life."

• Ohly's papers are in the Harry S. Truman Library, Independence, Mo. Information for this entry was drawn from Ohly's personal resumé, Jan. 1977; Steven L. Rearden, *The Formative Years, 1947–1950*, vol. 1 of *History of the Office of the Secretary of Defense*, ed. Alfred Goldberg (1984); a letter from Townsend Hoopes to Goldberg, 4 Mar. 1991; family members; and personal acquaintance. An obituary is in the *New York Times*, 11 Sept. 1990.

ALFRED GOLDBERG

OHR, George E. (12 July 1857–7 Apr. 1918), potter, was born George Edgar Ohr in Biloxi, Mississippi, the son of George Ohr, an Alsatian-born blacksmith, and Johanna Wiedman, who had emigrated from Württemberg, Germany. He was the second of five children. He attended the local elementary school and then a "German school" in New Orleans, but his formal education was not extensive. He learned the blacksmith trade from his father and worked in his father's shop until his mid-teens, when he went to New Orleans. There he worked for a couple of years for a ship's chandler and served on a sailing ship for one voyage. By the late 1870s he was back in Biloxi working for his father.

In 1879 Ohr was invited by his friend Joseph Fortune Meyer, an established potter, to return to New Orleans to learn that trade. Ohr wrote later that "when I found the potter's wheel I felt it all over like a wild duck in water" ("Some Facts in the History of a Unique Personality," *Crockery and Glass Journal*, 12 Dec. 1901, p. 123). He stayed long enough with Meyer to learn the craft. Then for two years he traveled around the country and worked as a journeyman potter. In 1882 he was back in New Orleans and probably working again with Meyer.

When Meyer's pottery closed in late 1883, Ohr headed for Biloxi with little in the way of savings but with an already large collection of his wares and no lack of self-confidence. Using his blacksmith background, he constructed his own kiln and other facilities and opened his first shop. He obtained his clay from the banks of the nearby Tchoutacabouffa River. Most of his creations were practical, such as pitchers and flowerpots. By 1885, when he exhibited at the Cotton Centennial Exposition in New Orleans, he had amassed about 600 wares. Ohr's pottery brought a mixed reception at the fair, and his unsold pieces were stolen while being shipped back to Biloxi. The need to create a new stock was magnified when he married Josephine Gehring of New Orleans in 1886 and began raising a family. In all, the Ohrs had seven children.

Hard work and moderate success enabled Ohr to build his second shop in 1888 on land owned by his father. Around this time Ohr heard again from Meyer, who was now operating kilns and throwing pots for the New Orleans Art Pottery. Meyer offered him regular employment, and by 1889 Ohr (without his family) had resettled in New Orleans. By early 1890, however, financial difficulties led the pottery to merge with the recently established Art League Pottery Club, run by William Woodward. Meyer remained with the new endeavor; Ohr returned to Biloxi after a short while.

Ohr's experience at the New Orleans Art Pottery was significant: Meyer's style was careful, consistent, and traditional, but Ohr also came into contact with more adventurous artists. From Meyer Ohr developed a taste for the brown and green glazes that characterize his later work. Over the next few years Ohr gradually moved from folk pottery (classic vessel shapes for practical uses) to an art pottery reflecting his eccentric but highly refined modernist breakdown of form and function. Ohr exhibited at the World's Columbian Exposition in Chicago in 1893. By the following year his Biloxi Art and Novelty Pottery had become a major tourist attraction. Always a nonconformist, Ohr sported an extravagant eighteen-inch moustache and promoted his increasingly unusual ceramic creations as "no two alike." On 12 October 1894, however, his shop was reduced to charred and shattered rubble when fire destroyed most of Biloxi's business district. Luckily his widespread renown as a local eccentric enabled him to rebuild immediately, and by the spring of 1895 Ohr opened the exotic-looking Biloxi Art Pottery.

After the fire Ohr began to pursue his aesthetic idiosyncracies further. He crimped, creased and folded otherwise conventional shapes to produce asymmetrical yet graceful forms of an incredible paper thinness. These beautiful but bizarre pieces seemed the inevitable product of an artist who now presented himself as the Mad Potter. At the Cotton States and International Exposition in Atlanta in the fall of 1895, Ohr exhibited the range of his work, from delicate twisted vases to folksy pitchers from which the water poured unexpectedly. To provide for his ever-increasing family, Ohr made occasional trips to New Orleans in the mid- and late 1890s to do work for Meyer, who was now at the Newcomb College pottery, one of the most important in the American Arts and Crafts movement. Without invitation, in 1899 Ohr shipped eight representative pieces of his work to the Smithsonian Institution, where they were neglected and damaged for more than eighty years. He also submitted some items to an exhibit of American ceramics held at the National Arts Club in early 1900. Adelaide Alsop Robineau was likely the author of a review in the *Keramic Studio* ("National Arts Club," Feb. 1900) that described Ohr's odd pieces and personality: "[T]he quaintest thing about him is his huge conceit. He adds a card with some legend inscribed to every piece, one of which describes himself as the only one and greatest variety potter in the world" (p. 212). Ohr's work was shown at the Exposition Universelle in Paris in 1900 and at the Pan-American Exposition in Buffalo the next year. Although he did not win any prizes at these events, he was mentioned with admiration by Edwin Atlee Barber in the revised edition of his authoritative *The Pottery and Porcelain of the United States* (1901). For the 12 December 1901 issue of the *Crockery and Glass Journal*, Ohr provided an enthusiastic if somewhat inaccurate sketch of his early years.

Ohr continued to produce pottery for the next five or six years. Still the showman, he also sought recognition for the artistry of his more revolutionary work. With this goal in mind, he brought his best pieces of art pottery to the Louisiana Purchase International Exposition held in St. Louis in 1904. He won a silver medal but did not sell anything. As Ohr's wife later recalled, "[N]obody really appreciated it. They were not willing to pay enough for it. It was art, high art, he considered, almost priceless" (*New Orleans Times-Picayune*, 1 Oct. 1922). By 1907 Ohr had virtually ceased doing pottery, and two years later he closed his shop and stored thousands of pots in a shed near his house, where they stayed until the early 1970s. Two of Ohr's

sons opened an automobile garage in 1910 in what had been their father's shop.

Ohr remained outspoken and outlandish for the remaining years of his life. One of his pet complaints focused on machine-made pottery, which he labeled fraudulent. Always a heavy smoker, Ohr died at home in Biloxi of lung cancer. In assessing Ohr's technique and achievement, Paul E. Cox, director of the Newcomb pottery, observed (in "Potteries of the Gulf Coast," *Ceramic Age*, Apr. 1935): "It is said that Ohr could work on the wheel whichever way it turned. Certainly he could throw wares of considerable sizes with walls much thinner than any other potter ever has accomplished. It is quite probable that George Ohr, rated simply as a mechanic, was the most expert thrower that the craft has ever known" (p. 140).

• The most comprehensive study of Ohr's life and pottery is Garth Clark et al., *The Mad Potter of Biloxi: The Art & Life of George E. Ohr* (1989); it also has the best collection of illustrations of Ohr's work. Ralph Kovel and Terry Kovel, "The Mad Potter of Biloxi," *Western Collector*, May 1972, pp. 18–20, was the first important article on Ohr; it remains a good study, as is the section on Ohr in *Kovels' American Art Pottery* (1993). See also Robert A. Ellison, Jr., "George Ohr: Small Wonders of a Giant's Vision," *Arts & Crafts Quarterly* 3 (Summer 1990): 18–23; Paul Evans, *Art Pottery of the United States* (1974); and *The George E. Ohr Exhibition Catalogue* (1983). An obituary is in the Biloxi *Daily Herald*, 8 Apr. 1918.

ANDREW RUBENFELD

O'KEEFFE, Georgia (15 Nov. 1887–6 Mar. 1986), artist, was born Georgia Totto O'Keeffe in Sun Prairie, Wisconsin, the daughter of Francis Calyxtus O'Keeffe, a farmer, and Ida Totto. O'Keeffe decided early to be an artist. In 1903 the O'Keeffes moved to Williamsburg, Virginia; in 1905 Georgia began to attend the Art Institute of Chicago. In 1907 she enrolled at the Art Students League in New York, where she studied with William Merritt Chase. At this period O'Keeffe encountered Alfred Stieglitz's gallery, at 291 Fifth Avenue. Stieglitz was a photographer, an art dealer, and an early champion of modern art. His gallery and opinion were central to the modernist movement in America.

In 1909 Georgia left school and began to work as an illustrator in Chicago. She then returned to Virginia and stopped painting altogether. The European-based system of teaching art involved copying the work of the masters. "I began to realize that a lot of people had done this same kind of painting before I came along," O'Keeffe said, "I didn't think I could do it any better" (Kuh, p. 189).

In 1912, at the University of Virginia summer school, O'Keeffe encountered the Oriental-based ideas of Arthur Wesley Dow, a Columbia University art professor. Dow's method was based on the creative participation of the student, and O'Keeffe began painting again. That winter she taught art in Amarillo, Texas, and the following summer at the University of Virginia. There she met Arthur Macmahon, a political scientist from Columbia University for whom she felt a strong attraction.

In the fall of 1915 O'Keeffe taught at Columbia College in rural South Carolina. Away from the aesthetic ferment of New York, O'Keeffe began to isolate her own artistic identity. At Thanksgiving she received a visit from Macmahon, for whom her feelings were steadily growing stronger. In the weeks following the visit, O'Keeffe reached a state of nearly ecstatic intensity. She moved beyond the traditions and conventions that had shaped her as an artist and translated her emotional experience into what was, finally and entirely, her own work.

O'Keeffe's drawings of December 1915 are charcoal abstractions. The images are abstract but drawn from nature; some are lyric, rounded and tender, some budding, some rushing and whiplike. These drawings are more like the German Expressionists, in which emotional and spiritual content was emphasized, than the more analytical and cerebral work of the French school. Although they reveal great technical skill, their power derives most importantly from emotional presence, which lies at the core of O'Keeffe's work.

When O'Keeffe returned to New York in the spring of 1916, Alfred Stieglitz showed her work at "291." The exhibition identified O'Keeffe both as a modernist and a member of the Stieglitz circle. This group would include John Marin, Arthur Dove, Marsden Hartley, Paul Strand, Charles Sheeler, Charles Demuth, and Ansel Adams.

That fall O'Keeffe taught in Canyon, Texas. Painting again in isolation, she produced another powerful series in response to the wide-open landscape. These works are semi-abstract, high-keyed in color, and spatially disorienting. In glowing, radiant watercolors she portrayed the great Texas sky and its dramatic atmospherics. O'Keeffe was experimenting with perspective and design, pattern and volume. The bold use of color, the voluptuous contours, and the sophisticated manipulation of space demonstrated her growing power and originality.

In 1917 Stieglitz showed O'Keeffe's work again. O'Keeffe and Macmahon had by now begun to drift apart, and Stieglitz was beginning to play an increasingly large part in O'Keeffe's life. In spring 1918 O'Keeffe fell ill and returned to New York. She was tended there by Stieglitz, who was twenty-three years her senior and married. That summer Stieglitz left his wife for O'Keeffe. Stieglitz and O'Keeffe would marry in 1924; they had no children.

During 1918–1919 O'Keeffe experimented with pure abstraction. Dow's approach made little distinction between realism and abstraction, and throughout her career O'Keeffe moved easily between the two. In *Music—Pink and Blue I*, a large oil of 1919, she uses voluptuous colors and orificial imagery: a trembling, lyrical, layered archway gives onto an ethereal space. In *Red and Orange Streak* (1919) the palette is earthy, dark, and harsh, and the forms are smooth and clean. In the early 1920s O'Keeffe executed a series of Dow exercises. Her subjects were organic—fruits, leaves, and vegetables. These images were representational, though vividly colored and increasingly simplified to produce clean stylized shapes. O'Keeffe was experimenting with space and volume, scale and perspective.

Stieglitz had closed his gallery with O'Keeffe's show in 1918, and during the early 1920s he arranged exhibitions elsewhere for himself and his artists. O'Keeffe's shows of 1916 and 1918 commanded interest, and in 1921 she and her work were again on exhibition, this time as subjects of Stieglitz's photographs. In 1923 and 1924 Stieglitz exhibited O'Keeffe's work, and in 1925 he opened the Intimate Gallery. For the next twenty years he showed O'Keeffe's work nearly every season.

O'Keeffe's fame, however, was complicated. The sensuality of her own work had aroused notice, and Stieglitz's photographs of her presented her not only as an artist standing next to her work but also as a sensuous nude model. O'Keeffe's sexuality became a matter of public speculation and general inquiry, much to her chagrin.

O'Keeffe had concentrated on small, close-up objects, painted on small canvases, but in the mid-1920s she began using larger canvases for the close-up images, working with a new set of premises. She was now drawing on another aesthetic source. The photographer Paul Strand had produced a brilliant series of abstract images around 1916 in which he used the camera lens to manipulate the image. Through magnification, tilting, and cropping, representational images became abstractions. O'Keeffe had experimented briefly with these ideas and had produced two magnified flower images. In the mid-1920s she began to explore magnification as a device more fully. Strand used magnification to strip the identity from the objects; O'Keeffe used it to increase the importance of the object and to exploit its emotional power. In the magnified flowers series, a voluptuous amplitude joins with a sense of overwhelming intimacy. The soft, yielding surfaces, the rapturous colors, and the hidden, vulnerable heart of the flower all infuse these paintings with great dramatic impact. The combination she produced, of femininity and power, was unique to O'Keeffe's work.

O'Keeffe and Stieglitz spent their winters in Manhattan and their summers at the Stieglitz family house at Lake George in upstate New York. She chafed at summers among the large and vociferous Stieglitz clan and began going alone to the Maine coast. In the summer of 1926, after a serious rift with Stieglitz, O'Keeffe spent four weeks in Maine. The result was a series of subdued and potent paintings, the most powerful of which were *Closed Clam Shell* and *Open Clam Shell*. In these the single magnified form, dignified and monumental, nearly fills the small canvas. The power here is emotional, as it is in the flowers, but the tone is very different. The palette here is cool and muted, restricted entirely to neutral grays and whites. The shells themselves are smooth and hard, their surfaces impenetrable. The revealed opening is barely there, or inexorably shut in a cool line of denial. Though the flower paintings suggest passionate vulnerability, the clam shells imply containment, prohibition, the closed and coupled self.

In 1926 O'Keeffe showed her first urban landscape, *New York with Moon*. She began to celebrate the smooth towering forms of the new skyscrapers. In these she used stylized and simplified images, sleek geometric forms, buildings without people, cars, or street life. In these works atmospherics are as important as the buildings themselves. Light, sky, wind, weather, and darkness—all are powerful compositional elements.

In 1929 O'Keeffe spent the summer in Taos, a village near Santa Fe, New Mexico. She found the wide southwestern horizon exhilarating and began to explore the dry magical landscape in her work. One of her first works there was the great *Black Cross, New Mexico*. The cross is somber and threatening, a symbol of prohibition. Hugely magnified, oppressive, it dominates the composition and nearly obliterates the earth and sky beyond it. The painting derives formal strength from the powerful cruciform. Behind the inexorable black geometry of the cross, however, lies voluptuous turbulence in the ripple of purple-red hills stretching out to the horizon. Here is a recurrent O'Keeffe theme: the dynamic juxtaposition of stern order and riotous passion.

New Mexico proved a rich source for O'Keeffe, and in the early 1930s she began another of her great series: the bones and antlers. "The bones seem to cut sharply to the center of something that is keenly alive on the desert even tho' it is vast and empty and untouchable—and knows no kindness with all its beauty" (O'Keeffe, exhibition catalog, An American Place, Jan. 1939). The bones are treated, compositionally, much as the flowers were: enlarged, centered, simplified, sometimes cropped. The smooth, osseous shapes, in O'Keeffe's hands, take on mythic overtones. They suggest an interior strength, tranquil, remote, and enduring.

In the early 1930s O'Keeffe's work was drastically interrupted. Stieglitz had begun a romantic liaison with Dorothy Norman in 1928. Tension between O'Keeffe and Stieglitz grew steadily and finally reached a climax in a professional dispute over O'Keeffe's mural commission at Radio City Music Hall. Stieglitz prevailed, and in late 1932 O'Keeffe developed increasingly severe psychological symptoms and was hospitalized in early 1933. Frightened by her condition, Stieglitz ended his affair with Norman.

O'Keeffe did not work again until early 1934, when she returned to New Mexico and discovered the Ghost Ranch near the village of Abiquiu. Some of her most powerful works were done here during the decade that followed. The soft collapsing forms, the yielding runoffs of pink sandstone beneath the high bluffs, the round mounds of red siltstone, and the clean sky were all part of a world to which she felt a mystical connection, one that she chronicled and adopted as her own. From 1935 to 1946 she painted version after version of this lyrical landscape, celebrating the rich glowing colors, the pellucid light, the sense of endless and crystalline space. During this period O'Keeffe continued to paint animal skulls as well. Calm, mystical, symmetrical, their shining iconic presences hang clean and centered in the vast radiant space of New Mexico. These paintings reverberate with the beauty, intimacy, and haunting distance that characterize some of O'Keeffe's best work.

In the early 1940s O'Keeffe began a new bone series celebrating the pelvis, a return to orificial imagery. "I like empty spaces," she said. "Holes can be very expressive" (Calvin Tomkins, "The Rose in the Eye Looked Pretty Fine," *New Yorker*, 4 Mar. 1974). In this series the ovoid shape is central and dominant. The paintings combine echoes of both birth and infinity; the clear sky behind the bones is deep and endless.

During this period O'Keeffe spent each summer at the Ghost Ranch; each fall she returned to Stieglitz in New York. O'Keeffe's shows received respect from the critics and enthusiasm from the public. In 1937 her exhibition drew a thousand people a week as her reputation grew steadily. She was given museum exhibitions and awarded honorary degrees. In 1942 the Whitney Museum of American Art in New York established a project to catalog and list her work. In 1943 she was given a one-woman retrospective at the Art Institute of Chicago and in 1946 a one-woman exhibition at the Museum of Modern Art in New York, the first ever given by that museum to a woman.

In 1946 Stieglitz died at the age of eighty-two. O'Keeffe spent the next three years in New York settling his estate. In 1949 she moved to New Mexico for good. Stieglitz's last gallery, An American Place, closed in 1950, with an exhibition of O'Keeffe's work.

During the 1950s O'Keeffe produced an austere series based on a door in the wall of her adobe house at Abiquiu. Large, handsome, and implacable, the works contain a certain majesty but little emotional power. Their strength is purely formal. This was to remain the case: after Stieglitz's death O'Keeffe's work lost the qualities that informed her greatest paintings. Absent now were the emotion, the yielding tenderness, the turbulent passion, and the cold rage that had given her earlier work such strength.

Both the mood and the subjects of O'Keeffe's work became increasingly remote, distant in both the physical and metaphysical sense. In 1958 she painted the whimsical and beguiling *Ladder to the Moon*, an image of transition in which a ladder hangs against the evening sky, halfway between earth and heaven, under a half-moon. It is literally a statement concerning a departure from the earth. O'Keeffe's last important works were the *Sky above Clouds* series of 1963–1965. These huge canvases derive from views seen from an airplane window. Rows of small puffy white clouds are laid out schematically against a calm sky. Peaceful and serene, the paintings suggest a state of sublime removal. In these paintings there is no earth at all, only sky.

O'Keeffe lost her central vision in the early 1970s, and thereafter her attempts to paint were negligible.

An assistant, Juan Hamilton, cared for her, and in 1984, when O'Keeffe was ninety-six years old and nearly blind, Hamilton arranged for her to sign a codicil that left him virtually all of her property. When O'Keeffe died in Santa Fe, her family contested the codicil, and Hamilton settled out of court. A nonprofit foundation was established to oversee the disposition of her works.

Georgia O'Keeffe was one of the great artists of the twentieth century. Her exploration of the formal and modernist concerns of her period is brilliantly demonstrated by her imaginative use of focus, scale, and perspective. She was also a breathtaking colorist, with a rich and vivid range of resonant hues. The greatest strength of O'Keeffe's work, however, lies in its emotional power: the central subject of her paintings is the wide, intense, highly charged spectrum of emotion itself.

• The largest collection of O'Keeffe material is in the Stieglitz Archive at the Collection of American Literature, Beinecke Rare Book and Manuscript Library, Yale University. An interview with O'Keeffe is in Katherine Kuh, *The Artist's Voice* (1962). An excellent selection of O'Keeffe's letters is in *Georgia O'Keeffe, Art and Letters*, ed. Jack Cowart et al. (1987). Her own book, *Georgia O'Keeffe* (1976), is a rather abstract but beautiful memoir illustrated by her work. Roxana Robinson, *Georgia O'Keeffe: A Life* (1989), is the most comprehensive biography, though Laurie Lisle's earlier work, *Portrait of an Artist* (1980; repr. 1986), is still a reliable source. Sarah Whitaker Peters, *Becoming O'Keeffe* (1991), examines the artist's work from 1915 to 1930. See also Charles Eldredge, *Georgia O'Keeffe* (1991); Lisa Mintz Messinger, *Georgia O'Keeffe* (1988); and Barbara Buhler Lynes, *O'Keeffe, Stieglitz and the Critics, 1916–1929* (1991). Permanent collections of O'Keeffe's work include those at the Museum of Modern Art, the Whitney Museum of American Art, and the Metropolitan Museum of Art, New York City; the Art Institute of Chicago; the Boston Museum of Fine Arts; the Philadelphia Museum of Art; and the National Gallery of Art, Washington, D.C. A lengthy obituary is in the *New York Times*, 7 Mar. 1986.

ROXANA ROBINSON

O'KELLY, Berry (c. 1860–14 Mar. 1931), businessman, was born in Chapel Hill, North Carolina, the son of slave parents. His father's name is unknown. His mother, Frances Stroud, died when O'Kelly was very young, and he was raised by members of her family. After emancipation, he attended local schools in Orange and Wake counties, North Carolina, and subsequently worked as a railroad freight and ticket agent. Frugal and hard-working, O'Kelly saved the wages he earned working as a store clerk in the all-black town of Mason Village, near Raleigh, North Carolina, and eventually bought a share of the business. By 1889 he was the sole owner of the general store, serving both Mason Village and Raleigh customers. Described as optimistic, genial, warm, and sympathetic, he was also a hard-nosed businessman and real estate investor. In 1890 Mason Village was renamed Method, and

O'Kelly became the town's postmaster, a position he held for more than twenty-five years. He married Chanie Ligon, who died childless in 1902.

By the early twentieth century O'Kelly had branched out into construction and brick manufacturing and invested in a Raleigh shoe store. The R. G. Dun and Company mercantile agency reference firm estimated his "pecuniary strength" in 1905 as among the best in Raleigh. In 1915 and 1918 O'Kelly was listed as owning a general store and a brick manufacturing enterprise, Dun and Company placing his pecuniary strength at between $35,000 and $50,000 and listing his credit rating as "high." In the 1920s he bought a brick building in Raleigh and leased commercial space to black businesses, headed both the Acme Realty Company and the Eagle Life Insurance Company, and invested in a black newspaper, the *Raleigh Independent*. He later served as an officer of the Raleigh branch of the Mechanics and Farmers Bank. His wealth and business achievements were remarkable in their day, equaled by only a small number of black southerners.

In the town of Method, O'Kelly was, according to one account, "general director of community affairs." Active in the African Methodist Episcopal church, he also served as chair of Method's primary school committee. In the 1910s and 1920s he helped develop the school into a much larger normal school and industrial education institution, the Berry O'Kelly Training School.

O'Kelly's success was aided by supportive black institutions, such as the Durham-based North Carolina Mutual Life Insurance Company from which he borrowed money when he needed ready cash. He was a member of the National Negro Business League, founded in 1900 by Booker T. Washington to promote black enterprise. By the time of his death in Wake County, amidst the Great Depression and despite a severe drop in land values, O'Kelly owned fifty-five tracts of land there, including thirty-seven in Raleigh, and several thousand acres of farmland in Virginia. An inventory of his holdings, excluding the Virginia land, which was heavily mortgaged, calculated the worth of his estate at between $145,000 and $156,000, making O'Kelly one of the wealthiest African Americans in North Carolina. He was survived by Marguerite Bell, whom he had married in 1923, and an infant daughter.

Despite his remarkable economic success, O'Kelly did not become a national black leader. Like other prosperous African Americans of his day, he devoted most of his energies to his business pursuits. Though active in local bond, road, and school elections, he remained aloof from party politics. His leadership qualities, however, were apparent, not only in his material success, but in his active participation in every aspect of community building in the African-American town of Method, North Carolina.

• Sources for O'Kelly's life are scattered. Elizabeth Davis Reid Murray reviewed much of what is available for her detailed article in William S. Powell, ed., *Dictionary of North*

Carolina Biography, vol. 4 (1991). See also the R. G. Dun records at Dun and Bradstreet, New York City; the records of the Superior Court, Wake County, Estate of Berry O'Kelly, 18 June 1931, at the Wake County Courthouse in Raleigh, N.C.; and an article in the *Wichita Searchlight*, 6 May 1911. Clement Richardson, ed., *The National Cyclopedia of the Colored Race* (1919), includes a brief essay on O'Kelly and a photograph. An obituary is in the *Raleigh News & Observer*, 26 Mar. 1931.

LOREN SCHWENINGER

O'KELLY, James (1735?–16 Oct. 1826), Methodist preacher and schismatic, was born probably in Ireland. Little is known of his background or early life until he moved to Surry County, Virginia, where he married Elizabeth Meeks about 1760. Apparently self-educated, he had become attached to the Methodist movement by the time of the Revolution. He was deeply committed to the cause of independence during the war and suffered hardship for his patriotism and for his incendiary preaching.

The first official mention of O'Kelly notes his appointment by the Methodist Conference in Leesburg, Virginia, in 1778 to preach on the New Hope circuit in North Carolina. Two years later he was moved to the Tan River circuit in North Carolina before receiving appointment in 1782 to southwestern Virginia, where he remained for ten years as presiding elder. His leadership was important enough that at the 1784 Christmas Conference in Baltimore, which instituted the Methodist Episcopal church, he was selected for ordination as elder.

During the next several years O'Kelly became increasingly anxious about the concentration of power in the hands of Francis Asbury, leading bishop of the new denomination. Open confrontation began in 1790 when he wrote a letter to Asbury complaining of the excessive use of authority. That same year O'Kelly wrote to Bishop Thomas Coke, now returned to England, to complain that Asbury would not convene a General Conference where his grievances might be addressed. Asbury relented in 1792 and convened a General Conference in Baltimore on 1 November.

Under pressure from many directions, Asbury proposed a new governing structure that included the conference. O'Kelly and his supporters proposed an amendment stating that "after a bishop appoints the preachers at conference to their several circuits, if anyone thinks himself injured by the appointment, he shall have the liberty to appeal to the conference and state his objections, and if the conference approves his objections, the bishop shall appoint him to another circuit." The amendment, which would have dramatically weakened episcopal powers, occasioned three days of bitter debate before it was defeated. O'Kelly and a number of followers left the conference, describing themselves as cast out. Jesse Lee, another leading preacher of the day, remarked to a colleague that he "was sorry to see the old man go off that way" because he "was persuaded he would not be quiet long; but he would try to be head of some party." Asbury and oth-

ers undertook to heal the breach, finally offering O'Kelly an annual stipend of £40 on condition that he not urge further divisions.

The division could not be healed, however, and the dissenters set up their own denomination, the Republican Methodists, a name intended to indicate the democratic principles underlying the rebellion. The effort to eradicate vestiges of individual authority soon led to a review of doctrine and practice among the Republican Methodists, who resolved to simplify both. "I am for Bible government, Christian equality, and the Christian name," O'Kelly declared. Accordingly, they abandoned their name, calling themselves simply "Christians," and adopted a democratic system of governance that divided power and responsibility between laity and clergy.

The schism was costly for the Methodist Episcopal church, which lost about 8,000 members to the new denomination over the next six years, mostly in Virginia and North Carolina. Several important leaders also sided with O'Kelly, including William McKendree, who remained with the dissenters for some months before he returned to the Methodists, ultimately becoming a bishop. The quarrel also cost the Methodist movement much prestige when O'Kelly initiated a pamphlet war with the publication of *The Author's Apology for Protesting against the Methodist Episcopal Government* (1798). Asbury provided material for Nicholas Snethen's *A Reply to an Apology . . .* (1800). The public feud continued with O'Kelly's *A Vindication of an Apology . . .* in 1801 and Snethen's *An Answer to James O'Kelly's Vindication of His Apology* later that year.

In addition to these polemical works, O'Kelly published a number of tracts, pamphlets, and books. The most famous was his *Essay on Negro Slavery* (1784), which asserted the principle of Christian equality against the practices of his day. Other works included *Divine Oracles Consulted* (1800), *The Christian Church* (1801), and *Letters from Heaven Consulted* (1822). He also compiled materials for the worship of his new denomination, including *Hymns and Spiritual Songs Designed for the Use of Christians* (1816).

O'Kelly died in Chatham County, North Carolina, where he resided in his later years. His movement ultimately left little mark on the Methodist Episcopal church. Asbury remained firmly in control until his death, and the power of the episcopacy in Methodism remained far greater than O'Kelly had hoped. O'Kelly's followers, representing the first important schism in Methodism, did not establish an enduring church. The movement began to diminish almost immediately, although some remained to reunite with the Methodist Episcopal church in 1934.

• O'Kelly has received much attention from Methodist historians. The best early biography is W. E. MacClenny, *The Life of Rev. James O'Kelly* (1910). Much more reliable is C. F. Kilgore, *The James O'Kelly Schism in the Methodist Episcopal Church* (1963). Frederick A. Norwood provides particularly good summaries of the controversy in *The Story* of *American Methodism* (1974) and in "James O'Kelly, Methodist Maverick," *Methodist History* (Apr. 1966): 14–28. A detailed and reliable account of the constitutional implications of O'Kelly's rebellion can be found in John J. Tigert, *A Constitutional History of American Episcopal Methodism* (1894), which includes a wealth of journal and diary commentaries from O'Kelly's contemporaries.

MICHAEL R. MCCOY

OKEY, John Waterman (3 Jan. 1827–25 July 1885), lawyer and judge, was born near Woodsfield in Monroe County, Ohio, the son of Colonel Cornelius Okey, a state politician, and Hannah Weir. Like most lawyers of his day, he did not attend college or law school. He received his education from both private instructors and local common schools and also attended the Monroe Academy. Okey then read law with a Woodsfield lawyer and was admitted to the bar in October 1849. In the same year he married May Jane Bloor; they had four children who survived infancy. After a few years of private practice, Okey was appointed a probate judge in Monroe County in 1853 and in 1856 was elected judge of the court of common pleas. He served until 1865 when he resigned and began the private practice of law in Cincinnati. He practiced law in Cincinnati for ten years, during which time he also published the *Digest of Ohio Reports* (1867, with Judge William Yates Gholson) and the *Municipal Code of Ohio* (1869, with Samuel Almond Miller).

In 1875, in recognition of Okey's ability and his interest in compiling Ohio law, Governor William Allen (1803–1879) appointed Okey and two others to a commission to revise, consolidate, and annotate all the Ohio statutes. This was the first comprehensive revision of Ohio statutes since 1805, and the commission took four years to complete its task. The commission's product, the *Ohio Revised Statutes of 1879*, remained in force, with amendments, for over thirty years. As the commission's work was proceeding, Okey was elected to the Ohio Supreme Court in 1877. He was reelected in 1882. In his eight years on the state supreme court, Okey published 170 written opinions, nine of which were subsequently cited by other courts more than a dozen times and were still being cited into the twentieth century. These opinions covered a wide range of issues typical of state litigation in that era. Several of his most influential opinions illustrate this range. In *Jewett v. Valley Railway Company* (1878), his most frequently cited opinion, Okey held that subscribers to a corporation's stock could be held liable for assessments, even though not all the stock had been subscribed to, if such assessments were permitted under the general incorporation law. This ruling protected creditors and made it easier for corporations to raise capital. He held that exempting cemetery associations from "taxation" did not exempt them from "assessments" in *Lima v. Cemetery Association* (1884), a result that allowed governments greater power to collect revenues. Finally, in *Oxford Township v. Columbia* (1882), Okey reaffirmed that municipalities are not exempt from statutes of limitation when they seek to determine ownership of real property, a decision that helped stabilize property titles in Ohio by providing a finite time in which the state could challenge titles.

In criminal cases Okey tended to write in support of defendants rather than the state. He held that a conviction for manslaughter must be reversed when the defendant's sister was prohibited from testifying that her brother did not make a threat, even though her testimony would have simply repeated what four other witnesses said (*Dickson v. State*, 1883). In *Mitchell v. State* (1884), Okey held that a defendant must be released on double jeopardy grounds when the judge at the first trial declared a mistrial over defendant's objection because of a misstatement in the original indictment.

Stylistically, Okey's opinions were short and concise statements of legal principles, typical of late nineteenth-century appellate opinions. They remain, however, remarkable in three respects. First, they often dealt with problems of statutory interpretation rather than the far more common issues of judge-made law. Okey was probably assigned these statutory cases because of his extensive knowledge of Ohio statutes gleaned from his work on the digests. Second, his opinions display a startling familiarity with the case law of other jurisdictions. It is not unusual in an opinion by Okey to see the case law of a dozen or more American jurisdictions and English precedents canvassed in deciding a disputed point of law. This sophistication did much to bring Ohio's law into harmony with the law of other states. Finally, Okey's well-written, well-reasoned opinions are remarkable because they only provide a gloss on Ohio law and do not state the law itself. In Ohio, from the late 1850s on, the supreme court adopted a rule that only the syllabus, the short statement of legal principles at the beginning of a case, states the court's decision. The opinion is merely the judge's views on the issues. Consequently, Okey carefully crafted his writing in the knowledge that it would be only of persuasive value and would not be definitive. He died in Columbus, Ohio.

• The most detailed account of Okey's life is "In Memoriam," *Ohio State Reports* 43 (1885), v–x. George Irving Reed, *Bench and Bar of Ohio*, vol. 1 (1897), pp. 31–32, presents a brief summary of his career. An obituary is in the *Cincinnati Commercial Gazette*, 26 July 1885.

ERIC A. CHIAPPINELLI

OKO, Adolph S. (5 Jan. 1883–3 Oct. 1944), librarian, Spinozist, and Judaica bibliographer, was born in Rudkov, Russia, to Tebel Oko, a cattle and grain merchant, and Deborah (maiden name unknown). Young Oko was educated in Germany before immigrating to the United States at the age of nineteen. He soon found work at the Astor Library (part of New York Public Library's Research Collection) working with Abraham Freidus and other American library leaders. It was at the Astor Library that Oko mastered the skills of librarianship. Four years later he was recruited to become the assistant librarian at Cincinnati's Hebrew Union College. The library had been founded along with the school in 1875 under Rabbi Isaac Mayer Wise as Reform Judaism's seminary and the first permanent Rabbinical college in the Americas. The library had grown from a collection of 154 volumes in its first year to an unorganized collection of textbooks and miscellaneous donations that Chancellor Kaufmann Kohler called a "haphazard collection without any real benefit to any" (Karf, p. 72).

Oko processed the collection, applying the library economy skills he learned in New York, and weeded out 14,000 of the 18,000 volumes originally in the library. In 1905 he married Etta Wesinger; they had two children. By 1907 he was the librarian at Cincinnati's Hebrew Union College, where he began to develop the collection into what would become one of the world's finest Judaica libraries. Oko excelled at fundraising to support the expansion of the library and the construction of two library buildings to house the growing collections. He also made significant purchases of Judaica collections and works on numerous trips to Europe and Asia, including one to Europe after World War I, which allowed him to obtain 18,000 items for the library. Included among his most notable acquisitions were manuscripts from the Jewish community in Kaifeng, China; the A. Freimann Collection of incunabula; and the Eduard Birnbaum collection of Jewish music.

Oko also became director of the HUC Museum, which in 1933 contained over 4,000 paintings and ceremonial objects and was housed in the old library building. An American pioneer in the acquisition of items of Jewish culture, the museum later became the Skirball Museum of Judaica.

Oko was an active writer of bibliographies and articles on Jewish philosophy. Many articles incorporating Jewish philosophy and his own freethinking appeared in the *Menorah Journal*, an influential literary magazine that he coedited from its founding in 1915. Some pieces, such as "Correspondence between a Bookman and a Jurist," appeared anonymously, while others are found under the pseudonym S. Baruch.

His main work, the *Spinoza Bibliography*, was not published until twenty years after his death, with the help of his wife and the Columbia University libraries. This massive work lists 17,000 items and was the most important reference work on Spinozana before World War II. Cambridge University Press also published his bibliography on Solomon Schechter in 1938. Shorter bibliographies appeared in the *HUC Monthly*, *Menorah Journal*, and other publications.

Spinoza was Oko's main scholarly interest, and he not only assembled one of America's best collections of Spinoza in the library but also accumulated a handsome one at home. Oko was a cofounder and the American secretary of the Societas Spinoza, which made Baruch Spinoza's house into a museum. Oko edited their *Chronicum Spinozanum* and often lectured and wrote on his favorite philosopher.

After his wife's death in 1924, Oko married Dorothy Kuhn, the former wife of an important Jewish philanthropist, in 1933. His new wife had obtained a Reno divorce from a major donor to the seminary, and her subsequent marriage to Oko created sufficient scandal for Oko to be asked to resign from HUC. At the time of Oko's resignation, the library was one of the world's outstanding collections of Judaica, containing around 100,000 manuscripts and volumes. This collection became even more significant following the destruction of many of the leading European Judaica collections during the Holocaust, only a few years later.

The couple then moved to England, where Oko devoted himself to his Spinoza bibliography; during this time their son was born. After the war forced them to return to the United States in 1938, Oko continued writing and became the editor of the *Contemporary Jewish Record* from 1942 until his death in New York City. In 1944 he wrote a history of the HUC Library and Museum, which also served as an influential survey of Judaica collections in American libraries.

• The Adolph S. Oko Papers, which include correspondence after his retirement, are housed in the American Jewish Archives, Hebrew Union College–Jewish Institute of Religion, Cincinnati, Ohio, along with other relevant records relating to the history of HUC. The Special Collections Departments of Columbia University; the Van Pelt Library, University of Pennsylvania; and Houghton Library, Harvard University, contain his correspondence with Dr. Carl Gebhardt, Lewis Mumford, and Richard Beer-Hoffman, respectively. Several articles in *Hebrew Union College Monthly*, 15 Apr. 1931, and *American Israelite*, 28 May 1931, focus on Oko and the new library building. Samuel E. Karf's *Hebrew Union College–Jewish Institute of Religion at One Hundred Years* (1976) offers insights into Oko and the history of the college. An obituary is in the *New York Times*, 4 Oct. 1944.

ANDREW B. WERTHEIMER

OKUN, Arthur Melvin (28 Nov. 1928–23 Mar. 1980), academic economist, policymaker, and presidential adviser, was born in Jersey City, New Jersey, the son of Louis Okun, a candy and tobacco wholesaler, and Rose Cantor. He attended Passaic (N.J.) High School and was an undergraduate at Columbia College in New York City, graduating in 1949 with a B.A. in economics. Seven years later he completed his Ph.D. at Columbia. Okun married Suzanne Grossman in 1951; they had three sons.

During his formative years at Columbia, Okun worked under the direction of Arthur F. Burns. He also came into contact with the works of economists A. G. Hart, J. M. Clark, F. C. Mills, and G. C. Means. Okun assimilated from this experience a strong empirical orientation and a "respect for the facts." One characteristic feature of Okun's later work was its persistence in confronting economic theory with empirical findings. Real-life observations and empirical generalizations always provided the basis for Okun's new hypotheses about economic behavior.

While working on his doctorate in 1952, Okun took an instructor position at Yale University, rising to the rank of full professor by age thirty-five (his rapid promotion was due in part to repeated attempts by Regents Professor of Economics Walter Heller to attract him to the University of Minnesota. At Yale he was James Tobin's "prize protégé" and was immersed in Keynesian doctrine in the belief that governments should actively manage the economy in order to achieve stabilization and economic growth objectives. Enlightened policy formation via the manipulation of discretionary monetary and fiscal instruments, supplemented by direct measures to hold down prices and costs, were expected to keep the economy on its growth path. Okun believed in a "sensible steering" of the economy. He eschewed the notion that the dials of policy could be manipulated with precision; he believed that the only objective should be to turn the right dials in the right direction and to make adjustments as circumstances warranted. He favored small, flexible, and frequent adjustments of policy instruments because he thought the economy would fare better if policymakers would use good judgment in diagnosing problems, forecasting trends, and prescribing solutions rather than adopting rigid formulas such as a balanced-budget requirement.

Tobin persuaded Okun to become in 1961–1962 a consultant and later a staff economist with the Council of Economic Advisers (CEA), an agency created in 1946 to provide economic advice to the president. Okun became a CEA member in 1964, replacing Walter Heller, and he took over as chair in 1968. His early contributions involved forecasting and fiscal policy and the development of what was later called "Okun's Law," first described by Okun in 1962 in "Potential GNP: Its Measurement and Significance" (reprinted in Pechman [1983]). In much of his work Okun attempted to translate theoretical ideas and concepts into operational guides or computational shortcuts of direct use to policymakers.

Okun's Law is an excellent example of the way Okun translated Keynesian theory into practical policy guidelines. In the early 1960s the CEA of the John F. Kennedy administration saw the need to stimulate a sluggish economy but had little guidance available as to how much the economy's output should be expanded to achieve certain unemployment targets. Okun found a shorthand approximation for the relationship between unemployment and output, showing that for every increase of three percentage points in the rate of economic growth above its long-term trend, unemployment would decline by one percentage point. This widely used rule of thumb continues to attract the interest of applied researchers and is featured in most macroeconomics textbooks. It is primarily through Okun's Law that generations have come across Okun's name.

Even after theoretical discussion has been transformed into operational policy proposals, it has to pass the test of public acceptance and political feasibility. Okun's efforts to develop simplified measures of the direction of budgetary policy (1970), government expenditure programs that would automatically scale down in times of prosperity (1970–1971), and tax-based income policies (1973–1974) were all attempts to translate theory into understandable and useful guidelines for direct policy.

When Okun became chair of the CEA in 1968 his main concern was to convince a reluctant President Lyndon Johnson that the funding of the Vietnam War was being inappropriately carried out. A 10 percent tax surcharge was passed by Congress in June 1968 to pay for the increased military expenditures and expanding domestic programs. To many observers this measure was far too late—Okun had urged that the same action be taken eighteen months earlier—and insufficient to stem the demand on the nation's resources.

When the Richard Nixon administration moved into Washington in January 1969 Okun prepared to move back to Yale, but he was persuaded to join the Brookings Institution as a senior fellow by its president, Kermit Gordon. He stayed at Brookings for the rest of his career, joining a group of topflight policy economists who moved easily between academia, the Brookings think tank, and government. These economists included Joseph Pechman, Charles Schultze, George Perry, Walter Salant, Edward Denison, Alice Rivlin, and Henry Aaron.

Okun's first book at Brookings was *The Political Economy of Prosperity* (1970). In addition to being a valuable personal history of his experiences with the CEA, the book was a case study of the use of Keynesian policies in the 1960s. His retrospective verdict was that the activist Keynesian policies of this period led to prosperity, while the difficulties that occurred toward the end of the decade reflected a failure to implement the recommended appropriate policies.

Perhaps Okun's greatest contribution while at Brookings was the founding (with George Perry) of the *Brookings Papers on Economic Activity* in 1972. This journal soon became one of the most frequently cited economic journals in the profession. The original aim of the journal was to provide timely and serious analysis of important policy issues in a form that was readable and understandable to the informed citizen. Individual studies have been widely cited in the literature and are often quoted in Congress.

During the 1970s Okun continued to be in the policy spotlight as a consultant to the Federal Reserve Board and a member of the *Time* Board of Economists. Politicians, the media, and the business community sought his advice, while his flair for metaphors and phrase making—the "leaky bucket," the "discomfort index," the "invisible handshake"—kept him in the public eye. His frequent appearances before congressional committees was another indication of his standing.

In regard to the thrust of his macro policies, "expansionist" does seem an apt tag for Okun. Between 1969 and 1979 he supported fiscal stimulus seven times, advocating restraint only in 1969–1970, 1973, and 1979.

He conceded, in retrospect, that greater monetary and fiscal restraint should have been applied during certain years in that period.

Okun quickly separates himself from the simplistic Keynesian textbooks on the application of fiscal policy. What is noteworthy about him is his persistent and innovative desire to make fiscal policy more practical and flexible in operation.

Beginning in the mid-1970s Okun shifted his attention to "innovative fiscal measures" that would hold down both inflation and unemployment. His views on inflation are also somewhat at odds with the cavalier attitude that Keynesians often portray. Okun was trenchant in his claims about the deleterious effects of inflation (even "anticipated" or "steady" inflation), which severely disrupted an economy based on the dollar yardstick in the 1970s. By late in the decade Okun seemed shaken by the virulence of inflation. The weapons Okun proposed to control it were direct measures to hold down prices and costs, which would then allow some relaxation of demand restraint. In that sense, they were alternatives to tough contractionary policies likely to generate high rates of unemployment. This was another theme in his work: the development of a more "humane" anti-inflation strategy.

In 1975 Okun published *Equality and Efficiency: The Big Tradeoff*, which quickly became a Brookings bestseller. The purpose of this work was to educate economists about the importance of equity in democratic solutions to national problems, and it reflected Okun's reaction to the public's apparent disillusionment with the welfare system. Okun examined the interaction between equity issues and efficiency concerns and reflected on the tasks that governments can be reasonably expected to do well.

Later in the 1970s, as he absorbed the lessons of the previous decade and acknowledged the economy's faltering performance, Okun became more cautious in his policy advice. He found it important to stress the changing evolution of the economy that made old remedies no longer applicable and created the need to develop new tools of economic management. Okun's doubts about the ability of forecasters to predict accurately the economy's movements also increased over the years.

This uncertainty led Okun to devote more and more of his intellectual resources to revising the Keynesian theoretical framework so that it again provided explanations consistent with empirical observations. This work resulted in two main articles, "Upward Mobility in a High Pressure Economy" (1973) and "Inflation: Its Mechanics and Welfare Costs" (1975) (both reprinted in Pechman [1983]), and in the posthumously published *Prices and Quantities: A Macroeconomic Analysis* (1981), which Okun regarded as his most important contribution to economic literature.

In these articles and the book, Okun tried to provide an empirically grounded theory of macroeconomics where labor and product markets failed to minimize unemployment and inflation. This occurred not because individuals and firms behaved irrationally, but because they were operating in the context of long-term contracts and business relationships where information was imperfect, transaction costs were high, and considerable uncertainty existed about prices, costs, and the quality of potential workers. As a result, prices and wages tended to be insufficiently flexible to clear markets so that output and employment carried the main burden of economic adjustment. Consequently, inflation persisted, and unemployment was excessive.

In the last years of his life Okun increasingly recognized the limited feasibility of pursuing a countercyclical fiscal policy as a stabilization device, but he persistently tried to make these instruments more flexible to override the political constraints on their use. However, an evaluation of the post–World War II record of monetary and fiscal policy could elicit only a judgment of mixed review from Okun in 1980. He acknowledged that "most of the credit for increased economic stability should go to the automatic stabilizers—both fiscal and financial—and their impact on private behavior" (letter to Martin Feldstein, 22 Jan. 1980).

Okun died of a heart attack at his home in Washington, D.C. He was one of America's better known economists, and his early death was much lamented. Gardner Ackley, a onetime chair of the CEA, regarded Okun as the best empirical economist and forecaster that he knew, while Geoffrey Harcourt thought that Okun surely would have been awarded a Nobel Prize had he lived longer. Paul Samuelson, who did win a Nobel Prize, acknowledged in 1983 that Okun was the wisest and most creative economic policy adviser of his time.

• Okun's papers are in the Lyndon Baines Johnson Presidential Library in Austin, Tex., as is an extensive interview by David McComb, dated 20 Mar. and 15 Apr. 1969. Another interview, dated 24 Feb. 1978, is published in E. C. Hargrove, ed., *Presidents and the Council of Economic Advisers: Interviews with CEA Chairmen* (1984). A collection of Okun's articles and a bibliography in J. A. Pechman, *Economics for Policy Making: Selected Essays of Arthur M. Okun* (1983). Evaluations of his contributions to economics and the policy process appear in J. Lodewijks, "Arthur Okun and the Lucasian Critique," *Australian Economic Papers* 27, no. 51 (1988): 253–71; Lodewijks, "Arthur M. Okun: Economics for Policymaking," *Journal of Economic Surveys* 2, no. 3 (1988): 245–64; and Lodewijks, "Arthur Okun's Contribution to the Macroeconomic Policy Debates," *Economic Analysis and Policy* 19, no. 2 (Sept. 1989): 141–66. Other appraisals are by E. S. Phelps, "Okun's Macro-Micro System," *Journal of Economic Literature* 19 (Sept. 1981), and in J. Tobin, *Macroeconomics, Prices and Quantities: Essays in Memory of Arthur M. Okun* (1983). Personal tributes of Okun are Brookings Institution, *In Memoriam: Arthur M. Okun* (1980); R. J. Gordon and R. E. Hall, "Arthur M. Okun: 1928–1980," *Brookings Papers on Economic Activity* 1 (1980); and Pechman, "Portrait: Arthur Okun," *Challenge* (May–June 1980). An obituary is in the *New York Times*, 24 Mar. 1980.

JOHN LODEWIJKS

OLCOTT, Chauncey (21 July 1860–18 Mar. 1932), actor, singer, and composer, was born John Chancellor Olcott in Buffalo, New York, the son of Mellen Whitney "Jack" Olcott, a horseman and stable operator, and Margaret Doyle. Olcott became interested in performing while growing up in Buffalo. He sang continually, influenced, he said, by his father's fine voice and his mother's stories of her Irish heritage. His first professional appearance was in blackface with Emerson and Hooley's Minstrels. He also appeared with Haverly's Original Mastodon Minstrels (he traveled to London with the company), Carncross's Minstrels, and Thatcher, Primrose, and West's Minstrels. In these companies Olcott sang sentimental songs and sometimes appeared in comic sketches.

Olcott made his legitimate theater debut in 1886 when he appeared in *Pepita; or, The Girl with the Glass Eyes*, a comic opera by Alfred Thompson, starring Lillian Russell. The performer who became known as "The Irish Comedian" made his debut as a Spanish youth. His next New York appearance came in August 1888, when he joined Denman Thompson's *Old Homestead*. Olcott sang in an offstage quartet and later played the role of the drunken son. In 1887 Olcott married Cora E. James. The two were divorced in 1895. They had no children.

After *The Old Homestead*, Olcott toured with comic opera companies. In 1889 he played the heroine's son in the J. C. Duff Opera Company's production of *Paola; or, The First of the Vendettas*. In May and June 1890 Olcott performed in revivals of *H.M.S. Pinafore* (as Ralph Rackstraw) and *The Mikado* (as Nanki-Poo). He then spent the 1890–1891 season with the McCaull Opera Company in Franz von Suppé's *Clover* and Carl Millocker's *The Seven Suabians*. After traveling to Europe to study voice, in 1891 he was hired by British performer/producer Charles Wyndham to appear in *Miss Decima*. This play set the course for the rest of Olcott's career. To perform the role of Chevalier Patrick Julius O'Flanagan, an Irish adventurer, he studied Irish dialect so he could use an authentic brogue. His success in the role started his notable career as a stage Irishman and Irish tenor.

Wyndham next used the popular tenor as Gnatbrain in the comic opera *Blue-Eyed Susan*. Olcott was again successful, and he soon had a long-term contract in England. However, when he returned to the United States for a vacation during the summer of 1892, he found an avenue to success in America in the person of producer Augustus Pitou. Pitou was a producer and playwright who most recently had presented William J. Scanlan, an American performer known for his Irish tenor voice, in a series of romantic plays with Irish themes and characters. Because of Scanlan's illness, Pitou was seeking a new leading man for his productions.

Olcott first appeared for Pitou in *Mavourneen*, a vehicle written for Scanlan by George H. Jessop and Horace Townsend. *Mavourneen* was typical of Pitou's Irish plays, which were described in the *New York Sun* (19 Mar. 1932) as "those in which the red-coated British soldier, the sneaky lawyer, the absentee landlord and the faithful priest were the figures about the hero, that broth of a boy who was ready to break into song at any minute." Olcott was a popular success in the play, and he toured in it across the country for over a year.

He next appeared in *The Irish Artist*, written by Pitou and Jessop, which made its New York premiere on 1 October 1894. This show, another sentimental melodrama, established Olcott as the successor to Scanlan.

Olcott made another important contribution to this show by writing several songs for it: "Katy Mahone" and "My Beautiful Irish Maid." Throughout his career, Olcott continued to write or cowrite songs for the shows in which he appeared.

Olcott appeared in Pitou's productions until the producer retired. He played New York City, usually at the Fourteenth Street Theatre in the 1890s, and toured the country almost continuously in Pitou's Irish-themed plays, including *The Minstrel of Clare* (a revival of *The Irish Minstrel* produced for Olcott in 1896), *Sweet Inniscarra* (1897), *A Romance of Athlone* (1899), *Garrett O'Magh* (1901), *Old Limerick Town* (1902), *Terence* (1904), *Edmund Burke* (1905), *Eileen Asthore* (1906), *O'Neill of Derry* (1907), *Ragged Robin* (1908), *Barry of Ballymore* (1911), and *Macushla* (1911).

Among his memorable songs were "My Wild Irish Rose" (from *The Romance of Athlone*), "Mother Machree," "Isle of Dreams," and "When Irish Eyes Are Smiling" (written with Ernest R. Ball, from *The Isle of Dreams* [1912]).

In 1897 Olcott married Margaret O'Donovan (she became known as Rita Olcott) from San Francisco, who was his partner until his death. She became involved in his career when she cowrote *Ragged Robin* with Rida Johnson Young in 1908. The Olcotts adopted a daughter.

Pitou retired after the season-long tour of Young's *Macushla* (1911–1912). After that Olcott continued to appear in Irish plays by other authors and producers, including Young (*The Isle of Dreams* [1912] and *Shameen Dhu* [1914], both staged by Henry Miller); Rachel Crothers (*The Heart of Paddy Whack* [1914] and *Once upon a Time* [1917]); and George M. Cohan (*Honest John O'Brien* [1916] and *The Voice of McConnell*, about a famous Irish tenor [1918]). He also appeared as the Irish soldier in J. Hartley Manners's *Out There!* (1918), an all-star Red Cross benefit production.

Olcott retired from the stage after his third tour of *Macushla* in 1920–1921, but he returned to the stage in 1925 to appear successfully as Sir Lucius O'Trigger in an all-star revival of Richard Brinsley Sheridan's *The Rivals*. On tour in November, however, he became ill and almost died. After this illness, Olcott never performed again. He lived a comfortable retirement, splitting his time between New York City and his winter home in Monte Carlo, where he died.

Chauncey Olcott was a tremendously popular matinee idol and box-office attraction. The productions in which he appeared, in addition to making him wealthy, helped create and perpetuate the heroic Irish stage character and the romantic Irish play on the American stage. He was acclaimed in New York City, but the true measure of his success came from the almost continual countrywide tours he made. Known for his beautiful, lyric tenor voice as well as his heroic and virtuous stage characters, he also composed several memorable Irish-American songs.

• The Billy Rose Theatre Collection, New York Public Library for the Performing Arts at Lincoln Center, has clippings, reviews, programs, photographs, and scrapbooks about Olcott. See also Chauncey Olcott, "Personal Reminiscences," *Theatre*, Feb. 1917, pp. 76–78, 124. Rita Olcott, *Song in His Heart* (1939), is a popular and sentimental biography of Olcott written by his second wife. Gerald Bordman, *American Musical Theatre: A Chronicle* (1978), briefly discusses all of Olcott's musical shows. Obituaries are in New York newspapers, 19 Mar. 1932.

STEPHEN M. VALLILLO

OLCOTT, Henry Steel (2 Aug. 1832–17 Feb. 1907), cofounder with Helena Blavatsky of the Theosophical Society and an important Western advocate of Buddhism, was born in Orange, New Jersey, the son of Henry Wyckoff Olcott, a businessman, and Emily Steel. He was raised in New York City. At sixteen, after the failure of his father's business, he worked on an uncle's farm in Ohio, where he took an interest in both Spiritualism, then at the height of its vogue, and agricultural science. In 1855 Olcott opened an agricultural school in New Jersey and as its director wrote several books and articles on farming. The school failed in 1859. He was assistant agricultural editor of the *New York Tribune* from 1858 to 1860. In 1860 Olcott married Mary Eplee Morgan; there were four children, two of whom died in infancy. During the Civil War he was appointed to serve the Union as an investigator of fraudulent military suppliers and given the title colonel, which he retained for the rest of his life.

Following the war, Olcott, now settled in New York, passed the bar exams to become a lawyer while continuing to write for newspapers. He divorced in the early 1870s. His interest in Spiritualism revived, providing a vehicle for an apparently deep-seated love of wonders and for his journalistic aspirations. In 1874 he visited, and wrote extensively about, spirit manifestations reported in Chittenden, Vermont. A book, *People from the Other World* (1875; reprint, 1972), resulted.

While in Chittenden, he met Helena Blavatsky, who had arrived in the United States the previous year. Upon their return to New York, the aristocratic Russian woman and the American, both with failed marriages behind them, established a close relationship based on their shared interest in occult matters. In 1875 they and others established the Theosophical Society, with Olcott as president, a position he kept for the remainder of his life. As he stated in his inaugural address as the society's president, Olcott believed that Theosophy, which intended to recover ancient wisdom underlying all of the world's religions, could lead people beyond the impasse caused in his view by the narrowness of both science and the established denominations of the day.

Olcott assisted Blavatsky in the production of her first major book, *Isis Unveiled* (1877). In 1878 the pair sailed for India, which they increasingly recognized as a great reservoir of the occult wisdom they sought and as the residence of many of the Masters of the Wisdom they believed were inwardly guiding them in their activities. They traveled extensively in India, Olcott lecturing and establishing branches of the Theosophical Society. Many native Indians, together with some Europeans, responded favorably to them, in part undoubtedly because, almost alone in this heyday of imperialism, Olcott and Blavatsky, though Westerners, displayed deep respect and appreciation for the traditional religions and cultures of Asia.

In 1880 in Ceylon (Sri Lanka), Olcott and Blavatsky formally became Buddhists. Taking this commitment seriously, though in tandem with Theosophy, Olcott raised money for Buddhist schools and represented the interests of Sinhalese Buddhists before their colonial overlords. But he believed further that if Buddhism was to take its place as an equal among the great religions of the world, it would need to develop a sense of its own unity and find ways to express its teaching in modern forms. To these ends, he devised a Buddhist flag, and in 1891 he helped Buddhists meeting at Theosophical headquarters at Adyar, near Madras, India, compose a catechism. Traveling to Buddhist lands as diverse as Theravada Burma or Sri Lanka and Mahayana Japan, he strove to promote inter-Buddhist meetings and understanding. He assisted a prominent Sinhalese Buddhist leader, Anagarika Dharmapala, to attend the World Parliament of Religions in Chicago in 1893, an event that was to play a very significant role in advancing interreligious dialogue.

As international president of the Theosophical Society during its early years of growth and burgeoning cultural influence (as a vehicle for Asian and esoteric spiritual ideas) in many parts of the world, Olcott found considerable scope for travel and activity. He also had numerous problems to contend with. In 1885 he managed to keep the society alive despite an adverse report, following an investigation, by a representative of the Society for Psychical Research accusing Blavatsky of psychic fraud. In 1888 he barely avoided a grievous split in the society—and between him and Blavatsky, now in Europe—over her desire to form a separate inner "Esoteric Section" in the society for occult study, a move he stoutly resisted but finally accepted in a modified form. Olcott was, however, unable to prevent schism in 1895 between most of the American section of the Theosophical Society, under William Q. Judge, and international headquarters in Adyar; the break was the culmination of a long-running dispute over Judge's claim to receive independent communications from the Masters. By the time of Olcott's death, "Adyar" branches of the Theosophical Society had been widely reestablished in the United States.

Olcott's importance as a nineteenth-century American missionary "in reverse"—for Buddhism rather than for Christianity—and so as a catalyst of the Hindu and Buddhist renaissance of his day, has been widely recognized, though to a greater degree in Asia than in the United States; he was not so much interested in spreading Buddhism to the West, except as a component of Theosophy, as in strengthening it in its Asian homeland, where it was under much pressure from missionaries, imperialists, and Western-style education. In Sri Lanka, "Olcott Day" is a national holiday, and stamps have been issued bearing his portrait. Appreciation of the world cultural significance of the Theosophical movement in the late nineteenth and early twentieth centuries seems to be growing, and as it does the stature of the society's first president can only increase. His charming *Old Diary Leaves* (6 vols., 1895–1935; repr. 1941–1975) are an important source for early Theosophical history.

• In addition to his own important autobiographical writings, material on Olcott can be found in Bruce F. Campbell, *Ancient Wisdom Revived: A History of the Theosophical Movement* (1980), and Josephine Ransom, *A Short History of the Theosophical Society* (1938). Though somewhat a work of apologetics, the major biography is Howard Murphet, *Hammer on the Mountain* (1972; reprinted as *Yankee Beacon of Buddhist Light: Life of Col. Henry S. Olcott*, 1988).

ROBERT S. ELLWOOD

OLDBERG, Arne (12 July 1874–17 Feb. 1962), pianist, composer, and teacher, was born in Youngstown, Ohio, the son of Oscar Oldberg, a pharmaceutical expert, and Emma Parritt. Oldberg began to play the piano at age five, taught by his father, a Swedish immigrant who was an excellent amateur musician.

In 1886 the family moved to the Chicago area, where Oscar Oldberg founded and became dean of the School of Pharmacy at Northwestern University. Arne then received piano lessons from August Hyllested from 1886 to 1890. He began composing, and at recitals in and around Chicago he usually included some of his own works.

In 1890, at age sixteen, he won the George M. Pullman Diamond Medal for the best piano playing outside the classes of the Chicago Musical College. The next year he was awarded the Ziegfeld Diamond Medal as best pianist in the teachers' certificate class. The *Chicago Herald* for 24 June 1891 speaks of him as "an accomplished pianist."

After graduating with honors from the Gottschalk Lyric School in Chicago in 1892, Oldberg went to Vienna to study with the legendary piano pedagogue Theodor Leschetizky from 1893 to 1895. He spent the first three years following his return to Chicago teaching piano privately and at the Chicago Conservatory as assistant to Leopold Godowsky. During the 1897 season he taught at Northwestern University.

During this time Oldberg took composition lessons with Wilhelm Middleschulte, Frederick Grant Gleason, and Adolph Koelling. In 1898 Oldberg made a second trip to Europe, this time to study composition at the Royal Academy of Art in Munich with Joseph Rheinberger, completing the three year course in one season. Upon his return to Chicago in 1899, he was appointed professor of music at Northwestern University, later professor of piano and composition, and then dean of the Graduate School of Music, a position he held until his retirement in 1941. In 1900 he married Mary Georgiana (maiden name unknown); they had five children.

During Oldberg's forty-two years at Northwestern, most of his time was devoted to teaching. Composing was done mostly during summer vacations in Colorado, and he continued to appear in public with the Los Angeles Philharmonic as a pianist and as a conductor of his own symphonies, concerti, and other compositions. He became a man of stature with a large following, and his influence was widely felt. Among his students were Howard Hanson, who founded and directed the Eastman School of Music, and John W. Schaum, author of one of the most widely used piano teaching methods in the United States.

During several summer sessions, beginning in 1930, Oldberg was a guest professor at the University of California at Los Angeles, and at Mount Saint Mary's College, also in Los Angeles.

After retiring from Northwestern University, Oldberg devoted himself exclusively to composing both new works and perfecting orchestral scores. He left approximately 100 compositions, of which about half were published by Clayton F. Summy, Chicago, and G. Schirmer, New York. There are some twenty-five orchestral works, including six symphonies, concerti, chamber music, sonatas, and piano pieces. His orchestral works have been performed by the Chicago, Minneapolis, Philadelphia, and Hollywood Bowl Symphonies.

Oldberg was honored and received prizes for his compositions. Symphony op. 23, no. 1 (1911) and Symphony op. 34, no. 2 (1915) were given national awards. In 1915 he was elected a member of the National Institute of Arts and Letters. In the summer of 1931 the Piano Concerto op. 43, no. 2 unanimously won the first prize at the Hollywood Bowl International Contest.

In 1958 Oldberg was among those honored at the sixtieth anniversary celebration of *Who's Who in America*. His biography had been listed in the book each year since its first edition was published in 1898. In 1959 he was awarded the Ohioana Career Medal in Music by the Kinney Cooper Ohioana Library Association in recognition of his achievements as a composer and a teacher.

After Oldberg's death in Evanston, Illinois, his music suffered neglect. Stylistically it belongs to the late-romantic period. The major piano works, especially the concerti and sonatas, are brilliant and technically very demanding, comparable to Rachmaninoff. As a pianist, Oldberg had the sparkling, virtuoso technique needed for their performance. The Piano Sonata in B-flat Minor, op. 28, was frequently played by Fannie Bloomfield Zeisler.

• As a leading American composer, Oldberg was asked to contribute representative scores to various music collections.

Nearly all material is now in the public domain. Important works are found in the Library of Congress, the Fleisher Collection of the Free Library in Philadelphia, and the Los Angeles County Museum of History, Science, and Art. Other holdings are at the Evanston Public Library; Northwestern University, an extremely rich source of archival material; Oberlin College, Eastman School of Music, the University of Utah, the University of Southern California, and De Pauw University. The Library of Congress also holds 112 holograph music manuscripts, approximately thirty published works, 236 letters from prominent contemporaries in the field of music, and more than 800 family and professional letters. A listing of nineteen shorter piano works by Oldberg is in John Gillespie and Anna Gillespie, *A Bibliography of Nineteenth-Century American Piano Music* (1984). Karlyen Tan, "The Life and Work of Arne Oldberg" (master's thesis, Univ. of Utah, 1993), is a useful source. Obituaries are in the *Northwestern University Alumni News*, Apr. 1962, and the *Evanston Review*, 22 Feb. 1962.

KEES KOOPER

OLD BRITON (1695?–21 June 1752), Miami (Piankashaw) war and village chief, was born in a Piankashaw village, probably on the St. Joseph River in southwestern Michigan. There is little information regarding Old Briton prior to 1745, although he was known to French officials in the Wabash Valley, who referred to him as "La Demoiselle" and indicated that he was a war chief living in a village led by Le Porc Epic, located near Kekionga, a large Miami village at modern Fort Wayne.

Angered over the high price of French trade goods, in 1747 Old Briton led a party of Miamis who sacked Fort Miamis, the French post at Kekionga, then fled to the Miami River in western Ohio, where he established a new village, Pickawillany, at the mouth of Loramie's Creek. Through Seneca intermediaries, Old Briton sought commercial and political ties with the British, and in July 1748 Miamis from Pickawillany led by Assapausa, Old Briton's son, journeyed to Lancaster, where they signed a treaty of "Friendship and Alliance" with the colony of Pennsylvania. British traders followed the Miamis back to Ohio, and Old Briton sent runners to villages in Indiana and Illinois, inviting other tribes to trade at Pickawillany.

Threatened by Pickawillany and the British trading activity, French officials sent a small expedition led by Pierre-Joseph Celoron down the Allegheny and Ohio rivers to Pickawillany in the summer of 1749, but Celoron's expedition was too small to force Old Briton and his followers back to Indiana. In December 1749 George Croghan, a trader from Pennsylvania, erected a log trading post at Pickawillany, and during the next two years the village's population increased, as Old Briton recruited Weas, Piankashaws, and other Indians into the British trade network.

French officials first threatened Old Briton, then attempted to bribe him to return to the Maumee, but he refused. In February 1751 the French sent a delegation of Ottawas to plead for the Miamis' return, but Old Briton declared that he "had taken our Brothers the English by the Hand." Angered by his refusal, in

November a small party of French soldiers killed an elderly Miami man and woman who were harvesting corn near Pickawillany but then fled back to Fort Miamis. In response Old Briton ceremoniously killed three captured French soldiers and cut the ears off another. Meanwhile Old Briton's followers continued to spread offers of a British political and commercial alliance to other tribes, and attacks on French traders increased.

In response, French officials at Detroit dispatched a large force of Ottawas, Potawatomis, and Ojibwas led by Ottawa métis Charles Langlade, who surprised Pickawillany on 21 June 1752. Most of Old Briton's warriors were absent hunting, and Old Briton fled to Croghan's fortified trading post but surrendered when Langlade promised to spare his life. Langlade violated his promise, killing Old Briton and boiling his body, which was devoured by Langlade's party. Old Briton's followers returned to Kekionga, and the pro-British alliance temporarily disintegrated.

Old Briton's career reflects the struggle of Native American leaders to develop positions of political independence between New France and the British colonies. Since French trade goods were both scarce and expensive, Old Briton and his followers solicited commercial ties with the British. Although they signed treaties with Pennsylvania, the isolation in western Ohio also provided a buffer against British hegemony. Ironically, however, the location also made them vulnerable to French retaliation.

• Correspondence and contemporary documents focusing on Old Briton can be found in *Collections of the Illinois State Historical Library*, vol. 29 (1940), and in *Minutes of the Provincial Council of Pennsylvania*, vol. 5 (1851). Journals of Celeron's expedition are in *Ohio Archaeological and Historical Publications*, 29 (1920): 331–450. *Journal of Captain William Trent*, ed. Alfred T. Goodman (1871), contains a contemporary account of Old Briton's death and Langlade's raid on Pickawillany. The most comprehensive discussion of Old Briton and his influence is R. David Edmunds, "Old Briton," in *American Indian Leaders: Studies in Diversity*, ed. Edmunds (1980). Richard White, *The Middle Ground: Indians, Empires, and Republics in the Great Lakes Region, 1650–1815* (1991), analyzes Old Briton's efforts within a broader frame of French–Native American relations and argues that Old Briton was attempting to establish a "republic" free from the French alliance that dominated most Native Americans in the region. Michael McConnell, *A Country Between: The Upper Ohio Valley and Its Peoples, 1724–1774* (1992), provides a good analysis of the events preceding Old Briton's attack on Fort Miamis and the role that the western Iroquois played in these events. Nicholas Wainwright, *George Croghan, Wilderness Diplomat* (1959), surveys the activities of British traders in the region.

R. DAVID EDMUNDS

OLDER, Fremont (30 Aug. 1856–3 Mar. 1935), editor and reformer, was born near Appleton, Wisconsin, the son of Emory Older, a farmer, and Celia Marie Augur. His father died in 1864 from an illness contracted in a Confederate prison camp, and Older lived for a few years with his grandparents as his mother was too poor to care for her two sons. His formal schooling came to an end at age twelve, after a few months in the preparatory department at Ripon College.

Taking an early interest in newspaper work, Older began his career at the age of thirteen as a printer's devil. In 1869 his mother remarried and moved to California, and Fremont, after working at a series of desultory jobs in eastern Wisconsin and the Upper Midwest, migrated there as well in 1873. Older joined the *San Francisco Morning Call* as a printer and during the ensuing ten years he labored on newspapers in Oakland, Santa Barbara, San Francisco, Bodie, and Redwood City as well as in Virginia City and Reno, Nevada. He returned to San Francisco for good in 1884, soon becoming the star reporter for the *Morning Call*, then city editor of the *San Francisco Post*.

While in Redwood City in the early 1880s Older had married Emma Finger. The match, which produced two children, soon ended in divorce. On 22 August 1893 he married Cora Baggerly in San Francisco. Shortly thereafter *Call* owner Robert A. Crothers brought him back to that paper once again, this time as city editor. When the *Call* was sold, Crothers bought the *San Francisco Evening Bulletin* and made Older managing editor. Along with his wife and brother-in-law, Older resurrected the nearly moribund *Bulletin*, transforming it into one of the West's most sensational and successful papers.

Idolizing Horace Greeley since boyhood, Older brought crusading zeal to his editorship, particularly by exposing the Southern Pacific Railroad and other corporations' powerful grip on politics in California. To counter the railroad machine's pervasive influence in San Francisco, Older convinced idealistic young millionaire James D. Phelan to run for mayor in 1895. Phelan's three enlightened terms were but an interlude from municipal corruption, however, as political boss Abraham Ruef rose to power behind the Union Labor party and mayor Eugene Schmitz in 1901.

A determined Older pounded away in the *Bulletin* at Ruef, Schmitz, and the graft-ridden board of supervisors. The Ruef machine's often violent efforts to silence Older only prodded the editor to dig harder to find evidence of bribery and officially sanctioned vice. Frustrated by his failure to convert rumors into proof, Older engaged the services of zealous prosecutor Francis J. Heney and Secret Service detective William J. Burns and secured the financial backing of former mayor Phelan and Rudolph Spreckels.

The graft prosecution commenced in 1906, only a few months after the great earthquake and fire of that year had destroyed San Francisco. Though Ruef and Schmitz were convicted, corporate bribe-givers closed ranks and obstructed further progress in the prosecution, which finally ground to a halt in 1911. Nonetheless, Older's fanatical devotion to rooting out corruption in San Francisco catalyzed political insurgency throughout the state. The progressive Republican triumph of 1910 ended Southern Pacific dominance in California and vaulted Hiram W. Johnson—a member of the prosecution team—into the governorship.

At the height of the prosecution, Older's life was threatened repeatedly and many among San Francisco's elite shunned and vilified him once the proceedings veered from city officials to powerful capitalists. At one point, when the prosecution was zeroing in on United Railroads president—and alleged bribe-giver—Patrick Calhoun, Older was "kidnapped" and placed on a Los Angeles-bound train. Word of Older's plight hit the streets within hours and the two "deputies"—ostensibly hired by Calhoun's minions—who accompanied Older on the train were arrested in Santa Barbara. Older returned to a hero's welcome in San Francisco.

The plight of Abraham Ruef, the only indicted figure to go to prison, agitated Older, who rued the fact that wealthier bribe-givers had escaped punishment. To the shock of both his enemies and friends, Older began an unsuccessful crusade for Ruef's release. Inspired by visits with Ruef at San Quentin and motivated by social Christian ideals, Older also took up the cause of prison reform and campaigned against the death penalty. While hardly a socialist, Older knew many radicals and supported labor unions. His publication of the "Oxman letters," which provided strong evidence that Thomas J. Mooney and Warren Billings—convicted of the 1916 San Francisco Preparedness Day bombing—had been framed, brought Older more opprobrium than ever and strained his relationship with the *Bulletin*'s owners.

In 1918 a beleaguered Older resigned from the *Bulletin* and was hired by William Randolph Hearst to edit the *Call*. From that post he renewed the fight on behalf of Mooney. Older's reporters unearthed damning evidence of perjury by the Mooney prosecution's chief witness, which led to a federal investigation that uncovered the frame-up. Although publication of the *Densmore Report* saved Mooney's life, it did not immediately get him out of prison despite nearly two decades of unceasing effort by Older.

The *Bulletin* never recovered from the loss of Older, hemorrhaging subscribers and money in increasingly alarming amounts until Hearst bought it and made Older president and editor in chief of the reconstituted *San Francisco Call-Bulletin* in 1929. Though as energetic a worker as ever, Older grew more depressed and pessimistic about the human condition in his last years, questioning the efficacy of crusades and causes. He died after suffering a heart attack at the wheel of his car near Stockton and was buried at "Woodhills," the Olders' Santa Clara County ranch. A dedicated practitioner of the "yellow journalism" that typified his era, Older nonetheless brought large doses of idealism and integrity to his craft while hiring and training such writers as John D. Barry, Kathleen Norris, and Rose Wilder Lane.

• Older's papers are housed in the Bancroft Library at the University of California, Berkeley. Fremont Older, *My Own Story* (1919; repr. 1926), briskly recounts his involvement with the graft prosecutions and years of selfless efforts to reform former convicts. Older, *Growing Up* (1931), is a short recounting of his hard-scrabble childhood and rise to prominence. Evelyn Wells, one of the many talented writers trained by Older, produced a full biography, *Fremont Older* (1936). An important work on Older is Robert Wilson Davenport, "Fremont Older in San Francisco Journalism: A Partial Biography, 1856–1918" (Ph.D. diss., Univ. of California, Los Angeles, 1969), which effectively places his career in political and journalistic context and traces his ideological influences. Miriam Allen deFord's short sketch in *They Were San Franciscans* (1941) is best avoided, but Oswald Garrison Villard's piece in *Some Newspapers and Newspaper-Men* (1923) is a generally perceptive and penetrating assessment written while Older was still alive. Also of some interest is one-time *Bulletin* editorial writer R. L. Duffus's meandering but entertaining memoir, *The Tower of Jewels: Memories of San Francisco* (1960). An obituary is in the *San Francisco Chronicle*, 4 Mar. 1935.

FRANK VAN NUYS

OLDFATHER, William Abbott (23 Oct. 1880–27 May 1945), classical scholar, was born at Urumiah, Persia (now Reza'iyeh, Iran), the son of Jeremiah M. Oldfather and Narcissa Rice, Presbyterian missionaries. In 1890 the family settled in Hanover, Indiana, and William graduated from Hanover College in 1899 (LL.D., 1933). He received the A.B. and A.M. degrees from Harvard (1901, 1902). In 1902 he married Margaret Agnes Giboney at Hanover; they had two children. From 1903 to 1906 Oldfather was instructor in classics at Northwestern University. In 1906 he matriculated at the University of Munich, by which he was awarded the Ph.D. in 1908. He returned to Northwestern for one year as assistant professor of Latin, but in 1909 he moved to the University of Illinois at Urbana-Champaign (full professor, 1915; head of the Department of the Classics, 1926–1945), where he taught until his death.

Oldfather's study at Munich was the critical formative experience of his life. There he learned exact German scholarly and historical method, and he also encountered German socialism. He was converted to both and retained all his life an ideal of precise and intensive scholarship, a view of antiquity as a cultural and historical whole, and an active commitment to social responsibility. In 1917 Oldfather and several colleagues at Urbana were accused by federal agents of Socialist and pro-German tendencies and disloyalty to the United States. All were exonerated. Oldfather always remained a champion of German scholarship and culture. He thus helped to professionalize American classical studies and worked against the post–World War I tendency toward provincialism. During World War II he was popularly but falsely suspected of Fascist leanings.

After World War I Oldfather secured American financial support and scholarly participation for such large German works as the *Thesaurus Linguae Latinae* and the Pauly-Wissowa *Real-Encyclopädie der classischen Altertumswissenschaft*. To the latter he contributed some 500 articles (more than any other American), chiefly on Locris, a district of ancient Greece that had been the subject of his Munich dissertation. His 150-column article ("Lokris") covering the history, mythology, archaeology, epigraphy, art, numismatics, and topography of the district is probably his single most important contribution to scholarship.

Oldfather was a tireless advocate of research and intellectual freedom in the United States. He was a charter member of the American Association of University Professors and served in the American Association for the Advancement of Science and the National Research Council. He was elected to the American Academy of Arts and Sciences in 1934. He served as Sather Professor at the University of California at Berkeley in 1934, where he lectured on "The Decline of Culture within the Roman Empire"; the lectures were never published. Oldfather was president of the American Philological Association in 1937–1938. During the 1930s he was active in organizations that sought to aid the Loyalists in the Spanish Civil War, and he supported the efforts of liberals to free the labor agitator Tom Mooney. During the early 1940s he was a member of the executive council of the American Committee for Democracy and Intellectual Freedom, which defended faculty members dismissed from the City College of New York for alleged Communist sympathies.

Always an advocate of cooperative scholarly projects, Oldfather gathered about him at Illinois a group of colleagues, assistants, and students that came to be known as the "Oldfather school." Under his direction the group produced indispensable *indices verborum* to Seneca's tragedies (1918), Apuleius (1934), and Cicero's letters (1938) and rhetorical works (posth., 1964). Large bibliographical projects undertaken by Oldfather were *Contributions toward a Bibliography of Epictetus* (1927; supplementary volume: posth., 1952), an uncompleted bibliography on the social life of antiquity, and the unpublished *Classica Americana*, aimed at noting all contributions to classical studies made in the Americas since colonial times.

Oldfather's phenomenal energy and enthusiasm were contagious, and his courses were among the most popular offered at Illinois—especially his large lecture course on ancient sports, in connection with which students engaged in track and field events on the main university quadrangle. Oldfather's forthright and combative personality won him many enemies, and his graduate students called him "der Herr" behind his back. Yet they gladly suffered his harangues and his cigar smoke; they sang, drank beer, hiked, boated, and played tennis and softball with him; and his broad and deep learning, inspiration, and unfailing support left an indelible mark on their careers. Of Oldfather's forty-six doctoral students, several were among the most significant American classical scholars of the next generation: Lloyd W. Daly, Richmond Lattimore, Levi Robert Lind, and J. B. Titchener. Oldfather drowned on a canoeing excursion with his graduate students near Urbana, leaving many major scholarly projects incomplete.

• Oldfather's papers are in the University Archives at the University of Illinois, Urbana-Champaign. His letters to A. S. Pease are in the Houghton Library at Harvard. A bibliography of his publications has been deposited in the Classics Library at the University of Illinois. In addition to the works mentioned in the text, Oldfather—often in collaboration with other scholars—produced many significant books and articles. With his colleague H. V. Canter he wrote *The Defeat of Varus and the German Frontier Policy of Augustus* (1915). Oldfather produced the Loeb Classical Library Epictetus (2 vols., 1926–1928) and (with colleagues) the Loeb Greek tacticians (1923). With his brother, the ancient historian Charles Henry Oldfather, he translated two works by Samuel Pufendorf, *Elementorum jurisprudentiae universalis* (1931) and *De jure naturae et gentium* (1934). With colleagues in the sciences he published a translation of Leonard Euler's *De Curvis Elasticis* (1933), and with his students he produced *Studies in the Text Tradition of St. Jerome's Vitae Patrum* (1943); similar volumes on Avianus and Epictetus were left unfinished at his death. Altogether, Oldfather's scholarly publications (aside from his articles in the *Real-Encyclopädie*) number more than 250. A list of dissertations directed by Oldfather is compiled by S. N. Griffiths, *Classical Journal* 74 (1978–1979): 149–53.

There is no full-scale biography. The best brief lives are Michael Armstrong, "A German Scholar and Socialist in Illinois: The Career of William Abbott Oldfather," *Classical Journal* 88, no. 3 (1993): 235–53, and John Buckler, "William Abbott Oldfather: 23 October 1880–27 May 1945," in *Classical Scholarship: A Biographical Encyclopedia*, ed. Ward W. Briggs and William M. Calder III (1990), pp. 346–52. See also William M. Calder III, "Ulrich von Wilamowitz-Moellendorff to William Abbott Oldfather: Three Unpublished Letters," *Classical Journal* 72 (1976–1977): 115–27; and Richmond Lattimore, "Memory of a Scholar (W. A. O. 1880–1945)," *New Republic*, 13 Nov. 1961, p. 15 = *Classical Journal* 57 (1961–1962): 271–72. Oldfather's scholarship in the context of post–World War I German-American relations is discussed by E. Christian Kopff, "Wilamowitz and Classical Philology in the United States of America: An Interpretation," in *Wilamowitz nach 50 Jahren*, ed. W. M. Calder III, H. Flashar, and T. Lindken (Darmstadt 1985), pp. 567–69, 577–79.

Obituaries are in the (Champaign-Urbana, Ill.) *News-Gazette* and *Evening Courier*, 28 and 29 May 1945. Scholarly obituaries include C. A. Forbes, "William Abbott Oldfather 1880–1945," *Classical Journal* 41 (1945–1946): 8–11; and A. S. Pease, "William Abbott Oldfather," *Transactions and Proceedings of the American Philological Association* 76 (1945): xxiv–xxvi.

MICHAEL ARMSTRONG

OLDFIELD, Barney (29 Jan. 1878–4 Oct. 1946), auto racer, was born Berna Eli Oldfield in Wauseon, Ohio, the son of Henry Clay Oldfield and Sarah Yarnell, farmers. In 1889 his parents moved to Toledo, and in 1893 he dropped out of school and went to work. After quitting several mundane jobs, he took up the dangerous but exhilarating sport of bicycle racing in 1894 and competed professionally throughout the Midwest as the self-proclaimed "Bicycle Champion of Ohio."

Winning cyclists were strong and fearless, attributes that automobile makers prized in test drivers, and in 1902 he was recruited by Tom Cooper, a former cycling competitor, and Henry Ford, a fledgling automaker, to drive the Cooper-owned, Ford-designed "999" against Alexander Winton, America's auto racing king. Neither Oldfield nor "999" had ever competed in an auto race; moreover, the car weighed 2,800 pounds and was steered by handlebars. Nevertheless, after two weeks of practice, Oldfield defeated Winton and three other competitors in a ten-mile race in Grosse Pointe, Michigan. Because winning races was the only way to demonstrate quantitatively the superiority of a particular automobile, the victory helped to establish Ford as a serious auto manufacturer; it also launched Oldfield's reputation as America's premier race driver.

Oldfield craved fame and fortune, and his relentless pursuit of both made his name synonymous with reckless speed. In 1903 he drove the first American sub-minute mile on a dirt track in Indianapolis. Later that year he killed a spectator in Detroit when he lost control of his car while steering with one hand and waving to the crowd with the other. Oldfield killed two more onlookers in a 1904 wreck in St. Louis and almost killed himself in a 1906 crash in Hartford. In 1909 he set the first track record at the Indianapolis Motor Speedway, future home of the Indianapolis 500, and in 1910 set a U.S. speed record of 131.7 miles per hour (mph) at Daytona Beach, Florida. In 1913 he killed his riding mechanic in a spectacular crackup in Corona, California. In 1916 he drove the first 100-mph lap on the Indianapolis track. In 1917 he almost drowned when he careened into an infield lake during one race, then almost burned to death when his car crashed and exploded during another. He set dirt-track speed records for all distances from one to fifty miles and boasted late in his career that Firestone tires were "my only life insurance."

At first glance, Oldfield's record as a competitor is surprisingly skimpy. In 1903, his first full year as an auto racer, he won the coveted title "Champion of the Championship Trail," the only year he would do so. In his two appearances in the Indianapolis 500, he placed fourth (1912) and fifth (1916). The reason is that Oldfield, as much a showman and hustler as he was a racer, avoided many top events because he preferred one-on-one match races, personal appearances, and exhibitions at small dirt tracks across the United States as the well-paid headliner of his own barnstorming troupe.

These exhibitions were carefully orchestrated; the standard scenario called for Oldfield, an unlit cigar clenched between his teeth, to win the first heat handily, lose the second heat by a car length, and, after trailing badly, win the last heat by the width of a tire. He raced against locomotives and airplanes, played himself in the Mack Sennett silent movie *Barney Oldfield's Race for a Life* (1913), and drove the first sub-minute mile on a farm tractor.

His incredible popularity as a barnstormer brought him into frequent conflict with the American Automobile Association, which had been the regulatory body of auto racing in the United States since 1902. The Association frowned on his appearances in unsanctioned events and in 1911 barred him from appearing in the inaugural Indianapolis 500 after he beat Jack Johnson, the heavyweight boxing champion, in a match race before thousands of spectators. Undeterred, he continued to flout Association rules and was banned for life from several sanctioned events.

During his racing career, Oldfield developed a cordial relationship with tire manufacturer Harvey Firestone that continued after Oldfield retired from racing in 1918. Seeking to capitalize on the ex-racer's popularity, Firestone made him president of the Oldfield Tire and Rubber Company, a Firestone subsidiary. Unfortunately, Oldfield was not interested in making tires and spent most of his time in Detroit's speakeasies. The negative publicity generated by Oldfield's many arrests forced Firestone to oust him from the company in 1922.

After trying unsuccessfully to manufacture tires on his own, Oldfield joined a Detroit investment firm. Aided by tips from "insider" friends, Oldfield amassed a paper fortune of more than $1 million, only to lose it all in the stock market crash of 1929. In 1931 he became a test driver for Hudson Motors. In 1933 he joined Plymouth Motors to promote their safe-driving campaign, but his effectiveness was compromised after he received several speeding tickets. He opened two saloons in California—in Van Nuys in 1937 and in Beverly Hills in 1941—both of which failed. At the time of his death, he lectured on auto safety for California's General Petroleum Corporation.

Oldfield's private life was every bit as bumpy as the dirt tracks on which he loved to race. In 1896 he married Beatrice Oatis; they divorced in 1906. In 1907 Oldfield married Rebecca Gooby "Bessie" Holland, whom he met in a hospital while convalescing after a wreck. Although his philandering did not perturb her, his drinking and barroom brawling did, and she reluctantly divorced him in 1924. Within a year Oldfield married Hulda Braden, and in 1931 they adopted a daughter and moved to Beverly Hills. The couple fought frequently and divorced in 1945. Two weeks after the breakup, a humbled and sober Oldfield remarried Bessie. His several marriages and countless affairs produced no children. He died in Beverly Hills.

Oldfield contributed significantly to the growth of the American automotive industry. As a competitor and lecturer, he helped to establish the reputation of several manufacturers. As a barnstormer, he served as a salesman of sorts by demonstrating to countless numbers of rural folk the power and glamour of the motorcar. In turn, Oldfield was transformed by the automobile; it provided him with fame, a livelihood, and, most importantly, the opportunity to indulge his passion for breakneck speed and flamboyant recklessness.

• Except for a few personal letters in private hands, Oldfield left no papers. His importance as a racing pioneer is assessed in David J. Abodaher, *Great Moments in Sports Car Racing* (1981); Ralph Hickok, *Who Was Who in American Sports* (1971); and Bill Libby, *Great American Race Drivers* (1970). William F. Nolan, *Barney Oldfield: The Life and Times of America's Legendary Speed King* (1961), presents a eulogistic account of Oldfield's life. His obituary is in the *New York Times*, 5 Oct. 1946.

CHARLES W. CAREY, JR.

OLDHAM, John (c. 1600–July 1636), trader, was born in Lancashire, England, of unknown parents. He first appeared in the historical record when he emigrated to Plymouth colony in 1623, arriving in July on the ship *Anne*. Like other non-Separatists (or "particulars") who desired to settle in the colony, he was required to sign an agreement accepting the authority of the government, even though he had paid his own passage. He did become a Separatist shortly after arriving, but Governor William Bradford himself expressed some doubt about Oldham's motives, saying of his conversion, "Now whether this was in hypocrisy, or out of some sudden pang of conviction, which I rather think, God only knows." Oldham was married and had children, but no details are known.

Oldham was well known for his temper and stubborn insistence on following his own path. In 1624 he joined forces with the newly arrived Reverend John Lyford to lead a faction of dissident settlers who began to work secretly against the Plymouth government. The two wrote several letters to some of the colony's enemies in England, hoping to gain leverage against the government, but a suspicious Bradford searched the ship before it left, discovered the letters, and read of the pair's intention to form their own church and "have the sacraments," apparently according to Lyford's "Episcopal calling." At first the governor did nothing with the information, but Oldham, perhaps emboldened by his anticipated support from England, became more contrary than ever, refusing to take his scheduled night watch and even drawing a knife against the captain (presumably Miles Standish) and calling him a "beggarly rascal." Bradford sent more men to quiet him, but Oldham only "ramped more like a furious beast than a man, and called them all traitors and rebels and other such foul language." Only a brief stint in jail calmed him down.

Shortly after this incident Oldham and Lyford did in fact establish their own church. Bradford and the Plymouth authorities decided the two had gone too far; the government tried and convicted them and in early 1625 banished them from the colony. Oldham flew into another rage during the trial when he discovered that Bradford had opened his letters. The governor allowed Oldham's family to remain in the colony until he could find a suitable home for them, but Oldham returned in March 1625 and again verbally excoriated the colony's leaders. The authorities jailed him and then personally escorted him out of town, forming "a guard of musketeers which he was to pass through, and every one was ordered to give him a thump on the breech with the butt end of his musket."

Oldham settled first at Nantasket (Hull) in Massachusetts and then on Cape Ann, where he established a successful Indian trade. During this time he seems to have undergone a change of attitude. On a trading voyage to Virginia his ship was in danger of sinking. According to Bradford, Oldham "did make a free and large confession of the wrongs and hurt he had done to the people and church here . . . [and] prayed to God to forgive him." He returned to Cape Ann and was employed as a trader by the Dorchester Company, founded in 1623 in an attempt to establish a permanent fishing village on the cape, until it went bankrupt in 1626. He also regained the Plymouth Colony's trust, returning in 1628 to escort the banished Thomas Morton back to England. While there, he sought commercial concessions from the fledgling Massachusetts Bay Company, but they rejected his proposal. In 1629 he purchased some land at the mouth of the Charles River from John Gorges, the son of Ferdinand Gorges, but the Bay Company refused to accept Gorges's claim to the land. In early 1630 Oldham and Richard Vines did receive a grant from the Council for New England for land on the Saco River in Maine, but Oldham showed no interest in developing the grant and settled instead in Watertown, Massachusetts. There he prospered; he became a freeman in 1631 and was elected a representative to the General Court in 1632 and 1634.

Still intent on pursuing riches, in September 1633 Oldham led a four-man scouting trip to the Connecticut River, returning with beaver, black lead, and hemp specimens. In the fall of 1634 he led a group of eight to Pyquag (later Wethersfield) on the Connecticut River, where he built shelters and explored the area in search of furs. That same year the Massachusetts General Court granted him 500 acres on the Charles River and made him one of the overseers of powder and shot for the colony. He had business relations with the Winthrop family. Though the Pequots rebuffed his attempts to open trade with them, the Narragansetts welcomed his overtures. In November 1634 they awarded him 500 bushels of corn and offered him possession of an island in Narragansett Bay if he would live among them. Finally, he was one of the messengers who delivered instructions from the Massachusetts government to John Winthrop, Jr., at the Fort Saybrook conference in July 1636 demanding, under threats of English revenge, that the Pequots and Western Niantics give further satisfaction for the 1634 death of John Stone.

Within a few days of the Saybrook conference, however, Oldham was dead. Captain John Gallop, sailing near Block Island, saw Oldham's ship, crowded with Indians. He investigated and found the trader's body. Gallop killed many of the Indians on board in revenge, but it seems clear that Oldham's killer was not among them. The circumstances of his death remain veiled; historians agree only that he had been on a trading mission to the island. John Winthrop claimed that Narragansett sachems conspired with the Block Island Indians to kill Oldham for attempting to trade with the Pequots the previous year. Yet at the time, the Narragansetts were at peace with the Pequots and allied with the Bay Colony. Historian Francis Jennings has argued that Oldham was the victim of something like a state execution by Narragansett sachems for an un-

known offense. It seems unlikely that historians will ever discover the truth.

The two leading Narragansett sachems, Canonicus and Miantonomo, were anxious to preserve their alliance with the Bay Colony, and they led some two hundred warriors to Block Island to take revenge for Oldham's death on the colony's behalf. They assured the English that they killed most of the assassins (though a few escaped to the Pequots), and they returned the two boys from Oldham's ship and his remaining goods. But Massachusetts authorities were not satisfied and subsequently launched reprisals against both the Block Island Indians and the innocent Pequots. These were the opening blows in the Pequot War.

Historians generally remember Oldham for his inadvertent role in the onset of this war. But his life also reminds us that not everyone who came to early New England was a cooperative, religiously motivated settler. Even after his change of heart in Virginia, Oldham sought wealth and prestige at least as much as religious peace.

• Though there is no study of Oldham's life, there are several excellent brief sources of information available. On his early years in Plymouth, see William Bradford, *Of Plymouth Plantation, 1620–1647*, ed. Samuel Eliot Morison (1952). On his later activities, begin with Francis Jennings, *The Invasion of America: Indians, Colonists, and the Cant of Conquest* (1975), and then consult the differing interpretations in Alden T. Vaughan, *New England Frontier: Puritans and Indians, 1620–1675* (1965), and Vaughan, "Pequots and Puritans: The Causes of the War of 1637," *William and Mary Quarterly*, 3d ser., 21 (1964): 256–69. Also see James Kendall Hosmer, ed., *Winthrop's Journal: "History of New England," 1630–1649*, vol. 1 (1908). The quotations are from Bradford, *Of Plymouth Plantation*, pp. 149, 151, 165, and 165–66.

RONALD P. DUFOUR

OLDHAM, Williamson Simpson (19 June 1813–8 May 1868), Confederate congressman, was born in Franklin County, Tennessee, the son of Elias Oldham and Mary Bratton, poor farmers. He was one of fourteen children. His formal education was rudimentary, for farm chores permitted him to attend school only during the winter. Nevertheless, he felt self-confident enough at the age of eighteen to open his own school. After two years he left teaching to read law and work in the office of the clerk of district court in Franklin County. He was admitted to the bar in 1836 and moved to Fayetteville, Arkansas.

Oldham entered politics and was elected to the Arkansas House of Representatives in 1838, when he was twenty-five years old. He failed to be reelected in 1840 but won again in 1842 and became Speaker of the house. Two years later he was elected by the legislature to be an associate justice of the state supreme court, a position he held for four years.

Oldham failed in a run for the U.S. Congress in 1846 and the Senate in 1848. Upset and afflicted with tuberculosis, he resigned his judgeship and moved to Texas, settling in Austin in 1849. He built a new legal practice and accumulated a substantial estate, including three slaves, worth $85,000 in 1860 (1860 Manuscript Census). He also engaged in civic promotion and was president of the Austin Railroad Association.

Oldham is significant primarily for his political activity just before and during the Civil War. He purchased a share of the *Texas State Gazette* in 1854 and wrote editorials preaching a strict states' rights gospel. He claimed that slaves were essential to the South and that the federal government had no power to legislate on the question of slavery in the territories. He campaigned for the successful Democratic candidate for governor against Sam Houston in 1857 and failed to get congressional nominations in 1858 and 1859. Discouraged, he moved to Brenham, Texas, in 1860.

As the secession crisis approached in 1860, Oldham supported John C. Breckinridge for the presidency. He was one of the leaders of the effort to call a secession convention, in spite of the opposition of Governor Houston. When the convention met in February 1861, Oldham was a representative of Washington County and voted for secession. He was elected to the Provisional Congress of the Confederacy. The Texas legislature later elected him to the Senate of the permanent Congress. He served in the Confederate Congresses from 2 March 1861 until the final adjournment on 18 March 1865.

Oldham supported the Confederacy to the last, but he strongly disagreed with many of the policies of Confederate president Jefferson Davis, notably suspension of the writ of habeas corpus and conscription, because he feared the unconstitutional expansion of the power of the central government. Conscription required some sort of exemption system, but to Oldham that too was an imposition on state sovereignty. He also opposed legislation in March 1862 that would place acreage restrictions on the planting of cotton in order to encourage production of foodstuffs. Oldham's ideas were so extreme that one historian asserts, "He could not understand the meaning of 'military necessity'" (King, p. 127).

Except for measures that he feared would strengthen the central government at the expense of the states, however, Oldham was willing to resort to any action that would bring victory. Among the extreme measures he favored were arson attacks on New York City and, contrary to other accounts, the enlistment of slave soldiers. He admitted that arson was not in accord with civilized warfare but asserted that it was acceptable "against savages who discard the moral code recognized by all civilized nations" (Oldham, "Last Days of the Confederacy," De Bow's Review, Sept. 1870, p. 741). During the last session of the Confederate Congress, 7 November 1864 to 18 March 1865, Oldham served on a joint committee "to inquire into our present and future means of public defense" (*Journal of the Confederate Congress*, vol. 4, p. 416). He agreed with the committee report that the Confederacy had the resources "to enable us to continue the struggle for an indefinite period of time," but he believed the Congress and the people had become so "war weary" as to be "desperate," "hopeless," and willing to accept defeat (Oldham, "Last Days of the Confederacy," *De Bow's Review*, Oct. 1869, pp. 865–66).

After the collapse of the Confederacy, Oldham went to Mexico. There he wrote "Last Days of the Confederacy," which was serialized in *De Bow's Review* (Oct. 1869-Sept. 1870). He learned photography in order to earn a living, but when the Maximilian government collapsed in 1866, he moved to Canada. He soon returned to the United States but ignored pleas of friends to apply for a pardon. Oldham was never reconciled to Confederate defeat. After the war he argued in "True Cause and Issues of the Civil War" (*De Bow's Review*, Aug.-Sept. 1869) that the conflict occurred when "war was made upon the Southern States by the Federal Government, or rather by the Northern States, using the Federal Government for the execution of their unconstitutional and revolutionary purposes" (p. 743).

Oldham returned to Texas in 1866, settled in Houston, and resumed the practice of law. Within a few years, he died in Houston from a prolonged case of typhoid. Oldham was an Episcopalian and a vestryman in that church for many years. He was married three times: to Mary Vance McKissick, 1837–1849, with whom he had five children; to Anne S. Kirk, 1850–1857; and to Agnes Harper in 1857.

Oldham seriously misjudged the staying power of the Confederacy and often undermined the Confederate war effort by his support of states' rights policies. Nevertheless, he understood better than most of the Confederate leadership the role of civilian morale. Opposing conscription and suspension of habeas corpus mainly because of their harmful effects on civilian morale and loyalty, he understood, as many others did not, that the war effort would fail if it oppressed the population. He believed the Confederacy lost the war because of problems of morale and noted in retrospect that, as a result, "the country was subjugated and prepared for submission upon any terms or conditions" (Oldham, "Last Days," *De Bow's Review*, Jan. 1870, p. 53).

• The University of Texas Library, Austin, has the largest collection of Oldham's papers, which include a typescript of his unpublished "Memoirs of Williamson S. Oldham, Confederate Senator, 1861–1865." He also coauthored, with George W. White, *A Digest of the General Statute Laws of the State of Texas . . .* (1859). The best modern sketch of Oldham is Laura N. Harper, "Williamson Simpson Oldham," in *Ten Texans in Gray*, ed. W. C. Nunn (1968). The best contemporary sketch is E. Fontaine, "Hon. Williamson S. Oldham," *De Bow's Review*, ser. 2, vol. 7 (Oct. 1869): 873–80. Fontaine knew Oldham personally, and if his article is somewhat adulatory, it is also fairly detailed. See also Alma Dexta King, "The Political Career of Williamson Simpson Oldham," *Southwestern Historical Quarterly* 33 (Oct. 1929): 112–33, which illustrates by its frequent reference to the writing of Fontaine and Oldham himself that little work has been done on this Confederate politician. For the significant portion of Oldham's political career, see Senate, *Journal of the Congress of the Confederate States of America, 1861–1865*, vols. 1–4,

58th Cong., 2d sess., 1904–1905, S. Doc. 234; and the "Proceedings of the . . . Confederate Congress" (title varies), *Southern Historical Society Papers* 44–50 (1923–1953).

RICHARD E. BERINGER

OLDS, Irving Sands (22 Jan. 1887–5 Mar. 1963), lawyer and industrialist, was born in Erie, Pennsylvania, the son of Clark Olds, a lawyer, and Livia Elizabeth Keator. Olds graduated from Erie High School in 1903 and earned a bachelor's degree from Yale University in 1907 and a law degree from Harvard University in 1910. After graduating from law school, Olds worked in Washington for a year as secretary to Associate Justice of the Supreme Court Oliver Wendell Holmes, Jr. Olds was admitted to the Pennsylvania bar in 1910 and to the New York bar in 1912. In 1911 he joined the New York law firm of White and Case, where he became a partner six years later.

From 1915 to 1917, while Europe was embroiled in World War I but America was still neutral, Olds served as counsel to the export department of J. P. Morgan and Company, advising on war purchases that Britain and France made in the United States. In 1917, after the United States entered the war, he became counsel for the purchasing department of the British War Mission to the United States. In that same year he married Evelyn Foster of New York City; they had no children. In 1918 he served in Washington as special assistant to Assistant Secretary of War Edward Stettinius, Sr. After the war Olds resumed his work with White and Case, building a reputation as a top corporate lawyer.

In October 1936 Olds joined the U.S. Steel Corporation as a member of the board of directors and as a member of the corporation's finance committee. In 1938 he was appointed special counsel to the corporation while the government's Temporary National Economic Committee examined U.S. Steel as part of its antitrust investigations. Olds's services in this capacity were extremely valuable to U.S. Steel; he proved to be an affable, eloquent spokesman for the company, and the three-volume study that he produced was praised as one of the most thorough and insightful ever made of U.S. Steel and the American steel industry. Olds was critical of the government's concern that U.S. Steel constituted a monopoly and, noting the company's contribution to the Allied effort in World War I, once commented that he could not comprehend "the logic or equity of representatives of our Government soliciting and welcoming aid of the larger groups of the country in times of national peril, and then assailing them as too large and powerful when the days of emergency have passed" ("Half a Century of United States Steel," p. 10).

When Edward Stettinius, Jr., resigned as chairman of the board of U.S. Steel in 1940 to work for the National Defense Commission in Washington, Olds was elected the new chairman. The steel company enjoyed heady times while Olds was chairman. Steel production soared during World War II, and after the war Olds continued to expand the company's production and operations. As board chairman Olds also pursued a liberal labor policy, and the company made important concessions to its workers during a 1946 strike.

Olds retired from the chairmanship of U.S. Steel in 1952 but continued to serve as a director and as a member of the finance committee. He also resumed work as a senior partner with the White and Case law firm in Manhattan, serving with them until his death.

During his retirement Olds and other prominent retired corporate board chairmen, including Alfred P. Sloan, Jr., of General Motors, urged business and industry to support private higher education in the United States through the Council for Financial Aid to Education, which was created in 1952 and which Olds served as board chairman. Olds took a special interest in his alma mater, Yale University. He served as a trustee of the Yale Corporation, the school's governing body; he was a member-at-large of the Yale Alumni Board and a member of its executive committee; from 1944 to 1947 he was chairman of the National Yale Alumni Placement Service; and from 1959 to 1961 he was president of the Yale University Council.

Olds died in New York City.

• Olds was interested in colonial America and in American naval history and wrote a book, *United States Navy, 1776–1815* (1942). He also authored *Bits and Pieces of American History* (1951), which was printed in a limited edition of 500 registered copies. This work featured his collection of historical paintings and included portraits of American naval commanders, such as John Paul Jones.

Olds's arguments on the deleterious economic effects and inefficacy of price controls appear in his essay, "The Price of Price Controls," *Reader's Digest*, Nov. 1952. Olds also delivered numerous addresses on business, economic, and historical topics. His 1951 address at New York City at a National Newcomen Dinner of the Newcomen Society of England was published as an essay, "Half a Century of United States Steel."

The USX Corporation archives contain biographical sketches, speeches, and annual reports of Irving Olds, as well as a tribute to Olds in Fred LePell, "The Nicest Man I Ever Met" (1980), who worked for Olds for nine years in U.S. Steel's Public Relations Department. An obituary is in the *New York Times*, 6 Mar. 1963.

YANEK MIECZKOWSKI

OLDS, Leland (31 Dec. 1890–3 Aug. 1960), statistician, journalist, and government regulatory official, was born in Rochester, New York, the son of George Daniel Olds, a professor of mathematics at the University of Rochester, and Marion Elizabeth Leland. In 1891 his father became chair of the mathematics department at Amherst College and eventually president of the college in 1924. Inspired by conservationist Gifford Pinchot and Theodore Roosevelt, Olds spoke at his high school commencement on the "use of natural resources for the benefit of the people."

A magna cum laude graduate of Amherst in 1912, Olds pursued graduate work in economics and sociology first at Harvard and then at Columbia. While at these universities, he also searched for ways in which he might apply Christian principles to industrialized society. Influenced by Henry George's *Progress and Poverty* and Charles Sheldon's *In His Steps*, he worried that "our civilization might be going the way of those before it in which justice and mercy and consideration of the poor were sacrificed to the worship of Mammon." Olds's postgraduate experience in a social settlement in the south end of Boston solidified his belief in the redemptive power of the Sermon on the Mount rather than in the ideas of Karl Marx, whom Olds rejected for failing to recognize spiritual values. After spending two years at Union Theological Seminary, he served briefly as a minister in a low-income section of Brooklyn.

In 1917 Olds found work that combined his graduate studies with his interest in the working class; he prepared a report on British labor policies during World War I for the Council of National Defense. He then served as a statistician for the Shipbuilding Labor Adjustment Board and as an administrator of awards for the National War Labor Board, where he formed an association with Frank P. Walsh, the noted labor attorney, and W. Jett Lauck, a labor economist and author. From this work he developed a lifelong commitment to unionization and collective bargaining. His experience in Pennsylvania during the 1919 steel strike convinced him that industrial unionism was needed as a counterbalance to the destructive materialistic tendencies within laissez-faire capitalism.

After the war Olds assisted Lauck in several cases before the Railway Labor Board and then became head of the American Federation of Labor's research bureau for two years. The open shop campaign of the railroads in the early 1920s alienated Olds, particularly because of his commitment to union recognition and to a living wage, as defined in 1919 by Father John Ryan and the Catholic bishops. With the demise of the research bureau in 1922, Olds joined the Federated Press, a labor news agency, as its industrial editor, a position he retained until 1929. His articles, more than 1,800 in number, analyzed economic data supportive of the labor movement, whose main purpose, he believed, was "to transfer the ownership of the great social enterprises from the small financial oligarchy to the people themselves." The tone of the articles reflected Olds's discontent with capitalism as it existed in the 1920s and his willingness to examine alternatives to that system, including nationalization of industry, labor cooperatives, and Soviet experiments, provided they were undertaken within the context of an evolving democratic and industrial society. Olds's articles received a wide distribution throughout the labor press, including the *Daily Worker*, a Communist newspaper. In 1924 he married Maud Agnes Spear, with whom he would have four children. They resided in Northbrook, Illinois.

In 1929, with the Federated Press losing its financial support, Walsh urged Olds to move to New York where Governor Franklin Roosevelt was interested in utility regulation. Olds served as an economist for the Community Councils of the City of New York during their campaign for stronger public power regulation.

His work led to his appointment as executive secretary of the newly created New York Power Commission, where he served from 1931 to 1939. This experience convinced him that "regulation of public services is an alternative to public ownership" because it could require the natural monopolies in the utility industry to provide maximum use of power at minimum rates. To balance the lack of competition among utilities he also encouraged municipal ownership of utilities and championed governmental development, transmission, and sale of hydroelectric power on a wholesale basis. The commission also began negotiations with Canada toward common development of the St. Lawrence seaway.

In 1939 President Roosevelt rewarded Olds with an appointment to the Federal Power Commission. As chairman of the commission from 1940 to 1946, Olds took pride in the agency's ability to get utilities to adopt a uniform accounting procedure that enabled them to gather data from all over the country and find ways to lower their rates. During World War II the FPC emphasized expanding power facilities to support military production. This enormous growth in kilowatts did not, in Olds's mind, lead to a problem of underutilization after the war but rather fostered the rapidly expanding sale of appliances and economic recovery. Olds was reappointed to the FPC during 1944 in spite of questions regarding his possible affinity for Marxism and complaints from a few state commissions that the FPC was usurping their power.

Olds's career had peaked during the pro-regulatory era of the New Deal, but the advent of the Cold War posed a serious threat to liberals and left-wingers in government. In 1949, at the height of the Red Scare, President Harry S. Truman submitted Olds's reappointment to the Senate. At the confirmation hearings Representative John Lyle of Texas presented numerous examples of Olds's left-wing rhetoric from his articles for the Federated Press as evidence that he was a Communist sympathizer; Olds denied that he had ever been a Communist or a Marxist. All the leaders of the opposition to Olds's renomination, Lyle and Senators Lyndon Johnson of Texas and Robert Kerr of Oklahoma, were from gas-producing states; they used redbaiting to oppose Olds, but the real issue was the power of the FPC to regulate wellhead prices for natural gas.

The Natural Gas Act of 1938 had permitted the FPC to regulate the price of gas sold in interstate commerce but not wellhead prices until a 1947 Supreme Court case opened the possibility of reinterpreting the act. Olds, who had repeatedly reassured wellhead producers during World War II that the FPC had no power to regulate them, then drafted a report in cooperation with another commissioner asserting otherwise. In response Kerr, a millionaire oil and gas producer, introduced a bill to exempt independent producers from FPC control, which Olds vigorously opposed before the Senate just prior to his confirmation hearings. Despite Truman's vigorous efforts to defend Olds as a champion of the people under siege by corporate interests and a *Washington Post* editorial of 29 September 1949 supporting him as "vigilant in squeezing the water out of utility accounts and vigorous in pressing for gas- and electric-rate reductions," the Senate rejected Olds's confirmation, 53–15. President Truman struck back with a veto of the Kerr Bill. The FPC, however, did not regulate wellhead prices until after a favorable Supreme Court decision in 1954.

The battle over Olds' renomination was part of the continuing war in the twentieth century between disciples of government regulation and advocates of marketplace determination as the best means of guaranteeing fair pricing for the consumer. Olds was an unswerving proponent of using regulatory agencies and government ownership to protect the consumer against monopolistic or oligopolistic price fixing by public utilities and pipeline companies. He did not foresee, however, the deleterious effect of extending government price fixing to the speculative and highly competitive business of gathering a natural resource. In the late 1970s Congress started deregulation of the natural gas industry, a process that lasted until 1993, as a remedy for the shortness of supply and high prices bedeviling Americans in the midst of an energy crisis.

For the remainder of his presidency Truman employed Olds as an expert on natural resources. After Truman's defeat in 1952, Olds became a consultant for the Public Affairs Institution and spoke on numerous occasions against the Eisenhower administration's favoritism toward big business and its attacks on the Tennessee Valley Authority. Olds died of a heart attack in Bethesda, Maryland.

• The Franklin D. Roosevelt Library at Hyde Park, N.Y., is the depository for the Leland Olds Papers. Besides his numerous articles for the Federated Press, quite a few of which are included in the 1949 Senate subcommittee hearings on his confirmation, Olds wrote "The Temper of British Labor," *Nation*, 19 Apr. 1919, pp. 601–3; "Yardstick and Birchrods," *Harper's*, Nov. 1935, pp. 648–59; and "The Economic Planning Function under Public Regulation," *American Economic Review* 48 (May 1958): 553–61. As a state and federal commissioner Olds wrote numerous reports, the most important of which were *Inquiry on Cooperative Enterprise in Europe* (1937), which demonstrated his commitment to worker and consumer cooperatives, and *Natural Gas Investigation . . . Report of Commissioner Leland Olds and Commissioner Claude L. Draper* (1948). Especially revealing for any study of Olds are the records of the subcommittee hearings on his confirmation before the Senate Committee on Interstate Commerce: *Leland Olds' Reappointment to Federal Power Commission: Hearings* (1944), and *Reappointment of Leland Olds to Federal Power Commission: Hearings* (1949). Joseph P. Harris probes the meaning of these hearings from a political science viewpoint in "The Senatorial Rejection of Leland Olds," *American Political Science Review* 35 (Sept. 1951): 672–94. Older works on the issue of public power include Thomas K. McGraw, *TVA and the Power Fight, 1933–39* (1971), and Philip J. Funigiello, *Toward a National Power Policy* (1973). For an analysis of public power issues dependent on more recent economic theory, see Douglas D. Anderson, *Regulatory Politics and Electric Utilities* (1981); Peter M. VanDoren, *Politics, Markets, and Congressional Policy Choices* (1991); and Richard H. K. Vietor, *Energy Policy in America Since 1945: A Study of Business-Government Relations* (1984). Also see Olds's obituary in the *New York Times*, 5 Aug. 1960.

WILLIAM D. JENKINS

OLDS, Ransom Eli (3 June 1864–26 Aug. 1950), pioneer automobile manufacturer, was born in Geneva, Ohio, the son of Pliny Fisk Olds, a blacksmith and machinist, and Sarah Whipple. Olds's father was involved in several businesses and farmed for a few years before moving in 1880 to Lansing, Michigan, where he and another son, Wallace, opened a machine shop.

Ransom Olds attended high school in Lansing before dropping out in order to work full-time in the family business, P. F. Olds & Son. In 1885 he bought out his brother's interest. Although he was only twenty-one, Olds soon assumed the dominant role in the company. P. F. Olds & Son had built a few wood- and coal-burning steam engines but the limited success it had enjoyed was based largely on repair work. Olds turned around the company's fortunes by encouraging his father and brother to develop a small, easy-to-operate steam engine that, by using a gasoline burner, could achieve the desired pressure much faster than traditionally fueled engines. Ransom Olds's belief that there would be a market for such an engine among businesses that needed power only intermittently was borne out by sales of about 2,000 engines between 1887 and 1892. In 1896 company sales totaled $29,000, nearly six times those of 1885, and the original plant had been twice expanded.

Olds married Metta Woodward in 1889; two of the couple's children survived infancy. P. F. Olds & Son was incorporated in 1890. Ransom Olds was the general manager, and his control of the company was clearly evident by the middle of the decade as he came to own most of the stock and his father prepared to retire as president.

The company still did repair work and made a variety of products, but, as Olds later put it, engines were the "bread and butter" of their business. It may have been his desire to explore new uses for these engines that initially led him into automotive experiments. A crude three-wheeled vehicle, powered by a one-horse-power Olds steam engine, which he tested in 1887, performed poorly. A larger, more elaborate steamer with twice the power of the earlier one attracted the attention of a writer for *Scientific American*. The reporter's favorable description of the vehicle's performance appeared in 1892, probably the first indication in a national publication of any automotive work in Michigan. The story, which was reprinted in *The Hub*, a carriage industry trade journal, caused the Francis Times Company of London in 1893 to purchase the Olds steamer. This may have been the first sale of an American-made horseless carriage to a foreign buyer.

Olds's experience convinced him that steam engines entailed too many problems for them to be a practical source of power for road vehicles. Exhibits at the World's Columbian Exposition in Chicago, which he visited in the summer of 1893, helped turn his attention to a better power source, the internal combustion gasoline engine. Returning to Lansing, he began work on his version of such an engine—a revision of existing models—that he and a staff member, Madison F. Bates, patented in 1896. The engine was an instant success, boosting company sales in 1897 by nearly 50 percent over the previous year's totals and necessitating still another factory addition.

Despite the success of the engines, Olds had come to feel that the "big venture" in his life would be the motor vehicle, and thus he resumed the experiments he had left off several years earlier. In Europe companies such as Peugeot, Benz, and Daimler had been producing automobiles since the late 1880s, but in the United States the commercial phase of automotive development had barely begun in 1896 when thirteen Duryea Motor Wagons were the first domestically made cars to be sold. Thus Olds was in a position to be in at the start of a major new industrial development. On 11 August 1896 he gave the first public demonstration of a carriage supplied by a Lansing factory and powered by a one-cylinder, five-horsepower Olds gasoline engine mounted beneath the body. Olds was quite satisfied with the results and the next month applied for a patent on certain features of a vehicle in which his object was to "meet most of the requirements for the ordinary uses on the road without complicated gear or requiring engine of great power and to avoid all unnecessary weight."

Although Olds hoped to move quickly into production and sale of the car he had developed, no significant numbers of Olds-built automobiles were available for several years. The strong demand for the Olds engine made it seem too risky to divert sufficient resources in Olds's existing production facilities to the assembling of cars. Thus, on 21 August 1897, a separate Olds Motor Vehicle Company was organized by Olds, but the money outside investors furnished was not enough to support a separate automobile factory. Finally, on 8 May 1899, as a result of a commitment of some $200,000 by Samuel L. Smith, a Detroiter who had made a fortune through real estate and copper mining investments, the Olds Motor Vehicle Company and the Olds engine operations were merged into the Olds Motor Works, with Smith and his associates controlling most of the stock. The Olds engines continued to be manufactured in Lansing, but a new plant was built in Detroit where the automobiles were to be produced. Little public enthusiasm was generated for the several models that Olds and his staff came up with, including an electric car, until the end of 1900 when they hit upon a small car, using the carriage style known as a runabout to which a distinctive curved-dash front was added. The first Olds vehicle bearing the Oldsmobile label, the curved-dash Olds was soon the most popular car of its day. Despite a disastrous fire, which held up production for several weeks in the spring of 1901, about 425 cars were produced that year. By 1902 the Olds Motor Works was the leading auto company in the country, and by 1904, when production topped 5,000, it was clearly the world's leading motor car producer.

Olds is entitled to the major credit for his company's success. At $650, the curved-dash Olds was not the cheapest car on the market, but the fact that it outsold all other cars, including some lower-priced runabouts other companies had available, was a testimony to the strength of Olds's organization. To keep up with the demand, unprecedented by that day's standards, Olds took the first steps toward improving the efficiency of his assembly operations. By moving along the vehicles that were being assembled on wooden platforms mounted on casters, with workers assigned specific tasks along the route and the parts they needed nearby in bins, Olds foreshadowed some of Henry Ford's mass-production advances of later years. Olds's success stimulated others to try to duplicate his achievements. A number of former employees of the Olds Motor Works and those who had supplied parts for the Oldsmobile formed their own companies such as Maxwell, Hupmobile, and Hudson. Most of these new companies were in or near Detroit. The Ford Motor Company's first model in 1903, a runabout that was initially called the Fordmobile, testified to the impact of the curved-dash Olds.

However, Ransom Olds's connections with the Olds Motor Works were deteriorating. In order to obtain the money he had needed to get into auto production, he had had to surrender financial control to outsiders, while continuing to direct manufacturing operations. But trouble started in 1901 when Olds moved from Detroit back to Lansing to oversee the operation of the new plant that was built there after the fire that had destroyed much of the Detroit factory in March. Samuel Smith's son Fred took over the day-to-day management of the rebuilt Detroit plant, and, while Olds officially remained in overall managerial control, a rift developed when Fred Smith began to try to change some of Olds's policies regarding production procedures. Olds angrily objected, but with only a minority stock interest there was little he could do to prevent the board of directors in January 1904 from turning the general manager's job over to Fred Smith.

By summer Olds had sold all of his stock and had resigned his position on the board of the Olds Motor Works. Meanwhile, he took an active role in the organization of a new company in Lansing, incorporated on 16 August 1904 and named the Reo Motor Car Company, using Olds's initials after Fred Smith and the Olds Motor Works had threatened to sue if the company employed the Olds name in its title. Olds, who this time retained a majority stock interest in the company, moved quickly to develop not only a new runabout model but also a heavier, more powerful touring car that would withstand the pounding cars took on the wretched roads of the period. It was this model, costing $1,250, twice the cost of the runabouts, that was primarily responsible for Reo's success. By 1907 it was one of the top four or five producers in the country. Meanwhile, sales of the Olds Motor Works declined sharply, as Fred Smith moved too quickly away from the inexpensive little runabouts with which the company's name had been associated.

Once Olds had demonstrated that he could repeat his earlier successes in a company he controlled, he lost the incentive to remain as active in the business as he had been in the past. By 1907 he was leaving more and more of the details to his staff, and instead indulged his love for travel and boating. Thus, while William C. Durant, who organized General Motors, acquired control of the Olds Motor Works in 1909 and began to refurbish the Oldsmobile image, Reo failed to live up to the promise of its early years. Olds continued to maintain some interest in the company and was probably mainly responsible for the decision in 1911 to begin producing trucks, a move that enabled the Lansing factory to continue work for nearly forty years after automobile production was ended in 1936. Olds gave up the title of general manager in 1915 and stepped down as president in 1923 to take on the largely honorary title of chairman. Meanwhile he dabbled in other interests, developing one of the first powered lawn mowers, working on diesel engines, and investing in real estate in Michigan, Florida, and elsewhere. The Great Depression caused him to resume a more active role in the direction of Reo, but when his fellow directors rejected the ideas he put forward to revitalize the company in 1934 he relinquished his managerial position and in 1936 resigned as director.

Olds died at his Lansing home. His reputation had long since been overshadowed by the achievements of others, particularly Henry Ford. To a great extent, Olds, by failing to maintain the hands-on control of his company that had gained him his early recognition, had only himself to blame for his declining stature. Nevertheless, that early period of activity, short as it was, had provided the example that was mainly responsible for the great boom that made Michigan the center of the auto industry.

• The papers of Ransom E. Olds are in the Historical Collections of Michigan State University, East Lansing. Nearly all the records are for the period after 1900. The same collection has the records of the Reo Motor Car Company from 1904 to its end in 1975. Among biographies, Duane Yarnell, *Auto Pioneering: A Remarkable Story of Ransom E. Olds, Father of Oldsmobile and Reo* (1949), was paid for by Olds and was based on his faltering recollections. Glenn A. Niemeyer, *The Automotive Career of Ransom E. Olds* (1963), is the first biography to be based on a study of the Olds papers. George S. May, *R. E. Olds: Auto Industry Pioneer* (1977), is the most extended treatment of the subject. Obituaries in the *Lansing State Journal* and *New York Times*, both 27 Aug. 1950, reflect inaccuracies that were long accepted in assessments of Olds's accomplishments.

GEORGE S. MAY

O'LEARY, Daniel (29 June 1846?–29 May 1933), pedestrian, was born in the village of Carrigroe, County Cork, Ireland, the son of a farmer. His parents' names are not known. Raised amid widespread famine and desolation, O'Leary worked on his father's farm until age twenty, when he immigrated to the United States.

Unable to find employment in New York City, he moved to Chicago, Illinois, and secured a job in a lumberyard. During the winter of 1866 O'Leary moved to Bolivar County, Mississippi, where he picked cotton. In 1868 he returned to Chicago and became a door-to-door book salesman. After achieving modest success as a book canvasser, the Chicago fire of 1871 wiped out many of his clients and left O'Leary with a $3,000 debt in idle inventory and unpaid bills. After the fire he started peddling his books in the Chicago suburbs. In addition to walking several miles from house to house, O'Leary began and ended each day by walking ten to fifteen miles from the city to the suburbs. He maintained this regimen for nearly two years, building the physical stamina that would enable him to become a long-distance race walker.

In 1873 O'Leary became interested in competitive long-distance walking after hearing several businessmen discussing the accomplishments of then-champion pedestrian Edward Payson Weston, who was planning to walk 500 miles in six days. Believing that he was capable of such a feat, O'Leary began training for long-distance race walking. On 14 July 1874 he made his pedestrian debut in Chicago, walking 100 miles in 23 hours, 17 minutes. Within a month O'Leary walked 105 miles in 23 hours, 38 minutes. After this performance he challenged Weston to a race, but the latter declined, maintaining that O'Leary's lack of reputation as a pedestrian did not warrant such a challenge. Determined to show that he deserved recognition alongside Weston, O'Leary purposely surpassed the latter's record for 24 hours, walking 116 miles in 23 hours, 12 minutes, 53 seconds, in Philadelphia, Pennsylvania, in March 1875. Although this performance clearly established O'Leary as one of the world's leading pedestrians, Weston still refused to confront him on the track, saying that O'Leary had not demonstrated his ability in the six-day race. In response to Weston, O'Leary won a 500-mile race over six and a half days in Chicago in May 1875. After O'Leary's victory, Weston agreed to compete against him in a six-day race in November. A month prior to their meeting, however, O'Leary walked 100 miles in 18 hours, 53 minutes, 40 seconds, establishing an American record. On 20 November 1875 O'Leary defeated Weston, 503⅓ to 451¼ miles, in their much publicized six-day race.

By defeating Weston, O'Leary claimed the title of "Champion Pedestrian of the World." British sports writers, however, neither recognized O'Leary's achievement nor appreciated Weston's accomplishments, maintaining that both pedestrians could not duplicate their performances under the scrutiny of British judges. In response to these charges, Weston sailed to England in January 1876 to challenge Britain's best pedestrians, none of whom were any contest for him. He explained to London journalists, however, that O'Leary had defeated him by "foul play" and that the hostile Chicago audience had thrown pepper in his face and threatened to kill him. Infuriated by Weston's remarks, O'Leary in October 1876 traveled to England to confront Weston once more. Upon arriving in London, he walked 502 miles in six days. By January 1877 the financial backers of Weston and O'Leary worked out a contract for a six-day race to be held at the Agricultural Hall in London. On 7 April 1877 O'Leary triumphed over Weston, covering 520 miles, and defended his title as the world champion pedestrian.

After the Weston-O'Leary race, Sir John Astley, Weston's financial backer, inaugurated a series of six-day races for what was called the "Long Distance Challenge Championship of the World." Popularly known as the Astley Belt races, the winner would receive a championship belt, donated by Astley and worth £100; a purse of £500; a percentage of the gate receipts; and other prizes. If the athlete won three consecutive races, the belt would become the athlete's permanent property. The first Astley Belt competition was held at the London Agricultural Hall in November 1877. O'Leary, who covered 520 miles, won the race and a total of $3,750 in prize money. Returning to Chicago with the belt, he declared that the next Astley Belt race would have to take place in the United States. In 1878 O'Leary defended the title against John Hughes, an up-and-coming Irish-American pedestrian. In addition to the Astley Belt race, O'Leary had competed in seven other pedestrian events that year, walking a total of 3,110 miles. Despite a brief respite from competition in Hot Springs, Arkansas, after the Astley Belt race, O'Leary failed to defend the championship in March 1879 against Charles Rowell of Great Britain. Many sportswriters attributed his failure to defend the belt to O'Leary's thirst for alcohol rather than exhaustion from an arduous year of competition.

Shortly after losing the Astley Belt to Rowell, O'Leary announced his retirement from long-distance race walking. In October 1879 he initiated a series of six-day races known as the O'Leary Belt Championship of America. The purpose of these races was to develop a long-distance walker capable of bringing the Astley Belt back to the United States. Nicholas Murphy won the first O'Leary Belt with a performance of 501 miles. In March 1880 O'Leary came out of retirement and competed against Weston in a six-day race in San Francisco, California, defeating Weston 516 to 490 miles. The second O'Leary Belt was held in April 1880, and Frank Hart, an African American and O'Leary protégé, won the race in a world record of 564 miles. In the first 24 hours of the race, Hart established a world record of 130 miles. On 7 December 1885 O'Leary and Weston began a two-month, 2,500-mile race from Newark, New Jersey, to Chicago, Illinois. After three weeks O'Leary began using various kinds of stimulants and, during the final week of the race, collapsed after completing 2,292 miles and failed to finish the race. Weston won the race, arriving in Chicago on 6 February 1886. Although O'Leary never avenged this loss to Weston, he continued to give professional walking exhibitions to support his wife and three children. In 1902 O'Leary walked 187 miles between Boston, Massachusetts, and Albany,

New York, in 45 hours. In 1904, he walked 535 miles between New York City and Toronto, Ontario, Canada, in nine days. In 1907 O'Leary walked a mile at the beginning of each hour for 1,000 consecutive hours in Cincinnati, Ohio. At age 35 he started the custom of walking 100 miles in 24 hours on his birthday. O'Leary continued this feat until age 75, completing 100 miles in 23 hours, 54 minutes. O'Leary walked until a tumor in his hip forced him to stop in 1932. He died in Los Angeles, California.

• For the history of pedestrianism and the contributions of O'Leary, consult John Cumming, *Runners and Walkers: A Nineteenth Century Sports Chronicle* (1981), and Tom Osler and Ed Dodd, *Ultra-Marathoning: The Next Challenge* (1979). Obituaries are in the *New York Times*, the *New York Herald Tribune*, and the *Los Angeles Times*, all 30 May 1933.

ADAM R. HORNBUCKLE

O'LEARY, James Lee (8 Dec. 1904–25 May 1975), pioneer in neuroanatomy and neurophysiology, was born in Tomahawk, Wisconsin, the son of James O'Leary, an engineer turned lawyer, and Mary Whalen. Shortly after O'Leary was born, his mother developed a lung infection, and the family had to move to a drier climate. He grew up in San Antonio, Texas. O'Leary's father died when the boy was eleven, and his mother began a real estate business to provide for her children. O'Leary did quite well in school and at the age of sixteen entered the University of Chicago. In 1925 he received his bachelor's degree, and under the influence of Robert R. Bensley of the department of anatomy, he was drawn toward research. With Bensley's assistance, he received a scholarship to study anatomy and entered the doctoral program at Chicago, remaining in the laboratories of Bensley. Other influential professors at Chicago included G. W. Bartelmez and C. J. Herrick, who directed him toward neurology. O'Leary was one of the first students to obtain a degree from the university's joint M.D.-Ph.D. program. After completing the requirements for his doctorate in 1928, he was offered a position at Washington University in St. Louis as an assistant professor of anatomy. O'Leary received his medical degree in 1931 after performing his clinical work at Chicago during the summers.

At Washington University, O'Leary joined George Holman Bishop and Peter Heinbecker in studying the connection between neuron size, function, and conduction rate. O'Leary was fortunate to join these neurologists at a time when specialties in neuroanatomy and neurophysiology were just beginning to be recognized. O'Leary's foundation in neuroanatomy was quickly supplemented by histological training under the direction of Raphael Lorente de No, who taught him the Golgi staining technique used in studying nerve cells, and by neurophysiological instruction during research projects with Bishop. Much of this early time was spent studying the effects of evoked potentials—electrical signals from the brain generated in response to external stimuli such as light, sound, and touch—using electroencephalography (EEG). From 1932 until 1934 O'Leary held the position of assistant professor of anatomy, rising to associate professor of neuroanatomy (1934–1942). He then served in the medical corps during World War II. He was assigned to duty at Mason General Hospital in Brentwood, New York, where he established standards for EEG operation, including duration of testing and placement of electrodes for various purposes, and was head of the EEG department. During this period he also gained experience in psychiatry, because most neurological programs were still focused on neuropsychiatry rather than anatomy or physiology. He attained the rank of lieutenant colonel before returning to Washington University in 1946 as an associate professor of neurology. In 1939, prior to entering the army, O'Leary had married Nancy Lucas Blair; they had two children.

After his return to St. Louis, O'Leary began studying induced epilepsy using EEG. During this time it became possible to monitor the slow voltage changes of the brain using improved EEG equipment, and O'Leary and Sidney Goldring studied these effects extensively. In 1947 O'Leary joined forces with Irwin Levy, a neurologist at Barnes Hospital in St. Louis, to establish a training program for medical students and fellows in neurology and neurosurgery. Students and trainees alike received thorough instruction in both clinical and laboratory neuroscience. In 1963 the neurology training program achieved departmental status within the medical school. O'Leary served as head of the department from its inception until 1970, and actively as professor of neurology from 1947 until his death in St. Louis.

O'Leary's interdisciplinary training fostered an enduring interest in the connection between brain and mind. He authored a number of reviews evaluating the current knowledge and future directions in neurology as related to identifying a link between neuronal activity and behavior, and advocating the continuation of research toward this ultimate goal. He promoted the idea of investigating the neurophysiological component of consciousness, likening the search for the mind within the brain to atomic physicists' search for fundamental matter (*Brain* [1965]). His most detailed review is in the two-part "Cerebral Universe," published in *The Journal of Nervous and Mental Disease* (1965). His fascination with the philosophy of this search for the consciousness underlying the action of neurons is evident in his statement in *Brain* (1965): "Paradoxically, man is unique for having achieved a brain sufficiently rational to doubt its own existence" (p. 779). These essays also document his transition from neuroanatomist to neurophysiologist as he envisioned the function rather than the structure of the neurons as of primary importance in the elucidation of the foundations of behavior.

O'Leary established himself as a leading authority in neurophysiology and epilepsy. He assisted in the formation and setting of rules for the Certification Board of the American EEG Society, and in the alteration of these rules to limit certification of persons with-

out medical degrees. He served as president of the American EEG Society and received its William G. Lennox Award in 1968. The American Neurological Association, which he also served as president, honored him with its highest recognition, the Jacoby Award, in 1971. He consulted for both the National Institute of Neurological Diseases and the National Multiple Sclerosis Society. He authored *Science in Epilepsy: Neuroscience Gains in Epilepsy Research*, with Sidney Goldring (1976), which was published shortly after his death. O'Leary has been described as possessing remarkable commitment and integrity, and he did much by example to promote Washington University as an early leader in the field of neuroscience.

• O'Leary's papers are held by the Archives of the Becker Medical Library at Washington University School of Medicine in St. Louis. A brief biographical sketch is in Russell N. DeJong, *A History of American Neurology* (1982), expanded in Robert B. Aird, *Foundations of Modern Neurology: A Century of Progress* (1994). O'Leary's own book with Goldring, *Science in Epilepsy: Neuroscience Gains in Epilepsy Research* (1976), contains a great deal of information concerning the history of epilepsy research, and most sections end with comments by O'Leary. The reviews by O'Leary lend insight into his philosophical stand on the mind-brain duality; see especially "Matter and Mind: Pursuit of Inaccessibles?," *Brain* 88 (1965):777–86, and "Cerebral Universe," *Journal of Nervous and Mental Disease* 141 (1965): 1–15, 135–54. Obituaries by William Landau appear in *Transactions of the American Neurological Society* 101 (1976): 311–14, and *Journal of the Neurological Sciences* 28 (1976): 255–57.

JOANNA B. DOWNER

OLIN, Stephen (2 Mar. 1797–16 Aug. 1851), college president and Methodist Episcopal minister, was born in Leicester, Vermont, the fifth child of Lois Richardson and Henry Olin, a state legislator and eventually lieutenant governor. Although exposed to Methodist instruction as a child, he showed no particular inclination toward the ministry while at Middlebury College, instead preparing himself for the law and studying philosophy. He graduated in 1820, but too ill to deliver the valedictory, Olin went south for his health and in January 1821 took up a teaching position at Tabernacle Academy, a Methodist institution in the Abbeville district of South Carolina. Health concerns would continue to haunt him. Boarded with a Methodist family and expected to exercise religious leadership, Olin devoted himself to studying the Bible and religious books and to prayer. A conversion experience followed, as did the decision to become a preacher, both detailed in his sustained correspondence with three classmates from Middlebury who also were pursuing the ministry.

Olin entertained a professorship of mathematics and natural philosophy at Middlebury, study at Princeton Seminary, and becoming an Episcopalian, but instead he became junior itinerant to the Rev. James E. Glenn and in January 1824 joined the South Carolina Conference in the Methodist Episcopal church. Appointed to Charleston for what would prove to be his only stint in the parish, he served until July, unable to preach because of diseased lungs (inflammatory bilious fever), for which he was prescribed a grain of mercury a day. In 1825, while stationed at Charleston, Olin launched the *Wesleyan Journal*; then, in 1826, despite ill health, he assumed the professorship of belles-lettres at Franklin College (now the University of Georgia), a post he held for seven years, during which he was ordained deacon (1826) and elder (1828). In 1827 he married Mary Ann Bostick of Milledgeville, Georgia.

Inaugurated as president of Randolph-Macon College in Virginia in 1834, Olin began to exercise national leadership on behalf of Methodism, advocating the church's role in education, missionary work, and theology, about which he made early, important statements. His growing prominence was signaled by three honorary degrees. In 1837, his health again broken, he and his wife sailed for Europe and the Middle East, a trip encapsulated in *Travels in Egypt, Arabia Petraea, and the Holy Land* (2 vols., 1843). While they were abroad, his wife died. Olin attended the Methodist Centenary Conference, and, still abroad, he was elected president of Wesleyan University in Middletown, Connecticut.

Too ill on his return to exercise the office, Olin relinquished the presidency to Nathan Bangs and effectively assumed it only in 1842. Wesleyan, at that time the flagship educational institution of the church, afforded Olin a national platform. Much in demand, he gave speeches and published articles (especially in the *Christian Advocate*); he appeared before annual conferences and frequently delivered sermons. Of particular note was his role at the Methodist Episcopal General Conference of 1844, where the church split over slavery, the precipitating debate centering on whether or not Bishop James O. Andrew of Georgia, a slaveholder, should be removed from the episcopacy. Enjoying a following in both North and South and having a great fondness for the South and southerners, Olin attempted a conciliatory role. He argued that slaveholding was "no disqualification for the ministerial office" (conceding that he had once owned slaves) and defended Bishop Andrew as "pre-eminently fitted to hold that office" and "as one of the greatest benefactors of the African race." In the end Olin realized, however, that the feeling against slavery made it "impracticable for Bishop Andrew to exercise his functions at present" and voted for the Finley motion that called for the suspension of those functions. Once the sectional division was a fact, Olin attempted both publicly and privately to sustain fraternal relations between the churches, making a pilgrimage to the South in 1845, partly for that reason and partly for the sake of his health. In the meantime—in 1843—he had remarried; he and his second wife, Julia M. Lynch, had two children, both sons.

In 1846 Olin traveled to Europe again for his health but also as a delegate from the New England and New York conferences to the organizing meeting of the Evangelical Alliance in London. There, too, he attempted to act on behalf of both the southern and the northern Methodists, effectively resisting ultraism, i.e., an abolitionist plank. He sought a similar conciliation at the organizing of an American Alliance in New York in the spring of 1847.

On Wesleyan's behalf, Olin pressed Methodists and particularly annual conferences for financial support, charging them to accept education as a sacred duty or risk the loss to other denominations of their sons, the church's elite. It was a call to which the church responded and through which he played a key role in the transformation of Methodism. From this period come his published sermons as well as the addresses made on important issues facing the church; both sets of writings were posthumously collected in *The Works of Stephen Olin, D.D., LL.D., Late President of the Wesleyan University* (2 vols., 1853). Elected to both the 1848 and the 1852 General Conference, Olin died in Middletown before the latter was held. Abel Stevens, the historian of Methodism, termed him "the most intrinsically great man, tak[ing] him 'all in all,' that American Methodism has produced."

• On Olin's life, see Matthew Simpson, *Cyclopedia of Methodism* (1878); the article by the editor, Nolan B. Harmon, in *The Encyclopedia of World Methodism* (1974); and [Julia Olin et al., eds.] *The Life and Letters of Stephen Olin* (2 vols., 1853); the *Life and Letters* includes the memorial article by Abel Stevens, reprinted from the *Methodist Quarterly Review* 34 (July 1852): 450–57. Olin's wife also oversaw the posthumous publication of three of his other works: *Youthful Piety* (1853), *Greece and the Golden Horn* (1854), and *College Life: Its Theory and Practice* (1867).

RUSSELL E. RICHEY

OLIPHANT, Elmer Quillen (9 July 1892–3 July 1975), college athlete, professional football player, and administrator, was born in Bloomfield, Indiana, the son of Marion Ellsworth Oliphant, a businessman, and Alice Quillen. At age nine he moved with his family to Washington, Indiana, and attended Washington High School for three years. After his father was swindled out of a large sum of money by his partner in the lumber business, Oliphant transferred to Linton High School in Linton, Indiana, so he could work in his father's coal mine and help pay the family's expenses. He was an all-state end in football at Linton and an outstanding runner on the track team. Oliphant graduated in 1910 and enrolled at Purdue University.

Oliphant worked at a variety of jobs to put himself through college. He still had time to participate in four sports and win 12 varsity letters. Oliphant made All-Western Conference as a baseball outfielder and as a football halfback in addition to being named a Helms Athletic Foundation All-America guard in basketball. He once scored the winning basket from a sitting position in a game against Wisconsin after being knocked down to the floor. During the 1912 football season he scored 43 points against Rose Polytechnic Institute (later Rose-Hulman Institute of Technology) with five touchdowns and 13 consecutive extra points. One of the outstanding dropkickers in football history, Oliphant kicked with a broken ankle a field goal that enabled Purdue to tie Illinois, 9–9, in 1912. The following year he helped lead the Boilermakers to a 4–1–2 record, its best since 1905. At 5′8″ and 178 pounds, Oliphant hit with the momentum of a medium-sized tank, often running over would-be tacklers. He graduated from Purdue in 1914 with a degree in mechanical engineering and gained an appointment to the U.S. Military Academy.

Because of the intercollegiate eligibility rules of the time, Oliphant was allowed to compete in varsity athletics at the service academy. During his first season at West Point, Oliphant played sparingly for the national champion Army team. Some writers have speculated that Oliphant received limited playing time because his egotistical personality irritated West Point coach Charles Daly and some of the players. The following three years, however, Oliphant dominated the Army offense and led the Cadets to records of 5–3–1, 9–0, and 7–1. In addition to winning the 1916 national championship, Army also won both games played against archrival Navy during those years. Oliphant was a consensus All-America halfback in 1916 and 1917. He set longstanding West Point records for most touchdowns (six) and most points scored (45) in one game (against Villanova in 1916) and most points scored (125) in one season set in 1917. In all, Oliphant won 12 varsity letters at West Point while participating in football, baseball, basketball, track, hockey, and boxing. He was also captain of the football and baseball teams. As the first cadet to earn varsity letters in four major sports, Oliphant was awarded a special letter containing a gold star and three stripes. On graduation day, 12 June 1918, he married Barbara "Bobbie" Benedict; they had no children.

After graduation, Oliphant served for one year in the U.S. Cavalry at Fort Sill, Oklahoma. He returned to West Point in 1919 as a physical education instructor, a position he held until 1922. West Point superintendent Douglas MacArthur appointed him as Army track coach in 1921. In his two years at this post, Oliphant coached the Cadets to two undefeated seasons. While serving at West Point, he played two seasons of professional football. In 1920 Oliphant played for the Rochester Jeffersons, a "road team" in the newly organized American Professional Football Association (APFA), renamed the National Football League in 1922. The Jeffersons played only one game against APFA competition that year, which they lost to the Buffalo All-Americans, 17–6. The following year Oliphant was signed by Buffalo, which fielded a very competitive team. With Oliphant leading the way, the All-Americans won their first six games before being tied in a game with the Akron Pros. Two weeks later, Buffalo defeated George Halas's Chicago Staleys (later the Bears) 7–6 to lead the APFA. Although the All-Americans finished the season in first place, they agreed to one final game with Chicago at Wrigley Field. The Staleys won that contest 10–7 and later claimed the APFA championship, but Buffalo contended that the second Chicago contest was merely a postseason exhibition game. During the winter the

league awarded the championship to Chicago. Oliphant led the league in scoring with 47 points and made all of his 26 extra point attempts. In 1922 he left military service and became athletic director at Union College.

After one year at Union, Oliphant took a position with the Metropolitan Life Insurance Company. Over the years he became one of the highest paid executives with the company. He retired in 1957, two years before being selected to the College Football Hall of Fame. In 1969 General Motors established the Elmer Q. Oliphant Scholarship in his honor. He died in New Canaan, Connecticut.

• A newspaper clipping file on Oliphant is at the Professional Football Hall of Fame, Canton, Ohio. The best published sources on Oliphant are L. H. Baker, *Football: Facts and Figures* (1945); Howard Roberts, *The Big Nine: The Story of Football in the Western Conference* (1948); Mervin Hyman and Gordon S. White, Jr., *Big Ten Football: Its Life and Times, Great Coaches, Players and Games* (1977); Alexander M. Weyand, *Football Immortals* (1962); David S. Neft and Richard M. Cohen et al., *Pro Football, the Early Years: An Encyclopedic History, 1895–1959* (1987). An obituary is in the *New York Times*, 6 July 1975.

JOHN M. CARROLL

OLIPHANT, Herman (31 Aug. 1884–11 Jan. 1939), legal educator and federal administrator, was born in Forest, Indiana, the son of Albert G. Oliphant, a farmer and livestock trader, and Martha Jane Richardson. Oliphant spent his early years on the family farm. After grade school, a year's work for his father and as a member of a bridge gang convinced Oliphant to continue his education, first at Danville Normal School and later at Marion Normal College, from which he graduated in 1907 with an A.B. Oliphant married Julia Sims, also of Forest, in 1905; their marriage produced five children. In order to finance his studies and support his family, Oliphant taught English at Marion College until 1911 while continuing his studies in philology, Greek, and philosophy at Indiana University. He obtained an A.B. from that institution in 1909 and pursued graduate studies for two more years. In 1911 Oliphant declined the offer of a fellowship to study philology at Indiana University and instead began legal studies at the University of Chicago Law School. He continued to teach English and mathematics in the evening to support his family and received a J.D. with honors in 1914.

Oliphant immediately accepted a position as an instructor at the law school. In 1915 he was made an assistant professor, in 1916 an associate professor, and in 1919 a full professor. He took pains to develop his teaching technique and made particularly effective use of hypothetical legal cases to enliven classroom discussion and to stimulate independent thought among his students.

In 1921 Oliphant accepted a position as professor of law at the Columbia University Law School in New York City and assumed his duties in 1922, teaching the first-year course in contracts. During his tenure at

Columbia he taught a variety of subjects within his specialization of commercial law, including the law of public utilities, problems of contract law, the law of marketing, and trade regulations. In 1924 and 1925 he shared in the direction of the graduate seminar in the law of business organizations.

Oliphant's legal philosophy can best be described as functionalist or realist. The legal realist movement in the 1920s and 1930s was in part a reaction against the legal formalism of the late nineteenth century, which presumed objective and immutable principles of truth and justice and which still pervaded the appellate courts in the 1920s, and against the "case method" of legal instruction, the content of which seemed increasingly abstracted from the social, economic, and political conditions of society. The legal realists, Oliphant among them, believed that the law could be made more scientific and socially relevant through the application of social scientific methods of statistical and quantitative analysis. Such studies would, they felt, place the law and its rules in a broader social context and provide a functional guideline for both legislators and the courts. As early as 1922 Oliphant reorganized his trade regulations course at Columbia along realist lines. He was among the faculty members who supported curricular reforms at the law school that would have integrated legal studies with the social sciences and created a new "sociological jurisprudence."

The faculty movement for curricular reform at the Columbia Law School reached its peak in 1928, when the appointment of a new dean who resisted the reform impulse led Oliphant and several of his colleagues to resign. Oliphant subsequently accepted an appointment as professor of law in the Institute of Law at Johns Hopkins University in Baltimore, Maryland, where he joined other prominent legal realists such as Hessel E. Yntema in creating a pioneering center for legal research. In 1932 the Institute of Law became the foundation for the New York Law Society and continued as a center for legal research.

Oliphant developed and publicized his ideas in numerous articles and addresses, perhaps the best known of which was his presidential address to the annual meeting of the Association of American Law Schools, "A Return to Stare Decisis" (*American Bar Association Journal* 14 [1928]: 71–76, 107, 159–62). His liberal views became widely known through his writings, his active involvement in the American Bar Association and Association of American Law Schools, and his help in preparing the brief for an important case denouncing so-called "yellow-dog," or company, contracts and the indiscriminate use of labor injunctions by the courts (*Interborough Rapid Transit Co. v. William Green et al, Brief for Defendants*, 1928).

Oliphant also earned repute as a government administrator. During World War I he served as assistant director of War Trade Intelligence and later as assistant director of the Industrial Relations Division of the Emergency Fleet Corporation. However, his greatest public service contributions were made during Franklin D. Roosevelt's administration, when he helped shape the fiscal policies and legislative program of the New Deal.

In March 1933 Oliphant was appointed general counsel to the Farm Credit Administration under Henry Morgenthau. In late 1933 and early 1934 he served as general counsel to the secretary of the Treasury before both he and Morgenthau were moved to the Treasury Department in 1934; there he continued to serve as general counsel.

Oliphant's realist theories and his belief that the law should be used as an instrument of public policy found favor with both Morgenthau and Roosevelt. In early 1935 Oliphant proposed a controversial tax on undistributed corporate profits in order to combat the concentration of economic power in large corporations; this measure became law the following year. In 1938 the president appointed him a member of the Temporary National Economic Committee, a joint legislative and executive body responsible for investigating economic concentration with a view to strengthening federal antitrust policies. As one of the administration's chief fiscal advisers, Oliphant supported New Deal measures such as the devaluation of the dollar, the purchase of silver, and the establishment of a revolving stabilization fund. Oliphant suffered a heart attack in late 1938 and later died at the Naval Hospital in Washington, D.C.

Oliphant's life was spun from three significant threads. His career as an educator was contemporary with the rise of the modern law school and the academic rather than practicing legal educator. His realist legal philosophy represented both a reaction to late nineteenth-century conservatism and an attempt to integrate the social sciences with legal studies to create a sociological jurisprudence that would serve the needs of society. Last, his government service represented an effort to use the theories of legal realism to combat the crisis posed by the Great Depression.

• Oliphant discussed the theory of legal realism in "Current Discussion of Legal Methodology" and "Study of the Operation of the Rules of Law," *American Bar Association Journal* 7 (1921): 241–43, and 9 (1923): 497–500, respectively. Oliphant's works on commercial law for use in law schools include *A Case Book of Business Law* (1920) and *Cases on Trade Regulation* (1923). Useful biographical accounts are in Julius Goebel, Jr., *History of the School of Law, Columbia University* (1955); and Franklin S. Pollock, "Memorial," *Association of the Bar of the City of New York Year Book* (1937): 432–36. Incidental references are in Fleming James, Jr., "The Work of the New York Law Society," *Georgetown Law Journal* 27 (1939): 680–96; and Allen S. Everest, *Morgenthau, the New Deal, and Silver* (1950). An obituary with a list of his publications is in the *New York Times*, 12 Jan. 1939.

MARK WARREN BAILEY

OLIVER, Andrew (28 Mar. 1706–3 Mar. 1774), merchant and public official, was born in Boston, Massachusetts, the son of Daniel Oliver, a merchant, and Elizabeth Belcher. Oliver was a British-American "creole," a member of the generation of colonial aristocrats in the early eighteenth century who were so well assimilated into their New World environment that they devoted their energies to making colonial institutions, economies, and cultural life functional, self-perpetuating, and more fully Anglicized.

From his father Oliver inherited a successful merchant firm, while politically he followed in the footsteps of his maternal grandfather, Massachusetts and New Jersey governor Jonathan Belcher. Having graduated from Harvard with an A.B. in 1724, Oliver received his M.A. in 1727 after defending in Latin the proposition that "precepts of moral law are obligatory under the Christian dispensation." In 1728 he married Mary Fitch, whose dowry included extensive land on the outskirts of Boston; they had three children. She and two of their children died in 1732, leaving him to rear their surviving son, Andrew. The grieving Oliver spent 1733 and 1734 in England making valuable political and mercantile contacts with friends and associates of his uncle Jonathan Belcher.

In 1734 he married Mary Sanford, Thomas Hutchinson's sister-in-law; they had fourteen children. Oliver and his brother and business partner Peter became leaders of the Hutchinson-Oliver faction, which dominated provincial Massachusetts politics until the eve of the American Revolution. Like other established merchants, Oliver strongly opposed the Massachusetts land banks of the 1730s and 1740s and served as a director of the Silver Bank, which sought to restrict currency to notes backed by specie.

Oliver was chosen as the Boston town auditor in 1737, and from that time on he held many burdensome local offices, including justice of the peace, collector of taxes, and overseer of the poor. He was a member of committees responsible for cordwood collection, almshouse management, inspection of public schools, and surveillance of petty criminals in poor neighborhoods. In 1764 the Boston town meeting elected him moderator; thereafter, his involvement in Boston affairs declined. In 1756 he served as a temporary justice of the superior court.

More significant was his legislative service. He represented Boston in the Massachusetts House of Representatives from 1743 to 1746, when the house elevated him to the Massachusetts Council. As part of his duties in the house, he served as the director of the provincial lottery. On the council he served on committees dealing with finance and public charity, dipping into his own pocket to pay for projects he advocated such as street paving, care for the indigent, and public schooling. In 1748 he represented the province in a conference with the Iroquois in Albany, and in 1754 he served at another Indian conference at Casco Bay (now in Maine). The press of work in his business prevented him from attending the Albany Congress later that year, although he did find time to help resettle some Acadian refugees. In 1764 the privy council appointed him to a commission investigating a boundary dispute between New Jersey and New York. In 1756 his old friend Lieutenant Governor William Phips secured Oliver's appointment as secretary of the province, an office he held until 1771 when he was elevated to lieutenant governor.

Oliver was a staunch Congregationalist—trinitarian and Calvinist in theology—and a member of Old South Church in Boston all his life. His contribution toward the cost of church bells for Christ Church in Boston may have been the basis of the myth that he defected to Anglicanism. A leader in the effort to send Congregationalist missionaries among the Indians, he tried to heal the breach between the rival Indian missionary efforts of the (Anglican) Society for the Propagation of the Gospel in Foreign Parts and the (Congregationalist) Society for Propagating the Gospel in New England and Adjacent Parts, which he served for many years first as treasurer and then as secretary. Oliver tried to support the creation of Eleazar Wheelock's missionary school for Indians in Lebanon, Connecticut (a forerunner of Wheelock's school in New Hampshire that became Dartmouth College). But Oliver became embroiled in an acrimonious dispute with Wheelock about financial matters. Oliver's fractious dealings with dissenters were symptomatic of the difficulty of bringing New England Indians under the sway of the region's pious and commercially aggressive elite.

Oliver suffered from deep emotional wounds as the political power of the Hutchinson-Oliver faction waned and the financial position of the family mercantile business declined. Appointed stamp distributor for Massachusetts without his knowledge, he reluctantly accepted the post from which he expected "to reap private benefit." He had heard a rumor that Benjamin Franklin was angling for the same post in Pennsylvania and reasoned that if Franklin could weather criticism over association with the new tax, he could as well. Franklin shrewdly secured the post for his crony, John Hughes, and dissociated himself from the Stamp Act in his famous if ambiguous testimony before the bar of the House of Commons. Although privately opposed to the act, Oliver made the egregious tactical mistake of appearing in early August in public with Jared Ingersoll, stamp distributor for Connecticut. On 14 August 1765, Oliver, the devil, and "Jack Boot" (Lord Bute) were hanged in effigy from the Liberty Tree in Boston. On the breast of his effigy was the confession:

> Fair Freedom's glorious cause I meanly quitted,
> betrayed my country for the sake of pelf,
> But ah! at length the devil hath me outwitted,
> instead of stamping others have hanged my self.

On his right arm were the identifying initials, "A. O."; on his left arm was the celebratory observation, "What greater joy did New England see, than a stampman hanging from a tree" (Shipton, p. 394).

The language was both ritually meaningful and historically significant. The creole elite of mid-eighteenth-century Massachusetts had indeed been identified with the preservation of liberty, but as the Hutchinson-Oliver faction reached for and attained political dominance after 1760, its leaders forfeited the generalized approbation with which Massachusetts repaid its hardworking commercial and landowning leadership. The "joy" of destroying Oliver's reputation for honesty and patriotism was a freshly minted sentiment in 1765 and thus all the more effective. The mob that gathered to view and jeer his effigy on 14 August then marched to the waterfront, where it dismantled his mercantile office on the dock and sawed off the sign bearing an image of Oliver's head. The drunken crowd carried the sign to Fort Hill, where it ritually burned Oliver's visage. The demonstrators then went to his nearby mansion and uprooted his famous garden of fruit trees and flower beds. Goaded by shouts of abuse from Oliver's servants and friends inside the house, the crowd broke down the doors and garden windows and demolished his looking glasses, china, and tea service. Witnesses believed that the crowd would have physically assaulted Oliver had they found him; they only dispersed on being told that Oliver had found safety with Governor Bernard in Castle William (when he was in fact in a neighbor's house).

With remarkable insight, Oliver viewed the crowd as a surrogate for the entire populace: he called his ordeal that of "a single man against the whole people for 36 hours" (Shipton, p. 395). On 17 December 1765 Oliver awoke to find Boston plastered with broadsides demanding his resignation. Standing in the rain under the tree on which he had been hanged in effigy, with the radical Ebenezer Mackintosh at his side, Oliver read a statement prescribed by the demonstrators: "I hereby . . . declare that I never have . . . or [will] take any measures for enforcing the Stamp Act in America, which is so grievous to the people" (Shipton, p. 399). In 1767 the general court finally agreed to compensate Oliver £172 for the damage that the mob did to his property on the condition that the offenders receive immunity from prosecution. Because the privy council disallowed the act, probably because of its immunity provisions, Oliver never recouped the loss.

In the aftermath of the Boston Massacre in 1770, the royal council—now dominated by enemies of the Crown—demanded the removal of British troops from Boston. As the province secretary, Oliver wrote in the minutes of the meeting that "divers gentlemen of the council . . . were of opinion that it was the determination of the people to have the troops removed." The council changed the minutes to show that the people "were so exasperated and incensed, on account of the inhuman and barbarous destruction of a number of inhabitants by the troops" that they demanded the troop withdrawal (Shipton, p. 403). Acting governor Hutchinson asked Oliver to put his account of the council meeting into writing—an account that found its way into print in London under the title *A Fair Account of the Late Unhappy Disturbance at Boston in New England* (1770), as did several indiscreet Oliver letters about colonial discontent and imperial vacillation. In 1771 the council reprimanded Oliver for disclosing secret council business to royal officials in England. In a calculated rebuke to the province, George III personally commended Oliver.

When Hutchinson was finally elevated to the governorship in 1771, Oliver succeeded him as lieutenant governor. Oliver sought the post in part because its new royal salary of £300 compensated him for years of poorly paid service as provincial secretary. That tainted salary, in addition to his long association with the Hutchinson-Oliver faction, destroyed his credibility and subjected him throughout 1773 to vituperative attacks that shortened his life. He suffered a stroke and died two days later in Boston.

• The largest body of Oliver's personal papers is in the Hutchinson-Oliver papers in the British Library, London (transcripts are at the Massachusetts Historical Society in Boston). Clifford K. Shipton's long entry, "Andrew Oliver," is in *Sibley's Harvard Graduates*, vol. 7 (1945): 383–413.

ROBERT M. CALHOON

OLIVER, Andrew (13 Nov. 1731–6 Dec. 1799), jurist and scientist, was born in Boston, Massachusetts, the son of Lieutenant Governor Andrew Oliver and Mary Fitch. A scion of wealth and power, Oliver developed early into a dilettante. At Harvard College he pursued extracurricular studies in French and such arts as music, astronomy, and cryptography. He also developed skill as a jeweler, and his letters often contain comic verse. Graduating with the class of 1749, Oliver continued study toward master's degrees at Yale (1751) and Harvard (1752). John Adams in his diary, while busily trying to find his own career, characterized Oliver in 1758 as a "trifler." Adams noted Oliver's skill in mathematical games and languages but condemned him for having no larger purpose for his life than becoming a "famous Decypherer." Unlike Adams, Oliver was lighthearted and content throughout his life—even when surrounded by tumultuous events.

Oliver married Mary Lynde, the daughter of Chief Justice Benjamin Lynde, in 1752; they had one child. The Olivers lived most of their lives in Salem, the Lyndes' hometown. After serving in minor public offices, Oliver was appointed judge of the inferior court of common pleas for Essex County on 19 November 1761. As county judge, Oliver oversaw the collection of taxes, adjudicated small disputes, and generally acted as county administrator. In 1762 he was also elected as one of Salem's two representatives to the Massachusetts General Court.

In political matters Oliver could be counted on to vote against taxes and duties, but he sided with his relative, Lieutenant Governor Thomas Hutchinson, in 1767 and lost his seat in the assembly. In 1774 Oliver was appointed to the colony's Mandamus Council but quickly resigned when he discovered that a Tory position made him a target of patriot anger. Back in Salem, he tried to regain the approval of the local patriot leaders by declaring that he was ready to join "in the service of my native Country, and for the Support and Vindication of the constitutional Rights, Liberties, and Privileges of British Americans." The declaration rang hollow in patriot ears since he also asked to be excused from the next militia meeting "if the Weather should prove unfavorable" since it put him "at the Risk of a fit of the Gout" (Pickering mss., Massachusetts Historical Society, vol. 1).

Oliver had little concern for revolutionary politics, and when the war began he gave up his job as judge and laid low. While other Olivers and Lyndes went into exile as Loyalists, he remained in Salem committed only to his hobbies—especially his scientific interest in air. "Air," he would write in his only book (1772), "is a grand medium of Nature, through which an all-bountiful providence conveys to us many of the conveniences, comforts, and delights of life." We "are more indebted" to air "than is generally imagined."

Oliver was much interested in science and even published a short description of an epidemic among the Indians of Martha's Vineyard and Nantucket (*Philosophical Transactions of the Royal Society* 54 [1764]: 386–88). In the early 1770s, however, after observing and reading about a comet of 1769, Oliver focused his attention long enough to produce three good scientific studies. The most influential and best was *An Essay on Comets in Two Parts* (1772), in which he offered an innovative explanation for the formation of comet tails and a rational foundation for the older idea that comets were inhabited. His speculations were deduced "from the known properties of air." Oliver's *Essay* was popular enough to be translated into French (1777) and eventually reprinted in Boston in 1811 with Harvard professor John Winthrop's *Two Lectures on Comets*.

Offering experiments, citing sources, and using mathematical calculations, Oliver proposed that comet tails were made up of air, the density of which changed according to the distance from the sun. The air of the tail could support life, and the changing density kept the temperature constant enough to keep that life from freezing or burning. As a man of the Enlightenment, Oliver hoped his *Essay* would discourage the popular notion that comets were "heralds sent forth to denounce the wrath of Heaven." Oliver offered a more "respectable" reason for comets that was "worthy" of a God "who has made nothing in vain."

Oliver's study of air continued over the next few years. He was elected to the American Philosophical Society on 15 January 1773. Two papers he read to the society in 1774 were eventually published: "A Theory of Lightening and Thunder Storms" and "Theory of Water Spouts" (*Transactions of the American Philosophic Society* 2 [1786]: 74–117). Both papers relied heavily on the work of Benjamin Franklin, Joseph Priestly, and European scholars. The first argues that electrical charges reside in air, not clouds, and that the movement and density of air is the key factor for understanding thunderstorms. The second offers a more complex explanation of water spouts than the merely electrical explanation most often given in the eighteenth century. In both cases, as with his study of comet tails, Oliver applied his observations on the properties and characteristics of fluids (he considered air a fluid) to natural phenomena.

Scientific activity in America decreased with the onset of the Revolution, but Oliver joined with John Adams and John Winthrop in the creation, in Massachusetts, of the American Academy of Arts and Sciences. Oliver's own scientific activity, however, succumbed to his illness and diminished finances. He spent the 1780s and 1790s mostly confined to his house, enjoying the conversation of friends. He died in Salem.

• Oliver papers are in the Massachusetts Historical Society, Boston, and the Essex Institute, Salem. Among these, some poems and letters are published in the Massachusetts Historical Society, *Proceedings*, 2d ser., 3 (1886–1887), and in Stephen T. Riley and Edward W. Hanson, eds., *The Papers of Robert Treat Paine* (1992). Oliver's publications and other sources of biographical information are cited fully in Clifford Shipton, *Sibley's Harvard Graduates*, vol. 12 (1962), pp. 455–61. Brook Hindle discusses Oliver in his context and mentions Oliver's description of the Indian epidemic in *The Pursuit of Science in Revolutionary America, 1735–1789* (1956), and Donald K. Yeomans describes Oliver's explanation of comet tails in *Comets: A Chronological History of Observation, Science, Myth, and Folklore* (1991), p. 164.

RICK KENNEDY

OLIVER, Andrew (14 Mar. 1906–20 Oct. 1981), lawyer and art historian, was born in Morristown, New Jersey, the son of William Hutchinson Pynchon Oliver, a lawyer, and Lydia Winthrop Seabury. Following preparation at the Mesa Ranch School near Phoenix, Arizona, Oliver entered Harvard College with the class of 1928, earning his A.B. degree before continuing at Harvard Law School, from which he received the L.L.B. degree in 1931.

After serving for a year as a clerk for his uncle, Judge Samuel Seabury (1873–1958), during his investigation of corruption in New York City government, Oliver entered the firm of Alexander & Green in New York City, with which he remained throughout his legal career, giving his attention to corporate, real estate, trust, and estate matters. He became a partner in 1944 and retired in 1970.

Among Oliver's lifelong interests was the Episcopal church, which he served as a layman in various capacities. While he was on the vestries of both the Church of the Resurrection and Trinity Church in New York, his interests ranged far beyond his own parish. He was a trustee and treasurer of the Protestant Episcopal Society for the Promotion of Religion and Learning in the State of New York, a trustee of the Home for Old Men and Aged Couples and of the Corporation for the Relief of Widows and Children of Clergymen of the Protestant Episcopal Church, and was invested as an officer of the American Society of the most Venerable Order of the Hospital of St. John of Jerusalem, an organization that dates back to the time of the crusades. Also active in the Episcopal Diocese of New York, Oliver served as chancellor of the diocese from 1961 to 1970. The religious organization that interested him most, however, was the General Theological Seminary, which he served as a trustee for nineteen years, accomplishing much to improve the financial condition of the seminary and seeking to make it the finest institution for the training of clergymen. It was for him a family institution, for both of his grandfathers had been professors there. After his work on the planning, financing, and construction of a new library and other facilities, Dean Lawrence Rose described him as "the most valuable, devoted, hard-working member of the Board, either clerical or lay, and unfailingly wise in his counsel." In 1970 he was awarded the degree of Doctor of Canon Law.

Upon retirement from the practice of law, Oliver moved to Boston, where he immersed himself in a new career as well as in the service of a number of learned societies. His interest in history had previously been expressed at the New-York Historical Society, of which he was first vice president. In Massachusetts he was at various times president of the Essex Institute, a trustee of the Boston Athenaeum, chairman of the Associates of the John Carter Brown Library, president of the Colonial Society of Massachusetts, and corresponding secretary of the Massachusetts Historical Society. In each of these organizations his tactful sagacity and willingness to work made him a valuable member. A memorial trustee minute of the Boston Athenaeum could have stood for any of the organizations Oliver served when it stated in part: "Andrew Oliver had a clear concept of the purpose of this institution and his part in it. He thought the Athenaeum was an organization full worthy of a major role in the years ahead. His energies and his excellent mind, as well as his heart, were devoted to our making logical and prompt steps toward that goal."

Even while Oliver practiced law in New York, the seeds of his second career as an art historian germinated. In 1960 he published a catalog of ancestral portraits, *Faces of a Family*. When this meticulously researched volume came to the attention of Lyman Butterfield, editor of the Adams papers, he conceived the idea of having Oliver write two volumes on Adams portraits to complement the volumes of Adams papers. The result was two erudite but eminently readable books: *Portraits of John and Abigail Adams* (1967) and *Portraits of John Quincy Adams and His Wife* (1970). For the rest of his life, Oliver produced a steady stream of books, articles, and reviews, principally in the area of American historical portraiture. In addition to the Adams volumes he wrote *Auguste Edouart's Silhouettes of Eminent Americans, 1839–1844* (1977) and *The Portraits of Chief Justice John Marshall* (1977). With this scholarly interest in portraiture, it was natural for Oliver to be appointed a commissioner of the National Portrait Gallery.

Praised by those who knew him for his enormous capacity for friendship, Oliver was welcomed into the Tavern Club, a group of artistic and literary Bostonians, of which he became president. He also served as chairman of the Walpole Society, a small but dedicated group of scholar-collectors of American antiquities. Among his talents was the ability to write occasional poetry, and the annals of these two clubs contain many examples of Oliver's deft creations.

While Oliver was not ostentatious, he was an elegant gentleman who loved tradition and ceremony. It was therefore fitting that on the occasion of Her Majesty Queen Elizabeth II's bicentennial visit to Boston, Andrew Oliver, descendant and namesake of the Loyalist lieutenant governor Andrew Oliver (1706–1774), was chosen to receive the queen in the council chamber of the Old State House, representing the Loyalists.

In 1936 Oliver was married to Ruth Blake, and they had three children. Despite his many obligations, professional, charitable, and scholarly, Oliver was a devoted family man, finding the time to read to his children, regale them with stories, and teach them in a semi-Socratic manner. All his transactions, whether with family, friends, or associates, were characterized by consideration, kindness, and unfailing good humor. He died in Boston.

• A collection of Andrew Oliver's occasional verse, *Special Occasions*, was published in 1990. The most complete information on him is contained in a memorial volume bearing his name, privately published in 1983 but available in any of the institutions mentioned above. In addition to several essays about him, the memorial volume contains a complete bibliography of his books, reviews, and articles as well as a list of the organizations with which he was affiliated. Information may also be found in the Reports of the Harvard Class of 1928. An obituary is in the *Boston Globe*, 22 Oct. 1981.

ELTON W. HALL

OLIVER, Henry William (25 Feb. 1840–8 Feb. 1904), ironmaster and businessman, was born in Dungannon, Ireland, the son of Henry W. Oliver, a harnessmaker, and Margaret Brown. His parents emigrated and settled in Pittsburgh in 1842. Henry—usually known as Harry—received a common school education and at age thirteen became a messenger at the National Telegraph Company, thanks to former schoolmate Andrew Carnegie. Their lives were often intertwined. In 1855 Oliver began working for Clark and Thaw, pioneers in the freight-forwarding business, before joining Graff, Bennett and Company, ironmakers, as a shipping clerk in 1859. He served with the Twelfth Pennsylvania Volunteers for ninety days in 1861 and as an emergency volunteer in 1863. He married Edith A. Cassidy in 1862, and the couple had one daughter.

Oliver entered business himself in 1861 as a partner in Martin, Oliver and Bickle, operating a small puddling mill in Kittanning, Pennsylvania. Then in January 1863 he joined Lewis, Oliver & Phillips, a new partnership making nuts and bolts. William Lewis ran the shop, John Phillips handled shipping, and Oliver was salesman and office manager. Oliver's brothers David and James joined LO&P in 1866; a rolling mill and expanded product lines were added. By 1880, with sales topping $4 million and 3,000 employees, the firm was one of the largest makers of iron specialities. Lewis retired in 1880, and the firm was restyled Oliver Brothers and Phillips, before being incorporated in 1888 as Oliver Iron and Steel Company.

During this period of dynamic growth in Pittsburgh, Oliver steadily gained stature among the city's business elite. He was appointed a director of the Homeopathic Hospital (1866), the Dollar Savings Bank (1869), and the Central Passenger Railway, a horsecar line (also 1869). He held a common council seat from 1871 to 1882 and was council president in 1871 and 1872. He also gained visibility in state and national politics, as a four-time delegate to Republican conventions (1872, 1876, 1888, and 1892) and a member of the platform committees. A presidential elector in 1880, he lost a bid for the U.S. Senate in 1881. He vigorously backed high tariffs and served on President Chester A. Arthur's tariff commission in 1882.

In business and politics, Oliver's genial personality served him well, inspiring especially the confidence of backers and bankers. His optimism and demeanor were supported by enormous energy and a keen sense of business opportunities. Oliver, like many businessmen, often operated perilously near financial ruin but proved to be a master juggler. As his horizons expanded, he became a pioneer in big business and realized that success in any given field was beginning to require both growth and a willingness to take on new activities.

For example, although Oliver was in the iron business, he worked to improve transportation, as evidenced by his promotion of the Davis Island dam on the Ohio River in the early 1880s. Railroads attracted even more attention, for most businessmen in Pittsburgh believed the Pennsylvania Railroad's freight rates were too high. Oliver was unusual in doing something about it; beginning in 1875, he promoted the Pittsburgh and Lake Erie Railroad (P&LE) and later helped it build a branch to the Connellsville coal fields. His strategy became apparent in 1883 when he arranged for the New York Central, a competing trunk line, to purchase the P&LE and reach Pittsburgh.

Oliver had similar plans for the Pittsburgh and Western Railroad. In 1879 he acquired a small line running north from Pittsburgh and used it to develop another rail connection to the Midwest. As president from 1889 to 1893 and chairman until 1901, Oliver added branch lines across Ohio and then constructed the Pittsburgh Junction Railroad (1883–1884) to link the new line to the Baltimore & Ohio Railroad. His goal seems to have been the creation of a shorter western route for the B&O, which acquired the Pittsburgh and Western in 1893 and absorbed it in 1901.

Oliver also pushed construction of the Fairport Docks on Lake Erie in 1890 as a coal and iron terminal, raising funds from iron producers in Pittsburgh and Youngstown, Ohio. He argued that this facility would promote competition and bring lower railroad rates. For similar reasons Andrew Carnegie built his Pittsburgh, Bessemer and Lake Erie Railroad in 1897. Oliver, however, also formed the American Transportation Company to ship coal and iron on the Great Lakes.

Oliver also expanded the range of activities conducted within his own firms, joining those pioneers who were creating larger, vertically integrated firms to take advantage of the lower costs associated with large-scale operations. First he expanded his line of finished iron and steel goods, then integrated backward to produce his own iron and steel, and finally acquired raw materials and transportation systems. This progression became clear after 1881, as Oliver opened, with his brothers and brothers-in-law, a new wire mill in Pittsburgh, acquired a barbed wire plant in Illinois, and built the Pittsburgh Wire Nail Company in 1882. Then in 1887 they built a new rod mill (previously rods, from which wire was drawn, were imported from Europe) and combined four plants into a single firm, known after 1894 as the Oliver Wire Company.

Oliver also tried to produce steel in 1882, but the experimental process he backed proved a costly failure, and the recession of 1883 placed him in serious financial straits. After he recovered, Oliver began to lease or purchase existing plants to produce his own iron and steel. In 1886 he acquired the Rosena Furnace in New Castle, Pennsylvania, bought Hainsworth Steel in Pittsburgh in 1889, and purchased the Edith Furnace in Pittsburgh in 1891. He further expanded in 1890 by building connections to the Schurz Bridge Building Company and opening the Monongahela Tin Plate Company a year later.

Oliver also underwrote development of steel freight cars, after the plans of inventor Charles Schoen caught his imagination. Oliver moved Schoen, who began producing pressed steel parts for railroad cars in 1888, to Pittsburgh in 1891 and in 1895 became the largest stockholder in the Schoen Pressed Steel Car Company. The company thrived after Carnegie ordered 600 steel hopper cars in 1896; by 1899, with orders for 15,000 cars, Schoen's firm and a leading competitor were joined into the Pressed Steel Car Company. At that point Oliver started a new firm to produce forged-steel car parts, and in 1901 he launched a rival car-building company with Andrew Mellon.

Many business leaders were integrating their firms, connecting materials production and fabrication. But Oliver took the next step and reached backward to control mineral resources. He organized the Monongahela Natural Gas Company, for example, to serve his plants in 1889. Then in 1891 he started leasing coal mines and building coke plants near Uniontown, Pennsylvania, imitating Carnegie, who had gained control of Henry Clay Frick's coal company in 1882. Oliver was far ahead of other steel men, however, in attempting to control iron ore resources. He was the first Pittsburgh ironmaster to grasp the potential of Minnesota's Mesabi range, visiting northern Minnesota in 1892. He instantly recognized the cost advantages of open-pit mining, leased the Mountain Home Mine from developer Lon Merritt (earlier dismissed by Carnegie and Frick), and organized the Oliver Iron Mining Company.

Oliver took a huge gamble because Mesabi iron ore required major changes in smelting practice and equipment. Moreover, the depression of 1893 constricted credit, and even Oliver Iron and Steel was forced into receivership. Oliver pressed ahead, leasing a second mine, but by 1894 he was desperate for capital and turned to Carnegie. His old friend, however, opposed owning iron mines and distrusted Oliver's enthusiasm. "Oliver's proposal is just like him—nothing in it," Carnegie wrote in 1892 (Bridge, p. 259). But when Frick, now Carnegie's partner, proposed that Oliver give Carnegie a half interest in Oliver Mining in return for a $500,000 loan, Carnegie relented and Oliver agreed.

By 1895 Oliver Mining produced half the Mesabi ore and continued to expand. Doing so required Oliver to dance a delicate minuet with Carnegie and John D. Rockefeller, the main force on the Mesabi range. Because of his lake-shipping interests, Rockefeller had backed iron exploration in Minnesota; the depression left him in control of several mines and the Duluth, Missabe, and Northern Railroad. Oliver discounted fears of Carnegie's partners that Rockefeller would move into steel, and in 1895 he negotiated an advantageous arrangement for both parties. Oliver Mining leased Rockefeller's mines, agreed to produce 600,000 tons per year at a reduced royalty, and promised to ship that ore plus 600,000 tons from Oliver's mines on Rockefeller's railroad and ore boats.

Shortly thereafter Carnegie insisted on controlling Oliver Mining and bought all but one-sixth of the stock in 1897. But Oliver remained president, and through 1899 he continued to lease mines, expanding to the Vermilion, Gogebic, and Marquette ranges in Michigan and Wisconsin. Again Carnegie resisted, but Oliver and others eventually convinced him of the value of controlling iron ore. Oliver even provoked a crisis with Rockefeller by acquiring additional Mesabi mines, a breach of the 1895 contract. Although that problem was negotiated away, Oliver further reduced Rockefeller's influence by organizing for Carnegie the Pittsburgh Steamship Company in 1900 to break Rockefeller's stranglehold on lake shipping.

Carnegie, never willing to admit poor judgment, recognized Oliver's accomplishment grudgingly, no doubt coloring subsequent assessments of Oliver. For example, Carnegie's 1912 testimony to a congressional committee investigating U.S. Steel acknowledged his resistance to Oliver's plans, adding, "Fortunately I woke up in time. . . . Harry Oliver, my fellow telegraph messenger, was one of the brightest men Pittsburgh ever could boast of, and he saw far ahead, and went up to that region and loaded himself with ore leases" (Wall, p. 598). But Carnegie next emphasized that only Carnegie Steel had been able to "carry the treasure safely through" (Jordan, p. 62). It would be more accurate to say that Oliver's leases, purchases, creative financing, and complex negotiating and Carnegie's money won the day. But Carnegie did not exaggerate when referring to Oliver Mining as a treasure. In 1901 U.S. Steel paid Oliver $17 million for his one-sixth share; more important, Oliver secured the future for first Carnegie and then U.S. Steel with that high-grade iron ore.

While building his iron empire, Oliver remained active on several other fronts through the 1890s. He brought Oliver Iron and Steel out of receivership in 1895 and remained chairman of the board until his death. He sold Oliver Wire and Monongahela Tin Plate to two different large trusts, and in 1896 he combined other properties (Edith Furnace, Hainsworth Steel Company, his coal leases, and his share of Oliver Mining) into a single integrated firm, Oliver & Snyder Steel. William P. Snyder, a pig-iron broker, operated the company, the industry's third largest coke producer. Oliver later invested in other Snyder ventures related to Crucible Steel. He also had a hand in mining activities, helping to organize the Pittsburgh Coal Company in 1899, the nation's largest coal company. He became a partner in the Chemung Mining Company, another Minnesota venture that acquired long-term leases on smaller mines, then sold them to U.S. Steel in 1903. Finally, Oliver was involved in the Calumet and Arizona Mining Company (later Phelps-Dodge) in Bisbee, Arizona.

Pittsburgh always remained Oliver's home, and he had extensive real estate holdings there, worth an estimated $12 million by 1904. He also planned a huge office building that was built and named for him after his death. And with his brother George he owned four Pittsburgh newspapers. He died in Pittsburgh.

The *Pittsburgh Dispatch* labeled Oliver "One of Pittsburgh's leading captains of industry," but he never escaped Carnegie's shadow. Frick commented in 1897 that "Mr. Oliver is a valuable man, properly controlled, but if he is allowed to run loose, he would soon wreck the credit of any concern he attempts to do business with" (Wall, p. 606). This was Carnegie's view also, but the *Dispatch* added, "He was a man who could dig a hole for himself better and find a way out easier than any other Pittsburgher of his time." Some talked about "Oliver luck," yet his iron-mining efforts proved him to be a shrewd judge of business prospects, a diplomatic negotiator, a skilled financial manipulator, and even a ruthless operator. Oliver understood the radical changes confronting his industry, and his visions shaped the future of the steel industry.

• No Oliver papers appear to have survived, and Henry Oliver Evans, *Iron Pioneer, Henry W. Oliver* (1942), is the only biography—a flattering, reasonably accurate account. Two biographical sketches with bibliographies are Terry Reynolds, "Henry W. Oliver," in *Iron and Steel in the Nineteenth Century: Encyclopedia of American Business History and Biography*, ed. Paul A. Paskoff (1989), and John H. Ingham's entry on Oliver in *Biographical Dictionary of American Business Leaders*, vol. 3 (1983). To understand Oliver's relationship with Andrew Carnegie and his efforts on the Mesabi iron range, see Joseph Frazier Wall, *Andrew Carnegie* (1970), and James H. Bridge, *The Inside History of the Carnegie Steel Company: A Romance of Millions* (1903). Some information on the steel railroad freight car firm can be found in John H. White, Jr., *The American Railroad Freight Car: From the Wood-Car to the Coming of Steel* (1993). A valuable obituary is in the *Pittsburgh Dispatch*, 8 Feb. 1904.

BRUCE E. SEELY

OLIVER, King (11 May 1885–8 Apr. 1938), cornetist and bandleader, was born Joseph Oliver in or near New Orleans, Louisiana, the son of Jessie Jones, a cook; his father's identity is unknown. After completing elementary school, Oliver probably had a variety of menial jobs, and he worked as a yard man for a well-to-do clothing merchant. He appears to have begun playing cornet relatively late, perhaps around 1905. For the next ten years he played in a variety of brass bands and large and small dance bands, coming to prominence about 1915. Between 1916 and 1918 Oliver was the cornetist of trombonist Edward "Kid" Ory's orchestra, which was one of the most highly regarded African-American dance orchestras in New Orleans. Early in 1919 Oliver moved to Chicago and soon became one of the most sought-after bandleaders in the cabarets of the South Side black entertainment district.

In early 1921 Oliver accepted an engagement in a taxi-dance hall on Market Street in San Francisco, and he also played in Oakland with his old friend Ory and perhaps in local vaudeville as well. After a stop in Los Angeles, he returned to Chicago in June 1922, beginning a two-year engagement at the Lincoln Gardens. After a few weeks, Oliver sent to New Orleans for his young protégé Louis Armstrong, who had been Oliver's regular substitute in the Ory band some five years earlier. With two cornets (Oliver and Armstrong), trombonist Honore Dutrey, clarinetist Johnny Dodds, string bassist William Manuel Johnson, drummer Warren "Baby" Dodds, and pianist Lillian Hardin (soon to marry Armstrong), King Oliver's Creole Jazz Band made a series of recordings for the Gennett, OKeh, Columbia, and Paramount labels (some thirty-seven issued titles), which are regarded as supreme achievements of early recorded jazz. (Other musicians substitute for the regulars on a few of these recordings.) There is ample evidence that a great many musicians, black and white, made special and repeated efforts to hear the band perform live.

By early 1925 Oliver was leading a larger and more up-to-date orchestra with entirely new personnel. This group was the house band at the flashy Plantation Cafe (also on the South Side) and as the Dixie Syncopators made a series of successful recordings for the Vocalion label. Oliver took his band to the East Coast in May 1927, but after little more than a month, it dispersed. For the next four years Oliver lived in New York City, touring occasionally and making records for the Victor Company at the head of a variety of ad hoc orchestras; these are widely considered inferior to his earlier work.

His popularity waning and his playing suffering because of his chronic gum disease, Oliver spent an unprosperous six years between 1931 and 1937 incessantly touring the Midwest and the Upper South. Savannah, Georgia, became his headquarters for the last year of his life; he stopped playing in September 1937 and supported himself subsequently by a variety of odd jobs. He died in Savannah of a cerebral hemorrhage; he was buried in Woodlawn Cemetery in New York City. The Reverend Adam Clayton Powell officiated and Louis Armstrong performed at the funeral service. He was survived by his wife Stella (maiden name unknown) and two daughters.

Oliver is the most widely and favorably recorded of the earliest generation of New Orleans ragtime/jazz cornetists, most influential perhaps in his use of straight and plunger mutes; aspects of Louis Armstrong's style clearly derive from Oliver. Oliver's best-known contributions as a soloist are his three choruses on "Dipper Mouth Blues," copied hundreds of times by a wide variety of instrumentalists on recordings made during the next twenty years. His major achievement, however, remains the highly expressive and rhythmically driving style of his band as recorded in 1923–1924. While the band owed its distinctiveness and energy, like all early New Orleans jazz, to the idiosyncratic musical talents of the individual musicians, its greatness was undoubtedly the result of Oliver's painstaking rehearsals and tonal concept.

• Laurie Wright, *"King" Oliver* (1987), is an exceptionally detailed discography and chronicle of Oliver's life, lavishly illustrated with photographs and other documents relating to the artist. For additional important bibliography see the article by Lawrence Gushee on Oliver in the *New Grove Dictionary of Jazz*, ed. Barry Kernfeld (1988). A lengthy obituary is in the *Chicago Defender*, 16 Apr. 1938.

LAWRENCE GUSHEE

OLIVER, Peter (17 Mar. 1713–12 Oct. 1791), colonial merchant, iron manufacturer, and jurist, was born in Boston, Massachusetts, the son of Daniel Oliver, a merchant, and Elizabeth Belcher, daughter of Governor Jonathan Belcher. Disciplined twice at Harvard, first for the theft of a goose and later a turkey, he graduated at the head of his class in 1730, a recognition of his social lineage. In 1733 he received an M.A. by arguing against the proposition that tautology is an ornament of oratory. In the same year he married Mary Clark, daughter of another prominent Boston merchant, Richard Clark. The couple joined Old South Church, where Oliver had inherited his father's rented pew. They had six children who survived infancy.

Oliver and his older brother, Andrew, inherited their father's mercantile firm. In 1744, in partnership with a leading Boston attorney, Jeremiah Gridley, Oliver bought an iron works on the Nemasket River and moved it to Middleborough. Powered by eight water wheels, it was the first rolling mill in the western hemisphere and became by the 1750s one of the largest iron works in North America. Oliver significantly increased his already substantial fortune producing cannon for Massachusetts in King George's War. In 1758 Oliver bought out Gridley's interest.

Preferring the life of a country squire at Middleborough to that of a Boston merchant, Oliver became an expert on scientific agriculture. He published and wrote an appendix for the third edition of Jared Eliot, *Essays Upon Field Husbandry* (1761). In recognition, the British Society for Promoting Agriculture elected him to membership.

In 1744 Oliver became a justice of the peace in Plymouth County, and in 1748 he became judge of the Plymouth court of common pleas. He supervised construction of the Plymouth County courthouse and served as guardian of the Titticut and Mattakeeset Indians. His elevation to the Massachusetts Superior Court in 1756 was widely applauded. Both Oliver and the public delighted in the ostentation of his riding judicial circuit in a coach emblazoned with his coat of arms and driven by postilions and outriders dressed in scarlet livery. After he served terms in the Massachusetts House of Representatives from 1749 to 1751, his fellow legislators elevated him to the council in 1759. He remained on the council until denied reelection in 1766. His public support for the Stamp Act, the growing unpopularity of his brother Andrew Oliver who was then the Stamp Distributor, and the public demonization of his brother-in-law, Lieutenant Governor Thomas Hutchinson, all contributed to his ouster.

Superficially fitting the mold of a New England Tory—haughty, opinionated, wealthy, privileged—Oliver differed temperamentally from the rest of the Hutchinson-Oliver faction. Not viscerally combative, he insulated himself during the Stamp Act crisis in bluff good humor, cultivating, as he said, his potatoes in Middleborough. He wryly requested that Hutchinson inform King George III that, during the riots, he had allowed Crown officials to hide in his pigeon house: "if I am not a man of the first consequence, then there is no man of any consequence at all. I expect a very great reward for my services" (Shipton, p. 744).

The Boston Massacre trials destroyed Oliver's imperturbability. In his capacity as a superior court judge, he presided over the trials of Captain Thomas Preston and the British soldiers directly involved in the shooting. Hutchinson found Oliver to be the only superior court judge who refused to be intimidated by popular outcry against the British troops. Oliver's summary to the jury that the soldiers acted in self-defense did almost as much as John Adams's defense of the accused to win acquittals for all but two of the defendants and conviction on lesser charges for those not acquitted. In 1772, on Hutchinson's recommendation, Oliver became chief justice of the superior court and in 1773 began receiving part of his salary from the Crown under a plan intended to insulate Massachusetts royal officials from political pressure from the legislature. Oliver tried to allay criticism of this arrangement by privately offering a compromise: if the legislature would reimburse him for the £2,000 he had spent out-of-pocket in support of his judicial duties, he would petition the king for permission to decline the Crown salary, or would resign from the bench. By Oliver's account, the assemblymen to whom he broached this offer told him to keep the Crown salary and remain chief justice.

Throughout the summer of 1773 protests against Crown judicial salaries mounted and other judges discreetly declined their royal stipends. Only Oliver refused. In September jurors in Boston and Worcester refused to serve in his court. The House of Representatives voted 92 to 8 to impeach Oliver for accepting his Crown salary and asked the council and governor to remove him from office.

When his brother Andrew died in March 1774, Oliver dared not attend the funeral in Boston. As it was, the mourners who marched to the cemetery did so amid jeers and insults. Had Oliver remained in seclusion in Middleborough, the uproar might have subsided. Instead, he took his place on the bench when the superior court next met in Charles Town in April. The grand juries there denounced him for "sitting as Chief Justice . . . while . . . under impeachment."

In May Oliver asked fellow justice Edmund Trowbridge whether the rest of the court would support him by rebuking and fining obstreperous jurors. Trowbridge hedged his answer by suggesting that, for his own safety, Oliver stay away when the court next met at Plymouth. Oliver agreed but insisted on performing his regular duty of presiding over the court in Boston on 30 August. A crowd of more than one thousand people surrounded the courthouse, restrained only by the presence of British troops. When the jurors refused to serve under Oliver, he and other judges filed out of the courthouse amid the hissing of the crowd. In November 1774 he was dragged bodily from the courtroom, only to return the next day under armed guard. With Boston under virtual martial law, the work of the court ceased.

Unable to return to Middleborough, Oliver remained besieged in Boston for more than a year. He buried his wife in Boston in March 1775, served on Governor Thomas Gage's appointed royal council, and sailed first to Halifax and then to London when the British evacuated the city in March 1776.

The impact of these confrontations on Oliver was traumatic. Confident of his superior virtue and dedication to his colony's well-being, he struggled to find pattern and explanation in the blur of rebellious events. His sometimes vitriolic but also penetrating history, *The Origin and Progress of the American Rebellion*, chronicled intimidation, trickery, and violence by patriot leaders and groups. He reported a particularly telling instance:

[the] clerk of an Episcopal Church at East Haddum in Connecticut, a man of 70 years of age, was taken out of his bed in a cold night, and beat against his hearth by men who held him by his arms and legs, . . . then laid across his horse without . . . clothes and drove to a considerable distance in that naked condition. His nephew, Dr. Abner Beebe, a physician, complained of the bad treatment of his uncle, and spoke very freely in favor of government, for which he was assaulted by the mob, stripped naked, and hot pitch was poured upon him, . . . then carried to a hog sty and rubbed over with hog's dung. They threw the hog's dung in his face and rammed some of it down his throat, and in that condition exposed him to a company of women. (Oliver, p. 157)

The passage resonates with Hobbesian rage, and it preserves with cinematic realism a tableau of ritual humiliation of those who stood in the path of rebellion and refused to yield to the logic of popular sovereignty.

When the British army evacuated Boston Oliver sailed with it. He reached exile in London on 23 June. He traveled extensively in England in 1776 and kept a detailed and perceptive diary of his experiences. The first important Loyalist refugee to abandon London, he moved to Birmingham, England, in the spring of 1778. He was soon joined there by several other Hutchinson and Oliver kinfolk. In 1780 he accepted the proffered governorship of a new Loyalist colony in Maine, which was to have been called "New Ireland." However, the legal difficulty of annulling prior land grants in the region scuttled the project. Oliver died in Birmingham.

• Oliver's papers are in the Hutchinson-Oliver papers, British Library. Oliver's history of the American Revolution languished in manuscript until 1961 when it was published as, *The Origin and Progress of the American Rebellion: A Tory View*, ed. Douglass Adair and John A. Schutz. Clifford K. Shipton, "Peter Oliver," in *Sibley's Harvard Graduates*, vol. 8 (1951), pp. 737–62 is a superb brief biography. See also Robert M. Calhoon, *The Loyalists in Revolutionary America, 1760–1781* (1973); L. Kinvin Wroth and Hiller B. Zobel, eds., *The Legal Papers of John Adams* (3 vols., 1965); Bernard Bailyn, *The Ordeal of Thomas Hutchinson* (1974); and Peter Hoffer and N. E. H. Hull, *Impeachment in America, 1635–1805* (1984). William H. Harrison's paper, "The First Rolling Mill in America," delivered to the 1881 meeting of the American Society of Mechanical Engineers, was published in 1975 in the *Middleborough Antiquarian*.

ROBERT M. CALHOON

OLIVER, Sy (17 Dec. 1910–27 May 1988), jazz arranger, composer, and trumpeter, was born Melvin James Oliver in Battle Creek, Michigan, the son of Melvin Clarence Oliver, a music teacher, concert singer, and choir director. His mother (name unknown) was a music teacher and a church organist. Oliver studied piano from age six but without any special interest in it. Raised in Zanesville, Ohio, from age ten, he decided to play trumpet. He bought a cheap cornet and learned so quickly that he was soon performing with local bands. He switched from cornet to its close cousin the trumpet early on. His father had a stroke, and Oliver in his sophomore year in high school began playing professionally with Cliff Barnett's Club Royal Serenaders to help support himself.

Upon graduating from high school Oliver joined Zack Whyte's Chocolate Beau Brummels in 1927 (or perhaps early in 1928). While with Whyte he acquired his nickname: "I was playing with a bunch of idiots that didn't understand anybody that spoke English. . . . One of them nicknamed me 'Psychology' for no reason except that it was a big word and sounded ridiculous" (Jones, p. 170). Oliver also explained that he began writing arrangements out of frustration with the bandmembers' inability to memorize what was supposed to be played. Despite these frustrations, he praised the band's musical talent highly, and he remained with Whyte until late in 1930, when he spent a few months, extending into 1931, helping Alphonso Trent reconstruct a big band library (collection of instrumental parts) after Trent lost his music in a nightclub fire in Cleveland. In 1931 Oliver returned to Whyte but also played briefly in drummer Speed Webb's big band. During this period his home base was Columbus, Ohio, where he worked as a teacher and a freelance arranger, while making further intermittent returns to Whyte's band.

In 1933 Oliver married Lillian Clark Farnsworth; they had two children. That same year he joined Jimmie Lunceford's orchestra. He intended merely to travel with Lunceford to New York, where he would enroll in school, but the orchestra was such a sensation in New York that Oliver stayed on, becoming for many listeners Lunceford's most significant musician. Oliver sang with the band, and he played many trumpet solos, as heard and seen in the film short *Jimmie Lunceford and His Dance Orchestra* (1936), but his performances were far less significant than his writing. Throughout his early career Oliver had a reputation as an impossibly impatient, tactless, and ill-tempered man, but Lunceford recognized that this contentiousness was due in part to Oliver's quick and creative musicality. Under Lunceford's direction, which was disciplinary and inspirational rather than directly musical, Oliver's creativity reached its peak. Among his best arrangements are his own compositions "Stomp It Off" (1934), "For Dancers Only" (1937), and "Le Jazz Hot," (1939); his versions of the popular songs "My Blue Heaven" (1935), "Margie" (1938), and "'Tain't What You Do (It's the Way That You Do It)" (1939); and above all his reworking of "Organ Grinder's Swing" (1936). In this arrangement of a childlike folk tune (familiar from the lyrics "I like coffee, I like tea") is merely the launching point for a creative exploration of stark and unusual instrumental groupings and contrasts, inspired in part by Duke Ellington's "Mood Indigo" and all presented within the context of a lilting rhythmic bounce and politely bluesy harmonies.

Tiring of the rigors of the traveling musician's life, Oliver left Lunceford in mid-1939, again with the intention of going to school in New York, but instead he immediately joined Tommy Dorsey's orchestra as an arranger when Dorsey made a spectacular offer of a $5,000 raise in salary and no obligation to tour with the band. Oliver's arrangements of "On the Sunny Side of the Street" and his own "Opus No. 1" were perhaps the finest swing tunes that Dorsey's big band performed. These were probably written in 1943, but owing to the musicians union's recording ban then in force, Dorsey did not cut studio versions of these titles until late the following year, by which time Oliver was in his second year as an army bandleader, in which capacity he resumed playing trumpet from 1943 to 1945.

After leading his own band in New York in 1946, Oliver worked for record companies as a music director and supervisor, initially in a decade-long association with Decca. He wrote and conducted arrangements for such notables as Lionel Hampton, Billie Holiday, Louis Armstrong, Ella Fitzgerald, Sammy Davis, Jr., Jackie Gleason, Pearl Bailey, Gene Kelly, Judy Garland, Frank Sinatra, and Danny Kaye.

In December 1967 Oliver traveled to Paris, where he became musical director at the Olympia Theater (1968 to Feb. 1969). Back in New York he resumed playing trumpet to lead a nonet that debuted at the Downbeat in April 1969 and then held residencies at the Riverboat, the Rainbow Grill, and the Americana. Oliver reorchestrated his well-known big-band arrangements and also arranged many other popular songs for the nonet, as heard on the album *Yes, Indeed!*, recorded in Paris in 1973. In 1974 Oliver returned to Europe with the memorial Tommy Dorsey band under trombonist Warren Covington's direction. From 1974 to 1984 Oliver's nonet held a residency at the Rainbow Room on top of the RCA building in New York. The group also performed at jazz festivals. In the mid-1970s he was one of four musical directors of the short-lived New York Jazz Repertory Orchestra, pioneering an effort to keep jazz masterpieces alive long before the formation of the Lincoln Center Jazz Orchestra. He retired in 1984. Oliver died in New York City.

One of the best arrangers of the swing era, in his finest pieces Oliver exhibited an interest in drawing novel sound combinations from a conventional big band and had the talent to do so without sacrificing a sense of orchestral balance and relaxed swing.

• A large collection of scores, parts, and memorabilia is held at the New York Public Library for the Performing Arts, Lincoln Center. Oliver gave a few arrangements to the Carl Haverlin-Broadcast Music, Inc., Archives in New York; see Jon Pareles, "Oliver Donates Notes to Jazz Archive," *New York Times*, 22 Apr. 1984. For interviews, see George Simon, "Sy Oliver: The Most Surprised Party is Me"! *Metronome* 62 (Feb. 1946): 23, 41; Bill Coss, "Triple Play," *Metronome* 77 (Nov. 1960): 40–41, 48–50; Henri Renaud, "Sy Oliver à Paris," *Jazz Hot*, no. 245 (Dec. 1968): 41; Stanley Dance, "The Return of Sy Oliver," *Jazz Journal* 23 (Sept. 1970): 2–5, repr. in Dance, *The World of Swing* (1974), pp. 125–34; John S. Wilson, "Sy Oliver's 9-Piece Band at Riverboat," *New York Times*, 3 July 1970; Wilson, "Sy Oliver," *International Musician* 69 (Jan. 1971): 7, 17; Claude Carrière: "Welcome, Sy Oliver," *Jazz Hot*, no. 294 (1973): 16–17; Max Jones, "Oliver: The Insider," *Melody Maker* 49 (27 Apr. 1974): 58, 66, repr. in Jones, *Talking Jazz* (1987), pp. 170–75; Brian Priestley, "Sy Oliver," *Into Jazz* 1 (1974); Zane Knauss, *Conversations with Jazz Musicians* (1977), pp. 150–177; and Dempsey J. Travis, *An Autobiography of Black Jazz* (1983). Albert McCarthy traces Oliver's affiliations in *Big Band Jazz* (1974). For detailed musical assessment of his contributions to Lunceford and Dorsey, see Gunther Schuller, *The Swing Era: The Development of Jazz, 1930–1945* (1989). A catalog of recordings with Oliver as leader is Charles Garrod, *Sy Oliver and His Orchestra* (1993). An obituary is in the *New York Times*, 28 May 1988.

BARRY KERNFELD

OLLOKOT (Dec. 1844?–30 Sept. 1877), Nez Percé war chief, whose name has also been spelled "Ollicut" or "Alokut," was the son of Tuetakis (Old Joseph), the head of a band of upper Snake River Nez Percés, and Etoweenmy. His older brother was Heinmah-Tooyalatkekht (Chief Joseph). The name Ollokot, meaning Frog, was taken from his paternal grandfather, a Cayuse leader. Ollokot was probably born at the Presbyterian mission near Lapwai Creek, Idaho, where his father then resided and where Ollokot was baptized "Joseph." In 1847, when the mission closed, Tuetakis returned to his traditional range, wintering at the mouth of the Grande Ronde River in Washington and spending summers in the Wallowa Valley in Oregon. When he died in 1871 he left his sons with the tasks of preserving their homeland from the encroachments of white settlers and resisting attempts to force the band to move to a reservation created at Lapwai by a fraudulent treaty of 1863. The treaty had not been signed by the headmen of several important Nez Percé bands, including the Grande Ronde–Wallowa band, and Tuetakis had regarded the treaty as invalid, refusing to move or to accept annuities under it.

Ollokot and Chief Joseph shared the band leadership, Ollokot serving as the war chief and his brother handling the civil duties. Ollokot, the more impassioned of the two, also managed much of the political debate (a relative once acknowledged that Ollokot "had more influence because he was the better speaker"). Whites dealing with the brothers repeatedly mixed them up, and further confusion arose because both were widely called "Joseph." Some referred to Chief Joseph as "Young Joseph" to distinguish him from his father, while others applied the same name to Ollokot to differentiate him from his older brother. Local settlers referred to them as "the Joseph boys." Disentangling the roles of the chiefs is thus difficult, and much that has been popularly attributed to Chief Joseph was actually done by Ollokot. Apparently it was Ollokot who helped rescue a pioneer family from the swollen Wallowa River in June 1875 and negotiated with Lieutenant Albert G. Forse, who was sent to the valley in 1876 when relations between the Indians and whites deteriorated.

Ollokot assisted Chief Joseph in protesting U.S. penetration into the Wallowa Valley after 1871, using maps that he created to illustrate his band's use of the region. When the U.S. government ordered all Nez Percés onto the Lapwai reservation in 1877, Ollokot arranged a meeting between General Oliver Otis Howard and the nontreaty bands in a futile search for alternatives. When conflict subsequently broke out, Ollokot's popularity with the warriors, his fighting ability, and his position as war chief of the largest band allowed him to play a major role during the Nez Percés' retreat from Idaho over the Bitterroot Mountains and across Montana into Canada. It was under his leadership that the Indians defeated Captain David Perry's superior force at White Bird Canyon (17 June 1877), fought troops under Colonel John Gibbon at the Big Hole (9–10 Aug.), and forestalled General

Howard's advance by attacking his camp at Camas Meadows (20 Aug.). The Indians were finally cornered in the Bear Paw Mountains, close to the Canadian line, and Ollokot was killed. Chief Joseph surrendered, simply referring to his brother as "he who led the young men."

Ollokot was married twice. His first wife was Aihits Palojami (Fair Land), with whom he had two sons who survived infancy. Following her death, he married Wetatommi; their only child died in infancy.

Over six feet tall, elegant, lithe, and handsome, Ollokot was, as General Howard testified, intelligent, "frank, open-hearted, and generous . . . full of fun and laughter." Nez Percés chiefly remembered his prowess as a warrior ("always in lead of every fight"), but his other talents suggest that had he survived he would have become one of the tribe's most important leaders.

• References to Ollokot are scattered and fragmentary. Important Indian testimony can be found in Duncan McDonald, "The Nez Perce, the History of Their Troubles and the Campaign of 1877," *New North-West*, 26 Apr. 1878–28 Mar. 1879, reprinted, with an introduction and notes by Merle W. Wells, in *Idaho Yesterdays* 21, no. 1 (1977): 2–15, 26–30, and no. 4 (1978): 2–10, 18–28; Edward S. Curtis, *The North American Indian*, vol. 8 (1911); Lucullus V. McWhorter Papers, Washington State University Library, especially the interview with Ollokot's wife Wetatommi (folder 170); and McWhorter, *Yellow Wolf* (1940) and *Hear Me, My Chiefs!* (1952). Other significant primary material is in Henry Clay Wood, *Supplementary to the Report on the Treaty Status of Young Joseph* (1878); Oliver Otis Howard, *Nez Perce Joseph* (1881); Cyrus Townsend Brady, *Northwestern Fights and Fighters* (1907); and *The Minutes of the Synod of Washington* (1936). Among secondary works, Alvin M. Josephy, Jr., *The Nez Perce Indians and the Opening of the Northwest* (1965); Grace Bartlett, "Ollokot and Joseph," *Idaho Yesterdays* 21, no. 1 (1977): 22–25, and *The Wallowa Country, 1867–1877* (1984); and Mark H. Brown, *The Flight of the Nez Perce* (1967), are particularly useful.

JOHN SUGDEN

OLMSTEAD, Albert Ten Eyck (23 Mar. 1880–11 Apr. 1945), historian, was born in Troy, New York, the son of Charles Olmstead, a farmer and storekeeper, and Ella Blanchard. Olmstead attended Cornell University on a scholarship, receiving his A.B. in 1902 and remaining for postgraduate study under Nathaniel Schmidt. After receiving an A.M. in 1903, he was among the students and faculty from Cornell who accompanied Schmidt to Jerusalem when Schmidt became director of the American School of Oriental Research there. Olmstead held the Thayer Fellowship at the Jerusalem School in 1904–1905. Awarded a Ph.D. from Cornell in 1906, he returned to the Near East with a fellowship from the American School of Classical Studies in Athens. In 1907–1908 he served as the director of the Cornell University Expedition to Asia Minor and the Assyro-Babylonian Orient, a small contingent of young men who recorded archaeological sites and ancient inscriptions in remote areas of Anatolia and Mesopotamia.

On his return to the United States, Olmstead taught Greek and Latin at the Princeton (N.J.) Preparatory School in 1908–1909. He joined the faculty of the University of Missouri in 1909 and taught ancient history there until 1917, when he moved to the University of Illinois as professor of ancient history and curator of the Oriental Museum. In 1913 Olmstead married Cleta Ermine Payne, a collaborator and colleague; they had three children. In 1929 he became a professor of Oriental history at the University of Chicago's Oriental Institute, where he remained until his death.

His doctoral dissertation, *Western Asia in the Days of Sargon of Assyria, 722–705 B.C.*, published in 1908, was extraordinary in its time for presenting a methodical critique of the textual sources as the basis for a synthesis of political history. Critical method and historical synthesis remained the central themes of Olmstead's later work. Olmstead's foremost treatment of method is his classic monograph on *Assyrian Historiography* (1916). At a time when the propagandistic annals of Assyrian kings were sometimes used naively in modern histories, the most polished propaganda being treated as the best historical source, Olmstead's monograph showed how principles of text-criticism and source-criticism were to be applied not only to the statements of the Assyrian kings themselves, but also to later Babylonian records of Assyrian history and to still later classical accounts that survived only in flawed epitomes quoted by the church fathers. His subsequent treatments of text-criticism, source-criticism, and method ranged from essays on the Hebrew and Greek texts of Old Testament books to evaluations of sources for the history of the Near East in late antiquity and a personal retrospective survey ("History, Ancient World, and the Bible: Problems of Attitude and of Method," *Journal of Near Eastern Studies* 2 [1943]: 1–34).

A series of detailed articles on sources and problems in Assyrian and Babylonian history laid the foundations for the first of his large historical syntheses, *History of Assyria* (1923). It was explicitly modeled on James Henry Breasted's *History of Ancient Egypt* (1905) in its aim to bring an ancient civilization to life, not as part of the background of the Bible, but as an autonomous historical entity in an accessible style. Breasted's work was also the nominal model for Olmstead's *History of Palestine and Syria* (1931), which put Old Testament historical sources into a common framework with Mesopotamian and West Semitic epigraphic evidence. His *Jesus in the Light of History* (1942) strove to treat New Testament accounts in the historical context of the Roman Near East. Shorter synthetic works include articles surveying the history of the neo-Babylonian kingdom in Mesopotamia and the vital social and political history of the Near East in the mid-third century A.D. Olmstead's final large work, *History of the Persian Empire*, was published posthumously in 1948. Relying heavily on Greek and Latin authors for the narrative political history of the Achaemenid state, he strove again (with mixed success) to interpret the facts of the narrative in a context of social and cultural history that did not come from Greek and Latin views of a barbarian Orient, but from the modern study of the ancient Near East, reaching back millennia into the histories of ancient Egypt and Mesopotamia. Articles from the last few years of Olmstead's life and obituaries of Olmstead refer to still more general historical books in progress: one on the history of New Testament times and another on the history of the Near East in late pre-Islamic times.

Olmstead repeatedly called for a change of emphasis and disciplinary context in the modern study of ancient Near Eastern history, away from cultural exposition in departments of philology and toward political history and comparative study in departments of history. In 1910 he was one of a group of young scholars who founded a section on ancient history in the American Historical Association. The contemporary impact of his publications was recognized in his elections as president of the American Oriental Society in 1922 and president of the Society for Biblical Research in 1941. Shortly before his mandatory retirement, Olmstead died in Chicago.

Few contemporaries and successors have encompassed as much of the pre-Islamic Near East as did Olmstead in historical research and exposition. While his approach may sometimes seem quaint and outdated, his emphasis on relationships between philology and history and his concern for breaking through the disciplinary boundaries that isolate categories of privileged sources from a broader context of historical connection remain at the center of ancient Near Eastern research. His large historical books have been superseded by substantive progress in research, changes in assumptions about humankind and history, and historiographic standards that have grown more stringent as factual knowledge has become more precise. Some of his books are targeted as historical baselines for rejection, amendment, or rebuttal, but few of them have been replaced by works of comparable scope. His essays on historiography and method, which abound in statements of startling vitality, are his most durable work.

• Obituaries of Olmstead are in the *Bulletin of the American Schools of Oriental Research* 99 (Oct. 1945) and the Olmstead memorial issue of the *Journal of Near Eastern Studies* 5, no. 1 (1946), both by John A. Wilson; and in the *New York Times*, 12 Apr. 1945.

MATTHEW W. STOLPER

OLMSTED, Denison (18 June 1791–13 May 1859), astronomer, was born in East Hartford, Connecticut, the son of Nathaniel Olmsted and Eunice Kingsbury, farmers. Olmsted obtained a broad education at an early age, which included instruction in arithmetic by Governor John Treadwell. He entered Yale College in 1809 and completed an A.B. in 1813. Financial difficulties caused Olmsted to temporarily cease his studies, and from 1813 to 1815 he taught at the Union School in New London. In 1815 he became a tutor at Yale, which allowed him to continue his studies in the-

ology at the college, but his career plans changed suddenly in 1817 when he was offered a professorship in chemistry at the University of North Carolina. After several months of intensive training in the sciences under Benjamin Silliman, who was professor of chemistry and natural history at Yale, Olmsted began teaching at North Carolina in 1818. That same year Olmsted married Eliza Allyn; the couple had seven children. After her death Olmsted married Julia Mason in 1831.

At Olmsted's instigation, North Carolina established its first state geological survey in 1822, and in the following year he was appointed state geologist and mineralogist. Under his guidance an extensive survey was made of North Carolina's natural resources; this work formed the basis for a number of papers that he subsequently published on the geology of that state. In 1825 Olmsted returned to Yale to become professor of mathematics and natural philosophy. In 1836, at Olmsted's request, a separate professorship was established in mathematics; Olmsted then became professor of astronomy and natural philosophy.

During his tenure at Yale, Olmsted greatly improved science instruction at the college by conducting experiments during his lectures and by introducing laboratory exercises for the students. The lack of good science textbooks prompted Olmsted to write a number of general works on natural philosophy and astronomy, including his *Introduction to Natural Philosophy* (1831–1832), *Compendium of Natural Philosophy* (1833), *Introduction to Astronomy* (1839), *A Compendium of Astronomy* (1839), and *Rudiments of Natural Philosophy and Astronomy* (1844). He also wrote a more popular work, *Letters on Astronomy, Addressed to a Lady* (1840), which he composed at the request of the Massachusetts Board of Education. Several of these textbooks went through many editions and remained in use until the turn of the century.

Olmsted contributed to a number of sciences ranging from physics to meteorology. In 1830 he published in the *American Journal of Science and Arts* a new theory on the causes of hail that rejected the idea that atmospheric electricity was its primary cause. He suggested, instead, that hail was produced when a body of warm humid air suddenly mixed with a body of extremely cold air high in the atmosphere. The eventual success of this theory derived from its ability to explain many of the observed characteristics of hailstorms.

It was in astronomy, however, that Olmsted made his most important contributions. His investigations fell into three main areas: shooting stars, the aurora, and the zodiacal light.

A spectacular display of shooting stars on 13 November 1833 led Olmsted to formulate a theory of shooting stars that became the foundation for the currently accepted theory of meteor showers. The event was unusual both for the numbers of meteors seen and for the fact that they appeared to radiate from a single point in the sky. To explain these observations Olmsted proposed the existence of a "nebulous body" similar to a comet as the source for these meteors. He calculated that the orbit of this nebulous body around the sun brought it near the earth and that as material from this body was drawn by gravitation into the earth's atmosphere, it "took fire" and burned away. Olmsted's explanation of the phenomenon allowed for the possibility of the event reappearing annually, which he observed it to do for the next five years. One of Olmsted's students, Edward C. Herrick, later refined this theory and demonstrated the existence of other meteor showers.

Shortly after completing his theory of shooting stars, Olmsted turned his attention to the problem of the aurora. Again he was concerned with establishing its origin and physical causes. He disagreed with those who thought the aurora was a terrestrial phenomenon and with the idea that it was produced by electricity. He argued, instead, that the aurora originated outside the earth's atmosphere. This led Olmsted to theorize that the aurora occurs when a nebulous body of light, flammable, semitransparent magnetic matter, revolving around the sun, is drawn by the earth's gravity into the atmosphere. Thus, there were certain analogies for Olmsted between meteors and the aurora in that they both were caused by nebulous bodies coming into contact with the earth's atmosphere.

Within the context of these ideas, Olmsted proposed in 1851 an explanation for the zodiacal light. Once more he invoked a "nebulous body," orbiting the sun along a path slightly inclined to the ecliptic, as its cause. In fact, he suspected that both the November meteor shower and the zodiacal light might be caused by the same object.

Olmsted taught at Yale until his death. His skills as a teacher and contributions as a researcher were widely acknowledged, and his ideas regarding hail, meteor showers, and the aurora influenced many later theories. Olmsted was also an active member of the American Association for the Advancement of Science. He died in New Haven, Connecticut.

• Olmsted's papers are in the Yale University Library (NUCMC 74-1197). Many of Olmsted's most important papers appeared in the *American Journal of Science and Arts*, and among those the most notable are his "Observations on the Meteors of November 13th, 1833," 26 (1834): 132–74; "On the Cause of the Meteors of November 13th, 1833," 29 (1836): 376–83; "On the Meteoric Shower of November, 1836," 31 (1837): 386–95; and "Observations on the Zodiacal Light, with an Inquiry into Its Nature and Constitution, and Its Relations to the Solar System," 12 (1851): 309–22. His theory explaining the aurora appeared in "On the Late Periodical Visitation of the Aurora Borealis," *Proceedings of the American Association for the Advancement of Science* 4 (1850): 51–56. A complete bibliography of Olmsted's works is given in Franklin B. Dexter, *Biographical Sketches of the Graduates of Yale College* (1912): 594–600. For a modern assessment of Olmsted's astronomical work, see Theodore R. Treadwell, "Denison Olmsted, an Early American Astronomer," *Popular Astronomy* 54 (1946): 237–41.

MATTHEW R. GOODRUM

OLMSTED, Frederick Law (26 Apr. 1822–23 Aug. 1903), landscape architect and travel writer, was born in Hartford, Connecticut, the son of John Olmsted, a dry goods merchant, and Charlotte Hull. Olmsted's mother died when he was three, and between the ages of seven and fifteen he received most of his schooling from ministers and private academies outside Hartford. In 1837, when he was about to enter Yale College, severe sumac poisoning weakened his eyes, leading to a decade of desultory education at the hands of a civil engineer and several farmers, interspersed with seven months with a dry goods firm in New York City, a year-long voyage to China, and a semester at Yale. In 1848 his father bought him a farm on Staten Island, where he lived for the next eight years, practicing scientific agriculture with special interest in tile drainage of soils. He read widely in these years, being especially influenced by Horace Bushnell, Thomas Carlyle, and John Ruskin. Spurred by his father's love of natural scenery, he read many of the classic eighteenth-century British writers on landscape.

In 1850 a six-month walking tour of the British Isles and the Continent led to publication of Olmsted's first book, *Walks and Talks of an American Farmer in England*. During the trip he visited Birkenhead Park near Liverpool, which he enthusiastically described in an article in A. J. Downing's *Horticulturist*. During a second tour in 1856 he saw designed landscapes in Italy and the German states, visited the new parks of Paris, and while living in London for six months became familiar with many of the parks in that region. A three-month official visit to English and Parisian parks in 1859 completed his early study of European park administration and design.

In December 1852 Olmsted began the first of two trips through the slaveholding South that lasted a total of twelve months. Between February 1853 and June 1854 he wrote sixty-four letters for the *New York Times* describing his travels. From these he wrote three volumes of description and analysis: *A Journey in the Seaboard Slave States* (1854), *A Journey through Texas* (1856), and *A Journey in the Back Country* (1860). They comprise the most extensive and detailed description of the society of the antebellum South by a contemporary observer. Assisted by the antislavery advocate Daniel Reaves Goodloe, Olmsted also published in 1861 a two-volume compilation titled *The Cotton Kingdom*. In his first series of letters of 1853–1854, Olmsted concluded that all elements of southern society suffered from the existence of slavery. He was particularly troubled by the lack of towns and the exchange of services and knowledge that they facilitated. His analysis had considerable influence on the developing free soil doctrines of the Republican party. Olmsted's experiences in the South caused him to dedicate himself to raising the cultural level of the North in order to demonstrate the superiority of free-labor society. As he reported to his friend Charles Loring Brace in a letter of 1 December 1853, he wished to foster popular institutions of culture that would enable all classes to acquire "refinement and taste and the mental & moral capital of gentlemen." The letters he wrote in 1854 and 1857 describing his second trip, through Texas and the "backcountry" from November 1853 to

August 1854, expressed increasing concern about the threat of slavery expansion to free-labor society in the trans-Mississippi West. He befriended Adolf Douai, editor of the antislavery *San Antonio Zeitung*, and solicited funds for him in the North. During the "Bleeding Kansas" furor of 1855–1857 Olmsted raised funds to purchase weapons for the defense of the free soil settlement of Lawrence, worked with the New England Emigrant Aid Society to establish antislavery settlers in northern Texas, and wrote an impassioned introduction to an edition of *Englishman in Kansas* (1857), the reminiscences of an English reporter, Thomas H. Gladstone.

From 1855 to 1857 Olmsted pursued a publishing career as a partner in the firm of Dix & Edwards and managing editor of *Putnam's Monthly Magazine*, which published original literary works, including pieces by Herman Melville and Henry David Thoreau and featured antislavery editorials by the magazine's sub rosa editors Parke Godwin and George W. Curtis. When the publishing venture failed in the summer of 1857, Olmsted's literary connections helped secure him the position of superintendent of Central Park in New York City. At that time the new board of park commissioners rejected the plan for the park adopted by the previous board and launched a design competition. Olmsted prepared the winning entry with the English-born architect Calvert Vaux. Their plan, "Greensward," was notable for its emphasis on the experience of landscape and for sinking the four required transverse roads below the line of sight. From early 1859 to June 1861 Olmsted was architect in chief of the park, organizing the work and directing a force of as many as 4,000 men. During this time he and Vaux redesigned the interior circulation system of the park, creating three entirely separate sets of ways—walks, bridle paths, and carriage drives.

In 1859 Olmsted married Mary Perkins Olmsted, the widow of his brother John Hull Olmsted, with whom she had three children. One of them was John Charles Olmsted, whom he adopted and who became his partner in 1884. Olmsted and his wife had two children, including Frederick Law Olmsted, Jr., who was a partner in the Olmsted firm from 1898 to his retirement in 1949.

In 1861 Olmsted's reputation as an administrator led to his appointment as the chief executive officer of the U.S. Sanitary Commission, which was charged with overseeing the camp conditions and health of the volunteer soldiers in the Union army, the vast majority of its troops. Olmsted organized a sanitary inspection system, took part in reorganizing the Army Medical Bureau, and directed a fleet of Sanitary Commission hospital ships during the Peninsula Campaign of 1862. He created a national relief system that drew from all states and distributed medicine and clothing throughout the army. In this role he demonstrated his ability to make comprehensive plans and to define the detailed steps needed to carry them out; he also demanded broad administrative powers and displayed an impatience with official superiors. His frustration with

the commission's executive committee and difficulties with independent sanitary commissions based in midwestern cities led him to resign his post in the summer of 1863.

At the same time, Olmsted was actively involved in planning for the Reconstruction that would follow the war. His antebellum observation of slaves convinced him that he was one of the best qualified men in the North to direct policy concerning the freedmen. He wrote the legislation establishing the Port Royal experiment in the South Carolina sea islands in 1862 and was disappointed that he was not put in charge of that undertaking. In order to strengthen the Lincoln administration after the Emancipation Proclamation, he helped organize the Union League Clubs of New York and Philadelphia. He also attempted to found a journal that would gain support for abolition of slavery as an aim of the war. His associate in this venture was Edwin L. Godkin, who became editor of the new publication, the *Nation*, when funding became available while Olmsted was in California in 1863–1865. During late 1865 and early 1866, a time of crisis, he provided important help to Godkin as assistant editor of the *Nation*.

During the last two years of the Civil War, instead of participating in the war and planning for Reconstruction, Olmsted was general manager of the vast Mariposa gold mining estate in the foothills of the Sierra Nevada. He justified this change as a way to secure economic independence, but the salary and stocks the owners offered him were as ephemeral as the played-out veins of gold on the estate. The company failed within two years of his arrival in California, but his western sojourn did expand his landscape design career. He served as chairman of the first commission in charge of the Yosemite Valley and Mariposa Big Tree Grove, planned a system of public pleasure grounds for San Francisco and a campus for the College of California at Berkeley that was not carried out, and designed his only cemetery—Mountain View in Oakland. At this time he began to develop a water-conserving style of landscape design suitable for the semiarid American West. While at Mariposa he closely studied the young society of the California gold mining camps and wrote a treatise on the effect of immigration and the frontier on American institutions and national character.

In the fall of 1865 Olmsted returned to New York City to join with Vaux in planning Prospect Park in Brooklyn and resume work on Central Park. He believed that he was turning to an urban frontier that was as challenging as the slaveholding South or mining-camp West: the eastern metropolis was essentially a new society, the most "heart-hardening and taste-smothering" place of all.

From this time forward Olmsted and Vaux consistently used the title "landscape architect" to describe themselves. Prospect Park was the single most important commission during the years of their partnership, 1865–1872. Especially notable is the Long Meadow, a classic passage of pastoral scenery with gracefully modulated terrain of greensward, scattered groves of trees, and indefinite boundaries that create a sense of unlimited space. Such landscape, Olmsted believed, was a specific medical antidote to the artificiality of the built city. He designed the scenery to relieve stress and subordinated all elements of the design to the central purpose of affecting those in it by an "unconscious" process, powerful and regenerating.

In 1868 Olmsted and Vaux began to design the park system of Buffalo, New York, their first comprehensive and unified system and one that Olmsted revised and expanded over the next twenty years. An innovation that the two men introduced in Brooklyn and Buffalo was the "parkway," a 200-foot-wide strip of green open space that connected elements of the park system, as in Buffalo, or ran between the major park and distant parts of the city as in Brooklyn. The parkway contained separate ways for different means of travel—walks, bridle paths, cycleways—while its distinctive feature was a central smooth-surfaced drive for use solely by carriages. The concept, and term, saw greatly expanded use in the twentieth century in the form of landscaped parkways for private vehicles that excluded commercial trucks as the original parkways had excluded carts and wagons. Olmsted also had a special conception of what a park should be—a place especially designed for the restorative experience of nature. All elements of a park should support that purpose, for as Olmsted urged in a review of the management of Central Park that he and Vaux prepared in 1872, "The Park throughout is a single work of art, and as such, subject to the primary law of every work of art, namely, that it shall be framed upon a single, noble motive, to which the design of all its parts, in some more or less subtle way, shall be confluent and helpful." At the same time, he recognized the need to provide for the gathering of large crowds and thus carefully planned peripheral areas for promenades, playgrounds, concert areas, and picnic groves. For him a park was meant to offer all residents of a city a common meeting ground free of the competitiveness of daily life. He preferred to devise a distinctive landscape character for each major element of a park system and wished to create citywide centers for particular activities. This can be seen in the two major sections of the original plan for the Chicago South Park (now called Washington and Jackson parks) and in the variety of spaces in the park systems he planned in Rochester and Louisville. His most varied system was in Boston, encircling the old city from the Charles River to the harbor at Marine Park. The circuit included Franklin Park, the Arnold Arboretum, the ponds of Jamaica Park and Leverett Park, the stream valley of the Riverway, the tidal marsh scenery of the Back Bay Fens, and several connecting parkways. Olmsted moved to the Boston suburb of Brookline in 1882, enabling his firm to devote close attention to the development of the park system there.

Another aspect of Olmsted's intent to create community was the residential suburbs that he planned. He was convinced that the "more openly built city" of the future would separate place of work from place of residence, providing families with freestanding homes set in grounds that would enhance both the domestic amenity and the taste of the residents. Riverside, Illinois, which he planned in 1868–1869 with Vaux, is the most fully realized and best preserved of his communities. It is a classic demonstration of his use of curving streets to produce a permanent residential community that would resist by its physical plan the encroachment of commercial and industrial uses. The streets with their "gracefully-curved lines, generous spaces, and the absence of sharp corners" were intended "to suggest and imply leisure, contemplativeness and happy tranquillity," in contrast to the "ordinary directness of line" and "eagerness to press forward" of ordinary town streets ("Preliminary Report upon the Proposed Suburban Village at Riverside, Near Chicago" [1868]). The streets formed a continuous public open space that was expanded by thirty-foot setbacks of houses. The streets were lined by sidewalks, since convenient access to scenery on foot was to be a key element of suburban life. Olmsted reserved the entire floodplain of the Des Plaines River in Riverside for public open space. Combined with two village commons, the roadsides, and the numerous green triangles at the intersection of streets that were to serve as neighborhood play areas for young children, over one-third of the community's 1,600 acres was to be public open space. Olmsted also called for communal facilities for gas, water, and sewerage by which needs of the residents could be met in an efficient and thorough way. His other major suburban community was Druid Hills in Atlanta, while his largest project of city planning was the laying out of the street system of the Bronx with the engineer J. J. R. Croes.

The residential community was also important to Olmsted because of the setting it provided for each family to develop its own domestic surroundings. He planned numerous "open air apartments" so that domestic activities could be moved outdoors. In the grounds he designed, he hoped that people would practice gardening characterized not by floral display but rather by unified compositions with subtle variety, intricacy, and delicacy of effect.

Olmsted planned academic campuses, most notably Stanford University and Lawrenceville School, and laid out the grounds of residential institutions, including McLean Asylum in Belmont, Massachusetts, where he spent the last five years of his life. He designed the grounds and terraces of the U.S. Capitol and planned the site of the World's Columbian Exposition of 1893. In the 1880s he was a leader in the campaign to create a scenic reservation at Niagara Falls and collaborated with Vaux in preparing a plan for the reservation. His last great project was George W. Vanderbilt's estate, "Biltmore," near Asheville, North Carolina, where he planned a naturalistic approach road and a series of spaces adjoining Richard Morris Hunt's great mansion. He also convinced Vanderbilt to establish the first significant demonstration of scientific forestry in this country and to begin construction, never completed, of the largest arboretum in the world.

Olmsted retired in 1895, having devoted the previous thirty years to establishing landscape architecture as both an art and a profession. He collaborated closely with other professions, especially engineers and architects, his work and friendship with H. H. Richardson being most notable. He always sought to make a clear differentiation between his art and that of the gardener, emphasizing the difference in scale of projects and the landscape architect's avoidance of decoration and display. Over a period of thirty-seven years he and his partners designed twenty major urban parks, more than one hundred other public recreation grounds, did planning for fifty-five academic campuses and residential institutions, and designed fifty residential communities and subdivisions and the grounds of some two hundred private estates. In number of commissions and extent of influence Olmsted far exceeded all other American landscape designers of his time and is rightly known as the founder of American landscape architecture.

• The major manuscript collections of Olmsted's papers are the Frederick Law Olmsted Papers and the Olmsted Associates Records, both in the Manuscript Division of the Library of Congress. The Frederick Law Olmsted National Historic Site in Brookline, Mass., has extensive holdings of plans and historic photographs. A selective letterpress edition of Olmsted's writings is *The Papers of Frederick Law Olmsted*, ed. Charles Capen McLaughlin and Charles E. Beveridge et al. (1977–). The most complete and reliable biography is Laura Wood Roper, *FLO: A Biography of Frederick Law Olmsted* (1973). A shorter assessment of Olmsted as a landscape architect is Beveridge and Paul Rocheleau, *Frederick Law Olmsted: Designing the American Landscape* (1995). The best study of Olmsted's work in a single city is Cynthia Zaitzevsky, *Frederick Law Olmsted and the Boston Park System* (1982). A work that places Olmsted's career in its larger American setting is David Schuyler, *The New Urban Landscape: The Redefinition of City Form in Nineteenth-century America* (1986). Dana F. White and Victor Kramer, eds., *Olmsted South: Old South Critic/New South Planner* (1979), presents a variety of articles relating to the subject.

CHARLES E. BEVERIDGE

OLMSTED, Frederick Law, Jr. (24 July 1870–25 Dec. 1957), landscape architect, planner, and public servant, was born on Staten Island, New York, the son of Frederick Law Olmsted, the progenitor of the profession of landscape architecture in the United States, and Mary Cleveland Perkins Olmsted, the widow of Olmsted's brother. Called Henry Perkins at birth, he was renamed Frederick Law Olmsted, Jr., at about age four by his father and thereafter informally known as "Rick." Since his father worked from home, Olmsted was immersed in the family business from his earliest years. He traveled with his father to job sites and on European study trips and helped out in the office during school vacations. In 1881 the senior Olmsted moved the family to Brookline, Massachusetts, where the Olmsted firm continued in practice for nearly a century. Frederick Olmsted received his A.B. in 1894

from Harvard, having planned his course of study with the expectation of becoming a landscape architect.

Olmsted spent thirteen months on George Vanderbilt's estate, "Biltmore," in Asheville, North Carolina, serving his final apprenticeship on what would be the elder Olmsted's final commission. Under pressure from his aging, ailing father, including threats not to take him into the family firm, Olmsted questioned his own assumption that he would take up his father's profession. However, at Biltmore he reaffirmed that landscape architecture was both his destiny and the correct career choice. Reconciling himself to the inevitable identification and comparisons with his famous father, Olmsted took pride in acknowledging his professional legacy, for the rest of his life often quoting his father and fondly pointing to parental influence on his work.

In 1896 Olmsted returned to Brookline as an official member of the Olmsted firm; the following year the senior Olmsted's retirement was announced. In 1898 Olmsted joined his half brother, John Charles, in partnership, renaming the office Olmsted Brothers. That same year Olmsted became the landscape architect for the Boston Metropolitan Park System, a title he held until 1920. He also had long-term relationships with park systems in Baltimore, Chicago, and Washington, D.C.

At the turn of the century Olmsted played a prominent role in two landmark events for the profession of landscape architecture in this country. In 1899 he became a founding member of the American Society of Landscape Architects and later served two terms as president (1908–1909, 1919–1923). The following year he was appointed instructor in landscape architecture at Harvard, creating the first university course on the profession in this country. He was named Charles Eliot Professor of Landscape Architecture in 1903 and continued to lecture at the university, as his other responsibilities permitted, until 1917.

Olmsted focused on the problems of an increasingly urbanized United States during the first two decades of his career. In 1901 he came to national prominence when he assumed what would have been his father's place, had he been well, on the Park Improvement Commission for the District of Columbia, commonly known as the McMillan Commission. Charged with interpreting L'Enfant's vision for the nation's capital for the twentieth century, Olmsted worked with his father's compatriots from the Chicago World's Columbian Exposition to transform Washington into a work of civic art and to devise a comprehensive plan for its future development. Olmsted's particular contribution was his visionary blueprint for a comprehensive park and parkway system for the entire metropolitan region. As the commission's youngest member, Olmsted alone lived to see the plan unfold. For decades he remained its guardian, serving on the two federal bodies responsible for overseeing development in the capital city, the Commission of Fine Arts (1910–1918) and the National Capital Park Planning Commission (1926–1932).

The McMillan report, with its promise that the "City Beautiful" could be achieved through the art and science of comprehensive planning, had a galvanizing effect on municipal art societies and civic improvement associations in cities and towns around the country. Olmsted found himself in great demand to advise new quasi-official planning boards and citizen associations on civic improvement; between 1905 and 1915 he produced planning reports for Detroit, Utica, Boulder, Pittsburgh, New Haven, Rochester, and Newport. He also applied the emerging principles of comprehensive planning to suburban settings, creating master plans for new sections of Roland Park, a Baltimore suburb (from 1902); for Forest Hill Gardens, a model garden community sponsored by the Russell Sage Foundation (1909) outside of New York City; and for the industrial town of Torrance, California (1911–1912, largely unrealized). Many of the features of his suburban plans had an enduring influence, including the concept of neighborhood-centered development, the differentiation of streets by function, the importance of common open and recreational spaces, and the need for continuing maintenance and aesthetic oversight to preserve the quality of the community.

During this period Olmsted was constantly on the move, establishing a lifelong pattern of relentless business travel comparable, he joked, "to that of a commercial bagman." Vacations were a busman's holiday since landscape architecture, Olmsted once pointed out to a client, was the one profession from which it was impossible to escape. He married Sarah Hall Sharples in 1911; they had one child. He even used his honeymoon as an opportunity to visit the Panama Canal Zone, where he would advise on landscape issues.

In 1910 Olmsted was chosen to head the National Conference on City Planning, a yearly gathering of design professionals, social reformers, and laymen looking for solutions to the country's urban problems. As one of the few planners to practice successfully in both the "City Beautiful" and the "City Efficient" eras, Olmsted gave presidential speeches to the group that helped lay the theoretical foundation for a new profession. He came to view the city plan not as a fixed map for future generations to follow, but rather as an organic, flexible document that must evolve, adapting to changing priorities and conditions. As such, the proper custodians of the plan, he said, were not outside experts or temporary planning commissions; rather, planning must become a regular function of municipal government.

In 1917 Olmsted was instrumental in organizing the American City Planning Institute, a professional society for planning practitioners, and he was elected its first president. As this organization's representative, he offered the planning profession's services to the government during World War I. Olmsted served on the Commission on Emergency Construction and was appointed manager of the Town Planning Division of the U.S. Housing Corporation (1917–1919), notable as the first direct federal participation in building worker housing.

With his brother's death in 1920, Olmsted became the senior partner in the firm, then the largest office of landscape architecture in the world. He devoted much of the rest of his professional life to public service, consulting on issues of conservation, preservation, and the appropriate uses of forests and parks. The 1916 bill establishing the National Park Service incorporated key language by Olmsted setting aside park lands for all time as places protected from development and preserved for human enjoyment. He advised the National Park Service on managing Yosemite National Park (1928–1940, 1951–1956), controlling the Potomac River Basin (1944), and conserving the water and scenic resources of the Colorado River Basin (1941–1955). On the state level, he conducted surveys to choose land for inclusion in the California state park system in 1929 and 1949 and devised the master plan for California's Save-the-Redwoods League.

In 1921 Olmsted was asked to advise on the preparation of a regional plan for the New York area, and his plan for Fort Tryon Park, a great urban park on the bluffs above New York City, also dates from this period. From 1921 to 1928 he served on the Department of Commerce's Advisory Committee on City Planning, which was responsible for the 1927 Standard City Planning and Enabling Act. Olmsted also designed two suburban communities in the 1920s: Palos Verdes Estates in California and the Mountain Lake Club in Lake Wales, Florida.

Olmsted's pace of work slowed considerably after his sixty-fifth birthday in 1935; however, he remained a partner in the firm until his official retirement on 31 December 1949. He died in Malibu, California.

For fifty years Olmsted was an acknowledged leader in two professions concerned with the interrelationship of people and their environment. His public service and private commissions placed him at the forefront of every major event in the planning, park, and conservation movements. Whether in urban, suburban, or wilderness settings, Olmsted always sought, he said, to harmonize use and beauty. His approach was practical and down-to-earth, like the man himself. Yet in contrast to the technocrats whom he feared might come to dominate the design professions, Olmsted created work that displayed the breadth of vision and artistry that were his true inheritance from his illustrious father. An appreciation appearing in *Landscape Architecture* (Apr. 1958) hailed Olmsted as a generalist "living in a period of intensifying specialization. . . . He set a standard, dignity and social usefulness for his profession higher than any previously defined. In this, we think, his true greatness is to be found."

• The project files and office records of the Olmsted firm, which contain copies of the majority of Olmsted's planning and park reports and citations for his numerous journal articles, are in the Manuscript Division of the Library of Congress. Plans, photographs, and other graphic material remain at "Fairsted," the Olmsted home and office in Brookline, Mass., now operated by the National Park Service as the Frederick Law Olmsted National Historic Site. Publications related to Olmsted's work as an urban planner include his speeches to the National Conference on City Planning, which appear in its yearly proceedings, and his introduction to *City Planning*, ed. John Nolen (1916). Olmsted coedited with Theodora Kimball a book on his father's career, *Frederick Law Olmsted: Landscape Architect, 1822–1903* (1922). The sole published overview and assessment of Olmsted's career is Edward Clark Whiting and William Lyman Phillips, "Fredrick Law Olmsted, 1870–1957: An Appreciation of the Man and His Works," *Landscape Architecture* 48 (Apr. 1958): 145–56. On Olmsted's early years see Susan L. Klaus, "'A Better School Could Scarcely Be Found.' Frederick Law Olmsted, Jr., at Biltmore," *National Association for Olmsted Parks Workbook Series*, no. 5 (1995); and Klaus, "'Such Inheritance as I Can Give You.' The Apprenticeship of Frederick Law Olmsted, Jr.," *Journal of the New England Garden History Society* 3 (Fall 1993): 1–7. For Olmsted as an urban planner see Klaus, "Efficiency, Economy, Beauty: The City Planning Reports of Frederick Law Olmsted, Jr., 1905–1915," *Journal of the American Planning Association* 57 (Autumn 1991): 456–70. An obituary is in the *New York Times*, 27 Dec. 1957.

SUSAN L. KLAUS

OLMSTED, Gideon (12 Feb. 1749–8 Feb. 1845), seaman and privateersman, was born in East Hartford, Connecticut, the son of Jonathan Olmsted and Hannah Meakins, farmers. Little is known of his early life. Olmsted went to sea sometime in 1770 and soon became captain of a small vessel trading from Connecticut to the West Indies. At the outbreak of the Revolution, Olmsted, along with several brothers and cousins, joined the East Hartford militia company and marched to Boston to take part in the siege. With the British evacuation of Boston in March 1776 Olmsted returned home. In the spring of 1777 he married Mabel Roberts; they had no children. In July he purchased the sloop *Seaflower* then anchored at Westerly, Rhode Island. After loading cargo, Olmsted sailed to Guadeloupe. On 6 April 1778, while en route home to Connecticut, Olmsted and his sloop were captured by the British privateer *Weir*. *Seaflower* was sent to New York and condemned while Olmsted and some of his crew were kept confined aboard the *Weir*. Confinement lasted barely a month. By mid-May the British had released Olmsted and his men and they were ashore at Cape Français on the island of Hispaniola.

Olmsted and his crew left Cape Français and made their way to Port-au-Prince, where he was offered command of the newly fitted out French privateer *Polly*. Toward midday on 8 July 1778, not far off the coast of Jamaica, *Polly* engaged the British sloop of war *Ostrich*. The two vessels were fairly matched and the battle turned into a slugfest. Olmsted's crew worked their guns with greater speed and accuracy. Gradually *Polly* took the advantage and toward early evening it appeared that *Ostrich* was close to surrender. Olmsted's apparent victory turned to a quick defeat when another British vessel, *Lowestoffe's Prize*, suddenly hauled into view and joined the fray. In less than one hour Olmsted surrendered.

Ostrich and *Lowestoffe's Prize* hauled *Polly* into Jamaica, where she was condemned while the captain and his men were confined to jail. Within a few days the Americans were put aboard a British vessel, the sloop *Active*, bound for New York, where their captors intended to confine them aboard one of the notorious prison hulks moored in the harbor. Off the New Jersey coast Olmsted and some of his crew managed to overwhelm their guards and take control of *Active*. They immediately set a course for the American port of Egg Harbor only to have bad luck strike again. *Active* was overtaken by two American vessels out of Philadelphia, *Convention* and *Le Gerard*, who, despite vigorous protests from Olmsted, took *Active* as their prize. *Active* was sold at Philadelphia and Olmsted received only one-quarter of the proceeds. Enraged, he went to the Pennsylvania Court, where he demanded all the proceeds for himself and his men. His cause was denied. He then appealed to the Continental Congress.

Although the states were ordinarily very jealous of their power, since late 1775 they had allowed appeals to Congress in matters concerning traditional matters of admiralty jurisdiction. At first such appeals had been heard by special committees, but on 30 January 1777 they had created a standing committee of five members to hear all such appeals. The committee found in Olmsted's favor, but the Pennsylvania authorities rejected the committee's authority. The Congress had no power to force the state into submission. Beaten in court, Olmsted returned to Connecticut and resumed his privateering career. For the remainder of the Revolution he commanded several privateers and enjoyed considerable success taking numerous prizes. He was again taken prisoner in 1782 while in command of *Virginia*. It was his last command of the war.

After the war Olmsted returned to Connecticut and resumed his career as a merchant. However, he never forgot the loss of the *Active*. He believed that the courts of Pennsylvania had done him a great injustice. In 1790 he resumed his attempt at justice. Using the new judicial structure created by the federal constitution, he carried his appeal out of Pennsylvania to the United States Supreme Court. The case soon became celebrated and was destined to set important precedents in American maritime law by clearly establishing the preeminence of federal jurisdiction in these matters. The court found in his favor and ordered the state of Pennsylvania to compensate Olmsted. The state still resisted. In 1809 President James Madison interceded and requested that the state adhere to the law. Olmsted finally triumphed and received his due.

Litigation did not occupy all Olmsted's time. In 1793, to avoid violating American neutrality, he concocted a subterfuge by which he became a French citizen and using that cover he commissioned his schooner *Hector* as a privateer under the French flag. In July of that year he captured a British vessel and brought it as a prize into Wilmington, North Carolina. Since the United States was at peace, the federal court refused to allow any proceedings against the vessel. This was Olmsted's last voyage as a privateersman. He returned to Philadelphia and for the next few years sailed as a merchant captain in the West Indies and Canaries trade. Sometime after 1800 Olmsted apparently returned to East Hartford, Connecticut, where he remained until his death there.

• Records of court appeals are in the Papers of the Continental Congress, item 29 in the National Archives microfilm. Also useful are Louis F. Middlebrook, *Captain Gideon Olmsted, Connecticut Privateersman, Revolutionary War* (1933); Middlebrook, *History of Maritime Connecticut during the American Revolution, 1775–1783* (1925); and William M. Fowler, Jr., "A Connecticut Yankee in a Pennsylvania Court," Connecticut Historical Society, *Bulletin* 37: 59–63.

WILLIAM M. FOWLER, JR.

OLNEY, Richard (15 Sept. 1835–8 Apr. 1917), lawyer, U.S. attorney general, and secretary of state, was born in Oxford, Massachusetts, the son of Wilson Olney and Eliza Butler. His paternal grandfather, also named Richard, was prominent in the small community, having founded the town's first textile mill and bank. A dominating personality, Olney's grandfather largely controlled the lives of his children even as adults, except for those who broke with him. Wilson Olney remained subservient, working in his father's counting house and later clerking in the Oxford Bank. Young Richard's personality more closely resembled his grandfather's and that of his ambitious and driving mother rather than his father's.

Olney was educated at Brown College, 1851–1856, and Harvard Law School, 1856–1858. He was admitted to the bar of Suffolk County in April 1859 and found his first employment with Judge Benjamin F. Thomas of Boston. Within two years he married the judge's daughter Agnes (6 Mar. 1861), and on Thomas's death in 1876, he inherited the judge's practice. The Olneys had two children.

At first Olney specialized as his father-in-law had in wills and trust estates. Although not especially lucrative, the practice brought him into contact with leading Brahmin families, the so-called "proper Bostonians." Increasingly, these clients entrusted him with their business affairs. Between 1876 and 1879 Olney successfully reorganized the financially distressed Eastern Railroad Company of Massachusetts. In the process he became the firm's general counsel and a member of its board of directors. In 1884, when the Boston & Maine Railroad leased the Eastern, Olney became that company's attorney and moved to its board of directors. His work there centered on legal problems involved in forging the firm's near monopoly over rail traffic in northern New England. Success in that venture made Olney one of Boston's leading railroad lawyers.

After 1886 Boston interests in control of the Chicago, Burlington & Quincy Railroad began turning to Olney for advice. In 1889 he became that line's general counsel and a member of its board. For the most part, his efforts were aimed at thwarting "Granger laws" (state measures for regulating railroads and their rates) and later the federal Interstate Commerce Act.

In appointing the cabinet for his second term (1893–1897), President Grover Cleveland selected Olney as attorney general. The Boston lawyer's only previous excursions into politics had been a one-year term in the Massachusetts legislature in 1874 and an unsuccessful bid for the state's attorney generalship in 1876. Unlike his colleagues, Olney prepared for cabinet meetings by looking into any important matter likely to arise, not just those related to his own department. As a consequence, he soon became all but indispensable to the president.

Olney played a significant role in almost every major issue of the second Cleveland administration. He argued against both the annexation of Hawaii and using force to restore Queen Liliuokalani to her throne; he worked for repeal of the Sherman Silver Purchase Act; he urged American neutrality in the Cuban struggle for independence from Spain; and he used federal court injunctions backed by the army to halt the march of Jacob S. Coxey's armies of the unemployed on Washington in 1894.

His most celebrated and controversial act as attorney general was suppressing the Chicago railroad boycott and strike of 1894 (better known as the Pullman strike). The affair began as a sympathetic boycott in support of a strike by American Railway Union (ARU) affiliates at the Pullman Company near Chicago. The ARU boycotted all Pullman sleeping cars on the nation's railroads. The major railroad companies centered in Chicago, already organized in the General Managers' Association (GMA), agreed to discharge any employee who boycotted sleeping cars. The ARU in turn struck every railroad that discharged one of its members. Within days railroad traffic in the area and across much of the nation was brought to a standstill. Olney forcefully moved against the boycott-strike. On advice of the GMA, he named a Chicago railroad lawyer to represent the Justice Department in Chicago. He ordered all U.S. attorneys and marshals to protect the movement of trains carrying mail or interstate commerce. He authorized the special attorney in Chicago to seek a blanket injunction against Eugene V. Debs, president of the ARU, and "all other persons whomsoever," forbidding them from aiding, abetting, encouraging, or promoting the strike in any way. When those measures failed, Olney advised Cleveland that nothing remained but for the president to call out the army to enforce the injunction. Illinois governor John Peter Altgeld protested that this action unconstitutionally infringed on the sovereignty of Illinois. Cleveland, allegedly working from a draft prepared by Olney, replied tersely that he was enforcing federal law and that Illinois was part of the United States.

It was not generally known at the time, but Olney was involved in a serious conflict of interest. Until the end of the strike he continued to receive his regular salary, an amount greater than what he was paid as attorney general, for services rendered as general counsel of the Burlington, one of the railroads directly involved in the strike. When the issue was raised, he quietly stopped the salary but continued as the line's general counsel. It is unlikely, however, that the source of his private income determined his conduct during the strike: his whole professional career had been on the side of large corporations and railroads. Nonetheless, even in that era he was guilty of a breach of ethics, if not of law.

During Olney's tenure as attorney general, the Justice Department brought three major cases before the U.S. Supreme Court. Olney regarded *In re Debs*, growing out of the Pullman strike, as the most important and personally argued that case before the high court. A sweeping unanimous decision, based largely on Olney's brief, upheld the blanket injunction and in effect outlawed strikes against railroads carrying either interstate commerce or the mail for the next quarter-century.

In *United States v. E. C. Knight et al.* (the sugar trust case), the Court so narrowly construed the Sherman Antitrust Act as to render it useless against trusts for at least a decade. Olney advanced the case, fully expecting the Court to invalidate the law, which he thought was worthless. In a similarly restrictive interpretation of the Constitution, the Court in *Pollock v. Farmers' Loan & Trust Company* struck down the income tax, closing off that source of revenue until adoption of the Sixteenth Amendment in 1913. As the government's advocate, Olney regarded the case as very important and hated losing, but, as he said, he took comfort in not himself having to file a return.

Upon the death of Secretary of State Walter Q. Gresham in 1895, Cleveland promoted Olney to that post. Neither Olney's manner nor his temperament was well suited to the norms of international diplomacy. He issued ultimatums and made demands on sovereign nations much as if they were opponents in litigation. He told the Spanish minister that if a frequently deferred claim of the United States was not paid, he would urge the president to lay the matter before Congress, implying that a resort to force might follow.

Most notorious was his similar ultimatum to Great Britain demanding submission of the long-standing boundary dispute between British Guiana and Venezuela to arbitration by the United States. Charging that Britain's claim violated the Monroe Doctrine, he asserted that the "infinite resources" and "isolated position" of the United States rendered it "master of the situation and practically invulnerable as against any or all other powers." When the deadline for replying passed, Olney helped Cleveland draft a message to Congress, asking for authority to draw the proper boundary line and if necessary to use armed force to uphold it. Britain subsequently accepted arbitration, and the war fever precipitated by the message died down. Although his initiation of the crisis needlessly risked war, his subsequent handling of the affair contributed to a reasonable settlement.

Twice Olney's admirers unsuccessfully urged his candidacy for the presidency, first in 1896, again in 1904. Those favoring him were never numerous, and he regarded office-seeking as unseemly. Further, Cleveland's coy handling of a possible third term in 1896 blocked all conservative Democratic candidates until too late to halt William Jennings Bryan's steam-roller. After two failed bids by Bryan, too few remembered Olney, who by 1904 was sixty-nine years old.

In his postcabinet years, Olney occasionally wrote or spoke on foreign policy and labor topics. For the most part, however, he practiced law until his retirement in 1908. In 1913 President Woodrow Wilson offered him appointments as ambassador to Great Britain and membership on the Federal Reserve Board, both of which he declined. He died in Boston.

• The bulk of Olney's personal papers are in the Richard Olney Papers, and important correspondence with the president is in the Grover Cleveland Papers, both in the Manuscript Division of the Library of Congress. Professional correspondence is in the Olney and Charles E. Perkins collections, Burlington Railroad Archives, Newberry Library, Chicago. Official correspondence and records are in the files of the Justice and State departments at the National Archives. Articles published by Olney include "International Isolation of the United States," *Atlantic Monthly* 81 (May 1898): 577–88; "Growth of Our Foreign Policy," *Atlantic Monthly* 85 (Mar. 1900): 289–301; "Recent Phases of the Monroe Doctrine," *Boston Herald*, 1 Mar. 1903; "Discrimination Against Union Labor—Legal?" *American Law Review* 42 (Mar.-Apr. 1908): 161–67; and "National Judiciary and Big Business," *Boston Herald*, 24 Sept. 1911. There are two biographies: Henry James, *Richard Olney and His Public Service* (1923), and Gerald G. Eggert, *Richard Olney: Evolution of a Statesman* (1974). An obituary is in the *Boston Globe*, 10 Apr. 1917.

GERALD G. EGGERT

OLSEN, Fred (28 Feb. 1891–2 Nov. 1986), industrial chemist and art collector, was born in Newcastle upon Tyne, England, the son of Fredrick Olsen, a textbook publisher, and Elizabeth Young. In 1906 Olsen's father retired and purchased a farm in Ontario, Canada. After working for a few years in Quebec lumber camps Olsen applied for a scholarship to the University of Toronto. He hoped to study classics in order to enter the church or become a teacher. To his surprise he ranked first in chemistry in the scholarship examination. He received bachelor's and master's degrees in chemistry in 1916 and 1918. He married Florence Quittenton in 1917 in Drummondville, Quebec, where he was a chemist for Aetna Explosives; the couple had two children. The Canadian government loaned him to the United States as an explosives expert for the duration of World War I, and he spent 1917–1918 in Emporium, Pennsylvania, at the Aetna Explosives plant and research laboratory. Before the war had ended, Aetna Explosives became overextended and went into receivership, and Olsen decided to remain in the United States.

In 1919 Olsen became chemical coordinator for U.S. Army Ordnance at the Picatinny Arsenal in New Jersey. He became an American citizen in 1922. At Picatinny he was an expert on smokeless powder, a colloidal nitrocellulose invented in the 1880s that outperformed black powder, the standard propellant explosive. Its manufacture was a complex and hazardous process that involved the nitration of pure cellulose and the conversion of the product into a colloidal gel, and the gel into grains of different sizes for blending into a uniform product. Its instability plagued World War I attempts to manufacture it. At Picatinny Olsen received important patents for the stabilization and storage of the powder, its gel structure, and control of its rate of burning.

In 1929 Olsen became director of research and development for the explosives division of Olin Industries, East Alton, Illinois. He remained with Olin until his retirement in 1956. In 1947 he became a member of the board of directors, and in 1948 he persuaded the company to move the research division to New Haven, Connecticut, believing it a more attractive location to recent science graduates. He lived in nearby Guilford, Connecticut, for the rest of his life. He guided a research group of about five hundred and had an important role in determining company policy.

Olsen held forty-five patents in cellulose chemistry involving the preparation of high-grade cellulose and of smokeless powder. In 1933 he received a patent for a new type of smokeless powder that required a novel and superior manufacturing process; the entire procedure took place underwater. Known by its trademark name, Ball Powder, it could be granulated as small spheres that were controlled in size to meet the ballistic requirements of a weapon. The powder was more stable, and the process less hazardous and about five times faster than conventional methods. Ball Powder became the standard propellant for military small-arms ammunition, small-caliber cannons, and sporting ammunition and has been basic to powder making ever since.

Another of Olsen's major innovations was the isolation of high-grade cellulose from wood pulp. The only source of quality cellulose was cotton linters, the fuzz that clung to the cottonseed after the removal of the staple cotton. During the 1920s and 1930s the demand for commercial products made from the chemical processing of cellulose increased so much that cotton linters became an insufficient source. Olsen explored, as an alternative, the use of wood pulp, which had a much smaller proportion of cellulose than cotton, and whose noncellulosic constituents had to be separated without degrading the quality of the cellulose. His task took on more urgency when, at the start of World War II, the U.S. Army commandeered all the available supply of cotton cellulose in order to make smokeless powder. Olsen overcame the inadequate supply by introducing during the war an efficient method of obtaining cellulose from paper pulp derived from the abundant southern pine.

A second wartime innovation was Olsen's discovery that certain dyes drove out the impurities that were bound to nitrocellulose and made it unstable. Gunpowder that was rendered more stable by this process also retained its hitting power whether in torrid or frigid zones. From 1943, American troops used it in the cartridges they fired.

In 1941 Olsen found another outlet for his energies. His son's Christmas gift, a book of reproductions of the paintings of Paul Klee, transformed him into a compulsive art collector. Although he at first found

Klee's paintings to be crude and trivial, he came to appreciate the creations of modern artists, and at the 1945 New York Armory Show he bought his first painting, a German expressionist work. His collection grew to include such modernists as Pablo Picasso, Joan Miró, Hans Hofmann, and Robert Motherwell. He then became an expert on the nonwestern art that had influenced the modernists and collected Egyptian, Persian, Chinese, Coptic, African, Tibetan, and especially pre-Columbian American art.

To share his enthusiasm for art with young people, Olsen divided his collection into six modern and six ancient collections and circulated them at no cost among colleges throughout the United States. In the 1950s he established the Olsen Foundation and over the rest of his life gradually donated or sold the collections to museums. He donated his magnificent pre-Columbian collections, two of the best in North America, to the art galleries of the University of Illinois and Yale.

In 1954 the Olsens traveled to Antigua in search of a winter vacation home. From 1957 on, they lived six months in Antigua and six months in Guilford. In 1955 Olsen uncovered on the island striking pottery painted in geometric designs—the work of the island Arawaks who had once populated the Caribbean. Olsen recreated the society and culture of the Arawaks in two 1974 books, *On the Trail of the Arawaks* and *Indian Creek*, personal and readable accounts of his efforts to trace the Arawaks throughout the Caribbean and their migration from their ancestral home in South America. Arawaks lived in Venezuela, Surinam, and Guyana, and he went there to learn about their society. In their mid-seventies Olsen and his wife were traveling by dugout canoe along the tributaries of the Orinoco River, still on the trail of the Arawaks. Olsen donated part of his large collection of Arawak ceramic and stone artifacts to the Peabody Museum of Natural History at Yale and sold part to the Pre-Columbian Art and Rare Book Gallery in Miami.

Olsen died in Guilford. He was a quiet and affable person, a major figure in the development of explosives, an art enthusiast who made ancient and modern art of high quality available to the public, and an amateur archeologist who contributed to the history of the Caribbean and Americas.

• Olsen's chemical publications appear in the journals *Army Ordnance* and *Industrial and Engineering Chemistry* from 1921 to 1943. He revealed the origin and development of his interest in art collecting in *Art News* 50 (Nov. 1951): 10. Theodore R. Olive describes Olsen's most important innovation in explosives in "Ball Powder Process Upsets Explosives Industry Tradition," *Chemical and Metallurgical Engineering* 53 (Dec. 1946): 92–96. George Kubler analyzes Olsen's gift to Yale in the illustrated essay "The Olsen Collection of Pre-Columbian Art," *Yale Art Gallery Bulletin* 24 (Oct. 1958): 9–25. Peter Hulme discusses Olsen's Arawak findings and places them in the context of Caribbean archeology and history in *Colonial Encounters: Europe and the Native Caribbean* (1986). Articles based on interviews with Olsen are in the *New Haven Regis-*

ter, 5 Apr. 1953 and 1 Dec. 1968, and by Walter Sullivan in the *New York Times*, 11 Apr. 1968. An obituary is in the *New York Times*, 10 Nov. 1986.

ALBERT B. COSTA

OLSEN, Ole (6 Nov. 1892–26 Jan. 1963), and **Chic Johnson** (5 Mar. 1891–26 Feb. 1962), comedians, were born John Sigvard Olsen and Harold Ogden Johnson, respectively, in Peru, Indiana, and Englewood, Illinois. Olsen was the son of Gustave Olsen and Catherine (maiden name unknown). Johnson's parents' names are unknown. Both attended Northwestern University, Olsen graduating in 1912.

The pair first met in 1914, most likely in a music publisher's office in Chicago. At the time Olsen played violin, sang with illustrated slides, and did a ventriloquist act with the College Four quartet, while Johnson advertised himself as the greatest ragtime pianist in the Midwest. When the pianist in the College Four quit, Johnson became his replacement. By 1915 Olsen and Johnson had formed their own comedic musical act, finally receiving some acclaim in "Mike Fritzel's Frolics," a nightclub floor show in Chicago. Billed as "Two Likeable Lads Loaded with Laughs," they moved into vaudeville, first for five years on the Pantages circuit for $250 a week and then on the Keith-Orpheum circuit for $2,500 a week. Though neither was truly the comic or the straight man/stooge, they were physically distinguishable: Olsen was lithe and taller than the roly-poly Johnson, who, with his shrill, high-pitched laugh, seemed the more outrageous of the two. Early in their careers both comics married, and they often used family members in their shows. Olsen married Eileen O'Dare in 1913, and Johnson married Catherine Creed in 1918. The Olsens had three children, the Johnsons, two.

By the early 1920s Olsen and Johnson headlined all over the United States as well as in England and Australia in an act that changed little during the rest of their careers. In 1926, while in Australia, they toured in the shows *Tip Toes* and *Tell Me More*, returning to the United States the same year to appear in Los Angeles in the first revue of their own, *Monkey Business*, which they subsequently toured.

Billed now as "The Mad Monarchs of Monkey Business" and usually successful on the road, especially in small cities throughout the Midwest, the duo nonetheless was forced to turn to other entertainment avenues, the result of film's increasing popularity and the decline of vaudeville. In 1930 they appeared in their first film, Warner Brothers' *Oh Sailor Behave!*, followed by two other Warner Brothers films, *Fifty Million Frenchmen* and *Gold Dust Gertie* (both 1931). After only modest success in films, the team returned to the stage, first with tours of *Atrocities of 1932* and *Everything Goes* and then with their 1933 Broadway debut at the Apollo Theater as replacements for Jack Haley (Ole) and Sid Silvers (Chic) in the musical *Take a Chance*. Subsequently, after buying a 50 percent interest, they toured the musical, despite critical disapproval for the use of vaudeville comics in legitimate

musical roles. When their show closed in New York, Olsen and Johnson were introduced to radio by Rudy Vallee and presented "Comedy News" over WABC.

With the basic concept for their brand of vaudeville revue well developed (described by film historian Leonard Maltin as "freewheeling, madcap comedy with no holds barred" [*Movie Comedy Teams*, p. 258]), Olsen and Johnson found the ultimate name for their show while appearing in Buckeye, Arizona, at the Fiesta del Sol, which was locally known as "Helzapoppin." They simply added another "l". While on the West Coast they also initiated a radio show over station KFI in Los Angeles and made two more films, this time low-budget efforts for Republic Pictures (*Country Gentlemen*, released in January 1937, followed by the September 1937 release of *All Over Town*).

Failing again to gain a solid footing in films, Olsen and Johnson turned once more to the lunatic *Hellzapoppin*, their "screamlined revue." New York producer Lee Shubert saw the show on tour in Philadelphia in 1938, persuaded the team to expand the revue from one hour to a full evening's entertainment, and with a budget of $15,000 brought the production to New York, where it opened on 22 September at the 46th Street Theater, subsequently moving to the larger Winter Garden. Although condemned by critics as lowbrow, unsophisticated, and vulgar, the show was promoted vigorously by columnist Walter Winchell and ran 1,404 performances before it closed on 17 December 1941.

Over the next several years Olsen and Johnson produced three Broadway shows without appearing in them: *The Streets of Paris* (June 1939), *Snookie* (June 1941), and *Count Me In* (Oct. 1942). Their next appearances together on stage were in thinly veiled imitations of *Hellzapoppin: Sons o' Fun*, for 300 performances; *Laffing Room Only* (1945); *Funzapoppin*, with some 200 performers (1949); *Pardon Our French* (1950); and an aquatic show at Flushing Meadow Park, New York, *Hellzasplashin* (1959), their final theatrical appearance together. During this period the comics made one last foray into films, beginning with a stultified adaptation of *Hellzapoppin* in 1941, termed by the *New York Times* "a jerky sequence of third-rate gags punctuated by gunfire," followed by *Crazy House* (1943), *Ghost Catchers* (1944), and *See My Lawyer* (1945). Their final film appearance was in a 1957 travelogue called *It's a Tough Life*.

Never successful on radio because of their visual humor, Olsen and Johnson were more effective on television, though their antics were severely limited by the medium. They were signed by NBC as a summer replacement for Milton Berle in 1949 and appeared in "Fireball Fun for All" (1949–1950) and "All Star Revue" (1951). During the 1940s and 1950s Olsen and Johnson continued to tour at home and abroad, including record-breaking appearances in *Grandstand Gayeties* at the Canadian National Exposition in 1948 and 1949 and a brief renewal of their nightclub career at New York's Latin Quarter in 1956.

Olsen and Johnson were partners for forty-seven years. They specialized in a form of ridiculous slapstick comedy that they termed "gonk" (hokum with raisins), never since duplicated. The duo emerged from the last years of vaudeville to prove, as comedy historian Joe Franklin notes, that "rambunctious, nonsensical buffoonery" did not die with vaudeville but survived briefly in the anti-intellectual comedy of these seasoned professionals. At the end of their performances, the comic duo would propose this toast, a suitable unofficial motto to their careers: "May you live as long as you want and may you laugh as long as you live." Johnson died in Las Vegas, Nevada, Olsen in Albuquerque, New Mexico. In 1963 Olsen's body was shipped to Las Vegas from Kansas, where it had been interred, and now lies next to Johnson's in the Palm Mausoleum.

• Clippings are in the New York Public Library for the Performing Arts. Early biographical sketches are in the *New Yorker*, 28 Jan. 1939 and 9 July 1949. Career particulars can be found in *Who Was Who in the Theatre* (1978). See also *Joe Franklin's Encyclopedia of Comedians* (1985 ed.); Leonard Maltin, *Movie Comedy Teams* (1985); and Anthony Slide, *The Encyclopedia of Vaudeville* (1994), for assessments of their comedic material and performances. Johnson's obituary is in the *New York Times* and the London *Times*, both 28 Feb. 1962; Olsen's is in the *New York Times*, 1 Apr. 1963 (it was delayed by a newspaper strike), the London *Times*, 28 Jan. 1963, and *Variety*, 30 Jan. 1963.

DON B. WILMETH

OLSON, Charles John (27 Dec. 1910–10 Jan. 1970), poet and essayist, was born in Worcester, Massachusetts, the son of Karl Joseph Olson, a postman, and Mary Hines. A gifted student, Olson distinguished himself early at Classical High School in Worcester; in his senior year he took third place in the National Oratorical Contest, winning a ten-week trip to Europe, where he met the Irish poet William Butler Yeats. He attended Wesleyan University in Middletown, Connecticut, from 1928 to 1932, graduating Phi Beta Kappa, and completed an M.A. in English there a year later. For two years he was an English instructor at Clark University in Worcester. In 1936 he entered the graduate program in American studies in its inaugural year at Harvard University but left in the spring of 1939 without finishing doctoral work on a study of Herman Melville. A year later he received the first of two Guggenheim Fellowships (a second followed in 1948) to write a book about Melville, a draft of which he completed in his mother's house in Worcester.

Like other bright youths of the depression years, Olson was drawn to politics and the Franklin D. Roosevelt revolution. He joined the American Civil Liberties Union in New York in 1941 and worked his way up the ranks of the Democratic party to become assistant chief of the foreign language section of the Office of War Information (OWI), an agency set up to monitor and protect U.S. minorities as ethnic tensions built during World War II. In August 1941 he began living with Constance Wilcock in a common-law marriage; they had one child.

A promising political career was cut short in 1944 because of Olson's dispute over the censorship of his news releases at the OWI, the forerunner of the U.S. Information Agency. Olson lingered briefly in other offices of the Democratic party until 1945, when Roosevelt died and an era of liberalism in Washington came to an end. Olson declared himself a "post-liberal" soon after and retreated briefly to Key West, Florida, to dedicate himself to poetry.

Olson brought wide learning in the sciences and history to the writing of poetry; he challenged old assumptions about form and lyric content and widened the boundaries of verse discourse to include mythology, psychohistory, geography, comparative culture, and the methodical analysis of social events gleaned from his years at Harvard. After 1950, when his work became better known, the experimental tradition had a new master to whom many younger poets were attracted.

Olson first drew attention to himself with the publication in 1947 of his study of Melville, *Call Me Ishmael*, which had evolved from his master's thesis at Wesleyan into a wide-ranging critique of American culture. Olson perceived Melville's central work, *Moby-Dick*, as a new myth of the West narrating the long era of planetary wanderings begun in Sumeria and ending with the death of the whaling captain, Ahab. The narrator, Ishmael, the lone survivor of the tale whom Olson hails as post-individual man, serves as the counter to the egocentric and imperial Ahab. The title of the study declares Olson's identification with Ishmael.

Ishmael was Olson's ideal observer, a figure more interested in the life around him than in himself. Olson is at pains to demonstrate Ishmael's close scrutiny of life, achieved through disinterested curiosity. The body of work following *Call Me Ishmael* was Olson's attempt to apply Ishmael's selfless attention to poetry, essays, a few plays, and his long poem, *The Maximus Poems*, on which he spent the better part of his writing life.

In 1949 Olson published one of his finest poems, "The Kingfishers," which weaves themes relating to Aztec religion, modern Mexico, archaeology, and world events and in which the poet renounces his European heritage and embraces the Indian cultures of the New World. The poem ushered postmodernism into being, a radical new mode of poetic expression that embraced the tenets of modernism, objectivism, and related movements stemming from Whitman's poetry, and which hailed the return of native cultures at the end of European colonialism.

To explain his method of writing "The Kingfishers," Olson published a manifesto titled *Projective Verse* in 1950; in this statement he set forth the main principles of his projective mode. In brief, it reorients meter to the breathing of the poet in the act of composition and places sound before sense in the construction of the phrase. The projective poem took on a sprawling appearance on the page as it attempted to transpose (project) the flow and mingling of words in the poet's mind onto paper. Olson praised the typewriter as a tool for registering the process by which language formed in the imagination.

A second part of the essay explored the attitude, which he called "objectism," or the role of poet as mere object among other objects in nature, required for writing such poetry. Olson rejected humanism's tendencies to privilege the human observer and to demote surrounding nature as resources and implements. Objectism was Olson's term for Ishmael's selfless scrutiny of life, which he now found in Aztec and Mayan art, where human subjects are cast among the flowers and animals of everyday life.

Soon after publication of *Projective Verse*, Olson made his pilgrimage to the Yucatan Peninsula to study Mayan temples and artifacts. Letters to the poet Robert Creeley, collected in *Mayan Letters* (1953), report Olson's researches into Mayan hieroglyphs, which he began to translate, and his conviction that objectism rested on sound aesthetic principles.

Olson's speculations about Mayan thought follow Ezra Pound's arguments regarding the Chinese written character, and both poets concluded that pictographic languages stand closer to nature than do the more abstract, and egocentric, languages of the modern West. Western humanism ignores the interplay of nature, reducing consciousness to logic. "If man is active, it is exactly here where experience comes in that it is delivered back, and if he stays fresh at the coming in he will be fresh at his going out. If he does not, all that he does inside his house is stale, more and more stale as he is less acute at the door" (*Human Universe and Other Essays*, p. 10).

Indeed, for Pound, William Carlos Williams, the lesser poets of the objectivist movement of the 1930s, and Olson and postmodern writers of the 1950s, nature was an active field of events expressing a plurality of souls in matter. Pound's ideogram was the shorthand verse recognition of spiritual forms in nature; Olson's projective poem was a similar expression of the poet's perceptions of living matter. The reanimation of nature as ensouled and self-cohering was the motive of experimental poetry from the beginning of modernism to Olson's time.

Many short poems followed the publication of *Projective Verse*, variously collected in *In Cold Hell* (1953), *The Distances* (1960), *Archaeologist of Morning* (1970), and *The Collected Poems of Charles Olson* (1987). Not all were cast in the projective mode, however, which worked best with large subjects like war, death, and the nature of history, where the poet introduces many separate themes and draws them together through a chain of connecting perceptions. Smaller subjects inspired fresh language but little experiment in form.

Human Universe and Other Essays, published in 1965, brought together most of Olson's reviews, essays, and speculations on objectism and its animistic roots in non-Western thought. "Human Universe," the title essay, comments at length on Mayan myth and its relevance to contemporary poetry; in "The Gate and the Center," Olson gives more shape to his argument in *Call Me Ishmael* that human migration formed a stage of human history where Western alienation from nature formed and gave rise to the individual.

In 1948 Olson replaced Edward Dahlberg on the faculty of Black Mountain College, an innovative arts school in rural North Carolina, where he joined such illustrious artists and thinkers as Buckminster Fuller, choreographer Merce Cunningham, painters Franz Kline and Josef Albers, and poets Robert Duncan and Robert Creeley. From 1951 to the school's demise in 1956, Olson was rector. During those years he set in motion the literary movement known as Black Mountain poetry. At Black Mountain his verse experiments, researches into Mayan art and religion, and his theories on history and myth drew admiring students and gained wide recognition among fellow poets. In 1956 he separated from Connie Wilcock and began a new common-law relationship with a Black Mountain music student, Augusta Elizabeth "Betty" Kaiser; they had one child.

From the mid-1940s on, Olson was preoccupied with writing a long poem to be called *The Maximus Poems* on the origins of America and its long cultural background reaching back to Mesopotamia. He chose as his speaker the itinerant mystic and writer Maximus, who had lived on the Phoenician coast in the fourth century A.D. and thus occupied a geographical locus parallel to Olson's on the Gloucester coast of North America. Like many long works of the twentieth century, Olson's engaged the present and informed it by means of ancient cultural paradigms: myths, cultural morphologies, and the archetypal events underlying the civilizations of the Western descent.

The project was slow in forming, but by 1953 much of the first volume of the work had been written, and part of it, *The Maximus Poems 1–10*, was published. Another installment, *Maximus 11–22*, followed in 1956, with the complete first volume appearing in 1960 as *The Maximus Poems*. The second volume, *Maximus IV, V, VI* was issued in 1968, but the final volume, *The Maximus Poems: Volume Three*, appeared posthumously in 1975, reconstructed from among Olson's working drafts by a former student, George F. Butterick, and by Charles Boer, a colleague at the University of Connecticut. Like its predecessors, Pound's *The Cantos* and Williams's *Paterson*, Olson's epic remained unfinished at the poet's death, with various drafts pointing to an ongoing text.

The overall structure of the poem is complete, however, and shows a poem growing out of the work of its forebears and steadily evolving its own unique, if sometimes chaotic, structure. *The Maximus Poems* narrates the beginnings of a fishery off Cape Ann that became the Plymouth Bay colony and then Massachusetts. Olson dissects the historical records to show how a small community of fishermen was taken over by

British investors, and thus America itself came under corporate control at its inception.

In the next volume, *Maximus IV, V, VI*, Olson employs "field composition," the use of the page as a landscape on which to represent the play of forces in nature. He called his method "reenactment," and the cascade of words, numbers, and documents maps phases of Western migration, the origins of Gloucester, and the growth and decay of American culture. The shape of history is organic. The upside-down lotus representing the spread of the cosmos in Hindu mythology appears in the poem as a motif of the organicity of all events.

The Maximus Poems, Volume Three, though edited by other hands, follows the logic of the preceding books to close the epic. Maximus explores modern Gloucester through eyes that have witnessed the rise and fall of civilizations elsewhere. The poems, or "letters" as they are sometimes called in the text, are by turns elegiac and contentious, but elegant in their grasp of myth in everyday life. The grand cosmic design is partly revealed in the minutiae of the town, and Maximus, like T. S. Eliot's Tiresias, bears a memory that is the "history of time."

Olson left Black Mountain College in 1957 to write in Gloucester, and from 1963 to 1965 he taught modern literature at the State University of New York at Buffalo. In January 1964 Olson's second wife was killed in a car crash, which stunned him and haunted his poetry toward the end. Work on the *Maximus* cycle slowed in the final years of his life, but his reputation as an innovator and thinker was secure despite the critical controversies raging around him. American poetry would never be the same after him. In 1969 he was invited to teach at the University of Connecticut, but after several sessions he was stricken with liver cancer and was forced to withdraw. He died in New York.

• Olson's papers are housed in two major depositories, the Olson Archive of the University of Connecticut and the Humanities Research Center at the University of Texas, Austin. Other works by Olson are *Causal Mythology* (1969), *The Fiery Hunt and Other Plays* (1977), and *The Post Office: A Memoir of His Father* (1974). Olson's reading list for poets is in *A Bibliography on America for Ed Dorn* (1964). *Selected Writings*, ed. Robert Creeley (1966), and *Additional Prose*, ed. George F. Butterick (1974), reprint short works. *The Special View of History*, ed. Ann Charters (1970), and *Muthologos: The Collected Lectures and Interviews*, ed. Butterick, contain his work on history. *Charles Olson and Ezra Pound: An Encounter at St. Elizabeths* (1975) reprints his notes on Pound. Biographies include Tom Clark, *Charles Olson: The Allegory of a Poet's Life* (1991) and Charles Boer, *Charles Olson in Connecticut* (1975), on the last days. Studies include Ed Dorn, *What I See in the Maximus Poems* (1960), Sherman Paul, *Olson's Push* (1978), Robert von Hallberg, *Charles Olson: The Scholar's Art* (1978), Paul Christensen, *Charles Olson: Call Him Ishmael* (1979), and Don Byrd, *Charles Olson's Maximus* (1980). Olson's correspondence is in *Letters for Origin*, ed. Albert Glover (1969); *Charles Olson and Robert Creeley: The Complete Correspondence*, ed. Butterick (1980–); and *In Love, in Sorrow: The Complete Correspondence of Charles Olson and Edward Dahlberg*, ed. Christensen (1990).

PAUL CHRISTENSEN

OLSON, Floyd Bjornstjerne (13 Nov. 1891–22 Aug. 1936), governor of Minnesota, was born in Minneapolis, Minnesota, the son of Paul Olson, a railroad worker, and Ida Marie Nelson. Olson grew up in the impoverished section of North Minneapolis, and his close association with poverty as a child profoundly influenced his later career in politics. After completing high school in Minneapolis, where he distinguished himself in debate and acting, Olson attended the University of Minnesota in its prelaw curriculum for one year in 1910. He left for financial reasons and worked at a series of jobs in Alaska, the Canadian Northwest, and as a dock worker in Seattle, where he briefly joined the militant Industrial Workers of the World. He returned to Minneapolis in 1913 and resumed his legal studies at night at the Northwestern Law College while working days as a legal clerk. He graduated at the head of his class in 1915 and joined the law firm of Frank Larrabee and Otto Davies. In 1917 he married Ada Krejci, with whom he had one daughter.

In May 1919, at the age of twenty-eight, Olson was appointed assistant county attorney for Hennepin County, reflecting his burgeoning political skills. He twice, in 1918 and 1920, unsuccessfully sought the Democratic nomination for congressman from Minnesota's Fifth Congressional District, yet he remained popular enough with Hennepin County Republicans to gain appointment to the prominent position of county attorney. Taking office in 1920, he held the position for the next ten years, easily winning reelection in 1922 and 1926. As the leading prosecuting attorney for the state's most populous county throughout the 1920s, Olson enjoyed high visibility and steadily increasing stature as an honest, hard-working public official who was not afraid to tackle difficult cases. He led an investigation into the activities of the Ku Klux Klan in 1923 and obtained several indictments against local Klan leaders. He also frequently prosecuted in libel, labor, coal pricing, and municipal graft cases and became well respected for representing the best interests of the people against the power of money and influence.

Olson joined the fledgling Minnesota Farmer-Labor Association, which gained strength in the years immediately following World War I as the farm economy deteriorated. His impressive speaking abilities and his hard-earned reputation as someone interested in the welfare of the common person made him highly attractive to the Farmer-Laborites, who hoped he could meld the disparate rural and urban elements of the party and lead them to victory. As the Farmer-Laborite candidate in the 1924 gubernatorial election, he lost by 40,000 votes to the Republican candidate, Theodore Christianson. Olson remained affiliated with the Farmer-Labor Association but declined to run in the 1928 election.

The onset of the depression in 1929 produced a swift decline in Minnesota's economy and led Olson to believe the Farmer-Laborites could win in the 1930 election. He ran a conservative campaign for governor, emphasizing his interest in appointing to office people who were nonpartisan and committed to the welfare of all Minnesotans. He won by nearly 200,000 votes and carried all but five counties. Although he would be reelected twice, Olson's party never controlled the Minnesota legislature. Throughout his three terms as governor, he constantly fought the more conservative elements in the legislature. Despite this, he signed a number of bills relating to expanding public works, regulating securities, encouraging cooperative enterprises (a favorite of the Farmer-Laborites), and conservation of natural resources. Much of Minnesota's legislation anticipated Franklin D. Roosevelt's New Deal, which began in 1933. Olson greatly admired Roosevelt, and during his last two terms as governor his state's program mirrored the New Deal. He gained passage of a mortgage moratorium, a state income tax, allocation of $15 million in direct relief to the destitute, and congressional reapportionment in recognition of the steady migration from rural to urban areas taking place in Minnesota since World War I. In 1934 Olson tackled a disruptive trucker's strike by declaring martial law after the strikers accepted his demand that they agree to mediation of the conflict. The employers sought an injunction of Olson's action, but the governor's position was upheld by the Minnesota Federal Court.

By 1934 Olson declared that he was not a liberal but a radical, and he called for the abolition of capitalism and the socialization of all means of production. Despite the belief of many that he should challenge Franklin Roosevelt in 1936, he supported Roosevelt for reelection, believing that having a Democrat in the White House willing to listen would best serve Farm-Laborite party interests to expand governmental services on behalf of the downtrodden. Olson instead began his campaign for the 1936 Senate contest. Late in 1935, however, he was diagnosed with pancreatic cancer, to which he succumbed at the Mayo Clinic in Rochester, Minnesota.

Olson was a pragmatic politician, whose words were often more radical than his deeds. His popularity with voters and his reputation for personal generosity and honesty enabled him to work effectively with an often hostile legislature in passing numerous laws that expanded the role of state government in the lives of Minnesotans. Olson believed government should function for the benefit of the many, not the few, and he devoted his life to that end.

• Olson's papers are in the Minnesota Historical Society, which also contains manuscripts relating to the Minnesota Farmer-Labor Association. Though dated, the best biography remains George H. Mayer, *The Political Career of Floyd B. Olson* (1951). Also useful is John S. McGrath and James J. Delmont, *Floyd Bjornsterne Olson: Minnesota's Greatest Liberal Governor, A Memorial Volume* (1937). Olson's early career is covered in Steven Donald Jansen, "Floyd Olson: The Years Prior to His Governorship, 1891–1930" (Ph.D. diss., Univ. of Kansas, 1985). Olson's political abilities are analyzed by Kenneth L. Berger, "A Rhetorical Analysis of the Public Speaking of Floyd B. Olson" (Ph.D. diss., Univ. of Minnesota, 1955). An obituary is in the *New York Times*, 23 Aug. 1936.

EDWARD A. GOEDEKEN

OLSON, Harry Ferdinand (28 Dec. 1901–1 Apr. 1982), acoustical engineer, was born in Mount Pleasant, Iowa, the son of Frans O. Olson and Nelly Benson, farmers. He became interested in electricity while in high school and designed and built all the components for a steam-driven direct current generator and an amateur radio station. He matriculated at the University of Iowa, where he studied electrical engineering, receiving his B.E. degree in 1924. As a graduate student at Iowa, he experimented with acoustic wave filters in solids and atom beams and received his M.A. in 1925 and Ph.D. in physics in 1928.

Olson moved from Iowa to New York City to join the research department of the Radio Corporation of America (RCA) as an acoustical researcher. In 1930 he was assigned to the RCA Photophone Division's engineering department, but he returned to the research department two years later, the same year he received his E.E. degree from Iowa. Charged with developing a replacement for the omnidirectional microphones then being used to record sound for "talking" motion pictures, he invented a bidirectional microphone that could pick up the same volume level at twice the distance. In 1930 he also patented a unidirectional "ribbon" microphone; its diaphragm consisted of a piece of magnetic tape that could pick up actors' voices without also picking up extraneous noise and echoes resulting from the acoustical design of the sound stage. This microphone was quickly adopted for use in virtually all applications of sound recording and radio broadcasting.

In 1935 Olson married Lorene E. Johnson, with whom he had no children. He had become, in 1934, the director of acoustical research for RCA Manufacturing Company. Under his supervision, the company continued to develop a variety of specialized microphones for commercial and military applications, as well as high-quality commercial sound reproduction equipment, such as the double voice coil loudspeaker and the multiple flare horn. In 1942 Olson was made director of RCA's newly formed Acoustical Research Laboratory in Princeton, New Jersey, in facilities constructed according to his specifications. One of its first customers was the U.S. government, for which Olson directed several research projects related to underwater warfare. The most important projects involved the development of improved sonar transducers for detecting submarines, and acoustic proximity fuses for detonating depth charges when they came within range of an enemy submarine. He also developed an ultrasensitive stethoscope for use in medical research.

After World War II Olson turned his attention to the reproduction of music. He was particularly interested in why most listeners seemed to prefer recorded music with an upper frequency cutoff of 5,000 hertz, even though the partial tones of most musical instruments had frequencies as high as 15,000 hertz. He soon discovered that what listeners objected to was not the higher frequencies per se, but rather the nonlinear distortion produced with higher frequencies by the sound reproduction systems of the day. In 1948 he invented a jewel-tipped vacuum tube for picking up sounds from a phonograph record. The vibrations the jewel picked up as it tracked along the record's grooves were converted by the tube into electrical impulses that could then be amplified without distortion. This apparatus served as the prototype for high-fidelity pickups and stimulated the development of high-fidelity phonographs and records. Olson also began experimenting with synthetic music, and in 1955 he and Herbert Belar demonstrated the RCA Electronic Music Synthesizer. Constructed from vacuum tubes and relay switches, the synthesizer was capable of reproducing the characteristic frequency, intensity, timbre, growth, steady state, decay, portamento, vibrato, and deviations of virtually any voice or musical instrument, either singly or in ensemble.

Meanwhile, Olson continued to work with microphones. In 1949 he developed the single element cardioid microphone, an instrument that outperformed the unidirectional microphone because it could pick up sounds in narrower bands of wavelengths. This feature led to its widespread adoption in both the television and motion picture industries. In the early 1950s he collaborated with researchers at the 3M Corporation in order to improve magnetic tape and recording heads so that prerecorded color television signals could be broadcast, a feat successfully performed in 1955. He and Belar also developed a phonetic typewriter in 1957, and in 1962 a complete speech-processing system, which included a speech analyzer, translator, typer, and synthesizer. In 1967 he became vice president of acoustical and electromechanical research. He retired that same year but continued to serve RCA as a consultant until the early 1970s.

Olson authored seven books and more than 130 scientific papers related to acoustical engineering, the physics of music, and sound reproduction. He was active in the affairs of the Acoustical Society of America (ASA) and served as a member of its executive council (1937–1940), vice president (1942–1944), and president (1953–1954); he was also associate editor of the *Journal of the Acoustical Society of America* for thirty years. He helped to found the Audio Engineering Society and served as its president in 1960. He received the National Association of Manufacturers' Modern Pioneer Award (1940), the Audio Engineering Society's John H. Potts Gold Medal (1952) and its Emile Berliner Award (1965), the Society of Motion Picture and Television Engineers' Samuel L. Warner Medal (1955), the City of Philadelphia's John Scott Medal and the Institute of Radio Engineers Professional Group on Audio's Achievement Award (1956), the American Society of Swedish Engineers' John Erics-

son Medal (1963), the Institute of Electrical and Electronics Engineers' Mervin J. Kelly Medal (1967) and its Lamme Gold Medal (1970), the Consumers Electronics Award (1969), and the ASA's first Silver Medal (1974) and its Gold Medal (1981). He was elected to the National Academy of Sciences in 1959. He died in Princeton.

Olson was a pioneer in the field of acoustical engineering. He held more than one hundred patents related to the design of microphones, loudspeakers, and stereophonic components, and he established RCA Acoustical Research Laboratory as a driving force in the discovery, engineering, and development of innovative methods for reproducing and amplifying sound.

• Olson's publications include *Acoustical Engineering* (1957), *Dynamical Analogies* (2d ed., 1958), and *Music, Physics, and Engineering* (1966). A biography, including a bibliography and a partial list of his patents, is Cyril M. Harris, "Harry F. Olson," National Academy of Sciences, *Biographical Memoirs* 58 (1989): 407–23. An obituary is in the *New York Times*, 4 Apr. 1982.

CHARLES W. CAREY, JR.

OLSON, Sigurd Ferdinand (4 Apr. 1899–13 Jan. 1982), writer and conservationist, was born in Chicago, Illinois, the son of Lawrence J. Olson (born Lars Jakob Olsson), a Swedish Baptist minister, and Ida May Cedarholm. He spent most of his childhood in northern Wisconsin, where he formed his lifelong attachment to nature and outdoor recreation. Olson earned a bachelor of science degree from the University of Wisconsin in 1920. He returned briefly in 1922 for graduate work in geology and earned a master's degree in zoology (animal ecology) from the University of Illinois in 1932. Meanwhile, in 1921 he married Elizabeth Dorothy Uhrenholdt; they had two children.

From 1923 to 1936 Olson taught at a high school and then at a junior college in Ely, Minnesota, in the northeastern part of the state. In 1936 he became dean of the Ely Junior College, a position he held until he resigned in 1947 to become a full-time writer and professional conservationist.

Ely remained Olson's home for the rest of his life. An iron-mining town on the Vermilion Range, it was located at the edge of the Quetico-Superior, several million acres of lakeland wilderness straddling the border between the United States and Canada. Olson traveled and guided there for many years, and he grew convinced that wilderness provided spiritual experiences vital to modern civilization. This conviction formed the basis of both his conservation and writing careers.

Olson became an active conservationist in the 1920s, fighting to keep roads and then dams out of the Quetico-Superior. In the 1940s he spearheaded a precedent-setting fight to ban airplanes from flying into the area; the conflict propelled him to the front ranks of the conservation movement. Olson served as wilderness ecologist for the Izaak Walton League of America from 1948 until his death, as vice president and then president of the National Parks Association from 1951 to 1959, as vice president and then president of the Wilderness Society from 1963 to 1971, and as an adviser to the National Park Service and to the secretary of the interior from 1959 to the early 1970s. He helped draft the 1964 Wilderness Act, which established the U.S. wilderness preservation system. He played an important role in the establishment of Alaska's Arctic Wildlife Refuge and helped to identify and recommend other Alaskan lands ultimately preserved in the Alaska National Interest Lands Conservation Act of 1980. Among his many other activities, he played key roles in the establishment of Point Reyes National Seashore in California and Voyageurs National Park in Minnesota. In recognition of his work, four of the five largest U.S. conservation organizations—the Sierra Club, the Wilderness Society, the National Wildlife Federation, and the Izaak Walton League—gave Olson their highest awards.

Often pictured with a pipe in his hand and a warm yet reflective expression on his weathered face, Olson became a living icon to many environmentalists, "the personification of the wilderness defender," according to former Sierra Club president Edgar Wayburn. He was trusting and sentimental but also a strong leader who could bring together warring factions of environmentalists. "I think he always kept his eye on the star, and he didn't get down here where we more common folks deal more with personalities," said former Wilderness Society president Ted Swem. "He made wilderness and life sing," said George Marshall, a former president of both the Sierra Club and the Wilderness Society. And yet in Olson's hometown of Ely, where many residents blamed wilderness regulations for the poor local economy, he was jeered and hanged in effigy. And, until he left the junior college in 1947, Olson often felt trapped in his career and sometimes despaired of his chances to achieve his dream of writing full time.

Olson's large and at times almost worshipful following derived in part from personal charisma but especially from the humanistic philosophy that he professed in nine popular books, in magazine articles, and in numerous speeches and interviews. He had a way of writing and speaking about the natural world that touched deep emotions in his audiences, and many responded with heartfelt letters. An excerpt from his bestselling first book, *The Singing Wilderness* (1956), shows his unpretentious, yet lyrical, style:

The movement of a canoe is like a reed in the wind. Silence is part of it, and the sounds of lapping water, bird songs, and wind in the trees. It is part of the medium through which it floats, the sky, the water, the shores. . . . There is magic in the feel of a paddle and the movement of a canoe, a magic compounded of distance, adventure, solitude, and peace. The way of a canoe is the way of the wilderness, and of a freedom almost forgotten. It is an antidote to insecurity, the open door to waterways of ages past and a way of life with profound and abiding satisfactions. When a man is part of his canoe, he is part of all that canoes have ever known.

In 1974 Olson received the Burroughs Medal, the highest honor in nature writing. His other books include *Listening Point* (1958), *The Lonely Land* (1961), *Runes of the North* (1963), *Open Horizons* (1969), *The Hidden Forest* (1969), *Wilderness Days* (1972), *Reflections from the North Country* (1976), and *Of Time and Place* (1982). He died in Ely.

Olson believed that the psychic, as well as physical, needs of humanity were rooted in the Pleistocene environment that dominated the evolutionary history of our species. This conviction, combined with his single-minded focus on spiritual values, distinguished him from other leading philosophers of the wilderness-preservation movement. Olson was a humanist influenced by the literary naturalists W. H. Hudson and John Burroughs as well as by many other thinkers and social critics of the nineteenth and twentieth centuries, including Ralph Waldo Emerson and Henry David Thoreau, Aldous Huxley and Julian Huxley, Pierre Teilhard de Chardin, Lewis Mumford, and Carl Jung. Olson argued that people could best come to know their true selves by returning to their biological roots. As he said at a Sierra Club conference in 1965:

I have discovered in a lifetime of traveling in primitive regions, a lifetime of seeing people living in the wilderness and using it, that there is a hard core of wilderness need in everyone, a core that makes its spiritual values a basic human necessity. There is no hiding it. . . . Unless we can preserve places where the endless spiritual needs of man can be fulfilled and nourished, we will destroy our culture and ourselves.

• Olson's papers are at the Minnesota Historical Society in St. Paul. His memoir, *Open Horizons* (1969), also is an important source. David Backes, *A Wilderness Within: The Life of Sigurd F. Olson* (1996), provides the most complete assessment. Olson's conservation activities in the Quetico-Superior wilderness receive attention in Backes, *Canoe Country: An Embattled Wilderness* (1991). Jim Dale Vickery, *Wilderness Visionaries* (1986), includes a chapter on Olson. Another important source is the introduction by his son Robert Keith Olson to *The Collected Works of Sigurd F. Olson, The Early Writings: 1921–1934*, ed. Mike Link (1988). Important articles include Frank Graham, Jr., "Leave It to the Bourgeois," *Audubon*, Nov. 1980, pp. 28–39; Dorothy Boyle Huyck, "Sig Olson: Wilderness Philosopher," *American Forests*, May 1965, pp. 46–47, 72–74; and the Autumn 1981 issue of *Naturalist*, dedicated to Olson. The best widely available obituaries are in the *Minneapolis Tribune*, 14 Jan. 1982, and *Living Wilderness*, Spring 1982.

DAVID BACKES

OLSSON, Olof (31 Mar. 1841–12 May 1900), Lutheran clergyman and theological professor, was born in Karlskoga, Sweden, the son of Anders Olsson, a farmer, and Britta Jonsdotter. Olsson's family life was characterized by fervent Christian faith and practice. His mother had been especially affected by the nineteenth-century pietistic religious revival with its emphases upon conscious religious experience, reading of the Scriptures, prayer, and conventicles (meetings held by laity). Although critical of the established church, she did not advocate schism.

Olsson displayed early signs of intellectual and musical ability. He was tutored by his mother, attended a folk school near Karlskoga, and studied privately for a year with a parish clerk and organist. At age seventeen, he came under the influence of Rev. Dr. Peter Fjellstedt, who, as the leader and pioneer of nineteenth-century missionary activity, traveled extensively. On an 1858 visit to Karlskoga, Fjellstedt persuaded Olsson to give his life to missions. That year, Olsson enrolled in the Fjellstedt Mission Institute in Stockholm. Although Fjellstedt believed that a year at the mission school at Leipzig would benefit Olsson, the school's rigid orthodoxy and high church style was too severe a contrast to the warm piety of Olsson's background. In early 1860, Olsson returned to his home for a brief period of healing and spent some time working in Vall, where the pietists had established an orphanage and a private school. There he met Anna Lisa Jonsdotter, whom he married in 1864; they had seven children.

Olsson enrolled at Uppsala University in the autumn of 1860 and was ordained in December 1863. Between 1863 and 1869, he served three successive parishes: Brunskog, Persberg, and Sunnemo. Though well received for his abilities as preacher, teacher, and musician, he came into conflict with his bishop, the ecclesiastical hierarchy, and many of his fellow pastors for his pietistic emphasis.

Several factors turned Olsson's attention to America: he was interested in missions; America was looked upon as a field for missionary activity by the pietists; and from Fjellstedt he had gained a deep interest in Native Americans. (On an 1876 visit to the Delaware tribe near Chetopa, Kansas, Olsson proposed, without success, that the Augustana Lutheran Synod begin a mission among these people.) Finally, he saw in America "framtidslandet," the land of the future. In 1869 the Olssons emigrated to America with 200 other people, of whom about 100 were from his own parish of Sunnemo. They settled in central Kansas around Lindsborg.

Olsson founded Bethany Lutheran Church in August 1869. Intended as a "pure church," where only people with a vital Christian experience could be members, it affiliated a year later with the Augustana Lutheran Synod, which had been founded by Swedish Lutheran immigrants in 1860. Conflict soon erupted between the Bethany pietists and an anticonfessional group who followed the neo-pietistic route of a more subjective type of Christian faith and worship. This group broke away and formed an Evangelical Covenant congregation in 1873 and 1874. Although Olsson remained more pietistic than some of his fellow Augustana Lutheran pastors, he had a closer kinship with his fellow pastors than with the more radical neo-pietists. The controversy in Lindsborg produced in Olsson a deepened loyalty to the Lutheran Confes-

sions, especially Luther's *Small Catechism* and the *Augsburg Confession*, in which he found the strength that he needed.

Olsson also played an important role in the political arena. In 1870–1871 he was the superintendent of schools in McPherson County. There is no evidence that his position as clergyman caused political tensions; his ability and skills apparently equipped him well to occupy this important office. He also served as a Republican representative to the state legislature in 1871 and 1872.

In 1876 Olsson became professor of theology at Augustana College and Theological Seminary in Rock Island, Illinois, where, except for two brief periods in 1879–1880 and 1891, during which he traveled to Europe, he spent the remainder of his life. In 1891 he became president of the college and seminary. He served in this office until his death.

As pastor, preacher, theologian, and author, Olsson won distinction and wide respect. Among his writings, *Vid korset. Betraktelser öfver frälsningen i Kristus* (*At the Cross: Meditations on Salvation in Christ*) (1887) was especially influential. In it he stated the doctrine of the Atonement on the basis of the Lutheran Confessions over against the views of the group in Lindsborg who had formed the Evangelical Covenant congregation. Olsson believed that, according to the Lutheran Confessions, sin is a violation of God's righteousness and only through God's work in Christ's suffering and death can humanity be reconciled with God. The Evangelical Covenant congregation considered the death of Christ powerful enough to stimulate within the believer love great enough to effect a reconciliation; they thus believed that humanity plays a greater part in reconciliation.

Olsson organized a choir at Bethany Lutheran Church and is said to have transcribed the notes into numbers so that musically inexperienced choir members could sing parts. He was also the major force in the establishment of oratorio societies at both Augustana and Bethany Colleges. Each of these groups has continued annual renditions of Handel's *Messiah* and other sacred works for over a hundred years.

During his presidency of Augustana College and Seminary, Olsson presided over significant changes. The Oratorio Society was incorporated into the Conservatory of Music; English began to displace Swedish; and women became increasingly important on the campus. Whereas before this time the course of study had centered around the classics and languages, now parallel courses—classical and scientific—were established. A normal department was inaugurated to prepare teachers for public as well as parochial schools. A varsity football team was begun in 1893, and physical education was expanded.

Olsson died in Rock Island, Illinois. His rich poetical and musical gifts, his piety based on the Lutheran Confessions, and his writings have continued to influence Augustana and Bethany Colleges. For historians who seek not only to understand the genius of the Augustana Lutheran Synod (or "Church," since 1948) but also to better interpret American and world Lutheranism, to which Augustana made significant contributions, Olsson's work is significant.

• Olsson's papers are in the Augustana College Library, Rock Island, Ill. Among his most significant theological works, whose readership included both Swedish Americans and readers in Sweden, are *Betraktelser vid korset* (*Meditations on the Cross*) (1878), *Grundragen af en sann medborgares karakter* (*Basic Traits of a True Citizen's Character*) (1883), *Det Kristna hoppet. Tröstens ord i lidanet och sorgen* (*The Christian Hope: The Word of Comfort in Suffering and Sorrow*) (1887), *Reformation, Socinianism and Waldenstromianism* (1880), and *Wid korset. Betraktelser för den stilla veckan* (*At the Cross: Meditations for Holy Week*) (1940), which was translated into English by Daniel Nystrom as *Salvation in Christ* (1942). Olsson's travel diaries are *Helsningar från fjerran. Minnen från en resa genom England och Tyskland år 1879* (*Greetings from Afar: Memories from a Journey through England and Germany in the Year 1879*) (1880) and *Till Rome och hem igen* (*To Rome and Home Again*) (1890). Biographical works include Johannes A. Nyvall, "Doktor Olsson," *Korsbaneret. Kristlig Kalendar for 1901* (*Banner of the Cross: Christian Calendar for 1901*), ed. J. G. Dahlberg, 22 (1901): 141–66; and Ernst William Olson, *Olof Olsson: The Man, His Work, and His Thought* (1941). See also Emory Lindquist, *Vision for a Valley: Olof Olsson and the History of Lindsborg* (1970).

EMMET E. EKLUND

O'MAHONEY, Joseph Christopher (5 Nov. 1884–1 Dec. 1962), U.S. senator, was born in Chelsea, Massachusetts, the son of Irish immigrant parents, Denis O'Mahoney, a furrier, and Elizabeth Sheehan. One of eleven children, he attended Columbia University (1905–1907) and received the LL.B. degree from Georgetown University in 1920. He married Agnes Veronica O'Leary in 1913; they had no children.

O'Mahoney worked as a newspaper reporter for the Boulder (Colo.) *Herald* from 1908 to 1916 then moved to Wyoming to become the Cheyenne *State Leader*'s city editor. Originally a Theodore Roosevelt Progressive, he switched to the Democratic party in 1916. When the newspaper's owner, Democratic governor John B. Kendrick, became a U.S. senator in 1917, O'Mahoney went along as his executive secretary. He served as vice chairman of the Democratic party's state committee from 1922 to 1930. An unsuccessful candidate for the U.S. Senate in 1924 and 1928, O'Mahoney played a leading role in writing the party platform at the 1932 Democratic National Convention, and in the ensuing campaign he served as the national campaign committee's vice chairman. The new Democratic administration rewarded his efforts by appointing him first assistant U.S. postmaster general in 1933. Senator Kendrick died later that year, and O'Mahoney was appointed to serve the remainder of his term. He was elected for a regular term in 1934 and reelected in 1940 and 1946.

In his long and distinguished senatorial career, O'Mahoney served on the Appropriations, Judiciary, and Interior committees, chairing the last from 1949 to 1952. A consistent supporter of issues of importance to his Wyoming constituents, he sponsored or supported legislation that dealt with oil, livestock, and land and water policy. Remaining faithful to his progressive principles during the 1930s, he supported much of the New Deal, especially federal intervention in the economy to destroy trusts, aid agriculture, and harness water power. Like other western progressives, however, he balked at the dramatic expansion of the federal government's authority and questioned the need for so much welfare-state legislation. The antimonopoly bill he cosponsored with Idaho senator William Borah, a demanding measure that never came close to passage, required a more rigorous application of antitrust laws than President Franklin D. Roosevelt was willing to countenance. He failed to endorse Roosevelt's Court-packing plan because he felt that the addition of more justices would not curtail the Supreme Court's abuse of power. Instead, he favored unanimous decisions before the Supreme Court could exercise its power of judicial review. Believing that suffrage alterations required constitutional amendment, he deviated from liberal orthodoxy by opposing anti–poll tax legislation.

O'Mahoney became best known as the bête noire of monopoly capitalism, supporting government supervision and regulation of large-scale corporations in behalf of small businesses and consumers. In 1938 he introduced the resolution creating the Temporary National Economic Committee (TNEC), an ad hoc body composed of six congressmen and six representatives from the executive branch, and chaired the committee during its existence from 1938 to 1941. His skillful handling of the committee, especially his probing yet cordial interrogation of hostile witnesses, won high praise from the press and the admiration of his congressional colleagues.

As a result of the committee's deliberations, O'Mahoney proposed a series of reforms, including more rigorous enforcement of antitrust laws; tax reduction to bolster small businesses and encourage new entrepreneurial ventures; mandatory national charters for corporations conducting interstate transactions to protect consumers; and the selection of goals for economic growth by a national assemblage of agriculture, business, labor, and consumer representatives. President Harry S. Truman subsequently incorporated some of the TNEC recommendations, such as a full-employment law and a peacetime Fair Employment Practices Commission, into his Fair Deal program. After his pioneering work on the TNEC, he focused his efforts in the Senate on dismantling monopolies, encouraging small-business enterprises, regulating insurance companies, and creating new ways for the federal government to manage the national economy. O'Mahoney cosponsored the Employment Act of 1946, establishing the Joint Congressional Economic Committee, which he chaired for three terms, and the Council of Economic Advisers.

During the Cold War years O'Mahoney played a prominent Senate role in addressing other major policy issues. In 1945 he introduced a resolution calling for an international agreement prohibiting the use of atomic weaponry. O'Mahoney lost to Republican

Frank A. Barrett in 1952. When Wyoming's other senator, Lester C. Hunt, died in 1954, O'Mahoney was elected to fill the vacant seat and simultaneously elected to the full term ending 3 January 1961. He strongly opposed the controversial Dixon-Yates contract in 1955, which would have allowed a private consortium proposing the construction of a power plant in Memphis, Tennessee, to achieve a monopoly. He contested Lewis Strauss's confirmation as secretary of commerce in 1959 because he objected to Strauss's performance as chairman of the Atomic Energy Commission, particularly his stance against public power in the controversial Dixon-Yates affair. O'Mahoney worked successfully to include a provision in the 1957 Civil Rights Act for jury trials in civil-rights cases, an addition requested by southerners and supported by many western Democrats to curb the growth of federal power, and he labored throughout the 1950s on behalf of statehood for Alaska and Hawaii. After suffering a stroke in 1959, the courtly, highly respected senator retired in 1961. He died at the Bethesda, Maryland, Naval Medical Center.

• O'Mahoney's papers are located in the University of Wyoming's Western History Research Center. There is a transcript of an interview with him in Columbia University's Oral History Collection. There is no O'Mahoney biography, but an important part of his senatorial career is covered in Frank Alan Coombs, "Joseph Christopher O'Mahoney: The New Deal Years" (Ph.D. diss., Univ. of Illinois at Urbana-Champaign, 1968). An obituary is in the *New York Times*, 2 Dec. 1962.

ROGER BILES

O'MAHONY, John (1816–6 Feb. 1877), political leader, was born in Mitchelstown, County Cork, Ireland, the son of Daniel O'Mahony, a landowner. He obtained his primary education at Hamblin's School in Middletown, County Cork, and was admitted in 1833 to Trinity College, Dublin. The death of his father and his older brother brought his studies to an abrupt end, as O'Mahony returned to "Ballycurkeen House," the family estate, in 1835 to manage the property he inherited.

The O'Mahony family was well known in Cork, not only for its affluence and its connection to the chieftainship of the clan but also for its support of Irish Catholic nationalism. O'Mahony's father and uncle had long been staunch opponents of the earls of Kingston, the dominant Protestant gentry family of the county, and had played a part in the abortive Irish rebellion of 1798. Coming as he did from such a family, it is not surprising that O'Mahony would be drawn to "Young Ireland," the romantic nationalist movement for independence, or that his involvement in this movement would eventually draw him into armed resistance to British rule. In 1848 he used his local prestige to gather a body of armed men, whom he led in the short-lived anti-British insurrection masterminded by William Smith O'Brien. This brief rebellion had longstanding consequences for O'Mahony; with a price on his head, he made over all of his property to his sister and fled to exile in Paris. There, in the company of fellow rebel and Young Irelander James Stephens, O'Mahony eked out a penurious living from remittances and language tutoring while partaking of the radical culture of the Parisian working class, fresh from its own 1848 rising.

In 1853 O'Mahony moved to New York, New York. The following year he helped found a paramilitary organization, the Robert Emmet Monument Association, named for an Irish poet and martyr of the 1798 rebellion. The association, which was founded to exploit Britain's difficulties in the Crimean War to Irish advantage, disbanded when the conflict ended in 1855 but served as the model for another group that emerged a few years later, the Fenian Brotherhood. The Fenians were the American branch of a society of the same name founded in Ireland by Stephens in 1858. Stephens realized that America, with its large population of Irish immigrants, would be an important recruiting ground for the cause of Irish independence from Great Britain and made O'Mahony the brotherhood's "head centre," in charge of fundraising and recruitment in the United States. Although his relationship with Stephens was often competitive and acrimonious, O'Mahony was a great success as a Fenian leader: He raised about £80,000 from the United States and Canada for the Fenian cause between 1860 and 1867; transformed small, relatively insignificant Irish-American groups into the Fenian Brotherhood; and recognized that Irish Americans were an important constituency for anti-British activism. During the Civil War he raised and commanded the largely Irish Ninety-ninth New York Regiment, recruited Irish Americans to join several other Union regiments, and garnered many donations to the Fenian cause.

Despite these successes, the American Fenians began to chafe under O'Mahony's autocratic leadership, and at the annual Fenian Congress in 1865, the members drew up a new constitution that retained him as president but also installed a senate to check his powers. A few months later a quarrel over the sale of Fenian bonds led to a split in the brotherhood, both sides of which claimed use of the name. The anti-O'Mahony faction installed W. R. Roberts as president and made plans for an invasion of English Canada, hoping to force Britain to negotiate over Ireland's status within the empire. The two factions reconciled in April 1866, and O'Mahony reluctantly organized a raid on Campobello Island, New Brunswick, in an attempt to regain his position as head of the Fenians. O'Mahony did not personally take part in the raid, which failed when James "Red Jim" MacDermott, O'Mahony's secretary who was actually a British spy, betrayed the plans to the Canadian government. This military maneuver ended in utter disaster for the Fenians and for O'Mahony, whose offer of resignation was immediately accepted by Stephens.

The American Fenian Brotherhood went into eclipse, superseded in the following years by the wealthier and far better-organized Clan na Gael. In 1872 an attempt to revive the brotherhood called

O'Mahony out of retirement and reinstated him as head centre. Although he held the title until just before his death, O'Mahony was unable to restore the brotherhood's former prestige and prosperity, and his last years were spent in great poverty in New York, where he died. He never married. Ironically, his glorious reputation was restored immediately after his death, when rival Irish nationalist groups competed to offer the most impressive tributes to him. His body was sent from New York to Ireland, where his burial at Glasnevin Cemetery, Dublin, on 4 March 1877 was the occasion of an enormous and majestic memorial demonstration.

Under O'Mahony's leadership, the Fenians commanded the loyalty of the post-famine Irish immigrants in the United States; he molded them into a powerful, self-defined voluntary organization that linked the causes of Irish freedom with the antislavery movement and support of the Union in the Civil War. Despite the many reversals and great poverty he suffered, O'Mahony was regarded after his death as an important architect of what became known as the Irish Republican Army and as the founder of the organization's financial and political support in the United States.

• O'Mahony's career receives significant attention in a number of histories of the Fenian movement, including R. V. Comerford, *The Fenians in Context* (1985); Leon O'Broin, *Fenian Fever: An Anglo-American Dilemma* (1971); and John Newsinger, *Fenianism in Mid-Victorian Britain* (1994). He also appears in the memoirs of several Irish nationalists, including John O'Leary, *Recollections of Fenians and Fenianism* (1896), and Joseph Denieffe, *Personal Narrative of the Irish Revolutionary Brotherhood* (1883). O'Mahony's obituary is in the *New York Herald*, 7 Feb. 1877, and the New York *Irish World*, 17 Feb. 1877.

NATALIE ZACEK

O'MALLEY, Walter Francis (9 Oct. 1903–9 Aug. 1979), baseball executive, was born in New York City, the son of Edwin J. O'Malley, a businessman and politician, and Alma Feltner. After having been elected to several class offices, he graduated with honors in engineering from the University of Pennsylvania in 1926. His father's business reverses in the late 1920s forced O'Malley to drop out of Columbia University Law School, but by attending evening classes he obtained a law degree from Fordham University in 1930. In 1931, he married Katherine Hanson, a childhood sweetheart; the couple had two children.

O'Malley, a self-characterized "hustler," quickly established himself as a successful engineer, businessman, and lawyer. Apart from hard work, savvy, and a penchant for risk-taking, his joviality, charm, legal expertise, and Tammany Hall political connections aided him in obtaining part ownership of (among other firms) the J. P. Duffy Company (building materials), the Long Island Railroad, the Brooklyn Borough Gas Company, the New York Subway Advertising Company, and Trommer breweries. As an attorney, he represented several large banking enterprises, and in

that capacity he became chief counsel of the Brooklyn Dodgers' baseball franchise in 1943. In transactions in 1944 and 1945, he, along with John L. Smith and Branch Rickey, obtained 75 percent of the Dodgers' stock. In 1950, O'Malley gained complete control of the club by purchasing Rickey's stock for $1.05 million and other outstanding shares for about $1 million.

During O'Malley's ownership of the Dodgers from 1950 until his death in 1979, no club in the major leagues was more consistently successful. The club won National League championships in 1952, 1953, 1955, 1956, 1959, 1963, 1965, 1966, 1974, 1977, and 1978 as well as the World Series in 1955, 1959, 1963, and 1965. O'Malley's teams initially owed much of their success to Rickey, who had established the Dodgers' farm system and pioneered in recruiting black players, but O'Malley soon made his own mark. Unlike many owners whose interests were outside of baseball, O'Malley, on assuming the presidency of the Dodgers, became a full-time baseball executive. He handled all business matters while delegating player development and field management to others. No other franchise exhibited more continuity in personnel or constancy in strategy than the Dodgers. Emil "Buzzy" Bavasi served as the club's general manager for eighteen years, and Walter Alston managed the Dodgers on the field for twenty-three seasons.

Amid a storm of controversy, O'Malley in 1958 initiated major league baseball's expansion to the West Coast. Although in the early 1950s Brooklyn's franchise had been the most profitable in baseball, after 1952 attendance averaged less than half that of the Braves who had moved from Boston to Milwaukee in 1953. For the Dodgers to compete successfully with the Braves and to remain in Brooklyn, O'Malley insisted, he needed a new ballpark that was more accessible to automobiles. While New York authorities dallied, Los Angeles offered O'Malley a 300-acre site for a ballpark in downtown Los Angeles with easy access to several freeways. In the meantime, O'Malley convinced Horace Stoneham, owner of the New York Giants, to move his club to San Francisco so that the two teams could continue their long-time rivalry and reduce the travel costs of the other National League teams. Since the Dodgers had become the single most important symbol in giving Brooklyn its distinctive identity, the borough's fans long afterward felt betrayed by O'Malley.

On the acreage furnished by Los Angeles, O'Malley built his own ballpark, Dodger Stadium, which, when completed in 1962, cost $18 million. A magnificent park, it seated 56,000 fans, had parking spaces for 16,000 cars, and featured a giant electric scorecard. O'Malley spent more than a million dollars on landscaping; he had olive and palm trees planted in the parking lots and installed a Japanese garden in center field. At Dodger Stadium, the last baseball facility built by private funds, the Dodgers regularly attracted more than two million fans per season, and in 1979 broke a major league record by passing the three million mark. By then no other franchise exceeded the worth of the Dodgers. In 1970, O'Malley turned the presidency of the club over to his son, Peter, while he remained chairman of the board of directors.

O'Malley's power extended far beyond the Dodgers, although it fell short of making him "the real boss [of all] of baseball," as claimed by Bill Veeck, then owner of the Chicago White Sox, as well as by sportswriters and subsequent historians of the game. Unlike professional football, major league baseball was not a close-knit economic cartel. Only with excruciating reluctance did the owners yield any of their power. Even the artful O'Malley was unable to have his way on some issues dear to him. For example, he failed to block the adoption of the amateur draft in 1965, which provided that teams could sign amateur players to contracts in reverse order of their previous season's standings. The draft, along with player free agency in 1976, would encourage in the 1980s a new era of team parity on the playing field. Furthermore, the other owners repeatedly rebuffed O'Malley's proposals for league realignment and expansion.

Yet from the 1950s through the 1970s, no one exceeded O'Malley's influence in shaping the history of baseball. He served on the major leagues' five-man owner's executive council for twenty-eight years where he was chiefly responsible for negotiating baseball's radio and television contracts. Apart from building the most successful franchise both on and off the field and introducing big league baseball to the West Coast, O'Malley was instrumental in getting, respectively, Ford Frick, William D. Eckert, and Bowie Kuhn elected as commissioner of baseball. Each commissioner invariably deferred to him on the more important issues.

• Both the National Baseball Hall of Fame Library in Cooperstown, New York, and the *Sporting News* Library in St. Louis, Missouri, contain newspaper and magazine clipping files on O'Malley. No manuscript collections are known to exist. Neither does O'Malley have a biography, but see especially Neil J. Sullivan, *The Dodgers Move West* (1987), Don Kowet, *The Rich Who Own Sports* (1977), Harold Parrott, *The Lords of Baseball* (1975), David Quentin Voigt, *American Baseball*, vol. 3 (1983), and Benjamin G. Rader, *Baseball: A History of America's Game* (1992). Obituaries are in the *New York Times*, 10 and 13 Aug. 1979, and the *Sporting News*, 25 Aug. 1979.

BENJAMIN G. RADER

OMLIE, Phoebe Jane Fairgrave (21 Nov. 1902–17 July 1975), aviator, was born in Des Moines, Iowa, the daughter of Andrew Fairgrave and Madge Traistor (or Traister). Phoebe Fairgrave graduated from Mechanic Arts High School in St. Paul, Minnesota, in 1920 and began work as a stenographer in a downtown business office. Within weeks she made a decision that would determine the course of her life: she wanted to earn a living in the aviation business. To begin this venture, she visited the Curtiss Northwest Company at a St. Paul airfield, which was offering civilian flight training in a surplus Curtiss JN-4D Jenny, and asked for her first airplane ride. Reluctant pilots laughed and

walked away, until one agreed to take her up. Encouraged by his friends to shake her up a bit, the pilot instead succeeded in further whetting her appetite for flying. She promptly bought the aircraft with a $3,500 inheritance from her grandfather and began to learn the art of parachute jumping, reasoning that this was her best avenue into aviation. Aerial barnstorming acts were the most visible aviation business and about the only one open to women. Her first jump was made on 17 April 1921, and only three months later, on 10 July, she set a women's altitude record by jumping from 15,200 feet. With stunt pilot Glenn Messer, she established the Fairgrave and Messer Flying Circus and learned a repertoire of aerial acts, including wingwalking, trapeze work from the wings and landing gear, double parachute jumps (cutting away the first parachute, freefalling, and opening a second chute), and air-to-air and ground-to-air transfers. Stunt work for the movies included a part in *The Perils of Pauline*. Vernon C. Omlie served as her flight instructor and joined the troop as well. They married in 1922 and had no children.

The Omlies eked out a meager existence and Messer soon departed, leaving the Omlies to establish themselves. During their southern tour of 1922, they settled in Memphis, Tennessee, to begin a flying school, combining that with exhibition flying for the next several years. They supported the dedication of the local Aero Club's airport, Armstrong Field, in 1926 and established their own commercial venture, Mid-South Airways, on site.

As a pilot for Mid-South Airways, Phoebe Omlie was required to master the new qualifications established by the Air Commerce Act of 1926 for commercial pilots, and on 30 June 1927 she became the first American woman to receive a commercial transport license (#199) from the Department of Commerce. She earned the first U.S. woman's airplane and engine mechanical license (#422) as well. Mid-South Airways started the South's first passenger service in 1928, selling tickets for and maintaining a privately owned Stinson Detroiter that took three weekly round trips to Chicago. The Omlies were nationally recognized in 1927 for their mercy flights and rescue missions over the flooded Mississippi River Valley and were instrumental in creating the Memphis Municipal Airport, dedicated in 1929.

Omlie took a new direction in 1928, as the only woman pilot on the grueling National Reliability Air Tour, sponsored by Henry Ford, for a $12,000 prize and the Edsel Ford trophy. Flying in a Monocoupe 70, *Chiggers*, she covered 6,300 miles, 32 cities, and 13 states in one month, received a perfect score for navigation, and became the first woman to fly over the Rocky Mountains. She became a Monocoupe distributor for Don Luscombe, president of Mono-Aircraft, Inc., of Moline, Kansas, and performed as one of the Monocoupe Rockets, a racing and publicity team comprised of Omlie, Florence Klingensmith, Cornelius Barnett "Scotty" Burmood, and Roy "Stub" Quinby. Later, Omlie recalled her position as a "special assistant to Don Luscombe," but whatever her actual title, she provided enormous exposure for the light but powerful Monocoupe. On 29 June 1929 she flew to an altitude of 24,500 feet, establishing a women's altitude record, a mark that was never made official because of a questionable barograph reading. Later that summer Omlie won the Women's National Air Derby in the light-plane class, flying 2,723 miles from Santa Monica, California, to Cleveland, Ohio, in a Monocoupe 113 Special named *Miss Moline*. She then won two closed-course races at the National Air Races in Cleveland. She was again the winner of two closed-course races at the 1930 National Air Races, and, as the winner of the 1930 Dixie Derby, Omlie flew a 1,575-mile course through nine states. Her landmark year as a racing pilot was 1931, when she won the women's division of the 1931 National Sweepstakes Derby from Santa Monica to Cleveland and was named overall winner of the derby by a racing point system, thus besting fifty-six men and women pilots. Cash prizes from city, state, and national races gave Omlie a substantial income for these depression years.

Franklin Delano Roosevelt was running for president in 1932, and Omlie vigorously campaigned for him, flying more than 20,000 miles in 16 states. As a result, in 1933, Omlie was rewarded with an appointment as special assistant of Air Intelligence of the National Advisory Committee for Aeronautics (NACA, the forerunner of the National Aeronautics and Space Administration [NASA]), where she guided the development of tri-cycle landing gear for airplanes at Langley Field, Virginia. For her contribution to this program and her overall dedication to aviation, syndicated writer Mary Margaret McBride named Omlie one of the ten outstanding women of the United States.

Omlie moved from NACA to conceive and direct the National Air Marking Program for the Works Progress Administration and Bureau of Air Commerce. The program identified towns and cities from the air as aids to navigation. Each state was blocked off into sections of twenty square miles, with the name of the nearest town painted on the roof of a building at fifteen-mile intervals. She established a network of 16,000 navigation aids in 48 states during her three-year tenure and appointed several women pilots to the program, including Blanche Noyes, who succeeded her as director. Eleanor Roosevelt named Omlie as one of the ten outstanding women for the year in 1935.

Tragedy intervened in 1936 when Omlie's husband Vernon was killed in an airline crash. Omlie returned to Tennessee to launch a statewide flight training program, including the passage of the Tennessee Aviation Act of 1937, which provided aviation training in the public vocational schools. The next year she established the Tennessee Civilian Pilot Training Program, also returning to flight instruction herself, and campaigned for Roosevelt. In 1941 the president appointed her as the Civil Aeronautics Administration representative to the Office of Education to promote national ground training programs. Women had been dropped from pilot training programs in favor of men

with the onset of World War II, but women pilots and the CAA still felt they could be useful as instructors. Omlie returned home briefly, in 1942, to spearhead an experimental training program, the Tennessee Aviation Research Instructor School for Women. Ten female flight instructors graduated from a course that included 62 hours of flying, 216 hours of ground school, and 162 hours of flight instructors ground school. The CAA immediately petitioned Congress to establish more schools, but it was turned down. Omlie continued to work for the CAA as private flying specialist in education, safety, and training programs until 1952, when she turned against government programs on the basis of the overregulation of aviation.

Suddenly, after thirty-one years in aviation, Phoebe Fairgrave Omlie, pioneer female aviator, racing pilot, and government aeronautics adviser, completely withdrew from aviation. She tried and failed at cattle ranching in Mississippi and then traded the ranch for a restaurant, which was later destroyed by a tornado. In 1961 she returned with few resources to Memphis, where she pursued a variety of local issues and an interest in international business for a decade, finally leaving for Indianapolis in 1970. Her last five years were beset with alcoholism and cancer. Omlie died in Indianapolis.

• Information on Omlie's life can be found in various aviation periodicals and newspaper articles of the 1920–1940 era and in books on the subject of women in aviation. The National Air and Space Museum has a small biographical file (CO-054000-01) and photographic file (CO-54000-99). Sally Knapp, *New Wings for Women* (1946), features a chapter on Omlie's early career. Omlie's career is followed in the Smithsonian Studies in Air and Space, no. 5, *U.S. Women in Aviation 1919–1929*; no. 6, *U.S. Women in Aviation 1930–1939*; and no. 7, *U.S. Women in Aviation 1940–1985*. An excellent periodical article is H. Glenn Buffington, "Phoebe Fairgrove [sic] Omlie," *Journal of the American Aviation Historical Society* 13, no. 3 (Fall 1968): 186–88. *Southern Aviation* featured two articles on Omlie in Apr. and July 1932. Omlie's stint with Mono Aircraft is detailed in James Zazas, *Visions of Luscombe: The Early Years* (1993), and her work in the Tennessee Civilian Pilot Training Program is detailed in Gene Slack, "Tennessee's Airwomen," *Flying*, May 1943, pp. 46–47, 128–32.

DOROTHY S. COCHRANE

ONASSIS, Jacqueline Kennedy (28 July 1929–19 May 1994), First Lady and cultural icon, was born in East Hampton, Long Island, New York, the daughter of John "Black Jack" Bouvier, an independently wealthy stock speculator, and Janet Lee. Jacqueline's father was a scion of the wealthy and respected Bouvier family. A notorious playboy, he lost most of his inherited wealth in the Great Depression, shortly after Jacqueline's birth. In 1936 the combination of his infidelities and financial irresponsibility resulted in his separation and later divorce from Jacqueline's mother.

From 1947 to 1951 Jacqueline Bouvier studied French literature at Vassar College, the Sorbonne, and George Washington University. After graduating from George Washington in May 1951 she took a job as a photographer for the *Washington Times-Herald*. One of her early photographic subjects was Massachusetts senator John F. Kennedy. After a brief courtship, they were married on 12 September 1953. In 1955 she suffered a miscarriage, and in 1956 she gave birth by cesarean section to a still-born child, one month premature. One year later her daughter, Caroline, was born. Within four years, her husband became the thirty-fifth president of the United States. Shortly before her husband was inaugurated in 1961, she gave birth to their second and last child, John.

John and Jacqueline Kennedy were both exceptionally attractive and intelligent people, and their union only added to their mystique. However, the senator's new wife preferred to avoid active involvement in politics, a practice she continued until almost the end of their marriage. Although she was not a "political wife" in the traditional sense, her beauty, poise, and even her aloofness were substantial political assets to her husband—assets he only grew to fully appreciate while in the White House.

A First Lady at the age of thirty-two, Jacqueline Kennedy was renowned for her beauty and fashion sense. The clothes she wore often spawned fashion trends; a famous example was the pillbox hat, which she made an overnight sensation. Although she did not often travel with the president, when she did interest in her and what she was wearing often overshadowed interest in him, once prompting the president to introduce himself in France as "the man who accompanied Jacqueline Kennedy to Paris."

As First Lady Jacqueline Kennedy also took an interest in "restoring" (as opposed to redecorating) the White House. She had it placed on the National Register of Historic Places. She also wrote and edited the first White House guidebook, which was sold to tourists. The proceeds from the book were used to help finance her restoration of the White House with historic antiques. She also made the White House a symbol of American cultural renewal by scheduling performances of ballet, Shakespearean drama, and classical music; the most notable of these events was the rare live performance of cello virtuoso Pablo Casals. During this period guests at White House dinners included artists such as Igor Stravinsky, Aaron Copland, Isaac Stern, and Tennessee Williams.

In November 1963 Jacqueline Kennedy agreed to do a rare thing: accompany her husband on a domestic political trip to Texas. On 22 November 1963, as she was riding by his side in Dallas, Texas, she saw her husband shot and killed. Film of the assassination shows her risking her life by climbing onto the back of their moving limousine to help pull a secret service agent into the car. She cradled her husband's head in her lap as he was rushed to Parkland Hospital. Within ninety minutes she was on the presidential airplane with her dead husband. In order to help legitimize Vice President Lyndon Johnson's transition to power, she was asked to stand next to him while he took the oath of office. Throughout the plane ride back she re-

fused to change her bloody clothes. "No," she repeatedly said, "I want them to see what they've done."

During the following three days of the funeral, Jacqueline Kennedy's bearing and dignity helped to focus the nation's grief and made her the most famous woman in the world. As one member of the British nobility said at the time, she had "given the American people from this day on the one thing they always lacked—majesty" (Manchester, p. 580). In a famous interview with T. H. White a week after the assassination, she spoke of how her husband used to like to have her play records before they would go to bed. She remembered, in particular, a line from the broadway musical *Camelot*, "Don't let it be forgot, that once there was a spot, for one brief shining moment that was known as Camelot." White, in reworking his interview notes, keyed in on this phrase, repeating it four times in a one-page article. The Kennedy administration was from then on remembered as Camelot.

After the assassination, Jacqueline Kennedy saw Robert Kennedy, the president's brother, as a strong, male role model for her children. When Robert Kennedy was assassinated in 1968, however, she became disillusioned with America and left the country. "I hate this country," she reportedly said. "I despise America and I don't want my children to live here anymore. If they're killing Kennedys, my kids are number one targets. . . . I want to get out of this country" (Heymann, p. 486). That same year she married Greek billionaire and shipping tycoon Aristotle Onassis. It was a testimony to her power as a national icon that large segments of the American public felt personally hurt and betrayed by her remarriage. During the 1960s and 1970s she was the subject of constant and obsessive media speculation. Between 1963 and her death, literally thousands of articles appeared on her in the tabloid and other presses. Paparazzi found that they would be paid huge amounts of money for any picture of her, in any pose; even pictures of her with her windblown hair across most of her face fetched enormous sums.

In 1975, while on a skiing trip in New Hampshire, Jacqueline Onassis was informed that her husband was in critical condition. She declined to travel to his deathbed. Shortly, thereafter, while in New York, she received word that Aristotle Onassis had died. At his death, Onassis's estate was valued at more than $1 billion. Soon a fight developed between Jacqueline Onassis and Onassis's daughter Christina over the division of the estate. Jacqueline Onassis fought for and won a $26-million settlement. Having achieved financial security for herself and her children, she kept the name Onassis, moved to New York, and took a job as an editor at Doubleday and Co. for the modest salary of $10,000 a year. For the last fifteen years of her life, she lived with diamond trader Maurice Tempelsman but never married again.

Jacqueline Kennedy Onassis died in New York City. Her death was a national event, generating front-page cover stories in most of the major newspapers and magazines in America. President Bill Clinton and his wife, Hillary, made a joint public statement from the Jacqueline Kennedy Garden at the White House mourning her loss.

Two years after Onassis's death, in May 1996, her two surviving children, John and Caroline, held an auction of some of her belongings to help pay their inheritance taxes (an action that had previously been suggested by their mother). For several days headlines across the nation reported how even the most mundane items connected with Jacqueline and John F. Kennedy fetched astronomical sums. Three of her old silk pillows sold for $25,300; one of John Kennedy's old cigar boxes went for $574,500; even a string of fake pearls set off ferocious bidding, resulting in a sale price of $211,500. The public desire to treat the Kennedy family detritus with the reverence usually reserved for holy relics showed, more powerfully than ever, the continuing impact that Jacqueline Kennedy Onassis and the myth of Camelot had on America.

• At the time of her death, there were twenty-two biographies of Jacqueline Kennedy Onassis and more references to her in the *Reader's Guide to Periodical Literature* than any other living woman. John H. Davis, *The Bouviers: Portrait of an American Family* (1969), is a fine account of her family and childhood. A useful biography is C. David Heymann, *A Woman Named Jackie* (1989). For Jacqueline as First Lady, her former personal secretary Mary Barelli Gallagher's *My Life with Jacqueline Kennedy* (1969) is an important inside source. For the Kennedy assassination and Jacqueline Kennedy's role in the funeral, William Manchester's *The Death of a President: November 20–November 25, 1963* (1967) is the classic account. The interview with T. H. White was published in *Life* magazine on 6 Dec. 1963. A transcript of White's interview notes (which are substantially different from the published account) is available at the John Fitzgerald Kennedy Library in Boston, under "Camelot Documents." Jacqueline Kennedy Onassis as an object of obsessive tabloid speculation is perhaps best represented by Irving Shulman, *Jackie! The Exploitation of a First Lady* (1967). For Jacqueline as a cultural icon, see Wayne Koestenbaum, *Jackie under My Skin* (1995), called by the *New York Times* the first attempt to apply the literary technique of deconstruction to an actual human subject. An obituary appears in the *New York Times*, 20 May 1994.

RICHARD BRADLEY

OÑATE, Juan de (c. 1551–c. 3 June 1626), frontiersman and colonial administrator, was born in Nueva Galicia, Mexico, the son of Cristóbal de Oñate, a provincial governor, and Doña Cathalina de Salazar. Cristóbal de Oñate is noted for discovering and developing the silver mines at Zacatecas, Mexico. Little is known of Juan's childhood except that he followed his father's lead, discovering the rich mines at Zichú, Charcas, and San Luis Potosí and became renowned on the northern frontier of New Spain for fighting the Chichimecas. In August 1595 he was confirmed as guarda mayor de la Casa de la Moneda de Potosí. He married and had two children with Isabel Tolosa, a descendent of both Cortés and Montezuma.

Oñate's greatest prominence came as founder, governor, and captain general of New Mexico. He became interested in New Mexico as early as 1583 when Viceroy Luis de Velasco received orders to appoint someone to explore and colonize the area. In return for heavy investment from his family's business, Oñate was awarded the contract and received privileges as *adelantado* on 21 September 1595. Troubles with a new viceroy delayed his expedition for almost two years, and Oñate's contract was almost canceled. In August 1597 he received final authorization and departed on the expedition with a company of several hundred soldiers and colonizers and ten Franciscan missionaries.

Striking north across the Chihuahua desert, he crossed the Rio Grande downriver from present-day El Paso, Texas, and took formal possession "of all the kingdoms and provinces of New Mexico" on 30 April 1598. By autumn of the same year he had "peopled" New Mexico with settlements reaching as far as 350 miles upriver from his initial entry point, a capital had been established at San Juan, and missionaries had been disbursed. Pacification of the Indians was accomplished by 1599 with the loss of a considerable number of Oñate's party, including his nephew, who was killed during the rebellion of Acoma.

The colony did not prosper. As early as 1598 the governor turned his attention to exploration and neglected the development of agriculture or livestock. According to his contract, Oñate was ordered to try to discover the imaginary northwest passage. He was also consumed with finding gold and riches to support his colony and recoup his investment in the enterprise of New Mexico. His explorations reached as far north as modern Kansas and west to the Gulf of California, but he failed to find either treasure or the legendary passage.

By 1601 complaints of mismanagement and cruelty to the Indians reached the viceroy from the colony. Although soldiers and missionaries were sent to the colony in 1605, the reinforcements were not enough. Oñate tried to pressure Mexican officials into supplying additional aid by resigning in 1607, but the viceroy called his bluff, replacing him with Don Pedro Peralta as governor and ordering Oñate to return to Mexico within three months to stand trial for mismanagement, disobedience, and misrepresentation of the value of New Mexico. After a lengthy trial, in 1614 he was fined 6,000 ducats, permanently expelled from the colony of New Mexico, and banished from Mexico City for four years.

Oñate appealed his verdict, but he failed to win a pardon from the king. He also failed to get appointed to office anywhere in the colonies. In 1624 he was finally appointed royal inspector of the mines in Spain, where he died during a tour of inspection.

• Archival information on his early life is in AGS, Charcas, 63, N. 65. Printed sources on Oñate include Marc Simmons, *The Last Conquistador: Juan de Oñate and the Settling of the Far Southwest* (1991); and George P. Hammond and Agapito Rey, eds., *Don Juan de Oñate, Colonizer of New Mexico, 1596–1628* (2 vols., 1953). A contemporary account by a member of the expedition is in translation, Gaspar Pérez de Villagrá, *History of New Mexico by Gaspar Pérez de Villagrá, Alcalá, 1610,* trans. Gilberto Espinosa (1933). Earlier important sources include *Colección de Documentos Inéditos, Relativos al Descubrimiento . . . de América,* vol. 16 (1871), as well as Beatrice Q. Cornish, "The Ancestry and Family of Juan de Oñate," in H. M. Stephens and H. E. Bolton, *The Pacific Ocean in History* (1917), and Bolton's own *Spanish Borderlands* (1927). Information on his trial is in G. P. Hammond, "The Conviction of Don Juan de Oñate, New Mexico's First Governor," in *New Spain and the Anglo-American West: Historical Contributions Presented to Herbert Eugene Bolton,* vol. 1 (1923), pp. 67–79.

JULIA C. FREDERICK

ONDERDONK, Benjamin Tredwell (15 July 1791–30 Apr. 1861), Episcopal bishop, was born in New York City, the son of John Onderdonk, a physician, and Deborah Ustick. His parents were members of the Episcopal church, and the future bishop probably attended Columbia Grammar School (then firmly under church auspices). He graduated from Columbia College in 1809, having matriculated when he was barely fifteen years old.

After graduation, because there was as yet no seminary for the education of Episcopal priests in the United States, Onderdonk began to study for the ministry of the Episcopal church under Bishop John Henry Hobart. In 1812 Onderdonk was made a deacon by Bishop Hobart, who about two years later ordained him a priest in Newark, New Jersey. Hobart had a residence in that state and often participated in Episcopal church affairs there until the diocese of New Jersey was formed in 1815. Onderdonk married Eliza Moscrop in 1813; they had seven children.

Although he was only twenty-three years old when ordained, Onderdonk came rapidly into prominence under the appreciative eye of his mentor, Bishop Hobart. Soon after ordination he became an assistant minister at Manhattan's powerful Trinity Church. In 1816 he was made secretary of the diocesan convention, a position that both kept him in the limelight and gave him a taste of political maneuvering. In 1818 he was elected a deputy to the General Convention of the Episcopal Church, and three years later he joined the faculty of the newly created General Theological Seminary in New York City. When Hobart died suddenly in 1830, Onderdonk preached at his funeral. Several weeks later he was elected fourth bishop of New York by a diocesan convention that is said to have remembered that Bishop Hobart had hoped his protégé would succeed him.

Onderdonk quickly grasped the challenge before him. Using Hobart's auxiliary organizations, he applied his superior managerial skills to make them more efficient for growth of the Episcopal church. By buckboard and canal boat, Onderdonk tirelessly traveled throughout his diocese, which initially embraced the entire state of New York. He attracted priests to work with him, and Episcopal churches sprang up in cities, towns, and hamlets across the state. In 1830, 140 priests attended the diocesan convention; eight years later, the number had nearly doubled. The Episcopal church was so firmly established in the distant parts of New York that in 1838 a separate diocese of western New York was set off from the original diocese, the first time in the history of the American Episcopal church that a diocese was thus divided.

Onderdonk and Hobart's other followers also laid the groundwork in the diocese of New York, and in the General Theological Seminary, for that reawakening of Anglicanism's heritage that eventually was named the Oxford Movement. Oxfordians called for the American Episcopal church to join with its parent body, the Church of England, in forwarding its Catholic and pre-Reformation integrity. Onderdonk believed that his church was a continuation of what he called the "primitive Catholic" church, and he refused to join with Protestant bodies such as the American Bible Society.

Onderdonk failed to perceive, however, that other Episcopalians preferred their Protestant heritage and, moreover, were uneasy about a drift toward Catholicism at a time when many Catholics were immigrating to the United States from Ireland and Germany. The seeds of Onderdonk's eventual downfall, however, lay not so much in what he believed as how he chose to promote those beliefs. Whereas Hobart charmed most of his hearers, Onderdonk seemed to bludgeon them into compliance. "He had great executive talent [but] ruled the diocese with a rod of iron," commented one contemporary. While many observers praised Onderdonk for his fearlessness, sagacity, and ready wit, his closest friends perceived trouble ahead because of his social gaffes and "familiarity and coarseness of manners." These, together with Onderdonk's stubborn refusal to acknowledge the sincerity of his enemies, combined to bring about the tragic events of 1844.

The year before, Onderdonk had stirred controversy by ordaining Arthur Carey, a youth suspected of Roman Catholic tendencies. At the same time, an eccentric priest, James Richmond, began to collect stories of the bishop's alleged misbehavior—tales about Onderdonk's supposed drunkenness and familiarity with women—that had been circulating in the church for some time. Supported by four women who said they would testify against the bishop, Richmond went to the general convention in Philadelphia in September 1844. There, several evangelical bishops, opponents of Onderdonk's Catholic tendencies, engineered a trial against him on charges of "immorality and impurity."

The trial began in November 1844 at St. John's Chapel in lower Manhattan. Onderdonk's position was jeopardized by the fact that his brother, Bishop Henry Ustick Onderdonk of Pennsylvania, had recently been accused of drunkenness and had confessed to stave off deposition. Benjamin Onderdonk's supporters among the bishops agreed to a suspension penalty in order to save him deposition. In so doing, however, they unwittingly sprang a trap on their friend, for there then existed no machinery for lifting that penalty. As a result, Onderdonk—who never ceased to maintain his innocence—was doomed to live the rest of his life in inactivity and virtual disgrace. The verdict was announced on 2 January 1845.

The diocese of New York, which overwhelmingly supported Onderdonk, was astounded by the outcome of the trial. The bishop was seen as a victim of evangelical persecutors. Onderdonk wrote a defense immediately after the trial and sent it to his brother bishops, but it fell on deaf ears. Later, several friends attempted to bring a lawsuit to have Onderdonk restored, but he forbade them, arguing that he did not want the secular law to be the judge of church law. Two attempts to have Onderdonk reinstated by the general convention also failed.

Onderdonk seldom stirred from his house after his suspension, except to attend church almost daily. The General Theological Seminary was loyal to the bishop and refused to remove him from its faculty, but he did not hold classes there, knowing that to do so would arouse hostility against himself and the seminary. Onderdonk died in Manhattan. The best appraisal of his life is probably that of George Templeton Strong, who noted in his diary when Onderdonk died that the bishop "just missed a great career and an honored name."

• The General Theological Seminary in New York City has much printed material on Onderdonk, and some manuscripts, in its collection. The New York Genealogical and Biographical Society also has some material, as does the Archives of the Episcopal Church, Seminary of the Southwest, Austin, Tex. Almost nothing pertaining to Benjamin Onderdonk is in the Archives of the Diocese of New York, but letters and other manuscripts are in the Archives of the Diocese of Maryland, in Baltimore. An account of Onderdonk's episcopate in New York is found in James Elliott Lindsley, *This Planted Vine* (1984).

JAMES ELLIOTT LINDSLEY

ONDERDONK, Henry Ustick (16 Mar. 1789–6 Dec. 1858), Protestant Episcopal bishop and controversialist, was born in New York City, the son of John Onderdonk, a noted physician, and Deborah Ustick. He was the elder brother of Benjamin Tredwell Onderdonk. He graduated from Columbia College in 1805 and studied medicine in both Edinburgh and London, receiving an M.D. from the University of Edinburgh. Returning to America in 1911, he married Eliza Carter, and they had nine children, eight of whom survived infancy. He practiced medicine in New York and was associate editor of the *New York Medical Magazine* from 1814 to 1815. During these years he decided to abandon the profession of medicine and studied for the ministry of the Episcopal church under Bishop John Henry Hobart. He was ordained deacon in 1815 and priest in 1816. Between 1816 and 1820 he served in Canandaigua, New York, and built up a congregation. Theologically he aligned himself with Hobart and the high church party within the Episcopal church and shared their emphasis on the necessity of an episcopally ordained ministry for the proper ordering of a church. From his early ministry he displayed a flair for ecclesiastical apologetics, and his *An Appeal to the Religious Public* (1818) was an able discussion of Episcopal theology and practice. Many of his other writings defended the high church idea of baptismal regeneration and set forth the implications of this teaching in contrast to the conversion-centered piety of American evangelicals.

In 1820 he was called as rector of St. Ann's Church, Brooklyn, New York, and in 1827 was elected assistant bishop of the diocese of Pennsylvania. He became bishop of the diocese in 1836 upon the death of William White. His election was a close and hotly contested one between the high church and low church factions of the diocese (the latter of which desired a theology and piety more in line with American and English evangelicalism) and was protested by a large minority of clerical and lay delegates who objected to his exclusive theology. The ill feelings created by the election were to mar his later episcopate.

During his years as bishop Onderdonk published a number of works that attempted to further refine his high church theological position. *An Essay on Regeneration* (1835) examined the question of baptismal regeneration. *Episcopacy Tested by Scriptures* (1830) and *Episcopacy Examined and Reexamined* (1835), which emerged out of a controversy with the Presbyterian theologian Albert Barnes, defended the biblical origin of the office of the bishop. Other important treatises were collected in *Sermons and Episcopal Charges* (2 vols., 1851).

In the early 1840s his high church teachings led him to express sympathy for the proponents of the Oxford Movement and their attempt to reassert the catholic nature of the Church of England. His support for the Oxford Movement precipitated a public controversy with John Henry Hopkins, bishop of Vermont, over the nature of the British Reformation. His support for the controversial Oxford Movement exacerbated the theological tensions within his diocese.

Onderdonk never possessed a strong physical constitution and continually suffered from intestinal problems. By the 1840s he had become addicted to the brandy that had been medically prescribed to relieve this condition, and this, coupled with his aggressively high church theology, created a scandal within his diocese. Both contemporaries and later scholars have argued about which issue was key in the scandal, but because many of his low church Episcopal critics also were temperance advocates, the two issues undoubtedly were intertwined. In 1844 he was forced to resign as bishop. The House of Bishops of the Protestant Episcopal church suspended him indefinitely from all his canonical duties, a suspension that was not lifted until 1856, when his ministry was restored due to his "exemplary conduct," and his authority to discharge episcopal functions was never restored. He continued to reside in Philadelphia until he died. In addition to his theological writings, he composed a number of hymns that were very popular during the nineteenth century.

• Onderdonk's other works include *Family Devotions from the Liturgy* (1835) and *Thoughts on Some of the Objections to Christianity* (1835). Some important correspondence is found in the Seabury Correspondence at the General Theological Seminary Library, New York. There is no full biography of Onderdonk, but sketches can be found in W. S. Perry, *The Bishops of the American Church* (1897), and J. W. Twelves, *A History of the Diocese of Pennsylvania* . . . (1969). See also Elmer Onderdonk, *Genealogy of the Onderdonk Family in America* (1910).

ROBERT BRUCE MULLIN

O'NEAL, Edward Asbury, III (26 Oct. 1875–26 Feb. 1958), farm organization leader, was born near Florence, Alabama, the son of Edward Asbury O'Neal II and Mary (maiden name unknown), plantation owners. O'Neal was raised on the plantation, located in the Tennessee Valley region of northern Alabama, which he managed following his graduation from Washington and Lee College in 1898. He married Julia Camper in 1904, and they had three children.

Earlier members of O'Neal's aristocratic family had included distinguished military officers and two Alabama governors. O'Neal himself was oriented to public service, particularly to the mission of improving southern agriculture. Although educated in the liberal arts, he subsequently took short courses in agriculture and became an enduring supporter of the state agricultural research institutions. He was also a persistent advocate of converting to agricultural uses the Muscle Shoals hydroelectric facilities that had been developed to make explosives for military use. Ultimately he supported U.S. Senator George William Norris's proposal to use these and other resources for regional development under a public corporation, the Tennessee Valley Authority, which was created in 1933.

O'Neal was an early leader of his county's and Alabama's Farm Bureaus, which had been organized under a new Agricultural Extension Service to help farmers adopt a more scientific agriculture. Farm Bureau leadership in the South was dominated by large land owners like O'Neal and in other regions by technologically progressive farmers who were also ready to protect the interests of the larger commercial farms. O'Neal became the South's principal leader in the emerging American Farm Bureau Federation (AFBF) and one of the major strategists in efforts by the Farm Bureau to enact federal farm programs. On a key issue O'Neal, as head of the Farm Bureau's "legislative committee," moved the organization to support an active governmental role in managing farm prices, as embodied in the McNary-Haugen bill. Under AFBF leadership this bill was passed by Congress in 1927 and again in 1928 but was vetoed each time by President Calvin Coolidge.

The AFBF in its fifth year (1925) chose O'Neal as its national vice president, although southern membership was still comparatively tiny. He was advanced to the presidency in 1931 with the support of midwestern leader Earl Smith. Under O'Neal's guidance during his sixteen-year presidency of the Farm Bureau, two great farming regions—the South and the Midwest—were brought into political coalition, enabling the creation of a truly national farm organization and the enactment of comprehensive federal farm programs, including the Agricultural Adjustment Act of 1933, the Soil Conservation and Domestic Allotment Act of 1936, and the Agricultural Adjustment Act of 1938.

O'Neal also helped establish an autonomous, bipartisan process for agricultural policy making, in which the leading actors were farm organizations, congressional agriculture committees, and the Department of Agriculture, with the White House being expected to play only a supportive role. O'Neal as a leader was bold in initiatives, genial in his relationships, and consistent in his goals but always prepared for compromise.

O'Neal gained the confidence of other farm organization leaders and formed intimate personal ties with President Franklin Roosevelt, Secretary of Agriculture Henry A. Wallace, and congressional agriculture leaders. One of O'Neal's techniques was to call timely meetings of principal legislators, lobbyists, and bureaucrats, at which he was often able to orchestrate collective action. As a lobbyist he was a policy impresario, serving at some congressional hearings as an unofficial master of ceremonies. Under O'Neal the AFBF developed techniques to mobilize grass-roots members that contributed to its status as one of the most respected and powerful Washington lobbies.

The AFBF under O'Neal proved flexible in pursuing its membership and organizational interests, allying with the early Roosevelt administration against business interests that opposed government's role in setting agricultural prices and then breaking with the administration over agencies or programs that might jeopardize the Farm Bureau's influence at the grass roots or in Washington. The Farm Bureau also undermined efforts to help subsistence farmers and farm workers under the Farm Security Administration and other programs. In World War II, O'Neal countered administration efforts to prevent farm price increases, even while convincing farm interests to accept some price controls (albeit at "incentive" levels well above the previous goal of "parity," a calculated standard for adequate net farm income).

In 1947 O'Neal resigned from the AFBF presidency, citing his advanced age and the need for new perspectives. The AFBF, under succeeding leadership, abandoned its longtime approval of supported prices fixed at levels based upon "parity," thereby sacrificing its Midwest-South axis and engendering conflict with other farm organizations and within the congressional agriculture committees. O'Neal rejected calls for his reelection to the AFBF presidency from those who wished to return the Farm Bureau to its former centrality as coalition leader. He died in Florence, Alabama.

In the principal study of the Farm Bureau during O'Neal's presidency, Christiana McFadyen Campbell characterized O'Neal's importance in the history of farm politics as follows: "O'Neal's skill as a mediator was superbly used at an opportune time in history. Probably more than any other one person, he accomplished the healing of 'that ancient breach' between Midwestern and Southern farmers. The fact that the breach reopened later does not detract from his contribution to an epoch in history" (p. 194).

• The Oral History Collection of Columbia University contains recollections by O'Neal and also by other agricultural leaders who worked with him. The roles of O'Neal and other leaders are described within a comprehensive history of policy making in Christiana McFadyen Campbell, *The Farm Bureau and the New Deal: A Study of the Making of National Farm Policy, 1933–1940* (1962). More detail on O'Neal's activities is provided in an official history of AFBF by Orville Merton Kile, *The Farm Bureau through Three Decades* (1948). John Mark Hansen views O'Neal's Farm Bureau as a ground breaker in *Gaining Access: Congress and the Farm Lobby, 1919–1981* (1991). P. O. Davis lauds O'Neal's enthusiasm for agricultural research in *One Man . . . Edward Asbury O'Neal, III* (1945). An obituary is in the *New York Times*, 27 Feb. 1958.

DON F. HADWIGER

O'NEALL, John Belton (10 Apr. 1793–27 Dec. 1863), legislator and judge, was born near Bush River, Newberry District, South Carolina, the son of Hugh O'Neall, a merchant, and Anne Kelly. Both of O'Neall's parents were members of the Society of Friends. He studied at the Newberry Academy, where he was pushed, according to O'Neall, "much too rapidly," reading classical Latin authors without understanding them. He also worked in his father's mercantile store but, his father "deprived of his reason," it ended in bankruptcy. However, Belton was helped by his uncle and later was graduated in 1812 from South Carolina College (later the University of South Carolina). This was followed by the study of law in the office of John Caldwell in Newberry and admission to the bar in 1814.

In 1818 O'Neall married Helen Pope. They had three daughters, but all died young. To use O'Neall's description: "in the death of all their children," they drank "the cup of sorrow to its dregs." Aside from the law, where he made his greatest contribution, O'Neall was involved in a number of other public endeavors. He served in the South Carolina legislature on different occasions during the years from 1816 to 1828, becoming house Speaker toward the end of that time. He then was elected an associate judge, with circuit duties in the South Carolina jurisdictional scheme. Two years later O'Neall was raised to the court of appeals, and thereafter he was to serve at the appellate level until the Civil War, becoming chief justice of the state in 1859. In addition to his judicial duties, he served as a trustee of South Carolina College, the president of the Newberry Baptist Bible Society from 1837 to the Civil War, the president of the Newberry District Agricultural Society from 1839 on, and president of the Greenville and Columbia Railroad from 1847 to 1853.

His work on the various appellate courts of South Carolina covered numerous legal and equitable issues,

but no cases loomed larger than *The State ex relatione Ed. M'Cready v. B. F. Hunt, Col 16th Reg't, So. Ca. Militia* and its companion *The State ex relatione James M'Daniel v. Thom. M'Meekin, Brg. Gen'l. 6th Brigade So. Ca. Militia* (both 1834). These cases grew out of the 1832 nullification movement. Nullifiers, led by John C. Calhoun, argued that since the federal government was a creation of the states, the states themselves could rule on the constitutionality of federal laws. South Carolina's nullification movement was sparked by a desire to end the oppression of the federal tariff laws, but beneath that struggle was a deeper concern to protect the state's system of slavery from a powerful central government. The ultimate threat of the nullifiers was secession from the Union. The cases that arose out of the struggle involved the loyalty oath prescribed by the nullifiers in South Carolina to all militia officers, which Unionists feared might be understood to require the pledging of one's primary allegiance to the state instead of the federal government.

The majority of the court of appeals ruled the state oath of allegiance unconstitutional in the highly charged political atmosphere. The case involved profound questions of political allegiance and obedience. O'Neall held that allegiance and obedience were interchangeable and that the sovereign people had created a union of two constitutions and two governments, federal and state, and allegiance (interchangeable with obedience) was due to both. The nullifiers, conversely, had declared that sole allegiance was due to the state, and obedience only, not allegiance, was due to the federal government. The *M'Cready* decision, striking down the loyalty oath, was a sharp rebuke to the nullifiers, and they in turn abolished the court of appeals, which had had law and equity jurisdiction, and divided its responsibilities. O'Neall was assigned to the law side of the appellate system, where he served thereafter.

O'Neall was a delegate to the Nullification Convention, where he associated with the Union party and worked unsuccessfully against nullification of the federal tariffs. As early as October 1832, however, he seemed to concede that the forces of disunion had the greater momentum. He advised Judge David Johnson, who sat with him on the court of appeals, in a despairing letter that it was time to say to "the dominant party" that it should "go on" as the Unionists would "neither paralyze y'r efforts nor delay y'r actions." As late as 1859 in a nonlegal set of sketches titled *The Annals of Newberry, Historical, Biographical and Anecdotal*, however, O'Neall still referred to nullification as a "dangerous experiment" and described himself as "one who is heartily tired of the incessant war of politics." It should be no surprise that he did not favor secession and declared himself in *The Annals* as "sick at heart with the intestine divisions by which this best of all governments is threatened to be rent asunder."

Another area of law with which any southern judge had to deal was that involving slavery. O'Neall addressed the subject in ways others avoided. In 1848 he presented a significant work, *The Negro Law of South*

Carolina, to the state agricultural society. This work was a survey of the law in his state, but it was also much more. O'Neall, himself a slaveowner, critically evaluated the law and suggested numerous reforms. Although born into a Quaker family, he did not reject slavery even though he wrote dispassionately, if not favorably, about the Friends' rejection of the institution as "irreligious." He suggested a number of reforms to existing law: that it might be wise to attach slaves to the soil when it came time to partition an estate in order to keep families together; that the existing rigorous restrictions on the right of masters to free slaves were unnecessary, ungenerous, and unwise; that slaves ought to be allowed to read and write, especially to understand the Gospel; and that the lives of slaves ought to be protected by law far better than they were at present. Such proposed reforms indicate that O'Neall sought to preserve the patriarchal social order he often described in his own judicial opinions.

In his personal life he was abstemious, at least after 1832–1833. He had long deplored the liquor trade, but it was not until 1832, in a somewhat mysterious experience, that he stopped drinking himself. It was, he claimed, "to save a friend" that he gave up liquor completely, and the next year he stopped using tobacco. Thereafter, he became one of the most vocal of all temperance advocates in the South and certainly in South Carolina. By 1841 he was the president of the South Carolina Temperance Society, the president of the Sons of Temperance in the state in 1850, and the president of the Sons of Temperance of North America. He published an antiliquor column titled "Drunkard's Looking-Glass" in the *South Carolina Temperance Advocate* and produced a *Course of Lectures on . . . Temperance* (1852). His attitude might be summed up in a note he added to a handwritten piece involving an 1815 criminal case, one of the first cases with which he was involved: "Drunkeness [*sic*] the cause of crime!!!"

O'Neall retired from the bench during the secession crisis (there is no direct evidence that he did so because of the crisis: he was already in his late sixties). He died in Newberry.

• A small but useful collection of the letters of John Belton O'Neall is in the South Caroliniana Library, Columbia. Other letters written by O'Neall are scattered among the personal papers of other southern jurists. Besides the works already mentioned, O'Neall published *Biographical Sketches of the Bench and Bar of South Carolina* (2 vols., 1859). Each of his major works contains useful information about O'Neall himself. See also A. E. Keir Nash, "Negro Rights, Unionism, and Greatness on the South Carolina Court of Appeals: The Extraordinary Chief Justice John Belton O'Neall," *South Carolina Law Review* 21 (1969): 141–90. The role of the court during the hectic nullification episode can be followed in William W. Freehling, *Prelude to Civil War: The Nullification Controversy in South Carolina, 1816–1836* (1966). The complex jurisdictional history of the court and the legal environment within which the judges worked can be seen in Donald Senese, "Legal Thought in South Carolina, 1800–1860" (Ph.D. diss., Univ. of South Carolina, 1970).

THOMAS D. MORRIS

O'NEILL, Buckey (2 Feb. 1860–1 July 1898), lawman, newspaper editor, and soldier, was born William Owen O'Neill, probably in St. Louis, Missouri, although his birth record is lost, and he gave variously St. Louis and Ireland as his birthplace. He was the son of Irish immigrant parents, John Owen O'Neill and Mary McMenimin, and was raised in Washington, D.C., where his father, disabled from wounds he received during the Civil War, worked for the Treasury Department.

O'Neill, who apparently had experience as a printer's apprentice in Washington, made his way to Phoenix, Arizona Territory, in 1879, where he found a job as a typesetter with the *Phoenix Herald* and worked occasionally as a special deputy for Phoenix marshal Henry Garfias. It was in Phoenix in this first year that he earned the nickname "Buckey." He had become a habitué of Phoenix's saloons where gambling was licensed and consisted of such games as roulette, monte, draw poker, 7-up, and O'Neill's particular favorite, faro. He became something of a local legend for his daring play at the game, and anyone who placed "go for broke" bets at the faro table, in gambling parlance, "bucked the tiger."

After a year with the *Herald* and a year of wandering, during which he worked briefly on the *Tombstone Epitaph*, O'Neill traveled to the Arizona territorial capital of Prescott, which would become his home. A mining town in the northwest central part of the territory, Prescott in 1882 had a population of about 5,000 and a reputation as the "toniest" of territorial towns.

O'Neill worked for the *Arizona Miner*, becoming its editor in 1883. He was an officer in the local militia group called the Prescott Grays and periodically served as court reporter to the circuit judge in Globe, 150 miles to the southeast. In 1885 he launched his own newspaper in Prescott, the *Hoof and Horn*, a magazine-sized journal devoted to cattle and stock growers' interests. A year later he married Pauline Marie Schindler, the daughter of an army officer. Their only child died in infancy. An avowed Republican in a Democratic stronghold, he was elected probate judge for Yavapai County in 1887.

O'Neill, in addition to attending to his duties as judge and newspaper editor, invested in real estate, especially in tracts of land around Phoenix, where the territorial capital was moved in 1889; wrote about irrigation issues; and published short stories with western settings in the *San Francisco Examiner* and various territorial newspapers.

In 1888 O'Neill was elected sheriff of Yavapai County. His most famous exploit as the chief lawman for the vast county occurred within three months of his taking office, when four cowboys with the Aztec Land and Cattle Company robbed a railroad safe at Canyon Diablo, east of Flagstaff. O'Neill formed a posse and in a three-week, 600-mile search in four territories ran the outlaws to bay in Wah Weep Canyon in southern Utah. He returned three of them to the county jail in Prescott, the fourth one escaping temporarily. The Canyon Diablo case made O'Neill an Arizona legend.

His renown grew after his relief and law enforcement work during the Walnut Creek Dam tragedy of February 1890, in which many mining camps and their populations disappeared in a catastrophic flood.

In the 1890s O'Neill twice ran unsuccessfully for Congress as a Populist. He explored the Grand Canyon, was a pioneer developer of the famed Bright Angel Trail and of a rail link to the canyon, uncovered copper deposits near the canyon's South Rim, and accumulated considerable wealth from an onyx mine partnership near Prescott. He served briefly as adjutant general of Arizona Territory and in 1897, the year he and Pauline adopted a son, was elected mayor of Prescott.

After the United States declared war against Spain on 25 April 1898, O'Neill answered Washington's call to arms. Working with others, he became a driving force behind and subsequently captain of Troop A of the Arizona contingent of the First U.S. Volunteer Cavalry Regiment, the regiment commanded by Colonel Leonard Wood and later by Lieutenant Colonel Theodore Roosevelt (1858–1919) that came to be known as the "Rough Riders." After a brief training period in San Antonio, Texas, the regiment joined the other units of the U.S. Army's Fifth Corps in Tampa, Florida. On 22 June 1898 the force's transports arrived at their debarkation point of Daiquiri on the southern coast of Cuba, sixteen miles from its chief objective, the city of Santiago de Cuba.

O'Neill was in front of his troops at the skirmish at Las Guásimas on 24 June, a confused engagement in which the Rough Riders first encountered their Spanish enemy. O'Neill had a proclivity for standing up, pacing, and smoking cigarettes in front of his crouched and dug-in troopers, even during the most furious enemy sniper fire. Although he escaped injury at Las Guásimas, his luck soon failed.

On 1 July 1898, preparatory for a frontal assault on the long San Juan Hill complex, the Rough Riders were placed in front of a secondary ridge named "Kettle Hill" for the sugarcane pots on its summit. Kettle Hill was heavily fortified, laced with entrenchments, and protected by snipers, who poured a rain of Mauser bullets down upon the American ranks. O'Neill, perhaps to give assurance to his troops, perhaps in misguided disdain for the enemy, strode before his soldiers, stopping occasionally to roll a cigarette. At about ten A.M., as he stopped to chat with a fellow officer, he was struck in the head by a sniper bullet and died instantly.

He was buried near where he fell, but his remains were disinterred and reburied at Arlington National Cemetery on 1 May 1899.

In 1907 a bronze statue "To the Memory of Captain William O. O'Neill" and "In Honor of" the Rough Riders of 1898 was unveiled in front of the Yavapai County Courthouse in Prescott, the work of Solon Borglum, brother of Gutzon Borglum, the Mount Rushmore sculptor.

• Few genuine O'Neill papers are extant. A scattering of his letters, principally to his friend James H. McClintock, are on file with the Arizona Historical Society in Tucson; the Phoenix Public Library has a valuable collection of McClintock papers, many of which touch on his association with O'Neill; and the Sharlot Hall Museum in Prescott has collected letters, papers, newspaper clippings, and records of its most distinguished historical figure. Microfilm records of the newspapers with which O'Neill was associated are generally available through public or university libraries in Arizona, including some of O'Neill's *Hoof and Horn*. The National Archives has O'Neill's war service records, pension petitions, and the records of the adoption of his son. Ralph Keithley, *Buckey O'Neill* (1949), is a sketchy, fictionalized novel-biography about O'Neill, and Dale L. Walker, *Death Was the Black Horse: The Story of Rough Rider Buckey O'Neill* (1975), reprinted as *Buckey O'Neill, the Story of a Rough Rider* (1983), remains the only full treatment of his life.

DALE L. WALKER

O'NEILL, Eugene (16 Oct. 1888–27 Nov. 1953), dramatist, was born Eugene Gladstone O'Neill in New York City, the son of James O'Neill, an actor, and Mary Ellen "Ella" Quinlan. His oldest brother, James, Jr., became a minor actor. A second brother, Edmund Burke, died in infancy. His father was a major star, whose performance as Edmond Dantès in *Monte Cristo*, Charles Fechter's adaptation of Dumas's *The Count of Monte Cristo*, made him a matinée idol. He played the melodrama over 4,000 times to the ultimate detriment of his promise as a tragedian who might have equaled the great Edwin Booth. With his early life governed by the tours of his father's company, O'Neill lived in hotels, having no permanent home except for a summer cottage in New London, Connecticut. Called "Monte Cristo Cottage," it became the setting for Eugene's finest tragedy, *Long Day's Journey into Night* (completed in 1941; produced in 1956).

In that play, O'Neill portrayed the dark, troubled side of his family. After his birth his mother had been given morphine to ease her pain, and she became an addict. O'Neill dramatized her as "Ella Tyrone," a drifting ghostlike creature who distances herself from her family with the drug. His father, called "James Tyrone," is haunted by the waste of his talent. James, Jr., called "Jamie," is an alcoholic who makes nightly rounds of bars and brothels. O'Neill's own character, "Edmund," is a drifter. The interrelationship of the four provided much of O'Neill's finest theater, both in *Long Day's Journey into Night* and in several of his earlier plays.

O'Neill's formal education included preparatory years in eastern Catholic schools and two dilatory semesters (1906–1907) at Princeton University, after which he left at the university's request. In 1909 he married Kathleen Jenkins, whom he had made pregnant. Their son, Eugene Jr., was born in 1910. Both saw the marriage as a mistake; they were divorced in 1912. Although he later came to know and admire his son, O'Neill saw his wife and baby only once in this period.

Between 1909 and 1912 he became a picaresque wanderer embarking on what he would later call "a seeking flight." His adventures took him on a gold-prospecting trip to Honduras, a voyage as a seaman on a Norwegian barque to Buenos Aires, and trips to England on both a tramp freighter and a passenger liner, where he earned the rank of able-bodied seaman. Ashore he lived at a New York waterfront establishment run by James Condon, known as "Jimmy the Priest." Part saloon and part flophouse, it provided the setting for *Anna Christie* (1920/1921) and *The Iceman Cometh* (1939/1946).

In 1912, at a nadir of alcoholic despair, O'Neill attempted suicide. Saved by his roommate, he returned to New London and worked for a time as news reporter, columnist, and occasional staff poet for the New London *Telegraph*. His health deteriorated, and on Christmas Eve 1912 he entered Gaylord Farm Sanatorium in Wallingford, Connecticut, to be treated for tuberculosis. The case was considered arrested by the following June, and he went back to New London, fired by his reading during his treatment with a new resolution: "To be an artist or nothing."

In the sanatorium, O'Neill had read much of the new drama from Europe: plays by George Bernard Shaw, Henrik Ibsen, August Strindberg, Gerhart Hauptmann, Eugène Brieux, J. M. Synge, and other theatrical innovators. Together with such novelists as Joseph Conrad and Jack London and poets like Ernest Dowson, Charles Baudelaire, and Algernon Charles Swinburne, these playwrights helped him define his concerns as a would-be artist of the theater.

In 1913–1914 O'Neill wrote several one-act plays of little consequence. Of these, *The Web*, *Thirst*, *Recklessness*, *Warnings*, and *Fog* were published in 1914 in a privately printed collection entitled *Thirst and Other One-Act Plays*. In each he attempted to show men and women as victims of an "ironic fate," a blind controlling force that doomed its victims. The same idea, significantly altered, is present in the only important achievement of these years, *Bound East for Cardiff*, a short play concerning the death of Yank, a stoker on a tramp freighter, the S.S. Glencairn. Here the ironic fate lies in the power of the sea, which holds the sailors in thrall. Should a sailor try to leave the sea, as Yank does, he will be punished for his apostasy. However, if sailors are obedient to the sea and follow its dictates without willful rebellion, the sea will protect them as a mother protects her children. Sailors, O'Neill suggests, are bound to the sea and to one another in a destiny the sea creates. This concept, together with the poetic realism of the dialogue and the simplicity of the narrative, marked the first time O'Neill's true voice was heard.

O'Neill entered Harvard in the fall of 1914 to study playwriting in a newly instituted course taught by Professor George Pierce Baker—English 47, known as "The 47 Workshop." Although he learned technical details of the craft of conventional playwriting, nothing he wrote proved to be of consequence. Leaving Harvard in 1915, he returned to New York City,

where he became friendly with the artists, anarchists, and drifters who frequented the bars and cafes in Greenwich Village. He began to drink heavily and wrote little.

In June 1916 he went to Provincetown, Massachusetts, where he met the poet George Cram Cook, Susan Glaspell (Cook's wife), John Reed, and other writers caught up in the foment of the new century. As a summer amusement they staged locally written one-act plays, among them *Bound East for Cardiff*, on an improvised stage in a shed built on a wharf. The power of the play gave the vacationers an unexpected cause: to create a theater. They banded together as "The Provincetown Players," and in the fall, in a converted brownstone house on Macdougal Street in Greenwich Village, they began to present bills of plays by American playwrights who were responding to new theories of theater arts. The Provincetown Playhouse became O'Neill's workshop. In the next years O'Neill wrote most of his one-act plays for their stage: *Before Breakfast* (1916), a monologue modeled after Strindberg's *The Stronger*, was followed by four short sea plays—*Ile* (1917) and the three that completed his account of life on the S.S. Glencairn, *The Long Voyage Home* (1917), *In the Zone* (1917), and *The Moon of the Caribbees* (1918). In 1918 he also wrote *The Rope*, a melodramatic version of the story of the prodigal son; *Shell Shock*, a sketch about a victim of a wartime offensive; *Where the Cross Is Made*, a story of buried treasure and the madness of an old sea captain; and *The Dreamy Kid*, a short tragedy about a Negro gangster, notable because the Players, contrary to standard theatrical practice, cast blacks in the central roles. Several of the plays were published in literary magazines such as *Seven Arts* and the *Smart Set*, whose editors, George Jean Nathan and H. L. Mencken, O'Neill had come to know.

In 1918, in addition to the one-act plays, O'Neill completed *Beyond the Horizon*, a four-act tragedy of life on a New England farm. Accepted by a Broadway producer, J. D. Williams, it became O'Neill's first fully professional production, and its success was unexpectedly rewarding. It was received with critical enthusiasm and in 1920 won O'Neill the first of his four Pulitzer Prizes.

O'Neill's personal life had changed substantially from the delinquent ways he had followed a few years earlier. In 1918 he married a young writer, Agnes Boulton, and in 1919 the couple went to live in an abandoned U.S. Coast Guard station at Peaked Hill Bar on Cape Cod. On the Cape his second son, Shane Rudraighe, was born (1919). Earlier difficulties between O'Neill and his father were smoothed over, but in 1920 James O'Neill died of cancer. Ella, who had overcome her morphine habit in 1914, took charge of the complexities of her husband's estate. She was aided by Jamie, who gave up drinking to be with her.

O'Neill's productivity in these years was extraordinary. In 1919 he wrote *The Straw*, a full-length play based on his experiences in the tuberculosis sanatorium; *Chris Christophersen*, a sea play in four acts; and several one-act plays he later destroyed. The following year he revised *Chris Christophersen*, which had failed in an out-of-town tryout, retitling it *Anna Christie*. He also completed *Gold*, a full-length version of his one-act play *Where the Cross Is Made*; *Diff'rent*, the portrait of a frustrated New England spinster; and most notably *The Emperor Jones*. *Gold* failed in its 1921 production, but *Diff'rent* (in the same year) had a respectable run, while *The Emperor Jones*, produced in 1920, was an exciting, exceptionally successful theatrical event. Audiences responded to the constant throbbing of the tom-toms that pursued the black Pullman-car porter, the self-proclaimed emperor of a Caribbean island, as he fled from the vengeance of the natives he had victimized. The relatively short drama provided the first starring role in a modern play for a black actor, Charles Gilpin. Later, in London, the young Paul Robeson would assume the role memorably.

The immediately succeeding years saw a repeated pattern of failure balanced by great success. *The Straw* (1919/1921) and a domestic drama, *The First Man* (1921/1922), failed; but O'Neill received his second Pulitzer Prize for *Anna Christie*, and *The Hairy Ape* (1921/1922), an account of the attempt of a Neanderthal stoker to find his place in the world, proved as startling as *The Emperor Jones*. He also completed a poetic account of Ponce de Leon's search for the Fountain of Youth, *The Fountain* (1922/1925), and *Welded* (1923/1924), a drama, reminiscent of Strindberg's *The Dance of Death*, that told of a playwright and an actress bound in a love-hate relationship. Both plays failed in production, but the latter pointed the way toward the psychological concerns of O'Neill's mature dramas of the late 1920s and 1930s.

His work achieved increasing success with critics and the public, and O'Neill received a gold medal from the National Institute of Arts and Letters in 1923; but his personal life was beset with tragic difficulties. Ella O'Neill, in Los Angeles to resolve problems of James's estate, died suddenly. Jamie at once resumed drinking, and on the night *The Hairy Ape* opened, the train bearing O'Neill's mother's body and his drunken brother arrived in New York. Jamie was committed to a sanatorium, where he died in November 1923. The circumstances of Ella's death provided the climax of O'Neill's last completed play, *A Moon for the Misbegotten* (1943/1947).

Although O'Neill continued to drink heavily, his creative energy did not wane. In the winter of 1923–1924 he completed his study of the marriage of a young black student to a white woman, *All God's Chillun Got Wings* (1923/1924), and his tragedy concerning incest and murder on a rocky New England farm, *Desire Under the Elms* (1924/1924). Both plays, the first dealing with miscegenation, the second with incest, had difficulties with censors.

In 1923 he joined critic Kenneth Macgowan and stage designer Robert Edmond Jones to manage two theaters in Greenwich Village, the old Provincetown Playhouse and the Greenwich Village Theatre. Calling the organization "The Experimental Theatre," the triumvirate staged rarely seen or new experimental plays, such as *The Great God Brown* (1925/1926), which used masks to differentiate the inner and outer levels of personality.

In 1924 the O'Neills visited Bermuda, where, in May 1925, their daughter Oona was born. A year later O'Neill bought "Spithead," a handsome home on Little Turtle Bay. There several events of importance transpired. After a short period of psychoanalysis, O'Neill, sensing the conflict between his drinking and his writing, gave up alcohol; with one or two falls from grace, he abstained for the rest of his life. He began work on three plays of great scale: *Marco Millions* (1925/1928), an eight-act retelling of Marco Polo's adventures in China; *Lazarus Laughed* (1926), a massive choral drama that attempted to set forth a theology for the modern world through an imaginative account of the life of Lazarus after his awakening in the tomb; and *Strange Interlude*, a nine-act drama of a woman's life, in which, through asides, the characters speak aloud their inmost thoughts. *Lazarus Laughed*, whose cast numbered in the hundreds, attracted no professional producer, but *Marco Millions*, shortened to three acts, was lavishly and successfully staged in January 1928, as was *Strange Interlude* in the same month. Both productions were undertaken by the Theatre Guild, which thereafter remained O'Neill's producer. *Strange Interlude* was one of the most successful productions of the decade. It ran for over 400 performances in New York and won O'Neill his third Pulitzer Prize. Several companies toured it through the United States, and it played to great success in Europe. The published text became a bestseller of over 100,000 copies.

In his personal life, changes were imminent. Since 1921 O'Neill had become friendly with his older son, and the boy visited Bermuda to their mutual pleasure. In 1926 he again met actress Carlotta Monterey, who had appeared as Mildred in *The Hairy Ape*. In 1928, when he went to New York to oversee rehearsals of *Strange Interlude* and *Marco Millions*, the two fell in love. O'Neill determined to leave his family in Bermuda and go with Carlotta to Europe. After a short tour to the Far East, he and Carlotta settled in France at Le Plessis, a chateau near Tours. There, in 1928, he completed work on *Dynamo*, which he planned as the first play of a trilogy entitled "Myths for the God-Forsaken." After *Dynamo* failed in its 1929 Theatre Guild production, O'Neill turned to another large work, a trilogy based on the Greek tragic legend of the House of Atreus, *Mourning Becomes Electra*. During this time his wife obtained a divorce, and in July 1929 O'Neill and Carlotta were married in Paris. They returned to the United States in 1931, as the trilogy, which required six drafts, went into production.

The success of *Mourning Becomes Electra* was substantial, and O'Neill continued to work at increasingly large concepts. In 1932 he began the second play of the *Dynamo* trilogy, which proved difficult. This play, finally titled *Days without End* (1933/1934), also required six revisions. Its story of a man's quest for faith appears to have been generated by O'Neill's concern with his lapsed Catholicism. The protagonist is played by two actors, who represent his need for and his denial of God. It was a failure when produced in 1934.

As a release from the problems of the religious play, O'Neill wrote his endearing comedy, *Ah, Wilderness!* (1932/1933), which looked nostalgically at his boyhood, burying the truth of his family's life at Monte Cristo Cottage under a charming tale of a young man's coming of age in a small Connecticut town in 1906. The play was written rapidly and smoothly and required little revision.

Late in 1934, as O'Neill worked on the third play of "Myths for the God-Forsaken," another project, astonishing in its scope, demanded his attention. He conceived of what grew in final plan to be an eleven-play cycle concerned with the failure of the American dream. Ultimately titled *A Tale of Possessors Self-Dispossessed*, it traced the history of two families from the revolutionary war to the middle 1930s. The cycle's theme was the betrayal of the bright promise of America by the greed of its inhabitants. In exemplary episodes set in locales around the world—a post-road tavern in 1828, a clipper ship rounding the Horn, a San Francisco saloon, a construction site on the first transcontinental railroad, Paris hotel rooms, a Buddhist temple in China, a Detroit automobile plant—O'Neill repeatedly asked the question found in Mark 8:36: "For what shall it profit a man, if he shall gain the whole world and lose his own soul?"

The work progressed in a handsome villa, "Casa Genotta," which O'Neill and Carlotta built in 1932 on Sea Island, Georgia. As he wrote, however, his health deteriorated, and ultimately they left Sea Island. In 1936 they went west to visit a friend of his, novelist Sophus Keith Winther, in Seattle. There O'Neill learned that he had won the Nobel Prize for literature. He and Carlotta traveled south to the San Francisco Bay area, Carlotta's girlhood home. There he was stricken with an acute attack of appendicitis with severe complications, requiring an extended stay in an Oakland hospital. On recovering, O'Neill determined to remain in the area and in 1937 built a new home, "Tào House," in the hills near the small town of Danville.

The period between 1937 and 1944, when he left Tào House, were years of both great creative fulfillment and personal hardship. O'Neill was at times incapacitated by illness, most notably an increasingly intense tremor that often made writing impossible. Shane and Oona, who had been left in their mother's care but whom he had seen on occasional visits, both became problems. At school, Shane did poorly and seemed to have no firm purpose in life. In 1942 Oona had been named debutante of the year at the Stork Club in New York and had gone to Hollywood to seek a screen career. There she met and married Charles Chaplin, whose personal and political life had darkened his reputation. Her actions earned her father's unrelenting hostility. On the other hand, he took pride in his older son, who had completed a doctorate at

Yale in classics and had been hired there as an instructor.

Tào House provided a remote, walled fastness wherein O'Neill, sealed away from interruption by its thick walls and by Carlotta's protective guardianship, turned to writing his best plays. Central to his attention was the cycle. He was physically able to complete only one part, *A Touch of the Poet* (1942/1958). Working intensely over the long line of the cycle, O'Neill wrote scenarios running to 20,000 words and completed long first drafts of many. When it became clear that he could not live to finish them, he destroyed the unfinished scenarios and drafts except for an unrevised version of *More Stately Mansions*, the sequel to *A Touch of the Poet*, and a detailed scenario of *The Calms of Capricorn*, the next play in the series.

As relief from the work on the cycle, in 1939 O'Neill completed a noncycle play, *The Iceman Cometh*, set in a saloon such as he had known in his youth. Here, Hickey, a traveling salesman, comes on an annual "periodical," but instead of hosting a drunken party for the derelicts, as he has done in previous years, he attempts to rid them of their "pipe dreams," the illusions they cling to that give them life. A long, difficult, and intense work, it has become one of the major dramas of the century.

Allied to it is *Hughie* (1942/1964), the only completed play of a cycle of one-act plays planned under the working title "By Way of Obit." In it, a desperate, lonely Broadway rounder tells his life story to a nearly mute night clerk in a run-down New York hotel. Like *The Iceman Cometh*, the play maintains that the life-lie, the self-created illusion of personal value, is essential to all persons.

The Tào House plays also include two works based on O'Neill's family life: *Long Day's Journey into Night*, which depicts his family as it existed in Monte Cristo Cottage shortly before he was sent to the tuberculosis sanatorium, and *A Moon for the Misbegotten*, which, in portraying an abortive romance between Jamie and a heavy-bodied farm girl, recalls Ella's death and Jamie's desperate attempt to find forgiveness for his dereliction while bringing her body on the train to New York.

O'Neill's power of creative concentration was never so evident as he fought off the tremor and the allied illnesses that threatened to make his writing impossible. He began several other noncycle plays, but illness prevailed. Tào House, increasingly isolated by the shortages occasioned by World War II, presented nearly insoluble problems, and finally in 1945 he returned to New York. The Theatre Guild produced *The Iceman Cometh* in 1946 and followed it with *A Moon for the Misbegotten*, which, after some censorship troubles, closed out of town in 1947. With this play O'Neill's theatrical career ended.

Although his illness and frustration at being unable to write created tension in his marriage, ultimately O'Neill and Carlotta resolved their differences, and he became almost entirely dependent on her. Eugene, Jr., turned to alcohol and committed suicide in 1950.

Shane, who had been committed to prison on a narcotics charge, followed him as a suicide in 1977. O'Neill made no attempt to communicate with Oona, but her marriage to Charles Chaplin proved a happy one. The two had eight children. Oona died in 1991.

In 1948 the O'Neills refurbished a cottage at Marblehead Neck in Massachusetts but moved in 1951 to a suite in the Shelton Hotel in Boston. Eugene appointed Carlotta his executor and donated many of his manuscripts and papers to Yale University. He died in the hotel and was buried at Forest Hills Cemetery in Boston.

For a time he dropped from the roster of major dramatists. However, Carlotta arranged for the premieres of his last plays, including *A Touch of the Poet*, *Hughie*, and *Long Day's Journey into Night*, in Stockholm, where their success led to New York productions and the reestablishment of his reputation. *Long Day's Journey into Night* posthumously won O'Neill his fourth Pulitzer Prize.

Throughout his life, until he was silenced by illness, O'Neill's career was characterized by an unsurpassed energy. He was never without plays in progress and turned from one to another with ease, letting one project rest and ripen while he worked on another. Several times he was responsible for opening two plays in the space of a month or less, a phenomenon made possible by his absolute familiarity with the technical demands of theater.

O'Neill wrote nothing quickly, with the possible exception of *Ah, Wilderness!* Writing was meditative and fanatically private. His letters discuss work in progress only as he came to the final form of the play in question. He composed his plays in handwriting so small that it sometimes requires a magnifying glass to decipher it. It resembles a personal code to which few were given the key. The scenarios and overly long first drafts were intensive investigations of a play's psychological content. The surviving draft of *More Stately Mansions* contains dialogue sequences whose speeches run to several hundred words, as O'Neill explored the desires and reactions of his characters.

O'Neill was unafraid to break conventional molds. In draft, the styles of the plays shifted between realism and expressionism—whatever seemed needed to ferret out the psychological truth of the characters. The length of his plays, from the one-act *Hughie* to the four-plus hours of *The Iceman Cometh*, suggests his refusal to accede to the norms of the commercial theater. He said once that he wanted to see how much an audience could bear and in his later work aimed to transform an audience from spectator to participant in the action. To this end, he experimented with many devices—masks, soliloquies, patterns of sound and of silence, significant music, carefully worked-out designs of light and dark. He set particular store by the monologue. Most of *The Emperor Jones* is an extended monologue. Voices speaking alone in silence are heard in *Desire Under the Elms*, *Marco Millions*, *Strange Interlude*, *Lazarus Laughed*, *The Iceman Cometh*, *A Moon for the Misbegotten*, and *Long Day's Journey into Night*.

These passages are always psychologically revealing, but in performance they also provide a lyricism comparable to great passages of poetic drama.

The concept of ironic fate, the central theme of his early short plays, acquired a more profound philosophical base when, as in *Desire Under the Elms*, O'Neill took from Friedrich Nietzsche the concept of opposing Apollonian and Dionysian ways of being. He found in the latter concept a philosophical underpinning for his idea that human beings are controlled by a force to which they belong by birth. The plays of the late 1920s and early 1930s are all influenced by Nietzsche, Schopenhauer, and other philosophers and by American naturalists such as Frank Norris and Jack London, who held similar views of man's nature and destiny.

At first O'Neill dramatized what he called "belonging" by showing his protagonists searching for their source; the Emperor Jones flees back to a primitive crocodile god, and Yank, the Hairy Ape, finds his home in the crushing embrace of the great ape in the Central Park zoo. O'Neill also explored the tragic fate of those who separate themselves by an act of will from their center of belonging, as does Robert Mayo, in *Beyond the Horizon*, when he stays on his farm rather than follow his destiny to sea. In *Strange Interlude*, the men whose lives center around heroine Nina Leeds are torn between their need for her maternal power and for an egotistical "God the Father." In *Lazarus Laughed*, O'Neill attempted to frame a quasi-scientific religion for a world in which, as Nietzsche had asserted, God was dead. The ill-fated "Myths for the God-Forsaken" depicted in *Dynamo* a god in the dynamo's power. In *Days without End*, O'Neill looked at organized religion as a way for one to find a center.

After the failure of *Dynamo* and *Days without End*, O'Neill turned from specifically theological themes to a more existential view of the human condition, perhaps best set forth in *The Iceman Cometh*, where the drunken bums of Harry Hope's saloon cling to their "pipe dreams" in order to retain a semblance of life amid almost total despair.

In the two autobiographical plays at the end of his career, O'Neill's own life was partly reflected in the desperate attempts of his characters to find some meager salvation. Such as it is, salvation is intimately bound with the memory of something that can assuage pain and provide a sense of blessing. Edmund Tyrone, in *Long Day's Journey into Night*, compares such memory to "a saint's vision of beatitude." For those incapable of sainthood, memory is a small and often painful remedy, but it is enough to offer a kind of salvation to the characters and perhaps to the playwright himself.

• The major collection of O'Neill manuscripts, letters, and memorabilia is in the Beinecke Rare Book and Manuscript Library at Yale University. Other substantial collections can be found in the Berg Collection at Columbia University; the New York Public Library Manuscript Collection; the Museum of the City of New York; the libraries of Cornell University, Harvard University, the University of Pennsylvania, Princeton University, and the University of Virginia; and the library of the Eugene O'Neill Foundation, Tao House, Danville, Calif.

The Library of America edition of O'Neill's dramatic writings, *Complete Plays*, ed. Travis Bogard (3 vols., 1988), is definitive; it contains the most accurate texts and chronology available, and its notes link O'Neill firmly with his theatrical productions. Important fugitive writings appear in *The Unknown O'Neill*, ed. Bogard (1988). See also the following O'Neill titles: *Poems, 1912–1944*, ed. Donald Gallup (1980); *Work Diary*, transcribed by Gallup (2 vols., 1981); and *"The Calms of Capricorn"*, transcribed by Gallup (2 vols., 1981).

O'Neill's published correspondence appears in several volumes: *Selected Letters of Eugene O'Neill*, ed. Bogard and Jackson R. Bryer (1988); *"The Theatre We Worked For": The Letters of Eugene O'Neill and Kenneth Macgowan*, ed. Bryer (1982); *"As Ever Gene": The Letters of Eugene O'Neill to George Jean Nathan*, ed. Nancy L. Roberts and Arthur W. Roberts (1987); and *"Love and Admiration and Respect": The O'Neill-Commins Correspondence*, ed. Dorothy Commins (1986).

Significant biographies are Arthur Gelb and Barbara Gelb, *O'Neill* (1962; rev. ed., 1973), and Louis Sheaffer, *O'Neill, Son and Playwright* (1968) and *O'Neill, Son and Artist* (1973). Several bibliographies have also been published.

Analysis of O'Neill's work can be found in Judith Barlow, *Final Acts* (1985); Bogard, *Contour in Time* (1972; rev. ed., 1988); Barrett H. Clark, *Eugene O'Neill, the Man and His Plays* (1926; rev. ed., 1947); Edwin Engle, *The Haunted Heroes of Eugene O'Neill* (1953); Michael Manheim, *Eugene O'Neill's New Language of Kinship* (1982); John Henry Raleigh, *The Plays of Eugene O'Neill* (1965); and Ronald H. Wainscott, *Staging O'Neill* (1988).

TRAVIS BOGARD

O'NEILL, James (14? Oct. 1846?–10 Aug. 1920), actor, was probably born in Kilkenny, Ireland, though precise dating cannot be established because corroborative birth records do not exist, and James himself gave varying dates. He was the son of Edward O'Neill (or O'Neil), an illiterate day laborer, and Mary (or Mary Ann); her maiden name is also O'Neill. Emigrating from Kilkenny in 1850, the O'Neill family settled in Buffalo, New York, where around 1856 James's father, apparently in despair, deserted his family and returned to Ireland, to die bizarrely by accidental poisoning. The O'Neills subsisted in such appalling poverty that James's mother and sisters became scrubwomen and seamstresses, and at the age of eleven, James was forced to leave school and work as an apprentice filemaker at fifty cents a week. After being twice evicted for nonpayment of rent, Mary O'Neill moved her family to Cincinnati in 1857–1858 at the suggestion of one of her daughters. According to his unreliable romanticized autobiography, James continued to work as a filemaker and then unsuccessfully tried his hand at selling newspapers. At some unspecified date during the Civil War, he migrated to Norfolk, Virginia, to work for a brother-in-law in the military uniform business. There, he claimed, he had a tutor and frequented the theater. It is certain that he had no formal education after the age of eleven.

He returned to Cincinnati in 1865, where his entrée to the stage was totally accidental. One night in September he was drafted as a supernumerary because of a theatrical strike at the National Theatre, which was adjacent to his favorite billiards saloon. The play was the melodrama *The Colleen Bawn*, by the Irish-American playwright Dion Boucicault. Almost immediately O'Neill became a company member, at twenty-five cents a performance. By the end of the year he had listed himself in the city directory as "actor."

He learned by doing, working his way up from super through utility player, "walking gentleman," juvenile lead, and finally leading man, honing his skills in stock companies in St. Louis, Baltimore, and Cincinnati. The handsome charm of "the black-mustachioed Adonis," and above all his "golden voice," mocked by his son, Eugene O'Neill, in *Long Day's Journey*, made him an attractive stage personality. O'Neill worked hard to lose his brogue and largely succeeded, though some reviewers always castigated him for it. He is said to have had the ability to vary the pitch of his voice by two or three tones and was able to project without apparent effort. He attracted the attention of such famous actors as Edwin Booth, Edwin Forrest, Joseph Jefferson (1829–1905), and others who both praised and taught this eager, talented young man.

His first appointment as leading man was for the season of 1870–1871 at the Academy of Music in Cleveland, where he met Thomas Quinlan, a prosperous stationer and the father of his future wife, Ella. A relentless self-improver, O'Neill read widely and mastered some fifty roles in his first year in Cleveland, though he never overcame his difficulty in memorizing (Matlaw, in Ranald, p. 564). In 1872 he became leading man at McVicker's Theatre in Chicago, the premiere house of that bustling city, honing his skills in the classical repertory. In 1874 he moved to Hooley's Opera House, Chicago's other major company.

During his years in Chicago (1872–1875), he matured as an artist, starring with Booth. As recorded in *Long Day's Journey*, O'Neill never forgot the occasion when, alternating with Booth as Iago and Othello, the senior actor praised him: "That young man is playing Othello better than I ever did." Reviewers agreed with this judgment, something for which O'Neill forever reproached himself when he thought of what might have been. During this period one actress was alleged to have killed herself for love of him, and a young woman named Nettie Walsh bore a son, claiming O'Neill as the father. He denied both the child and the marriage, but over the years paid temporary alimony and made a settlement on a paternity suit (even though the suit was dismissed).

By 1875 he was leading man in San Francisco; then, in 1876 he moved to Palmer's Union Square Theatre in New York. At St. Ann's Church in 1877 he married Mary Ellen "Ella" Quinlan, shy, sheltered, convent educated, and not yet twenty. They had three children. The popular couple went to San Francisco, where their first son, James Jr. ("Jamie") was born in 1878. His wasted life is recounted in Eugene's *A Moon for the Misbegotten* (1943). In San Francisco from 1877 to 1883, O'Neill was enormously popular, but his great disappointment was the successful religious opposition to his portrayal of Jesus Christ in *The Passion* (1879). O'Neill, who always considered himself a devout (though not totally observant) Roman Catholic, cited early alleged priestly ambitions and the purity of his matrimonial life as qualifications for the role, but they proved insufficient, and later production attempts were also unsuccessful. Later, O'Neill said that this play, roundly condemned as blasphemous by clerics of assorted denominations in San Francisco and later in New York, ruined his theatrical reputation and signified the end of his career as a serious actor.

After the San Francisco debacle he moved to New York, where in 1883 he met his nemesis when he replaced the ailing Charles Thorne as leading man in Charles Fechter's adaptation of the Dumas novel *The Count of Monte Cristo*. It was to haunt his existence. His enormous success in the role depressed him, and he castigated himself for becoming enslaved by it. His fear of the poorhouse militated against his giving up on a sure thing, so he played it relentlessly, giving more than six thousand performances over three decades, finally performing a cut-down version in vaudeville. Throughout these years O'Neill toured in *Monte Cristo* in virtually every city and town in the United States and Canada, crossing and recrossing the North American continent. The play was one of the era's greatest hits, and "the world is mine," its best-known line, shouted exultantly as he beat his way out of the waves, became a household phrase. Whenever he essayed other roles—and he tried many, including Hamlet—audiences clamored for his return to *Monte Cristo* and back he went into it. He bought the property, protecting his legal right to play it and thereby winning the financial security his immigrant fear of inevitable destitution demanded. He was now a star, important enough in 1895 to be one of those actor-managers who unsuccessfully challenged the hegemony of the Klaw Erlanger theater syndicate.

Like many a landless Irishman, O'Neill invested heavily and widely in real estate in a number of cities, but he bought only one home, Monte Cristo Cottage, in New London, Connecticut, in 1884. There the family spent summers in what was usually their only yearly residence together. In 1885, while O'Neill was on tour accompanied by his wife, their second child died of measles at the age of two. Ella was devastated and afterward underwent two abortions before giving birth to Eugene. Ella and James could not bear long separations, and during their 43-year marriage they were rarely apart for more than three months, always living in hotels. Because O'Neill's wife usually joined him on his frequent tours, the boys were sent at an early age to boarding schools, an act the hypersensitive Eugene perceived as rejection.

As a result of her difficult pregnancy with Eugene and complications resulting from his birth, Ella quite innocently became addicted to morphine. Unlike Eugene's fictional depiction of the situation in *Long Day's Journey into Night*, O'Neill tried to help and spent a small fortune on sanitoria for his beloved Ella, who eventually found her own cure through a sojourn in a Brooklyn convent about 1914. To be sure, the hard-drinking O'Neill always pinched pennies, but his generosity to friends, fellow actors, and even his two troublesome sons was legendary. He did not stint on their education at Fordham and Princeton, respectively, and when they dropped out he supported both of them, grudgingly at times, but still doing his paternal duty. He even gave them positions in his touring company, where they disgraced themselves by appearing drunk onstage. He secretly paid Eugene's salary as a cub reporter in New London (1912), financed his year in George Pierce Baker's playwriting course at Harvard (1913–1914), and underwrote his first published collection of one-act plays (1914). Certainly O'Neill did send Eugene to the Fairfield County State Tuberculosis Sanitorium in 1912, believing, with the pessimistic experience of the Irish, that the disease was incurable, but when Eugene left after two days, his father paid for an expensive private sanitarium.

All this time, and particularly after 1904, he was trying to shed *Monte Cristo*, a role that satisfied him less and less and that he realized was making him a laughingstock. For this reason, in 1912 he cut short his tour in its truncated vaudeville version. He repeatedly appeared in other vehicles, including *The Two Orphans*, *The White Sister*, *Virginius* (an adaptation of John Webster), and *Julius Caesar*. He also accepted subordinate roles in biblical spectacles like *Joseph and His Brethren* and *The Wanderer*. In fact, a study of his roles offers a history of the American theatrical scene from 1868 to 1917, with its classical roles, escapism, romanticism, and particularly its melodrama. Critics and reviewers celebrated his innovative "naturalism" onstage, but his 1912 filmed performance as Monte Cristo (still extant) demonstrates that he still practiced the old-fashioned histrionics of the period.

No longer a matinee idol, too permanently associated with *Monte Cristo*, and unable to trust his recalcitrant memory, the old trouper decided in 1917 that his day was over, and he retired. Indeed, it had been a long and financially successful career. He divided his time between Monte Cristo Cottage and apartment hotels in New York, where he and Ella were well-known opening nighters. He also remained a sociable theatrical presence at the Lambs', Friars', and Green Room clubs.

Before his death in New London, O'Neill had seen a performance of his son's first Broadway success (and first Pulitzer Prize winner), *Beyond the Horizon*, and realized that with it the theater of his livelihood had been turned upside down. His comment to his now reconciled son at the time summarizes his own theatrical philosophy: "People come to the theatre to forget their troubles, not to be reminded of them. What are you trying to do—send them home to commit suicide?" (Basso, quoted by Sheaffer [1968], p. 477).

O'Neill's obituaries generally concentrated on his considerable though now outdated achievements and did not mention his son's success. Today, however, he is chiefly remembered as the father of Eugene O'Neill, prize-winning dramatist, whose portrayal of his father as a miserly skinflint in *Long Day's Journey into Night* has overshadowed the magnitude of his flawed success.

• James O'Neill's papers are deposited at the Museum of the City of New York. His holograph autobiography is at The Players, New York City. Currently, no full-length biography of James O'Neill exists, though Myron Matlaw's manuscript is being completed. Other important materials are to be found in the standard biographies of Eugene O'Neill, notably Doris Alexander, *The Tempering of Eugene O'Neill* (1962), Arthur Gelb and Barbara Gelb, *O'Neill* (1962, repr. 1973), and Louis Sheaffer's two volumes, *O'Neill: Son and Playwright* (1968) and *O'Neill: Son and Artist* (1973). Further biographical information can be found in Matlaw, "Robins Hits the Road: Trouping with O'Neill in the 1880's," *Theatre Survey* 29 (1988): 175–92, and Edward L. Shaughnessy, "Ella, James, and Jamie O'Neill," *The Eugene O'Neill Review* 15, no. 2 (1991): 5–92. Ancillary biographical details are in Margaret Loftus Ranald, *The Eugene O'Neill Companion* (1984). Though occasionally an O'Neill "sendup" of his interviewer, the following should not be overlooked: Hamilton Basso, "The Tragic Sense" (profile of Eugene O'Neill), *New Yorker*, 28 Feb., 6 Mar., and 13 Mar. 1948. A discussion of the text of *The Count of Monte Cristo* may be found in Matlaw, "English and American Dramatizations of *Le Comte de Monte Cristo*," *Nineteenth Century Theatre Research* 7 (1979): 39–73. Obituaries are in the *New York Times*, 11 Aug. 1920, the *Boston Pilot*, 14 Aug. 1920, and the *New York Dramatic Mirror*, 21 Aug. 1920.

MARGARET LOFTUS RANALD
MYRON MATLAW

O'NEILL, Rose Cecil (25 June 1874–6 Apr. 1944), illustrator and writer, was born in Wilkes-Barre, Pennsylvania, the daughter of William Patrick O'Neill, a bookseller, and Alice Asenath Cecelia Smith, a former schoolteacher. At the time of her birth, the O'Neill family occupied "Emerald Cottage," a picturesque home with cupids and wreaths of roses ornamenting the ceiling in the octagonal living room. It is possible that these cupids, imprinted on her memory, later inspired her famous "Kewpie" illustrations of plump infants with tiny wings. In 1878 her family moved to Omaha, Nebraska, and at the age of thirteen, O'Neill, who attended parochial school, won a prize, awarded by the *Omaha World Herald*, for a solemn illustration of temptation leading down into the abyss. Within a year, O'Neill had begun selling drawings to magazines and newspapers, and she continued to do so until her death.

Before her twentieth birthday, O'Neill began pursuing a career as a writer as well as an illustrator. In 1893 she packed up her novel "Calesta," the story of a nun, and took it to New York, where she hoped to find a publisher. The novel did not sell, but New York magazines began purchasing her illustrations. O'Neill remained in New York, residing and enrolling in classes at the convent of the Sisters of St. Regis. By 1894 O'Neill's father had moved with her mother and four siblings to an isolated property called "Bonniebrook" in the Ozark hills near Branson, Missouri.

In 1896 O'Neill married Gray Latham, a Virginia aristocrat, who had met her in Omaha and courted her in New York. Subsequently, during times of stress and heartache, she retreated to Bonniebrook, as she did in 1901, after her divorce from Latham. Harry Leon Wilson, a writer and editor, courted her at Bonniebrook and married her in 1902. Neither marriage produced children. Rose maintained strong ties to her Bonniebrook family, especially her younger siblings, Callista and Clarence.

Both O'Neill and Wilson enjoyed a period of intense creativity between 1902 and 1907. She published *The Loves of Edwy: Tale and Drawings* in 1904 and illustrated Wilson's *Lions of the Lord* (1903), *The Seeker* (1904), and *The Boss of Little Arcady* (1905). Booth Tarkington became a close friend of the couple, spending time with them in Italy in 1905. O'Neill's high spirits clashed with Wilson's serious view of life, although she expressed great sadness after separating from him in 1907. Throughout her remaining years she called him "the Beloved." One of her best poems, "Established," published in the *Master-Mistress* in 1922, apparently refers to her parting from Wilson.

In her retreat at Bonniebrook after her second marriage ended, O'Neill began drawing her famous Kewpie characters. The sweet, adventurous Kewpies first appeared in *Ladies' Home Journal* in 1909. Instantly popular, the Kewpies illustrations accompanied stories in *Woman's Home Companion* beginning in 1910 and *Good Housekeeping* beginning in 1914. By 1913 the chubby winged infants, with their impish faces and rakish tufts of hair, had become a commercial phenomenon decorating soap, fabric, and stationery. Kewpie dolls of various sizes and materials, including bisque and celluloid, netted O'Neill millions of dollars in royalties. Kewpie comic strips ran in newspapers through the mid-1930s.

By 1918, after a period in Europe, O'Neill established a home and studio at 61 Washington Square, New York City, and acquired the sobriquet "Rose of Washington Square." She and Callista opened their various homes in New York, Westport (Conn.), and Capri to a wide array of acquaintances and friends. O'Neill, an ample blonde with a soft, Kewpie-like face, dressed dramatically in flowing red velvet and often went barefoot.

In contrast to the sunny sentimentality embodied in the Kewpies, beginning in the early 1900s, O'Neill produced a series of Titans, or monster drawings, depicting the tragic tension between the physical and spiritual aspects of human existence. With titles such as *The Faun Weeps Finding Himself the Father of a Human Infant*, these allegorical drawings reminded critic Talbot Faulkner Hamlin of the visionary art of William Blake. Nevertheless, wrote Hamlin, O'Neill's drawings clearly belonged to the twentieth century. Their modernity rested not in subject matter but in feeling. Hamlin wrote:

This modernity of subject is not a matter of drawing modern *things*. Indeed one wonders if Rose O'Neill ever drew a single modern object. It is something much more important, for it is something much deeper; it is a matter of expressing modern emotions, and especially the deepest and most disturbing of them all: the duality, the conflict between our physical heritage and our complex sophisticated culture. (Hamlin, p. 423)

O'Neill exhibited the monster drawings in 1921 at the Galerie Devambez in Paris and in 1922 at the Wildenstein Galleries in New York, receiving generally favorable notice from the critics.

As the Kewpies cavorted through the pages of popular magazines, O'Neill produced prose and poetry with mystical, brooding qualities. The poems collected in *Master-Mistress* dwelt on the sad ambiguities of love and sex. Her novel *Garda* (1929) told a strange story, drawn from her Irish heritage, of unbearable love between a twin brother and sister.

O'Neill won a lasting place in American popular culture with her rakishly modern, but innocent, Kewpies. Her passionate monster drawings, poetry, and fiction faded quickly from the public memory. She spent the last eight years of her life in her three-story home at Bonniebrook, where she and Callista attended their mother in her last days. During these years, O'Neill continued selling illustrations to magazines, creating in 1940 the character of a little laughing Buddha figure called "Ho-Ho." She also published poems in the *Ladies' Home Journal* and other magazines. After her death at Springfield, neighbors dug her grave near an Ozark stream.

• Lyons Memorial Library, College of the Ozarks, Point Lookout, Mo., holds a collection of O'Neill's unpublished manuscripts and letters. O'Neill published several books in addition to those mentioned above; these include *The Goblin Woman* (1930), *The Kewpie Kutouts* (1914), *The Kewpie Primer* (1916), *The Kewpies and Dotty Darling* (1912), *The Kewpies and the Runaway Baby* (1928), *The Kewpies: Their Book* (1913), and *The Lady in the White Veil* (1909). Maude M. Horine published a booklet, *Memories of Rose O'Neill*, in 1950. In 1985 the Springfield Art Museum, Springfield, Mo., published an exhibit catalog titled *Through Rose-Colored Glasses: The Drawings and Illustrations of Rose Cecil O'Neill*. Book-length biographies include Rowena G. Ruggles, *The One Rose* (1964); Ralph A. McCanse, *Titans and Kewpies: The Life and Art of Rose O'Neill* (1968); and Shelley Armitage, *Kewpies and Beyond: The World of Rose O'Neill* (1994). Of special note for its appreciation of O'Neill's more serious works of art is Talbot Faulkner Hamlin, "Mystic Vision in Modern Drawings: The Art of Rose O'Neill," *Arts and Decoration*, Apr. 1922, pp. 422–23ff. Obituaries are in the *New York Times*, 7 Apr. 1944, and the *Saturday Review*, 3 June 1944.

BONNIE STEPENOFF

O'NEILL, Thomas Philip "Tip" (9 Dec. 1912–5 Jan. 1994), politician, was born Thomas Philip O'Neill, Jr., in Cambridge, Massachusetts, the son of Thomas Philip O'Neill, Sr., a minor city official, and Rose Ann Tolan. O'Neill's parents reared him Irish American, Catholic, and Democratic. He earned his nickname from a baseball player, James Edward "Tip" O'Neill of the St. Louis Browns. (Young Tip loved

baseball and became a lifelong fan of the Boston Red Sox.) After attending parochial schools, O'Neill graduated from Boston College in 1936. He participated in politics for the first time in 1928, campaigning for the Democratic presidential nominee, Alfred E. Smith. In 1935 O'Neill narrowly lost a race for the Cambridge City Council, but a year later he was elected to the Massachusetts House of Representatives. In 1941 he married Mildred "Millie" Miller; they had five children.

O'Neill's liberal philosophy and leadership skills emerged during his service in the Massachusetts state house. He used government to improve the lives of his ethnic, working-class constituents. "All politics is local," he proclaimed. O'Neill remembered once standing in front of Harvard University, "As I watched privileged sons of America drinking their champagne, I dreamed of bringing my own people—and *all* Americans who weren't born into wealth or advantage—into the great American tent of opportunity" (*Man of the House*, p. 378). To achieve that end, he supported a series of social programs known in Massachusetts as the "Little New Deal." Occasionally O'Neill went against the wishes of voters. In 1937 he moved to repeal a popular law requiring state teachers to take a loyalty oath. Impressed with O'Neill's courage, Democrats elected him minority leader in 1944. O'Neill thereupon launched a campaign to wrest control of the state house from the Grand Old Party. In 1948 he became the first Democrat in 140 years to assume the Speakership of the Massachusetts house. Four years later Bay State voters sent him to the U.S. House of Representatives.

Congressman O'Neill blended parochialism with liberal principles and party loyalty. To protect Boston's status as a commercial center, O'Neill unsuccessfully opposed construction of the St. Lawrence Seaway. In 1958 he advanced a bill to establish Cape Cod National Seashore. Two years later, O'Neill supported the candidacy of Senator John F. Kennedy for the Democratic presidential nomination. Kennedy had previously held O'Neill's House seat. During the 1960s O'Neill voted for most of the social welfare, civil rights, housing, and education reform legislation proposed by Presidents Kennedy and Lyndon B. Johnson.

Gregarious, witty, and opinionated, O'Neill became acquainted with the nation's leading politicians. He befriended John Kennedy, whom he thought "had a radiance that made people glow when they were in his company." Hardly a sycophant to the Kennedys, O'Neill disliked Attorney General Robert F. Kennedy, whom he deemed "a self-important upstart and a know-it-all." O'Neill particularly respected Johnson's political skills, stating, "Johnson worked instinctively. If Kennedy's political style was in his head, Johnson's was in his blood." A fierce partisan, he sharply disparaged the caliber of the opposition's leaders. "Dwight Eisenhower," O'Neill joked, "did more for the game of golf than any other individual except Arnold Palmer and Jack Nicklaus." Of then vice president Richard

M. Nixon, he remarked, "I used to play poker with him and any guy who could screech over losing 40 bucks I always knew shouldn't be president" (*New York Times*, 7 Jan. 1994).

As a member of the House, O'Neill rose steadily. He followed the advice of his fellow Democrat, Speaker Sam Rayburn, "If you want to get along, go along." In 1955 Rayburn named O'Neill to the powerful House Rules Committee. Otherwise, O'Neill shunned the spotlight, worked to build coalitions through compromise, and became a protégé of then majority leader (later Speaker) John W. McCormack (D.-Mass.).

A combination of independence, patronage, and fate eventually propelled O'Neill to the Speakership of the House. O'Neill earned the respect of younger liberals when in 1967 he broke with President Johnson over the Vietnam War. In 1971 Speaker Carl Albert (D.-Okla.) and Majority Leader Hale Boggs (D.-La.) elevated O'Neill to majority whip. After Boggs died in an airplane accident in 1972, O'Neill became majority leader. To reclaim Congress's power to declare war, Majority Leader O'Neill backed the War Powers Act of 1973. He quietly urged the House to investigate the Watergate scandal and favored President Nixon's impeachment. When Albert retired as Speaker in 1976, Democrats elected O'Neill to succeed him. O'Neill served as Speaker of the House from 1977 to 1987, when he retired from Congress.

As Speaker, O'Neill pressed for congressional reform. In the aftermath of Watergate, O'Neill forced the House to adopt a stringent code of ethics. He also made the lower chamber more inclusive and open. O'Neill oversaw expansion of the whip organization from a small clique to a leadership group encompassing one-third of the Democratic caucus. He formed ad hoc task forces to give younger representatives a voice and allowed the Democratic caucus to debate policy. According to critics, such changes encouraged independence, weakened party discipline, and eroded the Speaker's powers. Yet O'Neill retained much of his authority, partly because he donned a partisan demeanor and used the Speakership as a platform for national leadership. In 1979 he permitted live, televised coverage of House proceedings on the congressional cable network C-SPAN. O'Neill's six-foot two-inch, 280-pound frame; thick, snowy hair; bulbous, pink nose; and cabbage ears became familiar to millions of Americans. He even appeared on the popular television comedy "Cheers," set in a bar in Boston.

Otherwise, O'Neill's tenure as Speaker proved frustrating. Democratic president Jimmy Carter, a Washington outsider, distanced himself from O'Neill, the quintessential "old pol." Carter often failed to consult the Speaker and resisted courting members of Congress. "When it came to the politics of Washington, D.C.," O'Neill recalled, "he never really understood how the system worked." The Speaker pushed through the Congress the administration's energy conservation bill and loan to the Chrysler Corporation, even though relations between the White House and Capitol Hill remained chilly. O'Neill particularly re-

sented slights from Carter's chief of staff, Hamilton Jordan. "As far as Jordan was concerned," he remembered, "a House Speaker was something you bought on sale at Radio Shack." Believing that Carter's early concession of defeat in 1980 had cost Democratic candidates votes, O'Neill roared at one White House staffer, "You guys came in like a bunch of jerks and I see you're going out the same way."

O'Neill's frustrations multiplied when Ronald Reagan entered the White House in 1981. The Speaker despised the Republican president's calls for increased defense spending, tax reductions for wealthy citizens, and curtailment of programs such as food stamps and college loans designed to aid low- and middle-income Americans. Assuming the role of opposition leader, O'Neill attacked Reagan as "Herbert Hoover with a smile" and "a cheerleader for selfishness." Republicans in turn ridiculed O'Neill. Representative John LeBoutillier (R.-N.Y.) called the Speaker "big, fat, and out of control—just like the federal government." During a time of recession, many Americans backed the charismatic Reagan. Assisted by a GOP–controlled Senate and a coalition of Republicans and conservative Democrats in the House, Reagan secured passage of his agenda in 1981.

Relations between O'Neill and Reagan were not entirely adversarial. The Speaker made certain that the president's proposals received consideration by the full House and not remain bottled up in committee. O'Neill opposed the administration's program to aid Nicaragua's anti-Communist rebels, but he nonetheless endorsed Reagan's deployment of troops in Lebanon in 1982. The Speaker also cooperated with the White House in passing the Tax Reform Act of 1986. O'Neill and Reagan—two ebullient Irishmen who came from humble origins and loved sports—claimed to be friends when the workday had ended. Yet the Speaker remained adamant that the president was "out of touch with how regular Americans live and the problems they face. His whole world is Hollywood." Citing the need for new leadership, O'Neill retired from the House in 1987.

Out of office, O'Neill pursued business ventures and relaxed. He cashed in on his celebrity status by publishing his memoirs and appearing in television commercials to peddle Miller Lite Beer, American Express credit cards, and Hush Puppies shoes. The former Speaker died in Boston.

O'Neill's career bridged two eras. He entered public service when liberalism was in full flower and departed after it fell from favor. An old school partisan who strolled through ethnic neighborhoods, "schmoozed" with fellow "pols," and reveled in anecdotes, the Speaker retired as politics came to revolve around independence, public relations, and thirty-second television sound bites. "He helped usher in a new age in the House," asserted political scientist Lynne P. Brown, "without ever being a new age politician." O'Neill's constituency, urban, working-class immigrants, gradually moved to the suburbs and assumed a middle-class identity. In that respect, liberals like

O'Neill helped to bring many disadvantaged citizens into "the great American tent of opportunity."

• O'Neill's papers are in the John J. Burns Library at Boston College, Boston, Mass. The Burns Library also possesses the papers of O'Neill's close friend, Representative Edward Boland (D.-Mass.). For O'Neill's career, consult his memoirs, *Man of the House* (1987) and *All Politics Is Local* (1994). Also helpful is Paul R. Clancy, *Tip: A Biography of Thomas P. O'Neill, Speaker of the House* (1980). His contributions to the Speakership are covered in James C. Garland, "The Socialization to Partisan Legislative Behavior," *Western Political Quarterly* 41, no. 2 (1988): 391–400; Daniel J. Palazzolo, "Majority Party Leadership and Budget Policymaking in the House of Representatives," *Congress and the Presidency* 19, no. 2 (1992): 157–74; "The Shrinking Speaker," *New York Times*, 8 Jan. 1994; and Janet Hook, "O'Neill Changed Speaker's Role and Helped Remake House," *Congressional Quarterly Weekly Report*, 8 Jan. 1994, pp. 16–17. For O'Neill's changing constituency, see Adam Clymer, "When O'Neill Was Young, and City Hall Was Irish," *New York Times*, 9 Jan. 1994. Obituaries are in the *New York Times* and the *Washington Post*, both 7 Jan. 1994.

DEAN J. KOTLOWSKI

ONIZUKA, Ellison S. *See* Challenger Shuttle Crew.

ONSAGER, Lars (27 Nov. 1903–5 Oct. 1976), chemist and physicist, was born in Oslo, Norway, the son of Erling Onsager, a barrister of the Supreme Court of Norway, and Ingrid Kirkeby. He was raised in Oslo, where he studied literature, philosophy, fine arts, and the Norwegian epics. In the fall of 1920 he entered Norges Tekniske Høgskole (Norwegian Institute of Technology) in Trondheim. At age twenty, while still a student, he proposed a correction to the theory of strong electrolytes recently published by Peter Debye and Erich Hückel. This theory explained the properties of solutions of strong electrolytes (salts whose solutions are good conductors of electricity) in terms of the electrical interactions of ions in solution. Onsager improved this theory by taking into account a factor Debye and Hückel had neglected—Brownian motion. In 1925 he received his Ch.E. (chemical engineering degree) and remained as a resident scientist at Trondheim in 1925–1926.

In 1925 Onsager traveled to Denmark, Germany, and Zürich, Switzerland, where he spent several months at the Eidgenössische Technische Hochschule (Federal Institute of Technology) with Debye, the future Nobel chemistry laureate, and his assistant Hückel. Debye was so impressed with Onsager's correction to his theory that he made him his research assistant for almost two years (1926–1928). At Zürich, Onsager organized his results on the theory of electrolytes for publication, broadened his knowledge of physics, became acquainted with many leading physicists, and rowed in crew races on the Zürchersee (Lake Zürich).

In 1928 Onsager accepted a position as associate in chemistry at Johns Hopkins University in Baltimore, Maryland, where he was assigned to teach freshman chemistry. The students complained that he could not present his lectures in suitably elementary terms.

Throughout his career, the challenges in his lectures, even to experts, were formidable. He habitually omitted intermediate steps in mathematical derivations and assumed that his audience was as intelligent as he. After one semester he was dismissed, and he spent the spring of 1929 working independently on reciprocal relations—research that was to win him the Nobel Prize for chemistry almost four decades later.

In 1929 Charles A. Kraus appointed Onsager research instructor at Brown University in Providence, Rhode Island, where he remained for five years. He had no undergraduate teaching duties but taught a graduate course in statistical mechanics, which his students called "Advanced Norwegian I," or "sadistical mechanics," as his strong accent made the difficult subject even more of a challenge. He began his more than three-decades-long collaboration on electrolytes with Raymond M. Fuoss, then a graduate student. During his first year at Brown University, Onsager submitted a Norwegian abstract for a meeting of the Scandinavian Physical Society on simultaneous irreversible processes under nonequilibrium conditions (for example, the dissolving of a cold lump of sugar in hot tea, whereupon heat is conducted to a cold body from a hot body, while simultaneously sugar molecules diffuse throughout the tea). Onsager showed that the reciprocal relations between simultaneous irreversible reactions are mathematically equivalent to a more general principle of least dissipation, stating that the rate of increase in entropy (a measure of the disorder of a system) in coupled irreversible processes is at a minimum. His two-part article "Reciprocal Relations in Irreversible Processes" (*Physical Review* 37 [1931]: 405–26; 38 [1931]: 2265–79) was ignored at the time, and when he submitted it for his doctoral dissertation at Trondheim, it was judged unacceptable. Onsager was three decades ahead of his time; irreversible thermodynamics, the heart of his 1931 reciprocal relations (now sometimes called the fourth law of thermodynamics), became fashionable only during the 1960s and is universally recognized as of great value in chemistry, physics, biology, and technology. Onsager received the Nobel Prize for chemistry in 1968 "for the discovery of the reciprocal relations bearing his name, which are fundamental for the thermodynamics of irreversible processes." Because the two *Physical Review* articles were only twenty-two and fifteen pages long, this work is one of the shortest ever to be awarded a Nobel Prize.

While at Brown, Onsager sent Debye a manuscript for publication in *Physikalische Zeitschrift*, of which Debye was an editor, describing a correction to Debye's formula for the dielectric constant of polar molecules (those with permanent dipole moments). Debye did not approve, and the so-called Onsager formula was not published until John G. Kirkwood persuaded Onsager to rewrite the manuscript in English (*Journal of the American Chemical Society* 58 [1936]: 1486–93). Debye accepted Onsager's correction only many years later.

When Kraus suggested that Onsager carry out experimental work in addition to theoretical analysis, Onsager, with his five years' experience as a chemical engineering student, attempted the separation of isotopes (forms of elements with the same number of protons but different numbers of neutrons), but he required a platinum tube three stories high, and the work was never completed. During World War II the separation of uranium isotopes was a crucial step in the production of the atomic bomb.

In 1933, at the height of the Great Depression, Onsager's position at Brown was eliminated. He spent several weeks of his summer in Europe with Hans Falkenhagen of the University of Cologne, with whom he had been corresponding about electrochemistry. There he met Falkenhagen's sister-in-law, Margarethe Arledter, daughter of a renowned pioneer in the art of paper making, whom he in 1933 married in Cologne; the couple had four children.

In the fall of 1933 Onsager and his wife returned to the United States, where he accepted the prestigious Sterling fellowship (1933–1934), which did not require any teaching duties, at Yale University. Because the position was a postdoctoral fellowship and Onsager had no doctorate, Yale waived the course requirements and awarded him a Ph.D. (1935) on the basis of a paper, as much mathematical as chemical, "Solutions of the Mathieu Equation of Period 4π and Certain Related Functions." Although he used the results in the article "Initial Recombination of Ions" (*Physical Review* 54 [1938]: 554–57), he never published his dissertation. At Yale he was assistant professor of chemistry (1934–1940), associate professor (1940–1945), and J. Willard Gibbs Professor of theoretical chemistry (1945–1972), a position named after the father of statistical mechanics, the field in which Onsager was the greatest twentieth-century practitioner.

Because Onsager did not become a U.S. citizen until 1945, he did not take part in any military work during World War II. He spent these years analyzing a problem in physics that many thought insoluble—whether statistical mechanics could theoretically account for phase transitions of matter. Using obscure branches of mathematics such as quaternion and spinor algebra and the theory of elliptical functions, he demonstrated that the specific heat of a ferromagnetic system rises to infinity at the transition point. Many consider this solution of the so-called two-dimensional Ising model, first proposed by Swedish physicist Gustaf Ising, Onsager's most spectacular achievement and one of the decade's most important contributions to nuclear physics (*Physical Review* 65 [1944]: 117–49).

Onsager's visiting professorships included the University of California, San Diego (1961); Rockefeller University (1967–1968); the University of Göttingen (1968); and the University of Leiden Lorentz professorship (1970). He was awarded seven honorary doctorates and, in addition to the Nobel Prize, the American Academy of Arts and Sciences' Rumford Medal (1953), the Royal Netherlands Academy of Sciences' Lorentz Medal (1958), the American Chemical Society's G. N. Lewis Medal (1962), the J. G. Kirkwood Medal (1962), the J. W. Gibbs Medal (1962), the T. W. Richards Medal (1964), the P. W. Debye Medal (1965), Yeshiva University's Belfer Award in pure science (1966), and the President's National Medal of Science (1968).

In 1971 Onsager reached Yale's official retirement age of sixty-eight. Although he could retain his office and continued governmental research support and salary, Yale's rule that retired faculty could not be principal investigators on research grants led him in 1972 to accept an offer of distinguished university professor from the University of Miami's Center for Theoretical Studies, where he continued his work with several postdoctoral research fellows until his death. He also joined the university's Neurosciences Research Program.

Onsager's interests were so wide that his graduate students, who were never numerous and were usually physicists rather than chemists, were often in entirely different scientific areas. Thus he never had a "group" or founded a "school." He preferred working problems out himself to reading the solutions of others, and he urged his students to do the same. His erudition was phenomenal; he read widely and translated several Norse epics into English. He enjoyed gardening, swimming, and carpentry on his New Hampshire farm. He died at his home in Coral Gables, Florida.

According to John G. Kirkwood, "Onsager's scientific work is characterized not only by mathematical virtuosity but also by profound physical insight and intuition" (Kirkwood, p. 300). In his Nobel presentation speech, Stig Claesson of the Royal Swedish Academy of Sciences told Onsager, "You have made a number of contributions to physics and chemistry. For example, your equation for the conductivity of solutions of strong electrolytes, your famous solution of the Ising problem, making possible a theoretical treatment of phase changes, or your quantisation of vortices in liquid helium. However, your discovery of the reciprocal relations takes a special place. It represents one of the great advances in science during this century."

• Onsager's letters, research notes, and papers are preserved on microfilm in the archives of Yale University's Sterling Library. His Nobel acceptance address, "The Motion of Ions: Principles and Concepts," is in *Nobel Lectures: Chemistry 1963–1970* (1972). Biographical articles include John G. Kirkwood, "The Scientific Work of Lars Onsager," American Academy of Arts and Sciences, *Proceedings* 82 (Dec. 1953): 298–300; H. Christopher Longuet-Higgins and Michael E. Fisher, "Lars Onsager," *Biographical Memoirs of Fellows of the Royal Society* 24 (1978): 443–71, which contains a complete list of Onsager's publications and a bibliography of shorter biographies; and "Lars Onsager," in *Nobel Prize Winners*, ed. Tyler Wasson (1987), which contains a portrait. Obituaries include *Chemical and Engineering News* 54, no. 43 (18 Oct. 1976): 47, with a portrait, and the *New York Times*, 6 Oct. 1976.

GEORGE B. KAUFFMAN

OOSTERBAAN, Bennie (24 Feb. 1906–25 Oct. 1990), college athlete and coach, was born Benjamin Gaylord Oosterbaan, the son of Benjamin Oosterbaan, a Muskegon, Michigan, postmaster, and Harriet Dick. Oosterbaan starred in four sports at Muskegon High School. He was selected as a forward on the 1922–1923 Interscholastic All-America basketball team, all-state in basketball in his senior year, and all-state as a football end in his junior and senior years. He also played baseball and won a state track and field championship in the discus. During the time he played at Muskegon High, the team won four football and three basketball state championships.

The low-key but self-confident Oosterbaan was to become one of the University of Michigan's greatest all-around, multisport athletes. At 6'2" and nearly 200 pounds, he was a highly effective end, receiving passes from quarterback Benny Friedman. Oosterbaan was an All-America choice from 1925 to 1927; in 1927 he also was Michigan's team captain. The 1925 Michigan team won seven games, losing only by a point to Northwestern, and claimed the Western Conference championship. Oosterbaan earned nine letters in varsity football, basketball, and baseball and was an All-America basketball selection in 1927 (when Michigan was conference champion) and in 1928.

After graduating, Oosterbaan had to decide between professional football or baseball contracts or remaining at Michigan as an assistant football coach under Harry G. Kipke. He eschewed the professionals and from 1928 to 1938 served under Kipke. He married Delmas Cochlin in 1933; the couple adopted one child.

In 1938, when Fritz Crisler became head football coach, Oosterbaan moved to the head basketball coaching position for eight years while continuing as one of Crisler's assistants. In 1946 Crisler made him the offensive backfield coach. Under his direction, the team regained its national reputation in 1946 and 1947 for a powerful and high-scoring offense. The 1947 Wolverines went undefeated, including a 49–0 win over Southern California in the Rose Bowl, and outscored their opponents 394 to 53 to claim the top Associated Press ranking and a national championship. After Crisler resigned in March 1948, he recommended Oosterbaan for the head coaching job. Oosterbaan had his doubters, however, since many believed that he lacked sufficient experience as well as Crisler's intensity. He faced the prospect of maintaining a fourteen-game unbeaten streak and fulfilling the expectations created by Crisler's ten-year Michigan record of 71–16–3. Nonetheless, Oosterbaan quietly went about establishing himself as the new head coach and building a strong relationship with his players.

He initially enjoyed remarkable success. His 1948 team continued the unbeaten streak and won the national championship; he was honored as coach of the year by the American Football Coaches Association. Oosterbaan's 1949 team extended the win streak to twenty-five games by winning its first two games before losing to Army. While the Wolverines had excel-lent seasons, sharing the conference title in 1949, winning it in 1950, and finishing with 7–2 records in 1955 and 1956, they also experienced lackluster seasons, suffering losing records in 1951 and 1958. Oosterbaan's 1950 team, however, won the Rose Bowl over the University of California.

Oosterbaan's coaching career at Michigan from 1948 through 1958 spanned a new era of intercollegiate football that brought more competitive and questionable national recruiting, a rules change in 1953 that temporarily sidetracked platoon football, the rise of new national football powerhouses, the development of new offensive systems, the Rose Bowl pact that assured the Big Ten winner of a bowl appearance, and more competition and parity within the conference. Oosterbaan responded to these changes with an easygoing style that challenged his players' intelligence and inspired them to maintain a tradition of excellence and sportsmanship. He was beloved by his players, who remained loyal to him long after they left the campus. Part of his appeal was that he refrained from bullying and histrionics and had a sense of fairness. His teams won 63, lost 33, and tied 4. He announced his pending resignation as head coach before the injury-plagued season of 1958, in which his team compiled a 2–6–1 record. From 1959 to 1972 he served as supervisor of public and alumni relations in the athletic department. He died in Ann Arbor.

• Oosterbaan's papers covering 1921 to 1981 are located in the Michigan Historical Collections at the Bentley Historical Library, University of Michigan. Biographical information on Oosterbaan can be found in *Who's Who in American Sports* (1928); *Current Biography* (1949); and Walter W. Ruch's "Michigan's Unexpected Hero," *Saturday Evening Post*, 9 Oct. 1949. Information on his playing and head coaching careers can be found in Allison Danzig, *The History of American Football: Its Great Teams, Players, and Coaches* (1956); John D. McCallum, *Big Ten Football Since 1895* (1976); Mervin D. Hyman and Gordon S. White, Jr., *Big Ten Football: Its Life and Times, Great Coaches, Players and Games* (1977); Will Perry, *The Wolverines: A Story of Michigan Football* (1974); Kenneth L. Wilson and Jerry Brondfield, *The Big Ten* (1967); and Tom Perrin, *Football: A College History* (1987). Jack Saylor's obituary article in the *Detroit Free Press*, 27 Oct. 1990, is a moving and detailed tribute. See also John Barton's obituary in the *Muskegon Chronicle*, 26 Oct. 1990.

DOUGLAS A. NOVERR

OPDYKE, George (7 Dec. 1805–12 June 1880), merchant and politician, was born in Kingwood Township, Hunterdon County, New Jersey, the son of George Opdyke and Mary Stout, farmers. Educated at district schools, he became a teacher at sixteen, at eighteen clerked in a store, and at twenty borrowed $500 and went with a friend to Cleveland, Ohio, where they operated a store catering to Irish canal workers. Barely making back their investment, the pair proceeded to New Orleans, where, discovering that slave clothing could be sold at a 100 percent markup, they opened a new store and made their fortune.

In 1829 Opdyke returned triumphantly to New Jersey to marry Elizabeth Hall Stryker, whose family had twice before rejected him for lacking sufficient prospects. The couple had six children. In 1832 he transferred his business to New York, although he continued to sell in the South, and carried on a successful wholesale trade in clothing and dry goods as well as importing and manufacturing woolens.

With the completion of a commuter railroad to New Jersey in 1837, Opdyke moved to Newark, where he systematically devoted his leisure time to reading, study, and self-improvement. Described by the diarist George Templeton Strong as a "pushing, intriguing man, fond of power and position" (*Diary*, vol. 3 [1952], p. 168), Opdyke demonstrated his newly acquired learning by publishing *Treatise on Political Economy* (1851), in which he argued for paper money (in limited amounts), free trade, and the end of slavery.

A nominal Democrat, Opdyke was moved to political activism by the slavery issue. Convinced of the moral and economic unsoundness of the institution by his residence in Louisiana, Opdyke considered it essential to halt the institution's spread. Abandoning the Democratic party, he helped write the Free Soil party's platform in 1848 and was an unsuccessful candidate for Congress the same year.

In 1853 Opdyke, now a millionaire, moved back to New York to become more involved in politics and civic affairs. Affiliating with the new Republican party, he ran twice for the state assembly, being successful in his second attempt in 1858. In the legislature he took a leading role on banking and insurance measures. He was a member of numerous social and charitable organizations and from 1858 to his death was a member of the chamber of commerce, serving as its vice president for eight years.

Frustrated by the New York Republican party's domination by former Whigs William Seward and Thurlow Weed, who seemed indifferent to the metropolis, Opdyke adhered to a faction led by the *Tribune* editor Horace Greeley. As a delegate to the Republican National Convention in 1860, Opdyke backed Abraham Lincoln against Seward and contributed $20,000 to Lincoln's campaign.

In 1861 Opdyke took advantage of divisions among local Democrats to win election as mayor of New York with little more than 34 percent of the vote. He had been defeated for the same post two years earlier. He faced a solidly Democratic city council and county board of supervisors and, after the 1862 elections, a hostile state government as well. With few powers and little popular authority and facing all the problems associated with the ongoing Civil War, Opdyke used stinging veto messages to portray Democrats as corrupt and wasteful while proposing "reforms," such as consolidating New York with its suburbs and enlarging mayoral powers, that would aid Republicans.

In 1863 the divided city exploded in the draft riots. The mayor followed a moderate strategy, neither declaring martial law, which he felt would inflame the mobs, nor supporting the city council's proposal to pay the $300 commutation fee for any New York draftee who could not afford to buy his way out of service. (Opdyke's own son had paid the fee when drafted.) As a symbol of Republicanism and the war effort (he manufactured uniforms), Opdyke's home was threatened twice by mobs, and his factory was destroyed. Opdyke supported financial compensation for riot victims when order was finally restored, leading Weed, whom Opdyke had constantly attacked as corrupt, to accuse him of conflict of interest. Opdyke filed a libel suit against Weed when he left office in 1864. Although the trial resulted in a hung jury, most observers felt that revelations that Opdyke had engaged in fraudulent business transactions and war profiteering seriously damaged his reputation.

Opdyke, who had constantly badgered the Lincoln administration to assign more troops to New York and assume the city's war-related financial burdens, was part of the Radical Republican effort to call a second convention to replace Lincoln with Salmon P. Chase in 1864. Chair of an allegedly anti-Lincoln National War Committee of the Citizens of New York, he remained allied with party Radicals until their endorsement of African-American suffrage after the war.

In 1866 Opdyke published *Official Documents, Addresses, etc., of George Opdyke Mayor of the City of New York during the Years 1862 and 1863* to justify his actions as mayor. In the same year he was elected to a convention to revise the state constitution, where he promoted compulsory school attendance and spoke frequently on issues affecting cities and commerce. The constitution was rejected by the public, and he served on the constitutional commission in 1872–1873 that proposed more limited changes.

In 1867 Opdyke retired from selling dry goods and with his sons established a banking house that concentrated on railroad financing. Although heavily hit by the financial panic of 1873, the firm survived. Opdyke continued to write on political topics for newspapers until his death at his home in the city.

• Papers from Opdyke's term as mayor are in Mayoralty Correspondence Papers, Municipal Archives, city of New York. Charles Wilson Opdyke, *The Op Dyck Genealogy* (1889), written by a son, is an important source. On his mayorship see Ernest A. McKay, *The Civil War and New York City* (1990). On the draft riots see Iver Bernstein, *The New York City Draft Riots* (1990). An obituary is in the *New York Times*, 13 June 1880.

PHYLLIS F. FIELD

OPECHANCANOUGH (fl. 1607–1646), foremost Pamunkey (Virginia Algonquian) leader, was responsible for the uprisings of 1622 and 1644 against the English colonists in Virginia. There are no definitive details about his origins, parentage, or date or place of birth and death, but English contemporaries believed that he was the brother of Powhatan and lived to be 100 years old.

Opechancanough (O-pe-chan'-can-o; O-pa-can'-can-o) was the first "patriot chief" to recognize and resist English colonization as a serious threat to Indian lifeways in the Chesapeake Bay region. When Jamestown was founded in 1607, he was the most dominant *werowance* (regional chieftain) in the Powhatans' thirty-tribe alliance, subordinate only to Powhatan/Wahunsonacock in the governance of Tsenacommacah, a domain encompassing the current boundaries of Virginia's coastal plain and containing up to 20,000 people. Opechancanough's considerable influence derived from his position as the heir to Powhatan's matrilineal title of *mamanatowick* (paramount chief) as well as from his command of the Pamunkeys, the most populous and powerful of the Powhatans. From his capital complex in the center of Tsenacommacah (the clustered villages of Menapucunt, Uttamussak, and Kupkipcock near present-day West Point), Opechancanough could reputedly mobilize between 300 and 1,000 accomplished warriors.

As a powerful Indian leader and indefatigable foe of English colonization, Opechancanough has been the object of biased or fanciful portrayals for the past three centuries. White historians have been obsessed with the unknowable details of his early life as a key to understanding his inveterate hatred of the English, while refusing to acknowledge the colonists' culpability for provoking his violent defense of the Powhatan homeland. In 1705 Virginia colonist Robert Beverley claimed that Opechancanough—"a Man of large Stature, noble Presence, and extraordinary Parts, . . . perfectly skill'd in the Art of Governing"—was "a Prince of a Foreign Nation," who had come to Virginia from the Spanish domains in America. Historian Carl Bridenbaugh revived a similar legend in 1981, arguing that Opechancanough was the Don Luis who had been captured by the Spanish in 1561, been educated abroad as a Christian, came back to Virginia with a Jesuit expedition in 1570, and soon thereafter murdered the missionaries. Such unprovable speculations divert attention from the more significant and verifiable role that Opechancanough played from 1607 to 1646 and ignore the gradual evolution of his justifiable hostility toward the Jamestown colonists.

Between May 1607 and August 1609 Opechancanough dutifully obeyed Powhatan's cautious policy of befriending the small group of white strangers until their intentions as useful allies or dangerous enemies became clear. Opechancanough was first mentioned in English accounts when, on 26 May 1607, he feasted with the leading colonists near present-day Richmond while a Powhatan attack force was testing the defenses of James Fort far downriver. In December Opechancanough and a Pamunkey hunting party captured Captain John Smith (c. 1580–1631) and took him to Powhatan, setting up the Englishman's famous "rescue" (that is, ritual adoption ceremony) by Powhatan's daughter, Pocahontas.

For nearly two years, the powerful personalities of Powhatan and Smith dominated Anglo-Algonquian relations, while Opechancanough played a constricted role as the loyal accommodationist who sent personal gifts and much-needed food supplies to the Jamestown garrison and quietly endured the offensive behavior of the arrogant colonists. In January 1609, however, the English earned the undying enmity of Opechancanough when Captain Smith invaded his home village to steal vital winter maize reserves at gunpoint and physically abused him and his son in front of their fellow warriors.

The growth of Opechancanough's personal animosity was perhaps pivotal in transforming the Powhatan policy of initial hospitality into one of ultimate hostility, for the tense and tenuous peace ended soon after this incident. In August 1609 the First Anglo-Powhatan War—England's first war with American Indians—erupted with devastating, retaliatory attacks against distant encampments of colonists. Three months later, Opechancanough's Pamunkeys inflicted the worst defeat and highest casualties that the English suffered on a single day in this war when they killed two-thirds of a fifty-man force and nearly captured their ship. That bloody debacle so shocked and intimidated the colonists that they chose to endure the subsequent Powhatan siege of James Fort rather than confront the Indians in combat. Refusing to leave the disease-ridden confines of their palisade until March 1610, the English suffered a mortality rate of 65 percent during the infamous winter "Starving Time."

After claiming 600 or more lives, the First Anglo-Indian War ended in a draw between exhausted combatants and a truce symbolized by the diplomatic marriage of John Rolfe and Pocahontas. The power of the aged Powhatan, from whom the English had wrested much James River territory, was now eclipsed by the leadership of the more vigorous Opechancanough, whose Pamunkeys had neither suffered defeat nor loss of lands in the war. As early as the spring of 1613, five years before the death of Powhatan, Jamestown officials already regarded Opechancanough as the Indians' "chief Captaine," who was in "commaund of all the people."

From at least 1618 to 1646 Opechancanough enjoyed power and prestige as the "great Kinge" of the Powhatans, although another brother, Opitchapam/Itoyatin, temporarily claimed the title of mamanatowick and contested for control. Opechancanough's ability to inspire and reinvigorate the disillusioned remnants of Powhatan's old tribal alliance, with the assistance of the mystical warrior-prophet "Jack of the Feather," resulted in a cultural and military revitalization of the Virginia Algonquians by 1620. The success of Opechancanough's unifying policies, in response to the aggressions of the mushrooming and land-hungry English population, became shockingly evident on 22 March 1622. In the famous Powhatan Uprising or "Great Massacre," warriors from different and distant Algonquian tribes simultaneously attacked English settlements all along the James River; when this single day of cathartic slaughter was over, some 330 colonists—representing one-fourth of Virginia's white population—lay dead.

Over the course of the ensuing Second Anglo-Powhatan War (1622–1632) and a decade thereafter, Opechancanough became the most hated and hunted public enemy in Virginia. The "bloody Monster" proved so elusive that rumors of his death were frequently believed. The Powhatans adopted the use of muskets and boldly confronted the English in open-field combat, but their intertribal alliance was compromised by old Indian enemies that supported the colonists. A truce was called in 1632, but with their grievances unresolved, the Powhatans soon realized that they suffered as much deprivation and dispossession during periods of peace as they did in wartime. Alarmed by the rapid decline of his people, Opechancanough orchestrated a third major uprising in April 1644, allegedly because he believed the colonists were divided and distracted by the English civil war. His warriors killed an estimated 500 colonists but failed to dislodge the now-dominant white population of 8,000.

Ending a manhunt that had lasted a quarter-century, Governor Sir William Berkeley (1606–1677) finally captured the "Great generall of the Salvages" in late 1645 or early 1646, using veteran cavalry and frontier tactics developed over decades of Anglo-Powhatan forest warfare. According to Beverley's 1705 account, Opechancanough was an aged invalid when Berkeley transported him to Jamestown on a litter, "his Flesh . . . all macerated, his Sinews slacken'd, and his Eyelids . . . so heavy that he could not see." Within two weeks of his capture, Opechancanough was assassinated by one of the governor's soldiers, who so resented "the Calammities the Colony had suffer'd by this Prince's Means, [that he] basely shot him thro' the Back."

Long known as "a great Captaine" and "cunning Prince" who "did always fight," Opechancanough "continued brave to the last Moment of his Life." Shortly before his death, he even expressed his "high Indignation" to Governor Berkeley at being "meanly . . . exposed . . . as a Show" to his hated enemies in the very colonial capital that he had long tried to destroy. After his passing, all remaining Powhatans endured the confinement and degradation of reservation life as subordinate, tribute-paying survivors of a once-dominant people.

As the last traditional Powhatan werowance from the pre-European era of a free Indian Virginia, Opechancanough employed both accommodation and aggression to preserve the lives and lifeways of his people against insurmountable odds. His farsighted fear of, and consistent opposition to, British imperialism proved prophetic, for no Indian group along the Atlantic Coast—neither the friends nor the foes of the colonists—survived the seventeenth century with their sovereignty or territory intact. The death of Opechancanough, the archetype of later and better-known patriot chiefs, symbolized the end of independence for indigenous peoples in the Chesapeake, whose creative freedom and cultural diversity had long enriched America.

• The most complete and accessible primary English accounts of Opechancanough's early career are Philip L. Barbour, ed., *The Complete Works of Captain John Smith* (3 vols., 1986); Barbour, ed., *The Jamestown Voyages under the First Charter, 1606–1609* (2 vols., 1969); Ralph Hamor, *A True Discourse of the Present Estate of Virginia* (1615), ed. A. L. Rowse (repr. 1957); and Susan Myra Kingsbury, ed., *Records of the Virginia Company* (4 vols., 1906–1935). His activities in the 1640s are briefly mentioned in *A Description of the Province of New Albion* (1648) and *A Perfect Description of Virginia* (1649), both collected in Peter Force, comp., *Tracts and Other Papers Relating Principally to the Origin, Settlement, and Progress of the Colonies in North America*, vol. 2 (1836; repr. 1963). Additional commentary, based on later hearsay, is found in Robert Beverley's *History and Present State of Virginia* (1705), ed. Louis B. Wright (1947). Recent biographical accounts include J. Frederick Fausz, "Opechancanough: Indian Resistance Leader," in *Struggle and Survival in Colonial America*, ed. David G. Sweet and Gary B. Nash (1981); and Carl Bridenbaugh's two works, *Jamestown, 1544–1699* (1980), chap. 2, and *Early Americans* (1981), chap. 1.

The only known "portrait" of Opechancanough is a European engraving of a generic Indian in Captain John Smith's *Generall Historie of Virginia, New-England, and the Summer Isles* (1624), between pp. 20 and 21.

J. FREDERICK FAUSZ

OPIE, Eugene Lindsay (5 July 1873–12 Mar. 1971), pathologist, was born in Staunton, Virginia, the son of Thomas Opie, a surgeon, and Sallie Harman. Opie received his bachelor's degree from the Johns Hopkins University in 1893. Before entering the new Johns Hopkins Medical School in 1894, he spent one year at the Baltimore College of Physicians, of which his father was dean. Opie's application to enter the second year of the first class of the Johns Hopkins Medical School was at first denied, but the faculty finally accepted him, and he graduated in 1897. While a medical student, Opie was drawn to laboratory medicine; contact with physician William Henry Welch inspired him to become a pathologist. While examining a microscopic section of pancreatic tissue, Opie asked Welch what the strange-looking pink cells in the section were. Welch answered that these cells had been described recently, but no one knew what their function was. Opie's finding of the absence of these cells, the islands of Langerhans, in diabetic patients, was the first evidence indicating when the hormone-controlling sugar metabolism was formed. Opie continued his studies on the pathologic physiology of the pancreas and demonstrated that hemorrhagic pancreatitis was related to reflux of bile into the pancreatic ducts.

During the Spanish-American War in 1898 Opie, along with William George MacCallum, volunteered to accompany injured soldiers from military hospitals in the South to those in the North. While performing this duty, these two young Hopkins interns learned much that they would later use in studies of yellow fever and malaria. William Sidney Thayer drew Opie's and MacCallum's attention to malaria, and they worked out the life cycle of the malaria parasite in Baltimore bird populations. Opie stayed at Hopkins for seven years after graduation as an assistant in bacteriology to William Henry Welch.

In 1902 Opie married Gertrude Lovat Simpson; they had four children. She died in 1909, and in 1916 Opie married her sister, Margaret Elizabeth Simpson.

Opie joined the Rockefeller Institute in 1904 and remained there until 1910. There he studied the enzymes involved with tubercle formation and observed the beneficial effect of injected leucocytes on tuberculous pleurisy in experimental animals. He also aided in organizing a laboratory at the Presbyterian Hospital to allow the staff to investigate the diseases they were treating.

In 1910 Opie accepted a position at Washington University Medical School in Saint Louis, acting as its dean from 1912 to 1915. He began studies on the pathological physiology of tuberculosis. He also studied the factors that result in liver necrosis and found that diet warded off necrosis produced by alcohol, phosphorus, and chloroform. He also studied the local anaphylactic phenomenon in tuberculosis. His World War I service in France with the Barnes Hospital, Washington University Medical Unit, brought important studies on pneumonia, influenza, trench foot, and tuberculosis, including an emphasis that the crowding of beds in the military was an important factor in the spread of disease.

In 1923 Opie was appointed director of the Henry Phipps Institute in Philadelphia as well as the chairman of the department of pathology at the University of Pennsylvania. Here he organized a study of the mode of transfer of tuberculosis and demonstrated the importance of X-rays in early diagnosis of that disease. Opie found that heredity, nutrition, and, particularly, transmission by intimate contact with infected family members were important factors in the epidemiology of tuberculosis. Opie also emphasized that the rapid spread of tuberculosis through lymph nodes in children resulted from their lack of immunity. A similar spread in adults was not seen because the adults had immunity from previous exposure to the tuberculosis bacillus. Noticing the different susceptibilities among races, he extended his epidemiological studies to Jamaica and found that Jamaicans were more susceptible to tuberculosis than blacks in the United States.

Opie remained in Philadelphia until 1932, when he was chosen to fill the chair of pathology at the Cornell Medical School and to be chief pathologist of New York Hospital. On his retirement at the age of sixty-five, he rejoined the faculty of the Rockefeller Institute and continued working there until 1970. During the 37-year period of his retirement he wrote more than forty papers, dealing mainly with carcinogenesis, water balance, and osmotic pressure in human tissues. He died in Bryn Mawr, Pennsylvania.

• Opie wrote about his own career in "The Peripatetic Education of a Pathologist," *Medical Clinics of North America* (1957): 935–52. Biographical sketches by others include Peyton Rouse, "An Inquiry into Certain Aspects of Eugene L. Opie," *Archives of Pathology* 34 (1942): 1–6; D. Murray Angevine, "Comments on the Life of Eugene Lindsay Opie," *Laboratory Investigation* 12 (1963): 2–7; Edmond R. Long, "Eugene Lindsay Opie, July 5, 1873–March 12, 1971," National Academy of Sciences, *Biographical Memoirs* 47 (1975): 293–320; and Angevine, "Eugene Lindsay Opie, M.D.: July 5, 1873–March 12, 1971," *Archives of Pathology* 92 (1971): 145–46. See also John G. Kidd, "Citation and Presentation of the Academy Medal to Eugene L. Opie," *Bulletin of the New York Academy of Medicine* 36 (1960): 228–34. Obituaries are in the *New York Times*, 13 Mar. 1971, and the *Baltimore Sun*, 14 Mar. 1971.

DAVID Y. COOPER

OPOTHLE YOHOLO (1780s?–Mar. 1863), Creek leader, was born at Tuckabatchee, Creek Nation (near present-day Montgomery, Ala.), the son of Davy Cornell and a Tuckabatchee woman, perhaps of the Potato clan. Descended from Joseph Cornells, who had entered the Creek Nation as a Carolina trader, the family was large, well connected, and influential when Opothle Yoholo was born. Opothle Yoholo's name, more correctly spelled Hoboihithli Yoholo, is best understood as a title. Creek men commonly received new names at various stages in their lives to commemorate achievements, denote changes in rank, and/or describe new responsibilities. Opothle Yoholo's name translates as Good Child Singer or Crier. The meaning of Good Child is not clear, but it was prestigious and honorific; Yoholo refers to the song or cry uttered by the officials who managed the important Black Drink Ceremony. Because the names of adult men changed, it is very hard to follow them through the historical record. Opothle Yoholo's name first appears in the documents in the mid-1820s, but there is no way to be sure that he was not mentioned earlier under a different name.

Opothle Yoholo had achieved significant stature in the Creek Nation by the mid-1820s. As speaker for Big Warrior (Tustunnuggee Thlucco), chief of Tuckabatchee and of the Upper Creeks, Opothle Yoholo was at the center of Creek political affairs. His duties included participating in governing council deliberations, announcing council decisions to the public, and representing Big Warrior in talks with other native groups and the United States. In negotiations with federal commissioners during the winter of 1824–1825, Opothle Yoholo emerged as a prominent voice of opposition to the sale of the Creek lands claimed by Georgia. In the absence of Big Warrior, Opothle Yoholo presented the council's rejection and coordinated its arguments with the commissioners. During the critical months following those talks, the commissioners bribed several headmen to sign a treaty, the council ordered the execution of the leading chiefs involved in the fraud, and the Creeks negotiated a new treaty in Washington. All of this occurred in the midst of a Creek leadership vacuum marked by the death of Big Warrior and the extreme age and ill health of his opposite number, Little Prince (Tustunnuggee Hopoie), chief of the Lower Creeks. Thus Opothle Yoholo was catapulted into a far more active leadership role than was normal for one in his office.

During the next several years, Opothle Yoholo led the effort of the Creeks to resist removal to the West. Resistance took several forms. To forge a united opposition, Opothle Yoholo was instrumental in an attempt to restructure council government in order to centralize its political authority and thus block voluntary emigration. Opothle Yoholo was also a central figure in the repeated attempts of the council to negotiate alternatives to removal. When all efforts failed, Opothle Yoholo masterminded a scheme to allot the lands of the Creek Nation to its citizens, hoping thereby to gain the right of the Creeks to remain in their eastern homes. This plan also failed, and in 1836 Opothle Yoholo led some 15,000 Creeks on the trek to Indian Territory.

Since 1828, despite the council's efforts to prevent them, several thousand Creeks had moved on their own to Indian Territory and had settled in the Arkansas River valley. Led by the relatives and associates of William McIntosh, one of the chiefs executed in 1825 for signing the fraudulent Treaty of Indian Springs, many continued to harbor ill will toward those, such as Opothle Yoholo, who had participated in the council decision to kill McIntosh. To prevent trouble, Opothle Yoholo and about 8,000 Creeks avoided the already established settlements and occupied the Canadian River valley. Separated by some fifty to eighty miles of prairie, the two groups began the process of rebuilding the nation.

Opothle Yoholo remained the recognized leader of the Canadian River Creeks until his death. He served only one four-year term as principal chief, however, preferring instead a less prominent position. At times of crisis, however, he emerged to assume a leadership role. In the mid-1850s, for example, the Creeks came under heavy government pressure to abandon their principle of common land ownership in exchange for the allotment of the nation into privately held individual tracts. Opothle Yoholo assumed a central role in opposition, citing both tradition and the failed allotment experiment in the East.

Opothle Yoholo tended to be culturally conservative, and both contemporaries and scholars have understood him to have been a powerful force against Creek adoption of Anglo-American cultural norms. But Opothle Yoholo was flexible and adaptive. He early recognized the value of western education and in 1826 enrolled his eight-year-old son in the famous Kentucky boardingschool for Indians, the Choctaw Academy. (Although Opothle Yoholo had a wife and other children, nothing is known about them.) He also participated actively in the market economy. He owned many slaves, managed a large plantation and ranching operation, and invested in several stores and trading posts. One, close to his plantation on the Canadian River near North Fork Town, was at the crossing of the Texas Road (the main artery between Kansas and Texas) and the road that ran west from Fort Smith, Arkansas, to California. The latter was a main thoroughfare during the gold rush, and Opothle Yoholo, along with other Creek entrepreneurs, profited handsomely in supplying the gold seekers. On the eve of the Civil War, Opothle Yoholo was widely reputed to be the richest Creek in Indian Territory.

During the early summer of 1861, Albert Pike, an agent of the Confederate government, held talks at North Fork Town with representatives of many Indian Territory tribes. Recognizing the strategic importance of Indian Territory, the Confederacy was anxious to conclude treaties of alliance with the tribes. Creek delegates agreed to such an alliance in July. Though not present at the negotiations, Opothle Yoholo let it be known that he opposed the Confederate alliance, arguing that the Confederacy represented the same southerners who had evicted the Indians from their homes twenty-five years before. Furthermore, Opothle Yoholo believed that the treaties binding the Creek Nation to the United States should be respected. Hoping to avoid involvement on either side, Opothle Yoholo recommended that the Creek Nation stand neutral. Like-minded Creeks began to coalesce around Opothle Yoholo and a close associate, Oktaharsars Harjo (Sands); they established a camp that grew to several thousand people, mostly Creeks but also including Seminoles and several hundred slaves. In November 1861, fearing an attack by Confederate Creeks, Opothle Yoholo led the group of men, women, children, huge herds of horses and cattle, plus wagons and carriages of every description laden with food and household goods, north. On the way the Confederates attacked three times. Opothle Yoholo's party defeated them in the first two engagements, but in the third, the 26 December 1861 Battle of Chustenahlah, the Confederates smashed the refugees, scattering their herds and driving the survivors afoot into a blizzard. Forced to abandon all their possessions, Opothle Yoholo's people made their way to the Verdigris River in southeastern Kansas, where Union agents housed them in a makeshift tent encampment. Somehow Opothle Yoholo, in his eighties, survived the ordeal. Once a neutralist, by this time he and his followers were dedicated Unionists, and several hundred men joined the Union army. Opothle Yoholo and the noncombatants were moved in the spring to scattered locations, including a large but badly furnished and poorly supplied camp near Leroy, Kansas. Living in a tent made of rotten cloth open at both ends and sleeping on the frozen ground, the old speaker succumbed to the winter of 1862–1863.

• A few primary sources can be found in the Indian Office correspondence files at the National Archives, Record Group 75. John B. Meserve, "Chief Opothleyahola," *Chronicles of Oklahoma* 9 (Dec. 1931): 440–53, is the only published biographical sketch. Opothle Yoholo's early career can be followed in Michael D. Green, *The Politics of Indian Removal: Creek Government and Society in Crisis* (1982), and in Angie Debo, *Road to Disappearance* (1941). For his life in Indian Territory, in addition to Debo, see Grant Foreman, *The Five Civilized Tribes* (1934). For the Civil War period, see Annie Able, *The Slaveholding Indians*, vols. 1 and 2 (1915, 1919), and articles by Edwin C. Bearss, "The Civil War Comes to Indian Territory, 1861: The Flight of Opothleyahola," *Journal of the West* 11 (Jan. 1972): 9–42; Kenny A. Franks, "Operations against Opothleyahola, 1861," *Military History of Texas and the Southwest* 10 (1972): 187–96; and Carter Blue

Clark, "Opothleyahola and the Creeks during the Civil War," in *Indian Leaders: Oklahoma's First Statesmen*, ed. H. Glenn Jordan and Thomas M. Holm (1979).

MICHAEL D. GREEN

OPPEN, George August (24 Apr. 1908–7 July 1984), poet, was born in New Rochelle, New York, the son of George August Oppenheimer, a diamond merchant, and Elsie Rothfeld. The Oppenheimers were wealthy, assimilated Jews who in 1927 shortened the family name to Oppen. When Oppen was four, his mother committed suicide. His father remarried in 1917, and the family moved to San Francisco the following year.

After a car accident in which one of his passengers was killed, Oppen was expelled from military academy for drinking in 1925. The next year he entered Oregon State University at Corvallis, where he met Mary Colby. Following his suspension and Colby's expulsion from school for violating the curfew, they hitchhiked to New York, marrying in Dallas, in 1927. The couple rejected the comfortable world of Oppen's parents and chose a life of independence.

In 1928 he met Louis Zukofsky and Charles Reznikoff. Zukofsky's "Objectivist" issue of *Poetry* (Feb. 1931) established the three of them along with William Carlos Williams and Carl Rakosi as Objectivists, but like Zukofsky, Oppen denied they formed a movement, insisting that objectivism referred to the necessity of form in a poem. However, all of them shared the conviction that the poet must be faithful to the world of facts.

With the small income he received on turning twenty-one, the Oppens went to France (1929) and established To Publishers (1931), which issued Zukofsky's *An 'Objectivists' Anthology*, Williams's *A Novelette and Other Prose*, and, in one volume, Ezra Pound's *How to Read* and *The Spirit of Romance* (1932). Financial difficulties led to the press's collapse before it could fulfill one of its primary goals, the publication of Pound's collected prose.

Before returning to the United States in 1932, Oppen went to Rapallo where he met Pound, who included Oppen in his *Active Anthology* (1933). Back in Brooklyn, Oppen joined Zukofsky, Reznikoff, and Williams in setting up the Objectivist Press, which published Williams's *Collected Poems 1921–31* (preface by Wallace Stevens, 1934), three books by Reznikoff, and Oppen's *Discrete Series* (preface by Pound, 1934). According to Oppen, the title of his volume refers to a mathematical series of terms, "each of which is empirically derived, each one of which is empirically true." Each poem gives a separate image from the perspective of the poet. This adherence to the concrete world was, for Oppen, a measure of sincerity and a consistent feature of his poetry. The book received few reviews, but Pound praised him as "a serious craftsman," and in a 1934 review for *Poetry*, Williams wrote, "by a sharp restriction to essentials, the seriousness of a new order is brought to realization."

The Objectivist Press issued its last book in 1936, but in response to the rise of fascism and the depression, Oppen had given up poetry and joined the Communist party a year earlier. He and his wife worked with the unemployed in New York City, agitating for basic social services, and Oppen helped organize industrial workers and direct-action strikes in Utica, New York. Although he adhered to Marxist historical materialism, Oppen later characterized his politics in the 1930s as liberal and antifascist.

With the end of the depression, he became less involved with politics. In 1940 the Oppens had a daughter, and two years later he was inducted into the army after deliberately forfeiting his work exemption as a machinist. He saw action in Europe from October 1944 to 22 April 1945, when artillery hit his foxhole, seriously wounding him and killing two others. He refers to this event in the third of "Some San Francisco Poems," "Of Hours," "The Myth of the Blaze," and "Semite." He was awarded the Purple Heart.

After the war, he moved to Redondo Beach, California, where he worked as a contractor and a custom carpenter. Although the Oppens were no longer politically active, they remained party members, and the FBI interviewed them in May and June 1949. Fearing possible imprisonment, the Oppens a year later moved to Mexico City, where they remained until 1958, making a few short visits to the United States before returning permanently in 1960.

During his years of political activity and exile, Oppen wrote no poetry. He said he "didn't believe in political poetry or poetry as being politically efficacious." In May 1958 he wrote his first new poem since 1934, "Blood from a Stone." His second book, *The Materials*, appeared in 1962 to largely excellent reviews and was followed by the equally successful *This in Which* (1965). These works express his belief that "true seeing is an act of love." His reemergence made him an important link for younger poets to the tradition of Pound and Williams. Oppen entered literary life by giving frequent public readings and enjoying a wide circle of literary friends.

On 31 May 1966 the FBI did its final report on the Oppens, which concerned their travel plans; the couple went to France and Belgium that summer, and in 1967 they moved to San Francisco. Public recognition came with the 1969 Pulitzer Prize for *Of Being Numerous* (1968). The title poem, a sequence of forty sections, explores the idea of humanity in a world of multiplicity. The poems express Oppen's belief in the absolutely singular.

More honors followed, including a symposium on the Objectivists at the University of Wisconsin in 1968. Oppen was named one of "Four Major American Poets" at the San Francisco Museum of Modern Art in 1973 and was poet in residence at Mishkenot Sh'ananim, Jerusalem, in 1975. On his return from Israel, Oppen's health began to decline. His *The Collected Poems of George Oppen* (1975) was nominated for the 1976 National Book Award, and in 1977 he completed his last collection, *Primitive* (1978). Later honors included lifetime recognition awards from the American Academy and Institute of Arts and Letters and from the National Endowment for the Arts. In December 1982 he received the PEN/West Rediscovery Award. That same year he was diagnosed as having Alzheimer's disease. He died two years later in Sunnyvale, California. His work remains highly regarded for its clarity, craftsmanship, and philosophical respect for the singularity of things in a world of multiplicity. Many younger poets committed to the modernist tradition acknowledge his influence.

• Oppen's papers are located at the Archive for New Poetry, University of California, San Diego. Books not mentioned above include *Alpine: Poems* (1969) and *Seascape: Needle's Eye* (1972). An indispensable document for the history of the Objectivists and Oppen's poetic theory is *The Selected Letters of George Oppen* (1990), which contains a valuable introduction and chronology by its editor, Rachel Blau DuPlessis. Oppen wrote only one essay, "The Mind's Own Place," *Kulchur* 3 (1963). Selections from his notebooks have appeared in *Ironwood* 26 (1985): 5–31; *Conjunctions* 10 (1987): 186–208; *Iowa Review* 18, no. 3 (1988): 1–17; and in three issues of *Sulfur*—25 (1989): 10–43; 26 (1990): 135–64; and 27 (1990): 202–20.

No biography has been written, but Mary Oppen's *Meaning a Life: An Autobiography* (1978) is important for understanding their relationship and their political activities. An account of To Publishers and the Objectivist Press can be found in *Pound/Zukofsky: Selected Letters of Ezra Pound and Louis Zukofsky*, ed. Barry Ahearn (1987). Charles Tomlinson, in *Some Americans: A Personal Record* (1981), offers a view of the enmities that developed between Oppen and Zukofsky. An invaluable interview conducted by L. S. Dembo first appeared in *Contemporary Literature* 10 (1969) and is reprinted in *The Contemporary Writer* (1972).

Bibliographies of secondary criticism can be found in a special issue of *Paideuma* 10, no. 1 (1981) devoted entirely to Oppen and in *George Oppen: Man and Poet* (1981), which contains interviews with the Oppens as well as essays and memoirs. Oppen is featured in *Ironwood* 5 (1975) and 26 (1985). Critical discussions of his work are available in Hugh Kenner, *A Homemade World: The American Modernist Writers* (1975); Michael Heller, *Conviction's Net of Branches: Essays on the Objectivist Poets and Poetry* (1985); John Freeman, ed., *Not Comforts/But Visions: Essays on the Poetry of George Oppen* (1985); L. S. Dembo, *The Monological Jew: A Literary Study* (1988); and Joseph M. Conte, *Unending Design: The Forms of Postmodern Poetry* (1991). An obituary is in the *New York Times*, 9 July 1984.

JOSEPH G. KRONICK

OPPENHEIM, James (24 May 1882–4 Aug. 1932), author and editor, was born in St. Paul, Minnesota, the son of Joseph Oppenheim and Matilda Schloss. His father, a businessman, served in the Minnesota legislature before moving the family in 1884 to New York City, where he died in 1888. Oppenheim attended public schools in the city and came under the influence of Felix Adler, who encouraged the development of a system of rigorous moral scrutiny. This early influence later shaped thematic concerns and the treatment of character in his fiction. He enrolled at Columbia University as a special student in 1901, registering for courses in psychology and sociology, while also performing social work at the Hudson Guild Settlement. In 1905 he married Lucy Seckel of New York City;

they had two sons. From 1905 to 1907 he taught at the Hebrew Technical School for Girls, where he also served as superintendent, a position he left when his increasing radicalism conflicted with the outlook of the school's board.

Shortly after leaving his teaching post, Oppenheim began to contribute poems and short stories to popular magazines. His poems appeared in *American Magazine*, *Current Literature*, *Outlook*, and *Century*; they reflected his idealism and political concerns. His early poems were collected in *Monday Morning and Other Poems* (1909). Later collections, such as *Songs for a New Age* (1914), also indicate his engagement with emerging poetic philosophies of his day, including imagism, and the influence of Whitman. He continued to write poetry throughout his career.

Oppenheim's short stories appeared in *Harper's*, *The Delineator*, *American Magazine*, *Colliers*, and the *Ladies' Home Journal*. A collection of stories, *Dr. Rast*, published in 1909, focused on the experiences of an idealistic doctor working on the East Side of New York who attempts to minister to the physical and emotional needs of his immigrant patients. Many of the stories also reveal the economic tensions that afflicted laborers and the conflicts that developed between immigrant parents and their more assimilated children. Oppenheim's fiction continued in this vein with *Pay Envelopes* (1911), a collection of stories about Austro-Hungarian steelworkers in Pennsylvania, as well as episodes of New York City life. In *The Nine-Tenths* (1911), he created a middle-class American who undergoes political awakening through his encounters with immigrant laborers; this novel includes episodes of the Triangle Shirtwaist Company fire and depicts the political activity of labor organization. While all of these works contain romanticized views of laborers and optimistic religious sentiment, they form part of the emerging body of labor fiction that laid the groundwork for the significant labor and protest novels of the 1930s. *Idle Wives* (1914), another novel that presented views of upper-middle-class and working-class experiences, caused Oppenheim personal turmoil; his wife sued him for divorce following its publication, charging that he had libeled her by using her as a model for one of his characters. In addition to poetry and fiction, Oppenheim wrote what he termed "poetic dramas," and his *Night: A Poetic Drama in One Act* was produced by the Provincetown Players in 1917 and published in *Flying Stag: Plays for the Little Theater* in 1918.

Oppenheim felt that the high point of his literary career occurred in 1916 with the establishment of the *Seven Arts*, a literary magazine that he cofounded with Waldo Frank and Paul Rosenfeld. Oppenheim served as its editor and published the work of many emerging as well as established writers, including Amy Lowell, Sherwood Anderson, Stephen Vincent Benét, Theodore Dreiser, and John Dos Passos. The advisory board for the journal included Kahlil Gibran, Louis Untermeyer, Van Wyck Brooks, and Robert Frost, who also contributed selections. The magazine, reflecting Oppenheim's own views, became increasingly assertive in its support of pacificism, strenuously objecting to the entry of the United States into World War I. This position cost the *Seven Arts* the support of its financial backers, and when it ceased publication in 1917 Oppenheim felt defeated.

Seeking personal renewal and a new direction for his career, Oppenheim resumed his study of human psychology, profoundly influenced by the work of Carl Jung. Earlier he had published advice pieces in magazines, but his renewed interest led to more serious study, as well as a desire to popularize Jung's theories. For a time he worked as a practicing analyst and published works such as *The Psychology of Jung* (1925), *A Psychoanalysis of the Jews* (1926), and *American Types: A Preface to Analytic Psychology* (1931). Neither this career nor his literary activity brought Oppenheim financial security, and in the last years of his life he struggled against poverty. During this time he married Linda Gray of Boston, Massachusetts, who cared for him during his final illness. Oppenheim died of tuberculosis in New York City. Though he wrote in a number of genres, Oppenheim did not achieve mastery in any of them; instead, his work is of interest for its historical and sociological content, rather than its artistic merit.

• Oppenheim's papers are held in the New York Public Library. Other works by Oppenheim include *The Pioneers: A Poetic Drama in Two Acts* (1910), *Wild Oats* (1910), *The Olympian: A Story of the City* (1912), *The Rise of Kirby Trask* (1913), *The Beloved* (1915), *War and Laughter* (1916), *The Book of Self* (1917), *The Solitary* (1919), *The Mystic Warrior* (1921), *The Golden Bird* (1923), *Your Hidden Powers* (1923), *The Sea* (1924), *Lyrics to the Olympian Deities* (1925), published under the pseudonym James Jay; and *Behind Your Front* (1928). An assessment of his work is Charles Hackenberry, "James Oppenheim" in *Twentieth-Century American-Jewish Fiction Writers*, vol. 28 of the *Dictionary of Literary Biography*. A chapter about him appears in Paul Rosenfeld, *Men Seen* (1925). An obituary is in the *New York Times*, 5 Aug. 1932.

MELISSA MCFARLAND PENNELL

OPPENHEIMER, Frank Friedman (14 Aug. 1912–3 Feb. 1985), physicist, was born in New York City, the son of Julius Oppenheimer, a wealthy clothing and textile merchant, and Ella Friedman, an artist. He was the younger brother of J. Robert Oppenheimer, who directed the Los Alamos Scientific (now National) Laboratory in developing the atomic bomb. Although the Oppenheimer brothers shared many common interests and experiences, such as sailing and traveling throughout Europe and the American Southwest, Frank developed independent skills as a musician and horseman. After graduating from the Fieldston School in New York City in 1930, he entered Johns Hopkins University and graduated with a bachelor of science degree in physics in 1933. An inheritance enabled him to study physics at the Cavendish Laboratory at Cambridge University in England from 1933 to 1935, and at the Istitudo di Arceti in Florence, Italy, in 1935.

Oppenheimer entered the California Institute of Technology in the fall of 1935 and graduated with a doctorate in physics in 1939. He married Jacquenette Nundell in 1936.

After graduation from Caltech, Oppenheimer joined the physics faculty at Stanford University as an assistant professor. He remained in that position until 1940, when he became a research assistant in the Radiation Laboratory at the University of California at Berkeley. Operated by Ernest O. Lawrence since the early 1930s, the Radiation Laboratory had made significant contributions to the development of nuclear physics through the use of the cyclotron, a device invented by Lawrence for the electromagnetic separation of radioactive elements. As part of the Manhattan Project to develop nuclear weapons during World War II, the Radiation Laboratory developed the calutron for the electromagnetic separation and enrichment of uranium. Oppenheimer worked on the development of this technology at the Radiation Laboratory and on its implementation at the Y-12 Plant in Oak Ridge, Tennessee. In 1943 he joined his brother and other scientists at the secluded weapons laboratory at Los Alamos, New Mexico, where he worked as an assistant to Kenneth T. Bainbridge on the preparation of Trinity, the nuclear weapon test site near Alamogordo, New Mexico. Oppenheimer set up the monitoring instrumentation at the site and participated in the first experimental explosion of a nuclear device on 17 July 1945, operating a monitoring and evacuation site south of the Trinity test site.

After the war's end, Oppenheimer returned to the University of California at Berkeley as a member of the physics department. He moved to the physics faculty at the University of Minnesota in 1947 and embarked on landmark studies of cosmic radiation. At that time scientists knew little about the origin and mechanics of cosmic radiation, which distributed energy levels thousands of times greater than known cyclotron energies. Enrico Fermi had postulated that atoms could reach such energies by equipartition with stars. To confirm Fermi's hypothesis the rays had to be captured and studied at high altitude. Oppenheimer, with the support of the U.S. Navy, studied high-altitude cosmic radiation with instruments carried aloft by balloons. In 1948 he and another physicist shared the discovery that primary rays represented a sampling of the energy spectrum of the entire periodic table.

Oppenheimer's cosmic radiation research ended abruptly in 1949, following his testimony before the House Committee on Un-American Activities (HUAC) regarding his political activities during the late 1930s. As a graduate student at Caltech he had joined other campus intellectuals in support of left-wing political ideas and activities. Oppenheimer, mainly through the influence of his wife, came to believe that socially-conscious individuals could effect change through political action and organization. Consequently, he joined the American Communist party in 1937 but quit in 1941 after joining the Manhattan Project. Although Oppenheimer admitted to HUAC that he had not been entirely truthful to wartime security investigators about his involvement with the American Communist party, he courageously refused to answer questions about the political activities of his friends and associates. In separate testimony, his wife insisted upon answering only questions that pertained to her own political past. Even though HUAC brought no action against Oppenheimer, the University of Minnesota fired him. In 1954, when the Atomic Energy Commission suspended J. Robert Oppenheimer's security clearance, Frank's testimony proved particularly damaging because they shared many of the same friends and political associates.

Oppenheimer left Minneapolis and settled in a ranching community near Pagosa Springs, Colorado. From 1949 to 1959 he raised cattle for a living. In 1957 the local elementary school teacher resigned, and Oppenheimer took over the position; the next year he became the science teacher at Archuleta County High School in Pagosa Springs. In 1959 Oppenheimer became a research associate at the University of Colorado, Boulder, teaching a summer course for high school science teachers. That opportunity led to him becoming a science teacher and educational consultant for the Jefferson County Public Schools. In 1961 Oppenheimer joined the physics faculty of the University of Colorado and returned to full-time research in particle physics. At Colorado, however, he gained national acclaim for his innovative teaching techniques. In his teaching laboratory Oppenheimer provided the instruments for investigating physical phenomena, but he encouraged students to ask their own questions and formulate independent solutions. With the support of the National Science Foundation, he and Malcolm Correll, a colleague in the physics department, transformed the physics curriculum along these lines. In 1970 Oppenheimer extended this method of teaching physics to the public through the development of the Exploratorium in San Francisco, California. After studying science museums throughout the world, he designed the Exploratorium so that visitors could participate directly in its exhibits and learn about nature through experience rather than observation and lecture. Oppenheimer served as director of that Exploratorium and of another in Denver until his death in Sausalito, California.

Although overshadowed by that of his brother, Oppenheimer's scientific career was nonetheless remarkable. While his role in the development of history's first nuclear weapons was minor, he made brilliant contributions to understanding the mechanics of cosmic radiation; these probably would have been greater had he not been ostracized for his youthful politics. Oppenheimer, like many others, was blacklisted from his profession, at least for a period. His dismissal from the University of Minnesota, however, did not deter his interest in science nor in teaching, and he gained lasting fame as an innovative educator.

• Material on Oppenheimer is in the archives of Johns Hopkins University, Baltimore, Md.; the California Institute of Technology, Pasadena; the University of Minnesota, St. Paul; and the University of Colorado, Boulder. For information on his childhood and relationship with J. Robert Oppenheimer, consult James W. Kunetka, *Oppenheimer: The Years of Risk* (1983), and Denise Royal, *The Story of J. Robert Oppenheimer* (1969). His role in the Manhattan Project is described in Kunetka, *City of Fire: Los Alamos and the Atomic Age, 1943–1945* (1979). His testimony before HUAC is detailed in Richard Rhodes, *Dark Sun: The Making of the Hydrogen Bomb* (1995). Obituaries are in *Leonardo* 18 (Nov. 1985); the *New York Times*, 5 Feb. 1985; *Newsweek* and *Time*, both 18 Feb. 1985; and, *Physics Today* 38 (Nov. 1985).

ADAM R. HORNBUCKLE

OPPENHEIMER, J. Robert (22 Apr. 1904–18 Feb. 1967), theoretical physicist and director of the Los Alamos Laboratory (Manhattan Project), was born Julius Robert Oppenheimer in New York City, the son of Julius Oppenheimer, a wealthy textile importer, and Ella Friedman, a painter. Although the family was of Jewish descent, they had no religious affiliations. The boy, known as Robert, grew up in a sumptuous Manhattan apartment whose walls were decorated with paintings by Vincent van Gogh, Paul Cézanne, and Paul Gauguin. In the summers he went sailing at the family estate on Long Island. He became interested in mineral collecting and sent letters to the New York Mineralogy Club, which, unaware that their learned correspondent was only twelve years old, invited him to present a paper. It was a success. Frail and bookish, he fared less well among people his own age, who often teased and occasionally tormented him. In 1921 Oppenheimer graduated from the Ethical Culture School of New York at the top of his class.

In the summer of 1921 Oppenheimer contracted dysentery on a prospecting trip to Europe. The illness prevented him from entering Harvard that fall. His father resolved to toughen the boy by sending him with a tutor to the West, where he rode horses and delighted in the outdoors. He grew especially fond of the broad mesas of New Mexico, an attachment that figured prominently later in his life.

In 1922 Oppenheimer enrolled at Harvard, where he took an intense program that ranged from math and sciences to philosophy and Eastern religions and French and English literature. Among the sciences, he preferred chemistry because it "starts right at the heart of things." He was nevertheless granted advanced standing to work with experimental physicist Percy Bridgeman. Oppenheimer graduated summa cum laude in 1925. Despite his evident success as a scholar, he was plagued with doubts. In a letter to a friend, Oppenheimer concluded a listing of his feverish academic pursuits with the abrupt phrase "and wish I were dead." As an adult he recalled that, during his adolescent and college years, nearly everything about him aroused "a very great sense of revulsion and wrong."

More anxieties were to follow. During his final semester at Harvard, Oppenheimer applied to study with Ernest Rutherford at the Cavendish Laboratory in Cambridge, England. Rutherford thought Oppenheimer's credentials inadequate and turned him down. Oppenheimer then applied to Joseph John Thomson at the Cavendish. Thomson accepted Oppenheimer as a research student and gave him the task of preparing thin films of beryllium. Oppenheimer regarded the work as "a terrible bore" and pronounced himself "so bad at it that it is impossible to feel that I am learning anything."

Oppenheimer's inadequacies as an experimental researcher hardened his resolve to turn to theoretical physics. In 1926 he studied with Max Born at the University of Göttingen in Germany, from which he received his doctoral degree in March 1927. From 1927 through 1928 he was a National Research Council Fellow. The following year he received offers to teach at Caltech and the University of California at Berkeley. He accepted both and for many years divided his time between Pasadena and Berkeley. He attracted a host of brilliant young students and did much to establish the West Coast as one of the nation's most important centers of advanced physics.

Oppenheimer's theoretical work during the late 1920s and through the 1930s has been unfairly dismissed as second rate. In 1927, working closely with Born, he solved a knotty problem involving calculations pertaining to subatomic particles. Oppenheimer concluded that the vibration and spin of protons could be ignored in theoretical calculations because the mass of the proton was incomparably greater than and essentially unaffected by the electron. The concept became known as the Born-Oppenheimer approximation. The next year Oppenheimer demonstrated that, when electrons were excited by a weak electric field, they could "tunnel" their way through the electrostatic forces that bound them to a nucleus. During the early 1930s Oppenheimer and his students applied the conservation laws of energy to posit the existence of a high-energy particle that complemented the electron; the positron was discovered by others in 1932. Oppenheimer's 1939 paper "On Continued Gravitational Contraction" predicted black holes, dying stars whose gravitational pull exceeded their energy production.

In 1936 Oppenheimer met Jean Tatlock, a psychiatry student, and they made plans to marry, although they were not to do so. Like many intellectuals during the Great Depression, they were drawn to radical causes. Tatlock joined the Communist party, and the couple increasingly moved in leftist circles. With the death of his father in 1937, Oppenheimer became wealthy, and he contributed to several left-wing organizations. In 1939 he fell in love with Katharine "Kitty" Puening Harrison, a biologist and widow of a Communist killed during the Spanish civil war. She, too, had belonged to the Communist party. They married in November 1940 and had two children.

About this time Oppenheimer began to sever his ties with many leftist friends and organizations. This may have been partly in response to chilling revelations about Joseph Stalin, but Oppenheimer was also strengthening his credentials so as to play a major role in the development of the atom bomb. Even before the Japanese attacked Pearl Harbor, American scientists were mobilizing under federal auspices to design such a device. Oppenheimer was initially excluded from the select circle of government scientists who were studying the matter. Ernest O. Lawrence, director of the radiation laboratory at the University of California, confided that they worried about his "leftwandering activities." Oppenheimer reassured Lawrence that there would be "no further difficulties" with radical affiliations and proceeded to prove his worth in tangible ways. At Berkeley he assembled a team of "luminaries," including the brilliant theoreticians Edward Teller and Hans Bethe, both émigrés from nazism, and put them to work on various problems pertaining to atom bomb development.

In August 1942 the U.S. Army was given charge of the entire atomic bomb mission, which became known as the Manhattan Project. Its director, General Leslie A. Groves, wanted Lawrence to direct the bomb design unit, but Lawrence was indispensable to the staggeringly difficult work of separating fissionable uranium from its chemically indistinguishable isotope. Groves settled on Oppenheimer, who, though lacking a Nobel Prize, possessed charisma and indisputable "genius," as Groves put it. In September Oppenheimer signaled his interest in the position by calling for a central laboratory wholly devoted to bomb design. The following month Groves offered him the job, and he accepted it.

Oppenheimer and Groves were an unlikely team, but the crass, mulish general and the suave, cerebral physicist worked together effectively. Groves insisted that the scientists be sequestered in a remote facility and that their access to scientific information be limited to what was necessary for their narrow individual tasks. Oppenheimer agreed with the first point and even proposed that the laboratory be located in one of the desolate haunts he had explored twenty years earlier in New Mexico. But he reasoned that, if the entire unit were virtually imprisoned within the compound's fences, no need would exist to fetter inquiry among the scientists within. Groves accepted this compromise and began construction of the facility at Los Alamos, New Mexico.

Oppenheimer went about the work of recruiting scientists, appealing variously to their love of physics, their patriotism, and their fear of the Nazis. He succeeded admirably, and in April 1943 brought to Los Alamos a collection of energetic and talented scientists whose average age was twenty-five. As director, Oppenheimer eventually supervised over 1,500 people, mediating the demands of the military bureaucracy and the free spirits of the scientists, solving innumerable theoretical and practical problems, and for the most part extinguishing the emotional sparks caused by the collision of powerful egos under tremendous pressure. Bethe recalled that Oppenheimer was intellectually "superior" to everyone else at Los Alamos: "He knew and understood everything that went on in the laboratory, whether it was chemistry or theoretical physics or machine shop." Teller disagreed and was angered that Oppenheimer had chosen Bethe instead of him to head the Theoretical Division. Increasingly, Teller withdrew from the laboratory's work. Oppenheimer removed him from the bomb design team, softening the blow by encouraging him to pursue theoretical issues pertaining to a possible fusion, or hydrogen, bomb.

Oppenheimer's indefatigable efforts in the laboratory were shadowed by troubling personal and security issues. In June 1943 Tatlock asked to meet her former fiancé, and Oppenheimer spent an evening at her home in San Francisco. He had been followed by army counterintelligence officials, whose superiors recommended that Oppenheimer be dismissed as a security risk. Groves invoked his broad powers to overrule them, and Oppenheimer stayed. In August, in an episode that has never been fully explained, Oppenheimer went to security officials and told them that a friend had approached project scientists, including himself, to discuss a plan to gather information about the project and transmit it to the Soviet Union. Oppenheimer reassured the officials that he had squelched the initiative but refused to divulge the friend's name until ordered to do so by Groves. The friend, Haakon Chevalier, a romance language instructor, was quietly dismissed from the University of California. In January 1944 Tatlock committed suicide. The army intelligence report on the Chevalier episode concluded that Oppenheimer posed no real security threat because he was "deeply concerned with gaining a worldwide reputation" and wanted desperately to keep his job. He did, but the matter was not forgotten.

At the Los Alamos Laboratory, Oppenheimer's charge was made yet more demanding: he would be obliged to design two different bombs. The first, a "gun assembly" prototype, fired two subcritical pieces of enriched uranium at each other. At the moment of impact, they attained critical mass and initiated a chain reaction. But the huge Manhattan Project plants at Oak Ridge, Tennessee, and elsewhere would not produce enough fissionable uranium for a single bomb until the summer of 1945. Although plutonium offered an alternative and more plentiful source of fissionable material, that artificial element was so unstable that it would predetonate and fizzle if used in the gun-assembly design. Oppenheimer's objective was to design a bomb that would bring subcritical masses of plutonium together within the tiniest fraction of a second. Seth Neddermeyer proposed coating a hollow sphere of plutonium with high explosives, which would implode instantaneously upon detonation. George Kistiakowsky devised a high-explosive lens that would focus the shock wave and squeeze the plutonium into a critical mass the size of an eyeball. The success of this device was demonstrated on 16 July 1945, when a plutonium bomb, the world's first nuclear device, was exploded at Alamogordo, New Mexico. Oppenheimer, watching from the distance, intoned a phrase from Hindu scripture in the *Bhagavadgita*, "I am become death, the shatterer of worlds." On 6 August the "gun-assembly" uranium bomb, nicknamed

"Little Boy," destroyed the Japanese city of Hiroshima; three days later a plutonium bomb, "Fat Man," obliterated Nagasaki. Japan surrendered.

Oppenheimer celebrated the end of the war and the success of the Manhattan Project, but the death toll and chilling descriptions of radiation sickness had a sobering effect. He informed government officials that most scientists in the project would not continue to pursue such work. "I feel we have blood on our hands," he told President Harry S. Truman. "Never mind. It'll all come out in the wash," Truman replied. In October Oppenheimer resigned from Los Alamos.

Oppenheimer nevertheless remained an important figure in atomic policy. He served as the guiding light of the Acheson-Lilienthal committee, which proposed that the United States relinquish its nuclear monopoly to avoid a nuclear arms race with the Soviet Union. Issued in early 1946, the committee report recommended creation of a United Nations atomic energy commission to supervise the use of fissionable material throughout the world. Groves denounced the plan, and Truman rejected it as unworkable. The nuclear arms race was now on.

From 1947 through 1952 Oppenheimer directed the Institute for Advanced Study at Princeton, which became a leading center of theoretical physics and attracted notable scholars in the social sciences and humanities. He also chaired the General Advisory Committee (GAC) of the Atomic Energy Commission (AEC), the U.S. agency responsible for the control and development of fissionable materials. When the Soviet Union detonated an atom bomb in 1949, Teller and Lawrence lobbied feverishly to develop the hydrogen bomb. In October the GAC, with Oppenheimer as chair, repudiated the hydrogen bomb as a weapon of "genocide" and argued that it was so indiscriminately destructive as to be militarily worthless; the GAC recommended against its development. The Joint Chiefs of Staff disagreed, as did Truman, who in early 1950 authorized a crash program to build the hydrogen bomb.

In May 1953 President Dwight D. Eisenhower asked Lewis Strauss to chair the Atomic Energy Commission. Strauss accepted on the condition that Oppenheimer, whom he regarded as a security risk, be dismissed. Strauss was given the job and immediately moved to revoke Oppenheimer's security clearance, thereby severing him from the commission's work. Strauss even dissuaded Senator Joseph McCarthy from barging in on so delicate a matter. Unaware of the impending battle or fatalistically resigned to it, Oppenheimer and his wife dined with the Chevaliers in Paris. This remarkable indiscretion infuriated Eisenhower and further emboldened Strauss.

On 21 December Strauss accused Oppenheimer of disloyalty and presented a list of the charges against him. Oppenheimer refused to resign, demanded a hearing, and hired a lawyer. Strauss arranged for the Federal Bureau of Investigation (FBI) to tap Oppenheimer's phones, and detailed transcripts of Oppenheimer's discussions with his lawyer were provided to

Strauss, a gross and illegal violation of Oppenheimer's rights. The AEC lawyers were predictably well prepared when the hearing began on 12 April 1954. After Oppenheimer had described Chevalier's initial approach to him as relatively innocuous, Strauss's lawyers cited Oppenheimer's far more incriminating description of events eleven years earlier, which, unbeknownst to Oppenheimer, had been tape-recorded by intelligence officers. Oppenheimer admitted that his original story was a "lie" concocted in a moment of "idiocy." Many scientists and public officials attested to Oppenheimer's loyalty and indisputable service to the nation, but Teller provided the final blow. After acknowledging Oppenheimer's loyalty, Teller said that he had serious doubts about Oppenheimer's judgment, leftist leanings on political matters, and opposition to the hydrogen bomb: "I would feel personally more secure if public matters would rest in other hands." On 27 May the security board affirmed Oppenheimer's loyalty but denied him security clearance. The AEC canceled his contract.

Though shaken, Oppenheimer continued to direct the Institute for Advanced Study and to write on the relation of Western culture to science. He bought a house in the Virgin Islands and spent time sailing. In 1963 the AEC conferred on him the Enrico Fermi Award. In 1966 he resigned from the institute. He died in Princeton.

In 1994 Pavel A. Sudoplatov, a retired KGB (Soviet intelligence agency) general, published an autobiography that claimed that Oppenheimer had passed atomic secrets to the Soviet Union. Some American conservatives found in these charges confirmation of earlier accusations. Liberals and the scientific community generally dismissed the aging spymaster's reminiscences as self-serving and riddled with obvious errors. Virtually no documentary evidence exists that Oppenheimer knowingly betrayed his country. Yet the pieces of his life have never been assembled in a way that provides a clear picture of the man and his motivations. Oppenheimer was driven by titanic ambition yet tormented by self-doubt; he cultivated deep and profound moral sensibilities, yet he became entangled in deceitful personal and professional relations; he repeatedly spoke of our "common bond with other men everywhere" (1945 speech to the Association of Los Alamos Scientists) yet worked tirelessly on a weapon that resulted in hundreds of thousands of civilian deaths. He was, ultimately, a brilliant scientist and a leader of scientists who thrust himself into the very center of human affairs, where he fashioned a complex and elusive role. His performance usually inspired and stimulated most scientists, but it often baffled and occasionally infuriated politicians, military leaders, and the public. No one doubted, however, that it forever changed their lives.

• Oppenheimer's papers are at the Library of Congress. Material is also available at the Bancroft Library of the University of California at Berkeley; the California Institute of Technology Archives; the Center for History of Physics of the American Institute of Physics, New York City; the Harvard University Archives; the Los Alamos National Laboratory, Records Division; and the National Archives. Many of Oppenheimer's letters are published in *Robert Oppenheimer: Letters and Recollections*, ed. Alice Kimball Smith and Charles Weiner (1980). Oral interviews are in the Archives for History of Quantum Physics, Niels Bohr Library, American Institute of Physics. Oppenheimer's books include *Science and Common Understanding* (1954), *The Open Mind* (1955), and *The Flying Trapeze: Three Crises for Physicists* (1961). The transcript of the 1954 security hearing appears verbatim in *In the Matter of J. Robert Oppenheimer: Transcript of Hearings before Personnel Security Board, Washington, D.C., April 12, 1954 through May 6, 1954* (1954). See also Philip M. Stern, *The Oppenheimer Case: Security on Trial* (1971). Biographical accounts from his associates are in Hans A. Bethe, *Three Tributes to J. Robert Oppenheimer* (1967); I. I. Rabi et al., *Oppenheimer* (1969); and John S. Rigden, "J. Robert Oppenheimer: Before the War," *Scientific America* 273, no. 1 (July 1995). The conservative position on Sudoplatov's charges is in Eric Breindel, "The Oppenheimer File," *National Review*, 30 May 1994. Rebuttals are in Priscilla Johnson McMillan, "The Sudoplatov File: Flimsy Memories," *Bulletin of the Atomic Scientists*, July–Aug. 1994. The full context of the atom bomb project and its aftermath is presented in Richard Rhodes, *The Making of the Atom Bomb* (1986) and *Dark Sun* (1994). An obituary is in the *New York Times*, 19 Feb. 1967.

MARK C. CARNES

OPPER, Frederick Burr (2 Jan. 1857–27 Aug. 1937), cartoonist, was born in Madison, Ohio, the son of Lewis Opper, a craftsman and small businessman, and Aurelia Burr. Leaving school at age fourteen, he found work on his hometown newspaper, the *Madison Gazette*, where, in addition to his duties as a printer's apprentice, he did cartooning. Determined to become a national cartoonist, he mailed out humorous drawings to a number of publications, big and small, and made sales to *Scribner's, St. Nicholas, Century*, and other magazines.

On the strength of these sales, Opper settled in New York City as a staff artist for *Wild Oats*, a humor magazine, where he remained for a year (1877–1878) before moving to *Leslie's Magazine* (1878–1881). He then joined *Puck*, the leading satiric publication of the day. There his cartoons and continuing series, such as *Streets of New York, The Age of Handbooks*, and *The Suburban Resident*, in which he satirized the trends and fads of the times, established him as one of the preeminent cartooning talents of the late nineteenth century.

Opper's work for *Puck* brought him to the attention of William Randolph Hearst, who in 1899 lured him to his chain of newspapers. Since 1897 Hearst had been developing his color comic supplement, the *American Humorist*, and in Opper he found an artist who could significantly contribute to that nascent American art form that was only then beginning to be called "the comics."

Opper's initial effort in the field proved a masterstroke. It was *Happy Hooligan*, which first appeared in the pages of the *American Humorist* in March 1900. A ragged Irish tramp with the moon face of a clown and a tin can for a hat, Happy was a luckless innocent who fell victim to his generous impulses; his various misadventures were always the result of half-baked attempts at winning sympathy from ungrateful strangers or correcting wrongs that almost invariably landed him in jail. Happy remained true to his name, however, and smiled through every misfortune. Happy prefigured the character of the pathetic little tramp that Charlie Chaplin was later to make his own, and like Chaplin's tramp, Happy in the end won his girl, the pert Suzanne, even in the face of her father's and society's opposition. *Happy Hooligan* was Opper's most popular and enduring creation, lasting until 1932.

The success of *Happy Hooligan* persuaded Opper to continue his comic-page experiments. In 1902 he created *Alphonse and Gaston* about two ludicrously polite Frenchmen later joined by their Parisian friend Leon. Attired in nineteenth-century dandy clothes, they never once lost their good manners, despite every conceivable catastrophe. Their constant scraping and bowing and their repeated exchanges of courtesy constituted most of the strip's appeal. "After you, my dear Alphonse," "No, after *you*, my dear Gaston," which recurred like a leitmotiv, have now passed into the language.

Another Opper creation that withstood the test of time is Maud, the unforgiving mule with the devastating kick. She first appeared as an occasional relief for Happy Hooligan and Alphonse and Gaston as early as 1904, and she first displayed her kicking prowess on Si, the old farmer who had bought her and was showing her off to his wife, Mirandy. This turned into a weekly ritual, and the feature became *And Her Name Was Maud!*, with the mule demonstrating her propulsive skills on all and sundry. Among Opper's other comic-page offerings were *Howson Lott* (a variation on the theme of the suburban resident), *Mr. Dubb* (about yet another meek little man), and *Our Antediluvian Ancestors*, the first of the caveman comics that have enlivened American popular culture in the twentieth century.

Along with his comic series Opper contributed innumerable political cartoons to Hearst's daily newspapers. He soon became the most feared pen artist of his era. His attacks on President William McKinley, portrayed as a puppet in the hands of "the Trusts" because of his perceived ties to moneyed interests, were the most savage perpetrated against an American president since Thomas Nast's depictions of Andrew Johnson. He was no more lenient toward Theodore Roosevelt (whom he derisively nicknamed "Little Teddie"); his criticism changed to admiration, however, when "Teddie" decided to take on the trusts. Opper's editorial cartoons were often organized in comic-strip format, sometimes running under their own titles, such as *Mr. Trusty, The Cruise of the Piffle*, and the well-known satires *Willie and Poppa* and *Willie and Teddie*.

In 1882 Opper had married Nellie Burnett, with whom he had two children. In addition to his considerable output as a cartoonist, he illustrated a number of books, including Bill Nye's comic *History of the United States*, Finley Peter Dunne's *Mr. Dooley's Philosophy*, and an anthology of short stories by Mark Twain. Despite ill health and failing eyesight he continued to work until Hearst forced his retirement at the age of seventy-five; he spent the last years of his life in semiseclusion in New Rochelle, New York, where he died.

Throughout his long career Opper enjoyed considerable success. His political drawings earned him great respect among readers and with his peers who bestowed on him the title of "Dean of American cartoonists." His comic-page creations were reprinted in book format and were adapted into animated cartoons, stage plays, and Broadway musicals. He is considered one of the founding fathers of the medium, a status he shares with Rudolph Dirks, Richard Outcault, and James Swinnerton. Coming to the field at age forty-two, he was able to use his cartooning experience to good effect, perfecting character and stylizing situations in the service of a single vision and a dynamic narrative. His influence on other comic artists, like Rube Goldberg, Milt Gross, and "Tad" Dorgan, was considerable during his lifetime, and in many respects it has extended well beyond his death.

• There is no full-length biography of Frederick Opper. All histories of comic art contain substantial discussions of the man and his work; see notably Coulton Waugh, *The Comics* (1947), Stephen Becker, *Comic Art in America* (1959), Pierre Couperie and Maurice Horn, *A History of the Comic Strip* (1968), Jerry Robinson, *The Comics: An Illustrated History* (1974), and Judith O'Sullivan, *The Great American Comic Strip* (1990). Lengthy entries on Opper and many of his creations can also be found in Horn, ed., *The World Encyclopedia of Comics* (1976), *The World Encyclopedia of Cartoons* (1980), and *Contemporary Graphic Artists*, vol. 2 (1987), and in Ron Goulart, ed., *The Encyclopedia of American Comics* (1990). A chapter devoted to Opper is included in Richard Marschall, *America's Great Comic-Strip Artists* (1989). An obituary is in the *New York Times*, 28 Aug. 1937.

MAURICE HORN

OPTIC, Oliver. *See* Adams, William Taylor.

OPUKAHAIA (c. 1792–17 Feb. 1818), Hawaiian student and first Hawaiian convert to Christianity, known as Henry Obookiah, was raised at Kealakekua Bay on the island of Hawaii. His mother was Kamohoula; his father's name is unknown. About 1802, during the wars of Kamehameha the Great, Opukahaia saw both of his parents killed before his eyes. When he tried to flee with his youngest brother on his back, an opposing chief's spear killed his infant brother. Opukahaia was spared and was taken captive, however, and for a time he lived in the household of the chief who had killed his parents. A year later, one of Opukahaia's uncles found where his nephew was living, and at his uncle's request, Opukahaia was allowed to return to his own people. In his uncle's home, the young man was trained as a kahuna (priest).

In 1808, Opukahaia persuaded Captain Brintnal, an American sea captain, to take him along when he returned to New England. Although Opukahaia would have enjoyed a special place as a kahuna had he remained, the internecine warfare between the chiefs that had resulted in the death of his parents made his life on the islands seem too precarious. With his uncle's reluctant consent, Opukahaia left the Hawaiian islands for the United States and a new life. Opukahaia worked for his passage aboard Brintnal's ship, the *Triumph*, and the sea captain took special interest in him, teaching him to speak English and to navigate. The crew also taught him how to climb the rigging, sight a star, skin a seal, and use the compass. Because the crew had trouble pronouncing his name, they called him Henry; for the rest of his life, he called and signed himself Henry Obookiah. During the trip, Obookiah became good friends with Thomas Hopu, another Hawaiian boy on the *Triumph*. When the ship finally docked at New York about a year after leaving Hawaii, Captain Brintnal invited both boys to live with him in New Haven, Connecticut.

From the Brintnal home, Obookiah visited Yale College, where he met Edwin Dwight, a Yale student. Dwight henceforth became a local patron, inviting Obookiah to his home to study. Obookiah proved to be a very bright pupil, and other Yale students joined Dwight's efforts, teaching Obookiah to read and write and instructing him in geography, history, arithmetic, literature, languages, and the Bible. Through the students' efforts, Obookiah was invited to live in the home of the president of Yale, Timothy Dwight (1752–1817), Edwin Dwight's father. Each summer, Obookiah and Hopu worked on farms around New Haven to earn their room and board.

Obookiah became a Christian, being accepted into the Church of Christ in Torringford and rejecting the Hawaiian gods of his youth. This conversion, as well as his experiences at Yale, inspired him with the desire to bring his newfound academic knowledge and Christian faith to Hawaii. In 1815 he began to preach at various churches around New Haven, calling for a special mission to the islands. The next year he enrolled in a special foreign mission school established in Cornwall by the American Board of Commissioners for Foreign Missions (ABCFM). Obookiah was an exemplary student, translating the Book of Genesis into Hawaiian and working on a Hawaiian dictionary, spelling book, and grammar text. A devout convert, praying both privately and publicly for a mission to Hawaii, he enjoyed a wide circle of influential friends within the ABCFM. Before the mission he sought could be organized, however, Obookiah contracted typhus and died in the Congregational parsonage near the school, where he was buried. His funeral drew many mourners from both the school and the wider Cornwall community.

Members of the ABCFM who had nursed Obookiah until his death felt compelled to honor his hopes for the mission to Hawaii. Their intentions were reinforced when Edwin Dwight, inspired by his friend's death, edited and published *The Memoirs of Henry Obookiah* (1818). Widely circulated throughout New England, the book publicized Obookiah's dying wish for a Hawaiian crusade and encouraged many congregationalists to contribute funds toward the expedition.

The first company of missionaries bound for Hawaii left Boston a year after Obookiah's death. The party included four Hawaiians educated at the Foreign Mission School, among them Thomas Hopu and George Kaumualii, the son of the king of Kauai. Arriving in Hawaii in 1820, the missionaries learned that the old Hawaiian religion had only recently been overthrown through the leadership of two of the former king's wives, Kaahumanu and Keopuolani. The missionaries interpreted this event as a miracle and a sign of God's faith in their endeavors. Many Hawaiians would eventually be converted to Christianity and the dreams of Obookiah realized.

Obookiah had willingly embraced a foreign culture and faith, sacrificing his life in the process, to further arouse New England's evangelical concern for the Sandwich islanders, and perhaps his training as a kahuna had laid the foundation for his religiosity. On his tomb in Connecticut is written: "He was eminent for piety and missionary zeal. . . . He died without fear, with a heavenly smile on his Countenance and glory in his soul."

In the summer of 1993 Obookiah's remains were exhumed from his grave in Cornwall, Connecticut, and reinterred at Kahikolu Church Cemetery in Napoopoo, Hawaii.

• See Edith Wolfe, *The Story of Henry Obookiah/Opukahaia* (1974); Gavan Daws, *Shoal of Time: A History of the Hawaiian Islands* (1968); Bingham papers, Hawaiian Mission Children's Society, Honolulu; Hiram Bingham, *Residence of Twenty-one Years in the Sandwich Islands*, Hartford (1847); and ABCFM Reports, 1820–1870, Boston, Mass.

BARBARA BENNETT PETERSON

ORBISON, Roy (23 Apr. 1936–6 Dec. 1988), singer and songwriter, was born Roy Kelton Orbison in Vernon, Texas, the son of Orbie Lee Orbison, an oil-field driller, and Nadine Schultz, a nurse. His early musical experiences centered around country and western music. Orbison performed regularly on country and western radio programs by the age of eight. Attending high school in Wink, Texas, he led a band of fellow students called the Wink Westerners, whose repertoire ranged from western swing and country and western, notably the songs of Hank Williams and Lefty Frizzell, to Tin Pan Alley pop and even the big band repertoire of the 1940s. He continued to play with the group in college, first at North Texas State in 1954 where he briefly studied geology, and in 1955 at the Texas State Teacher's College at Odessa.

Envying the success of his fellow Odessa student Pat Boone and that of Elvis Presley, both at that time riding the crest of early rock 'n' roll popularity, Orbison transformed his group into the Teen Kings, a rockabilly-oriented rock 'n' roll band. With the assistance of Norman Petty, a frequent collaborator of fellow Texan Buddy Holly who later also composed with Orbison, he recorded "Ooby Dooby," a song composed by two upperclassmen at North Texas State. This recording became a regional hit and eventually brought him to the attention of Sam Phillips, who had guided Presley's early career. Phillips signed him to his label, Sun Records, but Orbison's preference for singing ballads in a style that drew from mainstream pop as well as country and western never meshed well with the classic rockabilly that Phillips and most of his artists preferred, and his relationship with the label was not commercially successful.

Orbison's success in the late 1950s was more as a songwriter than as a performer. His song "Claudette," named for his wife Claudette Hestand, whom he had married in 1956 and with whom he had three children, became a hit for the Everly Brothers in 1958, and he began writing songs for the Acuff-Rose publishing company in Nashville, Tennessee.

He returned to recording in 1960 and achieved great success with a new style and a repertoire based largely on songs of unrequited love and plaintive laments, including "Only the Lonely" (1960), "I'm Hurtin'" (1960), "Crying" (1961), and "It's Over" (1964). From 1960 to 1966 Orbison placed twenty-two singles in the *Billboard* magazine Top Forty charts, with his popularity peaking in 1962–1964.

Orbison was widely known and respected for his distinctive vocal style. A natural baritone, he displayed a three-octave vocal range and made effective use of falsetto. Dubbed by the media as the "Caruso of rock," the range and purity of his voice, along with his use of vibrato and the emotional intensity with which he so frequently performed, led many to refer to his performance style as operatic. However, his demeanor on stage was unusually staid. Lacking the charismatic good looks of Elvis Presley or the other teen idols of the early 1960s, he increasingly adopted a solitary and mysterious posture, often dressing in black outfits on stage and wearing dark glasses for most public appearances. In the mid-1960s, he had a featured role in the film *The Fastest Guitar Alive* but made no further attempts to pursue a film career.

His songs, many of which he coauthored with Joe Melson or Bill Dees, periodically exhibited characteristics of the rockabilly- and Latin-tinged, or "Tex Mex," styles of the 1950s, e.g., "Only the Lonely" and "Blue Bayou" (1963). He also embraced the more mainstream rhythm-and-blues-influenced rock 'n' roll style of the early 1960s in songs such as "Mean Woman Blues" (1963) and in his last major hit, "Oh, Pretty Woman" (1964), coauthored by Dees. A number of his cowritten songs were considered unusually complex for the period, often containing a number of different sections rather than the simple alternation of chorus and verse that was typical of the early and mid-1960s. Also, his exploitation of gradually increasing dramatic tension in songs such as "Running Scared" was considered unique and innovative for the period. Nevertheless, his highly emotional style and the subject matter of his songs seemed increasingly out of place in the progressive rock era of the late 1960s, and

his American record sales plummeted. His popularity remained high in Canada, England, and Australia, however, and his annual European tours continued to be successful into the late 1960s.

Orbison divorced Claudette Orbison in 1965 but remarried her within a year. He stopped composing after her death in 1966, and other family tragedies kept him relatively inactive until 1970, when he married Barbara Wellnoener-Jacobs, with whom he had two children.

Orbison had no new hits in the 1970s, his repertoire drawing mostly on his songs from the early 1960s. His albums of songs by country legend Hank Williams and noted songwriter Don Williams in the late 1960s and early 1970s were critically well received but had little commercial impact. In 1978 he was sidelined for almost two years as he recovered from open heart surgery. While he had little commercial success with his own recordings in the 1970s, a number of popular singers openly paid homage to Orbison as an important influence, and some had significant success with their remakes of his songs, including Linda Ronstadt, with her 1977 version of Orbison's 1963 hit "Blue Bayou."

In 1980 his career was buoyed by the receipt of the recording industry's Grammy award for the Best Country Performance by a Duo or Group, for his recording of his song "That 'Lovin' You' Feeling Again" with Emmylou Harris. In this period, he also toured with the Eagles, a popular country-rock group. In September 1982 Orbison brought a partially successful suit against his manager, Wesley Rose, who also served as president of the Acuff-Rose publishing company with which Orbison had been associated since 1958, in an attempt to win a larger share of his song-publishing income.

In 1985 Orbison recorded a moderately successful double album of remakes of a number of his early hits, and in the same year the use of his 1963 song "In Dreams" for the soundtrack of the film *Blue Velvet* played an important role in bringing him back into public consciousness. In January 1987 he was inducted into the Rock-and-Roll Hall of Fame by his long-time admirer Bruce Springsteen, who subsequently joined him for a television special a few months later. Following this, Orbison began work on what was to be his last new solo album, *Mystery Girl*, released after his death.

In the late 1980s Orbison joined forces with Bob Dylan, George Harrison, Tom Petty, and Jeff Lynne to form the recording group the Traveling Wilburys, whose album *Traveling Wilburys, Vol. I* met with great success. Orbison continued to tour as a soloist until his death of a heart attack in Hendersonville, Texas. After his death, the *Traveling Wilburys, Vol. I* rose to number four on the *Billboard* album charts, eventually earning a Grammy award as the best album of the year. Orbison's album *Mystery Girl* rose to number five on the charts, posthumously providing Orbison with his greatest commercial success in over two decades.

In a career spanning more than three decades, Orbison achieved an enduring reputation as one of the premier rock 'n' roll singers to emerge in the early 1960s. His distinctive vocal style, combined with the poignant sentiments expressed in many of his best-known songs, made him the acknowledged master of ballads of unrequited or lost love in the 1960s.

• The most sympathetic view of Orbison's career is provided by Alan Clayson, *Only the Lonely: Roy Orbison's Life and Legacy* (1989). Also providing useful biographical information is Ellis Amburn, *Dark Star: The Roy Orbison Story* (1990). A substantial and informative interview and obituary describing Orbison's career and ideals appeared in *Rolling Stone*, 26 Jan. 1989; an obituary is in the *New York Times*, 8 Dec. 1988.

TERENCE J. O'GRADY

ORD, Edward Otho Cresap (18 Oct. 1818–22 July 1883), soldier, was born in Cumberland, Maryland, the son of James Ord, a farmer, former Jesuit, and veteran of the War of 1812, and Rebecca Cresap. The family moved to Washington, D.C., in 1819, where James Ord became a local magistrate (1821–1837). Educated at home by his father, Edward Ord received an appointment to the U.S. Military Academy at West Point in 1835. Ord befriended William T. Sherman and Henry W. Halleck and graduated seventeenth in a class of thirty-one in 1839.

The young second lieutenant, assigned to the Third Artillery, fought the Seminole Indians in Florida (1839–1842). Ord discovered the hardships and brutality of frontier warfare and became an adept fighter. During the Mexican War, Ord sailed for the Pacific Coast on 14 July 1846, arriving in Monterey Bay on 27 January 1847 to discover California already in American hands. Ord witnessed the chaotic conditions caused by the gold rush and made significant surveys of possible California railroad routes. Returning East in 1851, Ord disliked his posting in Boston. He secured an assignment with the Coast Survey with orders for California in 1853.

In 1854 Ord married Mary Mercer Thompson, daughter of a prominent San Francisco lawyer and former Virginia congressman; seven of their thirteen children reached maturity. Though he softened his proslavery sentiments after passage of the 1854 Kansas-Nebraska Act, Ord remained a Democrat. Later, during the Civil War, his prewar sentiments caused some Republican congressmen to doubt Ord's loyalty and demand his removal from the army. Halleck and Sherman protected him. Indeed, in summer 1863 Sherman captured Jefferson Davis's personal papers in Mississippi and, before sending the materials to Washington, culled the collection, removing embarrassing letters that Ord had addressed to Davis.

Ord commanded a company in California in 1855. Land disputes with American Indians caused hostilities, and Ord participated in several American Indian expeditions in Washington Territory and Oregon. He again proved himself a relentless fighter, gaining valuable command experience under difficult conditions.

Assigned to duty at Fort Monroe, Virginia, in 1859, site of the army artillery school, Ord assisted in suppressing John Brown's (1800–1859) raid on Harpers Ferry, Virginia (now West Virginia), and witnessed Brown's hanging. He wrote after the hanging that southern Democrats would be justified in electing their own president, "so hurrah for their nominee" (Cresap, p. 59). Despite such statements, Ord remained a strong Unionist, opposing secession. In January 1861 he made these feelings known to Washington authorities, suggesting ways to strengthen Federal positions in the South. Captain Ord returned to the Pacific Coast in March 1861.

Ord wanted to fight when war broke out. With political and professional friends in Washington, he secured an appointment as brigadier general of volunteers as of 14 September. Given command of a brigade in the Army of the Potomac, Ord captivated the nation by defeating Confederate James E. B. Stuart in a large skirmish at Dranesville, Virginia, on 20 December. Lack of Union victories magnified Ord's accomplishment at Dranesville and won him promotion to major general of volunteers as of 2 May 1862. Ord briefly commanded a division in the Department of the Rappahannock before transferring to Union forces in Tennessee commanded by Halleck.

Ord's abilities caught Major General Ulysses S. Grant's attention during the battles of Iuka (19 Sept.) and Corinth (3–4 Oct.), Mississippi. Ord's aggressive pursuit and engagement of Confederate forces during the battle of the Hatchie (5 Oct.) won Grant's lasting admiration. Seriously wounded on 5 October, Ord spent the winter recuperating.

Ord arrived at Vicksburg, Mississippi, to take command of the XIII Corps on 18 June 1863, when Grant relieved the troublesome political general John A. McClernand. "Ord placed in the command of the 13th Army Corps has proven a very great relief to me," Grant wrote. "The change is better than 10 000 reinforcements" (Simon, vol. 9, p. 146).

In March 1864 Grant assigned Ord to lead an expedition into the Shenandoah Valley. "[Franz] Sigel is as jealous as the devil at my having come here, and I really think on that account that [William W.] Averell will do *better* than I can," Ord wrote to Grant in April (Simon, vol. 10, p. 235). Ord privately suspected that the expedition might fail and asked to be relieved. Grant complied and later selected Ord to replace another troublesome corps commander on 21 July, giving him the XVIII Corps, Army of the James. Grant described Ord as "skillfull in the management of troops, and brave and prompt" (Simon, vol. 11, p. 192). Ord repaid this confidence, assaulting and capturing Fort Harrison, Virginia, on 29 September and receiving another serious wound.

When Ord returned to duty, Grant again used him to replace a political general, Benjamin F. Butler (1818–1893), on 8 January 1865. As Army of the James commander, Ord played a significant role in the final battles around Petersburg beginning on 29

March and witnessed the surrender of Robert E. Lee at Appomattox on 9 April.

Mustered out of volunteer service on 1 September 1866, Ord was rewarded for wartime services with promotion to brigadier general, U.S. Army, as of 26 July. He commanded the Fourth Military District (Ark. and Miss.) during the early stages of Congressional Reconstruction. His connection to the Democratic party coupled with his opposition to both suffrage and civil rights for African Americans made Reconstruction duty distasteful. Grant transferred Ord to California in early 1868. He commanded the Department of the Platte from 11 December 1871 until 6 April 1875 and the Department of Texas from 11 April 1875 until his retirement, 6 December 1880. While in Texas, Ord quarreled with General Philip H. Sheridan, and this quarrel, coupled with Ord's public endorsement of the Democratic presidential candidate in 1880, hastened his retirement.

Ord then worked on railroad development schemes in Mexico in association with Grant. En route to Vera Cruz he contracted yellow fever and died in Havana, Cuba.

Three times during the Civil War Grant demonstrated his confidence in Ord by using him to replace vexatious commanders. Ord, "a doer rather than a thinker" (Cresap, p. 345), met the challenge in each case. His most notable achievements occurred under Grant's direct guidance. Ord demonstrated little independent initiative but had few peers as an assault commander.

• The largest collection of Ord's papers is in Bancroft Library, University of California, Berkeley, with smaller collections at Stanford University and Georgetown University. The National Archives, Washington, D.C., contains Ord's voluminous official correspondence and reports, especially Record Group 94, Records of the Adjutant General's Office, 1780–1917; Record Group 108, Records of the Headquarters of the Army; and Record Group 393, Records of United States Army Continental Commands, 1821–1920. Many of his Civil War dispatches and reports are printed in *The War of the Rebellion: A Compilation of the Official Records of the Union and Confederate Armies* (128 vols., 1880–1901), vol. 129 (index). The only biography, Bernarr Cresap, *Appomattox Commander: The Story of General E. O. C. Ord* (1981), contains an excellent bibliography. The link between Ord and Grant is documented in John Y. Simon, ed., *The Papers of Ulysses S. Grant* (18 vols., 1967).

DAVID L. WILSON

ORD, George (4 Mar. 1781–24 Jan. 1866), naturalist, writer, and lexicographer, was born in Philadelphia, Pennsylvania, the son of George Ord, a retired sea captain who in 1798 became a ship chandler and rope maker, and Rebecca Lindemeyer. Educated in Philadelphia, Ord devoted himself from an early age to the study of science and literature. He entered his father's rope-making business in 1800 and continued the business after his father's death in 1806; he retired from the business in 1829 to devote more time to his avoca-

tional interests. In 1804 Ord married Margarette Biays, with whom he had three children, only one of whom survived infancy.

At age twenty-four Ord befriended the Scottish poet and naturalist Alexander Wilson, fifteen years his senior, who was then embarking on his great life work, *American Ornithology; or, The Natural History of the Birds of the United States*. After Wilson's death in 1813, Ord completed the eighth volume of the *Ornithology*. In 1814 he published the ninth and final volume from Wilson's notes and added a biography of his friend, which he later expanded into the book *Sketch of the Life of Alexander Wilson* (1828; repr. 1871). His first wife having died in 1808 or 1810, Ord remarried in 1815, but his second wife's name is unknown. They had one daughter who died in infancy.

In 1817 Ord became a member of the American Philosophical Society, where he later served as secretary, vice president, librarian, treasurer, and councillor. He was elected a fellow of the Linnaean Society of London in 1825. From 1851 to 1858 he served as president of the Academy of Natural Sciences of Philadelphia, to which he had been elected a member in 1815.

In addition to *Life of Wilson*, Ord wrote memoirs of fellow naturalists and academy members Thomas Say (1834) and Charles A. Lesueur (1849). Throughout his career he kept detailed scientific diaries (since lost) and published articles in numerous scientific periodicals, including London's *Magazine of Natural History*, the *Transactions of the American Philosophical Society*, and the *Journal of the Academy of Natural Sciences of Philadelphia*. Among his most important contributions was an anonymous account of the zoology of North America for the second American edition of William Guthrie's *Geographical, Historical, and Commercial Grammar* (1815). In a scientific paper of 1815, Ord named the grizzly bear *Ursus horribilis Ord*, a name later declared invalid by taxonomists because of the priority of an earlier name, *Ursus arctos* (Linnaeus, 1758). Ord had hoped to publish his own account of the mammals of North America to parallel Wilson's work on birds and had even commissioned some of the plates for the volume, but he was forced to abandon the expensive project because of serious financial reversals from his bad railroad investments.

Although Ord devoted most of his time to scientific pursuits, with a particular focus on birds and mammals, he also had a fascination with words and for forty years studied philology independently. In later life he donated his lexicographic manuscripts to Robert Latham of London, who included Ord's work in the 1870 edition of Johnson's dictionary. Ord also helped to enlarge *Noah Webster's Dictionary*.

Despite Ord's many personal accomplishments, Ord is best remembered for his animosity toward Wilson's most famous ornithological rival, John James Audubon. As Wilson's close friend, biographer, and executor, Ord may have felt threatened by Audubon's considerable talent when he burst onto the ornithological scene a decade after Wilson's death. After their first meeting at the Academy of Natural Sciences in 1824,

Ord aggressively campaigned against Audubon, using his significant influence to try to prevent Audubon from realizing success in scientific circles in the United States and abroad. Famed for his sharp tongue in defaming others, Ord made many assertions about Audubon's morals, intelligence, and integrity that today would almost certainly be considered libelous. In letters to friends and associates, he called the younger naturalist a "charlatan," an "impudent pretender," and a "contemptible imposter." To Charles Lucien Bonaparte, the influential ornithologist and nephew of Napoleon, Ord declared Audubon's *Ornithological Biography* "the biggest hodgepodge of stupidity and lies that I have ever seen." Though his campaign was unsuccessful in the end, it caused Audubon great distress and slowed his acceptance by some members of the scientific community.

As his dealings with Audubon reveal, Ord was a man of quick temper and strong opinion. He opposed industrialization and "the gaudiness of wealth." He mistrusted emerging technology such as the transatlantic telegraph, which he classed "among the most stupendous follies which ever incited the gullibility of man." An outspoken nationalist, he advocated limits to immigration. "What other country but ours would be so stupid as to permit other countries to impose the burden of maintaining their poor?" he wrote. His correspondence with English naturalist Charles Waterton reveals that he was a devout Catholic, though whether from birth or by conversion is unclear. Ord was a stern and often irascible figure who, according to a contemporary observer, "was very much respected but not very much loved." An "elegant belles-lettres scholar" who "shone in conversation" with those he liked, Ord could be shy, reserved, and even hostile toward strangers. He is said to have "detested children."

Ord outlived many of his friends and, turning more misanthropic with each year, eventually became a virtual recluse. In the last decade of his life he "renounced all the active pleasures of society," deriving what pleasure he could "from the fruits of literature." After his death in Philadelphia, Ord's extensive library of scientific works went to the College of Physicians of Philadelphia and the remainder of his estate, estimated at between $16,000 and $40,000, to the Pennsylvania Hospital for the Insane, where his wife had been institutionalized for most of their marriage. His son predeceased him by one year. Ord is buried near his old friend Alexander Wilson at Gloria Dei ("Old Swedes") Church in Philadelphia.

• George Ord's extensive notes and journals appear to have been lost, but there are useful collections of his letters at the American Philosophical Society, the Academy of Natural Sciences of Philadelphia, and the Houghton Library at Harvard University. A biographical sketch by Samuel Rhoads, although poorly written, is in *Cassinia: A Bird Annual, Vol. 12, 1908* (1909). References to Ord appear in Clark Hunter, *The Life and Letters of Alexander Wilson* (1983), and Walter Faxon, "Early Editions of Wilson's Ornithology," American Ornithologists Union, *Auk* 17 (Apr. 1901): 216–18. A brief but revealing firsthand reminiscence of Ord can be found in

Frank L. Burns, "Miss Lawson's Recollections of Ornithologists," *Auk* 34 (July 1917): 275–82. An obituary is in the *Philadelphia Public Ledger*, 26 Jan. 1866 but, curiously, not in any of the publications of the two institutions to which he devoted most of his intellectual life, the Academy of Natural Sciences of Philadelphia and the American Philosophical Society.

ROBERT MCCRACKEN PECK

ORDRONAUX, John (3 Aug. 1830–20 Jan. 1908), medico-legalist, was born in New York City, the son of John Ordronaux, a businessman, and Elizabeth Charreton. The elder John Ordronaux, a native of France, had commanded an American privateer during the War of 1812 and remained after the war in the United States, where he acquired and operated a sugar refinery. On his father's death in 1841, eleven-year-old John was adopted by John Moulton of Roslyn, New York, who assumed the rest of his upbringing.

After finishing primary education in Roslyn, Ordronaux completed a liberal arts degree at Dartmouth College in 1850 and a law degree at Harvard Law School in 1852. Admitted to the bar in 1853, he practiced law for two years in Taunton, Massachusetts, before returning to New York City. Ordronaux also became interested in medicine during the 1850s and mastered enough classical medical theory to justify the award of an M.D. from the National Medical College of Washington, D.C. (now George Washington University), in 1859. In 1861 Columbia College appointed him to teach medical jurisprudence, or legal medicine, a subject that became the principal focus of the rest of his professional life. He occupied a chair in that subject at Columbia until 1897 and at various times through 1908 taught medical jurisprudence at National Medical College, Dartmouth, the University of Vermont, and Boston University as well as Columbia.

The state of New York in 1861 appointed Ordronaux examining surgeon to inspect Civil War recruits in Brooklyn, the first of several governmental appointments that he would hold during the next three decades. In conjunction with examining soldiers, Ordronaux published two works on military medicine that were widely used by other doctors during the Civil War. Those studies launched a publishing career that would eventually include dozens of articles and several books on various aspects of the general subject of medical jurisprudence. Many of those publications had national significance, particularly in the areas of expert testimony and mental impairment. Perhaps the best known of his major books appeared in 1869, *The Jurisprudence of Medicine in Its Relation to the Law of Contracts, Torts and Evidence*. Ordronaux also published translations of classical Latin poetry and of early Roman health codes.

During the 1870s, along with most other American medico-legalists of the time, Ordronaux became deeply involved in issues associated with insanity. This was an era when medical theories about insanity were in flux and as a result, so were the judicial and legal implications of insanity. Ordronaux published extensively on the hotly debated new diagnoses of moral insanity and temporary insanity, the insanity defense in various legal proceedings, and the disposition of the criminally insane. He resented what he regarded as manipulation of the insanity defense by ambitious lawyers and well-paid expert witnesses. In this context Ordronaux became a strong advocate for expert juries in medico-legal cases, especially cases involving insanity, because he did not consider ordinary citizens capable of making difficult medical distinctions or rendering scientific judgments.

In 1873 a politically divided session of the New York state legislature attempted to solve some of the tangled legal problems associated with insanity by creating a Lunacy Commission, the first of its kind in the country. The commission was designed to expedite judicial proceedings that involved insanity and to oversee some of the legal aspects of the state's insane asylums. Ordronaux was appointed to head the commission. But his ten-year stint as New York commissioner in lunacy proved frustrating and contentious. He crossed professional swords with other practitioners prominent in the field, notably William A. Hammond; he broke with the state's asylum superintendents, who resented both his criticisms and his implied authority over their domain; and he was forced repeatedly to defend his commission before ideologically hostile and financially tightfisted legislators. When Ordronaux stepped down in 1882, little had been accomplished.

Through the rest of the 1880s and 1890s Ordronaux resumed his professional research and writing, which culminated in 1891 with the publication of *Constitutional Legislation in the United States*, his most ambitious foray into political theory and his last major treatise.

A longtime friend noted Ordronaux's "almost morbid prudence in expenditure," despite considerable wealth, and Ordronaux's compulsive attention to his own personal health, which affected his diet, clothing, and sleeping habits. The bacteriological theory of disease was introduced to American physicians during the last decades of the nineteenth century, and Ordronaux embraced it with such fervor that he disinfected his paper money and kept tarred rope (tar was thought to kill bacteria) in his purse.

Ordronaux's career spanned a major transition in the history of American professions. In his somewhat holistic approach to professional issues and in his failure as a medico-legal officer of the state, he echoed earlier developments that were coming to an end. In his own formal education, in his commitment to university training as a professor, and especially in his many well-researched scholarly publications, he prefigured twentieth-century patterns. He died in Glen Head, New York. He had never married and left no close relatives.

• While some of his letters and poetry exist in other manuscript collections, no major repository of Ordronaux's private papers seems to have survived. But Ordronaux's many publications document his intellectual interests and professional contributions. The *Index-Catalogue of the Library of the Surgeon General's Office* (5 ser., 1880–1961) is the best place to locate most of those publications. Ordronaux's stormy term as New York commissioner in lunacy may be followed in his reports to the legislature and in several articles that appeared during the 1870s and 1880s in the *Albany Law Journal*. Because both authors knew Ordronaux personally, G. Alder Blumer's entry in the *Dictionary of American Biography* and Thomas Hall Shastid's entry in *American Medical Biographies* contain original material of a personal nature; the quotation in the text is from Blumer. James C. Mohr, *Doctors and the Law: Medical Jurisprudence in Nineteenth-Century America* (1993), discusses Ordronaux's place in the evolution of his principal field. An informative obituary is in the *New York Tribune*, 21 Jan. 1908.

JAMES C. MOHR

ORDWAY, John (c. 1775–c. 1817), soldier and member of the Lewis and Clark expedition, was born in Dumbarton, New Hampshire. Sergeant John Ordway is one of the least known of the noncommissioned officers of the Meriwether Lewis and William Clark expedition, despite being the most diligent journal-keeper with the Corps of Discovery. He made an entry for every single day the explorers went out, from 14 May 1804 to 23 September 1806. Like so many men of the party, however, Ordway lived an obscure life before and after his brief season of glory and left little trace of himself beyond his expedition years.

Ordway joined the expedition from Captain Russell Bissell's company of First Infantry at Fort Kaskaskia, Illinois, and was placed on the party's roll on 1 January 1804. It is apparent, however, that he was in active service to the expedition some time before that date. Ordway was the only one of the original sergeants to come from the regular army with that rank, and probably for that reason he often took care of the paperwork and was in charge when the captains were absent. Ordway served as top sergeant at the wintering camp of 1803–1804 at Wood River, Illinois, across the Mississippi River from St. Louis. During the captains' absences during that period he had to deal with a sometimes rowdy contingent, bored by camp life and straining at military discipline. Lewis and Clark were clearly pleased with his performance and more than once praised his leadership and judgment at Wood River. Ordway seldom appears in the captains' journals except in references to his carrying out some useful duty, attesting again to his reliability.

His excitement at the prospect of the historic journey is apparent in a letter he wrote to his "Honored Parence" shortly before the party set out: "I am now on an expidition to the westward. . . . We are to ascend the Missouri River with a boat as far as it is navigable and then to go by land, to the western ocean, if nothing prevents." He expected to receive a "great Reward," of "15 dollars pr. month and at least 400 ackers of first Rate land, and if we make Great Discoveries as we expect, the united states, has promised to make us Great Rewards more than we are promised."

Lewis and Clark purchased Ordway's three-volume expedition journal for $300 after the endeavor. In 1810 the notebooks were given to Nicholas Biddle when he prepared a narrative account of the expedition. Biddle found Ordway's journal to be his most valuable resource after the diaries of the two captains. He kept the notebooks, which were rediscovered among his papers in 1913. The sergeant's journal was first published in 1916. Ordway does not record the detailed information that the captains did nor their wealth of scientific data. The events of each day were the sergeant's primary concern, yet he shows evidence of curiosity and an interest in the things and people around him. He noted, for instance, that the grizzly bear was one "which the natives and the french tradors call white but all of the kind that we have seen is of a light brown only owing to the climate as we suppose." Only later did Lewis and Clark come to understand the variety of coloration in grizzlies. While among the Flathead Indians on the Montana–Idaho border, Ordway observed that they had "the Stranges language of any we have ever yet Seen. they appear to us as though they had an Impedement in their Speech or brogue on their tongue. we think perhaps that they are the welch Indians." Ordway revived once more the old legend of elusive Welsh Indians in the deep interior of the continent.

After the expedition Ordway accompanied Lewis and a party of Indians to Washington, D.C., and then returned to New Hampshire, having taken his discharge. In 1809 he settled in Missouri, became prosperous, and married (date unknown). He and his wife, Gracy, had died by 1817, apparently with no survivors.

• Information about Ordway's service in the Lewis and Clark expedition is in Gary E. Moulton, ed., *The Journals of the Lewis and Clark Expedition* (8 vols., 1983–); Donald Jackson, ed., *Letters of the Lewis and Clark Expedition with Related Documents, 1783–1854*, 2d ed. (2 vols., 1978); and Milo Milton Quaife, ed., *The Journals of Captain Meriwether Lewis and Sergeant John Ordway Kept on the Expedition of Western Exploration, 1803–1806* (1916). The best biographical sketch is in Charles G. Clarke, *The Men of the Lewis and Clark Expedition: A Biographical Roster of the Fifty-one Members and a Composite Diary of Their Activities from All Known Sources* (1970).

GARY E. MOULTON

O'REILLY, Alejandro (1723?–23 Mar. 1794), first Count O'Reilly and Spanish general, was born Alexander O'Reilly at Baltrasna, County Meath, Ireland, the son of Thomas Reilly, a Catholic Irish nobleman and Rose McDowel. His place of birth is usually incorrectly listed as Dublin; his exact date of birth is unknown, but he was baptized on 24 October 1723. His parents took him to Spain while he was a child. He received some education in the Colegio de las Escuelas Pias at Zaragoza. At age ten O'Reilly became a cadet in the Hibernia Regiment. He participated in the regiment's Italian campaigns of 1734–1736 and 1740–1748, rising to the rank of sergeant major. During these campaigns he came to the attention of a fellow Irish expatriate, Ricardo Wall, later minister of foreign affairs for Carlos III. Wounded at the battle of Camposanto (8 Feb. 1743), O'Reilly limped for the rest of his life.

Between 1748 and 1762 O'Reilly studied tactics with the Austrian and French armies and was promoted to colonel on the personal recommendation of Louis XV of France. When he returned to Spain he was given command of one of the armies that invaded Portugal in 1762. Afterward he was promoted to the rank of brigadier general (*maestre de campo*) and made inspector general of the army.

In 1763 O'Reilly accompanied the Conde de Ricla when the latter took an army to reestablish Spanish control of Havana following the British occupation (1762–1763). O'Reilly established a trained, disciplined militia and wrote the ordinances for it. He also wrote a report on the political and economic situation in Cuba that influenced Carlos III's decision of 1765 to allow "free trade" between Spain's major ports and the Spanish Caribbean islands. From Cuba O'Reilly was sent to Puerto Rico, where he carried out a similar militia reform and drafted a similar report. For his Cuban service he was promoted to major general (1763). He became a member of the military order of Alcántara in 1765.

Returning to Spain, O'Reilly married Rosa de las Casas y Aragorri, sister of General Luis de las Casas, later captain general of Cuba. The couple had five children. O'Reilly also got deeper into court politics, securing the favor of Carlos III and Jerónimo Grimaldi, by then secretary of state. After the Hat and Cloak Riots in Madrid in 1766, O'Reilly commanded the troops that restored order. In 1767 he was promoted to lieutenant general. He wrote the army ordinance of 1768.

O'Reilly was the obvious choice to lead the expeditionary army ordered to Louisiana after the revolt of 1768 that deposed Governor Antonio de Ulloa. Moving with great speed and secrecy, O'Reilly sailed for Havana. There he took advantage of the results of the military reforms he had promoted five years before to raise a force of 2,056 soldiers. Sailing in twenty-one mostly small ships on 6 July 1769, the expedition dropped anchor inside the mouth of the Mississippi River on 20 July. O'Reilly occupied New Orleans on 18 August. Within days he had arrested the leaders of the rebellion, confiscated their property, and turned their cases over to Felix del Rey, a prosecutor brought along for the occasion. The cases were concluded on 20 October; four days later O'Reilly signed the suggested sentences. The next day, at 3 P.M., five of the six leaders were shot (the sixth had died of natural causes while under arrest). Six others were sent to Havana to serve sentences of various lengths. All eventually were allowed to go to France.

During the rest of 1769 and the first two months of 1770, O'Reilly carried out a sweeping replacement of French with Spanish institutions and legal systems, although he retained many provisions of the French slave code. New Orleans received a cabildo, or town council; a budget and tax code were decreed; the trade decree of 1768, which had directly caused the rebellion, was put into force, but with limited trade to Havana to provide additional opportunities for profit for Louisiana planters and merchants. Indian relations, church matters, and every aspect of governmental concern as then conceived received his attention. Most of his decrees remained in force until the end of the Spanish regime in Louisiana in 1803.

When he returned to Spain in 1770, O'Reilly was rewarded with a pension and the post of inspector general of the Army of America. Using that office, he extended the militia reform to Santo Domingo and New Granada. In 1771 Carlos III named him Conde de O'Reilly and Visconde de Cavan, effective 28 January 1772. He was made the governor of Madrid and its district. With royal support, he founded the Military Academy of Ávila for the training of infantry officers.

O'Reilly's fortunes turned in 1775 when he commanded a disastrous attack on Algiers in which his force suffered 4,500 casualties out of 22,000 men and withdrew without besieging the city. His enemies at court forced Carlos III to exile him to Andalucia, where he served as captain general until 1786, playing an important role in sending troops that took part in Bernardo de Gálvez's conquests of Mobile and Pensacola. As governor of Cadiz, 1780–1786, he directed major capital improvements in the city. Returning to court, his involvement in a plot to overthrow the conde de Floridablanca led to his exile to Galicia in 1792, to conduct inspections. That done, he retired to Valencia. He was recalled to active duty in 1794 to lead the army of Catalonia against the French, but he died at Bonete, Murcia, on the way to his post. He is buried in Bonete.

O'Reilly was taller than average, of robust build, with blue eyes and a somewhat prominent nose. Confident, even arrogant, he was a better politician and staff officer than a field commander. In Louisiana, he is remembered for the execution of the rebels of 1768 rather than for the far more important reforms he imposed or for his efforts to loosen the restrictive trade policy (as New Orleanians perceived it) that had provoked the rebellion.

• Biographical data can be found in Bibiano Torres Ramírez, *Alejandro O'Reilly en Las Indias* (1969); David K. Texada, *Alejandro O'Reilly and the New Orleans Rebels* (1970); Vicente Rodríguez Casado, *Primeros Años de la dominación Española en la Luisiana* (1942); and David K. Bjork, "Alejandro O'Reilly and the Spanish Occupation of Louisiana, 1769–1770," in *New Spain and the Anglo-American West*, ed. George Hammond, vol. 1 (1932). The significance of O'Reilly's activities in Cuba are discussed in Allan J. Kuethe, *Cuba, 1753–1815: Crown, Military, and Society* (1986). His activities in Louisiana are also described in John P. Moore, *Revolt in Louisiana: The Spanish Occupation 1766–1770* (1976), pp. 190–225. O'Reilly's years at Cadiz are covered by Pablo Antón Sole, *El Cadiz de Conde de O'Reilly* (1969). For his lineage see Eric Beerman, "Un bosquejo biográfico y

genealógico del general Alejandro O'Reilly," *Hidalguía* 24 (Mar.–Apr. 1981): 225–44; and John O'Hart, ed., *Irish Pedigrees*, vol. 1 (1915), pp. 743, 747.

PAUL E. HOFFMAN

O'REILLY, John Boyle (28 June 1844–10 Aug. 1890), writer, was born in Castle Dowth, near Drogheda, County Meath, Ireland, the son of William David O'Reilly, a schoolmaster, and Eliza Boyle. Educated by his father, O'Reilly early gained newspaper experience by working, beginning at age eleven, first as an apprentice for the Drogheda *Argus* until 1858, and then as a compositor and reporter at the *Guardian* in Preston, Lancashire, England. At age nineteen he joined the English army (Tenth Hussars) in order to urge its Irish soldiers to support the revolutionary Fenian movement, which sought to liberate Ireland from English rule. Because of his success in gaining recruits for the Fenian cause, in 1866 O'Reilly was court-martialed for treason and was sentenced to death, a sentence ultimately commuted to imprisonment for twenty years. After months of solitary confinement at Millbank prison, he was transferred to Portsmouth and then to Dartmoor prison, from which he tried unsuccessfully to escape. In 1867 he was sent, with other political prisoners, to a penal colony in Bunbury, near Fremantle, in Western Australia; during the voyage, he helped edit the ship journal. With the assistance of Father Patrick McCabe, he escaped and left Australia on the American whaler *Gazelle* in February 1869. In November, after numerous adventures at sea, he arrived in Philadelphia, Pennsylvania, aboard the *Bombay* and received naturalization papers. The next month, under the sponsorship of the Fenian society, he lectured in New York. He settled in Boston, Massachusetts, where he began his new life.

Soon after arriving in Boston, O'Reilly joined the staff of the Boston *Pilot*. Although strongly pro-Ireland, he criticized the Fenian raid into Canada in June 1870. With the *Pilot* he instilled pride among Irish Americans by arguing that they could significantly influence the emancipation of Ireland. In 1872 he married Mary Murphy, by whom he had four daughters. He published his first volume of verse, *Songs from the Southern Seas*, in 1873.

O'Reilly remained a faithful Fenian, going so far as to help plan with other members of the Clan na Gael, in 1875, a rescue of the six Fenians remaining in the Bunbury jail; the plan was successfully executed the following year. O'Reilly became editor of the *Pilot*—a position he retained for the rest of his life—and in 1876 he and Archbishop John J. Williams of Boston purchased it from the financially distressed Patrick Donahoe. Under Williams and O'Reilly, the *Pilot* became the major Irish-American newspaper.

In 1878 O'Reilly published the second of his four volumes of verse, *Songs, Legends and Ballads*; the other two are *The Statues in the Block* (1881) and *In Bohemia* (1886). His poetry is characterized by energy and vividness but not by craftsmanship. Also in 1878 O'Reilly began serial publication of "Moondyne Joe" in the *Pilot*; it appeared in 1879 as the novel *Moondyne*, which concerns a convict who escapes imprisonment in Western Australia and becomes a social reformer. O'Reilly's only other novel was the futuristic *The King's Men* (1884), a collaborative effort with Robert Grant, Frederic J. Stimson (as J. S. of Dale), and John T. Wheelwright in which King George V flees to America during a democratic revolt and the Irishman O'Donovan Rourke, president of the British republic, deals with various royalist uprisings. O'Reilly, an avid athlete, also wrote *Ethics of Boxing and Manly Sport* (1888), an autobiographical and sentimental review of the history of boxing that details the value of it and such sports as rowing and swimming.

O'Reilly championed the downtrodden, and not only the Irish. He actively supported African Americans and became a friend of Frederick Douglass. O'Reilly's revolutionary temperament stemmed from his fiery, romantic spirit. Fundamentally, though, he was a social idealist who believed in the precepts of democracy, including a strong conviction that all people should be free and treated justly.

O'Reilly received two honorary doctorates, one from Notre Dame (1881) and the other from Georgetown University (1889). He died at his home in Hull, Massachusetts, from an accidental overdose of chloral, a medication for insomnia, and is buried at the Holywood Cemetery in Brookline, Massachusetts.

• O'Reilly edited *Poetry and Songs of Ireland* in 1889; his *Poems and Speeches* appeared in 1891. For information about O'Reilly, see James Jeffrey Roche, *Life of John Boyle O'Reilly* (1891); William G. Schofield, *Seek for a Hero* (1956); and Francis G. McManamin, *The American Years of John Boyle O'Reilly* (1959; rev. ed., 1976). Also see John R. Betts, "The Negro and the New England Conscience in the Days of John Boyle O'Reilly," *Journal of Negro History* 51 (1966): 246–61.

BENJAMIN FRANKLIN V

O'REILLY, Leonora (16 Feb. 1870–3 Apr. 1927), labor organizer and progressive reformer, was born in New York City, the daughter of John O'Reilly, a printer, and Winnifred Rooney, a garment worker. Leonora's father died a year after she was born, and she spent her childhood watching her mother struggle to earn a wage that would support the household. Following a few years in elementary school, Leonora joined her mother in the garment trades, taking a job at a collar factory at age eleven.

Winnifred O'Reilly instilled in Leonora an appreciation for the role of organized labor in the lives of workers and specifically in the lives of women workers. Leonora learned these lessons at her mother's knee, in union meetings, and under the tutelage of family friends such as John Baptist Hubert and Victor Drury. She joined the Knights of Labor in 1886 when she was sixteen and began her lifelong career as a labor activist, organizer, educator, and feminist. In the same year she joined the Knights of Labor, O'Reilly began to attend meetings of the Comte Synthetic Circle, a Lower East Side self-education group led by printer and labor activist Edward King. Books, ideas, and so-

cial reform movements were discussed in this group, and O'Reilly's informal education was substantially advanced in this setting, which became a source of intellectual support for the balance of her life.

O'Reilly's young leadership abilities were fostered as a founding member in 1886 of the Working Women's Society, which brought women workers together to improve working conditions through fact sharing and legislation. Her work with the society attracted the attention of Louise Perkins, a prominent and wealthy social activist and labor sympathizer, who became a mentor and lifelong friend to O'Reilly. With Josephine Shaw Lowell, Perkins introduced her to the Social Reform Club, an important organization in New York comprised of easterners who were prominent in social reform work. O'Reilly joined the club in 1894 and through it expanded her circle of supporters and influence.

O'Reilly's garment trades work continued as she gained prominence as a labor organizer. She was made forewoman of the shirtwaist shop where she worked in 1894, and she continued organizing women shirtwaist workers and establishing links with the leadership of the United Garment Workers. In the fall of 1897 O'Reilly established an experimental cooperative shirtwaist shop at the Henry Street Settlement House, with the support of Lillian Wald. This venture, which lasted for only a year, took her out of the toil of the shop and into the education of workers, which became a major interest for the rest of her life.

With the support of Louise Perkins, O'Reilly pursued a domestic arts course at Pratt Institute in Brooklyn (1898–1900) and at the same time took on the job of head resident at Asacog House, a Brooklyn social settlement. She went on to teach machine sewing at the Manhattan Trades School for Girls in 1902 and held that post until 1909.

O'Reilly was a founding member of the New York chapter of the Women's Trade Union League (WTUL) (1903) and a member of the first board of the organization. The WTUL represented the causes that were most important to Leonora O'Reilly: working conditions for women, unionism, and industrial education. Through the league O'Reilly met Mary Dreier and her sister Margaret Dreier Robins, two prominent and wealthy social reformers who were so impressed with O'Reilly's fire that they convinced her to accept an annual annuity so she could be a full-time activist. According to Edward T. James, an editor of the NWTUL papers, during the years following her acceptance of the annuity (1909–1914) her "public career reached its peak."

Her main mode of expression and influence was public speaking, and she used her eloquent and passionate speeches to fire up support for her causes. She was a leader in the Shirt Waistmakers' strike of 1910–1911; she organized the 1911 protest surrounding the Triangle Shirt Waist Fire; also in 1911 she helped found the New York City Wage Earner's Suffrage League; and she was among the founders of the National Association for the Advancement of Colored

People in 1909. She campaigned for equity for girls and women in vocational education, arguing before the Federal Commission on Vocational Education in April 1914 that it was unreasonable to "put the girl off in a corner making bows when she might make a much better carpenter than the boy." Her work in vocational education resulted in her appointment to the Advisory Board on Vocational Education of the New York City Board of Education.

While her interests expanded to include peace activities just before World War I, and she traveled to The Hague in 1915 to attend the International Congress of Women as the representative of the NWTUL, O'Reilly steadily curtailed her public activities in the next twelve years because of ill health. She resigned from the NWTUL in September 1915 because of nagging differences of perspectives between herself and league leadership; however, she remained in touch with NWTUL friends. One of her last known public activities was to assist Robins in the organization of the International Conference on Working Women in Washington, D.C. She died in Brooklyn of heart disease.

Leonora O'Reilly, who never married, is best known for her work as a feminist labor activist. Her ability to inspire was a remarkable talent, as evidenced by Margaret Dreier Robins's tribute upon hearing of her death: she was "a great and glorious rebel."

• The most complete source of information on Leonora O'Reilly is her collection of papers (sixteen boxes), part of the National Women's Trade Union League Papers, Schlesinger Library, Radcliffe College. Ellen Condliffe Lagemann's biographical essay, "Leonora O'Reilly," is in *A Generation of Women: Education in the Lives of Progressive Reformers* (1979). Also helpful is Mary J. Bularzik, "The Bonds of Belonging: Leonora O'Reilly and Social Reform," *Labor History* 24, no. 1 (1983): 60–83. An obituary is in the *New York Times*, 4 Apr. 1927.

JANE BERNARD-POWERS

ORKIN, Ruth (3 Sept. 1921–16 Jan. 1985), photographer and filmmaker, was born in Boston, Massachusetts, the daughter of Sam Orkin, a toy-boat manufacturer, and Mary Ruby, a former silent-screen actress and cellist. She grew up, however, near Los Angeles, California, and attended Beverly Hills High School and then Eagle Rock High School, graduating in 1939. Orkin briefly attended Los Angeles City College, where she majored in photojournalism.

Orkin first became interested in photography at age ten when she was given a 39-cent Univex camera. When she was twelve, her mother gave her a darkroom set enabling her to develop pictures on her own. Throughout her teenage years, her interest in photography intensified, and in 1937 she won a prize in a *Women's Home Companion* photography contest. She continued to develop her own pictures and even mixed her own chemicals after requesting the formulas from Kodak. Still photography, however, was not her first love; it was film. She attended with her mother show openings at Grauman's Egyptian in Hollywood and

filled her diary with details of movies she had seen. Although she was an autograph-seeker, Orkin soon decided that photographs of movie stars and celebrities were more interesting. Her first celebrity photograph was of Burgess Meredith taken on Hollywood Boulevard in 1937. Also as a teen, she succeeded in capturing Howard Hughes on film by anticipating his camera-shyness and positioning herself at a side door while the press waited for him to exit at the front. "In order to get to that side door, I had to crawl under the dais. Because I was wearing bobby socks and carrying a $1 Brownie, no one bothered me" (*Popular Photography*, June 1977, p. 109). Orkin's interest in film was more than just an infatuation with celebrity; she wanted to make movies as a career. But running a camera required membership in the Cinematographers' Union, and the union did not allow women members. In 1982 Orkin told an interviewer that she would not have become a still photographer if she had been allowed in the union.

Since her real interest was in film, Orkin saw her early experiences with photography as little more than a hobby. Another hobby was bicycle riding. After graduating from high school, she cycled across the country (she actually took automobile and train rides for the long hauls), staying at youth hostels and photographing her travels with a $16 Pilot 6 single-lens reflex. Orkin's journey earned her the attention of the media, and the teenage photographer was photographed often, her picture appearing in three of Chicago's newspapers while she was there.

Orkin's enjoyment behind the lens as a teenager led her to the Los Angeles Library, where she spent much time looking through camera annuals. At age eighteen, she determined that she would need a 35-mm camera to capture the types of pictures she wanted to take, but she could not afford one. It was at this time that she discovered the work of Morris Engel, whose ability to take candid, "real" photographs she admired. "I remembered his name," she was to recall. "In fact, I memorized it. On the streetcar coming home, I kept saying 'Morris Engel' because it was a lot easier than Alfred Eisenstaedt" (*Darkroom Photography*, Sept.–Oct. 1982, p. 22). Orkin and Engel eventually met and married in 1952; they would have two children.

In 1943 Orkin went to work for MGM as a messenger, becoming the first female hired in such a capacity. After six months in this position, she should have advanced to apprentice, but since she was a woman and did not have union support, she was not promoted. She soon left the studio, her hopes of running a camera in the film industry thwarted. She joined the Women's Auxiliary Army Corps (WAAC) after seeing a billboard promising training in filmmaking. Unfortunately, instead of being sent to Astoria, Long Island, for the training, she was sent to Fort Oglethorpe, Georgia, where no one knew anything about the moviemaking offer. She was discharged in the fall of 1943 (for an earlier back injury), once again having gained no experience in film.

Orkin moved to New York following her discharge from the army. As she pondered a vocation, she tried to find a way to include one of her hobbies in her professional work. "I wasn't good enough to be a professional cellist (she had taken lessons as a youth and learned, in part, from watching her mother play); cinematography was out . . . I couldn't make a living bicycling. So . . . only photography was left" (*A Photo Journal*, p. 29). In her first job as a photographer, Orkin took pictures in a nightclub in Queens, New York. She also assisted other photographers, took jobs photographing children in Manhattan's Central Park West, and freelanced for specialized publications such as *Publishers Weekly* and *Musical Courier*. In 1945 she received her first assignment for a major publication, the *New York Times*; she was hired to photograph Leonard Bernstein with his first orchestra, the New York City Symphony. Photographing Bernstein in this setting recalled for Orkin her love of classical music, an interest she had developed as a teenager. Soon thereafter, she wrote to the Boston Symphony Orchestra about taking photographs at the Tanglewood Music Festival to be held the summer of 1946; she was basically told not to bother. She went to Tanglewood anyway, easily got on the grounds, and soon had newspaper and magazine reporters asking her to take pictures to go along with their articles. Orkin considered Tanglewood her best school of all. "[It] was a dream come true. It was like the Hollywood Bowl, the Peter Meremblum Orchestra, a summer camp, a holiday resort, and a working and money-making experience all rolled into one. I couldn't have been more stimulated, prolific, or happy" (*A Photo Journal*, p. 30). She spent the next two summers at Tanglewood doing the same work, photographing some of the greatest musicians of the time, including Isaac Stern and Gregor Piatigorsky.

During her first summer at Tanglewood, Orkin worked with a Rolleiflex camera that she found difficult to use. With the money that she earned that summer and borrowing the rest, she was finally able to buy a 35-mm camera, a Contax, which she said led to "a whole new world of seeing" (*A Photo Journal*, p. 31). After double-exposing the first roll, she sold the second roll to *Look*, her first picture story in a national magazine. During the remainder of the 1940s and into the 1950s, Orkin enjoyed success as a freelancer, working for such publications as *Coronet*, *Ladies' Home Journal*, *Life*, *Collier's*, and *This Week*. Her work was praised by critics, editors, and curators alike. In 1947 she took a sequence of photographs titled "Jimmy, the Storyteller" to the Museum of Modern Art and days later received a flattering letter from Edward Steichen, the director of photography there. Orkin sent additional pictures to Steichen over the following years, and in 1955 another sequence, "The Cardplayers," was chosen for inclusion in the historic collection and book *The Family of Man*. Both "Jimmy, the Storyteller" and "The Cardplayers" are street scenes of children from Orkin's neighborhood; to Steichen they were "full of human expression" (*A Photo Journal*, p.

31). Orkin was included in all the museum's group photography shows until Steichen left in 1962.

Orkin's most intense period of shooting was from 1947 to 1952. She photographed such celebrities as Marlon Brando, Montgomery Clift, and Ava Gardner and continued to shoot candid photographs of "real" people. In 1951 *Life* magazine hired her to travel with the Israeli Philharmonic during its first American tour. She followed this assignment by traveling to Israel, where she spent two and a half months taking pictures that were eventually published in *Pageant*, *Modern Photography*, *Cosmopolitan*, *This Week*, and the ASMP Annual. She left Israel and went to Europe, where she spent five months. Her best-known photograph, "American Girl in Italy," was taken on this trip. This picture shows a beautiful American woman, a friend of Orkin's, walking along a Florence street looking somewhat nervous about the stares she is attracting from admiring men. This photograph, a "posed-candid," appeared in *Cosmopolitan* with a lengthy article titled "Don't Be Afraid to Travel Alone."

Also during the 1950s Orkin realized her dream of making a movie when she codirected, cowrote, and edited (with her husband) two 35-mm feature films, *Little Fugitive* (1953) and *Lovers and Lollipops* (1956). *Little Fugitive*, the story of a seven-year-old boy who thinks that he shot his brother and runs away to Coney Island, was nominated for an Academy Award, won the top prize at the 1953 Venice Film Festival, and was credited with influencing the New Wave cinema of France. After making these films Orkin returned to still photography. In 1959 her first child was born, and she dedicated herself to raising her family. She continued, however, to take pictures, many from her fifteenth-floor apartment window overlooking Central Park. Some of these pictures were collected in her books, *A World through My Window* (1978) and *More Pictures from My Window* (1983). By the end of the 1950s Orkin was voted one of the top ten female photographers in America.

In the 1960s Orkin mostly photographed her young children and scenes from her window, although she did accept some assignments, including one for *Horizon* magazine in 1963 to photograph a rising comedian, Woody Allen. In 1967 she was diagnosed with cancer but continued to take pictures and exhibit her work. She had solo shows in 1977 and 1981 at Witkin Gallery and a permanent exhibition at the Rizzoli bookstore, both in New York City. She also taught part-time at New York's School of Visual Arts. Orkin died at her home in New York. After her death, a twenty-year retrospective of her work was held at Witkin Gallery (1994) and "American Girl in Italy" was part of a traveling exhibition on women photographers (1997).

Ruth Orkin, a self-taught, critically acclaimed photographer, succeeded in breaking into photojournalism when women represented only a small percentage in the profession. Her work was featured in many top magazines and newspapers of the time and has continued to attract national attention. Orkin's photographic equipment was always simple, yet her pictures were in demand in part because of her ability to push their sale. "You've got to be able to convince people you're better than someone else if you want to succeed," she said. "You've got to have a lot of ego" (*Darkroom Photography*, Sept.–Oct. 1982, p. 23).

• Orkin's papers are not part of a formal collection but are housed in her Central Park West apartment and controlled by her estate. Orkin's pictorial autobiography, *A Photo Journal* (1981), provides a good timeline for her career. A brief biographical sketch is in Naomi Rosenblum's *A History of Women Photographers* (1994). An interview with Orkin appears in *Darkroom Photography*, Sept.–Oct. 1982, pp. 18–25, 29, and a retrospective on her life and work is featured in *Popular Photography*, June 1977, pp. 100–109, 144, 158. Obituaries are in the *New York Times*, 17 Jan. 1985, and *Popular Photography*, May 1985. A short film on Orkin's life and work is *Ruth Orkin: Frames of Life*, written, produced and directed by her daughter, Mary Engel. The film is in Engel's possession.

LISABETH G. SVENDSGAARD

ORONTONY, Nicholas (c. 1695–1750), headman of the Eronhisseronon matriclan of the Wyandots' Andiawich (Turtle) phratry, was born probably in or near the composite Huronian village the Jesuits had established at St. Ignace, on Michigan's Upper Peninsula. "Orontony" (a French corruption of the Huronian "Rontondi"), literally meaning "to make a tree," was ordinarily rendered in English as "War Pole." This title/name was bestowed in matrilineal succession on sequential incumbents of the headmanship of the Wyandots' second-ranking Turtle clan. The early life and antecedents of Orontony are undocumented. Certainly, he was baptized Nicholas, perhaps by the Reverend Armand de la Richardie, S.J., sometime after that missionary arrived at Detroit in 1728.

In 1747 Richardie's assistant and successor, the Reverend Pierre Potier, characterized Orontony as a "one-armed man." If Orontony had been crippled while serving in one of the numerous French-initiated Wyandot attacks on their Mississippi Valley Indian adversaries such as the Chickasaw, a common experience during his early manhood, then this disabling wound may help account for the great bitterness he displayed toward the French during the last decade of his life. There were, however, larger geopolitical factors at work in the anti-French, Wyandot separatist movement identified with Orontony's stewardship.

In the half century following the New York Iroquois' devastation of the Huronians' Ontario Peninsula homelands until 1701, many of the few survivors of these Northern Iroquoian tribes found refuge west of Lake Michigan. These refugees included most surviving Tionnontate (called Petuns or Tobacco Hurons by the French), fewer Wendats (called Hurons), and even fewer "Neutrals." French authorities denominated these displaced peoples "Hurons of the West," not distinguishing between their prior, autonomous tribal identities, and encouraged their amalgamation into a single integrated community under French political-economic and Jesuit ecclesiastical management. Eventually, soon after Cadillac founded Detroit, these "Hurons of the West" were pressured into resettling in several villages near that vital outpost to aid the French in blocking the expansion of British interests into the North American interior. They were also regularly enlisted in French forays against hostile tribes in the Mississippi Valley, required in order to maintain effective communications between New France and the Louisiana colony. In this period, these Huronians' closest native allies were the Algonquian Ottawa.

During youth and early manhood, Orontony knew the considerable stresses that resulted from French political-religious hegemony, the increasingly conflicted relationships between the many disparate tribes assembled near Detroit, and—in particular—the growing antipathy between these Huronians and their closest native associates and benefactors, the Ottawa, whom the Huronians' leaders regularly sought to exploit and manipulate. Orontony also experienced internal discord between catholicized and pagan Huronian factions and between the numerically superior Tionnontate (Petuns) and the fewer Wendat (Hurons). This discord was exacerbated by the favoritism shown the Tionnontate component by French authorities and the Jesuits, who were promoting the Tionnontates' leading chief, Sasteretsi, as "King of the Hurons."

During his early adult years Orontony also witnessed some of the intermittent British penetrations of the upper country, efforts made to establish trading relationships with the interior tribes. So he became aware of the disparity in prices and quality between French and English trade goods, which gave him some incentive for an English connection. He was also involved in the earliest Tionnontate-Wendat inroads into then-depopulated northwestern Ohio. Until the early 1720s, some years after the New York Iroquois threat had been eliminated, the Ohio country was nearly vacant of enduring human settlements. Hence, for the displaced Huronians, Ohio offered especially rich opportunities, including long-fallow farm lands; little-hunted populations of buffalo, elk, and deer; an abundance of beaver and other fur-bearing animals; a chance for the Huronians to establish a rich territory of their own under their control; a way for dissidents vexed with the French to escape their overlordship; improved geographic access for productive ties to English traders and colonial officials; and a means of establishing a paramount tribal polity in an area being resettled by other peoples—such as the Seneca (called Mingo), Miami, Shawnee, and Delaware—then also moving in from several directions.

Orontony's political career turned on strategies adopted both to meet these challenges and to resolve the stresses caused by French domination and the growing antagonism of former Ottawa allies. In the end, he and his associates, among these principally Angirot (headman of the Wendats' fourth-ranking Turtle clan), successfully forced a schismatic split among the so-called Hurons of the West. Most of the Wendat elements of this composite independently settled into and established their control over and ownership of northwestern Ohio. There, in diplomatic negotiations with Anglo-American colonial officials, they effectively reasserted their long-submerged separate Wendat political identity; and they quickly became known by the anglicized version of an older ethnonym, Wyandot, a name they insisted on.

These developments did not emerge in a preplanned fashion under Orontony's or anyone's direction. They began soon after the Huronians had been brought to the Detroit area, with initial explorations of Northwest Ohio and then exploitation of this area as winter hunting grounds. There followed the establishment of extended-family–sized horticultural plots and seasonal settlements, all at first mainly in the Lower Sandusky River plains. Neither did the eventual schism and large-scale migration into Ohio mature without efforts to explore alternative solutions. In the mid-1730s the Huronians, for instance, made a separate peace with the Chickasaw and Choctaw, annoying their French masters, and antagonizing the Ottawa, Potawatomi, and Chippewa, whose raiding parties the Huronians betrayed to the Mississippi Valley tribes. Because of Ottawa counterthreats, the bulk of the Huronians still near Detroit had to fortify their villages. Then, in 1738, Orontony and other leaders petitioned the French for permission to migrate to the St. Lawrence (where other Huron refugees were located), there to settle on Jesuit-managed *reductiones*. Since French authorities already had ample "domiciled" Indians located in several of these utopian communes, this appeal was rebuffed; the Huronians were wanted for service at Detroit.

The Wyandot immigrating into Ohio did not at first assemble in one locale. Some moved beyond the Sandusky region farther east, to the Cuyahoga, the Upper Ohio, and the Forks of the Muskingum rivers. Whether based at Sandusky under Orontony and Angirot or elsewhere, they intensified trade and political relationships with the British and soon became well known to such influential merchants as George Croghan and Andrew Montour. In 1745 a substantial Wyandot delegation met with Croghan and Montour at Logstown. They explained their plan to break away from the French, invoked the memory of an alleged fifty-year-old agreement with New York's governor, boastfully exaggerated the number of gunmen they could field in support of British interests, falsely claimed that the Delaware were allied with them and under their influence, called for a political-economic alliance, and insisted on being called "Wondot" (as Croghan first spelled this name), not Hurons.

That this step represented a sharp, permanent break with the French became evident from ensuing events. Following diplomatic representations to the Pennsylvanians, Orontony and his associates, in company with some Ottawa and Potawatomi, began plotting a direct, major assault on the French at Detroit during 1747. Although his plans were betrayed to the French,

who thwarted them, Orontony's Wyandot did attack and destroy the Jesuit *reductione* on Bois Blanc Island. They killed some unwary French traders, engaged in other hostile acts, and eventually established themselves as a separate tribal society in northwestern Ohio, more closely linked to their new British allies. Subsequently, they aided the British in their prolonged contest for control of the North American interior. To the last, Orontony remained violently anti-French and anti-Jesuit. Reportedly, his last dying wish was for his people to murder the Reverend Richardie. In his last years he conducted diplomatic negotiations with Sir William Johnson and New York colonial officials. He did not live long enough to see the fruition of his labors, dying in 1750, reportedly of smallpox.

Orontony was known for his opposition to French hegemony during the 1740s, for fomenting an anti-French intertribal Indian alliance and promoting an attack on Fort Pontchartrain at Detroit, for promoting separate Wyandot tribalism and settlement of Northwest Ohio, and for establishing diplomatic-economic ties to the English colonies, primarily Pennsylvania and New York. In these respects, by seeking a course independent of the supremacy of one European-American power in the Western Great Lakes region through casting alliances with a rival dominion, he was a forerunner of the now better known Pontiac and Tecumseh of later decades.

For almost a century after Orontony's death, the Ohio Wyandot flourished, becoming the recognized landholders of much of the region and the central point of intertribal diplomatic dealings. They invited numerous Delaware and Shawnee to live in association with them, and by the time of the American Revolution they were recognized as the paramount native polity in the region. However, by helping to dilute French power and by establishing strong ties to the British seaboard colonies and promoting secure overland trade with them at a critical moment in the history of the region, Orontony also contributed his share to the eventual French defeat at British hands and to the subsequent colonization of the Ohio country by Americans. These later developments, in 1843, led to the Wyandots' final displacement and removal, first to Kansas and then to Oklahoma. One of the Wyandots' leaders in this last migration was a successor to Orontony called Warpole by Americans; by 1843 he was a deacon of the Methodist Episcopal church and a thirty-third-degree Mason.

• For more background on the career of Nicholas Orontony and details concerning his life, see James A. Clifton, "The Re-emergent Wyandot: A Study of Ethnogenesis on the Detroit River Borderland, 1747," in *The Western District*, ed. K. G. Pryke and L. L. Kulisek (1983); W. A. Hunter, "Orontony," in *Dictionary of Canadian Biography*, vol. 3; Richard White, *The Middle Ground* (1991); and Lucien Campeau, *La Mission des Jesuites chez Les Hurons* (1987). Readers may consult these published works for full citations of the much-scattered primary source documentation of Orontony's life.

JAMES A. CLIFTON

ORR, Alexander Ector (2 Mar. 1831–3 June 1914), merchant, was born in Strabane, County Tyrone, Ireland, the son of William Orr (occupation unknown) and Mary Moore. Although Orr's parents had arranged a career for him with the East India Company, an accident in which he was injured delayed these plans. As part of his recuperation, Orr traveled to the United States in 1850 and visited Richmond, Washington, D.C., Baltimore, and Philadelphia. After returning to Ireland, Orr persuaded his parents to allow him to live permanently in the United States. In 1851 he arrived in New York City, where he lived and worked.

On his arrival Orr found employment as a clerk in local commission houses. In 1857 he married Juliet Buckingham Dows, daughter of Amzi Dows who was associated with the David Dows & Co. firm, one of the largest grain dealers in the country. They had three children. Orr began working for his father-in-law's firm in 1858. In 1861 he became a partner, and in 1863 he represented the firm on the floor of the Produce Exchange. Later he participated in the construction of the firm's $8-million grain elevator adjacent to Pacific Street in Brooklyn.

In 1872 Orr's first wife died; the following year, he married Margaret S. Luquer. His business activity increased markedly in the 1870s. He participated in the reorganization of the Produce Exchange from 1871 to 1872 and served as its president from 1887 to 1888. For many years he was the chairman of its committee for arbitration, and he helped organize its Benefit Assurance Society and its Gratuity Association. Orr was the secretary of the building committee that erected the Produce Exchange's new $3-million office building.

Orr's business success brought him to the attention of New York governor Samuel J. Tilden, who in 1875 appointed him to the four-member commission created by the New York legislature to investigate corruption in the canal business. The commission determined that during the previous five years several contractors had received fraudulent payments. Orr's association with Tilden grew closer, and in 1876 he served as one of Tilden's presidential electors. After Tilden's death in 1886, Orr became a trustee of the Tilden Trust, funds of which were used to build the New York Public Library main branch at Fifth Avenue in 1911.

In local borough politics, the Democrat Orr nominated Republican Seth Low for mayor of Brooklyn in both 1881 and 1883. Orr also played an instrumental role in reorganizing the Brooklyn Civil Service Commission. He held important positions with the Chamber of Commerce of the State of New York, including the offices of vice president (1889–1894) and president (1894–1899). During this period he paid particular concern to financial matters, bankruptcy reform, customs administration, and rapid transit.

Known widely for his integrity, in 1894 Orr was appointed a member of the Rapid Transit Commission (RTC), an agency created by the legislature to design a transit system for New York City; the RTC was also responsible for hiring a firm to build and operate the proposed system. Orr was elected chairman of the RTC at its first meeting and continued in this position until 1907, when the Public Service Commission assumed the responsibilities of the RTC.

After confronting a number of unwilling large financial institutions, Orr finally arranged financing for the construction of the New York subway system through financier August Belmont II. The main system, on which work was begun in 1900, was twenty-one miles long and cost $35 million. The first trains began operations in 1904, and Orr made a public presentation at the opening. The journal *World's Work* noted, in the article "Saving Civilization in New York by the Subway," "The subway in New York City, which brings in a new epoch in urban travel, has been built—in New York, too—without scandal; and very much of the credit for this historic achievement belongs to Mr. Alexander E. Orr, the president of the Rapid Transit Commission. He will long be held in honor for this incalculable contribution to democratic civilization" ([Mar. 1904]: 4512). The *New York Times* credited Orr "more than any other one man" for the "conception and planning of subway communication" (5 June 1914).

In January 1906 Orr was elected president pro tem of the New York Life Insurance Company, and he remained in this office until June 1907. He was installed as president briefly to allay potential worries of policyholders after the insurer's previous president was forced to resign in response to allegations of the Charles Evans Hughes investigation looking into corruption in life insurance companies operating in New York.

At one point during his active business and civic career, Orr served on twenty-nine boards, including the Brooklyn Library, Packer Collegiate Institute, the Long Island Historical Society, and Greenwood Cemetery Corporation. He also served on the board that arbitrated disputes between the city and Brooklyn Bridge contractors. He played an active role in the Reformation of Juvenile Delinquents and the Long Island State Hospital and served as vice president of the Academy of Music and Art Association. He was a member of the Anti-Vice Commission and the American Geographical Society. He also belonged to the Protestant Episcopal church and served for almost fifty years as the treasurer of the Long Island diocese of the church. He was one of the incorporators and trustees of the Garden City Cathedral.

Orr's second wife died in 1913, and less than a year later he died at his Brooklyn home, leaving an estate worth $5 million. The New York Chamber of Commerce, in recognition of Orr's life and services, appointed a committee of fifteen prominent people to attend his funeral, including John Pierpont Morgan (1867–1943). His pallbearers included former mayor Low and financier Belmont.

• For additional information on Orr's life and work, see Lawrence F. Abbot, *The Story of NYLIC: A History of the Origin and Development of the New York Life Insurance Company from 1845 to 1929* (1930); Alexander Clarence Flick, *Samuel J. Tilden: A Study in Political Sagacity* (1939); John E. Bigelow, ed., *The Writings and Speeches of Samuel J. Tilden* (2 vols., 1885) and *Letters and Lit. Memorials of Samuel J. Tilden* (2 vols., 1908); *Rapid Transit in N.Y. City and in Other Great Cities* (1905), prepared by the city's chamber of commerce; and *Catalogue of Portraits in the Chamber of Commerce* (1924), which includes a sketch and the copy of a portrait of Orr painted by A. H. Munsell, his son-in-law. Also see the annual reports during Orr's era of the New York State Chamber of Commerce and its monthly *Bulletin* (particularly the obituary in June 1914). A privately printed memorial, *In Memory of A. E. Orr*, was published in 1917; other obituaries and memorials are in the *New York Times*, 4–6 and 10 June 1914, and the *Brooklyn Daily Eagle*, 3 and 4 June 1914.

CHRISTOPHER CASTANEDA

ORR, Gustavus John (9 Aug. 1819–11 Dec. 1887), educator, was born in Orrville, Anderson County, South Carolina, the son of James Orr, and Ann Anderson. He grew up near Jefferson, Jackson County, Georgia, where his widowed father remarried and established himself as a nonslaveholding cotton farmer. After brief sessions at small country schools and an apprenticeship at age sixteen to a village merchant, Orr entered Maryville Seminary in East Tennessee at the age of twenty, transferred to Franklin College of the University of Georgia in 1841, and graduated from Emory College in Oxford, Georgia, with honors in 1844. He joined the college's preparatory school faculty in 1845 but returned home in 1846 to study law and supported himself as principal of the Jefferson town academy. In 1847 he married Eliza Caroline Anderson; they had ten children. After their wedding the couple undertook management of the Covington Seminary for girls. In 1849 Orr apparently abandoned plans to become a lawyer and accepted election to the chair of mathematics at Emory College.

In November 1859 Orr was appointed to a joint Georgia-Florida team that surveyed the disputed boundary between the two states. With the outbreak of the Civil War, Orr and a friend founded a shoe factory to supply the Confederate army, to which he was able to devote himself full time after Emory College closed in November 1861. When the tax act of April 1863 was passed by the Confederate Congress, Orr was appointed tax collector for the Seventieth District of Georgia, a position that he held through the war and one that resulted in his temporary disenfranchisement under the Reconstruction government.

After the war he worked briefly in an Atlanta business before serving as president of the financially troubled Southern Masonic Female College for three years. He then accepted the mathematics professorship at Oglethorpe University in Atlanta in 1870, where he remained until he was appointed state school commissioner in 1872.

Orr's major accomplishment lay in breaking ground for a system of publicly financed schools in Georgia, a state that had the highest illiteracy rate in the nation, as well as a reduced tax base at one-fourth of its prewar level, a population that was half emancipated slaves, and a strong antipathy among whites to both taxation and northern interference in southern affairs. Orr became a mediator among rival interests in his own state as well as between northern educators, philanthropists, and legislators and southern politicians and educators. He urged greater northern understanding of, and responsibility for, the unique problems that emancipation and the war had created and encouraged Georgians to recognize that their future depended on schooling for both black and white children.

Orr was a member of the committee of the new Georgia Teachers Association, which drafted public schooling legislation for the first session following the Constitutional Convention of 1867–1868. Because of federal intervention in the seating of representatives, however, the committee decided not to risk association of the public school bill with a government that incurred the wrath of most prominent Georgians and instead produced a "Report on a System of Public Schools for the State of Georgia," written by Orr and published in March 1870. The report clearly influenced the first Georgia public school law, which, passed in 1870, outlined a state system of publicly funded, racially segregated schooling under local control and included state-funded normal schools or departments in universities and colleges. Implementation of that law was blocked, however, by both resistance to the Reconstruction government's state school commissioner and his misuse of state schooling funds. When Orr was appointed state school commissioner in January 1872, he inherited a $300,000 debt and little public support, but his appointment in March 1872 as agent for the philanthropic Peabody Fund demonstrated northern confidence in his judgment and enabled him to maximize use of Peabody monies. He delayed the opening of schools for a year and began a public relations campaign to build on Georgia's own pre–Civil War public school legislation and to chart a course toward universal public schooling that could gain broad support: racially segregated schools with modest goals for length of school term and curriculum that were controlled at the county level by men of property. His dual role helped focus northern resources on Georgia's needs but undoubtedly contributed to his already heavy workload: he personally received and answered 4,450 letters in his first two years as state school commissioner and for the first five years in office traveled continually throughout the state to promote education and the local taxation legislation to support it.

Although increases to school fund income were added through taxes on liquor sales, convict labor, dogs, and railroad income, the empowering legislation for county taxation (which did not pass until 1904) eluded Orr, and he turned his energies to securing federal funding. Invited by the U.S. commissioner of education to attend the December 1877 organizational meeting of the National Education Association's Department of Superintendence, he returned home to help organize city and state superintendents into the

Southern Educational Convention, which supported national aid to states without federal controls on its use. His presentations to the NEA in 1879 and 1880 on southern educational needs brought him widespread recognition as the spokesman for the South. In 1881, as incoming NEA president (a one-year post), Orr successfully invited the general convention to meet in Atlanta that year, a meeting for which he primed his Georgia colleagues by pointing out the association's support of a policy that assured Georgia priority because of its high illiteracy rate but no disturbance of its segregated system. It was a major effort at North-South dialogue on the nature and support of public schooling.

Although Orr's drive for funding included support for teacher education, he did not consider college-level coursework necessary for teachers and instead favored establishing normal schools for whites and blacks that were separate from the universities. Failing to secure either the removal of the Peabody-supported normal school to Atlanta when its Nashville accommodations appeared threatened or the establishment of a normal school at Milledgeville, in 1882 he was able to launch three summer institutes for teachers throughout the state and struggled to increase their numbers over the next four years.

Eight months before his death, Orr made a direct appeal to Georgia's voters through a circular entitled "Read and Ponder," which pointed out that one-third of the population could not write their names, that 285,000 of the total 310,000 students in schools attended only three months a year or less, and that Georgia gave less support to schools than any other state in the nation. With legislation pending to authorize a tax of one dollar per $1,000 of assessed property value, which would provide four months of school for everyone, he pled: "The property is yours, the children are yours, the representatives are yours. . . . Should this state of things continue?" Although the answer remained "yes" until the twentieth century, Orr had laid the foundations for change. Historian Oscar Joiner remarked that Orr "literally was worked to death" overseeing the nearly 7,000 schools that had been established during his sixteen years in office, managing Peabody Fund affairs in Georgia, and personally providing teacher education to the state with virtually no funding in his relentless crusade to focus northern and southern energies alike on the educational needs of the postwar South. Orr died in Atlanta.

• The most detailed biography of Orr, which draws on family documents as well as published sources and provides an extensive bibliography, is by Orr's granddaughter Dorothy Orr, *Gustavus John Orr, Georgia Educator 1819–1877* (1971). His place in Georgia's educational history is recounted in Oscar H. Joiner et al., *A History of Public Education in Georgia 1734–1976* (1979), and Dorothy Orr, *A History of Education in Georgia* (1950). His work as State School Commissioner is documented in the Georgia *Annual Reports of the Department of Education to the General Assembly* (1872–1886).

KATHLEEN CRUIKSHANK

ORR, H. Winnett (17 Mar. 1877–11 Oct. 1956), orthopedic surgeon, was born Hiram Winnett Orr in West Newton, Pennsylvania, the son of Andrew Wilson Orr, a dentist, and Frances Josephine Winnett. After graduation from West Newton High School in 1892, Orr traveled to Lincoln, Nebraska, to live and study medicine with his uncle, Hudson J. Winnett. A medical career had been planned for young Orr, and his uncle had agreed to provide financial assistance for his education. Orr studied at the University of Nebraska and assisted Winnett in his practice. After graduation in 1895, Orr entered the University of Michigan, where he earned his medical degree in 1899. He had applied for an internship in Cleveland, Ohio, but Winnett was ill and needed help with his practice, so Orr returned to Lincoln.

Orr began his career with enthusiasm and energy. In addition to his practice he became managing editor of the *Western Medical Review* in 1899, a position he held until 1909. From 1900 to 1915 he taught a class on medical history and literature at the University of Nebraska. He was also librarian of the Nebraska State Medical Society (1900–1912). These early efforts established a course that extended beyond medical practice to writing, teaching, innovation, and contributions to medical literature and librarianship. One such contribution was "Medical Bibliography" in the *Western Medical Review* (1904). In 1974 Bernice M. Hetzner, former director of the University of Nebraska Medical Center library, called it "the beginning of medical library work in Nebraska."

In 1904 Orr left Winnett and their practice for a few months to train for a specialty. He had decided on pediatrics, but while in Chicago he met John Ridlon, an orthopedic surgeon and professor at Northwestern University. Orr was impressed with Ridlon's work and decided to switch to orthopedic surgery. He returned to Lincoln armed with a new specialty and ready for new opportunities. One soon presented itself.

While Orr was in Chicago, Lenore Perkey, a homeopathic practitioner in Nebraska, had begun to stimulate public interest in caring for crippled children. At the time, there were no facilities in Nebraska for their care. A chance encounter on a street corner between Perkey and Orr resulted in Orr's becoming involved with her cause and eventually led to the establishment, in 1905, of the Nebraska Orthopedic Hospital. The facility was created to provide state care for crippled children and was only the third institution of its kind in the United States. Lord of Omaha was chief surgeon, and Orr was superintendent and assistant physician.

In addition to these responsibilities, Orr helped to establish a public hospital, Lincoln General, and became chief surgeon for its orthopedic division. He also served as chief consultant and orthopedic surgeon at Bryan Memorial and Veterans' Administration hospitals. He continued these duties rather routinely until 1917, when the United States entered World War I. Joel E. Goldthwait called for volunteers to form a party of twenty orthopedic surgeons to assist Sir Robert Jones, the famous orthopedic surgeon of Liverpool, England. Orr volunteered, received the commission of captain, and was assigned to Cardiff in South Wales. Later he was transferred to the American Expeditionary Force in Savenay, France.

The war was a unique opportunity for Orr to practice and learn more about orthopedic surgery. He brought to each situation the fundamentals Ridlon had taught him: treatment by rest, fixed traction, healing in correct position, and preservation of function. Orr found that gunshot wound fracture created a most serious problem because the accepted method for treating these wounds was directly opposed to orthopedic principles. Physicians considered the wound the priority and applied a combination of wet chemical compresses and antiseptic irrigation, known as the Carrel-Dakin technique; however, this method disturbed the fracture and provided no rest. Debates were common as orthopedists urged uninterrupted rest. Orr and others advocated early splinting of the fractures and even plaster-of-Paris casts to immobilize these injuries. They argued that the body's natural healing properties would cure the wound. When these methods were applied, orthopedists reported successful healing of both fracture and wound; still, the issue was intensely debated.

Orr was discharged with the rank of lieutenant colonel in 1919. At home he continued to promote the methods he and his colleagues had used in the war. Orr advocated pin fixation in plaster, infrequent dressing, drainage, and rest as treatment for osteomyelitis, compound fractures, and other infected wounds, but criticism of the technique continued. Often denounced as a "quack" for using such methods, he also vied with others for recognition in the development of the technique. Another doctor, J. Trueta, used similar methods during the Spanish Civil War, and the Russians were experimenting with the technique based on the success Nikolai Pirogoff had through enclosing open wounds in plaster during the Crimean War. Orr felt that others claimed too much responsibility for developing what he maintained was his method. Today the technique bears Orr's name and is still both debated and used. One criticism is the increased risk of contracture, or limited use after healing (see Jacquelin Perry, "Contractures: A Historical Perspective," *Clinical Orthopaedics and Related Research*, no. 219 [June 1987]: 8–14); however, John F. Connolly wrote in the *Nebraska Medical Journal* (Feb. 1984), "The Orr technique has proven superior to other methods of external skeletal fixation. . . . To a great extent this has become a treatment of choice for U.S. military wounds but is less widely recognized in civilian practice" (p. 48).

In addition to his medical career, Orr was an avid book collector and established several important collections. The H. Winnett Orr Historical Collection of more than 2,000 volumes documents medical history and military medicine and contains more than 450 rare books and classics of medicine. Originally housed at the American College of Surgeons in Chicago, in 1974 the collection was placed on permanent loan in the Rare Books Room of the McGoogan Library of Medicine at the University of Nebraska Medical Center. Orr also collected more than 1,000 books on Anne of Brittany, a fifteenth-century French monarch with a congenital hip dislocation who captured Orr's fancy and professional curiosity.

Throughout Orr's life of service to medicine, medical literature, librarianship, and his adopted state, he received numerous awards and honors. He was an active member of the American Orthopedic Association, the American College of Surgeons, and the Nebraska State Medical Society.

Orr married Grace Douglass in 1904; they had five children. He died in Rochester, Minnesota. Though controversial at times, Orr's contributions to orthopedic surgery endure in the eponymous Orr method.

• Orr's papers are in the McGoogan Library of Medicine at the University of Nebraska Medical Center in Omaha. His major works include *Osteomyelitis and Compound Fractures and Other Infected Wounds: Treatment by Method of Drainage and Rest* (1929), *Wounds and Fractures: A Clinical Guide to Civil and Military Practice* (1941), and *On the Contributions of Hugh Owen Thomas of Liverpool, Sir Robert Jones of Liverpool and London, John Ridlon, M.D., of New York and Chicago to Modern Orthopedic Surgery* (1949). Important biographical sources include Sumner L. Koch, "Dr. H. Winnett Orr, 1877–1956," *Bulletin of the American College of Surgeons* 42 (1957): 118–21; L. Margueriete Prime and Kathleen Worst, *A Catalogue of the H. Winnett Orr Historical Collection and Other Rare Books in the Library of the American College of Surgeons* (1960); and Phyllis M. Japp and John F. Connolly, "H. Winnett Orr and the Nebraska Orthopaedic Hospital," *Nebraska Medical Journal* 70 (1985): 401–8.

MAGGIE YAX

ORR, James Lawrence (12 May 1822–5 May 1873), Speaker of the House of Representatives, governor of South Carolina, and Confederate States senator, was born in Craytonville, Pendleton District (now Anderson County), South Carolina, the son of Christopher Orr, a merchant, and Martha McCann. After a conventional education in the local schools, he began the study of law at the University of Virginia in 1839. Following the death of his favorite mentor there, he returned to South Carolina, read law in a local firm, and was admitted to the bar in 1843. A year later he married Mary Jane Marshall, a union that produced seven children. For two years he edited the *Anderson Gazette*, espousing orthodox Democratic party doctrine, including strict economy in government and the notion that slavery was essential to republicanism, which advocates personal independence (for whites) resting on a sound economic basis. Elected to the state legislature in 1844, he soon abandoned journalism and joined J. P. Reed in a highly successful law partnership, a venture that enabled him to devote most of his time and energies to his true vocation, politics.

In his two terms at the statehouse in Columbia, Orr was an able champion of upcountry economic interests and an adherent to the moderate Calhoun line on national issues. Although he upheld the right of secession, he was wary of precipitate moves in that direction and joined John C. Calhoun in opposing Robert Barnwell Rhett's attempt to revive the nullification question. Easily elected to Congress in 1848, he sought to dampen South Carolina's separatist tendencies as the sectional crisis deepened. An ardent defender of states' rights, Orr nonetheless argued that the South could best defend slavery by remaining within the Union. Hence, he sought an accommodation with conservative and moderate northern Democrats, in which the "special interests" of the South would be somehow protected. At home he promoted modest industrial development as a means of freeing the South from its heavy dependence upon agriculture, strengthening republicanism, and giving southerners more leverage in Washington. Assuming leadership of the strongest element in the state Democratic organization, he became, as his friend William Gilmore Simms put it, "simply a *national* man" and a recognized force in national politics. With the support of northern Democrats he was elected Speaker of the House of Representatives in 1857, a position that also made him a long-shot contender for his party's presidential nomination three years later.

By 1860, however, South Carolina had become irrevocably committed to secession, and Orr, if for no other reason than to protect his power and influence at home, went with the tide that led to disunion. He led the state's delegation out of the National Democratic Convention in 1860, signed the ordinance of secession, and plunged full tilt into the politics of the new Confederacy. Although he served briefly in the military, his most effective contribution to the cause was as a Confederate States senator, an office he held from December 1861 until the end of the war. Perhaps because he put great value on individual rights (for whites only, of course), he clashed with Jefferson Davis repeatedly over restrictive measures the Richmond government resorted to as the conflict lengthened. The most serious differences between the two men arose from Orr's judgment, almost from the start of the war, that the South was doomed to defeat. An early advocate of a negotiated peace, he blamed Davis for bringing on the ultimate Confederate catastrophe by adamantly resisting all efforts to seek a settlement that might effect some rearrangement of the Union to the South's benefit.

Orr quickly accepted the results of the war. An outspoken "conciliationist," he wrote in 1865 that "there can be no wrong or disorder in our accepting facts as they exist, and yield to national authority." As his state's first elected postwar governor, he advised whites to show "kindness, humanity and justice" in dealing with their former slaves, and he worked to soften the Black Codes and extend some civil rights, including limited suffrage, to the freedmen. Yet he also advised the state legislature to reject the Fourteenth Amendment, thereby helping measurably to delay the national reconciliation he so desired.

Orr foresaw military Reconstruction and the new role of blacks in state government, and he advised his friends to join him in accepting the inevitable. Few followed his lead, however, especially when he joined the Radical party in the hope of influencing its policies. After leaving the governorship, he sat for several years as a circuit judge, still vainly trying to temper conservative resistance to Reconstruction. In 1872 President Ulysses S. Grant named him minister to Russia, but he served in that capacity only a few months before he died of pneumonia in St. Petersburg.

More than most other southern leaders of the time, Orr understood northern public opinion and had at least some sense of national political trends. Skilled as he was, however, he was unable to break the grip of race prejudice that underlay the response of most white South Carolinians to Reconstruction. Part of the problem was his own ambivalence in matters racial. As prejudiced as any of his contemporaries, he nonetheless recognized that the postwar South could never return to its old ways. His search for a "reasonable accommodation" was a sincere one, doubtless; but it also opened him to charges of opportunism, as he shifted from one position—and party—to another. His antebellum ideological base was republicanism, but in the turmoil of the war and Reconstruction years, it slipped away, leaving him politically rootless and unable to fulfill the promise of his early career.

• Source materials include the Orr papers and pamphlets in the South Caroliniana Library of the University of South Carolina, the Orr-Patterson papers at the University of North Carolina–Chapel Hill, and the governorship papers at the South Carolina Archives. The only biography is Roger P. Leemhuis, *James L. Orr and the Sectional Crisis* (1979). For specific aspects of Orr's career see also Lacy K. Ford, Jr., *Origins of Southern Radicalism: The South Carolina Upcountry, 1800–1860* (1988); Stephen A. Channing, *Crisis of Fear: Secession in South Carolina* (1970); Francis B. Simkins and Robert H. Woody, *South Carolina during Reconstruction* (1932); and Joel Williamson, *After Slavery: The Negro in South Carolina during Reconstruction, 1861–1877* (1965).

JOHN G. SPROAT

ORR, Jehu Amaziah (10 Apr. 1828–9 Mar. 1921), jurist and legislator, was born in Craytonville, South Carolina, the son of Christopher Orr, a merchant, and Martha McCann. In 1843 he moved with his parents to Chickasaw County, Mississippi, where his father, a slaveholder, had purchased land. Orr developed an interest in politics and the legal profession at an early age. Residing in Houston, the county seat, he read law under the guidance of Winfield Scott Featherston, a young lawyer and an aspiring Democratic politician. At the age of seventeen Orr went to the Democratic convention in Jackson to promote Featherston's candidacy for a state office. Leaving home in 1846 to broaden his educational horizon, he studied in the liberal arts at Erskine College in South Carolina and in 1847 transferred to the College of New Jersey in Princeton. He received a bachelor of arts in 1849; he later returned to Princeton and received a master of arts in

1857. In June 1849 he was licensed to practice law and formed a partnership in Houston with Featherston, who then represented the district in Congress. Also the new owner and editor of a local newspaper, Orr actively supported his law partner's successful bid for reelection in 1849. With the protection of slavery in the territories an issue in the campaign, Orr asserted that the federal judiciary, rather than the Whig "doctrine of congressional interference," provided "the safest and surest protection" for the slaveholder (*Houston Patriot*, 7 Oct. 1849).

Orr moved rapidly up the ladder of success to achieve prominence in Mississippi's legal and political circles. At the age of twenty-one, he secured the elective post of secretary of the state senate and served two years. He then represented his county in the state house of representatives for a two-year term. From 1854 to 1856 he filled a presidential appointment to the office of the federal district attorney for the northern district of Mississippi. In 1856 he attended the Democratic National Convention and also served as a presidential elector. A strong advocate for the educational interests of Mississippi, he assumed the duties of school commissioner in Chickasaw County in 1857. In 1852 he married Elizabeth Ramsay Gates; they had three children. After Elizabeth's death in 1857, Orr married Cornelia Ewing Van DeGraaf in December of that year. They had two children.

By 1860 Orr had acquired a large plantation and owned forty-eight slaves. He attended the Mississippi convention in January 1861 and voted for the ordinance of secession. Appointed in April 1861 to fill a vacated seat in the Provisional Confederate Congress, he sponsored measures to increase the efficiency of the army and strengthen the economy. At the end of the term in February 1862 he recruited a regiment of 1,400 men, who elected him colonel in command. After serving in the Mississippi campaigns of 1862 and 1863, Orr resigned his commission to enter the Second Confederate Congress in April 1864. Lacking confidence in Jefferson Davis, he voted against most of the Confederate president's nominees and proposals. A member of the Foreign Affairs Committee and prominent in the peace movement, he blamed Davis for the failure of the Hampton Roads conference in February 1865, when three Confederate emissaries met with President Abraham Lincoln and Secretary of State William H. Seward to discuss proposals to end the war. Orr reasoned that, because Davis insisted that the Confederate government's legitimacy be recognized prior to negotiations, Lincoln had no choice but to refuse the terms. Returning to Mississippi to report to the legislature, Orr received a chilly response for his criticism of Davis.

After the war Orr trimmed his sails to accommodate the prevailing political breezes. In the summer of 1865 he and his older brother James L. Orr, governor of South Carolina, took part in a conference in New York City with Horace Greeley and other moderate Republicans to discuss the restoration of the southern states to their former status in the Union. Convinced that partial enfranchisement of the former slaves would be in the South's best interest, Orr urged that policy upon his return to Mississippi, but most white leaders considered his views too radical.

Orr moved to the larger city of Columbus in 1868 to expand his law practice. In 1870 he was appointed to a district circuit judgeship. In 1876, for the first time in the postwar era, he supported the Democratic presidential candidate and canvassed for the party ticket. In the same year the governor and most white leaders in Orr's judicial district recommended him for reappointment, but he failed to win confirmation in the state senate.

Orr continued to have an active interest in state politics, but he never sought another elective office. He served on the board of trustees of the University of Mississippi for over thirty years, retiring in 1904. A successful lawyer, he represented the Mobile and Ohio Railroad Company and other important corporate clients and practiced law on a limited basis past his ninetieth birthday. In later years Orr advocated woman suffrage and denounced the new breed of demagogic politicians who exploited the race issue. He died at the home of his daughter in New York City.

In a paper read before the Mississippi Bar Association in 1908, Orr asserted that U.S. senator and fellow Mississippian L. Q. C. Lamar's leadership in restoring sectional harmony helped the postwar South more than anything else. "We have a long line of illustrious men reflecting honor upon Mississippi in the Senate of the United States," he declared, "and at the head of that list, pre-eminent in the grandeur of his character, stands the name of L. Q. C. Lamar." Although never achieving the fame of Lamar, Orr also worked to restore sectional harmony in the postwar era, and he compiled a remarkable, honorable record that linked the Old South to the New.

• The largest collection of Orr's papers is in the Southern Historical Collection at the University of North Carolina at Chapel Hill. "Reminiscences of J. A. Orr" and several letters are in the Orr papers at the Mississippi Department of Archives and History in Jackson. Articles by Orr are "Life of Hon. James T. Harrison," *Publications of the Mississippi Historical Society* 8 (1904): 187–200; "A Trip from Houston to Jackson, Miss., in 1845," *Publications of the Mississippi Historical Society* 9 (1906): 173–78; and "Reminiscence of a Few Mississippi Lawyers," *Reports of the Mississippi Bar Association* 16 (May 1908): 58–65. See also Reuben Davis, *Recollections of Mississippi and Mississippians* (1889); Cleo Hearon, "Mississippi and the Compromise of 1850," *Publications of the Mississippi Historical Society* 14 (1914): 58; *Biographical and Historical Memoirs of Mississippi* 2 (1891): 536–40; Frank A. Montgomery, *Reminiscences of a Mississippian in Peace and War* (1901); Dunbar Rowland, *Mississippi* 3 (1907): 623–33; Richard E. Beringer, "The Unconscious 'Spirit of Party' in the Confederate Congress," *Civil War History* 18 (Dec. 1972): 312–33; and William C. Harris, *The Day of the Carpetbagger: Republican Reconstruction in Mississippi* (1979). An obituary is in the *Columbus Dispatch*, 13 Mar. 1921.

THOMAS N. BOSCHERT

ORRY-KELLY (31 Dec. 1897–26 Feb. 1964), costume designer, was born Orry George Kelly in Kiama, New South Wales, Australia, the son of William George Kelly, a tailor, and Florence Evalean Purdue. After studying art in Australia and working briefly as a banker, Orry-Kelly immigrated to New York City in 1923, hoping to become an actor. In the mid-1920s he waited tables and worked as a clerk, acting only on occasion. He did, however, find work painting for scenic studios, decorating apartments, and designing silent film titles. It was in New York that he received his entrée into the career—as a costume designer—that would dominate his professional life. In the late 1920s he began designing costumes, and occasionally scenery, for Broadway productions, including *Boom Boom*, starring his close friend and roommate Cary Grant, vaudeville productions, and musical revues, such as *Padlocks of 1927* and *George White's Scandals*. He also designed gowns for shows starring actress Ethel Barrymore. The success of his designs on Broadway, particularly those for the Shubert Brothers, led to his being asked to design for two seasons at the St. Louis Municipal Opera. Orry-Kelly then returned briefly to New York to manage night clubs, but in 1931 he relocated to California to work in the entertainment industry, where the effects of the depression were not as severe.

From 1932 to 1943 Orry-Kelly was the chief designer, under exclusive contract, at Warner Brothers First National Studios. While in Hollywood he acquired the hyphen in his name, most likely owing to a mistake made during the drafting of his initial contract, which he retained because of its distinctive nature. His extraordinary talent was a match for that of fellow Hollywood designers Adrian at Metro-Goldwyn-Mayer and Travis Banton at Paramount Pictures. Orry-Kelly, Adrian, and Banton all created glamorous contemporary clothing for movies that were seen by, and that influenced, more women than did the couture designs from Paris. Movies influenced society dramatically in the 1930s, in part because the Great Depression meant that most Americans could experience elegance only through the silver screen.

Orry-Kelly's first major motion picture, *The Rich Are Always with Us* (1932), starring Ruth Chatterton, was followed by hundreds more, including *Casablanca*, *The Maltese Falcon*, *Jezebel*, *Dark Victory*, *George Washington Slept Here*, *Arsenic and Old Lace*, *Now, Voyager*, *That Certain Woman*, *The Man Who Came to Dinner*, and *No Time for Comedy*. Among the movies he designed were a few costume dramas, notably *The Private Lives of Elizabeth and Essex*, *The Corn is Green*, and *The Little Foxes*, all starring Bette Davis, and *The Dolly Sisters*, featuring Betty Grable. His real talent lay in creating glamorous contemporary fashions for movie characters. Davis, Rosalind Russell, Delores Del Rio, Joan Fontaine, Kay Francis, Marilyn Monroe, Ingrid Bergman, and Olivia de Havilland were among the glamorous stars in the thirties, forties, fifties, and sixties whose images were burnished by Orry-Kelly's high-quality designs. Most accounts of Orry-Kelly's career acknowledge that Jack Warner, the head of Warner Brothers, hired him because the stars and leading contract players at the studio admired his classy, understated designs. He was particularly adept at hiding actresses' flaws and enhancing their physical attributes. Even after he left Warner Brothers Orry-Kelly returned to design for Bette Davis, who insisted on wearing his creations, so much did she value and trust his ability not only to create appropriate character choices but also to flatter her figure.

Many of the gowns that Orry-Kelly designed for the movies became popular fashions for American women. Even though he regularly disavowed any desire to design mass-market or couture clothing, preferring to concentrate on fashions for the screen, his designs and his fashion advice appeared regularly in the periodicals *Photoplay*, *Modern Movies*, and *Screenland*. Through "Studio Styles," Warner Brothers marketed retail clothing adapted from movie designs, further enhancing Orry-Kelly's reputation as a designer of glamorous clothing as well as movie fashions. Orry-Kelly asserted, "The essential thing in dress for all women is to have clothes that are personal, that reflect their own individual personality. Any style trend I have started gained popularity because I introduced something that was becoming to a certain star and right for the part she was playing, not because I had the millions of women who might copy it in mind" (Lyn Miller, "They Wear What They . . . ").

Although Orry-Kelly served only a few months in the armed forces after being drafted in 1942, it was as an army air force private that he gained U.S. citizenship in April 1943. Following his return to Hollywood Orry-Kelly terminated his exclusive relationship with Warner Brothers. He was under contract at Twentieth Century–Fox Studios from 1944 to 1946 and at Universal Studios from 1948 to 1950, and he later worked as a freelance designer for Metro-Goldwyn-Mayer, United Artists, and Mirisch among others, also returning on occasion to Twentieth Century–Fox, Universal Studios, and Warner Brothers. The movies he designed during this phase of his career, including *Irma La Douce*, *Pat and Mike*, *Auntie Mame*, and *Sweet Bird of Youth*, are marked by his trademark quality and glamour.

Orry-Kelly received three Academy Awards for best costume design for *An American in Paris* (1951, shared with Irene Sharaff and Walter Plunkett), *Les Girls* (1957), and *Some Like It Hot* (1959), and he was also nominated for another for *Gypsy* (1962). At the time of his death in Hollywood he was working on his autobiography, *Women I've Undressed*, designing costumes for the movie *Kiss Me, Stupid*, and enjoying his longtime avocation, painting. Exhibits featuring his mixed-media works of art were held in New York in the 1950s and in Los Angeles in the early 1960s.

During his career Orry-Kelly designed costumes for over three hundred films and at the same time influenced trends in American fashion. Throughout the history of movies, couture designers had always inspired costumes, but Orry-Kelly, along with Adrian and Travis Banton, dominated film costume design during the thirties and early forties and established a specialization in costume design for movies.

• Original designs are in the collections of the Los Angeles County Museum of Art, Warner Brothers Corporate Archive at Warner Brothers Studio, the Warner Brothers Studio Facilities Star Wardrobe (including costumes actually worn in movies), the Shubert archive, and the Costume Designer's Guild. For additional information on Orry-Kelly and articles by and about him, see Lyn Miller, "You Wear What They Tell You," *Movie Classic*, Sept. 1935, pp. 40–41, 78; Elizabeth Leese, *Costume Design in the Movies* (1991); Ann Lee Morgan, ed., *Contemporary Designers* (1986); W. Robert Lavine, *In a Glamorous Fashion* (1980); David Chierichetti, *Hollywood Costume Design* (1976); Bobbi Owen, *Costume Design on Broadway* (1987); James Vinson, ed., *Writers and Production Artists*, vol. 4 of *The International Dictionary of Films and Filmmakers* (1987); and Susan Perez Prichard, *Film Costume, An Annotated Bibliography* (1981). Obituaries are in *Variety*, 4 Mar. 1964, and the *New York Times*, the *New York Herald Tribune*, and the Los Angeles *Herald Examiner*, all 27 Feb. 1964.

BOBBI OWEN

ORTH, Godlove Stein (22 Apr. 1817–16 Dec. 1882), congressman, was born in Lebanon, Pennsylvania, the son of Gottlieb Orth and Sarah Steiner, farmers. He attended local schools and Pennsylvania College in Gettysburg before studying law under James Cooper in Gettysburg. Orth was admitted to the bar in 1839 and that same year relocated to Lafayette, Indiana. In 1840 he married Sarah Elizabeth Miler, who died nine years later. Orth addressed political rallies in Indiana in 1840 to promote the election of William Henry Harrison as president, earning him recognition among leaders of Indiana's Whig party. In 1843 he was elected to the state senate, where he served as president pro tempore in 1845. He remained in the senate until 1848. That year he supported Zachary Taylor, the Whig nominee for president, and he was also a presidential elector on the Taylor-Fillmore ticket. In 1850 he married Mary Ayers. An antislavery Whig until the party collapsed in the early 1850s, Orth became active in the Indiana Know Nothing party in 1854 and 1855. The next year he helped organize in his state the new Republican party, endorsing its stand against slavery and its economic policies.

In 1861 Governor Oliver P. Morton selected Orth as one of Indiana's five representatives to a conference in Washington to arrange a peaceful resolution of the differences between North and South. Convinced that war was inevitable, Orth returned to Indiana to urge preparedness. During the Civil War, he supported President Abraham Lincoln's prosecution of the conflict. Upon learning in 1862 of a possible invasion of southern Indiana by Confederate forces, Orth organized a company of volunteers in two hours, became captain of approximately 200 men, and commanded the U.S. ram *Hornet*, in which he cruised the Ohio River on the borders of Indiana, Illinois, and Kentucky.

In 1862 Orth won election as a Republican to the U.S. House of Representatives. He served in that capacity from 1863 to 1871, from 1873 to 1875, and again from 1879 until his death. Although not a particularly prominent member of Congress, Orth earned recognition for his work on the Private Land Claims, Ways and Means, Civil Service Reform, and Foreign Affairs committees. He endorsed the Thirteenth, Fourteenth, and Fifteenth Amendments to the Constitution while supporting strong Reconstruction measures against the South and favoring the impeachment of President Andrew Johnson in 1868. The next year he helped secure the Speakership for James G. Blaine of Maine and over the next few years sought to obtain from European governments the right of expatriation, advocated the annexation of Santo Domingo, and framed legislation to reorganize the diplomatic and consular system. In 1874 Orth declined to seek renomination to the House. The following year President Ulysses S. Grant appointed him envoy extraordinary and minister plenipotentiary to Austria-Hungary, where he remained until his return to Indiana in 1876.

Described by the *Indianapolis News* on 15 February 1876 as "one of the best post-politicians and strongest electioneers in the state," Orth received his party's gubernatorial nomination. Immediately thereafter stories surfaced about his rumored connection with a group of swindlers who had speculated in Venezuelan bonds and claims arising under a treaty in 1866 between Venezuela and the United States. A congressional investigation in the early 1870s had revealed that Orth acted as legal counsel for the speculators. In 1876 Orth persistently refused to answer questions about this affair, preferring instead to defend Republican policies. His silence on the subject aroused the suspicions of a hostile Democratic press and reformist Republicans. Public pressure on Orth to withdraw his candidacy mounted steadily. After Morton withdrew his support and several newspapers attacked his integrity, Orth dropped out of the race.

Although forced to retreat under fire in 1876, Orth reentered politics two years later, when he was elected to the Forty-sixth Congress. The majority of people in his congressional district entertained no reservations about his honesty, and a House investigatory committee later declared that Orth had no criminal connections with the Venezuelan claims. He won reelection in 1880. Vindicated by his constituents, Orth emerged once again as a spokesman for Indiana Republicanism, advocating tariff protectionism, pensions for veterans, and a sound monetary system.

Orth died in Lafayette while serving as a member of the House of Representatives. He was a midwestern legislator and strong partisan who expressed interest in foreign service and in the success of Republicans in his state and nation.

• A small collection of Orth's letters are in the Indiana Historical Society Library and the Indiana State Library in Indianapolis. The latter collection has some letters to Schuyler Colfax regarding state and national political issues. Other letters are in the papers of William H. English, Indiana Historical Society Library and the University of Chicago Library; Benjamin Harrison, Library of Congress; William Henry Smith, Ohio Historical Society Library; and Liver Morton and George W. Julian, Indiana State Library. Orth's speeches are in the *Congressional Globe* and *Congressional Record*, 1863–1871, 1873–1875, and 1879–1882. Additional information is in O. B. Carmichael, "The Campaign of 1876 in Indiana," *Indiana Magazine of History* 9 (1913): 276–97; and *The Indiana Republican Hand Book for the Campaign of 1876* (n.d.). Obituaries are in the *Indianapolis Sentinel* and the *New York Times*, 17 Dec. 1882.

LEONARD SCHLUP

ORTIZ, Manuel (2 July 1916–31 May 1970), boxer, was born in Corona, California, the son of Mexican immigrants Juan Ortiz and Madelena Villanueva. He grew up in California's Imperial Valley, where his formal education ended after one year of high school. He went to work picking beans for two dollars per day, later becoming a truck driver. In 1937, while attending an amateur boxing program in Brawley, California, Ortiz was prevailed upon to act as a substitute for a boxer who failed to appear. Although untrained, and with no previous boxing experience, he won impressively. This began a short but highly successful amateur boxing career; Ortiz became the Southern California amateur flyweight champion and then won the National Golden Gloves flyweight championship in Boston, Massachusetts.

In February 1938 Ortiz became a professional boxer under the management of Noel Johnson. For the first two years he progressed slowly against good opposition, as he won 17 fights and lost 10. By 1940 he was fighting in main events, and on 5 April 1940 he scored his first major victory with a knockout of Jackie Jurich, the eighth-ranked world flyweight, in Hollywood. In 1941, with Tommy Farmer as his manager, Ortiz became a consistent winner and moved up to the bantamweight division. After defeating several contenders, including Tony Olivera, Rush Dalma, and Kenny Lindsay, he outpointed champion Lou Salica in 12 rounds in Hollywood on 7 August 1942, and he won recognition as world bantamweight champion from the National Boxing Association. However, the New York State Athletic Commission continued to recognize Salica as champion, claiming that the title could not be put at stake in a fight not scheduled for 15 rounds.

Ortiz was an active champion. In 1943 he won eight defenses of his bantamweight championship, including a knockout of Salica on 10 March in Oakland, California, that made Ortiz the undisputed titleholder. In 1944 he made four more successful defenses, including two hard-won 15-round decisions over Olivera and Mexican Ernesto Aguilar, both in Los Angeles. As the first Mexican American to hold a world boxing title, the handsome, curly-haired Ortiz became a popular hero to both Mexican Americans and Mexicans.

An aggressive fighter with a hard punch in either fist, Ortiz was also a clever defensive boxer who recovered quickly if hit hard. A good strategist, he often started slowly, taking two or three rounds to estimate his opponent's strength and ability, after which he maintained relentless pressure and remained strong in the late rounds. Because of his aggressiveness, his fights were almost always exciting.

In 1945, although Ortiz was married (his wife's name is unknown) and had three children, he served in the U.S. Army for several months and made no title defenses. After being discharged late that year, he successfully defended the bantamweight championship in 1946 against Luis Castillo, Jurich, and Lindsay. A loss later in the year to featherweight Carlos Chavez was only his second defeat in five years, the other having come in 1944 when he lost a close 10-round decision to Willie Pep in Boston.

On 6 January 1947 Ortiz lost his bantamweight title to Harold Dade by a 15-round decision in San Francisco. Dade, previously a featherweight, had reduced to the bantamweight limit of 118 pounds but retained his strength. Ortiz, by then, was himself experiencing trouble in making the bantamweight limit. On 11 March Ortiz regained the championship by winning a close decision from Dade in Los Angeles. Later in the year he made successful defenses again Kui Kong Young in Honolulu and Tirso del Rosario in Manila, but he was also knocked out for the only time by featherweight Manny Ortega in a nontitle fight in El Paso, Texas.

In 1948 and 1949 Ortiz defended his title successfully twice more, against Memo Valero in Mexico City and Dado Marino in Honolulu. But he lost six nontitle fights during this time, and it was evident that he was losing speed and quickness. On 31 May 1950 he faced a much faster and younger challenger, Vic Toweel, in Johannesburg, South Africa, and lost his championship after 15 thrilling rounds. He had only seven more fights, losing five, before retiring in 1951.

While champion, Ortiz owned a 500-acre ranch near El Centro, California, and various other businesses. His prosperity disappeared soon after he left the ring. He became an alcoholic, his wife divorced him, he lost his property, and he descended into a hand-to-mouth existence. In 1953 and again in 1955 he made brief, unsuccessful ring comebacks. His health declined and he died of a liver ailment in San Diego.

Ortiz's success undoubtedly inspired numerous young men of Mexican descent to enter the ring, and many world champions came from that ethnic group in the decades to follow. Despite the losses that he suffered early in his career and after 1946, Ortiz won 95 of 127 fights, scoring 49 knockouts. He was inducted into the International Boxing Hall of Fame in 1996.

• Ortiz's complete boxing record is available in Herbert G. Goldman, ed., *The 1986–87 Ring Record Book and Boxing Encyclopedia* (1987). Useful articles from *The Ring* magazine are Gene Vinassa, "The Fighting Champ," Aug. 1943, pp. 9, 43; and the anonymous "Manuel Ortiz," Aug. 1985, p. 24. His fight with Vic Toweel is detailed by Chris Greyvenstein in *The Fighters: A Pictorial History of South African Boxing from 1881* (1981). See also Donald Woods, "Ortiz to Retire

Next Spring—Still Champion or Otherwise," *Boxing News*, 19 Oct. 1949, p. 5. Descriptions of his major fights are available in *The Ring* and in Los Angeles area newspapers. An obituary by Nat Loubet is in *The Ring*, Sept. 1970, pp. 31, 59.

LUCKETT V. DAVIS

ORTON, Edward Francis Baxter (9 Mar. 1829–16 Oct. 1899), geologist, was born in Deposit, Delaware County, New York, the son of Samuel Gibbs Orton, a Congregational minister, and Clara Gregory. The family lived in two small towns in New York State until 1833, when his father became pastor of the Presbyterian church in Ripley, New York, on Lake Erie. The boy enjoyed the rural life of farming communities. He was tutored by his father, a stern and inflexible Calvinist, and he attended academies in nearby Westfield and Fredonia.

When he was sixteen, Orton entered Hamilton College as a sophomore and received an M.A. in 1848. He intended to go into the ministry but over the next few years began having serious doubts about Calvinistic religion, with its emphasis on the innate sinfulness of humans. Orton taught for a year at an academy in Erie, Pennsylvania, and then entered Lane Theological Seminary in Cincinnati, Ohio, in 1849 but left because of eye trouble. He taught natural sciences at the Delaware Literary Institute in Franklin, New York, was a student at Harvard's Lawrence Scientific School for six months in 1852, and then went on to Andover Seminary. He married Mary M. Jennings in 1855; they had four children.

Ordained as a Presbyterian minister, Orton served as pastor of a church in Downsville, New York, in 1856 and later that year became professor of natural sciences at New York State Normal School in Albany. Objections arose to his "liberal tendencies in theology," so in 1859 Orton resigned his ministry. At about this time he changed to the Unitarian religion. He served as principal of Chester Academy in Orange County, New York, until 1865. Invited by his close friend, the Reverend Austin Craig, who had become acting president of Antioch College in Yellow Springs, Ohio, Orton went there in 1865. He considered the move westward a great release from bigotry: "The prison doors are at last opened for me" (quoted in White, p. 199).

Orton was successively principal of the preparatory department, professor of natural history, and in 1872 president of Antioch. He began geologic researches in Ohio, at first for teaching purposes. In 1869 he was asked to participate in the just-established Second Geological Survey of Ohio that was directed by John Strong Newberry of Columbia University.

When Ohio began to organize an Agricultural and Mechanical College as a land-grant college in the early 1870s, Orton accepted an offer in 1873 to become its first president, as well as professor of geology. Some of the already established colleges in Ohio considered the Agricultural and Mechanical College "an unwelcome interloper," according to Orton's biographer Israel

Charles White, who credited Orton with "infinite tact, patience, labor and wise leadership" in the early years. He was granted considerable autonomy by the board of trustees. "The curriculum was planned," said Orton's biographer John J. Stevenson, "not with a view to bringing the greatest number of students at the earliest moment, but with a view to the advantage of the state and of higher education" (p. 208). The number of students and the scope of the college increased quickly, so that in 1878 it was renamed Ohio State University. When Orton stepped down as its president in 1881, he continued as professor of geology until his death. Orton's wife died in 1873, and two years later he married Anna Davenport Torrey; they had two children.

For the state geological survey, Orton was first assigned to describe the geology of the southwestern quarter of Ohio. When Newberry ended his work in 1874, Orton continued with fieldwork and edited reports on the regions that had been studied. In 1882 he was instructed by the state legislature to complete those reports under a third establishment of a geological survey, and the next year he was appointed state geologist, while continuing at the university. He held that appointment for the rest of his life. Newberry had tended to emphasize his own interests in paleontology, an expensive subject to illustrate in reports and not of practical importance. Orton, "ever in close sympathy and touch with the common people" (said White, p. 201), recognized the value to the state of determining its economic materials, so he first concentrated his efforts on iron ores, building stones, lime, gypsum, clays, and coal. He published the results quickly in Ohio state survey reports. He differed with Newberry in adopting the analysis of the stratigraphy of the coal beds that had been determined by Israel Charles White along the boundary of Pennsylvania and Ohio. In the 1884 report of the Ohio survey Orton gave what geologist John J. Stevenson called a "masterly presentation of the whole Carboniferous series in Ohio" (p. 211) that very much clarified the geologic relationships with adjoining states. After 1884, when natural gas and oil had become significant in the country, he put special emphasis on those resources and coordinated the information with nearby states. He supported White again in his anticlinal theory on the nature of the origin of oil and gas, which helped to convince other geologists. Orton was requested by geologists of state surveys in Kentucky and New York to examine their potential oil and gas fields. He began urging the conservation of mineral resources but was not especially successful in convincing the public.

Orton's geologic competence was chiefly in painstaking and exact observation. His biographer G. K. Gilbert noted, "His contributions to theory came late, were few in number, and were broadly founded on the facts of his own observation. He never entered the field of speculation" (p. 546).

A modest person of courteous manners and keen consideration for others, Orton was noted by colleagues as one who showed good judgment in dealing with people of all stations and a person with a fine command of written and spoken language. He enjoyed speaking to farmers' groups and teachers' institutes. At Ohio State University he continued his liberal religious viewpoint by giving Sunday lectures for students who chose not to attend local churches.

Orton was president of the Geological Society of America in 1897 and president of the American Association for the Advancement of Science in his final year. He died in Columbus, Ohio.

• Records of Orton and his presidency of the college are in the Ohio State University Archives. He published about 100 papers on geology, many of them in reports of the Geological Survey of Ohio. Biographies include G. K. Gilbert, *Bulletin of Geological Society of America* 11 (1900): 542–50, with bibliography; John J. Stevenson, *Journal of Geology* 8 (1900): 205–13; and I. C. White, *American Geologist* 25 (1900): 197–210, with bibliography.

ELIZABETH NOBLE SHOR

ORTON, George Washington (10 Jan. 1873–26 June 1958), athlete, coach, and educator, was born in Stratbury, Ontario, Canada, the son of Oliver Henry Orton and Mary Ann Irvine. Although crippled by a childhood accident, he restored his ambulatory ability through exercise, especially running. Reminiscing about his origins as a runner, Orton said that many boys "beat me in the dashes, but as the route became long, I killed off my adherents." Recognizing that distance running was his "forte," he practiced regularly and developed into one of the premier athletes of the late nineteenth century.

Orton graduated from the Guelph Collegiate Institute in Ontario in 1889 and entered the University of Toronto. From 1890 to 1892 he dominated the half-mile and mile runs in the annual University of Toronto Varsity Games and represented Toronto in athletic meets throughout Canada and the United States. Orton captured the Canadian mile-run championship in 1892. His winning time of 4 minutes, 21.8 seconds marked a Canadian national record, falling short of the world record by only 3.4 seconds. He also won the first of six Amateur Athletic Union (AAU) mile-run titles in 1892 and the first of seven AAU two-mile steeplechase championships in 1893 in the United States.

As a graduate student at the University of Pennsylvania, Orton captured the Intercollegiate American Amateur Athletic Association (IC4A) mile-run championship in 1895 and 1897. His 1895 winning performance of 4 minutes, 23.4 seconds remained the meet record for twelve years. Also in 1895 he played a role in the development of the University of Pennsylvania Relay Carnival. Orton won the AAU cross-country title in 1897 and 1898 and the AAU ten-mile championship in 1899. As a member of a University of Pennsylvania track and field contingent representing the United States in the 1900 Summer Olympic Games in Paris, France, he won the gold medal in the 2,500-meter steeplechase and set a world record of 7 minutes, 34.4 seconds. He also took third place in the 400-meter intermediate hurdles and fifth in the 4,000-meter steeplechase.

Orton epitomized the scholar-athlete ideal at both the Universities of Toronto and Pennsylvania. After graduating second in his undergraduate class with a bachelor's degree in modern languages in 1893, he earned master's and doctoral degrees in philosophy in 1894 and 1896, respectively. At age twenty-three he was one of the youngest recipients of the doctorate from the University of Pennsylvania. Fluent in nine languages, Orton became a teacher and administrator in Philadelphia area preparatory schools. He served as a language instructor at Eastbury Academy from 1897 to 1900, Blight School from 1901 to 1902, and Episcopal Academy from 1902 to 1905. He also served as the headmaster of the Banks Preparatory School from 1905 through 1908. Orton married Edith Wayne Martin of Philadelphia in 1899. They had two daughters.

Orton also coached track and field, founded youth summer camps and recreational programs, and authored books on athletic training. He established two camps in the White Mountains of New Hampshire for young boys, Camp Tecumseh in 1902 and Camp Iroquois in 1916. Orton, who coached track and field at Episcopal Academy from 1902 to 1905, won praise from the *Philadelphia Ledger* in 1905 for lifting the city's interscholastic sports "up to the standard of any section of the country." At the same time, he founded the Philadelphia Children's Playground Association. In 1905 A. G. Spalding & Bros. published his *Athletic Training for School Boys*, which outlined the training regimen and technique required for success in track and field.

In 1909 Orton resigned as the headmaster of the Banks Preparatory School and resumed coaching track and field full time at Episcopal Academy. He later coached track at the University of Pennsylvania (approximately 1912–1916, perhaps intermittently). In 1916 Orton organized the sports program of the Sesquicentennial Independence Celebration and from 1928 to 1934 served as the director of the Municipal Stadium. As Stadium director, he campaigned to resume the Army-Navy football game and to secure the event permanently for Philadelphia. In 1932 Orton's marriage ended in divorce, and he retired after 1934. A member of the Academy of American Poets, Orton served as the recording secretary of the Rose Tree Fox Hunting Club and wrote a history of that organization. He died in Center Harbor, New Hampshire.

Although Orton never considered himself more than "a fair runner," he arguably stands as the best combination miler/steeplechaser of the late nineteenth century. No athlete won as many AAU mile or steeplechase titles until Joie Ray captured the mile eight times in the 1910s and 1920s and Joseph McCluskey garnered the steeplechase nine times in the 1930s and 1940s. As a pivotal figure in the development of sporting and recreational opportunities for young boys, Orton reflected the sporting ideology of the Progressive Era. Social and educational reformers, such as Orton were concerned about the decreasing role of the family and the church in preparing youth, especially boys and young men, for adult roles and responsibilities.

They saw organized sports and outdoor activities as a way to manage and supervise urban youth and instill adult attitudes and patterns of conduct in them. The Army-Navy football game, which is played annually at Philadelphia, is a lasting tribute to Orton's efforts to promote major sporting events in that city.

• The archives of the University of Pennsylvania and the University of Toronto contain biographical files on Orton. Statistical information on Orton's performances is found in Frank G. Menke, *The Encyclopedia of Sports*, 4th ed. (1969), and David Wallechinsky, *The Complete Book of the Olympic Games*, rev. ed. (1988). For Orton's place in the history of athletics, see Roberto L. Quercetani, *A World History of Track and Field Athletics* (1964). An obituary is in the *New York Times*, 27 June 1958.

ADAM R. HORNBUCKLE

ORTON, Helen Fuller (1 Nov. 1872–16 Feb. 1955), author, was born at the Fuller family farmhouse between Sanborn and Pekin, New York, the daughter of Merritt Bond Fuller, a schoolteacher and gentleman farmer, and Lucy Ann Taylor, a former schoolteacher. Helen was educated at home by her parents until she was almost eight years old. She then attended a rustic country school for a year before her parents sent her to middle school in Pekin. For high school, she traveled twenty miles a day to Lockport, New York, graduating in 1893. She taught elementary school in Lockport until 1895, when she married Jesse F. Orton, a law student and economics instructor at the University of Michigan at Ann Arbor. After moving to Michigan, she audited history, economics, and psychology courses at the university. When her husband completed his degree in 1897, they moved to Grand Rapids, where three of their four children were born. In 1908 the family moved back to New York, settling in Elmhurst, Long Island. Although she never worked as a journalist, Orton took advantage of the family's proximity to New York City and unofficially studied journalism at Columbia University.

Orton did not begin writing fiction until 1920, when she was forty-eight years old and her children were grown. Once started, she wrote deliberately and methodically. For three months, Orton wrote one children's story a week until she had fifteen stories, largely based on her childhood on the Fuller family farm. Her first collection of stories, *Prince and Rover of Cloverfield Farm* (1921), sold well and was well received. Orton continued to write prolifically, averaging more than a book a year for the next thirty-four years.

After writing five collections of farm stories for children, most of which were set in the 1880s of her own childhood, Orton began to indulge her passion for historical research. Using old letters, diaries, maps, town records, and manuscripts, she produced her own version of New York history, concentrating on the migration of people like her own ancestors, the original New England settlers who later moved into western New York. Instead of focusing her historical fictions on famous people or grand historic events, Orton celebrat-

ed the heroism and mystery of ordinary life as rich material for study and moral emulation.

Much of Orton's historical fictions had elements of suspense that served as a "hook" for young readers who might not otherwise be interested in early American history. In *The Treasure in the Little Trunk* (1932), for example, the 1825 opening of the Erie Canal is the central historic event. A young girl from New England who is traveling west by wagon must sell a cherished string of gold beads to a traveler headed back east in order to save her mother's life. Mysteriously, the beads reappear the day the canal opens, and readers thus learn how the opening of the canal closed the cultural and physical distance between east and west as it reduced the travel time between eastern cities and western outposts from weeks to days. Similarly, in *Mystery at the Little Red Schoolhouse* (1941), a gold coin disappears and no one knows whether a traveling peddler, a little chipmunk, an orphan girl, or the school prankster has taken it. As they search for the coin, the children realize that the coin's story is more important than its monetary value because the coin was given to their teacher by Abraham Lincoln and is thus a symbolic link to a great American president and a way of holding American history in the palm of one's hand.

Readers, both adult and juvenile, enjoyed Orton's particular mix of history, mystery, and nature-laden nostalgia for a nineteenth-century pre-urban America. While an occasional reviewer noted that Orton's stories seemed "simple and so old-fashioned as to be almost naive" (*New York Times*, 17 Feb. 1955), most reviewers familiar with historical fiction for children applauded Orton's exceptionally lifelike details, dialogue, and the spirit of history captured in all her work. Because of her commercial success, well-articulated theory of what children's fiction should be, and personal appeal, Orton was a popular lecturer, often invited to speak at writer's conferences or to read her work at schools.

During her lifetime, Orton's book sales totaled more than a million copies. Throughout the 1930s and 1940s Orton's books were popular both in the United States and England. Many were also published as foreign-language editions for markets abroad. An active member of the Authors League of America, the Daughters of the American Revolution, and the New York Historical Association, Orton continued to write children's histories and mysteries and to lecture about writing juvenile fiction until her death in Queens, New York.

• Most biographical information about Helen Fuller Orton comes from information she submitted to various publications during her lifetime. Orton provided the *Wilson Library Bulletin* 8 (Feb. 1934): 320–21 with a collection of autobiographical notes, which although fragmentary are also the best source of information about Orton's professional life and personal interests. Some of these notes merely record factual information about religion, ancestry, and papers presented. Other notes are more detailed, providing information about Orton's opinions about subjects ranging from the need for effective movie censorship for films frequented by children to the benefits of educating children at home. Another source of biographical information about Orton comes from a 1946 article, "All Children Love A Secret," by Helen Dean Fish, Orton's editor at J. B. Lippincott, in the *Wilson Library Bulletin* (Oct. 1946): 166, 170. This article discusses Orton's narrative technique and theory of children's fiction, often quoting the author directly. An autobiographical sketch solicited by Stanley J. Kunitz and Howard Haycraft, editors of *The Junior Book of Authors* (1951), pp. 233–34, provides Orton's most polished nonfictional account of her early life at the Fuller family farm, and while it reveals a great deal about Orton's early life it tells very little about her later interests or activities. Orton's obituary in the *New York Times*, 17 Feb. 1955, provides the most detailed information about her not found in any of her autobiographical sketches.

DARCY A. McLAMORE

ORTON, James (21 Apr. 1830–25 Sept. 1877), naturalist, explorer, and educator, was born in Seneca Falls, New York, the son of Azariah Giles Orton, a theologian and scholar, and Minerva Squire. His father earned a meager salary as a country parson, and his family had few material advantages, but young Orton received much intellectual stimulation and support at home. He exhibited a keen interest in science, particularly natural history and mineralogy. While still in his teens he began to write about the things he observed on the numerous field trips he took near his rural home. After attending a boarding school in Oxford, New York, he went to Williston Seminary because his family felt he should prepare for the ministry. Maintaining his interest in the natural sciences, however, he wrote and published *The Miner's Guide and Metallurgist's Directory* (1849).

The beginning of Orton's college career was delayed because of his poor health and financial constraints. When he entered Williams College in 1851, the ministry was his goal, but he was still drawn to natural history and spent his spare time on field trips exploring Nova Scotia and Newfoundland, as well as regions near the college. His activities caught the eye of Mark Hopkins, the president of Williams, who encouraged Orton to pursue the natural sciences.

After graduating from Williams in 1855, Orton attended the Andover Theological Seminary and spent several years studying in Europe. He was ordained in 1860 as a pastor in the same parish in Greene, New York, served by his father twenty-five years earlier. He served various congregations in New York and also in the sea coast community of Thomaston, Maine—sea air was recommended as a tonic for his poor health. Orton married Ellen E. Foote of Williamstown, Massachusetts, in 1859; they had four children.

An opportunity arose in the natural sciences when Orton replaced a friend and former classmate at Williams, Henry Ward, who had taken a leave of absence in 1866 from his position as curator of the museum at the University of Rochester. Orton's service as instructor of natural science at the university was so rewarding that he decided to give up the ministry to devote the remainder of his life to scientific investigation and teaching.

Through his association with the Lyceum of Natural History at Williams College, Orton was selected to lead an 1867 expedition to the Andes to determine whether the fossils there were marine in origin or had been deposited by the action of glaciers. When he returned home in 1869, he was appointed professor of natural history at Vassar College. While analyzing his data, Orton saw the significance of his discovery of marine shells at Pebas, Peru; it confirmed that Charles Darwin was correct about the marine origin of the fossils, and Orton became a staunch supporter of the Darwinian theory of evolution. He dedicated *The Andes and the Amazon* (1870) to Darwin, modeling it after Darwin's *Journal of Researches*. Darwin was grateful for this tribute and support, and he wrote to compliment Orton on his discovery of marine fossils. Some of the specimens collected by Orton were deposited at the Smithsonian Institution, the sponsor of the expedition, and the rest were given to the Academy of Natural Sciences of Philadelphia, the Boston Society of Natural History, the Peabody Academy of Science, and Vassar College.

Orton returned to South America in 1873 to continue his exploration of the Andes. He traveled from Para to Lake Titicaca to collect additional samples of fossils, flora, and fauna, as well as Incan artifacts. When he returned to Vassar to resume his teaching duties, he incorporated his observations and his data into a revision of *The Andes and the Amazon* (3d ed., 1876). His observations in natural history, geology, meteorology, and ethnology added to his reputation as one of the leading authorities on South American natural science.

Despite his poor health, Orton planned to return to South America on another journey of exploration, hoping that the high altitudes of Peru and Bolivia would improve his worsening pulmonary condition. The expedition began auspiciously when Edward Drinker Cope of Philadelphia agreed to finance it in return for the specimens collected. However, despite Cope's support and Orton's careful planning, the trip proved disastrous. Some of the former soldiers and native workers hired to assist the expedition deserted the group, and the weather turned unbearably cold. Orton suffered a severe pulmonary hemorrhage; he died as the party reached the shores of Lake Titicaca. After Orton's death there was further misfortune; the material collected during this ill-fated journey was lost before it reached New York, so the fruits of his last exploration could not be shared by other naturalists.

In his short life Orton added considerable information to the biogeography of the Andes, and his experience set a standard for future explorations of South America. His observations of the geology, climate, flora, and fauna of the Andes were the most comprehensive since the work of Alexander von Humboldt. Orton's support for Darwin's theory of evolution was noteworthy because many American naturalists did not readily embrace Darwinian evolution. Therefore, his work helped make the concept of evolution more acceptable in the United States.

• Orton's correspondence with Charles Darwin is preserved in the Darwin papers at the Cambridge University Library and in the History of Science Collections, University of Oklahoma. Some notes for his revised edition of *The Andes and the Amazon* are at the De Golyer Library, University of Oklahoma. Orton's other works include *Underground Treasures: How and Where to Find Them* (1872); *The Liberal Education of Women, the Demand and the Method, Current Thoughts in America and England* (1873); and *Comparative Zoology, Structural and Systematic, for Use in Schools and Colleges* (1876), an innovative text that emphasizes function as well as structure. The natural history of Orton's journeys are discussed in two articles in *Proceedings of the Academy of Natural Sciences of Philadelphia* by Edward Drinker Cope, "An Examination of the Reptilia and Batrachia Obtained by the Orton Expedition to Ecuador and the Upper Amazon, with Notes on Other Species," vol. 20 (1868): 96–140, and "On Some Batrachia and Nematognathi Brought from the Upper Amazon by Professor Orton," vol. 26 (1874): 120–37; articles in *Proceedings of the Boston Society of Natural History*, Philip Reese Uber, "Notices of the Hemiptera Obtained by the Expedition of Prof. James Orton in Ecuador and Brazil," vol. 12 (1869): 321–27; George Dale Smith, "List of Coleoptera Collected by Professor James Orton in Ecuador and Brazil," vol. 12 (1869): 327–30; and Samuel Hubbard Scudder, "Notes on Orthoptera Collected by Professor James Orton on Either Side of the Andes of Equatorial South America," vol. 12 (1869): 330–45. Biographical sources include two articles in *Bulletin of the Pan American Union*, Edward Albes, "An Early American Explorer," vol. 39 (1914): 1–13; and I. K. Macdermott, "An International Dedication Ceremony," vol. 55 (1922): 117–28; Edward Orton, *An Account of the Descendants of Thomas Orton of Windsor, Connecticut, 1641* (1896); Susan R. Orton, "A Sketch of James Orton," *Vassar Quarterly* 1 (1916): 1–8; and Jesse Leonard Rosenberger, *Rochester: The Making of a University* (1927). Obituaries are in the *New York Times*, 8 Nov. 1877, and the *New York Tribune*, 31 Oct. 1877.

JOEL S. SCHWARTZ

ORTON, William (14 June 1826–22 Apr. 1878), president of Western Union Telegraph Company, was born in Cuba, Allegany County, New York, the son of Horatio Orton, a teacher, and Sarah Carson. William attended district schools before attempting to follow in his father's footsteps. It is unclear whether William actually attended the State Normal School in Oswego, New York, or merely passed an examination before the Regents of Education, but he obtained a teaching degree in 1846. During the period before this examination he supported himself by working in a printing establishment. Orton's initial introduction to telegraph technology came during the preparation of his thesis on the new electromagnetic telegraph of Samuel Morse, which he accompanied with a model of his own construction.

After receiving his degree Orton taught at a small school in Livingston County, New York. He also clerked in the Geneva, New York, bookstore of the Derby and Company publishing firm of which he was to become a partner. In 1852 he moved to Buffalo to open a branch of the firm, Derby, Orton, and Miller.

That same year he married Agnes Gillespie; the couple had eight children. In 1856 he founded a publishing house in New York City, which failed after two years, a casualty of the panic of 1857. At that time he became managing clerk for the booksellers Gregory & Company. Orton, who had begun to study law, became involved in Republican politics and won election to the New York Common Council in 1861. The following year President Abraham Lincoln appointed him an internal revenue collector for the city. In early 1865, at the behest of former treasury secretary Samuel Chase, President Andrew Johnson appointed him internal revenue commissioner.

It was at this point that Orton saw an opportunity that would significantly change his life. The directors of the newly organized United States Telegraph Company, impressed by the managerial skills he had shown while working for the Internal Revenue Service, appointed him president of the company in October 1865. Orton soon discovered, however, that the company faced a precarious competitive position. He therefore entered into negotiations with the industry leader, Western Union, which resulted in a consolidation with the larger company. Orton, who became a Western Union vice president with the merger, succeeded to the company's presidency in 1867.

Orton reorganized Western Union to consolidate the telegraph lines of its former principal competitors, United States Telegraph and American Telegraph, turning it into the country's first truly national telecommunications network. One of his first important decisions was to hire British telegraph engineer Cromwell F. Varley to investigate the condition of the company's lines. Following Varley's suggestions, Western Union undertook an extensive program of line reconstruction and improvement. To accomplish this Orton also began to reduce the corporate debt created by consolidation by suspending dividend payments and putting profits into a program of technical improvement. He also reorganized the company's administrative structure to meet the needs of its national network.

Although Orton lacked familiarity with the telegraph industry at the time of his appointment as president of United States Telegraph, he quickly gained crucial insights into the business of telegraphy, which became the basis of his management of Western Union. Orton believed that the principal customers of the telegraph were businessmen and that they considered quality of service to be more important than price. He thought that the best way to improve his company's competitive position was to increase the volume of its business by improving the condition of its wires in order to increase their capacity and by expanding the number of new lines operated by the company in order to attract additional customers. To accomplish this he promoted technical innovation, declaring in an 1869 public statement that it was in Western Union's interest "to adopt every improvement whereby the dispatch of business within a given time can be materially increased" or that might reduce the need to build new wires with their large construction and repair costs. He actively supported the work of several inventors, including Thomas Edison.

To coordinate the way in which the company investigated and adopted new technologies, Orton reorganized its technical administration by establishing the office of electrician under the direction of George Prescott, a leading telegraph engineer. Prescott's office played an important role in the commercial introduction of new inventions acquired by Western Union and worked to increase the operating efficiency of its network. Perhaps the most important of these was the duplex telegraph, developed by Joseph Stearns, which allowed two messages to be sent simultaneously in opposite directions over a single wire. This invention proved so valuable that Orton told the company's executive committee that he would not sell it for a million dollars. Although he created an institutional framework for evaluating any improvements the company might adopt, Orton himself made the final decisions about new inventions. When confronted with conflicting opinions from his experts, he trusted to his own judgment.

As Orton's obituary in the company-sponsored *Journal of the Telegraph* noted, the Western Union president "was not content to understand merely the business and financial management, for which his previous experience had especially qualified him, but he was determined to familiarize himself with the telegraphic art, and the scientific principles upon which that art is based." Orton's insights into the technology of telegraphy became an essential component of Western Union's competitive strategy as he focused on inventions such as the duplex. This enabled the company to increase the number of messages sent over its wires without replacing its basic Morse telegraph system, thus retaining the corporation's investment in trained operators and equipment.

Orton's grasp of telegraph technology proved particularly important when Western Union was challenged by Jay Gould through the Atlantic and Pacific Telegraph Company. Gould's entry into the telegraph industry was part of his larger effort to challenge railroad baron Cornelius Vanderbilt, who also owned a controlling interest in Western Union. Gould combined telegraph lines on his own railroad system with those of a number of small telegraph companies to quickly build a major competitor to Western Union. One of these small companies was using Thomas Edison's automatic telegraph system, which Orton had rejected in the belief that automatic machinery was more expensive to build and maintain, was more liable to go out of order, and did not obviate the need for skilled operators to provide the prompt, reliable, and accurate service he felt was essential to business customers. At the same time Orton had informally supported Edison's efforts to develop a quadruplex system that would double the number of messages sent by duplex.

Orton had failed to reckon, however, with Edison's dire financial situation at the end of 1875 (the result of the panic of 1873), which caused the inventor to sell his rights in the quadruplex to Gould. Though Orton had not secured Edison's rights, Western Union did have rights to the invention from George Prescott, the company's chief engineer whom Edison had brought in as a partner. Orton was thus able to install the quadruplex system on Western Union lines while Gould's telegraph managers opted for the automatic instead. Orton's judgment was soon proved right as the quadruplex became an integral part of the Western Union system while the automatic fell into disuse when Edison returned to the Western Union fold. This time, though, Orton made sure that Edison's inventions were secured under a formal contract with Western Union.

Besides working long hours to improve Western Union's competitive position, Orton also labored to blunt the criticism of those who considered Western Union a dangerous monopoly. Particularly significant were his appearances before congressional committees considering the creation of a federally owned postal telegraph system, based on European models, that would replace or compete with Western Union. Through his efforts the company successfully lobbied to defeat several postal telegraph bills. These efforts combined with his rigorous administration of Western Union took their toll, however, causing his early death by apoplexy at his home in New York City.

William Orton was the principal architect of Western Union's competitive strategies during the 1860s and 1870s. Particularly significant were his administrative reorganization of the company and his active promotion of technological innovation. Under his guidance Western Union became the dominant company in the telegraph industry and one of the most important corporations in the country.

• Letters and other documents by Orton appear in Thomas E. Jeffrey et al., *Thomas A. Edison Papers: A Selective Microfilm Edition* (1985–). His letterbooks are in the Western Union collection at the archives of the National Museum of American History, Smithsonian Institution, which also contains pamphlets authored by Orton as well as the company's annual reports and minutebooks. Orton's efforts as Western Union president are extensively discussed in Paul Israel, *From Machine Shop to Industrial Laboratory: Telegraphy and the Changing Context of American Invention* (1992), and James D. Reid, *The Telegraph in America* (1879). Obituaries are in the *Journal of the Telegraph* 11 (1878): 129–31, and the *New York Times, New York Herald, New York Tribune,* and *New York Daily Graphic,* all on 23 Apr. 1878.

PAUL B. ISRAEL

ORY, Kid (25 Dec. 1890?–23 Jan. 1973), jazz trombonist, bandleader, and composer, was born Edward Ory in La Place, Louisiana, of Creole French, Spanish, African-American, and Native American heritage. His father was a landowner; the names and other details of his parents are unknown. Ory first spoke French. The family made weekend visits to New Orleans, thirty miles away, where Ory had many opportunities to hear musicians. He built several instruments before acquiring a banjo at age ten, shortly before his mother died.

His father having become an invalid, Ory took over the support of his younger sisters and then, after the younger ones went to live with relatives, an older sister. He apprenticed as a bricklayer, caught and sold crawfish, and worked as a water boy for field hands. At age thirteen he began performing in public with his own band. He started to play trombone—first a valved instrument and then a slide trombone—at around age fourteen. Not long afterward the legendary cornetist Buddy Bolden asked Ory to join his band, but Ory was too young to accept the offer.

Ory fulfilled a promise to his parents that he would take care of the older sister until he was twenty-one, and on that birthday (c. 1911) he moved to New Orleans. He married Elizabeth "Dort" (maiden name unknown) in 1911; they had no children. From about 1912 to 1919 he led what was widely regarded as the best band in New Orleans. His sidemen included Mutt Carey on trumpet, King Oliver or Louis Armstrong on cornet, Johnny Dodds, Sidney Bechet, Big Eye Louis Nelson, or Jimmie Noone on clarinet, and Ed Garland on string bass.

Having asked his wife if she would rather live in Chicago or California, Ory came west in October 1919. Carey and Garland joined his new band, which worked mainly in Los Angeles and San Francisco as Kid Ory's Brownskinned Babies and Kid Ory's Original Creole Jazz Band, the latter also known as the Sunshine Orchestra. In Los Angeles in June 1922, as Spikes' Seven Pods of Pepper, this group recorded "Ory's Creole Trombone" and "Society Blues." Ory's trombone solo is crude and unswinging, but the performances nonetheless have historical significance as some of the first instrumentals made by an African-American jazz band.

Around late October 1925 Ory traveled to Chicago to record with Armstrong and to join Oliver at the Plantation Cafe. He initially worked as an alto saxophonist until trombonist George Filhe finished out his six-week notice to Oliver. Over the next two years he was involved in many of the greatest early jazz sessions. With Armstrong, Ory recorded his own composition "Muskrat Ramble" (1926), which was titled "Muskat Ramble" on original issues by the producer and publisher Walter Melrose, who thought "muskrat" offensive. "Muskrat Ramble" became a staple of the traditional jazz repertory. Ory also recorded "Drop That Sack" (1926) with Louis Armstrong and his wife, pianist Lil Armstrong, who led the session; with pianist Jelly Roll Morton's Red Hot Peppers, "Dead Man Blues," "Doctor Jazz," and "Smokehouse Blues" (all 1926); with the New Orleans Wanderers, "Perdido Street Blues" and "Gate Mouth" (also 1926); with Louis Armstrong, "Potato Head Blues," "S.O.L. Blues," and an updated rendition of "Ory's Creole Trombone" (all 1927); and with Oliver's Dixie Syncopators, "Every Tub" (1927).

Ory started on Oliver's tour to New York City in May 1927, but he returned to Chicago by early June. He joined Dave Peyton's orchestra and then transferred to Clarence Black's group at the Savoy Ballroom, at which point he composed "Savoy Blues," recorded with Armstrong in December. Ory left Black in 1928 to become a member of the Chicago Vagabonds at the Sunset Cafe. He remained into 1929. He returned to Los Angeles in 1930. His last job was with Leon René's band in the show "Lucky Day" in San Francisco in the early 1930s.

Leaving music, Ory sorted mail at the Santa Fe Railroad post office, ran a chicken ranch in Los Angeles, worked as a cook, and served as a custodian at the city morgue. He resumed playing in 1942 as a member of clarinetist Barney Bigard's group in Los Angeles. Bigard categorically denied a fairly unimportant but nonetheless oft-told story, that Ory initially played string bass in the group, but clarinetist Joe Darensbourg remembered that Ory played bass pretty well.

In any event, Ory was soon back on trombone. He gave concerts with cornetist Bunk Johnson in San Francisco in 1943. In February 1944 he broadcast on Orson Welles's show as a member of a cooperative seven-piece traditional jazz group that included Carey, Noone, Garland, and drummer Zutty Singleton. Welles's show was a great success, and the group returned weekly for many months. Noone died in April, and Bigard was among several new bandmembers. The band became Ory's, and he recorded under his name, with clarinetist Omer Simeon for Bigard on "Get out of Here" and "Blues for Jimmie" (both 1944), and Darnell Howard taking Simeon's place for "Maryland, My Maryland," "Down Home Rag," and "Maple Leaf Rag" (all 1945). These discs are among the central recordings of the New Orleans jazz revival.

Ory's band held extended runs at the Jade Room on Hollywood Boulevard in Hollywood, beginning in April 1945, and at the Beverly Cavern in Los Angeles from 1949 to 1953. Among his sidemen were Howard, Darensbourg or Bigard, and drummer Minor Hall. In rather bitter remembrances of Ory, Bigard reported that he helped the trombonist secure royalties for "Muskat Ramble." Ory received $8,000 immediately, followed by quarterly checks for several hundred dollars. Bigard said that Ory bought a house and changed for the worse, leaving his wife in an underhanded manner, remarrying, and treating his sidemen badly. Ory married Barbara (maiden name unknown) around 1952; they had one daughter.

Ory recorded the album *Kid Ory's Creole Jazz Band, 1954* and from 1954 to 1961 ran his own club, On the Levee, in San Francisco. He also had a role in the movie *The Benny Goodman Story* (1955), and he toured Europe in 1956 and England in 1959. In July 1961 he moved back to Los Angeles and resumed bandleading at the Beverly Cavern. From 1964 onward he reduced his activities to performances on the riverboat at Disneyland, and in 1966 he retired to Hawaii. Ory suffered a serious bout of pneumonia in 1969. Four years later he died in Honolulu, Hawaii.

Writer Martin Williams supplied a remembrance: Ory was stiff or standoffish with everyone, but if you had a pretty girl with you, a kind of Creole graciousness would come out. . . . He was always a frugal man, you know. He always saved money and lived well. And he usually did his own business management and booking. Ory has the mentality of a French peasant, with all the charm that that implies, and all the shrewdness and stinginess and caginess too.

In the mid-1920s Ory was a shaky, awkward, coarse soloist by comparison with his frequent companions Armstrong and Dodds, but he excelled in collective improvisations, offering definitive examples of the raucous, sliding technique known as "tailgate trombone" within the New Orleans jazz style. He played the instrument open and muted, mainly using a cup mute. During his second career, he sometimes sang; his manner was entertaining but utterly unremarkable, save for the occasional use of Creole patois rather than English. While retaining his formidible ensemble skills, he became a smoother trombone soloist, and he expanded his collection of mutes to achieve a variety of timbres.

• Taped interviews by Nesuhi Ertegun and Bob Campbell (20 Apr. 1957; also transcribed) and by Bill Russell and Richard Allen (26 Aug. 1958) are at Tulane University. There is no lengthy or accurate study of Ory's life, and one must rely upon the somewhat inconsistent and casual surveys by Alma Hubner, "Ory: That New Orleans Trombone," *Jazz Notes*, no. 60 (Jan. 1946): 4–9, 18; Jane Greenough, "What Did Ory Say," *Record Changer* 6 (Nov. 1947): 5–6, 12; Marili Ertegun, "Just Playing Music I Love, Says Kid Ory," *Down Beat* 18 (10 Aug. 1951): 2, 16, 19; Bertha Wood, "New Orleans Music," in *Just Jazz*, ed. Sinclair Traill and Gerald Lascelles (1957); Giltrap and Dixon, *Kid Ory* (c. 1958); Samuel B. Charters, *Jazz: New Orleans, 1885–1963: An Index to the Negro Musicians of New Orleans*, rev. ed. (1963; repr. 1983); Geoffrey Marne, "The Kid Ory Story," *International Musician* 63, no. 6 (Dec. 1964): 18–19, 30; and Martin Williams, *Jazz Masters of New Orleans* (1967; repr. 1979). Further small details and some sense of the larger context may be gained from Donald M. Marquis, *In Search of Buddy Bolden: First Man of Jazz* (1978; repr. 1980); Barney Bigard, *With Louis and the Duke* (1985); Joe Darensbourg with Peter Vacher, *Telling It Like It Is* (1987), American edition published as *Jazz Odyssey: The Autobiography of Joe Darensbourg*; Walter C. Allen and Brian A. L. Rust's *"King" Oliver*, rev. ed. (1987); and Gene Anderson, "Johnny Dodds in New Orleans," *American Music* 8 (1990): 405–40, which provides a detailed yearly summary of Ory's band personnel during 1912–1919. Obituaries are in the *New York Times*, 24 Jan 1973; *Melody Maker*, 3 Feb 1973, p. 18; and *Bulletin du Hot Club de France*, no. 225 (1973): 3.

BARRY KERNFELD

OSBON, B. S. (16 Aug. 1827–6 May 1912), maritime journalist, was born Bradley Sillick Osbon in Rye, Westchester County, New York, the son of Abiathar Mann Osbon, a Methodist minister, and Elizabeth Sillick. Osbon attended common schools in New York, excelling only in geography and history. An unruly youngster, he repeatedly ran away from home in search of adventure, first at the age of eleven to work on Hudson River canal boats, then at thirteen to sail on the *Cornelia* for a run from New York to Liverpool, England. Following his return, he studied navigation in a private school in Brooklyn, New York, and served on storeships in the U.S. Navy. He mustered out of the navy to join a whaling expedition in 1847, sailed into the Arctic and Antarctic oceans, served in the Anglo-Chinese navy during a layover in Hong Kong in 1851, and returned to the United States in 1852. A year later, he joined the Argentine navy, resigning to serve as quartermaster of a steamship in 1857, and ended his merchant marine career in 1858.

His journalism career began on the lecture circuit on which he embarked to earn a living, recounting his farflung sailing adventures. Newspaper editors in the towns Osbon visited frequently asked him to write about his adventures for publication, a congenial task for which he discovered he had some talent. He contributed to many New York City newspapers, joining the newly founded penny paper *New York World* in 1860 as a $9-a-week reporter.

Osbon's celebrated journalistic reputation was based on his eyewitness accounts of Civil War naval battles, beginning with the Confederate bombardment of Fort Sumter at Charleston, South Carolina, in April 1861. Serving as a clerk and signal officer aboard the U.S. cutter *Harriet Lane*, Osbon observed the bombardment, siege, and surrender of the fort. His lengthy descriptive dispatch on 12 April 1861 to the *New York World* tersely began: "The ball is opened—war is inaugurated." The *New York Herald's* managing editor, Frederic Hudson, was so impressed with the *World's* reportage that he hired Osbon for the $25-a-week position of *Herald* naval editor.

Osbon received a roving commission from U.S. Secretary of the Navy Gideon Welles that allowed him to accompany the Union naval expedition to Port Royal, South Carolina, in October 1861. His dispatches to the *Herald* described the daily maneuverings of the ships and the fighting. The 29 October dispatch concluded: "We are now in the heart of the enemy's country where first the disunion fires were lighted and where the aristocracy of the Southern chivalry dwelt in fancied security."

Admiral David Farragut appointed Osbon fleet signal officer on the flagship *Hartford* for the 1862 Union assault on New Orleans. "No duty could have been more congenial to my tastes or more suited to my position as correspondent," Osbon recalled in his memoirs, *A Sailor of Fortune* (p. 171). "It brought me into the closest touch with the Flag Officer, and gave me the most initmate knowledge of every movement of the fleet." Osbon's 10 May *Herald* dispatch reported his eyewitness account of Confederate forts' attack of Farragut's fleet south of New Orleans: "The river and its banks were one sheet of flame and the messengers of death were moving with lightning swiftness in all directions. . . . Shot, shell, grape and cannister filled the air with deadly missiles. It was like the breaking up of a thousand worlds—crash—tear—whiz!"

The ironclad monitor *Montauk*'s assault on Fort McAllister, on the Ogeechee River in Georgia, was the last major Civil War naval battle Osbon covered for the *New York Herald*. Although the *Montauk* was struck seventy-one times without major damage, Osbon suffered broken ribs and a knee injury. He reported in the *Herald*'s 13 March 1863 edition: "Your correspondent was at the instant of impact on one knee writing a paragraph in his notebook . . . and I tumbled over against the side of the narrow pilot house, when, to my surprise, I was struck by a piece of iron bolt (weighing about one pound) first on the shoulder and then on the knee."

Osbon resigned from the *Herald* in 1864 to set up his own news syndicate specializing in maritime and naval affairs. One of the stories he offered to his newspaper clients dealt with a planned Union attack on Wilmington, North Carolina. The *Boston Daily Advertiser* and the *Philadelphia Press* published the article on 19 December 1864, five days before the assault. The articles were reprinted in newspapers in the Confederate capital of Richmond, Virginia, prompting Assistant Secretary of the Navy Gustavus Fox to charge Osbon with violating the Fifty-Ninth Article of War for giving information to the enemy. Osbon was arrested at his New York City office on 1 January 1865, confined to the Capitol Prison in Washington, D.C., and acquitted and released six months later.

Following his release from prison, he reestablished his news bureau and worked for the New York Associated Press in New Orleans in 1867. He married Eliza Balfour in 1868 and traveled to Le Havre, France, to attend the Maritime Exposition, returning to the United States in 1871 to found the weekly *Nautical Gazette*. He sold the newspaper in 1884. For the remainder of his life, he was engaged in many unsuccessful business projects. His major source of income, when he died at the Post-Graduate Hospital in New York City, was a $20-a-month government pension.

Osbon's participatory reportage provided daring eyewitness accounts of the Civil War's major naval battles, earning him one of the most celebrated reputations among war correspondents in the nineteenth century. Forty years after the South surrendered, Osbon was "content with the memories of the vanished days. Yet the smell of powder puts it all before me and makes me long sometimes for the flash and roar of battle—to feel the deck lift and rock to the thunder of heavy guns" (Paine, p. 331).

• Osbon wrote two books dealing with maritime affairs, *Visitors' Hand Book; or, How to See the Great Eastern* (1860) and *Handbook of the United States Navy* (1864). He edited *Cruise of the U.S. Flagship Hartford, 1862–1863: Being a Narrative of All Her Operations since Going into Commission, in 1862, until Her Return to New York in 1863. From the Private Journal of William C. Holton* (1863). Albert Bigelow Paine, *A Sailor of Fortune: Personal Memoirs of Captain B. S. Osbon* (1906), is an important source. Louis M. Starr, *Bohemian Brigade: Civil War Newsmen in Action* (1954), J. Cutler Andrews, *The North Reports the Civil War* (1955), and Bernard A. Weisberger, *Reporters for the Union* (1953), are useful. Brief obituaries of Osbon appear in the *New York Times* and the *New York Herald*, 7 May 1912.

A. J. KAUL

OSBORN, Chase Salmon (22 Jan. 1860–11 Apr. 1949), governor of Michigan, journalist, and entrepreneur, was born in Huntington County, Indiana, the son of George Augustus Osborn and Margaret Ann Fannon, hydropathic physicians. Osborn was named by his abolitionist-oriented parents after Ohio's then-U.S. senator and soon-to-be Abraham Lincoln's secretary of the Treasury, Salmon P. Chase. His largely rural boyhood was a mixture of both modest affluence and poverty. He began studies at Purdue University (c. 1873–1876) but never completed them, choosing instead around 1878 to enter the newspaper business in Illinois, Wisconsin, and finally Sault Ste. Marie, Michigan. He married Lillian G. Jones of Milwaukee in 1881. They had six children, four of whom lived to maturity. In 1887 he, with a partner, bought the *Sault Ste. Marie News*, and Osborn became the sole owner before the end of the century.

In 1890 he was appointed postmaster, but his tenure was cut short by the Democrats when they returned to national power in 1893. In 1895 Governor John Rich appointed him state game and fish warden. This position provided excellent opportunities for Osborn, who used its patronage and statewide visibility to lay the foundation for greater political activity.

An unsuccessful race for Congress (1896), two highly publicized terms as state railroad commissioner (1899–1903), an unsuccessful attempt to win the Republican nomination for governor in 1900, service as delegate to the 1908 National Conservation Congress and the Republican National Convention, and finally appointment to the University of Michigan's Board of Regents (1908–1911) were the preliminary steps to Osborn's successful campaign to win the Republican gubernatorial nomination in 1910. During these years he also built a modest fortune through his iron ore discoveries, timber lands, and an expanding newspaper business.

When Osborn announced his candidacy for the Republican nomination for governor on 16 October 1909, a host of followers—old-time professional politicians, associates from the newspaper world, and many personal friends—hurried to join his campaign. Most important of these was Osborn's successor as editor of the *Sault Ste. Marie Evening News*, Frank Knox, who later achieved fame in politics as vice presidential nominee in 1936 and secretary of the navy in World War II. Knox energetically managed Osborn's strenuous campaign, which saw Osborn travel 12,000 miles in Michigan's first full-scale automobile campaign. He made hundreds of speeches spelling out his progressive program that he called the "New Deal." His colorful campaigning and reform program brought him a substantial plurality over his Republican rivals in the primary, followed by an easy victory in the November election.

A few days after his inauguration, Osborn presented his program to the legislature in what Senator Robert M. La Follette called a "strong state paper." He called for stricter child and female labor laws, more state regulation of business, improved primary election laws, the initiative, referendum, and recall, and a workmen's compensation act—in fact practically all of the reforms associated with the Progressive movement of that time.

Though the legislature was Republican-controlled, its members did not share Osborn's reform spirit. Thus the new governor had a hard time getting his program enacted. But from his struggles with the legislature in its regular 1911 session and two special sessions in 1912 emerged a substantial program of reform. His most important and most lasting accomplishment was the enactment of Michigan's first workmen's compensation law.

The legislature passed other laws protecting and enlarging the rights of labor and expanding the state's power over railroads, express companies, telephone companies, banks, insurance companies, and saloons. Important tax legislation granted more power to the state tax commission, set up an expert reappraisal of mines, and authorized a commission to review the entire tax structure of the state. In addition, the Sixteenth Amendment to the U.S. Constitution was ratified, introducing the federal income tax. Measures expanding popular government were advanced with the passage of a presidential primary law, the extension of the state primary law, and legislation enabling Michigan voters to vote on woman suffrage.

Osborn also took an active part in national politics. He was a major leader to get former president Theodore Roosevelt to oppose William Howard Taft for the 1912 Republican presidential nomination, although he never joined the new Bull Moose party. The active campaigning of this party coupled with tepid support from conservative Republicans resulted in Osborn's defeat when he sought reelection in 1914. He never again held public office, though he spoke out in favor of the League of Nations after World War I and the United Nations after World War II. He took organized labor's side during the sit-down strikes at Michigan's auto plants during 1937. He wrote a number of books and traveled extensively. His first wife having died, he was aided in these activities in his later years by Stella "Nova" Lee Brunt, whom he married in 1949 shortly before his death at his winter home in Worth County, Georgia.

In 1920 Osborn wrote of himself: "Because of Osborn's independence and temperamental Liberalism, he was charged with being erratic, not a few called him crazy, and everybody agreed to the fact that he would not stand hitched." No better brief characterization of Michigan's twenty-seventh governor could be written. He fitted no well-defined pattern, and the only consistent theme running throughout his life was independence of thought and action.

• The Chase S. Osborn Papers in the Michigan Historical Collections, Bentley Historical Library of the University of Michigan, comprise some 179 feet and 267 volumes of manuscripts, including correspondence, diaries, business and miscellaneous papers, addresses, and scrapbooks of newspaper articles. These materials are supplemented by thirteen boxes of Osborn manuscripts in the State Archives, Michigan Department of State, Lansing. Other correspondence appears in various collections at the Bentley Library. Robert M. Warner, "Chase S. Osborn and the Progressive Movement" (Ph.D. diss., Univ. of Michigan, 1958), covers Osborn's governorship and political activities. See also Osborn's autobiography, *The Iron Hunter* (1919), and Stella Brunt Osborn, *An Accolade for Chase S. Osborn* (1940). Warner, "Chase S. Osborn and the Presidential Campaign of 1912," *Mississippi Valley Historical Review* (Sept. 1959): 19–45, and *Chase Salmon Osborn, 1860–1949* (1960), a pamphlet, detail aspects of Osborn's career.

ROBERT M. WARNER

OSBORN, Fairfield (15 Jan. 1887–16 Sept. 1969), naturalist and leader in conservation, was born Henry Fairfield Osborn, Jr., in Princeton, New Jersey, the son of Henry Fairfield Osborn, a professor of comparative anatomy at Princeton University, and Lucretia Perry. When the boy was four, his father became professor of biology at Columbia University, and the family moved to New York City. In his room in the family's brownstone he "gave vent to these very great inner longings to be surrounded by animals" (*New Yorker*, 9 Mar. 1957, p. 24). The senior Osborn soon became closely associated with the American Museum of Natural History and the New York Zoological Society. The family spent considerable time in the Hudson River highlands at Garrison, New York, and moved in an affluent social circle in New York City.

Osborn attended the Groton School in Massachusetts and in 1905 entered Princeton University. After receiving a B.A. in 1909, he went to Cambridge University for a year of graduate study in biology. He then spent several years in various jobs, including working in freightyards in San Francisco and laying railroad track in Nevada. He married Marjorie Mary Lamond, an artist, in 1914 in London; they had three daughters.

In 1914 Osborn became treasurer of a company that manufactured labels and the next year treasurer of the Union Oil Company. During World War I he was captain of a field artillery unit of the American Expeditionary Force. He then became a partner in a New York City investment banking firm, Redmond and Company, with which he continued until 1935. He accompanied his father on several scientific expeditions in the United States and one to Egypt. The reawakening of his interest in animals began with his appointment in 1923 as a trustee and member of the executive board of the New York Zoological Society (NYZS), with which his father had been associated from its founding in 1895. The younger Osborn first concerned himself with increasing membership in the society. In 1935 he briefly joined the banking firm of Maynard, Oakland, and Lawrence, but that same year he became secretary of the NYZS and resigned from his business obligations. He was responsible for a popular exhibit by the society at the New York World's Fair in 1939.

In 1940 Osborn became president of the NYZS, which operated the 261-acre New York Zoological Park (popularly known as the Bronx Zoo) and the New York Aquarium. From its beginning the society had urged scientific research and preservation of wildlife. Osborn carried these aims much further than his predecessors, and he expanded the society's education programs. Another founding concept of the society had been to display animals in natural surroundings, but not until Osborn's presidency was much of that done. His administration saw the creation of an African plains exhibit, an enlarged facility for apes, a penguin pool, and a flight cage for tropical birds. Osborn was able to obtain funds for some projects from his wealthy acquaintances. During World War II he edited *The Pacific World* (1944), a handbook for U.S. servicemen on the plants and animals of the Pacific islands.

Osborn's concern for conservation came to the forefront in 1948, when his book *Our Plundered Planet* was published. Its primary message was that humans must learn to cooperate with nature by conserving natural resources and protecting living creatures. His book effectively presented major concerns of the impact of increasing human population on wildlife and also emphasized that civilization was imperiled by its overuse of natural resources. Translated into thirteen languages and widely read, it received a special citation of the Gutenberg Award (1948) and was named the outstanding book of 1948 by the National Education Association.

Also in 1948 Osborn was the primary founder and first president (until 1961) of the Conservation Foundation, first a section of the NYZS and later an independent organization. Its aim was education on conservation, about which it published books, produced films, and sponsored conferences. With Laurance S. Rockefeller, in 1948 he helped to establish Jackson Hole Wildlife Park at Moran, Wyoming, with field research facilities for wildlife biologists. It was later included in Grand Teton National Park. Osborn's involvement in conservation led to his being appointed a member of the Advisory Committee on Conservation of the U.S. Department of the Interior (1949–1950), an advisory expert on the United Nations Scientific Conference on Conservation and Utilization of Resources Preparatory Committee (1949), and a member of the board of trustees of the National Parks Association (1951–1954). His second book, *The Limits of the Earth* (1953), emphasized problems of overpopulation. Osborn wrote many articles on conservation in *Animal Kingdom*, published by the NYZS, and in other magazines.

The NYZS had operated an aquarium at Battery Park in Manhattan since 1902, and by the 1930s it was in need of repair or replacement. That facility closed in 1941, and a new site was selected at Coney Island in Brooklyn. World War II and postwar financial problems delayed construction, but the new aquarium finally opened in 1957. At Osborn's urging, it included research laboratories; when these were expanded in 1967, they were named the Osborn Research Laboratories.

Another interest of Osborn's was animal behavior. With Detlev Wulf Bronk of the Rockefeller Institute, in 1965 he established the Institute for Research in Animal Behavior, later a facility of Rockefeller University.

Osborn resigned as president of the NYZS in 1968 but continued as chair of its board of trustees until his death in New York City. Among his many awards were the Prix Manley Bendall from the Institut Océanographique in Monaco (1957), the first Conservation Medal awarded by the San Diego Zoological Society (1966), the Gold Medal of the NYZS (1966), and the Audubon Medal of the National Audubon Society (1968). Colleagues appreciated his keen interest in all kinds of animals as well as his sense of humor and his informality.

• Osborn's archival records are at the Wildlife Conservation Society in New York City and include a draft bibliography. A biographical sketch is Laurance S. Rockefeller, "My Most Unforgettable Character," *Reader's Digest*, Oct. 1972, pp. 137–41. A brief feature on Osborn is "Full Circle," *New Yorker*, 9 Mar. 1957, pp. 23–24. The history of the New York Zoological Society is in William Bridges, *Gathering of Animals* (1974). Obituaries are in the *New York Times*, 17 Sept. 1969, and *Animal Kingdom*, Oct. 1969, pp. 28–29.

ELIZABETH NOBLE SHOR

OSBORN, Harold Marion (13 Apr. 1899–5 Apr. 1975), track and field athlete and Olympic gold medal champion, was born in Butler, Illinois, the son of Jesse Osborn and his wife Emma (maiden name unknown), farmers. "I was a farmer's son and ran three miles to and from school each day," he wrote, "and I spent dozens of hours a week strengthening my only above average physical skills." At the University of Illinois, he managed a modest 6'2½" high jump at the end of his sophomore year (1920), and he jumped an inch higher the following year. At the 1922 Drake Relays he established an American intercollegiate record of 6'6". Osborn helped his university track team win indoor and outdoor Big Ten titles in 1920, 1921, and 1922, helping his team score points in the long jump, hurdles, and 16-pound shot put as well in the high jump. He graduated from Illinois in 1922. In 1923 he joined the Illinois Athletic Club and won the Amateur Athletic Union (AAU) national championship decathlon with a record 7,351.89 points.

On the eve of the 1924 Olympic Games to be held in Paris, the blond, bespectacled, 5'10", 172-pound Osborn was considered the best American in both the decathlon and the high jump. He did not disappoint and won both Olympic gold medals, the only athlete to accomplish the feat. The *New York Times* reported that "Osborn's jumping was faultless" as he cleared 1.98 meters (6'6"). Several days later, he won the arduous decathlon, despite trailing the other American, Emerson Norton, through nine of the ten events. The seven-hour event lasted into darkness, where Osborn scored twice as many points as Norton in the 1,500-meter run, enabling Osborn to win a second gold medal. His 7,710.775 was a world record.

Earlier in 1924, at the U.S. Olympic Trials, Osborn high jumped 6'8¼", a world record. From 1925 through 1928 he competed and won 100 competitions in the decathlon, high jump, shot put, long jump, hurdles, and standing long and high jumps. He faltered at the 1928 Olympic Summer Games in Amsterdam, finishing fifth in the high jump. Osborn married Ethel Calderwood of Canada in 1927. In the following year, she won the Olympic high jump, the marriage ended in divorce, and in late 1928 Osborn married Estelle Bordner, with whom he had four children.

During the 1930s Osborn competed nearly full time in indoor and outdoor events, eventually participating in thirty-five AAU championships and winning twenty-five American, Canadian, British, and European titles, including six world records, one of them, a 5'6" standing high jump in 1936, at age 37. In 1937 he graduated from the Philadelphia College of Osteopathy and established a practice in Champaign, Illinois, eventually becoming president of that state's osteopathy association.

During World War II Osborn served as assistant track coach at Virginia Polytechnic Institute and at the University of Illinois. His twenty years as an athlete proved him to be one of the most durable and versatile track and field performers of the century. A determined competitor, Osborn was never once reprimanded for unsportsmanlike conduct. In 1974 he became a charter member of the American Track and Field Hall of Fame. In *Athletics of Today* (1929), F. A. M. Webster called Osborn's training regimen, "the epitome of the scientific method," a dedicated scholar-athlete. The U.S. Olympic track coach R. L. "Dink" Templeton described Osborn as a "very robust individual with nearly infinite capacities for hard work." Osborn died in Champaign where he had spent so much of his life as a student, as an athlete, and in his professional practice.

• Osborn's brief autobiography appears in R. L. Templeton, ed., *The High Jump* (1930), pp. 150–63. The best analysis of his place in decathlon history can be found in Frank Zarnowski, *The Decathlon* (1989), pp. 54–56. Also see Bill Mallon and Ian Buchanan, *Quest for Gold: The Encyclopedia of American Olympians* (1984), pp. 331–32, and the *New York Times*, 8 July 1924, p. 15, and 13 July 1924, pp. 1 and 25. Obituaries appear in the *Chicago Tribune*, 6 Apr. 1975, and the *New York Times*, 7 Apr. 1975.

JOHN A. LUCAS

OSBORN, Henry Fairfield (8 Aug. 1857–6 Nov. 1935), paleontologist and science administrator, was born in Fairfield, Connecticut, the son of William Henry Osborn, a businessman, and Virginia Reed Sturges. The Osborn and Sturges families belonged to New York's mercantile elite, and Henry Fairfield Osborn grew up in a household that was wealthy and well connected to powerful political and financial figures in nineteenth-century New York. Osborn's parents were devout Presbyterians, and the emphasis on reconciling religion and science would have an important bearing on Osborn's work.

Osborn followed his family's Scottish Presbyterian interests and attended Princeton University from 1873 to 1877. His father, president of the Illinois Central Railroad, intended Osborn to enter the family business. But Osborn, influenced by Princeton president James McCosh, became interested in an academic career. Following his graduation in 1877, he participated in a university-sponsored expedition to the western states and spent the following year studying fossils collected on that trip. He also took McCosh's graduate courses in philosophy and psychology. At McCosh's urging, Osborn did additional work in biology, taking courses with John Call Dalton at Columbia College of Physicians and Surgeons and William Henry Welch at New York's Bellevue Hospital. In 1879 he traveled to England to study with the zoologist Thomas Henry Huxley and the Cambridge embryologist Francis Maitland Balfour. Following his return, Osborn wrote a dissertation, received an Sc.D. degree from Princeton in 1881, and that same year was hired by Princeton to teach comparative anatomy and embryology. In 1881 he married Lucretia Perry, with whom he had five children.

Osborn spent ten productive years at Princeton. He continued his research in several fields of biology, including neuroanatomy, paleontology, and embryology. Although separate disciplines today, those fields were then linked as part of the study of animal morphology (structure) that focused on establishing evolutionary relationships among organisms. In 1886 Osborn's embryological work defining the evolutionary relationship between marsupials and placental mammals was attacked by the German biologist Emil Selenka. In light of Selenka's criticisms Osborn retracted his interpretation and abandoned research in embryology and neuroanatomy, claiming that he lacked the technical facility for doing laboratory research in those fields. He continued to teach those subjects, and through his influence several Princeton graduate students were able to publish their master's theses in Charles Otis Whitman's new *Journal of Morphology*. But in his own work Osborn turned to vertebrate paleontology and began to publish on fossil mammals and evolution. Advice and support from his father led Osborn in 1886 to reduce his teaching load and hire collectors and artists to assist with that research. Osborn did little fieldwork, but discoveries by his Princeton colleague William Berryman Scott and Scott's students provided specimens for his analysis. Scott and Edward Drinker Cope, a noted American paleontologist, also influenced Osborn's ideas on vertebrate evolution and classification. In the 1880s Osborn embraced Cope's neo-Lamarckian interpretation that evolution occurred by the use or disuse of parts and that such changes were passed on from an organism to its progeny. He later adopted Scott's views that a guiding force was responsible for the linear, cumulative patterns of change found in the fossil record. Osborn was not a first-rate scientist or an original thinker, but an ability to recognize problems and raise resources for their analysis enabled him to develop research programs in neuroanatomy, embryology, and vertebrate paleontology at Princeton.

Osborn operated in similar fashion, though on a larger scale, when he accepted a joint appointment at Columbia University and the American Museum of Natural History, both in New York City, in 1891. Seth Low, the new president of Columbia, was eager to transform a mediocre college into a major metropolitan university and hired Osborn to establish a biology department. Osborn developed a program that reflected his interest in animal morphology. While he taught vertebrate morphology and evolution, he hired Edmund Beecher Wilson to offer similar courses on invertebrates. Through his appointments of Bashford Dean and John I. Northrup, two faculty members in Columbia's School of Mines, and his own lectures to the College of Physicians and Surgeons, Osborn strategically linked the new department to other academic units in the university. He obtained financing that enabled Columbia faculty and students to do research at marine biology laboratories at Woods Hole, Massachusetts, and Naples, Italy. He helped develop Columbia's new biology laboratory; established a field biology laboratory at Port Townsend, Washington, and a teacher's summer school on Long Island; and initiated the prestigious Columbia lecture series in biology. As the first dean of the School of Pure Science, he made graduate education, research, and publication a priority and laid the foundations for what soon became a first-rate biology department. By 1897 Osborn had given up his administrative duties at Columbia, but he continued to teach there until 1910 and remained actively involved in departmental affairs for the rest of his life.

During the 1890s, while still active at Columbia, Osborn became increasingly involved in developing public institutions for biology in New York. As president of the executive committee of the New York Zoological Society, he selected the site and chose the director for the Bronx Zoo in 1896, and two years later he presided over its public opening. Even more significant were his efforts at the American Museum of Natural History. Appointed curator of a new program in vertebrate paleontology in 1891, Osborn quickly created a leading world center for that science. With financial support from museum trustees, notably his uncle J. Pierpont Morgan and Morris K. Jesup, a wealthy railroad securities broker and the museum's president, Osborn hired a large, diversified staff to carry out his and the trustees' objectives. Under his direction, collectors launched a series of annual expeditions that established an excellent fossil collection. By 1897 his program had expanded beyond the collection of mammals, and his assistants were excavating dinosaur remains in Montana and Wyoming. Ten years later Osborn sponsored an expedition to the Fa-

yûm of Egypt, and by the 1920s his interest in the search for fossil humans led to the museum's Central Asiatic Expeditions to the Gobi Desert in Mongolia.

Osborn also promoted the development of museum displays. In the 1880s Osborn had concentrated on research and publication, but in New York he embraced the museum trustees' interest in public education. He directed laboratory assistants to develop innovative means for exhibiting extinct animals in lifelike poses. His department was soon displaying fossil vertebrates in greater variety and larger numbers than any other institution in the United States. When fossil remains of gigantic sauropod dinosaurs were discovered in Wyoming and Montana in the late 1890s, Osborn made an all-out effort to present those creatures to the public. The American Museum was not the first institution to display dinosaurs, but the mountings of *Brontosaurus* in 1905 and *Tyrannosaurus rex* in 1910 were so popular that other natural history museums followed suit. Osborn directed his associates to publish popular guides and to create bronze miniatures, life-size restorations, and watercolor reproductions of prehistoric life. Charles R. Knight, an artist commissioned by Osborn, painted murals that defined the public perception of dinosaurs, mammoths, and fossil hominids for over fifty years.

In 1908 Osborn became museum president and promoted expeditions and exhibits on a grand scale. His interest in paleoanthropology led to the exploration of Cro-Magnon and Neanderthal sites in Europe and the development of a large Hall of the Age of Man. He actively supported Roy Chapman Andrews's explorations in Mongolia, and he sent other expeditions to the Congo, Micronesia, and Canada's Northwest Territories. Discoveries from those expeditions were displayed in large dioramas, habitat groups, and exhibit halls throughout the museum. The most famous was the Theodore Roosevelt Memorial, a project that was conceived by Osborn and required the construction of an entire new wing of the museum. Highlighted by the African Hall, which included habitat groups and a dramatic life-size herd of charging elephants constructed by the taxidermist Carl Akeley, the entire structure was a monument to Roosevelt, who had studied and hunted animals in Brazil, Africa, and North America. Through his connections, enthusiasm, and ability to orchestrate large projects involving thousands of dollars and dozens of people, Osborn made the American Museum the largest and most famous science museum in the country.

A wealthy and powerful figure, Osborn ran his program in vertebrate paleontology, and later the entire museum, as an aristocrat. He did not engage in the day-to-day scientific work of collecting, cleaning, or mounting fossil specimens but supervised those activities. His assistants, including scientists trained in zoology and paleontology, were at his beck and call, expected to drop their endeavors at any moment to assist with his research. A personal staff of artists, secretaries, and editorial assistants helped with his myriad scientific and administrative activities. Yet Osborn took most of the credit for his publications and the museum's achievements. He determined which expeditions, exhibits, and research projects were funded and which weren't, and by the 1920s the entire museum was a reflection of his personal interests and enthusiasms.

While engaged in administrative activities, Osborn also published extensively. He wrote on the evolution and classification of almost all families of fossil mammals and published technical and popular articles on dinosaurs. He was the author of several voluminous studies of fossil vertebrates, though all were done with help from his assistants. William Diller Matthew did much of the research and writing for Osborn's 1918 monograph, "The Equidae of the Oligocene, Miocene, and Pliocene of North America." William King Gregory wrote much of Osborn's two-volume work, *The Titanotheres of Ancient Wyoming, Dakota, and Nebraska* (1929). Osborn examined, described, and classified specimens in those and other works, but primarily he coordinated the efforts of an army of individuals who contributed to his publications.

Osborn also published prolifically on evolutionary biology. By 1896 he had developed a theory that explained evolution as the gradual unfolding of a hereditary potential that guided change in determinate, linear directions. Osborn's interest in evolution, biogeography, and functional morphology influenced Matthew and Gregory, who not only aided in his studies, but made important contributions in their own right. On the one hand, Osborn's belief that variations accumulated in a very slow, orderly, and predictable manner led him to reject the random, discontinuous changes associated with genetic mutations and fostered antagonism between paleontologists and geneticists at Columbia. On the other hand, his belief that evolution demonstrated plan and purpose led him to reject the claims of William Jennings Bryan and the Fundamentalists. Following the Scopes trial in 1925, he sought to reconcile science and religion with a theory of human evolution that denied mankind's ape ancestry.

Osborn's evolutionary interpretation also upheld conservative political and social values. His early evolutionary studies were conducted in the religious context at Princeton. In later years, as he solidified his ties with New York elites, he condemned twentieth-century social developments. Repelled by the nation's growing urbanization and ethnic pluralism, he adopted conservationist objectives, becoming a leader in the Audubon Society, the American Bison Society, and the Save the Redwoods League. His concern for the preservation of flora and fauna led Osborn to glorify the outdoor activities of the field biologist and condemn the experimental biologist who worked indoors in urban laboratories. Only the scientist who did first-hand work in the field could understand nature and nature's laws. Osborn's concern for the preservation of nature also extended to the white Anglo-Saxon Protestant elite to which he belonged. A proponent of eugenics, he viewed unrestricted immigration as a threat to public health and human survival. In *Men of the Old Stone Age* (1915) he claimed that humanity had declined after Cro-Magnon because of the onset of civilization and racial mixing. Based on his studies of fossils, which indicated that heredity controlled evolution, Osborn maintained that only those of a particular ancestry should guide human evolution. He termed his evolutionary theory aristogenesis.

The American Museum of Natural History reflected his worldview. Explorations were more than a basis for new discoveries; they were an opportunity to celebrate nature and escape the potentially debilitating effects of civilization. For those who could not participate in explorations, massive displays offered similar lessons. Exhibits of dinosaurs or titanotheres indicated the power of nature's creations; the Hall of the Age of Man and the Hall of Public Health implicitly suggested the threats posed by unrestricted immigration. Osborn made the museum a world leader, but it also reflected evolutionary and hereditarian ideas that grew out of the social concerns felt by the elite class to which he belonged.

The force of Osborn's scientific interpretations and institutional power eventually waned. While his views on variation, evolution, and inheritance had considerable support in the 1890s, by the decade beginning with 1910 significant new developments in genetics and other fields of experimental biology led most scientists to ignore or dispute his interpretations. Even Matthew and Gregory, who had assisted with his publications and tacitly supported his interpretations, began to criticize Osborn. By the 1920s leaders within the museum also were reacting against the excesses of the Osborn era. In 1933 he was pressured to resign as president and was hard-pressed to obtain support for his research. By the time of his death in Garrison, New York, biologists and paleontologists were supplanting his interpretations, and American Museum administrators were defining very different priorities for their institution. Yet Osborn remains a major figure in early twentieth-century paleontology, one who published prolifically and established the American Museum as a leading center for exploration, exhibition, and research in that field.

• Most of Osborn's papers are in the Central Archives in the Library of the American Museum of Natural History. That archive also possesses Osborn's official correspondence as museum president. The museum's Department of Vertebrate Paleontology possesses additional collections of Osborn correspondence as well as materials pertaining to his monographs and books. A separate collection of the Osborn papers is in the New-York Historical Society.

Osborn's bibliography comprises over 900 publications. His principal books include: *From the Greeks to Darwin: An Outline of the Idea of Evolution* (1894), *The Age of Mammals in Europe, Asia, and North America* (1910), *The Origin and Evolution of Life* (1917), *The Earth Speaks to Bryan* (1925), *Creative Education in School, College, University and Museum* (1927), *Man Rises to Parnassus* (1927), and *Cope: Master Naturalist. The Life and Writings of Edward Drinker Cope* (1931). His technical monographs include: "The Equidae of the Miocene, Oligocene, and Pliocene: Iconographic Type Revision," *Memoirs of the American Museum of Natural History*, n.s., 2 (1917): 1–217; and, with Charles C. Mook, "*Camarasaurus, Amphicoelias*, and other Sauropods of Cope," *Memoirs of the American Museum of Natural History*, n.s., 3 (1921): 247–387; *The Titanotheres of Ancient Wyoming, Dakota, and Nebraska* (2 vols., 1929); and *Proboscidea: A Monograph of the Discovery, Evolution, Migration and Extinction of the Elephants and Mastodonts of the World* (1936–1942).

The most recent biographical study is Ronald Rainger, *An Agenda for Antiquity: Henry Fairfield Osborn and Vertebrate Paleontology at the American Museum of Natural History, 1890–1935* (1991). See also William King Gregory, "Henry Fairfield Osborn," *National Academy of Sciences, Biographical Memoirs* 19 (1938): 53–119. Osborn is discussed in John Michael Kennedy, "Philanthropy and Science in New York City: The American Museum of Natural History, 1868–1968" (Ph.D. diss., Yale Univ., 1968); and Geoffrey Hellman, *Bankers, Bones and Beetles: The First Century of the American Museum of Natural History* (1968).

RONALD RAINGER

OSBORN, Paul (4 Sept. 1901–12 May 1988), playwright and screenwriter, was born Paul Romaine Osborn, in Evansville, Indiana, the son of Edwin Faxon Osborn, a Baptist minister and social reformer, and Laura Bertha Judson. When Osborn was one year old he moved with his parents to Kalamazoo, Michigan. Though popular fiction and visits to the theater were forbidden by his religiously strict father, young Osborn became an avid reader and worked for a time as an usher at Kalamazoo's Fuller Theatre. After graduating from Central High school in 1919, he spent one year at Kalamazoo College, then transferred to the University of Michigan, where he began an enduring friendship with Robert Frost, who was then poet in residence at the university. Receiving a bachelor's degree in English in 1923 and a master's degree in psychology in 1924, Osborn stayed on at the University of Michigan for two more years as an instructor of rhetoric.

Bored by academic life, Osborn began co-writing plays with a fellow instructor and thus discovered his talent for writing dialogue. In 1926 he won a scholarship to George Pierce Baker's playwriting workshop at Yale University and within a few months had sold his first full-length play, *Hotbed*, to Broadway producer Brock Pemberton. Not interested in a formal study of the theater, Osborn did not return to Yale for a second year. Instead, he moved to New York City, where he supported himself with odd jobs, including gate tender for the Long Island Railroad, while waiting for *Hotbed* to be produced. In March 1928 he married New Yorker Florence Louchheim. The couple had no children.

Osborn's first Broadway effort, *Hotbed*, was a heavy-handed drama about an overzealous clergyman who discovers his daughter is having an affair with a college professor. Basing the play on his experience as the child of a minister, and on his years as a college instructor, Osborn used the play to lash out at narrow-minded religious fanatics and spineless academics. *Hotbed* reached Broadway in November 1928 but survived for only nineteen performances. Osborn's sec-

ond Broadway effort, *A Ledge* (1929), was also short-lived. Following the advice of his wife, Osborn resumed work on an unfinished play, *The Vinegar Tree*, a Philip Barry–style society comedy about a flighty middle-aged woman's dalliance with a man she mistakenly thinks is an old flame. Starring Mary Boland, it opened at the Playhouse in New York City on 8 November 1930. John Anderson in the *New York Evening Journal* (19 Nov. 1930) called the play "a gay and giddy comedy" and added that Osborn "reveals throughout a sense of dialogue and pace that makes most of his play deftly amusing." *The Vinegar Tree* ran for the rest of the season and established Osborn as a leading young playwright. A film version of the play, *Should Ladies Behave?* (1933), featured Alice Brady and Lionel Barrymore.

After the failure of the comedies *Oliver, Oliver* (1934) and *Tomorrow's Monday* (1936, summer stock only), Osborn accepted an offer from producer Dwight Deere Wiman to write a stage adaptation of Lawrence Edward Watkin's novel *On Borrowed Time*, a heartwarming tale of a garrulous old man who keeps the Angel of Death at bay so that his orphaned grandson will not be left in the care of a puritanical aunt. Directed by Joshua Logan and starring Dudley Digges, *On Borrowed Time* opened at the Longacre Theatre on 3 February 1938. The success of this adaptation and the failure of his next original work, *Morning's at Seven* (1939), led Osborn to write more adaptations. He eventually came to be regarded as one of the most skilled adapters of novels for the stage and motion pictures. His stage adaptations include *The Innocent Voyage* (1943, from Richard Hughes's *A High Wind in Jamaica*), *A Bell for Adano* (1944, from the novel by John Hersey), *The Point of No Return* (1951, from the novel by John P. Marquand), and *The World of Suzie Wong* (1958, from the novel by Richard Mason). An original Osborn play written during this period, *The Maiden Voyage* (1957), loosely based on Greek myths, closed before reaching Broadway.

Notable among Osborn's film adaptations are *The Young in Heart* (1938, from I. A. R. Wylie's *The Gay Banditti*), *Madame Curie* (1943, from Eve Curie's biography of her mother), *Cry Havoc* (1943, from the novel by A. R. Kenward), *The Yearling* (1946, from the novel by Marjorie Kinnan Rawlings), *Portrait of Jennie* (1948, from the novel by Robert Nathan), *South Pacific* (1958, from James Michener's *Tales of the South Pacific*), and *Wild River* (1960, from Borden Deal's *Dunbar's Cove* and William Bradford Huie's *Mud on the Stars*). His screenplays for *East of Eden* (1955, from the novel by John Steinbeck) and *Sayonara* (1957, from the novel by James Michener) earned Academy Award nominations. "Sometimes I wish I'd never done an adaptation. I liked to write original plays so much more, but the adaptations were so easy. Someone would come up and ask me to do one, and since I wasn't doing anything else, I'd end up doing it," the blunt but soft-spoken Osborn told the *New York Times* in 1980.

A popular revival in 1980 of the 1939 failure *Morning's at Seven* did much to restore Osborn's reputation as an original playwright. The play tells the homely but affecting story of four midwestern sisters in late middle age who live with their families in neighboring houses and get up every morning at seven prepared to deal with whatever fate has in store. Its revival, directed by Vivian Matalon, starred Maureen O'Sullivan, Teresa Wright, Nancy Marchand, and Elizabeth Wilson. "A human comedy that is warm, antic, wise and utterly endearing," wrote T. E. Kalem in *Time* (21 Apr. 1980). Harold Clurman, in *The Nation* (3 May 1980), called the play "Chekhov on an American back porch." The success of *Morning's at Seven* led to major New York revivals of other Osborn works, including *Oliver, Oliver* at the Manhattan Theatre Club and *Tomorrow's Monday* at the Circle Repertory Theatre, both in 1985; *The Vinegar Tree* at the York Theatre Company in 1988; and *On Borrowed Time*, with George C. Scott, at the Circle-in-the-Square in 1991.

Divorced from Florence Louchheim in 1938, Osborn married actress and writer Millicent Green in 1939. They had a daughter. Having lost most of his sight to a degenerative eye disease and finding writing by dictation unworkable, Osborn wrote little in the last two decades of his life. He died at Mount Sinai Hospital in New York City.

Osborn was interested in exploring the conflicting emotions within ordinary people. His works take a sharp but often affectionate look at American family life and helped to lay the groundwork for later naturalistic playwrights such as Horton Foote and Lanford Wilson.

• Osborn's papers, which consist of scripts, correspondence, clippings, posters, and scrapbooks, are at the State Historical Society of Wisconsin in Madison. A good source of information on Osborn is Earl Charles Lammel, "Paul Osborn: A Professional Biography" (Ph.D. diss., Ohio State Univ., 1973). *World Authors, 1980–1985* (1991) offers an essay on Osborn. See also Michiko Kakutani, "40 Years Late, Osborn Has a Hit," *New York Times*, 14 Apr. 1980, and Stephen Harvey, "Renaissance of a Neglected Playwright," *New York Times*, 3 Nov. 1985. An obituary is in the *New York Times*, 13 May 1988.

MARY C. KALFATOVIC

OSBORN, Sarah Haggar Wheaten (22 Feb. 1714–2 Aug. 1796), revival leader and educator, was born in London, England, the daughter of Benjamin Haggar, a brazier, and Susanna Guyse. She came to New England in 1722 and by 1729 was settled in Newport, Rhode Island, where she lived for the rest of her life. In 1731, before she was eighteen, Sarah went against her parents' wishes and married Samuel Wheaten, a sailor, who died at sea two years later. Left with an infant son to support, Sarah took over the direction of a small school and, despite chronic ill health, ran a school almost continuously until she reached her sixties.

After years of soul searching, Sarah joined the First Congregational Church in Newport in 1737. Her life was permanently changed during 1740–1741 when she participated in revivals and heard the preaching of George Whitefield and Gilbert Tennent. Sarah later wrote: "A number of young women, who were awakened to a concern for their souls, came to me, and desired my advice and assistance, and proposed to join in a society, provided I would take care of them." Sarah, along with her close friend Susanna Anthony, led this female society as it continued to meet at least once a week throughout her lifetime. It was one of the few female prayer societies to survive the period of the Great Awakening, and it continued into the nineteenth century as the "Osborn Society." Sarah Wheaten Osborn's leadership of the female society fostered women's autonomy and independence, encouraged intellectual and benevolent activity, and helped pave the way for the female associations of the nineteenth century.

In 1742, a year after her first school failed, Sarah accepted a proposal of marriage from Henry Osborn, a widower with three grown sons. Henry's health and business failed a few months after their marriage, and he never worked steadily again. Shortly afterward Sarah opened another school to support the family and this time was successful. After 1758 she began to board students in her home. The school grew large, often including up to seventy students, male and female, black and white, including poor children.

Although some members of the community criticized Sarah Osborn for her work as a teacher because the school took time away from her family responsibilities, these criticisms were mild compared to those she received regarding her role as the focus of the Newport revival of 1766–1767 and her work with free blacks. In 1766 an "Ethiopian Society," probably made up of free blacks, began to meet weekly in the Osborn home, as did a group of up to forty-two slaves. At one point more than seventy blacks attended the revival in Osborn's home to read, sing, and converse about religious matters. Groups of whites including young women and men, as well as heads of households, Baptist men and women, and several children's groups also met at the Osborn home. In July 1766 over 300 people attended the weekly meetings; by January 1767 these numbers had reached 525. Understandably, Osborn was initially astonished at the numbers who flocked to her home: "I was affrighted at the throng and Greatly feared that it would be as the river Jordan overflowing all the banks." The Newport revival of 1766–1767 was the first revival led by a woman until the twentieth century to include both blacks and whites of both sexes and all ages.

Although it was considered socially acceptable for women in the eighteenth century to lead other women and teach children of both sexes, Osborn was clearly aware that in venturing to provide for the spiritual life of men and older boys she was moving beyond her ascribed role. Although she pleaded with clergy to assist her with the revival, she met with a mixed response. A friend and colleague to numerous clergy, Osborn corresponded for nearly forty years with Joseph Fish, a minister in Stonington, Connecticut. Although generally supportive of Osborn's work, Fish was concerned about her leadership of the revival and work with blacks, and encouraged her to develop more "feminine" interests. While she responded to Fish respectfully, Osborn argued her work was essentially an extension of the female role of Christian instruction and refused to give it up, believing she would "starve" without the stimulation of the meetings in her home. The meetings "refresh recruit and enliven my Exhausted spirits," she wrote Fish. "Would you advise me to shut up my Mouth and doors and creep into obscurity?"

As Sarah Osborn's health began to deteriorate further in the 1770s, it was another minister, Samuel Hopkins (1721–1803), who shared most intimately in her work until the end of her life. Osborn and the female society were instrumental in securing Hopkins's call to Newport, and he almost immediately began to participate in her work with blacks. Although Osborn had been working with blacks in Newport for almost twenty years before receiving consistent assistance from any minister, Hopkins continued her work in a more public fashion through his role as an antislavery advocate.

Sarah Osborn remained in Newport while the British occupied the city during the revolutionary war. Although a patriot by inclination, Osborn tended to see the American Revolution in religious rather then political terms, praying for the repentance and conversion of the new nation. During the war when Hopkins and other ministers fled Newport, members of the First Congregational Church continued to worship in the Osborn home, thus assuring the survival of Congregationalism in that city.

Sarah Osborn's life bespeaks the centrality of women to eighteenth-century evangelical culture. Her experience of the revivals of the Great Awakening suggests religion as a primary motivating factor for American women, allowing them to transcend constricting gender roles. Revivals such as the one Osborn led in 1766–1767 caused disruptions of the social structure, giving women opportunities to exercise religious leadership. Moreover, evidence of Osborn's alliances with ministers supports the existence of working partnerships between men and women in the eighteenth century, while her friendship with Samuel Hopkins encouraged the growth of antislavery activity in America.

During the last twenty-five years of her life, Osborn's health gradually deteriorated, though she continued her work with the female society and as a mentor to ministers of the First Congregational Church to the end. She died in Newport.

• Sarah Osborn's diaries are in the Beinecke Rare Book and Manuscript Library, Yale University; the Newport Historical Society, R.I.; and the Connecticut Historical Society, Hartford. Osborn's correspondence is in the Sarah Osborn Letters Collection at the American Antiquarian Society; the Samuel Hopkins Papers, Andover Newton Theological School, Franklin Trask Library; the Simon Gratz Collection, Historical Society of Pennsylvania, Philadelphia; and the Silliman Family Papers, Sterling Memorial Library, Yale University. See also Samuel Hopkins, comp., *Memoirs of the Life of Mrs. Sarah Osborn* (1799), and Elizabeth West Hopkins, comp., *Familiar Letters Written by Mrs. Sarah Osborn and Miss Susanna Anthony* (1807). Sarah Osborn's tract, *The Nature, Certainty and Evidence of True Christianity* (1755), is her only known work to be published during her lifetime. Secondary sources include Mary Beth Norton, "'My Resting Reaping Times': Sarah Osborn's Defense of Her Unfeminine Activities, 1767," *Signs* 2, no. 2 (1976): 515–29; Barbara E. Lacey, "The Bonds of Friendship: Sarah Osborn of Newport and the Reverend Joseph Fish of North Stonington, 1743–1779," *Rhode Island History* 45, no. 4 (1986): 127–36; and three articles by Sheryl A. Kujawa: "The Great Awakening of Sarah Osborn and the Female Society of the First Congregational Church in Newport," *Newport History* 65 (Spring 1994): 133–53, "The Teacher as Reformer: Sarah Osborn, 1714–1796," *Union Seminary Quarterly Review* 47 (1993): 89–100, and "Religion, Education, and Gender in Eighteenth-Century Rhode Island: Sarah Haggar Wheaten Osborn, 1714–1796," *Rhode Island History* 52 (May 1994): 35–48.

SHERYL A. KUJAWA

OSBORN, Thomas Andrew (26 Oct. 1836–4 Feb. 1898), lawyer, politician, and diplomat, was born in Meadville, Pennsylvania, the son of Carpenter Osborn and Elizabeth Morris. Nothing is known about what his parents did for a living. Osborn learned the printing trade in Meadville and attended the preparatory department of Allegheny College from 1855 to 1857. He read for the law in 1856. In 1857 he moved to Pontiac, Michigan, where he was admitted to the bar. He left Pontiac in late 1857 and settled in Lawrence, Kansas, where he worked as a print compositor and occasional acting editor of the *Kansas Herald of Freedom*. In 1858 he opened a law office in nearby Elwood and was elected attorney for Doniphan County.

A Republican and a Free Stater, Osborn held strong antislavery views. In 1862, only twenty-six years old, he was elected president pro tempore of the Kansas Senate and presided at the impeachment of Governor Charles Robinson, the secretary of state, and the state auditor. Later in 1862 he was elected lieutenant governor of Kansas. President Abraham Lincoln appointed Osborn U.S. marshal in 1864, but President Andrew Johnson removed him in 1867 because he opposed administration policies. He apparently returned to law practice until he ran for governor in 1872.

In 1870 Osborn married Julia Delahay, daughter of federal judge Mark W. Delahay. They had one child. In 1873 Osborn began the first of two two-year terms as the sixth governor of Kansas, his governorship coinciding with the whole of the depression of 1873 to 1877. His administration successfully urged laws prohibiting lotteries, creating a state board of education, establishing a state insane asylum, and providing for biennial rather than annual legislative sessions. He handled the major crises of his administration—drought, a grasshopper plague, scandals about the misuse of state funds, and the impact of the depression of 1873—with ability. Calling a special session of the legislature, Osborn supervised efficient relief operations during the destructive "grasshopper year" of 1874. Faced with disturbances between settlers and American Indians on Kansas's southern border, he managed to avoid warfare. In 1874 and 1876 he undertook prompt measures to steady financial markets and avoid a financial crisis when successive state treasurers mismanaged state funds. One resigned; the other, accused of forgery with state bonds, fled but was arrested in Chicago and returned to Kansas. During his terms as governor, he encouraged foreign immigration and settlement in Kansas.

In 1877 Osborn unsuccessfully campaigned for the U.S. Senate. Afterward President Rutherford B. Hayes appointed him minister to Chile on 31 May 1877. He and Thomas Ogden Osborn (no relation), U.S. minister to Argentina, were instrumental in arranging a settlement of the longstanding dispute between Chile and Argentina over the Patagonian boundary, the southernmost tip of South America. He failed to arrange a peaceful settlement of the Tacna-Arica conflict—over control of the rich coastal areas of Bolivia and Peru—between Chile on one side and Peru and Bolivia on the other. Chile's modern military won the war, stripped Bolivia of its only seacoast, and took the coastal provinces Tacna and Arica from Peru. Although the U.S. government wished to remain neutral in the conflict, rising foreign concern about the disruption of economic and commercial activity disturbed U.S. officials, who also looked askew at a total Chilean victory. In mid-1880 Osborn suggested that it might be time for mediation in the dispute. While the subsequent exchanges of views did not produce an immediate settlement, the fighting wound down in the early 1880s. (The treaty was eventually signed in 1883.) Appointed minister resident to Brazil by President James A. Garfield on 19 May 1881, Osborn presented his recall on 28 July 1881.

Osborn presented his credentials in Brazil on 17 December 1881. He easily obtained Brazil's agreement to attend the Pan-American peace conference scheduled for Washington, D.C., in the fall of 1882, but the conference was canceled after Garfield's assassination when President Chester Arthur named Frederick Theodore Frelinghuysen to succeed Secretary of State James G. Blaine. No significant issues disturbed relations between the United States and Brazil, but Osborn did report on the tension between Brazil and its neighbors Argentina and Uruguay. In appreciation of his service, the Brazilian government awarded Osborn the Grand Cross of the Order of the Rose. He was recalled on 11 July 1885, apparently in the normal rotation of patronage at the change of administrations.

Osborn returned to Topeka, Kansas, where he engaged in banking, mining, real estate, railroads, and politics. He headed the Kansas delegation to the 1888 Republican National Convention and that year was elected state senator from Shawnee County, serving two terms. In 1894 he became a director of the Atchison, Topeka, and Santa Fe Railroad, a position he held until his death. Osborn died in Meadville, Pennsylvania, where he was visiting his birthplace after attending an Atchison, Topeka, and Santa Fe board meeting in New York.

• The U.S. State Department's microfilmed records contain Osborn's official correspondence from Chile (microfilm M10, reels 29–31) and from Brazil (microfilm M121, reels 47 and 48). Some of his official correspondence is published in U.S. State Department, *Papers Relating to the Foreign Relations of the United States, 1882* (1884). Osborn has not yet attracted a biographer. A sketch of Osborn is in John E. Findling, ed., *Dictionary of American Diplomatic History* (1989). His domestic political career is sketched in Daniel Webster Wilder, *The Annals of Kansas* (1886), Frank W. Blackmar, *Kansas: A Cyclopedia of State History* (2 vols., 1912), William Frank Zornow, *Kansas: A History of the Jayhawk State* (1957), and Robert W. Richmond, *Kansas: A Land of Contrasts*, 3d ed. (1989). His career in Chile is described briefly in Henry Clay Evans, *Chile and Its Relations with the United States* (1927), Herbert Millington, *American Diplomacy and the War of the Pacific* (1948), David Pletcher, *The Awkward Years: American Foreign Relations under Garfield and Arthur* (1962), Jay Kinsbruner, *Chile: A Historical Interpretation* (1973), and William F. Sater, *Chile and the War of the Pacific* (1986). An obituary is in the *New York Times*, 5 Feb. 1898.

THOMAS SCHOONOVER

OSBORN, William Henry (21 Dec. 1820–2 Mar. 1894), merchant, railroad executive, and philanthropist, was born in Salem, Massachusetts, the son of William Osborn and Anna Henfield Bowditch, farmers. After a few years at local schools Osborn, at the age of thirteen, became a clerk in a Boston firm, the East India House of Peele, Hubbell & Company. Bright and quite capable, by age sixteen he was representing his firm in Manila, Philippine Islands. While still in his twenties Osborn set up his own import-export business in Manila. The new firm prospered and by the early 1850s he had made a small fortune. He left the Philippines, toured Europe, and returned to the United States in 1853.

In New York City Osborn met Jonathan Sturges, an import merchant with whom he had done business while in Manila, and in December 1853 Osborn married Sturges's daughter, Virginia Reed Sturges. After a European honeymoon the couple made their home in New York City; they had four children. Sturges, one of the incorporators of the Illinois Central (IC) Railroad and still active in the affairs of the company, introduced his son-in-law to the directors of the line. Osborn became interested in the IC, and he was elected a director on 11 August 1854, a position he would hold until 1877. He was elected vice president in June 1855 and president of the railroad on 1 December 1855. The IC had been aided by a federal land grant in 1850, but its position when Osborn joined the board in 1854 was precarious. It was an unfinished, disconnected road of about 300 miles, had a floating debt of $2.5 million, and was facing a scandal involving its first president, Robert Schuyler. In 1854 the 34-year-old Osborn was without any railroad experience, but he soon mastered the details of railroad management, financial matters in particular.

Osborn insisted that the IC should be completed with short-term loans rather than by assessing the stockholders up to the par value of their stock. When the road was finished in September 1856, the wishbone-shaped 705-mile line ran from Cairo, Illinois, north to Dunleith in the northwestern corner of the state, with a second line to Chicago. It had cost $26 million to build and was reported to be the longest railroad in the world. When the panic of 1857 caused a serious reduction in freight traffic, Osborn knew he had little chance of renewing the $4 million of short-term obligations. He avoided receivership by assessing the stock up to par, convincing the foreign bondholders of the road's future, and using his own credit to support the obligations of his road. The worst of the crisis passed during 1858 and 1859, and by 1860 freight traffic was up a third over that of 1857. The IC paid its first dividend in 1861.

When the Civil War started in 1861, Cairo, at the mouth of the Ohio, was one of four rail gateways to the South. The north-south IC route was like a gun pointed down the Mississippi toward the lower Confederacy. Osborn made the Illinois Central a funnel to the South as troops and supplies were gathered at Cairo to support General Ulysses S. Grant's campaign against Forts Henry and Donelson. Total IC revenue doubled during the war. Osborn paid off $2 million of funded debt, and dividends rose to $6 in 1863, $8 in 1864, and $10 in 1865. During the war the IC sold over 800,000 acres of its land grant for about $9 million. Osborn urged his land agents to sell the land in small parcels so that they could be cultivated, adding to the value of adjacent acres. Osborn retired as president in 1865 with the Illinois Central in excellent financial shape.

Osborn had little interest in extending the IC westward into Iowa, but he was eager to find a rail connection south of Cairo. In the late 1850s he had convinced George Peabody of London to help finance the completion of the Mississippi Central, a 238-mile line connecting Jackson, Tennessee, with Canton, Mississippi. South of Canton, the New Orleans, Jackson & Great Northern provided rail service to New Orleans. Both southern roads were badly worn and damaged during the Civil War. By 1870 both lines had been acquired and modestly restored by Colonel Henry S. McComb, a northerner from Delaware. In 1872 Osborn inspected the two southern lines belonging to McComb. Once back in Illinois Osborn persuaded his fellow IC directors to loan $16 million to McComb, the money to be used to pay old debts and to upgrade the two roads south of Jackson, Tennessee. About $3 million of the total loan was to be spent in building a 104-mile extension from Jackson north to East Cairo, Kentucky. The depression following the panic of 1873 pushed both of McComb's roads into receivership. Osborn headed up an Illinois Central group that purchased the two lines in 1877.

In November 1877 the two recently acquired lines were merged into the Chicago, St. Louis & New Orleans Railroad. Osborn became president of the new consolidated line, and seven of the twelve board members were IC men. Late in 1882 the IC negotiated a 400-year lease of the Chicago, St. Louis & New Orleans. Soon thereafter Osborn retired from the presidency of the southern lines. Not long before his retirement Osborn was able to sell a major issue of IC bonds at a very low interest rate of 3.5 percent. Osborn was a stern man and sometimes had a sharp tongue, but he had given nearly three decades of devoted and skillful service to the Illinois Central.

In retirement Osborn turned to a life of philanthropy. While residing in Chicago, he and his wife were active in sponsoring a library and an employees' relief association for railroad workers. In New York City Osborn liberally supported the New York Hospital, Bellevue Training School for Nurses, and the Society for the Relief of the Ruptured and Crippled. Also in retirement he greatly enlarged his own excellent library and art collection. Much of his retirement was spent at "Castle Rock," his Garrison, New York, estate. Osborn died in New York City.

• Many letters and other material concerning Osborn are located in the Illinois Central Archives (1851–1906), Newberry Library, Chicago. Osborn's career with the IC is reviewed in Carlton J. Corliss, *Main Line of Mid-America: The Story of the Illinois Central* (1950), and John F. Stover, *History of the Illinois Central Railroad* (1975). Additional material on Osborn's railroad years is in Thomas C. Cochran, *Railroad Leaders, 1845–1890: The Business Mind in Action* (1953). Osborn's role in extending the IC line south of the Ohio River is also told by Stover in *The Railroads of the South, 1865–1900: A Study in Finance and Control* (1955). An obituary is in the *New York Tribune*, 4 Mar. 1894.

JOHN F. STOVER

OSBORNE, Estelle Massey Riddle (3 May 1901–12 Dec. 1981), nursing leader, was born Estelle Massey in Palestine, Texas, the daughter of Hall Massey and Bettye Estelle (maiden name unknown). At the time of her birth, many black Americans lived in conditions of poverty and sickness similar to slave days. Because black doctors were scarce, black nurses provided the bulk of health care for their communities. Thus for working-class and poor black women, nursing offered an appealing way to embark on a profession, to enter the middle class and gain prestige, and to help others of their race at a time when segregation was common and racism virulent.

As a young woman, Osborne considered becoming a dentist like her brother. He dissuaded her, however, arguing that she did not have enough money for dental training and that in any case, nursing was a more suitable job for a woman. At the time, the profession was racially segregated across much of the nation. In 1920, after briefly attending Prairie View College in Prairie View, Texas, Osborne enrolled at the nursing school based at the racially segregated Homer G. Phillips Hospital in St. Louis, Missouri; she graduated in 1923 and later scored 93.3 percent on the Missouri state nursing exam. Named head nurse of a large ward at the hospital, she became the first black administrator there.

In 1927 Osborne moved to New York City, where she enrolled in Teachers College at Columbia University. Three years later she earned a bachelor of science degree in nursing education. In 1931 (supported by a grant from the Julius Rosenwald Fund) she obtained a master's degree in nursing education—the first black American nurse to do so. She became an instructor at Harlem Hospital and later served as educational director at Freedmen's Hospital in Washington, D.C. In the mid-1930s she returned to St. Louis and became the first black nursing director at Homer G. Phillips Hospital. She also participated in a Rosenwald-funded study of health and welfare in the rural South.

At that time, white-run southern nursing schools and colleges rejected black students, whereas most northern schools set a quota on the number of black applicants that were admitted. The professional societies were no less segregated. Black nurses were denied membership in seventeen state affiliates of the American Nurses' Association and in the National League of Nursing Education. In addition, salaries for black nurses were markedly lower than those for whites. The National Association of Colored Graduate Nurses (NACGN), founded in 1908, tried to defend the rights of black nurses but was hampered by its tiny membership—only 175 members in 1933. The following year, Osborne was elected president.

Mabel Keaton Staupers was Osborne's choice as NACGN's first executive secretary. Their energetic collaboration would do much to rejuvenate the organization and thereby mobilize the NACGN toward the goal of opening up the profession to black nurses. As women, Osborne and Staupers had much in common. Both had been married to black doctors, then divorced, then remarried; neither had any children. An associate described both women as "flamboyant"; Osborne was "tall, had a high sense of fashion, wore exquisite jewelry, was noted for her hats, and her sense of grooming and dress" and would have appeared "perfectly at home in *Vogue* or *Harper's Bazaar*" (Hine, p. 121). Together the two women toured the eastern and midwestern states, where they met with black nurses and observed their working situations. As Hine has recorded they encountered "dozens of moribund state affiliates, disillusioned nurses, and a generally uninformed public . . . The overwhelming majority of black nurses neither belonged to nor apparently identified with the NACGN" (Hine, p. 121).

Throughout her five-year tenure as NACGN president, Osborne wrote articles decrying the serious shortage of black nurses, particularly in the South. "Hundreds of miles of rural areas are untouched by Negro nurses in both the North and the South," she reported in the *Journal of Negro Education* in 1937. "If a county has money to employ but one or two nurses the preference is given to the white nurse, irrespective of the size of the Negro population." In addition, many black nurses received poor training. Osborne charged that of the more than one hundred "so-called

training schools for Negro nurses" then in operation, only twenty-six were accredited by the National League of Nursing Education.

During World War II Osborne served on the NACGN Special Defense Committee, which fought racial discrimination in the hiring of military nurses. She also became consultant to the National Nursing Council for War Service. In 1943 her friend and congresswoman Frances Bayne Bolton of Ohio pushed through the bill authorizing the creation of the U.S. Cadet Nurses Corps as an arm of the U.S. Public Health Service. The bill's antidiscrimination clause marked a major step forward for black nurses. However, although the war effort had afforded blacks greater economic opportunities, the battle for fair treatment of black nurses was far from won. In August 1945, the last month of the war, Osborne pointed out (with co-author Josephine Nelson) in the *American Journal of Nursing* that there were only 8,000 registered black nurses in the United States—2.9 percent of the total number—even though blacks made up 10 percent of the population.

In 1946 Osborne became the first black member of the nursing faculty at the New York University School of Education, a post she held until 1952. Also in 1946 she received the Mary Mahoney Award from the NACGN, named for the first black registered nurse trained in the United States, and became associate general director of the National League for Nursing; she held that post until 1967. Having gained a national reputation, Osborne served as secretary of the New York state committee supporting Progressive party candidate Henry A. Wallace's 1948 presidential campaign. That same year she became the first black member elected to the board of directors of the American Nurses' Association, a position she held for four years. In 1949 she was an ANA delegate to the International Congress of Nurses held in Stockholm, Sweden. In 1952 she was elected first vice president of the National Council of Negro Women, which she had helped to found in 1935 and which she had served previously as second vice president.

In the late 1940s and early 1950s, with the emergence of the civil rights movement, opportunities for black nurses improved dramatically. By 1949, as Osborne reported in the *Journal of Negro Education*, 354 U.S. nursing school had adopted a nondiscrimination policy, compared to only 29 in 1941; and over the same eight-year period, the number of southern nursing associations that refused to accept black nurses as members had been cut almost in half. These gains were seemingly so significant that in 1951 NACGN officials voted to disband the organization because they believed it had achieved its primary goals. At the group's final meeting, however, Osborne cautioned her colleagues about continuing inequalities in preliminary education and the problem of segregated and inadequately supported nursing schools; about salary differentials on the basis of race; about fewer job opportunities and resistant barriers to advancement. "Frequently there is merely token or no representation of Negro nurses in the policy-making areas at the highest levels of participation," Osborne said, linking the NACGN's unfinished work with the "unfinished business of democracy" (Carnegie, 1986, p. 100).

In 1959 New York University honored Osborne by presenting her its Nurse of the Year award. In 1978 she became the first black nurse to be recognized as an Honorary Fellow by the American Academy of Nursing. That same year—another sign of how much American nursing had changed since her youth—the American Nurses' Association elected its first black president, Barbara Nichols. Osborne died in Oakland, California. In 1984 the American Nurses' Association inducted her into its Hall of Fame.

• An oral history interview conducted by Patricia Sloan is filed at the M. Elizabeth Carnegie Nursing History Archive at Hampton University School of Nursing, Hampton, Va. Osborne's many articles include "The Training and Placement of Negro Nurses," *Journal of Negro Education* 4 (1935); "Sources of Supply of Negro Health Personnel—Section C: Nurses," *Journal of Negro Education* 6 (1937); "Negro Nurses: The Supply and Demand," *Opportunity: Journal of Negro Life* 15 (Nov. 1937); "The Negro Nurse Looks toward Tomorrow" (with Josephine Nelson), *American Journal of Nursing* 45 (Aug. 1945); "Status and Contribution of the Negro Nurse," *Journal of Negro Education* 18 (Summer 1949); and "Integration in Professional Nursing" (with Mary E. Carnegie), *Crisis* 69 (Jan. 1962). Several of her articles are reprinted in *The History of American Nursing*, ed. Susan Reverby (1985). A memorial statement, including biographical details, was issued by the American Academy of Nursing after Osborne's death; it is reprinted in Mary Elizabeth Carnegie, *The Path We Tread—Blacks in Nursing, 1854–1984* (1986). Osborne's career is discussed in a book by Mabel Keaton Staupers, *No Time for Prejudice* (1961). A key source on black nursing history is Darlene Clark Hine, *Black Women in White* (1989); see in particular chapter eight, which details the battles for black nurses' rights during the Second World War. An obituary is in the *New York Times*, 17 Dec. 1981.

KEAY DAVIDSON

OSBORNE, Mary (17 July 1921–4 Mar. 1992), jazz guitarist and singer, was born Mary Orsborn in Minot, North Dakota. Although her parents's names are unknown, it is known that both played the guitar. Her mother also sang, and her father, a barber, led ragtime and country string bands. She took up the ukulele at age four, violin during first grade in grammar school, and guitar at age nine. The following year she joined her father's group, in which she played banjo. From age eleven to age fifteen, while attending school, she performed twice weekly on local radio station KLPM. At age twelve she began working professionally, leading an all-girl hillbilly, dinner music, and light classical trio in Bismarck, North Dakota. As a teenager she sang and played jazz in nightclubs.

Osborne joined the trio of pianist Winifred McDonnell (or McDonald; sources disagree), including bassist and violinist Mary Wood, in Bismarck, at age fifteen; in the trio she performed on string bass as well as singing and playing guitar. At age seventeen she heard the electric guitarist Charlie Christian at a local club

and was overwhelmed by his talent. Immediately she purchased an electric instrument and amplifier and began modeling her soloing after his swinging single-note lines. While touring, McDonnell's trio broadcast on KDKA in Pittsburgh, Pennsylvania; then they all joined Buddy Rogers's band. Osborne continued touring with McDonnell, finally arriving in New York City, where Rogers disbanded and she found work on radio, at recording sessions, and in clubs on Fifty-second Street.

Osborne became romantically involved with trumpeter Ralph Scaffidi, who secured a job for her in Dick Stabile's band. Receiving scarcely any opportunity to play solos with Stabile, she left to work in other bands, most notably with Joe Venuti for eight months. Venuti was reportedly so taken by her playing that he featured her constantly, to the exclusion of others in the band, and offered her use of his late partner Eddie Lang's guitar if she would stay.

Osborne married Scaffidi in 1942; they had three children. When he was drafted in 1942, she resumed her freelance activities in Chicago, Illinois, where she recorded with violinist Stuff Smith. In 1944 she sat in with tenor saxophonist Coleman Hawkins and pianist Art Tatum during a concert at the Academy of Music in Philadelphia, Pennsylvania, and in January 1945 she was recorded in concert in New Orleans, Louisiana.

Moving to New York City, she formed a trio with pianist Sanford Gold and bassist Frenchy Couette (or Cauette) for a year-long engagement at Kelly's Stable. This opportunity led to further radio and club work and a recording contract. Her recordings as a leader included "Mary's Guitar Boogie" and "The One I Love Belongs to Someone Else" (c. 1946). Her finest recordings with others included "Spotlite" and "Low Flame" from a session with Hawkins (1946); "Allen's Alley" from that same session, but without Hawkins himself participating; and "Low Ceiling" (a retitled "How High the Moon") from among three tracks with pianist and singer Beryl Booker's trio (1946). She also recorded two sessions with pianist Mary Lou Williams (c. 1945 and 1946). Osborne's trio continued until 1949, with Jack Pleis replacing Gold. She then worked as a soloist, making appearances on Arthur Godfrey's television show.

From 1952 to 1962 or 1963 she was a studio musician at CBS in New York, performing in Elliott Lawrence's quartet on Jack Sterling's radio show in the morning, playing on Ted Steele's television show in the afternoon, and recording at night, including trombonist and vibraphonist Tyree Glenn's album *Tyree Glenn at the Embers* (1957) and her own album *Girl and Her Guitar* with pianist Tommy Flanagan (1959; reissued as *Now and Then* with additional performances from c. 1981). In 1962 she studied classical guitar with Alberto Valdez Blaine, and she resumed playing in clubs, while also teaching students.

In 1968 Osborne and Scaffidi settled in Bakersfield, California. She taught at workshops for his Osborne Guitar Company (later, Osborne Sound Laboratories), manufacturer of Rosac amplifiers. She also performed with her own quartet four nights a week at the local Hilton Hotel, taught both in school and privately, and began to give concerts, appearing at the Newport and Concord jazz festivals in the early 1970s. At times she led a family jazz band, including her husband on trumpet and her son on bass.

Osborne recorded the bop album *Now's the Time* as a member of pianist Marian McPartland's quintet during a performance in Rochester, New York, in 1977. She went to New York again in 1981 to perform at the Kool Jazz Festival and in 1990 for an engagement at the Village Vanguard nightclub. She also performed at the Classic Jazz Festival in Los Angeles, California, in 1989 and 1990, the Playboy Jazz Marathon in Hollywood, California, in 1990, and the Los Angeles Airport Hilton in 1991. She died in Bakersfield.

In a genre dominated by male instrumentalists, Osborne was among the few women players who sustained a career with leading jazz musicians, and she was the only woman who made a significant mark as a swing guitarist. She was also one of the first female electric guitarists. Her playing followed Christian's innovative style closely, except for a personalized manner of substituting rhythmically stuttering lines for Christian's characteristic smoothness.

• Surveys of Osborne's career include Leonard Feather, "Mary Osborne: A TV Natural," *Down Beat*, 18 May 1951, pp. 4–5; Leonard Ferris (presumably a pseudonym for Feather), "Mary Osborne: A Unique Role in Jazz Guitar History," *Guitar Player* 8 (Feb. 1974): 10, 30–31; Sally Placksin, *American Women in Jazz: 1900 to the Present: Their Words, Lives, and Music* (1982); Linda Dahl, *Stormy Weather: The Music and Lives of a Century of Jazzwomen* (1984); and Feather, *The Jazz Years: Earwitness to an Era* (1986). Obituaries are in the *Los Angeles Times*, 5 Mar. 1992; the *New York Times*, 6 Mar. 1992; and *Jazz Journal International* 45 (Sept. 1992): 17 and 19.

BARRY KERNFELD

OSBORNE, Thomas Burr (5 Aug. 1859–29 Jan. 1929), chemist and biochemist, was born in New Haven, Connecticut, the son of Arthur Dimon Osborne, an attorney and banker, and Frances Louisa Blake. Osborne attended Yale University and received his bachelor's degree in 1881. A year in Yale's medical school was not to his liking, so Osborne enrolled in the graduate school to study chemistry in 1882. One year later he was employed as a laboratory assistant in analytical chemistry, a post that enabled him to pursue his own research and publish three papers, the last of which served as his dissertation for the doctorate degree, awarded in 1885 ("The Quantitative Determination of Niobium," *American Journal of Science* 30 [1885]: 329–37). While in the chemistry program, Osborne came under the tutelage of Samuel W. Johnson, a pioneer agricultural chemist in the United States. With Johnson's support, Osborne stayed on at the Sheffield Scientific School for an additional year as an instructor and researcher in analytical chemistry. In May 1886 Johnson, concurrently director of the Connecticut Agricultural Experiment Station (CAES) in New Haven, appointed Osborne to the staff of the station's chemistry department, where he would remain for his entire professional career, becoming head of that department in 1902. Osborne's ties to Johnson were strengthened by his marriage to Johnson's daughter, Elizabeth Annah, in June 1886.

Two years later, at Johnson's request, Osborne began his chemical studies of the proteins of the seeds of plants used extensively as human food and animal feed, a subject that dominated his research over the next forty years. His first publication in this area dealt with the proteins of oats (1891). His last paper on the topic was concerned with chemical structures of proteins (1928). Osborne proved to be Johnson's most eminent pupil in both the high quality and quantity of research projects and publications. "They were in daily contact for nearly thirty years, Johnson the scholar, . . . Osborne . . . the careful experimenter" (Vickery, p. 265). By 1901 the "careful experimenter" had come to the conclusion that ultimate chemical analysis (that is, analysis for carbon, oxygen, hydrogen, and sulfur) was not an adequate measure of the purity and specificity of proteins found in seeds. Using the newest techniques, he initiated attempts to break proteins down into their amino acids, units then coming to be seen as the building blocks of proteins.

As of 1908, Osborne had isolated proteins from more than thirty different plant seeds (including those of oats, maize, wheat, rye, barley, and various beans) and was beginning to accumulate data on the amino acid composition of many of these proteins. It is not surprising to find that Osborne wondered whether such differences as he was finding implied differences in the nutritive properties of the proteins. Events of the following year, 1909, turned Osborne's work into new directions. First, the efforts of twenty years of research were published in his book, *The Vegetable Proteins* (1909; 2d ed., 1924), in which he summed up the methods of extraction, analysis, purification, and classification of proteins from seeds. Second, the death of his mentor, Samuel Johnson, deprived Osborne of his closest scientific confidant. A cooperative alliance with Lafayette B. Mendel, Yale's preeminent physiological chemist, was formed, and the two men set out to investigate the nutritive and physiological properties of proteins and amino acids. Mendel, although thirteen years younger than Osborne, gradually assumed Johnson's role of scholar while Osborne continued on as the careful experimenter.

Beginning in August 1909, feeding experiments were carried out using the albino rat as the principal subject. Although animal feeding experiments had been done by other researchers for more than fifty years, no long-term, systematic approach using small animals with short reproductive cycles had been conducted until Elmer V. McCollum developed the first such rat colony to study nutrition at the University of Wisconsin in 1907. Osborne and Mendel modeled their colony, in part, along the lines of McCollum's. In sum, what chemical analysis could not do in 1909 could probably be done through animal feeding experiments, namely, discover the nutritive properties of different proteins. Averaging nearly five publications annually over the next twenty years, Osborne and Mendel became a "scientific name" as their efforts revealed both qualitative and quantitative needs for various proteins and amino acids in the diets of their experimental animals. Some proteins, for example, were found to be capable of supporting normal growth while others served only to maintain animals at constant weight; some proved to be totally ineffective in supporting life at all. These characteristics, amply demonstrated by 1911, became the substance of Osborne and Mendel's first publication in the field, *Feeding Experiments with Isolated Food-Substances* (Carnegie Institution of Washington, Pub. No. 156 [2 vols., 1911–1912]).

In later years, Osborne and Mendel discovered the absolute need of the animal for two amino acids, lysine and tryptophan. Their persistence in refining dietaries led them to the independent discovery of vitamin A. By 1917 they had confirmed the existence of vitamin B but suspected it to be a complex of more than one substance. Furthermore, their comprehensive research shed new light on the mineral and trace mineral requirements of animals. The overall importance of their endeavors was understood by other investigators in nutrition who initiated their own studies using the albino rat as the experimental animal. Even a superficial examination of publications in the *Journal of Biological Chemistry* alone between 1910 and 1920 shows the rapid spread of animal feeding experiments in many laboratories in the United States.

Within the laboratory he supervised at the CAES, Osborne was known as an aloof, domineering individual, cautious to the extreme in both his professional and personal lives. These characteristics, as well as his enormous persistence, are readily discernible in his published papers, his correspondence, and his laboratory notebooks. Caution and persistence also are apparent in the flowcharts he prepared, often on grocery wrapping paper common at that time, to illustrate, stepwise, methods of obtaining purified proteins and amino acids, methods that frequently required many months to bring to completion. Osborne employed a similar tactic to clarify methodologies described by other researchers in their publications. One of these, for example, showing Casimir Funk's preparation of a substance rich in vitamin B, consists of diagrams on sheets of note paper, glued together to form a chart, five inches wide and more than eight feet in length. This level of thoroughness and persistence has been preserved by the historical tradition of the CAES; the station's permanent collection includes not only written materials but also samples of proteins and amino acids prepared by Osborne, some of which date back to the last years of the nineteenth century.

Thomas Burr Osborne's life was totally committed to chemistry, and for his accomplishments he received numerous awards (Gold Medal of the Paris Exposition in 1900, for example) as well as honorary degrees. He retired from the CAES in mid-1928 and died about seven months later at his home in New Haven, survived by his wife and one of their two children. His legacy to biochemistry lies principally in his work that revealed the chemical diversities among the proteins of plant seeds, followed by efforts that illuminated the biochemical differences of these same proteins when fed to growing animals (the albino rat in particular). Add to these accomplishments his role in elaborating and confirming the vitamin hypothesis and it becomes clear why, nearly seventy years after his death, Osborne's name has continued to appear in bibliographies attached to various publications on nutrition.

• Osborne's papers, correspondence, notebooks, and sample materials are located in the Thomas Burr Osborne Collection of the biochemistry department at the Connecticut Agricultural Experiment Station, New Haven. Some important works by Osborne are "The Proteids or Albuminoids of the Oat-Kernel," *American Chemistry Journal* 13 (1891): 327–47, 385–414; "A Review of Hypotheses of the Structure of Proteins," *Physiological Reviews* 8 (1928): 393–446; "The Relation of Growth to the Chemical Constituents of the Diet," *Journal of Biological Chemistry* 15 (1913): 311–26; and "The Anaphylactogenic Activity of Some Vegetable Proteins, V," *Journal of Infectious Diseases* 14 (1914): 377–84. An excellent overview of Osborne's life is by Hubert B. Vickery in National Academy of Sciences, *Biographical Memoirs* 14 (1931): 261–304. Other secondary literature includes Stanley L. Becker, "Butter Makes Them Grow: An Episode in the Discovery of Vitamins," CAES *Bulletin* 767 (Jan. 1977). Significant obituaries include Vickery and L. B. Mendel in *Science* 69 (1929): 385–89; Mendel in *Journal of Biological Chemistry* 81 (1929), on two unnumbered pages preceding p. 1; and H. D. Dakin in *Journal of the Chemical Society* (London) (1929): 2974–76. A tribute to Osborne was published as "Thomas B. Osborne: A Memorial," CAES *Bulletin* 312 (Feb. 1930): 275–394.

STANLEY L. BECKER

OSCEOLA (1802?–30 Jan. 1838), Seminole war leader (*tastanagi*), was born in Alabama, probably the son of a white trader, William Powell, and a mestizo Creek woman (name unknown), who was the granddaughter of a Scot, James McQueen, and the niece of Peter McQueen, the head warrior of Tallassee on the Tallapoosa. Osceola spent his youth with McQueen's band, which fled to Florida after the defeat of the Creeks by the United States in 1814. In 1818 the boy was captured by Andrew Jackson's troops during their invasion of Florida but was evidently soon released. He and his band became part of the Seminole people, but little is known of his early career. Sometimes he was known as "Billy Powell," but his adult Indian name, better rendered "Asi-yaholo," suggests that he was a singer at the black-drink ceremonies. He possessed a few hereditary claims to distinction, but it was as a warrior that he principally earned renown, and he was also called the "Talcy (Tallassee) tustenuggee."

Friction between the Seminoles and the expanding American settlements in northern Florida increased. Following an agreement at Camp Moultrie (1823) the United States attempted to confine the Indians to a reservation, and after 1827 Osceola found employment at Fort King helping to keep the Seminoles within the agreed boundaries. In 1830 the Indian Removal Act made provision to encourage eastern Indians to relocate west of the Mississippi, and the United States made use of treaties negotiated with some Seminoles at Payne's Landing (1832) and Fort Gibson (1833) to legitimize removing the Indians from Florida to lands assigned the Creeks in present-day Oklahoma. The treaties were disputed by many Seminoles, who resented the threat to their lands in Florida, feared a loss of autonomy if they were placed with the Creeks, and also were concerned for the security of the blacks in Seminole country. Blacks enjoyed a greater status and freedom with the Seminoles, and it was believed that removal would expose them to slave-owning whites and Indians.

Osceola had relatively little standing among the Seminoles before 1834 and was then seen, in the words of one contemporary, as "an upstart in the nation." He emerged as the most vociferous opponent of removal, however, and by dramatic and intimidating displays captured the rebellious mood rising in the Seminole towns, persuading or silencing many senior chiefs. In October 1834, during discussions with the American agent Wiley Thompson, he stiffened resistance to proposals for removal and by June of the following year had become so brazen that Thompson had him imprisoned. Osceola affected to accept removal to secure his freedom but within months was planning armed resistance. In November he murdered Charley Emathla, a proremoval leader who had signed the agreements of Payne's Landing and Fort Gibson.

Hostilities with the Americans broke out in December 1835. Osceola has been credited with capturing a baggage train at Kanapaha on the eighteenth and with helping to plan the annihilation of Major Francis L. Dade's column in central Florida on 28 December. He almost certainly led the force that killed Wiley Thompson and three others at Fort King the same day. There followed the so-called Second Seminole War, in which Indians and associated blacks resisted superior numbers of better-armed troops in protracted guerrilla warfare in the difficult terrain of the Florida peninsula. Osceola was a leader in some of the first major engagements. He was slightly wounded in the defeat of Brigadier General Duncan L. Clinch's 750-strong army on the Withlacoochee River in western Florida on 31 December 1835, and the next year he helped ambush 1,000 men under Major General Edmund Pendleton Gaines near the same spot and pin them down for nine days (27 Feb.–6 Mar. 1836).

Osceola made an important contribution to prolonging resistance in staging a coup against the Seminoles' principal leader, Micanopy, in 1837. Major General Thomas S. Jesup had concluded a truce with the Indians, who appeared ready to assemble at Tampa Bay for removal. Osceola seems to have considered relocating too and drew rations at Fort Mellon in May as he made his way to Tampa; but when the United States began to prevaricate about fully honoring Jesup's

pledges to the Seminoles that the blacks among them would be secure, many Indians swung back to opposing removal. On 2 June the militants, led by Sam Jones (?–1867) and Osceola, captured the shipment center at Tampa, deposed Micanopy, and led several hundred Indians back into the interior. Although some Seminoles continued to surrender and emigrate, Osceola and others returned to the armed struggle.

In October 1837 Osceola and Coa Hadjo offered to treat with Brigadier General Joseph M. Hernandez and arranged to confer at an Indian camp near Fort Peyton on Moultrie Creek, near St. Augustine. Their motives are unclear. Jesup feared that the Seminoles hoped to seize hostages for the release of an important Indian leader called Philip, held at St. Augustine, or even to attack the town itself. However, Osceola's party flew a white flag over the camp and showed no aggression when Hernandez arrived for the parley on 21 October. Deploying 250 soldiers, Hernandez, acting on the orders of Jesup, arbitrarily seized Osceola, Coa Hadjo, and eighty-one followers and imprisoned them at Fort Marion in St. Augustine. A further fifty or so of Osceola's party, including his two wives (one was named Che-cho-ter; the other's name is unknown) and two children, subsequently also surrendered; but a full report of Hernandez's treachery was carried back to the Indian camps by the warrior Coacoochee, who escaped from Fort Marion, and it probably helped revitalize the more determined opponents of removal.

Osceola was sent to Fort Moultrie, Charleston, where he was imprisoned with Micanopy, Philip, and some 200 other Seminoles. Because of his stand and treacherous capture he had become a celebrity, and George Catlin and others painted his portrait. They found a man in his mid-thirties, of medium height, spare, with expressive features and a ready and "pleasant smile." Capable of being violently assertive, he was generally affable and resigned and left an impression that enhanced his standing among Americans. Osceola was then also seriously ill, latent malaria aggravating quinsy, and he died in confinement only days after Catlin had completed his portrait. His body, beheaded by a post surgeon, was buried outside Fort Moultrie.

Osceola has been much lionized and sometimes debunked. There is no evidence that he held wide political views or any military abilities that Seminoles would have considered unusual. Although the American press fixed upon him, there were other important leaders in the Indian struggle, including the Mikasuki holy man (Arpeika) Sam Jones and warriors such as Alligator of the Alachua and Coacoochee of the St. Johns Seminoles. However, Osceola's reputation as a key figure withstands any fair evaluation. His courageous, determined, and impassioned attack upon removal made him a strong man upon whom weaker ones relied and helped create a climate of opinion among the Seminoles that overshadowed the views of many senior but more moderate leaders. At a time of crisis he supplied example, energy, and spirit to Seminole resistance.

• Although lacking essential contextual information, the best biography of Osceola is Mark F. Boyd, "Asi-Yaholo or Osceola," *Florida Historical Quarterly* 33 (1955): 249–305, itself one of several useful papers that form the "Osceola Double Number" of the *Florida Historical Quarterly* 33 (1955): 159–306. A popular biography is William Hartley and Ellen Hartley, *Osceola: The Unconquered Indian* (1973). For additional scholarly comment, see Kenneth W. Porter, "The Episode of Osceola's Wife: Fact or Fiction?" *Florida Historical Quarterly* 26 (1947–1948): 92–98; Edwin C. McReynolds, *The Seminoles* (1957); John K. Mahon, *History of the Second Seminole War* (1967); and J. Leitch Wright, Jr., *Creeks and Seminoles* (1986). The considerable industry that has developed around Osceola is discussed in Patricia R. Wickman, *Osceola's Legacy* (1991), and Theda Perdue, "Osceola: The White Man's Indian," *Florida Historical Quarterly* 70 (1992): 475–88.

JOHN SUGDEN

OSGOOD, Frances Sargent Locke (18 June 1811–12 May 1850), poet and editor, was born in Boston, Massachusetts, the daughter of Joseph Locke, a merchant, and his second wife, Mary Ingersoll Foster. She was apparently educated at home. She wrote under various names: Florence, Ellen, Kate Carol, and her married name. Her first poem was published in *Juvenile Miscellany* in 1825. She married the painter Samuel Stillman Osgood in October 1835 and lived with him in England from 1835 to 1839. She had her first daughter in 1836 and published two volumes of poetry, *A Wreath of Wild Flowers from New England* (1838) and *The Casket of Fate* (1839), both favorably received in London and later reissued in the United States. The Osgoods returned to Boston, where a second daughter was born in 1839, and then moved to New York City. Osgood became an editor at the *Ladies Companion* and soon was contributing poems to major journals of her day. Within the next five years, she published *Flower Gift* (1840); *The Snow-Drop, a New Year Gift for Children* (1842); *The Rose: Sketches in Verse* (1842); *Puss in Boots; or, The Marquis of Carabas* (1844); and *The Flower Alphabet in Gold and Colors* (1845).

From 1844 to 1847 Osgood was separated from her husband. In 1845 she met Edgar Allan Poe and Rufus Wilmot Griswold. Osgood and Poe began a relationship that still puzzles scholars. Her short story "Ida Grey," published in *Graham's Magazine* in August 1845, is considered autobiographical. Gossip was fueled by the birth in 1846 of Osgood's third daughter, who died soon after birth. Whether or not the Poe-Osgood relationship was sexually consummated, they did share a poetic interchange, as is evidenced by Osgood's "To a Dear Little Truant, Who Wouldn't Come Home" (1846), in which Osgood seeks Poe's return to New York City in the spring during which the breeze murmurs " 'like a lute.' " At any rate, the affair was over by the time Osgood's husband left for the California goldfields in 1849. Samuel Osgood returned to New York City shortly before Frances Osgood died of consumption in New York City.

Osgood was a member of a group of New York literati who wrote both poetry and prose, edited journals and collections, and often supported themselves and their families. Although they were often forced to rely on male editors and mentors, Osgood and her friends represented an artistically ambitious and culturally questioning counterbalance to the canonical writers of the American Renaissance.

Unfortunately, Osgood's art and reputation have been submerged by her relationship with Poe. This was not the case in her own time, however. Osgood was the only woman discussed in *The Living Authors of America* (1850) by the Englishman Thomas Powell. Her work appeared in various anthologies of poetry by American women published in the 1840s and early 1850s by Griswold (1847), Thomas Buchanan Read (1848), and Caroline May (1848). Her prose is represented in John S. Hart's *The Female Prose Writers of America* (1852). After Osgood's death, Mary E. Hewitt edited a memorial volume whose contributors included Griswold, Nathaniel Hawthorne, Sarah Helen Whitman, and William Gilmore Simms. Published in 1851 as *The Memorial, Written by Friends of the Late Mrs. Osgood*, it was reprinted in 1854 as *Laurel Leaves*. Her reputation had diminished by the end of the century, but her name resurfaced for serious study as women scholars of the late twentieth century, such as Mary G. De Jong, Cheryl Walker, and Emily Watts, rediscovered her poetry.

The topics of Osgood's poetry and prose center upon domesticity—home, children, gardens or woods (as opposed to wilderness), heterosexual love, poetry, and friendships between women. In poetry, she contributed to the expansion and evolution of American verse by using metaphors of the home, by presenting children as proper topics for adult poetry, and by introducing the consciously subversive celebration of witches and witchery that continued in several forms throughout the poetry of American women into the twentieth century.

Feminist scholars have recently been interested in a number of Osgood's poems that are sometimes brief and epigrammatic expressions of the failure of love or that are indirect comments on the dominant literary theories and cultural assumptions of her day. In the first category are such poems as "Forgive and Forget," Untitled ("Have I caught you at last, gentle rover?"), and "The Lily's Delusion"—cynical and ironic poems, collected in the 1850 *Poems*. In the second category of poems, Osgood gently confronts the nature (and Transcendentalist) poets of her day. The poet-speaker in "May-Day in New England" is probably the only poet in early nineteenth-century America unable to find a wildflower during a spring walk in the woods. Flowers represented universal truth for the Transcendentalists, were the teacher of morals for Bryant, a portion of American identity for Whitman, and for Poe a pattern of symbols. In Osgood's work, the poet's estrangement from nature, as well as the poet's subsequent discovery of a wildflower in her daughter's cheek, suggests an estrangement from the dominant poetic tradition as well as a valuing of humanity over nature.

An allegorical poem, "A Flight of Fancy," indicates Osgood's awareness of the contemporary Romantic theories of fancy, imagination, and reason, as she elevates fancy to a positive poetic principle, undoubtedly a female poetic principle, indeed a witch in disguise. Female Fancy, who talks a language that is "melodious" and "new," represents women's poetry. Reason, who, according to Judge Conscience, has been corrupted by Fancy, is confined to jail and falls asleep. Osgood's depiction of a sleeping Reason, who has been separated from Fancy and confined by Conscience, suggests her frustration with the patriarchal (and probably matriarchal) norms, which kept poetry in separate male and female spheres. That Fancy is a witch (an image that still reverberated in the American consciousness) implies an association of women's poetry, or at least Osgood's poetry, with subversion of critical and cultural norms.

The most misunderstood and least explored qualities of Osgood's art are her prosody and her use of painterly scenes. Her husband was a painter, and her volumes of poetry are illustrated. Her prosody was praised in her own day by Poe and others as "spontaneous" and "light"; however, she was sophisticated in her selection of stanzaic and metrical patterns. Before Emily Dickinson, she used the common or short (hymnal) measure ironically for poems that are not pious, as, for example, the pending adultery in "Oh! hasten to my side, I pray." Before James Russell Lowell, she used anapestic tetrameter for literary criticism—a meter more appropriate for her "A Flight of Fancy" than to his "A Fable for Critics." Somewhat like Emerson, she experimented with short, uneven lines, such as the dimeters of "Song" ("I cannot forget him") and "Ah! Woman Still." In the prosodic confusion of early nineteenth-century American poetry—certainly a defining period—Osgood's poetry may yet be seen as having been integral to the development of American poetry.

• Osgood's papers are housed in the Boston Public Library with those of Rufus Wilmot Griswold, her literary executor. In addition to those mentioned above, important biographical sources include T. O. Mabbott, "The Children of Frances S. Osgood," *Notes and Queries* 160, no. 2 (10 Jan. 1931): 27–28; John Evangelist Walsh, *Plumes in the Dust: The Love Affair of Edgar Allan Poe and Fanny Osgood* (1980); and Cheryl Walker, "Legacy Profile: Frances Osgood, 1811–1850," *Legacy* 1 (Fall 1984): 5–7. See also biographies of Poe by Arthur Hobson Quinn (1941) and Kenneth Silverman (1991). For critical analyses, see Mary G. De Jong, "Her Fair Fame: The Reputation of Frances Sargent Osgood, Woman Poet," *Studies in the American Renaissance*, ed. Joel Myerson (1987); Cheryl Walker, *The Nightingale's Burden: Women Poets and American Culture before 1900* (1982); and Emily Stipes Watts, *The Poetry of American Women from 1632 to 1945* (1977).

EMILY STIPES WATTS

OSGOOD, Jacob (16 Mar. 1777–29 Nov. 1844), religious leader, was born in South Hampton, New Hampshire, the son of Philip Osgood and Mehitable Flanders, farmers. He wrote later that his parents "were poor and were not able to give me much learning." When Jacob was about twelve, the family moved to Warner, New Hampshire. In 1797 he married Miriam Stevens; they had eight children. Shortly after his marriage, Jacob purchased from his father a 100-acre farm on a hill north of town. He farmed that land until his death.

In his brief autobiography, Osgood described his religious experiences beginning at around age twenty-five, and he dated his conversion to October 1805. He started in the Congregational church, where both he and his wife sang in the choir, and began to preach locally. For a time he joined the Free Will Baptists—who placed greater importance on conversion, adult baptism, and emotional revivals—until the elders objected to his testimony when he claimed to have divine authority. Osgood asserted that his prayers could bring misfortune or healing; he also challenged, and expressed contempt for, the Baptist clergy and subscribed to a militant pacifism that differed from the beliefs of the Free Will Baptists. In 1812 he founded his own sect, which grew to include members living in Warner and surrounding towns.

The Osgoodites believed in the power of prayer. They treated the sick with prayer and the laying on of hands, and they believed that their prayers could bring rain in time of drought. They opposed doctors, lawyers, and paid clergymen, and as pacifists they refused to participate in military training or to pay war taxes. This refusal cost Osgood and his followers many fines, which they also refused to pay. They frequently had property seized as a result and saw themselves as suffering persecution for their faith.

On 1 July 1820 Osgood and several followers were jailed for refusing to serve in the militia. Osgood wrote that "the jail was like paradise to us . . . We kept the jail full of the glory of God" (Osgood, p. 12). In jail Osgood enjoyed plenty to eat and drink, and he met and worshiped with his followers; he also began to write his autobiography. After eleven days the authorities decided to release Osgood, but he refused to leave without his brethren and had to be carried from the prison—a difficult task, since he weighed well over 300 pounds. A few of his followers were kept in jail until 1821. For Osgood and his followers, persecution and imprisonment strengthened their faith and offered opportunities to demonstrate the power of God. Osgood claimed that "one officer defied the God I worshipped to kill him, and my flesh trembled on my bones, and I told him that God would take him out of the way, and he did no more work till he was carried to the grave" (Osgood, p. 13). Osgood's autobiography is filled with accounts of his followers being persecuted by the authorities, and of his persecutors experiencing God's judgment in the form of grasshoppers, storms, illness, or injuries. They prayed that God would smite their enemies and believed they saw those prayers answered.

Osgoodite worship services were usually held in members' homes. Contemporaries described meetings as disorganized prayer, exhortation, and song, with everyone participating. Osgood "always preached, prayed and sung, sitting in his chair, keeping his eyes closed the whole time and one hand on the side of his face. After every one had said something and there was a lull, Elder Osgood would abruptly close the exercises by saying,—'If there's no more to be said, meeting's done'" (F. M. Colby, p. 109).

In 1817, and again in around 1830, Osgood and his followers held a number of "great revivals" in New Hampshire. Most of his followers were rural farmers, uncomfortable with railroads and other technological improvements. Many of their hymns were very partisan, supporting Democrats and including among their targets Whigs, Republicans, abolitionists, colleges, "hireling" clergy, rival religious denominations, and the temperance movement. Other hymns described members' suffering and imprisonment and celebrated their deliverance from or victory over their enemies. Osgood wrote a number of the hymns himself, and they served as an effective means of spreading and reinforcing his beliefs.

Contemporaries described Osgood as a religious enthusiast, an effective speaker, and a powerful singer who had led a singing school in Warner prior to his conversion. They noted his generosity, saying that in time of hardship he shared his harvest with needy neighbors, regardless of their creed. They also noted his willingness to rebuke anyone whom he believed deserved it.

In June 1844 Osgood began to foretell his coming death. He fell ill and died five months later in Warner. After his death, his followers were led by Nehemiah Ordway and Charles Colby. Their numbers ceased to grow; meetings continued for several decades, but with decreasing frequency, and they ceased completely before 1890. The Osgoodites had no ties with other religious groups and, in keeping with their antiestablishment beliefs, founded no institutions. They can be understood as a local, colorful manifestation of the Second Great Awakening.

• Osgood's autobiography was originally published as *The Christian Experience of Jacob Osgood* (1867). An expanded version is Charles H. Colby, ed., *The Life and Christian Experience of Jacob Osgood with Hymns and Spiritual Songs* (1873). A vivid description of Osgood is in Frederick Myron Colby, "Rambles about a Country Town," *Granite Monthly* 14 (Apr. 1892): 105–11. Kenneth Scott, "The Osgoodites of New Hampshire," *New England Quarterly* 16, no. 1 (1943): 20–40, provides a good overview and citations to other nineteenth-century accounts of Osgood and his followers. Louis Billington, "Northern New England Sectarianism in the Early Nineteenth Century," *Bulletin of the John Rylands University Library of Manchester* 70, no. 3 (1988): 123–34, provides useful religious context.

ELIZABETH MCKEE WILLIAMS

OSGOOD, Samuel (3 Feb. 1748–12 Aug. 1813), merchant and politician, was born in Andover, Massachusetts, the son of Peter Osgood, a farmer and town official, and Sarah Sprague Johnson. After graduating in 1770 from Harvard and relinquishing his earlier hope of becoming a minister, Osgood returned to Andover and entered the mercantile business, in which he be-

came successful, with his brother Peter. In 1775 he married Martha Brandon; it was a childless marriage terminated by her death in 1778.

Osgood commenced public service in 1774 with participation in the Essex County Convention, one of a number of similar gatherings called to protest the Intolerable Acts of 1774 and the suspension of the Massachusetts charter. From 1775 he served in the Massachusetts provincial congress. When the revolutionary war broke out, he captained the Andover, Massachusetts, Minute Men, served as aide-de-camp and assistant quartermaster to General Artemas Ward, and rose to the rank of colonel. As the war began to wind down in New England, Osgood resumed civilian service. He was appointed justice of the peace of Essex County in 1776 and served three terms in the Massachusetts provincial congress in 1776, 1779, and 1780. He was also elected to the Massachusetts constitutional convention of 1779–1780—the first convention whose members were elected by the people of a state for the sole purpose of writing a constitution—and to the first state senate seated under the resulting Massachusetts Constitution of 1780.

In 1781 Osgood entered his long service at the national level when he was elected Massachusetts delegate to the Continental Congress; he was reelected for successive annual terms in 1782 and 1783. No doubt in part for his business experience, the Congress chose him to be a director of the Bank of North America, founded in 1781 and the first bank to receive a charter from Congress. Because of his fear of concentrated financial power, he was also a moving force in 1784 behind successful efforts to replace the powerful superintendent of finance, Robert Morris, with a three-man board of treasury commissioners. That same year, at the expiration of his third term as delegate, Osgood was forced by provision of the Articles of Confederation to leave Congress. In 1785 Congress chose him to be one of the three treasury commissioners, a post he occupied until the organization of the new constitutional government in 1789. Between his service as congressional delegate and commissioner of the treasury, he served one year, in 1785, as an elected member of the Massachusetts House of Representatives, in which he was appointed to a committee to prepare a claim on lands in central and western New York State in a dispute between the two states, which was not settled until 1786.

Osgood had difficulty making up his mind about the Constitution of 1787. At first he was an antifederalist, if only a mild one, citing as the new Constitution's chief defect its provision for exclusive congressional jurisdiction over a large capital city. Then he came to favor the Constitution, in part because he was convinced that suitable amendments, like those that became the Bill of Rights, would be attached to it. He was thus soon found urging ratification by New York so that its representatives to the new government could push for amendments in the first federal Congress.

George Washington, after having resided in Osgood's New York residence at the time of his inauguration, appointed him in 1789 first postmaster general of the United States. The appointment was no doubt in part a result of Osgood's change of view from antifederalist to federalist as well as of his standing in the business communities of Massachusetts and New York. Although Osgood framed plans for his young department, he did not remain in office to see to their enactment by Congress. Instead, he resigned in 1791, choosing to remain in New York, where he had moved permanently in 1785, when the government moved to Philadelphia.

From then on, Osgood began a gradual, enduring shift toward opposition to the Federalist party of Washington and Alexander Hamilton. His conversion was no doubt assisted by his second marriage, in 1786, to the wealthy widow Maria Bowne Franklin of New York City. She was linked by marriage to the powerful family of George Clinton and DeWitt Clinton, the former being first governor of the state and leader of the antifederalist opposition to the Constitution, the latter being George Clinton's nephew, a rising figure in the state, and, like his uncle, by the mid-1790s a Democratic-Republican. The marriage produced six children, four of whom lived to adulthood. Osgood's association with the Clintons may help explain both his vacillation about the new Constitution and his attractiveness to Washington when considering members of his first administration.

Although chosen in 1792 by the New York legislature to the electoral college, where he cast his vote for Washington's reelection to a second term, Osgood that same year served on political committees seeking George Clinton's reelection as governor. The next year he helped welcome French minister Edmond Charles Genêt, the bête noire of Federalists, to New York City. After Thomas Jefferson's election as president in 1801, Osgood successfully worked to influence the incoming administration to transfer patronage in New York State to Governor Clinton and away from Aaron Burr. At the same time Osgood was alerting the president, with whom he had served in the Confederation Congress, of Burr's scheming. Having been elected to the New York assembly in 1800, in which he sat until 1803 and of which he was chosen Speaker in 1801, Osgood accepted appointment from Jefferson as supervisor of internal revenue for the District of New York. Then in 1803, with the agreement of DeWitt Clinton, he became naval officer of the port of New York, a post he held until his death in New York City.

A Congregationalist who retained a lifelong interest in theological studies, he was the author in 1794 of *Remarks on the Book of Daniel and on the Revelations*, in 1807 of *A Letter upon the Subject of Episcopacy*, and in 1811 of *Three Letters on Different Subjects*. Osgood also helped organize a free school for poor children and the American Academy of Fine Arts.

Osgood's career illustrates the complexity and fluidity of ideological commitments in the early republic, especially among the mercantile gentry of New York. Though reconciled to the new constitutional government, to which he had at first been lukewarm, and

then firmly secured to it by his appointment as postmaster general, he soon drifted into partisan opposition to its Federalist custodians, more it seems out of personal associations than deep political convictions.

• A small collection of Osgood's papers is in the New-York Historical Society. Other letters and documents are to be found in various collections in the New York Public Library, the Massachusetts Historical Society, and the Massachusetts Archives. A brief autobiographical text is "Sketch of the Life of Samuel Osgood . . . Written by Himself," *Magazine of American History* 21 (1889): 324–28. A full-length biography of Osgood has yet to be published.

JAMES M. BANNER, JR.

OSGOOD, William Fogg (10 Mar. 1864–22 July 1943), mathematician, was born in Boston, Massachusetts, the son of William Osgood, a physician, and Mary Rogers Gannett. The young Osgood studied at the Boston Latin School and entered Harvard in 1882. For the first two years he pursued the classics but was won over to mathematics by Benjamin Osgood Peirce and Frank N. Cole. He graduated summa cum laude, the second in his class, and remained at Harvard for an additional year to obtain his M.A. in 1887. Receiving a Harris and Parker fellowship, he studied with Felix Klein from 1887 to 1889 at the University of Göttingen. He then spent the 1889–1890 academic year at the University of Erlangen, where he obtained his Ph.D. in 1890 from Max Noether with a dissertation on Abelian integrals.

In 1890 Osgood married Therese Anna Amalie Elise Ruprecht of Göttingen, Germany; they had three children. Following their marriage the Osgoods returned to Harvard, where he successively served as an instructor (1890–1893), assistant professor (1893–1903), professor (1903–1933), and finally as William Byerly's successor as Perkins Professor of Mathematics from 1913 to 1933. For several months in 1922 he also was acting dean of the Graduate School of Arts and Sciences at Harvard, and following his retirement he taught for two years (1934–1935) at the National University of Peking. He married Céleste Phelps Morse, the former wife of his Harvard colleague Marston Morse, in 1932, after his first marriage ended in divorce.

Osgood was highly honored and respected during his lifetime; he was elected a member of the National Academy of Sciences in 1904, served as eighth president of the American Mathematical Society (1905–1906), and had the rare distinction of being twice colloquium lecturer of the American Mathematical Society (1898, 1913). In 1903, in a poll conducted by *American Men of Science* of leaders in science in America, he was rated third out of eighty in mathematics. He was an editor of the *Annals of Mathematics* (1899–1902) and of the *Transactions of the American Mathematical Society* in 1910. However, he had little taste for administrative detail and preferred to devote his energy to research and teaching duties. He was an inspiring teacher, and together with his colleague Maxime Bôcher, he was a major force in the development of the

Harvard mathematics program from 1894 to 1914. Because of his interest in working on what he called "problems with a pedigree," he produced only four Harvard doctorates. Notwithstanding this paucity of doctoral students, Osgood was a great teacher who was devoted to his students and especially concerned with their success and finding them suitable academic positions.

Osgood's primary research interest lay in classical analysis; he was the preeminent function theorist of his generation in the United States. His activities enriched much of the analysis in vogue at the turn of the century, i.e., the theory of convergence (1896–1897), complex function theory (1896), differential equations (1898), the calculus of variations (1901), and the theory of the Riemann integral (1902–1903). Two especially noteworthy results were his proof of the Riemann mapping theorem (1901, with a generalization in 1913) and the construction of a Jordan curve of positive area (1903). The former had eluded the efforts of a number of distinguished European experts since its formal announcement in 1851, and Osgood's proof was the first satisfactory one. Osgood contributed an influential survey article, "Allgemeine Theorie der analytischen Functionen einer und mehrer komplexen Größen," to the prestigious *Encyklopädie der Mathematischen Wissenschaften* (1901), and this focused his interest in complex analysis. Ultimately this led to his masterpiece *Lehrbuch der Funktionentheorie*, which appeared in three volumes (1907, 1924, 1929) and effectively encompassed the entire field of classical analysis. The latter volumes of this treatise, together with his colloquium lectures *Topics in the Theory of Functions of Several Complex Variables* (1914), were the first book-length expositions of this subject. His activities in this area began with two important notes (1899, 1900), and, together with F. Hartogs, he must be regarded as one of the founders of the theory of several complex variables. Indeed, in this theory one finds an Osgood lemma, the Osgood condition, an Osgood theorem, and the Osgood-Braun theorem. He also did important work on the theory of uniformization of an algebraic function (1913) and the mathematical theory of the gyroscope (1922). In addition, his exemplary textbooks, *A First Course in the Differential and Integral Calculus* (1907), *Plane and Solid Analytic Geometry* (with William C. Graustein, 1921), *Elementary Calculus* (1921), *Introduction to Calculus* (1922), *Advanced Calculus* (1925), *Functions of Real Variables* (1936), *Functions of a Complex Variable* (1936), and *Mechanics* (1937), were deservedly popular and widely used. Following his return from China, Osgood resided in Belmont, Massachusetts, where he died.

Osgood's importance lies in his deep loyalties to mathematics and to Harvard University, and he made distinguished contributions to both without thought of personal ambition. His mathematical style was incisive and striking in its power and precision. All of his writings are models of systematic methodology and lucid thought.

• Osgood's retiring address as president of the American Mathematical Society, "The Calculus in Our Colleges and Technical Schools," *Bulletin of the American Mathematical Society* 13 (June 1907), is unusual for its elementary character and pedagogical content. His memorial tribute to his colleague Maxime Bôcher in *Bulletin of the American Mathematical Society* 25 (Apr. 1919), contains valuable comments that reflect Osgood's views on research and the teaching of mathematics. The biographical notice by R. C. Archibald appearing in *A Semicentennial History of the American Mathematical Society, 1888–1938* (1938) includes a complete list of Osgood's doctoral students and publications. Obituary notices are in *Science* 98 (5 Nov. 1943), the *Bulletin of the American Mathematical Society* 50 (Mar. 1944), and the *New York Times*, 23 July 1943.

JOSEPH D. ZUND

O'SHAUGHNESSY, Michael Maurice (28 May 1864–12 Oct. 1934), hydraulic engineer, was born in Limerick, Ireland, the son of Patrick O'Shaughnessy and Margaret O'Donnell. In 1884 he received a bachelor of engineering degree from the Royal University, Dublin, graduating with honors. Deciding to emigrate to the United States, he came to California in 1885 and became an assistant engineer with the Sierra Valley & Mohawk Railroad. The Southern Pacific Railroad employed him for two years, but by the early 1890s he had found a home in San Francisco and was designing water systems for the city. He surveyed the extension of Market Street over Twin Peaks Mountain to the Pacific Ocean and the extension of Protero Avenue along the bay shore to the county line, but, because of the vagaries of San Francisco politics, he was never paid for this work. O'Shaughnessy married Mary Spottiswood of San Francisco in 1890; they had five children.

During the 1890s O'Shaughnessy was involved in a variety of hydraulic projects for various employers, including the Spring Valley Water Company, which supplied water to San Francisco. From 1899 to 1906 he designed and constructed twenty water supply systems and three aqueducts, each about ten miles in length, for Hawaiian sugar plantations. Returning to the mainland, he became chief engineer of the Southern California Mountain Water Company in San Diego. During this time he supervised the construction of the thirteen-mile-long Dulzura Conduit and the Morena Rock Fill Dam.

O'Shaughnessy preferred to work with private corporations rather than in public service, but in 1912 Mayor James Rolph of San Francisco persuaded him to take the post of chief engineer for the city, a position he held for the next twenty years. The tasks he faced were challenging, the more so as he could have made much more money in the private sector. O'Shaughnessy, whose long-term view of the city's infrastructure included much more than its water supply, felt that San Francisco's public transportation network should be a single system providing uniform service at a reasonable price throughout the city. The transportation system could be used to encourage growth in given areas through construction of new lines ahead of residential development. Careful design of the system would produce cost-effectiveness. O'Shaughnessy thus supervised the expansion of the city's streetcar system by building new lines into areas with no previous service, using funds derived from operating income and by assessing properties along the right-of-way. Between 1915 and 1927 O'Shaughnessy created the municipal streetcar system that formed the basis of San Francisco's future public transportation network.

In addition to modernizing the railway system, O'Shaughnessy supervised a new fire system, sewers, streets, highways, bridges, and tunnels. Much of this construction was done over the areas destroyed by the 1906 earthquake and fire. Under his leadership the city built a main sewer line under Golden Gate Park to the Pacific Ocean.

All of these accomplishments, however, paled before the challenge of the construction of the city's water-supply system from the Hetch Hetchy Valley. Shortly after O'Shaughnessy became chief engineer of San Francisco, the city won its long battle for the damming of the Hetch Hetchy Valley in Yosemite National Park. As city engineer, O'Shaughnessy assumed responsibility for the network of dams, tunnels, and aqueduct that would bring water and power to San Francisco. In 1912 he had toured the Hetch Hetchy Valley and campaigned for approval of the project. He also played a major role in persuading Congress to pass the Raker Act, which gave San Francisco the right to construct the project over public lands.

O'Shaughnessy began surveying the valley site in the spring of 1914. Consistent with his view of long-term planning, the entire project took more than twenty years to complete. O'Shaughnessy supervised construction of the 344-foot-high dam that would bear his name; a 68-mile-long railroad; the 137.4-mile aqueduct; 85 miles of tunnels, some requiring drilling through solid granite; a power plant at Moccasin Creek; several smaller dams and hydroelectric plants; and transmission lines. Anticipating victory in the political battle over Hetch Hetchy, San Francisco voters had approved a $45 million bond issue in 1910. Before the project was half completed, however, the money was exhausted. O'Shaughnessy found himself as a major public official campaigning for additional bond issues in 1924 and 1928. Some critics suggested that his initials, M. M., stood for "More Money." O'Shaughnessy proudly stated that the project remained free from graft. He also noted that the engineering problems were simple compared to the political problems.

The total cost of the Hetch Hetchy project has been estimated at $100 million. When completed, it produced a daily capacity of 400 million gallons of water. O'Shaughnessy had retired in 1932 but continued to work on the project as a consulting engineer. On 12 October 1934, sixteen days before water was to be officially turned into the aqueduct, O'Shaughnessy died in San Francisco of a heart attack. On 28 October, the day of the celebration, the city posthumously awarded him a gold medal recognizing his contributions.

During his professional career O'Shaughnessy served as a consultant to other cities, including Portland, Detroit, and Seattle, as well as private corporations. He wrote a pamphlet, *The Hetch Hetchy Water and Power Project* (1921), and contributed "San Francisco's Municipal Railway" to *Municipal Railways in the United States and Canada*, edited by Delos F. Wilcox (1922). His article "Construction of the Morena Rock Fill Dam" (American Society of Civil Engineers, *Transactions* 75 [1912]: 27–51), was awarded the society's James Laurie Prize. In 1932 O'Shaugnessy addressed the California Historical Society on "The Water Supply of San Francisco" (*California Historical Society Quarterly* 11 [1932]).

O'Shaughnessy is memorialized by the naming of a San Francisco city street and the O'Shaughnessy Dam in Hetch Hetchy Valley in his honor. His leadership in modernizing the infrastructure of San Francisco and in overseeing one of the great construction projects of the early twentieth century secured his reputation as one of the most important civil engineers in American history. He ignored the political controversies surrounding the Hetch Hetchy project, focusing instead on the technological and engineering challenges, which he successfully overcame.

• O'Shaughnessy's vision for modernizing San Francisco is described in Robert W. Cherny, "City Commercial, City Beautiful, City Practical: The San Francisco Visions of William C. Ralston, James D. Phelan, and Michael M. O'Shaughnessy," *California History* 73 (Winter 1994–1995): 296–307. Obituaries are in the *San Francisco Examiner*, 13 and 14 Oct. 1934; *San Francisco Chronicle*, 13 Oct. 1934; *New York Times*, 13 Oct. 1934; American Society of Civil Engineers, *Transactions* 100 (1935): 1710–13; *Engineering News-Record*, 18 Oct. 1934; and *California Historical Society Quarterly* 13 (1934): 415–16.

ABRAHAM HOFFMAN

OSHKOSH (1795–30 Aug.? 1858), chief of the Menominee Indians, was born in Old King Village at the mouth of the Menominee River, where present-day Marinette, Wisconsin, and Menominee, Michigan, are located. His parents' names are unknown. His grandfather was Chief Cha-wa-non, and Tomah, his grandfather's adviser, taught Oshkosh and accompanied him to the council fires and on the warpath. In the War of 1812 Oshkosh and one hundred Menominee warriors served under Tomah's command in the British forces. Menominees took part in the capture of Fort Michilimackinac in 1812, the attack on Fort Stephenson in 1813, and a second Michilimackinac expedition and the capture of Prairie du Chien in 1814.

Few descriptions of Oshkosh exist. Canadian artist Paul Kane, who painted Menominee, provides the best physical description of the chief. He says, "Although a small man, his appearance, while speaking, possessed dignity, his attitude was graceful, and free from uncouth gesticulation." Kane also refers to Oshkosh's "fine flow of native eloquence, seasoned with good sense."

Oshkosh's family of twelve members, eight of whom were male, comprised the largest family in the tribe. Oshkosh was married three times. With Bamban-ni (Flying across the Sky), Oshkosh had three children. Following her death, Oshkosh married Shaka-noni-u (Decorated with Plumes), and after her death, Tono-ko-kum, with whom he had one child. Oshkosh was succeeded by his nephew, Ernest Oshkosh, who became first chief in 1858.

Oshkosh accepted the position of grand chief in 1827 at the Butte des Morts treaty site in Wisconsin. He inherited the problems of the tribe, including continued relations with the 160 French and British traders within the tribe and in Green Bay, a settlement of the land crisis with New York Indians who had been removed to Wisconsin, and the need to deal effectively with the newly established hegemony of the United States in the territory of the Menominee.

There was considerable mixed marriage with the traders. The mixed-blood relationship became an issue in 1848, when the treaty of that year, in which the Menominee ceded all of their land to the state of Wisconsin, called for treaty money to be paid to persons of mixed blood. In compliance with the treaty, Oshkosh and the Menominee chiefs compiled the first list of persons with mixed Menominee and other blood, most common of which was French. The Menominee objected to giving the mixed bloods treaty money, however. More than 700 such Indians had their names inscribed on the Menominee roll and received treaty payments. It was not until 1938 that the stipulation of at least one-quarter Menominee blood for enrollment as Menominee became the rule.

The land crisis with the New York Indians was shrewdly negotiated by Chief Oshkosh and Grizzly Bear in 1832, after four previous treaty agreements had been rejected by the Menominee. The terms of the settlement gave 500,000 acres of land on the southwestern side of the Fox River to the New York Indians—Stockbridge, Munsee, Brothernton, and Oneida—while the Menominee retained 500,000 acres on the northeastern side of the river.

Direct American relations with the Menominee began with a pledge of allegiance given at Fort Michilimackinac on 27 June 1816. Oshkosh and a company of Menominee warriors first served in the U.S. Army in 1827 during the Winnebago War and then in 1832 under General Winfield Scott during Black Hawk's War. Besides the mixed-blood issue, the treaty of 1848 called for the removal of the Menominee from Wisconsin.

Oshkosh successfully fought off attempts to remove the Menominee from their traditional lands. He refused to go to Washington, and he went with the Menominee delegation that inspected the Crow Wing River land in Minnesota in the spring of 1850, a proposed site for Menominee habitation. Oshkosh insisted that the very existence of the tribe depended on wild game, wild rice, and a peaceful environment. None of those things existed along the Crow Wing River. There was no game to hunt, no wild rice, and the presence of Sioux and Chippewa Indians posed a threat to a peaceful environment.

On their return, the Indians refused to give the agents an answer but insisted on going to Washington to address the issue. Oshkosh, with William Powell interpreting, told President Millard Fillmore why the Crow Wing site would not be a suitable home for the Menominee and implored the president to give the Menominee more time. Fillmore granted the request. In the meantime, friends of the Indians began petitioning the government on their behalf. In 1852 the Wisconsin legislature petitioned the president to grant the Menominee "a tract of land set apart for them . . . on the Wolf and Oconto Rivers." This request was honored, and in 1854 the Menominee Reservation was created along the beautiful, wild Wolf River, where the majority of the tribe resided at that time. The final settlement came in 1856 following the settlement of some preemption claims and Stockbridge Indian claims. The dream of Oshkosh and the Menominee people came true. The chief's death on the reservation, however, following a drunken brawl with his sons, brought sadness to the Menominee people. Oshkosh died knowing his people would continue to walk on the land of their ancestors and that "even the poorest region in Wisconsin was better than the Crow Wing."

• For more information on Oshkosh, see Walter Hoffman, *The Menomini Indians*, U.S. Bureau of American Ethnology, *Fourteenth Annual Report, 1892–93* (1896); Paul Kane, *The Wanderings of an Artist among the Indians of North America from Canada to Vancouver Island and Oregon through the Hudson's Bay Company Territory and Back Again* (1850, repr. 1925); Felix Keesing, *The Menomini Indians of Wisconsin: A Study of Three Centuries of Cultural Contact and Change* (1939); Publius V. Lawson, *Story of Oshkosh, His Tribe and Fellow Chiefs* (n.d.); Patricia K. Ourada, *The Menominee Indians: A History* (1979); Ourada, *The Menominee* (1990); Frank E. Stevens, *The Black Hawk War* (1903); and William Wood, ed., *Select Documents of the Canadian War of 1812* (2 vols., 1850; repr. 1988).

PATRICIA K. OURADA

OSLER, Sir William (12 July 1849–29 Dec. 1919), physician, educator, and historian, was born in Bond Head, Ontario, Canada, the son of Featherstone Lake Osler, an Anglican priest, and Ellen Free Pickton, both of Cornwall, England. William's father left Britain's Royal Navy for an evangelical calling in the backwoods of early nineteenth-century Ontario. In 1837 the Oslers came to their new home in Bond Head, forty miles north of Toronto. The young Osler was a proficient scholar, caught in the common mid-nineteenth-century dichotomy between science and church. Ultimately, another Anglican priest, the Reverend W. A. Johnson, settled the matter by nourishing Osler's interest in natural science. Microscopy replaced the ministry. As early as 1869, Osler's first published work analyzed microscopic forms in a pond near his home.

All his life Osler remained an assiduous and discriminating reader. At home, he delved deeply into religious writings and the thinking of many of the major theologians. But outside the home he immersed himself in the classics, especially in Sir Thomas Browne (1605–1682), whose *Religio Medici* became a lifetime favorite, Thomas Carlyle, and the agnostic, Thomas Huxley.

Osler's formal education began at Trinity College, in Toronto, where he planned to study divinity. After one year, however, much influenced by one of his preceptors in studies of nature, James Bovell, a physician, he switched to medicine. Probably it was Bovell who urged Osler to leave the Toronto School of Medicine after his first two years, and he transferred in 1870 to McGill Medical College, from which he graduated in 1872.

After graduation Osler decided to become an ophthalmologist. His well-to-do brother Edmund provided him with the means to pursue a lengthy trip to Europe. (Soon after he left Montreal, another ophthalmologist settled in Montreal, and Osler's training shifted to what later would be identified as general medicine combined with pathology.) In London Osler recorded observations on the blood platelets that were among his most original scientific achievements. He continued his studies on the Continent, especially in Germany and Austria. This casual approach to postgraduate study, much dependent on letters of introduction and a knowledge of European languages, was all that was available at the time. A generation later, Osler and his colleagues at Johns Hopkins would devise the first version of the formal, carefully regulated system that is now the model for postgraduate training in any medical specialty.

When Osler returned to Canada in 1874 he had no position. He moved into the family home in Dundas. In that small town he worked as a general practitioner briefly and also did a locum tenens for a physician in nearby Hamilton. But soon McGill wrote offering him the position of lecturer in the Institutes of Medicine for the 1874–1875 academic year, which was about to begin. Osler moved back to Montreal where he spent ten uncommonly productive years.

Osler rose rapidly to the rank of full professor and became a great favorite with his students. He was appointed pathologist to the smallpox hospital, a potentially dangerous responsibility. He practiced privately, reputedly with little income. His small store of published articles began to swell prodigiously as he published extensively in clinical medicine, pathology, and veterinary medicine. His reputation as a skilled clinician of great common sense and tact, as a brilliant pathologist, and as a charismatic teacher spread, first in Canada, but soon across the continent and in Britain. He played a role in introducing modern methods of teaching physiology, performed hundreds of autopsies, and made numerous museum preparations of important specimens, some of which survive and are still in use.

In 1884 Osler was named professor of clinical medicine at the University of Pennsylvania. He was a great success in the United States. From 1885 to 1889 he consolidated his reputation as one of the bright stars of medical North America. This came about because of a combination of superior clinical care, painstaking work in the postmortem room, extensive publication, and great personal charm and generosity. In 1888 he was named to head the medical department when the Johns Hopkins School of Medicine began to gather its core of leaders. Osler was appointed first to be chief of medicine in Johns Hopkins Hospital, which opened before the medical school; he moved to Baltimore in 1889. The founders, whose role was decisive in making Hopkins almost immediately the best medical school in North America, were William S. Halsted, William H. Welch, Howard A. Kelly, and Osler.

Osler remained in Baltimore from 1889 to 1905. In terms of longstanding influence, Osler's most important activities at Hopkins were threefold: the educational programs at the medical school and hospital, the publication of his textbook of medicine, and the evolution of a body of disciples whose impact on medicine in the English-speaking world carried forward Osler's ideas and ideals for at least two generations into the future.

The educational reforms were not unique to Hopkins, though many of them flowered there more luxuriantly than in most centers. An undergraduate degree was required of medical candidates. Women were admitted from the beginning (albeit reluctantly on the part of some faculty members). Students were put into close and frequent contact with patients from their third year on. Internships and, ultimately, formalized programs in postgraduate education were created to assure thorough training for specialists in the various fields of medicine. These innovative approaches became the standards of medical education for most of the twentieth century.

Osler's textbook, *The Principles and Practice of Medicine*, was first published in 1892; triennial revisions were published throughout Osler's lifetime and for two decades afterward. Beginning with the eighth edition in 1912, Thomas McCrae became second author; he continued his involvement with the book after Osler's death. Osler's lucid, jargon-free style, incorporation of pertinent historical content, and unstinting credit to other practitioners helped to make the text preeminent in its field for many years. French, German, Spanish, Portuguese, Russian, and Chinese translations appeared.

In one regard Osler's textbook stood alone in presenting an unvarnished view of the inefficacy of most drugs then in use. Instead of advocating the typical multiconstituent remedies of the time, Osler declared candidly that few drugs were specific cures. This was an accurate assessment at that time, though it led to Osler's being characterized as a therapeutic nihilist by some critics. *The Principles and Practice of Medicine* was immensely successful, contributing much to the education of tens of thousands of physicians and providing Osler with a generous income.

One additional and totally unanticipated consequence stemmed from the remarkable readability of this scientific textbook. Frederick Gates, a member of John D. Rockefeller's philanthropic staff, read every word and categorized it as "one of the very few scientific books that are possessed of high literary quality" (Cushing, vol. 1, p. 454). More important, he came to understand how ineffective the medical profession was in curing diseases about which too little was known. Soon after, the Rockefeller Institute for Medical Research was created, and Gates stated unequivocally that it had its origin "in Dr. Osler's perfectly frank disclosure of the very narrow limitations of ascertained truth in medicine as it existed in 1897" (Cushing, vol. 1, p. 456).

During the Johns Hopkins years, Osler's interest in medical history became manifest. Not only did he refer to historical antecedents in his text, but increasingly he directed students to seek out original publications and to learn about the important contributors to the genesis of the medical profession. He helped to found a medical-historical society at Hopkins, and he began to publish a series of insightful historical essays, most of them elucidating the lives and contributions of individual practitioners, famous and obscure.

In 1892 Osler married Grace Linzee Revere Gross, the widow of his Philadelphia colleague and friend, Samuel W. Gross. The Oslers had two children. The first died within weeks of birth; the second was killed at the age of twenty-two while serving with the Royal Artillery in Flanders in August 1917.

Eventually, Osler's career in Baltimore began to overwhelm him. He was constantly in demand to travel across the continent, consulting in obscure cases, teaching, and lecturing, in addition to his numerous duties at Johns Hopkins. The possibility of a breakdown began to worry him. But just at this time, his outstanding reputation in Britain led in 1904 to perhaps the most prestigious appointment in medicine, that of regius professor at Oxford University. After discreet inquiries as to his availability, a formal invitation was issued by King Edward VII. Osler accepted the honor with enthusiasm.

Osler's departure from Baltimore was surrounded by controversy. Making his farewell address at Johns Hopkins University on 22 February 1905, Osler chose as his motif Anthony Trollope's novel *The Fixed Period* (1882). Why this particular book should have been on Osler's mind is unknown, but the choice proved unfortunate. Trollope recommended that older persons should be put to death because of their uselessness to society. Evidently Osler used the idea in a lighthearted attempt to persuade his American colleagues that they should not mourn his departure. By Trollopean standards, at fifty-six Osler's career was essentially washed up. His attempt at humor failed. The American yellow press claimed that Osler seriously proposed that older persons be chloroformed. He could not have been more misjudged, having always

been supportive of the aged, whether family, friends, or patients. A few suicides were found with newspaper clippings about Osler's lecture in their pockets. Some plans to memorialize him in Baltimore were canceled. Briefly, the verb "to oslerize" came into use as a synonym for "to kill by chloroforming."

Osler did not move to Oxford seeking dignified semiretirement. On the contrary, he flung himself into medical and medical-historical affairs in Britain with vigor and enthusiasm. The family purchased an elegant home at 13 Norham Gardens, a short walk from the university. Without any deliberate intention but because of natural warmth, generosity, and graciousness, the Oslers transformed their home into an important social focus, particularly for visiting Canadians and Americans.

Osler began his labors as a professor of medicine with no students to teach; Oxford University students did their clinical work in London. But he had patients, postgraduate students, and fellow physicians, and he soon was teaching as well as pursuing his many other interests. He became as busy in Oxford as he had been in Baltimore. He helped create societies and journals. He campaigned vigorously for public health measures of all kinds. He enlarged his historical pursuits by expanding his own library, adding many treasures to what ultimately became one of the great medical libraries. Osler wrote on clinical, pathological, historical, and bibliographic topics. In recognition of his accomplishments, he was knighted in 1911.

During World War I, Osler's exertions were redoubled. He was a colonel in the Royal Army Medical Corps, serving as consultant in Great Britain and in France. He became ill in the autumn of 1919 after a long, cold, wet ride in an automobile. Despite temporary improvements in his condition, he developed empyema of the lung. He predicted the date of his own death in Oxford, England, accurately.

Osler's various scientific contributions were solid but not epoch-making. He was especially interested in cardiac disease of all kinds and endocarditis in particular. A paper on chronic infectious endocarditis published in 1909 contained his description of what still are termed "Osler's nodes." Other eponyms include Osler-Weber-Rendu disease, or hereditary telangiectasia, and Osler-Vaquez disease, or polycythemia vera. Typically, in the last instance his article cited the priority of Vaquez (and several other authors) in reporting similar cases. Osler did much veterinary work, and while in Montreal he first described an organism causing canine bronchitis; subsequently it was named *Syphranuri osleri*.

Osler's great strength was clinical teaching. He stated, "I desire no other epitaph . . . than the statement that I taught medical students in the wards, as I regard this as by far the most useful and important work I have been called upon to do" ("The Fixed Period," p. 22). Osler repeatedly urged that the medical student be taken out of the lecture rooms and put "in the outpatient department—put him in the wards" ("The Hospital as a College," in *Aequanimitas*, p. 331). Today, of course, medical students commonly begin to see patients during their first year in medical school.

Osler's collection of rare books was bequeathed to McGill University. Its organization was unusual, Osler categorizing his books in terms of their perceived importance in delineating medical progress or in their contribution to such ancillary areas as literature and medicine, biography, bibliography, incunabula, and manuscripts. Ultimately, a decade after his death, a description of the collection was published as the *Bibliotheca Osleriana* (1929), the great catalog of his library.

Osler's literary output was prodigious. His published bibliography approaches 1,500 entries. He wrote a few books in addition to his textbook, several monographs on subjects such as neurology, abdominal tumors, and angina pectoris, and his biographically oriented general medical history, *The Evolution of Modern Medicine* (1921). He also edited a multiauthor seven-volume "System," *Modern Medicine: Its Theory and Practice* (1907–1910).

In addition to Osler's scientific books and articles, he produced a corpus of writings that is literary, historical, educational, philosophical, and in some instances inspirational. These essays are significant because they are the items of Osleriana that continue to be read, dispensing Oslerian ideals to later generations. They provide sensible advice for students and practitioners. One of his favorite themes was to urge students to be systematic: "faithfully followed day by day system may become at last engrained in the most shiftless nature, and at the end of a semester a youth of moderate ability may find himself far in advance of the student who works spasmodically, and trusts to *cramming*" ("Teacher and Student," in *Aequanimitas*, p. 35).

Osler was not a true philosopher. He described himself as being handicapped in philosophy because "cheerfulness was always breaking in." Nevertheless, his literate essays such as "A Way of Life," "The Master-Word in Medicine," and "The Student Life" provide insight into Oslerian values.

For many physicians and educators today, Osler's influence exists because of his embodiment of a fragile tradition of humanism in medicine. Osler did not practice humanist as an intellectual discipline, it simply was a part of his character.

By the early years of this century, Osler saw clearly the danger that untrammeled science held for medicine. He fought against whole-time clinical teaching, fearing that those teaching medical students would be scientists rather than humanistic physicians. Osler did not oppose scientific progress; he was himself too much influenced by science to do that. What he feared was science at the expense of art. Science and the humanities, in Osler's phrase, should be "twin berries on one stem."

Osler remains influential today for several reasons. His magnificent library at McGill University in Montreal is a permanent and highly useful memorial. The efforts of Osler and his Hopkins colleagues in medical education have been perhaps the most substantial and ubiquitous contribution, since methods they devised a century ago, though amended over the years, nevertheless continue as the basic model for training physicians. Finally, though less tangibly, Osler's humanistic approach to medicine continues to attract physicians and students who share his conviction on the need to couple the scientific education of physicians with deep appreciation for the humane approach to their patients.

• The chief archival holdings on Osler are held at McGill University, Johns Hopkins University, and Oxford University. The largest repository is that at McGill and includes the material collected by Harvey Cushing for his Pulitzer Prize–winning biography. Osler's views on clinical teaching are in "The Fixed Period," in *Sir William Osler, 1849–1919: A Selection for Medical Students*, ed. Charles G. Roland (1982), and "On the Need of a Radical Reform in Our Methods of Teaching Senior Students," *Medical News* 82 (1903): 49–53. An example of his advice to students is "Teacher and Student," in *Aequanimitas* (1906). Three books provide an entry to Osler's life and career: Harvey Cushing, *The Life of Sir William Osler* (2 vols., 1925); Richard L. Golden and Roland, eds., *Sir William Osler: An Annotated Bibliography with Illustrations* (1988); and Earl Nation, Roland, and John P. McGovern, eds., *An Annotated Checklist of Osleriana* (1976). In the decades since Osler's death, many books and articles have been written about him. Nation, Roland, and McGovern cite almost 1,400 entries, and the number increases annually. The family of Featherstone and Ellen Osler, including William, is described in Anne Wilkinson, *Lions in the Way: A Discursive History of the Oslers* (1956).

CHARLES G. ROLAND

OSTENACO (fl. 1741–1777), Cherokee chief, warrior, and orator, also known as Outacite, was born probably in the first decade of the eighteenth century. The identities of his parents are not known. He was first associated with the Overhill towns of Hiwassee and later Tomotly (in present-day Monroe and Polk counties in Tennessee). Outacite means "mankiller," and although there were numerous "mankillers" in the various Cherokee towns, the most famous was the individual normally referred to in the colonial records and histories as Ostenaco or Judd's Friend. (Aside from mention of a daughter, nothing about his having a family is on record.) Ostenaco must have won his title of mankiller very early because by 1741 he had distinguished himself sufficiently to be named as one of the guardians of the young teenager Ammonscossittee. This young Cherokee inherited from his father, Moytoy of Tellico, the title of emperor of the Cherokee nation.

In the early 1750s Ostenaco provided protection to several English traders and was invited by Governor James Glen of South Carolina to visit Charleston for a conference concerning a trade embargo placed on the Cherokees. Ostenaco is credited with influencing Glen to lift that embargo.

Although trade was reintroduced and new regulations were passed to aid the Cherokees, tension remained against the South Carolinians. Against the advice of Ostenaco, the young emperor went to Virginia, where he sought to establish trade with the rivals of Carolina. This trip was not only a failure but cost the young emperor much of his prestige as the neighboring town of Chota sought to regain its preeminence among the Cherokee nation.

By the mid-1750s Ostenaco warned the English that French influence had made serious inroads into the Overhill towns and that all the Cherokees there, except himself, would join their cause. When the English-French rivalry culminated in the French and Indian War, Ostenaco led more than a hundred Cherokees under the command of Major Andrew Lewis. The Cherokees participated in the abortive Sandy Creek expedition against the Shawnee towns along the Ohio River sent to retaliate for General Edward Braddock's defeat. George Washington reported that the Indians were "more serviceable than twice their number of white men." Later, Virginia governor Robert Dinwiddie invited Ostenaco to Williamsburg, where he rode in the governor's coach in a long parade.

When in the late 1750s some Virginian frontiersmen killed a number of Cherokees, their clansmen retaliated. In 1759 a number of chiefs went to Charleston to prevent the outbreak of war between the Cherokees and English and a new trade embargo. Governor William Henry Lyttelton, however, arrested the peace delegation and held them hostage at Fort Prince George (near present-day Clemson, S.C.). This action erupted into the Cherokee War of 1760–1761, and Ostenaco helped lay siege to Fort Loudoun (in present-day Tennessee). Peace was eventually established but not before two expeditions under Colonel Archibald Montgomery and Colonel James Grant devastated the Cherokee Middle Settlements of western North Carolina. To cement the peace, Lieutenant Henry Timberlake carried the news to the Cherokees and spent several months among them as the personal guest of Ostenaco. When Timberlake returned to Williamburg, he was accompanied by Ostenaco and a Cherokee delegation. While there, Ostenaco met young Thomas Jefferson and was given a tour of William and Mary. When Ostenaco was shown a portrait of King George III, he commented that it had long been a desire of his to see the king himself and that he would not "depart . . . [from Williamsburg] till I have obtained my desires." Arrangements were made, and Timberlake and Thomas Sumter accompanied three Cherokees (Ostenaco, Pouting Pigeon, and Stalking Turkey) to London on Captain Peter Blake's *Epreuve*. After several weeks' delay, the Cherokees had their audience with George III. Ironically they were presented to the king by Lord Eglinton, otherwise known as Colonel Archibald Montgomery, who had led an attack against the Cherokees in 1760. Oliver Goldsmith visited Ostenaco while he was in London, and the court painter, Sir Joshua Reynolds, painted a group portrait. Ostenaco was also the subject of a separate portrait, which became a feature illustration of the Royal Magazine. The trip cemented Ostenaco's loyalty to the British. When he returned, his daughter had given birth to a son, who was named Richard Timberlake after his father.

A few years later Ostenaco was among the Cherokee leaders present for marking the boundary line between the Cherokees and South Carolina. He was also one of the signatories of the Treaty of Peace and Friendship at the congress held in Augusta in 1763. In 1769 he agreed, along with the Cherokee leader Saluy, to reopen boundary negotiations with Virginia. Two years later Ostenaco and other chiefs agreed to cede land in return for cancellation of Cherokee trading debts. After these events Ostenaco does not seem to be very visible.

In 1775, prior to the American Revolution, Ostenaco was one of the few older chiefs who refused to participate in the tremendous land cession to Richard Henderson, a North Carolina judge and speculator. The cession involved most of modern-day Kentucky and a portion of middle Tennessee. Instead Ostenaco, siding with Dragging Canoe, separated himself from other Cherokees and began new settlements along the Tennessee-Alabama border, the inhabitants of which were soon known as the Chickamauga Cherokees. These Cherokees resisted the American takeover of their tribal lands for more than seventeen years (1777–1794). Ostenaco probably died before 1780. His grandson Richard Timberlake accepted a reserve in Hamilton County, Tennessee, by a treaty with the Cherokees in 1819. This treaty allowed individual Cherokees to remain on ceded land and apply for 640 acres and citizenship. Ostenaco's grandson and others who accepted the reserves became the core of the group known as the Eastern Band of Cherokees.

• The most complete biographical sketch of Ostenaco is E. Raymond Evans, "Notable Persons in Cherokee History: Ostenaco," *Journal of Cherokee Studies* 1 (Summer 1976): 41–54. A briefer account can be found in J. Norman Heard, *Handbook of the American Frontier: Four Centuries of Indian-White Relationships*, vol. 1: *The Southeastern Woodlands* (1979). Ostenaco's activities can be traced in Samuel Cole Williams, ed., *Lieut. Henry Timberlake's Memoirs, 1756–1765* (1948); John P. Brown, *Old Frontiers: The Story of the Cherokee Indians from Earliest Times to the Date of Their Removal to the West, 1838* (1938); David H. Corkran, *The Cherokee Frontier: Conflict and Survival, 1740–1762* (1962); and M. Thomas Hatley, *The Dividing Paths: Cherokees and South Carolinians through the Era of Revolution* (1993).

WILLIAM L. ANDERSON

OSTEN SACKEN, Carl Robert Romanovich von der (21 Aug. 1828–20 May 1906), entomologist and diplomat, was born in St. Petersburg, Russia; his parents' names are unknown. A member of the Russian nobility, he received some education in St. Petersburg. His serious interest in insects began at age eleven, when another young nobleman introduced him to the subject while Osten Sacken was visiting Baden Baden with his family. In 1849 he joined the Russian diplomatic corps, and prior to receiving an American posting, Osten Sacken published several papers on insects, one of them an account of the species to be found in the suburbs of St. Petersburg. In 1856 he traveled to Washington, D.C., where he took up his duties as secretary to the Russian legation. During the two-month trip, he stopped to visit some of Europe's leading entomologists, including Hermann A. Hagen, then living in Konigsberg. In the mid-1860s Osten Sacken was instrumental in recommending that the zoologist Louis Agassiz invite Hagen to Harvard, where Hagen became the first American incumbent of a chair in entomology. In 1862 Osten Sacken was named the Russian consul general in New York City, a post he held until 1871.

Osten Sacken was primarily a student of flies, mosquitoes, and their allies, and while in the United States he worked diligently to categorize the North American species of these insects found north of Panama. Much of this work was done in collaboration with the Vienna, Austria, entomologist Hermann Loew, to whom he sent many specimens for study. In 1858 the Smithsonian Institution published Osten Sacken's *Catalogue of the Described Diptera of North America*; a second edition appeared in 1878. Between 1862 and 1873 Osten Sacken and Loew completed four volumes of their *Monographs of the Diptera of North America*, which also were published by the Smithsonian. In addition to publishing his own work, Osten Sacken also translated and edited a number of Loew's manuscripts into English, probably the one of many languages after his native Russian in which he was most proficient. His papers on North American insects appeared in various journals, including one four-part series on gall insects that was published between 1861 and 1865 in the *Proceedings of the Entomological Society of Philadelphia*.

After leaving the Russian diplomatic service in 1871, Osten Sacken made several trips to Europe and to Russia, partly for the purpose of research in European museum collections. From 1873 to 1875 Osten Sacken spent much of his time at the Museum of Comparative Zoology at Harvard, working with Hagen and other entomologists on the insect collections there. From late 1875 until the fall of 1876 Osten Sacken traveled in the western United States, collecting insects in the Rocky Mountains and in California. His account of western Diptera was published by the Smithsonian in 1877, and the California varieties were later described in a bulletin of the U.S. Geological and Geographical Survey of the Territories, published in 1887.

Returning to Europe in 1877, Osten Sacken spent much of the remaining three decades of his life in Heidelberg, Germany. It was arranged that he and his longtime colleague Loew, then very ill, would carry out Osten Sacken's plan of contributing their jointly accumulated collections of North American Diptera to the Museum of Comparative Zoology at Harvard. Osten Sacken personally superintended the packing and shipment of this material to Cambridge, Massachusetts. In response, the museum then sent Loew a substantial honorarium. In appreciation for this thoughtful gesture, Osten Sacken then presented much of his personal collection of American insects to

Harvard; a smaller collection went to the American Entomological Society in Philadelphia. Most of his Russian and European specimens were later presented to the zoology museum in St. Petersburg.

Osten Sacken remained active, publishing a number of short but valuable papers, maintaining an extensive correspondence with entomologists in various parts of the world, and working up a catalog of world Diptera outside of Europe. In 1894 he went back to Russia, where he served for a time in the Russian Foreign Office. Toward the end of his life, he made humorous references to himself as "the grandfather of American Dipterology," an honor that he truly deserved. Shortly before his death, he completed *Record of My Life Work in Entomology*, an autobiography. The first and second parts were published in Cambridge in 1903 and the third part in Heidelberg in 1904. Osten Sacken died in Heidelberg.

• Osten Sacken's papers are at the Museum of Comparative Zoology, Harvard University. Biographical sketches include E. O. Essig in *A History of Entomology* (1931); Arnold Mallis, *American Entomologists* (1971); and Clark A. Elliott, *Biographical Dictionary of American Science: The Seventeenth through the Nineteenth Centuries* (1979). See also the obituaries by J. M. Aldrich and C. W. Johnson in *Entomological News*, Oct. 1906, and by G. H. Verrall in *Entomologist's Monthly Magazine*, Oct. 1906.

KEIR B. STERLING

OSTENSO, Martha (17 Sept. 1900–24 Nov. 1963), writer, was born in Haukeland, Norway, the daughter of Sigurd Brigt, a businessman, and Lena Tungeland. In 1902 her parents immigrated to the United States and settled in Minnesota. Ostenso began writing at an early age; the *Minneapolis Journal* regularly published her work on its juvenile page, even occasionally paying her. The Ostensos moved frequently around Minnesota, then to South Dakota, and finally, when Ostenso was fifteen, to Brandon, Manitoba, Canada. Profoundly affected by the harsh life of the settlers of the northern prairies, she later wrote, "The story of my childhood is a tale of seven little towns in Minnesota and South Dakota. Towns of the field and prairie all, redolent of the soil from which they had sprung and eloquent of that struggle common to the farmer the world over." There on the prairies "was human nature stark, unattired in the convention of a smoother, softer life. A thousand stories are there, still to be written."

In 1918 Ostenso entered the University of Manitoba in Winnipeg, where she met her future husband, Douglas Leader Durkin, a writer on the faculty there. Durkin was married to his first wife at that time. After leaving the university, Ostenso taught school for a year in rural Manitoba before moving permanently to the United States. Settling in New York, she worked as a social worker for the Bureau of Charities in Brooklyn from 1920 until 1923. This exposure to the grim poverty of urban life, she claimed, made her appreciate rural life. During that time she resumed work on a novel she had begun while in Winnipeg. In 1921 she enrolled in a fiction writing course at Columbia University, where she renewed her acquaintance with Durkin, who had separated from his wife. Ostenso and Durkin were unable to marry until 1944 because his wife would not grant him a divorce. However, at this time they established both a personal relationship and a professional, collaborative writing relationship that continued until her death. They lived in a variety of locations, including New Jersey and Minneapolis, before eventually settling in Brainerd, Minnesota.

Although Ostenso is primarily known for her novels, her first published book was a volume of poetry, *A Far Land* (1924). Clara Thomas has persuasively argued that "several of its works pre-figure her strongest fictional themes, the death-in-life of the spirit of man and his terrible isolation" (p. 40). Certainly these themes reappear in *Wild Geese*, her first novel. Set in Manitoba, *Wild Geese* tells the story of the Gare family as they struggle under the tyranny of their autocratic father, Caleb Gare, who regards his wife and children as virtual slaves and considers the prairie as an adversary to be conquered. Two visitors to the district spur Caleb's wife and children to a justified rebellion, but Caleb is ultimately responsible for his own defeat and death because of his greed and cruelty.

For this work Ostenso won the $13,500 *Pictorial Review*, Dodd, Mead & Company, and Famous Players-Lasky Corporation prize for the best first novel of 1925. *Wild Geese* is, indeed, Ostenso's best work: its plot is original, and its stark depiction of the struggle for survival on a small family farm is powerful. It suffers, however, from melodrama and Ostenso's heavy-handed use of symbols. Scholars frequently group *Wild Geese* with Robert J. C. Stead's *Grain* (1926), Philip Grove's *Settlers of the Marsh* (1925), and Sinclair Ross's *As for Me and My House* (1941) in the genres of Canadian prairie fiction and western realism. Yet critics have also recognized in *Wild Geese* elements of the grotesque and the romance.

Wild Geese remains Ostenso's best-known and most critically acclaimed novel, but several critics have questioned its authorship. Based on his correspondence with relatives of both Durkin and Ostenso, Peter E. Rider argues that *Wild Geese* was essentially a collaborative project between Durkin and Ostenso. Because Durkin was already a published author, he was ineligible for the novel contest. Ostenso had the outline of a novel, however, and Rider postulates that Durkin was able to contribute valuable technical experience to its production. Rider claims that this partnership continued for several of the novels that were published under Ostenso's name, and he concludes that "the proportion that each contributed to the novels is hard to distinguish, but both their talents were undoubtedly an integral part of the final products" (p. xvii). Ostenso herself frequently credited Durkin with assistance, calling him "my severest critic and most exacting collaborator" (*Minnesota Writers*, p. 249).

Ostenso's well-received and commercially successful later novels, such as *The Mad Carews* (1927) and *The Stone Field* (1937), differ greatly in style from *Wild Geese*. As Ostenso matured, her writing became

smoother and more consistent, but her plots lost much of their originality; many, in fact, are rather conventional romances. The differences in style in these later works may lend weight to the argument that Durkin collaborated most heavily with Ostenso on *Wild Geese*. Yet these later novels still share common themes, foremost among them the value of an agrarian lifestyle. Ostenso exposes the dangers of alienation from the earth and isolation from others; her characters struggle to balance the powerful needs of the individual against those of the community. Her novels are also notable for their portrayals of strong-willed, independent female characters, such as Judith Gare in *Wild Geese* and Marcia Vorse Gunther in *The Young May Moon* (1929), as well as for their frank treatment of female sexuality.

Ostenso's novels and short stories continued to be popular in the United States throughout her career (her shorter works, which were published in a variety of magazines and journals, have never been collected). She was never as popular in Canada, however, and was essentially forgotten in the United States after her death. Modern Canadian critics have only recently begun to give her the attention she deserves.

Ostenso may be best known in popular culture for her only notable work of nonfiction, *And They Shall Walk: The Life Story of Sister Elizabeth Kenny* (1943). Written in collaboration with Kenny, the Australian nurse who pioneered physical therapy treatments for victims of polio, this work was filmed in 1946 as *The Sister Kenny Story*, starring Rosalind Russell.

Ostenso wrote only three novels in the last twenty years of her life, none of which achieved critical acclaim. She died suddenly after traveling with Durkin to visit his two sons in Seattle, Washington.

• Ostenso's other major works include *The Dark Dawn* (1926), *The Waters under the Earth* (1930), *Prologue to Love* (1932), *There's Always Another Year* (1933), *The White Reef* (1934), *The Mandrake Root* (1938), *Love Passed This Way* (1942), *Milk Route* (1948), *The Sunset Tree* (1949), and *A Man Had Tall Sons* (1958).

Dick Harrison, *Unnamed Country: The Struggle for a Canadian Prairie Fiction* (1977), contains a bibliography of both primary and secondary sources of Canadian fiction. See also John Moss, *A Reader's Guide to the Canadian Novel* (1981). Ostenso has an autobiographical sketch in Carmen Nelson Richards, ed. *Minnesota Writers* (1961). Additional biographical information is available in Grant Overton, *The Women Who Make Our Novels*, rev. ed. (1928); Clara Thomas, "Martha Ostenso's Trial of Strength," in *Writers of the Prairies*, ed. Donald Stephens (1973); and Peter Rider, introduction to *The Magpie*, by Douglas Durkin (repr. 1974). An obituary is in the *New York Times*, 26 Nov. 1963.

KAREN A. WEYLER

OSTERHAUS, Peter Joseph (4 Jan. 1823–2 Jan. 1917), army officer and diplomat, was born in Koblenz, Germany, the son of Anton A. Osterhaus. His mother's name is not known. After attending a military school in Berlin, he served as a gentleman volunteer in the Prussian Twenty-ninth Infantry Regiment. In 1846 he married Natilda Born; they had five children. When a wave of revolutions swept Germany in 1848, Osterhaus sided with those striving to give Germany a unified, liberal government. They failed, and many, like Osterhaus, fled to America the following year. Osterhaus settled in Belleville, in southwestern Illinois, and got a job in a dry goods store. In the next two years he moved first to Lebanon, Illinois, where he ran a general store, and then to St. Louis, Missouri, where a large German-American population made social conditions pleasant for the Osterhauses. In St. Louis he obtained employment as a bookkeeper for a hardware wholesaler.

When the Civil War came, Osterhaus, like the numerous other German Americans of the St. Louis area, cast his lot with the Union. He enlisted as a private in the Twelfth Missouri Volunteer Infantry and participated in Captain Nathaniel Lyon's seizure of prosecession Missouri militia at Camp Jackson. Later, he raised a company of Missourians and became its captain. When combination with other companies raised this formation to battalion strength (Osterhaus's Missouri Battalion), he became its major, on 27 April 1861. His battalion, which sometimes was considered part of the Second Missouri Regiment, took part in the battle of Wilson's Creek on 10 August of that year. At the end of that month, however, it was mustered out of service, and Osterhaus was temporarily out of the service too. That December he was commissioned colonel of his old Twelfth Missouri. By March 1862, though still only a colonel, he was commanding a division in General Samuel R. Curtis's Army of Southwest. He led his division in action at the crucial battle of Pea Ridge, 6–8 March. Promotion to brigadier general followed that June, and Osterhaus continued to command various divisions within the Army of the Southwest throughout the remainder of 1862 and well into 1863. In the spring of 1863 his troops became part of General Ulysses S. Grant's army in his campaign to take Vicksburg, Mississippi. As Grant drove the Confederate forces backward into the doomed city, fierce clashes occurred at Champion's Hill (16 May) and Big Black River (17 May). In the latter of these Osterhaus, commanding a division of General William T. Sherman's XV Corps, was lightly wounded by a shell fragment. He returned to duty two days later, taking part in the Vicksburg siege as well as in Sherman's capture of Jackson, Mississippi, after the fall of the river bastion.

That fall Osterhaus's division accompanied Sherman, now commanding the Army of the Tennessee, on his march to the aid of the beleaguered Army of the Cumberland at Chattanooga, Tennessee. In Grant's November offensive, Osterhaus's division was detached to the command of General Joseph Hooker. The German led his troops in the successful assaults on Lookout Mountain and Missionary Ridge, crushing the Confederate left flank and capturing thousands of prisoners. It was probably Osterhaus's finest hour as a general. Thereafter he continued in the Army of the Tennessee, now under General James B. McPherson, as a part of Sherman's force operating against Atlanta during the summer of 1864. Despite the disapproval of Sherman (who believed Osterhaus had engaged in high-level wirepulling to get promotion), Osterhaus was promoted to major general to date from 23 July, the day after the Army of the Tennessee's ordeal in the hard-fought battle of Atlanta. After the fall of that city in September 1864, Osterhaus continued in division command throughout the march to the sea. When on 13 December 1864 XV Corps commander General John A. Logan was temporarily transferred to Tennessee, Osterhaus succeeded to command of the corps. By 8 January Logan was back, and the German reverted to his previous command. Thereafter, Osterhaus was transferred to the Gulf Coast to serve as chief of staff to General Edward R. S. Canby, who was driving to take Mobile, Alabama.

Osterhaus's last important wartime service involved the final Confederate surrender. At New Orleans, on 26 May 1865, Osterhaus, acting on behalf of Canby, met with Confederate general Simon B. Buckner (1823–1914), who in turn represented Confederate Trans-Mississippi commander General Edmund Kirby Smith. The resulting agreement arranged for the surrender of all remaining organized Confederate troops. After the war Osterhaus continued in district command in Mississippi until January 1866, when he was mustered out of the service. He was one of the best of the many foreign-born generals to have served the Union during the Civil War.

Osterhaus's first wife having died in November 1863, he married her sister, Amalia Born, the following July. This second marriage produced three children.

In June 1866 Osterhaus was appointed U.S. consul for Lyon, France, where he served until August 1877. He astutely analyzed the economic effects in France of the treaty that ended the Franco-Prussian War in 1871. Returning to the United States as a private citizen, he went back to St. Louis and the hardware business, this time in manufacturing and exporting. In 1898 he was appointed deputy U.S. consul for Mannheim, Germany, where he served until his retirement in 1900. In 1905 Congress, by special vote, added him to the army's retired list as a brigadier general, allowing him to collect a pension. He died in Duisburg, Germany, and was buried there.

• For more information on Osterhaus see Peter Cozzens, *The Shipwreck of Their Hopes* (1994); Ulysses S. Grant, *Personal Memoirs* (1885–1886); E. B. Long and Barbara Long, *The Civil War Day by Day: An Almanac, 1861–1865* (1971); James Lee McDonough, *Chattanooga—A Death Grip on the Confederacy* (1984); John F. Marszalek, *Sherman: A Soldier's Passion for Order* (1993); U.S. War Department, *The War of the Rebellion: A Compilation of the Official Records of the Union and Confederate Armies* (128 vols., 1880–1901); and Ezra Warner, *Generals in Blue: The Lives of the Union Commanders* (1964).

STEVEN E. WOODWORTH

OSTERHOUT, Winthrop John Vanleuven (2 Aug. 1871–9 Apr. 1964), general physiologist, was born in Brooklyn, New York, the son of John Vanleuven Osterhout, a Baptist minister, and Annie Loranthe Beman. After losing his mother and infant sister to typhoid fever in 1873, the boy lived with his grandmother in Baltimore, Maryland, until 1879, when he rejoined his father (now living with his third wife) in Providence, Rhode Island.

Winthrop grew up bookish, unathletic, and fond of literature. He entered Brown University in 1889, soon familiarizing himself with most of the books in the university library. By 1893, when he received his B.A., botany had become his main interest.

At the urging of H. C. Bumpus, Brown professor of botany, Osterhout attended W. A. Setchell's summer botany course at Woods Hole, Massachusetts, in 1892. During field trips with Setchell, Osterhout learned much about large-celled fresh-water algae, whose advantages as experimental organisms he would exploit in his experimental work in the 1920s. Osterhout was also intellectually stimulated by the great experimental biologists in residence there, including T. H. Morgan; E. G. Conklin; Frank Lillie; and Jacques Loeb, who later became Osterhout's close friend. From 1893 to 1895 he earned his living teaching botany at Woods Hole and at Brown, where he earned an M.A. in 1894.

Osterhout spent the academic year of 1895–1896 in Bonn, Germany, as a graduate student of plant cytologist Eduard Strasburger. There he helped elucidate the mechanism of mitotic spindle formation in the dividing cells of the horsetail (*Equisetum*). The spindle is responsible for chromosome separation. He also worked on the cytology and reproduction of *Batrachospermum*, a freshwater red alga. The resulting publications helped establish Osterhout's reputation as an observer and experimenter.

On his return to the United States in 1896, Osterhout accepted a position as instructor of botany at the University of California at Berkeley, where Setchell was now professor of botany. There, under Setchell's supervision, Osterhout obtained his Ph.D. in 1899. That same year he married Anna Maria Landstrom; they had two daughters.

Osterhout benefited by contact with the great European scientists who came to Berkeley on extended visits: Svante Arrhenius from Sweden; Hugo De Vries from Holland; and Wilhelm Ostwald from Germany. But the German-born Loeb, who came to Berkeley in 1902 and stayed for eight years, had the greatest influence in shifting Osterhout's orientation from morphology and cytology to physiology and physical chemistry.

Osterhout, promoted to assistant professor in 1901 and to associate professor in 1907, had become interested in the effects of dissolved salts on plant cells, a subject of practical importance in agriculture. He had observed that plants, attached to the hulls of river steamers that sailed from fresh to salt water, survived great changes in salt concentration, whereas small changes of salt concentration in the laboratory were sufficient to injure or kill such plants.

About 1911–1912 Osterhout focused his study of ionic effects on the permeability of cell membranes to salts. He discussed the problem with Loeb, who had previously demonstrated, in animal cells, opposing permeability effects of sodium salts to those of calcium and potassium salts. Osterhout now showed that the plant cell membrane was permeable to salts, and that it too exhibited "salt antagonism." Sodium salts increased membrane permeability; calcium salts had an opposite effect. Solutions in which the salts existed in ratios similar to that in sea water were tolerated by cells over a wide concentration range. Osterhout also observed that cells injured by unbalanced solutions recovered on being restored to their normal environment if the injury had not been too great or too prolonged. He also showed that sodium, which had generally been believed to be needed by animals but not by plants, was necessary for plant life.

In 1905 Osterhout published *Experiments with Plants*, which went through six editions in as many years, was illustrated by his friend Luther Burbank, and was translated into Dutch and Russian within a few years of its first appearance. Twenty years later, it was still used in elementary botany courses. The success of his book, like that of his lectures, rested in part on his ingenuity in devising simple experiments: using readily available materials, such as seeds, corks, lamp chimneys, umbrella ribs, etc., to illustrate basic concepts of plant physiology. In 1910 he published, with E. W. Hilgard, the widely used *Agriculture for Schools of the Pacific Slope*.

That same year Osterhout accepted an assistant professorship at Harvard University and was elected the following year a fellow of the American Academy of Arts and Sciences. Obliged by a low salary to supplement his earnings by outside teaching, he nevertheless found a rich intellectual atmosphere at Harvard. He soon became friends with noted zoologist George Howard Parker and with Theodore Richards, the United States's first Nobel laureate in chemistry. By 1910 Osterhout could renew his collaboration with Loeb, who had come east, to the Rockefeller Institute, in New York. Osterhout now also resumed his connection with Woods Hole Marine Biological Laboratory (MBL), where he worked until 1922. He was elected a trustee of MBL in 1922 and remained on the board for nearly thirty years.

At Harvard, where Osterhout's career advanced rapidly, he had become a professor of botany by 1913. In 1917 he was made a member of the American Philosophical Society and two years later was elected to the National Academy of Sciences.

In 1919 Loeb and Osterhout co-founded the *Journal of General Physiology*, published by the Rockefeller Institute, on whose board of scientific directors Osterhout served from 1920 to 1926. When Loeb died in 1924, Osterhout continued, as sole editor of the journal until shortly before his own death.

Osterhout was often invited to present endowed series of lectures, whose published versions constitute his principal book-length publications. His Colver Lectures at Brown in 1922, published in 1924 as *The Nature of Life*, stressed analogies between biological phenomena and those found in the inorganic world. His Lowell Lectures, in Boston, on the role of water in the nonaqueous surface layer of cytoplasm, were published as *Injury, Recovery and Death in Relation to Conductivity and Permeability* (1923). His 1925 Sedgwick Memorial Lectures, at the Massachusetts Institute of Technology, appeared in print as *Some Fundamental Problems of Cellular Physiology* (1927).

In 1922 Osterhout received a Rockefeller Institute grant of $10,000 to study marine plants in Bermuda. With a capable young staff, Osterhout now studied the chemistry of large algal cells, some of which appear to be little more than a thin coating of protoplasm surrounding a huge cell vacuole. He showed that the vacuolar liquid differed greatly in ionic content and in acidity from that of the ambient liquid in which the cells flourished, implying that processes other than passive diffusion were involved.

By 1920 Osterhout was developing techniques for observing changes in cell permeability by recording electrical conductivity of columns of stacked segments of Laminaria (kelp). Relating these data to changes in ambient salt concentrations and ultimately to processes of injury, recovery, and death, Osterhout evolved the view that the deaths of cells and of multi-celled organisms was not instantaneous. He deduced that the physical changes in membrane permeability and loss of cell function associated with death occur continually during life and are accompanied by growth and recovery processes. When the balance is altered beyond repair, death occurs gradually, at different rates in various parts of the organism.

Osterhout remained at Harvard until 1925, when he left to head the Rockefeller Institute division of general physiology, a position left vacant by Loeb's death. He remained thereafter at Rockefeller, being granted emeritus status in 1939. Among his more famous assistants at Rockefeller was W. M. Stanley, the future Nobel laureate.

The early 1930s were years of personal crisis for Osterhout. By 1931, he was afflicted by glaucoma, from which he ultimately went blind. He suffered a severe heart attack (atrial fibrillation) in 1933. That same year his first marriage ended in divorce and he married Marian Irwin, who had been his assistant at Rockefeller for about eight years.

Recognition of Osterhout's contributions included honorary memberships in scientific societies in Scotland, Germany, and Sweden. He died in New York City.

• Osterhout's papers are at the American Philosophical Society, Philadelphia, Pa., and at the Rockefeller Archive Center, North Tarrytown, N.Y. Useful data on Osterhout's professional life can be found in G. W. Corner, *A History of the Rockefeller Institute* (1964). Obituaries are in the *New York Times*, 10 Apr. 1964, and *Brown Alumni Monthly*, May 1964.

CHARLES H. FUCHSMAN

OSTROMISLENSKY, Iwan Iwanowitch (8 Sept. 1880–16 Jan. 1939), organic and medicinal chemist, was born in Moscow, Russia, the son of Ivan Ostromys-

lenskii, an officer in the Imperial Guard, and Olga Ivanova. After graduating from a Moscow military academy in 1895, Ostromislensky studied at the University of Moscow for three years. In 1899 he entered the University of Zurich, where he earned a Ph.D. in 1902 and an M.D. in 1906. Before returning to Russia in 1907 he received a diploma in chemical engineering from Karlsruhe Polytechnic. From 1907 to 1911 he was an assistant professor of chemistry at Moscow University. He then abandoned teaching to devote himself to research in a private laboratory. In 1916 the Scientific Institute in Moscow appointed him director of its chemotherapy division; in 1917 he became professor of chemistry at the University of Nizhni Novgorod in the Russian city of that name.

Ostromislensky's most notable research, conducted while he was in Russia, began in 1911 with investigations into the chemistry of rubber and culminated in an extraordinary series of twenty journal articles published in 1915. These not only described a new vulcanization process that substituted organic peroxides and other chemicals for sulfur but also made important advances in the development of synthetic rubbers, a project that had assumed urgency for the Russian government during World War I. In particular, Ostromislensky succeeded in using butadiene and vinyl chloride as monomers, or building blocks, in the synthesis of polymers that have many of the properties of natural rubber. As part of this research he developed novel methods of preparing butadiene from alcohol on an industrial scale and developed methods for making polyvinylchloride (PVC) from its vinyl chloride monomers; these methods laid the groundwork for the commercial production of PVC.

A czarist, Ostromislensky fled Russia in 1921, following the Bolshevik victory in the civil war. After a brief period in Riga, Latvia, he came to the United States on the invitation of the U.S. Rubber Company to join its research staff in New York. Ostromislensky found that U.S. Rubber was primarily interested in his vulcanization process. The company did allow him to continue his research on vinyl chloride and butadiene, and his studies resulted in about thirty U.S. patents. Nevertheless, the company did not regard his investigations as having great significance and in 1925 vetoed further research in this area. He left U.S. Rubber to form in 1926 the Ostro Research Laboratory in New York City and dedicated himself to chemotherapy and the development of new pharmaceuticals. In the 1930s he was associated with several pharmaceutical laboratories as well as serving as consultant to Eastman Kodak on the uses of PVC.

Ostromislensky's work was essential to the American synthetic rubber industry. His 1926 patent that described a variety of plasticizers and additives to make flexible PVC prompted companies such as DuPont, B. F. Goodrich, and Union Carbide to develop the substance into a practical material. During the 1930s, PVC found use as a plastic, insulator, film, lacquer, and in such consumer items as coating for rainwear, vinyl floor tile, and gramophone records. Ostromislensky's research on butadiene overcame the limitation that butadiene polymerized into an inferior rubber. He developed methods to prepare styrene and its polymerization into polystyrene. He pioneered the use of styrene as a copolymer with butadiene. American companies made polystyrene in the 1930s, and Union Carbide used his patents in developing buna rubber in the early 1940s. This butadiene-styrene copolymer was made in tonnage quantities in World War II.

In 1926 Ostromislensky resumed the work on medicinal chemistry that he had initiated in Moscow. In 1914 he had devised a theory of chemotherapy that guided him in his search for novel pharmaceuticals. He elaborated this theory in the United States in *The Scientific Basis of Chemotherapy* (1926). Using chemical ideas about the binding of chemically active portions of drugs, toxins, and antitoxins, he modified organic substances to obtain what he hoped were better drugs to replace existing ones. For example, he prepared organoarsenicals with less toxic side effects to replace salvarsan, the antibacterial agent used to treat syphilis. He received more than sixty U.S. patents, which were divided about equally between rubber and polymer discoveries and medicinal ones. His hopes that his drugs would be commercially successful, however, were not realized.

Ostromislensky and his wife Olga (maiden name unknown) had two children. He became a U.S. citizen in 1930. Dedicated to the cause of Russian culture in America, he was president of the National League of Americans of Russian Origin and a founder with Russian composer Sergei Rachmaninoff of the Circle of Russian Culture. He died in New York City from coronary artery disease. As the first chemist to propose exploiting PVC as a synthetic rubber and film, and the first to copolymerize a diene with styrene, Ostromislensky contributed substantially through his work to the development of the synthetic rubber and polymer industry in the United States.

• Library listings may be found under the modern transliteration: Ostromyslenskii, Ivan Ivanovich. On Ostromislensky's contributions to rubber and polymer chemistry, see Glenn Babcock, *History of the United States Rubber Company* (1966); Harry Barron, *Modern Synthetic Rubbers* (1944); and Morris Kaufman, *The History of PVC* (1969). Obituaries are in the *New York Times*, 19 Jan. 1939; *India Rubber Journal*, 18 Feb. 1939; and the *Rubber Age*, Feb. 1939.

ALBERT B. COSTA

O'SULLIVAN, James Edward (26 June 1876–15 Feb. 1949), builder, was born in Port Huron, Michigan, the son of James O'Sullivan, a building contractor and local political leader, and Anna Waller. His parents were Irish immigrants who had come to the United States by way of Canada, first settling in Detroit and finally Port Huron. He graduated from the University of Michigan with a B.A. degree in 1902, attended law school there, and was admitted to the Michigan bar in

1903. He also worked at the same time in his father's contracting firm. In 1905 he married Pearl Twiss, with whom he had three children.

O'Sullivan moved to Seattle in 1905 to open a law practice, but because of depressed times he instead became the foreman of a construction project. Then, from 1906 to 1910, he taught history and political science at the State Normal School in Bellingham, Washington.

Admitted to the Washington state bar in 1910, he moved to Ephrata and began a law practice. At this same time he developed a lifelong interest in irrigating what was then known as the Big Bend Country and is now known as the Columbia Basin. This interest caused him to move back and forth between his family home in Michigan and the state of Washington for the next nineteen years. When his father died in 1915, O'Sullivan returned to Port Huron to become president and general manager of the family business. Nevertheless, he continued his interest in Washington State and maintained his private holdings in the Basin at both Ephrata and Moses Lake.

He returned to Washington in 1919 to resume his work in private irrigation and to lead the local effort to convince the state and federal governments to build Grand Coulee Dam on the Columbia River and to fund the Columbia Basin Federal Reclamation Project. At the time, agriculture and business in the Basin were experiencing an "era of drought and depression," and they viewed federal irrigation as the solution to their troubles. Those in favor of this plan were nicknamed "the pumpers." As their leader, O'Sullivan wrote numerous articles in the *Wenatchee World* on the subject. These were forwarded to Washington, D.C., and were largely responsible for causing the U.S. Bureau of Reclamation to investigate the Grand Coulee proposal, when most authorities at the state and federal level favored irrigating the Basin from the more distant Pend Oreille River. This latter plan would have directly benefited private interests in Spokane, especially the Washington Water Power Company, which opposed the building of a huge federal dam along the Columbia.

Between 1920 and 1929 O'Sullivan was back in Michigan again, tending to the family contracting business. Still, he kept himself well informed and never lost sight of his vision for irrigating the Columbia Basin. In 1929 O'Sullivan completed his family business in Michigan and returned to eastern Washington to revive the effort to build Grand Coulee Dam and to develop the land of the Basin. During 1929–1933 O'Sullivan helped organize the Columbia River Development League, became its executive secretary, and successfully lobbied throughout the Pacific Northwest and in Washington, D.C. He worked during this time without salary, depending on donations of money, meals, and lodging. His first breakthrough came when the Army Corps of Engineers "308" or "Butler" Report was released in 1932. This report persuaded the federal government to approve the concept of a dam at Grand Coulee, which would be part of an overall regional plan for the Columbia River. In 1933 O'Sullivan helped secure the creation of a Washington State Columbia Basin Commission to lobby Congress for funding and then became its executive secretary, a post he held until the state commission ended in 1937. In this position he worked assertively for the construction of a "high" rather than a "low" dam at Grand Coulee. A low dam would have provided only electricity while a high dam would also provide sufficient water for the proposed Columbia Basin Project. Grand Coulee Dam was completed in 1941 at a cost of nearly $64 million, but construction of the Columbia Basin Project was delayed until after World War II.

During the last decade of his life, O'Sullivan anticipated the construction of the Columbia Basin Project. He helped organize the Quincy–Columbia Basin Irrigation District in 1939 and became its secretary. In 1940 he was appointed a consultant to the federal Bonneville Power Administration, and in 1948, four years before the opening of the Columbia Basin Project, the dam on the Potholes Reservoir was renamed O'Sullivan Dam in his honor. He died in Spokane, never having received financial gain for his years of commitment. In 1986 the Washington State Historical Society inducted him into its Washington State Centennial Hall of Honor along with 100 other outstanding citizens.

• The James O'Sullivan Papers are located at the library of Gonzaga University in Spokane, Wash. George Sundborg, *Hail Columbia: The Thirty Year Struggle for Grand Coulee Dam* (1954), a sympathetic account of O'Sullivan's role, is based on the above papers and is the best printed source for this subject. Other published works that deal with O'Sullivan include C. C. Dill, *Where Water Falls* (1970); Rufus Woods, *The 23 Year Battle for Grand Coulee Dam* (1944); and two articles by Martin and Rita Seedorf, "Drought, Depression and Dreams: Grant County's Struggle for Water," *Columbia Basin Daily Herald*, 28 Apr. 1983, and "James O'Sullivan, the 'Pumpers' and the Fight for Grand Coulee Dam, 1918–1933," *Pacific Northwest Forum* 3 (Winter–Spring 1990).

MARTIN F. SEEDORF

O'SULLIVAN, John Louis (13 Nov. 1813–24 Mar. 1895), lawyer, journalist, and legislator, was born aboard a British man-of-war off the coast of Gibraltar, the son of John Thomas O'Sullivan, a U.S. diplomat and sea captain, and Mary Rowly. Descended from a long line of colorful Irish expatriates and soldiers of fortune, in childhood O'Sullivan eagerly absorbed tales of the family's adventures. The romantic twist of his birth aboard an enemy ship during the War of 1812 was repeated throughout his life's uneven course. Julian Hawthorne, son of author Nathaniel Hawthorne, observed of his father's close friend, "His faith and enthusiasm in 'projects' knew no bounds; he might be deceived and bankrupted a hundred times, and would toe the mark the next time with undiminished confidence. He was continually, and in the quietest way, having the most astonishing and cataclysmic adventures."

The death of O'Sullivan's father at sea in 1825 indirectly led to the son's most successful and best-remembered venture, the *United States Magazine and Democratic Review*. Founded in 1837 at Washington, D.C., the *Democratic Review* likely was funded by the family's successful claim against the U.S. government in connection with Captain O'Sullivan's death. Twenty-three-year-old John Louis O'Sullivan, a graduate of Columbia College (1831) and an attorney, saw the magazine as an opportunity to advance the principles of the radical Jacksonian Democrats and the cause of a democratic, American literature. Contributors included Hawthorne, Ralph Waldo Emerson, Henry David Thoreau, John Greenleaf Whittier, William Cullen Bryant, and a then-unknown Walter Whitman. Among O'Sullivan's essays for the *Democratic Review*, "The Democratic Principle" (1 [Oct. 1837]: 1–15), "Democracy" (7 [Mar. 1840]: 215–29), and "The Great Nation of Futurity" (6 [Nov. 1839]: 426–30), best express his romantic, democratic idealism. In the inaugural issue he declared "that high and holy DEMOCRATIC PRINCIPLE . . . designed to be the fundamental tenet of the new social and political system created by the American experiment" as the magazine's ideological foundation. "Democracy must finally triumph," he wrote in "Democracy." "[Its] essence is justice. . . . [Its] object is human progress. . . . The movement of man . . . must be onward." Ill health and financial crisis led O'Sullivan to yield editing duties in 1839 to his brother-in-law Samuel Langtree, the magazine's cofounder. While practicing law in New York City, O'Sullivan continued to contribute articles to the magazine and successfully gained election to the New York state assembly in 1840. At the end of that year, he took over sole editorship of the *Democratic Review*, moved it to New York City, and suspended publication for six months while he served the first of two terms in Albany.

An aggressive, articulate reformer, O'Sullivan pushed for change on many fronts, most notably seeking to abolish capital punishment in New York State. As chairman of a special committee to investigate the matter, he wrote *A Report in Favor of the Abolition of Punishment of Death by Law* (1841). O'Sullivan-sponsored measures to end the death penalty, however, failed by narrow margins during both of his legislative terms. Historians of the movement have termed his role in the cause essential to its near-success.

During the presidential campaign of 1844, John Louis O'Sullivan and Samuel J. Tilden founded and edited the *New York Morning News*, a paper boosting the campaign of James K. Polk. O'Sullivan also hammered editorially against the nativist administration of Mayor William Harper. In editorials in the *News* and the *Democratic Review*, O'Sullivan outlined his vision of continental expansion summarized in the phrase "manifest destiny." O'Sullivan's expansionism was essentially peaceful, and his first editorials in the *News* on the Mexican War questioned the circumstances of its initiation. By June 1846, because of investor dissatisfaction with his management style, O'Sullivan was ousted as editor of the *News* and shortly thereafter disposed of his interest in the *Democratic Review*.

In October 1846 O'Sullivan married Susan Kearny Rodgers. They had no children. For the next few years, he pursued a number of enterprises, including two attempted invasions of Cuba in association with General Narciso Lopez. A New York City jury acquitted him in March 1852 after he was indicted and tried for violating the Neutrality Act. Still affiliated with the Van Buren wing of the New York Democracy, O'Sullivan represented that faction in patronage negotiations with president-elect Franklin Pierce. In 1854 he was appointed U.S. consul to Portugal and served until removed by President James Buchanan in 1858.

After his finances were depleted by his filibustering and failed business enterprises, O'Sullivan spent much of his final years in economic struggle. Living in Europe during the Civil War, he served the Confederacy as a propagandist and negotiator. Returning to the United States in the early 1870s, he promoted Spiritualism. In 1889 O'Sullivan suffered a stroke and finally succumbed to related complications in a New York City residential hotel in 1895.

O'Sullivan played a leading role in promoting the early career of Hawthorne. Under his editorship, the *Democratic Review* was the leading voice of literary Young America, and his optimistic, romantic nationalism helped give rise to the political Young America movement of the early 1850s. His *Democratic Review* and *News* editorials provide valuable insights into the ideological foundations of radical, northern Democratic thought in antebellum America.

• No central collection of John L. O'Sullivan papers exists, though his letters are in the Martin Van Buren and James K. Polk Papers, Library of Congress; Samuel J. Tilden Papers, New York Public Library; Benjamin F. Butler Papers, Yale University; George Bancroft Papers, Massachusetts Historical Society; and scattered in other collections. O'Sullivan's attempt at autobiography is in Florence Addicks, "A Genealogical History of the O'Sullivan Family," Genealogical Society of Pennsylvania. In addition to the anti–capital punishment report, O'Sullivan's published works include *Nelson Jarvis Waterbury: A Biographical Sketch* (1880) and *Union, Disunion, and Reunion: A Letter to General Franklin Pierce* (1862). O'Sullivan appears in Philip English Mackey, *Hanging in the Balance: The Anti–Capital Punishment Movement in New York State, 1776–1861* (1982); Perry Miller, *The Raven and the Whale: The War of Words and Wits in the Era of Poe and Melville* (1956); James R. Mellow, *Nathaniel Hawthorne in His Times* (1980); Edward Haviland Miller, *Salem Is My Dwelling Place: A Life of Nathaniel Hawthorne* (1991). Works focusing on O'Sullivan are Sheldon H. Harris, "John L. O'Sullivan and the Election of 1844 in New York," *New York History* 41 (July 1960): 278–98, and "John L. O'Sullivan Serves the Confederacy," *Civil War History* 10 (1964): 275–90; Julius W. Pratt, "John L. O'Sullivan and Manifest Destiny," *New York History* 14 (July 1933): 213–34, and "The Origin of Manifest Destiny," *American Historical Review* 32 (1926–1927): 129–56. Works on O'Sullivan and the *Democratic Review* are Landon Edward Fuller, "The *United States Magazine and Democratic Review*, 1837–1859: A Study of Its History, Contents, and Significance" (Ph.D. diss., Univ. of

North Carolina, 1948); Sheldon H. Harris, "The Public Career of John Louis O'Sullivan" (Ph.D. diss., Columbia Univ., 1958); and Robert Dean Sampson, "'Under the Banner of the Democratic Principle': John Louis O'Sullivan, the Democracy, and the *Democratic Review*" (Ph.D. diss., Univ. Of Illinois, 1995).

ROBERT D. SAMPSON

O'SULLIVAN, Mary Kenney (8 Jan. 1864–18 Jan. 1943), labor organizer, was born in Hannibal, Missouri, the daughter of Michael Kenney, a railroad machinist, and Mary Kelly, both of whom were Irish immigrants. Kenney attended school only through the fourth grade when she began to work as an apprentice dressmaker. In 1878 her father died and fourteen-year-old Kenney became the sole support of her invalid mother. She went to work in a book bindery, a trade she followed for the next dozen years in binderies in Hannibal and Keokuk, Iowa. In the late 1880s the Keokuk bindery closed and Kenney and her mother moved to Chicago. She soon found work there but was increasingly faced with the limitations of her craft in which women bindery workers were generally confined to the lesser skilled and lower paid facets of production. She soon turned to trade unionism as a way to relieve some of the inequities women faced as wage earners at the end of the nineteenth century.

Kenney joined the Women's Federal Labor Union No. 2703, an American Federation of Labor (AFL) affiliate. She was soon elected as a delegate to the Chicago Trades and Labor Assembly, thus becoming an active member of that city's labor movement. That movement, however, was dominated by male trade unionists who did not always support the active participation of women given their goal of a family wage earned by a male breadwinner. Within Chicago's vibrant social reform community, however, Kenney found support for her efforts. When she organized the Women's Bindery Union No. 1 (probably c. 1890), the only place Kenney could find as a meeting place was a room above a saloon, which was not an appropriate place for respectable wage-earning women, especially for Kenney, who was an ardent prohibitionist. She then turned to Jane Addams of Hull House, who not only offered Kenney a place to meet but provided the funds to print the meeting notices.

By the early 1890s Kenney was a resident of Hull House and continued her organizing efforts among women bookbinders as well as women garment makers. She also organized the Jane Club, a cooperative apartment building for working women, near Hull House. In 1892 AFL president Samuel Gompers asked the 28-year-old Kenney to become the first woman organizer for the AFL. She went east, organizing women collar makers in Troy, New York, before going to Boston in 1892. There she spent several months organizing women bindery workers, garment workers, and shoe workers. As in Chicago, Kenney relied on both the labor and the social reform communities, establishing ties with the Boston Central Labor Union and with Denison House, a settlement connected with the College Settlement Association. Kenney soon realized that organizing women was a slow process given the perception that women worked only briefly before marriage and the reality that women were generally confined to low-paid unskilled work often not represented by a trade union. After only six months, the AFL executive committee decided that it did not pay to keep a woman organizer in the field, and Mary Kenney was fired. She returned to Chicago where she once again joined the Hull House community, assisting Florence Kelley in her efforts to gain passage of the Illinois Factory Bill of 1893, which regulated the hours and conditions of labor for women and child workers.

In 1894 Kenney returned to Boston and married John O'Sullivan, an AFL labor organizer and labor editor for the *Boston Globe*. Now known as Mary Kenney O'Sullivan, she continued her labor organizing while having four children, one of whom died in infancy, during the next eight years. Often working with her husband, Kenney O'Sullivan organized women silk weavers and rubber workers as well as garment workers, and both O'Sullivans held office in the Boston Central Labor Union. She also renewed her connections with Denison House, where she and her husband lived for a time in the late 1890s, and was active in the Women's Educational and Industrial Union, which had been formed in 1878. In 1902 John O'Sullivan died, and Kenney O'Sullivan was once again the sole support of dependents, this time her three children, who ranged in age from four years to seven months. She become the manager of a model tenement and ran a girls' summer camp in Winthrop, Massachusetts, for Denison House.

Still hoping to improve the conditions of labor for wage-earning women, Kenney O'Sullivan joined with settlement-house worker William English Walling and several other trade unionists and social reformers in founding the national Women's Trade Union League (WTUL) in 1903. Established as a cross-class alliance, the WTUL sought to organize women into existing unions and lobby for protective labor legislation. Kenney O'Sullivan served the national league as secretary and vice president and was a leader in the Boston branch of the WTUL as well. However, when the WTUL did not support the 1912 strike of 15,000 textile workers in Lawrence, Massachusetts, Kenney O'Sullivan left in disgust the organization she had helped create. In 1914 she was appointed one of five women factory inspectors for the Massachusetts Board of Labor and Industries, retiring in 1934 at the age of seventy.

In addition to trade unionism for women, Kenney O'Sullivan had long been an advocate of woman suffrage, and with the outbreak of World War I she became a pacifist. In 1926, with the financial assistance of several friends, she went to Dublin, Ireland, as a delegate to the annual Women's International League for Peace and Freedom. During the 1920s she also wrote an autobiography that stands as a testament to the lifelong efforts of one working-class woman to im-

prove the conditions of labor for countless others. She died of heart disease in her West Medford, Massachusetts, home in 1943.

• Mary Kenney O'Sullivan's autobiography is part of the papers of the National Women's Trade Union League held by the Schlesinger Library, Radcliffe College; a small collection of her other personal papers is also in the Schlesinger Library. On Kenney O'Sullivan's early life and her labor organizing in Chicago, see Meredith Tax, *The Rising of the Women: Feminist Solidarity and Class Conflict, 1880–1917* (1980). On the formation of the Women's Trade Union League and Kenney O'Sullivan's role, see Nancy Schrom Dye, *As Equals and as Sisters: Feminism, the Labor Movement, and the Women's Trade Union League of New York* (1980). An obituary is in the *Boston Globe*, 19 Jan. 1943.

KATHLEEN BANKS NUTTER

O'SULLIVAN, Timothy H. (1840–14 Jan. 1882), photographer, was born on Staten Island, New York, or in Ireland, the son of Jeremiah O'Sullivan and Ann (maiden name unknown). The details of his early life and education are unknown.

O'Sullivan's career probably began as an apprentice operator in Mathew Brady's daguerreotype studio in New York City. As photographic methods advanced, Brady utilized new materials and formats and hired individuals such as Alexander Gardner, a Scottish photographer who was an expert in the wet-collodian process, to manage his Washington, D.C., studio, where as an assistant O'Sullivan was responsible for mixing chemicals. When the Civil War broke out, Brady and his associates were in an ideal position to photograph the people and landscape of the war. As a member of Brady's Photographic Corps, O'Sullivan photographed military sites and personnel in the field. This task was made particularly challenging by the photographic process that necessitated the construction of a portable darkroom. The resulting photographs were exhibited and sold through Brady's studios in Washington and New York and through E. H. & T. Anthony, a supplier of photographic materials.

Between December 1861 and May 1862 O'Sullivan followed General William Tecumseh Sherman through South Carolina, photographing the army as well as the South Carolina landscape. Upon returning to Washington O'Sullivan found that Gardner had left Brady's studio to establish his own business as a studio photographer. Gardner, who also received assignments from the military, hired O'Sullivan and assigned him to copy and field work. Copy work included taking photographs of maps and making prints, which were used by officers in the field. Over a three-year period O'Sullivan photographed soldiers before and after battle, the machinery of war, and the devastating aftermath of pivotal battles such as Antietam, Fredericksburg, Gettysburg, and Appomattox. The resulting photographs were sold in various formats through Gardner's studio, to publishers such as Philip and Solomons in Washington and to other photographers such as Brady. O'Sullivan's and Gardner's Civil War photographs were included in a two-volume work, *Gardner's Photographic Sketchbook of the War*, published by Gardner in 1866.

Following his experience on the field of battle, O'Sullivan participated in a number of important scientific and military surveys of the western United States. In 1867 he joined the unit assigned to carry out the Fortieth Parallel Survey, funded by the War Department and led by geologist Clarence King. O'Sullivan had already mastered many of the challenges of field photography and continued to refine his visual and technical skills. His subjects ranged from eerie tufa formations around Pyramid Lake, Nevada, to the dangerous subterranean mining operations near Virginia City, Nevada. In 1868 he returned to Washington to print his negatives. He rejoined the expedition, which was by then in Salt Lake City, Utah, in 1869 and spent the season photographing Utah and Wyoming. When the Fortieth Parallel Survey ended in late 1869, O'Sullivan returned to Washington and shortly afterward joined an expedition sponsored by the navy to Panama. In 1870 he again found employment as an expedition photographer, this time on the Geographical and Geological Explorations and Surveys West of the 100th Meridian led by Lieutenant George Wheeler, who recognized the importance of O'Sullivan's previous western experience and gave him both independence and authority within the expedition. The first season with Wheeler proved particularly grueling as it began in Nevada, crossed Death Valley, California, and proceeded up the Colorado River two hundred miles against the current to the Grand Canyon. After spending the 1872 season in Nevada with King, O'Sullivan rejoined Wheeler's expedition in 1873, photographing sites such as Canyon de Chelly and Pueblo Indians and their architecture. Between expeditions, he found time to court Laura Virginia Pywell, and the two were married in 1873.

In 1874, after spending the winter in Washington printing negatives from both the King and Wheeler expeditions, O'Sullivan traveled west for the last time. He spent the first part of the season with Wheeler photographing the landscape as well as Native Americans in New Mexico and Colorado. On his own, he traveled through Utah to Shoshone Falls, Idaho. After his final field season, he returned to Washington to continue printing the enormous body of negatives he had produced over the previous seven years.

O'Sullivan's prints initially accompanied reports by expedition leaders, but he also made sets of prints from the King and Wheeler expeditions for the American Geographical Society, which were sent to the 1873 Vienna Exposition. In addition, a set of photographs from the Wheeler expedition was printed for the Centennial Exhibition in Philadelphia, Pennsylvania. In 1874 O'Sullivan received funding, approved by the secretary of war, to print official sets of the photographs from the Wheeler expedition. Both full prints and stereographs were printed, and the prints were mounted with captions.

The years between 1876 and O'Sullivan's death were distressing professionally and personally. His wife became pregnant in 1876, but the child was stillborn, and the couple never had children. O'Sullivan worked for the photographic firm of Armstrong and Co. or independently, but unlike earlier years he did not participate in major private or government-funded projects. He was hired as photographer for the Department of the Treasury in 1880 but a year later learned that he had tuberculosis and resigned his position. In October 1881 his wife died of tuberculosis. Four months later O'Sullivan died in his parents' Staten Island, New York, home, also of tuberculosis.

During his short lifetime and afterward, O'Sullivan was praised for his ability to make technically and visually compelling photographs under physically strenuous circumstances. On the battlefields of the Civil War, in the unbearable heat of the Nevada mines, or in the often inhospitable landscapes of the Great Basin and the Southwest, he not only adapted but excelled, producing some of the most powerful images of the American West. His work continues to be the subject of scholarship and exhibition.

• O'Sullivan's work is in the following collections: the American Geographical Society Collection, University of Wisconsin, Milwaukee; the National Archives; the Smithsonian Institution; the Library of Congress; the New York Public Library; the New-York Historical Society; the Museum of Modern Art; the Metropolitan Museum of Art; the International Museum of Photography, Rochester, N.Y.; and the Art Institute of Chicago. Joel Snyder, *American Frontiers: The Photographs of Timothy H. O'Sullivan, 1867–1874* (1981), contains a biographical essay as well as an essay on O'Sullivan's aesthetics and a thorough list of primary and secondary sources. The position of O'Sullivan's work within the history of photography in general is discussed in Beaumont Newhall, *The History of Photography* (1982), and within the history of western landscape photography specifically in Weston Naef and James Wood, *Era of Exploration: The Rise of Landscape Photography in the American West, 1860–1885* (1975). In his volume of essays, *Reading American Photographs: Images as History, Mathew Brady to Walker Evans* (1989), Alan Trachtenberg discusses O'Sullivan's Civil War images and expedition photographs.

KATHLEEN L. BUTLER

OSWALD, Eleazer (1755–30 Sept. 1795), newspaper publisher, was born in Falmouth, England, the son of a sea captain; his parents' names are not known. At the age of fifteen, soon after his father disappeared, Oswald left England for New York City, where he apprenticed himself to printer John Holt of the *New-York Journal, or General Advertiser*. He absorbed printing quickly and was welcomed into the Holt family, marrying Holt's daughter Elizabeth.

Oswald joined Benedict Arnold's 1775 expedition to Canada. Oswald and twenty-eight men captured two British ships on Lake Champlain, but he was captured himself on the last day of 1775 and was not able to return to active service until exchanged for a British prisoner in May 1777.

Oswald served with distinction at the Battle of Monmouth in 1778. He was admired as a practical mathematician, locating cannon at Fishkill, on a Hudson River bluff, so that he could shell British ships below; answering fire that either embedded itself in the bluff or whistled harmlessly overhead.

By 1778 Oswald was furious with the military hierarchy, including General George Washington, believing that he was denied proper seniority in his rank of lieutenant colonel. In 1779 Congress accepted Oswald's resignation.

Once a civilian, Oswald joined William Goddard's printing and papermaking business in Baltimore, helping to publish Goddard's *Maryland Journal*. The partnership was jolted in 1779 by the aftermath of their newspaper's publication on 6 July of "Some Queries, Political and Military," the pseudonymous work of another disgruntled officer, General Charles Lee, attacking the revered General Washington. On 8 July 1779 a thirty-man mob broke into Goddard's bedroom and forced Goddard to publish an apology.

After asking protection from Maryland's governor, Goddard then retracted his recantation. By 11 July Oswald had challenged Colonel Samuel Smith, a Baltimore magistrate who led the mob, to a duel, an honor Colonel Smith declined. The partnership with Goddard ended in 1781, and Oswald moved to Philadelphia.

The first issue of the *Independent Gazetteer* appeared on 13 April 1782. Rumors had spread that Goddard—despised for having published his attack on Washington—was Oswald's silent partner. Oswald disavowed any connection in his first issue.

Oswald suspected other Philadelphia printers—notably Francis Bailey, who had established his *Freeman's Journal* a year earlier—of starting the rumors and accused the other printers of a "biass [sic] of interest."

The *Independent Gazetteer* at first was close to the powerful and unscrupulous Robert Morris, superintendent of finance for the United States, for it published articles of "A Revolutionist" in support of land speculators. From its first issue, the newspaper was immersed in Pennsylvania politics, generally taking the side of the Republican faction and of Robert Morris and interests favoring creation of a national bank. This put Oswald's paper on a collision course with Bailey's *Freeman's Journal*.

The *Independent Gazetteer* wasted little time in testing whether the English common-law doctrine of seditious libel, which made effective criticism of government or its officers a crime, remained in force in revolutionary Pennsylvania. The second issue, 20 April 1782, ran a series of essays signed "Whiggish Curiosity" that culminated in accusing a Constitutionalist faction leader, Pennsylvania vice president James Potter, of embezzling state currency. Although libel charges were threatened, none was filed until late in 1782, when Oswald ran afoul of Pennsylvania chief justice Thomas McKean.

The imperious McKean had been criticized by newspapers for plural officeholding; he served simultaneously as a member of the Continental Congress from Delaware. McKean, writing under the transparent pen-name of "Jurisperitus," warned printers that "it is not for men of glass to throw stones." Oswald's *Independent Gazetteer* ignored the warning, criticizing McKean for levying an "enormous" £80 fine (the equivalent of an artisan's wages for a year) on Colonel John Proctor. The colonel had beaten an election inspector who had dared to ask for proof that the officer had signed Pennsylvania's loyalty oath.

McKean charged Oswald with libel in a warrant for the printer's arrest issued on 12 October 1782. The printer wrote to General John Lamb of New York, saying, "The infamous English law doctrine of Libels being introduced by the more infamous Judges and Lawyers, in an American Court. O tempora! O mores!" Early in 1783, however, a grand jury thwarted the irate McKean by refusing to indict Oswald. After McKean again asked the grand jury to consider charges, the jurors presented him with a memorial criticizing his behavior. When McKean refused to hear the memorial, the jurors adjourned to a tavern after taking their remonstrance to David Hall and William Sellers's *Pennsylvania Gazette* for publication.

In November 1782, early in Oswald's confrontation with McKean, the *Independent Gazetteer* published one of the earliest American repudiations of seditious libel. A correspondent using the pseudonym "Junius Wilkes" declared that Pennsylvania's 1776 constitution protected publications about the conduct of public servants, even if those publications turned out to be false. "[W]hen they even appear false and groundless it is rather an inconvenience . . . a kind of *damnum absque injuria* [harm without injury in the legal sense]."

That article by "Junius Wilkes" was an important attack on the Blackstonian definition of freedom, which forbade prepublication censorship but allowed postpublication punishment for attacks on government or government officers. The *Independent Gazetteer*'s correspondent, on the other hand, argued that "the danger is precisely the same to liberty, in punishing a person *after* the performance appears to the world, as in preventing its publication in the first instance." Other *Independent Gazetteer* contributors, including "Koster," advocated making truth a defense in libel cases, and "Candid" urged indemnifying publications that contained errors of fact "not proceeding from design."

Paradoxically, Oswald was a better advocate than a practitioner of freedom. Mathew Carey's *Pennsylvania Journal* responded to a political attack in the *Independent Gazetteer* with *The Plagi-Scurriliad*, a poem dedicated to Oswald. The poem pointed to close similarities between writings published in the *Independent Gazetteer* and the works of famed English writers, John Wilkes's *New Briton* and the Junius Papers. Carey unwisely met Oswald on the dueling grounds in 1786 and was severely wounded in the thigh.

Oswald, aligned with Pennsylvania conservatives—including some nationalists-to-be such as Robert Morris in the early 1780s—initially seemed to approve the proposed Constitution of 1787. The *Independent Gaz-*

etteer, however, became the leading newspaper fighting against adoption of the new constitution. It published twenty-four of the "Centinel" essays by Pennsylvania leader Samuel Bryan, as well as many other Antifederal writings. The "Centinel" writings should be read in conjunction with the Federalist's "Publius" essays—better known as the Federalist Papers—to better understand the revolutionary era. Complaints published by the Antifederalists should not be undervalued. Antifederalist fears about liberties not mentioned in the body of the Constitution—including freedom of speech, press, assembly, and petition and the right to trial by jury—threatened to prevent ratification. A political concession by the Federalists—a promise to add a bill of rights—finally overcame opposition to ratification.

As the leading Antifederalist publisher, Oswald added new enemies to the old. In 1788 Andrew Brown, his former partner in the *New York Journal*, started the *Federal Gazette* with Federalist support. Oswald's paper termed Brown an embezzler, a British army deserter, and a coward. Brown brought a libel action. The *Independent Gazetteer* claimed Brown was a tool of Oswald's enemies, including Dr. Benjamin Rush, whose brother sat on Pennsylvania's supreme court.

Oswald's enemies soon joined the attack. Pennsylvania Supreme Court Chief Justice McKean charged Oswald with contempt of court, found him guilty (no jury trial was required in contempt cases), fined him £10, and sentenced him to a month in jail. This confrontation, in *Respublica v. Oswald*, led an unsuccessful vote in the Pennsylvania legislature to impeach Chief Justice McKean. Oswald's struggles with courts and judges arguably resulted, in part, in language in the Pennsylvania Constitution of 1790 stating that juries should decide whether publications were libelous, and making truth (when "proper for public information") a defense against criminal libel charges involving public officials.

In 1792, when in England on business, Oswald volunteered for service in the French Revolution, serving as an artillery colonel at the 1793 Battle of Gemape, and later made an abortive trip to Ireland to encourage rebellious striving there. Back in France, he quarreled over back pay and the loss of a horse, returning to New York in 1794. While Oswald played the soldier of fortune and after his death in the early 1790s, his wife Elizabeth published the *Independent Gazetteer*. After his death she published the paper for a year before selling it to Joseph Gales.

Oswald died of yellow fever in New York after visiting a stricken friend, Major Charles Tillinghast. He was forty years old, this printer whom McKean had called "a seditious turbulent man." He published some of the early arguments against seditious libel and for a freedom of the press broad enough to protect criticism of government. He fought for his own rights, perhaps, more than for the rights of others, but the Antifederalist diatribes he published helped make possible the Bill of Rights.

• The sparse Oswald papers are in Miscellaneous Manuscripts at the Library of Congress; additional letters from Oswald may be found in the John Lamb Papers at the New-York Historical Society. The best biographical treatment is in Joseph Towne Wheeler, *The Maryland Press 1777–1790* (1938); see also Leona M. Hudak, *Early American Women Printers and Publishers 1639–1820* (1978). Pennsylvania and national politics of Oswald's times are variously described in Robert L. Brunhouse, *The Counter-Revolution in Pennsylvania 1776–1790* (1942); Jackson Turner Main, *The Antifederalists: Critics of the Constitution* (1961), and Thomas R. Meehan, "The Pennsylvania Supreme Court in the Law and Politics of the Commonwealth, 1776–1790" (Ph.D. diss., Univ. of Wisconsin, 1960). For an assessment of Oswald's contributions to defining press freedom, see Leonard W. Levy, *Emergence of a Free Press* (1985); Dwight Teeter, "The Printer and the Chief Justice: Seditious Libel in 1782–1783," *Journalism Quarterly* 45 (Summer 1968): 235–42, 260; and "Decent Animadversions," in Donavan Bond and W. Reynolds McLeod, eds., *Newsletters to Newspapers: Eighteenth-Century Journalism* (1977).

DWIGHT L. TEETER, JR.

OSWALD, Lee Harvey (18 Oct. 1939–24 Nov. 1963), alleged assassin of President John F. Kennedy, was born in New Orleans, Louisiana, the son of Robert E. Lee Oswald, a collector of insurance premiums, and Marguerite Claverie, a telephone operator and sales clerk. Because his father died two months before his birth, forcing his mother to work, Lee, together with his brother Robert and half brother John Pic spent much of his early childhood in orphanages. In 1945 Marguerite married Edwin A. Ekdahl and moved to Fort Worth, Texas. This marriage did not last, however, and Lee had a difficult time, being shuffled from place to place and from school to school. When Lee was thirteen, they moved to New York City. Because of repeated truancy violations, he was confined to a youth house for six months. A psychological evaluation found him of above average intelligence but tense, withdrawn, and shy. In early 1954 Marguerite moved back to New Orleans, where Lee attended school, participated in the local squadron of the Civil Air Patrol, and became interested in Marxism. In July 1956 they moved back to Fort Worth, and three months later Lee Harvey Oswald joined the marines.

Because of his high intelligence test scores, Oswald was assigned to a marine air radar unit that operated in the supersecret Central Intelligence Agency–controlled U-2 spy plane section at the Atsugi Air Force Base in Japan. Oswald's access to classified information about the U-2, his mysterious disappearances from his unit for several days at a time, and his learning the Russian language during his two-and-a-half-year stint in the marines have given rise to speculation that he had been recruited by a branch of American intelligence. No positive evidence of Oswald's links to U.S. intelligence has ever been produced, although the destruction of the Defense Department's intelligence files on Oswald and the withholding of millions of pages of documentary evidence on the Kennedy assassination by the CIA, the Federal Bureau of Investigation, and other government agencies leave the question open.

On 3 September 1959 Oswald received a hardship discharge, ostensibly because he had to help his ailing mother. In reality, he visited her for only one day and on 17 September boarded a freighter bound for Europe. On 15 October Oswald arrived in Moscow and at the end of the month entered the American embassy, where he renounced his American citizenship and declared his intention to reside permanently in the U.S.S.R. The only evidence of Oswald's life in the U.S.S.R. consists of an alleged "Historic Diary." The suspicious nature of the diary, replete with misspellings and grammatical mistakes uncharacteristic of Oswald's other writings, and the many erroneous dates it contains leave its authenticity unresolved. In March 1961, while living in Minsk and working at an electronics plant there, Oswald married Marina Prusakova, the niece of a colonel in the KGB. On 2 June 1962 Oswald, disillusioned with the U.S.S.R., left for the United States with his wife and child, arriving in Fort Worth two weeks later.

Oswald worked at a photographic company for a few months but lost his job and failed to find another. In Fort Worth and Dallas, Lee and Marina Oswald made friends with George and Jeanne DeMorenschildt, both of whom had extensive backgrounds in intelligence activities. In March 1963 Oswald purchased a Mannlicher-Carcano 6.5mm rifle through the mail, and some writers claim that he used the weapon in an attempt on the life of retired army major general Edwin A. Walker, although conclusive evidence of the incident has never been developed. The following month he moved to New Orleans, where he got a job at a coffee company. During his five months in New Orleans, Oswald outwardly posed as a Marxist and a staunch supporter of Fidel Castro's regime in Cuba. However, all of his known acquaintances of the time were men of extremist anti-Communist, right-wing views. On 25 September 1963 Oswald took a bus to Mexico City, where he spent a week visiting the Soviet and Cuban embassies. On 1 October he arrived in Dallas, where he rented a room by himself. In the middle of the month he got a job as an order filler at the Texas School Book Depository.

Although Lee and Marina lived apart, he often visited her at the Irving residence of Ruth Paine, especially after their second child was born. On 21 November Oswald made an unusual weekday visit to the Paine home, supposedly to obtain curtain rods to install in his room. On the morning of 22 November Oswald, carrying a package in a brown paper bag, rode to work with fellow depository employee Buell Wesley Frazier. He was last observed on the building's first floor at about 12:20 P.M., ten minutes before the assassination of President Kennedy. At the time of the assassination, a spectator named Howard L. Brennan observed a man, whom he later identified as Oswald, fire a shot at the presidential limousine. Two other witnesses saw Oswald in a second-floor lunchroom less than two minutes after the assassination, and he was

also identified as taking a Dallas bus and a taxi minutes later. At 1:00 he was spotted entering and then leaving his rooming house. Fifteen minutes later, witnesses saw Oswald at the scene of the murder of Dallas police officer J. D. Tippit, and running away from the scene. Observed entering a nearby movie theater at 1:45, Oswald was arrested there minutes later. Taken to Dallas police headquarters, he vehemently denied complicity in either the Kennedy assassination or the Tippit murder. At 11:20 A.M. on 24 November 1963, as Oswald was being led into the basement of police headquarters to be transferred to the more secure Dallas county jail, Jack Ruby, a Dallas nightclub owner, bolted from a crowd of police and reporters and fired one shot into Oswald's abdomen. Oswald was rushed to Parkland Hospital but died during surgery because of massive internal hemorrhaging.

President Lyndon B. Johnson appointed a commission headed by Chief Justice Earl Warren to allay public concerns about the Kennedy and Oswald assassinations. In September 1964 the commission issued its report, which found Lee Harvey Oswald solely responsible for the murder of President Kennedy, the simultaneous wounding of Texas governor John B. Connally, and the murder of Officer Tippit. The Warren Commission in particular emphasized that it found no evidence of a conspiracy. In finding Oswald guilty, the commission pointed to the eyewitness identification of him as the sixth-floor gunman, the discovery of his rifle and cartridge cases on the sixth floor, the medical evidence proving that all shots came from the rear, and Oswald's shooting of Officer Tippit. The best case for the argument that Oswald was the sole assassin has been made by Gerald Posner in *Case Closed* (1993). However, under pressure from Johnson to conduct a hasty inquiry, and handicapped by the destruction of evidence by various federal agencies and the suppression of several million pages of documents relating to the assassination, the Warren Commission failed to resolve conclusively the question of Oswald's responsibility.

In the opinion of the present writer, the evidence makes it likely that shots were fired by two assassins, prima facie proof of a conspiracy. A film of the shooting made by spectator Abraham Zapruder demonstrates that Kennedy and Connally could not have been wounded by two separate shots fired from Oswald's bolt-action rifle, as the Warren Commission contended in its controversial "single bullet theory." A bullet from Oswald's rifle allegedly found on Connally's stretcher at the hospital was in such pristine condition that most authorities agree that it could not have inflicted the wounds on the two men. The explosive impact of the fatal shot on the president's head and the sharp backward movement of the head indicate that the bullet was fired from in front. The sighting of Oswald in a second-floor lunchroom only ninety seconds after the assassination makes it virtually impossible for him to have fired the shots from the sixth floor. The incompetence of the autopsy on Kennedy leaves many medical questions unanswered.

• Oswald left no collection of papers. His "Historic Diary," address book, personal letters, and other paraphernalia are in the National Archives, Records of the President's Commission on the Assassination of President Kennedy, RG 272. These, together with the assassination records of all federal agencies, will be gathered in the President John F. Kennedy Assassination Records Collection in the National Archives. Although the collection will contain a considerable amount of material unrelated to Oswald, it will become the center of primary source material on him. Of the many studies of the assassination, the most significant dealing with Oswald include Edward Jay Epstein, *Legend: The Secret World of Lee Harvey Oswald* (1978), which provides a stimulating account of Oswald's possible ties to American intelligence agencies; Don DeLillo, *Libra* (1988), a fascinating novel in which Oswald is the central character; Michael L. Kurtz, *Crime of the Century: The Kennedy Assassination from a Historian's Perspective* (1982), which raises serious questions about Oswald's guilt, and "Lee Harvey Oswald in New Orleans: A Reappraisal," *Louisiana History* 21 (1980): 7–22, which documents Oswald's "double life" in New Orleans; Priscilla Johnson McMillan, *Marina and Lee* (1977), which covers their personal relationship from Marina's perspective; Gerald Posner, *Case Closed: Lee Harvey Oswald and the Assassination of JFK* (1993); and Norman Mailer, *Oswald's Tale: An American Mystery* (1995). President's Commission on the Assassination of President Kennedy, *Report of the President's Commission on the Assassination of President Kennedy* (1964), commonly called the Warren Report, details some parts of Oswald's life and the commission's case against him. U.S. House of Representatives, Select Committee on Assassinations, *Report of the Select Committee on Assassinations* (1979), concludes that Oswald and another gunman fired shots and emphasizes the "probability" of a conspiracy.

MICHAEL L. KURTZ

OTERO, Miguel Antonio (21 June 1829–30 May 1882), politician and businessman, was born in Valencia, New Mexico, then a province of the Mexican Republic, the son of Don Vicente Otero and Dona Gertrudis Chaves y Argon. Vicente Otero was primarily a farmer and merchant but also filled local judicial positions under the Mexican government. Miguel Antonio Otero entered St. Louis University, St. Louis, Missouri, in September 1841 and continued his education there until the outbreak of the Mexican-American War in May 1846, at which time his parents sent for him. In 1847 he enrolled at Pingree College, located in Fishkill on the Hudson, New York. Within a short time he became a teacher at the college and also an assistant to the principal. In 1849 Otero commenced the study of law, first with James Thayer, an attorney living in Fishkill on the Hudson, then with a General Sanford in New York City during the winter of 1849–1850, and finally with Trusten Polk in St. Louis, Missouri, from 1851 to 1852. Otero was admitted to the Missouri bar in the spring of 1852, immediately after which he returned to New Mexico, now a U.S. territory. That same year he took a herd of sheep, presumably the property of his brother, Antonio José Otero, overland to California.

After his return from California, Miguel Otero began a law practice in Albuquerque, New Mexico, but shortly accepted the position of private secretary for William Carr Lane, territorial governor of New Mexico, serving in that capacity until the end of Lane's term in 1853. In September 1852 Otero was elected to the New Mexico territorial legislature. He represented Valencia County in the house during the Second Legislative Assembly, convened in December 1852. According to his son, Miguel A. Otero, Jr., Otero supposedly served as the attorney general for New Mexico Territory for a period during Governor David Meriwether's administration, 1853–1857; however, Miguel Otero is not listed as such in the first edition of the *New Mexico Blue Book* (1882).

After declining a presidential appointment as U.S. district attorney for New Mexico Territory, Otero was elected New Mexico's delegate to Congress in 1855. He held this seat for three consecutive terms, from 1855 to 1861. In 1857 he married Mary Josephine Blackwood; they had four children, three of whom survived to adulthood. A Democrat, Otero persuaded the New Mexico legislature to pass a slave code in 1859, thus aligning the territory with southern interests. He also endeavored as delegate to get a transcontinental railroad routed through New Mexico and made an attempt to secure statehood for the territory. In September 1859 Otero fought a bloodless duel with John S. Watts, a former associate justice of the New Mexico Supreme Court and a political adversary.

In 1861 President Abraham Lincoln appointed Otero secretary for New Mexico Territory. Lincoln had previously offered Otero the post of U.S. minister to Spain, which Otero declined. Because of Otero's known Southern leanings, he was not confirmed in his post by the U.S. Senate, thus he only served as secretary from April to September. According to one short biography, Otero "never favored secession, but sympathized with the South" (Speer and Brown, p. 31). However, New Mexico historian Ralph E. Twitchell charges that Otero was involved in a "conspiracy" that would have enabled the Confederacy to seize control of the forts and military supplies in the Southwest. Twitchell also states that Otero "secured the distribution of an address, in Spanish and English, throughout the territory inciting the people to rebellion" (Twitchell, *Old Santa Fe* [1925], p. 369). Neither effort, if they indeed occurred, succeeded.

After the loss of his secretarial appointment, Otero focused his attention on business pursuits. He moved to Kansas City, Missouri, in 1862, where he had formed a partnership with David V. Whiting. Whiting & Otero, as the firm was called, conducted a forwarding and commission business out of Kansas City and later New York City as well. In 1864, after apparently severing his business ties with Whiting, Otero moved to Leavenworth, Kansas. There he was a silent partner in C. R. Morehead & Co., also a forwarding and commission firm. While at Morehead & Co., Otero became acquainted with bookkeeper John Perry Sellar, and in 1867 the two started their own forwarding and commission business at Fort Harker, Kansas, then the western terminus of the Union Pacific Eastern Division (afterward the Kansas Pacific). The Otero & Sellar firm relocated as the railroad built west, moving to the railheads of Hays City, Kansas, in 1867, Sheridan, Kansas, in 1869, and Kit Carson, Colorado Territory, in 1870.

By about 1870 the name of the firm had changed to Otero, Sellar & Co., and it had an additional partner, New Mexican merchant José Leandro Perea. A credit report for November 1871 reveals that both Otero and Perea had recently retired from the business, with Sellar remaining as the sole proprietor. According to a subsequent report, Sellar chose to leave the firm name unchanged because of Otero's popularity with New Mexican traders, who made up a large portion of the firm's customers. Yet there is also evidence that Otero continued to maintain an intimate connection with the business after 1871, which eventually located in Las Vegas, New Mexico, in 1879 (the firm was reorganized as Gross, Blackwell & Co. two years later).

In the 1870s Otero worked aggressively as an agent of the Atchison, Topeka, and Santa Fe Railroad (AT&SF) to bring its line into New Mexico. Otero helped organize the New Mexico and Southern Pacific Railroad, a subsidiary of the AT&SF, which obtained for the railroad the crucial right of way through the territory. In December 1878, in Raton Pass on the Colorado–New Mexico border, Otero was given the honor of driving the ceremonial spike in the first rail laid on New Mexico soil. In addition to his railroad interests during the 1870s and early 1880s, Otero also invested in mining, banking (he was an organizer and first president of the San Miguel National Bank, Las Vegas), a hot springs resort, and a telephone company.

Otero died suddenly at his home in Las Vegas, New Mexico, of complications resulting from pneumonia. Despite his numerous business endeavors, he was "comparatively a poor man" at the time of his death (Otero, p. 287). However, Otero had wielded considerable influence over the political affairs of New Mexico Territory throughout most of his life, particularly up to the Civil War, and as a forwarding and commission merchant and railroad representative, he facilitated the territory's commercial and industrial development. Perhaps his greatest legacy, though, was his son, Miguel Otero, Jr., who became New Mexico's first Hispanic territorial governor in 1897.

• Otero's personal papers do not appear to have survived. Business records of his forwarding and commission business, Otero, Sellar & Co., are in the Gross, Kelly and Company Collection (#96B), Special Collections, University of New Mexico Library, Albuquerque, N.Mex. Credit reports on Miguel Otero and Otero, Sellar & Co. appear in the N.Mex. and Colo. volumes, R. G. Dun & Co. Collection, Baker Library, Harvard University Graduate School of Business Administration. A short history of Otero, Sellar & Co. is in Daniel T. Kelly, *The Buffalo Head: A Century of Mercantile Pioneering in the Southwest* (1972). A volume that provides much information and many personal insights on Otero's life and character is his son's autobiography, Miguel Antonio Otero, Jr., *My Life on the Frontier, 1864–1882* (1935). A detailed biographical sketch of Otero is in William S. Speer and John Henry Brown, eds., *The Encyclopedia of the New West* (1881). For an obituary, see the *(Denver, Colo.) Rocky Mountain News*, 2 June 1882.

MARK L. GARDNER

OTERO-WARREN, Nina (23 Oct. 1882–3 Jan. 1965), suffragist, politician, and author, was born María Adelina Isabel Emilia Otero in Los Lunas, New Mexico, the daughter of Eloisa Luna and Manuel B. Otero, ranchers. Nina grew up within one of the oldest and most traditional New Mexican households. Women were expected to learn the domestic arts and eventually marry well in order to run households of their own. Her family, on both her mother's and her father's side, was composed of the most prominent citizens, politicians, and ranchers of the territory; they claimed to be descendants of the original Spanish settlers of New Mexico. Nina's traditional Hispano and Catholic upbringing proscribed a life of domesticity akin to the life her mother and grandmother had known.

Her father's untimely and violent death, at the hands of a Texas cattleman over disputed property rights, however, thrust the Otero family along a different course early in Nina's life. Eloisa Luna Otero was left a young widow with a large hacienda and three small children to manage. A few years after her husband's death, Nina's mother married an Anglo merchant, Alfred M. Bergere, who took over the family affairs. Bergere's connections to the dominant Anglo merchant class, combined with Nina's impeccable pedigree as a descendant of the most prominent families in New Mexico, placed Nina on solid footing within New Mexican society.

After a brief time at Maryville College of the Sacred Heart in Saint Louis, Nina returned to New Mexico. She and her family moved to Santa Fe in 1897, when territorial governor Miguel A. Otero, Nina's second cousin, appointed her stepfather as a clerk to the First New Mexico Judicial District. After ten years as a young socialite in Santa Fe, Nina met and married army lieutenant Rawson D. Warren. They moved from Santa Fe to his post near Grants, New Mexico. Nina disliked the post's remote location, the pettiness of army existence and her limited control over her own life. After just one year of marriage, she returned to Santa Fe, proclaiming herself a widow. In reality, however, she quietly divorced Warren and went about the rest of her life and career as Nina Otero-Warren. She never married again and never had children.

Upon her return to Santa Fe, Otero-Warren began her political career by involving herself in Republican politics and aiding the Congressional Union's efforts for woman suffrage in New Mexico. It was through her political good sense, lobbying, and connections that the state was one of the first to ratify the Nineteenth Amendment. After women began voting in the state, Otero-Warren made her first foray into electoral politics. In 1918 she was elected superintendent of public schools in Santa Fe County, a post she held for eleven years. She also ran as the Republican nominee for the U.S. House of Representatives, a race she lost in 1922.

One of Otero-Warren's deepest concerns was the poor level of education New Mexicans received and the incredibly high illiteracy rate throughout the state. She believed that education was the path to power and success for New Mexico's Hispano children, and she insisted that they be offered the highest level possible. Consequently, as superintendent she lobbied the state legislature for a program of school reform that included longer school years, bilingual education, and higher pay for teachers.

Nina received her first federal appointment in 1922 when she was asked to oversee the Indian schools in the state. She quit that post only two years later. Nevertheless, Otero-Warren remained county superintendent and was involved in federal literacy efforts during the depression, serving as the director of literacy education with the Civilian Conservation Corp and the Works Progress Administration.

In the early 1930s Otero-Warren took a break from her public life by homesteading a ranch, which she called "Las Dos." Her intention was to create a retreat just outside of Santa Fe where she could be free of her social obligations in order to write a book about her childhood and recount old stories she had heard. The book, *Old Spain in Our Southwest* (1936), told of Nina's early days and the history of her family when they were among the most notable citizens of New Mexico. Through the book she hoped to remind all Americans about the Spanish legacy of the American Southwest. The book, with its idealized and romantic portrayals of New Mexican hacienda life, was a literary and historical success and placed Otero-Warren firmly among the literati crowd gathering in northern New Mexico.

With the arrival of World War II, Nina returned to Santa Fe to aid in the war effort. She became the Santa Fe County director of the Office of Price Administration and was responsible for monitoring the price of consumer goods and enforcing the price ceilings established by the federal government. After the war she divided the last twenty years of her life between her familial home in Santa Fe and her ranch at Las Dos. She also opened a successful real estate business, while simultaneously guiding the extensive holdings of her familial estate. She died in Santa Fe. Otero-Warren emerged from the sheltered home of her family's ranch in Los Lunas, New Mexico, to become one of the most politically, socially, and culturally savvy persons in Santa Fe during the first half of the twentieth century.

• There is no separate collection of Otero-Warren's papers, although many of her letters, as well as other documents pertaining to her family business, can be found in the A. M. Bergere Family Papers at the State Records Center and Archives, Santa Fe, N.Mex. A recent biography is Charlotte Whaley, *Nina Otero-Warren of Santa Fe* (1994), which comprehensively covers the major events of Otero-Warren's public life. See also Elizabeth Salas, "Ethnicity, Gender and Divorce: Issues in the 1922 Campaign by Adelina Otero-Warren for the U.S. House of Representatives," *New Mexico Historical Review* (Oct. 1995). An obituary is in the *Santa Fe New Mexican*, 4 Jan. 1965.

MARIA MONTOYA

OTEY, James Hervey (27 Jan. 1800–23 Apr. 1863), first Episcopal bishop of Tennessee and first chancellor of the University of the South, was born in Bedford County, Virginia, the son of Isaac Otey and Elizabeth Mathews, farmers. He was graduated from the University of North Carolina at Chapel Hill in 1820 and stayed on as tutor in ancient languages for another year. Religion had little influence on his early life, but his duties required that he conduct morning chapel. Obtaining a copy of the Episcopal Book of Common Prayer, he found that it met his spiritual needs, and in the next six years he completed his studies for the Episcopal priesthood under the tutelage of future Bishop William Mercer Green of Mississippi, then the chaplain of the university at Chapel Hill, and John Stark Ravenscroft, the memorable first bishop of North Carolina.

In 1821 he married Eliza Davis Pannill; they had six children who survived to adulthood, and he grieved enormously over the three who died. He and his wife first went in 1821 to Tennessee, where he taught at Harpeth Academy in Franklin, living on tuition, and continued theological studies under Green. He was ordained priest in North Carolina in 1827 and returned to Franklin to teach, again at Harpeth, while also holding church services there, in Nashville, and in Columbia. He and two other clergymen organized the diocese of Tennessee in 1829.

Otey was an imposing figure, six feet four inches tall, proficient in classical languages and the country fiddle, and possessed of spiritual depth. He has no rival for the title "Father of the Episcopal Church in Tennessee." He was elected bishop at the fifth annual convention of the diocese in 1833 and consecrated in Philadelphia in 1834. His resolutions espousing education appeared at every official gathering of the convention, and his personal influence was felt in the diocese for as long as he lived. He traveled by stagecoach, but mostly on horseback, from end to end of the longest diocese east of the Mississippi River—500 miles from Memphis to Bristol—usually twice a year. He also had jurisdiction at various times between 1834 and 1859 in the states of Alabama, Florida, Kentucky, Mississippi, Louisiana, Arkansas and the Indian Territory, and Texas. His long absences from his wife are recorded heartbreakingly in his letters and diary.

In 1838 the General Convention hurt his work grievously by plucking his strongest priest and kindred spirit, the wealthy Leonidas Polk, and assigning him as bishop to some of Otey's extradiocesan territory, including Louisiana, Arkansas, and the Republic of Texas. Following the departure of Polk, Otey ranged unassisted through the diocese for fourteen years from his base in Columbia, Tennessee, before moving to Memphis in 1852. He grew to know his clergy intimately, achieving a remarkable unity among them. Matthew Fontaine Maury, commodore of the Confederate navy and "pathfinder of the seas," was not the least of his students. During this period, his lay leaders insisted he take a trip for his health. In 1851 he went to England, where he not only benefited physically but had a rare emotional experience. At Holy Communion in the Royal Chapel of St. James he found himself kneeling next to the aged duke of Wellington. The touch of history was not lost on him.

In politics Otey was a Whig and an opponent of division of the Union. As secession drew closer, he wrote pleading letters to his friend Stephen Elliott, the aristocratic and cultured first bishop of Georgia, as well as to Polk, by then bishop of Louisiana, vainly urging them to stand by the Union. In 1861, with secession inevitable, he tried to avert war, directing a letter to Secretary of State William Seward, saying in effect that the South in no way contemplated attacking the North and urging him to help stop any attack on the South. Once the war began, however, Otey became an ardent supporter of the Confederacy.

Although he was unable to build all the schools he sought for his diocese, including the never-opened Madison College (1837), he became a key figure, with Polk and Elliott, in the founding of the University of the South in Sewanee, Tennessee, in 1857. They planned for it to be the first modern university in the United States, equal to the best in Europe. As senior bishop in the federated dioceses, and with the title of chancellor, Otey presided over meetings of the board of trustees from 1857 to 1861. In 1868, five years after his death, the university opened with nine students and four professors. The first academic building on the 10,000-acre domain on the Cumberland Plateau was named for him.

Otey referred to himself as a Catholic churchman, called high church at the time and emphasizing formality in ritual and more stress on the Book of Common Prayer than on preaching. He was an effective speaker but not in harmony with the two-hour tirades of the Bible-thumping evangelists who prevailed among the Protestant right-wing fundamentalists. He believed that man was empowered by God to interpret literal word-by-word passages into intellectually respectable concepts. He accepted historical context, scholarship, and reason as components of biblical study. If Methuselah was said to have been 900 years old, it simply meant that he was an old man, whether 90 or 900. The flood and the ark were allegorical. He drew from the New Testament rather than the Old. He attracted intellectuals to his congregations, which were larger in influence than in numbers, and he preached a living Christ who exemplified charity, love, mercy, and forgiveness of sins rather than hellfire and damnation. The Golden Rule was a cornerstone of his teaching. Faith in God was his absolute.

Otey had met in Memphis a young medical school professor, the brilliant Connecticut-born Huguenot Charles Todd Quintard, and through him had the rare opportunity of bringing to the ministry his own successor, whom he instructed in theology. Because

Quintard (bishop from 1865 to 1898) had the same experience with his successor, Thomas Frank Gailor (bishop from 1898 to 1935), the diocese of Tennessee enjoyed for more than 100 years the remarkable continuity of three strong personalities linked spiritually and intellectually. Otey died in Memphis and was buried in St. John's Churchyard, Ashwood.

Otey was a towering figure in Tennessee, in the increasingly cohesive Episcopal church in the South, and on the national scene in the House of Bishops. His desire for unity found continued expression through the labors of Quintard, who at the General Convention of 1865 helped to heal the wounds of war. The Episcopal church became the only non-Roman Catholic denomination in the South to reunite with its northern brethren when the battle lines disappeared. Otey laid the foundation for that reunion.

• Manuscript material by Otey in the Archives of the University of the South includes microfilm of his diary, proceedings of the board of trustees, and other papers. Additional Otey papers are located in the Southern Historical Collection, University of North Carolina, Chapel Hill; the Archives of the Episcopal Church in Austin, Tex.; and the General Theological Seminary Library in New York City. For other important archival information see the journals of the dioceses of Tennessee, Alabama, Arkansas, Florida, Kentucky, Louisiana, and Mississippi and the journals of the General Convention of the Protestant Episcopal Church. The records of the Domestic and Foreign Missionary Society of the Protestant Episcopal Church in the United States of America (PECUSA) are available at the Episcopal Church Archives in Austin. The manuscript proceedings of the board of trustees are in the University of the South Archives; abstracts for 1857–1861 were published in Telfair Hodgson, ed., *University of the South Papers*, ser. A, no. 1 (1888).

The most scholarly biography is Donald Smith Armentrout, *James Hervey Otey, First Episcopal Bishop of Tennessee* (1984). Published in the year of Otey's death was James Craik, *The Right Reverend James Hervey Otey, D.D., LL.D., Late Bishop of Tennessee* (1863). Otey's friend and mentor, the Rt. Rev. William Mercer Green, *Memoir of the Right Reverend James Hervey Otey, D.D., LL.D.* (1885), includes extracts from the bishop's diary, from letters, and some addresses and sermons; the memoir also gives the most intimate details about Bishop Otey's relationships with his family, his priests, and other bishops. Moultrie Guerry, *Men Who Made Sewanee* (1932), devotes the first chapter to Bishop Otey, whose 1832 diocesan resolution Guerry considered the "real origin" of the University of the South. Several articles on Bishop Otey and his work can be found in issues of the *Historical Magazine of the Protestant Episcopal Church*, now *Anglican and Episcopal History*. Arthur Ben Chitty, *Reconstruction at Sewanee* (1954), records Otey's part in establishing the University of the South until his death. A few diocesan histories also are important, especially Margaret B. McDonald, *White Already to Harvest* (1975, Ark.); Hodding Carter and Betty W. Carter, *So Great a Good* (1955, La.); and Arthur H. Noll, *History of the Church in the Diocese of Tennessee* (1900).

ARTHUR BEN CHITTY

OTHER DAY, John (1819?–30 Oct. 1869), Christian farmer chief of the Wahpeton Dakotas who became famous for leading white settlers to safety during the Dakota War of 1862, was born in southern Minnesota, the son of Scarlet Bird (Zitkadanduta), a war shaman. His mother's name is not known. His Indian name was Anpetutokeca; he was also known as Good Sounding Voice, or Hotonhowaste.

Other Day was a Wahpeton but lived for a time among the Mdewakanton division of the tribe with his father. Later, when his uncle Curly Head was a Wahpeton chief, he became associated with the Wahpetons of Lac qui Parle. Living near Joseph Renville's trading fort, Other Day became a select member of Renville's warrior society, the Tokadans (Kitfoxes). He also attended Dr. Thomas Williamson's mission school in 1838. On 3 July 1839 he participated in the battle of the St. Croix with the Ojibways and distinguished himself for rescuing a wounded comrade. (His father was killed by the Ojibways on the same day.) He also led several war parties against the Ojibways and killed five of the enemy. Missionary Stephen Riggs commented that Other Day was "foremost in everything . . . [and] physically . . . does not know what fear is." Of his hunting skills, fur trader Henry H. Sibley said Other Day "was classed by the fur traders [as] among those who could be safely trusted . . . as reliable and honest."

Yet, for all his skills as a hunter and warrior, Other Day was "a desperate character" who led a troubled life. During drunken fights, he killed several fellow Dakotas. Riggs also felt that Other Day was "very licentious" for having had "a good many wives." Other Day's instability was further demonstrated in 1841 when he attempted to commit suicide when asked to take sides in a dispute.

In spite of his desperado reputation, Other Day achieved fame of a positive nature during the Inkpaduta Outbreak of 1857. He and Paul Mazakutemani rescued captive Abbie Gardner from Inkpaduta's band, for which Other Day received a $400 reward in St. Paul on 27 June 1857. Later he joined a detachment of U.S. soldiers that pursued and killed Inkpaduta's son.

In the late 1850s Other Day became head farmer of a Wahpeton band with about fifteen families. He represented them in a delegation to Washington and was a signer of the Treaty of 1858, which ceded half of their reservation to the United States. Riggs complained, however, that Other Day also "signalized himself in debauchery" on the trip. He in fact brought a white woman home with him to the reservation; she was a hotel waitress by one account, and a prostitute by another.

During the following year Other Day was converted to Christianity. After he and his white wife were married (21 Mar. 1859) by Riggs, they were admitted to a mission church. At his baptism Other Day took the name "John." He thereafter dressed as a white man, kept his hair cut, lived in a house, and had the largest stock of cattle among his people. Other Day attributed his change of character to his conversion: "It is the religion of Jesus Christ alone; but for this, I should have been the bloodiest of murderers." Riggs wrote to his mission board, "May he be as famous in serving Christ as he has been in serving the Devil."

When the Dakota War of 1862 broke out on 18 August, Other Day immediately warned the whites at the Upper Agency of the danger of Indian attack. He told the hostile faction, "If you are counseling the death of the whites, kill me also. I will not live." At the approach of dawn on 19 August he urged the whites to flee with him. The party, consisting of sixty-two people, entrusted their lives to Other Day's care and skill, and they managed to reach Shakopee safely. Other Day was afterward brought to St. Paul, where a ceremony was held in his honor. He said in part, "At the present time I have fallen into great evil and affliction, but have escaped from it. . . . I attribute it to the mercy of the Great Spirit."

Other Day afterward joined the U.S. forces under Colonel Henry H. Sibley as a scout and participated in the battle of Wood Lake (23 Sept. 1862). In 1866 the government awarded him $2,500—five times more than any other "friendly" Dakota received. The following year he signed the Sisseton and Wahpeton treaty in Washington (19 Feb. 1867). Failing in his efforts to farm near Henderson, Minnesota, he moved to the Sisseton Reservation in South Dakota, where he died of tuberculosis. He was buried in an unkempt plot near Big Coulee Creek, but his remains were later moved (1926) to Ascension Church, 15 miles south of Sisseton.

Other Day was certainly a notable warrior and among the few pioneers of his tribe to accept Christianity and adopt farming and cattle raising for an occupation. Because the Dakotas were divided in their prosecution of the war of 1862, they viewed him either as a traitor or a hero; the whites generally considered him their foremost friend during the war.

• Short biographies of Other Day include Henry H. Sibley, "Sketch of John Other Day," *Minnesota Historical Collections* 3 (1880): 99–102, and Thomas Hughes, *Indian Chiefs of Southern Minnesota* (1927). The chief is also biographied in two important manuscript letters, Stephen R. Riggs to Selah B. Treat, 21 Mar. and 11 Apr. 1859, American Board of Commissioners for Foreign Missions Papers, Minnesota Historical Society, St. Paul. His statements about the war were recorded in Henry B. Whipple, *Lights and Shadows of a Long Episcopate* (1912), and *St. Cloud Democrat*, 4 Sept. 1862. His speeches appear in Mark Diedrich, comp., *Dakota Oratory* (1989). An obituary is in the *St. Paul Daily Pioneer*, 7 Nov. 1869. See also Doane Robinson, "John and Paul," *Monthly South Dakotan* 3 (Oct. 1900): 205–08.

MARK F. DIEDRICH

OTIS, Arthur Sinton (28 July 1886–1 Jan. 1964), psychologist and author, was born in Denver, Colorado, the son of George Frank Otis and Margaretta Jane Sinton. Mathematics was always an area of interest to Otis, and upon entering Stanford University he studied civil engineering for two years before changing his major to psychology. He received an A.B. in 1910.

Otis then undertook graduate work in education and psychology at Stanford, from which he received an M.A. in 1915 and a Ph.D. in 1920.

As a graduate student, Otis studied under Lewis Terman, a pioneer in the development of intelligence tests in the United States, who was busy working on a revision of the Binet-Simon scale of intelligence, a French intelligence test that had recently been translated into English. Terman involved a number of his graduate students including Otis in his work and in 1916 published the Stanford-Binet Intelligence Scale. One difficulty with the Stanford-Binet was that it had to be individually administered, making it impractical for group testing purposes. In response to this, and as his dissertation topic, Otis developed a group test of intelligence that could be administered and scored relatively quickly. In developing the measure, Otis included elements of the Stanford-Binet as well as measures of educational achievement. Familiar with the construction of academic tests, especially tests of reading, he was able to incorporate his knowledge of answer formats used in early reading achievement tests into the scaling and scoring of responses for his group intelligence test. For each question, a number of alternative answers was presented and the examinee was instructed to circle the correct one. This system, which would come to be recognized as the multiple choice format, made test responding and scoring easier and more time efficient.

Terman was impressed enough by Otis's work that in 1917 he brought it to the attention of a committee of psychologists who were working to develop mental tests for evaluating army recruits during World War I. Under the direction of psychologist Robert Yerkes, the committee developed the Army Alpha and Army Beta tests of intelligence. Otis's work was evident in the format, administration, and scoring of these group intelligence tests. By the end of the army testing program, more than 1.7 million men had been tested and a new era in mental testing had begun. Otis served in the army for two years; the first in the Army Sanitary Corp and the second as director of research in the psychology division of the Surgeon General's Office in Washington, D.C. In 1919 he was honorably discharged from the army and served briefly as an instructor at Stanford. After receiving his Ph.D. in 1920, he served for a year as a development specialist for the U.S. War Department.

Otis's work with Terman was instrumental in helping him launch his career. In 1918 Terman persuaded the World Book Company to publish Otis's group test under the title "the Otis Group Intelligence Scale." The test went through six revisions and from 1967 was published under the title "the Otis-Lennon School Ability Test." Not only did Terman advocate the publishing of Otis's test, he also recommended Otis for the position of editor of tests and mathematics at World Book, a position Otis held from 1921 to 1944. During this time World Book (which merged with Harcourt Brace Jovanovich in 1960) became a major producer of intelligence and achievement tests. Otis, who did not share Terman's belief in the native endowment of intelligence, considered his mental ability test to be a test of scholastic aptitude, which was based on many complex and interacting factors, such as social and economic conditions, all of which could affect performance. While at World Book, Otis authored or coauthored numerous educational books in mathematics, including *Statistical Method in Educational Measurement* (1925), *Modern Plane Geometry* (1926), *Child Accounting Practice* (1927), *Modern Solid Geometry* (1928), *First Steps in Teaching Number* (1929), *Modern School Arithmetic* (1929), *Primary Arithmetic through Experience* (1939), *The First Number Book* (1939), and *Second Number Book* (1940).

Otis served in the military again during World War II as a consultant to the Bureau of Aeronautics for the U.S. Navy from 1944 to 1945 and then as a consultant to the Civil Aeronautics Administration from 1945 to 1948. During these years his interest in aeronautics led to the publication of two books, *Elements of Aeronautics* (1941) and *The Airplane Power Plant* (1944), and he wrote scripts for a series of educational movies about aviation. Upon retiring in 1948, he took up flying as a hobby, earning a private pilot's license and purchasing a plane, which he flew across the United States. In retirement, Otis remained an active writer concerned with an eclectic range of topics. For example, in 1954 he wrote two books about ground transportation, *Reducing Traffic Congestion* and *Financing Highway Transportation*, while in 1957 he challenged Albert Einstein's theory of relativity in *The Conceptual Interpretation of the Einstein Theory of Relativity: Is It Valid?* His final book, dealing with tax code issues, was *Added Revenue without Burden: A New Plan of Taxation* (1957). Also strongly interested in music, Otis composed the fight song for the Stanford University football team in 1910 and in 1954 wrote and composed the musical "Love among the Stars," which was probably never produced.

Otis had married Jennie Theresa Minnick in 1919; they had no children and were later divorced. He was married a second time, to Edna Farmer Jackson. Otis died in St. Petersburg, Florida.

Otis played a pivotal role in bringing mass testing of intelligence and in particular, of scholastic aptitude, to American society. Original in his approach to item selection and scoring, he also brought to his work a psychometric rigor that was often missing in the development of mental tests during the early decades of the twentieth century. From the testing of intelligence of recruits in World War I to the testing of school ability in children today, the influence of Arthur Otis continues to be felt.

• For information regarding Otis's development of the Group Intelligence Scale see Franz Samelson's chapter, "Was Early Mental Testing (a) Racist Inspired, (b) Objective Science, (c) A Technology for Democracy, (d) The Original Multiple-Choice Exams, (e) None of the Above? (Mark the RIGHT Answer)," in *Psychological Testing and American Society, 1890–1930*, ed. Michael M. Sokal (1987). See also Henry L. Minton, *Lewis M. Terman: Pioneer in Psychological Testing* (1988). An obituary is in the *New York Times*, 2 Jan. 1964.

DAVID B. BAKER

OTIS, Bass (17 July 1784–3 Nov. 1861), artist, was born in Bridgewater (now East Bridgewater), Massachusetts, the son of Josiah Otis, a physician, and Susanna Orr. Few definite facts are known about his early childhood and youth, but family stories and the comments of painter and art historian William Dunlap suggest that he was apprenticed to a scythe maker. This was the trade of his grandfather Hugh Orr and other relatives, so Otis may have been apprenticed into a family business. However, he eventually pursued an interest in art that had manifested itself when as a boy he had made chalk drawings on the bellows of a forge. His first real training in painting came when he worked with a coach painter; he later studied with Gilbert Stuart while living in Boston between about 1805 and 1808, according to the testimony of his family. Otis then moved to New York City, where he may have worked for a time as an assistant to painter John Wesley Jarvis.

With his arrival in Philadelphia in 1812, Otis's career as a painter began to flourish. He was elected to the Society of Artists of the United States in 1812, and in the same year eight of his portraits were included in the combined exhibition of the Society of Artists and the Pennsylvania Academy of the Fine Arts. His work regularly appeared in the Philadelphia exhibitions thereafter, and he was elected an academician in the Pennsylvania Academy in 1824. One of Otis's most famous early works showed a scene inside a metal-working shop, probably a reflection of his years as an apprentice. In 1813 he married Alice Pierie of Philadelphia, and they had six children.

Otis was granted a patent in 1815 for the perspective protractor, an artist's tool. In the same year he began painting a series of portraits for an ambitious publishing venture undertaken by Philadelphia publisher Joseph Delaplaine, titled *Delaplaine's Repository of the Lives and Portraits of Distinguished American Characters*. This enterprise took the two men in 1816 to Virginia and Washington, D.C., where Otis painted portraits of Thomas Jefferson and James and Dolley Madison. Otis's notebook lists twenty-four portraits produced for Delaplaine's project, although only one of these, the Jefferson portrait, was reproduced in the *Repository* before publication ceased in 1818. Some of Otis's paintings for the project were exhibited in Philadelphia in a gallery owned by Delaplaine, which subsequently formed part of Rubens Peale's New York museum.

As early as 1818 Otis may have been experimenting with lithographic techniques. In 1819 Samuel Brown provided him with samples of lithographic stone, and Otis soon produced what is generally regarded as the first lithograph made in America, a scene of a building at water's edge. The print was included in the July 1819 issue of the *Analectic Magazine*, accompanying a description of the lithographic process. Despite this early start Otis seems to have produced only a few other lithographs. In this same general period he also made a number of engravings, often working in aquatint. Most of these were portraits.

Otis's notebook of accounts for the years 1819 to 1826 reveal a thriving and varied painting business. He occasionally painted landscapes and did some commercial work, including flags and transparencies. He also executed commissions for copies of portraits of celebrities such as George Washington, Lafayette, and Napoleon. The notebook also lists portraits of Philadelphia merchants, bankers, attorneys, and their families, sometimes after the death of the subject. One of Otis's most famous postmortem portraits was of Philadelphia financier Stephen Girard. William Dunlap, referring to Otis's generally middle-class clientele, wrote in 1834, "Mr. Otis, as a portrait painter, has strong natural talents, and a good perception of character. Many of his heads are well coloured. At one period he painted many portraits in Philadelphia, but they were all of one class; if not so originally, he made them so" (vol. 2, p. 227). Nonetheless, there was a considerable demand for Otis's services; in the period covered by the notebook alone, he produced more than three hundred portraits. Some of the better-known ones are those of John Neagle, the Reverend Shepard Kosciusko Kollock, Victor Marie du Pont, John Greenleaf Whittier, John C. Frémont, and the Reverend James Abercrombie. In the year before his death Otis painted a self-portrait that is now owned by the American Antiquarian Society.

Apart from brief residences in Boston, Massachusetts, in 1837 and in Wilmington, Delaware, in 1839, Otis had lived and worked in Philadelphia almost continuously from 1812 until 1846. His wife Alice died in 1842, and in 1846 Otis relocated with his family to Boston, where he lived until about 1858. He then returned to Philadelphia, residing there until his death.

• Otis's manuscript notebook containing his accounts from 1819 to 1826 is in the American Antiquarian Society. A transcription and a biography can be found in Thomas Knoles, "Bass Otis, Philadelphia Portrait Painter," *Proceedings of the American Antiquarian Society* 103 (1993): 179–253. *Bass Otis: Painter, Portraitist, and Engraver* (1976), an exhibition catalog, contains a biography and reproductions of many of Otis's paintings. For a nineteenth-century view and assessment, see William Dunlap, *A History of the Rise and Progress of the Arts of Design in the United States* (1834). Otis's collaboration with Joseph Delaplaine is studied in Gordon Hendricks, "'A Wish to Please, and a Willingness to Be Pleased,'" *American Art Journal* 2 (1970): 16–29. On Otis's lithographic work, see Philip J. Weimerskirch, "Lithographic Stone in America," *Printing History* 11 (1989): 2–15.

THOMAS KNOLES

OTIS, Brooks (10 June 1908–26 July 1977), classical philologist and literary critic, was born in Boston, Massachusetts, the son of Edward Otis, a doctor, and Marion Faxon. Like his father before him, Otis attended Phillips Exeter Academy, from which he graduated in 1925, and proceeded to Harvard (B.A., 1929). He received his M.A. in Latin from Harvard in 1930 and taught classical languages for two years (1930–1932) at Earlham College in Indiana. He returned to Harvard, where he earned his Ph.D. in classical philology in 1935 with a dissertation written in Latin under the direction of Edward Kennard Rand on the manuscripts of Ovid's *Metamorphoses*. While at Harvard he edited with Reuben Brower, also a graduate student, a journal of liberal Christian thought, the *New Frontier*, from 1933 to 1935.

Otis took a position in 1935 at small Hobart College (later Hobart and William Smith Colleges) in upstate Geneva, New York, as assistant professor of classics and lecturer in sociology. In 1937 he married Christine Battle Cheney, with whom he had five children. Otis held the Hobart Professorship of Classics from 1939 to 1957. Like most classicists, Otis had been brought up discussing and comparing a set of canonical authors in Greek and Latin literature. Both Otis's research and teaching impressed on him the difficulty of comparing authors who had lived hundreds of years apart, such as Homer (eighth century, B.C.) and Virgil (first century, B.C.) or Demosthenes (fourth century, B.C.) and Cicero (first century, B.C.). Inspired by Paul Alexander, with whom he taught survey courses on the ancient world, Otis began to study the Greek and Latin fathers of the fourth century, A.D., especially the Greek Cappadocian fathers Basil of Caesarea, Gregory of Nazianzen, and Gregory of Nyssa and the Latin fathers Ambrose, Jerome, and Augustine. These great authors wrote at the same time on the same problems, while preserving the distinctive traits of their different Greek or Latin cultures. Using the insights he had gained from the fourth-century fathers to study the pagan Augustan age, Otis puzzled over the dilemma faced by poets trying to write great poetry based on a mythology that was not believed in "Ovid and the Augustans" (*Transactions of the American Philological Association* 69 [1938]: 194–205). By the mid-1950s he had written a long manuscript on the Augustan epic. He was also a key figure in creating the Western civilization–based curriculum for which Hobart was long distinguished and was chairman of the Division of the Humanities as well as of the Department of Classics.

In 1955 Stanley Millett, assistant professor of politics, gave a talk at the college chapel that the local community interpreted as communist, and in December 1956 the executive committee of the trustees of the school told Millett that he would not receive tenured reappointment the following year. In January 1957 a request to the new president, Louis S. Hirshson, for a faculty investigation was rejected, and the Board of Trustees reaffirmed its decision. The faculty had decided to resign en masse if an investigation was not begun, and on 13 April Otis and one other professor did so. Otis long remembered the experience of calling his colleagues that day only to discover that no other senior faculty had resigned.

A visiting professorship at the American University in Beirut, Lebanon, was hastily improvised. Otis then procured a professorship and the position of executive head of the department of classics at Stanford University, which he held from 1958 to 1963. From 1964 until 1970 he was Olive H. Palmer Professor of Humanities. It was at Stanford that Otis published his most important work. His seminal essay, "Cappadocian Thought as a Coherent System" (*Dumbarton Oaks Papers* 12 [1958]: 95–124), used the methods and attitudes of contemporary literary criticism to show the theological unity behind the various writings of the great defenders of Trinitarian orthodoxy in the fourth century, A.D., Greek East, the Cappadocian fathers Basil of Caesarea, Gregory of Nazianzen, and Gregory of Nyssa. Two large sections of his manuscript on the Augustan epic, *Virgil: A Study in Civilized Poetry* (1963) and *Ovid as an Epic Poet* (1966; 2d ed., 1970), were also published. In 1966 he founded the Intercollegiate Center for Classical Studies in Rome.

Otis never disguised the major influences on his thinking: the insights into Greek and Latin sensibilities discovered by comparing the fourth-century Christian fathers, and the German literary criticism of the twentieth century, e.g., that of Richard Heinze, Viktor Pöschl, Friedrich Klingner, Günther Jachmann, and Erich Burck. Otis felt that an important difference between Greek and Latin literature was that the Greek strove to present action in "objective" terms, while Latin authors tended to introduce the character's "subjective" point of view. *Virgil* shows the poet's development in re-creating Greek literature, especially Homer, in Latin verse, as he learned to deploy the distinctively Roman "subjective" and "empathetic-sympathetic style," Otis's terms for Virgil's contribution to the natural tendencies of the Latin sensibility. The book used stylistic and structural analysis to reinforce its points. *Virgil* appeared one year before Georg Nicholaus Knauer's *Die Aeneis und Homer* (1964) and Michael Putnam's *The Poetry of the Aeneid: Four Studies in Imaginative Unity and Design* (1964). Together, these three books dominated work on Virgil for the next generation. *Ovid* met with less approval, but it initiated a massive literary critical reassessment of Ovid, who had attracted much less serious discussion than Virgil. *Ovid* began from the premise of Richard Heinze that the *Metamorphoses* was a true epic. Many have argued that the poem is rather an anti-epic and that Otis's readings of Ovid were often too serious. In the introduction to the second edition, Otis called one of his own interpretations "stupid." The book included a magistral assessment of Ovid's sources, of value even to those who do not accept the book's premise or methods.

Facing mandatory retirement at age sixty-five, Otis became Paddison Professor of Classics at the University of North Carolina at Chapel Hill, where the retirement age was seventy and where the appointment of several senior scholars had raised the stature of the classics department. At Chapel Hill Otis continued to work on the Christian fathers and initiated a long study of the problem of evil and theodicy from Greek tragedy to the fourth-century fathers. The first part, a book on Aeschylus, *Cosmos and Tragedy*, was published in 1981. It has not proved as influential as his work on Virgil and Ovid. Otis retired from his regular teaching duties in 1977 and died in Chapel Hill that same summer. His work remains a model of successfully combining creative literary criticism with traditional philological methods.

• Otis's many publications on classical authors, Christian fathers, and modern literary and social problems are widely scattered. The unpublished writings of his later years are in the possession of the Department of Classics of the University of North Carolina at Chapel Hill. Otis's dissertation, "De Lactantii qui dicitur Narrationibus Ovidianis," was summarized in *Harvard Studies in Classical Philology* 46 (1935): 209–11, and it appeared in part as "The Arguments of the So-called Lactantius," in *Harvard Studies in Classical Philology* 47 (1936): 131–63. Information on the Millett affair is based on research done in Geneva, N.Y., by Ward W. Briggs, Jr. (see his foreword to the 1995 repr. of *Virgil*); articles in the *New York Times*, 14 and 21 April 1957; and E. Christian Kopff's personal discussions with Brooks and Christine Otis.

E. CHRISTIAN KOPFF

OTIS, Charles Rollin (29 Apr. 1835–24 May 1927), inventor and manufacturer, was born in Troy, New York, the son of Elisha Graves Otis, a machinist and manufacturer, and Susan A. Houghton. Otis attended schools in Halifax, Vermont, and Albany, New York. He inherited his father's passion for mechanics, and at age thirteen he began to work in the Hudson Manufactory, his father's machine shop. He grew interested in steam engines and at the age of fifteen became an engineer at a bedstead factory in Bergen, New Jersey, where his father had moved the family to work as master mechanic of the factory.

Although Otis dreamed of becoming an engineer on an ocean or river steamer, he became more focused on the elevator business after his father established an elevator shop in Yonkers, New York. Seeing a bright future in this business, Otis urged his father to concentrate on manufacturing safety elevators, which used a special device to prevent the elevator from falling in case its cable broke. At the time such a safety elevator was unavailable anywhere on the world market. Otis served as a foreman at his father's elevator factory and in 1860 he and his younger brother Norton reorganized the firm as the Otis Brothers Elevator Company. In 1861 Charles married Caroline F. Boyd of New York City. The couple had two adopted daughters. When their father died that same year, the two brothers were determined to carry on his work in the elevator business. Charles improved a steam hoisting engine that his father had originally developed, and the engine soon became a standard in the elevator industry.

The company endured a brief slump at the outset of the Civil War but soon afterward began to record steady profits. Charles oversaw operations at the Yonkers plant while Norton frequently traveled to stimulate sales. In 1867 the company, which until then had been a partnership, was organized as a stock company,

with Charles as president and Norton as treasurer. The two brothers eventually bought all of the company's stock and became sole owners. In 1882 they sold their interests and retired, but they soon regained control of the company. Charles once again became president and served in that capacity until he retired for good in 1890. By the late 1880s Otis Brothers and Company was the premier elevator manufacturer in the world, shipping its products throughout the United States as well as to many countries overseas, including Austrialia, Britain, and China.

Otis served as superintendent of the Westminster Sunday School in Yonkers from 1881 to 1884, and he chaired a committee that oversaw construction of the church's new building. In 1886 he received an appointment on the Yonkers Board of Education and served there for more than a decade. He also supported establishment of a Yonkers Young Men's Christian Association chapter and served as vice president of its board of directors.

Like his father and brother, Otis was an active inventor and developed many devices to improve the functioning of elevators, including a special governor, which was designed to stop an elevator if it hit an excessive speed. His name appears on a total of thirty-one elevator patents.

During the last years of his life Otis lived in East Northfield, New York, and at a winter home in Sommerville, South Carolina, where he died. His wife had died in 1923. After his death his second cousin, Margaret Otis Nesbit, who had served as his nurse in Sommerville, challenged Otis's will, claiming that she and Otis had married in November 1926. After months of legal wrangling, Nesbit received an award of $130,000 from Otis's estate (whose total value was $461,000).

Otis presided over the remarkable growth of his family's elevator company and thus helped to develop the elevator industry itself. The elevator has remained one of the most important inventions of the nineteenth century, for it made practical the construction of tall buildings by making access to higher floors quick and easy.

• The Otis Elevator Company Historic Archives in Farmington, Conn., maintains articles and information on Charles Otis. The company archives also contain a diary that he kept from 1858 to 1887. Obituaries are in the *Yonkers Herald* and the *Yonkers Statesman*, both 25 May 1927.

YANEK MIECZKOWSKI

OTIS, Elisha Graves (3 Aug. 1811–8 Apr. 1861), inventor and manufacturer, was born in Halifax, Vermont, the son of Stephen Otis, a farmer, justice of the peace, and state legislator, and Phoebe Glynn. Stephen Otis was a successful farmer with a natural aptitude for mechanics, and he made no objection when his youngest son, Elisha, asked to leave home at the age of nineteen. Elisha Otis, who left high school without graduating, joined his brother Chandler Otis, a builder in Troy, New York. In 1834 Elisha Otis married Susan A. Houghton, with whom he had two children. After four or five years in Troy, Otis's health broke following a bout with pneumonia, and he turned to transporting goods between Troy and Brattleboro, Vermont. In 1838 he built a gristmill on the Green River in Vermont but was unable to make a living from it. He transformed it into a sawmill and manufactured carriages and wagons, at which he was more successful. His wife died in 1842, and three years later he married Elizabeth A. Boyd. They had no children. When his health failed again in 1845, Otis and his family moved to Albany, New York, where he took a job as a mechanic with Otis Tingley & Co., a bedstead manufacturer. In his three years with Tingley he devised several labor-saving machines, including one that automatically produced the wooden rails that connected the sides and ends of a bedstead without the use of a woodturner's lathe.

After accumulating some capital, Otis left the bedstead company and rented a small brick building with water power. There he set up a business doing general jobbing work and manufactured machinery such as the automatic rail-turning device he had invented while working for Tingley. He prospered for three years. When the city of Albany took possession of the stream supplying him with power, however, he was forced to give up his shop, and in 1851 he took a job in Bergen, New Jersey, with Josiah Maize, a former partner of Tingley. Maize had established a bedstead business in Bergen and contracted with Otis for a rail turner and other machinery. The next year Otis was put in charge of moving Maize's business to Yonkers, New York. While installing the machinery of the new factory, he developed a hoist in which he incorporated several new features, including an automatic ratchet device to hold the platform in place in case the hoist rope broke. His new mechanism was so effective that he received unsolicited orders for three of his "safety hoisters" from manufacturers in New York City. He gave up his plan to take his family to California to prospect for gold and opened a small machine shop as a sideline to his job with the Yonkers Bedstead Manufacturing Company. When Maize's business failed in 1854, Otis borrowed some money, enlarged his shop, and went into the elevator business full time, offering his safety elevator for $300.

Otis received no orders during the first four months of 1854 and determined to promote his invention. He set up one at the American Institute Fair then taking place in the Crystal Palace in New York City under the management of P. T. Barnum and demonstrated it personally with a combination of showmanship and mechanical expertise. He explained the mechanism while standing on a platform that was raised by a rope to a height of thirty or forty feet, and at the conclusion of his speech he slashed the supporting rope. The viewers gasped when the platform remained in place, and Otis solemnly swept off his tall hat, bowed, and announced, "All safe, gentlemen, all safe." In May 1854 the *New York Tribune* reported that his demonstration of "an Elevator, or machine for hoisting goods" attracted attention "for the apparent daring of the inventor." Within the year Otis received orders for his freight elevators from the states of New York, South Carolina, and Massachusetts. His sales in 1854 amounted to only $2,975, but the next year they reached $5,605. In 1856 he sold twenty-seven elevators for a total of $13,488. On 23 March 1857 he installed an enclosed belt-driven elevator designed to carry people as well as freight in the new five-story china and glassware shop of E. V. Haughwout and Co. on the corner of Broome Street and Broadway in New York City. Still priced at $300, the world's first passenger elevator opened new possibilities for building construction, permitting the erection of structures of great height. As Donald Dale Jackson noted, "Otis' invention and other improvements in elevator technology would ultimately transform the face of the urban world: they would create vertical cities. . . . The elevator made possible the soaring, dramatic skylines that have come to exemplify the 20th century" (Jackson, p. 210).

Otis was a model of Yankee ingenuity. In the great American tradition of self-taught tinkerer, he designed his inventions completely in his mind without resorting to models or sketches. In addition to patents issued for his safety elevator in 1854 and a steam-powered model in 1861, he received others for a railroad car braking system in 1852, a steam plow in 1857, and a new baking oven in 1858. In 1865 his older son secured three more patents on his father's steam hoisting engine.

A tall, imposing figure with a full beard, Otis was described by his son Charles as "an ardent patriot . . . prominent in local public affairs . . . , a man of determined purposes, an earnest temperance worker, an old-school abolitionist, very active and energetic, throwing his whole soul into everything he undertook" (*E. G. Otis, Inventor*). An impractical businessman whose restless mind was always on new inventions, Otis left his sons Charles Otis and Norton Otis a plant and stock worth only about $5,000 and debts amounting to $8,200 when he died of diphtheria in Yonkers. By 1953, the centennial year of his revolutionary invention, however, the Otis Elevator Company was still the undisputed leader in the field, with a history of sales topping $2 billion.

• Information on Otis and the company he founded is in Charles R. Otis, *E. G. Otis, Inventor, Originator of Otis Safety Elevator Business, 1811–1861* (1911); "The First Safe Elevator," *Otis Bulletin*, Nov. 1948, pp. 6–7; *The First 100 Years* (1951); and *Tell Me about Elevators* (1991), all issued by the Otis Elevator Company. See also L. A. Peterson, *Elisha Graves Otis, 1811–1861* (1945); R. A. Weller, "World's Fair Stunt that Lifted Skylines," *Nation's Business*, Jan. 1971, pp. 82–83; and Donald Dale Jackson, "Elevating Thoughts from Elisha Otis and Fellow Uplifters," *Smithsonian*, Nov. 1989, pp. 210–34.

DENNIS WEPMAN

OTIS, Eliza Ann (16 Aug. 1833–12 Nov. 1904), journalist and poet, was born in Walpole, New Hampshire, the daughter of Charles T. Wetherby, a woolens manufacturer and Congregational minister, and Nancy Hyde. Eliza was a studious little girl who loved literature and especially poetry. Her first published poem appeared in the *Congregationalist* when she was only sixteen. She attended schools in New Hampshire and was graduated from the Castleton Seminary in Vermont in 1856. After graduation, Eliza joined her parents in Lowell, Ohio, where Charles Wetherby had established Wetherby Academy. While working as a teacher at her father's academy Eliza Wetherby met Harrison Gray Otis, a student four years her junior, who had already begun a career as a printer's apprentice. On 11 September 1859 they were married, probably by her father.

The young married couple moved to Louisville, Kentucky, where Harrison Otis joined the staff of the *Louisville Journal*. When the Civil War broke out two years later, he enlisted as a private in the Twelfth and later the Twenty-fourth Ohio Infantries, rising to the rank of lieutenant colonel before the war's end. To ease her loneliness during the war years Otis lived in a boardinghouse with three other young women. She saw her husband only once, when he was wounded and she visited him in the hospital.

After the war the Otises moved to Marietta, Ohio, and began to publish their first newspaper, the *Washington County News*. It was not a financial success, so they moved again, this time to Washington, D.C., where Otis's husband served as foreman of the Government Printing Office. By this time the family had grown with the birth of a daughter. A son born earlier had died in infancy. While in Washington, Otis gave birth to two more daughters, but she also found the time to return to writing poetry and feature stories.

A trip to California in 1874 had convinced Harrison Otis of the possibilities of success in southern California, which he called "the fattest land I ever was in." Discouraged by government work, he resigned his position in 1876 to accept an offer to publish a new newspaper in the little town of Santa Barbara, California. In 1876 the Otises and their three daughters moved west. Eliza Otis welcomed the chance to contribute to the struggling *Santa Barbara Press*. In 1878 she took a three-month trip to the Yosemite Valley and wrote a series of letters describing her adventures. When her politically active husband accepted an appointment as special agent of the Treasury Department in Alaska, Otis took on the position of editor to keep the newspaper going. During her husband's absence, she wrote the entire paper and occasionally even set type. She also wrote an article for the *Ohio State Journal* on the Southern California Horticultural Fair of 1879 and completed a book manuscript, which was never published.

Harrison Otis had come to believe that Santa Barbara was too small a town for his ambitions, and in 1882 he sold the *Santa Barbara Press* and invested his funds in the newly created *Los Angeles Times*, of which he became editor in chief. Four years later the Otises bought out their partner and took total control of the *Times*.

Although Eliza Otis did not take part in the day-to-day business of the *Times*, she continued to contribute to the paper. She wrote letters, sermons, children's stories, essays, poetry, and editorials. She wrote the regular columns "Woman and Home," "Our Boys and Girls," "Susan Sunshine," and "The Saunterer." She wrote strong editorials, often as a defender of such "good causes" as women's education, kindergarten, social welfare of women, and women's legal rights. Poetry remained her favorite form of expression, and she published a volume of her poems, *Echoes from Elf-Land*, in 1890. She was a member of the Friday Morning Club, the women's club that was involved in many educational and social reform movements in Los Angeles. As a strong advocate for women's rights and education, she wrote in the *Times* of 14 October 1889 that women must "learn business methods and their relation with the laws of the land. They must learn the value of time and money." After her death in Los Angeles, a book of her poetry and other writings was published as *California, Where Sets the Sun* (1905).

• Correspondence between Eliza Otis and Harrison Otis is in the archives of the *Los Angeles Times*. Midge Sherwood, "Eliza Ann Otis, Co-Founder of the *Los Angeles Times*," *Pacific Historian* 28, No. 3 (1984): 45–53, gives a brief but excellent account of Otis's life and argues her importance as cofounder of the *Los Angeles Times*. Otis is given short shrift in histories of the *Times*, such as Robert Gottlieb and Irene Wolt, *Thinking Big: The Story of the Los Angeles Times, Its Publishers and Their Influence on Southern California* (1977), which mentions her only twice, or Marshall Berges, *The Life and Times of Los Angeles: A Newspaper, a Family and a City* (1984), which devotes just seven pages to Harrison Otis's relationship with his wife. Short biographical articles on Eliza Otis appear in Rockwell D. Hunt, *California and Californians* (1926), and *The Los Angeles County Pioneer Society Historical Record and Souvenir* (1923). An obituary notice, along with publication of several of Otis's poems, appears in the *Los Angeles Times*, 13 Nov. 1904, and a long, detailed obituary and tribute is in the *Los Angeles Times*, 16 Nov. 1904, the day after her funeral.

VIRGINIA ELWOOD-AKERS

OTIS, Elwell Stephen (25 Mar. 1838–21 Oct. 1909), lawyer and soldier, was born in Frederick, Maryland, the son of William Otis, a civil engineer, and Mary Ann Catherine Late. Elwell graduated from the University of Rochester in 1858 and from Harvard Law School in 1861. His career as a lawyer was shortened by the Civil War. On 13 September 1862 he was commissioned a captain in the 140th New York Infantry Regiment, and his unit was with the Union V Corps, Army of the Potomac, for all of its battle operations during the war. Otis was promoted to lieutenant colonel on 23 December 1863. After the battle of Spotsylvania in May 1864, he took command of the 140th, whose commanding officer was killed in action. However, Otis did not stay with the regiment throughout the war. On 1 October 1864, near Petersburg, Virginia, he received a bullet-inflicted head wound that was serious enough to prohibit his return to combat. He was released from service on 24 January 1865. His battle record merited the brevet ranks of colonel and brigadier general of volunteers.

After the war, Otis settled on a military career rather than returning to legal practice. He accepted an appointment as lieutenant colonel in the Twenty-second Infantry in 1867 and joined the unit in the Dakota Territory, where he engaged in several actions against the American Indians. In 1870 he married Louise Seldon; they had two children. In 1874 Otis was reassigned as assistant inspector general of the Department of Dakota. His wife died on 24 April 1876. Later in 1876 he returned to the West with the Twenty-third Infantry Regiment and participated in the repression of the tribes involved in the 1876 massacre of General George A. Custer's command. In the bitter winter of that year Otis and General Nelson A. Miles exacted revenge on the Indians. However, Otis was not without sympathy for the plight of Native Americans. He understood that the army was a tool used by the U.S. government to ensure prosperity on newly settled western lands but also, if need be, to suppress labor unrest so the nation's industrial progress would be uninterrupted. His ideas concerning Indians are expressed in his book, *The Indian Question*, published in 1878. In that same year he married Louise Bowman McAlester; they had three children.

Otis was promoted to full colonel on 8 February 1880 and began an entirely new phase of his career. He assumed command of the Twentieth Infantry and was promptly sent with a contingent of his regiment to Fort Leavenworth, Kansas, to found a school for army officers. He thus participated in a major change in the army, an expansion of the officer education program that was based mainly on established European practices. Otis was at the center of an ultimately successful program to professionalize an officer corps that had been intellectually stultified by dreary duty at small, widely scattered posts in the American West. Otis was the commandant of the School of Application from 1881 until June 1885. His subsequent service before the Spanish-American War included recruiting duty and, after his promotion to brigadier general, a stint as the commander of the Department of the Columbia, headquartered in Vancouver, Washington.

The beginning of the Spanish-American War found Otis in the Department of Colorado. He was quickly promoted to major general of volunteers on 4 May 1898 and ordered to San Francisco, where he assisted in the deployment of American forces to the Philippines. Troops first sailed on 25 May, then Otis followed in July. Arriving in Manila on 21 August, he became the commander of the VIII Corps, heading all U.S. combat forces in the Philippines. Eight days later he became commander of the Department of the Pacific and military governor of the Philippines.

The American control of the Philippines was not destined to be obtained without blood, and Otis became embroiled in another war, this one against Filipino insurgents. Many Filipinos felt they had not resisted Spanish rule to suffer under American masters, and

on 4 February 1899 open fighting broke out between the U.S. Army and insurgent forces seeking independence. Otis, who had been absorbed in managing a largely successful transition from Spanish to American rule, directed immediate offensive operations to suppress the rebellion. When he was relieved of his duties by General Arthur MacArthur on 5 May 1900, fighting was still going on, but the United States had finally put in enough troops to ensure that American control would be extended throughout most of the islands' populated regions.

Returning to the United States, Otis was promoted to major general in the regular army on 16 June 1900. His last tour of duty was as commander of the Department of the Lakes. He retired on 25 March 1902 and died in Rochester, New York.

Otis was a transitional figure in American history. He began his military career during the Civil War, when the country was essentially agricultural, and finished it when the United States had far-flung colonial possessions, was rapidly becoming a major factor in international affairs, and was well on the way to becoming the world's greatest industrialized nation. Like most of his countrymen, he equated these changes to progress. Otis placed his stamp on the professionalization of the U.S. Army's officer corps and America's methods of governing other peoples. Mostly, he was instrumental in seeing that Washington's aims were not thwarted by separatist southerners, Indians, rioting laborers, or foreign insurgents.

• Otis's thoughts on the army's role in quelling strife is revealed in his article, "The Army in Connectin with the Labor Riots of 1877," *Journal of Military Service Institute* (1884). His own report of most of his service in the Philippines is in *Report of Major General E. S. Otis, U.S. Volunteers, on Military Operations and Civil Affairs in the Philippine Islands*. The Otis family history is in W. A. Otis, *A Genealogical and Historical Memoir of the Otis Family in America* (1924). His military career is highlighted in the *Official Army Register* (1909). His work at Fort Leavenworth is detailed in *Historical Sketch of the U.S. Infantry and Cavalry School, Fort Leavenworth Kansas* (1895). An obituary is in the *New York Times*, 23 Oct. 1909, the *Army and Navy Journal*, 23 Oct. 1909, and the Rochester *Democrat and Chronicle*, 21 Oct. 1910.

ROD PASCHALL

OTIS, George Alexander (12 Nov. 1830–23 Feb. 1881), U.S. Army medical officer, was born in Boston, Massachusetts, the son of George Alexander Otis, a lawyer, and Anna Maria Hickman. His mother remained for some time in Boston after his father died in 1831 before returning to her native Virginia, and Otis attended Boston Latin School before entering school in Fairfax County, Virginia. He received a B.A. from Princeton College in 1849 and entered medical school at the University of Pennsylvania that same year, after spending the summer studying with a local physician. He married Pauline Clark Baury in 1850; they had two children. In 1851 Otis received both an M.A. from Princeton and his medical degree from the University of Pennsylvania. He then studied ophthalmic and general surgery in Paris, France, until the spring of 1852, when he returned to the United States and opened a private practice in Richmond, Virginia.

In the spring of 1853 Otis provided the necessary financing and joined another physician to start publishing the *Virginia Medical and Surgical Journal*, in which he included many abstracts and translated articles from French medical literature. In 1854, having concluded that his practice in Richmond would not provide him with the experience as a surgeon that he desired, Otis moved to Springfield, Massachusetts, where the growing population and the presence of manufacturing offered more promise. He continued for some years thereafter, however, to serve as a corresponding editor for the *Virginia Medical and Surgical Journal*.

With the outbreak of the Civil War, Otis joined the Twenty-seventh Massachusetts Volunteers as surgeon. In this capacity he served in campaigns in Maryland, Virginia, and North Carolina. While on detached duty in the Department of the South he made the acquaintance of Charles H. Crane, the department's medical director, who soon thereafter became Surgeon General Joseph K. Barnes's chief assistant. In June 1864 Otis resigned from the Twenty-seventh Massachusetts Volunteers to accept an appointment as assistant surgeon, U.S. Volunteers, in which capacity he could be assigned wherever his services were needed. Not long thereafter he renewed his acquaintance with Crane, who had him detailed to assist the curator of the newly established Army Medical Museum, John H. Brinton, then deeply involved in collecting anatomical specimens representative of Civil War wounds or illustrative of damage done by disease. In October 1864 Otis was appointed to succeed Brinton as curator, in which position he served sixteen years, longer than anyone else has ever served.

Otis was mustered out of the wartime army in 1866 but immediately accepted an appointment as first lieutenant and assistant surgeon in the Regular Army Medical Department. Within weeks he had been promoted to captain. He was also granted brevet ranks of captain, major, and lieutenant colonel in recognition of his wartime services. From this time onward his professional life centered on the museum. He was assigned particular responsibility for those sections of the museum concerned with surgery and photography. Among his ambitions was collecting skulls "from the oldest burial places in our own and other countries." His efforts on the museum's behalf led to the transfer to the Army Medical Museum of all human skeletons held by the Smithsonian Institution.

Otis's numerous publications in this period covered a range of subjects and included many monographs published by the Medical Department in the form of circulars. Surgeon General Barnes's concern that guidelines be established concerning evacuation during the campaigns of the Indian War led him to order Otis to conduct research into the way the problem had been managed in the past. The result was Otis's circular *A Report to the Surgeon General on the Transport of Sick and Wounded by Pack Animals* (1877), which, appearing after the debacle at Little Bighorn in 1876, was based in part on the experiences of surgeons involved in that campaign against the Sioux.

Otis's greatest contribution, however, was undoubtedly his work as editor of the three-part surgical volume of the massive and widely respected *Medical and Surgical History of the War of the Rebellion*, which was based on specimens and records collected for the museum. For this effort, Otis oversaw a large team of clerks and technicians who collected and organized Civil War medical records. The first part was published in 1870, the second in 1876, but in May 1877, before the final part of the surgical volume had been completed, Otis was crippled by a paralytic stroke. Although he never ceased his efforts thereafter and was promoted to major in March 1880, his work had to be finished after his death by David Lowe Huntington, who also succeeded Otis as curator of the museum.

Otis, "a man of culture and social instincts, but always interesting and instructive, and one of the most delightful companions" (*Boston Medical and Surgical Journal* 104 [1881]: 261), was also apparently a shy man, especially in the presence of those he did not know well. As a result, despite his achievements, he worked in the shadow of more aggressive or politically astute colleagues. Nevertheless, his work was widely respected. His authority in the field of surgery was recognized by his being asked to handle the coverage of that topic in the four-volume *Johnson's New Universal Cyclopaedia*, edited by Frederick A. P. Barnard and Arnold Guyot (4[1878]: 1678–86). The wide range of his interests and the breadth of his influence were reflected in his membership in many scientific organizations in the United States and Europe, among them the Academy of Natural Sciences of Philadelphia, the Massachusetts Medical Society, the Virginia Medical Society, the Anthropological Society in the District of Columbia, for which he also served as vice president, and the Philosophical Society of that city. He became a foreign member of the Medical Society of Norway in 1870 and a foreign corresponding member of the Surgical Society of Paris in 1875. He died in Washington, D.C.

• Letters to and from Otis are in the Armed Forces Institute of Pathology in Washington, D.C., and scattered throughout the correspondence held in RG 112, Papers of the Surgeon General, at the National Archives. In addition to the works already cited, he wrote circulars for the Medical Department, including *Drawings, Photographs and Lithographs Illustrating the Histories of Seven Survivors of the Operation of Amputation at the Hipjoint, during the War of the Rebellion, together with Abstracts of These Seven Successful Cases* (1867), *Report on Excisions of the Head of the Femur for Gunshot Injury* (1869), *Histories of Two Hundred and Ninety-six Surgical Photographs Prepared at the Army Medical Museum* (1871), *A Report of Surgical Cases Treated in the Army of the United States from 1865 to 1871* (1871), and *A Report on a Plan for Transporting Wounded Soldiers by Railway in Time of War* (1875). He also contributed articles to journals, beginning with eight articles written between 1853 and 1856 for the *Virginia Medical and Surgical Journal*.

References to Otis and his work can be found in Robert S. Henry, *The Armed Forces Institute of Pathology: Its First Century, 1862–1962* (1964), and Wyndam D. Miles, *A History of the National Library of Medicine, the Nation's Treasury of Medical Knowledge* (1982). Obituaries are in several contemporary medical journals, among them *Transactions of the American Medical Association* 329 (1881): 529–34, and the *Evening Star*, 23 Feb. 1881.

MARY C. GILLETT

OTIS, Harrison Gray (8 Oct. 1765–28 Oct. 1848), politician, lawyer, and businessman, was born in Boston, Massachusetts, the son of Samuel Allyne Otis, a merchant and the first secretary of the U.S. Senate, and Elizabeth Gray. "Harry," as he was called, enjoyed the privileges of economic comfort and social elevation, including his family connection to two famous revolutionary figures: his paternal aunt Mercy Otis Warren and his uncle James Otis. As a child Harry experienced the effects of the American Revolution directly when his family fled to the countryside during the British siege of Boston (1775–1776). Otis attended Harvard College from 1779 to 1783, graduated at the top of his class, and received his master's degree three years later. After training with Boston lawyer John Lowell, Otis entered the bar in 1786.

In 1786 Otis served as a captain in the Independent Light Infantry, a militia company formed in the shadow of Shays's Rebellion, and the following year he received a commission as a major in the Suffolk County militia. In the late 1780s and early 1790s Otis's law practice grew. Esteemed by contemporaries as a man of eloquence and urbanity, he took his place among Boston's social elite. He delivered the Fourth of July oration in Boston in 1788 and participated prominently in town meetings. He married Sally Foster in 1790; they had eleven children.

Along with several business partners, Otis purchased Copley Pasture on Beacon Hill in 1795. The investment enriched him greatly and led to the development of Boston's most fashionable residential district, where Otis himself lived. He was a leading participant in other real estate ventures associated with the growth of Boston in this era, including the purchase in 1803 of what became South Boston. He was also one of the original proprietors of the Boston Bank and invested significant sums in New England's growing textile industry, including the Taunton Manufacturing Company, in which he had an interest of about $100,000 by 1823.

Otis's political career began with his election on the Federalist ticket as a representative to the Massachusetts General Court in 1796 after two failed campaigns in 1794 and 1795. Also in 1796, President George Washington appointed him a U.S. district attorney for Massachusetts, and he became a director of the Boston branch of the United States Bank. Otis resigned as district attorney to run for national office and was elected in November 1796 to the U.S. House of Representatives, where he served from 1797 to 1801. As a spokesman for the Federalist party, Otis advocated a strong central government, friendly relations with Great Britain, and hostility to France. Described by his predecessor in Congress, the prominent Massachusetts Federalist Fisher Ames, as "ardent and ambitious," Otis entered the fray with the opposing Republican party. In his first congressional speech, he spoke out against a Republican statement that seemed to excuse the French government's refusal to receive the new American minister to France, Charles Cotesworth Pinckney, calling the statement "an absurd and humiliating apology" to France. "The tide of conquest has deluged Europe," he added, warning his fellow congressmen of Napoleon's victories. "It may well swell the great Atlantic and roll towards our shores, bringing upon its troubled surface the spirit of revolution, which may spread like a pestilence" (*Annals of Congress*, 5th Cong., vol. 7, 108). This speech furthered Otis's reputation as an orator and helped cement his affiliation with his party.

Like other Federalists, Otis supported the Alien and Sedition Acts of 1798 and defended the latter in a congressional speech. He also spoke in favor of restrictions on naturalization of foreign-born persons, saying he did "not wish to invite Hordes of wild Irishmen, nor the turbulent and disorderly of all parts of the world, to come here with a view to disturb our tranquillity, after having succeeded in the overthrow of their own Governments" (*Annals of Congress*, 5th Cong., vol. 7, 430). This nativist stance was typical of New England Federalists, largely because immigrants tended to vote for Republicans, but it also reflected Otis's elitist views. Unlike Thomas Jefferson and his party, who celebrated democracy, Otis and other Federalists feared that, as Otis wrote to South Carolina Federalist John Rutledge, the "popular current" might "overflow its banks & bear down opposition" (Morison, *Harrison Gray Otis*, p. 173). In 1800, after Otis chose not to run for a third term, John Adams appointed him as a U.S. district attorney in Massachusetts, but Otis was turned out of office by Jefferson the next year.

For the next fifteen years, with the Federalist party on the decline nationally, Otis confined himself to state and regional politics. He was a leader of the Massachusetts Federalist party and a constant member of the General Court of Massachusetts, where he served as both a state representative (1802–1805, 1813–1814) and a state senator (1805–1813, 1814–1817). He served as the speaker of the Massachusetts house in 1804–1805 and as the president of the state senate in 1805–1806 and 1808–1811. In 1808, as the moderator of the state Federalist legislative caucus, Otis helped organize what some historians have called the first national presidential nominating convention, which nominated Charles Cotesworth Pinckney on the Federalist ticket. New England Federalists had hoped that Pinckney's victory would bring an end to the 1807 embargo, which severely hurt New England commerce. James Madison's triumph and the Republican Congress's passage of the Enforcement Act (Jan. 1809) spurred many New Englanders to call for nullification of the federal commercial restrictions. The more temperate Otis was among those who favored a convention "for the purpose of procuring amendments to the Constitution essential to our best interests . . . [which might] avert violent commotions & civil war" (Banner, p. 356). After the embargo was repealed in March 1809, tensions eased and no convention was held.

The most significant political event of Otis's life was the Hartford Convention of 1814. The dissatisfaction New Englanders had long felt with the federal government's policies came to a head during the War of 1812. Radicals advocated nullification of Madison's embargo of 1813, the negotiation of a separate peace with Britain, and secession from the Union. In October 1814 the Massachusetts General Court adopted Otis's report, calling for a meeting of New England states in order to "lay the foundation for radical reform in the national compact, by inviting to a future convention a deputation from all the States of the Union" (Banner, p. 324). The convention of twenty-six prominent New England Federalists met in secret session from mid-December to early January 1814–1815, and Otis served on all of the convention's important committees. The final report, probably written by Otis, asked the federal government for the right to appropriate federal revenues to pay for state-organized defense against the British and recommended the adoption of seven Constitutional amendments designed to strengthen New England's relative power by weakening that of the West and South. Compared with the furor in which it took place and with the desires of radical Federalists, the outcome of the Hartford Convention was moderate. But in the eyes of many contemporaries, the convention was tainted with treason and secession. Otis's involvement compromised his remaining political career.

From 1810 to 1812 and from 1814 to 1825, Otis served on the Board of Overseers for Harvard College and was a Fellow of the Corporation from 1823 to 1825. From 1814 to 1818 Otis served as the judge for the Boston Court of Common Pleas, also known as Town Court.

Otis declined the Federalist nomination for governor in 1816, wishing to return to private life, but early the next year the Massachusetts legislature elected him to the U.S. Senate. When Republican President James Monroe visited New England that year, Otis chaired the Federalist committee on arrangements and personally hosted a party in Monroe's honor, thus doing his part to initiate the "Era of Good Feelings." This social success was not matched in the Senate: Otis's effort to obtain federal reimbursement for costs Massachusetts had incurred in its defense during the War of 1812 failed in part because his association with the Massachusetts Federalist party and the Hartford Convention had hurt his credibility in Congress. He responded to criticisms against him by publishing the first of his several defenses of the convention in the *National Intelligencer* in 1820. Although he originally voted with the majority in rejecting the Tallmadge amendment to restrict slavery from Missouri, Otis later spoke against the extension of slavery in the West and in favor of the citizenship rights of free blacks. He resigned from the Senate in 1822.

That same year, after Boston was incorporated as a city, Otis ran in the first mayoral race but lost when a rivalry with Josiah Quincy led to the election of John Phillips. In 1823 he ran for governor of Massachusetts. The Hartford Convention was one of the major issues in the campaign that contributed to Otis's defeat, which he later said was "a mortification, and a severe disappointment to me at the time" (*The Stay and the Staff Taken Away*, p. 21).

Otis reentered public life in 1829, when he was elected as the third mayor of Boston. Although Otis was always a moderate who personally opposed radical antislavery agitation, as mayor he rejected appeals from southern leaders to suppress the antislavery literature that originated in Boston, particularly David Walker's *Appeal* (1829) and William Lloyd Garrison's periodical, the *Liberator*. Otis articulated his own views on slavery in an editorial in the *Boston Courier* in 1832, in which he suggested that federal monies be appropriated to fund the colonization of slaves to Africa.

With the demise of the Federalist party on the state as well as the national level, Otis became an ardent Whig. He corresponded with Henry Clay during the 1840 presidential campaign and in 1848 wrote a letter that appeared in the *Boston Atlas* in favor of the Whig presidential nominee Zachary Taylor.

Otis died in his Beacon Street house in Boston. At the time of his death he was one of the wealthiest residents of the city. The Reverend Samuel Lothrop remembered him in his funeral oration as a distinguished citizen and a man of "courteousness and urbanity" and "brilliancy and versatility" of talents. Otis represents a class of people—social conservatives born of the prerevolutionary elite—who dominated the politics and society of the early national era in New England and who played a role on the national stage as well, but who lost influence and importance as the nation moved toward a more democratic political and social order. As a leader in the Massachusetts Federalist party and the Hartford Convention, Otis's moderate nature and concern for social stability helped temper the more radical impulses among his fellow Federalists.

• Otis's papers are at the Massachusetts Historical Society and are also available on microfilm. Materials relating to Otis as a student, overseer, and fellow of Harvard College can be found in the Harvard University Archives. An important group of Otis's letters is held in the John Rutledge Papers at the University of North Carolina, Chapel Hill. Several of his public letters and speeches are available on microfilm in the Early American Imprints Series. See especially his *Letter . . . [to] William Heath* (1798), *Eulogy on General Alexander Hamilton* (1804), and *Mr. Otis's Speech in Congress, on the Sedition Law* (1819). For defenses of the Hartford Convention, see *Letters Developing the Characters and Views of the Hartford Convention* (1820) and *Otis' Letters in Defence of the Hartford Convention* (1824). The biography by Samuel Eliot Morison, *Harrison Gray Otis, 1765–1848: The Urbane Federalist*

(1969), is a revision of Morison's fuller and more politically oriented account, *The Life and Letters of Harrison Gray Otis, Federalist, 1765–1848* (1913), which includes transcriptions of a number of letters to and from Otis. For an insightful account of Massachusetts Federalism and the forces leading to the Hartford Convention, see James M. Banner, Jr., *To the Hartford Convention: The Federalists and the Origins of Party Politics in Massachusetts, 1789–1815* (1970). An analysis of Federalist ideology may be found in Linda Kerber, *Federalists in Dissent* (1970), and an analysis of Federalist politics is in David Hackett Fischer, *The Revolution of American Conservatism* (1965). The funeral oration delivered by Samuel Kirkland Lothrop was printed as *The Stay and the Staff Taken Away: A Sermon Preached . . . on the Death of the Hon. Harrison Gray Otis* (1848). Obituaries are in the *Boston Evening Transcript*, 28 Oct. 1848, and the *Boston Daily Advertiser*, 30 Oct. 1848.

EVA SHEPPARD

OTIS, Harrison Gray (10 Feb. 1837–30 July 1917), editor and publisher, was born in a log cabin in Washington County, Ohio, the son of Stephen Otis, a farmer, and Sarah Dyar. He was named for a distant relative, who had been a leader of the Federalist party in Massachusetts. Although the elder Harrison Gray Otis (1765–1848) flourished at the opposite end of the nineteenth century as well as of the country, his political philosophy was similar to the conservatism that his namesake was to espouse.

The youngest of sixteen children, Otis described his parents as "staunch, stalwart, intelligent, God-fearing people of the Methodist faith, and neither rich nor poor." Growing up as an Ohio farmboy, Otis received little formal education. He began his career as a printer in 1851, working first as an apprentice and then a journeyman in printing offices and small country newspapers in Ohio, Illinois, Iowa, and Kentucky. In 1859 he married Eliza Wetherby. They had three children. Their daughter Marian was married to publisher Harry Chandler.

During the Civil War, Otis enlisted as a private in the Ohio Volunteers and fought in more than a dozen engagements. He was wounded twice and discharged as a brevet lieutenant colonel. After the war, he drifted through a variety of minor government positions, including a stint as a treasury agent in Alaska from 1879 to 1881.

In 1882 Otis moved to Los Angeles and began his long career as editor and publisher of the *Los Angeles Times*. From the beginning, Otis was an unabashed booster of his adopted city. "I enter upon my journalistic duties in Los Angeles," he wrote in his first editorial, "with a profound faith in the future development and sure destiny of the city!"

Otis believed that the key to the future growth and prosperity of Los Angeles was the leadership of vigorous individuals like himself. As a corollary to his ardent individualism, Otis maintained an unwavering opposition to organized labor. He made the watchword of the *Times* "industrial freedom"—the freedom of workers not to join a union and the freedom of employers to discharge them if they did. In 1890 Otis succeeded in breaking the local printers' union by announcing a wage cut and lockout. Under his leadership, Los Angeles became the country's citadel of the open shop. Otis's individualism also led him to oppose, on occasion, the bureaucratic power of California's mightiest corporation, the Southern Pacific Railroad. The president of the railroad in the 1890s, Collis P. Huntington, favored the building of a federally funded deep-water harbor at Santa Monica, where the Southern Pacific owned sufficient land to prevent competing railroads from gaining access. Otis and other local interests fought successfully for the building of the harbor at San Pedro, relatively free of Southern Pacific control.

During the Spanish-American War, Otis interrupted his career in journalism by re-enlisting and serving in the Philippines as an active combat commander during 1898 and 1899. Following his discharge as a brevet major general, he returned to his post at the *Times*. He later commented that the turn of the century found him "doing my part in the never-ending conflict, either military or civil, which seems to be my destiny. The sword had been laid aside, and the pen was again in full swing." Otis was convinced that the military plan of organization was an ideal plan for society as a whole. The good worker—just like the good soldier—never went on strike or disobeyed an order. Otis preferred to be addressed as "the General" and ran the *Times* like a field officer, calling his staff "the phalanx" and his mansion on Wilshire Boulevard "the Bivouac."

Otis and Edward H. Harriman of the Southern Pacific and Henry E. Huntington of the Pacific Electric formed in 1903 a real estate syndicate known as the Los Angeles Suburban Homes Company. The syndicate's holdings in the San Fernando Valley, just north of Los Angeles, greatly appreciated in value when the Pacific Electric extended interurban rail service into the area. The syndicate also benefited from the construction of a municipal aqueduct, designed to bring water to southern California from the Owens Valley. The first public knowledge of the proposed aqueduct came in an enthusiastic article in the *Times* on 29 July 1905. Otis spearheaded the move to build the canal, winning approval of a bond issue by the voters of Los Angeles. Construction of the aqueduct began in 1908 and was completed five years later.

When the metal trades workers of Los Angeles launched a strike on 1 June 1910, Otis and the *Times* grandiloquently denounced it as an assault on "the cradle of industrial freedom." The strike was the largest work stoppage the city had ever known, and it attracted nationwide attention because the whole future of the open shop seemed at stake. Early on the morning of 1 October, an explosion destroyed the *Times* building, killing twenty employees and injuring seventeen others. Otis called the blast "the crime of the century" and blamed it on the agents of organized labor. Six months later a professional dynamiter and two officials of an ironworkers' union were arrested and charged with the crime. Samuel Gompers and other national labor leaders rallied to the defense of the accused. When the union officials confessed their guilt, on 1 December 1911, organized labor across the country was demoralized. The result in Los Angeles was thirty more years of dominance by the open shop.

No single individual had a greater impact on the history of southern California in the late nineteenth and early twentieth centuries than did Harrison Gray Otis. Praised by some as a visionary and damned by others as a reactionary, his influence on the political, economic and cultural development of the region was unparalleled. He died in Hollywood.

• The editorial library of the *Los Angeles Times* has a large collection of newspaper clippings and other source material on the life of Harrison Gray Otis. Especially useful are Otis's own unpublished memoir, "Milestones" (1913), and a typescript of "Western History Material" compiled at the request of Charles F. Lummis for the Los Angeles Public Library. Richard C. Miller, "Otis and His *Times*," (Ph.D. diss., Univ. of California, Berkeley, 1961), offers a penetrating and critical analysis. For the *Times* viewpoint, see *The Forty-Year War for a Free City: A History of the Open Shop in Los Angeles* (1929), a special supplement issued in pamphlet form. An institutional history is available in Marshall Berges, *The Life and Times of Los Angeles* (1984). Kevin Starr, *Inventing the Dream: California through the Progressive Era* (1985), and James J. Rawls and Walton Bean, *California: An Interpretive History* (1993), offer overviews of Otis's career in southern California. See also W. D. Showalter, "General Otis: A Fighter with Sword and Pen," *Editor and Publisher* 49 (1917): 1–2, and obituaries in the *San Francisco Chronicle* and *Los Angeles Times*, 31 July 1917.

JAMES J. RAWLS

OTIS, James (2 Feb. 1725–23 May 1783), politician, was born in West Barnstable, Massachusetts, the son of Colonel James Otis and Mary Allyne. James Otis, Sr., was the political "boss" of Barnstable County (Cape Cod), the colonel of its militia, and a longtime representative and leader of the Massachusetts General Court. James Otis, Jr., graduated from Harvard College in 1743, although he complained to his father of its "miserable, despicable, and arbitrary government." He then studied law with the noted Boston lawyer Jeremiah Gridley, practiced locally, and in 1755 married the wealthy heiress Ruth Cunningham. She sympathized with the Loyalists during the American Revolution, as did her father, Captain Nathaniel Cunningham. Their three children reflected the parental disagreement: a son died in a British prison in 1777, a daughter married a lieutenant in the British army, while the other daughter wed the son and namesake of General Benjamin Lincoln.

After his marriage Otis moved to Boston, where his father's connections with Governors William Shirley and Thomas Pownall obtained for him appointments as justice of the peace (1756) and deputy advocate general of the vice admiralty court (1757), the latter worth £200 a year. Yet Otis did not rise through nepotism alone. He studied law deeply, published a work titled *The Rudiments of Latin Prosody* (1760), wrote an unpublished work on Greek prosody, frequented politi-

cal, legal, and literary circles in Boston, and gained a superb reputation as a lawyer, which impressed both future patriot John Adams and future Loyalist Thomas Hutchinson, who "never knew fairer or more noble conduct in a pleader, than in Otis," who "defended his causes solely on their broad and substantial foundations" rather than technical points of law (Tudor, p. 36).

However, the friendship between Hutchinson and Otis did not last long. Governor William Shirley had promised Otis's father, then Speaker of the assembly, the first vacancy on the Massachusetts Superior Court, which became available when Chief Justice Stephen Sewall died in September 1760. Hoping that incoming governor Francis Bernard would honor his predecessor's commitment, Otis approached Lieutenant Governor Hutchinson and asked support for his father. There are two versions of what happened next. Otis thought that Hutchinson pledged his help, then double-crossed him by accepting the post himself. Hutchinson's version was that he only agreed not to seek the position, that he put in a good word for Otis, and only reluctantly accepted it when Bernard assured him he would never choose Otis. Either way, the battle lines were drawn between the two powerful families and their supporters. Hutchinson also claimed that Otis then swore he would set the province aflame or perish in the attempt, an allegation Otis and the patriots vehemently denied.

Hutchinson and Otis clashed again almost immediately. The Boston mercantile community was enraged at a recent crackdown on illegal trade by Customs Commissioner Charles Paxton. Paxton relied on Writs of Assistance (general search warrants that permitted him to search anywhere) to secure convictions. Merchants brought suit in the superior court, now headed by Hutchinson, to have the procedure declared illegal. Otis relinquished his vice admiralty position to take the case, which he shared with Oxenbridge Thacher without a fee, in December 1760. The following February he presented the argument, which 82-year-old John Adams, remembering an event he had witnessed over a half-century previously, forever immortalized: "Otis was a flame of fire! . . . He hurried away everything before him. American independence was then and there born; the seeds of patriots and heroes were then and there sown" (Adams, vol. 10, p. 247).

Yet what Otis said and its significance will never be exactly known. Adams's notes of the trial indicate that Otis stressed two points. First, the Writs of Assistance were "the worst instrument of arbitrary power, the most destructive to English liberty, and the fundamental principles of the Constitution." As such, the Act of Parliament authorizing the writs was against both the Constitution and equity and hence void; it was then the duty of "the executive courts . . . to pass such acts into disuse" (Adams, vol. 2, pp. 521–22). Otis was grasping at straws because it was difficult to deny that an act of Parliament had binding force. Hutchinson ignored constitutional issues, inquired whether British courts authorized similar writs, and assumed the Massachusetts Superior Court possessed equal power. Ironically, when the British attorney general finally ruled on the writs in 1766, he ignored both Otis's and Hutchinson's reasoning and merely asserted that the act of Parliament concerning the writs did not apply to the colonies. The impact of Otis's speech is also open to question: few people heard it, it was not published and only publicized in the nineteenth century, and natural law's superiority to man-made law had been invoked previously, as in the right to resist naval impressment following the great riot of November 1747 in the *Independent Advertiser*. Yet undoubtedly Otis's powerful challenge to the sovereignty of Parliament and his defense of constitutional rights beyond the reach of any power initiated the discussion for the revolutionary era.

Two months after the writs case, Otis won election to the Massachusetts House of Representatives from Boston: the 1761 returns ousted Hutchinson's and Bernard's "court" supporters from three of the town's four seats. After 1764 they would never hold any of them. Otis won election each year until 1769 and then again in 1771, when his deepening insanity forced him to retire. In 1762 he published the first of his major political writings, *A Vindication of the Conduct of the House of Representatives*. At issue was the trivial sum of £72, which Governor Bernard had spent to send the province sloop off to Maine to protect shipping in wartime. But for Otis, this unauthorized expenditure during the recess of the house violated the principle that "a House of Representatives, here at least, bears an equal proportion to the governor, as the House of Commons to the King," who could not spend a shilling the Commons had not appropriated. In *The Rights of the British Colonies Asserted and Proved* (July 1764), he went even further: "The very act of taxing, except over those who are represented, appears to me to be depriving them of one of their most essential rights as freemen; and if continued, seems to be in effect an entire disfranchisement of every civil right." Otis argued that even the Acts of Trade and Navigation, which the colonies usually acknowledged in return for protection they received from British ships and arms, were in effect a tax on trade and hence illegal. In *A Vindication of the British Colonies* (Mar. 1765), Otis mocked the idea that lawmakers from one part of the empire could "virtually" represent in Parliament those who did not actually vote for them: "as to any personal knowledge they have of us," we are "as perfect strangers . . . as the savages of California." We have "no more share, weight or influence than the Hottentots have in . . . China, or the Ethiopians in . . . Great Britain." Through these works and other pamphlets, newspaper articles, and speeches in the Boston Town Meeting and Massachusetts General Court that circulated by word of mouth, Otis was perhaps the most influential advocate in Massachusetts, if not America, of the position that Britain had no right to tax or even legislate for unrepresented colonists and that unconstitutional law was no law at all.

Yet despite these bold pronouncements Otis earned a reputation among Boston radicals as "a reprobate, an apostate, and a traitor" (Adams, vol. 10, p. 295). The same Otis who denied Parliament's right to legislate for the colonies also wrote in "A Vindication of the British Colonies": "God forbid these colonies should ever prove undutiful to their mother country! . . . Were these colonies left to themselves tomorrow, America would be a mere shambles of blood and confusion, before little petty states could be settled." While it was reasonable and expedient for Parliament to honor colonial rights, Parliament was the "supreme judge from whose determination there is no appeal." At the Stamp Act Congress, to which he was one of three Massachusetts delegates, Otis counseled remonstrance, not resistance. He did so again, successfully, to Samuel Adams's dismay, when the redcoats landed in Boston in 1768.

"How can such inconsistencies and prevarications be reconciled to honesty, patriotism, and common sense?" wrote the *Boston Evening Post* on 5 May 1766. It is a question that has vexed historians to this day. Those charitably inclined stress that Otis mentally struggled far more than most of his radical contemporaries with how natural rights could be reconciled with social order. A politician of the old school who achieved prominence before the revolutionary crisis, he appreciated the benefits of the British Empire and legal system, which had done well by him and his family. His encroaching madness, aggravated by heavy drinking and a savage beating by Customs Commissioner John Robinson in September 1769, may have been due to the strain of balancing liberty and authority.

On the other hand, Otis's attitude toward Bernard and Hutchinson changed dramatically from 1763 to early 1765, when Otis's father was appointed probate judge and chief justice of the Court of Common Pleas of Barnstable County. In fact, Otis's career in Boston might have been jeopardized, and he would have lost his assembly seat in the 1765 elections, had not Loyalist Samuel Waterhouse gone overboard in attacking him. The vehicle was a satirical poem, "Jemmibullero," which appeared in the *Evening Post* on 13 May 1765 and which won Otis some sympathy. The poem read in part: "So Jemmy railed at upper folks when Jemmy's DAD was out. / But Jemmy's DAD now has a place so Jemmy's turned about." But Otis redeemed himself by supporting the Stamp Act Congress's majority and opposing the congress president, Massachusetts's Timothy Ruggles, in insisting that the congress protest the act as a violation of American rights, instead of asking for repeal as a matter of favor or referring the mode of protest to the provincial legislatures. From then until his madness set in, Otis was a firm patriot.

Otis's final years were tragic. He drank to excess, raved like a lunatic, broke the windows in the Boston townhouse, and ran about firing his gun. His relatives petitioned Hutchinson in his capacity as judge of probate to remand him to their custody. Despite occasional periods of rationality, he had little to do with the revolutionary movement after 1770. He charged into the American ranks at the battle of Bunker Hill but somehow survived. He died, as he both predicted and desired, when a bolt of lightning struck him at the house of Isaac Osgood in Andover, Massachusetts. The contradiction between liberty and sovereignty that tore apart the British Empire also destroyed the mind of James Otis. In addition he was divided between the conventional, patronage politics that enriched and advanced his family and the ideological struggle of an age of revolution. Otis, like Moses, was fated to glimpse the Promised Land but never enter into it.

• Otis's papers are at the Massachusetts Historical Society and Butler Library of Columbia University. His pamphlets are printed in University of Missouri, *Studies*, vol. 4, ed. C. F. Mullett (1929). Those written until 1765 are more easily obtained in Bernard Bailyn and Jane Garrett, eds., *Pamphlets of the American Revolution*, vol. 1, *1750–1765* (1965). Of Otis's contemporaries, the shrewdest, if critical observations, are found in the papers of Francis Bernard, Houghton Library, Harvard University, and of Thomas Hutchinson, vols. 25–27, the Massachusetts Archives; the writings of John Adams, *Works* (10 vols., 1850–1856); and various papers published since 1961 by the Adams Papers Project at the Massachusetts Historical Society. The standard biography is still William Tudor, *The Life of James Otis* (1823), although it is usefully supplemented by John J. Waters, Jr., *The Otis Family in Provincial and Revolutionary Massachusetts* (1968). Partial to Otis is James R. Ferguson, "Reason in Madness: The Political Thought of James Otis," *William and Mary Quarterly*, 3d ser., 36 (1979): 194–214. Critical are Ellen E. Brennan, "James Otis: Recreant and Patriot," *New England Quarterly* 12 (1979): 691–725, and Clifford K. Shipton, *Sibley's Harvard Graduates*, vol. 11 (1960), pp. 247–87. Oliver M. Dickerson, "Writs of Assistance as a Cause of the American Revolution," in *The Era of the American Revolution*, ed. Richard B. Morris (1939), pp. 40–75, downplays their role; Joseph R. Frese, "James Otis and the Writs of Assistance," *New England Quarterly* 30 (1957): 496–508, rehabilitates it.

WILLIAM PENCAK

OTT, Mel (2 Mar. 1909–21 Nov. 1958), baseball player and manager, was born Melvin Thomas Ott in Gretna, Louisiana, the son of Charles Ott, an oil refinery worker, and Caroline Miller. Ott grew up outside New Orleans in the town where he was born. The handsome, brown-eyed youngster completed most of the credits for his high school degree before joining the New York Giants' baseball club. He received his diploma belatedly, after he led the Giants to victory in the 1933 World Series. Ott married Mildred Wattigny of Gretna in 1930. The couple had two children.

Ott's storybook career with the Giants began in September 1925 when wealthy Louisiana lumberman Harry Williams, a friend of manager John McGraw, sent the 16-year-old sandlot catcher to him in New York. McGraw converted the stocky, 165-pound teenager into an outfielder in 1926 and kept him with the Giants to polish his skills rather than sending him to the minor leagues for the usual apprenticeship. After

becoming the Giants' regular right fielder in 1928, Ott attained full stardom a year later. Despite a considerable height and weight disadvantage, he remained one of baseball's major run producers and best all-around players through World War II.

The novelty of his extreme youth as an established major league star and the consistently high level of his performance impressed others. Ott gained attention with his distinctive batting style. His level, lefthanded swing was preceded by a quick raising and lowering of his front leg just before his upper body moved into the pitch. "Master Melvin," as the writers nicknamed him, explained that this instinctive mannerism compensated in part for his relatively small size by providing him with extra leverage as he attacked the ball.

Ott's ability to pull the ball sharply proved ideal for the Polo Grounds, the Giants' home field, which had a short, 257-foot right field wall. He also hit well on the road, attaining a much higher batting average in other National League parks than at the Polo Grounds over his career. During his first nine seasons as a regular, Ott batted an impressive .343 away from home. The 1929 season was his best, as he set National League road records for runs batted in (87) and runs scored (79). Altogether, Ott led the National League both in home runs and in walks six times, batted in more than 100 runs in each of nine seasons, and compiled a .304 lifetime average over 22 seasons. He averaged .295 in three World Series, hitting four home runs and batting in 10 runs. He also played in 11 All-Star games. When he retired as a player, Ott held National League career records for home runs (511), runs batted in (1,860), runs scored (1,859), and walks (1,708), all of which have been broken. He was elected to the National Baseball Hall of Fame in 1951.

Ott also excelled defensively. He was adept at fielding drives off the angled right field wall at the Polo Grounds, and opposing players quickly learned to respect his superb throwing arm. He was rated the premier National League defensive right fielder for most of his career. An extremely versatile player, Ott played capably at third base several seasons.

Ott's career records do not completely reflect his value to the Giants. For much of the 1930s he was the Giants' major offensive threat. The club relied primarily on tight defense and the solid pitching of lefthander Carl Hubbell and righthanders Hal Schumacher and Freddie Fitzsimmons in winning consistently during those years. During Ott's playing career the Giants won pennants in 1933, 1936, and 1937 and won the World Series in 1933. Ott led the Giants in home runs for 18 consecutive years and in runs batted in for 11 of those seasons. Accordingly, opposing pitchers pitched to him carefully, which accounts for his many bases on balls.

Ott replaced Bill Terry as the Giants' manager shortly before the United States entered World War II. Giants' fans were elated at his selection, but many considered him "too nice" to be a successful manager. Their concern was borne out. Weak pitching, bad luck, and Ott's inability to rouse sluggish players handicapped him. His teams compiled a lackluster .467 record over six and a half seasons as manager, winning 464 games and losing 530, despite the presence of such stars as first baseman Johnny Mize, catchers Ernie Lombardi and Walker Cooper, outfielders Joe Medwick, Willard Marshall, and Bobby Thomson, and righthanded pitcher Larry Jansen. The Giants finished in the first division only twice during the six full seasons Ott managed. He was replaced in July 1948 by Leo Durocher, who was intensely disliked by Giants' followers but a much more aggressive manager.

A few years before Durocher replaced Ott, the two men contributed unwittingly to an American idiom. Before a game between Ott's last-place Giants and manager Durocher's Brooklyn Dodgers, Durocher commented loudly to baseball writers, "Do you know a nicer guy than Mel Ott? Or any of the other Giants? Yet, those nice guys are in last place!" Durocher's remark triggered the familiar tough-guy expression, "Nice guys finish last."

Ott was widely respected and loved as much for his warm character and strong sense of sportsmanship as for his achievements on the field. New York area baseball writers took the unusual step of naming him an honorary member of the local chapter of the Baseball Writers Association of America. Fans voted him the most popular right fielder *and* third baseman in 1938, as he shuttled between both positions. In 1940 more than 53,000 people crowded into the Polo Grounds on "Mel Ott Night" in one of the most impressive tributes given a New York player.

Years after Ott left the baseball scene, aficionados recalled his strong sense of sportsmanship. Unlike some other managers and players, Ott, a proud southerner, treated Jackie Robinson of the Brooklyn Dodgers with respect and fairness during Robinson's difficult breaking of major league baseball's color line in 1947. Giants' players followed Ott's instructions to treat rookie Robinson exactly as they would any other player. Former Brooklyn Dodgers' broadcaster Red Barber, in his *1947— When All Hell Broke Loose in Baseball*, wrote, "And let it be noted that Mel Ott, a former Giant hero of genuine worth, and his players did not give Robinson a hard time in any way."

"The Little Giant" died in New Orleans at age forty-nine as a result of an automobile accident.

• Milton J. Shapiro, *The Mel Ott Story* (1959), is a biography aimed at youthful readers. Details of his career with the New York Giants appear in Fred Stein, *Under Coogan's Bluff* (1979); Fred Stein and Nick Peters, *Giants Diary* (1987); Mike Shatzkin, ed., *The Ballplayers* (1990); and David Porter, ed., *BDAS Baseball* (1987). Up-to-date compilations of his playing records are in John Thorn and Pete Palmer, eds., *Total Baseball* (1989); also Rick Wolff, ed., *The Baseball Encyclopedia*, 8th ed. (1990). Another retrospective article appeared in the *Sporting News*, 12 June 1971. Obituaries are in the *New York Times*, 22 Nov. 1958, and the *Sporting News*, 3 Dec. 1958.

FRED STEIN

OTTENDORFER, Anna Behr Uhl (13 Feb. 1815–1 Apr. 1884), newspaper owner and philanthropist, was born in Würzburg, Bavaria, the daughter of Eduard Behr, a storekeeper of modest background, and a mother whose name is unknown. Little is known of Anna Behr's early life in Germany. She immigrated in 1837 to the United States, where she joined her brother on a farm in Niagara County, New York.

In 1838 Anna Behr married Jakob Uhl, another immigrant from Bavaria who worked as a printer in New York City. In 1844 Uhl acquired his own print shop in New York; a year later, he purchased the *New-Yorker Staats-Zeitung*, a German-language newspaper for which he had been the printer. Together the couple developed the weekly paper, which had been founded in 1834, into a daily, and saw its circulation grow as the city's German population expanded. It became the principal German-language organ for the Democratic party in New York City. Although occupied with the raising of the couple's six children, Anna Uhl played an active role in the business management of the paper. After Jakob Uhl died in 1852, she refused to sell the paper and took over control of its publication. She relied for assistance on Oswald Ottendorfer, who had been a staff member of the paper since 1851 and whom she married in 1859. The Ottendorfers had no children.

From 1859 onward, Anna Ottendorfer left most of the editorial functions of the newspaper to her husband while continuing to play a strong part in the paper's business management. Virtually every business day until shortly before her death found her in the newspaper's offices. The *Staats-Zeitung* prospered in the years during and after the Civil War and became the preeminent German-language journal of New York City and the most widely circulated German paper in the United States. By the early 1870s the newspaper rivaled in circulation the city's major English-language newspapers such as the *New York Times* and the *New York Tribune*. The *Staats-Zeitung* occupied an imposing five-story Victorian structure built especially to house it at "Printer's Square" on Park Row, where the other major New York newspapers were located. As proprietor of the largest German newspaper in the country, Anna Ottendorfer became the most influential woman in German-language journalism in the United States.

The newspaper's prosperity by the 1870s brought considerable social status to Anna Ottendorfer, both within the German community and in New York society generally. It also allowed her to devote herself to philanthropy at the same time that her husband became involved in the politics of the city. The principal objects of her charitable activity were the welfare of women and children and the fostering and preservation of German language and culture. In 1875 her benefactions established the Isabella Home (named for her deceased daughter) for aged German women in Astoria, New York. In 1881 she contributed $35,000 for German education in memory of her late son Hermann Uhl; these gifts supported the national German-

American Teachers' Seminary in Milwaukee and various German-language schools in New York City. She also established a fund at the New York Normal School for prize awards for scholarship in German. In 1882 the German Hospital of New York City opened a new Women's Pavilion at Seventy-seventh Street and Fourth Avenue through a gift of $100,000 from Anna Ottendorfer. In 1882 and 1883 she made extensive contributions for the relief of flood victims in Germany; in gratitude for these efforts she was awarded a medal by Empress Augusta of Germany.

At the time of Anna Ottendorfer's death, work was being completed on a new building for the German Dispensary, a branch of the German Hospital for outpatients at Ninth Street and Second Avenue. She had paid for the building and its land and also acquired adjacent tracts of land to house the Ottendorfer Branch of the New York Free Circulating Library. She had donated the land and the building for the library; benefactions from her husband furnished it and stocked it with 8,800 volumes, about half of them in German. Both the new dispensary and the library were opened after her death in 1884. Her will bequeathed an additional $250,000 to various charities, bringing the total of her charitable gifts to at least $750,000.

Anna Ottendorfer died at her home on East Seventeenth Street in New York City. Her funeral was judged by the *New York Times* to be the largest ever held for a woman in New York City. The flags at City Hall were flown at half-mast, over two hundred carriages joined the procession, and the principal eulogy was delivered by Carl Schurz, the most prominent German-American leader of the day.

• Files of the *New-Yorker Staats-Zeitung* during Anna Ottendorfer's career are in the New York Public Library. Detailed information about the paper can be found in Karl J. R. Arndt and May E. Olson, *The German Language Press of the Americas*, vol. 1, *History and Bibliography, 1732 to 1955* (3d rev. ed., 1976). A biographical memoir by Heinrich A. Rattermann, "Ein deutsch-amerikanische Philanthropin: Frau Anna Ottendorfer," is in *Deutsche Pionier* 16 (1884): 293–301. An article about the dedication of her library is in the *New York Times*, 7 Dec. 1884. The *Staats-Zeitung* published a memorial volume, *Zur Erinnerung an Anna Ottendorfer* (1884). A lengthy obituary appeared in the *Sonntagsblatt der New-Yorker Staats-Zeitung*, 6 Apr. 1884. Other obituaries are in the *New York Times*, 2, 5 Apr. 1884, and in *Harper's Bazar*, 3 May 1884.

JAMES M. BERGQUIST

OTTENDORFER, Oswald (26 Feb. 1826–15 Dec. 1900), German-American newspaper publisher, was born in Zwittau, on the Bohemian border of Austria, the son of Vincenz Ottendorfer, a moderately prosperous cloth manufacturer, and Catherine Neumeister. Ottendorfer enrolled at age twenty at the University of Vienna and then went to study law at Prague, where he became involved in the liberal movements that became active in the revolutions of 1848. He took part in military efforts to free Schleswig-Holstein from Danish rule and later was in Vienna for the short-lived uprising of October 1848. After its collapse he fled across the border of Saxony to Leipzig. When the revolutionary forces were defeated at Dresden in May 1849, he fled to Jena and then enrolled briefly at the university in Heidelberg (1849–1950). Sought by Austrian authorities for his revolutionary activities, he embarked for America, arriving in New York City on 26 October 1850.

Initially unskilled in the English language, he worked for a time in a champagne factory and in a pharmacy. In the spring of 1851 Ottendorfer took a position in the business office of the *New Yorker Staats-Zeitung*, a Democratic German-language newspaper established in 1834 and owned since 1845 by Jakob Uhl. When Uhl died in 1852, his widow Anna took over operations, and Ottendorfer took an active part in the business affairs of the paper. He assumed the editorship in 1858, and in 1859 he married Anna Uhl. They had no children.

From 1859 to 1900 Ottendorfer served as both editor and publisher of the paper, while his wife maintained its business operations until her death in 1884. The *Staats-Zeitung* became America's largest German-language newspaper, with a daily circulation approaching 60,000 in the last decades of the century. The Ottendorfers applied to the *Staats-Zeitung* many of the mass-journalistic techniques being introduced by the American press at large, such as more illustrations and feature articles, special Sunday editions, and new technologies such as the rotary press and the linotype.

Although many refugees of the 1848 German revolutions joined the Republican party in the years leading up to the Civil War, Ottendorfer and the *Staats-Zeitung* remained loyal to the Democrats, supporting Stephen A. Douglas for the presidency in 1860. During the war Ottendorfer was an active force in the New York City Union Democrats, in opposition to the "Peace Democrats" of Fernando Wood, northern Democrats who were sympathetic to the Confederate cause. In the postwar years he supported various reform Democratic movements against the city's Tammany Hall organization, and he was prominent among the political forces that joined in late 1871 to oppose the "ring" of William Marcy Tweed. After the defeat of Tweed, Ottendorfer served as a city alderman from 1872 to 1874 and ran unsuccessfully for mayor in 1874 on behalf of one faction of the Democrats. A supporter of Democratic president Grover Cleveland, Ottendorfer broke with the Democratic party in 1896 when populist free-silver forces under William Jennings Bryan took control of it. Although a "reformer," Ottendorfer represented both the conservative businessman's wing of the Democratic party and the well-to-do elite leadership of New York City's German community, elements somewhat remote from working-class and radical Germans. Ottendorfer was benefactor to many of the charitable and cultural institutions of New York City, of its German community, and of his native town of Zwittau. He died in New York City.

• The best documentation of Ottendorfer's career in America appears in the newspaper files of the *New Yorker Staats-Zeitung*. Detailed information about the paper can be found in Karl J. R. Arndt and May E. Olson, *The German Language Press of the Americas*, vol. 1, *History and Bibliography, 1732 to 1955*, 3d rev. ed. (1976); see also Carl Wittke, *The German Language Press in America* (1957). Ottendorfer's role as a New York City German leader is discussed in Stanley Nadel, *Little Germany: Ethnicity, Religion and Class in New York City, 1845–80* (1990). The most complete obituary was published in the *Sonntagsblatt der New Yorker Staats-Zeitung*, 16 Dec. 1900. The *Staats-Zeitung* also published a memorial volume, *Zur Erinnerung an Oswald Ottendorfer* (1900). Another obituary is in the *New York Times*, 16 Dec. 1900.

JAMES M. BERGQUIST

OTTERBEIN, Philip William (3 June 1726–17 Nov. 1813), German Reformed clergyman, was born at Dillenburg, in the Duchy of Nassau, now in Germany, the son of John Daniel Otterbein, a teacher at the Latin School at Dillenburg and later pastor at Fronhausen and Wissenbach, and Wilhemina Henrietta Hoerlen. In addition to his father, his grandfather, uncle, five brothers, and four nephews were clergymen, and his sister married a pastor. Otterbein was educated at the new Reformed University of Herborn by professors whose Calvinism was modified by Dutch pietistic influences. After completing his studies in 1748, he taught briefly in Berg, a county in the lower Rhine Valley, and in 1749 succeeded his brother as vicar at Ockersdorf, near Herborn. He remained there until 1752 when the Reverend Michael Schlatter came to Europe from Pennsylvania to obtain support for German Reformed congregations in America. Otterbein responded to his plea for missionaries and received an enthusiastic endorsement from his professors and approval from church officials.

Despite having initially accepted a five-year tour, his extraordinarily active ministry kept him in America until his death sixty-one years later, except for a short visit to his family in 1770–1771. His first American parish was at Lancaster, from which he served also smaller congregations at Pequa and Blaser's, as well as supplying ministry at Reading and Conewago, all in Pennsylvania. From 1758 until 1760 he supplied two congregations in the Tulpehocken region and occasionally provided pastoral care to Reformed congregations in the Monocasy region in neighboring Maryland. In 1760 he moved to that area and became pastor of the Frederick congregation but ministered also to other Reformed settlers in the vicinity and in Virginia, sometimes traveling 300 miles a month. From 1765 until 1774 he was the pastor of congregations in and around York, Pennsylvania. His last and longest pastorate was with the Second Reformed Church in Baltimore, which he served from 1774 until his death.

Judged by several standards, Otterbein's ministry was effective. Other parishes requested his ministry, including the prestigious but contentious parish in Philadelphia. Congregations at Lancaster, Frederick, and Baltimore erected new buildings during his pastorates. He initiated practices that reflected his pietis-

tic background in the lower Rhine River Valley of the German Palatinate, and at least some of his parishioners responded. At Lancaster, he insisted that prospective communicants meet with him before receiving the sacrament. In the Tulpehocken congregations and at Frederick, he conducted prayer meetings. While serving the Baltimore congregation, he and five other Reformed clergymen, known as the "United Ministers," introduced the "class system" to develop intense personal spirituality in Reformed congregations in the Pipe Creek region, northwest of Baltimore. Throughout his ministry he traveled widely into the interior, often preaching at "big meetings" in barns and fields.

Although Otterbein belonged throughout his life to the German Reformed Church, he frequently cooperated with religious leaders of other denominations. In 1774 he began a lifelong friendship with the Methodist missionary to America Francis Asbury, who shared his enthusiasm for evangelism. A decade later Otterbein participated in Asbury's consecration as superintendent of American Methodists. In 1767, at a big meeting near Lancaster, he met the Mennonite bishop Martin Boehm, with whom he later led itinerant preachers to serve pastorless people in rural areas of Pennsylvania, Maryland, and Virginia. In 1789 Otterbein chaired a meeting of his colleagues in his parsonage in Baltimore, including seven ordained ministers and seven lay preachers; nine were Reformed and five were of Mennonite background. By 1800 this group, which thereafter held annual meetings, had developed into the "United Brethren," led by Otterbein and Boehm. Possibly because of illness, Otterbein did not attend after 1805. Shortly before his death he and a Methodist minister formally ordained three of the United Brethren to the ministry, which suggests that by this date the group was evolving into a separate denomination. At Otterbein's memorial service on 17 November 1813, Methodist, Lutheran, and Episcopal clergymen officiated, but no Reformed.

Otterbein's ministry aroused intense opposition in some quarters because of his alleged departure from traditional church practices and beliefs. Reformed church officials initially refused to give Otterbein permission to move from York to Baltimore in 1774, hoping that they could unite the two congregations there, which Otterbein's presence would render unlikely. Otterbein's defiance left them with no alternative but to approve. In particular, the Reformed leadership disapproved of his carelessness about ecclesiastical boundaries. Lutheran pastor Henry Melchior Muhlenberg charged that Otterbein proselytized among Lutherans in York. The "big meetings" in which Otterbein participated attracted people from various congregations, leading his successor at Frederick to declare that his prayer meetings were inconsistent with Reformed procedures and to refuse his request to preach in the church when he returned to that area. Twice colleagues charged Otterbein with doctrinal heresy because of his differences with theologian John Calvin on predestination. Otterbein defended his views, stating that he believed in election to grace—

that is, that God calls but not that God condemns. The Reformed church's administrative bodies consistently defended Otterbein and cleared him of all charges. His theology was consistent with the church's Heidelberg Catechism, and his practices were well known among Reformed pietists in Europe.

Otterbein devoted his life to the church; he had no family in America. Although he married Susan LeRoy of Lancaster in 1762, she died six years later, after a long and expensive illness. They had no children. Otterbein did not marry again.

In many ways, Otterbein was an unusual churchman. He was highly educated—knowledgeable in theology and competent in Hebrew, Greek, Latin, French, Dutch, English, and German. Yet, he was able to serve and communicate with unlettered colleagues and audiences in frontier settlements. Unlike many other evangelists, he did not have a powerful voice but awakened the spirituality of his hearers through the clarity and validity of his message and through the example of his personal piety. Despite the accolades of his followers, he remained a modest man. No doubt it was this that caused him to direct that his papers be burned shortly before his death in Baltimore, Maryland. Consequently, only one published sermon, *Die Heilbringende Menschwerdung und Der Herliche Sieg Jesu Christi Deu Teufel Und Tod* (The glorious victory of Jesus Christ over death and the devil that brings salvation to mankind) (1760), outlines of several others, and a few letters survive. Although he never separated from the Reformed church and continued to attend its synod meetings until ill health may have prevented travel after 1806, much that he did during his ministry led to the departure of many of his colleagues and followers to form the Church of the United Brethren in Christ (now a part of the United Methodist church) shortly after his death, and probably even before.

• Otterbein's few remaining papers appear in Arthur C. Core, *Philip William Otterbein: Pastor, Ecumenist* (1968), with interpretive essays by Core, William J. Hinke, Raymond W. Albright, and Paul H. Eller. A. W. Drury, *Life of Philip William Otterbein* (1884), is a full-scale biography. Paul William Milhouse has written a biographical sketch, *Philip William Otterbein: Pioneer Pastor to the Germans in America* (1968). J. Steven O'Malley has treated the Otterbein family of Reformed clergymen in *Pilgrimage of Faith: The Legacy of the Otterbeins* (1973). Sketches of Otterbein's career can be found in Henry Harbaugh, *Fathers of the German Reformed Church*, vol. 2 (1857), pp. 53–76; William J. Hinke, *Ministers of the German Reformed Congregations in Pennsylvania and Other Colonies in the Eighteenth Century*, ed. George W. Richards (1951), pp. 71–75; and Charles H. Glatfelter, *Pastors and People: German Lutheran and Reformed Churches in the Pennsylvania Field*, vol. 1: *Pastors and Congregations* (1980), pp. 101–3.

JOHN B. FRANTZ

OTTLEY, Roi (2 Aug. 1906–1 Oct. 1960), journalist, was born Vincent Lushington Ottley in New York City, the son of Jerome Peter Ottley, a real estate broker in Harlem, and Beatrice Brisbane. His parents were both immigrants from the West Indies. Ottley grew up in Harlem in the 1920s, during the period known as the Harlem Renaissance. As a young person, Ottley witnessed the great expansion of black participation in cultural and intellectual activities, as well as in politics and entertainment. He watched the parades held by black nationalist Marcus Garvey and his supporters in the Universal Improvement Association. He also attended the largest black church in the United States, the Abyssinian Baptist Church in Harlem, where Adam Clayton Powell, Sr., was the minister.

Ottley attended public schools in New York City; a city sprinting championship in 1926 won him a track scholarship to St. Bonaventure College in Olean, New York. He began his career in journalism at St. Bonaventure drawing cartoons and illustrations for the student newspaper. In 1928 he studied journalism at the University of Michigan. Although he never earned an undergraduate degree, Ottley briefly studied law at St. John's Law School in Brooklyn and writing at Columbia University, City College of New York, and New York University.

Ottley sought employment as a newspaper writer during the Great Depression. In 1932 he began writing for the *Amsterdam News*, an African-American newspaper published in New York City. At the same time he worked for the New York Welfare Department and in the Abyssinian Baptist Church relief program providing free meals. He was fired from his job as editor of the sports and theater pages of the *Amsterdam News* in 1937, ostensibly for his support of a new labor union, the New York Newspaper Guild. Ottley then began working for the Federal Writers Project, a Works Progress Administration program under the New Deal. The program provided work for unemployed writers during the Great Depression. Ottley became one of the supervisors of a project that researched and wrote a history of the experience of black people in New York. The result of this project, *The Negro in New York*, edited by Ottley and William J. Weatherby, was not published until 1967, after Ottley's death, by the New York Public Library from the Federal Writers Project research collection that had been deposited by Ottley in the Schomburg Collection.

Ottley used the material from the Federal Writers Project as the basis for his first book, *"New World A-Coming": Inside Black America* (1943). This history of black people in New York City covers the period from the first appearance of eleven black slaves in 1626 to a discussion of African-American opinion concerning America's entrance into World War II. The book was published in the middle of World War II, as race riots erupted in Detroit and Harlem, and black Americans demanded that the United States practice democracy at home by ending racial discrimination. More than a history, the book attempted to explain the condition of black people in contemporary society and to explain their demands as well. Ottley warned that the black American's "rumblings for equality in every phase of American life will reverberate into a mighty roar in the days to come. For the Negro feels that the day for talking quietly has passed" (p. 344). "*New World A-Coming*" won the Life in America Prize, the Ainsworth Award, and the Peabody Award.

After the Federal Writers Project ended in 1940, Ottley began freelance writing for several periodicals and newspapers. During World War II he was a war correspondent in Europe and North Africa for the New York newspaper *PM*, for *Liberty* magazine, and for the *Pittsburgh Courier*. When he returned to New York after the war, he continued freelance writing, contributing articles to African-American publications, including the *Negro Digest*, *Jet*, and *Ebony*.

In 1948 Ottley's second book, *Black Odyssey*, a history of African Americans in the United States, was published. Both *Black Odyssey* and "*New World A-Coming*" were noteworthy because they attempted to present the experiences of black people from their own perspective using original documents and interviews. In *Black Odyssey*, Ottley presented the position that the United States must extend full civil rights to all of its citizens. His history stressed the international implications of American racial discrimination in the post–World War II climate, in which the United States sought to maintain its position as a model for democracy around the world. A third book, *No Green Pastures* (1951), based on Ottley's experience as a war correspondent, is primarily a record of his observations and feelings as he traveled in Europe, Egypt, and Israel from 1944 through 1946. The thesis of *No Green Pastures* was that black Americans should not delude themselves into thinking that they would find less racial discrimination in Europe.

In 1950 Ottley moved to Chicago, Illinois, and began writing for the black weekly newspaper, the *Chicago Defender*. After his previous marriages, to Mildred M. Peyton and to Gladys Tarr, had ended in divorce, in 1951 Ottley married Alice Dungey, a librarian at the *Defender*; the couple had one child. In 1953 he began writing regular bylined articles for the *Chicago Tribune* on issues that concerned African Americans. During this period Ottley also hosted a radio interview program. In 1955 he published *The Lonely Warrior*, his biography of Robert S. Abbott, the founder of the *Chicago Defender*. Although Ottley had never met Abbott, he believed that Abbott had been one of the greatest influences on African-American thought in his position as the founding editor of one of the nation's most widely read black newspapers.

At the time of his death in Chicago, Ottley had nearly finished his first book of fiction about an interracial marriage, *White Marble Lady*. His wife edited and published the book in 1965.

• Material collected during the Federal Writers Project under Ottley's supervision is in the Schomburg Collection at the New York Public Library in Harlem. Biographical information on Ottley is in "Ottley Sees New World A'Coming," the *New York Post*, 7 Apr. 1944; "What Became of Roi Ottley?" *Sepia*, Sept. 1960; and the *Chicago Defender*, 21 May 1955. An incomplete list of his published articles is in the *Kaiser Index to Black Resources, 1948–1986* (1992). Obituaries are in the *Amsterdam News*, the *New York Times*, and the *Chicago Tribune*, 2 Oct. 1960. An obituary is also in the *Chicago Defender*, 8 Oct. 1960.

JENIFER W. GILBERT

OTTO, Bodo (1711–12 June 1787), physician and surgeon, was born in Hanover, Germany, the son of Christopher Otto and Maria Magdalena Menschen (or Nienecken). Otto's father, whose patron was the count of Oberg, was controller for the district of Scharzfels. Otto was baptized on 20 July 1711 in the royal chapel of the castle of the elector of Hanover.

After serving as apprentice to Albrecht Heinrich Klarig of the barber-surgeons guild of Hildesheim, Otto studied medicine under several surgeons at Hamburg, where for a time he attended the Hamburg lazaretto, and was then commissioned a surgeon in the duke of Celle's dragoons. He settled in Luneberg and on 13 June 1736 was admitted by examination to the "College of Surgeons." In the same year he married Elizabeth Sanchen, with whom he had one child. After her death in 1738, he married at Luneberg Catharina Dorothea Dahncken in 1742; they had four children, of whom one died in infancy.

Otto left Luneberg in 1748 and soon became chief surgeon for the district of Scharzfels at Lauterberg. Although he is said at this time to have "frequented the physical, anatomical and botanical lectures of two eminent professors" at Göttingen, he did not receive a medical degree. Otto's father died in 1752, and for that or another reason Otto left Germany for Pennsylvania, where a brother-in-law had already settled. He arrived at Philadelphia on 7 October 1755 and two months later, on 16 December, announced that he had opened a medical practice with Reimer Landt. An advertisement for their services mentioned in particular their treatment of gout, rheumatism, venereal diseases, cancers, old fistulas, fractures, dislocations, "and all kinds of wounds." In February 1756 the partners separated. Otto moved out of the city to Germantown, where he practiced until 1759 or 1760, when he moved to Cohansey in Cumberland County, New Jersey. He practiced there until 1766. He then returned to Philadelphia, where he was a member of the immigrant aid German Society, founded in 1764, and supported John Christopher Kunze's seminarium, or pre-theological school, founded in 1772. In 1773 Otto moved to Reading, Pennsylvania, where he took over the apothecary shop of Adam Simon Kuhn, and he was associated with Reading for the remainder of his life. After the death of his second wife in 1765, Otto had married Maria Margaretta (or Margaretha) Paris, a native of Strasburg, in 1766. They had no children.

In Reading, Otto became a leading citizen, an active layman in the Lutheran church, and apparently a successful physician and surgeon. Almost nothing, however, is known about his medical practice, which was pretty well confined to the German communities of Pennsylvania. Nor is anything known of his medical ideas: his only publications were announcements and advertisements in German language newspapers. Pastor Henry Melchior Mühlenberg, for whose loss of hearing Otto had once prescribed, described him as "a certain refined, courteous chirurgeon." Otto had several apprentices, among them Jonathan Elmer and his sons Frederick and John Augustus, all of whom became, like their preceptor, surgeons in the Continental army.

Otto firmly supported the revolutionary movement in America from its beginning. He appears to have publicly opposed the Stamp Act in 1765 and ten years later was chosen a member of the Berks County Committee of Safety. In 1776 he was one of the representatives of the county to the Pennsylvania Provincial Conference that issued a call for a convention to draft a new form of government. Despite his age—he was sixty-five in 1776—he volunteered as surgeon to the Berks County battalion of the Flying Camp and served at the battle of Long Island (27 Aug.), where he lost "all his Medicines, and other Usefull Utentials" (Continental Congress Papers, National Archives). In the winter of 1776–1777 Otto was in charge of military patients in the Bettering House in Philadelphia, and on 17 February 1777 he was ordered to Trenton, New Jersey, to establish a smallpox inoculation hospital for Continental troops. With the rank of senior surgeon in the hospital, he served in the summer and fall in a military hospital at Bethlehem, Pennsylvania, and in the winter of 1777–1778 in hospitals at or near Valley Forge. From 1778 until the end of the war he was in charge of the hospital at Yellow Springs, a few miles from Valley Forge, to which soldiers with lingering illnesses or requiring lengthy rehabilitation were sent.

At Yellow Springs Otto faced the usual difficulties and problems of war hospitals. Medicines, instruments, blankets, straw, and other necessities and comforts were usually in short supply. He often had to plead for money to buy fresh provisions for his patients. But his administration of Yellow Springs appears to have been honest and efficient; he received no harsh criticism of the kind directed at other hospitals and surgeons, and, although he testified voluntarily in support of William Shippen, Jr., director-general of the hospital, he took no part in the acrimonious and destructive quarrels among physicians John Morgan, Benjamin Rush, and Shippen over their direction of the hospital between 1777 and 1781. An army chaplain who visited Yellow Springs several times in 1778 and 1779 reported that the hospital was "clean and airy," the patients "well provided for, and the gentlemen take good care of the sick" (Gibson [1937], p. 306). In the reorganization of the army medical services of 1780 Otto was reappointed hospital physician and surgeon of the Continental hospitals.

In the early fall of 1781, even before the cessation of hostilities, Congress, to the dismay of John Cochran, director-general of the hospital, ordered that the hospitals at Boston, Albany, and Yellow Springs be "broken up." Cochran directed Otto to keep himself in readiness to accept posting to another hospital where he might be needed. But no such need arose, and on 1 February 1782 Otto retired from the service. Forced to sell the certificates of his retirement pay, as he explained in a petition to Congress, he "has Ever Since been Obliged to Shift for Necessarys for himself and Familie."

Within two weeks of his retirement Otto once again began practice in Philadelphia, but in October 1782 he moved to Baltimore, where he opened an apothecary shop. Still seeking a steady practice and income, he returned in the summer of 1784 to Reading, where he operated an apothecary shop with his son John until his death there.

• There is no known large collection of Otto papers, but references are scattered throughout several archives. The principal biographical source is James E. Gibson, *Dr. Bodo Otto and the Medical Background of the American Revolution* (1937), based on surviving family papers and a substantial documentation concerning the administration of the Hospital Department of the Continental army. See also Gibson, "Bodo Otto, Senior Hospital Physician and Surgeon of Valley Forge," *Berks County Historical Review* 2 (1936): 10–15. A few references to Otto are in the *Journals* of Henry M. Muhlenberg, trans. and ed. Theodore G. Tappert and John W. Doberstein (1942–1958). James Sproat's diary, with its references to the Yellow Springs hospital, is in *Pennsylvania Magazine of History and Biography* 27 (1903). Announcements in the German newspapers of Otto's several residences can be located through Edward W. Hocker, *Genealogical Data Relating to the German Settlers of Pennsylvania and Adjacent Territory* (1980).

Some biographers of Bodo Otto have confused him with his contemporary John Matthew Otto, a Moravian physician of Bethlehem, Pa. John Otto, not Bodo, was a member of the American Philosophical Society and the physician who treated the injured son of the American Indian chief Tattamy.

WHITFIELD J. BELL, JR.

OTTO, John Conrad (15 Mar. 1774–26 June 1844), physician, was born near Woodbury, New Jersey, the son of Bodo Otto, a physician, and Catherine Schweighauser. Both his father and paternal grandfather were medical officers in the revolutionary war. His grandfather, Bodo Otto, was in charge of the hospital at Valley Forge during the trying winter of 1778. His father died at age thirty, leaving behind a wife and three children, of whom John was the youngest.

Otto graduated with an A.B. from the College of New Jersey (now Princeton) in 1792 and in the following year apprenticed himself to Benjamin Rush. He soon became one of Rush's favorite students and afterward a close lifelong friend. In 1796 he received his M.D. from the University of Pennsylvania, submitting a graduation thesis on epilepsy. He returned to this subject in 1828, when he mistakenly thought he had found a therapy to cure or greatly mitigate the disease in some cases if treated during its early stages ("Case of Epilepsy Successfully Treated," *North American Medical and Surgical Journal* [July 1828]: 153–59).

After graduation Otto settled in Philadelphia, where he established a successful medical practice but did not engage in surgery or obstetrics. He was present during the yellow fever epidemics that savaged Philadelphia in the late 1790s and early 1800s and was stricken with the disease in 1798. In that year Otto was elected a physician to the Philadelphia Dispensary, a position he held until 1803. In 1802 he married Eliza Tod, the daughter of a prominent merchant. They had nine children, one of whom, William Tod Otto, became a distinguished jurist and assistant secretary of the interior during President Abraham Lincoln's administration.

John Otto secured a place for himself in medical history in 1803, when he provided the first definitive clinical diagnosis of hemophilia, noting that females are not affected but may transmit the disease to their male children ("An Account of an Hemorrhagic Disposition Existing in Certain Families," *Medical Repository* [1803]: 1–4). In 1805 he described four fatal cases of hemorrhage in the male children of an Easton, Maryland, family, the deaths resulting from "trifling injuries" such as a pin prick and a shallow cut (*Philadelphia Medical Museum* [1805]: 286–88). Otto's work was confirmed by other medical practitioners in America and Europe, and in 1828 the German physician Johann Lucas Schönlein named the condition "hemophilia." For centuries familial bleeders were described intermittently, but Otto was the first to describe the features of family transmission and to establish the condition as a clinical model.

Otto's career was similar to that of other elite physicians in the early nineteenth century; it included public service and membership in the city's most prestigious medical institutions. When Rush died in 1813, Otto succeeded him as one of the attending physicians of the Pennsylvania Hospital, a position he held for twenty-two years. Medical students from all areas of the United States received clinical training at the hospital, and it was through this position that Otto exerted great influence on medicine and became nationally prominent. In addition to his work at the Pennsylvania Hospital, Otto was affiliated with several other public charities. For twenty years he was the Orphan Asylum physician. He also provided medical care for the residents of the Magdalen Asylum.

In 1819 he was elected a fellow of the College of Physicians of Philadelphia and for the next two decades played an active role in its affairs. He served as censor for many years, a position that entrusted him with wide and varied oversight of college business. He was vice president of the college during the last four years of his life.

In 1832 Otto was chosen chair of a committee of twelve leading Philadelphia physicians appointed to defend the city against an expected onslaught of cholera. This was the first wave of cholera to hit the United States, and it struck Philadelphia hard, killing 750 persons in the months of July and August. Under Otto's direction, the committee cleansed the city of filth and established hospital facilities in which to isolate and treat cholera patients. A grateful city gave Otto a silver ceremonial pitcher for his services.

Otto lived a quiet life centered around his work and family. He read the Bible every day and rarely participated in the city's lively social whirl. One of Otto's biographers described him as a "man of the highest principles with a keen sense of duty, of a simple way of life yet with ease of manners, . . . content with the regard of his professional brethren and the patients that made up his rather small practice" (Krumbhaar, p. 139). Otto's interest in various other intellectual endeavors is evidenced by his membership in the American Philosophical Society.

Otto died in Philadelphia. Best known to his contemporaries for his bedside teaching and case histories, he is still remembered for his description of hemophilia, one of the earliest significant contributions to medical science by an American.

• A partial bibliography of Otto's writings is in Edward B. Krumbhaar, "John Conrad Otto and the Recognition of Hemophilia," *Bulletin of the Johns Hopkins Hospital* (Jan. 1930): 123–40. See also Isaac Parrish's memoir in *Summary of the Transactions of the College of Physicians of Philadelphia* (1845), pp. 305–18.

STUART GALISHOFF

OUIMET, Francis Desales (5 Aug. 1893–2 Sept. 1967), amateur golfer, was born in Brookline, Massachusetts, the son of Louis Ouimet, a gardener, and Mary Ellen Burke. While attending Putternam School, Francis would cross the fairways of the Country Club in Brookline, the first country club in the United States, searching for golf balls and clubs. At age eleven Francis followed in his older brother Wilfred's footsteps and became a caddie at the Country Club. In 1908, as a freshman at Brookline High School, Ouimet won the Greater Boston Interscholastic Championship, as well as leading his high school team to a championship that same year.

After graduating from high school in 1912, Ouimet worked as a salesman at the sporting goods store Wright and Ditson in Boston. By this time he had established himself as a promising young amateur in the Boston area. After failing to qualify for the U.S. Amateur championship for three years from 1910 to 1912 (each time by one stroke), Ouimet reached the final of the Massachusetts State Amateur, only to lose by a narrow margin. However, in May 1913 Ouimet won the first of his six state amateur championships.

After successfully establishing himself as a reputable amateur golfer in his home state, Ouimet shocked the world by winning the U.S. Open Championship that same year. Although the tournament was played at the Country Club, Ouimet's "home course," he was not considered a threat to win the most prestigious tournament outside of the British Open. After tying the heavily favored Harry Vardon and Edward "Ted" Ray in regulation, the twenty-year-old Ouimet soundly defeated the British veterans in the eighteen-hole playoff. Overnight, Ouimet had become the United States' first domestic golf hero.

In 1914 Ouimet fortified his reputation by winning the French Amateur championship. One of the highlights of Ouimet's amateur career would be his capturing of the U.S. Amateur championship later that same year at the Ekwanok Country Club in Manchester, Vermont. In 1915 Ouimet and amateur golfer and friend Jack Sullivan opened their own sporting goods store. As a result, the United States Golf Association (USGA) stripped Ouimet of his amateur status for engaging in business connected with the game of golf. Ouimet, who had initially acquiesced with the decision, entered and won the 1917 Western Amateur. Only after Ouimet was inducted into the armed forces in 1918 did the USGA reinstate Ouimet's amateur status for his apparent severance with the sporting goods company. That same year he married Stella Mary Sullivan, Jack Sullivan's sister; the couple would have two children.

Ouimet also established himself as a formidable Walker Cup player from 1922 to 1934 and as nonplaying captain during the years 1936–1949. His individual singles record in this competition was an impressive four wins, two defeats, and two matches halved, while his foursome record was a respectable five wins and three defeats. Yet Ouimet may forever bear the stigma of being the first Walker Cup captain to lose the series of transatlantic matches to Great Britain in 1938. After the matches resumed in 1947 with the end of the Second World War, Ouimet's team recaptured the Walker Cup by a convincing score of 8–4. During this time he endured six semifinal losses in the U.S. Amateur; in 1931 he captured his second U.S. Amateur championship, the last of his major championship victories.

Having entered the investment business in 1919, Ouimet worked as a stockbroker at the investment firm of Brown Brothers Harriman in Boston from 1954 until his death. He was a charter inductee into the PGA Golf Hall of Fame in 1949. His reputation as both a golfer and captain of numerous Walker Cup teams led to Ouimet's induction as captain of the Royal and Ancient Golf Club at St. Andrews, Scotland, on 1 May 1951, the first American to receive this honor. He died in Newton, Massachusetts.

Ouimet was considered by a vast majority of his fellow competitors and the media to be a true gentleman. Characterized by his cleancut appearance, he became the epitome of equanimity, especially on the golf course. Ouimet's victory over Vardon and Ray in the 1913 U.S. Open was perhaps a defining moment of golf in America; the number of golfers in the United States rose from over 300,000 just prior to Ouimet's astounding victory to more than 2.5 million only a decade later. Writers who called this triumph "the shots heard round the world" did not understate the legacy that Ouimet left behind.

• Ouimet wrote three books: *Golf Facts for Young People* (1921); *A Game of Golf* (1932); and *The Rules of Golf* (1948). Details of his heroics at Brookline in 1913, as well as reports regarding his other golfing exploits and some personal information, can be found in Herbert Warren Wind's *The Story of American Golf: Its Champions and Its Championships* (1956) and Charles Price's *The World of Golf: A Panorama of Six Centuries of the Game's History* (1962).

JASON W. PARKER

OURAY (c. 1830–24 Aug. 1880), leader of the Tabeguache Ute Indians (now the Uncompahgre Utes), was born in Taos, New Mexico, the son of Guera Mureh, a Jicarilla Apache who had been captured by the Utes when he was a child, and a Ute woman whose name is not known. Ouray was a talented young man. He became proficient in the use of Spanish and later learned English. He herded sheep in northern New Mexico as a young man and then departed from northern New Mexico to live with his tribe in west central Colorado.

Ouray married a member of the Tabeguache band. His five-year-old son was taken in a Sioux raid north of Denver. Later, Ouray's wife died, and he married Chipeta, one of the most famous of the Utes. Chipeta was sixteen years of age, and Ouray was about ten years older. They did not have children.

Ouray gained recognition in 1863 when a treaty was negotiated between the Tabeguache band and the U.S. government that defined the boundaries of that group. The treaty was ratified by the Senate but never implemented. Ouray emerged as a leader because of his ability to use Spanish and English. From that time on, the U.S. government recognized Ouray for his ability to deal on behalf of the Indians; therefore, to the government he became Chief Ouray. He was a leader to be sure, useful to his band, but his own people never recognized Ouray as a chieftain with chieftaincy powers.

In 1868 during the discussions leading to a second treaty, in which the Utes ceded all but 16 million acres of their land, the federal government recognized Ouray as the leading spokesman for all of the seven Ute bands. Because of Ouray's language skills he was the speaker for the tribe during the negotiations. Naturally, the government negotiators considered him the leader. Also, Ouray was somewhat compliant in his dealings with the federal government, and that made him popular among the federal officials. It should not be interpreted that this popularity was correspondingly great among the Tabeguache Utes, to say nothing of the other six bands of the Ute people. Chipeta's family, especially her brothers, were very influential among the Tabeguache, and Ouray's association with them gave him some importance.

Prospectors violated the treaty of 1868 by intruding into the San Juan Mountains. The U.S. government refused to prevent such incursions into Ute lands. When the prospectors found gold, the government decided it would be better to take the land rather than try to protect it for the Ute. But the Ute were reluctant to negotiate. A delegation of ten Utes, including Ouray and Chipeta, went to Washington, D.C., in 1872 at the invitation of the government. Then the government officials offered to find Ouray's son in return for negotiations. In September 1873 the Utes finally met with government commissioners and worked out an agreement that ceded the San Juan region and other mineral rich areas to the United States. The Ute retained hunting rights to the ceded lands and were to receive a perpetual trust that would yield $25,000 annually to be used for the tribe's benefit. Ouray influenced the other Ute leaders to sign this agreement.

The federal officials did attempt to find Ouray's son, but the boy thought to be he was with the southern Arapahoes and refused to acknowledge his connection to Ouray and the Ute.

Later, Ouray became an important national figure. In northwestern Colorado an argument between Nathan Meeker, the Indian agent, and the Ute of that area led to armed conflict. The argument arose over the issue of whether or not the Ute would become farmers. The Ute were solidly opposed to the idea, while Meeker was insistent. The Indians killed Meeker in the altercation. The army entered the conflict, and troops from Fort Steele, Wyoming, moved into the area of the Ute reservation along the White River. The war known as the Ute War of 1879 broke out. The Ute killed the leader of the army troops, Major Thomas Tipton Thornburg, and badly mauled his detachment in fighting along the banks of the Milk River in northwestern Colorado. Ouray intervened on behalf of the Ute and negotiated a peace that prevented the government from sending a reinforced army against the Ute, probably saving many lives.

Ouray attempted to keep the Ute people in Colorado on the reservation, but he was not able to do so. Therefore, in the final stages of Ouray's life, some rather tragic things occurred to the Utes of the Tabeguache band, including their removal to a remote section of Utah. Ouray was in declining health. The government acknowledged his service by providing him with a pension, a house, a wagon, and a team of horses. These were all trappings of white civilization and alienated Ouray from his people.

Also, after the Meeker affair, Ouray lost influence over the Ute. He suffered from nephritis and could not stop the removal of his band from the new state of Colorado to Utah Territory. He was a significant participant in the creation of the Agreement of 1880. For the Ute this agreement was tragic in many ways. The U.S. government expelled the Ute from Colorado, both those who had rebelled against Meeker and the Tabeguache, who had been guiltless and who, in fact, had intervened on behalf of the federal government. The U.S. army headed by Colonel Ranald S. McKenzie of Texas fame rounded up all the Utes who lived north of the San Juan Mountains in Colorado and drove them across the Colorado River, through the Bookcliff Mountains, and into the Uintah basin of Utah. But Ouray was not with them. He had died of nephritis in western Colorado and was buried near Ignacio, Colorado.

Ouray was at once a heroic and a tragic figure. He learned well, he acted in the way that he felt was best for his people, but the government of the United States used him callously.

• Since Ouray played a central role following the Meeker affair and acted as spokesman for his part of the Ute tribes, contemporary newspaper and magazine accounts are abundant. Denver newspapers are detailed, national publications such as *Harper's Weekly* contain important sources, and numerous articles can be used from *Colorado Magazine*. A standard account of Ouray and his role in the history of Colorado is in Robert Emmitt, *The Last War Trail: The Utes and the Settlement of Colorado* (1954). See also Fred A. Conetah, *A History of the Northern Ute People* (1982).

FLOYD A. O'NEIL

OUTCAULT, Richard Felton (14 Jan. 1863–25 Sept. 1928), cartoonist, was born in Lancaster, Ohio, the son of well-to-do parents, J. P. Outcault and Catherine Davis. After graduating from McMicken Academy in Cincinnati, where he majored in art, Outcault was hired to do mechanical drawings for Thomas Edison. For the Paris Exposition of 1889–1890, the inventor sent Outcault to France to supervise the installation of his company's exhibits. While there, Outcault changed the spelling of the family name, adding a second *u*.

Upon returning to the United States, Outcault continued working for Edison and made frequent trips to Lancaster to court the granddaughter of a leading banker, Mary Jane Martin. They were married in December 1890 and settled in Flushing, Queens, New York. There Outcault pursued his career as a draftsman, making technical drawings for *Electric World* and *Street Railway Journal*, and began also to indulge his penchant for humor, submitting cartoons to the weekly humor magazines *Puck*, *Judge*, *Life*, and the somewhat more risqué *Truth*.

In the fall of 1894, Outcault joined the staff of Joseph Pulitzer's *New York World* to provide the content of the paper's newest innovation, a weekly full-color comic magazine supplement for the Sunday edition, patterned after the weekly humor magazines. When the supplement debuted on 18 November, its cover was a full-page comic strip by Outcault. The comedy arose from the antics of a clown and his dog and an anaconda; when the dog is devoured by the snake, the clown cuts open the serpent's belly to permit the dog's legs to emerge and leads the creature off. Prophetically, the page was titled, "The Origin of a New Species." It was the first Sunday comic supplement, and its success would breed imitation by virtually every newspaper in the land, resulting in the growth and development of a new art form, the newspaper comic strip. The first of the imitations would be launched a year later by William Randolph Hearst's *New York Journal*, then engaged in journalism's most celebrated circulation war with Pulitzer's *World*. Comics would be on the front line in the battlefield.

For his weekly comic picture, Outcault soon revived a series he had started in *Truth*. Taking inspiration from a popular song ("Down in Hogan's Alley" was the opening line of "Maggie Murphy's Home," a musical number in Edward Harrigan's play *O'Reilly and the Four Hundred*), Outcault titled his series *Hogan's Alley* and burlesqued city life by focusing on its cluttered and squalid slums, which he infested with a manic assortment of raggedy urchins, juvenile toughs, and enough stray dogs and cats to start a pound. The cartoons rejoiced in a hearty vulgarity, often finding comedy in violence and casual cruelty. In the midst of a field of nondescript ragamuffins, one stood out: he had a head as round and naked as a billiard ball, surmounted on either side by giant ears, and his only raiment was a long, dirty nightshirt on which Outcault often lettered some saucy comment about the mayhem at hand. The kid began making sporadic appearances on 17 February 1895, but it was not until early the next year that he became a permanent resident of Hogan's Alley. On 5 January 1896 the *World*'s printers, experimenting with a new quick-drying yellow ink, chose the kid's nightshirt as the best testing ground, and the Yellow Kid was christened. He quickly became the star attraction of the *Sunday World*. No matter what the disturbance in Hogan's Alley, the Yellow Kid was there, his vaguely Oriental visage baring its two teeth at the reader in a grin at the same time vacuous and knowing—the leering capstone above whatever irreverent commentary was emblazoned on the signal flare of his yellow billboard shirtfront. So popular was the Yellow Kid that he became the first merchandized comic strip character, appearing on buttons, cracker tins, cigarette packs, ladies' fans, and a host of other artifacts of the age.

Hearst, seeing how successfully the Yellow Kid sold papers, hired Outcault away from the *World* and used the Yellow Kid to launch his weekly, the *American Humorist*, on 18 October 1896. Pulitzer engaged George Luks to continue drawing *Hogan's Alley* (starring the Kid) for the *Sunday World*. Circulation drives for both papers splashed the Yellow Kid and his vacant grin on posters all over town. Thus Outcault's hapless waif became the most conspicuous combatant in the battle for readers. Those watching the warfare from the sidelines took to calling the two papers "the Yellow Kid journals," or "the yellow journals." And the kind of sensation-mongering journalism the warring papers practiced was thereafter dubbed "yellow journalism."

Within a year, the Yellow Kid's popularity began to wane; Luks's last Kid page appeared on 1 August 1897, and Outcault returned to the *World* in early 1898 to begin several new features, all about city kids—*The New Bully*, *The Casey Corner Kids*, and *The Kelly Kids*. He also sold two short-lived features to the *Philadelphia Inquirer*: *The Country School* and *The Barnyard Club*. By early 1900, Outcault was contributing regularly to the *New York Herald*, launching two new series, *Pore Li'l Mose*, about a black kid prankster, and *Buddy Tucker*, about a bellhop. Then on 4 May 1902 Outcault started another cartoon feature in the *Herald* that would bring him fame and fortune greater than had been generated by the renowned Yellow Kid.

The title character in *Buster Brown* was an incarnation of Frances Hodgson Burnett's Little Lord Fauntleroy with long curly hair and knee pants, a city kid but not a slum urchin. Although not as vulgar and violent as the Kid, Buster was nonetheless an incorrigible scamp. Every weekly installment involved him in some juvenile mischief and ended with his heartfelt resolution to reform, a moral aspect of the feature that appealed to parents. Buster became a national fad, and Outcault licensed his name to promote a vast array of products—musical instruments, cigars, cooking stoves, clothing, raisins, and shoes.

Outcault owned Buster Brown and was therefore able to take the character, his pet dog Tige, and his girlfriend Mary Jane with him when he rejoined the Hearst organization in 1906. His first *Buster* for Hearst appeared on 14 January; the feature lasted well into the 1920s, although Outcault had by then left its production mostly to assistants as he concentrated on merchandising his creations, to which end he founded an advertising agency that operated out of Chicago. Outcault devoted the last decade of his life to painting, retiring entirely from the newspaper comic strip field, which he was so instrumental in creating. He died at his home in Flushing.

• Outcault published several books that reprint the Buster Brown comic strips or are inspired by them: *Buster Brown's Pranks* (1905), *Buster Brown's Resolutions* (1906), *Buster, Mary Jane, and Tige* (1908), *Buster Brown, the Busy Body* (1909), *Real Buster and the Only Mary Jane* (1909), *Buster Brown in Foreign Lands* (1912), *Buster Brown—The Fun Maker* (1912), and *Buster Brown and His Pets* (1913). The Yellow Kid gave his name to a magazine that published fifteen issues in the late 1890s; original art for several of the covers is archived at the Bird Library of Syracuse University. Details of Outcault's life are in *The Encyclopedia of American Comics* (1990; under entries for Outcault, the Yellow Kid, and Buster Brown), and Gordon Campbell, "The Yellow Kid and Buster Brown," *Cartoonist PROfiles* 51 (Sept. 1981): 44–49. Roy L. McCardell, "Opper, Outcault, and Company: The Comic Supplement and the Men Who Made It," *Everybody's Magazine* 30 (June 1905), describes the history of the Sunday comic supplement and Outcault's part in it. An obituary is in the *New York Times*, 26 Sept. 1928.

ROBERT C. HARVEY

OUTERBRIDGE, Eugenius Harvey (8 Mar. 1860–10 Nov. 1932), merchant and civic leader, was born in Philadelphia, Pennsylvania, the son of Alexander Ewing Outerbridge, a shipping executive, and Laura C. Harvey. A member of a prominent and wealthy family that included the brothers Alexander Ewing Outerbridge, a metallurgist, and Sir Joseph Outerbridge of Bermuda, Eugenius Outerbridge was educated at Ury House, a private school in Philadelphia. At the age of sixteen he took a job with Harvey & Company, a long-established import-export firm belonging to his mother's family, in St. John's, Newfoundland. After two years he returned to the United States as the New York agent for the company, and in 1881 the New York office was reorganized as Harvey & Outerbridge, with Outerbridge as the sole resident partner. In 1923, when it was incorporated, he became its president. In addition to his thriving import and export business, Outerbridge was active in numerous other business ventures. He became the president, treasurer, and managing director of the Pantasote Leather Company in New York and New Jersey and was vice president and managing director of the Agasote Millboard Company of New York. In 1891 he married Ethel Boyd;

they had two children. Their son, Kenneth Boyd Outerbridge, became the president of Harvey & Outerbridge after Eugenius Outerbridge's death.

Outerbridge's commercial interests brought him a wide association with the business community in New York, and he was very active in civic and philanthropic affairs. He was a director of numerous banks, including Seaman's Bank for Savings, the National Park Bank of New York, and Chase National Bank, of which he was a member of the advisory committee. He was also a director of the Delaware & Hudson Co., the Society Realty Co., and beginning in 1906, the Equitable Life Assurance Society. Among the many service organizations to which he contributed his time were the United Hospital Fund, of which he was a trustee, the National Employment Exchange, which he served as secretary and director, the New York Produce Exchange, and the Regional Plan Association.

Other organizations of which Outerbridge was an active member included the Century Association, the Pennsylvania Society, Pilgrims of the United States, St. George's Society, the Economic Club of New York, and the Merchant's Association, and he was a governor of the Union Club and the Bankers Club. Outside of the business community he was a member of the Academy of Political and Social Science of Philadelphia, the Academy of Political Science of New York, the National Institute of Social Science, and the French Institute of New York. Extensively engaged in church work, he was a vestryman and the chairman of the rebuilding committee of St. James Episcopal Church in New York.

From its inception in 1909, Outerbridge worked as the chairman of the Committee of One Hundred, a civic body dedicated to municipal reform, with a particular emphasis on public transportation. His service to the Chamber of Commerce of the State of New York was especially notable. He was a member from 1903 until his death, serving as its president for two terms in 1916–1917, its vice president in 1924–1925 and 1927–1928, chairman of its Special Committee on National Defense, and a member of many other committees during his twenty-nine years with the chamber.

Outerbridge is best remembered for his work for the Port of New York, whose post–World War I congestion and jurisdictional conflicts over the adjacent shorelines of New Jersey were a source of many problems for the city's trade. His experience as an importer and exporter and his wide-ranging commercial affiliations led to his appointment in 1917 to the newly formed New York–New Jersey Port and Harbor Development Commission, established to resolve these problems. When the New York Port Authority Commission was created in 1921, he was appointed its first chairman. He brought all his influence and managerial skill to integrating the harbor facilities of New York and New Jersey because, as the General Counsel of the Port Authority noted shortly after his death, "The larger interests of both, as he saw them, lay in continuous, combined effort, for their own and the nation's good."

Known as "the Father of the Port Authority," Outerbridge served as its chairman until 1924, working diligently and without remuneration for the construction of the system of bridges and tunnels that connect New York and New Jersey in the harbor area. His curious surname, which originated in sixteenth-century England with reference to the family residence near the outer bridge on a river outside Sheffield, provided the authority with a rare opportunity for a play on words in honoring him by naming its first project the Outerbridge Crossing. Spanning the Arthur Kill between Perth Amboy, New Jersey, and Tottenville, Staten Island, the four-lane cantilever bridge, opened in 1928, is the outermost bridge in the Port of New York.

A resident of Staten Island for the last twenty years of his life, Outerbridge died in New York City. Twenty days later the Committee of the Whole of the Port Authority of New York read into its minutes a tribute naming the bistate agency's first president "the Builder of a Great Port."

• Information about Outerbridge is in publications of the Port Authority of New York and New Jersey, including "Outerbridge Crossing Named for First Port Authority Chairman," press release of Apr. 1967, and "Memorial to the Hon. Eugenius H. Outerbridge," Board Minutes of 1 Dec. 1932, pp. 218–221, which are available from the office of the Freedom of Information Administrator of the Port Authority of New York and New Jersey. Obituaries are in the *New York Times*, 11 Nov. 1932, and the *New York Herald Tribune*, 12 Nov. 1932.

DENNIS WEPMAN

OVERBECK, Margaret (3 July 1863–13 Aug. 1911), artist and ceramist, was born near Hamilton, Ohio, the daughter of John Arehart Overpeck, a farmer and cabinetmaker, and Sarah Ann Borger. (The American *p* in the father's surname was changed back to the German *b*.) Margaret was joined in the effort to develop art pottery by three of her sisters: **Hannah Borger Overbeck** (14 Mar. 1870–28 Aug. 1931), **Elizabeth Gray Overbeck** (21 Oct. 1875–1 Dec. 1936), and **Mary Frances Overbeck** (28 Jan. 1878–20 Mar. 1955), who were born on their parents' farm in Jackson Township, Wayne County, Indiana, just north of Cambridge City.

From a modest but imaginative family, the girls attended the local grade and high schools and were embarking on higher studies and careers at the time the Arts and Crafts movement was gaining momentum. The sisters' artistic endeavors attracted attention long before they were able to establish their own ceramics studio. In 1891 the local newspaper noted that "the Misses Overbeck have meritous works of art in their gallery." "Misses" may refer to Margaret and her older sister Ida, who operated a photography studio by 1887, and perhaps Hannah, too. Another long article of the time describes one of Margaret's early still-life paintings and praises her abilities. Margaret studied under Indiana and Ohio artists J. H. Sharp, L. H. Meakin, Lewis Cass Lutz, Vincent Nowattny, Otto

W. Beck, and Thomas Noble, as well as with Arthur Dow of Columbia University and Marshall Fry.

When she was nearly thirty years old, Margaret enrolled in four classes during the 1892–1893 term of the Cincinnati Art Academy: watercolor, wood carving, head studies from life and casts, and oil painting from still life. (Her 1895 oil portrait of her mother can be seen in the Overbeck Museum in Cambridge City.) In February 1895 Margaret went to Zanesville, Ohio, to work as a decorator at Lonhuda/Weller Pottery until a disastrous fire in May. The next school term she taught art at Sayre Institute in Lexington, Kentucky; in 1897 she was in charge of the art department at Megguier Seminary in Boonville, Missouri. In the 1898–1899 term she returned to the Cincinnati Art Academy to take the life (from models) class. From 1899 to 1911 Margaret taught drawing, watercolor, and china painting at DePauw University, Greencastle, Indiana.

Hannah worked with Ida in the latter's photography studio before attending Indiana State Normal School (now Indiana State University) at Terre Haute. After her graduation in 1894, Hannah was a public school teacher in western Indiana. Then she spent several months (perhaps studying) in Germany, returning home in 1903.

Like other women potters of the time, Margaret, Hannah, and Mary began their ceramics careers with china painting. By 1903 their work was exhibited in Cincinnati and their china-painting designs were being published in *Keramic Studio Magazine*. Their work earned honors and awards from the magazine from 1903 to 1916. The December 1906 issue carried Mary's blue and gold design of a camel and palms for a child's table set of mug and bowl, which won first prize. Nearly the entire March 1907 issue was devoted to twenty-five of Margaret's designs, paintings, and sketches and her commentaries. She wrote, "When the highest degree of utility is reached, the elements of beauty have been attained." The June 1913 issue contained five full pages of Hannah's bleeding heart designs and her directions for painting them. Her dinner set with orange blossom design in the April 1915 issue was awarded first prize. Altogether, Margaret contributed to seventeen, Hannah to forty-seven, and Mary to twenty-two issues of this national publication.

Margaret spent the 1907–1908 school year recovering from severe head injuries she had suffered in an auto accident in Chicago in August 1907. In the summer of 1908, seemingly recovered, she organized and taught classes in design at nearby Richmond, and that fall she returned to her position as supervisor of art and drawing at DePauw. From January to March 1909 the three sisters' china painting was included in the annual exhibit of the Woman's Art Club of Cincinnati at the art museum. During 1909 and 1910 Elizabeth studied ceramics with the noted Charles Fergus Binns at the New York State School of Clayworking in Alfred. Binns is considered the father of studio ceramics, and Elizabeth is one of seven of his students identified as making their own contribution to the American art pottery movement.

After some experimental work with clay, glazes, and firing, the sisters originated Overbeck Pottery in 1911. It was an answer to Margaret's pensive desire expressed in the March 1907 issue of *Keramic Studio Magazine*: "Oh! that we could be our own potters!" This first art pottery studio in Indiana for the making of "handmade decorative ware" was established in the frame Federal-style house at 520 East Church Street that had been the Overbeck family home since 1883. The design studio was in a south room; the workshop at the rear was used for straining and mixing the slips and clays; the basement had south and west windows, natural light for the potter's wheel. A separate small, square frame kiln house for firings still stands just outside the west workshop door. The dining room furniture displayed their finished wares for sale.

The sisters were highly dependent on one another. Margaret, the visionary and catalyst for the pottery, was artist and teacher to her younger sisters. Hannah's strong sense of design enhanced all the pottery that was produced from her drawings. Elizabeth, following her year of study with Binns, became the technician for the art pottery studio. She developed the glazes and colors for which their products became widely known, worked the clays, and operated the potter's wheel. Elizabeth is described as being tidy and cheerful. A teacher and scholarly lecturer, she was offered the opportunity to establish a school of ceramics at Indiana University in Bloomington, but she declined, preferring the home studio setting. Mary, having studied under Margaret for her early training, was a potter, designer, and decorator for the family operation, and she assisted Elizabeth with the firings. For a time, Mary taught in Boulder, Colorado, as well as in her hometown and in nearby Centerville. She studied under Marshall Fry and, with Margaret, spent the summer of 1905 at Ipswich, Massachusetts, studying under Arthur Dow of Columbia University. Unfortunately, Margaret never got to reap the rewards of the art pottery studio. The head injury she suffered four years before may have contributed to her untimely death, at home, at age forty-eight.

The sisters united their efforts toward a common goal to achieve quality in technical and aesthetic aspects, not quantity. Their philosophy was "borrowed art is dead art." Originality and experimentation were emphasized. The Overbecks adhered to the ideals of the American Arts and Crafts movement: objects must be at once simple, beautiful, functional, and handwrought. Overbeck art pottery is characterized by highly stylized motifs drawn from nature. Hannah's designs were largely floral, while Mary used geometric animals, birds, and human figures. They used the techniques of glaze inlay, incising, and carving to decorate their pieces; a conjoined OBK cipher was used to mark their works. Their glazes (ranging from the early soft matt to the later bright gloss) and slips (in colors of grape, hyacinth blue, turquoise, raspberry, green, and earth tones) became their finest developments.

Dr. Kathleen Postle, author of *The Chronicle of the Overbeck Pottery* published by the Indiana Historical Society in 1978, lists the products of their kiln in four categories:

1. The functional or conventional pieces: jars, dinnerware, pitchers, tiles, candlesticks, tea and coffee pots.
2. Representational sculptures: small figurines drawn from real life, from models, or from photographs of both human and animal subjects, such as a Quaker pair, an historical personage, a family group or pet.
3. Grotesques: caricaturized sculptures created with a sense of humor and fantasy, depicting a local personality or well-known figure, or an animal.
4. Vases and bowls: the important pieces made on consignment.

As early as 1914 the three sisters were commissioned to produce two fourteen-inch stoneware trophy vases bearing GFWC in the floral design of the body for the national convention of the General Federation of Women's Clubs in Chicago. Probably designed by Hannah, the vases were made by Elizabeth and decorated by Mary (see Bowman, p. 168, color photo). The following year an eighteen-inch Overbeck earthenware vase of copper brown with panels of a conventionalized nasturtium design in blue-black glaze (now in the Overbeck Museum) was exhibited at the San Francisco Panama-Pacific International Exposition (see Postle, p. 37, pl. 4). In 1917 a large commemorative wall plaque about 18″ × 24″, composed of a dozen ceramic tiles showing a distant village beyond three trees, was commissioned for Joseph Moore School in Richmond, Indiana (now in Richmond schools' administration building).

The peak designing years for Hannah were 1910 through 1916. For the rest of her life she suffered from crippling acute neuritis (inflammation of the nerves), but she continued to design, even from her bed. She filled five notebooks with her designs, which include details of plants and trees from roots and leaves to flowers and seeds, and drawings of insects. Mary also filled two notebooks with designs. This portfolio of motifs was used through the years by the sisters in decorating their art pottery. Well known for the bookplates she designed, Mary also painted in oil and watercolors and did illustrations. Her prizewinning cover designed in 1916 for the program booklet of the Cambridge City Helen Hunt Club (a GFWC club) is still in use for the club's annual book. Mary, said by her nephew to be the most outgoing of the three sisters, was also probably the public relations person, since Hannah was disabled and Elizabeth was intent on her technical work. As the Overbecks' fame increased, pilgrimages were made to the family home by many art groups, who were always graciously received. In the early 1920s summer classes for small groups were held in the home studio.

The sisters' collections won many prizes in Indianapolis during the 1910s and 1920s at the annual John Herron Art Institute exhibitions. The Art Association of Indianapolis notes in its February 1918 *Bulletin* that it had acquired six pieces: a large jar with handles, a tall vase, a large bowl, two smaller vases, and a small jar. In 1928 the Overbeck multipiece collection won first prize at John Herron. One hundred and fifty-two ceramic favors were created for the state convention of the Altrusa Clubs in the fall of 1929. During the 1930s their pottery took many prizes in the Applied Arts Division of the Indiana State Fair. Their thirty-piece tea set with glossy oyster glaze and black matt handles won first place in the Fine Arts Division of the 1933 Century of Progress Exhibition in Chicago (see Postle, p. 40, pl. 7).

After Hannah's death at age sixty-one at home, Elizabeth and Mary were commissioned to produce a pair of large sixteen-inch vases that stand on black matt bases and are topped by hand-molded black matt horse finials, making the overall height twenty-three inches and the diameter eight inches. The vases (now in the Overbeck museum) have a deep turquoise glaze over a white porcelain-like body, with carved horses and geometrical lines of turquoise (see Postle, p. 80, fig. 35). These were early products of the Public Works of Art Project (PWAP) of the federal government, which supplemented the income of artists across the nation during the Great Depression. Another PWAP commission consists of five round, colorful tiles about seven inches in diameter depicting children with a teacher and at play. These tiles were set in the wall of the first-grade room during construction of the Central Elementary School in 1935 in Cambridge City. (The building was sold, so the tiles were removed in the summer of 1995 to be placed in a new elementary school building.)

Production and recognition peaked in the late 1920s and early 1930s before Elizabeth died at home at age sixty-one. She had been named a fellow of the American Ceramic Society eight months before her death and was a member of the Helen Hunt Club for forty-two years as well as a member of the Cincinnati Woman's Art Club. Upon her death it was remarked that "the real light of the household has gone out." Postle writes that Elizabeth brought more recognition to their art pottery than did her sisters.

Mary worked alone for eighteen years. Her later clay work was mostly small, sturdy ceramic figurines and pins, hand-built and hand-decorated. The 1943 Ceramic Trade Directory lists her production at 600 pieces annually. Mary's death at home at age seventy-seven brought an end to the creation of purely American Arts and Crafts pottery by this exceptional family of women artists. The year before she died, Mary was honored for being a 45-year member of the Helen Hunt Club. During their lives, the sisters' involvement in the creative arts was constant. Described as charming but modest and retiring, none of the four married.

During a 43-year period the Overbeck Pottery Studio, altogether a women's enterprise, produced literally thousands of unique artworks for buyers all across the nation. Most pieces were sold from the sisters' home or from the L. S. Ayres department store in Indianapolis. In his foreword to Postle's book, noted art pottery author Paul Evans writes, "What is evident in the Overbecks' pottery is a respect for the material they used and the integrity of the designs they employed. The two blended to form a unique, artistic object which reflects [the Overbecks'] skill and artistic ideals, an achievement which has earned for them an important place in the art history of the United States."

Their many first-place awards for china painting designs in *Keramic Studio Magazine* and for artworks in exhibitions around the United States, including San Francisco, Chicago, and Syracuse, New York, during the 1920s and 1930s verify that the talents of Margaret, Hannah, Elizabeth, and Mary were highly regarded during their lifetimes.

The resurgence of interest in the American Arts and Crafts movement beginning in the 1980s brought a growing appreciation of the Overbeck works of art by art galleries, museums, art auction houses, and collectors all across the nation. Compared with the output of commercial potteries of the time (such as Rookwood, Grueby, and Newcomb) Overbeck pottery, because of its indigenous uniqueness and limited production, became highly desirable and increasingly valuable. In assessments of the American Arts and Crafts movement the Overbeck sisters are counted among the most gifted craftspersons, such as the Stickleys, the Roycrofters, Louis Comfort Tiffany, and Frank Lloyd Wright. Their extraordinary works of art will continue to be appreciated by future generations.

• The Overbeck Museum, established in the Cambridge City public library in 1972 by Arthur and Kathleen Postle, has a comprehensive collection of the Overbecks' art pottery and artworks, including oil paintings, fabrics, lace, metalwork, and jewelry, plus ribbons and awards. Other collections of the art pottery are maintained at the Indianapolis Museum of Art, the Wayne County Historical Museum in Richmond, the Richmond Art Museum, Ball State University's Art Gallery in Muncie, and the American Ceramic Society, Columbus, Ohio. In 1976 the Overbeck family home (restored by Jerry and Phyllis Mattheis as their private residence) was listed on the National Register of Historic Places. Kathleen R. Postle, *The Chronicle of the Overbeck Pottery* (1978), is the definitive source of basic information concerning the Overbecks and their work; it includes a complete listing of contributions to *Keramic Studio Magazine* (1903–1916) and a comprehensive bibliography. See also Paul Evans, *Art Pottery of the United States* (1974); Elisabeth Cameron, *The Encyclopedia of Pottery and Porcelain, 1800–1960* (1986), pp. 252–53; Don Johnson, "Overbeck Pottery," *Today's Collector*, Oct. 1994, pp. 1, 42–47; Richard Zakin, "The Overbeck Studio," *Ceramics Monthly*, Summer 1994, pp. 48–51. With regard to the Overbecks' place within the Arts and Crafts movement, see Wendy Kaplan, *"The Art That Is Life": The Arts and Crafts Movement in America, 1875–1920* (1987); Ted M. Volpe and Beth Cathers, *Treasures of the American Arts and Crafts Movement, 1890–1920* (1988); and Leslie Greene Bowman, *American Arts and Crafts: Virtue in Design* (1990). For information on the Overbecks within the context of their state, see Mary

Q. Burnet, *Art and Artists of Indiana* (1921), and Esther Griffin White, *Indiana Bookplates* (1910), with the artists' early biographies included in the appendix.

PHYLLIS (RESH) MATTHEIS

OVERMAN, Lee Slater (3 Jan. 1854–12 Dec. 1930), lawyer and senator from North Carolina, was born in Salisbury, North Carolina, the son of William Overman, a wealthy cotton merchant and mill owner, and Mary Slater. He attended Trinity University (now Duke University), where he received a B.A. in 1874. Then the young, ambitious North Carolina patrician taught school, read for the bar, and entered politics. Overman attached himself to Zebulon Baird Vance, one of the state's leading opponents of Reconstruction, and became his private secretary when Vance was elected governor in 1876. In 1879, when Vance went to the U.S. Senate, Overman moved on to the senator's successor, Thomas J. Jarvis. In 1878 he had married Mary Marrimon; they had five children.

Although Overman, like many of his peers, favored regional industrial development, he did not always support the New South, free-swinging entrepreneurship of the post-Reconstruction era. He favored government regulation in the public interest, and while he did introduce a plan to privatize the management of state-owned railroads into the legislature, he also proposed that they be placed under a regulating commission. Although, perhaps through the influence of his wife, he became a prohibitionist, he generally conformed to the views of his social circle and those of the moderate wing of his party. Gradually rising in North Carolina Democratic politics, he served in the state house of representatives from 1883 through 1899 and was elected Speaker in 1893. He lost out on his first try for the Senate in 1895 against the Populist candidate, Jeter C. Pritchard, but succeeded him when the Republican-Populist fusion movement splintered at the turn of the century in a battle over the place of African Americans in North Carolina society. Overman, who had always supported racial segregation and African-American disfranchisement, entered the U.S. Senate in 1903.

In the Senate Overman's social attitudes continued to be representative of his section, but his economic positions seemed to make him something of a progressive. He supported government regulation of corporate interests and labor reform. Despite his large interests in the North Carolina textile industry with its traditional protectionist attitude toward the home market, he favored downward revision of the tariff and encouraged the expansion of American overseas trade. After the election of 1912, he became a firm supporter of President Woodrow Wilson and his "New Freedom" program to unseat "monopoly capitalism" and restore competition. As chairman of the powerful Rules Committee and as a ranking member of the Judiciary and Appropriations committees, Overman advocated banking and currency reform and promoted the passage of the Federal Reserve Act of 1913. Not unfriendly to white working people, in the same year he backed the establishment of an independent Department of Labor and in 1914 helped lead the Senate fight to pass the Clayton Anti-Trust Act.

Foreign affairs were never among Senator Overman's primary concerns. From 1914 to 1917 he followed President Wilson's lead. He was not in the forefront of the fight for preparedness, but he did support the legislative compromises that resulted in the National Defense Act of 1916. He voted for the war resolution, which passed the Senate on 4 April 1917, and steadily supported the administration during the conflict. In February 1917, when for several weeks it seemed that control of the war effort might be wrested from the president's hands by insurgent Democrats led by George E. Chamberlain, Overman introduced legislation, drafted in the War Department, to strengthen executive control. Known as the Overman Act, it was enacted into law on 20 May 1918 and authorized President Wilson to coordinate or consolidate executive offices in any way necessary to win the war. Although often cited as an important piece of war legislation, it was really significant only in that it legalized measures the Wilson administration had been pressing forward since January 1918.

After the war the senator was active in the investigation of German and Bolshevik propaganda and played a role in bringing on the so-called Red Scare that plagued American politics in 1919 and 1920. He was also one of the group of Democrats led by Senator Gilbert M. Hitchcock of Nebraska who would not break ranks and loyally supported President Wilson through the fight over the League of Nations and the Treaty of Versailles. Overman thus shared some responsibility for the failure to accept even the mild reservations that might have brought the Senate to consent to the treaty.

Reelected in 1920 and again in 1926, Overman was a fixed star in the firmament of North Carolina Democratic politics. With his silvery locks, dignified carriage, and characteristic accent, he was described by several observers as a representative southern politician of his day. He served his state and its traditional social order until his death at home in Salisbury two years into his fifth term in the U.S. Senate.

• The most significant collection of Overman papers is at the Duke University Library in Durham, N.C. C. Van Woodward, *The Origins of the New South 1877–1913* (1951), is still the single best history of the region between the end of the Civil War and the beginning of the Great War. For Overman's career during those years, the best source is Arthur S. Link, *Woodrow Wilson and the Progressive Era 1910–1917* (1954). For background to the Overman Act and the senator's wartime and immediate postwar activities, see Daniel R. Beaver, *Newton D. Baker and the American War Effort 1917–1919* (1966), David A. Lockmiller, *Enoch H. Crowder: Soldier, Lawyer and Statesman* (1955), Seward W. Livermore, *Politics Is Adjourned: Woodrow Wilson and the War Congress* (1966), and Robert K. Murray, *Red Scare: A Study in National Hysteria 1919–1920* (1955). An obituary is in the *New York Times*, 14 Dec. 1930.

DANIEL R. BEAVER

OVERTON, John (9 Apr. 1766–12 Apr. 1833), attorney, judge, and politician, was born in Louisa County, Virginia, the son of James Overton, a small planter, and Mary Waller. At age twenty-one he migrated to Mercer County, Kentucky, and read law for two years before taking up practice in Nashville on the raw Tennessee frontier. From a few rows of crude cabins on the Cumberland River, the town's population exploded to nearly 6,000 during Overton's lifetime. Upon his arrival, he took up residence in a boardinghouse run by the widow of Colonel John Donelson, a woman of considerable property. By a twist of fortune, one of his fellow boarders was another struggling lawyer, the young Andrew Jackson. Thus began a lifelong friendship and political association that advanced both men beyond what either might have achieved alone.

Overton and Jackson both made a fortune in land speculation, the most direct way to fast wealth in the trans-Appalachian West. To that end they forged a business partnership in May 1794, agreeing to share equally in any profits or losses from their investments. Within a year they controlled some 50,000 undeveloped acres, including 5,000 acres on a fortuitously located bluff overlooking the Mississippi River—the future site of Memphis, purchased in 1794 for just $500. Much of their speculation involved lands still in the hands of native tribes. Believing that being truthful is good business, Overton advised his sometimes impulsive partner to be "candid and unreserved" with purchasers, to hide nothing "with respect to the Situation and quality of the Land" (*Papers of Andrew Jackson*, vol. 1, p. 54). Well-timed transactions eventually made Overton one of the richest men in Tennessee, with enough capital to conduct a banking enterprise in addition to a law practice and a vast cotton plantation, "Traveller's Rest," a 2,300-acre estate six miles south of Nashville. While serving as a watering hole for prominent men—among them Sam Houston, John Eaton, and Jackson—the Overton property featured a cotton gin for service to neighboring planters, extensive orchards, a fruit tree nursery, large flocks of sheep as a local source of raw wool, and a fledgling vineyard.

Contempt for enemies and devotion to friends were two of Overton's more salient character traits, probably reflecting his rough-and-tumble environment. The world, as he saw it, was divided between decent and loathsome people. "It too frequently happens," he declared to Jackson in 1806, "that the honest, unsuspecting part of society will be infested with reptiles, the heads of which must be sought after and bruised so as to be secure from their poison" (*Papers of Andrew Jackson*, vol. 2, p. 100). In that battle, he regarded "Old Hickory" as the premier champion. Overton by nature was less hotheaded than his famous cohort, preferring to take the high road in disputes, and he implored Jackson to avoid settling quarrels by the manly art of dueling: "No man . . . doubts your personal courage and you would gain more by not noticing any thing that these people may say, than otherwise" (*Papers of Andrew Jackson*, vol. 2, p. 109).

Beyond his private legal practice, the bulk of which was land litigation, Overton moved steadily through a series of bureaucratic and judicial appointments. From 1795 to 1804 he served as the supervisor of federal revenue collections for the Tennessee district. In 1804 he replaced Jackson on the Superior Court of Tennessee, keeping that seat until George Campbell's resignation in November 1811 created a place for him, by legislative appointment, on the Tennessee Supreme Court, at a hefty salary of $1,500 annually. Though prestigious, the Tennessee high court post was burdensome. The court's two judges rode a circuit that included sittings in Clarksville, Nashville, Carthage, Knoxville, and Jonesboro. Opinions had to be given in writing. On the road much of the time—over 1,500 miles a year by Overton's estimate—it is no mystery that Overton chose bachelorhood during his days on the bench. Drawing on his own business experience, he frequently adjudicated cases involving property disputes and helped write a number of land statutes that emerged from the state legislature during the period. In 1813 and 1817 he published *Tennessee Reports*, two volumes covering cases tried from 1791 to 1816. These compilations represented the first formal record of state decisions, freeing Tennessee attorneys and judges from exclusive reliance on English and North Carolina court precedents. He retired from the court in 1816.

Always politically active, Overton's involvement intensified in the years following the panic of 1819. As in other western states, the crisis brought urgent appeals for debtor relief. The Tennessee legislature responded with a state loan office, which was authorized to issue fresh notes for payment of creditors. This inflationary expedient incensed the state banking community, and that included Overton as the head of the Bank of Tennessee in Nashville. He and his political allies—the Blount-Overton faction—deplored the loan office and governmental relief efforts in general as improper state intervention in private enterprise. Along with fellow bankers Hugh Lawson White, Pleasant M. Miller, and William B. Lewis, Overton represented an antigovernment position that foreshadowed some Jacksonian public policies of the 1830s. Even so, the commercial elite in Tennessee was not necessarily opposed to Nicholas Biddle's Bank of the United States prior to 1832, and Overton himself sat on the board of its Nashville branch.

Overton married Mary McConnell White May, the widow of Knoxville physician Francis May, in 1820; they had three children, among whom was John Overton, Jr., who fought for the Confederacy during the Civil War. His wife also had five children from her first marriage.

In 1821 Overton's political clique expanded to a committee of eighteen, the so-called Nashville Junto, whose purpose was to promote Jackson for the presidency. Overton assumed the roles of campaign manager and press agent for "Old Hickory," coordinating with nascent Jackson movements in other states and answering slanderous attacks by political enemies. By 1827 a network of offshoot "Jackson Committees" proliferated throughout the West, each raising money, sponsoring rallies, and distributing appeals to voters. After Jackson's triumph in the election of 1828, Overton declined a personal share of the spoils of victory; advancing age and failing eyesight now restricted his activities. He remained Jackson's confidant, however, and made annual trips to visit the president in Washington—an exhausting twenty-day trip by river and over land. Little over a month after his old friend's second inauguration, Overton died peacefully at Traveller's Rest.

• The Overton papers are at the Tennessee Historical Society in Nashville. The Tennessee State Library and Archives holds some Overton letter books and family materials. A little of his correspondence is published in Fletch Coke, ed., *Dear Judge: Selected Letters of John Overton of Traveller's Rest* (1978). Although Overton deliberately burned much of his correspondence with Jackson, the development of their friendship remains visible in the multivolume *The Papers of Andrew Jackson*, ed. Sam B. Smith et al. (1980–). On Overton's Tennessee milieu, Thomas P. Abernethy, *From Frontier to Plantation in Tennessee* (1932), remains useful. For his contributions to Jackson politically, see Robert V. Remini, *Andrew Jackson and the Course of American Freedom, 1822–1832* (1981). An obituary is in the *Nashville Republican and State Gazette*, 17 Apr. 1833.

JOHN R. VAN ATTA

OVINGTON, Mary White (11 Apr. 1865–15 July 1951), civil rights reformer and a founder of the National Association for the Advancement of Colored People (NAACP), was born in Brooklyn, New York, the daughter of Theodore Tweedy Ovington, a china and glass importer, and Ann Louise Ketcham. Mary attended a Unitarian church, where the minister's abolitionist sermons strengthened views she had acquired from her family. She valued heroism above all else, especially that of slaves who had escaped to freedom.

Ovington attended Packer Collegiate Institute from 1888 until 1891, when she entered Radcliffe College. In 1893, after an economic depression detrimentally affected her father's business, Ovington left school and became the registrar of the Pratt Institute in Brooklyn. Visiting a model tenement in New York City, she realized the depth of poverty among working-class immigrants and accepted an offer to open a settlement there, which became the Greenpoint Settlement of the Pratt Institute Neighborhood Association. Although the settlement program grew under Ovington's leadership as head resident, she remained dissatisfied with the results. Upon her resignation in 1903, she felt little was being done to benefit the elderly, to educate the youth, or to provide intellectual stimulation.

Her experiences at Greenpoint, however, were not wasted. Ovington made contacts with other reformers and worked to improve conditions for workers, joining organizations such as the Brooklyn Consumers' League to fight for better wages and hours for retail clerks. At the Social Reform Club she lobbied for legislation and reforms for workers. Although she did not officially join the Socialist party until 1905, she took an active interest in socialism and wrote that it "taught" her "to look below the surface of a problem to the cause." In her work at Greenpoint she discovered that racial prejudice was very much alive, and a presentation at the club by Booker T. Washington revealed the extent of that prejudice. Washington spoke of how blacks in the North faced discrimination, were unemployed, and lived in poverty. His speech set the course for Ovington's future. She decided not to marry and to open a black settlement.

In 1903 Ovington contracted typhoid fever. After a year-long recovery she began in earnest to raise interest in her idea for the black settlement. Advised by friends and associates to learn more about African Americans before tackling their problems, she started research on blacks in New York City, receiving a fellowship from the Greenwich House for the study. Her extensive research taught her much about the problems of African Americans and their struggles against both prejudice and poverty. She corresponded with and asked the advice of W. E. B. Du Bois, a prominent black leader whom she met in 1904, and she worked with the National League for the Protection of Colored Women and the Committee for Improving the Industrial Condition of Negroes.

In 1906, on assignment for the *New York Evening Post*, she attended the meeting of the Niagara Movement, an organization advocating a radical approach for full citizenship of African Americans as well as woman suffrage and freedom of speech. There she again met Du Bois; their meeting reinforced a growing friendship. In 1908 Ovington became the only white woman living in Manhattan's Tuskegee Apartments, where she hoped to start her settlement. Enriched by people who respected her as much as she respected them, Ovington reluctantly left after eight months, unable to obtain financial support for a settlement, or for herself. A short time later, when a friend opened the Lincoln Settlement for blacks, Ovington was asked to help. While her research kept her from being at the settlement daily, she managed to put together a program to assist with neighborhood problems. Her studies on blacks eventually resulted in the 1911 publication of *Half a Man: The Status of the Negro in New York*, which explored the problems of blacks in housing and employment. In her book she called for racial tolerance and justice.

After reading a newspaper article on race riots in Springfield, Illinois, in 1908 Ovington wrote to the author, William English Walling. Her letter resulted in meeting Walling and the formation of a small committee. In early 1909 the committee placed a newspaper advertisement inviting others to the National Conference on the Negro to form a National Negro Committee. The advertisement, titled "The Call," was signed by fifty-three people, both black and white, most of whom Ovington had contacted. The resulting conference was well attended. A second meeting established the NAACP whose objectives were to uphold the freedoms that the African American had won through constitutional amendments and to "defend him against race prejudice."

Ovington served as acting executive secretary of the NAACP board from 1910 to 1911. She served in various board positions, including acting chair from 1917 to 1919, and she was chair of the NAACP board from 1919 until 1932, when she resigned to become treasurer. Ovington remained with the NAACP for nearly forty years, helping to keep the organization intact through her ability to mediate differences and serve as a buffer between a sometimes difficult Du Bois, who initially joined as director of publicity and research, and other members. In all capacities she endeavored to fight against discrimination through her efforts to create an organization, raise money, expand the NAACP throughout the country, and keep all races working together by formulating policy. She was never paid for her work except for a small stipend she received while hospitalized in the 1940s.

As a feminist she attempted unsuccessfully during her tenure to secure voting rights for black women. Fruitless efforts to get antilynching bills passed led Ovington to a new course of action at the NAACP: to get matching federal aid for black and white schools. Although it meant a falling out with Du Bois, she kept her stance that integration should be the NAACP's key directive when Du Bois asked for black participation in a program of voluntary segregation in 1934. She refused to support radical economic plans by the Committee on Future Plan and Program, arguing that it would lessen the NAACP's support among the black middle class.

Ovington retired from the NAACP in 1947 and died four years later in Newton Highlands, Massachusetts. She believed wholeheartedly in the work done by the NAACP and that it was "functioning for those eternal rights of liberty and opportunity and equality that make men great." She brought blacks to prominent board positions but felt disappointed that when she retired total integration had not been achieved. Unbiased, never self-absorbed, she worked behind the scenes, always downplaying her involvement. Her greatest abilities were in bringing varying personalities and temperaments together—no matter what their race, class, or gender—into a network building toward integration and tolerance for one another.

• The Mary White Ovington Papers are located in the Archives of Labor History and Urban Affairs, Wayne State University, Detroit, Mich. Papers of the NAACP are located at the Library of Congress. Ovington's own recollections are in *The Walls Came Tumbling Down* (repr. 1969); and Ralph E. Luker, ed., *Black and White Sat Down Together: The Reminiscences of an NAACP Founder* (1995). In addition to *Half a Man*, Ovington wrote *Hazel* (1913) and *Zeke: A Schoolboy at Tolliver* (1931), novels for children; *The Upward Path: A Reader for Colored Children*, with Myron Thomas Pritchard (1920); *The Shadow* (1920), a novel for adults; *The Awakening* (1923); *Portraits in Color* (1927); and *Phillis Wheatley: A Play* (1932). Her short story "White Brute" is in the *Masses*,

Oct.–Nov. 1915, pp. 17–18. Her magazine articles include "The Status of the Negro in the United States," *New Review*, Sept. 1913, pp. 744–49; "Socialism and the Feminist Movement," *New Review*, Mar. 1914, pp. 143–47; and "The United States in Porto Rico," *New Republic*, 8 July 1916, pp. 244–46, and 15 July 1916, pp. 271–73. Also helpful are B. Joyce Ross, *J. E. Spingarn and the Rise of the NAACP, 1911–1939* (1972), and a biography by Daniel W. Cryer, "Mary White Ovington and the Rise of the NAACP" (Ph.D. diss., Univ. of Minnesota, 1977). Ovington's obituary is in the *New York Times*, 16 July 1951.

MARILYN ELIZABETH PERRY

OWEN, Chandler (5 Apr. 1889–2 Nov. 1967), journalist and politician, was born in Warrenton, North Carolina; his parents' names and occupations are unknown. He graduated in 1913 from Virginia Union University in Richmond, a school that taught its students to think of themselves as men, not as black men or as former slaves. Migrating to the North, where he lived for the remainder of his life, Owen enrolled in Columbia University and the New York School of Philanthropy, receiving one of the National Urban League's first social work fellowships. In 1915 he met another southern transplant, A. Philip Randolph, with whom he formed a lifelong friendship. The pair studied sociology and Marx, listened to streetcorner orators, and joined the Socialist party, working for Morris Hillquit's campaign for mayor of New York City in 1917. Concerned about the exploitation of black workers, Owen and Randolph opened a short-lived employment agency and edited a newsletter for hotel workers, which was the predecessor for their later Marxist-oriented monthly magazine, the *Messenger*, which they edited from 1917 to 1928.

World War I and the postwar red scare propelled Owen into the most significant years of his life. During this period he had his most significant influence on black affairs and was at his most influential in attracting white attention to black issues. He and Randolph believed that capitalists had caused the war and that the working masses of all nations, including African Americans, were being sacrificed for purposes that would bring them no benefit. They admired the Russian revolution and therefore exempted Russia from their censure. The first issue of the *Messenger* in 1917 expressed these themes and the view, shared by many blacks, that World War I was a "white man's war." Subsequent articles argued that blacks could hardly be expected to support a war to "make the world safe for democracy" when they suffered lynching and discrimination. An article in the July 1918 *Messenger* entitled "Pro Germanism Among Negroes" prompted the post office department to cancel the magazine's second class mailing permit, and for the remainder of the war Owen and Randolph printed their most radical essays in pamphlet form. Both men declared themselves conscientious objectors. Randolph escaped military service because he was married, but Owen was inducted in late 1918 and served to the end of the war.

The Department of Justice and army intelligence watched Owen and Randolph closely. They were charged with treason in the summer of 1918 for allegedly impeding the war effort, but the judge dismissed the charges, refusing to believe the two young African Americans were capable of writing the socialist and antiwar essays offered as evidence. During the rest of the war, and throughout the red scare, the Justice Department's Bureau of Investigation (later renamed the Federal Bureau of Investigation) monitored Owen and Randolph's activities and writings, burglarized their offices, and unsuccessfully sought their prosecution. J. Edgar Hoover, head of the Justice Department's antiradical campaign, charged that Owen and Randolph's *Messenger* was "the most dangerous Negro magazine" and the worst example of black radicalism. Hoover and other guardians of the racial status quo objected particularly to its admiration for Russian bolshevism, enthusiasm for the Industrial Workers of the World, legitimization of armed self defense against lynchers and rioters, and demand for social equality between the races. Hoover hoped to prosecute Owen and Randolph in 1919, using the wartime Espionage Act, but was thwarted when federal attorneys argued that a jury was unlikely to convict them.

Surveillance of Owen and Randolph by infiltrators and the bureau's first black agents continued into the 1920s. The pair coined the term "New Crowd Negroes" to describe their own generation, which rejected not only the racial accommodationism once promoted by Booker T. Washington, but also the leadership of W. E. B. Du Bois, whom they considered to be insufficiently militant. They continued to promote the Socialist party, Owen running unsuccessfully for the New York state assembly in 1920. The post office refused to restore the magazine's second-class rate until 1921, when the *Messenger* resumed full publication, devoting much of its energy to the campaign against the West Indian Pan-Africanist Marcus Garvey. Owen and Randolph were totally opposed to Garvey's rejection of a future in the United States for blacks; they believed that integration and full civil rights should be the goals for all American blacks. In January 1923 Owen wrote a controversial public letter to Attorney General Harry M. Daugherty, signed by seven other prominent blacks, urging the government to speed up its prosecution of Garvey, charging him with worsening race relations and encouraging violence against his opponents.

After the red scare (1919–1920) Owen became disillusioned with socialism, moved to Chicago in 1923, and for a time was managing editor of the *Chicago Bee*, a black newspaper that supported Randolph's efforts to organize a Pullman porter's union. Changing his political course, Owen joined the Republican party and ran unsuccessfully for the House of Representatives in 1928. For the rest of his life he worked in journalism and public relations, for a number of years writing a column for the *Chicago Daily News*. During World War II Owen wrote a patriotic government pamphlet, *Negroes and the War* (1942), five million copies of which were distributed to civilians and soldiers. He wrote speeches for presidential candidates

Wendell Willkie and Thomas Dewey and campaigned for Dwight Eisenhower in 1952. Owen's longstanding Republicanism was only interrupted in 1964 when he felt he could not support Barry Goldwater and instead backed Lyndon Johnson. Never married, he died in Chicago.

During Chandler Owen's most powerful years, from 1917 to 1923, he was a witty, iconoclastic, knowledgeable, and persuasive speaker whose *Messenger* editorials likewise exposed racism and dissected the defects in American society. With A. Philip Randolph, he helped define black militancy for their generation. After the mid-1920s Owen's racial influence declined. Some friends admired his journalism and oratory, while others disdained him as an influence peddler who played the role of "Negro spokesman" for white politicians. In fact, Owen had little impact on the black community after World War II.

• There is neither a full biography of Owen nor a significant extant body of his personal papers. Theodore Kornweibel, Jr., *No Crystal Stair: Black Life and the Messenger, 1917–1928* (1975), charts his most productive years and makes use of interviews with several of Owen's contemporaries. The same author's *Federal Injustice: The Red Scare Campaigns Against Black Militancy, 1918–1925* (1995) uses FBI and other federal records to detail Owen's militancy. Also see Jervis Anderson, *A. Philip Randolph: A Biographical Portrait* (1972) and Theodore Kornweibel, Jr., ed., "Federal Surveillance of Afro-Americans (1917–1925): The First World War, the Red Scare, and the Garvey Movement" (1986), a 25-reel microfilm collection containing dozens of FBI documents on Owen.

THEODORE KORNWEIBEL, JR.

OWEN, David Dale (24 June 1807–13 Nov. 1860), geologist, was born at Braxfield House, on the upper Clyde, in New Lanark, Scotland, the son of Robert Owen, an industrialist, philanthropist, and social reformer, and Anne Caroline Dale, the daughter of David Dale, Glasgow's former Lord Provost. Advised by his father to study chemistry for its usefulness in science and in "the arts, and manufactures," David Dale Owen followed the educational paths of his elder brothers Robert Dale and William. Dale, as he was commonly known, passed from private tutors to the Lanark Academy and then, with his younger brother Richard, to Philipp Emanuel von Fellenberg's "progressive" school at Hofwyl, near Bern, Switzerland. During the three years the two younger Owens spent at Hofwyl (1824–1826) and with chemist Andrew Ure at Glasgow's Andersonian Institution (1826–1827), their father purchased "Harmonie on the Wabash" from Indiana's Harmonie Society community. Robert Owen, in partnership with geologist-philanthropist William Maclure of Philadelphia, tried but failed to create a second communal utopia at "New Harmony" through "moral science," useful education, and industry. David and Richard Owen reached New Harmony in January 1828, eight months after their father and Maclure had divided their property and left the town. Owen and Maclure's social, economic, and scientific experiment continued in their absence. Their libraries remained in New Harmony with Owen's sons while Thomas Say and Charles-Alexandre Lesueur continued as the town's principal naturalists.

The lack of work for a practicing chemist in New Harmony led David Dale Owen to pursue greater skills in art, printing, and natural history. In 1830 Owen left the village's print shop for New York City, where his brother Robert Dale and Frances Wright edited the *Free Enquirer*. There, Owen met Henry Darwin Rogers, geologist and formerly professor of chemistry at Dickinson College. Owen and Rogers sailed in 1831 for England, where they resided with Owen's parents in London. Owen attended Edward Turner's chemistry lectures and studied geology at London University and met Charles Lyell and other members of the city's Geological Society. Returning in 1833 to New Harmony, Owen established a laboratory and museum for research and teaching in chemistry and geology. In 1835 Owen enrolled at Cincinnati's Ohio Medical College, whose faculty included John Locke, a chemist-geologist trained at Yale by Benjamin Silliman. Owen spent part of 1836 aiding former New Harmonist Gerard Troost's geological survey for the state of Tennessee.

In March 1837 Owen, now an M.D., married Caroline Charlotte Neef, the daughter of Maclure's protégé Francis Joseph Nicholas Neef, a principal Pestalozzian teacher at New Harmony; they would have four children. In the same month, Owen began a career as a government-sponsored geologist. Seeking internal improvements and economic development, Indiana joined the twelve other state governments that founded geological surveys earlier in the boom years of the 1830s. Also in 1837, Indiana's governor appointed Owen state geologist at the urging of state legislator and fellow Democrat Robert Dale Owen and George William Featherstonhaugh, the Army Topographical Bureau's U.S. geologist. Owen completed two years' work, identifying and mapping the state's coal and other mineral resources, before resigning to accept federal employment with the Treasury Department's General Land Office (GLO).

Early in February 1839 Congress renewed its request to the executive branch for "a plan for the sale of the public mineral lands" and authorized surveys to gather information about "their location, value, productiveness, and occupancy" (U.S. Congress, 25th, 3d session, *Congressional Globe* 7, p. 175) in order to end misappropriation of and restore revenues from the Midwest's lead and other ore deposits. Fellow Hoosier and Democrat James Whitcomb, GLO's commissioner, asked Owen to map and assess quickly the geology, minerals, soils, and timber of some 11,000 square miles in the Dubuque and Mineral Point Land Districts in adjacent parts of Iowa, Wisconsin, and Illinois. Principal Assistant Owen, his deputy Locke, and the 139 aides they trained at New Harmony, between September 1839 and April 1840 completed field work, maps, and a text report, a volume that Congress reissued in 1844 with Owen's 1:344,000-scale map of the districts. In the 1840s Owen also arranged the mineral and fossil collections William Maclure had gathered and used principally to map the geology of the United States, served as secretary to the American Association of Geologists and Naturalists, and hosted Lyell's visit to New Harmony. During his four-year term in Congress, Robert Dale Owen introduced the legislation that established the Smithsonian Institution in 1846 and promoted David Dale Owen's ideas about the design of and materials for the Smithsonian's "castle" building.

In March 1847 Congress established the Chippewa and Lake Superior Land Districts for lands purchased from native peoples in the upper Midwest. David Dale Owen's reputation and his elder brother's influence with Robert Montgomery Young, another Democrat serving as GLO commissioner, gained him an appointment as U.S. geologist to survey the Chippewa lands, located in Wisconsin and Iowa north of those he had examined in 1839. During 1847–1852 Owen, his chief assistant Joseph Granville Norwood, and their new 26-person team mapped, evaluated, and reported on the district's 46,000 square miles (at a scale of 1:625,000) and additional parts of adjacent Minnesota and Iowa, as well as the Nebraska Territory flanking the Missouri and White rivers (at 1:1,225,000 overall). Owen then was named the state geologist of Kentucky (1854), Arkansas (1857), and Indiana (1859), although his brother Richard actually did most of the work in their home state. In 1860 Owen's new (and fourth) laboratory at New Harmony, whose construction cost him $10,000, replaced the long-used facilities in the Harmonist granary-mill. David Dale Owen, aided by his sister Jane Fauntleroy and his eldest son Alfred, completed the Kentucky and Arkansas reports in the new building before succumbing there to malaria, rheumatism, and overwork. He died at New Harmony. In 1862 Richard Owen reported the results of their investigations in Indiana.

In addition to the significant results of his four state surveys, David Dale Owen, "a master of reconnaissance geology" and "an artist of uncommon skill" (Rabbitt, p. 81), and his teams mapped, analyzed, and classified the coals, metal ores, and other resources of more than 200,000 square miles of public lands in the upper Mississippi Valley—"the largest area geologically mapped in detail in the United States before the 1870s" (Nelson in Patton, p. 232). The value of Owen's well-organized and mission-oriented work far exceeded Featherstonhaugh's less-focused reconnaissances in the 1830s, fully equaled the results of the best contemporary state surveys, and nearly reached the quality of John Wells Foster, Josiah Dwight Whitney, Locke, and James Hall's survey of the Lake Superior Land District. During these years topographic maps replaced GLO plats or other planimetric bases in Owen's geologic cartography. As his "compass" for mineral-resource evaluations, Owen established by 1842 a preliminary structural and fossil-based stratigraphic framework for the region's Paleozoic rocks and compared the latter with the European and other American usages. Owen's surveys also provided some basic studies in geomagnetism and paleontology, as well as new techniques of illustrating fossils, but units from Hall's "New York" stratigraphic scheme replaced Owen's cautious scheme of nongeographic names and lettered and numbered strata. Most of Owen's federal collections deposited at the Smithsonian and the Maclure-Owen specimens purchased by Indiana University were destroyed by fire.

Among other legacies, Owen thoroughly trained his younger assistants—Norwood, Edward Travers Cox, John Evans, Peter Lesley, Fielding Bradford Meek, Richard Owen, Charles Christopher Parry, and Benjamin Franklin Shumard—in geology, paleontology, and scientific illustration. All these individuals subsequently served with distinction in state and (or) federal surveys.

• Record Group 49 (Bureau of Land Management) at the National Archives and Records Administration's Archives II facility in College Park, Md., contains documents from Owen's GLO reconnaissances. Other manuscript materials are held privately by Owen's descendants in New Harmony and in the archives of the Indiana Commission on Public Records at Indianapolis, Purdue University at Lafayette, and Maclure's Workingmen's Institute at New Harmony. The institute's Owen items include his letters and memoranda of a plan for the Smithsonian and its buildings. *U.S. Geological Survey Bulletins* 30 (1885): 247–51 and 746 (1923): 804–5 list Owen's principal publications; most of these data also are available on CD-ROM as part of the American Geological Institute's "GeoRef" online bibliographical database.

The only major biography is Walter B. Hendrickson, *David Dale Owen: Pioneer Geologist of the Middle West* (1943). Mary C. Rabbitt, *Mineral, Lands, and Geology for the Common Defence and General Welfare*, vol. 1: *Before 1879* (1979), places Owen's work in the context of federally sponsored geology before the Civil War. Additional perspective is provided by Markes E. Johnson, "Geology in American Education: 1825–1860," *Geological Society of American Bulletin* 88 (1987): 1192–98; Herman R. Friis, "The David Dale Owen Map of Southwestern Wisconsin," *Prologue—The Journal of the National Archives* 1 (Spring 1969): 9–28; articles by Anne Millbrooke, Clifford M. Nelson, and John B. Patton in Patton's "The New Harmony Geologic Legacy (Field Trip 11)," in *Field Trips in Midwestern Geology*, vol. 1, ed. Robert H. Shaver and Jack H. Sunderman (1983), pp. 225–43; and Clifford M. Nelson, "Paleontology in the United States Federal Service, 1804–1904," *Earth Sciences History* 1 (1982): 48–57. Also see N. Gary Lane, "New Harmony and Pioneer Geology," *Geotimes* 22, no. 2 (Sept. 1966): 18–20, 22; Henry H. Gray's introduction to and commentary on the reprint (*Indiana Geological Survey Bulletin* 61, 1987) of Owen's 1839 reports of his geological reconnaissance of the state in 1837 and 1838; and the articles in Robert H. Shaver, "Field Guide and Recollections. The David Dale Owen Years to the Present. A Sesquicentennial Commemoration of Service by the Geological Survey," *Indiana Geological Survey Special Report* 44 (1987). Unsigned obituary notices by Owen's contemporaries appeared in 1861 in Owen's *Fourth Report of the Geological Survey of Kentucky, Made during the Years 1858 and 1859* (pp. 323–30) and in the *American Journal of Science and Arts*, 2d ser., 31: 153–55.

CLIFFORD M. NELSON

OWEN, Maribel Yerxa Vinson (12 Oct. 1911–15 Feb. 1961), figure skater and coach, was born in Winchester, Massachusetts, the daughter of Thomas A. Vinson, a lawyer, and Gertrude Cliff. Growing up in a skating family, Maribel seemingly began her life on the ice. Her father had competed in North American skating competitions in the 1890s using the "Old American" style of skating and was a runner-up in international competitions in Canada. He gave Maribel piggyback rides across the ice at the age of two, and she first skated at the age of three at an outdoor rink in Cambridge. Maribel won her first championship at the age of eleven, winning the ladies' singles at the Cambridge Skating Club in Boston. At twelve she won the Junior Nationals held in Philadelphia, Pennsylvania, after being promised a meal of lobster, her favorite food, if she did well. In 1925, at the age of fourteen, Maribel placed third in the National Seniors competition, behind Beatrix Loughran (later Harvey) and Theresa Weld. She shook off this loss, going on to capture nine U.S. ladies' senior singles championships, including six in a row from 1928 to 1933. After graduating cum laude from Radcliffe College in 1933, she returned to the ice to win three more ladies' senior singles titles, holding the championship from 1935 through 1937.

Owen was also a well-known pairs skater. She teamed with Thornton Coolidge to win the 1927 U.S. junior pairs title as well as the 1928 and 1929 U.S. senior pairs titles. Following Coolidge's retirement, Owen competed with George Hill to win the U.S. pairs championship in 1933 and 1935–1937, as well as the 1935 North American pairs title. In international competition, Owen never received the highest honors as a singles skater, however, as she had to compete with the formidable Norwegian skater Sonja Henie. Henie, who had competed in her first Olympics at the age of eleven, performed jumps and spins that most of the other competitors, including Owen, could not match. She did, however, frequently make a run at Henie and always stayed near the top of her field, earning a fourth-place finish at the St. Moritz Olympic Games in 1928.

Owen also won the silver at the World Championships held in London in 1929. King George V and Queen Mary attended a presentation put on by the medal winners following the competition. Because of poor ice conditions, nearly all the skaters fell or simplified their routines in the exhibition. When Owen skated, she brought the capacity crowd to roaring laughter by bowing to the royal guests after falling in front of their ice-side box seats.

Owen won the bronze in the 1930 World Championships and was fourth there in 1931, before winning her last medal, a bronze at the 1932 Winter Games in Lake Placid, New York. She later represented the United States at the 1936 Olympics held in Garmisch, Germany, but did not earn a medal.

In 1937 Owen became a professional skater after receiving numerous monetary offers. One of the best-known skaters of her era, she began a touring ice show called the "Gay Blades," a very successful show that toured famous hotels around the world. It was during this period that she met her future husband, Canadian skating great Guy Owen. The two married in 1938 but were divorced in 1949.

Owen began teaching skating in Berkeley, California, in 1940 after the birth of the first of her two daughters and eventually coached both children to national and international fame. Daughter Maribel paired with Dudley Richards to win the 1961 National Senior Pairs Championship, while daughter Laurence (Laurie) was the North American and U.S. ladies' singles champion in that same year. Owen also coached other internationally known skaters, including 1944 U.S. ladies' singles champion Gretchen Merrill, four-time American pairs title winners Nancy Roulliard and Ronald Ludington, and Tenley Albright, the first American figure skater to win the Olympic Gold Medal. Rouillard and Ludington also went on to win the bronze medals at the 1959 World Championships and at the 1960 Olympic Games. During the mid-1950s Owen returned to Boston. In her coaching career, she found time to teach the fundamentals of figure skating to more than 4,000 pupils, including housewives and businessmen.

In the early 1930s Owen had begun a second career as a writer. She was the first female sportswriter to report for the *New York Times*, writing commentaries and essays on skating competitions beginning in September 1933. She also wrote a weekly column titled, "Women in Sports." Owen used her expert writing ability to author three informative books for the general public: *The Primer of Figure Skating* (1938), *Advanced Figure Skating* (1940), and *The Fun of Figure Skating* (1960).

Owen's life ended in a tragic accident. She, her two daughters, and the entire U.S. skating contingent were killed in a plane accident near Brussels, Belgium, en route to Prague, Czechoslovakia, for the 1961 World Figure Skating Championships, which were canceled on account of the accident. Owen was named to the U.S. Figure Skating Association Hall of Fame in 1976.

• An interview with USFSA research associate Diane Kreider, 11 Jan. 1984, provided extremely useful information. In addition to Owen's own three books already mentioned, other helpful sources are "Maribel Vinson Owen," *Skating*, Apr. 1961; "Maribel Vinson Owen," *Skating*, June 1977; and Bill Mallon and Ian Buchanan, *Quest for Gold: The Encyclopedia of American Olympians* (1984). An obituary, along with other articles about the plane crash, is in the *New York Times*, 16 Feb. 1961.

KURT ZIMMERMAN
SHARON KAY STOLL

OWEN, Robert Dale (9 Nov. 1801–24 June 1877), reformer and congressman, was born in Glasgow, Scotland, the son of Robert Owen, an industrialist and social reformer, and Ann Caroline Dale. Owen's early life was spent in New Lanark, Scotland, where his father managed the textile mills of his maternal grandfather. At the age of thirteen he toured factories that employed child laborers and from eighteen to twenty-two attended a progressive school in Hofwyl, Switzerland. These experiences stirred in him an early interest in social reform and confirmed for him his father's conviction that education offered the potential for overcoming social divisions that were based on class, economic status, and gender. He returned to New Lanark to help teach workers' children and to write *An Outline of the System of Education at New Lanark* (1824).

In 1825 Owen left Scotland for New Harmony, Indiana, the socialist community that his father had founded in 1825 as a utopian experiment. By the time New Harmony collapsed in 1827, Owen had acted as teacher, school superintendent, and editor of the *New Harmony Gazette*, a freethought journal. He had also established a partnership with Frances Wright, another Scottish reformer, who had founded a small community at Nashoba, Tennessee. Nashoba was at first intended to teach slaves who had been bought or donated for the purpose to learn to live in freedom in preparation for settlement in Africa. Wright later saw it as a place where blacks and whites could learn to live together. Owen's somewhat romantic friendship with Wright ended in permanent estrangement in 1836, but in the intervening years Owen participated in Nashoba, traveled to Europe with Wright, and moved with her to New York City in 1829. There he edited the *Free Enquirer*, another freethought periodical that took a stand against organized religion and clergy, and supported a variety of reform movements, primarily on behalf of women and workers. Owen and Wright also opened a Hall of Science, which offered freethought lectures, a library, medical advice, and inexpensive literature for workers. Here he met Mary Jane Robinson, whom he married in 1832; they had six children.

In 1830 Owen published the first birth control tract in America, *Moral Physiology*, an early manifestation of what was to be a continuing concern in his career for women's rights, particularly in the areas of property ownership, suffrage, and more liberal divorce laws. Controversial from their inception, Owen's opinions from his freethought years, particularly those about religion and birth control, would continue to be an issue at various times in his political career, although by the late 1830s he himself espoused more moderate views and described himself as less "ultra in my notions of moral and political reform."

In 1832 Owen left the editorship of the *Free Enquirer*, and after spending six months in Europe, he and his wife returned to New Harmony in 1833 to establish a permanent home. In 1836 he announced his candidacy for the lower house of the Indiana legislature. Elected to three successful terms, he decided to forego a fourth but quickly became the Democratic candidate for the U.S. House of Representatives from the First District, a mostly rural, Whig-dominated constituency. He was defeated but won election to the House in 1843, after having withdrawn from the Senate race in 1842. He made several more attempts to become a U.S. senator but was always disappointed.

The issues that Owen took up during his state and national political careers demonstrate his move from reformer to politician (Leopold [1940], p. 157). As an Indiana legislator, he secured surplus federal funds for public education and worked to increase legal rights for married women, such as control of their own property. In the U.S. House, captured by the growing spirit of expansionism in the West and apparently convinced by fellow westerners in Congress that American democracy offered the optimum form of society, Owen functioned as a proponent of Manifest Destiny in his efforts to bring about the annexation of Oregon and Texas. He introduced the bill that constituted the Smithsonian Institution, chaired its building committee, and worked as a regent, though unsuccessfully, to make its primary mission popular scientific and agricultural education.

Defeat in his race for a third House term, which he attributed to overconfidence, prompted Owen's return to Indiana in 1847. Between then and 1853, when President Franklin Pierce appointed him a diplomat to the Kingdom of the Two Sicilies at Naples, Owen served as trustee of Indiana University and as a prominent member of the Indiana constitutional convention in 1850. There he continued his efforts, again unsuccessfully, to obtain more legal rights for married women. "Women," he said, "want less flattery and more justice." His publications during these years reflected the diversity of his interests and included *Hints on Public Architecture* (1849) and *A Brief Practical Treatise on the Construction and Management of Plank Roads* (1850).

Although Owen had been exposed to spiritualism by his father, he only began to take it seriously in Naples, at the home of the Russian ambassador. Based on a belief that the dead could communicate with the living, the movement emphasized spirit phenomena as a scientific and therefore rational basis for religious belief. Spiritualists were highly optimistic about human nature and progress and were often involved with other reform movements, such as women's rights. While all of these things appealed to Owen, he considered himself a Christian spiritualist, in spite of his former agnosticism, and kept a distance from the more radical factions. In 1860 he published *Footfalls on the Boundary of Another World*, an extensive study of spontaneous rather than evoked spirit phenomena. The sequel, *The Debatable Land Between this World and the Next*, appeared in 1872.

Owen never again held elected public office after he returned to the United States in 1858, but he played several roles, which were national in scope, that related to the Civil War and Reconstruction. An ardent peace advocate who favored compromise over war, he nevertheless accepted in May 1861 the job of ordering war goods for Indiana's troops. In 1861 Secretary of War Edwin M. Stanton appointed Owen ordnance commissioner, and in 1863 he was named chair of the American Freedmen's Inquiry Commission. Owen's final report for the commission, *The Wrong of Slavery*, the *Right of Emancipation, and the Future of the African Race in the United States* (1864), was credited with influencing the establishment of the Freedmen's Bureau.

In the last years of his life, Owen supported himself by writing. One of his most successful efforts was the autobiography of his first twenty-seven years, *Threading My Way* (1874), which was first serialized in the *Atlantic Monthly*. In 1874–1875 he wrote another series for the *Atlantic Monthly* mostly about spiritualism, but its reception was marred by a nationwide scandal—the exposure of a medium, Katie King, whom Owen had endorsed. Owen spent time in an insane asylum in 1875 because of emotional and physical exhaustion although popular accounts attributed this to a loss of religious faith. A widower since 1871, Owen married Lottie Walton Kellogg in 1876 and died a year later at her Lake George home.

Historians tend to divide Owen's life and thought into three periods: the early years as a reformer and freethinker, which were heavily influenced by his father; the middle years that he devoted to Indiana and national politics; and the last twenty years, which were dominated by his involvement in spiritualism. His sympathetic stance toward the rights of women persisted throughout his life, but he was never particularly successful at bringing about legislative changes. His dislike of slavery and concern for blacks was also a constant theme but was manifested in different ways throughout his life: from early sympathy for African colonization, to legislative participation in excluding blacks from Indiana, to the radical support of emancipation and suffrage of his later years. The agnosticism of his young adulthood was eventually replaced by a fervent dedication to spiritualism. Owen's biographer, Richard Leopold, suggests that the mutability of Owen's thoughts and positions may account for the relative historical obscurity of a man who was so prominent in his own era. For religious and social historians, however, Owen's many writings on education, birth control, freethought, women's rights, emancipation, religion (both as an agnostic and as a spiritualist), and the conflict between science and religion, provide insights into the complexities of the issues in which he was involved.

• Owen's papers are held in a variety of places. Richard Leopold, *Robert Dale Owen: A Biography* (1940), a well-documented biography, provides the locations of Owen's papers and a bibliography of books, magazine articles, pamphlets and tracts, reports, poetry, and selected speeches and letters. Elinor Pancoast and Anne E. Lincoln, *The Incorrigible Idealist: Robert Dale Owen in America* (1940), is a briefer, somewhat anecdotal biography. Arthur Bestor, *Backwoods Utopias: The Sectarian Origins and the Owenite Phase of Communitarianism in America, 1663–1829*, rev. ed. (1970), supplies background for understanding the first part of Owen's life and the New Harmony experiment. John G. Sproat, "Blueprint for Radical Reconstruction," *Journal of Southern History* 23 (1957): 25–44, includes Owen's participation in the American Freedmen's Inquiry Commission. Richard Leopold, "The Adventures of a Novice in Research: New Harmony and Indianapolis, 1935," *Indiana Quarterly Magazine of History* 74 (1978): 1–22, provides a more recent perspective on his 1940 biography. See also Howard Kerr, *Mediums and Spirit-Rappers and Roaring Radicals: Spiritualism in American Literature 1850–1900* (1972), pp. 121–54; and Nella Fermi Weiner, "Of Feminism and Birth Control Propaganda (1790–1840)," *International Journal of Women's Studies* 3 (1980): 411–30.

MARY FARRELL BEDNAROWSKI

OWEN, Ruth Bryan. *See* Rohde, Ruth Bryan Owen.

OWEN, Stephen Joseph (21 Apr. 1898–17 May 1964), football player and coach, was born in Cleo Springs, Indian Territory (now Okla.), the son of James Rufus Owen, a farmer, and Isabella Doak, the area's first schoolteacher. Steve Owen, who grew to be nearly six feet in height and 220 pounds by the time he was sixteen years of age, graduated from Aline (Okla.) High School and then enrolled in the Student Army Training Corps (SATC) at Phillips University in Enid, Oklahoma, where he played football. With the end of World War I, Owen continued at Phillips as a regular student and held down a place at tackle on Coach Johnny Maulbetsch's successful football team.

Owen coached for a year at Phillips and worked for a time in the oil fields before joining the Kansas City Cowboys of the infant National Football League (NFL) in the 1924 season. His strength and size—he weighed 240 pounds, which was very heavy for that day—impressed the New York Giants, who purchased Owen's contract from Kansas City for $500. It was an unusually high price for a lineman, Owen recalled, but "I had seen fat hogs go for more than they paid for me. . . . In those days, a fat hog was a lot more valuable than a fat tackle." Owen was a good buy for the Giants, however, for he became a fixture at tackle for several seasons and made unofficial all-league teams in 1926, his first with the Giants, and 1927. He remained in New York in the offseasons to work at a coalyard belonging to Giants' owner Tim Mara. The two often discussed football, and after soliciting Owen's thoughts about a new coach for the 1932 season—the team already had had four coaches since its founding in 1925—Mara surprised Owen and the New York media, who had speculated about what established coach the Giants might hire, by appointing Owen to the vacancy. Owen and Mara finalized the deal by shaking hands, and for nearly twenty-five years a handshake was the only security Owen had as the Giants' head coach.

Owen rewarded Mara's judgment, stressing the basics of blocking and tackling and displaying keen insight in evaluating personnel. Even though the Giants had an indifferent record in his first season at the helm, the team rebuilt quickly to win three consecutive Eastern Division championships, adding to the 1934 divisional title the league championship as well. The 1933 season was the last in which Owen also played. The 1934 title game became memorable when the Giants, claiming the Eastern Division title with an indifferent 8–5 record, faced the juggernaut Chicago

Bears for the league championship. Playing on a frozen field at New York City's Polo Grounds, neither team could do much offensively, but the Bears held a 10–3 lead at halftime. Meanwhile, Owen, responding to a suggestion that sneakers might provide better traction on the frozen turf, had sent a man to try to collect sufficient sneakers for their needs from the locker room of the Manhattan College basketball team. With the sneakers Giants quarterback Ed Danowski and his receivers had the traction to evade the Bears' secondary defenders, and the Giants established a league record by scoring 27 points in the fourth quarter to gain a 30–13 victory.

When the team declined badly in 1936, Owen again revamped the team's personnel and surprised observers by abandoning the conventional single-wing offense for a variant of it that became known as the "A formation." In the A formation the Giants lined up with an unbalanced line and retained the power blocking of the single-wing but could employ more trapping and pulling blocks and provide more options for the backs who took stations behind the weak side of the line. Utilizing the A formation and some talented new personnel, Owen's Giants captured a league championship in 1938, with what he regarded as his best team, and added divisional titles in 1939, 1941, 1944, and 1946. In 1935 Owen married Miriam Virginia Sweeny. The couple had no children.

In 1950 Owen surprised the football world when the Giants faced the highly rated passing attack of the Cleveland Browns, led by star quarterback Otto Graham and several of the NFL's finest receivers. Owen had the Giants line up in a conventional 6–1–4 defense, but as soon as the ball was centered he dropped the two ends back to cover the Browns' outside receivers. During this time coaching staffs were small, and Owen, who did not like to plan the details of a defense, told his players—several of whom, like defensive back Tom Landry, were World War II veterans and hence were unusually mature—to complete the planning and determine individual responsibilities for the linemen and pass defenders. With as many as seven men having coverage responsibilities, the Giants stymied the Browns' great passing attack and earned for the new alignment the name "umbrella defense." Owen had already hired a clever assistant, former quarterback Allie Sherman, to replace the outdated A formation with the T formation, which by 1950 was almost universally used in the NFL. Owen also had acquired good new personnel, including quarterback Charlie Conerly, running backs Kyle Rote and Frank Gifford, and defensive backs Landry and Emlen Tunnell, but was unable to win any more championships.

The Giants slipped in 1952, absorbing the worst defeat in the franchise's history, a 63–7 loss to the Pittsburgh Steelers, while suffering five defeats in a 12-game schedule. Owen's emphasis on defense and a 3–9 record in 1953 left Giants fans disgruntled, and the owners decided to make a coaching change after the season, asking Owen to take a position in the front office. As the Giants' coach he had compiled a lifetime record of 151 wins, 100 losses, and 17 ties, and he had made an enormous contribution to making the Giants a viable enterprise in New York.

Owen wished to be back on the sidelines, however, and in 1955 he left New York to join the coaching staff of Baylor University. In 1956 and 1957 he served as line coach with the Philadelphia Eagles, after which he spent five years coaching for Toronto and Calgary in the Canadian Football League. Owen's final position in football was a scout for the Giants.

Owen died in Oneida, New York. He was posthumously selected to the Professional Football Hall of Fame in 1966, an honor well deserved by a man who had won distinction as a player and who as a coach won six divisional and two league titles.

• A clipping file for Owen is in the Professional Football Hall of Fame, Canton, Ohio. Owen wrote one book, *My Kind of Football*, with Joe King (1952), as well as "I'd Rather Coach Professionals," *Street and Smith's Sport Story Magazine*, Nov. 1940. See also George Sullivan, *Pro Football's All-Time Greats* (1968); Dave Klein, *The New York Giants: Yesterday, Today, Tomorrow* (1973); Jack Hand, *Heroes of the NFL* (1965); Gerald Eskenazi, *There Were Giants in Those Days* (1976); Jordan A. Deutsch et al., *Pro Football: The Early Years, An Encyclopedic History, 1895–1959* (1978); Tom Landry with Gregg Lewis, *Tom Landry: An Autobiography* (1990); Frank Graham, "Steve Owen: The Man behind the Giants," *Sport*, Dec. 1947; Stanley Grosshandler, "Steve Owen: The Great Innovator," *Football Digest*, Mar. 1973; and George Strickler, "Defense Came First with Steve Owen," *Football Digest*, Nov. 1971. An obituary is in the *New York Times*, 18 May 1964.

LLOYD J. GRAYBAR

OWENS, Jesse (12 Sept. 1913–31 Mar. 1980), Olympic track champion, was born James Cleveland Owens in Oakville, Alabama, the son of Henry Owens and Mary Emma Fitzgerald, sharecroppers. Around 1920 the family moved to Cleveland, Ohio, where the nickname "Jesse" originated when a schoolteacher mispronounced his drawled "J. C." A junior high school teacher of physical education, Charles Riley, trained Owens in manners as well as athletics, preparing him to set several interscholastic track records in high school. In 1932 the eighteen-year-old Owens narrowly missed winning a place on the U.S. Olympic team. Enrolling in 1933 at Ohio State University, Owens soared to national prominence under the tutelage of coach Larry Snyder. As a sophomore at the Big Ten championships, held on the Ann Arbor campus of the University of Michigan, on 25 May 1935 he broke world records in the 220-yard sprint, the 220-yard hurdles, and the long jump, and equaled the world record in the 100-yard dash.

Scarcely did the success come easily. As one of a handful of black college students at white institutions in the 1930s, Owens suffered slurs on campus, in the town of Columbus, and on the athletic circuit. Personal problems also intruded. Just over a month after his astounding athletic success at Ann Arbor, Owens was pressured to marry his high school sweetheart, Minnie

Ruth Solomon, with whom he had fathered a child three years earlier. Academic difficulties added to his ordeal. Coming from a home and high school bare of intellectual aspirations, Owens found it impossible to perform well academically while striving for athletic stardom. For two years at Ohio State he stayed on academic probation; low grades made him ineligible for the indoor track season during the winter quarter of 1936.

Allowed again to compete during the spring quarter outdoor track season, Owens set his sights on winning a place on the 1936 Olympic team. His great obstacle was a less-heralded but strong Temple University athlete, Eulace Peacock. A varsity football running back, Peacock had already beaten Owens in five of their previous six head-to-head sprints and long jumps. At the Penn Relays in late April, however, the heavily muscled Peacock snapped a hamstring that kept him limping through the Olympic trials.

At the Berlin Olympics in early August 1936, Owens tied the world record in the 100-meter sprint and broke world records in the 200-meter sprint, the long jump, and the 4-by-100-meter relay to win four gold medals. On the streets, in the Olympic village, and at the stadium his humble demeanor and ready smile mesmerized foes and friends alike. German filmmaker Leni Riefenstahl fell under his spell, making him the centerpiece of her long, artistic film *Olympia* (1936). German chancellor Adolf Hitler ceremoniously attended the games to cheer for German athletes. In the most enduring of all sports myths, Hitler supposedly "snubbed" Owens, refusing to shake his hand after his victories; Hitler allegedly stormed out of the stadium enraged that Owens's athleticism refuted the Nazi dogma of Aryan superiority. Although this account of Hitler's behavior caters to our sense of justice, it has no basis in fact. Reported over and over, it quickly became enshrined as one of the great moral minidramas of our time.

After the Berlin games, Owens incurred the wrath of Olympic and Amateur Athletic Union (AAU) officials when he returned home to capitalize on various commercial offers rather than complete an exhibition tour of several European cities; the tour had been arranged to help pay the expenses of the U.S. team. He left the tour in London, provoking the AAU to ban him from future amateur athletic competition. Supported in his decision by Snyder, Owens returned to the United States to cash in on numerous endorsement offers. Most of the offers proved bogus, however, but from Republican presidential candidate Alf Landon he received a goodly sum to campaign for black votes. Shortly after Landon's defeat, Owens was selected as the Associated Press Athlete of the Year, and on Christmas Day 1936, he won a well-paid, highly publicized race against a horse in Havana, Cuba. Various other fees for appearances and endorsements brought his earnings during the four months following the Berlin Olympics to about $20,000.

For the next two years he barnstormed with several athletic groups, supervised playground activities in Cleveland, and ran exhibition races at baseball games. In 1938 he opened a dry-cleaning business in Cleveland, but within the year it went bankrupt. Now with three daughters and a wife to support, he nevertheless returned to Ohio State hoping to finish his baccalaureate degree. He gave up that dream just a few days after Pearl Harbor, and during World War II he held several short-term government assignments before landing a job supervising black workers in the Ford Motor Company in Detroit.

With the onset of the Cold War, in the late 1940s Owens enjoyed a rebirth of fame. In 1950 he was honored by the Associated Press as the greatest track athlete of the past half century. Moving to Chicago, he served briefly as director of the South Side Boys' Club, the Illinois State Athletic Commission, and the Illinois Youth Commission, and emerged as an effective public speaker extolling patriotism and athleticism to youth groups, churches, and civic clubs. In 1955 the U.S. State Department tapped him for a junket to India, Malaya, and the Philippines to conduct athletic clinics and make speeches in praise of the American way of life. At government expense, in 1956 he went as a goodwill ambassador to the Melbourne Olympics, then served for a time in President Dwight D. Eisenhower's People-to-People Program. Republican to the marrow, Owens largely ignored the civil rights movement.

Deprived of White House patronage when the Democrats returned to power in 1960, he linked his name to a new public relations firm, Owens-West & Associates, in Chicago. While his partner managed the business, Owens stayed constantly on the road addressing business and athletic groups. For several years he carelessly neglected to report his extra income and in 1965 was indicted for tax evasion. He pleaded no contest and was found guilty as charged by a Chicago federal judge. At the sentencing, however, the judge lauded Owens for supporting the American flag and "our way of life" while others were "aiding and abetting the enemy openly" by protesting the Vietnam War. To his great relief, Owens was required merely to pay his back taxes and a nominal fine.

At the Mexico City Olympics in 1968, the politically conservative Owens reacted in horror to the demonstrative black-power salutes of track medalists Tommie Smith and John Carlos. He demanded of them an apology, but they saw him as a traitor to his race. Two years later, in a book ghostwritten by Paul Neimark, *Blackthink: My Life as Black Man and White Man* (1970), Owens savagely attacked Smith, Carlos, and others of their ilk as bigots in reverse. He argued that indolence, rather than bias, kept blacks from advancing in this society: "If the Negro doesn't succeed in today's America, it is because he has chosen to fail" (p. 84). In response to hostile reactions from black readers and reviewers, Owens again collaborated with Neimark to rephrase his principles in more moderate terms published in *I Have Changed* (1972). Two more Neimark-Owens potboilers, *The Jesse Owens Story* (1970) and *Jesse: A Spiritual Autobiography* (1978), blended reminiscences with prescriptions of the work ethic, patriotism, and religious piety as means to success.

Owens's own success in the 1970s came largely from contracts with major corporations. Atlantic Richfield Company (ARCO) owned his name for exclusive commercial use and sponsored annual ARCO Jesse Owens games for boys and girls. At business conventions and in advertisements, Owens also regularly represented Sears, United Fruit, United States Rubber, Johnson & Johnson, Schieffelin, Ford Motor Company, and American Express. His name was made all the more useful by a bevy of public awards. In 1972 he finally received a degree from Ohio State, an honorary doctorate of athletic arts. In 1974 he was enshrined in the Track and Field Hall of Fame and honored with a Theodore Roosevelt Award from the National Collegiate Athletic Association for distinguished achievement since retirement from athletic competition.

To his black critics, the aging Owens was an embarrassment, a throwback to the servile posture of Booker T. Washington; to his admirers, his youthful athleticism and enduring fame made him an inspiration. On balance, his inspirational achievements transcended race and even politics. In 1976 he received the Medal of Freedom from Republican president Gerald Ford for serving as "a source of inspiration" for all Americans; in 1979 Democratic president Jimmy Carter presented Owens a Living Legends award for inspiring others "to reach for greatness." Within the next year, Owens died in Tucson, Arizona.

• William J. Baker, *Jesse Owens: An American Life* (1986), is primarily based on extensive year-to-year coverage in the *Chicago Defender*, oral interviews, and Barbara Moro's transcript of interviews with Jesse Owens and Ruth Owens in 1961; the transcript is in the Illinois State Historical Library, Springfield. The four books that Owens collaborated on with ghostwriter Paul Neimark are essential for understanding how Owens would like to be remembered but are filled with factual inaccuracies that contribute to the Jesse Owens myth. For the context of his Olympic feats, Richard D. Mandell, *The Nazi Olympics* (1971), and Duff Hart-Davis, *Hitler's Games: The 1936 Olympics* (1986), are essential. William O. Johnson, Jr., *All That Glitters Is Not Gold: The Olympic Game* (1972), provides a critical assessment of the older Owens. An obituary is in the *New York Times*, 1 Apr. 1980.

WILLIAM J. BAKER

OWENS, John Edmond (2 Apr. 1823–7 Dec. 1886), actor and manager, was born in Liverpool, England, the son of Owen Griffith Owen (later changed to Owens) and Mary Anderton, both of Welsh origins. In 1828 the Owens family emigrated to the United States, joining other family members who had preceded them in Philadelphia, where young Owens received his limited formal education. Introduced to the theater at an early age and disenchanted with his employment as a pharmacy clerk, Owens determined upon a career on the stage. He made his acting debut at seventeen, under-taking bit parts at William E. Burton's Arch Street Theater. Within a year he graduated to feature roles, largely in the popular comedies of the day.

Dividing his time between Philadelphia and Baltimore, Owens had by the mid-1840s established himself as a promising young comedian whose touring activities ultimately took him to the Mississippi Valley. In the provincial theaters of the South and West he came to be acclaimed for the first time as a star performer. The brilliant American actor Joseph Jefferson saw him perform in New Orleans in 1846 and later pronounced Owens "the handsomest low comedian I had ever seen," commanding "lively expression" and producing a "great flow of animal spirits" (Jefferson, p. 65). The theater critic William Winter concurred. "His comic power was elemental," Winter wrote, "and [its] natural manifestations . . . inevitably resulted in comic effect" (Winter, vol. 1, p. 218).

In 1849 Owens married Mary C. Stevens of Baltimore (number of children unknown). She wrote his biography—in part a defense of Owens against all who came to be critical of her husband's abilities. Meanwhile, the actor continued to build his reputation by performing many of the roles with which he would come to be identified, including (especially) Solon Shingle in Joseph S. Jones's *The Peoples' Lawyer*, Caleb Plummer in the Dion Boucicault adaptation of Dickens's *Cricket in the Hearth*, and all of the stereotyped "Yankee" characters so popular in the mid-nineteenth-century United States. He also performed several of the major Oliver Goldsmith character parts as well as Shakespearean roles, including both Dromios in *Comedy of Errors*.

By the early 1850s Owens had begun his managerial career, managing stock companies first in Baltimore, then in New Orleans, Cincinnati, and the other river towns. He proved to be an able manager, careful in selecting his stock companies and their repertoires and constantly attentive to all technical details. In New Orleans he was a special favorite both as actor and manager, and he brought the Crescent City several of the best seasons offered there prior to the outbreak of the Civil War during his managerial stints in the late 1850s. His annual managerial appearances in New Orleans in those years led him eventually to claim the city as "my winter home." As a theater manager, he also demonstrated a certain courage when, in 1855, he produced *Uncle Tom's Cabin* in Baltimore, choosing to play Tom himself in the only recorded performance of the Harriet Beecher Stowe classic south of the Mason-Dixon Line.

In 1882, after years of near-constant touring that saw him perform in every major playhouse in the United States and London, Owens joined the repertory company of the Madison Square Theatre in New York. There he remained a popular success despite the fact that he had cut back considerably on his stage appearances. Increasingly poor health necessitated his retirement in 1885. His financially successful career had enabled him in 1853 to purchase a small country estate in Aigburth Vale, Maryland, some six miles from Baltimore, which he made his retirement residence. Over the years he had augmented and improved his land holdings, and he enjoyed entertaining his friends and family on the estate until the time of his death there.

Without a doubt, Owens was a genuine comic type, with great flexibility of facial features (a close friend, the actress Clara Morris, noted in particular his expressive eyes), lively body movement, and excellent comic timing. He was also given to improvisation, some of which may have been overstated and inappropriate, thus incurring some of the negative criticism that marked the latter phase of his career. Nonetheless, he was clearly among the most popular comic character actors of the nineteenth-century American stage, long remembered by his many fans as without peer in his field.

• While scattered, biographical material on Owens is substantial, beginning with the loving memoir of his wife, Mary C. Owens, *Memories of the Professional and Social Life of John E. Owens* (1892). Most of the theatrical memoirs of the time comment on Owens, including Joseph Jefferson, *The Autobiography of Joseph Jefferson* (1890), and Clara Morris, *Life on the Stage* (1901) and *Stage Confidences* (1902). William Winter makes credible critical judgments in *The Wallet of Time* (2 vols., 1913). The New Orleans years are best treated in John S. Kendall, *The Golden Age of the New Orleans Theater* (1952), and James H. Dormon, *Theater in the Antebellum South* (1967). Obituaries are in the *New York Times*, 8 Dec. 1886, and the *New York World*, 11 Dec. 1886.

JAMES H. DORMON

OWENS, Michael Joseph (1 Jan. 1859–27 Dec. 1923), inventor and glass manufacturer, was born in Mason County, West Virginia, the son of Irish immigrants John Owens, a coal miner, and Mary Chapman. Although impoverished and little-educated, Owens was blessed with a talent for tinkering that matured into a tremendous mechanical ability. After leaving school at the age of ten, Owens moved from his rural birthplace to Wheeling, West Virginia, a bustling manufacturing center on the National Road that boasted several glass factories. There he secured an apprenticeship with J. H. Hobbs, Brockunier and Company, one of the nation's leading manufacturers of consumer glassware, and by age fifteen he had mastered the craft of glassblowing—a task that he would later revolutionize with his inventions.

At Hobbs the outspoken Owens assumed a leadership position in the American Flint Glass Workers' Union, participating in a strike in eastern Massachusetts that resulted in the closure of Edward Drummond Libbey's firm, the New England Glass Company, in 1888. Ironically, when Libbey moved his business, renamed the Libbey Glass Company, to Toledo, Ohio, later that year in the hope of avoiding labor troubles, Owens left Wheeling and secured a position as a blower of lamp shades in the new works.

Within a few months, Owens and Libbey were on their way to establishing the relationship that would transform glassmaking not only in Toledo but throughout the nation and the world. Whether he impressed or cajoled Libbey is unknown, but Owens soon assumed the duties of blowing-room foreman and plant supervisor at Libbey's glass factory, which used handicraft methods to produce high-quality consumer products, including cut glassware. In 1889 he married Mary McKelvey; they had two children. In 1893 Owens managed the Libbey Glass Company's display of glassblowing, cutting, and engraving at the World's Columbian Exposition in Chicago. During slow periods at the fair, Owens pondered ways to mechanize the process of glassblowing, a trade still dominated by highly skilled, well-paid artisans who worked in small groups, or shops, assisted by numerous helpers. Back in Ohio, Owens created several devices for expediting tumbler and lamp-chimney production, which he patented on behalf of his employer. These accomplishments persuaded Libbey to finance the Toledo Glass Company in 1896, a firm dedicated to developing and promoting Owens's equipment in the tumbler and lighting fields. Through a series of agreements, the Toledo Glass Company licensed other American glass companies to use Owens's tumbler and chimney machines, reaping considerable profits from those inventions.

The founding of the Toledo Glass Company marked a new era in Owens's relationship with Libbey, for this company acknowledged the men as equal partners with the complementary skills of inventor-mechanic and business strategist. As Owens's ideas matured into workable, patentable, and profitable machines, he depended on Libbey and other Toledo investors to establish a network of firms to use, manage, sell, and license his inventions. Owens's investments primarily lay in the Toledo Glass Company, the Owens Bottle Machine Company (established in 1903), and the Libbey-Owens Sheet Glass Company (established in 1916).

Owens's interests gradually shifted away from semi-automatic equipment for producing tumblers and chimneys to automatic equipment for making containers, leading to his greatest technical achievement: the so-called Owens bottle machine. In 1898 and 1899 Owens directed the construction of several new gathering and blowing machines, all designed to do jobs that had been performed by unionized glassblowers. When perfected, the Owens motor-powered bottle machine gathered molten glass from a furnace, transferred the gob to a mold, puffed hot air into the mold to shape the bottle, and severed the finished piece onto a conveyor headed for the annealing, or cooling, oven. A typical Owens machine was equipped with from six to twenty arms, each capable of blowing a container; a fifteen-arm machine could do as much work as thirteen to fifty-four skilled glassworkers, depending on the size and shape of the product. As Owens anticipated, the automatic bottle machine significantly increased a glass factory's production while reducing its direct labor costs, sometimes by more than 80 percent. Once Owens perfected his equipment, Libbey secured the capital for the Owens Bottle Machine Company and incorporated to build the machines and to license them to established American bottle factories. In 1919 the firm's name was changed to the Owens Bottle Company, and in 1929 it merged with the Illinois Glass Company to form the Owens-Illinois Glass Company.

Owens's final technical achievement was the perfection of the Colburn sheet-drawing process for the continuous production of windowpanes. Until the early twentieth century, panes were cut from enormous blownglass cylinders that had been split open, flattened, and annealed. For decades various entrepreneurs had experimented with making panes from drawn sheet glass, but without success. The most successful of these inventors was Irving W. Colburn, whose factory in western Pennsylvania suffered from a lack of glassmaking, mechanical, and financial expertise. Fascinated with Colburn's work, Owens threatened to leave the Owens Bottle Machine Company in 1912 unless his partners in the Toledo Glass Company purchased Colburn's patents and his bankrupt company. Libbey acquiesced, and Owens spent the next four years tinkering with Colburn's patents, using his knowledge of glassmaking to perfect the sheet-drawing process. In 1916 Owens, Libbey, and their partners formed the Libbey-Owens Sheet Glass Company to make window glass from the newly perfected automatic process.

A temperamental character, Owens devoted most of his time to his work, having few interests beyond glassmaking. In contrast to Libbey, Owens saved little of his fortune, often complaining about a lack of funds. In a manner befitting a life dedicated to work, Owens died suddenly in his office in Toledo, leaving little behind except his inventions—one of the greatest mechanical legacies of industrial America.

• The major repository of Owens's business and personal papers is the Corporate Archives of the Owens-Illinois Glass Company in Toledo, Ohio. The best accounts of Owens's career are Warren Candler Scoville, *Revolution in Glassmaking: Entrepreneurship and Technological Change in the American Industry, 1880–1920* (1948), and Dennis Michael Zembala, "Machines in the Glasshouse: The Transformation of Work in the Glass Industry, 1820–1915" (Ph.D. diss., George Washington Univ., 1984). To place Owens in the context of his industry, see Pearce Davis, *The Development of the American Glass Industry* (1949), and George E. Barnett, *Chapters on Machinery and Labor* (1926). Obituaries are in the *Toledo News-Bee*, 27 and 28 Dec. 1923, and the *New York Times*, 28 Dec. 1923.

REGINA LEE BLASZCZYK

OWENS, Ruby Agnes. *See* Texas Ruby.

OWENS-ADAIR, Bethenia Angelina (7 Feb. 1840–11 Sept. 1926), physician, feminist, and social reformer, was born in Van Buren County, Missouri, the daughter of Thomas Owens and Sarah Damron, farmers. In 1843 the family moved to Oregon's Clatsop Plains. Fond of the outdoors, Owens preferred helping her fa-

ther work with horses to doing domestic work. By age eleven, she had received only three months of schooling.

In 1853 Owens helped her father drive their stock to Roseberg, Oregon, where the family settled in the Umpqua Valley. She was proud that her father called her "my boy" because of her skills. At fourteen, she married Legrand Hill, her father's laborer. The relationship was not happy; four years later she separated from her husband, successfully suing for the custody of their son. Her prosperous father offered to support her, but she was determined to get an education. She milked cows, did housework, and took in wash to support herself and her son while she attended school in Astoria. For nine difficult years she combined study, teaching, and sometimes other jobs to advance her education while she maintained her independence. By saving every scrap of money, she was able to build herself a small house.

In 1867 she moved to Roseberg where her parents lived. A relative helped her start a millinery business that was successful until she was challenged by a trained milliner. Characteristically, Owens went to San Francisco to learn the millinery trade from experts; she returned in 1870 to great success. Her persistence and hard work allowed her to send her son to the University of California, Berkeley, the following year.

Owens was also involved in her community, holding offices in local organizations, becoming an active member of the Woman's Christian Temperance Union and a believer in woman suffrage, even helping to arrange Susan B. Anthony's visit to Roseberg in 1871. She was a prolific writer of newspaper articles, often concerning temperance and women's rights, many of them for Abigail Scott Duniway's paper, the *New Northwest*. She fervently believed that women should have opportunities equal to those enjoyed by men.

After gaining skills in nursing, Owens began studying anatomy medical books and determined to become a physician. Her parents, supportive of her other endeavors, objected to formal medical schooling. Nevertheless, she attended Eclectic Medical University in Philadelphia, receiving a degree in 1874. Returning to Oregon to practice with a male physician, she and her partner also owned a store with a millinery business in one half and drugs in the other. In 1875 she adopted a fourteen-year-old girl who later became a physician.

On her son's graduation from Willamette Medical College in 1877, Owens began to want a degree from a regular school of medicine for herself because many did not respect eclectic training. She desired to be "second to no physician in the state." Although friends who previously supported her now loudly objected, Owens attended the University of Michigan in 1878 and, two years later, had graduated. Following a summer of clinical work in Chicago, she returned to Michigan, where she did postgraduate work in medicine, surgery, therapeutics, homeopathy, history, and literature and then made a tour of European hospitals.

Engaged in a respected, orthodox practice and specializing in diseases of the eye and ear, Owens's practice quickly grew on her return in 1881 to Oregon, where she was one of the first woman physicians. Three years later she met a childhood acquaintance, West Point graduate Colonel John Adair, whom she married on 24 July 1884. In 1887 the death of an infant daughter caused the couple to move to a farm near Astoria that Owens-Adair helped manage while still practicing medicine. They adopted two sons. Although her practice was thriving, Owens-Adair began to suffer with severe rheumatism, so the family moved to North Yakima, where her son was a physician. Here she practiced until her retirement in 1905. Colonel Adair died in 1915.

Around the turn of the century Owens-Adair had become interested in eugenics sterilization, associating heredity with high rates of crime and insanity. In 1907 she proposed a bill to require the sterilization of epileptics, criminals, the insane, and the retarded, except those excused by a review board, in the states of Washington and Oregon. The bill was criticized and rejected then, but in part because of Owens-Adair's persistent advocacy, eugenics sterilization bills were passed in Washington in 1909 and in Oregon in 1925. Her efforts on behalf of eugenics reflected the nation's social concerns, as did her activities related to temperance and woman suffrage.

Owens-Adair was a woman of vigor and strong convictions. Sentimental, intelligent, even driven, she possessed the stamina to pursue her goals to fruition. She dedicated a great deal of time and energy to her interests in women's health and education, medicine, temperance, woman suffrage, and eugenics. A frequently sought after and well-respected lecturer, she addressed groups all over Oregon. Although her view on eugenics was controversial even then, her interests reflected her times and her accomplishments mirrored her belief that women could do everything. Owens-Adair died in Astoria, Oregon.

• Eight letters from Jesse Applegate to Bethenia Owens, 1869–1878, are at the Oregon Historical Society, Portland. For an interview with Owens-Adair, see Fred Lockley, "In Earlier Days" (n.d.), located in the University of Washington Special Collections Pacific Northwest Collection, Oregon Biography Pamphlet File O. The principal biographical source on Owens-Adair is her autobiography, *Dr. Owens-Adair: Some of Her Life Experiences* (1906). Her other writing includes *Human Sterilization* (1909), *Human Sterilization: Its Social and Legislative Aspects* (1922), and *The Eugenic Marriage Law and Human Sterilization* (1922). Files of the *New Northwest*, 1871–1887, include many articles by Owens-Adair. See also Elwood Evans et al., *History of the Pacific Northwest: Oregon and Washington*, vol. 2 (1889); Nancy Wilson Ross, *Westward the Women* (1944), which is based on Owens-Adair's autobiography; and Helen Markely Miller, *Woman Doctor of the West: Bethenia Owens-Adair* (1960), a biography for children. An obituary is in the *Astoria Evening Budget*, 13 Sept. 1926.

SANDRA VARNEY MACMAHON

OWINGS, Nathaniel Alexander (5 Feb. 1903–13 June 1984), architect, was born in Indianapolis, Indiana, the son of Nathaniel Owings, a fine-wood importer, and Cora Alexander. After his father's death in 1914, his mother supported the family by working as an accountant. In 1920 Owings won a Rotary Club trip to Europe, where he saw the cathedrals of Notre Dame, Chartres, and Mont-Saint-Michel. The experience determined his course in life. In 1921 he began studies in architecture at the University of Illinois but left after a year on account of illness. He returned to school, attending Cornell University, where he graduated in 1927 with degrees in architecture and engineering. He began his career in the New York architecture firm of York and Sawyer. In 1931 he married Emily Hunting Otis; they had four children.

A charismatic figure, described by colleagues as ebullient, competent, and devoted, as well as a radical thinker and a buccaneer, Owings would soon prove his ability to make big plans happen when, upon invitation from his brother-in-law Louis Skidmore, the chief of design for the 1933 Chicago World's Fair, he moved to Chicago to become the fair's development supervisor. Planned before the stock market crash of 1929, the initially grand event was reduced by depression-era scarcity. In charge of concessions, both their coordination and design, Owings learned how to make bold gestures with the simplest of manufactured materials, such as beaverboard. His designs were strongly influenced by modern European precedents as interpreted by American architects like Raymond Hood. "A Century of Progress," as the fair was called, was an economic success as well as one of the first coherent displays of modern architecture in the United States.

In 1936 Owings formed a partnership in Chicago with Skidmore. Three years later they were joined by structural engineer John Merrill. The firm of Skidmore, Owings and Merrill set the standard for the large-scale, corporate practice of architecture and represents one of Owings's most important accomplishments. Aspiring to be a "modern 'Gothic Builders Guild,'" as Owings explained in his memoir *The Spaces in Between* (1978), the firm advocated teamwork and anonymity. The concept of group practice as devised by Owings, which revolved around a team consisting of a partner, a project manager, and a designer, was to prove as important as any of the firm's designs.

Decentralized early, with a New York office opened in 1937, Skidmore, Owings and Merrill gained a reputation for bigness through commissions for hotels, air bases, and even towns. The firm prospered during World War II and the great building boom that followed. After Lever House (1952) in Manhattan, the firm became known for its celebrated International Style designs. In *The Spaces in Between*, Owings wrote, "I as an individual cannot point to any major building for which I am solely responsible." Indeed, his skill was as a facilitator, cajoler, and motivator of both designer and client, a role he compared to that of a symphony conductor whose orchestra is filled with accomplished musicians and supreme soloists often in need of direction.

Owings played an integral part in the completion of Skidmore, Owings and Merrill's large governmental commissions, often becoming involved in legislative matters. Projects such as the design of the secret nuclear town of Oak Ridge, Tennessee (1942–1946), where uranium was refined for the first atomic bomb, and the $152.5 million Air Force Academy in Colorado Springs (1954–1962), along with a term as chairman of the Chicago Plan Commission (1948–1951), honed his political skills and changed his design philosophy. Owings began to question the modernist aesthetic his firm had helped popularize through glass-and-steel structures such as Lever House. "Is it, indeed, the personal touch of humanity that we have imprisoned and denied in our glass boxes?" he asked in 1983. Following the governmental commissions, he became an advocate of urban planning that was not only sensitive to human interests but also to architectural preservation and the natural environment. Rather than destroying the built or natural environment for new structures, he believed that old cities could be reorganized more cheaply, more efficiently, and more quickly than building new ones. Part of his urban renewal program included the creation of open spaces in and around densely populated cities, an idea explored in his 1969 book *The American Aesthetic.*

Owings implemented his approach to urban planning in a variety of cities, including Chicago, Baltimore, San Francisco, and Washington, D.C. In Baltimore he prevented an interstate highway from bisecting the city and the harbor. By working with a team of architects and engineers in developing workable alternatives and in obtaining the public consensus, he persuaded developers to reroute the road. The maneuver saved the city's waterfront, which later became a popular commercial district with access to the harbor. His most enduring urban design contribution occurred in Washington, D.C., where he was appointed in 1962 by President John F. Kennedy to the President's Advisory Council of Pennsylvania Avenue. Through steady determination, wise prodding, and savvy political combativeness, Owings oversaw the avenue's rebirth and the enrichment of the Great Mall from the Capitol to the Lincoln Memorial. His innovations include the underground placement of the highway in front of the Capitol and the design of the Capitol Reflecting Pool and Constitution Gardens. He also conceived of returning the Mall to pedestrians. For his efforts, ultimately spanning a twenty-year period and four presidential administrations, Owings received the Conservation Service Award of the Department of the Interior. This 1968 honor commended him for having restored the vision of the original Pierre Charles L'Enfant plan of 1791.

In 1953 Owings and his wife were divorced, and that same year he married Margaret Wentworth Millard and established residency in California's Big Sur. They had no children. The change coincided with Owings's emergence as an articulate and aggressive voice for conservation. At a time when few people were concerned about the environment, he and his new wife led a successful campaign against development in Big Sur. He rated this act as one of his greatest accomplishments, maintaining that architecture was nothing without land.

Toward the end of his life, as a resident of Santa Fe, New Mexico, Owings championed a crusade to save the region's adobe churches. He led the effort to preserve and restore structures such as the Church of San José de Gracia de las Trampas. After his retirement from Skidmore, Owings and Merrill in 1976, Owings continued to support his favorite causes until his death in Santa Fe.

Architect, urban designer, and environmentalist, Owings dedicated his life to the advancement of a built environment that harmonized with nature and the past. In 1983 the American Institute of Architects recognized his achievements by awarding him their prestigious Gold Medal. Lauded in the award citation for his "drive, imagination and sense of mission," Owings will be long remembered for the legacy of buildings, urban designs, and protected lands he left behind.

• A biography, bibliography, résumé, and chronology of Owings's life can be obtained from the firm of Skidmore, Owings and Merrill. For a complete listing of periodicals see Dale E. Casper, *Nathaniel Alexander Owings, Architect: Journal Literature, 1967–1987* (1988). For discussions of the firm's early history see Ernst Danz, *Architecture of Skidmore, Owings and Merrill, 1950–1962* (1963), and Christopher Woodward, *Skidmore, Owings and Merrill* (1970). The later period is considered in Arthur Drexel and Axel Menges, *Architecture of Skidmore, Owings and Merrill, 1963–1973* (1974). An obituary is in the *New York Times,* 14 June 1984.

LISA A. TORRANCE

OWSLEY, Frank Lawrence (20 Jan. 1890–21 Oct. 1955), historian, was born in rural Montgomery County, Alabama, the son of Lawrence Monroe Owsley, a farmer who rented land to African-American sharecroppers, and Annie Scott McGehee. In childhood Owsley spent much time listening to aging Confederate veterans; as an adult he cherished these remembrances of the old South and the Civil War. The stories and recollections of his mother also intensified Owsley's love for his native land.

Owsley began his education in a one-room schoolhouse. He attended the Fifth District Agricultural School in Wetumpka, Alabama, from 1906 to 1909, earning a high school diploma and beginning college-level studies. He then enrolled at Alabama Polytechnic Institute (now Auburn University), intending to become a farm demonstration agent. Instead, he fell under the influence of the historian George Petrie, a graduate of Herbert Baxter Adams's seminars at Johns Hopkins University and a proponent of the new scientific history. Finishing his baccalaureate in 1912, Owsley returned to the Fifth District Agricultural School to teach history and Latin. In 1914 he returned to Alabama Polytechnic Institute to complete a master's degree in history. Determined to become a professional historian, he began additional graduate studies in 1916 at the University of Chicago, working under the noted southern historian William Edward Dodd. Although Owsley enjoyed working with Dodd, he was grieved when other Chicago professors disdained his Alabama diplomas and required him to complete a second master's degree. Despite the delay, and a brief interruption for World War I military service, he completed requirements for the Ph.D. in 1919.

Owsley's Chicago experiences were crucial to the formation of his historical perspective. He believed that the history faculty, heavily influenced by pronorthern and neoabolitionist sentiments, presented an erroneous interpretation of the South. An emotional pro-Confederate, Owsley deeply resented the attitudes of northern people in general toward his beloved region. In 1924 he received his doctorate magna cum laude and then set forth on his lifelong mission to revise the conception of the South.

Owsley taught for one year at Birmingham-Southern College before joining the history faculty of Nashville's Vanderbilt University in 1920. On 24 July of that year he married Harriet Fason Chappell, who assisted him as a researcher and collaborator in many projects. They had two children.

During his Vanderbilt tenure Owsley gained a reputation as a warm, inspiring teacher, equally congenial to undergraduate and graduate students. His students found him cheerful and fun-loving. One later recalled, "Those of us who studied with the Owsleys were taught by example, never by precept, that history is serious business—but joyous!" Owsley directed almost forty doctoral dissertations. He supported his students, even those who challenged his own interpretations.

At times Owsley found himself at odds with the Vanderbilt administration. He was also unhappy with Vanderbilt Library's refusal to establish a manuscripts depository. Given the opportunity to return home, he joined the faculty at the University of Alabama in 1949. There he assisted in founding the university's graduate program in history and served as chairman of the history department, at some sacrifice of his research activities. In 1955 he resigned as chairman to begin work on an exhaustive study of northern Civil War diplomacy. Granted a Fulbright Fellowship as a researcher and lecturer at St. John's College, Cambridge University, he arrived in England in September 1956, only to suffer a fatal heart attack the next month.

For more than thirty years Owsley profoundly influenced the development of southern historical research. His historical philosophy was motivated by his understanding that the South was a distinctive region with a unique culture. Responding to what he perceived as attacks upon the South by hostile northerners, liberals, industrialists, proabolitionist historians, civil rights activists, and Communists, he dedicated his teaching and writing to fighting the prejudices and misconceptions these elements created. He became convinced that the future of American civilization de-pended on the survival of southern regionalism. Owsley, like his mentor Dodd, was committed to the importance of the common white man. Envisioning himself as a Jeffersonian, he idealized the independence and individuality he saw as characteristic of the South's rural people. In much of his writing he emphasized the contributions and significance of the common man in southern history, attributing the shape and course of southern history to the independent small farmers, or yeomen, rather than to the slave-holding aristocrats. Unlike Dodd, who saw class conflict in the old South, Owsley argued for consensus, claiming that the yeomen rarely looked on the large planters as their oppressors.

Owsley's scholarly output reflected this dedication to southern regionalism. The historian Fred Arthur Bailey divided Owsley's career into three overlapping phases. In the first, from 1925 to 1931, he concentrated on internal divisions, which he interpreted as the root of southern problems. From 1930 to 1940 Owsley railed against forces he thought threatened the South, including liberal reformers, industrialists, and northern intellectuals. In the final phase, from 1936 to 1949, a period culminating in the publication of *Plain Folk of the Old South* (1949), Owsley dedicated his energy to creating a more positive image of antebellum southern society.

Owsley produced three significant books, four textbooks, numerous scholarly articles, book reviews, and forewords to the works of other historians. Two of his major works came early in his career: *State Rights and the Confederacy* (1925) and *King Cotton Diplomacy* (1931). In the former Owsley lamented the Confederacy's failure to achieve a spirit of nationalism, arguing that dedication to the states' rights ideology was the chief cause of southern defeat. In the second, which was heralded as a significant contribution to American diplomatic history, Owsley theorized that English neutrality had been based more on the profits its industry acquired as a result of the American conflict and less on considerations of morality.

During the second phase of his career Owsley published polemical essays attacking those he considered enemies of the South. In 1930 he associated with a group of Vanderbilt intellectuals known as the Southern Agrarians. United in their opposition to northern and liberal scholarship, this group published a volume titled *I'll Take My Stand* (1930). Owsley contributed "The Irrepressible Conflict," in which he lashed out at the North for attempts to dominate the South spiritually and economically. Three years later he expanded these themes in "Scottsboro, the Third Crusade: The Sequel to Abolition and Reconstruction," presented before the American Historical Association and then published in the *American Historical Review* (1 [1933]: 257–85). Condemning northern race reformers as the "grandchildren of abolitionists and reconstructionists," he announced that the South was white man's country and that African-Americans must accommodate to that reality. In 1935 he published "The Pillars of Agrarianism" (*American Historical Re-*

view 4: 529–47), advocating a return to the economic independence of subsistence agriculture as a means of protecting the common people against the modern corporation. Serving as president of the Southern Historical Association in 1940, Owsley gave a convention address which castigated the North for assuming it represented the entire nation and for violating what he called "the comity of section." He leveled the blame for this attitude on northern abolitionists, whom he described as more vulgar and obscene than Nazi propagandists.

Owsley's lasting fame as a historian rests on his third book, *Plain Folk of the Old South*, one of the most influential works on southern history ever written. Pioneering the use of quantitative techniques, based largely on the examination of manuscript federal census returns, tax and trial records, and local government documents and wills, *Plain Folk* argued that southern society was not dominated by planter aristocrats, but that yeoman farmers played a significant role in it. The religion, language, and culture of these common people created a democratic "plain folk" society. Although *Plain Folk* was not without its detractors, who criticized its statistical methods, Owsley had fundamentally altered the historical portrait of southern society.

Thirty years after his death Owsley's position among American historians remained secure. During his lifetime he was often seen as reactionary in his defense of southern culture and tradition, especially his lifelong commitment to the South as white man's country. Owsley remained unperturbed by criticism. His scholarly work and his support of prosouthern political and social causes (such as the maintenance of segregation) demonstrated an unwavering attachment to a white South. In his last years, however, he appeared more moderate; for example, he refused to support his close friend Donald Davidson's anti-black campaign in Nashville. The harsh evaluation of Owsley by late twentieth-century scholars may be overdrawn; Owsley was complex, and his words, especially in private correspondence, could be more shocking than his rather gentle public persona.

Although much of Owsley's work has been challenged, *Plain Folk* has retained scholarly interest. His emphasis on the yeoman greatly affected later scholars, notably Grady McWhiney and Forrest McDonald. Works by James Oakes and Orville Vernon Burton emphasize the economic opportunities for the southern middle class and yeomen. Owsley's example of quantitative methods and systematic study of neglected sources has been followed by the new social historians, who have concentrated on the study of local communities through the examination of census returns and tax records. Finally, historians of rural America recognize Owsley as an early leader in attempts to understand agrarian society. His emphasis on the culture of ordinary events presaged much more recent literature. With his wife Harriet, he was one of the first historians to explore seriously the role of women in rural and southern society.

Critics acknowledge Owsley's pioneering efforts at demographic research but point out that he overemphasized the size of the southern landholding class while excluding the large class of poor landless and slaveless southerners. He also neglected the tremendous economic imbalance of the region. Furthermore, Owsley assumed that shared economic interests united southern farmers without considering the vast difference inherent in the planters' commercial agriculture versus the yeomen's subsistence.

Despite his reactionary and fire-eating attributes, Owsley has continued to influence historians. His challenging the orthodox conception of the South reminds the historian to be cautious in accepting traditional points of view. His persistent dedication to altering the image of the South eventually led to the revision of the standard northern interpretation. The Southern Historical Association instituted the Frank L. and Harriet C. Owsley Award, given for distinguished books in southern history.

• Nineteen boxes of Owsley's private papers are deposited in the Joint University Libraries, Nashville. There are also Owsley letters in the Wendell Holmes Stephenson Papers, Duke University; William E. Dodd Papers, Library of Congress; Andrew Nelson Lytle Papers and Donald Davidson Papers, Joint University Libraries, Nashville; Robert Penn Warren Papers and *American Review* Papers, Yale University; and Allen Tate Papers, Princeton University. Important articles by Owsley include "Local Defense and the Downfall of the Confederacy," *Mississippi Valley Historical Review* 11 (Mar. 1925): 492–525; "The Confederacy and King Cotton: A Study in Economic Coercion," *North Carolina Historical Review* 6 (Oct. 1929): 371–97; and two articles with Harriet C. Owsley, "The Economic Basis of Society in the Late Ante-Bellum South," *Journal of Southern History* 6 (Feb. 1940): 24–25, and "The Pattern of Migration and Settlement on the Southern Frontier," *Journal of Southern History* 11 (May 1945): 147–76. Treatments of his life and significance include Fred Arthur Bailey, "Plain Folk and Apology: Frank L. Owsley's Defense of the South," *Perspectives on the American South: An Annual Review of Society, Politics, and Culture*; M. E. Bradford, "What We Know for Certain: Frank Owsley and the Recovery of Southern History," *Sewanee Review* 78 (1970): 664–68; Benarr Cresap, "Frank L. Owsley," in *The Encyclopedia of Southern History*, ed. David Roller and Robert Twyman (1979); Grady McWhiney, "Historians as Southerners," *Continuity* 9 (Fall 1984): 1–32; and Harriet Chappell, *Frank Lawrence Owsley: a Memoir* (1990). An important obituary by Thomas D. Clark is in *The Journal of Southern History* 23 (1957): 143–45.

ORVILLE VERNON BURTON

OXNAM, Garfield Bromley (14 Aug. 1891–12 Mar. 1963), Methodist bishop, ecumenical leader, and social reformer, was born in Sonora, California, the son of Thomas Henry Oxnam, a Cornish immigrant mining engineer, and Mary Ann "Mamie" Jobe. His father's religious enthusiasm found expression as a Methodist lay minister and his mother's intense piety suffused the Oxnam home in Los Angeles, assuredly influencing his teenage decision to pledge his life to Christ. Forced to leave high school because of his father's ill health and financial reverses, Oxnam both clerked and attended a business school before entering the University of Southern California, then a Methodist institution. At USC he earned solid grades, athletic renown, and repute as a campus leader.

After graduating with a B.A. in 1913, Oxnam entered Boston University School of Theology. He received the Bachelor of Sacred Theology degree in 1915 and did postgraduate study at Harvard and the Massachusetts Institute of Technology. Marriage in 1914 to Ruth Fisher, a woman whose warmth and graciousness complemented her husband's intense, driving nature, much to the advancement of his career, provided forty-eight years of companionship; they had three children.

Returning to California in 1916, Oxnam was ordained in the Methodist Episcopal church, first serving a struggling rural church in Poplar. The years 1917 to 1927 were largely devoted to fulfilling a youthful dream, the creation of the Church of All Nations. Located in polyglot East Los Angeles and serving forty-two ethnic groups, Mexicans predominating, the church was open to people of all faiths or none. All Nations embraced a chapel, clinic, dining hall, day care center, lending library, community house, and a camp in the Sierras for a boys' club of 1,000. Oxnam also opened its doors to labor union meetings, and because he supported longshoremen in their bitter 1923 strike he came under vicious conservative attack. Indeed, beginning in 1922 the Los Angeles office of the Bureau of Investigation (forerunner of the Federal Bureau of Investigation) began sending ominous reports to Washington; ultimately Oxnam's FBI file, of which he was unaware, numbered more than four hundred muddled pages. During this decade of involvement with All Nations, Oxnam also taught at the University of Southern California, spent months traveling worldwide, served as a delegate to Methodist General Conferences and on denominational committees, lectured endlessly, and wrote articles and three books—two of them, *The Mexican in Los Angeles* (1920) and *Russian Impressions* (1926), of continuing interest to scholars.

With All Nations firmly established, Oxnam accepted a call in 1927 to teach at Boston University School of Theology and the following year accepted an invitation to become president of Indiana's DePauw University. He remembered the DePauw experience as the "eight happiest years of our lives." Popular with the students, who found him imposing yet approachable, he made many wise, hard decisions in the teeth of the depression. Nevertheless, it was a lively time. Groups of patriots raged at his abolition of the Reserve Officers' Training Corps unit and criticized him for allegedly exposing students to "sex, Sovietism, and socialism." Concurrently, within the faculty some members were angered by what they considered their president's authoritarianism and were ashamed when in 1934 DePauw was censured by the American Association of University Professors for Oxnam's dismissal of tenured professors without proper hearings. (The censure was not lifted until after his departure.)

In 1936 Oxnam was elected bishop of the Methodist Episcopal church, which in 1939 united with the Methodist Episcopal church, South, and the Methodist Protestant church to form the newly named Methodist church, becoming the nation's largest and most muscular Protestant denomination. Then the youngest bishop, Oxnam marched on to become almost certainly the most puissant member of the Council of Bishops. He was assigned to increasingly more prestigious areas: Omaha, 1936–1939; Boston, 1939–1944; New York, 1944–1952; and Washington, D.C., 1952–1960. He early adopted the exhausting practice of visiting every church in the area to which he was appointed, some 5,000 in all. As secretary of the Council of Bishops from 1939 to 1956, Oxnam transformed its casual periodic meetings into regularized formal meetings to consider agendas he set. He also arranged for the council to meet in Washington with Presidents Franklin D. Roosevelt, Harry S. Truman, and Dwight D. Eisenhower and their cabinets. He originated a plan that required the bishops to visit foreign fields. He was instrumental in moving Westminster Seminary from rural Maryland to Washington as Wesley Seminary and in securing unprecedented General Conference funds to establish the School of International Service at American University. He chaired the church's divisions of educational institutions and foreign missions and chaplains. He conceived and led the massive Methodist Crusade for a New World Order, designed to persuade Methodists of the wisdom of American leadership in forming the United Nations; for this he received the personal thanks of Roosevelt and Truman.

Oxnam served as president of the Federal Council of Churches from 1944 to 1946. Although not a pacifist and believing the war against the Axis powers was just (his two sons were in uniform), he engaged the Federal Council in securing governmental protection for conscientious objectors. Nevertheless, when a handful of respected Protestant leaders condemned the relentless bombing of Germany and the obliteration of Hiroshima and Nagasaki, Oxnam as Federal Council president defended the stern, tragic deeds as necessary. During the war and postwar years Oxnam was consumed by the Federal Council's famed Commission on a Just and Durable Peace, led by Presbyterian layman John Foster Dulles. Even after Dulles later emerged as a Cold War warrior, Oxnam's initial admiration for him remained inexplicably undimmed.

When in 1950 the Federal Council became the larger National Council of Churches, Oxnam was a founder and leader. His widening participation in the ecumenical movement led to his election in 1948 as a president (one of six and the only American) of the newly formed World Council of Churches. Among his contributions to the World Council none was more valuable than his securing the reluctant permission of the Eisenhower administration for delegates from behind the Iron Curtain to enter the United States in 1954 to attend the great Second Assembly at Evanston, Illinois; without that permission Canada of necessity would have become the host country. Oxnam's leadership in the Federal, National, and World councils, as indeed in his own Methodist church, reveals an irenic spirit, to be sure, but also a less lovely passion for giant enterprises—corporate structures, bureaucratic values, and rationalized efficiency—characteristic of the secular world in which churches found themselves.

The U.S. government called on Oxnam frequently, most notably in early 1945 as official visitor to army and navy chaplains in Europe and in late 1945 as chairman of a commission to study relief and refugee conditions in defeated Germany. The commission's report to President Truman played a role in shaping America's occupation policies.

Oxnam's early concern for laboring Americans never slackened as he defended their rights in addresses before union conventions and testimony before congressional committees, served on the Public Review Board of the United Automobile Workers, and mediated numerous strikes. Despite accusations to the contrary, he never moved further to the left than the Americans for Democratic Action, an organization he helped found. His awareness of America's deepest sin, racism, however, came tardily, but by the mid-1940s his sense of contrition led to an increasing commitment to rooting out that sin. With words and deeds he challenged segregation in Methodism, in all Christian churches, and in society at large. Quite another observation must be made of his relations with Roman Catholics, or more precisely, the Catholic hierarchy. Every point of tension between Protestantism and Catholicism sparked in Oxnam grave anxiety, which he expressed in unmeasured language, in taut meetings with President Truman, and in the founding in 1948 of Protestants and Other Americans United for the Separation of Church and State, of which he was the first president. In judging Oxnam's keelhauling of the Catholic church, it is well to remember that the controversy raged before Vatican II and that, in any case, many other leaders of both faiths were also guilty of uncharitableness.

Oxnam became a considerable public figure. He was widely sought as a speaker, averaging close to three hundred addresses annually. In addition to a torrent of articles and news columns, he edited five books and wrote seventeen. While some were winsome statements of his liberal religious beliefs, none were deeply informed by biblical scholarship or theological study, subjects of little interest to this apostle of muscular Christianity.

Oxnam's finest hour, though not without ambiguity, came on 21 July 1953 when he appeared at his own request before the House Un-American Activities Committee (HUAC) to answer Representative Donald Jackson's charge on the floor of Congress that Oxnam was "to the Communist front what Man O'War was to thoroughbred horse racing." The ten-hour hearing was filmed for abbreviated television showing, and the press coverage was extensive. Although the committee members remained intractable (other than acknowl-

edging that he was not a Communist party member), Oxnam's brave and masterful performance helped alert the national public to the questionable motives and dangerous methods of HUAC in particular and of McCarthyism in general. Ravaged by Parkinson's disease, Oxnam retired in 1960. He died in White Plains, New York.

A quintessential Methodist, Oxnam honored the truth of the Social Gospel's dictum, "We rarely sin against God alone." His career was characterized by energy, enterprise, ceaseless activity, vaulting visions, and ambitious goals for Methodism, America, the world—and G. Bromley Oxnam. Not many years were to pass before it became clear that his reach had exceeded his grasp. Few Methodists would condemn him for that.

• Oxnam willed a massive collection of his papers to the Library of Congress. The second largest group of materials is housed at Wesley Theological Seminary. His two most autobiographical books are *I Protest* (1954) and *A Testament of Faith* (1958). Extensive information relating to Oxnam's political activities can be found in the papers of Presidents Truman and Eisenhower, John Foster Dulles, David E. Lilienthal, Charles P. Taft, and Myron C. Taylor. A full biography is Robert Moats Miller, *Bishop G. Bromley Oxnam: Paladin of Liberal Protestantism* (1990). Wayne Lowell Miller's "A Critical Analysis of the Speaking Career of Bishop G. Bromley Oxnam" (Ph.D. diss., Univ. of Southern California, 1961) is a fine study. The *Encyclopedia of World Methodism* contains an insightful sketch by Albea Godbold. An obituary is in the *Christian Advocate*, 28 Mar. 1963.

ROBERT MOATS MILLER

OZAWA, Takao (15 June 1875–16 Nov. 1936), central figure in naturalization test case, was born in Sakurai village, Ashigara-Kami District, Kanagawa Prefecture, Japan. Ozawa arrived in San Francisco at the age of nineteen. There he worked while putting himself through school and graduated from Berkeley High School. He then attended the University of California for three years. In 1906 he discontinued his studies and moved to Hawaii, where he was employed as a salesman by the Theo H. Davies Company, a large Honolulu dry goods wholesale dealer. He was married to Masako Takeya, who was also a Japanese immigrant. They had five children, all born, raised, and educated in Honolulu.

Ozawa was a highly assimilated Japanese immigrant. He read, spoke, and wrote English fluently. Indeed, throughout his life he insisted that English, and only English, be spoken in his household. He never spoke Japanese to his children and had them educated exclusively in American public schools. His wife, who had lived in Hawaii since the age of nine, was also an assimilated Japanese. Thus most of her upbringing was on the islands. Reflecting their complete adaptation to American culture, the Ozawa family ate only American foods and even dispensed with the practice of eating with chopsticks.

Desiring American citizenship, Ozawa filed a petition for naturalization on 16 October 1914 in Honolulu. Twelve years earlier, he had filed his petition of intent to naturalize in Alameda County, California. Ozawa satisfied all the nonracial requirements for naturalization. He met the five-year continuous residency requirement. His personal character and fluency in English satisfied the requirements related to moral fitness and knowledge of the English language. His case revolved primarily around the legal question of whether or not Ozawa, as a Japanese, could meet the racial requirement, specified in Section 2169 of the Act of 1906, that only "a free, white person" was eligible for naturalization.

Ozawa was unsuccessful at the lower court level. On 25 March 1916 Judge Charles F. Clemons of the U.S. District Court of the Territory of Hawaii ruled that Ozawa, though otherwise eminently qualified, was not eligible for naturalization because he failed to satisfy the racial requirement of Section 2169. Classified as a member of the Mongolian race, he was not a so-called free, white person, and was therefore disqualified. Ozawa immediately appealed his case to the Ninth Circuit Court, which in turn referred the case to the U.S. Supreme Court on 31 May 1917.

Japanese immigrant leaders on the Pacific Coast financially supported Ozawa in his appeal. The state of California had enacted the 1913 Alien Land Law, which prohibited so-called aliens ineligible for citizenship from purchasing agricultural land and restricted the leasing of such land to three years. Because all Japanese immigrants were automatically subject to this 1913 enactment, Japanese immigrant leaders viewed the acquisition of naturalization rights as the fundamental solution to the 1913 California Alien Land Law

and its subsequent 1920 amendment as well as to the other alien land laws enacted after 1921 by other western states.

In 1922 the Supreme Court heard the Ozawa case and confirmed the lower court ruling that, as a member of the Mongolian race, Ozawa was ineligible for citizenship. This ruling validated the racial requirement for naturalization and assured that Japanese immigrants would continue to be political pariahs within the American body politic.

Ozawa died without realizing his lifelong ambition to become an American citizen. During the Second World War, his only son, George Yshio Ozawa, an American by birth, volunteered for military service and was killed in action in Italy as a member of the famed Japanese-American combat unit, the 100th Infantry Battalion. After the passage of the Walter-McCarran Act of 1952, Japanese immigrants finally became eligible for citizenship. Ozawa's daughters fondly remember their mother, after she became a naturalized American, returning home "waving a little American flag" and saying, "If only [Takao] were here now."

• The best sources for information on the Ozawa case are Consulate General of Japan, *Documental History of Law Cases Affecting Japanese in the United States, 1916–1924*, vol. 1 (1925), pp. 1–20; Yuji Ichioka, "The Early Japanese Immigrant Quest for Citizenship: The Background of the 1922 Ozawa Case," *Amerasia Journal* 4, no. 2 (1977): 1–22; and Ichioka, *The Issei: The World of the First Generation Japanese Immigrants, 1885–1924* (1988), pp. 210–26.

YUJI ICHIOKA

P

PACA, William (31 Oct. 1740–13 Oct. 1799), lawyer and officeholder, was born on the Bush River near Abingdon in Baltimore (later Harford) County, Maryland, the son of John Paca, a planter, local officeholder, and delegate to the lower house of the Maryland General Assembly, and Elizabeth Smith. The Paca family was English, the Maryland progenitor arriving in the colony about 1660. At age twelve, Paca entered the Academy and Charity School in Philadelphia, which three years later became the College of Philadelphia. Paca took his B.A. in 1759 and studied law in the office of Stephen Bordley, a prominent Annapolis lawyer. Soon after arriving in Annapolis in 1759, Paca became a founding member of the Forensic Club, a group of "young Gentlemen" that met twice each month to debate politics, morality, and natural law.

In 1760 or 1761, Paca visited London, where he studied briefly at the Inns of Court. Returning to Maryland, he was admitted to practice law before the Annapolis Mayor's Court in October 1761. In 1762, after submitting a thesis, Paca was awarded an M.A. from the College of Philadelphia. This was an unusual educational achievement for a Marylander at the time, especially for one who was not training for the ministry. In June 1763, Paca began his law practice after qualifying as an attorney before the Anne Arundel and Baltimore county courts.

In 1763 Paca married Mary Chew, who possessed a considerable fortune. Four days after their marriage, the Pacas purchased two large city lots in Annapolis upon which they built, largely with Mary's wealth, the provincial capital's first great five-part Georgian mansion, including a two-acre pleasure garden in the English natural style.

Paca's political career began in 1765–1766 when he and Samuel Chase organized the Anne Arundel County Sons of Liberty and led the opposition to the Stamp Act in Annapolis. In 1767, Paca was one of two delegates elected without opposition to represent Annapolis in the lower house of the General Assembly. There Paca became a leader in defending the rights of the colonists. He opposed the Townshend Acts of 1767, and led the fight against Governor Robert Eden's Fee Proclamation of 1770. In each of these political controversies, Paca worked closely with Chase, and their individual strengths complimented each other. Chase was a fiery orator, who on a moment's notice could raise a mob in the streets; Paca excelled at formulating strategy and at writing closely reasoned newspaper essays and legal briefs. Together, Paca and Chase formed a potent political force in opposition to both British policies and perceived abuses by Maryland's proprietor. The Anglican rector, Jonathan Boucher, loyal defender of both king and pro-prietor, considered Paca and Chase the "two chief demagogues" among Maryland patriots.

In 1774, Paca was elected as a Maryland delegate to the first Continental Congress. He continued to serve in Congress until 1777. Paca joined with the other Maryland delegates in voting for independence from Britain on 2 July 1776, and in August 1776 signed the engrossed, or parchment, copy of the Declaration of Independence specially prepared for members' signatures.

Paca's successful public career contrasted with his private life. Mary Chew died in 1774. She had borne him three children; only one, John Philemon, survived to adulthood.

In August 1775 while he was representing Maryland in Congress, Paca and a woman named Levina, described as a "mustee" or person of mixed race, had a daughter. When the child, named Hester, was a month old, Paca had her baptized in Philadelphia's Christ Church. Nothing more is known of Levina. When Paca moved back to Maryland in 1781, he left Hester at a prominent Philadelphia boarding school for young ladies under the care of the eminent physician Benjamin Rush. She probably died before her father; he did not mention her in his will.

Paca fathered another natural daughter, who was probably born in 1777. Named Henrietta Maria, her mother was Sarah Joice, an Annapolis resident. Paca provided generous support for both mother and daughter, and bequeathed Henrietta Maria land, slaves, livestock, and cash in his will.

In February 1777, Paca married his second wife, Anne Harrison of Philadelphia, who at twenty was sixteen years his junior. Her father, a wealthy merchant and landowner, had been mayor of Philadelphia. Anne died three years after her marriage to Paca, leaving him a son who died in 1781. Like his first wife, Anne Harrison left Paca an "affluent fortune," including valuable property in Philadelphia.

In 1777, Paca led efforts on Maryland's Eastern Shore to raise a militia to oppose the British incursions into Chesapeake Bay and to put down local Tory insurrections. An ardent Anglican, Paca accused "scoundrel Methodist Preachers" of fomenting Loyalist opposition. Despite his firm support for independence, Paca refused to be tyrannized by what he considered illegal actions by patriot forces. When an American officer demanded that he surrender horses needed for a cavalry unit, Paca told him "if he attempted to seize any of my Horses I would blow his Brains out."

In 1777 and 1779–1780, Paca sat in the new state senate. In 1778, he was appointed a judge of the General Court, and in 1780 he was appointed by Congress as a judge of the Court of Appeals for Admiralty and Prize Cases.

In 1782, the General Assembly elected Paca to the first of three consecutive one-year terms as governor of Maryland. As the state's chief executive during the transition period between war and peace, Paca dealt with both the enormous state debt and the lack of public confidence in the economy and government. Paca advocated "the principle of public support for the ministers of the Gospel," even though Maryland's state constitution of 1776 embraced disestablishment. He also supported the cause of higher education, helping to convince the General Assembly in 1783 to charter Maryland's first college, Washington College, in Chestertown.

During Paca's tenure as chief executive, Annapolis became the temporary seat of the confederation government. Paca directed the completion and outfitting of the rooms in Maryland's new state house where Congress would hold its sessions. On 23 December 1783, General George Washington appeared before Congress, which was sitting in the Maryland Senate chamber, to resign his commission as commander in chief. Three weeks later, on 14 January 1784, Congress there approved the Treaty of Paris formally ending the War of Independence.

After completing his third term as governor and ineligible to succeed himself, Paca returned to Wye Island in Queen Anne's County on Maryland's Eastern Shore. His first wife had inherited half of the island, and Paca had maintained his legal residence there since 1774.

In 1786, the voters of Queen Anne's County elected Paca to the lower house of the Maryland General Assembly. Simultaneously, senate electors chose Paca as a member of the state's fifteen-man senate. Paca declined the senate post, choosing to represent Queen Anne's County in the lower house. There, with his old ally Samuel Chase, Paca led the effort to pass a paper money bill to aid those suffering the effects of the postwar economic depression. Faced with strong senate opposition Paca and Chase appealed directly to the voters, urging them to adopt instructions directing the senate to pass a paper money bill. The tactic backfired. Senators argued that the call for constituent instructions jeopardized their independence as members of a separate branch of the legislature. The public agreed, and the paper money bill failed. Paca never again stood for election to the Maryland General Assembly.

In early 1787, Paca declined appointment as one of Maryland's delegates to the Philadelphia convention to revise the Articles of Confederation. When the proposed U.S. Constitution adopted by the convention became public in the fall of 1787, Paca opposed it because it lacked a bill of rights.

Most Marylanders supported the proposed Constitution, including Paca's Queen Anne's County neighbors. In an apparent effort to prevent Paca and Chase (who had recently moved from Anne Arundel County to Baltimore Town) from winning election as Antifederalist delegates to Maryland's ratification convention, the General Assembly in the fall of 1787 passed a requirement that convention delegates reside in their county of election.

Despite this law, shortly before the election for delegates to Maryland's ratification convention, Paca returned to Harford County on the Western Shore, the place of his birth, to run for election on an Antifederalist slate. Although Paca had never before stood for election in Harford County, his slate won easily. He joined eleven other Antifederalists in Maryland's ratification convention, including Chase, who had returned to his political base in Anne Arundel County.

Maryland's ratification convention assembled in the state house in late April 1788. Paca had drawn up twenty-two amendments to the proposed Constitution, most of them drawn verbatim from Maryland's own state Declaration of Rights of 1776. Paca's amendments were the first systematic and comprehensive proposal for a bill of rights to come before any state ratification convention.

Federalists dominated the Maryland convention seventy-six delegates to twelve, however, and they refused Paca's request to introduce or even discuss his proposed amendments. When it became clear that Maryland would ratify the Constitution by a large majority, Paca proposed a deal that the Federalists accepted. He voted for the Constitution in exchange for the establishment of a committee authorized to review his amendments.

The amendments committee, chaired by Paca, met for two days. Despite a nine to four majority of Federalists, the committee approved thirteen proposed amendments. The Federalist majority in the convention prevented these amendments from being formally presented, however, and on 28 April 1788, the delegates voted sixty-three to eleven for unconditional ratification. True to his word, Paca voted with the majority.

Despite the agreement that required him to vote for ratification of the Constitution, Paca joined his fellow Antifederalists from the convention in publishing a defense of the amendments they believed were necessary to preserve individual rights and a role for the states. Virginia Antifederalists used the Maryland document as a source for some of the amendments in the proposed bill of rights that they presented in June to that state's ratification convention.

Paca's objections to the Constitution were mollified when Congress in 1789 proposed a federal Bill of Rights, and he soon became a firm supporter of the federal government. In 1789, Paca assumed his last public office when he accepted President Washington's offer to become the first judge of the federal district court for Maryland.

Except for attending court sessions, Paca spent the last ten years of his life in virtual retirement on his Wye Island estate. He had great wealth, accumulated from his law practice and his two marriages. In the late 1780s, he began the construction of "Wye Hall," a five-part country house with French-inspired ornamentation on his Wye Island estate. Designed by architect Joseph Clark with gardens designed by Luke O'Dio, it was one of the finest houses in America when completed.

Paca died at Wye Hall and was buried on the grounds. When his son, John Philemon, later solicited comments about his father, none described Paca with more sensitivity than Charles Willson Peale, the Maryland-born artist who had painted a full-length image of him in the 1770s. Peale remembered Paca as "a handsome man, more than 6 feet high, of portly appearance, being well educated and accustomed to the best company, he was graceful in his movements and complacent to every one; in short his manners were of the first polish."

• Personal papers of William Paca are scarce, and if a family archive existed it was probably destroyed when Wye Hall burned in 1879. Paca's public career can be traced and his substantial landholdings can be reconstructed from public records at the Maryland State Archives in Annapolis. The Maryland State Papers series at the Maryland State Archives has much material relating to Paca's service in the Continental Congress and as governor of the state. The only full-length biography of Paca is Gregory A. Stiverson and Phebe R. Jacobsen, *William Paca, A Biography* (1976), although his family history and public career are outlined in the Paca sketch in Edward C. Papenfuse et al., *A Biographical Dictionary of the Maryland Legislature, 1635–1789* (2 vols., 1979–1985), 2:632–35. Some interesting material can be found in Albert Silverman, "William Paca, Signer, Governor, Jurist," *Maryland Historical Magazine* 37 (1942): 1–25. Paca's opposition to the proposed U.S. Constitution and his proposed constitutional amendments are discussed in Gregory A. Stiverson, "Maryland's Antifederalists and the Perfection of the U.S. Constitution," *Maryland Historical Magazine* 83 (1988): 18–35. The history of the restored Paca house and gardens in Annapolis is covered in Jean B. Russo, *William Paca House & Garden* (1990).

GREGORY A. STIVERSON

PACE, Edward Aloysius (3 July 1861–26 Apr. 1938), Catholic priest and scholar, was born in Starke, Florida, the son of George Edward Pace, a Methodist planter and manufacturer of turpentine, and Margaret Kelly, a Catholic and daughter of the comptroller of the Port of Halifax, Nova Scotia. The first of eight children, Pace attended Duval High School in Jacksonville (1872–1876) and St. Charles College in Ellicott City, Maryland, a preparatory seminary (1876–1880, A.B.). He then became a seminarian at the North American College in Rome, studying philosophy (1880–1882) and theology (1882–1886, S.T.D.) at the Urbanian College. One of his professors was Francesco Satolli, a promoter of the Thomistic revival. Pace was ordained priest on 30 May 1885 for the Diocese of St. Augustine.

Pope Leo XIII recommended Pace, who had been rector of the cathedral in St. Augustine, to be the first rector of the Catholic University of America (opened in 1889), and in 1888 Pace returned to Europe to prepare himself to teach philosophy. Considering a knowledge of science essential for this purpose, he took courses in biology at the University of Louvain and in chemistry and physiology at the Sorbonne before proceeding to Leipzig, where he became a student of psychology under Wilhelm Wundt and of physiology under Karl Ludwig. He was only the third American and the first Catholic priest to study under Wundt. Having written a dissertation titled *Das Relativitätsprincip in Herbert Spencer's psychologischer Entwicklungslehre: eine kritische Studie* (The principal of relativity in Herbert Spencer's psychological theory of development: A critical study), he received the degrees of doctor of philosophy and master of fine arts magna cum laude in 1891. Thereupon he was appointed to the faculty of the Catholic University, where he remained until he retired in 1935.

Pace was named professor of psychology in 1891, and in that year he established a psychological laboratory, the second of its kind in the United States and the first among Catholic universities or colleges in the world. In 1892 he was among the first five men elected to membership by the twenty-six charter members at the founding of the American Psychological Association. In most of his early articles he dealt with experimental psychology, either reporting his laboratory findings or attempting to justify the science in the eyes of Catholics by showing its harmony with the faith. In this way, in spite of some early suspicions of his orthodoxy, he helped to bring his co-religionists into the modern age. Even after he was named professor of philosophy in 1894, he maintained a keen interest in psychology, continuing his critical search for empirical data bearing on basic philosophical problems. In 1901 he began editing the series "Psychological Studies from the Catholic University of America." In 1904 he was chairman of the experimental psychology section at the International Congress of Arts and Sciences held during the Universal Exposition in St. Louis. From 1904 to 1908 he collaborated in editing the *Psychological Review*, and in 1926 he became the first editor of "Studies in Psychology and Psychiatry."

When the School of Philosophy, comprising several departments of arts and sciences, was established in 1895, Pace was appointed its first dean; he served in that office until 1899 and again in 1906–1914 and 1934–1935. In 1900 he was a delegate of the university at the founding of the Association of American Universities, and in 1924 he traveled to Louvain to represent it at the first meeting of what was to become the International Federation of Catholic Universities. He also held other positions in the university administration, most notably vice-rector (1925–1935).

As professor of philosophy Pace advanced the neo-scholastic movement, the revival of the philosophy of St. Thomas Aquinas, in the United States through his teaching and writing. He was a founding member of the American Philosophical Association (1893). In 1926, with James H. Ryan, he organized the American Catholic Philosophical Association and was its first president; he also became co-founder and coeditor of its journal, *The New Scholasticism* (1927–1936). With his mastery of the text of the Thomistic corpus, his clear understanding of the mind of St. Thomas, and his grasp of the fundamental principles of the Thomistic synthesis and world view, he was the most distinguished American exponent of that school of philosophy in the first third of the twentieth century.

Using philosophy for the theory and psychology for the method, Pace also developed the discipline of education. He was founder (1899) and director of the Institute of Pedagogy, out of which the university's department of education evolved. He collaborated in the launching of a Teachers' Institute for Sisters in San Francisco and an Institute of Pedagogy in New York City, where he traveled once a week for several years to teach. In 1911, in collaboration with Thomas E. Shields of the Catholic University, he established the *Catholic Educational Review* and became its first editor. He was also an adviser to various national Catholic educational organizations. In 1914 he helped to found Catholic Sisters College near the Catholic University of America for the training of teachers in Catholic schools. In 1925–1926 he was chairman of the American Council on Education, and in 1929 he was made a member of the National Advisory Committee on Education by President Herbert Hoover.

In other ways too Pace was engaged and recognized outside his university. In the late 1890s he helped to found Trinity College for women in Washington, D.C., and after it was opened in 1900 he taught there for many years. In 1904 he became one of the founders and editors of the *Catholic Encyclopedia*, a sixteen-volume international work of reference (1907–1914), to which he contributed thirty-seven articles. In recognition of his labors he was honored by Pope Pius X with the medal *Pro Ecclesia et Pontifice*. In 1919 he was commissioned to compose a joint pastoral letter for the American hierarchy; it was the first national pastoral issued since 1884 and has never been exceeded for comprehensiveness. In the following year (1920) Pope Benedict XV conferred on him the title of prothonotary apostolic. He became professor emeritus in 1935. He died in Washington, D.C.

With his fair hair and youthful features, Pace had the appearance of a southern gentleman and professional scholar. He was gifted with a pleasant personality, a serene disposition, and a courteous demeanor, and he was highly cultured. Although he was an original and creative thinker and a pioneer and leader in many fields, he was not rash. As a teacher and writer he was noted for the lucidity of his style, which was unaffected and marked by order and logic. He strove to integrate Catholic theology, scholastic metaphysics, and contemporary science. Specifically in education he endeavored to improve methods of teaching religion, to develop programs and courses for seminarians and for graduate students in philosophy and psychology, and to advise and encourage other educators. In the three areas of his intellectual specialization, his was an enduring influence, especially on American Catholics.

• Pace's papers are deposited at the Catholic University of America. His nearly 300 writings are scattered in many periodicals and reference works. Besides his dissertation cited above, his best-known book is *Lectures on Methods of Teaching Religion* (1928). See also the biographical sketch by James H. Ryan in the festschrift for Pace's seventieth birthday, *Aspects of the New Scholastic Philosophy*, ed. Charles A. Hart (1932), and the one by John K. Ryan in *The New Scholasticism* 35 (1961): 141–51. He is the subject of a doctoral dissertation in philosophy written by William P. Braun, C.S.C., "Monsignor Edward A. Pace, Educator and Philosopher" (Catholic Univ. of America, 1968). He is included in *Catholics in Psychology: A Historical Survey* by Henryk Misiak and Virginia M. Staudt (1954) and is frequently mentioned by C. Joseph Nuesse in *The Catholic University of America: A Centennial History* (1990).

ROBERT TRISCO

PACE, Harry Herbert (6 Jan. 1884–26 July 1943), entrepreneur, was born in Covington, Georgia, the son of Charles Pace, a blacksmith, and Nancy Francis. Pace's father died when he was an infant, but he was nonetheless able to secure a good education. He finished elementary school in Covington by the time he was twelve and seven years later graduated as valedictorian of his class at Atlanta University.

Pace learned the trade of printer's devil as a youth and worked in the Atlanta University printshop. After graduation he took a job in a new firm established by a group of prominent blacks in Atlanta. Pace served as foreman and shop manager, but the venture was unsuccessful and soon closed. In 1904 Pace became an instructor at the Haines Institute in Augusta, Georgia, where he remained for only a year when W. E. B. Du Bois, who had been one of his teachers at Atlanta University, persuaded him to join him in launching the *Moon Illustrated Weekly*, a magazine for blacks published in Memphis, Tennessee. Du Bois served as editor of the journal, which commenced publication in December 1905, and Pace was its manager. Although the venture was relatively short-lived, it was one of the earliest efforts at a weekly magazine for blacks and provided Pace with a favorable introduction to the rising African-American business community of Memphis.

When the *Moon* folded in July 1906 Pace was offered a position as professor of Latin and Greek at Lincoln University in Jefferson City, Missouri, where he remained for a year. In 1907 Robert R. Church, president of Solvent Savings Bank in Memphis, asked the young man to join the bank as cashier. Pace proved himself an excellent businessman. Within four years he had increased the bank's assets from $50,000 to $600,000, turning it into an exceedingly profitable venture.

In 1912 Heman Perry, the owner of Standard Life Insurance Company of Atlanta, offered Pace the position of secretary of the firm, which was just being organized. Perry and Pace put herculean efforts into the company, and in 1913 Standard Life became the first black insurance company organized solely for the purpose of selling ordinary life insurance and the third African-American insurance firm to achieve legal reserve status. Standard Life grew rapidly over its first ten years. Pace installed rigorous business systems at Standard, but these exacting regulations did not suit the entrepreneurial personality of Perry, causing the two men to clash often over Perry's cavalier attitude. Nonetheless, Pace managed to work with Perry until the summer of 1917, when petty friction while Pace was on his honeymoon with Ethlynde Bibb, with whom he had two children, finally exploded into a confrontation that caused Pace to leave Standard Life.

Pace headed for New York City, where in 1918 he joined William C. Handy, the great composer and compiler of the blues, in establishing Pace and Handy Music, a sheet music publishing company. The two had been associated with each other since 1907 in the music industry in Memphis, where Pace had often written lyrics to accompany songs written by Handy. Pace and Handy Music was a dynamic and successful business in New York for a number of years. Pace, who served as its first president, stayed with the company until 1921. Handy continued to run the company as Handy Brothers Music Company until the 1950s.

Pace and Handy's greatest success was with "St. Louis Blues," written earlier by Handy, which became a huge hit. But Pace was frustrated. White-owned record companies would buy their songs and then record them using white artists. In March 1921 Pace started his own record firm, Black Swan Records, the first to be owned by blacks in the United States. Pace did not have an easy time getting the firm established because white-owned companies set up obstacles, preventing him, for instance, from purchasing a record-pressing plant for a time. Ultimately, however, he set up recording studios, a pressing laboratory, and obtained other supplies necessary to produce records. The future for Black Swan Records seemed bright in 1922–1923, but the advent of radio as a popular, and much cheaper, means of transmitting music destroyed the prospects of the company and threatened to send even white record firms into bankruptcy. As a result Pace decided to sell his firm to Paramount Records in 1925. Although many of Pace's artists, such as Ethel Waters, continued to be recorded, much of the authenticity of earlier black music was lost. Most importantly, blacks were largely shut out of the management side of the record business.

In 1925 Pace moved back into the insurance industry, participating in the organization of Northeastern Life Insurance Company in Newark, New Jersey, and serving as its president. Although the firm struggled in its first couple of years, Pace operated it fairly successfully until 1929, when he began talking with Truman K. Gibson about the possibility of merging Northeastern with Supreme Life and Casualty of Columbus, Ohio. Supreme Life had large holdings of industrial insurance, with salesmen trained to sell it, while Pace's Northeastern had an excellent investment portfolio and first-rate management. Neither firm, however, had been profitable in 1928, so they began seeking another company that had larger cash reserves. They merged with Liberty Life Insurance of Chicago, one of the largest and most successful black companies in the country. The new firm, called Supreme Liberty Life Insurance, had combined capital of $400,000, insurance in force of $25 million, total assets of over $1.4 million, and 1,090 employees. Pace was named president and chief executive officer in the new company.

The early years of Supreme Liberty Life were ones of struggle. Just after the merger in 1929, the devastating Great Depression struck, and the situation for Supreme Liberty was more desperate than for many insurance firms because the company relied more heavily on the ordinary life insurance market. These policies were expensive, so poor blacks, who suffered greatly from the depression, were more likely to allow them to lapse. To deal with these crushing problems, Pace focused the firm more on the industrial insurance market. This was successful, and Supreme Liberty became increasingly profitable in the late 1930s. This recovery was based largely on a system called "mass production," in which largely untrained agents were sent out to write as many policies as they could without requiring any financial settlement at the time of signing. After the policy had been processed and issued, the agent would then try to get the client to sign it, stressing the very small weekly premiums to be paid. This technique allowed a rapid expansion of Supreme Liberty's industrial holdings. This expansion, however, was very expensive. Supreme Liberty's lapse rate was the highest among black firms, and the expense of collecting premiums on policies in force was also high. Although this did little to enhance the reputation of Supreme Liberty, the total insurance in force increased from $16.6 million in 1930 to $83.1 million by 1944.

After the American entrance into World War II, with black employment and wages rising rapidly, Supreme Liberty began to sell the more profitable ordinary life insurance. But this new era was faced by Gibson after Pace's death in Chicago. Pace was a member of the National Negro Insurance Association, serving as its president in 1928–1929. Partially because of this position, he became an influential writer on insurance issues among blacks and wrote a number of articles for the African-American insurance industry that appeared in major African-American publications.

Pace was the founder or cofounder of an impressive number of important African-American companies, at times introducing blacks into industries where they previously had no standing. He networked with most of the prominent African Americans of the time, to the extent that he operated at the very apex of the status and power pyramids in the black communities of Memphis, Atlanta, New York City, and Chicago at various points in his life.

• Neither family nor business papers of Harry Pace are known to exist, but portions of his correspondence can be found in several collections. A number of references to Pace, along with the words to one of his early songs appear in the W. C. Handy Collection at the Memphis–Shelby County Public Library. At least two letters from Pace to Booker T. Washington are in the Booker T. Washington Papers at the Library of Congress. Most interesting and useful, however, are a number of letters between Pace and Robert L. Vann concerning Black Swan Records in the Percival L. Prattis Collection at the Moorland-Spingarn Research Center at Howard University. Pace's articles appeared in a number of newspapers and magazines. The most significant were "The Possibilities of Negro Insurance," *Opportunity*, Sept. 1930; "The Attitude of Life Insurance Companies Toward Negroes," *Southern Workman*, Jan. 1928; "The Business of Insurance Among Negroes," *Crisis*, Sept. 1926; and "The Business of Insurance," *Messenger*, Mar. 1927. Only two issues of the *Moon Illustrated Weekly* survive; they are held at the Memphis–Shelby County Public Library.

For additional information consult Paul G. Partington, "The *Moon Illustrated Weekly*—the Precursor of *The Crisis*," *Journal of Negro History* (July 1963): 206–16; Miriam DeCosta-Willis, "DuBois' Memphis Connection," *West Tennessee History Society Papers* 42 (Dec. 1988): 30–38; Harry C. Pace, "A New Business Venture," *Crisis* 8 (Jan. 1914): 143; W. C. Handy, *Father of the Blues* (1941); Ethel Waters, *His Eye Is on the Sparrow* (1950); Robert C. Puth, "Supreme Life: The History of a Negro Life Insurance Company," *Business History Review* (Spring 1969): 1–21; and "From Enforced Segregation to Integration: Market Factors in the Development of a Negro Life Insurance Company," in *Business Enterprise and Economic Change: Essays in Honor of Harold F. Williamson*, ed. Louis F. Cain and Paul J. Uselding (1973), pp. 280–301. Obituaries are in the *Chicago Defender* and *Amsterdam News*, both 31 July 1943.

JOHN N. INGHAM

PACH, Walter (11 July 1883–27 Nov. 1958), artist and art critic, was born in New York City, the son of Gotthelf Pach, a photographer, and Frances Wise. The elder Pach was the official photographer for the Metropolitan Museum of Art and by bringing Walter to the museum while he worked, Gotthelf Pach introduced his son to art at an early age. Pach grew up in a comfortable, middle-class home with one brother, Alfred. He graduated with a bachelor of arts degree from the College of the City of New York in 1903. Thereafter he received artistic training in Manhattan under Leigh Hunt, William Merritt Chase, and Robert Henri. He also studied at the Académie Ranson in Paris. Between 1903 and 1910 Pach was the agent for the Chase European Summer School.

Although he lived in New York City most of his life, Pach resided abroad frequently. He was in Paris intermittently between 1903 and 1913 and from 1929 through 1932, and he lived in Mexico City in 1922 and during 1942 and 1943. In February 1914 he married Magdalene Frohberg of Dresden, Germany, whom he had met in Florence in 1907. The couple had one son. Magdalene Pach died in 1950; in 1951 Pach married Nikifora Loutsi of Greece.

Walter Pach was a seminal figure in the history of early twentieth-century American art. His importance lies in his roles as an art critic, historian, lecturer, agent, and champion of modernism. Pach played a pivotal part in the organization of the famous International Exhibition of Modern Art, better known as the Armory Show. This event, held in New York, Chicago, and Boston in 1913 and 1914, was the first large-scale exhibition to bring avant-garde European paint-ing and sculpture to America, thereby changing the course of art in the United States.

While living in Paris during the early 1900s, Pach became friends with several of the most advanced painters and sculptors of the time. He was instrumental in securing the loan of works from artists such as Henri Matisse, Odilon Redon, Marcel Duchamp, and Constantin Brancusi and became, in essence, the European agent for the Armory Show. As a publicist, chief salesperson, and lecturer during the show's run in America, Pach helped promote and disseminate the ideas of modernism to large audiences. During the course of the exhibition he met John Quinn and Walter Arensberg, individuals who, through Pach's assistance, amassed two of the earliest and most significant collections of modern art in the United States.

During World War I Pach acted as a liaison between some of the European artists and American galleries and collectors. He borrowed pieces from Georges Rouault, André Derain, Raoul Dufy, Raymond Duchamp-Villon, and others for display at various venues in New York and Philadelphia, and he was the representative for the Carroll Galleries of New York. With the war raging on the Continent, this was a critical time for modernism and its proponents. Through Pach's efforts avant-garde European artists found not only a place to exhibit their works but individuals to purchase them.

Pach was also a staunch supporter of American and Mexican painters and sculptors of his day. He formed close bonds with John Sloan, Maurice Prendergast, Arthur B. Davies, Diego Rivera, and José Orozco and wrote articles on some of these artists. In addition to arranging shows at commercial galleries, Pach helped found and was treasurer of the Society of Independent Artists. From 1917 to 1944 this New York organization held annual exhibitions that promoted all styles of foreign and American art.

Pach devoted a substantial amount of his career to writing. Some of his major works include *George Seurat* (1923), *Raymond Duchamp-Villon, sculpteur* (1924), *The Masters of Modern Art* (1924), *Ananias, or the False Artist* (1928), *Queer Thing, Painting* (1938), *Ingres* (1939), and *The Classical Tradition in Modern Art*, published posthumously in 1959. In addition to these books, Pach contributed numerous articles to newspapers and magazines such as the *New York Times*, *Scribner's Magazine*, the *Dial*, the *Freeman*, the *Century*, *L'Amour de l'Art*, and *Gazette des Beaux-Arts*. His piece on Cézanne in *Scribner's Magazine* (Dec. 1908) was the first serious discussion of the artist to appear in English. Pach also translated several books, among them Elie Faure's five-volume *History of Art* (1921–1930) and *The Journal of Eugene Delacroix* (1937).

Between 1906 and his death, Pach lectured extensively throughout the United States. His topics covered the history of art in general, with an emphasis on modernism. He was an instructor at the University of California, Berkeley (Summer 1918), the National University of Mexico in Mexico City (Summer 1922 and 1942–1943), New York University (1924, 1926–

1928), the Art Students League in Manhattan (Fall 1932), Columbia University (Summer 1935, Fall 1936, 1937–1938), and the College of the City of New York (1949–1958). Through these activities Pach introduced modern as well as other art to a broad range of the populace.

Although most renowned for his work as critic and speaker, Pach considered himself first and foremost an artist. He created and exhibited numerous paintings, watercolors, and etchings, and his style ranged from realistic to abstract. Most of his mature works are either still lifes or portraits. Several of his works are in the collections of the Metropolitan Museum of Art, the New York Public Library, and the Museum of Modern Art, New York. In the 1910s, 1920s, and 1930s Pach's works received favorable reviews. However, in the last two decades of his life the realistic style and subject matter of his art were considered outdated.

The history of American art and art criticism would have been quite different without the work of Walter Pach. He not only championed the art of his own time, stating in an article for the *Atlantic* (May 1950), "Art must be modern because life must be modern," but he also had a comprehensive knowledge of the history of art. His books, articles, and lectures discussed a wide range of subjects, from ancient Mexican and Native American art to early twentieth-century European and American modernism. Pach firmly believed in the power of art to shape and affect people's lives. Throughout his career he strove to promote an understanding of and appreciation for the art of different nations and eras. He fought to make art a vital part of life in America. As John Quinn, Pach's friend and colleague, remarked, "I believe that before very long his contributions would come to be regarded as the best art criticism that we would have." Walter Pach died in New York City.

• Walter Pach's papers are in the Archives of American Art, Smithsonian Institution, Washington, D.C. William C. Agee, "Walter Pach and Modernism: A Sampler from New York, Paris, and Mexico City," *Archives of American Art Journal* 28 (1988): 2–10, gives an overview of the contents of the Pach papers. Pach's publications, in addition to those mentioned in the text, include *Odilon Redon* (1913), *A Sculptor's Architecture* (1913), *An Hour of Art* (1930), *Vincent Van Gogh, 1853–1890: A Study of the Artist and His Work in Relation to His Times* (1936), *Masterpieces of Art, New York World's Fair* (1940), and *The Art Museum in America* (1948). Bennard B. Perlman, "Walter Pach (1883–1958) and Magda Pach (1884–1950)," in *Exhibition of the Art of Walter and Magda Pach* (1988), discusses Pach's life and career. A publication that specifically analyzes Pach's art criticism is Sandra Phillips, "The Art Criticism of Walter Pach," *Art Bulletin* 65 (Mar. 1983): 106–22. An obituary is in the *New York Times*, 28 Nov. 1958.

LAURETTE E. McCARTHY

PACHECO, Romualdo (31 Oct. 1831–23 Jan. 1899), governor, congressman, and diplomat, was born José Antonio Romualdo Pacheco in Santa Barbara, California, the son of José Antonio Romualdo Pacheco, a Mexican soldier, and Ramona Carrillo. Within two months of the boy's birth, his father was killed in combat during the internal conflicts in the period following the end of Spanish rule near Los Angeles, and his mother subsequently married John Wilson, a Scottish sea captain. In 1838 Pacheco and his older brother sailed on the *Don Quixote* to the Hawaiian Islands to attend an English school. Pacheco returned to California in 1843 and immediately went to sea on one of his stepfather's ships to learn navigation, accompanied by a tutor, Thomas B. Parker of Massachusetts. The youth left this endeavor in 1848 to work on the large estates owned by his wealthy mother and stepfather in San Luis Obispo County. He was a successful rancher and businessman by 1850, when he took the oath of allegiance accepting U.S. citizenship, a choice granted to him by the terms of the Treaty of Guadalupe Hidalgo, which ended the Mexican War in 1848. Two years later California entered the Union, and Pacheco's interests turned to politics and government.

Pacheco's first political office was that of superior court judge of San Luis Obispo County, which he held from 1853 to 1857. In the latter year he was elected a state senator, serving until 1862 in the ninth and tenth legislative sessions. His district comprised San Luis Obispo and Santa Barbara counties. Pacheco entered politics as a Democrat, but the election of Abraham Lincoln as president in 1860, the secession of eleven southern states in 1860–1861, his abhorrence of slavery, and his loyalty to the Union impelled Pacheco to change political affiliations. When he successfully sought reelection to the state senate in 1861, he ran as a member of the Union party.

The year 1863 was a turning point in Pacheco's career. During those twelve months, he joined the Republican party, was appointed state treasurer to fill a vacancy, and received the nomination for state treasurer, to which office he was elected, defeating Thomas Findley, a Democrat. He also obtained a commission as brigadier general of the California State Militia from Governor Leland Stanford. In addition, that year Pacheco married Mary Catherine McIntire, who was among the first published women writers of California. Her works included plays and novels. They had two children, one of whom died at age seven.

Pacheco in 1867 lost a reelection bid for state treasurer to Antonio Coronel, but he returned to the state senate in 1869. In 1871 Pacheco was nominated at the Republican State Convention for lieutenant governor to run on the ticket headed by Newton Booth. They won election on 6 September and took office on 8 December 1871. As lieutenant governor, Pacheco served, as ex officio warden of the San Quentin penitentiary and tried to clean up the deplorable living conditions there. When the state legislature selected Booth to fill a seat in the U.S. Senate, Lieutenant Governor Pacheco inherited the governorship.

Pacheco's brief gubernatorial term, lasting from 27 February 1875 to 9 December 1875, was basically uneventful but filled with promise. He enjoyed the distinction of being California's first native governor. During his ten months in office, Pacheco granted sixty pardons from the state prison and seventeen from county jails. He recommended a statewide policy on irrigation, recognized the necessity for the state to control corporations, advocated expenditures for public schools, urged more buildings for the University of California, favored new facilities for the state government, supported the development of the Yosemite Valley, and sought to build a harmonious society in California between the native Spanish-speaking groups, on the one hand, and settlers from various regions, on the other. His progressive attitude was reflected in his message to the legislature, "There would be less crime and misery, less convict labor wasted, and fewer pensioners on the public bounty, if the opportunity were given to many to properly learn even the rudiments of those arts and sciences which enable a man or woman to command fair wages for honest labor" (*Journals of the Senate and Assembly*, app., 4th Assembly, 21st sess., pp. 15–16). The governor also believed in a low rate of taxation to alleviate the financial burdens of the people.

Although Pacheco sought the nomination for governor at the Republican State Convention in Sacramento in June 1875, he withdrew from the contest when he realized that he would not receive the coveted prize because of intraparty divisions. He ran instead as an independent candidate for lieutenant governor but lost to Democrat James A. Johnson. Even in defeat Pacheco garnered more votes than the Republican candidates for governor and lieutenant governor.

Pacheco's defeat in 1875 opened the door to other political opportunities. In 1876 he ran for California's Fourth District seat in the U.S. House of Representatives, receiving 19,104 votes, one more vote than that obtained by his Democratic opponent, Peter D. Wigginton, the incumbent, who contested the results. Some of the returns from precincts in Monterey County were questionable. Pacheco petitioned for a writ of mandamus after the California secretary of state refused to declare him the winner. The California Supreme Court thereupon ordered the secretary of state to issue a certificate of election to Pacheco, who took the oath of office on 17 October 1877, upon the approval of Representative James A. Garfield, Republican floor leader. A House committee, however, recommended seating Wigginton, and the full House, on a partisan vote, later concurred with this report. Returning to California to enhance his political base, Pacheco ran again for the elusive House seat in 1878 and won the election. He secured reelection in 1880, serving in the lower chamber from 1879 to 1883. Pacheco chaired the Committee on Private Land Claims in the Forty-seventh Congress and worked to improve farm conditions.

Following the expiration of his term, Pacheco returned to his home in California, where he remained a prominent resident. For a time he was a San Francisco stockbroker, a partner in the firm of Hale and Pacheco.

In 1890 President Benjamin Harrison summoned Pacheco to serve as envoy extraordinary and minister plenipotentiary to the Central American republics. On 1 July 1891 he was appointed minister plenipotentiary to Honduras and Guatemala, where he worked to stabilize relations between those two countries. He served until 21 June 1893, three months after the inauguration of President Grover Cleveland. After his return to California, Pacheco lived quietly in retirement at the home of his brother-in-law, Henry R. Miller, in Oakland, where he died.

An important political figure in California, Pacheco spanned the Spanish and American periods of California's history. He was the first native governor of California, the state's first native congressman, and its first native son who served as minister to a neighboring country.

• Pacheco left no personal papers. Some of his letters are in the Benjamin Harrison Papers at the Library of Congress. His speeches are in the *Congressional Record* from 1877 to 1883. The main work on Pacheco is Peter Thomas Conmy, *Romualdo Pacheco, 1831–1899: Distinguished Californian of the Mexican and American Periods* (1957). Other useful works include Ronald Genini and Richard Hitchman, *Romualdo Pacheco: A Californio in Two Eras* (1985); R. Hal Williams, *The Democratic Party and California Politics, 1880–1896* (1973); *Papers Relating to the Foreign Relations of the United States* (1890–1891); Theodore Hittell, *History of California* (1885–1897); Annie L. Morrison and John H. Haydon, *History of San Luis Obispo County and Environs* (1917); and Winfield J. Davis, *History of Political Conventions, 1849–1892* (1893). An obituary is in the *Oakland Tribune*, 24 Jan. 1899.

LEONARD SCHLUP

PACKARD, Alpheus Spring, Jr. (19 Feb. 1839–14 Feb. 1905), zoologist, was born in Brunswick, Maine, the son of Alpheus Spring Packard, a professor of Greek and Latin at Bowdoin College, and Frances Elizabeth Appleton. He received an A.B. from Bowdoin College in 1861 and an M.D. from Maine Medical School in 1864. While still a child, Packard had begun to study natural history. He studied insect morphology and classification at the Lawrence Scientific School and Museum of Comparative Zoology, Cambridge, Massachusetts, under Louis Agassiz from 1861 to 1864 and from 1862 to 1864 was an assistant at the Museum of Comparative Zoology. After a brief expedition to Labrador, he served ten months in the Civil War as assistant surgeon in a Maine unit. He occupied several positions between 1865 and 1878: acting custodian and librarian of the Boston Society of Natural History, curator of the Peabody Academy of Science at Salem, and lecturer at Maine State Agricultural College, Massachusetts Agricultural College, and Bowdoin College. In 1867 he married Elizabeth Derby Walcott; they would have four children. That year he also cofounded the *American Naturalist*, originally a popular science journal. In 1869 Packard published *Guide to the Study of Insects*, essentially a summary of current knowledge of entomology. Highly successful, by 1884 it had appeared in eight editions.

Deeply religious, and adhering to the idealist morphology he had learned from Agassiz, Packard was slow to be convinced of evolution. By 1871, however, study of the embryological development of *Limulus* (the horseshoe crab) had caused him to follow Edward Cope and Alpheus Hyatt in accepting a theory of evolution based on the acceleration and retardation of development, in which changing physical conditions of life led to evolutionary change. Agassiz's principle of recapitulation, whereby the life history of each organism recapitulates the history of life, was recast in evolutionary terms: recapitulation occurs because each stage of an organism's life history results from the inheritance of characteristics acquired in response to conditions present at that stage.

During the 1870s, Packard studied zoology and entomology at various institutions and government agencies. Between 1871 and 1873 he served as state entomologist of Massachusetts, preparing annual reports on "injurious and beneficial" insects. In summer 1873, he taught at Agassiz's Anderson School of Natural History, on Penikese Island off the coast of Massachusetts. In 1874, with the Geological Survey of Kentucky, he investigated the fauna of the Mammoth Cave and other caves. In 1875–1876 Packard was connected with the United States Geological and Geographical Survey, which published in 1876 his 600-page *Monograph of the Geometrid Moths*. In 1877 he became secretary of the new U.S. Entomological Commission; this involved study of locusts and other insect pests, culminating with a large monograph, *Insects Injurious to Forest and Shade Trees* (1881, 1890). In 1878 Packard became professor of zoology and geology at Brown University, a post he held until his death in Providence, Rhode Island.

As his career developed, Packard's studies in evolution became prominent. Research on the blind fauna of Mammoth Cave and other caves had helped convince him that the physical environment was the chief agent of evolution, inducing organisms to become better adapted to their environment. Evolution was therefore progressive, and hence compatible with his religious convictions, because it demonstrated, he once wrote, the guidance of "an infinite intelligence and will." Indeed, as Packard noted in *Our Common Insects* (1873), "the evolution theory . . . revealing to us the mode in which the Creator of the Universe works in the world of matter, [forms] an immeasurably grander conception of the order of creation and its Ordainer, than was possible for us to form before these laws were discovered and put to practical use." He accordingly drew away, after the 1870s, from the theories of Cope and Hyatt, which postulated nonadaptive evolutionary trends. He summarized his work on cave fauna in *The Cave Fauna of North America* (1888).

By the 1890s, Packard had firmly associated his views on evolution with those of Chevalier de Lamarck, writing in 1901 a biography, *Lamarck, the Founder of Evolution, His Life and Work*. He also coined the term "neo-Lamarckism," thereby helping to establish, with Cope and Hyatt, the distinctive identity of this first American school of evolutionary theory. His advocacy of neo-Lamarckism and his criticism

of theories of evolution by natural selection became increasingly strident, reflecting a polarization between these rival schools of evolutionary theory. While involved in this theoretical dispute, Packard nevertheless continued other work. In 1898 he published his *Textbook of Entomology*, a substantial college-level survey of the discipline. Through this and other books, Packard had perhaps his widest influence. One colleague observed that "as a teacher through books he has taught more students than any other American entomologist" (Cockerell, p. 204).

Packard also gained an increasingly distinguished reputation within the zoological research community. In 1872 he was elected to the National Academy of Sciences. In 1889 he was elected an honorary president of the International Zoological Congress. In 1898 he served as vice president of the section of zoology of the American Association for the Advancement of Science.

Packard's work reflected several aspects of nineteenth-century American entomological and zoological study. In his work in insect taxonomy and classification, he described many new genera and species. His studies of comparative anatomy and embryology placed him within a tradition of classical morphology, once significant but of waning importance by the time of his death. His work illustrated the continuing influence of Agassiz's ideas on his students. His use of cave fauna as evidence for neo-Lamarckian evolution stimulated interest in them among other zoologists; this interest declined after his death, even as the neo-Lamarckian school faded in the early decades of the twentieth century. Overall, the diversity of his scientific career—marked by work in several distinct fields of study and of interest not only to specialists, but to amateur naturalists and those concerned with insect pests—typified a pattern that by the close of his life was becoming rare among scientists.

• No known collection of Packard's papers exists. An early assessment, with complete bibliography, is T. D. A. Cockerell, "Biographical Memoir of Alpheus Spring Packard 1839–1905," *Biographical Memoirs of the National Academy of Sciences* 9 (1920): 180–236. See also Stephen Bocking, "Alpheus Spring Packard and Cave Fauna in the Evolution Debate," *Journal of the History of Biology* 21 (1988): 425–56. A useful obituary is A. D. Mead, "Alpheus Spring Packard," *Popular Science Monthly* 67 (1905): 43–48.

STEPHEN BOCKING

PACKARD, Elizabeth Parsons Ware (28 Dec. 1816–25 July 1897), mental health reformer, was born in Ware, Massachusetts, the daughter of Samuel Ware, a minister, and Lucy Parsons. Although her family moved from town to town in western Massachusetts during her childhood, she received an education at the Amherst Female Seminary in classics, literature, and mathematics that prepared her to teach in a number of local private schools by the age of sixteen. At nineteen, she suffered from what was then called "brain fever," and her symptoms of violent headaches and visionary-like trances led to her commitment at the new public asylum for the insane in Worcester, Massachusetts. Within six weeks, the asylum superintendent discharged her as cured. Three years later, she married Theophilus Packard, a renowned minister of the Congregational church in nearby Shelburne; they had six children.

The Packards moved from Massachusetts to various states in the Midwest, finally settling in Manteno, Illinois. Both Theophilus's ambitions and his disapproval of Elizabeth's behavior contributed to the peripatetic nature of their lives. He was discomfited by her ventures into the community to carry out missionary activities, her travels on her own for extended periods, and her expressions of religious views contrary to his. Her spiritualist and Swedenborgian ideas especially clashed with his traditional views about Calvinism. Elizabeth's challenge to the Calvinist doctrines of depravity, her insistence on the right of the individual to interpret Scripture, and her outspokenness led her husband to commit her to the Illinois Hospital for the Insane in 1860.

Never discouraged by refusals of writs of habeas corpus, the interception of her letters, or any other seeming institutional malevolence, Elizabeth finally convinced the hospital trustees of her sanity. She was released in 1863, only to suffer virtual imprisonment in her home by her husband. Although released through a writ of habeas corpus from the room where her husband locked the doors and nailed shut the windows, Elizabeth still had to withstand a five-day trial to prove her sanity. When the trial ended in January 1864, she was a free but penniless woman. Her husband had confiscated all the family resources and taken their children back to Massachusetts. Realizing that the statutes that limited the legal rights of married women and other dependents offered her no redress, she set out to change those laws.

Elizabeth Packard argued that the insane were the "most exposed, defenseless, unprotected class of human beings on God's footstool." She had learned that the law offered "not even a shadow of protection, to the oppressed," and especially none to married women who had no recourse against arbitrary actions by their husbands. Thus, she set out to change asylum commitment procedures and the postal rights of patients. Beginning in Illinois in 1865, she argued that deviant behavior, not deviant ideas or opinions, should constitute a definition of insanity and that a jury should determine whether a patient should be confined. Illinois passed this jury law in 1872.

Meanwhile, Packard also took her crusade to Iowa, Massachusetts, Connecticut, New York, New Jersey, Pennsylvania, Maryland, and Washington, D.C. Facing the opposition of many in the now powerful and highly organized psychiatric profession (the forerunners of the American Psychiatric Association), she won battles for monthly visiting teams to asylums in Massachusetts, Iowa, and Maine. In Iowa, the "Packard Law" also guaranteed that patients' mail would not be intercepted by asylum officials and that at least one woman would be a member of the visiting team. In Illinois, Myra Bradwell's petition for the right of married women to their wages benefited from Packard's arguments about the vulnerability of married women. Packard lobbied legislators, wrote books, garnered newspaper publicity, and addressed any interested audience on the justice of her causes. There is some evidence that she continued her crusade in areas as farflung as Nebraska, Minnesota and the Washington Territory well into the 1880s.

In 1869 Packard had persuaded the courts to grant her custody of her three youngest children. She supported her family and her reform activities on the income she derived from her writings. At first she wrote about her specific circumstances, as in her 1860 "Mrs. Packard's reproof to Dr. McFarland for his abuse of his patients, and for which he called her hopelessly insane," but by the late 1860s she had expanded her concerns. In 1864 she wrote *The Exposure on Board the Atlantic & Pacific Car of the Emancipation for the Slave of Old Columbia*, a religious treatise; in 1865, *Great Disclosure of Spiritual Wickedness!! In High Places, with an Appeal to the Government to Protect the Inalienable Rights of Married Women*; and in 1866, *Marital Power Exemplified in Mrs. Packard's Trial . . . or, Three Years' Imprisonment for Religious Belief*. Nearly 30,000 copies of her works were sold even before she wrote *The Prisoner's Hidden Life* in 1868 (reissued as *Modern Persecution, or Insane Asylums Unveiled* in 1871) and *The Great Drama; or, the Millennial Harbinger* in 1892. Packard was an accomplished lobbyist as well. When she traveled to promote legislation to guarantee the rights of the insane, she first contacted the prominent citizens of the community and convinced them to purchase her relevant works. She then took up residence in a hotel in the vicinity of the meeting place of the legislature and talked with the delegates individually and in groups, selling her books to them as well.

Packard remained active until the late 1880s, testifying before the Minnesota legislature as late as 1889. She spent her later years living with her son and his wife in California, while caring for her daughter Lizzie. When Lizzie's mental health failed, Elizabeth decided to return with her to Illinois to live but died upon reaching Chicago.

Elizabeth Packard successfully fought for personal liberty laws and against wrongful confinement in a number of states. The "Packard Law," though no longer mandatory after a few decades had at least brought the plight of married women and dependents to the attention of the American public. For forty years, the psychiatric profession had to combat popular suspicions raised by Packard's crusade. Nearly two decades after her death, prominent psychiatrists were still questioned by the public and asylum governing boards regarding commitment procedures and the jury law. In the 1930s, her issues were revived briefly by Albert Deutsch (*The Mentally Ill in America*, 1937) in his insider's view about the need for reform, and in the 1960s antipsychiatry movement she once again gained repute with dissidents like Thomas Szasz

(*Law, Liberty, and Psychiatry,* 1963) and Phyllis Chesler (*Women and Madness,* 1972).

• The fullest account of the life and work of Elizabeth Packard is Barbara Sapinsley, *The Private War of Mrs. Packard* (1991), which includes a complete list of Packard's books. Myra Samuels Himelhoch, "Elizabeth Packard: Nineteenth-Century Crusader for the Rights of Mental Patients," *Journal of American Studies* 13, no. 3 (1979): 343–75, written with Arthur H. Shaffer, is an equally discerning analysis of Packard's crusade. (The biographical sketch by John Chynoweth Burnham in *Notable American Women* is an interpretation drawn largely from the unexamined assumptions of the nineteenth-century psychiatrists who opposed her work.) Obituaries are in the *Chicago Tribune* and the *Boston Transcript,* 28 July 1897.

CONSTANCE M. McGOVERN

PACKARD, Francis Randolph (23 Mar. 1870–18 Apr. 1950), physician and medical historian, was born in Philadelphia, Pennsylvania, the son of John Hooker Packard, a distinguished surgeon, and Elisabeth Wood, the daughter of nationally known physician Horatio C. Wood. After attending Rugby Academy in Philadelphia, Packard was a pre-medical student in the biological department of the University of Pennsylvania from 1887 to 1889 and obtained an M.D. in 1892 from the university's Department of Medicine. Unable to obtain a residency immediately at the Pennsylvania Hospital, he was invited to the new Johns Hopkins Hospital by the eminent internist William Osler, who had taught Packard's brother at Pennsylvania before moving to Baltimore in 1889. Packard worked in the pathological laboratory and observed Osler's clinical practice. When residencies opened up simultaneously in Philadelphia and Baltimore, Packard returned, on Osler's advice, to his native city, where he eventually intended to practice.

After completing his residency at the Pennsylvania Hospital in 1894–1895, Packard began his private practice in 1895, specializing after 1898 in otorhinolaryngology. He also taught at the Philadelphia Polyclinic and College for Graduates in Medicine, serving as its dean from 1899 to 1901, and briefly at the University of Pennsylvania Department of Medicine (1900–1902). At the age of thirty-four, he became chief of the nose and throat service at Pennsylvania Hospital, one of the six hospitals with which he had become affiliated. In 1899 he married Christine B. Curwen, who died two years later, and in 1906 he married Margaret Horstman, with whom he had four children. During World War I, Packard served as an army surgeon in Belgium.

Like his mentor Osler, Packard exemplified the Victorian ideal of a gentleman-physician who was a bibliophile and scholar as well as an active practitioner. His medical writings, which numbered forty-two publications and included a *Text-book of Diseases of the Nose, Throat and Ear, for the Use of Students and General Practitioners* (1909), continued through 1925, while his writings on the history of medicine, begun in 1898, resulted in seven books and ninety-seven articles over the course of his life. Packard's last article, published in the *Archives of Internal Medicine* in 1949 as "William Osler in Philadelphia, 1884–1889," coincidentally took his role model as its subject.

An avid reader, Packard was interested in English and French history and literature and was an active promoter of the history of medicine, particularly that of the United States. He frequently read historical papers at medical society meetings and was one of the founders in 1905 of the Section on Medical History of the College of Physicians of Philadelphia, an institution in which he played prominent roles throughout his professional life. Having obtained the sponsorship of publisher Paul B. Hoeber, he created in 1917 one of the first American medical history journals, the *Annals of Medical History,* which he edited until its demise in 1942. With a lavish format designed and financed by Hoeber, it contained mostly biographical and classical literary topics relating to medicine and surgery.

Packard is best known for his *History of Medicine in the United States* (1901), which he described as "a collection of facts and documents relating to the history of medical science in this country from the earliest English colonization to the year 1800, with a supplemental chapter on the Discovery of Anaesthesia." In 1931 the rewritten second edition, consisting of two volumes, extended the history to the early twentieth century. Packard's purpose was not to create a scholarly synthesis but, as he wrote, "to present to those interested as much material bearing on the history of medicine in America as he could collect, in the fond hope that some more capable hands may be found to fill out the gaps."

To further stimulate interest in medical history Packard published a new edition of William MacMichael's *The Gold-headed Cane* (1827), with an introduction by Osler, in 1915, and issued Sir John Harington's *School of Salernum* (the English version of "Regimen Sanitatis Salernitanum," of which Osler owned the original manuscript). His other books included *Life and Times of Ambroise Paré* (1921), *History of the Pennsylvania Hospital Unit (Base Hospital No. 10, U.S.A.) in the Great War* (1921), *Guy Patin and the Medical Profession in Paris in the Seventeenth Century* (1925), and *Some Account of the Pennsylvania Hospital from Its First Rise to the Beginning of the Year 1938* (1938).

Packard was active in many of Philadelphia's cultural institutions as well as its dining and literary clubs. He served as president of the Medical Library Association in 1913, the American Laryngological Association in 1930, the College of Physicians of Philadelphia from 1931 to 1933, and the American Otological Society in 1936. In 1942 he gave the third Garrison Lecture at the annual meeting of the American Association of the History of Medicine, a lecture "given by persons distinguished for contributions to medical history." He died in Philadelphia.

As physician, bibliophile, and literary scholar, Packard was one of the most successful advocates and promoters of medical historiography in the United States in the early twentieth century.

• The College of Physicians of Philadelphia is the repository of Packard's library and personal papers. The most comprehensive biographical account, which includes a detailed curriculum vitae and bibliography, is W. B. McDaniel 2d, "Francis R. Packard and His Role in Medical Historiography," *Bulletin of the History of Medicine* 25 (1951): 66–85. Memories of personal associations with Packard by Frederick Fraley, George W. Coates, Edward B. Krumbhaar, and McDaniel are contained in the "Proceedings of the Section on Medical History Devoted to the Late Francis R. Packard and the 200th Anniversary of the Pennsylvania Hospital," *Transactions and Studies of the College of Physicians of Philadelphia*, 4th ser., 19 (1951): 75–84. Packard's association with Osler is discussed in Samuel X. Radbill, "'Dear Packard,' Francis Packard's Osler Connection," *Transactions and Studies of the College of Physicians of Philadelphia*, 5th ser., 6 (1984): 223–29. Many specific details of his medico-historical work can be found in Whitfield J. Bell, Jr., "Practitioners of History: Philadelphia Medical Historians before 1925," *Bulletin of the History of Medicine* 50 (1976): 89–91. Obituaries are by John H. Gibbon in *Transactions and Studies of the College of Physicians of Philadelphia*, 4th ser., 18 (1951): 131–32, and Richard H. Shryock in *Bulletin of the Medical Library Association* 38 (1950): 424–25.

GENEVIEVE MILLER

PACKARD, Frederick Adolphus (26 Sept. 1794–11 Nov. 1867), editor and Sunday school advocate, was born in Marlboro, Massachusetts, the son of Reverend Asa Packard, a Congregational minister, and Nancy Quincy. Packard graduated from Harvard with honors in 1814, having been prepared at the school of his uncle Hezekiah Packard. He then read law in Northampton, Massachusetts, in 1816 and practiced in Springfield until 1829. In addition to practicing law, Packard was also the editor and owner of the *Hampshire Federalist*, a weekly scientific, religious, and literary journal. While in Springfield he married Elizabeth Dwight Hooker (1822), the daughter of a local judge. They would eventually have four children, including a prominent physician (John Hooker Packard) and a classical scholar (Lewis Richard Packard).

Packard became involved with the Sunday school of the Congregational church in Springfield, overseeing the selection of books he thought particularly suitable for youth. As a result of these activities, he was sent in 1828 to a national convention of the recently formed American Sunday School Union (ASSU), where one of its managers, Joseph Dulles, asked him to become an editor of their publications. Even though his law practice in Springfield was prospering and the financial position of the ASSU was tentative, he considered the prospect a call from God and accepted, relocating to Philadelphia in 1829. Packard took over the duties of Frederick W. Porter, who then involved himself with the business affairs of the union. For many years Packard and Porter assumed the lion's share of the union's daily management. Packard's dedication and stamina were evident in the vast output of publications that soon issued from the offices of the ASSU. He

eventually edited more than 2,000 volumes, many of them written by him, though it is difficult to determine the exact number of these since he refused out of modesty to allow his name to be placed on the publications. He was an indefatigable proselytizer for the Sunday school and its related literature, maintaining that Sunday schools were useful even in areas without a ministry as a means of stimulating religious interest in the population.

Packard's attempt to introduce a specially compiled library of 121 books into the common schools brought him into conflict with Horace Mann, then secretary of the Board of Education of Massachusetts. In 1837 Mann succeeded in getting the Massachusetts legislature to levy a tax for the provision of libraries in the schools. Packard, trying to steer the ASSU through very difficult financial times, saw an opportunity to distribute his religious literature and reduce the Sunday School Union's $50,000 debt. He wrote to Mann in March of 1838 offering the library for inclusion in the schools and included one volume, Abbot's *The Child at Home*, for approval. Believing that the book met the requirements of nonsectarianism and unaware of Mann's personal experience with Calvinist doctrine, he must have been shocked by the unequivocal and detailed rejection that was returned to him. Mann listed four specific objections that Universalists in particular would have. These included damnation for all sins regardless of their severity and the portrayal of God as severe and unyielding rather than loving. He also pointed to the inconsistency of claiming on the one hand the depravity of all children while on the other maintaining that they would be naturally drawn to virtue. Mann found the passage, "If you are not loved, it is good evidence that you do not deserve to be loved," especially offensive, taking him back, no doubt, to the cruel remarks made by a Calvinist minister presiding at his brother's funeral. Having drowned before being "saved," his brother was pronounced lost forever. Mann would neither forget nor forgive this incident and clearly was not about to have such doctrine introduced into the fledgling common school system.

Stung, Packard replied that Mann was also guilty of inconsistency in maintaining that it was possible to impart religious morality without reference to some particular tenets. They also exchanged charges over whether Mann had said or implied that children should not be religiously indoctrinated until they were sufficiently able to draw their own conclusions. Mann denied this charge, but they clearly differed on the nature of religious teaching permissible in the schools. Packard made his charges against Mann's alleged attempt to exclude religious morality from the public schools in two anonymous letters to the *New York Observer* in October 1838. In these and other letters, he urged the adoption of the library, appealing directly to the people and the Massachusetts General Assembly. His vitriolic attacks backfired in the assembly, however, creating more sympathy for Mann than opposition. Packard's attack also generated an otherwise unlikely coalition of Catholic support for Mann's nonsectarian position. In his arguments for adoption Packard urged district or teacher control over matters of text selection. Given his argument that Protestantism, not simply Christianity, was the only acceptable sectarian influence for American schools, thus providing a bulwark against encroaching Catholicism, he must have reasoned that few if any individual districts would come under Catholic control.

By 1841 only fifty of the 1,000 libraries published had been sold, and Packard was concentrating his attention on the Sunday schools. In 1849, twice offered the position of president of the newly formed Girard College for Orphans in Philadelphia, he refused despite the higher salary and position it would have provided. In light of his dispute with Mann, this offer was ironic, considering the unequivocal provision in benefactor Stephen Girard's will that sectarian teachers or ministers were to be banned from even setting foot on school grounds. In 1850 Packard surveyed business and educational leaders on the nature of reading material that they had read in their youth. From this he drew up a list of works that were to be modified and adapted to the Sunday School Union's needs. Many of these he substantially rewrote himself. The vast network of Sunday schools provided an enormous readership, with several of his own works distributed in excess of one million copies. He also served as an editor of the *Journal of Prison Discipline* and as a board member of Girard's school. Among his major publications were *The Teacher Taught* (1839), in which he outlined proper teacher behavior, including the avoidance of "anything that borders on the queer"; *The Union Bible Dictionary* (1839); *Religious Instruction in the Common Schools* (1841); *The Great Aim of the Sunday School Teacher* (1843); *The Rock* (1861); *The Daily Public School in the United States* (1866), in which he attacked the inefficiencies of the system and urged a return to basics; and a *Life of Robert Owen* (1866), in which he condemned Owen's emphasis on proper environmental factors in child rearing rather than instruction in moral precepts.

Afflicted with painful cancer of the lip, Packard worked daily almost until the end, passing away at his home in Philadelphia. He had a profound influence on generations of children growing up in the nineteenth century. His rigid moralism, self-discipline, and social conservatism were amply expressed in the many publications of the Sunday School Union and thereby conveyed to millions of youth and adults. Rarely mentioned in social, intellectual, or educational histories of the nineteenth century, Packard's legacy is well captured in this statement from his obituary in the *New York Times*, "There does not survive him one whose influence on the minds of a large class of American readers can at all compare with his."

• Packard's manuscripts are in the collection of the American Sunday School Union preserved by the Presbyterian Historical Society in Philadelphia. The best discussion of Packard and the American Sunday School Union can be found in Edwin Wilbur Rice, *The Sunday School Movement 1780–1917, and the American Sunday-School Union 1817–1917* (1971), and Anne M. Boylan, *Sunday School: The Formation of an American Institution, 1790–1880* (1988). Raymond B. Culver, *Horace Mann and Religion in the Massachusetts Public Schools* (1929), provides insights into the conflict between Packard and Mann. Background information on contemporary developments in the public schools is provided by Lawrence Cremin, *The American Common School: An Historical Conception* (1951), and William Kailer Dunn, *What Happened to Religious Education? The Decline of Religious Teaching in the Public Elementary School 1776–1861* (1958). Histories of the Sunday school movement include E. H. Byington, "Historical View of Sabbath Schools," *Congregational Quarterly* 7 (1865): 26–29; Frank Glenn Lankard, *A History of the American Sunday School Curriculum* (1927); and Robert W. Lynn and Elliott Wright, *The Big Little School: Sunday Child of American Protestantism* (1971). Obituaries are in the *New York Times*, 12 Nov. 1867, and *Sunday-School World* 7 (Dec. 1867).

TED D. STAHLY

PACKARD, James Ward (5 Nov. 1863–20 Mar. 1928), automobile manufacturer, was born in Warren, Ohio, the son of Warren Packard, a hardware store, lumber mill, and iron mill owner, and Mary E. Doud. He graduated from Lehigh University in 1884 with a degree in mechanical engineering.

Although Packard is best known for the automobile that bears his name, his early engineering work was in the electrical industry. After graduation, he worked for the Sawyer-Mann Electric Company of New York City and was soon made foreman of its incandescent lamp department. His interest in research and product development would lead eventually to his obtaining over forty electrical patents. His first patent was for a magnetic circuit, which was followed by patents for testing devices, a lamp socket, a rheostat, and improved vacuum pumps for incandescent lamp bulbs, among others. In 1889, he patented the Packard lamp, significantly improving bulb reliability. With the 1889 sale of the Sawyer-Mann Electric Company to Westinghouse, Packard returned in 1890 to Warren, Ohio, where he and his older brother, William Doud Packard, incorporated the Packard Electric Company on 5 June 1890. The company served as a contractor for arc and incandescent light plants and advertised the manufacture of a wide variety of electric products.

Early in 1891 Packard persuaded some former New York City associates to invest capital in a new company, The New York and Ohio Company, set up in Warren to manufacture Packard's incandescent lamps and transformers. Packard himself served as general superintendent.

The New York and Ohio Company was the base from which the Packard Motor Car Company was developed. In 1895 Packard secured a French DeDion-Bouton tricycle, a crude gasoline vehicle, which he called a "thing of pain and sorrow." His strong commitment to mechanical excellence motivated him to develop a better vehicle, and on 16 May he engaged Edward P. Cowles to begin work on a "motor wagon," but little progress was achieved during the next two years. In the meantime, on 13 August 1898, Packard took delivery of an automobile built by Alexander Winton, who was just beginning production in Cleveland, but the vehicle seldom ran properly and he made many trips to the Winton factory through June 1899 in attempts to get the quality results he expected. Winton reportedly took offense and told Packard that if he could build a better car, he should do so.

Packard's response was to resume work on his own automobile and to secure the help of two of Winton's ablest assistants, George Weiss and William A. Hatcher, who agreed to leave Winton to join Packard to develop "a practical Motor Vehicle." Work was begun immediately, the first engine was tested on 30 October, and the completed one-cylinder car was successfully tested on 6 November. Before the year was over the Automobile Department of the New York and Ohio Company was organized. On 13 April 1900, the first production automobile was shipped; a total of forty-nine were produced that first year, and they promptly won a reputation for the quality and reliability of Packard's design and manufacture. William Doud Packard later recalled that he and his brother initially had great difficulty in securing parts that met their rigorous quality standards, leading them to recognize the need to make most of their parts themselves.

This early, strong commitment to quality assured the initial success of the Packard automobile and became its hallmark. Extensive driving trips were made to demonstrate the product reliability and quality to a larger national public. The Automobile Department of the New York and Ohio Company was separately incorporated on 20 August 1900 as the Ohio Automobile Company; incorporation became official on 10 September. James Ward Packard served as president of the board and general manager and William Doud Packard as treasurer.

In an attempt to break into the national market, the company demonstrated several cars at the first national automobile show held in New York City, 3–10 November 1900. There the car came to the attention of several prominent eastern buyers. A New York City branch was established immediately, followed early the next year by branches in Boston and Newport. In September 1901, the New York to Buffalo endurance run enabled the Packards to demonstrate again the reliability of their automobile. Although the event was cut short by the assassination of President McKinley, all five Packards entered successfully completed the run. In contrast, over half of the eighty entries failed to finish. This highly publicized demonstration quickly established a national reputation for quality and significantly increased Packard sales.

The car came to the attention of Henry Bourne Joy, a prominent Detroit businessman, who purchased one during his visit to the 1901 New York Auto Show, and promptly pronounced it "one of the best in the country." In January 1902, Joy purchased 250 shares of Ohio Automobile Company stock and began to exercise significant influence in the company. On 13 October 1902, the Ohio Automobile Company was official-

ly renamed the Packard Motor Car Company, and the sale of 2,500 additional shares was authorized; these were purchased by Joy and his wealthy Detroit friends.

The Packards needed the extra capital Joy and his friends provided for major expansion; the result, however, was that the Packards became minority stockholders in their own company. Their associates, Weiss and Hatcher, promptly resigned, and James Ward resigned as president on 16 June 1902, but the board of directors did not accept his resignation; he remained as president, plant manager, and board member. However, by 11 September 1903, Joy had become general manager and James Ward became a largely honorary president.

In October 1903 a new Detroit factory was completed, and production was moved from Warren to Detroit. With the move, Packard was no longer closely involved with the Packard automobile, choosing instead to remain in Warren to devote closer attention to the Packard Electric Company and the New York and Ohio Company (eventually absorbed by General Electric). In 1904 he married Elizabeth Achsah Gillmer. Packard remained titular president of the Packard Motor Car Company until 1909, board chairman until 1912, and board member until 1915, and he continued to be a major stock holder throughout his life. He also continued his experimentation in electrical and automotive engineering, securing numerous patents in both fields.

Packard later turned his attention to philanthropic activities and to building extensive collections of watches, typewriters, adding machines, and other mechanical and electrical devices. His largest gift was to Lehigh University for a new and well-equipped engineering laboratory. He also gave them the first automobile he built.

James Ward Packard's uncompromising commitment to engineering excellence and his ability to refine mechanical and electrical products laid the groundwork for the early success of the Packard automobile, which would ultimately become known around the world as a high-quality product. Packard died in Cleveland, Ohio.

• There is no public collection of Packard's personal papers, although his diaries remain with the family. The Packard Electric Company retains its business records in Warren, Ohio. The definitive work on the automobile and the company, Beverly Rae Kimes, ed., *Packard: A History of the Motor Car and the Company* (1978), contains the most detailed information available on the early life of James Ward Packard, based on his personal diaries and on those of his brother. For published early references on the early Packard automobile, see Frank T. Snyder, Jr., "Packard—The Early Days 1899–1910: A Study in References," *Antique Automobile*, Nov.-Dec. 1973, pp. 48–53. For a photographic record of some of the company's most distinguished products, see George H. Dammann and James A. Wren, *Packard* (1996), and Hugo Pfau, *The Coachbuilt Packard* (1973; repr. 1992). For additional information on Packard corporate history, see A. H. Allen, "Motors, Machines, Men—and Millions," *Steel*, 9 May 1949, pp. 61–76. For a large selection of Packard magazine advertising from 1901 to 1945, see Otto A. Schroeder, ed., *Packard: Ask the Man Who Owned One* (1974). An obituary is in the *New York Times*, 21 Mar. 1928.

CARL F. W. LARSON

PACKARD, Silas Sadler (28 Apr. 1826–27 Oct. 1898), pioneer business educator, was born in Cummington, Massachusetts, the son of Chester Packard, a mill operator and mechanic, and Eunice Sadler. The family had resided in Massachusetts since the first Packard settled in Hingham in 1638. Chester Packard succumbed to the "Ohio Fever" in 1833, and the family moved to the vicinity of Fredonia, in Licking County, Ohio. After a number of irregular terms in district schools, Packard had a year of secondary school at the Granville Academy. That concluded his formal education. He began teaching at seventeen, as a writing master in Eden, Ohio, after learning the craft from an itinerant instructor of penmanship. While teaching at a district school in Delaware County, Ohio, the following year, he learned the art of portrait painting in just three weeks of lessons from a traveling artist. In the fall of 1845 he crossed the Ohio River into Kentucky, where, for the next two and a half years, he taught school and painted portraits. Packard apparently thought his paintings lacked artistic merit for, many years later, he dryly remarked that "the houses that harbor them are absolutely free from rats."

Packard resumed the teaching of penmanship in 1848 at Bartlett's Commercial College in Cincinnati and soon added bookkeeping to the subjects he taught. Packard married Marion Helena Crocker, a pupil of his at Bartlett's College in Cincinnati, on 6 March 1850. This union produced two children, but neither survived him. After a year's teaching in Adrian, Michigan, he next taught at the Lockport, New York, Union School. He soon followed an early and lasting interest in writing, moving to nearby Tonawanda and starting a weekly newspaper, the *Niagara River Pilot*, in 1853.

It was in Western New York that Packard began a long association with Henry B. Bryant and Henry D. Stratton, who had founded their first business college in Cleveland, Ohio, just a few years earlier. They persuaded Packard to head their recently established school in Buffalo. The association was a fruitful one, and between 1856 and 1858 Bryant and Stratton dispatched Packard to Chicago, Illinois, and Albany, New York, to initiate classes in those cities. (By the time Stratton's death in 1867 brought an end to expansion, the Bryant and Stratton chain numbered more than fifty business colleges.) Packard next moved to New York City in 1858, this time as a partner with Stratton, not an employee. With Bryant and Stratton capital, he founded Packard's Business College in two upper-floor rooms in the Cooper Union Institute. Packard purchased Bryant's and Stratton's interests in the school and became sole proprietor in 1867. He continued to head the school until his death. Packard's Business College became Packard Junior College in the 1940s. When the school closed its doors just four years short of its centennial, graduates numbered more than 100,000.

In 1858 Packard's interest in writing joined Packard with his friend Elihu Burritt and with Stratton to launch *Bryant and Stratton's American Merchant and Nautical Magazine*. The magazine met general approval but nonetheless survived for only a year. After the death of his first wife, he married Lottie Hill, an 1864 graduate of and faculty member at Packard College, on 24 April 1884. He died in New York City.

Packard was a pioneer among business educators. A prolific author, he wrote and frequently revised numerous texts on bookkeeping and accounting, penmanship, business arithmetic, shorthand, and business school education, many of them published by his own Packard Publishing Company. Packard's texts were widely used, both in Bryant and Stratton schools and by other business colleges, well into the twentieth century. Successful textbooks disseminated his methods throughout the nation. He was also a frequent contributor to a large number of other publications on a wide variety of topics.

Packard was the first president of the organization that became the Business Educators Association of America, using its national convention in New York in 1878 to outline a "course of procedure that was the keynote to the work that has been done in business colleges throughout the country." Packard wrote frequently on business education and was widely read by others in the field. He clearly understood the value of publicity and used it effectively to elevate the status of business education. Generally conservative in political and social outlook, he nevertheless advocated a greater role for women in business. Packard College was among the first schools to offer training in stenography and in the use of the newly invented typewriter. He contributed importantly to the establishment of professional standards for the licensing of certified public accountants in New York, and he was a leader in most of the principal professional organizations of business educators.

• Packard's papers and those of Packard Junior College are lodged with the New-York Historical Society. Biographical information is available in Silas Sadler Packard, *My Recollections of Ohio, a Paper Read before the Ohio Society of New York, Monday Evening, May 12, 1890* (pub. by the society), and "Silas S. Packard; Chairman of the Governing Committee of the Ohio Society," *National Magazine*, Dec. 1891, pp. 205–8. His career is discussed in Thomas L. Cahalan, "Silas Sadler Packard, Pioneer in American Business Education" (Ph.D. diss., New York Univ., 1955), which contains a substantial bibliography of Packard's writings. An obituary is in the *New York Tribune*, 28 Oct. 1898.

LEONARD F. RALSTON

PACKARD, Sophia Betsey (3 Jan. 1824–21 June 1891), educator and home missionary, was born in New Salem, Massachusetts, the daughter of Winslow Packard and Rachel Freeman, farmers. During Packard's childhood she and her family attended the Baptist church in North Prescott, a town near New Salem.

She received a diploma from the Charlestown (Mass.) Female Academy in 1850, then taught at a number of New England schools before accepting in 1854 the position of preceptress and teacher at the New Salem Academy. There she met Harriet Giles, a twenty-year-old senior student and "assistant pupil." Vowing to establish a school of their own, the two women became lifelong friends and co-workers. They later taught at schools in the villages of Petersham and Orange, Massachusetts, before opening their own school in 1859 at Fitchburg, fifty miles northwest of Boston. Trustees of the Connecticut Literary Institution in Suffield, Connecticut, soon persuaded Packard, however, to accept the position as preceptress at their school. Giles also joined the faculty of this Baptist-controlled institution, and both women remained there from 1859 to 1864.

The Oread Collegiate Institute in Worcester, Massachusetts, founded in 1849 and unique in that it offered college-level training to young women, was the next place of employment for the two friends. From 1864 to 1867 Packard served as executive head of the institute, sharing the position first with the Reverend John Shepardson, pastor of the Baptist church of Petersham, Massachusetts, and then with Harris R. Greene, principal of Worcester High School. Although Giles attributed Packard's resignation in 1867 to her failing health, the inability of Packard and Greene to work together successfully also was a factor. Giles left Oread in the same year, and both women settled in Boston.

Packard next took an office job with the Empire Life Insurance Company of Boston in 1868. Finding this work unsatisfactory because she was not working actively in Christian service, Packard remained only until 1870, when she became the pastor's assistant at the Shawmut Avenue Baptist Church. Although Packard's new salary was only one-fourth what she earned at the insurance company, the work was more in keeping with her experience as teacher and promoter of Christian ideals. When in 1873 Packard's pastor moved to Boston's Tremont Temple, one of the leading Baptist churches in the country, she transferred her church membership to Tremont and remained as his assistant until 1878.

Packard played a pivotal role in 1877 in organizing the Woman's American Baptist Home Mission Society (WABHMS), an auxiliary of the American Baptist Home Mission Society (ABHMS). Predominantly made up of New England women, the WABHMS sought to educate former slaves, Indians, and the increasing number of immigrants entering the United States. Packard served first as treasurer of the organization before being elected WABHMS corresponding secretary in 1878.

Wishing to learn more about the recipients of WABHMS aid, Packard traveled to the South in 1880, gathering information on the condition of "colored women and girls." She focused her efforts in Georgia, where she noted that although every sixth person was Baptist the ABHMS had established a school for "colored boys but not for colored Baptist girls." To allevi-

ate the appalling conditions that she saw, Packard petitioned the WABHMS for money to start a school for "Negro women and girls" in the South. After deliberating for almost a year, the WABHMS members finally granted Packard's request, and in 1881 both she and Giles moved to Atlanta, Georgia. With the enthusiastic support of the African-American community and the help of the Reverend Frank Quarles, Packard and Giles welcomed eleven students to the first class of the Atlanta Baptist Female Seminary held in the basement of Reverend Quarles's Friendship Baptist Church. Rapidly increasing enrollment forced a move in 1883 to larger accommodations, nine acres of land and five frame buildings formerly used as Union barracks during the Civil War. In 1882 Packard's former pupil from the Connecticut Literary Institution, the Reverend G. O. King, pastor of the Wilson Avenue Church in Cleveland, Ohio, had invited Packard and Giles to speak to his congregation about their school. Church member John D. Rockefeller (1839–1937), after hearing their talk, offered them financial support if Packard and Giles continued their educational work. In recognition of Rockefeller as the school's earliest and most consistent supporter, trustees renamed the institution Spelman Seminary in 1884 in tribute to the abolitionist parents of Rockefeller's wife, Laura Spelman Rockefeller.

During her ten years as seminary principal, Packard saw student enrollment increase to over 400 and supervised the addition of several campus buildings. Packard offered students an education that she believed would "uplift the colored race" by educating its future mothers and teachers. With a curriculum focused initially on industrial training and teacher education, Spelman students attended classes in nursing, teaching, printing, or domestic work. As student preparation improved, Packard expanded the academic courses, including mathematics, English grammar and literature, geography, and natural philosophy. Packard relied on religious studies and activities to build student character. Both the school's motto, "Our Whole School for Christ," and Packard's encouragement to students to consider Christ their "personal friend" and guide as they went out to work among their own people during the summer months emphasized the importance of religion at Spelman. Packard also considered neatness, cleanliness, industry, and economy necessary virtues of all Spelman students and held them to a strict code of behavior.

Packard's tenure at Spelman predated the ongoing debate at the turn of the century between Booker T. Washington with his advocacy of industrial training for African Americans and W. E. B. Du Bois and his focus on classical education for future leaders of the race. Yet it is unlikely that Packard would have taken a stand on either side. Her focus on women's education was reflected in an early letter to John D. Rockefeller in which she wrote, "The salvation of the race and our country depends upon the Christian training of these girls who are to be the future mothers and educators." Educated mothers ensured strong families and hence a stable African-American community. The teaching profession enabled African-American women to contribute to the economic stability and growth of their communities. In this regard, Packard failed to offer new roles to African-American women who had traditionally understood their importance as mothers and providers. Yet Packard's goal of creating a curriculum that would eventually offer both industrial studies and classical academic courses to girls and young women allied her more closely with African-American women educators such as Anna Julia Cooper and Nannie Helen Burroughs than with prominent male educators of the day. Sophia Packard died in Washington, D.C., and was buried in Silver Lake Cemetery, Athol, Massachusetts.

• Letters from Sophia Packard to John D. Rockefeller and various members of the General Education Board are in the Rockefeller Family Collection, the General Education Board Collection, and the Spelman Fund Collection in the Rockefeller Archive Center, North Tarrytown, N.Y. Information pertaining to Packard's tenure at Spelman is in the records of the Spelman College Archives, Atlanta, Ga. The comprehensive history of Spelman College as well as biographical information and bibliographic sources on Packard are found in Florence Matilda Read, *The Story of Spelman College* (1961), and Beverly Guy-Sheftall and Jo Moore Stewart, *Spelman: A Centennial Celebration, 1881–1981* (1981). See also Lynn D. Gordon, "Race, Class, and the Bonds of Womanhood at Spelman Seminary, 1881–1923," *History of Higher Education Annual* 9 (1989); Janice M. Leone, "The Mission of Women's Colleges in an Era of Cultural Revolution, 1890–1930" (Ph.D. diss., Ohio State Univ., 1989); and Martha B. Wright and Anna M. Bancroft, eds., *History of the Oread Collegiate Institute* (1905).

JANICE M. LEONE

PACKER, Asa (29 Dec. 1805–17 May 1879), railroad builder, was born in Groton, Connecticut, the son of Elisha Packer and Desire (maiden name unknown). The absence of family resources limited Packer's schooling and forced him to seek training as a tanner's apprentice in North Stonington. After the death of his sponsor, Elias Smith, Packer turned unsuccessfully to farming. Then in 1822 he set out for the village of Brooklyn, Susquehanna County, located in northeastern Pennsylvania, where he resumed his apprentice status under the tutelage of his cousin, Edward Packer, a carpenter. Upon finishing his training, Packer practiced his trade in Susquehanna County, where he maintained a home in Springville, and spent one year in New York City. After several fruitless years of farming or working as a carpenter, Packer finally abandoned these pursuits in 1833. He married Sarah Blakeslee in 1828. They had three children.

Packer migrated to Mauch Chunk, now Jim Thorpe, located astride the Lehigh River in northeastern Pennsylvania. There he encountered a booming economy precipitated by the completion of the Lehigh Canal and the ensuing exploitation of anthracite coal deposits in the area. Packer quickly engaged in canal boat hauling and soon had two boats in operation. By 1835 the boat business had turned such substantial

profits that Packer withdrew from the actual operation and shifted a portion of his growing capital into commerce by purchasing the E. W. Kimball's general store in Mauch Chunk. Packer than opened a boat construction business that capitalized on his past occupational and entrepreneurial experiences. By the late 1830s he had expanded his activities to include construction of a series of canal locks from Mauch Chunk north to White Haven.

Packer branched out into mining and the coal trade speculation that flourished as a result of the great demand for energy in Philadelphia. He mined and shipped anthracite coal for the Lehigh, Coal, and Navigation Company, the major firm in the region. Eventually, Packer opened his own coal-mining business in the nearby Nesquehoning area, from where he hauled coal to Philadelphia. During the 1840s Packer expanded the scope of these activities sufficiently to claim the occupation of a coal dealer and, by 1850, to have accumulated $100,000 in real and personal property.

His operations in the coal and canal industries won Packer widespread recognition in the region. During the 1840s he used this prominence to win two terms (1841–1842, 1842–1843) in the Pennsylvania House of Representatives, where he used his political influence to organize in 1843 Carbon County, of which Mauch Chunk served as the county seat. After completing this service, Packer secured a gubernatorial appointment as associate judge of Carbon County for a five-year term. A lifelong member of the Democratic party, Packer represented his party and his district in the U.S. Congress from 1852 to 1854.

In 1851 Packer capitalized on an opportunity to buy the majority of the stock in a railroad venture. Organized in 1846 by Philadelphian Edward R. Biddle and investors from adjacent Lehigh and Northampton counties, the Delaware, Lehigh, Schuylkill and Susquehanna Railroad faced the expiration of its charter when Packer took control, and he immediately confronted the formidable task of construction. He was convinced that a railroad could prosper as an independent carrier rather than as a feeder for the main freight hauler of the day, the canal. With legislative approval Packer renamed the company the Lehigh Valley Railroad (LVRR) in 1853. Within two years, he completed the 46-mile route from Mauch Chunk to Easton at the confluence of the Lehigh and Delaware rivers. He secured rolling stock on lease from the Central Railroad of New Jersey and relied on his local mining activities and those of his kinsmen and entrepreneurial allies, who included bankers, merchants, and coal operators. These men helped sustain Packer's operations and enabled him to survive the initial hazards of construction and operation of a new enterprise.

Packer sought out new business in other sections of the anthracite coal mining regions. By 1866 he had constructed 161 miles of track and consolidated these into one railroad system that touched many areas of the anthracite coal fields. The value of the railroad stock made Packer one of the richest men in Pennsylvania and facilitated his nomination as a gubernatorial candidate for his party in 1869, a bid he eventually lost in the autumn election.

Despite his successes in Mauch Chunk, Packer realized the limitations of a community surrounded by mountains. In 1854 he began efforts to purchase thirty-five acres in South Bethlehem as a potential site for a terminus of the LVRR. Packer eventually decided to make the community the chief site for his railroad in the Lehigh Valley. He also invested in the Bethlehem Iron Company, incorporated by his distant kinsman Charles Brodhead of Easton in 1859. By 1863 the Bethlehem Iron operation produced solely for the LVRR and benefited from the rail company's tremendous growth. Soon the iron operation placed second behind the LVRR as the largest company in the Lehigh Valley. The combination of iron production and a major rail company quickly industrialized South Bethlehem. Members of Packer's entrepreneurial network began to migrate from Mauch Chunk down the Lehigh River to South Bethlehem. While Packer remained in Mauch Chunk, by 1870 his capital and resources had departed for the new community.

Packer's money moved to South Bethlehem in other ways that also contributed to the prosperity and economic health of the community. He made significant donations to St. Luke's Hospital and on his death bequeathed $300,000 to the institution. Even more important, Packer decided to build a university in South Bethlehem that could train young men for careers in business, in particular, mining and transportation. In 1865 he bought fifty-six acres as a site for Lehigh University and made a sizable contribution to ensure its survival. In his will, Packer set aside $1.5 million as a permanent endowment for the university.

Packer's activities contributed in significant ways to industrializing the Lehigh Valley. His coal operations, railroads, and other capital investments facilitated the transformation of the Lehigh Valley as an undeveloped region into a thriving economic area with diversified industrial activities. He also made the LVRR one of the major anthracite carriers in the northeast stretching to New York, New Jersey, and the eastern seaboard. At his death the LVRR included 658 miles of track, recorded $53 million in capital, and hauled more than four million tons of anthracite a year. It also made Packer the richest man in Pennsylvania.

• Because Packer left few papers for scholars to use in studying his entrepreneurial activities, his life must be reconstructed from county histories, census materials, and other local records. Packer memorabilia and records can be found in the rare book room at Lehigh University Library and the Canal Museum in Easton, Pa. Biographical accounts include Milton Sturat, *Asa Packer, 1805–1879* (1938), and W. Ross Yates, *Asa Packer: A Perspective* (1983). The most effective study of his business career appears in Burton W. Folsom, *Urban Capitalists: Entrepreneurs and City Growth in Pennsylvania's Lackawanna and Lehigh Valleys, 1800–1920* (1981), chap. 8. Obituaries are in the *Philadelphia Public Ledger*, 19 May 1879, and the *New York Times*, 18 May 1879.

EDWARD J. DAVIES II

PADDOCK, Charles William (11 Aug. 1900–21 July 1943), track and field athlete, was born in Gainesville, Texas, the son of Charles Hood Paddock, a railroad executive, and Lulu Robinson. In 1907 his father moved the family to Pasadena, California, where Charles became a competitive runner in high school. He then entered the University of Southern California but soon left school to join the army during World War I, receiving a commission as second lieutenant of field artillery. In 1919, while still serving in the army, he won the 100-meter and 200-meter races at the Inter-Allied Games at Paris, setting his first world record at the longer distance. After leaving the army, he returned to southern California and received his baccalaureate degree in 1922.

As a university student Paddock had an unparalleled series of record-equaling and record-breaking performances. On 10 July 1920 at New York City he equaled the world record for the 100 meters. In 1921 he reached his peak form, shattering world records at various distances. In one memorable afternoon at Redlands, California, he broke four world records, including the 100-meter sprint by 1/5 of a second, the 200-meter by 2/5 of a second, the 300-yard by 2/5 of a second, and the 300-meter by two seconds; he also tied the world record for 100 yards. So amazing were Paddock's performances that the eastern-based American Athletic Union (AAU) refused to accept the timekeeper's results at Redlands because "it was impossible for any human being to run that fast." Indeed, it was years before some of Paddock's records were accepted by the AAU, and others set at distances less frequently run in competition were never regarded as official. In all, Paddock broke or equaled 94 world records and was often referred to as "the world's fastest human" during the 1920s.

Paddock became one of the best-known and most controversial figures in the history of running athletics. His practice of concluding his races with dramatic leaps and outspread arms annoyed the ruling figures of amateur athletics. The hesitancy of AAU officials to accept his records led to an almost endless series of quarrels between Paddock and his backers on the one hand and the eastern athletic establishment on the other. In general, Paddock ignored the attempts of the AAU to regulate his competitive appearances. He was accused of professionalism when he wrote paid journalistic reports on events in which he participated and when he spoke publicly and made films in relation to running competition. But he defended himself effectively and maintained his public support.

Physically, Paddock was rather stocky with a deep chest, muscular build, and thick, powerful legs. He was affable, energetic, enthusiastic, and spoke and wrote with a flair. As a public speaker, as an author of articles in *Collier's*, the *Saturday Evening Post*, and other magazines, and as a newspaper reporter, he extolled athletic competition and good sportsmanship. He also wrote two books: his autobiography, *The World's Fastest Human* (1932), and *Track and Field* (1933).

Paddock represented the United States in the 1920, 1924, and 1928 Olympics, winning the gold medal for the 100 meters in 1920 and silver medals for the 200 meters in 1920 and 1924. His last world record was set in 1927 at the nonstandard distance of 250 meters. He retired from competition in 1929, still the holder or co-holder of records at 100 yards, 100 meters, 200 meters, 220 yards, 300 yards, and 300 meters, and various other short distances down to 60 meters. Paddock's best time at 100 meters was 10.4 seconds; in the 1990s the world record was slightly less than ten seconds. At 200 meters, his best effort was 20.2 seconds, compared to the 1990s world record of slightly less than twenty seconds.

In December 1930 Paddock married Neva Prisk Melaby, the previously married daughter of newspaper publisher Charles H. Prisk, and they had two children. He became vice president and general manager of the *Pasadena Star-News* Publishing Company and vice president of the *Long Beach Press-Telegram* Publishing Company, owned by his father-in-law, and held these positions until his death. In July 1942 he entered the U.S. Marine Corps and was commissioned as a captain, becoming the aide of Major General William P. Upshur. He died with Upshur when their airplane crashed near Sitka, Alaska.

Historically, Paddock may be regarded as the amateur equivalent of Babe Ruth and Jack Dempsey during the 1920s, a colorful personality with high public visibility in a period during which sports rose to new heights of popularity. He was, perhaps, the person who most popularized the sprint events in running. Furthermore, he initiated the rebellion against unqualified amateurism, which eventually led to the weakening of the boundary between professionals and amateurs in sports.

• Paddock described his track career in an autobiography, *The World's Fastest Human*. His record setting performances are listed in the annual editions of *T. S. Andrews World's Sporting Annual* (1920–1930). Two informative articles are "World's Fastest Sprinter—from California," *Literary Digest*, 25 June 1921, pp. 48, 50–51, and "The International War over Paddock," *Literary Digest*, 28 July 1923, pp. 46, 48–49. An obituary is in the *New York Times*, 23 Aug. 1943.

LUCKETT V. DAVIS

PADOVER, Saul K. (13 Apr. 1905–22 Feb. 1981), social scientist, historian, and writer, was born Saul Kussiel Padover in Vienna, Austria, the son of Keva Padover and Fanny Goldmann. His mother was a native Austrian, his father a U.S. citizen. Keva Padover's Jewish forebears had originated in Padua, Italy (the surname is derived from the alternative spelling "Padova"), and moved to Austria in the early nineteenth century before migrating later in the century to Memphis, Tennessee. Keva Padover was born there but moved to Austria as a young man.

After Saul's birth his father returned to the United States and settled in Detroit. Saul and his older brother were raised by their mother in Vienna until the three joined Keva Padover in 1920. Saul attended pub-

lic schools in Detroit and completed his secondary education in 1925. He then enrolled at Wayne (now Wayne State) University, also in Detroit, where he majored in English and history and edited the literary magazine. After graduating with honors in 1928, Padover did graduate work at Yale University for a year, then continued his studies in both American and European history at the University of Chicago, receiving a master's degree in 1930 and a doctorate two years later.

Padover had begun his academic career while still in graduate school, teaching during the summers of 1930 and 1931 at West Virginia State College. In 1933 he joined the history department of the University of California, Berkeley, as a research associate and remained there for three years. In 1936–1937 he traveled in Europe as a Guggenheim fellow and did research in Paris, Vienna, and London.

In 1938 Padover turned from academic life to government service when he became personal assistant to Secretary of the Interior Harold L. Ickes. He held that post for five years while also serving for a time as a consultant to the department's Office of Facts and Figures and heading its Research Unit on Territorial Policy in 1942–1943. He then served in London as the principal policy analyst for the Federal Communications Commission before becoming an intelligence officer in the Office of Strategic Services in 1944 with the rank of lieutenant colonel.

Padover entered Normandy soon after D-Day and served for the duration of the war with U.S. forces in France and Germany. The secret intelligence he gathered was of major importance to the Allied initiative and led to the creation of a denazification policy that won praise from General Dwight D. Eisenhower. Padover's wartime service earned him a Bronze Star with five battle stars and a special citation from President Harry S. Truman.

Returning to civilian life as a Rockefeller Fellow in 1945–1946, Padover focused his scholarly attention on the occupation of postwar Germany. In 1946 he traveled to that country as an adviser to the U.S. War Department. That year he also became a columnist and foreign correspondent for *PM*, a New York City newspaper. In 1947 he rejoined academia as a lecturer at the New School for Social Research in New York City; a year later he was named to the school's graduate faculty. He remained with the New School for more than thirty years, serving as dean of its School of Politics from 1950 to 1955 and as distinguished service professor from 1971 until his death.

During his long career Padover also served as a visiting professor of American politics at the Sorbonne in Paris (1949) and at Columbia University (1954–1955), and as a Fulbright professor at the University of Tokyo (1960). In addition, he made several trips to Southeast Asia over the years as a State Department lecturer.

Besides his teaching and research, Padover wrote or edited more than forty books as well as numerous articles on major figures and events in American and European political history. At the time of his death, an estimated three million copies of paperback editions of his books had been sold throughout the world. Padover won praise from both academic critics and the general reading public for presenting balanced yet engaging views of all his subjects, which included Alexander Hamilton, James Madison, Louis XVI of France, and Joseph II of Austria. He was most widely known, however, as a leading authority on Marx and Jefferson, and the majority of his books concerned these two figures.

Padover's *Thomas Jefferson on Democracy* (1939), a collection of excerpts from Jefferson's letters and other writings, was translated into more than two dozen languages and became an international bestseller. *Jefferson* (1942; rev. ed., 1952) is considered an outstanding shorter biography of the third U.S. president, and *The Complete Jefferson* (1943; repr. 1969) was for many years the only one-volume edition of Jefferson's major writings. Padover's many works on Marx included *Karl Marx: An Intimate Biography* (1978); he also edited *The Essential Marx* (1979), and he was the editor and translator of the seven-volume Karl Marx Library (1972–1977).

Padover was married to Irina Raben in 1942; she died several years later. He married his second wife, Margaret Thompson Fenwick, a screenwriter, in 1957. There were no children from either marriage. Padover died in a New York City hospital several days after suffering a stroke.

• Padover's manuscripts are in the Rare Book Collection of the New York Public Library; the Library of Congress; the Libraries of the State University of New York, Albany; and the New York Historical Archives, Cornell University. Padover's correspondence with Max Lerner and John Collier is in the Lerner and Collier collections, Manuscripts and Archives, Yale University. A collection of photocopies and reprints of Padover's articles is on file at the Raymond Fogelman Library at the New School for Social Research. Biographical information on Saul K. Padover can be found in *Current Biography Yearbook 1952*; *Contemporary Authors*, new rev. ser., vol. 2 (1981); and *Who Was Who in America*, vol. 7 (1981). An obituary appears in the *New York Times*, 24 Feb. 1981.

ANN T. KEENE

PAFF, Michael (?–10 June 1838), art dealer, was born in one of the states that constituted the Holy Roman Empire. No other facts about his birth or his parentage are known. Nor is it known that he ever married. Although the paucity of information about his life is discouraging, at least it may be said that none of the other art dealers of his time left a more complete record.

Paff arrived in the United States as an adult in 1784. By 1797 he had set himself up in business in New York as the co-owner, with his brother John, of a music shop. One of their rivals in the trade was John Jacob Astor, who had sailed to New York on the same ship. The brothers stocked pianos, music boxes, and sheet music, some of which was published under their own imprint. From time to time they also sold paintings

and engravings on consignment. They were so successful that in 1802 they were able to buy out Astor. By 1811 Michael Paff was on his own. For the first time, he was listed in the *New-York Register and City Directory* without John and with the words "picture gallery" after his name.

The following year marked the beginning of Paff's rise in the art community. For many years he had been forming a collection of paintings. In March 1812 he issued a prospectus in which he noted that although the United States could boast that among her sons were such distinguished painters as John Trumbull and Benjamin West, "it was Beyond the Atlantic that their genius unfolded itself," not at home as it might have done had fine pictures been on hand for them to study. Paff proposed to enlighten the public by putting just such works on view. This was to be a money-making venture; visitors to his gallery would pay an entrance fee. The catalog that he issued was primarily a roll call of famous European names, including Rubens, Rembrandt, Correggio, and Titian. But, given the poor state of connoisseurship at the time, it is unlikely that Paff had actually acquired original works by most, if any, of the masters in the catalog.

Neither the prospectus nor the catalog indicates that the paintings were for sale. Yet if on his debut as a gallery owner Paff was unwilling to sell the works in his collection, by 1818, if not before, he was in the picture trade. Early in that year he made an offer, at $10,000, of a selection of works to the Academy of the Fine Arts—an offer that was rejected, but with a note of thanks. In July of the same year he advertised the gallery in the *National Advocate*. Art lovers who visited it would find pictures "worthy of their attention . . . at the smallest expense." To this he added, "Old Paintings restored to their original lustre, or purchased at their utmost value."

Unlike merchants of art in the colonial era and the early republic who sold art alongside such household items as furniture and toys, Paff sold nothing but art. The frequent mention of his gallery in the press and in guides to the city attests to its importance, as does the very fact that he was a pioneer in the trade. Although the gallery was described by the painter Daniel Huntington as "a dimly lighted and musty den," Paff demonstrated his love of art by gracing its exterior with a plaster Cupid holding not the traditional bow and arrows but a palette and brushes. Inevitably some of his customers, like the prominent wholesale merchant and collector Luman Reed, discovered that their purchases were not the works of the great masters they were purported to be. But it is less likely that Paff intended to cheat the public than that his iconophilia led him to overestimate the value of his wares. Reminiscing about him in the *New York Times* some sixty years after his death, C. L. Beaumont, the son of the obscure dealer John P. Beaumont, wrote, "He would wash, scrape, study, and ponder over an old painting; would sit up nights with it consulting books, and when he had made a discovery, his enthusiasm carried him off the earth." Michelangelo seems to have figured in his fantasies above all other artists. Having read that no works had been recorded for a certain period in Michelangelo's life, he became convinced that one of his holdings was from that master's hand. Beaumont, recreating the accent that Paff never lost, reports him as saying, "Vot vos he doing all dot time, my poy? He vos paint dot picter." A *Last Supper* in the gallery he took to be by Michelangelo because the number of stones painted across the floor in the scene amounted to ten, the number of letters in the artist's surname, Buonarotti.

Despite the uneven quality of his goods, Paff prospered. No sales records of the gallery are known to exist, but the fact that he remained in business for twenty years as an engaging public figure attests to his success. His own belief in the worth of his acquisitions and the warmth with which he expressed it were his major assets. Another asset was his quaint appearance. "He was," wrote Beaumont, "a little, old, white-faced Schwartzwalder, in a broad-brimmed, low-crowned hat and a short-waisted, long, full-skirted coat, a merry, happy, good-natured man." Paff died in New York.

• No biography of Paff exists, nor is it likely that enough information about his life will surface to provide the basis for one. Nor has an obituary come to light. On his career in the music business, see Rita Susswein Gottesman, *The Arts and Crafts in New York* (2 vols., 1959, 1965). See also Daniel Huntington, *Asher B. Durand: A Memorial Address* (1887), and, on Paff's death, Philip Hone, *Diaries*, ed. Allan Nevins (1927).

MALCOLM GOLDSTEIN

PAGE, Ann Randolph Meade (3 Dec. 1781–28 Mar. 1838), Episcopal slavery reformer, was born at "Chatham," the family home in Stafford County, Virginia, the daughter of Col. Richard Kidder Meade, aide-de-camp of General George Washington, and Mary Fitzhugh Grymes. She grew up on "Lucky Hit," her parents' plantation in Frederick (now Clarke) County, Virginia. She was raised in an educated gentry family of English descent. As an evangelical, her mother taught her children not only reading and writing but also what evangelicals cherished—the importance of self-denial, simple living and service to slaves in contrast to what the gentry sought—a fashionable living reminiscent of the English nobility with servants to indulge their needs.

In 1799 Ann Meade married her cousin Matthew Page, a wealthy planter and member of Virginia's House of Delegates; they had two daughters. On his 2,000-acre estate outside Berryville he built a mansion, which he named "Annfield" in honor of his bride. By the time of his death, he owned 200 slaves. Following her marriage, Page felt a tension between the gentry world of her husband and the evangelical values of her mother. After an agonizing faith struggle, she experienced conversion and dedicated herself to serving slaves. A female slave helped her gain assurance of salvation.

Emulating her mother, Page grew in the contemplative life. As a mystic, Page practiced the continual presence of God, desired union of her will with God, and saw visions. She adopted the practice of writing out her prayers and journal entries. These provide a rare look into the interior life of a female who struggled over her conflicting roles as plantation mistress and slavery reformer. "O that slavery's curse might cease!" became her passionate prayer. "Thou seest how thy grace has taught me to desire above all earthly things, the abolition of slavery." On another occasion she prayed for "a peaceful end to slavery throughout the earth—that lurking device of Satan to destroy men's soul, . . . that enchantment of the evil one!" (Page Papers, Clarke County Historical Association). While her husband would not allow her to free family slaves, he did permit her to educate, evangelize, and care for them.

Sensing a calling as an emancipator, she exclaimed that God had summoned her "to stir up my soul to redress the injuries of this depressed people." She declared, "I have long by God's grace, devoted myself peculiarly to . . . the African race, to which all the Lord's dealings with me from early youth have been evidently calling me" (Andrews, p. 45).

When the American Colonization Society formed in 1816, she supported its aims of emancipating slaves for resettlement in Liberia, since she felt that colonization would break the evil power of slavery and that blacks were not safe from persecution and exploitation as long as they stayed in the United States. A supporter of the Frederick Colonization Society and treasurer of the Child's African Missionary Society, she persuaded neighboring children to raise money to benefit emancipated slaves in Liberia. She encouraged her brother William Meade and her son-in-law Charles Wesley Andrews to serve as agents of the society and to emancipate their slaves. Her letters to her cousin Mary Lee Fitzhugh Custis reveal the commitment of these two women to the Liberian scheme. Her cousin's daughter Mary Anna Randolph Custis was born at "Annfield" and later married Robert Edward Lee, who emancipated his slaves for Liberian colonization.

With her husband's permission, Page taught slaves to read in her plantation school even though this practice incited opposition from her neighbors. In a letter to the New York abolitionist Gerrit Smith, she shared her dream that "our southern darkness may be so dissipated as to have universal reading instead of oral instruction given" African Americans (Page to Smith, 13 Aug. 1834, Gerrit Smith Papers).

Once her husband died in 1826, Page wanted to emancipate all family slaves, but his executors sold more than 100 slaves to pay off debts, despite her objections. However, she was free to emancipate slaves she had inherited from the dower interest of the estate, and she let them choose where they would like to enjoy their freedom. They selected Liberia, and before her death Page sent thirty-three slaves to that country. But her emancipation scheme brought her trials. Neighbors began to "persecute her," and the emancipations left her in dire financial straits. Discouraged by the defeat of the gradual emancipation plan in the Virginia House of Delegates in 1831, she wrote "To the Lord let us look to overrule all" (Page to Custis, 11 Feb. 1832, Charles Wesley Andrews Papers). She argued, "I earnestly desire to fix on a plan for the most speedy and advantageous delivery of these slaves from bondage" (Andrews, p. 27). Unlike some Southerners, she complimented the work of northern abolitionists: "The abolition society will I trust do good by exciting alarm and consideration in our southern region" (Page to Smith, 13 Aug. 1834, Gerrit Smith Papers). After her death at "Annfield," her daughter Sarah Page Andrews continued emancipating and colonizing her slaves.

Charles Wesley Andrews published posthumously a memoir of Page in 1844 in which he held up his mother-in-law as a model emancipator for Southern slaveholders to emulate. Many Virginians told him that "they had never felt any particular interest in the condition of slaves, or had their consciences awakened respecting them, until they heard of the efforts of Mrs. Page" (Andrews, p. 55). Her unpublished papers reveal stronger antislavery sentiments than those found in the more cautious memoir by Andrews.

Her brother Bishop William Meade, who had entered the Episcopal priesthood at her urging, looked to her as a spiritual guide on matters concerning his private life, slavery reform, and church affairs as he labored for the revival of the Diocese of Virginia. Both were intensely evangelical. Seldom did anyone visit her house without receiving a tract or some word of witness from her about the Christian faith.

Jane Rendall depicted Page as an early nineteenth-century feminist. Other research revealed Page as a strong female who filled religious roles usually confined to men: she preached to her slaves, argued with men about the evils of slavery, corresponded with slavery reformers, condemned the sexual exploitation of black women, and championed literary instruction of slaves. Donald G. Mathews called her "one of the most redoubtable women in Southern history" ("Telling an Untold Story") whose obsession as an evangelical was "to convert and free her slaves" (*Religion in the Old South*, p. 17). Her journal and prayer entries constitute a striking contribution to Anglican spirituality as they unveil the deepest yearnings of a contemplative who fought injustice wherever it surfaced.

• Page's papers, including her prayers, journals, and letters may be found in the Charles Wesley Andrews Papers, William R. Perkins Library, Duke University; Mary Lee Fitzhugh Custis Papers, Virginia Historical Society; Gerrit Smith Papers, George Arents Research Library of Syracuse University; American Colonization Society Papers, Library of Congress; and the Ann Randolph Meade Page Papers, Clarke County Historical Association, Berryville, Va. The standard early biography is C. W. Andrews, *Memoir of Mrs. Anne R. Page* (1844; 2d ed., 1856); the 1856 edition was reprinted in 1987 in the Women in American Protestant Religion Series, 1800–1930, vol. 8. The most complete modern assessments are Arthur D. Thomas, Jr., "'O That Slavery's Curse Might

Cease' Ann Randolph Meade Page: The Struggle of a Plantation Mistress to Become an Emancipator," *Virginia Seminary Journal* 45 (Dec. 1993): 56–61; Thomas, "The Second Great Awakening in Virginia and Slavery Reform, 1785–1837" (Ph.D. diss., Union Theological Seminary in Virginia, 1981); and Peter Kent Opper, "The Mind of the White Participant in the African Colonization Movement, 1816–1840" (Ph.D. diss., Univ. of North Carolina at Chapel Hill, 1972). For an evaluation of her as an early feminist and significant southern woman, see Jane Rendall, *The Origins of Modern Feminism: Women in Britain, France, and the United States, 1780–1860* (1985); Rosemary Radford Ruether and Rosemary Skinner Keller, eds., *Women and Religion in America* (1981), 1:31–32, which has a typographical error listing her as Mrs. Ann Page Randolph; Donald G. Mathews, *Religion in the Old South* (1977); and Mathews, "Telling an Untold Story: The Current Scholarship, Southern Episcopal Church Women," an unpublished paper dated 2 June 1995 and held at St. Mary's School, Raleigh, N.C. Much important information on her early life and relationship to her brother may be found in David Lynn Holmes, Jr., "William Meade and the Church of Virginia, 1789–1829" (Ph.D. diss., Princeton Univ., 1971); and John Johns, *A Memoir of the Life of the Right Rev. William Meade* (1867). Works analyzing her role in Liberian colonization include Patricia Elizabeth Hickin, "Antislavery in Virginia, 1831–1861" (Ph.D. diss., Univ. of Virginia, 1968), and Bell I. Willey, ed., *Slaves No More: Letters from Liberia 1833–1869* (1980). An obituary is in *African Repository*, Apr. 1838, p. 127.

ARTHUR DICKEN THOMAS, JR.

PAGE, Charles Grafton (25 Jan. 1812–5 May 1868), scientist, inventor, and government official, was born in Salem, Massachusetts, the son of Jere Lee Page, a sea captain, and Lucy Lang. He graduated from Harvard College in 1832 and Harvard Medical School in 1836. After concluding his residency at Massachusetts General Hospital in Boston, he set up practice in Salem. Throughout this period, however, Page's consuming interest was natural philosophy, especially the science of electricity. At the age of ten he had designed an electrostatic machine, and at the age of twenty-two he published his first paper in Benjamin Silliman's *American Journal of Science*, the first of more than forty. In many of these papers he described inventions that were made and sold as laboratory apparatus by his collaborator, Daniel Davis, Jr., the first American to manufacture devices for demonstrating electromagnetic phenomena. By the late 1830s Page had caught the notice of William Sturgeon in London, who broadcast his work in England and on the Continent via his *Annals of Electricity, Magnetism, and Chemistry*. "I know of no philosopher more capable of close reasoning on electro-magnetic and magnetic electrical physics than Professor Page," Sturgeon later wrote (*Scientific Researches, Experimental and Theoretical . . .* [1852], p. vii).

In 1838 Page's family moved to Fairfax County, Virginia, and he spent all of his last thirty years either in or near Washington, D.C., becoming an intimate of such diverse celebrities as Daniel Webster, Samuel F. B. Morse, and Joseph Henry. Henry, who came to Washington in 1846 to head the new Smithsonian Institution, had taken note of Page's work many years before, repeating several of his key experiments. Though his scientific reputation ultimately transcended Page's, each man has precisely the same number of citations in the 1800–1863 volume of the *Royal Society Catalogue of Scientific Papers.*

While Page continued to develop apparatus for basic research in electromagnetism on into the 1840s, he was also confronted with the necessity of making a living and in 1842 he took a job as an examiner at the U.S. Patent Office, one of the few institutions outside academia that employed people on the basis of their scientific competence. It also paid examiners handsomely (Page's starting salary was $1,500, later raised to $2,500) and permitted them remarkable latitude. In 1844 he married Priscilla Sewall Webster; they had four children. Page devoted much of his time—as well as a $20,000 federal appropriation secured on his behalf by Senator Thomas Hart Benton of Missouri—to an effort to propel vehicles by means of electric power. Eventually Page built a battery-powered railroad locomotive that managed to complete a test run between Washington and Bladensburg, Maryland, in 1851. But the basic idea of powering a locomotive by means of wet-cell batteries was technically unsound. The politicians who helped Page secure his federal appropriation may not have understood this, but many scientists felt that Page himself should have realized the whole project was doomed.

This was one of several episodes that tarnished Page's public image after midcentury. In the 1860s he persuaded Congress to enact a measure authorizing him to obtain a patent on the induction coil, even though that device had been in public use for many years, and even though Patent Office employees were not ordinarily permitted to hold patents. While his claim to having invented the coil was defensible, the patent was supposed to be merely honorific. Later, however, Page's heirs exploited it for a substantial cash gain, and the legal wrangles that dragged on long afterward left a decidedly negative impression of Page in the popular mind.

Likewise detrimental to his standing in the American scientific community was his central role in the movement to "liberalize" patent examinations—that is, to establish standards that were less rigorous about the novelty of inventions. Idealizing the virtues of the practical mechanic while casting aspersions on the value of abstract scientific principles, partisans of this movement often argued their case in language that carried strong overtones of anti-intellectualism. Page worked for the Patent Office for a decade, until 1852, during which time he also held a professorship at Columbian College (now George Washington University) and served as a consultant to inventors like Morse. In 1852 he resigned his government position to go into business as a patent agent. He also coedited a periodical called the *American Polytechnic Journal,* which joined forces with other proponents of "liberalization"—notably the New York journal *Scientific American*—to exert pressure on the Patent Office to assess questions of novelty more leniently. This campaign was eminently successful. In 1851 fewer than one in three applications received by the office resulted in letters patent; by the time Page rejoined the examining corps in 1861 the proportion had risen to more than seven in ten.

Page was a versatile and prolific experimentalist, and he also proved to be an adept promoter and effective reformer. Beyond that, he is significant as a focal point for studying the evolution of American patent policy, the genesis of federal involvement in private research and development, and the complex interplay among scientists, inventors, politicians, and bureaucrats in mid-nineteenth-century Washington. The federal government played a striking role in practically every phase of Page's career. He spent seventeen years in its employ plus another nine dealing with the Patent Office as an agent. He also obtained two extraordinary governmental dispensations, a special appropriation in 1850 and a special patent in 1867.

Page was paradoxical. Despite his passion for investigating and elucidating natural phenomena, he could pursue privileged self interest with single-minded devotion and involve himself in numerous situations that would later have been termed conflicts of interest. Eventually he exemplified the fate that awaited even a onetime insider who failed to heed the rules of professional etiquette set forth by the like-minded group of men who established the National Academy of Sciences in 1863. For more than a century after his death in Washington, D.C., historians largely ignored his substantial contributions to electrical science. Insofar as they did address his career, they tended to cast him either as a schemer or a shortsighted zealot. Perhaps there was something of both qualities in him, but he was also a natural philosopher to be ranked with the best in America during the eighteenth and nineteenth centuries. "Franklin, Henry, and Page," declared an electrical journal a few years after he died, "may be regarded as exponents of pure science of whom any country should be proud" (*Journal of the Telegraph,* 16 June 1878).

• There is no collection of Page papers, but substantial quantities of his correspondence can be found in the Joseph Henry Papers at the Smithsonian Institution, the Samuel F. B. Morse Papers at the Library of Congress, and especially the Records of the United States Patent Office in the National Archives. Franklin L. Pope's "The Inventors of the Electric Motor," published in five parts in the *Electrical Engineer* 11 (1891), includes a series of letters exchanged between Page and another electrical inventor, Thomas Davenport of Brandon, Vt. Page himself published more than 100 articles between 1834 and 1868 as well as two noteworthy books, *Psychomancy: Spirit Rappings and Table Tippings Exposed* (1853) and *History of Induction: The American Claim to the Induction Coil and Its Electrostatic Developments* (1867). His wife, Priscilla Sewall Webster, in 1886 published a book of *Personal Reminiscences.* The best sketch of Page's career by a contemporary scientist is Jonathan Homer Lane, "Charles Grafton Page," *American Journal of Science,* 2d ser., 48 (1869): 1–17. The only analytical study is Robert C. Post, *Physics, Patents, and Politics: A Biography of Charles Grafton Page* (1976), which may be supplemented, for detail, with three articles by Post, "The Page Locomotive: Federal Sponsorship of Invention in Mid-19th-Century America," *Technology and Culture* 13 (1972): 140–69; "Stray Sparks from the Induction Coil: The Volta Prize and the Page Patent," *Proceedings of the Institute of Electrical and Electronics Engineers* 114 (1976): 1279–87; and "'Liberalizers' vs 'Scientific Men' in the Antebellum Patent Office," *Technology and Culture* 17 (1976): 24–54. The relationship between Page and his instrument maker is elucidated in Roger Sherman, "Charles Page, Daniel Davis, and Their Electromagnetic Apparatus," *Rittenhouse: Journal of the American Scientific Instrument Enterprise* 2, no. 2 (1988): 34–47. The context of Page's Washington career is elaborated in A. Hunter Dupree, *Science in the Federal Government* (1957), and Nathan Reingold, ed., *Science in Nineteenth Century America* (1964).

ROBERT C. POST

PAGE, Geraldine (22 Nov. 1924–13 June 1987), actress, was born in Kirksville, Missouri, the daughter of Leon Elwin Page, an osteopath, and Pearl "Maize" (maiden name unknown), a descendant of Edgar Allan Poe. Her first exposure to the legitimate theater occurred at age seventeen, when her drama coach took the drama club of Englewood Methodist Church, of which Page was a member, to the Goodman Theater to see Luigi Pirandello's *Right You Are If You Think You Are*. She was fascinated.

After graduation from high school Page enrolled in the Goodman Theater School. She completed the three-year curriculum in 1945 and from 1946 to 1949 played in stock companies in the Midwest. In the winter of 1949–1950 she moved to New York, where she took acting lessons from Uta Hagen. She mingled with the Actors' Studio's young crowd and joined the small group of actors and actresses that formed around director José Quintero, who starred her in such off-Broadway successes as *Ethan Frome* and *The Glass Menagerie*.

She first attracted attention with her performance in Quintero's production of Tennessee Williams's *Summer and Smoke* (1952), appearing opposite Lee Richardson. It had a successful off-Broadway run at Greenwich Village's Circle in the Square, then moved to a Broadway theater, ostensibly in order to accommodate larger audiences. Although she received the New York Drama Critics award for her performance in this play, Page was not recognized as a Broadway actress until her role in *Midsummer* (1953), where her performance received rave reviews.

Movies followed. She appeared in *Taxi* (1953) with Dan Dailey. Next she costarred with John Wayne in *Hondo* (1953), for which she received an Academy Award nomination for best actress in a supporting role. It was the first of her seven Academy Award nominations. For the next eight years Page was occupied with the Broadway stage and repertory theater. In 1954 Page married Alexander Schneider, the first violinist with the Budapest String Quartet. They were divorced after three years. In the early 1960s she married actor-director Rip Torn; they had three children.

Page was cast next in Terrence Rattigan's *Separate Tables* (1957–1958), then took the play on tour. When she came back to New York, Page received her second big break when she was cast in Tennessee Williams's *Sweet Bird of Youth* (1958–1959), for which she received the New York Drama Critics award and a Tony Award nomination. Page later said that this part had taken much more effort than anything else she had ever done. In 1961, back in Hollywood, she filmed *Summer and Smoke* and the next year the movie version of *Sweet Bird of Youth*, in which she costarred with Torn and Paul Newman; Richard Brooks directed. She received her second and third Academy Award nominations for her performances in these two films. In 1963 she created another memorable role in the film *Toys in the Attic*. That same year Page costarred with Jason Robards in Quintero's production of Eugene O'Neill's *Strange Interlude*. In 1966 she was offered the lead role in Edward Albee's *Who's Afraid of Virginia Woolf?*, which she turned down in her very characteristically outspoken way: "He [Albee] is a wonderful plagiarist. He has wonderful taste in the people he steals from, mainly [August] Strindberg."

Also in 1966 Page appeared on television in "A Christmas Memory," for which she received an Emmy Award. She received a second Emmy for her performance in "The Thanksgiving Visitor" (1967). Both television productions were based on Truman Capote stories.

Page spent 1967 in Hollywood, making three films: *You're a Big Boy Now*, for which she received her fourth Academy Award nomination; *Monday's Child*; and *The Happiest Millionaire*. Page continued to divide her career between Broadway and Hollywood, interspersing it with frequent appearances in regional and stock theaters. She remained a strong proponent of the method school of acting. Together with her husband she founded the repertory Sanctuary Theater. She appeared under Torn's direction in William Shakespeare's *Richard III*, *Macbeth*, and *Hamlet*, as well as in Jean Giraudoux's *The Madwoman of Chaillot* and several Henrik Ibsen and Strindberg plays.

Page next made four more films: *The Beguiled* (1971); *J. W. Coop* (1972); *Pete and Tillie*, for which she received her fifth Academy Award nomination (1972); and *Happy as the Grass Was Green / Hazel's People* (1973). She returned to Broadway to star in *Absurd Person Singular* (1974–1975), for which she received a Tony award nomination. Over the rest of the decade Page made three more films, each of which became a landmark. In *The Day of the Locust* (1975) she gave one of her most outstanding performances. *Nasty Habits* (1976), a film critical of the Catholic church, aroused the fury of church prelates. Woody Allen's film *Interiors* (1978) won her a sixth Academy Award nomination.

Page did not slow down in the 1980s. In February 1980 she appeared at the Kennedy Center in Washington, D.C., in James Prideaux's *Mixed Couples*, which costarred Julie Harris, Torn, and Michael Higgins. Page then went to Hollywood to appear in the film

Harry's War (1981), returning to Broadway to play Zelda Fitzgerald in Tennessee Williams's *Clothes for a Summer Hotel* (1980–1981). She was in Hollywood again for *Honky Tonk Freeway* (1981). On Broadway, she took the lead in *Mixed Couples* (1981–1982) and then returned to Hollywood to do *I'm Dancing as Fast as I Can* (1982). She topped this uninterrupted streak of successes with her performance in *Agnes of God* (1982) on Broadway, for which she was again nominated for a Tony Award.

During her remaining years Page appeared in six more films: *The Pope of Greenwich Village* (1984); *The Bride, Walls of Glass* (1985; also known as *Flanagan*), *White Nights*, and *The Trip to Bountiful* (all 1985); and *My Little Girl* (1986). Page received her seventh Academy Award nomination and, at long last, the coveted Oscar itself, for her role in *The Trip to Bountiful*.

Page received a Tony ward nomination for her last Broadway appearance, in a revival of Noël Coward's *Blithe Spirit* (1987). After she failed to appear in Saturday matinee and evening shows, it was announced to the audience after the last curtain that she had died in her Chelsea townhouse in Greenwich Village of a heart attack.

Page dedicated her life to acting. She was identified primarily with plays by Tennessee Williams, method acting, and indefatigable support of repertory theater. She appeared in twenty-eight films, thirty-two Broadway plays, as well as memorable performances in teleplays of the most prestigious television playhouses, and innumerable repertory, stock, and regional performances. In 1983 she was inducted into the Theater Hall of Fame.

• Page did not write an autobiography. Chapters dedicated to her in essay collections are sometimes very flimsy. However, the press was very kind to her and published many interviews and biographical portraits of the actress. The most noteworthy include articles in the *New York Times Magazine*, 2 Feb. 1953 and 29 Mar. 1959; Hedda Hopper's syndicated column of 20 Aug. 1961; Vincent Canby, "Seven Years after Her Film Discovery, Geraldine Page May Be 'Accepted,'" *Variety Weekly*, 15 Nov. 1961; Bill Davidson, "Geraldine Page: Diamond Who Likes It Rough," *Saturday Evening Post*, 17 Nov. 1962; the *New York Times*, 9 Apr. 1967; John Simon, "Damsels Inducing Distress," *New York*, 7 Apr. 1980; David Galligan, "Geraldine Page Stars in New Shepard Play and 'Bountiful' Film," *DramaLogue*, 19 Dec. 1985; and Simon Bauner, "Hollywood's Gentler Giant," *The Times* (London), 4 June 1986. Obituaries are in the *New York Times*, 15 June 1987, and in *Variety Weekly* (N.Y. ed.), 17 June 1987.

SHOSHANA KLEBANOFF

PAGE, Hot Lips (27 Jan. 1908–5 Nov. 1954), jazz trumpeter and singer, was born Oran Thaddeus Page in Dallas, Texas. His parents' names are unknown. His father, who worked in the moving business, died in 1916. His mother taught school and gave Page his first music lessons. He played piano, clarinet, and saxophone before taking up trumpet when he was twelve.

Page played in adolescent bands locally before touring in carnival and minstrel shows during the summer after he turned fifteen. At some point he toured on the Theater Owners' Booking Association circuit, in which setting he accompanied blues singers Bessie Smith and Ida Cox. By one account Page attended high school in Corsicana, Texas, but dropped out to work in a Texas oil field; by another, he organized bands while attending a college in Texas. Accompanying blues singer Ma Rainey, he toured to New York for performances at the Lincoln Theater in Harlem.

By the late 1920s Page had become one of the first trumpeters to make a career of patterning his playing and singing after Louis Armstrong. From early 1928 to 1930 he was a member of bassist Walter Page's southwestern band, the Blue Devils, with whom he recorded solos on "Blue Devil Blues" and "Squabblin'" in November 1929. Along with others from the Blue Devils, Page had transferred into the Kansas City–based big band of Bennie Moten by October 1930, when he made his first recordings under Moten, including "That Too, Do." Page was unquestionably the finest soloist in Moten's band, as heard for example on "The Blue Room" and "Milenberg Joys," from a magnificent recording session of December 1932 that the group made in the midst of an otherwise disastrous trip east.

As work for Moten declined in 1933, Page found work with Moten's former pianist Count Basie, playing in Basie's Cherry Blossom Orchestra in Little Rock, Arkansas, and in the Southwest from 1933 into 1934. The group gradually dissolved. Page returned to Kansas City in 1934. After Moten's death in April 1935, Page formed a quintet that included tenor saxophonist Herschel Evans and pianist Pete Johnson. He also worked as a freelancer with Basie's new band, of which he became a member while they were at the Reno Club in Kansas City in 1936. At this now legendary venue, Page participated in broadcasts on WXBY that led to Basie's discovery and subsequent fame. In what has been deemed one of the worst career moves in the history of jazz, Page excluded himself from this success in the summer of 1936 when he was persuaded by Armstrong's manager, Joe Glaser, to leave Basie and to work instead as a soloist. Page led an assortment of bands in New York from 1937 on, but often he just participated in jam sessions for lack of steady work. Many have speculated that Glaser made this move to undermine Page, thus protecting Armstrong from one of his most direct competitors.

Before organizing his own band in New York, Page joined trumpeter Louis Metcalf's big band in the autumn of 1936 for performances at the Renaissance Casino in Manhattan and the Bedford Ballroom in Brooklyn. Page's first big band performed in August 1937 at Small's Paradise in Harlem and in May 1938 at the Plantation Club, a white's-only venue, but it broke up a month later. He then formed a group at the Brick Club, which became in effect a venue for out-of-work musicians, playing for whatever they could take in at the door; this too did not last.

Page recorded "Skull Duggery" as a leader in 1938, participated in the Spirituals to Swing concert at Carnegie Hall on 23 December, and in June 1939 recorded "Cherry Red" with pianist Pete Johnson and His Boogie Woogie Boys, featuring singer Joe Turner. Later that year he led another band at Kelly's Stable and the Golden Gate Ballroom in New York. In January 1940 he recorded "Gone with the Gin." He toured as the featured soloist with tenor saxophonist Bud Freeman's big band in July 1940, joined clarinetist Joe Marsala in October, and then formed another short-lived big band for a stand at the West End Theater Club in November, in which month he recorded "Piney Brown Blues" with Turner and "Lafayette" and "South" under his own name.

Page returned to Kelly's Stable as the leader of a septet from May 1941 into the summer. He then joined clarinetist Artie Shaw's big band in August 1941 and soon made a hit with his singing and trumpeting on "Blues in the Night" and "St. James Infirmary." Like others of his era, including singer Billie Holiday and trumpeter Roy Eldridge, Page suffered from racist taunts as the African-American star in a white band. In any event the association was short-lived, as Shaw broke up the band in January 1942 to enlist in the navy.

Page once again led an unsuccessful big band. Writer Greg Murphy reports, "The pattern of Lips' life now reflected the increasing frustration with big bands that seemed accident prone, compensated by large intakes of alcohol and throwing himself into the jam session without restraint." From summer 1943 on he usually led small groups, while forming big bands for special occasions. His playing and singing are featured on "Uncle Sam Blues," made with Eddie Condon (Mar. 1944), and "I Keep Rollin' On" (June 1944), the latter session as a leader also including one of his finest instrumentals, "Pagin' Mr. Page." He participated in several of Condon's weekly concerts at Town Hall in New York in May and June 1944. At year's end he recorded "The Sheik of Araby" under his own name.

Page performed with Don Redman at the Apollo Theater in the summer of 1945, and that July he recorded under the pseudonym Papa Snow White with reed player Sidney Bechet. In the spring of 1946 he accompanied Ethel Waters in New York. That year Page's first wife died; her name and details of the marriage are unknown.

This period of Page's career was recalled by record store owner and producer Milt Gabler, who ran a swing style session at Jimmy Ryan's on 52d Street in competition with a concurrent bebop session: "There was only one musician who played both jams: Hot Lips Page. He would play one set in our place and run across the street and play theirs" (Shaw, p. 248).

Page continued to lead a small band. Between March and August 1949 he performed occasionally on Condon's television program "Floor Show" and early in May he went to Paris to participate in the first Festival International de Jazz. That same year Page and singer Pearl Bailey recorded a hit record pairing together "The Hucklebuck" and "Baby, It's Cold Outside" (1949), but its success did much more for her

career than for his. Page married Elizabeth (maiden name unknown) around 1950. Whether his son was from the first or second marriage is unknown.

Page worked mainly as a freelance soloist during the 1950s. He toured Europe from July to October 1951 and again in the summer of 1952, and held a residency at the downtown location of Cafe Society in New York from May to June 1953. By this time his health was failing. He suffered a heart attack late in 1953 and another in October 1954, shortly before his death in New York City.

Perhaps Page's most devoted fan was jazz writer Dan Morgenstern, who well captured his essential qualities:

Lips Page was one of the most powerful trumpeters in jazz history. When he wanted to, he could make walls shake. But he could also play softly and tenderly, and everywhere in between. His tone was broad and brilliant, with a wide but pleasing vibrato. He was a master of the growl and of the plunger mute—only trombonist Tricky Sam Nanton could approximate the depth of feeling evoked by Page on a minor blues. . . . Yet he could also make swinging, stinging sounds with a Harmon mute, or make a romantic ballad bloom the way an Armstrong or a Hawkins can.

As a singer, Page excelled at the blues. According to Morgenstern, "He had a marvelous sense of humor. . . . He could also be savage and scathing. . . . And in the wee hours of the morning, when most of the blowing was done, Page could sit and sing the blues, happy and sad at once, making up new verses or remembering some good old ones, in a way that no witness will ever forget" (*Music '65*, p. 84).

• Surveys and interviews are by Kay C. Thompson, "Kansas City Man: Hot Lips Page," *Record Changer* 9 (Dec. 1949): 9, 18–19; Henry Kahn, "That's How Mr. Page Swings—Like a Pendulum," *Melody Maker* 27 (28 July 1951): 3; Dan Morgenstern, "Hot Lips Page," *Jazz Journal* 15 (July 1962): 4–6, 40 and (Aug. 1962): 2–4; Morgenstern, "Three Forgotten Giants," *Down Beat's Music '65* (1964): 80–84; Greg Murphy, "The Forgotten Ones: Hot Lips Page," *Jazz Journal International* 34 (Aug. 1981): 12–13; and Morgenstern, "Oran Hot Lips Page: A Trumpet King in Harlem," *Village Voice*, 28 Aug. 1990, pp. 73–74. See also Ross Russell, *Jazz Style in Kansas City and the Southwest* (1971); Albert McCarthy, *Big Band Jazz* (1974); Arnold Shaw, *The Street That Never Slept* (1971; repr. as *52nd Street: The Street of Jazz* [1977]); Stanley Dance, *The World of Count Basie* (1980); John Chilton, *Who's Who of Jazz: Storyville to Swing Street*, 4th ed. (1985); Chris Sheridan, *Count Basie: A Bio-Discography* (1986), pp. 7–19; John Chilton, *Sidney Bechet: The Wizard of Jazz* (1987); and Nat W. Pearson, Jr., *Goin' to Kansas City* (1987). For a catalog of recordings, see Morgenstern et al., "Hot Lips Page on Record," *Jazz Journal* 15 (Nov. 1962): 13–15 and (Dec. 1962): 17–18. For musical analysis, two useful sources are Gunther Schuller, *Early Jazz: Its Roots and Musical Development* (1968) and *The Swing Era: The Development of Jazz, 1930–1945* (1989). Obituaries are in the *New York Times*, 7 Nov. 1954, and *Melody Maker* 30 (20 Nov. 1954): 7.

BARRY KERNFELD

PAGE, John (17 Apr. 1743–11 Oct. 1808), planter, revolutionary leader, and governor of Virginia, was born at "Rosewell" plantation, Gloucester County, Virginia, the son of Mann Page II and Alice Grymes, planters. Page's grandmother, Judith Carter Page, gave him intellectual guidance during his childhood. In 1752 Page attended Abingdon Parish glebe school but disliked the teacher, William Yates. For the next four years Page studied with a tutor, William Price, whom he credited with teaching him the ideas of classical republicanism and the Whig political principles of the seventeenth-century English revolutions. Page attended the College of William and Mary from 1757 to 1763. There he formed a lifelong friendship with Thomas Jefferson and, like Jefferson, developed an abiding interest in natural science under the tutelage of William Small. Page observed the transit of Venus in 1769, helped found the Virginia Society for the Promotion of Useful Knowledge in 1772, and became its president in 1774. He also became a member of the American Philosophical Society. Charles Willson Peale, the Philadelphia scientist and museum director, counted him a friend.

Page's father conveyed Rosewell plantation to him in 1765, the year in which Page married Frances Burwell. They had twelve children. Defeated in Gloucester for the House of Burgesses in 1769, Page won as the College of William and Mary's representative in 1771. In 1773 the governor, John Murray, earl of Dunmore, obtained Page's appointment to the Virginia Council, but the two soon fell out over Page's opposition to British policies. Although Page believed that his oath as councillor obliged him to advise Dunmore in May 1774 to dissolve the House of Burgesses for its support of Massachusetts after the Boston Tea Party, Page joined the movement to halt trade with Great Britain and force repeal of Parliament's punitive acts against the northern colony. In the spring of 1775, when Dunmore seized the powder stored in the Williamsburg public magazine, Page advised the governor to return it. Dunmore thereafter excluded Page from council meetings and instituted proceedings to oust him. A newspaper exchange in 1774 with a professor of William and Mary, Samuel Henley, over Henley's alleged Unitarianism also alienated the governor and brought Page fame as a lay theologian.

Page provided administrative backbone for the Revolution in Virginia as vice president of the Committee of Safety under Edmund Pendleton in 1775 and early 1776 and, after independence, from 1776 to 1780 as president of the executive council and lieutenant governor during Patrick Henry's three terms as governor and Jefferson's first. Henry's frequent illnesses often placed day-to-day responsibility for the government on Page. Friends drew him into an unsuccessful campaign against Jefferson for governor in 1779, but with no significant policy differences between them, the campaign did not affect their friendship. The following year Jefferson sought Page to succeed him, but Page declined. When the capital moved from Williamsburg to Richmond in 1780, Page resigned as

councillor. For most of 1781 he served as a militia officer during the British invasion of Virginia. He represented Gloucester in the House of Delegates from 1781 to 1788, except for 1784, when he served on the Pennsylvania-Virginia boundary commission, and 1787, when his wife died.

After the war Page's religious convictions merged with his political Whiggism and admiration for classical republicanism to form a vision of a Christian republic. With the establishment of political freedom, he thought, all rational citizens would turn to Christianity. He opposed Jefferson's Statute for Religious Freedom and proposed instead a general religious assessment for all Protestant denominations instead of just the Anglican church. He played a major role in restructuring the Anglican denomination as the Protestant Episcopal church. At the Virginia Episcopal conventions in 1785 and 1786 and the national Episcopal convention in Philadelphia in September 1785, he espoused broadly defined, latitudinarian positions to persuade evangelical members, on one side, to remain within the church and, on the other, to reconcile rational, scientific ideas of the Enlightenment with orthodox doctrine. Dismissing suggestions that he take orders and become Virginia's first bishop, he endorsed the elevation of William and Mary's president, the Reverend James Madison.

Page's position on ratification of the federal constitution balanced his Whig politics with a deepening concern for stability in the new nation. He welcomed the Annapolis Convention's call in 1786 to amend the Articles of Confederation and strengthen the continental government, but he opposed ratification of the Constitution, proposed the next year by the Philadelphia Convention, without first adding a bill of rights. He also thought the new Constitution gave too much authority to the central government and regarded some provisions as too reminiscent of the British constitution. Eventually the other James Madison, the founding father, convinced Page to accept ratification without amendment on Madison's promise to seek a bill of rights immediately afterward. Because of Page's support for the Constitution, he lost campaigns in 1787 for both the ratifying convention and the governorship, but after ratification he won election to the first Congress in 1789. In New York he met and in 1790 married Margaret Lowther of Scotland, whose literary inspiration led to joint publication of the poem *Dodsley* in 1793. They had eight children.

Page's enthusiasm for the federal administration waned under Secretary of the Treasury Alexander Hamilton's proposals for a strong central economic program. Still, Page led the Gloucester militia against the 1794 Whiskey Rebellion, when Pennsylvania farmers rose against a federal excise. Page's conversion to Jeffersonianism thwarted his reelection to Congress in 1797 but returned him to the House of Delegates in 1797 and 1800. He worked hard for Jefferson in the 1800 presidential campaign. Page won the Virginia governorship in 1802, serving three terms until 1805. In the wake of the abortive Virginia slave uprising in

1800 known as Gabriel's Rebellion, Page's administrations focused on revamping the militia, procuring munitions, and building a prison in case of a recurrence. Page's ambivalence toward slavery paralleled Jefferson's: both decried the existence of the institution, but both remained slaveholders. Aside from supporting manumission bills as a delegate and speculating on colonization of freed slaves outside Virginia, Page did not challenge the system.

Wartime interruption of the tobacco trade and Page's neglect of his affairs for public service gravely diminished his fortune, once among Virginia's greatest. The cost of maintaining Rosewell, the largest eighteenth-century Virginia mansion, financially burdened him throughout his life, as did support of his numerous progeny. When the tobacco trade did not return to tidewater Virginia after the war as he expected, he began selling his lands and reduced his slaveholdings from 162 in 1783 to around 35 at his death. He died in Richmond.

• Collections of Page papers are at Duke University, the University of Virginia, and in the Executive Letterbooks and Papers, Virginia State Library. Much Page correspondence is scattered in collections of other revolutionary leaders, particularly the Tucker-Coleman collection at the College of William and Mary; the Lee papers at the University of Virginia, the Virginia Historical Society, and the American Philosophical Society; and in *The Papers of Thomas Jefferson*, ed. Julian P. Boyd et al. (1950–), and *The Papers of James Madison*, ed. William T. Hutchinson et al. (1962–). A definitive biography with a complete bibliography is Theodore B. McCord, Jr., "John Page of Rosewell: Reason, Religion, and Republican Government from the Perspective of a Virginia Planter, 1743–1808" (Ph.D. diss., American Univ., 1991).

JOHN E. SELBY

PAGE, Leigh (13 Oct. 1884–14 Sept. 1952), physicist, was born in South Orange, New Jersey, the son of Edward Day Page, a merchant, and Cornelia Lee. Page attended the Friend's Seminary in New York City before entering Yale University, where he intended to study mechanical engineering. He received a Ph.B. in 1904 from the Sheffield Scientific School at Yale, and then embarked on a five-year hiatus from his studies, during which he worked on a ranch in Colorado, was a mechanical engineer in New York, and taught mathematics and physics in a preparatory school in New Jersey. He returned in 1909 to Yale, where he served from 1910 as an assistant instructor and from 1912 as an instructor in physics. He received a Ph.D. in physics in 1913, with a dissertation, "The Photoelectric Effect," written under the direction of Henry A. Bumstead. He became an assistant professor in 1916, and then served as the first J. Willard Gibbs Professor of Mathematical Physics from 1922 until his death. Page was a fellow of the American Physical Society and a member of the Connecticut Academy of Arts and Sciences. During World Wars I and II he served as a civilian with the U.S. Army and Navy respectively. In 1910 Page married Mary Edith Cholmondeley Thornton; they had one son and two daughters.

Page was one of the few American physicists of his generation whose primary research and teaching interests lay in theoretical physics. As such he was highly regarded by his contemporaries, and his teaching gave great stability to the Yale program following the unexpected death of Bumstead in 1921. In 1918, on the hundredth anniversary of the *American Journal of Science* (which had been founded by Benjamin Silliman at Yale), Page contributed a two page review article, "A Century's Progress in Physics." His research interests were largely devoted to electrodynamics and its applications, with occasional forays into relativity (the special theory), and atomic structure (as described by the old quantum theory). He never accepted the new quantum theory, i.e., the post-1925 theories, and many of his efforts were directed at attempting to obtain quantum theory as a consequence of electrodynamics and relativity theory. He also participated in the writing of two National Research Council Bulletins: "General Survey on the Present Status of the Atomic Structure Problem" (1921) and "The Molecular Spectra of Gases" (1926). Altogether he produced some seventy publications that appeared in scientific journals.

Page's most important results in theoretical physics were concerned with giving derivations of electrodynamics from various viewpoints. The first one employed relativity and electrostatics (1912), and the second, relativity and an emittor postulate (1914), to derive Maxwellian electrodynamics. The latter became known as the emission theory of electrodynamics and was treated in detail in his book, *An Introduction to Electrodynamics from the Standpoint of Electron Theory* (1922), and his graduate text, *Electrodynamics* (1940), written with his colleague Norman I. Adams, Jr. Page also wrote an influential textbook, *An Introduction to Theoretical Physics* (1928), which for many years was employed in a required course for Yale graduate students in physics. One of the first of its kind in the United States, the book gives an impressive image of Page as a teacher. However, in its later (1935 and 1952) editions, it remained severely classical, clearly demonstrating Page's preference for classical theories. He also wrote an elementary text, *Principles of Electricity* (1931), in collaboration with Adams. Page's last major work in theoretical physics was his 1936 publication of a "New Relativity" (*Physical Review* 49 [1 Feb. 1936]: 254–68, and 49 [15 Mar. 1936]: 466–69), which claimed that Albert Einstein's special theory was "too restrictive" to include all possible motions of material particles. (This theory was inspired by Edward A. Milne's 1935 discovery of kinematic relativity, which Page's son was studying at Oxford University with Milne.) In the same volume of the journal, Howard P. Robertson demonstrated that Page's "new theory" was in fact merely a very special and artificial case of Einstein's general theory of relativity. In his final years Page continued his search for an electrodynamic explanation of quantum theory, but none of this research was ever published.

Despite his nonacceptance of much of modern physics, Page remained a well-respected and valued member of the American physics community. Through his scholarship and teaching he made an invaluable contribution to the physics program at Yale at a time when his talents were sorely needed, and throughout the remainder of his life he continued to serve with distinction. Page remained active until his death in Randolph, New Hampshire. In 1954 his widow established an annual $1,000 Leigh Page Prize to be awarded for outstanding work by a Yale graduate student in physics.

• A listing of Page's publications is in *Poggendorffs biographisch-literarisches Handwörterbuch, Bänden* V, VI (1926, 1938). Obituaries are in *Science* 117 (20 Mar. 1953): 289–90, and the *New York Times*, 17 Sept. 1952. The former contains a brief description of his final attempts to reconcile electrodynamics and quantum theory.

JOSEPH D. ZUND

PAGE, Logan Waller (10 Jan. 1870–9 Dec. 1918), highway engineer and government administrator, was born in Richmond, Virginia, the son of Legh R. Page and Page Waller (occupations unknown). His family was well off, and several relatives were noted public servants, including a cousin Walter Hines Page, publisher of *World's Work* and ambassador to Great Britain, and another cousin, who was ambassador to Italy. Page received a fine education at the Powder Point School and Bear Island Academy and attended Virginia Polytechnic Institute from 1887 to 1889 without earning a degree. He enrolled at the Lawrence Scientific School at Harvard in 1889 and entered the first specialized highway engineering course in the country, conceived and directed by geology professor Dr. Nathaniel S. Shaler. An early "good roads" enthusiast, Shaler was determined to place road work on a scientific basis. To that end, as the first head of the Massachusetts Highway Commission, formed in 1891 as the first in the country, Shaler appointed Page geologist and testing engineer for the commission in 1893. In 1903 Page married Shaler's daughter, Anne P. Shaler.

Shaler was Page's uncle as well, but Page proved the correct choice for the job. Harvard permitted the Highway Commission to use Shaler's laboratory, and Page systematically began to gather information about road materials. He made the first petrographic studies of rock for roads and published a comprehensive report on road-building stone in 1898. A greater contribution was his role in transferring physical-testing machinery and materials-testing procedures to this country from France, where the world's leader in road building, the Corps des Ponts et Chausées (Corps of Bridges and Roads) had introduced them. Page visited Paris to study French techniques in 1897–1898 and then made minor improvements upon his return. Overall, his efforts eventually convinced most state highway departments to routinely test road-building materials.

In 1900 Page joined the Bureau of Chemistry in the U.S. Department of Agriculture as chief of the Division of Tests, where he worked primarily with the Office of Public Road Inquiry (OPRI), an agency charged with disseminating information about road building. He continued to improve materials-testing procedures, adopting chemical tests. Page also cooperated with the American Society for Testing Materials (ASTM) to disperse construction specifications and materials standards. By 1904 Page's laboratory was performing more than 1,000 analyses annually, building a knowledge base that led to numerous technical circulars and bulletins. These efforts greatly strengthened the office's reputation as the leading American source of technical information on highways.

Page's activities were in keeping with the reform efforts of the dawning Progressive era, which trusted technical experts with authority in the belief they would eliminate inefficiency, waste, and political corruption. Following this pattern, Page was promoted in 1905 to head the renamed Office of Public Roads (OPR). The previous director, Martin Dodge, had permitted a few unscrupulous promoters to reap illegal financial rewards while promoting good roads. Moreover, Dodge had lobbied Congress and breached other ethical norms. Congress angrily added a clause to the OPR's appropriation in 1905 requiring an engineer or scientist to head the office.

Page immediately embarked on a model Progressive reform program. First, he established strict ethical guidelines for all staff and helped the Post Office bring mail fraud charges against the most unethical road promoters. Second, he argued convincingly that highway policy should rest on sound technical information and made sure that the OPR was the leading source of technical assistance in the country. He expanded advisory programs and the testing laboratory, and he himself engaged in research until about 1910. He was also elected a member of the American Society of Civil Engineers in 1909, having served on several of its committees for years.

The third phase of Page's program logically followed from the second: the key to efficient highway programs was control by engineers. Like other reformers, Page assumed that scientific training created decision makers resistant by definition to corruption. He encouraged state legislatures to create highway departments headed by engineers, drafted a model bill, and permitted federal engineers to testify in the states; the bills usually passed. He also launched a postgraduate training program in the office for highway engineers and assigned federal engineers to short periods of service with state and county agencies to teach efficient management and construction procedures.

Finally, he conducted an extensive educational program on the value of good roads. Page's message combined an abhorrence of inefficiency with a belief that better roads were an instrument of social justice, permitting rural Americans to enjoy the same life as town dwellers. Page initiated a lecture program spreading this gospel of good roads and cooperated with numerous organizations favoring road improvements. In 1913 he revived the Good Roads Trains, an idea first utilized in 1901–1902 to carry the message to rural Americans via special trains containing displays, models, and lecturers.

After 1910 Page sought to channel public support for better roads into legislative action. Apparently contradicting his belief that road-building decisions should be kept out of the political arena, Page played an important role in shaping federal highway legislation. The key was his self-image as an objective, incorruptible engineer serving the general public. Even as he helped form a lobbying organization (the American Highway Association) in 1910, he argued repeatedly that his office played no role in political decisions. Moreover, Page largely shaped the first bill providing federal funds for post roads in 1912 and the more comprehensive Federal-Aid Road Act of 1916. The latter established the federal-aid policies that still guide American highway programs, with state and federal governments sharing costs and responsibilities. Page worked closely with congressmen and committees, provided technical information and staff assistance, and even helped draft the bill, which embraced his vision of post roads for rural Americans rather than a national highway system built directly by the federal government as proposed by the automobile industry. While hard to accept at face value, this image of apolitical expertise is central to understanding Page's accomplishments and the Progressive faith in expertise.

Obscure now, in his time Page was a recognized reform leader. In 1909 newspaperman E. W. Scripps commented, "Although he is a Government officer and a member of the bureaucracy I consider him one of the most able, effective and enthusiastic of all of our citizens; he is doing for our roads what [Gifford] Pinchot is doing for our forests." In keeping with his combined technical/social reform program, in 1915 Page's office was renamed the Office of Public Roads and Rural Engineering and was assigned responsibility for irrigation, drainage, and other rural programs.

During World War I, Page chaired the U.S. Highways Council, which coordinated efforts to facilitate highway transportation. Materials shortages and other factors delayed work on the new federal-aid roads system, however, and critics attacked Page's plan of administration. In December 1918 he was attending the annual meeting of the American Association of State Highway Officials in Chicago, in part to answer complaints, when he was stricken by a heart attack and died unexpectedly. Page's primary legacy was the federal-aid highway system, for few Progressive Era reforms lasted as long as the system and principles of highway administration he helped establish.

• Like many engineers, Page's work was his life. For the best source of information about him, see the correspondence files of the Bureau of Public Roads in Record Group 30, Records of the Bureau of Public Roads, National Archives, Washington National Record Center, Suitland, Md. The letter from Scripps is from this material: File 104, General Correspondence, 1893–1916. One should also examine the annual reports of the Office of Public Roads from 1905 to 1917. The archival records and government documents provide the basis of Bruce E. Seely, *Building the American Highway System: Engineers as Policy Makers* (1987), which traces the evolution of the Bureau of Public Roads and Page's role. See also "The United States Office of Public Roads," *Engineering Record* 62 (17 Dec. 1910): 709–11. Page's publications include *The Testing of Road Materials* (1901); *Roads, Paths, and Bridges* (1912), numerous government reports, and articles in both popular and technical journals, such as *Scientific American, Collier's, Engineering News, Transactions of the American Society of Civil Engineers*. Biographical sketches can be found in U.S. Department of Agriculture, Bureau of Public Roads, *Annual Report of the Bureau of Public Roads* (1919); John M. Goodell, "Logan Waller Page," *Engineering News-Record* 81 (12 Dec. 1918); Goodell, "An Apostle of Good Roads: Logan Waller Page," *American Review of Reviews* 59 (Mar. 1919): 302–4; "Memoir of Logan Waller Page," *Transactions of the American Society of Civil Engineers* 83 (1919–1920): 2305–9; and "Logan Waller Page," *Engineering and Contracting* 50 (18 Dec. 1918): 577–78. An obituary is in the *New York Times*, 10 Dec. 1918.

BRUCE E. SEELY

PAGE, Mann (1691–24 Jan. 1731), planter and government official, was born in Gloucester County, Virginia, the son of Matthew Page, a planter and member of the council of Virginia, and Mary Mann, heiress of John Mann of "Timberneck," Gloucester County. Mann Page inherited wealth and extensive lands from his parents and his grandfather, who had established the family's social and political position by the time of his death in 1691. The third-generation representative of the family in Virginia, Page was sent back to England to be educated at Eton, where he was admitted in 1706. Three years later, in July 1709, he entered St. John's College, Oxford, although it is not known how long he stayed. By 1711 he had returned to Virginia and married Judith Wormeley, the daughter of Ralph Wormeley II of "Rosegill," Middlesex County. With this marriage, Page allied himself with another leading colonial Virginia family. In March 1714 Governor Alexander Spotswood recommended him for appointment to the council as "a young gentleman of a liberal education, good parts, and a very plentiful estate, whose father and grandfather both had the honor of the same post." In December 1716 Judith Wormeley Page died. By 1718 Page had married Judith Carter, the daughter of Robert "King" Carter of "Corotoman," Lancaster County. Once again, Page had allied himself with one of the colony's elite families. His second father-in-law would prove an invaluable connection in helping Page obtain extensive land grants. Page had six children from his second marriage as well as three from his first. Two of the children died in infancy.

Spotswood's high opinion of Page was well rewarded. Page was one of the governor's few steadfast supporters on the council during attempts by other councillors, including Robert Carter, to have Spotswood dismissed. Page was a member of the short-lived Virginia Indian Company that the governor promoted to encourage trade with the Indians. Page was also involved with his father-in-law in a scheme to mine copper in northern Virginia. Although the plan proved unsuccessful, it allowed the two men to extend their landholdings, until Page was one of the largest landowners in Virginia. Carter thought highly of his son-in-law and declared, "You are blest with so steady a head and so tenacious a memory that I never doubt your punctual performance of all particulars that you are at any time pleased to take into your command." During the administration of Governor Hugh Drysdale, Page continued on the council and, by virtue of that position, on the General Court. Drysdale also appointed him county lieutenant.

A later governor, William Gooch, had a less favorable opinion of Page. Writing the Board of Trade some years after Page's death, Gooch stated that the councillor had "almost ruined his Family by taking up Land, in order to be respected as the richest man in the Country." Later critics claimed that building "Rosewell," a grand house, wreaked havoc on the family's fortunes as well and loaded Page's heir, Mann Page II, with debts that he could only resolve by selling entailed lands. Contemporaries also questioned Page's business practices and criticized his personality after his relatively early death at Rosewell, possibly from gout. Carter confessed to his son-in-law's creditors that "Colo Pages books . . . appear to be kept in a very Confused negligent manner," and in praising the son in December 1744 Governor Gooch damned the father with the comment that "the son . . . is a very worthy Man, and the reverse of his Father's temper."

Page's mansion, Rosewell, begun sometime between 1721 and 1726, became his monument. Located in Gloucester County on a tract west of Carter's Creek and north of the York River, the house rivaled the Governor's Palace in Williamsburg in size and swagger. The academic symmetry of Rosewell, the use of marble tile in the stair hall, and a double-pile plan underscored Page's claim to leadership among the colony's elite. In employing two cupolas on the lead roof of the dwelling, Page may have meant to include the royal governors among the architectural rivals with whom he was competing. The house was gutted by fire in 1916 and now lies in ruins. The site is under the protection of the Rosewell Foundation, which seeks to preserve Page's architectural legacy.

• Few Page family papers survive, and Gloucester County records burned during the Civil War. Many aspects of Page's life are gleaned from a variety of sources, including the William Gooch Papers, Public Record Office, London; Robert "King" Carter Diary and Letterbooks, no. 3807, Manuscripts Department, University of Virginia Library; and Robert Carter Letterbooks, Virginia Historical Society. For secondary accounts of Page and Rosewell, see Betty Crowe Leviner, "The Pages and Rosewell," Museum of Early Southern Decorative Arts, *Journal* (May 1987), and Leviner, "Rosewell Revisited," Museum of Early Southern Decorative Arts, *Journal* (Nov. 1993). See also Leonidas Dodson, *Alexander Spotswood, Governor of Colonial Virginia, 1710–1722* (1932), and Richard L. Morton, *Colonial Virginia*, vol. 2 (1960), for political views of Page.

BETTY CROWE LEVINER

PAGE, Ruth (22 Mar. 1899–7 Apr. 1991), dancer and choreographer, was born in Indianapolis, Indiana, the daughter of Lafayette Page, a brain surgeon, and Marian Heinly, a professional pianist and founder of the Indianapolis Symphony Orchestra. Having decided at the age of five to become a ballerina, Ruth waited until she was twelve to begin professional training. Her early instruction included ballet lessons with Andreas Pavley and Serge Oukrainsky and fancy and skirt dancing with Anna Stanton. After meeting fifteen-year-old Ruth, world-famous ballerina Anna Pavlova encouraged her mother to allow Ruth to take summer ballet classes in Chicago with Pavlova's company. Soon afterward Ruth Page joined the Anna Pavlova company on a tour of Latin America. On her return she attended the French School for Girls, a boarding school in New York, while studying dance under Adolph Bolm and Ivan Clustine. She performed in a Bolm revue in 1917.

In December 1919 Page debuted as a dancer in Chicago in the leading role of *The Birthday of the Infanta*, choreographed by Bolm and based on an Oscar Wilde story. Page danced with Bolm's company the following year, traveling with them to London, where she studied with Enrico Cecchetti, Pavlova's teacher. Page became *première danseuse* of Bolm's Ballet Intime and made several U.S. tours with the company. Bolm and Page appeared together in *Danse Macabre* (1922), Francis Brugiers's dance film, the first of its kind with synchronized sound. From October 1922 to March 1924 Page danced the principal role in Irving Berlin's *Music Box Revue*, performing in New York City the first year and on the U.S. tour in the second. She became the prima ballerina for the avant-garde company Chicago Allied Arts, a position that gave her an opportunity to experiment with choreography. In 1924 Page choreographed and danced in the jazz piece *The Flapper and the Quarterback*, a duet with Paul Dupont, and *Oak Street Beach*, an ensemble piece portraying the subculture thriving on the Chicago beach. In 1925 Page married Thomas Hart Fisher, a wealthy lawyer and dance enthusiast.

Following her marriage Page worked for a short time in Diaghilev's Ballets Russes, but she left the company to join Bolm in Buenos Aires, where she danced the lead roles in *Le Coq d'Or* and *Petrouchka*, performing with the Municipal Opera Company. She worked with the Metropolitan Opera Company in New York from 1926 to 1928 as guest soloist and, beginning in 1926, spent seven summers in Chicago as *première danseuse*, choreographer, and ballet mistress of the Ravinia Opera Company. In Washington, D.C., Page took the leading role in the premiere of Stravinsky's *Apollon Musagète*, choreographed by Bolm, on 27 April 1928.

At the end of 1928 Page set out on a three-month tour of the Far East; her appearances included a performance at the enthronement ceremony of Emperor Hirohito. In 1930, at the invitation of the Soviet Government, she traveled to Moscow to present a series of American dances to workers' groups. She choreographed several pieces for the Century of Progress Exposition in Chicago in 1933, including *Guiablesse*, to African-American composer William Grant Still's score, performed by an all African-American company (excepting Page) and starring Katherine Dunham. The following year Page returned to the Far East and also toured in Europe and the United States. These tours showcased original dances created with Harald Kreutzberg, an innovator in German modern dance. Their work together was dramatic, playful, inventive, concrete rather than abstract, and neither classical nor serious in conception. In stints from 1934 to 1937, 1942 to 1943, and in 1945, she was *première danseuse* and ballet director for the Chicago Opera Company, the first such company to present all-ballet evenings. Among the works featured were her *Hear Ye! Hear Ye!* (1934), with music by Aaron Copland, and *An American Pattern* (1937), with music by Jerome Moross.

While Page worked as director of Chicago's Federal Theater Dance Project in 1938 and 1939, she also established with Bentley Stone the Page-Stone Ballet, with which she toured Latin America and the United States. The Page-Stone company lasted until 1946, when Stone entered the military. Working in conjunction, Page and Stone produced the overwhelmingly successful ballet *Frankie and Johnny* (1938) for the Federal Dance Project.

In 1939 Page began choreographing operas into ballets, a genre that would become her trademark. Her first efforts translated Bizet's *Carmen* into the ballet *Guns and Castanets* (1939), set in modern-day, civil-war–torn Spain. She was later to choreograph Verdi's *Il Trovatore* (renamed *Revenge*, 1951); Rossini's *The Barber of Seville* (renamed *Susanna and the Barber*, 1956); Verdi's *La Traviata* (renamed *Camille*, 1957); Johann Strauss, Jr.'s operetta *Die Fledermaus* (1961) and Oscar Straus's operetta *The Chocolate Soldier* (renamed *Bullets and Bonbons*, 1965); three more productions of *Carmen* (1959, 1962, and, called *Carmen and José*, 1972); and Gounod's *Faust* (renamed *Mephistophela*, 1963). In an interview with *Dance Magazine*, Page explained her interest in the relationship between opera and dance: "I felt that the dancing body could successfully express the drama and emotion conveyed by the voice of the singer and that the dramatic ideas of the composer and the librettist could be expressed in dance as well as in song" (Feb. 1961, p. 24).

In the late 1940s Page began to work more frequently in Europe. She was a guest dancer and choreographer for the Ballets Russes de Monte Carlo from 1946 to 1950, for the Royal Festival Ballet in 1953, and for Les Ballets des Champs-Elysées from 1948 to 1951, creating and dancing in the ballets *Billy Sunday* (1946; Ballet Russe de Monte Carlo, 1948), *Impromptu au Bois* (1951; her 1934 *Gold Standard* renamed), and *Revanche* (1951), as *Revenge* was named in France. In 1950 she and her Chicago group traveled to Paris, where they appeared as Les Ballets Américains, presenting a series of original and highly innovative dances. Audiences were at first taken aback by the unconventionality of her performances, which mixed diverse dance styles and incorporated a plethora of often only loosely connected ideas, but critical and popular appreciation for her work soon grew. Page choreographed *Minnie Moustache* (1956), a French musical about the Gold Rush and settlement of the American West, especially for her French audiences. Her other experiments of the late 1940s included combining dance with poetry recitals.

Page became ballet director of the new Chicago Lyric Opera in 1954 and remained with the company until 1969. They performed her ballet *The Merry Widow*, derived from Franz Lehar's operetta, on Broadway in 1955, with Alicia Markova dancing the lead role. Ruth Page's Chicago Opera Ballet was organized by Page in conjunction with the Chicago Lyric Opera; it has continued as a group of dancers performing with the opera during its regular season and on tour. Page worked as ballet director of the company from its inception in 1956 to 1966. She then founded, in 1966, Ruth Page's International Ballet, for which she served as choreographer and director until its demise in 1970, and the Ruth Page School of Dance in Chicago in 1971. Page embarked on a lecture tour entitled Ruth Page's Invitation to Dance in 1971 and 1972. Her later choreography includes a version of *The Nutcracker* (1965), *Carmina Burana* (1966), *Bolero* (1968), *Dancer's Ritual* (1969), *Alice in the Garden* (1970), *Catulli Carmina* (1973), and *Alice in Wonderland* and *Alice Through the Looking Glass* (1978). Honors bestowed on Page include a citation from the Ballet Guild of Chicago (1977), the Mahariski Award from Columbia University (1977), the Association of Dance Costumers Award (1978) for outstanding service to dance, the Community Arts Foundation Award (1978), the Dance Magazine Award (1980), two medals of merit from the city of Chicago, and the Illinois Gubernatorial Award in 1985. She received honorary degrees from Indiana University (1983), De Paul University (1984), and the University of Illinois (1985). After the death of her first husband in 1969, Page married André Delfau, an artist and designer, in 1983. She died in Chicago of respiratory failure.

Ruth Page was one of the best-known and most influential ballet dancers and choreographers of her time. Relentlessly innovative, she often mixed dance styles within a performance, incorporating, for example, classical ballet, jazz, and modern and ethnic dance in a single piece, creating original and unusual effects but occasionally overwhelming audiences with too many disparate ideas. Page also combined dance with other art forms, including opera and poetry. She is remembered for her uniquely American perspective, which was evinced in ballets with Americana themes and in the commissioning of music from American composers, including George Gershwin, Aaron Copland, Clarence Loomis, and Jerome Moross. Page did much to popularize dance, especially in her native Chicago. Her vast energy and excellent organizational abilities made her a superb founder and director of ballet companies. However, her continuing loyalty to Chicago, while it greatly enhanced the area's cultural offerings, had the drawback of limiting Page's personal career by distancing her from the major focal points of ballet performance and culture in Europe and New York.

• Page published two books: *Page By Page* (1980), a memoir, and *Class: A Selection of Notes on Dance Classes Around the World, 1916–1980* (1985), compiled by Andrew Mark Wentink from Page's notebooks. A comprehensive biographic source for Page's life is John Martin's *Ruth Page: An Intimate Biography* (1977). Articles on Ruth Page appear in *Dance Magazine*, Feb. and Dec. 1961. She is mentioned in Anatole Chujoy's *Dance Encyclopedia* (1949) and Olga Maynard's *The American Ballet* (1959). An obituary appears in the *New York Times*, 9 Apr. 1991, and the *Los Angeles Times*, 10 Apr. 1991.

ELIZABETH ZOE VICARY

PAGE, Thomas Jefferson (4 Jan. 1808–26 Oct. 1899), naval officer and explorer, was born in Shelly, Gloucester County, Virginia, the son of Mann Page, a plantation owner, and Elizabeth Nelson. Page's varied and interesting career began in 1827 when he was appointed to the U.S. Naval Academy (aboard a ship in New York) by President John Quincy Adams in recognition of the services of his grandfathers, both distinguished Virginia governors. One of them, John Page, was a friend of Thomas Jefferson, hence his own name. He graduated as midshipman with honors and was assigned to the *Erie* in the Caribbean. He was soon recognized as an adventuresome and capable mariner. In 1833 (10 June) he passed the exams for promotion, but the promotion was delayed for some time. In the same year he was assigned to work on a coastal survey with the Swiss engineer Ferdinand Hassler. During the nine years on the survey he acquired much scientific knowledge and developed a sense of methodical investigation. In 1838 he married Benjamina Price in Washington, D.C. They had seven children. On 20 December 1839 he was promoted to lieutenant. When the survey work finished in 1842, Page joined the *Columbus* and spent two years in the Mediterranean and Brazil. In 1844 he was sent to work at the Naval Observatory under Matthew Maury, with whom he later maintained a strong friendship and an interesting correspondence.

In 1848 Page was given command of the brig *Dolphin*, which was part of the Far East fleet. He proved himself to be "alive, energetic and brave." In the three years he sailed in the Orient he recognized the commercial importance of that region and suggested to Secretary of the Navy William Alexander Graham that the China seas be surveyed. The idea was accepted, and Congress appropriated money for the construction of an adequate ship. However, Graham's successor, John Pendleton Kennedy, chose Commander Cadwalader Ringgold to head the expedition. In September 1852 Kennedy offered Page command of a ship under Ringgold or the possibility of leading a scientific and commercial expedition to the La Plata region of South America. Page eagerly accepted the second offer and was also empowered by Secretary of State Edward Everett to arrange a commercial treaty with Paraguay.

For the journey Page was given the *Water Witch*, the only side-wheel steamer man-of-war the navy ever had. He set sail on 8 February 1853, and he and his crew (including his twelve-year-old second son, John) spent the next three years charting and traveling some 3,300 miles on rivers and 4,400 on land. His ship was the first foreign vessel to ascend the Paraná and Paraguay rivers and to enter and explore the Chaco region of Paraguay and the Mato Grosso province of Brazil. He met and dealt with important men of the time: Andrés Santa Cruz of Peru and Bolivia, Hilarión Ortiz of Bolivia (both in exile), Justo José de Urquiza of the Argentine Confederation, whose life he saved and who later became president, and Carlos Antonio López of Paraguay. The expedition made extremely valuable contributions to natural science (botany, zoology, mineralogy, and geology) and geography and opened the way for commercial treaties with Paraguay and Argentina. Even more might have been accomplished but for the foolish and undiplomatic actions of Edward Hopkins, a commercial agent who used his position to further his own interests, and Page's unwise support of him, which caused López to ban the *Water Witch* from Paraguay territory (3 Oct. 1854). When a second in command tried to navigate the river between Paraguay and Argentina, the ship was fired on and one man was killed (1 Feb. 1855). Page's protests and demands for satisfaction went unheeded, but the United States responded by promoting him to commander (14 Sept. 1855). Two years later President James Buchanan authorized a retaliatory mission, and Page was fleet captain of nineteen ships under Commodore William Branford Shubrick. Paraguay quickly apologized, paid for losses, and signed a commercial treaty. Meanwhile Page's report to the secretary of the navy was published in 1856, and this he later turned into a book, *La Plata, the Argentine Confederation, and Paraguay* (1859).

From March 1859 to October 1860 Page made a second expedition to the La Plata region, exploring mainly the estuary itself and some Argentine rivers. He was organizing his notes and charts for a second report when Fort Sumter was fired on in April 1861. Because he was, in the words of Captain Samuel Barron, "a good officer and a high-strung Southern patriot," Page chose to enter the Confederate service and began instructing the water battery in the use of nine-inch guns. General John Bankhead Magruder reported that Page had "successfully applied the resources of his genius and ripe experience to the defense of Gloucester Point" (Va.) and two months later he was given command of the heavy batteries at Chapin's Bluff and Balls Bluff, Virginia.

In 1863 Page, now both colonel of artillery and commander, was sent to Europe to negotiate the return of the ironclad *Sphynx*, built in France for the Confederacy but sold to Denmark. There followed nearly two years of intrigue and repeated delays and it was not until January of 1865 that Page finally sailed from Copenhagen to France on the rechristened *Stonewall*. Forced to stop in El Ferrol, Spain, for repairs, he finally arrived in Nassau in May only to learn that the war was over and with it his naval career.

He decided to go to Argentina where he was still something of a hero and spent some years in Entre Ríos on a cattle ranch that belonged to his old friend Urquiza. Later, the Argentine government sent him to England to supervise the construction of two ironclads and two gunboats for the new national fleet. In 1880 Page and most of his family moved to Florence, Italy, and lived with his daughter, the Countess Spinola. After the count died the family moved to Rome, where Page spent his last years in blindness, died, and is buried.

• In addition to known reference works, further information on Page can be found in Edward W. Callahan, ed., *List of Officers of the Navy of the United States and of the Marine Corps. from 1775 to 1900* (1901); J. Thomas Scharf, *History of the Confederate States Navy* (1887, repr. 1969); and Richard Page, *Genealogy of the Page Family in Virginia* (1883, repr. 1972). A partial biography is found in the *Southern Historical Society Papers*, vol. 27, pp. 219–31, written shortly after his death in 1899. The works that most reveal Page's character, temperament, and thought are those related to his 1853–1856 expedition. Most important are *Letters etc. from Lt. T. J. Page Commanding United States Steamer Water Witch: Exploration and Survey of the Rivers of La Plata, Paraguay and Parana and Their Tributaries, January 6, 1853, and August 4, 1856*, found in the National Archives, Military and Naval Branch office, record group 45. Two works by Page himself are significant, *Report of the Exploration and Survey of the River "La Plata" and Tributaries* (1856), and *La Plata . . .* mentioned in the text. All of this material has been coordinated with other sources in Robert D. Wood, *The Voyage of the Water Witch* (1985). The expedition is also covered in a more summary fashion in Vincent Ponko, *Ships, Seas and Scientists: U.S. Naval Exploration and Discovery in the Nineteenth Century* (1974). Page's Civil War activities can be found in *Official Records of the Union and Confederate Navies in the War of the Rebellion*, ser. 2, vol. 2, and James D. Bulloch, *The Secret Service of the Confederate States in Europe* (1959). On his mission and all the difficulties he had over the *Stonewall*, see his article in the *Southern Historical Society Papers*, vol. 7 (1879), pp. 263–80.

ROBERT D. WOOD

PAGE, Thomas Nelson (23 Apr. 1853–1 Nov. 1922), author, was born at "Oakland," his family's plantation in Hanover County, Virginia, the son of John Page, an attorney, and Elizabeth Burwell Nelson. Only twelve when the Civil War ended, Page saw the Old South firsthand during his most impressionable years. Idealizing the prewar South, he remained until his death a staunch defender of the old regime. As a Virginia gentleman he received a classical education, and while attending Washington College (1869–1872) he knew and

revered its president, Robert E. Lee. After reading law and tutoring in Kentucky, Page studied law at the University of Virginia (1873–1874). He then practiced law in Virginia country courts for several years, before establishing a successful practice in Richmond (1876–1893).

At first, his success as a lawyer left Page little opportunity to pursue his interest in writing. In April 1884, however, *Century Magazine* published "Marse Chan," a dialect story of old Virginia that was well received and brought Page national attention as a spokesman for the Old South and as a local color writer. In 1886 he married Anne Seddon Bruce. The following year, his "Marse Chan," "Meh Lady," "Unc Edinburg's Drowndin'," and three other stories largely in black dialect were republished in book form as *In Ole Virginia*. Page did his part to promote better relations between the North and South in tales such as "Meh Lady," a love story of a Union soldier and a Virginia planter's daughter. Even though this theme was a conventional one in the 1880s, Page's handling of it was superior to that found in many stories by northern writers who had little understanding of southern life.

Page's *Befo' de War* (with A. C. Gordon), a collection of dialect verse, and his *Two Little Confederates*, a novella that views the Civil War and its aftermath through the eyes of two boys, were published in 1888. Following his wife's death in the same year, Page immersed himself in business affairs, first mining in Colorado (1889) and then in Europe (1891). Finding himself with some reputation in England, he enjoyed there the social life of a writer. Economic difficulties, however, forced him to return to Richmond and embark with the best-selling author F. Hopkinson Smith on a lecture tour that served to enhance his literary reputation at home.

In 1893, after his marriage to Florence Lathrop Field, the widow of Marshall Field's brother Henry, Page gave up the practice of law completely in order to devote full time to his writing. Moving to Washington, D.C., and maintaining a summer residence at York Harbor, Maine, the Pages entertained often, including among their guests men of affairs as well as artists and writers. As part of international society, they traveled regularly to Paris, London, Rome, and the Riviera. During the nineties, Page further established himself as a man of letters and a sought-after lecturer and dinner guest. He encouraged younger writers and was especially supportive of southern writers struggling to achieve literary recognition.

In 1892 Page published a collection of essays and articles, *The Old South*, the first of several such volumes that would earn him the reputation of being very knowledgeable about the details of everyday life in antebellum Virginia. *The Burial of the Guns* (1894) includes the story "Little Darby," which provides an illuminating insight into Page's social creed. The protagonist, Little Darby, is a poor, illiterate boy, descended from good English stock, who saves a Confederate army. Though Page denied the importance of caste, that importance is implicitly recognized in the story. And throughout his work, Page celebrates stamina and personality derived from long-rooted ancestry.

Page's *Social Life in Old Virginia*, a collection of essays and social studies, appeared in 1897. His first novel, *On Newfound River* (1891), is a story of Virginia before the Civil War based on an event in the lives of his first wife's family. It is interesting but hardly on a level with his second, *Red Rock* (1898), a novel of Reconstruction. Northern misperceptions of southern life and character had long irritated Page, and much of his earlier work had been designed to refute them. *Red Rock* was in effect a belated reply to *Uncle Tom's Cabin*. With the Civil War and Reconstruction viewed as tragic by northerners and southerners alike by the end of the nineteenth century, *Red Rock* found a large and sympathetic audience throughout the country. With reconciliation as one of its themes, the novel begins effectively, but the narrative soon bogs down, for Page was unable to handle effectively a long and complicated plot.

Though critics were not impressed, Page's third novel, *Gordon Keith* (1903), was a popular success, partly because it deals, somewhat sentimentally, with the New South rather than the Old. Nevertheless, the opening sentence—"Gordon Keith was the son of a gentleman"—typifies Pages point of view by invoking the values of an earlier day. In a series of magazine articles written in the first few years of the twentieth century, Page turned to nonfiction and appraised southern blacks in what he saw as realistic terms. Collected as *The Negro: The Southerner's Problem* in 1904, these sometimes reactionary pieces treat blacks as a stumbling block to the South's social and economic development. More of Page's essays on antebellum Virginia were published in *The Old Dominion* in 1908, the same year in which he was elected to the American Academy of Arts and Letters.

A very different Page is revealed by *John Marvel, Assistant* (1909), his last novel except for the posthumous and unfinished *Red Riders* (1924). Set for the most part in a large midwestern city, it is a "problem" novel (a type Page said he detested) and represents a medley of the topics that drew Page's interest during his Washington period: racial intolerance, social reform, and politics. Though not a good novel, *John Marvel* does reveal a Page who had at last developed a national outlook on public life.

By 1910 Page had decided that most editors wanted little more from him than a string of antebellum Marse Chans, so he turned increasingly to politics. In 1912 he helped unite Virginia's delegates to the Democratic National Convention behind Woodrow Wilson, whose idealistic objectives he supported. The following year Wilson appointed Page ambassador to Italy, a post he held successfully until 1919. Frustrated by the Treaty of Versailles, he returned home and began writing again. Mrs. Page died suddenly in 1921. Page died at Oakland the following year.

Through his numerous stories and novels, Page succeeded in getting many northerners to recognize the "glories" of the Old South while reassuring white southerners that they had an origin and history of which to be proud. With his emphasis on the need for sectional reconciliation and his depiction of antebellum plantation life, Page assured himself a secure position in the history of southern fiction. Yet in his very depiction of plantation life he revealed inadvertently the serious shortcomings of the Eden he so steadfastly praised.

• An extensive collection of Page manuscripts is held by Duke University, and a collection of material dealing primarily with his ambassadorship to Italy is at the College of William and Mary. Works by Page other than those mentioned in the text include *Among the Camps* (1891); *Elsket and Other Stories* (1891); *Pastime Stories* (1894); *The Old Gentleman of the Black Stock* (1897); *Two Prisoners* (1898); *Bred in the Bone* (1904); *The Coast of Bohemia* (1906); *Under the Crust* (1907); *Robert E. Lee, the Southerner* (1908); *Robert E. Lee, Man and Soldier* (1911); *The Land of the Spirit* (1913); *Italy and the World War* (1920); *Dante and His Influence* (1922); and, published posthumously, *North African Journal, 1912, with Letters along the Way* (1970); *On the Nile in 1901* (1970); *Mediterranean Winter, 1906: Journal and Letters* (1971). Pertinent works on Page are Roswell Page, *Thomas Nelson Page: A Memoir of a Virginia Gentleman* (1923); Harriet Holman, "The Literary Career of Thomas Nelson Page, 1884–1910" (Ph.D. diss., Duke Univ., 1947); Theodore Gross, *Thomas Nelson Page* (1967); Lucinda MacKethan, "Thomas Nelson Page: The Plantation Arcady," in *The Dream of Arcady: Time and Place in Southern Literature* (1980).

L. MOODY SIMMS, JR.

PAGE, Walter (9 Feb. 1900–20 Dec. 1957), jazz bassist and bandleader, was born Walter Sylvester Page in Gallatin, Missouri. His parents (names unknown) stressed learning, and in 1917 their son graduated from Lincoln High School in Kansas City with a sound musical education gained primarily from the teaching of Major N. Clark Smith, a man responsible for training a number of jazz musicians of the era. Page attended Kansas State Teacher's College from 1917 to 1920 but did not complete a degree in music education. From there, he entered the freewheeling Kansas City jazz scene.

Page's first professional experience occurred in 1918 with the Bennie Moten Orchestra, playing rhythm tuba, the popular dance-band predecessor to string bass. He also played the bass and baritone saxophone, as well as the sousaphone. Some bandleaders preferred the sousaphone for dance numbers because it could be heard more clearly than a string bass. Page stayed with Moten until 1923.

During the mid-1920s Page traveled throughout Oklahoma and Texas, playing in a number of small bands with names like the Jeter-Pillars Club Plantation Orchestra. It was a hectic life, and in 1927 he returned to Kansas City and the relative stability of Moten's band, where he now played bass, his instrument of choice. This second round with Moten lasted until 1929. In that year, he broke away and formed his own band, Walter Page's Blue Devils.

The Blue Devils were destined to become an important and influential band in the history of jazz. Page enlisted William "Count" Basie as his pianist, altoist Buster Smith, tenor sax player Lester Young, trumpeter Oran "Hot Lips" Page (although some disagreement exists about their actual sibling relationship, Hot Lips Page claimed to be Walter Page's younger half brother), trombonist and arranger Eddie Durham, trombonist Dan Minor, drummer Alvin Burroughs, and vocalist Jimmy Rushing. With his formal musical training, Page taught many of his musicians to read and to play in a disciplined band setting. In their heyday (1929–1931), the Blue Devils were considered the finest band in the Southwest. As was the custom then, bands frequently "battled" one another—contests designed to demonstrate a group's skills and ability to play virtually any arrangement. The Blue Devils took on all comers, including such unlikely contestants as the bands of Lawrence Welk and Vincent Lopez. More often than not, Page's group was victorious. Although the Blue Devils were recorded in 1929, when the best members were still present (some scholars, however, argue that Basie was not the pianist in these sessions but instead Willie Lewis was), the recording quality is such that Page can barely be heard.

In 1929 Moten successfully hired away some of the leading players from the group and employed them in his own orchestra. Page could not effectively replace them; he ultimately turned the band over to James Simpson in 1931 and rejoined Moten for a third time. He stayed until 1935. Moten had died earlier in 1935 as a result of a botched tonsillectomy, but Page and others struggled to keep the aggregation together. In 1934 Count Basie had formed his own band, and Walter Page became its bassist in late 1935 or early 1936. He would remain with Basie until the fall of 1942, with another stint in 1946–1948. It was with the Basie band that Page achieved his greatest fame and influence. Nevertheless, he also toured or recorded with Sidney Bechet, Jimmy Rushing, Jimmy McPartland, Eddie Condon, Harry James, Benny Goodman, and many others from the late 1930s until his death.

Although Page was initially influenced by bassist Wellman Braud, whom he first heard in 1917, he quickly moved beyond Braud's traditional style and became an important innovator on the instrument. Probably the major contribution of Page and the Blue Devils, along with Moten's band (and, later, Basie's), was the introduction of Kansas City swing, a loose, riff-based dance music (a riff is a musical phrase of just a few notes repeated in varying tones by different sections of the band, sometimes as a background to a soloist or vocalist and sometimes as foreground material in its own right, as exemplified by a number of Basie arrangements).

Working with Basie drummer Jo Jones, Page discovered that the bass could lead a band and that the drums (particularly cymbals) could complement that lead. Jones, Page, Basie, and guitarist Freddie Green experimented with ever greater simplification. Page's bass counted off the beats but did little else, and yet there was a sense of the rhythm, a shading of the notes, along with unexpected emphases. Before their experi-

ments, standard jazz rhythm was usually a 2/4 that was driven by the drummer; Page introduced a more flowing 4/4 that was led by the string bass. That rhythmic smoothness, coupled with repeated riffs, became the trademark of the Kansas City sound. In addition, Page pioneered the "walking" or "strolling" bass, now a standard fixture in many jazz aggregations. The end result was a forward-driving propulsion that could carry an entire band.

During his lifetime, Page was nicknamed "the Big One" (or "Big 'Un") and "Horse" because of his size and strength with the unwieldy bass. He was also called "Big Four" for his powerful walking 4/4 bass line. It is said that he could drive a band without drums, although there is unfortunately not much evidence of this on record. He felt that the rhythm section should be a team and that the bass player should constantly push the band. He built on a simplification—a paring down—of previous styles, and he demonstrated that swinging jazz need not be played loudly—the swing would still be felt or sensed. His numerous recordings with the Count Basie orchestra, wherein "the All-American Rhythm Section" of Basie, Jones, Green, and Page propelled the band, give the best examples of his prowess. He rarely soloed, but he was a great influence on the evolution of the string bass in jazz. Page died in New York City.

• Most reputable jazz histories acknowledge Page's contributions to both the music and the instrument. Best among these are Gunther Schuller's *Early Jazz: Its Roots and Musical Development* (1968) and *The Swing Era: The Development of Jazz, 1930–1945* (1989), both for discussions of Page, but also for their coverage of Kansas City swing. Stanley Dance's *The World of Count Basie* (1980) and sections of *Jazz*, ed. Nat Hentoff and Albert McCarthy (1959), are also illuminating. The extensive recordings made by the Count Basie band from the mid-1930s until the late 1940s give good coverage to "the All-American Rhythm Section." They can be found on both the Decca and Columbia labels in all formats. The technical quality of most of the extant Blue Devils and Bennie Moten sides is such that Page's contributions are difficult to hear and appreciate.

WILLIAM H. YOUNG

PAGE, Walter Hines (15 Aug. 1855–21 Dec. 1918), writer and diplomat, was born in Cary, North Carolina, the son of Allison Francis Page, a builder, and Catherine Frances Raboteau. Able to recall the Civil War, he grew to adulthood during the troubled years of Reconstruction. It was in fact a reaction to southern provincialism, bitterness, and absorption in the "Lost Cause" that would provide a leitmotif to Page's early professional activities.

The fact that the war had ruined his father's business limited his options for higher education, but Walter did get to college. After one year (1871–1872) at tiny Trinity College (now Duke University), Page spent three years at Randolph-Macon in Ashland, Virginia, graduating in classical studies in 1875, and one year (1876–1877) as a graduate fellow in Greek at the new Johns Hopkins University in Baltimore. The Baltimore experience did much to broaden his intellectual vision and help sort out professional choices; at least he knew that he did not wish to be a "professional Greek." He wanted to become a journalist.

Journalism, as Page later would remark, did not seem anxious to admit him. With no jobs opening up, he taught English in 1878–1879 at Male High School in Louisville, Kentucky, where he began contributing to a new weekly magazine, *The Age*. After a year of newspaper work with the St. Joseph (Mo.) *Gazette*, he resigned in 1881, took a tour of the South, and wrote articles about places he visited. Much to his delight, major newspapers in New York, Chicago, and Boston published the essays. In 1882–1883 he worked as a writer and literary editor for the New York *World*, but when he seemed to be on his way in journalism, he suddenly returned to North Carolina. In 1883 he started his own newspaper, the Raleigh *State Chronicle*. Page called for a new South to forget the Civil War, broaden its vision, and reform agriculture rather than, in the manner of most advocates of a "new" South, rush headlong into industrialization. Adverse reaction to his editorials confirmed some of Page's worst notions about the backwardness of his home state and the South in general. With a growing family to care for— he had married a North Carolinian, Willia Alice Wilson, in 1880, and the Pages would produce four children—he resigned the newspaper in 1885 and turned again, permanently he now believed, to the North.

In the publishing world of the Northeast Page's career moved steadily forward. Between 1887 and 1895 he worked for a new magazine, *Forum*, first as business manager and next as editor. Finding brief jobs with established firms, in 1898 he worked with Houghton Mifflin in Boston, where he edited the prestigious journal *Atlantic Monthly*, followed by a few months at the House of Harper. The climax of his career came in 1900, when he joined forces with Frank N. Doubleday to found the publishing firm of Doubleday, Page and Company. Page directed most of his attention in the partnership to a new journal of literary and current affairs, *World's Work*, which he edited from 1900 until he joined the government in 1913.

In the course of this long career Page wrote numerous articles, editorials, and essays. After 1900 he authored three books: *The Rebuilding of Old Commonwealths* (1902), a collection of his speeches; *A Publisher's Confession* (1905), a trade publication; and *The Southerner* (1909), his only novel. His clear, direct prose was best suited to short pieces and letters; it was as editor and publisher that Page most effectively left a mark on his time. His work stood as an expression of the flowering of periodical literature and the connection between journalism and politics and reform in the early twentieth century. Page's publications revealed a nation on the make, anxious to cleanse its politics, solve its economic problems, and stand up and be noticed in world affairs. While more conservative than the popular "muckraking" periodicals of that age, *World's Work* typified important aspects of the Progressive movement. Although he had become a con-

firmed expatriate, he never lost sight of North Carolina, and his journal often dealt with the need to bring the South into the mainstream of national social and economic currents. In New York's publishing circles Page acquired the status, influence, and contacts that led him into the final and most famous aspect of his life.

Page's reputation in history grew largely from his activity as U.S. ambassador to Great Britain in the years 1913 to 1918, the time of the First World War, particularly during 1914–1917, when as a neutral, the United States struggled with deadly challenges thrown up by the war in Europe. Appointment to that high post probably should be classified as a political payment, a reward for assistance in the political career of President Woodrow Wilson. Yet the people who called Page to government—Wilson and his adviser, Edward M. "Colonel" House—knew that they were picking an individual who, while dreadfully short on knowledge of foreign affairs, was honest and talented, a literary man who should fit well into the British capital. Diplomatic experience was no prerequisite for an ambassadorial appointment in that day.

An Anglophile when he went to London, Page enjoyed moving in the swirl of the world's largest empire. These were impressive men he met, especially Foreign Secretary Sir Edward Grey, with whom he most frequently dealt. When the war began Page had no difficulty accepting the British view that they were fighting for survival against a brutal and greedy foe. He argued that the United States, the most powerful neutral nation, should cause Britain no difficulty in its efforts to keep goods—including American goods— from going to Germany, even though the practices might be vexing and inconvenient. His appeals to Wilson that the United States go to war with Germany, which began in 1915, were as impassioned and eloquent as those urging nonaction in reaction to Allied violation of American neutral rights. The most controversial and perhaps most-remembered aspect of his ambassadorship involved his practice, made public after the war, of collaborating with Grey on how best to circumvent complaints from Washington about British restrictions on American trade. If a charge of disloyalty, made by postwar critics of American intervention, seems excessive, it is fair to say that Page became a more vigorous spokesman for Britain to the United States than for the United States in London.

In the end Page received the outcome he wanted, but one scarcely could call it a personal victory. War with Germany came nearly two years after Page began to urge that step. If the United States declined to challenge the British blockade, it probably was not because Page recommended that policy. The ambassador did indeed "protest too much" and thereby lost his effectiveness. Wilson did not stop reading Page's cables, but he ignored the advice; after a point he stopped opening the long personal letters that Page spent so much time in composing. The president nonetheless never got around to replacing his unhappy ambassador in London, and Page stayed on until nearly the end of the war, when ill health brought him home. He died where he insisted on being at the end of his life, back home in Pinehurst, North Carolina. At the time of his death the momentous Paris peace conference was about to start.

Page did not establish a model for future diplomats to follow, but his career in foreign policy is nonetheless worthy of attention. His ambassadorship stood as a statement for a vigorous foreign policy based on Anglo-American cooperation and encompassing earlier American intervention in the war. But for all the attention it received, his influence in foreign policy did not match that of the writer and journalist, the work he did in New York before his ambassadorship. In a final way the literary man won out over the diplomat. Long after his ambassadorship, and the war, had ended, Page's writing lived on in his moving letters from wartime London. A publishing bonanza of the 1920s and perhaps the best American memoir of the world war, Burton J. Hendrick's three-volume *The Life and Letters of Walter Hines Page* (1922–1926) tells the story of a man of literary excellence rather than a master of the art of diplomacy.

• Page's papers are in Houghton Library, Harvard University. Some letters and other materials appear in other collections, especially the papers of Edward M. House, Yale University Library, and the papers of Woodrow Wilson, in the Library of Congress and Princeton University Library. Lists of Page's speeches and writings are in John Milton Cooper, Jr., *Walter Hines Page: The Southerner as American 1855–1918* (1977), which deals in depth with his preambassadorial career, and Robert J. Rusnak, *Walter Hines Page and the World's Work* (1982). Burton J. Hendrick, *The Training of an American: The Earlier Life and Letters of Walter Hines Page* (1928), was a publishing sensation that, along with his previous work on Hines, won two Pulitzer Prizes in the 1920s. Although these volumes were classified as biography, their chief appeal came from Page's exceptional letters, many of which were published in full. Different insights on Page came from Charles Seymour, ed., *The Intimate Papers of Colonel House* (4 vols., 1926–1928), especially the first two volumes, and Sir Edward Grey, *Twenty-Five Years, 1892–1916* (2 vols., 1925). Page's diplomatic experiences are the focus of Ross Gregory, *Walter Hines Page: Ambassador to the Court of St. James's* (1970). References to various stages of both of Page's careers appear in Arthur S. Link's major biography, *Wilson* (5 vols., 1947–1965).

ROSS GREGORY

PAGE, William (23 Jan. 1811–30 Sept. 1885), portraitist, was born in Albany, New York, the son of Levi Page, a plane maker, and Tamer Gale Dunnell. In 1819 the family moved to New York City, where Page studied at Joseph Hoxie's Latin school. His love of the antique world was one of several interests fostered by his education. In 1825 Page began working in the law office of Frederick De Peyster, who noticed that the boy was more interested in drawing than in law. Page soon began training in art with the New York artist James Herring. In 1826 he began studying with Samuel F. B. Morse. Unlike the commercial atmosphere of Herring's workroom, the environment of Morse's stu-

dio at the American Academy of the Fine Arts was infused with artistic idealism. At the academy, Page drew antique casts, from which he acquired a "love for the antique he never lost," wrote his biographer Joshua Taylor. As a teenager Page also considered a career in the ministry, and from 1827 to 1828 he embarked on religious training at Phillips Academy in Andover, Massachusetts, followed by the less religiously rigorous Amherst College.

In 1828, at age seventeen, Page submitted miniatures to the National Academy, and at twenty-one he made his first trip to Europe, having determined on a career in the arts. In 1833 he married Lavinia Twibill; they had three children. He received a few portrait commissions and turned to engraving to supplement his income. By the 1840s he was recognized as a rising New York painter and had written a series of essays on his theories of color in art (*Broadway Journal* [1845]). His range of interests was suggested by a skillful narrative painting, *The Young Merchants* (1842, Pennsylvania Academy of the Fine Arts), acquired by the Philadelphia publisher and art collector Edward L. Carey; a contemplative, veiled erotic subject picture, *Cupid and Psyche* (1843, Fine Arts Museums of San Francisco); and such incisive charcoal drawings as a *Self-Portrait* (1843, Princeton Art Museum) and *James Russell Lowell* (c. 1843, Grolier Club, N.Y.). Lowell, who had met Page during his brief residence in Boston, dedicated a volume of his poems to the artist in 1843. From this period, companion portraits of two little girls, possibly Page's daughters Anne Page (c. 1837 or 1838, Metropolitan Museum of Art) and Mary Page (early 1840s, Metropolitan Museum of Art), reveal the skill and sensibility that so impressed Lowell. The serious faces of the children are free from conventionalized sentimentality common to treatment of this theme at mid-century, yet Page's subtle color and masterful study of light passing through translucent skin contribute to an impression of directness and vulnerability.

Page hoped that close study of Titian's paintings would improve his own theories of color; so with his his second wife, Sara Daugherty Page (he had been divorced from his first wife c. 1841), he traveled to Italy in 1850 and remained there for more than a decade. In Florence Page attempted to shed the last vestiges of American Puritanism and absorbed the mystical philosophy of Martin Swedenborg from the teachings of a close friend, the American sculptor Hiram Powers. The Pages settled in Rome in 1852, and at one time they shared a villa with the poets Elizabeth Barrett Browning and Robert Browning who fondly referred to the artist as "that noble Page." Page created a portrait of Robert Browning the following year (1853, Baylor University, Waco, Texas). He was prominent in an expatriate artistic circle including the sculptor Thomas Crawford and the actress Charlotte Cushman, whose portrait (1853, National Portrait Gallery) was one of the first to establish his reputation in Rome. A year earlier Page's extravagant second wife decamped with an Italian count, leaving Page in straitened financial circumstances with his three daughters by his first marriage. Yet his artistic reputation was undiminished. Robert Browning advised American sculptor Harriet Hosmer in 1854 to listen to Page's remarks, "for it is real life blood you will get out of him, real thoughts and facts, nothing like sham or conventionalism" (Vance, p. 227).

Page's *Venus Guiding Aeneas and the Trojans to the Latin Shore* (c. 1857–1862, National Museum of American Art), one of several versions of the theme, depicted an unashamedly naked Venus, signifying "health and beauty." Even though the composition was overburdened by theory and the pose was labored, the painting successfully toured the United States. However, because of the nudity of Venus, it was rejected by the Paris Salon and refused as a gift to the Boston Athenaeum.

Page had met a beautiful young American widow, Sophia Candace Stevens Hitchcock, an art and news journalist who traveled to Rome with Bertha Olmsted. Hitchcock and Page married in October 1857. His originality, forceful draftsmanship and geometric relationships of "the true proportions of the human figure" alluded to by Browning (Vance, p. 229) are best expressed in paintings titled *Mrs. William Page* and a companion *Self-Portrait* (1860–1861, Detroit Institute of Arts). The hooded, full-length figure of Mrs. Page stands before the Colosseum. Page's choice of an eighteenth-century print as the source for his view of the Colosseum signified the timelessness of the classical world. The composed intellectuality of *Mrs. William Page* dominates the canvas, which also features Page's self-portrait in his studio, shown with an ancient sculpture in the background.

Page's theories of color stressed the "middle tint," built by glazing the canvas with black until he arrived at a middle value, followed by successively glazed highlights with gradual applications of colored pigments to achieve unified tonality. These painstaking methods, Page wrote, "may seem only a road to destruction," since some of his effects were fugitive.

In 1860 the Pages returned to the United States and rejoined New York art circles. In 1865 the new building of the National Academy of Design was opened; there, Page was an active exhibitor and teacher. He believed in disciplined study from nature and advocated administrative reforms to encourage a more nationally representative point of view at the academy. Page found himself at the center of a "party of reform," and after having been proposed as a candidate three times, he was elected president of the National Academy from 1871 to 1873. He worked tirelessly at painting and his administrative duties at the academy, resulting in permanent damage to his health. Despite this, he completed his *Portrait of Shakespeare* (1873, Folger Shakespeare Library) and published his researches in 1874 on a possible German death mask of Shakespeare that had preoccupied him for years, and he continued to labor on a few commissions until a final collapse in 1877.

William Page painted religious, mythological, and genre subjects, but his reputation rests primarily on portraiture. Although Page's paintings were sometimes flawed by the chemistry of his investigations into Venetian color, his individualistic theories and paintings are a mix of noble failures and notable achievements. He died at his home on Staten Island, New York.

• The William Page Papers and Page Family Papers, including diaries, letters, photographs, and drawings, are in the Archives of American Art, Smithsonian Institution. The authoritative study of the artist's life and work is Joshua Taylor, *William Page: The American Titian* (1957). See also Kathleen Luhrs, ed., *American Paintings in the Metropolitan Museum of Art*, vol. 1: *A Catalogue of Works by Artists Born by 1815* (1994), for information about portraits of his daughters; Garnett McCoy, "William Page and Henry Stevens: An Incident of Reluctant Art Patronage," *Archives of American Art Journal* 30 (1990): 15–21, about Page's *Venus Guiding Aeneas* and its United States tour; McCoy, "I Am Right and You Are Wrong (Charles Briggs's Letters Written in the 1840s to William Page)," *Archives of American Art Journal* 28 (1988): 13–18; and William L. Pressly, *A Catalogue of Paintings in the Folger Shakespeare Library* (1993), pp. 308–10. Lois Dinnerstein, "The Significance of the Colosseum in the First Century of American Art," *Arts Magazine*, June 1984, pp. 116–20, includes a brief biography of Sophia Stevens Hitchcock Page and nineteenth-century critical commentary on the portrait *Mrs. William Page*. William Vance, *America's Rome*, vol. 1: *Classical Rome* (1989), discusses Page and the expatriate circle.

ANNE SUE HIRSHORN

PAIGE, Satchel (7 July 1906–8 June 1982), Negro League baseball pitcher and Hall of Famer, was born Leroy Robert Paige in Mobile, Alabama, the son of John Paige, a gardener, and Lulu (maiden name unknown), a washerwoman. Paige acquired his nickname as a youth after rigging a sling for toting satchels for travelers from the Mobile train station. He joined his first organized team, at the W. H. Council School, at age ten and soon developed a reputation as one of Mobile's best schoolboy players. But he also gained notoriety with the truant officer for frequently playing hooky and getting into gang fights. When he was twelve, Paige was committed to the Industrial School for Negro Children at Mount Meigs, Alabama, after he stole a handful of toy rings from a store. Paige later reflected that the five and a half years he spent at Mount Meigs "did something for me—they made a man out of me . . . and gave me a chance to polish up my baseball game."

The slender, 6'3½" Paige joined the semipro Mobile Tigers for the 1924 season. By his own account, he won thirty games and lost only one that year. Two years later, the peripatetic Paige jumped to the Chattanooga Black Lookouts of the Negro Southern League. Sold to the Birmingham Black Barons of the Negro National League in 1927, he moved on to the Nashville Elite Giants of the Negro Southern League in 1931. The team left Nashville for Cleveland that year, but the depression hurt attendance, and the club folded before season's end.

That left Paige a free agent, of which he took advantage by selling his services to Gus Greenlee's Pittsburgh Crawfords. Greenlee, who ran the numbers in Pittsburgh's Hill District from his Crawford Grill, had taken on a black sandlot club the year before and was intent on remaking them into the top black club in the country.

Greenlee recruited some of the best players in the nation, including future Hall of Famers Josh Gibson, Cool Papa Bell, Oscar Charleston, and Judy Johnson. He built Greenlee Field, the finest black-owned stadium in the country, for the Crawfords to play in, and he resurrected the Negro National League, which had collapsed in 1931. With Gibson and Paige, the Crawfords had not only black baseball's best battery, but its two most marketable and highly paid players. Paige, who had filled out to 180 pounds, pitched for the Crawfords and also hired himself out on a freelance basis to semipro teams through the 1933 season. (It was not uncommon for a black pro club to add a semipro player, usually a pitcher, when playing an unusually heavy schedule of games. Negro League players also sold their services on an ad hoc basis.) After a contract dispute with Greenlee, Paige left the Crawfords for a white semipro club in Bismarck, North Dakota, in 1935, returning for the 1936 season.

He did not stay for long. During spring training in New Orleans the following year, he was seduced by a lucrative offer to pitch for Ciudad Trujillo, a club in Santo Domingo associated with Dominican Republic dictator Rafael Trujillo. Paige said in his autobiography that he was offered $30,000 for his services and for recruiting eight other players, with the division of the money up to him. Gibson, Bell, and a half-dozen other Crawfords joined him, decimating the Crawfords but winning the island championship for Ciudad Trujillo.

Branded an outlaw by the Negro National League, Paige barnstormed with the Trujillo All-Stars on his return to the United States. Barnstorming meant traveling from town to town, usually living on buses, playing against teams of white major leaguers or local semipros, and splitting the proceeds at the gate. Greenlee then sold Paige's contract to the Newark Eagles, but he refused to report. Instead, he pitched in the Mexican League during the 1938 season, until a sore arm caused him to return to the United States.

Paige's career seemed over, and most black teams declined to bid for his services. Finally, Kansas City Monarchs' owner J. L. Wilkinson signed him to play for the Monarchs' second team, which barnstormed through the Northwest and Canada. Still a draw at the gate, Paige was advertised to pitch every game. Relying more on guile than his once-famous fastball, he would pitch for three innings before retiring to the bench. But as the summer wore on, his arm came back, and he reported to spring training with the Monarchs' regular club for the 1940 season.

For the next nine seasons, with Paige as their ace, the Monarchs challenged the Homestead Grays as black baseball's best team. A regular at the Negro League East-West All-Star game, Paige was known for his "bee ball" (you could hear it but not see it), pinpoint accuracy, and hesitation pitch. During the 1942 Negro League world series, he won three of the Monarchs' four victories over the Grays.

In 1948, Paige made his long-awaited debut in the major leagues. Cleveland Indians' owner Bill Veeck signed him during the 1948 pennant drive, and the forty-two-year-old "rookie" responded with six victories and only one defeat. Some 201,000 fans attended his first three starts, as the Indians set night game attendance records at home and in Chicago. Paige pitched for the Indians through the 1949 season, but he lost his spot on the roster after Veeck sold the team. His record that year was 4–7, with a 3.04 ERA and five saves. Paige returned to the long bus rides through the night that characterized independent baseball, pitching for the Philadelphia Stars and for remnants of the Kansas City Monarchs.

He returned to the majors in 1951, reunited with Veeck, by then the owner of the St. Louis Browns. Paige won 12 games in 1952 for the hapless Browns and was selected to the American League All-Star team. After the 1953 season, Paige once again returned to barnstorming, but he was soon back in the minors, with stays at Miami in the International League (1956–1958) and Portland of the Pacific Coast League (1961). His last major league appearance came with the Kansas City Athletics in 1965. The Athletics' owner, Charles O. Finley, who signed Paige to help him qualify for a major league pension, put a rocking chair in the bullpen for the 59-year-old pitcher, who hurled three shutout innings against the Boston Red Sox. He is thought to be the oldest player to appear in a major league game.

Paige ended his career in 1967, riding the bus with black baseball's last team, the Indianapolis Clowns. He coached for the Atlanta Braves the following season. His major league statistics of 28 wins, 31 losses, 476 innings pitched, and a 3.29 ERA were only a belated addition to the numbers he put up during five decades on the mound.

Negro League and independent baseball records are incomplete, but, by his own account, Paige threw an estimated 55 no-hitters and won more than 2,000 of the 2,500 games in which he pitched. Many of the games were against semipro opposition. "I had that suit on every day, pretty near 365 days out of the year," he said. Paige told his biographer that he reckoned he had pitched before about 10 million fans. Given his constant travels and ability to pitch virtually every day, it is likely that more fans personally witnessed Paige play than any other ballplayer.

Paige is perhaps most popularly remembered for the all-star aggregations of Negro Leaguers he led in exhibition games against teams of major league stars during the 1930s and 1940s. In these encounters, which sometimes matched Paige versus Dizzy Dean or another Hall of Fame pitching opponent, the Negro Leaguers more than held their own. His feats in such games became part of baseball mythology. Many a fan recounts a story about a game in which Paige intentionally walked the bases loaded with major leaguers, told his fielders to sit down, and then struck out the side.

Paige married Janet Howard in 1934, but they divorced in 1943. He later married Lahoma Brown in 1974 and had six children with her.

Paige, who toured with the Harlem Globetrotters and appeared in a motion picture, *The Wonderful Country*, which starred Robert Mitchum, offered six rules as his guide to longevity:

1. Avoid fried meals, which angry up the blood.
2. If your stomach disputes you, lie down and pacify it with cool thoughts.
3. Keep the juices flowing by jangling around gently as you move.
4. Go very light on the vices, such as carrying on in society. The social rumble ain't restful.
5. Avoid running at all times.
6. Don't look back. Something might be gaining on you.

Satchel Paige embodied life in baseball's Negro Leagues. Black baseball's best-known performer, the lanky righthander barnstormed his way across the United States, Canada, and into the Caribbean basin in a career that spanned half a century. By combining showmanship and incredible durability with magnificent talent, Paige became one of baseball's most enduring legends. In 1971, he was the first Negro League player elected to baseball's Hall of Fame. "To tell you the truth," Paige said in 1981, "all over Cuba, Santo Domingo, Puerto Rico, South America, everywhere I played, I had bouquets on my shoulder . . . I just could pitch. The Master just give me an arm. . . . You couldn't hardly beat me." He died in Kansas City, Missouri.

• The best biography of Paige is John B. Holway, *Josh and Satch: The Life and Times of Josh Gibson and Satchel Paige* (1991). See also Leroy Satchel Paige, *Maybe I'll Pitch Forever*, as told to David Lipman (1962), and Rob Ruck, *Sandlot Seasons: Sport in Black Pittsburgh* (1987).

ROB RUCK

PAIN, Philip (c. 1647–c. 1667), poet, is known only as the author of a collection of poems, *Daily Meditations: or, Quotidian Preparations for, and Considerations of Death and Eternity* (1668). According to the title page the poems were "Begun *July* 19. 1666. By *Philip Pain*: Who lately suffering Shipwrack, was drowned." This date is attached to the first meditation, the last being dated "August 3," 1666. It is assumed that Pain died not long after, perhaps in 1667, but before 3 September 1668, when the printer, Marmaduke Johnson, referred to the volume in a legal proceeding. How or when the verses found their way to the printer is unknown. The introductory poem is signed "P. P.," and in Meditation 50 there is a pun on his name: "O my Soul, must I / Go from *PAIN* here, to Pain eternally."

No appropriate person (Pain, Paine, Payne) has been identified in either colonial or British records, and thus the validity of the name has been questioned, particularly that of the first name, which, it has been suggested, may be the printer's expansion of the "P." attached to the poem; even the initial may be a printer's error. The birth date derives from the implication, both in the poem and in "A Postscript to the Reader," that the author was young when he died. If he were twenty in 1667, his birth date would be 1647. The author appears to be Anglican rather than Puritan, neither a strict Calvinist nor an Arminian, as has been alleged.

The publication history of the volume and editorship are confused. The first edition of 1668 was published in Cambridge, Massachusetts, by Johnson; another edition appeared in 1670 with some textual changes and the printers given as "S. G." and "M. J." (that is, Samuel Green and Marmaduke Johnson). But a further edition, calling itself the second edition, appeared in 1682. In the first printing, "A Postscript to the Reader" was signed "J. T."; in the second, "M. J." "J. T." is unidentified, and it has been supposed that Johnson was either admitting or falsely appropriating authorship of "A Postscript." An eighteenth-century manuscript transcription from an edition in the Curwen Family Papers, Essex Institute, Salem, Massachusetts, does nothing to solve any of these problems. Indeed, there is a complication in that "A Postscript" is signed "J. S. Israel."

The volume is apparently the first collection of poems published in the colonies (Anne Bradstreet's *The Tenth Muse* [1650] having been printed in London), and, if Pain was born in the colonies, the first collection by a native of America. It consists of an introductory poem, "The Porch," in eleven iambic pentameter couplets; sixty-four six-line stanzas in iambic pentameter with couplet rhyme, each labeled "Meditation" and numbered consecutively; and "A Postscript to the Reader," seven six-line stanzas of iambic pentameter, rhyming *ababcc*. The three divisions parallel those in George Herbert's *The Temple* ("The Church-Porch," "The Church," and "The Church Militant"). *The Temple* was available in eight editions from Cambridge or London between 1633 and 1660. While the church year is important to Herbert's ordering of his poems in "The Church," Pain dates his meditations. Each day is represented by a page of four stanzas, with the date and the day of the week (the first day being Sunday). At the bottom of each page appears an iambic pentameter couplet, aphoristically summing up and ending that day. Sixteen days of meditation are thus recorded, organized around a "week" of four days and yielding a sequence of four weeks, or a month, for the whole.

Built on the mystic triad of the purgative way, the contemplative way, and the unitive way, these meditations deal with preparation for and consideration of death and eternity as their title says. While progress through Herbert's *Temple* will bring one to be the temple of God, Pain's meditations will bring one to accept death and be ready for salvation. Citations on the title page (Job 30:23 and Eccles. 12:1) indicate this hoped-for result. "The Porch" presents the entry into the meditations, and this is emphasized by the framing arched doorway printed around it. The poem is built on mystic symbols of resurrection and Christ, thus pointing the way to overcome mortality and fears of death. It capsulates the subject of the meditations and the resolution in God's salvation for the worthy. "A Postscript to the Reader" reprises some of the images of the meditations and remarks that their publication is intended to show the author's grace rather than his wit. It is difficult, however, to assign the poem to Johnson with any assurance, despite the initials.

Aside from the influences of the Bible and Herbert, the poems reflect John Donne (some of his language, images, and poetic devices) and Francis Quarles (his language and emblematic style). The scholarship that has been addressed to the collection has often been negative, casting the poetry as little more than versified religious doctrine and flat, sometimes padded versification. But a closer examination of the structures, imagery, allusion, and poetic devices should yield a higher estimate for an apparently young and early American poet.

• In 1936 two facsimile editions of the 1668 edition of *Daily Meditations* were published, one by the Massachusetts Historical Society and the other by the Henry E. Huntington Library, San Marino, Calif.; the latter was edited, with an introduction, by Leon Howard. An eighteenth-century transcription is in the Curwen Family Papers in the Essex Institute, Salem, Mass. Selections from *Daily Meditations* are included in Harrison T. Meserole, ed., *Seventeenth-Century American Poetry* (1968), with an introduction. For discussion of Pain in light of other seventeenth-century poets, see Thomas E. Johnston, Jr., "American Puritan Poetic Verses: Essays on Anne Bradstreet, Edward Taylor, Roger Williams, and Philip Pain" (Ph.D. diss., Ohio Univ., 1968); John T. Shawcross, "Some Colonial American Poetry and George Herbert," *Early American Literature* 23 (1988): 28–51; and Donald E. Stanford, "The Imagination of Death in the Poetry of Philip Pain, Edward Taylor, and George Herbert," *Studies in Literary Imagination* 2 (1976): 53–67.

JOHN T. SHAWCROSS

PAINE, Albert Bigelow (10 July 1861–9 Apr. 1937), author and Mark Twain's literary executor, was born in New Bedford, Massachusetts, the fifth child of Samuel Estabrook Paine, a Vermont storekeeper, and Mercy Coval Kirby. The Paine family soon moved to Xenia, Illinois, where Paine attended school and worked in the village store. At twenty he traveled to St. Louis and learned photography. For ten years he sold photographic supplies in Fort Scott, Kansas. In 1885 he married Wilhelmina Schultz. The sale of a story to Richard Harding Davis at *Harper's Weekly* led to his move to New York City and the full-time pursuit of a writing career.

Paine's direction as a writer was at first uncertain. He wrote undistinguished verse as well as a Hawthornian romance, *The Mystery of Evelin Delorme* (1894), and a Poe-like tale of adventure at the South Pole, *The Great White Way* (1901). *The Bread Line: A Story of a Paper* (1900), an early and significant piece of near autobiography, concerns the attempts made by four New York "bohemian" journalists to succeed in the crassly corporate, market-driven world of magazines. The book also portrays the writers' increasing anxieties about the city's growing underclass.

From 1899 to 1909 Paine served as an editor of *St. Nicholas*, a prestigious children's magazine. He wrote a number of successful works for this audience, including the many "Hollow Tree" stories and books. After his first marriage had ended, Paine married Dora Locey in 1892; they had four children—all girls. The family's early adventures in search of the perfect home were detailed in three explicitly autobiographical works: *The Van Dwellers* (1901), *The Commuters* (1904), and *Dwellers in Arcady* (1919). The books retain interest for their depiction of middle-class, turn-of-the-century ideals of, respectively, city, suburban, and Connecticut country life. The volumes are increasingly sentimental, but each also documents Paine's condescension toward an unending series of stereotyped laborers upon whom he depends in order to set up house, including professional movers, drunken Irish janitors, female house servants who eat too much, lazy black boys and cleaning ladies, "unskilled and unfaithful" ethnic carpenters, and masons who abscond with cash advances. "Work was my problem," Paine wrote—"somebody to do it."

Much of Paine's later work fell under the shadow of Mark Twain. He edited many volumes of Twain's writings, and wrote the three-volume *Mark Twain: A Biography* (1912). The biography remains his most-read work, and it is a legitimate classic of its genre, deeply colored by Paine's unusual, personal relationship with its subject. Paine was twenty-six years Twain's junior but by the time their collaboration began in 1906 he was already a well-known author because of his *Thomas Nast: His Period and His Pictures* (1904). Paine called the older man "Mr. Clemens." He moved his family into Twain's home, tucked Twain into bed at night and read to him, and managed many general family matters as a kind of majordomo. Paine planned and played the music at the funeral of Jean Clemens, Twain's daughter; he also tended Twain in his final illness, made his funeral arrangements and then put pen to paper. Paine's portraits of Twain are the defining moments in the popular conception of the man. Paine wrote that the youthful Twain was a "tender-hearted, romantic, devil-may-care lad, loathing application and longing only for freedom," and that as an adult Twain "had a natural instinct for the right, but, right or wrong, he was for the underdog."

Some of Paine's work as Twain's literary executor has been criticized in recent years. His composite and, in places, fabricated text for Twain's *The Mysterious Stranger, A Romance* (1916) has been called an "editorial fraud" in which Paine "secretly tried to fill Mark Twain's shoes." Shortly after Twain's death, Paine and Clara Clemens prevented publication of a scathing satire on bureaucratic enterprise, "The International Lighting Trust" (1909), that Twain already had sent to his publisher. On the other hand, Paine deserves high marks for his edition of Twain's *Mark Twain's Autobiography* (2 vols., 1924), which, unlike later presentations of these materials, stuck closely to Twain's original intentions.

The experience of four years with Twain affected much of Paine's later writing. Many of his subsequent works are in the realm of homage or pastiche, in which Twain's complex, ambivalent responses to his world are greatly simplified. Paine followed Twain's *The Innocents Abroad* (1869) with *The Ship-Dwellers: A Story of a Happy Cruise* (1910), in which he attempted to "follow the track" of Twain by making painfully imitative wisecracks about the group of "reprobates" with whom he sails. Twain had written of the corporate boss and community outlaw Slade in *Roughing It* (1872); Paine responded with a book about a far less ambiguous, rough-and-tumble lawman who also brought order to the frontier in *Captain Bill McDonald, Texas Ranger: A Story of Frontier Reform* (1909). And Paine tried to trump Twain in the line of Joan of Arc studies with his *Joan of Arc, Maid of France* (2 vols., 1925). He achieved a measure of success in this case, and the French government made Paine a chevalier in the Legion of Honor in recognition of his scholarship. In both *Joan* and *Life and Lillian Gish* (1932), Paine's worship of pure little girls closely followed that of his mentor into questionable territory. Though Gish was an adult film star, for example, Paine's fascination was with her ability to freeze time—to portray a version of her former "exquisite," childlike, and "Christ-like beauty of innocence, of sinlessness."

Paine's sentimental, romantic sensibility was counterbalanced in two privately contracted biographies celebrating individuals who consolidated American business enterprise. *George Fisher Baker* (1920) profiled one of the most powerful of American bankers, and Paine's biography of Theodore N. Vail, *In One Man's Life* (1921), applauded the "great work" and leadership abilities of the American Telephone & Telegraph executive who sought to "organize a grand telephonic system" through long-wire extensions between cities.

Paine's favorite among his own books was *Jan the Romantic* (1928), a bildungsroman about a budding writer of mixed British and French descent making his way between the early part of the century and the end of World War I. Jan's nature propels him gypsy-like across France with a wealthy patron who speaks for Paine when he says that modern times "are worse, less fine spiritually. With all our resources we cannot today build a cathedral. Mechanical growth means spiritual decline: That is axiomatic. We are on the down grade." It is a deeply felt, antimodernist book, and similar to much of his fiction and autobiography in its search for a natural place sealed off from the "greed and struggle" of modern life.

Paine served for many years on the Pulitzer Prize Committee. His last major work consisted of editing *Mark Twain's Notebook* and writing *The Family Mark Twain*, both published in 1935. Paine died in New Smyrna, Florida, en route to his home in New York.

• Paine's other important works as an editor of Twain are *Mark Twain's Speeches* (1910); *Mark Twain's Letters* (2 vols., 1917); *Moments with Mark Twain* (1920), a selection of Paine's favorite passages from Twain; and *Europe and Elsewhere* (1923), a collection of miscellaneous pieces. All of this editorial work has been or will be superseded by the University of California editions of Twain's writing. After Paine's death, some of his works for children were collected in *The Hollow Tree and the Deep Woods Book* (1938) and *The Hollow Tree Snowed-In Book* (1938).

No major article on Paine exists, and a number of short pieces, including his *New York Times* obituary (10 Apr. 1937), contain errors about his work. For material on Paine as an editor of Twain, see William M. Gibson's introduction to Mark Twain's *The Mysterious Stranger* (1969) and John S. Tuckey's introduction to Mark Twain's "The International Lighting Trust," *Fables of Man*, ed. John S. Tuckey (1972).

SCOTT MICHAELSEN

PAINE, John Knowles (9 Jan. 1839–25 Apr. 1906), composer, organist, and teacher, was born in Portland, Maine, the son of Jacob Small Paine, a proprietor of a music store, and Rebecca Beebe Downes. The family was highly musical. Paine's grandfather, John K. H. Paine, was an organ builder, bandmaster, and music dealer who had been a fife-major in the War of 1812; his uncle David was an organist, composer, and music teacher; his uncle William was a trombonist and hymn tune writer; and his sister Helen Maria became a noted contralto soloist and vocal teacher in Portland.

Paine's first music teacher was Hermann Kotzschmar, an immigrant from Germany who was trained in Dresden and who directed several musical organizations in Portland in addition to playing the organ at the First Parish Church. When Paine was seventeen years old his father died, and his two uncles took over the family music store, where Paine set himself up as a piano teacher. He soon became active in other local musical affairs, being elected organist of the Haydn Association (a choral group) in 1857. But Kotzschmar recognized young Paine's outstanding musical gifts and began to urge him to continue his studies in Europe. To this end he organized a series of benefit concerts by the Orchestral Union, featuring Paine and several vocal soloists, which, along with some of the income from his sister Helen's teaching, generated sufficient funding to send the nineteen-year-old Paine to Germany to begin his studies in Berlin. One of his traveling companions was Alexander Wheelock Thayer, an early biographer of Beethoven, who helped him to find accommodations and teachers, among them Gustav Teschner, Friedrich Wieprecht, and the noted organist and composer Karl August Haupt. Paine was soon playing organ recitals, some of which included his own compositions.

Upon Paine's return in 1861 he stayed briefly in Portland, where he gave a recital at the First Parish Church and presented his old teacher with one of his choral compositions. In the fall of that year he moved to Boston and accepted the position of organist at the West Church, which had just installed a fine new organ. In 1862 he was offered the position of teacher of sacred music at Harvard University, which included directing music in the college chapel. He combined these duties with his work at the West Church, playing the organ for the weekday services at Harvard and training the choir there, but in 1864 he left the church to devote himself entirely to work at Harvard, where he had begun a series of lectures in addition to his other duties, although he continued to give occasional organ recitals at West Church and other venues, such as Tremont Temple. In 1863 a large German organ was installed in Boston Music Hall, and Paine was the youngest of the six organists who played the opening recital in the fall of that year. His playing, especially of Bach, was much praised, and he later played several solo recitals there.

Although Paine worked zealously to improve the quality of his musical courses at Harvard, they carried no academic credit. What did gain him some recognition was his work with choral and orchestral music among the students. For a "Commemoration Day" observance following the end of the Civil War in 1865, he marshaled a sixty-voice mixed chorus, a thirty-voice male chorus, and an orchestra of twenty-six players to perform music by Bach, Cherubini, and himself. In 1866 he organized a series of successful organ and choral concerts to raise funds for the repair of the chapel organ.

Paine again visited Europe in 1866, this time in company with a student, a promising young tenor named George L. Osgood, who was to study for three years in Germany and Italy. Paine spent a short time in England, then crossed to Germany, his goal being a performance of his recently composed *Mass*. Despite some difficulties, it was ultimately performed in February 1867 at the Singakademie in Berlin, where it received favorable notices in the press. Paine returned the following month to resume his duties at Harvard and to take on additional responsibilities as teacher of piano, organ, church music, harmony, and counterpoint at the recently opened New England Conservatory of Music in Boston.

Paine's reputation as composer, performer, and teacher was growing, although his work at Harvard still had no academic status. When music-loving Charles William Eliot was elected president of Harvard in 1869, one of his first acts was to confer upon Paine the degree of master of arts, thereby giving him the credentials necessary for holding a professorship. In September 1869 Paine married Mary Elizabeth Greeley, like himself a native of Portland; they had no children. Among President Eliot's early reforms was the revival of the University Lecture Series, and in 1870 and 1871 Paine was asked to give a series of eighteen lectures on the history of music, in which he displayed his admiration for Bach, Beethoven, Mendelssohn, and Schumann while disparaging the excesses of some of the more recent "wild dreamers" such as Wagner (whom he later grew to appreciate) and Liszt. His

lectures were well attended, not only by the students and faculty of Harvard, but by some of the more notable musical figures of the Boston area. Eliot also elevated Paine's courses in theory, composition, and history to the status of elective credit courses, and in 1875 a full professorship of music was established, to which Paine was appointed.

Despite the growing amount and complexity of Paine's academic duties, he continued to compose, although he seems to have begun to cut back on giving organ recitals. The *Mass*, which had been premiered in Berlin, was followed by another large-scale choral work, the oratorio *St. Peter*. Modeled somewhat after the passions of Bach and the oratorios of Mendelssohn, it had its first performance at the New England Conservatory in 1872. It was received with some reservations by critics, for while J. S. Dwight praised its originality, others found it cold and academic. Some piano pieces brought out at around the same time (including *Vier character-Stücke*) seem to have been better received as was his *Symphony in C minor*, first performed by the Theodore Thomas Orchestra in 1876. The *Symphony* was the first of several large-scale orchestral works written by Paine during the 1870s. Perhaps most popular of all of Paine's compositions in this period was his *Centennial Hymn*, written to a John Greenleaf Whittier text for the celebration of the American Centennial in 1876. During the same year Paine's *Sonata for Piano and Violin in B minor* and *Overture to "As You Like It"* also received their first performance and were warmly acclaimed.

During the 1880s, Paine continued to produce large-scale symphonic works. His *Second ("Spring") Symphony* was first performed in March 1880, and it proved popular. Equally successful was his incidental music to *Oedipus Tyrannus*, first performed in the following year. These works established Paine as a major composer in the eyes of critics, and in the following years he turned his attention to somewhat shorter works, including Sonata for Violin and Piano in B minor cantatas and shorter choral pieces, and several piano works. Many of his early organ works were being published for the first time; his *Deux Préludes*, written during his early Boston years, did not appear in print until 1892. Not all of his mature output was serious, however; his students were delighted with the levity of his little choral setting of an advertisement for a popular nostrum (*Radway's Ready Relief*), and his *Fuga giocosa* for piano, based on a childhood baseball chant, "Over the fence is out, boys."

Although some of Paine's larger organ and piano solos continued to appear on recital programs, and his anthems were doubtless performed at many churches, it is the performance of his symphonic works that is best documented. They appeared regularly on concert programs in Boston, New York, Chicago, Cincinnati, and elsewhere. The earlier works were joined in the 1890s by the tone poem *An Island Fantasy*, his last major symphonic work, and the cantata *Song of Promise*, commissioned for one of the Cincinnati May Festivals, along with such "occasional" pieces as the *Columbus*

March and Hymn written for the Columbian Exposition of 1892. In addition to prestigious commissions, Paine also received many honors in his later years, but he did not rest on his laurels. During the 1890s he branched out again into a hitherto unexplored medium with his opera, *Azara*. Despite praise by some critics, the work never obtained a fully staged performance in Paine's lifetime, although excerpts were performed, and the Cecilia Society presented a slightly abridged concert performance the year after Paine's death.

In 1903 Paine and his wife made one final trip to Europe, where he represented Harvard at the unveiling of a Wagner monument in Berlin and attended the accompanying festival, at which his own *Oedipus Tyrannus* overture was performed. During Paine's later years the Harvard music department had hired two additional professors, and from 1899 to his retirement in 1905 Paine reduced his own duties to teaching only the history course and giving occasional lectures. From this vantage point he could look back on a career that had brought music at Harvard from a minor and nonessential activity to a fully recognized academic component with its own faculty and plans on the drawing board for its own building, later to be named Paine Hall. He had counted among his pupils many who had gone on to distinguish themselves in the fields of composition, performance, and music criticism, including Arthur Foote, Daniel Gregory Mason, Walter R. Spalding, Frederick S. Converse, Hugo Leichtentritt, Carl Ruggles, John Alden Carpenter, and Mabel Daniels.

The reason for Paine's retirement was his deteriorating health; he had been a diabetic for a number of years. But even in retirement he remained active as a composer, and at the time of his death in Cambridge he was working on a major tone poem titled *Lincoln*, a tribute to a president whom he had always admired. His book, *The History of Music to the Death of Schubert*, was completed during his final years but not published until 1907. Paine's well-attended funeral was held in the Harvard chapel.

By the time of his death the popularity of Paine's compositions had waned significantly, being considered too old-fashioned in style by some of the critics and certain younger composers. Although some of his shorter and more utilitarian pieces have been performed from time to time, it was not until the final decades of the twentieth century that performers and audiences rediscovered the worth of some of his large-scale compositions, many of which (including the *Mass*, both symphonies, and various chamber works and organ works) are now obtainable on records. Among the most active latter-day promoters of Paine's music are composer and conductor Gunther Schuller and Harvard University organist Murray Somerville.

• Many of Paine's unpublished manuscripts are in the libraries of Harvard University; certain of his organ works from this source were published for the first time in 1995. Paine is now mentioned in most standard sources and books on American music, but an extensive study is John C. Schmidt, *The Life and Works of John Knowles Paine* (1980), which includes a complete list of his compositions. Much information on Paine's family and early years is found in George T. Edwards, *Music and Musicians of Maine* (1928), and his Harvard career is chronicled in Walter R. Spaulding, *Music at Harvard* (1935). An appreciative account by a former student is M. A. DeWolfe Howe, "John Knowles Paine," *Musical Quarterly* 25 (July 1939): 257–67. Obituaries are in the *Portland Post*, 25 Apr. 1906, and the *Boston Evening Transcript*, 26 Apr. 1906.

BARBARA OWEN

PAINE, Martyn (8 July 1794–10 Nov. 1877), physician and medical educator, was born in Williamstown, Vermont, the son of Elijah Paine, a U.S. senator from 1795 to 1801, and Sarah Porter. Paine received his early education from private tutors—including Francis Brown, who later became the president of Dartmouth College—and continued his studies at a preparatory school in Atkinson, Vermont. He graduated from Harvard College in 1813 with an A.B. and again from Harvard in 1816 with an M.D. While at Harvard he was apprenticed to John Warren until Warren's death two years later, after which he completed his medical training with Warren's son. Paine wrote his medical thesis on inflammation, in which he claimed that "most diseases are inflammatory in origin and demand antiphlogistic treatment."

After medical school Paine moved to Canada, where he practiced medicine. In 1822 he returned to New York City. In 1825 he married Mary Ann Weeks; they had one daughter and two sons. (One of his sons apparently committed suicide just before graduating from Harvard, and to commemorate him Paine published a *Memoir of Robert Troup Paine* in 1852.) Paine was active in the cholera outbreak of the early 1830s and published his first book, *Letters on the Cholera Asphyxia* (1832), which contained letters on his experience with the disease in New York written to Warren in Boston. The first two volumes of his *Medical and Physiological Commentaries* were published in 1840, with a third volume published in 1844.

Along with Gunning S. Bedford, A. Sidney Doane, Charles A. Lee, and Alfred C. Post, Paine founded the Medical College of the University of New York City in 1841, after overcoming opposition to the new medical school from the College of Physicians and Surgeons. He was its first professor of the Institutes of Medicine and Materia Medica and occupied the chair until 1850, when he became a professor of therapeutics and materia medica. He was an uninspiring teacher, prone to reading his lectures. Other members of the original faculty included Bedford, John W. Draper, Valentine Mott, Granville S. Pattison, and John Revere. Paine published *A Therapeutic Arrangement of the Materia Medica* (1842) and *Materia Medica and Therapeutics* (1848), which went through three editions. In 1847 Paine traveled to Europe, where he realized that medical science might treat diseases common to humanity but could not improve upon local diet. That year he also published the *Institutes of Medicine*, which went through nine editions. Paine based his *Institutes* upon two principles: solidism (the doctrine that disease results from changes in the solid parts of the body) and vitalism (the doctrine that a vital principle or life force is the cause, not the result, of life). His favorite treatment for many diseases was bloodletting. For example, to treat his case of acute pneumonia, Paine had himself bled so extensively that his attending physician, James C. Bliss, refused to bleed him further. But Paine insisted and was bled another twenty ounces. When discussing the outbreak of the Civil War with Samuel W. Francis, Paine claimed that the "disease is of a highly inflammatory character; and the only remedy—copious, frequent, and heroic *bloodletting*" (Francis, p. 64).

In the 1850s Paine was personally involved in the repeal of a New York state law that made dissection of a human cadaver a criminal offense. On 4 June 1853 Draper, then president of the university, wrote Paine a letter, requesting Paine to travel to Albany to lobby for the passage of the "anatomical bill." At first Paine rejected the request but accepted it later in the year. For three months he met individually with members of the New York House of Assembly, where there was strong opposition to the bill. He explained to the members of the assembly the importance of the bill's passage, and it eventually passed 67 to 43, narrowly meeting the needed two-thirds majority. Although there was strong opposition to the bill from many sectors in the community, after its passage in 1854 it was readily accepted by all.

By confession Paine was an Episcopalian. He was a strong opponent of tobacco and alcohol use. Besides his major works cited above, Paine also presented his vitalistic views in *Discourse on the Soul and the Principle of Instinct, Physiologically Distinguished from Materialism* (1848) and *Organic Life As Distinguished from Chemical and Physical Doctrines* (1849). In 1856 he published *On Theoretical Geology*, in which he defended the Mosaic accounts of the creation and flood against uniformitarian geology. In 1859 Paine also defended, in several *New York Medical Press* editorials, the superiority of medical education available in America over that available in England. He was also involved in other controversies, including the founding of the American Medical Association to reform U.S. medical education and the introduction of the quantitative method into medicine. He retired from his position at the university in 1867 and became an emeritus professor. He died in New York City.

During his career, Paine was active in physiological research and contributed to the discovery of the reflex action of nervous tissue. He was a member of a number of professional societies, including the New York Academy of Medicine, medical societies of Leipzig and Sweden, and the Montreal Natural History Society. In an assessment of Paine, contemporary physician Samuel D. Gross wrote: "Paine touched few subjects which he did not exhaust, or which he did not adorn. He was a closet man, a strong thinker, and a bookworm, reading much and digesting well what he read.

A man of fortune, he had an abundance of leisure, never allowed himself to be annoyed by the practice of medicine, mixed little in society, and was seldom seen at places of amusement. His life was a life of introspection" (Gross, p. 388).

• The Paine Collection is at the Ehrman Library of the New York University Medical Center Archives and the Bobst Library of the New York University Archives. For biographical information on Paine, see "Prof. Martyn Paine, M.D.," *Medical Recorder* 12 (1877): 735; Samuel W. Francis, "Biographical Sketches of Distinguished Living New York Physicians: I. Martyn Paine, M.D., LL.D.," *Medical and Surgical Reporter* 15 (1866): 63–67; and Samuel D. Gross, *Autobiography of Samuel D. Gross, M.D., with Sketches of His Contemporaries*, vol. 2 (1887): 388–90. An obituary is in the *New York Times*, 12 Nov. 1877.

JAMES A. MARCUM

PAINE, Robert (12 Nov. 1799–19 Oct. 1882), Methodist bishop, was born in Person County, North Carolina, the son of James Paine, a magistrate, and Nancy Williams. His family moved to Giles County, Tennessee, in 1814. Before entering Cumberland College of Nashville in October 1817, he experienced a religious conversion at a Methodist camp meeting revival in Giles County. This event led Paine into the ministry, and he received a Methodist preacher's license in 1818. In his early ministry, Paine traveled as a circuit preacher chiefly in southern Tennessee and northern Alabama. In 1824 he married Susanna Beck, who died in 1836. His second wife, Amanda Shaw, lived only a few months after their 1837 marriage. His final wife, Mary Eliza Millwater, whom Paine married in 1839, died in 1904. Two sons were born during his first marriage; five sons and three daughters, during his third.

Paine was ordained in the Methodist Episcopal church by the Tennessee Conference, first as a deacon in 1821 and then as an elder in 1823. From 1823 to 1829 he served as a presiding elder, primarily overseeing Methodist preachers in the Nashville area. Between 1824 and 1844 he was a six-time delegate to the Methodist Episcopal church's quadrennial General Conference, the denomination's governing assembly. In 1830 he became the first president of Methodist La Grange College in Franklin County, Alabama (later the University of North Alabama, Florence). During his tenure at La Grange (1830–1846), Paine served the college as both an administrator and a professor, teaching a range of subjects, from moral science to geology.

Paine was one of the founders, in 1845, of the Methodist Episcopal Church, South, a regional denomination that resulted from the schism between northern and southern Methodists brought on by the slavery debate during the 1830s and 1840s. At the 1844 General Conference in New York, Paine served on the Committee of Nine. The committee established guidelines for slaveholding annual conferences to withdraw from the Methodist Episcopal church, with the hope that both sides would amicably separate. This agreement was the basis for the Louisville Convention (Louisville, Ky.) held in May 1845. Paine was one of the leaders at this convention that established the Methodist Episcopal Church, South. He was also a delegate, in 1846, at the denomination's first General Conference in Petersburg, Virginia, where he was elected bishop.

While he was a bishop, Paine supervised Methodist annual conferences throughout the South. Before the Civil War he promoted church mission work to plantation slaves. Although a slave owner, he resisted resolutions in the South in favor of secession. He told President James Buchanan in 1860 that he had not voted in a presidential election for thirty years, observing that he wanted "to reserve my influence for moral and religious ends" (quoted in Rivers, p. 142). During the Civil War, Paine preached in Confederate army camps, supervised army chaplains, and turned his home in Aberdeen, Mississippi, into a hospital for wounded soldiers—at points avoiding capture by Union soldiers.

After the war Paine stressed the humane treatment of African Americans, but his views on race relations nonetheless mirrored the patterns of institutional segregation that characterized postwar Reconstruction in the South. In 1870 Paine and other southern Methodist bishops supervised the formation of the Colored Methodist Episcopal church (renamed Christian Methodist Episcopal church in 1956), a denomination consisting largely of former slave members of the Methodist Episcopal Church, South.

Paine also supported a variety of lay and educational reforms within American Methodism. He endorsed the 1866 decision of the Methodist Episcopal Church, South to allow lay delegates to vote at the General Conference. In his later years he advocated the founding of Methodist colleges, universities, and seminaries in the South. In 1882 Paine College in Augusta, Georgia, was founded by the Methodist Episcopal Church, South and the Colored Methodist Episcopal church. This school became one of the historically African-American colleges associated with the United Negro College Fund.

Paine died at his longtime residence of Aberdeen, Mississippi, only a few months after his retirement as a bishop. His leadership had helped to bring stability and growth to the Methodist Episcopal Church, South. His successes as a pastor, college president, and bishop mark him as an important figure of nineteenth-century southern Methodism.

• Selected papers can be found at the University of North Alabama, Florence. Paine's only published book was *The Life and Times of William McKendree* (1869), a biography of an early nineteenth-century Methodist itinerant preacher and bishop who had been one of Paine's mentors during his early ministry. R. H. Rivers, *Life of Robert Paine* (1884), is the only full-length biography. Emory Bucke, ed., *The History of American Methodism*, vol. 2 (1964), provides a significant overview of Paine's career within American Methodism. William Lindsey McDonald, *Beginnings of the University of North Alabama: The Story of Florence Wesleyan University* (1991), gives a useful sketch of Paine's early life through his tenure as La Grange College president.

CHRISTOPHER H. EVANS

PAINE, Robert Treat (11 Mar. 1731–11 June 1814), lawyer, Massachusetts attorney general, and signer of the Declaration of Independence, was born in Boston, Massachusetts, the son of Thomas Paine, a merchant, and Eunice Treat. Shortly before Paine's birth, his father had left the ministry for a mercantile career that soon flourished, providing comfortable circumstances for the family. Paine followed the traditional Boston elite educational path from Boston Public Latin School to Harvard College, where he graduated with the class of 1749. At about the same time, his father lost his fortune; following graduation, Paine was forced to seek his own way without the benefit of a family business.

Paine taught school briefly in Lunenburg, Massachusetts, and in Boston. In 1751 he began a series of mercantile ventures that took him to North Carolina, the Azores, and Spain, followed by a whaling voyage to Greenland in 1754. After leaving the sea Paine determined to study law and moved to Lancaster, Massachusetts, where various relatives were active in the county court system. While in Lancaster Paine accepted an offer to preach for six weeks in the nearby district of Shirley. In the autumn of 1755 when his kinsman Colonel Samuel Willard led a regiment on the Crown Point Expedition, Paine failed to obtain an officer's commission but was appointed regimental chaplain. He followed the regiment to New York on the futile campaign, which was abandoned in December 1755. Paine resumed informal legal studies in Lancaster and in 1756 returned to Boston where he studied more formally with Benjamin Prat. On 6 May 1757 Paine was admitted to practice before Suffolk County bar.

In the mid-eighteenth century, the courts still traveled the circuit of Massachusetts's counties, which included the district of Maine. As a result Paine spent much of his time on the road throughout his entire career as lawyer, attorney general, and judge, developing a wide acquaintanceship throughout Massachusetts. At first he maintained a law office in Boston, but in 1761 Paine moved to Taunton, the seat of Bristol County, where only one other lawyer practiced regularly. In 1770 he married Sally Cobb, daughter of a locally prominent iron manufacturer. The couple had eight children, including Robert Treat Paine, Jr., later a well-known poet.

Paine's first major case also came in 1770. The town of Boston hired him as one of the prosecuting attorneys for the Boston Massacre trials, in opposition to John Adams. Paine's service at these trials brought him into Boston's radical political sphere, and in 1773 the town of Taunton elected him as its delegate to the house of representatives. As a member of the Massachusetts General Court, Paine was prominent in the struggles that began to separate the province from Crown authority.

Paine was one of the five-man delegation chosen to represent Massachusetts at the Continental Congress in 1774. When he returned the next year to the Second Continental Congress, which created the Continental army, Paine became deeply involved in the pragmatic work of supplying the army as chairman of the cannon committee and was active in other committee work to encourage production of saltpeter needed for gunpowder. By early 1776 dissension within the Massachusetts delegation over the move toward independence separated conservative Paine from the radical John Adams and Samuel Adams. A ploy to remove Paine from the delegation failed, and the Massachusetts General Court again returned him to Congress. As instructions from the legislature changed to support independence, Paine moved into that camp and so voted in July 1776. Throughout the rest of the year he continued his heavy commitment to committee work, concentrating on facilitating the production of cannon until Philadelphia was evacuated in December, when Paine returned home to Taunton.

In 1777 Paine was again elected to the Continental Congress but chose instead to remain in Boston as a member of the house of representatives, which he served as Speaker. As his last congressional duty, Paine in December chaired a committee to investigate the failure of the Rhode Island Expedition, an abortive attack on British-held Newport. In June he had been elected attorney general for Massachusetts. As state prosecutor, Paine resumed traveling the circuit of the superior court. One of his major responsibilities was the confiscation of loyalist estates to help finance the continuing war. Although he initiated many libels against these properties, few were ever fulfilled, and the result of all these actions was negligible. More important was Paine's work on the legislature's committee to revise the state's laws in accordance with the new 1780 constitution. Paine's conservatism was reflected in the new legal structure's faithfulness to its colonial precedents. His conservatism again showed itself when Paine acted as chief prosecutor in the treason trials following the suppression of Shays's Rebellion in 1787.

In 1780 Paine moved his family to Boston, where he was increasingly involved in the social and intellectual world of the new republic. That same year he was a founding member of the American Academy of Arts and Sciences and also joined the First Church of Boston, which he eventually followed into Unitarianism.

In 1789 Paine wrote to Vice President John Adams and unsuccessfully requested a federal judgeship. The next year he did accept an associate justiceship of the Massachusetts Supreme Judicial Court, a position that he had twice previously rejected, refusing to serve as a junior member of that court. Although embittered by the fact that he was never appointed chief justice, Paine remained on the bench until 1804 when he retired because of increasing deafness. He died at his Boston home and was buried among many of Boston's revolutionary generation in the town's Granary Burying Ground.

Robert Treat Paine's major contributions followed from his character traits of pragmatism and conservatism. His dedication to the letter of the law often overshadowed the spirit of the times, and his insistence on the older system of hierarchy in preference to the newer meritocracy, which often promoted men junior to Paine in age, education, or professional standing, left him mired in an outdated philosophy. Although involved in government positions for more than thirty years, Paine generally distanced himself from politics and provided a stabilizing if somewhat reactionary course of leadership.

• Paine's papers, many of which appear in the *Collections of the Massachusetts Historical Society*, vols. 87 and 88, ed. Stephen T. Riley and Edward W. Hanson (1992), are at the Massachusetts Historical Society. The most complete study of Paine's life and career is Edward W. Hanson, "'A Sense of Honor and Duty': Robert Treat Paine (1731–1814) of Massachusetts and the New Nation" (Ph.D. diss., Boston College, 1992). Clifford K. Shipton's sketch of Paine appears in *Sibley's Harvard Graduates* 12: 462–82. A more sympathetic approach is taken by Stephen T. Riley, "Robert Treat Paine and John Adams: A Colonial Rivalry," in *Sibley's Heir: A Volume in Memory of Clifford Kenyon Shipton*, vol. 59 (1982), pp. 415–29.

EDWARD W. HANSON

PAINE, Robert Treat, Jr. (9 Dec. 1773–13 Nov. 1811), poet and lawyer, was born Thomas Paine in Taunton, Massachusetts, the son of Robert Treat Paine, Sr., a legislator, jurist, and signer of the Declaration of Independence, and Sally Cobb. The younger Paine legally changed his name to Robert Treat in 1801, adopting the name of a brother who had died in 1798. Contemporary Boston Federalists said he wanted to avoid mistaken identification with the "infidel" author of the *Age of Reason*.

After the family moved to Boston, Paine, a precocious child, was sent to the Boston Latin School, where he excelled. At age twelve, under the pseudonym of "Cerberus," he attacked his father in a long, scathing poem. Probably he reflected the familial neglect his mother had expressed during the prolonged absences of Robert Treat Paine, Sr., during the American Revolution. This diatribe presaged a lifelong breach with his father.

Entering Harvard in 1788, Paine excelled in Latin, Greek, and rhetoric. His rhymed translations from the Greek won him attention, but he was a maverick and was frequently punished for missing requisite prayers or recitations. Sharp minded and confident, he was conspicuous in a student brawl in his senior year and "greatly aggravated" college authorities "by the indecent and imprudent manner in which he pretended to justify himself" (Faculty Records, bk. 6, p. 128). The result was a four-month suspension, though he was readmitted after public censure in chapel. Later, for graduation ceremonies, he composed and read a valedictory poem as well as one titled "Nature and Progress of Liberty."

Paine attempted a mercantile career in James Tisdale's firm, soon giving up his clerkship when writing verses for the *Massachusetts Magazine* took precedence. He carried on a poetical romance in the journal with Sarah Wentworth Morton, a Boston poet, with pieces such as "The Laurelled Nymph—Addressed to Philenia." The interchange between "Menander" and "Philenia" reflected an increasing public interest in indigenous literary accomplishment, although Paine and other poets still imitated English models.

Boston's burgeoning theater business, gradually freed from shackling legal restrictions and public hostility in the early 1790s, became the center of Paine's activities in 1792–1793. He joined the Board Alley Theatre, then became active in the splendorous Boston Theatre in Federal Street, recently designed by Charles Bulfinch. Competing in a contest to write a prologue in verse for the opening performance on 3 February 1794, he won a gold medal. Although his poem was praised as "highly creditable to the poet's genius" (William W. Clapp, Jr., *A Record of the Boston Stage* [1853], p. 22), he acknowledged a need to eliminate bombastic phraseology. His interest in drama was matched by his infatuation with actress Elizabeth Baker, the sixteen-year-old daughter of actor parents. Paine's marriage to Baker in 1795 led his father to bar him from his house.

Paine founded the *Federal Orrery*, a biweekly newspaper, in October 1794, encouraged by Boston Federalists. Its spirited pages went beyond political issues to promote drama and to print numerous poetic efforts. In 1796 he sold the *Orrery* to Benjamin Sweetser after his acerbic satirical thrusts in a poem, "The Jacobiniad," condemning Jeffersonian Republicans, led to a mob attack and a beating by the son of an affronted victim.

Requested by Harvard's President Joseph Willard in 1795 to present a commencement poem, Paine returned to receive his A.M. degree and produced *The Invention of Letters: A Poem . . . on the Day of Annual Commencement*, in part a panegyric to Harvard as the "blest seat of letters" with its "sacred walls." Typically, he overstepped bounds by refusing the president's demand to delete searing lines comparing the "Jacobins" to a "green-eyed monster." The poem was popular with Federalist readers, and two editions were published, for which Paine received the large sum of $1,500.

With an unusually facile mind, Paine was able to dazzle his contemporaries with inspired poems often written on the spur of the moment. For a period he also wrote highly regarded theater criticism. Drink and increasing debts, however, undermined his productivity, but his Harvard Phi Beta Kappa poem in 1797, "The Ruling Passion," was considered by his friends as "the most perfect of all his poetical productions" (Prentiss, p. 43).

Paine captured the surge of patriotism during the 1798 crisis with France by writing several very popular nationalistic songs. Responding to the request of the Massachusetts Charitable Fire Society, he wrote

catchy lyrics for "Adams and Liberty." The poet expressed a postrevolutionary hope: "Mid the reign of mild peace, / May your nation increase, / With the glory of Rome, / And the wisdom of Greece." President John Adams was present at Boston's Haymarket Theatre on 5 June 1798 and heard the song in "Tempo Gusto." A newspaper publisher, Major Benjamin Russell, strongly insisted that George Washington's name be included. Paine instantly responded with a laudatory stanza. The song was published in at least eleven editions before 1800. Later Paine wrote the lyrics for "Adams and Washington" as well as "The Green Mountain Farmer."

Paine's popularity led to frequent politically tinged invitations for commemorative speeches. In 1799 he delivered an oration glorying in the dissolution of the Franco-American Alliance. Denouncing France, in *An Oration Written at the Request of the Young Men of Boston* he declaimed about the defeat of "Gallic perfidy" that restored freedom to America. On reading a copy, Thomas Boylston Adams, a son of President John Adams, maintained that it "seems to labor in several places rather unpleasantly."

Paine's eulogy on the death of Washington in 1799, *An Eulogy on the Life of General George Washington* (1800), given in Newburyport, was more sedate, emphasizing the president's high principles, his intelligence, and "the robust vigor of his virtue." Most of Paine's literary work was evoked by the occasion of the moment. In 1804, under the name of Robert Treat Paine, Jr., he wrote an ode, "The Spirit of the Vital Flame," for the Humane Society. His "Spain, Commerce, and Freedom," honoring Spanish patriots, elicited comments in the *Port Folio* (Dec. 1809, p. 497) that it was "undoubtedly written in the true spirit of an oracle . . . sublime, prophetic, and unintelligible."

Encouraged by friends, Paine belatedly studied law under Massachusetts chief justice Theophilus Parsons and was admitted to the bar in 1802. He was a successful attorney but lacked persistence, drifting back to his old ways of drinking and dissolute living. He planned a collection of his works, but the desire was unfulfilled in his lifetime. One of his last publications was an epilogue to William Charles White's tragedy, *The Clergyman's Daughter* (1810). As late as 1810 Robert Treat Paine, Sr., urged his son to reform, but Paine, in ill health, returned to his father's house, only to die in an attic room.

Despite his talents, widely admired in his own time, Paine was quixotic. He was unable to make his way in a milieu that barely recognized the professional writer. As Thomas Boylston Adams perceptively noted in 1799, "A Professional Poet cannot live here by his trade." In 1818 William Cullen Bryant harshly but directly assessed Paine's poetic accomplishment, writing that "the brilliancy of Paine's poetry is like the brilliance of frost work—cold and fantastic. . . . He was a fine, but misguided genius" (Bryant, p. 205). Though not a profound thinker, Paine made a distinctive contribution through his popular and patriotic verse.

• The papers of Robert Treat Paine, Sr., are at the Massachusetts Historical Society, Boston. Selections from the collection, focusing on the era of the Revolution, are in Stephen T. Riley and Edward W. Hanson, eds., Massachusetts Historical Society *Collections* 87 and 888 (1992). Faculty Records bks. 5 and 6, Harvard University Archives, are informative about Paine's college activities. Charles Prentiss, ed., *The Works in Verse and Prose of the Late Robert Treat Paine, Jr.* (1812), is a collection of Paine's literary output and includes a lengthy biographical sketch. The work was reviewed in the *Port Folio*, May 1813. William Cullen Bryant, "American Poetry," *North American Review* 7 (1818): 198–211, is starkly critical of Paine as a poet. Lewis Leary, "The First Published Poem of Thomas Paine," *New England Quarterly* 43 (Mar. 1970): 130–34, illustrates Paine's early conflict with his father. Paine's work is scattered. Various unattributed pieces are in the *Federal Orrery* and the *Massachusetts Magazine*. Among the poet's separately published pieces are *An Ode Written . . . for the Faustus Association* (1807), *A Monody on the Death of Lieut. General Sir John Moore* (1811), and a poem in *An Account of the Great Fire . . . at Newburyport . . . 31 May, 1811*. Paine's popular songs were frequently printed and can be traced in Clifford Shipton and Robert Mooney, eds., *National Index of American Imprints* (1969). The literary scene of Paine's day is brought out in Lawrence Buell, *New England Literary Culture: From Revolution to Renaissance* (1986).

WINFRED E. A. BERNHARD

PAINE, Thomas (29 Jan. 1737–8 June 1809), author of political pamphlets of the Age of Revolution, was born Thomas Pain in Thetford, England, the son of Joseph Pain, a Quaker corset maker, and Frances Cocke, an Anglican. Enrolled by his parents in 1743 at the Thetford Grammar School, Paine left school seven years later to begin an apprenticeship in his father's shop. In 1756 he ran away to enlist on the privateer *Terrible*, commanded by Captain William Death. Hours before the ship sailed from London, Paine's father persuaded him to abandon his plans, a fortunate turn of events since the ship was nearly destroyed by a French vessel, and most of its crew perished. In 1757 Paine served for six months on the privateer *King of Prussia*.

In the winter of 1757–1758, Paine lived in London. "The natural bent of my mind was to science," he later wrote, and he attended popular scientific lectures offered by Benjamin Martin and James Ferguson. Although the popular Newtonianism circles in which Paine now moved had no overt political content, the scientific mentality inculcated a deep respect for freedom of inquiry and the conviction that all human institutions should be judged before the bar of reason, a principle Paine would later apply with devastating results to the British system of government and the principle of hereditary rule.

After working as a journeyman corset maker in Dover, Paine moved in 1759 to Sandwich, where he opened his own shop. That year he married Mary Lambert, an orphan employed as a domestic servant. She and their child died in childbirth in 1760. Local tradition claims that Paine preached as a Methodist in Sandwich. After his wife's death, he returned to Thetford to study for the excise officers' examination. In 1762 he was appointed a supernumerary officer in Lincolnshire and two years later received a permanent position there. In 1765 Paine was dismissed from the service for filing a report without actually examining the goods. Over the next three years, he worked as a corset maker, taught school in London, and won reinstatement in the excise service, assigned to a position in Lewes in 1768. In 1771 he married Elizabeth Ollive, the daughter of a local shopkeeper. They had no children.

Apart from being quite dangerous, since smugglers were prone to resort to violence to avoid apprehension, the position of revenue officer, as Paine later wrote, put him in a unique position "to see into the numerous and various distresses" of ordinary people in Britain in the 1760s, a decade of rising prices, falling real wages, and sporadic food riots. In Lewes he became a member of the White Hart Evening Club, which met regularly at a local inn to discuss political issues. Paine was considered the best debater in the group with an unusually deep fund of political knowledge, according to fellow member William Lee, the editor of a local newspaper. During this period, Paine certainly read the works of Joseph Priestley and James Burgh, advocates of liberty of conscience and parliamentary reform, and he may well have been influenced by the republican traditions that flourished in Lewes. Paine's name appears in records of local government meetings and of church vestry activities distributing poor relief. The only significant piece of writing that can definitively be attributed to Paine before his departure for America was *The Case of the Officers of Excise* (1772), a plea for higher salaries for revenue officers. Parliament took no action on the request, but Paine had finally found his calling as a political pamphleteer.

In 1774 Paine's life seemed to hit rock bottom. He was dismissed from the excise service for being absent from his post without permission. Soon afterward, his household possessions were sold at public auction, and he and his wife signed a formal separation agreement, via which Paine received £35 in lieu of future claims against her property. In London his friend George Lewis Scott, a member of the excise board, introduced Paine to Benjamin Franklin. In October, carrying a letter of introduction from Franklin, Paine set sail for Philadelphia, one of the countless Britons in these years to seek a new life in America. At age thirty-seven he had already lived half his life with no hint of the prominence he would achieve.

Thanks to his letter from Franklin, Paine soon secured the position of editor of the *Pennsylvania Magazine*, a periodical published by Philadelphia bookseller Robert Aitken. Paine contributed poems and essays of his own, but since none was signed, scholars disagree over exactly which pieces are his. No conclusive evidence confirms that a March 1775 essay condemning slavery was written by Paine, although he later supported abolition in Pennsylvania. As the struggle between the American colonies and Great Britain accelerated and war broke out at Lexington and Concord,

Paine gravitated to a group of advocates of the American cause, including John Adams, Benjamin Rush, David Rittenhouse, Timothy Matlack, Thomas Young, and James Cannon. By the end of 1775, these men had concluded that American independence was inevitable. Rush suggested that Paine write a pamphlet supporting the idea, though he urged him to avoid using the word itself so as to avoid frightening those who believed open avowal of independence would unleash a movement for democratic change within the colonies.

Its author listed only as "an Englishman," *Common Sense* appeared in January 1776. It quickly became one of the most successful and influential pamphlets in the history of political writing, selling, by Paine's estimate, some 150,000 copies. Paine directed that his share of the profits be used to buy supplies for the Continental army. The pamphlet offered not only a powerful argument for American independence but an attack on the British Constitution and the principle of hereditary rule. Its main purpose, Paine later wrote, was "to bring forward and establish the representative system of government."

The most striking passages in *Common Sense* contained Paine's powerful attack on the "so much boasted Constitution of England" and the principle of monarchial government. "Of more worth is one honest man to society, and in the sight of God," he wrote, "than all the crowned ruffians that ever lived." King George III was "the royal brute of England," who, by corrupt influence, had "eaten up the virtue of the House of Commons." Far preferable would be a democratic system based on frequent elections, with citizens' rights protected by a written constitution.

Paine then turned to the issue of independence. "There is something absurd," he wrote, "in supposing a continent to be perpetually governed by an island." Within the British empire, America's prospects were limited; independent, its "material eminence" and political greatness were certain. Toward the close, Paine outlined a breathtaking vision of the historical importance of the American Revolution. "We have it in our power," he wrote, "to begin the world over again." In a world "overrun with oppression," America alone would be the home of freedom, "an asylum for mankind."

Adams, who resented that Paine received much of the credit for converting Americans to the cause of independence, later claimed that *Common Sense* was simply "a tolerable summary of the argument which I had been repeating again and again in Congress for nine months" (*Adams, Diary and Autobiography*, ed. Butterfield, vol. 3, p. 333). Nothing in it was new, Adams believed, except "the phrases, suitable for an emigrant from New Gate, such as 'the royal brute of England.'" To some extent, Adams was correct. What was unique in Paine was not so much the originality of his ideas but his mode of expressing them. He was the pioneer of a new style of political writing designed to extend political discussion beyond the narrow bounds of the eighteenth century's "political nation." He assumed knowledge of no authority but the Bible and avoided the florid language common in pamphlets addressed to educated readers. His literary style conveyed the same democratic message as his political argument—anyone could grasp the nature of politics and government. All it required was common sense.

For the next several years, Paine threw himself into the cause of independence. In the spring of 1776, under the pseudonym "the Forester," he published a series of articles in the Philadelphia press responding to critics of *Common Sense*. Shortly after Congress adopted the Declaration of Independence, he joined a Philadelphia militia company and became secretary to General Daniel Roberdeau. He served with the force defending Perth Amboy, New Jersey, and in September became aide-de-camp to General Nathanael Greene. After the evacuation of Fort Lee, Paine joined the forces of George Washington retreating across New Jersey. To help revive American morale, in December Paine published *The American Crisis*, which began with the famous words, "These are the times that try men's souls."

Between 1777 and 1783 Paine published twelve more *Crisis* essays, commenting on political and military events and arousing support for the war. He also served in a number of government posts, among them secretary to the commission appointed by Congress to negotiate with Indian tribes and secretary to the Committee on Foreign Affairs of Congress. In this latter capacity, he became involved in an acrimonious controversy involving Silas Deane, a Connecticut merchant Congress had sent to France to purchase war supplies. In 1778 Paine wrote a series of newspaper articles accusing Deane of financial improprieties. Imprudently referring to secret diplomatic correspondence between France and the United States, Paine's articles caused considerable embarrassment in Congress, and he was forced to resign his post with the Committee for Foreign Affairs. Despite the controversy, he was chosen in 1781 to accompany Colonel John Laurens to Europe on a mission to obtain further financial and material aid from France.

During these years, Paine was also deeply involved in the internal affairs of Pennsylvania, where a popular movement led by his associates Young, Matlack, and Cannon in 1776 inspired the drafting of a new, democratic constitution that eliminated the office of governor, abolished imprisonment for debt, called for the establishment of schools with low fees, and allowed all men who paid taxes to vote. In 1777 Paine was elected to the Committee of Correspondence of the Whig Society, an organization established to defend the new constitution against conservative attacks. In a series of letters in the Pennsylvania press, he praised the new frame of government and gave voice to the egalitarian impulse unleashed by the War for Independence. "Wherever I use the words *freedom* or *rights*," Paine wrote, "I desire to be understood to mean a perfect equality of them." All men, he insisted, should vote, except those who had "voluntarily" surrendered their independence by working as personal servants, a definition of democracy even broader than that in the constitution he was defending.

In 1779 Paine became involved in the controversy surrounding efforts to control prices in wartime Philadelphia. In May he was elected to two extralegal committees, one charged with regulating the prices of goods like coffee, rice, and sugar, the other with investigating the affairs of the prominent merchant Robert Morris, who was accused of holding goods from the market to profit from rising prices. As the effort to regulate prices collapsed amidst the refusal of merchants and farmers to bring goods to market at regulated prices, Paine became persuaded that price controls were counterproductive. In *Common Sense* he had insisted it was the destiny of an independent America to trade freely with the entire world. He had distinguished sharply between society and government—the former "in every state a blessing," the latter "a necessary evil." The events of 1779 reinforced Paine's commitment to economic laissez faire and the idea that, if left to follow its own natural laws, unfettered commerce would produce a prosperity in which all classes would share.

In the 1780s Paine's writings increasingly concerned themselves with the economic policies of the new nation and the need to strengthen national authority. *The Crisis Extraordinary*, published in October 1780, urged the state governments to levy new taxes to support the war effort. *Public Good*, which appeared in December 1780, argued against the western land claims of Virginia, insisting that all such territory belonged to the federal government. Paine insisted that his position was not influenced by the fact that he owned 300 shares in the Indiana Company, which stood to profit if Virginia's claims were disallowed.

Public Good also called for the convening of a "Continental convention" to draw up a new federal Constitution with a stronger central government. Since *Common Sense*, Paine had been a strong American nationalist. In 1782 he entered into a secret agreement with Washington, Robert R. Livingston, and Morris, via which Paine was paid to write in support of fiscal policies promoted by Morris, the federal government's superintendent of finance, to restore the national credit. His pieces included articles calling on Rhode Island to approve a plan whereby Congress would be empowered to levy taxes on imports. Paine also accepted payment from the French minister to the United States for an article calling for joint negotiations involving the United States, Britain, and France to end the war. In 1786 he wrote a pamphlet, *Dissertations on Government; the Affairs of the Bank; and Paper Money*, supporting the rechartering of the Bank of North America, with which Morris was associated, and opposing the issuing of paper money not backed by specie. Paine also received $3,000 from Congress for his services to the Revolution and, from the New York legislature, the confiscated estate of a New Rochelle Loyalist.

In his writings on the bank, Paine insisted that a central financial institution was essential for promoting the roads, bridges, and other improvements necessary for American economic development. In 1786, re-

turning to his scientific interests, he began work on a design for a wrought-iron bridge. His model was exhibited in Philadelphia in January 1787, but he failed to secure funding for the project from the Pennsylvania Assembly. In April Paine embarked for Europe, traveling to France and England to raise funds for his bridge project. In France he struck up a friendship with Thomas Jefferson, then serving as American ambassador. In Britain he became acquainted with Edmund Burke and was made an honorary member of the Society for Constitutional Information, a group of genteel advocates of parliamentary reform. For the next three years he shuttled back and forth between England and France, devoting most of his time to promoting his plan for an iron bridge.

The publication in 1790 of Burke's *Reflections on the Revolution in France* led Paine to resume his vocation as a political writer and to embark on the most turbulent phase of his career. Early in 1791 Paine published his answer to Burke's attack on the French Revolution, *Rights of Man*. Dedicated to Washington, the pamphlet was part vindication of events in France, part elaboration of the principles of republican government Paine had earlier supported in the United States. Rejecting Burke's invocation of precedent and tradition to condemn the Revolution, Paine, as in *Common Sense*, called for a radical break with the past in Britain as well as France. "It is an age of revolutions," he wrote, "in which everything may be looked for." A year later he published his boldest work, *Rights of Man, Part the Second*, again assailing British political institutions and calling on the Old World to recast government in the American image. In chapter five he unveiled a plan for a rudimentary welfare state, financed by progressive taxation on property, in which each poor family would receive direct grants from the government to educate its children, workers would receive retirement benefits after age sixty, and public employment would be provided for the "casual poor." Paine denounced the aristocracy as unproductive "drones" and insisted working men and women were the backbone of society.

Rights of Man, Part the Second became a central text of the British radical tradition. For the first time, the demand for political reform had been linked with a social program to alleviate the plight of the poor. The pamphlet sold some 200,000 copies by the end of 1792 and inspired an upsurge of radical politics among the "lower and middling class" of British society. The government's response was to unleash a wave of political repression. Paine was indicted, and he left for France, where he had been elected a member of the National Convention as a mark of respect for his defense of the Revolution against Burke. He arrived in France in September 1792 and took his seat in the Convention, voting for the formal abolition of the monarchy. In December he was convicted *in absentia* of seditious libel and declared an outlaw in the land of his birth.

Unlike in the United States and England, Paine, who spoke little French, found it impossible to find his bearings in revolutionary Paris. He gravitated to the

Girondin group, who spoke English, admired the American Revolution, and opposed the execution of King Louis XVI. Influenced by his Quaker background, Paine in January 1793 spoke in the Convention against execution. After the fall of the Girondin leaders and the rise of the Jacobins, Paine was arrested and imprisoned in the former Luxembourg palace. He remained there from December 1793 until the following November.

While in prison, Paine completed *The Age of Reason* (1794), an attack on organized Christianity and the idea of the divine inspiration of the Bible. A second part appeared in 1795. Although Paine, a deist, insisted, "I believe in one God, and no more; and I hope for happiness beyond this life," *The Age of Reason* made his name anathema among the clergy and devout Christians on both sides of the Atlantic. In 1795 he published an intemperate open letter to Washington, reproaching the president for allegedly failing to secure Paine's release from prison. Actually, American ambassador Gouverneur Morris did little to aid Paine, whose release came after Morris was succeeded by James Monroe. In 1796 Paine published another attack on the American president, accusing him of treachery and hypocrisy and even denouncing his generalship during the War for Independence. In the following year appeared his last pamphlet of enduring importance, *Agrarian Justice*, in which he noted that private property in land deprived millions of men of their natural right to a portion of the soil. Unlike François Noël Babeuf, who had recently used similar logic to demand the outlawing of private property in general, Paine proposed that each individual reaching adulthood be given a sum of £15 as compensation for the loss of his or her natural inheritance. *Agrarian Justice* established Paine as a pioneer of the land reform tradition, which in the United States stretched down to Henry George almost a century later.

In 1802, at the invitation of Jefferson, who was now president, Paine returned to the United States. But *The Age of Reason* had embittered many of his former allies against him, and his insistence on continuing his deist writings, contributing numerous essays to *The Prospect*, edited by deist Elihu Palmer, made him an embarrassment to the administration, much of whose political support came from evangelical Christians. Paine returned to his farm in New Rochelle and sank into obscurity. In 1806 New Rochelle election officials refused to allow him to vote on the grounds that he was not an American citizen. In 1808 he moved to Greenwich Village. By the time of his death in New York, Paine had been largely forgotten. Only six mourners attended his funeral. Even after his death, one final indignity awaited him. In 1819 the British journalist and reformer William Cobbett disinterred his remains and took them to England, hoping to build a memorial to Paine there. After Cobbett's death, Paine's bones were lost.

Of the men who made the American Revolution, none had a more remarkable career than Paine, even though he always remained something of an outsider in America. When Franklin remarked to Paine, "Where liberty is, there is my country," Paine replied, "Where liberty is not, there is my country" (Keane, p. xiii). Paine's profound influence on American events was acknowledged by friends and opponents alike, but after his death he was excluded from the group of revolutionary leaders canonized in American popular culture. His memory was kept alive primarily by succeeding generations of radicals, who rediscovered him again and again as a symbol of revolutionary internationalism, free thinking, and defiance of existing institutions. More than any other individual, Paine set an example of the radical cast of mind—his aforementioned revolutionary internationalism and defiance of existing institutions, his rationalism and faith in human nature, and his belief in casting off the burden of the past and remaking institutions. As a political writer, he did much to usher in the world and the language of modern politics. "I know not," Adams observed in 1806, "whether any man in the world has had more influence on its inhabitants or affairs for the last thirty years than Thomas Paine."

• No complete edition of Paine's writings exists. The fullest collection is Philip S. Foner, ed., *Complete Writings of Thomas Paine* (1945), although Moncure Conway, *Writings of Thomas Paine* (1894–1896), remains useful. Paine's major pamphlets and some previously unpublished articles are collected in Eric Foner, ed., *Paine*, Library of America ed. (1995). The most complete biography is John Keane, *Tom Paine: A Political Life* (1995). Among other biographies that retain value are Conway, *The Life of Thomas Paine* (1892); A. O. Aldridge, *Man of Reason: The Life of Thomas Paine* (1959); Audrey Williamson, *Thomas Paine: His Life, Work, and Times* (1973); and David Freeman Hawke, *Paine* (1974). Works covering particular aspects of his career include Eric Foner, *Tom Paine and Revolutionary America* (1976); Aldridge, *Thomas Paine's American Philosophy* (1984); Gregory Claeys, *Thomas Paine: Social and Political Thought* (1989); and Jack Fruchtman, Jr., *Thomas Paine, Apostle of Freedom* (1994). Bernard Vincent, *Thomas Paine ou la religion de la liberté* (1987), is the first French biography and a long overdue attempt to assess Paine's role in the French Revolution.

ERIC FONER

PAINTER, Theophilus Shickel (22 Aug. 1889–5 Oct. 1969), experimental zoologist and university president, was born in Salem, Virginia, the son of the Reverend Franklin Verzelius Newton Painter, a professor of modern languages at Roanoke College, Virginia, and Laura Shickel. Painter grew up in a deeply religious and scholarly household, and, because he was a sickly child, he was taught at home. He enrolled in Roanoke College in 1904 and received his B.A. in 1908. Roanoke College at that time offered little instruction in the sciences, so, being attracted to the study of chemistry, Painter took advantage of a scholarship for graduate studies at Yale University. There, Professor L. L. Woodruff provided Painter his first opportunity for using a microscope, which inspired Painter to change his graduate major to biology. He received his M.A. in 1909 and his Ph.D. in 1913. His doctoral thesis in experimental biology, a field then being pioneered by biologists like Thomas Hunt Morgan, was "Spermatogenesis in Spiders," directed by the spider expert Alexander Petrunkevitch. He published his first scientific paper, "On the Dimorphism of *Maevia vittata*," in 1913, and his thesis in 1914, both in the *Zoologische Jahrbücher*.

In 1914 Painter undertook a year of postgraduate studies with Theodore Boveri at the University of Würzburg and at the Naples Marine Zoological Station, thus establishing himself on the leading edge of international cytogenetic research. He returned to the United States to take up duties as an instructor of zoology at Yale for two years. He also taught summer courses (1914 and 1915) in marine invertebrate zoology at the Marine Biology Laboratory in Woods Hole, Massachusetts. One of his students there was Mary Anna Thomas, whom he married in 1917; they had four children.

At Woods Hole Painter also met John Thomas Patterson, then chair of the zoology department at the University of Texas at Austin (UT), who offered him an adjunct professorship; he accepted the post and remained at the University of Texas for the rest of his career. After Painter, Patterson recruited Herman Joseph Muller in 1920, who stayed at UT until 1936; the three of them formed the kernel of an innovative, widely influential "Genetics Group."

American participation in World War I led Painter into military service as a reserve officer in the U.S. Army from 1917 to 1919. This interruption in his research delayed his promotion to associate professor until 1921. He became a full professor and a member of the graduate faculty in 1925.

Painter's early papers continued work begun in Europe and Woods Hole, but after a paper on lizards, he turned to mammalian (including human) spermatogenesis. Throughout the rest of the 1920s he studied a variety of mammals—monkeys, opossums, and rodents, among others—but he is best known for his work on the human chromosome, announced in *Science* in 1922 and followed by a longer article in the *Journal of Experimental Zoology* (vol. 37, 1923). This work helped establish the XY type of sex distinction in humans and forty-eight as the number of human chromosomes. (It was not until 1956 that improved staining techniques allowed J. H. Tijo and A. Levan to give the correct number as forty-six.) By 1929 Painter was collaborating with Muller in studying mutations generated by radiation in *Drosophila melanogaster* (fruit fly), a continuation of Muller's Nobel Prize–winning work. This collaboration resulted in a paper now considered classic, "Parallel Cytology and Genetics of Induced Translocation and Deletions in Drosophila," which helped to establish the synthesis (previously hypothetical) of the Mendelian theory of inheritance with the chromosome theory. Painter augmented this line of development during the 1930s in a series of papers drawing on his discovery of the giant salivary gland chromosomes in a late larval stage of the fruit fly. The large size of these chromosomes and innovative preparation and staining techniques developed by Painter greatly accelerated work in cytogenetics.

By the end of the 1930s Painter had begun to accrue honors. He was awarded the Elliot Medal of the National Science Foundation in 1933; Yale conferred an honorary doctorate in 1936; and in 1939 he was elected to membership in the American Philosophical Society and became a University of Texas Distinguished Professor.

In 1944 a clash of wills (the issue was academic freedom) between the UT regents and university president Homer Price Rainey, a political and social liberal, resulted in Rainey's being fired. The regents asked Painter to act as president of the university while chairing a search committee for a new one; in 1946 Painter was appointed to the post. Painter's position as a distinguished member of the faculty exerted a stabilizing influence that helped to buffer the faculty from reactionary state politics. Shortly after his appointment, Painter, as president of UT, became involved as codefendant in an early postwar civil rights action commonly known as *Sweatt v. Painter*. In that case an African-American World War II veteran and postal worker named Heman Marion Sweatt brought a suit that he might be admitted to the UT Law School because there were no law schools in Texas for black students. Finding itself in violation of the "separate but equal" constitutional provision, the regents and Painter attempted to create a law curriculum especially for Sweatt in Houston. Although this stratagem was upheld in the lower courts, the Supreme Court eventually found in favor of Sweatt, and he was admitted to the law school.

In 1952 Painter resigned from the presidency of the university in order to return to teaching and research. In the process, he embarked upon a severe regime of study in order to catch up on the literature. By 1953 he was publishing original research once again, and he continued to do so past his retirement in 1966. Throughout his career Painter was known as an enthusiastic teacher of undergraduate as well as graduate students, and he was an active member of many organizations, including the American Society of Zoologists and the Genetics Society. He died in Fort Stockton, Texas, just after returning from a hunting trip.

• A considerable amount of material on Painter can be found in various files of the Center for American History, University of Texas at Austin; these are especially useful for the term of Painter's presidency of the university. This article relied on Bentley Glass, "Theophilus Shickel Painter, August 22, 1889–October 5, 1969," National Academy of Sciences, *Biographical Memoirs* 59 (1980): 309–37, which contains an extensive bibliography of Painter's scientific articles. See also Garland E. Allen, "Painter, Theophilus Shickel," in *Dictionary of Scientific Biography* 10 (1974): 276–77, and the pamphlet *The Genetics Group*, published around 1951 by the University of Texas Department of Zoology. For an overview of the case of *Sweatt v. Painter* see Lynn Hughes, "The Sociological Implications of *Sweatt v. Painter*," *Touchstone* 5 (1986): 77–88.

JOSÉ ALFREDO BACH

PAL, George (1 Feb. 1908–2 May 1980), animator, film producer and director, and special effects expert, was born in Cegled, Hungary, the son of George Pal and Maria (maiden name unknown), entertainers in a traveling theater. Pal studied architecture at the Budapest Academy of Arts. After graduation he was hired by Hunnia Films of Budapest to draw subtitles and posters for silent films. Interested in animated cartoons, Pal learned the basic techniques from George Feld, a Hungarian who had been a Hollywood editor. In 1930 he married Zsoka Grandjean; they would have two children, both born in the United States.

In 1931, after a few months of independent work as a cartoonist, Pal was hired by the Berlin-based UFA Studio, the most prestigious in Germany. In 1932 Pal opened his own studio in Berlin, and it soon became a successful enterprise. At about this time a Cologne cigarette company commissioned Pal to create an animated cartoon featuring its products. Instead of animating drawings Pal shot real cigarettes, moving them frame by frame. This stop-motion technique was an instant success.

Investigated by the Gestapo in 1933 because they were foreign nationals, the Pals moved first to Prague and then to Paris. During this period Pal designed a stop-motion camera that was easily transported in a suitcase. He and his wife moved to Holland in 1935, when Philips Radio commissioned him to produce some commercials there. More work for European companies soon followed. Granted an American visa in 1939, the Pals settled in Hollywood, where they became friends with renowned animator Walter Lantz, who later sponsored their American naturalization. Impressed by Pal's work, Barney Balaban, president of Paramount Pictures, offered him a contract to supply puppet shorts for the Hollywood studio. Throughout the 1940s Pal and his team of creative artists and artisans produced more than forty animated fiction shorts, or Puppetoons, "color cartoons in three dimensions" as he fondly referred to them. Pal had coined the word "Puppetoons" as an amalgamation of the words "puppet" and "cartoons." In 1943 he received a special Academy Award for the animation techniques he had developed.

The Puppetoons were wooden puppets constructed with rubber-covered wire arms and legs for walking, to make them pose easily. Each puppet had several replacement parts, particularly heads, to achieve a wide range of expressions. They were animated against papier-mâché and cardboard sets. Pal and his story-sketch artist, Jack Miller, wrote the stories. Each short required an average of six weeks for production. One of his most successful creations was the Screwball Army, characters composed of nuts and bolts that constituted Pal's humorous parody of the totalitarian Nazi regime, a recurrent theme throughout his work. The Screwball Army appeared in the Academy Award nominees *Tulips Shall Grow* (1942) and *Bravo Mr. Strauss* (1943). Interested in American black folktales, Pal created Jasper, a naive black boy, and his two friends, Professor Scarecrow and Blackbird. About a dozen shorts featuring these characters were produced, including the Academy Award nominee *Jasper and the Beanstalk* (1945). The shorts drew some bitter criticism for what was considered a perpetuation of black stereotypes. To counter this critique, Pal made *John Henry and the Inky Poo* (1946), based on a black folktale in which the protagonist was not a comical, naive character. This short also received an Academy Award nomination. During World War II Pal made many training films for the army and navy Signal Corps.

In 1948 Pal closed his puppet studio and then became a film producer. His first feature was *The Great Rupert*, produced in 1949 and released in 1950, a comedy fantasy directed by Irving Pichel that featured an animated wooden squirrel. It was followed by *Destination Moon*, also released in 1950, a pioneer technicolor science fiction adventure also directed by Pichel. Its remarkable special effects earned the film an Academy Award. Made as an independent production for less than $600,000, the film grossed $5.5 million. Pal's next production was *When Worlds Collide* (1951), made for Paramount Pictures and based on the popular science fiction classic by Philip Wylie and Edwin Balmer. Directed by Rudolph Mate, this story of scientists preparing for a world cataclysm earned an Academy Award for its special effects. In 1953 Pal produced the H. G. Wells classic *The War of the Worlds*, directed by Byron Haskin, also for Paramount, at a cost of $1.2 million. This science fiction thriller vividly chronicles Martians invading the Earth. It was the third Pal production to receive an Academy Award for special effects. *Houdini* (1953), a film about the legendary magician that was directed by George Marshall, was a box office success for Paramount and helped to establish the career of actor Tony Curtis. Pal's next production for Paramount was *The Naked Jungle*, produced and released in 1954 and directed by Haskin. Actor Charlton Heston stars in this South American jungle adventure about a plantation invaded by an army of Marabunta ants. Pal returned to the science fiction genre in *The Conquest of Space* (1955), again directed by Haskin for Paramount. Based on a book by Willy Ley and Chesley Bonestell, this film about the first trip to Mars did not reach the level of previous Pal productions.

Pal made his directorial debut with *Tom Thumb* (1958), a film for children shot in England for Metro-Goldwyn-Mayer (MGM) that included some delightful Puppetoon sequences. Produced by Pal for $900,000, the picture received an Academy Award for special effects. Next MGM commissioned Pal to produce and direct *The Time Machine*, produced in 1959 and released in 1960, an entertaining adaptation of the classic H. G. Wells fantasy novel about a scientist who invents a time travel machine. Made for $850,000, the picture brought Pal his fifth Academy Award for special effects. It was followed by *Atlantis, the Lost Continent* (1960), produced and directed by Pal for MGM. This science fiction fairy tale about the destruction of the legendary island was a critical disappointment. His next production for MGM, directed by Henry Levin, was *The Wonderful World of the Brothers Grimm* (1962), shot in the new multiscreen process Cinerama. Filmed largely on location in Germany, the picture combines the lives of the famous writers with four of their fairy tales. Pal included Puppetoons in a toy shop sequence and created a fabulous fire-breathing dragon. Mary Wills's costumes earned the film an Academy Award. Pal's next production, which he also directed, was *7 Faces of Dr. Lao* (1964), based on the 1935 novel by Charles G. Finney. The film is a fairy tale about the magical effects of a circus of mythical beasts run by the strange Dr. Lao in a small Arizona town. An Academy Award went to William Tuttle for his makeup creations. The box office failure of the picture affected Pal's career. A few years passed before he was able to produce his next film, *The Power* (1968), a science fiction thriller about an evil supergenius who kills by unconventional means, directed by Haskin for MGM. *Doc Savage, the Man of Bronze* (1975) was Pal's last film. Directed by Michael Anderson for Warner Brothers, at a cost of $1.5 million, the film marked the screen debut of the popular pulp hero created by Lester Dent ("Kenneth Robeson") in the 1930s.

Pal died at his home in Beverly Hills, California. Like many talented European émigrés working in Hollywood, Pal brought a humanistic worldview to bear on his work, showing his faith in the capacity of people to do good and battle evil. He made a unique contribution to the entertainment industry with pioneering developments in three-dimensional stop-motion animation in the 1940s, with Puppetoons, and with special effects in classic 1950s science fiction films.

• The George Pal Papers are in the Arts Library, Special Collections, University of California, Los Angeles. They consist of twenty-one boxes of scripts for cartoons and films that Pal produced and directed, including some original artwork. The UCLA Film and Television Archive holds more than nine feature films and thirty of Pal's Puppetoons and animated shorts in 35 mm., including *Destination Moon*, *When Worlds Collide*, and *The War of the Worlds* (1953). The most complete biography of Pal, including extensive analysis of his animation work and feature films, is Gail Morgan Hickman, *The Films of George Pal* (1977). Pal's science fiction films are discussed in the context of the genre in John Brosnan, *Future Tense: The Cinema of Science Fiction* (1978). The obituary in *Variety*, 7 May 1980, provides an overall assessment of Pal's career as an animator, producer, and director.

MARÍA ELENA DE LAS CARRERAS-KUNTZ

PALEY, William S. (28 Sept. 1901–26 Oct. 1990), broadcasting executive, was born in Chicago, Illinois, the son of Samuel Paley, a cigar manufacturer, and Goldie Drell. Paley received a B.S. from the University of Pennsylvania in 1922. He then went into his family's successful cigar business. In 1927 he became interested in broadcasting when his family business began advertising over a Philadelphia radio station. In 1928, when the financially troubled Columbia Phonographic Broadcasting System, then consisting of twenty-two affiliates and sixteen employees, came up for sale, the Paley family purchased it for $400,000. It was renamed the Columbia Broadcasting System (CBS), with William Paley as its president.

Paley, who until the purchase of CBS had not been highly regarded as a businessman, soon showed great acumen as the head of the fledgling network. Aware of the fact that the programming his network offered was not as popular as that of its major rival, NBC, Paley offered stations across the country free programming in exchange for an option on advertising time on their evening schedules. This practice would eventually become the industry standard.

Paley also showed imagination in luring advertisers to CBS, including allowing them to mention prices on the air. In addition, early on he gave evidence of what would be his strongest asset, choosing talent for the new network. Within a short period he launched the radio careers of young singers such as Bing Crosby, Kate Smith, and Morton Downey.

In 1932 Paley married Dorothy Hart Hearst; they adopted two children and divorced in 1947. That same year Paley married Barbara "Babe" Cushing Mortimer; they had two children.

Despite Paley's early success (he sold Paramount a half share in CBS for $5 million in 1929), CBS still lagged behind NBC, particularly in the area of programming. As a result, Paley decided to make a major effort in the field of broadcast journalism, where NBC did not hold such a commanding lead. He hired in 1930 Edward Klauber, a former editor for the *New York Times*, as his right-hand man; in 1933 he recruited former United Press reporter Paul White to head the CBS News division. CBS News began to rival NBC.

Nevertheless, it was not until 1935, when Edward R. Murrow was hired as the CBS director of talks, that CBS News really came of age. Murrow was dispatched to London in 1937. In 1938, on the heels of Adolf Hitler's invasion of Austria, CBS launched the first broadcast—by William L. Shirer and others—of what would become "CBS World News Roundup." Murrow also hired a group of reporters, including Eric Sevareid, Howard K. Smith, Richard C. Hottelet, and Charles Collingwood, whose reporting changed the nature of broadcast news.

During World War II Paley served in the Psychological Warfare Division of the Office of War Information. After the war he was determined to capture the lead in entertainment programming from NBC. In 1948 he lured to CBS some of NBC's brightest stars, including Jack Benny, George Burns and Gracie Allen, and Red Skelton. "Paley's Raid," as it became known in the broadcasting industry, became the basis of CBS's lead in entertainment programming for the next twenty years.

That lead became strongest during the rise of network television. At first Paley was unwilling to get involved in television, but under prodding from Frank Stanton, whom he had appointed CBS president in 1946, he soon realized the potential of the new technology. He used the stars he had taken from NBC, along with shows such as "I Love Lucy," "Gunsmoke," "The Ed Sullivan Show," and "Arthur Godfrey and His Friends," and CBS became known in industry circles as the "Tiffany network."

The network's reputation for high quality was also a result of Paley's other public activities. He worked to aid the Museum of Modern Art, serving on its board from 1937 and as its president from 1968 to 1972; he also amassed a substantial art collection of his own. He led in the building of the architecturally distinguished CBS headquarters in Manhattan and in the founding of the Museum of Broadcasting (subsequently renamed the Museum of Television and Radio). In addition, CBS, which through most of its history had lagged behind NBC in technological development, was introducing new electronics products, including the long-playing record and the first version of color television.

In 1974 the Columbia Broadcasting System changed its name to CBS, Inc., acknowledging the fact that it was no longer just a broadcasting company but a mass media conglomerate. The corporation owned magazines (such as *Woman's Day*), the publishing house of Holt, Rinehart and Winston, Columbia Records, and even (from 1964 to 1973) the New York Yankees. Although many people expected Paley to retire, he kept the reins of the company, ignoring his own retirement edict, which he had used to force the exit of his heir-apparent Frank Stanton in 1973.

In rapid succession Paley hired, then fired, a series of presidents and chief executive officers: Arthur Taylor in 1976, John Backe in 1980, and Thomas Wyman in 1986. The last firing occurred during a period when CBS was fighting a takeover bid from Ted Turner, as well as an effort by Senator Jesse Helms to get conservatives to buy stock and take over CBS. In order to oust Wyman, Paley allied himself with investor Laurence Tisch who, as head of Loew's Corporation, owned 25 percent of CBS stock. With Wyman gone, Tisch took over the real power in the company; Paley was reinstalled but was largely inactive as executive committee chair.

As one of the founders of modern broadcasting, Paley tried to balance demands for mass entertainment with the need for artistic and informational programming. He also created an image of leadership in this new, immensely powerful industry that was consonant with the traditional elite of American society. He died in New York City.

• Paley's autobiography, *As It Happened: A Memoir* (1979), is somewhat inadequate as a guide to his life. Much more substantial and critical is Sally Bedell Smith, *In All His Glory: The Life of William S. Paley: The Legendary Tycoon and His Brilliant Circle* (1990). Also critical and more analytic is David Halberstam, *The Powers That Be* (1979). Robert Metz, *CBS: Reflections in a Bloodshot Eye* (1975), emphasizes the dark side of Paley. A. M. Sperber, *Murrow: His Life and Times* (1986), is informative on the Murrow-Paley relationship. Gary Paul Gates, *Air Time: The Inside Story of CBS News* (1978), is a good history of that division.

ALBERT AUSTER

PALFREY, John Gorham (2 May 1796–26 Apr. 1881), clergyman, author, and politician, was born in Boston, Massachusetts, the son of John Palfrey, an unsuccessful merchant and shipmaster, and Mary Sturges Gorham. After his mother's death in 1802, his father left him (the eldest) and his four brothers with relatives. Two years later his father moved permanently to New Orleans, taking only his four youngest sons with him, and became a plantation owner and slaveholder. Meanwhile, left behind, young John attended the Berry Street Academy in Boston and Phillips Exeter Academy in Exeter, New Hampshire, where he was a charity student. With no encouragement and little financial support from his father, Palfrey attended Harvard as a scholarship student, graduating in 1815. He studied at the Harvard Divinity School from 1816 to 1818, graduated and was ordained in 1818, and served as pastor of the prestigious Unitarian Church at Brattle Square, Boston, from 1818 until 1831. He developed into a respected religious, social, and intellectual leader known throughout Boston and beyond.

Palfrey broadened his intellectual interests in 1820 by becoming a member of the editorial board of the *Christian Disciple*. In 1822 he became its editor, changed its name to the *Christian Examiner*, and published some of his sermons in it as well as many separate articles and reviews on matters of church history and theology. In 1823 he married Mary Ann Hammond, with whom he had six children. He resigned from his editorial position in 1825 to turn to his first extensive scholarly task, publishing in 1828 his translation and edition of *The New Testament in the Common Version, Conformed to Griesbach's Standard Greek Text*, based on Johann Jakob Griesbach's monumental three-volume work of 1775–1776 written in Jena, Germany. Palfrey's edition, which reveals enormous scholarly diligence and profundity, was designed to present the New Testament in a popular text, critically sound, but not bound to the phraseology of the King James version.

In 1831 Palfrey became professor of sacred literature at Harvard, dean of the faculty of the divinity school, and its executive chairman. He taught and was an innovative administrator at Harvard until 1839. The year 1831 also saw the publication of his *Harmony of the Gospels . . .* , in which Palfrey collated the four gospels, edited them, and arranged them in chronological order for the benefit of less experienced readers. He published *Academical Lectures on the Jewish Scriptures and Antiquities* in 1838, the first of four such volumes of lectures; the second was published in 1840 and the third and fourth in 1852. These lectures concern Old Testament linguistics, history, and literary style. His elaborate annotations demonstrate his knowledge of Greek, Hebrew, Syriac, and much else.

In 1839 Palfrey turned full-time to editing the *North American Review*, which he had purchased three years earlier for $2,000 from Edward Everett. Palfrey also turned his attention to writing about historical, literary, and sociopolitical issues, and began to enliven his writings with touches of satire. Among the approximately thirty essays and thirty briefer critical notes Palfrey wrote and published in the *Review*, he praises New England extravagantly for its racial homogeneity, rationalizes its old Puritan leaders' known religious intolerance somewhat casuistically on the grounds of political expediency, and praises the eloquence of English parliamentarians at the expense of his most disliked political target—the Congress of the United States. Seeking to improve politics, at least at the state level, Palfrey ran as a Whig for a seat in the Massachusetts state legislature, won, and served in 1842 and 1843. After he sold the nearly bankrupt *Review* for very little money to the philosopher-editor Francis Bowen in 1842, Palfrey continued both his literary and his political careers. He published historical reviews, while also serving from 1843 to 1847 as Massachusetts secretary of state. Fiercely energetic, he prepared the massive *Statistics on the Condition and Products of Certain Branches of Industry in Massachusetts*, which, published in 1846, concerns statewide agricultural and industrial production and includes demographic tables.

A dramatic event made Palfrey an active, even heroic, abolitionist. He had long opposed slavery theoretically, but in 1843 his father's death in Louisiana left him and his proslavery brothers inheritors of slaves. Palfrey went to Louisiana in 1844 to take legal possession of some twenty slaves as his share of the estate. Three of the slaves were legally freed at once because of old age. After much difficulty and expense, he transported the remaining seventeen to freedom in Boston in 1845. Although he wanted no publicity, influential and vocal persons, notably the scholar-educator Cornelius Conway Felton and the politician Charles Sumner publicized the facts and Palfrey was soon extolled as "a practicing abolitionist." He proceeded to lecture and write extensively in favor of the antislavery movement. In 1846 he and two friends bought the *Boston Whig*. He wrote frequently for it and gathered some two dozen of his contributions, which combined historical scholarship and invective against the South, into his *Papers on the Slave Power . . .* (1846). He was elected to the U.S. Congress but served only one term (1847–1849) because he offended his Whig party supporters by associating with Free Soilers and other radicals. Defeated for reelection as a Free Soil candidate, and then as a Free Soil candidate for governor in 1851, he tried to remain a behind-the-scenes political force but devoted his energies successfully thereafter only to renewed research and publication. His monograph, *The Inter-State Slave Trade* (1855), castigates the Old South—Virginia, North Carolina, and South Carolina—for breeding and selling slaves to planters in the New South—Alabama, Mississippi, and Texas—and thus encouraging the spread of slavery. Early in 1856 Palfrey and his wife traveled to London, where he delved deeply into Privy Council and Board of Trade records relevant to aspects of New England history. Sumner, Francis Parkman, and Richard Henry Dana, Jr., among other friends, offered social and professional leads. Palfrey

visited Holland and France before returning home late in 1856.

Palfrey's historical work followed, including *History of New England during the Stuart Dynasty*, volume 1 (1858), volume 2 (1860), and volume 3 (1864), and *History of New England from the Revolution of the Seventeenth Century to the Revolution of the Eighteenth*, volume 4 (1875), and volume 5, edited by his son Francis W. Palfrey and published posthumously (1890). Palfrey abridged the first three volumes as *A Compendious History of New England . . .* (volumes 1 and 2, 1866, and volume 3, 1872). His work displays the virtue of unremitting thoroughness. Offputting to modern readers is Palfrey's theory—no longer admired or even tenable—that New England became the superior region that it did, and its people the wonders that they were, because of its racial homogeneity and the concomitant respect its citizens, who were descendants of the best blood in England, always had for hard work and honestly accumulated property. Indeed, Palfrey opined that the later influx of Irish and German immigrants operated to the detriment of New England. Despite his abhorrence of slavery, he never could accept African Americans as his social, political, or intellectual equals. And he thought Native Americans were savage heathens—indolent, vicious, and utterly lacking in any capacity for civilization. Singling out King Philip of the Wampanoag tribe, Palfrey labeled him "a squalid savage, whose palace was a pig sty."

Palfrey downgraded the early Pilgrims for tolerantly separating themselves from the theological and, consequently, the political, commercial, and social advantages that the Puritans enjoyed by sensibly remaining on decent terms with Old World Anglicanism as long as possible. He deplored any wrenching of the sociopolitical fabric of seventeenth-century New England, whether caused by Indians, by Roger Williams ("obnoxious to the government"), by Anne Hutchinson (who "threatened . . . anarchy"), or by "alleged witches." Calling the 1692 witchcraft trials in Salem a "tragedy," he partly accounted for them as resulting from the contagious delusions and even willful histrionics of teenage females and from competing adults motivated by "vindictiveness and malice." He sarcastically called Cotton Mather, a leading advocate of witch-hanging, "always infallible in his own eyes." Palfrey managed a lame rationalization: in a time of near-universal belief in "a possible demoniacal agency," New England authorities slaughtered far fewer witches than did their confreres in Europe.

Palfrey did not enjoy sizable royalties from any of his publications, but his finances improved when he was appointed postmaster of Boston from 1861 to 1867. Light duties in that office interfered very little with his ongoing scholarship, on which he continued to work for a decade after President Andrew Johnson replaced him with an ex–Union Army general. Physical weakness finally forced Palfrey to desist. He died peacefully in the library of his residence in Cambridge, Massachusetts. Palfrey's theological scholarship has been superseded and his *History of New Eng-*

land downgraded when not entirely ignored, but his dogged conscientiousness remains an example of the best that New England produced.

• Most of Palfrey's papers are in the American Antiquarian Society at Worcester, Massachusetts, the Boston Public Library, the Massachusetts Historical Society in Boston, the Connecticut Historical Society in Hartford, the Houghton Library at Harvard University, the Department of Archives and Manuscripts at Louisiana State University, and the Library of Congress in Washington, D.C. Henry Adams includes complimentary comments about his friend Palfrey in *The Education of Henry Adams* (1918). Frank Otto Gatell, *John Gorham Palfrey and the New England Conscience* (1963), the standard critical biography, contains a definitive primary bibliography. James Truslow Adams, *The March of Democracy: A History of the United States*, vol. 2, *A Half-Century of Expansion* (1932), is typical of twentieth-century historians who regard Palfrey's historical work as provincial and antiquated. Van Wyck Brooks, *The Flowering of New England 1815–1865* (1936), calls Palfrey "a 'Christian lawyer' in his theology and a theologian in his literature." Perry Miller, *The New England Mind from Colony to Province* (1953), dismisses Palfrey as pompous. However, Christine Leigh Heyrman, in "Spectors of Suppression, Society of Friends: Dissent and the Devil in Provincial Essex County," in David D. Hall et al., eds., *Saints & Revolutionaries: Essays on Early American History* (1984), pp. 38–74, defends Palfrey. Obituaries are in the *Boston Evening Transcript*, 27 Apr. 1881, and the *New York Times*, 28 Apr. 1881.

ROBERT L. GALE

PALMER, Albert Marshman (27 July 1838–7 Mar. 1905), theater manager and entrepreneur, was born in North Stonington, Connecticut, the son of Reverend Dr. Albert Gallatin Palmer, a Baptist minister, and Sarah Amelia Langworthy. He was educated at the Suffield Institute and graduated in 1860 from the New York University Law School but soon turned his attention to politics.

Sheridan Shook, the collector of Internal Revenue for New York, made Palmer his chief deputy before 1869. He held this post until 1871, when he was hired as head bookkeeper at Shook's new Union Square Theatre. The next summer Palmer began his theatrical career by taking over the management of the theater from Robert W. Butler under Shook's plan to create a first-class "home of the drama" out of the former roadhouse. Palmer began his tenure by continuing the practice of running combination bills, including the successful Voke's Family comedy troupe. However, with a bit of luck and astute timing, Palmer enticed Agnes Ethel, one of the leading actresses from Augustin Daly's company, to join the Union Square Theatre. She brought with her a new play, *Agnes*, composed for her by Victorien Sardou, which opened on 17 September 1872 and became the first major, long-running hit of Palmer's management career.

In 1873 Palmer decided to form a stock company "capable of realising the romantic school of drama" (Strang, p. 207) to compete with Lester Wallack's company, which was devoted to high comedy, Edwin Booth's tragedy, and Augustin Daly's light comedy.

Palmer's company over the years included many of the leading players of the day, such as Clara Morris, Kate Claxton, Maude Granger, Annie Russell, J. H. Stoddart, McKee Rankin, James O'Neill, Richard Mansfield, and F. F. Mackay. The repertory of the company consisted primarily of foreign plays, classics such as *The London Assurance, School for Scandal*, and *Caste* (all 1872), as well as adaptations such as *Led Astray* (1873), *The Danicheffs* (c. 1877), *A Parisian Romance* (1883), and Palmer's greatest success, *The Two Orphans* (1874). In addition, he achieved some success with new American plays, including Bartley Campbell's *Peril* and *My Partner* (both 1874) and Bronson Howard's *The Banker's Daughter* (1878).

In partnership with Shook, Palmer also managed the Brooklyn Theatre from 1874 until 1876, when it was destroyed by fire. Despite his inexperience at the beginning, the ten years Palmer spent at the Union Square Theatre proved to be his greatest, and this period, in conjunction with that of his closest competitors, Wallack and Daly, is considered "one of the brightest chapters in the history of the New York stage" (Odell, vol. 9, p. 200). Palmer epitomized the qualities of theater managers of his day. He was a shrewd but honest businessman with a sharp eye for new and potentially lucrative talent, discovering and promoting many of America's premier performers of the period. His was not only a theater of high capital return, however; it was also one of "dignity and form" where standards of public taste were met with "culture, refinement, and scholarship" (Hornblow, p. 261).

After a disagreement with Shook, Palmer left the Union Square Theatre in 1883 and spent the next few months in Europe. In September 1884 he joined the Mallory Brothers in management of the Madison Square Theatre (formerly Fifth Avenue Theatre). His opening production, in contrast with the very serious, and somewhat dour, naturalism of the previous manager, David Belasco, was the rollicking farce, *The Private Secretary*. The success of Palmer's approach can be measured by this production's remarkable 200-night run and by the rising prestige of the Madison Square company in general over the succeeding years, eventually supplanting the "Union Square Theatre as the hub of New York's theatrical activity" (Durham, p. 358).

Also in 1884, Palmer attempted, with the help of Harrison Grey Fiske and M. B. Leavitt, to build a new theater further uptown. The group, however, was unable to secure the appropriate pieces of property on Forty-second Street near Sixth Avenue, and the venture folded. Palmer maintained his interest in this part of town, however, and finally secured management of Wallack's Theatre at Broadway and Thirtieth Street in July 1888, paying more than $300,000 in the bargain (Durham, p. 359) and renaming it Palmer's Theatre. Palmer managed both the Madison Square Theatre and Palmer's Theatre until 1891, when he moved his successful company to the uptown site.

During this period Palmer engaged as literary and artistic adviser Augustus Thomas, who provided the play that opened the 1891–1892 season at Palmer's, the phenomenally successful *Alabama*. It was one of the first American plays that Palmer had produced in years, and in his autobiography Thomas recounts Palmer's doubts and fears about the play's viability. This hesitation reflects the generally held assessment of Palmer as an intelligent manager but one who was rather conservative in his repertory. Indeed, it was this cautiousness that caused Palmer to turn down the money-making *Paul Kauvar* when Steele MacKaye offered it to him in 1875 (Percy MacKaye, *Epoch: The Life of Steele MacKaye*, vol. 1 [1927], p. 241). Palmer's conservative attitude toward preserving the stock-company system (which was losing ground to the combination-house system) compounded with rapidly changing public taste to make the 1890s increasingly difficult for him. Despite major productions of celebrated plays such as Sidney Grundy's *The Broken Seal* (1892), Bronson Howard's *Colonel Carter of Cartersville* (1892) and *Aristocracy* (1892–1893), and Oscar Wilde's *Lady Windermere's Fan* (1893), Palmer found himself forced to book more and more touring combinations to sustain his theater and was finally obliged to give up control of Palmer's Theatre in 1896.

Between 1893 and 1896 Palmer also leased the Garden Theatre at Madison Avenue and Twenty-seventh Street in partnership with Edmund C. Stanton. This venture, however, suffered the same difficulties as his own house despite the success of Paul M. Potter's *Trilby* in 1895. Impresario Charles Frohman took over the Garden Theatre in 1896.

Palmer's last theater management project was his lease of the brand-new Great Northern Theatre in Chicago in the fall of 1896. His plans to establish a stock company there, however, failed, and he returned to New York in 1897 heavily in debt. Palmer then spent three years managing tours for Richard Mansfield. In 1903, after having withdrawn from professional life for some time because of failing health, Palmer was hired to manage the Herald Square Theatre for Frohman.

In addition to management, Palmer contributed to the theater industry in general. He initiated the practice of paying for the use of foreign plays, and he sought a court decision to protect his rights to use unprinted foreign plays for which he had paid; this action led, in 1891, to the institution of copyright obligations on foreign plays. He was one of the founders of the Actor's Fund of America and served as its president from 1885 to 1897. He was also involved in the creation of the Player's Club in 1888. Palmer considered it one of his greatest honors to have been offered the position of president (shepherd) of the New York supper club, the Lambs, after Wallack's death in 1888 (MacKaye, vol. 2, p. 109). Due to business and personal obligations, however, he gracefully turned down the honor. He died in New York City.

• Palmer's papers and notebooks are held in the Harvard Theatre Collection; the New York Public Library for the Performing Arts, Lincoln Center; the Walter Hampden-Edwin Booth Theatre Collection and Library, The Players, New York; and the Princeton University Library. See also Pat M. Ryan, "A. M. Palmer, Producer: A Study of Management Dramaturgy, and Stagecraft in the American Theatre, 1872–1896" (Ph.D. diss., Yale Univ., 1959). For excellent coverage of theaters managed by Palmer, including extensive bibliographies, see Weldon Durham, *American Theatre Companies*, vol. 2 (1987), pp. 325–34 (Madison Square Theatre), pp. 359–64 (Palmer's Company), and pp. 491–99 (Union Square Theatre). Arthur Hornblow, *A History of the Theatre in America* (1919), pp. 260–78, recounts the history of the Union Square Theatre. Palmer wrote a biography of Charles R. Thorne, Jr., that is included in Frederic E. Makay and Charles Wingate, eds., *Famous American Actors of Today* (1896), pp. 221–30. See also Montrose J. Moses, *The American Dramatist* (1925); Lillian Hall, *Catalogue of Dramatic Portraits in the Theatre Collection of the Harvard College Library* (1931), p. 290; Lewis Strang, *Players & Plays of the Last Quarter Century* (1903); George C. D. Odell, *Annals of the New York Stage* (1927–1949); and Augustus Thomas, *The Print of My Remembrance* (1922). An obituary is in the *New York Times*, 8 Mar. 1905.

GLEN NICHOLS

PALMER, Alice Elvira Freeman (21 Feb. 1855–6 Dec. 1902), educator and college president, was born at Colesville, Broome County, New York, the daughter of James Warren Freeman and Elizabeth Josephine Higley, farmers. Both parents came from well-to-do families with interests in lumber, dairy farming, and land. Alice's father enrolled in medical school in 1861, completed the M.D. in 1864, and moved the family to Windsor, New York. Alice enrolled in Windsor Academy in 1865, graduating in 1872.

At Windsor, Alice met Thomas Barclay, a Yale theology student teaching part time to pay for his college expenses. Barclay encouraged her intellectual curiosity and served as her mentor. Over time, the two became close, and by 1869 they were engaged to be married. But by 1871 Alice had broken the engagement to pursue her dream of attending college.

In June 1872 Palmer and her father traveled to the University of Michigan to meet with President James Angell. He found the seventeen-year-old very bright and socially adept but unable to pass the examinations for full admission. Impressed by her determination and talent, Angell overrode his admissions committee and admitted her "on condition." Palmer studied hard over the summer in Windsor, and the next fall, after further tutoring in Ann Arbor, she was granted full admission.

A serious and hard-working student, Palmer was also charismatic and popular among students and faculty alike. She was often invited to various social and academic events, and, although Michigan had few women students, she was selected as one of four senior class speakers at her commencement in 1876. She had paid for her education by tutoring others and teaching school in the local area, suspending her enrollment in classes completely in her junior year to earn money as principal of a high school in Ottawa, Illinois, after a recommendation by Angell.

Palmer's first position after graduation was at Lake Geneva Seminary, a private secondary school in Wisconsin. She returned to Michigan for graduate work in history during the summer. She declined an offer to teach mathematics at Wellesley College and instead became principal at East Saginaw High School in Michigan in the fall of 1877. Her father declared bankruptcy in 1877 after losing the family funds in a mining investment. In response, Palmer moved her family to Saginaw and paid for a rented house from her principal's salary. In 1879 her younger sister Estelle became ill and died. The loss forced her to reconsider her own career aspirations, and in June of that year she finally accepted a third offer from Wellesley College, this time to teach history.

As a young faculty member, Palmer soon became a favorite of Wellesley students. Word of her dedication to her students and to the institution spread quickly within the Wellesley community. Soon she counted Henry and Pauline Durant, her employers and cofounders of the college, among her admirers as well. After Henry Durant's death in 1881, Pauline Durant offered Palmer the presidency, which she accepted.

Palmer served Wellesley in a manner that was both graceful and determined. Her vision of women's education differed from that of the Durants, and under her direction Wellesley slowly changed from a small school dedicated to the promotion of Christian domesticity to a respected academic institution for the education of women in science, education, and the arts. Palmer is generally credited with Wellesley's rapid rise to become one of the elite women's colleges.

At the time Palmer assumed the presidency of Wellesley in the 1880s, debate still raged over the education of women. Many leading academicians, including Charles Eliot at Harvard, seriously questioned the value and certainly the necessity of higher education for women. While the debate would continue for generations to come, Palmer attempted an academic conciliation at Wellesley. She valued the intellectual challenges she had found at Michigan and encouraged both faculty and students under her supervision to aspire to high levels of academic achievement. She hoped to create a combination of female values and virtue infused with higher learning; a combination some have referred to as a "cultural hybrid." Few women would compete with men for employment, even with college degrees, but Palmer believed in the ability of women to provide an important moral compass within their families and communities, shaping the world through their example. Wellesley women were educated to lead, not follow. Although women might not be bank presidents or heads of state, Palmer believed they could clearly lead and direct social causes and be a strong influence in their own homes, armed with keen intellects and the best scholarship available.

The dualism of maintaining a womanly character as well as appealing to the intellect was both a personal and professional challenge for Palmer throughout her life. To soften the academic rigor she extolled at Wellesley, she developed the "cottage system," building small, comfortable houses in which students and faculty could find opportunity to study, socialize, and even retreat from the challenges of the academic life. She eventually moved to a cottage and frequently participated in college activities, which endeared her to students and later created a personal mythology built on her benevolent and caring actions.

Palmer's administrative expertise may have been one of her greatest skills. She was able to delegate very little, in large part because of her personal importance to students, faculty, peers, and benefactors to the college. In a quiet way, she typically achieved every goal she set for herself at Wellesley. Unfortunately, the demands often threatened her health. Debilitated by chronic respiratory illnesses, including a near fatal bout with tuberculosis, Palmer often pushed herself to exhaustion in her dedication to running the college. But she drew strength from her successes. She managed to return to Michigan in the summer of 1882 to complete her Ph.D. in history.

Under Palmer's direction, the Wellesley board of trustees was reconstituted over time and assumed a greater responsibility for the college than they had been allowed under the Durants. New faculty were selected for their expertise and skill rather than their pious nature. Palmer instituted a policy of faculty review and granted tenure after three successful years on the Wellesley campus. Admissions standards were elevated, and the curriculum was expanded. As a charter member of the Association of Collegiate Alumnae (ACA) in 1882, Palmer saw great benefit in women collectively supporting the education of other women. She was very active in the ACA and encouraged the establishment of Wellesley Alumnae Clubs to support the college and to help recruit students.

In eight years, Palmer and Wellesley College became national leaders in women's education. True to her alma mater, she actively recruited other Michigan women to Wellesley as faculty. Angell had been instrumental in Palmer's early career, recommending her for her first three positions, and even claimed a key role in her Wellesley appointment. Palmer followed the same course, staying in close contact with Michigan and giving other women graduates her support. Beyond her Michigan connections, she helped many other women establish themselves in faculty and administrative roles in higher education during the late nineteenth century. As a pioneer in the advancement of women's higher education, Palmer was less forceful than some other women's rights figures and avoided calling attention to herself, preferring to let her work speak for itself. Her warm personality and subtle manner often belied her leadership skills, which were singular. She was extremely successful in orchestrating a variety of diverse opinions and drawing new benefactors to her causes.

Alice Freeman first met Harvard philosopher George Herbert Palmer at the home of Wellesley faculty member Eben Horsford in 1884, but their personal interests in each other grew after a dinner party at the home of Mary Claflin, a Wellesley trustee and wife of the former governor, in the summer of 1886. After an extended courtship, they were married in December 1887 at Claflin's Boston home.

At the insistence of her future husband, Palmer resigned as president of Wellesley in the fall of 1887 in anticipation of her marriage. However, she continued to serve as a national figure for women's education. A popular and gifted speaker, she was in constant demand. She worked hard to open Harvard to women but was unsuccessful. When Eliot agreed to a coordinate college, the Annex (later Radcliffe), Palmer helped to raise funds to support the new institution. No children were born to Alice and George Palmer. However, the couple later took in young Lucy Sprague, eventually a national figure in women's and elementary education herself, as a companion for Alice.

In the early 1890s William Rainey Harper, president of the new, coeducational University of Chicago, lobbied both Palmers to join his faculty. Backed by John D. Rockefeller's fortune, Harper sought a prestigious faculty, and he was determined to have a national figure in women's education oversee the female students. Although her husband refused to leave Cambridge for Chicago, Palmer saw the offer as both a duty and a challenge. She convinced her close friend and fellow charter member of the Association of Collegiate Alumnae, Marion Talbot, to join her. Palmer agreed to be dean of women and professor of history when Chicago opened in 1892 but only for twelve weeks a year. Talbot would be her assistant and remain on campus year long. The arrangement worked for three years. Together, the two women created a hospitable climate for women at Chicago, borrowing freely from the successes Palmer had introduced at Wellesley, including a variant of the cottage system.

Unable to maintain her professional and personal commitments in Chicago and Boston, Palmer resigned as dean in 1895 and returned to Boston. Nonetheless, she and Talbot had made their mark on the new university. Talbot remained as dean of women and professor in domestic sciences until her retirement in 1925.

In Boston, Palmer continued her leadership in women's education, giving speeches, consulting, and lending her name to various enterprises. The Palmers entertained many notable national and international figures. Twice they traveled to Europe. On the second trip, in 1902, Alice Palmer became ill with abdominal distress. Surgery revealed congenital problems. She grew weaker and finally died from complications in Paris, with her husband and Lucy Sprague in attendance. She was cremated, and her ashes were returned to the United States.

Palmer was eulogized in many memorial services after her death. Special tributes were held at the Universities of Chicago and Michigan, as well as Wellesley and in her adopted home of Boston. George Herbert Palmer published a biography as a celebration of her life in 1908 and in it noted, "At her death I received nearly two thousand letters from statesmen, schoolgirls, clerks, lawyers, teachers, country wives, outcasts, millionaires, ministers, men of letters—a heterogeneous and to me largely an unknown company, but alike in feeling the marvel of her personality and the loss her death had caused them. Few women of her time, I have come to think, were more widely loved" (Palmer, pp. 1–2). A significant figure in women's higher education, Palmer was one of the new generation of college-educated women who began to assume leadership roles in the late nineteenth and early twentieth centuries.

• Palmer's letters and papers are located in archival collections at Wellesley College and the University of Chicago, as well as intermingled with G. H. Palmer's papers at Harvard. Some of her addresses are available as printed documents. A collection of essays and poems on marriage was published posthumously by George Palmer as *A Marriage Cycle* (1915). Biographies of Palmer include George Herbert Palmer, *The Life of Alice Freeman Palmer* (1908), which was written after her death, while a later biography, Ruth Bordin, *Alice Freeman Palmer: The Evolution of a New Woman* (1993), presents a more objective and detailed perspective. Alice Fleming, *Alice Freeman Palmer: Pioneer College President* (1970), is also available. A rigorous and insightful view of Palmer and a few of her famous peers is found in Roberta Frankfort, *Collegiate Women: Domesticity and Career in Turn-of-the-Century America* (1977). Institutional histories of Wellesley and the University of Chicago mention her positions and contributions as do numerous books on women's colleges and women's education, including Helen Horowitz, *Alma Mater: Design and Experience in the Women's Colleges from Their Nineteenth Century Beginnings to the 1920s* (1984), and Patricia Palmieri, *In Adamless Eden* (1995).

ROBERT SCHWARTZ

PALMER, Alonzo Benjamin (6 Oct. 1815–23 Dec. 1887), physician, teacher, and author, was born in Richfield, Otsego County, New York, the son of Benjamin Palmer and Anna Layton, farmers. Although his father died when he was nine years old, Palmer obtained an adequate early education in Oswego, Otsego, and Herkimer. He studied medicine at the College of Physicians and Surgeons of the western district of New York at Fairfield, Herkimer County, from which he graduated in 1839.

Soon after graduation Palmer moved to Tecumseh, Michigan. During his twelve years there he built up a busy practice. In 1843 he married Caroline Augusta Wright, who died in 1846. Palmer found time to attend postgraduate studies during the winter of 1847–1848 in New York City, and the following winter in Philadelphia. In 1850 he relocated to Chicago, Illinois, where he became an associate of Nathan Davis in general practice. In 1852 Palmer was appointed city physician in Chicago and was thus in charge of the cholera hospital during the 1852 epidemic. The hospital treated about 1,500 cholera victims that year. Palmer's experience in this epidemic laid the groundwork for his paper "Observations on the Cause, Nature and Treatment of Epidemic Cholera" (1854), the first of his many contributions on the disease.

In 1852 Palmer was also appointed professor of anatomy at the Medical School of the University of Michigan, but owing to a lack of funding he never occupied the chair. Two years later he became professor of materia medica, therapeutics, and diseases of women and children. He moved to Ann Arbor, Michigan, to take up his academic duties. In 1860 he was reassigned to the chair of pathology and the theory and practice of medicine, a position he occupied until his death. He also served as the editor of the *Peninsular Journal of Medicine and the Collateral Sciences* and its successor, the *Peninsular and Independent Medical Journal*, from April 1853 to March 1860. In 1860 he became vice president of the American Medical Association.

During the Civil War, Palmer served briefly from April to September 1861 as surgeon in General Richardson's Brigade and in the Second Michigan Infantry. He was present during several engagements, including the first battle of Manassas. He resigned his commission after this brief service to resume his duties at the university.

An active instructor who enjoyed lecturing, Palmer was said to have prepared, in one year, 196 lectures, about half of which were new. He was well liked by his colleagues at the several institutions where he taught during the last two decades of his life. From 1864 to 1867 he was professor of pathology and practice of medicine in the Berkshire Medical Institution, Pittsfield, Massachusetts. From 1869 to 1879 he was professor of the practice of medicine at Bowdoin College, Maine. These positions did not interfere with his work at the University of Michigan because the classes in Michigan ended in March, and he was free thereafter to lecture at other institutions from April to June. Palmer married his second wife, Love M. Root of Pittsfield, in 1867.

Palmer was president of the Michigan State Medical Society in 1872. That same year, he became dean of the medical department at the University of Michigan, holding that position for all but one year until his death. He was also president of the United States Medical Society (1872 and 1873) and an honorary member of the New York and Maine Medical societies.

Palmer's prolific writings reflect his varied career. His principal work was the two-volume *Treatise on the Science and Practice of Medicine, and the Pathology and Treatment of Internal Diseases* (1882). This was preceded by *Lectures on the Sulphate of Quinine* (1858) and *Epidemic Cholera: Its Pathology and Treatment* (1866), and followed by *A Treatise on Epidemic Cholera and Allied Diseases* (1885) and *The Temperance Teachings of Science* (1886). The last, a general work on the effects of alcohol and narcotics on the body, demonstrated Palmer's advocacy of temperance; it was endorsed by the Woman's Christian Temperance Union and circulated widely. Apart from his more technical medical work, Palmer also wielded his pen against the practice of homeopathy, which he felt was a scandalous form of quackery; his works on that topic include *Four Lectures on Homeopathy* (1869) and *Homeopathy: What Is It?* (1881).

Palmer died in Ann Arbor from septicemia. He had no children by either wife.

Not a medical innovator, Palmer's contribution and significance lies in his influence on his students both through his writings and through his teaching. His contributions, especially to the study of cholera and his reaction to homeopathy, are of particular note. His textbook on temperance had international appeal and wide circulation.

• Much information on Palmer's life is in obituaries in contemporary medical journals, including *Medical Record*, Dec. 1887; *Journal of the American Medical Association*, 31 Dec. 1887; and *Physician and Surgeon*, June–Aug. 1888. A newspaper obituary is in the *Detroit Free Press*, 24 Dec. 1887. His wife, Love M. Root Palmer, wrote *Memorial of Alonzo Benjamin Palmer* (1890). Much of his writing appears in the *Transactions of the Michigan State Medical Society*, as well as in the volumes cited in the text.

DANIEL J. MALLECK

PALMER, A. Mitchell (4 May 1872–11 May 1936), attorney general and congressman, was born Alexander Mitchell Palmer in Luzerne County, Pennsylvania, the son of Samuel Bernard Palmer, a lumberyard owner and bridge builder, and Caroline Albert. A Quaker, Palmer attended Swarthmore College, graduating in 1891, first in his class and class president. In college he evidenced the prejudice against immigrants then common among white native-born Protestants. Certain judicial reforms, he declared, would "insure justice . . . to the lowest foreigner who comes to our free land as well as to the highborn American through whose veins course the blood of the Pilgrim fathers."

Palmer worked as an attorney in Stroudsburg, the county seat of Monroe County, Pennsylvania, where his family had long been active in Democratic politics. In 1898 he married Roberta Bartlett Dixon, daughter of the president of the Easton [Md.] National Bank; they had one child. Palmer was elected to Congress in 1908 by the largest majority the steel-, coal-, slate-, and wool-producing district ever had given a congressional candidate.

Palmer rose rapidly to leadership in the Pennsylvania Democratic party and in Congress. Progressive reformers in the state party engineered his election as Pennsylvania's Democratic National Committee member in 1912, defeating the incumbent, longtime party boss James Guffey. Palmer's high status in Pennsylvania—which would have more votes in the 1912 Democratic National Convention than any state but New York—gave him sudden eminence in Congress. Democratic congressional leaders already had decided to elevate Palmer in recognition of his eloquence as a speaker, his skill in political maneuvering, his complete party loyalty, and his affability, and they appointed him to the influential Ways and Means Committee.

Palmer served as Woodrow Wilson's floor leader at the 1912 Democratic National Convention. After Wilson's nomination and election and Palmer's reelection, the president-elect, unaware that Palmer was a Quaker, offered him a place in the cabinet as secretary of war. Palmer declined, declaring in a letter to Wilson, "As a [pacifist] Quaker War Secretary I should consider myself a living illustration of a horrible incongruity." Instead, Wilson used Palmer as his chief link to the House of Representatives. In June 1913 Wilson helped arrange Palmer's election as chairman of the powerful five-man Executive Committee of the Democratic National Committee.

Palmer introduced a series of progressive measures in Congress, the most far-reaching of which was a child labor bill. This measure prohibited interstate commerce in goods manufactured even in part by children under fourteen or in the products of mines or quarries that employed children under sixteen. Wilson's chief biographer, Arthur S. Link, stated, "The Palmer bill was the most momentous measure of the progressive era, for its adoption [by the House of Representatives] marked a turning point in American constitutional history—the use of the commerce power to justify almost any form of federal control over working." If Palmer's bill had become law and then been approved by the Supreme Court, virtually no limits would have existed to national regulation of economic activity. However, President Wilson opposed the bill as unconstitutional, and although it passed the House by a vote of 233 to 43 on 15 February 1915, Wilson's opposition helped defeat the measure in the Senate.

Palmer's voting record on labor issues was rated as perfect by the American Federation of Labor (AFL). He spoke in favor of a quarry inspection bill and helped initiate a federal investigation into labor conditions in the Bethlehem Steel Company, whose main plant was in his district. He also pleased most U.S. women by introducing woman suffrage legislation.

As a member of the Ways and Means Committee, Palmer helped write the Underwood Tariff Bill, which reduced rates in almost every classification. A schedule prepared by Palmer placed most forms of iron and steel and their products on the tariff-free list, an action which had profound repercussions on his political career in Pennsylvania, the largest producer of these products.

In 1914 Palmer planned to run for governor of Pennsylvania, a race in which the tariff would be a negligible factor. Instead, President Wilson persuaded him to serve as the Democratic candidate for the U.S. Senate seat held by Republican state boss Boies Penrose, one of the Senate's most reactionary members. Despite Penrose's reputation for bribery, graft, voting fraud, and immorality, Palmer lost by a large margin. Penrose received huge majorities in wards where workers predominated, because they agreed with him that low tariffs would lead to increased foreign competition and lost American jobs. Palmer's later opposition to organized labor as attorney general probably had as one of its sources this refusal of workers to vote for him despite his record as labor's friend.

Palmer returned to his private law practice, but within two years, at the urging of Democratic party leaders, Wilson appointed him to the office of alien property custodian, which administered enemy-owned property in the United States. Businesses under Palmer's control supplied the government with hundreds of products, including munitions, medicines, ships, ball bearings, medical and engineering instruments, and magnetos for airplane and automobile motors. Despite favoritism and fraud in the sale of German properties, Palmer was not held legally responsible for the illegal acts of his subordinates.

By the time Palmer took over the position of attorney general from Thomas W. Gregory, Americans were affected by a series of crises in 1919: runaway prices, nationwide strikes, revolutions throughout much of Europe, and signs of a serious threat from radicals at home. With President Wilson first preoccupied with the peace treaty then incapacitated by strokes, the attorney general, under whose jurisdiction the major domestic crises fell, was obliged to find solutions. Because the peace treaty had not yet been signed, Palmer decided that he could make use of extraordinary wartime powers.

To deal with soaring postwar prices, Palmer began legal proceedings against hoarders, especially of food and clothing. A majority of wartime state food administrators and county Fair Price Committee members responded to his call to resume their posts under the authority of the Justice Department. However, the attorney general had no control over most labor, commodity, or interest costs or over foreign producers, and prices continued to rise rapidly until the worldwide speculative bubble burst in the summer of 1920.

Palmer shocked organized labor by obtaining injunctions under the wartime Lever Act, which ended strikes by mine and railroad workers. AFL president Samuel Gompers denounced the November 1919 injunction that forced leaders of the United Mine Workers union to withdraw their strike order as "so autocratic as to stagger the human mind." Palmer paralyzed cabinet opposition to the injunctions by assuring members that his intelligence division, headed by J. Edgar Hoover, had collected proof that the strike was part of a worldwide communist conspiracy.

In August 1919 Palmer gave Hoover responsibility for interpreting the purposes and gauging the strength of U.S. radical organizations. By fall Hoover had reported that radicals posed a real threat to overthrow the U.S. government. Actually, Hoover had been unnecessarily frightened by reading radical literature. Little possibility existed that the virtually unarmed and disorganized American radical organizations could mount a serious uprising in 1919–1920.

The pressure on Palmer grew. In October 1919 the Senate passed a resolution demanding that Palmer inform the U.S. Senate if he had taken legal action against radicals, "and if not, why not." Palmer declared to Congress later, "I was shouted at from every editorial sanctum in America . . . ; I was preached upon from every pulpit; I was urged . . . throughout the country to do something and do it now." So the attorney general, who already was a candidate for president, agreed to his advisers' plans for the deportation of alien radicals. The Immigration Act of 1917 as amended in 1918 made any alien anarchist, no matter how pacific his or her beliefs, and anyone who belonged to an organization that advocated violence against the government deportable. The Labor Department, under whose jurisdiction enforcement of immigration laws fell, agreed to provide warrants for the arrest of alien anarchists and Communists.

The first of the mass roundups swept up members of the Union of Russian Workers, whose written manifesto advocated anarchy. However, the radical authors of that manifesto had returned to Russia, leaving behind an organization with almost wholly social and educational functions. In November 1919 members of the union throughout the country were arrested by Justice Department agents with assistance from local police. Most arrests were made without warrants. Witnesses reported beatings of those who protested, among them U.S. citizens and nonmembers attending inoffensive meetings in union halls. Some of those arrested spent up to four months in prison awaiting a deportation hearing.

Beginning 2 January 1919 well over 3,000 suspected members of the Communist and Communist Labor parties were arrested under the direction of the Justice Department. At least that many more suspects were taken into custody and held for periods of up to several months before they were released. Even Hoover, who was in charge of the matter, was unable later to estimate for a Senate investigating committee how many arrests were made without warrants, though that appears to have occurred in the majority of cases. These Palmer Raids constituted, at the time, perhaps the most widespread violations of civil liberties in U.S. history. Nevertheless, the former critics of Palmer's inactivity now applauded him.

In March 1920 Secretary of Labor William B. Wilson fell ill, and Assistant Secretary Louis F. Post became acting secretary. Post, though not a radical, was sympathetic with the plight of aliens held without good cause or due process. He released aliens held on evidence seized improperly and those belonging to groups whose leaders had transferred their memberships to the Communist party without their knowledge. He lowered bail for those with jobs and families, despite Hoover's protests. By April Post had decided 1,600 cases, canceling arrests in over 70 percent of them.

The House Committee on Rules, informed by Palmer about what was delaying deportations, began impeachment proceedings against Post but, after listening to the acting secretary, took no action. Meanwhile, some of America's most prominent attorneys, including Charles Evans Hughes; Harlan Fiske Stone; Roscoe Pound, dean of the Harvard Law School; Harvard law professors Felix Frankfurter and Zechariah Chafee, Jr.; and Ernst Freund of the University of Chicago Law School, spoke out against the Palmer Raids and signed a report criticizing them.

By mid-1920 public opinion had turned against Palmer, but the furious opposition to him from organized labor played an even larger role in defeating his otherwise strong campaign for the 1920 Democratic presidential nomination. He entered the convention a close second to Ohio governor James M. Cox in the number of pledged delegate votes. However, the leading Democratic politicians who originally had favored his nomination chose to withhold the votes at their command rather than risk losing labor support during the fall election campaign.

Palmer's first wife died in 1922. The following year he married Margaret Fallon Burrall, with whom he did not have any children.

At the request of his friend Franklin D. Roosevelt, Palmer wrote the original draft of the 1932 Democratic platform, with help from Cordell Hull. Roosevelt and Palmer then revised it, and with the exception of a few planks, the Democratic convention adopted their version. Palmer was working on the 1936 platform when he died in Washington, D.C. Most Americans associated Palmer with the "red scare" and labor injunctions. To those who had served Wilson, however, his name was linked to a period of glorious achievement.

• Palmer's personal letters were destroyed. Most of his official correspondence is in the papers of Woodrow Wilson, Princeton University Library; and the Alien Property Custodian Records and the Justice Department Records, both in the National Archives. His biography is Stanley Coben, *A. Mitchell Palmer: Politician* (1963; repr. 1972). See also Arthur S. Link, *Wilson: The New Freedom* (1956); Robert K. Murray, *Red Scare: A Study in National Hysteria, 1919–1920* (1955); and Richard Gid Powers, *Secrecy and Power: The Life of J. Edgar Hoover* (1987). An obituary is in the *New York Times*, 12 May 1936.

STANLEY COBEN

PALMER, Bartlett Joshua (10 Sept. 1882–27 May 1961), chiropractor, was born in What Cheer, Iowa, the son of Daniel David Palmer, the "Discoverer of Chiropractic," and Louvenia Landers. An indifferent student, he left school at an early age and spent a year traveling with an entertainer hypnotist as a professional "hypnotic subject." In 1902 he graduated as a doctor of chiropractic from his father's Palmer Infirmary and Chiropractic Institute in Davenport, Iowa, and became its secretary and "adjuster in chief" when his father fled west to avoid prosecution for practicing medicine illegally. Universally known as "B. J.," Palmer gained full control of the school in 1906 after his father was convicted and jailed by the Scott County court for practicing medicine without a license. Palmer had also been indicted for "publicly professing to heal and cure without having procured and filed a certificate of the Board of Medical Examiners," but court records show no formal disposition of his case. In 1904 he married Mabel Heath, who soon became a chiropractor and his invaluable helpmate in running his school; they had one son.

Much to his father's dismay, Palmer designated himself as the "Developer of Chiropractic," republished in 1910 their jointly authored 1906 *Science of Chiropractic*, with himself as sole author, and took chiropractic in a theoretical direction of which his father disapproved, one that made Palmer the spokesman until his death for "straight" (i.e., unmixed with medical or physiotherapeutic modalities) chiropractic. He graduated thousands of chiropractors from his Palmer School of Chiropractic and led the fight against organized medicine, which always opposed laws licensing chiropractors and instigated their arrest and suits against them when they practiced unlicensed medicine. In 1906 he organized the Universal Chiropractors Association to defend chiropractors charged in court; by 1916 membership had grown to more than 2,500. He traveled the country lecturing and testifying on behalf of chiropractic in courts and legislatures.

Palmer pioneered advertising chiropractic, once claiming that he had developed chiropractic with printer's ink. Author of hundreds of pamphlets and more than thirty books, including *Radio Salesmanship* (1942), he owned powerful radio stations in Davenport and Des Moines and what he called "the prettiest little print shop in America," which produced thousands of brochures for sale to practicing chiropractors. A persuasive and charismatic figure, his lecturing style captivated students, alumni, and the public. In an interview with the writer one of his 1912 graduates observed that "B. J. had the students so they could hardly wait to get into practice, to carry chiropractic to the world and to get sick people well. He filled us with enthusiasm and self-confidence. We knew that we had the power to do these things right in the palms of our hands. We were 'miracle men.' I wanted to be a pioneer, a leader, a martyr if necessary. I wanted to be B. J.'s representative in Boston." On the walls of the Palmer School were seventy-five plaques dedicated to the "Early Martyrs" of chiropractic who had been convicted and sent to jail. A medical critic, F. F. Farnsworth, after hearing him lecture described him thus: "as egotistic as a Chinese God and as ignorant as an African cannibal."

In 1924 Palmer stunned the profession by introducing a new diagnostic instrument, the neurocalometer (NCM), designed to detect spinal subluxations by measuring heat differentials on the skin between two sides of a vertebra. His insistence that it be used and that it be rented from his school at a high price split the profession and led to the decline of his influence. Palmer School enrollment fell from 2,300 in 1921 to fewer than 400 in 1927, and the school nearly went bankrupt.

A creator of controversy throughout his life, Palmer remained the leader of straight chiropractors, who objectified their solidarity in 1941 by organizing the International Chiropractors Association. Although he remained president of the Palmer School, he always left its day-to-day management to others. Until 1949 he opposed lengthening the curriculum at the Palmer School from three years of six months each to four

years of nine months each, and he continued to lecture and write on behalf of "pure, straight, and unadulterated" chiropractic. He died from a peptic ulcer, for which he characteristically refused medical treatment, in Sarasota, Florida, near his beloved Circus Hall of Fame, to which he had donated a very large circus bandwagon.

Without B. J. Palmer chiropractic might not have survived as a separate and distinct form of healing. Although his salesmanship infuriated medical authorities and his rigidly straight philosophy alienated many chiropractors, he succeeded in inspiring all chiropractors to struggle against what he defined as "medical oppression" and to seek favorable licensing legislation in all jurisdictions. This was finally achieved in 1974, when chiropractic also received federal authorization for its Council on Chiropractic Accreditation to accredit its colleges, and chiropractors began receiving fee reimbursements under Medicare. Modern chiropractic is very much his legacy.

• Palmer's papers are in the archives of the Palmer College Library in Davenport. For contemporary evaluations see Elbert Hubbard, *The New Science; or, The Fine Art of Getting Well and Keeping So* (1913), and F. F. Farnsworth, "B. J. Palmer, Chiropractor," *West Virginia Medical Journal* (Jan. 1921): 252–55. See also Russell Gibbons, "Assessing the Oracle at the Fountainhead: B. J. Palmer and His Times, 1902–1961," *Chiropractic History* 7, no. 1 (1987): 9–14; W. Heath Quigley, "Last Days of B. J. Palmer: Revolutionary Confronts Reality," *Chiropractic History* 9, no. 2 (1989): 11–19; and Walter I. Wardwell, *Chiropractic: History and Evolution of a New Profession* (1992).

WALTER I. WARDWELL

PALMER, Benjamin Morgan (25 Jan. 1818–28 May 1902), pastor and first moderator of the Presbyterian Church in the Confederate States of America, was born in Charleston, South Carolina, the son of the Reverend Edward Palmer, Presbyterian pastor, and Sarah Bunce. Palmer studied under the Reverend J. B. Van Dyke at the Waterloo Academy before traveling north to Amherst College in Massachusetts in 1832. At Amherst, he played chess with Henry Ward Beecher and befriended John Holmes Bocock and Stuart Robinson, who became influential Presbyterian ministers. Palmer stood first in his class but was expelled during the spring of his second year after refusing to reveal the secret proceedings of a student literary society. As he later confessed, "It was an uncanny time for Southern men to trim their sails for Northern seas" (quoted in Johnson, p. 48).

Palmer returned to South Carolina in 1834 and taught in McPhersonville and Mt. Pleasant before resuming his formal education. From 1837 to 1838 he studied at the University of Georgia, where he graduated with first honors. In 1839 he entered Columbia Theological Seminary in Columbia, South Carolina, where he frequently heard James Henry Thornwell preach at the nearby First Presbyterian Church. Palmer graduated in 1841, and in April the Presbytery of Charleston licensed him to preach. He preached three months at Anderson, South Carolina, before accepting a call to the First Presbyterian Church of Savannah, Georgia. In October 1841 he married Mary Augusta McConnell; they had six children. They set off for Savannah, and on 6 March 1842 the Presbytery of Georgia ordained Palmer. Less than fifteen months later, he left Savannah and returned to Columbia in 1843 to follow in Thornwell's footsteps as pastor of the First Presbyterian Church. In 1847 he joined mentor Thornwell and George Howe, his father-in-law, as founding editors of the *Southern Presbyterian Review*, intended as a southern counterpart to the *Princeton Review*. In 1852 Oglethorpe University awarded Palmer the doctor of divinity degree. The Columbia congregation thrived under Palmer and opened a new building in 1853. Palmer declined calls to pulpits in Charleston, Baltimore, Cincinnati (twice), and Philadelphia, and refused the chair of Hebrew at the Danville (Ky.) Theological Seminary. In 1853 he accepted a call to his alma mater, Columbia Theological Seminary.

At Columbia, Palmer served as provisional instructor in ecclesiastical history and polity in 1853, concurrent with his pastoral duties. In 1854 he was formally elected to the position, and he resigned his pastorate the following year. He still found time to preach, however, and traveled weekly to Orangeburg, South Carolina, throughout 1856. When Palmer toured the Southwest for a seminary fundraising tour, the First Presbyterian Church of New Orleans, Louisiana, heard him preach and persuaded him to serve as its pastor. He resigned his professorship and left for New Orleans in December 1856. Within a few months, his new congregation had erected a new building. He spent the rest of his life in New Orleans, declining subsequent calls to Princeton Theological Seminary, Southwestern Presbyterian University, and Columbia Theological Seminary.

Palmer rose to national prominence on the eve of the Civil War. In his 1860 Thanksgiving Day sermon, he abandoned his staunch support of Thornwell's doctrine of the "spirituality of the church" and its consequent aversion to political issues such as slavery. He declared the South's "providential trust" to "conserve and to perpetuate the institution of domestic slavery," based upon its duty to itself, to its slaves, to the civilized world, and to God. Because Lincoln's election had betrayed the national trust, Palmer declared, "I throw off the yoke of this union as readily as did our ancestors the yoke of King George III." His sermon was frequently reprinted and widely circulated throughout the South.

After the onset of the Civil War, southern Presbyterians convened to establish the Presbyterian Church in the Confederate States of America. When the first general assembly convened on 4 December 1861 in the First Presbyterian Church of Augusta, Georgia, Palmer preached the opening sermon and was unanimously elected moderator. He served as a chaplain to the Confederate army and, when Thornwell died, briefly assumed his chair of systematic theology at Co-

lumbia (1862–1863). Palmer's books and personal belongings were burned during Sherman's march.

Palmer returned to New Orleans in 1865 and resumed his pastoral duties. He founded the weekly *Southwestern Presbyterian* with Dr. Henry Martin Smith and Dr. Thomas R. Markham in 1868. He helped establish Southwestern Presbyterian University and served as a director from its founding until his death. He resisted reunion with the northern Presbyterian church and fought for the ouster of the theistic evolutionist professor James Woodrow from Columbia Theological Seminary. He advocated strict sabbath observance in Louisiana, sought relief of persecuted Russian Jews, and led the fight against the state lottery.

In 1888 Palmer's wife died. In early May 1902 he was struck by a street car and died shortly thereafter in New Orleans. Several prominent Protestant, Catholic, and Jewish civic leaders spoke glowingly of Palmer at his memorial service.

• Palmer's papers are in the Presbyterian Church (U.S.A.) Archives at Montreat (N.C.), Duke University, the University of South Carolina, the Historical Society of Pennsylvania, Louisiana State University, and Austin Presbyterian Theological Seminary. Palmer's six books include *The Life and Letters of James Henley Thornwell, D.D., LL.D.* (1875) and *The Broken Home; or, Lessons in Sorrow* (1890), a personal testimony to his grief at the early death of four of his children and his wife. Many of his sermons were printed verbatim or summarized in daily papers; several were compiled and published. He wrote extensively for the *Southwest Presbyterian Review*, the *Southwestern Presbyterian*, and the *Presbyterian Quarterly*. His publications are listed in Harold B. Prince, *A Presbyterian Bibliography: The Published Writings of Ministers Who Served in the Presbyterian Church in the United States during Its First One Hundred Years 1861–1961, and Their Locations in Eight Significant Theological Collections in the U.S.A.* (c. 1983). Palmer's principal biography is T. C. Johnson, *The Life and Letters of Benjamin Morgan Palmer* (1906). Other studies include Richard T. Hughes, "A Civic Theology for the South: The Case of Benjamin M. Palmer," *Journal of Church and State* (Autumn 1983): 447–67, and Doralyn J. Hickey, "Benjamin Morgan Palmer: Churchman of the Old South" (Ph.D. diss., Duke Univ., 1962). Obituaries are in the *New Orleans Daily Picayune*, 29 May 1902, and the *Presbyterian Quarterly* 16, no. 1 (July 1902): 77–92.

DAVID B. MCCARTHY

PALMER, Bertha Honoré (22 May 1849–5 May 1918), Chicago society leader and reformer, was born in Louisville, Kentucky, the daughter of Henry Hamilton Honoré, a hardware and cutlery importer, and Eliza Jane Carr. Following Bertha's sixth birthday the family arrived in Chicago, where her father became a real estate developer and helped to expand the town on Lake Michigan into a bustling city. Religiously affiliated with the Disciples of Christ church in her early years, she later became an Episcopalian.

Educated at St. Xavier's Academy and Dearborn Seminary in Chicago, Bertha graduated in 1867 from the Visitation Convent School in Georgetown, D.C., one of six students to receive highest honors. Her intense curriculum included studies in ancient and modern geography, chemistry, meteorology, botany, and philosophy. She had an interest in politics, and when the Civil War broke out she joined in patriotic duty by helping her family work for the Sanitary Fairs of 1863 and 1865.

She debuted in Chicago society and attended rounds of concerts, parties, and picnics. Musically inclined, she played the harp and continued to read and study. Men considered her "clever," but the man who won her heart was Potter Palmer, a Quaker and a wealthy man twenty-three years her senior. They married in 1870. Known as the "first merchant prince of Chicago," Potter Palmer moved to the city from upstate New York in 1852 and had garnered his wealth in dry goods, real estate, and cotton trading. Upon marriage the couple moved into the recently built Palmer House, which burned to the ground during the Great Chicago Fire of 1871. Also destroyed in the fire were the Grand Pacific Hotel, the Sherman House, and Crosby's Opera House, all owned by the Palmers. Undaunted, the couple began rebuilding their fortunes and started a family. They had two sons.

As she rose to social prominence in the city, Bertha Palmer opened the doors of her home to celebrities and statesmen as well as factory girls and millinery workers. One of her goals was to elevate the city with artistic and cultural refinements, and she became one of the instigators in Chicago's "upward movement." At the Fortnightly, Bertha discussed intellectual and artistic topics with other club members. With her husband, she joined the Contributors' Club, an association consisting of writers and patrons that had its own magazine for members' literary productions. The Palmers also aided the artistic side of the city with contributions to the Chicago Academy of Design. Her interest in art led to her association with painter Mary Cassatt, who advised her to begin buying French Impressionist art of Degas, Renoir, and Monet, which she did in the late 1880s. Palmer willed many of these paintings to the Chicago Art Institute upon her death.

Interested in philanthropy and reform, Palmer sponsored the annual charity ball and joined the Chicago Woman's Club, where she encouraged other members to participate in rejuvenating the city. Always a visible figure, she arrived at Jane Addams's Hull-House in furs and feathers to attend meetings. A supporter of unions, she often held meetings of the Women's Trade Union League in her home and helped in the successful organizing of Chicago millinery workers. Between 1892 and 1896 she pursued the increasing opportunities for women's education as a trustee of coeducation at Northwestern University. Although not completely against woman suffrage, she detested the militancy of the movement.

Palmer's talents at organization were evidenced during the 1893 World's Columbian Exposition held in Chicago. In her role as chairman of the Board of Lady Managers of the World's Columbian Exposition, she laid out plans for a Woman's Building, which she intended to be an exclusively female project so as to elevate the status of women. Palmer oversaw the operations and commissioned a woman architect to design the building. Mary Cassatt painted murals along with other female muralists. Other interior motifs were completed by women sculptors, painters, wood carvers, and decorators. Also in evidence were many labor-saving inventions, such as the first gas range, to help in domestic duties.

In her dedication speech of the Woman's Building, Palmer protested against the treatment of women that kept them inadequately educated, poorly paid, and in forced dependence. After the exposition Palmer took the cause of women workers much more seriously, expanding her views to worldwide problems and sometimes demonstrating a sympathetic view toward socialism.

Following the world's fair, Palmer accepted a position for a short term as vice president of the Chicago Civic Federation (later the National Civic Federation), which organized to clean up Chicago's vice-ridden areas and do away with corruption. In 1900 President William McKinley appointed her to represent the United States as the only woman on the board of commissioners to the Paris Exposition. A staunch Democrat, Palmer campaigned for her son Honoré Palmer in his successful bid for city alderman in both the 1901 and 1903 elections.

After the death of her husband in 1902, Palmer traveled, spending most of her time in London and Paris until she bought property in Florida. She moved to Osprey near Sarasota in 1910. Until her death in Osprey she pursued an active life of overseeing the farming, growing citrus fruits, and breeding cattle on her ranch, which she called "The Oaks." By the time of her death she had doubled the fortune her husband had left her. Once called the "nation's hostess" and an unofficial goodwill ambassador for the United States, Bertha Honoré Palmer's wealth enabled her to help those less fortunate than she.

• Bertha Palmer's papers are located at the Chicago Historical Society and the Sarasota County, Fla., Historical Commission. A biography of her was written by Ishbel Ross, *Silhouette in Diamonds: The Life of Mrs. Potter Palmer* (1960). World's Columbian Exposition materials on Palmer are in *Addresses and Reports of Mrs. Potter Palmer* (1894). Other information is in Dixon Wecter, *The Saga of American Society* (1937); Bernard Duffey, *The Chicago Renaissance in American Letters* (1954); Bessie L. Pierce, *A History of Chicago*, vol. 3 (1957); Hugh D. Duncan, *Culture and Democracy* (1965); David Lowe, *Lost Chicago* (1975); Emmett Dedmon, *Fabulous Chicago* (1981); June Skinner Sawyers, *Chicago Portraits* (1991); and Donald L. Miller, *City of the Century: The Epic of Chicago and the Making of America* (1996).

MARILYN ELIZABETH PERRY

PALMER, Daniel David (7 Mar. 1845–20 Oct. 1913), founder of chiropractic, was born in a log cabin on the shore of Lake Scugog, about thirty miles west of Toronto, Canada, the son of Thomas Palmer, a rural Ontario teacher and postmaster, and Catherine McVay. Growing up on the harsh Ontario frontier when Upper

Canada was still a crown colony of the British Empire, Palmer had few opportunities for advancement. He wrote that "I was cradled in a piece of hemlock bark" by his German-English father. In 1865, while the Civil War was still raging in the United States, Daniel and his older brother Thomas left home to seek employment in one of the port cities of the Great Lakes. According to Thomas Palmer's autobiography, they walked for thirty days before reaching Buffalo "with their meager belongings packed in a carpet bag and two dollars borrowed from friends."

After securing passage to Detroit and eventually Chicago, the brothers split, Thomas traveling first to Iowa and then to the Indian Territory, where eventually he became editor and publisher of the *Oklahoma Guardian*, the territory's most popular newspaper. In 1866 Daniel settled in New Boston, Illinois, where he farmed and became an apiarist. According to his grandson, David Palmer, "Soon he was one of the largest bee-keepers in the United States and yearly sent large shippings of honey to New York City." Daniel Palmer married Abba Lord in 1871 in New Boston. She died in childbirth the next year.

In 1874 Palmer married Louvenia Landers McGee, who he wrote was "a New Orleans gentlewoman and a widow of a Confederate officer who had left her war-torn and confiscated Louisiana plantation." From this union, in their new home near What Cheer, Iowa, were born three children. Three years later, Louvenia Palmer died. For several years, Palmer owned a mercantile store in What Cheer before moving to Burlington and later to Davenport, where about 1885 he "established an office to practice natural magnetic healing on the fourth floor of the Ryan Building." Palmer married Martha Henning in 1885, which may have ended in divorce. Palmer married again in 1888 to Villa Thomas. She died in 1905, and Palmer then married Mary Hudler later the same year. There were no children from these marriages.

For the next decade, Palmer embarked on a personal quest into the then undefined borders of medicine, the biological sciences, and health. The era of frontier medicine was disappearing, but alternative schools were still popular, with eclectic and homeopathic institutes and hospitals more numerous than those of the "regular" schools in the Midwest. Palmer, by his own account, studied under Paul Caster, who was teaching the magnetic healing concepts advanced by the German physician Friedrich Anton Mesmer, a pioneer in hypnosis.

Magnetic healing was a popular hands-on form of therapeutics, usually employed by nonmedical practitioners. Eclectic physicians were a botanical-based medical sect that was popular after the Civil War, while homeopathy, a German dissent to regular medicine, was based on the theory that disease is cured by remedies that produce in healthy individuals symptoms that resemble those of the sick. Palmer eventually rejected all these alternative teachings when he evolved his concept of spinal adjustment.

Although advertisements placed by Palmer in local directories between 1887 and 1891 announced that he "Cures with His Magnetic Hands," it is probable that he offered a primary health service to his patients. One chiropractic historian, A. August Dye, wrote that turn-of-the-century druggists in Davenport recalled Palmer writing prescriptions, and an early associate reported that he also attended "accouchements" (obstetrics).

The burning controversy of early chiropractic—the allegation that Palmer had "stolen" its concepts from Andrew Taylor Still's osteopathy—may never be resolved to the satisfaction of historians. Secondary accounts by the son-in-law of Still and by Palmer's son Bartlett Joshua "B. J." Palmer offer contradictory views as to Palmer's being in Kirksville, Missouri, the seat of osteopathy, prior to 1895. Both founders apparently had met at a Clinton, Iowa, Spiritualist camp prior to 1906, but the proximity of Davenport and Kirksville—a day's journey down the Mississippi and overland—suggests that Palmer also explored this new reform school of healing as well. Indeed, some of the terms familiar to early osteopathy emerged in Palmer broadsides.

In any event, Palmer dates the first adjustment to 18 September 1895 in his Ryan Building offices, administered to a black janitor Harvey Lillard, and later refined to an "art, science and philosophy" that was named "chiropractic" by one of his early patients, Samuel H. Weed, a Greek scholar and clergyman.

Involved in a near-fatal railroad accident in 1897 at Fulton, Missouri, Palmer wrote that "I then determined to teach the science and art as fast as it was unfolded." The first school, known as the Chiropractic School and Cure, began in converted classrooms on the fourth floor of the Ryan Building, and the first two graduates (1898) were physicians—Andrew P. Davis and William A. Seeley. In time it became the Palmer Institute and Chiropractic Infirmary, where inpatients were housed, but with few students, an improbable future, and little more than an idea to sustain it. There were fifteen graduates by 1902, including his son B. J.

Palmer began what amounted to a decade-long wandering in 1902, leaving the school in the care of B. J. because of threatened prosecutions by both creditors and a now-disgruntled medical community who saw his institution as a cause for concern. The itinerant went to the West Coast, first to Portland, Oregon, where he began the Portland College of Chiropractic, then to California, where he conducted classes and clinics at Santa Barbara.

The schools were unsuccessful, and he returned to Davenport, where he was arrested, tried, and convicted by a Scott County, Iowa, court for practicing medicine without a license—the first of many such prosecutions that would embrace three generations of chiropractors. Difficulties over the management of the school were resolved by his son, who had shown a greater administrative talent, through an agreement that transferred whole ownership to B. J. in 1906. The transfer resulted in a bitter split between father and son, which would last until the senior Palmer's death. B. J. Palmer incorporated the Palmer School of Chiropractic the same year. The senior Palmer again left Davenport after serving twenty-three days in jail, taking part of his osteological collection, his library, and a cash settlement.

Palmer settled in Oklahoma, then in Indian Territory, and following a brief mercantile career joined with Alva A. Gregory, a physician who had obtained a chiropractic degree from the Carver College of Oklahoma City, an institution launched by Palmer's one-time attorney Willard Carver. Their venture, the Palmer-Gregory College of Chiropractic, was also of short duration. Palmer went to Oregon, where he opened another college. Again, Palmer's disposition was not toward partnerships, and he resumed his own institution, the D. D. Palmer School of Chiropractic, which also failed. Soon he retired to private practice and a voluminous correspondence with his followers, detractors, colleagues, and friends.

It was during this 1908–1910 period that Palmer prepared his notes, diaries, correspondence, and unpublished papers and combined them with a new text for the 1,000-page tome that would be known both as *The Chiropractor's Adjuster* and the *Science, Art and Philosophy of Chiropractic*, published in Portland in 1910. Historian Chittenden Turner said that the book "flayed allopathy in particular, denounced the use of drugs and discussed the cure of almost every disease from abasia to zymosis." In 1914 Palmer's widow published his last book as *The Chiropractor*.

On occasion, Palmer would journey to Los Angeles and Davenport and be in residence as a visiting professor ("Old Dad Chiro," as he preferred it) at the Ratledge College, the Davenport School of Chiropractic, and the Universal Chiropractic College in Davenport—the latter two affiliations causing still greater enmity between father and son.

Palmer's journeys took him throughout California and the Midwest. In 1912 Frank Elliott, a pioneer graduate of the Palmer School who later became a radio executive, found him practicing on South Grand Avenue in Los Angeles and became a family intermediary between father and son, resulting in Palmer's return to Davenport in the summer of 1913. After a brief reconciliation, the senior Palmer left B. J.'s residence and took rooms near the Universal College a short distance away, where he also gave lectures.

The accident that occurred during the school homecoming and Lyceum parade that August, in which Palmer was struck by an automobile erroneously said to have been driven by his son, gave rise to persistent rumors of patricide, largely inspired by B. J.'s own enemies and rivals. Three coroner's juries were unable to return bills of particulars against B. J., and a regular physician who attended the elder Palmer at his death in Los Angeles two months after the accident testified that the cause of his death—typhoid fever—was unrelated to injuries suffered in Davenport. Palmer's ashes resided in a huge bust along with that of his son on the campus of the Palmer College in Davenport for many decades before being moved to a family plot.

The world's first chiropractor was somewhat of an enigma, with his public life in healing spanning fifteen years at the end of the nineteenth century and just more than the first decade of the twentieth century. Palmer's followers considered him the classic innovative thinker whose concepts were rejected by mainstream science and medicine, suffering ostracism and even imprisonment for his beliefs. His critics—which included most of the medical community—dismissed him as little better than a pretender and a quack, purporting that his theory of the adjustment of the spine was a panacea for the ills of the human body.

Palmer's absence of formal training in medicine and the basic sciences have not deterred all who have studied him. In 1985 a French historian of medicine, Pierre Louis Gaucher-Perslherbe, wrote that "Palmer was a splendid self-taught anatomist and physiologist . . . who did not use a single word that might be unfamiliar, defining it in precise detail."

• Palmer's early correspondence, papers, journals, and manuscripts are in the B. J. Palmer Special Collections at the David D. Palmer Health Sciences Library, Davenport, Iowa. More information on Palmer and the history of chiropractic can be found in August Dye, *The Evolution of Chiropractic* (1939); Pierre Louis Gaucher-Perslherbe, *La Chiropratique: Contribution à l'histoire d'une discipline marginalisée* (1987), and *Chiropractic: Early Concepts in Their Historical Setting* (1994); Russell W. Gibbons, "Evolution of Chiropractic: Medical and Social Protest in America," in *Modern Developments in the Principles and Practice of Chiropractic*, ed. Scott Haldemann (1979); Verne Gielow, *Old Dad Chiro: A Biography of D. D. Palmer* (1981); Dennis Peterson and Glenda Wiese, *Chiropractic: An Illustrated History* (1995); Chittenden Turner, *The Rise of Chiropractic* (1931); and Walter Wardwell, *Chiropractic: The History and Evolution of a Profession* (1982). An obituary is in the *Los Angeles Times*, 21 Oct. 1913.

RUSSELL W. GIBBONS

PALMER, Erastus Dow (2 Apr. 1817–9 Mar. 1904), sculptor, was born in Pompey, Onondaga County, New York, the son of Erastus Palmer, a carpenter, and Laurinda Ball. When Palmer was nine years old, his family moved to Utica, New York, where he learned the rudiments of carpentry from his father. By 1834 he was ready to pursue his own career, and that year he moved to Dunkirk, New York, to establish his trade as a woodcarver and joiner. Among the projects in which he was involved were the design and carving of a circular staircase for a rural church near Dunkirk and a decorative wooden frieze for his own house. In 1839 he married a local woman, Matilda Alton, but she soon died from complications in childbirth; the baby, named Edward Alonzo, died soon thereafter. In 1840 Palmer returned to Utica.

Palmer continued to practice the carpenter's trade for several years, but 1846 marked a turning point. A neighbor showed him a cameo portrait that evidently had been brought back from Europe. The delicacy of the carving impressed Palmer, and he determined to try his own hand at the art. His first work in this medium was a portrait of his second wife, Mary Jane Seaman, whom he had married in 1843, and with whom he eventually had three children. Palmer showed the cameo to a friend, who in turn showed it to the lawyer Thomas R. Walker. Walker praised it, and in gratitude, Palmer executed a portrait of Walker. His career as a sculptor thus began.

Walker persuaded Palmer that, having so quickly mastered the art of cameo cutting, he should turn to large-scale sculpture. To that end, Walker financed a trip to New York City in September 1846; there Palmer purchased materials and tools for modeling. He carried letters of introduction from Walker that allowed him to meet the sculptor and marble carver Robert Launitz and the painter and president of the National Academy of Design, Samuel F. B. Morse. In 1847 Walker introduced Palmer to Edward Salisbury, an educator and art patron of New Haven, Connecticut, who showed Palmer his personal art collection, which included several examples of contemporary American neoclassic sculpture. That same year Palmer worked for a time in Albany, and he returned briefly to New York City in 1848.

During the late 1840s the influence of neoclassicism, the dominant aesthetic in American and European sculpture at the time, became apparent in Palmer's work. In 1848 he created his first ideal subject, *Virginia* (private collection, Wayzata, Minn.), a shell cameo with its subject taken from *Paul et Virginie*, a popular novel by Bernardin de Saint-Pierre; and the following year he carved his first full-length figure, *Mariner's Wife* (Albany Institute), a relief sculpture of a partially nude female figure seated in a landscape. His reliefs became more three-dimensional when he created *Flora* (1849, unlocated), a sculpture in very high relief. This work has been seen as a transitional one in Palmer's oeuvre, for shortly after carving *Flora*, he began producing sculptures in the round. This shift was probably made not due to the sculptor's deteriorating eyesight, as has been traditionally thought, but because he knew that it was the larger works that would bring him notice and possibly fame.

In 1849 Palmer moved to Albany, probably in search of attention that he hoped would come in the form of patronage, both public and private. Shortly thereafter he modeled the first work to bring him public notice, a bust of his daughter, which he called *Infant Ceres* (private collection, Santa Barbara, Calif.). The procedure Palmer utilized here became typical of his work: he often carved an image of someone he knew in a fairly realistic manner and then gave the sculpture an allegorical or classical title. One of Palmer's biographers has called this method a "curious joining of classical tradition and the artist's own immediate American life" (Webster, p. 22).

Palmer achieved artistic maturity during the 1850s. In 1852 he built a studio near the State Capitol in Albany and began to employ studio assistants. Several of them worked for him for a number of years, and under Palmer's influence and with his generous support became professional sculptors in their own right. One was Launt Thompson, who not only assisted Palmer but also became such a close friend to the family that Palmer named one of his children, in part, after Thompson: Walter Launt Palmer, who also became an artist, specialized first in portraiture and later in landscape painting. With the help of his assistants, Palmer was able to accept more commissions, many of which were for portrait busts.

Like that of most of his contemporaries, notably Hiram Powers, Palmer's style was closest to the idealization of the ancient Greeks when he created literary and allegorical works, but it was closer to the realism of the ancient Romans when he executed portraits. This is seen in his early cameos and relief portraits but especially in his busts, such as that of Erastus Corning (1854–1855, Albany Institute); another fine example is his bust of Commodore Matthew Perry (1859, Naval Historical Display Center, Washington Naval Yard, Wash.), wherein he also shows his expertise at using drapery for both formal and symbolic purposes.

During the 1850s Palmer's studio became the center of artistic activity in Albany, a sort of salon where younger artists could observe the working life of a successful, professional artist, and where they could exchange ideas about art. Among those who frequented the studio during this decade were the sculptors Thompson, Richard Henry Parks, Jonathan Scott Hartley, and Charles Calverley; and the painters George Henry Boughton, Homer Dodge Martin, and Will Hickok Low. Palmer could count among his close friends other contemporary artists such as the painters James M. Hart and his brother William Hart, Jervis McEntee, John Frederick Kensett, Charles Loring Elliott, and especially Frederic Edwin Church, with whom Palmer's son Walter began studying in 1870.

During the 1850s, too, Palmer sought a wider audience. He sent works to public exhibitions such as the prestigious annual exhibitions at New York's National Academy of Design, an organization to which Palmer had been elected an honorary member in 1849. In 1853 he sculpted his first full-length free-standing figure, *Indian Girl*, or *The Dawn of Christianity* (Metropolitan Museum of Art), commissioned by the wealthy New York politician and art collector Hamilton Fish. With the example of Hiram Powers's immensely popular *The Greek Slave* in mind, Palmer used a nude model as his starting point, idealized the figure, and gave the statue an obvious didactic moral: the marble depicts a beautiful young American Indian who gazes in wonder and awe at a small Christian cross that she has evidently found in the wilderness.

The positive public reaction to the *Indian Girl* encouraged Palmer to accept the invitation of a group of New Yorkers, which included Hamilton Fish, the artist Asher B. Durand, and the author William Cullen Bryant, to mount a one-man show in that city. The exhibition opened in October 1856 in a building owned by the Church of the Divine Unity, located on Broadway at the center of the New York art world. The *Indian Girl* was displayed in the center of the main gallery, where it was accompanied by eleven of Palmer's other marbles, including reliefs, busts, and medallions.

The exhibition was a tremendous critical and popular success and led to several major commissions for Palmer. The most important of these came from Fish and resulted in Palmer's best-known work, *The White Captive* (1857–1859, Metropolitan Museum of Art), also probably inspired by *The Greek Slave*. Palmer's *Captive* was shown at William Schaus's commercial gallery in New York and became, with Frederic Church's painting *Heart of the Andes*, one of the most popular works of the 1859–1860 season. Three thousand people saw Palmer's marble sculpture in the first two weeks of its exhibition, and it received much attention in the press. Palmer was at the peak of his career.

Unfortunately, that peak coincided with the Civil War. While the war itself inspired one of Palmer's most beautiful and classicizing relief sculptures (*Peace in Bondage*, 1863, Peabody Institute, Baltimore), patronage for his works declined during and after the national calamity. He created only two works between 1867 and 1872, one of which, *Angel of the Sepulchre*, was commissioned by Robert L. Banks for his family lot in the Albany Rural Cemetery.

To this point in his career Palmer had used marble almost exclusively for his sculptures. But in 1873, when the State of New York commissioned him to execute a full-length statue of the statesman Robert R. Livingston, he developed a new interest in bronze. In planning for the Livingston statue, which he and his patrons decided should be cast in the more durable material, Palmer made a long-delayed trip to Europe; it was, in fact, his first visit. He sailed from New York in April 1873; visited England, Belgium, Germany, and Italy; and was in Paris early the following year. There he rented a studio in which to model the figure of Livingston. The finished product was cast at the Barbedienne foundry and shipped to America in 1874. Palmer produced two bronze casts, one of which was presented by New York to the U.S. Capitol in Washington for display in Statuary Hall; the other was placed in the New York State Court of Appeals in Albany. A version in plaster is owned by the Albany Institute of History and Art. Palmer returned to America that same year, and he returned to Europe only one more time briefly in 1886, when he visited one of his daughters, who was then living in England.

By that time, though, Palmer was nearly seventy years old. The neoclassic style in which he had worked most of his life had long since gone out of fashion on both sides of the Atlantic and been replaced with a style influenced by the achievements of contemporary French sculptors rather than those of the artists of ancient Greece and Rome and of the Renaissance. Classicizing idealization was replaced by a more active realism, marble was supplemented by bronze, and Palmer and his contemporaries were superseded by a new generation of sculptors who included Augustus Saint-Gaudens and Daniel Chester French. Because of these changes in taste, Palmer's own art and style had little

lasting effect on American sculptors who came after him. He died in Albany.

Nevertheless, it should not be thought that Palmer left no artistic legacy. He was a member of the second generation of professional American sculptors who, following the lead of Horatio Greenough, Hiram Powers, and Thomas Crawford, created works, mostly in marble, with allegorical, mythological, and literary subjects in the style of neoclassicism. During his lifetime much was made of the fact that, unlike most American sculptors of his generation, Palmer did not go to Europe to study and work. This, it was thought, allowed his style to develop in a peculiarly American manner; staying at home left his art pure and uncorrupted by undue European influence. Whatever might be thought of that, it cannot be denied that Palmer's presence in the United States, and especially in a city other than a major metropolis such as Boston, New York, or Philadelphia, had a healthy impact on an important segment of the next generation of American artists—artists who came of age after the Civil War, and who helped take American art through the end of the nineteenth century and to the brink of modernism.

• Correspondence from and to Palmer, as well as other related papers, can be found at the Albany Institute of History and Art, Albany, N.Y.; the Wells College Library, Aurora, N.Y.; the Archives of American Art, Smithsonian Institution; and the New York Public Library, New York City. Of any public repository of art, the Albany Institute has the largest collection of Palmer's sculptures. J. Carson Webster, *Erastus D. Palmer* (1983), includes a catalogue raisonné of the artist's work and an extensive bibliography, and reproduces all known letters written by Palmer. Webster also reprinted Palmer's writings on art, including the most complete expression of the sculptor's art theory, originally published as "Philosophy of the Ideal," in *Crayon* 3 (Jan. 1856): 18–20. An interview with Walter Launt Palmer, which includes useful information about the sculptor's early life, Albany studio, and travels, is in the DeWitt Lockman Papers at the New-York Historical Society and on microfilm at the Archives of American Art, Washington, D.C. Among the better contemporary accounts of Palmer is Henry T. Tuckerman, "The Sculptor of Albany," *Putnam's Magazine* 7 (Apr. 1856): 394–400, which was revised for Tuckerman's *Book of the Artists* (1867), pp. 355–69; and an interesting section on Palmer and his influence on younger artists can be found in Will H. Low, *A Painter's Progress* (1910), pp. 32–40. The best-known painted portrait of Palmer is Tompkins H. Matteson's *The Studio of Erastus Dow Palmer, Albany, N.Y.* (1857; Albany Institute), which shows the artist working on a bust with a number of other works and two studio assistants nearby. An early daguerreotype (1842) and a later photograph (1860) of him are reproduced in Webster's monograph; the National Portrait Gallery, Washington, owns a photograph of Palmer by Mathew Brady.

DAVID B. DEARINGER

PALMER, George Herbert (19 Mar. 1842–7 May 1933), philosopher and teacher, was born in Boston, Massachusetts, the son of Julius A. Palmer, a businessman, and Lucy Manning Peabody. Palmer grew up in a household that was modest economically but richly endowed in the religious traditions of the Puritans and Congregationalists. In spite of ill health, he entered Phillips Academy, Andover. Two years later, eye problems interrupted his studies. When medical treatment failed, Palmer, at age fifteen, took a recommended sea voyage to Egypt with his older brother. The trip did not improve his sight, and assuming his education to be finished, Palmer on his return took a position in a dry goods store.

After further medical treatment, Palmer studied with a tutor for a year and, as he recalled, "crawled" into Harvard in 1860. Unimpressed with the rigid curriculum and poor teaching, Palmer spent his Harvard years reading widely in poetry, philosophy, and history with like-minded peers. He encountered the philosophy of John Stuart Mill, which became the first major influence on his own thought. Upon graduating in 1864, Palmer taught high school for a year in Salem, Massachusetts. In 1865 he began advanced studies in philosophy at Andover Theological Seminary, where he would receive the B.D. in 1870. From 1867 to 1869 Palmer studied in Germany at the University of Tübingen with Christian Sigwart. Frequent ill health interrupted his studies, and he returned home without a German Ph.D.

In 1870 Palmer began his long tenure at Harvard when Charles W. Eliot appointed him tutor in Greek, despite Palmer's knowing little of the language. Two years later, following a resignation, Eliot appointed him instructor in philosophy. Palmer supplemented his income by taking private students and serving as curator of the Gray Collection of Engravings. He was promoted to assistant professor in 1873, professor in 1883, and Alford Professor in 1889. He retired in 1913 but served Harvard as an overseer until 1919. He remained a familiar figure on campus, living in Harvard Yard until his death.

Palmer was married twice. He was acquainted with his first wife, Ellen Margaret Wellman of Brookline, Massachusetts, for many years before their marriage in 1871. She encouraged his teaching and scholarship, especially his translation of the *Odyssey* (1884). She died in 1879. He was married to Alice Elvira Freeman, then president of Wellesley College, from 1887 until her death in 1902. Both marriages were childless.

Palmer was an innovative teacher and academic administrator. He pioneered the approach of teaching philosophy from original texts, rather than from a standard textbook. His Philosophy IV: A Theory of Ethics Considered Constructively "became a model for philosophical instruction in the United States" (Kuklick, p. 239). Instead of employing traditional rote learning, Palmer both presented his own theories of ethics and encouraged critical thinking in his students. As its long-time chair, he was instrumental in building the Harvard philosophy department into the best in the United States, having among its faculty William James, Josiah Royce, George Santayana, and Hugo Münsterberg. Rather than create a "school" of philosophy, Palmer recalled that they "avoided 'breeding-in' and directly aimed at diversity" in appointments (*Autobiography of a Philosopher*, p. 51).

Palmer also fostered the growth of professional philosophy in the United States with his judicious and widely respected recommendations of his students to academic positions.

As a philosopher, Palmer recognized his limitations. His strengths were ethics and criticism. He recalled that "criticism became my sacred word" (*Autobiography of a Philosopher*, p. 125). Palmer's early interest in Mill waned under the influence of German idealism. His German studies had introduced him to Kant's philosophy, and for six summers in the 1870s and 1880s he studied with Scottish Hegelian Edward Caird. Under these idealistic influences he developed an ethics of self-realization, which he set forth in his Philosophy IV course at Harvard and in a series of books: *The Field of Ethics* (1901), *The Nature of Goodness* (1903), *The Problem of Freedom* (1911), and *Altruism: Its Nature and Varieties* (1919).

Palmer believed that it was possible to develop a rational ethical scheme. Ethics was a prescriptive science in which humans analyzed what could occur in the future. This process was never completed; individuals were always engaged in the process of self-realization. Freedom, for Palmer, lay in the ability to move beyond a purely sequential analysis of future events, in which past events determined the future, to antesequential causation. The intersection of various sequential chains of events provided humans with the freedom to choose how to proceed. Each intersection of events provided at least one moral choice not determined by prior events. The ethical individual had the freedom at this intersection to make the one rational moral choice available. Goodness, in Palmer's scheme, was an appropriate relationship to external objects and a proper adjustment of all the objects' internal relationships. Both extrinsic goodness and intrinsic goodness were relationships that could be developed. For humans, goodness was a process of self-realization that took a lifetime of development. Unlike his Harvard colleagues, Palmer devoted little of his scholarship to developing the idealistic metaphysics underlying his ethical theories. He was more interested in "applying his ethics to the Cambridge world around him" through his teaching and educational administration (Kuklick, p. 227).

Palmer stressed the importance of teaching, for the good teacher provided the student with the tools necessary to achieve self-realization. "The function of education was self-realization," and educational institutions should be designed to foster it (Kuklick, p. 236). Palmer was proud of the role he played in helping Eliot transform Harvard and its philosophy department into the kind of institution that progressively improved its ability to encourage self-realization among its faculty and students. Although his ethics are now seldom studied, Palmer's efforts to transform the teaching of philosophy, to build the Harvard philosophy department, and to remake Harvard into a modern university have had lasting influence.

• Palmer's papers are at Wellesley College. His *Autobiography of a Philosopher* (1930), also published as the introduction to George P. Adams and William Pepperell Montague, *Contemporary American Philosophy* (1930), remains the major source for Palmer's life. See also Harvard University Department of Philosophy, *George Herbert Palmer, 1842–1933: Memorial Addresses* (1935). Arthur J. Linenthal, *Two Academic Lives: George Herbert Palmer and Alice Freeman Palmer* (1995), contains a brief autobiographical sketch and an annotated bibliography of writings by and about Palmer. The most complete modern treatment of Palmer's contribution to philosophic thought and the making of the Harvard philosophy department is Bruce Kuklick, *The Rise of American Philosophy: Cambridge, Massachusetts, 1860–1930* (1977). Obituaries are in the *Boston Transcript* and the *New York Times*, both 8 May 1933.

DANIEL J. WILSON

PALMER, James Shedden (13 Oct. 1810–7 Dec. 1867), naval officer, was born in New Jersey. No information is available on his parents or his education before becoming a midshipman in the U.S. Navy on 1 January 1825, nor is information available on his early years in the navy. He never married. In 1836 Palmer was promoted to lieutenant. During 1838, while serving aboard the *Columbia* in the Far East, he participated in operations aimed at suppressing piratical activities against American commerce from Sumatra. During the war with Mexico, Palmer commanded the schooner *Flirt*, blockading the Mexican coast. He was promoted to commander in 1855.

At the outbreak of the Civil War, Palmer was serving in the Mediterranean aboard the steam sloop *Iroquois*, which was at first assigned to the blockade of Savannah. In September 1861 Palmer was ordered to locate and capture or destroy the Confederate commerce raider *Sumter*. The raider, commanded by Raphael Semmes, had earlier eluded the blockaders off New Orleans and escaped to sea. After a four-month search, Palmer found the *Sumter* taking on coal at St. Pierre on the French island of Martinique in the West Indies. Palmer was faced with a dilemma. If he chose to anchor in the harbor, French regulations would allow Semmes a 24-hour head start whenever he chose to leave. Instead, Palmer attempted to provoke Semmes into starting a fight by entering the harbor at night, then returning to his former position outside the harbor. When this strategy failed, Palmer was compelled to blockade the fifteen-mile wide harbor, hoping to catch the *Sumter* trying to escape to open sea. Despite his vigilance, the *Sumter* was able to get away only a day before the arrival of another powerful Federal warship, the *Dacotah*. Navy Secretary Gideon Welles held Palmer responsible for the serious setback and removed him from command until an investigation could be completed. The subsequent court of inquiry exonerated Palmer, and by early 1862 he was once again commanding the *Iroquois*.

On 8 May 1862 Palmer commanded a force of sailors and marines that occupied the city of Baton Rouge, and five days later he commanded the force that occupied Natchez, Mississippi. These operations led to a major naval attack on Vicksburg commanded by Admiral David Farragut. During the action, under heavy fire from the Confederate batteries, Palmer deliberately ordered the engines of the *Iroquois* stopped to allow the ship to drift to within supporting distance of the flagship *Hartford* with Farragut aboard. Farragut at first admonished Palmer for disobeying his orders until Palmer told him, "I thought you had more fire than you could stand, and so I came down to draw off a part of it." Farragut was so impressed by Palmer's "coolness and bravery" under fire that he gave him command of the *Hartford*. Soon afterward Farragut was transferred to the West Gulf Squadron, and he left Palmer in command of all Federal naval forces on the Mississippi. In July 1862 Palmer was promoted to captain; he became a commodore the following year. From November 1864 until January 1865 Palmer replaced Farragut as commander of the West Gulf Squadron. During the battle of Mobile Bay he was in command of the First Division at New Orleans.

After the war, in December 1865, Palmer became commander of the West Indies Squadron. He was promoted to rear admiral in 1866. The following year, after an earthquake and tidal wave devastated St. Thomas in the Virgin Islands, Palmer launched an all-out effort to save lives. But when a yellow fever epidemic struck, he became a casualty.

Palmer was a brave and resourceful officer in whom Admiral Farragut placed complete confidence. Dignified and reserved, his fellow officers nicknamed him "Piecrust Palmer" because of his practice of wearing formal dress with kid gloves before engaging the enemy.

• No Palmer papers have been located. Palmer's official Civil War correspondence is in RG 45 (National Records Collection), National Archives, and *The Official Records of the Union and Confederate Navies in the War of the Rebellion* (30 vols., 1894–1922). See also Loyall Farragut, *The Life of David Glasgow Farragut* (1879), and Raphael Semmes, *Memoirs of Service Afloat during the War between the States* (1869). An obituary is in the *New York Times*, 22 Dec. 1867.

NORMAN C. DELANEY

PALMER, Joel (4 Oct. 1810–9 June 1881), Oregon territory superintendent of Indian affairs, was born in Elizabethtown, Canada, the son of Ephraim Palmer, a farmer, and Anna Phelps, ninth-generation Americans who left Canada during the War of 1812 and settled in Lowville, New York. His Quaker parents bound him out when he was twelve to a Quaker family in Jefferson, New York. There he attended school for three months, his only formal education.

At the end of his apprenticeship in 1826, Palmer moved to Philadelphia, helped construct canals, and in 1830 married Catherine Caffee, who died shortly after giving birth to a daughter. In 1836 he married Sarah Ann Derbyshire, a Quaker orphan whose trust fund enabled the couple to weather the failure of most of his business ventures and with whom he had seven more children.

In 1836 the family moved to the Quaker community of Laurel, Indiana, where Palmer was awarded a contract to dig a section of the Whitewater Canal, only to see the collapse of state finances in 1837 terminate the project. Palmer was twice elected as a Democrat to represent Franklin County in the state legislature (1843–1845), where he served on the internal improvements and banking committees.

Palmer caught "Oregon fever" in 1845. Leaving his family behind, he captained a large company of wagons across the plains to the Pacific. Here he met his first American Indians, who proved easier to get along with than the disputatious whites. He told his story in his highly regarded *Journal of Travels over the Rocky Mountains to the Mouth of the Columbia River* (1847). In 1847 he brought his family across the plains, again as captain of a large company. Finding that his original claim had been "jumped," he tried different sites before founding, in 1850, Dayton, Oregon, where he resided the rest of his life.

Shortly after Palmer's return to Oregon, the Whitman massacre by the Cayuse Indians sparked a decade of warfare in which Palmer played a major role. In the subsequent Cayuse War, Palmer was appointed commissary general and peace commissioner.

If population pressure already threatened the Indians, the discovery of gold in California in 1848 and small strikes in Oregon in the 1850s caused a demographic explosion that severely strained resources. Palmer spent several months prospecting in California and came away convinced that an impoverished, transient, violent element among the miners was the main cause of friction with the natives.

Indian relations in Oregon suffered from the fact that westward migration had outpaced government. Federal authorities were supposed to negotiate treaties with the Indians for their lands before white settlement, but on the West Coast settlement preceded treaties. The Mexican War had yielded to the United States more than one million square miles and over 100,000 Indians, but the federal bureaucracy was undermanned and caught unprepared. As the white population increased, small wars erupted in southern Oregon in 1851 and 1853.

In February 1853 Palmer was appointed Oregon's superintendent of Indian affairs. He was the fifth man in eleven years to hold the thankless post. While he sympathized with the Indians, he believed they were doomed to extinction unless protected by the federal government, provided with reservations, educated in schools, and furnished with farm equipment. He hoped they could eventually regain their autonomy and practice local self-government. Unfortunately, the lack of funds forced Palmer to renege on many of his promises to the Indians.

Palmer negotiated nine treaties in 1854 and 1855. In May 1855 he joined Isaac I. Stevens in a council with thousands of Cayuse, Walla Walla, Yakima, and Nez Percé. He pleaded with the Indians to be realistic: "Can you prevent the whites from coming? . . . Like the grasshoppers on the plains . . . you cannot stop them. Our chief cannot stop them, we cannot stop them." Although fifty-six chiefs begrudgingly signed away 60,000 square miles, their mood was belligerent.

In September 1855 the Yakima War broke out in upper Oregon, and in October the Rogue River War was fought in the south. Territorial governor George L. Curry announced that the natives were united in a war to the death and called out four companies of volunteers, promising them generous compensation. While Palmer conceded that the natives were the aggressors in the north, he felt that the danger in the south was vastly exaggerated. He charged that the volunteers' reckless attacks were driving neutral Indians into fighting. To keep the war from spreading, he tried to safeguard the noncombatant natives and deputized sixty civilian guards to watch them until they could be sent to reservations. He wrote to General John E. Wool, who shared his views, that the Rogue River War had been "forced upon these Indians against their will . . . by a set of reckless vagabonds . . . who regard the treasury of the United States as a legitimate object of plunder." In fact, Oregon eventually billed the federal government $4,449,949 to reimburse its volunteers.

Palmer's solicitude for the natives outraged Oregon militants. The Oregon legislature censured him in December 1855, and when his correspondence with Wool was leaked to the press, the legislators demanded his recall. He was removed on 23 February 1856, and at the battle of Big Meadows on 25 May 1856 soldiers decisively defeated the southern tribes, who surrendered and moved to reservations.

Indian superintendents were caught in a clash of cultures that often left them beaten and bruised. Thousands of Oregonians apparently appreciated Palmer's peacekeeping efforts, however, for in 1862 he won election as a Union Democrat to the Oregon legislature, where he was chosen Speaker of the House and in 1864 was elected to the state senate. During the Civil War Union Democrats merged with Republicans, and after the war Palmer, who had opposed both slavery and secession, switched his partisan allegiance. In 1870 he ran for governor as a Republican and was narrowly defeated.

In 1871 Palmer was appointed Indian agent at the Silentz reservation, but bitter denominational attacks that he was not evangelizing the Indians quickly drove him from office. His last years were relatively obscure; he died in Dayton.

Although Palmer ultimately failed to prevent war, protect the natives, and force their acculturation, it is easy to imagine that despite all the death and suffering in frontier Oregon, conditions would have been worse without his efforts. While true to the interests of the United States, he believed it was in the national interest to deal humanely with the natives. His career was best summarized by frontier army doctor Rodney Glisan, who wrote that Palmer "stood like a wall of adamant between the two races in their numerous quarrels" (*Journal of Army Life* [1874], p. 364).

• Palmer's papers are in the Oregon Historical Society and the University of Oregon, Eugene. His official correspondence is in various published Senate and House documents in the late 1850s and in the microfilmed Bureau of Indian Affairs Oregon Superintendency Records. Full-length studies include Stanley Sheldon Spaid, "Joel Palmer and Indian Affairs in Oregon" (Ph.D. diss., Univ. of Oregon, 1950), and Terence O'Donnell, *An Arrow in the Earth: General Joel Palmer and the Indians of Oregon* (1991). An obituary is in the (Portland) *Morning Oregonian*, 10 June 1881.

STEVEN J. NOVAK

PALMER, John McAuley (13 Sept. 1817–25 Sept. 1900), governor of Illinois and U.S. senator, was born in Scott County, Kentucky, the son of Louis D. Palmer and Ann Hansford Tutt, farmers. His Palmer forebears had been farmers and artisans, while the Tutts were generally more prosperous. His father was a Jacksonian Democrat whose opposition to slavery prompted the family's move, when John was fourteen, to farmland between Edwardsville and Upper Alton, Illinois. In 1834 young Palmer left home to attend Alton Seminary (later Shurtleff College) in Upper Alton for two years. Traveling through west-central Illinois as a clock peddler from 1836 to 1838, he met future political allies Lyman Trumbull and Stephen A. Douglas and witnessed mob violence against opponents of slavery. After teaching school for a year in Fulton County, he settled in Carlinville to study law and was admitted to the bar in 1839. A successful and prominent attorney, he was often in court with Abraham Lincoln and other celebrated lawyer-politicians of central Illinois. In 1842 he married Malinda Ann Neely, with whom he had ten children. Following Malinda's death from tuberculosis in 1885, he married Hannah Lamb Kimball, a Springfield widow, in 1888.

A Democrat since childhood, Palmer was elected probate justice of the peace in 1843. He was subsequently elected as a delegate to the state constitutional convention in 1847, county judge in 1848, and state senator in 1852. During his successful campaign for reelection to the senate in 1854, he exhibited an independence that would mark the remainder of his career. Rebuffing pressure from Democrats to support the Douglas policy on slavery in Kansas and Nebraska, Palmer ran instead as an Anti-Nebraska Democrat. This ended his friendship with Douglas and presaged an equally stormy sixteen-year Republican affiliation. In 1856 he presided at the new party's state convention, and at the Republican National Convention he attempted to secure the vice presidential nomination for Abraham Lincoln. Recognized as a leading Illinois Republican, he ran unsuccessfully for Congress in 1859 and helped Lincoln win nomination and election as president the next year.

Civil War military duty further revealed Palmer's qualities of leadership and combativeness. Enlisting as a colonel shortly after Fort Sumter, he served courageously in several battles and reached the rank of major general. However, he criticized the arrogance of some West Point officers, feuded with General William T. Sherman, and antagonized both civil and army officials as Lincoln's military commander in Kentucky. By war's end his ardent views on African-American enfranchisement and Reconstruction placed him in the Radical wing of his party.

Moving from Carlinville to Springfield in 1867, he resumed practicing law and reentered politics, winning election as governor in 1868. He antagonized many in his party during his administration by consistently vetoing special-interest legislation and championing states' rights over federal encroachment. The latter position was particularly evident in his protest against the unsolicited assignment of U.S. troops to Chicago after the 1871 fire. Disenchanted with Republican corruption, he helped organize the Liberal Republican movement in 1872. Palmer devoted the next decade to family and legal matters, returning to public life as an unsuccessful candidate in several U.S. Senate contests and the 1888 gubernatorial race. The final phase of his political career began with his 1891 election to the U.S. Senate as a Democrat supporting Grover Cleveland. Despite scant legislative accomplishments, he gained national standing in the party and was a favorite-son presidential contender in 1892. When William Jennings Bryan and the free-silver cause gained the party leadership in 1896, he formed a splinter group that became the National or Gold Democrats. Nominated as their presidential candidate, the 79-year-old Palmer endorsed his Republican opponent, William McKinley, before Democratic audiences. He gained less than 1 percent of the popular vote but helped McKinley win as many as six states. Leaving the Senate at the completion of his term in 1897, he wrote two books during his retirement.

Quick to judge and disinclined to compromise, Palmer wandered the nineteenth-century political landscape in search of a suitable party home. Labeled "a conscientious turncoat" by his biographer, he rose to leadership positions and high elective office in both major parties, and he spearheaded three notable splinter movements, Anti-Nebraska Democrats, Liberal Republicans, and Gold Democrats. Similarly inconsistent on national versus state power and other issues, he was nevertheless a steadfast champion of African-American rights, labor rights, and some political reforms. As governor he vetoed many private and special bills aimed at granting favors to corporations and utilities; later he publicly favored the popular election of senators. His independence resulted in meager personal accomplishments but won praise for his principled behavior. He died in Springfield.

• Palmer's papers and letters are in the Illinois State Historical Library, Springfield. Palmer edited *The Bench and Bar of Illinois* (2 vols., 1899) and wrote *Personal Recollections of John M. Palmer: The Story of an Earnest Life* (1901). His grandson, George Thomas Palmer, wrote a sympathetic biography, *A Conscientious Turncoat: The Story of John M. Palmer, 1817–1900* (1941). See also Virginia Rose Grollemond, "The Administration of Governor John M. Palmer of Illinois, 1869–1873" (M.A. thesis, Univ. of Ill., 1955). A good modern monograph is J. Rogers Hollingsworth, *The Whirligig of Poli-*

tics: The Democracy of Cleveland and Bryan (1963). Also informative are Horace Samuel Merrill, *Bourbon Democracy of the Middle West, 1865–1896* (1953), and Paul J. Kleppner, *The Cross of Culture: A Social Analysis of Midwestern Politics, 1850–1900* (1970).

CULLOM DAVIS

PALMER, John McAuley (23 Apr. 1870–26 Oct. 1955), army officer and military intellectual, was born in Carlinville, Illinois, the son of John Mayo Palmer, a lawyer, and Ellen Clark Robertson. After graduation from the U.S. Military Academy in 1892, Lieutenant Palmer joined the Fifteenth Infantry Regiment. In June 1893 he married Maude Laning, who bore him two children. His army assignments included the Chicago railroad strike of 1894, the fast-vanishing Indian frontier in Arizona, occupation duty in Cuba, service with the relief expedition to China during the Boxer Rebellion, a faculty assignment at West Point, a stint as governor of the Lanao District in Mindanao in the Philippines, and two student years at the Staff College, Fort Leavenworth, Kansas, where he became a fast friend of a younger contemporary, Lieutenant George Marshall.

His duty on the Army General Staff from 1911 to 1913 marked the turning point in Palmer's career. There he earned favorable notice when he proposed a tactical reorganization of the U.S. Army, but his plan was not adopted. After further assignments in the Pacific, he returned to the general staff in 1916 in time to participate in the planning for possible U.S. entry into World War I, including provision for a compulsory manpower draft. Selected by General John J. Pershing in 1917 as chief of operations for the American Expeditionary Force (AEF), he sailed to France on the steamer *Baltic* with the advance party where he helped lay out the basic AEF war plan. Following a breakdown from overwork, he accompanied a military mission to Italy in December 1917 to plan for U.S. support after the disastrous retreat of the Italian army at Caporetto. Back in France, rested and recovered, he took command, as a colonel, of the Fifty-eighth Brigade, Twenty-ninth Infantry Division, successfully breaking through the German front beyond Verdun in October 1918. Although Pershing recommended Palmer for an advance to brigadier general, the armistice stopped all such promotions.

He returned to the United States as Pershing's special emissary to the general staff, which was then laying plans for the postwar army. Palmer joined the War Plans Division of the general staff where he found himself at odds with the chief of staff, Peyton C. March. March favored a large regular army backed by a wartime draft to provide the necessary manpower. Palmer, by contrast, favored a small regular army with a large reserve component of citizen soldiers prepared in peacetime via universal military training and organized into units under reserve officers. Palmer presented his views before the Senate Military Affairs Committee and made such a favorable impression with his carefully thought-out concept of the kind of army best suited to a democratic nation that he was invited to serve as a special advisor to the committee, much to the dismay of General March. In this capacity, Palmer was one of the principal architects of the National Defense Act of 1920, the legislation that laid the foundation for the army that fought World War II.

He articulated his underlying conception clearly and simply: "If we . . . invest all our military budget in regular troops we should have only a handful upon mobilization for a great war. The same amount of money uniformly and consistently applied to a Citizen Army of adequate size will result in an economical and impregnable system of national defense" (Palmer MSS, Library of Congress, notebook 18, p. 110).

Although Congress declined to enact universal military training, the Defense Act of 1920 that finally emerged did reflect Palmer's conception of a small regular army to serve as a force in being and source of doctrine, plus a ready reserve of National Guardsmen and at least a cadre of organized reserve citizen soldiers that could incorporate wartime draftees into tactical units faster and more effectively than would be possible without an experienced cadre. The objective was to avoid the makeshift organizations of 1917 and 1918 by building an ordered and experienced framework that could mobilize all or any necessary part of the nation's manpower in time of need.

A crucial aspect of Palmer's contribution was his recognition that to elicit the best service from citizen soldiers, they must be given opportunities to rise to levels of command limited only by their individual abilities. To this end, the entire command structures of the Organized Reserve as well as the National Guard were to be entrusted to reserve officers. Palmer's experiences in France in a National Guard division had persuaded him that only by such an arrangement would the best energies and full potential of citizen soldiers be unleashed. To insure a proper regard for local loyalties and political sensitivities when effecting the necessary postwar reorganization, the 1920 act included a section calling for mixed committees of regulars and citizen soldiers to preside over the process.

When General Pershing became chief of staff in 1921, he appointed Palmer as a special assistant to help implement the 1920 act. Promoted to brigadier general in November 1922, Palmer served as a brigade commander in Panama from 1923 until his retirement in 1926. In retirement, however, he continued his crusade to persuade the regular army, as he had already persuaded George Marshall, that even without universal military training, which Congress had rejected, a principal function of the regulars should be to prepare in peace the volunteer reservists for the role they would play in war. To this end, during his retirement he wrote several books using historical examples to illustrate his convictions. Best known among these was *America in Arms* (1941), which subsequently had substantial impact on the army when officially distributed by the War Department as a paperback. With the outbreak of war in Europe in 1939, he joined the leaders of the Military Training Camps Association, an organization largely comprising veteran civilian officers produced by the Plattsburg, New York, training camps program of World War I. Among these, most prominent were Julius Ochs Adler of the *New York Times,* New York attorney Grenville Clark, and former upstate New York senator James W. Wadsworth in successfully pushing Congress to enact the Selective Service Act of 1940, the first peacetime compulsory training mandate.

In November 1941, just before Pearl Harbor was attacked, Chief of Staff George Marshall recalled General Palmer to active duty to serve as a special advisor on the citizen components. As Marshall explained to Secretary of War Henry Stimson, he saw Palmer as "the civilian conscience" of the U.S. Army. Marshall, ever sensitive to the physical limitations of his seventy-year-old colleague, had Palmer set up his office in the Library of Congress, not in the Pentagon, so that he could think and plan in peace and quiet. In this capacity as military elder statesman, Palmer remained on active duty until 1946. He served on committees, wrote articles, and testified before Congress in support of a democratic, territorial (that is, locally organized as was the National Guard), citizen reserve led by citizen soldiers who had proved themselves competent to lead. His philosophy was articulated officially in War Department Circular 347 of 25 August 1944 and manifestly influenced Marshall's final report to the nation on the U.S. Army in World War II, which called, unsuccessfully as it turned out, for legislation to implement universal military training. Though repeatedly rebuffed and frustrated, to the day of his death in Washington, D.C., Palmer's driving concern was to awaken the nation to the need for a military establishment suited to the genius of a democratic people.

• The bulk of Palmer's papers are in the Manuscript Division of the Library of Congress, but the U.S. Military Academy and the National Archives have some official papers. Palmer's writings include *An Army of the People* (1916); a chapter in *Ways to Peace,* ed. E. E. Lapp (1924); *Statesmanship and War* (1927); *Washington, Lincoln, and Wilson: Three War Statesmen* (1930); *General Von Steuben* (1937); and *America in Arms* (1941). I. B. Holley, Jr., *General John M. Palmer: Citizen Soldiers and the Army of a Democracy* (1982), is a full biography. An obituary appears in the *New York Times,* 27 Oct. 1955.

I. B. HOLLEY, JR.

PALMER, Lizzie Pitts Merrill (8 Oct. 1838–28 July 1916), philanthropist and founder of the Merrill-Palmer Institute, was born in Portland, Maine, the daughter of Charles Merrill and Frances Pitts. Charles Merrill made his fortune in Maine lumber and in the 1850s brought his family to Michigan to expand his business to the pine forests of the Midwest. In 1855 seventeen-year-old Lizzie Pitts Merrill married Thomas Witherell Palmer, the son of a prosperous Michigan family and a business associate of her father. The couple settled just outside Detroit on a 600-acre farm

that Thomas Palmer had inherited from his mother. The Palmers later (1895) donated this land to the city of Detroit, and it is now known as Palmer Park.

In 1878 Thomas Palmer began a career in politics with his election to the Michigan State Senate. In 1883 he was elected to the U.S. Senate, where he gave the first speech on the floor of the Senate advocating suffrage for women. In Washington, D.C., during her husband's term Lizzie Palmer gained a reputation for being an excellent hostess. In 1889 Thomas Palmer was appointed American ambassador to Spain, a position he resigned the following year. The Palmers, who had no children, returned from Spain with the young son of a Spanish military officer, whom they later adopted. Although the Palmers invited other children into their home over the years and helped educate several of them, Harold Palmer was the only child they legally adopted. In 1892 Thomas Palmer was appointed president of the Chicago World's Columbian Commission.

After her marriage Lizzie Palmer became a prominent patron of the Detroit Institute of Art and, with her husband, founded the Michigan branch of the Society for the Prevention of Cruelty to Animals (presumably in the early 1870s). The Palmers built a log cabin on their estate outside the city in 1887 and furnished it with colonial heirlooms from the Merrill, Palmer, and Witherell families. They were well known in Detroit for throwing lavish parties at the cabin for prominent guests. This cabin later became part of Palmer Park and was open to the public for many years.

Lizzie Palmer had always been susceptible to illness, and in her later years she spent much of her time in "Larchmont Manor," a family estate on Long Island Sound in New York, where she felt more comfortable. On 1 June 1913, while at this manor, she heard of her husband's death. Three years later Lizzie Palmer also died, leaving behind an unconditional bequest to found the Merrill-Palmer Institute.

Despite her illness, Palmer became increasingly interested in social issues in the years before her death. In 1915, for example, she worked with the Detroit Welfare League to bring prison reform to Michigan by appointing a board of managers to oversee prison conditions. The spirit of progressive reform is reflected in the words that begin her last will and testament: "I hold profoundly the conviction that the welfare of any community is divinely, and hence inseparably, dependent upon the quality of its motherhood, and the spirit and character of its homes." To carry out this conviction Palmer endowed over $3 million to establish the Merrill-Palmer Motherhood and Home Training School in Detroit after her death. In her will Palmer envisioned the school as an institution in which "girls and young women of the age of ten years or more shall be educated, trained, developed and disciplined with special reference to fitting them mentally, morally, physically and religiously for the discharge of the functions and service of wifehood and motherhood, and the management, supervision, direction and inspiration of homes . . . " In 1918 the Merrill-Palmer corporation, made up of twelve leading men and women of Detroit, was formed to carry out the terms of the will. The corporation hired innovative educator Edna Noble White, who, by the early 1920s, had built the Merrill-Palmer Motherhood and Home Training School into a world-renowned center of study on child development.

In its early years the institute founded one of the first nursery schools and ran an infant laboratory, play group, summer camp, and guidance service for parents. The school, which changed its name to the Merrill-Palmer Institute of Human Development and Family Life in 1960, continued its research and training activities for many years. In 1981 the Merrill-Palmer Institute ceased to operate independently and became associated with Wayne State University. However, for many decades it stood as a leader in childhood education, teacher training, and family research, expanding the legacy of service and community involvement left by Lizzie Palmer.

• For information on the Merrill-Palmer Institute see the papers at the Archives of Labor History and Urban Affairs, Walter P. Reuther Library, Wayne State University. Information on the Palmer, Witherell, and Merrill families can also be found among the Merrill-Palmer papers. Palmer's life is discussed in George B. Catlin, *The Story of Detroit* (1923); Friend Palmer, *Early Days in Detroit* (1960); and Nicholas P. Georgiady et al., *Michigan Women* (1967). Also see "Lizzie Merrill Palmer to Help Welfare League," *Detroit News*, 8 Jan. 1916.

VICTORIA W. WOLCOTT

PALMER, Phoebe Worrall (18 Dec. 1807–2 Nov. 1874), Methodist lay revivalist and author, was born in New York City, the daughter of Henry Worrall, an engineer, and Dorothea Wade. Converted in England under John Wesley's preaching in 1785, her father set up a staunch Methodist home when he emigrated to America in 1792. Nothing is known of her education, but Phoebe embraced her parents' Methodist faith as a child and adhered to it all her life. In 1827 she married Walter Clarke Palmer, a physician and a lay leader in the Methodist Episcopal Church; they had six children. Although based in New York City, she traveled extensively, holding meetings in places as widely separated as California, Louisiana, Quebec, and Scotland. Palmer began her career as a theologian by penning religious verse, then branched out to write articles and books. Filling in for her husband at a Methodist class-meeting launched her as a revivalist, and she eventually crossed the continent and the Atlantic to preach the good news. As a feminist, she first spoke at a women's prayer meeting and later produced a full-scale defense of women's ministries. As a humanitarian, she distributed tracts in poor neighborhoods and later established one of the nation's first settlement houses. Her three surviving children all went into professional Christian service.

The turning point in Palmer's life came on the evening of 26 July 1837, when she totally consecrated her life to God. Three of her children had died in infancy. As she grieved over her loss, she became convinced that God had taken her children because she had loved them more than she loved the Lord. She resolved to resign to God everything that she held dear and to obey the Lord ungrudgingly. Resolving to give to the Lord the time she would have spent with her children, she thought of her commitment as the "living sacrifice" that God required and felt completely cleansed from her sin, made holy, and filled with love for God and her neighbor. She believed that she had experienced the "entire sanctification" that her Methodist heritage had taught her to expect. Though Palmer never thought of herself as a theologian and considered "theology" a complex, human substitute for God's simple truth, her seventeen books, which appeared between 1841 and 1875, as well as the *Guide to Holiness*, a periodical that she edited from 1864 to 1874, explicated her theology. Some male Methodist leaders refused to take her seriously as a theologian, but to the bishops, professors, and editors who joined two hundred lay people at the weekly meetings in her home, to the thirty-seven thousand who subscribed to her magazine, and to the hundreds of thousands who read her books, she was an important teacher of theological truth.

Palmer simplified and popularized John Wesley's doctrine of "entire sanctification," modifying it in six ways. Wesley had taught that the Lord could work in a believer's heart, cleansing it from sin and instilling perfect love for God and neighbor. Palmer changed Wesley's teaching by, first, identifying entire sanctification with the baptism of the Holy Spirit. What the first Christians experienced at Pentecost (Acts 2:1–22) was available for every believer. Second, she taught that the baptism of the Holy Spirit brings "power from on high" to enable one to live a victorious life and to bring revival to the church. Third, she described sanctification as an instantaneous event rather than a gradual process. She proclaimed in capitals, "THERE IS A SHORTER WAY!," and reduced the quest for sanctification from an arduous labor to a simple, three-step process: first, consecrate oneself entirely to God; second, believe God keeps his promise to sanctify what is consecrated; and third, bear witness to what God has done. Because sanctification was so simple to obtain, her fifth modification of Wesley's doctrine insisted that entire sanctification should occur near the beginning of a Christian's spiritual life, rather than being a goal to be reached sometime in the future. Sixth, she held that one needed no evidence other than the biblical text to be assured of entire sanctification. If one followed the steps the Bible laid out, one could be sure of entire sanctification. Methodists, Baptists, Presbyterians, Congregationalists, and Anglicans accepted her ideas, and later her thought gave theological direction to such holiness groups as the Wesleyan Methodists, the Free Methodists, the Church of the Nazarene, the Salvation Army, and the Keswick Movement. While she herself never spoke in tongues, her emphasis on Pentecost and Spirit baptism helped to pave the way for the Pentecostal and Charismatic movements. These groups now number more than a hundred million adherents worldwide, and most teach a variation of her theology.

Palmer's career as a revivalist began in 1837, and by the following year she had begun to speak in camp-meetings and protracted revival services. She ultimately participated in more than 300 of these events. In 1857 reports of Palmer's success in revival services in Canada stimulated the transatlantic prayer revival that brought 2.5 million members into the churches of Britain and America. She and her husband followed the revival to Great Britain in 1859 and spent the next four years in full-time ministry. When they returned to the United States, Walter abandoned his medical practice and served as publisher for the *Guide to Holiness*, which Palmer edited. Besides preaching and writing, she civilized and systematized the methods of frontier Methodist revivalism, adapting them to the city. Her emphasis on lay ministry helped to transform revivalism from the clergy-centered, small-town campaigns waged by Charles G. Finney to the lay-organized, city-wide crusades led by Dwight L. Moody.

Palmer's zeal for the salvation of souls led her in 1837 to begin to distribute religious tracts to people who would never hear the gospel in a church. She went from "cellar to garret" to distribute tracts and speak to people about their souls. Her visits to the poor also made her aware of their other needs, and along with her physician husband, she began providing food, medical care, medicines, and money. The Palmers even adopted a boy who needed their aid. In addition to these personal ministries, Palmer organized others to aid the poor and in 1847 became an officer in the Ladies' Home Missionary Society of the Methodist Episcopal church. In this role she began the Five-Points Mission in New York's worst slum. Five years earlier Charles Dickens had visited the Five Points under the protection of two policemen. Palmer, however, regularly went alone into the same area to visit people and knew their spiritual and physical needs firsthand. After several years of agitation, in 1850 she persuaded the other board members of the society to buy and then demolish the "Old Brewery," which dominated the Five Points, and to establish a home, school, workroom, and chapel in its place. This mission house at Five Points was one of Protestantism's first efforts to meet the needs of the poor in urban America's slums. Its ministry set the pattern for the social ministry of many urban churches for the rest of the nineteenth century. By example and by argument Palmer also advanced the cause of women's rights. In her roles as preacher, writer, and editor she showed that women could excel at tasks usually reserved for men. Her book *Promise of the Father* (1859) was one of the first defenses of women's ministries in the church. She died in New York City.

• The Walter and Phoebe Palmer Collection at the New York Public Library is almost valueless because it consists of letters people wrote to the Palmers and not the letters the Palmers wrote themselves. Four of Palmer's most significant works are: *The Way of Holiness* (1845), *Faith and Its Effects* (1852), *Incidental Illustrations of the Economy of Salvation* (1855), and *Promise of the Father* (1859). The first published biography is Richard Wheatley, *The Life and Letters of Mrs. Phoebe Palmer* (1876). Also useful is Harold E. Raser, *Phoebe Palmer: Her Life and Thought* (1987), which sets Mrs. Palmer's work against the background of social trends in nineteenth-century America. The most complete modern biography is C. E. White, *The Beauty of Holiness: Phoebe Palmer as Theologian, Revivalist, Feminist, and Humanitarian* (1986).

CHARLES EDWARD WHITE

PALMER, Potter (20 May 1826–4 May 1902), merchant and developer, was born in Potter's Hollow, Albany County, New York, the son of Benjamin Palmer, an owner of stock farms, and Rebecca Potter. He attended only elementary school and by age eighteen was working as a clerk in a Durham, New York, store; two years later he was in charge. At age twenty-one he opened his own dry goods store nearby in Oneida, then after almost three years moved west to Lockport. After a year there, he sold out and, with $6,000 in capital, headed for Chicago. Palmer believed that the greatest opportunities would emerge in the rapidly developing West; he expected Chicago would be at the heart of that development, that it would become the distribution center for the whole region—thus offering not only larger opportunities in retail, but also unique ones in wholesale. He persuaded his father and some family friends to let him "have their capital for investing purposes," augmenting his own resources. In 1852 he opened a dry goods store on Lake Street, then Chicago's commercial center.

From the start, Palmer's approach differed strikingly from that of other retailers, whose stores he described as "small and cramped, badly ventilated and on the tavern plan. You could buy codfish or calico in them." He instead "struck out for a large and distinctive dry good store and began bidding for the wholesale trade from the wilderness." Palmer was among the first to appreciate the importance of attractive displays of goods and the value of heavy advertising—his displays and advertisements were uncommonly large and included prices for comparison. He also offered higher quality goods than anyone else believed could find a market in frontier Chicago. His enterprise thrived; in 1857 he opened a grand four-story store, though warned by "several kind friends" that he "would be ruined in a year." And when the financial crisis of 1857 hit, Palmer turned it to his advantage, buying up huge inventories of goods at distress prices, then offering the goods at prices below those of all his competitors as recovery set in.

Palmer also introduced a revolutionary approach to dealing with customers. He offered to let them take goods on approval, thus having the opportunity to inspect goods before buying. To this he added the opportunity for established customers to "charge" purchases (payment due the first of the month) and the more revolutionary concept of guaranteed satisfaction, inviting customers to exchange or return goods for a full refund when dissatisfied. His impact was so dramatic that soon most Chicago merchants adopted the "Palmer system;" Macy's head came to Chicago to learn the details and carried the concept back to New York City. Palmer also built strong relationships with suppliers, opened a New York City office to handle purchasing, contracted directly with many manufacturers, traveled abroad to buy imported goods directly, and, to secure the best prices, bought in volume and often for cash.

Palmer was among the first to appreciate the impact the Civil War would have on business. Believing prices must rise strongly with the disruption of supplies and military demand, he bought huge inventories of wool and cotton textiles as well as other goods. Working from New York City, he was magnificently successful. But the war was not simply an opportunity to make profits; Palmer, though a Democrat, was an ardent supporter of the Union, gladly paid his federal income tax, bought heavily in government war bonds, and in January 1864 publicly promised to donate the entire profits from a day of sales to support needy soldiers' families. The importance of the New York City business led Palmer to make his residence there from 1864.

Though only thirty-eight, Palmer was exhausted; his doctor advised him to retire from active management. Thus in early 1865 Marshall Field and Levi Leiter, who had risen from clerks to partners at competitor Cooley, Farwell & Co., took over the Palmer enterprise, creating Field, Palmer, and Leiter (later Marshall Field & Co.). (The Palmer name referred to Milton, Potter's brother, who owned a share of the new company and was a general partner; he withdrew in 1867.)

Three years later, after much European travel and with his health restored, Palmer moved back to Chicago to concentrate on real estate. He believed the Lake Street commercial district, running east-west along the reeking Chicago River, was in decline; he decided to invest heavily in the north-south State Street artery, then a narrow, irregular, ill-drained, ill-paved, and utterly uninviting street. He bought virtually every property for three-quarters of a mile, moved some buildings back, replaced others with modern structures, and transformed the street into a wide, well-paved, handsome boulevard. He built a particularly magnificent marble-fronted store at State and Washington streets, the first establishment in Chicago illuminated with gas lights; Field & Leiter leased it in 1868 for $1,000 a week and after 1871 for the princely sum of $70,000 annually. In four years, by 1871, Palmer's efforts had brought all of Chicago's principal stores to State Street, and he had redefined its business district. In 1870 he married Bertha Honoré, with whom he was to have two children, both sons.

On 8 October 1871 the great Chicago fire began its devastating sweep across the city. Palmer lost more than thirty commercial properties. Urged on by his new wife, he was among the first to begin rebuilding. He secured a loan of $1.7 million from Connecticut Mutual Life Insurance—the largest loan ever made up to that time to an individual—to finance the effort. He also sold many of his commercial lots to give primary attention to rebuilding the Palmer House in magnificent style. Fireproof, built without wooden laths or partitions, with a stunning iron façade, marble staircases, and beautiful frescoes, with 600 guest rooms, plus another 100 rooms for meetings, and costing over $2 million, when finished two years later it was probably the finest hotel in North America.

Palmer's last major impact on Chicago was developing the area north of Chicago Avenue and east of Rush Street, an area then largely of dunes and swamp. He helped lay out Lake Shore Drive, played a central role in transforming the adjacent lands into an appealing area, and built his own magnificent residence there. North Lake Shore Drive and the adjacent parks remain one of the defining features of Chicago.

Palmer never occupied public office, though in 1870 President Ulysses S. Grant offered him a position in his cabinet. Palmer was one of the original incorporators of the Chicago Board of Trade; was important in developing the park system on Chicago's south side, for which he served as commissioner; and helped plan the World's Columbian Exposition, on whose board of directors he served as vice president. He was an active member of the Disciples of Christ church.

Palmer had an enduring impact on American retailing practices; his innovations still resonate in the late twentieth century. And perhaps no individual had more influence in establishing the spatial pattern of modern downtown Chicago and its special orientation toward Lake Michigan. Palmer died at his home on Lake Shore Drive.

• There is a collection of Potter Palmer Papers at the Chicago Historical Society. Extensive records of Marshall Field & Co. are in the corporate archives in Chicago. See also *System* 10 (July 1906): 22–24; John William Ferry, *A History of the Department Store* (1960); and Robert W. Twyman, *History of Marshall Field & Co., 1852–1906* (1954). Obituaries are in the *New York Times*, 5 May 1902, and the *Chicago Daily Tribune*, 5 and 7 May 1902.

FRED CARSTENSEN

PALMER, Sarah Worrall Lankford (23 Apr. 1806–24 Apr. 1896), Methodist laywoman, was born in New York City, the daughter of Henry Worrall, an engineer, and Dorothea Wade. Like her more famous younger sister, Phoebe Palmer, Sarah Palmer was a vigorous proponent of the doctrine of entire sanctification. There is no record of her education. In 1831 she married Thomas Lankford, a builder.

Sarah had been converted as a teenager at a camp meeting in 1819 and, when the event returned the next summer, professed entire sanctification at the age of fourteen. (She later had other religious experiences that she called "sanctification," so her chronology on this issue is confusing.) As a fifteen-year-old she was elected superintendent of the female section of the local Methodist Episcopal Sunday School, and later, in 1833, she led a prayer meeting in her church. Besides these leadership roles she had an extensive ministry of visitation among the poor. In 1836 she and her husband, Walter Palmer, began to share a house with her sister, Phoebe, and her husband in a comfortable neighborhood in New York's Lower East Side.

Shortly after moving into this new home, Sarah began the famous "Tuesday Meeting for the Promotion of Holiness." The format she established remained the same for the next sixty years. People would gather in her home, recount their religious experiences, and hear the leader teach Scripture. Then various people would lead the group in prayer. The gathering started as a meeting for women only, but in 1839 Sarah allowed men to attend. In 1840 Sarah's husband pursued a business opportunity in Caldwell, New York, so Sarah moved with him to that city fifty miles up the Hudson. Phoebe Palmer inherited leadership of the Tuesday Meeting, but on the occasions when she left town to hold evangelistic services, Sarah returned to lead the gathering. In the late 1840s and through the 1850s, as Phoebe's evangelistic travels lengthened, Sarah led the meetings throughout the summer. When Phoebe and her husband went to England from 1859 to 1863 sole leadership of the Tuesday Meeting reverted to Sarah. Most of the leaders of the Methodist Episcopal church attended the meeting whenever they happened to be in New York, and they were joined by college presidents, ministers, and editors from various denominations. In addition to these religious leaders, laywomen and laymen would often swell the attendance to 200. Many professed entire sanctification at the meeting and 238 similar Tuesday Meetings were established across the United States and Canada as well as in places as far away as England, India, and New Zealand.

Thomas Lankford died in 1871, and Phoebe Palmer died in 1874. In 1876 Sarah married Phoebe's widower, Walter, and moved back to New York. Together they continued to hold the Tuesday Meeting in their home. They also continued to publish the *Guide to Holiness*, which Phoebe had edited until her death. In addition, Sarah led various camp meetings, notably in Ocean Grove, New Jersey, during the summers from 1877 to 1895. After Walter died in 1883, the estate of Sarah's father, which had been tied up in court for decades, came to her. She used the money to support the New York House of Refuge on Randall's Island and various ministries of the Methodist Episcopal church. She left large bequests to the home and to foreign missionary societies of that denomination upon her death in New York City at the age of ninety.

Sarah Palmer is important as a woman who publicly taught male leaders of various Protestant denominations while backing up her leadership role with a life of service to the needy. By filling in for her better-known sister, she enabled Phoebe to extend her ministry across the continent and across the Atlantic without diminishing her home base in New York City. Sarah's philanthropy aided various missionary projects and allowed the *Guide to Holiness* to keep being published for more than twenty years after her sister's death.

• The only biography is J. A. Roche, *The Life of Mrs. Sarah A. Lankford Palmer* (1898). Her contribution is noted in her sister's biography by C. E. White, *The Beauty of Holiness: Phoebe Palmer as Theologian, Revivalist, Feminist, and Humanitarian* (1986).

CHARLES EDWARD WHITE

PALMER, Sophia French (26 May 1853–27 Apr. 1920), professional nurse, was born in Milton, Massachusetts, the daughter of Simeon Palmer, a physician, and Maria Burdell Spencer. Details of Palmer's early years and education are limited.

In 1876, at the age of twenty-two, Palmer entered the Boston Training School for Nurses (later the Massachusetts General Hospital School of Nursing). Upon graduating from the two-year program, she took on the private care of patients with nervous or mental illnesses, beginning in 1878 with those of the well-known physician/alienist S. Weir Mitchell of Philadelphia. Her private care cases involved traveling to California, where she stayed for a few years. Upon her return to the East, Palmer developed her organizational skills by establishing nurses' training schools, first in 1883 at St. Luke's in New Bedford, Massachusetts, and later, in 1889, at the Garfield Memorial Hospital in Washington, D.C.

Considered a born crusader, and described as restless, impatient, and "like a spirited race horse held by the reins of tradition," Palmer found her niche in nursing journalism. In 1896, while still employed as director of the Rochester (N.Y.) City Hospital (later known as Rochester General), she studied journalism in preparation for the work that would occupy her until the time of her death. From 1893 to 1895 she served as editor of the *Trained Nurse and Hospital Review*, and in 1900 she helped to establish, and assumed editorial responsibility for, the *American Journal of Nursing*, the first publication to be owned and edited by nurses. She remained its editor through the first two decades of its development.

Known for her gifts of logical analysis as well as her outspoken editorials, Palmer was influential in the promotion of a variety of nursing reforms. Her diverse interests often put her in the forefront of innovation. For example, her participation in the 1893 Congress of Nurses at the World's Columbian Exhibition in Chicago catalyzed the establishment of the first national professional organization for women, the Society of Superintendents of Training Schools for Nurses (later the National League for Nursing). In 1896 this society established the Associated Alumnae, now the American Nurses Association. Palmer was instrumental in securing state registration for nurses and served as the first president of the New York State Board of Nurse Examiners, a body that emphasized upgrading schools through inspections rather than focusing on the practice of individuals.

In 1906, though unmarried, Palmer adopted an eight-year-old daughter, Elizabeth A. Palmer, who died in 1917 after a long struggle with tuberculosis. The circumstances surrounding the adoption remain unclear, probably because of Palmer's insistence on privacy in her personal life.

Although her pioneering efforts were instrumental to nursing's move toward professionalization, Palmer was criticized for her militant, intimidating, and unfair journalism, often by Lavinia Dock, a contemporary challenger who served as an associate editor of the *American Journal of Nursing* throughout Palmer's twenty years as editor in chief. Provoking outrage through her editorials and her selective inattention to contemporary issues, Palmer was steadfast in her belief that the journal remain neutral in political issues and was soundly criticized by those who disagreed. For example, there was no mention of Margaret Sanger, whose crusade for voluntary motherhood ultimately developed into the planned parenthood movement. And although Dock's special crusade, the National Women's Suffrage Movement, was gaining extraordinary momentum during her tenure as editor, it was never treated in the journal, which was read almost exclusively by women.

Of all the wide-ranging activities that contributed to her success as a leader, Palmer's stewardship of the *American Journal of Nursing* had the broadest impact. Her last editorial, which was published in the same issue in which her death was announced, marked a new and promising era for nursing. It included highlights from meetings with the Rockefeller Foundation, which led to the Goldmark Report of 1923, a landmark study on the education of nurses that supported the establishment of independent university schools of nursing. This editorial also included comments on the shortage of nurses and a recommendation of the reorganization bill for the army, which would provide nurses in the military with rank, benefits, and recognition. Palmer died in Forest Lawn, New York.

Through her commitment and efforts, Palmer established schools for nursing, was instrumental in creating two major nursing organizations, and helped obtain state registration as a route to credibility for nursing practice. The journal provided a very public forum for her to speak out on every aspect of nursing's development, and through it she was an impressive presence to be reckoned with by those who sought to give form and substance to organized nursing.

• Publications by Palmer include editorials in *Trained Nurse and Hospital Review* (June–Dec. 1895) and in the *American Journal of Nursing* (1900–1920) as well as "Editor's Miscellany" in the *American Journal of Nursing* (1900–1907; 1911; 1912). Palmer also wrote six articles for these journals: "Alumnae Associations," *Trained Nurse and Hospital Review* 14 (Apr. 1895): 201; "Present Work and Future Possibilities of the Trained Nurse in the Care of the Sick Poor in Their Homes," *Trained Nurse and Hospital Review* 15 (Sept. 1895): 114; "Effect of Registration upon the Educational Standards of Training-Schools," *American Journal of Nursing* 7 (Mar. 1907): 428; "The Essential Features of a Bill for the State Registration of Nurses, and How to Pass It," *American Journal of Nursing* 7 (Mar. 1907): 428; "Efficiency in Hospital Management, the Need of the Personal Equation in Service versus Public Pride in Equipment," *American Journal of Nursing* 8 (Jan. 1908): 252; and "State Societies, their Organization and Place in Nursing Education," *American Journal of Nursing* 9 (Sept. 1909): 956. See especially Palmer's first editorial in the *American Journal of Nursing* 1, no. 1 (Oct. 1900), and her last, vol. 20, no. 7 (Apr. 1920). T. E. Christy, "Portrait of a Leader," *Nursing Outlook* 23 (Dec. 1975): 746–51, provides biographical details. An obituary is in *American Journal of Nursing* 20, no. 7 (Apr. 1920).

OLGA MARANJIAN CHURCH

PALMER, Walter Walker (27 Feb. 1882–28 Oct. 1950), physician and educator, was born in Southfield, Massachusetts, the son of Henry Wellington Palmer and Almira Roxana Walker, farmers. After completing his secondary education at Mount Hermon Academy in 1901, he matriculated at Amherst College and received a B.S. in 1905. He spent the next year teaching mathematics at Milton Academy and then enrolled in the Harvard University Medical School, where he received an M.D. in 1910. For the next five years he was affiliated with Boston's Massachusetts General Hospital, the first year as an intern and then two years each as a Henry P. Walcott Fellow and a resident physician.

In 1913 Palmer was persuaded to take on the additional duties of instructor of physiological chemistry at Harvard by Lawrence Joseph Henderson, the Harvard biochemist who discovered the chemical processes by which the human body's acid-base balance is maintained. Although Palmer had originally intended to open his own general practice, he soon decided that teaching and research were more alluring and began collaborating with Henderson on a study of the intensity of urinary acidity in normal and pathological conditions.

In 1915 Palmer moved to New York City, where he became an assistant in medicine at the Rockefeller Institute for Medical Research. He broadened his investigations concerning acid-base balance by studying how this balance is upset by pathological conditions such as diabetes and nephritis, a form of kidney disease. He also investigated the functions of the thyroid gland and developed a more accurate method for determining the amount of hemoglobin, the iron-carrying pigment of the red blood cells that carries oxygen from the lungs to the tissues, present in the bloodstream.

In 1917 Palmer returned to teaching, as associate professor of medicine at Columbia University's College of Physicians and Surgeons. He also joined the staff at Presbyterian Hospital as an associate attending physician and acting director of medical service. With the exception of a brief sojourn at Johns Hopkins University, where he was associate professor of medicine at the medical school and associate visiting physician at the hospital from 1919 to 1921, he continued at Columbia and Presbyterian for the next thirty years. In 1921, the year before he married Francesca de Kay Gilder, with whom he had three children, he was appointed Bard Professor of Medicine and promoted to director of medical service. Shortly thereafter he was joined by several of his former colleagues from Johns

Hopkins, who helped him develop Columbia's department of internal medicine into one of the finest in the world. He also played an important role in developing Columbia's medical clinic into one of the foremost teaching and research organizations in the United States by helping to found in the late 1920s the New York Medical Center, a joint venture of Columbia and Presbyterian. In 1938, following the merger of the governing boards of Presbyterian and the Neurological Institute, he took on the additional duties of the institute's medical director. In 1947 he retired from Columbia and Presbyterian and became the director of the New York Public Health Research Institute, a position he held until his death.

Toward the end of his career Palmer became a spokesman for increasing the resources allocated to medical research. In 1945 he chaired the medical advisory committee, one of four committees convened at the request of President Franklin D. Roosevelt by Vannevar Bush, director of the Office of Scientific Research and Development (OSRD), to investigate ways to employ the scientific lessons learned during World War II for peaceful purposes. Palmer's committee recommended that the government take an active role in medical research by establishing a federally funded national foundation to initiate and coordinate medical research. This recommendation became part of the so-called Vannevar Bush Report, which argued forcefully in favor of greater government participation in basic scientific research and ultimately resulted in the establishment of the National Science Foundation in 1950. In 1949 Palmer was elected president of the American College of Physicians, and in this capacity he urged that the high quality of American clinical research and medical training be maintained by the creation of more career positions in the basic and clinical sciences.

Palmer served in the U.S. Army Medical Reserve Corps as a first lieutenant from 1917 to 1919 and as a major from 1926 to 1931. During World War II he was chairman of the National Research Council's committee on drugs and supplies and a member of OSRD's advisory committee. He served as president of the Harvey Society of New York City in 1926–1927, a member of the National Board of Medical Examiners from 1921 to 1943, editor in chief of the Neilson Loose Leaf System of Medicine, and a member of the American Medical Association's council of pharmacy and chemistry. He also served on the editorial staffs of *Journal of Biological Chemistry*, *Archives of Internal Medicine*, and *Archives of Medicine* and chaired the advisory committee of the *American Journal of Medicine*. He died at his farm in Tyringham, Massachusetts.

As a biochemical researcher Palmer contributed to a better understanding of the human body's biochemistry. As a teacher and administrator he contributed significantly to the development of several of the country's foremost medical research institutions.

• Palmer's papers have not been located. His involvement with the Vannevar Bush Report is discussed in Vannevar

Bush, *Science—The Endless Frontier: A Report to the President on a Program for Postwar Scientific Research* (1945; repr. 1960). An obituary is in the *New York Times*, 29 Oct. 1950.

CHARLES W. CAREY, JR.

PALMER, William Adams (12 Sept. 1781–3 Dec. 1860), lawyer and anti-Mason, was born in Hebron, Connecticut, the son of Stephen Palmer and Susannah Sawyer, farmers. Palmer as a boy suffered from an accident to his hand that made it difficult for him to do farm work. After receiving an education in the public schools of Hebron, he decided to pursue a legal career. He went to work in a law office in Hebron, moved in 1800 to Chelsea, Vermont, to continue his legal training, and two years later was admitted to the Vermont bar. Palmer's practice for the next five years was conducted in Derby and surrounding villages. In 1806 he moved to St. Johnsbury.

Palmer met with success in his legal career and occupied several judicial posts. While in St. Johnsbury, he was elected in 1807 as judge of probate for Caledonia County. To execute the responsibilities of this position, he went that year to live on a farm near the country seat at Danville, which became his permanent home for the rest of his life. Between 1811 and 1817 he again served as probate judge, and between 1807 and 1815 he was also clerk of the county court. In 1816 he was elected a justice of the Vermont Supreme Court and held this position for one year. In 1813 he married Sarah Blanchard of Danville; they had seven children, of whom five survived to maturity.

Palmer also became active in both state and national politics. He was elected twice as a Democratic-Republican representative to the lower house of the Vermont legislature (1811–1812, 1818). After James Fisk resigned from the U.S. Senate in October 1818, Palmer was chosen to replace him and then was elected for a full term, starting in 1819. That year Palmer voted for Missouri's admission to the Union as a slave state; he encountered resentment from his constituents and attempted to justify his vote in light of an argument for states' rights. In the Senate Palmer backed bills for internal improvements and supported legislation for a protective tariff. After his return from Washington, in 1825 and in 1826 he was elected as a representative to the lower house of the Vermont legislature. During these two years he gave his support to bills financing the building of roads and canals.

Between 1826 and 1834 Palmer played an important role in Vermont politics. An anti-Masonic movement arose there after William Morgan was murdered in 1826, allegedly by Masons from Canandaigua, New York, after he threatened to divulge the secrets of the order. Opposition to Freemasonry spread quickly and received Palmer's support. By 1829 Palmer, serving that year as a state assemblyman, helped to organize the first annual convention of Vermont's anti-Masonic party in Montpelier. He also attacked the power of the Masonic elite in Vermont politics and in its court system: he spoke against Masonry's tight grip over banking and business in Vermont and against the order's

exploitation of the state's agricultural system. Palmer ran as the anti-Masonic candidate for governor in 1830, opposing the National Republican and Mason Samuel C. Crafts and the Democrat Ezra Meech. He came in second behind Crafts during the popular election. Because no candidate had secured a popular majority, the state legislature had to choose a governor and decided on Crafts. Palmer suffered another defeat in 1830, when the legislature denied him election to the U.S. Senate.

Palmer experienced political success during the next four years, however; he became the anti-Masonic governor of Vermont. Members of the state legislature during the 1831 and 1832 runoff elections chose him rather than Crafts or Meech. Palmer generally appointed members of his party to judicial and county administrative posts, but as a result of majority measures in the state legislature, he was required to approve the appointments of Thomas Hutchinson and Stephen Royce, Jr., both Masons, as justices of the state supreme court. He was also compelled by votes of the assembly to name a few Masons to serve as county sheriffs.

After his victory over Meech by popular vote in the 1833 gubernatorial election, Palmer took action against Masons. He proposed a law, approved by the state assembly on 7 November 1833, that stipulated that any person administering an oath in a secret organization would be fined between fifty and one hundred dollars. Palmer was chosen by the legislature as governor in 1834. That year he succeeded in having the legislature pass a law to suspend the civil charter of the Masonic Grand Lodge of Vermont.

In his later life, Palmer's political fortunes declined. After the state assembly in 1835 was unable to elect a governor after sixty-three rounds of voting, the frustrated Palmer resigned as governor; he was replaced by his lieutenant governor, the Whig Silas Jennison. When the anti-Masons formed a coalition with the Vermont Whigs in 1836, Palmer ran as a Democrat for governor that year, but he lost to Jennison. In 1836 and 1837, however, he was elected to the Vermont Senate. He retired from political life in 1838 but briefly reappeared as a delegate to the 1850 state constitutional convention. He died in Danville.

Palmer was closely associated with the legacy of anti-Masonry in early nineteenth-century America. He denounced Masonry's secrecy, ritualism, and elitism, and as governor he opposed Masonry for its alleged control of Vermont's political and judicial machinery; his laws had a devastating effect on Freemasonry in Vermont for more than a decade.

• Significant primary sources relating to Palmer's terms as governor appear in *Records of the Governor and Council of the State of Vermont*, vol. 8 (1880). A chronology of his life is in *Biographical Directory of the American Congress, 1774–1961* (1961). For his political career see J. M. Comstock, *A List of Civil Officers of Vermont from 1777 to 1918* (1918); and A. M. Hemenway, *The Vermont Historical Gazetteer*, vol. 1 (1868). See also R. A. Wheeler, *History of the Town of Stonington, County of New London, Connecticut* (1900); J. G. Ullery, *Men*

of Vermont (1894): and Lee S. Tillotson, *Ancient Craft Masonry in Vermont* (1920). The most comprehensive analysis of Palmer's career is William Preston Vaughn, *The Anti-Masonic Party in the United States, 1826–1843* (1983). For Palmer's involvement in Vermont's anti-Masonic party, consult Randolph A. Roth, *The Democratic Dilemma: Religion, Reform, and the Social Order in the Connecticut River Valley of Vermont, 1791–1850* (1987); Paul Goodman, *Towards a Christian Republic: Antimasonry and the Great Transition in New England, 1826–1836* (1988): Steven C. Bullock, *Revolutionary Brotherhood: Freemasonry and the Transformation of the American Social Order, 1730–1840* (1996); Philip A. Grant, Jr., "The Antimasons Retain Control of the Green Mountain State," *Vermont History* 34 (1966): 169–87; and Donald J. Ratcliffe, "Antimasonry and Partisanship in Greater New England, 1826–1836," *Journal of the Early Republic* 15 (Summer 1995): 199–239.

WILLIAM WEISBERGER

PALMER, William Jackson (18 Sept. 1836–13 Mar. 1909), railroad builder, was born in Leipsic, Delaware, the son of John Palmer, a farmer and merchant, and Matilda Jackson. He attended Quaker schools and Philadelphia public schools through age sixteen, when he entered business, gaining experience in coal mining and railroad construction.

The direction of Palmer's career was set in 1858, when he became private secretary to J. Edgar Thompson, president of the Pennsylvania Railroad and one of the early leaders in the development of the American railroad system. Four years in Thompson's employment were an education in the problems and possibilities of railroad construction and management.

Palmer, as a brigadier general, fought all four years of the Civil War on behalf of the Union. In 1861 he raised a troop of cavalry and fought in the western theater in the Nashville and Shiloh campaigns. He then recruited the Fifteenth Pennsylvania Cavalry regiment, which he led at Antietam. Later captured by Confederate forces, he was exchanged in time to participate in the battles at Chickamauga, Missionary Ridge, and Atlanta.

In 1865 Palmer became treasurer and construction manager for the eastern division of the new Union Pacific Railroad (after 1869 the Kansas Pacific Railroad), building from Kansas City to Denver. He also assisted construction of the Denver Pacific from Denver to Cheyenne. The work confirmed his skills as a railroad executive and introduced him to the undeveloped resources of Colorado and the Southwest. Palmer married Mary Lincoln Mellen in 1870. They would have three children.

That same year Palmer organized the Denver and Rio Grande Railroad. His plan was to build from Denver south to Santa Fe, with a possible extension to Mexico City. "I thought how fine it would be to have a little railroad a few hundred miles in length," he wrote, "all under one's own control with one's friends, to have no jealousies and contests and differences, but be able to carry out harmoniously one's view about what ought and ought not to be done" (Fisher, p. 177). Palmer envisioned his railroad as the main street of a self-sufficient economic region, with a main line running along the base of the Rocky Mountains and spurs into the major valleys and over the key passes. He expected the transcontinental lines to detour north and south around the great mass of the Colorado mountains, leaving his railroad to develop and benefit from the mineral wealth of the Rockies. The Denver and Rio Grande reached Pueblo in 1872 and the base of La Veta Pass in 1876.

The next four years saw a bitter and complex battle between Palmer and the new Santa Fe Railroad, which had run a line up the Arkansas River to Pueblo. The two railroads battled for dominance in the Southwest by contesting control of key routes. The Santa Fe won the race over La Veta Pass and the easiest access to New Mexico. The two lines fought to a standoff in the Royal Gorge of the Arkansas River, the logical route from Pueblo to the silver-mining city of Leadville. Palmer gained control of the route in June 1879, implementing a U.S. Supreme Court decision by ousting Santa Fe employees at gunpoint. In 1880 the two companies agreed to divide the territory. The Denver and Rio Grande took the area north of the thirty-sixth parallel and west of its Denver-Trinidad line; the Santa Fe took the territory to the east and south. The agreement turned the Denver and Rio Grande into a Colorado railroad that threw 1,300 miles of rail line over the southern and central portions of the state by 1883. Much of the mileage was narrow gauge, to facilitate construction through narrow canyons and precipitous terrain.

Palmer's vision was social as well as economic. He spoke of the opportunity to create a new commonwealth and condense the progress of centuries. The railroad was not just "a mode of making money, but a large-scale model way of conjoining that with usefulness on a large scale solving a good many vexed social problems" (Anderson, p. 15).

He acted on this conviction through town promotion and industrial development. He laid out South Pueblo as an industrial center (1872) and organized the Colorado Coal and Iron Company (later Colorado Fuel and Iron) to manufacture steel rails (1880). To complement the industrial center at Pueblo, he envisioned the "Fountain Colony," later Colorado Springs, as a model community. Two-thirds of the revenues from land sales were to be reserved for community improvements and expenses. As it developed in the 1870s, Colorado Springs became a summer resort and permanent home for members of the upper middle class rather than an ideal city for the working class. Palmer's community contributions included founding Colorado College in Colorado Springs in 1874 and providing much of its support.

In 1883 Palmer resigned from his railroad and took on the presidency of the Rio Grande Western, a separate corporation that he had previously organized to connect Colorado railroads to Salt Lake City. He invested in Utah coal mining and operated the Rio Grande Western until 1901, when it was sold to the Denver and Rio Grande. He also helped to plan and build portions of the Mexican national railway between Mexico City and the United States.

When he died in Colorado Springs, Palmer was recognized as one of the leading architects of the "Rocky Mountain Empire." He was both a railroad builder and community builder who managed to maintain personal integrity while operating in the cutthroat world of nineteenth-century railroad tycoons.

• The standard biography of Palmer is John S. Fisher, *Builder of the West: The Life of General William Jackson Palmer* (1939). Shorter treatments of his career include George L. Anderson, *General William Jackson Palmer: Man of Vision*, Colorado College Studies, no. 4 (1960), and Brit Allen Store, "William Jackson Palmer: The Technique of a Pioneer Railroad Promoter in Colorado, 1871–1880," *Journal of the West* 5 (Apr. 1966): 263–74. Palmer is a central figure in Robert Athearn, *Rebel of the Rockies: A History of the Denver and Rio Grande Western Railroad* (1962), and Herbert O. Brayer, *William Blackmore: A Case Study in the Economic Development of the West* (2 vols., 1949).

CARL ABBOTT

PAN, Hermes (10 June 1905–19 Sept. 1990), dancer and film choreographer, was born Hermes Panagiotopoulos in Memphis, Tennessee, in 1905 (though he would later claim it was 1911 and then 1913), the son of Spiros Panagiotopoulos, the Greek counsel to the southern states, and Maria (maiden name unknown). Pan was raised in Nashville, where he received dance training, mostly in tap and the ballroom and social forms, becoming a specialist in the Charleston through the informal training his family's black chauffeur gave him and his sister Vasso. Shortening their last name to Pan, Vasso and Hermes performed exhibition ballroom dancing on the vaudeville circuit and finally reached New York. Hermes Pan made his debut on Broadway as a chorus dancer in 1929 in *Top Speed*, which also marked the debut of Ginger Rogers in a featured role. He moved to Los Angeles in 1931 with his sister to continue their dance act in nightclubs and to teach in private dance studios.

Pan joined RKO Studios in 1933 as camera dance assistant to Dave Gould, the dance director for the studio, on the film *Flying Down to Rio*, which introduced Fred Astaire and Ginger Rogers as a dancing team to movie audiences. Pan assisted Astaire on his solo routines and came up with the idea of Fred and Ginger "dancing head to head" in "The Carioca." This dance was so successful that Astaire insisted Pan work on all his films. Hal Borne, the rehearsal pianist for most of the series, said, "Hermes was terribly instrumental in everything Fred did. He was really Fred's alter ego. His ideas for choreography was [*sic*] exactly what Fred wanted." Eventually Pan was to work with Astaire on seventeen films, including Astaire's last musical, *Finian's Rainbow*, in 1968.

Pan remained at RKO until 1939 and was solely responsible for all the chorus work in the Astaire-Rogers series, including "The Continental" for *The Gay Divorcee* (1934), "The Piccolino" in *Top Hat* (1935), and "The Yam" in *Carefree* (1938). For the famous duets, owing to Rogers's hectic schedule Astaire would work out the steps and partnering with Pan playing Rogers's part, and then Pan would teach it to Rogers before the filming began. Pan also dubbed in the tap sounds for Rogers in all the movies. Pan won an Academy Award for Best Dance Direction in 1937 (the last year such an award was given) for the "Stiff Upper Lip" number featured in *Damsel in Distress*, where Astaire, Gracie Allen, and George Burns dance through the labyrinth of a fun house in an amusement park.

Pan's last film for RKO was also the last in that studio's series for Astaire and Rogers, *The Story of Vernon and Irene Castle* (1939). After helping Astaire on the film *Second Chorus* at Paramount in 1940, Pan went under contract to 20th Century–Fox, where he worked on musicals with Alice Faye, Carmen Miranda, Sonja Henie, and Rita Hayworth. However, it was Betty Grable, the studio's biggest star, with whom he worked most closely, staging ten of her musicals from 1941 to 1948. These included *Moon over Miami* (1941), where he appeared on screen as Grable's partner in the "Kindergarten Conga"; *Springtime in the Rockies* (1942), with its elaborate "Pan American Jubilee" finale; *Coney Island* and *Sweet Rosie O'Grady* (both 1943), where he again danced with Grable on the screen; and *That Lady in Ermine* (1948), his last film with Grable and for Fox.

During these years Pan worked once more with Astaire, on loan to Paramount for the musical *Blue Skies* (1946), and then was reunited with Astaire and Rogers on their last film together when Pan did the choreography for *The Barkleys of Broadway* (1949) at MGM. He accepted a long-term contract with that studio whereby he especially worked for producers Jack Cummings and Arthur Freed. With Astaire he did *Three Little Words* (1950), for which he devised many of the vaudeville routines, especially the ingenious "Mr. and Mrs. Hoofer at Home" for Astaire and Vera-Ellen, and *Silk Stockings* (1957), the choreographic credits for which he shared with Eugene Loring.

Pan also worked with other MGM stars, including Esther Williams in *Texas Carnival* (1951) and *Jupiter's Darling* (1955) and Ann Miller in *Lovely to Look At* (1952) and *Hit the Deck* (1955). Probably his best-remembered film during this period was *Kiss Me Kate* (1953), for which he had to devise dances that worked in 3-D, though the film was released "flat."

Although movie musicals had begun to decline by the late 1950s, Pan continued to work almost continuously, albeit on a freelance basis. These later musicals were mostly screen transfers of Broadway musicals and included *Pal Joey* (1957) for Rita Hayworth and Frank Sinatra (which also marked Pan's last appearance as a dancer on the screen); *Porgy and Bess* (1959); *Can-Can* (1960), which featured Shirley MacLaine and Juliet Prowse in the high-stepping title song; *Flower Drum Song* (1961); and *My Fair Lady* (1964). During this period he also staged the elaborate "Entrance to Rome" and dances for the epic *Cleopatra* (1963) starring Elizabeth Taylor and worked with Astaire on all three of his television specials in 1958,

1959, and 1960. His last choreographic achievements for film musicals were, unhappily, on two expensive failures: *Darling Lili* (1969), starring Julie Andrews, and *Lost Horizon* (1973). He continued to work in films, however, staging dances in nonmusical films such as the *Pink Panther* series.

Besides his Academy Award, Pan won two Emmy Awards for *An Evening with Fred Astaire* (1958) and *Astaire Time* (1960), a National Film Award for achievement in cinema (1980), and a special award from the Joffrey Ballet (1986). He died at his home in Beverly Hills.

Pan's work on the screen is often difficult to assess since he was so closely associated with Astaire and seemed to be quite happy remaining in his shadow. In a 1972 interview with John Kobal, Pan said he had "absorbed an awful lot from [Astaire], subconsciously even, and from his style. On the other hand, I'm certain that he has gotten certain things from me." Pan bore a striking resemblance to Astaire and was sometimes used as a double in some of the long shots in the RKO films. Perhaps this was why he was never interested in a performing career; he later said his onscreen partnering of Hayworth and Grable at Fox was "more by accident. There were just no trained men around to dance with them." One of Pan's major assets was obviously his adaptability: he could create interesting numbers that showcased the superior dancing abilities of Astaire, or just as easily showcase the more limited abilities of Grable, or devise spectacular settings for the specialized talents of the skating Sonja Henie or the swimming Esther Williams. He was also the only dance director–choreographer in Hollywood to work continuously for nearly four and a half decades and for every major studio.

• Pan's work with Fred Astaire is discussed in some detail in John Mueller, *Astaire Dancing* (1985), and to a lesser extent in Arlene Croce, *The Fred Astaire and Ginger Rogers Book* (1972). Highly complimentary references to him are in both Astaire's autobiography, *Steps in Time* (1959), and Ginger Rogers's *Ginger* (1991). A perceptive interview with Pan is included in John Kobal, *People Will Talk* (1985), and the same author takes a more extensive look at Pan's post-RKO career in *Gotta Sing Gotta Dance* (1971; rev. ed., 1983). All of the Rogers and Astaire movies are available on Turner Home Video, some of the Betty Grable films on Fox Video, and most of the MGM musicals on MGM/UA. Some of these are on laser disk with rare footage of deleted musical numbers. Interviews with Pan are in a number of television documentaries, including *The RKO Story* (Turner Home Video), and on tape by Ronald L. Davis for the SMU Oral History Project on the Performing Arts. An obituary is in *Dance Magazine*, Jan. 1991, pp. 30–32.

FRANK W. D. RIES

PANCAKE, Breece Dexter (29 June 1952–8 Apr. 1979), writer, was born in Milton, West Virginia, the son of Clarence Robert Pancake, a chemical company employee, and Helen Frazier. Known more commonly as Breece D'J Pancake, he acquired this unique form of his given name partly by accident. When he converted from Methodism to Catholicism (1977), he chose John as his confirmation name, and the complete name he planned to use when he published his stories was Breece D. J. Pancake. After a typesetter altered the punctuation, Pancake deliberately let the mistake stand.

As a young man Pancake loved hunting and fishing, and he traveled extensively (frequently by hitchhiking) in the western United States and Mexico. After high school he worked part time as a short-haul truck driver, a member of a road construction crew, and a short-order cook. Such experiences would provide material for his gritty, working-class fiction.

During the summer and fall of 1970 Pancake attended West Virginia Wesleyan College, where he became interested in drama and folk music. Because of his father's chronic illness and a desire to be closer to home, he transferred in 1971 to Marshall University in Huntington, West Virginia. There he was fiction editor of the student literary magazine, and in 1974 he earned a B.A. degree with a major in English.

Pancake considered attending law school but instead took a teaching job at Fork Union Military Academy in August 1974. The next year he moved to Staunton Military Academy, where he taught English and served as department chair. Meanwhile he enrolled in some graduate classes in English at the University of Virginia. In 1977 he resigned his teaching position and moved to Charlottesville as a full-time student. There he studied creative writing under John Casey, Richard Jones, James Alan McPherson, and Peter Taylor. Pancake was fiction consultant to the editor of the *Virginia Quarterly Review* and taught undergraduate classes in composition and fiction writing. He received a Governor's Fellowship (1976) and a Hoyns Fellowship in Fiction Writing (1978), and he won a Jefferson Society Fiction Award in 1977.

Meanwhile Pancake's stories began to appear in journals of limited circulation like *Rivanna* and the *Declaration* (a student publication at the University of Virginia). His work first attracted national attention in December 1977, when his story "Trilobites" was published in the *Atlantic Monthly*. Phoebe-Lou Adams, an editor at the magazine, commented that this story provoked more favorable reader responses than that of any other new writer in her memory. Pancake published only two more stories before his death: "In the Dry" in the *Atlantic Monthly* (Aug. 1978) and "Time and Again" in *Nightwork* (Sept. 1978).

Shortly before his twenty-seventh birthday Pancake died from a self-inflicted shotgun wound near his apartment on the Farmington Estate outside Charlottesville. Except for one course in German, he had completed the requirements for an M.A. in English with a concentration in creative writing. At the time of his death Pancake was working on additional short stories and a novel focusing on the lives of West Virginia coal miners. Another uncompleted project was a play based on his experiences teaching at military schools and tentatively titled "Toy Soldier."

After Pancake's death the *Atlantic Monthly* published two more of his stories, and still another ap-peared in *Antaeus*. A posthumous volume of stories collected by his former teacher John Casey was published in 1983. This collection contained six previously published stories (with minor changes) along with six new stories. The book was nominated for a Pulitzer Prize and has been translated into German and Portuguese. A play titled *Hollow*, which incorporated several Pancake stories and details of his life, was produced by Mark Rance in Mount Hope, West Virginia (1990).

Even though Pancake's literary output was limited, his stories have been compared favorably to those of Ernest Hemingway and Flannery O'Connor. Most of Pancake's stories are set in his native West Virginia, and his protagonists are usually frustrated adolescents or defeated older men who are trapped by environment or personal history. For example, in Pancake's best-known story, "Trilobites," the main character searches his drought-stricken farm for fossils. Just as these tiny "stone animals" are covered by layers of soil and rock, he feels buried in the sediment of past events. If employed at all, Pancake's characters typically hold dead-end, minimum-wage jobs, and away from work they are drawn to the blood and violence of barroom brawls, hunting, and cockfights. Characteristic story titles like "Time and Again" or "The Way It Has to Be" suggest repetitive, compulsive behavior or a sense of futility. In "A Room Forever" the narrator uses a bleak rented room as a metaphor for the human condition and observes that he has been "inside too long." When he examines the situations of those around him, however, he knows that "they can't run away from it or drink their way out of it or die to get rid of it." Critic Ellesa Clay High says this story "exemplifies what Pancake does best: a dark fictional frieze of those hanging on the fringes . . . those who somehow survive on the other side of pain and despair."

• Most of Pancake's manuscripts and letters are in the possession of his mother, Helen Pancake. Some materials left with John Casey are now in the University of Virginia Library. The most useful sources of biographical information are Cynthia Kadohata, "Breece D'J Pancake," *Mississippi Review* 18, no. 1 (1989): 35–61, and Thomas E. Douglass, "The Story of Breece D'J Pancake," *Appalachian Journal* 17, no. 4 (1990): 376–90 (but dates of birth and death given by Douglass are incorrect). The best critical evaluation is Geoffrey Galt Harpham, "Short Stack: The Stories of Breece D'J Pancake," *Studies in Short Fiction* 23, no. 3 (1986): 265–73. See also Albert E. Wilhelm, "Poverty of Spirit in Breece Pancake's Short Fiction," *Critique: Studies in Modern Fiction* 28, no. 1 (1986): 39–44, and Ellesa Clay High, "A Lost Generation: The Appalachia of Breece D'J Pancake," *Appalachian Journal* 13, no. 1 (1985): 34–40.

ALBERT E. WILHELM

PANCOAST, Henry Khunrath (26 Feb. 1875–20 May 1939), physician and educator, was born in Philadelphia, Pennsylvania, the son of Seth Pancoast, a physician, and Susan George. In 1892 Pancoast graduated from Friends Central School in Philadelphia. He had decided to study medicine like his father, but the untimely death of both his parents necessitated his working in a bank before entering medical school. In 1896 he worked as a radiographer with Charles Lester Leonard in the first X-ray department in the United States, established by the University of Pennsylvania in the William Pepper Chemical Laboratory. Pancoast received his M.D. from the medical school of the University of Pennsylvania in 1898.

From 1901 to 1904 Pancoast served as assistant instructor in clinical surgery and assistant demonstrator in surgery at the School of Medicine of the University of Pennsylvania, where he continued to pursue his interest in radiology. Pancoast's expertise in X rays was rewarded in May 1902, when he was appointed radiographer of the university hospital, succeeding Leonard. During the same year he published his first radiological paper, "Cervical Rib." In 1903 he married Clara L. Boggs; they had no children.

Pancoast was elected to membership in the American Roentgen Ray Society in 1903, and at that meeting he presented his findings on the therapeutic effects of the X rays. Pancoast's results were based the use of X rays in the treatment of nearly 100 cases. This study was one of the first attempts at X ray dosage control to be undertaken in the United States, and through it Pancoast attained national recognition among radiologists. In 1905 he became a charter member of the Philadelphia Roentgen Ray Society, which was formed under the leadership of Leonard. With C. B. Worden, J. Sailer, and G. Davis, Pancoast demonstrated, in 1906, that bismuth subnitrate (a chemical compound used in early X-ray diagnostics and therapies) was toxic. These findings led to the general adoption of bismuth subcarbonate and bismuth oxychloride for radiographic purposes. In 1911 Pancoast was elected secretary of the American Roentgen Ray Society, and the following year he became president of the Philadelphia Roentgen Ray Society. Also in 1912 he became professor of radiology in the medical school of the University of Pennsylvania. Four years later he was a charter member of the American Radium Society.

Pancoast became secretary of the American Radium Society in 1917 and, with T. G. Miller and H. R. M. Landis, published "A Roentgenologic Study of the Effects of Dust Inhalation upon the Lungs," one of the earliest studies of pneumoconiosis, a lung disease caused by dust inhalation. In 1918 Pancoast was commissioned assistant surgeon, lieutenant junior grade, in the Medical Corps of the U.S. Navy, serving during World War I. In 1919 he was elected president of the American Radium Society and retired to the navy's inactive list. He became an active member of the Radiological Society of North America in 1922 and the following year was elected a Fellow of the American College of Radiology. Also in 1923 he was appointed consulting physiologist to the U.S. Bureau of Mines in connection with his research on the effects of dust inhalation. Pancoast served as chancellor of the American College of Radiology from 1924 to 1928 and in 1925 published with E. P. Pendergrass an important contribution on the study of pneumoconiosis. In 1932

Pancoast was appointed chairman of the Section on Radiology of the American Medical Association, serving on the board of directors and as a member of the Executive Committee of the American Society for the Control of Cancer.

In 1933 Pancoast published "The Widening Field of Radiology and the Future of Radiology as a Medical Specialty." On 25 September 1933 he was elected president of the First American Congress of Radiology and, three days later, the first president of the American College of Radiology. He died at his home in Merion, Pennsylvania.

Pancoast's contributions to radiology are reflected in part by his published papers, which number more than a hundred. The moderation and care that characterized his exposition of scientific problems were evident even in his earliest work. While he came to know the enormous scope and value of radiography, his opinions were based on ample experimental evidence observed through the years. Pancoast's pioneering efforts with X rays helped to develop and establish the science of radiology.

• The primary biographical source on Pancoast is his autobiographical "Reminiscences of a Radiologist," *American Journal of Roentgenology* (Feb. 1938). Obituaries are in *Radiology* (Aug. 1939), the *Journal of Industrial Hygiene and Toxicology* (Sept. 1939), and the *New York Times*, 22 May 1939.

LUTHER W. BRADY

PANCOAST, Joseph (23 Nov. 1805–7 Mar. 1882), anatomist and surgeon, was born in Burlington, New Jersey, the son of John Pancoast and Ann Abbott. Pancoast's forebears on his father's side had accompanied William Penn from England to America. Pancoast received his medical degree in 1828 from the University of Pennsylvania. He married Rebecca Abbott in July 1829; the couple had one child. He opened a surgical practice in Philadelphia and joined other bright young doctors in the Philadelphia Association of Medical Instruction.

In 1831 Pancoast became director of the Philadelphia School of Anatomy, was elected a physician to the Philadelphia Hospital and its children's hospital in 1834, and became a visiting surgeon there from 1838 to 1845. For a span of thirty-six years, Pancoast held in succession the two most important chairs at the Jefferson Medical College: the chair of surgery (1838–1840) and the chair of anatomy (1841–1874). From 1854 to 1864 he was also a member of the staff of the Pennsylvania Hospital.

As a surgeon Pancoast was an equal in skill and boldness to George McClellan, his predecessor in the hospital. His clinics were always eagerly attended by the students, who were sometimes allowed to participate in practical work. When military medical representatives visited the United States, they were directed by the Military Bureau of the War Department to observe Pancoast's innovative surgical techniques. He developed numerous new procedures, including an operation for remedying exstrophy of the bladder, a condition in which the bladder turns itself inside out as a result of weak or missing vesicals on the anterior wall; an operation for soft and mixed cataracts; a procedure for draining pus from the pleural cavity; an operation for obstruction of the nasal duct; and an operation for bad cases of strabismus, a muscular disability of the eyes rendering them unable to focus on a single point simultaneously and often resulting in crossed eyes. His surgical expertise and knowledge of human anatomy in general made him a confident, lucid teacher, whose aim was to teach anatomy of the living, not that of the dead.

In addition to his practical contributions to surgery, Pancoast published a number of works. His greatest contribution to medical literature was his *Treatise on Operative Surgery* (1844). He also translated several foreign medical books from Italian into English, revised three editions of *System of Anatomy* (1839, 1843, and 1846) by Caspar Wistar and William Horner, and contributed many articles to the *American Journal of Medical Sciences*, the *Medical Examiner*, and the *American Medical Intelligencer*. He had been in retirement for eight years when he died in Philadelphia.

• Contemporary sources regarding Pancoast and his work include *Poulson's American Daily Advertiser* (Philadelphia, Pa.), 4 July 1829; the *Boston Medical and Surgical Journal* (16 Mar. 1882); the *Medical News*, 18 Mar. 1882; and the *Philadelphia Medical Times*, 25 Mar. 1882. See also Samuel W. Gross, *Autobiography*, vol. 2 (1887); W. S. Miller, "Master Surgeons of America: Joseph Pancoast," *Surgery, Gynecology, and Obstetrics* 50 (May 1930): 921–23; J. W. Crosky, *History of Blockley* (1929); Joseph W. Holland, *The Jefferson Medical College of Philadelphia* (1909); and George W. Gould; *The Jefferson Medical College: A History 1826–1904* (1904). An obituary is in the *Philadelphia Public Ledger*, 8 Mar. 1882.

DAVID Y. COOPER

PANGBORN, Clyde Edward (28 Oct. 1894–29 Mar. 1958), aviation pioneer, was born in Bridgeport, Washington, the son of Max J. Pangborn and Frances Opel Lamb, farmers. While he was a small boy, Pangborn's family moved to Idaho, where he was educated, graduating from St. Marie's High School in 1914. Although he studied civil engineering at the University of Idaho, he left school without graduating and worked for a time as a forest ranger and a deputy sheriff in Shoshone County.

Pangborn was initiated into aviation when he enlisted in the U.S. Army Air Service on 19 December 1917, after the United States entered World War I. During flight training at Eberts Field, Arkansas, and Love Field, Texas, he quickly demonstrated great skill and composure at the controls. He received his pilot rating in November 1918, too late for service in the war. Not content to go back to his earlier life, he secured work in the Air Service as an instructor pilot at Ellington Field, Texas, and as a result was able to keep flying until March 1919, when he was mustered out of the military.

Pangborn was still unwilling to give up airplanes, and he became one of the legendary barnstormers who emerged just after World War I. He made a living as a gypsy flyer, traveling the backwaters of the United States, exhibiting his aircraft, and giving rides to locals. Equipped with a war surplus JN-4 "Jenny" trainer, Pangborn roamed the country in search of thrills and money enough to survive and keep flying. Pangborn spent much of his time in the Pacific Northwest—which was not the prime location for barnstorming—and in California. In 1921 he and Ivan R. Gates formed the Gates Flying Circus, and for the next seven years they made the circuit around the country, journeying more than 125,000 miles. They made a respectable living during the 1920s, but as the decade ended the depression and the increasing commonness of airplanes combined to wipe out their barnstorming business.

Pangborn next attempted to launch the New Standard Aircraft Corporation of Paterson, New Jersey, but the depression also ended that effort. He then went to work for the Bergen County, New Jersey, police department as a pilot. That lasted only a short time, however, and in 1930 he tried barnstorming again. He also ventured into air racing, and on 28 July 1931, Pangborn and Hugh Herndon, Jr., set out to break an around-the-world flight record recently set by Wiley Post and Harold Gatty. Although they got as far as Khabarovsk in the Soviet Union, delays forced them to abandon the attempt.

With the around-the-world flight a bust, the two fliers decided to set a speed record during the return trip from Asia across the Pacific Ocean to the United States. Unfortunately, during the flight from Khabarovsk to Tokyo, Pangborn and Herndon flew over Japanese military installations, and they were arrested as spies upon entering Japan. It took weeks to sort out the diplomatic problems, and Pangborn's mother even enlisted the help of Senator William E. Borah (R.-Idaho) to gain their release. They were finally fined $1,025 each and allowed to leave Japan, taking off on 3 October 1931. From Samishiro Beach, Japan, to Wenatchee, Washington, Pangborn and Herndon made the first nonstop flight across the Pacific in 41 hours and 13 minutes.

In 1932 Pangborn went to New York City to work for Clarence D. Chamberlin as an aeronautical engineer and test pilot, but in less than a year he left that job to sell Fairchild Aircraft Company airplanes in South America. In 1934 he and Roscoe Turner, a famous air racer and aviation advocate, flew a modified Boeing 247D—a revolutionary, twin-engined, all-metal monoplane that helped bring about the airline revolution of the 1930s—from London to Australia in the MacRobertson Race. They left on 20 October and landed 92 hours, 55 minutes, and 38 seconds later in Melbourne after flying 11,325 miles. Even so, they finished second in the race, following closely behind the record-setting De Havilland "Comet."

For the next twenty years Pangborn drifted around the aviation industry in a variety of capacities. He flew demonstration aircraft for the Burnelli Company in 1935–1936 and worked for a short while as a test pilot for the Bellanca Aircraft Company. Connections with these European firms ensured that he traveled throughout the Continent, witnessing firsthand the emergence of fascism and the troubles that erupted into war. Just as Germany invaded Poland in 1939, Pangborn returned to the United States, bringing with him Swana Beauclaire Duval, a French fashion designer whom he had married in 1937. They had no children. Once back in the United States, Pangborn recruited American fliers for the Royal Air Force (RAF), helping them enter Canada where they could legally enlist to fight with the British. Several members of the RAF's Eagle Squadron, the unit made up of Americans that fought in the battle of Britain, were recruited by Pangborn. He was also instrumental in organizing the shipment of aircraft and air weapons to Britain in 1940 and 1941. He later served in the war as a pilot transporting war matériel from the United States to the Allies in Europe.

Following World War II Pangborn returned to Europe and worked for Burnelli demonstrating their twin-engined "flying wing" aircraft. This aircraft, however, proved to be a disappointing design because of aerodynamic instability. He also worked as a test pilot and consultant for several other aeronautical firms, especially Lear Aviation. He died in New York City.

Pangborn's career was not unlike many other second-level fliers of his generation. He was able to make a life in the industry but never on the scale of Charles A. Lindbergh (1902–1974) or Eddie Rickenbacker. He was a capable airman, recognized as such both by the public and his fellow aviators. The record-setting flights he made between 1931 and 1934 were highlights of his career, but his service in 1940 and 1941 on behalf of the British opposing Nazi Germany may have been his greatest contribution.

• The Pangborn collection at Washington State University has more than 100,000 items relating to his career. There is also material relating to him in the National Air and Space Museum, Smithsonian Institution, Washington, D.C.; the North Central Washington Museum Association, Wenatchee; and the William E. Borah Collection in the Library of Congress. A biography of Pangborn is Carl M. Cleveland, *"Upside-Down Pangborn": King of the Barnstormers* (1978). A short sketch of his career can be found in Ronald W. Hoagland, ed., *The Blue Book of Aviation* (1942). On barnstorming see K. C. Tessendorf, *Barnstormers and Daredevils* (1988), and Don Dwiggins, *The Barnstormers: Flying Daredevils of the Roaring Twenties* (1968). Other aspects of his career are discussed in Richard P. Hallion, *Legacy of Flight: The Guggenheim Contribution to American Aviation* (1977); Cecil R. Roseberry, *The Challenging Skies: The Colorful Story of Aviation's Most Exciting Years, 1919–1939* (1966); and Terry Gwynn-Jones, *Farther and Faster: Aviation's Adventuring Years, 1909–1939* (1991). An obituary is in the *New York Times*, 30 Mar. 1958.

ROGER D. LAUNIUS

PANOFSKY, Erwin (30 Mar. 1892–14 Mar. 1968), art historian, was born in Hannover, Germany, the son of Arnold Panofsky, a man of independent means whose family made its money in the mining district of Silesia,

and Caescilie Solling. Panofsky grew up in Berlin, where he attended the Joachimsthalsche Gymnasium. At the University of Freiburg he studied law before turning to study art history under the supervision of Wilhelm Vöge and received his doctorate in 1914 with a revision of an essay on German artist Albrecht Dürer's relation to the art theory of the Italian Renaissance, which had earlier won him the Hermann-Grimm Prize. A riding accident relieved him of completing military service during World War I, thus enabling him to study at the University of Berlin with medieval art historian Adolf Goldschmidt. In 1916 he married Dorothea "Dora" Mosse, a member of the important Berlin publishing family, with whom he would have two sons.

In 1920 Panofsky was invited to head the art history department of the newly created University of Hamburg; he served as junior faculty member there from 1921 to 1926 and as chaired professor from 1926 to 1933. In 1931 Panofsky began to teach alternating semesters as a visiting professor at New York University and was in the United States when he learned of his dismissal from Hamburg in 1933 as a result of the Nazi expulsion of Jews from government offices. During the 1934–1935 academic term, he taught at both Princeton University and at New York University's Institute of Fine Arts. In 1935 he was named as the first permanent professor of the School of Historical Studies of the newly founded Institute for Advanced Study at Princeton. During the 1947–1948 academic year he taught as the Charles Eliot Norton Professor at Harvard University, giving the lectures that later would be published as his masterful study, *Early Netherlandish Painting* (1953). While at Princeton he continued to teach at the Institute of Fine Arts in New York and in 1962, upon his retirement from the Institute for Advanced Study, was named to the Samuel F. B. Morse Chair of the Institute of Fine Arts. Dorothea Panofsky died in 1965, and in 1966 he married art historian Gerda Soergel. Panofsky died two years later in Princeton, New Jersey.

Frequently described as the most important art historian of the twentieth century, Panofsky was an energetic participant in early twentieth-century German efforts to establish the methodological identity of the young discipline of art history, and after his emigration he assumed a fundamental role in the professionalization of art history in the United States. Over his career, Panofsky trained a long line of prominent art historians, including William S. Heckscher, Walter Horn, H. W. Janson, Lotte Brand Philip, and Edgar Wind.

As a young scholar, Panofsky wrote a series of important methodological essays engaging the work of two of the pioneers of his discipline, Alois Riegl and Heinrich Wölfflin. In three of his essays, "Das Problem des Stils in der bildenden Kunst" (1915), "Der Begriff des Kunstwollens" (1920), and "Uber das Verhältnis der Kunstgeschichte zur Kunsttheorie" (1925), Panofsky, like other German scholars, was engaged in a neo-Kantian enterprise: just as other neo-Kantians sought transcendental categories of human thinking in philosophy or science, Panofsky made the same effort in the realm of art. He explained that the "salvation of scientific study of art was that it always must acknowledge that art is art and not just any sort of historical object." In tandem with his student Edgar Wind, who offered "form" and "fullness" as bipolar categories in his dissertation, Panofsky wrote that art resides between the poles of artistic power to give form and the sensual data of perception. In *Idea* (1924), Panofsky studied the interaction of those two poles not so much as they were reflected in artistic production as in two strands of neo-Platonic aesthetic philosophy.

In Hamburg, Panofsky became closely associated with philosopher Ernst Cassirer and even attended Cassirer's university lectures. During the 1920s Cassirer was producing his *Philosophy of Symbolic Forms*, in which he expanded Kant's "Copernican revolution"— the belief that knowledge of the world, even empirical knowledge, was structured by the human mind—into an analysis of all cultural phenomena as human creations or "symbolic forms." In a tribute to Cassirer's philosophy, Panofsky wrote one of his most important essays, "Die Perspektive als 'symbolische Form'" (1927). In this essay, Panofsky analyzed the development of Renaissance perspective as the creation not of objective perspective, since it was not an exact replica of physiological experience, but rather of a conventional or symbolic form that conditioned modern artistic representation. Related to his earlier discussions of fullness and form, Panofsky emphasized perspective's mediating role: it provided order but, ultimately, it was the visual world that it ordered.

In Hamburg, Cassirer and Panofsky were both closely associated with the group of scholars that formed around Aby Warburg's Renaissance studies research institute, the Warburg Library. Dedicated to the study of the "afterlife of antiquity," the library grew out of the thematic concerns of Warburg's art history. Warburg's associates often adopted his *Typengeschichte*, or history of types, by which he studied the complicated transformations of certain types, such as Salome or Judith, on their circuitous route from the classical past to Renaissance art and attempted to decode the cultural significance of these transformations. Panofsky's *Hercules am Scheidewege* (1930), a study of the topos of Hercules' choice between two Venuses at the crossroads, is one of the consummate examples of the Warburgian tracing of types.

The history of types is, however, part of Warburg's larger methodological development of "iconology," which involves the cultural and intellectual decoding of images, often using close readings of literary texts likely to have influenced, sometimes indirectly, the artist under consideration. Warburg's iconology required that the art historian be part philologist, working closely with a wide range of literary sources, often obscure medieval treatises on science and magic.

Panofsky became the principal emissary of Warburg's iconology to the United States and eventually became its principal proponent internationally. To an American academic discipline with few of the rigors of art history in Europe, iconology became a path to the professionalization of art history in the United States, and Panofsky's *Studies in Iconology* (1939), with its "introductory" setting out a definition of iconology, became one of the key guides for a generation of art historians. The introductory sets out three levels of interpretation. The first is a pre-iconographical level, by which an art historian identifies the subject matter and the expressional character of a gesture (Panofsky uses the example of a hat being removed); the second is iconographical, by which, for example, St. Bartholomew is identified by his knife; the third, or iconological, level is "apprehended by ascertaining those underlying principles which reveal the basic attitude of a nation, a period, a class, a religious or philosophical persuasion—unconsciously qualified by one personality and condensed into one work" (p. 7). Although Panofsky refers in his introductory to Cassirer's symbolic analysis, his iconological enterprise in the United States concentrated mostly on the philosophical and theological decoding of art. Thus, for example, in expounding his theory of "disguised symbolism" in *Early Netherlandish Painting*, Panofsky deciphered religious symbols hidden in the naturalistic paintings of the van Eyck brothers and other Netherlandish paintings.

For American art historians, Panofsky's method stood as an extremely intellectualized art history by comparison to the connoisseurship practiced by many American art historians before World War II. If Panofsky took pleasure in publishing footnotes with untranslated Greek quotations, his erudition was an inextricable part of his position in the American academic environment. In the midst of a mid-century American emphasis on the humanities and the value of culture, Panofsky wrote an essay on "The History of Art as a Humanistic Discipline" (1940), tying his discipline to the tradition of the humanities and the humanities to human dignity.

Because of the philosophical and literary erudition that is so important to his work, Panofsky has often been placed at the contextual end of the contextual/formal divide within art history and criticized for a tendency to overintellectualize art. Nevertheless, style was a significant part of his analysis. It played an important role in *Early Netherlandish Painting* as it did in *The Life and Art of Albrecht Dürer* (1943), in which he painstakingly described the burin movements of Dürer's engravings. In terms of stylistic or formal analysis, Panofsky saw the connoisseur as closely tied to the art historian, writing that the connoisseur might be "defined as a laconic art historian, and art historian as a loquacious connoisseur" ("The History of Art as a Humanistic Discipline," *Meaning in the Visual Arts* [1955], p. 20). Panofsky also wrote often about artists' attempts to "solve" artistic problems. In that connection one of the recurring motifs of his art history was the seeming stylistic retrogression that was required in order for artists to move to the next stage of artistic evolution, an idea Panofsky used, for example, in his analysis of the work of Roger van der Weyden in *Early*

Netherlandish Painting. But despite Panofsky's sensitivity to style and his deep interest in formal problems, his art history is likely to remain the exemplar of art history born of immense intellectual erudition and humanistic scope.

• Panofsky's papers are in the Archives of American Art, Washington, D.C. Important works by Panofsky not cited above are *Dürers 'Melencolia I'*, with Fritz Saxl (1923), *Renaissance and Renascences in Western Art* (1960), and *Tomb Sculpture: Four Lectures on Its Changing Aspects from Ancient Egypt to Bernini* (1964). For a sharp sketch of Panofsky's personality, see William S. Heckscher, "Erwin Panofsky: A Curriculum Vitae," in Panofsky, *Three Essays on Style* (1995). On Panofsky's early theoretical essays, see Michael Ann Holly, *Panofsky and the Foundations of Art History* (1984). Also on Panofsky's theory and method, see Christine Hasenmueller, "Panofsky, Iconography, and Semiotics," *Journal of Aesthetics and Art Criticism* 36 (Spring 1978): 289–301; Michael Podro, *The Critical Historians of Art* (1982); Silvia Ferretti, *Cassirer, Panofsky, and Warburg*, trans. Richard Pierce (1989); and Joan Hart, "Erwin Panofsky and Karl Mannheim: A Dialogue on Interpretation," *Critical Inquiry* 19 (Spring 1993): 534–66. On Panofsky's fascination with the Renaissance within the context of American cultural politics, see Carl Landauer, "Erwin Panofsky and the Renascence of the Renaissance," *Renaissance Quarterly* 47 (Summer 1994): 255–81. An obituary is in the *New York Times*, 16 Mar. 1968.

CARL LANDAUER

PANTON, William (1745?–26 Feb. 1801), merchant-adventurer, was born on the family farm on the Mains of Aberdour some eight miles west of Fraserburgh, Aberdeenshire, Scotland, the son of John Panton and Barbara Wemyss, farmers. Nothing is known about his education in Scotland. Panton came to America in 1765 and served as an apprentice with John Gordon and Company, merchants and Indian traders, of Charleston. In 1774 he and Philip Moore formed a partnership that lasted for several years. He next joined with Thomas Forbes in the firm of Panton, Forbes and Company, with offices in South Carolina and Georgia. Panton and Forbes, however, were Loyalists, and the American Revolution soon forced them to move to St. Augustine, British East Florida.

In December 1775 Governor Patrick Tonyn of East Florida designated Panton the official trader for the Creeks. In 1778 Indian agent Colonel Thomas Brown appointed Panton to handle presents to the Creeks and Cherokees. The Indian trade was a substantial part of Panton, Forbes and Company's business during those years, but the company also sold food and merchandise to the residents and Loyalist refugees in East Florida.

Panton returned to Georgia briefly during the Loyalist reoccupation and was elected to the Commons House of Assembly in 1780. He represented Frederica and St. James Parish. His stay was short, however, and he soon returned to St. Augustine. As a result of his Loyalist stand, the Georgia Council of Safety declared Panton "dangerous to the liberties of America." His properties and those of his partners, valued at more than £25,000, were confiscated.

In 1782 or early 1783 Panton, John Forbes, William Alexander, John Leslie, and Charles McLatchy pooled their assets and formed Panton, Leslie and Company. They continued their business with the Indians and others but were faced with the alarming news that the Floridas would soon be returned to Spain. Panton and his partners wanted to remain in the Floridas, and Governor Tonyn recommended to the Spaniards that the company should stay as a means for controlling the Indians. Governor Vicente Manuel de Zéspedes, after his arrival in East Florida, was impressed by the cooperation of the company in supplying gifts to him for the Indians. Alexander McGillivray, the Creek chief, also appealed to Spanish officials on behalf of the Creeks that the company stay. McGillivray became a silent partner in the company about 1784. Thus Zéspedes recommended that the company be permitted to remain in the Spanish Floridas until it could be replaced by a Spanish company. That time never arrived.

Panton soon departed for the Bahamas and left the company business in East Florida under the management of John Leslie. After a brief stay in the islands, Panton came to Pensacola and opened a trading post there. From his new base of operations in West Florida, Panton, in cooperation with McGillivray, soon acquired a virtual monopoly of the Indian trade of the southeastern Spanish borderlands. At its peak, the company had eight or nine trading posts stretching from Nassau to New Orleans to Chickasaw Bluffs (by 1802, Memphis Bluffs).

About one thing there is little doubt, Panton did not like the United States. He is known to have urged the Indians to turn their weapons on its citizens when caught in Indian territory. Panton managed, tenuously at times and not single-handedly to be sure, to keep the southeastern Indians in the Spanish camp. As a result, the United States was prevented from expanding westward a few years longer than might otherwise have been possible. In 1793 Panton forced an end to the Creek-Chickasaw war by threatening to cut off trade with the Creeks. Such examples of Panton's influence over the Indians was noted by the United States and brought forth praise from Spain. The company reached its pinnacle of success about 1793, but the death of Alexander McGillivray in that year signaled troubled times for the company.

William Augustus Bowles, an adventurer and merchant, had already appeared on the scene to plague the company. Bowles's 1792 and 1800 raids on the company's St. Marks trading post cost Panton and his associates thousands of dollars. The United States and Spain ended their boundary dispute in the Treaty of San Lorenzo in 1795 and established the West Florida–United States border at thirty-one degrees north latitude. This placed many of the company's most important customers, the Indians, in United States territory. At almost the same time the United States decided to implement the factory system for trade with the Indians. The factors, or persons in charge of the trading posts, were U.S. government employees. The system provided the Indians with goods at cost in order to compete commercially with foreign traders such as Panton, Leslie and Company. As it turned out, however, the company retained a competitive edge, and U.S. Indian agent Benjamin Hawkins and Panton became good friends.

In 1797 the outbreak of war between Spain and Great Britain—Panton's company received most of its supplies from England—greatly increased the company's risks and seriously reduced profits. In February 1801 Panton, ill and discouraged, decided, on the advice of medical practitioners, to effect a change of climate. Aboard the *Shark*, en route to Nassau, Panton died.

In spite of the disappointments of his last years, Panton had indeed succeeded as a merchant-adventurer. In his personal life, he lived sumptuously as a bachelor in his imposing brick mansion in Pensacola and was noted for his lavish hospitality. Business associates, traders, and visitors to Pensacola were treated to a wide assortment of imported foods and beverages. Panton knew the advantage of a well-placed gift, and Spanish officials often were the objects of his favor. He spent $18,000 annually on entertainment and gifts, which he considered a necessary business expense. Panton was also noted for his generosity, and on more than one occasion he came to the financial aid of family and friends.

Panton was articulate and straightforward, if not truthful, a man of action, versatile, self-confident, bold, and possessed of a good business head—a man to fit Adam Smith's mold of the eighteenth-century British entrepreneur.

Notwithstanding reports to the contrary, neither Panton nor the firm he represented was ever worth $1 million. His will provided in excess of £10,000 to various friends and members of the family. Unfortunately, much of the firm's profits were in the form of debts owed to it by the Indians and the Spanish government. The total amount due the company reached well over $200,000. If Panton played a major role in making the money for the company as he obviously did, it was left to his successor, John Forbes, to collect it.

• The Papers of Panton, Leslie and Company, some 200,000 plus pages, which includes several documentary collections, are located in the John C. Pace Library, University of West Florida, Pensacola. There is a 26-reel microfilm edition of selected documents and a 764-page guide, *The Papers of Panton, Leslie and Company* (1986). Those interested in the microfilm collection should contact Research Publications, Inc., 12 Lunar Drive, Woodbridge, Conn. 06525. The most complete bibliography and biography of William Panton is William S. Coker and Thomas D. Watson, *Indian Traders of the Southeastern Spanish Borderlands: Panton, Leslie & Company and John Forbes & Company, 1783–1847* (1986). See also the following publications by Coker, which are not included in the Coker-Watson bibliography: "Entrepreneurs in the British and Spanish Floridas, 1775–1821," in *Eighteenth-Century Florida and the Caribbean*, ed. Samuel Proctor (1976); and "Indian Traders of the Southeastern Spanish Borderlands: A Spanish, French and English Documentary Project," in *The Hispanic Experience in North America*, ed. Lawrence A. Clayton (1992); "The Columbian Exchange in the Floridas: Scots, Spaniards, and Indians, 1783–1821," *Colonial Latin American Historical Review* 3 (Summer 1994): 305–25; and "The Papers and History of Panton, Leslie and Company and John Forbes and Company," *Florida Historical Quarterly* 73, no. 3 (Jan. 1995): 353–58.

WILLIAM S. COKER

PAPANICOLAOU, George Nicholas (13 May 1883–19 Feb. 1962), anatomist, oncologist, and endocrinologist, was born in Coumi (or Kyme), Greece, the son of Nicholas Papanicolaou, a physician, and Mary Critsutas. After early schooling in Coumi, he attended Gymnasium in Athens and then studied medicine at the University of Athens. After receiving his M.D. degree in 1904, he completed his mandatory military service (1904–1906). He returned to Coumi, where he joined his father briefly in the practice of medicine, before leaving for further education in Germany. In 1910 he received the Ph.D. in zoology at Munich. His thesis, entitled "Sex Determination and Sex Differentiation," had been completed under the supervision of Richard Goldschmidt.

Papanicolaou returned to Greece to marry Mary Andromaque Mavroyeni in September 1910. The couple had no children.

By 1911 Papanicolaou was in Monaco, working as an assistant at the Oceanography Museum. He was the physiologist with the Prince of Monaco's oceanographic expedition in that year. The Balkan wars of 1912 and 1913 brought Papanicolaou back to Greece; he served as a second lieutenant in the Greek Army Medical Corps.

In 1913 Papanicolaou came to the United States. With the help of Thomas Hunt Morgan, the distinguished geneticist then at Columbia University, Papanicolaou obtained a part-time assistantship in the pathology department at New York Hospital, an affiliate of Cornell Medical College. Reference to Papanicolaou's doctoral dissertation had appeared in Morgan's recently published book, *Heredity and Sex* (1910). In September 1914 he transferred to the medical school, where, as assistant in research biology, he worked with Charles R. Stockard, head of the anatomy department. In 1916 Papanicolaou became instructor in clinical anatomy.

His research at this time developed out of his studies in Munich on ovogenesis—the metabolic process whereby the female produces fertile egg cells—and on parthenogenesis, the development of an organism from an unfertilized egg cell. Work on mammalian ova was hindered by an inability to determine precisely the time of ovulation. Papanicolaou suggested that changes in the vaginal secreta would provide useful indicators. He and Stockard were able to correlate such physical and cytological changes with the course of the guinea pig's oestrus cycle. Papanicolaou followed these findings with studies on the effects of fluids from ovarian cysts and of corpus luteum extracts on the endometrium (uterine lining).

Papanicolaou became assistant professor in 1923 and a naturalized American citizen in 1927. By 1923 his work on ovulation cycles was extended to human subjects and focused on early detection of pregnancy.

In human vaginal smears, Papanicolaou had from time to time seen cancerous cells indicative of cervical carcinoma. He presented his findings in a paper, "New Cancer Diagnosis," at the Third Conference on Race Betterment (1928). The paper had little immediate effect, since cervical biopsy was widely accepted as the reliable diagnostic procedure for the disease. Later the great value of Papanicolaou's observations would be realized and would profoundly alter medical practice.

Papanicolaou continued his studies of oestrus, especially of the correlation of hormonal levels with cytological changes in the reproductive tissues. His 1933 article, "The Sexual Cycle in the Human Female as Revealed by Vaginal Smears" (*American Journal of Anatomy* 52, supp. [May 1933]: 519–637), helped establish that the sexual rhythm in the human female extends into the postmenopausal years.

In 1937 Papanicolaou was promoted to be associate professor of clinical anatomy. Two years later, the great change in the role of Papanicolaou's work in the diagnosis and treatment of cancer came with the appointment of Joseph C. Hinsey to head the anatomy department at the Medical College. Hinsey was impressed with the need for early detection of cancer if treatment were to be effective. The vaginal smear method could detect cervical cancer earlier than other currently used procedures. He persuaded Papanicolaou to resume his work on the diagnosis of uterine cancers and to collaborate with Herbert F. Traut of the Department of Obstetrics and Gynecology. Hinsey made funds available to support the research, which was directed at perfecting the technique, confirming its validity, and training others to perform and interpret the tests. In 1941 Papanicolaou and Traut published their important paper, "The Diagnostic Value of Vaginal Smears in Carcinoma of the Uterus," in the *American Journal of Obstetrics and Gynecology* (42 [Aug. 1941]: 193–206). The paper generated much interest, and financial support became available, principally from the Commonwealth Fund, which published Papanicolaou and Traut's book, *The Diagnosis of Uterine Cancer by the Vaginal Smear* (1943). The book stressed the fact that uterine carcinomas are exfoliative; they continually shed superficially placed cells into the vaginal secreta, where they can be identified, even in the earliest stages of cancer development. The smear tests were not to be regarded as the ultimate diagnosis; when positive, they should be followed by confirmatory biopsy.

Traut left New York in 1943 for the University of California, and Andrew Marchetti replaced him as Papanicolaou's chief collaborator. Papanicolaou was promoted to full professor in 1947. In 1948 the Commonwealth Fund published *The Epithelia of the Woman's Reproductive Organs* by Papanicolaou, Traut, and Marchetti. Between 1941 and 1952, the Common-

wealth Fund expended $124,000 in support of Papanicolaou's work. With widespread use of the vaginal smear procedure, now informally named the "Pap test," research funding became available from other sources, especially the National Institutes of Health and the American Cancer Society.

In 1950 Papanicolaou became director of the Papanicolaou Research Laboratory at the medical school and consultant to numerous hospitals, laboratories, and research centers. He extended his studies to cancers of the male genital tract, the lungs, and the urinary and gastrointestinal systems. A sputum test, a form of "Pap smear," was used in early detection of lung cancer among smokers. His magisterial *Atlas of Exfoliative Cytology* was published in 1954, with supplements appearing in 1957 and 1960.

Papanicolaou received many honors at home and abroad, including the Borden Award of the Association of American Medical Colleges (1948); the Amory Prize of the American Academy of Arts and Sciences (1948); the Lasker Award of the American Public Health Association (1950); and the Honor Medal of the American Cancer Society (1952). He was honored in the country of his birth with the Royal Order of George I (1951) and the Cross of the Grand Commander of the Royal Order of the Phoenix (1953).

On retiring from Cornell University Medical School in 1961 with the title professor emeritus, Papanicolaou moved to Florida to become director of the Cancer Institute of Miami, which was renamed the Papanicolaou Cancer Research Institute. Three months after assuming the directorship, he died of a heart attack.

Papanicolaou's principal contribution to public health remains the "Pap test" for early detection of uterine cancers. The use of this test, and the prompt treatment it made possible, has resulted in a marked decrease in the death rate from the disease.

• Papanicolaou was the author of more than 100 journal articles. Obituaries are in the *New York Times*, 20 Feb. 1962; *Acta Cytologica* 6 (1962): 483–86; and *Anatomical Record* 143 (1962): 276–78.

CHARLES FUCHSMAN

PAPP, Joseph (22 June 1921–31 Oct. 1991), theater producer, director, and administrator, was born Joseph Papirofsky in Brooklyn, New York, the son of Samuel Papirofsky, a trunk maker, and Yetta Miritch, a garment worker. Both parents were Jewish immigrants from Eastern Europe. Encouraged by teachers in local public schools, young Joseph Papirofsky developed an enthusiasm for English literature, especially the works of Shakespeare. After graduating from Eastern District High School in 1938, he applied to Brooklyn College but was not admitted because of poor grades in science and mathematics. He then worked at a series of jobs and became active in the Communist party. From 1942 to 1946 he served in the U.S. Navy, spending most of this time in an entertainment unit. After discharge from the navy, Papirofsky enrolled at the Actors' Laboratory Workshop in Los Angeles, using veteran's benefits to pay expenses. At the Actors' Lab, which had been founded by former members of the politically left wing Group Theater of the 1930s, he gained valuable experience in fundamentals of stage direction and nonprofit theater management. He stayed with the Actors' Lab until it ceased operations in May 1950, and then joined a touring company of *Death of a Salesman* as assistant stage manager and understudy.

In 1951 Papirofsky settled in New York City and found work at CBS-TV in early 1952. He spent eight years at CBS-TV, stage managing such programs as "Studio One" and "I've Got a Secret." In his spare time, the energetic Papirofsky directed theater productions for little or no salary. In 1954 he founded the nonprofit Shakespeare Workshop at Emmanuel Church on Manhattan's Lower East Side, and it was during this period that he began using the name Papp (it was legally changed in 1959). Initial productions at the Shakespeare Workshop drew little attention from critics or the public. In the summer of 1956 Papp obtained permission from the city of New York to mount free outdoor theater productions at the East River Park Amphitheater and offered *Julius Caesar* and *The Taming of the Shrew*. The experiment was a great success.

In 1957 Papp moved his Shakespeare Workshop outdoor productions to Central Park. This move, to a higher-profile location, was not authorized by the city. A battle ensued between youthful, idealistic Papp (who was still employed full time as a stage manager at CBS-TV) and Robert Moses, New York City's powerful parks commissioner. Moses wanted the Shakespeare Workshop to charge admission so the city could be reimbursed for security and other maintenance costs. Papp, an unrelenting advocate of public funding for the arts, refused to charge audiences even a modest amount. This David-versus-Goliath–style fight earned Papp and his Shakespeare Workshop much publicity and public sympathy. The dark-haired young producer's "matinee idol" looks and compelling personality did not hurt his cause. A court decision in 1959 allowed the free summer "Shakespeare in the Park" to continue. The next year the Shakespeare Workshop changed its name to the New York Shakespeare Festival. Papp resigned from his job at CBS in early 1959 to become the Festival's full-time administrator. Actually, Papp had been fired from CBS a few months earlier after he was called before the House Un-American Activities Committee (HUAC) and refused to answer questions about his past associations with the Communist party. The Radio and Television Directors Guild, the labor union to which Papp belonged, had him reinstated in November 1958, but by this time he had lost interest in the job.

The Delacorte Theater, a permanent outdoor amphitheater in Central Park (funded by the city and by publisher George Delacorte), was built primarily to house the Shakespeare Festival. It opened in 1962 with a production of *The Merchant of Venice*, starring George C. Scott. Performers such as Scott, Colleen Dewhurst, James Earl Jones, and later Raul Julia, Meryl Streep, Kevin Kline, and Sam Waterston often appeared in Festival productions, but Papp never employed a regular company of actors. Not intimidated by British traditions, Papp's Shakespearean productions avoided the overly reverential, Anglophilic attitude often taken by Americans toward Shakespeare. Multiracial casts and updated settings were often used, and American accents were not disguised. The Festival also gave special performances for public school students and operated a mobile unit that took plays to locations around the city.

Papp added a second venue to his operations when the Shakespeare Festival acquired the slated-for-demolition Astor Library in Lower Manhattan in 1966. The next year the renovated Astor Library opened as the nonprofit Public Theater, a multistage facility showcasing the work of new playwrights (confusingly, Papp continued to call his organization the New York Shakespeare Festival though it now produced a wide range of material and was no longer a seasonal festival). Shakespeare in the Park continued under Papp's auspices at the Delacorte, but developing new talent was now the producer's major interest, and the Public Theater became his base of operations. Within a few years Papp was one of the most powerful figures in the New York theater and the Festival was a magnet for ambitious young writers and performers. The intense and indefatigable Papp kept a watchful eye over his theatrical enterprises, rarely taking a day off. He closely monitored the work of his directors and occasionally took over directorial duties entirely. A master of public relations and fundraising, the outspoken Papp and his provocative productions were "good copy" for journalists covering the increasingly lackluster theater scene of the 1970s.

Throughout his career Papp disparaged the commercial theater as "bourgeois" and irrelevant. Although the Public Theater was not free (unlike the Delacorte), ticket prices were kept within the range of modest-income theatergoers. Papp believed that funding for the arts was a basic civic responsibility. He fondly recalled band concerts at Brooklyn's Prospect Park during his childhood. These free outdoor concerts drew listeners who were unlikely to enter a concert hall. It was this kind of unintimidating, democratic atmosphere that Papp attempted to recapture in Festival productions.

Despite his contempt for the commercial theater, in the early 1970s Papp began transferring some of his Public Theater and Delacorte Theater productions to big-time Broadway houses, maintaining that these were especially remarkable works that deserved a wider audience. Skeptics claimed that Papp had simply lost his idealism and was behaving in the power-hungry manner of a conventional "impresario." The success of many Festival productions on the Great White Way indicated that the typical white, middle-class, middle-aged theatergoer was not as narrow-minded as Papp thought (or, perhaps, his productions were not as adventurous as he thought). If Papp was often criticized by some for being too avant-garde, others found him not avant-garde enough. From 1973 to 1977 Papp and the New York Shakespeare Festival managed the Vivian Beaumont and Forum (now the Mitzi E. Newhouse) theaters at Lincoln Center. When pressure to fill seats slanted him toward blatantly crowd-pleasing ventures, such as a sellout 1975 production of Ibsen's *A Doll's House* featuring movie star Liv Ullmann, Papp decided to end the Festival's association with Lincoln Center.

Reflecting Papp's notions of worthwhile theater, the New York Shakespeare Festival focused on plays dealing with contemporary social issues. Lightweight entertainments and plays mainly about personal relationships were mostly avoided. Works by unknown writers were preferred to that of established dramatists. Over the years, hundreds of Festival productions of varying quality and content were mounted at the Delacorte, the Public, and Lincoln Center. Many were raw works by outsiders, including racial minorities and women, whose voices were ignored by mainstream producers. Some were polished professional pieces that might have found backing with a commercial producer. "I try to judge the entire work and say: Isn't it an interesting evening in the theater?" Papp once said. "That's the most important thing."

Among the notable works to originate at the New York Shakespeare Festival were the "rock" musical *Hair*, which inaugurated the Public Theater in 1967; Charles Gordone's *No Place to Be Somebody* (Pulitzer Prize, 1970); David Rabe's *The Basic Training of Pavlo Hummel*, *Sticks and Bones*, and *Streamers*; a popular musical version of Shakespeare's *Two Gentlemen of Verona*; Jason Miller's *That Championship Season* (Pulitzer Prize, 1973); a much-admired production of *Much Ado About Nothing*, set in the "Gibson Girl" era of the early twentieth century; the backstage musical *A Chorus Line* (Pulitzer Prize, 1976), which ran on Broadway for a record-breaking fifteen years, its profits financing dozens of less commercial Festival productions; Miguel Pinero's *Short Eyes*; Gretchen Cryer and Nancy Ford's "feminist" musical *I'm Getting My Act Together and Taking It on the Road*; Ntozake Shange's *For Colored Girls Who Have Considered Suicide/When the Rainbow Is Enuf*; *Runaways* by Elizabeth Swados; a revival of Gilbert and Sullivan's *The Pirates of Penzance*, with pop music star Linda Ronstadt; *True West* by Sam Shepard; *The Normal Heart* by Larry Kramer; and a musical version of Dickens's *The Mystery of Edwin Drood* by Rupert Holmes.

Not personally profiting from any of his theatrical ventures, Papp drew a relatively modest salary from the New York Shakespeare Festival budget. Expensive cigars were his major indulgence. Only in the last decade or so of his life, when his now international reputation brought invitations from theaters around the world, did he take extensive vacations. A short man whose erect posture and commanding presence made him seem larger than he really was, Papp was completely absorbed in his work and was never a model husband or father. He was married four times: to

Brooklyn neighbor Betty Ball from 1941 to 1946 (divorced; one child); to Actors' Laboratory receptionist Sylvia Ostroff from 1946 to 1951 (divorced; one child); to actress-turned-psychotherapist Peggy Bennion from 1951 to 1974 (divorced; two children); and to Gail Merrifield, the Public Theater's director of play development, from 1976 to his death. He also had an out-of-wedlock child, whom he acknowledged, from a relationship during his U.S. Navy service. Joseph Papp died at his home in Greenwich Village.

• The papers of Joseph Papp and the papers of the New York Shakespeare Festival are at the New York Public Library for the Performing Arts, Lincoln Center. Helen Epstein, *Joe Papp: An American Life* (1994), is an "authorized" but honest biography written by a journalist friend of Papp with the cooperation of Papp's widow, Gail Merrifield. Stuart W. Little, *Enter Joseph Papp: In Search of a New American Theater* (1974), closely examines Papp's working methods, with a focus on the early 1970s. Robert A. Caro, *The Power Broker* (1974), a biography of New York parks commissioner Robert Moses, has a chapter about Papp's fight to stay in Central Park. See also Barbara Lee Horn, *Joseph Papp: A Bio-Bibliography* (1992); Christine E. King and Brenda Coven, *Joseph Papp and the New York Shakespeare Festival: An Annotated Bibliography* (1988); and Yoko Hashimoto, "Joseph Papp and the New York Shakespeare Festival" (Ph.D. diss., Univ. of Michigan, 1972). A detailed obituary is in the *New York Times*, 1 Nov. 1991.

MARY C. KALFATOVIC

PAREJA, Francisco (15??–15 June? 1628?), priest and missionary, was born in Aunon, diocese of Toledo, Spain. Nothing is known about his birth, parentage, or life before his arrival in Florida in 1595 except that he entered the Franciscan Order of Friars Minor in the order's province of Castile.

Pareja came to Florida with about a dozen other friars to work in the catechization and conversion of its aboriginal peoples. He began his missionary work in 1595 among a subgroup of the Timucua Indians known as Mocama at the mission of San Juan del Puerto on Fort George Island at the mouth of the St. Johns River, which is part of today's city of Jacksonville. From his base at San Juan he served the inhabitants of nine other settlements a little over one-half mile to six and one-half miles away. He spent most of his missionary career at that post except for numerous expeditions to other Timucua-speaking groups in the interior of north Florida and on the coastal mainland of south Georgia.

Pareja also served on a temporary fill-in assignment at Cumberland Island's San Pedro Mocama mission in 1597. While there he witnessed an abortive attack the Guale made on the mission with the intent of killing the island's friars and Christian natives, and he was among the first Franciscans to learn that a number of the friars with whom he had arrived in Florida were killed as a result of a nativist uprising in 1597 among the Guale of North Georgia's coast.

Pareja's renown is based on his intense study of the Timucua's language. It led to his publishing the first known books in the language of an Indian group living within the territory of the present-day United States. The linguist Julian Granberry noted that Pareja's contributions in the Timucua language contributed significantly to making the Timucua language "one of the best-attested extinct native American languages." Between 1612 and 1627 he arranged to have printed in Mexico five volumes in the Timucuan and Castilian languages, copies of which are extant. He published other volumes that do not appear to have survived. The titles (in translation) of the surviving works are *Catechism in the Castilian and Timuquana Language in Which Is Contained What Can Be Taught to the Adults Who Are to Be Baptized* (1612), *Catechism and Brief Exposition of the Christian Doctrine, Very Useful and Necessary Alike for Spaniards as Well as Natives, in the Castilian and Timuquana Language, in the Form of Questions and Answers* (1612), *Confessor's Manual in the Castilian and Timuquana Language with Some Counsels to Encourage the Penitent* (1613), *Rules and Pronunciation in the Timuquana Language and Castilian* (1614), and *Catechism and Examination for Those Going to Communion: In the Castilian and Timuquana Language* (1627). Granberry observed that "Pareja's five extant works constitute over 2,000 pages of Timucua text."

It is not known whether Pareja went to Mexico during the 1612–1614 period when the first four of his extant works were published. The prevalence of literate Timucuans that marked the first half of the seventeenth century is a measure of the influence of his works among the natives and of the dedication of the friars who taught the natives to read and write in their own language.

By 1609 at the latest Pareja had begun to rise to a position of leadership among Spanish Florida's Franciscans, holding the title of *custodio* or superior while still serving at San Juan. When the Florida-Cuba district of the Franciscans became a province in 1612, Pareja was chosen as senior definitor or provincial counselor. At the chapter for the province held in 1616, Pareja's Franciscan brethren elected him their provincial on the first ballot. The visiting Franciscan official who supervised the chapter proceedings characterized Pareja as a "man of great sanctity and of incredible zeal for the salvation of souls as his works and writings . . . give testimony" (Oré, p. 69).

Pareja was conservative in his approach to admitting neophytes to receive communion. After seven years of work at San Juan, he observed that there were "native men and women who receive communion because they are advanced in their knowledge of Christian things and know enough, although those who receive communion are not numerous" (Letter to Blas de Montes, 14 Sept. 1602). He belonged to the school of friars who advocated punishment of Indians who did not fulfill the obligations they assumed on becoming Christians and forcible repatriation of those who fled from their mission village to escape peer pressure to conform. He was not timid about criticizing Spanish governors who did not adequately support the friar's work or whom he felt were treating natives with undue harshness.

Little is known of Pareja's life after his 1616 election to a three-year term as provincial, nor is it known whether he continued to work among the natives during those years. He left Florida for Mexico sometime after 1626, where he joined the Franciscan province of the Holy Gospel.

• Correspondence of Francisco Pareja may be found in the Archivo General de las Indias, Seville, Spain. Pareja receives considerable attention in Luís Gerónimo de Oré, O.F.M., *The Martyrs of Florida (1513–1616)*, trans. Geiger (1936). See also John H. Hann, *A History of the Timucua Indians and Missions* (1996); Hann, *Missions to the Calusa* (1991); Hann, *Summary Guide to Spanish Florida Missions and Visitas with Churches in the Sixteenth and Seventeenth Centuries* (1990; repr. 1990); Maynard Geiger, O.F.M., *Biographical Dictionary of the Franciscans in Spanish Florida and Cuba (1528–1841)* (1940); Geiger, *The Franciscan Conquest of Florida (1573–1618)* (1937); and John Gilmary Shea, *The Catholic Church in Colonial Days* (1886). Pareja's work with the Timucua language receives the fullest treatment in Julian Granberry, *A Grammar and Dictionary of the Timucua Language* (1993). Lucien Adam and Julian Vinson, *Arte de la Lengua Timvqvana, Compuesto en 1614 por el Pe Francisco Pareja* (1886), is a republication in France of Pareja's grammar, *Rules and Pronunciation in the Timuquana Language and Castilian* (1614).

JOHN H. HANN

PARENTI, Tony (6 Aug. 1900–17 Apr. 1972), jazz clarinetist and saxophonist, was born Anthony Parenti in New Orleans, Louisiana. Both of his parents (names unknown) were from Sicily, where his father had been a musician in the Italian Peasant army. Parenti started playing violin and then switched to clarinet, which he studied at the St. Phillip School and with Professor Joseph Taverno, in whose concert band he played for eighteen months. In 1914 he started playing in a jazz band led by Alfred "Baby" Laine, son of bandleader Jack "Papa" Laine, while also substituting for clarinetist Alcide "Yellow" Nunez in another Laine band that included drummer Johnny Stein and cornetist Nick La Rocca, soon to become leader of the Original Dixieland Jazz Band (ODJB). In 1915 Parenti worked with cornetist Johnny De Droit's group at the Cave in the Grunewald Hotel, played in a trio on the SS *Majestic* docked at Lake Pontchartrain, and accompanied silent films at the Triangle and Alamo theaters. In 1916 he worked at Pup's Café and that same year was asked by Stein and La Rocca to go to Chicago with Stein's newly formed quintet, but because of his age he had to turn their offer down. The clarinetist who did go north with this band was the considerably older Nunez, who, with his immediate successor in the ODJB, Larry Shields, was an important influence on Parenti's conception of jazz style.

Parenti worked regularly for De Droit and other leaders until 1922, when he formed his own Symphonic Dance Orchestra for a yearlong residency at the Cave. Now doubling on alto and baritone saxes as well as clarinet, in 1924 he took an eight-piece band into the Liberty Theater and the La Vida Dance Hall (formerly Pup's), while in 1925 he also played clarinet in the Saenger Theater Symphony Orchestra. His 1925–1928 records were all made in New Orleans with his regular working personnel and show a gradual change in style. Whereas the earlier performances are very much in the traditional New Orleans "hot dance band" style, by 1928, with cornetist John Hyman (Johnny Wiggs) on "In the Dungeon" and "When You and I Were Pals," the influence of such New York–based jazzmen as Red Nichols, Miff Mole, and Jimmy Dorsey is clearly evident. The hotter style of Louis Armstrong is heard on "Gumbo" and "You Made Me Like It, Baby," recorded only a few months later with trumpeter Leon Prima, older brother of the more famous Louis Prima. Parenti himself exhibits digital dexterity and self-assurance throughout these records but almost nothing in the way of inventiveness, sensitivity, or swing. By way of contrast, the 1922–1925 records by the New Orleans Rhythm Kings with clarinetist Leon Roppolo, as well as those by such other white bands as the New Orleans Owls and the Halfway House Orchestra, present far better examples of early Dixieland. Parenti's band is itself quite impressive on almost every number recorded, but the leader's faulty pitch and "corny" phrasing invariably weaken the overall performances. Other white New Orleans clarinetists of the mid to late 1920s, such as Charlie Scaglioni, Cliff Holman, and Charlie Cordella, and the light-skinned Creole Sidney Arodin, were demonstrably better jazzmen than Parenti, and their records readily bear this out. However, with the exception of Arodin, because of their limited recorded exposure they never received the credit that came Parenti's way. Parenti continued working locally with his group at the Strand Theater and other prime locations through December 1928, when he disbanded and moved to New York.

Because of his classical training and experience in theater orchestras, Parenti had no difficulty in joining the relatively small but active clique of radio and recording studiomen. Starting in January 1929, he substituted regularly for Benny Goodman in Ben Pollack's band at the Park Central Hotel and freelanced with the popular radio and dance orchestras of Henry Busse, B. A. Rolfe, Paul Ash, Don Voorhees, Mike Markel, and Meyer Davis. During this same year he was on record dates with Adrian Schubert, Fred Rich, and Jack Pettis. In June 1929 he recorded a virtuosic clarinet solo with piano accompaniment, "Old Man Rhythm," which shows marked improvement over his earlier work but still has more flash than substance.

In the months following the stock market crash, like many other qualified dance band musicians, Parenti turned to radio for his primary income. In early 1930 he joined the staff of CBS, where he played on a wide variety of musical programs, including one featuring his own saxophone quartet. There is no indication that he played any jazz at all for the next several years, for in 1935 he joined the Radio City Music Hall Symphony Orchestra under the direction of Erno Rapee, a position he held for four years. Throughout 1936, along with several other studio-employed jazzmen, he was

present on possibly two dozen or more commercial recordings by Jack Shilkret, another society dance band leader. Even though the swing era was at its height by 1938–1939, when Parenti finally broke away from the security of the Music Hall and his studio jobs, his style was probably too outdated to fit in with the leading swing bands of the day. Instead, he joined his old friend, New Orleans trombonist George Brunies, in Ted Lewis's distinctly third-rate novelty band, where he remained through 1945. He was featured on Lewis's "Tiger Rag" and "Jazz Me Blues" from May 1941.

In January 1946 Parenti started working with Brunies and Wild Bill Davison at Eddie Condon's newly opened club in Greenwich Village. In June he worked with Brunies at Nick's and in November led a trio at Jimmy Ryan's on Fifty-second Street, later returning to first Nick's and then Condon's. In 1946 he also appeared at a Jazz at Town Hall concert and recorded with Brunies and Condon, while in 1947, along with Joe Sullivan and George Wettling, he recorded with cornetist Doc Evans. In November 1947 he recorded six classic rags with Davison, Jimmy Archey, Ralph Sutton, Baby Dodds, and others for Circle, a small label started by jazz historian Rudi Blesh, who also produced the "This Is Jazz" radio series. Although Parenti never played on the show, his firsthand experience with and continued interest in ragtime did inspire Blesh to research and publish the pacesetting 1950 history *They All Played Ragtime*, and in that sense he may be said to have helped spark the ragtime revival.

In December 1947 Parenti went to Chicago to work with Muggsy Spanier and remained there to play with Miff Mole through January 1949. Upon his return to New York, Parenti recorded another series of rags in a trio context for Circle and freelanced around town, frequently appearing at Stuyvesant Casino. In August, again with Davison and Archey, and with the driving rhythm section of Art Hodes, Pops Foster, and Arthur Trappier, he recorded his best straight jazz session yet, for the newly formed Jazzology label. Parenti's playing, undoubtedly inspired by the incendiary Davison and the powerfully propulsive slapped bass of Foster, easily compensates for its earlier shortcomings. In 1950 he moved to Miami, where he worked into 1954 with the Five Saints, a Dixieland band led by drummer "Preacher" Rollo Laylan, recording with them between 1951 and 1953 and taking time off in 1952 to play seven weeks with the Dukes Of Dixieland.

In 1954 Parenti moved back to New York, where he worked afternoons at the Metropole with a trio including New Orleans drummer Zutty Singleton. In 1955, when clarinetist George Lewis's band was playing at Childs' Paramount on Broadway, Parenti, while continuing his regular daytime job, replaced the ailing Lewis for two weeks. Another important recording date took place in October 1955, when Parenti, Davison, and Foster, this time with Lou McGarity, Hank Duncan, and Singleton, taped an equally commendable second album for Jazzology. In 1956, along with trumpeter Phil Napoleon and three veteran members of the ODJB, Parenti appeared on Garry Moore's "I've Got a Secret." After a period working in upper New York State, Boston, and Toronto, in April 1958 he played with Louis Armstrong and Jack Teagarden on an NBC-TV "Timex Jazz Special." In 1962 and 1963 Parenti led his own Deans Of Dixieland at Condon's, after which, from late 1963 to 1969, he led another trio with Singleton at Jimmy Ryan's. In June 1969 he appeared at the New Orleans Jazz Festival and continued to remain active, for a time playing at his own short-lived club and then Ryan's through 1971. He died in New York.

Parenti's basic style never varied from the classic Dixieland of his formative years, but his playing did improve over time. Along with the cultivation of a powerful sound and an even more assured technique, he also developed a more sensitized approach to blues feeling, rhythm, and intonation, although he was not always consistent in this latter respect. Parenti had long been a devoted proselytizer of ragtime and used his extensive collection of rare sheet music as the source of his arrangements for both trio and the standard six-piece jazz band instrumentation. Significantly, this music suited his rhythmic style far better than the swing-oriented jazz that most of his New York colleagues were playing in the 1960s, for he did not have to alter his natural way of phrasing in order to perform it authentically. Although never a major jazz clarinetist, Parenti's reputation ultimately rests on the role he played in reviving and maintaining ragtime.

• There are no biographies of Parenti, and his name is mentioned only in passing in a few of the major jazz histories. A rather exaggerated, one-sided picture of the importance of early white New Orleans jazzmen is in H. O. Brunn, *The Story of the Original Dixieland Jazz Band* (1960); Burton Peretti, *The Creation of* Jazz (1992), is a more objective discussion of the racial and musical relationships and differences between black and white jazzmen in New Orleans. There are quite a few references to Parenti's bands and the musicians he played with in Al Rose and Edmond Souchon, *New Orleans Jazz: A Family Album* (1978), but he is referred to only briefly in Samuel B. Charters and Leonard Kunstadt, *Jazz: A History of the New York Scene* (1962). Also see Nat Shapiro and Nat Hentoff, *Hear Me Talkin' to Ya* (1955), and Tom Bethel, *George Lewis: A Jazzman from New Orleans* (1977), for direct quotations. There is nothing written on his post–New Orleans career except what is found in the liner notes of his albums for Jazzology. Discographical listings are in Brian Rust, *Jazz Records, 1897–1942* (1982), and Walter Bruyninckx, *Traditional Jazz Discography, 1897–1988* (6 vols., 1985–1989) and *Swing Discography, 1920–1988* (12 vols., 1985–1989). An obituary is in the *New York Times*, 18 Apr. 1972.

JACK SOHMER

PARET, Jahail Parmly (3 Oct. 1870–24 Nov. 1952), tennis player, journalist, and author, was born in Bergen Point, New Jersey, the son of Henry Paret, a wealthy clothing merchant, and Anna Elizabeth Parmly, later the editor of *Harper's Handy Book for Girls* (1910). Named for his maternal grandfather, Paret so disliked his first name that he constantly reduced it to a first initial and preferred to be called by his middle name. He graduated in 1886 from Grammar School 68 in New York City.

Paret started playing lawn tennis in 1883 and, a year later, won his first tournament, a minor event for boys held in Central Park. He played in greater New York City tournaments from 1887 through 1894, earning little distinction until he won the 1893 Staten Island and the 1894 Nyack Open singles titles. By then he already displayed journalistic skills, a family trait, and began writing about sports for newspapers and periodicals. His article "Scientific Tennis," published in the 24 September 1892 issue of *Harper's Weekly*, marked him as an astute observer of the mechanics of tennis strokes. Despite later being a serious contender for the U.S. championship, he always would be better known for his contributions to tennis literature.

From 1895 through 1902 Paret competed in many tournaments along the U.S. eastern seaboard and, in 1898, in western Europe. He was a sound, intelligent player, and his performances improved dramatically. During these years he ranked nationally among the top tennis players, his highest ranking being fourth in 1899. Paret's high point came in the 1899 U.S. singles championship as he upset higher-ranking players Malcolm Chace, Bob Huntington, Leo Ware, and Dwight Davis, in that order, to win the all-comers title. He lost the challenge round to Malcolm Whitman, the defending champion, 6–1, 6–2, 3–6, 7–5, but James Dwight, the tournament referee and the acknowledged authority on tennis, thought that, had Paret won the fourth set, he would also have taken the fifth set and the U.S. crown. Paret's next most impressive victories were the 1902 U.S. indoor singles title and, in the southern championship, two singles and seven doubles titles.

Neither a hard hitter nor a spectacular shot maker, Paret relied on strategy, steadiness, endurance, and correct positioning on the court. He would rush to the net behind both first and second serves so quickly that a standing joke was that he once, at the net, was hit in the back by his own serve. After his December 1901 marriage to Laura Marion Wilson, with whom he would have one son, Paret moderated his heavy tournament schedule but continued to compete regularly for several decades. His final victory probably came at age fifty-nine when he won a Connecticut club championship. Paret also excelled as a tennis instructor. His coaching of Bessie Moore, Juliette Atkinson, and Marion Jones, done mainly at the New York Tennis Club, materially helped them win their U.S. women's championships during the 1890s and 1900s.

Paret edited a number of publications, including *Sportsman's Magazine* (1896–1897); *Spalding's Lawn Tennis Annual* (1897, 1900–1903); *Lawn Tennis*, the official U.S. National Lawn Tennis Association bulletin (1901–1903); and the *Goodrich Hand-book of Lawn Tennis for 1905* (1905). He also wrote feature articles covering tennis instruction, history, reviews of competition, critical analyses, and current developments. These writings appeared frequently from the early 1890s through the early 1920s in *Harper's Weekly* and

Outing and occasionally in *Colliers* and a few other magazines. From 1915 to 1951 a total of thirty-seven articles by Paret appeared in *American Lawn Tennis*, the leading U.S. tennis periodical of that time.

Paret's first book, *The Woman's Book of Sports* (1901), was followed by *How to Play Lawn Tennis* (1902), a volume in Spalding's Athletic Library that was republished seven times by 1912. *Lawn Tennis, Its Past, Present, and Future* (1904), a volume in the American Sportsman's Library, contained the first American bibliography of English-language lawn tennis literature. Paret then provided textbooks for various levels of expertise, from beginners to advanced players. These works eventually became the first four volumes of the Lawn Tennis Library, sponsored by *American Lawn Tennis* and its editor, S. Wallis Merrihew, who wrote volume six, *The Quest of the Davis Cup* (1929). Merrihew and Paret had intended to complete the series by collaborating on volume five, *History and Champions of Our Day*, and volume seven, *Lawn Tennis Encyclopedia*, but never did. From 1933 to 1940 Paret either wholly or partially wrote a new series of large magazine-sized paperbound instruction manuals published by *American Lawn Tennis*.

Divorced from his first wife, Paret married Rachelle Hamilton Osborne in November 1931. For many years Paret also owned and managed a stationer and printing company. He retired from business in 1937, although he remained in tennis journalism, and moved, first, to Cadboro Bay, British Columbia, Canada, and then to Pasadena, California, where he died.

At a time when young gentlemen of leisure played in strictly amateur tournaments, most ceased aggressive competition after a few years to pursue other occupations. Paret differed from his peers in that respect. His fascination with the sport and his inherited affluence caused him to maintain extremely close lifetime ties to tennis. Besides competing as a first-class player who won more than 100 trophies and being an excellent teacher, Paret endured as an outstanding tennis journalist for sixty years. His numerous, respected books were reprinted many times through several editions, were distributed throughout the English-speaking world, and were translated into several foreign languages. The Japanese version of *Methods and Players* became a standard text in Japan. After the death of James Dwight in 1917, Paret became generally regarded as the most knowledgeable authority on the game in the United States.

• Paret wrote the following textbooks: *Lawn Tennis for Beginners* (1916, 1926); *Mechanics of the Game . . .* (1926); *Psychology and Advanced Play . . .* (1927); and *Methods and Players of Modern Lawn Tennis* (1915, 1922, 1931). A number of his articles appeared in *Country Life, Harper's Bazaar,* and *St. Nicholas* magazines. Very little information is available about Paret's personal life and activities, except for coverage of his tennis matches in newspapers and tennis trade periodicals. "The Lawn Tennis Career of Paret," in *How to Play Tennis,* ed. Stephen Wallis Merrihew (1936), is useful, as is his entry in *Who Was Who in America,* vol. 5, p. 553. Descriptions of Paret's matches in the 1899 U.S. singles championship are in *Wright & Ditson Lawn Tennis Guide for 1900,* pp. 42–46, and J. P. Paret, ed., *Spalding's Lawn Tennis Annual for 1900,* pp. 14–18. For a more general context, see E. Digby Baltzell, *Sporting Gentlemen: Men's Tennis from the Age of Honor to the Cult of the Superstar* (1995). An obituary by Edward C. Potter is in *Racquet,* Jan. 1953, p. 30.

FRANK V. PHELPS

PARHAM, Charles Fox (4 June 1873–29 Jan. 1929), evangelist and Pentecostal theologian, was born near Muscatine, Iowa, the son of Ann Maria Eckel and William M. Parham, farmers. In 1878 the family moved to more prosperous fields in Cheney, Kansas, but Charles was afflicted with poor health: probably encephalitis in childhood and definitely rheumatic fever that recurred intermittently throughout his lifetime. In a reversal of the usual sequence, he felt called to preach before he had a conversion experience. While studying at Southwest Kansas College (1890–1893) he reaffirmed his commitment to preaching, finally leaving school to become a Methodist supply pastor before completing his degree. By 1895 Parham refused to accept the ecclesiastical supervision common to Methodist bishops and launched an independent ministry. The following year he married Sarah Eleanor Thistlethwaite; the couple had six children.

During a bout of illness while at college Parham claimed to have been healed through faith, and he placed heavy emphasis on divine healing in all later evangelical efforts. In 1898 he established Beth-el Healing Home in Topeka, Kansas, which offered lodging, Bible study, and faith training for people seeking cures to physical and spiritual ills. The following year he began publishing *Apostolic Faith,* a weekly journal that appeared sporadically over the next few decades. Alongside divine healing, Parham stressed the experience of an indwelling presence of the Holy Spirit. Using the biblical event of Pentecost in Acts 2:1–47 as a guideline, he held that baptism by the Holy Spirit was a postconversion experience, an additional level of Christian attainment and one manifested by such outward gifts as prophecy, healing, and the ability to speak or interpret tongues. Parham understood the gift of tongues to be xenolalia, an inspired ability to speak a recognizable language. This instantaneous expertise would, he hoped, initiate a new global missionary effort and rapidly prepare the way for Christ's return to earth. Few of his followers shared this specific interpretation of Holy Spirit baptism because when people seemed to speak under divine influence they did so in no known tongue. This form of utterance, known as glossolalia, used speech understood by no one except those whom God allowed to interpret it. Such experiences were impressive, however, and between 1901 and 1903 Parham's popularity spread as he engendered Pentecostal revival experiences with increasing publicity and growing thousands of supporters.

In 1905 Parham taught Bible classes in Houston, Texas. Among those he trained as missionary evangelists was William Seymour, a black minister interested in holiness and healing. A year later Seymour was the central figure at the Azusa Street Mission in Los Angeles when Pentecostal phenomena there drew national attention. By then Parham was at the height of his popularity, naming himself the "Projector" of Pentecostalism. He avoided sensationalist displays and criticized other revival leaders for exhibiting crude physical aberrations in their services, but sometimes it was difficult for observers to distinguish between what he called acceptable enthusiasm and what he condemned as excessive emotionalism.

Parham's influence remained strong as through his preaching he laid theological foundations for what some began calling Assemblies of God. These tenets included a stress on personal holiness or sanctification, divine healing, power of the Holy Spirit displayed through glossolalia, and a fervent missionary impetus. The preacher and teacher also tried to become the organizer. Parham tried to harness the religious enthusiasm of his followers through federated assemblies and to secure his own authority over them.

This move to establish more formal lines of power proved Parham's undoing. His attempts often aroused suspicion and resistance. Separate movements under various leaders split Pentecostalism into separate institutional forms. Then in 1907 Parham was arrested in San Antonio, Texas, on charges of sodomy. Details of the homosexual scandal were vague and imprecise, and all charges were eventually dropped without explanation, but denominational rivals used damaging press releases to ruin Parham's reputation. He spent the last two decades of his life in relative obscurity in Baxter Springs, Kansas, where he died (of heart damage due to rheumatic fever) almost unknown to a second generation of Pentecostals. Still, he conceptualized speaking in tongues as evidence of a new level of Christian experience and gave his movement a separate identity from Holiness emphases, which laid greater importance on perfectionist ethics. An initial architect of modern Pentecostalism, Parham insisted that Holy Spirit baptism was a demonstrable experience, and such a missionary impulse has been crucial to Pentecostal growth around the world.

• Parham published two volumes of sermons, and these have been reprinted in modern editions: *Kol Kare Bomidbar: A Voice Crying in the Wilderness* (1902; repr. 1944, 1985) and *The Everlasting Gospel* (1919; repr. 1985). Another primary source is Robert Parham, ed., *Selected Sermons of the Late Charles F. Parham and Sarah E. Parham* (1941). For biographical information see Sarah E. Parham, *The Life of Charles F. Parham* (1930; repr. 1985), and James R. Goff, Jr., *Fields White unto Harvest: Charles F. Parham and the Missionary Origins of Pentecostalism* (1988). An obituary is in the *New York Times*, 31 Jan. 1929.

HENRY WARNER BOWDEN

PARISH, Peggy (14 July 1927–19 Nov. 1988), bestselling children's author, was born Margaret Cecile Parish in Manning, South Carolina, to Herman Parish and Cecile Rogers. Her mother died when Parish was very young. Brought up near the Black River in the small southern town of Manning, with little exposure to culture, she did not experience a wider world until college. According to Parish, Manning was a place "where everybody knew everybody," and life centered around church and school. Although her father's occupation is unknown, Parish once remarked that he had no formal education beyond the fourth grade. Both the Parish children, however, were given a college education, and her brother Stanley became a physician. Because she was a sickly child, Parish felt that her family went out of their way to read to her, fostering a lifelong love of books. Parish received a B.A. from the University of South Carolina in 1948 with a major in English that reflected her love of reading. She then pursued graduate study at George Peabody College for Teachers (now Vanderbilt University) in 1950. During her writing career Parish produced over forty children's books, including works of fiction, nonfiction, craft books, and mysteries.

Her love of children, the encouragement she received from her family, and her energetic, lively personality first led Parish to a career in teaching. While visiting her brother and his wife and two children in Kentucky, where he was working as a doctor in a coal-mining area, Parish was persuaded to try her hand at teaching locally. She remained as a teacher in Kentucky for two years and continued with teaching positions in Oklahoma and Texas. After moving to New York City, she worked for the Girl Scouts before landing a teaching position. She spent fifteen years as a third grade public school teacher at the Dalton School in Manhattan, New York. Parish also worked as a creative dance instructor from 1948 to 1952 and briefly in advertising.

Parish's experiences as a teacher led her in turn to a prolific writing career. She once observed, "Children have always been my life, so writing stories for children came naturally." While teaching at the progressive, experimental Dalton School, she had difficulty finding the types of books she wanted for her students, so she decided to produce her own instead. Her first book was initially rejected, but after a parent from the Dalton School introduced her to an editor at Harper, her writing career was launched. Parish credited her talented and patient editor for her success, and her first story was accepted for publication in 1961.

Parish's most famous character, a comically literal-minded maid named Amelia Bedelia, grew out of the author's fascination with words, their often double meanings, and her own sense of humor. The first Amelia Bedelia book was published by Harper in 1963. Parish once told an interviewer, "I guess that loving mischief as much as Amelia and I do shows. I simply enjoy laughing at life." Apparently, many children and their parents and teachers shared her views, for Parish's children's books had a combined sale of over 7 million copies.

Amelia Bedelia appeared in eleven books, in which the playful maid pursued her penchant for following directions to the letter. These adventures included cutting up pieces of sponge to make a sponge cake, planting electric light bulbs instead of flower bulbs, and "dusting" the furniture with talcum powder, among a variety of other comic mishaps. Amelia Bedelia's long suffering employers, Mr. and Mrs. Rogers, bear Parish's own mother's maiden name. One of Parish's most successful books in the series, *Teach Us, Amelia Bedelia* (1977), was dedicated to her first-grade teacher, who introduced her to the "magic of words."

To celebrate Amelia Bedelia's twenty-fifth birthday in 1988, publishers Harper and Row and Greenwillow mounted a year-long schedule of celebratory events. Children were encouraged to write letters and create drawings for the fictional character, and thousands responded. The last book in the series, *Amelia Bedelia's Family Album* (1988), also appeared during the same year. Characters in the book included Amelia Bedelia's relatives, cousin Calvin, described as a boxer (he packed boxes), and Aunt Clara, a bookkeeper (she never returned a book). A reviewer in *Horn Book* maintained that even after twenty-five years, Amelia Bedelia's "humor and appeal are as fresh as ever."

In addition to the Amelia Bedelia stories, Parish produced a mystery series featuring two brothers and a sister, Bill, Jed, and Liza, who appeared in such books as *Key to the Treasure* (1966) and *Pirate Island Adventure* (1975). The popular series featured word puzzles and codes, which challenged young middle school readers. She also authored several craft books, praised for their clear directions on how to make such children's items as costumes, games, mobiles, and holiday decorations.

Parish, who never married, returned to Manning, South Carolina, in 1972, where she continued to write, teach creative writing, and appear before library associations and children's educational groups. She also appeared as a children's book reviewer on a South Carolina television program, "Carolina Today," and pursued her hobbies of sewing elaborate children's clothing, gardening, and raising her pet cats. She died suddenly in Manning.

Parish exhibited a lifelong interest in teaching children to read and was proud that her books were used in many schools. Through her enormously popular Amelia Bedelia series, Parish introduced hundreds of thousands of beginning American readers to the delights of reading and language.

• A collection of Parish's manuscripts is in the Kerlan Collection, University of Minnesota, Minneapolis. Information about Peggy Parish is in *Something about the Author* (1993); *Children's Literature Review* (1991); *Fourth Book of Junior Authors and Illustrators* (1978); and *Famous Children's Authors* (1988). Obituaries are in the *New York Times*, 22 Nov. 1988, and *Publishers Weekly*, 23 Dec. 1988.

JEANNE ABRAMS